America's Registry
of
Outstanding Professionals
6th Edition

32 Bond Street
Westbury, NY 11590

This edition of America's Registry was prepared by

Publishers
Jack M. Pizzo
Anthony T. Pizzo

President
Jack M. Pizzo

Chief Operating Officer
Anthony T. Pizzo

Vice President
Cynthia M. Grey

Vice President of Operations
Frank M. Colletti

Controller/Accounting Manager
Maureen McShane

Systems Program Managers
Christopher Wierzbicki
Christopher Ziminski

Senior Editor
Ana B. Hanley

Associate Editors
Ann Marie Barone
Hope Anderson

Senior Research Directors
Jodi Kay
Patricia Mason
Ann Stevens
Scott Stone
Rich Winston

Associate Research Directors

Tim Flynn
Grace Forman
Tina Hanson
Maria Laurentz
Doug Lawson
Susan McGrath
Vanessa Mingo
John Moxin
Steve Pine
Alex Reiff
Michael Reyer
Mary Sanders
Mark Silver
Deborah Stewart
James Tucker

America's Registry
of
Outstanding Professionals
6th Edition

 For information regarding this edition or any upcoming editions, address America's Registry of Outstanding Professionals, 32 Bond Street, Westbury, NY 11590.

ISBN 978-1-890347-17-8
ISSN 1942-0579

Printed in U.S.A.

IMPORTANT NOTICE

America's Registry reserves the right to omit any biographical information not in accordance with its style, format and/or standards set forth by the editorial staff. In the event of any errors in the publication, the sole responsibility of America's Registry will be to correct such errors in succeeding editions of the same publication. Such corrections are in lieu of any other compensation. America's Registry disclaims all other liability for loss, incidental or consequential damage, whether arising from negligence, or any other cause, to any party for errors in printing.

In Memoriam

This edition of America's Registry of Outstanding Professionals is dedicated to the memory of one of the founding directors of this publication, Ann Stevens.

Ann was one of the original research directors appointed to this project more than 7 years ago when the registry was in its infancy. As a result of her hard work and perseverance, America's Registry grew to become a well known and respected directory of professionals.

We extend our deepest sympathy to Ann's family and dedicate this edition of America's Registry to Ann with fondest memories of one of our own.

Table of Contents

Preface

America's Registry represents a cross-section of corporate America, listing the biographies of men and women of achievement in all the major professions throughout the United States and abroad. The listings do not include religion, marital status or political affiliations unless such information is an integral part of the biographee's listing.

Subsequent editions of America's Registry will reflect the growth and changes in our members' professional lives.

Information Key

America's Registry is comprised of 4 parts. The first section is the V.I.P. section which highlights some of our outstanding biographees who have demonstrated exceptional leadership and achievement in their chosen field or profession. In this section we encourage information of a more personal nature such as spouse and children's names, along with an expanded work history and career accomplishments section.

The next section of the book divides our members by S.I.C. codes into 15 different categories and then each member is listed alphabetically. The full biographical profile appears in this section.

The third section is an alphabetical listing that also includes their S.I.C. code and section number for cross reference.

Lastly, there is a geographical index. It lists all members by location with their S.I.C. code so that their biography can be located quickly by cross referencing the section number.

V.I.P. Biographies

The V.I.P. section of America's Registry of Outstanding Professionals highlights those biographees who have shown exceptional achievement in their respective profession or industry. Along with a listing of educational background, career accomplishments, work history and other pertinent information, the biographies include details of a more personal nature such as spouse's and children's names.

In addition to appearing in the regular section of the registry, the biographies are showcased here in a half page format.

ACHOLONU, ALEXANDER D.W.

Alcorn State University
Dept. of Biological Science
1000 ASU Dr., #843
Alcorn State, MS 39096

Industry: Education **Born:** November 30, 1932, Imo State, Nigeria **Univ./degree:** B.S., Howard University, 1958; M.S., Prairie View A&M University, 1961; Ph.D., Colorado State University, 1964; Continuing Education Certificate, Tulane University, School of Public Health, Tropical Medicine and Hygiene, 1994 **Current organization:** Alcorn State University **Title:** PhD, FAS, OON, Professor **Type of organization:** University **Major product:** Higher education **Area of distribution:** Alcorn State, Mississippi **Expertise:** Parasitology, microbiology **Honors/awards:** Top 100 Educators of 2005; International Educators of the Year, 2003; 2000 Outstanding Intellectuals of the 21st Century, 2002 ,U.K.; Cited as a Great Mind of the 21st Century; Universal Award of Accomplishment; Who's Who of American Teachers, 2005; President, Sigma XI Research Honor Society, Southern University Chapter, 1968-69; Beta Beta Beta Biological Honor Society **Published works:** 80+ scientific publications, 2 books, 1 booklet, 4 book chapters **Affiliations:** Vice Chair, Mississippi Academy of Sciences, Zoology and Entomology Section; American Ecological Society; American Society of Parasitologists; Council Member, Executive Board, World Federation of Parasitologists; Nigerian Association of Medical Scientists; Science Association of Nigeria; Nigerian Society for Microbiology; American Society of Parasitologists; Mississippi Academy of Sciences; Ecological Society of America; National Association of African American Studies **Hob./spts.:** Physical fitness, photography, dancing **SIC code:** 82 **E-mail:** chiefacholonu@yahoo.com

ADAMS, RICHARD C.

Charter Steel
4300 E. 49th St.
Cuyahoga Heights, OH 44125-1004

Industry: Steel **Born:** Pittsburgh, Pennsylvania **Univ./degree:** B.S., Metallurgy, University of Pennsylvania **Current organization:** Charter Steel **Title:** Manager of Quality/Technical Services **Type of organization:** Manufacturing **Major product:** Steel **Area of distribution:** National **Expertise:** Management, quality control **Affiliations:** A.S.Q.; A.S.M.; A.I.S.I.; I.F.I **SIC code:** 33 **E-mail:** adamsr@chartersteel.com

ADAMS JR., WILLIAM J. (BILL)

7940 Caledonia Dr.
San Jose, CA 95135

Industry: Machinery **Born:** February 9, 1917, Riverdale, California **Spouse:** Marijane E. Leishman Adams **Married:** December 26, 1939 **Children:** W. Michael Adams, 63; John P. Adams, deceased at 52 **Univ./degree:** B.S.M.E. Magna Cum Laude, Santa Clara University, California, 1937 **Title:** P.E., FMC Corp. (Retired) **Work history:** General Electric Co., Schenectady, NY, Engineer-in-Training, 1937-38; Garwood Industries, Detroit, MI, Design Engineer of earth-moving scraper and controls, 1939-40; GE Aeronautics Equipment Division, Schenectady, NY, Design Chief Project Engineer of the first remote controlled gun turrets for the B-29, A-26 and other high altitude aircraft, 1940-45; FMC corporation, San Jose, CA, 1 yr. Chief Project Engineer, Central Engineering Dept.; 7 yrs. Chief Engineer, Bolens Division, wide range of outdoor power equipment; 17 yrs., Central Engineering Laboratories, Asst. General Mgr. on advanced machinery R&D, technical support to FMC Divisions, Industrial Design Center and engineering management; 5 yrs., Director of Planning & Ventures for Woodlands Equip. Div.; 4 yrs, Director of New Business Venture, Central Engr. Labs., 1946-80; Consultant Engineering, New Product and Business Dev., 1980-1990 **Type of organization:** Manufacturing **Major product:** Machinery **Area of distribution:** International **Expertise:** Mechanical engineering (Mechanical CA ME7672, Retired); Agricultural engineering (Agricultural CA AG234, Retired) **Honors/awards:** Listed in Who's Who in America; Listed in Who's Who in Science and Engineering; Distinguished Engineering Alumnus Award, Santa Clara University, 1991; Outstanding Engineering Service Award, Santa Clara University, 2003; Silicon Valley Engineering Council Hall of Fame, 1998 **Published works:** Technical papers and presentations; 2 books; 12 U.S. and 15 foreign patents **Affiliations:** Life Fellow, American Society of Mechanical Engineers; Fellow, American Society of Agricultural Engineering; Life Member, Society of Automotive Engineers **Hob./spts.:** Travel, fly-fishing, skiing, hunting **SIC code:** 35

ALFRED, KARL S.

20 Brandywood Dr.
Pepper Pike, OH 44124

Industry: Healthcare **Born:** Norway **Spouse:** Mollie Bombach **Married:** 1951 **Children:** Peter, 62; Richard, 63, Step-daughter, Patricia Alleman, 66 (6 grandchildren and 3 great-grandchildren) **Univ./degree:** 5AB, University of Virginia, Pre-Med, 1938; M.D., Downstate Medical Center (SUNY), Brooklyn, New York, 1942; Internship, Mountainside Hospital, Montclair, New Jersey; Residency, University Hospitals, Cleveland **Current organization:** Karl S. Alfred, M.D., L.F.A.C.S. **Title:** M.D./Life Fellow, American College of Surgeons (Retired) **Work history:** Chief of Orthopedic Surgery St. Vincent Charity Hospital, Cleveland for 32 years; Served 2 terms as president of the medical staff, several years on the executive staff and 14 years as a member of the Board of Trustees of the hospital. **Type of organization:** Private practice **Major product:** Patient care, medical consultation, medical meetings **Area of distribution:** International **Area of Practice:** Orthopaedic surgery consulting, lecturing **Honors/awards:** Lectureship in his Honor and Teacher of the Year, Cleveland Clinic Orthopaedic Department (3 times); Special Honors Award for Many Years of Service with Distinction, Cleveland Academy of Medicine, 1989; Charles Hudson Award for Distinguished Service, 1994; Presented with a plaque in recognition for all the contributions to the Dept. of Orthopaedic Surgery in the capacity of Affiliate Faculty, the Cleveland Clinic Education Foundation, 1960-88; Honors for many years of distinguished service to St. Vincent Charity Hospital, its patients and to the mission of the hospital, St. Vincent Charity Hospital's Society of St. Luke, 2004; Edward F. Myers Award as Outstanding Hospital Trustee, Center for Health Affairs **Published works:** 5 publications to journals, 7 exhibits and lectures delivered nationally and internationally **Affiliations:** Lt. Commander, US Navy Medical Corps., American Medical Association; Life Fellow, American College of Surgeons; Fellow, American Academy of Orthopaedic Surgeons; Clinical Orthopaedic Society; Mid-America Orthopedic Society; International College of Surgeons; Norwegian American Orthopedic Society; Professor, Cleveland Clinic; Member, Board of Directors, Cleveland Academy of Medicine (8 years); Cleveland Orthopedic Society **Hob./spts.:** Travel, sports, swimming, walking **SIC code:** 80

AUCELLA, LAURENCE F.

90 Oakleaf Dr.
Waterbury, CT 06708

Industry: Education, research **Born:** July 24, 1959, Waterbury, Connecticut **Univ./degree:** B.A., Behavioral Science, Edu., Anna Maria College, 1982; M.Ed., Dev. and Edu. Psych, Boston College, 1984; CAS, 6th Yr. Counseling, Univ. of Bridgeport, 1992; M.S., Research & Measurement, Southern CT State U., 1996; Ed.D., U. of Bridgeport, 1997 **Current organization:** Crosby High School **Title:** School Counselor **Work history:** Student Teacher in a resource room at Chandler Street School, Worcester, MA, 1981; While attending Boston College, he interned at Boston Children's Hospital (Developmental Evaluation Unit), the Boston Veterans Administration Hospital (Aphasia Unit) and the Hale Reservation (summer camp for children); After graduation in 1984, he returned home to Connecticut and received a position as a Drug and Alcohol Counselor for the Morris Foundation; After remaining there for 14 months, he became a School Counselor for Waterbury Adult Education in Jan. 1986, a position he still holds albeit on a part-time evening basis; In Jan. 2001, he was hired as an Elementary School Counselor at Rotella Magnet School in Waterbury; At the present time he works as a School Counselor at Crosby High School during day hours and at adult education in the evening. **Type of organization:** High school **Major product:** Education, research **Area of distribution:** Waterbury, Connecticut **Expertise:** Counseling, research **Published works:** "Cerebral Dominance, English as a Second Language, Methodologies, Theory, Learning and Acquisition for the Adult ESL Student", 1997, Description: xi, 247 p.: tables, figures; 23cm, Note: Includes bibliographical references p. 239-247, Subject: Cerebral dominance, OCLC # ocm39113526; "Principles of Cerebral Lateralization" (a work in progress) **Affiliations:** A.P.A.; A.C.A.; A.S.A.; President of La Casa Bienvenida in Waterbury, CT; Adjunct Faculty (teaches Thesis Proposal), Albertus Magnus College, New Haven, CT; School Counselor in E.S.L. Program, Waterbury Adult Education, Waterbury, CT **Career accomplishments:** Providing the optimal guidance and knowledge of the entire life development in terms of biological, psychological, spiritual, emotional and philosophical, as it is essential for the school counselor to recognize that organisms react as a whole **Hob./spts.:** Reading, book collecting **SIC code:** 82 **E-mail:** aucella_laurence@hotmail.com

BAILEY II, JAMES B.

Denver Public Schools
2800 W. Seventh Ave.
Denver, CO 80204

Industry: Education/Communications **Born:** April, 17, 1957, Denver, Colorado **Spouse:** Susan Elizabeth Miller **Married:** December 17, 1983 **Children:** Alison O., 19; Trisha A., 18 **Univ./degree:** Business/Education, Western State College, 1977; Federal Aviation Administration Airframe and Powerplant Mechanic licensed Emily Griffith Opportunity School, 1980 **Current organization:** Denver Public Schools Transportation **Title:** Communications Technician Chief **Work history:** Denver Public Schools 1982-present; Part-time Teacher Para, Emily Griffith Opportunity School Aircraft Training Center (Airframe and Powerplant mechanic teaching electronics of the aircraft, 1985-93); Vulcan Tool Representative (TRW), 1981-82; Mobile Accessories Inc., Service Manager - Mechanic (R.V.'S), 1981; Pioneer Airways, Airframe/Powerplant Mechanic, 1981 **Type of organization:** Large City (Denver) public schools system **Major product:** Transportation, safety and security services; elementary and secondary schools education communication needs **Area of distribution:** Denver, Colorado **Expertise:** Technician (two-way communications); FCC Licensed with Radar Endorsement 1983; Certified NABER Technician 1984; Senior Member, ACT 1988; PCIA Certified Communications Technician 2000; A plus Computer Certified; Maintain Large School public two-way communications systems - currently working on a new radio network to connect all Denver Public Schools to a central security dispatch center and construction of a new Transportation Dispatch Center **Honors/awards:** Communication needs for 7 school districts transportation central command station for World Youth Day with the Pope, John Paul II, 1993 **Published works:** Photographs in: The International Library of Photography; Timeless Treasures Book and America at the Millennium, Best Photos of the 20th Century **Affiliations:** APCO Association of Public-Safety Communication Officials International **Career accomplishments:** Communications at the 1993 PGA Senior Golf Open, Cherry Hills Country Club; Taping golf event with ABC Television; Bill McCartney Promise Keepers 1993 and 1994 Boulder, Colorado; Care to Dare Pathfinders 1994 Bandemare Speedway Colorado; Now working on a new type voice over IP for making computer desktop into a dispatch console via Ethernet; This system will operate two-way radio communications from each school at Denver Public Schools **Hob./spts.:** Photography, bee keeping **SIC code:** 82 **E-mail:** busybeeboy@msn.com

BATCHELOR, PHILLIP A.

Gresham, Smith and Partners
3595 Grandview Pkwy.
Suite 300
Birmingham, AL 35243

Industry: Engineering **Born:** December 13, 1967, Haleyville, Alabama **Univ./degree:** Attended 2 years, study in Engineering Drafting Technology, Beville State Community College **Current organization:** Gresham, Smith and Partners **Title:** Senior Project Supervisor/Firm Associate **Type of organization:** Consulting firm **Major product:** Consulting (architecture/engineering) **Area of distribution:** National **Expertise:** Roadway engineering **Affiliations:** A.S.C.E.; Served in active duty, U.S. Army, 1986-96 **Hob./spts.:** Family, football, history **SIC code:** 87 **E-mail:** pbatc@gspnet.com **Web address:** www.gspnet.com

BEAHAM III, GORDON T.

Faultless Starch/Bon Ami Co.
1025 W. Eighth St.
Kansas City, MO 64101

Industry: Consumer goods **Born:** February 2, 1932, Kansas City, Missouri **Univ./degree:** M.B.A., Harvard Business School **Current organization:** Faultless Starch/Bon Ami Co. **Title:** Co-Chairman & Co-CEO **Type of organization:** Manufacturing, distributing **Major product:** Commercial laundry products, lawn and garden hardware **Area of distribution:** International **Expertise:** Marketing **Affiliations:** G.M.A.; B.E.N.S. **Hob./spts.:** Swimming, golf, grandchildren, chess **SIC code:** 28 **E-mail:** gbeaham@faultless.com

BERRY, CHARLENE HELEN

Dulcimer Evente
49614 Oak Street
Plymouth, MI 48170

Industry: Entertainment **Born:** January 4, 1947, Highland Park, Michigan **Univ./degree:** B.S.E., 1968; M.A., 1970; M.S.L.S., 1974, W.S.U., MI; CMT, 1998 EMF; D.Min, U.S.C.; Diplomate, Specs Howard, 1992; Diplomate, I.M.I., 1997; D. Min. (Honorary), Destiny Christian University, 2008 **Current organization:** Dulcimer Evente **Title:** Chief Executive Officer/Owner **Work history:** Academic Librarian, Madonna University, 1980-; Church Organist, 1980-; Notary Public, Wayne County, 1992-; Performer, 1985-; Band Leader, Downriver Dulcimer, 1987-89; Band Leader, Dulcimae, 1991-; Ordained Music Minister, Gospel Lighthouse Min., 1991-; Pastor, Healing Light Atonement Min., 1998-; Radio Show, Dulcimer World, WPON AM1460, Fri 7-8 PM **Type of organization:** Music **Major product:** Live and pre-recorded music (tapes and CD's) **Area of distribution:** National **Expertise:** Special music for special people, original compositions, improvisations; Endorsed Artist, Christian Music Presenters **Honors/awards:** Listed in, Who's Who Worldwide Global Registry; World Who's Who of Women; Dictionary of Int'l Biographies; Int'l Who's Who of Intellectuals; Who's Who in the World; Who's Who in the Midwest; Who's Who in America; 2000 Notable American Women; Most Admired Men & Women of the Year; Int'l Directory of Distinguished Leadership; Int'l Who's Who of Professional and Business Women; Michigan Touring Arts Directory; 20th Century Award of Achievement; Int'l Order of Merit; Star of the Stars Music Award, 2006; Silver Medal Winner, Christian Music Connection, 2006; Businesswoman of the Year, 2003, 2004; Ronald Reagan Award, 2004 **Published works:** Dulcimer Delights, v.1, 1991; Marches, Waltzes, Free Composition and Solo Symphony, v.2, 1993; Hammering the Hammer Dulcimer, video, 1994 **Affiliations:** B.P.W.; A.A.U.W.; American Federation of Musicians; American Guild of Organists; Gospel Music Association; Fellow, American Biological Institute; Life Fellow, International Biological Association; Deputy Governor American Biog. Inst. Res. Association **Career accomplishments:** Leader in the current revival of the hammer dulcimer and the development of hammering techniques, performance and practice **Hob./spts.:** Landscape painting, photography **SIC code:** 79 **E-mail:** cberry@dulcimerworld.com **Web address:** www.dulcimerworld.com

BONFIGLIO, RICHARD S.

The Law Firm of Richard S. Bonfiglio, Esq.
238-92nd St.
Brooklyn, NY 11209-5702

Industry: Law **Born:** January 22, 1952, Brooklyn, New York **Univ./degree:** B.A., Accounting and Tax, Pace University, 1973; J.D. Fordham University School of Law, 1984 **Current organization:** The Law Firm of Richard S. Bonfiglio, Esq. **Title:** Attorney **Type of organization:** Law firm **Major product:** Legal services **Area of distribution:** New York **Area of Practice:** Civil trial, tax, trusts, estates **Affiliations:** American Bar Association; New York State Bar Association; New York State Trial Lawyers Association; American Trial Lawyers Association **Hob./spts.:** Family, golf, deep sea fishing **SIC code:** 81 **E-mail:** suedoctor@aol.com

BOYER, SELENA L.

Wyeth Laboratories
206 N. Biddle St.
Marietta, PA 17547-0304

Industry: Vaccines **Born:** September 28, 1960, Lancaster, Pennsylvania **Univ./degree:** B.S., Biology, Mansfield State University, 1982 **Current organization:** Wyeth Laboratories **Title:** Training Supervisor **Type of organization:** Manufacturing **Major product:** Vaccines **Area of distribution:** Georgia **Expertise:** Vaccines-production training GMP's **Affiliations:** A.S.T.D.; P.D.A. **SIC code:** 28 **E-mail:** boyers60@comcast.com **Web address:** www.wyeth.com

CARRO PAGÁN, CARLOS J.

Advanced Cardiology Center
P.O. Box 331788
Ponce, PR 00733-1788

Industry: Healthcare **Born:** Puerto Rico **Univ./degree:** M.D., University of Santo Domingo, 1978; Cardiology Degree, Ponce School of Medicine, 1986 **Current organization:** Advanced Cardiology Center **Title:** Cardiologist **Type of organization:** Medical office **Major product:** Patient care **Area of distribution:** Puerto Rico **Area of Practice:** Cardiology, internal medicine **Published works:** 6 articles **Affiliations:** A.M.A.; Puerto Rico Board of Physicians **Hob./spts.:** Golf, fishing **SIC code:** 80 **E-mail:** carropagancarlosj@prtc.net

CASTRO, FRANCISCO A.

Newark Public Schools
2 Cedar St.
Newark, NJ 07102

Industry: Education **Born:** December 14, 1948, Santo Domingo, Dominican Republic **Univ./degree:** B.S., Fairleigh Dickinson University **Current organization:** Newark Public Schools **Title:** Supervisor Engineer **Type of organization:** Public school district **Major product:** Education **Area of distribution:** Newark, New Jersey **Expertise:** Engineering **Affiliations:** A.E.E. **Hob./spts.:** Sports **SIC code:** 82 **E-mail:** fcastro@nps.k12.nj.us

CHANG, DAVID DAH-CHUNG

Building & Safety Dept.
City of Los Angeles
9746 Sunflower St.
Alta Loma, CA 91737

Industry: Government **Born:** September 18, 1954, Taiwan **Univ./degree:** B.S./M.S., Civil Engineering, National Cheng Kung University; M.S., Structural Engineering, U.C.L.A. **Current organization:** Building & Safety Dept., City of Los Angeles **Title:** Plan Check Supervisor **Work history:** International ICC Existing Building Code Committee Vice Chair, 1999-2002; ICC International Building Code Interpretation Committee, 2003-2007 **Type of organization:** Government/ building and construction **Major product:** Building codes and building permits **Area of distribution:** California **Expertise:** Engineering, building codes **Affiliations:** A.S.C.E.; American Concrete Institute; Structural Engineers Association of California; Vice Chair International of Existing Building Code Committee; A.T.C. (Applied Technical Council); E.E.R.I. (Earthquake Engineering Research Institute) **Career accomplishments:** Presentation Speaker for SEAOC Seminars; President of National Cheng Kung University Alumni Association of Southern California; President of National Cheng Kung University Alumni Foundation of Southern California **Hob./spts.:** Physical fitness, reading, travel **SIC code:** 95 **E-mail:** david.chang@lacity.org

CHONG, EDWIN K.P.

Colorado State University
1373 Campus Delivery
Ft. Collins, CO 80523-1373

Industry: Education **Born:** February 2, 1966, Malaysia **Spouse:** Yat-Yee Chong **Children:** Madeleine, 6; Isaac, 4 **Univ./degree:** B.E., Honors, 1987, University of Adelaide, South Australia; M.A., Electrical Engineering, 1989; Ph.D., Electrical Engineering, 1991, Princeton University **Current organization:** Colorado State University **Title:** Professor, Dept. of Electrical and Computer Engineering/Professor, Dept. of Mathematics **Work history:** Purdue University, 1991-2001 **Type of organization:** University **Major product:** Higher education, research **Area of distribution:** International **Expertise:** Electrical and computer engineering **Honors/awards:** Numerous including, Outstanding IEEE Branch Counselor and Advisor Award, 1993; IEEE Section Recognition Award (IEEE Central Indiana Section), 1994; National Science Foundation Faculty Early Career Development Award, 1995; Tarkington Hall Certificate of Appreciation, 1996; Frederick Emmons Terman Award by American Society for Engineering, 1998; Purdue University Faculty Scholar Award, 1999; IEEE Control Systems Society Distinguished Lecturer, 2001-03; Elected to Full Member of Sigma Xi, 2002; Elsevier Best Paper Award, 2004 **Published works:** 2 books, "An Introduction to Optimization", 1996, ISBN 0-471-08949-4, xiii+409 pp and "An Introduction to Optimization, 2nd Edition", 2001, ISBN 0-471-39126-3, xvi+477 pp, John Wiley & Sons Inc., New York, NY; 200 journal papers, conference proceedings and presentations and book chapters; Papers on philosophy, theology and alologetics **Affiliations:** Fellow, I.E.E.E. **SIC code:** 82 **E-mail:** ekpchong@yahoo.com **Web address:** www.edwinchong.us

CHRISTMAN, LUTHER P.

5535 Nashville Hwy.
Chapel Hill, TN 37034

Industry: Medical **Born:** February 26, 1915, Summit Hill, Pennsylvania **Univ./degree:** M.S., Clinical Psychology, Temple University, 1950; Ph.D., Sociology/Anthropology, Michigan State University, 1966 **Title:** Professor Emeritus, Vanderbilt University; Dean Emeritus, Rush University **Type of organization:** University **Major product:** Higher education **Area of distribution:** National **Expertise:** Nursing, sociology **Affiliations:** Fellow, American Association for the Advancement of Science; President, American Assembly for Men in Nursing **Career accomplishments:** He was refused admission to the Army Nurse Corps in World War II because he was a man. Despite this, he gained qualifications in psychology and his research led to high level appointments in university nursing faculties. He became the first male to hold the joint appointments of Dean of Nursing and Hospital Director of Nursing. He developed the Rush Model of nursing that gained him an international reputation as a nursing leader. His strategic plans for the development of the nursing profession entailed a critique of its organization, policies, practices, education and female domination that challenged nursing leaders, physicians and hospital administrators alike. **Hob./spts.:** Gardening, wild birds, travel, hiking **SIC code:** 82 **E-mail:** lchristman@united.net

CLAYCOMB, STEPHEN H.

Middle Tennessee Pediatrics and Adolescent Medicine, PC
1405 Baddour Pkwy.
Suite 101
Lebanon, TN 37087

Industry: Healthcare **Born:** October 4, 1961, Pine Bluff, Arkansas **Univ./degree:** M.D., University of Arkansas **Current organization:** Middle Tennessee Pediatrics & Adolescent Medicine, PC **Title:** M.D., President **Type of organization:** Pediatric health care practice **Major product:** Patient care **Area of distribution:** Lebanon, Tennessee **Area of Practice:** Pediatrics **Published works:** 1 article **Affiliations:** A.M.A; A.A.P; T.M.A **Hob./spts.:** Swimming and coaching swimming **SIC code:** 80 **E-mail:** shclaycomb@msn.com

COWDEN, RONALD R.

(In Memoriam)
Mobile, AL 36606

Industry: Basic biomedical research **Born:** July 9, 1931, Memphis, Tennessee **Univ./degree:** Ph.D., Zoology, University of Vienna **Current organization:** Coastal Biomedical Laboratory **Title:** Director/Professor **Type of organization:** Private research **Major product:** Research in cell biology **Area of distribution:** International **Expertise:** Cell biology, cytochemistry **Published works:** 125 publications **Affiliations:** A.S.C.B.; A.S.D.B.; T.H.S.; R.M.S. **Hob./spts.:** Grand opera, big game hunting **SIC code:** 87 **E-mail:** tiffron@comcast.net

CRAIN, FRANCES UTTERBACK

255 N. Avalon St.
Memphis, TN 38112-5101

Industry: Healthcare **Born:** December 28, 1914, Crawfordsville, Indiana **Spouse:** James W. Crain (Deceased) **Married:** September 13, 1937 **Children:** James Michael Crain, May 9, 1942; Patrick Desmond Crain, July 23, 1943 **Univ./degree:** B.A., Nutrition, University of Illinois, 1935 **Current organization:** Shelby County, Oakville Healthcare Center **Title:** Dietitian (Retired) **Work history:** Dietician, University of Illinois, 1936-37; Therapeutic Dietician, Indianapolis City Hospital, 1937-38; Chief Dietician, Alexian Brothers Hospital, St. Louis, Missouri, 1941; Executive Director, Memphis Dairy Council, Memphis, Tennessee, 1947-61; Chief Dietician, Shelby County Hospital, Memphis, Tennessee, 1969-74; Chief Dietician, Shelby County Penal Farm and Chief Dietician, Oakville Health Care Center, Memphis, Tennessee, 1974-1980 **Type of organization:** Healthcare center **Major product:** Healthcare, nutrition **Area of distribution:** Memphis, Tennessee **Area of Practice:** Nutrition **Honors/awards:** 1955 Memphis Career Woman of the Year; 1976 Tennessee Outstanding Dietitian; 1977 Tennessee Outstanding Dietician; Salvation Army Certificate of Appreciation; 2003 Frances Crain Book Fund established by Memphis area Nutrition Council & Memphis District Dietetic Assoc. **Published works:** Book, "Of Weeds and Views", 2000; "To Your Taste - Butter", National Dairy Council, 1958; Weekly food feature article for The Commercial Appeal, Memphis, TN, 1952-61 **Affiliations:** Numerous including: President, Memphis District Dietetic Association, 1949-50; President, Tennessee Dietetic Association; District Governor Quota Club International; President Shelby County Retirees Organization, 1987-89 **Career accomplishments:** Employed by Shelby County in 1969. Thereafter, her time was split between Shelby County Hospital and Shelby County Penal Farm. After becoming full time at Shelby County Hospital, she was retained on a consulting basis at Shelby County Penal Farm until retirement in 1980. **Hob./spts.:** Scrabble, home maintenance **SIC code:** 80 **E-mail:** fran255@aol.com

CREASY, JEFF L.

Vanderbilt University
Dept. of Radiology
21st & Garland
Nashville, TN 37232

Industry: Healthcare/education **Born:** November 14, 1954, Vestal, New York **Univ./degree:** B.S., Michigan State University, 1976; M.D., University of North Carolina at Chapel Hill, 1980 **Current organization:** Vanderbilt University, Dept. of Radiology **Title:** M.D./Associate Professor **Type of organization:** University hospital **Major product:** Medical care, teaching **Area of distribution:** Tennessee **Area of Practice:** Neuroradiology **Affiliations:** A.S.N.R.; R.S.N.A.; A.R.S. **Hob./spts.:** Photography **SIC code:** 80

CREIGHTON, JOHN W.

105 Park Dr.
Port Barrington, IL 60010

Industry: Publishing **Univ./degree:** General Motors Certified, Chicago Tech Institute **Title:** Editorial Director, Irving Cloud Publications (Retired) **Type of organization:** Publishing **Major product:** Magazine publications **Area of distribution:** National **Expertise:** Editorial consulting **Affiliations:** Board Member, Catholic Transfiguration Parish; Life Member, Society of Automotive Engineers.; Past Member, Chicago Press Club; Knights of Columbus **Hob./spts.:** Woodworking **SIC code:** 27

DAY, RICHARD A.

University of Cincinnati
Dept. of Chemistry
ML 0172
Cincinnati, OH 45221-0172

Industry: Education **Born:** April 4, 1931, Kellogg, Iowa **Univ./degree:** B.S., Iowa State University, 1953; Ph.D., Organic Chemistry, Massachusetts Institute of Technology, 1958 **Current organization:** University of Cincinnati **Title:** Professor **Type of organization:** University **Major product:** Higher education, research ("Beta-Lactams") **Area of distribution:** International **Expertise:** Biochemistry **Published works:** 100+ (articles, reviews and book chapters) **Affiliations:** A.C.S.; A.S.M.B.; A.S.M.S. **Hob./spts.:** Archeo-astronomy, music, travel, gardening **SIC code:** 82 **E-mail:** richard.day@uc.edu

DIETZ, ALMA

2929 Memory Lane
Kalamazoo, MI 49006-5534

Industry: Pharmaceuticals **Born:** November 29, 1922, Holyoke, Massachusetts **Univ./degree:** B.A., American International College; Graduate work in botany, University of Michigan **Current organization:** Independent consultant **Title:** Microbial Taxonomist, Specialty-Actinomycetes **Work history:** Lab Instructor, AIC, 1944-46; Microbial Taxonomist and Culture Curator in infectious disease research, The Upjohn Co., Kalamazoo, Michigan; Retired from the Upjohn Co. in 1990; served as a consultant and has given lectures and presentations nationally and internationally **Type of organization:** Private consulting practice **Major product:** Antibiotics **Area of distribution:** International **Expertise:** Microorganisms **Honors/awards:** 2004 AIC Alumni Achievement Award; honored in 1981 with the Upjohn Co.'s prestigious W.E. Upjohn Award for her extensive contributions to the advancement of science through activities associated with culture collections of living organisms **Published works:** 80+ publications, 5 U.S. patents, provided the descriptions and identifications of the strains in 66 other U.S. patents; Editor of the Japanese Journal of Antibiotics **Affiliations:** American Mycological Society; American Society for Microbiology; Society of Industrial Microbiology; Editorial Board of Japanese Journal of Antibiotics; U.S. Federation for Culture Collections; active in local Episcopal Church; served on the Board of Directors of the Arcadia Neighborhood Association in Kalamazoo **Career accomplishments:** Numerous contributions to the field of industrial microbiology **Hob./spts.:** Golf, gardening **SIC code:** 87 **E-mail:** admicrotax@aol.com

DRESCHER-LINCOLN, CAROLYN KAY

Bionique Testing Laboratories, Inc.
156 Fay Brook Dr.
Saranac Lake, NY 12983

Industry: Biopharmaceuticals **Born:** April 13, 1950, Columbus, Ohio **Univ./degree:** B.S., Biology, Lebanon Valley College, 1972; Ph.D., Microbiology, University of Pittsburgh School of Medicine and Dental Medicine, 1979; Thesis Committee chaired by Julius S. Youngner, D.Sc. **Current organization:** Bionique Testing Laboratories, Inc. **Title:** Director, Technical Services **Work history:** Teaching Ass't. Dept. of Microbiolgy, Univ. of Pittsburgh S.O.M., 1974-75; Instructor, Dept. of Micorbiology, Univ. of Pittsburgh S.O.M.1976-78; **Type of organization:** Biotech company **Major product:** Mycoplasma testing and problem solving **Area of distribution:** International **Expertise:** Chief Scientific Officer, medical microbiology, in vitro cell biology **Honors/awards:** Esther Teplitz Award for Teaching Excellence, University of Pittsburgh, 1977; Guest Lecturer for Technical Seminar Series sponsored by Life Technologies, Inc. Johns Hopkins Genetics CORE Research Facility, 1994 **Published works:** 1 chapter in Methods in Cell Biology, Vol. 57; 8 scientific papers; numerous publications and lectures including: Dresher-Lincoln, C.K., P. Jargiello, T.J. Gill III amd H.W. Kunz, 1980 Analysis of the Giemsa-banding patterns of the chromosomes from rats carrying the genes of the growth and reproduction complex (GRC). J. Immunogentics 7:427-430 **Affiliations:** American Society for Microbiology; American Association for the Advancement of Science; International Organization for Mycoplasmology **Career accomplishments:** All of her scientific endeavors, starting with the establishment of her first cell culture lines as part of her senior research project at Lebanon Valley College to the present, have been utilized by others to further scientific discovery and application across specialty boundaries. To date, all of her bench work, whether experimental or analytical, has been repeated and verified by others and then served as a factual foundation for further basic research and/or as factual stepping stones to today's release of numerous cell culture derived biomedical products manufactured by the client companies that she serves. **Hob./spts.:** Family, reading, sketching, home projects/woodworking, baseball, cross-country skiing **SIC code:** 87 **E-mail:** clincoln65@hotmail.com **Web address:** www.bionique.com

EICHBAUM, BARLANE RONALD

12065 Stoney Brook Dr.
Reno, NV 89511

Industry: Applied Research & Development **Born:** September 1, 1926, New Brunswick, New Jersey **Spouse:** Beatrice Roth **Married:** August 26, 1950 **Children:** Susanne Bashista, Nancy Radford, Virginia Anderson; Grandchildren: David Bashista, Jimmy Bashista, Kristen Bashista, Timothy Anderson, Brian Chapin; Great Grandchildren: Alex Bashista, Luke Bashista, Dominik Bashista **Univ./degree:** B.S., Rutgers University; M.S., Ceramic Engineering, Texas University; Ph.D., Rutgers University **Title:** Materials Processing Engineer/Scientist and Environmental Scientist **Work history:** B29 Gunner, WWII, 1944-46; US Signal Corps, Res. Engr. 1953-56; IBM Research Lab. Solid State Res. Engr., 1956-59; Ford Motor Co. (Aeronutronic & Philco Research & Dev. Labs.); Asst. Dir. Of Res., 1959-65; AMP Inc. Dir. Of Dev., 1965-67: Gulton Ind. Dir Ceramic & Materials Res., 1967-68; Lear Ind. Inc., Chief Scientist, 1968-70; Environmental & Materials Processing Consultant, 1970-75; US Bureau of Mines Res. Lab. R&D on Automation of Materials Processing equipment & Environmental Studies and cleanup of mining pollution, 1975-95; Semi retired and materials and environmental pollution consulting, 1995-present **Major product:** Advanced components for: computers, industrial and military equipment; materials processing for new systems; environmental programs and studies to reduce pollution **Area of distribution:** International **Expertise:** Inorganic Materials Science/Engineering and Environmental Science **Honors/awards:** Foote Minerals 1st Award; Ferro Enamels Award; IBM ERAD Award; Materials in Design Engineering Award; Ford Motor Co. Awards for directing: 1) BIAX High Speed Memory Element Development and Production and 2) Advanced High Speed Thin Film Memory Prototype for NSA; Who's Who in: Electronic Industry; The East; The West; Commerce & Industry; American Men & Women in Science and Royal Blue Book of Great Britain; Fellow, American Institute of Chemists **Published works:** Over 60 publications, patents and presentations in the fields of ceramic and inorganic processing; solid state and electronic component development; studies on external and internal combustion engines and air pollution; automated metal extraction technology and water pollution clean-up studies **Career accomplishments:** His accomplishments have been possible with the help of his GI Bill of Rights for his Engineering education, with prayer to God, working with and with the assistance of many excellent scientific associates. He has had many accomplishments in the field of Applied Research & Development in the development of advanced computers, NASA equipment, military equipment and industrial automated processing equipment **Hob./spts.:** Family activities, genealogy, travel, Christian activities; Founding Member, Reno Christian Fellowship; patriotic events **SIC code:** 87 **E-mail:** eichbaum2@aol.com

ESSENHIGH, ROBERT H.

Ohio State University
Mechanical Engineering Dept.
201 W. 19th Ave.
Columbus, OH 43210

Industry: Education **Born:** April 29, 1928, Hightown, Lancashire, United Kingdom **Univ./degree:** Ph.D., University of Sheffield, United Kingdom, 1959 **Current organization:** Ohio State University **Title:** E.G. Bailey Professor of Energy Conversion/Professor of Mechanical Engineering **Type of organization:** Research, teaching university **Major product:** Higher education, research, science and engineering **Area of distribution:** International **Expertise:** Combustion science, engineering and teaching **Published works:** 100 articles, 20 book chapters **Affiliations:** American Society of Mechanical Engineers; American Association for the Advancement of Science; A.C.S. **Hob./spts.:** Sailing, flying in small planes **SIC code:** 82 **E-mail:** essenhigh.1@osu.edu **Web address:** www.rclsgi.eng.ohio-state.edu/~essenhigh/hier

FLECKENSTEIN, EDWARD A.

39 King Ave.
Weehawken, NJ 07086

Industry: Publishing/history **Born:** November 27, 1919, Weehawken, New Jersey **Univ./degree:** A.B., Economics, Fordham University, 1941; J.D., Fordham University School of Law, 1943 **Current organization:** Edward A Fleckenstein, Chairman/Weehawken Township Historical Commission **Title:** Commission Head/Writer **Type of organization:** Publishing/historical commission **Major product:** Legal services/articles **Area of distribution:** National **Expertise:** Writer **Published works:** Articles on historical accounts, cultural and political matters **Affiliations:** Trustee, Fritz Reuter Life Care Center; Board Member, Palisades Medical Center; Corresponding Editor, Der Volksfreund / People's Friend of Buffalo, NY **Career accomplishments:** Chairman of the Weehawken Housing Authority and involved with its holding of pageants and cooperation with other historical and genealogical organizations and its collecting books and documents on local history **Hob./spts.:** Photography, writing **SIC code:** 27

FORBES, SARAH E.

Women's Complete Health Care
Forbes Enterprises
12420 Warwick Blvd.
Bldg. #5
Newport News, VA 23606

Industry: Healthcare **Born:** May 4, 1928, Currituck, North Carolina **Univ./degree:** B.A., University of Rochester; M.D., Medical College of Virginia, 1954 **Current organization:** Women's Complete Health Care/Forbes Enterprises **Title:** M.D. **Type of organization:** Private practice **Major product:** Ob/Diag., Gynecology, complete female healthcare, primary care and geriatrics **Area of distribution:** Newport News, Virginia **Area of practice:** Obstetrics, gynecology, entrepreneurial services **Area of Practice:** Obstetric consults, gynecology **Honors/awards:** The Medallion Award, The Boys and Girls Club; American Medical Association Physician Recognition Award; The YWCA Twin Award Tribute to Women in Business and Industry; Woman of the Year for the Peninsula Award; The Forty Year S.P.C.A. Presidential Award **Affiliations:** F.A.C.O.G.; A.M.A.; Medical Society of Virginia; Newport News Medical Society; President, Virginia Peninsula Boys & Girls Club **Career accomplishments:** Owner of Windmill Point Restaurant & Rentals on the Ocean Cottages, Nags Head, North Carolina, SEBROF Corporation Construction Co., Mary B. Forbes Land Corporation, Newport News, Virginia **Hob./spts.:** Philanthropy, sailing, nature lover **SIC code:** 80 **E-mail:** sforbes@visi.net **Web address:** www.rentalsontheocean.com or www.windmillrestauran

FRAGOMENI, JAMES M.

College Park Station
P.O. Box 211074
Detroit, MI 48221-5074

Industry: Education **Born:** September 24, 1962, Columbus, Ohio **Univ./degree:** B.S., Metallurgical Engineering, 1985, University of Pittsburgh; M.S.E., Mechanical Engineering, 1989; Ph.D., Mechanical Engineering, 1994, Purdue University **Current organization:** University of Detroit Mercy **Title:** Adjunct Instructor **Work history:** Engineering Consultant, Engineering and Science Consulting Services, 2005-2007; Assistant Professor, Mechanical Engineering, University of Detroit Mercy, 2000-2004; Assistant Professor, Mechanical Engineering, Ohio University, 1997-2000; Assistant Professor, Aerospace Engineering & Mechanics, University of Alabama, 1995-2000; NASA Faculty Research Fellow, Marshall Space Flight Center, 1996-1997 **Type of organization:** University **Major product:** Higher education **Area of distribution:** International **Expertise:** Lightweight alloys for aerospace; Research emphasis is on characterizing the mechanical behavior and microstructures of high strength light weighting aluminum-lithium alloys as a function of the material processing, manufacturing and chemistry **Honors/awards:** Diploma of Expertise, American Biographical Institute, 2005; Marquis Who's Who in Science & Engineering, 8th ed. 2005-06; AcademicKey's Who's Who in Engineering Education, 2002; AFOSR Summer Research Faculty Fellow, 1998; NASA Summer Research Faculty Fellow, 1996, 1997; Order of Engineer, 1989; Honor Societies: Pi Tau Sigma; Sigma Xi; Omicron Delta Kappa; Tau Beta Pi; Phi Eta Sigma; Honors from the American Biographical Institute (ABI): Lifetime Fellow; Lifetime Deputy Governor, 2005 - present; Ambassador of Grand Eminence, A.G.E., 2005-present; Man of the Year, 2005 and 2006; Great Minds of the 21st Century, 2006; American Hall of Fame, 2006; International Peace Prize, 2006; Ambassador General of the United Cultural Convention, 2006-present; Lifetime Achievement Award, United Cultural Convention, 2006 **Published works:** Recent Journal Publications: "Effect of Heat Treating on the Microstructure and Fatigue Behavior of a Ti-6wt.%Al-4wt.%V ELI Alloy", Journal of Advanced Materials, Vol. 33, No. 3, pp. 18-25, July 2001; "Characterizing the Brittle Fracture and the Ductile to Brittle to Ductile Transition of Heat-Treated Binary Aluminum-Lithium Alloys", Engineering Transactions, Vol. 49, No. 4, pp. 573-598, Dec. 2001 **Affiliations:** American Society for Engineering Education; American Society for Materials; Material Society; Engineering Society for Detroit; Society for Manufacturing Engineers; Michigan Education Association; American Society for Quality; American Society for Mechanical Engineers **Career accomplishments:** Advanced research in characterizing the mechanical behavior and microstructures of aluminum lithium aerospace alloys as a function of the material processing, manufacturing and chemistry **Hob./spts.:** Physical fitness, skiing, photography, scuba diving, archery, tennis **SIC code:** 82 **E-mail:** jamesmark88@yahoo.com **Web address:** www.jamesmatsci.org

FRONTELA, ODALYS P.

Miami Dade Health & Rehabilitation Services, Inc.
3233 Palm Ave.
Hialeah, FL 33012

Industry: Healthcare **Born:** October 12, 1959, Cuba **Children:** Hamlet Sanchez, 15 **Univ./degree:** M.D., University of Costa Rica, 1988 **Current organization:** Miami Dade Health & Rehabilitation Services, Inc. **Title:** M.D., F.A.C.P. **Type of organization:** Hospital/clinic **Major product:** Patient care **Area of distribution:** Florida **Area of practice:** Internal medicine **Area of Practice:** Internal medicine **Affiliations:** F.M.A.-P.A.C.H.A.; A.C.P.-A.S.I.M.; A.C.P.E.; A.M.A.; A.M.P.A.C.; Diplomate, American Board of Internal Medicine **Hob./spts.:** Family, travel, sports **SIC code:** 80 **Phone:** (305)826-0660 **Fax:** (305)825-0245 **E-mail:** ofrontela@aol.com

GATES-BELLER, CHERYL K.

Cheryl K. Gates-Beller, BSMNS, RN, C
Independent Healthcare Provider
609 Gender Rd.
Canal Winchester, OH 43110

Industry: Healthcare **Born:** April 8, 1944, Chillicothe, Ohio **Univ./degree:** Diploma, Riverside-White Cross School of Nursing, Columbus, OH, 1965; B.S., Management of Nursing Services. College of Mount St. Joseph, Cincinnati, OH, 1995; Legal Nurse Consulting, Kaplan College, Boca Raton, FL; Medical Consulting Network, Columbus, OH **Current organization:** Self-employed independent healthcare provider **Title:** Clinician, IV Specialist, Case Management, Supervisor American Nursing Care, Columbus, OH **Type of organization:** Independent healthcare provider **Major product:** Nursing care **Area of distribution:** Central Ohio **Area of Practice:** ANCC Medical-Surgical Certification, Chemo Certification **Affiliations:** American Nursing Association; Ohio Nursing Association; Cross Alumni Association; College of Mount St. Joseph Association and Business Alumni-Honorary **Hob./spts.:** Physical fitness, reading **SIC code:** 80 **E-mail:** ckbeller@bright.net

GAVRILESCU, TUDOR H.

SUNY Downstate Medical Center
450 Clarkson Ave., Box 24
Brooklyn, NY 11203

Industry: Healthcare **Univ./degree:** M.D., Romania, 1967; Ph.D., Romania, 1982 **Current organization:** SUNY Downstate Medical Center, Brooklyn, New York **Title:** M.D., Ph.D., F.A.C.O.G., Clinical Associate Professor, Director of Gynecology **Work history:** In August 2004 he was appointed Clinical Associate Professor in the Department of Obstetrics and Gynecology at SUNY Downstate Medical Center, University Hospital of Brooklyn; He also maintains a private practice in gynecology; For appointments, call (718) 363-2907 or 2908 **Type of organization:** University hospital and faculty, private practice **Major product:** Women's healthcare **Area of distribution:** Long Island, New York **Area of practice:** Obstetrics/Gynecology (Board Certified), gynecologic surgery, vaginal surgery, laparoscopic surgery **Area of Practice:** Obstetrics/Gynecology (Board Certified), gynecologic surgery, vaginal surgery, laparoscopic surgery **Published works:** Articles **Affiliations:** A.C.O.G; American Society of Laparoscopic Surgeons **Hob./spts.:** Tennis, gardening **SIC code:** 80 **E-mail:** tudororia@hotmail.com

GEWONT, MARGARET

Fitzgerald's Motel
530 Broadway
Wisconsin Dells, WI 53965-1500

Industry: Hospitality **Born:** January 18, 1954, Zakopane, Poland **Spouse:** Eugene Tokarczyk **Married:** July 26, 1979, City Hall, Zakopane, Poland; July 29, 1979, church, Witów, Poland **Children:** Sgt. Andrew Peter Andrew, USMC, October 12, 1979; Katherine Marie Tokarczyk, March 10, 1984 **Univ./degree:** M.S., Jagiellonian University, Kraków, Poland; M.S., DeKalb University, Kennedy Western University; Richard Daley College **Current organization:** Fitzgerald's Motel **Title:** General Manager **Work history:** Fitzgerald Motel, Wisconsin **Type of organization:** High-end motel **Major product:** Hotel accommodations **Area of distribution:** Wisconsin Dells, Wisconsin **Expertise:** Daily operations oversight **Affiliations:** Catholic Church **Hob./spts.:** Reading, hiking, biking, skiing **SIC code:** 70 **Web address:** www.fitzgeraldsmotel.com

GOLDSTEIN, SAUL I.

SemiTech
9215 Clark Circle
Twinsburg, OH 44087

Industry: Consulting **Born:** 1935, Brooklyn, New York **Univ./degree:** B.S.E.E., Newark College of Engineering; M.S., Business, Pace College **Current organization:** SemiTech **Title:** Electronic Engineering Consultant **Type of organization:** Consulting **Major product:** Electronic engineering **Area of distribution:** International **Expertise:** Electronic engineering consultation **Affiliations:** I.E.E.E. **SIC code:** 87 **E-mail:** goldsi@earthlink.net

HADDAWAY, ROBERT M.

RMH Cable TV, Inc.
7301 R.R. 620 North
Suite 155,197
Austin, TX 78726

Industry: Cable television **Born:** March 6, 1959, Louisville, Kentucky **Current organization:** RMH Cable TV, Inc. **Title:** President **Type of organization:** Cable television sales and installations contract company **Major product:** Sales and installation cable television subscriptions **Area of distribution:** Texas **Expertise:** Marketing **Affiliations:** T.C.A.; C.T.A. **Hob./spts.:** Golf, snorkeling **SIC code:** 48

HARTSAW, WILLIAM O.

1407 Green Meadow Rd.
Evansville, IN 47715

Industry: Education/Engineering **Univ./degree:** B.S., Engineering, 1946; M.S. Engineering, Purdue University; Ph.D., Engineering, University of Illinois **Title:** Distinguished Professor Emeritus (Retired), University of Evansville **Type of organization:** University **Major product:** Higher education **Area of distribution:** Evansville, Indiana **Expertise:** Mechanical engineering, Dean of Engineering, teaching, public speaking, consulting **Affiliations:** American Society of Mechanical Engineers; Heating and Refrigeration Association **Hob./spts.:** Solar energy enthusiast **SIC code:** 82 **E-mail:** wo@hartsaw.net

HASSAN, SYED T.

National Physical Therapy Services
12701 Telegraph Rd.
Suite 209
Taylor, MI 48180

Industry: Healthcare **Born:** January 30, 1939, Bihar, India **Univ./degree:** B.S., General Science, University Bihar, India, 1959; M.S., Glass Engineering, University of Sheffield, UK, 1964 **Current organization:** National Physical Therapy Services **Title:** Administrator **Type of organization:** Private practice **Major product:** Physical therapy **Area of distribution:** National **Area of Practice:** Operations management, glass and ceramics engineering; pioneered tinted glass in Pakistan, 1978 **Honors/awards:** Inbo Asahi Japan Scholarship, 1959 **Affiliations:** Chairman, Pakistan Standard Institute; A.C.S.; G.I. **Hob./spts.:** Family, soccer **SIC code:** 80 **E-mail:** tahirgilani@yahoo.com

HUGHES, ALEXANDRA O.

11 E. 80th St., #2A
New York, NY 10021

Industry: Entertainment **Born:** January 30, 1957, New York, New York **Univ./degree:** B.F.A., Bennington College, 1973; B.M.F.A., The Julliard School of Music, 1978; M.A., The Julliard School of Music, 1979 **Current organization:** Self employed **Title:** Opera Singer, Artistic Liaison to the Nuage France Foundation (www.nuage-france.org) **Major product:** Opera, recital and orchestral engagements, crossover popular events, recordings **Area of distribution:** International **Expertise:** Mezzo soprano **Honors/awards:** Acclaimed by critics worldwide for her performances in "Tristan und Isolde" (Brangaene), Honolulu Star Bulletin, Opera, Opera News; "Das Rheingold" (Fricka), Seattle Post Intelligencer, Seattle Times, Opera, London Observer; "Werther" (Charlotte), Opernwelt, Das Orchester, Sudkurier; "Hansel und Gretal" (Hansel), Opera, Seattle Post Intelligencer; "Der Rosenkavalier" (Octavian), Opera, Montreal Gazette, The Suburban; "Ariadne auf Naxos" (Komponist), Badische Zeitung, Basler Zeitung, Sudkurier, Sudwest Presse; "Carmen" (Carmen), Openwelt, Seattle Gay News; "Samson and Dalila" (Dalila), Fyns Stiffende Odense; "The Turn of the Screw" (Mrs. Grose), The New York Times, The Philadelphia Enquirer, Opera News, New York Magazine; Performing venues worldwide include Carnegie Hall, San Francisco Opera, Seattle Opera Co., New York City Opera Co., Canadian Opera Co., Montreal Opera, Live from Town Hall with Garrison Keillor, Cabrillo Festival, St. Paul Chamber Orchestra, New Orleans Opera, Opera Omaha, Detroit Opera, Pierpont Morgan Library, Hyde Collection, Brooklyn Bargemusic Series, Philadelphia Museum of Art, Grand Theatre Geneva, Opera de Marseille, Giverny, Basle Opera Switzerland, American Choral Society Soloist in Paris, Finnish National Opera, Odense Symphony Orchestra as well as the Aspen Music Festival and Cologne Philharmonic Orchestra **Published works:** Recordings: Finnish National Opera, Richard Wagner, "Die Walküre, Act II, Scene II"; "You Must Remember This From Gershwin to Lerner and Lowe"; "Alexandra Hughes, Monteverdi Excerpts"; "Alexandra Hughes, Mezzo Soprano"; "Alexandra Hughes, American Music in the time of Thomas Eakins"; "Alexandra Hughes, Italian Arias & Duets" **Hob./spts.:** Physical fitness, the outdoors, sailing, painting; fluent in English, French and German **SIC code:** 79 **E-mail:** alexamezza@aol.com **Web address:** www.alexandrahughes.com

HURTADO, JON R.

Elite Financial Design, LLC
30100 Telegraph Rd.
Suite 480
Bingham Farms, MI 48025

Industry: Financial **Born:** Detroit, Michigan **Univ./degree:** B.A., Business, University of Michigan **Current organization:** Elite Financial Design, LLC **Title:** President/CEO **Type of organization:** Financial design company **Major product:** Wealth accumulation investments, insurance, asset accumulation, recruiting and marketing strategies **Area of distribution:** National **Expertise:** Wealth accumulation, insurance investment, asset accumulation, recruitments, advertising, marketing and strategies **Honors/awards:** Businessman of the Year, House Leadership Committee, 2006; Michigan Businessman of the Year, National Congressional Committee, 2005; National Congressional Committee Leadership Award, 2005; GAMA Leadership and Management Award, 2005 and 2006; Top Partner Award, New York Life, 2003; Top Recruitment Award, New York Life, 2003; Member, National Register's Who's Who for Business Executives; BIA Spike Award for Management and Recruiting Achievement, 2000 **Affiliations:** G.A.M.A.; B.I.A, **Career accomplishments:** Created a number of successful companies. Elite Financial began operations in November of 2003. By mid 2004 had become a multi-million dollar financial services enterprise. Has worked successfully to put together a team to make initial public offerings. Has managed over $100 million of revenue generated from major companies with 2500 employees. **Hob./spts.:** 3 time World Bench Press Champion; 3 time World Power Lifting Champion **SIC code:** 67 **E-mail:** jonhurtado394@msn.com

JACOBY JR., NEIL H.

1434 Midvale Ave.
Los Angeles, CA 90024

Industry: Estate management **Born:** October 20, 1940, Chicago, Illinois **Univ./degree:** B.A., Astronomy, 1965; M.S., Engineering, 1969; Post M.S. Studies, Mathematical Economics, Optimization Theory, Statistics, 1970-72, University of California at Los Angeles **Current organization:** Self-employed **Title:** Property and Investment Manager **Work history:** Lecturing and demonstrating scientific exhibits, Griffith Observatory, 1962; Computer Program Consultant, Western Data Processing Center, 1966-67, Research Assistant in Control Systems, 1967, Teaching Assistant in Astrodynamics, 1968, School of Engineering and Applied Science, Research Assistant in Statistical Analysis of U.S. Corporate Business, 1970-71, Research Assistant Mathematical Economics, 1971-72, Graduate School of Management, University of California at Los Angeles; Staff Scientist, Computer Science Corporation, 1972-76; Systems Analyst, Satellite Control Program, 1977-78, Orbital Analysis, 1979-80, National Oceanographic System Satellite, 1980-81, System Development Corporation **Type of organization:** Estate management **Major product:** Maintenance and management of family estate and investments, astrodynamics problem solving **Area of distribution:** Los Angeles, CA **Expertise:** Management, engineering, astrodynamics **Honors/awards:** Alpha Gamma Sigma (Junior College Honor Society) **Published works:** Numerous including, "Generation of Prag Satellite Lifetime Model Coefficients for Selected Sets of Restraints," System Development Corporation, 1980; Co-author "Preliminary Orbit Determination Method Having No Co-Planar Singularity, "Celestial Mechanics, 1977; Co-author, "Technical Memorandum on the Deep Space Surveillance Satellite," Computer Science Corporation, 1975 **Affiliations:** Sr. Member, A.A.S.; A.I.A.A.; American Association for the Advancement of Science; New York Academy of Sciences; Board of Directors, Homeowners of South Westwood, Inc.; Member, International Biographical Association; Marquis Who's Who **Hob./spts.:** Swimming, surfing, jogging, physical fitness **SIC code:** 73 **E-mail:** neiljacoby@yahoo.com **Web address:** www.geocities.com/researchtriangle/facility/2435

JAMES, JEANNETTE ADELINE

3068 Badger Rd.
North Pole, AK 99705-6117

Industry: Government **Born:** November 19, 1929, Maquoketa, Iowa **Spouse:** James Arthur James **Married:** February 16, 1948 **Children:** James Jr., Jeannie, Alice Marie **Univ./degree:** Attended Merritt Davis School of Commerce; University of Alaska **Current organization:** Alaska Legislature, Administration **Title:** Representative, Advisor **Work history:** Birds Eye Division, General Foods, 1956-66; Pacific Fence & Wire, 1966-69; 1969-present, self-employed business services **Type of organization:** State legislature **Major product:** Legislature, public service **Area of distribution:** Alaska **Expertise:** Accounting, economics, communication, business owner, foster parent **Affiliations:** Rotary; Alaska Miners Association; Greater Fairbanks Chamber of Commerce; North Pole Community Chamber of Commerce; Emblem Club; Women of the Moose **Career accomplishments:** Awards: Arctic Alliance for People, "Community Service Award" 2001; Who's Who in the 21st Century, "Outstanding contribution in the field of business, communication, government" 2001; Alaska Outdoor Council, "Legislator of the Year" 2000; Alaska Chapter of Safari Club Int., "Outstanding courage fighting for continued equality of all Alaska citizens" 2000; National Rifle Assoc., "Defender of Freedom Award" 1994; Golden Heart Shootist Society, Life Membership 2002; University of Alaska-Anchorage, "Tireless Efforts to enact negotiated rulemaking legislation" 2002; Prince William Sound Community College, "Outstanding support" 1996; Alaska Municipal League, "Friend of Municipalities" 1996; International Register of Profiles, 1981; Alaska Psychology Assoc., "Friend of Psychology" 2001; Tanana Valley Sportsmen, "Appreciation-support for rights of Alaskans to protect themselves" 1994; National Federation of Independent Business, "Guardian of Small Business" 1998; Fairbanks Republican Women, "Woman of the Year" 2002; Alaska State Legislature Citation 2003; Alaska Farm Bureau, "Legislator of the Year" 1994; Alaska Farmers Union Life Member 2001; Who's Who in Executives and Professionals 1994-95; Strathmore's Who's Who, Leadership & Achievement Life Member; ABI, "Great Minds of the 21st Century, Business, Communication and Government" 2001 **Hob./spts.:** Bowling, arts and crafts, music, children **SIC code:** 91 **E-mail:** usually@acsalaska,net **Web address:** www.repjames.org

JANES, JANET E.

3278 Cragmoor Ave.
Toledo, OH 43614

Industry: Medical **Current organization:** Owens Medical College **Title:** Professor (Retired from Medical College of Ohio Hospital) **Type of organization:** Hospital/community college **Major product:** Medical services **Area of distribution:** Ohio **Area of Practice:** Administration, education, operating room, sterile processing **Affiliations:** Governor's Commission of Nursing; President, A.O.R.N.; Member, Board of Regents **Hob./spts.:** Gardening **SIC code:** 80 **E-mail:** hayden1@buckeye-express.com

JOHNSON, JANE PENELOPE

P.O. Box 8013
Garden Side Branch
Lexington, KY 40504-3010

Industry: Writing/poetry **Born:** July 1, 1940, Danville, Kentucky **Spouse:** William E. Johnson **Married:** July 15, 1958 **Children:** Buddy Johnson; Robbie Johnson **Univ./degree:** Famous Writers School Graduate, Westport, Connecticut, 1967; Honorary Doctor of Letters, London, England, 1993 **Current organization:** Penny Johnson (Pen Name) Free-Lance Writer **Title:** Freelance Songwriter/World Renowned Poet **Major product:** Poems, songs, gospel songs **Area of distribution:** International **Honors/awards:** Most Admired Woman of the Decade; International Woman of the Year, Cambridge, England; 3 time award winner, Woman of the Year, American Biographical Institute; The National Library of Poetry; Listed, International Who's Who of Intellectuals; "Sing Hosanna" CD sent to U.S. troops in Iraq and around the world, Christmas, 2005; Penny's songs No.1 out of 18; Hilltop Records, Hollywood, California; Who's Who of International Poets "Goldpin" sent to Penny Johnson for excellence in poetry and vision; Appointment - Genius Laureate, USA by Janet M. Evans, President, A.B.I.; Inclusion in 500 Greatest Genius Laureates of the 21st Century; Life Member, American Hall of Fame; Marquis Who's Who in the World, 2007; Lifetime Achievement, A.B.I. **Published works:** Books, "Anthology, Treasured Poems of America"; Noble Laureate" from A.B.I.; "Songs of Honour", worldwide - Penny's poem "Introspection" included according to Nigel Hillary, U.K., 2006-07; "A Penny for Your Thoughts", Penny Johnson, Published by Authorhouse, Bloomington, Indiana, 06-30-04- I.S.B.N. #1-4184-2489-7; Currently in Print-A Poetry book warmly written to lift you up and give you hope **Affiliations:** International Order of Merit; World Literary Academy; Deputy Governor, American Biographical Institute of North Carolina; Laureate Founder - International Society of Poets - Advisor, Nobel House - Empire State Bldg. Poetry Office, U.K. - Paris and Tokyo Publishing **Hob./spts.:** Piano, singing, dancing, walking, swimming **SIC code:** 89 **E-mail:** pennyspoems@yahoo.com **Web address:** www.poetry.com

JONES, ROGER J.

Latham & Watkins, LLP
Sears Tower, Suite 5800
233 South Wacker Dr.
Chicago, IL 60806-6401

LATHAM&WATKINS LLP

Industry: Law **Born:** January 17, 1951, Buffalo, New York **Spouse:** Karen Krawczyk **Married:** May 2, 1970 **Children:** Robert E. Jones, 1970; Deanna E. Mustafa, 1977; 4 grandchildren **Univ./degree:** B.A., Mathematics and History, 1973; M.A., History, 1976; Ph.D., History, 1979; J.D., 1983, State University of New York at Buffalo **Current organization:** Latham & Watkins, LLP **Title:** Partner **Work history:** Tax and ERISA Associate-Phillips, Lytle, Hitchcock, Blaine & Huber 1984-86; Tax Associate-Mayer, Brown & Platt 1987-90; Partner, Tax Controversy Practice-Mayer, Brown, Rowe & Maw, 1991-2005; Partner, Tax Controversy Practice, Latham & Watkins, LLP, 2005-present; Adjunct Professor-Chicago-Kent College of Law 1994-99 **Type of organization:** Law firm **Major product:** Legal services, general practice **Area of distribution:** International **Area of practice:** Federal and state tax law, tax litigation, appellate advocacy **Area of Practice:** Federal and state tax law, tax litigation, appellate advocacy **Honors/awards:** Chambers USA-America's Leading Lawyers for Business, 2004-2007; Illinois Super Lawyers, 2005, 2006, 2007; International Tax Review, World Directory of Tax Advisors, 2001; Phi Beta Kappa, 1973; Sea Grant Fellowship, 1981-83; Teaching Fellowships, 1973-75, 1982-83 **Published works:** "The Life of John Morton, Archbishop of Canterbury and Chancellor of England", "Intercompany Pricing: Getting it Right and What Happens if You Don't", "Staying out of the Lion's Den - U.S. Tax Practice" **Affiliations:** American Bar Association; Illinois Bar Association; New York Bar Association; admitted in Illinois, New York; admitted to U.S. Supreme Court; U.S. Courts of Appeals - 2nd, 6th, 7th, 8th, 9th, 10th and 11th Circuits; U.S. Tax Court, Court of Federal Claims **Career accomplishments:** Frequent speaker at seminars, symposia and conferences on varied tax topics; Editor, International Trade and Business Law Annual 1999-present; Member, Dean's Advisory Council, John Lord O'Brien Law School, S.U.N.Y. at Buffalo 1999-present; have litigated more than 45 Federal and state tax cases, including The Limited, Inc. v. Commissioner, Nestlé Holdings Inc. v. Commissioner, Tele-Communications Inc. v. Commissioner, Westreco Inc. v. Commissioner and Continental Illinois Corp. v. Commissioner **Hob./spts.:** Horseback riding, skiing, hiking **SIC code:** 81 **E-mail:** roger.jones@lw.com **Web address:** www.lw.com

KARSH, JEROME W.

Karsh Consulting P.C.
650 S. Cherry St.
Suite 115
Denver, CO 80246

Industry: Financial **Born:** January 16, 1936, Denver, Colorado **Univ./degree:** M.B.A., Business Administration, University of Denver, 1967; B.S., Finance, University of Denver **Current organization:** Karsh Consulting P.C. **Title:** Chairman of the Board **Type of organization:** Accounting firm **Major product:** Full service public accounting firm **Area of distribution:** National **Expertise:** Business valuations; litigation support; qualified as an Expert Witness in over 2000 court cases; CPA license **Honors/awards:** Reference in "Best Lawyers in America Directory of Experts" **Affiliations:** Colorado Society of Certified Public Accountants; American Institute of Certified Public Accountants **Hob./spts.:** President, U.S. Billiards Association **SIC code:** 87 **E-mail:** jkarsh@karshcpa.com

KATZ, ELLEN H.

Mentor Talk, Inc.
96 Fifth Ave.
Suite 4D
New York, NY 10011-7607

Industry: Business/Education **Born:** January 7, 1935, Long Beach, New York **Univ./degree:** B.S., Home Economics Education, Brooklyn College, City Univ. of New York, 1956; M.S., Secondary Education, Hofstra Univ., 1962; Ph.D., Home Economics in Higher Education, New York Univ., 1992 **Current organization:** Mentor Talk, Inc. **Title:** President/Partner **Work history:** Business experience: Scholastic Magazines, New York, NY, Curriculum Designer, 1973; Coats & Clarke Inc., New York, NY, Hotline Supervisor, 1973-74; Consolidated Edison Co. of New York, Coordinator of Program Dev. & Training, Consumer Affairs, 1975-80; Senior Specialist, Energy Services, 1980-97; Mentor Talk, Inc., New York, NY, President/Partner, 2003-present; Teaching experience: since 1956; most recent, Queens College, City Univ. of New York, Adjunct Assistant Professor, 2003; Brigham Young Univ., Visiting Professor, 2000-01; **Type of organization:** Educational services/career services **Major product:** Career services (career networking, career placement, resume preparation) and educational services (workshops/seminars/classes/research) in career management, career mentoring, career counseling and advice **Area of distribution:** International **Expertise:** Career management and peer review, career mentoring and networking (especially young women), career counseling, career placement, resume preparation, design and implementation of business/education internship programs **Honors/awards:** Assoc. of Home Appliance Manufacturers ALMA Award, 1975, 1976, 1977, 1978; Certificate of Appreciation, Field Study Program, College of Human Ecology, Cornell Univ., 1979; Education Scholastic Research Award, New York Univ., 1988; Certificate of Merit Award, Bureau of Human Services, N.Y. City Public Schools, 1988; Who's Who Among Students in American Univ. and Colleges, 1990; Certificate of Appreciation for Sensitivity and Assistance to Older New Yorkers, N.Y. State Dept. for the Aging, 1990; Honorary Member, Women's Int'l Network of Utility Professionals, 1997; Challenge '96 Team Award Winner, Consolidated Edison Co. of N.Y., 1997 **Published works:** Rowley, M. & Katz., E. (1992), "An Evaluation of Changing Expectations and Perceptions of Professional Organizations", Journal of the Utah Academy of Sciences, Arts and Letters; Katz, E., Dalton, S., Giacquinta, J. (1994), "Status Risk Taking and Receptivity of Home Economics Teachers to a Statewide Curriculum Innovation" (based on doctoral thesis), Home Economics Research Journal; Katz, E., Rowley, M. Eggert, D., Williams, J.D. (pending), "A Model Supporting the Need for Accountability of Professional Organizations in Meeting Different Member Expectations of Benefits", ERIC ED; 31 collective works, articles, journals, papers **Affiliations:** Nat'l Assoc. of Women Business Owners; Nat'l Assoc. of Female Executives; Women's Int'l Network of Utility Professionals; Amer. Assoc. of Family and Consumer Services; Amer. Educ't'l Research Assoc.; Advisory Committee, Eleanor and Lou Gehrig MDA/ALS Center, Columbia Presbyterian Medical Center, NYC; Student/Alumni Networking Events, New York Univ; The Woodhull Institute of Ethical Leadership **Career accomplishments:** Numerous awards and listings from professional organizations and universities **Hob./spts.:** Swimming, reading **SIC code:** 87 **E-mail:** katzl@verizon.net **Web address:** www.mentortalk.com

KEENAN, TERRANCE

435 Sterling St.
Newtown, PA 18940

Industry: Philanthropy **Born:** February 1, 1924, Philadelphia, Pennsylvania **Univ./degree:** B.A., Yale University, 1950 **Current organization:** The Robert Wood Johnson Foundation **Title:** Special Program Consultant **Type of organization:** Philanthropic foundation **Major product:** Health and healthcare grant making **Area of distribution:** National **Expertise:** Program design and implementation, financial services, business development, project management, communications; frequent lecturer and public speaker on medical education **Honors/awards:** Served in U.S. Naval Air Corps in World War II **Published works:** Articles, journals, short fiction books **Hob./spts.:** Walking, gardening **SIC code:** 86 **E-mail:** tkeenan@rwjf.org **Web address:** www.rwjf.org

KRISHNAMURTHY, VENKATARAMU

University of Michigan/VA Hospital
UHB1 D530
1500 East Medical Center Dr.
Ann Arbor, MI 48109

Industry: Healthcare **Born:** May 10, 1971, Sagar, India **Univ./degree:** M.D., Post Graduate Institute of Medical Education and Research, Chandigarh, India, 1997; Residency, Radiology, India, 1994 **Current organization:** University of Michigan/VA Hospital **Title:** M.D./Radiologist/Clinical Assistant Professor **Type of organization:** University/VA hospital **Major product:** Medical education/VA patient care **Area of distribution:** International **Area of Practice:** Interventional radiology, interventional oncology, peripheral vascular interventions; Radiology (Board Certified) **Honors/awards:** Silver Medal for Diagnostic Radiology, PGI; Henry H. Lerner Award, Teaching Excellence, University of Michigan, 2005; Fellowship, Abdominal Imaging, University of Miami, 2001; Fellowship, Vascular Interventional Radiology, Indiana University Hospital, 2001-02 **Published works:** 10 publications, 1 book chapter **Affiliations:** Radiological Society of North America; I.R. Lexicon Committee; American Roentgen Ray Society **Hob./spts.:** Reading **SIC code:** 80 **E-mail:** venkatking@hotmail.com

LE, KIM N.
Kim N. Le, D.D.S.
990 U.S. Hwy. 287N, #112
Mansfield, TX 76063

Industry: Healthcare **Born:** March 14, 1970, Binh Buong, Viet Nam **Univ./degree:** B.S.; D.D.S., Baylor College of Dentistry, 1998 **Current organization:** Kim N. Le, D.D.S. **Title:** D.D.S. **Type of organization:** Private practice **Major product:** Dental care **Area of distribution:** Texas **Area of Practice:** Implants, dentures, cosmetics **Affiliations:** A.D.A.; A.C.P. **Hob./spts.:** Swimming, hiking **SIC code:** 80 **E-mail:** drngale99@yahoo.com

MALANI, ASHOK K.
Heartland Regional Medical Center
53 Faraon St.
St. Joseph, MO 64506

Industry: Healthcare **Born:** December 17, 1969, Jabcharla, India **Univ./degree:** Biology, St. Joseph Junior College, Hyderabad, India, 1986; M.B.B.S., Osmania University, India, 1992 **Current organization:** Heartland Regional Medical Center **Title:** M.D./M.S./F.R.C.S. **Type of organization:** Hospital **Major product:** Patient care **Area of distribution:** St. Joseph, Missouri **Area of Practice:** Hematology, oncology, treatment of cancer and blood disorders **Hob./spts.:** Writing, movies, tennis, photography **SIC code:** 80

MANTA, ROBYN A.
Anzalone Law Offices
98 S. Franklin St.
Wilkes-Barre, PA 18701

Industry: Law **Born:** January 8, 1964, Wilkes-Barre, Pennsylvania **Spouse:** Jude Roth **Married:** October 22, 1994 **Univ./degree:** Certified, Paralegal, Penn State University, 1996; A.S., Business Management, Center for Degree Studies, 2003 **Current organization:** Anzalone Law Offices **Title:** Office Manager/Paralegal **Work history:** Legal Secretary/Receptionist/Computer Operator, Griffith, Aponick & Musto Law Offices, 1983-85; Legal Secretary to William F. Anzalone, Principal, Hourigan, Kluger, Spohrer & Quinn, P.C., 1985-91; Office Manager/Legal Secretary, William F. Anzalone, Esq., 1991-present **Type of organization:** Law firm **Major product:** Legal services **Area of distribution:** National **Area of Practice:** Paralegal, IT consultation, office management, Notary Public **Honors/awards:** Numerous including, "Name the Employee Newsletter" contest winner, Hourigan, Kluger, Spohrer & Quinn; Distinguished Typing Award from Lisa Gialanella, Wilkes-College Nursing Dept.; Letter of Appreciation from Gerard McHugh Jr., Esquire re. coordinating and scheduling legal agenda; Letter of Appreciation from Nancy Wozniak, Administrative Assistant, Hourigan, Kluger, Spohrer & Quinn re. extra effort given during phone crisis; Acknowledgement and Thank You from Wilkes-Barre Chapter of UNICO Annual East-West Football Game **Affiliations:** Paralegal Division, A.T.L.A.; Pennsylvania Association of Notaries; Advisory/Scholarship Board **Hob./spts.:** Reading **SIC code:** 81 **E-mail:** robyn.manta@anzalonelaw.com **Web address:** www.anzalonelaw.com

MASTERSON, THOMAS E.
1417 S. Minnesota Ave.
Sioux Falls, SD 57105

Industry: Healthcare **Born:** March 10, 1949, Windom, Minnesota **Univ./degree:** M.D., University of Minnesota, 1975 **Current organization:** Medical X-Ray Center **Title:** M.D. **Type of organization:** Medical facility **Major product:** Patient care **Area of distribution:** Sioux Falls, South Dakota **Area of Practice:** Interventional radiology **Affiliations:** S.I.R.; A.C.R; R.S.N.A.; A.M.A.; S.D.M.A. **Hob./spts.:** Reading, basketball **SIC code:** 80 **E-mail:** tmasterson@sio.midco.com

MATHRE, OWEN B.

Chem/Qual Consulting
119 Westgate Drive
Wilmington, DE 19808-1427

Industry: Chemicals/quality **Born:** November 26, 1929, Kendall County, Illinois **Univ./degree:** B.A., Harvard College; Ph.D., University of Minnesota **Current organization:** Chem/Qual Consulting **Title:** President **Type of organization:** Business services firm **Major product:** Information, consulting services **Area of distribution:** National **Expertise:** Quality control and quality systems **Affiliations:** 50 year member, American Chemical Society; A.W.W.A.; P.S.A. **Hob./spts.:** Photography, gardening, fishing **SIC code:** 28 **E-mail:** omathre@magpage.com

MCMULLIN, GARY D.

Telmar Distributing Co.
16781 Noyes Ave.
Irvine, CA 92606

Industry: Telecommunications **Born:** April 9, 1937, Kansas City, Missouri **Univ./degree:** B.S., Engineering, University of California at Los Angeles, 1959 **Current organization:** Telmar Distributing Co. **Title:** Executive Vice President **Type of organization:** Testing and distributing company **Major product:** Transmission, distribution and switching circuit cards **Area of distribution:** International **Expertise:** Management consultant, engineer and lecturer **Honors/awards:** Dean's Advisory Board, Elgin Community College; Motorda Science Advisory Board, 1978-79, Department of Navy Fellowships (two); L.A. City Goals Project **Affiliations:** American Society for Quality Control; Certified Quality Engineer **Hob./spts.:** Cosmology, evolution, quantum mechanics, hiking, fishing, opera, classical music **SIC code:** 50 **E-mail:** gary.mcmullin@telmarnt.com **Web address:** www.tlmr.com

MCRAE, GEORGE E.

Mount Tabor Missionary Baptist Church
1701 N.W. 66th St.
Miami, FL 33147

Industry: Religion **Born:** August 13, 1941, Florida **Univ./degree:** B.A., Bethune Cookman College, 1976; M.Div., Morehouse School of Religion, 1984; D.Min., Columbia Theological Seminary, 1993 **Current organization:** Mount Tabor Missionary Baptist Church **Title:** Pastor **Type of organization:** Church **Major product:** Religious services, education **Area of distribution:** Miami, Florida **Expertise:** Spiritual leadership **Affiliations:** Florida General Baptist Convention Inc. **Hob./spts.:** Salt and freshwater fishing **SIC code:** 86 **E-mail:** Tabor1701@aol.com

MEANOR, H. CURTIS

Podvey, Sachs, Meanor, Catenacci, Hildner, Cocoziello & Chattman
1 Riverfront Plaza
8th floor
Newark, NJ 07102

Industry: Law **Born:** October 6, 1929, Cleveland, Ohio **Univ./degree:** LL.B., Rutgers University Law School, 1955 **Current organization:** Podvey, Sachs, Meanor, Catenacci, Hildner & Cocoziello **Title:** Attorney **Type of organization:** Law firm **Major product:** Legal services **Area of distribution:** New Jersey and New York metropolitan area **Area of Practice:** Arbitration and mediation of complex cases **Honors/awards:** When nominated to the U.S. District Court, District of New Jersey, was rated exceptionally well-qualified by unanimous vote by the American Bar Association Committee on Judiciary **Affiliations:** Life Member, American Law Institute; A.A.A.; C.P.R.; Judge of the Superior Court, Law Division (4 years); Judge of the Superior Court, Appellate Division (1 year); Judge of the U.S. District Court, District of New Jersey (8½ years) **Hob./spts.:** Golf **SIC code:** 81 **E-mail:** hmeanor@podveysachs.com

MILLER, LINCOLN P.

Lincoln P. Miller, M.D.
1500 Pleasant Valley Way
Suite 201
West Orange, NJ 07050

Industry: Medical **Born:** October 27, 1957, New York, New York **Spouse:** Nancy B. Kalkin **Married:** September 22, 1992 **Children:** Graham 9, Georgia 8, Dorothea 4 **Univ./degree:** M.D., University of Tel Aviv Sackler School of Medicine, 1985 **Current organization:** New Jersey Medical School **Title:** Associate Professor **Type of organization:** Medical school **Major product:** Medical education **Area of distribution:** National **Expertise:** Board Certified, Internal Medicine, 1988; Board Certified, Infectious Diseases, 2000 **Honors/awards:** National Research Council; Senior Associateship Award, 1992, 1994 **Affiliations:** American Society of Microbiology; American College of Physicians **Hob./spts.:** Running, bird watching **SIC code:** 82 **E-mail:** millerlpnyc@aol.com

MINKWITZ, MARGARET C.

Zeneca Pharmaceuticals
1800 Concord Pike
Wilmington, DE 19856-5437

Industry: Pharmaceuticals **Born:** June 30, 1946, Corning, New York **Spouse:** Vernon C. Minkwitz **Married:** September, 1990 **Children:** Catherine Flavin, Richard Cecce, Leanna Coates, Florence Cecce; Grandchildren: Christina, Michael, Rebecca and Matthew Flavin, George H. Coates V **Univ./degree:** A.A.S., Corning Community College; B.S., 1980, Elmira College; M.S., 1983; Ph.D., 1986, Cornell University **Current organization:** AstraZeneca **Title:** Director, Biostatistics Products Team Leader **Work history:** Pharmaceutical industry since Ph.D., Biostatistician at Dupont; Biostatistics team leader ICI, Zeneca, Associate Director in Medical Affairs managing statistics, data management and medical writing at Zeneca, Director, biostatistics product team leader for anti-infective products and central nervous system products at AstraZeneca; Responsibilities include insuring statistical resource available to provide statistical input for clinical trials (protocol development through reporting), FDA interactions and publications **Type of organization:** Pharmaceutical company, research and development of prescription drugs **Major product:** Prilosec®, Zestril®, Diprivan®, Merrem®, Nolvadex®, Rhinocort®, Accolate®, Zomig® **Area of distribution:** International **Expertise:** Biostatistics, project management, management **Published works:** Co-author of 15 articles in various medical journals for Accolate® and 2 for Merrem® **Affiliations:** American Statistical Association, International Biometrics Society, Past Secretary, Vice President, President, Symposia Chairman for the Delaware Chapter of the American Statistical Association **Career accomplishments:** Responsible for statistical support of the US marketing approval for Accolate® including participation in the FDA advisory panel 1996; managed 30 staff supporting Zeneca marketed products, producing significant number of scientific publications to support the marketed products **Hob./spts.:** Singing, AstraZeneca singers, St. Mary of the Assumption choir; sewing, knitting, needlework **SIC code:** 28 **E-mail:** margaret.minkwitz@astrazeneca.com **Web address:** www.astrazeneca.com

MIZUSHIMA, MASATAKA
523 Theresa Dr.
Boulder, CO 80303

Industry: Education **Born:** March 30, 1923, Tokyo, Japan **Spouse:** Tsuboi Yoneko **Married:** December, 1955 **Children:** Nanko, 50; Naomi, 48; Nori, 47, Nobuko, 46; Nieret, 43 **Univ./degree:** Degree Rigakushi, Chemistry, 1946; Degree Rigakuhakushi, Sc. Dr. in Physics, 1951; Ph.D., 1952, University of Tokyo; **Current organization:** University of Colorado at Boulder **Title:** Professor of Physics Emeritus **Work history:** Research Assistant in Physics, University of Tokyo, 1957-52; Research Associate in Physics, University of Tokyo, 1947-52; Research Associate in Physics, Duke University, 1952-55; Assistant Professor of Physics, University of Colorado, 1955-58; Associate Professor of Physics, University of Colorado, 1958-60; Professor of Physics, University of Colorado, 1960-89; Physicist, National Bureau of Standards, Boulder, 1955-63; Visiting Professor: University of Tokyo, Japan, 1964; University of Rennes, France, 1964; Institute of Atomic Physics, Romania, 1969-70; University of Nijmegan, Netherlands, 1972; University of Tokyo, Japan, 1972; Honorary Fellow, University College, London, England, 1979-80; Visiting Professor, University of Electro-Communication, Tokyo, Japan, 1980-81, 1987, 1989; Visiting Professor, Nagoya University, Japan, 1986; Visiting Researcher, ATR Optical and Radio Communication Research Laboratories, Osaka, Japan, 1987, 1989; Professor Emeritus of Physics, University of Colorado, 1989-present **Type of organization:** University **Major product:** Higher education, research **Area of distribution:** International **Expertise:** Physics, general relativity, molecular spectroscopy **Published works:** 86 in molecular spectroscopy including 3 books and 41 in general relativity **Affiliations:** American Chemical Society **Career accomplishments:** 20 Ph.D.'s **Hob./spts.:** Music, geology **SIC code:** 82 **E-mail:** mizushima@colorado.edu **Web address:** www.colorado.edu

MOLLOY, JOHN F.
404 S. Via de los Campos
Tucson, AZ 85711

Industry: Law **Born:** August 18, 1917, Los Angeles, California **Spouse:** Barbara (Bobbi) Boyer **Married:** September 13, 2002 **Children:** John Joseph Molloy, Eva Josephine Bansner (deceased), Marjorie Letson, Karen Sebring, Thomas A. Molloy, M.D., Craig William Molloy **Univ./degree:** B.A., with Distinction, 1939; J.D. with High Distinction, 1944, University of Arizona, J.D., with Distinction, University of Kansas City, 1939 **Current organization:** Board of Directors, Emeritus - The National Law Center for Inter-American Free Trade **Title:** Judge/Author **Work history:** Navy Pilot, 1941-1945, retired with rank of Captain; Law Firm of Hall, Catlin and Molloy, 1946-1957; Pima County Superior Court Judge, 1957-1961; State of Arizona Court of Appeals, 1961-1967; Chief Judge of the Court of Appeals, 1967-1969; President, Molloy, Jones and Donahue, 1969-1991; National Law Center for Inter-American Free Trade, 1991-present **Major product:** Legal services **Area of distribution:** Arizona **Area of Practice:** Trial law, writing **Honors/awards:** Honorary Doctor of Laws, University of Arizona, 1986; Distinguished Citizen Award, University of Arizona, 1994 **Published works:** Book, "The Fraternity", Lawyers and Judges in Collusion, published by Paragon House; Authored over 300 decisions for the Arizona Court of Appeals as well as the final Miranda decision for the Arizona Supreme Court **Affiliations:** A.B.A.; Arizona Bar Association; American Trial Lawyers Association; American Board of Trial Advocates **Career accomplishments:** Founded Pima County Court of Conciliation, 1960; President of Arizona Judges Association, 1965; President of the Marshall Foundation for 26 years; President of the Tucson YMCA, 1966-1968; Appointed to the State Board of Regents by Governor Raul Castro, 1976; Commander of American Legion Post 7, 1949-1951; Visiting Professor of the University of Arizona Law School; Served on the Boards on the Arizona Health Sciences Center, The Sarver Heart Center, The Little Chapel of All Nations, El Pueblo Health Center, Arizona Children's Home, Child Guidance Clinic and the St. Elizabeth of Hungary Clinic; President of the largest law firm in the State of Arizona **Hob./spts.:** Tennis, hunting **SIC code:** 81 **E-mail:** johnfmolloy@aol.com

NEFF, MICHAEL A.

Michael A. Neff, P.C.
5 W. 86th St., #6B
New York, NY 10024

Industry: Law **Born:** September 4, 1940, Springfield, Illinois **Univ./degree:** J.D., Columbia University **Current organization:** Michael A. Neff, P.C. **Title:** President **Type of organization:** Law firm **Major product:** Legal services **Area of distribution:** New York, New York **Area of Practice:** Adoption law **Affiliations:** American Bar Association (Family Law Section); National Association of Council for Children; American Association of Adoption Attorneys (Pending) **Hob./spts.:** Writing, training **SIC code:** 81 **E-mail:** maneffpc@aol.com

NEWSOME, JAMES L.

Norwood Clinic
1528 Carraway Blvd.
Birmingham, AL 35234

Industry: Healthcare **Born:** October 28, 1955, Marietta, Georgia **Univ./degree:** M.D., Medical College of Georgia, 1980; Fellowship, Surgical Autopsy Pathology, 1986-87; Fellowship, Cytopathology, Sloan Kettering, 1987 **Current organization:** Carraway Methodist Med. Center/Norwood Clinic **Title:** Chair, Dept. of Pathology **Type of organization:** Hospital and clinic **Major product:** Patient care **Area of distribution:** Birmingham, Alabama **Area of Practice:** Anatomic and clinical pathology, hospital administration **Honors/awards:** Physician's Recognition Award, A.M.A. **Published works:** 2 articles in "Birmingham News" **Affiliations:** Fellow, College of American Pathologists; A.M.A.; International Academy of Cytology; Alabama State Medical Association **Hob./spts.:** Orchid cultivation, scuba diving **SIC code:** 80 **E-mail:** jnews91126@aol.com

NOLAN, MARC A.

Progressive Medical Assoc.
90 East End Ave.
New York, NY 10028

Industry: Healthcare **Univ./degree:** M.D., George Washington University **Current organization:** Progressive Medical Assoc. **Title:** Doctor **Type of organization:** Private practice **Major product:** Patient care **Area of distribution:** New York, New York **Area of Practice:** Cardiology, diagnosis and treatment of adult heart conditions **Published works:** Scholarly articles, peer reviews **Affiliations:** Fellow, American College of Cardiology; Diplomate, The Certification Board of Nuclear Cardiology; Diplomate, American Board of Internal Medicine; American Society of Nuclear Cardiology; American Medical Association **SIC code:** 80 **E-mail:** brianbeck911@hotmail.com **Web address:** www.pmanyc.com

OJAKAAR, LEO

8 Jacqueline Dr.
Hockessin, DE 19707

Industry: Elastomers research and technology **Born:** April 26, 1926 **Univ./degree:** Ph.D., Chemistry, Virginia Polytechnic Institute, 1974 **Title:** Ph.D., E.I. DuPont DeNemours & Co. (Retired) **Type of organization:** Manufacturing, research and technology **Major product:** Kalrex, viton, polymers research and technology **Area of distribution:** International **Expertise:** Research Chemist **Affiliations:** A.C.S.; Sigma Xi **Hob./spts.:** Music **SIC code:** 28

OVERGAARD, WILLARD M.
2023 South Five-Mile Rd.
Boise, ID 83709-2316

Industry: Education **Born:** October 16, 1925, Montpelier, Ohio **Spouse:** Lucia C. (Cochrane) Died: August 10, 2002 **Married:** June 14, 1946 **Children:** Eric Willard, born 1951; Mark Fredrik, born 1957; Alisa Claire, born 1959 **Univ./degree:** B.A., Liberal Arts, University of Oregon, 1949; M.A. Scandinavian Area Studies, University of Wisconsin, 1955; Ph.D., Political Science-Public Law, University of Minnesota, 1969 **Current organization:** Boise State University (Retired 1994) **Title:** Professor Emeritus of Public Law **Work history:** Assistant Professor of International Affairs, George Washington University, 1964-67; Associate Professor & Chairman, Dept. of Political Science & Director, International Studies Institute, Westminster College, New Wilmington, PA, 1970-72; Professor of Public Law, Dept. of Political Science, Boise State University, 1972-94, also Chairman of Dept. of Political Science, 1972-87; Academic Director, Master of Public Administration Degree Program, 1975-85; Director, Taft Institute Seminars for Public School Teachers, 1985-87; Member of Humanities Council, Interdisciplinary Studies in Humanities, 1976-87; Coordinator, Legal Assistant Program, 1990-95; Other professional experience: Instructor of Soviet and International Affairs, U.S. Army Intelligence School, Europe, 1956-62 and Director of Intelligence Research Training Program, 1958-61; Political Analyst, Senior Research Staff, Operations Research Inc., U.S. Army Institute of Advanced Studies, Carlisle, PA, 1967-70; Military Service: U.S. Army Air Corps, 1943-45; U.S. Army-Military Intelligence Officer, 1951-54, U.S. Army Reserve, rank of Major, 1969 **Type of organization:** College/University and special educational programs **Major product:** Higher education **Area of distribution:** National and international **Expertise:** Public law and public affairs (U.S.A. and international) **Honors/awards:** Numerous including, Selected for Who's Who in America, annually, 1988-2005; Men of Achievement, International Biographical Centre, Cambridge, England, 1977; Fulbright Scholarship, Graduate Study, University of Oslo, Norway, 1949-50 **Published works:** Many including, Co-author, "The Communist Bloc in Europe" 1959; Author, "The Schematic System of Soviet Totalitarianism", 3 vols. 1961 **Affiliations:** Associate Member, A.B.A.-Legal Education, Administrative Law, Alternate Dispute Resolutions Sections; Life Member, Reserve Officers Association (Major, USAR, Retired); American Legion **Career accomplishments:** Organized newly created Dept. of Political Science; Designed and implemented a Master of Public Administration Graduate Degree Program **Hob./spts.:** Research law; foreign languages with general language fluency in Danish, Norwegian, Swedish and German; working knowledge of Russian, Spanish, French and Icelandic **SIC code:** 82 **E-mail:** wgaard@velocitus.net

PATEL, BHAILAL (BOB) L.
New Falls Motel
201 Lincoln Hwy.
Fairless Hills, PA 19030

Industry: Hospitality **Born:** July 2, 1947, Virol, India **Univ./degree:** M.S., Biochemistry, University of Scranton, Pennsylvania **Current organization:** New Falls Motel **Title:** President **Type of organization:** Motel **Major product:** Lodging **Area of distribution:** Pennsylvania **Expertise:** Management, development **Hob./spts.:** Travel, cricket, swimming **SIC code:** 70

PUTNAM, REX G.

Entergy Nuclear
17265 River Rd.
Kiliona, LA 70057

Industry: Nuclear power utility **Born:** July 22, 1958, Dallas, Texas **Univ./degree:** M.S., Electrical Engineering, Naval Post Graduate School **Current organization:** Entergy Nuclear **Title:** Systems Engineer Supervisor **Type of organization:** Engineering **Major product:** Waterford 3 nuclear power plant **Area of distribution:** National **Expertise:** I&C systems, control systems **Affiliations:** I.E.E.E.; American Nuclear Society **Hob./spts.:** Sailing **SIC code:** 87 **E-mail:** rputnam@entergy.com

QUINT, BRYAN S.

Booz Allen Hamilton
1299 Farnam St.
Omaha, NE 68102

Industry: Consulting/engineering **Univ./degree:** B.A., History, California State University, Sacramento, 1970; M.S., Systems Management, University of Denver, Colorado, 1972 **Current organization:** Booz Allen Hamilton **Title:** Usstratcom Market Lead **Type of organization:** Consulting firm **Major product:** Systems engineering, modeling and simulation **Area of distribution:** International **Expertise:** Engineering, marketing **Affiliations:** National Contracts Management Association; Armed Forces Communication & Electronics Association **Hob./spts.:** Gardening **SIC code:** 87 **E-mail:** quint_skip@bah.com

REY, AYLED

Dept. of Veterans Affairs Medical Center
1 Veterans Plaza
San Juan 00927, PR

Industry: Medical **Univ./degree:** M.D., Universidad Central Del Este, 1976 **Current organization:** Dept. of Veterans Affairs Medical Center **Title:** M.D., Chief Section of Internal Medicine **Type of organization:** University hospital **Major product:** Patient care **Area of distribution:** San Juan, Puerto Rico **Area of practice:** Internal Medicine, Nephrology **Area of Practice:** Internal Medicine, Nephrology **Hob./spts.:** Family **SIC code:** 80

RIVERA, HECTOR L.

GlaxoSmithKline
S.B. Pharmo PR, Inc.
P.O. Box 11975
Cidra 00739-1975, PR

Industry: Pharmaceuticals **Born:** August 3, 1975, Amityville, New York **Univ./degree:** B.S., Electrical Engineering, University of Puerto Rico **Current organization:** GlaxoSmithKline **Title:** Validation Scientist **Type of organization:** Manufacturing **Major product:** Prescription drugs and medicines **Area of distribution:** Puerto Rico **Expertise:** Verify process **Affiliations:** S.H.P.E. **Hob./spts.:** Tennis **SIC code:** 28 **E-mail:** hector.l.rivera@gsk.com

ROBERTS, EVELYN FREEMAN

Young Saints Scholarship Foundation (Inc. 1967)
2000 Wellington Rd.
Los Angeles, CA 90016-1825

Industry: Education in performing arts **Born:** February 13, 1919, Cleveland, Ohio **Spouse:** Thomas S. (Tommy) Roberts **Children:** Evelyn Anita Roberts, Ernest F. Roberts, Lisa F. Roberts (all deceased), Claire E. Freeman, 64 **Univ./degree:** B.A., Music, Cleveland Institute of Music, 1941; Attended U.S.C. and U.C.L.A. **Current organization:** Young Saints Scholarship Foundation (Inc. 1967) **Title:** President/CEO **Work history:** Worked in the music industry as a performer (piano/electric organ), arranger and composer (recordings, television, movies, stage during the 1950's, 60's and 70's). Worked with such stars as Frankie Laine, Peggy Lee, Louis Prima, Dean Martin, Leslie Uggams, Danny Kaye and Eddie Albert Played shows (Hollywood) at the Moulin Rouge, bandleader at Ciro's and her own club "The Upstairs" on Sunset Strip; Las Vegas: Dunes Desert Inn Hotels; Composed and arranged (as Musical Director) all music for Young Saints appearances at the Nixon White House, 4 Jonathan Winters TV shows, the Ed Sullivan Show, the Andy Griffith Special, performances with community symphony orchestras and the 1984 Olympics. **Type of organization:** Nonprofit (501)(C)(3) **Major product:** Program of free training in performing arts and related technical skills for "at risk" youth **Area of distribution:** Los Angeles, California **Expertise:** Professional musician/educator (training, performing with equal emphasis) **Honors/awards:** Numerous plaques, citations, proclamations from 2 governors, 3 mayors, Congress, state and local officials; Others from community and civic groups; Recipient of Los Angeles Music Week Award, 2003; Induction into the Watts Walk of Fame "Promenade of Prominence", 2006 **Published works:** "Come to Me My True Love" Recorded by Giselle MacKenzie and others); "The Jelly Coal Man" (Recorded by Frankie Laine and others); "Didn't it Rain" and other spirituals **Affiliations:** National Academy of Recording Arts and Sciences (N.A.R.A.S); American Society of Composers, Authors and Publishers (A.S.C.A.P); Songwriters Guild of America; Life Member, American Federation of Musicians (AFL-CIO) **Career accomplishments:** Many recordings, published songs (own publishing, Morrisania music) appearances on TV shows, movies; Successful seminars (4) on the history of black music **Hob./spts.:** Music, record collecting, lecturing, teaching music history **SIC code:** 82 **Phone:** (323)734-5379 **Fax:** (323)734-4997

ROBERTSON, RESA L.

1120 North Walnut St.
Hutchinson, KS 67501

Industry: Healthcare **Born:** March 15, 1952, Arkansas City, Kansas **Spouse:** David L. Robertson **Married:** June 4, 1983 **Children:** Joshua Metteal Robertson, DOB February 4, 1985; Jacob Lee Robertson, DOB May 27th, 1987; Jonathan David Robertson, DOB October 23, 1989 **Univ./degree:** B.S.N., Southwestern College, 2002; M.S.N., Family Nurse Practitioner Specialization, Wichita State University, 2005 **Current organization:** Hutchinson Clinic **Title:** A.R.N.P. **Work history:** Nurse Manger of Cancer and Blood Care, P.C. Ponca City, Oklahoma, 1998-2004; Pediatric Oncology Nurse Practitioner for the Solid Tumor Service, M.D. Anderson Cancer Hospital, Houston, Texas, 1981-1991; Pediatric Oncology Nurse, M.D. Anderson Cancer Hospital, Houston, Texas, 1979-1980; Registered Nurse at Arkansas City, Kansas, 1974-1978 **Type of organization:** Clinic **Major product:** Patient care **Area of distribution:** Hutchinson, Kansas **Area of Practice:** Oncology, 20 years experience **Honors/awards:** National Society of Collegiate Scholars, 2004; Sigma Theta Tau International, Honor Society of Nursing, 2003 - present; Oncology Nursing Society, 1999 - present **Published works:** Numerous including: Jaffe, M.D., N. Raymond, M.D., K., Robertson R.N. P.N.P., R., Effective of cumulative courses of intra-arterial cis-diammenedichloroplatin-II on the primary tumor in osteosarcoma, CANCER, Vol. 63, No 1, January1, 1989; Jaffe, N., Cangir, A., Wallace, S., Robertson, R., Treatment of pediatric bone and soft tissue sarcoma with intra-arterial cis-diammenedichloroplatin-II (CDP)., Contr. Oncol., Vol. 29, pp. 292-305 **Affiliations:** Sigma Theta Tau; Oncology Nursing Society **Career accomplishments:** Speaker to local college nursing students; Transcriptionist of Kansas and local cancer support groups on cancer awareness and detection of breast cancer. Served as preceptor for the advancement of other nurse practitioner students and physician assistants for the care and management of oncology patients. **Hob./spts.:** Cooking, gardening, walking, outdoor gardening **SIC code:** 80 **E-mail:** resalou@cox.net

ROMANKIW, LUBOMYR T.

IBM T.J. Watson Research Center
P.O. Box 218
Yorktown Heights, NY 10598

Industry: Computers and communications **Born:** April 17, 1931, Lviv, Western Ukraine **Univ./degree:** B.Sc., Chemical Engineering, University of Alberta, Canada, 1955; M.Sc., Ph.D., Metallurgy and Materials, Massachusetts Institute of Technology, 1962 **Current organization:** IBM T.J. Watson Research Center **Title:** IBM Fellow/ Chief Scout of Plast-Scout Movement in Ukraine and Diaspora **Type of organization:** Research and development **Major product:** Computers and electronic components **Area of distribution:** International **Expertise:** Electrochemical technology, micro fabrication, magnetics **Honors/awards:** Numerous including the Perkin Gold Medal of the Society of Chemical Industries, 1993 **Published works:** 57 patents, 120+ published inventions, 150+ scientific papers including "Thirty Years of Thin Film Magnetic Heads for the Hard Disk Drives", J. Magn. Soc. Japan, Vol. 24, pp. 1-4, 2000 and "Think Small-One Day It May Be Worth A Billion" Interface (Electrochemical Society), pp. 17-20, 56-57, 1993), 5 book chapters, edited 10 volumes of symposia proceedings in the areas of Magnetic Materials, Processes and Devices and Electrochemistry in Electronics **Affiliations:** Electrochemical Society; ISE; ECS; AESF; IEEE; SPIE; Shevchenko Scientific Society; Ukrainian Engineering Society; Engineering Academy of Ukraine **Career accomplishments:** Dr. Romankiw started the Scout movement for boys and girls in the Ukraine after Ukraine gained independence in 1991. The Scout organization is raising new Western oriented citizens to integrate into the Western world. As Chief Scout, Dr. Romankiw is actively working not only to bring the Ukrainian youth in the world of Scouting traditions of God and country, help to others and obeying Scout laws and leadership, but is engaged in fundraising to support Scouts in Ukraine via the Plast Conference, Inc.-Chief Scout Fund, a USA nonprofit, tax exempt 501(c)(3) organization whose address is: P.O. Box 303, Southfield, NY 10975 **Hob./spts.:** Boy Scouts, fundraising, violin, singing **SIC code:** 87 **E-mail:** romankiw@us.ibm.com **Web address:** www.ibm.com

ROSARIO, ISMAEL TORRES

Hato Rey Hematology Oncology Group
C-8 Calle Honduras
Oasis Gardens
Guaynabo 00969-3452, PR

Industry: Healthcare **Born:** January 26, 1956, Honduras, Puerto Rico **Univ./degree:** B.S., 1987; M.D., 1982, San Juan City Hospital **Current organization:** Hato Rey Hematology Oncology Group **Title:** MD **Type of organization:** Group practice **Major product:** Patient care/medical research **Area of distribution:** International **Area of practice:** Oncology **Area of Practice:** Oncology **Affiliations:** F.A.C.P.; American College of Oncology; National Cancer Institute **Hob./spts.:** Family **SIC code:** 80 **E-mail:** ismael531@aol.com

SANDERSON, JASON H.

74 Piscassic Rd.
Newfields, NH 03856

Industry: Religion **Born:** April 7, 1966, West Burke, Vermont **Univ./degree:** Theological Training **Current organization:** St. Jude's Liberal Catholic Church **Title:** Father **Type of organization:** Liberal Catholic Church **Major product:** Religious service and outreach programs **Area of distribution:** International **Expertise:** Athletes outreach ministry, African missions **Affiliations:** Member, Masons **Hob./spts.:** Writing, reading mysteries, wrestling **SIC code:** 86 **E-mail:** luchepadre@comcast.net

SCHARF, JONATHAN

Exton Dental Health Group
101 J.R. Thomas Dr.
Exton, PA 19341-2652

Industry: Dentistry **Born:** July 18, 1947, New York, New York **Univ./degree:** D.M.D., University of Pennsylvania School of Dental Medicine, 1972 **Current organization:** Exton Dental Health Group **Title:** Dentist **Work history:** Maintained a private practice in Exton, Pennsylvania for thirty years; Served as a continuing education course reviewer for the Pennsylvania Academy of General Dentistry; Currently the new technologies media spokesperson for the national organization **Type of organization:** Private practice **Major product:** Dental care **Area of distribution:** International **Area of Practice:** Cosmetic dental care **Honors/awards:** Included in: Who's Who in Medicine, 1990, Who's Who Among Outstanding Americans, 1994, Who's Who in Dentistry, 1995; President's Awards for outstanding contributions to The American Academy of Cosmetic Dentistry; Voted "Best of the Main Line", Main Line Today, 2003; Best Dentists in America:, 2004, 2005, 2006 **Published works:** Interviews and clinical photographs in Glamour, Woman's World, American Health Magazine; Consulting Editor for Cosmetic Dentistry for the GP, Cosmetic Dentistry Update, Dentistry Today; Member of editorial team of the Esthetic Dentistry Research Group, (Reality) **Affiliations:** American Dental Association; Pennsylvania Dental Association; Chester-Delaware County Dental Association; Academy of General Dentistry; International Association for Orthodontics; American Equilibration Society; Past President, American Academy of Cosmetic Dentistry; Diplomate, American Board of Aesthetic Dentistry **Career accomplishments:** Established the American Academy of Cosmetic Dentistry Educational Endowment Fund; Has created smiles for television and media personalities as well as corporate executives throughout the Main Line, Philadelphia and the Greater Delaware Valley; Visiting Associate Professor, Dept. of Esthetic Dentistry, University of Buffalo School of Dental Medicine; Has trained dentists internationally in Cosmetic Dental Technology, Cosmetic Dental Practice Management and Fiber Reinforcement in Dentistry **SIC code:** 80 **E-mail:** drjscharf@aol.com

SIEGEL, BARRY D.

Recruitment Enhancement Services
7676 Hillmont
Houston, TX 77040

Industry: Professional services **Born:** November 9, 1942, New York, New York **Spouse:** Barbara (Bobbie) Siegel, maiden name Stasko **Children:** Debbie Psifidis, Niki Warren **Univ./degree:** B.S., Business Management, Fairleigh Dickinson University, 1964 **Current organization:** Recruitment Enhancement Services **Title:** President **Type of organization:** Provider of solutions for staffing functions **Major product:** Recruitment Process Outsourcing **Area of distribution:** National **Expertise:** Recruitment marketing, recruiting, hiring process re-engineering, staffing technology **Honors/awards:** Recognized as 'Inventor of Recruitment Process Outsourcing', 'One of the 100 Superstars of Human Resource Outsourcing', HRO Today Magazine **Published works:** "The Keys to Successful Recruiting and Staffing", published by Weddle's, www.weddles.com, ISBN: 1-928734-17-0. Book is about making smart investments in talent acquisition. He has drawn on his 30+ years of experience to craft a roadmap for organizations that realize the importance of preparing now for the competition they will face for top talent in the future. Those that follow his advice will be well positioned to compete for the best talent and, as a consequence, better able to implement brands with power and distinction. He has also written a white paper entitled "The Business Case for Recruitment Process Outsourcing", available at www.resjobs.com **Affiliations:** S.H.R.M. **Career accomplishments:** Joined Bernard Hodes Group in 1971 as an Account Executive and progressed to Account Supervisor, Creative Director, Branch Manager, Regional Manager, Vice President, Senior Vice President, Executive Vice President and President of Interactive and Staffing Solutions. He still holds the last title at Bernard Hodes Group, along with serving as President of Recruitment Enhancement Services **Hob./spts.:** Music, tennis **SIC code:** 73 **E-mail:** bsiegel@resjobs.com

RECRUITMENT
ENHANCEMENT
SERVICES

An Omnicom Group Inc. Company

SIEW, SHIRLEY

Michigan State University
Dept. of Pathology
East Fee Hall, A-634
East Lansing, MI 48824

Industry: Medical **Born:** March 12, 1925, South Africa **Univ./degree:** M.D.; Ph.D., Witwatersrand University, South Africa, 1963 **Current organization:** Michigan State University **Title:** M.D./Ph.D./Professor **Type of organization:** University **Major product:** Medical services **Area of distribution:** International **Area of Practice:** Pathology **Published works:** 90 articles, 3 book chapters **Affiliations:** F.A.C.C.; A.M.A. **SIC code:** 80 **E-mail:** shirley.siew@ht.msu.edu **Web address:** www.ht.msu.edu

SIMMS, WILLIAM A.

Arnett, Draper & Hagood
2300 First Tennessee Plaza
Knoxville, TN 37929

Industry: Law **Born:** February 18, 1946, Lebanon, Tennessee **Univ./degree:** B.A., Political Science, University of the South, Sewanee, Tennessee, 1969; J.D., University of Tennessee Law School, Knoxville, Tennessee, 1971 **Current organization:** Arnett, Draper & Hagood **Title:** Managing Partner **Work history:** Trial Lawyer, Arnett, Draper & Hagood from 1972 to present **Type of organization:** Law firm **Major product:** Legal services **Area of distribution:** Tennessee **Area of Practice:** Trial practice, product liability, insurance defense, construction, aviation **Honors/awards:** Best Lawyers in America, 2007; Strathmore's Who's Who **Published works:** "A Practical Guide to Discovery and Personal Injury Cases", Tennessee Bar Association sponsored seminar on Practical Discovery, November, 1966; "Discovery Tactics and Tips: Depositions", Knoxville Bar Association sponsored seminar, October, 2002; "Ethical Considerations", National Business Institute sponsored seminar entitled Litigating to Win Through Advanced Trial Advocacy, June, 2007 **Affiliations:** I.A.D.C.; F.D.C.C.; President, Tennessee A.B.O.T.A., 2004; T.D.L.A.; A.B.A.; T.B.A.; K.B.A.; Fellow, Tennessee Bar Foundation and Knoxville Bar Foundation **Hob./spts.:** Hunting, shooting, fishing **SIC code:** 81 **E-mail:** bsimms@adhknox.com **Web address:** www.adhknox.com

STAHLHUTH, GAYLE

East Lynne Theater Co.
121 Fourth Ave.
West Cape May, NJ 10016

Industry: Entertainment/Arts **Born:** August 11, Indianapolis, Indiana **Spouse:** Lee O'Connor **Married:** November 8, 1981 **Univ./degree:** B.A., Theatre, University of Indianapolis, 1972 **Current organization:** East Lynne Theater Co. **Title:** Artistic Director **Work history:** Since 1999, directing most of the productions, choosing season, etc. **Type of organization:** Equity professional theatre company **Major product:** Plays (early American playwrights and adaptations about America's theatrical heritage) **Area of distribution:** National **Expertise:** Acting, playwriting, directing, producing **Honors/awards:** Applause Award, New Jersey Theatre Alliance, 1998; Grants: New York State Foundation for Arts; Utah Arts Council; Mid-Atlantic Arts Foundation; New Jersey Humanities Council **Published works:** Play, "Beast in the Jungle"; Article (Backstage), "The Leach Diaries: The First Four Years" **Affiliations:** Actors Equity Association; Screen Actors Guild; American Federation of TV and Radio Artists; Active Member, Dramatists Guild **Career accomplishments:** For her work as an actor, playwright and director, listed among 200 artists of varied disciplines in the National Endowment for the Arts "Directory of Community Artists"; Commissions from Pennsylvania Stage Company and Theatre Works/USA; Perform off-Broadway, regional theatre, film and TV; One-person shows throughout the country **Hob./spts.:** Bicycling, swimming, fishing, model trains **SIC code:** 79 **E-mail:** gaylestahl@aol.com **Web address:** www.eastlynnetheater.org

STANSBERY, DAVID HONOR

32 Amazon Place
Columbus, OH 43214

Industry: Research/Teaching **Born:** May 5, 1926, Upper Sandusky, Ohio **Spouse:** Mary Lois Pease **Married:** June 16, 1948 **Children:** Michael D., 54; Mark A., 52; Kathleen M., 50; Linda C., 48 **Univ./degree:** B.S. Cum Laude, 1950; M.S., 1953; Ph.D., Zoology, 1960, Ohio State University **Current organization:** Ohio State University (Retired) **Title:** Professor Emeritus/Curator Emeritus/Ecologist, Malacologist **Work history:** 1956-62, Instructor, Ohio State University; 1960-1962 Associate Editor, 1962-1965, Editor-in-Chief, Ohio Journal of Science;1962-66, Assistant Professor, Ohio State University; 1962-72, State Curator of Natural History, Ohio State Museum, Ohio Historical Society; 1966-71, Associate Professor, Ohio State University; 1973-74, Visiting Scientist, National Museum of Natural History, Smithsonian Institution; 1972-present, Senior Research Associate, Ohio Historical Center, Ohio Historical Society; 1971-91, Professor of Zoology, Ohio State University; 1970-94, Curator of Crustacea, Ohio State University; 1970-92, Curator of Bivalve Mollusks, Ohio State University; 1970-92, Director, Museum of Zoology, Ohio State University; 1987-91, Visiting Professor, Upper Cumberland Biological Station, Tennessee Technological University; 1988, Visiting Professor, Auburn University, Auburn, AL; 1992, Visiting Scientist, Huazhong Agricultural University, Wuhan, Hubei, P.R. China; 1992-present, Curator of Mollusks, Ohio State University; 1991-present, Professor Emeritus, Ohio State University **Type of organization:** University **Major product:** Teaching, research and service **Area of distribution:** International **Expertise:** Teaching, research, publishing, editing, administration **Honors/awards:** The Ohio Conservation Achievement Award, Ohio Dept. of Natural Resources, 1974; The Oak Leaf Award, The Nature Conservancy, 1977; The Osborn Award, The Ohio Biological Survey, 1999; Life Achievement Award, Society for the Conservation of Freshwater Mollusks, 1999 **Published works:** Numerous articles, 4 book chapters, 1 book (in press) **Affiliations:** Fellow, American Association for Advancement of Science; Fellow, Ohio Academy of Science; American Malacological Society; National Board Member, The Nature Conservatory; Visiting Scientist, Smithsonian Institution; Freshwater Mollusk Conservation Society **Career accomplishments:** Numerous offices held, governing boards, etc. for professional organizations; Authored 223 journal articles and reports between 1952 and 1988; Gave 206 presentations, seminars and guest lectures between 1961 and 1988 (detailed records not kept after 1988) **Hob./spts.:** Family, geology, linguistics, history of science **SIC code:** 82 **E-mail:** stansbery.1@osu.edu

STUCKEY, RONALD L.

RLS Creations
P.O. Box 3010
Columbus, OH 43210

Industry: Printing/publishing **Born:** January 9, 1938, Bucyrus, Ohio **Univ./degree:** B.S., Cum Laude, Biology, Heidelberg College, Ohio, 1960; M.A., Botany, 1962, University of Michigan; Ph.D., Botany, 1965, University of Michigan **Current organization:** RLS Creations **Title:** Owner **Work history:** Professor of Botany, The Ohio State University, 1965-1991 **Type of organization:** Printing and distributing **Major product:** Books, post cards **Area of distribution:** National **Expertise:** Editor, publisher, botanist, teacher **Honors/awards:** Professor Emeritus, Botany, The Ohio State University, 1991; Centennial Honoree, Ohio Academy of Science, 1991; Distinguished Service Award, F.T., Stone Laboratory of The Ohio State University, 1995; Herbert Osborn Ohio Biological Survey Award, 2002; Ohioana Library Book Award, 2003 **Published works:** Numerous scientific books, journal articles, biographical essays, chapters, abstracts; Books, "Edwin Lincoln Mosley (1865-1948)", "Emanuel D. Rudolph's Studies in the History of North American Botany", "Lost Stories" and other books **Affiliations:** International Association for Plant Taxonomy; Botanical Society of America; Past President, 1995; Past Secretary, 1996-99, Ohio Academy of Science; Southern Appalachian Botanical Club; International Bluegrass Music Association; Past President, The Ohio State University Chapter of Sigma Xi, 1981; Past President, The Ohio Academy of Medical History, 1981 **Career accomplishments:** 26 years of teaching Botany; publications of numerous botanical works; as a researcher and author, he is an internationally recognized authority on the identification and geographical distribution of aquatic and wetlands plants in North America **Hob./spts.:** Writing, family and local history, bluegrass festivals **SIC code:** 27

SZUEBER, JUNE ALAINE

672 Crystal Creek Rd.
Perris, CA 92571

Industry: Fine art **Born:** March 25, 1925, Wyoming **Univ./degree:** B.A., Art and Education, Blue Mountain College **Current organization:** Self-employed **Title:** Artist/Educator **Major product:** Fine arts education **Area of distribution:** California **Expertise:** Realistic, fantasy paintings; Volunteer teacher, St. James Catholic School **Honors/awards:** Volunteer of the Year, 2005 **Affiliations:** Riverside Community Artists Association **Hob./spts.:** Community volunteering **SIC code:** 89 **E-mail:** art.teach@verizon.net **Web address:** www.yessy.com and www.artbyjuneszueber.com

TOKARCZYK, EUGENE J.

Fitzgerald's Motel
530 Broadway
Wisconsin Dells, WI 53965-1550

Industry: Hospitality **Born:** March 1, 1950, Jablonka, Poland **Univ./degree:** M.S., Jagiellonian University, Poland **Current organization:** Fitzgerald's Motel **Title:** Manager **Type of organization:** High-end motel **Major product:** Hotel accommodations **Area of distribution:** Wisconsin Dells, Wisconsin **Expertise:** Daily operations oversight **Affiliations:** Catholic Church **Hob./spts.:** Hiking, reading **SIC code:** 70

VON ESCHEN, ROBERT L.

3445 Gladstone Lane
Amarillo, TX 79120-0020

Industry: Consulting **Married:** Widowed **Children:** Eric L., Marc A.; Grandchild: Steven A. **Univ./degree:** B.S.E.E., Montana State University; International Law Studies, University of Liberia; US Federal Regulations, Glendale Community College; Computer Programming, Lakeland Community College; Computer Programs, MicroAge Corp. **Current organization:** BWXT Pantex **Title:** Consultant Engineer **Work history:** As an International Consultant Engineer worked, lived or traveled in most of the U.S. states and 33 foreign countries, in construction management, field engineering, startup engineering, technical investigation or auditing. Most projects were fossil fuel, diesel, combined-cycle, hydro-electric and nuclear electrical power generating facilities, also industrial projects and currently the management of the USDOE Pantex Plant; Assigned as Resident Site Manager for construction management and startup of the West Phoenix Combined Cycle Units 1, 2 & 3, plus the replacement of the Logo Oil Refinery electrical distribution system and Resident Project Manager for development of Pantex Performance Based Assessment Program; Current employment, the last 10 years, has included duties as a Performance Based Assessment Program Engineer, an Internal Program Auditor, the Manager of Maintenance Scheduling, Condition Assessment Survey Inspections, Predictive Maintenance and Facility Betterment, a Facility Maintenance Deficiency Inspector, Predictive Maintenance Specialist, the Hoisting & Rigging Program Administer and a Project Reliability Engineer **Type of organization:** Engineering consulting **Major product:** Facility (O&M) management, engineering **Area of distribution:** International **Expertise:** Technical investigation-audits, inspections, predictive maintenance **Honors/awards:** Listed in Marquis Who's Who-43 publications, 1994 thru 2004; International Biographical Centre (Cambridge, England)-7 publications, 1995 thru 2002; America's Registry, 2002; Many Boy Scouts of America Awards including Silver Beaver **Affiliations:** Institute of Electrical and Electronics Engineers; National Society of Professional Engineers; Texas Society of Professional Engineers; National Defense Industrial Association; Masonic Lodge; Scottish Rite; Shriners; BPO Elks; NRA; Society of American Military Engineers; Association of Former Intelligence Officers **Career accomplishments:** Many technical investigation certifications, a multitude of computer training, plus publication of many manuals, training plans and project standards or Procedures **Hob./spts.:** World travel, writing, coin/stamp collecting **SIC code:** 87 **E-mail:** bobve@amaonline.com

WAGNER, A. JAMES

National Centers for Environmental Prediction, NOAA
5200 Auth Rd.
Camp Springs, MD 20746

Industry: Government **Born:** April 12, 1934, Greenwich, Connecticut **Univ./degree:** B.A., Physics, Wesleyan University, 1956; M.S., Meteorology, M.I.T., 1958 **Current organization:** National Centers for Environmental Prediction, NOAA **Title:** Senior Forecaster **Type of organization:** Government/science service and research **Major product:** Weather and climate forecasts **Area of distribution:** National **Expertise:** Long-range weather forecasts **Published works:** Articles in journals **Affiliations:** Past Board Member, Washington Academy of Science; American Meteorological Society; National Weather Association **Hob./spts.:** Music, reading, photography **SIC code:** 89 **E-mail:** james.wagner@noaa.gov **Web address:** www.ncep.noaa.gov

WAGONER, DONALD G.

Technology Consultant
531 Buckthorn Way
Louisville, CO 80027

Industry: Computers, telecommunication **Born:** September 25, 1946, Kansas **Spouse:** Michele Aroele **Married:** 1981 **Children:** David. 23; Kevin, 19; Hannah, 16 **Univ./degree:** B.S.E.E., University of Illinois, 1972 **Current organization:** Semi retired consultant, IT **Title:** Technology Consultant **Work history:** US Army; IBM; AT&T; Firmware design of IBM SNA products, Architect and Designer of Global encrypted data/voice network **Major product:** Disaster backup and recovery, Global ATM/Frame Relay Network, security **Expertise:** Capacity planning, AI, programming, security, backup, Data Mining, very large network architecture and design **Honors/awards:** Listed in Strathmore's Who's Who **Affiliations:** I.E.E.E.; Tau Beta Pi; Eta Kappa Nu **Career accomplishments:** Built largest IDNX/Timeplex network; Designed and built IBM disaster backup business; Built IBM network that saved IBM $700 million a year; Designed Global network that became the AT&T Frame Relay/ATM Global Internet **Hob./spts.:** tennis, karate, classical guitar **SIC code:** 73 **E-mail:** dgwagoner@msn.com

WEINTRAUB, NEIL

ITT Technical Institute
7955 N.W. 12th St.
Miami, FL 33126

Industry: Education **Born:** April 30, 1934, Brooklyn, New York **Univ./degree:** M.Ed., American Intercontinental University, 2004; B.S., ITT Technical Institute **Current organization:** ITT Technical Institute **Title:** Master Instructor **Type of organization:** College **Major product:** Higher education **Area of distribution:** National **Expertise:** Electronic engineering technology, math, physics **Affiliations:** N.A.R.T.E.; E.T.A.; A.S.E.E. **SIC code:** 82 **E-mail:** docproff@aol.com

WETTERNACH, EDNA P.

445 W. Wilson
Madison, WI 53703

Industry: Real estate **Born:** June 22, 1920, Webb, Iowa **Univ./degree:** B.A., Cedar Falls, Iowa Teachers College; B.A., Business Management & Accounting **Current organization:** The Dowling Apartment Building **Title:** Owner/Manager **Work history:** Assistant Sales Manager, Cecil Whitbone, San Francisco, California; Controller for the Volkswagen distributor in Bremerton, Washington; Sales Representative, Niagara Therapeutic Co. **Type of organization:** Real estate management **Major product:** Rentals **Area of distribution:** Madison, Wisconsin **Expertise:** Project management **Honors/awards:** Received national honors for being the "Top Salesperson Worldwide for a Month", Niagara Therapeutic Co., 1972; Preservation Award Winner, Madison Trust for Historic Preservation, 2003 (for long term care of the historic Dowling Apartments); listed in National Register's Who's Who in Executives and Professionals; nominated by the Governing Board of Editors of the American Biographical Institute for inclusion in the Tenth Commemorative Edition of 2,000 Notable American Women; the Dowling Apartment Building is listed with the State and National Historical Society (it is over 80 years old) **Affiliations:** Daughters of the Nile; Daughters of the American Revolution **Hob./spts.:** Dancing, aerobics, travel, reading, fishing **SIC code:** 65

WINTRINGHAM, NEIL A.

New Dawn Minerals & Exploration
742 Cedarbrook Rd.
Bridgewater, NJ 08807-1209

Industry: Minerals/consulting **Born:** May 1922, Glen Ridge, New Jersey **Children:** Nina Dougherty, Karen Bice, Drew, Jill Kennedy; Grandchildren: Andrew, Christopher, Jonathan, Rebecca Dougherty, Alexander **Univ./degree:** B.S., Chemistry; M.S., Geology, Cornell University, New York **Current organization:** New Dawn Minerals and Exploration **Title:** Mineralogist/ Earth Science Education Consultant **Work history:** 20 years in chemical industry as research and development chemist, technical staff assistant, supervisor of information services and technical editor of paper; 23 years teaching high school biology, general science, earth science, chemistry, physics and geology; 2 years Adjunct Professor, Earth Science Education, Kean University and Rutgers University **Type of organization:** Consulting/exploration **Major product:** Economic mineralogy, earth science education **Area of distribution:** Northeastern U.S. **Expertise:** Mineralogy, pegmatites, earth science education; consultant, editor, author **Honors/awards:** Numerous including, Distinguished Service, New Jersey Earth Science Education, NJSTA Presidential Award, 1993; Outstanding Earth Science Teacher, NAGT, 1986; Elected Honored Member of Leidy Microscopical Society, 2004-05 **Published works:** Author/editor of several books and many technical papers including, Handbook for a Week With Maine Minerals, 3 editions; Mineralogy of the Franklin Limestone, 1961, 1989; New Jersey Oriented Earth Science: A Selected Bibliography, 1991; Maine Checklists and Guidebooks-The Collector's Literature: A Review and Personal Evaluation, 1992, 1993, 2000; Frequent presenter of papers and workshops at New Jersey Science Convention; Frequent lecturer at various mineral clubs and adult groups **Affiliations:** Numerous including, American Chemical Society-Emeritus; Friends of Mineralogy, Director Penn. Chapter; Friends of the Rutgers Museum; Geological Association of New Jersey; Mineralogical Society of America; National Association of Geoscience Teachers; Legion of Honor Member, Society of Mining Engineers **Career accomplishments:** Earth Science Education awards; association with Maine Geological Survey **Hob./spts.:** Micromineralogy **SIC code:** 14

WOLFENSON, AZI U.
PROA Project Promotion AG
3601 N.E. 207th St., #1205
Aventura, FL 33180

Industry: Consulting engineering **Born:** August 1, 1933, Riskani, Romania **Spouse:** Rebeca Sterental **Married:** January 10, 1983 **Children:** Ida, born 1958 (deceased 1994); Jeannette, born 1960; Ruth, born 1962; Moises, born 1966; Alex, born 1970; Michael Ben, born 1989; 9 grandchildren **Univ./degree:** Mech. and Elect. Engineer, 1955; Industrial Engineer, 1967, Univ. Nacional de Ingenieria, Peru; M.S., Industrial Engineering, 1966, Univ. of Michigan; Ph.D., Engineering, Mgmt., 1983, Pacific Western Univ.; Ph.D., Engineering Energy, 1985, Century Univ. **Current organization:** Montecristo Editores/La Razon Newspaper **Title:** Ph.D. Engineering/President/Founder-Director **Work history:** Proj. Mgr., Corporacion Financiera de Desarrollo (COFIDE), 1971-73; Pres., DESPRO project development and consulting firm, 1973-76; Exec. Pres., Electro-Peru, 1976-80; Founder & G.M., La Republica, 1981; Pres., PROA Project Promotion AG, 1982-2005; Correspondent, La Republica, 1982-92; Pres., Board of Editora Sport, 1993-2004; Founder Director, Newspaper, "La Razón", 2001-present **Type of organization:** Engineering consulting **Major product:** Energy, communications **Area of distribution:** International **Expertise:** Energy, management, project promotion and development **Honors/awards:** Numerous state, city and assoc. medals, distinguishes, diplomas and awards including, Appointed Deputy, 1991; Senator, High Chamber, 1996, Int'l Parliament for Safety and Peace; Medal and Diploma for Distinguished Services, Pres. of Peru and Minister of Energy and Mines, 1980; Medal of Recognition, So. Amer. Electrical Development, 1979-80; Exec. of the Year, Gente Magazine, 1979; Medal of Honor from Capítulo de Ingeniería Eléctrica, CIP Peru, Dec. 2003; Special Award, Gente Magazine, Lima, Peru, 2006 **Published works:** Numerous including, El Gran Desafio 1981; co-author, Hacia una Politica Econòmica Alternativa 1982 **Affiliations:** A.S.M.E.; A.I.I.E.; I.I.E.; MTM Assoc.; A.S.E.E.; A.M.A.; A.I.M.; A.E.P.; Amer. Soc. for the Advancement of Science; Institute of Administrative Mgmt.; A.N.S.; Alumni Associations of the Michigan, Pacific Western and Century Universities; F.I.P.E.; F.I.M.E.; F.I.A.M.; F.I.E.E.; Fellow, British Institute of Mgmt.; Peruvian Assoc. of Journalists; PEN Club Int'l; Swiss Assoc. of Writers; Peruvian Circle of Sport Journalists **Career accomplishments:** Dean of Engineering, Executive President of Electro-Peru, responsible for all the electricity in Peru; Founder of very successful newspapers in Peru **Hob./spts.:** Reading, stamp collecting, art collecting, soccer **SIC code:** 87 **E-mail:** aziwolfenson@aol.com

WONG, BARON C.K.W.
Wahiawa Specialty Clinic
128 Lehua St.
Ground floor
Wahiawa, HI 96786

Industry: Healthcare **Born:** December 1, 1970, Kailua, Hawaii **Univ./degree:** B.S. with Distinction, Biology, University of Hawaii, 1992; M.D., John A. Burns School of Medicine, 1997; Training: Internal Medicine Residency, Geriatric Fellowship Program, 2001 **Current organization:** Wahiawa Specialty Clinic **Title:** M.D./Consultant at Wahiawa General Hospital **Work history:** 1997-2000, Clinical Teaching Assistant, University of Hawaii Internal Medicine Residency Program, Honolulu, HI 96813; 2002-present, Assistant Clinical Professor, University of Hawaii Geriatric Medicine Fellowship Program, Honolulu, HI 96817; The Queen's Medical Center/Out-Patient Center, 130 Punchbowl St., Honolulu, HI 96813; Castle Medical Center, 640 Ulukahiki St., Kailua, HI 96734; St. Francis Medical Center-West, 91-2141 Ft. Weaver Rd., Ewa Beach, HI 96706; St. Francis Medical Center-Liliha, 2226 Liliha St., Honolulu, HI 96817; Kalihi-Palama Health Center, 915 N. King St., Honolulu, HI 96817; University of Hawaii Geriatrics Program, 347 N. Kuakini St., Honolulu, HI 96817 **Type of organization:** Hospital, medical centers, clinics **Major product:** Patient care **Area of distribution:** Hawaii **Area of Practice:** American Board of Geriatric Medicine (Board Certified, 2001); American Board of Internal Medicine (Board Certified, 2000); Diplomate of the American Board of Hospital Physicians; Diplomate of the American College of Ethical Physicians; American Board of Medical Specialties; Member and Fellow of the American Board of Hospital Physicians **Honors/awards:** Home Care Physician of the Year, Healthcare Association of Hawaii, Homecare and Hospice Division, 2004; America's Top Physicians Award, 2003; Inclusion, State License Documentation, 2003 and 2006; 2000 Outstanding Intellectuals of the 21st Century, 2004; Outstanding Physician Nominee, The Queen's Medical Center, 2002; Physician's Recognition Award, 2002-03, American Medical Association; James A. Orbison Resident of the Year Award, 1999-2000, University of Hawaii Internal Medicine Residency Program; Mission Effectiveness Award, St. Francis Medical Center **Published works:** Numerous articles and presentations at state/institutional meetings **Affiliations:** American Medical Association; American College of Physicians-American Society of Internal Medicine; American Geriatric Association; Alpha Omega Alpha Medical Honor Society; Hawaii Medical Association; Honolulu County Medical Society; American Association of Family Physicians; American Medical Association-Political Action Committee; Diplomate, Fellow and Member of the American Board of Hospital Physicians; Diplomate of American College of Ethical Physicians, American Board of Medical Specialties, American Biographical Institute, International Biographical Centre **Career accomplishments:** Clinical Teaching for Geriatric Fellows, Medical Residents and Medical Students **Hob./spts.:** Tennis, reading, jogging, spending time with family **SIC code:** 80 **E-mail:** baronwong@hotmail.com

WOODWARD, NEIL W.

Advanced Colon & Rectal Surgery
4200 W. Memorial Rd.
Suite 909
Oklahoma City, OK 73120

Industry: Healthcare **Univ./degree:** M.D., University of Oklahoma, 1956 **Current organization:** Advanced Colon & Rectal Surgery **Title:** M.D. **Type of organization:** Private medical practice **Major product:** Health services **Area of distribution:** Oklahoma **Area of Practice:** Colon and rectal surgery **Affiliations:** Delegate, Oklahoma State Medical Association; Oklahoma County Medical Society **Hob./spts.:** Pilot instructor **SIC code:** 80 **E-mail:** drnww@aol.com

ZAVER, ALLA G.

3 Eliot Hill Rd.
South Natick, MA 01760

Industry: Government/healthcare **Born:** December 26, 1923, Harbin, Manchuria **Univ./degree:** MB. BS (Bachelor of Medicine & Bachelor of Surgery, equivalent to M.D. as per Mass. Medical Board of Registration), Australia University of Queensland Medical School **Current organization:** Social Security Administration **Title:** M.D.; SSA Regional Medical Advisor **Type of organization:** Federal government **Major product:** SSA **Area of distribution:** Region I, New England 6 states, report to Baltimore **Expertise:** Internal medicine, cardiology **Honors/awards:** Outstanding Public Service Award, Social Security Administration, U.S. Dept. of Human Resources (HEW), 1982; Certificate of Appreciation, American Heart Association; Certificate of Appreciation, American Heart Association, Massachusetts Affiliate and Greater Boston, 1989; Active Member Recognition, New York Academy of Sciences, 1984 **Published works:** 8 articles, 5 abstracts including- Zaver, A.G., Nadas, A.S.: Five Congenital Cardiac Defects, A study of the Profile and Natural History, Atrial Septal Defec Secundum Type, Supplement to Circulation 32:#6, 1965, American Heart Association Monography No 12; Zaver, A.G.: Pulmonary Arterial Hypertension, International Anesthesiology Clinics, Pediatric Anesthesia 1:69 August 1962, Little, Brown & Company, Boston, MA; Alla G. Zaver, M.B., B.S., M.R.A.C.P., M.R.C.P. (London), Cardiac Problems in Adolescents, The Medical Clinics of North American, March 1965, Vol 49, No 2, W.B. Saunders Company **Affiliations:** Fellow, Royal Australian College of Physicians MRACP 1956, Fellow PRACP 1973; Member, Royal College of Physicians, London (MRCP), 1957; Fellow, American College of Physicians (FACP), 1965; Fellow, American College of Cardiology (FACC), 1974; American Heart Association; Massachusetts Medical Association; Former Affiliations: British Medical Society; American Association for the Advancement of Science; American Society of Law and Medicine **Career accomplishments:** American Heart Association, chaired many projects and committees while Director of the ICU including Chair of the hospital Quality Assurance Committee **Hob./spts.:** Gardening, nature, music **SIC code:** 94 **E-mail:** agzaver@comcast.net

ZHOU, PING
Stanford University
Hansen Lab
Stanford, CA 94305

Industry: Research/aerospace **Born:** April 21, Beijing, China **Univ./degree:** B.S., University of Chemical Technology at Beijing, China, 1969 **Current organization:** Stanford University, Hansen Lab **Title:** Engineer **Type of organization:** University **Major product:** Higher education **Area of distribution:** National **Expertise:** Gravity Probe B Mission, Accelerometers **Honors/awards:** Chinese Academy of Science 2nd Class Achievement **Published works:** Over 40 publications **Affiliations:** ASM-International, Materials Research Society **Hob./spts.:** Reading, hiking **SIC code:** 87 **E-mail:** ping@relgyro.stanford.edu

Agriculture, Forestry and Fishing

AYALA, PIEDAD L.
Industry: Agriculture **Born:** August 11, 1962, Mexico **Current organization:** Ayala Corp. **Title:** Owner/CEO **Type of organization:** Agricultural corporation **Major product:** Provides laborers to ranchers and farmers **Area of distribution:** California **Expertise:** Farm labor contractor **Affiliations:** M.I.M.E.S.C.A. **Hob./spts.:** Fishing **SIC code:** 2 **Address:** Ayala Corp., 21510 S. Chateau Fresno Ave., Riverdale, CA 93656 **E-mail:** piedadayala8@hotmail.com

CLAYBAUGH, WILLIAM J.
Industry: Agriculture **Born:** September 26, 1951, Henderson, Nebraska **Univ./degree:** Kisswkee College, 1971; B.S., Animal Science, Iowa State University, 1973 **Current organization:** TWJ Farms & Feeds **Title:** Treasurer/Partner **Type of organization:** Manufacturing company **Major product:** Feed **Area of distribution:** Nebraska **Expertise:** Computers **Honors/awards:** Nebraska Delegate to AFBF Beef Advisory Committee, 1988, 1995 **Affiliations:** American Farm Bureau; Nebraska Farm Bureau; Northeast Nebraska Cattleman; National Cattleman Beef Association; Nebraska Poultry Industries; Wayne Country Farm Bureau; U.S. Chamber of Commerce; Nebraska Chamber of Commerce; Past President, Carroll Community Club; Co-chairman, Carroll Centennial Committee; President of Volunteer Association, Carroll Volunteer Fire Department; Administrative Board, Board of Trustees, Wayne First United Methodist Church; Board Member, Providence Medical Center Foundation **Career accomplishments:** Farm produces 800 acres corn, 650 soybeans, 125 acres oats, 125 acres alfalfa, 400 acres grassland, 65 head registers Polled Hereford cows, 370,000 laying hen operation (producing 7.5 million dozen eggs), 15, 000 tons poultry feed, 5,000 tons hog feed, 2,500 cattle, dairy, sheep feed per year **Hob./spts.:** Selling and breeding cattle, research, working on the Internet **SIC code:** 2 **Address:** TWJ Farms & Feeds, 301 Lincoln St., Carroll, NE 68723-0216 **E-mail:** billclay@hunter.net

DEUPREE, JEFF
Industry: Food **Univ./degree:** B.S., Genetics, University of California, 1992 **Current organization:** Delicato Family Vineyards **Title:** Laboratory & Quality Assurance Manager **Type of organization:** Vineyard **Major product:** Wine/grapes **Area of distribution:** International **Expertise:** Chemistry **SIC code:** 1 **Address:** Delicato Family Vineyards, 12001 S. Highway 99, Manteca, CA 95336 **E-mail:** ideupree@delicato.com

DICRUTTALO, ARIC A.
Industry: Forestry **Born:** November 9, 1962, Gloversville, New York **Univ./degree:** A.S., Applied Science, 1983; B.S., Science, 1985, Syracuse University **Current organization:** National Grid **Title:** Supervisor Capital Region Forestry **Type of organization:** Forestry service **Major product:** Vegetative management **Area of distribution:** International **Expertise:** Vegetative management, forestry, arborist **Affiliations:** International Society of Arborists **Hob./spts.:** Fishing, golf, arboriculture **SIC code:** 8 **Address:** National Grid, 558 3rd Ave. Ext., Rensselaer, NY 12144 **E-mail:** aric.dicruttalo@us.ngrid.com **Web address:** www.nationalgrid.com

DREITZLER III, RALPH F.
Industry: Agriculture/equestrian training **Born:** December 11, 1953, Bellevue, Washington **Current organization:** Raflyn Farms, Inc. **Title:** President **Type of organization:** Riding school **Major product:** Equestrian training and instruction **Area of distribution:** U.S. and Canada **Expertise:** Dressage **Honors/awards:** F.E.I. Gold medal **Published works:** Book, "Basics of Dressage" **Affiliations:** U.S. Dressage Federation; Canadian Equestrian Federation; American Horse Council **Hob./spts.:** Flying, boating, scuba diving, the outdoors **SIC code:** 7 **Address:** Raflyn Farms, Inc., 7014 180th St. S.E., Snohomish, WA 98296 **E-mail:** raflyn@aol.com

FINCH, GEORGIA L.
Industry: Education, Trade/Technical and Agriculture **Born:** December 9, 1934, Altoona, Pennsylvania **Current organization:** American School of Dog Grooming/ Majestic Kennels/ Stallion Road Stud Farm **Title:** Owner, Director/Instructor, Breeder **Type of organization:** Dog grooming instruction and dog, horse, Miniature Horse, peacock breeding and retail sales **Major product:** Dog grooming and instruction; breeding and sales of Borzoi and Miniature Schnauzers, all colors including rare white and toy size Schnauzers; breeding and sales of Black Arabians, Miniature Horses and peacocks, all colors including rare white and brown cafe au lait **Area of distribution:** National **Expertise:** Dog grooming and instruction; breeding dogs, showing/judging and breeding horses, Miniature Horses and peafowl **Affiliations:** Better Business Bureau, Past BCOA, Award Chairman, many dog and horse organizations **Hob./spts.:** Showing dogs, horseback riding, art and woodworking, wave runners, classic Cadillac's, c/w dancing **SIC code:** 7 **Address:** 22 Jacobstown Rd., Bldg. #2, New Egypt, NJ 08533

GREEN, CHARLES E.
Industry: Agriculture **Born:** January 23, 1943, Chester, Montana **Univ./degree:** B.S., Microbiology, 1965; Ph.D., Generics, 1970, Montana State University **Current organization:** Seminis Vegetable Seeds **Title:** Senior Vice President, Research **Type of organization:** Development, manufacturing, marketing **Major product:** Seeds and plants **Area of distribution:** International **Expertise:** Molecular, cellular and whole plant biology **Honors/awards:** Father of the Year, Northern California District, National Diabetes Association, 2006 **Hob./spts.:** Travel, woodworking, the mountains **SIC code:** 1 **Address:** Seminis Vegetable Seeds, 37437 State Hwy 16, Woodland, CA 95695 **E-mail:** ed.green@seminis.com **Web address:** www.seminis.com

HUNTER SR., MAXCY P.
Industry: Agriculture **Born:** May 30, 1927, Laurens, South Carolina **Univ./degree:** B.S., Husbandry, Clemson University, 1951 **Current organization:** M.P. Hunter & Sons, Inc. **Title:** President **Type of organization:** Agricultural construction/design services **Major product:** Grading, paving, demolition **Area of distribution:** South Carolina **Expertise:** Administration, breeding beef cows **Affiliations:** State Director, Farm Bureau; VFW; American Legion; Past President, Lion's Club; Masons; Shriners; Trustee, Laurens County School District **Hob./spts.:** Bird hunting, fishing **SIC code:** 7 **Address:** M.P. Hunter & Sons, Inc., 19448 Hwy. 221 North, Laurens, SC 29360

ISIDORO, EDITH ANNETTE
Industry: Nursery/native plants **Born:** October 14, 1957, Albuquerque, New Mexico **Univ./degree:** B.S., Horticulture, 1981; M.S., Horticulture, 1984, New Mexico State University, **Current organization:** Garden of Edith **Title:** Owner **Type of organization:** Native plant nursery **Major product:** Native flowering perennials, ornamental grasses **Area of distribution:** Fallon, Nevada **Expertise:** Horticulture **Published works:** 2 articles **Affiliations:** American Association of University Women; American Society of Horticulture Science **Hob./spts.:** Flute **SIC code:** 1 **Address:** Garden of Edith, 3900 Sheckler Rd., Fallon, NV 89406 **E-mail:** eaim@phonewave.net

KAYE, DOROTHY R.
Industry: Farming **Born:** October 3, 1927, Laclede, Missouri **Spouse:** Joseph I. Kaye, Jr. **Married:** March 26, 1950 **Children:** Cynthia C. Kay Reisinger, 53; Gayle Leah Kaye Allen, 52; Lesa Elaine Kaye Haley, 46; Alicyn Ann Kaye Ehrich, 43 **Title:** Farm Owner & Manager, Kaye Ranch (Retired) **Type of organization:** Ranch **Major product:** Feeder cattle, soybeans, corn **Area of distribution:** National **Expertise:** Irrigation crops, livestock, farm management **Published works:** 3 articles published in Missouri Ruralist, Farmers Electric and Farm Journal **Affiliations:** Former Member, A.B.W.; Board Member, F.C.E.; Board Member, Farm Bureau; Associate Member, American Business Women; University of Missouri Extension Councils & Advisory Committee; Missouri Republican Party; Lifetime Member, United Methodist Church **Career accomplishments:** Expanded the farm acerage - paid for 625 acres since 1972; Installed three Center Pivots of Irrigation; A terrace program on all 1400 acres **Hob./spts.:** Family, spending time with her grandchildren, sewing, flower gardening, M.U. football, basketball **SIC code:** 2 **Address:** Kaye Ranch, R.R.I. Box 56, Sumner, MO 64681

LEWIS, JERRY A.
Industry: Agriculture **Born:** March 3, Concord, New Hampshire **Univ./degree:** B.A., University of New Hampshire, 1962 **Current organization:** Lewis Family Organic Farms **Title:** Owner **Type of organization:** Farm **Major product:** Organic vegetables and herbs **Area of distribution:** Lynchburg, Virginia **Expertise:** Raising organic food **Affiliations:** Retired, U.S. Navy **Hob./spts.:** Gardening, travel, golf **SIC code:** 1 **Address:** 8069 Leesville Rd., Lynch Station, VA 24571-2139 **Phone:** (434)665-1423 **E-mail:** organicjal@aol.com

MITCHELL, ROBERT M.
Industry: Landscape architecture **Born:** March 5, 1953, Miami, Florida **Univ./degree:** B.L.A. Magna Cum Laude, University of Florida, 1975; M.L.A., Harvard University College of Graduate Design, 1977 **Current organization:** Vanasse & Daylor, LLP **Title:** Director of Landscape Architecture **Type of organization:** Land development services **Major product:** Landscape architecture **Area of distribution:** National **Expertise:** Landscape and site design, expert in subtropical native plants **Honors/awards:** Design Award of the Decade, City of Walnut Creek **Published works:** Published in Miami Herald Landscape Architecture Magazine **Affiliations:** Past Section Chair; American Society of Landscape Architects; Council of Landscape Architectural Registration Boards **Hob./spts.:** Golf, photography, **SIC code:** 7 **Address:** Vanasse & Daylor, LLP, 12730 New Brittany Blvd., Ft. Myers, FL 33907 **E-mail:** bmitchell@vanday.com **Web address:** www.vanday.com

OLSON, ANTHONY T.
Industry: Agriculture **Born:** December 27, 1976, Perry, Iowa **Univ./degree:** A.S., Iowa Central Community College **Current organization:** Gold-Eagle Cooperative **Title:** Electrician **Type of organization:** Manufacturing **Major product:** Feed grain, corn, beans, animal feed **Area of distribution:** Iowa **Expertise:** Industrial electrician, PLG programmer **Honors/awards:** Honorary Member, Phi Beta Kappa **Hob./spts.:** Auto racing, golf **SIC code:** 7 **Address:** 805 W. Broadway, Eagle Grove, IA 50533 **E-mail:** newmanroy@yahoo.com

POLLEY, ROBERT D.
Industry: Veterinary medicine **Born:** January 2, 1948, Leavenworth, Kansas **Univ./degree:** D.V.M., Kansas State University, 1976 **Current organization:** Meadowbrook Veterinary Clinic **Title:** D.V.M. **Type of organization:** Veterinary practice **Major product:** Veterinary services **Area of distribution:** Peoria, Illinois **Expertise:** Small animal medicine **Affiliations:** Illinois State Veterinary Medical Association; American Veterinary Medical Association; American Animal Hospital Association **Hob./spts.:** Hunting **SIC code:** 7 **Address:** Meadowbrook Veterinary Clinic, 1624 W. War Memorial Dr., Peoria, IL 61614 **E-mail:** meadowbrookvet@sbcglobal.net **Web address:** www.meadowbrookvet.com

RAY, SHAWN C.
Industry: Professional service **Born:** May 6, 1982, Kannapolis, North Carolina **Current organization:** Shawn C. Ray Co. **Title:** Owner/Operator **Type of organization:** Home services and maintenance **Major product:** Landscaping, interior design, painting, electrical maintenance **Area of distribution:** Kannapolis, North Carolina **Expertise:** Operations and management **Affiliations:** Better Business Bureau; National Arbor Day Foundation; PGA Partner Club **Hob./spts.:** Golf **SIC code:** 7 **Address:** Shawn Ray Co., 6611 Bealgray Rd., Kannapolis, NC 28081 **E-mail:** shawn@shawnrayinc.com

ROBERTS, JERRY D.
Industry: Farming **Born:** August 13, 1936, Bono, Indiana **Current organization:** W.S. Roberts & Sons, Inc. **Title:** President **Type of organization:** Farm **Major product:** Cattle, corn and soybeans **Area of distribution:** International **Expertise:** Management, operations **Affiliations:** County Commissioner **Hob./spts.:** Family activities **SIC code:** 2 **Address:** 10974 Spangler Hill Rd., Campbellsburg, IN 47108

ROBINSON, RANDAL
Industry: Food **Born:** December 4, 1950, Clayton, New Mexico **Current organization:** 21st Century Grain Processing **Title:** Director of Marketing and Sales **Type of organization:** Farmer owned cooperative **Major product:** Wheat flour and food corn **Area of distribution:** Southwest area and Mexico **Expertise:** Sales, marketing **Affiliations:** Paet County President for Texas Farm Bureau; Past Representative for Texas Young Farmers and Ranchers **Hob./spts.:** Family, water and snow skiing, travel, whitewater rafting, calf roping **SIC code:** 1 **Address:** 21st Century Grain Processing, P.O. Box 570, Campas, TX 79015 **E-mail:** randal.robinson@21stcenturygrain.com

SANDERSEN, PAUL
Industry: Landscaping **Born:** July 25, 1959, Montrose, Colorado **Current organization:** Horticulture Unlimited **Title:** Construction Supervisor **Type of organization:** Landscape design service **Major product:** Commercial and residential landscape installation **Area of distribution:** Tucson, Arizona **Expertise:** Management **Affiliations:** Tucson Chamber of Commerce **Hob./spts.:** Fishing **SIC code:** 7 **Address:** Horticulture Unlimited, 3237 N. Richey Blvd., Tucson, AZ 85716 **E-mail:** paul@horticultureunlimited.com **Web address:** www.horticulturelimited.com

SCHILLING, TAMARA J. CRAIG
Industry: Agriculture **Born:** October 17, 1967, Charleston, Illinois **Univ./degree:** B.S., Communications, University of Illinois, 1990 **Current organization:** Monsanto **Title:** Business Team Leader **Type of organization:** Manufacturing, research **Major product:** Corn, soybeans, herbicides technology **Area of distribution:** International **Expertise:** Biotechnology **Affiliations:** Illinois Farmers Bureau; Chemical Fertilizer Association **Hob./spts.:** Family, travel, antiques **SIC code:** 1 **Address:** Monsanto, 800 N. Lindbergh Blvd., St. Louis, MO 63141-7843 **E-mail:** tamara.j.craig.schilling@monsanto.com **Web address:** www.monsanto.com

SELLERS, DON R.
Industry: Production agriculture **Born:** January 16, 1961, Belle Glade, Florida **Univ./degree:** B.S., Animal Science, Auburn University, 1985 **Current organization:** U.S. Sugar Corp. **Title:** Area Manager **Type of organization:** Integrated Agri-Business **Major product:** Sugar **Area of distribution:** Okeechobee, Florida **Expertise:** Sugar cane management; Certified crop advisor **Affiliations:** American Society of Sugar Cane Technologists **Hob./spts.:** Salt water fishing, hunting **SIC code:** 1 **Address:** U.S. Sugar Corp., 2720 N.E. 54th Trail, Okeechobee, FL 34972 **E-mail:** dsellers@ussugar.com **Web address:** www.ussugar.com

TULLOS, RICHARD
Industry: Poultry **Univ./degree:** B.S., Mississippi State University, 1995 **Current organization:** Pilgrim's Pride Co. **Title:** Live Production Manager **Type of organization:** Agriculture/poultry producer **Major product:** Poultry **Area of distribution:** International **Expertise:** All aspects of live production **Affiliations:** A.P.E.N.A. **Hob./spts.:** Hunting, fishing **SIC code:** 2 **Address:** 2881 Rocky Head Rd., Enterprise, AL 36330 **E-mail:** rick.tullos@pilgrimspride.com

WHEELOCK, VICTOR W.
Industry: Food **Born:** September 21, 1956, Chambersburg, Pennsylvania **Current organization:** Wheelock Hatchery Inc. **Title:** President **Type of organization:** Hatchery **Major product:** Chickens **Expertise:** Raising chickens, eggs **Hob./spts.:** Flowers, gardening, planting, U.S. coins, reading, history, hunting **SIC code:** 2 **Address:** Wheelock Hatchery Inc., 2170 Wayne Rd., Chambersburg, PA 17201 **E-mail:** wheel064254@earthlink.net **Web address:** www.wheelockgenealogy.com

Mining

ANDERSON, DAVE
Industry: Mining (stone) **Born:** Milton, Wisconsin **Univ./degree:** B.S., Environmental Health and Safety, University of Wisconsin, Whitewater, 1996 **Current organization:** Halquist Stone Co., Inc. **Title:** Vice President **Type of organization:** Mining, manufacturing, distributing **Major product:** Building and landscape products **Area of distribution:** National **Expertise:** Human resources, public relations, environmental health and safety, strategic planning **Affiliations:** Management Resources Association **Hob./spts.:** Sports, golf **SIC code:** 14 **Address:** Halquist Stone Co., Inc., N51 W23563 Lisbon Rd., Sussex, WI 53089 **E-mail:** davea@halquiststone.com

BOGGS, CRAIG
Industry: Coal Mining **Born:** January 7, 1970, Logan, West Virginia **Univ./degree:** B.B.A., Accounting, Pikeville College, 1993 **Current organization:** Marfork Coal Company, Inc. **Title:** Human Resources Director **Type of organization:** Coal Mining and processing **Major product:** Processing and shipping of coal **Area of distribution:** International **Expertise:** Human resources **Published works:** Editor, company newsletter **SIC code:** 12 **Address:** Marfork Coal Company, Inc., Route 3/1, Whitesville, WV 25209 **E-mail:** cboggs1@earthlink.net

BRITTON, ANDY B.
Industry: Mining **Born:** September 18, 1971, Ely, Nevada **Univ./degree:** Certificate, Heavy Maintenance Planning, Universal Technical Institute **Current organization:** BHP Nevada Mining Co. **Title:** Environmental Specialist III/Coordinator Knowledge Services **Type of organization:** Copper mine **Major product:** Copper concentrate **Area of distribution:** Nevada **Expertise:** Computer networking, environmental compliance **Affiliations:** President, Whitepine Bristlecone Bowman; Whitepine Little League; Whitepine County Deputy Sheriff **Hob./spts.:** Hunting, fishing, camping, travel, golf **SIC code:** 10 **Address:** BHP Nevada Mining Co., P.O. Box 382, Ruth, NV 89319 **E-mail:** andy.b.britton@bhpbilliton.com **Web address:** www.bhpbilliton.com

BURGER, MARTHA A.
Industry: Energy **Univ./degree:** M.B.A., Oklahoma University **Current organization:** Chesapeake Energy Corp. **Title:** Treasurer and Senior Vice President, Human Resources **Type of organization:** Energy producer **Major product:** Natural gas exploration and production **Area of distribution:** Oklahoma **Expertise:** Finance, human resources **SIC code:** 13 **Address:** 2608 W. Country Club Dr., Oklahoma City, OK 73116-4217 **E-mail:** mburger@okenergy.com

CALDWELL, PAUL L.
Industry: Energy **Born:** March 17, 1947, Chandler, Oklahoma **Univ./degree:** B.S.M.E., Oklahoma State University, 1970; M.B.A., University of Denver, 1978 **Current organization:** Mobil Producing **Title:** Managing Director (Retired) **Type of organization:** Oil exploration and production **Major product:** Crude oil and natural gas **Area of distribution:** International **Expertise:** Business management, Registered P.E. in Colorado, California and Oklahoma **Honors/awards:** 1999 Black Engineer of the Year in U.S.A. **Affiliations:** S.P.S.; A.S.E. **Hob./spts.:** Hunting, fishing, golf, outdoor activities **SIC code:** 13 **Address:** RR 1 Box 2204, Chandler, OK 74834 **E-mail:** plcjr@aol.com

CARTY, J.D.
Industry: Natural gas and oil **Born:** January 22, 1968, Paintsville, Kentucky **Current organization:** J.D. Carty Resources, LLC **Title:** Owner **Type of organization:** Drilling contractor/producer **Major product:** Leasing property, contract natural gas and oil drilling **Area of distribution:** Kentucky **Expertise:** Drilling, natural gas and oil production **Hob./spts.:** Trail riding horses **SIC code:** 13 **Address:** J.D. Carty Resources, LLC, 2936 Coon Creek Rd., Salyersville, KY 41465 **E-mail:** jdcartyres@foothills.net

EKPE, EMMANUEL R.
Industry: Petroleum **Born:** August 30, 1963, Kumba **Univ./degree:** M.S., Chemical Engineering, University of Benin, Nigeria **Current organization:** Mobil Producing Nigeria **Title:** Machinery Engineer **Type of organization:** Exploration and production **Major product:** Crude oil, gas, ngl and condensate **Area of distribution:** International **Expertise:** Engineering **Affiliations:** A.F.E. **Hob./spts.:** Preaching **SIC code:** 13 **Address:** Mobil Producing Nigeria, 3225 Gallows Rd., Fairfax, VA 22037 **E-mail:** emmanuel.r.ekpe@exxonmobil.com

ELAM, JACK G.
Industry: Petroleum **Born:** August 25, 1921, Glendale, California **Univ./degree:** B.S., M.S., Geology, University of California at Los Angeles; Ph.D., Geology, Rensselaer Polytechnic Institute, 1960 **Current organization:** Jack G. Elam, Inc. **Title:** Oil Operator/Geologist **Type of organization:** Oil well operations **Major product:** Oil **Area of distribution:** International **Expertise:** Oil exploration **Honors/awards:** Public Service Award, A.A.P.G.; Dedicated Service Award, Local Geological Society **Published works:** 50 publications, 1 book **Affiliations:** A.A.P.G.; G.S.A.; S.I.D.E.S.; S.E.P.M.; West Texas Geological Society **Hob./spts.:** Singing, dancing **SIC code:** 13 **Address:** Jack G. Elam, Inc., 219 N. Main St., Midland, TX 79701 **E-mail:** jelam2501@aol.com

ENZE, CHARLES R.
Industry: Oil and gas/petroleum **Born:** May 13, 1953, South Dakota **Univ./degree:** B.S., Civil Engineering, South Dakota School of Mines and Technology, 1975 **Current organization:** Shell International Exploration and Production **Title:** V.P., Offshore Engineering and Projects **Type of organization:** Petroleum development **Major product:** Development of Hydrocarbons **Area of distribution:** International **Expertise:** Engineering and project management **Affiliations:** A.S.C.E.; S.P.E. **Hob./spts.:** Golf, bird watching **SIC code:** 13 **Address:** Shell International Exploration & Production, 200 N. Dairy Ashford, Houston, TX 77079 **E-mail:** crenze@shellus.com

MINING

FALLON, JAMES K.
Industry: Petroleum **Born:** September 27, 1980, Los Angeles, California **Univ./degree:** B.S.M.E., Tulane University, 2002 **Current organization:** Exxon Mobil **Title:** Mechanical Contract Engineer **Type of organization:** Refining **Major product:** NGL, gasoline, diesel **Area of distribution:** International **Expertise:** Engineering **Affiliations:** A.S.M.E.; Louisiana Professional Engineering and Land Surveying Group **Hob./spts.:** Athletics, outdoor activities, volunteering **SIC code:** 13 **Address:** 6195 N. Major Dr. Apt. 208, Beaumont, TX 77713 **E-mail:** james.k.fallon@exxonmobil.com

FOGEL, JENNIFER L.
Industry: Mining **Born:** April 15, 1976, Los Angeles, California **Univ./degree:** B.S.Zoology, University of Texas, Austin, 1998 **Current organization:** US Borax Inc. **Title:** Technical Associate **Type of organization:** Mining company **Major product:** Borates **Area of distribution:** International **Expertise:** Business development **Published works:** IRG Conference; Forest Products Journal, 2002 **Affiliations:** I.R.G.; F.P.S.; A.A.A.S. **Hob./spts.:** Kickboxing, piano **SIC code:** 14 **Address:** US Borax Inc., 26877 Tourney Rd., Valencia, CA 91355 **E-mail:** jennifer.fogel@borax.com

HALES, DAVID A.
Industry: Top soil, minerals **Born:** September 16, 1949 **Current organization:** David A. Hales Inc. **Title:** President **Type of organization:** Surface mining company **Major product:** Top soil, fill dirt, sand **Area of distribution:** Quinlan, Texas **Expertise:** Surface mining **Hob./spts.:** Arrowhead hunting **SIC code:** 14 **Address:** David A. Hales Inc., 3459 Hwy. 276 West, Quinlan, TX 75474

HIRSCHFELD, ALAN R.
Industry: Mining/construction **Univ./degree:** B.S., Geological Science, University of Florida, Miami, 1985 **Current organization:** Haines and Kibblehouse Group **Title:** Senior Hydrogeologist **Type of organization:** Quarrying and retail **Major product:** Production and sale of aggregates and architectural stone **Area of distribution:** East Coast, U.S. **Expertise:** Public relations, geology, hydrogeology, environmental resolution **Affiliations:** A.E.G. **Hob./spts.:** Sports, coaching hockey, church **SIC code:** 14 **Address:** 219 Laureen Rd., Schwenksville, PA 19473 **E-mail:** hirschfeldl219@comcast.net

HOLGATE, BRAD B.
Industry: Petroleum **Univ./degree:** B.A., Business Administration, Weber State University 1995 **Current organization:** Flying J. Inc. **Title:** Director of Procurement **Type of organization:** Diesel fuel/retail **Major product:** Exploration, retail, refining, transportation of fuel **Area of distribution:** National and Canada **Expertise:** Procurement, contract negotiations **Hob./spts.:** Astronomy, woodworking **SIC code:** 13 **Address:** Flying J. Inc., 1104 Country Hill Dr., Ogden, UT 84403 **E-mail:** brad.holgate@flyingj.com

HURTTE, JAMES E.
Industry: Mining/Processing **Born:** December 14, 1951, Taylorville, Illinois **Univ./degree:** B.S., Mining Engineering, University of Missouri, 1974 **Current organization:** IMC Phosphates Co. **Title:** Safety Manager, Florida Operations **Type of organization:** Mining/processing **Major product:** Fertilizer, phosphate and acid **Area of distribution:** International **Expertise:** Safety management, human resource management, production management, engineering, certified safety professional **Honors/awards:** Listed in Who's Who in the Midwest and Who's Who in Emerging Leaders in America; Team member on Underground Mine Rescue Teams that won Illinois, Kentucky and Ohio State Rescue Contests **Affiliations:** A.S.S.E. **Hob./spts.:** Church, fishing, hunting, coaching youth baseball **SIC code:** 14 **Address:** IMC Phosphates Co., P.O. Box 2000, Mulberry, FL 33860 **E-mail:** jehurtte@imcglobal.com

JAIN, DILIP
Industry: Refractory raw materials **Born:** October 10, 1947 **Univ./degree:** M.S., Ceramic Engineering, Virginia Polytechnic Institute; B.S., Ceramic Engineering, India **Current organization:** Kyanite Mining Co. **Title:** V.P. Technology and Asia Sales **Type of organization:** Mining/manufacturing **Major product:** Kyanite and mullite **Area of distribution:** International **Expertise:** Quality control, R&D, marketing, plant operations **Affiliations:** I.C.I.; A.C.S.; A.S.T.M.; I.S.I. **Hob./spts.:** Reading, golf, travel **SIC code:** 10 **Address:** Kyanite Mining Co., 30 Willis Mountain Lane, Dillwyn, VA 23936 **E-mail:** dilipjain@kyanite.com **Web address:** www.kyanite.com

KLIMA, DENNIS V.
Industry: Oil **Born:** September 9, 1951, Sterling, Kansas **Current organization:** Klima Well Service, Inc. **Title:** President **Type of organization:** Oil services company **Major product:** Oil well services **Area of distribution:** Claflin, Kansas **Expertise:** Well servicing, work over **Affiliations:** A.I.F.; A.E.S.C.; National Federation of Independent Business **Hob./spts.:** 60739 **SIC code:** 13 **Address:** Klima Well Service, Inc., 610 W. Front St., Claflin, KS 67525

KNOX, GORDON SHELDON
Industry: Oil **Born:** November 19, 1924, Denver, Colorado **Univ./degree:** B.S., Geology, University of Oklahoma, 1946 **Current organization:** Knox Industries, Inc. **Title:** President/CEO **Type of organization:** Oil exploration and production **Major product:** Oil, gas **Area of distribution:** Midland, Texas **Expertise:** Geology **Affiliations:** Midland Country Club **Hob./spts.:** Golf, swimming **SIC code:** 13 **Address:** Knox Industries, Inc., 203 W. Wall St., S.W., Midland, TX 79702 **E-mail:** knox@marshill.com

MORITZ, WILLIAM R.
Industry: Energy **Born:** August 14, 1957 **Univ./degree:** A.S., Science, Vermont College, Texas, 1978 **Current organization:** Resource Energy Service Corp. **Title:** Drilling Manager **Type of organization:** Mining **Major product:** Oil and gas drilling **Area of distribution:** National **Expertise:** Mining and drilling **Honors/awards:** Phi Beta Kappa **Affiliations:** American Petroleum Institute; Society of Petroleum Engineers; American Association of Drilling Engineers **Hob./spts.:** Fishing, golf **SIC code:** 13 **Address:** Resource Energy Service Corp., 60 Copano Ridge Rd., Rockport, TX 78382 **E-mail:** wmoritz@renscousa.com **Web address:** www.renscousa.com

MORRISON, CHERYL L.
Industry: Oil and gas **Univ./degree:** B.S., Petroleum Engineering, University of Alabama, 1979 **Current organization:** Chevron Texaco **Title:** Project Manager **Type of organization:** Oil and gas integrated company **Major product:** Oil and gas production, refining and environmental remediation **Area of distribution:** International **Expertise:** Engineering, petroleum **Published works:** 1 article **Affiliations:** Society of Petroleum Engineers **Hob./spts.:** Travel, sightseeing **SIC code:** 13 **Address:** Chevron Texaco, 6001 Bowinger Canyon Rd., San Ramon, CA 94583 **E-mail:** cmorrison@chevrontexaco.com

MUTAMA, KUDA R.
Industry: Gold mining **Born:** December 1, 1963, Melsetter, Rhodesia/Zimbabwe **Univ./degree:** Ph.D., University of British Columbia, Vancouver, 1995 **Current organization:** Barrick Goldstrike Mines, Inc. **Title:** Senior Engineer **Type of organization:** Mining company **Major product:** Gold production **Area of distribution:** International **Expertise:** Thermo-dynamics/fluid mechanics **Published works:** 12 articles **Affiliations:** A.S.M.E. **Hob./spts.:** Reading, technology development, astronomy and cosmology **SIC code:** 14 **Address:** Barrick Goldstrike Mines, Inc., 505 Copper St., #1202, Elko, NV 89801 **E-mail:** kmutama@bgmi.com

NIELSON, WENDELL KEITH
Industry: Consulting **Born:** September 27, 1947, Payson, Utah **Univ./degree:** B.S., Economics, Weber State University, 1969 **Current organization:** Nielsen Land Services **Title:** Manager **Type of organization:** Oil and gas exploration/pipeline right of way **Major product:** Land and agriculture consultation **Area of distribution:** Southeastern U.S. **Expertise:** Landowner relations **Affiliations:** American Association of Professional Landmen; Environmental Assessment Association; National Wildlife Federation; World Wildlife Federation **Hob./spts.:** Professional skydiving, scuba diving; Pilot **SIC code:** 13 **Address:** 207 Montgomery Dr., Lafayette, LA 70506 **E-mail:** wknielson@aol.com

POGGIO, PHILIP J.
Industry: Quarry/mining **Born:** July 1, 1953, Wallingford, Connecticut **Univ./degree:** B.S., English, Quinnipiac College, 1973 **Current organization:** Fairfield Resources Management Inc. **Title:** Operations Manager **Type of organization:** Manufacturing/mining **Major product:** Crushed stone and aggregates **Area of distribution:** Connecticut **Expertise:** Operations management **Affiliations:** National Stone Association; Veterans of Foreign Wars; American Legion **Hob./spts.:** Archery, rifle practice, photography **SIC code:** 14 **Address:** Fairfield Resources Management Inc., 98 Laurel Hill Rd., Brookfield, CT 06804 **E-mail:** frmisales@snet.net

POWELL, SAMUEL S.
Industry: Mining/minerals processing **Born:** November 23, 1959, Louisville, Georgia **Current organization:** Imerys Pigments **Title:** Electrical Construction Supervisor **Type of organization:** Mining **Major product:** Calcium carbonate **Area of distribution:** International **Expertise:** Electrical **Hob./spts.:** Auto repair and restoration **SIC code:** 10 **Address:** 805 N. U.S. Hwy. 221, Adrian, GA 31002 **E-mail:** ssp@imerys.com

RIDER, BOBBY E.
Industry: Mining **Born:** December 25, 1941, Pensacola, Florida **Univ./degree:** B.S., Transportation, University of Alabama, 1965 **Current organization:** Vulcan Materials Co. **Title:** Manager, Safety and Health **Type of organization:** Mining facility **Major product:** Crushed aggregate, asphalt **Area of distribution:** National **Expertise:** Developing and implementing safety and health programs **Honors/awards:** Executive of the Year, International Society of Mining Professionals, 2006; Georgia's Miner of the Year, Georgia Mining Association, 1995 **Published works:** Several safety articles **Affiliations:** University of Alabama Alumni; International Society of Mine Safety Professionals; American Society of Safety Engineers **Hob./spts.:** RV travel, golf, University of Alabama sports fan **SIC code:** 14 **Address:** Vulcan Materials Co., 1 Glenlake Pkwy. N.E., Suite 600, Atlanta, GA 30328 **E-mail:** riderb@vmcmail.com **Web address:** www.vulcanmaterialscompany.com

RYAN, JULIAN G.
Industry: Oil **Born:** October 6, 1913, Medora, Illinois **Univ./degree:** B.S., Chemistry, University of Illinois, 1935 **Title:** Research Engineer, Shell Development Co. (Retired) **Type of organization:** Oil development **Major product:** Oil and gas production **Area of distribution:** National **Expertise:** Fuel and lubricant research **Published works:** Article **Affiliations:** American Chemical Society; Society for American Engineers **SIC code:** 13 **Address:** 664 Halloran Ave., Wood River, IL 62095

SON, ADELINA J.
Industry: Oil & Gas **Univ./degree:** Ph.D., Chemistry, University of Illinois **Current organization:** Champion Technologies **Title:** Dr./Manager **Type of organization:** Manufacturing **Major product:** Chemicals **Area of distribution:** International **Expertise:** Analytical chemistry, materials testing (analytical, physical) **Honors/awards:** Several patents including: US Pat. 5,117,058 Cationic Amide/Ester Compositions as Demulsifiers (May 26, 1992); US Pat. 4,536.297 Well Drilling and Completion Fluid Composition (Aug. 20,1985); US Pat. 4,526,693 Shale and Salt Stabilizing Drilling Fluid (July 2, 1985); Service Award, American Petroleum Institute, 2005; Outstanding Filipino Scientist, Houston, Texas, 1994 **Published works:** Numerous including: Son, A.J. Paper No. 07618, Corrosion 2007; Son, A.J., Paper No. 04373, Corrosion, 2004; Son, A.J. and Sitz, C. Proceedings, International Symposium for Ion Chromatography, San Diego, Ca. (2003) **Affiliations:** American Petroleum Institute; American Chemical Society; American Society for Testing and Materials **Hob./spts.:** Musician **SIC code:** 13 **Address:** Champion Technologies, 3130 FM 521, P.O. Box 450499, Fresno, TX 77245 **E-mail:** adelina.son@champ-tech.com **Web address:** www.champ-tech.com

TATE, JACK M.
Industry: Oil and gas **Born:** October 24, 1946, Carthage, Mississippi **Univ./degree:** A.A.S., Accounting and Business, Hinds College, 1967 **Current organization:** Diversified Land Management **Title:** President **Type of organization:** Oil and gas exploration **Major product:** Oil and gas acquisition **Area of distribution:** National **Expertise:** Oil and gas exploration **Affiliations:** A.A.P.L.; L.A.P.L. **Hob./spts.:** Football **SIC code:** 13 **Address:** Diversified Land Management, 132 Trace Cove Dr., Madison, MS 39110 **E-mail:** geoagent46@aol.com

WAGNER, HANS
Industry: Oil and gas exploration **Born:** February 17, 1952, Holland **Univ./degree:** B.S., Mechanical Engineering, Holland **Current organization:** SBM-IMODCO, Inc. **Title:** Manager of Procurement **Type of organization:** Main contractor **Major product:** Floating production systems **Area of distribution:** International **Expertise:** Mechanical engineering, contracts **Hob./spts.:** Music, tennis **SIC code:** 13 **Address:** SBM-IMODCO, Inc., 1255 Enclave Pkwy., Suite 400, Houston, TX 77077 **E-mail:** wagnerhans@sbmimodco.com

WINTRINGHAM, NEIL A.
Industry: Minerals/consulting **Born:** May 1922, Glen Ridge, New Jersey **Children:** Nina Dougherty, Karen Bice, Drew, Jill Kennedy; Grandchildren: Andrew, Christopher, Jonathan, Rebecca Dougherty, Alexander **Univ./degree:** B.S., Chemistry; M.S., Geology, Cornell University, New York **Current organization:** New Dawn Minerals and Exploration **Title:** Mineralogist/Earth Science Education Consultant **Type of organization:** Consulting/exploration **Major product:** Economic mineralogy, earth science education **Area of distribution:** Northeastern U.S. **Expertise:** Mineralogy, pegmatites, earth science education; consultant, editor, author **Honors/awards:**

Numerous including, Distinguished Service, New Jersey Earth Science Education, NJSTA Presidential Award, 1993; Outstanding Earth Science Teacher, NAGT, 1986; Elected Honored Member of Leidy Microscopical Society, 2004-05 **Published works:** Author/editor of several books and many technical papers including, Handbook for a Week With Maine Minerals, 3 editions; Mineralogy of the Franklin Limestone, 1961, 1989; New Jersey Oriented Earth Science: A Selected Bibliography, 1991; Maine Checklists and Guidebooks-The Collector's Literature: A Review and Personal Evaluation, 1992, 1993, 2000; Frequent presenter of papers and workshops at New Jersey Science Convention; Frequent lecturer at various mineral clubs and adult groups **Affiliations:** Numerous including, American Chemical Society-Emeritus; Friends of Mineralogy, Director Penn. Chapter; Friends of the Rutgers Museum; Geological Association of New Jersey; Mineralogical Society of America; National Association of Geoscience Teachers; Legion of Honor Member, Society of Mining Engineers **Career accomplishments:** Earth Science Education awards; association with Maine Geological Survey **Hob./spts.:** Micromineralogy **SIC code:** 14 **Address:** New Dawn Minerals & Exploration, 742 Cedarbrook Rd., Bridgewater, NJ 08807-1209

Contractors

ACHEK, DAN M.
Industry: Construction **Univ./degree:** M.A., Construction, 1979; M.E., 1982, Baalbeck College; B.A., Architecture, University of Oklahoma, 1988 **Current organization:** Achek Design & Construction **Title:** President **Type of organization:** Building contractor **Major product:** Design and construction, residential/commercial **Area of distribution:** Tri-state **Expertise:** Architectural engineering and construction **Honors/awards:** National Tax Credit Award for Outstanding Design for the Station House Apartments; Historic Preservation Award for Restoration of the Station House Apartments, Preservation Alliance for Greater Philadelphia; Building Excellence Award for Multi-housing Design of Villa Del Caribe; Building Excellence Award for Commercial Building Design of Station House Apartments; Building Excellence Award for Multi-Housing Design on the Rittenhouse School Apartments, Norristown, Pennsylvania; Outstanding College Students of America **Hob./spts.:** Basketball, volleyball, tennis, swimming, reading **SIC code:** 15 **Address:** Achek Design & Construction, 1009 Jones Rd., Gulph Mills, PA 19428 **E-mail:** dachek@comcast.net

ALBARANO, JOHN J.
Industry: Construction **Born:** June 21, 1928, Lilly, Pennsylvania **Univ./degree:** B.S., Penn State, 1952 **Current organization:** Albarano Construction Inc. **Title:** President/Founder **Type of organization:** Construction **Major product:** Commercial and multifamily construction **Area of distribution:** National **Expertise:** Design, build, lease, manage commercial construction **Affiliations:** P.E.A.P.; W.B.S.A. **Hob./spts.:** Amateur collegiate boxing **SIC code:** 15 **Address:** Albarano Construction Inc., 201 Basin St., Williamsport, PA 17701 **E-mail:** jalbarano@suscom.net

AL-BIRMANI, MAAD S.
Industry: Construction **Born:** February 23, 1957, Baghdad, Iraq **Univ./degree:** B.S.C.E., University of the District of Columbia, 1985; M.S., Structural Engineering, University of Maryland, 1987 **Current organization:** Cecco Inc. **Title:** President **Type of organization:** General contractor **Major product:** Construction **Area of distribution:** Virginia **Expertise:** Construction, structural engineering **Affiliations:** Past Vice President, University of the District of Columbia; A.S.C.E. Chapter **Hob./spts.:** Family **SIC code:** 15 **Address:** Cecco Inc., 10804 Sunset Hills Rd., Reston, VA 20190 **E-mail:** cecco4u@hotmail.com

ANDERSON, JOEL
Industry: Construction/Metal products and services **Born:** December 11, 1957, Provincetown, Massachusetts **Univ./degree:** Mechanical Engineering, HB Ward Technical, 1974; Engine Theory & Operation, Wayne Diesel Academy, 1975; Hydraulics, Theory & Operation, N.Y.S. Institute of Fluid Power, 1985; Business Administration, HCI, 2001 **Current organization:** Global Welding & Fabrication Service, Inc., D/B/A Anderson Construction Services **Title:** President/CEO **Type of organization:** Construction/Manufacturing/repair service **Major product:** Pre-engineered structures, steel, stainless steel, aluminum **Area of distribution:** International **Expertise:** State of Florida Certified General Contractor, structural and equipment problem solving **Affiliations:** R.P.C.A.; A.A.R.S; A.A.P.R.C.O.; S.B.C.C.I.; Chamber of Commerce; Special Advisor to Chairman, President's Business Advisory Council Representing Florida Small Businesses **Hob./spts.:** Gymnastics, private piloting, boating, community volunteer activities **SIC code:** 15 **Address:** Global Welding & Fabrication Service, Inc., D/B/A Anderson Construction Services, 1690-A N. Hercules Ave., Clearwater, FL 33765 **E-mail:** joela@globaleval.com **Web address:** www.globaleval.com

ANDERSON, KEITH A.
Industry: Construction **Born:** Klamath Falls, Oregon **Current organization:** Homes of Merit **Title:** General Manager **Type of organization:** Home builder **Major product:** Homes **Area of distribution:** National **Expertise:** Homes, modules **Hob./spts.:** Golf, riding Harley's **SIC code:** 15 **Address:** Homes of Merit, 1915 S.E. State Rd. 100, Lake City, FL 32025 **E-mail:** kanderson@championhomes.net

ARZOUMANIAN, JAGHIK
Industry: Construction **Born:** January 30, 1958, Urmieh, Iran **Univ./degree:** B.S.E.E. with Honors, New York Polytechnic Institute, 1981; M.S., Mathematics/Operations and Research, DePaul University, 1990 **Current organization:** Arzoumanian & Co./Construction by Design **Title:** Vice President **Type of organization:** Architectural design and build company **Major product:** Unique, custom designed homes and commercial projects **Area of distribution:** Chicago and North Shore Suburbs, Illinois **Expertise:** Finance, project management, computer presentations **Hob./spts.:** Golf, travel, theatre, the arts **SIC code:** 15 **Address:** Arzoumanian & Co./Construction by Design, 8707 Skokie Blvd., Suite 204, Skokie, IL 60077 **E-mail:** jaghik@comcast.net

ATTARDO, MICHAEL
Industry: Construction **Born:** December 16, 1947, Palermo, Sicily **Current organization:** PGF Group LLC/MFD Builders and Developers **Title:** Executive Vice President, PGF Group LLC; Founder/President, MFD Builders and Developers **Type of organization:** Builders and developers (construction) **Major product:** General contracting (residential and commercial); specializing in fire and water restoration, dance and recording studios and heating and A/C design **Area of distribution:** New Jersey, New York, Pennsylvania **Expertise:** Commercial, industrial and residential construction **Honors/awards:** Recording Studio and Dance Studio, New York City **Hob./spts.:** Family, bicycling **SIC code:** 15 **Address:** PGF Group LLC/MFD Builders and Developers, 10 Daned Rd., Emerson, NJ 07630 **E-mail:** mfddevelopers@aol.com

AZOFF, CHARLES J.
Industry: Construction **Born:** September 27, 1957, Boston, Massachusetts **Univ./degree:** B.B.A., Business Law, Babson College **Current organization:** CJA Custom Remodeling **Title:** President **Type of organization:** Design, build **Major product:** Custom remodeling, renovation and house building **Area of distribution:** Massachusetts **Expertise:** Residential remodeling **Affiliations:** Society for Human Resource Professionals; Northeast Human Resources Association **Hob./spts.:** NASCAR, football, scuba diving, photography **SIC code:** 15 **Address:** CJA Custom Remodeling, 253 Winter St., Whitman, MA 02382 **E-mail:** chuck@azoff.net **Web address:** www.azoff.net

BABBITT, MERRI WEST
Industry: Plumbing contracting **Born:** November 16, 1963, Warner Robins, Georgia **Current organization:** West Plumbing Sales & Service, Inc. **Title:** Vice President **Type of organization:** Contracting **Major product:** Plumbing sales, service **Area of distribution:** Warner Robins, Georgia **Expertise:** Master Plumber **Affiliations:** Chamber of Commerce; Home Builders Association; Better Business Bureau **SIC code:** 17 **Address:** West Plumbing Sales & Service, Inc., 104 Constitution Dr., Warner Robins, GA 31088 **E-mail:** mbabbitt@alltel.net

BADER, TERRY
Industry: Construction **Born:** January 22, 1958, Farmington, New Mexico **Current organization:** Bryant Electric **Title:** Owner **Type of organization:** Electrical contractor **Major product:** Electrical contracting **Area of distribution:** Texas **Affiliations:** N.F.P.A.; I.E.C. **Hob./spts.:** Gardening **SIC code:** 17 **Address:** Bryant Electric, P.O. Box 3464, San Angelo, TX 76902 **E-mail:** bryelec@wcc.net

BAIRD, JAMES L.
Industry: Building services **Born:** April 21, 1947, Chestnut Hill, Pennsylvania **Univ./degree:** M.B.A., University of Pennsylvania, 1978 **Current organization:** Washington Gas Energy Systems/ACI **Title:** Chief Executive Officer/President **Type of organization:** Contracting **Major product:** Heating, ventilation and air conditioning **Area of distribution:** Reisterstown, Maryland **Expertise:** Engineering, executive marketing and sales **Published works:** AFHRAE Journal, 1999 **Affiliations:** AFHRAE, AEE **Hob./spts.:** Children, golf **SIC code:** 17 **Address:** Washington Gas Energy Systems/ACI, 14 Brian Daniel Ct., Reisterstown, MD 21136 **E-mail:** jbaird@washgas.com

BAKER, BYRON W.
Industry: Construction **Born:** June 11, 1956, Covington, Louisiana **Univ./degree:** B.S.M.E. Candidate, University of Texas at Austin **Current organization:** Global Industries, LLC **Title:** Senior Vice President of Operations **Type of organization:** Marine construction **Major product:** Offshore construction services **Area of distribution:** International **Expertise:** Engineering, oil exploration, operations **Published works:** 6 articles **Hob./spts.:** Family, sports, travel, big game hunting, college football **SIC code:** 16 **Address:** Global Industries, LLC, 8000 Global Dr., Carlyss, LA 70665 **E-mail:** byronb@globalind.com **Web address:** www.globalind.com

BARR, RAYMOND E.
Industry: Construction **Born:** December 6, 1966, Philadelphia, Pennsylvania **Univ./degree:** B.S., Civil/Construction Engineering, Temple University, 1991 **Current organization:** Fletcher-Harlee Corp. **Title:** Project Manager **Type of organization:** Construction **Major product:** Industrial and commercial buildings **Area of distribution:** Pennsylvania **Expertise:** Engineering and construction management **Affiliations:** A.S.C.E. **Hob./spts.:** Family, car enthusiast, avid sports fan **SIC code:** 15 **Address:** Fletcher-Harlee Corp., 240 New York Dr., Ft. Washington, PA 19034 **E-mail:** raymondbarr@msn.com

BELDYK, RICHARD M.
Industry: Construction/steel bridges **Born:** September 25, 1959, Wilmington, Delaware **Univ./degree:** B.M.E., University of Delaware, 1982 **Current organization:** Ohio Bridge Corp. **Title:** Engineer **Type of organization:** Manufacturing/construction **Major product:** Design/build steel bridges **Area of distribution:** National **Expertise:** Engineering **Affiliations:** A.S.M.E.; A.S.S.E.; N.F.P.A.; Society of Fire Protection Engineers **Hob./spts.:** Amateur radio, camping, backpacking **SIC code:** 16 **Address:** Ohio Bridge Corp., 201 Wheeling Ave., Cambridge, OH 43725 **E-mail:** rich_beldyk@member.asse.org **Web address:** www.usbridge.com

BENITEZ QUIÑONES, OLGA M.
Industry: Construction development **Born:** June 18, 1977, San Juan, Puerto Rico **Univ./degree:** B.S., Accounting, University of Puerto Rico **Current organization:** Ensenada Construction Corp. **Title:** Controller **Type of organization:** Construction and housing developers **Major product:** Urban housing **Area of distribution:** National

Expertise: Accounting **Affiliations:** Golden Key Association; Alumni, University of Puerto Rico **Hob./spts.:** Science fiction, going to the beach, family activities **SIC code:** 17 **Address:** Ensenada Construction Corp., 701 Ponce de Leon Ave., Suite 211, San Juan, PR 00907 **E-mail:** benolga@coqui.net

BLALOCK, STEVEN A.
Industry: Construction **Born:** July 1, 1970, Birmingham, Alabama **Current organization:** Gary C. Wyatt General Contractor **Title:** Director of Operations/Partner **Type of organization:** Commercial construction **Major product:** Construction of theaters, churches, hotels, condos, school, office buildings **Area of distribution:** Southeastern U.S. **Expertise:** Oversight, administration and field operations **Affiliations:** Associated Builders and Contractors **Hob./spts.:** Hunting **SIC code:** 15 **Address:** Gary C. Wyatt General Contractor, 4527 Southlake Pkwy., Birmingham, AL 35244 **E-mail:** sblalock@gcwyatt.com

BOISVERT, JAMES P.
Industry: Construction **Born:** June 3, 1950, Lowell, Massachusetts **Univ./degree:** Attended Lowell Technological Institute **Current organization:** Kyoto House **Title:** Sole Proprietor/Owner **Type of organization:** Traditional Japanese craft/residential and commercial services **Major product:** Fine Japanese structures, gardens, ponds **Area of distribution:** Massachusetts **Expertise:** Sukiya style living design and building **Published works:** Featured in Vineyard Style Magazine and Cape Cod Magazine **Hob./spts.:** Swimming, scuba diving, basketball **SIC code:** 17 **Address:** Kyoto House, 20 Winslow Dr., Mashpee, MA 02649

BOLTON, ROBERT F.
Industry: Construction **Born:** October 18, 1942, Dunlop, Iowa **Univ./degree:** Attended Professional Institute, Phoenix, Arizona and Verde School of Real Estate, Sedona, Arizona **Current organization:** Bolton Building & Development Co. **Title:** Owner **Type of organization:** Home building and development **Major product:** Residential construction and remodeling **Area of distribution:** Camp Verde, Arizona **Expertise:** Custom home building, remodeling, real estate investing **Affiliations:** National Home Builders Association; United Methodist Church **Hob./spts.:** Reading history/current events, furniture building **SIC code:** 15 **Address:** Bolton Building & Development Co., 2206 W. Park Verde Rd., Camp Verde, AZ 86322-7902 **E-mail:** boltonrfb@yahoo.com

BOWERS, ROBERT E.
Industry: Construction **Current organization:** Bowers Construction **Title:** Owner **Type of organization:** Construction **Major product:** Buildings **Area of distribution:** Pennsylvania **Expertise:** 21 years estimating, day-to-day operations **Affiliations:** Home Builders Association **Hob./spts.:** Golf, hunting **SIC code:** 15 **Address:** Bowers Construction, 183 Grandview Rd., Hamburg, PA 19526 **E-mail:** hummgbrdlover@comcast.net

BOWINGS, TODD
Industry: Construction **Born:** February 5, 1970, Baltimore, Maryland **Univ./degree:** A.A., Electronic Technician, Essex Community College, Maryland, 1990 **Current organization:** Blumenthal-Kahn Electric Limited Partnership **Title:** Executive Manager **Type of organization:** Electrical contractor **Major product:** Electrical construction/service **Area of distribution:** Maryland **Expertise:** Management **Affiliations:** Masonic lodge **Hob./spts.:** Family, golf, fishing, sports **SIC code:** 17 **Address:** Blumenthal-Kahn Electric Limited Partnership, 10233 S. Dolfield Rd., Owings Mills, MD 21117 **E-mail:** tbowings@bkelp.com **Web address:** www.bkelp.com

BOYCHENKO, ERWIN B.
Industry: Real estate **Born:** January 13, 1954, San Francisco, California **Univ./degree:** B.S., Business Administration/Accounting, California State University at Northridge, 1976; Screen Writing Certificate, UCLA, 2001 **Current organization:** Currey-Riach Co. **Title:** Vice President of Finance **Type of organization:** Land developers/general contractors **Major product:** Land development/commercial and new home development **Area of distribution:** California **Expertise:** Accounting, finance **Hob./spts.:** Photography, writing, tennis, golf **SIC code:** 15 **Address:** Currey-Riach Co., 23480 Park Sorrento, Suite 206B, Calabasas, CA 91302 **E-mail:** curyrich@pacbell.net

BRAME, W. EDWARD
Industry: Construction/remodeling **Born:** February 10, 1940, Evansville, Indiana **Univ./degree:** University of Evansville, 1963; University of Cincinnati, 1965 **Current organization:** Ballwin Siding & Construction Co., Inc. **Title:** President **Type of organization:** Private contractor **Major product:** Home improvements **Area of distribution:** Greater St. Louis , Missouri **Expertise:** Administration, sales **Honors/awards:** National or Regional Contractor of the Year (6 times), National Association of the Remodeling Industry **Affiliations:** N.A.R.I., Home Builders Association; (HBA) West County Chamber of Commerce **Hob./spts.:** Golf, hunting, fishing **SIC code:** 15 **Address:** Ballwin Siding & Construction Co., Inc., 255 Old State Rd., Ellisville, MO 63021 **E-mail:** sales@ballwinsidingandconst.com **Web address:** www.ballwinsidingandconst.com

BRANDLI, OWEN E.
Industry: Construction **Born:** April 8, 1959, Warroad, Minnesota **Univ./degree:** B.A., Business Administration, University of North Dakota, 1981 **Current organization:** Standard Pacific Homes **Title:** Vice President, Operations **Type of organization:** Builder **Major product:** Home production **Area of distribution:** California **Expertise:** Operations, land development, construction, purchasing, warranty **Hob./spts.:** Motorcycling; owns small almond orchards **SIC code:** 15 **Address:** Standard Pacific Homes, 5172 Kiernan Ct., Suite B, Salida, CA 95368 **E-mail:** obrandli@stanpac.com **Web address:** www.stanpac.com

BRODERICK, JASON L.
Industry: Construction **Born:** May 26, 1978, Vancouver, British Columbia **Univ./degree:** B.S., Marketing, Florida State University **Current organization:** Broderick Builders Inc. **Title:** Vice President **Type of organization:** Construction, C-Corp **Major product:** Residential remodeling and construction **Area of distribution:** Nashville, Tennessee **Expertise:** Systems analysis **Published works:** Presentation, "How to Choose a Contractor", Annual Home Show, Nashville, Tennessee **Affiliations:** N.A.H.B.; Remodelers Council **Hob./spts.:** Playing drums, music **SIC code:** 15 **Address:** 5800 California Ave., Nashville, TN 37209 **E-mail:** jason@broderickbuilders.com **Web address:** www.broderickbuilders.com

BROWN, EDWARD B.
Industry: Construction contracting **Born:** January 19, 1969, Cape Cod, Massachusetts **Univ./degree:** B.S., Wentworth University, Boston, 1996 **Current organization:** Goodfellow Bros., Inc. **Title:** Division Manager **Type of organization:** Heavy civil contractor **Major product:** Civil work **Area of distribution:** National **Expertise:** Construction management **Hob./spts.:** Golf, beach, 3 children **SIC code:** 16 **Address:** Goodfellow Bros., Inc., 87 Mile Marker N. Mauka, Kailua Kona, HI 96740 **E-mail:** edb@gbimaui.com

BUELOW, JOHN A.
Industry: Construction **Born:** October 6, 1948 **Current organization:** John Buelow Excavating **Title:** Owner **Type of organization:** Construction contractor **Major product:** Excavating, sewer water, septic **Area of distribution:** MN, WI, TX, UT **Expertise:** Excavating, sewer water, septic **Affiliations:** Board of Directors, M.O.S.C.A.; Historical Equipment Contractors Association **Hob./spts.:** Family, white water rafting, travel **SIC code:** 17 **Address:** John Buelow Excavating, 13254 20th St. North, Stillwater, MN 55082

BUGBEE, ROBERT S.
Industry: Contracting **Born:** August 2, 1952, Jericho, Vermont **Univ./degree:** A.S., Champlain College **Current organization:** Bugbee Insulation Inc. **Title:** Owner **Type of organization:** Contractor **Major product:** Commercial and residential insulation **Area of distribution:** Vermont **Expertise:** Daily operations oversight **Affiliations:** H.B.A. **Hob./spts.:** Skiing, fishing, hunting, tennis, golf, racquetball **SIC code:** 17 **Address:** Bugbee Insulation Inc., 15 North Main St., Jericho, VT 05465

BURKS, WESLEY D.
Industry: Construction **Current organization:** Penhall Co. International **Title:** Project Manager **Type of organization:** Bridge removal contractors **Major product:** Highway rehabilitation, concrete cutting **Area of distribution:** International **Expertise:** Engineering **Hob./spts.:** Deep-sea fishing **SIC code:** 17 **Address:** Penhall Co. International, 6940 Oakridge Pkwy., Austell, GA 30168 **E-mail:** wburks@penhall.com

BURNETTE, KENNETH T.
Industry: Home Improvement **Born:** June 2, 1948, Washington, D.C. **Current organization:** The Burnette Group, LLC (dba Kenstruct 4U) **Title:** President **Type of organization:** General contractor **Major product:** Residential remodeling **Area of distribution:** Washington, D.C. **Expertise:** Carpentry **Affiliations:** N.A.R.I. **Hob./spts.:** Fishing, swimming, horseback riding, camping **SIC code:** 15 **Address:** The Burnette Group, LLC (dba Kenstruct 4U), 3114 Westover Dr. S.E., Washington, DC 20020-3720 **E-mail:** kenstruct4@aol.com

BUSH, THOMAS J.
Industry: Construction **Born:** April 9, 1942, La Porte, Indiana **Current organization:** Bush Builders & Remodeling **Title:** Owner **Type of organization:** Construction contractor **Major product:** Home building and repair **Area of distribution:** Wisconsin **Expertise:** Kitchen and bath remodeling; Certified Electrician **Affiliations:** N.A.R.I. **Hob./spts.:** NASCAR, reading **SIC code:** 15 **Address:** Bush Builders & Remodeling, 6329 248th Ave., Salem, WI 53168-9771 **E-mail:** bushbuilders@yahoo.com

CARTER, WILLIAM P.
Industry: Construction **Current organization:** Carter Glass Co., Inc. **Title:** Vice President, Sales **Type of organization:** Glazing contractor **Major product:** Glass glazing, aluminum systems, skylights **Area of distribution:** Missouri **Expertise:** Custom designed projects **SIC code:** 17 **Address:** Carter Glass Co., Inc., 1608 Locust

St., Kansas City, MO 64108 **E-mail:** billcarter@carterglass.net **Web address:** www.carterglass.com

CASANI, DAVID P.
Industry: Real estate **Born:** March 29, 1942, Philadelphia, Pennsylvania **Univ./degree:** Attended St. Joseph's University **Current organization:** Turnberry Associates **Title:** Senior Projects Manager **Type of organization:** Real estate developer **Major product:** Luxury condominiums **Area of distribution:** Aventura, Florida **Expertise:** Hi-rise construction management **Affiliations:** O.S.H.A.; National Fire Protection Association; National Safety Council **Hob./spts.:** Cooking, reading, home improvement projects **SIC code:** 15 **Address:** Turnberry Associates, 19501 Biscayne Blvd., Aventura, FL 33180 **E-mail:** casanid@turnberry.com **Web address:** www.turnberry.com

CASHMARECK, JOSEPH J.
Industry: Construction **Born:** August 22, 1943, Shamokin, Pennsylvania **Univ./degree:** B.S., Engineering, Bucknell University, 1964 **Current organization:** S.A. Cashmareck Engineering **Title:** President **Type of organization:** General construction **Major product:** Buildings, site work foundations **Area of distribution:** Delaware **Expertise:** Engineering **Affiliations:** A.B.C. **Hob./spts.:** Airplane flying, gardening, wood working **SIC code:** 15 **Address:** 231 Salt Forest Lane, Rehoboth Beach, DE 19971

CASPER, MARIE
Industry: Construction/education **Born:** March 26, 1924, Honesdale, Pennsylvania **Univ./degree:** M.A. Equivalency, Penn State University, 1988 **Current organization:** Simply Elegant Homes & Construction Co., Inc./Western Wayne School District **Title:** Corporate Secretary/Teacher **Type of organization:** Builder/school district **Major product:** Custom homes/elementary and secondary school education **Area of distribution:** Waymart, Pennsylvania **Expertise:** Secretarial duties/teaching **Affiliations:** Monroe County Builders' Association; National Education Association; Better Business Bureau **Hob./spts.:** Vocal music, needle work, sports **SIC code:** 17 **Address:** Simply Elegant Homes & Construction Co., Inc., Western Wayne School District, P.O. Box 937, Kresgeville, PA 18333

CASTILLO, ERNEST E.
Industry: Excavation **Born:** January 28, 1957, Raton, New Mexico **Current organization:** EMC Enterprises, City of Raton **Title:** President, Landfill Manager **Type of organization:** Municipality/excavation **Major product:** Excavation, heavy equipment, landfill management **Area of distribution:** New Mexico **Expertise:** Heavy equipment, management, federal and state regulations **Hob./spts.:** Drag racing, 69 Mach/Mustang **SIC code:** 17 **Address:** EMC Enterprises, City of Raton, HCR 63 Box 507, House 131, Raton, NM 87740-9709

CHESLOCK, STAN
Industry: Architecture **Born:** June 22, 1953, Richmond, Virginia **Title:** Director of Construction Services **Type of organization:** Home builder/construction **Major product:** Single and multifamily homes **Area of distribution:** California **Expertise:** Product design, estimating, purchasing, operations, business development **Affiliations:** B.I.A.; N.A.H.B. **Hob./spts.:** Home renovations, physical fitness **SIC code:** 15 **Address:** 4919 Longview Way, El Cajon, CA 92020 **E-mail:** stancheslock@att.net

CHESTEEN, BENNIE M.
Industry: Plumbing, sheet metal, electrical **Current organization:** C&C and Son Mechanical Inc. **Title:** President/Owner **Type of organization:** Contracting **Major product:** Heating and air conditioning **Area of distribution:** International **Expertise:** Sales, service and installation **Affiliations:** E.A.A.; A.O.P.O **Hob./spts.:** Flying aircraft **SIC code:** 17 **Address:** C&C and Son Mechanical Inc., 5141 Easley St., Millington, TN 38053 **E-mail:** comfortco1@aol.com

CHETRAM, RISHIRAM
Industry: Construction/electric **Born:** February 8, 1954, Guyana, South America **Univ./degree:** Diplomate, Electrical Engineering, City and Guilds of London, 1976 **Current organization:** Joey Electrical Co., Inc./J.N.R. Construction & Installations, Inc. **Title:** President/Master Electrician/Licensed Construction Contractor/Notary **Type of organization:** Electrical contracting, general contracting **Major product:** Electrical services **Area of distribution:** Queens Village, New York **Expertise:** Electrical Installations, maintenance, contracting **Affiliations:** Five Boroughs Electrical Contractors Association **Hob./spts.:** Travel, basketball, boxing **SIC code:** 17 **Address:** Joey Electrical Co., Inc./J.N.R. Construction & Installations, Inc., 214-75 Jamaica Ave., Queens Village, NY 11428

CLUSTER JR., EDWIN A.
Industry: Electrical contracting **Born:** September 23, 1951, Baltimore, Maryland **Current organization:** Primo Electric Co. **Title:** V.P. of Operations **Type of organization:** Electrical contracting company **Major product:** Contracting services **Area of distribution:** National **Expertise:** Operations **Affiliations:** Chairman of the Board, Associated Builders and Contractors **Hob./spts.:** Scuba diving instructor, antique cars **SIC code:** 17 **Address:** Primo Electric Co., 220 Eighth Ave. N.W., Glen Burnie, MD 21061 **E-mail:** ecluster@primoelectric.com

COLE, LARRY J.
Industry: Construction **Born:** May 8, 1958, Quincy, Illinois **Univ./degree:** B.S., Business Administration/Administration and Justice, Minor in Accounting, Culver-Stockton College, 1980 **Current organization:** Cole Construction Co., Inc. **Title:** President **Type of organization:** General contractor **Major product:** New home construction **Area of distribution:** Missouri **Expertise:** Marketing, supervision **Hob./spts.:** Waterskiing, hunting **SIC code:** 15 **Address:** Cole Construction Co., Inc., 808 College St., Canton, MO 63435

COLLIER, HENRY
Industry: Electrical contracting **Born:** March 9, 1949, Akron, Ohio **Current organization:** Court Electric, Inc. **Title:** President **Type of organization:** Construction **Major product:** Commercial, industrial, networks **Area of distribution:** Ohio **Expertise:** All phases of electrical and network hardware contracting **Affiliations:** Former Board Member, A.S.A. **Hob./spts.:** Golf, skiing, biking **SIC code:** 17 **Address:** Court Electric, Inc., 317 Julien Ave., Akron, OH 44310 **E-mail:** emailhc@netscape.net

COLLINS JR., DENVER
Industry: Construction **Born:** October 2, 1932, Akron, Ohio **Univ./degree:** B.S., Civil Engineering, Ohio State University, 1956 **Current organization:** Marshal C. Rardin & Sons, Inc. **Title:** President **Type of organization:** Contracting firm **Major product:** Highway construction **Area of distribution:** Ohio **Expertise:** Civil engineering **Honors/awards:** President, Higher Contracting Association; Hall of Fame, Ohio Contracting Board of Directors **Affiliations:** A.R.T.W.A. **Hob./spts.:** Hunting, golf **SIC code:** 16 **Address:** Marshal C. Rardin & Sons, Inc., 2715 Mogadove Rd., Akron, OH 44312

CONSIDINE III, EUGENE J.
Industry: Construction **Born:** August 19, 1960, Kingston, Pennsylvania **Univ./degree:** A.S., Automotive Technology, Johnson College **Current organization:** Home Building Specialists **Title:** Owner/President **Type of organization:** General contractor **Major product:** New home construction **Area of distribution:** Pennsylvania **Expertise:** Custom homes, high-end construction **Affiliations:** Better Business Bureau **Hob./spts.:** Fishing, hunting **SIC code:** 15 **Address:** Home Building Specialists, 70 Updyke Rd., Hunlock Creek, PA 18621 **E-mail:** homebuildingspecialists.@aol.com **Web address:** www.homebuildingspecialists.com

COOK, DUANE J.
Industry: Construction **Born:** Junction City, Kansas **Univ./degree:** A.S., General Business/Drafting and Design, Mississippi Gulf Coast College, 1981; B.S., Construction Engineering, University of Southern Mississippi, 1991 **Current organization:** Rod Cooke Construction, Inc. **Title:** Project Manager **Type of organization:** Construction **Major product:** Construction services **Area of distribution:** Mississippi and Alabama **Expertise:** Management of daily operation of projects, working with superintendent of projects and architects **Honors/awards:** Who's Who International, 1996 **Hob./spts.:** Service to God and community **SIC code:** 15 **Address:** P.O. Box 2428, Pascagoula, MS 39569 **E-mail:** djcook8099@aol.com

COSTELLO, JOHN M.
Industry: Construction **Born:** May 6, 1957, Cincinnati, Ohio **Univ./degree:** B.S., Business Administration, Wilmington College, 1980 **Current organization:** Costello Painting & Building Restoration Inc. **Title:** President **Type of organization:** Construction **Major product:** Historical restoration, hotel renovations **Area of distribution:** National **Expertise:** Management **Affiliations:** Allied Construction Industries; Better Business Bureau; Association of Building Contractors **Hob./spts.:** Photography, travel **SIC code:** 15 **Address:** Costello Painting & Building Restoration Inc., 1113 Halpin Ave., Cincinnati, OH 45208 **E-mail:** jcostello5@cinci.rr.com

CROWDER JR., JOHN L.
Industry: Construction **Univ./degree:** B.S., Engineering Geology, Tennessee Tech University, 1995 **Current organization:** Olympian Construction **Title:** Senior Project Manager **Type of organization:** Construction **Major product:** Commercial construction **Area of distribution:** National **Expertise:** Medical facility project management, troubleshooting **SIC code:** 15 **Address:** Olympian Construction, 814 Church St., Suite 200, Nashville, TN 37203 **E-mail:** johnc@olympianconstruction.com **Web address:** www.olympianconstruction.com

CUMMINGS, JAMES O.
Industry: Construction **Born:** October 11, 1971, Durham, North Carolina **Univ./degree:** B.S., Industrial Engineering, Florida State University, 1994 **Current organization:** Peter R. Brown Construction, Inc. **Title:** Project Manager **Type of organization:** Commercial general contractor **Major product:** Construction management/design, build **Area of distribution:** Florida **Expertise:** Industrial engineering **Affiliations:**

I.I.E. **Hob./spts.:** Golf **SIC code:** 15 **Address:** 1475 S. Belcher Rd., Largo, FL 33771 **E-mail:** cummingsj@peterbrownconst.com

DANIEL, T. MAUREEN
Industry: Electrical **Born:** Aruba **Current organization:** Helix Electric, Inc. Constructors/Engineers **Title:** Director of Safety **Type of organization:** Electrical construction **Major product:** Electrical installation and management **Area of distribution:** California, Nevada, Arizona **Expertise:** Safety training, management of all jobsite safety activities, incident/accident investigation and reporting, field inspection, compliance and improvement of safety activities. **Affiliations:** Vice President, San Diego Chapter, American Society of Safety Engineers **Hob./spts.:** Golf, swimming, snorkeling **SIC code:** 17 **Address:** Helix Electric, Inc. Constructors/Engineers, 8260 Camino Santa Fe, San Diego, CA 92121 **E-mail:** tcmd@cox.net

DARNELL, LEON J.
Industry: Electrical **Born:** January 10, 1953, Blue Earth, Minnesota **Univ./degree:** A.S., Mesa Community College **Current organization:** Lee's Electric, Inc. **Title:** President **Type of organization:** Electrical contracting **Major product:** New construction electrical services **Area of distribution:** Apache Junction, Arizona **Expertise:** Operations, personnel **Affiliations:** N.I.F.B. **Hob./spts.:** Fishing, hunting **SIC code:** 17 **Address:** Lee's Electric, Inc., 461 W. Apache Trail, #147, Apache Junction, AZ 85220 **E-mail:** leelectricinc@aol.com

DARWISH, MITCH (MUETAZ)
Industry: Construction **Born:** September 15, 1962, Damascus, Syria **Univ./degree:** B.S, Kansas State University, 1989 **Current organization:** Creative Home Interiors **Title:** President/Project Manager **Type of organization:** General contractor/engineering **Major product:** Building construction **Area of distribution:** International **Expertise:** Construction **Affiliations:** Building Trades Association **Hob./spts.:** Bowling, pool, swimming, dining, reading **SIC code:** 15 **Address:** Creative Home Interiors, 701 E. Ball Rd., Suite 101, Anaheim, CA 92805 **E-mail:** mitchdarwish@yahoo.com **Web address:** www.creativehomeinteriors.com

DAUGHERTY, DAVID R.
Industry: Excavation/plumbing **Born:** June 16, 1965, Orleans, Indiana **Current organization:** Daugherty's Services, Inc. **Title:** President **Type of organization:** Contracting **Major product:** Excavation and plumbing **Area of distribution:** Indiana **Expertise:** Operations and management **Affiliations:** Indiana Land Improvement Contractors Association **Hob./spts.:** NASCAR races, fishing, riding **SIC code:** 17 **Address:** Daugherty's Services, Inc., 180 N. Roosevelt St., Orleans, IN 47452

DAUGHERTY, DIANA K.
Industry: Excavation and plumbing **Born:** January 18, 1968, Paoli, Indiana **Current organization:** Daugherty's Services, Inc. **Title:** Co-Owner **Type of organization:** Contracting **Major product:** Excavation and plumbing **Area of distribution:** Indiana **Expertise:** Operations, management **Hob./spts.:** Camping, walking, NASCAR **SIC code:** 17 **Address:** Daugherty's Services, Inc., 180 N. Roosevelt St., Orleans, IN 47452 **E-mail:** dsinc@iquest.net

DAVID, ROBERT E.
Industry: Construction **Born:** August 27, 1922, Darlington, South Carolina **Univ./degree:** Ph.D., University of South Carolina; Ph.D., Lander College **Current organization:** Malu Developers, Inc. **Title:** President **Type of organization:** Builder **Major product:** Construction **Area of distribution:** National **Hob./spts.:** Spending time with his family, horses, baseball **SIC code:** 15 **Address:** Malu Developers, Inc., P.O. Box 3, Camden, SC 29020

DAVILA, ANGEL T.
Industry: Construction **Born:** May 31, 1970, Puerto Rico **Univ./degree:** Engineering, Purbo University, Puerto Rico, degree pending **Current organization:** Gire Construction Inc. **Title:** President **Type of organization:** Construction **Major product:** Home building **Area of distribution:** National **Expertise:** 15 years general construction, restoration, re-construction **Affiliations:** Disabled American Veterans; Sigma Beta; **Hob./spts.:** Basketball, mountain climbing **SIC code:** 15 **Address:** Gire Construction Inc., P.O. Box 1496, Juncos, PR 00777 **E-mail:** davilaa391@aol.com

DAVIS, DONALD F.
Industry: Construction **Born:** Houma, Louisiana **Univ./degree:** B.S., Business Administration, University of Phoenix **Current organization:** Beverly Industries, Inc. **Title:** Operations Manager **Type of organization:** Construction company **Major product:** Construction, trucking **Area of distribution:** Louisiana **Expertise:** Estimating, project management, pricing **Hob./spts.:** Fishing, hunting **SIC code:** 15 **Address:** Beverly Industries, Inc., 1214 River Rd., Bridge City, LA 70094 **E-mail:** donaldd@beverlyinc.com

DAWSON, PATRICK H.
Industry: Telecommunications **Born:** March 3, 1946, Morgantown, West Virginia **Univ./degree:** B.S., University of West Florida, 1969 **Current organization:** VT Milcom **Title:** Commercial Program Manager (Retired) **Type of organization:** Contractor/telecommunications and electrical OSP/ISP installer **Major product:** Software, hardware **Area of distribution:** National **Expertise:** Marketing, engineering **Affiliations:** D.I.C.S.I. **SIC code:** 17 **Address:** Milcom Systems Corp., 119 Industrial Blvd., Pensacola, FL 32505 **E-mail:** patdawson@vtmilcom.com **Web address:** www.vtmilcom.com

DECASTRO, WILSON R.
Industry: Bituminous concrete installation **Born:** June 6, 1961, Colombia, South America **Univ./degree:** A.S., Civil Engineering, Wentworth Technical Institute, 1979 **Current organization:** Wildeca Corp. **Title:** President/Owner **Type of organization:** Construction **Major product:** Paving, resurfacing, repairs **Area of distribution:** Massachusetts **Expertise:** Operations management **Published works:** Articles **Affiliations:** Latin-American Culture Club **Hob./spts.:** Soccer, baseball **SIC code:** 17 **Address:** Wildeca Corp., P.O. Box 365677, Hyde Park, MA 02136

DEL RÍO TORRES, HÉCTOR L.
Industry: Construction **Born:** May 3, 1952, San Juan, Puerto Rico **Univ./degree:** A.A., Engineering/Highway Construction, University of Puerto Rico **Current organization:** Tamrio, Inc. **Title:** President **Type of organization:** General contractor **Major product:** Roads/bridges/site preparation **Area of distribution:** Puerto Rico **Expertise:** Engineering/operations **Affiliations:** A.E.C.; A.G.C.; C.E.S. **Hob./spts.:** Sailing, fishing **SIC code:** 16 **Address:** Tamrio, Inc., P.O. Box 455, Mayagüez, PR 00681 **E-mail:** tamrio@coqui.net

DERISO, DAVID C.
Industry: Construction **Born:** November 22, 1953, Americus, Georgia **Univ./degree:** B.A., Business Administration, Shorter College, 1994 **Current organization:** Realty Construction Corp. **Title:** President **Type of organization:** General Contractor **Major product:** Residential and commercial multidwelling construction **Area of distribution:** National **Expertise:** Real estate development and construction **Affiliations:** Home Builders Association; Atlanta Apartment Association **Hob./spts.:** Golf, reading, running **SIC code:** 15 **Address:** Realty Construction Co., 11800 Wills Rd., Suite A, Alpharetta, GA 30004 **E-mail:** dderiso@realtyconstruction.com **Web address:** www.realtyconstruction.com

DIETZ, GREG G.
Industry: Construction **Born:** July 16, 1962, Chicago, Illinois **Univ./degree:** B.S., Electrical & Computers, James Madison University, 1985; M.S., Electrical & Computers, Marquette University, 1989 **Current organization:** Greenheck **Title:** Software Architect **Type of organization:** Manufacturing **Major product:** Air movement equipment **Area of distribution:** International **Expertise:** Engineering **Hob./spts.:** Running **SIC code:** 17 **Address:** Greenheck, 400 Ross Ave., Schofield, WI 54476 **E-mail:** greg.dietz@greenheck.com

DIGLIO, LUANNE L.
Industry: Construction **Born:** August 15, 1964, New Haven, Connecticut **Univ./degree:** Electrical/construction trade school **Current organization:** Diglio Electrical Contractors, LLC **Title:** Owner **Type of organization:** Contractor **Major product:** Electrical/construction contracting **Area of distribution:** Northford, Connecticut **Expertise:** Electrical **Affiliations:** Also owns: Diggers Harley Svcs., Diggers Motor Sports, Diggers Graphics **Hob./spts.:** Racing, volleyball **SIC code:** 17 **Address:** Diglio Electrical Contractors, LLC, 1065 Middletown Ave., Northford, CT 06472

DODSON, J.S. STEVE
Industry: Construction equipment **Born:** May 28, 1949, Memphis, Tennessee **Current organization:** Steve Dodson Construction Co./Nu-Corp International Technologies Inc./C.S.I. **Title:** Owner/President/Director of Construction & Commercial Property Development **Type of organization:** Construction firm **Major product:** Construction services, manufacturing equipment, R&D of Waste Stream Technology - State of the Art/Crude Oil Recovery and Oil Recovery Specialties **Area of distribution:** National/International **Expertise:** Management **Honors/awards:** Active Duty U.S. Army, 1967-1973 **Hob./spts.:** Scuba diving, duck hunting, sport fishing **SIC code:** 17 **Address:** Steve Dodson Construction Co./Nu-Corp International Technologies Inc./C.S.I., 28 Chase St., Suite A, Byhalia, MS 38611 **E-mail:** sdodsonnucorp@aol.com

DOLBERG, RONEN
Industry: Landscaping/concrete paving **Born:** September 21, 1961, Israel **Univ./degree:** Ph.D., Engineering, Israeli University, Tel Aviv, 1987 **Current organization:** Ackerstone, Inc. **Title:** Operations Manager **Type of organization:** Manufacturing **Major product:** Concrete pavers **Area of distribution:** International **Expertise:** Operations, paving, administration **Affiliations:** U.N.I.; I.C.P.I. **Hob./spts.:** Basketball, boating, soccer, sports **SIC code:** 16 **Address:** Ackerstone, Inc., 13296 Temescal

Canyon Rd., Corona, CA 92883-5299 **E-mail:** plantmanager@ackerstone.com **Web address:** www.ackerstone.com

DOLLESCHAL, THOMAS
Industry: Construction **Born:** November 18, 1959, Berlin, Germany **Current organization:** D. Thomas Construction **Title:** Owner **Type of organization:** Contractor **Major product:** Residential remodeling **Area of distribution:** California **Expertise:** Residential remodeling **Hob./spts.:** Swimming **SIC code:** 15 **Address:** D. Thomas Construction, 1801 Paseo Azul, Rowland Heights, CA 91748 **E-mail:** ibld9@adelphia.net

DUPRÉ, ROBERT
Industry: Real estate **Born:** September 15, 1934, Brooklyn, New York **Univ./degree:** B.B.A., Long Island University **Current organization:** Innovative Project Specialists **Title:** President **Type of organization:** Builders **Major product:** Residential and commercial development **Area of distribution:** Rancho Mirage, California **Expertise:** Property selection and marketing **Affiliations:** U.S.P.T.A. **Hob./spts.:** Boating, tennis **SIC code:** 15 **Address:** Innovative Project Specialists, P.O. Box 1734, Rancho Mirage, CA 92270

EDMONDS, RYAN M.
Industry: Construction **Born:** August 17, 1974, Augusta, Georgia **Univ./degree:** B.S., Construction, Clemson University, 1997 **Current organization:** Beers Skanska, Inc. **Title:** Project Manager **Type of organization:** General contractor **Major product:** General contracting and construction management **Area of distribution:** International **Expertise:** Healthcare facilities $10-100 million **Hob./spts.:** Outdoor activities, fishing, golf, musical instruments **SIC code:** 15 **Address:** Beers Skanska, Inc., 1303 Johnston Willis Dr., Richmond, VA 23235 **E-mail:** ryan.edmonds@beers.skanska.com

EDWARDS, DWAYNE
Industry: Painting **Born:** July 1, 1960, Austin, Texas **Current organization:** J.D. Edwards Painting Inc. **Title:** President **Type of organization:** Painting and wall covering contractor **Major product:** Painting and paper hanging **Area of distribution:** Manassas, Virginia **Hob./spts.:** Hunting **SIC code:** 17 **Address:** J.D. Edwards Painting Inc., 9288 Prince William St., Suite 107, Manassas, VA 20110 **E-mail:** jdepaint@aol.com

EVERETT, MATT
Industry: Contracting **Born:** December 28, 1961, Royal Oak, Michigan **Univ./degree:** B.S., Biology/Pre-Med, University of South Florida, 1984 **Current organization:** Paul Davis Restoration of Fox Valley **Title:** Owner **Type of organization:** General contracting **Major product:** Restoration of buildings **Area of distribution:** Wisconsin **Expertise:** Management, marketing, sales **Affiliations:** I.A.Q.A.; A.I.C.; Valley Home Builders Association **Hob./spts.:** Golf **SIC code:** 15 **Address:** Paul Davis Restoration of Fox Valley, 1555 S. Commercial St., Neenah, WI 54956 **E-mail:** meverett@new.rr.com

FAHNESTOCK, JEFFREY S.
Industry: Painting/Construction **Current organization:** Colorworld Painting **Title:** Owner **Type of organization:** Contractor **Major product:** Painting, construction **Area of distribution:** Virginia **Expertise:** Painting **Hob./spts.:** Stock car and dirt track racing **SIC code:** 17 **Address:** Colorworld Painting, 24 S. Pleasant Valley Rd., Winchester, VA 22601

FENTRESS, PHILLIP B.
Industry: Construction **Title:** Owner **Type of organization:** General contractors **Major product:** Commercial construction **Expertise:** Insurance **SIC code:** 15 **Address:** 6006 E. 38th St., c/o Dee Fentress, Indianapolis, IN 46226 **E-mail:** info@fentressbuilders.com

FIOCCHI, JOHN J.
Industry: Construction **Born:** October 30, 1959, Portland, Oregon **Current organization:** WE-BE Construction, Inc./WE-BE Homes LLC **Title:** President/CEO **Type of organization:** General contractor/home builder **Major product:** New home construction/remodeling **Area of distribution:** Oregon **Expertise:** Investment properties, home building **Hob./spts.:** Community and church activities **SIC code:** 15 **Address:** WE-BE Construction, Inc./WE-BE Homes LLC, 5420 S.E. 41st Ave., Portland, OR 97202 **E-mail:** webehomes.msn.com

GAINES, DAVID J.
Industry: Construction **Born:** May 23, 1956, Syracuse, New York **Current organization:** Muirfield Homes, Inc. **Title:** President/CEO **Type of organization:** Home builder **Major product:** Custom homes **Area of distribution:** Pawleys Island, South Carolina **Expertise:** Construction **Affiliations:** S.B.I.C.; South Carolina Homes and Gardens; National Association of Home Builders **SIC code:** 15 **Address:** Muirfield Homes, Inc., 239 Business Center Dr., Pawleys Island, SC 29585 **Web address:** www.muirfieldhomes.com

GALLENSTEIN, PAUL C.
Industry: Contractors/developer **Born:** March 13, 1965, Cummington, Kentucky **Univ./degree:** M.S., Civil Engineering, University of Kentucky, 1991 **Current organization:** Gallenstein Companies, LLC **Title:** Civil Engineer/President **Type of organization:** Contractors/developer **Major product:** Commercial, industrial, residential buildings **Area of distribution:** Kentucky **Expertise:** Developing real estate **Honors/awards:** Chamber of Commerce in Kentucky **Published works:** Magazine articles, papers **Affiliations:** A.S.C.E.; A.G.C.; H.B.A. **Hob./spts.:** Camping, fishing, biking **SIC code:** 15 **Address:** Gallenstein Companies, LLC, 25 Crestview Hills Mall Rd., Crestview Hills, KY 41017 **E-mail:** paulgallenstein@msn.com

GANS, BARRY
Industry: Construction/plumbing and heating **Born:** June 6, 1942, Brooklyn, New York **Current organization:** National Plumbing & Heating Corp. **Title:** President **Type of organization:** Plumbing and heating contractor **Major product:** Plumbing and heating **Area of distribution:** Manhattan, Brooklyn, Queens, New York, Staten Island **Expertise:** Operations **Affiliations:** Building Trades Association **SIC code:** 17 **Address:** National Plumbing & Heating Corp., 1956 E. Eighth St., Brooklyn, NY 11223 **E-mail:** national10@aol.com

GODWIN, KIMBERLY H.
Industry: Construction **Born:** July 12, 1960, Keokuk, Iowa **Current organization:** Arlington Beaches Roofing, Inc. **Title:** President/Owner **Type of organization:** Contractor **Major product:** Roofing **Area of distribution:** Florida **Expertise:** Residential re-roofing **Honors/awards:** Nominated by the Small Business Advisory Board for a Dinner with President Bush, 2006 **Affiliations:** The Florida Roofing, Sheet Metal and Air Conditioning Contractors Association **Hob./spts.:** Hunting **SIC code:** 17 **Address:** Arlington Beaches Roofing, Inc., 1327 Tutter St., Jacksonville, FL 32211

GOMEZ, CARLOS J.
Industry: R&D Construction **Born:** June 26, 1962, Patagonia, Arizona **Univ./degree:** B.A., University of South Carolina **Current organization:** Subcrews.com, Extreme Framing, Rock Development **Title:** President **Type of organization:** Builder, developer **Major product:** Housing **Area of distribution:** National **Expertise:** Marketing, development **SIC code:** 15 **Address:** Subcrews.com, 21009 Brinkley St., Cornelius, NC 28031 **E-mail:** cgomez@subcrews.com **Web address:** www.subcrews.com

GONZALEZ, RICHARD M.
Industry: Construction **Born:** November 15, 1970, Miami, Florida **Univ./degree:** Boca Raton Community College **Current organization:** EMF Drywall, Inc. **Title:** President/CEO **Type of organization:** Construction contractor **Major product:** Drywall framing and painting **Area of distribution:** Florida **Expertise:** New construction **Hob./spts.:** Scuba diving **SIC code:** 17 **Address:** EMF Drywall, Inc., 773 S. Kirkman Rd., #112, Orlando, FL 32811 **E-mail:** michael@emfdrywall.com

GOODRUM, NORMAN RAY
Industry: Construction **Born:** February 1, 1956, Colorado Springs, Colorado **Current organization:** Quality Services, Inc. **Title:** General Contractor **Type of organization:** Contracting **Major product:** Commercial and industrial construction **Area of distribution:** Washington **Expertise:** Site and concrete work **SIC code:** 15 **Address:** Quality Services, Inc., 2757 Pacific Ave. S.E., Suite 22B, Olympia, WA 98501 **E-mail:** qsi@tds.net

GREEN, DAVID P.F.
Industry: Construction **Born:** May 3, 1947, Raleigh, North Carolina **Univ./degree:** A.A., Business, Wyngate, UNC at Chapel Hill and Nelson Stousland School of Securities, 1968 **Current organization:** Green & Co. Builders **Title:** President/Owner **Type of organization:** General Contractor **Major product:** Residential custom building **Area of distribution:** Raleigh, North Carolina **Expertise:** Customer service, management, craftsmanship **Hob./spts.:** Deep-sea fishing, hunting **SIC code:** 15 **Address:** Green & Co. Builders, (James Bryce Moore Building Co.), 5621 Timber Ridge Dr., Raleigh, NC 27609-4140

GREINER, THOMAS
Industry: Construction **Current organization:** Greiner Construction **Title:** Owner **Type of organization:** Construction company **Major product:** Residential framing and commercial building **Area of distribution:** Indiana **Expertise:** Framing **Affiliations:** Indiana Home Builders Association **SIC code:** 15 **Address:** Greiner Construction, 2305 Cailynn Dr., Terre Haute, IN 47802

GRIEGO JR., JAVIER
Industry: Construction **Born:** September 4, 1972, El Paso, Texas **Univ./degree:** A.S., Applied Science, El Paso Community College, 1992 **Current organization:** Classic American Homes **Title:** Chief of Design **Type of organization:** Private contractor **Major product:** Single family homes **Area of distribution:** Texas **Expertise:** Architectural design **Hob./spts.:** Photography, drawing, golf **SIC code:** 15 **Address:**

Classic American Homes, 11240 Vista Del Sol Dr., STEA, El Paso, TX 79936 **E-mail:** javirgo72@excite.com

GRIFFIN, DWAYNE
Industry: Engineering/construction **Born:** May 5, 1970, Clanton, Alabama **Univ./degree:** B.S.M.E., University of Alabama at Birmingham, 1992 **Current organization:** Lee Co. **Title:** Project Manager **Type of organization:** Mechanical contractor **Major product:** Designing/building mechanical and plumbing systems **Area of distribution:** National **Expertise:** Mechanical engineering, design, finance, project management **Affiliations:** A.S.H.R.A.E.; A.S.M.E. **Hob./spts.:** Scuba diving, hunting, sports, travel **SIC code:** 17 **Address:** Lee Co., 3825 Lorna Rd., Suite 212, Hoover, AL 35244 **E-mail:** dgriffin@leecompany.com **Web address:** www.leecompany.com

GUERRA, RAUL IVAN
Industry: Construction **Born:** February 24, 1948, Guayaquil, Ecuador **Univ./degree:** B.A., University of Madrid, Spain, 1974 **Current organization:** Total Apartments, Turnkey & Maintenance **Title:** President **Type of organization:** Construction firm **Major product:** Building, renovations, restoration, refurbishing **Area of distribution:** Southeast U.S. **Expertise:** Operations, management **Hob./spts.:** Fishing, camping **SIC code:** 15 **Address:** Total Apartments, Turnkey & Maintenance, 12780 Providence Rd., Alpharetta, GA 30004 **E-mail:** totalapt@aol.com

GUILLORN, GERARD J.
Industry: Construction services **Born:** October 11, 1954, Newark, New Jersey **Univ./degree:** B.S., Ryder University, 1976 **Current organization:** Sordoni Skanska, Inc. **Title:** Vice President **Type of organization:** Construction management **Major product:** Pharmaceuticals, biotechnology **Area of distribution:** National **Expertise:** Business development, marketing **Affiliations:** I.S.P.E.; B.I.O.; I.D.R.C.; I.F.M.A. **Hob./spts.:** Golf, family **SIC code:** 17 **Address:** Sordoni Skanska, Inc., 400 Interpace Pkwy., Parsippany, NJ 07054 **E-mail:** jerry.guillorn@sordoni.com

GUY, TROY D.
Industry: Construction **Born:** February 14, 1962, Miami, Florida **Current organization:** Antamex **Title:** Superintendent Iron Worker **Type of organization:** Contractor/union **Major product:** Glass curtain walls/installment **Area of distribution:** Miami, Florida **Expertise:** Superintendent, Union iron worker Local 272 **Affiliations:** A.P.A. **Hob./spts.:** Shooting pool **SIC code:** 15 **Address:** 10791 N. Kendall Dr., Apt. B302, Miami, FL 33176-1474 **E-mail:** troyd.guy@aol.com

HARDEN, KEMPER H.
Industry: Construction **Born:** March 30, 1954, Chester, Montana **Current organization:** Kemper Drywall, Inc. **Title:** President **Type of organization:** Contracting **Major product:** Drywall installation **Area of distribution:** Tigard, Oregon **Expertise:** Custom homes; License and bonded in Oregon **Affiliations:** Home Builders Association **SIC code:** 15 **Address:** Kemper Drywall, Inc., 8900 SW Burnham St., Tigard, OR 97223 **Web address:** www.kemper-drywall.com

HARKINS, DWAIN E.
Industry: Construction **Current organization:** Kokosing Construction **Title:** Master Mechanic/Welder **Type of organization:** Commercial construction **Major product:** Heavy highway construction, welding **Area of distribution:** Ohio **Expertise:** Construction, jobsite maintenance **Affiliations:** N.R.A. **Hob./spts.:** Hunting **SIC code:** 16 **Address:** 1021 Third St., Brilliant, OH 43913 **E-mail:** cgb234a@prodigy.net

HARRIS, MICHAEL J.
Industry: Construction **Born:** May 12, 1967, San Antonio, Texas **Univ./degree:** B.A., Auburn University, 1991 **Current organization:** M.J. Harris, Inc. **Title:** President, C.E.O. **Type of organization:** Construction contractor **Major product:** Building, general contracting **Area of distribution:** National **Expertise:** Building science **Affiliations:** I.E.B.; A.S.A.; A.B.C. **Hob./spts.:** Hunting **SIC code:** 15 **Address:** M.J. Harris, Inc., 1 Riverchase Ridge, Suite 300, Birmingham, AL 35244 **E-mail:** michaelh@mjharris.com **Web address:** www.mjharris.com

HATFIELD, ROGER L.
Industry: Construction **Born:** March 18, 1968, Kansas City, Missouri **Univ./degree:** B.S., Mechanical Engineering, University of Missouri, 1991 **Current organization:** Midwest Mechanical Contractors, Inc. **Title:** Operations Manager/Support Services **Type of organization:** Construction **Major product:** Mechanical contractor **Area of distribution:** National **Expertise:** Hydronic heating and cooling **Affiliations:** A.S.H.R.A.E. **Hob./spts.:** Cars, home improvement **SIC code:** 17 **Address:** Midwest Mechanical Contractors, Inc., 4550 W. 109th St., Overland Park, KS 66211 **E-mail:** rhatfield@mmccorps.com

HAWKINS, SAM O.
Industry: Construction **Born:** November 21, 1945, San Francisco, California **Current organization:** Fluor-Ameco **Title:** Senior Director Operations **Type of organization:** Contractor **Major product:** Mining, construction, government services **Area of distribution:** International **Expertise:** Project start-up and execution, site procurement, logistics, training, presentations, heavy equipment engineering **Affiliations:** Served in U.S. Army (Vietnam for 2 1/2 years) **Hob./spts.:** Travel **SIC code:** 15 **Address:** Fluor-Ameco, 2106 Anderson Rd., Greenville, SC 29661 **E-mail:** sam.hawkins@ameco.com

HAYES, CARMEN R.
Industry: Civil construction **Born:** July 23, 1952, Havana, Cuba **Univ./degree:** B.S., Biology, 1977; M.S., Biology, 1978, University of Havana, Cuba; M.B.A., 1997, Troy University, Florida **Current organization:** Behety-Hayes Construction Co. **Title:** CEO **Type of organization:** Highway and building construction **Major product:** Concrete, road and culvert **Area of distribution:** National **Expertise:** Commercial concrete, real estate **Hob./spts.:** Water sports, sailing, travel **SIC code:** 16 **Address:** Behety-Hayes Construction Co., 3678 Union Hill Rd., Bonifay, FL 32425-9092 **E-mail:** behehay@hotmail.com

HAYES-CALVERT, LIDA
Industry: Construction **Title:** President **Type of organization:** Painting contractor **Major product:** Painting, wallcovering, special coatings **SIC code:** 17 **Address:** S&L Painting and Decorating, Inc., 1011 W. Northwest Blvd., Winston-Salem, NC 27101 **E-mail:** lidasl@aol.com **Web address:** www.sandlpaintinginc.com

HAYWARD, ROBERT C.
Industry: General construction **Born:** Milwaukee, Wisconsin **Univ./degree:** A.S., Chicago Technical College **Current organization:** Hayward Quality Builders **Title:** President/Owner **Type of organization:** Construction and environmental rehabs **Major product:** Residential housing and light commercial **Area of distribution:** Camp Douglas, Wisconsin **Expertise:** Marketing, management **Hob./spts.:** Hunting, fishing **SIC code:** 15 **Address:** Hayward Quality Builders, N10098 Second Ave., Camp Douglas, WI 54618-9727 **E-mail:** hayward@mwt.net

HEIL JR., FRANCIS C.
Industry: Mechanical contracting/construction **Born:** October 15, 1932, Philadelphia, Pennsylvania **Univ./degree:** B.S., Drexel University, 1963 **Current organization:** Herman Goldner Co., Inc. **Title:** Project Engineer **Type of organization:** Contractor **Major product:** Mechanical construction-new and renovation **Area of distribution:** Philadelphia, Pennsylvania **Expertise:** Mechanical engineering/construction **Published works:** 2 articles **Affiliations:** N.S.P.E.; Supervisor, National Environmental Balancing Bureau, (Air and Water, 1972; Sound Vibration, 1977) **SIC code:** 17 **Address:** Herman Goldner Co., Inc., 7777 Brewster Ave., Philadelphia, PA 19153 **E-mail:** franifrane@aol.com

HENTHORN, GARY W.
Industry: Construction **Born:** November 29, 1952, Ottawa, Kansas **Univ./degree:** B.S., Safety, Central Missouri State University **Current organization:** Berkel & Co. Contractors, Inc. **Title:** Corporate Safety Manager **Type of organization:** Contracting **Major product:** Deep auger-cast foundation piles **Area of distribution:** National **Expertise:** Writing safety policy and procedures **Affiliations:** A.S.S.E. **Hob./spts.:** All sports, avid Chiefs fan **SIC code:** 17 **Address:** Berkel & Co. Contractors, Inc., 2649 S. 142nd St., Bonner Springs, KS 66012 **E-mail:** ghenthorn@berkelapg.com

HERDEN, RICHARD J.
Industry: Construction **Born:** May 6, 1954, Milwaukee, Wisconsin **Current organization:** Electrical Associates Inc. **Title:** President/Master Electrician **Type of organization:** Electrical contractor **Major product:** Residential, commercial and industrial electrical installations **Area of distribution:** Wisconsin **Expertise:** Project management **Affiliations:** I.A.E.; N.F.P.A. **Hob./spts.:** Scuba diving, snowmobiling **SIC code:** 17 **Address:** 5565 S. 110th St., Hales Corners, WI 53130 **E-mail:** eairick@aol.com

HILL, JEFFREY H.
Industry: Carpentry/construction **Born:** December 23, 1947, Phillsburg, New Jersey **Current organization:** J. Hill Carpentry **Title:** Owner **Type of organization:** General construction contractor **Major product:** Restoration of residential, historical and industrial buildings **Area of distribution:** New Jersey **Expertise:** Restoration **Honors/awards:** Strathmore's Who's Who, County Awards and Citations **Published works:** Numerous articles **Affiliations:** Member, New Jersey Building Association **Hob./spts.:** Bowling, snowmobiling, waterskiing, coaching - baseball, soccer, football and basketball **SIC code:** 15 **Address:** J. Hill Carpentry, 189 Jonestown Rd., Oxford, NJ 07863

HOGAN, THOMAS S.
Industry: Construction **Born:** June 30, 1927, Queens, New York **Univ./degree:** B.S., Physics/Chemistry/Math, Fordham University, 1948 **Current organization:** The Enterprise, Inc. (Retired from Hilton Hotels Corp., associated with the Waldorf-Astoria and 25 yrs at the Hilton New York as the Director of Catering) **Title:** President **Type of organization:** Construction **Major product:** Sound barriers along sides of highways **Area of distribution:** New York **Expertise:** Administration, marketing and business

development **Hob./spts.:** Boating, museums, theatre **SIC code:** 16 **Address:** The Enterprise, Inc., 180 E. 79th St., New York, NY 10021 **E-mail:** piertom@aol.com

HOLT, R. JED

Industry: Construction/environmental (water/waste) **Born:** December 30, 1947, Mt. Vernon, Illinois **Spouse:** Nettie **Married:** April 1, 1983 **Children:** Amie, Jason **Univ./degree:** B.S., Civil Engineering, Rose-Hulman Institute of Technology, Indiana, 1970 **Current organization:** Bowen Engineering Corp. **Title:** President **Type of organization:** General/mechanical contractor **Major product:** Municipal, environmental, industrial construction **Area of distribution:** Indiana, Kentucky, Illinois, Ohio **Expertise:** Construction operations, management; Professional Engineer in Indiana **Affiliations:** Trustee, Education and Construction Division, Member, Contract Administration Committee, American Water Works Association; Past President, Indiana Chapter, American Concrete Institute; Board Member, Past President, Director, Indiana Chapter, Associated General Contractors; Past Director, Indiana Constructors; Board Member, Top Notch; American Society of Mechanical Engineers; Mechanical Contractors Association; Military Service: Indiana National Guard, 1971-76 **Career accomplishments:** Construction foreman and superintendent before graduating college; Project Superintendent of the $44 million U.S. 41 Highway improvements from Kentland, Indiana to State Road 63 at age 25; Developed state approved training programs and has chaired a task force to develop design - build legislation in Indiana; Attended the AGC Advanced Management Program, the Executive Development Program at the Wharton School and the Top Management Briefing of the American Management Association **Hob./spts.:** Fishing, boating, reading, swimming **SIC code:** 17 **Address:** Bowen Engineering Corp., 10315 Allisonville Road, Fishers, IN 46038 **E-mail:** jedh@bowenengineering.com

HOOD, MARK

Industry: Heating, ventilation and air conditioning **Born:** June 2, 1958, Hinsdale, Illinois **Current organization:** A&M Heating and Air Conditioning, Inc. **Title:** Owner **Type of organization:** Contracting **Major product:** Installation of heating and air conditioning **Area of distribution:** Wisconsin **Expertise:** Business management, commercial and residential; CFC Licensed; Freon Certified; 4 year trade school in sheet metal **Affiliations:** Local 265 **Hob./spts.:** Restoring old boats and cars **SIC code:** 17 **Address:** 437 Main St., Wausaukee, WI 54177

HORAN, BRIAN J.P.

Industry: Construction **Born:** October 10, 1960, South Haven, Michigan **Current organization:** Badger, Inc. **Title:** Vice President/Chef Operations Officer **Type of organization:** Excavation **Major product:** Material sales, underground utilities, site work **Area of distribution:** Michigan **Expertise:** Customer service **Affiliations:** Sheriff's Dept., Search & Rescue, Dover Township, South Haven **Hob./spts.:** woodworking, canine search and rescue **SIC code:** 16 **Address:** Badger Inc., 74150 Tenth Ave., South Haven, MI 49090 **E-mail:** badger4909@yahoo.com

HUNSDON, SIMEON A.

Industry: Electrical construction **Born:** April 11, 1946, Ticonderoga, New York **Current organization:** Hour Electric Co., Inc. **Title:** President **Type of organization:** Electrical contractor **Major product:** Electrical services **Area of distribution:** New York **Expertise:** Commercial/industrial electrical wiring **Affiliations:** B.B.B.; N.E.C.A.; New York State Rural Electric Cooperative Association; National Federation of Independent Business **Hob./spts.:** Harness racing **SIC code:** 17 **Address:** Hour Electric Co., Inc., 30 East St., Ft. Edward, NY 12828 **E-mail:** hourelectric@capital.net

HUNT, KERRY M.

Industry: Construction **Born:** January 9, 1962, Lubbock, Texas **Current organization:** D&K Hunt Electric **Title:** Owner **Type of organization:** Electrical contractor **Major product:** Electrical installation and repair **Area of distribution:** Texas **Expertise:** Estimation **Affiliations:** N.E.C.A.; Habitat for Humanity **Hob./spts.:** ATV's, golf, skiing **SIC code:** 17 **Address:** D&K Hunt Electric, 8217A Valencia, Lubbock, TX 79424

HUNTER, SHAWN A.

Industry: Communications **Born:** December 22, 1973, Ravenna, Ohio **Univ./degree:** A.A., Electrical Engineering, ITT Technical Institute, Ohio, 1994 **Current organization:** Rauland-Borg Corporation of Florida **Title:** RCDD/Project Engineer **Type of organization:** Contractors **Major product:** Installation of low voltage communications for school and hospital **Area of distribution:** Florida **Expertise:** Project design, management, regulatory communications distribution **Affiliations:** B.I.C.S.I. **Hob./spts.:** Family, automotive racing, golf **SIC code:** 17 **Address:** Rauland-Borg Corporation of Florida, 620 Douglas Ave., Suite 1316, Altamonte Springs, FL 32714 **E-mail:** shawn.hunter@rauland-fl.com

IVY, DAVID J.

Industry: Construction **Born:** November 4, 1961, Quitman, Mississippi **Univ./degree:** B.S., Architectural Engineering Technology, University of Southern Mississippi **Current organization:** Polk Construction Corp. **Title:** Vice President **Type of organization:** General contractor **Major product:** Commercial construction (new and existing), schools, hospital, churches, universities **Area of distribution:** Mississippi, Louisiana **Expertise:** Construction management, estimating, operations **Affiliations:** Associated Builders and Contractors **Hob./spts.:** Fishing, hunting, whitewater rafting **SIC code:** 15 **Address:** Pok Construction Corp., 3708 Hwy. 589 South, Sumrall, MS 39482 **E-mail:** davidivy@bellsouth.net

JACOBS II, JAMES H.

Industry: Construction/excavation **Born:** January 24, 1977 Murfreesboro, Tennessee **Current organization:** Jacobs Construction & Jacobs Group **Title:** Owner **Type of organization:** Contractor **Major product:** Building roads/site work **Area of distribution:** International **Expertise:** Commercial and residential development **Hob./spts.:** Baseball, basketball, show horses **SIC code:** 16 **Address:** Jacobs Construction, 6655 Jacobs Rd., Murfreesboro, TN 37127

JAMES, DANNY L.

Industry: Construction **Born:** June 17, 1953, Gassaway, West Virginia **Current organization:** The Lane Construction Corp. **Title:** Mechanical Supervisor **Type of organization:** Construction **Major product:** Asphalt and construction **Area of distribution:** National **Expertise:** Mechanical, paving specialist **Affiliations:** Company affiliation, N.A.P.A. **SIC code:** 16 **Address:** 2506 Manor Ct., Apt. 1A, Fredericksburg, VA 22403 **E-mail:** dljames@laneconstruct.com

JARVIS, PHILLIP D.

Industry: Construction **Born:** June 24, 1969, Murray, Utah **Univ./degree:** B.A., Business Administration, University of Central Florida, 1998 **Current organization:** Burgoon Berger Construction Corp. **Title:** Corporate Estimator **Type of organization:** General contractor **Major product:** Single family homes **Area of distribution:** Florida **Expertise:** Purchasing, estimating **Hob./spts.:** Boating, fishing, the beach, target shooting **SIC code:** 15 **Address:** Burgoon Berger Construction Corp., 4520 Dixie Hwy. N.E., Palm Bay, FL 32905 **E-mail:** pjarvis@burgoonberger.com

JOHNSON, NEAL

Industry: Development and Construction **Born:** April 8, 1973, British Columbia, Canada **Univ./degree:** B.A.Sc., Civil (Structural) Engineering, University of Waterloo, Canada, 1998 **Current organization:** Williams Island Associates, Inc. **Title:** Construction Manager **Type of organization:** Land development **Major product:** Luxury hi-rise condominium and hotel **Area of distribution:** South Florida **Expertise:** Project Management; Florida State Licensed General Contractor **Affiliations:** Canadian Professional Engineering Society **Hob./spts.:** Fishing, scuba diving, snow skiing, general fitness **SIC code:** 15 **Address:** 1621 Bay Road, #601, Miami Beach, FL 33139 **E-mail:** deve8@bellsouth.net **Web address:** www.williamsisland.com

JORGENSEN, GARY L.

Industry: Construction **Born:** January 19, 1943, Cedar Falls, Iowa **Current organization:** Johnson Lake Const. Services, Inc. **Title:** President **Type of organization:** Construction, contracting **Major product:** Commercial, industrial, alternate heat, propane construction **Area of distribution:** Minnesota **Expertise:** Administration, sales, marketing **Affiliations:** V.F.W.; American Legion; Minnesota Propane Gas Association **Hob./spts.:** Football, travel, fishing, hunting **SIC code:** 17 **Address:** Johnson Lake Const. Services Inc., 38745 State Hwy. #38, Deer River, MN 56636 **E-mail:** jlcsinc@paulbunyan.net

JOYCE, ROBERT (BOB)

Industry: Construction **Born:** Hammond, Indiana **Current organization:** McCartin McAuliffe Mechanical Contractor, Inc. **Title:** Project Manager / Stud Welding Division **Type of organization:** Industrial mechanical contractor **Major product:** Mechanical contracting **Area of distribution:** National **Expertise:** Paper mills, solid waste (within the power industry), stud welding **Affiliations:** Solid Waste Association of North America **Hob./spts.:** Golf **SIC code:** 17 **Address:** McCartin McAuliffe Mechanical Contractor, Inc., 4508 Columbia, Hammond, IN 46327 **E-mail:** bjoyce@mccartingrp.com

KEMBERLING, EDWARD

Industry: Electrical **Born:** May 4, 1944, Harrisburg, Pennsylvania **Current organization:** Cherokeeman Electric **Title:** Owner **Type of organization:** Sole proprietorship **Major product:** Residential and commercial wiring **Area of distribution:** Pennsylvania **Expertise:** Electrical **Affiliations:** I.B.E.W.; Member, Glory to God in The Highest Church, Harrisburg, Pennsylvania **Hob./spts.:** Martial arts **SIC code:** 17 **Address:** Cherokeeman Electric, 729 N. Hanover St., Lebanon, PA 17046

KEUSCH, JOHN

Industry: Construction **Univ./degree:** B.A., Business Administration, University of New Hampshire, 1969 **Current organization:** Centex Homes **Title:** Customer Service Manager **Type of organization:** Home builder **Major product:** Residential home construction **Area of distribution:** New Jersey **Expertise:** Customer service, consulting

(35 years in industry) **Published works:** 2 articles in Builders Magazine **Affiliations:** A.H.A.; N.H.B. **Hob./spts.:** Golf **SIC code:** 15 **Address:** 511 Roby Rd., Sutton, NH 03278 **E-mail:** builderadvice@mcttelecom.com

KING, RICHARD J.
Industry: Construction **Born:** May 14, 1943, Elmont, Maine **Current organization:** Richard J. King, Inc. **Title:** President **Type of organization:** General contracting **Major product:** Log home construction, excavating **Area of distribution:** National **Expertise:** Supervising operations **Affiliations:** Lion's Club; Lamoine Chamber of Commerce **Hob./spts.:** Fishing, hunting **SIC code:** 15 **Address:** Richard J. King, Inc., 721 Douglas Hwy., Lamoine, ME 04605 **E-mail:** dickking@adelphia.net **Web address:** www.rjkinginc.com

KING JR., CHARLES N.
Industry: Construction **Univ./degree:** B.S., Electrical Engineering Technology, Northeastern University **Current organization:** Delta Electric & Construction Co., Inc. **Title:** President **Type of organization:** General contracting **Major product:** Building and electrical construction **Area of distribution:** Virgin Islands **Expertise:** Electrical construction and maintenance **Affiliations:** General Contractors Association; The Home Builders Association **Hob./spts.:** Playing pool, softball **SIC code:** 15 **Address:** Delta Electric & Construction Co., Inc., 6-GB Peter's Rest, Christiansted, VI 00820 **E-mail:** deltaelec@viaccess.net

KNOX, LARRY D.
Industry: Construction **Born:** January 21, 1951, Clay Center, Kansas **Univ./degree:** M.B.A., University of Dallas, 1998 **Current organization:** Bob Moore Construction, Inc. **Title:** Vice President **Type of organization:** General contractor **Major product:** Commercial construction **Area of distribution:** National **Expertise:** Pre-construction services **Affiliations:** A.S.P.E.; A.S.C.E. **Hob./spts.:** Golf, hunting **SIC code:** 15 **Address:** Bob Moore Construction, Inc., 1110 N. Watson Rd., Arlington, TX 76011 **E-mail:** larryknox@earthlink.net

LANDIS SR., DONALD R.
Industry: Construction **Born:** October 17, 1943, Norristown, Pennsylvania **Univ./degree:** Attended Georgia Tech **Current organization:** Tiernan and Patrylo Design Group **Title:** Process Engineering Director **Type of organization:** Design and build **Major product:** Engineering and construction **Area of distribution:** National **Expertise:** Mechanical Engineering **Hob./spts.:** Woodworking, wood carving, metal working **SIC code:** 15 **Address:** Tiernan and Patrylo Design Group, 665 Hwy. 74 South, Suite 100, Peachtree City, GA 30269 **E-mail:** dlandis@tpdesignbuild.com

LANTHIER, BERTHA H.
Industry: Construction **Title:** President **Type of organization:** Residential contractor **Major product:** New construction of residences **Expertise:** Design, marketing **SIC code:** 15 **Address:** Premiere Estate Corp., 108 Wills Dr., Lafayette, LA 70506 **E-mail:** balanthier@bellsouth.net

LESINS, JANIS E.
Industry: Construction **Born:** April 23, 1953, Mannheim, Germany **Univ./degree:** B.S. Candidate, Thermo-Nuclear Physics, Stockton State College **Current organization:** J&P Building Contractors, Inc. **Title:** President **Type of organization:** Building contractors **Major product:** Commercial buildings **Area of distribution:** New Jersey **Expertise:** Design, build, plan specifications **Affiliations:** C.S.I. **Hob./spts.:** Fishing, golf, reading science fiction **SIC code:** 15 **Address:** J&P Building Contractors, Inc., P.O. Box 682, Minotola, NJ 08341 **E-mail:** yonis@jpbuildingcontractors.com

LOCH, BRADLEY J.
Industry: Construction **Born:** May 26, 1972, Stillwater, Minnesota **Univ./degree:** B.S., Business Administration, 1997; M.S., Business Taxation, 2002, University of Minnesota; J.D., 2000, William Mitchell College of Law **Current organization:** AHR Construction Inc. **Title:** Counsel/Vice President **Type of organization:** Construction **Major product:** Residential homes **Area of distribution:** Shoreview, Minnesota **Expertise:** Residential real estate counsel **Affiliations:** A.B.A.; M.S.B.A.; American Land Title Association **Hob./spts.:** Rock music, theatre, movies, gardening **SIC code:** 15 **Address:** 5840 Hodgson Rd., Shoreview, MN 55126 **E-mail:** bradleyloch@earthlink.net

LOCKE JR., CARL E.
Industry: Construction **Born:** September 8, 1958, Bartow, Florida **Univ./degree:** M.A., Construction, University of Florida, 1990 **Current organization:** SEMCO Construction, Inc. **Title:** President **Type of organization:** Construction firm **Major product:** Commercial and industrial construction **Area of distribution:** Bartow, Florida **Expertise:** Construction management **Affiliations:** A.G.C.; F.H.B.A.; C.I.L.B. **Hob./spts.:** Golf, coaching Little League baseball **SIC code:** 15 **Address:** SEMCO Construction, Inc., 205 Century Blvd., Bartow, FL 33830 **E-mail:** celockejr@semco.com

LOPES, PAUL
Industry: Construction **Born:** February 19, 1971, Portugal **Current organization:** K-7 Construction Corp. **Title:** General Manager **Type of organization:** Construction **Major product:** Renovations, new homes **Area of distribution:** New York **Expertise:** Building, management **Affiliations:** Building Trades Association **Hob./spts.:** Baseball, hockey **SIC code:** 15 **Address:** K-7 Construction Corp., 61 Fairfield Ave., Mineola, NY 11501 **E-mail:** asemlimite@aol.com

LUNDSTRUM, ROBERT L.
Industry: Home building **Born:** June 9, 1971, Des Moines, Iowa **Current organization:** Jerry's Homes Inc. **Title:** General Manager **Type of organization:** General contractor **Major product:** Single and multi-family homes **Area of distribution:** Urbandale, Iowa **Expertise:** Management **Affiliations:** H.B.A.; N.M.C. **Hob./spts.:** Family, golf, racing, collectibles **SIC code:** 15 **Address:** Jerry's Homes Inc., 3301 106th Circle, Urbandale, IA 50322 **E-mail:** bob@jerryshomes.com **Web address:** www.jerryshomes.com

LUTZ, CHARLES E.
Industry: Plumbing & design **Born:** December 31, 1932 **Univ./degree:** Ph.D., Massachusetts Institute of Technology, 1949 **Current organization:** Vik-kel Corp. **Title:** Ph.D./Professional Engineer **Major product:** Plumbing & design **Area of distribution:** Pennsylvania **Expertise:** Engineering **Hob./spts.:** Raising beef cattle **SIC code:** 17 **Address:** Vik-kel Corp., 459 Lincoln Way, Jeannette, PA 15644-3044

MACE, LOUIS L.
Industry: Heavy construction/engineering **Born:** March 5, 1935, Burns, Oregon **Univ./degree:** M.B.A., George Washington University **Current organization:** S.J. Groves & Sons Co. **Title:** Past President (Retired) **Type of organization:** Construction **Major product:** Construction of highway, bridges, dams and industrial plants **Area of distribution:** Idaho **Expertise:** Civil engineering **Affiliations:** A.S.C.E. **Hob./spts.:** Skiing, golf **SIC code:** 16 **Address:** 226 Red Devil Dr., Hailey, ID 83333 **E-mail:** loumace@aol.com

MADARAS, MICHAEL
Industry: Construction **Born:** October 29, 1969, Mesa, Arizona **Univ./degree:** B.S., Finance, Western International University, Phoenix, Arizona **Current organization:** Read Homes, Inc. **Title:** Purchasing Manager **Type of organization:** Home builder **Major product:** Single-family homes **Area of distribution:** Arizona **Affiliations:** National Home Builders Association **Hob./spts.:** Golf, hunting **SIC code:** 15 **Address:** Read Homes, Inc., 7742 E. Florentine Rd., Prescott Valley, AZ 86314 **E-mail:** mmadaras@readhomes.com

MAIO, WILLIAM J.
Industry: Telecommunications **Born:** April 3, 1971 **Current organization:** Jolen Electric & Communications, Inc. **Title:** Electric PM Estimator **Type of organization:** Contracting **Major product:** Electrical/low voltage installations **Area of distribution:** National **Expertise:** Estimating/as-built design **Affiliations:** N.E.C.A., N.F.P.A. **Hob./spts.:** Family, softball, spectator sports **SIC code:** 17 **Address:** Jolen Electric & Communications, Inc., 309 Garnet Dr., New Lenox, IL 60451 **E-mail:** bmaio@jolenelectric.com

MAKRIS, GUS
Industry: Construction/Real Estate Development **Born:** New York, New York **Current organization:** Aspen Contracting Corp. **Title:** President **Type of organization:** Construction Management **Major product:** New homes and commercial **Area of distribution:** New Jersey **Expertise:** Business management **Affiliations:** N.J.S.B.A.; N.J.B.A.; N.A.H.B. **Hob./spts.:** Family, boating, skiing **SIC code:** 15 **Address:** Aspen Contracting Corp., 2211 Route 88 East, Brick, NJ 08724 **E-mail:** gmakris@aspencontractingcorp.com

MALONEY, WILLIAM A.
Industry: Construction **Born:** March 13, 1941, Mount Vernon, New York **Current organization:** Vista Electrical Contractors, Inc. **Title:** President/CEO **Type of organization:** Electrical contractor **Major product:** Power and control wiring for industry **Area of distribution:** New York & New Jersey metro area **Expertise:** Operations, administration **Honors/awards:** Jack Miller Network, Outstanding Networker, 1999-2003; Associated Builders & Contractors of Northern New Jersey, 1st Vice President, 1991-92 & Distinguished Leadership Award; Associated Builders and Contractors, Director of Education 1985-86 and Outstanding Service Award **Affiliations:** Jack Miller Network; Associated Builders & Contractors; International Association of Electrical Inspectors **Hob./spts.:** Golf, skiing **SIC code:** 17 **Address:** Vista Electrical Contractors, Inc., 745 W. Nyack Rd., West Nyack, NY 10994 **Phone:** (845)353-3313 **Fax:** (845)353-3678 **Web address:** www.vistaelectric.com

MANNING, PAUL O.
Industry: Construction **Born:** December 29, 1955, Oak Park, Illinois **Univ./degree:** B.Arch., University of Illinois, 1977 **Current organization:** Raimondo Construction

Co. **Title:** Chief Operating Officer **Type of organization:** General contractor **Major product:** Building construction **Area of distribution:** New Jersey **Expertise:** Architect, operations **Affiliations:** Urban Land Institute; C.S.I. **Hob./spts.:** Racquetball, church **SIC code:** 15 **Address:** Raimondo Construction Co., 540 Bergen Blvd., Ft. Lee, NJ 07024 **E-mail:** pmanning@craimondo.com

MAPLE, THOMAS JAIMMISON
Industry: Construction **Born:** Indianapolis, Indiana **Univ./degree:** B.S., Construction Technology, Purdue University **Current organization:** The Estridge Companies **Title:** Director of Estimating and Purchasing **Type of organization:** Home builder **Major product:** New residential homes - single family **Area of distribution:** Indiana **Expertise:** Purchasing and estimating **Affiliations:** B.A.G.I.; American Purchasing Society **Hob./spts.:** Golf, speaks fluent Spanish **SIC code:** 15 **Address:** The Estridge Companies, 1041 W. Main St., Carmel, IN 46032 **E-mail:** maplej@estridge.net

MARDICK, BRUCE L.
Industry: Construction **Born:** March 3, 1954, Climax, Colorado **Univ./degree:** B.A. University of Colorado, 1977 **Current organization:** Metropolitan Builders **Title:** Vice President **Type of organization:** Home building **Major product:** Single family/multi family housing **Area of distribution:** Colorado **Expertise:** Construction management **Affiliations:** H.B.A. **Hob./spts.:** Mountain biking, backpacking, hiking, rock climbing, fly-fishing, sailing **SIC code:** 15 **Address:** Metropolitan Builders, 2696 S. Colorado Blvd., Suite 430, Denver, CO 80222 **E-mail:** b.mardick@metropolitanhomes.net **Web address:** www.metropolitanhomes.net

MARKS, J. CRAIG
Industry: Construction **Born:** September 9, 1958, Opelousas, Louisiana **Current organization:** Professional Service Industries **Title:** CS Department Manager **Type of organization:** Contracting **Major product:** Construction **Area of distribution:** Jefferson, Louisiana **Expertise:** Account management **Affiliations:** A.C.I.; A.S.C.E. **Hob./spts.:** Fishing, hunting **SIC code:** 15 **Address:** Professional Service Industries, 724 Central Ave., Jefferson, LA 70121 **E-mail:** craig.marks@psiusa.com

MARTELL, ROBERTO
Industry: Construction **Born:** April 29, 1961, Matanzas, Cuba **Current organization:** Martell Construction Inc. **Title:** Vice President/Owner **Type of organization:** Construction contractor **Major product:** Building and renovation **Area of distribution:** Miami, Florida **Expertise:** General contracting **Affiliations:** B.B.B. **SIC code:** 15 **Address:** Martell Construction Inc., 9870 SW 70th St., Miami, FL 33173 **E-mail:** robertmartell@bellsouth.net

MARTINEAU-ROBINSON, MICHELLE
Industry: Building **Univ./degree:** B.A. Candidate **Current organization:** SMS Custom Home Builders **Title:** Executive Vice President **Type of organization:** Manufacturing/construction **Major product:** High quality housing manufacturing/commercial contractor **Area of distribution:** Idaho **Expertise:** Management, oversees administration, sales, marketing **Hob./spts.:** Gardening, camping, fishing **SIC code:** 15 **Address:** 574 Canyon Dr., Pocatello, ID 83204 **E-mail:** mark@cableone.net

MARTINELLO, EUGENE THOMAS
Industry: Custom and production home builder **Born:** February 2, 1953, East Brunswick, New Jersey **Current organization:** ICI Homes, Inc. **Title:** Director of Cost Operations **Type of organization:** Certified builders **Major product:** Corporate management of production, semi-custom and custom home building **Area of distribution:** Florida **Expertise:** Cost management, supply chain management, computer and digitized estimating systems, public relations; Florida State Certified Residential Contractor with 35 years experience **Affiliations:** Northeast Florida Builders Association **Hob./spts.:** Saltwater fishing, archery **SIC code:** 15 **Address:** ICI Homes, Inc., 5150 Belfort Rd., Bldg. #700, Jacksonville, FL 32256 **E-mail:** gmartinello@icihomes.com **Web address:** www.icihomes.com

MASSEY, TERRY L.
Industry: Carpentry **Born:** October 31, 1957, Wyandotte, Michigan **Current organization:** M&K Inc. **Title:** President **Type of organization:** Contracting **Major product:** Custom cabinets, furniture, houses **Area of distribution:** National **Expertise:** Master carpenter **Hob./spts.:** Coaching baseball, carpentry **SIC code:** 17 **Address:** 147 Berkeley Rd., Leesville, SC 29070

MATARAZZO, CHARLES T.
Industry: Construction **Born:** February 9, 1958, New Jersey **Current organization:** Matarazzo Excavating & Masonry, LLC **Title:** President **Type of organization:** Contracting company **Major product:** Excavation and masonry **Area of distribution:** Asbury, New Jersey **Expertise:** Septic system installation and repairs **SIC code:** 17 **Address:** Matarazzo Excavating & Masonry, LLC, 1024 Rt. 173, Asbury, NJ 08802 **E-mail:** matarazzoexcatavingllc@netlink.com

MCDONALD, JIM
Industry: Construction **Born:** August 21, 1942, Torrington, New York **Univ./degree:** B.S.M.E., Cleveland University, 1969; C.D.S.; C.D.M. **Current organization:** Sunland Asphalt, Inc./Marine Engineering, LLC **Title:** Shop Superintendent/President **Type of organization:** Contractor **Major product:** Asphalt, seal coating **Area of distribution:** Arizona **Expertise:** Design engineering, custom and specialty asphalt equipment **Published works:** 3 patents **Affiliations:** N.T.A.; A.M.T.A.; V.V.H.P.A.; V.V.A.; Vietnam Veteran, served in active duty, U.S. Army, 1960-1966; Lions Club; Veterans Club **Hob./spts.:** Drag boat racing **SIC code:** 17 **Address:** Marine Engineering, LLC, 808 W. Detroit St., Chandler, AZ 85225 **E-mail:** jimm@sunland-inc.com

MCGEE, ROBERT F.
Industry: General contracting **Born:** May 30, 1962, Boston, Massachusetts **Univ./degree:** B.S., Mechanical Engineering, Northeastern University, 1987 **Current organization:** D.F. Pray General Contractors **Title:** Project Manager **Type of organization:** Construction **Major product:** Retail builders **Area of distribution:** Seekonk, Massachusetts **Expertise:** Mechanical engineering **Affiliations:** Institute of Store Planners **Hob./spts.:** Swimming, camping, soccer, skiing **SIC code:** 15 **Address:** D.F. Pray General Contractors, 25 Anthony St., Seekonk, MA 02771

MCNEILL, T. KEITH
Industry: Plumbing **Born:** August 31, 1952, Tallahassee, Florida **Current organization:** Keith McNeill Plumbing Contractor Inc. **Title:** President **Type of organization:** Contractor **Major product:** Plumbing services **Area of distribution:** Florida **Expertise:** Commercial and residential plumbing **Affiliations:** Local CC; Tallahassee Builders Association; F.T.H.C.C.; N.T.H.C.C. **SIC code:** 17 **Address:** Keith McNeill Plumbing Contractor Inc., 3505 N. Monroe St., Tallahassee, FL 32303 **E-mail:** keithmcneill@comcast.net

MERCHEL, ROBERT G.
Industry: Recreation **Born:** September 21, 1943 **Univ./degree:** B.S., Math, 1968; M.Ed., Math, 1973, Wayne State University **Current organization:** Summer Fun Pools, Inc. **Title:** President **Type of organization:** Swimming pool contractor, designer and dealer **Major product:** Custom gunite pools and spas **Area of distribution:** Southeastern Michigan **Expertise:** Business management, estimates, building/service **SIC code:** 17 **Address:** Summer Fun Pools, Inc., 39473 Mound Rd., Sterling Heights, MI 48312 **E-mail:** summerfunpoolsinc@hotmail.com **Web address:** www.summerfunpools.com

MERKEL, DAVID W.
Industry: Heavy construction **Born:** September 19, 1958, Illinois **Current organization:** Bulk Transport Corp. & Brown Inc. **Title:** General Manager **Type of organization:** Construction firm **Major product:** Excavation, mill services **Area of distribution:** Indiana **Expertise:** Operations management, supervision **Hob./spts.:** NASCAR, golf **SIC code:** 17 **Address:** Bulk Transport Corp. & Brown Inc., 720 W. Hwy. 20, Michigan City, IN 46360 **E-mail:** dmerkel@bibtc.com

MICAMES, SYLVINA K.
Industry: Construction/engineering **Born:** March 5, 1978, Mayaguez, Puerto Rico **Univ./degree:** B.S., Civil Engineering, University of Puerto Rico, 2001 **Current organization:** Vissepó & Diez Construction Corp. **Title:** Estimator **Type of organization:** General contractors **Major product:** Construction **Area of distribution:** Western Puerto Rico **Expertise:** Civil engineering **Affiliations:** Past Member, A.S.C.E.; Colegio de Ingenieros of A.S.C.E. **Hob./spts.:** Tennis **SIC code:** 15 **Address:** Vissepó & Diez Construction Corp., P.O. Box 3607, Mayaguez, PR 00681 **E-mail:** sylvinamicames@hotmail.com

MILLER, STEVEN J.
Industry: Construction **Born:** July 26, 1983, Fontana, California **Current organization:** Varner Construction, Inc. **Title:** Project Manager/Estimator **Type of organization:** Contractor **Major product:** Grading **Area of distribution:** Southern California **Expertise:** Project management, estimating earth work/quantities, training **Hob./spts.:** Music (plays the guitar), swimming **SIC code:** 17 **Address:** Varner Construction, Inc., 5694 Mayfield Ave., San Bernardino, CA 92407 **E-mail:** stevem@varnerinc.com **Web address:** www.varnerinc.com

MOE, GREGORY G.
Industry: Environmental remediation **Born:** April 13, 1960, Grafton, North Dakota **Univ./degree:** Liberal Arts, University of North Dakota; Photography, Hennepin Technical Institute; Certified, Asbestos, Lead, Contractor Supervision & Project Design, State of Michigan; Certified, Mold Remediation, McCrone Institute **Current organization:** Taplin Contracting, LLC **Title:** General Manager **Type of organization:** Environmental contractor **Major product:** Remediation contracting **Area of distribution:** Michigan **Expertise:** Lead, asbestos, mold, project design, supervision, inspection, abatement **Affiliations:** Boys & Girls Clubs of Kalamazoo **Hob./spts.:** Photography **SIC code:** 17 **Address:** Taplin Contracting, LLC, 5100 W. Michigan

Ave., Kalamazoo, MI 49006 **E-mail:** greg@taplonenvironmental.com **Web address:** www.taplonenvironmental.com

MONNOT, JAMES MICHAEL
Industry: Construction **Born:** August 15, 1944, Gridley, California **Current organization:** Zachary Construction Corp. **Title:** Equipment Director **Type of organization:** Construction company **Major product:** Construction projects **Area of distribution:** International **Expertise:** Equipment management **Affiliations:** A.C.E.M. **Hob./spts.:** Ultra light flying, kayaking, camping **SIC code:** 15 **Address:** Zachary Construction Corp., 527 Logwood, San Antonio, TX 78244 **E-mail:** monnotj@zachary.com

MUJICA, ALEXANDER
Industry: Construction **Born:** August 2, 1974, San Juan, Puerto Rico **Univ./degree:** B.S., Civil Engineering, University of Massachusetts, 1997 **Current organization:** Levitt Homes Corp. **Title:** Project Manager **Type of organization:** Developer/contractor **Major product:** New home construction, land development **Area of distribution:** Puerto Rico **Expertise:** Civil engineering, cost estimating, scheduling, contracting **Affiliations:** Society of Engineers of Puerto Rico **Hob./spts.:** Golf **SIC code:** 15 **Address:** Levitt Homes Corp., Tabonuco B-5, Galeria San Patricio, #207, Guaynabo, PR 00968 **E-mail:** almujica@libertypr.net

NAMOUCHI, RIADH
Industry: Construction **Born:** May 3, 1964, Beja, Tunisia **Univ./degree:** M.S., Mechanical Engineering, University of Illinois, 1990 **Current organization:** Caterpillar, Inc. **Title:** Six Sigma Black Belt **Type of organization:** Manufacturing **Major product:** Construction and mining equipment **Area of distribution:** International **Expertise:** Engineering, quality assurance **Affiliations:** A.S.M.E.; A.S.E. **Hob./spts.:** Soccer, football, tennis **SIC code:** 17 **Address:** Caterpillar, Inc., 27th St. & Pershing Rd., DE-AG2, Decatur, IL 62525 **E-mail:** namouchoe@yahoo.com

NELSON, ROBERT A.
Industry: Plumbing and heating **Born:** Elizabeth, New Jersey **Univ./degree:** Master Plumber, University of Dayton, Ohio 1998 **Current organization:** Bob Nelson Plumbing & Heating, Inc. **Title:** President, Master Plumber **Type of organization:** Contracting **Major product:** Residential, commercial and industrial plumbing and heating services **Area of distribution:** New Jersey **Expertise:** Operations management, business development **Affiliations:** ANSWERS-Monmouth County Rescue & Recovery Dive Team, Oakhurst, NJ; Member, Better Business Bureau; Building Trades Association; Monmouth County League of Master Plumbers **Hob./spts.:** Scuba diving **SIC code:** 17 **Address:** Bob Nelson Plumbing & Heating, Inc., 3430 Sunset Ave., #23, Ocean, NJ 07712 **E-mail:** bnplumbing@optonline.net **Web address:** www.bobnelsonplumbing.com

NICKS, RONALD L.
Industry: Construction **Born:** February 3, 1952, Sparta, Wisconsin **Univ./degree:** Mechanical Design, Western Wisconsin Technical College at La Crosse **Current organization:** Nicks Construction, Inc. **Title:** Owner **Type of organization:** Contracting and design/build firm **Major product:** Home building **Area of distribution:** Wisconsin **Expertise:** Designed and constructed commercial facilities and residential buildings across the state of Wisconsin, including office buildings, day care centers, multiple residential housing units, as well as homes **Affiliations:** Founding Principal and Investor, CEO, Stonic Energy LLC ; Has served on Board of Appeals for the City of Tomah; Has served as Vice President for Tomah Area Contractor's Association; Lions Club of Tomah (former President); Board of Directors for regional chapter, Habitat for Humanity; Business Advisory Council, National Republican Committee **Hob./spts.:** Golf, fishing, travel **SIC code:** 15 **Address:** Nicks Construction. Inc., P.O. Box 697, Tomah, WI 54660

NORMAN, LEWIS J.
Industry: Construction **Current organization:** Theophilus, Inc. **Title:** President, Owner **Type of organization:** Contracting **Major product:** Excavating, site development **Area of distribution:** Mount Dora, Florida **Expertise:** Has owned and operated an excavating company for 22 years **SIC code:** 17 **Address:** Theophilus, Inc., 21902 State Rd. 46, Mount Dora, FL 32757 **E-mail:** ljnorman@theophilus.com

NORMAN, SCOTT A.
Industry: Construction **Born:** June 17, 1961, Bakersville, California **Current organization:** Herzog Contracting Corp. **Title:** Chief Estimator **Type of organization:** Railroad contractor **Major product:** Construction management **Area of distribution:** International **Expertise:** Mass transit contracting **Affiliations:** American Society of Professional Estimators **Hob./spts.:** Family activities, skiing, coaching baseball **SIC code:** 17 **Address:** Herzog Contracting Corp., 600 S. Riverside Rd., St. Joseph, MO 64507 **E-mail:** scottn@herzogcompanies.com **Web address:** www.herzogcompanies.com

OCHOA, MIRIAM E.
Industry: Construction **Type of organization:** Construction firm **SIC code:** 15 **Address:** Solution Services Inc., 3105 Mt. Pleasant St. N.W., Suite 200, Washington, DC 20010 **E-mail:** miriam@dynamericamc.com

ODEN, JEREMY H.
Industry: Construction remodeling **Born:** October 7, 1968, Birmingham, Alabama **Univ./degree:** B.A., Christian Administration, Counseling, Asbury College **Current organization:** O&O Construction **Title:** Co-Owner **Type of organization:** Construction remodeling **Major product:** Vinyl siding, roofing, window replacement **Area of distribution:** Alabama **Expertise:** Marketing, management **Honors/awards:** Alabama State Representative, 11th District, (Cullman, Morgan) **Affiliations:** Eva Lions' Club; Arrites Oden Masonic Lodge; Huntsville Scottish Rite; Decatur York Rite; Huntsville Shrine Association; Board Member, Asbury Alumni Association **Hob./spts.:** Fishing, gunsmith, hunting **SIC code:** 15 **Address:** P.O. Box 185, Eva, AL 35621 **E-mail:** jhoden@hiwaay.net

PAOLINI, GARY D.
Industry: Construction **Born:** August 31, 1964, Buffalo, New York **Univ./degree:** B.A., Oxford University,1986, B.S., University of Maryland **Current organization:** Space Innovation, LLC **Title:** CEO **Type of organization:** Development services **Major product:** General contracting, architectural mill work **Area of distribution:** National **Expertise:** Architectural mill work **Honors/awards:** Architectural Digest Recognition Award **Hob./spts.:** Golf, water sports **SIC code:** 15 **Address:** Space Innovation, LLC, 9215 Solon Dr., SuiteA-5, Houston, TX 77064 **E-mail:** spaceinnov@avl.com

PARK, JANET R.
Industry: Construction **Born:** May 20, 1962, Riverside, California **Univ./degree:** A.S., Oklahoma State University, 1990; B.S., Business Management, Laturna University, 1995 **Current organization:** Kimball Hill Homes **Title:** Purchasing Manager **Type of organization:** Home builder **Major product:** Single family homes **Area of distribution:** Dallas, Texas **Expertise:** Construction, training, QA, purchasing, estimating, Licensed Real Estate Home Inspector **Published works:** Internal construction manual **Hob./spts.:** Jewelry making, bowling, swimming, physical fitness **SIC code:** 15 **Address:** Kimball Hill Homes, 3010 LBJ Fwy., Suite 1100, Dallas, TX 75234 **E-mail:** jpark@direcway.com

PAVAO, PETER
Industry: Construction Management **Born:** Sao Miguel, Azores Portugal **Current organization:** P.J. Keating Co. **Title:** Senior Project Manager **Type of organization:** Roadway and highway road construction/Manufacturing of construction earth products **Major product:** Asphalt and aggregate manufacturing, general contracting **Area of distribution:** National **Expertise:** Licensed construction supervisor in Massachusetts; Surveying and construction layout, heavy utility construction and site work **Affiliations:** C.P.I. Institute; Construction Technology & Rutgers University, Radon Mitigation **Hob./spts.:** Deep sea fishing, boating, running, reading **SIC code:** 16 **Address:** 138 Renaud St., Fall River, MA 02721 **E-mail:** ppavao@pjkeating.com **Web address:** www.pjkeating.com

PELLETIER, JAMES L.
Industry: Construction **Current organization:** J.P. Construction, Inc. **Title:** President **Type of organization:** General contractor **Major product:** Specialized concrete foundations - industrial satellites and foundation **Area of distribution:** National **Expertise:** Communications construction **Affiliations:** Home Builders Association **Hob./spts.:** Big game fishing **SIC code:** 17 **Address:** J.P. Construction, Inc., 291 Sharon Church Rd., Loganville, GA 30052 **E-mail:** jpconstructioninc@msn.com

PETERS, MARK C.
Industry: Construction **Born:** November 20, 1961, Evansville, Indiana **Univ./degree:** B.S., Finance, University of Southern Indiana, 1985 **Current organization:** Hazex Construction Co., Inc. **Title:** Controller **Type of organization:** Construction firm **Major product:** Site excavation, concrete structures **Area of distribution:** Henderson, Kentucky **Expertise:** Accounting **Hob./spts.:** Tennis, golf, coaching (soccer, baseball, basketball), attending youth activities **SIC code:** 15 **Address:** Hazex Construction Co., Inc., 1890 Madison St., Henderson, KY 42420 **E-mail:** mpeters@hazex.com

PETERS, SCOTT W.
Industry: Construction **Born:** December 14, 1974, Brookville, Pennsylvania **Univ./degree:** A.S., Specialized Technology, Bradley Academy for the Visual Arts, 1995 **Current organization:** New Era Building Systems, Inc. **Title:** Regional Sales Manager **Type of organization:** Construction **Major product:** Modular housing **Area of distribution:** National **Expertise:** Design, sales **Hob./spts.:** Freelance design **SIC code:** 15 **Address:** New Era Building Systems Inc., 451 Southern Ave., Strattanville, PA 16258 **E-mail:** speters_newera@hotmail.com

PFINGSTEN, DAVID R.
Industry: Construction **Born:** April 10, Orange, California **Univ./degree:** B.S.C.E., Texas A&M University **Current organization:** EBCO Commercial, Ltd. **Title:** Project Administrator **Type of organization:** General contractor, construction **Major product:** Commercial construction (schools, hotels, hospitals, etc.) **Area of distribution:** Texas **Expertise:** Civil engineering **Published works:** Article **Affiliations:** A.S.C.E.; N.S.P.E.; N.P.S. **Hob./spts.:** Carpentry, coin and stamp collecting, camping, water sports **SIC code:** 15 **Address:** EBCO Commercial, Ltd., 305 W. Gillis, Cameron, TX 76520 **E-mail:** dave@ebco1.com

PHALORE, PARMINDER S.
Industry: Construction **Born:** Kenya, Africa **Univ./degree:** B.S.C.E., London University, 1984 **Current organization:** Flora Construction Inc. **Title:** President **Type of organization:** General contracting/construction management **Major product:** General contracting, construction, fire restoration (residential, commercial)) **Area of distribution:** Michigan **Expertise:** Engineering **Hob./spts.:** Reading, sports **SIC code:** 15 **Address:** Flora Construction Inc., 8850 Strathmoor St., Detroit, MI 48228 **E-mail:** phalore@msn.com **Web address:** www.floraconstruction.com

POMBRIANT, KEVIN C.
Industry: Construction **Born:** October 25, 1966, Vernon, Connecticut **Univ./degree:** B.S., Project Management, Southern Maine Technical College, 1992 **Current organization:** Partners in Construction **Title:** Chief Estimator **Type of organization:** Construction **Major product:** Residential home builders **Area of distribution:** Massachusetts **Expertise:** Chief estimator, project management **Affiliations:** NHAB **Hob./spts.:** Computer design **SIC code:** 15 **Address:** Partners in Construction, 5 Hills Dale Ave., Burlington, MA 01803 **E-mail:** pombriant@att.net

RATLIFF JR., ROBERT B.
Industry: Specialty construction **Born:** October 24, 1950, Narrows, Virginia **Univ./degree:** B.S., Mechanical Engineering, Virginia Polytechnic Institute, 1973 **Current organization:** Pike Electric, Inc. **Title:** Vice President **Type of organization:** Construction **Major product:** Powerline construction and maintenance **Area of distribution:** 7 states **Expertise:** Management **Affiliations:** National Society of Professional Engineers; Professional Engineers of North Carolina **Hob./spts.:** Golf, college football **SIC code:** 17 **Address:** 100 Pike Way, Mount Airy, NC 27030 **E-mail:** bratliff@pike.com

RAYBURN, JASON R.
Industry: Construction **Born:** March 20, 1974, Ohio **Current organization:** Jason Rayburn Construction Inc. **Title:** President **Type of organization:** Construction company **Major product:** Concrete and masonry **Area of distribution:** Florida **Expertise:** Room additions **Hob./spts.:** Fishing **SIC code:** 17 **Address:** Jason Rayburn Construction Inc., 4731 Alcen St., New Port Richey, FL 34652

RAYMOND, FRANK J.
Industry: Construction **Born:** July 11, 1933, Chicago, Illinois **Current organization:** Raymond Enterprises **Title:** Owner **Type of organization:** General contractor **Major product:** New constructions, remodels, renovations - commercial/residential **Area of distribution:** Texas **Expertise:** Restorations, new uses for old buildings **Hob./spts.:** Church work - Chaplain (nursing homes, jails, Bible studies), new church starts-church planter, woodworking, gardening, vocal performing, agriculture, livestock-cattle **SIC code:** 15 **Address:** Raymond Enterprises, 225 Old 290 West, P.O. Box 774, Dripping Springs, TX 78620-0774 **E-mail:** kayraytex@cs.com

RIVERA, MANUEL
Industry: Construction **Born:** October 30, 1977, Caguas, Puerto Rico **Univ./degree:** B.S., Civil Engineering **Current organization:** M.R. Construction Inc. **Title:** Civil Engineer **Type of organization:** Construction **Major product:** Urban development **Area of distribution:** Puerto Rico **Expertise:** Civil engineering **Affiliations:** American Society of Civil Engineers **Hob./spts.:** Boating, diving **SIC code:** 15 **Address:** PMB 616-200 Ave., Rafael Cordero St., #140, Caguas, PR 00725-3757 **E-mail:** manuelrivera@mail.com

RODRIGUEZ, ROBERTO M.
Industry: Construction/real estate **Born:** February 18, 1955, Havana, Cuba **Univ./degree:** M.B.A., Master of Business Administration, 1981; M.B.T., Master of Business Taxation,1992; Ph.D., Educational Policy and Administration, 1998, University of Minnesota **Current organization:** AHR Construction Inc. **Title:** Comptroller **Type of organization:** Construction **Major product:** Homes **Area of distribution:** Minnesota **Expertise:** Accounting and finance **Affiliations:** Institute of Management Accountants; Society of Agriculture; U.S. Achievement Academy **Hob./spts.:** Travel, bicycling, reading, music, theatre **SIC code:** 15 **Address:** ERA Beartooth Realty, LLC, 11916 Davenport Ct. N.E., Blaine, MN 55449 **E-mail:** rbrtrod@earthlink.net

RODRIQUEZ JR., RAFAEL
Industry: Construction **Univ./degree:** B.S., 2006 **Current organization:** DynAmerica Construction Inc. **Title:** President **Type of organization:** Construction firm **Major product:** Residential and commercial property improvements **Area of distribution:** Washington, D.C. **Expertise:** General construction **Affiliations:** S.B.A.; M.C.S. **SIC code:** 15 **Address:** DynAmerica Construction Inc., 3105 Mount Pleasant St. N.W., Suite 200, Washington, DC 20010 **E-mail:** rafael@dynamericainc.com

ROMINE II, RICHARD L.
Industry: Construction **Born:** January 3, 1970, Morristown, Tennessee **Current organization:** Romine & Associates Contracting and Design **Title:** Owner **Type of organization:** General contractor **Major product:** Remodeling and new construction of commercial and residential structures **Area of distribution:** National **Expertise:** Construction, general management **Hob./spts.:** Golf, photography **SIC code:** 15 **Address:** Romine & Associates Contracting and Design, 108 Bristol Dr., Lascassas, TN 37085 **E-mail:** richard@richardromine.net **Web address:** www.richardromine.net

ROSS, ERIC A.
Industry: Construction **Born:** September 11, 1961, Mineola, New York **Spouse:** Lauren **Married:** May 31, 1986 **Univ./degree:** B.A., Mathematics, Hope College, Holland Michigan, 1983; B.E., Engineering Science, Hofstra University, Hempstead, New York, 1985 **Current organization:** MC² (Management Computer Controls, Inc.) **Title:** Senior Engineer, Integrated Solutions Group **Type of organization:** Construction **Major product:** Heavy highway construction **Area of distribution:** International **Expertise:** Civil engineering, cost estimating, project management, new client development, contract administration; Licensed Professional Engineer; Certified Professional Estimator; National Guest Lecturer, (AGC/ASPE) **Honors/awards:** Who's Who Professional of the Year, 2006 **Affiliations:** American Society of Civil Engineers; American Society of Professional Estimators; Construction Institute; Construction Specifications Institute; Michigan Association of Planning; National Eagle Scout Association; National Society of Professional Engineers; Project Management Institute **Career accomplishments:** Actively involved with bidding/estimating of earthwork, underground utilities (sanitary, storm and water mains), concrete paving, cast in-place concrete structures, asphalt paving. As low bidder successfully completed projects totalling in excess of 60 million dollars; Developed construction parametrics to assist construction companies **Hob./spts.:** Golf, ballroom dancing, volleyball, sailing **SIC code:** 16 **Address:** MC² (Management Computer Controls, Inc.), 5100 Poplar Ave., Suite 3400, Memphis, TN 38137-3400 **E-mail:** eross@mc2-ice.com **Web address:** www.mc2-ice.com

RUDY, GARY E.
Industry: Heavy construction **Univ./degree:** M.B.A., University of Redlands **Current organization:** Duran & Venables, Inc. **Title:** Safety Director **Type of organization:** Contracting **Major product:** Excavation, paving **Area of distribution:** California **Expertise:** Heavy construction safety management **Affiliations:** National Utility Contractors Association ; American Society of Safety Engineers **Hob./spts.:** Skiing, bicycling, scuba diving **SIC code:** 16 **Address:** Duran & Venables, Inc., 261 Bothelo Ave., Milpitas, CA 95035 **E-mail:** gary@dvpave.com

SANDERS, MILAGROS G.
Industry: Construction **Born:** June 5, 1943, Philippines **Current organization:** Sanders Construction Co., Inc. **Title:** President **Type of organization:** Contracting **Major product:** Drainage, materials and supplies **Area of distribution:** Mount Holly Springs, Pennsylvania **Expertise:** Local government contracts **Affiliations:** Disadvantaged Minority Contractors **Hob./spts.:** Golf **SIC code:** 17 **Address:** Sanders Construction Co., Inc., P.O. Box 108, Mount Holly Springs, PA 17065 **E-mail:** fsanders1943@comcast.net

SCHLAM, STEVE
Industry: Construction **Born:** November 21, 1952, Cleveland, Ohio **Univ./degree:** B.A., Business, Kent State University, 1979 **Current organization:** Diamond Built Homes, LLC **Title:** Managing Member **Type of organization:** Developer, homebuilder **Major product:** Homes **Area of distribution:** Oregon **Expertise:** Overall management **Hob./spts.:** Baseball, fishing **SIC code:** 15 **Address:** Diamond Built Homes, LLC, 1516 S.W. Highland Ave., Redmond, OR 97756 **E-mail:** steve@diamondbuilthomes.com **Web address:** www.diamondbuilthomes.com

SCHMIDT, MICHAEL N.
Industry: Home builder/developer **Born:** April 26, 1959, Northridge, California **Univ./degree:** Attended Los Angeles Valley College, Business Management **Current organization:** M.B.K. Homes, Ltd. **Title:** Vice President of Construction **Type of organization:** Home builder **Major product:** New homes **Area of distribution:** Southern California **Expertise:** Operations and management **Published works:** Fourth in Customer Satisfaction, J.D. Powers, 2003 **Affiliations:** B.I.A.; A.G.C.; N.A.H.B.; Regional Commissioner and Board Member, A.Y.S.O. Executive Board of Directors **Hob./spts.:** Travel, community volunteering, family **SIC code:** 15 **Address:** M.B.K.

Homes Ltd., 175 Technology Dr., Irvine, CA 92618 **E-mail:** mikeschmidt@mbk.com **Web address:** www.mbkhomes.com

SCHOEFFLER, JULIE A.
Industry: Construction **Born:** November 20, 1954, Thibodaux, Louisiana **Univ./degree:** A.S., Office Administration, Nicholls State University, 1974 **Current organization:** Affordable Concepts, Inc. **Title:** Office Manager **Type of organization:** Construction **Major product:** Commercial and industrial construction **Area of distribution:** Nevada **Expertise:** Daily operations oversight; Notary Public **Honors/awards:** Citizen of Distinction, 2003 **Affiliations:** CMA Business Credit Services **Hob./spts.:** Baseball, football, sewing, reading **SIC code:** 15 **Address:** Affordable Concepts, Inc., 2975 W. Lake Mead Blvd., Suite 102, North Las Vegas, NV 89032 **E-mail:** jschoeffler@acilv.com

SCHOENDORF, JOHN D.
Industry: Construction **Born:** September 21, 1944, Jamaica, New York **Current organization:** Sawing High Construction **Title:** President/Owner **Type of organization:** Construction company **Major product:** Home and business remodeling **Area of distribution:** Bainbridge Island, Washington **Expertise:** Engineering and remodeling: Certified remodeling contractor **Affiliations:** National Home Builders Association **Hob./spts.:** Hiking, free mountain climbing (no ropes), family **SIC code:** 15 **Address:** Sawing High Construction, P.O. Box 798, Suquamish, WA 98392

SELL, GEORGE A.
Industry: Construction **Born:** May 21, 1972, Eau Claire, Wisconsin **Univ./degree:** B.S., Construction Management, University of Wisconsin, 1999 **Current organization:** Pulte Homes **Title:** Superintendent **Type of organization:** Contracting **Major product:** Residential home building **Area of distribution:** Minnesota **Expertise:** Construction superintendent **Affiliations:** N.H.A.B. **Hob./spts.:** Hunting, fishing, golf **SIC code:** 15 **Address:** Pulte Homes, 815 Northwest Pkwy., Suite 140, Eagan, MN 55121 **E-mail:** g.sell@pulte.com

SELVAGGIO, MICHAEL A.
Industry: Construction **Born:** March 8, 1961, Danbury, Connecticut **Current organization:** Lehr Construction Corp. **Title:** Project Manager **Type of organization:** Construction **Major product:** Interior renovation **Area of distribution:** New York, New York **Expertise:** Project coordinator **Hob./spts.:** Family, sports, coaching Little League **SIC code:** 15 **Address:** Lehr Construction Corp., 902 Broadway, New York, NY 10010 **E-mail:** michael_selvaggio@lehrco.com **Web address:** www.lehrco.com

SHAW, MICHAEL D.
Industry: Custom building, steel building **Born:** March 31, 1959, Fort Kent, Maine **Current organization:** MDS Building Inc. D/B/A/ Atlantic Builders **Title:** President **Type of organization:** Building contractors **Major product:** High end custom building, residential and commercial **Area of distribution:** Maine/coastal Maine **Expertise:** General contracting **Published works:** Magazine and newspaper articles **Affiliations:** A.S.A.; Rotary Club; American Forest & Paper Association; Registered Maine Guides Association **Hob./spts.:** Extreme sports **SIC code:** 15 **Address:** MDS Building Inc. D/B/A/ Atlantic Builders, P.O. Box 136, Surry, ME 04684 **E-mail:** atlanticbuild@acadia.net

SHAW, RON D.
Industry: Construction **Born:** February 21 1957, Los Angeles, California **Univ./degree:** A.A., Orange County College, 1979 **Current organization:** Shaw & Sons, Inc. **Title:** President **Type of organization:** Construction firm **Major product:** Architectural concrete **Area of distribution:** California **Expertise:** Concrete, construction, building **Honors/awards:** ACI Awards; Cornerstone Awards **Published works:** 1 book, "Shaw & Sons Architectural/Concrete Guide" **Hob./spts.:** Boating, dirt bikes, hiking **SIC code:** 17 **Address:** Shaw & Sons, Inc., 829 W. 17th St., Suite 5, Costa Mesa, CA 92627 **Web address:** www.shawconstruction.com and www.lithocrete.com

SHEPHERD, CHARLES L.
Industry: Construction **Born:** April 23, 1939, Portland, Oregon **Current organization:** Sun Country Homes **Title:** President **Type of organization:** General contractor, architect **Major product:** Custom coastal homes **Area of distribution:** Hudson, Florida **Expertise:** Construction management **Hob./spts.:** Scuba diving, pilot **SIC code:** 15 **Address:** Sun Country Homes, 9632 Katy Dr., #D-3, Hudson, FL 35667-4363 **E-mail:** info@suncountrygroup.com

SHEPHERD, RONNIE G.
Industry: Construction **Born:** July 25, 1957, Owensboro, Kentucky **Current organization:** Thompson Homes **Title:** Construction Foreman **Type of organization:** New home construction **Major product:** Complete building process of residential homes **Area of distribution:** Owensboro, Kentucky **Expertise:** Construction management and supervision **Hob./spts.:** Hunting **SIC code:** 15 **Address:** Thompson Homes, 316 Frederica St., Owensboro, KY 42301 **E-mail:** scshepherd@aol.com

SIDDIQUI, JAY A.
Industry: Electrical contracting **Born:** October 18, 1954 **Univ./degree:** B.S., Electricity; B.S., Power; M.A., Southeastern Oklahoma University, 1981 **Current organization:** Meco Electric Co., Inc. **Title:** President **Type of organization:** Electrical engineers/contractors **Major product:** Electrical design and building **Area of distribution:** New York, New Jersey **Expertise:** Electrical engineering, power and controls **Honors/awards:** Business Achievement Award from Mayor Guiliani **Affiliations:** A.S.S.E.; A.S.Q.; N.E.C.A.; I.E.E.E.; Local No. 3 **SIC code:** 17 **Address:** Meco Electric Co., Inc., 56 West St., Staten Island, NY 10310 **Phone:** (718)273-3900 **Fax:** (718)273-5900 **E-mail:** siddmeco@aol.com

SLAGEL, THOMAS R.
Industry: Residential construction **Born:** January 23, 1957, Pittsburgh, Pennsylvania **Univ./degree:** B.S., Business Administration/Accounting, Clarion University, Pennsylvania, 1979 **Current organization:** M/I Schottenstein Homes, Inc. **Title:** Vice President of Purchasing **Type of organization:** Construction/builders **Major product:** Single family detached and attached homes **Area of distribution:** Virginia **Expertise:** Purchasing, cost estimating, accounting **Hob./spts.:** Spending time with his kids, golf, bowling **SIC code:** 15 **Address:** 12401 Hampton Crossing Dr., Chesterfield, VA 23832 **E-mail:** tslagel@parkerorleans.com

SMITH, PHILLIP E.
Industry: Nonprofit housing developer **Born:** October 11, 1956, Youngstown, Ohio **Univ./degree:** B.S., Sociology and Psychology, Malone College, 1978 **Current organization:** Youngstown Choice Homes **Title:** President **Type of organization:** Housing developer **Major product:** Homes **Area of distribution:** Ohio **Expertise:** Housing development; Certified, Housing Credit Professional **Affiliations:** National Urban League **Hob./spts.:** Golf, travel **SIC code:** 15 **Address:** Youngstown Choice Homes, 2733 Market St., Youngstown, OH 45507

SMITH, STEWART R.
Industry: Construction **Born:** October 8, 1957, Los Angeles, California **Univ./degree:** B.S. **Current organization:** U.S. Home **Title:** Senior Construction Manager **Type of organization:** Home builder **Major product:** New home construction **Area of distribution:** California **Expertise:** Construction management **Hob./spts.:** Archery, hunting, fishing **SIC code:** 15 **Address:** U.S. Home, 2366 Gold Meadow Way, Suite 200, Gold River, CA 95670 **E-mail:** stewart.smith@lennar.com

SMITH JR., LOUIS C.
Industry: Plumbing **Born:** March 26, 1947, Newport News, Virginia **Univ./degree:** M.A.T., Biology, Murray State University, 1972 **Current organization:** L.C. Smith Plumbing & Heating Co., Inc. **Title:** President **Type of organization:** Service **Major product:** Plumbing and heating services **Area of distribution:** Henderson, Kentucky **Expertise:** Repair and remodeling; Journeyman Plumber License; Master Plumber License; Certified Massage Therapist **Honors/awards:** President's Environmental Youth Award (as sponsor of Water Watch Program at HCSJHS); Who's Who Among America's Teachers; National Register's Who's Who in Executives & Professionals; National Republican Congressional; Committee Business Advisory Commission; National Register's Who's Who in Executives & Businesses; Strathmore's Who's Who; 2004 Presidential Election Registry; NRCC Business Advisory Council "Businessman of the Year" in Kentucky; Ronald Reagan Gold Medal; 2004 Metropolitan Registries **Affiliations:** K.R.T.A.; K.A.E.E.; Board Member, K.S.T.A., 1982-83; N.E.A.; S.D.E.A.; H.E.A.; International Massage Association; Honorary Co-Chair, Republican Presidential Business Commission **Hob./spts.:** Gardening, fishing, travel **SIC code:** 17 **Address:** L.C. Smith Plumbing & Heating Co., Inc., 857 Madison St., Henderson, KY 42420

SOLARES, ANDRES J.
Industry: Construction **Born:** January 28, 1946, Havana, Cuba **Univ./degree:** B.S.C.E., University of Havana, Cuba, 1968; Diploma with distinction, Port & Shipping Administration, University of Whales, United Kingdom, 1970; Post Graduate, Management of the National Economy, ESDE, 1987; Post Graduate, Investment Management, 1987 **Current organization:** Talmac, Inc. **Title:** President **Type of organization:** General contracting firm **Major product:** Masonry & Stucco for large commercial projects **Area of distribution:** Florida **Expertise:** Management and engineering **Honors/awards:** Challenge Award, Contractor Resource Center; Republican of the Year, 2001; Businessman of the Year, 2003 through N.R.C.C.; Republican Gold Medal, 2002 **Published works:** Book, Investigaciones sobre la Industria de la Construccion, Cuba, 1981; numerous articles published in The Miami Herald, Diario de las Americas & Ahora Magazine **Affiliations:** C.A.A.C.E.; A.A.G.C.; P.B.C. **Hob./spts.:** Baseball, travel, politics **SIC code:** 17 **Address:** Talmac, Inc., 10411 N.W. 28th St., C-106, Miami, FL 33172 **E-mail:** andressolares@aol.com

SPANN, MITZI
Industry: Construction **Born:** June 24, 1968, Dixon, Tennessee **Current organization:** Spann Builders, LLC **Title:** Owner **Type of organization:** Building contractor **Major product:** Custom home building **Area of distribution:** Burns, Tennessee **Expertise:**

Home building **Affiliations:** Chamber of Commerce; Home Builders Association; State Commissioner Board of Home Improvements **Hob./spts.:** Golf, stained glass **SIC code:** 15 **Address:** Spann Builders, LLC, 2000 Spencer Mill Rd., Burns, TN 37029 **E-mail:** spannbldr@aol.com **Web address:** www.spannbuilders.com

STAGEMEYER, BILL DALE
Industry: Construction **Born:** July 4, 1958, Sundance, Wyoming **Univ./degree:** A.A., Commercial Arts, 1980, Casper, Wyoming **Current organization:** B.D.S. Development Inc. **Title:** President **Type of organization:** General contractor **Major product:** Custom high end kitchen remodeling **Area of distribution:** Arizona **Expertise:** Building and design specialist, project management, business development and customer care **Hob./spts.:** 4-wheeling, boating, rock climbing **SIC code:** 15 **Address:** B.D.S. Development Inc., 1528 E. Jasmine, Mesa, AZ 85203 **E-mail:** bdsscs@aol.com

STAUFFER, CHRIS
Industry: Construction **Born:** November 28, 1932, Front Wayne, Indiana **Current organization:** Chris Stauffer Homes, Inc. **Title:** President **Type of organization:** Private contractor **Major product:** Residential homes **Area of distribution:** Indiana **Expertise:** Home building, land development **Honors/awards:** Sagamore of the Wabash World Record Cross Country Bicycle Challenge, Coast to Coast, 70 year olds, 7 days/16 hours/31 minutes, 2002 **Hob./spts.:** Bicycling **SIC code:** 15 **Address:** Chris Stauffer Homes, Inc., 10808 Coldwater Rd., Ft. Wayne, IN 46845 **E-mail:** chrisstaufferhomes@verizon.net **Web address:** www.chrisstaufferhomes.com

STORY, JEFF D.
Industry: Heavy construction **Born:** March 16, 1961, Henderson, Texas **Current organization:** Aker Kvaerner Industrial Constructors **Title:** Mechanical Superintendent **Type of organization:** Industrial constructors **Major product:** Construction for oil and gas, pulp and paper, electrical power industries **Area of distribution:** International **Expertise:** Construction management **Hob./spts.:** Bowling, fishing, waterskiing **SIC code:** 17 **Address:** Aker Kvaerner Industrial Constructors, 1501 W. Derby Ave., Auburndale, FL 33823 **E-mail:** jeff.story@akerkvaerner.com

SWIFT, RALPH M.
Industry: Construction **Current organization:** Swift Construction & Development **Title:** Owner **Type of organization:** Contractor **Major product:** Land/lot development **Area of distribution:** California **Expertise:** Development **SIC code:** 15 **Address:** Swift Construction & Development, 8850 Auburn Folsom Rd., Granite Bay, CA 95746 **E-mail:** RMSwift@surewest.net

TAGLIAFERRI, PAUL J.
Industry: Construction **Born:** Brooklyn, New York **Univ./degree:** B.S., Economics and Business Management, Dowling College **Current organization:** Lorich Building Corp. **Title:** Senior Project Manager **Type of organization:** Construction **Major product:** Construction management **Area of distribution:** New York **Expertise:** Business management/economics **SIC code:** 15 **Address:** Lorich Building Corp., 15 Rave St., Hicksville, NY 11801 **E-mail:** pjtag124@aol.com

THOMAS, DANIEL E.
Industry: Construction/financial services **Born:** February 13, 1963, Livingston, Montana; Raised and educated in Billings, Montana **Univ./degree:** B.S., Psychology, 1985; B.S., Business Management and Accounting, 1988, Rocky Mountain College, Billings, Montana; M.B.A. Candidate, University of Phoenix **Current organization:** Lueck Masonry, Inc. **Title:** President and Chief Financial Officer **Type of organization:** Sub contractor **Major product:** Masonry **Area of distribution:** Colorado **Expertise:** Accounting and finance **Affiliations:** Construction Financial Management Association; Rocky Mountain Masonry Institute; Timberline Users Group; American Biographical Institute USA; Institute of Management Accounts; National Register's Who's Who; Strathmore's Who's Who; International Association of Business Leaders **Hob./spts.:** Gardening, cooking, reading, music **SIC code:** 17 **Address:** Lueck Masonry, Inc., 2000 West 60th Ave., Denver, CO 80221 **E-mail:** danielthomas1066@aol.com

THOMPSON, JEFF P.
Industry: Construction **Born:** January 24, 1943, Texas **Univ./degree:** A.S., Business Administration, San Antonio College **Current organization:** Zachery Construction Co. **Title:** Equipment Superintendent **Type of organization:** Construction firm **Major product:** Power plants, roads, bridges **Area of distribution:** International **Expertise:** Power plant construction equipment **Published works:** Safety articles **Affiliations:** N.R.A., 82nd Airborne **SIC code:** 16 **Address:** Zachery Construction Co., 527 Logwood Ave., San Antonio, TX 78221 **E-mail:** thompsonjp@zachery.com

TWEDDLE, THOMAS J.
Industry: Construction **Univ./degree:** Attended Penn State University for Architecture **Current organization:** Tweddle Construction **Title:** President **Type of organization:** Construction contractor **Major product:** Residential and commercial construction **Area of distribution:** Montgomery, Bucks & Philadelphia Counties **Expertise:** Fine Finish Carpentry, custom kitchens and baths, historic renovations, construction management **Honors/awards:** Whole House Renovation Award (Chrysalis Award), 2000-2001 **Affiliations:** National Home Builders Association; Who's Who of America; United States Power Squadron **Hob./spts.:** Sport fishing, bowling, boating **SIC code:** 15 **Address:** Tweddle Construction, 1425 Tallyho Rd., Meadowbrook, PA 19046 **E-mail:** ttweddle@aol.com

UPHAM, FRANK A.
Industry: Construction **Current organization:** SD Deacon Corp. of Oregon **Title:** Safety Director **Type of organization:** General contractor **Major product:** Commercial construction **Area of distribution:** West coast **Expertise:** Safety compliance, fall protection, excavating protection **Honors/awards:** Safety Professional of the Year, 2003-04 **Affiliations:** American Society of Safety Engineers **Hob./spts.:** Harley Davidson motor cycles, fishing, hunting, sailing **SIC code:** 15 **Address:** SD Deacon Corp. of Oregon, 0720 SW Bancroft, Portland, OR 97239 **E-mail:** frank.upham@deacon.com **Web address:** www.deacon.com

VALENTINE II, NOAH
Industry: Residential construction **Born:** May 29, 1951, Winchester, Indiana **Univ./degree:** A.A., Computer Engineering, Tampa Technical School, 1992 **Current organization:** Rainbow Springs Const. Corp. (a.k.a. Podia Construx) **Title:** Senior Estimator **Type of organization:** Land development and building **Major product:** Custom homes **Area of distribution:** Florida **Expertise:** Estimating **Affiliations:** International Executive Guild **SIC code:** 15 **Address:** Rainbow Springs Const. Corp. (a.k.a. Podia Construx), 9207 S.W. 193rd Circle, Dunnellon, FL 34432 **E-mail:** noah@tvrs.com

VAN DORST, ROY M.
Industry: Construction **Born:** November 3, 1947, California **Univ./degree:** Engineering, California State Polytechnic University **Current organization:** California Homes **Title:** Director of Development **Type of organization:** Development and construction **Major product:** Single-family homes and apartments **Area of distribution:** California **Expertise:** Engineering and site development **Hob./spts.:** Hunting, fishing **SIC code:** 15 **Address:** California Homes, 3202 W. March Lane, Suite A, Stockton, CA 95219 **E-mail:** rvandorst@californiahomes2000.com

VARNADOE, HARRY F.
Industry: Commercial grading/underground utilities **Born:** May 8, 1945, Lumber City, Georgia **Current organization:** Harry Varnadoe Grading & Piping, Inc. **Title:** President/Owner **Type of organization:** Sub contractor **Major product:** Fire, water, domestic storm drains, grading, hauling, sanitary, sewer **Area of distribution:** Fairburn, California **Expertise:** President/Owner **SIC code:** 16 **Address:** Harry Varnadoe Grading & Piping, Inc., 6925 Roosevelt Hwy., Fairburn, GA 30213 **E-mail:** hvarnadoehug&p@fairburn.com

VÁZQUEZ, HIPOLITO A.
Industry: Construction **Born:** January 12, 1969, Mayaguez, Puerto Rico **Univ./degree:** B.S., Civil Engineering, University of Puerto Rico, 1992 **Current organization:** Oriental Sand & Gravel **Title:** Plant Manager **Type of organization:** Sand quarry **Major product:** Sand **Area of distribution:** Puerto Rico **Expertise:** Civil engineering **Affiliations:** A.S.C.E.; Puerto Rico College of Engineering **SIC code:** 17 **Address:** Oriental Sand & Gravel, P.O. Box 9022708, San Juan, PR 00902-2708 **E-mail:** flh04@coqui.net

VERNON, CLIFFORD J.
Industry: Electrical **Born:** January 22, 1922, Shamung, New York **Current organization:** Line Construction Contractors/Buffalo Electric and Bradley & Williams **Title:** Journeyman Electrician/Published Poet (Retired) **Type of organization:** Electrical contracting firm **Major product:** Electrical services **Area of distribution:** National **Expertise:** Foreman, General Foreman and Superintendent **Published works:** Book, "Grandfather's Politically Incorrect Poems for the 21st Century", Barnes & Noble Book Store and Christian Arrowhead Book Store **Affiliations:** A.P.S.; served in U.S. Signal Corps 1943-1947 (WWII Veteran) **SIC code:** 17 **Address:** 5405 Rt. 26, #3, Whitney Point, NY 13862

WADDELL, KEVIN D.
Industry: Environmental construction **Univ./degree:** B.S., Civil Engineering, University of Kansas, 1993 **Current organization:** Redford Construction, Inc. **Title:** P.E., Project Manager **Type of organization:** Utility construction **Major product:** Waterlines, sanitary sewers, storm water/drainage systems **Area of distribution:** Missouri, Kansas **Expertise:** Civil engineering/construction management **Affiliations:** American Waterworks Association; Licensed P.E. in Kansas & Texas **Hob./spts.:** Golf, collecting sports cards **SIC code:** 15 **Address:** Redford Construction, Inc., P.O. Box 1065, Raymore, MO 64083 **E-mail:** kwaddell3@cs.com

WAGNER, WILLIAM T.
Industry: Manufactured housing **Born:** June 16, 1956, Lewistown, Pennsylvania **Univ./degree:** A.S., Civil Engineering, Harrisburg Area Community College **Current organization:** Marlette Homes **Title:** Market Development Manager **Type of organi-**

zation: Manufacturing **Major product:** Mobile and modular homes **Area of distribution:** Pennsylvania, New York, Virginia, West Virginia **Expertise:** Sales **Affiliations:** Secretary, New York Housing Association **Hob./spts.:** Volleyball, football, golf, home remodeling, furniture building **SIC code:** 15 **Address:** Marlette Homes, 30 Industrial Park Rd., Lewistown, PA 17044 **E-mail:** billwa@clayton.net

WALD, TERRY A.
Industry: Construction **Born:** November 4, 1955, Bismarck, North Dakota **Current organization:** T&M Electric **Title:** President/Owner **Type of organization:** Electrical contracting **Major product:** Electrical wiring **Area of distribution:** Bismarck, North Dakota **Expertise:** Electrical wiring for residential and commercial properties **Affiliations:** Bismarck Chamber of Commerce; Bismarck Homebuilders Association **Hob./spts.:** Hunting, fishing **SIC code:** 17 **Address:** T&M Electric, 8301 Apple Creek Rd., Bismarck, ND 58504 **E-mail:** viper8301@hotmail.com

WANCATA, GEORGE R.
Industry: Construction **Born:** July 1, 1942, Cleveland, Ohio **Univ./degree:** A.A., Business, Ohio University **Current organization:** Crane Certification Services, Inc. **Title:** President **Type of organization:** Construction **Major product:** Heavy equipment/crane inspections **Area of distribution:** National **Expertise:** Crane inspections, operations **Affiliations:** Lifetime Member, Operating Engineers **Hob./spts.:** Family, gardening **SIC code:** 17 **Address:** 8076 Richard Rd., Broadview Heights, OH 44147-1241 **E-mail:** info@cranecert.com **Web address:** www.cranecert.com

WEBSTER, JEAN H.
Industry: General construction/Architecture **Born:** September 6, 1942, Barthelemy, West Indies **Univ./degree:** B.Arch., Bennett College, England, 1962 **Current organization:** Authentic Design & Construction Co. **Title:** Owner **Type of organization:** Construction **Major product:** Custom homes **Area of distribution:** Virgin Islands **Expertise:** Marketing, engineering, operations **Affiliations:** American Design and Drafting Institute; Virgin Islands General Contractors Association **Hob./spts.:** Sailing, baseball, fishing **SIC code:** 15 **Address:** Authentic Design & Construction Co., P.O. Box 8301, St. Thomas, VI 00801-1301 **E-mail:** errolw@viaccess.com

WEEKLEY III, E. WALTER
Industry: Construction **Born:** December 15, 1962, Atlanta, Georgia **Univ./degree:** B.S.; B.A., The Citadel, Military College of South Carolina **Current organization:** WeWil Construction Co., Inc. **Title:** President **Type of organization:** General contractor **Major product:** New home construction, custom and spec **Area of distribution:** South Carolina **Expertise:** Construction and business management **Hob./spts.:** Competitive tennis, fishing, hunting **SIC code:** 15 **Address:** WeWil Construction Co., Inc., 925-B Wappoo Rd., Charleston, SC 29407

WENGER SR., BRUCE D.
Industry: Residential construction **Born:** November 2, 1967, Framingham, Massachusetts **Univ./degree:** B.A., Economics, Hampden-Sydney College, 1989 **Current organization:** Parker & Orleans Homebuilders **Title:** Director of Construction Services **Type of organization:** Construction **Major product:** Single family homes **Area of distribution:** Virginia **Expertise:** Administration, marketing, purchasing **SIC code:** 15 **Address:** Parker & Orleans Homebuilders, 711 Moorefield Park Dr., Suite E, Richmond, VA 23236 **E-mail:** bwenger@parkerorleans.com

WHITE, MARC
Industry: Construction **Born:** November 16, 1955, Birmingham, Alabama **Univ./degree:** B.S., Education, New Mexico State University, 1981 **Current organization:** Homes by Marc LLC **Title:** Owner **Type of organization:** Contractor **Major product:** New residential homes, land development **Area of distribution:** Las Cruces, New Mexico **Expertise:** Planning, design, management **Affiliations:** President, Las Cruces Home Builders Association; Las Cruces Realtors Association **Hob./spts.:** Golf, travel **SIC code:** 15 **Address:** Homes by Marc LLC, 3551 Cactus Gulch Way, Las Cruces, NM 88011 **E-mail:** marchomes@zianet.com

WILGUS, PATSY C.
Industry: Construction **Born:** Hattiesburg, Mississippi **Univ./degree:** Accounting, Management, University of Southern Mississippi **Current organization:** Larry Johnson & Co. **Title:** Partner, Officer Manager, Real Estate Agent **Type of organization:** Construction **Major product:** Specialty home construction **Area of distribution:** Mississippi **Expertise:** Operations management, bookkeeping, business development **Affiliations:** H.B.R.; N.A.R.; H.B.A.; Eastern Star; D.A.C. **Hob./spts.:** Family, sewing, quilting **SIC code:** 15 **Address:** Larry Johnson & Co., 11 Carriage Lane, Hattiesburg, MS 39402 **E-mail:** patsycwilgus@comcast.net

WILLIAMS, FRED T.
Industry: Electrical construction **Born:** July 18, 1957, Bridgeport, Connecticut **Current organization:** Paul Dinto Electrical Contractors Inc. **Title:** Project Manager **Type of organization:** Electrical contracting **Major product:** Electrical installation and design **Area of distribution:** Connecticut **Expertise:** Electrical project management **Hob./spts.:** Time with family, boating **SIC code:** 17 **Address:** Paul Dinto Electrical Contractors Inc., 121 Turnpike Dr., Middlebury, CT 06762 **E-mail:** fwilliams@pauldintoelec.com

WILSON, MARK M.
Industry: Construction **Born:** June 29, 1942, Granite Falls, Minnesota **Univ./degree:** Rocky Mountain College, 1967 Post Graduate, Business, Biology, Psychology **Current organization:** Duininck Bros. **Title:** Estimator **Type of organization:** Producing, planning, manufacturing **Major product:** Grading, asphalt, rock products **Area of distribution:** Minnesota **Expertise:** Engineering, estimating, management **Hob./spts.:** Fishing, hunting, all sports **SIC code:** 17 **Address:** Duininck Bros., 8070 Hwy. 23 N.E., Spicer, MN 56288

WOODWARD SR., CHARLES L.
Industry: Construction **Born:** May 27, 1954, Coral Gables, Florida **Current organization:** Paladin Concrete Services, LLC **Title:** Owner/Managing Member **Type of organization:** Concrete construction firm **Major product:** Concrete construction **Area of distribution:** Arizona **Expertise:** Concrete service **Affiliations:** Northwest Arizona Better Business Bureau; Kingman Chamber of Commerce **Hob./spts.:** Golf, fishing **SIC code:** 17 **Address:** Paladin Concrete Services, LLC, HC 32 Box 3186, Kingman, AZ 86401 **E-mail:** paladin1@frontiernet.net

WRIGHT, ALAN MICHAEL
Industry: Construction **Born:** February 16, 1949, Wichita, Kansas **Univ./degree:** B.S., Construction Science, Kansas State University, 1971 **Current organization:** Mid-South Partitions Tulsa, Inc. **Title:** Vice President **Type of organization:** Contractor **Major product:** Commercial, interiors **Area of distribution:** Tulsa metropolitan area **Expertise:** Project management, marketing **Affiliations:** B.B.B.; National Federation of Independent Business; Republican National Committee; National Republican Congressional Committee; Heritage Foundation; Oklahoma Republican State Committee; Kansas State University Alumni Association **Hob./spts.:** Golf, lake activities, travel, politics, reading **SIC code:** 15 **Address:** Mid-South Partitions Tulsa, Inc., 5835 S. Garnett Rd., Tulsa, OK 74146 **E-mail:** wright.msp@tulsacoxmail.com

YANINAS, GERALD E.
Industry: Building construction **Born:** January 29, 1950, Nanticoke, Pennsylvania **Current organization:** Barr & Barr, Inc. **Title:** Superintendent **Type of organization:** Construction firm **Major product:** Building construction **Area of distribution:** Mid-Atlantic and Northeast U.S. **Expertise:** Superintendent of construction; continually employed in construction industry since 1967 **Published works:** Home Magazine, 1987; Global Architecture **Affiliations:** A.S.T.M.; Construction Specification Institute; Door and Hardware Institute; American Concrete Institute; Concrete Reinforcing Steel Institute; N.F.P.A.; Financial Secretary and Past President of Tatra of Luzerne County, Pennsylvania **Hob./spts.:** Automobiles, designed and self-built his home **SIC code:** 15 **Address:** Barr & Barr, Inc., 110 Yeager Rd., Mountaintop, PA 18707-9729 **E-mail:** jyaninas@barrandbarr.com

YOUNG, JOHN F.
Industry: Construction **Born:** June 18, 1956, Columbus, Ohio **Univ./degree:** B.S., Construction, University of New Mexico **Current organization:** Blue Sky Builders, Inc. **Title:** Project Manager **Type of organization:** General contracting **Major product:** Commercial construction **Area of distribution:** New Mexico **Expertise:** Project management **Affiliations:** N.M.S.E.A.; A.S.C.E. **Hob./spts.:** Mountain biking, skiing, reading, alternative energy **SIC code:** 15 **Address:** 98 County Rd. 119, Espanola, NM 87532 **E-mail:** portyoung@cybermesa.com

ZEHEB, SHERRY S.
Industry: Construction **Born:** April 2, 1962, Richmond, Virginia **Current organization:** Parker & Orleans Homebuilders **Title:** Construction Services Coordinator **Type of organization:** Construction **Major product:** Single family homes **Area of distribution:** Virginia **Expertise:** Construction plan review, distribution and service coordination **Hob./spts.:** Running **SIC code:** 15 **Address:** Parker & Orleans Homebuilders, 711 Moorefield Park Dr., Suite H, Richmond, VA 23236 **E-mail:** szeheb@parkerorleans.com

Manufacturing

ABALOS, DANIEL M.
Industry: Aerospace **Univ./degree:** B.S., Operations, 1979 **Current organization:** Thales Avionics **Title:** Director, Operations **Type of organization:** Manufacturing, product development **Major product:** Avionics **Area of distribution:** International **Expertise:** Daily operations, management, manufacturing **Hob./spts.:** Softball, hiking **SIC code:** 37 **Address:** 2415 Via Sedona, San Clemente, CA 92673 **E-mail:** dan.abalos@thales-ifs.com

ABEYTA, MIKE
Industry: Electronics **Born:** March 21, 1958, Long Beach, California **Current organization:** BI Technologies **Title:** Facility supervisor **Type of organization:** Manufacturing **Major product:** Electronic devices for steering **Area of distribution:** International **Expertise:** Facility management, safety and HAZMAT training **Hob./spts.:** Physical fitness, spectator sports enthusiast **SIC code:** 36 **Address:** BI Technologies, 4200 Bonita Place, Fullerton, CA 92835 **E-mail:** mikeabeyta@bitechnologies.com **Web address:** www.bitechnologies.com

ADAM, JOHN M.
Industry: Beverages **Born:** May 26, Callicoon, New York **Univ./degree:** A.S., Electronics, Management Process Diploma, Rochester Institute of Technology **Current organization:** Cadbury Schweppes America's Beverages **Title:** Maintenance Manager **Type of organization:** Manufacturing **Major product:** Juices **Area of distribution:** National **Expertise:** Troubleshooter **Affiliations:** A.F.E. **Hob./spts.:** Motorcycle riding, working on small motors **SIC code:** 20 **Address:** Cadbury Schweppes America's Beverages, 4363 Route 104, Williamson, NY 14589 **E-mail:** john.adam@cs-americas.com

ADAMS, CHRISTOPHER
Industry: Research instrumentation **Born:** June 9, 1976, Columbus, Ohio **Univ./degree:** B.S., Biology, Minor, Chemistry, Bowling Green State University, 1999 **Current organization:** Columbus Instruments **Title:** Assistant Sales Manager/Marketing Manager **Type of organization:** Manufacturing/distributor **Major product:** Research instrumentation **Area of distribution:** International **Expertise:** Sales, marketing **Hob./spts.:** Computer graphic design, music **SIC code:** 38 **Address:** Columbus Instruments, 950 N. Hague Ave., Columbus, OH 43204 **E-mail:** cadams@colinst.com **Web address:** www.colinst.com

ADAMS, RICHARD C.
Industry: Steel **Born:** Pittsburgh, Pennsylvania **Univ./degree:** B.S., Metallurgy, University of Pennsylvania **Current organization:** Charter Steel **Title:** Manager of Quality/Technical Services **Type of organization:** Manufacturing **Major product:** Steel **Area of distribution:** National **Expertise:** Management, quality control **Affiliations:** A.S.Q.; A.S.M.; A.I.S.I.; I.F.I **SIC code:** 33 **Address:** Charter Steel, 4300 E. 49th St., Cuyahoga Heights, OH 44125-1004 **E-mail:** adamsr@chartersteel.com

ADAMS JR., WILLIAM J. (BILL)
Industry: Machinery **Born:** February 9, 1917, Riverdale, California **Spouse:** Marijane E. Leishman Adams **Married:** December 26, 1939 **Children:** W. Michael Adams, 63; John P. Adams, deceased at 52 **Univ./degree:** B.S.M.E. Magna Cum Laude, Santa Clara University, California, 1937 **Title:** P.E., FMC Corp. (Retired) **Type of organization:** Manufacturing **Major product:** Machinery **Area of distribution:** International **Expertise:** Mechanical engineering (Mechanical CA ME7672, Retired); Agricultural engineering (Agricultural CA AG234, Retired) **Honors/awards:** Listed in Who's Who in America; Listed in Who's Who in Science and Engineering; Distinguished Engineering Alumnus Award, Santa Clara University, 1991; Outstanding Engineering Service Award, Santa Clara University, 2003; Silicon Valley Engineering Council Hall of Fame, 1998 **Published works:** Technical papers and presentations; 2 books; 12 U.S. and 15 foreign patents **Affiliations:** Life Fellow, American Society of Mechanical Engineers; Fellow, American Society of Agricultural Engineering; Life Member, Society of Automotive Engineers **Hob./spts.:** Travel, fly-fishing, skiing, hunting **SIC code:** 35 **Address:** 7940 Caledonia Dr., San Jose, CA 95135

AFFUL, JOHN KOFI
Industry: Consumer products **Born:** September 28, 1959, Ghana, West Africa **Univ./degree:** B.S., Chemistry & Biology, Illinois State University **Current organization:** Proctor & Gamble Mfg. Co. **Title:** Site Environmental Leader **Type of organization:** Manufacturing **Major product:** Metamucil **Area of distribution:** International **Expertise:** Environmental control, DOT/HAZ-MAT Coordinator **Affiliations:** Former Member, A.C.S. **Hob./spts.:** Ping-pong, watching basketball, football and playing soccer (Illinois State University) **SIC code:** 28 **Address:** Proctor & Gamble Mfg. Co., Environmental Dept., 2050 S. 35th Ave., Phoenix, AZ 85009 **E-mail:** afful.jk@pg.com **Web address:** www.pg.com

AGRAWAL, OM P.
Industry: Electronics **Born:** India **Univ./degree:** M.B.A., University of Santa Clara, 1985; Ph.D., Iowa State University, 1974 **Current organization:** Lattice Semiconductor **Title:** Vice President and Chief Technical Officer **Type of organization:** IC Manufacturing **Major product:** Semiconductors (PLDs) **Area of distribution:** International **Expertise:** New product development with focus on new innovative architectures **Honors/awards:** 83 patents; "Inventor of the Year" Award, Silicon Valley Intellectual Property Lawyers Association, 2000; Significant Achievement Award, AMD, 1999; Most Prolific Author Award, AMD, 1992 **Published works:** 60+ technical papers; Co-Author, "High Speed Memory Systems" with Dr. A.V. Pohm **Affiliations:** A.C.M. **Hob./spts.:** Music, hiking **SIC code:** 36 **Address:** Lattice Semiconductor, 2680 Zanker Rd., San Jose, CA 95134 **E-mail:** om.grawal@latticesemi.com

AGRILLO, TED
Industry: Publishing **Univ./degree:** A.S., Graphic Arts Design, New York Institute of Technology, 1966 **Current organization:** Grasshopper Productions **Title:** President **Type of organization:** Manufacturing/distributor **Major product:** Novelty children's books **Area of distribution:** National **Expertise:** Oversees daily operations **Affiliations:** Bookbinders Guild of New York **SIC code:** 27 **Address:** Grasshopper Productions, 1858 Hempstead Turnpike, East Meadow, NY 11554 **E-mail:** grasshopper.productions@att.net

AGUAYO, PEDRO
Industry: Cement **Univ./degree:** B.S., Electrical Engineering, Colima University, Mexico **Current organization:** Holcim (US) Inc., Ada Plant **Title:** Area Manager **Type of organization:** Manufacturing **Major product:** Cement **Area of distribution:** National **Expertise:** Process engineering, production, quality management **Hob./spts.:** Soccer, fishing, bicycling **SIC code:** 32 **Address:** Holcim (US) Inc., Ada Plant, 14500 CR 1550, Ada, OK 74820 **E-mail:** pedro.aguayo@holcim.com

AGUIÑAGA, MAGDALENA
Industry: Electronics **Born:** September 25, 1974, Toluca, Mexico **Univ./degree:** M.I.B., École Superior de Management, France, 2001 **Current organization:** Alpine Electronics of America **Title:** Sr. Buyer **Type of organization:** Manufacturing **Major product:** Electronics **Area of distribution:** International **Expertise:** Purchasing of raw materials for manufacturing and packaging **Hob./spts.:** Volunteer hospital work **SIC code:** 36 **Address:** 701 Via Vista, Pharr, TX 78577 **E-mail:** iosoyfeliz@hotmail.com

AHRONI, JOSEPH M.
Industry: Electrical products **Born:** March 24, 1920, Seattle, Washington **Univ./degree:** Officers School, California **Current organization:** General Enterprises, Inc. **Title:** President **Type of organization:** Manufacturing, distribution, importing **Major product:** Christmas lighting products **Area of distribution:** International **Expertise:** Engineering **Affiliations:** New York Academy of Science; American Association for the Advancement of Science **Hob./spts.:** Sports **SIC code:** 36 **Address:** General Enterprises, Inc., 6554 Fifth Place So., Seattle, WA 98108-3434

AKOPIAN, PAUL
Industry: Medical equipment **Born:** September 25, 1944, Soviet Union **Univ./degree:** Ph.D., Academy of Sciences of the USSR, 1975 **Current organization:** Integrated Surgical Systems **Title:** Operation & Engineering Director **Type of organization:** Designing and manufacturing of medical equipment **Major product:** Medical equipment **Area of distribution:** International **Expertise:** Research and development, engineering **Published works:** 10 articles **Affiliations:** American Society of Orthopedic Surgeons; Boy Scouts of America **Hob./spts.:** Mountain climbing, skiing **SIC code:** 38 **Address:** Integrated Surgical Systems, 1850 Research Park Dr., Davis, CA 95616 **E-mail:** pakopian@ultimatehc.com **Web address:** www.robodoc.com

ALAIGH, POONAM
Industry: Pharmaceuticals **Born:** November 19, 1964, Pakistan **Univ./degree:** M.D., Lady Harding Medical School, 1987; M.S., Healthcare Policy and Management, Stonybrook University, 1997 **Current organization:** Glaxo Smith Kline **Title:** Senior Medical Director/M.D. **Type of organization:** Manufacturing, research and development **Major product:** Pharmaceuticals **Area of distribution:** International **Expertise:** Internal medicine, vascular disease **Published works:** Multiple publications **Affiliations:** A.C.P.; A.M.A. **Hob./spts.:** Music, reading, hiking **SIC code:** 28 **Address:** Glaxo Smith Kline, 1600 Vine St., Philadelphia, PA 19102 **E-mail:** poonam.alaigh@gsk.com

ALBERICO, STEVEN P.
Industry: Engineering/nuclear power **Born:** September 29, 1956, Joliet, Illinois **Univ./degree:** B.S.M.E., University of Illinois, 1978 **Current organization:** Exelon Corp., La Salle Station **Title:** Project Manager **Type of organization:** Generation plant **Major product:** Electric power **Area of distribution:** Illinois **Expertise:** Engineering, project management, turbine generators **Affiliations:** N.S.P.E **Hob./spts.:** Biking (former organizer of the Round, Illinois bike ride event), skiing **SIC code:** 36 **Address:** 208 Beechwood Dr., Minooka, IL 60447 **E-mail:** steve.alberico@exeloncorp.com

ALBRECHT, CHRISTOPHER S.
Industry: Food service marketing **Born:** October 10, 1966, Santa Ana, California **Univ./degree:** B.B.A., Florida State University **Current organization:** Gulf States Food Service Marketing, LLC **Title:** Food Service Marketing Representative **Type of organization:** Manufacturing/distributing **Major product:** Food products **Area of distribution:** Louisiana **Expertise:** Marketing **SIC code:** 20 **Address:** Gulf States Food Service Marketing, LLC, P.O. Box 338, Metairie, LA 70004 **E-mail:** lanole@cox.net

ALBRECHT, E. DANIEL
Industry: Metals/ceramics **Born:** February 11, 1937, Kewanee, Illinois **Univ./degree:** Ph.D., University of Arizona, 1964 **Current organization:** Buehler International, Inc. **Title:** Chairman Emeritus **Type of organization:** Manufacturing, R&D **Major product:** High temperature ceramics and composites **Area of distribution:** International **Expertise:** Product design, corporate executive organization specialist **Hob./spts.:** Botany, gardening, golf, trustee of museum **SIC code:** 32 **Address:** 5219 N. Casa Blanca Dr., #55, Paradise Valley, AZ 85253-6201 **E-mail:** edasantafe@aol.com

ALCÓN, SILVIA
Industry: Cosmetics **Born:** June 18, 1971, Barcelona, Spain **Univ./degree:** B.A., Economics, Fordham University, 1993 **Current organization:** L'Oreal **Title:** Senior Manager, Creative Package Development **Type of organization:** Manufacturing, distributing, marketing **Major product:** Cosmetics **Area of distribution:** International **Expertise:** Development **Hob./spts.:** Music, reading, travel **SIC code:** 28 **Address:** L'Oreal, 575 Fifth Ave., 20th floor, New York, NY 10017 **E-mail:** salcon@us.loreal.com **Web address:** www.loreal.com

ALDERSON, STEVEN R.
Industry: Sales **Born:** August 28, 1948, St. Louis, Missouri **Current organization:** Alderson Industrial Sales, Inc. **Title:** President **Type of organization:** Manufacturing **Major product:** Power transmissions and electrical products **Area of distribution:** Mid-western U.S. **Expertise:** Practical engineering, power transmission **Published works:** Newspaper and magazine articles **Affiliations:** M.A.N.A.; P.T.R.A. **Hob./spts.:** Motorcycle enthusiast **SIC code:** 39 **Address:** Alderson Industrial Sales, Inc., 1 Ronda Dr., Florissant, MO 63031 **E-mail:** steve@aldersonsales.com **Web address:** www.aldersonsales.com

ALELYUNAS, YUN W.
Industry: Pharmaceuticals **Born:** July 6, 1960, Beijing, China **Univ./degree:** Ph.D., Physical Organic Chemistry, UOR, 1988; B.S., Chemistry, Nanka University **Current organization:** AstraZeneca **Title:** Scientist **Type of organization:** Manufacturing, research & development **Major product:** Pharmaceuticals **Area of distribution:** International **Expertise:** Chemistry **Published works:** 10 + technical journals, 5 abstracts **Affiliations:** A.A.P.S.; A.C.S.; A.L.A. **Hob./spts.:** The outdoors, hiking, travel, reading, camping **SIC code:** 28 **Address:** AstraZeneca, 1800 Concord Pike, Wilmington, DE 19803 **E-mail:** yun.alelyunas@astrazeneca.com **Web address:** www.astrazeneca.com

ALLEN, JERRY L.
Industry: Food **Univ./degree:** Aviation Maintenance Degree **Current organization:** Gibbon Packing Inc. **Title:** Plant Electrician **Type of organization:** Manufacturing **Major product:** Red meat processing **Area of distribution:** National **Expertise:** Electrical **Affiliations:** National Horse Association; National Rifle Association **SIC code:** 20 **Address:** Gibbon Packing Inc., 218 E. Hwy. 30, Gibbon, NE 68840 **E-mail:** jerryallen@gibbonpacking.com

ALLEN, JOAN M.
Industry: Electronic assembly **Born:** Danbury, Connecticut **Univ./degree:** A.S., Radio/TV Broadcasting, Connecticut School of Broadcasting, 1979 **Current organization:** AB Electronics, Inc. **Title:** Vice President/Owner **Type of organization:** Manufacturing **Major product:** PCB, cable assembly **Area of distribution:** Danbury, Connecticut **Expertise:** Sales/materials management **Honors/awards:** C.C.D. **Affiliations:** N.F.I.B.; D.E.C.A. (public speaker); C.C.D. **Hob./spts.:** Family **SIC code:** 36 **Address:** AB Electronics, Inc., 22 Shelter Rock Lane, Danbury, CT 06810 **E-mail:** abelectronics@aol.com

ALLEN, RICHIE S.
Industry: Cosmetics **Born:** June 6, 1966, North Carolina **Univ./degree:** Executive Development Center, North America **Current organization:** Paris Perfumes of America **Title:** President **Type of organization:** Manufacturing **Major product:** Perfumes, cosmetics **Area of distribution:** International **Expertise:** Operations, management **Hob./spts.:** Computers **SIC code:** 28 **Address:** Paris Perfumes of America, 200 Eastwood Rd., Chapel Hill, NC 27514 **E-mail:** richieallen@hotmail.com

ALLISON, EARL S.
Industry: Textiles **Born:** September 14, 1945, Concord, North Carolina **Univ./degree:** B.A., North Carolina State University, 1967 **Current organization:** Tubular Textile Machinery Corp. **Title:** Vice President Research & Development Engineering **Type of organization:** Manufacturing **Major product:** Finishing machinery for knits **Area of distribution:** International **Expertise:** R&D patent law **Hob./spts.:** Golf, fishing, arrowheads, custom tractors **SIC code:** 35 **Address:** Tubular Textile Machinery Corp., Hargrave Rd. at I-95, P.O. Box 2097, Lexington, NC 27293-2097 **E-mail:** sallison@tubetex.com

ALMANZA, ERASMO ELI
Industry: Office products **Born:** April 8, 1973, Valle Hermos, Mexico **Univ./degree:** M.S., Neuvo Leon State University, Mexico, 2001 **Current organization:** Cardinal Brands, Inc. **Title:** General Maintenance Superintendent **Type of organization:** Manufacturing **Major product:** Office products **Area of distribution:** McAllen, Texas **Expertise:** Engineering, maintenance **Hob./spts.:** Fishing **SIC code:** 39 **Address:** Cardinal Brands, Inc., 3218 Daytona Ave., McAllen, TX 78503 **E-mail:** erasmoalmanza@yahoo.com

ALTMAN, ROBERT M. & VICTORIA L.
Industry: Professional lighting **Current organization:** Altman Stage Lighting Co., Inc. **Title:** CEO/President/Owner **Type of organization:** Manufacturing **Major product:** Theatrical, TV, film and architectural lighting **Area of distribution:** International **Expertise:** Daily operations **SIC code:** 36 **Address:** Altman Stage Lighting Co., Inc., 57 Alexander St., Yonkers, NY 10701 **E-mail:** www.altmanltg.com

ALTSHULER, GREGORY B.
Industry: Medical technology **Born:** July 12, 1948 St. Petersburg, Russia **Univ./degree:** D.Sc., Optic Engineering; Ph.D., Laser Physics, Institute of Fine Mechanics and Optics, St. Petersburg, 1972 **Current organization:** Palomar Medical Technologies, Inc. **Title:** Vice President of Research **Type of organization:** Manufacturing, R&D **Major product:** Medical lasers & optics **Area of distribution:** International **Expertise:** Laser physics & optic engineering research **Published works:** 75 patents/inventions (10 pending), 150+ papers, two books **Affiliations:** S.P.E.; Optical Society of America **SIC code:** 38 **Address:** Palomar Medical Technologies, Inc., 82 Cambridge St., Burlington, MA 01803 **E-mail:** galtshuler@palmed.com

ALVAREZ JR., TIRSO R.
Industry: Automotive **Born:** December 26, 1948, San Antonio, Texas **Current organization:** GMC **Title:** Power Vehicle Operator/Stockhandler **Type of organization:** Manufacturing and service **Major product:** Automobiles and diesel engines and equipment/warehouse service parts operations **Area of distribution:** International **Expertise:** Journeyman Diesel Motor Technician **Affiliations:** A.M.A.; U.A.W. **Hob./spts.:** Fishing, automotive, films **SIC code:** 37 **Address:** 2599 Walnut Ave., Unit 229, Signal Hill, CA 90755-3672 **Phone:** (562)802-5335 **Fax:** (810)236-3166 **E-mail:** tralvarezjr@aol.com **Web address:** www.gm.com

ALVAREZ-MENA BONNET, MAXIMO
Industry: Food **Born:** November 18, 1955, Havana, Cuba **Univ./degree:** M.B.A., Inter-American University, 1983 **Current organization:** Empresas La Famosa **Title:** General Manager **Type of organization:** Manufacturing/distributing **Major product:** Juice, sauces, beans, canned foods **Area of distribution:** International **Expertise:** Management and international marketing **Affiliations:** B.A.U.S; M.D.A.; M.I.D.A. **Hob./spts.:** Sports, hiking, scuba diving **SIC code:** 20 **Address:** Empresas La Famosa, Carr. 865 Esq. 866, Bo. Candelaria Arenas, Toa Baja, PR 00949 **E-mail:** mralvarezmena@empresaslafamosa.com **Web address:** www.empresaslafamosa.com

ANDERSON, CORY M.
Industry: Power **Born:** October 20, 1971, Holdrege, Nebraska **Univ./degree:** B.A., Engineering, University of Nebraska, 1995 **Current organization:** National Dynamics **Title:** Engineer **Type of organization:** OEM **Major product:** Boilers, heat generators **Area of distribution:** International **Expertise:** Engineering, organizing projects, boiler design for power plant installations **Affiliations:** A.S.M.E. **Hob./spts.:** Sports, outdoor activities, computer games **SIC code:** 34 **Address:** National Dynamics, 6940 Cornhusker Hwy., Lincoln, NE 68510 **E-mail:** canderson@aqua-chem.com

ANDERSON, KATHERINE J.

Industry: Food seasonings **Born:** June 25, 1933, Osceola, Arkansas **Children:** Michael, Larry and Roy **Univ./degree:** Attended Mississippi Industrial College **Current organization:** Andy's Seasoning, Inc. **Title:** President **Type of organization:** Manufacturing **Major product:** Seasoned salt, fish and chicken breading, other batters and breadings **Area of distribution:** National **Expertise:** Marketing **Honors/awards:** Top 25 Female Business Owners of St. Louis, Missouri, 1998; St. Louis Argus Distinguished Citizen Award, 1998; Women in Vision Female Entrepreneur of the Year Award, 1999; Distinguished Woman Business Owner of the Year Award, 2000-NAWBO **Affiliations:** Minority Business Council; St. Louis, Regional Commerce Growth Association; National Association of Female Executives; National Alliance of Business; Agape Christian Center; I.B.P.O.E. of W. (Elks); U.S. Chamber of Commerce **SIC code:** 20 **Address:** Andy's Seasoning, Inc., 2829 Chouteau Ave., St. Louis, MO 63103 **Web address:** www.andysseasoning.com

ANDERSON, KRISTIN MARIE

Industry: Control systems **Born:** January 16, 1974, Jacksonville, Florida **Univ./degree:** B.S., Mechanical Engineering, University of Florida, 1997 **Current organization:** DRS Training and Control Systems **Title:** Mechanical Engineer II **Type of organization:** Design, development, manufacturing **Major product:** Design and production of complex electronic control systems used in military shipboard, ground and air weapon systems. **Area of distribution:** International **Expertise:** Design and analysis **Honors/awards:** Above and Beyond TQM Award; Teamword TQM Award **Hob./spts.:** Astronomy, writing **SIC code:** 36 **Address:** 412 Nordic Lane N.W., #E, Ft. Walton Beach, FL 32548 **E-mail:** kanderson@drs-tcs.com **Web address:** www.drs.tcs.com

ANDERSON, WAYNE B.

Industry: Motors **Born:** March 7, 1944, Kingston, Ontario **Current organization:** Xtreme Energy **Title:** Project and Production Manager **Type of organization:** Design and manufacturing **Major product:** DC - brushless, slotless motors **Area of distribution:** International **Expertise:** Manufacturing management **Hob./spts.:** Playing chess, RC radio, boats, planes, skiing **SIC code:** 35 **Address:** Xtreme Energy, 9543 International Court North, St. Petersburg, FL 33716 **E-mail:** wayne.anderson@xtreme-energy.com **Web address:** www.xtreme-energy.com

ANDERSON IV, CHARLES W.

Industry: Communications **Born:** September 17, 1974, Jackson, Mississippi **Univ./degree:** A.B.A. Candidate, Hines Community College **Current organization:** Shiers Communication Specialists, Inc. **Title:** President **Type of organization:** Manufacturing/distributing **Major product:** Cable TV systems, fiber optics, closed circuit security **Area of distribution:** National **Expertise:** Engineering **Affiliations:** Disco & Marte **Hob./spts.:** Hunting, fishing, motocross **SIC code:** 36 **Address:** Shiers Communication Specialists, Inc., 3532 Manor Dr., Suite 2, Vicksburg, MS 39180 **E-mail:** shierscomm@aol.com

ANDO, SADAHIRO

Industry: Laser printer/business and office machines **Univ./degree:** B.S., Engineering and Computer Science, University of California at Berkley, 1976 **Current organization:** Xerox International Partners **Title:** Director, Product Engineering **Type of organization:** Manufacturing **Major product:** Laser printer/multi-function devices **Area of distribution:** International **Expertise:** Engineering **Affiliations:** I.E.E.E. **SIC code:** 35 **Address:** Xerox International Partners, 3400 Hillview Ave., Bldg. 4, Palo Alto, CA 94304

ANDRECOLA, PAUL N.

Industry: Eco-friendly colloidal cleaners **Born:** Philadelphia, Pennsylvania **Univ./degree:** B.S., Engineering, Rowan University; M.S., Engineering, M.I.T., 1980 **Current organization:** InventeK, PG Technologies **Title:** President **Type of organization:** Manufacturing **Major product:** Eco-friendly colloidal cleaners, application apparatus **Area of distribution:** International **Expertise:** Engineering and formulation, sales, management, overall operations; P.E. License, 1983 **Affiliations:** U.N.I.C.O.; Society of Automotive Engineers, A.A.E.S.; A.A.E.E. **Hob./spts.:** Funny car drag racing, engine building **SIC code:** 28 **Address:** InventeK, 4021 King Ave., Pennsauken, NJ 08109 **E-mail:** mrfixxitpe@comcast.net

ANDREWS, ANDREW PETER

Industry: Engineering **Born:** October 12, 1979, Krakow, Poland **Univ./degree:** B.S., Engineering, DeVry University, 2001 **Current organization:** General Electrical **Title:** Engineer **Type of organization:** Manufacturing **Major product:** Electrical products **Area of distribution:** International **Expertise:** Field engineering **Hob./spts.:** Flying **SIC code:** 36 **Address:** 5010 McClelland Dr., #311, Wilmington, NC 28405 **E-mail:** andrew.andrews@med.ge.com

ANDREWS, SANDA L.

Industry: Eyewear **Born:** November 11, 1952, Toledo, Ohio **Current organization:** Toledo Optical Lab., Inc. **Title:** Administrative Manager **Type of organization:** Manufacturing **Major product:** Eyeglasses, optical wholesale **Area of distribution:** Ohio **Expertise:** Human resources, accounting, credit **Hob./spts.:** Gardening, outdoor activities, dancing, clubbing **SIC code:** 38 **Address:** Toledo Optical Lab., Inc., 1201 Jefferson Ave., Toledo, OH 43604 **E-mail:** sam2542003@yahoo.com

ANGENEND, VICKIE R.

Industry: Telecommunications/construction **Born:** December 15, 1958, Orange, Texas **Univ./degree:** Attended Lamar University for Management, Beaumont, Texas **Current organization:** Microwave Networks Inc./Waterfilled Barriers **Title:** Director of Human Resources/Owner (Waterfilled Barriers) **Type of organization:** Manufacturing **Major product:** Wireless transmission equipment, safety products **Area of distribution:** International **Expertise:** Human Resources **Affiliations:** Society for Human Resource Management, HR Houston **Hob./spts.:** Golf, community service, crafts **SIC code:** 36 **Address:** Microwave Networks Inc., 4000 Greenbriar Dr., Stafford, TX, 77477, Waterfilled Barriers, 9201 Fairbanks N. Houston Rd, Houston, TX 77064 **E-mail:** vangenend@houstonrr.com **Web address:** www.waterfilledbarriers.com

ANTHONY, JASON C.

Industry: Paper converting **Univ./degree:** B.S., Mechanical Engineering Technology, Pennsylvania State University, 2001 **Current organization:** Exopack LLC **Title:** Facility Process/Maintenance Engineer **Type of organization:** Manufacturing **Major product:** Multiwall paper bags **Area of distribution:** International **Expertise:** Mechanical design and engineering, equipment modification **SIC code:** 26 **Address:** Exopack LLC, 3 Maplewood Dr., Hazleton, PA 18202 **E-mail:** jason.anthony@exopack.com

APPEZZATO, MARC R.

Industry: Printing **Born:** January 22, 1973, Rahway, New Jersey **Univ./degree:** A.A., Union County College, New Jersey, 1995; B.S., Graphic Technology, Kean College, New Jersey, 1997 **Current organization:** Ideal Jacobs Corp. **Title:** Graphic Designer **Type of organization:** Screen printing **Major product:** Display panels for computer hardware **Area of distribution:** National **Expertise:** Preparation of drawings for printing **Published works:** Photography published **Affiliations:** Epsilon Pi Tau **Hob./spts.:** Photography, interior design, writing **SIC code:** 27 **Address:** Vantage Custom Classics, 100 Vantage Dr., Avenel, NJ 07001 **E-mail:** mrock_1@yahoo.com

ARAMBULA, JESSE

Industry: Automotive interior systems **Born:** February 21, 1943, Phoenix, Arizona **Univ./degree:** B.S., Engineering, Arizona State University **Current organization:** Lear Corp., Electronic Systems Division **Title:** Senior Electrical Engineer **Type of organization:** Manufacturing **Major product:** Electronic body control modules **Area of distribution:** International **Expertise:** Engineering **Affiliations:** I.E.E.E. **Hob./spts.:** Softball, walking, fishing, mentoring **SIC code:** 37 **Address:** Lear Corp., Electronics Systems Division, 415 Patriot St., Canton, MI 48188

ARCHER, CLAIRE

Industry: Power tools **Born:** September 30, 1976, Middlesborough, England **Univ./degree:** B.Eng. with Honors, University of Nottingham, England **Current organization:** Black and Decker **Title:** SEC Design Manager **Type of organization:** Manufacturing and design **Major product:** Outdoor power tools **Area of distribution:** International **Expertise:** Design engineering, systems involvement, training **Hob./spts.:** Golf. outdoor sports, travel **SIC code:** 36 **Address:** Black and Decker, 4409 Wanda Ave., McAllen, TX 78503 **E-mail:** claire.archer@bdk.com **Web address:** www.blackanddecker.com

ARNESON, ROB J.

Industry: Packaging **Born:** July 31, 1963, Sycamore, Illinois **Current organization:** SCA Consumer Products/Alloyd Co. Inc. **Title:** Machinery/Parts and Services Manager **Type of organization:** Manufacturing **Major product:** Custom thermoformer and machinery **Area of distribution:** International **Expertise:** Machinery production, management **Affiliations:** P.M.M.I. **Hob./spts.:** Antique cars **SIC code:** 35 **Address:** SCA Consumer Products/Alloyd Co. Inc., 1401 Pleasant St., Dekalb, IL 60115 **E-mail:** rob.arneson@sca.com

ARSLAN, GÜNER
Born: March 21, 1973, Pinneberg, Germany **Univ./degree:** Ph.D., University of Texas, 2000 **Current organization:** Silicon Labs **Area of distribution:** National **Published works:** Journals, 10 conference papers **Affiliations:** I.E.E.E. **Hob./spts.:** Soccer, reading **SIC code:** 36 **Address:** Silicon Labs, 7000 W. William Cannon Dr., Austin, TX 78735 **E-mail:** garslan@cicada-semi.com

ARTHUR, WILLIAM P.
Industry: Writing **Born:** August 17, 1949, Anamosa, Iowa **Univ./degree:** B.A., Speech, University of Minnesota, 1971 **Title:** Author **Area of distribution:** International **Expertise:** Author **Honors/awards:** Outstanding Achievement in Amateur Photography, International Society of Photographers **Published works:** "Time and Chance", a satirical novel about newspapers featuring dinosaur species as journalists **Affiliations:** American Legion; University of Minnesota Alumni Association **Hob./spts.:** Collecting baseball cards, running **SIC code:** 27 **Address:** End of the Trail Enterprises, 804 Old Settlers Trail, Unit I, Hopkins, MN 55343 **E-mail:** williamarthur952@aol.com

ARTHUR JR., NELSON B.
Industry: Tobacco **Born:** July 12, 1945, Richmond, Virginia **Univ./degree:** A.S., Electronic Drafting Technology, Virginia Commonwealth University, 1972 **Current organization:** Philip Morris, USA **Title:** Instrument Electrical **Type of organization:** Manufacturing **Major product:** Tobacco products **Area of distribution:** International **Expertise:** Instrumentation and electronic maintenance **Affiliations:** I.S.A. **Hob./spts.:** Computers, photography, physical fitness **SIC code:** 21 **Address:** 9000 Canvasback Circle, Chesterfield, VA 23838 **E-mail:** ben.n.arthur@pmusa.com

ASHRAF, MUHAMMAD
Industry: Chemicals **Born:** November 5, 1955 Pakistan **Univ./degree:** M.S., Applied Chemistry, Pakistan, 1980 **Current organization:** Comstar International, Inc. **Title:** Plant Manager **Type of organization:** Manufacturing **Major product:** Specialty chemical products **Area of distribution:** International **Expertise:** Engineering, management **Affiliations:** C.S.U.S.A. **Hob./spts.:** Cricket, field hockey **SIC code:** 28 **Address:** Comstar International Inc., 20-45 128th St., College Point, NY 11356

ASHTON, DALE CARL
Industry: Mining and Metals **Born:** July 11, 1943, Lehi, Utah **Spouse:** Deanne Ashton (Peterson) **Married:** November 9, 1962 **Children:** Annette, Corrie, Dayton, Tiffany, Danielle, Brooklann **Univ./degree:** B.S., Civil Engineering, University of Utah, 1971 **Current organization:** U.S. Magnesium, LLC **Title:** Senior Project Engineer **Type of organization:** Smelting and refining **Major product:** Magnesium metal **Area of distribution:** National **Expertise:** Registered Structural Engineer and Registered Civil Engineer; Expert Witness **Career accomplishments:** While working for U.S. Magnesium, he has concentrated on improving the structural integery of the process equipment used to purify the molten magnesium metal; All equipment used to purify and transport the metal must be able to withstand temperatures in the range of 1300 degrees F; This has been a great challenge as materials and construction methods used to contain metal at these temperatures are very specialized; During his employment he has greatly improved both equipment material and construction methods which have reduced operating costs and improved production **Hob./spts.:** Reading in several scientific fields, fishing on a good lake or stream **SIC code:** 33 **Address:** U.S. Magnesium, LLC, 238 N. 2200 West, Salt Lake City, UT 84116-2921 **E-mail:** dashton@usmagnesium.com **Web address:** www.usmagnesium.com

AVILA, JOEL C.
Industry: Healthcare **Born:** December 26, 1971, Manila, Philippines **Univ./degree:** B.S.M.E., Norwich University; M.B.A., Regis University **Current organization:** Pride Mobility Products **Title:** Manufacturing Engineer **Type of organization:** Manufacturing **Major product:** Powered wheelchairs and scooters **Area of distribution:** International **Expertise:** Engineering **Affiliations:** Society of American Military Engineers **Hob./spts.:** Bodybuilding **SIC code:** 38 **Address:** 182 Susquehanna Ave., Exeter, PA 18643 **E-mail:** javila@pridemobility.com

AWAD, HUSSAM M.
Industry: Polymers **Born:** August 30, 1964, Alexandria, Egypt **Univ./degree:** B.S., Chemical Engineering, University of Tennessee, 1995 **Current organization:** Tiepet, Inc. **Title:** Production Manager **Type of organization:** Manufacturing **Major product:** PET resin, bottle grade **Area of distribution:** International **Expertise:** Chemical engineering **Hob./spts.:** Tennis, soccer **SIC code:** 30 **Address:** Tiepet, Inc., 801 Pineview St., Asheboro, NC 27203 **E-mail:** hawad@asheboro.com

AZAD, ABDUL-MAJEED
Industry: Fuel cell components **Born:** August 15, 1959, Jamshedpur, India **Univ./degree:** Ph.D., University of Madras, 1990 **Current organization:** Nextech Materials, Ltd. **Title:** Research Scientist **Type of organization:** Manufacturing **Major product:** Solid oxide fuel cell components; raw materials and finished products pertaining to fuel cells **Area of distribution:** International **Expertise:** Scientific research **Honors/awards:** NASA Certificate of Recognition, May 2002 **Published works:** 77 research articles **Affiliations:** American Ceramic Society; American Chemical Society; American Biographical Institute **Hob./spts.:** Creative writing **SIC code:** 39 **Address:** NexTech Materials, Ltd., 720-I Lakeview Plaza Blvd., Worthington, OH 43085 **E-mail:** azad@nextechmaterials.com **Web address:** www.nextechmaterials.com

BACKHAUS, STACY J.
Industry: Machinery **Born:** Manitowoc, Wisconsin **Univ./degree:** Attending Lakeshore Technical College **Current organization:** Kaufman Manufacturing **Title:** Production Coordinator **Type of organization:** Manufacturing **Major product:** MTO, ETO machines **Area of distribution:** International **Expertise:** Production, management **Honors/awards:** Phi Beta Kappa, National Scholars Honors Society **Affiliations:** Secretary, APICS; St. Nazianz Lions Club; Village Trustee, St. Nazianz **Hob./spts.:** Volunteer work, reading, football, cooking **SIC code:** 35 **Address:** Kaufman Manufacturing, 547 S. 29th St., Manitowoc, WI 54221 **E-mail:** sbackhaus@kaufmanmfg.com

BADII, NADER "NATE"
Industry: Medical devices and service **Born:** January 26, 1957, Mashad, Iran **Univ./degree:** B.S.M.E., West Virginia University, 1979; M.B.A., National University, 2000 **Current organization:** Cardinal Health **Title:** Principal Mechanical Engineer **Type of organization:** Manufacturing **Major product:** Infusion pumps **Area of distribution:** International **Expertise:** Engineering, problem solving, continuous improvement **Affiliations:** Project Management Institute; American Society for Quality; Cardinal Committees, Safety Ergonomics and Continuous Improvement **Hob./spts.:** Study of philosophy, humanities, democracy **SIC code:** 38 **Address:** 9190 Activity Rd., San Diego, CA 92126 **E-mail:** nate.badii@cardinal.com

BAILEY, DOUGLAS B.
Industry: Transportation **Born:** October 12, 1972, Shelbyville, Kentucky **Univ./degree:** A.S., Mechanical Engineering, University of Pennsylvania (ICS), 2001 **Current organization:** Shelby Industries **Title:** Director of Engineering **Type of organization:** Manufacturing **Major product:** Trailer accessories, couplers, winches and jacks **Area of distribution:** National **Expertise:** Engineering, project management, mechanical design **Affiliations:** National Association of Trailer Manufacturers **Hob./spts.:** Coaching football, basketball, soccer and baseball **SIC code:** 37 **Address:** Shelby Industries, 175 McDaniel Rd., Shelbyville, KY 40065 **E-mail:** doug@shelbyindustries.com **Web address:** www.shelbyindustries.com

BAILEY, NANCY A.
Industry: Automotive **Born:** April 14, 1977, Greenfield, Indiana **Univ./degree:** B.S., Agricultural & Biological Engineering, Purdue University, 2000 **Current organization:** Rieter Automotive North America **Title:** Process Engineer **Type of organization:** Manufacturing **Major product:** Automotive sound insulation **Area of distribution:** National **Expertise:** Engineering **Affiliations:** A.S.A.E. **Hob./spts.:** Horseback riding, camping, fishing **SIC code:** 37 **Address:** Rieter Automotive North America, 101 W. Oakley Ave., Lowell, IN 46356 **E-mail:** nancy.bailey@rieterauto.com

BALAN, MIRCEA
Industry: Valves **Born:** July 23, 1965, Romania **Univ./degree:** M.S.M.E., George Asache University, Romania, 1989 **Current organization:** AOP Industries **Title:** Engineering Manager **Type of organization:** Manufacturing **Major product:** High pressure gate valves and well head components **Area of distribution:** International **Expertise:** Design engineering **Published works:** 4 patents (Romania) **Affiliations:** Quality Committee, A.O.P. **Hob./spts.:** Travel, computers, reading **SIC code:** 35 **Address:** AOP Industries, 2101 S. Broadway, Moore, OK 73160 **E-mail:** balanm@aopind.com

BALLARD, RAYMOND V.
Industry: Concrete **Born:** June 26, 1939, Alex, Oklahoma **Current organization:** Goddard Ready Mix Concrete Co., Inc. **Title:** Vice President, Sales/General Manager **Type of organization:** Manufacturing **Major product:** Ready mix concrete - residential and commercial **Area of distribution:** Oklahoma **Expertise:** Sales, management, trouble shooting, truck driving **Affiliations:** Square dance clubs **Hob./spts.:** Square dancing, woodworking, RVing **SIC code:** 32 **Address:** Goddard Ready Mix Concrete Co., Inc., 3101 N.E. Tenth St, Oklahoma City, OK 73117 **E-mail:** goddardc@aol.com

BARIA, NOSHIR
Industry: Pharmaceutical **Born:** January 16, 1939, Navsari, India **Univ./degree:** B.E., Mechanical & Electrical Engineering, University of Karachi **Current organization:** Pfizer Inc. **Title:** Senior Manager, Pfizer Global Engineering **Type of organization:** Manufacturing **Major product:** Pharmaceuticals **Area of distribution:** Global **Expertise:** Process plant design & facility planning **Hob./spts.:** Woodworking, shipbuilding **SIC code:** 28 **Address:** Pfizer Inc., 235 E. 42nd St., New York, NY 10017

BARNES, MICHAEL RAY
Industry: Concrete/masonry **Born:** November 13, 1968, Charleston, South Carolina **Univ./degree:** M.B.A., Marketing/Management, Keller School of Management, 2001 **Current organization:** Euclid Chemical Co. **Type of organization:** Manufacturing

Major product: Admixtures, concrete repair products, curing and sealing compounds, grouts, sealants and coatings **Area of distribution:** International **Affiliations:** N.S.P.E.; A.S.C.E.; C.S.I.; A.C.P.A. **Hob./spts.:** Scuba diving, mountain biking **SIC code:** 28 **Address:** Euclid Chemical Co., 7506 E. Independence Blvd., Charlotte, NC 28227 **E-mail:** barnesmr@euclidchemical.com **Web address:** www.euclidchemical.com

BARRETT, MICHAEL L.
Industry: Labels **Born:** North Carolina, 1982 **Univ./degree:** B.S., Mechanical Engineering, North Carolina State University, 2004 **Current organization:** Acucote Inc. **Title:** Process & Plant Engineer **Type of organization:** Manufacturing **Major product:** Pressure sensitive labels **Area of distribution:** National **Expertise:** Engineering management **Affiliations:** A.S.M.E. **SIC code:** 28 **Address:** Acucote Inc., 910 E. Elm St., Graham, NC 27253 **E-mail:** mikeb@acucote.com **Web address:** www.acucote.com

BARRINGER, D. MARTIN
Industry: Dental supplies **Born:** June 23, 1976, Gastonia, North Carolina **Univ./degree:** B.A., Marketing; B.S.B.A., Health Care Management, Appalachian State University **Current organization:** Dentsply Supply International **Title:** Alliance Account Executive **Type of organization:** Manufacturing/distributing **Major product:** Full line of dental supplies **Area of distribution:** North Carolina and Virginia **Expertise:** Business development, marketing, management, sales **Hob./spts.:** Spectator sports, basketball, kick boxing **SIC code:** 38 **Address:** 3900 Knickerbocker Pkwy., #P, Raleigh, NC 27612 **E-mail:** rockmb44@hotmail.com

BARTEL, KARL C.
Industry: Electronics/communications **Univ./degree:** B.S.E.E., South Dakota School of Mines and Technology, 1968 **Current organization:** Polyphaser **Title:** Senior Design Engineer **Type of organization:** Manufacturing **Major product:** Lightning protection devices **Area of distribution:** International **Expertise:** Engineering, electronics **Hob./spts.:** Mechanics, working on restoring classics **SIC code:** 36 **Address:** Polyphaser, 2225 Park Place, Minden, NV 89423 **E-mail:** kbartel@polyphaser.com

BARTOLETTI, JEFFREY F.
Industry: Industrial controls **Born:** May 29, 1967, Albany, New York **Univ./degree:** B.S., Electrical Engineering, Penn State University **Current organization:** GE Fanuc Automation **Title:** Market Development Manager **Type of organization:** Manufacturing **Major product:** Automation systems and enterprise software **Area of distribution:** International **Expertise:** Sales and marketing **Affiliations:** A.I.S.T.; Advisory Board, Montgomery County Community College **Hob./spts.:** Volunteer work, boating **SIC code:** 35 **Address:** GE Fanuc Automation, 640 Freedom Business Center, King of Prussia, PA 19406 **E-mail:** jeff.bartoletti@ge.com

BASTIEN, GILBERT J.
Industry: Testing products **Born:** Los Angeles, California **Univ./degree:** M.S., Mechanical Engineering, University of Southern California, 1969 **Current organization:** Screening Systems, Inc. **Title:** Halt and Hass Specialist, SR **Type of organization:** Manufacturing **Major product:** Testing systems **Area of distribution:** International **Expertise:** Engineering **Affiliations:** A.S.M.E.; I.E.E.E.; I.E.S.T. **Hob./spts.:** Golf **SIC code:** 36 **Address:** Screening Systems, Inc., 7 Argonaut, Aliso Viejo, CA 92256 **E-mail:** gbastien@scrsys.com

BATKY, RICHARD T.
Industry: Jewelry **Born:** January 17, 1947, Budapest, Hungary **Current organization:** Batky Jewelers **Title:** President **Type of organization:** Manufacturing, retail **Major product:** Gold, platinum, diamonds, emeralds, rubies; exclusive designs, expert restoration and remounting **Area of distribution:** International **Expertise:** Art, design, manufacturing; Designer-Master Jeweler **Affiliations:** D.D.C.; J.B.T.; Polygon **Hob./spts.:** Tennis, chess **SIC code:** 39 **Address:** Batky Jewelers, 5600 W. Lovers Lane, #120, Dallas, TX 75209 **E-mail:** rbatky@aol.com **Web address:** www.batky.com

BAZNER, ROBERT A.
Industry: Automotive **Born:** July 4, 1962, Hamtramck, Michigan **Current organization:** Veltri Metal Products **Title:** Engineering Manager **Type of organization:** Manufacturing **Major product:** Sheet metal stampings and assemblies **Area of distribution:** International **Expertise:** Engineering **Hob./spts.:** Golf, home improvement **SIC code:** 34 **Address:** Veltri Metal Products, 4336 Coolidge Hwy., Royal Oak, MI 48073 **E-mail:** bbazner@veltrimetal.com **Web address:** www.veltrimetal.com

BEAHAM III, GORDON T.
Industry: Consumer goods **Born:** February 2, 1932, Kansas City, Missouri **Univ./degree:** M.B.A., Harvard Business School **Current organization:** Faultless Starch/Bon Ami Co. **Title:** Co-Chairman & Co-CEO **Type of organization:** Manufacturing, distributing **Major product:** Commercial laundry products, lawn and garden hardware **Area of distribution:** International **Expertise:** Marketing **Affiliations:** G.M.A.; B.E.N.S. **Hob./spts.:** Swimming, golf, grandchildren, chess **SIC code:** 28 **Address:** Faultless Starch/Bon Ami Co., 1025 W. Eighth St., Kansas City, MO 64101 **E-mail:** gbeaham@faultless.com

BEAM, EARL G.
Industry: Textiles **Born:** September 28, 1955, Lock Haven, Pennsylvania **Univ./degree:** B.S., Lock Haven University **Current organization:** Berwick Offray LLC **Title:** Senior Buyer **Type of organization:** Manufacturing **Major product:** Ribbon and bows **Area of distribution:** International **Expertise:** Purchasing **Affiliations:** I.S.M.; A.P.I.C.S. **Hob./spts.:** Hunting, fishing, motorcycling, golf **SIC code:** 22 **Address:** Berwick Offray LLC, 2015 W. Front St., Berwick, PA 18603 **E-mail:** earl.beam@berwickoffray.com

BEARD, JOHN D.
Industry: Chemicals **Born:** August 31, 1951, Kenosha, Wisconsin **Univ./degree:** M.S., Chemical Engineer, Mississippi State University, 1977 **Current organization:** Southern Ionics, Inc. **Title:** Safety, Quality and Environmental Manager **Type of organization:** Manufacturing **Major product:** Inorganic chemicals **Area of distribution:** Mississippi **Expertise:** Safety and engineering **Honors/awards:** The George Westinghouse Signature Award of Excellence, 1987 **Affiliations:** A.C.S.; A.I.C.H.E.; A.W.W.A. **Hob./spts.:** Bass fishing **SIC code:** 28 **Address:** Southern Ionics, Inc., 201 Commerce St., West Point, MS 39773 **E-mail:** jbeard@southernionics.com

BEAVER, GEORGE W.
Industry: Automotive **Born:** August 1, 1964, Lincoln Park, Michigan **Univ./degree:** B.S., Design Engineering, Sienna Heights University, 1993; M.S., Administration, Central Michigan University, 1998 **Current organization:** ITT Industries Fluid Handling Systems **Title:** Product Design and Engineering Services Manager **Type of organization:** Manufacturing **Major product:** Fluid handling systems **Area of distribution:** International **Expertise:** Management of the Product Development and Design Engineering Group plus the Corporate Reliability Laboratory **Honors/awards:** Taguchi Case Study Award Recipient, I.T.T., 1987 **Published works:** SME technical papers **Affiliations:** Society of Automotive Engineers; Society of Manufacturing Engineers; American Society for Quality **Hob./spts.:** Camping, hiking, travel **SIC code:** 37 **Address:** ITT Industries Fluid Handling Systems, 2110 Executive Hills Ct., Auburn Hills, MI 48326 **E-mail:** george.beaver@itt.com

BEDEY, RICHARD F.
Industry: Packaging/converting **Born:** Toledo, Ohio **Univ./degree:** B.S., Aeronautic Engineering, Kent State University **Current organization:** Mac Tac **Title:** Plant Engineer **Type of organization:** Manufacturing **Major product:** Pressure sensitive labels **Area of distribution:** International **Expertise:** Asset engineering **Hob./spts.:** Flying, golf **SIC code:** 26 **Address:** Mac Tac, 2576 Norcross Dr., Columbus, IN 47201 **E-mail:** rfbedey@bemis.com

BEERS, TIMOTHY M.
Industry: Transportation **Born:** June 3, 1968, Turney, Missouri **Current organization:** Herzog Contracting Corp. **Title:** Shop Manager **Type of organization:** Manufacturing **Major product:** Railroad equipment **Area of distribution:** National **Expertise:** Design, welding, fabrication, engineering **Hob./spts.:** NASCAR, farming, horseback riding **SIC code:** 37 **Address:** Herzog Contracting Corp., 6001 Easton Rd., St. Joseph, MO 64507 **E-mail:** timbeers@herzogcompanies.com

BEIDEL, BRIAN S.
Industry: Industrial equipment **Born:** March 20, 1977, Chambersburg, Pennsylvania **Univ./degree:** B.S., Mechanical Engineering, Pennsylvania State University, 2000 **Current organization:** Ingersoll-Rand (IR):Club Car **Title:** mechanical Design Engineer **Type of organization:** Manufacturing **Major product:** Golf and utility vehicles **Area of distribution:** National **Expertise:** Engineering **Affiliations:** Pi Tau Sigma **Hob./spts.:** Golf, basketball, NASCAR **SIC code:** 37 **Address:** Ingersoll-Rand (IR):Club Car, 1704 Woodhill Trail, Augusta, GA 30909 **E-mail:** brian-beidel@irco.com

BEITEL, BAY H.
Industry: Agriculture/oil field **Born:** August 20, 1973, Long Island, New York **Univ./degree:** A.S., Agriculture Economics, Howard College, 1995 **Current organization:** Adroit Industries, Inc. **Title:** President/CEO **Type of organization:** Manufacturing **Major product:** Bearings, housings, oilfield parts **Area of distribution:** National **Expertise:** Engineering, accounting **Affiliations:** N.F.I.B. **Hob./spts.:** Golf, horses **SIC code:** 39 **Address:** Adroit Industries, Inc., 9803 E. County Rd. 7540, Slaton, TX 79364 **E-mail:** adroitind@aol.com

BELLACICCO, JOSEPH
Industry: Food **Born:** April 10, 1930, New York, New York **Current organization:** Joe Bellacicco Enterprise Inc. **Title:** President **Type of organization:** Manufacturing **Major product:** Bakery products and machinery **Area of distribution:** International **Expertise:** Design and invention of bakery products **Hob./spts.:** Machine design **SIC code:** 35 **Address:** 95-01 43rd Ave., Elmhurst, NY 11373 **E-mail:** joebellacicco@hotmail.com

BELLIS, TERRY
Industry: Steel **Born:** July 21, 1946, Natchez, Mississippi **Univ./degree:** B.S., Business Administration, Mississippi College, 1968 **Current organization:** Steel Service Corp. **Title:** Maintenance Manager **Type of organization:** Manufacturing **Major product:** Structural steel **Area of distribution:** National **Expertise:** Maintenance and repair **Hob./spts.:** Tree farming, fishing **SIC code:** 33 **Address:** Steel Service Corp., 2260 Flowood Dr., Flowood, MS 39215-1144 **E-mail:** tbellis@steelservicecorp.com **Web address:** www.steelservicecorp.com

BENDER, MICHELE ANN MORETTI
Industry: Manufacturer of durable/consumer goods **Born:** February 20, Newark, New Jersey **Univ./degree:** B.A., Speech and Theater, Montclair State University, Upper Montclair 1976; Pursuing MBA/HR degree through Baker College, Michigan online program **Current organization:** Titan Tool Inc. **Title:** Sr. H.R. Generalist/ Manager **Type of organization:** Manufacturing and distributing **Major product:** Manufacturing of spray paint equipment for contractor usc - part of the "Decorative Finishings" Division (consumer and contractor) for Wagner Spray Tech US and parent company Wagner located in Germany. **Area of distribution:** International **Expertise:** Human Resources, Training and Development, Performance Management, Staffing, Workers' Compensation, OSHA Compliance, ISO Compliance Management, Employee Relations, Special Project and Event Management; PHR Certification **Honors/awards:** First Place, US Dance Champion, 1978; Represented the US in World Dance Championsip held in Germany, 1978; Employee of Choice Award for Safety, Tital Tool, 2002 **Affiliations:** International Member, Society for Human Resource Management (SHRM); Former Proprietor, Moretti Art of Dance School, Nutley, NJ; Member of Employer Association of New Jersey **Hob./spts.:** International ballroom dancing, golf **SIC code:** 28 **Address:** Titan Tool Inc., 107 Baver Dr., Oakland, NJ 07430 **E-mail:** and5678@optonline.net **Web address:** www.titantool.com

BENNETT, R. RANDALL
Industry: Fluid power **Born:** July 6, 1955, Akron, Ohio **Current organization:** Nass Controls **Title:** Vice President **Type of organization:** Manufacturing **Major product:** Solenoids, connectors **Area of distribution:** International **Expertise:** Engineering **Affiliations:** Fluid Power Association; National Fluid Power Association **Hob./spts.:** Reading, hockey, church related activities, school activities/Band Booster **SIC code:** 36 **Address:** Nass Controls, 51509 Birch St., New Baltimore, MI 48047 **Phone:** (586)725-6610 **Fax:** (586)725-5802 **E-mail:** randy.bennett@nasscontrols.com

BENSIEK, WILLIAM F.
Industry: Fabricated metal products **Born:** June 2, 1933, St. Louis, Missouri **Univ./degree:** B.S.M.E., University of Missouri, 1955; M.S., Applied Physics, 1971; M.B.A., 1975, Lynchburg College **Current organization:** BWX Technologies **Title:** Senior Principal Engineer **Type of organization:** Manufacturing **Major product:** Nuclear test reactor components **Area of distribution:** National **Expertise:** Engineering **Hob./spts.:** Fly-fishing, home improvement, gardening, hiking, photography, travel **SIC code:** 34 **Address:** BWX Technologies, 1750 Mt. Athos Rd., Lynchburg, VA 24504

BENSON, DANIEL E.
Industry: Paper conversion machinery **Univ./degree:** Attended Johns Hopkins University **Current organization:** Sherwood Tool Inc. **Title:** Assembly Manager **Type of organization:** Manufacturing **Major product:** Machinery **Area of distribution:** International **Expertise:** Project management **Hob./spts.:** Fishing, fitness **SIC code:** 35 **Address:** Sherwood Tool Inc., 10 Main St., Kensington, CT 06037 **E-mail:** danbenson@att.net

BENZ, GEORG R.
Industry: Medical devices **Born:** September 14, 1947, Suffern, New York **Univ./degree:** B.S., Mechanical Engineering, Pennsylvania State University, 1985 **Current organization:** Invivo Research Inc. **Title:** Director of Mechanical Engineering and Document Control/Q.S. Management Representative **Type of organization:** Manufacturing **Major product:** Patient vital signs monitors and systems **Area of distribution:** International **Expertise:** Mechanical engineering **Affiliations:** A.S.M.E.; A.S.Q. **Hob./spts.:** Radio controlled model airplanes, computers, softball, golf **SIC code:** 38 **Address:** Invivo Research Inc., 12601 Research Pkwy., Orlando, FL 32826 **E-mail:** gbenz@invivocorp.com

BERENS, WAYNE H.
Industry: Public seating **Current organization:** Irwin Seating Co. **Title:** Maintenance Lead Person **Type of organization:** Manufacturing **Major product:** Public seating for theaters, auditoriums, stadiums, arenas **Area of distribution:** National **Expertise:** Maintenance of plant facilities **Affiliations:** Jordan College; Grand Rapids Junior College **SIC code:** 25 **Address:** Irwin Seating Co., 3251 Fruitridge, Walker, MI 49544 **E-mail:** berensco@irwinseating.com

BERGERON, PIERRE
Industry: Security and telecommunications **Born:** May 6, 1957, Montreal, Canada **Univ./degree:** B.S., College of St. Therese, 1995 **Current organization:** Tech Laboratories Inc. **Title:** MIT/PLM **Type of organization:** Manufacturing and distributing **Major product:** Intrusive detection system and network switch **Area of distribution:** International **Expertise:** Engineering, marketing; Accounting Certificate **Affiliations:** Association for Choice for Information Management Professionals **Hob./spts.:** Golf, reading **SIC code:** 36 **Address:** Tech Laboratories Inc., 955 Belmont Ave., North Haledon, NJ 07508 **E-mail:** pierrebergeron@techlabsinc.com

BERGFORS, GORDON A.
Industry: CNC machinery-automation **Born:** February 27, 1963, Oak Park, Illinois **Univ./degree:** A.A.S., Wake Technical Community College **Current organization:** ShopBot Tools, Inc. **Title:** Secretary/Treasurer; Vice President of Product Development **Type of organization:** Manufacturing **Major product:** Industrial machinery and tools, CNC routers **Area of distribution:** International **Expertise:** Computer programming and product development **Published works:** Articles **Affiliations:** I.E.E.E.; Phi Beta Kappa **Hob./spts.:** Cub Scouts, mountain biking, kayaking, cooking **SIC code:** 35 **Address:** ShopBot Tools, Inc., 3333-B Industrial Dr., Durham, NC 27704 **E-mail:** gordon@shopbottools.com

BERLIN, RONALD G.
Industry: Medical devices **Born:** November 21, 1953, St. Louis, Missouri **Univ./degree:** M.B.A., Whele School of Business, Canisius College, 1987 **Current organization:** Stryker Howmedica Osteonics **Title:** Vice President of Global Supply Chain **Type of organization:** Manufacturing **Major product:** Orthopaedic implants **Area of distribution:** International **Expertise:** Supply chain, purchasing **Affiliations:** N.A.P.M. **SIC code:** 38 **Address:** 7 Grandview Rd., Central Valley, NY 10917 **E-mail:** rberlin@howost.com **Web address:** www.howost.com

BERNARD, EDWIN I.
Industry: Aerospace **Born:** April 18, 1946, Calcutta, India **Univ./degree:** B.S., Engineering, 1969 **Current organization:** Northrop Grumman **Title:** Display System Engineer **Type of organization:** Manufacturing **Major product:** Situation awareness for military **Area of distribution:** International **Expertise:** Engineering **Affiliations:** Chair, Society for Information Display, Los Angeles Chapter; Royal Academy of Music **Hob./spts.:** Toastmaster, piano **SIC code:** 37 **Address:** Northrop Grumman, 21240 Burbank Blvd., Woodland Hills, CA 91367 **E-mail:** edwin.bernard@northropgrumman.com

BEVERLY, LEAH A.
Industry: Oil field equipment and services **Univ./degree:** A.A., North Harris College, 1991 **Current organization:** Brandt-A Varco Co. **Title:** Sr. Product Designer **Type of organization:** Design & Manufacturing **Major product:** Various oil field equipment i.e. Solids Control, Waste Management and auxiliary equipment **Area of distribution:** International **Expertise:** R&D Engineering, Product design, Product Value engineering, Product packaging design, Electro-mechanical packaging design, technical writer of research, report and operational and maintenance manuals **Published works:** Technical papers, trade journal articles, manuals, newsletters and as a hobby, public service information articles **Hob./spts.:** My children, home building, charcoal and oil paintings of American wildlife and western sconces, amateur archaeology, water sports and "the Wind in my Face" **SIC code:** 35 **Address:** Brandt- A Varco Co., 2800 N. Frazier, Conroe, TX 77303 **E-mail:** 1bayse@varco.com **Web address:** www.varco.com

BHOGAL, KIRPAL SINGH
Industry: Postal automation **Born:** December 10, 1944, Phagwara, India **Univ./degree:** M.S., Electrical Engineering, Mid West College of Engineering, Illinois, 1976 **Current organization:** Siemens Dematic Postal Automation L.P. **Title:** Engineering Specialist/ Scientist **Type of organization:** Manufacturing **Major product:** Sorting machines for postal automation **Area of distribution:** International **Expertise:** Engineering, research & development **Hob./spts.:** Public relations, social work, reading **SIC code:** 35 **Address:** Siemens Dematic Postal Automation L.P., 2910 Avenue F, Arlington, TX 76011-5214 **E-mail:** kirpal.bhogal@aol.siemens.com

BIGGERT, CHARLES "TONY" A.
Industry: Oil **Born:** October 2, 1959, Las Vegas, Nevada **Current organization:** NuDawn Metal Fabrication **Title:** C.E.O. **Type of organization:** Manufacturing **Major product:** Oil **Area of distribution:** International **Expertise:** Production equipment, risers, tilt-up, sub-sea development **Affiliations:** American Welding Society **Hob./spts.:** Auto racing, deep sea and salt water fishing **SIC code:** 29 **Address:** NuDawn Metal Fabrication, 18606 Cedar Edge Dr., Spring, TX 77379 **E-mail:** nudawnmetalfab@aol.com

BILGEN, MEHMET V.
Industry: Printing/graphics **Title:** Co-Owner/Graphic Artist **Type of organization:** Copy-print shop **Major product:** Printing, design **Expertise:** Graphic art **SIC code:** 27 **Address:** Copy Shoppe, LLC, 122 Prospect Hill Rd., East Windsor, CT 06088 **E-mail:** copyshop02@aol.com

BISHOP, BRETT A.
Industry: Injection molding **Born:** February 23, 1962, Richmond, Indiana **Current organization:** Vandor Corporation **Title:** Director of Purchasing **Type of organization:** Manufacturing **Major product:** Wire spools, specialty - die cutting thermoforming **Area of distribution:** International **Expertise:** Procurement and planning **Hob./spts.:** Golf **SIC code:** 30 **Address:** Vandor Corporation, 4251 W. Industries Rd., Richmond, IN 47374 **E-mail:** brett.bishop@vandorcorp.com

BLANCHFIELD, PHILLIP EDWARD
Industry: Machinery **Univ./degree:** Associates Degree, Mechanical Design, Northwest Technical College, 1964 **Current organization:** Creative Machine Design, Inc. **Title:** President **Type of organization:** Manufacturing **Major product:** Paper machines **Area of distribution:** National **Expertise:** Design and engineering **Affiliations:** A.S.M.E. **Hob./spts.:** Boating, building and finishing furniture **SIC code:** 35 **Address:** Creative Machine Design, Inc., N. 962 Towerview Dr., Greenville, WI 54942 **E-mail:** creativemachinedesign@msn.com

BLANKENSHIP, TERRY T.
Industry: Aerospace **Born:** July 19, 1943, Winston-Salem, North Carolina **Univ./degree:** A.S., Education, Gilford Technical Community College **Current organization:** B/E Aerospace Inc. **Title:** Manager of Training **Type of organization:** Manufacturing **Major product:** Aerospace parts **Area of distribution:** International **Expertise:** Interior aircraft parts **Honors/awards:** Academic All American **Hob./spts.:** Sports, photography **SIC code:** 37 **Address:** B/E Aerospace Inc., 1455 Fairchild Rd., Winston-Salem, NC 27105 **E-mail:** terry_blankenship@beaerospace.com

BLETHEN, MARVIN R.
Industry: Mining **Born:** December 14, 1958, Madison, West Virginia **Univ./degree:** B.S., Mining Engineering West Virginia University; M.S., Mining Engineering, University of Idaho; M.B.A., Troy State University **Current organization:** WHIBCO, Inc. **Title:** Vice President of Engineering and Real Estate **Type of organization:** Mining **Major product:** Sand and gravel/foundry materials **Area of distribution:** National **Expertise:** Supervision of engineers; P.E. certifications from Alabama, West Virginia, Ohio, Pennsylvania, Kentucky, New Jersey **Affiliations:** Society of Mining Engineers **Hob./spts.:** Family, golf **SIC code:** 32 **Address:** WHIBCO, Inc., 87 Commerce St. East, Bridgeton, NJ 08302 **E-mail:** mblethen@whibco.com **Web address:** www.whibco.com

BLYAKHMAN, YEFIM M.
Industry: Chemicals **Born:** December 11, 1937, Leningrad, Russia **Univ./degree:** Ph.D., Leningrad Institute of Technology, Russia, 1965; D.Sc., Plastic Polymer Science Research Organization, Russia, 1973 **Current organization:** Huntsman, Inc. **Title:** Senior Staff Scientist **Type of organization:** Manufacturing **Major product:** Structural composites for aerospace **Area of distribution:** International **Expertise:** Research and development **Published works:** 20 articles and 30 patents in the U.S.; 400 articles and 250 patents in Russia **Affiliations:** A.C.S.; S.A.M.P.E. **Hob./spts.:** Travel, swimming, volleyball **SIC code:** 28 **Address:** 4705 Henry Hudson Pkwy., Apt. 2L, Bronx, NY 10471-3237 **Web address:** www.huntsman.com

BOBO, FRANK E.
Industry: Textile **Born:** July 21, 1917, Gray Court, South Carolina **Univ./degree:** B.S., Chemistry and Chemical Engineering, Clemson University **Current organization:** Mallen Industries **Title:** Vice President **Type of organization:** Manufacturing **Major product:** Knitted fabric **Area of distribution:** National **Published works:** 6 articles **Affiliations:** President, National Association of Hosiery Manufacturers; Manufacturing Council of America; Past President, Kiwanis International **Hob./spts.:** Symphony, church activities **SIC code:** 22 **Address:** Mallen Industries, 6836 Jimmy Carter Blvd., Norcross, GA 30071

BODDY, DAVID D.
Industry: Packaging **Born:** September 9, 1939, Johannesburg, South Africa **Univ./degree:** Empire Graduate School of Business **Current organization:** Precision Valve Corp. **Title:** Executive Vice President International **Type of organization:** Manufacturing **Major product:** Aerosol valves **Area of distribution:** International **Expertise:** General management **Affiliations:** Alumnus, Empire Graduate School of Business **Hob./spts.:** Cooking, jazz, travel **SIC code:** 38 **Address:** Precision Valve Corp., 700 Nepperhan Ave., Yonkers, NY 10702

BONAR, DARREN P.
Industry: Plastics **Born:** March 13, 1966, Parkersburgh, West Virginia **Current organization:** Standard Corp. **Title:** Maintenance Scheduler **Type of organization:** Manufacturing **Major product:** Plastics **Area of distribution:** National **Expertise:** Training, team leadership, program design, project management, all aspects of maintenance **Hob./spts.:** Playing drums, Dungeons and Dragons role playing games **SIC code:** 30 **Address:** Standard Corp., 251 Arrowhead Rd., Little Hocking, OH 45742 **E-mail:** darren.p.bonar@usa.dupont.com

BONEV, PANAYOT I.
Industry: Semiconductors **Born:** September 26, 1948, Sofia, Bulgaria **Univ./degree:** M.S.M.E., 1971; M.S., Electronic Engineering, 1988, Technical University of Sofia **Current organization:** Rubicon Technology **Title:** Engineer **Type of organization:** Manufacturing **Major product:** Semiconductors **Area of distribution:** International **Expertise:** Micro electrical engineering **Published works:** Publications in the field of Management and Technology of Installation Works for big industrial projects such as nuclear stations, thermo electrical power stations, oil refineries, metallurgy and cement plants (Magazine of Bulgarian Society of Scientists) **Affiliations:** B.S.S. **Hob./spts.:** Soccer, electronics, history, political science **SIC code:** 36 **Address:** Rubicon Technology, 9931 Franklin Ave., Franklin, IL 60131 **E-mail:** panayotbonev@yahoo.com

BOOK, DONALD C.
Industry: Electrical **Born:** July 6, 1938, Williamsport, Pennsylvania **Univ./degree:** B.S.M.E., Pennsylvania State University, 1960 **Current organization:** Worldwide Electric Co., Inc. **Title:** National Sales Manager/V.P. Electric Motors **Type of organization:** Manufacturing/importing **Major product:** Electric motors, controls, reducers **Area of distribution:** National **Expertise:** Sales and marketing **Affiliations:** S.M.E. **SIC code:** 36 **Address:** Worldwide Electric Co., Inc., 240 Prospect Rd., Sugarloaf, PA 18249 **E-mail:** wwelectric@frontiernet.net

BOSWELL, ROBERT C.
Industry: Automotive **Born:** June 29, 1944, Washington D.C. **Univ./degree:** B.S.M.E., 1971; B.S., Business Management, 1974, Lawrence Technological University; M.S., Engineering Management, University of Detroit, 1998 **Current organization:** ATEO/Ford Motor Co. **Title:** Product Engineer/CAE Analyst **Type of organization:** Manufacturing and automotive design **Major product:** Transmission NVH and FEA Analysis **Area of distribution:** International **Expertise:** Automotive design engineering, consulting, quality control, webpage designing **Affiliations:** Toastmasters; Engineering Society of Detroit; Director, Webmaster, S.A.E., Detroit Section **Hob./spts.:** Computers, skiing, walking, running **SIC code:** 37 **Address:** Ford Motor Co., 36200 Plymouth Rd., MD 26, Livonia, MI 48150-1442 **E-mail:** robertboswell@comcast.net; rboswel1@ford.com

BOUTOUSSOV, DMITRI
Industry: Medical **Born:** May 11, 1963, St. Petersburg, Russia **Univ./degree:** Ph.D., St. Petersburg Technical University, Russia, 1990 **Current organization:** Biolase Technology **Title:** Ph.D., Director of Engineering **Type of organization:** Manufacturing **Major product:** Laser systems **Area of distribution:** International **Expertise:** Engineering **Published works:** 20 articles **Affiliations:** S.P.I.E. **Hob./spts.:** Family, hockey, windsurfing **SIC code:** 38 **Address:** Director of Engineering, Biolase Technology, 981 Calle Amanecer, San Clemente, CA 92673 **E-mail:** boutoussov@earthlink.net

BOWIE, MICHAEL R.
Industry: Shipbuilding **Born:** March 4, 1960, Lewiston, Maine **Univ./degree:** A.S., Architecture and Civil Engineering, Central Maine Vocational Technical Institute **Current organization:** Bath Iron Works **Title:** IT Manager **Type of organization:** Manufacturing **Major product:** Battleships **Area of distribution:** International **Expertise:** Information technology outsourcing **Affiliations:** Town/City politics **Hob./spts.:** Golf **SIC code:** 37 **Address:** Bath Iron Works, 700 Washington St., Bath, ME 04530 **E-mail:** mike.bowie@biw.com

BOYD, ROBERT T.
Industry: Automotive **Born:** February 23, 1953, Whittier, California **Univ./degree:** Master Technician, Ford Motor Co., 2003 **Current organization:** Costa Mesa Lincoln Mercury **Title:** Master Technician **Type of organization:** Manufacturing **Major product:** Automobiles **Area of distribution:** California **Expertise:** Master Technician, Ford Motor Co., 2003 **Affiliations:** Automotive Society of Engineers; Professional Technicians Society **Hob./spts.:** Boating, bicycling, mine exploration **SIC code:** 37 **Address:** Costa Mesa Lincoln Mercury, 2626 Harbor Blvd., Costa Mesa, CA 92626 **E-mail:** notlegally@msn.com

BOYD SR., DAROLD A.
Industry: Metals **Univ./degree:** B.A., Business Management, University of New Orleans, 1987 **Current organization:** Evans Industries, Inc. **Title:** Safety Quality Production Manager **Type of organization:** Manufacturing **Major product:** Industrial containers (55 gallon metal drums) **Area of distribution:** Louisiana **Expertise:** Business management, industrial safety **Hob./spts.:** Golf **SIC code:** 34 **Address:** Evans Industries, Inc., 1255 Peters Rd., Harvey, LA 70058 **E-mail:** dboyd@evansind.com

BOYER, SELENA L.
Industry: Vaccines **Born:** September 28, 1960, Lancaster, Pennsylvania **Univ./degree:** B.S., Biology, Mansfield State University, 1982 **Current organization:** Wyeth Laboratories **Title:** Training Supervisor **Type of organization:** Manufacturing **Major product:** Vaccines **Area of distribution:** Georgia **Expertise:** Vaccines-production training GMP's **Affiliations:** A.S.T.D.; P.D.A. **SIC code:** 28 **Address:** Wyeth Labora-

tories, 206 N. Biddle St., Marietta, PA 17547-0304 **E-mail:** boyers60@comcast.com **Web address:** www.wyeth.com

BRADLEY, STEVEN S.
Industry: Chemical **Born:** May 14, 1974, Washington, D.C. **Univ./degree:** B.S.M.E., Clemson University, 1997 **Current organization:** Exxon Mobil **Title:** Machinery Engineer **Type of organization:** Manufacturing **Major product:** Plastic **Area of distribution:** International **Expertise:** Mechanical engineering, machine design, troubleshooting, quality control, consulting **Affiliations:** A.S.M.E. **Hob./spts.:** Restoring classic cars, golf **SIC code:** 30 **Address:** Exxon Mobil, 11675 Scotland-Zachary Hwy., Baton Rouge, LA 70807 **E-mail:** steven.s.bradley@exxonmobil.com

BRADY, TIMOTHY D.
Industry: Publishing **Born:** March 24, 1952, Albuquerque, New Mexico **Current organization:** Write Up the Road Publishing **Title:** Trucker's Advocate/Publisher/Author/Speaker/Radio Commentator/Columnist/Retired Owner-Operator **Type of organization:** Publisher/On-Line Book Store/Speakers Bureau **Major product:** "Books, stories, photos of the American road and the lives along it" **Area of distribution:** National **Expertise:** Transportation technology, highway safety, trucking business information **Honors/awards:** American Moving & Storage Association Super Van Operator of the Year, 2002; OverDrive Magazines March 2003 Trucker of the Month, Midnight Trucking Network Million Miler Club (2.3 million miles, no accidents, no tickets); multiple driver and exemplary service awards from over 20 years with United Van Lines **Published works:** "Driven 4 Profits (An Owner/Operator's Guide to Keeping More of the Money You Earn)", 2002; "Romancing the Road (A Slice of Trucking Life with a Romantic Turn)", 2002; "You Know You're Married to a Trucker When..", 2003; "Gearing Up 4 Profits (An Owner/Operator's Guide to Load Profitability)", 2004; "Quick & Simple Recordkeeping for Owner/Operators", 2004 **Affiliations:** Lifetime Member, O.O.I.D.A. (Owner-Operator Independent Drivers Association); S.P.A.N. (Small Publishers Association of North America) **Hob./spts.:** Trained professional chef; onetime youngest member of Chef du Cuisine; archery, golf **SIC code:** 27 **Address:** Write Up the Road Publishing, P.O. Box 69, Kenton, TN 38233 **E-mail:** info@writeuptheroad.com **Web address:** www.writeuptheroad.com

BRAGAGNOLO, JULIO A.
Industry: Solar electric power (photovoltaics) **Born:** October 6, 1941, Buenos Aires, Argentina **Univ./degree:** Ph.D., Physics, 1973 **Current organization:** NPC America Corp. **Title:** Vice President **Type of organization:** Manufacturing **Major product:** Manufacturing equipment **Area of distribution:** International **Expertise:** Science/engineering **Affiliations:** A.I.P. **Hob./spts.:** Physical fitness, swimming, watching soccer, reading **SIC code:** 35 **Address:** NPC America Corp., 390 Briar Lane, Newark, DE 19711 **E-mail:** julio@npcgroup.net **Web address:** www.npcgroup.net

BRANDT, GERD RALF
Industry: Automotive **Born:** February 8, 1959, Hueckelhoven, Germany **Current organization:** Blessing Clamping Devices **Title:** General Manager **Type of organization:** Manufacturing **Major product:** Chucks **Area of distribution:** International **Expertise:** Engineering, sales **Affiliations:** S.M.E. **SIC code:** 37 **Address:** Blessing Clamping Devices, 1225 Equity Dr., Troy, MI 48084 **E-mail:** ralfbrandt@comcast.net

BRATISAX, LIZ A.
Industry: Food **Born:** November 12, 1963, Bethpage, New York **Univ./degree:** B.S., Nutrition, Long Island University, CW Post Campus, New York, 1995 **Current organization:** George Weston Bakeries, Inc. **Title:** Senior Analytical Researcher **Type of organization:** Manufacturing **Major product:** Baked goods **Area of distribution:** National **Expertise:** Analytical/microbiology **Affiliations:** International Food Technologists **Hob./spts.:** Cooking, snowmobiling **SIC code:** 20 **Address:** George Weston Bakeries, Inc., 30 Inez Dr., Bay Shore, NY 11706 **E-mail:** lbratisax@gwbakeries.com

BRAULT, MICHAEL J.
Industry: Wireforming/shape memory alloys **Born:** Bristol, Connecticut **Current organization:** Ultimate NiTi Technologies **Title:** General Manager, R&D **Type of organization:** Manufacturing **Major product:** Nickel titanium wire products **Area of distribution:** International **Expertise:** Engineering, product development **Affiliations:** A.S.M.; S.M.E.; N.R.R.P.T. **SIC code:** 34 **Address:** 200 Central St., Bristol, CT 06010 **E-mail:** mbrault@ultimateniti.com

BRAY, LONNIE T.
Industry: Machinery **Born:** March 31, 1944, Baltimore, Maryland **Current organization:** Kenlee Precision Corp. **Title:** Manufacturing Manager **Type of organization:** Manufacturing **Major product:** Machine parts **Area of distribution:** National **Expertise:** Operations management of manufacturing/process organization, training **Affiliations:** Kenlee Executive Committee **Hob./spts.:** Bowling, bicycling, physical fitness **SIC code:** 35 **Address:** Kenlee Precision Corp., 1701 Inverness Ave., Baltimore, MD 21230 **E-mail:** lbray@kenlee.com

BREAUX, MATTHEW LANE
Industry: Packaging **Born:** May 12, 1971, Lafayette, Louisiana **Univ./degree:** B.S., University of Louisiana, Lafayette, 1993 **Current organization:** C&G Containers **Title:** Vice President, Sales **Type of organization:** Manufacturing/distributing **Major product:** Packaging, science ware **Area of distribution:** International **Expertise:** Consulting, sales, regulatory; Certified Hazardous Materials Management, Texas A&M University **Affiliations:** L.A.C.H.M.M.; Institute of Hazardous Materials Management **Hob./spts.:** Hunting, fishing, golf **SIC code:** 26 **Address:** C&G Containers, 152 Easy St., Lafayette, LA 70506 **E-mail:** lanebreaux@cgcontainers.com **Web address:** www.cgcontainers.com

BRENNAN, JOHN W.
Industry: Marine/petroleum/consulting **Born:** October, 16, 1952, Mobile, Alabama **Univ./degree:** B.S., Mechanical Engineering, University of New Orleans, 1993 **Current organization:** John Brennan & Associates **Title:** Manager **Type of organization:** Manufacturing/service **Major product:** Remote operated vehicles and underwater intervention tooling **Area of distribution:** International **Expertise:** Research, design, development and support operations for ROV's; systems integration onto marine vessels **Affiliations:** A.S.M.E. **Hob./spts.:** Fishing, hunting **SIC code:** 37 **Address:** John Brennan & Associates, 645 E. Marlin Ct., Gretna, LA 70056 **E-mail:** john.brennan@oceanrobotics.biz

BREWER, KATHRYN A.
Industry: Aerospace **Univ./degree:** M.S., Business Administration, Pepperdine University, 2004 **Current organization:** Acromil Corp. **Title:** COO/CFO **Type of organization:** Manufacturing **Major product:** Airframe components **Area of distribution:** National **Expertise:** Precision machining **SIC code:** 37 **Address:** Acromil Corp., 18421 Railroad St., City of Industry, CA 91748 **E-mail:** kbrewer@acromil.com

BREWER, RICHARD LYNN
Industry: Semi-conductors **Born:** September 28, 1944 **Univ./degree:** B.S., University of Houston, 1971 **Current organization:** Trace Detect, Inc. **Title:** CEO/President **Type of organization:** Manufacturing **Major product:** Trace metal analyzers **Area of distribution:** International **Expertise:** Start-ups **Published works:** Patents, papers **Hob./spts.:** Golf, fly-fishing **SIC code:** 36 **Address:** Trace Detect, Inc., 180 N. Canal St., Seattle, WA 98103 **E-mail:** richardb@tracedetect.com **Web address:** www.tracedetect.com

BRICE, MICHAEL R.
Industry: Chemicals **Born:** May 13, 1963, New York, New York **Univ./degree:** B.A., History, Union College, 1985 **Current organization:** Superior Printing Ink Co., Inc. **Title:** President/Chief operating Officer **Type of organization:** Manufacturing **Major product:** Lithographic printing ink **Area of distribution:** National **Expertise:** Over 18 years experience in the printing industry, specializing in all areas of corporate management, plant development, staff management, production, sales, research and development, marketing; active in lecturing and public speaking at conferences and seminars **Affiliations:** N.A.P.M.; Metro New York Printing and Ink Association; Graphic Arts Professionals; The Image Committee **Hob./spts.:** Spending time with family, charity work, travel, tennis, hiking, coaching children's soccer, basketball and baseball **SIC code:** 28 **Address:** Superior Printing Ink Co., Inc., 70 Bethune St., New York, NY 10014 **E-mail:** mbrice@superiorink.com **Web address:** www.superiorink.com

BRIDGES, TERRENCE
Industry: Lighting **Born:** December 2, 1958, Torrance, California **Univ./degree:** M.S., Industrial Design, California State University at Long Beach, 1996 **Current organization:** Vista Professional Outdoor Lighting **Title:** Design Engineer **Type of organization:** Manufacturing **Major product:** Architectural lighting **Area of distribution:** National **Expertise:** Engineering **Hob./spts.:** Professional football, ballroom dancing, owns a product design business **SIC code:** 36 **Address:** Vista Professional Outdoor Lighting, 1765 Fred Ave., Simi Valley, CA 93065 **E-mail:** tnbridges1765@prodigy.net

BRIGGS, KEVIN B.
Industry: Fire equipment **Born:** October 18, 1961, Valparaiso, Indiana **Current organization:** Task Force Tips Inc. **Title:** Materials Manager **Type of organization:** Manufacturing **Major product:** Nozzles/foam equipment **Area of distribution:** International **Expertise:** Purchasing/inventory control; Certified, ISO9001 Internal Auditor; Disc Management Strategies **Affiliations:** American Purchasing Society **Hob./spts.:** Golf, cooking **SIC code:** 34 **Address:** Task Force Tips Inc., 2800 Evans Ave., Valparaiso, IN 46383 **E-mail:** kbb@tft.com **Web address:** www.tft.com

BRIGHT, REX
Industry: Pharmaceutical **Born:** April 8, 1940, Kansas City, Missouri **Univ./degree:** B.A., Drury University, 1962 **Current organization:** SkinMedica, Inc. **Title:** President, C.E.O. **Type of organization:** Manufacturing **Major product:** Vaniqa Cream **Area of distribution:** National **Expertise:** General management **Affiliations:** A.A.D.; N.A.C.D.S.; Biocom; Vistage International **SIC code:** 28 **Address:** SkinMedica, Inc.,

5909 Sea Lion Place, Carlsbad, CA 92010 **E-mail:** rbright@skinmedica.com **Web address:** www.skinmedica.com

BRINKSMA, JAMES M.
Industry: Telecommunications **Born:** January 8, 1974, Hackensack, New Jersey **Univ./degree:** B.S., 1999; M.B.A., 2003, Information Systems, Norwich University-University of Maryland **Current organization:** Ciena **Title:** Regional Manager Systems Engineering **Type of organization:** Manufacturing, equipment provider **Major product:** D.W.D.M. Optical Switching **Area of distribution:** International **Expertise:** Systems engineering **Affiliations:** I.E.E.E.; International Society of Optical Engineering **Hob./spts.:** Family, skydiving, rock climbing, golf **SIC code:** 36 **Address:** Ciena, 200 Schulz Dr., Red Bank, NJ 07701 **E-mail:** jimb@ciena.com **Web address:** www.ciena.com

BRITT, NADINE M.
Industry: Publishing **Born:** December 9, 1957, Queens, New York **Univ./degree:** B.A., Communication Arts, Marymount University, 1979 **Current organization:** Penguin Group USA **Title:** Production Director **Type of organization:** Publisher **Major product:** Books **Area of distribution:** International **Expertise:** Novelty books/production/manufacturing **Published works:** Featured in Book Tech Magazine, 2000 **Affiliations:** Bookbinders' Guild of New York **Hob./spts.:** Bicycle riding, reading **SIC code:** 27 **Address:** Penguin Group USA, 345 Hudson St., New York, NY 10014 **E-mail:** nadine.britt@us.penguingroup.com **Web address:** www.us.penguingroup.com

BROUGH, M. JOSEPH
Industry: Physical fitness **Born:** December 11, 1963, Salt Lake City, Utah **Univ./degree:** M.B.A., University of Utah, 1987 **Current organization:** Icon Health & Fitness **Title:** Chief Operating Officer **Type of organization:** Manufacturing **Major product:** Exercise equipment **Area of distribution:** International **Expertise:** Manufacturing, daily operations oversight **Affiliations:** Leader, Boy Scouts of America; Foundation for North American Wild Sheep **Hob./spts.:** Hunting, hiking **SIC code:** 39 **Address:** Icon Health & Fitness, 1500 S. 1000 West, Logan, UT 84321 **E-mail:** broughj@iconfitness.com

BROWER, KEN
Industry: Automotive **Born:** October 18, 1962, Queens, New York **Univ./degree:** B.S., Chemical Engineering, Virginia Polytechnic Institute, 1984 **Current organization:** Collins & Aikman **Title:** Plant Manager **Type of organization:** Manufacturing **Major product:** Floor mats **Area of distribution:** International **Expertise:** Engineering **Hob./spts.:** Family **SIC code:** 37 **Address:** Collins & Aikman, 8281 Country Rd. 245, Holmesville, OH 44633 **E-mail:** ken.brower@colaik.com

BROWN, CHRISTIAN D.
Industry: Automotive **Born:** December 26, 1972, Chillicothe, Ohio **Univ./degree:** B.S., Electrical Engineering, Ohio University, 1997 **Current organization:** International Crankshaft Inc. **Title:** Primary Electrical Engineer **Type of organization:** Manufacturing **Major product:** Automotive crankshafts **Expertise:** Automation/safety/training **Affiliations:** I.E.E.E. **SIC code:** 37 **Address:** 121 E. Chapin Way, Georgetown, KY 40324 **E-mail:** tugood2B@excite.com

BROWN, DAVID W.
Industry: Recreational vehicle **Univ./degree:** B.S., Political Science, Kansas State University, 1970 **Current organization:** King of the Road RV, Div. of Chiefind **Title:** National Sales and Marketing Manager **Type of organization:** Manufacturing **Major product:** Fifth wheels and motorhomes **Area of distribution:** National **Expertise:** Marketing, sales management **Hob./spts.:** Outdoor sports, golf, skiing, fly-fishing **SIC code:** 37 **Address:** King of the Road RV, Div. of Chiefind, 1313 Road G., York, NE 68467 **E-mail:** brownsofriverside@hotmail.com

BROWN, JEFFREY C.
Industry: Aerospace **Born:** June 4, 1956, Cooper, Texas **Univ./degree:** B.B.A., Management, University of Texas of the Permian Basin, West Texas, 1987 **Current organization:** Cytec Engineered Materials **Title:** Materials & Logistics Manager **Type of organization:** Manufacturing **Major product:** Composites **Area of distribution:** International **Expertise:** Operations, materials **Affiliations:** A.P.I.C.S.; Noon Exchange Club of Garland, Texas **Hob./spts.:** Woodworking, golf, bowling, sports **SIC code:** 30 **Address:** Cytec Engineered Materials, 4300 Jackson St., Greenville, TX 75402 **E-mail:** jeff_brown@ft.cytec.com

BROWN, MARCIA
Industry: Interior decorating **Born:** October 2, 1937 **Univ./degree:** A.S., Interior Design, Chicago Institute of Interior Decorating and Design, 1967 **Current organization:** Harmony Interiors **Title:** Owner **Type of organization:** Manufacturing **Major product:** Custom window treatments **Area of distribution:** National **Expertise:** Interior decorating **Affiliations:** Dunn and Bradstreet **Hob./spts.:** Sewing, yard sales, antiquing, gardening **SIC code:** 22 **Address:** 432 Priscilla St., Salisbury, MD 21804 **E-mail:** marciabrown15@aol.com

BROWN, NAN
Industry: Steel equipment **Born:** Crossville, Tennessee **Univ./degree:** A.A., Roane State Community College **Current organization:** Manchester Tank & Equipment **Title:** Production Manager **Type of organization:** Manufacturing **Major product:** Propane cylinders **Area of distribution:** International **Expertise:** Management **Honors/awards:** Phi Beta Kappa Honors Program **Hob./spts.:** Travel, numismatics (coin collecting) **SIC code:** 34 **Address:** Manchester Tank & Equipment, 1383 Industrial Blvd., Crossville, TN 38555-5426 **E-mail:** nbrown@mantank.com

BROWN, ROBERT
Industry: Fabrication **Born:** July 16, 1958, Decatur, Illinois **Current organization:** Charles Industries, Ltd. **Title:** Model Shop Machinist **Type of organization:** Manufacturing **Major product:** Telecom/marine equipment **Area of distribution:** National **Expertise:** Prototyping **Hob./spts.:** Skydiving, scuba diving, billiards, waterskiing **SIC code:** 34 **Address:** Charles Industries, Ltd., 201 Shelhouse Rd., Rantoul, IL 61866 **E-mail:** RBrown@charlesindustries.com **Web address:** www.charlesindustries.com

BROWN, RODGER A.
Industry: Medical devices **Born:** August 24, 1950, Beatrice, Nebraska **Univ./degree:** Attended University of Alaska **Current organization:** Neoprobe Corp. **Title:** V.P., RA/QA **Type of organization:** Manufacturing **Major product:** Medical devices **Area of distribution:** International **Expertise:** Regulatory affairs and quality assurance **Affiliations:** R.A.P.S.; A.S.Q.; Association for the Advancement of Medical Instrumentation **Hob./spts.:** Photography, fly-fishing **SIC code:** 38 **Address:** Neoprobe Corp., 425 Metro Place North, #300, Dublin, OH 43017 **E-mail:** rbrown@neoprobe.com

BROWN, WILLIAM F.
Industry: Broadcast communications **Born:** March 29, 1961, Braintree, Massachusetts **Univ./degree:** B.S.E.E., Worchester Polytech Institute, 1996 **Current organization:** Microwave Radio Communication **Title:** Lead Engineer **Type of organization:** Manufacturing/sales **Major product:** Microwave broadcast systems **Area of distribution:** International **Expertise:** Embedded systems design **Affiliations:** I.E.E.E. **Hob./spts.:** Science robotics, German sports cars **SIC code:** 36 **Address:** 30 Worthen St., Chelmsford, MA 01824 **E-mail:** wfbrown@mrcbroadcast.com **Web address:** www.mrcbradcast.com

BRUINSMA, DANIEL G.
Industry: Automotive **Born:** July 5, 1967, Rochester, New York **Univ./degree:** B.S., Environmental Engineering, North Carolina State University, 1994 **Current organization:** Michelin **Title:** Industrial Engineer **Type of organization:** Manufacturing **Major product:** Radial tires **Area of distribution:** International **Expertise:** Administration, management **Hob./spts.:** Golf, fishing **SIC code:** 37 **Address:** Michelin, 51201 21st St., Tuscaloosa, AL 35401

BRUNT, MICHAEL T.
Industry: Electronics **Born:** September 29, 1972, Kosciusko, Mississippi **Univ./degree:** B.S.E.E., Mississippi State University **Current organization:** CM Solutions, Inc. **Title:** Quality Manager **Type of organization:** Manufacturing **Major product:** Electronics for automotive, medical and government industries **Area of distribution:** National **Expertise:** Test engineering/quality **Hob./spts.:** Mountain biking, music **SIC code:** 36 **Address:** CM Solutions, Inc., 2674 S. Harper Rd., Corinth, MS 38835 **E-mail:** m_brunt@comcast.net

BRUNTZ, SAMUEL H.
Industry: Aluminum scrap recycling and rolling mill **Born:** March 31, 1950, London, Kentucky **Spouse:** Judy Cooksey **Married:** November 11, 1980 **Children:** Ronald, 17; Melissa, 12 **Univ./degree:** B.S., Metallurgical Engineering, University of Kentucky **Current organization:** Commonwealth Aluminum Lewisport, Inc. **Title:** Senior Environmental Engineer **Type of organization:** Manufacturing **Major product:** Painted and bare aluminum coils **Area of distribution:** National **Expertise:** Environmental engineering, Registered Environmental Manager with the National Registry of Environmental Professionals **Honors/awards:** University of Kentucky, Department of Metallurgical Engineering Student of the Year, 1972-73 **Published works:** Numerous air pollution permit applications **Affiliations:** Air and Waste Management Association **Career accomplishments:** Development of dry scrubbing efficiency modifications at 2 aluminum delacquering operations, participation in development of regulations at

the Federal and State level and successful management of numerous stack test projects mandated by Federal and State agencies **Hob./spts.:** His parrots, playing in a local brass band **SIC code:** 33 **Address:** Commonwealth Aluminum Lewisport, Inc., Kentucky Hwy. 1957, Lewisport, KY 42351 **E-mail:** rem833@aol.com

BRUST, DAVID J.
Industry: Telephone directories **Born:** June 22, 1952, Streator, Illinois **Current organization:** R.R. Donnelley **Title:** Technical Supervisor **Type of organization:** Manufacturing **Major product:** Telephone directories **Area of distribution:** International **Expertise:** Printing **Affiliations:** American Legion **Hob./spts.:** Golf, boating **SIC code:** 27 **Address:** R.R. Donnelley, 801 N. Union St., Dwight, IL 60420 **E-mail:** dave.brust@rrd.com

BRUTON, KIMBERLY C.
Industry: Pharmaceutical **Born:** December 14, 1969, Mount Sterling, Kentucky **Univ./degree:** B.S., Biology, Transylvania University, 1992 **Current organization:** Elan Holding **Title:** Manufacturing Manager **Type of organization:** Manufacturing **Major product:** Sustained release drugs **Area of distribution:** International **Expertise:** Management, production process, training **Hob./spts.:** Reading, community service, missionary work **SIC code:** 28 **Address:** Elan Holding, 1300 Gould Dr., Gainesville, GA 30504 **E-mail:** kim.bruton@elan.com **Web address:** www.elan.com

BRYAN, EDDIE R.
Industry: Petrochemicals **Born:** March 21, 1966, Tulsa, Oklahoma **Univ./degree:** B.S., Engineering, Oklahoma State University, 1992 **Current organization:** Boyle Manufacturing **Title:** Chief Engineer **Type of organization:** Manufacturing **Major product:** Auxiliary equipment for mechanical seals **Area of distribution:** National **Expertise:** Engineering **Affiliations:** A.S.M.E. **Hob./spts.:** Sailing **SIC code:** 35 **Address:** Boyle Manufacturing, 930 E. 36th St., Tulsa, OK 74105 **E-mail:** erbryan@boylemfg.com

BUCKLEY, ROGER L.
Industry: Microwave and RF components **Born:** May 22, 1964, Miami, Florida **Univ./degree:** B.S., Finance, University of South Florida **Current organization:** TRAK Microwave Corp. **Title:** Materials Manager **Type of organization:** Manufacturing **Major product:** RF/microwave systems/subsystems/components **Area of distribution:** International **Expertise:** Purchasing, inventory control **Affiliations:** A.P.E.X. **Hob./spts.:** Soccer, fishing **SIC code:** 36 **Address:** TRAK Microwave Corp., 4726 Eisenhower Blvd., Tampa, FL 33634 **E-mail:** rbuckley@trak.com **Web address:** www.trak.com

BUCKNER, RANDY C.
Industry: Automotive **Born:** October 21, 1964, Trenton, Michigan **Univ./degree:** B.S., Wayne State University, 1987 **Current organization:** T.I. Automotive Group **Title:** Engineer **Type of organization:** Tube manufacturing **Major product:** Single wall tubes **Area of distribution:** International **Expertise:** Engineering/electrical **Published works:** 1 article **Affiliations:** S.M.E. **Hob./spts.:** Hockey, repairing electronics **SIC code:** 30 **Address:** 17655 Robert St., Melvindale, MI 48122 **E-mail:** rbuc102828@aol.com

BUFFUM, STANLEY G.
Industry: Appliances **Current organization:** Appliance Controls Group Inc. **Title:** Manufacturing/Automation Engineer **Type of organization:** Manufacturing **Major product:** Components for gas range industry **Area of distribution:** National **Expertise:** Engineering; Certified through the American Vacuum Society **Hob./spts.:** Woodworking, water sports **SIC code:** 36 **Address:** Appliance Controls Group Inc., 525 Elm Place, Princeton, IL 61356 **E-mail:** sbuffum@harper-wyman.com

BUONGIORNO, JOSEPH P.
Industry: Food **Born:** April 5, 1947, Hoboken, New Jersey **Univ./degree:** M.S., Structural Engineering, New Jersey Institute of Technology, 1972 **Current organization:** Kraft Foods North America **Title:** Manager of Building Infrastructure **Type of organization:** Manufacturing **Major product:** Multiple food products **Area of distribution:** National **Expertise:** Engineering **Affiliations:** A.S.C.E.; A.C.I.; S.P.C. **SIC code:** 20 **Address:** Kraft Foods North America, 200 DeForest Ave., East Hanover, NJ 07936 **E-mail:** jbuong@optonline.net

BURAAS, KAREN W.
Industry: Boats/fiberglass products **Current organization:** U.S. Technology & Science Corp. **Title:** President/Owner **Type of organization:** Manufacturing **Major product:** Building revolutionary boats **Area of distribution:** International **Expertise:** Stretch R-V's **SIC code:** 37 **Address:** U.S. Technology & Science Corp., 210 N.E. 102 St., Miami Shores, FL 33138 **E-mail:** kwburaas@aol.com

BURDICK, ANDY P.
Industry: Aerospace **Born:** October 1, 1942, Warsaw, New York **Univ./degree:** B.S., Business Management, Alfred University **Current organization:** Senior Operations Inc. **Title:** Sr. Estimator/Planner **Type of organization:** Manufacturing **Major product:** Hot air duct systems **Area of distribution:** National **Expertise:** Estimating, cost analysis **Affiliations:** Past Member, American Welding Association **Hob./spts.:** Church **SIC code:** 37 **Address:** Senior Operations Inc., 2980 N. San Fernando Blvd., Burbank, CA 91504 **E-mail:** a.burdick@senioraerospace.com

BURGOS, FRANCISCO J.
Industry: Pharmaceuticals **Univ./degree:** B.S., Chemistry, InterAmerican University, Rio Piedras, Puerto Rico, 1984; M.A. Candidate, Universidad Metropolitana, Puerto Rico **Current organization:** Bristol Meyers-Squibb **Title:** Environmental Affairs Manager **Type of organization:** Manufacturing **Major product:** Prescription drugs and medicines **Area of distribution:** International **Expertise:** Handles all compliance issues **Affiliations:** W.E.F.; American Chemical Society **Hob./spts.:** Drums, music **SIC code:** 28 **Address:** Chalet de Bairoa Gorrion Rd., #119, Caguas, PR 00727-1269 **E-mail:** francisco.burgos@bms.com

BURNS, BYRON L.
Industry: Automotive **Born:** August 9, 1956, Peru, Indiana **Current organization:** Vibracoustic N.A. **Type of organization:** Manufacturing **Major product:** Bushing motor mounts **Area of distribution:** International **Expertise:** Lean manufacturing **Honors/awards:** Greenbelt Sigma, 2002 **Hob./spts.:** Boating **SIC code:** 37 **Address:** Vibracoustic N.A., 1497 Gerber St., Ligonier, IN 46767 **E-mail:** blb@fngp.com

BUTLER, CONNOR M.
Industry: Computer hardware **Born:** December 15, 1974, Glendale, Arizona **Univ./degree:** B.S., Mechanical Engineering, University of Arizona **Current organization:** Intel Corp. **Title:** Project Engineer **Type of organization:** Manufacturing **Major product:** Semiconductors **Area of distribution:** International **Expertise:** Design/build management from inception to completion **Hob./spts.:** Fishing **SIC code:** 36 **Address:** Intel Corp., 4500 S. Dobson Rd., OC4-009, Chandler, AZ 85248 **E-mail:** connor.m.butler@intel.com

BYERLY, RODRICK R.
Industry: Petrochemicals **Univ./degree:** B.S., Biochemistry, Lemoore University, 1977 **Current organization:** Chevron Phillips Chemical Co. **Title:** Chemist, Supervisor **Type of organization:** Manufacturing, distributing **Major product:** Alpha olefins, polyethylene, plastics **Area of distribution:** International **Expertise:** Customer service, personnel development, analytical test development **Hob./spts.:** Family, preaching the Gospel **SIC code:** 28 **Address:** Chevron Phillips Chemical Co., 9500 Interstate 10 East, Baytown, TX 77521 **E-mail:** byerlrr@cpchem.com **Web address:** www.cpchem.com

CAIN, ADAM
Industry: Aerospace **Born:** April 27, 1976, Amherst, Ohio **Current organization:** Parker Hannifin **Title:** Model Maker **Type of organization:** Manufacturing/engineering **Major product:** Fuel pumps **Area of distribution:** International **Expertise:** Prototyping, moldmaking **Hob./spts.:** Flying **SIC code:** 37 **Address:** Parker Hannifin, 711 Taylor, Elyria, OH 44035 **E-mail:** adam427427@yahoo.com

CAIN, STEVEN M.
Industry: Steel **Univ./degree:** B.S., Management, Southeastern Oklahoma State University , 1995 **Current organization:** North Texas Steel Co., Inc. **Title:** Environmental/Safety Manager **Type of organization:** Manufacturing **Major product:** Structural and bridge components **Area of distribution:** Texas **Expertise:** Environmental, health, safety compliance **Affiliations:** N.A.S.P.; E.P.A.; O.S.H.A. **Hob./spts.:** Sports, the outdoors **SIC code:** 33 **Address:** North Texas Steel Co., Inc., 412 W. Bolt St., Ft. Worth, TX 76110 **E-mail:** smcain@ntxst1.com

CALMBACHER, CHARLES W.
Industry: Medical devices **Born:** June 14, 1951, Bronx, New York **Univ./degree:** B.S., Biology,1973; M.S., Biology, 1975; Ph.D., Biology, 1979, Fordham University **Current organization:** Theragenics Corporation **Title:** Ph.D/Corporate Environmental, Health and Safety Officer **Type of organization:** Manufacturing **Major product:** Brachytherapy seeds **Area of distribution:** National **Expertise:** Certified Industrial Hygienist; Industrial hygiene and safety; Environmental compliance **Honors/awards:** The Humanitarian Service Medal during the Cuban refugee crisis, 1980; National Science Foundation Award for his doctoral research in Biosystematics, 1975 **Published works:** 60+ articles **Affiliations:** American Industrial Hygiene Association, Publications Committee; Sigma XI **Hob./spts.:** Reading, plays the bagpipes, builds and races cars, ham radio **SIC code:** 38 **Address:** Theragenics Corporation, 5203 Bristol Industrial Way, Buford, GA 30518 **E-mail:** calmbacc@theragenics.com **Web address:** www.theragenics.com

CAMERLENGO, EMILIANO
Industry: Food **Born:** January 27, 1964, Altavilla, Irpina, Italy **Current organization:** Ferrero Inc. **Title:** Vice President, Manufacturing **Type of organization:** Manufacturing **Major product:** Food **Area of distribution:** National **Expertise:** Management

Hob./spts.: Soccer, basketball **SIC code:** 20 **Address:** Ferrero Inc., Carr #1 Km 29.4, Caguas, PR 00725 **E-mail:** emilianocamerlengo@ferrero-inc.com

CAMPBELL, COLIN D.
Industry: Industrial machinery design **Born:** January 12, 1978, Flemington, New Jersey **Univ./degree:** M.S.M.E., Virginia Tech **Current organization:** PCA Mechanical Engineering LLC **Title:** Mechanical Engineer **Type of organization:** Manufacturing and consulting think tank **Major product:** Innovative concept design and manufacturing **Area of distribution:** National **Expertise:** Computer/mathematical modeling, computer animations/video computing, simulations, 3D CAD modeling, electronic hardware/software design, machinery design **Honors/awards:** Phi Theta Kappa; Golden Keg; Paul C. Torgerson Leadership Award **Hob./spts.:** Church Youth Director; building with Lego MindStorms **SIC code:** 39 **Address:** 271 Laymantown Rd., Troutville, VA 24175 **E-mail:** colin.campbell@pca-research.com **Web address:** www.colincampbellonline.com

CAMPBELL, TONY L.
Industry: Textile **Born:** July 7, 1962, Harrisonburg, Virginia **Univ./degree:** A.S., Liberal Arts **Current organization:** Transprint USA **Title:** Purchasing Manager **Type of organization:** Printing **Major product:** Head transfer paper, designing prints **Area of distribution:** International **Expertise:** Printing (25 years experience) **Hob./spts.:** Kayaking, riding motorcycles, drag racing, photography **SIC code:** 26 **Address:** Transprint USA, 1000 Pleasant Valley Rd., Harrisonburg, VA 22801 **E-mail:** tony@transprintusa.com **Web address:** www.transprintusa.com

CANADAY, D. CHARLENE
Industry: Glass **Born:** August 4, 1932, Sissonville, West Virginia **Title:** Traffic Manager, Owens-Illinois, Inc. (Retired) **Type of organization:** Manufacturing **Major product:** Glass bottles **Area of distribution:** National **Expertise:** Traffic management **Hob./spts.:** Travel **SIC code:** 32 **Address:** 32 Woodlawn Ave., Clarion, PA 16214

CANTILLO, RONELIO N.
Industry: Printing **Born:** December 3, 1964, Philippines **Current organization:** Midweek Printing Inc. **Title:** Pre-Press Manager **Type of organization:** Publication **Major product:** Newspapers/commercial work **Area of distribution:** Hawaii **Expertise:** Pre-press operations **Hob./spts.:** Surfing, A.B. graphics **SIC code:** 27 **Address:** Midweek Printing Inc., 45-525 Luluku Rd., Kaneohe, HI 96744 **E-mail:** rcantillo@starbulletin.com

CARLINO, LAURA ANN
Industry: Specialty foods **Born:** May 29, 1964, Abruzzo, Italy **Univ./degree:** Attended Villanova University **Current organization:** Carlino's Specialty Foods Inc. **Title:** Secretary, Vice President **Type of organization:** Manufacturing and retailer **Major product:** Italian specialty foods and catering **Area of distribution:** Pennsylvania **Expertise:** Food styling, customer service, personell relations **Affiliations:** Board of Directors, National Hemophilia Association **Hob./spts.:** Family, reading, travel **SIC code:** 20 **Address:** Carlino's Specialty Foods Inc., 2612-16 E. County Line Rd., Ardmore, PA 19003 **Web address:** www.carlinosmarket.com

CARLSON, JOHN "DAVID"
Industry: Material Processing Technologies **Born:** December 28, 1951, Elgin, Illinois **Univ./degree:** B.S., South Illinois University, 1974 **Current organization:** Eirich Machines, Inc. **Title:** Test Manager **Type of organization:** Manufacturing **Major product:** Material processing machinery **Area of distribution:** International **Expertise:** Material processing system design, development, testing, quality improvement **Honors/awards:** Baxter Travenol Laboratories Co-inventor Patent Award, 1977; SAE "Outstanding Young Member" Award, 1986; Listed in Marquis "Who's Who in the Midwest", 1986-1987 **Published works:** 1 patent **Affiliations:** Member, American Society for Quality **Hob./spts.:** Travel, photography **SIC code:** 35 **Address:** 1401 Andover Dr., Mundelein, IL 60060 **E-mail:** dcarlson@eirichusa.com

CARLSON, KEVIN R.
Industry: Paper **Univ./degree:** B.A., Business, The Citadel, South Carolina, 1986 **Current organization:** Smurfit-Stone Container Corp. **Title:** Plant Manager **Type of organization:** Manufacturing **Major product:** Corrugated containers **Area of distribution:** International **Expertise:** Plant management **Affiliations:** Alumni Association, The Citadel **Hob./spts.:** Family, water sports, outdoor activities **SIC code:** 26 **Address:** Smurfit-Stone Container Corp., 501 Zschokke St., Highland, IL 62249 **E-mail:** kcarlson2@smurfit.com

CARMICHAEL, JENNIFER W.
Industry: Luggage **Univ./degree:** B.S., Business Administration, Western Washington University, 1998 **Current organization:** Skyway Luggage Co. **Title:** Executive Vice President **Type of organization:** Manufacturing, distributing **Major product:** Luggage, casual bags, backpacks **Area of distribution:** National **Expertise:** Client satisfaction, management **Affiliations:** Board Member, W.S.E.E.C.; T.G.A. **SIC code:** 22 **Address:** Skyway Luggage Co., 30 Wall St., Seattle, WA 98121 **E-mail:** carmichaeljw@aol.com

CARNLEY, JOHN RICHARD
Industry: Shipbuilding **Born:** October 17, 1950, Mojave, California **Univ./degree:** A.A., Jackson County Junior College, 1972 **Current organization:** Friede Goldman Halter, Moss Point Yard **Title:** Program Manager **Type of organization:** Manufacturing **Major product:** Oceanographic research vessels **Area of distribution:** National **Expertise:** Program management (government project engineering) **Hob./spts.:** Hunting, Rock n' Roll music **SIC code:** 37 **Address:** Friede Goldman Halter, Moss Point Yard, 5801 Elderferry Rd., Moss Point, MS 39563 **E-mail:** j.carnley@fgh.com

CARONE, GREGORY W.
Born: July 24, 1959, Grove City, Pennsylvania **Univ./degree:** B.S., Point Park College, Pennsylvania **Current organization:** Technical Precision, Inc. **Title:** President **Type of organization:** Manufacturing **Major product:** Tooling for powdered metals industry **Area of distribution:** International **Expertise:** Engineering, marketing **Hob./spts.:** Coaching Jr. High School Basketball **SIC code:** 34 **Address:** Technical Precision, Inc., 2343 Perry Hwy., Hadley, PA 16130 **E-mail:** techprec@earthlink.net

CARPIO, FRANCISCO
Industry: Test equipment **Born:** August 25, 1938, Santa Fe, Argentina **Univ./degree:** M.E., Universidad Del Litoral, Argentina, 1963 **Current organization:** DIT-MCO International **Title:** Director of Special Products Group **Type of organization:** Manufacturing **Major product:** Testing equipment **Area of distribution:** International **Expertise:** Director of SPG Division of DIT-MCO International **Hob./spts.:** Swimming, travel **SIC code:** 38 **Address:** DIT-MCO International, 5612 Brighton Terrace, Kansas City, MO 64130 **E-mail:** fcarpio@ditmco.com

CASHION, BARBARA WEATHERFORD
Industry: Plastics/metals **Born:** April 2, 1937, Russellville, Alabama **Univ./degree:** M.A., Business Education, University of North Alabama **Current organization:** Cashion Thermoplastics, Inc. **Title:** President **Type of organization:** Manufacturing **Major product:** Plastics and metals **Area of distribution:** Alabama **Expertise:** Business administration **Affiliations:** A.E.A.; N.E.A. **Hob./spts.:** Genealogy **SIC code:** 30 **Address:** Cashion Thermoplastics, Inc., P.O. Box 400, Red Bay, AL 35582

CASTLE, KEITH L.
Industry: Paper **Born:** July 16, 1945, Port of Spain, Trinidad **Current organization:** Global One Resources **Title:** President/CEO **Type of organization:** Distribution **Major product:** Paper products and general supplies **Area of distribution:** International **Expertise:** Marketing **Affiliations:** N.A.A.C.P.; Veterans Benefits Program; Roxbury Community College Foundation **Hob./spts.:** Golf **SIC code:** 26 **Address:** Global One Resources, 15 Hallowell St., Boston, MA 02120 **E-mail:** kcastle863@aol.com

CASWELL, GREG
Industry: High tech electronics **Born:** June 13, 1947, Somerville, New Jersey **Univ./degree:** B.S.E.E., Rutgers University, 1976; B.A., Business Management, St. Edwards University, 1984 **Current organization:** Silicon Hills Design **Title:** Technical Sales Director **Type of organization:** Manufacturing **Major product:** Contract design and assembly **Area of distribution:** International **Expertise:** Technical sales **Honors/awards:** TRACOR Technical Innovation Award, 1984; ISHM, Technical Achievement Award, 1986; ISHM, Fellow of the Society Award, 1993; ISHM, Daniel C. Hughes Award, 1995 **Published works:** 200 technical papers **Affiliations:** I.M.A.P.S. (2001 President of International Society) **Hob./spts.:** Genealogy **SIC code:** 36 **Address:** Silicon Hills Design, 8504 Cross Park Dr., Austin, TX 78754 **E-mail:** greg@siliconhills.com **Web address:** www.siliconhills.com

CAVALLO, JOHN F.
Industry: Combustion technology **Born:** August 26, 1951, Brooklyn, New York **Current organization:** ERB-Ensign **Title:** President **Type of organization:** Manufacturing **Major product:** Industrial burners **Area of distribution:** International **Expertise:** Marketing, administration **Affiliations:** B.E.M.A.; B. & C.M.A. **Hob./spts.:** Snowmobiling **SIC code:** 35 **Address:** ERB-Ensign, 101 Secor Lane, Pelham Manor, NY 10803 **E-mail:** jfc@erbensign.com **Web address:** www.erbensign.com

CAVANZON, LUIS C.
Industry: Automotive **Univ./degree:** B.S., International Business, Itesm Technical University, 1998 **Current organization:** Delphi Corp. **Title:** Supply Chain Management **Type of organization:** Manufacturing **Major product:** Electrical systems **Area of distribution:** International **Expertise:** International business **SIC code:** 36 **Address:** Delphi Corp., 48 Walter Jones Blvd., Mail Station 30-A, El Paso, TX 79912 **E-mail:** luisc.c.cavanzon@delphi.com

CENTERS, JOEY D.
Industry: Automotive **Born:** February 21, 1965, Berea, Kentucky **Univ./degree:** B.A., Berea College, 1988 **Current organization:** Hayes-Lemmerz, Motor Wheel Division

Title: Manager **Type of organization:** Manufacturing **Major product:** Commercial highway brake drums and brake hubs **Area of distribution:** National **Expertise:** Materials Specialist **Hob./spts.:** Softball, hunting, fishing **SIC code:** 34 **Address:** Hayes-Lemmerz, Motor Wheel Division, 160 Glades Rd., Berea, KY 40403 **E-mail:** jcenters@hayes-lemmerz.com

CERIO, FRANK M.
Industry: Semiconductors **Born:** June 9, 1964, Providence, Rhode Island **Univ./degree:** B.S. with Honors, Chemistry, Worcester Polytechnic Institute; Ph.D. with Honors, Chemistry, Boston University **Current organization:** Tel Technology Center, America **Title:** Process Development Manager **Type of organization:** Manufacturing and development **Major product:** Semiconductor equipment **Area of distribution:** International **Expertise:** Engineering technology, development of new applications **Published works:** 20 articles, several patents on ionized physical vapor deposition **Affiliations:** American Chemical Society, Past Member **Hob./spts.:** Travel, 10K runner, numismatics **SIC code:** 36 **Address:** Tel Technology Center, America, 255 Fuller Rd., Suite 244, Albany, NY 12203 **E-mail:** frank.cerio@us.tel.com

CHAMBLY, LAWRENCE R.
Industry: Electrical systems **Born:** April 25, 1938, Chicago, Illinois **Univ./degree:** Attended Pasadena College **Current organization:** USA Harness/New Concepts **Title:** Founder/ V.P. Sales/President/Chairman/CEO **Type of organization:** Manufacturing **Major product:** Electrical systems and harnesses **Area of distribution:** International **Expertise:** Marketing, manufacturing **Affiliations:** S.A.E.; Treasurer, Director, Founder, W.H.M.A. **Hob./spts.:** Fishing, golf **SIC code:** 36 **Address:** USA Harness/ New Concepts, 1201 E. Coke Rd., Winnsboro, TX 75294 **E-mail:** larry@usaharness.com

CHAMPAGNE, LORETTA A.
Industry: Oil/Cosmetics **Born:** February 26, 1949, Lake Charles, Louisiana **Univ./degree:** Certification in Computer Programming, Sowela Technical School, 1980 **Current organization:** CITGO Petroleum Corp./Avon **Title:** Laboratory Secretary/Representative **Type of organization:** Gasoline and oil distributor/cosmetics distributor **Major product:** Oil refining/cosmetics **Area of distribution:** International/Louisiana **Expertise:** Secretarial/sales marketing **Hob./spts.:** Gardening, reading **SIC code:** 29 **Address:** CITGO Petroleum Corp./Avon, 4401 Louisiana Hwy. 108, Westlake, LA 70669 **E-mail:** lorettachampagne120@cs.com

CHAN, JOHNI
Industry: Computer hardware/software **Born:** December 5, 1967, Hong Kong, China **Univ./degree:** Ph.D., Electrical Engineering, Stanford University **Current organization:** I-Bus Corp. **Title:** President/CEO **Type of organization:** Manufacturing **Major product:** High availability platforms **Area of distribution:** International **Expertise:** Engineering **Hob./spts.:** Tennis **SIC code:** 36 **Address:** I-Bus Corp., 3350 Scott Blvd., Bldg. 54, Santa Clara, CA 95054 **E-mail:** jchan@ibus.com

CHANEY, MARK R.
Industry: Defense/Aerospace **Born:** November 12, 1948, Ogden, Utah **Univ./degree:** M.S., Science of Administration, Michigan State University, 1989 **Current organization:** Raytheon TSC **Title:** Senior Analyst **Type of organization:** RDT&E, manufacturing **Major product:** Missles, radar, sensors, technical support **Area of distribution:** International **Expertise:** Marketing, program development **Affiliations:** A.U.S.A.; A.A.I.A.; N.D.I.A.; R.O.A. **SIC code:** 36 **Address:** Raytheon TSC, 529 Michigan Ave., Elizabethtown, KY 42701 **E-mail:** mark.chaney@knox.army.mil

CHANG, CRAIG H.
Industry: Aerospace/chemical **Born:** May 19, 1939, Tainan, Taiwan **Univ./degree:** Ph.D., Physical Chemistry, Rice University, 1967 **Current organization:** Honeywell International, Inc. **Title:** Ph.D., Senior Principal Scientist **Type of organization:** Manufacturing **Major product:** Chemicals and aerospace components **Area of distribution:** International **Expertise:** Research and development **Published works:** 50+ scientific journals, articles **Affiliations:** A.C.S.; A.A.A.S. **SIC code:** 28 **Address:** 511 Revere lane, Palatine, IL 60067 **E-mail:** craig.chang@honeywell.com

CHANG, HAN
Industry: Semiconductors **Born:** August 19, 1965, Taipei, Taiwan **Univ./degree:** B.S., Aerospace Engineering, 1987, National Cheng Kung University; M.S., Applied Math, 1991; M.S., Engineering, 1993; Ph.D., Engineering, 1993, Brown University **Current organization:** Philips AMS **Title:** Applications Manager **Type of organization:** Manufacturing, R&D **Major product:** Metrology **Area of distribution:** International **Expertise:** Product promotion, semiconductor processing, technical project management **Published works:** 17 papers, 2 patents **Hob./spts.:** Tennis **SIC code:** 36 **Address:** Philips AMS, 12 Michigan Ave., Natick, MA 01760 **E-mail:** hanchieh_chang@yahoo.com **Web address:** www.ams.phillips.com

CHAPLIN, VINCENT B.
Industry: Automotive **Univ./degree:** B.S., South Carolina State University, 1986 **Current organization:** ABB Inc. **Title:** Senior Engineer **Type of organization:** Manufacturing **Major product:** Robotics Automation **Expertise:** Engineering **Hob./spts.:** Photography, jazz music, travel **SIC code:** 37 **Address:** ABB Inc., 1250 Brown Rd., Auburn Hills, MI 48326 **E-mail:** vincent.b.chaplin@us.abb.com

CHATALBASH, RUTHIE C.
Industry: Decorative glass **Born:** January 6, 1963, Bronx, New York **Title:** Owner **Type of organization:** Manufacturing **Major product:** Stained decorative glass design and manufacturing **Area of distribution:** New York **Expertise:** Stained glass design and construction **Hob./spts.:** Stained glass, art, sports, cooking **SIC code:** 32 **Address:** 563 Forest Ave., Massapequa, NY 11758 **E-mail:** grosso25@optonline.net

CHAUDHURI, RATAN K.
Industry: Chemicals **Born:** September 9, 1945, Varanasi, India **Univ./degree:** B.S., 1967; M.S., 1969; Ph.D., Pharmacology/Chemistry, 1973, Banaras Hindu University **Current organization:** EM Industries **Title:** Technical Director **Type of organization:** Manufacturing **Major product:** Cosmetic ingredients **Area of distribution:** International **Expertise:** Research and development **Honors/awards:** 57 Chemical Patents **Published works:** 70+ publications **Affiliations:** S.C.C.; A.C.S. **SIC code:** 28 **Address:** EM Industries, 7 Skyline Dr., Hawthorne, NY 10532 **E-mail:** rchandhuri@emindustries.com

CHELLAPPA, MUTHUKRISHNAN
Industry: Electronic equipment **Born:** March 29, 1945, Nanguneri, India **Univ./degree:** M.S.E.C.E., University of Texas, 1985 **Current organization:** JMAR Precision Systems, Inc. **Title:** Vice President, Sales & Product Management **Type of organization:** Manufacturing **Major product:** Non-contact inspection systems **Area of distribution:** International **Expertise:** Technical sales and product management **Affiliations:** American Association for Quality Control **Hob./spts.:** Tennis **SIC code:** 36 **Address:** JMAR Precision Systems, Inc., 9207 Eton Ave., Chatsworth, CA 91311 **E-mail:** kmuthkrishnan@jmar-psi.com

CHEN, BRYAN HSI-CHING
Industry: Military/aerospace **Born:** December 1, 1966, Taipei, Taiwan **Univ./degree:** B.S., Taiwan, 1989; M.S., 1993; Ph.D., 1997, University of California at San Diego **Current organization:** General Atomics **Title:** Senior Materials Scientist **Type of organization:** Manufacturing, R&D **Major product:** Aerospace, military products **Area of distribution:** International **Expertise:** Engineering, science **Published works:** 15+ technical publications **Affiliations:** American Ceramic Society; A.S.M. International; National Defense Industrial Association **Hob./spts.:** Travel, movies, tennis **SIC code:** 37 **Address:** General Atomics, 3550 General Atomics Ct., San Diego, CA 92121 **E-mail:** bryan.chen@gat.com

CHENOWETH, JOHN E.
Industry: Agricultural equipment/machinery **Born:** May 1, 1954, Decatur, Illinois **Univ./degree:** B.S.M.E. with Honors, University of Illinois, 1976; M.B.A. with Honors, St. Ambrose University, 1983 **Current organization:** Deere & Co. **Title:** Senior Engineer **Type of organization:** Manufacturing **Major product:** Agricultural equipment/machinery **Area of distribution:** International **Expertise:** Manufacturing process and design **Honors/awards:** Machinery Design Award, University of Illinois, 1976 **Affiliations:** Society of Manufacturing Engineers; American Society of Mechanical Engineers **Hob./spts.:** Hosta growing, basketball, antiques **SIC code:** 35 **Address:** Deere & Co., 1 John Deere Place, Moline, IL 61265 **E-mail:** chenoweth.john@johndeere.com **Web address:** www.johndeere.com

CHERETTE, MYRLAIN
Industry: Pharmaceutical **Born:** March 10, 1972, Port-au-Prince, Haiti **Univ./degree:** B.S., Mechanical Engineering, New Jersey Institute of Technology, 1996 **Current organization:** Schering Plough Co. **Title:** Project Engineer **Type of organization:** Manufacturing **Major product:** Pharmaceuticals **Area of distribution:** National **Expertise:** Engineering **Affiliations:** A.S.M.E. **Hob./spts.:** Music, playing the bass **SIC code:** 28 **Address:** 27 Laurel Ave., Irvington, NJ 07111 **E-mail:** myrlain.cherette@spcorp.com

CHEUK, MOON
Industry: Hardware/software **Born:** May 25, 1951, Hong Kong, China **Univ./degree:** B.S.E.E., San Diego State University, 1974; M.S.E.E., California State University at Los Angeles, 1977 **Current organization:** Econolite Control Products **Title:** Vice President of Engineering **Type of organization:** Manufacturer **Major product:** Traffic control, electronic hardware and software **Area of distribution:** International **Expertise:** Engineering, system design, project management, product development, strategic planning, team leadership **Hob./spts.:** Photography, reading **SIC code:** 36 **Address:** Econolite Control Products, 3360 E. La Palma Ave., Anaheim, CA 92806 **E-mail:** mcheuk@aol.com

CHILUMULA, AJAYA K.
Industry: Semiconductors **Born:** June 24, 1980, Hyderabad, India **Univ./degree:** M.S.E.E., Clemson University, 2003 **Current organization:** Micron Technology **Title:** Test Engineer **Type of organization:** Manufacturing/distributing **Major product:** Memory products **Area of distribution:** International **Expertise:** Design and test engineering **Affiliations:** I.E.E.E. **Hob./spts.:** Photography **SIC code:** 36 **Address:** Micron Technology, 8000 S. Federal Way, Boise, ID 83707 **E-mail:** ajay.kc@gmail.com

CHINNICI, ROY R.
Industry: Accessories **Born:** January 16, 1944; Brooklyn, New York **Univ./degree:** B.S., Business, Murray State University, 1966 **Current organization:** V. Fraas **Title:** Vice President **Type of organization:** Manufacturing **Major product:** Cold weather products **Area of distribution:** International **Expertise:** Men's, women's and children's cold weather accessories **Affiliations:** Board Member, Accessory Council **Hob./spts.:** Skiing, fishing **SIC code:** 23 **Address:** V. Fraas, 58 W. 40th St., New York, NY 10018 **E-mail:** rchinnici@frass.com **Web address:** www.fraas.com

CHMURA, MICHAEL A.
Industry: Electronics **Born:** August 23, 1957, Chicago, Illinois **Univ./degree:** B.S., Industrial Technology, Northern Illinois University, 1981 **Current organization:** MGE UPS Systems Inc. **Title:** V.P. Sales & Marketing **Type of organization:** Manufacturing **Major product:** Uninterruptible power supplies (UPS) systems **Area of distribution:** International **Expertise:** Sales, market analysis, product design, development **Hob./spts.:** Golf, camping **SIC code:** 36 **Address:** MGE UPS Systems Inc., 2300 N. Barrington Rd., Suite 200, Hoffman Estates, IL 60195 **E-mail:** mike.chmura@mgeups.com **Web address:** www.mgeups.com

CICON, RAYMOND T.
Industry: Welding **Born:** November 3, 1960, Susquehanna, Pennsylvania **Current organization:** Raymond's Mobile Welding **Title:** President **Type of organization:** Private business **Major product:** Welding, fabricate, special orders, diesel engine repair **Area of distribution:** Pennsylvania **Expertise:** Welding-stainless steel, aluminum, steel and diesel engine repairs **Affiliations:** First Baptist Church of Susquehanna; Small Business Voice for Congress **Hob./spts.:** Remote control airplanes and helicopters **SIC code:** 33 **Address:** Endless Mountain Stone Co., P.O. Box 273, Susquehanna, PA 18847 **E-mail:** Raymond@nep.net

CIMINO, STEPHEN M.
Industry: Telecommunications **Univ./degree:** B.S., Graham University, 1981 **Current organization:** Pace Micro Technology America **Title:** Director of National Accounts **Type of organization:** Manufacturing **Major product:** CATV hardware **Area of distribution:** National **Expertise:** Engineering, sales **Affiliations:** S.C.T.E. **SIC code:** 36 **Address:** Pace Micro Technology America, 10952 Baroque Lane, San Diego, CA 92124 **E-mail:** scimino@san.rr.com

CIRINO, SEPIDEH SALLY
Industry: Electronics **Born:** September 19, 1962, Tehran, Iran **Current organization:** First Phase Components/Adiva Manufacturing **Title:** President **Type of organization:** Manufacturing/distributing **Major product:** Semiconductors **Area of distribution:** International **Expertise:** Marketing, business development, strategic alliances **Hob./spts.:** Swimming, charity work **SIC code:** 36 **Address:** First Phase Components, 21 Spectrum Pointe Dr., Lake Forest, CA 92630 **Web address:** www.firstphase.com

CIUCCI, CHRIS P.
Industry: Automotive **Born:** November 27, 1971, Camp Hill, Pennsylvania **Univ./degree:** A.S., Advanced Automotive Automated Technology, Harrisburg Area Community College, 1995; B.A. Candidate, Management, Old Dominion University **Current organization:** Johnson Controls **Title:** Engineering Manager **Type of organization:** Manufacturing **Major product:** Automotive interiors **Area of distribution:** International **Expertise:** Engineering **SIC code:** 37 **Address:** Johnson Controls, 3824 Cook Blvd., Chesapeake, VA 23328 **E-mail:** christopher.p.ciucci@jci.com **Web address:** www.johnson.com

CIZEK, DAVID W.
Industry: Soft drink beverages **Born:** November 6, 1958. Nebraska **Univ./degree:** A.S., Electronics, Northeast Technical College, 1979 **Current organization:** Wis-Pak of Norfolk, Inc. **Title:** Quality Assurance Manager **Type of organization:** Manufacturing **Major product:** Soft drink beverages (Pepsi, Dr. Pepper. 7-Up) **Area of distribution:** National **Expertise:** Process analysis, troubleshooting, operations **SIC code:** 20 **Address:** Wis-Pak of Norfolk, Inc., 1400 W. Tahazouka Rd., Norfolk, NE 68701 **E-mail:** cizek@telebeep.com

CLARK, RAMONA
Industry: Printing **Born:** August 19, 1955, Joplin, Missouri **Current organization:** Offset Press Ink & Frame Shoppe **Title:** President **Type of organization:** Print products broker **Major product:** Printing and design **Area of distribution:** Springdale, Arkansas **Expertise:** Brokering printing services **Hob./spts.:** Camping, 4-wheeling **SIC code:** 27 **Address:** Offset Press Ink & Frame Shoppe, 3801 W. Huntsville Ave., Springdale, AR 72762

CLARK, RANDY RAY
Industry: Food **Born:** August 14, 1962, Jefferson, Iowa **Univ./degree:** B.A., B.S., Drake University, 1983 **Current organization:** Shari Candies, Inc. **Title:** Vice President of Operations **Type of organization:** Manufacturing/distribution **Major product:** Candy **Area of distribution:** National **Expertise:** Corporate management, business development, marketing, sales, manufacturing process improvement, quality assurance and client relations, lecturing and public speaking at colleges and universities **Affiliations:** I.F.T. **Hob./spts.:** Spending time with family, camping, tennis **SIC code:** 20 **Address:** Shari Candies, Inc., 1804 N. Second St., Mankato, MN 56001 **E-mail:** rclark@hickorytech.net

CLAXTON, SHARON Y.
Industry: Automotive **Univ./degree:** B.S.M.E., Tennessee State University, 1996 **Current organization:** Saturn Corp. **Title:** Operations Module Advisor **Type of organization:** Manufacturing **Major product:** Cars/sport utility vehicles **Area of distribution:** International **Expertise:** Engineering/operations **Honors/awards:** Rising Star Award, 2002 **Affiliations:** S.M.E.; A.S.M.E. **Hob./spts.:** Reading, travel, physical fitness **SIC code:** 37 **Address:** Saturn Corp., P.O. Box 1500, Spring Hill, TN 37174 **E-mail:** sharon.y.claxton@gm.com

CLEGG, PAUL
Industry: Defense and aerospace electronics **Born:** February 28, 1954, Fort Dix, New Jersey **Univ./degree:** B.A., Literature, Reed College, Oregon, 1972 **Current organization:** Raytheon Co., Network Centric Systems (NCS) **Title:** Director of Human Resources **Type of organization:** Design and development **Major product:** Communications, radars, combat systems **Area of distribution:** International **Expertise:** Human resource **Hob./spts.:** Music, reading, running, sports **SIC code:** 36 **Address:** Raytheon Co., Network Centric Systems (NCS), 1001 Boston Post Rd., Marlborough, MA 01752 **E-mail:** paul_clegg@raytheon.com

CLEVER, DAVID A.
Industry: Commercial equipment **Born:** February 24, 1943, Columbus, Ohio **Univ./degree:** B.S., Engineering, Ohio State University, 1967 **Current organization:** John Deere Technology Center **Title:** Senior Standards Engineer **Type of organization:** Manufacturing **Major product:** Machinery for agriculture, forestry, construction, lawn and garden **Area of distribution:** International **Expertise:** Standards and standardization **Affiliations:** A.S.A.E.; S.E.S.; S.A.E. **Hob./spts.:** Woodworking, time with his children **SIC code:** 35 **Address:** Deere & Co., One John Deere Place, Moline, IL 61265-8098 **E-mail:** cleverdavida@johndeere.com

CLONTZ, JEREMY M.
Industry: Automotive **Born:** October 16, 1975, Flint, Michigan **Univ./degree:** B.S.M.E., Kettering University/GMI, 1998 **Current organization:** Cardinal Machine Co. **Title:** Engineering Manager/Quality Manager **Type of organization:** Manufacturing **Major product:** Full design machine tool **Area of distribution:** International **Expertise:** Engineering management, sales, global consulting; developed and implemented their QS9000 TE Supplement System **Hob./spts.:** Church involvement, leadership and motivational reading **SIC code:** 35 **Address:** Cardinal Machine Co., 860 Tacomac St., Clio, MI 48420 **E-mail:** jeremyc@cardinalmachine.biz **Web address:** www.cardinalmachine.biz

COELHO, SILVERIO
Industry: Electrical **Born:** September 22, 1966, Portugal **Univ./degree:** B.E.E., Catholic University, 1988 **Current organization:** Eaton Corp. **Title:** Senior Sales Engineer **Type of organization:** Manufacturing **Major product:** Electrical control and distribution products **Area of distribution:** International **Expertise:** Sales, marketing and engineering **Hob./spts.:** Little League Baseball (Coach/Manager), travel **SIC code:** 36 **Address:** Eaton Corp., 379 Thornall St., 8th floor, Edison, NJ 08837 **E-mail:** silcoelho@eaton.com

COLBORN, GENE L.
Industry: Healthcare publishing, clinical anatomy research **Born:** November 23, 1935, Springfield, Illinois **Univ./degree:** M.S., Anatomy, 1965; Ph.D., Medical Sciences, 1967; Wake Forest University Bowman Gray School of Medicine **Current organization:** GELCO Medical Publishing, LLC **Title:** President/Professor Emeritus, Anatomy & Surgery, Clinical Professor of Surgery **Type of organization:** Publishing company **Major product:** Medical texts **Area of distribution:** National/international **Expertise:** Clinical anatomy and surgery **Honors/awards:** Medical Educator of the Year, Medical College of Georgia, Ross University School of Medicine and American University of the Caribbean; Regents Award in Education **Published works:** 125 articles, books, Co-Author of "Surgical Anatomy"; Author, "Clinical Gross Anatomy" **Affiliations:** Editorial Board Member, American Association of Clinical Anatomy; Associate Editor, Journal of Clinical Anatomy **Hob./spts.:** Music, roses, chess, Sudoku, woodworking,

opera performance **SIC code:** 27 **Address:** GELCO Medical Publishing, LLC, 178 Creekview Ct., Martinez, GA 30907 **E-mail:** glcolb@yahoo.com

COLBORN, KENNETH L.
Industry: Electric cable assemblies **Born:** May 2, 1929, Glendale, Los Angeles, California **Univ./degree:** B.S., Finance, University of Southern California, 1951 **Current organization:** Teletronic Div. of DCX-CHOL, Inc. **Title:** Consulting Engineer **Type of organization:** Manufacturing **Major product:** Electric cable assemblies for the military **Area of distribution:** International **Expertise:** Electrical Engineer, wire expert, marketing, estimating, process production **Affiliations:** U.S. Navy Commander, 1948-72 (Korean and Vietnam wars) **Hob./spts.:** Volunteer community woodworking for schools and churches **SIC code:** 36 **Address:** Teletronic Div. of DCX-CHOL, Inc., 12831 S. Figueroa St., Los Angeles, CA 90061-1157 **E-mail:** debbief@dcxchol.com

COLBY, ROBERT A.
Industry: Electronics **Born:** January 16, 1958, Hauppauge, New York **Univ./degree:** B.S., Union College, New York, 1980 **Current organization:** Thomson Multimedia Inc. **Title:** Group Leader **Type of organization:** Manufacturing **Major product:** Electronics **Area of distribution:** International **Expertise:** Engineering, process control, software, project management **Published works:** 30+ articles **Affiliations:** I.E.E.E.; I.S.A.; A.S.M.E.; Tau Beta Pi; Eta Kappa Nu **Hob./spts.:** Camping, sailing, outdoor activities **SIC code:** 36 **Address:** Thomson Multimedia Inc., 1002 New Holland Ave., Lancaster, PA 17601 **E-mail:** colbyr@tce.com **Web address:** www.thomson.com

COLETTA, FRANCES A.
Univ./degree: Ph.D., St. Louis University, 1987 **Current organization:** Swan Food Co. **Title:** Nutrition Consultant **Area of distribution:** International **Expertise:** Nutritionist/consultant **Honors/awards:** President's Award, Team for New Products **Affiliations:** American Dietetic Association; American Society for Nutritious Sciences **Hob./spts.:** Gourmet cooking **SIC code:** 20 **Address:** 233 E. Elm St., Fremont, MI 49412 **E-mail:** f.coletta@comcast.net

COLLINS, DUANE Z.
Industry: Automotive **Born:** January 19, 1966, Indiana **Univ./degree:** B.S., Electrical Engineering, Purdue University, 1990 **Current organization:** Delphi **Title:** Chief Engineer **Type of organization:** Manufacturing **Major product:** Automotive components **Area of distribution:** International **Expertise:** Engineering, management, budget, design, customer relations, pricing **Hob./spts.:** Sports, music, family time **SIC code:** 37 **Address:** 6455 Loma De Cristo, El Paso, TX 79912 **E-mail:** dzcollins@hotmail.com

COLWELL, MELVIN P.
Industry: Flow control systems **Born:** April 13, 1946, Baltimore, Maryland **Univ./degree:** A.Sc., Mechanical Engineering, Pennsylvania State University, 1973; BSc., Technical Management/Mechanical Engineering, University of Maryland, 1986; M.B.A., Frostburg State University, 1995 **Current organization:** Tyco Valves & Controls **Title:** Manager of Engineering **Type of organization:** Manufacturing **Major product:** Valves and controls **Area of distribution:** International **Expertise:** Operations management, engineering management, quality assurance management; Six Sigma Tested and Certified **Honors/awards:** YMCA Service to Youth Award **Affiliations:** American Society of Mechanical Engineers; Penn State Alumni Association **Hob./spts.:** Playing softball, bowling, all outdoor activities **SIC code:** 34 **Address:** Tyco Valves & Controls, 9700 West Gulf Bank Rd., Houston, TX 77040 **E-mail:** mcowell@tycovalves.com **Web address:** www.tycovlaves.com

COMANITA, V. JOHN
Industry: Chemical **Born:** July 14, 1951, Romania **Univ./degree:** M.S., Chemical Engineering, Purdue University, 1975; M.B.A., Case Western Reserve University, 1981 **Current organization:** Ferro Corp. Specialty Plastics Group **Title:** Vice President **Type of organization:** Manufacturing **Major product:** Compounds and colorants **Area of distribution:** International **Expertise:** Marketing **Affiliations:** Case Western Reserve University, Weatherhead School of Management **Hob./spts.:** Skiing, soccer, sailing, waterskiing **SIC code:** 28 **Address:** Ferro Corp. Specialty Plastics Group, 1000 Lakeside Ave., Cleveland, OH 44114 **E-mail:** comanita@ferro.com **Web address:** www.ferro.com

COMBS, THOMAS MICHAEL
Industry: Pharmaceuticals/cosmetics/laboratory/medical **Born:** July 28, 1946, New Brunswick, New Jersey **Univ./degree:** M.S., Physics, University of Georgia, 1971; B.S., Physics, Seton Hall University, 1968 **Current organization:** American Engineering & Equipment Co. **Title:** Manager/Engineer **Type of organization:** Manufacturing, distributing, research & development **Major product:** Laboratory equipment, controls **Area of distribution:** International **Expertise:** Physics, engineering **Honors/awards:** Milliken Science Award; Castle/Sybron Achievement Award; SCI Technical Excellence Award **Affiliations:** A.I.P., A.A.M.I. **Hob./spts.:** Woodworking, gardening, canoeing, tennis, photography, stamps and coins **SIC code:** 28 **Address:** American Engineering & Equipment Co., P.O. Box 430, York Haven, PA 17370 **E-mail:** aeec@surfbest.net **Web address:** www.aeec.itctv.com

CONLEY, GREGORY D.
Industry: Industrial controls systems/engineering **Born:** 1970, Virginia **Univ./degree:** B.S., Computer Science, Whittefield University **Current organization:** ABB **Title:** Industrial Engineer/Architect Manager **Type of organization:** Manufacturing **Major product:** Oil, pharma, automotive, water, chemical, consumer goods **Area of distribution:** International **Expertise:** Marketing, management, sales, project engineering **Affiliations:** Member, Presidential Business Commission; Chair, The State of Ohio; Member, President Bush's Committee **Hob./spts.:** Golf, boating **SIC code:** 39 **Address:** ABB, 664 Tremain Place, Medina, OH 44256 **E-mail:** greg.conley@us.abb.com

CONNELLY, LETINA MARIE
Industry: Information technology **Born:** May 11, 1965, Australia **Univ./degree:** B.S., Mathematics & Statistics, Australian National University **Current organization:** IBM **Title:** Director of Pervasive Strategy and Solutions **Type of organization:** Manufacturing/IT service **Major product:** Hardware, software and services **Area of distribution:** International **Expertise:** Marketing and strategy, project management, design and implementation of sales programs, business development; active lecturer on an international level **Published works:** Write-ups, press interviews **Hob./spts.:** Theatre, fine dining, walking, biking, golf, travel **SIC code:** 36 **Address:** IBM, Rt. 100, Bldg. 3, Office 2J-29, Somers, NY 10589 **E-mail:** letinac@us.ibm.com

CONNORS, DANA M.
Industry: Industrial equipment **Born:** March 10, 1960, Albuquerque, New Mexico **Current organization:** Humboldt Controls & Fabricating Co. LLC **Title:** Plant Manager **Type of organization:** Manufacturing **Major product:** Industrial equipment **Area of distribution:** National **Expertise:** Engineering (equipment design) **Hob./spts.:** Fishing, hunting **SIC code:** 35 **Address:** Humboldt Controls & Fabricating Co. LLC, 1303 22nd St. North, P.O. Box 127, Humboldt, IA 50548 **E-mail:** dconnors@humboldtfabrication.com

COOK, PEGGY A.
Industry: Manufacturing/engineering **Born:** May 16, 1969, Warren, Michigan **Univ./degree:** B.S., Central Michigan University **Current organization:** Oetiker Inc. **Title:** Engineering, Drawing Control **Type of organization:** Manufacturing **Major product:** Clamps for various applications **Area of distribution:** International **Expertise:** Engineering **Hob./spts.:** Snowmobiling, bowling, NASCAR **SIC code:** 38 **Address:** Oetiker, Inc., 3305 Wilson St., Marlette, MI 48453 **E-mail:** pcook@us.oetiker.com

COOK, STEVEN THOMAS
Industry: Machinery **Born:** January 21, 1955, Dayton, Ohio **Current organization:** Dayton Systems Group **Title:** Vice President/CTO **Type of organization:** Manufacturing **Major product:** Special machines and tooling **Area of distribution:** International **Expertise:** Mechanical and electrical engineering **Published works:** Write-up **Affiliations:** A.S.M.E. **Hob./spts.:** Family, physical fitness, sports **SIC code:** 35 **Address:** Dayton Systems Group, 3003 Southtech Blvd., Miamisburg, OH 45342 **E-mail:** scook@dsgtech.com **Web address:** www.dsgtech.com

COPERTARI, DIEGO M.
Industry: Ceramics **Born:** September 7, 1977. Argentina **Univ./degree:** M.B.A., University of Akron **Current organization:** Koch Knight, LLC **Type of organization:** Manufacturing, engineering, construction **Major product:** Ceramics, acid proof construction **Area of distribution:** International **Expertise:** Sales, marketing, technical sales **Affiliations:** N.S.H.; M.B.A.; B.G.S. **Hob./spts.:** Jogging, tennis, golf **SIC code:** 32 **Address:** 5385 Orchard View Dr. S.E., East Canton, OH 44730 **E-mail:** dcopertari@yahoo.com

CORTNER, GARY D.
Industry: Food **Born:** March 21, 1946, Butte, Montana **Univ./degree:** B.S., University of Washington **Current organization:** Pristine Alaska Seafoods, LLC **Title:** Managing Director **Type of organization:** Manufacturing **Major product:** Cold water seafood **Area of distribution:** International **Expertise:** Management, industrial engineering, production engineering **Published works:** Numerous articles **Hob./spts.:** Building and remodeling homes, hunting, fishing, boating **SIC code:** 20 **Address:** Annette Island Packing Co., 100 Tait St., P.O. Box 468, Metlakatla, AK 99926 **E-mail:** dcoceansbest@gmail.com

COSGROVE JR., WILLIAM J.
Industry: Engineering **Born:** February 13, 1963, Upland, Pennsylvania **Spouse:** Margarita Rose Buczkowski **Married:** September 3, 1994 **Children:** Ryan Patrick, 3; twins Lauren Elizabeth and Evan Joseph, 1 **Univ./degree:** B.S., Electrical Engineering, University of Missouri, 1985; M.S., Electrical Engineering, California State University, Northridge, 1991 **Current organization:** Raytheon Space & Airborne Systems **Title:** Senior Principal Engineer **Type of organization:** Manufacturing **Major product:** Aerospace and defense **Area of distribution:** International **Expertise:** Electrical engi-

neering **Honors/awards:** Strathmore's Who's Who V.I.P. Member **Published works:** "A Survey of Finite Impulse Response Digital Filter Design", January, 1991 **Affiliations:** I.E.E.E.; Computer and Signal Processing Societies **Career accomplishments:** One of the youngest Raytheon Company employees ever promoted to a Program Manager position **Hob./spts.:** Football, billiards **SIC code:** 36 **Address:** Raytheon Co., Point Mugu Engineering Center, P.O. Box 42202, Port Hueneme, CA 93044-4502 **E-mail:** wjcosgrove@raytheon.com

COSTA, ALEX
Industry: Shutters **Born:** September 10, 1977, Ecuador **Univ./degree:** B.S., Architecture, Art Institute of Fort Lauderdale, 2004 **Current organization:** SSMF, Inc. **Title:** Vice President, Wholesale Division **Type of organization:** Manufacturing, retail, distributing **Major product:** Accordion shutters, steel, glass **Area of distribution:** Sunrise, Florida **Expertise:** Sales, design for commercial projects, manufacturing **Affiliations:** American Shutter System Association **Hob./spts.:** Soccer, golf **SIC code:** 34 **Address:** SSMF, Inc., 5011 N. Hiatus Rd., Sunrise, FL 33351 **E-mail:** alex@ssmfinc.com **Web address:** www.ssmfinc.com

COSTELLO, LAWRENCE B.
Industry: Consumer products **Born:** January 30, 1948, Riverside, New Jersey **Univ./degree:** B.S., Administration & Finance, Rider University, 1971; P.M.D, Harvard University, 1983 **Current organization:** American Standard Companies **Title:** Sr. Vice President, Human Resources **Type of organization:** Manufacturing **Major product:** Air conditioning systems, bathroom and kitchen products, vehicle control systems **Area of distribution:** International **Expertise:** Senior corporate management, human resources, business development, talent development, training, long term planning, strategic analysis **Honors/awards:** Was on the front cover of "HR Executive Magazine", 2003; HR Workforce Magazine interview, 2003 **Affiliations:** Advisory Board Member, Rutgers University MBA Program **Hob./spts.:** Reading, sailing, cycling, motor sports racing, golf **SIC code:** 39 **Address:** American Standard Companies, One Centennial Ave., Piscataway, NJ 08855 **E-mail:** lcostello@americanstandard.com

COURSON, JIMMY O.
Industry: Food **Born:** Lakeland, Ga **Univ./degree:** A.S., Electrical Engineering, Valdosta Technical Institute, 1972 **Current organization:** Miller Brewing Co. **Title:** Electrical Engineering **Type of organization:** Manufacturing **Major product:** Beer **Area of distribution:** Georgia **Expertise:** Engineering **Hob./spts.:** Hunting, fishing **SIC code:** 20 **Address:** Miller Brewing Co., 405 Cordele Rd., Albany, GA 31705 **E-mail:** courson.jimmy@mbco.com

COURTNEY, JOHN L.
Industry: Manufacturing pesticide products **Born:** November 19, 1961, Arkansas **Univ./degree:** M.S., Environmental Engineering, University of Arkansas, 1986 **Current organization:** BASF Corp. **Title:** Manager, Environmental Services **Type of organization:** Manufacturing **Major product:** Agricultural products, pesticides **Area of distribution:** National **Expertise:** Environmental engineering; process safety; Certified, Hazardous Material Management, CHMM **Honors/awards:** Strathmore's Who's Who **Affiliations:** N.P.S.A.; A.C.C. **Hob./spts.:** Family, jogging, hiking, biking, church **SIC code:** 28 **Address:** BASF Corp., 26 Davis Drive, Research Triangle Park, NC 27709 **E-mail:** courtnj@basf.com

CRAFT, BARBARA-BENITA
Industry: Automotive **Born:** March 25, 1952, Oxford, Mississippi **Univ./degree:** B.S.W., Wayne State University; M.A., Industry and Organization Psychology, University of Detroit; M.Ed., University of Detroit **Current organization:** UAW-Ford Auto Alliance International **Title:** Education & Training Coordinator **Type of organization:** Manufacturing **Major product:** Mazda 6 automobile **Area of distribution:** National **Expertise:** Overseeing budget, education benefits and establishing education programs **Published works:** Ford World Magazine, University of Detroit publications **Affiliations:** Officer, Kappa Delta Phi; American Psychological Association **Hob./spts.:** Writing, dance, research, film and lecture **SIC code:** 37 **Address:** UAW-Ford Auto Alliance International, 1 International Dr., Flat Rock, MI 48134 **E-mail:** bcraft@ford.com

CRAINE, MARC H.
Industry: Semiconductors **Born:** April 6, 1954, New York **Univ./degree:** Marketing **Current organization:** MGI Products, Inc. **Title:** Sales Engineer/Facility Manager **Type of organization:** Manufacturing **Major product:** Semiconductors **Area of distribution:** International **Expertise:** Marketing **Hob./spts.:** Golf, fishing, hunting **SIC code:** 36 **Address:** MGI Products, Inc., 6392 Deere Rd., Syracuse, NY 13206 **E-mail:** mcraine@mgiproducts.com

CRANDALL, ARIZONA WIGGINS
Industry: Community volunteering/publishing **Born:** March 5, 1944, Holland, Georgia **Univ./degree:** Nashville Christian Institute; Attended, Medgar Evers College & Meharry School of Nursing; Hefftey and Brown Secretarial School **Current organization:** Interfaith Hospital, Women's Auxiliary-Democratic Caucus **Title:** Author/Teacher/Counselor **Major product:** Writing, publishing, education **Area of distribution:** National **Expertise:** Creative artistic design, community services, counseling **Honors/awards:** Benevolence Award, Brooklyn Church of Christ; Award for Community Service, Concerned Women of Brooklyn, 1998; Congressional Recognition Award for Outstanding Community Service, awarded by Congressman Ed Towns; Volunteer Achievement Award, United Funds Hospital Auxiliary, 2000; Women's Caucus Award for Outstanding Community Service; Humanitarian Award, National Association of Negro Professional Business Women: Certificates of Merit; 8 Community Awards; Achievement Award; Humanitarian Award; DeCosta Headly, State Committee Leader, Achievement Award **Published works:** "Silent Memories-Desperate Hours" **Affiliations:** I.H.W.A.; Black Women in Publishing; St. John Hospital Center; Interfaith Hospital Center; Founder & Secretary of the Board, Brownsville Recreation Center; Director , JHS 275 Youth Board (Retired); Former Secretary, PTA, JHS 275 **Hob./spts.:** Interior design, teaching arts and crafts, writing, reading **SIC code:** 27 **Address:** 620 Schenectady Ave., Brooklyn, NY 11203 **E-mail:** arizonawiggins@aol.com

CRECCA, KIP JOSEPH
Industry: Medical/surgical equipment **Univ./degree:** B.A., Political Science/International Affairs, SUNY Binghamton, 1988 **Current organization:** Stryker Corp. **Title:** Territory Manager **Type of organization:** Manufacturing **Major product:** Medical/surgical equipment **Area of distribution:** International **Expertise:** Sales, marketing medical/surgical devices **Honors/awards:** Presidents Advisory Council Member **Hob./spts.:** Avid rugby player **SIC code:** 38 **Address:** Stryker Corp., 3730 McKinley St. N.W., Washington, DC 20015 **E-mail:** kip.crecca@verizon.net

CREIGHTON, JOHN W.
Industry: Publishing **Univ./degree:** General Motors Certified, Chicago Tech Institute **Title:** Editorial Director, Irving Cloud Publications (Retired) **Type of organization:** Publishing **Major product:** Magazine publications **Area of distribution:** National **Expertise:** Editorial consulting **Affiliations:** Board Member, Catholic Transfiguration Parish; Life Member, Society of Automotive Engineers.; Past Member, Chicago Press Club; Knights of Columbus **Hob./spts.:** Woodworking **SIC code:** 27 **Address:** 105 Park Dr., Port Barrington, IL 60010

CROMACK, ROBERT D.
Industry: Cable television equipment **Born:** March 8, 1943, Greenfield, Massachusetts **Univ./degree:** B.A., University of Texas at El Paso, 1980 **Current organization:** Motorola, Inc. **Title:** Corporate Vice President/Director, Supply Chain **Type of organization:** Manufacturing **Major product:** Cable television equipment **Area of distribution:** International **Expertise:** Supply chain-manufacturing, procurement, logistics, distribution **Honors/awards:** Inner Circle, U.S. Senate **Published works:** Write-ups **Hob./spts.:** Tennis, gardening, plants **SIC code:** 36 **Address:** Motorola, Inc., 101 Tournament Dr., Horsham, PA 19044 **E-mail:** robert.cromack@mot.com

CROUCH, JEFFREY KEITH
Industry: Emergency vehicles **Born:** May 12, 1960, Decatur, Illinois **Univ./degree:** M.B.A., Alabama A&M University, 1996 **Current organization:** Cast Products, Inc. **Title:** Vice President **Type of organization:** Manufacturing **Major product:** Aluminium castings **Area of distribution:** International **Expertise:** Marketing **Affiliations:** F.A.M.A.; A.A.A.; N.T.E.A. **Hob./spts.:** Golf, skiing **SIC code:** 33 **Address:** Cast Products, Inc., 18675 N. Jefferson St., Athens, AL 35614 **E-mail:** jeff@getcpi.com

CROWELL, CURTIS
Industry: Diesel engines **Born:** Dunkirk, New York **Current organization:** Cummins Engine Co. **Title:** Test Cell Software Developer **Type of organization:** Manufacturing **Major product:** Diesel engine and repair parts **Area of distribution:** International **Expertise:** Fuel system technology, test cell programming **Hob./spts.:** Singing for St. Peter and Paul Roman Catholic Church **SIC code:** 39 **Address:** Cummins Engine Co., 4720 Baker St., Lakewood, NY 14750 **E-mail:** curt.c.crowell@cummins.com

CUEVAS, HENRY A.
Industry: Metallurgy **Born:** June, 9, 1955, Dominican Republic **Univ./degree:** B.S., Electrical Engineering, Dominican Republic **Current organization:** Consarc Corp. **Title:** Field Service Engineer **Type of organization:** Manufacturing & Design **Major product:** Furnaces **Area of distribution:** Global **Expertise:** Field Service **Published works:** Trade Journals **Hob./spts.:** Baseball, golf **SIC code:** 33 **Address:** Consarc Corp., 1171 Liberty St., Camden, NJ 08104 **E-mail:** hcuevas@consarc.com

CUNNINGHAM, DONALD S.
Industry: Material handling manufacturing **Born:** September 2, 1963, Batavia, New York **Current organization:** Unidex Corp. **Title:** General Manager **Type of organization:** Manufacturing **Major product:** Material handling equipment and systems **Area of distribution:** International **Expertise:** Operations, production **Affiliations:** Board Member, United Way; CEO Roundtable Member; Town Councilman **Hob./spts.:** Family, hot rods, softball **SIC code:** 35 **Address:** Unidex Corp., 2416 N. Main St., Warsaw, NY 14569 **E-mail:** dcunningham@unidex-inc.com

CURRAN, J. STEVEN
Industry: Life science **Born:** December 14, 1961, Needham, Massachusetts **Univ./degree:** B.S., Chemicals, Worcester Polytechnic Institute, 1984 **Current organization:** Applied Biosystems **Title:** Director of Manufacturing **Type of organization:** Manufacturing **Major product:** Genomic and proteomic **Area of distribution:** International **Expertise:** Manufacturing **Honors/awards:** Managers Award, Milli Por Award for Innovation, 1993 **Affiliations:** A.I.C.H.E.; A.C.S. **SIC code:** 38 **Address:** Applied Biosystems, 251 Albany St., Cambridge, MA 02139 **E-mail:** curranjs@appliedbiosystems.com

D'ANDREA, JOSEPH
Industry: Electronics/interconnect electronics **Born:** July 8, 1946, Jersey City, New Jersey **Univ./degree:** B.A., Marketing, 1979; Dual M.B.A.-Master of Marketing and Master of Business Administration, Fairleigh Dickinson University **Current organization:** Printed Circuits Corp. **Title:** Sales Manager **Type of organization:** Manufacturing **Major product:** PCB/PCBA FAB/EMS services **Area of distribution:** National **Expertise:** Oversees sales, marketing **Affiliations:** I.E.E.E.; I.P.C. Design Council; S.M.T.A. Atlanta, GA; Gwinnett Chamber of Commerce **Hob./spts.:** Tennis, golf **SIC code:** 36 **Address:** Printed Circuits Corp., 4467 Park Dr., Suite E, Norcross, GA 30093 **E-mail:** joed@pcc-i.com **Web address:** www.pcc-i.com

D'ANDREA, MARCELLO
Industry: Food **Born:** January 10, 1969, Toronto, Ontario, Canada **Univ./degree:** B.S.M.E., Ryerson Polytechnic Institute, Toronto, Canada **Current organization:** Nestlé **Title:** Engineering Manager **Type of organization:** Manufacturing/sales/marketing **Major product:** Commercial foods **Area of distribution:** National **Expertise:** Confectionary Engineer, capital investments **Affiliations:** Association of Professional Engineers of Ontario **Hob./spts.:** Golf, hockey **SIC code:** 20 **Address:** Nestlé, 800 N. Brand Blvd., Glendale, CA 91203 **E-mail:** marcello.dandrea@us.nestle.com

DANIEL, MORGAN A.
Industry: Cedar wood products **Born:** July 31, 1972, Huntsville, Alabama **Univ./degree:** B.S., Human Resources, Faulkner University, 2003 **Current organization:** Giles & Kendall, Inc. **Title:** Human Resources Manager **Type of organization:** Manufacturing **Major product:** Cedar closet liners, cedar oil **Area of distribution:** International **Expertise:** Administration, human resources **Affiliations:** Northern Alabama Society for Human Resources; Society for Human Resource Management **Hob./spts.:** Biking, photography, family, scrapbooking, movies **SIC code:** 24 **Address:** Giles and Kendall, Inc., 3470 Maysville Rd., Huntsville, AL 35811 **E-mail:** mdaniel@cedarsafeclosets.com

DANIELS, CHARLES E.
Industry: Wood products **Title:** Procurement Forester **Type of organization:** Manufacturing **Major product:** Lumber **Expertise:** Procurement **SIC code:** 24 **Address:** Allegheny Wood Products, Inc., 2130 S. Dennis St. Ext., Enfield, NC 27823 **E-mail:** cdaniels@alleghenywood.com

DASGUPTA, TRIDIB R.
Industry: Dental products for Dentist (Clinical) & Dental Laboratory (Technical) **Born:** May 9, 1947, Calcutta, India **Univ./degree:** B.S., Engineering (Metallurgy), Banaras Hindu University, India, 1968; M.S., Metallurgical Engineering, Indian Institute of Science, India, 1971 **Current organization:** Ivoclar Vivadent Inc. **Title:** Director of Material Research **Type of organization:** Research, Manufacturing, Marketing & Sale of Dental Material **Major product:** Dental Material & Equipment for Dental Laboratory and Clinical products and Equipment for Dentist **Area of distribution:** International **Expertise:** Metallurgical Engineering, Continuous Casting Process/Project Leader **Affiliations:** A.S.M.; I.A.D.R.; I.P.M.I. **Hob./spts.:** Coaching soccer, photography, travel, cooking **SIC code:** 38 **Address:** Ivoclar Vivadent Inc., 175 Pineview Dr., Amherst, NY 14228-2231 **E-mail:** tridib.dasgupta@ivoclarvivadent.us.com

DAUPHINAIS, GORDON ROBERT
Industry: Concrete products **Born:** September 21, 1967, Saskatchewan, Canada **Univ./degree:** A.S., Aircraft Maintenance Engineering, Southern Alberta Institute of Technology (SAIT) **Current organization:** Kobra Molds, LLC **Title:** Vice President **Type of organization:** Manufacturing **Major product:** Molds/Interlocking pavingstones **Area of distribution:** International **Expertise:** Operations/project management **Hob./spts.:** Boating, fishing, guitar, music, theatre, travel **SIC code:** 32 **Address:** 7823 North Fork Dr., West Palm Beach, FL 33411 **E-mail:** grdauphinais@aol.com

DAVES SR., RAYMOND A.
Industry: Appliances **Born:** June 17, 1957, Birmingham, Alabama **Univ./degree:** B.S., Biology and Math, Livingston University, 1985; B.S., Biological Engineering, Mississippi State University, 1986 **Current organization:** General Electric **Title:** Advanced Quality and Manufacturing Engineer **Type of organization:** Manufacturing **Major product:** Ranges and other major appliances **Area of distribution:** International **Expertise:** Quality **Affiliations:** A.S.C. **Hob./spts.:** Woodworking **SIC code:** 36 **Address:** General Electric, 1507 Broomtown Rd., LaFayette, GA 30728 **E-mail:** raymond.daves@appl.ge.com

DAVIDOCK, STEVEN
Industry: Steel **Born:** May 3, 1972, Bucks County, Pennsylvania **Univ./degree:** B.S., Civil Engineering, The Pennsylvania State University **Current organization:** U.S. Steel **Title:** Project Engineer **Type of organization:** Manufacturing **Major product:** Steel **Area of distribution:** National **Expertise:** Engineering, project management **Affiliations:** A.I.S.E.; P.M.I.; C.I.I.; I.P.A. **SIC code:** 33 **Address:** U.S. Steel, One N. Broadway, MS 11-1, Gary, IN 46402 **E-mail:** ssdavidock@uss.com

DAVIDOVICH, MARTHA
Industry: Pharmaceuticals **Born:** Romania **Univ./degree:** M.S., Organic Chemistry, CUNY, 1978 **Current organization:** Bristol-Myers Squibb **Title:** Sr. Research Scientist **Type of organization:** Manufacturing/R&D **Major product:** Pharmaceuticals **Area of distribution:** International **Expertise:** Material science characterization **Affiliations:** A.C.S.; I.C.D.D. **Hob./spts.:** Travel, music **SIC code:** 28 **Address:** Bristol-Myers Squibb, 1 Squibb Dr., Bldg. 107, New Brunswick, NJ 08901 **E-mail:** martha.davidovich@bms.com

DAVIS, TRUMAN R.
Industry: Petroleum **Born:** September 3, 1949, Stamford, Texas **Current organization:** D&D Hydraulic Casing Tong Services **Title:** Owner/President **Type of organization:** Manufacturing/distributing **Major product:** Hydraulic casing tongs **Area of distribution:** International **Expertise:** Administration/marketing/design **Hob./spts.:** Scuba diving, airplane pilot **SIC code:** 35 **Address:** D&D Hydraulic Casing Tong Services, 375 T&P Lane, Abilene, TX 79602 **E-mail:** randyddtongs@aol.com

DE GUZMAN, ENRIQUE G.
Industry: Metal **Born:** July 8, 1958, Philippines **Univ./degree:** B.S., Electronics and Communications Engineering, Manila, Philippines, 1979 **Current organization:** Western Metal **Title:** Project Engineer **Type of organization:** Manufacturing **Major product:** Metal framing **Area of distribution:** National **Expertise:** Automation design **Affiliations:** S.M.E. **Hob./spts.:** Bowling, scuba diving **SIC code:** 34 **Address:** Western Metal, 988 N. Turner Ave., #283, Ontario, CA 91764 **E-mail:** edegu74962@aol.com

DE KOE, CORNELIS W.
Industry: Aerospace **Born:** January 9, 1965, Haarlem, The Netherlands **Univ./degree:** B.S., Dutch College for Aviation, 1985 **Current organization:** Honeywell **Title:** Staff Engineer-Systems **Type of organization:** Manufacturing **Major product:** Electronic controls **Area of distribution:** International **Expertise:** Engineering, customer service **Hob./spts.:** Cars, car racing, electronics, fine dining **SIC code:** 36 **Address:** 11100 N. Oracle Rd., #M226, Tucson, AZ 85737 **E-mail:** cornelis.dekoe@honeywell.com

DEAN, DAVID R.
Industry: Pharmaceuticals/neutraceuticals **Univ./degree:** B.A., Chemistry, California State University, Northridge, 1979 **Current organization:** Selected Supplements **Title:** QA Manager **Type of organization:** Manufacturing **Major product:** Vitamins, dietary supplements **Area of distribution:** International **Expertise:** Analytical chemistry, quality assurance **Affiliations:** A.C.S.; American Society for Quality **Hob./spts.:** Classic car restoration, outdoor sports, photography **SIC code:** 28 **Address:** Selected Supplements, 5800 Newton Ave., Carlsbad, CA 92008 **E-mail:** drddavedean7@cs.com

DEAVER, EDWARD W.
Industry: Cement **Born:** February 18, 1960, Charleston, South Carolina **Univ./degree:** B.S., Civil Engineering, University of South Carolina, 1997 **Current organization:** Holcim (US) Inc. **Title:** Tech Service Engineer **Type of organization:** Manufacturing **Major product:** Cement and GGBFS production **Area of distribution:** International **Expertise:** Engineering/marketing **Affiliations:** A.S.C.E.; N.S.P.E.; C.R.M.C.A.; A.S.T.M.; C.C.M.A.; S.C.A.; A.C.P.A. **Hob./spts.:** Family, hunting, NASCAR racing **SIC code:** 32 **Address:** Holcim (US) Inc., 1501 Main St., Suite 725, Columbia, SC 29201 **E-mail:** edward.deaver@holcim.com **Web address:** www.holcim.com

DEBAN, ARMAND CHARLES
Industry: Electronics **Born:** January 15, 1959, Niagara Falls, New York **Univ./degree:** B.S., University of Buffalo, 2001 **Current organization:** Vishay Thin Film, Inc. **Title:** Divisional Environmental, Health and Safety Manager **Type of organization:** Manufacturing **Major product:** Electronic components, passives (resistors) **Area of distribution:** International **Expertise:** Engineering, environmental, health and safety **Affiliations:** C.P.E.A.; C.H.M.M. **Hob./spts.:** Soccer, hockey, golf, home improvements **SIC code:** 36 **Address:** Vishay Thin Film, Inc., 2160 Liberty Dr., Niagara Falls, NY 14304 **E-mail:** armand.deban@vishay.com

DEBELIUS, CHRISTOPHER AUGUST
Industry: Electronics **Univ./degree:** B.S., Marine Engineering **Current organization:** Intel Corp. **Title:** Senior Engineer **Type of organization:** Manufacturing **Major product:** Semiconductors **Area of distribution:** New Mexico **Expertise:** Engineering, process **Hob./spts.:** Sailing **SIC code:** 36 **Address:** P.O. Box 44102, Rio Rancho, NM 87124 **E-mail:** christopher.a.debelius@intel.com

DECOU, HAL H.
Industry: Construction materials **Born:** August 18, 1956, Montrose, Pennsylvania **Univ./degree:** B.S., Electrical Engineering, California State Polytechnic University, Pomona, 1980 **Current organization:** Cemex **Title:** Electrical Field Engineer **Type of organization:** Manufacturing **Major product:** Cement **Area of distribution:** International **Expertise:** Electrical engineering **Hob./spts.:** Building hot rods, fishing **SIC code:** 32 **Address:** Cemex, 16888 E St., Victorville, CA 92394-2999 **E-mail:** hdecou@cemexusa.com

DEL CASTILLO, DAMARYS Y.
Industry: Food **Born:** October 20, 1971, Mayaguez, Puerto Rico **Univ./degree:** B.S., University of Puerto Rico. Mayaguez Campus, College of Agriculture **Current organization:** Goya De Puerto Rico Inc. **Title:** Quality Control Director **Type of organization:** Manufacturing, distributing **Major product:** Canned beans and juices **Area of distribution:** International **Expertise:** Agronomist **Affiliations:** Puerto Rico College of Agronomists **Hob./spts.:** Reading, scuba diving **SIC code:** 20 **Address:** Goya De Puerto Rico Inc., Street #28, Corner 5, Luchetti Industrial Park, Bayamón, PR 00959 **E-mail:** dcastill@goya.com

DEL PRATO, THOMAS A.
Industry: Chemicals **Born:** September 17, 1960, Philadelphia, Pennsylvania **Univ./degree:** B.S., Chemical Engineering, Drexel University **Current organization:** Matheson Trigas **Title:** Director of Engineering **Type of organization:** Manufacturing **Major product:** High purity gases for semiconductor market **Area of distribution:** International **Expertise:** UHP design, process and project engineering **Published works:** Trade journal articles **Affiliations:** A.I.C.H.E. **Hob./spts.:** Outdoor activities **SIC code:** 28 **Address:** Matheson Trigas, 1920 W. Fairmont Pkwy., LaPorte, TX 77571 **E-mail:** tdelprato@matheson-triagas.com

DEMANOSOW, VASYL
Industry: Connectors **Born:** December 27, 1951, Torrington, Connecticut **Univ./degree:** A.S.M.E., Waterbury State University **Current organization:** Deringer-Ney **Title:** Senior Die Designer **Type of organization:** Manufacturing **Major product:** Electrical, connectors **Area of distribution:** National **Expertise:** Mechanical engineering, die design **Hob./spts.:** Fly-fishing, motorcycle riding **SIC code:** 36 **Address:** Deringer-Ney, 2 Douglas St., Bloomfield, CT 06002 **E-mail:** wdemanosow@deringerney.com

DEMENT, DEREK G.
Industry: Custom injection molding **Born:** January 29, 1980, Rochester, New York **Current organization:** Webster Plastics **Title:** Purchasing coordinator/Material Dept. Supervisor **Type of organization:** Manufacturing **Major product:** Custom injection molding for specific clientele **Area of distribution:** National **Expertise:** Purchasing management **Affiliations:** I.S.M.; A.P.I.C.S.; National Association of Purchasing Management-Rochester, Inc. **SIC code:** 30 **Address:** Webster Plastics, 83 Estates Dr. West, Fairport, NY 14450 **E-mail:** derek@websterplastics.com **Web address:** www.websterplastics.com

DHALIWAL, BALBIR K.
Industry: Cosmetics **Born:** January 1, 1947, India **Univ./degree:** Ph.D., Chemistry and Biochemistry, Northern Illinois University at Dekalb, 1982 **Current organization:** Jevlon Inc. **Title:** President **Type of organization:** Contract manufacturing and private label manufacturing **Major product:** Cosmetics, toiletries, perfumes and over the counter drugs **Area of distribution:** International **Expertise:** Chemistry, biochemistry, formulation development **Honors/awards:** First Prize in Mathematics in Undergraduate Studies; Research scholarship from National Institute of Health for Doctoral Program; Approval from State of Illinois Department of Public Health to serve as Director of Clinical Laboratories, November, 1991 **Published works:** Kinetic study of alkaline transitions of Cytochrome C Peroxidase, Biochimica et Biophysica Acta, volume 827, 1985 page 174-182 **Hob./spts.:** Badminton **SIC code:** 28 **Address:** Jevlon Inc., 6404 Denali Ridge Dr., Plainfield, IL 60586-1496

DIAZ, ALEX
Industry: Pharmaceutical **Born:** October 30, 1975, Caguas, Puerto Rico **Univ./degree:** B.S., Mechanical Engineering, Turabo University **Current organization:** URL/Mutual Pharmaceuticals **Title:** Project Engineer **Type of organization:** Manufacturing **Major product:** Pharmaceuticals **Area of distribution:** Pennsylvania **Expertise:** Engineering **Hob./spts.:** Reading, computers, baseball **SIC code:** 28 **Address:** URL/Mutual Pharmaceuticals, 1100 Orthodox St., Philadelphia, PA 19124 **E-mail:** adiaz75@msn.com

DIAZ-VEGA, LUIS
Industry: Pharmaceuticals **Born:** January 9, 1969, Chicago, Illinois **Univ./degree:** B.S.E., University of Puerto Rico **Current organization:** Wyeth Pharmaceutical Co. **Title:** Technology and Processing Manager **Type of organization:** Manufacturing **Major product:** Drugs, prescription medicines **Area of distribution:** International **Expertise:** Scientist, supervisor, quality control **Affiliations:** C.A.P.T.E.C.H. **Hob./spts.:** Basketball, baseball **SIC code:** 28 **Address:** Wyeth Pharmaceutical Co., State Rd. #3, km 142.1, Guayama, PR 00784 **E-mail:** diazl2@wyeth.com

DICKERSON, RANDY L.
Industry: EPS manufacturing **Born:** May 15, 1974, Bradenton, Florida **Current organization:** Polysource, Inc. **Title:** Materials Manager/ Health & Safety Coordinator **Type of organization:** Manufacturing **Major product:** Color EPS bicycle helmets **Area of distribution:** International **Expertise:** Purchasing, logistics - ISO coordinator **SIC code:** 39 **Address:** Polysource, Inc., 555 E. Statler Rd., Piqua, OH 45356 **E-mail:** rdickerson@polysource.com **Web address:** www.polysource.com

DICKINSON, KIRK
Industry: Food and kindred products **Born:** March 13, 1962, Newfane, New York **Current organization:** Morrison Milling Co. **Title:** Project Research Technician **Type of organization:** Manufacturing **Major product:** Dry baking mixes, flour **Area of distribution:** National **Expertise:** Equipment implementation, machine specialist **Affiliations:** A.I.B. **Hob./spts.:** Family, fly-fishing, flying kites **SIC code:** 20 **Address:** Morrison Milling Co., 319 E. Prairie, Denton, TX 76202 **E-mail:** kdickinson@morrisonmilling.com **Web address:** www.morrisonmilling.com

DICKSON, RICHARD L.
Industry: Consumer products **Univ./degree:** B.S., Economics, 1990, University of Maryland **Current organization:** Senior Vice President, Worldwide **Title:** Mattel, Inc. **Type of organization:** Manufacturing **Major product:** Brands, categories beyond toys **Area of distribution:** Worldwide **Expertise:** Marketing **Honors/awards:** Brand Week Marketer of the Year **Published works:** Write-ups about him - Brand Week Toy News **SIC code:** 39 **Address:** Mattel, 333 Continental Blvd., El Segundo, CA 90245 **E-mail:** dicksonr@mattel.com **Web address:** www.mattel.com

DIXON, JOHN J.
Industry: Holographic equipment **Born:** October 4, 1956, New York, New York **Univ./degree:** A.A., York College, 1976 **Current organization:** Holman Technology Inc. **Title:** CEO **Type of organization:** Manufacturing **Major product:** Holographic equipment, services and products **Area of distribution:** International **Expertise:** Modern holography **Affiliations:** I.M.H.A. **SIC code:** 39 **Address:** Holman Technology Inc., 5B Marlen Dr., Hamilton, NJ 08691 **E-mail:** jdixon@holmtech.com

DOBBERFUHL, EVAN G.
Industry: Automotive accessories **Born:** January 13, 1943, Green Bay. Wisconsin **Current organization:** Cequent Trailer Products **Title:** Senior Manufacturing Engineer **Type of organization:** Manufacturing **Major product:** Screw jacks **Area of distribution:** International **Expertise:** Engineering, automation, manufacturing cells **Honors/awards:** Listed in International Who's Who of Professionals **Published works:** Hydraulics & Pneumatics Magazine **Affiliations:** Society of Manufacturing Cells, Past Secretary **Hob./spts.:** Classic cars, hiking, travel **SIC code:** 37 **Address:** Cequent Trailer Products, 1050 Indianhead Dr., Mosinee, WI 54455 **E-mail:** mcsevan@mtc.net

DOBROWSKI, GEORGE H.
Industry: Communications **Born:** October 12, 1946, Manchester, New Hampshire **Univ./degree:** M.S., Electrical Engineering, Northwestern University, 1981 **Current organization:** Conexant Systems **Title:** Director, Technology and Product Planning; Previously CTO of start-up Ficon Technology **Type of organization:** Manufacturing, R&D **Major product:** Semiconductors, software **Area of distribution:** International **Expertise:** Engineering and strategic marketing **Published works:** Co-author of 2 books, "ATM and SONET Basics", published 2000 and "Principles of Signaling for Cell Relay and Frame Relay", published 1995; author of numerous articles and conference papers; frequent speaker **Affiliations:** I.E.E.E.; Board of Directors, DSL Forum **Hob./spts.:** Skiing, golf **SIC code:** 36 **Address:** Conexant Systems, 100 Schultz Dr., Red Bank, NJ 07701 **E-mail:** george.dobrowski@conexant.com

DOMANSKI, MICHAEL J.
Industry: Petroleum **Born:** May 11, 1943, Edinburgh, Scotland **Univ./degree:** M.A., Edinburgh University, Scotland, 1964; Business Diploma, London Graduate School of Business **Current organization:** Tidelands Oil Production Co. **Title:** President **Type of organization:** Manufacturing **Major product:** Oil and gas production **Area of distribution:** California **Expertise:** Marketing, finance, general management **Affiliations:** Director, C.I.P.A.; Board Member, Business College of California State University at Long Beach **SIC code:** 29 **Address:** Tidelands Oil Production Co., 301 E. Ocean Blvd., Long Beach, CA 90802

DONLEY, BRIAN J.
Industry: Food **Born:** August 15, 1959, Battle Creek, Michigan **Univ./degree:** A.S., Drafting & Design, 1985; A.S., General Studies, 1989; Kellogg Community College; B.S., Production Technology, Western Michigan University, 1995 **Current organization:** Kraft Foods North America **Title:** Senior Project Manager **Type of organization:** Manufacturing **Major product:** Cereal **Area of distribution:** International **Expertise:** Project management **Honors/awards:** Graduated with honors **Hob./spts.:** Spectator sports, roller skating **SIC code:** 20 **Address:** Kraft Foods North America, 275 Cliff St., Battle Creek, MI 49014 **E-mail:** bdonley@kraft.com

DOYAL, RANDELL KEITH
Industry: Packaging **Born:** February 25, 1976, Hobbs, New Mexico **Current organization:** Atlantis Plastics **Title:** QA Supervisor **Type of organization:** Manufacturing **Major product:** Stretch film **Area of distribution:** National **Expertise:** Quality control **Hob./spts.:** Hunting, fishing **SIC code:** 26 **Address:** Atlantis Plastics, 6940 W. 76th St., Tulsa, OK 74131 **E-mail:** keith.doyal@atlantisplastics.com

DREES, THOMAS C.
Industry: Pharmaceuticals, blood products **Born:** February 2, 1929, Detroit, Michigan **Univ./degree:** M.B.A., Ph.D., Business, University of the Pacific, Stockton, California, 1981 **Current organization:** Sanguine Corp., Drees International Inc. **Title:** Chairman/CEO **Type of organization:** Manufacturing, R&D, National & International sales **Major product:** Synthetic blood **Area of distribution:** National & International **Expertise:** Management, marketing **Published works:** 1 book, 50 articles, 50 journals **Affiliations:** A.B.R.A.; A.B.C.; National Health Review; U.S. Congress Office of Technology **Hob./spts.:** Golf, history, biographies **SIC code:** 28 **Address:** Sanguine Corp., Drees International Inc., 101 E. Green St., #11, Pasadena, CA 91105 **Phone:** (626)405-0079 **Fax:** (626)405-1041

DRY, RANDALL
Current organization: Orgo-Thermit Inc. **Title:** General Manager, Rail Services **Type of organization:** Manufacturing **Major product:** Thermit welding for railroads and crane tracks **Area of distribution:** International **Expertise:** Management **Affiliations:** American Railway Engineering & Maintenance of Way Association **Hob./spts.:** Football (college and pro) **SIC code:** 33 **Address:** Orgo-Thermit Inc., 3500 Colonial Dr. North, Manchester, NJ 08759 **E-mail:** randy.dry@orgothermit.com **Web address:** www.orgothermit.com

DUNBAR, CATHERINE L.
Industry: Pallets **Born:** Riverside, California **Univ./degree:** A.S., Parks Thornton College, 1994 **Current organization:** L&R Pallet Service Inc. **Title:** Office Manager **Type of organization:** Manufacturing **Major product:** Manufacturing and distribution of pallets **Area of distribution:** National **Expertise:** Administration, paralegal **Hob./spts.:** Fishing, hunting, NFL Football (Broncos), NASCAR **SIC code:** 24 **Address:** L&R Pallet Service Inc., 3855 Lima St., Denver, CO 80239 **E-mail:** cdunbear@aol.com

DUNN, MERVIN
Industry: Transportation **Born:** October 7, 1953, Dayton, Ohio **Univ./degree:** M.S., Operational Management, Eastern Kentucky University, 1986 **Current organization:** Commercial Vehicle Group **Title:** President/CEO **Type of organization:** Manufacturing **Major product:** Interior trim, seating, controls, wipers and mirrors for commercial vehicle manufacturers **Area of distribution:** International **Expertise:** Administration **Affiliations:** A.S.Q.C.; N.A.M. **Hob./spts.:** Golf, motorcycling **SIC code:** 37 **Address:** Commercial Vehicle Group, 6530 W. Campus Oval, New Albany, OH 43054 **E-mail:** merv.dunn@cvgrp.com

DURAND, STEVEN C.
Industry: Steel **Born:** January 14, 1962, Pomona, California **Current organization:** Dixie Metal Products, Inc. **Title:** Plant Manager **Type of organization:** Manufacturing **Major product:** Structural steel **Area of distribution:** Florida **Expertise:** Daily operations oversight **Affiliations:** National Rifle Association; Board of Directors, Ocala Sportsman's Association **Hob./spts.:** Shooting **SIC code:** 34 **Address:** Dixie Metal Products, Inc., 442 S.W. 54th Ct., Ocala, FL 34474 **E-mail:** steved@dixiemetals.com **Web address:** www.dixiemetals.com

DURST, JOHN
Industry: Commercial machinery **Born:** February 5, 1947, Salem, Oregon **Current organization:** Master Machine, Inc. **Type of organization:** Machine manufacturing and repairs **Major product:** Equipment manufacturing and paper machine services **Area of distribution:** National **Expertise:** Paper machine equipment **Hob./spts.:** Camping, fishing, hunting **SIC code:** 35 **Address:** 486 Oregon Street, Lebanon, OR 97355

DUVALL, RONALD M.
Industry: Glass **Born:** April 17, 1961, Monroe, Michigan **Univ./degree:** A.S., Business, Monroe College, 1980 **Current organization:** Guardian Ind. **Title:** Maintenance Manager **Type of organization:** Manufacturing **Major product:** Raw glass **Area of distribution:** International **Expertise:** Plant maintenance **Affiliations:** Steel Society **Hob./spts.:** Hunting, fishing **SIC code:** 32 **Address:** Guardian Ind., 14600 Romine Rd., Carleton, MI 48177 **E-mail:** rduvall@guardian.com

DVORAK, DALE A.
Industry: Cosmetics **Born:** January 17, 1953, Chicago, Illinois **Univ./degree:** M.B.A., Boston University, 1978 **Current organization:** Shiseido America, Inc. **Title:** Sr. Vice President of Operations **Type of organization:** Manufacturing **Major product:** Cosmetics **Area of distribution:** International **Expertise:** Engineering, operations management **Affiliations:** New Jersey Chamber of Commerce **Hob./spts.:** Weightlifting, running **SIC code:** 28 **Address:** Shiseido America, Inc., 366 Princeton Hightstown Rd., East Windsor, NJ 08520 **E-mail:** ddvorak@sai.shiseido.com

EAGLE, KEMPER E.
Industry: Aerospace/Automotive **Born:** June 5, 1940, Harrisonburg, Virginia **Univ./degree:** B.S., Chemistry, Randolph-Macon College, 1962; M.S., Chemistry, American University, 1972 **Current organization:** Atlantic Research Corp. **Title:** Laboratory Manager **Type of organization:** Manufacturing **Major product:** Rocketry, tactical components, airbags **Area of distribution:** National **Expertise:** Analytical Chemist **Published works:** 3 conference papers/abstracts **Affiliations:** American Chemical Society **Hob./spts.:** Flyfishing, tennis, photography **SIC code:** 37 **Address:** Atlantic Research Corp., 5945 Wellington Rd., Gainsville, VA 20155 **E-mail:** eagle@arceng.com **Web address:** www.arceng.com

EARNEST, JOHN I.
Industry: Aerospace/avionics **Born:** September 16, 1942, Greenville, Tennessee **Univ./degree:** B.S., Industrial Technology, East Tennessee State University, 1965 **Current organization:** Kidde Aerospace **Title:** Test Engineer **Type of organization:** Manufacturing **Major product:** Safety systems **Area of distribution:** International **Expertise:** Test Engineer - electronics **Affiliations:** I.E.E.E. **Hob./spts.:** Fishing, the outdoors **SIC code:** 37 **Address:** Kidde Aerospace, 4200 Airport Dr., Wilson, NC 27896 **E-mail:** john.earnest@wkakti.com

EAST, LEONARD B.
Industry: Automotive parts **Born:** March 24, 1960, Chicago, Illinois **Univ./degree:** A.A.B., Business Management, Edison Community College **Current organization:** Greenville Technology Inc. **Title:** Production Assistant Manager **Type of organization:** Manufacturing **Major product:** Interior and exterior automotive parts **Area of distribution:** International **Expertise:** Manufacturing **Honors/awards:** Published in the National Dean's List, 2003 **Affiliations:** International Honor Society **Hob./spts.:** Golf, reading, hunting **SIC code:** 37 **Address:** Greenville Technology Inc., 5755 State Route 571 E, Greenville, OH 45331 **E-mail:** brian_east@gtioh.com

EATON, CHRISTOPHER A.
Industry: Appliances **Born:** August 19, 1951, Fairbanks, Alaska **Univ./degree:** B.S., Mechanical Engineering, Louisiana Tech, 1973; M.S., Systems Engineering, University of West Florida, 1975 **Current organization:** Sunbeam Products, Inc. **Title:** Advance Manufacturing Engineer **Type of organization:** Manufacturing **Major product:** Household appliances **Area of distribution:** International **Expertise:** Engineering, manufacturing, tooling engineering, occupational health/safety, quality assurance, project management, team leadership **Affiliations:** Served over 10 years with the U.S. Marine Corps as a Naval Aviator **Hob./spts.:** Golf, boating, scuba diving, cross country driving, charity work **SIC code:** 36 **Address:** Sunbeam Products, Inc., 95 W. L. Runnels Industrial Dr., Hattiesburg, MS 39401 **E-mail:** eatonc@sunbeam.com

EBRIGHT, SCOTT R.
Industry: Engineering **Born:** July 11, 1964, Sunbury, Pennsylvania **Univ./degree:** B.S., Engineering, Pennsylvania State University, 1986 **Current organization:** Prototype Machinery, Inc. **Title:** President **Type of organization:** Manufacturing **Major product:** Custom automation machinery **Area of distribution:** International **Expertise:** Project management, engineering **Hob./spts.:** Music, drummer for "The Cash Crew" (Johnny Cash's younger brother's band) **SIC code:** 35 **Address:** Prototype Machinery, Inc., 202 Ridge Ave., Milton, PA 17847

ECKLUND, ROBERT L.
Industry: Optical **Born:** May 14, 1970, St. Petersburg, Florida **Univ./degree:** A.S., National Aviation Academy, 1996 **Current organization:** Essilor of America **Title:** Process Technician **Type of organization:** Manufacturing, research and development **Major product:** Lenses **Area of distribution:** National **Expertise:** Engineering **Affiliations:** Coastal Conservation Clean Up Association **Hob./spts.:** Licensed aviation mechanic, travel, robotics **SIC code:** 38 **Address:** Essilor of America, 5459 Seventh Ave. North, St. Petersburg, FL 33710 **E-mail:** recklund@tampabay.rr.com

EDIE, MICHAEL J.
Industry: Automotive **Born:** February 18, 1949, Glen Falls, New York **Univ./degree:** B.S., Economics, St. John Fisher College, 1970 **Current organization:** Hayes Lem-

merz International **Title:** Vice-President, Logistics and Global Materials **Type of organization:** Manufacturing/distributing **Major product:** Automotive parts/wheels **Area of distribution:** International **Expertise:** Supply chain management **Affiliations:** N.P.O.; C.L.M. **Hob./spts.:** Fox hunting, horseback riding **SIC code:** 37 **Address:** Hayes Lemmerz International, 15300 Centennial Dr., Northville, MI 48167 **E-mail:** medie@hayes-lemmerz.com

EHLERS, PETER B.
Born: June 25, 1968, Toronto, Ontario, Canada **Univ./degree:** B.S., University of Toronto, 1992; M.B.A. Candidate, Xavier University **Current organization:** Swagelok Corp. **Area of distribution:** International **Affiliations:** S.A.E.; A.S.M.E. **Hob./spts.:** Playing and coaching hockey, golf, reading, is a Six Sigma Black Belt **SIC code:** 29 **Address:** ., 8795 Brent Dr., Cincinnatti, OH 45231 **E-mail:** peter.ehlers@swagelok.com **Web address:** www.swagelok.com

EHRLICH JR., MANUEL H.
Industry: Chemicals **Born:** September 25, 1942, Allentown, Pennsylvania **Univ./degree:** B.S., Chemistry, Drexel University, 1965; M.S., Chemical Engineering, New York University, 1971; M.A., Counseling Psychology for Business and Industry, 1986; M.S., Education, 1988, Columbia University **Current organization:** International Specialty Products **Title:** Vice President Health, Safety, Security **Type of organization:** Manufacturing **Major product:** Specialty chemicals **Area of distribution:** International **Expertise:** Chemistry, labor relations, counseling, security **Published works:** Articles **Affiliations:** N.F.P.A.; American Society for Testing and Materials; National Safety Council **Hob./spts.:** Photography, ice skating, woodworking **SIC code:** 28 **Address:** Responder Corp., P.O. Box 58, Montville, NJ 07470 **E-mail:** manyehrlich@aol.com **Web address:** www.responder.com

ELIAS, TOUMA M.
Industry: Computers **Born:** January 2, 1945 **Univ./degree:** Ph.D., Cranfield Institute of Technology, United Kingdom **Current organization:** Konnektia Technologies, Inc. **Title:** President/CEO **Type of organization:** Manufacturing **Major product:** Computers **Area of distribution:** International **Expertise:** Engineering, management **Affiliations:** Electrical Engineering Society **Hob./spts.:** Physical fitness, running, weights **SIC code:** 35 **Address:** Konnektia Technologies, Inc., 9833 Pacific Hts. Blvd., Suite C, San Diego, CA 92121 **E-mail:** toumaelias@hotmail.com **Web address:** www.konnektia.com

ELLIOTT, DONALD C.
Industry: Petroleum **Born:** January 19, 1948, Beaumont, Texas **Univ./degree:** B.S.E.E., Oklahoma State University, 1971 **Current organization:** ConocoPhillips **Title:** Staff Engineer **Type of organization:** Mining/manufacturing **Major product:** Petroleum products **Area of distribution:** International **Expertise:** Automation, automatic safety systems **Affiliations:** Instrument Society of America **Hob./spts.:** Photography, Jazz **SIC code:** 29 **Address:** ConocoPhillips, 600 N. Dairy Ashford, Houston, TX 77079 **E-mail:** don.c.elliott@conocophillips.com **Web address:** www.conocophillips.com

ELLISON, BARBARA M.
Industry: Pharmaceuticals **Born:** September 11, 1954, New Milford, Connecticut **Univ./degree:** B.S., Chemistry, Central Connecticut State University, 1976; M.B.A., Fairleigh Dickinson University, 1988 **Current organization:** Novartis Pharmaceuticals Corp. **Title:** Executive Director/County Manager **Type of organization:** Manufacturing **Major product:** Pharmaceuticals **Area of distribution:** International **Expertise:** Quality assurance, compliance and administration **Affiliations:** I.S.P.E.; P.D.A. **Hob./spts.:** Reading, sewing **SIC code:** 28 **Address:** Novartis Pharmaceuticals Corp., 1 Health Plaza, Room 105/3W048, East Hanover, NJ 07936 **E-mail:** barbara.ellison@pharma.novartis.com

ELLISON, JESSE J.
Industry: Food **Born:** Brownsville, Tennessee **Current organization:** Nashville Bun Co. **Title:** Sanitation Manager **Type of organization:** Manufacturing **Major product:** Muffins, buns, general food products **Area of distribution:** South U.S. **Expertise:** Administration of sanitation and hygiene **Hob./spts.:** Hunting, fishing **SIC code:** 20 **Address:** Nashville Bun Co., 2975 Armory Dr., Nashville, TN 37204 **E-mail:** littlee704@hotmail.com

EMERSON, JAMES S.
Industry: Aerospace **Current organization:** Lockheed-Martin Missiles & Fire Control **Title:** Lead Plant Design Engineer **Type of organization:** Manufacturing **Major product:** Missiles and control systems **Area of distribution:** Texas **Expertise:** Facilities engineering **Affiliations:** Chair and Trustee of Long Range Planning Committee **Hob./spts.:** Golf, tennis, high school umpire **SIC code:** 37 **Address:** Lockheed-Martin Missiles & Fire Control, 1701 W. Marshall Dr., Grand Prairie, TX 75051 **E-mail:** steve.emerson@mco.com

ENGELKING, MICHAEL E.
Industry: Automotive **Born:** October 6, 1946, Seymour, Indiana **Univ./degree:** B.S., Business Administration, North Carolina Wesleyan College, 1992 **Current organization:** Consolidated Diesel Co., Inc. **Title:** Manager, Advanced Manufacturing Engineering **Type of organization:** Manufacturing **Major product:** Diesel engines **Area of distribution:** International **Expertise:** Engineering **Hob./spts.:** Golf, boating **SIC code:** 37 **Address:** Consolidated Diesel Co., Inc., 9377 US 301, Whitakers, NC 27891 **E-mail:** mike.e.engelking@cummins.com

ENO, MOSES
Industry: Metal finishing **Born:** December 7, 1957, London, England **Univ./degree:** B.S. Michigan State University; M.S., Environmental Science, Alabama A&M University **Current organization:** UPI/UPC **Title:** Vice President **Type of organization:** Manufacturing **Major product:** Metal finishing, which includes: plating, anodizing, painting and silkscreening **Area of distribution:** National **Expertise:** Engineering **Affiliations:** Metal Finishing Organization; Automotive Design Production; West News Organization **Hob./spts.:** Golf, running **SIC code:** 34 **Address:** UPI/UPC, 3400 Stanwood Blvd. N.E., Huntsville, AL 35811 **E-mail:** meno@knology.net

ESPARZA, JORGE L.
Industry: Automotive **Born:** May 11, 1968, Zaragoza-Coahuila, Mexico **Univ./degree:** A.S., Business Management, Southwest Texas Jr. College, 2002 **Current organization:** Alcoa Fujikura Ltd. **Title:** Senior Quality Engineer **Type of organization:** Manufacturing **Major product:** Electrical distribution systems **Area of distribution:** International **Expertise:** Business management, quality control **Honors/awards:** Leadership Award for Outstanding Management Students **Affiliations:** A.S.Q. **Hob./spts.:** Woodworking, carpentry, landscaping **SIC code:** 36 **Address:** Alcoa Fujikura Ltd., 1 Cienegas Rd., Del Rio, TX 78840 **E-mail:** jorge.esparza@alcoa.com

ESTES, LONNIE W.
Industry: Automotive **Born:** August 28, 1973, Versailles, Kentucky **Univ./degree:** Diploma, Quality Control, Kentucky Vocational Tech School, 1997 **Current organization:** Ohio Automotive of America **Title:** Quality Engineer **Type of organization:** Manufacturing **Major product:** Trim products (door locks, check links, window reg.) **Area of distribution:** International **Expertise:** Quality assurance, quality control **Affiliations:** A.S.Q.; Served in active duty, U.S. Army, 1993-94 **Hob./spts.:** Golf, playing music (drums and bass) **SIC code:** 37 **Address:** Ohio Automotive of America, 1030 Hoover Blvd., Frankfurt, KY 40601 **E-mail:** lestes@ohiamerica.com

ETIENNE, JEAN CLAUDE
Industry: Crystal and glass artware **Univ./degree:** B.A., Scientology, 1975; B.S., Electrical Engineering, Technical Foundation University **Current organization:** Crystal Clear Industries **Title:** Manager, Design & Development **Type of organization:** Manufacturing **Major product:** Fine crystal, chandeliers, lamps, handcut vases and bowls **Area of distribution:** National **Expertise:** Design and development, engineering **Affiliations:** Clergy Association **SIC code:** 32 **Address:** Crystal Clear Industries, 300 Indsutrial Ave., Ridgefield, NJ 07660 **E-mail:** jetienne@crystalclear.com

EVANS, CHARLES D.
Industry: Commercial & consumer equipment **Univ./degree:** B.A., Montana State University; M.B.A., University of Dubuque **Current organization:** John Deere Horicon Works **Title:** Manager - Human Resources **Type of organization:** Manufacturing **Major product:** Lawn and garden - golf equipment **Area of distribution:** International **Expertise:** Human resources **Affiliations:** Rotary; Board of Directors, Y.M.C.A.; President, Flyway Area Labor- Management Council; S.H.R.M. **Hob./spts.:** Bird hunting, fly fishing, running, skiing, golf **SIC code:** 35 **Address:** John Deere Horicon Works, 203 East Lake Street, Horicon, WI 53032 **E-mail:** tx03322@deere.com

EVANS, ROBERT E.
Industry: Biotechnology **Born:** March 9, 1955, Baltimore, Maryland **Current organization:** Guilford Pharmaceuticals Inc. **Title:** Facilities Manager **Type of organization:** Research and development **Major product:** Drug development **Area of distribution:** National **Expertise:** Project management, environmental planning, facilities maintenance and engineering **Affiliations:** Board Member, N.A.P.E., Baltimore Chapter; Vice President, Association for Facilities Engineering, Baltimore Chapter **Hob./spts.:** Spending time with family, fishing **SIC code:** 28 **Address:** Guilford Pharmaceuticals Inc., 6611 Tributary St., Baltimore, MD 21224 **E-mail:** evansb@guilfordpharm.com

EWING, DAVID R.
Industry: Aerospace **Born:** June 6, 1944, Walters, Oklahoma **Univ./degree:** M.S., Contract and Acquisition Management, Florida Institute of Technology **Current organization:** Aerojet **Title:** Director, Supply Chain/Material Management **Type of organization:** Manufacturing **Major product:** Solid rocket motors **Area of distribution:** National **Expertise:** Materials management/procurement **Affiliations:** Past Adjunct Professor, Florida Institute of Technology **Hob./spts.:** Golf **SIC code:** 37 **Address:** Aerojet, Highland Industrial Park, P.O. Box 1036, Bldg. 2SH10, Camden, AR 71701 **E-mail:** david.ewing@aerojet.com

FALLS, JAMES HAROLD
Industry: Chemicals **Born:** March 7, 1943, Chase City, Virginia **Univ./degree:** B.S., Chemistry, Campbell University, 1965 **Current organization:** CF Industries, Inc. **Title:** Chief Chemist **Type of organization:** Manufacturing **Major product:** Fertilizer products **Area of distribution:** Worldwide **Expertise:** Analytical methods in fertilizer **Published works:** Articles in journals **Affiliations:** AOAC International; American Chemical Society; Association of Fertilizer and Phosphate Chemists; International Fertiliser Society **Hob./spts.:** Family, stamp collecting, reading **SIC code:** 28 **Address:** CF Industries, Inc., P.O. Drawer L, Plant City, FL 33564 **E-mail:** jhfalls@cfifl.com

FARRIS, CHESTER A.
Industry: Energy/solar panels and modules **Born:** March 5, 1954, Fort Worth, Texas **Current organization:** Shell Solar LP **Title:** President **Type of organization:** Manufacturing **Major product:** Solar panels and modules **Area of distribution:** International **Expertise:** Operations, management **Affiliations:** S.E.I.A.; N.A.D.C. **Hob./spts.:** Fishing, boating, windsurfing **SIC code:** 39 **Address:** Shell Solar LP, 4650 Adohr Lane, Camarillo, CA 93012 **E-mail:** chet.farris@shell.com

FAUTEUX, JOSEPH
Industry: Aviation **Born:** December 26, 1939, Montreal, Canada **Current organization:** Can-Ame, Inc. **Title:** President **Type of organization:** Aircraft mechanics shop **Major product:** Aircraft parts (titanium, stainless steel) and service **Area of distribution:** National **Expertise:** Machinist **Hob./spts.:** Coaching hockey **SIC code:** 37 **Address:** Can-Ame, Inc., 101 Derby Ave., Seymour, CT 06483 **E-mail:** joseph_fauteux@sbcglobal.net **Web address:** www.canameincmachineshop.com

FAWLEY, MARY JULIA
Industry: Synthetic products **Born:** November 15, 1958, Boston, Massachusetts **Univ./degree:** A.S., Liberal Studies, Mount Saint Clare College, Iowa, 1981 **Current organization:** Atwood & Thompson Inc. **Title:** President **Type of organization:** Manufacturing-fabrication, installation **Major product:** Custom made countertops, shower stalls, vanities **Area of distribution:** National **Expertise:** Residential and commercial custom countertops, management, operations **SIC code:** 30 **Address:** Atwood & Thompson Inc., 9172 Birch St., Spring Valley, CA 91977 **E-mail:** atwoodbob@aol.com

FAZIO, JOSEPH C.
Industry: OEM products **Born:** Syracuse, New York **Univ./degree:** B.S., Mechanical Engineering, Syracuse University, 1990 **Current organization:** Tuthill Pump Group **Title:** Senior Mechanical Engineer **Type of organization:** Manufacturing **Major product:** Magnetically coupled gear pumps **Area of distribution:** International **Expertise:** Mechanical engineering, FEA 3D simulation, tribology **Affiliations:** A.S.M. **Hob./spts.:** Skiing, hiking, travel, history, reading **SIC code:** 35 **Address:** Tuthill Pump Group, 5143 Port Chicago Hwy., Concord, CA 94520-1216 **E-mail:** jfazio@tuthill.com

FEDESNA, KENNETH J.
Industry: Amusement games **Born:** October 14, 1949, Chicago, Illinois **Univ./degree:** M.S., Electrical Engineering, Illinois Institute of Technology **Current organization:** Cashbox Games, Inc. **Title:** President/CEO **Type of organization:** Developer and manufacturer **Major product:** Coin operated games **Area of distribution:** International **Expertise:** Management **Hob./spts.:** Boating, waterskiing, collecting Lionel trains **SIC code:** 39 **Address:** Cashbox Games, Inc., 4 Oneida Lane, Hawthorn Woods, IL 60047 **E-mail:** kfedesna@comcast.net

FEDOROWICZ, JEFFREY A.
Industry: Automotive **Born:** October 1, 1966, Milwaukee, Wisconsin **Univ./degree:** B.S., Chemical Engineering, University of Wisconsin, 1988 **Current organization:** J.F. Filtration Consulting **Title:** Owner **Type of organization:** Consulting **Major product:** Consulting services **Area of distribution:** United States and Canada **Expertise:** Engineering, project management and design **Published works:** 1 SAE paper of fuel filtration; 2 AFS papers on crankcase filtration; Patents: 5 patents on crankcase filtration; Patent numbers: 6,247,463; 6,478,018; 6,478,019 + 2 applied for **Affiliations:** S.A.E.; N.F.P.A.; A.F.S. **Hob./spts.:** Golf, travel, coaching youth softball **SIC code:** 37 **Address:** J.F. Filtration Consulting, 1801 W. Hwy. 51, Stoughton, WI 53589 **E-mail:** jeff_fedorowicz@ameritech.net

FELMAN, ESFIR
Industry: Microwave and RF **Born:** November 12, 1946, Novgorod, Russia **Univ./degree:** M.S. **Current organization:** Trompeter - Semflex **Title:** RF Engineer **Type of organization:** Manufacturing **Major product:** Connectors and adaptors for the RF microwave industry **Area of distribution:** International **Expertise:** Microwave RF engineering **SIC code:** 36 **Address:** 18319 Collins St., #8, Tarzana, CA 91356 **E-mail:** esfir.felman@trompeter.com

FERANDES, GARY W.
Industry: Aerospace **Born:** October 18, 1959, Baltimore, Maryland **Univ./degree:** A.S., Harford Community College, 1995 **Current organization:** Lockheed Martin NE&SS **Title:** Mechanical Staff Engineer **Type of organization:** Manufacturing **Major product:** DOD Products **Area of distribution:** International **Expertise:** Electronic packaging design **Honors/awards:** National Deans List **Hob./spts.:** Volleyball **SIC code:** 37 **Address:** Lockheed Martin NE&SS, 2323 Eastern Blvd., Baltimore, MD 21220 **E-mail:** gary.w.ferandes@lmco.com **Web address:** www.lmco.com

FERGUS, RENEE
Industry: Biotechnology **Born:** November 18, 1976, Passaic, New Jersey **Univ./degree:** B.S., Chemistry, Fairleigh Dickinson University, 1998 **Current organization:** SAIC-NCI Frederick **Title:** QC Analyst II **Type of organization:** Manufacturing/development **Major product:** Biopharmaceuticals **Area of distribution:** International **Expertise:** Quality control **Affiliations:** A.C.S. **Hob./spts.:** Taking classes **SIC code:** 28 **Address:** SAIC-NCI Frederick, P.O. Box B, Bldg 434, Frederick, MD 21702 **E-mail:** rfergus@mail.ncifcrf.gov

FIGG, DENNIS R.
Industry: Printing **Current organization:** Rapid Impressions, Inc. **Title:** Plant Manager **Type of organization:** Commercial printer **Major product:** High end printing and bindery **Area of distribution:** National **Expertise:** Daily operations oversight **Affiliations:** Lithographers Club of Chicago **Hob./spts.:** Camping **SIC code:** 27 **Address:** Rapid Impressions, Inc., 2206 Parkes Dr., Broadview, IL 60155 **E-mail:** rsmlitho@comcast.net

FIGUEREDO, LISA M.
Industry: Publishing **Born:** March 18, 1961, Tampa, Florida **Univ./degree:** A.S., Commercial Art, Tampa Tech Institute, 1995 **Current organization:** Cigar City Magazine, Inc. **Title:** Owner/President/Publisher **Type of organization:** Publishing **Major product:** Magazine on Tampa history **Area of distribution:** National **Expertise:** Publishing **Affiliations:** West Tampa Chamber of Commerce; Rotary Club; Lions Club **Hob./spts.:** Skiing, playing the guitar, drawing **SIC code:** 27 **Address:** 306 N. Glen Ave., Tampa, FL 33609 **E-mail:** publisher@cigarcitymagazine.com

FISCHER, JUDY K.
Industry: Food **Univ./degree:** B.A., Business, Kennedy-Western University, 1998 **Current organization:** Sargento Foods, Inc. **Title:** Senior Packaging Engineer **Type of organization:** Manufacturing **Major product:** Packaged cheeses **Area of distribution:** International **Expertise:** Package engineering; CPP Certified, Green Belt Certified Six Sigma **Honors/awards:** 1 patent **Affiliations:** P.M.M.I.; I.O.P.P. **Hob./spts.:** Golf, cooking, travel **SIC code:** 20 **Address:** Sargento Foods, Inc., 305 Pine St., Elkhart Lake, WI 53020 **E-mail:** jufische@sargento.com

FISHER, JASON S.
Industry: Electronics **Born:** February 23, 1970, Glasgow, Scotland, United Kingdom **Univ./degree:** B.A.S.E.E.T., Bachelor of Applied Science in Electronics Engineering Technology, ITT Technical Institute, Utah, 1994 **Current organization:** Elma Electronics **Title:** Systems Engineer **Type of organization:** Original equipment manufacturer **Major product:** Enclosures **Area of distribution:** International **Expertise:** Environmental testing and documentation **Affiliations:** ITT Technical Institute **Hob./spts.:** Family nature walks **SIC code:** 36 **Address:** Elma Electronics, 44350 Grimmer Blvd., Fremont, CA 94538 **E-mail:** jasonf@elma.com

FIX, KENNETH C.
Industry: Safety products **Born:** May 21, 1959, Pittsburgh, Pennsylvania **Univ./degree:** B.S.M.E., University of Pittsburgh, 1995 **Current organization:** Mine Safety Appliances Co. **Title:** Manufacturing Process Engineer **Type of organization:** Manufacturing **Major product:** Hard hats, air systems for fire services **Area of distribution:** International **Expertise:** Manufacturing engineering **Hob./spts.:** Golf **SIC code:** 39 **Address:** Mine Safety Appliances Co., 3880 Meadowbrook Rd., Murrysville, PA 15668 **E-mail:** ken.fix@msanet.com

FLACH, JUERGEN K.
Industry: Healthcare/research **Born:** July 30, 1942, Darmstadt, Germany **Univ./degree:** M.S., Ph.D., 1976, University Darmstadt **Current organization:** Roche Diagnostics Corp. **Title:** Vice President for International Business, Roche Applies Sciences **Type of organization:** Manufacturing, distribution **Major product:** Biochemical reagents and instruments **Area of distribution:** International **Expertise:** Marketing in Bioscience **Hob./spts.:** Travel, skiing, European handball, jazz, ballet **SIC code:** 38 **Address:** Roche Diagnostics Corp., 9115 Hague Rd., Indianapolis, IN 46256 **E-mail:** juergen.flach@roche.com **Web address:** www.ind.roche.com

FLECKENSTEIN, EDWARD A.
Industry: Publishing/history **Born:** November 27, 1919, Weehawken, New Jersey **Univ./degree:** A.B., Economics, Fordham University, 1941; J.D., Fordham University School of Law, 1943 **Current organization:** Edward A Fleckenstein, Chairman/ Weehawken Township Historical Commission **Title:** Commission Head/Writer **Type of organization:** Publishing/historical commission **Major product:** Legal services/ articles **Area of distribution:** National **Expertise:** Writer **Published works:** Articles on historical accounts, cultural and political matters **Affiliations:** Trustee, Fritz Reuter Life Care Center; Board Member, Palisades Medical Center; Corresponding Editor, Der Volksfreund / People's Friend of Buffalo, NY **Career accomplishments:** Chairman of the Weehawken Housing Authority and involved with its holding of pageants and co-operation with other historical and genealogical organizations and its collecting books and documents on local history **Hob./spts.:** Photography, writing **SIC code:** 27 **Address:** 39 King Ave., Weehawken, NJ 07086

FLORUS, LIONEL
Industry: Medical supplies **Born:** March 29, 1956, Port-au-Prince, Haiti **Univ./degree:** A.A., Business Management, La Guardia Community College, 1985; B.S. **Current organization:** Propper Manufacturing Co. **Title:** Vice President, Operations **Type of organization:** Manufacturing **Major product:** Medical and sterilization products **Area of distribution:** International **Expertise:** Operations management, productivity, training, presentations **Honors/awards:** Outstanding Service Award, Propper Manufacturing, 1988 **Affiliations:** Executive Committee, Propper Manufacturing Co. **Hob./spts.:** Tennis, basketball, travel **SIC code:** 38 **Address:** Propper Manufacturing Co., 36-04 Skillman Ave., Long Island City, NY 11101 **E-mail:** lflorus@nyc.rr.com **Web address:** www.proppermfg.com

FLOYD JR., ROBERT P.
Industry: Filters **Born:** November 5, 1936, Mullins, South Carolina **Current organization:** Bon-Aire Filters Inc. **Title:** President **Type of organization:** Manufacturing **Major product:** Air filters **Area of distribution:** International **Expertise:** Sales and filter design **Affiliations:** Mason **Hob./spts.:** Salt water fishing, boating **SIC code:** 35 **Address:** Bon-Aire Filters Inc., P.O. Box 67, Marietta, NC 28362 **E-mail:** filterbonair67@bellsouth.net **Web address:** www.bon-airefilters.com

FOOR, STEVEN M.
Industry: Automotive **Born:** August 13, 1957, Altoona, Pennsylvania **Current organization:** RTI Technologies, Inc. **Title:** IT Manager **Type of organization:** Manufacturing **Major product:** Automotive fluid recycling, automotive service equipment **Area of distribution:** Global **Expertise:** IT- wiring/cabling/repairs, management **Hob./spts.:** Camping, football **SIC code:** 37 **Address:** RTI Technologies, Inc., 10 Innovation Dr., York, PA 17402 **E-mail:** smf@rtitech.com **Web address:** www.rtitech.com

FOURIE, HUGO
Industry: Oil and gas **Born:** August 25, 1973, Fochville, South Africa **Univ./degree:** B.S., Accounting, 1994; B.S., Computer Science, 1996; M.S., Accounting, 1998, University of Houston & University of Phoenix **Current organization:** Agar Corp., Inc. **Title:** Controller **Type of organization:** Manufacturing **Major product:** Hydrocarbon/water/gas measurement and control devices **Area of distribution:** International **Expertise:** Accounting **Hob./spts.:** Horseback riding, travel, tennis, computers, movies, painting **SIC code:** 38 **Address:** Agar Corp., Inc., 5150 Tacoma Dr., Houston, TX 77041 **E-mail:** hfourie@mail.agarcorp.com **Web address:** www.agarcorp.com

FOX, DAVID G.
Industry: Food **Born:** May 31, 1941, Portland, Indiana **Univ./degree:** Teaching Credential, University of California, Santa Cruz, 1982 **Current organization:** McCormick & Co., Inc. **Title:** Maintenance Work Leader **Type of organization:** Manufacturing **Major product:** Consumer and retail spices **Area of distribution:** International **Expertise:** Team leader of ten mechanics in #2 consumer plant in company; HVAC certified **Honors/awards:** National Level One Ranking **Affiliations:** Association for Facilities Engineer; Chamber of Commerce; Old Town Association; Co-Owner of Side Pocket Billiards **Hob./spts.:** Camping, freshwater fishing, golf, restoring golf cars **SIC code:** 20 **Address:** 13348 Jackson St., Salinas, CA 93906 **E-mail:** david_fox@mccormick.com

FRANK, STEPHEN A.
Industry: Paper **Born:** June 17, 1951, Daggett, Michigan **Current organization:** International Paper **Title:** Lead Person **Type of organization:** Manufacturing **Major product:** Corrugated paper, boxes, displays **Area of distribution:** International **Expertise:** Maintenance, installation, trouble shooting, repair **Affiliations:** American Legion **Hob./spts.:** Hunting, fishing **SIC code:** 26 **Address:** International Paper, N143W6049 Pioneer Rd., Cedarburg, WI 53012-2857 **E-mail:** safrank51@aol.com

FRANKS, JOHN L.
Industry: Electrical **Born:** March 4, 1971, Kalamazoo, Michigan **Univ./degree:** A.S., Kalamazoo Valley Community College, 1993 **Current organization:** HECO, Inc. **Title:** Shipping Manager **Type of organization:** Repair, distributing **Major product:** Electric motors **Area of distribution:** Michigan, Indiana, Illinois and Ohio **Expertise:** Shipping and receiving, transportation **Affiliations:** National Rifle Association; National Wild Turkey Federation **Hob./spts.:** Shooting, hunting, fishing, camping, sports **SIC code:** 37 **Address:** HECO, Inc., 3509 S. Burdick St., Kalamazoo, MI 49001 **E-mail:** jfranks@hecoinc.com

FREEMAN, TAMI M.
Industry: Sheet metal **Born:** July 28, 1977, Lubbock, Texas **Current organization:** GST Manufacturing, Ltd. **Title:** Office Manager **Type of organization:** Manufacturing **Major product:** Sheet metal goods **Area of distribution:** National **Expertise:** Purchasing/accounts payable **Hob./spts.:** Music, songwriting **SIC code:** 33 **Address:** GST Manufacturing, Ltd., 1109 Foch St., Ft. Worth, TX 76107 **E-mail:** tfreeman@gstmanufacturing.com

FREIDHOFF, CARL B.
Industry: Aerospace **Born:** May 5, 1959, Pittsburgh, Pennsylvania **Univ./degree:** B.S., Chemistry, University of Miami, 1981; M.A., Chemical Physics, 1984; Ph.D., Chemical Physics, 1987, Johns Hopkins University **Current organization:** Northrop Grumman ES **Title:** Senior Technical Advisor **Type of organization:** Manufacturing and development **Major product:** Military electronics and sensor systems **Area of distribution:** International **Expertise:** Microelectromechanical systems, micro sensors, chem-bio sensor systems, chem bio sonar systems, **Honors/awards:** Northrop Grumman Presidential Leadership Finalist **Affiliations:** I.E.E.E.; A.V.S.; S.P.I.E.; M.R.S. **Hob./spts.:** Fishing, camping, sailing, hiking **SIC code:** 37 **Address:** Northrop Grumman ES, 7323 Aviation Blvd., MS 1111, Linthicum, MD 21090 **E-mail:** carl.freidhoff@ngc.com

FREIJI, GEORGE I.
Industry: Packaging **Born:** Lebanon **Univ./degree:** B.S., Southern Illinois University **Current organization:** Hilex Poly Co., LLC **Title:** Plant Manager **Type of organization:** Manufacturing **Major product:** Plastics **Area of distribution:** National **Expertise:** Management **Affiliations:** Board Member, Central Pennsylvania Workforce Development Corp. **Hob./spts.:** Car restoration, ice hockey **SIC code:** 30 **Address:** Hilex Poly Co., LLC, 606 Old Curtin Rd., Milesburg, PA 16853 **E-mail:** george.freiji@hilexpoly.com

FRITZ, FRANK D.
Industry: Commercial laundry equipment and services **Born:** Washington, Iowa **Univ./degree:** B.A., Accounting, Coe College **Current organization:** The Dexter Company **Title:** Vice President, Finance/Secretary/Treasurer **Type of organization:** Manufacturing **Major product:** Commercial laundry equipment, foundry castings **Area of distribution:** National **Expertise:** Finance and accounting **Affiliations:** A.I.C.P.A.; Iowa Society of C.P.A.'s **Hob./spts.:** Golf, running, fan of college football and college basketball **SIC code:** 35 **Address:** The Dexter Company, 2211 W. Grimes Ave., Fairfield, IA 52556 **E-mail:** ffritz@dexter.com

FRUMENTO, MICHAEL J.
Industry: Hazardous waste **Born:** September 3, 1969, Philadelphia, Pennsylvania **Univ./degree:** A.S., Applied Science, U.S. Navy **Current organization:** Pollution Control Industries **Title:** Maintenance Director **Type of organization:** Manufacturing **Major product:** Recycling hazardous waste into solvents **Area of distribution:** National **Expertise:** Management, maintenance **Hob./spts.:** Fishing, hunting **SIC code:** 39 **Address:** Pollution Control Industries, 4343 Kennedy Ave., East Chicago, IN 46312 **E-mail:** mfrumento@pollutioncontrol.com **Web address:** www.pollutioncontrol.com

GABRIEL, GEORGE P.
Industry: Construction materials **Born:** September 18, 1923, Scranton, Pennsylvania **Univ./degree:** B.S., Chemical Engineering, Penn State University, 1949 **Current organization:** Atlas Minerals and Chemicals, Inc. **Title:** Chairman, Board of Directors **Type of organization:** Manufacturing **Major product:** Construction materials **Area of distribution:** International **Expertise:** Engineering **Published works:** 6 technical articles **Affiliations:** N.A.C.E.; A.S.T.M.; National Society of Professional Engineers **Hob./spts.:** Oil painting, art, model doll houses and ships **SIC code:** 39 **Address:** Atlas Minerals and Chemicals, Inc., P.O. Box 38, 1227 Valley Rd., Mertztown, PA 19539 **E-mail:** geopgabriel@aol.com

GADBERRY, DAVID
Industry: Conveyor systems **Born:** June 22, 1962, Stanton, California **Univ./degree:** B.S.M.E, University of California at Irvine,. 1988 **Current organization:** Can Lines, Inc. **Title:** Engineering Manager **Type of organization:** Manufacturing **Major product:** Custom designed conveyors for the food industry **Area of distribution:** International **Expertise:** Engineering management, custom design work **Honors/awards:** Miller Brewing Supplier of the Year, 2002 **Affiliations:** American Society of Mechanical Engineers **Hob./spts.:** International surfer; environmental volunteer **SIC code:** 35 **Address:** Can Lines, Inc., 9839 Downey-Norwalk Rd., Downey, CA 90241-7039 **E-mail:** dave@canlines.com **Web address:** www.canlines.com

GALLO, RALPH B.
Industry: Premium eyewear and apparel **Univ./degree:** Rochester Institute of Technology; Rochester Business Institute; Orange Coast College; Irvine Valley College **Current organization:** Oakley, Inc. **Title:** Technical Support Project Manager **Type of organization:** Manufacturing **Major product:** Premium sunglasses, sports eyewear, prescription eyewear, apparel, footwear, watches **Area of distribution:** International **Expertise:** Vacuum technology, water purification, electrical and mechanical engineering, accounting **Affiliations:** A.V.S.; I.S.A.; N.F.P.A. (NEC) **Hob./spts.:** Tennis, basketball, bike riding, beach, local theatre, travel, reading **SIC code:** 23 **Address:** Oakley, Inc., 1 Icon, Foothill Ranch, CA 92610-3000 **E-mail:** ralphg@oakley.com

GANIEANY, DEBBIE
Industry: Wood **Title:** Human resources **Type of organization:** Manufacturing **Major product:** Plywood **Expertise:** Human resources **SIC code:** 24 **Address:** Eagle Veneer Inc., 220 W. 16th St., Junction City, OR 97448 **E-mail:** debbie.ganieany@eagleveneer.com

GANS, ROBERT A.
Industry: Biotechnology **Born:** July 16, 1941, Port Chester, New York **Univ./degree:** M.B.A., Stanford University, 1968 **Current organization:** Genway Biotech, Inc. **Title:** Executive VP, CFO, QA Manager **Type of organization:** Manufacturing/producing **Major product:** Proteins and antibodies, custom services and catalog products **Area of distribution:** International **Expertise:** Finance, QA, human resources **Hob./spts.:** Skating, golf, history **SIC code:** 28 **Address:** Genway Biotech, Inc., 6777 Nancy Ridge Dr., San Diego, CA 92121 **E-mail:** rgans@genwaybio.com **Web address:** www.genwaybio.com

GARCIA, EDGAR
Industry: Sheet metal **Born:** April 21. 1958, Tenares, Dominican Republic **Current organization:** N.I.C. **Title:** Facilities manager **Type of organization:** Manufacturing **Major product:** Fabricated metal products **Area of distribution:** Washington **Expertise:** Machine maintenance **Hob./spts.:** Skiing, fishing **SIC code:** 33 **Address:** N.I.C., 23518 63 Ave. S.E., Woodinville, WA 98072 **E-mail:** edgar.garcia@nicmfg.com

GARCIA, RAUL
Industry: Automotive **Born:** November 3, 1965, Mexico City **Univ./degree:** B.A., Monterrey Technological Institute, 1989 **Current organization:** Automotive Lighting Co. **Title:** Sales Manager **Type of organization:** Manufacturing **Major product:** Auto lighting **Area of distribution:** International **Expertise:** Sales **Affiliations:** Society of Auto Engineering **Hob./spts.:** Family, travel **SIC code:** 37 **Address:** Automotive Lighting Co., 37484 Interchange Dr., Farmington Hills, MI 48335 **E-mail:** raul_garcia_o@hotmail.com

GARCÍA-LLAMAS, JOSÉ
Industry: Medical devices **Born:** August 24, 1951, Humacao, Puerto Rico **Univ./degree:** B.S.C.E., University of Puerto Rico; M.B.A., Turabo University, 1987 **Current organization:** Fisher Diagnostic **Title:** Engineer **Type of organization:** Manufacturing **Major product:** Diagnostic reagents **Area of distribution:** International **Expertise:** Engineering/maintenance **Affiliations:** Past Member, International Society for Pharmaceutical Engineering **SIC code:** 38 **Address:** Fisher Diagnostic, 8365 Valley Pike, Middletown, VA 22645 **E-mail:** jose.garcia@fishersci.com **Web address:** www.fishersci.com

GARNER, JOSEPH N.
Industry: Biopharmaceuticals **Univ./degree:** Ph.D., Molecular Biology, University of Maryland, 2002 **Current organization:** Advanced Product Enterprises LLC **Title:** C.O.O./C.F.O. **Type of organization:** Manufacturing **Major product:** Biodefense mechanisms **Area of distribution:** National **Expertise:** Operations **Affiliations:** A.S.PE.T.; American Society of Microbiology **Hob./spts.:** Golf **SIC code:** 28 **Address:** Advanced Product Enterprises LLC, 5716 Industry Lane, Suite F, Frederick, MD 21704-5110 **E-mail:** garner@ape-bio.com

GARRETT, ROBBY P.
Industry: Furniture **Born:** May 31, 1960, Vicksburg, Mississippi **Current organization:** Standard Furniture **Title:** Plant Manager **Type of organization:** Manufacturing **Major product:** Bedroom furniture **Area of distribution:** National **Expertise:** Promotional/residential furniture **Affiliations:** U.S. Golf Association; Director, Monroe Chamber of Commerce; AL Supporter, Hope Village for Children, Meridian, Mississippi **Hob./spts.:** Golf, fundraising, sports, Mississippi State University **SIC code:** 25 **Address:** Standard Furniture, 57 Chamber St., Frisco City, AL 36445 **E-mail:** robby.garrett@sfmco.com

GAUDETTE, CHRISTOPHER J.
Industry: Food **Born:** January 29, 1971, Lebanon, New Hampshire **Univ./degree:** M.B.A., Southern New Hampshire University **Current organization:** Cedar's Mediterranean Foods Inc. **Title:** C.F.O. **Type of organization:** Manufacturing, distributing **Major product:** Hommus - Mediterranean cuisine **Area of distribution:** National **Expertise:** Business accounting, reporting, administration **Hob./spts.:** Golf **SIC code:** 20 **Address:** Cedar's Mediterranean Foods Inc., 50 Foundation Ave., Ward Hill, MA 01835 **E-mail:** cgaudette@cedarsfoods.com

GEER, JAMES R.
Industry: Oil refining **Born:** October 22, 1952, San Diego, California **Univ./degree:** A.S., Industrial Maintenance, Southwest Tennessee University, 1981 **Current organization:** Williams Refining & Marketing Co., LLC **Title:** Maintenance Coordinator **Type of organization:** Refinery **Major product:** Refining crude oil **Area of distribution:** Tennessee **Expertise:** T/A planning **Hob./spts.:** Golf **SIC code:** 29 **Address:** Williams Refining & Marketing Co., LLC, 543 W. Mallory, Memphis, TN 38109 **E-mail:** james.geer@williams.com

GENTRY, THOMAS W.
Industry: Building materials **Born:** January 28, 1949, Macon, Georgia **Univ./degree:** B.S., Accounting, Cameron University, 1977; M.B.A., University of Central Oklahoma, 1979; U.S. Army Command and General, General Staff College, 1983 **Current organization:** Georgia-Pacific Sweetwater Gypsum Plant **Title:** Human Resources Manager **Type of organization:** Manufacturing **Major product:** Wall board **Area of distribution:** International **Expertise:** Certified S.P.H.R , public administration, leadership, consulting; Market Based Management; Gainsharing **Honors/awards:** Appointed to North Carolina Governor's Advisory Council for Industry and Business, 1998-2002; Orange County, North Carolina, Executive Steering Committee for the Aged **Affiliations:** Society for Human Resource Management; North Carolina County Parks and Recreation Advisory Committee; Orange County, North Carolina, Executive Steering Committee for the Aged; US Army Lt. Col., 1969-1990 **Hob./spts.:** FIFA referee, licensed soccer coach (international), fishing **SIC code:** 24 **Address:** Georgia-Pacific Sweetwater Gypsum Plant, 310 FM 1856, Sweetwater, TX 79556 **E-mail:** tgee1949@yahoo.com

GERACI, JOSEPH
Industry: Metals reroll **Born:** June 15, 1953, Montreal, Canada **Univ./degree:** Quality Management Studies, Waterbury State Technical College **Current organization:** Somers Thin Strip **Title:** Rolling Supervisor **Type of organization:** Manufacturing **Major product:** Steel and copper light gauge strips **Area of distribution:** International **Expertise:** Quality assurance, slitting and rolling; safety and quality training and seminars; Statistics Certification; CPR and Safety Certifications **Published works:** Quality Assurance Manual; American Society for Metals **Affiliations:** Association of Quality Assurance Management **Hob./spts.:** Golf, bowling **SIC code:** 33 **Address:** Somers Thin Strip, 215 Piedmont St., Waterbury, CT 06720-0270 **E-mail:** jgeraci@olin.com

GHEITH, MOHAMMED F.
Industry: Cosmetics **Univ./degree:** B.A., Dominican College; M.A., Loyola University **Current organization:** William H. Cooper & Co. **Title:** Owner **Type of organization:** Manufacturing **Major product:** Cosmetics **Area of distribution:** National **Expertise:** Marketing **SIC code:** 28 **Address:** William H. Cooper & Co., 816 N. Spaulding Ave., Chicago, IL 60651-4133 **E-mail:** gheith@wmh.cooper.com **Web address:** www.wmh.cooper.com

GIFFUNI, MIGUEL F.
Industry: Beauty supplies **Born:** February 12, 1956, Salerno, Italy **Univ./degree:** Mechanical Engineering, Simon Bolivar University, 1977 **Current organization:** Magiff International, Inc. **Title:** Founder/CEO **Type of organization:** Manufacturing **Major product:** Nail care products **Area of distribution:** International **Expertise:** Beauty supplies **Published works:** Articles **Hob./spts.:** Power sailing, boxing **SIC code:** 39 **Address:** Magiff International, Inc., 8406 N.W. 17th St., Miami, FL 33126 **E-mail:** miguelgiffuni@aol.com **Web address:** www.magiff.com

GILES, SCOTT D.
Industry: Automotive **Born:** February 6, 1977, New Albany, Indiana **Univ./degree:** B.S.E.E., Purdue University, 1999 **Current organization:** Delphi Automotive **Title:** Manufacturing Test Engineer **Type of organization:** Manufacturing **Major product:** Automotive electronics **Area of distribution:** National **Expertise:** Engineering **Honors/awards:** Quality Performance Award, 2002; Leadership in Execution and Attitude Demonstration Award, 2003; Six Sigma/Black Belt Cert., 2003 **Hob./spts.:** Soccer **SIC**

code: 37 **Address:** 1901 S. Goyer, #122, Kokomo, IN 46902 **E-mail:** scottdougg@aol.com

GILILLAND, EARL R.
Industry: Concrete products/construction **Born:** December 8, 1950, Denver, Colorado **Current organization:** Rinker Materials-Hydro-Conduit Div. **Title:** Asset Manager **Type of organization:** Manufacturing **Major product:** Concrete products **Area of distribution:** International **Expertise:** Shipping and maintenance **Hob./spts.:** Woodworking, fishing, hunting **SIC code:** 32 **Address:** Rinker Materials-Hydro-Conduit Div., P.O. Box 370, Grand Island, NE 68802 **E-mail:** egililland@rinker.com **Web address:** www.rinker.com

GLEITER, JOHN H.
Industry: Semiconductors **Born:** May 8, 1961, Cincinnati, Ohio **Univ./degree:** B.S., Business, Finance and Marketing, Emory University **Current organization:** Broadcom Corp. **Title:** Director, Business Development **Type of organization:** Manufacturing **Major product:** Semiconductors **Area of distribution:** International **Expertise:** Marketing **Affiliations:** A.O.P.A.; Sports Car Club Association; E.A.A. (Experimental Aircraft Association) **Hob./spts.:** Boating, flying **SIC code:** 36 **Address:** Broadcom Corp., 4385 Rivergreen Pkwy., Duluth, GA 30096 **E-mail:** jgleiter@broadcom.com

GLOVER, TRUDY B.
Industry: Hardwoods **Born:** Winchester, Kentucky **Univ./degree:** PHR, Human Resources Certification Institute, 1996 **Current organization:** The Freeman Corp. **Title:** Human Resources Manager & Safety Director **Type of organization:** Manufacturing **Major product:** Fine hardwood veneers (cherry, walnut, oak) **Area of distribution:** National **Expertise:** Human Resources, safety administration **Affiliations:** Board Member, F.I.W.C.F.; Society for Human Resource Management **Hob./spts.:** Target shooting, swimming, outdoor activities **SIC code:** 24 **Address:** The Freeman Corp., 415 Magnolia St., Winchester, KY 40392 **E-mail:** tglover@freemancorp.com

GLOWINSKI, MICHAEL E.
Industry: Analytical instruments **Born:** January 20, 1962, Danbury, Connecticut **Current organization:** Wilk's Enterprises, Inc. **Title:** Mechanical Designer **Type of organization:** Manufacturing/research & development **Major product:** Infrared based analyzers **Area of distribution:** National **Expertise:** Mechanical design, technical drawing **Hob./spts.:** Restoring vintage computers **SIC code:** 38 **Address:** Wilk's Enterprises, Inc., 140 Water St., Norwalk, CT 06854 **E-mail:** mglowinski@wilksir.com

GODDARD, KELLY E.
Industry: Concrete **Born:** May 19, 1962, Oklahoma City, Oklahoma **Univ./degree:** B.B.A., Central State University, 1984 **Current organization:** Goddard Ready Mix Concrete Co., Inc. **Title:** President **Type of organization:** Manufacturing **Major product:** Ready mix concrete - residential and commercial **Area of distribution:** Oklahoma **Expertise:** Financial management; Certified Concrete Technician, Certified Miner, MSHA **Honors/awards:** Outstanding Young Women of America; First woman in Oklahoma to become a Certified Concrete Technician **Affiliations:** N.R.M.A.; C.O.H.B.A.; Oklahoma Ready Mix Concrete Association; Midwest City and Choctaw Chambers of Commerce; Oklahoma and National Homebuilders Association; Oklahoma Safety Council **Hob./spts.:** Church activities; acting with the Whodunit Dining Room Mystery Theater **SIC code:** 32 **Address:** Goddard Ready Mix Concrete Co., Inc., 3101 N.E. Tenth St., Oklahoma City, OK 73117 **E-mail:** goddardc@aol.com

GODEN, PAUL ALEXANDER
Industry: Aerospace **Born:** June 30, 1956, Santa Monica, California **Univ./degree:** B.S.B.A., Accounting, University of Southern California, 1978 **Current organization:** The Mexmil Co. **Title:** Senior Financial Analyst **Type of organization:** Manufacturing/fabrication **Major product:** Insulation systems **Area of distribution:** International **Expertise:** Financial forecasting, human resources **Honors/awards:** Summa Cum Laude, National Honor Society, Governor's Award **Affiliations:** A.I.C.P.A.; C.A.S.C.P.A.; University of Southern California Alumni Association **Hob./spts.:** Spectator sports, songwriting, music, physical fitness **SIC code:** 39 **Address:** 319 W. Lambert Rd., #40, Brea, CA 92821 **E-mail:** paul.goden@mexmil.com **Web address:** www.mexmil.com

GOMEZ, MIGUEL A.
Industry: Plastics **Born:** October 7, 1941, Puerto Rico **Univ./degree:** M.B.A., Inter-American University, 1978 **Current organization:** Western Manufacturing Services, Inc. **Title:** CEO **Type of organization:** Manufacturing **Major product:** Molders of plastic products for pharmaceutical and electronics industries **Area of distribution:** Aguadilla, Puerto Rico **Expertise:** Engineering **Hob./spts.:** Baseball, basketball **SIC code:** 30 **Address:** Western Manufacturing Services, Inc., Montana Industrial Park, Rt. 107 Km 0.5, Aguadilla, PR 00605 **E-mail:** gomezm@coqui.net

GOMEZ, PABLO F.
Industry: Pharmaceutical **Born:** August 25, 1972, Bogotá, Colombia **Univ./degree:** M.S., Structural Engineering, Virginia Tech University **Current organization:** Baxter Health Care Corp. **Title:** Senior Principal Engineer **Type of organization:** Manufacturing **Major product:** Medication **Area of distribution:** International **Expertise:** Automation and projects **Hob./spts.:** Golf, computers, construction projects **SIC code:** 28 **Address:** Baxter Healthcare Corp., 250 Rd. 144 Km 20.6, Jayuya, PR 00664 **E-mail:** pablo_f_gomez@baxter.com

GOMEZ-MANCILLA, BALTAZAR
Industry: Pharmaceuticals **Born:** September 4, 1957, Toluca, Mexico **Univ./degree:** M.D., U.A.E.M, Mexico, 1982; Ph.D.; Laval University, Quebec, Canada **Current organization:** Pharmacia Corp. **Title:** Director, Clinical Genomics and Biobanking **Type of organization:** Manufacturing, distributing **Major product:** Pharmaceuticals **Area of distribution:** International **Expertise:** Research, pharmacogenomics **Published works:** 40 publications **Affiliations:** A.A.N. **Hob./spts.:** Motorcycles, scuba diving, running **SIC code:** 28 **Address:** Pharmacia Corp., 526 Jasper St., Kalamazoo, MI 49007 **E-mail:** baltazar.gomez-mancilla@pharmacia.com

GONZALEZ, EDGAR S.
Industry: Food **Born:** December 3, 1954, Peru **Univ./degree:** B.S.C.E., Peru **Current organization:** Nellson Nutraceutical **Title:** Sanitation manager **Type of organization:** Manufacturer **Major product:** Nutrition bars **Area of distribution:** National **Expertise:** Food safety **Hob./spts.:** Soccer, guitar **SIC code:** 20 **Address:** Nellson Nutraceutical, 5801 Ayala Ave., Irwindale, CA 91706 **E-mail:** arequipaedgar@yahoo.com **Web address:** www.nellsonni.com

GONZALEZ, RICARDO F.
Industry: Automotive **Born:** April 21, 1960, Matamoros, Mexico **Univ./degree:** B.S., Technical Institute, Mexico **Current organization:** Summit Polymers Inc. **Title:** Injection Molding Manager **Type of organization:** Manufacturing **Major product:** Custom molding **Area of distribution:** International **Expertise:** Engineering, consulting, manufacturing (Lean) **Hob./spts.:** Baseball **SIC code:** 30 **Address:** Summit Polymers Inc., 5845 S. Padre Island Hwy., Brownsville, TX 78521 **E-mail:** rgonzale@summitpolymers.com

GONZÁLEZ, WANDA I.
Industry: Chemicals **Born:** October 27, 1955, Ponce, Puerto Rico **Univ./degree:** B.S., Chemical Engineering, University of Puerto Rico, 1979 **Current organization:** ISP-Freetown Fine Chemicals, Inc. **Title:** Site General Manager **Type of organization:** Manufacturing **Major product:** Amphetamines, suntan lotion, skin care products, dyes for photos and inkjet printers **Area of distribution:** International **Expertise:** Producing environmentally safe products, operations, management **Affiliations:** A.I.C.H.E.; Greater Four River United Way **Hob./spts.:** Family, theatre, ballet, reading **SIC code:** 28 **Address:** ISP-Freetown Fine Chemicals, Inc., 238 S. Main St., Assonet, MA 02702 **E-mail:** wgonzalez@ispcorp.com **Web address:** www.ispcorp.com

GORGY, DIANE L.
Industry: Healthcare products **Univ./degree:** M.S., Industrial Engineering, New Jersey Institute of Technology, 1984 **Current organization:** Johnson & Johnson Consumer Products Co. **Title:** Project Manager, Contract Manufacturing **Type of organization:** Manufacturing **Major product:** Healthcare and personal care products, cosmetics **Area of distribution:** International **Expertise:** Contract project and account management **Hob./spts.:** Antiques **SIC code:** 28 **Address:** Johnson & Johnson Consumer Products Co., 199 Grandview Rd., Skillman, NJ 08558 **E-mail:** dgorgy1@cpcus.jnj.com

GORTAREZ, SERGIO F.
Industry: Metals **Born:** April 1, 1980, Mexicali, Mexico **Current organization:** All Metals Bar Grinding, Inc. **Title:** President **Type of organization:** Processing plant **Major product:** Centerless grind metal round products **Area of distribution:** National **Expertise:** Marketing and sales **Hob./spts.:** Basketball, golf **SIC code:** 34 **Address:** All Metals Bar Grinding, Inc., 7625 E. Rosecrans Ave., #10-11, Paramount, CA 90723 **E-mail:** allmetalsgrinding@comcast.net

GOTTSCHALK, SHELIA
Industry: Printing **Born:** October 26, 1960, Laurent, France **Univ./degree:** B.S., Human Resources, MidAmerica Nazarene University, 1996 **Current organization:** Hallmark Cards Inc. **Title:** Technical Quality Planner II **Type of organization:** Manufacturing **Major product:** Printing, social expression **Area of distribution:** National **Expertise:** Quality, 2D and 3D displays **Hob./spts.:** Softball **SIC code:** 27 **Address:** Hallmark Cards Inc., 2501 McGee St., Kansas City, MO 64141-6580 **E-mail:** sgotts1@hallmark.com **Web address:** www.hallmark.com

GOVARDHAN, SUBODH M.
Industry: Aerospace **Born:** October 29, 1965, Indore, India **Univ./degree:** Ph.D., Materials Engineering, Auburn University, 1996 **Current organization:** Eaton Corp. **Title:** Senior Manufacturing Engineer **Type of organization:** Manufacturing **Major**

product: Aerospace fluid conveying systems; connectors, hose assemblies **Area of distribution:** International **Expertise:** Welding, brazing, metallurgy, engineering **Published works:** 2 journal articles, 10 conferences **Affiliations:** American Welding Society **SIC code:** 37 **Address:** Eaton Corp., 300 S.East Ave., Jackson, MI 49203 **E-mail:** subodhmgovardhan@eaton.com

GRAVES, AARON L.
Industry: Aluminum **Title:** IPS Supervisor **Type of organization:** Manufacturing **Major product:** Pre-cast refractory shapes **Expertise:** Problem resolution **SIC code:** 34 **Address:** Permatech Inc., 911 E. Elm St., Graham, NC 27253 **E-mail:** aaron.graves@permatech.net **Web address:** www.permatech.net

GREEN, RICHARD B.
Industry: Sculpture, design **Born:** April 18, 1946, Barrie, Ontario, Canada **Univ./degree:** A.O.C.A., Ontario College, 1969 **Current organization:** Richard Green Sculptures **Title:** Owner **Type of organization:** Manufacturing **Major product:** Sculpture **Area of distribution:** International **Expertise:** Bronze sculpture **Honors/awards:** Anne and Jim Goodnight Award of Excellence; **Published works:** Works in permanent collections of Coldwell Banker and numerous private collections; numerous articles **Affiliations:** Cary Visual Arts; Triangle Artists Group; Member, Sculptor Society of Canada; International Sculpture Center; Fine Arts League of Cary; Rotary Club; Originated and organized Muskoka Autumn Studio Tour **Hob./spts.:** Motorcycling, boating **SIC code:** 39 **Address:** 418 Warren Ave., Cary, NC 27511 **E-mail:** richardgreensculpture@msn.com **Web address:** www.richardgreensculpture.com

GRIBBLE, LOWELL L.
Industry: Professional Service **Born:** July 2, 1910, Aurora, Oregon **Univ./degree:** B.S., Liberal Arts, Willamet University, Salem, Oregon **Current organization:** Ultrasonic Predictable Maintenance **Title:** President **Type of organization:** Problem solving **Major product:** The Ffudic System **Area of distribution:** International **Published works:** Articles **Hob./spts.:** Spending time with family, grandchildren, golf **SIC code:** 36 **Address:** Ultrasonic Predictable Maintenance, 340 Gilmore St., Heppner, OR 97836

GRIFFIN, RICHARD C.
Industry: Refractories **Born:** May 1, 1953, Grantha Lincoln Shire, England **Univ./degree:** M.S., Ceramic Science Engineering, Rutgers University, 1990 **Current organization:** Minteq International Inc. **Title:** Senior Research & Development Engineer **Type of organization:** Manufacturing **Major product:** Refractory materials **Area of distribution:** International **Expertise:** Product research **Affiliations:** A.C.S.; Iron & Steel Society **Hob./spts.:** Coaching soccer and baseball **SIC code:** 39 **Address:** Minteq International Inc., 640 N. 13th St., Easton, PA 18042 **E-mail:** richard.griffin@mineralstech.com

GRIGORE, VIORICA
Industry: Nutraceutical **Born:** June 10, 1950 Liteni, Romania **Univ./degree:** M.S., University of Romania, 1978 **Current organization:** J.W.S. Delavau Co., Inc. **Title:** Chemist **Type of organization:** Manufacturing **Major product:** Vitamins **Area of distribution:** International **Expertise:** Quality control chemist **Affiliations:** A.S.C.P. **Hob./spts.:** Hiking, physical fitness **SIC code:** 28 **Address:** J.W.S. Delavau Co., Inc., 10101 Roosevelt Blvd., Philadelphia, PA 19154-2105 **E-mail:** vgrigore@delavav.com

GRIMES, DEBRA R.
Industry: Consumer product design/development **Born:** October 16, 1970, Oakland, California **Current organization:** Coit Road Incubator **Title:** President/Chief Operating Officer **Type of organization:** Manufacturing/recreational helmets and insoles **Major product:** Manufacturing, consumer product design, development, helmets **Area of distribution:** International **Expertise:** Engineering, administration, management **Honors/awards:** Multiple patent holder **Affiliations:** Founder, President, Chief Operating Officer, Team Wendy, Inc. and Perfect Impressions, Inc., Cleveland Heights; Founder, Donor, National Helmets for Disabled Children and Adults; A.S.T.M.; S.P.E.; S.A.E. **Hob./spts.:** Flyfishing, travel, sports **SIC code:** 30 **Address:** Coit Road Incubator, 12819 Coit Road, Cleveland Heights, OH 44108 **E-mail:** debbie@teamwendy.com **Web address:** www.teamwendy.com

GRINDE, JAMES E.
Industry: Transportation **Born:** January 31, 1948, South Dakota **Univ./degree:** B.S., Math and Physics, Augustana College, South Dakota, 1971 **Current organization:** QAI Precision Products **Title:** VP Engineering **Type of organization:** Manufacturing/importation **Major product:** Suspension design and components, off road vehicles **Area of distribution:** International **Expertise:** Product development/design **Affiliations:** S.A.E.; A.S.M.E.; A.S.I.M.A. **Hob./spts.:** Boating **SIC code:** 37 **Address:** QAI Precision Products, 21730 Hanover Ave., Lakeville, MN 55044 **E-mail:** jgrinde@qual.net

GRINDROD, PAUL
Industry: Food **Born:** April 5, 1925, Oconomowoc, Wisconsin **Univ./degree:** Ph.D., Chemical Engineering, University of Wisconsin at Madison **Title:** Principal Scientist, Oscar Mayer/Kraft (Retired) **Type of organization:** Manufacturing, distribution, research **Major product:** Packaged retail meats **Area of distribution:** International **Expertise:** Packaging, research and development **Published works:** 31 patents **Hob./spts.:** Skiing, biking **SIC code:** 20 **Address:** 4221 Esch Lane, Madison, WI 53704-4287 **E-mail:** grinderski@aol.com

GROSHEK, SCOTT M.
Industry: Chemicals **Univ./degree:** M.S., University of Wisconsin, 1999 **Current organization:** Rayovac Corp. **Title:** Senior Project Engineer **Type of organization:** Manufacturing **Major product:** Alkaline batteries **Area of distribution:** International **Expertise:** Capital projects **SIC code:** 28 **Address:** Rayovac Corp., 100 Rayovac Ct., Fennimore, WI 53809 **E-mail:** groshek@rayovac.com

GROSS, JEFFREY A.
Industry: Dies & Castings **Born:** January 13, 1954, Sharon, Pennsylvania **Univ./degree:** B.S. Candidate, Mechanical Engineering, Youngstown State University **Current organization:** Ellwood Engineered Castings **Title:** Journeyman Millwright/Electrician **Type of organization:** Manufacturing **Major product:** Automotive stamping dies/ingot molds **Area of distribution:** National **Expertise:** Mechanical and electrical industrial maintenance **SIC code:** 27 **Address:** 1463 George St. Ext., Hermitage, PA 16148-1956 **E-mail:** jag11354@hotmail.com

GROSVENOR, STEVEN
Industry: Optical media **Born:** January 18, 1960, Scranton, Pennsylvania **Univ./degree:** A.A., Engineering, Lincoln Tech, Pennsylvania, 1980 **Current organization:** Cinram **Title:** Senior Director of Manufacturing **Type of organization:** Manufacturing **Major product:** CDs and DVDs **Area of distribution:** International **Expertise:** Manufacturing **Affiliations:** Video Software Dealers Association; Society of Plastics Engineers **Hob./spts.:** Hunting, fishing, computers **SIC code:** 36 **Address:** Cinram, 1400 E. Lackawanna St., Olyphant, PA 18448 **E-mail:** steve.grosvenor@cinram.com

GRUNLEE, JOHN C.
Industry: Batteries **Born:** December 9, 1959 **Univ./degree:** B.S., Mechanical Engineering, Illinois Institute of Technology, 1985 **Current organization:** Duracell/The Gillette Co. **Title:** Project Engineering Manager **Type of organization:** Manufacturing **Major product:** Batteries **Area of distribution:** International **Expertise:** Manufacturing and systems engineering, team leadership **Affiliations:** S.A.E.; I.I.E. **Hob./spts.:** Sailing **SIC code:** 36 **Address:** Duracell/The Gillette Co., 208 Copper Top Lane N.E., Cleveland, TN 37312 **E-mail:** jgrunlee@bellsouth.net

GUERRA, ALBERT
Industry: Electronics **Born:** May 28, 1961, Torino, Italy **Univ./degree:** B.S., Nuclear Engineering, IT IS - GB Pininfarina, Italy, 1980 **Current organization:** International Rectifier **Title:** Director of Business Unit Appliance Products **Type of organization:** Manufacturing **Major product:** Semiconductors **Area of distribution:** International **Expertise:** Engineering, management, business development **Hob./spts.:** Classical music, tennis, jogging **SIC code:** 36 **Address:** International Rectifier, 222 Kansas St., El Segundo, CA 90245 **E-mail:** aguerra1@irs.com

GULER, FATIH
Industry: Commercial electronics **Born:** May 13, 1957, Turkey **Univ./degree:** M.A., University of Turkey, 1984 **Current organization:** Arichell Technologies, Inc. **Title:** Vice-President of Engineering **Type of organization:** Design and manufacturing **Major product:** Hydraulic controls **Area of distribution:** International **Expertise:** Engineering **Published works:** Patents **Affiliations:** International Who's Who **Hob./spts.:** Woodworking **SIC code:** 35 **Address:** Arichell Technologies, Inc., 55 Border St., West Newton, MA 02465 **E-mail:** fatihg@arichell.com

GUMBS SR., RODNEY A.
Industry: Electronics **Born:** July 25, 1956, Perth Amboy, New Jersey **Univ./degree:** A.A., Electronics, San Joaquin Delta College **Current organization:** Photronics Inc. **Title:** Senior Data Prep Technician **Type of organization:** Manufacturing **Major product:** Photo mask making **Area of distribution:** International **Expertise:** Photo mask making for the semiconductor industry **Hob./spts.:** Golf, tennis **SIC code:** 36 **Address:** Photronics Inc., 15 Secor Rd., Brookfield, CT 06804 **E-mail:** rodneygumbs@sbcglobal.net

GUSTAFSON, FREDERICK A.
Industry: Pharmaceutical **Born:** August 22, 1938, Melrose Park, Illinois **Univ./degree:** B.S., Chemistry, Biology, University of Illinois; M.B.A., Loyola University **Current organization:** Abbott Laboratories **Title:** Vice President, Corporate Regulatory Affairs **Type of organization:** Manufacturing **Major product:** Prescription drugs and devices **Area of distribution:** International **Expertise:** Regulatory affairs **Affiliations:** Lifetime Member, Parental Drug Association **Hob./spts.:** Computers, reading, dogs, sports

SIC code: 28 **Address:** 28532 N. Skycrest Dr., Ivanhoe, IL 60060 **E-mail:** gandggus@comcast.net

GUTIERREZ, EDMO
Industry: Construction **Born:** August 3, 1956, Monterrey, Mexico **Univ./degree:** M.B.A., Monterrey Tech Institute, 1986; M.S., International Management, IPADE, 1989 **Current organization:** Cemex Inc./Kosmos Cement Co. **Title:** Plant Manager **Type of organization:** Manufacturing **Major product:** Cement **Area of distribution:** International **Expertise:** International management, engineering **Affiliations:** P.C.A.; A.C.I. **Hob./spts.:** Equestrian sports **SIC code:** 32 **Address:** Cemex Inc./Kosmos Cement Co., 15301 Dixie Hwy., Louisville, KY 40272 **E-mail:** edmo.gutierrez@cemex.com

GUYER, KEITH G.
Industry: Trade show exhibits **Born:** Boston, Massachusetts **Univ./degree:** B.S., Nicholas College, 1985 **Current organization:** Access TCA, Inc. **Title:** Senior Account Executive **Type of organization:** Manufacturing/marketing **Major product:** Design, production and management of custom trade show exhibits, events, road shows and corporate demo centers **Area of distribution:** International **Expertise:** Marketing, sales **Affiliations:** I.E.A.; E.D.P.A. **SIC code:** 39 **Address:** Access TCA, Inc., 1 Main St., Whitinsville, MA 01588 **E-mail:** kguyer@accesstca-bos.com **Web address:** www.accesstca.com

GUZZI, JOSEPH
Industry: Aerospace **Born:** January 10, 1960, Pittsburgh, Pennsylvania **Univ./degree:** B.S.M.E., Point Park College, 1995 **Current organization:** Federal Express **Title:** Engineer **Type of organization:** Aircraft provider for delivery services **Major product:** Delivery services **Area of distribution:** International **Expertise:** Engineering **Published works:** United Airlines manuals, repair manuals for airbus aircraft **Affiliations:** A.S.M.E. **Hob./spts.:** Blues music, playing guitar and harmonica, car racing, bungee jumping, sky diving **SIC code:** 37 **Address:** Federal Express, 3502 South High School Rd., Indianapolis, IN 46280 **E-mail:** mafguzzi@ad.com

GVILLO, FREDRICK H.
Industry: Pharmaceuticals **Univ./degree:** B.S., Agriculture, Illinois State University, 1971 **Current organization:** Schering/Berlex Biosciences **Title:** Head Corporate Research Administrator **Type of organization:** Manufacturing/research **Major product:** Drugs, medicines **Area of distribution:** International **Expertise:** Administration **Affiliations:** Past Member, American Health Institute **SIC code:** 28 **Address:** Schering/Berlex Biosciences, 2600 Hilltop Dr., Richmond, CA 94806 **E-mail:** fred_gvillo@berlex.com

HAALAND, ANDREW C.
Industry: Aerospace **Born:** February 28, 1964, Chicago, Illinois **Univ./degree:** B.S., Chemical Engineering, University of California at Santa Barbara, 1986; M.B.A., Utah State University, 1996 **Current organization:** ATK Thiokol Propulsion **Title:** Manager, Propulsion Technology Business Development **Type of organization:** Manufacturing **Major product:** Rocket motors **Area of distribution:** International **Expertise:** New business development **Published works:** 30+ articles, 3 patents **Affiliations:** American Institute of Aeronautics and Astronautics **Hob./spts.:** Woodworking, skiing, restoring old cars **SIC code:** 37 **Address:** 1665 Creekside Lane, Park City, UT 84098 **E-mail:** andrew.haaland@atk.com **Web address:** www.atk.com

HAAS, JAMES R.
Industry: Oilfield **Born:** September 13, 1950, New Braunfels, Texas **Current organization:** Vetco Gray Inc. **Title:** Shipping/Receiving Supervisor **Type of organization:** Manufacturing **Major product:** Subsea/surface/tubular oilfield equipment **Area of distribution:** International **Expertise:** Inventory control management, logistics **Affiliations:** Energy Traffic Association **Hob./spts.:** Fishing, hunting **SIC code:** 35 **Address:** Vetco Gray Inc., 12221 N. Houston Rosslyn Rd., Houston, TX 77086 **E-mail:** jim.haas@vetco.com

HADLEY, JOHN L.
Industry: Batteries **Born:** February 19, 1952, Schenectady, New York **Univ./degree:** B.S., Chemistry, Ursinus College, 1974 **Current organization:** Rayovac Corp. **Title:** Alkaline Technical Manager **Type of organization:** Manufacturing **Major product:** Batteries **Area of distribution:** International **Expertise:** Product engineering and marketing **Honors/awards:** ASQ Certified Quality Engineer, 1985 **Affiliations:** A.N.S.I. C-18 Standards Committee; I.E.C. TC-35 Standards Committee **Hob./spts.:** Cycling, home brewing **SIC code:** 36 **Address:** Rayovac Corp., 601 Rayovac Dr., Madison, WI 53711-2497 **E-mail:** hadley@rayovac.com

HAFERKORN, GARY A.
Industry: Seafood **Born:** March 19, 1958, Bellingham, Washington **Univ./degree:** B.S., Biology, Western Washington University, 1981 **Current organization:** Trident Seafoods Corp. **Title:** Corporate Quality Assurance Manager **Type of organization:** Manufacturing **Major product:** Fresh and frozen seafood products **Area of distribution:** International **Expertise:** Quality assurance for the Northwest region; Latin American import/export liaison; training and presentations **Affiliations:** Institute of Food Technologies **SIC code:** 20 **Address:** Trident Seafoods Corp., 2825 Roeder Ave., Bellingham, WA 98225-2053 **E-mail:** garyh@tridentseafoods.com

HAHN, PETER S.
Industry: Pharmaceuticals **Born:** Sept. 1, 1958, South Korea **Current organization:** Ross Products Division/Abbott Laboratories **Title:** Senior Process Engineer **Type of organization:** Manufacturing **Major product:** Pediatric and medical nutritionals **Area of distribution:** National **Expertise:** Aseptic engineering and processing **Honors/awards:** Abbott Lab Engineering Excellence Award, 1999 **Affiliations:** President of the Korean Catholic Community, Columbus, Ohio **Hob./spts.:** Tennis, fishing **SIC code:** 28 **Address:** Ross Products Division/Abbott Laboratories, 585 Cleveland Ave., Columbus, OH 42315 **E-mail:** peter.hahn@abbott.com

HALE, CECIL H.
Industry: Chemicals **Born:** June 12, 1919, Kilgore, Texas **Univ./degree:** Ph.D., Physical Chemistry, Purdue University, 1948 **Current organization:** Sachem, Inc. **Title:** Board Director **Type of organization:** Manufacturing **Major product:** Tetramethylammonium hydroxide **Area of distribution:** International **Expertise:** Chemical research and development **Published works:** 6 patents, 8 articles **Hob./spts.:** Bridge, tennis, UTX athletics **SIC code:** 28 **Address:** Sachem, Inc., 821 Woodward St., Austin, TX 78704

HALL, DAVID A.
Industry: Fluid controls **Born:** January 10, 1959, Kirkland, Missouri **Current organization:** DynaQuip Controls **Title:** Plant Manager **Type of organization:** Manufacturing **Major product:** Ball valves/automated ball valves **Area of distribution:** International **Expertise:** Plant/program management **Hob./spts.:** Golf **SIC code:** 34 **Address:** DynaQuip Controls, 10 Harris Industrial Park, St. Clair, MO 63077 **E-mail:** dave@dynaquip.com

HALL, GAIL D.
Industry: Chemicals **Born:** January 6, 1954, Glen Falls, New York **Univ./degree:** B.S., Marketing & Management, Siena College, New York, 1988 **Current organization:** ChemStation New England **Title:** Chemical Management Specialist **Type of organization:** Manufacturing **Major product:** Bulk chemicals **Area of distribution:** National **Expertise:** Marketing, sales **Honors/awards:** Dean's List, Adirondack Community College; Presidential Scholar, Siena College; top sales for ChemStation New England, 1996-2002; National Sales Recognition, Corp. ChemStation; National Sales Award, Corp ChemStation **Hob./spts.:** Biking, kayaking, snowshoeing **SIC code:** 28 **Address:** 1496 John Fitch Blvd., South Windsor, CT 06074 **E-mail:** gdh33@aol.com

HALL, SCOTT DAVID
Industry: Heating, air-conditioning and refrigeration **Born:** January 7, 1953, LaCrosse, Wisconsin **Univ./degree:** B.S., Education, University of Wisconsin at LaCrosse, 1976 **Current organization:** Trane (American Standard) **Title:** Manager, Trane OEM Compressors **Type of organization:** Manufacturing **Major product:** Refrigeration compressors **Area of distribution:** International **Expertise:** Sales, marketing **Published works:** 2 articles, 1 U.S. Patent **Affiliations:** A.S.H.R.A.E. **Hob./spts.:** Family, reading, travel, New York Yankees fan **SIC code:** 35 **Address:** Trane (American Standard), 3600 Pammel Creek Rd., La Crosse, WI 54601 **E-mail:** shall@trane.com **Web address:** www.trane.com

HALLADAY, HENRY E.
Industry: Aerospace **Born:** February 21, 1939, Minneapolis, Minnesota **Univ./degree:** B.S.E.E.; M.S.E.E.; Ph.D., Electrical Engineering, University of Minnesota **Current organization:** Boeing **Title:** Senior Technical Fellow **Type of organization:** Manufacturing/research & development **Major product:** Aerospace systems **Area of distribution:** International **Expertise:** Electrical/electronic engineering **Hob./spts.:** New technology, network devices, digital video **SIC code:** 37 **Address:** 3230 110th Ave. S.E., Bellevue, WA 98004 **E-mail:** henry.e.halladay@boeing.com

HALLDORSSON, BRYNJAR
Industry: Printed circuit boards **Born:** June 15, 1947, Keflavik, Iceland **Univ./degree:** University of Iceland **Current organization:** American Testing Corp./Perfectest **Title:** Director of Engineering **Type of organization:** Manufacturing **Major product:** Test equipment **Area of distribution:** International **Expertise:** Engineering **Hob./spts.:** Family, nature walks, licensed pilot **SIC code:** 36 **Address:** American Testing Corp./Perfectest, 18348 Redmond Way, Redmond, WA 98052 **E-mail:** bhalldorsson@perfectest.com

HAMILTON, BELINDA S.
Industry: Textiles **Born:** May 7, 1952, Springfield, Missouri **Univ./degree:** B.S., Business, University of Missouri, 1976 **Current organization:** W-C Designs **Title:** Senior Vice President/Sales Manager **Type of organization:** Manufacturing/design **Major product:** Table linen **Area of distribution:** National **Expertise:** Advertising,

marketing, sales **Hob./spts.:** Horseback riding, tennis **SIC code:** 22 **Address:** 29391 Christiana Way, Laguna, CA 92677

HAMILTON, KEVIN S.
Industry: X-ray technologies **Born:** May 26, 1955, Omaha, Nebraska **Univ./degree:** B.S., Engineering, Ohio Institute of Technology, 1979; Certified Industrial Radiographer **Current organization:** Yxlon International, Inc. **Title:** Engineer, Application, Radiation Safety Coordinator **Type of organization:** Manufacturing/services **Major product:** Non-destructive testing equipment/industrial x-rays **Area of distribution:** International **Expertise:** Engineering, radiation safety **SIC code:** 38 **Address:** 633 Lakewood Blvd., Akron, OH 44314 **E-mail:** kevin.hamilton@yxlon.com

HAMMOND, DONALD E.
Industry: Metals **Born:** July 27, 1949, Martinsburg, West Virginia **Current organization:** CMC Sheet Metal **Title:** Executive Vice President **Type of organization:** Contractor **Major product:** Commercial sheet metal fabrication and installation **Area of distribution:** Maryland **Expertise:** Administration **Affiliations:** M.S.A., Washington Building Congress **Hob./spts.:** Golf, race cars, antique cars **SIC code:** 33 **Address:** CMC Sheet Metal, 1208 Marblewood Ave., Capitol Heights, MD 20743 **E-mail:** dhammond@cmcsheetmetal.com

HANEY, MICHAEL P.
Industry: Automotive/machinery **Born:** September 9, 1960, Rochester, New York **Univ./degree:** A.S., Electrical Mechanical Technology **Current organization:** Calvary Automation Systems **Title:** Sr. Project Manager **Type of organization:** Manufacturing **Major product:** Automated assembly systems **Area of distribution:** International **Expertise:** Automation systems **Hob./spts.:** Hockey, volleyball, baseball, tennis **SIC code:** 35 **Address:** Calvary Automation Systems, 45 Hendrix Rd., West Henrietta, NY 14586 **E-mail:** mhaney@calvauto.com

HANS, KARL
Industry: Agriculture **Born:** October 20, 1956, Fort Wayne, Indiana **Univ./degree:** A.S., Digital Electronics, Ivy Tech **Current organization:** Murray Equipment Inc. **Title:** Control Engineer **Type of organization:** OEM **Major product:** Fertilizer and chemical batching systems **Area of distribution:** National **Expertise:** PLC Programming and electrical schematic creation **Published works:** Trade journals **Hob./spts.:** Restoring classic cars and hot rods **SIC code:** 38 **Address:** Murray Equipment Inc., 2515 Charleston Place, Ft. Wayne, IN 46808 **E-mail:** khans@murrayequipment.com **Web address:** www.murrayequipment.com

HANS, MARK L.
Industry: Tool and die **Born:** July 4, 1950, Salem, Ohio **Univ./degree:** B.S., Accounting, Kent State University, Ohio, 1972 **Current organization:** TruCut Inc. **Title:** Application Engineer **Type of organization:** Manufacturing **Major product:** Stamping dies **Area of distribution:** Ohio **Expertise:** Figure process and estimating **Affiliations:** P.M.A. **Hob./spts.:** Family, golf **SIC code:** 35 **Address:** TruCut Inc., P.O. Box 338, Sebring, OH 44672-0338 **E-mail:** mhans@trucut.com

HANSEN, NORM B.
Industry: Agriculture **Born:** March 14, 1953, Fresno, California **Univ./degree:** Licensed Electrician, Sate of California; Licensed California Contractor, Fresno City College, 1974 **Current organization:** Anderson Clayton Corp. **Title:** Automation Engineer **Type of organization:** Cotton ginning **Major product:** Cotton storage, cotton marketing and cotton bales **Area of distribution:** National **Expertise:** PLC and SCADA Systems, Automation Engineering **Affiliations:** California Cotton Ginners Association **Hob./spts.:** Skiing, scuba diving **SIC code:** 22 **Address:** Anderson Clayton Corp., 7060 N. Marks, Fresno, CA 93711 **E-mail:** normh@andersonclayton.com **Web address:** www.andersonclayton.com

HANSON, CALBERT D.
Industry: Chemical **Born:** August 3, 1970, Jamaica **Univ./degree:** B.S., Mechanical Engineering, University of the West Indies, 1990; M.B.A., Florida International University, 2002 **Current organization:** Jamalco **Title:** Raw Material Superintendent **Type of organization:** Manufacturing **Major product:** Alumina **Area of distribution:** International **Expertise:** Engineering **Affiliations:** J.I.E. **Hob./spts.:** Lawn tennis **SIC code:** 28 **Address:** Jamalco, P.O. Box 28528, Miami, FL 33102-8528 **E-mail:** calberthanson@hotmail.com

HANSON, DAVID L.
Industry: Automotive **Born:** August 13, 1968, Dansville, New York **Univ./degree:** B.S.M.E.; Alfred University, 1990 **Current organization:** Trico Products **Title:** Director of Engineering **Type of organization:** Manufacturing, Research and Development **Major product:** Windshield wiper systems **Area of distribution:** International **Expertise:** Automotive R&D, Product Development, Manufacturing, Project Management and Strategic Planning **Hob./spts.:** Automotive design, computers, football, basketball, hockey, fishing and touring/experiencing different cultures **SIC code:** 37 **Address:** Trico Products, 3255 W. Hamlin Rd., Rochester Hills, MI 48309-3231 **E-mail:** dave.hanson@tricoproducts.com

HAROONI, SOLAIMAN M.
Industry: Electronics **Born:** October 2, 1971, Kabul, Afghanistan **Univ./degree:** B.S.E.E., San Jose State University, 1996 **Current organization:** Amplifiers/National Semiconductor Corp. **Title:** Senior Product Engineer **Type of organization:** R&D, manufacturing **Major product:** Semiconductors **Area of distribution:** International **Expertise:** Engineering **Affiliations:** I.E.E.E. **Hob./spts.:** Travel, basketball **SIC code:** 36 **Address:** Amplifiers/National Semiconductor Corp., 2900 Semiconductor Dr., M/S C2-693, Santa Clara, CA 95051 **E-mail:** solaiman.m.harooni@nsc.com

HAROUNA, ABDOU
Industry: Aerospace **Born:** January 1, 1968 **Univ./degree:** B.Tech., Agricultural Engineering, Federal University of Technology, Nigeria; M.B.A., Averett University, 2004 **Current organization:** Easton Aerospace **Title:** Supply Chain Manager **Type of organization:** Manufacturing **Major product:** Aerospace fluid conveyance products **Area of distribution:** National **Expertise:** Operations management over purchasing, production planning and shipping, strategic sourcing **Honors/awards:** Cavalier of Merit for Outstanding Service to His Country, President of Nigeria, 1993 **Published works:** University thesis on genetic engineering (published in Nigeria) **Affiliations:** Association of Operations Management; A.P.I.C.S.; Council of Supply Chain Management Professionals **Hob./spts.:** Black Belt in Tae Kwon Do, reading world politics **SIC code:** 38 **Address:** Easton Aerospace, 2500 W. Argyle St., Jackson, MI 49202-1845 **E-mail:** abdouxharouna@eaton.com **Web address:** www.eaton.com

HARPER JR., WILLIAM L.
Industry: Plumbing products **Born:** February 12, 1958, Washington D.C. **Univ./degree:** B.B.A., Administration/International Affairs, Pittsburgh State College, 1981 **Current organization:** BrassCraft Mfg. Co. **Title:** Director of Service Parts and Development **Type of organization:** Manufacturing/distributor **Major product:** Water supply parts and components **Area of distribution:** International **Expertise:** Marketing, sales **Honors/awards:** Patent **Hob./spts.:** Reading, football **SIC code:** 34 **Address:** BrassCraft Mfg. Co., 39600 Orchard Hill Place, Novi, MI 48375 **E-mail:** wharper@brasscrafthq.com

HARRIS, EDWIN D.
Industry: High fructose corn syrup **Born:** December 2, 1953, Childress, Texas **Univ./degree:** B.S., Electrical Engineering, Texas Tech University, 2002 **Current organization:** Cargill **Title:** Project Engineer **Type of organization:** Manufacturing **Major product:** High fructose corn syrup **Area of distribution:** National **Expertise:** Engineering **Affiliations:** I.E.E.E. **Hob./spts.:** Snow and water skiing **SIC code:** 20 **Address:** Cargill, 129 Floyd, Dumas, TX 79029 **E-mail:** eddie_harris@cargill.com

HARTMAN, FREDERICK R.
Industry: Medical **Born:** December 8, 1948, Lebanon, Pennsylvania **Univ./degree:** B.S., Electrical Engineering, DeVry Institute of Technology, Chicago, 1970 **Current organization:** Johnson & Johnson **Title:** Principal Engineer **Type of organization:** Manufacturing **Major product:** Medical devices **Area of distribution:** International **Expertise:** Electrical engineering **Published works:** Article in Fortune Magazine **Affiliations:** I.E.E.E.; I.S.A. **Hob./spts.:** Pilot, skiing, reading **SIC code:** 38 **Address:** Johnson & Johnson, 199 Grandview Rd., SG-240, Skillman, NJ 08558 **E-mail:** fhartma@cpcus.jnj.com

HATCH, KENNETH F.
Industry: Industrial controls **Born:** September 27, 1939, Oakland, California **Univ./degree:** Ph.D., Electrical Engineering, Massachusetts Institute of Technology, 1971 **Current organization:** KLA-Tencor **Title:** Principal Engineer **Type of organization:** Manufacturing **Major product:** Industrial controls **Area of distribution:** International **Expertise:** Engineering **Affiliations:** Past Member, I.E.E.E. **Hob./spts.:** Amateur radio, golf, pool **SIC code:** 36 **Address:** KLA-Tencor, 1 Technology Dr., Milpitas, CA 95035 **E-mail:** k_hatch@kla-tencor.com

HAUCK, KATHRYN M.
Industry: HVAC **Born:** August 19, 1959, Milwaukee, Wisconsin **Univ./degree:** B.S., Engineering, University of Missouri, 1987 **Current organization:** Armstrong Air Conditioning **Title:** Marketing Manager **Type of organization:** Manufacturing **Major product:** HVAC **Area of distribution:** National **Expertise:** Engineering and marketing **Published works:** Poems, articles **Affiliations:** P.M.I.; A.SH.R.A.E.; American Society of Gas Engineers; President, Gateway Chapter St. Louis **Hob./spts.:** Equestrian, photography **SIC code:** 34 **Address:** Armstrong Air Conditioning, 421 Monroe, Bellevue, OH 44811 **E-mail:** kathrynn.hauck@aac-inc.com **Web address:** www.aac-inc.com

HAWKINS, RICHARD A.
Industry: Consumer goods/automotive/lasers **Born:** May 8, 1960, Sacramento, California **Univ./degree:** B.S.E.E., California Polytechnic Institute, 1996 **Current**

organization: OSRAM Opto-Semiconductor **Title:** Electronic Design Engineer **Type of organization:** Manufacturing/R&D **Major product:** Light emitting diodes and organic LED's, IR devices **Area of distribution:** National **Expertise:** Electronic design engineering, system testing **Affiliations:** S.P.I.E.; Society of Information Displays; Society of Photonics **Hob./spts.:** Fly-fishing, camping walking **SIC code:** 36 **Address:** OSRAM Opto-Semiconductor, 3870 N. First St., San Jose, CA 95134 **E-mail:** rich.hawkins@osram-os.com

HAYES, KEN R.
Industry: Medical instruments **Univ./degree:** A.S., Design/Drafting, New England Tech, 1991 **Current organization:** Depuy a J&J Co. **Title:** Tool Designer **Type of organization:** Manufacturing **Major product:** Medical instruments **Area of distribution:** Massachusetts **Expertise:** Engineering **Affiliations:** A.S.M.E. **SIC code:** 38 **Address:** Depuy a J&J Co., 61 John Vertente Blvd., New Bedford, MA 02721

HAYES, MARY ESHBAUGH
Industry: Publishing **Born:** September 22, 1928, Rochester, New York **Univ./degree:** B.A., Syracuse University, New York, 1950 **Current organization:** The Aspen Times **Title:** Contributing Editor **Type of organization:** Newspaper publishing **Major product:** News **Area of distribution:** Colorado **Expertise:** Reporter, Columnist **Honors/awards:** Colorado Woman of the Year for Writing and Photography, 1987; Listed in Marquis Who's Who in America, Who's Who in the West, Who's Who in American Women and Who's Who in the Media **Published works:** Books, "Aspen Potpourri Cookbook" and "The Story of Aspen"' **Affiliations:** Board Member, A.H.S.; Board Member, Les Dames D'Aspen; C.P.W.; N.P.W. **Hob./spts.:** Swimming, cross-country skiing **SIC code:** 27 **Address:** The Aspen Times, 310 E. Main St., Aspen, CO 81611 **E-mail:** meh@sopris.net

HAYWARD, JR., THOMAS Z.
Industry: Fabricated metal **Univ./degree:** J.D., Northwestern University, 1965; M.B.A., University of Chicago, 1970 **Current organization:** TCR Corp. **Title:** Chairman/CEO/Esquire **Type of organization:** Manufacturing **Major product:** General heat treated and fabricated metal products **Area of distribution:** International **Published works:** Articles **Affiliations:** E.C.C.; A.B.A. **SIC code:** 33 **Address:** TCR Corp., 3703 S. Route 31, Crystal Lake, IL 60012-1412 **E-mail:** thayward@tcindustries.com

HEARD, L. DARRELL
Industry: Concrete **Born:** September 16, 1962, Oklahoma City, Oklahoma **Current organization:** Goddard Ready Mix Concrete Co., Inc. **Title:** Vice President, Administration **Type of organization:** Manufacturing **Major product:** Ready mix concrete - residential and commercial **Area of distribution:** Oklahoma **Expertise:** Administration - day to day operations **Hob./spts.:** Golf, lake sports **SIC code:** 32 **Address:** Goddard Ready Mix Concrete Co., Inc., 3101 N.E. Tenth St., Oklahoma City, OK 73117 **E-mail:** goddardc@aol.com

HEDRICK II, ROGER L.
Industry: Electronics **Born:** June 9, 1952, Fort Worth, Texas **Univ./degree:** B.S., Mechanical Engineering, General Motors Institute, 1975 **Current organization:** Kimball Electronics **Title:** Mechanical Engineer **Type of organization:** Manufacturing **Major product:** Printed circuit assemblies **Area of distribution:** International **Expertise:** Gauge and product design **Hob./spts.:** Bowling, golf, mission projects **SIC code:** 36 **Address:** Kimball Electronics, 9780 N. 900E, Dubois, IN 47527 **E-mail:** rhedrick@kimball.com

HEITZMAN, JO
Industry: Food service technology **Born:** April 8, 1961, Mt. Pleasant, Iowa **Univ./degree:** B.S., Food Science & Home Economics Education, Iowa State University, 1983 **Current organization:** Enodis **Title:** Global Account President, MacDonald's **Type of organization:** Manufacturing **Major product:** Food service equipment and technology **Area of distribution:** International **Expertise:** Account management **Honors/awards:** Outstanding Sales, Frymaster, 1998 **Published works:** 1 patent, conveyer microwave oven **Affiliations:** National Association of Food Service Equipment **Hob./spts.:** Gourmet cuisine **SIC code:** 35 **Address:** Enodis, 2227 Welbilt Blvd., Trinity, FL 34655

HELGET, BRUCE A.
Industry: Semiconductors **Born:** November 21, 1973, New Ulm, Minnesota **Univ./degree:** A.A., Southwestern College, 1995 **Current organization:** The Futurestar Corp. **Title:** Mechanical Designer **Type of organization:** Manufacturing **Major product:** Teflon flow meters **Area of distribution:** International **Expertise:** Engineering **Affiliations:** American Drafting & Design Association **Hob./spts.:** Motorcycling **SIC code:** 36 **Address:** The Futurestar Corp., 6529 Cecilia Circle, Minneapolis, MN 55439 **E-mail:** bhelget@futurestarcorp.com **Web address:** www.futurestarcorp.com

HELLARD, RANDY L.
Industry: Food **Born:** January 23, 1958, Mount Holly, North Carolina **Univ./degree:** Certified, Yarn Manufacturing, North Carolina Vocational Technical School, 1977 **Current organization:** Land O'Lakes Purina Feed **Title:** Manufacturing Supervisor **Type of organization:** Manufacturing **Major product:** Livestock feed **Area of distribution:** National **Expertise:** Scheduling, production **Affiliations:** Democratic Party of Georgia **Hob./spts.:** Fishing, golf **SIC code:** 20 **Address:** Land O'Lakes Purina Feed, 1125 Purina Dr., Gainesville, GA 30501 **E-mail:** rhellard@landolakes.com **Web address:** www.landolakes.com

HENDERSON, DAVID C.
Industry: Electronics/aviation **Born:** September 5, 1970, Gardenia, California **Current organization:** Southern Avionics Co., Inc. **Title:** Purchasing Manager **Type of organization:** OEM **Major product:** Non-directional radio beacons **Area of distribution:** International **Expertise:** Procurement **Affiliations:** Institute for Supply Management **Hob./spts.:** Fishing, tennis, writing **SIC code:** 36 **Address:** Southern Avionics Co., Inc., 5000 Belmont St., Beaumont, TX 77707 **E-mail:** davidchenderson@hotmail.com

HENDERSON, JOHN D. "DOUG"
Industry: Mechanical transport **Born:** August 17, 1946 **Univ./degree:** B. S., Engineering Technology **Current organization:** Thyssen Krupp Elevator Manufacturing, Inc. **Title:** Sr. Engineer **Type of organization:** Manufacturing, sales and service **Major product:** Elevator equipment **Area of distribution:** International **Expertise:** Engineering **Affiliations:** Air Force Veteran **SIC code:** 35 **Address:** P.O. Box 66, Middleton, TN 38052 **E-mail:** doug.henderson@thyssenkrupp.com **Web address:** www.thyssenkrupp.com

HENRICH, PATRICK J.
Industry: Food **Born:** January 23, 1961, Counsil Bluffs, Iowa **Current organization:** Well's Dairy **Title:** Sanitation Manager **Type of organization:** Manufacturing **Major product:** Ice cream **Area of distribution:** National **Expertise:** Sanitation **Hob./spts.:** Boating, coaching softball **SIC code:** 20 **Address:** Well's Dairy, 1191 18th St. S.W., P.O. Box 1310, Le Mars, IA 51031 **E-mail:** pjhenrich@bluebunny.com

HERBST, ROBERT J.
Industry: Waste water treatment **Born:** February 24, 1947, Oakland, California **Current organization:** Screen Lore Corp. **Title:** Project Manager **Type of organization:** Manufacturing **Major product:** Wastewater treatment equipment **Area of distribution:** National **Expertise:** Design and development of wastewater treatment technology **Affiliations:** W.Q.S. **Hob./spts.:** Fishing, motorcycles **SIC code:** 35 **Address:** Screen Lore Corp., 2345 S. Federal Blvd., Suite 160, Denver, CO 80219 **E-mail:** bobherbst@allwest.net

HERDLEIN, THOMAS A.
Industry: Metals **Current organization:** Allvac **Title:** Laboratory Supervisor **Type of organization:** Manufacturing **Major product:** Specialty metals **Area of distribution:** International **Expertise:** Laboratory management **Honors/awards:** "Recognition of Quality", Certified Engineer, 2006 **Affiliations:** A.S.T.M. **Hob./spts.:** Guitar **SIC code:** 33 **Address:** Allvac, 695 Ohio St., Lockport, NY 14094 **E-mail:** tomasherdlein@allvac.com **Web address:** www.allvac.com

HERING, ROBERT TIMOTHY
Industry: Electronics manufacturing **Born:** April 26, 1961, New Jersey **Spouse:** Kimberly **Married:** March 23, 1985 **Children:** William James **Univ./degree:** B.S., Electrical Engineering, Trenton State College, New Jersey, 1989; M.S., Engineering Management, Drexel University, Pennsylvania, 1996; Ph.D., Begin. Engineering Management, Stevens Institute of Technology, New Jersey, 2004 **Current organization:** Metrologic Instruments **Title:** Director of Manufacturing Operations and Global Service Training **Type of organization:** Design and Manufacturing **Major product:** Bar code scanning solutions for point of sale and industrial applications **Area of distribution:** International **Expertise:** Engineering management driving technological innovation thru automation, lean manufacturing principles and global service training **Affiliations:** Institute of Electrical and Electronics Engineers (IEEE Society), 12 years **Career accomplishments:** In his 4.5 year tenure, established a satellite NA manufacturing plant which produced 30% of all NA products; championed Lean Manufacturing initiatives which permitted condensing all NA manufacturing operations into one main facility; developed a strong Automation and Test group for enhancing reliability, increasing thruput and capacity; reduced overall direct labor and floorspace, for producing a set of world class bar code scanning products; and finally began deploying a strategy for Global Service Training along with internet based tools for real time service center field issue updates and means for rapid feedback to global production facilities **Hob./spts.:** Traveling with family, antiquing, sci-fi television and movies, business related reading **SIC code:** 36 **Address:** Metrologic Instruments, 90 Coles Rd., Blackwood, NJ 08012 **Phone:** (856)374-5539 **Fax:** (856)239-2293 **E-mail:** b.hering@metrologic.com **Web address:** www.metrologic.com

HIGDON, ALAN
Industry: Tobacco **Born:** April 16, 1956, Owensboro, Kentucky **Univ./degree:** B.A., University of Evansville, 1990; Dale Carnegie graduate, AIB/HACCP Certified, Kraut-

hammer International **Current organization:** Swedish Match North America **Title:** Production Process Manager **Type of organization:** Manufacturing **Major product:** Smokeless tobacco products **Area of distribution:** International **Expertise:** ISO 9001 and ISO 14001 (lead auditor), Lean Manufacturing, Continuous Improvement, Performance Management **Honors/awards:** United Way Ambassador, 1995; International Cultural Management Program **Affiliations:** Labor Management Executive, Negotiating Committee, Environmental, Safety and Quality Committees, S.M.N.A. **Hob./spts.:** Motor coach camping, golf, crossword puzzles, landscape gardening **SIC code:** 21 **Address:** Swedish Match North America, 1121 Industrial Dr., Owensboro, KY 42301 **E-mail:** alan.higdon@smna.com **Web address:** www.smna.com

HILBERT, LARRY D.
Industry: Automotive **Born:** October 4, 1948, Wooster, Ohio **Univ./degree:** B.S.M.E., Indiana Institute of Technology, 1971 **Current organization:** Motor Coach Industries **Title:** Manufacturing Engineer **Type of organization:** Manufacturing **Major product:** Bus parts **Area of distribution:** Loudonville, Ohio **Expertise:** Engineering, safety **Hob./spts.:** Sports cars **SIC code:** 37 **Address:** Motor Coach Industries, 520 N. Spring St., Loudonville, OH 44842 **E-mail:** larry.hilbert@mcicoach.com

HILL, NATHAN
Industry: Pharmaceuticals **Born:** January 18, 1969, Bedford, Indiana **Current organization:** Baxter Pharmaceutical Solutions **Title:** Formulation Supervisor **Type of organization:** Manufacturing **Major product:** Pharmaceuticals **Area of distribution:** International **Expertise:** Formulation **Hob./spts.:** Family, music, spectator sports **SIC code:** 28 **Address:** Baxter Pharmaceutical Solutions, P.O. Box 19, Harrodsburg, IN 47434 **E-mail:** nathan-hill@hotmail.com

HILL, ROBERT MICHAEL
Industry: Textiles **Born:** September 13, 1958, Greenville, South Carolina **Univ./degree:** Graduate Work, College of Charleston and Southern University **Current organization:** CMI Enterprises **Title:** Executive VP; Corporate Director of Design **Type of organization:** Manufacturing/distributing **Major product:** Fabrics, vinyls, leathers **Area of distribution:** International **Expertise:** Marketing, R&D, design **Affiliations:** T.M.G.; National Registry of Who's Who in Executives and Professionals **Hob./spts.:** Riding horses, painting, tennis, the outdoors **SIC code:** 22 **Address:** CMI Enterprises, 100 S. Sunrise Way, Suite A, PMB 720, Palm Springs, CA 92262 **E-mail:** fabhill@aol.com

HIRCHE, ROBERT E.
Industry: Scientific instrumentation **Univ./degree:** B.S., Geology, Marietta College, Ohio, 1977 **Current organization:** ICMAS **Title:** President/Founder **Type of organization:** Manufacturer's representative firm **Major product:** Scientific instrumentation for physicists, chemists and material scientists **Area of distribution:** Southern U.S. **Expertise:** Sales, sales management, product launch **Affiliations:** American Vacuum Society; Microscopy and Microanalysis **Hob./spts.:** Boy Scouts, fishing **SIC code:** 38 **Address:** ICMAS, 354 Glascock St., Alcoa, TN 37701 **E-mail:** bob@icmas.com

HIRSCHBURGER, WOLFGANG
Industry: Power tools **Born:** November 29, 1965, Reutlingen, Germany **Univ./degree:** M.S., Electrical Engineering, University of Stuttgart, Germany; M.B.A., Kellogg School of Management, Evanston, Illinois, 2002 **Current organization:** Robert Bosch Tool Corp. **Title:** Director of Engineering **Type of organization:** Manufacturing/engineering **Major product:** Power tools **Area of distribution:** International **Expertise:** Engineering, engineering management, cross cultural work experience; multilingual (English, German, French) **Hob./spts.:** Skiing, golf, glider piloting **SIC code:** 36 **Address:** Lueftestr 8, 72762 Reutlingen, Baden-Württemberg, Germany **E-mail:** maexken@gmx.de/wolfgang.hirschburger@de.bosch.com

HOANG, LOC B.
Industry: Electronics **Univ./degree:** B.S.E.E., University of California at Berkeley, 1988; M.S.E.E., San Jose State University, 1993 **Current organization:** Silicon Storage Technology, Inc. **Title:** Director of Memory Design **Type of organization:** Manufacturing, research and development **Major product:** Makers of SuperFlash® technology products, designing and marketing a diversified range of non-volatile memory solutions, flash memory components, mass storage products and microcontrollers with on-chip flash memory **Area of distribution:** International **Expertise:** Project management, research and development **Honors/awards:** Silver & Gold Medal Recipient of the Winbond Electronics Corporation's Patent and Innovation Contest 1998 & 2000; Silver Medal Recipient of the International Biographical Centre's 2000 Outstanding Scientists of the 20th Century, 1999; Marquis Who's Who in Science and Engineering, 1999 edition; Strathmore Who's Who VIP Member, 2001 edition; Marquis Who's Who in America, 2000 edition **Published works:** "A 65ns 1Mb CMOS Alternate Metal Virtual Ground EPROM with Dual Reference Sensing Scheme and Word Line Voltage Regulator", International Symposium on VLSI Technology, Systems and Applications, May 1993, Taipei, Taiwan; Inventor/Co-inventor of 9 U.S. Patents: Row Decoder and Driver with Switched-Bias Bulk Regions, Semiconductor Memory Device with Dataline Undershoot Detection and Reduced Read Access Time, Electrically Byte Selectable and Byte Alterable Memory Arrays, Flash Cell Having Self-Timed Programming, Memory Device and Method of Operation, Semiconductor Memory Device with Reduced Read Disturbance, Semiconductor Memory Device with Reduced Read Disturbance, Semiconductor Memory Array with Buried Drain Lines and Methods Therefor; Semiconductor Memory Array Partitioned into Memory Blocks and Sub-blocks and Method of addressing, Semiconductor Memory Array with Buried Drain Lines and Processing Methods Therefor and other U.S. patents **Affiliations:** Institute of Electrical and Electronics Engineers **Hob./spts.:** Table tennis, movies, swimming **SIC code:** 36 **Address:** 5253 Rooster Dr., San Jose, CA 95136-3370 **E-mail:** lhoang@ssti.com **Web address:** www.ssti.com

HOCKERSMITH, JOHN P.
Industry: Asphalt road equipment **Born:** March 13, 1953, Shippensburg, Pennsylvania **Current organization:** Vogele America, Inc. **Title:** Quality Manager **Type of organization:** OEM **Major product:** Asphalt road equipment **Area of distribution:** International **Expertise:** Quality control management **Hob./spts.:** Fishing, camping, cycling **SIC code:** 35 **Address:** Vogele America, Inc., 1445 Sheffler Dr., Chambersburg, PA 17201 **E-mail:** jhockersmith@vogeleamerica.com

HODZIC, NIJAZ
Industry: Motion and control technologies and systems **Univ./degree:** M.M.E. Candidate, University of Illinois **Current organization:** Parker Hannifin Corp. **Title:** Product Engineer Design **Type of organization:** Manufacturing **Major product:** Custom hydraulic and pneumatic cylinders **Area of distribution:** National **Expertise:** Custom cylinder design, motion control and multi body systems dynamic **Published works:** Co-author, "Electrohydraulic Motion Control Systems" **Hob./spts.:** Art, oil painting, skiing **SIC code:** 36 **Address:** Parker Hannifin Corp., 800 N. York Rd., Bensenville, IL 60106-1183 **E-mail:** nhodzic@parker.com

HOEFT, WERNER H.
Industry: Integrated circuits **Born:** November 26, 1930, Elbing, Germany **Univ./degree:** B.S., Engineering, Polytechnic Institute of Berlin, Germany, 1955 **Current organization:** Pulsecore, A Division of Alliance Semiconductor **Title:** Director of Engineering **Type of organization:** Manufacturing **Major product:** Semiconductors **Area of distribution:** International **Expertise:** Engineering **Hob./spts.:** Photography, swimming **SIC code:** 36 **Address:** Pulsecore, A Division of Alliance Semiconductor, 2575 Augustine Dr., Santa Clara, CA 95054 **E-mail:** hoefflin@yahoo.com

HOFFMAN, SCOTT R.
Industry: Automotive **Born:** July 14, 1953, Rochester, New York **Univ./degree:** B.S.M.T., Purdue University, 1979 **Current organization:** Porter Engineered Systems **Title:** Test Laboratory Manager **Type of organization:** Manufacturing **Major product:** Seat recliners **Area of distribution:** International **Expertise:** Testing management - established and new products **Hob./spts.:** Classic car restoration **SIC code:** 37 **Address:** Porter Engineered Systems, 19635 U.S. 31 North, Westfield, IN 46074 **E-mail:** shoffman@porteres.com

HOFFMANN, CAROLA
Industry: Chemicals **Born:** April 12, 1969, Neuss, Germany **Univ./degree:** Diplomate, Universität Dortmund, Germany (MBA equivalent) **Current organization:** Ineos Styrenics **Title:** Manager, Human Resources **Type of organization:** Manufacturing **Major product:** Polystyrene **Area of distribution:** National and international **Expertise:** Human resource generalist **Affiliations:** Society for Human Resource Management; Ineos Leadership Team **Hob./spts.:** Reading, pet charities, travel **SIC code:** 28 **Address:** Ineos Styrenics, 25846 S.W. Frontage Rd., Channahon, IL 60410 **E-mail:** carola.hoffmann@ineosstyrenics.com **Web address:** www.ineosstyrenics.com

HOLLEY, KEVIN
Industry: Transportation equipment **Born:** May 7, 1965, Washington, Pennsylvania **Univ./degree:** B.S., Purdue University, 1988 **Current organization:** International Truck & Engine **Title:** Plant Manager **Type of organization:** Manufacturing **Major product:** Engines and trucks/school buses **Area of distribution:** International **Expertise:** Manufacturing leadership **Honors/awards:** Crane Chicago Business "40 under 40" **Hob./spts.:** Physical fitness, golf, reading **SIC code:** 37 **Address:** International Truck & Engine, 10400 W. North Ave., Melrose Park, IL 60160 **E-mail:** kevin.holley@nav-international.com **Web address:** www.nav-international.com

HOLMAN, SUSAN HARTJES
Industry: Medical devices **Born:** December 28, 1953, Appleton, Wisconsin **Univ./degree:** B.A., Biomedical Science; B.A., Biology, 1976, St. Cloud State University **Current organization:** Uroplasty, Inc. **Title:** C.O.O. (Chief Operating Officer) **Type of organization:** Manufacturing **Major product:** Urology devices **Area of distribution:** International **Expertise:** Quality, regulatory, microbiology, product development **Affiliations:** Regulatory Affairs Professionals Society; Senior member, American Society for Quality; Henrici Society **Hob./spts.:** Travel, gardening, golf **SIC code:** 38 **Address:** Uroplasty, Inc., 2718 Summer St. N.E., Minneapolis, MN 55413 **E-mail:** susan.holman@uroplasty.com

HOLOVACKO, THOMAS E.
Industry: Painting supplies **Born:** January 30, 1950, South Amboy, New Jersey **Current organization:** Hercules Inc. **Title:** Safety Supervisor **Type of organization:** Manufacturing **Major product:** Paint thinner **Area of distribution:** International **Expertise:** Safety awareness **Affiliations:** National Safety Council; National Chemical Council **Hob./spts.:** Bowling, P.B.A. **SIC code:** 28 **Address:** Hercules Inc., 50 South Minisink Ave., Parlin, NJ 08859 **E-mail:** tholovacko@herc.com

HOLOWAK, PETER C.
Industry: Telecommunications **Born:** October 14, 1955, Dallas, Texas **Univ./degree:** Technical Degree, Aerospace Maintenance Engineering, Texas AeroTech University, 1991 **Current organization:** IMS Connector Systems **Title:** Quality Management/Quality Assurance Engineer **Type of organization:** Manufacturing **Major product:** Telecommunications components, RF connectors, side switches, electric/mechanical **Area of distribution:** International **Expertise:** Quality assurance, engineering **Honors/awards:** International Who's Who of Professionals **Hob./spts.:** Flying, fishing, golf, dancing, driving **SIC code:** 36 **Address:** 2600 Preston Rd., #506, Plano, TX 75093 **E-mail:** viper223@ev1.net

HOOKS, GREG
Industry: Automotive **Born:** March 21, 1951, Dallas, Texas **Univ./degree:** B.S., Economics, University of Texas at Arlington **Current organization:** Curt Mfg., Inc. **Title:** CEO/President **Type of organization:** Manufacturing, distributing **Major product:** Leisure transportation, towing products **Area of distribution:** National **Expertise:** Sales **Hob./spts.:** Running, racquetball, physical fitness, travel **SIC code:** 37 **Address:** Curt Mfg., Inc., 6208 Industrial Dr., Eau Claire, WI 54701 **E-mail:** ghooks@curtmfg.com

HORII, NAOMI
Industry: Publishing **Born:** January 12, 1968, West Lafayette, Indiana **Univ./degree:** M.A., University of Missouri at Columbia, 1993 **Current organization:** Many Mountains Moving, Inc. **Title:** Director **Type of organization:** Nonprofit publishing, arts & literature **Major product:** Literary journal **Area of distribution:** National **Expertise:** Editing, writing **Affiliations:** Fellow, Colorado Council of the Arts; N.A.F.E.; Council of Literary Magazines **Hob./spts.:** Music, writing **SIC code:** 27 **Address:** Many Mountains Moving, Inc., 420 22nd St., Boulder, CO 80302 **E-mail:** naomi@mmminc.org **Web address:** www.mmminc.org

HOULE, RICHARD D.
Industry: HVAC **Born:** November 5, 1968, St. Paul, Minnesota **Univ./degree:** B.S.M.E., University of Minnesota, 1995 **Current organization:** Uponor Wirsbo **Title:** Director, Codes and Standards **Type of organization:** Manufacturing **Major product:** Cross linked polyethylene tubing **Area of distribution:** International **Expertise:** Engineering, codes and standards **Affiliations:** P.P.F.A.; P.P.I.; I.A.P.M.O.; A.S.T.M. **Hob./spts.:** Golf **SIC code:** 34 **Address:** Uponor Wirsbo, 5925 148th St. West, Apple Valley, MN 55124 **E-mail:** rhoule@uponrhsdna.com

HOUNSLEY, ROBERT C.
Industry: Automotive **Born:** May 2, 1958, Culver City, California **Current organization:** Walker Corp. **Title:** Tool Designer and Maker **Type of organization:** Manufacturing **Major product:** Metal stampings **Area of distribution:** International **Expertise:** Tool design, trouble shooting **Affiliations:** Boy Scouts of America **Hob./spts.:** Woodworking, building furniture and cabinets, crafts **SIC code:** 34 **Address:** Walker Corp., 1555 S. Vintage Ave., Ontario, CA 91761

HOYLE, KEITH M.
Industry: Biotechnology/pharmaceutical **Born:** Upland, Pennsylvania **Univ./degree:** M.S., Villanova University **Current organization:** Amgen, Inc. **Title:** Senior Technologist **Type of organization:** Manufacturing/R&D **Major product:** Pharmaceuticals **Area of distribution:** International **Expertise:** Research informatics **Published works:** Several articles for Molecular Pharmacology Journal **Hob./spts.:** Scuba diving **SIC code:** 28 **Address:** Amgen, Inc., 1 Amgen Center Dr., Thousand Oaks, CA 91360 **E-mail:** khoyle001@hotmail.com

HOYLE JR., FRED L.
Industry: Automotive **Born:** April 4, 1961, Columbus, Ohio **Univ./degree:** Graduate, North East Career Center, 1979 **Current organization:** Superior Die Tool & Machinery Co. **Title:** Chief Engineer/Product Development **Type of organization:** Manufacturing **Major product:** Sheet metal stamping/tooling **Area of distribution:** International **Expertise:** Engineering/product development **Affiliations:** A.S.M. **Hob./spts.:** Car shows **SIC code:** 33 **Address:** Superior Die Tool & Machinery Co., 2301 Fairwood Ave., Columbus, OH 43147 **E-mail:** fredh@superior-dietool.com

HRUSOVSKY, IRENE G.
Industry: Healthcare **Born:** Lake Forest, Illinois **Univ./degree:** M.D., University of British Colombia, 1969 **Current organization:** Eragen Biosciences, Inc. **Title:** President/CEO **Type of organization:** Manufacturing, research **Major product:** Drugs/devices **Area of distribution:** International **Expertise:** Executive business leadership **Affiliations:** American Academy of Pediatrics; American Cancer Society **SIC code:** 28 **Address:** 918 Deming Way, Madison, WI 53717 **E-mail:** ibrusovsky@eragen.com **Web address:** www.eragen.com

HUBBARD, RICHARD E.
Industry: Research and development, semiconductors **Born:** April 10, 1963, Blytheville, Arkansas **Univ./degree:** B.S., Liberal Studies and Mathematics, 1991; B.S.E.E., 1996, University of Central Florida; M.B.A., 2001, University of Texas at Austin **Current organization:** Texas Instruments, Inc. **Title:** Characterization Manager **Type of organization:** Research and development, manufacturing **Major product:** Semiconductors **Area of distribution:** International **Expertise:** Engineering, management **Published works:** 1 article **Affiliations:** President, United Methodist Men's Group **Hob./spts.:** Member of the United Methodist Church, spending time with family **SIC code:** 36 **Address:** Texas Instruments, Inc., 12500 TI Blvd., MS 8781, Dallas, TX 75243-0592 **E-mail:** r-hubbard2@ti.com

HUBSCH, LYNN DAVID
Industry: Ceramics **Univ./degree:** Los Angeles City College-2 years/School of Hard Knocks **Current organization:** Rappahannock Mudworks **Title:** Owner/Partner **Type of organization:** Manufacturing/design **Major product:** Wine stoppers and wine accessories, decorate whiteware ceramics and porcelain, creation and development of new products **Area of distribution:** National and International **Expertise:** Custom sculpted items, stone and clay, creative/artistic problem solving **SIC code:** 32 **Address:** Rappahannock Mudworks, 6581 Commerce Ct., Warrenton, VA 20187 **E-mail:** mudworks@rapmud.com **Web address:** www.rapmud.com

HUDSON, GLENN R.
Industry: Aerospace **Born:** May 10, 1932, High Point, North Carolina **Univ./degree:** B.S.M.E., Indiana Institute of Technology **Current organization:** Equipment & Supply, Inc. **Title:** Engineering Manager **Type of organization:** Manufacturing **Major product:** Military aircraft equipment **Area of distribution:** North Carolina **Expertise:** Engineering **Hob./spts.:** Scuba diving, skydiving, flying airplanes, boating, travel **SIC code:** 37 **Address:** Equipment & Supply, Inc., 4507 Highway 74W, Monroe, NC 28110 **E-mail:** ghudson2@carolina.rr.com

HUDSON, THOMAS L.
Industry: Automotive **Born:** January 18, 1961, Park Ridge, Illinois **Univ./degree:** B.S.M.E., Kennedy Western University **Current organization:** Littelfuse **Title:** Manufacturing Engineer **Type of organization:** Manufacturing **Major product:** Automotive parts **Area of distribution:** International **Expertise:** Equipment rebuilding, training, product line maintenance **Affiliations:** Society of Engineers **SIC code:** 37 **Address:** Littelfuse, 800 E. Northwest Hwy., Des Plaines, IL 60016

HUGGINS, STANLEY
Industry: Machinery manufacturing **Born:** March 4, 1956, Creston, South Carolina **Univ./degree:** Associates Degree, Orangeburg Technical College, 1988 **Current organization:** KCV-MD **Title:** Engineering Supervisor **Type of organization:** Manufacturing **Major product:** Bearings **Area of distribution:** Orangeburg, South Carolina **Expertise:** Engineering **Hob./spts.:** Golf, sports **SIC code:** 35 **Address:** KCV-MD, P.O. Drawer 967, Orangeburg, SC 29115 **E-mail:** s.huggin@koyocorp.com

HUMMEL, MYRON F.
Industry: Transportation equipment **Univ./degree:** B.S., Mathematics, Mary Christ College, 1984 **Current organization:** Caterpillar Inc., Technical Services Division **Title:** Senior Design Engineer **Type of organization:** Manufacturing **Major product:** Diesel engines, research and development **Area of distribution:** Illinois **Expertise:** Facilities engineering **Affiliations:** A.S.M.E.; A.F.F.; Chapter President, A.S.P.E. **SIC code:** 37 **Address:** 1137 W. Cedar Ct., Chillicothe, IL 61523-1318 **E-mail:** mfhummel@mtco.com **Web address:** www.mtco.com

HUMMEL, PETER
Industry: Automotive **Born:** March 2, 1967, Stuttgart, Germany **Univ./degree:** M.B.A., Informatics Economy, University of Cooperative Education **Current organization:** Behr America, Inc. **Title:** Senior Network Manager/Electronic Business Engineer **Type of organization:** Manufacturing **Major product:** Air conditioning and cooling systems for vehicles **Area of distribution:** International **Expertise:** Information technology, IT security, IT management **Affiliations:** A.O.P.A. **Hob./spts.:** Family, flying (Licensed Pilot), shooting **SIC code:** 37 **Address:** Behr America, Inc., 1600 Webster St., Dayton, OH 45404 **E-mail:** peter.hummel@us.behrgroup.com **Web address:** www.behrgroup.com

HUNT, KENNETH R.
Industry: Automotive **Born:** June 7, 1947, Detroit, Michigan **Univ./degree:** B.S., Mechanical Engineering, Lawrence University, 1971 **Current organization:** Sportrack Automotive **Title:** Corporate tooling manager **Type of organization:** Manufacturing development **Major product:** Roof luggage racks, exterior plastic components **Area**

of distribution: Sterling Heights, Michigan **Expertise:** Tooling, engineering **Affiliations:** S.A.E. **Hob./spts.:** Boating, bowling, specialty building **SIC code:** 37 **Address:** Sportrack Automotive, 12900 Hall Rd., Suite 200, Sterling Heights, MI 48313 **E-mail:** khunt@AASLLC.com

HUNTER, CARLOS
Industry: Steel **Born:** February 4, 1960, Mexico **Univ./degree:** E.M.B.A., Sullivan University, 2005 **Current organization:** North American Stainless **Title:** New Installations Manager **Type of organization:** Manufacturing **Major product:** Stainless steel **Area of distribution:** International **Expertise:** Engineering **Hob./spts.:** Bicycling **SIC code:** 33 **Address:** North American Stainless, 6870 Hwy. 42 East, Ghent, KY 41045-9615

HURD, MARVIN L.
Industry: Aerospace **Born:** June 5, 1932, Cherokee, Iowa **Univ./degree:** M.S., Automatic Control, Dynamics and Mechanical Engineering, University of Washington, 1963 **Current organization:** The Boeing Co. **Title:** Engineer/Scientist 4 **Type of organization:** Manufacturing **Major product:** Aircraft and aerospace vehicles **Area of distribution:** International **Expertise:** Engineering analysis and algorithm development **Hob./spts.:** Hiking, flyfishing **SIC code:** 37 **Address:** 1005 Harbor Ave. S.W., #502, Seattle, WA 98116-1773 **E-mail:** marvlh@aol.com

HURT, DAVID T.
Industry: Technology **Born:** October 8, 1940, Glassville, Kentucky **Current organization:** VIP, Inc. **Title:** President **Type of organization:** Printing company **Major product:** Processing manuals **Area of distribution:** National **Expertise:** Data compression algorithm **SIC code:** 27 **Address:** VIP, Inc., 3029 E. Washington St., Bldg. K, Indianapolis, IN 46201 **E-mail:** dhurt@hurtsvip.com **Web address:** www.hurtsvip.com

HUTCHENS, ANDREW W.
Industry: Food **Born:** July 14, 1973, Cold Water, Michigan **Univ./degree:** B.S., Elementary Education, Grand Valley State University, Michigan, 1996 **Current organization:** Sara Lee Foods **Title:** Quality Assurance Manager **Type of organization:** Manufacturing **Major product:** Deli and food service meat items **Area of distribution:** International **Expertise:** Quality processes, process design, food safety **Hob./spts.:** Flyfishing, rock climbing, backpacking **SIC code:** 20 **Address:** Sara Lee Foods, 8300 96th Ave., Zeeland, MI 49464 **E-mail:** andrew.hutchens@saralee.com

HUTCHENS, GAIL R.
Industry: Plastics **Born:** Bentonville, Arkansas **Current organization:** Techmer PM **Title:** Analytical Services Supervisor **Type of organization:** Manufacturing **Major product:** Colors and additives **Area of distribution:** International **Expertise:** Analytical chemistry **Hob./spts.:** Scuba Instructor; First Responder Instructor; photography **SIC code:** 30 **Address:** Techmer PM, 1 Quality Circle, Clinton, TN 37716 **E-mail:** ghutchens@techmerpm.com **Web address:** www.techmerpm.com

HUTTO, MERL G.
Industry: Appliances **Univ./degree:** M.B.A., George Washington University **Current organization:** Mastercraft Ind. Inc. (Retired) **Title:** Independent Consultant Mortgage Management **Type of organization:** Manufacturing **Major product:** Commercial vacuum cleaners and floor polishers **Area of distribution:** International **Expertise:** Engineering **Affiliations:** U.S. Military Academy at West Point **Hob./spts.:** Politics **SIC code:** 35 **Address:** 7 Partridge Rd., Cornwall-on-Hudson, NY 12520 **E-mail:** mgh23aol.com

HYDER, MUNIR
Industry: Chillers and refrigeration and process heat exchangers **Born:** Karachi, Pakistan **Univ./degree:** B.S., Mechanical Engineering, NED University of Engineering and Technology, Pakistan, 1981 **Current organization:** Ketema LP **Title:** Product Engineer **Type of organization:** Manufacturing **Major product:** Packaged chillers and heat exchangers **Area of distribution:** National **Expertise:** Engineering **Affiliations:** A.S.H.R.A.E. **Hob./spts.:** Cricket **SIC code:** 38 **Address:** Ketema LP, 2300 W. Marshall Dr., Grand Prairie, TX 75051 **E-mail:** mhyder@ketemalp.com

IMMEL, BRIAN D.
Industry: Plastics **Born:** February 5, 1962, Lancaster, Pennsylvania **Current organization:** Lancaster Mold Inc. **Title:** Senior Designer & Estimator **Type of organization:** Manufacturing **Major product:** Plastic injection molds **Area of distribution:** National **Expertise:** Design and estimating, trade show presentations **Affiliations:** Society of Manufacturing Engineers; Society of Plastic Engineers **Hob./spts.:** Hunting, fishing, travel **SIC code:** 30 **Address:** Lancaster Mold Inc., 2501 Horseshoe Rd., Lancaster, PA 17601 **E-mail:** bimmel@lancastermold.com **Web address:** www.lancastermold.com

INGLES, WALLACE WAYNE
Industry: Forestry **Born:** June 7, 1958, Winnfield, Louisiana **Current organization:** Ingles Logging **Title:** Owner **Type of organization:** Contractor **Major product:** Harvesting timber **Area of distribution:** Louisiana **Expertise:** Logging **Honors/awards:** Certified Master Logger **Published works:** Featured in Southern Loggin' Times, December 1993 **Hob./spts.:** Family, hunting, fishing, the outdoors, sponsor for Ducks Unlimited **SIC code:** 24 **Address:** Ingles Logging, 396 Horseshoe Rd., Winnfield, LA 71483 **E-mail:** wingleslogging@aol.com

INIKORI, SOLOMON OVUEFERAYE
Industry: Oil/gas **Born:** March 27, 1964, Warri, Delta State, Nigeria **Univ./degree:** B.Eng., Mechanical Engineering, University of Nigeria, Nsukka, Nigeria, 1988; M.Eng., Mechanical Engineering, University of Benin, Benin-City, Nigeria, 1993; Ph.D., Petroleum Engineering, Louisiana State University, 2002 **Current organization:** Shell International Exploration and Production, Inc. **Title:** Senior Reservoir Engineer **Type of organization:** Exploration and production company **Major product:** Oil and gas **Area of distribution:** International **Expertise:** Reservoir engineering (oil exploration) **Honors/awards:** First Place, Ph.D. Division, S.P.E., Gulf Coast Section Student Paper Contest, April 2002; First Place, Ph.D. Division, S.P.E., International Student Paper Contest, October 2002; College of Engineering Exemplary Dissertation Award, Louisiana State University and A&M College, May 2003 **Published works:** S.P.E. and A.S.M.E. conference proceedings **Affiliations:** Society of Petroleum Engineers International (SPE); American Society of Mechanical Engineers, Petroleum Division (ASME) **SIC code:** 29 **Address:** Shell International Exploration and Production, Inc., 200 N. Dairy Ashford, Room WCK 2113, Houston, TX 77079 **E-mail:** solomon.inikori@shell.com **Web address:** www.shell.com

IOERGER, MICHAEL J.
Industry: Heavy equipment **Born:** March 24, 1963, Illinois **Univ./degree:** B.A., Business Management, Bradley University, 1992 **Current organization:** Caterpillar, Inc. **Title:** Purchasing Manager **Type of organization:** Manufacturing **Major product:** Engines and earth moving equipment **Area of distribution:** International **Expertise:** Business management **Hob./spts.:** Basketball, baseball, family **SIC code:** 37 **Address:** 539 State Rt. 116, Metamora, IL 61548 **E-mail:** mtelc@mtco.com

IPPOLITO, NICHOLAS M.
Industry: Aerospace **Born:** September 8, 1966, Tempe, Arizona **Current organization:** Foresight Technologies **Title:** Lead Programmer **Type of organization:** Manufacturing **Major product:** Aerospace/semiconductor hardware **Area of distribution:** Arizona **Expertise:** CNC programming/engineering **Hob./spts.:** Plays bass guitar, golf, camping **SIC code:** 36 **Address:** Foresight Technologies, 1401 S. McClintock Dr., Tempe, AZ 85281 **E-mail:** nippolito6266@earthlink.net

IRWIN, TIMOTHY S.
Industry: Electronics **Born:** December 9, 1962, Canton, Illinois **Univ./degree:** B.S.M.E., University of Illinois, 1985 **Current organization:** Bently Nevada **Title:** Machinery Management Engineer **Type of organization:** Electronic equipment **Major product:** Asset care of rotating machinery **Area of distribution:** South Carolina **Expertise:** Mechanical engineering, rotating machinery **Affiliations:** A.S.M.E.; Vibration Institute **Hob./spts.:** Archery **SIC code:** 36 **Address:** 13 Aberdeen Way, Elgin, SC 29045 **E-mail:** tim.irwin@bently.com

ISAAC, DARLENE
Industry: Lumber **Born:** November 22, 1958, Prestonsburg, Kentucky **Univ./degree:** Attended Shawnee State College **Current organization:** Ohio Valley Lumber **Title:** Controller **Type of organization:** Manufacturing **Major product:** Lumber and logs **Area of distribution:** International **Expertise:** Accounting, financial operations **Hob./spts.:** Basketball, football, horseback riding, reading **SIC code:** 24 **Address:** Ohio Valley Lumber, 16523 St. Rt. 124, Piketon, OH 45661 **E-mail:** darlene@ohiovalleylumber.com

ISMAILOV, MURAD MARIPHOVICH
Industry: Automotive/aerospace **Born:** March 1, 1960, Moscow, Russia **Univ./degree:** Flight Control and Aerodynamics, Moscow State Technical University, Moscow, 1983; Ph.D., Mechanical Engineering Issued by Government; Doctorate, Mechanical Engineering Issued by Government, 1993 **Current organization:** Combustion Dynamics Corp. **Title:** Director of Automotive Research and Development **Type of organization:** Development and manufacturing **Major product:** Diesel injection systems **Area of distribution:** International **Expertise:** Combustion engineering **Affiliations:** Society of Automotive Engineers; American Society of Mechanical Engineers; Russian Academy of Sciences; Japanese Society of Mechanical Engineers **Hob./spts.:** Swimming, parachuting, volleyball, guitar, piano, philosophy **SIC code:** 37 **Address:** Combustion Dynamics Corp., 499 Park Ave., 20th floor, New York, NY 10022 **E-mail:** muradcdc@aol.com; muradcdc@yahoo.com

IWASAKI, TERUO
Industry: Automotive **Born:** March 13, 1966, Tokyo, Japan **Univ./degree:** B.S., Business Administration, Tokyo International University, 1988 **Current organization:** TS Trim Industries, Inc. **Title:** Senior Manager, Business Planning **Type of organization:** Manufacturing **Major product:** Automobile interior parts **Expertise:**

Business planning, administration **Hob./spts.:** Golf, movies **SIC code:** 37 **Address:** TS Trim Industries, Inc., 6380 W. Canal St., Canal Winchester, OH 43110 **E-mail:** thomas_iwasaki@tstrim.com

JACKSON, STEPHEN J.
Industry: Pharmaceuticals **Born:** July 16, 1962, Philadelphia, Pennsylvania **Univ./degree:** B.S., Marine Engineering Systems, U.S. Merchant Marine Academy, 1984 **Current organization:** Hotpack Corp. **Title:** Electrical Engineer **Type of organization:** Manufacturing **Major product:** Original equipment manufacturer **Area of distribution:** International **Expertise:** Engineering (mechanical & electrical) **Published works:** Co-author of book with Clarence Jones, "Programmable Logical Controls Complete Guide to Technology" **Affiliations:** I.S.A. **Hob./spts.:** Construction **SIC code:** 28 **Address:** Hotpack Corp., 10940 Dutton Rd., Philadelphia, PA 19053 **E-mail:** jacksons@hotpack.com **Web address:** www.hotpack.com

JACOBSEN, LEIF Y.
Industry: Packaging **Born:** September 1, 1936, New York, New York **Univ./degree:** B.A., History, Hope College, Michigan, 1960 **Current organization:** Wrap-It Packaging Products, Inc. **Title:** President **Type of organization:** Marketing and sales **Major product:** Protective packaging equipment and materials **Area of distribution:** Midwestern United States **Expertise:** Operations, sales **Affiliations:** I.O.P.P. **Hob./spts.:** Sailing, swimming **SIC code:** 26 **Address:** Wrap-It Packaging Products, Inc., 22 Nicholson Ct., Dayton, OH 45459 **E-mail:** wrapitpkg@aol.com

JAMES JR., ARTHUR S.
Industry: Aluminum **Born:** December 6, 1973, Sarasota, Florida **Current organization:** Casual Creations/Progressive Screens Inc./Unique Technology **Title:** President **Type of organization:** Manufacturing **Major product:** Outdoor furniture, motorized screens, screen doors **Area of distribution:** National **Expertise:** Management **Affiliations:** Aluminum Association of Florida **Hob./spts.:** Boating **SIC code:** 34 **Address:** Casual Creations/Progressive Screens Inc./Unique Technology, 1300 Hardin Ave., Sarasota, FL 34243 **E-mail:** artjames@myway.com **Web address:** www.casualcreations.com

JANA, WILLIAM A.
Industry: Automotive **Born:** January 5, 1963, Springfield, Massachusetts **Univ./degree:** B.A., Cum Laude, Pastoral Studies, Bob Jones University, 1984; A.A., Computer Science, Greenville Technical College, 1988; Post-Grad Certification, University of California at Berkeley **Current organization:** International Logistics/Michelin North America **Title:** International Export Manager **Type of organization:** Manufacturing **Major product:** Tires and transportation services **Area of distribution:** International **Expertise:** Logistics and information services **Honors/awards:** Michelin North America "CEO Excellence Award, 2001; Michelin Mexico Customer Service "Strategic Partner Award", 2000; Michelin North America "Outstanding IT Leadership Award", 1999; MetLife Golden Nameplate Recipient for repeated outstanding service to clients 1994-95 **Published works:** Featured in AT&T Mexico Client Quarterly (2000); Featured in Michelin's quarterly magazine "Project Office" in the Project Manager Spotlight, 1997 **Affiliations:** The Logistics Institute; Warehousing Education and Research Council **Hob./spts.:** Volleyball, billiards, travel, biking, reading **SIC code:** 37 **Address:** Michelin North America, 1 Parkway South, Greenville, SC 29615 **E-mail:** william.jana@us.michelin.com **Web address:** www.michelin.com

JANG, JIN-WOOK
Industry: Semiconductors **Born:** December 7, 1967, Seoul, South Korea **Univ./degree:** Ph.D., Material Science, Seoul National University **Current organization:** Motorola Semiconductor Products Sector **Title:** Ph.D. **Type of organization:** Manufacturing **Major product:** Semiconductor products **Area of distribution:** International **Expertise:** Engineering **Published works:** Journal articles, 1 book chapter **SIC code:** 36 **Address:** Motorola Semiconductor Products Sector, 2100 E. Elliot Rd., MD EL725, Tempe, AZ 85284 **E-mail:** j.jang@motorola.com

JANG, KYUNG J.
Industry: Food **Born:** January 10, 1963, Seoul, Korea **Univ./degree:** B.S.M.E., 1991; M.S.M.E., 1994; Ph.D., Mechanical Engineering, 1999, Iowa State University **Current organization:** IMI Cornelius **Title:** Design Engineer/Test Lab Supervisor **Type of organization:** Manufacturing **Major product:** Commercial/industrial ice machines and beverage dispensers **Area of distribution:** International **Expertise:** Engineering **Published works:** 5 articles, 1 abstract **Affiliations:** Former member, A.S.H.R.E. **Hob./spts.:** Energy conservation, artificial necro network project **SIC code:** 20 **Address:** IMI Cornelius, 2421 15th St. S.W., P.O. Box 1527, Mason City, IA 50402 **E-mail:** kenj@cornelius.com

JAYNE, THOMAS G.
Industry: Paper **Born:** November 2, 1951, Appleton, Wisconsin **Univ./degree:** M.S., Chemistry, Institute of Paper Chemistry, 1975 **Current organization:** International Paper Co. **Title:** Manager Environmental Services **Type of organization:** Manufacturing **Major product:** Paper **Area of distribution:** International **Expertise:** Environmental regulatory services **Honors/awards:** Recognition Award; Recognition Pollution Prevention Award from state of Wisconsin **Published works:** TAPI Journal **Affiliations:** Wisconsin Paper Council **Hob./spts.:** Traveling, watching sports events **SIC code:** 26 **Address:** International Paper Co., 600 Thilmany Rd., Kaukauna, WI 54130 **E-mail:** thomas.jayne@ipaper.com

JEWETT, SCOTT Y.
Industry: Control products and systems **Born:** April 12, 1955, Cleveland, Ohio **Univ./degree:** M.B.A., John Carroll University, Ohio, 1987 **Area of distribution:** International **Expertise:** Project engineering **Affiliations:** A.I.C.H.E. **Hob./spts.:** Travel, tennis, hiking **SIC code:** 38 **Address:** ABB, 29801 Euclid Ave., Wickliffe, OH 44092 **E-mail:** scott.jewett1@aol.com

JIMMERSON SR., RONALD BYRON
Industry: Automotive/furniture/containers **Born:** April 11, 1944, Muskegon, Michigan **Univ./degree:** Special Social Work Program, Western Michigan University, 1976 **Current organization:** Cascade Engineering, Inc. **Title:** Human Resource Manager **Type of organization:** Manufacturing **Major product:** Plastic injection molding parts for automotive, furniture and container **Area of distribution:** International **Expertise:** Human resource **Published works:** 1 article in "Grand Rapids Press" **Affiliations:** S.H.R.M.; Workforce Development; Exodus Correctional; City Hope Ministries; Employers Advisory Council for Interurban Transportation (ITP); member, Family Support America Roundtable **Hob./spts.:** Tennis, ministry **SIC code:** 37 **Address:** Cascade Engineering, Inc., 5251 36th St. S.E., Grand Rapids, MI 49512-2011 **E-mail:** jimmersonr@cascadeng.com **Web address:** www.cascadeng.com

JOHNSTON, EARL B.
Industry: Paper **Born:** September 23, 1953, Jerome, Idaho **Univ./degree:** Hydraulics, Pneumatics, Lane Community College; B.S. Candidate, Mechanical Engineering, University of Wisconsin, Madison **Current organization:** Weyerhaeuser Container Board **Title:** Fluid Mechanical Technician **Type of organization:** Manufacturing **Major product:** Paper **Area of distribution:** National **Expertise:** Mechanical engineering, analyzing/eliminating pipe vibrations, carpentry, OSHA standard welding, mobile equipment operating, piping apprenticeship program developing, hydraulics, pneumatics, research and development; Certified General Contractor; Certified, Steam & Condensate Systems; 23 years experience Journeyman Mechanic **Affiliations:** A.W.P.P.W. **Hob./spts.:** Snow skiing, fishing, travel, hunting, camping, Oregon Ducks Football **SIC code:** 26 **Address:** Weyerhaeuser Container Board, 785 N. 42nd St., Springfield, OR 97478 **E-mail:** earl.johnston@weyerhaeuser.com

JONES, THOMAS L.
Industry: Automotive supplies **Born:** June 8, 1963, Mansfield, Ohio **Univ./degree:** M.S., Science and Project Development, University of Detroit at Mercy, 2001 **Current organization:** Visteon Corp. **Title:** Product Design Engineer **Type of organization:** Manufacturing **Major product:** Product design and instrumentation **Area of distribution:** International **Expertise:** Plastics design **Affiliations:** American Society of Manufacturing Engineers **Hob./spts.:** Computer games, animation, ceramic dragon collectibles **SIC code:** 37 **Address:** Visteon Corp., 16630 Southfield, Suite 1100B, Allen Park, MI 48101 **E-mail:** tjones56@visteon.com

JORDAN, EARNEST M.
Industry: Food **Born:** September 18, 1945, Louin, Mississippi **Univ./degree:** B.S., Industrial Electronic Technology, Southern Illinois University, 2003 **Current organization:** Loders Croklaan **Title:** Total Productive Maintenance Coordinator **Type of organization:** Manufacturing **Major product:** Oils for food **Area of distribution:** International **Expertise:** Instrumentation, efficiency, quality **Hob./spts.:** Chess, sports, recreation, travel **SIC code:** 20 **Address:** Loders Croklaan, 24708 W. Durkee Rd., Channahon, IL 60410-5249 **E-mail:** slam-d07@prodigy.net

JORDAN, FRANK J.
Industry: Food **Born:** June 1, 1956 **Current organization:** Delmonte Foods **Title:** Corporate Manager Loss Prevention **Type of organization:** Manufacturing **Major product:** Consumer foods **Area of distribution:** National **Expertise:** Health and safety **Hob./spts.:** Scuba diving, power boating **SIC code:** 20 **Address:** Delmonte Foods, 1075 Progress St., Pittsburgh, PA 15212 **E-mail:** frank.jordan.@delmonte.com

JORGENSEN, POUL
Industry: Aerospace **Born:** April 13, 1931, Toronto, Canada **Current organization:** Mini-Flex Corp. **Title:** President **Type of organization:** Manufacturing **Major product:** Miniature metal bellows **Area of distribution:** National **Expertise:** Engineering and management **Hob./spts.:** Golf, art **SIC code:** 37 **Address:** Mini-Flex Corp., 2472 Eastman Ave., Unit 29, Ventura, CA 93003

JOSEPH, MITCHELL J.
Industry: Beverage **Born:** June 3, 1947, Youngstown, Ohio **Univ./degree:** B.A., Arts & Sciences, Youngstown State University **Current organization:** Chill-Can, Inc. **Title:** Chairman/CEO **Type of organization:** Manufacturing/distributing/research and

development **Major product:** Worldwide chilling technology **Area of distribution:** International **Expertise:** Marketing, patents **Affiliations:** Ellis Island Medal of Honor, Awarded Kentucky Colonel, 1985 **Hob./spts.:** Golf **SIC code:** 20 **Address:** Chill-Can, Inc., 27612 Fargo Rd., Laguna Hills, CA 92653

JOST, MICHAEL B.
Industry: Industrial process control instrumentation **Born:** January 4, 1965, St. Cloud, Minnesota **Univ./degree:** Ph.D., Material Science, University of Minnesota, 1992 **Current organization:** Invensys Foxboro **Title:** Vice President, Measurement & Instruments Division **Type of organization:** Manufacturing, engineering **Major product:** Process control instrumentation **Area of distribution:** International **Expertise:** Executive management (marketing, engineering) **Published works:** 19 referee articles and technical journals **Affiliations:** I.S.A.; A.V.S. **Hob./spts.:** Fishing, hunting **SIC code:** 38 **Address:** Invensys Foxboro, 33 Commercial St., N04-3A, Foxboro, MA 02035 **E-mail:** mjost@foxboro.com **Web address:** www.foxboro.com

JOY, DAVID L.
Industry: Hair care products **Born:** February 10, 1959, Glenridge, New Jersey **Current organization:** Dax Hair Care **Title:** President **Type of organization:** Manufacturing **Major product:** Pomades, Dax Wax **Area of distribution:** International **Expertise:** Corporate management **Hob./spts.:** Family, snowmobiling, dirt biking **SIC code:** 28 **Address:** Dax Hair Care, 120 New Dutch Lane, Fairfield, NJ 07004 **E-mail:** djoy@imperialdax.com

JUDGE JR., JOHN J.
Industry: Robotics **Born:** February 14, 1943, Holyoke, Massachusetts **Current organization:** R.O.V. Technologies, Inc. **Title:** President/CEO **Type of organization:** Manufacturing/service **Major product:** Wet/dry robotics and vision systems for the nuclear industry **Area of distribution:** National **Expertise:** Robotics, vision systems, operations, remote tooling, field operations **Honors/awards:** National Republican Committee Business Man of the Year, 2003; Tip Award, Nuclear Energy Institute, 2003 **Published works:** 10 articles **Affiliations:** Robotics for Hazardous Environments; Eagle Alliance; Chairman, National Republican Congressional Committee for Business Advisory Council; Project Management Institute **Hob./spts.:** Golf, heavy equipment restoration, pedigree grasses for golf courses **SIC code:** 36 **Address:** R.O.V. Technologies, Inc., 616 Franklin Rd., Vernon, VT 05354 **E-mail:** mail@rovtech.com **Web address:** www.rovtech.com

JUHL, WILLIS RAY
Industry: Agriculture **Born:** October 29, 1929, Bowesmont, North Dakota **Current organization:** Natural Way Mills - Trust **Title:** Co-Trustee **Type of organization:** Grain mill **Major product:** Organic food **Area of distribution:** National **Expertise:** Flour, cereals, whole grain, stone milling **Hob./spts.:** Travel, vacations, camping **SIC code:** 20 **Address:** Natural Way Mills - Trust, 24509 390th St. NE, Middle River, MN 56737 **E-mail:** naturalwaymills@wiktel.com **Web address:** www.naturalwaymills.com

KANTHAMNENI, SUDHAKAR
Industry: Oil country tubular goods **Born:** August 10, 1947, India **Univ./degree:** M.S., Industrial Engineering, University of Iowa, 1975 **Current organization:** Maverick Tube Corp. **Title:** Vice President of Manufacturing and Technology **Type of organization:** Manufacturing **Major product:** Oil country tubular goods **Area of distribution:** International **Expertise:** Engineering and operations **Published works:** Thesis **Affiliations:** P.T.A.; A.S.T.M. **Hob./spts.:** Baseball, football, tennis **SIC code:** 33 **Address:** Maverick Tube Corp., 16401 Swingley Ridge Rd., Suite 700, Chesterfield, MO 63017 **E-mail:** sk@maverick-tube.com

KARASIEWIZ, EUGENE B.
Industry: Metal **Born:** February 22, 1936, Austria **Univ./degree:** A.S., Business Administration, Union College, 1980 **Current organization:** Wm. Steinen Mfg. Co. **Title:** General Foreman of Manufacturing/Chief Heating Lab Technician **Type of organization:** Manufacturing **Major product:** Oil burner and industrial nozzles **Area of distribution:** International **Expertise:** Manufacturing production, R&D, combustion testing; Certified ICS **Honors/awards:** Certificate of Achievement from Dayton Progress Corp., Subject-Die Repair and Standardization Principles, 1970; Certificates of Achievement from R.W. Beckett Corp., Subject-The Installation, Adjustment, Servicing and the Combustion Efficiency Measurement of Oil Burners, 1992 and Subject-Additional Training in Installation, Adjustment, Servicing and the Combustion Efficiency Measurement of Oil Burners, 1996; National Education Program, sponsored by N.D.R.A. and conducted by R.W. Beckett Corp., Subject-Residential Burner Program, 2004 **Hob./spts.:** Photography, audio files, fishing, skiing, swimming, target shooting **SIC code:** 34 **Address:** Wm. Steinen Mfg. Co., 29 E. Halsey Rd., Parsippany, NJ 07054

KARDYS, JAN L.
Industry: Publishing **Born:** June 12, 1954, Hartford, Connecticut **Univ./degree:** B.A., English Literature, Elmira College, 1976 **Current organization:** Black Hawk Enterprise, LLC **Title:** President **Type of organization:** Book publishing service **Major product:** Reviewing contracts **Area of distribution:** National **Expertise:** Reviewing publishing laws **SIC code:** 27 **Address:** Black Hawk Enterprise, LLC, 16 Black Hawk Rd., Scarsdale, NY 10583 **E-mail:** jankardys@aol.com

KARDYS, JOSEPH A.
Industry: Pharmaceuticals **Born:** January 11, 1925, Chicopee, Massachusetts **Univ./degree:** B.S., Science and Math Education; M.A., Organic Chemistry **Current organization:** Pfizer **Title:** Organic Chemist (Retired) **Type of organization:** Manufacturing, research and development **Major product:** Drugs **Area of distribution:** International **Expertise:** Organic chemistry, drugs, vitamins, technical writing **Hob./spts.:** Grandchildren, reading **SIC code:** 28 **Address:** 75 Rope Ferry Rd., Waterford, CT 06385-2617

KARNIK, SHASHANK P.
Industry: Automotive **Univ./degree:** M.B.A., York College, 1992; M.S., University of Michigan, 1996 **Current organization:** Faurecia Interior Systems **Title:** Director of Engineering **Type of organization:** Development and manufacturing **Major product:** Automotive interior systems **Area of distribution:** International **Expertise:** Engineering **Affiliations:** S.A.I.; Society of Plastic Engineers **SIC code:** 37 **Address:** Faurecia Interior Systems, 34405 W. Twelve Mile Rd., Suite 343, Farmington Hills, MI 48331 **E-mail:** skarnik@detroit.faurecia.com

KASER, BRYAN M.
Industry: Surgical instruments **Born:** January 27, 1973, Morgantown, West Virginia **Univ./degree:** B.S., Business, Baldwin-Wallace College, 1996 **Current organization:** Ethicon Endo-Surgery **Title:** Surgical Sales **Type of organization:** Manufacturing **Major product:** Surgical instruments (disposable) **Area of distribution:** N. Royalton, Ohio **Expertise:** Sales, training **Hob./spts.:** Golf, running, weightlifting **SIC code:** 38 **Address:** 14812 Thornton Dr., North Royalton, OH 44133 **E-mail:** bkaser@eesus.jnj.com **Web address:** www.ethiconendo.com

KAUBLE, THOMAS P.
Industry: Automotive **Born:** August 27, 1966, Kokomo, Indiana **Univ./degree:** B.S.M.E., Purdue University, 1989; M.B.A., Wesleyan University, 1994 **Current organization:** Truck Accessories Group **Title:** Director of Engineering **Type of organization:** Manufacturing **Major product:** Limousines, ambulances, hearses **Area of distribution:** International **Expertise:** Engineering, R&D, management **Published works:** 2 patents **Hob./spts.:** Physical fitness, swimming, biking, jogging, golf, travel, reading **SIC code:** 37 **Address:** Accubuilt, 2550 Central Point Pkwy., Lima, OH 45804-3890 **E-mail:** tpkauble@aol.com **Web address:** www.accubuilt.com

KAUFFMAN, WILLIAM J.
Industry: Building products **Born:** January 9, 1945, Chicago, Illinois **Univ./degree:** B.S., Chemistry, Juniata College, Pennsylvania, 1966; Ph.D., Organic Chemistry, University of New Hampshire, 1969 **Current organization:** Armstrong World Industries **Title:** Intellectual Property Manager **Type of organization:** Manufacturing **Major product:** Research and development, floor products **Area of distribution:** International **Expertise:** Innovation, patent strategy **Published works:** 30 US patents, 10 technical publications **Affiliations:** American Chemical Society; Society of Plastics Engineers; National Science Foundation **Hob./spts.:** Baseball, golf, racquetball, gardening **SIC code:** 24 **Address:** Armstrong World Industries, 226 Hershey Dr., Manheim, PA 17545 **E-mail:** wjkauffman@armstrong.com

KAUFMAN, ANDREW J.
Industry: Industrial tools, surgical devices **Born:** November 28, 1960, Patterson, New Jersey **Univ./degree:** B.S., Electrical Engineering, Devry Institute of Technology, 1980 **Current organization:** Triangle Manufacturing Co., Inc. **Title:** Production Manager **Type of organization:** Manufacturing **Major product:** Industrial tools, surgical devices **Area of distribution:** International **Expertise:** Production and inventory management **Affiliations:** A.P.I.C.S. **Hob./spts.:** Skiing, hiking, camping, bicycling, guitar, travel **SIC code:** 38 **Address:** Triangle Manufacturing Co., Inc., 116 Pleasant Ave., Upper Saddle River, NJ 07458 **E-mail:** akaufman@trianglemfg.com

KAYE, KEVIN J.
Industry: Engineering **Born:** September 3, 1964, Daytona Beach, Florida **Univ./degree:** University of Missouri, St. Louis **Current organization:** Ocean Optics Inc. **Title:** Senior Photonics Applications Engineer **Type of organization:** Manufacturing **Major product:** Photonics **Area of distribution:** International **Expertise:** Engineering applications **Affiliations:** Laser Institute of America; Optical Society of America **Hob./spts.:** Surfing, golf **SIC code:** 38 **Address:** Ocean Optics Inc., 830 Douglas Ave., Dunedin, FL 34698 **E-mail:** kjkaye@knology.net

KEITH, ANDREA L.
Industry: Edible oils, emulsifiers, encapsulates **Born:** September 10, 1963, Joliet, Illinois **Univ./degree:** B.S., Chemistry, Bradley University, 1985; M.B.A., 1995; M.A., Organizational Behavior, 1997, Illinois Benedictine University **Current organization:**

Loders Croklaan **Title:** Business Development Manager **Type of organization:** Manufacturing **Major product:** Edible oils, emulsifiers, encapsulates **Area of distribution:** International **Expertise:** Sales and marketing **Published works:** 1 article, "Food Processing", The Magazine of Strategy, Technology and Trends **Affiliations:** I.F.T.; A.A.P.S.; A.O.C.S.; A.A.C.C. **Hob./spts.:** Fitness, crocheting **SIC code:** 20 **Address:** Loders Croklaan, 24708 W. Durkee Rd., Channahon, IL 60410 **E-mail:** andrea.keith@croklaan.com

KELLY, DAVID L.
Industry: Commercial construction **Born:** November 14, 1939, Sacramento, California **Univ./degree:** B.S.C.E., California State University, Sacramento, 1963 **Current organization:** Meadow Burke Products **Title:** Vice President, Chief Engineer **Type of organization:** Manufacturing **Major product:** Construction materials and accessories **Area of distribution:** International **Expertise:** Engineering; P.E. (Australia, Canada, California, Washington, Texas) **Honors/awards:** 17 US patents **Published works:** Several articles **Affiliations:** M.C.A.; A.C.I. **SIC code:** 39 **Address:** Meadow Burke Products, 231-A Lathrop Way, Sacramento, CA 95815-4214 **E-mail:** dkellype@meadowburke.com **Web address:** www.meadowburke.com

KENNEALLY, DANIEL J.
Industry: Welding **Born:** October 17, 1950, Ireland **Current organization:** Kk Welding Inc. **Title:** President **Type of organization:** Manufacturing **Major product:** Welding and lead fabrication **Area of distribution:** Hyde Park, Massachusetts **Expertise:** Lead fabrication and welding repair **Affiliations:** Local C.C. **Hob./spts.:** Reading, golf, soccer **SIC code:** 34 **Address:** Kk Welding Inc., 107 Providence St., Hyde Park, MA 02136 **E-mail:** dkenna552@aol.com

KERN, ROBERT R.
Industry: Automotive **Born:** October 1, 1946, West Bend, Wisconsin **Univ./degree:** B.S.M.E., University of Wisconsin, 1969 **Current organization:** General Motors Corp. **Title:** SEMA Relations Manager **Type of organization:** Manufacturing **Major product:** Automotive vehicles **Area of distribution:** International **Expertise:** Engineering, product development of aftermarket products **Honors/awards:** "Man of the Year," 2004, National Sports Compact Council **Affiliations:** S.A.E.; S.B.E. **Hob./spts.:** Classical vehicle restoration, tennis, boating **SIC code:** 37 **Address:** General Motors Corp., 100 Renaissance Center, Detroit, MI 48265 **E-mail:** rob_eagle2@yahoo.com

KEVO, IVAN
Industry: Food **Born:** June 9, 1946, Apatin, Yugoslavia **Univ./degree:** B.S., Mechanical Engineering, Zagreb Mechanical Technical School, Croatia, 1964; B.S., Aeronautical Engineering, Aerospace Institute of Chicago, 1975 **Current organization:** Fair Oaks Farms **Title:** Plant Engineer **Type of organization:** Manufacturing **Major product:** Pork sausages **Area of distribution:** International **Expertise:** Manufacturing, process development and management **Affiliations:** Board Member, R.E.T.A. **Hob./spts.:** Fishing, hunting **SIC code:** 20 **Address:** Fair Oaks Farms, 7600 95th St., Pleasant Prairie, WI 53158 **E-mail:** ikevo@osigroup.com **Web address:** www.usigropu.com

KEY, BARRY T.
Industry: Conveyor terminals and structures **Born:** July 15, 1968, Jasper, Alabama **Univ./degree:** B.S.M.E., University of Alabama, 1993 **Current organization:** Continental Conveyor & Equipment Co. **Title:** Senior Engineer **Type of organization:** Manufacturing **Major product:** Conveyor terminals and structures **Area of distribution:** National **Expertise:** Engineering **Affiliations:** A.S.M.E. **Hob./spts.:** Golf, fishing **SIC code:** 35 **Address:** Continental Conveyor & Equipment Co., 438 Industrial Dr., Winfield, AL 35594 **E-mail:** bkey@continentalconveyor.com

KEY, MICHAEL J.
Industry: Automotive **Born:** August 17, 1968, Danville, Illinois **Current organization:** Master Guard/Flex-N-Gate **Title:** Paint Coordinator **Type of organization:** Manufacturing **Major product:** Rear stop bumpers and truck accessories **Area of distribution:** International **Expertise:** Paint **Affiliations:** Prairie Chapel Church; 32 Degree Mason **Hob./spts.:** Playing guitar and singing, deer hunting **SIC code:** 37 **Address:** Master Guard/Flex-N-Gate, 1200 E. Eighth St., Veederburg, IN 47987 **E-mail:** mikek@flex-n-gate.com

KEYES, CHARLES R.
Industry: Medical devices **Born:** Hudson, Massachusetts **Univ./degree:** A.S., Psychology, Worcester, Massachusetts **Current organization:** Biotech Manufacturing Center of Texas, Inc. **Title:** Medical Extrusion Engineer **Type of organization:** Manufacturing/engineering/medical incubator **Major product:** Medical devices, medical extrusions, molding, assembly, dipping **Area of distribution:** National **Expertise:** Engineering - medical extrusions **Published works:** 3 articles **Affiliations:** The Plastics Society **Hob./spts.:** Writing **SIC code:** 38 **Address:** Biotech Manufacturing Center of Texas, Inc., 1704 Enterprise St., Athens, TX 75751 **E-mail:** charleskeyes@earthlink.net **Web address:** www.bmc-texas.org

KIEN, TAI T.
Industry: Medical devices **Born:** April 14, 1970 Tra Vinh, Vietnam **Univ./degree:** B.S., Plastics Engineering, University of Massachusetts **Current organization:** Innovative Medical Design **Title:** R&D Engineer **Type of organization:** Manufacturing **Major product:** Medical devices **Area of distribution:** International **Expertise:** Innovative products **Honors/awards:** 2 patents **Hob./spts.:** Soccer, fishing **SIC code:** 38 **Address:** Innovative Medical Design, 31 Westech Dr., Tyngsboro, MA 01879 **E-mail:** taikien_imd@yahoo.com

KILAR, ANDREW D.
Industry: Food **Univ./degree:** Dale Carnegie Training Seminar **Current organization:** Stonyfield Farm **Title:** Processor II **Type of organization:** Manufacturing **Major product:** Yogurt **Area of distribution:** National **Expertise:** R&D, processing **Hob./spts.:** Continuing education **SIC code:** 20 **Address:** Stonyfield Farm, 10 Burton Dr., Londonderry, NH 03053 **E-mail:** adkilar@hotmail.com

KILLIAN, MICHAEL R.
Industry: Construction Management **Born:** December 22, 1976, Bloomsburg, Pennsylvania **Univ./degree:** B.S., Business Administration, Bloomsburg University of Pennsylvania, 2000 **Current organization:** J.A. Jones Engineering & Construction Co. **Title:** Project Engineer **Type of organization:** Construction management **Major product:** Construction **Area of distribution:** International **Expertise:** Engineering **Hob./spts.:** Softball, biking, fishing **SIC code:** 28 **Address:** J.A. Jones Engineering & Construction Co., 270 Davidson Ave., The Tower, Somerset, NJ 08873 **E-mail:** michael.killian@hotmail.com

KIMMEL, MARK E.
Industry: Food **Born:** September 25, 1951, Johnstown, Pennsylvania **Univ./degree:** B.S., Food Service, Purdue University; C.C.P.S. Certificate, Culinary Institute of Hyde Park, New York **Current organization:** Stanislaus Food Products **Title:** Senior Vice President **Type of organization:** Manufacturing **Major product:** Fresh packed canned tomatoes and tomato products **Area of distribution:** National **Expertise:** Quality control, research and development, production and sales in food processing **Affiliations:** A.Q.S.; C.L.F.P.; R.C.A.; A.C.F.; Past President, F.P.S.A. **Hob./spts.:** Golf, woodworking, fishing **SIC code:** 20 **Address:** Stanislaus Food Products, 1202 "D" St., Modesto, CA 95354

KIMMEL, ROBERT I.
Industry: Publishing **Born:** January 28, 1923, Uniontown, Pennsylvania **Univ./degree:** Bucknell University **Current organization:** The Paxton Herald / Communications Systems Design Associates **Title:** Manager / Technical Consultant **Type of organization:** Publishing / Engineering Design and Sales - Satellite System Phone Equipment and Satellite Phone Service **Area of distribution:** Central Pennsylvania / 7 Middle Atlantic States **Honors/awards:** American Red Cross Life Saver Medal **Published works:** "Emergency Communications During the 3-Mile Island Accident", "Effect of Speed Control Radar on Pacemakers"; Retired Dir., Communications Div., Pennsylvania State Police **Affiliations:** Executive Director, Greater Edgemont Senior Center; Board of Directors, Salvation Army; Life Member, American Legion; Board of Directors, American Legion Post 272; Past President, Pennsylvania Engineers Society; Past President, St. Marks Lutheran Church; Past President, Atlantic Chapter Public Safety Communications Officers; Life Member, Pennsylvania Chiefs of Police Association **Hob./spts.:** Golf, photography, reading **SIC code:** 27 **Address:** The Paxton Herald, 101 Lincoln St., Harrisburg, PA 17112 **E-mail:** rikm1@juno.com **Web address:** www.communicationssytemsdesign.com

KINNEY, M. DAVID
Industry: Power sports machines **Born:** March 28, 1973, Waukesha, Wisconsin **Univ./degree:** B.S., University of Wisconsin **Current organization:** Polaris Ind. **Title:** Manufacturing Engineer, Coating **Type of organization:** Manufacturing **Major product:** Power sports vehicles, parts, accessories **Area of distribution:** International **Expertise:** Polymer engineering **Affiliations:** S.M.E. **Hob./spts.:** Hunting, fishing **SIC code:** 37 **Address:** 1900 Hwy. 71, Spirit Lake, IA 51360 **E-mail:** david.kinney@polarisind.com

KINNEY, TERRY A.
Industry: Automotive/appliance **Born:** February 15, 1952, West Branch, Michigan **Univ./degree:** B.S.M.E., Lake Superior State University, 1975 **Current organization:** Tawas Industries Inc. **Title:** Engineering Manager **Type of organization:** Manufacturing **Major product:** Automotive/appliance components **Area of distribution:** International **Expertise:** Mechanical/manufacturing engineering **Affiliations:** S.A.E. **Hob./spts.:** Carpentry, hunting, fishing, golf **SIC code:** 36 **Address:** Tawas Industries Inc., 905 Cedar St., Tawas City, MI 48763

KINSEY, RONALD A.
Industry: Construction/industrial electrical **Born:** October 22, 1957, Denver, Colorado **Current organization:** MYR Group Inc. **Title:** Safety Supervisor **Type of organization:** Contractor **Major product:** Utility power construction **Area of distribution:**

National **Expertise:** Electrical engineering and safety **Affiliations:** I.E.E.E.; National Safety Council **Hob./spts.:** Auto racing **SIC code:** 36 **Address:** MYR Group Inc., 612 E. Bridgeport Pkwy., Gilbert, AZ 85296 **E-mail:** rkinsey@myrgroup.com

KIPFERL, ROBERT J.
Industry: Electronics **Born:** August 8, 1965, Elmira, New York **Univ./degree:** OSHA Certified, UCI University, 1996; Backflow Prevention Protector Certified, Orange County Health Agency, 1998; Certified Industrial Treatment Operator, C.W.A.E. **Current organization:** Sanmina-SCI Corp. **Title:** EHS Operations Manager **Type of organization:** Manufacturing **Major product:** Printed circuit boards, EMS products **Area of distribution:** Costa Mesa, California **Expertise:** Environmental, health and safety operations **Affiliations:** C.W.E.A. **Hob./spts.:** Golf, hotrod cars **SIC code:** 36 **Address:** Sanmina-SCI Corp., 2945 Airway Ave., Costa Mesa, CA 92626 **E-mail:** robert.kipferl@sanmina.com **Web address:** www.sanmina.com

KIRBY, THOMAS E.
Industry: Computers **Born:** October 14, 1952, Winnsboro, Louisiana **Univ./degree:** B.S., Instrumentation, Macanese State University, 1990 **Current organization:** Corning, Inc. **Title:** Automation Engineer **Type of organization:** Manufacturing **Major product:** Flat panel display glass **Area of distribution:** International **Expertise:** Engineering **Affiliations:** I.S.A. **Hob./spts.:** Automotive electronics **SIC code:** 35 **Address:** Corning, Inc., 680 E. Office St., Harrodsburg, KY 40330 **E-mail:** kirbyte@corning.com **Web address:** www.corning.com

KIRKITADZE, MARINA D.
Industry: Pharmaceuticals **Born:** July 8, 1969, Russia **Univ./degree:** B.S., Physics & Biophysics, Tbilisi State University, Republic of Georgia, 1991; Ph.D., Biological Sciences, Institute of Protein Research, Russian Academy of Sciences, 1996; M.B.A., Global Management, University of Phoenix; 2007 **Current organization:** Sanofi Pasteur Ltd. **Title:** Senior Scientist **Type of organization:** Manufacturing **Major product:** Vaccines **Area of distribution:** International **Expertise:** Protein Biochemistry and Biophysics **Honors/awards:** Edward R. and Anne G. Lefler Fellowship for project "Conformational dynamics of amyloid beta-protein fibrillogenesis", 2001, July 1-2002, June 30; George Soros Fellowship for postgraduate students (Grant form George Soros International Science Foundation No A96-806)1996; Scholarship to attend 8th International Conference on Alzheimer's Disease and Related Disorders (July 20-25, 2002, Stockholm, Sweden) **Published works:** 21 articles including, Co-author, "Amyloid b-protein assembly (Ab): Ab40 and Ab42 oligomerize through distinct pathways", Proc. Natl. Acad. Sci. 2003, 100: 330-335; "Central modules of the Vaccinia virus complement control protein are not in extensive contact", Biochem.J. 1999, 344: 167-175; "Independently melting modules and highly structured intermolecular junctions within complement receptor type 1", Biochemistry 1999, 38:7019-31; "A Molecular mechanisms initiating amyloid B-fibril formation in Alzheimer's disease", Acta Biochemica Polonica, 2005 **Affiliations:** Past Member, Biochemical Society (Russia); Protein Society (US); Society of Neuroscience (US); Present Member, Smithsonian Society (US); American Society for Biochemistry and Molecular Biology (US) **Hob./spts.:** History, geology, geography, Formula 1 **SIC code:** 28 **Address:** Sanofi Pasteur Ltd., 1755 Steeles Ave. West, Toronto, ON M2R3T4, Canada **E-mail:** Marina.Kirkitadze@sanofipasteur.com

KIRKPATRICK, TODD W.
Industry: Communications **Born:** May 12, 1973, Vernon, Alabama **Univ./degree:** B.S.M.E., Auburn University, 1996 **Current organization:** Continental Conveyor **Title:** Chief Engineer of Conveyor components **Type of organization:** Manufacturing **Major product:** Communication components **Area of distribution:** International **Expertise:** Engineering **Affiliations:** S.M.E.; Pi Tau Sigma; Tau Beta Pi; Golden Key National Honor Society **Hob./spts.:** Family, playing guitar, training quarter horses **SIC code:** 36 **Address:** Continental Conveyor, 438 Industrial Dr., Winfield, AL 35594 **E-mail:** tkirkpatrick@continentalconveyor.com

KLEIN, HERBERT G.
Industry: Publishing **Born:** April 1, 1918, Los Angeles, California **Univ./degree:** B.S., University of Southern California, 1940 **Current organization:** Copley Newspapers **Title:** V.P./Editor in Chief **Type of organization:** Publishing **Major product:** 9 daily and 30 weekly newspapers **Area of distribution:** National **Expertise:** Newspaper editing **Honors/awards:** Honorary Doctorate, University of San Diego **Affiliations:** Board Member, Greater San Diego Chamber of Commerce; Board Member, Holiday Bowl **Hob./spts.:** Sports, reading **SIC code:** 27 **Address:** Copley Newspapers, P.O. Box 8935, Rancho Santa Fe, CA 92067

KLINE, CHRIS H.
Industry: Truck equipment **Born:** June 1, 1970, Reading, Pennsylvania **Current organization:** Utility One Source **Title:** Quotation Specialist **Type of organization:** Distributor **Major product:** Aerial bucket trucks **Area of distribution:** Pennsylvania **Expertise:** Sales quotations **Affiliations:** N.T.E.A. **Hob./spts.:** Golf, travel **SIC code:** 37 **Address:** Utility One Source, 2706 Brodhead Rd., Bethlehem, PA 18020 **E-mail:** ckline@utilityonesource.com

KNIBB-CROOKS, ELEANOR R.
Industry: Apparel **Born:** July 3, 1948, Kingston, Jamaica **Univ./degree:** Attended Clarendon Private School **Current organization:** Design House **Title:** Owner **Type of organization:** Manufacturing **Major product:** Screen printing on clothes **Area of distribution:** National **Expertise:** Sales and marketing **Affiliations:** Ormond Beach Chamber of Commerce **Hob./spts.:** Cooking, gardening **SIC code:** 27 **Address:** Design House, 320 Division Ave., Unit A, Ormond Beach, FL 32174 **E-mail:** eleanor@designhouse.com

KOCHAT, HARRY
Industry: Pharmaceuticals **Born:** October 19, 1959, Trichur, India **Univ./degree:** Ph.D., Purdue University, 1988 **Current organization:** Bionumerik Pharmaceuticals **Title:** Senior Manager **Type of organization:** Drug discovery and manufacturing **Major product:** Anticancer drugs **Area of distribution:** International **Expertise:** Research and manufacturing **Honors/awards:** 76 patents; Best Scientist of the Year, Recognition Award From CSIR, 1999-2000 **Affiliations:** A.C.S. **Hob./spts.:** Tennis **SIC code:** 28 **Address:** Bionumerik Pharmaceuticals Inc., 8122 Datapoint, Suite 400, San Antonio, TX 78229 **E-mail:** harry.kochat@bnpi.com

KOCHEVAR, STEVEN D.
Industry: Instrumentation **Born:** September 27, 1961, Big Spring, Texas **Univ./degree:** B.S.E.E., University of Colorado, Denver, 2001; M.S. Candidate, Optical & Robotic Engineering **Current organization:** Particle Measuring Systems **Title:** Applications & Electrical Engineer **Type of organization:** Manufacturing, R&D **Major product:** Semiconductors and pharmaceuticals **Area of distribution:** International **Expertise:** Engineering **Published works:** 20 journal articles **Affiliations:** I.E.E.E. **Hob./spts.:** Computer design, travel **SIC code:** 36 **Address:** Particle Measuring Systems, 5475 Airport Blvd., Boulder, CO 80301-2339 **E-mail:** skochevar@pmeasuring.com

KOGAN, BORIS
Industry: Automotive **Born:** May 29, 1945, Ukraine **Univ./degree:** Ph.D., Mechanical Engineering, Moscow Automotive Research Center (NAMI) and Kalinin Polytechnic Institute; M.S.M.E., Samara Aircraft Institute, Russia **Current organization:** Green Bearing/Bearing Technologies Ltd. **Title:** Chief Engineer **Type of organization:** Manufacturing and Assembly, R&D **Major product:** Hub assembly, clutch release bearings **Area of distribution:** International **Expertise:** Engineering **Hob./spts.:** Travel, bicycling **SIC code:** 37 **Address:** Green Bearing / Bearing Technologies, Ltd., 9801 Harvard Ave., Cleveland, OH 44105 **Phone:** (216)883-7800 **Fax:** (216)381-4943 **E-mail:** kobosi2@att.net

KONLE, HANS P.
Industry: Machinery **Born:** July 17, 1956, Ellwangen, Germany **Univ./degree:** M.A., University of Karlsruhe, Germany, 1983 **Current organization:** Autoprod, Inc. **Title:** Engineering Manager **Type of organization:** Manufacturing **Major product:** Packaging machinery **Area of distribution:** International **Expertise:** Engineering **Affiliations:** S.S.A.; V.P., Tampa Bay Soaring Society **Hob./spts.:** Flying, soaring **SIC code:** 35 **Address:** 8060 Cypress Garden Ct., Seminole, FL 33777 **E-mail:** nenak@aol.com

KOOS, DANIEL A.
Industry: Semiconductor equipment **Born:** Chicago, Illinois **Univ./degree:** Ph.D., Physical Chemistry, University of Oregon, 1991 **Current organization:** Novellus Systems, Inc. **Title:** Ph.D. **Type of organization:** Manufacturing **Major product:** Semiconductor equipment, CMP machines, physical vapor deposition **Area of distribution:** International **Expertise:** Process engineering, cleaning applications **Affiliations:** E.C.S. **SIC code:** 36 **Address:** Novellus Systems, Inc., 300 N. 56th St., Chandler, AZ 85226 **E-mail:** daniel.koos@novellus.com

KOSAMIA, MOHAN
Industry: Rubber products **Born:** February 12, 1941, India **Univ./degree:** M.S., Organic Chemistry, Gujarat University, India, 1963 **Current organization:** Church & Dwight Virginia Co., Inc. **Title:** Manager, Technical Services **Type of organization:** Manufacturing **Major product:** Trojan condoms **Area of distribution:** National, International **Expertise:** Polymer science **Affiliations:** Chairman, ASTM D11.40.01 Committee; Member, American Chemical Society, Rubber Division **Hob./spts.:** Reading, music **SIC code:** 30 **Address:** Church & Dwight Virginia Co., Inc., 1851 Touchstone Rd., Colonial Heights, VA 23834 **E-mail:** mohan.kosamia@churchdwight.com **Web address:** www.churchdwight.com

KOTRCH, MARILYNN G.
Industry: Printing **Born:** August 19, 1940, Toronto, Ontario, Canada **Univ./degree:** Davenport University, Michigan, 1976 **Current organization:** MK Printing Co., Inc. **Title:** President, C.E.O. **Type of organization:** Custom printing **Major product:** Tags, labels **Area of distribution:** International **Expertise:** Printing consulting **Affiliations:** Sand Lake Chamber of Commerce **Hob./spts.:** Hunting **SIC code:** 27 **Address:** MK Printing Co., Inc., 12815 Hamilton Hills Dr., Gowen, MI 49326 **E-mail:** mkprinting@triton.net **Web address:** www.mkprinting.com

KOUKOURAKIS, NICK
Industry: Appliances **Univ./degree:** M.S., Mechanical Engineering, University of Akron, Ohio, 1988 **Current organization:** Maytag International **Title:** Director, International Floorcare **Type of organization:** Manufacturing **Major product:** Washers, dryers, drying cabinets **Area of distribution:** International **Expertise:** Product management, product plans and development **SIC code:** 36 **Address:** 9980 Derbyshire Ave., N.W., North Canton, OH 44720 **E-mail:** nick.koukourakis@maytag.com

KOVANGJI, MUHAMED
Industry: Paper **Born:** October 20, 1960, Prizren, Kosovo **Univ./degree:** M.S., University of Pristina, 1982 **Current organization:** Recycled Paperboard of Clifton, Inc. **Title:** Technical Director/Plant Engineer **Type of organization:** Manufacturing **Major product:** Recycled paper **Area of distribution:** International **Expertise:** Engineering **Hob./spts.:** Math, soccer, boxing **SIC code:** 26 **Address:** Recycled Paperboard of Clifton, Inc., One Ackerman Ave., Clifton, NJ 07011

KOWALIK, KRIS
Industry: Paper **Born:** August 12, 1959, Warsaw, Poland **Univ./degree:** Design & Manufacturing Degree, Warsaw, Poland, 1980 **Current organization:** Nielsen Bainbridge **Title:** Lead Plant Engineer **Type of organization:** Manufacturing **Major product:** Paper converting **Area of distribution:** New Jersey **Expertise:** Engineering **Hob./spts.:** Diving **SIC code:** 26 **Address:** Nielsen Bainbridge, 17 S. Middlesex Ave., Jamesburg, NJ 08831 **E-mail:** kkowalik@nbframing.com

KRAMER, BENJAMIN H.
Industry: Pharmaceuticals **Born:** November 12, 1956, Brooklyn, New York **Univ./degree:** M.D., New York Medical College 1982 **Current organization:** Pfizer **Title:** M.D./Senior Medical Director **Type of organization:** Pharmaceutical manufacturing **Major product:** Medicines, drugs **Area of distribution:** International **Expertise:** Allerg, immunology and pharmaceutical medicine **Published works:** 7 publications, 12 abstracts **Affiliations:** A.C.A.A.I., A.A.A.A.I **Hob./spts.:** Music, theatre, tennis, weight lifting, running **SIC code:** 28 **Address:** Pfizer, 235 E. 42nd St., New York, NY 10017 **E-mail:** kramb@pfizer.com **Web address:** www.pfizer.com

KRANER, EMIL
Industry: Semiconductors **Born:** September 15, 1953, Moldova, Russia **Univ./degree:** Moscow Institute of Airplane Design, 1976 **Current organization:** Technical Manufacturing Corp. **Title:** Ph.D. **Type of organization:** Manufacturing **Major product:** Vibration isolation systems **Area of distribution:** International **Expertise:** Engineering **Affiliations:** I.E.E.E. **Hob./spts.:** Family **SIC code:** 36 **Address:** Technical Manufacturing Corp., 15 Centennial Dr., Peabody, MA 01960 **E-mail:** ekraner@techmfg.com

KRAUS, BEV. J.
Industry: Electronics **Born:** October 28, 1957, Belle Plaine, Minnesota **Current organization:** Valtek Manufacturing Inc. **Title:** Owner/Manager **Type of organization:** Contract manufacturing **Major product:** Wire harnesses and electronic assembly **Area of distribution:** National **Expertise:** Contract electronic and wire assembly **SIC code:** 36 **Address:** Valtek Manufacturing Inc., 625 Slack Dr., Lesueur, MN 56058 **E-mail:** valtek@qwest.net

KRIDLER, DON
Industry: Steel **Born:** October 6, 1955, Salem, Ohio **Current organization:** V&M Star **Title:** Caster Maintenance Supervisor **Type of organization:** Manufacturing (steel mini mill) **Major product:** Seamless pipe **Area of distribution:** International **Expertise:** Maintenance **Honors/awards:** Car show award **Hob./spts.:** Hunting, cars **SIC code:** 33 **Address:** V&M Star, 2669 Martin Luther King Jr Blvd., Youngstown, OH 44510

KRUG, GREGORY F.
Industry: Biotechnology **Univ./degree:** B.S., Delaware Valley College of Science and Agriculture **Current organization:** Lampire Biological Laboratories, Inc. **Title:** President **Type of organization:** Manufacturing of diagnostic and pharmaceutical reagents **Major product:** Blood products, custom antibody production services **Area of distribution:** International **Expertise:** Corporate management **Honors/awards:** 2002 Achievement Award in Animal Science, Delaware Valley College Alumni Association **Affiliations:** American Association of Clinical Chemistry (AACC); American Association of Laboratory Animal Scientists (AALAS); American Chemical Association; American Society for Microbiology; Eastern Technology Council; Mid-Atlantic Region Society of Quality Assurance; Pennsylvania Farmers Association; Regional Biotechnology Council for Central Bucks; numerous community organizations including Bedford County Agriculture/Biotechnology Committee; Bedford County Development Association; Bedford County and Bucks County Chamber of Commerce **Hob./spts.:** Football, polo **SIC code:** 28 **Address:** Lampire Biological Laboratories, Inc., P.O. Box 270, Pipersville, PA 18947

KRUHOFFER, KURT
Industry: Pharmaceuticals **Born:** October 1, 1941, Frederiksberg, Denmark **Univ./degree:** M.B.A., Denmark, 1971, Handelshoejskolen i Aarhus **Current organization:** Leo Pharma, Inc. **Title:** Business Development **Type of organization:** Marketing **Major product:** Antibiotics, dermatologicals **Area of distribution:** Latin America **Expertise:** Marketing, management **Honors/awards:** Boersens Annual Award for Best Accounting Practice and Best Annual Report, Danish financial paper Boersen for best performance among companies in Denmark **Affiliations:** Pharmaceutical Association of Denmark; Danish Conservative Party **Hob./spts.:** Golf, squash, sailing **SIC code:** 28 **Address:** Leo Pharma, Inc., 61 N.W. 128th Ave., Plantation, FL 33325 **E-mail:** bufas@bellsouth.net

KRUMMECK, ROY C.
Industry: Furniture **Born:** April 12, 1959, Johannesburg, South Africa **Univ./degree:** B.A., Psychology, 1984; Higher Diploma in Education, 1986, University of the Witwatersrand **Current organization:** Kwalu, LLC **Title:** Marketing Manager **Type of organization:** Manufacturing **Major product:** Furniture **Area of distribution:** International **Expertise:** Marketing, advertising; team leader of website development, trade shows, training seminars **Published works:** Motivational writing **Affiliations:** South African Navy, 1977-85 (Reserves) **Hob./spts.:** Playing the guitar, Hogg touring, bicycling **SIC code:** 25 **Address:** Kwalu, LLC, 146 Woodlawn St., Ridgeland, SC 29936 **E-mail:** rkrummeck@kwalu.com

KUBICEK III, JOHN E.
Industry: Technology **Born:** January 9, 1960, Dallas, Texas **Univ./degree:** Technical Training **Current organization:** National Semi Conductor **Title:** Facility Coordinator **Type of organization:** Manufacturing **Major product:** Semiconductors **Area of distribution:** Arlington, Texas **Expertise:** Ultra pure water engineering **Honors/awards:** Served in The Air Force **Published works:** Paper, "Ultra Pure Magazine" **Affiliations:** T.P.M. **SIC code:** 36 **Address:** National Semi Conductor, Mail Stop B1100, 1111 W. Bardin Rd., Arlington, TX 76017 **E-mail:** john.kubicek@nsc.com

KUHNKE II, EARL W.
Industry: Hydraulic components **Born:** July 7, 1946, Boone, Iowa **Univ./degree:** M.S., Mechanical Engineering **Current organization:** Parker Hanson **Title:** Engineering Manager-Applications **Type of organization:** Manufacturing **Major product:** Industrial and mobile hydraulic valves and components **Area of distribution:** International **Expertise:** Hydraulic design of components and systems **Published works:** 6 patents **Affiliations:** A.S.M.E.; S.P.E.; F.T.S.; H.S.A. **SIC code:** 36 **Address:** 4415 Valley View Rd., #12, Edina, MN 55424 **E-mail:** ewkuhnke@hotmail.com

KUKRECHT, TATYANA
Industry: Wigs **Born:** July 4, 1933, Novi Sad, Yugoslavia **Univ./degree:** Wig making Apprenticeship, Salon Georgstaudt, 2005 **Current organization:** European Wigmaker at Tanya's Chalet **Title:** Owner **Type of organization:** Manufacturing **Major product:** Wigs, post-mastectomy supplies **Area of distribution:** International **Expertise:** Custom wigmaker, stylist, fashion shows **Honors/awards:** First Prize, Student Competition, Fantasy Hairstyling, 1961 **Published works:** 1 article, "Sarasota Tribunal" **SIC code:** 39 **Address:** European Wigmaker at Tanya's Chalet, 2135 Siesta Dr., Sarasota, FL 34239 **E-mail:** tanyaschalet@yahoo.com **Web address:** www.tanyaschalet.com

KUS, RICHARD W.
Industry: Automotive **Born:** March 26, 1954, Detroit, Michigan **Univ./degree:** A.S., Liberal Arts, Henry Ford Community College, 1995 **Current organization:** American Axle Inc. **Title:** Oil Analyst **Type of organization:** Manufacturing **Major product:** Front and rear axles **Area of distribution:** National **Expertise:** Preventive maintenance, oil analysis **Affiliations:** Registered Member, The Vibration Institute **Hob./spts.:** Softball, fishing, family **SIC code:** 37 **Address:** American Axle Inc., 1840 Holbrook St., Detroit, MI 48212 **E-mail:** kusr@aam.com **Web address:** www.aam.com

KUSTEK, MICHAEL J.
Industry: Pharmaceuticals **Born:** Brooklyn, New York **Univ./degree:** B.S., Chemistry, SUNY Fredonia; Ph.D., Physical Pharmaceutical Research, University of Connecticut, 1981 **Title:** Research Associate **Type of organization:** Manufacturing **Major product:** Drugs, medicines **Area of distribution:** National **Expertise:** Preformulation, dissolution testing; UNIX Certification, 2002 **Affiliations:** A.A.P.S. **Hob./spts.:** Bicycling, computers, the Internet **SIC code:** 28 **Address:** 19 Van Doren Ave., Somerville, NJ 08876 **E-mail:** mustbemikek@netscape.net

KUTZBERGER, STEVEN M.
Industry: Food **Born:** May 20, 1961, Baltimore, Maryland **Univ./degree:** A.A., Food Science, Essex Community College, 1989 **Current organization:** Washington Quality Foods/Wilkins-Rogers **Title:** Coatings Division Manager **Type of organization:** Manufacturing, research and development **Major product:** Batters and breading mixes **Area of distribution:** International **Expertise:** Product development, sales and marketing **Affiliations:** Past Treasurer, Maryland Chapter, IFT, 1998-2001 **Hob./spts.:** Softball, swimming, outdoor sports, travel **SIC code:** 20 **Address:** Washington Qual-

ity Foods/Wilkins-Rogers, 4501 Hollins Ferry Rd., Halethorpe, MD 21227 **E-mail:** s.kutzberger@att.net

LA BARBERA, JAMES M.
Industry: Packaging/engineering **Born:** August 12, 1974, North Hollywood, California **Univ./degree:** B.S.M.E., California State University, Northridge, 2002 **Current organization:** Air Packaging Technologies, Inc. **Title:** Packaging/R&D Engineer **Type of organization:** Manufacturing **Major product:** Custom protective packaging **Area of distribution:** International **Expertise:** Engineering (design, drafting, tooling and testing) **Honors/awards:** Served in Active Duty U.S. Army, 1993-95 **Affiliations:** A.S.M.E. **Hob./spts.:** Basketball, baseball, hiking, camping, skiing, rock collecting **SIC code:** 26 **Address:** 19240 Ranier St., Canyon County, CA 91351 **E-mail:** jlabar1228@aol.com

LABOY, OMAR
Industry: Pharmaceuticals **Born:** October 19, 1972, New York, New York **Univ./degree:** B.S., Chemistry, University of Puerto Rico at Mayaguez **Current organization:** IPR Pharmaceuticals, Inc. **Title:** Computer Validation Technologist **Type of organization:** Manufacturing **Major product:** Solid dosage prescription drugs **Area of distribution:** International **Expertise:** Computer system validation-laboratory systems **Affiliations:** A.S.Q.; C.Q.A.; C.S.Q.E.; I.E.E.E. **Hob./spts.:** Movies, reading **SIC code:** 28 **Address:** IPR Pharmaceuticals, Inc., P.O. Box 1985, Carolina, PR 00984 **E-mail:** omar.laboy@usa.net

LAFEVRE, TIMOTHY J.
Industry: Machinery **Born:** March 28, 1956, Mansfield, Ohio **Current organization:** Heartland Hydraulics, Inc. **Title:** President/G.M. **Type of organization:** Manufacturing and distribution (to support auto industry, steel industry, packaging industry, etc.) **Major product:** Fluid power distributor **Area of distribution:** National **Expertise:** Fluid power specialist, systems design and distribution **Affiliations:** F.P.D.A.; N.F.P.S.; N.R.A.; Amateur Trapshooting Association **Hob./spts.:** Trap shooting, hunting, Lake Erie Charter Captain **SIC code:** 35 **Address:** Heartland Hydraulics Inc., 136 Green Valley Dr., Howard, OH 43028 **E-mail:** timlafevre@heartlandhydraulics.com

LANDER, MICHAEL J.
Industry: Food **Born:** January 29, 1953, Sioux City, Iowa **Univ./degree:** 2 years of college **Current organization:** Tyson Foods Inc. **Title:** Assistant Operations Manager **Type of organization:** Manufacturing **Major product:** Boxed beef **Area of distribution:** Sioux City, Iowa **Expertise:** Operations **Hob./spts.:** Sports **SIC code:** 20 **Address:** 5401 Old Lake Port Rd., Sioux City, IA 51106 **E-mail:** mike.lander@tyson.com

LANIUS, JOEY D.
Industry: Metals **Born:** October 1, 1971, Nashville, Tennessee **Univ./degree:** B.S., Industrial Technology, Tennessee Tech, 1997; M.B.A., Western Kentucky University at Bowling Green, 2001 **Current organization:** Norandal USA **Type of organization:** Manufacturing **Major product:** Aluminum foil **Area of distribution:** National **Expertise:** Engineering **Published works:** Articles **Affiliations:** S.A.E. **SIC code:** 33 **Address:** Norandal USA, 400 Bill Brooks Dr., Huntington, TN 38344 **E-mail:** joey.lanius@norandal.com

LAPTEV, PAVEL N.
Industry: Electronics **Born:** June 12, 1962, Ryazan, Russia **Univ./degree:** M.S., Electronics Engineering, Moscow University of Electronics Engineering, 1986 **Current organization:** Tegal Corp., PVD Group **Title:** Director of Engineering **Type of organization:** Manufacturing **Major product:** Vacuum equipment, PVD **Area of distribution:** International **Expertise:** Engineering, physics **Published works:** 2 articles, 3 patent applications **Hob./spts.:** Electronics troubleshooting, radio, computers, programming **SIC code:** 36 **Address:** Tegal Corp., PVD Group, 320 Nopal St., Santa Barbara, CA 93103 **E-mail:** plaptev@tegal.com

LARRABEE, STAN
Industry: Glass containers **Born:** October 23, 1958, Worcester, Massachusetts **Univ./degree:** B.E.E., Worcester Polytechnic University, 1981 **Current organization:** Anchor Glass Container Corp. **Title:** Plant Engineer **Type of organization:** Manufacturing **Major product:** Glass bottles **Area of distribution:** National **Expertise:** Engineering **Affiliations:** Society of Manufacturing Engineers **Hob./spts.:** Building houses and furniture **SIC code:** 32 **Address:** Anchor Glass Container Corp., 83 Griffith St., Salem, NJ 08079 **E-mail:** larrabeestan@aol.com

LATTANZI, RICHARD E.
Industry: Communications **Born:** Evanston, Illinois **Univ./degree:** M.A., Thunderbird American Graduate School of International Management, 1972 **Current organization:** Raptor Networks Technology, Inc. **Title:** Documentation Manager **Type of organization:** Manufacturing **Major product:** Ethernet switches **Area of distribution:** International **Expertise:** Technical writing, documentation **Hob./spts.:** Personal writing, martial arts **SIC code:** 36 **Address:** Raptor Networks Technology, Inc., 65 Enterprise Rd., Aliso Viejo, CA 92656 **E-mail:** richard_lattanzi@hotmail.com

LAUGHLIN, CRAIG R.
Industry: Electronics **Born:** March 30, 1949, Logansport, Indiana **Univ./degree:** B.S., Zoology, University of Oklahoma **Current organization:** Dallas Semiconductor Corp. **Title:** Senior Plasma Process Engineer **Type of organization:** Manufacturing **Major product:** Semiconductors **Area of distribution:** International **Expertise:** Engineering **SIC code:** 36 **Address:** Dallas Semiconductor Corp., 4401 S. Beltwood Pkwy., Dallas, TX 75244-3292 **E-mail:** craig.laughlin@dalsemi.com

LAUGHLIN, R. BRUCE
Industry: Publishing **Born:** February 10, 1936, Portland, Maine **Current organization:** Hop Frog Publishing **Title:** President **Type of organization:** Publisher **Major product:** Books on glass craft **Area of distribution:** National **Expertise:** Glass crafting, writing **Published works:** Handbook for stroke victims **SIC code:** 27 **Address:** Hop Frog Publishing, 310 Hackmatack St., Manchester, CT 06040

LAW, ROBERT
Industry: Semiconductor **Born:** December 31, 1958, Taiwan **Univ./degree:** Ph.D., Northeastern University, 1986 **Current organization:** IBM **Title:** Senior Development Engineer/Scientist **Type of organization:** Research, development and marketing **Major product:** Chip. optical connectors **Area of distribution:** International **Expertise:** Engineer, plasma reaction engine diagnostics **Published works:** Article, Forum for Automotive Aerospace: Engine Control Diagnostics **Affiliations:** Society if Automotive Engineers; Combustion Institution **Hob./spts.:** Classical music, building and repairing objects **SIC code:** 36 **Address:** IBM, Hudson Valley Research Park, 2070 Route 52, Zip 81AB 330D, Hopewell Junction, NY 12533 **E-mail:** roblaw@us.ibm.com **Web address:** www.ibm.com

LAZOTT, JAMES B.
Industry: Scales **Born:** March 2, 1937, Manchester, New Hampshire **Univ./degree:** A.S.E.E., Franklin Institute of Boston, 1960 **Current organization:** Fairbanks Scales **Title:** Manufacturing Engineer **Type of organization:** Manufacturing **Major product:** Scales **Area of distribution:** International **Expertise:** Process engineering **Published works:** 3 patents **Affiliations:** I.C. Electrician, US Navy, 1954-58 **SIC code:** 35 **Address:** Fairbanks Scales, 2176 Portland St., Suite 1, St. Johnsbury, VT 05819 **E-mail:** jim.b.lazott@francor.com

LEATHERS, LEE E.
Industry: Aluminum **Born:** December 21, 1966, Mattoon, Illinois **Univ./degree:** M.S., Industrial Engineering, University of Louisville **Current organization:** Alcoa **Title:** Plant Manager **Type of organization:** Manufacturing **Major product:** Aluminum sheet products **Area of distribution:** International **Expertise:** Engineering **Affiliations:** Illinois Manufacturing Association; Quality Manufacturing Association **Hob./spts.:** Golf, hunting, fishing **SIC code:** 34 **Address:** Alcoa, 1 Customer Place, Danville, IL 61834 **E-mail:** lee.leathers@alcoa.com

LEE, ANSON L.
Industry: Electronic sensors for safety applications **Born:** October 16, 1961, Hong Kong, China **Univ./degree:** B.S., Industrial Technology, San Francisco State University, California, 1994 **Current organization:** Scientific Technologies Inc. **Title:** Production Manager **Type of organization:** Manufacturing **Major product:** Electronic sensors for safety applications **Area of distribution:** International **Expertise:** Management **Affiliations:** S.M.E. **Hob./spts.:** Golf, tennis, educational volunteering **SIC code:** 36 **Address:** Scientific Technologies Inc., 6550 Dumbarton Circle, Fremont, CA 94555 **E-mail:** anson_lee@sti.com **Web address:** www.sti.com

LEE, DONGHO
Industry: Computer hardware/software **Born:** Seoul, Korea **Univ./degree:** B.S., Electrical Engineering, Rensselaer Polytechnic Institute; M.S., Electrical Engineering, Cornell University, 1997 **Current organization:** IBM **Title:** Electrical Engineer **Type of organization:** Manufacturing, R&D **Major product:** Network systems, computers, servers **Area of distribution:** International **Expertise:** Engineering, integrated circuit design; New York State Licensed P.E., 2000 **Affiliations:** I.E.E.E.; I.E.E.; British Electrical Engineering Society; Cornell Society of Engineers **SIC code:** 36 **Address:** IBM, 1455 South Rd., Poughkeepsie, NY 12601 **E-mail:** ckt4ever@yahoo.com

LEE, JAMES W.
Industry: Recreational products **Born:** May 27, 1959, San Rafael, California **Current organization:** Mueller Recreational Products **Title:** Molding Manager **Type of organization:** Manufacturing **Major product:** Recreational products - cue racks, dart cabinets; billiard and dart mail order company **Area of distribution:** International **Expertise:** Molding **Hob./spts.:** Cars, deer hunting **SIC code:** 39 **Address:** Mueller Recreational Products, 4825 S. 16th St., Lincoln, NE 68512 **E-mail:** molding@poolndarts.com

LEE, LAURENCE Z.
Industry: Food **Born:** December 13, 1958, China **Univ./degree:** Ph.D., Food Science, Laval University, Canada **Current organization:** Primera Foods **Title:** Director, Research Development **Type of organization:** Manufacturing **Major product:** Food ingredients **Area of distribution:** National **Expertise:** Food chemistry/engineering **Affiliations:** A.A.C.C.; A.O.C.S **Hob./spts.:** Reading **SIC code:** 20 **Address:** Primera Foods, 72241 250th Ave., Hayfield, MN 55940 **E-mail:** llee@primerafoods.com

LEE, WAI MUN
Industry: Technology **Univ./degree:** B.S., Chemical Engineering, University of California, Berkeley, 1972 **Current organization:** DuPont Electronic Technologies **Title:** V.P., New Business & Technology Development **Type of organization:** Manufacturing, R&D **Major product:** Electronic chemicals **Area of distribution:** International **Expertise:** New business product development **Published works:** 50 patents **Affiliations:** I.E.E.E. **Hob./spts.:** Golf, camping **SIC code:** 36 **Address:** DuPont Electronic Technologies, 2520 Barrington Ct., Hayward, CA 94545 **E-mail:** wai.m.lee@usa.dupont.com

LEINBACH, STEVEN R.
Industry: Pharmaceuticals **Born:** September 15, 1955, El Khart, Indiana **Univ./degree:** M.S., Ohio State University, 1981 **Current organization:** Capsugel - Division of Pfizer **Title:** Supervisor Global Stability **Type of organization:** Manufacturing **Major product:** Gelatin capsules **Area of distribution:** International **Expertise:** Analytical chemistry **Honors/awards:** A.S.Q. Certifications: Certified Quality Engineer; Certified Quality Auditor; Certified Reliability Engineer; Certified Quality Manager **Affiliations:** A.S.Q.; I.S.P.E. **Hob./spts.:** Bicycling, music (trombone and trumpet), computer programming **SIC code:** 28 **Address:** Capsugel-Division of Pfizer, 525 Grace St., Greenwood, SC 29649 **E-mail:** sleinbach@earthlink.net

LEININGER, GREGORY J.
Industry: Automation **Born:** Red Bank, New Jersey **Current organization:** Motion Systems Corp. **Title:** Quality Control/Safety Manager **Type of organization:** Manufacturing (OEM) **Major product:** Ball drive actuators **Area of distribution:** International **Expertise:** Engineering (mfg.), quality, safety **Affiliations:** A.S.M.; A.S.Q. **Hob./spts.:** Skiing **SIC code:** 36 **Address:** Motion Systems Corp., 600 Industrial Way West, Eatontown, NJ 07724 **E-mail:** gmrlein@optonline .net

LENTO, MARKKU
Industry: Telecommunications **Born:** April 15, 1960, Finland **Univ./degree:** B.S., Telecommunications, Turun Teknillinen Opisto, Finland **Current organization:** Elektrobit, Inc. **Title:** Vice President and General Manager **Type of organization:** R&D, manufacturing and ODE **Major product:** Production automation, testing and CR&D **Area of distribution:** International **Expertise:** Executive management, telecommunications, international business **Hob./spts.:** Ice hockey **SIC code:** 36 **Address:** Elektrobit, Inc., Coppell Business Center I, 1201 S. Beltline Rd., Suite C100, Coppell, TX 75019 **E-mail:** markku.lento@elektrobit.com **Web address:** www.elektrobit.com

LEONARD, MITCHELL H.
Industry: Metal **Born:** May 4, 1954, Brooklyn, New York **Univ./degree:** B.S., Queens College, 1976 **Current organization:** Watson Metal Products Corp. **Title:** Production Manager **Type of organization:** Manufacturing **Major product:** Threaded rod **Area of distribution:** New Jersey **Expertise:** Engineering **SIC code:** 34 **Address:** 9 Borden Place, Livingston, NJ 07039 **E-mail:** mitch@watsonmetal.com **Web address:** www.watsonmetal.com

LEONE III, ALFIO
Industry: Plastics **Born:** December 28, 1948, Woodbury, New Jersey **Univ./degree:** A.A., Camden County College, New Jersey **Current organization:** Ronald Mark Associates, Inc. **Title:** Engineering Manager **Type of organization:** Manufacturing **Major product:** Custom sizing/plastics **Area of distribution:** International **Expertise:** Engineering **Affiliations:** I.B.E.W. **Hob./spts.:** Family, fishing, photography **SIC code:** 30 **Address:** Ronald Mark Associates, Inc., P.O. Box 355/N. Summit Ave., Pitman, NJ 08071 **E-mail:** rma_aleone@verizon.net

L'HÉNAFF, JEAN-JACQUES
Industry: Technology **Born:** February 11, 1970, Angers, France **Univ./degree:** B.A., Industrial Design, ESDI, 1992 **Current organization:** Terk Technologies **Title:** Vice President, Corporate Design **Type of organization:** Manufacturing **Major product:** Consumer electronics **Area of distribution:** International **Expertise:** Branding and design, industrial and technical design, project management, consulting, business development, strategic analysis and quality assurance **Honors/awards:** Lecturer and educator **Published works:** Articles **Affiliations:** Vice Chair, New York Chapter, I.D.S.A.; D.M.I. **Hob./spts.:** Sailing, travel **SIC code:** 36 **Address:** Terk Technologies, 63 Mall Dr., Commack, NY 11725 **E-mail:** jjl@terk.com

LI, LEPING
Industry: Semiconductor Equipment and Environmental Instrumentations **Univ./degree:** Ph.D., Chemical Physics, SUNY at Stony Brook, 1986; Post-Doctoral Research, Yale University, 1987-1989 **Current organization:** VIAS International/Eco Physics AG **Title:** Senior Research and Development Scientist/Eco Fellow **Type of organization:** Research, development and manufacturing **Major product:** Semiconductor Process Control Equipment **Area of distribution:** International **Expertise:** Laser Spectroscopy, Engineering, Sensor-Based Endpoint Detection and Control of Industrial Processes **Published works:** 30+ articles, peer reviews and book chapters, 55+ patents **Hob./spts.:** Foreign languages (Japanese, French) **SIC code:** 36 **Address:** IBM, 2070 Route 52, Hopewell Junction, NY 12533 **Phone:** (845)454-9888 **Fax:** (845)454-9888 **E-mail:** leping.li@viasint.com

LI, XIAO
Industry: Semiconductors **Born:** April 4, 1963, China **Univ./degree:** Ph.D., Material Science, Oregon State University **Current organization:** LSI Logic **Title:** Process Engineer **Type of organization:** Manufacturing **Major product:** Semiconductors **Area of distribution:** National **Expertise:** Engineering **SIC code:** 36 **Address:** 2245 River Heights Circle, West Linn, OR 97068 **E-mail:** xli@lsil.com

LIBERMAN, SERGIO
Industry: Electronic components for multimedia **Born:** July 21, 1957, Santo Angelo, Brazil **Univ./degree:** B.S., Electrical Engineering, Tel Aviv University **Current organization:** Freescale Semiconductor **Title:** Systems Architect **Type of organization:** Manufacturing, design **Major product:** Semiconductors **Area of distribution:** International **Expertise:** Chip design, signal processing, computer architect, digital audio **Published works:** 7 papers, 3 patents: US 6232903, US 5724038, US 20040243657 **Affiliations:** I.E.E.E.; Audio Engineering Society **Hob./spts.:** Reading, audio and music **SIC code:** 36 **Address:** Freescale Semiconductor, 7601 Rialto Blvd., #1921, Austin, TX 78735 **E-mail:** sergio.liberman@freescale.com

LIEBER, DANIEL N.
Industry: HVAC **Born:** November 22, 1978, Richmond, Virginia **Univ./degree:** B.S.M.E., Virginia Military Institution, 2001 **Current organization:** Buffalo Air Handling **Title:** Applications Engineer **Type of organization:** Manufacturing **Major product:** Custom air handlers **Area of distribution:** National **Expertise:** Engineering **Affiliations:** A.S.M.E.; A.S.H.R.A.E. **SIC code:** 34 **Address:** 4715 Boonsboro Rd., #45, Lynchburg, VA 24503 **E-mail:** danlieber@hotmail.com

LIGGETT, RICK
Industry: Pharmaceuticals **Univ./degree:** B.S., Eastern Kentucky University, 1994 **Current organization:** Martek Biosciences **Title:** Senior Operations Engineer **Type of organization:** Manufacturing **Major product:** DHA and ARA (Omega 3 fatty acids) **Area of distribution:** South Carolina **Expertise:** Downstream oil processing; international guest speaker **Affiliations:** A.O.C.S. **Hob./spts.:** Golf, fishing **SIC code:** 28 **Address:** Martek Biosciences, 1416 N. Williamsburg County Hwy., Kingstree, SC 29556 **E-mail:** ricky@martekbio.com

LILOIA, PAT C.
Industry: Pigments **Born:** February 15, 1976, Belleville, New Jersey **Univ./degree:** B.S. Chemistry, Armstrong Atlantic University **Current organization:** EMD Chemicals **Title:** Production Supervisor **Type of organization:** Manufacturing **Major product:** Pearl pigment **Area of distribution:** International **Expertise:** R&D **Hob./spts.:** Drag racing, golf, gardening **SIC code:** 28 **Address:** EMD Chemicals, 110 EMD Blvd., Savannah, GA 31407 **E-mail:** pliloia@emdchemicals.com **Web address:** www.emdchemicals.com

LIM, REGINA S.
Industry: Cosmetics **Born:** March 1, 1961, Philippines **Univ./degree:** B.S., Pharmacology, Philippine Women's University, 1982 **Current organization:** Product Quest Mfg., Inc. **Title:** Technical Director **Type of organization:** Manufacturing **Major product:** Health and beauty products **Area of distribution:** International **Expertise:** Management, skin care **Published works:** Book, "Sunscreen" **Affiliations:** Society of Cosmetic Chemists **Hob./spts.:** Singing, dancing **SIC code:** 28 **Address:** Product Quest Mfg., Inc., 330 Carswell Ave., Daytona Beach, FL 32117 **E-mail:** reginal@productquestmfg.com **Web address:** www.productquestmfg.com

LIN, DONGPING
Industry: Medical equipment **Born:** April 24, 1958, Beijing, China **Univ./degree:** Ph.D., Computer Engineering, University of Michigan, 1988 **Current organization:** Cardiac Science Inc. **Title:** Chief Software Architect, Chief Intellectual Property Officer **Type of organization:** Manufacturing **Major product:** Medical equipment, medical devices **Area of distribution:** International **Expertise:** Software, intellectual property **Affiliations:** A.H.A.; I.E.E.E.; A.A.M.I.; U.L.; N.A.P.E. **Hob./spts.:** Biking, swimming, basketball **SIC code:** 38 **Address:** Cardiac Science Inc., 16931 Millikan Ave., Irvine, CA 92606 **E-mail:** dlin_ca_2000@yahoo.com

LIU, HAIBIN
Industry: Telecommunications **Born:** November 18, 1953, China **Univ./degree:** Ph.D., Doctor of Engineering, Erlang-Neuberg University, Germany, 1993 **Current organization:** Bahn Networks, Inc. **Title:** VP of Engineering **Type of organization:** Manufacturing **Major product:** Broadband networking equipment **Area of distribution:** International **Expertise:** Engineering **Published works:** 2 papers, International Workshop for A.I. **SIC code:** 36 **Address:** Bahn Networks, Inc., 16109 Silverleaf Dr., San Lorenzo, CA 94580

LIVINGSTON, TIMOTHY E.
Industry: Automotive **Born:** August 28, 1965, Indianapolis, Indiana **Univ./degree:** B.S., Business, Indiana University, 1987 **Current organization:** International Crank Shaft Inc. **Title:** Quality Control Manager **Type of organization:** Manufacturing **Major product:** Crankshafts **Area of distribution:** International **Expertise:** Quality control, troubleshooting, customer relations **Affiliations:** American Society for Quality **Hob./spts.:** Family **SIC code:** 37 **Address:** International Crank Shaft Inc., 101 Carley Ct., Georgetown, KY 40324 **E-mail:** timl@icicrank.com

LIVSHITS, EUGENE
Industry: Pharmaceutical **Born:** June 2, 1952, Moscow, Russia **Univ./degree:** Ph.D., Analytical Chemistry, Moscow University, 1980 **Current organization:** Lannett Co., Inc. **Title:** Vice President **Type of organization:** Manufacturing **Major product:** Pharmaceuticals Rx **Area of distribution:** National **Expertise:** Technical affairs **Published works:** 20 scientific journals, 10 patents **Affiliations:** A.C.S.; G.P.H.A. **Hob./spts.:** Books, sports **SIC code:** 28 **Address:** Lannett Co., Inc., 9000 State Rd., Philadelphia, PA 19136 **E-mail:** eugene1pharm@hotmail.com **Web address:** www.lannettt.com

LLORCA-PONS, JUAN
Industry: Art furniture **Born:** April 10, 1927, Valencia, Spain **Current organization:** Llorca Art Furniture **Title:** President **Type of organization:** Manufacturing **Major product:** Restoration and design of art deco furniture **Area of distribution:** Florida **Expertise:** Artistic oriental lacquer, gold leafing, marquetry **Affiliations:** A.I.C. **Hob./spts.:** Racquetball **SIC code:** 25 **Address:** Llorca Art Furniture, 152 W. 25th St., Hialeah, FL 33010 **E-mail:** juanllorcapons@mindspring.com

LOCKE, J. PHILIP
Industry: Concrete **Born:** October 9, 1957, Beeville, Texas **Current organization:** Goddard Ready Mix Concrete Co., Inc. **Title:** Vice President, Fleet Maintenance **Type of organization:** Manufacturing **Major product:** Ready mix concrete - residential and commercial **Area of distribution:** Oklahoma **Expertise:** Fleet purchases, maintenance and evaluating products **Affiliations:** Lifetime member, NRA; Member, First Baptist Church, Choctaw **Hob./spts.:** Golf, skiing **SIC code:** 32 **Address:** Goddard Ready Mix Concrete Co., Inc., 3101 N.E. Tenth St., Oklahoma City, OK 73117 **E-mail:** goddardc@aol.com

LOCKWOOD, JORGE
Industry: Medical devices **Born:** March 24, 1967, San Juan, Puerto Rico **Univ./degree:** B.S.E.E., Polytechnic University of Puerto Rico **Current organization:** Baxter Healthcare, Aibonito **Title:** Manager I **Type of organization:** Manufacturing **Major product:** Medical devices and pharmaceuticals **Area of distribution:** National **Expertise:** Engineering **Hob./spts.:** Hockey, gym management **SIC code:** 38 **Address:** Baxter Healthcare, Aibonito, P.O. Box 1389, Suite 271, Aibonito, PR 00705 **E-mail:** jorge_lockwood@baxter.com

LOCKWOOD, STEPHEN J.
Industry: Food and beverage **Born:** March 22, 1957, Cleveland, Ohio **Univ./degree:** B.S., Mechanical Engineering, Purdue University, 1979 **Current organization:** Procter & Gamble Co. **Title:** Site Manager **Type of organization:** Manufacturing **Major product:** Food and beverage **Area of distribution:** International **Expertise:** Management **Affiliations:** N.S.P.E. **Hob./spts.:** Woodworking **SIC code:** 20 **Address:** Procter & Gamble Co., 1230 Tustin Ave., Anaheim, CA 92807 **E-mail:** lockwood.sj@pg.com

LOGAN, ANTHONY W.
Industry: Agriculture **Born:** December 2, 1949, Seattle, Washington **Univ./degree:** B.S., Physical Education, University of Washington **Current organization:** Cajun Sugar Co-op **Title:** Electrician **Type of organization:** Manufacturing; 3rd largest sugar mill in Louisiana **Major product:** Sugar **Area of distribution:** Louisiana **Expertise:** Trouble shooting, maintenance, computer and electrical repairs **Hob./spts.:** Sports, fishing off his boat **SIC code:** 20 **Address:** 1034 Eagle St., Franklin, LA 70538

LOGUE, HAROLD E.
Industry: Food **Current organization:** Flowers Baking Co. **Title:** Manufacturing Manager **Type of organization:** Manufacturing **Major product:** Baked foods **Area of distribution:** Georgia **Expertise:** Manufacturing **SIC code:** 20 **Address:** Flowers Baking Co., 300 S. Madison St., Thomasville, GA 31792 **E-mail:** ed_logue@flocorp.com

LOGUE, JOSEPH C.
Industry: Semiconductors **Born:** 1920, Philadelphia, Pennsylvania **Univ./degree:** B.E.E., 1944; M.E.E., 1949, Cornell University **Title:** CEO (Retired), Lorex **Type of organization:** Development, manufacturing **Major product:** Piezocon, process chemical control **Area of distribution:** International **Expertise:** Engineering, semiconductors **Affiliations:** Fellow, I.B.M.; Fellow, American Association for the Advancement of Science; National Academy of Engineering; Fellow, I.E.E.E. **Hob./spts.:** Combat shooting, photography **SIC code:** 36 **Address:** 52 Boardman Rd., Poughkeepsie, NY 12603 **E-mail:** jclogue@msn.com

LOLAKAPURI, LAXMI N.
Industry: Biomedical **Born:** December 15, 1977, India **Univ./degree:** B.S.M.E., 2000; M.S.M.E., University of Memphis, 2003 **Current organization:** Smith & Nephew, Inc. **Title:** Mechanical Engineer **Type of organization:** Manufacturing/design **Major product:** Knee and hip implants **Area of distribution:** National **Expertise:** Mechanical engineering, project management, strategic planning, product development **Published works:** Several articles in India **Affiliations:** A.S.M.E.; Phi Beta Delta **Hob./spts.:** Chess, cricket, reading **SIC code:** 38 **Address:** Smith & Nephew, Inc., 3571 Midland Ave., #4, Memphis, TN 38111 **E-mail:** sai.lolakapuri@smithnephew.com

LOPEZ-GONZALEZ, WALTTER
Industry: Building materials **Born:** August 24, 1963 **Univ./degree:** Ph.D., University of Madrid, Spain, 1992; Innovation Tech Management, Dodge University of Tampa, 2005 **Current organization:** Cemex **Title:** Ph.D. **Type of organization:** Manufacturing **Major product:** Cement and concrete **Area of distribution:** National **Expertise:** Building **Hob./spts.:** Spending time in the countryside **SIC code:** 32 **Address:** Cemex, 6725 78th St., Riverview, FL 33569

LOVE JR., JAMES L.
Industry: Aerospace **Current organization:** Bell Helicopter Textron **Title:** Principal Engineer **Type of organization:** Manufacturing **Major product:** Rotor wing aircraft **Area of distribution:** National **Expertise:** Engineering **Affiliations:** A.F.A.; A.H.S. **SIC code:** 37 **Address:** 101 Brandy Hill, Lorena, TX 76655 **E-mail:** jlove@bellhelicopter.textron.com **Web address:** www.bellhelicopter.com

LOVESEE, PATRICK A.
Industry: Food **Born:** April 21, 1963, Wausau, Wisconsin **Univ./degree:** B.S., Economics & Political Science, University of Wisconsin, 1985 **Current organization:** McCain Snack Foods **Title:** Director, Customer Satisfaction **Type of organization:** Manufacturing **Major product:** Food service appetizers **Area of distribution:** International **Expertise:** Customer service, logistics **Affiliations:** Council of Logistics Management; Supply Chain Council **Hob./spts.:** Family, hunting, fishing **SIC code:** 20 **Address:** 517 W. Rolling Meadows Lane, Appleton, WI 54913 **E-mail:** patrick.lovesee@mccain.com

LUCAS, CANDY Z.
Industry: Food **Born:** Portsmouth, Virginia **Univ./degree:** B.S., 1993; M.S., 1995, Natural Resource Management, Sul Ross State University **Current organization:** National Steak and Poultry **Title:** Senior Manager, Quality Assurance **Type of organization:** Manufacturing **Major product:** Steaks and poultry **Area of distribution:** National **Expertise:** Quality assurance, food safety, microbiology, consulting, auditing and training **Honors/awards:** Member, (DTA) Delta Tau Alpha, Agricultural National Honor Society; Who's Who Among Students in American Universities and Colleges, 1993-94 **Affiliations:** I.A.F.P.; N.E.H.A. **Hob./spts.:** Golf **SIC code:** 20 **Address:** National Steak and Poultry, 301 E. 5th St., Owasso, OK 74005 **E-mail:** CLucas@Nationalsteak.com

LUCAS, TIMOTHY W.
Industry: Heavy equipment **Born:** July 11, 1958, Gary, Indiana **Current organization:** Howell Tractor & Equipment, LLC **Title:** Service Manager **Type of organization:** Manufacturing **Major product:** Tractors and heavy equipment **Area of distribution:** Indiana **Expertise:** Oversees service department operations **Hob./spts.:** Camping, fishing, sports **SIC code:** 35 **Address:** Howell Tractor & Equipment, LLC, 480 Blaine St., Gary, IN 46406 **E-mail:** tlucas@howelltractor.com **Web address:** www.howelltractor.com

LUCKMAN, JOEL A.
Industry: Home appliances **Born:** November 25, 1975, Covington, Kentucky **Univ./degree:** M.S., Chemical Engineering, University of Kentucky, 2001 **Current organization:** Whirlpool Corp. **Title:** Project Engineer **Type of organization:** R&D **Major product:** Washers, dryers **Area of distribution:** International **Expertise:** Chemical engineering (separation science) **Affiliations:** A.S.M.E.; A.C.S.; A.I.C.H.E.; A.S.W.E. **Hob./spts.:** Outdoor activities **SIC code:** 36 **Address:** Whirlpool Corp., 750 Monte Rd., MD 5155, Benton Harbor, MI 49022 **E-mail:** joel_a_luckman@whirlpool.com

LUNSFORD JR., JOHNNY MYRL
Industry: Automotive **Born:** January 19, 1963, Roxboro, North Carolina **Current organization:** Kostal of America **Title:** Senior Project Engineer **Type of organization:** Manufacturing **Major product:** Automotive switches; engineering services **Area of distribution:** International **Expertise:** Engineering; Certified, Unigraphics and Catia **Affiliations:** Society of Automotive Engineers **Hob./spts.:** Golf, basketball, home improvements **SIC code:** 37 **Address:** Kostal of America, 25325 Regency Dr., Novi, MI 48375 **E-mail:** jmyrljr@yahoo.com

LUU, MELISSA MAI
Industry: Food and manufacturing automation **Born:** March 21, 1966, Vung Tau, South Vietnam **Current organization:** Hills Pet Nutrition, Inc. **Title:** Project/Controls Engineer **Type of organization:** Manufacturing **Major product:** Pet food **Area of distribution:** International **Expertise:** Electrical engineering **Hob./spts.:** Tennis, volleyball, the outdoors **SIC code:** 20 **Address:** Hills Pet Nutrition, Inc., 6041 S. Malt Ave., City of Commerce, CA 90040 **E-mail:** melissa_luu@colpal.com

LY, JOHN D.
Industry: Communications **Born:** February 8, 1962, Saigon, Vietnam **Univ./degree:** B.S., San Diego State University, 1986; M.S., National University, 1994 **Current organization:** Cisco System **Title:** Software Technical Leader **Type of organization:** Manufacturing **Major product:** Routers, switching communications **Area of distribution:** International **Expertise:** Engineering **Published works:** Patent pending **Affiliations:** I.E.E.E. **Hob./spts.:** Family **SIC code:** 36 **Address:** Cisco System, 170 W. Tasman Dr., San Jose, CA 95134 **E-mail:** jly@cisco.com

LYLE, DOUG
Industry: Product development **Univ./degree:** Ph.D., Mechanical Engineering/Materials, University of South Carolina, 1997 **Current organization:** Advanced Glass Fiber Yarns, LLC **Title:** Senior Research Associate **Type of organization:** Material supplier, manufacturing **Major product:** Producing glass fibers for use in electronic, industrial, ballistic and composite applications **Area of distribution:** International **Expertise:** Engineering, product development **Published works:** 1 book chapter **Affiliations:** A.P.C.; A.S.M.E.; I.P.C.; Sigma Pi Sigma; Phi Beta Kappa **Hob./spts.:** The beach, jogging, running, travel **SIC code:** 32 **Address:** Advanced Glass Fiber Yarns, LLC, 2558 Wagener Rd., Aiken, SC 29801-0499 **E-mail:** doug.lyle@agy.com

MADDOX, CRAIG M.
Industry: Concrete equipment **Univ./degree:** Northern Illinois University, 1978 **Current organization:** Blastcrete Equipment Co. **Title:** Vice President, Engineering **Type of organization:** OEM **Major product:** Concrete pumping equipment **Area of distribution:** International **Expertise:** Design, manufacturing **Affiliations:** A.P.I.C.S. **SIC code:** 35 **Address:** Blastcrete Equipment Co., 2505 Alexandria Rd., Anniston, AL 36202 **Web address:** www.blastcrete.com

MADDOX, DAVID P.
Industry: Furniture **Univ./degree:** B.A., Columbia University, Southern Tennessee, 1978 **Current organization:** Stanley Furniture Co. **Title:** Director of Engineering **Type of organization:** Manufacturing **Major product:** Wood household furniture **Area of distribution:** National **Expertise:** Environmental engineering **SIC code:** 25 **Address:** Stanley Furniture Co., P.O. Box 30, Stanleytown, VA 24168 **E-mail:** dmaddox@stanleyfurniture.com **Web address:** www.stanleyfurniture.com

MADISON, ERIC P.
Industry: Consumer goods **Born:** February 20, 1968, Washington, D.C. **Univ./degree:** M.B.A., Business Administration, Regis University, Denver, Colorado **Current organization:** Roper Corp. **Title:** Industrial Engineer **Type of organization:** Manufacturing **Major product:** Oven ranges **Area of distribution:** International **Expertise:** Lean manufacturing **Affiliations:** U.S. Army Reserves **Hob./spts.:** Restoring classic cars and Mustangs **SIC code:** 36 **Address:** Roper Corp., 1507 Broomtown Rd., Lafayette, GA 30728 **E-mail:** eric.madison@ge.com

MADREN, LUTHER B.
Industry: Textile **Born:** October 14, 1945, North Carolina **Current organization:** Culp Upholstery/Prints Division **Title:** Quality Manager **Type of organization:** Manufacturing/distributing **Major product:** Upholstery fabric **Area of distribution:** International **Expertise:** Quality assurance **Affiliations:** A.F.M.A. **Hob./spts.:** NASCAR, golf, fishing **SIC code:** 22 **Address:** 2804 Keck Dr., Burlington, NC 27215

MADRID, ANNA M.
Industry: Computer components and systems **Born:** March 16, 1966, Española, Mexico **Univ./degree:** M.S., Electrical Engineering, Arizona State University **Current organization:** Intel Corp./Components and Systems Materials Operation **Title:** Senior Materials Quality Engineer **Type of organization:** Manufacturing **Major product:** Semiconductors **Area of distribution:** International **Expertise:** Electrical and thermal engineering **Hob./spts.:** Reading **SIC code:** 36 **Address:** Intel Corp./Components and Systems Materials Operation, 5000 W. Chandler Blvd., Chandler, AZ 85226 **E-mail:** anna.m.madrid@intel.com

MAGRO JR., DANIEL LEE
Industry: Metals/cans **Born:** February 17, 1976, Baton Rouge, Louisiana **Univ./degree:** M.B.A., Strayer University, 2005 **Current organization:** Rexam Beverage **Title:** Finance Manager **Type of organization:** Manufacturing **Major product:** Beverage cans **Area of distribution:** National **Expertise:** Cost accounting **Hob./spts.:** Golf, reading **SIC code:** 34 **Address:** Rexam Beverage, 10800 Marina Dr., Olive Branch, MS 38654 **E-mail:** leemagro@yahoo.com

MAHFOUZ, MICHAEL A.
Industry: Daily newspaper **Born:** September 22, 1950, Dermott, Arkansas **Univ./degree:** B.S., Magna Cum Laude and Alpha Chi, Engineering, Arkansas Tech University, 1980; M.B.A., University of Texas at Dallas, 1997 **Current organization:** New York Daily News **Title:** Senior Director, Engineering **Type of organization:** Publishing **Major product:** Newspaper production **Area of distribution:** New York **Expertise:** Engineering **Honors/awards:** Navy Achievement Medal from Secretary of the Navy for cost savings, professional achievement, technical competence and exemplary leadership; Commendation for Achievement from Westinghouse Corp. Plant Manager for exceptional performance, leadership and nuclear plant knowledge **Hob./spts.:** Jogging, weightlifting **SIC code:** 27 **Address:** 125 Theodore Conrad Dr., Jersey City, NJ 07305 **E-mail:** mmahfouz@nydailynews.com **Web address:** www.nydailynews.com

MAIER, CURT M.
Industry: Chemical **Univ./degree:** B.S., Civil Engineering, University of Notre Dame, 1979; M.B.A., University of Phoenix, 1987 **Current organization:** Air Products & Chemicals, Inc. **Title:** General Manager **Type of organization:** Manufacturing **Major product:** Industrial gases **Area of distribution:** National **Expertise:** Marketing **Affiliations:** A.S.C.E.; American College of Healthcare Executives **SIC code:** 28 **Address:** Air Products and Chemicals, Inc., 7201 Hamilton Blvd., Allentown, PA 18195 **E-mail:** maiercm@apci.com **Web address:** www.apci.com

MALIK, RAM L.
Industry: High tech data storage **Born:** October 5, 1940, Sargodha, India **Univ./degree:** B.S., Mechanical Engineering, Punjab Engineering College, Chandigarh (Punjab) India; M.B.A., University of Minnesota Carlson School **Current organization:** Seagate **Title:** Staff Engineer **Type of organization:** Manufacturing **Major product:** Disk drives **Area of distribution:** International **Expertise:** Engineering **SIC code:** 35 **Address:** Seagate, 155 S. Milpitas Blvd., Milpitas, CA 95035 **E-mail:** ram.l.malik@seagate.com

MALINSKY, JOSEPH B.
Industry: Aerospace **Born:** February 7, 1948, Ukraine **Univ./degree:** M.S., Electronics Engineering, Kyiv International University of Civil Aviation, 1976 **Current organization:** ACS **Title:** Principal Engineer **Type of organization:** Manufacturing **Major product:** Aerospace electronics **Area of distribution:** International **Expertise:** Electrical engineering **Affiliations:** New York Academy of Science-1993 **Hob./spts.:** Travel, fishing **SIC code:** 36 **Address:** ACS, 7529 Standish Place, Suite 200, Rockwell, MD 20855 **E-mail:** joemalinsky@engineer.com

MALYAROV, ILYA
Industry: Medical diagnostics **Born:** May 22, 1952, Kiev, Ukraine **Univ./degree:** M.S.E., Institute of Technology, Kiev, Ukraine, 1979 **Current organization:** DPC Instrument System Division **Title:** Principal Engineer **Type of organization:** Manufacturing **Major product:** Blood analyzers **Area of distribution:** International **Expertise:** Engineering, conceptional design **Hob./spts.:** Photography, skiing, volleyball **SIC code:** 38 **Address:** 25 Brandon Ave., Livingston, NJ 07039 **E-mail:** imalyarov@dpconline.com

MANANSALA, MICHAEL C.
Industry: Electronics **Born:** Manila, Philippines **Univ./degree:** B.S., Electronics and Communications Engineering, University of the East Philippines, Manila, 1986 **Current organization:** Fujitsu Microelectronics **Title:** Project Manager **Type of organization:** R&D **Major product:** Semiconductors, fingerprint sensors **Area of distribution:** International **Expertise:** Engineering, design and development **Published works:** 1 patent **Affiliations:** I.E.E.E. **Hob./spts.:** Swimming **SIC code:** 36 **Address:** 1031 Clyde Ave., #1301, Santa Clara, CA 95054 **E-mail:** mmanasal@fma.fujitsu.com

MANDILAKIS, ROBERT D.
Industry: Laminators and supplies **Born:** July 30, 1954, Cleveland, Ohio **Current organization:** Graphic Laminating Inc. **Title:** Vice President of International Sales **Type of organization:** Manufacturing **Major product:** Laminators, laminating film and supplies **Area of distribution:** International **Expertise:** Business development and relations **Hob./spts.:** Travel, art, antiques **SIC code:** 35 **Address:** 28792 Woodmill Dr., West Lake, OH 44145 **E-mail:** bmandilakis@graphiclaminating.com

MANGAN, MATTHEW F.
Industry: Elevators/escalators **Born:** August 23, 1971, Lynn, MA **Univ./degree:** B.S., Wentworth Institute of Technology, 1994 **Current organization:** Thyssen Krupp Elevator Corp. **Title:** Regional Engineer **Type of organization:** Manufacturing **Major product:** Elevators, escalators **Area of distribution:** International **Expertise:** Engineering **Affiliations:** A.S.M.E. **Hob./spts.:** Car restoration, boating, skiing, fishing **SIC code:** 35 **Address:** Thyssen Krupp Elevator Corp., 601 Nursery Rd., Linthicum Heights, MD 21090 **E-mail:** matt.mangan@thyssenkruppelevator.com

MANQUERO, CARLOS
Industry: Electronics **Born:** July 10, 1950, El Paso, Texas **Univ./degree:** M.S., Physics, University of Texas at El Paso, 1974; M.B.A., University of Texas at Brownsville, 1993 **Current organization:** Spectrum Control Technology, Inc. **Title:** Quality Manager **Type of organization:** Manufacturing **Major product:** Ceramic capacitors **Area of distribution:** International **Expertise:** Statistical process control **Published works:** Thesis **Affiliations:** S.H.E.; A.S.Q.; J.C.S. **Hob./spts.:** Baseball **SIC code:** 36 **Address:** 12345 N. I-10 Service Rd., #308, New Orleans, LA 70128 **E-mail:** lemiii33@aol.com

MARCINIAK, JO B.
Industry: Food **Born:** March 26, 1947, Chicago, Illinois **Univ./degree:** M.B.A., Benedictine University, Illinois **Current organization:** Azteca Foods, Inc. **Title:** Quality Assurance Manager **Type of organization:** Manufacturing **Major product:** Tortillas and tortilla chips **Area of distribution:** International **Expertise:** Quality systems **Affiliations:** A.S.Q.; N.O.W. **Hob./spts.:** Bicycling, scuba diving, physical fitness **SIC code:** 20 **Address:** Azteca Foods, Inc., 5005 S. Nagle Ave., Chicago, IL 60638 **E-mail:** jo.marciniak@aztecafoods.com

MARK, LILLY
Industry: Pharmaceuticals **Born:** November 30, 1970, Montreal, Canada **Univ./degree:** B.S., Animal Sciences, Vanier College, Canada, 1996 **Current organization:** Purdue Pharma L.P. **Title:** Associate Scientist **Type of organization:** Biotech **Major product:** Drug discovery **Area of distribution:** International **Expertise:** Drug discovery, pain research, small animal surgery **Published works:** British Journal of Pharmacology **Hob./spts.:** Gardening, antiquing, cooking, avian behavior and care, reading **SIC code:** 28 **Address:** Purdue Pharma L.P., 6 Cedar Brook Dr., Cranbury, NJ 08512 **E-mail:** lilly.mark@pharma.com

MAROV, G.J.
Industry: Food science/beverage consulting **Born:** January 3, 1920, Unije, Croatia **Univ./degree:** B.S., Chemistry, City College of New York, 1942; M.S., Physical Chemistry, Columbia University, 1950 **Title:** Chief Chemist, PepsiCo. (Retired) **Type of organization:** Manufacturing **Major product:** Carbonated beverages **Area of distribution:** International **Expertise:** Technical consultant, soft drinks and related industries **Honors/awards:** U.S. Army, 1942-46, WW II Veteran awarded the Purple Heart **Published works:** Journal articles, papers **Affiliations:** A.C.S.; I.S.B.T.; A.W.W.A; S.I.T.; I.C.U.M.S.A. **Hob./spts.:** Family, fishing, gardening **SIC code:** 20 **Address:** 64-12 214th St., Bayside, NY 11364 **E-mail:** gjmarov@optonline.net

MARSH, CHARLES E.
Industry: Shipbuilding/repair **Born:** May 23, 1955, Washington, D.C. **Univ./degree:** B.A., Magna Cum Laude, Business and Computer Information Science, P.A.C.E., 1994 **Current organization:** Colonna's Shipyard **Title:** Director of Human Resources **Type of organization:** Specialty trade contractor **Major product:** Repair and building of ships **Area of distribution:** Virginia **Expertise:** Human resource generalist, workforce development **Published works:** Programs in curriculum development for shipbuilding industry **Affiliations:** Co-founder and Chairman, Governor's Maritime Task Force Committee; Adjunct Professor, Tidewater Community College; National Society for Human Resource Management; Hampton Roads Society for Human Resource Management; US Navy Chief Electrician (retired 1993) **Hob./spts.:** Hunting **SIC code:** 37 **Address:** Colonna's Shipyard, 400 E. Indian River Rd., Norfolk, VA 23523 **E-mail:** charlesmarsh@aol.com

MARSH, LEE
Industry: Electric and industrial communications products **Born:** December 7, 1949, El Paso, Texas **Univ./degree:** B.B.A., Operations Management, University of Texas at El Paso, 1980 **Current organization:** Woodhead LP **Title:** Director, Juarez Operations/ Audit Director Corporate Production System **Type of organization:** Manufacturing **Major product:** Electronic and industrial communications products and specialty electrical products **Area of distribution:** International **Expertise:** Operations management and development **Published works:** Article **SIC code:** 36 **Address:** Woodhead LP, 11501 James Watt, El Paso, TX 79936 **E-mail:** lmarsh@dominodaniel/woodhead.com

MARSHALL, CHRISTOPHER L.
Industry: Contractors/defense **Born:** December 25, 1965, Bedford, Pennsylvania **Univ./degree:** B.S., Electrical Engineering, Pennsylvania State University, 1988 **Current organization:** General Dynamics Amphibious Systems **Title:** Vetronics Systems Architect **Type of organization:** Defense contractor **Major product:** Military vehicles **Area of distribution:** International **Expertise:** Systems design **Affiliations:** I.E.E.E. **Hob./spts.:** Family, woodworking, restoring antique cars **SIC code:** 37 **Address:** General Dynamics, Amphibious Systems, 14041 Worth Ave., Woodbridge, VA 22192 **E-mail:** marshalc@gdls.com

MARTIN, CARL
Industry: Healthcare **Born:** March 6, 1962, Ephrata, Pennsylvania **Current organization:** Advanced Scientifics, Inc. **Title:** CEO **Type of organization:** Manufacturing **Major product:** Medical disposables **Area of distribution:** International **Expertise:** Marketing, business development **Affiliations:** D.O.E.; A.A.P.S.; P.A.C. **SIC code:** 38 **Address:** Advanced Scientifics, Inc., 163 Research Lane, Millersburg, PA 17061 **E-mail:** cmartin@advancedscientifics.com **Web address:** www.advancedscientific.com

MARTIN, STERLING A.
Industry: Lamination and steel stamping **Born:** August 13, 1937, Camden, New Jersey **Univ./degree:** Technical Diploma, Camden County Vocational **Current organization:** Thomson Lamination Co., Inc. **Title:** President/CEO **Type of organization:** Manufacturing **Major product:** Magnetic core lamination **Area of distribution:** International **Expertise:** Steel stampings for electric motors **Hob./spts.:** Woodworking, rebuilding and restoring Corvettes **SIC code:** 35 **Address:** Thomson Lamination Co., Inc., 504 E. Linwood Ave., Maple Shade, NJ 08052 **Web address:** www.tlclam.net

MARTIN, WILLIAM J.
Industry: Small motors **Born:** July 2, 1954, Tulsa, Oklahoma **Univ./degree:** B.S., General Engineering, 1976; M.S., Mechanical Engineering, 1988, University of Arkansas **Current organization:** Arkansas General Industries **Title:** Engineering Manager **Type of organization:** Manufacturing **Major product:** Fractional AC and DC motors **Area of distribution:** International **Expertise:** Engineering **Published works:** Master thesis **Hob./spts.:** Water sports **SIC code:** 36 **Address:** Arkansas General Industries, 102 Miller St., Bald Knob, AR 72010 **E-mail:** red_martin@argenind.com

MARTINDALE, WILLIAM A.
Industry: Ceramic injection molding **Born:** May 3, 1917, Spokane, Washington **Current organization:** Wunder-Mold, Inc. **Title:** President **Type of organization:** Manufacturing **Major product:** Industrial ceramics components **Area of distribution:** International **Expertise:** Manufacturing **SIC code:** 32 **Address:** Wunder-Mold, Inc., 4957 Allison Pkwy., Vacaville, CA 95688 **Web address:** www.wundermold.com

MARTINEZ, CONSTANTINO GUILLEN
Industry: Electronics **Born:** May 13, 1968, Mexico **Univ./degree:** B.S., Mechanical Engineering, 1988 **Current organization:** Panasonic AVG Networks **Title:** MPEIS Supervisor **Type of organization:** Manufacturing **Major product:** Television and satellite receiver sets **Area of distribution:** National **Expertise:** Equipment automation dedicated to production; all aspects of mechanical engineering, project management, staff management and quality control **Hob./spts.:** Weightlifting, camping, hiking, running, movies, music **SIC code:** 36 **Address:** Panasonic AVG Networks, 7625 Panasonic Way, San Diego, CA 92154 **E-mail:** martinezc1@panasonic.com

MARTINEZ, SARAH B.
Industry: Concrete **Born:** February 25, 1959, Taos, New Mexico **Univ./degree:** B.A., History and Government, Adams State University **Current organization:** Robert Medina & Sons Concrete & Sand Inc. **Title:** Corporate Treasurer **Type of organization:** Retail **Major product:** Concrete, aggregates **Area of distribution:** New Mexico **Expertise:** Finance **Hob./spts.:** Biking, travel **SIC code:** 32 **Address:** Robert Medina & Sons Concrete & Sand Inc., 915 E. Kit Carson Rd., Taos, NM 87571

MARTINI, SANDRO
Industry: Electronics **Born:** July 28, 1948, Mantua, Italy **Univ./degree:** B.S., Electrical Engineering, Politecnico University, Milan, Italy, 1972 **Current organization:** International Rectifier **Title:** Marketing Director **Type of organization:** Manufacturing **Major product:** Semiconductors **Area of distribution:** International **Expertise:** Marketing **Hob./spts.:** Art, skiing **SIC code:** 36 **Address:** 4335 Marina City Dr., #638E, Marina del Rey, CA 90292 **E-mail:** smartin1@irf.com

MASON, DAVID
Industry: Machining/grinding **Born:** September 30, 1963, Washington, D.C. **Current organization:** Surface Manufacturing **Title:** Journeyman Machinist **Type of organization:** Manufacturing **Major product:** Grinding, CNC lathes **Area of distribution:** National **Expertise:** Grinding **Affiliations:** National Tooling and Machining Association **Hob./spts.:** Softball, Auburn Little League, basketball, golf **SIC code:** 35 **Address:** Surface Manufacturing, 2025 Airpark Ct., Auburn, CA 95603 **E-mail:** davidbmason@hotmail.com

MASTRONARDI, PAUL
Industry: Publishing **Born:** March 24, 1959, Queens, New York **Univ./degree:** M.B.A., Finance, St. Johns University **Current organization:** Vibe/Spin Ventures, LLC **Title:**

Chief Financial Officer **Type of organization:** Publisher **Major product:** Magazines **Area of distribution:** National **Expertise:** Financial operations **Hob./spts.:** Softball, football **SIC code:** 27 **Address:** 34 Hawthorne Ave., Floral Park, NY 11001 **E-mail:** pmastron@aol.com

MATHAI, THOMAS P.
Industry: Pharmaceuticals **Born:** February 24, 1950, Kerala, India **Univ./degree:** B.S., Biology, 1971; B.S., Pharmaceutics, University of Karaka, India, 1976; B.S., Pharmaceutics, Long Island University, 1982 **Current organization:** Bristol Myers Squibb **Title:** Associate Director **Type of organization:** Manufacturing, research and development **Major product:** Pharmaceutical, chemical and drug products **Area of distribution:** International **Expertise:** Technical sources, research and development **Affiliations:** N.J.P.H.A. **Hob./spts.:** Cooking, travel, reading, theatre **SIC code:** 28 **Address:** Bristol Myers Squibb, 1 Squibb Dr., New Brunswick, NJ 08901 **E-mail:** thomas.mathai@bms.com **Web address:** www.bms.com

MATHRE, OWEN B.
Industry: Chemicals/quality **Born:** November 26, 1929, Kendall County, Illinois **Univ./degree:** B.A., Harvard College; Ph.D., University of Minnesota **Current organization:** Chem/Qual Consulting **Title:** President **Type of organization:** Business services firm **Major product:** Information, consulting services **Area of distribution:** National **Expertise:** Quality control and quality systems **Affiliations:** 50 year member, American Chemical Society; A.W.W.A.; P.S.A. **Hob./spts.:** Photography, gardening, fishing **SIC code:** 28 **Address:** Chem/Qual Consulting, 119 Westgate Drive, Wilmington, DE 19808-1427 **E-mail:** omathre@magpage.com

MATTE, PIERRE
Industry: Electronics **Born:** May 3, 1959, Marseille, France **Univ./degree:** M.B.A., IAE Grenoble, B.S.E.E., Enserg Grenoble **Current organization:** ST Microelectronics **Title:** Marketing Director **Type of organization:** Manufacturing **Major product:** Semiconductors **Area of distribution:** International **Expertise:** Marketing **Hob./spts.:** Soccer, tennis, skiing **SIC code:** 36 **Address:** ST Microelectronics, 10 Maguire Rd., Suite 130, Lexington, MA 02421 **E-mail:** pierre.matte@st.com

MAUCH, THEODORE A.
Industry: Power transmission **Born:** July 17, 1953, Saginaw, Michigan **Univ./degree:** B.A., Political Science and History, Saginaw Valley State University, 1976 **Current organization:** KTR Corp. **Title:** Regional Manager **Type of organization:** Manufacturing **Major product:** Couplings (Rotex, Bowex etc.) **Area of distribution:** International **Expertise:** Sales **Honors/awards:** Outstanding Graduate in History, Saginaw Valley State University **Affiliations:** Knights of Columbus **Hob./spts.:** Community and church work, baseball, reading **SIC code:** 35 **Address:** P.O. Box 9065, Michigan City, IN 46361-9065 **E-mail:** t.mauch@ktr.com **Web address:** www.ktr.com

MAVERLEY, WILLIAM
Industry: Pharmaceuticals **Born:** Ireland **Univ./degree:** M.S., Chemical Engineering, Bradford University, England, 1966 **Current organization:** Pfizer Inc. **Title:** Senior Manager, Engineering **Type of organization:** Manufacturing **Major product:** Pharmaceuticals **Area of distribution:** International **Expertise:** Chemical engineering **Honors/awards:** Silver Medal **SIC code:** 28 **Address:** Pfizer Inc., 235 E. 42nd St., New York, NY 10017 **E-mail:** william.maverley@pfizer.com

MAYHEW, EMILY A.
Industry: Nuclear power **Born:** September 28, 1943, Altavista, Virginia **Univ./degree:** B.A., Business, 1981; M.B.A., 1984, Lynchburg College **Current organization:** AREVA NP Inc. **Title:** Vice President, U.S. Region Quality **Type of organization:** Manufacturing **Major product:** Design, construction and service of nuclear power plants **Area of distribution:** International **Expertise:** Administration, quality **Honors/awards:** CVC Outstanding Alumnus of the Year, 2004; American Business Women, Top Ten National. 2004 **Published works:** "Do it Right the First Time - Design Quality In" papers for ASQ Conferences on Quality **Affiliations:** American Society for Quality; American Business Women's Association; Society of Mechanical Engineers; Blue Ridge Area Food Bank **Hob./spts.:** Reading, grandchildren, cruises **SIC code:** 36 **Address:** AREVA NP Inc., 3315 Old Forest Rd., Lynchburg, VA 24501 **E-mail:** emily.mayhew@areva.com **Web address:** www.areva.com

MCBRIDE, ROBERT ALBERT
Industry: Biotechnology **Born:** March 9, 1960, Woonsocket, Rhode Island **Univ./degree:** M.B.A., Bryant College, 1994 **Current organization:** Genzyme Corp. **Title:** Director, Global Training **Type of organization:** R&D **Major product:** Prescription drugs **Area of distribution:** International **Expertise:** Training/management **Affiliations:** W.A.C.; Naval Reserve Association; Commander, U.S. Naval Reserve **Hob./spts.:** Golf, weightlifting, basketball **SIC code:** 28 **Address:** Genzyme Corp., 500 Kendall St., Cambridge, MA 02142 **E-mail:** bob.mcbride@genzyme.com

MCBROOM, TERRY "DUKE" M.
Industry: Agriculture **Born:** February 5, 1954, Richmond, Virginia **Univ./degree:** Marine Biology and Chemistry **Current organization:** Crop Production Services **Title:** Sales/Operations Manager **Type of organization:** Manufacturing **Major product:** Farm, fertilizer, lawn products **Area of distribution:** National **Expertise:** Agriculture Specialist, management of all chemicals (liquid and dry fertilizer) and seed **SIC code:** 28 **Address:** Crop Production Services, P.O. Box 97, Sealston, VA 22547

MCCARTNEY, BRIAN E.
Industry: Automotive **Born:** January 26, 1965, Galion, Ohio **Univ./degree:** A.S., Draft Design, North Central State University, 1944 **Current organization:** Stoneridge Inc., Hi-State Lexington Division **Title:** Engineering Software Administrator **Type of organization:** Manufacturing **Major product:** Switches and sensors **Area of distribution:** International **Expertise:** System integration/CAD **SIC code:** 37 **Address:** 196 Holiday Hill, Lexington, OH 44904 **E-mail:** brian.mccartney@hst.stoneridge.com

MCCARTY, BRAD
Industry: Fertilizer/chemical **Born:** December 16, 1960, Borger, Texas **Univ./degree:** A.S., Estimating, Amarillo College, 1996 **Current organization:** XL Energy **Title:** Instrument Technician **Type of organization:** Manufacturing **Major product:** Fertilizer **Area of distribution:** Borger, Texas **Expertise:** Instrumentation **Affiliations:** I.S.A. **Hob./spts.:** Family, sports, travel, motorcycles, cars **SIC code:** 28 **Address:** XL Energy, Borger, TX 79007 **E-mail:** bmmccarty@agrium.com

MCCLAIN, LESS D.
Industry: Electronic, healthcare and industrial equipment **Born:** April 6, 1960, St. Francis, Kansas **Univ./degree:** B.S., Electronics, University of Wyoming, 1980 **Current organization:** Tyco International **Title:** Director of IS **Type of organization:** Manufacturing and service company **Major product:** Electronic, healthcare and industrial equipment **Area of distribution:** International **Expertise:** Information systems **SIC code:** 36 **Address:** Tyco International, 1 Town Center Rd., Boca Raton, FL 33486 **E-mail:** lmclain@tyco.com

MCCLINE, FRAGER
Industry: Computer technology **Born:** September 29, 1972, Shelby, Mississippi **Univ./degree:** B.S., Computer Science, Mississippi Valley State University, 1994; M.S., Information Systems Management, University of Mississippi, 2002 **Current organization:** Viking Range Corporation **Title:** Systems Analyst **Type of organization:** Manufacturing **Major product:** Appliances **Area of distribution:** National **Expertise:** Info technology, bar coding **Hob./spts.:** Video games, biking, football, family **SIC code:** 35 **Address:** Viking Range Corp., 111 Howard St., Greenwood, MS 38930 **E-mail:** fmccline@vikingrange.com

MCCOPPIN, ANTHONY S.
Industry: Medical devices **Born:** July 23, 1966, Troy, Ohio **Current organization:** Medrad, Inc. **Title:** Principal Technical Associate **Type of organization:** R&D, manufacturing **Major product:** Medical imaging products **Area of distribution:** National **Expertise:** New product development, engineering **Hob./spts.:** Classic cars **SIC code:** 38 **Address:** Medrad, Inc., One Medrad Dr., Indianova, PA 15051 **E-mail:** amccoppin@medrad.com

MCCOWAN, PHILIP E.
Industry: Tires **Born:** June 28, 1941, Shawnee, Oklahoma **Univ./degree:** B.B.A., 1971; J.D., Oklahoma City University, 1990 **Current organization:** Bridgestone Firestone North American Tire LLC OKC Plant **Title:** Environmental Coordinator **Type of organization:** Manufacturing **Major product:** Passenger and light truck tires **Area of distribution:** International **Expertise:** Environmental **Hob./spts.:** Pro bono legal work, golf **SIC code:** 30 **Address:** Bridgestone Firestone, North American Tire LLC OKC Plant, 2500 S. Council Rd., Oklahoma City, OK 73128 **E-mail:** mccowanphil@bfusa.com

MCDANIEL, JOHN SCOTT
Industry: Textiles **Born:** January 16, 1975, Greenville, South Carolina **Univ./degree:** B.S., BusinessEconomics, Erskine College, 1997; M.S., Textile Technology, The Institute of Textile Technology, 2001 **Current organization:** Milliken & Co. **Title:** Process Improvement Leader **Type of organization:** Manufacturing **Major product:** Yarn **Area of distribution:** Bostic, North Carolina **Expertise:** Improvement leader, manufacturing **Honors/awards:** 4 patents **Published works:** Thesis **Affiliations:**

Administrative Vice President, Spartanburg Jaycees.; Treasurer, Young Republicans Club **SIC code:** 22 **Address:** Milliken & Co., 153 Lower Fair Forest Church Rd, Union, SC 29379 **E-mail:** scott.mcdaniel@milliken.com

MCDONALD, ALAN J.
Industry: Food **Born:** December 10, 1965, Dobbs Ferry, New York **Univ./degree:** A.S., Culinary Arts, Johnson & Wales University, Rhode Island, 1985 **Current organization:** Heinz North America **Title:** Certified Executive Chef **Type of organization:** Manufacturing **Major product:** Food, sauces, soups, salad dressings, desserts, ketchup **Area of distribution:** International **Expertise:** Culinary arts **Affiliations:** A.C.F.; R.C.A. **Hob./spts.:** Wine tasting **SIC code:** 39 **Address:** Heinz North America, 2501 Twelve Oaks Lane, Colleyville, TX 76034 **E-mail:** alan.mcdonald@hjeinz.com

MCGILL, DAVID M.
Industry: Electrical **Born:** March 16, 1954, Knoxville, Tennessee **Univ./degree:** B.S., Industrial Engineering, Southern Illinois University; M.S., Industrial Engineering, North Carolina State University, 2003 **Current organization:** Crouse-Hinds Molded Products **Title:** Senior Manufacturing Engineer **Type of organization:** Manufacturing **Major product:** Electrical products **Area of distribution:** International **Expertise:** Engineering **Hob./spts.:** Family, scuba diving, motorcycle riding **SIC code:** 36 **Address:** Crouse-Hinds Molded Products, 4758 Washington St., La Grange, NC 28551 **E-mail:** david.mcgill@crouse-hinds.com **Web address:** www.crouse-hinds.com

MCGLADE, LARRY W.
Industry: Carpets **Born:** February 3, Indianapolis, Indiana **Univ./degree:** B.S.M.E., Purdue University, 1960 **Current organization:** Northwest Carpets, Inc. **Title:** Vice President, Sales and Marketing **Type of organization:** Manufacturing **Major product:** Carpeting, pad, cove base **Area of distribution:** International **Expertise:** Marketing, sales **Affiliations:** Carpet and Rug Institute; American Association of Manufacturers **Hob./spts.:** Spending time with his grandchildren, tennis, boating, water skiing, swimming **SIC code:** 22 **Address:** Northwest Carpets, Inc., 3358 Carpet Capital Dr., Dalton, GA 30720 **E-mail:** larry@northwestcarpets.net **Web address:** www.northwestcarpets.net

MCGOWAN III, VINCENT E.
Industry: Metals, construction **Born:** May 24, 1972, Cheverly, Maryland **Current organization:** CMC Sheet Metal **Title:** Vice President of Construction **Type of organization:** Manufacturing, construction **Major product:** Commercial sheet metal fabrication and installation **Area of distribution:** Maryland, Virginia, D.C. **Expertise:** Construction operations **SIC code:** 33 **Address:** CMC Sheet Metal, 1208 Marblewood Ave., Capitol Heights, MD 20743 **E-mail:** vmcgowan@cmcsheetmetal.com

MCLAREN, JAMES A.
Industry: Disinfectants and soaps **Born:** December 13, 1954, Summerville, New Jersey **Univ./degree:** B.S., Wildlife, Eastern New Mexico University, 1979 **Current organization:** Alden Scientific Division of Metrix **Title:** Chemist **Type of organization:** Manufacturing **Major product:** Disinfectants and soaps **Area of distribution:** International **Expertise:** QC, QA, production chemistry **Published works:** 2 Articles on wildlife, lectures **Affiliations:** National Wildlife Rehabilitation Association **Hob./spts.:** Wildlife photography, writing **SIC code:** 28 **Address:** Alden Scientific Division of Metrix, 360 Cold Spring Ave., West Springfield, MA 01089

MCMAHON, MICHAEL R.
Industry: Air tools **Born:** August 28, 1939, Grand Forks, North Dakota **Current organization:** McMahon Industries **Title:** President **Type of organization:** Manufacturing **Major product:** Air filter/air brush **Area of distribution:** National **Expertise:** Inventor **Affiliations:** Theatre, pipe organ music **Hob./spts.:** Theatre, pipe organ music **SIC code:** 39 **Address:** McMahon Industries, 8809 Siwanoy Ct., Santee, CA 92071 **E-mail:** mcmahon8@pacbell.net

MCMILLEN, DAVID G.
Industry: Industrial machinery **Born:** January 26, 1938, Louisville, Kentucky **Univ./degree:** M.B.A., Catherine Spalding University, 1969 **Current organization:** Waukesha-Pearce Industries, Inc. **Title:** Director, Credit and Collections **Type of organization:** Distributor and fabricator **Major product:** Industrial engines and generators, construction equipment **Area of distribution:** Texas **Expertise:** Finance **Published works:** Articles **Affiliations:** N.A.C.M. **Hob./spts.:** Banjo band, civic groups **SIC code:** 35 **Address:** Waukesha-Pearce Industries, Inc., 12320 S. Main St., Houston, TX 77035 **E-mail:** mcmild@waukesha-pearce.com

MECKERT, GEORGE W.
Industry: Recycling **Univ./degree:** B.S., Chemical Engineering, M.I.T., 1951 **Current organization:** Lehigh Technologies LLC **Title:** V.P., Engineering **Type of organization:** Manufacturing **Major product:** Powdered rubber, plastics, rubber compositions **Area of distribution:** National **Expertise:** Process engineering, material handling, plant design **Affiliations:** A.S.M.E.; A.S.T.M.; Agricultural Engineering Society **Hob./spts.:** Hiking, golf, fishing **SIC code:** 30 **Address:** Lehigh Technologies LLC, 146 Old Country Rd., Mineola, NY 11501 **E-mail:** gwmeckert@lehighllc.com

MEDDAUGH, TIMOTHY GRIDLEY
Industry: Power transmission products **Born:** April 26, 1945, Ithaca, New York **Current organization:** Emerson Power Transmission Corp. **Title:** Tool and Machine Designer **Type of organization:** Manufacturing and distribution **Area of distribution:** International **Expertise:** Machines that improve productivity by rapid assembly of precision engineered chain components with regular and continuous testing to verify quality. EPT Corp. is an ISO 9001 company **Honors/awards:** SME Chapter 157 Golden Anniversary Medal, 1982; SCCA NeDiv Steward of the Year, 1993; Glen Region Service Award, 1982; Glen Region Executives Award, 1993; Jim Burleigh Award, 1992 **Affiliations:** Society of Manufacturing Engineering (Past Chairman, 1st, 2nd and 3rd Vice Chairman, Treasurer and Program Chairman); Sports Car Club of America (Past and Current Glen Regional Executive, Competition Board Chairman, Director, National F & C and National Chief Steward) **SIC code:** 35 **Address:** Emerson Power Transmission Corp., 620 S. Aurora St., Ithaca, NY 14850 **E-mail:** TeGeMe@juno.com

MEI, GEORGE C.
Industry: Chemical **Born:** December 28, 1951, Taipei, Taiwan **Univ./degree:** Ph.D., Chemistry, Washington University, St. Louis, 1982 **Current organization:** OLIN Corp. **Title:** Sr. Engineering Associate **Type of organization:** Manufacturing **Major product:** Chemicals, brass, ammunition **Area of distribution:** International **Expertise:** Chemist **Affiliations:** I.P.S. **SIC code:** 28 **Address:** OLIN Corp., 427 N. Shamrock St., East Alton, IL 62024 **E-mail:** gcmei@corp.olin.com

MEIER, GARRY J.
Industry: Aerospace **Born:** September, 25, 1968 **Univ./degree:** B.S., Business, 2004 **Current organization:** Greater Machining & Manufacturing **Title:** Plant Manager **Type of organization:** Manufacturing **Major product:** Machining and sheet metal fabrication **Area of distribution:** International **Expertise:** Leadership and machining **Hob./spts.:** Motorcycles **SIC code:** 34 **Address:** Greater Machining & Manufacturing, 901 12th St. N.E., Independence, IA 50644 **E-mail:** jmeier@geater.com **Web address:** www.geater.com

MENDOZA, LUIS ALFONSO
Industry: Food **Born:** April 13, 1942, Cali, Colombia **Univ./degree:** B.S., Food Chemistry, Universidad del Valle, Colombia, 1964 **Current organization:** Y& S Candies/Hershey Food Corp. **Title:** Manager of Quality Assurance **Type of organization:** Manufacturing **Major product:** Twizzlers/licorice products/chocolate **Area of distribution:** International **Expertise:** Quality assurance **Affiliations:** City Councilman, City of Lancaster, Pennsylvania **Hob./spts.:** Fishing, travel, soccer **SIC code:** 20 **Address:** Y & S Candies/Hershey Foods Corp., 400 Running Pump Rd., Lancaster, PA 17603 **E-mail:** lmendoza@hersheys.com

MERTENS, FRED
Industry: Aerospace **Born:** February 6, 1949, Falfurrias, Texas **Current organization:** Honeywell International **Title:** Electrician **Type of organization:** Manufacturing **Major product:** Navigation systems **Area of distribution:** International **Expertise:** Maintenance, electrical **Affiliations:** International Association of Electrical Inspectors **Hob./spts.:** Missions work, inventions **SIC code:** 38 **Address:** 7404 149th Ave. N.W., Anoka, MN 55303 **E-mail:** fred_mertens@msn.com

MERTZ, CHRISTOPHER
Industry: Industrial pumps **Born:** February 9, 1977, Shreveport, Louisiana **Univ./degree:** B.S., Engineering, Kennedy-Western University, Villanova University, Grauton Institute of Technology **Current organization:** Keithville Machine Works, Inc. **Title:** Reliability Engineer **Type of organization:** Manufacturing/service **Major product:** Centrifugal pumps **Area of distribution:** Midwestern U.S. **Expertise:** Reliability engineering, fluid hydraulics and pump technology **Hob./spts.:** Building small scale steam engines **SIC code:** 35 **Address:** Keithville Machine Works, Inc., 3159 Stagecoach Rd., Keithville, LA 71047 **E-mail:** cmertzbsme@aol.com

MESHRI, DAYAL T.
Industry: Chemicals **Univ./degree:** Ph.D., Fluorine Chemistry, 1967 **Current organization:** Advance Research Chemicals Inc. **Title:** Ph.D., President, C.E.O. **Type of organization:** Manufacturing **Major product:** Specialty fluorine compounds **Area of distribution:** International **Expertise:** Fluorine chemistry **Affiliations:** American Chemical Society; American Academy of Sciences; American Institute of Science **SIC code:** 28 **Address:** Advance Research Chemicals Inc., 1110 W. Keystone Ave., Catoosa, OK 74015 **E-mail:** dr.meshri@fluorinearc.com **Web address:** www.fluorinearc.com

MEVES, VIRGINIA L.
Industry: Newspaper periodicals **Born:** March 23, 1927, Indianapolis, Indiana **Spouse:** Dr. Theodore F. Meves **Children:** Theodore James, Roderick Linn, Adrienne Teri, Lenore Ruth **Univ./degree:** R.N., Indiana University School of Nursing, 1948; Graduate work in Education, Marquette University, Wisconsin, 1957-58 **Current**

organization: Wisconsin Report Publishing Co., Inc./Education Service Council **Title:** Director/Editor/Publisher **Type of organization:** Publishing **Major product:** Newspapers, periodicals **Area of distribution:** International **Expertise:** Editing **Honors/awards:** Received the Congress of Freedom "Liberty Award", 1974, 1975 ,1976, 1977, 1978 **Published works:** Articles in the Wisconsin Report on "The Hidden Secrets of the Alpha Course" and "The Dark Agenda Behind Alpha"; Lectured on the status of the United States and all government functions emphasizing legality **Affiliations:** State Coordinator, Wisconsin Legislative and Research Committee, Inc.; Corresponding Secretary, Lutheran Medical Mission Assn., Milwaukee Chapter **Career accomplishments:** Has worked with the National Committee to Restore the Constitution; Helped to organize the Wisconsin Legislative and Research Committee Inc. and affiliate of the National Committee to Restore the Constitution; Her and her husband were Lutheran Medical Missionaries in Nigeria, West Africa, 1953-55; She was the Assistant Clinical Instructor, Milwaukee Lutheran Hospital, 1957-58; Organized and directed the Lutheran School for Medical Evangelism, Milwaukee, September, 1962; Served as consultant and committee member of Planning Committee on Teacher Education for Disadvantaged Pupils - State of Wisconsin (UW-M), 1968 **Hob./spts.:** Cooking, recipes, reading, missionary work **SIC code:** 27 **Address:** Wisconsin Report Publishing Co., Inc., 18310 Benington Dr., Brookfield, WI 53045-5419, Education Service Council, P.O. Box 271, Elm Grove, WI 53122-0271

MEYER, PAUL C.
Industry: Computer systems integration **Born:** May 22, 1947, Hicksville, New York **Univ./degree:** B.S., Suma Cum Laude, Accounting, C.W. Post College, 1974 **Current organization:** Real Time Division, Concurrent Computer Corp. **Title:** President **Type of organization:** Manufacturing **Major product:** Hardware, software **Area of distribution:** Florida **Expertise:** General management **Affiliations:** Republican National Committee **Hob./spts.:** Golf, tennis **SIC code:** 36 **Address:** Real Time Division, Concurrent Computer Corp., 2881 Gateway Dr., Pompano Beach, FL 33069 **E-mail:** pmeyer522@aol.com

MEYERSON, SEYMOUR
Industry: Chemicals **Title:** Research Consultant (Retired) **Type of organization:** Manufacturing **Major product:** Petroleum products and petrochemicals **Expertise:** Chemical research, mass spectrometry **SIC code:** 29 **Address:** 43 Vermont Ct., #A1, Asheville, NC 28806 **E-mail:** meyerson43@hotmail.com

MIAO, HELEN W.
Industry: Metals **Univ./degree:** M.S., Electrical and Computer Engineering, North Carolina State University, 1987 **Current organization:** Hitchiner Manufacturing Co., Inc. **Title:** Staff Controls Engineer **Type of organization:** Manufacturing **Major product:** Metal castings **Area of distribution:** International **Expertise:** Scada systems, PLC programs **Affiliations:** N.F.P.A. **Hob./spts.:** Reading, travel **SIC code:** 33 **Address:** Hitchiner Manufacturing Co., Inc., Elm St., P.O. Box 2001, Milford, NH 03055 **E-mail:** helenmiao@comcast.net

MICHAUD, WILLIAM G.
Industry: HVAC **Born:** August 10, 1960, Sudbury, Ontario, Canada **Current organization:** Siemens Building Technologies **Title:** Account Engineer **Type of organization:** Manufacturing, distribution, service **Major product:** HVAC control and engineering **Area of distribution:** International **Expertise:** Controls engineering, sales, design, installations **Honors/awards:** Served in active duty, U.S. Air Force, 1983-90 as an Air Traffic Controller **Hob./spts.:** Family, golf **SIC code:** 34 **Address:** Siemens Building Technologies, 31623 Industrial Rd., Livonia, MI 48150 **E-mail:** william.michaud@siemens.com **Web address:** www.siemens.com

MIKHAYLENKO, BORIS
Industry: Industrial control and automation **Born:** November 8, 1949, Kiev, Ukraine **Univ./degree:** M.S. Electronics, Kiev Technical University, 1979 **Current organization:** Advantech Automation Corp. **Title:** Senior Design Engineer **Type of organization:** Manufacturing **Major product:** Industrial computers **Area of distribution:** International **Expertise:** Engineering, project management, industrial solutions, strategic planning **Honors/awards:** 'The Inventor of the USSR', Medal, Gold and Bronze Medals of the USSR Industrial Achievements National Exhibition for New Technologies Products Design **Published works:** 56+ articles **Hob./spts.:** Spending time with his grandchildren, flying private plane, radio controlled planes **SIC code:** 36 **Address:** Advantech Automation Corp., 1320 Kemper Meadow Dr., Cincinnati, OH 45240 **E-mail:** boris.mikhaylenko@advantech.com **Web address:** www.advantech.com

MILLER, KEITH A.
Industry: Air conditioning/refrigeration **Born:** June 28, 1954, Miami, Florida **Univ./degree:** A.S., Arts, Miami Dade Community College, 1982 **Current organization:** E.M. Corson/Cors-Air **Title:** Sales Engineer **Type of organization:** Manufacturing **Major product:** Air conditioning and ventilations parts **Area of distribution:** Florida **Expertise:** Engineering, sales **Affiliations:** N.F.P.A.; A.S.H.R.A.E.; A.E.E. **Hob./spts.:** Fishing, scuba diving **SIC code:** 35 **Address:** E.M. Corson/Cors-Air, 2865 S.W. 30 Ave., Pembroke Park, FL 33330 **E-mail:** keith@cors.air.com

MILLER, LAWRENCE W.
Industry: Industrial turbo machinery **Born:** May 12, 1950, Portsmouth, Virginia **Univ./degree:** B.S.M.E., with Aerospace Option, University of Pittsburgh, 1973 **Current organization:** Elliott Turbo Machinery Co., Inc. **Title:** Senior Product Design Engineer **Type of organization:** Manufacturing **Major product:** Steam turbines and compressors **Area of distribution:** International **Expertise:** Engineering **Published works:** Book chapter, "Sawyer's Turbo Machinery Maintenance Handbook" **Hob./spts.:** Woodworking **SIC code:** 35 **Address:** Elliott Turbo Machinery Co., Inc., 901 N. Fourth St., Jeannette, PA 15644-1474 **E-mail:** lmiller@elliott-turbo.com

MILLICAN, CHARLIE A.
Industry: Chemicals **Born:** August 14, 1956, Houston, Texas **Univ./degree:** A.S., Instrumentation, Leigh College, 1978 **Current organization:** GE Automation Services Inc. **Title:** I/E Engineer **Type of organization:** Manufacturing **Major product:** Specialty chemicals **Area of distribution:** International **Expertise:** Engineering **Affiliations:** I.S.A. **Hob./spts.:** Baseball, coaching little league, motorcycles, dirt bikes **SIC code:** 28 **Address:** GE Automation Services Inc., 12000 Aerospace Ave., Suite 100, Houston, TX 77034 **E-mail:** houmad@rohmhaas.com **Web address:** www.ge.com

MILLS, LEON J.
Industry: Food **Born:** December 20, 1954, Green Bay, Wisconsin **Univ./degree:** A.S., Automated Manufacturing and Electrical Mechanical Engineering, Fox Valley Technical College, 1990 **Current organization:** Hillshire Farm & Kahn's/Division of Sara Lee **Title:** Project Engineer **Type of organization:** Manufacturing **Major product:** Smoked sausage and meats **Area of distribution:** International **Expertise:** Engineering **Hob./spts.:** Woodworking, gardening **SIC code:** 20 **Address:** N3124 Midway Ct., Clintonville, WI 54929 **E-mail:** leon.mills@saralee.com

MINERVINI, LEO
Industry: Process control **Born:** Hoboken, New Jersey **Univ./degree:** B.S.M.E., New Jersey Institute of Technology, 1993 **Current organization:** Westlock Controls, a Division of Tyco International **Title:** Vice President, Engineering **Type of organization:** Manufacturing **Major product:** Valve controls **Area of distribution:** International **Expertise:** Engineering **Affiliations:** I.S.A. **Hob./spts.:** Music, golf **SIC code:** 38 **Address:** Westlock Controls, a Division of Tyco International, 280 Midland Ave., Saddle Brook, NJ 07663 **E-mail:** leominervini@westlockcontrols.com

MINKWITZ, MARGARET C.
Industry: Pharmaceuticals **Born:** June 30, 1946, Corning, New York **Spouse:** Vernon C. Minkwitz **Married:** September, 1990 **Children:** Catherine Flavin, Richard Cecce, Leanna Coates, Florence Cecce; Grandchildren: Christina, Michael, Rebecca and Matthew Flavin, George H. Coates V **Univ./degree:** A.A.S., Corning Community College; B.S., 1980, Elmira College; M.S., 1983; Ph.D., 1986, Cornell University **Current organization:** AstraZeneca **Title:** Director, Biostatistics Products Team Leader **Type of organization:** Pharmaceutical company, research and development of prescription drugs **Major product:** Prilosec®, Zestril®, Diprivan®, Merrem®, Nolvadex®, Rhinocort®, Accolate®, Zomig® **Area of distribution:** International **Expertise:** Biostatistics, project management, management **Published works:** Co-author of 15 articles in various medical journals for Accolate® and 2 for Merrem® **Affiliations:** American Statistical Association, International Biometrics Society, Past Secretary, Vice President, President, Symposia Chairman for the Delaware Chapter of the American Statistical Association **Career accomplishments:** Responsible for statistical support of the US marketing approval for Accolate® including participation in the FDA advisory panel 1996; managed 30 staff supporting Zeneca marketed products, producing significant number of scientific publications to support the marketed products **Hob./spts.:** Singing, AstraZeneca singers, St. Mary of the Assumption choir; sewing, knitting, needlework **SIC code:** 28 **Address:** Zeneca Pharmaceuticals, 1800 Concord Pike, Wilmington, DE 19856-5437 **E-mail:** margaret.minkwitz@astrazeneca.com **Web address:** www.astrazeneca.com

MINTHORN, ELISABETH A.
Industry: Pharmaceutical **Born:** February 14, 1968, Silver Spring, Maryland **Univ./degree:** B.S., Biology/Chemistry, West Chester University, Pennsylvania, 1989

Current organization: GlaxoSmithKline Pharmaceuticals **Title:** Investigator **Type of organization:** Pharmaceutical/R&D **Major product:** Pharmaceuticals **Area of distribution:** International **Expertise:** Pharmacokinetics and Drug Metabolism scientist who provides leadership to project teams and devises strategies for selection/progression of drug candidates with optimum absorption, tissue distribution, metabolism and excretion properties **Published works:** 16 published articles and abstracts including: Davies, B.E., Minthorn, E.A., et al. The Pharmacokinetics of topotecan and its carboxylate form following separate intravenous administration to the dog. Pharm Res 14(10):1461-5, 1997: D.R. Mould, C.B. Davis, E.A. Minthorn, et al. Population PK/PD Analysis of Clenoliximab in Patients with Active Rheumatoid Arthritis. Clin Pharmacol Ther 66(3):246-57, 1999; T.K. Hart, R.M. Cook, P. Zia-Amirhosseini, E. Minthorn, et al. Preclinical Efficacy and Safety of Mepolizumab (SB-240563), a Humanized Anti-IL-5 Monoclonal Antibody, in Cynomolgus Monkeys. J Allergy and Clin Immunol 108(2): 250-257, 2001 (editor's choice); and other articles on topics such as pharmacology, pharmacokinetics and drug-transporter interactions **Affiliations:** American Association of Pharmaceutical Scientists (AAPS); Young Mathematicians Network; Dutch Society for Theoretical Biology **Hob./spts.:** Crafts, gardening, playing piano, dragon boat racing **SIC code:** 28 **Address:** GlaxoSmithKline Pharmaceuticals, 1250 S. Collegeville Rd., Collegeville, PA 19426 **E-mail:** elisabeth.a.minthorn@gsk.com **Web address:** www.gsk.com

MIRANDA, VICENTE
Industry: Communication systems **Born:** December 6, 1969, Tlacotalpan, Mexico **Univ./degree:** M.S., Electronic Engineering, Institute of Technology at Monterrey, Mexico, 1996 **Current organization:** Motorola **Title:** Test System Engineer **Type of organization:** Manufacturing **Major product:** Digital satellite receivers **Area of distribution:** International **Expertise:** Design test systems **Hob./spts.:** Family, travel, computers **SIC code:** 36 **Address:** Motorola, Prolongacion Ruiz Cortinez, Nogales, Sonora 84000, Mexico **E-mail:** vicente.miranda@motorola.com

MIRIANASHVILI, MARIAM
Industry: Communications **Born:** February 19, 1969, Tbilisi, Georgia (country) **Univ./degree:** Ph.D., Ehime University, Matsuyama, Japan, 2000 **Current organization:** California Eastern Laboratories **Title:** Senior Engineer **Type of organization:** Design and manufacturing **Major product:** Semiconductor components **Area of distribution:** California **Expertise:** Engineering and marketing **Published works:** "Coupled-Mode Analysis of Bent Planar Waveguides with Finite Claddings", Jpn. J. Appl. Phys. Vol. 37, 1998, pp.3651-3656; "Coupled-Mode Analysis of Loss in Bent Single-Mode Optical Fibers", Jpn. J. Appl. Phys. Vol. 39, 2000, pp.1468-1471 **Affiliations:** I.E.E.E.; O.S.A.; S.W.E. **Hob./spts.:** Travel, chess, tennis, music **SIC code:** 36 **Address:** California Eastern Laboratories, 4590 Patrick Henry Dr., Santa Clara, CA 95054 **E-mail:** mariageorgia@gmail.com

MIROLO JR., AMEDEO A.
Industry: Electrical **Born:** July 27, 1957, Columbus, Ohio **Univ./degree:** B.S., Industrial Education, Ohio State University, 1979 **Current organization:** SAIA Burgess Inc. **Title:** Sr. Manufacturing Engineer **Type of organization:** Manufacturing **Major product:** Electrical activators for military, consumer products postal and healthcare industries **Area of distribution:** International **Expertise:** Engineering **Affiliations:** Senior Member, S.M.E.; Epsilon Pi Tau **Hob./spts.:** Auto restoration, flying model airplanes **SIC code:** 36 **Address:** SAIA Burgess Inc., 801 Scholz Dr., Vandalia, OH 45377-3121 **E-mail:** al.mirolo@saiaburgessinc.com

MITCHELL JR., LENNERT J.
Industry: Pharmaceuticals/biotechnology **Born:** December 12, 1961, Los Angeles, California **Univ./degree:** B.S., California State University, Los Angeles, 1989 **Current organization:** Pfizer, Inc. **Title:** Senior Associate Scientist II **Type of organization:** Pharmaceuticals **Major product:** Prescription drugs **Area of distribution:** International **Expertise:** Medicine/chemistry **Honors/awards:** Best Undergraduate Thesis Award **Published works:** 1 article **Affiliations:** American Chemical Society **Hob./spts.:** Spending time with family, gardening **SIC code:** 28 **Address:** Pfizer, Inc., 10770 Science Center Dr., San Diego, CA 92121 **E-mail:** lennert.mitchell@pfizer.com

MODI, GITTU M.
Industry: Metal **Born:** December 31, 1951, Bombay, India **Univ./degree:** B.S., Chemistry and Metallurgy, Bombay University, 1965 **Current organization:** Brass Masters, Inc. **Title:** President **Type of organization:** Manufacturing **Major product:** Brass hardware for the building industry **Area of distribution:** National **Expertise:** Metallurgy **Hob./spts.:** Golf, chess **SIC code:** 34 **Address:** Brass Masters, Inc., 82-47 210th St., Hollis Hills, NY 11427 **E-mail:** modigittu@yahoo.com

MOEHRING, JOHN T.
Industry: Engineering **Univ./degree:** M.S., University of Minnesota **Current organization:** GE Aircraft Engines **Title:** Flight Safety Director **Type of organization:** Design and manufacturing **Major product:** Jet engine manufacturing and service **Area of distribution:** International **Expertise:** Engineering/aircraft accident investigation **Honors/awards:** The Flight, Propulsion Hall of Fame, 1999 **Published works:** I.S.A.S.I. Journal; Journal of Flight Safety Foundation **Affiliations:** S.A.E.; I.S.A.S.I. **SIC code:** 37 **Address:** GE Aircraft Engines, 8921 Paw Paw Lane, Cincinnati, OH 45236 **E-mail:** jtmoehfltsft@fuse.net

MOGHADAM, ALI (ALEX)
Industry: Healthcare equipment **Born:** March 21, 1959, Mashad, Iran **Univ./degree:** Ph.D., Biomedical Engineering, Western University, 2004 **Current organization:** ACI Corp. **Title:** Senior Transfer Technology Team Leader **Type of organization:** Manufacturing **Major product:** Endoscopy equipment **Area of distribution:** International **Expertise:** Medical Electronics **Published works:** ESD Fundamentals & Requirements, I.E.E.E. Magazine, 2004; CMOS vs. CCD Camera Application in Endoscopy Equipment, 24 X 7 Magazine, 2004 **Affiliations:** A.I.M.E.E.; I.E.E.E. **SIC code:** 38 **Address:** ACI Corp., 300 Stillwater Ave., Stamford, CT 06902 **E-mail:** amoghadam@acmicorp.com

MOLINA, EDWARD E.
Industry: Chemicals **Born:** January 5, 1952, Honduras **Univ./degree:** B.A., Lamar University, Beaumont, Texas, 2000 **Current organization:** Chevron Phillips Chemical Co. **Title:** Electrician **Type of organization:** Manufacturing **Major product:** Plastic feedstock **Area of distribution:** International **Expertise:** Electrical maintenance **Affiliations:** I.B.E.W. **Hob./spts.:** Golf, travel **SIC code:** 28 **Address:** 970 Sabine Dr., Bridge City, TX 77611 **E-mail:** molinee@cpchem.com

MONROE, JESSIE E.
Industry: Bedding **Title:** Shipping Manager **Type of organization:** Manufacturing/retail **Major product:** Raw material/home goods **Expertise:** Shipping **SIC code:** 22 **Address:** Hollander Home Fashions, 10750 Denton Dr., Dallas, TX 75220 **E-mail:** monroejess@aol.com

MONTEIRO, ROBSON S.
Industry: Nanotechnology **Born:** April 14, 1967, Ipatinga, Brazil **Univ./degree:** Ph.D., Chemical Engineering, Federal University of Rio de Janeiro, 1997 **Current organization:** Hyperion Catalysis International, Inc. **Title:** Ph.D. **Type of organization:** Manufacturing **Major product:** Carbon nanotubes **Area of distribution:** International **Expertise:** Research science **Affiliations:** A.I.C.E.; A.C.S.; N.Y.A.S. **Hob./spts.:** Tennis, classical music **SIC code:** 28 **Address:** Hyperion Catalysis International, Inc., 38 Smith Place, Cambridge, MA 02138 **E-mail:** rmonteiro@hyperioncatalysis.com

MONTENEGRO ALVARADO, JOSÉ M.
Industry: Pharmaceuticals **Born:** February 20, 1974, Ponce, Puerto Rico **Univ./degree:** B.S., Chemical Engineering, University of Puerto Rico, Mayaguez Campus, 1998; M.S., Chemical Engineering, University of Puerto Rico, Mayaguez Campus, 2001 **Current organization:** Pfizer Pharmaceuticals LLC, Global Manufacturing Division **Title:** Chemical Engineer **Type of organization:** Manufacturing **Major product:** Non sterile solid oral dosage forms **Area of distribution:** International **Expertise:** Pharmaceutical operations, process control, cGMP equipment qualification, computerized systems validation, fluid bed drying processes **Published works:** Master's thesis, Determination of Optimum Drying Endpoints of Pharmaceutical Granulations: Development of an Automated Pilot Unit **Affiliations:** National Society of Professional Engineers; American Institute of Chemical Engineers; College of Engineers and Land Surveyors of Puerto Rico; Institute of Chemical Engineers of Puerto Rico **Hob./spts.:** Reading, real estate prospects **SIC code:** 28 **Address:** Pfizer Pharmaceuticals LLC, Global Manufacturing Division, 211 Paseo del Puerto, Penuelas, PR 00624 **E-mail:** jose.m.montenegro.alvarado@pharmacia.com

MONTOYA, DANNY A.
Industry: Pharmaceutical injections **Univ./degree:** Journeyman Electrician Degree, New Mexico Journeyman's Association, 1989 **Current organization:** Cardinal Health **Title:** Senior Line Mechanic **Type of organization:** Manufacturing **Major product:** Pharmaceutical injections **Expertise:** Automation integration - robotics **SIC code:** 28 **Address:** 2127 Tapia Blvd. S.W., Albuquerque, NM 87105 **E-mail:** danny.montoya@cardinal.com

MOODY, JOHN W.
Industry: Paper manufacturers **Born:** August 22, 1945, Terrehaute, Indiana **Univ./degree:** Electrical Technology, I.V.T.C., 1975 **Current organization:** International Paper Co. **Title:** Plant Engineer/Maintenance Manager **Type of organization:** Manufacturing **Major product:** paper, corrugated boxes **Area of distribution:** International **Expertise:** Engineering, electrical trouble-shooting **Affiliations:** I.E.I.A.; Electrical League of Indiana **Hob./spts.:** Drawing, painting, travel **SIC code:** 26 **Address:** International Paper Co., 3904 W. Ferguson Rd., Ft. Wayne, IN 46809 **E-mail:** john.moody@ipaper.com **Web address:** www.ipaper.com

MOON, CARROLL L.
Industry: Waste compactors **Current organization:** SSI Shredding System, Inc. **Title:** Customer Service **Type of organization:** Manufacturing **Major product:** Waste compactors **Area of distribution:** Wilsonville, Oregon **Expertise:** Customer service

Affiliations: N.R.A. **Hob./spts.:** Power lifting, hunting, fishing **SIC code:** 35 **Address:** SSI Shredding System, Inc., 9760 S.W. Freeman Dr., Wilsonville, OR 97070 **E-mail:** cmoon@ssiword.com

MOORE, PAUL W.
Industry: Hydraulics **Born:** July 27, 1942, Hutchinson, Kansas **Univ./degree:** B.S., Pittsburg State University, Kansas, 1964 **Current organization:** Eaton Hydraulics **Title:** Manufacturing Manager **Type of organization:** Manufacturing **Major product:** Hydraulic piston and gear pumps **Area of distribution:** International **Expertise:** Management **Hob./spts.:** N.H.R.A. competition **SIC code:** 37 **Address:** Eaton Hydraulics, 3401 E. Fourth St., Hutchinson, KS 67501 **E-mail:** paulmoore@eaton.com

MOORE, RICK
Industry: Railcars **Born:** Kennett, Missouri **Current organization:** American Railcar Industries **Title:** Manager of Manufacturing **Type of organization:** Manufacturing **Major product:** Covered hopper cars **Area of distribution:** National **Expertise:** Administration **Hob./spts.:** Boating, late model dirt track racing **SIC code:** 37 **Address:** American Railcar Industries, 901 Jones Rd., Paragould, AZ 72450 **E-mail:** rmoore@americanrailcar.com

MORA, MICHAEL K.
Industry: Electronics **Born:** July 1, 1968, Albuquerque, New Mexico **Univ./degree:** B.S.E.E., 1991; M.B.A., University of New Mexico, 1996 **Current organization:** General Technology Corp. **Title:** Quality Assurance Manager **Type of organization:** Manufacturing **Major product:** Military electronics **Area of distribution:** International **Expertise:** Electrical Engineering, Quality Assurance **Honors/awards:** Certified Quality Manager; Employee of the Year, 1996 **Published works:** "High Speed Data Transfer Using GaAs", I.E.E.E. Magazine; "Quality Corner", Quality Press Magazine **Affiliations:** A.S.Q. **Hob./spts.:** Semi-Professional Football (linebacker), reading **SIC code:** 36 **Address:** General Technology Corp., 1450 Mission Ave., N.E., Albuquerque, NM 87107 **E-mail:** mora@gt-corp.com **Web address:** www.gt-corp.com

MORGANTI, RICHARD J.
Industry: Aerospace/energy **Born:** March 19, 1959, Boston, Massachusetts **Univ./degree:** B.S., Massachusetts Maritime Academy, 1982; M.S., Manufacturing, Boston University, 2003 **Current organization:** Spincraft **Title:** Vice President, Technology and Product Development **Type of organization:** Contract manufacturing **Major product:** Aerospace fuel tanks and domes/energy turbine components **Area of distribution:** International **Expertise:** Manufacturing engineering, project management, business development, quality control **Honors/awards:** Guest lecturer at Boston University; was a Launch Attendee at Space Flight Awareness, NASA, 2001 **Affiliations:** A.S.N.E.; A.S.M.; A.W.S.; S.A.E. **Hob./spts.:** Reading, golf, travel **SIC code:** 37 **Address:** Spincraft, 500 Iron Horse Park, North Billerica, MA 01862 **E-mail:** rmorganti@spincraft.net **Web address:** www.spincraft.net

MOTTER, WILLIAM A.
Industry: Flexible packaging **Born:** September 17, 1957, Kittanning, Pennsylvania **Univ./degree:** A.A.F., Electronics and Electrical Engineering Technology, Germania Community College **Current organization:** Cello-Foil Products Inc. **Title:** Maintenance Manager **Type of organization:** Manufacturing **Major product:** Printed packages **Area of distribution:** National **Expertise:** Electrical engineering **Hob./spts.:** Martial arts **SIC code:** 26 **Address:** Cello-Foil Products Inc., 1801 Oakhaven Dr., Albany, GA 31706 **E-mail:** bill.motter@cello-foil.com

MOURA, DOMINGOS G.
Industry: Medical instruments **Born:** August 31, 1961, Oporto, Portugal **Univ./degree:** A.S., Electronics, New Haven University, 1982; Certification, Quality Improvement, Worcester University, 2002 **Current organization:** Tyco Intl./U.S. Surgical **Title:** Quality Engineer **Type of organization:** Manufacturing **Major product:** Medical surgical instruments **Area of distribution:** International **Expertise:** Quality engineering **Hob./spts.:** Family and children, martial art of Kung Fu (Black Belt), travel, sports **SIC code:** 38 **Address:** Tyco Intl./U.S. Surgical, 195 McDermott Rd., North Haven, CT 06473 **E-mail:** domingos.moura@ussurg.com **Web address:** www.ussurg.com

MUCEK, JOSEPH
Industry: Machining parts **Born:** November 22, 1951, Janikowo, Poland **Univ./degree:** B.S., Agriculture, University of Poland, 1969; Attended Wright College for Mechanical Engineering **Current organization:** J.M. Quality Machining Inc. **Title:** President **Type of organization:** Manufacturing **Major product:** Machining parts and assembly **Area of distribution:** National **Expertise:** Engineering **Affiliations:** Oxford Club **Hob./spts.:** Family **SIC code:** 35 **Address:** J.M. Quality Machining Inc., 4275 S. Navajo St., Englewood, CO 80110 **E-mail:** jmucek5686@aol.com

MUI, MICHAEL YAMPUI
Industry: Pharmaceuticals **Born:** October 30, 1970, China **Univ./degree:** B.S., Sophie Davis Medical School, 1996 **Current organization:** Eli Lilly & Co. **Type of organization:** Manufacturing **Major product:** Drugs, pharmaceuticals **Area of distribution:** National **Expertise:** Sales, marketing **Hob./spts.:** Weight training, outdoor sports **SIC code:** 28 **Address:** Eli Lilly & Co., 265 Cherry St., #15D, New York, NY 10002 **E-mail:** mui_michael_y@lilly.com

MULFORD, FREDERICK MICHAEL
Industry: Material handling **Born:** April 21, 1972, Geneva, New York **Univ./degree:** Vocational-technical for auto mechanics and various mechanical courses including machine shop basic electricity, mechanical drawing, technical mechanics/surveying **Current organization:** Frazier Industrial Co. **Title:** Technical Support Supervisor **Type of organization:** Manufacturing **Major product:** Structural steel pallet rack **Area of distribution:** National **Expertise:** Equipment design **Honors/awards:** Technical Service Training, Swimming Pool and Spa Heaters; Pool/Spa Heater Installation & Repair Service Seminar, 1993; The National Spa and Pool Institute Professional training Seminars, 1992; participant, Boy's State **Hob./spts.:** Farming, camping, hunting, antique machinery (especially steam engines), metal working/fabrication, automobiles and woodworking **SIC code:** 34 **Address:** Frazier Industrial Co., 1291 Waterloo Geneva Rd., Waterloo, NY 13165 **E-mail:** mmulford@frazier.com

MULLALY, TERRY A.
Industry: Automotive **Born:** August 20, Canton, Ohio **Univ./degree:** A.S., Mt. Vernon College, 1974 **Current organization:** Flex Technologies, Inc. **Title:** IS Manager/C.C.P. **Type of organization:** Manufacturing **Major product:** Automotive parts **Area of distribution:** National/Global **Expertise:** I.T.; E.D.I.; R.P.G.; C.O.B.O.L. **Affiliations:** V.F.W.; American Legion; F.O.E.; Eagle Scouts; Past Member, I.C.C.P.; D.P.M.A. **Hob./spts.:** Poetry **SIC code:** 37 **Address:** Flex Technologies, Inc., P.O. Box 400, Midvale, OH 44653 **E-mail:** termultuous@yahoo.com

MULLIGAN, KEVIN T.
Industry: Pharmaceuticals **Born:** May 7, 1955 New York, New York **Univ./degree:** B.S., Chemistry, Marquette University, 1978; M.B.A., Fairleigh Dickinson University, 1982 **Current organization:** TYCO Healthcare **Title:** Director of Packaging Engineering **Type of organization:** Manufacturing **Major product:** Medical and pharmaceutical products **Area of distribution:** International **Expertise:** Chemical and package engineering **Published works:** 12+ technical journals **Affiliations:** I.O.P.P. **Hob./spts.:** All sports, coaching youth sports, travel, reading **SIC code:** 28 **Address:** TYCO Healthcare, 15 Hampshire St., Mansfield, MA 02048 **E-mail:** kevin.mulligan@tycohealthcare.com **Web address:** www.tycohealthcare.com

MULLINS, JEFFREY L.
Industry: Automated environmental control systems **Univ./degree:** B.S., Electrical Engineering, Michigan University, 1992 **Current organization:** Salmet Poultry Systems **Title:** Head of Engineering Design/Program **Type of organization:** Manufacturing, distributing **Major product:** Complete control systems (computer and field) **Area of distribution:** International **Expertise:** Engineering, programming, product improvement **Hob./spts.:** Robotics **SIC code:** 38 **Address:** Salmet Poultry Systems, 11177 Township Rd. 133, P.O. Box 5, West Mansfield, OH 43358 **E-mail:** jeff.mullins@salmet.us

MURARI, SHOBHA
Industry: Glass **Born:** September 20, 1962, Washington, D.C. **Univ./degree:** Ph.D., Organic Chemistry, University of Roorkee, India, 1988 **Current organization:** JPS Glass **Title:** Director of R&D **Type of organization:** Manufacturing **Major product:** Textile - glass fabric for construction and aerospace **Area of distribution:** International **Expertise:** Administration, research, new product development **Affiliations:** A.C.S. **SIC code:** 32 **Address:** JPS Glass, 101 Slater Rd., Slater, SC 29683

MURTHA JR., ROBERT C.
Industry: Engineering **Univ./degree:** Ocean Engineering, U.S. Naval Academy; M.S., Environmental Engineering, Johns Hopkins University **Current organization:** ACS Defense **Title:** Vice President **Type of organization:** Manufacturing **Major product:** Environmental air products for the defense sector and private industry **Area of distribution:** National **Expertise:** Environmental engineering, manufacturing design, strategic analysis, team leadership, business development with an emphasis on air products that protect from chemical and biological attacks **Affiliations:** A.S.C.E.; Member, Advisory Board for the Environmental Engineering Program at Johns Hopkins University; 5 years of service with the U.S. Marines **SIC code:** 36 **Address:** ACS Defense, 5290 Shawnee Rd., Alexandria, VA 22312 **E-mail:** robert.murtha@acs-inc.com **Web address:** www.acsdefense.com

MYHRE, KJELL E.
Industry: Consulting/manufacturing **Born:** March 9, 1930, Addis Ababa, Ethiopia **Univ./degree:** Ph.D., University of Palmer's Green, London, England **Current organization:** Century Technology Co. **Title:** President/Owner **Type of organization:** Manufacturing **Major product:** Sensors/instruments **Area of distribution:** International **Expertise:** Engineering **Honors/awards:** IR100 Award for Industrial Research, 1966 **Published works:** 6 patents **Affiliations:** A.S.M.; A.W.S.; A.A.M.I.; I.S.A.; S.E.S.A.

Hob./spts.: Skiing **SIC code:** 36 **Address:** Century Technology Co., 10831 Roy Croft St., Suite 32, Sun Valley, CA 91352 **E-mail:** myhrek@aol.com

MYRVIK, QUENTIN N.
Industry: Appliances **Born:** November 9, 1921, Minneota, Minnesota **Univ./degree:** M.S., Microbiology/Immunology, 1950; Ph.D., Microbiology/Immunology, 1952, University of Washington **Current organization:** Myrvik Enterprises **Title:** President **Type of organization:** Manufacturing/retailer **Major product:** Lamps, shades, vacuum cleaners, radio controlled clocks, weather stations **Area of distribution:** National **Expertise:** Product development, marketing **Published works:** 4 books, 150+ articles **Hob./spts.:** Travel, boating, organ music, digital photography, electronics **SIC code:** 36 **Address:** Myrvik Enterprises, 4583 Long Beach Rd., Southport, NC 28461 **E-mail:** quenmy@bcinet.net **Web address:** www.myrvikenterprises.com

NAGRABECKI, GREGORY
Industry: Plastic packaging **Born:** March 12, 1958, Darlowo, Poland **Univ./degree:** B.S., Mechanical Engineering, Poland, 1981 **Current organization:** Graham Packaging Inc. **Title:** Warehouse Manager **Type of organization:** Manufacturing **Major product:** H.D.P.E. plastic packaging **Area of distribution:** International **Expertise:** Computers, Microsoft Access, database development **Hob./spts.:** Travel, soccer **SIC code:** 30 **Address:** Graham Packaging Inc., 2900 Woodbridge Ave., Edison, NJ 08837 **E-mail:** gregory.nagrebecki@grahampackaging.com

NASON, JAY O.
Industry: Instrumentation design **Born:** November 29, 1966, Portland, Maine **Univ./degree:** B.S., Computers and Electrical Engineering, Western Polytechnic Institute, 1988 **Current organization:** Emerson Apparatus, Inc. **Title:** Electrical & Software Engineer **Type of organization:** Manufacturing **Major product:** Laboratory testing equipment **Area of distribution:** International **Expertise:** Engineering **Affiliations:** T.A.P.P.I. **Hob./spts.:** Hiking, waterskiing, computers, travel **SIC code:** 38 **Address:** Emerson Apparatus, Inc., 170 Anderson St., Portland, ME 04101 **E-mail:** jayn@emersonappartus.com **Web address:** www.emersonapparatus.com

NAUMANN, HANS J.
Industry: Railroad, automotive, machine building and tool & die **Born:** May 5, 1935, Dewitz, Germany **Univ./degree:** Masters Degree, Engineering, University of Hamburg, Germany, 1960; M.B.A., Rochester University, 1965 **Current organization:** Simmons Machine Tool Group/Niles-Simmons-Hegenscheidt G.M.B.H. **Title:** Chairman/CEO **Type of organization:** Manufacturing **Major product:** Machine tools **Area of distribution:** National and international **Expertise:** Management, decision maker **Affiliations:** S.A.E.; V.D.I.; A.S.M.E.; S.M.E. **Hob./spts.:** Boating, golf **SIC code:** 34 **Address:** Simmons Machine Tool Group, 1700 N. Broadway, Albany, NY 12204 **E-mail:** hnaumann@smtgroup.com **Web address:** www.smtgroup.com

NAZARIO-CANCEL, VICENTE
Industry: Security **Born:** June 24, 1953, Mayaguez, Puerto Rico **Univ./degree:** B.B.A., Accounting, Universidad InterAmericana, Puerto Rico, 1975 **Current organization:** Checkpoint Systems of Puerto Rico, Inc. **Title:** Vice President, Manufacturing, Caribbean Operations (Puerto Rico and Dominican Republic) **Type of organization:** Manufacturing **Major product:** Security/label; world leading provider of radio frequency (RF) based loss prevention systems to retail industry **Area of distribution:** International **Expertise:** International supply chain, manufacturing, marketing **Affiliations:** Board Member, Puerto Rico Purchasing & Logistics Council; A.P.I.C.S.; Manufacturing Association of Puerto Rico **Hob./spts.:** Fishing, cooking **SIC code:** 39 **Address:** Checkpoint Systems of Puerto Rico, Inc., Sabanetas Industrial Park, P.O. Box 7283, Ponce, PR 00732 **E-mail:** vnazario@checkpt.com **Web address:** www.checkpointsystems.com

NEAL, ROBERT M.
Industry: Chemicals/vitamins **Born:** Point Pleasant, West Virginia **Univ./degree:** Associates degree in welding Engineering **Current organization:** BASF Corp. **Title:** Project/Maintenance/EHS Coordinator **Type of organization:** Manufacturing/distributor **Major product:** Vitamin "C"/Vitamin "E" **Area of distribution:** International **Expertise:** Engineering/inspection/project management **Affiliations:** American Welding Society; American Petroleum Institute; North Carolina E.M.T.; VFW; A.F. & A.M. **Hob./spts.:** Scuba diving **SIC code:** 28 **Address:** BASF Corp., 101 Vitamin Dr., Wilmington, NC 28401

NEEDHAM, JONATHAN D.
Industry: Cosmetics **Born:** October 27, 1957, New Brunswick, New Jersey **Univ./degree:** B.S., Mechanical Engineering, Trenton State College **Current organization:** L'Oreal USA **Title:** Vice President of Manufacturing **Type of organization:** Cosmetics **Major product:** Hair products **Area of distribution:** International **Expertise:** Engineering **Affiliations:** Society of Packing Professionals **Hob./spts.:** Skiing, golf **SIC code:** 28 **Address:** L'Oreal USA, 222 L'Oreal Way, Clark, NJ 07066 **E-mail:** jneedham@us.loreal.com

NETHERTON, JOHN F.
Industry: Automotive **Born:** November 22, 1964, Medina, Idaho **Univ./degree:** B.S.M.E., Akron University, 1992 **Current organization:** Yusa Corp. **Title:** Process Engineer **Type of organization:** Manufacturing **Major product:** Engine mounts, hoses, frame bushings **Area of distribution:** International **Expertise:** Process improvements, mold design **Honors/awards:** 2 patents **Hob./spts.:** Family, cars, baseball, sports buff **SIC code:** 37 **Address:** Yusa Corp., 151 Jamison Rd. S.W., Washington Court House, OH 43160 **E-mail:** jnetherton@yusa-oh.com

NGUYEN, DAVID D.
Industry: Cryogenics **Born:** February 10, 1957, Vietnam **Current organization:** CVIP, Inc. **Title:** President/Owner **Type of organization:** Manufacturing **Major product:** Custom fabrication of modular skidded system and cryogenic equipment **Area of distribution:** International **Expertise:** Manufacturing engineering **Affiliations:** A.W.A.S.; A.S.M.E. **Hob./spts.:** Golf, tennis **SIC code:** 34 **Address:** CVIP, Inc., 801 Broad St., Emmaus, PA 18049 **E-mail:** daven@cvipinc.com **Web address:** www.cvipinc.com

NGUYEN, MAI V.
Industry: Oil and gas **Born:** October 20, 1969, Hue, Vietnam **Univ./degree:** B.S.M.E. with Honors, Polytechnic University, 1990; B.T.M.E., Algonquin College, 1994; M.B.A. Summa Cum Laude, Rushmore University, 2002; M.S.G.E. Summa Cum Laude, Kennedy Western University, 2004 **Current organization:** ATI/Firth Sterling Corp. **Title:** Design Engineer **Type of organization:** Design/manufacturing **Major product:** Carbide drill bits for oil and gas **Area of distribution:** International **Expertise:** Design engineering in computer numerical control machining, presentations and training; Registered Certified Engineer in technology (Canada) **Honors/awards:** Excellence Award for new solder compatibility and design, 2005 **Published works:** Articles and patents **Affiliations:** National Society for Professional Engineers **Hob./spts.:** Ice skating, roller blading, ice hockey, soccer, travel **SIC code:** 35 **Address:** ATI/Firth Sterling Corp., 4435 W. 12th St., Houston, TX 77055 **E-mail:** mnguyen@firthsterling.com **Web address:** www.firthmpd.com

NICHOLS, TAWANA M.
Industry: Consumer products **Born:** June 6, 1977, Richmond, Virginia **Univ./degree:** B.S., Accounting, Howard University, 1999 **Current organization:** The Clorox Co. **Title:** Financial Analyst **Type of organization:** Manufacturing **Major product:** Consumer products **Area of distribution:** International **Expertise:** Cost accounting **Affiliations:** American Institute of Certified Public Accountants; I.M.A. **Hob./spts.:** Travel, desktop publishing **SIC code:** 39 **Address:** The Clorox Co., 1221 Broadway, Oakland, CA 94612 **E-mail:** tawana.nichols@clorox.com

NIKOLAUS JR., FRANCIS J.
Industry: Food **Born:** June 16, 1947, Columbia, Pennsylvania **Current organization:** Y&S Candies, Inc. **Title:** Manager, Treatment Plant **Type of organization:** Manufacturing **Major product:** Candy **Area of distribution:** National **Expertise:** Management **Affiliations:** P.W.E.A. **Hob./spts.:** Fishing, hunting, his grandchildren **SIC code:** 20 **Address:** Y and S Candies, Inc., 400 Running Pump Rd., Lancaster, PA 17603-2269 **E-mail:** fnikolaus@hershey.com

NINKHAM, NOCK KHAMSAY
Industry: Automotive **Born:** March 1, 1969, Vang Vieng, Laos **Univ./degree:** B.S.M.E., University of Arkansas, 1995 **Current organization:** Superior Industries International, Inc. **Title:** Product Engineer **Type of organization:** Manufacturing **Major product:** OEM aluminum alloy road wheels **Area of distribution:** North America, Europe & Asia **Expertise:** Product engineering **Hob./spts.:** Fishing, basketball, hunting **SIC code:** 37 **Address:** Superior Industries International, Inc., 1901 Borick Dr., Fayetteville, AR 72701 **E-mail:** nninkham@hotmail.com/nninkham@supind.com **Web address:** www.supind.com

NISBET, JOHN JAMES
Industry: Healthcare products **Born:** November 23, 1952, Sarnia, Ontario, Canada **Univ./degree:** B. Com., With Honors, University of Guelph, 1976 **Current organization:** Healthpoint, Ltd. **Title:** Senior Director, International Business Development **Type of organization:** Manufacturing, marketing **Major product:** Pharmaceuticals, medical devices **Area of distribution:** International **Expertise:** International business development **Affiliations:** American Marketing Association; Canadian Healthcare Licensing Association; Licensing Executive Society **Hob./spts.:** Ice hockey, downhill skiing, waterspouts **SIC code:** 28 **Address:** Healthpoint, Ltd., 3909 Hulen St., Ft. Worth, TX 76107 **E-mail:** jay.nisbet@healthpoint.com **Web address:** www.healthpoint.com

NISBETT, EDWARD G.

Industry: Steel **Born:** February 24, 1929, Glasgow, Scotland **Spouse:** Barbara Nisbett **Married:** November 17, 1972 **Children:** Simon Nisbett, 39; Andrew Nisbett, 36 **Univ./degree:** B.Sc., Glasgow University, Scotland; ARTC, Royal Technical College, Glasgow **Current organization:** Edward G. Nisbett, Consulting Metallurgist **Title:** Consulting Metallurgist **Type of organization:** Consulting **Major product:** Metallurgical engineering **Area of distribution:** Worldwide **Expertise:** Failure analysis, (specialties crankshafts and pressure vessels), steel forgings, heat treatment, codes and standards **Published works:** Co-editor of Steel Forgings Symposium, ASTM STP903, 1984, Residual Elements in Steel, ASTM STP1042, 1987 and Second Symposium on Steel Forgings, STP1259, 1996; "Design, Manufacture and Safety Aspects of Forged Vessels for High Pressure Services," ASME Pressure Vessel & Piping Conference, 1979; "Metallographic Control of Heat Treatment," Metallography as a Quality control Tool Symposium, July , 1979; "Some Materials used for Construction of Forged Vessels for High Pressures in the U.S.A.," Proceedings of the VIIth International AIRAPT Conference, 1979; "The Role of Metallography in a Boiler Explosion," Proceedings of the 13th Annual Technical Meeting of the Metallographic Society, 1980; "Production and Properties of Heavy Walled Forged Vessel Shells in 9%Cr-1%Mo Alloy Steel," ASM "Ferritic Steels for High Temperature Applications," October, 1981; "The Effect of Residual Elements on the Tensile Strength of Heavy Carbon Steel Forgings, Heat Treated for Optimum Notch Toughness," ASTM STP 1042, 1987; "Improving the Notch Toughness of Nuclear Forgings in Carbon and Alloy Steels by Intercritical Heat Treatment," 8th International Forgemasters Meeting, October, 1997; Guest speaker **Affiliations:** Professional Engineer; Chartered Engineer; Fellow Institution of Materials; Fellow ASTM; Member ASME; Chairman ASTM Subcommittee on Steel Forgings and Billets; Chairman Subgroup on Ferrous Specifications on Section II of the ASME Boiler and Pressure Vessel Code **Career accomplishments:** Development of an iron powder metallic arc welding electrode manufactured in the UK, Primary materials and processing responsibility for high strength penetrator warheads for the U.S. Air Force, Forgings for offshore tension leg oil platforms, Investigation of boiler explosions, crankshaft failures and pressure vessel failures; Primary author of ASTM specifications for closed die crankshafts and high strength pressure vessels, Expert witness **Hob./spts.:** Camping, outdoor activities and bowling **SIC code:** 34 **Address:** Edward G. Nisbett, Consultant, 7052 Gandy Dr., Navarre, FL 32566-8716 **E-mail:** enisbett@bellsouth.net **Web address:** www.forgingexpert.com

NOTO, JAMIE T.

Industry: Pharmaceuticals **Born:** August 15, 1975, Brooklyn, New York **Univ./degree:** B.S., Microbiology, Hofstra University **Current organization:** Hoffman LaRoche **Title:** Scientist **Type of organization:** Manufacturing **Major product:** Pharmaceuticals **Area of distribution:** International **Expertise:** Microbiology **Published works:** Articles **Hob./spts.:** Mountain biking **SIC code:** 28 **Address:** Hoffman LaRoche, 2435 E. 28th St., Brooklyn, NY 11235 **E-mail:** jamie_noto@yahoo.com

OAKES, FRANK R.

Industry: Biomedical **Born:** October 21, 1950, Escondido, California **Univ./degree:** B.S., Marine Science, California Polytech, 1973 **Current organization:** Stellar Biotechnologies, Inc. **Title:** CFO/Research Director **Type of organization:** Manufacturer **Major product:** Marine products for the pharmaceutical industry **Area of distribution:** International **Expertise:** Business development/research **Hob./spts.:** Scuba diving **SIC code:** 28 **Address:** Stellar Biotechnologies, Inc., 417 E. Hueneme Rd., PMB #170, Port Hueneme, CA 93041 **E-mail:** liveoaks@aol.com

OAKS, CHARLES W.

Industry: Chemicals **Born:** November 14, 1952, Evanston, Wyoming **Univ./degree:** M.S., Human Resources, University of Utah, 1980 **Current organization:** Huntsman Corp. **Title:** Manager of Organizational Development **Type of organization:** Manufacturing **Major product:** Petrochemicals, polymers **Area of distribution:** International **Expertise:** Human resources **Affiliations:** Tri Chair, Chamber of Commerce **Hob./spts.:** Motorcycling **SIC code:** 28 **Address:** Huntsman Corp., 3040 Post Oak Blvd., Houston, TX 77056 **E-mail:** chuck_oaks@huntsman.com

OBERMAN, LAURENCE A.

Industry: IT **Born:** April 18, 1962, Johannesburg, South Africa **Univ./degree:** M.S.E.E., University of Witwatersrand, South Africa, 1995 **Current organization:** Hewlett Packard **Title:** Principal Software Engineer **Type of organization:** Manufacturing **Major product:** HPUX, Solaris, Tru64 Unix and Linux **Area of distribution:** International **Expertise:** UNIX and storage performance **Affiliations:** I.E.E.E.; Association for Computing Machinery **Hob./spts.:** Amateur ham radio operator, model railroads **SIC code:** 36 **Address:** Hewlett Packard, 74 Bjorklund Ave., Worcester, MA 01605 **E-mail:** online@photonlinux.com

O'BRIEN, SHAHLA M.

Industry: Pharmaceuticals **Born:** December 15, 1952, Tehran, Iran **Univ./degree:** M.S., Organic Synthetic Chemistry, SUNY Buffalo, 1985 **Current organization:** Boehringer-Ingelheim Pharmaceuticals, Inc. **Title:** Director **Type of organization:** Manufacturing **Major product:** Pharmaceuticals **Area of distribution:** International **Expertise:** Information technology **Affiliations:** A.C.S.; Q.A.I. **Hob./spts.:** Reading, photography, painting **SIC code:** 28 **Address:** Boehringer-Ingelheim Pharmaceuticals, Inc., 900 Ridgebury Rd., Ridgefield, CT 06877 **E-mail:** sobrien@rdg.boehringer-ingelheim.com

OBROCEA, MIHAIL

Industry: Pharmaceutical **Born:** February 16, 1959, Romania **Univ./degree:** M.D., Bucharest University, Romania, 1985 **Current organization:** Pfizer, Inc. **Title:** M.D., Associate Director **Type of organization:** Manufacturing **Major product:** Pharmaceuticals, oncology medications **Area of distribution:** International **Expertise:** Clinical development **Affiliations:** A.S.C.O.; A.A.C.R.; A.S.H.; A.C.P.; A.M.A. **Hob./spts.:** Soccer, tennis **SIC code:** 28 **Address:** Pfizer, Inc., 50 Pequot St., MS-6025-A3119, New London, CT 06320 **E-mail:** mihail_obracea@groton.pfizer.com

OCHOA, GILBERT A.

Industry: Silk-screening **Born:** November 1, 1956, El Paso, Texas **Current organization:** Orange County Nameplate Co., Inc. **Title:** Quality Assurance Manager **Type of organization:** Manufacturing **Major product:** Name plates, Scotchcals **Area of distribution:** National **Expertise:** Quality **Affiliations:** A.S.Q.; A.S.M. **Hob./spts.:** Basketball **SIC code:** 39 **Address:** 14210 Gandesa Rd., La Mirada, CA 90638 **E-mail:** gochoa@nameplates-ocn.com

OGREN, HERMAN A.

Industry: Aerospace **Born:** March 31, 1925, Kenosha, Wisconsin **Univ./degree:** Ph.D., University of Southern California, 1961 **Current organization:** Ogren Avionics **Title:** Professor of Biology (Retired) **Type of organization:** Manufacturing **Major product:** Home built airplanes **Area of distribution:** International **Expertise:** Airplane construction **Affiliations:** American Society of Mammalogists; Fish and Wildlife Research Institute **Hob./spts.:** Airplanes, wild animals, travel **SIC code:** 37 **Address:** Ogren Avionics, 1900 16TH Place, Kenosha, WI 53140

OHLY, EUGENE

Industry: Engineering **Current organization:** Evans Speed Equipment **Title:** Owner **Type of organization:** Machining **Major product:** High performance machine work **Area of distribution:** National **Expertise:** Engineering; high performance vehicles, race cars, airplanes, boats, antique cars **Published works:** Published in "Hot Rod Magazine" **SIC code:** 35 **Address:** Evans Speed Equipment, 2550 Seaman Ave., South El Monte, CA 91733

OJAKAAR, LEO

Industry: Elastomers research and technology **Born:** April 26, 1926 **Univ./degree:** Ph.D., Chemistry, Virginia Polytechnic Institute, 1974 **Title:** Ph.D., E.I. DuPont DeNemours & Co. (Retired) **Type of organization:** Manufacturing, research and technology **Major product:** Kalrex, viton, polymers research and technology **Area of distribution:** International **Expertise:** Research Chemist **Affiliations:** A.C.S.; Sigma Xi **Hob./spts.:** Music **SIC code:** 28 **Address:** 8 Jacqueline Dr., Hockessin, DE 19707

OLMSTEAD, KAY K.

Industry: Specialty pharmaceuticals **Born:** September 10, 1960, Seoul, South Korea **Univ./degree:** B.S., Chemistry, Yonsei University, Seoul, South Korea, 1981; Ph.D., Organic Chemistry, Johns Hopkins University, 1986; M.B.A., San Diego State University, 2000; 2 years, Post Doctorate, Stanford University **Current organization:** Santarus, Inc. **Title:** Director of Product Development **Type of organization:** Pharmaceutical development **Major product:** Products for the prevention and treatment of gastrointestinal diseases and disorders **Area of distribution:** National **Expertise:** Product development & management **Published works:** 20+ articles, 3 patents **Affiliations:** A.A.P.S.; American Chemical Society **SIC code:** 28 **Address:** Santarus, Inc., 10590 W. Ocean Air Dr., Suite 200, San Diego, CA 92130 **E-mail:** kolmstead@santarus.com **Web address:** www.santarus.com

OLSON, LANCE C.

Industry: Machinery **Born:** September 27, 1971, Menomonie, Illinois **Univ./degree:** B.S., Cum Laude, Manufacturing Engineering, University of Wisconsin, 1995 **Current organization:** John Deere Harvester Works **Title:** Manufacturing Engineer **Type of organization:** Manufacturing **Major product:** Combines, agricultural machinery **Area of distribution:** International **Expertise:** Process engineering, laser cutting sheet metal **Published works:** Company newsletter articles on laser technology **Affiliations:** Society of Manufacturing Engineers **Hob./spts.:** ATV's, snowmobiling, camping, hiking **SIC code:** 35 **Address:** John Deere Harvester Works, 1100 13th Ave., East Moline, IL 61244 **E-mail:** olsonlancec@johndeere.com **Web address:** www.johndeere.com

OLVIDO, GLORIA M.
Industry: Advertising/direct mail publication **Born:** Philadelphia, Pennsylvania **Univ./degree:** B.A., Communications, University of South Florida, 1997 **Current organization:** Pittsburgh Pennysaver **Title:** Major Accounts Manager **Type of organization:** Direct mail publication **Major product:** Pennysaver **Area of distribution:** Pittsburgh, Pennsylvania **Expertise:** Selling advertising to regional and national accounts **Hob./spts.:** Golf, reading, tennis **SIC code:** 27 **Address:** Pittsburgh Pennysaver, 460 Rodi Rd., Pittsburgh, PA 15235 **E-mail:** g.olvido@pittsburghpennysaver.com

OMILIAN, ROBERT A.
Industry: Automotive **Born:** August 30, 1958, Detroit, Michigan **Univ./degree:** M.B.A., University of Michigan, 1986 **Current organization:** Visteon Corporation **Title:** Director, Operations - Tax **Type of organization:** Manufacturing **Major product:** Electronics, climate control **Area of distribution:** International **Expertise:** Finance **Published works:** 3 articles **Hob./spts.:** Drawing portraits, photography, baseball **SIC code:** 37 **Address:** 10280 Fellows Hill Dr., Plymouth, MI 48170 **E-mail:** romilian@comcast.net

ORNELAS, EDWIN D.
Industry: Semiconductors **Born:** June 13, 1964, Albuquerque, New Mexico **Univ./degree:** B.A., Business, University of Phoenix, 2001 **Current organization:** Rodel, Inc. **Title:** Global CMP Technical Service Manager **Type of organization:** Materials and engineering supplier **Major product:** Semiconductor manufacturer/consumables supplier **Area of distribution:** International **Expertise:** Applications engineering **Published works:** Multiple technical publications **Hob./spts.:** Golf, coaching soccer and football, fishing **SIC code:** 36 **Address:** Rodel, Inc., 3804 E. Watkins St., Phoenix, AZ 85034 **E-mail:** eornelas@rodel.com

ORTIZ, LOIDA A.
Industry: Publishing **Born:** November 11, 1960 **Univ./degree:** M.S., Mass Communication, Florida State University **Current organization:** United Bible Societies **Title:** Publishing Director **Type of organization:** Religious publishing **Major product:** Translate, produce, print and distribute the Bible and other materials in different languages and format **Area of distribution:** International **Expertise:** Publishing **Affiliations:** E.C.P.A.; N.R.B. **Hob./spts.:** Reading **SIC code:** 27 **Address:** United Bible Societies, 1989 N.W. 88 Ct., Miami, FL 33172 **E-mail:** lortiz@sbu.org **Web address:** www.labibliaeb.com

ORTIZ LOPEZ, WILFREDO
Industry: Pharmaceuticals **Born:** June 18, 1971, Mayaguez, Puerto Rico **Univ./degree:** B.S., Mechanical Engineering, University of Puerto Rico, 1997 **Current organization:** Allergan Pharmaceuticals **Title:** Production Engineering Supervisor **Type of organization:** Manufacturing **Major product:** Pharmaceuticals, Botox, Alphagan (eyecare prescriptions) **Area of distribution:** International **Expertise:** Engineering, design **Hob./spts.:** Scuba diving, basketball **SIC code:** 28 **Address:** Allergan Pharmaceuticals, 8301 Mars Dr., P.O. Box 2675, Waco, TX 76702-2675 **E-mail:** wortiz1@hot.rr.com

OSBORNE, TIMOTHY M.
Industry: Chemicals **Born:** July 24, 1965, Marion, Virginia **Univ./degree:** M.S., Industrial Engineering, Columbia State University **Current organization:** Rhodia, Inc. **Title:** Maintenance Planner **Type of organization:** Manufacturing **Major product:** Specialty chemicals **Area of distribution:** International **Expertise:** Facilities and equipment engineering, efficiency, productivity, WCM **Honors/awards:** Albright & Wilson Americas, Outstanding Contributor to Production, 1996, Charleston, SC **Affiliations:** American Society of Non-Destructive Test Engineers (ANST); American Legion **Hob./spts.:** Home improvement, woodworking **SIC code:** 28 **Address:** Rhodia, Inc., 2151 King St. Ext., Charleston, SC 29405 **E-mail:** tim.osborne@us.rhodia.com **Web address:** www.rhodia.com

OSUALLA, NATHAN O.
Industry: Accounting/finance **Born:** November 12, 1955, Bendels Asaba, Nigeria **Univ./degree:** B.S., Accounting, John Brown University, 1996; M.B.A., Accounting, Alabama A&M University, 2001 **Current organization:** Sanmina-SCI Corp. **Title:** Operator **Type of organization:** Manufacturing **Major product:** Satellite TV circuit boards/service **Area of distribution:** Huntsville, Alabama **Expertise:** Accounting **Honors/awards:** Alpha Kappa Apha; Delta Sigma Theta **Affiliations:** Society of A.I.C.P.A. **Hob./spts.:** Reading, soccer, football, travel **SIC code:** 36 **Address:** 3617 Chasewood Dr., Apt. 11, Huntsville, AL 35805 **E-mail:** nosualla@msn.com

O'TOOLE JR., RAYMOND D.
Industry: Government **Born:** August 19, 1960, New York, New York **Univ./degree:** M.S., Systems Engineering, Virginia Polytechnic Institute, 1989 **Current organization:** U.S. Navy **Title:** Ship Design Manager **Type of organization:** Manufacturing **Major product:** Submarines, ships **Area of distribution:** National **Expertise:** Engineering **Affiliations:** A.S.M.E.; A.S.N.E.; S.N.A.M.E. **Hob./spts.:** Running **SIC code:** 37 **Address:** U.S. Navy, 4180 Fox Den Lane, Huntingtown, MD 20639 **E-mail:** otoolejrrd@navsea.navy.mil

OUDODOVA, ANNA
Industry: Injection molding **Born:** December 2, 1971, Kiev, Ukraine **Univ./degree:** B.A., Psychology, North Park University, 1997 **Current organization:** NYPRO Chicago **Title:** Human Resources Manager, Senior Staff Member **Type of organization:** Manufacturing **Major product:** Precision plastics for healthcare and industrial consumer industries **Area of distribution:** International **Expertise:** Recruitment and retention, training, organizational development, strategic planning, compliance, program development, coaching and lecturing **Affiliations:** Society for Human Resource Management **Hob./spts.:** Reading, dance, travel **SIC code:** 30 **Address:** NYPRO Chicago, 955 Tri-State Pkwy., Gurnee, IL 60031 **E-mail:** aoudodova2@yahoo.com **Web address:** www.nypro.com

PAGEL, BRUCE J.
Industry: Flexographic printing **Born:** Kokomo, Indiana **Univ./degree:** A.A., Flexographic Printing, Fox Valley Technical **Current organization:** Tufco Technologies, Inc. **Title:** Sales Manager **Type of organization:** Manufacturing **Major product:** Packaging, printing **Area of distribution:** International **Expertise:** Flexographic printing **Affiliations:** National Flexographic Association **Hob./spts.:** Camping, fishing, hunting **SIC code:** 27 **Address:** Tufco Technologies, Inc., 3161 S. Ridge Rd., Green Bay, WI 54304-3500 **E-mail:** brucepagel@sbcglobal.net

PALIHAKKARA, NIMAL N.
Industry: Medical instruments **Born:** April 26, 1948 **Univ./degree:** A.A., Westchester Community College **Current organization:** Harrick Scientific Corp. **Title:** R & D Technician **Type of organization:** Manufacturing **Major product:** Spectroscopy instruments and plasma cleaners **Area of distribution:** International **Expertise:** R&D in electronic, electrical and mechanical **Hob./spts.:** Photography, jogging, cricket **SIC code:** 38 **Address:** 81 King Dr., Poughkeepsie, NY 12603 **E-mail:** palihakkara@aol.com

PANAGIOTOU, THOMAI "MIMI"
Industry: Capital equipment **Born:** February 12, 1964, Thessaloniki, Greece **Univ./degree:** Ph.D., Mechanical Engineering, Northeastern University, 1995 **Current organization:** Microfluidics **Title:** Vice President, R&D **Type of organization:** Manufacturing **Major product:** Capital equipment for the chemical and pharmaceutical industries **Area of distribution:** International **Expertise:** R&D/engineering/customer liaison **Affiliations:** A.C.S.; S.A.E. **Hob./spts.:** Photography, hiking, travel **SIC code:** 35 **Address:** Microfluidics, 30 Ossipee Rd., Newton, MA 02464 **E-mail:** mimip@mfics.com

PAPAZOGLOU, ELISABETH S.
Industry: Chemicals **Born:** December 11, 1959, Kavala, Greece **Univ./degree:** Ph.D., Case Western Reserve University, Cleveland, Ohio, 1988 **Current organization:** Great Lakes Chemical **Title:** Technical Service Manager **Type of organization:** Technology **Major product:** Specialty additives/chemicals **Area of distribution:** International **Expertise:** Technology and marketing **Published works:** 40 Publications in the field of polymer specialty additives **Affiliations:** A.C.S.; S.P.E.; A.I.C.H.E. **Hob./spts.:** Swimming, tennis, dancing **SIC code:** 28 **Address:** Great Lakes Chemical, 1801 U.S. Hwy. 52, West Lafayette, IN 47906 **E-mail:** epapazog@glcc.com

PARAMADILOK, PRACHA
Industry: Food **Born:** December 7, 1948, Nakhon Si Thammarat, Thailand **Univ./degree:** B. Sc., Food Science and Technology, Kasetsart University, Bangkok, Thailand, 1971; M.Sc., Food Technology, New South Wales University, Sydney, Australia, 1978 **Current organization:** Schulze & Burch Biscuit Co. **Title:** Senior Line Coordinator **Type of organization:** Manufacturing **Major product:** Baked goods **Area of distribution:** Chicago, Illinois **Expertise:** Quality assurance **Affiliations:** American Association of Cereal Chemists; Institute of Food Technologists; Association of Official Analytical Chemists; Philadelphia Church **Hob./spts.:** Physical fitness, reading **SIC code:** 20 **Address:** Schulze & Burch Biscuit Co., 1133 W. 35th St., Chicago, IL 60609 **E-mail:** pracha.paramadilok@schulzeburch.com

PARANJPE, AJIT P.
Industry: Semiconductors/electrical equipment **Born:** September 22, 1962, Zurich, Switzerland **Univ./degree:** Ph.D., Mechanical/Electrical Engineering, Stanford University, 1989 **Current organization:** Torrex **Title:** Ph.D./V.P. of Technology **Type of organization:** Manufacturing **Major product:** Semiconductors **Area of distribution:** International **Expertise:** Technology development **Honors/awards:** 28 patents **Published works:** 30 peer-reviewed articles **Affiliations:** I.E.E.E.; A.V.S.; G.C.S. **Hob./spts.:** Swimming, travel, electronics **SIC code:** 36 **Address:** Torrex, 4777 Bennett Dr.,

Bldg. E, Livermore, CA 94550 **E-mail:** aparanjpe.torrex.com **Web address:** www.torrex.com

PARDO, PJ
Born: October 31, 1956, Havana, Cuba **Univ./degree:** M.S., Mercer College, 1993 **Current organization:** Global Project Solutions **Area of distribution:** International **Affiliations:** A.S.Q.; American Association of Tissue Banks; American Association of Blood Banks **Hob./spts.:** Scuba diving, reading, travel **SIC code:** 38 **Address:** 2446 N.W. 14th Place, Gainesville, FL 32605 **E-mail:** pjpardo@cox.net

PARIKH, DILIP J.
Industry: Printing **Born:** Bombay, India **Univ./degree:** M.S., Chemical Engineering, University of Massachusetts **Current organization:** Fort Dearborn Co. **Title:** Senior Director of Manufacturing Services **Type of organization:** Manufacturing **Major product:** Labels and packaging **Area of distribution:** International **Expertise:** Management, services **Published works:** 6 papers **Affiliations:** T.A.P.P.I.; A.F.T.M.; I.O.P.P. **Hob./spts.:** Reading, photography, travel **SIC code:** 27 **Address:** Fort Dearborn Co., 6035 Gross Point Rd., Niles, IL 60714 **E-mail:** dparikh@fortdearborn.com

PARSONS, DICK E.
Industry: Paper **Born:** April 27, 1949, Waterville, Maine **Univ./degree:** B.S.M.E., Maine Maritime Academy, 1971 **Current organization:** International Paper **Title:** Divisional Maintenance Manager **Type of organization:** Manufacturing **Major product:** Paper and corrugated boxes **Area of distribution:** International **Expertise:** Engineering; State of Maine Boiler License **Published works:** Internal publications **Affiliations:** T.A.P.P.I.; A.F.E. **Hob./spts.:** Painting, writing **SIC code:** 26 **Address:** International Paper, 6420 Poplar Ave., Tower 111, 9th floor, Memphis, TN 38197 **E-mail:** dick.parsons@ipaper.com

PARTHASARATHY, VINOD
Industry: Automotive **Born:** August 17, 1979, Bombay, India **Univ./degree:** B.E., Mechanical Engineering, University of East London **Current organization:** Freudenberg-Nok **Title:** Lean Systems Manager **Type of organization:** Manufacturing **Major product:** Seals for shock absorbers, steering and bearings **Area of distribution:** International **Expertise:** Engineering, lean systems; Six Sigma Black Belt **Honors/awards:** Winner of Outstanding Student Award at University of East London; Winner of Best Industrial Project Award at University of East London **Published works:** 4 patents pending **Affiliations:** I.E.E.E. **Hob./spts.:** Skydiving, volunteer work for the Republican party, writing **SIC code:** 37 **Address:** Freudenberg-Nok, 51 Growth Rd., Laconia, NH 03246 **E-mail:** vop@fngp.com **Web address:** www.vinnyswildworld.com

PARTRIDGE III, CLARENCE V.
Industry: Ship building and repair **Born:** April 7, 1980, Mobile, Alabama **Univ./degree:** B.S., Political Science, University of Montevallo, Alabama **Current organization:** Bender Shipbuilding & Repair Co., Inc. **Title:** Manufacturing Manager **Type of organization:** Manufacturing **Major product:** Ships **Expertise:** Management **Hob./spts.:** Physical fitness, golf, hunting, the beach **SIC code:** 37 **Address:** Bender Shipbuilding & Repair Co., Inc., 265 S. Water St., Mobile, AL 36601 **E-mail:** part@bendership.com **Web address:** www.bendership.com

PASCAVIS, KIMBERLEY JILL
Industry: Robotics **Born:** December 5, 1972, Oakland, California **Univ./degree:** B.S.M.E., Colorado State University, 2000 **Current organization:** CBW Automation **Title:** Mechanical Engineer **Type of organization:** Manufacturing **Major product:** Automation and robotics for plastics industry **Area of distribution:** International **Expertise:** Engineering **Affiliations:** A.S.M.E.; S.M.E. **Hob./spts.:** Skiing **SIC code:** 36 **Address:** CBW Automation, 3939 Automation Way, Ft. Collins, CO 80525 **E-mail:** kpascavis@cbwautomation.com **Web address:** www.cbwautomation.com

PATEL, ARVIND B.
Industry: Automotive **Univ./degree:** B.S., Electrical Engineering, India, 1972 **Current organization:** Q3 Stamped Metal Inc. **Title:** Plant Engineer and Safety Coordinator **Type of organization:** Manufacturing **Major product:** Automotive parts **Area of distribution:** National **Expertise:** Plant engineering and safety **Hob./spts.:** Swimming, walking **SIC code:** 37 **Address:** 1014 Snohomish Ave., Worthington, OH 43085 **E-mail:** apatel@q3inds.com

PATEL, LOKANATH
Industry: Construction and forestry **Born:** June 1, 1943, Sambalpur, Orissa, India **Univ./degree:** M.S., Ceramic Engineering, Virginia Polytechnic Institute, 1974; M.S., Metallurgical Engineering, University of Tennessee, 1977 **Current organization:** John Deere Dubuque Works **Title:** Metallurgical Engineer **Type of organization:** Manufacturing **Major product:** Farm equipment, tractors **Area of distribution:** International **Expertise:** Metallurgy, electron microscopy testing **Honors/awards:** Work Simplification Award, John Deere Dubuque Works, 1988 **Published works:** 2 thesis (on ceramics and stainless steel) **Affiliations:** Past Chair, Dubuque Chapter, American Society for Metals; President, Friends of India Association; Teaches Physics at Northeast Iowa Community College **Hob./spts.:** Investments, photography, philosophy, cooking **SIC code:** 35 **Address:** John Deere Dubuque Works, 18600 S. John Deere Rd., P.O. Box 538, Dubuque, IA 52004-0538 **E-mail:** patellokanath@johndeere.com

PATHOOMVANH, HEATHER J.
Industry: Electronics **Born:** February 14, 1969, Hartford, Connecticut **Univ./degree:** B.A., Accounting, San Diego, 1990 **Current organization:** Jem Electronics, Inc. **Title:** Quality Manager **Type of organization:** Manufacturing **Major product:** Electronics, cables, harnesses **Area of distribution:** International **Expertise:** Quality and production management **Affiliations:** A.S.Q.; Q.S.G.N.E. **Hob./spts.:** Sports, children **SIC code:** 36 **Address:** Jem Electronics, Inc., 23 National Dr., Franklin, MA 02038 **E-mail:** hpathoomvanh@jemelectronics.com

PAYNE, ARLIE JEAN
Industry: Publishing **Born:** October 9, 1920, Priest River, Idaho **Univ./degree:** M.A., University of Washington, 1967 **Current organization:** Family First Inc. **Title:** Editor/Publisher **Type of organization:** Publishing facility **Major product:** Newspaper **Area of distribution:** Nine Mile Falls, Tum Tum, Washington **Expertise:** Parent education/concern for education improvement **Honors/awards:** Washington State Crystal Apple for Support for Education **Published works:** "Climate for Learning", "We're Driving Our Kids Crazy" **Hob./spts.:** Spending time with her grandchildren, reading periodicals, health and nutrition **SIC code:** 27 **Address:** Family First Inc., 5978 Hwy. 291 #3, Nine Mile Falls, WA 99026 **E-mail:** lakespokanenewsforum@comcast.net **Web address:** www.whimsicaljeans@comcast.net

PEARSON, THOMAS F.
Industry: Food **Univ./degree:** B.S., Safety and Health Engineering, Columbia Southern University **Current organization:** DCUSL Danisco USA Inc. **Title:** Manager/Environmental, Health and Safety Engineer **Type of organization:** Manufacturing **Major product:** Flavorings **Area of distribution:** International **Expertise:** Safety **Affiliations:** American Society of Safety Engineers; World Safety Organization; Certified Instructor, American Red Cross **SIC code:** 20 **Address:** DCUSL Danisco USA Inc., 411 East Gano, St. Louis, MO 63147 **E-mail:** tom.pearson@danisco.com **Web address:** www.danisco.com

PELLETT, AL
Industry: Coatings **Title:** General Manager **Type of organization:** Manufacturing **Major product:** Inorganic protective coatings **Expertise:** Development and research for new products **SIC code:** 34 **Address:** Earthtech Inc., 121 E. Florida Ave., Appleton, WI 54911-1321 **E-mail:** awpellett@sbcglobal.net

PEPER, ALEX CHRISTIAN
Industry: Automotive **Born:** July 4, 1956, St. Louis, Missouri **Univ./degree:** B.S., Physics, University of Massachusetts at Lowell, 1992 **Current organization:** Car Code **Title:** President **Type of organization:** Manufacturing **Major product:** Diagnostic Equipment **Area of distribution:** International **Expertise:** Development **Affiliations:** S.A.E.; S.E.M.A. **Hob./spts.:** Biking **SIC code:** 37 **Address:** Car Code, 931 Summer Leaf Dr., St. Peters, MO 63376 **E-mail:** sales@obd-2.com **Web address:** www.obd-2.com

PERKINS, ROGER L.
Industry: Electronics **Born:** March 25, 1966, Cleveland, Ohio **Univ./degree:** B.S., Mechanical Engineering, University of Delaware, 1985 **Current organization:** Keystone Electronics, Inc. **Title:** Engineering Manager **Type of organization:** Manufacturing **Major product:** Electronics **Area of distribution:** International **Expertise:** Engineering, management **Affiliations:** S.M.E. **Hob./spts.:** Little League, real estate **SIC code:** 36 **Address:** 1735 Clover Lane, York, PA 17403-4013 **E-mail:** roger@keyelectro.com

PERLES, MARYANN
Industry: Food **Born:** September 24, 1969, Sunbury, Pennsylvania **Univ./degree:** B.S., 1996 **Current organization:** Bernardi Italian Foods **Title:** Micro Lab Technician **Type of organization:** Manufacturing **Major product:** Frozen Italian pasta **Area of distribution:** Pennsylvania **Expertise:** Biology/microbiology **SIC code:** 20 **Address:** Bernardi Italian Foods, 595 W. 11th St., Bloomsburg, PA 17815 **E-mail:** mperles@windsorfoods.com

PERRONNE, MICHAEL R.
Industry: Small gas engines **Born:** August 11, 1952, Plymouth, Wisconsin **Univ./degree:** B.A., Music, Lakeland College, Sheboygan, Wisconsin, 1974; B.S., Manufacturing Engineering, Milwaukee School of Engineering, 2001 **Current organization:** Tecumseh Products Co. **Title:** Senior Computer Numerical Control (CNC) Programmer/Engineer, Milwaukee, Wisconsin **Type of organization:** Manufacturing **Major product:** Small gas engines **Area of distribution:** International **Expertise:** CNC programming/manufacturing engineering **Affiliations:** Society of Manufacturing Engineers **Hob./spts.:** Woodworking, golf **SIC code:** 37 **Address:** Tecumseh Products Co.,

1604 Michigan Ave., New Holstein, WI 53061 **E-mail:** mperronne@tecumsehpower.com

PERRY, DONALD S.
Industry: Pharmaceuticals **Born:** November 18, 1953, Philadelphia, Pennsylvania **Univ./degree:** B.S., Electronic Engineering Technology, Temple University, 1978 **Current organization:** Glaxo Smith Kline Corp. **Title:** Metrology Supervisor **Type of organization:** Manufacturing **Major product:** Antibiotic medicines **Area of distribution:** National **Expertise:** Electronic instrumentation systems **Affiliations:** I.E.E.E.; I.S.A.; N.H.S. **Hob./spts.:** Coaching basketball **SIC code:** 28 **Address:** Glaxo Smith Kline Corp., 801 River Rd., Bldg. 16 AI-1696, Conshohocken, PA 19428 **E-mail:** donald.s.perry@gsk.com

PERRY, JOSEPH J.
Industry: Food **Born:** May 26, 1924, Dallas, Pennsylvania **Univ./degree:** B.S., Chemical Engineering, Pennsylvania State University; M.S., Chemical Engineering, Louisiana Sate University **Current organization:** Perry Apiaries **Title:** Owner **Type of organization:** Manufacturing **Major product:** Honey, beeswax, pollination **Area of distribution:** National **Expertise:** Honey production **Affiliations:** American Beekeepers Federation **SIC code:** 20 **Address:** Perry Apiaries, 4417 Somerset Rd., Lake Charles, LA 70605

PERSICO, DANIEL FRANCIS
Industry: Electronics **Born:** September 9, 1955, Boston, Massachusetts **Univ./degree:** Ph.D., Chemistry, University of Texas at Austin, 1984 **Current organization:** Kemet Electronics Corp. **Title:** V.P., Business Development **Type of organization:** Manufacturing, marketing **Major product:** Passive components, capacitors **Area of distribution:** International **Expertise:** Technology, international business **Affiliations:** American Chemical Society **Hob./spts.:** Golf, wine, cooking, travel, rugby **SIC code:** 36 **Address:** 11 Coach Lane, Simpsonville, SC 29681 **E-mail:** danpersico@charter.net

PERTLE, DAVID D.
Industry: Machine tools **Born:** August 18, 1944, Wichita, Kansas **Current organization:** Extrude Hone Corp. **Title:** Controls Designer **Type of organization:** Manufacturing **Major product:** Machine tools manufacturing and service **Area of distribution:** International **Expertise:** Controls design and service **Hob./spts.:** Racquetball **SIC code:** 34 **Address:** Extrude Hone Corp., P.O. Box 1000, Irwin, PA 15642 **E-mail:** davep@extrudehone.com **Web address:** www.extrudehone.com

PETIT, BRUNO JACQUES
Industry: Automotive **Born:** December 25, 1954, Montargis, France **Current organization:** Hutchinson **Title:** Vice President **Type of organization:** Manufacturing, business unit **Major product:** Rubber and plastic components **Area of distribution:** International **Expertise:** Management **Affiliations:** RMA **Hob./spts.:** Golf, painting, travel, hiking **SIC code:** 37 **Address:** Hutchinson, 1225 Livingston Hwy., Byrdstown, TN 38549 **E-mail:** bruno.petit@hutchinsonfts.com

PETRUSKA, GARY
Industry: Plastics **Born:** November 5, 1950, Youngstown, Ohio **Univ./degree:** A.S., Electrical Engineering, Youngstown State University, 1989 **Current organization:** Mar-Bal, Inc. **Title:** Corporate Plant Engineer **Type of organization:** Manufacturing **Major product:** Thermosetting materials **Area of distribution:** International **Expertise:** Engineering **Affiliations:** S.P.E. **Hob./spts.:** Motorcycling, boating **SIC code:** 30 **Address:** Mar-Bal, Inc., 16930 Munn Rd., Chagrin Falls, OH 44023 **E-mail:** garyp@mar-bal.com

PFEIFER, MAGGIE M.
Industry: Machinery **Current organization:** FMB Machinery USA **Title:** General Manager **Type of organization:** Manufacturing **Major product:** Heavy equipment machinery, bar feeders/sales and service **Area of distribution:** International **Expertise:** Machinery **Affiliations:** A.M.T.D.A. **SIC code:** 35 **Address:** FMB Machinery USA, 190 Fairfield Ave., West Caldwell, NJ 07006 **E-mail:** fmbmach@aol.com **Web address:** www.fmb-machinery.com

PHAM, DUC NGUYEN
Industry: Wireless communications **Born:** November 17, 1970, Vietnam **Univ./degree:** M.S., Electrical Engineering, San Jose State University; Dr.Eng., Santa Clara University **Current organization:** Micro Lambda Wireless Inc. **Title:** Product Manager **Type of organization:** Manufacturing and design **Major product:** RF and microwave components **Area of distribution:** International **Expertise:** Engineering **Affiliations:** New York Academy of Sciences; Sigma Xi: The Scientific Research Society **Hob./spts.:** Golf, tennis, football **SIC code:** 36 **Address:** Micro Lambda Wireless Inc., 1620 Karl St., San Jose, CA 95122 **E-mail:** dpham@microlambdawireless.com

PHAM, STEVEN
Industry: Food **Univ./degree:** A.S., Computer Technology **Current organization:** Sara Lee Food Service **Title:** Operation Manager **Type of organization:** Manufacturing **Major product:** Food **Area of distribution:** International **Expertise:** Packaging, troubleshooting, employee training **SIC code:** 20 **Address:** Sara Lee Food Service, 1201 Edwards Ave., Harahan, LA 70123 **E-mail:** spham@saraleecoffee.com

PHANEUF, PAUL-ERIC
Industry: Textiles **Born:** August 25, 1970, Montreal, Quebec, Canada **Current organization:** Donwalt Industries Inc. **Title:** Research & Development Director **Type of organization:** Manufacturing, R&D **Major product:** Textile machines, printers **Area of distribution:** International **Expertise:** Mechanical engineering, product design, consulting, industrial mechanics, strategic analysis, troubleshooting, research **Published works:** Technical papers, book chapters **SIC code:** 35 **Address:** Donwalt Industries Inc., 1009 Bucks Industrial Park, Statesville, NC 28625 **E-mail:** paule@donwalt.com

PHELPS, THOMAS E.
Industry: Valves/water **Born:** October 15, 1948, Kewanee, Illinois **Univ./degree:** Attending Black Hawk Community College, Law Enforcement **Current organization:** Henry Pratt Co. **Title:** Senior Inspector **Type of organization:** Manufacturing **Major product:** Valves and shut off valves for water industry **Area of distribution:** International **Expertise:** Quality assurance **Affiliations:** V.F.W.; American Legion; Served in active duty, U.S.M.C., 1966-70 **SIC code:** 34 **Address:** 207 Fourth St., P.O. Box 207, Manlius, IL 61338 **E-mail:** tphelps@henrypratt.com **Web address:** www.henrypratt.com

PIERSON, NOEL C.
Industry: Personal products **Born:** January 15, 1980, Florida **Univ./degree:** B.S., Accounting; B.A., Business Management, Hartwick College **Current organization:** Johnson & Johnson **Title:** Financial Analyst **Type of organization:** Manufacturing/healthcare **Major product:** Consumer products, medical devices & diagnostics, pharmaceuticals and nutritional products **Area of distribution:** International **Expertise:** Finance **Affiliations:** Willow Tru Inc. (WT); Institute of Management Accountants (IMA); Financial Women's Association (FWA); W.T.T.I. **Hob./spts.:** Outdoor activities, soccer, basketball, art **SIC code:** 28 **Address:** 45 Coneflower Lane, West Windsor, NJ 08550 **E-mail:** npierson@theima.org

PIOLANTI, ROBERTO
Industry: Electronics **Born:** May 15, 1969, Carrara, Italy **Univ./degree:** M.S., Electronics Design, University of Pisa, Italy **Current organization:** Magnetek **Title:** General Manager **Type of organization:** Manufacturing **Major product:** Power supplies **Area of distribution:** International **Expertise:** Engineering, management and operations **Hob./spts.:** Chess, tennis, music **SIC code:** 36 **Address:** Magnetek, 9738 Sari Place, North Hills, CA 91343 **E-mail:** robertopiolanti@magnetek.com

PISTILLI, MICHAEL F.
Industry: Building products **Born:** December 21, 1942, Chicago, Illinois **Univ./degree:** B.S., Chemistry, Saint Louis University, Illinois, 1965 **Current organization:** Prairie Material Sales, Inc. **Title:** Technical Director **Type of organization:** Manufacturing **Major product:** Concrete, cement **Area of distribution:** National **Expertise:** Chemistry, petrography **Published works:** 15 articles **Affiliations:** A.S.T.M.I.; American Chemical Society; American Concrete Institute **Hob./spts.:** Rock collecting, model railroading, basketball **SIC code:** 32 **Address:** Prairie Material Sales, Inc., 7601 W. 79th St., Bridgeview, IL 60455 **E-mail:** mpistilli@prairiegroup.com **Web address:** www.prairiegroup.com

PITTS, MARVIN H.
Industry: Commercial machinery **Univ./degree:** B.S., Engineering, University of Tennessee, 1974 **Current organization:** Pitts Engineering Works Division **Title:** President **Type of organization:** Manufacturing **Major product:** Concrete mixers and aggregate bins **Area of distribution:** International **Expertise:** Marketing **SIC code:** 35 **Address:** Pitts Engineering Works Division, 4420 Candora Ave., Knoxville, TN 37920 **E-mail:** pittsengineering@aol.com

PLATT, DANIEL F.
Industry: Engines **Born:** June 28, 1962, Ada, Minnesota **Univ./degree:** B.B.A., CIS, Occupational Sciences, Wayland University **Current organization:** Cummins Inc. **Title:** CBS Site Support-CNGE **Type of organization:** Manufacturing **Major product:** Natural gas engines **Area of distribution:** International **Expertise:** Local area networking **Affiliations:** M.C.S.E. Group; Cloris Community College Information Technology Steering Group **Hob./spts.:** Riding motorcycles, fishing, hunting **SIC code:** 37 **Address:** Cummins Inc., 409 S. Norris St., Clovis, NM 88101 **E-mail:** daniel.f.platt@cummins.com

POLLARD, BRYAN
Industry: Semiconductors **Born:** June 25, 1965, Cedartown, Georgia **Univ./degree:** B.S., Auburn University, 1988 **Current organization:** Intel **Title:** Staff Engineer **Type of organization:** Manufacturing/engineering **Major product:** Computer chips **Area of distribution:** Marlboro, Massachusetts **Expertise:** Engineering **Hob./spts.:** Cycling, video photography **SIC code:** 36 **Address:** Intel, 12 Bacher Circle, Marlboro, MA 01752 **E-mail:** bryanmpollard@comcast.net

POMERENKE, FREDERICK W.
Industry: Lighting **Born:** December 8, 1929, Valley Stream, New York **Current organization:** Westron Lighting Corp. **Title:** V.P., Sales and Marketing **Type of organization:** Manufacturing, distributing **Major product:** Energy saving lighting products **Area of distribution:** National **Expertise:** Energy expert, marketing **Affiliations:** Kiwanis Club; Elks Club; Chambers of Commerce **Hob./spts.:** Singing in the annual veterans' show, sponsoring youth sports **SIC code:** 36 **Address:** Westron Lighting Corp., 3590-C Oceanside Rd., Oceanside, NY 11572 **E-mail:** wc3590@aol.com

POOLE, CHARLOTTE A.
Industry: Commercial signs **Born:** Mount Airy, Maryland **Univ./degree:** B.A., Accounting, Business Management, University of Maryland, 1976 **Current organization:** Jack Stone Sign Co. Inc. **Title:** Controller **Type of organization:** Manufacturing, service **Major product:** Signs **Area of distribution:** Maryland, D.C. and Virginia **Expertise:** Accounting **Affiliations:** Peachtree Accounting Network **Hob./spts.:** Artwork, jigsaw puzzles, "Joy" Group, owns business (CAPAS) **SIC code:** 39 **Address:** Jack Stone Sign Co. Inc., 3131 Pennsy Dr., Landover, MD 20785 **E-mail:** cpoole@jackstone.net

POOLE, LEN E.
Industry: Automotive/consumer goods **Born:** February 1, 1974, Okinawa, Japan **Univ./degree:** B.S., Plastics Engineering, Ferris State University, Michigan, 1997 **Current organization:** DPI In-Mold Applications **Title:** Program Development Manager **Type of organization:** Manufacturer **Major product:** Decorative plastic parts **Area of distribution:** International **Expertise:** Sales, development with OEM's, design, tooling **Published works:** 2 articles in Injection Molding Magazine **Affiliations:** Society of Plastics Engineering **Hob./spts.:** Racing motorcycles, jet skiing **SIC code:** 30 **Address:** DPI In-Mold Applications, 1340 Monroe Ave. Northwest, Grand Rapids, MI 49505 **E-mail:** lpoole@displaypack.com **Web address:** www.dpi-inmold.com

POPOVICH, CRAIG A.
Industry: Entertainment **Born:** March 23, 1970, Youngstown, Ohio **Univ./degree:** B.F.A., College of Art and Design, Ohio, 1992 **Current organization:** Dark Horse Entertainment **Title:** President **Type of organization:** Manufacturing **Major product:** Special effects, custom prop and set fabrication **Area of distribution:** National **Expertise:** Prop and set design **Affiliations:** Chamber of Commerce **Hob./spts.:** Writing, waterskiing **SIC code:** 39 **Address:** Dark Horse Entertainment, 3822 N.E. 55th Place, Gainesville, FL 32609

PORTER, V. JAMES
Industry: Industrial/transportation components **Born:** July 1, 1960. Milwaukee, Wisconsin **Univ./degree:** B.S., Chemistry, Ball State University, 1984 **Current organization:** E-A-R Specialty Composites **Title:** Quality Manager **Type of organization:** Manufacturing **Major product:** Energy and noise control materials **Area of distribution:** National **Expertise:** Product quality improvement **Affiliations:** American Society for Quality **Hob./spts.:** Tennis, scuba diving **SIC code:** 37 **Address:** E-A-R Specialty Composites, 650 Dawson Dr., Newark, DE 19713 **E-mail:** jim_porter@aearo.com **Web address:** www.aearo.com

POTOCZEK, DON
Industry: Steel **Born:** July 27, 1963, Akron, Ohio **Current organization:** GS Steel Co. **Title:** President **Type of organization:** Steel service center **Major product:** Steel plate **Area of distribution:** National **Expertise:** Business management; ISO9001Compliant **Affiliations:** Better Business Bureau **Hob./spts.:** Golf, drag racing **SIC code:** 34 **Address:** GS Steel Co., 3400 Cavalier Trail, Cuyahoga Falls, OH 44224 **E-mail:** donpotoczek@gssteel.com

POWELL, MICHAEL L.
Industry: Lawn and garden equipment **Born:** September 10, 1952, Clinton, Missouri **Univ./degree:** Attended McKendree College **Current organization:** Billy Goat Industries **Title:** Warehouse Manager **Type of organization:** Manufacturing **Major product:** Outdoor power equipment **Area of distribution:** National **Expertise:** Shipping and receiving, scheduling **Affiliations:** American Legion **Hob./spts.:** Hunting, fishing, golf, softball **SIC code:** 36 **Address:** Billy Goat Industries, 1803 S.W. Jefferson, Lees Summit, MO 64082 **E-mail:** mikep@billygoat.com **Web address:** www.billygoat.com

POWELL, STEPHEN L.
Industry: Steel **Born:** July 13, 1949, Chester, Pennsylvania **Univ./degree:** B.S., Education & Social Sciences, Millersville University, 1972 **Current organization:** Powell Steel Corp. **Title:** President/CEO **Type of organization:** Manufacturing **Major product:** Structural and miscellaneous steel fabrication and erection **Area of distribution:** National **Expertise:** Marketing, operations **Affiliations:** Millersville University Advisory Board **SIC code:** 33 **Address:** Powell Steel Corp., 625 Baumgardner Rd., Lancaster, PA 17603 **E-mail:** spowell@powellsteel.com **Web address:** www.powellsteel.com

POWELL, STEVEN E.
Industry: Mold making **Born:** March 7, 1957, Weiser, Idaho **Current organization:** Sorenson Mold Inc. **Title:** Tooling Engineer **Type of organization:** Manufacturing **Major product:** Plastic injection molds **Area of distribution:** National **Expertise:** Design engineering and mold making **Hob./spts.:** Playing computer games with his children **SIC code:** 30 **Address:** Sorenson Mold Inc., 6645 S. 400 West, Salt Lake City, UT 84107 **E-mail:** spowell@sormold.com

PRESTON, JOHN F.
Industry: Automotive **Born:** December 16, 1952, Philadelphia, Pennsylvania **Univ./degree:** B.S., Southwest Missouri State University **Current organization:** GM Wentzville GMTG **Title:** Advisor **Type of organization:** Manufacturing **Major product:** Full size vans **Area of distribution:** International **Expertise:** Maintenance **Hob./spts.:** Hunting, fishing, horse races **SIC code:** 37 **Address:** 4810 County Rd., Fulton, MO 65251 **E-mail:** john.preston@gm.com

PRICE, SCOTT
Industry: Carpet **Born:** August 19, 1971, Georgia **Univ./degree:** B.S., Engineering, Georgia Tech, 1994 **Current organization:** Shaw Industries, Plant 15 **Title:** MOS Manager **Type of organization:** Manufacturing/distribution **Major product:** Modular carpet **Area of distribution:** National **Expertise:** Operations management, product testing, design engineering, lecturing and public speaking **Hob./spts.:** White water rafting, softball, basketball, golf **SIC code:** 22 **Address:** Shaw Industries, Plant 15, P.O. Box 429, Cartersville, GA 30120 **E-mail:** scott.price@shawinc.com

PRIGITANO, VINCENT
Industry: Packaging **Univ./degree:** M.B.A., University of New Haven, 1993 **Current organization:** Tape & Label Engineering **Title:** Chief Operating Officer **Type of organization:** Manufacturing **Major product:** Prime labels **Area of distribution:** National **Expertise:** Finance, operations **Affiliations:** F.I.C.P.A.; A.I.C.P.A. **SIC code:** 26 **Address:** Tape & Label Engineering, 2950 47th Ave. North, St. Petersburg, FL 33714 **E-mail:** vprigitano@webermarking.com

PRIME, REGINALD E.
Industry: Consumer products **Born:** January 26, 1960, San Diego, California **Univ./degree:** B.S., Environmental Engineering, University of Central Florida, 1986 **Current organization:** Coca Cola Enterprises Inc. **Title:** Manager, Corporate Environmental Engineering **Type of organization:** Manufacturing **Major product:** Soft drinks **Area of distribution:** National **Expertise:** Environmental engineering, consulting and marketing **Affiliations:** National Registry of Environmental Engineers; Academy of Certified Hazardous Materials Managers; Georgia Food Processors Association **Hob./spts.:** Golf, swimming, racquetball **SIC code:** 20 **Address:** Coca Cola Enterprises Inc., 2500 Windy Ridge Pkwy. SE, Atlanta, GA 30339-5677 **E-mail:** rprime@na.cokecce.com

PRINCE, RAYMOND J.
Industry: Electronics **Born:** August 30, 1957, Oak Park, Illinois **Univ./degree:** B.S.E.E., Illinois Institute of Technology, 1985 **Current organization:** MGE UPS Systems, Inc. **Title:** President, North America **Type of organization:** Manufacturing **Major product:** Uninterruptible power supplied (UPS) systems **Area of distribution:** International **Expertise:** Sales and marketing **Affiliations:** I.E.E.E.E. **Hob./spts.:** Golf, baseball, bowling **SIC code:** 36 **Address:** MGE UPS Systems, Inc., 1660 Scenic Ave., Costa Mesa, CA 92626 **E-mail:** ray.prince@mgeups.com **Web address:** www.mgeups.com

PROCTOR JR., JOHN C.
Industry: Automotive **Born:** October 6, 1974, Columbus, Ohio **Current organization:** Mosey Manufacturing Co., Inc. **Title:** Application Engineer **Type of organization:** Manufacturing **Major product:** Transmission (green) ring gears **Area of distribution:** International **Expertise:** Quoting new product/launching new product **Hob./spts.:** Family, coaching youth sports - Little League baseball and football **SIC code:** 37 **Address:** Mosey Manufacturing Co., Inc., 1700 North F St., Richmond, IN 47374 **E-mail:** proctor@moseymfg.com

PRUESSMANN, DIETMAR F.
Industry: Machines/tool and die **Born:** May 7, 1937, Dusibruge, Germany **Univ./degree:** B.A., M.A., 1962, Mechanical Engineering, Zimmermann University,

Germany **Current organization:** Coronado Machine, Inc. **Title:** President **Type of organization:** Manufacturing company **Major product:** Precision machinery, tool and die for aerospace, medical and oil industries **Area of distribution:** National **Expertise:** Engineering **Affiliations:** N.T.D.A.; S.M.E. **Hob./spts.:** Computers, opera **SIC code:** 35 **Address:** Coronado Machine, Inc., 1308 First St. N.W., Albuquerque, NM 87102 **E-mail:** dfp1144@qwest.net

PRYKANOWSKI, THOMAS
Industry: Hospitality **Born:** December 3, 1969, Princeton, New Jersey **Univ./degree:** A.S., Culinary Arts, 1990; B.A., Marketing, Johnson and Wales University, 1992 **Current organization:** BF Saul Co., Hotel Division **Title:** Corporate Director of Food and Beverage **Type of organization:** Hotel/management **Major product:** Restaurants, catering facilities **Area of distribution:** National **Expertise:** Food and beverage administration **Affiliations:** N.R.A.; Program Advisory Board Member, A.I.W. **SIC code:** 20 **Address:** BF Saul Co., Hotel Division, 7501 Wisconsin Ave., Suite 1500, Bethesda, MD 20814-6522 **E-mail:** thomas.prykanowski@bfsaulco.com **Web address:** www.bfsaul.com

PUCKETT, KENNETH D.
Industry: Automotive **Univ./degree:** Certified Journeyman Tool & Die Maker, U.S. Dept. of Labor, 1974 **Current organization:** Shiloh Industries Inc. **Title:** Tooling Engineer **Type of organization:** Manufacturing **Major product:** Metal stamping and assemblies **Area of distribution:** International **Expertise:** Tooling and process **Hob./spts.:** Hunting, fishing, Gospel music **SIC code:** 34 **Address:** 1030 Johnston Dr., White Bluff, TN 37187 **E-mail:** kdpuckett@shiloh.com

PURYEAR, JAMES W.
Industry: Sports equipment **Born:** October 12, 1959, Lawrenceburg, Tennessee **Univ./degree:** A.A., Industrial Management, Motlow State Community College, 1979 **Current organization:** Rawlings/Worth LLC **Title:** Distribution Manager **Type of organization:** Manufacturing and distributing **Major product:** Baseball and softball equipment **Area of distribution:** International **Expertise:** Distribution, quality, inventory control **Hob./spts.:** Hunting, golf, baseball **SIC code:** 39 **Address:** Rawlings/Worth LLC, 2100 N. Jackson St., Tullahoma, TN 37388 **E-mail:** jwpuryear@charter.net **Web address:** www.worthsports.com

PYLE, WARD J.
Industry: Machinery **Born:** May 1, 1969, Louisville, Kentucky **Current organization:** Toyota Industrial Equipment Manufacturing **Title:** Design Engineer **Type of organization:** Manufacturing **Major product:** Forklifts **Area of distribution:** International **Expertise:** Engineering, special design packages, design/production liaison **Hob./spts.:** Hunting, fishing, golf **SIC code:** 35 **Address:** Toyota Industrial Equipment Manufacturing, 5555 Inwood Dr., Columbus, IN 47202-2487 **E-mail:** w_pyle@hotmail.com

QIAO, YUNFEI
Industry: Electric power components/cables/transformer **Born:** May 28, Jilin, China **Univ./degree:** B.S., Materials Engineering, BUAA, China, 1985; M.S., Mechanical Engineering, China University of Mining and Technology, 1988; Ph.D., Materials Engineering, Stevens Institute of Technology, 2001 **Current organization:** IGC-SuperPower **Title:** Senior Materials Scientist **Type of organization:** Manufacturing and development **Major product:** Second generation HTS superconductor **Area of distribution:** International **Expertise:** Long-length super smooth metal substrates polishing technology development **Affiliations:** A.P.S.; A.S.M./T.M.S. **Hob./spts.:** Soccer **SIC code:** 36 **Address:** 450 Duane Ave., Schenectady, NY 12304 **Phone:** (518)346-1414 **Fax:** (518)346-6080 **E-mail:** yunfei_quiao@hotmail.com **Web address:** www.igc.com

QUINN, MICHAEL T.J.
Industry: Furniture **Born:** September 19, 1963, Lewistown, Pennsylvania **Univ./degree:** B.S., Manufacturing, Engineering Technology, Pennsylvania College of Technology, 1998 **Current organization:** Pulaski Furniture **Title:** Engineering Manager **Type of organization:** Manufacturing **Major product:** Curio, console, corner curio **Area of distribution:** International **Expertise:** Engineering, manufacturing **Published works:** Furniture Design Magazine **Hob./spts.:** Refinishing antique furniture, golf **SIC code:** 25 **Address:** Pulaski Furniture, 301 N. Madison Ave., Plant #1, Pulaski, VA 24301 **E-mail:** mquinn@pulaskifurniture.com

RAMIREZ, LUCAS M.
Industry: Pharmaceutical/biotechnical **Born:** September 19, 1973, Arecibo, Puerto Rico **Univ./degree:** B.S.M.E., Georgia Institute of Technology, 1995 **Current organization:** Ultra Pure Systems Inc. **Title:** Vice President **Type of organization:** Design/manufacturing/installation **Major product:** Process skids, piping and systems installation **Area of distribution:** Puerto Rico **Expertise:** Engineering, operations management, presentations **Affiliations:** Puerto Rico College of Engineering; International Association of Pharmaceutical Engineers **Hob./spts.:** Golf, reading **SIC code:** 34 **Address:** Ultra Pure Systems Inc., P.O. Box 8697, Bayamón, PR 00960 **E-mail:** lucas_ramirez@msn.com **Web address:** www.upsipr.com

RAMOS, ARCADIO
Industry: Pharmaceuticals **Born:** December 24, 1950, San Juan, Puerto Rico **Univ./degree:** B.S., Chemical Engineering, University of Puerto Rico, 1973 **Current organization:** Procter & Gamble Pharmaceuticals **Title:** Maintenance Manager **Type of organization:** Manufacturing **Major product:** Pharmaceutical products **Area of distribution:** International **Expertise:** Engineering, maintenance **Hob./spts.:** Ping-Pong, bowling, music **SIC code:** 28 **Address:** Procter & Gamble Pharmaceuticals, Hwy #2 Kilometer 45-7, Manati, PR 00674 **E-mail:** ramos.a.2@pg.com

RAMOS, JOHNNY
Industry: Metal **Born:** March 22, 1962, San Juan, Puerto Rico **Univ./degree:** M.A., University of Puerto Rico, 1992 **Current organization:** CNC 2000 Inc. **Title:** Owner **Type of organization:** Manufacturing **Major product:** Medical equipment, defense equipment **Area of distribution:** National **Expertise:** Medical equipment, defense equipment, marketing **Hob./spts.:** Golf, basketball, music, farming **SIC code:** 34 **Address:** CNC 2000 Inc., State Rd. 156 km 58.6, W. Industrial Park, Caguas, PR 00726 **E-mail:** jramos@cnc2000.com **Web address:** www.cnc2k.com

RAMOS MATOS, JOSÉ A.
Industry: Electric/industrial **Born:** August 5, 1976, Rio Piedras, Puerto Rico **Univ./degree:** B.S., Industrial Engineering **Current organization:** Caribe General Electric, Inc. **Title:** Plating Production and Process Leader **Type of organization:** Manufacturing **Major product:** Electroplating and finishing **Area of distribution:** International **Expertise:** Engineering, electroplating expert **Affiliations:** A.S.E.F. **SIC code:** 36 **Address:** Caribe General Electric, Inc., P.O. Box 14001, Arecibo, PR 00614-0011 **E-mail:** jose.ramos@ge.com

RANDEN, RONALD W.
Born: January 11, 1940, St. Louis, Missouri **Univ./degree:** B.S., Mechanical Engineering, University of Santiago, Chile, 1968 **Current organization:** Missouri Enterprises **Title:** Senior Vice President, Business Development **Area of distribution:** International **Affiliations:** Society of Manufacturing Engineers **Hob./spts.:** Hunting, fishing **SIC code:** 35 **Address:** Missouri Enterprises, 800 University Dr., Rolla, MO 65401 **E-mail:** r.randen@missourienterprises.com

RANDERIA, SURBALA B.
Industry: Nutraceutical **Born:** Bombay, India **Univ./degree:** M.S., Biochemistry, University of Bombay, 1963 **Current organization:** General Research Laboratory **Title:** Vice President **Type of organization:** Manufacturing **Major product:** Nutraceutical and food **Area of distribution:** National **Expertise:** Technical formulation, production, research and development **Hob./spts.:** Music **SIC code:** 28 **Address:** 7574 W. 82nd St., Playa del Rey, CA 90293 **E-mail:** meru4co@hotmail.com

RANEY, SAM
Industry: Food **Born:** October 15, 1947, Baton Rouge, Louisiana **Univ./degree:** B.A., General Studies and Psychology, Louisiana State University, 1991 **Current organization:** Imperial Sugar **Title:** Manager, Human Resources **Type of organization:** Refinery **Major product:** Sugar **Area of distribution:** National **Expertise:** Human resources, labor relations **Affiliations:** S.H.R.M. **Hob./spts.:** Golf, fishing, deer hunting **SIC code:** 20 **Address:** Imperial Sugar, 1230 S. 5th Ave., Gramercy, LA 70052 **E-mail:** sam.raney@imperialsugar.com

RASHEED, SYED A.
Industry: Cement **Born:** October 10, 1942, Bangalore, India **Univ./degree:** B.S., Chemistry, University of Karachi, 1964; M.S., Chemical Engineering, Century University, New Mexico, 2000 **Current organization:** TXI Riverside Cement Co. **Title:** Chief Chemist **Type of organization:** Manufacturing **Major product:** Various types of Portland cements **Area of distribution:** International **Expertise:** Quality control **Affiliations:** A.C.S.; A.S.Q.C. **Hob./spts.:** Cricket **SIC code:** 32 **Address:** TXI Riverside Cement Co., 1500 Rubidoux Blvd., P.O. Box 832, Riverside, CA 92509 **E-mail:** srasheed@txi.com

RASMUSSEN, ROBERT LEE
Industry: Automotive **Born:** April 7, 1954, Rochelle, Illinois **Current organization:** Rockford Products Tool Room **Title:** Journeyman Precision Machinist/Journeyman CNC Set Up Operator **Type of organization:** Manufacturing **Major product:** Cold formed front end suspension parts **Area of distribution:** International **Expertise:** Tooling **Affiliations:** A.S.M.E.; A.M.E. **Hob./spts.:** Fishing **SIC code:** 37 **Address:** Rockford Products Tool Room, Plant 3, 707 Harrison Ave., Rockford, IL 61104-7197 **E-mail:** popparaz1@aol.com

RATLIFF JR., HARVEY L.
Industry: Engineering **Born:** April 11, 1931, Amarillo, Texas **Univ./degree:** B.S., Petroleum Engineering, Texas Tech **Current organization:** Ratcliff Operating Corp.

Title: President, Owner **Type of organization:** Petroleum production company **Major product:** Production of crude oil **Area of distribution:** National **Expertise:** Petroleum exploration and production **Affiliations:** S.P.E.; P.P.R.A.; T.A.E.P. **Hob./spts.:** Painting, writing **SIC code:** 29 **Address:** Ratcliff Operating Corp., 112 W. Eighth Ave., Suite 708, Amarillo, TX 79101 **E-mail:** ratliff31@sbcglobal.net

REGAN, MICHAEL W.
Industry: Industrial equipment **Born:** May 28, 1952, Lafayette, Louisiana **Univ./degree:** B.S.N., 1984 **Current organization:** Crane Ceaux of Lake Charles, LLC **Title:** President, CEO **Type of organization:** Manufacturing/rental agency **Major product:** Crane rental agency with operators **Area of distribution:** Louisiana **Expertise:** Crane manufacturing and erection/heavy rigging and lifting **SIC code:** 35 **Address:** Crane Ceaux of Lake Charles, LLC, 2309 Hwy. 397, Lake Charles, LA 70615 **E-mail:** craneceaux@worldnet.att.net

REID, ROBERT
Industry: Plastics **Born:** August 17, 1947, Philadelphia, Pennsylvania **Univ./degree:** Diploma, Data Processing Institute, 1969; Diploma, Personal Computer Specialist , 1997; Diploma, P.C. Repair, 1999, International Correspondence Schools; IBM School, Certificate of Achievement **Current organization:** ABTec Inc. **Title:** Maintenance/Product Supervisor **Type of organization:** Manufacturing **Major product:** Plastic molding, electronic and medical products **Area of distribution:** Bristol, Pennsylvania **Expertise:** Maintenance, supervision of plant **Honors/awards:** Award given by the National Technology Transfer Institute, Controls Division for Troubleshooting Motor Controls, 1996; Award given by the National Technology Transfer Institute, Fluid Power Division for Hydraulics Technology, 1993 **Hob./spts.:** Coin collecting, stamp collecting **SIC code:** 30 **Address:** ABTec Inc., 2570 Pearl Buck Rd., Bristol, PA 19007 **E-mail:** witlewin@msn.com

REILLY, MARK J.
Industry: Food **Born:** August 1, 1963, Manchester, Iowa **Univ./degree:** B.S., Iowa State University, 1985; M.A., Business, University of Iowa, 2004 **Current organization:** General Mills (Cedar Rapids Plant) **Title:** Start-up Manager **Type of organization:** Manufacturing **Major product:** Snacks, cereal, fruit snacks, popcorn, frosting **Area of distribution:** International **Expertise:** Project installation and start-up **Published works:** 1 article **Hob./spts.:** Reading, farming **SIC code:** 20 **Address:** General Mills (Cedar Rapids Plant), 4800 Edgewood Rd., Cedar Rapids, IA 52406 **E-mail:** mark.reilly@genmills.com **Web address:** www.genmills.com

RETTEDAL, TICO
Industry: Electronics **Title:** Document Control Supervisor **Type of organization:** Manufacturing **Major product:** Video, audio, data transport **Expertise:** Document control **SIC code:** 36 **Address:** Video Products Group, 1380 Flynn Rd., Camarillo, CA 93012-8016 **E-mail:** trettedal@vpginc.com

REYES, JOSSUE
Industry: Medical devices **Born:** December 29, 1970, Ponce, Puerto Rico **Univ./degree:** B.S., Materials Management; M.S., Technology **Current organization:** Medtronic PR **Title:** IT Director **Type of organization:** Manufacturing/R&D **Major product:** Pacemakers, diabetes pumps, neuro stimulators **Area of distribution:** International **Expertise:** IT, network systems **Hob./spts.:** Swimming, travel, bowling **SIC code:** 38 **Address:** Medtronic PR, P.O. Box 6001, Villalba, PR 00766-6001 **E-mail:** jarcns@gmail.com

REYNOLDS, MARTHA
Industry: Automotive/heavy duty truck parts **Born:** June 29, 1959, Giles County, Virginia **Univ./degree:** A.S., Accounting, New River Community College **Current organization:** Imperial Fabricating Company of Virginia **Title:** Purchasing Manager **Type of organization:** Manufacturing **Major product:** Heavy duty truck parts **Area of distribution:** International **Expertise:** Purchasing and management **Hob./spts.:** Crafts, boating, fishing, hunting, cooking **SIC code:** 37 **Address:** Imperial Fabricating Company of Virginia, 4969 Stepp Place, Dublin, VA 24084 **E-mail:** mreynolds@imperialgroup.com **Web address:** www.imperialgroup.com

RHODES, ARTHUR W.
Industry: Financial consulting (small business) **Born:** May 11, 1917, Greenbrier, Tennessee **Univ./degree:** B.S., Electrical Engineering, Naval Academy; M.S., Business Administration, New York University, 1961 **Current organization:** Campel Associates, Inc. **Title:** President **Type of organization:** Manufacturing/distribution **Major product:** Manufacturing assembly and storage **Area of distribution:** International **Expertise:** Management, engineering **Published works:** Co-author, "Projects to Generate Electric Power More Efficiently" **Hob./spts.:** Woodworking, photography, sailing **SIC code:** 36 **Address:** Campel Associates, Inc., P.O. Box 2083, Darien, CT 06820-0083 **E-mail:** awrhodes@juno.com

RICE, FERILL J.
Industry: Home elevators/dumbwaiters **Born:** July 4, 1926, Hemingford, Nebraska **Current organization:** Rice Health Care/Waupaca Elevator Co., Inc. **Title:** Advertising Director **Type of organization:** Manufacturing **Major product:** Elevators and dumbwaiters exclusively for residential use **Area of distribution:** National **Expertise:** Management, advertising, Editor **Published works:** "Caught in The Butterfly Net", Fenton Art Glass, Collectors of America **Affiliations:** President, Past President and Co-founder, Fenton Art Glass Collectors of America **Hob./spts.:** Glass collecting **SIC code:** 35 **Address:** Rice Health Care, Waupaca Elevator Co., Inc., 1726 N. Ballard St., Appleton, WI 54914 **E-mail:** ferillr@ricemanagement.com **Web address:** www.waupacaelevator.com

RICKABAUGH, LELAND R.
Industry: Agriculture **Born:** May 15, 1944, Correctionville, Iowa **Current organization:** Wilson Trailer Co. **Title:** Quality Control Manager **Type of organization:** Manufacturing **Major product:** Semi-trailers **Area of distribution:** National **Expertise:** Quality control **Affiliations:** A.W.S. **Hob./spts.:** Fishing **SIC code:** 37 **Address:** Wilson Trailer Co., 4444 S. Lewis Blvd., Sioux City, IA 51106

RICKETSON, DAVID L.
Industry: Recreational vehicles **Born:** July 23, 1966, Grand Rapids, Michigan **Univ./degree:** B.S., Embery-Riddle Aeronautical University, 1990; M.B.A., Grand Valley State University, 2003 **Current organization:** Coachmen **Title:** Product Engineer **Type of organization:** Manufacturing **Major product:** Recreational vehicle **Area of distribution:** National **Expertise:** Engineering **Affiliations:** Society of Manufacturing Engineers **SIC code:** 37 **Address:** Coachmen, 418 Portage, Three Rivers, MI 49093 **E-mail:** dlricketson@earthlink.net

RIEMENSCHNEIDER, HERBERT H.
Industry: Chemicals **Born:** August 27, 1953, Buenos Aires, Argentina **Univ./degree:** Ph.D., Chemical Engineering, University of Stuttgart, Germany, 1983 **Current organization:** Degussa Corp. **Title:** Director of Technology and Process **Type of organization:** Manufacturing **Major product:** Specialty chemicals **Area of distribution:** International **Expertise:** Manufacturing **Published works:** 10 patents **Affiliations:** A.I.C.H.E.; Board of Directors, I.F.P.R.I.; Member, Executive Committee P.E.R.C./University of Florida **Hob./spts.:** Boating, hiking **SIC code:** 28 **Address:** Degussa Corp., 4301 Degussa Rd., Theodore, AL 36590 **E-mail:** herbert.riemenschneider@degussa.com

RILEY, TRACY L.
Industry: Ice merchandisers **Born:** January 4, 1964, Dumas, Arkansas **Current organization:** Leer Limited Partnership **Title:** Shipping Supervisor/Production Scheduler **Type of organization:** Manufacturing **Major product:** Freezer units **Area of distribution:** International **Expertise:** Forecasting, production scheduling (MRP) **Hob./spts.:** Fishing, hunting **SIC code:** 35 **Address:** Leer Limited Partnership, Hwy. 65 South, Dumas, AR 71639 **E-mail:** triley@leerlp.com

RINALDI, JAMES A.
Industry: Aerospace **Born:** November 23, 1960 Pennsylvania **Univ./degree:** B.S., Mechanical Engineering, University of North Carolina at Charlotte, 1998 **Current organization:** Kearfott Guidance & Navigation **Title:** Design Engineer **Type of organization:** Manufacturing **Major product:** Activators, guidance systems **Area of distribution:** National **Expertise:** Engineering **Affiliations:** A.S.M.E.; S.E.M. **Hob./spts.:** Pilot, dirt-bikes, hiking **SIC code:** 37 **Address:** Kearfott Guidance & Navigation, Route 70, Black Mountain, NC 28711 **E-mail:** rinaldi@asheville.kearfott.com

RIVERA, FELIX O.
Industry: Electronics **Born:** March 11, 1970, Bronx, New York **Univ./degree:** B.S., University of Puerto Rico, 1993 **Current organization:** Autoware **Title:** President **Type of organization:** Manufacturing **Major product:** Electronic equipment **Area of distribution:** International **Expertise:** Electronic equipment design **Affiliations:** Vice President, Committee of Young Entrepreneurs of Puerto Rico Manufacturing Associates **SIC code:** 36 **Address:** Autoware, A11 Ave. Degetau, Caguas, PR 00725 **E-mail:** felix@autowarepr.com **Web address:** www.autoware.com

RIVERA, HECTOR L.
Industry: Pharmaceuticals **Born:** August 3, 1975, Amityville, New York **Univ./degree:** B.S., Electrical Engineering, University of Puerto Rico **Current organization:** GlaxoSmithKline **Title:** Validation Scientist **Type of organization:** Manufacturing **Major product:** Prescription drugs and medicines **Area of distribution:** Puerto Rico **Expertise:** Verify process **Affiliations:** S.H.P.E. **Hob./spts.:** Tennis **SIC code:** 28 **Address:** GlaxoSmithKline, S.B. Pharmo PR, Inc., P.O. Box 11975, Cidra, PR 00739-1975 **E-mail:** hector.l.rivera@gsk.com

RIVERA, JOSE R.
Industry: Pharmaceuticals **Univ./degree:** B.S., Pharmacy Sciences, University of Puerto Rico, 1977; M.B.A. Candidate, Baylor University, Texas, 2005 **Current**

organization: Allergan Inc. **Title:** Director of Validation **Type of organization:** Manufacturing **Major product:** Ophthalmic eye drops **Area of distribution:** National **Expertise:** Validation, production, products transfers, project management, aseptic process **Hob./spts.:** Classic cars, reading, coin collecting **SIC code:** 28 **Address:** 9406 Pioneer Dr., Woodway, TX 76712 **E-mail:** doval78@hotmail.com

ROBERTS, JUDY D.
Industry: Dairy **Born:** July 27, 1953, Nancy, Kentucky **Univ./degree:** A.D., Applied Science, University of Kentucky **Current organization:** Southern Belle Dairy **Title:** Quality Compliance Director **Type of organization:** Manufacturing **Major product:** Dairy products **Area of distribution:** Somerset, Kentucky **Expertise:** Quality Compliance Officer **Affiliations:** Kentucky Association of Milk, Food and Environmental Sanitarians **Hob./spts.:** Collecting antiques **SIC code:** 20 **Address:** Southern Belle Dairy, 607 E. Bourne Ave., Somerset, KY 42501 **E-mail:** judy.roberts@southernbelledairy.com **Web address:** www.southernbelledairy.com

ROCKETT, A. GARY
Industry: Forest products **Born:** December 23, 1949, El Dorado, Arkansas **Univ./degree:** B.S., Louisiana Tech University, 1973 **Current organization:** Potlatch Corp. **Title:** Manufacturing Superintendent **Type of organization:** Manufacturing **Major product:** Random length southern yellow pine lumber **Area of distribution:** National **Expertise:** Department management, sawfiler, lumber quality control, high temp kilns **Honors/awards:** 20 years of service with Louisiana-Pacific - VPP **Hob./spts.:** Fox hunting, duck hunting **SIC code:** 24 **Address:** Potlatch Corp., 810 W. Pine St., P.O. Box 390, Warren, AR 71671 **E-mail:** gary.rockett@potlatchcorp.com **Web address:** www.potlatchcorp.com

ROCKROHR, RONALD L.
Industry: Electronics **Born:** January 25, 1960, Harvey, Illinois **Univ./degree:** B.S.E.E.T., DeVry Institute of Technology, 1981 **Current organization:** Mission Electronics, Inc. **Title:** Systems Engineer **Type of organization:** Audio/video system integration **Major product:** A/V systems **Area of distribution:** National **Expertise:** System design **Honors/awards:** CTS-D, CTS-I, CBTE, AMX ACE **Affiliations:** S.B.E.; I.C.I.A.; B.I.C.S.I. **Hob./spts.:** Radio control modeling, audio mixing **SIC code:** 36 **Address:** Mission Electronics, Inc., 11450 W. 79th St., Lenexa, KS 66214-1484 **E-mail:** ron@missionelectronics.com **Web address:** www.missionelectronics.com

RODERICK, WAYNE A.
Industry: Transportation **Born:** May 31, 1944, New Castle, Indiana **Univ./degree:** A.S., Machine Design, Springfield School of Technology, 1964 **Current organization:** Acro Trailer Co. **Title:** General Manager **Type of organization:** Manufacturing **Major product:** Tank trailers **Area of distribution:** International **Expertise:** Engineering, management **Hob./spts.:** Hunting, fishing **SIC code:** 37 **Address:** Acro Trailer Co., 2320 N. Packer Rd., Springfield, MO 65803-5097 **E-mail:** wroderick@acrotrailer.com

RODRIGUEZ, HENRY
Industry: Medical products **Born:** April 28, 1969, Newburg, New York **Univ./degree:** B.A., Marketing, Orange County Community College, New York, 1990 **Current organization:** Biomet Orthopedics **Title:** Managing Director **Type of organization:** Distributing **Major product:** Joint replacements **Area of distribution:** International **Expertise:** Marketing; sales for joint replacements **SIC code:** 38 **Address:** Biomet Orthopedics, P.O. Box 363926, San Juan, PR 00936-3926 **E-mail:** biomethr@coqui.net

RODRIGUEZ, LUIS E.
Industry: Pharmaceuticals **Born:** November 26, 1968, Ponce, Puerto Rico **Univ./degree:** B.S., Chemical Engineering, 1992; M.B.A., Industrial Management, University of Puerto Rico, 1996 **Current organization:** Wyeth Pharmaceutical Co. **Title:** Technology Specialist **Type of organization:** Manufacturing **Major product:** Pharmaceuticals **Area of distribution:** Puerto Rico **Expertise:** Validate and quality check equipment **Hob./spts.:** Travel **SIC code:** 28 **Address:** Wyeth Pharmaceutical Co., State Rd., #3, KM.142.1, Guayama, PR 00784 **E-mail:** rodrigla@wyeth.com

ROEDER, RICHARD L.
Born: January 14, 1938, Milwaukee, Michigan **Univ./degree:** B.S., University of Wisconsin, 1958 **Current organization:** FOF Inc. **Title:** President **Type of organization:** Manufacturing **Major product:** Pop up work tents and fabric air diffusion systems **Area of distribution:** International **Expertise:** Designing and developing new products **Hob./spts.:** Sailing, tennis, swimming **SIC code:** 35 **Address:** FOF Inc., 1505 Racine St., P.O. Box 904, Delavan, WI 53115 **E-mail:** dickroedoer@sbcglobal.net **Web address:** www.fabricairducts.com and www.popnwork.com

ROGERS, MILDRED A.
Industry: Food **Born:** November 12, 1952, Cheektowaga, New York **Univ./degree:** B.A., History, State University of New York at Buffalo, 1974 **Current organization:** General Mills Inc. **Title:** Electrician, AA, PLC Qualified **Type of organization:** Manufacturing **Major product:** Cereal **Area of distribution:** National **Expertise:** Certified Electrician, 1994 **Affiliations:** Church **SIC code:** 20 **Address:** General Mills Inc., 54 S. Michigan Ave., Buffalo, NY 14203 **E-mail:** electrichillie@yahoo.com

ROMAN, MARK
Industry: Defense electronics **Born:** December 11, 1953, New Brunswick, New Jersey **Univ./degree:** B.S., Electrical Engineering, College of New Jersey, 1978 **Current organization:** Raytheon **Title:** Test Engineering Manager **Type of organization:** Design and sustaining **Major product:** Radar systems **Area of distribution:** National **Expertise:** Test engineering **Hob./spts.:** Running, 1980 Olympic Marathon Candidate **SIC code:** 36 **Address:** Raytheon, 2106 Sonata Lane, Carrollton, TX 75007 **E-mail:** mark-roman@raytheon.com

ROMANO, JAMES J.
Industry: Medical **Born:** February 13, 1951, Bronx, New York **Univ./degree:** A.S., Electrical Engineering, New York Institute of Technology-1974 **Current organization:** Hill-Rom **Title:** Senior R&D Engineer **Type of organization:** Manufacturing **Major product:** Medical support surfaces **Area of distribution:** International **Expertise:** R&D engineering **Published works:** Medical journals; 35+ patents **Affiliations:** Navy 1969-75 **Hob./spts.:** Deep sea fishing **SIC code:** 38 **Address:** Hill-Rom, 4349 Corporate Rd., Charleston, SC 29405 **E-mail:** jj.romano@hill-rom.com

ROMERO-RAMSEY, MARILYN
Industry: Refining/chemicals **Born:** October 12, 1942, Port Arthur, Texas **Univ./degree:** Steno Degree, Port Arthur College **Current organization:** ATOFINA Petrochemicals, Inc. **Title:** Secretary III **Type of organization:** Manufacturing **Major product:** Oil and gas products, petrochemicals **Area of distribution:** International **Expertise:** Staff assistance, office management **Affiliations:** Muscular Dystrophy; Salvation Army; American Cancer Society **Hob./spts.:** Bowling, dancing, travel, interior decorating, time with family and friends **SIC code:** 29 **Address:** ATOFINA Petrochemicals, Inc., Hwy. 366 @ 32nd St., Port Arthur, TX 77642 **E-mail:** marilyn.romero-ramsey@atofina.com

ROPER, KEN
Industry: UV Chemistry **Born:** February 21, 1950, Oklahoma City, Oklahoma **Univ./degree:** Diplomate, Optical Dispensing, American College of Optics-Los Angeles, CA, 1978-79; Attended Goldenwest College, Huntington Beach, California, 1988-1990 **Current organization:** The UV Chemistry Co., Inc. **Title:** Production Manager, Purchasing Manager, Shipping/Receiving **Type of organization:** Manufacturing **Major product:** Adhesives and coatings for film screen, optical, air tanks, flooring silkscreen **Area of distribution:** International **Expertise:** HAZMAT Shipper Certified (every 3 years) all adhesives and coatings; American Board of Opticianry Certified (ABOC), 1994 **Honors/awards:** Supervisor of the Year, Heard Optical Co., 1986, 1988, 1990; Employee of the Month - Lightwave Energy Systems Co., Torrance, CA, 1998 **Affiliations:** American Chemical Society; Dispensing Opticians Association **Hob./spts.:** Friends, target shooting, camping, country music, jazz music, pool shooting, dancing **SIC code:** 28 **Address:** Lightwave Energy Systems Co. (LESCO), 23520 Telo Ave., Suite 8, Torrance, CA 90505 **E-mail:** ken@uvchemistry.com

ROSE, EDWARD E.
Industry: Aerospace **Univ./degree:** B.S.E.E., University of Bridgeport **Current organization:** Raytheon **Title:** Principal Design Engineer **Type of organization:** Manufacturing and research **Major product:** Avionics **Expertise:** Digital signal processing **Affiliations:** I.E.E.E.; Raytheon Black Employees Network **Hob./spts.:** Scuba diving, golf, tennis **SIC code:** 37 **Address:** Raytheon, 2501 W. University Dr., McKinney, TX 75070 **E-mail:** e-rose2@raytheon.com

ROSEN, CHARLES
Industry: Apparel **Born:** March 4, 1931, Minneapolis, Minnesota **Univ./degree:** M.S.I.E., Tome School of Engineering, 1952 **Current organization:** Blauer Manufacturing, Co., Inc. **Title:** V.P., Manufacturing **Type of organization:** Manufacturing **Major product:** Police, fire and EMS uniforms **Area of distribution:** National **Expertise:** Manufacturing, sourcing **Published works:** "Meteor Burst technique in the Propagation of Low Power Radio Waves", Gibbsville Press, New York, NY 1954 **Affiliations:** National Fire Protection Association; American Society for Quality; Institute of Industrial Engineers **Hob./spts.:** Naval history **SIC code:** 23 **Address:** Blauer Manufacturing, Co., Inc., 20 Aberdeen St., Boston, MA 02215 **E-mail:** crosen@blauer.com

ROSENBERG, J. IVANHOE
Industry: Snow removal equipment **Born:** October 30, 1919, Powell, Wyoming **Current organization:** Sno-Skat Mfg. Co. **Title:** President **Type of organization:** Manufacturing **Major product:** Snowplows **Area of distribution:** Colorado **Expertise:** Retired newspaper publisher; Former Denver City Councilman **Honors/awards:** Nominated to the Denver Press Club Hall of Fame **Affiliations:** National Inventors Congress; Board of Directors, Colorado Press Association; Denver Press Club **Hob./**

spts.: Auto racing **SIC code:** 37 **Address:** Sno-Skat, 316 Federal Blvd., Denver, CO 80219 **E-mail:** jivanhoeatwork@aol.com

ROUGHTON, BRYAN C.
Industry: Paint **Born:** June 16, 1958, Wichita, Kansas **Current organization:** Kwal Paint **Title:** V.P., Business Development **Type of organization:** Manufacturing/retail/wholesale/distribution **Major product:** Architectural coatings **Area of distribution:** National **Expertise:** Marketing **Hob./spts.:** Family, fishing, golf, hunting **SIC code:** 28 **Address:** Kwal Paint, 3900 Joliet St., Denver, CO 80239 **E-mail:** broughton@kwalhowells.com **Web address:** www.kwallhowells.com

ROY, GISELLE D.
Industry: Publishing **Born:** August 2, 1958, Wichita, Kansas **Univ./degree:** B.B.A., with Honors, University of California at Sacramento, 1984 **Current organization:** The Wichita Eagle/McClatchy Newspapers **Title:** Vice President, Human Resource Employment and Community Relations **Type of organization:** Publishing **Major product:** Newspapers **Area of distribution:** Central Kansas **Expertise:** Employment, labor relations, training, lecturing **Honors/awards:** Nominated, SHRM, 2006; Resource Professional of the Year, 2003; Powerful Women in Wichita Award, Wichita Women's Business Association; Community Service Award, Arthritis Foundation, 2003 **Affiliations:** Society for Human Resource Management; National Association of Minority Media Executives; Board of Directors, American Red Cross, Central Plains Region **Hob./spts.:** Reading, travel, community service **SIC code:** 27 **Address:** The Wichita Eagle/McClatchy Newspapers, 825 E. Douglas, Wichita, KS 67201 **E-mail:** groy@wichitaeagle.com **Web address:** www.kansas.com/mid/kansas

RUBIN, MAURICE (RICK) M.
Industry: Melting equipment **Born:** August 17, 1926, Milwaukee, Wisconsin **Current organization:** WRIB Manufacturing Inc. **Title:** Vice President **Type of organization:** Manufacturing **Major product:** Cupolas and related melting equipment **Area of distribution:** International **Expertise:** Management, operations **Hob./spts.:** University of Illinois Basketball, football **SIC code:** 35 **Address:** WRIB Manufacturing Inc., 28 Dixie Acres Rd., Danville, IL 61832 **E-mail:** wrib-mfg@k-inc.com

RUFUS, ISAAC B.
Industry: Floor covering **Born:** January 13, 1959, India **Univ./degree:** Ph.D., Chemistry, Indian Institute of Technology, 1990 **Current organization:** Mannington **Title:** Ph.D./Senior Scientist **Type of organization:** Manufacturing, research and development **Major product:** Floor covering **Area of distribution:** International **Expertise:** Polymers, research and development **Honors/awards:** 6 patents **Published works:** 3 book chapters, 23 journal articles **Affiliations:** American Chemical Society; Radtech Association **Hob./spts.:** Tennis, sports **SIC code:** 24 **Address:** Mannington, Research and Development Laboratory, 75 Mannington Mills Rd., Salem, NJ 08079 **E-mail:** isaacr@mannington.com **Web address:** www.mannington.com

RUMFIELD, STANLEY R.
Industry: Cement manufacturing **Born:** November 22, 1944, Phillipsburg, New Jersey **Univ./degree:** B.S.E., University of California at Berkeley, 1966 **Current organization:** Keystone Cement Co. **Title:** Manager of Maintenance **Type of organization:** Manufacturing **Major product:** Cement **Area of distribution:** National **Expertise:** Maintenance, engineering **Published works:** Articles **Affiliations:** I.E.E.E.; A.S.E. **Hob./spts.:** Family, fishing, hunting, golf **SIC code:** 32 **Address:** Keystone Cement Co., P.O. Box "A", Bath, PA 18045 **E-mail:** srumfield@keystone-cement.com **Web address:** www.keystone.cement.com

RUTH, WILLIAM A.
Industry: Stainless castings **Born:** February 27, 1940, Detroit, Michigan **Univ./degree:** A.S., Great Lakes College, 1960 **Current organization:** Temperform Corp. **Title:** Manager, Quality Systems **Type of organization:** Engineering **Major product:** Stainless castings **Area of distribution:** International **Expertise:** Foundry **Affiliations:** A.F.S., Engineers Society of Detroit; American Society of Safety Engineers; American Welding Society **Hob./spts.:** Photography, gardening **SIC code:** 33 **Address:** Temperform Corp., 25425 Trans-X Rd., Novi, MI 48376 **E-mail:** bruth@temperform.com **Web address:** www.temperform.com

RUTKOWSKI, RANDALL S.
Industry: Automotive/food **Born:** December 20, 1961, Dearborn, Michigan **Current organization:** Marathon Weld Group LLC **Title:** Senior Designer & President of Truline Design LLC **Type of organization:** Manufacturing **Major product:** Design and build special machines **Area of distribution:** National **Expertise:** Special machine design **Hob./spts.:** Hunting, automobile restoration **SIC code:** 35 **Address:** Marathon Weld Group LLC, 5750 Marathon Dr., Jackson, MI 49201 **E-mail:** rrutkowski@marathonweldgroup.com

RYDER, DEIRDRE
Industry: Printing and packaging equipment **Born:** December 17, New York, New York **Univ./degree:** B.A., Iona College, 1987 **Current organization:** VITS America, Inc. **Title:** Managing Director/President **Type of organization:** Manufacturing and distributing **Major product:** Sheeters and inline finishing equipment **Area of distribution:** International **Expertise:** Business management **Affiliations:** N.P.E.S; P.I.A. **SIC code:** 35 **Address:** VITS America, Inc., 200 Corporate Dr., Blauvelt, NY 10913 **E-mail:** deidrer@vitsamerica.com **Web address:** vitsamerica.com

RYSER, JEFF L.
Industry: Industrial equipment **Born:** November 10, 1969, Salina, Kansas **Univ./degree:** B.S., Industrial Design, Fort Hays State University, 1995 **Current organization:** Salina Vortex Corp. **Title:** Engineering Development Manager **Type of organization:** OEM **Major product:** Slide gate, diverter valves **Area of distribution:** International **Expertise:** Engineering, design, product development, supervision **Affiliations:** Past Member, S.M.E. **Hob./spts.:** Baseball, softball, mountain biking **SIC code:** 34 **Address:** 935 Hancock St,, Salina, KS 67401 **E-mail:** jryser@salinavortex.com

SAHETA, VISHAL S.
Industry: Petroleum **Born:** May 30, 1976, Bombay, India **Univ./degree:** B.S.M.E., Bombay University, 1997; M.S.M.E., Design/Mechanics, Purdue University, 2001 **Current organization:** Schlumberger **Title:** Development Engineer **Type of organization:** Manufacturing & design **Major product:** Oil field equipment **Area of distribution:** International **Expertise:** Engineering **Honors/awards:** Merit Scholarship, Bombay University **Published works:** 2 articles, 1 patent pending **Affiliations:** A.S.M.E. **Hob./spts.:** Photography, volunteering for Jr. Achievement Program for mentoring and tutoring, travel **SIC code:** 29 **Address:** 9801 Meadowglen Lane, #42, Houston, TX 77042 **E-mail:** vsaheta@slb.com **Web address:** www.slb.com

SAMMUT, VINCENT P.
Industry: Automotive **Born:** February 3, 1949, Rabat, Malta **Univ./degree:** M.B.A., University of Wisconsin, 1974 **Current organization:** New Venture Gear **Title:** Director Program Management **Type of organization:** Manufacturing **Major product:** Car and truck drive trains **Area of distribution:** International **Expertise:** Sales, marketing, product engineering **Hob./spts.:** Sailing, swimming, hiking **SIC code:** 37 **Address:** New Venture Gear, 1650 Research Dr., Troy, MI 48084 **E-mail:** vincent777@aol.com

SANDGATHE, HUGH JAMES
Industry: Chemical technology **Born:** March 21, 1970, Eugene, Oregon **Univ./degree:** B.S., Electrical Engineering, University of Washington, 1993 **Current organization:** John Zink Co., LLC **Title:** Facilities Engineer **Type of organization:** Manufacturing/R&D **Major product:** Burners, flares **Area of distribution:** International **Expertise:** Electrical engineering, controls programming **Affiliations:** Past Member, I.E.E.E. **Hob./spts.:** Family, downhill skiing, cross-country skiing **SIC code:** 38 **Address:** John Zink Co., LLC, R&D Test Center, 11920 E. Apache St., Tulsa, OK 74116-1309 **E-mail:** sandgath@kochind.com

SANICKI, SCOTT DAVID
Industry: Aerospace **Born:** July 18, 1978, Falmouth, Massachusetts **Univ./degree:** B.S.M.E.; 2000; M.S.M.E., 2002, University of Hartford, Connecticut **Current organization:** Pratt & Whitney **Title:** Engineer **Type of organization:** Manufacturing/engineering **Major product:** Aircraft engines **Area of distribution:** International **Expertise:** Acoustical engineering **Affiliations:** A.S.M.E.; S.A.E. **Hob./spts.:** Scuba diving, auto restoration, classic cars **SIC code:** 37 **Address:** Pratt & Whitney, 595 Goodwin St., East Hartford, CT 06108 **E-mail:** scott.sanicki@tw.utl.com **Web address:** www.tw.utl.com

SANTERRE, ADAM D.
Industry: Pharmaceuticals **Born:** January 19, 1971, Providence, Rhode Island **Univ./degree:** B.A., Chemistry, University of California at Davis, 1993 **Current organization:** Alza Corp. **Title:** Chemist III **Type of organization:** Manufacturing **Major product:** Pharmaceuticals **Area of distribution:** International **Expertise:** Laboratory leads **Hob./spts.:** Mountain climbing, skiing, basketball, guitar **SIC code:** 28 **Address:** Alza Corp., 700 Eubanks Dr., Vacaville, CA 95688 **E-mail:** adam.santerre@alza.com

SASIC, BORIS
Industry: Industrial equipment/electronics **Born:** 1963 **Univ./degree:** B.S.E.E., University of Belgrade, 1990 **Current organization:** Curtis Instruments Inc. **Title:** Power Conversion Group Leader **Type of organization:** Manufacturing **Major product:** Battery charges **Area of distribution:** International **Expertise:** Electronics engineering, design and manufacturing of power electronic equipment **Affiliations:** I.E.E.E. **Hob./spts.:** Photography, audio electronics **SIC code:** 36 **Address:** Curtis Instruments Inc., 200 Kisco Ave, Mount Kisco, NY 10549 **E-mail:** sasicb@curtisinst.com

SATZ, JEFFREY STEVEN
Industry: Telecommunications **Born:** February 10, 1972, Jackson Heights, New York **Univ./degree:** B.S.E.E., 1995; M.S.E.E., 1996, Rensselaer Polytechnic Institute **Current organization:** Nortel Networks **Title:** R&D Manager **Type of organization:** Manufacturing/distribution **Major product:** Telecom hardware and software **Area of distribution:** International **Expertise:** Engineering management **Honors/awards:**

Listed in Who's Who in America **Affiliations:** I.E.E.E.; MENSA **Hob./spts.:** Reading, walking, racquetball **SIC code:** 36 **Address:** 4456 Big Sky Dr., Plano, TX 75024-7281 **E-mail:** satzj@metronet.com

SAUCEDO, JERRY
Industry: Food **Born:** August 11, 1956 **Current organization:** Del Monte Fresh Produce N.A. Inc. **Title:** Safety and Loss Prevention Manager **Type of organization:** Manufacturing **Major product:** Fruits and vegetables **Area of distribution:** International **Expertise:** Safety, loss prevention, security; Certification in Homeland Security III; Certification in Highway Watch Training **Affiliations:** American College of Forensic Examiners; CHS - National Emergency Response Team (CHS-NERT) **Hob./spts.:** Competitive weight lifting, football, travel, reading **SIC code:** 20 **Address:** Del Monte Fresh Produce N.A. Inc., 1400 Parker St., Dallas, TX 75215 **E-mail:** jsaucedo@freshdelmonte.com **Web address:** www.freshdelmonte.com

SAWYER, MARK R.
Industry: Concrete **Born:** April 4, 1957, Plymouth, North Carolina **Univ./degree:** B.S. Candidate, Civil Engineering, Wilson Technical College **Current organization:** Old Castle/N.C. Products **Title:** Plant Manager **Type of organization:** Manufacturing **Major product:** Precast concrete, concrete pipe **Area of distribution:** International **Expertise:** Business management, quality assurance, quality control, budgeting; Certified Materials Engineer, American Concrete Institute, 1999 **Affiliations:** A.C.P.A.; A.C.I.; Founder and Board Member, Triangle Lightning Fast Pitch Girls Softball Team **Hob./spts.:** Coaching softball for daughter's team **SIC code:** 32 **Address:** Old Castle/N.C. Products, 916 Withers Rd., Raleigh, NC 27603-6095 **E-mail:** mark.sawyer@oldcastleprecast.com **Web address:** www.oldcastleprecast.com

SAYLOR, STEPHEN D.
Industry: Automotive **Born:** January 19, 1944, Seymour, Indiana **Current organization:** Alma Products Co. **Title:** Commodity Manager, P.E. **Type of organization:** Manufacturing **Major product:** Automotive components **Area of distribution:** International **Expertise:** Engineering **Affiliations:** Society of Manufacturing Engineers; P.M. #59 F. & A.M.; O.E.S.; Scottish Rite; A.T.A.; N.S.C.A. **Hob./spts.:** Woodworking, fishing, shot gun sports **SIC code:** 37 **Address:** 6237 McNeil Rd., St. John's, MI 48879 **E-mail:** stevesaylor@almaproducts.com

SCHAEFER, JEFF C.
Industry: Tooling components **Title:** Human Resources/Safety Coordinator **Type of organization:** Manufacturing **Major product:** Workholding components **Expertise:** Human resources, safety **SIC code:** 34 **Address:** TE-CO, 109 Quinter Farm Rd., Union, OH 45322 **E-mail:** hr@te-co.com

SCHAEFER, ROBERT F.
Industry: Government/healthcare **Born:** July 5, 1926, Glen Carbon, Illinois **Univ./degree:** M.D., St. Louis University School of Medicine, 1948 **Current organization:** Central Arkansas Veterans Health Care Centers **Title:** M.D./U.S. Army Captain, 109th Field Hospital, 1953-55 **Type of organization:** Government/Veterans Affairs hospital **Major product:** Patient care, education **Area of distribution:** Arkansas **Expertise:** Anatomic pathology **Honors/awards:** Best Physician in Arkansas, 2002; Best Physician in U.S.A., 1999; Queen Elizabeth Recognition of Services for Treatment of British Soldiers, 1953 **Affiliations:** Southern Medical Society **Hob./spts.:** Airplane piloting, fishing **SIC code:** 38 **Address:** Leawood Manor, 1524 Mountain Dr., Little Rock, AR 72227-5801 **E-mail:** schaefer.robert@little-rock.va.gov

SCHAIBLE, DEXTER E.
Industry: Agriculture, farm equipment **Born:** June 5, 1949, Quinter, Kansas **Univ./degree:** B.S., Agriculture, Kansas State University, 1971 **Current organization:** AGCO Corp. **Title:** Vice President of Engineering and Product Development **Type of organization:** Manufacturing **Major product:** Tractors, combines and hay equipment **Area of distribution:** International **Expertise:** Marketing, product development **Affiliations:** Agriculture Society of America **Hob./spts.:** Boating, waterskiing **SIC code:** 35 **Address:** AGCO Corp., 4205 River Green Pkwy., Duluth, GA 30096 **E-mail:** dexter.schaible@agcocorp.com **Web address:** www.agrocorp.com

SCHEFFLER, DANIEL AARON
Industry: Automotive **Born:** July 15, 1966, St. Joseph, Michigan **Univ./degree:** B.S.M.E., Western Michigan University, 1996 **Current organization:** Ford Motor Co. **Title:** Launch Engineer **Type of organization:** Manufacturing **Major product:** Automobiles **Area of distribution:** International **Expertise:** Manufacturing and process engineering **Affiliations:** A.S.M.E.; S.A.E.; USAF Reserves (3 years service) **Hob./spts.:** Time with E.A.A. and A.O.P.A. **SIC code:** 37 **Address:** 14617 Horger Ave., Allen Park, MI 48101 **E-mail:** dscheff1@ford.com **Web address:** www.dscheffler1@comcast.net

SCHELLER, MICHAEL J.
Industry: Food **Born:** April 26, 1966, Selma, Alabama **Univ./degree:** B.S., Chemistry, Institute of Technology, University of Minnesota, 2000; M.S. Candidate, Food Science, University of Minnesota **Current organization:** Land O'Lakes, Inc. **Title:** R&D Technologist **Type of organization:** Manufacturing **Major product:** Dairy food **Area of distribution:** International **Expertise:** Research and development, new products **Affiliations:** A.I.C.H.E.; American Chemical Society **Hob./spts.:** Musician, avid golfer **SIC code:** 20 **Address:** Land O'Lakes, Inc., 64101, Mail Stop 0050, St. Paul, MN 55164-0101 **E-mail:** mjscheller@landolakes.com

SCHERLIZIN, GEORGES
Industry: Labels **Born:** August 22, 1949, Belgium **Univ./degree:** B.S.M.E., E.C.A.M., Belgium, 1972 **Current organization:** Impressive Labels Inc. **Title:** President/COO **Type of organization:** Manufacturing **Major product:** Labels **Area of distribution:** International **Expertise:** Engineering **Hob./spts.:** Grandchildren **SIC code:** 26 **Address:** Impressive Labels Inc., 300 E. Fourth St., Safford, AZ 85546 **E-mail:** gscherlizin@cs.com

SCHERMER, TORSTEN A.
Industry: Adhesives **Born:** June 28, 1956, Hamburg, Germany **Univ./degree:** M.B.A., University of Hamburg, 1985 **Current organization:** tesa tape inc. **Title:** President/CEO **Type of organization:** Manufacturing **Major product:** Adhesive tapes **Area of distribution:** International **Expertise:** Management, operations, marketing, sales **Published works:** Has been featured in many articles **Affiliations:** Board Member, Pressure Sensitive Tape Council; Board of Directors of International Business Studies; Board Member, Advisors on Charlotte Chamber of Commerce **Hob./spts.:** Travel, politics, music, sports **SIC code:** 39 **Address:** tesa tape inc., 5825 Carnegie Blvd.,, Charlotte, NC 28209-4633 **E-mail:** tschermer@tesatape.com **Web address:** www.tesatape.com

SCHERMERHORN, JERRY D.
Industry: Electronic subsystems **Born:** January 23, 1944, Coffey County, Kansas **Univ./degree:** B.S., Physics, 1967; M.S., Physics, 1969, University of Illinois at Urbana-Champaign **Current organization:** Electro Plasma Inc. **Title:** Vice President/Technical Director **Type of organization:** Manufacturing **Major product:** Design/manufacturing electronic subsystems/plasma displays and human interface **Area of distribution:** International **Expertise:** Engineering management, new product interfacing development **Published works:** Numerous publications and patents in plasma displays **Affiliations:** I.E.E.E.; Society for Information Display **Hob./spts.:** Fencing, bicycling **SIC code:** 36 **Address:** Electro Plasma Inc., 4400 Martin-Moline Rd., Millbury, OH 43447 **E-mail:** perrycream@aol.com **Web address:** www.epiglobal.com

SCHILD, MICHAEL W.
Industry: Industrial operating service **Born:** June 3, 1977, Pittsburgh, Pennsylvania **Univ./degree:** B.S., Chemical Engineering, Penn State University, 2000 **Current organization:** US Filter/Process Solutions **Title:** Technical Process Engineer **Type of organization:** Design, manufacturing, operation of industrial equipment **Major product:** Petroleum/petrochemical waste oil treatment **Area of distribution:** National **Expertise:** Technical and developmental engineering **Published works:** 1 patent pending **Affiliations:** A.I.C.H.E.; Past Member, A.C.S. **Hob./spts.:** Martial arts, fishing, home remodeling, golf **SIC code:** 29 **Address:** US Filter/Process Solutions, 87 Oates Rd., Bldg. 1, Houston, TX 77013 **E-mail:** schildmw@usfilter.com **Web address:** www.usfilter.com

SCHLIEF, GERALD W.
Industry: Fuel **Born:** Houston, Texas **Univ./degree:** M.B.A., Finance, University of Utah, 1974 **Current organization:** ATP Oil & Gas Corp. **Title:** Senior Vice President **Type of organization:** Manufacturing **Major product:** Oil and gas **Area of distribution:** International **Expertise:** Senior Management, oil development **Affiliations:** American Institute of Certified Public Accountants **Hob./spts.:** Tennis, hunting, skiing **SIC code:** 29 **Address:** ATP Oil & Gas Corp., 4600 Post Oak Place, Suite 200, Houston, TX 77027 **E-mail:** jschlief@atpog.com **Web address:** www.atpog.com

SCHMIDT, JUNE A.
Industry: Consumer products **Born:** September 2, 1963, Parkston, South Dakota **Univ./degree:** Certified in Administration, Mitchell Vocational School **Current organization:** The Dial Corp. **Title:** National Account Manager-Lodging **Type of organization:** Manufacturing **Major product:** Personal care products, laundry care and home care **Area of distribution:** National **Expertise:** Sales/marketing **Affiliations:** Membership Committee, Dial Professional Women's Forum **Hob./spts.:** English Mastiff breed of dogs **SIC code:** 39 **Address:** The Dial Corp., 15501 N. Dial Blvd., Suite 1410, Scottsdale, AZ 85260 **E-mail:** schmidtj@dialcorp.com

SCOTT, JEFFREY B.
Industry: Aerospace **Current organization:** Turbine Maintenance Services, Inc. **Title:** Jet Engine Mechanic **Type of organization:** Maintenance, repair **Major product:** Turbojet engines **Area of distribution:** Miami, Florida **Expertise:** Mechanics **SIC code:** 37 **Address:** Turbine Maintenance Services, Inc., 8049 NW 66th St., Miami, FL 33166-2729

SEKHON, SHARNJIT K.
Industry: Computers and chassis related products **Born:** April 4, 1972, India **Univ./degree:** B.S., Industrial Engineering Technology, San Jose University **Current organization:** Elma Bustronics Corp. **Title:** Quality Assurance Manager **Type of organization:** OEM/design/manufacturing **Major product:** Computers and chassis related products **Area of distribution:** International **Expertise:** Industrial/manufacturing engineering **Affiliations:** Q.M.I. **Hob./spts.:** Painting, reading **SIC code:** 36 **Address:** Elma Bustronic Corp., P.O. Box 14511, Fremont, CA 94539 **E-mail:** ssekhon@bustronic.com **Web address:** www.bustronic.com

SELA, DEBORAH M.
Industry: Consumer products **Born:** May 29, 1979, Passaic, New Jersey **Univ./degree:** B.S., Mechanical Engineering, University of Maryland, 2001 **Current organization:** Unilever **Title:** Supply Chain Associate **Type of organization:** Manufacturing **Major product:** Home and personal care consumer products **Area of distribution:** International **Expertise:** Plant engineering/plant planning **Affiliations:** A.S.M.E. **SIC code:** 39 **Address:** 122 Aspen Glen Dr., Hamden, CT 06518 **E-mail:** deborahsela@yahoo.com

SENN, TAZE L.
Industry: Agriculture, formulators **Born:** October 16, 1917, Newberry, South Carolina **Univ./degree:** Ph.D., Biochemistry, University of Maryland, 1956 **Current organization:** Senn, Senn & Senn, LLC **Title:** President **Type of organization:** Manufacturing **Major product:** Plant growth stimulants, natural organics **Area of distribution:** National **Expertise:** Biophysiology, biochemistry, consulting **Honors/awards:** Numerous awards including, National Outstanding Horticultural Teaching Award, 1968; Spencer Award for Outstanding Achievement in Agriculture, 1979; Clemson University Centennial Professor Award, 1989; Listed in Who's Who in the South and Southwest, Who's Who in American Education **Affiliations:** Garden Club of South Carolina; Garden Club of America; American Society for Testing Materials; American Men of Science **Hob./spts.:** Football **SIC code:** 28 **Address:** Senn, Senn & Senn, LLC, 201 Strawberry Lane, Clemson, SC 29631 **Phone:** (864)654-8020 **Fax:** (864)654-5322 **E-mail:** tsenn@mindspring.com

SGAMBATI, BILL
Industry: Consumer electronics and music **Born:** New Jersey **Univ./degree:** A.A.S., Orange County Community College, 1976; B.A., Computer Science, Ramapo College, 1978 **Current organization:** Sony Electronics, Inc. **Title:** Systems Engineering Manager **Type of organization:** Manufacturing **Major product:** Electronics **Area of distribution:** International **Expertise:** Audio/video systems engineering **Hob./spts.:** Music recording, drums, band member of The Remnants **SIC code:** 36 **Address:** Sony Electronics, Inc., 1 Sony Dr., MD 1D2, Park Ridge, NJ 07656 **E-mail:** bill.sgambati@am.sony.com **Web address:** www.sony.com

SHAH, JAVEED I.
Industry: G.E. Energy **Born:** November 14, 1960, Hyderabad, India **Univ./degree:** B.E., Electronic Engineering. N.E.D. University of Engineering & Technology, Pakistan, 1982; M.S., Controls Engineering, King Fahd University of Petroleum & Minerals, Saudi Arabia, 1993 **Current organization:** General Electric/Performance Evaluation Services **Title:** Lead Instrument Specialist **Type of organization:** Manufacturing **Major product:** Gas/steam/turbine generators **Area of distribution:** International **Expertise:** Controls, instrumentation engineering **Published works:** 1 publication **Affiliations:** Pakistan Engineering Council **Hob./spts.:** Web surfing, travel **SIC code:** 36 **Address:** General Electric/Performance Evaluation Services, Bldg. 1 Bay 10, 100 Rotterdam Industrial Park, Rotterdam, NY 12306 **E-mail:** shah.javeed@ps.ge.com

SHAIN, RICHARD
Industry: Plating **Born:** March 3, 1958, Wichita, Kansas **Univ./degree:** B.S., Business, Friends University, 2000 **Current organization:** Kansas Plating, Inc. **Title:** Quality Assurance Manager **Type of organization:** Special processing service company **Major product:** Special processing for the aerospace industry **Area of distribution:** National, International **Expertise:** Quality assurance, operations oversight, auditing **Hob./spts.:** Son's sporting events **SIC code:** 33 **Address:** Kansas Plating, Inc., 1110 N. Mosley, Wichita, KS 67214-3043 **E-mail:** rlshain2004@yahoo.com **Web address:** www.kansasplating.com

SHAPIRO, ALAN M.
Industry: Printing **Born:** August 1, 1949, Minneapolis, Minnesota **Univ./degree:** B.S.; J.D., University of Minnesota, 1977 **Current organization:** Shapco Printing Inc. **Title:** President, Esquire **Type of organization:** Manufacturing **Major product:** Highest quality and technology printing, high-end color printing **Area of distribution:** National **Expertise:** Marketing **Honors/awards:** Inc. Magazine, 1999 ranked 87 in the Top 100 Fastest Growing Inner City Companies in the Nation **Published works:** 22 articles **Affiliations:** J.A.T.F. **Hob./spts.:** Physical fitness, running **SIC code:** 27 **Address:** Shapco Printing Inc., 524 N. Fifth St., Minneapolis, MN 55401 **E-mail:** ashapiro@shapco.com **Web address:** www.shapco.com

SHARP, DEAN
Industry: Chemicals **Born:** July 18, 1969 **Univ./degree:** Certificate Program, US Navy Nuclear Power School **Current organization:** Sensient Technologies **Title:** Director of Architecture **Type of organization:** Manufacturing **Major product:** Flavors, colors and scents **Area of distribution:** International **Expertise:** Public speaking, consulting, security of network infrastructure, data, telecommunications, budget writing and investments **Affiliations:** CISCO; Kentucky Colonel for the Loyal Order of Kentucky Colonels **Hob./spts.:** Writing **SIC code:** 28 **Address:** Sensient Technologies, 777 E. Wisconsin Ave., Suite 1100, Milwaukee, WI 53202 **E-mail:** dean.sharp@sensient-tech.com

SHAW, JOE
Industry: Machinery **Born:** June 6, 1966, Burkesville, Kentucky **Current organization:** Precision Machine & Tool, Inc. **Title:** President **Type of organization:** Manufacturing **Major product:** Tool and die, custom parts and machinery **Area of distribution:** National **Expertise:** Custom fabrication, tool and die **Hob./spts.:** Golf, coaching baseball **SIC code:** 35 **Address:** Precision Machine & Tool, Inc., 7560 Edmonton Rd., Glasgow, KY 42141 **E-mail:** precision@scrtc.com

SHENG, ROBERT S.
Industry: Industrial laboratory **Univ./degree:** B.S., Mechanical Engineering, National Taiwan University, 1969; B.S., Electrical Engineering, 1970; M.S., Electrical Engineering, 1972, University of Florida; M.B.A., Temple University, 1985 **Current organization:** Microtrac Inc. **Title:** President **Type of organization:** Manufacturing **Major product:** Analyzer products **Area of distribution:** International **Expertise:** Finance, marketing, engineering, corporate management **Published works:** Journal articles **Affiliations:** Forbe's Magazine, CEO Club **SIC code:** 38 **Address:** Microtrac Inc., 148 Keystone Dr., Montgomeryville, PA 18936 **E-mail:** bob_s@microtrac.com

SHIELDS, DANNY L.
Industry: Textiles **Born:** November 4, 1962, Greensboro, North Carolina **Univ./degree:** B.S., Textile Science, North Carolina State University, 1987 **Current organization:** Inman Mills **Title:** Process Engineer **Type of organization:** Manufacturing **Major product:** MJS Yarn, fabric **Area of distribution:** Inman, South Carolina **Expertise:** Process engineering **Affiliations:** A Squared/T Squared **Hob./spts.:** Hunting, fishing **SIC code:** 22 **Address:** Inman Mills, 1 First St., Inman, SC 29349 **E-mail:** hunterdaddy1@aol.com

SHIELDS, RONALD V.
Industry: Automotive **Born:** November 9, 1958, Toledo, Ohio **Univ./degree:** Certificate, Tool & Die Apprenticeship, Owens Community College, 1980 **Current organization:** Toledo Tool & Die Co. **Title:** Engineering Manager **Type of organization:** Manufacturing **Major product:** Metal stamping and assemblies **Area of distribution:** International **Expertise:** Engineering- design and build automotive stamping dies, welding, design fixture and process **Affiliations:** Society of Manufacturing Engineers; Precision Metal Forming Association **Hob./spts.:** Hunting, fishing **SIC code:** 33 **Address:** 266 State Rt. 300, Gibsonburg, OH 43612 **E-mail:** shields@toledotool.com **Web address:** www.ttd.cc

SHINN, HARRY L.
Industry: Furniture **Current organization:** Carolina Foam, LLC **Title:** Plant Manager **Type of organization:** Manufacturing **Major product:** Furniture **Area of distribution:** National **Expertise:** Daily operations management **Affiliations:** Catawba County Chamber of Commerce **Hob./spts.:** Golf, auto racing **SIC code:** 25 **Address:** Carolina Foam, LLC, P.O. Box 131, Maiden, NC 28650

SHUMAN, BRIAN
Industry: Electronics **Univ./degree:** B.S.E.E., Purdue University, 1994 **Current organization:** Belden Electronics Division **Title:** RCDD **Type of organization:** Manufacturing **Major product:** Product design and development of electronic wire and cable **Area of distribution:** National **Expertise:** Engineering, making presentations at trade shows **Published works:** Presentations **Affiliations:** I.E.E.E.; B.I.C.S.I. **Hob./spts.:** Martial arts, fishing, playing guitar, woodworking **SIC code:** 36 **Address:** 1011 S. Mineral Springs Rd., Centerville, IN 47330

SIEGEL, HOWARD M.
Industry: Healthcare communications equipment **Born:** Bronx, New York **Univ./degree:** B.A., New York University, 1955 **Current organization:** American Medical Alert Corp. **Title:** CEO/COB **Type of organization:** Manufacturing **Major product:** Emergency response systems **Area of distribution:** National **Expertise:** Marketing **Hob./spts.:** Tennis, golf **SIC code:** 38 **Address:** American Medical Alert Corp., 3265 Lawson Blvd., Oceanside, NY 11572 **E-mail:** howard.siegal@amac.com **Web address:** www.amac.com

SIERRA, CAROLINA G.
Industry: Pharmaceuticals **Born:** October 2, 1956, Cuba **Univ./degree:** M.D., Universidad Central del Este, Dominican Republic, 1983 **Current organization:** Glaxo Smith

Kline **Title:** M.D./Vice President of Medical Affairs and Healthcare Management **Type of organization:** Manufacturing/research and development **Major product:** Medications **Area of distribution:** International **Expertise:** Internal medicine, endocrinology **Published works:** 2 papers **Affiliations:** A.A.C.E.; A.A.P.S. **Hob./spts.:** Family, baseball **SIC code:** 28 **Address:** Glaxo Smith Kline, 1600 Vine St., MC 3F 0605, Philadelphia, PA 19102 **E-mail:** carolina.2.sierra@gsk.com

SILVER, ALAN H.
Industry: Telecommunications **Born:** January 23, 1958, Chicago, Illinois **Univ./degree:** A.S., University of Florida **Current organization:** PC Designs International, Inc. **Title:** President **Type of organization:** Design/manufacturing **Major product:** Electronics **Area of distribution:** International **Expertise:** Intellectual property **Honors/awards:** United States Patent **Published works:** Articles **Affiliations:** I.S.S.F.; L.E.S. **Hob./spts.:** Computers, movies, music **SIC code:** 36 **Address:** PC Designs International, Inc., 6075 N.W. 41st Dr., Coral Springs, FL 33067 **E-mail:** alsilco@aol.com

SILVERS JR., THERMAN CLARK
Industry: Foundry, brass **Born:** July 20, 1960, Poughkeepsie, New York **Univ./degree:** Mechanical Engineering courses , Isothermal College **Current organization:** Watts Regulator Inc. **Title:** Millwright **Type of organization:** Manufacturing **Major product:** Pressure valves **Area of distribution:** National **Expertise:** Supervision **Honors/awards:** Awarded a Metal from the National Science Foundation, 2000-2001 **Hob./spts.:** Playing guitar, singing, music **SIC code:** 34 **Address:** 113 Princess Dr., Forest City, NC 28043

SIMON, KEITH R.
Industry: Oil **Univ./degree:** B.S.N., 1977; B.S., Pre-Medicine, 1980, University of Louisiana **Current organization:** Sigma Coatings USA/Total **Title:** Int. Offshore Manager **Type of organization:** Manufacturing **Major product:** Protective coatings **Area of distribution:** International **Expertise:** Management, engineering **Published works:** 2 Trade Magazine article on the oil industry - World Oil & Offshore Magazines **Affiliations:** S.S.P.C.; N.A.C.E.; I.A.D.C. **Hob./spts.:** Snow skiing, hunting, football **SIC code:** 28 **Address:** 104 Pomerol Place, Lafayette, LA 70503-6527 **E-mail:** keith.simon@sigmacoatingsusa.com

SIMS, ROBERT K.
Industry: Machinery **Univ./degree:** B.S.M.E., Purdue University, 1998 **Current organization:** Engineered Machined Products, Inc. **Title:** Quality Assurance Manager **Type of organization:** Manufacturing **Major product:** Diesel engine sub-assembly components **Area of distribution:** National **Expertise:** Quality assurance **Affiliations:** President, Homeowners Association; Chemical Coaters Association; Kappa Alpha Psi **Hob./spts.:** Jogging, physical fitness **SIC code:** 35 **Address:** Engineered Machined Products, Inc., 5750 Kopetsky Dr., Suite A, Indianapolis, IN 46217 **E-mail:** bob.sims@emp-corp.com

SINGH, BARINDER P.
Industry: Power electronics **Born:** May 10, 1976, Chandigarh, India **Univ./degree:** Engineering Degree, Punjab Technical University; Rochester Institute of Technology **Current organization:** MKS Instruments-ENI Products Division **Title:** Mechanical Engineer **Type of organization:** Manufacturing, distributing **Major product:** RF & DC generators **Area of distribution:** International **Expertise:** Thermal engineering **Hob./spts.:** Golf, racquetball, music **SIC code:** 36 **Address:** MKS Instruments-ENI Products Division, 100 High Power Rd., Rochester, NY 14623 **E-mail:** barindersingh@mksinst.com **Web address:** www.mksinst.com

SINGH, JAGDAT
Industry: Metals **Born:** April 23, 1957, British Guyana, South America **Univ./degree:** M.E., The City and Guilds of London Institute, England, 1974 **Current organization:** J&F Manufacturing, Inc. **Title:** President/CEO **Type of organization:** Manufacturing **Major product:** Metal fabrication for department store display fixtures **Area of distribution:** National **Expertise:** Engineering **Honors/awards:** Manufacturer of the Year, United States Department of Commerce, 2004; 2 U.S. Patents **Hob./spts.:** Auto racing **SIC code:** 34 **Address:** J&F Manufacturing, Inc., 104-46 Dunkirk St., Jamaica, NY 11412 **E-mail:** jsingh@jfmfg.com

SISCO, DAVID R.
Industry: Hydraulic motors **Born:** Arkansas **Univ./degree:** A.A., Humanities/Social Sciences, Santa Monica College **Current organization:** Eaton Corp. **Title:** Facilities Manager **Type of organization:** Manufacturing **Major product:** Hydraulic motors **Area of distribution:** Oklahoma **Expertise:** Engineering **Hob./spts.:** RV'ing, camping **SIC code:** 35 **Address:** Eaton Corp., 8701 N. Harrison Ave., Shawnee, OK 74804 **E-mail:** daversisco@eaton.com

SKALKOS, GUS A.
Industry: Industrial products **Born:** September 14, 1952, Hamilton, Ohio **Univ./degree:** B.A., Political Science and International Business, Ohio State University; B.S., 1980 **Current organization:** Graftech International Ltd. **Title:** International Marketing Manager **Type of organization:** Manufacturing **Major product:** Fuel cell products, electronic thermal management **Area of distribution:** International **Expertise:** Marketing **Hob./spts.:** Sailboat racing **SIC code:** 34 **Address:** Graftech International Ltd., 11709 Madison Ave., Lakewood, OH 44107 **E-mail:** gus.skalkos@graftech.com

SLAUGHTER, KENNETH F.
Industry: Nutritional supplements **Born:** September 17, 1952, Philadelphia, Pennsylvania **Current organization:** Natural Alternatives International **Title:** Corporate Buyer **Type of organization:** Manufacturing **Major product:** Nutritional supplements **Area of distribution:** International **Expertise:** Packaging buyer, raw materials buyers, repetitive buyer, international shipments and purchase capital equipment **Hob./spts.:** Bass guitar **SIC code:** 28 **Address:** Natural Alternatives International, 1185 Linda Vista Dr., San Marcos, CA 92078 **E-mail:** kslaughter@nai-online.com

SLEIMAN, SAMIR
Industry: Electronics **Born:** September 5, 1956, Beirut, Lebanon **Univ./degree:** M.S., Engineering, Tulsa, Oklahoma, 1984 **Current organization:** Applied Materials Inc. **Title:** Sr. Engineering Manager **Type of organization:** Manufacturing **Major product:** Semiconductor equipment **Area of distribution:** International **Expertise:** Product safety engineering, hazardous energy analysis **Affiliations:** A.S.S.E.; A.I.C.E. **SIC code:** 36 **Address:** Applied Materials Inc., 974 E. Arques Ave., M/S 81204, Sunnyvale, CA 94086 **E-mail:** samir_sleiman@amat.com

SMITH, BARRY P.
Industry: Petroleum **Born:** October 19, 1955, Louisville, Kentucky **Univ./degree:** B.S., Mechanical Engineering, Ohio Northern University, 1977 **Current organization:** Marathon Ashland Petroleum LLC **Title:** Planning Supervisor **Type of organization:** Refiner **Major product:** Unleaded gasoline **Area of distribution:** Midwest United States **Expertise:** Maintenance **Affiliations:** American Society of Mechanical Engineers; National Society of Petroleum Engineers; American Welding Society **Hob./spts.:** Family, carpentry, golf, coaching youth sports **SIC code:** 29 **Address:** Marathon Ashland Petroleum LLC, 1307 S. Loop 197, Texas City, TX 77592 **E-mail:** bpsmith@mapllc.com

SMITH, DEL
Industry: Chemicals **Univ./degree:** M.B.A., Case Western University **Current organization:** E.C. Morris Corp. **Title:** Plant Engineer/Manager of E.C.I.S. **Type of organization:** Manufacturing **Major product:** Rubber and chemicals processing **Area of distribution:** National **Expertise:** Engineering, plant design and computer systems **Published works:** Articles **Hob./spts.:** Church activities **SIC code:** 28 **Address:** E.C. Morris Corp., 201 Quadral Dr., Wadsworth, OH 44281 **E-mail:** del@ecmorris.com

SMITH, JAMES W.
Industry: Packaging **Born:** October 9, 1940, Yakima, Washington **Current organization:** Shields Bag & Printing Co. **Title:** Technical Services Manager **Type of organization:** Manufacturing **Major product:** Flexible packaging **Area of distribution:** National **Expertise:** R&D, production **Affiliations:** S.P.E.; S.M.E. **Hob./spts.:** Golf, woodworking **SIC code:** 26 **Address:** Shields Bag & Printing Co., 1009 Rock Ave., Yakima, WA 98902 **E-mail:** jwsmith@shieldsbag.com

SMITH, JOSEPH D.
Industry: Chemicals/hydrocarbon equipment **Born:** January 30, 1957, Salt Lake City, Utah **Univ./degree:** Ph.D., Chemical Engineering, Brigham Young University, 1990 **Current organization:** John Zink Co., LLC **Title:** Director **Type of organization:** Manufacturing, R&D **Major product:** Chemicals, hydrocarbon equipment **Area of distribution:** National **Expertise:** Computational fluid dynamics **Published works:** Multiple articles **Affiliations:** A.I.C.E. **Hob./spts.:** Basketball, golf **SIC code:** 28 **Address:** John Zink Co., LLC, 7130 No. 194th East Ave., Awasso, OK 74055 **E-mail:** smith3j@kochind.com

SMITH, MARK W.
Industry: Electronics **Born:** May 5, 1957, Bristol, Tennessee **Univ./degree:** B.S., Physics, King College **Current organization:** Microporous Products L.P. **Title:** Electronics Engineer **Type of organization:** Polymer - manufacturing **Major product:** Battery separators **Area of distribution:** International **Expertise:** Programming, troubleshooting **Hob./spts.:** Amateur radio **SIC code:** 34 **Address:** Microporous Products L.P., 596 Industrial Park Rd., Piney Flats, TN 37686 **E-mail:** msmith@mplp.com

SMITH, PAUL C.
Industry: Aerospace **Born:** July 3, 1956, Brookfield, Connecticut **Univ./degree:** B.A., National University, San Diego, 1989 **Current organization:** EMF Corp. **Title:** President **Type of organization:** Manufacturing **Major product:** Nickel tooling and nickel abrasion strips **Area of distribution:** International **Expertise:** Engineering **Affiliations:** National Association of Manufacturers **Hob./spts.:** Tennis, golf, skiing

SIC code: 33 **Address:** EMF Corp., 3025 Janitell Rd., Colorado Springs, CO 80906 **E-mail:** psmithemfcorp@att.net

SMITH, PHILIP L.
Industry: Consumer products **Born:** December 23, 1956, Milen, Indiana **Univ./degree:** B.S., Microbiology, Purdue University, 1980 **Current organization:** Procter and Gamble Co. **Title:** Senior Scientist **Type of organization:** Manufacturing **Major product:** Personal care products, cleaning, food and beverage **Area of distribution:** International **Expertise:** Competitive and technical intelligence **Published works:** 30 abstracts **Affiliations:** Vice President, Ohio and Kentucky Radio Society **Hob./spts.:** Amateur radio **SIC code:** 28 **Address:** Procter and Gamble Co., 6300 Center Hill Ave., Suite E-110, Cincinnati, OH 45224 **E-mail:** smith.pl.3@pg.com **Web address:** www.pg.com

SMITH, WILLIAM "BILL"
Industry: Electronics/High Voltage **Born:** January, 3, 1938, Jersey City, New Jersey **Current organization:** Glassman High Voltage **Title:** Facilities Manager **Type of organization:** Manufacturing and assembly **Major product:** Power supply and assembly **Area of distribution:** International **Expertise:** Engineering, production, building and tooling; maintenance; construction and design; Trained in structural engineering, Bethlehem Steel Corporation **Honors/awards:** Builder of The Year for Middlesex County, New Jersey Builders' Association, 1984-1985, **Published works:** 3 home designs published in magazines **Affiliations:** Glassman-Fire Marshall; Knights of Columbus (Past Grand Knight) **Hob./spts.:** Baseball and travel **SIC code:** 36 **Address:** Glassman High Voltage, 124 W. Main St., P.O. Box 317, High Bridge, NJ 08829 **E-mail:** bill.smith@glassmanhv.com **Web address:** www.glassmanhv.com

SMITH, WILLIAM EDWARD
Industry: Aerospace **Univ./degree:** M.D., University of Kansas School of Medicine, 1988 **Current organization:** The Boeing Co. **Title:** Regional Health Services Manager **Type of organization:** Manufacturing **Major product:** Aerospace **Area of distribution:** International **Expertise:** Health and productivity, health services, management **Affiliations:** A.C.O.E.M.; American College of Physicians **SIC code:** 37 **Address:** 440 Shannaron Lane, Camano Island, WA 98282-7644 **E-mail:** william.e.smith@boeing.com

SNAPP, JOHN K.
Industry: Computerized components **Born:** June 12, 1956 **Univ./degree:** Ph.D., Computer Science, Ashford University, London, 2002 **Current organization:** Minolta Corp. **Title:** General Manager, Solutions Development **Type of organization:** Manufacturing, distributing **Major product:** Business office products and software **Area of distribution:** North America **Expertise:** Computer science and engineering with emphasis in Document Management **Affiliations:** A.C.M.; I.E.E.E.; A.F.S.M.I.; A.F.C.E.A.; I.A.W.M.D. **Hob./spts.:** Skiing, motorcycling **SIC code:** 36 **Address:** Minolta Corp., 100 Williams Dr., Ramsey, NJ 07446 **E-mail:** jsnapp@minolta.com

SOARES, LUIS C.G.
Industry: Automotive **Born:** December 8, 1966, Niteroi, Brazil **Current organization:** Casco Products Corp. **Title:** Logistics Manager **Type of organization:** Electronics supplier **Major product:** Power outlets, lighters, sensors **Area of distribution:** International **Expertise:** Logistics, lean manufacturing and Toyota production systems **Published works:** 1 article **Affiliations:** Professional Society of Business Administrators in Brazil **Hob./spts.:** Teaching in Brazil, Formula One, bike riding, walking, horseback riding **SIC code:** 37 **Address:** Casco Products Corp., 1098 Martin Luther King Jr. Dr., Marks, MI 38646 **E-mail:** luis.soares@cascoproducts.com

SOGHOMONIAN, ZAREH S.
Industry: Electric propulsion systems **Born:** June 21, 1967, Great Britain **Univ./degree:** Ph.D., University of Wales College Cardiff, U.K., 1996 **Current organization:** Wavecrest Labs LLC **Title:** Principal Electromagnetic Engineer **Type of organization:** Research & development/production **Major product:** Electric motors, electric propulsion systems, H.V. E.V. **Area of distribution:** National/International **Expertise:** Engineering, research & development, magnetics, electromagnetics, sensors magnetic materials, magnetic testing, magnetic systems **Honors/awards:** Recipient of a Century award and medal from Barons of Who's Who (USA), as part of the global 500 leaders of the last century in Science and Engineering **Published works:** Soft Magnetic Materials Conference/15 patents **Affiliations:** Senior Member, I.E.E.E., Washington DC Chapter; Industrial Electronics Conference / IECON 2006; I.E.E.E. Vehicle Power and Propulsion (VPP) Conference/2006; I.E.E.E. The Applied Power Electronics Conference/2007; Advisory Board Member, Illinois Institute of Technology; Who's Who in the World (USA), 1998, 1999, 2000, 2001, 2003, 2005, 2006; Who's Who in the World (USA) in Science and Engineering, 2000-01, 2005-06; Acceptance and Inclusion in the International Who's Who of Professionals, USA **Hob./spts.:** Cycling, jazz, Armenian history and culture, Armenian literature **SIC code:** 36 **Address:** Wavecrest Labs LLC, 45600 Terminal Dr., Sterling, VA 20166 **Phone:** (703)435-7102 **Fax:** (703)435-7103 **E-mail:** zareh.soghomonian@wavecrestlabs.com

SOMMERFELD, HOWARD R.
Industry: Railroad transportation **Univ./degree:** A.A.S., Electronics, DeVry College, 1967 **Current organization:** Cardwell Westinghouse **Title:** Manager of R&D Laboratory **Type of organization:** Manufacturing **Major product:** Draft gears, handbrakes, slack adjusters **Area of distribution:** International **Expertise:** R&D, new product development **Published works:** 10 patents and 15 pending; 2 articles **Affiliations:** Founder, It's Not Rocket Science, Ltd.; Chairman, Consumer Protection Commission of Oak Forest; Chairman, Draft Gear Manufacturer's Equipment Committee **SIC code:** 37 **Address:** Cardwell Westinghouse, 8400 S. Stewart Ave., Chicago, IL 60620 **E-mail:** hsommerfeld@inrsltd.com **Web address:** www.wabtec.com

SONDERMAN, THOMAS J.
Industry: Semiconductors, microprocessors **Born:** April 21, 1963, St. Louis, Missouri **Univ./degree:** B.S., Chemical Engineering, University of Missouri at Ralla, 1986; M.S.E.E., National Technological University, 1991 **Current organization:** Advanced Micro Devices **Title:** Director of Technology **Type of organization:** Manufacturing **Major product:** Semiconductors, microprocessors **Area of distribution:** International **Expertise:** Water fabrication technology, process control engineering **Published works:** 5 articles, 2 patents, 5 abstracts **Affiliations:** I.E.E.E.; A.I.C.E.; A.I.C.H.E. **Hob./spts.:** Golf, travel, coin collecting **SIC code:** 36 **Address:** Advanced Micro Devices, 5204 E. Ben White Blvd., Austin, TX 78741 **E-mail:** thomas.sonderman@amd.com **Web address:** www.amd.com

SOOD, SHASHI B.
Industry: Cooking ranges & barbeques **Born:** August 6, 1948, India **Univ./degree:** B.S.M.E.,Regional Engineering College, Cashmir, India, 1969 **Current organization:** Dynamic Cooking Systems, Inc. **Title:** Vice President of Manufacturing **Type of organization:** Manufacturing **Major product:** Cooking ranges and barbeques **Area of distribution:** International **Expertise:** Manufacturing **Affiliations:** American Society of Quality Control Engineers; American Society of Manufacturing Engineers **Hob./spts.:** Tennis, mountain biking **SIC code:** 34 **Address:** Dynamic Cooking Systems, Inc., 15951 Silvertip Lane, Fountain Valley, CA 92708 **E-mail:** shashisood@hotmail.com

SOTO, ALEXANDRA
Industry: Pharmaceuticals **Born:** Caguas, Puerto Rico **Univ./degree:** B.S., Chemistry, University of Puerto Rico **Current organization:** Bristol Myers-Squibb **Title:** Quality Control Laboratory Analyst **Type of organization:** Manufacturing **Major product:** Pharmaceuticals **Area of distribution:** Puerto Rico **Expertise:** Product Analysis; Quality Control; Compliance **Affiliations:** Puerto Rico Chemical Society **Hob./spts.:** Photography **SIC code:** 28 **Address:** Bristol Myers-Squibb, KM 77.5, Humacao, PR 00792 **E-mail:** alexandrasoto@aol.com

SOUTHEARD, RICHARD T.
Industry: Building products **Born:** July 23, 1962, Scottsboro, Alabama **Current organization:** Louisiana Pacific Corp. **Title:** Plant Manager **Type of organization:** Manufacturing **Major product:** Structural panels - OSB **Area of distribution:** National **Expertise:** Business management **Hob./spts.:** Golf, fishing, hunting **SIC code:** 24 **Address:** Louisiana Pacific Corp., 902 Main Ave. S.E., Hanceville, AL 35077 **E-mail:** richard.southeard.jr@lpcorp.com

SPANO, JOHN F.
Industry: Photo imaging **Born:** June 24, 1971, Newburgh, New York **Univ./degree:** B.E.E., Fairleigh Dickinson University **Current organization:** Konica-Minolta **Title:** Engineer **Type of organization:** Manufacturing **Major product:** Copier toner **Area of distribution:** National **Expertise:** Automation and controls, pneumatics, refrigerant **Hob./spts.:** Motorcycles, snowmobiling, rc planes **SIC code:** 28 **Address:** Konica-Minolta, 51 Hatfield Lane, Goshen, NY 10924 **E-mail:** buellxb9r@frontiernet.net

SPIES, RONALD H.
Industry: Automotive **Born:** April 5, 1946, Canton, Ohio **Univ./degree:** M.B.A., University of Connecticut, 1986 **Current organization:** General Motors **Title:** Manager Dealer Audit **Type of organization:** Manufacturing/corporate audit staff **Major product:** Motorized vehicles, cars and trucks **Area of distribution:** International **Expertise:** Identification and control of risk **Affiliations:** I.I.A.; A.S.E. **Hob./spts.:** Boating, sailing, motorcycling **SIC code:** 37 **Address:** General Motors, Renaissance Center, 3000 Jefferson Ave., Mail Stop 482-C 17D35, Detroit, MI 48265 **E-mail:** spiessrgi@aol.com

SPRADLIN, RANEÉ
Industry: Food **Born:** April 23, 1958, Tacoma, Washington **Univ./degree:** A.A.S. with Honors, Environmental Health and Safety Technology; Texas State Technical College, 2002; A.A.S. Candidate, Radiological Technology Safety Certification, B.S., Candidate, Industrial Hygiene and Safety, Tyler University **Current organization:** Cal-Maine Foods, Inc. **Title:** Safety Compliance Director **Type of organization:** Manufacturing, distributing **Major product:** Eggs **Area of distribution:** National **Expertise:** Certified Safety Compliance Specialist; new program development and training **Affiliations:**

Vice President, Health Physics Society, Student Chapter; Health Physics Inc., South Texas Chapter; American Society of Safety Engineers **Hob./spts.:** Hiking, reading, travel, outdoor activities **SIC code:** 20 **Address:** Cal-Maine Foods, Inc., 967 County Rd. 41, Flatonia, TX 78941 **E-mail:** raneespradlin@yahoo.com

SPROHAR, DANIEL S.
Industry: Oil **Born:** April 5, 1952, Rochester, Pennsylvania **Current organization:** Eckel Mfg. **Title:** Maintenance Technician **Type of organization:** Manufacturing **Major product:** Oil field tongs **Area of distribution:** International **Expertise:** Troubleshooting, maintenance of production machinery **Affiliations:** E.M.C. **SIC code:** 29 **Address:** Eckel Mfg., 8035 W. County Rd., Odessa, TX 79764 **E-mail:** jazziota9@cs.com

ST. GEORGE, ALFRED
Industry: Automotive **Born:** July 2, 1936, Brooklyn, New York **Univ./degree:** B.S., Mechanical Engineering, City University of New York, 1961 **Current organization:** Fasco DC Motors **Title:** Product Engineer **Type of organization:** Manufacturing **Major product:** DC Actuators **Area of distribution:** International **Expertise:** Engineering, gear systems **Affiliations:** 10 year Veteran, Toast Masters International **Hob./spts.:** Home gardener, reading, walking **SIC code:** 37 **Address:** 1354 Daylilly Dr., Holt, MI 48842 **E-mail:** asg_cfi@yahoo.com

STAEHLE, CHARLES M.
Industry: Marine **Born:** October 4, 1938, Lovell, Wyoming **Univ./degree:** B.S., Nuclear Engineering, Navy Nuclear Power Program, 1959; B.S., Physics, University of Oklahoma, 1963 **Current organization:** Submersible Systems Technology, Inc. **Title:** President **Type of organization:** Manufacturing, engineering **Major product:** Manned submersibles **Area of distribution:** National **Expertise:** U.S. Navy Captain, Submarine Service (retired), submarine operations maintenance and building since 1956, Chief Engineer, SST, special underwater equipment for deep ocean research **Published works:** 2 patents, 40+ journal articles **Affiliations:** Society of Naval Architects and Marine Engineers; Vice Chair, Marine Submersible Committee; American Bureau of Shipping; Marine Technology Society **Hob./spts.:** High fire rifle competitor, scuba diving, sailing, writing **SIC code:** 37 **Address:** Submersible Systems Technology, Inc., 3612 Reese Ave., Riviera Beach, FL 33404 **E-mail:** sst_mike@bellsouth.net **Web address:** www.submarinebuilders.com

STEINER, JOSEPH P.
Industry: Pharmaceuticals **Born:** September 15, 1961, Allentown, Pennsylvania **Univ./degree:** B.S., Biochemistry, 1983; M.S., Chemistry, 1984, Lehigh University; Ph.D., Johns Hopkins University, 1989; 4 years Post Doctorate; Attended Duke University, 1 year Post Doctorate **Current organization:** Guilford Pharmaceuticals Inc. **Title:** Principal Scientist **Type of organization:** Manufacturing **Major product:** Drugs for neurodegenerative diseases **Area of distribution:** International **Expertise:** Research **Published works:** 40+ articles, 100 abstracts, 6 book chapters, 50 patents **Affiliations:** Society for Neuroscience **Hob./spts.:** Gardening, weightlifting **SIC code:** 28 **Address:** Guilford Pharmaceuticals Inc., 6611 Tributary St., Baltimore, MD 21224 **E-mail:** steinerj@guilfordpharm.com **Web address:** www.guilfordpharm.com

STEINPREIS, STEVEN M.
Industry: Furnishings **Born:** December 4, 1956, Plymouth, Wisconsin **Current organization:** Bemis Manufacturing Co. **Title:** Operations Manager **Type of organization:** Manufacturing **Major product:** Toilet seats **Area of distribution:** International **Expertise:** Process engineering, administration, purchasing, M.I.S. **Affiliations:** S.M.E., American Management Association **Hob./spts.:** Bowling, golf, volunteering **SIC code:** 25 **Address:** Bemis Manufacturing Co., 300 Mill St., Dock Door 1, Sheboygan Falls, WI 53085 **E-mail:** steve.steinpreis@bemismfg.com

STENZEL, KAREN L.
Industry: Garage doors **Born:** October 24, 1951, Amboy, Illinois **Current organization:** Raynor Garage Doors **Title:** Materials Manager **Type of organization:** Manufacturing **Major product:** High-end garage doors (residential and commercial) **Area of distribution:** International **Expertise:** Materials management **Affiliations:** A.P.I.C.S. **Hob./spts.:** Tailoring, designing and sewing wedding dresses **SIC code:** 24 **Address:** Raynor Garage Doors, 1101 E. River Rd., Dixon, IL 61021 **E-mail:** kstenzel@raynor.com

STEPANEK, LESLIE A.
Industry: Semiconductor equipment **Born:** 1960, San Diego, California **Univ./degree:** B.S., Aeronautical Engineering, California Poly, SLO, 1983; M.S., Safety, University of Southern California, 1988 **Current organization:** Applied Materials, Inc. **Title:** Director, Corporate EHS **Type of organization:** Manufacturing, R&D, customer support **Major product:** Semiconductor, manufacturing equipment **Area of distribution:** International **Expertise:** Product safety management **Affiliations:** C.S.P. **Hob./spts.:** Ice hockey, travel, friends and family, photography **SIC code:** 36 **Address:** Applied Materials, Inc., 3535 Garrett Dr., Mail Stop 10071, P.O. Box 58039, Santa Clara, CA 95054 **E-mail:** leslie_stepanek@amat.com

STERN, MARGARET B.
Industry: Publishing **Born:** June 6, 1920, Brooklyn, New York **Univ./degree:** M.A., Early Childhood Education, Bank Street College of Education, 1979 **Current organization:** Structural Arithmetic Program **Title:** Author **Type of organization:** Educators publishing service **Major product:** Math materials, teachers guides and workbooks for K-3 **Area of distribution:** National **Expertise:** Author; tutoring children with learning disabilities **Honors/awards:** Recipient of Oxton Dyslexia Society Award, 1989; The Bank Street College of Education Award for Outstanding Accomplishments, 1998; Lectures on behalf of the AMAC organization **Affiliations:** I.D.A.; N.C.T.M. **Hob./spts.:** Oil and water painting **SIC code:** 27 **Address:** 754 N. Hollow Rd., Rochester, VT 05767 **E-mail:** structuralarith@aol.com **Web address:** www.sternmath.com

STEVENS, CRAIG T.
Industry: Metal finishing OEM **Born:** Grand Rapids, Michigan **Univ./degree:** M.B.A., Stamford Hill University **Current organization:** Walgren Co. **Title:** Technical Services Manager **Type of organization:** O.E.M. **Major product:** Automated anodize/plating **Area of distribution:** International **Expertise:** Engineering **Affiliations:** A.E.S.F. **SIC code:** 33 **Address:** Walgren Co., 3677 Sysco Ct., Grand Rapids, MI 49512 **E-mail:** craigs@walgren.com

STEWART, DAVID H.
Industry: Paint **Born:** July 11, 1940, Kane, Pennsylvania **Current organization:** Ace Hardware Corp./Paint Division **Type of organization:** Manufacturing company **Major product:** Trade sales paint - architectural water based and alkyd based paints, varnishes, stains and water sealers **Area of distribution:** International **Expertise:** Engineering and Maintenance Manager, overseeing construction **Affiliations:** Midwest Paint Society; Federation Society for Coatings Technology **Hob./spts.:** Boat racing, car racing **SIC code:** 28 **Address:** Ace Hardware Corp./Paint Division, 21901 S. Central Ave., Matteson, IL 60443 **E-mail:** dstewr@acehardware.com

STEWART, MARK W.
Industry: Confections **Born:** November 20, 1958, Chattanooga, Tennessee **Current organization:** Kraft Foods North America **Title:** Stockroom Coordinator **Type of organization:** Manufacturing **Major product:** Candy **Area of distribution:** International **Expertise:** Logistics, parts warehousing **Hob./spts.:** Golf, bowling **SIC code:** 20 **Address:** Kraft Foods North America, 3002 Jersey Pike, Chattanooga, TN 37422 **E-mail:** mark.stewart@kraft.com

STIER, ROGER E.
Industry: Chemicals **Born:** December, 1946, Hackensack, New Jersey **Univ./degree:** B.S., Biology and Chemistry, Fairleigh Dickinson University, 1968 **Current organization:** Noville **Title:** Technical Director **Type of organization:** Research and development **Major product:** Fragrances, flavors (oral hygiene products) **Area of distribution:** International **Expertise:** Oral hygiene research **Published works:** 12 patents, 2 articles **Affiliations:** A.A.P.S.; A.C.S.; A.A.A.S.; I.A.D.R.; Minister, New Apostolic Church **Hob./spts.:** Playing the organ **SIC code:** 28 **Address:** Noville, 3 Empire Blvd., South Hackensack, NJ 07606 **E-mail:** rstier@noville.com **Web address:** www.noville.com

STIGLIANO, STEVEN M.
Industry: Textile **Born:** May 15, 1963, Hoboken, New Jersey **Current organization:** Kabat Textile Corp./S.A.S. Apparel **Title:** Vice President/President **Type of organization:** Wholesale/manufacturing **Major product:** Evening wear fabric and finished garments **Area of distribution:** National **Expertise:** Project management, sales, marketing, business development, budget forecasting, strategic planning, quality assurance **Hob./spts.:** Family, gardening, tennis **SIC code:** 22 **Address:** Kabat Textile Corp., 247 W. 37th St., New York, NY 10018 **E-mail:** steven@kabatex.com

STOUT, EDWARD I.
Industry: Medical devices **Born:** March 2, 1939, Washington, Iowa **Univ./degree:** Ph.D., Organic Chemistry, University of Arizona, 1973 **Current organization:** Southwest Technologies Inc. **Title:** President/CEO **Type of organization:** Manufacturing **Major product:** Medical devices **Area of distribution:** International **Expertise:** Chemistry, research and development **Affiliations:** American Chemical Society; European Burn Association, Tissue and Wound Repair; International Burn Association **SIC code:** 38 **Address:** Southwest Technologies Inc., 1746 Levee Rd., North Kansas City, MO 64116 **E-mail:** estout@elastogel.com

STRAUB, DELROY F.
Industry: Plastics **Born:** May 19, 1962, Harrisburg, Pennsylvania **Current organization:** MI Plastics **Title:** Machine Repair Technician **Type of organization:** Manufacturing **Major product:** Plastic extrusions for windows and storm doors **Area of distribution:** Pennsylvania **Expertise:** Repair injection mold machines **Honors/awards:** Served in the U.S. Army for 15 years **Hob./spts.:** Fly-fishing **SIC code:** 30 **Address:** 1320 W. Main St., Valley View, PA 17983

STRAZA, GEORGE C. P.
Industry: Aerospace **Born:** December 3, 1955, Los Angeles, California **Univ./degree:** B.S., Mechanical Engineering, USC, 1979 **Current organization:** Aerovision **Title:** Inventor **Type of organization:** Manufacturing **Major product:** Jet engine seals **Area of distribution:** International **Expertise:** Inventor - knife edge seals, exotic metals **Hob./spts.:** Golf **SIC code:** 37 **Address:** Aerovision, 2235 Avenida Costa Este, Suite 100, San Diego, CA 92154 **E-mail:** george@aerovisionusa.com

STRICKLAND, EDWIN C.
Industry: Medical **Born:** January 27, 1952, Shreveport, Louisiana **Univ./degree:** B.S., Automotive Engineering Technology, Weber State College, Utah, 1975 **Current organization:** Hamilton Co. **Title:** Facilities Manager **Type of organization:** Manufacturing **Major product:** Medical devices-precision fluid handling systems, precision measuring syringes and miniature inert valves **Area of distribution:** International **Expertise:** Facilities management **Affiliations:** Knights of Columbus **Hob./spts.:** Family, golf **SIC code:** 38 **Address:** Hamilton Co., 4970 Energy Way, Reno, NV 89502 **E-mail:** estrickland@hamiltoncompany.com

STRZELCZYK, MARTIN A.
Industry: Ink **Born:** May 25, 1952, Berwyn, Illinois **Current organization:** Inx International Ink Co. **Title:** Risk Manager/Financial Analyst **Type of organization:** Manufacturing **Major product:** Ink for magazines, packaging **Area of distribution:** International **Expertise:** Accounting/insurance; CPA **Honors/awards:** Attained Advanced Toastmaster-Silver Level (ATM-S) **Affiliations:** Toastmasters International; Illinois CPA Society; Illinois Institute of Internal Auditors **Hob./spts.:** Family (married 18 years, 2 teenage daughters), fishing, sports, **SIC code:** 28 **Address:** Inx International Ink Co., 651 Bonnie Lane, Elk Grove, IL 60007 **E-mail:** marty.strzelczyk@inxintl.com

STUCKEY, RONALD L.
Industry: Printing/publishing **Born:** January 9, 1938, Bucyrus, Ohio **Univ./degree:** B.S., Cum Laude, Biology, Heidelberg College, Ohio, 1960; M.A., Botany, 1962, University of Michigan; Ph.D., Botany, 1965, University of Michigan **Current organization:** RLS Creations **Title:** Owner **Type of organization:** Printing and distributing **Major product:** Books, post cards **Area of distribution:** National **Expertise:** Editor, publisher, botanist, teacher **Honors/awards:** Professor Emeritus, Botany, The Ohio State University, 1991; Centennial Honoree, Ohio Academy of Science, 1991; Distinguished Service Award, F.T., Stone Laboratory of The Ohio State University, 1995; Herbert Osborn Ohio Biological Survey Award, 2002; Ohioana Library Book Award, 2003 **Published works:** Numerous scientific books, journal articles, biographical essays, chapters, abstracts; Books, "Edwin Lincoln Mosley (1865-1948)", "Emanuel D. Rudolph's Studies in the History of North American Botany", "Lost Stories" and other books **Affiliations:** International Association for Plant Taxonomy; Botanical Society of America; Past President, 1995; Past Secretary, 1996-99, Ohio Academy of Science; Southern Appalachian Botanical Club; International Bluegrass Music Association; Past President, The Ohio State University Chapter of Sigma Xi, 1981; Past President, The Ohio Academy of Medical History, 1981 **Career accomplishments:** 26 years of teaching Botany; publications of numerous botanical works; as a researcher and author, he is an internationally recognized authority on the identification and geographical distribution of aquatic and wetlands plants in North America **Hob./spts.:** Writing, family and local history, bluegrass festivals **SIC code:** 27 **Address:** RLS Creations, P.O. Box 3010, Columbus, OH 43210

STUDLEY, BRUCE C.
Industry: Power generation **Univ./degree:** M.S., Engineering Management, New Jersey Institute of Technology, 1986 **Current organization:** Foster Wheeler Power Group Inc. **Title:** Senior Vice President, Plant Operations **Type of organization:** Engineering/manufacturing **Major product:** Steam generation equipment, boilers and power plants **Area of distribution:** International **Expertise:** Power plant operations; Registered P.E. in New Jersey, New York, Florida **Published works:** 16 technical papers **Affiliations:** A.S.M.E.; N.S.P.E. **SIC code:** 34 **Address:** 110 High St., Randolph, NJ 07869 **E-mail:** bruce_studley@fwi.com

SUAREZ TORMO, ANTONIO
Industry: Food/beef **Born:** Madrid, Spain **Univ./degree:** B.S., Chemical Engineering, Texas A&M University, 2002 **Current organization:** Cargill **Title:** Utilities Superintendent **Type of organization:** Manufacturing **Major product:** Food products - beef **Area of distribution:** International **Expertise:** Energy, boiler and refrigeration systems **Affiliations:** A.C.S. **Hob./spts.:** Soccer, tennis, chess **SIC code:** 20 **Address:** Cargill, 4 Mile W. Hwy. 60, Friona, TX 79035 **E-mail:** antonio_suarez_tormo@cargill.com **Web address:** www.cargill.com/

SUBER, DEMETRIA L.
Industry: Food **Born:** September 27, 1969, Newark, New Jersey **Univ./degree:** B.S., Food Science, Rutgers University, 1992 **Current organization:** Chr. Hansen, Inc., Food Technology **Title:** Food Technologist **Type of organization:** Research and development/manufacturing **Major product:** Flavors and other food ingredients **Area of distribution:** International **Expertise:** Savory flavor development **Published works:** Poetry **Affiliations:** National Institute of Food Technologists, New York & Central New Jersey Chapters **Hob./spts.:** Writing, poetry, painting **SIC code:** 20 **Address:** Chr. Hansen, Inc., Food Technology, 1595 MacArthur Blvd., Mahwah, NJ 07430 **E-mail:** dsuber@chr-hansen-us.com **Web address:** www.chr-hansen-us.com

SUMMERLIN, TIMOTHY SCOTT
Industry: Adhesive tape **Univ./degree:** B.S., Graphic Design, Appalachian State University, 1994 **Current organization:** Shurtape Technologies, LLC **Title:** Packaging Specialist **Type of organization:** Manufacturing **Major product:** Packaging and adhesives systems **Area of distribution:** International **Expertise:** Vendor qualification, database maintenance, management, pre-press **Hob./spts.:** Football, baseball, reading, oil painting **SIC code:** 28 **Address:** Shurtape Technologies, LLC, 1506 Highland Ave. N.E., Hickory, NC 28601

SUNDAR, RAJ A.
Industry: Plastics/Polymers **Born:** March 1960, Guyana, South America **Univ./degree:** B.S., Chemistry, Pace University, 1987; Ph.D., Polymer Science, University of Southern Mississippi, 1994; M.T.M., Technology Management, Stevens Institute of Technology, 2002 **Current organization:** Ticona-A business of Celanese AG **Title:** Product Development Scientist **Type of organization:** Manufacturing **Major product:** Plastics/Polymers **Area of distribution:** International **Expertise:** R&D, product and process development, technical service, customer relations, polymer formulation/compounding/injection molding, extrusion/synthesis, six sigma-black belt **Affiliations:** A.C.S.; P.D.M.A. **Hob./spts.:** Sports **SIC code:** 30 **Address:** Ticona-A business of Celanese AG, 90 Morris Ave., Summit, NJ 07901 **Phone:** (908)598-4108 **Fax:** (908)522-7841 **E-mail:** raj.sundar@ticona.com

SUPRISE, KELLY J.
Industry: Poultry diagnostics **Born:** March 26, 1969, Green Bay, Wisconsin **Univ./degree:** B.S., Biology, University of Wisconsin, 1994 **Current organization:** Hy-Vac **Title:** Quality Assurance Manager **Type of organization:** Processing and testing **Major product:** Eggs, chicks **Area of distribution:** International **Expertise:** Laboratory testing, quality assurance **Hob./spts.:** Piano, NFL sports (football) **SIC code:** 20 **Address:** Hy-Vac, 2583 240th St., P.O. Box 310, Dallas Center, IA 50063 **E-mail:** ksuprise@hy-vac.com

SURESH, BABANNA
Industry: Electrical equipment **Born:** April 15, 1965, Bangalore, India **Univ./degree:** B.E.E., Bangalore University, 1989; M.E.E., Indian Institute of Science, India, 1998 **Current organization:** Virginia Transformer Corp. **Title:** Engineer **Type of organization:** Manufacturing **Major product:** Power and specialty transformers **Area of distribution:** International **Expertise:** High voltage engineering **Published works:** 2 articles **SIC code:** 36 **Address:** Virginia Transformer Corp., 220 Glade View Dr., Roanoke, VA 24012 **E-mail:** sureshb2000@hotmail.com **Web address:** www.virginiatransformer.com

SURLES, BETSY D.
Industry: Porcelain **Univ./degree:** B.S., Nutrition, Mary Washington College, Virginia **Current organization:** Main Street Studios **Title:** Director of Marketing **Type of organization:** Manufacturing, distributors **Major product:** Decorated porcelain and hand painted glass **Area of distribution:** National **Expertise:** Marketing **Honors/awards:** 1st Place Award In Novelties and Collectibles **Affiliations:** D.A.R.; American Red Cross **Hob./spts.:** Grandchildren, needlework **SIC code:** 32 **Address:** Main Street Studios, P.O. #33, Warrenton, VA 20186 **E-mail:** surles@infionline.net

SVOLOPOULOS, GREGORY A.
Industry: Medical **Born:** October 31, 1940, Ohio **Univ./degree:** B.S., University of Denver **Current organization:** Allied Health Care Corp. **Title:** Design & Manufacturing Engineer **Type of organization:** Medical manufacturing **Major product:** Respiratory therapy equipment **Area of distribution:** International **Expertise:** Respiratory care **Affiliations:** American Society of Mechanical Engineers **SIC code:** 38 **Address:** Allied Health Care Corp., 1720 Sublette Ave., St. Louis, MO 63110 **E-mail:** svolopg@alliedhpi.com

SWABEK, CARL G.
Industry: Aerospace **Born:** November 25, 1957, Youngstown, Ohio **Univ./degree:** M.E., University of Cincinnati, 1989 **Current organization:** GE Aircraft Engines **Title:** General Manager of Sales, Eastern U.S.A. **Type of organization:** Manufacturing **Major product:** Aircraft engines **Area of distribution:** International **Expertise:** Marketing and sales **Hob./spts.:** Golf, tennis, skiing **SIC code:** 37 **Address:** 141 Springfield Pike, Wyoming, OH 45215 **E-mail:** carl.swabek@ae.ge.com

SWEET, ROBERT H.
Industry: Jewelry **Born:** August 6, 1925, Hartford, Connecticut **Univ./degree:** M.B.A., Bryant College, 1949 **Current organization:** The Robbins Co. **Title:** Chairman of the Board Emeritus **Type of organization:** Manufacturing **Major product:** High quality award jewelry **Area of distribution:** International **Expertise:** Corporate management, sales, marketing, business development, strategic planning **Published works:** Interviews, television appearances **Affiliations:** Served in the U.S. Military during World War II **Hob./spts.:** Art, reading, architecture, family **SIC code:** 39 **Address:** 24 Central Park South, New York, NY 10019

SWIGERT, LEO J.
Industry: Paperboard/printing **Born:** January 28, 1948, Sheboygan, Wisconsin **Current organization:** Green Bay Packaging, Inc. **Title:** Printing Supervisor **Type of organization:** Manufacturing **Major product:** Folding cartons **Area of distribution:** International **Expertise:** Production management; Indentured Journeyman-State of Wisconsin; State Certified as Apprentice Instructor at Lakeshore Tech College; ISO 9000-2000 Auditor **Affiliations:** Graphics Advisory Committee Member, L.T.C. , Cleveland, Wisconsin; Graphics Advisory Committee Member, Northwest Tech College, Green Bay, Wisconsin **Hob./spts.:** Grandchildren, travel **SIC code:** 26 **Address:** Green Bay Packaging, Inc., 750 Cormier Rd., Green Bay, WI 54304 **E-mail:** Lswigert@gbp.com **Web address:** www.gbp.com

SYLVIA, ROBERT J.
Industry: Medium security locks **Born:** May 3, 1951, Newport, Rhode Island **Univ./degree:** B.S., Salve Regina University, 1982 **Current organization:** Hudson Lock, LLC **Title:** Senior Vice President, Operations **Type of organization:** Manufacturing **Major product:** Medium security locks **Area of distribution:** International **Expertise:** Operations, engineering, quality control, manufacturing **Hob./spts.:** Golf **SIC code:** 33 **Address:** Hudson Lock, LLC, 81 Apsley St., Hudson, MA 07149-1549 **E-mail:** robert.sylvia@hudsonlock.com

TAEGER, ROBERT E.
Industry: Engineering/environmental consulting **Born:** September 9, 1954, Tucson, Arizona **Univ./degree:** Assoc. Science Civil Engineering; Assoc. Science Welding **Current organization:** PBS&J **Title:** Project Manager, Environmental Compliance **Type of organization:** Consulting **Major product:** Environmental compliance/engineering **Area of distribution:** International **Expertise:** Environmental and civil engineering; Registered Environmental Manager, Registered Environmental Property Assesor, Certified Opacity Reader **Affiliations:** National Fire Protection Association; National Registry of Environmental Professionals; Texas Aggregate & Concrete Association; Oklahoma Aggregates Association; Society of Texas Environmental Professionals; Texas Association of Business and Commerce **Hob./spts.:** Woodworking, tennis, physical fitness **SIC code:** 32 **Address:** Martin Marietta Materials, Inc., 2277 Masch Branch Rd., Denton, TX 76207 **E-mail:** retaeger@pbsy.com

TAMASHIRO, TERRY YUKIO
Industry: Automotive **Born:** January 19, 1968, Hawaii **Univ./degree:** B.S.M.E., University of Hawaii, 1992 **Current organization:** Kavlico Corp. **Title:** Quality Engineering Supervisor **Type of organization:** Manufacturing **Major product:** Transducers **Area of distribution:** National **Expertise:** Mechanical engineering, quality assurance, project management, strategic analysis **Hob./spts.:** Computers, hiking, basketball **SIC code:** 37 **Address:** Kavlico Corp., 14501 Los Angeles Ave., Moorpark, CA 93021 **E-mail:** ttamashiro@kavlico.com

TANNER, OTIS L.
Industry: Gloves **Born:** December 5, 1923, Hoschton, Georgia **Univ./degree:** B.S., Piedmont College, 1949 **Current organization:** American Glove Co., Inc. **Title:** Owner **Type of organization:** Manufacturing **Major product:** Work gloves **Area of distribution:** Georgia **Expertise:** Manufacturing gloves since 1962 **Affiliations:** Former Member, Work Glove Institute **Hob./spts.:** Fishing, golf **SIC code:** 23 **Address:** American Glove Co., Inc., 98 Alpine St., Lyerly, GA 30730

TARANTO, THOMAS F.
Industry: Air system controls **Born:** February 8, 1954, Norwich, New York **Univ./degree:** B.S.M.E., Clarkson University, 1975 **Current organization:** ConservAIR Technologies LLP **Title:** Systems Engineer **Type of organization:** Manufacturing **Major product:** Compressed air system controls **Area of distribution:** International **Expertise:** Engineering, performance improvement/efficiency **Affiliations:** A.S.M.E.; Association of Energy Engineers **SIC code:** 38 **Address:** ConservAIR Technologies LLP, 8417 Oswego Rd., PMB-213, Baldwinsville, NY 13027 **E-mail:** TomTar@aol.com

TARVER, HARRISON P.
Industry: Electronic components **Born:** June 6, 1946, New York, New York **Univ./degree:** M.B.A., Business Management, Dowling College, 1993 **Current organization:** American Technical Ceramics Corp. **Title:** Vice President of Quality Assurance **Type of organization:** Manufacturing **Major product:** Ceramic capacitors, thin film circuits **Area of distribution:** International **Expertise:** Quality and reliability assurance systems, general management, engineering management **Honors/awards:** Delta Mu Delta, National Honor Society in Business Management **Affiliations:** EIA; ASQ **Hob./spts.:** Astronomy, ancient history **SIC code:** 36 **Address:** 35 Maple Wing Drive, Central Islip, NY 11722-4608 **E-mail:** htarver@atceramics.com

TATE, RICHARD M.
Industry: Textiles **Born:** June 2, 1977 **Univ./degree:** B.S.E.E., Rose-Hulman Institute of Technology, 1999 **Current organization:** Milliken & Co. **Title:** Senior Production Manager **Type of organization:** Manufacturing **Major product:** Automotive fabrics **Area of distribution:** Georgia **Expertise:** Engineering and management **Hob./spts.:** Golf **SIC code:** 22 **Address:** Milliken & Co., 1000 Elm St., LaGrange, GA 30240 **E-mail:** richard.tate@milliken.com

TAYLOR, PAUL E.
Industry: Metal **Born:** Nashville, Tennessee **Current organization:** TMRSS Custom Metal Fabricating **Title:** Owner **Type of organization:** Manufacturing **Major product:** Railings, gates, furniture **Expertise:** Product design, assembly **Hob./spts.:** Remote control aviation **SIC code:** 34 **Address:** TMRSS Custom Metal Fabricating, 3616 Hwy. 31-W, White House, TN 37188 **E-mail:** ptaylor22@aol.com

TEETOR, RONALD L.
Industry: Machinery **Born:** November 22, 1939, Lexington, Nebraska **Current organization:** Maytag Corp. **Title:** Tool & Die Supervisor **Type of organization:** Manufacturing **Major product:** Laundry products. washers and dryers **Area of distribution:** International **Expertise:** Administration, tool & die operations **Hob./spts.:** Golf, fishing **SIC code:** 36 **Address:** Maytag Corp., 200 Queensway St., Searcy, AR 72143-7421 **E-mail:** ron.teetor@amana.com

TENGGARDJAJA, FRANCIS D.
Industry: Transportation **Born:** August 1, 1948, Indonesia **Univ./degree:** M.S., Design, University of Trisakti, 1972; M.Eng., University of Toronto, 1977 **Current organization:** N/S Corp. **Title:** Vice President **Type of organization:** Manufacturing **Major product:** Vehicle washing equipment **Area of distribution:** International **Expertise:** Marketing, engineering **Hob./spts.:** Fishing, tennis **SIC code:** 35 **Address:** N/S Corp., 235 W. Florence Ave., Inglewood, CA 90301 **E-mail:** francist@nswash.com

TENNIMON, THOMAS W.
Industry: Compressed gas cylinders **Born:** October 29, 1959, Biloxi, Mississippi **Current organization:** Norris Cylinder Co. **Title:** Maintenance Manager **Type of organization:** Manufacturing **Major product:** Compressed gas cylinders **Area of distribution:** International **Expertise:** Project engineering, equipment efficiency, facilities, new equipment development **Hob./spts.:** Church activities; Certified Personal Trainer **SIC code:** 34 **Address:** Norris Cylinder Co., 1535 Fm 1845 South, Longview, TX 75603 **E-mail:** ttennimon@norriscylinder.com

THIRAKUL, VATHANA BELTRAN
Industry: Electronics **Born:** September 29, 1975, Laos **Univ./degree:** B.S., Electrical Engineering, Marquette University, 1997 **Current organization:** Zebra Technologies Corp. **Title:** Design Engineer **Type of organization:** Manufacturing **Major product:** Bar code label printer **Area of distribution:** International **Expertise:** Design **Affiliations:** I.E.E.E. **Hob./spts.:** Tennis, basketball, volleyball **SIC code:** 36 **Address:** Zebra Technologies Corp., 333 Corporate Woods Pkwy., Vernon Hills, IL 60061 **E-mail:** vtec29@yahoo.com

THOMAS, DOUGLAS GRAHAM
Industry: Electronics **Born:** August 18, 1938, Los Angeles, California **Univ./degree:** A.A., Business Administration, Glendale Community College, 1965 **Title:** Quality Assurance Systems and Administrative Specialist, General Technology Corp. (Retired)

Type of organization: Contract manufacturing **Major product:** Avionics and military products **Area of distribution:** International **Expertise:** Quality in workplace effectiveness **Honors/awards:** U.S. Military, Good Conduct Medal, various VN campaign medals and ribbons **Published works:** Newsletter Editor, "The Sandoval (County) Republican"; newsletter of the American Society for Quality, Albuquerque Section; "Menzia", newsletter of the Albuquerque Chapter of Mensa **Affiliations:** Treasurer, Albuquerque Chapter of NCMA; Vice Chair, Publicity Chair and Newsletter Editor, Albuquerque Section of ASQ and County Republican Party **Hob./spts.:** Internet networking, science fiction, movies, travel, helping job-seekers with resumes **SIC code:** 36 **Address:** 109 Dakota Morning Rd. N.E., Rio Rancho, NM 87124-2551 **E-mail:** douginrrnm@yahoo.com

THOMAS, HUEY L.
Industry: Telecommunications **Born:** June 1, 1962, Atlanta, Georgia **Univ./degree:** A.S., General Engineering, Southern Polytechnic State University, 1998; B.S., Industrial Engineering, Southern Polytechnic State University, 1999 **Current organization:** Lucent Technologies, Inc. **Title:** Property Manager **Type of organization:** Manufacturing **Major product:** Fiber optics **Area of distribution:** National **Expertise:** Engineering **Affiliations:** Society of Manufacturing Engineers; American Management Association; Institute of Industrial Engineers **Hob./spts.:** Football, computers, cars (Corvettes) **SIC code:** 33 **Address:** 3160 Brookview Dr., Marietta, GA 30068-3815 **E-mail:** thomas6011@prodigy.net

THOMAS, JOANN H.
Industry: Machines **Univ./degree:** A.A., Tennessee State College **Current organization:** Thomas Precision Machine **Title:** Owner **Type of organization:** Manufacturing **Major product:** Machine production for all industries **Area of distribution:** International **Expertise:** Engineering **Affiliations:** Pencil Makers Association **Hob./spts.:** Grandchild, rock masonry, horseback riding, reading **SIC code:** 35 **Address:** Thomas Precision Machine, 92 Stoneboro Rd., Fayetteville, TN 37334 **E-mail:** bobbythomas@cafes.net

THORNTON, JAMES C.
Industry: Forest products **Born:** September 11, 1950, Savannah, Georgia **Univ./degree:** B.S., University of South Carolina, 1984 **Current organization:** International Paper **Title:** Division Manager, Environment, Health & Safety **Type of organization:** Manufacturing **Major product:** Wood products (lumber, plywood) **Area of distribution:** International **Expertise:** Environmental compliance and safety leadership **Affiliations:** E.A.A.; Past Member, A.I.C.E.S. **Hob./spts.:** Golf **SIC code:** 24 **Address:** International Paper, 1201 W. Lathrop Ave., Wood Products Bldg., Savannah, GA 31415 **E-mail:** jim.thornton@ipaper.com **Web address:** www.ipaper.com

TIAN, CHENGUO
Industry: Metal **Born:** China **Univ./degree:** B.S., Central South University of Technology, China, 1982; M.S., Process Metallurgical Engineering, 1990; Ph.D., Process Metallurgical Engineering, McGill University, 1995 **Current organization:** Hydro Magnesium **Title:** Technical Service Engineer **Type of organization:** Manufacturing **Major product:** Magnesium metal **Area of distribution:** International **Expertise:** Metallurgy, metallurgical engineering, materials science and engineering manufacturing technology, molten mental refining and cleanliness control, high pressure die casting process optimization **Published works:** Technical papers in international journals and conferences including, C. Tian and D. Albright, "Fundamentals of Magnesium Melt Handling in Die Casting Foundries", Die Casting Engineer, May 2003; C. Tian, "Quality Assurance Indicators of Magnesium Alloy Ingots", IMA Educational Seminar, Anderson, IN, Oct. 23, 2002; C. Tian, G.A. Irons and D.S. Wilkinson, "Settling of Multi-Sized clusters of Alumina Particles in Liquid Aluminum", Metallurgical and Materials Transactions B., Vol. 30B, No. 4, 1999, pp.241-247 **Affiliations:** T.M.S., ASTM; North American Die Casting Association **Hob./spts.:** International politics, walking, sightseeing, reading **SIC code:** 33 **Address:** 43310 Silverwood Dr., Canton, MI 48188 **E-mail:** chenguo.tian@hydro.com **Web address:** www.hydromagnesium.com

TIMM, SANDRA R.
Industry: Electronic manufacturing services (EMS) **Born:** December 2, 1970, Melrose Park, Illinois **Univ./degree:** B.F.A., Liberal Arts, Cardinal Stritch University, 1992; B.S.E.E.T., Devry University, 1996; M.B.A. Candidate, Technology Management, University of Phoenix **Current organization:** Plexus Technology Group **Title:** Quoting Engineer **Type of organization:** Product realization services **Major product:** Automated test equipment (ATE) **Area of distribution:** International **Expertise:** Cost estimation engineering; Certified National First Responder **Hob./spts.:** Photography, volunteer work **SIC code:** 36 **Address:** Plexus Technology Group, 55 Jewelers Park Dr., P.O. Box 677, Neenah, WI 54957 **E-mail:** sandy.timm@plexus.com

TIMPSON, MARIA E.
Industry: Paper **Univ./degree:** B.S., Psychology, Curry College, 1982 **Current organization:** B-P Products **Title:** Production Manager **Type of organization:** Manufacturing **Major product:** Paper goods, die cut paper products **Area of distribution:** Connecticut **Expertise:** Production, shipping/receiving **SIC code:** 26 **Address:** B-P Products, 100 Sanford St., Hamden, CT 06514 **E-mail:** maria@b-pproducts.com **Web address:** www.b-pproducts.com

TOMA, JOSEPH R.
Industry: Aerospace, Aircraft, Missiles, Communications **Born:** March 6, 1927, Franklin, New Jersey **Univ./degree:** B.S., Seton Hall University, South Orange, New Jersey; Engineering, N.J.I.T., Newark, New Jersey **Current organization:** Astrolab Inc. **Title:** Chairman of the Board **Type of organization:** Design and manufacturing **Major product:** Microwave components, RF cable, RF connectors, RF cable assemblies, phase shifters, waveguide adaptors, waveguide clamps **Area of distribution:** International **Expertise:** Marketing, engineering **Affiliations:** I.E.E.E. **Hob./spts.:** Woodworking, travel **SIC code:** 36 **Address:** Astrolab Inc., 4 Powder Horn Dr., Warren, NJ 07059

TOMAINO, ANTHONY J.
Industry: Health & beauty aids **Born:** July 3, 1945, Redbank, New Jersey **Univ./degree:** B.S., Biology/Chemistry/Physics/Math, Monmouth College 1967; B.B.A., Accounting/Finance, Stockton State College, 1985 **Current organization:** E.T. Browne Drug Co. Inc. **Title:** Director of Purchasing **Type of organization:** Manufacturing **Major product:** Health & beauty aids **Area of distribution:** International **Expertise:** Operations **Affiliations:** , A.S.Q., S.C.C. **Hob./spts.:** Tennis, automobiles, music **SIC code:** 28 **Address:** E.T. Browne Drug Co. Inc., 440 Sylvan Ave., Englewood Cliffs, NJ 07632 **Web address:** www.palmerscocoabutter.com

TOMASCHKE, JOHN E.
Industry: Separation membrane **Born:** September 23, 1949, San Diego, California **Univ./degree:** B.S., San Diego State University, 1972 **Current organization:** Hydranautics **Title:** Director of Membrane Development **Type of organization:** Manufacturing **Major product:** Membrane filters **Area of distribution:** International **Expertise:** Polymer membrane chemistry **Published works:** Article in Encyclopedia of Separation Science; Co-Author, Ultra Pure Water Conference **Hob./spts.:** Wine-making, running **SIC code:** 38 **Address:** Hydranautics, 401 Jones Rd., Oceanside, CA 92054 **E-mail:** jtomaschke@hydranautics.com

TOMEI, WAYNE A.
Industry: Semiconductor **Born:** July 2, 1974, Benton, Illinois **Univ./degree:** B.S., Computer Engineering, University of Illinois, 1997 **Current organization:** LSI Logic Corp. **Title:** Physical Design Manager **Type of organization:** Manufacturer **Major product:** Application-specific integrated circuits **Area of distribution:** International **Expertise:** Physical design/ASIC layout **Affiliations:** I.E.E.E.; A.C.M.; N.S.P.E. **Hob./spts.:** Basketball **SIC code:** 36 **Address:** LSI Logic Corp., 8300 Norman Center Dr., Suite 730, Bloomington, MN 55437 **E-mail:** wtomei@lsil.com

TORRES, LINO J.
Industry: Electronics **Born:** Caracas, Venezuela **Univ./degree:** M.S., Systems Science Automation and Control, City University of London **Current organization:** Emerson Process Systems & Solutions **Title:** Director, Latin America **Type of organization:** Manufacturing **Major product:** Control systems **Area of distribution:** International **Expertise:** Engineering, marketing **Affiliations:** I.S.A. **Hob./spts.:** Hiking, photography, bicycling **SIC code:** 36 **Address:** Emerson Process Systems & Solutions, 8301 Cameron Rd., Austin, TX 78754 **E-mail:** lino.torres@emersonprocess.com

TOWLE, KENNETH L.
Industry: Christmas decorations **Born:** October 14, 1963, Lubbock, Texas **Univ./degree:** B.S., Eastern New Mexico University, 1988 **Current organization:** Christmas by Krebs Corp. **Title:** Director of Finance **Type of organization:** Manufacturing **Major product:** Christmas ornaments **Area of distribution:** International **Expertise:** Finance **SIC code:** 39 **Address:** Christmas by Krebs Corp., Dept. of Finance, 3911 S. Main St., Roswell, NM 88203 **E-mail:** lancet@christmasbykrebs.com **Web address:** www.christmasbykrebs.com

TRABER, JOHN W.
Industry: Building controls **Born:** July 31, 1950, Milwaukee, Wisconsin **Univ./degree:** B.S., Library Science, University of Wisconsin, 1974 **Current organization:** Siemens Building Technologies **Title:** HVAC Operations Supervisor **Type of organization:** Manufacturing **Major product:** HVAC controls **Area of distribution:** International **Expertise:** Teaching basic core HVAC class, engineering, field project manager classes **Affiliations:** A.S.H.R.A.Y. **Hob./spts.:** Woodworking, hunting, vegetable gardening, ice-skating, waterskiing, snow skiing **SIC code:** 38 **Address:** Siemens Building Technologies, 1000 Deerfield Pkwy., Buffalo Grove, IL 60089 **E-mail:** john.traber@siemens.com

TRACY III, THOMAS JAMES
Industry: Power **Born:** May 17, 1968, Indianapolis, Indiana **Univ./degree:** A.A., 1990; B.A., Psychology, 1993, West Virginia University **Current organization:** Tradewinds Power Corp. **Title:** President/CEO **Type of organization:** Manufacturing/distributors

Major product: Diesel engines and products including generator sets, power units and pump sets **Area of distribution:** International **Expertise:** Corporate management, strategic planning, business development, team leadership **Affiliations:** U. S. Chamber of Commerce **Hob./spts.:** Reading, fishing, surfing, snowboarding, football, physical fitness **SIC code:** 35 **Address:** Tradewinds Power Corp., 5820 N.W. 84th Ave., Miami, FL 33166 **Web address:** www.tradewindspower.com

TRAN, ERIK Q.
Industry: Healthcare **Born:** January 1, 1956, Danang, Vietnam **Univ./degree:** B.S., Chemical Engineering, University of California **Current organization:** Baxter Healthcare Corp. **Title:** Principal Engineer **Type of organization:** Manufacturing **Major product:** Infusion pumps **Area of distribution:** International **Expertise:** Chemical process development, medical device development **Published works:** Articles **Affiliations:** Society of Plastic Engineers; Past Member, American Institute of Chemical Engineers; Past Member, American Chemical Society **SIC code:** 38 **Address:** Baxter Healthcare Corp., 17511 Armstrong Ave., Irvine, CA 92614 **E-mail:** erik_tran@baxter.com

TRAN, KEVIN KHUONG
Industry: Semiconductors/memory devices **Born:** October 5, 1978, Saigon, Vietnam **Univ./degree:** B.S., Electrical Engineering, San Jose State University, 2001 **Current organization:** Micron Technology **Title:** Strategic Applications Engineer **Type of organization:** Manufacturing **Major product:** Networking and portable memory solution **Area of distribution:** International **Expertise:** Marketing/engineering **Affiliations:** I.E.E.E. **Hob./spts.:** Skiing, tennis, mountain biking **SIC code:** 36 **Address:** Micron Technology, 4440 Stone Canyon Dr., San Jose, CA 95136 **E-mail:** khuong_tran@hotmail.com

TRAN, THANH T.
Industry: Electronics **Born:** February 3, 1962, Vietnam **Univ./degree:** Ph.D., Electrical Engineering, University of Houston, 2001 **Current organization:** Texas Instruments Inc. **Title:** Senior Member, Technical Staff **Type of organization:** Manufacturing **Major product:** Semiconductors **Area of distribution:** International **Expertise:** Multimedia systems design and high speed DSP systems design **Honors/awards:** 18 issued patents; N.S.F. Panelist **Affiliations:** Senior Member, I.E.E.E.; Adjunct Faculty, Rice University **Hob./spts.:** Soccer **SIC code:** 36 **Address:** Texas Instruments Inc., 12203 Southwest Fwy., MS 722, Houston, TX 77477 **E-mail:** thanh-tran@houston.rr.com

TRIPPODI, GARY P.
Industry: Printing **Born:** May 11, 1947, Passaic, New Jersey **Univ./degree:** Certification, A.P.G. Maryland, Auto Mechanics; Certification, A&B Mechanics, Gas and Diesel Engines; Certification, Bergen Technical Trade School, Welding, Mechanic Shop, Print Reading **Current organization:** Adolph Gottscho, Inc. **Title:** Service Technician **Type of organization:** Printing equipment manufacturing **Major product:** Printing equipment/platen printer/hot stamping **Area of distribution:** National **Expertise:** Installation and trouble shooting **Honors/awards:** National Hero Award, F.B.I., 2001 **Affiliations:** Member, A.B.C.; A.S.P.C.A.; Humane Society; American and Foreign WWI and II; Vietnam Veterans; Local Law Enforcement; Blind Foundation **Hob./spts.:** Bowling, American Foundation of Metal Detection **SIC code:** 33 **Address:** Adolph Gottscho, Inc., 835 Lehigh Ave., Union, NJ 07083 **E-mail:** agiservice@gottscho.com

TROCONIS, MICHELLE D.
Industry: Plumbing fixtures (kitchen and bath) **Univ./degree:** B.A., Music, University of Texas, 1995; M.B.A., University of Illinois, 1999 **Current organization:** American Standard **Title:** Product Director **Type of organization:** Manufacturing **Major product:** Faucets **Area of distribution:** National **Expertise:** Marketing **SIC code:** 34 **Address:** 382 Finch Lane, Bedminster, NJ 07921 **E-mail:** mcyr99@yahoo.com

TSAI, JOHN J.
Industry: Media/publishing **Born:** September 9, 1942, Taiwan **Spouse:** Lois Lo **Married:** 1978 **Children:** David, 23, Jenny, 19 **Univ./degree:** B.S., National Taiwan University, 1965; M.S., Physics, College of William and Mary, Virginia, 1970; Ph.D., Ocean Physics, University of Miami, 1977; M.B.A., Florida International University, 1987 **Current organization:** Overseas Chinese News **Title:** Publisher/Editor **Type of organization:** Publishing corporation **Major product:** Newspaper **Area of distribution:** International **Expertise:** Publishing, editing **Honors/awards:** One Thousand Greatest Scientists, 2003; 21st Century Award for Achievement, 2001; International Man of Millennium, 2000; International Who's Who; Contemporary Who's Who **Published works:** Over 200 articles **Affiliations:** President, Chinese Amer. Press Institute; Asian Amer. Journalists Assoc.; Chairman, Miami/Kaoshiung Sister Cities Committee; Chairman, Board of Trustees, Global Alliance of Democracy and Peace, Florida Chapter; Miami-Dade County Asian Amer. Advisory Board; Amer. Geophysical Union; Acoustical Society of Amer.; Miami-Dade County Asian Pacific Rim/Taipei County Sister Cities Committee; Chinese Federation of Florida; Chinese Amer. Club of Miami **Career accomplishments:** First scientist in 1985 to study and observe the large amplitude internal soliton waves in Sulu Sea, Philippines, using acoustic remote sensing technique. Received both Distinguished Authorship Award from NOAA and Annual Award for an Outstanding Paper in Unclassified Journal from the Johns Hopkins University in 1986. Founded the Overseas Chinese News in 1990 and served as Publisher and Editor to make the newspaper the leading Chinese community newspaper in Florida **Hob./spts.:** Writing, publishing, stamp collecting, tennis **SIC code:** 27 **Address:** Overseas Chinese News, 8100 S.W. 92 Court, Miami, FL 33173 **Phone:** (305)274-4915 **Fax:** (305)274-1651 **E-mail:** tsai@ocn-miami.com **Web address:** www.ocn-miami.com

TUCKER, BARNEY A.
Industry: Chemicals **Univ./degree:** B.S., Agricultural Sciences, University of Tennessee, 1937 **Current organization:** Top Yield Industries, Inc. (sold to Cargill, 1986) **Title:** Chairman of the Board (Retired) **Type of organization:** Manufacturing **Major product:** Chemicals, agricultural chemicals (fertilizer) **Area of distribution:** Kentucky, Indiana, Tennessee, Ohio **Expertise:** Administration, construction, distribution, marketing **Honors/awards:** Served in active duty, U.S. Army 1941-46, World War II Veteran, Retired Major, field artillery; Recipient of the Bronze Star Medal; Listed in Who's Who in World Commerce & Industry; Who's Who in the South and Southwest, 1973-74; Served 10 Consecutive Governors of the Commonwealth from Lawrence Witherby to Wallace Wilkinson starting in 1953 **Affiliations:** Former Chairman, Kentucky State Board of Education; Former Sate President, R.O.A.; President, Kentucky State Chamber of Commerce; Member, Kiwanis Club; Former Chairman of the Board, Sayre School, Lexington; Major supporter and contributor to the Markey Cancer Center; Chairman, Board of Regents, Kentucky State University **SIC code:** 28 **Address:** 1628 Richmond Rd., Lexington, KY 40502

TUCKER, PHYLLIS A.
Industry: Publishing **Born:** July 26, 1952, Arkadelphia, Arkansas **Univ./degree:** M.S.E., Secondary Counseling, Henderson State University, 1976 **Current organization:** Holt, Rinehart & Winston **Title:** Secondary Sales Representative **Type of organization:** Publishing **Major product:** Secondary education textbooks **Area of distribution:** National **Expertise:** Sales, promotions **Affiliations:** Phi Delta Kappa **SIC code:** 27 **Address:** 2606 Twin Oaks Ct., Benton, AR 72015 **E-mail:** ptucker@hrw.com

TUDOR, MAURICIU
Industry: Electrical appliances **Born:** August 23, 1950, Bucharest, Romania **Univ./degree:** M.S., Power Engineering, Technical University of Romania, Bucharest, 1974 **Current organization:** Precision Quincy Corp. **Title:** Electrical Engineer **Type of organization:** Manufacturing **Major product:** Industrial ovens, dryers and software for control **Area of distribution:** International **Expertise:** Engineering, 15 years experience in wind energy **Published works:** 15 publications **Affiliations:** E.W.A.; A.W.A. **Hob./spts.:** Photography, fishing **SIC code:** 36 **Address:** Precision Quincy Corp., Electrical Dept., 1625 W. Lake Shore Dr., Woodstock, IL 60098 **E-mail:** mtudor@precisionquincy.com

TUMA, JERRY
Industry: Food **Current organization:** Quality Naturally Foods, Inc. **Title:** Vice President, R&D **Type of organization:** Manufacturing **Major product:** Bakery and food service **Area of distribution:** International **Expertise:** Product development/consulting **Affiliations:** S.C.I.F.T.S.; Past Member, American Society of Bakery Engineers **SIC code:** 20 **Address:** Quality Naturally Foods, Inc., 2284 Desert Forrest Lane, Bullhead City, AZ 86442 **E-mail:** jerrytuma@frontier.net

TUMEY, JIMMY F.
Industry: Paper **Born:** June 16, 1952, Arkansas **Univ./degree:** B.S., Chemical Engineering, Louisiana Technical University, 1978 **Current organization:** Domtar Industries, Inc. **Title:** Manager Paper Production **Type of organization:** Manufacturing **Major product:** Paper **Area of distribution:** National **Expertise:** Engineering **Hob./spts.:** Chess, reading, active member in First Baptist Church **SIC code:** 26 **Address:** Domtar Industries, Inc., 285 Hwy. 71 South, Ashdown, AR 71822 **E-mail:** jimmy.tumey@domtar.com

TURI, MORDECHAI
Industry: Textiles **Univ./degree:** M.A., Mechanical Engineering, Worster Poly Tech. Institute, 1966 **Current organization:** First Quality Nonwovens **Title:** Director of Technology **Type of organization:** Manufacturing **Major product:** Healthcare

products **Area of distribution:** International **Expertise:** Research and development **Published works:** Multiple papers **Affiliations:** I.N.D.A. **Hob./spts.:** Tennis, running **SIC code:** 22 **Address:** First Quality Nonwovens, 101 Green Mountain Rd., Hazleton, PA 18201 **E-mail:** mturi@fqnonwovens.com

TURNER, CARL L.
Industry: Aluminum extrusion **Born:** October 21, 1960, Tulsa, Oklahoma **Current organization:** Kaiser Aluminum **Title:** Operations Manager **Type of organization:** Aluminum plant **Major product:** Aluminum **Area of distribution:** National **Expertise:** Operations, controls **Hob./spts.:** Motorcycles, football, canoes, camping, coaching softball and baseball **SIC code:** 33 **Address:** Kaiser Aluminum, 4111 S. 74th East Ave., Tulsa, OK 74145 **E-mail:** carl.turner@ep.kaiseral.com **Web address:** www.ep.kaiseral.com

TURNQUEST, GERON A.
Industry: Salt **Univ./degree:** B.S.M.E., Prairie View A&M University, 1982 **Current organization:** Morton Bahamas, Ltd. **Title:** Vice President of Operations **Type of organization:** Manufacturing **Major product:** Salt (NaCl) **Area of distribution:** International **Expertise:** Engineering **Affiliations:** A.S.M.E. **Hob./spts.:** Music, reading **SIC code:** 20 **Address:** Morton Bahamas, Ltd., 450 Cargo Rd., Cape Canaveral, FL 32920 **E-mail:** gturnquest@batelnet.bs

TURSI JR., LOUIS H.
Industry: Sports equipment **Born:** March 7, 1961, Philadelphia, Pennsylvania **Univ./degree:** B.S., Food Marketing, St. Joseph's University, 1983 **Current organization:** The Top-Flite Golf Co. **Title:** Executive V.P., Sales & Marketing **Type of organization:** Manufacturing and distribution **Major product:** Golf balls, golf clubs **Area of distribution:** International **Expertise:** Sales and marketing **Affiliations:** N.G.F. **Hob./spts.:** Golf, baseball **SIC code:** 39 **Address:** The Top-Flite Golf Co., 425 Meadow St., Chicopee, MA 01013 **E-mail:** ltursi@topflite.com

ULVESTAD, ANNE E.
Industry: Publishing **Born:** October 19, 1953, Yonkers, New York **Univ./degree:** B.S., Nursing, Hunter College, 1971 **Current organization:** The World & I Magazine **Title:** Art/Graphics Director **Type of organization:** Magazine publishing **Major product:** 350 page monthly magazine **Area of distribution:** International **Expertise:** Graphic design **Honors/awards:** Listed in Who's Who Worldwide for Business Leaders; Women's Federation for World Peace Friendship Award **Published works:** Graphics in magazine **Affiliations:** American Institute of Graphic Design **Hob./spts.:** Biking, colonial time history **SIC code:** 27 **Address:** The World & I Magazine, 3600 New York Ave. N.E., Washington, DC 20002 **E-mail:** artdirector@worldandimag.com **Web address:** www.worldandi.com

UMSTED, NANCY
Industry: Food **Born:** June 15, 1965, Algona, Iowa **Univ./degree:** B.A., Management and Human Resources, University of Northern Iowa, 1988; M.B.A., Ball State University, 2004 **Current organization:** Country Maid, Inc. **Title:** Human Resource Manager **Type of organization:** Manufacturing **Major product:** Food, bread **Area of distribution:** National **Expertise:** Human resource management, policy development, training, labor relations **Published works:** The Employee Handbook Safety Programs **Affiliations:** Society for Human Resource Management; Board Member, E.S.O.P. Association **Hob./spts.:** Quilting, community service **SIC code:** 20 **Address:** Country Maid, Inc., P.O. Box 56, West Bend, IA 50597 **E-mail:** nancy.umsted@countrymaid.net

VAHEDIAN, FIROOZEH D.
Industry: Chemicals **Born:** August 27, 1955, Iran **Univ./degree:** M.S., Chemical Engineering, Teheran University, Iran, 1980 **Current organization:** Dupont/EKC Technology Inc. **Title:** Senior Project Engineer **Type of organization:** Manufacturing **Major product:** Specialty chemicals for semiconductors **Area of distribution:** International **Expertise:** Engineering **Affiliations:** A.I.C.H.E. **Hob./spts.:** Classic movies **SIC code:** 28 **Address:** Dupont/EKC Technology Inc., 2520 Barrington Ct., Hayward, CA 94545 **E-mail:** fdvahedi@ekctech.com

VAKILYNEJAD, MAJID
Industry: Pharmaceuticals **Born:** November 21, 1963, Iran **Univ./degree:** Ph.D., University of Alberta, Canada, 1995 **Current organization:** TAP Pharmaceutical Products, Inc. **Title:** Ph.D. **Type of organization:** Manufacturing **Major product:** Drugs, medicines **Area of distribution:** International **Expertise:** Pharmaceutical science **Published works:** 8 articles, 10 abstracts **Affiliations:** A.A.P.S.; C.P.A.; A.C.C.P. **Hob./spts.:** Movies **SIC code:** 28 **Address:** TAP Pharmaceutical Products, Inc., 675 N. Field Dr., Lake Forest, IL 60045 **E-mail:** majid.vakily@tap.com

VALENTIN, VICTOR X.
Industry: Electrical products **Born:** March 27, 1972, San Juan, Puerto Rico **Univ./degree:** B.S.M.E.; Polytechnic University of Puerto Rico, 1996 **Current organization:** Caribe GE Humacao **Title:** Facilities and Maintenance Engineer **Type of organization:** Manufacturing **Major product:** Electrical contacts **Area of distribution:** Puerto Rico **Expertise:** Engineering **Affiliations:** P.R.E.A. **SIC code:** 36 **Address:** 13930 S.W. 53rd St., Miramar, FL 33027 **E-mail:** victor.valentin@ge.com

VAN BECELAERE, ANDY
Industry: Sheet metal **Born:** June 16, 1978 **Univ./degree:** B.S., Engineering, University of Missouri, 2002 **Current organization:** Fabri-Tech Sheet Metal **Title:** Project Engineer **Type of organization:** Manufacturing **Major product:** Custom fabricated architectural sheet metal **Area of distribution:** Missouri **Expertise:** Engineering **SIC code:** 33 **Address:** Fabri-Tech Sheet Metal, 1200 S. Spring, St. Louis, MO 63110 **E-mail:** andy@fabri-tech.org

VAN SCHOONENBERG, ROBERT G.
Industry: Consumer and industrial products **Born:** August 18, 1946, Madison, Wisconsin **Univ./degree:** J.D., University of Michigan, 1974 **Current organization:** Avery Dennison Corp. **Title:** Executive V.P., General Counsel and Secretary **Type of organization:** Manufacturing **Major product:** Multiple consumer and industrial products **Area of distribution:** International **Expertise:** Mergers and acquisitions, law, corporate development **Affiliations:** A.C.C.A.; A.S.C.S. **SIC code:** 39 **Address:** Avery Dennison Corp., 150 N. Orange Grove Blvd., Pasadena, CA 91103 **E-mail:** rgvs@averydennison.com

VANDALEY, SHAWN W.
Industry: Electric vehicles **Born:** February 5, 1974, Somers Point, New Jersey **Current organization:** South Jersey Electric Vehicles **Title:** R&D Director **Type of organization:** Manufacturing **Major product:** Advanced electric vehicles and golf carts **Area of distribution:** New Jersey **Expertise:** Custom design and build, project management, trade show presentations **Affiliations:** Absecon Salt Water Sports Association **Hob./spts.:** Fishing **SIC code:** 37 **Address:** South Jersey Electric Vehicles, 1322 Doughty Rd., Egg Harbor Township, NJ 08234 **E-mail:** halibuthunter2@aol.com **Web address:** www.golfvehicles.com

VANDERBOEGH, DONALD W.
Industry: Training manuals **Born:** July 1, 1927, Michigan **Current organization:** Quality Basic, Inc. **Title:** CEO **Type of organization:** Manufacturing, customer assurance **Major product:** Business training and procedures manuals **Area of distribution:** National **Expertise:** Has worked as expediter, timekeeper, millwright, processing, salvage, inspector, floor inspector, supervisor, superintendent, quality engineer, manager, customer assurance quality system consultant, customer assurance systems implementation; Inventions: first bowling wrist brace, clothes dryer-reengineered, process control data collection system, electronic dryer upgrade **Published works:** "Basic Customer Assurance" manuals, "Alpha Class Training" curriculum, quality data collection work forms, suppliers "Quality Handbook"; Card games: "We The People" (teaches the Constitution), "United We Stand" (the discovery and settlement of America and its revolution) and other games; Entered a proposed redesign for a new World Trade Center; Developed a highway safety program to control drivers **Hob./spts.:** Showing others practical ways to resolve problems and/or innovate improvements **SIC code:** 27 **Address:** Quality Basic, Inc., 1582 Lakefront Dr., Mansfield, OH 44905 **E-mail:** gbink13@yahoo.com **Web address:** www.qualitybasic.com

VARGAS, JOSE M.
Industry: Petrochemicals **Born:** October 10, 1952, San Juan, Puerto Rico **Univ./degree:** Ph.D., Chemical Engineering, University of Pennsylvania, Philadelphia **Current organization:** ExxonMobil Chemical Co. **Title:** Global Process Associate **Type of organization:** Manufacturing/R&D **Major product:** Chemicals **Area of distribution:** International **Expertise:** Chemical engineering **Hob./spts.:** Photography, snorkeling, swimming **SIC code:** 28 **Address:** 18724 Manchac Highlands Dr., Prairieville, LA 70769 **E-mail:** jimvargas@cox.net

VARGAS, MADELLINE M.
Industry: Pharmaceuticals **Born:** February 11, 1962, Ponce, Puerto Rico **Univ./degree:** B.S., Biology, Catholic University of Puerto Rico **Current organization:** IVAX Pharmaceuticals, Inc. **Title:** QA, QC & Compliance Manager **Type of organization:** Manufacturing **Major product:** Cephalosporin **Area of distribution:** National **Expertise:** Quality assurance **Honors/awards:** Biology Honor Program, City University of New York **Affiliations:** P.B.A.; American Chemical Society **Hob./spts.:** Reading, handcrafting, knitting, swimming, snorkeling **SIC code:** 28 **Address:** IVAX Pharmaceuticals, Inc., 5127 Mt. Welcome, Christiansted St. Croix, VI 00820-4527 **E-mail:** madeline_vargas@ivax.com **Web address:** www.ivax.com

VARNER, MIKE G.
Industry: Business displays **Born:** April 11, 1961, Charleston, West Virginia **Current organization:** Advance Finishing and Display **Title:** Plant Manager **Type of organization:** Manufacturing **Major product:** Displays, design, printing, packing, shipping **Area of distribution:** Ohio **Expertise:** Distribution **Hob./spts.:** Architecture, landscaping, baseball, home improvement **SIC code:** 26 **Address:** Advance Finishing and

Display, 605 N. Wayne Ave., Cincinnati, OH 45215 **E-mail:** mikev@advancedisplay.com

VARZINO, ROBERT E.
Industry: Tools **Born:** February 15, 1963, Grayslake, Illinois **Univ./degree:** B.S., Economics, Illinois State University, 1987 **Current organization:** WMH Tool Group **Title:** Director of Marketing **Type of organization:** Manufacturing **Major product:** Tools **Area of distribution:** National **Expertise:** Marketing **Affiliations:** A.H.M.A. **SIC code:** 39 **Address:** WMH Tool Group, 2420 Vantage Dr., Elgin, IL 60510 **E-mail:** rvarzino@wmhtoolgroup.com **Web address:** www.wmhtoolgroup.com

VASHI, DIPAK M.
Industry: Chemicals **Born:** July 24, 1951, Gujarad, India **Univ./degree:** M.S., Chemistry, University of South Gujarat, India, 1974 **Current organization:** Engelhard Corp. **Title:** Application Chemist **Type of organization:** Manufacturing **Major product:** Polyolefin catalysts **Area of distribution:** International **Expertise:** Customer's application support **Honors/awards:** Company Recognition Awards **Affiliations:** A.C.S. **Hob./spts.:** Tennis **SIC code:** 28 **Address:** Engelhard Corp., 10001 Chemical Rd., Pasadena, TX 77507 **E-mail:** dipak.vashi@engelhard.com

VELEZ, JOSÉ M.
Industry: Foundry **Born:** November 9, 1947, San Juan, Puerto Rico **Univ./degree:** B.A., University of Puerto Rico, 1970 **Current organization:** PAC Foundries, Inc. **Title:** ASNT NDT Level III, Certificate #51606 **Type of organization:** Manufacturing **Major product:** Investment castings **Area of distribution:** USA, Europe **Expertise:** Non destructive testing (RT, PT, MT Methods) **Affiliations:** A.S.N.T.; A.W.A. **Hob./spts.:** Bicycling, photography, reading, computers **SIC code:** 33 **Address:** PAC Foundries, Inc., 11000 Jersey Blvd., Rancho Cucamonga, CA 91730 **E-mail:** jose.velez@cfi-pac.com

VELEZ-RAMIREZ, ANGEL Z.
Industry: Pharmaceuticals **Born:** February 19, 1975, Humacao, Puerto Rico **Univ./degree:** B.S., 1999; B.S.M.E., University of Puerto Rico **Current organization:** Wyeth Pharmaceutical Co. **Title:** Scientist II **Type of organization:** Manufacturing **Major product:** Solid dosage drugs **Area of distribution:** International **Expertise:** Validation and qualification of pharmaceutical equipments **Affiliations:** I.S.P.E. **Hob./spts.:** Tennis, guitar **SIC code:** 28 **Address:** P.M.B. 215, P.O. Box 4952, Caguas, PR 00726-4952 **E-mail:** veleza2@wyeth.com

VELTRI, ENRICO P.
Industry: Pharmaceuticals **Born:** January 12, 1954, Paterson, New Jersey **Univ./degree:** M.D., University of Medicine and Dentistry of New Jersey, 1979 **Current organization:** Schering - Plough Research Institute **Title:** Vice President **Type of organization:** Research and development **Major product:** Pharmaceuticals **Area of distribution:** National **Expertise:** Cardiology **Published works:** 54+ publications **Affiliations:** F.A.C.C.; N.A.S.P.E.; A.C.C.P. **Hob./spts.:** Soccer **SIC code:** 28 **Address:** Schering - Plough Research Institute, 2015 Galloping Hill Rd., Kenilworth, NJ 07033 **E-mail:** enrico.veltri@spcorp.com

VERHOFF, DONALD H.
Industry: Transportation equipment **Born:** July 4, 1946, Ohio **Univ./degree:** B.S., Engineering, Purdue University, 1973 **Current organization:** Oshkosh Truck Corp. **Title:** VP, Corp. Engineer/ Technology **Type of organization:** Manufacturing **Major product:** Specialty trucks and bodies **Area of distribution:** National **Expertise:** Engineering **Affiliations:** S.A.E.; S.P.E.; N.D.I.A. **Hob./spts.:** Boating, restoring cars and motorcycles **SIC code:** 37 **Address:** Oshkosh Truck Corp., 2307 Oregon St., Oshkosh, WI 54902 **E-mail:** dverhoff@oshtruck.com

VERHOFF, JONATHAN M.
Industry: Construction materials-residential **Born:** February 19, 1973, Wyma, Ohio **Univ./degree:** B.S., Mechanical Engineering, University of Cincinnati, 1996; M.S., Mechanical Engineering, Purdue University, 1999 **Current organization:** Owens Corning **Title:** Advanced Engineer **Type of organization:** Manufacturing **Major product:** Lightweight stone veneer **Area of distribution:** International **Expertise:** Research and development **Published works:** 3 journal articles, 4 conference papers, 1 patent **Affiliations:** S.A.E.; A.S.M.E.; S.M.E.; National Precast Concrete Association **Hob./spts.:** Golf, computer **SIC code:** 39 **Address:** Owens Corning, 2790 Columbus Rd., Room 20-2, Granville, OH 43023 **E-mail:** jonathan.verhoff@owenscorning.com **Web address:** www.owenscorning.com

VERHOFF, STEPHEN J.
Industry: Automotive **Born:** January 10,1977, Toledo, Ohio **Univ./degree:** B.S., Mechanical Engineering, G.M.I./Kettering University, 2000 **Current organization:** Faurecia Exhaust Systems **Title:** Product Engineer **Type of organization:** Manufacturing/research and design **Major product:** Exhaust systems **Area of distribution:** National **Expertise:** Engineering **Affiliations:** A.S.M.E.; Tau Beta Pi; Pi Tau Sigma **SIC code:** 37 **Address:** Faurecia Exhaust Systems, 543 Matzinger Rd., Toledo, OH 43612 **E-mail:** sverhoff@toledo.faurecia.com

VERMA, RAVINDRA S.
Industry: Rubber **Born:** September 26, 1961, Roorkee, India **Univ./degree:** B.S.E.E., I.TT.; M.S., Artificial Intelligence, Texas A&M University **Current organization:** Bridgestone Firestone **Title:** Computer Engineer/Systems Integrator **Type of organization:** Manufacturing **Major product:** Tires (car, truck, sport utility) **Area of distribution:** International **Expertise:** Computer integrated manufacturing **Published works:** AI Journal; Environmental Engineering Journal **Affiliations:** A.O.T.S.; I.E.E.E. **Hob./spts.:** Painting, acting, soccer **SIC code:** 30 **Address:** Bridgestone/Firestone, 1 Bridgestone Pkwy., Graniteville, SC 29829 **E-mail:** vermaravi@bfusa.com **Web address:** www.busa.com

VÉRTIZ, ALICIA M.
Industry: Auto components/subsystems/electronics/medical devices **Born:** Rosario, Argentina **Univ./degree:** M.V.D., National University of La Plata, Argentina **Current organization:** Delphi Corp. **Title:** Senior Staff Research Scientist **Type of organization:** Manufacturing **Major product:** Auto components, electronics, subsystems, electronics, medical devices, safety systems **Area of distribution:** National **Expertise:** Human factors, engineering; Certified Professional Ergonomist **Published works:** 11 patents, 20 technical publications **Affiliations:** S.A.E. **SIC code:** 36 **Address:** Delphi Corp., 5725 Delphi Dr., Mail Code 483-400-121, Troy, MI 48098 **E-mail:** alicia.m.vertiz@delphi.com

VICAIN, JANICE R.
Industry: Lighting **Born:** August 12, 1939, Greeley, Colorado **Current organization:** Progress Lighting **Title:** Account Manager **Type of organization:** Manufacturing **Major product:** Residential, commercial and industrial lighting **Area of distribution:** National **Expertise:** All types of lighting design; Lighting Specialist Certificate **Affiliations:** National Kitchen and Bath Association; American Lighting Association **Hob./spts.:** Interior design, lighting, gardening, golf **SIC code:** 36 **Address:** Progress Lighting, 3416 Klevner Way, Rancho Cordova, CA 95670 **E-mail:** jvicain@progress-lighting.com

VIDANES, FRED G.
Industry: Chemicals **Born:** April 25, 1944, Manila, Philippines **Univ./degree:** B.S., Chemical Engineering, MIT, 1969 **Current organization:** LPS Laboratories, Inc. **Title:** Environmental Manager **Type of organization:** Manufacturing **Major product:** Aerosol lubricants, electronic cleaners, degreasers **Area of distribution:** International **Expertise:** Environmental management, quality assurance **Affiliations:** A.S.Q.; A.C.S. **Hob./spts.:** Golf, fishing, boating, home improvements **SIC code:** 28 **Address:** LPS Laboratories, Inc., 4647 High Howell Rd., Tucker, GA 30084-5004 **E-mail:** fvidanes@yahoo.com

VILLON, SEBASTIEN D.
Industry: Medical devices **Born:** June 11, 1972, France **Univ./degree:** M.B.A. **Current organization:** Aircast **Title:** Product Manager **Type of organization:** Manufacturing **Major product:** Medical devices, leg-related braces **Area of distribution:** International **Expertise:** Marketing **Hob./spts.:** Friends **SIC code:** 38 **Address:** Aircast, 92 River Rd., Summit, NJ 07901 **E-mail:** sebastienv@aircast.com

VINCENT JR., RALPH
Industry: Pulp and paper **Born:** September 17, 1958, Franklin, Virginia **Univ./degree:** OSHA 1910 & 1926 Training; Special Government Employee (SGE); Level I & II Industrial Truck Operator Trainer; Attended Theocratic Ministry School; Graduate, International Paper's Corporate Health & Safety University **Current organization:** International Paper Co. **Title:** Safety Coordinator **Type of organization:** Manufacturing **Major product:** Printing and communication papers **Area of distribution:** National **Expertise:** Converting safety and health training, OSHA Safety Specialist **Honors/awards:** Advanced Safety Certificate, National Safety Council (NSC); Member, Strathmore's Who's Who **Affiliations:** Ordained Minister of Jehovah's Witnesses; Facilitator of Bible Studies Program at Southampton Corrections and Deerfield Corrections, Capron, Virginia; Diversity Council Chairman; International Paper Franklin Mill Representative **Hob./spts.:** Golf, fishing, gardening **SIC code:** 26 **Address:** International Paper Co., 34040 Union Camp Dr., Franklin, VA 23851 **E-mail:** ralph.vincent@ipaper.com

VINSON, GORDON T.
Industry: Automotive **Born:** February 23, 1953, Sturgis, Kentucky **Current organization:** Lawrence Manufacturing **Title:** Maintenance Manager **Type of organization:** Manufacturing **Major product:** Die castings **Area of distribution:** International **Expertise:** Maintenance, engineering **Hob./spts.:** Guitar, recording, family pets **SIC code:** 33 **Address:** Lawrence Manufacturing, 1301 Amistad St., San Benito, TX 78586 **E-mail:** gvinson@gibbsdc.com **Web address:** www.gibbsdc.com

VIRDEN, LAURENCE L.
Industry: Material handling **Born:** July 23, 1976, Detroit, Michigan **Univ./degree:** B.S., Electrical Engineering, Oakland University, 1999 **Current organization:** Siemens Dematic **Title:** Engineer **Type of organization:** Manufacturing and design **Major product:** Conveyors and AGVs **Area of distribution:** International **Expertise:** Engineering **Affiliations:** N.S.P.E.; I.E.E.E.; N.S.B.E. **SIC code:** 35 **Address:** Siemens Dematic, 38755 Hills Tech Dr., Farmington Hills, MI 48331 **E-mail:** virdenll@rapistan.com **Web address:** www.rapistan.com

VIVAS, MIGUEL A.
Industry: Pharmaceuticals **Born:** March 21, 1971, Latacunga, Ecuador **Univ./degree:** Attended, Universidad Tecnológica Equinoccial, Ecuador, 1998 **Current organization:** Arnet Pharmaceutical **Title:** Purchasing Manager **Type of organization:** Manufacturing **Major product:** Neutraceuticals **Expertise:** Administration, operations **Hob./spts.:** Soccer **SIC code:** 28 **Address:** Arnet Pharmaceutical, 2525 Davie Rd., Suite 330, Davie, FL 33317 **E-mail:** vivasm26@hotmail.com

VOGEL, SHARON S.
Industry: Chemicals **Born:** February 18, 1964, Parkersburg, West Virginia **Univ./degree:** B.S.E.E., West Virginia Institute of Technology, 1987; M.B.A., Marshall University, 2000 **Current organization:** Flexsys America, LP **Title:** Senior Instrument and Electrical Engineer **Type of organization:** Manufacturing **Major product:** Rubber chemical additives **Area of distribution:** International **Expertise:** Engineering **Hob./spts.:** Spending time with her daughter, reading, travel, golf **SIC code:** 28 **Address:** Flexsys America, LP, No. 1 Monsanto Rd., Nitro, WV 25143 **E-mail:** sharon.vogel@flexsys.com

WADE, MICHAEL J.
Industry: Steel **Born:** Hamilton, Ontario, Canada **Current organization:** Running Metal Coating Lines **Title:** Production Manager/6 Sigma Black Belt **Type of organization:** Manufacturing **Major product:** Coated coil sheet steel **Area of distribution:** National **Expertise:** Cost saving initiative **Affiliations:** A.I.S.I.; A.S.Q. **Hob./spts.:** Hockey, motorcycling **SIC code:** 33 **Address:** Six Sigma Black Belt, 3229 W. Meyers Rd., San Bernardino, CA 92407

WAKEFIELD, STEVEN B.
Industry: Electronics **Born:** July 9, 1974, Boston, Massachusetts **Univ./degree:** B.S., Mechanical Engineering, University of New Hampshire, 1996; M.S., Material Science, Northeastern University, 2003 **Current organization:** Tyco Electronics **Title:** Materials Development Engineer **Type of organization:** Development **Major product:** Electronics components **Area of distribution:** International **Expertise:** Materials engineer **Affiliations:** Tau Beta Pi **Hob./spts.:** Golf, travel, fishing **SIC code:** 36 **Address:** Tyco Electronics, 452 John Dietsch Blvd., North Attleboro, MA 02760

WALDRON, JIM
Industry: Forging **Born:** March 10, 1963, Jacksonville, Florida **Univ./degree:** M.B.A., Illinois Benedictine College, 1991 **Current organization:** Advanced Green Components **Title:** President **Type of organization:** Manufacturing **Major product:** Forgings and machined rings for bearings **Area of distribution:** International **Expertise:** Business administration **Hob./spts.:** Water skiing, golf, jogging **SIC code:** 34 **Address:** Advanced Green Components, 4005 Corporate Dr., Winchester, KY 40391 **E-mail:** waldronw@advgreen.com

WALDROP, DONNA F.
Industry: Glassware **Born:** February 11, 1957, Sallisaw, Oklahoma **Univ./degree:** B.S, Human Resource Development, University of Arkansas, 2000; M.B.A., Webster University, 2001 **Current organization:** Owens Corning **Title:** Advanced Human Resource Specialist **Type of organization:** Manufacturing **Major product:** Home building and construction products **Area of distribution:** International **Expertise:** Human resources department oversight, HR leader and staff member **Affiliations:** Society for Human Resource Management **Hob./spts.:** Music, band: "Steven Waldrop Family" **SIC code:** 32 **Address:** 171 Horizon Lane, Alma, AR 72921 **E-mail:** dfwaldrop@yahoo.com

WALENTOSKI, RICHARD E.
Industry: Mining equipment **Born:** October 3, 1946, Oil City, Pennsylvania **Univ./degree:** A.S., Business Management, University of Pittsburgh at Titusville **Current organization:** Joy Mining Machinery **Title:** Quality Assurance Person **Type of organization:** Manufacturing **Major product:** Underground mining equipment **Area of distribution:** International **Expertise:** Quality control **Affiliations:** International Association of Machinists and Aerospace Workers **SIC code:** 35 **Address:** Joy Mining Machinery, 120 Liberty St., Franklin, PA 16323-1066 **E-mail:** dwalento@joy.com **Web address:** www.joy.com

WALERYSZAK, MICHAEL M.
Industry: Industrial blades **Univ./degree:** B.A., Accounting/Finance, Youngstown State University, Ohio, 1979 **Current organization:** Crescent Manufacturing Co. **Title:** President/CFO **Type of organization:** Manufacturing **Major product:** Industrial and medical razor blades **Area of distribution:** International **Expertise:** Organizational and accounting **Affiliations:** Board of Director of Trustees, Fremont Country Club; Financial Executives International **Hob./spts.:** Golf, travel **SIC code:** 34 **Address:** Crescent Manufacturing Co., 1310 Majestic Dr., Fremont, OH 43470 **E-mail:** mwaleryszak@crescentblades.com

WALKER, FRANKLYN D.
Industry: Aerospace **Born:** September 4, 1948, Tahlcquah, Oklahoma **Univ./degree:** A.S., Aviation Technology, Texas Technical College, 1996 **Current organization:** L-3 Communication IS **Title:** Manufacturing Manager **Type of organization:** Manufacturing, research and development **Major product:** Aircraft modifications **Area of distribution:** International **Expertise:** Production management **Honors/awards:** Maintenance Technician of the Year for the Southwest Region, F.A.A., 1991 **Affiliations:** U.S. Army, 1968-88 **Hob./spts.:** The outdoors, hunting, fishing, travel **SIC code:** 37 **Address:** L-3 Communication IS, 7500 Maehr Rd., Waco, TX 76705-1632 **E-mail:** f_walker@isl-3com.com

WALLISER, MICHAEL A.
Industry: Printing **Born:** November 19, 1949, Libertyville, Illinois **Univ./degree:** Attended Triton College **Current organization:** Repacorp Label Products **Title:** Plant Manager **Type of organization:** Manufacturing **Major product:** Labels and tags **Area of distribution:** International **Expertise:** Management **Hob./spts.:** fishing, golf **SIC code:** 27 **Address:** 4670 Tipp Elizabeth, Tipp City, OH 45371-9480

WALSH, KEVIN D.
Industry: Consumer products **Born:** October 7, 1956, Derby, Connecticut **Univ./degree:** B.S., Microbiology; M.S., Microbiology, University of Connecticut **Current organization:** Cadbury Schweppes **Title:** Director, Biotechnology **Type of organization:** Manufacturing, R&D **Major product:** Food and beverages **Area of distribution:** International **Expertise:** Microbiology, biotechnology **Hob./spts.:** Golf, electronics **SIC code:** 20 **Address:** Cadbury Schweppes, 30 Trefoil Dr., Trumbull, CT 06611 **E-mail:** kevin.walsh@csplc.com

WANG, NAI SHU
Industry: Medical devices **Born:** November 25, 1946, Chong Qing, China **Univ./degree:** M.D., University of Medical Sciences, Chong Qing, 1970; Ph.D., Zoology/Medical Sciences, Ohio University, 1991 **Current organization:** Alfa Scientific Designs Inc. **Title:** President **Type of organization:** Manufacturing, research & development **Major product:** Rapid on-site in-vitro diagnostic devices, those detect Drug of Abuse, Fertility, tumor markers, infectious diseases, cardiac markers and other disorders **Area of distribution:** Global and US domestic market **Expertise:** Research, manufacturing **Honors/awards:** Minority Owned Small Business of the Year, 2002 **Affiliations:** San Diego US-Chinese Entrepreneurs Association **SIC code:** 38 **Address:** Alfa Scientific Designs Inc., 12330 Stowe Dr., Poway, CA 92064 **E-mail:** wnss@alfascientific.com

WANG, WENDAI
Industry: Electrical, aerospace, medical , power and transportation equipment **Born:** December 10, 1962, China **Univ./degree:** Ph.D., University of Arizona, 1998 **Current organization:** General Electric Co. **Title:** Senior Professional Engineer **Type of organization:** Research and Development **Major product:** Industrial and commercial products **Area of distribution:** International **Expertise:** Reliability engineering, project management, R&D, has lectured at seminars/conferences **Published works:** 30+ published works **Affiliations:** Society of Reliability Engineers **Hob./spts.:** Sports, movies, stamp collecting, coin collecting **SIC code:** 39 **Address:** General Electric Co., 1 Research Circle KWC 1633, Niskayuna, NY 12309 **E-mail:** wang@research.ge.com

WANG, ZORAH WU
Industry: Health and beauty products **Born:** January 8, 1949, Taiwan **Univ./degree:** M.S., Herbalogy, Harmony College, 1993 **Current organization:** Filmagic Inc./Nature's Dream **Title:** Executive Director **Type of organization:** R&D, manufacturing, distributing, exporting **Major product:** Health and beauty products **Area of distribution:** International **Expertise:** Health and beauty consulting **Published works:** Articles **Affiliations:** Professor, Harmony College **Hob./spts.:** Travel, church work, music **SIC code:** 28 **Address:** Filmagic Inc./Nature's Dream, 120 N. Fairway Lane, West Covina, CA 91791 **Web address:** www.naturesdream.net

WARD, FLORIAN M.
Industry: Food ingredients **Born:** Nueva Ecija, Philippines **Univ./degree:** B.S., Food Processing Technology; B.S., Pharmacy; M.S., Pharmaceutical Chemistry, University of the Philippines; Ph.D., Food Science, University of Washington **Current organization:** TIC Gums, Inc. **Title:** Senior Principal Scientist/Vice President R&D **Type of organization:** Manufacturing, R&D **Major product:** Food ingredients and pharmaceutical products **Expertise:** Food science, cosmetics and pharmaceuticals, inventing **Published works:** 5 book chapters, 25 trade journal articles, invented series of hydrocolloids **Affiliations:** A.A.C.C.; A.I.B.; American Chemical Society; Institute

of Food Technologists **Hob./spts.:** Reading, writing, travel **SIC code:** 28 **Address:** TIC Gums, Inc., 4609 Richlynn Dr., Belcamp, MD 21017 **E-mail:** fward@ticgums.com

WARD, LARRY
Industry: Plastic food containers **Born:** June 23, 1950, Columbus, Indiana **Univ./degree:** A.S., Business Management, Western Kentucky University, 1979 **Current organization:** Dart Container Corp. of Kentucky **Title:** Safety Coordinator **Type of organization:** Manufacturing **Major product:** Disposable food containers **Area of distribution:** Kentucky **Expertise:** Safety Professional **Hob./spts.:** Golf **SIC code:** 30 **Address:** Dart Container Corp. of Kentucky, 975 S. Dixie Hwy., Horse Cave, KY 42749 **E-mail:** lward@dart.biz **Web address:** www.dart.biz

WARD, PAMELA PEARDON
Industry: Semiconductors **Born:** August 18, 1958, Savannah, Georgia **Univ./degree:** A.S., Electronics Engineering, State Technical Institute at Knoxville, 1979; T.I.E., Materials Science, Sandia National Laboratory, 1990 **Current organization:** Peak Sensor Systems **Title:** Vice President & Director of R&D **Type of organization:** Manufacturing, supplier **Major product:** ProPak Plasma Monitor **Area of distribution:** International **Expertise:** Plasma physics **Honors/awards:** 19 patents **Published works:** 40 articles **Hob./spts.:** Musical instruments (guitar, keyboard), fishing, woodworking **SIC code:** 36 **Address:** Peak Sensor Systems, 6207 Pan American Fwy. N.E., Albuquerque, NM 87109 **E-mail:** ppward@peaksensor.com **Web address:** www.peaksensor.com

WARD, PATRICK T.
Industry: Construction **Born:** January 16, 1960, Chico, California **Univ./degree:** B.S.C.E., California State University at Chico, 1983 **Current organization:** North Valley Iron Works, Inc. **Title:** Vice President, R.M.O. **Type of organization:** Fabrication **Major product:** Structural steel and miscellaneous metals **Area of distribution:** National **Expertise:** Marketing, civil engineering **Affiliations:** A.S.C.E.; A.W.S.; I.C.C. **Hob./spts.:** Hunting, fishing, photography, golf **SIC code:** 34 **Address:** North Valley Iron Works, Inc., P.O. Box 258, Chico, CA 95927 **E-mail:** nviw.sunset.net

WARD, RICHARD A.
Industry: Flooring **Univ./degree:** B.S. Candidate, Safety Management, Kennedy Western University **Current organization:** Roppe Corp. **Title:** Safety Manager **Type of organization:** Manufacturing **Major product:** Flooring materials **Area of distribution:** Ohio **Expertise:** Safety, personnel **Affiliations:** A.A.S.E.; National Safety Council **Hob./spts.:** Golf **SIC code:** 24 **Address:** Roppe Corp., 1602 N. Union St., Fostoria, OH 44830 **E-mail:** rawarrd@roppe.com **Web address:** www.roppe.com

WARREN, DAVID A.
Industry: Industrial machinery **Born:** August 11, 1959, Albion, New York **Univ./degree:** A.A.S., 1995; B.S., 2000, Rochester Institute of Technology **Current organization:** Airtech Division of API **Title:** Process Innovation Engineer **Type of organization:** Manufacturing **Major product:** Compressors, steam turbines **Area of distribution:** International **Expertise:** Manufacturing processes, engineering; Certified Manager from the Institute of Certified Professional Managers, campus of James Madison University, Harrisonburg, VA **Affiliations:** A.S.M.E.; N.M.A. **Hob./spts.:** Soccer, golf, NASCAR **SIC code:** 35 **Address:** 1545 Bills Rd., Kent, NY 14477 **E-mail:** david_a_warren@dresser_rand.com

WASILKOWSKI, CHARLES W.
Industry: Chemical **Born:** Walnutport, Pennsylvania **Univ./degree:** Leadership and Technology related courses, seminars, training **Current organization:** Geo Specialty Chemicals **Title:** Maintenance Supervisor **Type of organization:** Manufacturing **Major product:** Pipe fitting **Area of distribution:** Pennsylvania **Expertise:** Offering consistent growth and contribution in positions that have provided a broad range of mechanical, plant maintenance, supervisory, teaching and team building skills; Certifications: Welding, Health and Safety, Emergency Response, Fire Protection, Mechanical **Affiliations:** National Safety Council **Hob./spts.:** Hunting, fishing, coaching little league baseball **SIC code:** 28 **Address:** Geo Specialty Chemicals, 2409 N. Cedarcrest Blvd., Allentown, PA 18104-9733 **Phone:** (610)782-2626 **Fax:** (610)782-2636 **E-mail:** charles.wasilkowski@geosc.com

WATANABE, HIDEO
Industry: Medical devices **Born:** Glendale, California **Univ./degree:** B.S., Chemistry, University of California at Los Angeles **Current organization:** Salter Lab, Inc. **Title:** Chemist **Type of organization:** Manufacturing **Major product:** Respiratory devices **Area of distribution:** National **Expertise:** Chemistry **Affiliations:** A.C.S. **SIC code:** 38 **Address:** Salter Lab, Inc., 220 W. C Street, Tehachapi, CA 93561

WATANABE, HIROKUNI
Industry: Photographic, medical and graphic design **Born:** January 5, 1941, Tokyo, Japan **Univ./degree:** Business Administration/Economic Policy Degree, Hitotsubashi University **Current organization:** Fuji Photo Film, Inc. **Title:** President **Type of organization:** Manufacturing/research and development **Major product:** Photographic, printing and medical media **Area of distribution:** International **Expertise:** Global management for manufacturing **Honors/awards:** PMAI Award for Distinguished Service in Photo Imaging, South Carolina Ambassador for Economic Development by the Governor of South Carolina **Affiliations:** Rotary Club **Hob./spts.:** Golf **SIC code:** 38 **Address:** Fuji Photo Film, Inc., 211 Pucketts Ferry Rd., Greenwood, SC 29648 **E-mail:** hwatanabe@fujigreenwood.com

WAUGH, DENNIS W.
Industry: Food **Born:** May 8, 1952, Wilmington, Delaware **Univ./degree:** Ph.D., Occupational Safety, Western State University, Missouri, 1995 **Current organization:** ConAgra Refrigerated Foods Group **Title:** V.P. Health, Safety and Security **Type of organization:** Manufacturing **Major product:** Processed foods **Area of distribution:** International **Expertise:** Health and safety **Affiliations:** World Safety Organization; National Safety Council; American Society for Industrial Security **Hob./spts.:** Bagpipe Band, bicycling, spectator sports **SIC code:** 20 **Address:** ConAgra Refrigerated Foods Group, 2001 Butterfield Rd., Downers Grove, IL 60515 **E-mail:** dwaugh@crfc.com

WEBER, STEPHEN A.
Industry: Medical devices **Born:** June 20, 1966, Allentown, Pennsylvania **Univ./degree:** B.S., Mechanical Engineering, Pennsylvania State University, 1988 **Current organization:** B. Braun Medical, Inc. **Title:** Engineering Manager, I.V. Systems **Type of organization:** Manufacturing **Major product:** Medical devise disposables **Area of distribution:** International **Expertise:** Engineering, development and manufacturing **Affiliations:** A.S.M.E. **Hob./spts.:** Skiing, tennis, fencing, volunteer work **SIC code:** 38 **Address:** B. Braun Medical, Inc., 901 Marcon Blvd., Allentown, PA 18109 **E-mail:** steve.weber@bbmus.com **Web address:** www.bbraunusa.com

WEBER, TROY M.
Industry: Chemicals **Born:** December 10, 1962, New Orleans, Louisiana **Current organization:** Nalco Chemical Co. **Title:** Instrument Technician **Type of organization:** Manufacturing **Major product:** Water treatment chemicals **Area of distribution:** International **Expertise:** Instrumentation maintenance **Affiliations:** I.S.A.-C.C.S.T. **Hob./spts.:** Camping, collectibles **SIC code:** 28 **Address:** Nalco Chemical Co., P.O. Draw I, Garyville, LA 70051 **E-mail:** tweber318@hotmail.com

WEESNER, BETTY J.
Industry: Publishing **Born:** January 22, 1926, Danville, Indiana **Univ./degree:** B.A., Indiana University, 1951 **Current organization:** Hendricks County Republican, Inc. **Title:** President, Treasurer and Editor **Type of organization:** Publishing **Major product:** Newspaper **Area of distribution:** Hendricks County, Indiana **Expertise:** Editor, Manager, Owner **Honors/awards:** First woman to be elected to the Danville High School Hall of Fame; Honorary Life Member, Danville Friends of Library **Affiliations:** H.S.P.A.; Daughters of the American Revolution; American Legion Auxiliary; Indiana Sheriff's Association; Indiana University Alumni Association **Hob./spts.:** Photography **SIC code:** 27 **Address:** Hendricks County Republican, Inc., 6 E. Main, Danville, IN 46122 **E-mail:** therepublican@sbcglobal.net

WEHAGE, NICHOLAS E.
Industry: Food **Born:** February 16, 1959, Portland, Oregon **Univ./degree:** M.A., Finance, Washington State University **Current organization:** Pizza Blends Inc. **Title:** Controller **Type of organization:** Manufacturing **Major product:** Pizza dough dry mix **Area of distribution:** Oregon **Expertise:** Accounting, management **SIC code:** 20 **Address:** Pizza Blends Inc., 5357 N. Marine Dr., Portland, OR 97203 **E-mail:** nickwehage@yahoo.com

WEI, WEI
Industry: Semiconductors **Born:** March 4, 1974, Shanghai, China **Univ./degree:** M.S., Electrical Engineering, University of Washington at Seattle, 1999 **Current organization:** Atmel Corp. **Title:** Project Leader **Type of organization:** Manufacturing and design **Major product:** Semiconductors **Area of distribution:** International **Expertise:** Engineering **Affiliations:** I.E.E.E. **Hob./spts.:** Painting, outdoor activities **SIC code:** 36 **Address:** Atmel Corp., 2325 Orchard Pkwy., San Jose, CA 95131 **E-mail:** wwei@atmel.com

WEIBLE, BURTON
Industry: Gas measurement and control equipment **Born:** June 25, 1955, Sacramento, California **Univ./degree:** B.S., Business Administration, Peru State College, 1995 **Current organization:** American Meter Co. **Title:** Die Cast Engineering Analyst **Type of organization:** Manufacturing **Major product:** Residual gas meters, gas measurement **Area of distribution:** National **Expertise:** Technical support **Affiliations:** North American Die Cast Association **Hob./spts.:** Hunting, camping, fishing **SIC code:** 38 **Address:** American Meter Co., 2221 Industrial Rd., Nebraska City, NE 68410 **E-mail:** bweible@americanmeter.com

WELLET, MICHAEL W.
Industry: Specialty chemicals **Born:** March 11, 1970; Livingston, New Jersey **Univ./degree:** B.S., Chemical Engineering, 1995; M.Eng., 2000, New Jersey Institute of

Technology; M.B.A., University of Texas, 2004 **Current organization:** Magnesium Elektron, Inc. **Title:** Senior Process Engineer **Type of organization:** Manufacturing **Major product:** Zirconium chemicals **Area of distribution:** International **Expertise:** Chemical engineering, P.E. in New Jersey, New York, Delaware, Maryland and Certified Plant Engineer nationally **Affiliations:** A.I.C.E.; A.C.S. **SIC code:** 28 **Address:** Magnesium Elektron, Inc., 500 Point Breeze Rd., Flemington, NJ 08822 **E-mail:** mwellet@meichem.com **Web address:** www.meichem.com

WENZEL, DORIS REPLOGLE
Industry: Publishing **Born:** February 11, 1940, Mattoon, Illinois **Univ./degree:** B.S., English/Theatre/Speech Communication, North Central University, 1981; M.A., Communications, Illinois State University, 1988 **Current organization:** Mayhaven Publishing **Title:** Owner/Publisher **Type of organization:** Publishing company **Major product:** Books **Area of distribution:** International **Expertise:** Author/Publisher **Published works:** Book, "10 Sisters, A True Story," and feature article in Family Circle Magazine **Affiliations:** Board Member, AFTRA; Abraham Lincoln Museum **Hob./spts.:** Art work, quilting, gardening, video production **SIC code:** 27 **Address:** Mayhaven Publishing, P.O. Box 557, Mahomet, IL 61853 **E-mail:** mohometpublishing@mchsi.com **Web address:** www.mayhavenpublishing.com

WEST, DARBY L.
Industry: Oil and gas equipment **Born:** January 13, 1938, Melrose, New Mexico **Spouse:** Angelina Loomis Padilla **Married:** February 9, 1980 **Children:** Rebecca, 43; Darby Jr, 42; John, 41; Carl 42; Isaac Jr., 40; Terry and Larry, 39; 16 grandchildren; 3 great grandchildren **Current organization:** L.I.P., Inc. **Title:** Vice President of Engineering **Type of organization:** Manufacturing company **Major product:** Natural gas dehydration and production units, various types of pressure vessels **Area of distribution:** National **Expertise:** Engineering **Affiliations:** Farmington Chapter, American Petroleum Institute; Elks **Hob./spts.:** Leather carvings, fishing, boating, golf, bowling **SIC code:** 35 **Address:** L.I.P., Inc., P.O. Box 1187, Bloomfield, NM 87413 **E-mail:** darbywest@msn.com

WEST, VIRGIL J.
Industry: Air filtration **Born:** Louisa, Kentucky **Univ./degree:** B.A., Mt. Vernon University **Current organization:** Columbus Industries Inc. **Title:** Plant Manager **Type of organization:** Manufacturing **Major product:** Air filtration **Area of distribution:** International **Expertise:** Project management, safety **Hob./spts.:** Spending time with family, golf **SIC code:** 35 **Address:** Columbus Industries Inc., 11545 St. Rt.41, West Union, OH 45693 **E-mail:** vwest@colind.net **Web address:** www.colind.net

WESTON, MATTHEW C.
Industry: Wet separation/dewatering **Born:** January 17, 1980 **Univ./degree:** B.S., Engineering, Oklahoma State University, 2002 **Current organization:** Andritz-Ruthner, Inc. **Title:** Mechanical Design Engineer **Type of organization:** Manufacturing **Major product:** Screens, belt presses, centrifuges **Area of distribution:** International **Expertise:** Design engineering **Affiliations:** A.S.M.E. **Hob./spts.:** Race cars, outdoor activities **SIC code:** 34 **Address:** Andritz-Ruthner, Inc., 1010 Commercial Blvd. South, Arlington, TX 76001 **E-mail:** mweston63@hotmail.com

WHARTON, JOSEPH B.
Industry: Consulting **Univ./degree:** M.B.A., Harvard Business School, 1965 **Current organization:** Joseph B. Wharton, Consultant **Title:** Director of Finance **Type of organization:** Consulting **Major product:** Agricultural chemicals; consulting to multiple industries, primarily manufacturing and professional services **Area of distribution:** National **Expertise:** Corporate finance **SIC code:** 28 **Address:** 330 W. Olympia Place, Suite 401, Seattle, WA 98119 **E-mail:** Wharton.joe@gmail.com

WHITE, NELSON H.
Industry: Publishing **Born:** October 29, 1938, Baltimore, Maryland **Univ./degree:** B.A., University of Redlands; Honorary D.D. & Th.D. **Current organization:** The Technology Group **Title:** Founder/Owner **Type of organization:** Sole Proprietorship **Major product:** Book publishing/sales **Area of distribution:** International **Expertise:** Personal safety and security **Published works:** 140 books **Affiliations:** Board member, European Knight Templer **Hob./spts.:** Pilot, pistol shooting, reading, travel **SIC code:** 27 **Address:** The Technology Group, Attn: Sheila Emery, 5069 Appian Way Rear, El Sobrante, CA 94803 **E-mail:** whtmagick@aol.com **Web address:** www.techgroupbooks.com

WHITE, VINCENT W.
Industry: Water treatment for semiconductors **Born:** May 12, 1958, San Antonio, Texas **Univ./degree:** A.S., Industrial Water Treatment, San Juan College, 1999 **Current organization:** AMD, Inc. **Title:** Plant Specialist, Lead Operator **Type of organization:** Manufacturing, R&D **Major product:** Semiconductor devices **Area of distribution:** International **Expertise:** Process water treatment, licensed plumber, licensed backflow prevention tester/repairman **Affiliations:** T.N.R.C.C. **Hob./spts.:** Fishing **SIC code:** 36 **Address:** 1331 Warrington Dr., Austin, TX 78753-4407 **E-mail:** vinswayn@ev1.net

WHITNEY, ALISON
Industry: Education **Born:** April 4, 1945 **Univ./degree:** B.A., With Honors, Humanities, University of California at Berkeley, 1967 **Current organization:** WhitneyWorks - AbuseAlert **Title:** President/Founder **Type of organization:** Publishing, educating **Major product:** Workbooks with cassette tapes, leadership training seminars, songs for young children **Area of distribution:** National/International **Expertise:** Writing, public speaking, teaching **Honors/awards:** Listed in Outstanding Young Women of America, 1978; Who's Who in the West, 1995-2003; Who's Who in the World, 1996-2003; Who's Who in American Education, 2004-2005 **Published works:** "Challenge of Being a Woman" (1976-2003); "Knowing You Are Loved", a study guide with cassette tape (1982-1990); "Activity Songs For Young Children", published by Gospel Light (1978-1992) **Affiliations:** C.B.E. (Christians for Biblical Equality); N.C.A.D.V. (National Coalition Against Domestic Violence); S.C.C.B.W. (Southern California Coalition of Battered Women); A.A.U.W., (American Association of University Women); Delta Gamma **Hob./spts.:** Spending time with friends, reading, lecturing, running, swimming, tennis, fine dining, movies, music, the beach **SIC code:** 27 **Address:** WhitneyWorks - AbuseAlert, 2345 Paseo Dorado, La Jolla, CA 92037 **E-mail:** a.whitney@earthlink.net

WHITTIMORE, JAMES RICKY
Industry: Automotive **Born:** December 25, 1956, Henderson, Tennessee **Current organization:** Saturn Corp. - A Division of General Motors **Title:** Operations Technician **Type of organization:** Manufacturing **Major product:** Automobiles **Area of distribution:** International **Expertise:** Parts, production **Affiliations:** United Auto Workers; Democratic National Committee **Hob./spts.:** Politics, the stock market, baseball, football, bowling, physical fitness **SIC code:** 37 **Address:** Saturn Corp. - A Division of General Motors, Hwy. 31, Springhill, TN 37174

WIGFALL, AUTHOR R.
Industry: Food **Born:** May 28, 1947, Fort Worth, Texas **Univ./degree:** B.A., Texas Southern University, 1969 **Current organization:** Robert Dairy Co. **Title:** Quality Assurance Manager **Type of organization:** Manufacturing **Major product:** Fluid milk, cultured products, DQ mix, juices **Area of distribution:** Nebraska **Expertise:** QA/QC **Hob./spts.:** Flight simulation, fishing, chess, basketball, son's soccer **SIC code:** 20 **Address:** Roberts Dairy Co., 2901 Cuming St., Omaha, NE 68131 **E-mail:** awigfall@robertsdairy.com

WILCOX, MARTIN H.
Industry: Marine **Univ./degree:** B.S.E.E., University of Pennsylvania, 1966 **Current organization:** Marine Sonic Technology, Ltd. **Title:** President **Type of organization:** Manufacturing **Major product:** Imaging Sonar **Area of distribution:** International **Expertise:** Engineering **Published works:** Articles **Affiliations:** M.T.S.; I.E.E.E. **SIC code:** 37 **Address:** Marine Sonic Technology, Ltd., 5508 George Washington Memorial Hwy., P.O. Box 730, White Marsh, VA 23183 **E-mail:** mwilcox@marinesonic.com

WILCOX, MICHAEL J.
Industry: Artificial vision systems and cameras **Born:** Detroit, Michigan **Univ./degree:** Ph.D., Biophysics, Purdue University **Current organization:** Hyperactivity Systems **Title:** CEO **Type of organization:** Manufacturing, R&D **Major product:** Artificial vision systems and cameras **Area of distribution:** National **Expertise:** Engineering and research **Published works:** Articles and book chapters **Affiliations:** S.P.I.E.; I.E.E.E.; Sigma Pi Sigma; Sigma Xi **Hob./spts.:** Camping, weightlifting, Harley Davidson motorcycles **SIC code:** 36 **Address:** Hyperacuity Systems, 6555 Delmonico Dr., #212, Colorado Springs, CO 80919 **E-mail:** mike.wilcox@usafa.af.mil

WILDE, PATRICK J.
Industry: Electronics **Born:** July 21, 1959, Decatur, Texas **Univ./degree:** B.S., Physics, North Texas State University, 1983 **Current organization:** Advanced Product Center/Raytheon **Title:** Project Manager **Type of organization:** Manufacturing/R&D **Major product:** Microwave components **Area of distribution:** National **Expertise:** Physics, project management **Honors/awards:** Patent in surface acoustic wave processing **Published works:** Articles **Affiliations:** I.E.E.E. **Hob./spts.:** Spending time with his grandchildren, hiking **SIC code:** 36 **Address:** Advanced Product Center/Raytheon, 13510 N. N. Central Expwy., Dallas, TX 75265 **E-mail:** p-wilde@raytheon.com **Web address:** www.raytheon.com

WILKENS, WILLIAM F.
Industry: Construction **Born:** May 9, 1963, Huron, South Dakota **Univ./degree:** B.S.E.E.; South Dakota School of Mines and Technology, 1985 **Current organization:** Rosco Manufacturing, a Leeboy Co. **Title:** Operations Manager **Type of organization:** Manufacturing **Major product:** Road maintenance equipment **Area of distribution:** National **Expertise:** Project engineering, operations management, factory automation, material handling, troubleshooting, customer relations, quality assurance, team leadership **Affiliations:** Rotary International **Hob./spts.:** Tennis, golf, gardening **SIC code:** 35 **Address:** Rosco Manufacturing, a Leeboy Co., 1001 S.W. First St., Madison, SD 57042 **E-mail:** billw@leeboy.com

WILKIE, JONATHAN P.
Industry: Electronics **Univ./degree:** B.S., Business, Menlo College, 1970 **Current organization:** Nicollet Technologies Corp. **Title:** President **Type of organization:** Manufacturing **Major product:** Custom magnetics **Area of distribution:** National **Expertise:** Product development **Published works:** Articles **Affiliations:** I.U.V.A.; F.T.A.; E.M.C.M.; N.A.M.; RadTech International **SIC code:** 36 **Address:** Nicollet Technologies Corp., 711 Fifteenth Ave. N.E., Minneapolis, MN 55413 **E-mail:** jwilkie@nictec.com **Web address:** www.nictec.com

WILLIAMS, DANIEL J.
Industry: Intrusion prevention systems **Univ./degree:** B.S., Education, Slippery Rock University, Pennsylvania, 1970 **Current organization:** 3COM/TippingPoint Technologies **Title:** Manager, New Production Introduction **Type of organization:** Manufacturing **Major product:** Network - based intrusion prevention equipment **Area of distribution:** International **Expertise:** Operations **Honors/awards:** A.P.I.C.S. **Affiliations:** President, Pflugerville Area Youth Soccer League **Hob./spts.:** Family, youth soccer **SIC code:** 36 **Address:** 3COM/TippingPoint Technologies, 7501 N. Capital of Texas Hwy., Bldg. B, Austin, TX 78731-1776 **E-mail:** danw@tippingpoint.com

WILLIAMS, OLLIE SHELTON
Industry: Machinery **Univ./degree:** Journeyman Degree, Craven County Community College **Current organization:** Robert Busch Corp. **Title:** Tool & Die Maker **Type of organization:** Contract manufacturing **Major product:** Tools, dies and holding devices **Area of distribution:** International **Expertise:** Tool and die prototype **SIC code:** 35 **Address:** P.O. Box 12062, New Bern, NC 28560

WILLIS, SIGMUND J.
Industry: Oil **Born:** December 22, 1957, Nassau, Bahamas **Univ./degree:** B.S., Management, LaSalle University , 2000 **Current organization:** Bahamas Oil Refining Co. Int. Ltd. **Title:** Marine Superintendent **Type of organization:** Oil terminal **Major product:** Oil storage/blending and transshipment **Area of distribution:** International **Expertise:** Marine operation and spill response **Affiliations:** B.M.A.; B.S.O.A.; International Maritime Organization; American Management Association **Hob./spts.:** Bahamas bowling team **SIC code:** 29 **Address:** Bahamas Oil Refining Co. Int. Ltd., 760 N.E. Seventh Ave., Dania, FL 33004 **E-mail:** sigmundwillis@hotmail.com

WILLIS JR., GEORGE A.
Industry: Pharmaceutical **Born:** February 2, 1962, Staten Island, New York **Univ./degree:** B.S. Wagner College, New York, 1984 **Current organization:** Bristol-Myers Squibb Co. **Title:** Sr. Clinical Supplies Scientist **Type of organization:** Manufacturing/R&D **Major product:** Pharmaceuticals **Area of distribution:** International **Expertise:** Clinical Supplies **Honors/awards:** Strathmore's Who's Who **Hob./spts.:** Fishing, part time chef at four star restaurant **SIC code:** 28 **Address:** Bristol-Myers Squibb Co., 1 Squibb Dr., Bldg. 107, Room 1560, New Brunswick, NJ 08903 **E-mail:** george_willis@bms.com

WILSON, DUANE P.
Industry: Dairy **Born:** January 15, 1954, Sioux City, Iowa **Current organization:** Wells Dairy Inc. **Title:** Sanitation Supervisor **Type of organization:** Manufacturing **Major product:** Ice cream, yogurt, dips **Area of distribution:** National **Expertise:** Sanitation **Hob./spts.:** Golf **SIC code:** 20 **Address:** Wells Dairy Inc., , Kingsley, IA 51028 **E-mail:** dpwilson@bluebunny.com

WILSON, WILLIE C.
Industry: Chemical (air separation) **Born:** December 12, 1947, Union Springs, Alabama **Univ./degree:** A.S., Business Administration; A.S., Computer Programming, Bryant & Stratton Business Institute; B.S., Computer Science **Current organization:** Praxair Inc. **Title:** Sr. Systems Operator **Type of organization:** Information technology **Area of distribution:** International **Expertise:** Computer systems operations **Affiliations:** Served in US Army 1967-70 **Hob./spts.:** Fishing, bowling, hunting, the outdoors **SIC code:** 28 **Address:** Praxair Inc., 175 E. Park Dr., Tonawanda, NY 14150 **E-mail:** williewilson@praxair.com **Web address:** www.praxair.com

WIRT, DARRELL A.
Industry: Cooking appliances **Born:** June 25, 1968, Memphis, Tennessee **Univ./degree:** B.S., Electrical Engineering, University of Memphis, 2000 **Current organization:** BSH Home Appliances **Title:** Microwave Engineer **Type of organization:** Manufacturing **Major product:** Microwave/built-in wall ovens **Area of distribution:** International **Expertise:** Engineering **Affiliations:** I.E.E.E.; S.M.E. **Hob./spts.:** Computer surfing, football **SIC code:** 36 **Address:** BSH Home Appliances, 100 Bosch Blvd., New Bern, NC 28562 **E-mail:** darrell.wirt@bshg.com

WOLAK, TIMOTHY E.
Industry: Automotive **Born:** December 6, 1960, Detroit, Michigan **Univ./degree:** B.S.E.E., General Motors Institute, 1984; M.B.A., Operations Management/Human Resources, Oakland University, 1995 **Current organization:** General Motors, Powertrain Division **Title:** Maintenance Manager **Type of organization:** Manufacturing **Major product:** Cars and trucks **Area of distribution:** International **Expertise:** Manufacturing management **Published works:** Undergraduate thesis **Hob./spts.:** Family, travel, sports **SIC code:** 37 **Address:** 2568 Locksley Ct., Troy, MI 48083 **E-mail:** tim.wolak@gm.com

WONDRASEK, ARTHUR W.
Industry: Fasteners **Born:** Illinois **Univ./degree:** B.S., B.A., Loyola University, Illinois, 1966 **Current organization:** QSN Industries **Title:** President **Type of organization:** Manufacturer/distributor **Major product:** Fasteners - screws, bolts **Area of distribution:** International **Expertise:** Management **Honors/awards:** Entrepreneurs of the Year **Affiliations:** Industrial Fasteners Institute; Chicago Entrepreneurs Society **Hob./spts.:** Golf **SIC code:** 34 **Address:** QSN Industries, 1441 N Wood Dale Rd., Wood Dale, IL 60191-1078 **E-mail:** artw@qsn.com **Web address:** www.qsn.com

WOOD, CONSTANCE S.
Industry: Publishing **Born:** November 18, 1947, Wooster, Ohio **Univ./degree:** M.A., Human Resource Management, Stafford University, 1996 **Current organization:** ProQuest Business Solutions **Title:** Senior Human Resources Manager **Type of organization:** Publisher **Major product:** Electronic republishing of technical reference materials for auto, power sports and outdoor power equipment industries **Area of distribution:** National **Expertise:** Human Resources Generalist **Affiliations:** United Way Venture Grant; Society for Human Resource Management **Hob./spts.:** Playing the drums, singing **SIC code:** 27 **Address:** ProQuest Business Solutions, 1909 Old Mansfield Rd., Wooster, OH 44691 **E-mail:** connie.wood@pbs.proquest.com

WOOD, LESLIE DAVE
Industry: Food **Born:** Dayton, Ohio **Current organization:** Camden Locker Plant **Title:** Owner **Type of organization:** Processor/manufacturing **Major product:** Process and packaging of beef, pork and sheep **Area of distribution:** Ohio **Expertise:** Management, operations, meat processing, butchering **SIC code:** 20 **Address:** Camden Locker Plant, 52 E. Central Ave., Camden, OH 45311

WOODS-HALEY, DEBRA A.
Industry: Electronics **Born:** October 22, 1968, Brooklyn, New York **Univ./degree:** B.S.E.E., New Jersey Institute of Technology **Current organization:** Control Instruments **Title:** Director of Sales **Type of organization:** Manufacturing **Major product:** Electro-mechanical safety systems **Area of distribution:** International **Expertise:** Sales, marketing **Affiliations:** I.S.A.; NJ Friends.org **Hob./spts.:** Music, playing the guitar, dancing **SIC code:** 36 **Address:** Control Instruments, 25 Law Dr., Fairfield, NJ 07004 **E-mail:** debwh@aol.com

WOODUM, R. C.
Industry: Woodworking **Born:** October 11, 1946, San Antonio, Texas **Current organization:** Texas Architectural Panel **Title:** President **Type of organization:** Manufacturing **Major product:** Architectural woodwork, veneer panels, conference tables, doors, reception desks **Area of distribution:** National **Expertise:** Architectural panel products **Affiliations:** A.I.A.; A.W.I. **Hob./spts.:** Boy Scouts **SIC code:** 24 **Address:** Texas Architectural Panel, 5713 Cottonwood St., Pearland, TX 77584 **E-mail:** randy@texaspanel.com **Web address:** www.texaspanel.com

WORKING, ROBERT S.
Industry: Automotive/industrial construction **Born:** April 16, 1950 **Current organization:** Sika Corp. **Title:** Maintenance Manager **Type of organization:** Manufacturing **Major product:** Expandable and non-expandable rubber based products **Area of distribution:** International **Expertise:** OEE, TPM, predictive/preventive maintenance **Affiliations:** S.P.E. **Hob./spts.:** Fishing, boating **SIC code:** 30 **Address:** Sika Corp., 14201 Botts Rd., Grandview, MO 64030 **E-mail:** working.bob@sika-corp.com

WRIGHT, JAY H.
Industry: Electronics service and facilities **Born:** April 11, 1952, Lebanon, Indiana **Univ./degree:** B.S., Engineering, Purdue University, 1980; M.S.E.E., Iowa State University, 1985; Ph.D., Biomedical Electronics, Harrington University, 1995 **Current organization:** Southwestern Electronics **Title:** President/owner **Type of organization:**

Micro Manufacturing, R&D, Sales **Major product:** Electronics sales and service **Area of distribution:** International **Expertise:** Certified electronics officer, Certified IT&T instructor, amateur radio class instructor **Published works:** 6 patents, 75 articles, inventor of electronography **Affiliations:** I.E.E.E.; N.E.S.D.A.; American Red Cross; President of IN Electronics Service Association **Hob./spts.:** Ham amateur radio, camping, scouting, water sports, boating **SIC code:** 36 **Address:** Southwestern Electronics, 2016 E. Main St., Danville, IN 46122 **E-mail:** jay@southwesternelec.com

WRIGHT, RON D.
Industry: Custom injection molding **Born:** January 6, 1956, St. Charles, Illinois **Univ./degree:** A.S., Construction and Design, Three Rivers Community College, 1979 **Current organization:** PMB Inc. **Title:** Tooling/Quality Manager **Type of organization:** Manufacturing **Major product:** Automotive fasteners/consumers products **Area of distribution:** International **Expertise:** Engineering, quality control, product development **Published works:** 5 patents **Affiliations:** Society of Plastics Engineers **Hob./spts.:** Fishing, hunting, canoeing, camping, softball **SIC code:** 30 **Address:** PMB Inc., 14 County Rd. 465, Poplar Bluff, MO 63901 **E-mail:** greenacres@semo.net

WU, WINTHROP
Industry: Computers **Born:** September 28, 1962, Alliance, Ohio **Univ./degree:** M.S., Computer Science, U.C.L.A., 1989 **Current organization:** ATI Research **Title:** Staff Engineer **Type of organization:** Design/manufacturing **Major product:** Computer graphic products **Area of distribution:** International **Expertise:** Engineering **Affiliations:** I.E.E.E. **Hob./spts.:** Tennis **SIC code:** 36 **Address:** ATI Research, 62 Forest St., Marlborough, MA 01752 **E-mail:** wuwinthrop@townisp.com

WUSTHOLZ, FREDERICK C.
Industry: Food **Born:** January 15, 1952, Hackensack, New Jersey **Univ./degree:** B.S., Food Science, Delaware Valley College, 1974 **Current organization:** DSM Food Specialties **Title:** Technical Affairs Manager **Type of organization:** Manufacturing **Major product:** Food ingredients **Area of distribution:** National **Expertise:** Development/marketing/sales of new products **Affiliations:** I.F.T. **Hob./spts.:** Reading, fine arts, tennis **SIC code:** 20 **Address:** DSM Food Specialists USA, Inc., 2675 Eisenhower Ave., Eagleville, PA 19403 **E-mail:** f.wustholz@aol.com

WYLIE, DAVID G.
Industry: Marine electronics **Born:** June 20, 1975, Houston, Texas **Univ./degree:** International College **Current organization:** Heinz Marine Electronics **Title:** General Manager **Type of organization:** Manufacturing, dealer/service **Major product:** Marine communications, navigation, radio and satellite communications **Area of distribution:** National **Expertise:** GPS systems **Affiliations:** Fort Myers Chamber of Commerce; Kiwanis Club **Hob./spts.:** Boating **SIC code:** 36 **Address:** Heinz Marine Electronics, 19190 San Carlos Blvd., Ft. Myers, FL 33931 **E-mail:** david.wylie.1975@hotmail.com **Web address:** www.heinzmarine.com

YOAKAM, ALICE BURNS
Industry: Printing, publishing **Current organization:** Panagraphics Printing **Title:** Partner **Type of organization:** Commercial printing **Major product:** Art and composition; printing, bindery, publishing **Area of distribution:** Local **Expertise:** Pre-press and management **Affiliations:** The Oxford Club; National Association of Female Executives; The Inventors Club **SIC code:** 27 **Address:** Panagraphics, Inc., 340 Western Rd., Unit 14, Reno, NV 89506 **E-mail:** babyb10495@aol.com

YODER, TIMOTHY L.
Industry: Food **Born:** March 14, 1961, Findlay, Ohio **Univ./degree:** Building Industry Certified, Findlay Vocational, 1979 **Current organization:** Oak State Products, Inc. **Title:** Production Manager **Type of organization:** Manufacturing **Major product:** Cookies, breakfast bars, inclusions **Area of distribution:** International **Expertise:** Production **Hob./spts.:** Sports **SIC code:** 20 **Address:** Oak State Products, Inc., 775 State Rt. 251, Wenona, IL 61377 **E-mail:** tim-yoder@oakstate.com

YOKELSON, TITUT N.
Industry: Nutritional products **Univ./degree:** B.S., Chemistry; D.Pharm., University of Montana **Current organization:** Nutritional Laboratories International **Title:** Ph.D./Vice President, R&D **Type of organization:** Manufacturing **Major product:** Nutritional supplements, tablets, capsules **Expertise:** Science, biochemistry, biophysics **Affiliations:** American Chemical Society **Hob./spts.:** Reading, dancing, kayaking **SIC code:** 28 **Address:** Nutritional Laboratories International, 1001 S. Third West, Missoula, MT 59801 **E-mail:** tyokelson@nutritionallabs.com

YOSHIDA, AKITO
Industry: Electronics **Born:** November 21, 1961, Yokohama, Japan **Univ./degree:** B.S., Physics, Tokyo University, 1984 **Current organization:** Amkor Technology **Title:** Senior Product Manager **Type of organization:** Manufacturing **Major product:** Semiconductor packaging **Area of distribution:** International **Expertise:** Engineering **Published works:** Numerous including, "Stacked Package-on-Package Design Guidelines", Chip Scale Review Magazine, July 2005; "Stackable CSP", Japan Semiconductor International Magazine, June 2005; "Board Level Reliability Study on Three-Dimensional Thin Stacked Package", IEEE, Electronic Components and Technology Conference, 2004; "Key Assembly Technology for 3-D Packaging-Stacked Die and Stacked Package", International Wafer-Level Packaging Congress, 2004; "Co-design", Advanced Packaging Magazine, June 2004 **Affiliations:** IEEE; IMAPS **Hob./spts.:** Hiking **SIC code:** 36 **Address:** Amkor Technology, 1900 S. Price Rd., Chandler, AZ 85248 **E-mail:** akitoyo@cox.net **Web address:** www.amkor.com

YOTT, MARK E.
Industry: Load transfer systems/construction **Born:** September 15, 1969, Kankakee, Illinois **Current organization:** American Highway Technology **Title:** Electrician **Type of organization:** Manufacturing **Major product:** Concrete reinforcement for roads **Area of distribution:** Illinois **Expertise:** Electricity, repair and maintenance of welding equipment **Hob./spts.:** Farm toy collecting **SIC code:** 32 **Address:** American Highway Technology, 2150 S. Route 45-52, Kankakee, IL 60901 **E-mail:** marke28@juno.com

YOUNG, MICHAEL JAMES
Industry: Network Storage **Born:** September 20, 1967, San Jose, California **Univ./degree:** B.S., Mathematics, Jacksonville University, 1992 **Current organization:** Net Helix, Inc. **Title:** CEO **Type of organization:** Manufacturing **Major product:** Storage virtualization appliance **Area of distribution:** International **Expertise:** Marketing **Hob./spts.:** Mountain biking **SIC code:** 39 **Address:** Net Helix, Inc., 85 Paloma Dr., Morgan Hill, CA 95037 **E-mail:** myoung@wildernessvoice.com

YUAN, LANG
Industry: Telecommunications **Born:** June, 2, 1974, Sichuan, China **Univ./degree:** M.S.M.E., Thermal Engineering, Jiangsu University, Chinas, 1999; M.S.M.E., Electronic Packaging and Thermal Management, University of Maryland, 2001 **Current organization:** Fujitsu Network Communications **Title:** Mechanical Design Engineer **Type of organization:** Manufacturing **Major product:** Electronics **Area of distribution:** International **Expertise:** Lead thermal design engineer; international lecturing **Honors/awards:** Outstanding Performance-Fujitsu, 2003 **Published works:** 8 articles; 1 patent approved and 1 pending **Affiliations:** American Society of Heating, Refrigerating and Air-Conditioning Engineers; I C D T '99 Committee **SIC code:** 36 **Address:** Fujitsu Network Communications, 2 Blue Hill Plaza, Pearl River, NY 10965 **E-mail:** langyuan@yahoo.com **Web address:** www.fujitsu.com

ZAIDI, SYED ISTAFA
Industry: Electronic instruments & control **Univ./degree:** M.S., Mechanical Engineering, University of Cincinnati, 1984 **Current organization:** Conductus, Inc. **Title:** Vice President, Operations **Type of organization:** Manufacturing **Major product:** Electronic components systems **Area of distribution:** International **Expertise:** Operations including manufacturing and quality **Published works:** Articles **SIC code:** 36 **Address:** 38694 Guardino Dr., Fremont, CA 94536 **E-mail:** syed.zaidi@conductus.com

ZARAKHOVICH, YURI A.
Industry: News **Born:** August 12, 1946, Ukraine **Univ./degree:** Ph.D., History, Institute of Oriental Studies, Russian Academy of Sciences **Current organization:** Time Magazine **Title:** Correspondent **Type of organization:** Magazine **Major product:** Media **Area of distribution:** International **Expertise:** Russian correspondent, Russian book translator **Hob./spts.:** Travel, lecturing **SIC code:** 27 **Address:** Time Magazine, 1271 Sixth Ave., Time-Life Bldg., New York, NY 10020 **E-mail:** yuri@time.ru **Web address:** www.timeeurope.com

ZHU, JAMES Z.
Industry: Voice and data communications **Born:** April 19, 1962, China **Univ./degree:** Ph.D., New Jersey Institute of Technology, 1996 **Current organization:** Vidanetwork Technologies, Inc. **Title:** CTO, PhD **Type of organization:** Manufacturing **Major product:** Software and communication equipment **Area of distribution:** International **Expertise:** Technical solutions, tele engineer, consulting and implementation of telecommunications **Affiliations:** I.E.E.E.; A.C.M. **Hob./spts.:** Soccer, tennis, swimming **SIC code:** 36 **Address:** Vidanetwork Technologies, Inc., 11 Revere Ave., Bridgewater, NJ 08807 **E-mail:** jzhu@vidanetwork.com **Web address:** www.vidanetwork.com

ZHU, NI
Industry: Medical devices **Born:** May 29, 1958, Dalian, China **Univ./degree:** M.S., University of Texas, 1991 **Current organization:** Retractable Technologies, Inc. **Title:** Product Development Manager **Type of organization:** Manufacturing **Major product:** Safety medical devices **Area of distribution:** International **Expertise:** Research and development **SIC code:** 38 **Address:** 4408 Brigade Ct., Plano, TX 75024

ZHU, YONG
Industry: Industrial automation/aerospace/computer systems **Univ./degree:** Ph.D., Industrial Automation Engineering, Zhejiang University, China **Current organization:** Antcom Corp. **Title:** Software Engineer **Type of organization:** Manufacturing

Major product: Software, microwave test systems **Area of distribution:** International **Expertise:** Engineering **Published works:** Scientific journals **SIC code:** 36 **Address:** 3612 Keystone Ave., #9, Los Angeles, CA 90034 **E-mail:** zhu_yong@yahoo.com **Web address:** www.antcom.com

ZIELKE, CHRISTOPHER
Industry: Electronics **Born:** January 23, 1952, Philadelphia, Pennsylvania **Univ./degree:** M.S., Physics, La Salle University, 1978 **Current organization:** Avnet Electronics **Title:** Engineering Director **Type of organization:** Manufacturing **Major product:** Semiconductors **Area of distribution:** International **Expertise:** Engineering **Affiliations:** I.S.A. **Hob./spts.:** Electronics **SIC code:** 36 **Address:** Avnet Electronics, 6321 San Ignacio Ave., San Jose, CA 95119 **E-mail:** chris.zielke@avnet.com

ZIELKE, RANDY H.
Industry: Automotive stampings **Title:** Controller **Type of organization:** Manufacturing **Major product:** Class "B" automotive parts **Expertise:** Finance **SIC code:** 37 **Address:** Hofley Mfg., 15500 12 Mile Rd., Roseville, MI 48066

ZILNER, CATHLEEN A.
Industry: Surgical **Univ./degree:** M.B.A., Indiana University of Pennsylvania, 1994 **Current organization:** Johnson & Johnson, Ethicon Endo-Surgery **Title:** Senior Territory Manager **Type of organization:** Manufacturing **Major product:** Surgical and medical devices **Area of distribution:** National **Expertise:** Surgical sales, management **Affiliations:** American College of Healthcare Executives, Harvard, Yale Princeton Club **Hob./spts.:** International travel, collecting art/sculpture, volunteer work: St. Vincent de Paul Society, St. Ignatius Church (feeding the poor, packing food, distribution of food, Bundle Sunday, Blanket Sunday) **SIC code:** 38 **Address:** Johnson & Johnson, Ethicon Endo-Surgery, 4545 Creek Rd., Cincinnati, OH 45242 **E-mail:** czilner@eesus.jnj.com

ZIMA, RICARDO
Industry: Electrical engineering **Born:** January 20, 1957, Brazil **Univ./degree:** B.S., Electrical Engineering/Economics; Masters, Marketing, ESPM University of São Paulo, Brazil; M.B.A., Keenan Flagler University, University of North Carolina, Chapel Hill **Current organization:** ABB Inc. **Title:** Proposal Manager **Type of organization:** Electrical engineering **Major product:** AIS and GIS substations **Expertise:** Industrial marketing of power systems **Published works:** Article, "The Mobile Substation", from "Mundo Elétrico", Brazil 07/87 **Affiliations:** Member, Beta Gamma Sigma **Hob./spts.:** Watching movies, fishing, swimming **SIC code:** 36 **Address:** ABB, Inc., 940 Main Campus Dr., Raleigh, NC 27606 **E-mail:** ricardozima@hotmail.com

ZIVIC, GEOFFREY A.
Industry: Printing **Born:** January 3, 1960, Joliet, Illinois **Current organization:** H.S. Crocker Co., Inc. **Title:** Pressroom Foreman **Type of organization:** Manufacturing **Major product:** Lidding **Area of distribution:** U.S., Canada, Mexico **Expertise:** Management, inventing **Hob./spts.:** Family, drawing, painting **SIC code:** 27 **Address:** H.S. Crocker Co., Inc., 12100 Smith Dr., Huntley, IL 60142 **E-mail:** geoffathscrocker@hotmail.com

ZOTT, F. ERIC
Industry: Chemicals **Born:** Mount Holly, New Jersey **Current organization:** Stepan Co. **Title:** Materials Team Leader **Type of organization:** Manufacturing **Major product:** Surfactants (detergents) **Area of distribution:** International **Expertise:** Purchasing **Hob./spts.:** Reading, gardening; Manager of Pee Wee Ice Hockey Team **SIC code:** 28 **Address:** Stepan Co., 2 Fourth St., Fieldsboro, NJ 08505 **E-mail:** fzott@stepan.com

ZWETTLER, ERICH F.
Industry: Automotive **Born:** February 6, 1977 **Univ./degree:** B.S.M.E., Southern Illinois University, 2001 **Current organization:** Dura Automotive Systems, Inc. **Title:** Product Engineer **Type of organization:** Manufacturing, design **Major product:** Seat adjuster assemblies, recliner assemblies, track slides **Area of distribution:** International **Expertise:** Mechanical engineering **Affiliations:** A.S.M.E. **Hob./spts.:** Amateur radio, education, golf, tennis, hiking, motorcycling, boating, tinkering **SIC code:** 37 **Address:** Dura Automotive Systems, Inc., 301 S. Simmons St., Stockton, IL 61085 **E-mail:** zwettler.e@duraauto.com

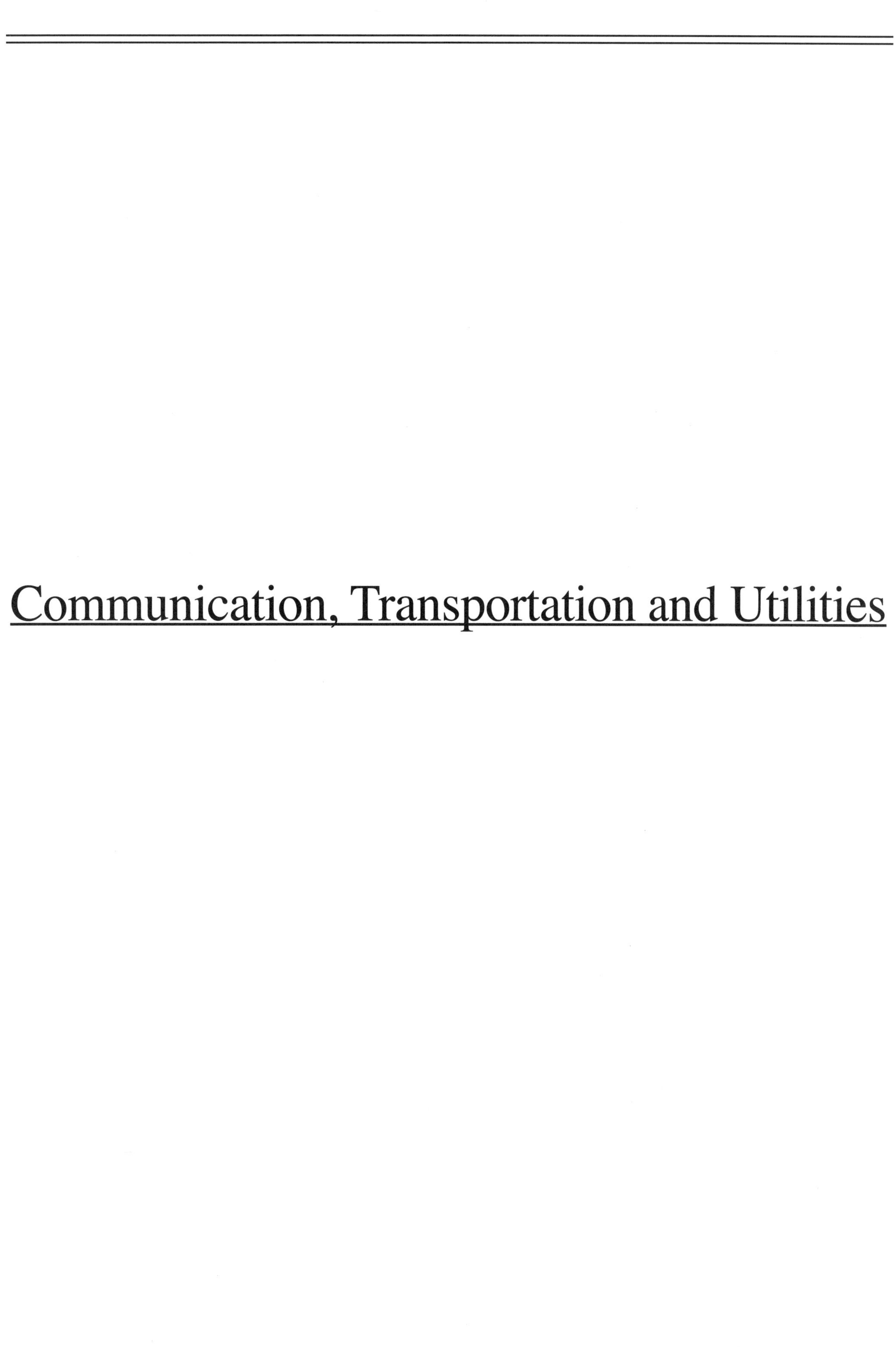

Communication, Transportation and Utilities

ADAMOVICH, DENNIS J.
Industry: Entertainment **Univ./degree:** B.A., Business, University of Southern Florida, 1986 **Current organization:** Turner Entertainment - Cartoon Network **Title:** Senior Vice President, Marketing **Type of organization:** Television network **Major product:** Television programming **Area of distribution:** National **Expertise:** Marketing **SIC code:** 48 **Address:** Turner Entertainment - Cartoon Network, 1050 Techwood Dr. N.W., Atlanta, GA 30318 **E-mail:** dennis.adamovich@turner.com

ADAMS, DOUG
Industry: Communications **Univ./degree:** Certificate, Richmond Technical Institute, 1977 **Current organization:** Adelphia Communications **Title:** Senior Technician **Type of organization:** Service provider **Major product:** Cable TV and Internet **Area of distribution:** North Carolina **Expertise:** Cable and fiber; community guest speaker **Affiliations:** N.C.T. **Hob./spts.:** Fishing **SIC code:** 48 **Address:** Adelphia Communications, 222 North Wilkinson Dr., Laurinburg, NC 28352 **E-mail:** doug.adams@adelphia.com

ALLEN, JERRY L.
Industry: Telecommunications **Born:** December 30, 1954, Lodi, Ohio **Univ./degree:** B.S., Mechanical Engineering, Tristate University, 1978 **Current organization:** TVC Communications Inc. **Title:** Vice President, Research & Development **Type of organization:** Distributing **Major product:** Fiber-optic construction materials **Area of distribution:** International **Expertise:** Mechanical engineering **Honors/awards:** Honorary Doctorate, Mechanical Engineering, Tristate University, 1998; Jerry L. Allen School of Engineering **Published works:** 9 patents **Hob./spts.:** Flyfishing **SIC code:** 48 **Address:** TVC Communications Inc., 600 Plum Creek Dr., Wadsworth, OH 44281 **E-mail:** jallen@tvcinc.com

ALTON, DAWN D.
Industry: Telecommunications **Born:** October 22, 1961, Sulphur, Louisiana **Univ./degree:** B.A., Management, Centennial University, 2001 **Current organization:** Centennial Wireless **Title:** Account Representative **Type of organization:** Telecommunications **Major product:** Wireless services **Area of distribution:** Louisiana **Expertise:** Sales, customer service **Honors/awards:** Salesperson of the Year, 2003 **Hob./spts.:** Travel, family, Internet access **SIC code:** 48 **Address:** Centennial Wireless, 7784 Colorado Ave., Ft. Polk, LA 71459 **E-mail:** dds4261@yahoo.com

ALVI, OBAID U.
Industry: Telecommunications **Univ./degree:** M.S., Computer Science, Texas A&M, 1985 **Current organization:** AT&T Wireless **Title:** Manager/Director **Type of organization:** Service provider **Major product:** Wireless/cell phones **Area of distribution:** National **Expertise:** Software architecture, management, retail distribution; P.E., 1988 **Affiliations:** I.O.U.G.; A.S.C.E. **Hob./spts.:** Volunteer work for local church **SIC code:** 48 **Address:** 645 Harvest Glen Dr., Richardson, TX 75081 **E-mail:** obalvlue@hotmail.com

ARMS, RUTH E.
Industry: Transportation **Born:** September 6, 1934, Englewood, Colorado **Univ./degree:** A.S., Management, Oklahoma State Community College, 1996 **Current organization:** R&R Shipping Services **Title:** Owner **Type of organization:** Shipping **Major product:** Small package shipping **Area of distribution:** International **Expertise:** Certified packing **Affiliations:** Neighbor for Neighbor **Hob./spts.:** Golf **SIC code:** 42 **Address:** R&R Shipping Services, 12316A North May Ave., Oklahoma City, OK 73120 **E-mail:** mailchute@sbcglobal.net

AVERKAMP, JOSEPH JOHN
Industry: Wireless telecommunications **Born:** May 27, 1958, Dubuque, Iowa **Univ./degree:** M.B.A., University of Chicago, 1992 **Current organization:** Sprint P.C.S. **Title:** Senior Director **Type of organization:** Communication provider **Major product:** Wireless services **Area of distribution:** International **Expertise:** Business development, engineering **Affiliations:** C.T.I.A.; S.A.E.; ITS America **Hob./spts.:** Golf **SIC code:** 48 **Address:** Sprint P.C.S., 6160 Sprint Pkwy., KSOPHIO414-4A375, Overland Park, KS 66224 **E-mail:** javerk01@sprintspectrum.com

BAHLOUL, WISSAM Y.
Industry: Shipping and trading **Born:** March 14, 1969, Beirut, Lebanon **Univ./degree:** B.S., University of Central Florida, 1995 **Current organization:** Global Shipping & Freight Int. **Title:** President/CEO **Type of organization:** Shipping company **Major product:** International shipping, freight, export services **Area of distribution:** International **Expertise:** International coordination **Hob./spts.:** Sports, travel, the outdoors **SIC code:** 47 **Address:** 4405 W. South Ave., #C, Tampa, FL 33614 **E-mail:** samtheeman30@hotmail

BAKER, DAVID W.
Industry: Utilities **Born:** April 18, 1949, Pontiac, Michigan **Univ./degree:** B.S., Engineering, Oakland University **Current organization:** DTE Energy **Title:** Director, Belle River and North Area Plants **Type of organization:** Electric utility **Major product:** Electrical energy **Area of distribution:** Michigan **Expertise:** Director of Engineering, Professional Engineer **Affiliations:** E.U.C.G. **Hob./spts.:** Golf, fishing, hunting, reading **SIC code:** 49 **Address:** 702 Fourth St., Marysville, MI 48040 **E-mail:** bakerd@dteenergy.com

BAR-COHEN, BARAK
Industry: Telecommunications **Born:** September 18, 1970, Boston, Massachusetts **Univ./degree:** M.B.A., Tuck School of Business, Dartmouth, 2000 **Current organization:** RCN Corp. **Title:** Vice President, Marketing & Public Relations **Type of organization:** Telecommunications **Major product:** Residential telecom services **Area of distribution:** National **Expertise:** Marketing/public relations/customer service **Affiliations:** New Jersey-Israel Commission **Hob./spts.:** Basketball, hiking **SIC code:** 48 **Address:** RCN Corp., 105 Carnegie Center, Princeton, NJ 08540 **E-mail:** barak.bar.cohen@rcn.net **Web address:** www.rcn.com

BARKER, STANLEY B.
Industry: Electrical utility **Born:** February 20, 1957, St. Louis, Missouri **Univ./degree:** Loss Control Internship Program from University of Nebraska at Lincoln, Certified OSHA Instructor **Current organization:** White River Valley Electric Cooperative, Inc. **Title:** Director of Safety and Training **Type of organization:** Electricity distribution cooperative **Major product:** Electricity **Area of distribution:** Branson, Missouri **Expertise:** Certified Loss Control Professional **Honors/awards:** Area Leadership, 2000 **Published works:** Loss Control Program "Means of Egress" **Affiliations:** N.R.E.C.A.; NUTSEA; Rotary International; Area Chamber of Commerce Board Member; Branson Board of Alderman **Hob./spts.:** Golf, target shooting **SIC code:** 49 **Address:** P.O. Box 969, Branson, MO 65615 **E-mail:** sbarker@whiteriver.org **Web address:** www.whiteriver.org

BARNEY, JO D.
Industry: Telecommunications **Current organization:** Adelphia Communications **Title:** Manager **Type of organization:** Telecommunications **Major product:** Cable television, telecom services **Area of distribution:** Charlottesville, Virginia **Expertise:** Analysis reporting **Affiliations:** C.T.E.; Women in Cable Television **Hob./spts.:** NASCAR, nature photography **SIC code:** 48 **Address:** Adelphia Communications, 675 Peter Jefferson Pkwy., Suite 450, Charlottesville, VA 22911 **E-mail:** jo.barney@adelphia.com

BARTLETT, JOE
Industry: Broadcasting/media **Born:** September 15, 1952, Albany, New York **Current organization:** WOR **Title:** News Director **Type of organization:** Radio **Major product:** News, current events, interviews **Area of distribution:** International **Expertise:** Radio broadcasting **Affiliations:** Past President and Current Member, Associated Press Broadcasters Association **Hob./spts.:** Golfing, coaching soccer, church activities **SIC code:** 48 **Address:** WOR, 1440 Broadway, New York, NY 10018 **E-mail:** joebartlett@wor710.com

BERLINER, WILLIAM
Industry: Marine **Born:** July 28, 1924, New York **Univ./degree:** B.S.M.E., Cornell University, 1949 **Current organization:** Berliner Technical Services **Title:** Owner **Type of organization:** Design, installation and maintenance **Major product:** Integrated navigation, communication and electrical systems **Area of distribution:** National **Expertise:** engineering **Affiliations:** C.M.T.A.; A.I.A.A.; A.B.Y.C. **Hob./spts.:** Boating, cruising, travel **SIC code:** 44 **Address:** Berliner Technical Services, P.O. Box 205, Essex, CT 06426 **E-mail:** btssx@cs.com

BERNARD, NEFTALI
Industry: Telecommunications, consulting, telemarketing, wireless communication **Born:** February, 1968, Puerto Rico **Univ./degree:** B.A., Accounting, University of Puerto Rico, 1991 **Current organization:** HD Group/Image Marketing Corp. **Title:** Vice President/Chief Operating Officer **Type of organization:** Telecommunications **Major product:** Telecommunication consulting, wireless equipment distribution **Area of distribution:** Puerto Rico **Expertise:** Business development, accounting, finance **Affiliations:** A.T.A.; Chamber of Commerce **SIC code:** 48 **Address:** HD Group/Image Marketing Corp., 318 Ponce de Leon Ave., Suite 3000, San Juan, PR 00901 **E-mail:** nbernard@hdgrouppr.com

BERRY, WILLIAM W.
Industry: Energy **Born:** May 18, 1932, Norfolk, Virginia **Univ./degree:** B.S., Electrical Engineering, Virginia Military Institute, 1954; M.A., Commerce, University of Richmond, 1964 **Current organization:** ISO New England **Title:** Chairman of the Board **Type of organization:** Wholesale electric **Major product:** Electrical power **Area of distribution:** New England **Expertise:** Operations Management **Affiliations:** Life Member, Institute of Electrical and Electronics Engineers; Member of the Board of Trustees and Ethyl Corp.; Member of the Board of Trustees, Science Museum of Virginia **Hob./spts.:** Sailing **SIC code:** 49 **Address:** 8001 Franklin Farms Dr., Suite 137, Richmond, VA 23229 **Phone:** (804)288-2271 **Fax:** (804)288-2272 **E-mail:** ww.berry@richmond.infi.net

BLACK, KEITH F.
Industry: Communications **Current organization:** Interact Private Cable **Title:** V.P. Operations **Type of organization:** Distributing **Major product:** Cable installation, warless internet networking **Area of distribution:** Florida **Expertise:** Executive management **Affiliations:** Hollywood Chamber of Commerce **Hob./spts.:** Golf, skiing, reading, travel **SIC code:** 48 **Address:** Interact Private Cable, 2201 W. Prospect Rd., Suite 100, Ft. Lauderdale, FL 33309 **E-mail:** keithipcable@aol.com

BLAHA, FRANK R.
Industry: Telecommunications **Born:** May 20, 1945, Oak Park, Illinois **Univ./degree:** M.B.A., Southern Methodist University, 1973 **Current organization:** Worldwide Translations **Title:** President **Type of organization:** Telecommunications **Area of distribution:** International **Affiliations:** A.I.S.P. **Hob./spts.:** Tennis, international travel **SIC code:** 48 **Address:** Spectrum Communications Systems, Inc., 2994 Marble Cliff Ct., Henderson, NV 89052 **E-mail:** fblaha@cox.net **Web address:** www.cox.net

BLAND, BRIAN
Industry: Television **Born:** September 11, 1977, Richmond, California **Current organization:** KCRT Television **Title:** Production Assistant **Type of organization:** City municipality **Major product:** Government programming **Area of distribution:** Richmond, California **Expertise:** Producing, directing, editing **Hob./spts.:** Hunting, fishing, biking, reading **SIC code:** 48 **Address:** KCRT Television, 2544 Barrett Ave., Richmond, CA 94804 **E-mail:** brianabland@yahoo.com

BOSTICK, ISAAC
Industry: Telecommunications **Born:** November 16, 1969, Covington, Georgia **Univ./degree:** Technical Degree, West Central Technical College, 1990 **Current organization:** Covington Cable TV **Title:** Senior Technician **Area of distribution:** Covington, Georgia **Hob./spts.:** Fishing, playing piano **SIC code:** 48 **Address:** Covington Cable TV, 1167 Pace St., Covington, GA 30014 **E-mail:** ibostick@covcatv.net **Web address:** www.corcatv.net

BOTT, TIMOTHY W.
Industry: Telecommunications **Born:** March 31, 1978, Orange, California **Univ./degree:** B.S., Business Administration, Western New England College, 2001 **Current organization:** Infonet Services Corp. **Title:** Web Developer **Type of organization:** Telecommunications **Major product:** Global communications services **Area of distribution:** International **Expertise:** Web application development **Hob./spts.:** Lacrosse **SIC code:** 48 **Address:** Infonet Services Corp., 321 S. Orange Grove Blvd., Pasadena, CA 91105 **E-mail:** timbott@timbott.net **Web address:** ww.timbott.net

BOUCHARD, BRUCE E.
Industry: Telecommunications **Born:** November 27, 1957, New Bedford, Massachusetts **Univ./degree:** Diploma, Automotive Repair, Rhode Island Trade Shop School; Electronic Technology, Microprocessor, Computer Processing Institute **Current organization:** Cingular Wireless **Title:** Operations Manager **Type of organization:** Wireless mobile carrier **Major product:** Mobile wireless service **Area of distribution:** National **Expertise:** Network management **Honors/awards:** Awarded Outstanding Service Technician for Isoetec Communication Inc., 1986; Awarded Outstand Employee of the year for Metro Mobile CTS, 1989 **Hob./spts.:** Computers, sports, coaching soccer **SIC code:** 48 **Address:** Cingular Wireless, 50 Royal Little Dr., Providence, RI 02904 **E-mail:** bruce.bouchard@cingular.com **Web address:** www.cingular.com

BRINKHOFF, HANS M. M.
Industry: Cruises **Born:** October 1, 1942, Nymegen, Netherlands **Univ./degree:** B.A., Hotel and Restaurant Management and Administration, Maastricht, Netherlands **Current organization:** Holland America Line **Title:** Director F.B. Operations **Type of organization:** Cruise ship operations **Major product:** All-inclusive vacation onboard cruise liner **Area of distribution:** International **Expertise:** Food and beverages, director of purchasing **Honors/awards:** Maitre de Table, Chaine des Rotisseurs; Knight of the Grand Order of the Dynasty; Les Disciples D'Auguste Escoffier **Published works:** Journals, trade magazine **Affiliations:** Marine Hotel Association **Hob./spts.:** Cooking, classical music and opera, Certified Diver **SIC code:** 44 **Address:** Holland America Line, 300 Elliott Ave. West, Seattle, WA 98119 **E-mail:** hbrinkoff@halw.com

BRITO, JEANETTE
Industry: Travel **Born:** February 24, 1974, New York, New York **Univ./degree:** B.A., Mercy College, 1997; M.B.A., Long Island University, 2000 **Current organization:** Royal Caribbean Cruise Co. **Title:** Financial Analyst **Type of organization:** Cruise company **Major product:** Cruises **Area of distribution:** International **Expertise:** Financial analyses **Honors/awards:** Delta Mu Delta **Affiliations:** National Association of Female Executives; Board Member, Farhand Housing **Hob./spts.:** Swimming, research on internet, volunteer **SIC code:** 44 **Address:** Royal Caribbean Cruise Co., 1050 Caribbean Way, Miami, FL 33132 **E-mail:** jbrito@rccl.com **Web address:** www.rccl.com

BROADWELL, GERRY L.
Industry: Transportation **Born:** May 27, 1954, Paducah, Kentucky **Current organization:** Old Dominion Freight Lines Inc. **Title:** Vice President, South Central **Type of organization:** Trucking company **Major product:** Freight trucking **Area of distribution:** National **Expertise:** General management, customer service **Hob./spts.:** Golf, fishing **SIC code:** 42 **Address:** Old Dominion Freight Lines Inc., 500 Old Dominion Way, Thomasville, NC 27630 **E-mail:** gerry.broadwell@odfl.com **Web address:** www.odfl.com

BROW, SCOTT J.
Industry: Telecommunications/semiconductors **Born:** March 17, 1969, Butte, Montana **Univ./degree:** B.S.M.E, University of Washington, 2000 **Current organization:** Motorola **Title:** Lead Product Engineer **Type of organization:** Telecommunications **Major product:** Wireless power amplifiers for cell phones **Area of distribution:** International **Expertise:** Product engineering/new product introduction to market **Published works:** Co-author, 1 article **Affiliations:** A.S.M.E. **Hob./spts.:** Golf, hiking, long distance running, professional baseball **SIC code:** 48 **Address:** Motorola, 2100 E. Elliott Rd., MDE4542, Tempe, AZ 85284 **E-mail:** scott.brow@motorola.com **Web address:** www.motorola.com

CABRERA, DOMINGO A.
Industry: Communications **Born:** San Diego, California **Univ./degree:** B.S., Business Management, University of Redlands, 1986; M.S., Organizational Management, University of Phoenix, 1989 **Current organization:** SBC-West Region **Title:** Area Manager **Type of organization:** Information technology **Major product:** Infrastructure for communications **Area of distribution:** California **Expertise:** Management **Hob./spts.:** Recording Engineer **SIC code:** 48 **Address:** SBC, 7337 Trade St., Suite 5670, San Diego, CA 92121 **E-mail:** dc1924@sbc.com

CAMPBELL, WINSTON A.
Industry: Transportation **Born:** May 31, 1948, Kingston, Jamaica **Univ./degree:** B.S., Electrical Engineering, University of Bridgeport, Connecticut, 1981 **Current organization:** M.T.A., New York City Transit Authority **Title:** Electrical Engineer **Type of organization:** Transit authority **Major product:** Transportation services **Area of distribution:** Bronx, New York **Expertise:** Electrical engineering **Affiliations:** I.E.E.E. **Hob./spts.:** Soccer **SIC code:** 47 **Address:** 1680 Metropolitan Ave., Apt. 5E, Bronx, NY 10462

CARDONA, JOSE
Industry: Waste **Born:** April 2, 1963, Aguadilla, Puerto Rico **Univ./degree:** M.S., Business Administration, University of Phoenix, 1997 **Current organization:** Service/utility **Title:** Vice President & General Manager **Type of organization:** Utility **Major product:** Waste collection and disposal **Area of distribution:** National **Expertise:** Business management **Hob./spts.:** Golf **SIC code:** 49 **Address:** Rd. #1 KM 27 1/2, Caguas, PR 00726 **E-mail:** jcardona@wm.com

CARMIGNANI, ISAAC
Industry: Postal **Born:** December 4, 1966, New York, New York **Univ./degree:** A.S., Electrical Engineering, New York City Technical School, 2005 **Current organization:** US Postal Service **Title:** Electronics Technician **Type of organization:** Postal service **Major product:** Mail delivery **Area of distribution:** National **Expertise:** Engineering/technical **Affiliations:** I.E.E.E.; A.A.S.; President of local P.T.A. **Hob./spts.:** Computers, audio **SIC code:** 43 **Address:** 20-76 19th St., #3A, Astoria, NY 11105 **E-mail:** thekrenim@earthlink.net

CARVEL, BERNARD J.
Industry: Natural gas L.D.C. **Born:** July 2, 1956, Massena, New York **Univ./degree:** B.S., Business Administration, University of Phoenix, 2002 **Current organization:** St. Lawrence Gas Co., Inc. **Title:** Manger, Distributions Operations **Type of organization:** Utility (L.D.C.) **Major product:** Natural gas **Area of distribution:** New York **Expertise:** Utility operations **Affiliations:** G.O.A.C.; Director, Local Chamber of Commerce, New York Gas Group **Hob./spts.:** Golf, softball, motorcycling **SIC code:** 49 **Address:** St. Lawrence Gas Co., Inc., 33 Stearns St., Massena, NY 13662 **E-mail:** bcarvel@stlawrencegas.com

CHAMBERS, LYNN A.
Industry: Wireless communications **Born:** July 25, 1953, Portsmouth, Virginia **Univ./degree:** Attended Penn State, Widener University & Delaware County Community College **Current organization:** T-Mobile USA **Title:** General Manager **Type of organization:** Distributor **Major product:** Cell phones, wireless products and services **Area of distribution:** National **Expertise:** Distribution **Hob./spts.:** Golf, fishing, spending time with friends **SIC code:** 48 **Address:** T-Mobile USA, 2996 Samuel Dr., Bensalem, PA 19020 **E-mail:** lynn.chambers@t-mobile.com **Web address:** www.t-mobile.com

CHANDHOK, VINAY B.
Industry: Telecommunications **Born:** November 15, 1952, Port Jefferson, New York **Univ./degree:** B.S.E.E. with Honors, Birla Institute, 1974; B.S.E.E., Carnegie Mellon,

1978; M.S.E.E., University of Bridgeport, 1986 **Current organization:** Nortel **Title:** Director, Business Development **Type of organization:** Business solutions **Major product:** IVR and web solution, web solutions **Area of distribution:** International **Expertise:** New business development **Published works:** Editor of 1 book **Affiliations:** Past Member, I.E.E.E. **Hob./spts.:** Reading, investing **SIC code:** 48 **Address:** Nortel, 4000 Veteran's Memorial Hwy., Bohemia, NY 11716 **E-mail:** vinaybc04@yahoo.com

CHÁVEZ, LINA L.
Industry: Utilities **Born:** July 25, 1980, Villahermosa, Tamaulipas, Mexico **Univ./degree:** B.S.E.E., Texas A&M University, 2002; M.B.A. Candidate, University of Phoenix **Current organization:** Brownsville Public Utilities Board **Title:** Power Quality Engineer **Type of organization:** Utility **Major product:** Electric power and water **Area of distribution:** Brownsville **Expertise:** Power quality equipment engineering and installation, public health fair presentations **Honors/awards:** Student of the Semester Year 2001, Texas A&M University **Affiliations:** I.E.E.E.; Student Hispanic Engineering Professionals; Mexican-American Student Association **Hob./spts.:** Charities, sports, reading **SIC code:** 49 **Address:** Brownsville Public Utilities Board, 1425 Robinhood St., Brownsville, TX 78521 **E-mail:** linachavez_9@hotmail .com

CLARK, KENNETH G.
Industry: Logistics/transportation **Born:** February 1, 1977, Baltimore, Maryland **Univ./degree:** B.A., Marketing/Small Business Management, Gettysburg College, 1999 **Current organization:** Kenneth Clark Co. **Title:** President **Type of organization:** General contractors for trucking, warehousing, import, export, packing **Major product:** Logistics services **Area of distribution:** International **Expertise:** Marketing **Hob./spts.:** Golf **SIC code:** 47 **Address:** Kenneth Clark Co., Inc., 10264 Baltimore National Pike, Ellicott City, MD 21042 **E-mail:** kclark@kennethclark.com **Web address:** www.kennethclark.com

COFFMAN, BRYAN J.
Industry: Communications **Univ./degree:** B.S., Technical Management, DeVry College, 2004 **Current organization:** Sprint **Title:** Sr. Tech Support Analyst **Type of organization:** Communications technology **Major product:** Telecommunications **Area of distribution:** National **Expertise:** Enterprise solutions - technical management **Hob./spts.:** Eagle Scouts **SIC code:** 48 **Address:** Sprint, 1310 E. 104th, Kansas City, MO 64131 **E-mail:** bryan.j.coffman@mail.sprint.com

COKER, WILLIAM B.
Industry: Government/Utilities **Univ./degree:** B.S.E.E., University of Nebraska, 1981 **Current organization:** Beatrice Board of Public Works **Title:** Electrical Engineer **Type of organization:** Municipal utility **Major product:** Electricity **Area of distribution:** Beatrice, Nebraska **Expertise:** Engineering, project management **Affiliations:** I.E.E.E.; Free Masons, K.Y.C.H. **SIC code:** 49 **Address:** Beatrice Board of Public Works, 500 N. Commerce, Beatrice, NE 68310 **E-mail:** bcoker@bpw.ci.beatrice.ne.us

CONNER, CHRIS S.
Industry: Cable/communications **Born:** October 7, 1980, Texas **Univ./degree:** B.B.A., LeTourneau University; M.B.A. Candidate, 2008 **Current organization:** Sudden Link Communications **Title:** Regional Customer Care Manager **Type of organization:** Cable **Major product:** Cable, Internet, telephony **Area of distribution:** Texas, Arkansas, California, Louisiana **Expertise:** Operations/sales - new products and services **Affiliations:** City Council; Boys and Girls Club; Meals on Wheels **Hob./spts.:** Movies, wine, dinning, soccer, tennis **SIC code:** 48 **Address:** Sudden Link Communications, 322 N. Glenwood Blvd., Tyler, TX 75702 **E-mail:** chris.conner@suddenlink.com **Web address:** www.suddenlink.com

CONOVER, DONNA D.
Industry: Transportation **Born:** February 21, 1953, Clarksville, Texas **Univ./degree:** A.A., Tarrant County Junior College, 1974 **Current organization:** Southwest Airlines Co. **Title:** Executive Vice President **Type of organization:** Airline **Major product:** Customer service **Area of distribution:** National **Expertise:** EVP, Customer service **Affiliations:** Society for Human Resource Management **Hob./spts.:** Skiing, reading, horseback riding, football, baseball **SIC code:** 45 **Address:** Southwest Airlines Co., 2702 Love Field Dr., Dallas, TX 75235 **E-mail:** donna.conover@wnco.com

CONTI, FRANK M.
Industry: Communications/entertainment **Born:** April 13, 1963, Bronx, New York **Univ./degree:** B.S., Computer Engineering, New York Technological Institute, 1985 **Current organization:** Infiniti Sales & Marketing **Title:** President **Type of organization:** Sales and marketing **Major product:** Digital non-linear video editing **Area of distribution:** New Jersey **Expertise:** Administration **Affiliations:** N.A.B.; W.E.V.A. **Hob./spts.:** Golf **SIC code:** 48 **Address:** Infiniti Sales & Marketing, 1 Bethany Rd., Suite 39, Hazlet, NJ 07730 **E-mail:** fconti@infinitisales.com

COPE, BRADFORD L.
Industry: Communications **Univ./degree:** A.A., Roane State Community College, 1990 **Current organization:** Paxson Communications **Title:** Chief Engineer **Type of organization:** Television broadcast network station **Major product:** Television station operations **Area of distribution:** National **Expertise:** Electrical engineering, satellite **Affiliations:** S.B.E. **Hob./spts.:** Music, guitar **SIC code:** 48 **Address:** 350 Myrtle Ave., Crossville, TN 38555 **E-mail:** bradcope@pax.net

CRIVELLARO JR., BENNIE G.
Industry: Government **Born:** January 21, 1959, Easton, Pennsylvania **Univ./degree:** A.S., Elgin Community College, 2002 **Current organization:** United States Postal Service **Title:** Supervisor, Maintenance Operations **Type of organization:** Post office **Major product:** Mail services **Area of distribution:** St. Charles, Illinois **Expertise:** Supervisory functions, all maintenance operations **Hob./spts.:** Woodworking, internet and computers **SIC code:** 43 **Address:** 50 Renaux Blvd., St. Charles, IL 60175 **E-mail:** bcrivell@email.usps.gov **Web address:** www.usps.gov

CUSSIGH, GUENTHER J.
Industry: Hospitality/travel **Born:** April 8, 1961, Konstanz, Germany **Univ./degree:** Master Chef, Vocational School of Miesbach, Germany, 1982 **Current organization:** Holland America Line **Title:** Corporate Executive Chef **Type of organization:** Cruise line/hotel **Major product:** Cruises **Area of distribution:** International **Expertise:** Menu development **Affiliations:** World Master Chefs Association **Hob./spts.:** Golf, music **SIC code:** 44 **Address:** Holland America Line, 300 Elliot Ave. West, Seattle, WA 98119 **E-mail:** gcussigh@hollandamerica.com

DE SOUZA, MICHELLE
Industry: Advertising **Born:** Detroit, Michigan **Univ./degree:** M.A., Organizational Management/Human Resources, University of Phoenix, 2001 **Current organization:** MDesign Media **Title:** Consultant/President **Type of organization:** Media agency **Major product:** Broadcasting, cable, print media, ad sales **Area of distribution:** Michigan **Expertise:** Broadcast marketing **Honors/awards:** Emmy Award Winner, Lifetime Achievement, 2002; Telly Award Winner, 2002 **Affiliations:** S.H.R.M.; N.A.T.A.S. **Hob./spts.:** Singing **SIC code:** 48 **Address:** MDesign Media, 950 Whitmore Rd., Suite 208, Detroit, MI 48203-4074 **E-mail:** mdeso2@hotmail.com

DEAN, DAVID ERIC
Industry: Utilities **Born:** October 6, 1954, Greenville, South Carolina **Univ./degree:** A.A., Wastewater Technology, Greenville Technical College **Current organization:** Broad Creek Public Service District **Title:** Operations Manager **Type of organization:** Public service district **Major product:** Water and sewer services for Palmetto Dunes Resort **Expertise:** Managing all aspects of operations **Affiliations:** Water Environment Federation; South Carolina Environment Association; American Waterworks Association **Hob./spts.:** Family, history buff, hunting, fishing, camping **SIC code:** 49 **Address:** Broad Creek Public Service District, 3 Marina Side Dr., Hilton Head, SC 29938 **E-mail:** edean5878@aol.com

DEBOER, TAMA M.
Industry: Telecommunications **Born:** March 5, 1968, Passaic, New Jersey **Univ./degree:** B.S., Magna Cum Laude, Political Science, Montclair State University, 2004; RETS Degree with Honors, Computer Repair Technician, 1991 **Current organization:** Verizon Communications **Title:** First Line Manager, Construction **Type of organization:** Communications **Major product:** Construction/phone service/FTTP (fiber to the premise) **Area of distribution:** International **Expertise:** Construction management **Affiliations:** Golden Key International Honor Society; Montclair State University Alumni Association **Hob./spts.:** Shopping, spectator baseball, domestic travel, scrapbooking **SIC code:** 48 **Address:** Verizon Communications, 445 Georges Rd., North Brunswick, NJ 08902 **E-mail:** tama.m.deboer/empl/nj/verizon.com **Web address:** www.verizon.com

DECKER, TERRY L.
Industry: Sanitation **Born:** September 2, 1959, Roaring Spring, Pennsylvania **Current organization:** TLD Enterprises, Inc. **Title:** President **Type of organization:** Trash removal and recycling company **Major product:** Non ferrous metals, clean-ups **Area of distribution:** Roaring Spring, Pennsylvania **Expertise:** Recycling **Hob./spts.:** Motorcycle drag racing **SIC code:** 49 **Address:** TLD Enterprises, Inc., 525B Cove Mountain Rd., Roaring Spring, PA 16673 **E-mail:** tdecker111@aol.com

DHUWARAHA, RAMA K.
Industry: Communications **Born:** May 22, 1974 **Univ./degree:** B.S., Electrical Engineering, University of Kentucky, 1998; M.B.A. Candidate, Purdue University, Indiana **Current organization:** Win Enterprises, Inc. **Title:** Vice President **Type of organization:** Broadband service provider **Major product:** Data connectivity **Area of distribution:** Kentucky **Expertise:** Engineering **Affiliations:** Director, Kentucky Internet Provider Association; L.Y.P.A. **SIC code:** 48 **Address:** Win Enterprises, Inc., 2265 Harrodsburg Rd., Suite 219, Lexington, KY 40504 **E-mail:** rama@winent.net

DIBIANCO, DONNA
Industry: Broadcasting **Born:** December 23, 1963, Hempstead, New York **Univ./degree:** A.A., Broadcasting, Santa Fe Community College **Current organization:** KAOS 89.3 FM@ The Evergreen State College **Title:** Operations Manager **Type of organization:** University radio station **Major product:** Broadcasting **Area of distribution:** National **Expertise:** Talent development, training and compliance **Hob./spts.:** Swimming, fine dining, dancing, cooking, skiing **SIC code:** 48 **Address:** KAOS 89.3 FM, Evergreen State College, 2700 Evergreen Pkwy., CAB 301, Olympia, WA 98505 **E-mail:** publicradiogoddess@yahoo.com

DOMEK, DOREEN
Industry: Travel **Born:** March 6, 1956, Chicago, Illinois **Univ./degree:** Interior Design and business Management course from Harper College **Current organization:** Apple Vacations **Title:** Chief Operating Officer **Type of organization:** Tour operator **Major product:** Wholesale travel packages to the Caribbean, Mexico, Hawaii **Area of distribution:** International **Expertise:** Quality assurance, management **Honors/awards:** Top Women and Travel awards multiple times **Affiliations:** Youth services, Children's advocate **Hob./spts.:** Cross country skiing and Golf **SIC code:** 47 **Address:** 101 Northwest Point Blvd., Elk Grove, IL 60007 **E-mail:** ddomek@applevac.com **Web address:** www.applevac.com

DOMINO, ROSEMARY
Industry: Environmental **Univ./degree:** B.S., California State University **Current organization:** D/K Environmental **Title:** Director, Environmental Affairs **Type of organization:** Hazardous waste/waste water treatment facility **Major product:** RCRA transfer, storage, treatment and disposal **Area of distribution:** California **Expertise:** Environmental compliance **Affiliations:** California Waste Association; California Society of Safety and Scrutiny Professionals **Hob./spts.:** Travel, gardening, landscaping **SIC code:** 49 **Address:** 10255 Tyhurst Rd., Garden Grove, CA 92840 **E-mail:** rdomino@asburyenv.com

DREES, LARRY J.
Industry: Transportation **Born:** July 6, 1949, Frostburg, Maryland **Univ./degree:** B.S., Chemistry and Math, Frostburg State University, Maryland, 1971 **Current organization:** CSX Transportation **Title:** Supervisor, Environmental Field Services **Type of organization:** Railroad transportation **Major product:** Rail cargo services **Area of distribution:** Maryland **Expertise:** Chemistry **SIC code:** 40 **Address:** CSX Transportation, 16 Offutt St., Cumberland, MD 21502 **E-mail:** mydrees@aol.com

EGERTON, CLARKE A.
Industry: Communications **Univ./degree:** B.S., Communication, Western Carolina University, 1983 **Current organization:** Cingular Wireless **Title:** Product Distribution Manager **Type of organization:** Wireless provider **Major product:** Wireless communications **Area of distribution:** National **Expertise:** Compliance **Affiliations:** Former Member, Junior Chamber of Commerce **Hob./spts.:** Photography, music **SIC code:** 48 **Address:** Cingular Wireless, 1130 Situs Ct., Suite 100, Raleigh, NC 27606 **E-mail:** clarke.egerton@cingular.com

ENGLAND, LONNIE K.
Industry: Broadcasting **Born:** February 15, 1965, Yakima, Washington **Univ./degree:** Degree in Broadcast Engineering Systems/Studio Design, Matsushita Engineering School, 1983; B.S., Electronics, Olympic University, 1985 **Current organization:** Apple Valley TV/KWCC-TV/KNEE-TV **Title:** Owner **Type of organization:** Broadcast facility **Major product:** Broadcasting **Area of distribution:** Washington **Expertise:** RF technology - operations **Published works:** Patent pending **Affiliations:** National Translator Association; Society of Broadcast Engineers **Hob./spts.:** Family, walking, snowmobiling **SIC code:** 48 **Address:** Apple Valley TV/KWCC-TV/KNEE-TV, 205 First St., Wenatchee, WA 98801 **E-mail:** lonnie@kwcctv.com **Web address:** www.kwcctv.com

EVANS, MARY C.
Industry: Energy **Current organization:** Southern California Edison **Title:** Project Analyst **Type of organization:** Private utility **Major product:** Energy **Area of distribution:** Southern California **Expertise:** Project analysis, training, employee development **Affiliations:** National Association for Female Executives; Dale Carnegie Instructor; Volunteer Chair, River Valley High School Site Council **Hob./spts.:** Travel, arts, writing **SIC code:** 49 **Address:** 7001 Kaiser Dr., Mohave Valley, AZ 86440 **E-mail:** evans@citlink.net

FERNBAUGH, PHILIP M.
Industry: Telecommunications **Born:** December 15, 1975, Shreveport, Louisiana **Current organization:** CP-TEL Network Services, Inc. **Title:** Network Operations Manager **Type of organization:** Competitive local exchange carrier (CLEC) **Major product:** Digital services **Area of distribution:** Louisiana **Expertise:** Voice/data/video design & implementation **Hob./spts.:** Golf **SIC code:** 48 **Address:** CP-TEL Network Services, Inc., 5909 Hwy. 1 Bypass, Natchitoches, LA 71457 **E-mail:** pfernbaugh@cp-tel.com

FISCHER, JEDD J.
Industry: Utilities **Born:** January 21, 1977, Columbus, Nebraska **Univ./degree:** B.S.M.E., University of Nebraska at Lincoln, 2001 **Current organization:** Nebraska Public Power District **Title:** Mechanical Engineer **Type of organization:** Public power utility **Major product:** Power generation **Area of distribution:** Nebraska **Expertise:** System and mechanical engineering **Affiliations:** A.S.M.E.; Order of the Engineer **SIC code:** 49 **Address:** Nebraska Public Power District, P.O. Box 98, Brownville, NE 68321-0098 **E-mail:** jjfisch@nppd.com

FISHER, JOAN F.
Industry: Telecommunications **Born:** August 29, 1954, Brooklyn, New York **Univ./degree:** M.B.A., Peter F. Drucker Management Center of the Claremont Graduate School **Current organization:** Comcast TVWorks **Title:** QA Engineer **Type of organization:** Interactive digital television **Major product:** ITV **Area of distribution:** California **Expertise:** Software quality assurance **Hob./spts.:** Tennis, squash, sculling **SIC code:** 48 **Address:** 391 Miller Ave., #202, Mill Valley, CA 94941 **E-mail:** joan_fisher@tvworks.com

FLETCHER, BRUCE D.
Industry: Telecommunications **Born:** September 15, 1956, Greenfield, Iowa **Univ./degree:** B.S., Computer Science, Electrical Engineering, Southwestern University, 1983 **Current organization:** MCI **Title:** Distinguished Technical Member **Type of organization:** Telecommunications **Major product:** Telecom services **Area of distribution:** International **Expertise:** Network design and engineering **Hob./spts.:** Golf, skiing **SIC code:** 48 **Address:** MCI, 2400 N. Glenville Dr., Richardson, TX 75082 **E-mail:** bruce.fletcher@wcom.com

FLIEGEL, DAMON
Industry: Transportation **Born:** April 5. 1977, Phoenix, Arizona **Current organization:** Aardvark Movers, Inc. **Title:** President **Type of organization:** Moving company **Major product:** Relocation services **Area of distribution:** Phoenix, Arizona **Expertise:** Apartment, home and office relocation **Affiliations:** N.F.I.B.; Better Business Bureau **Hob./spts.:** Basketball, astronomy **SIC code:** 42 **Address:** Aardvark Movers, Inc., 2225 W. Mountain View Rd., Phoenix, AZ 85021 **E-mail:** aardvark@eshelon.com **Web address:** www.aardvarkmovers.com

FOWLER, ROGER G.
Industry: Electric utility **Born:** March 12, 1955, Shreveport, Louisiana **Univ./degree:** Certified in Leadership and Supervision, Texas A&M University, 2000 **Current organization:** Claiborne Electric Cooperative **Title:** Operations and Maintenance Manager **Type of organization:** Cooperative **Major product:** Electricity **Area of distribution:** Homer, Louisiana **Expertise:** Supervising and coordinating work on powerlines; Louisiana linemen training program **Affiliations:** 4-H Club; Louisiana Superintendents and Foremen Association **Hob./spts.:** Fishing, scuba diving, hang gliding **SIC code:** 49 **Address:** Claiborne Electric Cooperative, 12525 Hwy. 9, Homer, LA 71040 **E-mail:** rogerfowler@claiborneelectric.org **Web address:** www.claiborneelectric.org

FRANK, RICHARD D.
Industry: Transportation **Univ./degree:** B.S., Accounting, California State University, 1991 **Current organization:** Titan Transportation & Engineering Contractors, Inc. **Title:** President **Type of organization:** Truck transportation **Major product:** Trucking (sand, gravel and asphalt) **Area of distribution:** National **Expertise:** Accounting, engineering **Affiliations:** C.P.A.A.; California Dump Truck Association; California Trucking Association **SIC code:** 42 **Address:** Titan Transportation & Engineering Contractors, Inc., 25225 Maitri Rd., Corona, CA 92883 **E-mail:** rfii@aol.com

FRAZER, EILEEN M.
Industry: Healthcare accreditation **Born:** May 20, 1946, Allentown, Pennsylvania **Univ./degree:** R.N. Diploma, Allentown Hospital School of Nursing and Muhlenberg College, 1967 **Current organization:** Commission on Accreditation of Medical Transport Systems **Title:** Executive Director **Type of organization:** Nonprofit **Major product:** Air transport accreditation **Area of distribution:** International **Expertise:** Air medical transport **Affiliations:** A.A.M.S.; A.S.T.N.A. **Hob./spts.:** Piano, writing poetry and short stories **SIC code:** 45 **Address:** Commission on Accreditation of Medical Transport Systems, 117 Chestnut Lane, Anderson, SC 29625 **E-mail:** efrazer@aol.com

GAIDIS JR., RICHARD A.
Industry: Entertainment **Born:** June 30, 1949, Salisbury, Maryland **Univ./degree:** B.S., Business, Delaware State University, 1973 **Current organization:** TALK America **Title:** MIS Director **Type of organization:** Radio station **Major product:** Radio broadcasting **Area of distribution:** National **Expertise:** Security **Affiliations:** P.A.D.I. **Hob./spts.:** Scuba diving (is an instructor), travel **SIC code:** 48 **Address:** TALK America, 126 Trafalgar Dr., Dover, DE 19904 **E-mail:** rgaidis@juno.com

GEORGE, DAVID L.
Industry: Telecommunications **Born:** September 19, 1963, Philadelphia, Pennsylvania **Univ./degree:** Two-year degree, Electronics, Ohio Institute of Technology, 1983; Honorary Graduate, Fiber Optic/System/Service/Installation Technology, National Cable Television Institute **Current organization:** Comcast Cable **Title:** FCC/OSHA Compliance Inspector **Type of organization:** Cable television, telecommunications **Major product:** MSO cable, internet **Area of distribution:** National **Expertise:** FCC/OSHA compliance **Hob./spts.:** Swimming, fishing, sports **SIC code:** 48 **Address:** Comcast Cable, 1555 Suzy St., Lebanon, PA 17046 **E-mail:** dave_george@cable.comcast.com

GERHART, DAVID C.
Industry: Energy **Univ./degree:** M.B.A., Alameda University, 2003 **Current organization:** NRG Energy **Title:** Plant Manager **Type of organization:** Power plant **Major product:** Power service **Area of distribution:** National **Expertise:** Safety, P&L, new business, facility oversight **Affiliations:** Council of Energy Advisors; American Society of Mechanical Engineers **Hob./spts.:** Golf, fishing, hiking, skiing **SIC code:** 49 **Address:** 6702 Rapids Rd., Lockport, NY 14094 **E-mail:** david.gerhart@nrgenergy.com **Web address:** www.nrgenergy.com

GIANNACI, ANTHONY T.
Industry: Government/transportation **Born:** February 10, 1959, Jersey City, New Jersey **Univ./degree:** B.S., Mechanical Engineering, New Jersey Institute of Technology, 1981 **Current organization:** N.J. Transit **Title:** DGM Facility Maintenance **Type of organization:** Transportation services **Major product:** Rail, bus and light rail operations **Area of distribution:** New Jersey **Expertise:** Engineering **Honors/awards:** Distinguished Achievement Awards **Affiliations:** P.A.L.; President, Athletic Booster Club **Hob./spts.:** Coaching Little League, football **SIC code:** 47 **Address:** N.J. Transit, 180 Boyden Ave., Maplewood, NJ 07040 **E-mail:** agiannaci@njtransit.com

GILMORE, WILLIAM E.
Industry: Utilities **Current organization:** Westar Energy **Title:** Machinist **Type of organization:** Utility company **Major product:** Electrical generation **Area of distribution:** Kansas **Expertise:** Power plant maintenance, project management, strategic planning, team leadership **Hob./spts.:** Computers, photography, riding Harley Davidsons, country and western music **SIC code:** 49 **Address:** Westar Energy, 25905 Jeffrey Rd., St. Marys, KS 66536 **E-mail:** oldhippie@starband.net

GOODWIN, CHARLES M.
Industry: Telecommunications **Univ./degree:** B.S., Computer Science, University of Toledo, 1982 **Current organization:** SBC Midwest Network Services **Title:** Manager, Results & Web Technology **Type of organization:** RBOC **Major product:** Wireless, local, LD phone service, broadband DSL **Area of distribution:** National **Expertise:** IT and web development **Affiliations:** I.W.A. Writers Guild **Hob./spts.:** Art collecting, hunting **SIC code:** 48 **Address:** SBC Midwest Network Services, 220 N Meridian St., Room 530, Indianapolis, IN 46204 **E-mail:** cg4185@msg.ameritech.com

GRUNBERG, KEITH A.
Industry: Telecommunications **Born:** July 10, 1962, Lebanon, Oregon **Univ./degree:** A.S., Electrical Engineering, 1984; A.S., Electromechanical Engineering, 1985; Shemeketa Community College **Current organization:** Rodban Northwest Network **Type of organization:** Telecommunications **Major product:** Service provider, voice, video and data transport **Area of distribution:** National **Expertise:** Design, engineering of high speed privatized data networks, sales, implementation, project management and support **Affiliations:** Society of Telecommunication Engineers **Hob./spts.:** Waterskiing, snow skiing, high school and college wrestling referee (21 yrs.) **SIC code:** 48 **Address:** Rodban Northwest Network, 803 Merlot Ave. N.E., Keizer, OR 97303 **E-mail:** kgrunberg@comcast.net

HADDAWAY, ROBERT M.
Industry: Cable television **Born:** March 6, 1959, Louisville, Kentucky **Current organization:** RMH Cable TV, Inc. **Title:** President **Type of organization:** Cable television sales and installations contract company **Major product:** Sales and installation cable television subscriptions **Area of distribution:** Texas **Expertise:** Marketing **Affiliations:** T.C.A.; C.T.A. **Hob./spts.:** Golf, snorkeling **SIC code:** 48 **Address:** RMH Cable TV, Inc., 7301 R.R. 620 North, Suite 155,197, Austin, TX 78726

HAHN, JOAN C.
Industry: Travel **Born:** May 9, 1933, Kemmerer, Wyoming **Univ./degree:** B.S., Speech & Drama, Brigham Young University, Utah, 1965 **Current organization:** Travel Passport **Title:** Owner; (Retired Drama Teacher, Cottonwood High School) **Type of organization:** Travel agency **Major product:** Broadway shows, theatre and cruises, European trips **Area of distribution:** International **Expertise:** International travel **Affiliations:** National Education Association; Utah Education Association; International Association of Travel Agents **Hob./spts.:** Fly-fishing, reading, embroidery **SIC code:** 47 **Address:** Travel Passport, P.O. Box 1336, Salem, UT 84653 **E-mail:** joanhahn@juno.com

HALLIVIS, ALBERTO
Industry: Shipping **Born:** June 26, 1960, Mexico City, Mexico **Univ./degree:** M.S., Business, Instituto Panamericano, 1999 **Current organization:** DHL Regional Services **Title:** Vice President, Sales & Marketing **Type of organization:** Transportation express **Major product:** International documents and parcels **Area of distribution:** International **Expertise:** Marketing **Published works:** 15 articles **Hob./spts.:** Golf, waterskiing, road cycling **SIC code:** 47 **Address:** 11301 Sea Grass Circle, Boca Raton, FL 33498 **E-mail:** alberto.hallivis@dhl.com

HAMILTON, VICKI W.
Industry: Communications **Born:** May 27, 1963, Chicopee Falls, Massachusetts **Univ./degree:** M.B.A., St. Louis University, 1994 **Current organization:** Cinema Screen Media **Title:** Senior Vice President, Shared Services and I.T. Operations **Type of organization:** Cable television network **Major product:** Cable television programming **Area of distribution:** National **Expertise:** Administration **Affiliations:** W.I.C.T.; N.A.M.I.C.; S.C.T.E.; N.B.M.B.A. Association **Hob./spts.:** Aerobics, weight training **SIC code:** 48 **Address:** Cinema Screen Media, 2121 New Market Pkwy., Suite 30, Marietta, GA 30067

HARRIS, MARK R.
Industry: Telecommunications **Born:** March, 1967, United Kingdom **Univ./degree:** First University of Lester **Current organization:** DSL Internet Corp. **Title:** Chief Financial Officer **Type of organization:** Broadband business to business **Major product:** VoIP phone services **Area of distribution:** Florida **Expertise:** Finance, fund raising, IPO's **Published works:** Financial Times **Affiliations:** I.C.A. **Hob./spts.:** Skiing, rugby, soccer **SIC code:** 48 **Address:** DSL Internet Corp., 5000 S.W. 75th Ave., Miami, FL 33155 **E-mail:** mrharris67@hotmail.com

HAWTHORNE, ROBERT C.
Industry: Aviation **Born:** Richmond, Virginia **Univ./degree:** B.A., Virginia Military Institute; M.A., Management, Central Michigan University; Ed.S., Troy State University, 1983 **Current organization:** Washington DC National Airport **Title:** General Manager **Type of organization:** Independent transportation company **Major product:** Disaster relief helicopter support; Jet transportation for VIP's, congressmen **Area of distribution:** International **Expertise:** Operations management, administration, helicopter and jet charter support **Affiliations:** N.B.A.A.; V.M.I.; U.S.A.F. **Hob./spts.:** Civil War history, stamp and coin collecting **SIC code:** 45 **Address:** Washington DC National Airport, Martinair c/o Hangar 7, Washington, DC 20001 **E-mail:** martinairdc@aol.com

HEBERT, MARK J.
Industry: Telecommunications **Current organization:** Houma Telephone Service, Inc. **Title:** President **Type of organization:** Telecommunications **Major product:** Phones and computers **Area of distribution:** National **Expertise:** Toshiba **SIC code:** 48 **Address:** Houma Telephone Service, Inc., 230 New Orleans Blvd., Houma, LA 70364 **E-mail:** ctsystems@bellsouth.net **Web address:** www.houmatelephoneservice.com

HEGER, JEFF B.
Industry: Communications **Univ./degree:** B.S., Engineering Management; M.B.A., University of North Carolina at Raleigh **Current organization:** Comcast **Title:** Director of Business Operations **Type of organization:** Service provider **Major product:** Cable TV, Internet, phone service **Area of distribution:** National **Expertise:** Management operations **Hob./spts.:** Golf, family activities **SIC code:** 48 **Address:** 250 Cannon Way, Warrenton, VA 20186 **E-mail:** jeff.heger@adelphia.net

HEGNA, WILLIAM L.
Industry: Magazine fulfillments **Born:** June 11, 1941, Spencer, Iowa **Current organization:** Communications Data Services (CDS) **Title:** Purchasing Specialist **Type of organization:** Magazine fulfillment **Major product:** Magazine billing and renewals **Area of distribution:** National **Expertise:** Purchasing **Honors/awards:** Region II Service Award, 2000 **Affiliations:** Member, N.A.P.M., 1991; Life Member, Iowa Chapter, Paralyzed Veterans of America; Business Forms Management Association; Institute for Supply Management **Hob./spts.:** Family, flying, travel **SIC code:** 48 **Address:** Communications Data Services (CDS), 1901 Bell Ave., Des Moines, IA 50315-1099 **E-mail:** bhegna@cdsfulfillment.com **Web address:** www.cdsfulfillment.com

HENNESSEY, DAN E.
Industry: Common carrier **Born:** February 11, 1939, Zanesville, Ohio **Univ./degree:** B.A., Muskingum College, 1960 **Current organization:** Putnam Truckload Direct **Title:** Chairman/CEO **Type of organization:** Trucking company **Major product:** Pick up and delivery **Area of distribution:** International (USA and Province of Ontario, Canada) **Expertise:** Expediting trucking service **Honors/awards:** Emeritus Board, Good Will; Ronald Reagan Republican Gold Medal Award, 2005 **Affiliations:** Rotary Club; 32nd Degree Mason; Past Chair /Board Member, Ohio Trucking Association; Past Chair/Board Member, Noon Rotary; Zanesville and Ohio Chamber of Commerce; Maysville South Business Association; Fuel Source Advisory Council of the Public Utilities Commission; Past Chair, Faith United Methodist Church **Hob./spts.:** Boating, fishing **SIC code:** 42 **Address:** Putnam Truckload Direct, 1705 Moxahala Ave., P.O. Box 2909, Zanesville, OH 43702-2909 **E-mail:** danH@MSM1sp.com **Web address:** www.putnamtruckload.net

HER, ZANG JU
Industry: Telecommunications **Univ./degree:** PhDEE, La Salle University, 1996 **Current organization:** Cingular Wireless **Title:** R.F. Engineer **Type of organization:** Telecommunications/PCS provider **Major product:** Design and optimization **Area of distribution:** National **Expertise:** Radio frequency, electrical engineering **SIC code:** 48 **Address:** 3931 Temple Ct., Merced, CA 95348 **E-mail:** zang.her@cingular.com

HILL, LEON A.
Industry: Trucking **Born:** January 3, 1955, Muscatine, Iowa **Current organization:** Schuster Co. **Title:** Corporate Director of Safety **Type of organization:** Trucking **Major product:** Transportation of goods **Area of distribution:** National **Expertise:** Safety and compliance **Affiliations:** N.S.C.; I.C.S.M. **Hob./spts.:** Golf, football **SIC code:** 42 **Address:** Schuster Co., 1345 Twelfth Ave. S.W., Le Mars, IA 51031 **E-mail:** lhill@schusterco.com

HOFFMAN JR., WILLIAM J.
Industry: Communications **Born:** January 10, 1962, Fort Lee, Virginia **Univ./degree:** B.S., Electrical Engineering, Officers Candidate School **Current organization:** Uniqua Technologies, Inc. **Title:** CEO **Type of organization:** Wireless service provider for Nextel **Major product:** Internet service and Nextel sales **Area of distribution:** National **Expertise:** Leadership, engineering, sales **Affiliations:** I.E.E.E.; C.T.I.A. **Hob./spts.:** Golf, skiing, jogging **SIC code:** 48 **Address:** Uniqua Technologies, Inc., 816 Curie Dr., Alpharetta, GA 30005 **E-mail:** wjhoffman@vectorlink.com

HOHN, JOHN J.
Industry: Telecommunications **Born:** January 2, 1976, Dover, New Jersey **Current organization:** Wireless Solutions International Inc. **Title:** CEO **Type of organization:** Telecommunications **Major product:** Wireless services **Area of distribution:** International **Expertise:** Engineering **Hob./spts.:** Snowboarding **SIC code:** 48 **Address:** Wireless Solutions International Inc., 3353 Gun Club Rd., Nazareth, PA 18064-8597 **E-mail:** john@wirelesssolutionsinc.com **Web address:** www.wirelesssolutions.com

HORSTMANN, JOHN V.
Industry: Utilities **Born:** August 3, Breese, Illinois **Univ./degree:** Attended Allied Institute of Technology for Industrial Tool Engineering **Current organization:** Certop Inc. **Title:** President **Type of organization:** Sanitary services/water and waste water treatment **Major product:** Contract operations of water and wastewater facilities **Area of distribution:** St. Louis, Missouri **Expertise:** Certified Operator (Water Supply System Operator Class A) and (Wastewater Plant Operator Class 1), consulting, training, **Honors/awards:** Water Operator of the Year **Published works:** Training videos **Affiliations:** Illinois Potable Water Operators Association; Past President, Southwest Central Water Operators Association; Past President, Southern Illinois Water Operators Association; Past President, New Baden, Illinois Jaycees **Hob./spts.:** Fishing, boating, travel **SIC code:** 49 **Address:** Certop Inc., 16923 Pollman Rd., Bartelso, IL 62218 **E-mail:** h2ohorstmann@yahoo.com

HOWARD SR., GEORGE DANNY
Industry: Municipal water utility **Born:** September 28, 1952, Leeds, Alabama **Current organization:** Leeds Water Works **Title:** Chief Operator **Type of organization:** Public utility **Major product:** Drinking water **Area of distribution:** Leeds, Alabama **Expertise:** Daily operations oversight **Affiliations:** Rural Water Works Association; National Water Works Association; American Water Works Association **Hob./spts.:** Collecting U.S. coins, restoring antique cars **SIC code:** 49 **Address:** Leeds Water Works, P.O. Box 100, Leeds, AL 35094

HSU, PING
Industry: Utilities **Born:** July 1, 1944, Hunan, China **Univ./degree:** M.S., University of Iowa; B.S., Ph.D., Civil Engineering, National Cheng Kung University **Current organization:** Southern Co. **Title:** Principal Engineer **Type of organization:** Utility **Major product:** Electricity, power plant design and operations **Area of distribution:** National **Expertise:** Nuclear power plant design and analysis, civil and structural engineering, project management, quality control **Published works:** Presented a paper at the ICONE seminar **Affiliations:** A.S.C.E.; A.S.M.E. **Hob./spts.:** Reading, music, travel **SIC code:** 49 **Address:** Southern Co., 42 Inverness Pkwy., Birmingham, AL 35242

HUBBARD, SHAWN ALLAN
Industry: Composite industry **Born:** October 3, 1976, Westfield, New York **Univ./degree:** B.S., Mechanical Engineering, Penn State Erie, The Behrend College, 1998 **Current organization:** VEC Technology **Title:** CAD Design Engineer **Type of organization:** Marine manufacturing **Major product:** Boats **Area of distribution:** Greenville, Pennsylvania **Expertise:** Engineering, Certified Composites Technician, 2002-2005 **Honors/awards:** National Honor Society of Leadership, Omicron Delta Kappa, '97 **Affiliations:** A.S.M.E. **Hob./spts.:** Basketball, baseball, football **SIC code:** 44 **Address:** VEC Technology, 639 Keystone Rd., Greenville, PA 16125 **E-mail:** hub33us@yahoo.com

HUNTER, GARY V.
Industry: Railroad transportation **Born:** March 5, 1954, Oakland, California **Univ./degree:** B.A., Business Administration, 1976; M.B.A., 1979, San Francisco State University, California **Current organization:** Railroad Industries Incorporated **Title:** Chairman/Chief Executive Officer; Other Affiliations: Chairman/Chief Operating Officer, Reno Pacific Rail Corporation; Trustee, Philip E. Kalthoff Estate **Type of organization:** Consulting firm **Major product:** Transportation consulting **Area of distribution:** National and international **Expertise:** Marketing, finance, operations, strategic planning, equipment planning **Honors/awards:** Awards - American Biographical Institute 2000 Notable American Men, 1992 and 1993; Citations - Who's Who Among Rising Young Americans, 1992 and 1993; Who's Who in Executives and Professionals, 1998-99 **Affiliations:** National Industrial Transportation League; Pacific Railway Club **Hob./spts.:** Physical fitness, fishing, sports **SIC code:** 40 **Address:** Railroad Industries Incorporated, 1105 Terminal Way, Suite 202, Reno, NV 89502 **E-mail:** railindinc@worldnet.att.net

ISKANDER, PETER A.
Industry: Telecommunications, wireless carrier **Born:** December 24, 1972, Columbus, Ohio **Univ./degree:** B.A., Business Management, Indiana State University **Current organization:** Verizon Wireless **Title:** Senior Financial Analyst **Type of organization:** Service provider **Major product:** Wireless voice and date products **Area of distribution:** International **Expertise:** Corporate finance, sales operations, training, consulting, strategic planning, business development, program implementation, human resources **Hob./spts.:** Family, golf, outdoor activities **SIC code:** 48 **Address:** Verizon Wireless, 250 E. 96th St., Suite 175, Indianapolis, IN 46240 **E-mail:** peter.iskander@verizonwireless.com

JACKSON, HOWARD L.
Industry: Utilities **Born:** August 13, 1953, Norfolk, Virginia **Current organization:** Citizens Gas & Coke Utility **Title:** Technical Trainer **Type of organization:** Distribution **Major product:** Natural gas **Area of distribution:** Indianapolis, Indiana **Expertise:** Training of field personnel **Hob./spts.:** Golf, camping **SIC code:** 49 **Address:** Citizens Gas & Coke Utility, 2150 Dr. Martin Luther King Jr. St., Indianapolis, IN 46202 **E-mail:** hjackson@cgcu.com

JACKSON, PAUL E.
Industry: Utilities **Born:** October 29, 1974, Nashville, Tennessee **Univ./degree:** B.A., Tennessee Technological University, 1998 **Current organization:** P.E.S. **Title:** Chief Operations Officer **Type of organization:** Distributing **Major product:** Electric power **Area of distribution:** Tennessee **Expertise:** Operations/engineering management **Hob./spts.:** Water sports, hiking, classical music **SIC code:** 49 **Address:** P.E.S., 128 S. First St., Pulaski, TN 38478 **E-mail:** ejackson@pulaskielectric.org

JAMES, RAY ALLAN
Industry: Transportation/education **Born:** May 31, 1958, Wichita Falls, Texas **Univ./degree:** A.A., 1987; B.S., 1990, University of Maryland-Pirmasens, West Germany; Masters Degree Candidate, Training & Development, Midwestern State University, Texas **Current organization:** T-Square Logistics, S.A.F.B./Burkburnett F.W.I.S.D. **Title:** Licensed Bus and Truck Driver/Dispatcher/Substitute Teacher; Poet and Songwriter **Type of organization:** Contractor/school district **Major product:** Transportation/ office education **Area of distribution:** International **Expertise:** Music, poetry, teaching; Licensed in Driver's Education, Behind-the-Wheel Instructor **Honors/awards:** Elected Official with Student Government at MSU as Senator 2005; National Deans List; International Who's Who of Professionals; International Poetry Hall of Fame; International Society of Poets; International Who's Who in Poetry; National Defense Service Medal; Good Conduct Medal; Army Service Ribbon; Overseas Service Ribbon; Sharpshooter Badge, etc. **Published works:** Numerous including, "A Touch of Mary Ann Hatfield", Lyrical Heritage, published by the National Library of Poetry, 1996; "The Sound of Poetry", 1996; "Almighty Joe", Best Poems of 1996; "A Pocket Full of Emotions", On The Threshold of a Dream, published by The National Library of Poetry; "Born Free", Outstanding Poets of 1994; "You'll Be Mine", "My Love for You", Garden of Thoughts, published by Creative Arts & Science Enterprise, 1993;

Songbook Anthology - numerous including, "I Got Friends in High Places", "My Love for You", "You'll Be Mine", "A Pocket Full of Emotion", "Let Me Tell You Now", Profiles in Music, Tin Pan Alley & Broadway Music Productions, 1993 **Affiliations:** N.S.W.A.; International Library of Poetry; Past Member, Talent Search of America; Past Member, Nashville's Songwriters Association **Hob./spts.:** Travel, weight training, teaching, tutoring **SIC code:** 47 **Address:** 105 Lindsey Dr., Wichita Falls, TX 76301 **E-mail:** rayajames@yahoo.com **Web address:** www.poets.com/rayallanjames.html and www.poetry.co

JEFFRIES, TIMOTHY H.
Industry: Telecommunications **Born:** July 16, Cincinnati, Ohio **Univ./degree:** A.A., Electrical Engineering, University of Kentucky, 1988 **Current organization:** ATIS **Title:** Vice President, Technology **Type of organization:** Communications **Major product:** Communications solutions **Area of distribution:** International **Expertise:** Administration, technology **Hob./spts.:** Family, basketball, reading **SIC code:** 48 **Address:** ATIS, 1200 G. St. N.W., Suite 500, Washington, DC 20005 **E-mail:** tjeff1125@comcast.net

JOHN, BRIAN B.
Industry: Travel **Born:** March 7, 1978, Grenada, West Indies **Univ./degree:** B.A., Business Administration, 2000; A.A., Hospitality, University of West Indies, 2001 **Current organization:** BJ Travel Services **Title:** Director of Operations/Manager **Type of organization:** Full service travel agency **Major product:** Leisure/luxury travel **Expertise:** Management **Hob./spts.:** Travel, basketball, soccer **SIC code:** 47 **Address:** BJ Travel Services, 167-A MacDougal St., Suite 1A, Brooklyn, NY 11233 **E-mail:** brian.john@bjtravelservices.com **Web address:** www.bjtravelservices.com

JOHNSON, Z. WAYNE
Industry: Transportation **Born:** August 9, 1951, Trenton, New Jersey **Current organization:** New Jersey Transit Corp. **Title:** Assistant Executive Director, Human Resources **Type of organization:** Public/private transportation service delivery **Major product:** Public transportation **Area of distribution:** National **Expertise:** Human resources, small business programs, training **Affiliations:** Regional Alliance for Small Contractors; American Public Transportation Association; The United Way **Hob./spts.:** Tennis, martial arts (Isshin Ryu 1st degree Black Belt; Shoto Kan, 2nd degree Black Belt; Bando-Masters, 5th degree ranking) **SIC code:** 41 **Address:** New Jersey Transit Corp., 1 Penn Plaza East, East Newark, NJ 07105-2246

KABROTH, KAROL
Industry: Transportation **Born:** August 26, 1949, Mechanicsburg, Pennsylvania **Current organization:** Carlisle Carrier Corp. **Title:** Director of Safety and Claims **Type of organization:** Tucking company **Major product:** Trucking **Area of distribution:** National **Expertise:** Truck safety and liability claims **Affiliations:** Pennsylvania Motor Truck Association; Pennsylvania Notary **Hob./spts.:** Rollerblading **SIC code:** 42 **Address:** Carlisle Carrier Corp., 6380 Brackbill Blvd., Mechanicsburg, PA 17055 **E-mail:** kkabroth@carlislecc.com **Web address:** www.carlislecc.com

KAYE, ANDY
Industry: Radio broadcasting **Born:** June 2, 1962, Chicago, Illinois **Univ./degree:** Graduate, Midwestern Broadcasting School, Chicago, 1982 **Current organization:** Lotus Broadcasting Corp. **Title:** News and Public Affairs Director/Human Resource Coordinator **Type of organization:** Radio station(s) **Major product:** News broadcasting **Area of distribution:** Nevada **Expertise:** Management; news and sports broadcasting **Honors/awards:** Nevada Broadcasters Hall of Fame, 2005 (NBA) **Affiliations:** Dept. Head, KOMP Human Resources and Public Affairs Dept.; Muscular Dystrophy Assoc.; Ronald McDonald House; Co-host, KOMP Rock & Roll Morning Show; Hosts a weekly public affairs program "Neon & Beyond" **Hob./spts.:** Mentoring, reading to school children, baseball, ice hockey **SIC code:** 48 **Address:** Lotus Broadcasting Corp., 8755 W. Flamingo Rd., Las Vegas, NV 89147 **E-mail:** andy@komp.com **Web address:** www.komp.com

KRIVOKAPIC, IVAN
Industry: Wireless communications **Born:** October 28, 1960, Belgrade, Yugoslavia **Univ./degree:** Ph.D., University of Belgrade, Yugoslavia, 1996 **Current organization:** Graviton **Title:** RF System Engineer **Type of organization:** R&D, production **Major product:** Wireless sensor networks **Area of distribution:** National/International **Expertise:** Engineering **Published works:** 4 papers (WIEEE transactions) **Hob./spts.:** Skiing, hiking **SIC code:** 48 **Address:** Graviton, 7665 Palmilla Dr., Suite 5039, San Diego, CA 92122 **E-mail:** ikrivokapic@graviton.com **Web address:** www.graviton.com

KRUGER, PAULA
Industry: Communications **Born:** July 31, 1950, Brooklyn, New York **Univ./degree:** B.A., Summa Cum Laude, Economics, full scholarship, C.W. Post-Long Island University, 1972; M.B.A., Summa Cum Laude, Concentration in Marketing, full scholarship, C.W. Post-Roth Graduate School of Business, 1976 **Current organization:** Qwest **Title:** Executive Vice President **Type of organization:** Premier provider of full service communications **Major product:** Telecommunications **Area of distribution:** National **Expertise:** Strategic call center leadership **Affiliations:** Junior Achievement, Qwest Women; Human Resources Committee, Girls, Inc.; National Society of Decorative Painters; Board Member, Technology Solutions Corp. **Hob./spts.:** Golf, skiing, decorative arts, reading **SIC code:** 48 **Address:** Qwest, 1801 California St., 52nd floor, Denver, CO 80202 **E-mail:** paula.kruger@qwest.com

KUMAR, ASHA L.
Industry: Communications/radio broadcasting **Born:** February 13, 1976, Warren, Ohio **Univ./degree:** The Ohio Center for Broadcasting, 1996 **Current organization:** Midwest Family Broadcast Group **Title:** Promotions Director **Type of organization:** FM radio stations: KQRA, KOSP, KKLH, KOMG **Major product:** Radio broadcasting **Area of distribution:** Missouri **Expertise:** Event coordinator, marketing, promotions, website designing **Affiliations:** Member, Board of Directors, The Springfield Arts Association; Development Center of the Ozarks **Hob./spts.:** Teaching dance (tap, jazz, ballet), local theatre **SIC code:** 48 **Address:** Midwest Family Broadcast Group, 319-B E. Battlefield, Springfield, MO 65807 **E-mail:** akumar@mwfmarketing.fm **Web address:** www.mwfmarketing.fm

KUNKEL, A. LEWIS
Industry: Transportation **Born:** January 20, 1951, Bluffton, Indiana **Univ./degree:** A.A., Aviation Management, Lewis University, 1971 **Current organization:** Sky Night, LLC **Title:** Aviation Manager **Type of organization:** Private jet corp. travel **Major product:** Travel **Area of distribution:** International **Expertise:** Air travel **Affiliations:** N.B.A.A.; A.O.P.A. **Hob./spts.:** Golf, skiing **SIC code:** 45 **Address:** Sky Night, LLC, 430 Airport Rd., Greeneville, TN 37745 **E-mail:** lkunkel@forwardair.com

LEE, PATRICK J.
Industry: Telecommunications **Univ./degree:** M.B.A., Fairleigh Dickinson University, 1999 **Current organization:** AT&T Corp. **Title:** Marketing Director **Type of organization:** Retail **Major product:** Telecommunications **Area of distribution:** International **Expertise:** Marketing **SIC code:** 48 **Address:** AT&T Corp., 1 AT&T Way 3C130C, Bedminster, NJ 07921 **E-mail:** leepj.@att.com

LEWIS-OGIUGO, RAYNELL M.
Industry: Transportation **Born:** December 11, 1967, Paincourtville, Louisiana **Univ./degree:** B.S., Information Technology, University of Phoenix, Pittsburgh, Pennsylvania, 2002; M.B.A., Technology Management, University of Phoenix, New Orleans, Louisiana, 2005 **Current organization:** FedEx **Title:** Senior Manager **Type of organization:** Delivery service **Major product:** Ground delivery **Area of distribution:** National **Expertise:** Client relations and negotiations, legal environment of business, logistics management, professional presentations, staff training and development **Hob./spts.:** Home restoration, singing **SIC code:** 42 **Address:** FedEx, 325 Jeannie St., Lake Charles, LA 70605 **E-mail:** raymarlo1967@yahoo.com

LICHNER, BRIAN P.
Industry: Telecommunications **Born:** April 25, 1960, Baker, Oregon **Univ./degree:** University of Alaska **Current organization:** GCI Cable Inc. **Title:** Regional Inside Plant Engineer **Type of organization:** Broadband communications **Major product:** Television transmission **Area of distribution:** Alaska **Expertise:** Engineering, administration, management of special projects **Affiliations:** Board Member, Alaska S.C.T.E.; Cable Labs (Cable industry testing facility); Council of Telecommunications Advisors **Hob./spts.:** Coaching softball, reading, travel, fishing, hunting, community volunteer **SIC code:** 48 **Address:** GCI Cable Inc., 5151 Fairbanks St., Anchorage, AK 99503 **E-mail:** blichner@gci.com

LIKHARI, GURMEET S.
Industry: Consulting **Univ./degree:** B.S., MIT, India **Current organization:** MobileComm Professionals, Inc. **Title:** President **Type of organization:** Telecommunications consulting **Major product:** Consulting services to major wireless carriers **Area of distribution:** International **Expertise:** Wireless telecommunications consulting services **SIC code:** 48 **Address:** MobileComm Professionals, Inc., 1255 W. 15th St., Suite 440, Plano, TX 75075 **E-mail:** glikhari@mcpsinc.com

LOGAN JR., JOHN C.
Industry: Communications **Born:** November 23, 1948, Dayton, Ohio **Univ./degree:** Ph.D., Mass Communications, Union Institute and University, Cincinnati, Ohio **Current organization:** WCSU - FM Radio, Central State University **Title:** General Manager **Type of organization:** Radio station **Major product:** Radio broadcasting **Area of distribution:** International **Expertise:** Broadcast communications **Honors/awards:** #1 Black College Student radio station **Published works:** 1 book entitled "Violent Music Causes Violent Kids" **Affiliations:** Kappa Alpha Psi Fraternity **Hob./spts.:** Music, flying airplanes **SIC code:** 48 **Address:** 2169 Cornwall Dr., Xenia, OH 45385-4709 **E-mail:** jloganphd1@aol.com

LOZANO, GRACIELA J.
Industry: Communications **Born:** March 11, 1964, Lima, Peru **Current organization:** Paradise Internet Services and Wireless Communications **Title:** President **Type of organization:** Internet service provider **Major product:** Internet access **Area of distribution:** National **Expertise:** Computer internet provider **Affiliations:** Rotary Club; Lions Club; Jaycees; Chamber of Commerce **Hob./spts.:** Golf **SIC code:** 48 **Address:** Paradise Internet Services and Wireless Communications, 1608 Dennis St., Key West, FL 33040

MADER, JUSTIN B.
Industry: Electrical power **Born:** June 13, 1970, Colby, Kansas **Univ./degree:** B.S., Nuclear Engineering, Kansas State University, 1995 **Current organization:** Wolf Creek Nuclear Power Plant **Title:** Nuclear Station Operator **Type of organization:** Nuclear power plant **Major product:** Electrical power **Area of distribution:** National **Expertise:** Designing trailers; production and manufacturing engineering **Affiliations:** A.N.S.; Formerly Product Engineer for Exiss Aluminum Trailers **Hob./spts.:** Flying aircraft **SIC code:** 49 **Address:** Exiss Aluminum Trailers, 900 Exiss Trailers Blvd., El Reno, OK 73099 **E-mail:** jumader@earthlink.net

MANRIQUEZ, RAMON
Industry: Aviation **Born:** May 3, 1956, Ensenada, Mexico **Univ./degree:** A.S., Aviation Management, Embry-Riddle Aeronautical University , 1984 **Current organization:** Global Exec Aviation **Title:** President **Type of organization:** Aviation charter company **Major product:** Aircraft management and charter **Area of distribution:** National/International **Expertise:** Operations, pilot **Affiliations:** N.B.A.A. **Hob./spts.:** Travel, computers **SIC code:** 45 **Address:** Global Exec Aviation, 3250 Airflite Way, Long Beach, CA 90807 **E-mail:** ramon@globalexecaviation.com

MARANO, MARK WILLIAM
Industry: Utilities **Born:** October 8, 1962, Mineola, New York **Univ./degree:** B.A., Business Administration, State University of New York at Oswego, 1984 **Current organization:** American Electric Power **Title:** Senior Vice President, Generation Business Services / President & CEO, Numanco, LLC (majority owned subsidiary of AEP) / President, USTI (wholly owned subsidiary of AEP) **Type of organization:** Electrical utility **Major product:** Electricity **Area of distribution:** Ohio, West Virginia, Michigan, Indiana, Oklahoma, Oregon, Texas, Arkansas, Louisiana **Expertise:** Business management **Honors/awards:** College Baseball Scholarship **Affiliations:** E.U.C.G.; A.A.C.E. **Hob./spts.:** Baseball, golf, tennis, outdoor activities **SIC code:** 49 **Address:** American Electric Power, 1 Riverside Plaza, 20th floor, Columbus, OH 43215 **E-mail:** mwmarano@aep.com **Web address:** www.aep.com

MARMON, JAMES J.
Industry: Transportation **Born:** May 18, 1971, Long Beach, California **Current organization:** J&J Drive Away, Inc. **Title:** CEO **Type of organization:** Transportation **Major product:** Transporting semi-tractors, service for truck dealers **Area of distribution:** National **Expertise:** Management, marketing **Hob./spts.:** Golf, travel, exotic fishing, coaching **SIC code:** 42 **Address:** J&J Drive Away, Inc., 6728 W. 153rd St., Lenexa, KS 66220 **E-mail:** jmarmon@jjdriveaway.com

MARTIN, DARREN J.
Industry: Broadcast communications **Born:** August 20, 1972, Mobile, Alabama **Univ./degree:** University of Southern Alabama **Current organization:** WPMI **Title:** Chief IT Engineer **Type of organization:** Broadcast **Major product:** Advertising **Area of distribution:** Alabama **Expertise:** IT Engineering **Affiliations:** Sol Circle Entertainment **Hob./spts.:** Disc jockey, baseball, basketball, home recording studio **SIC code:** 48 **Address:** WPMI, 661 Azalea Rd., Mobile, AL 36693 **E-mail:** dmartin@wpmi.com

MAYES, MARGARETTA L.
Industry: Utilities **Born:** September 18, 1972, Leesville, Louisiana **Univ./degree:** B.S., Computer Information Systems, Northwestern State University, Louisiana, 1995 **Current organization:** Beauregard Electric Co-op, Inc. **Title:** System Analyst **Type of organization:** Utility provider **Major product:** Electric power **Area of distribution:** DeRidder, Louisiana **Expertise:** Network administration **Affiliations:** Rotary International Club **SIC code:** 49 **Address:** Beauregard Electric Co-op, Inc., 1010 E. First St., DeRidder, LA 70634 **E-mail:** mmayes@beci.org **Web address:** www.beci.org

MCDOUGLE, BRIAN R.
Industry: Transportation **Born:** September 2, 1953, Falls Church, Virginia **Current organization:** Metropolitan Washington Airports Authority **Title:** Heavy Equipment Mechanic **Type of organization:** International airport **Expertise:** Diagnoses of electrical problems, hydraulics, air operated systems, diesel engine diagnose and repair, preference-medium and heavy duty truck; The 'hands on' learning and actual working as an apprentice in a 'place of business' started in 1965; Has received numerous certificates in years of profession, ASE Certified; Responsibilities: All required repairs and preventive maintenance on ambulances, 5 "Oshkosh" crash trucks (aircraft rescure). pumper trucks, ladder truck, hazmat unit, foam trailer and department light vehicles; Also perform 'break-down' calls out @ terminals on Mobile Lounges and minor repairs **Hob./spts.:** Motorcycle riding (customized 'Goldwing' with pull behind trailer), Siberian Husky's **SIC code:** 45 **Address:** 6872 Maplewood Dr., Bealeton, VA 22712 **E-mail:** toytractor91@aol.com

MERRIMAN, ERIC F.
Industry: Utilities **Born:** January 19, 1949, Tucson, Arizona **Current organization:** City of Stafford **Title:** Electrician Specialist **Type of organization:** Municipal utilities **Major product:** Electric, water, gas, sewers, line work-substations; 40 years experience **Area of distribution:** Stafford, Arizona **Expertise:** Electrical **Affiliations:** B.L.M. (government agency) **Hob./spts.:** Fishing, hunting, the outdoors **SIC code:** 49 **Address:** City of Stafford, 405 W. Discovery Park Blvd., P.O. Box 272, Safford, AZ 85546 **E-mail:** emerriman@gilaresources.com

MIARECKI, GALE A.
Industry: Energy **Born:** August 23, 1946, Chicago, Illinois **Current organization:** Fuel Handling, Yard Operations TVA **Title:** Manager of Methods and Processes, Human Performance and Training **Type of organization:** Power Plants **Major product:** Electrical Energy **Area of distribution:** Tennessee Valley **Expertise:** Development of processes, procedures, web based, interactive, on time reporting, emphasis on event analysis, root cause and replication for 11 plants, human behavior enhancement **Hob./spts.:** Physical fitness, walking, reading, antique car enthusiast **SIC code:** 49 **Address:** TVA Fuel Handling Operations, 13246 State Rte. 176, Drakesboro, KY 42337 **E-mail:** gamiarec@tva.gov

MICHAEL, MONICA L.
Industry: Transportation **Born:** July 1, 1966, Michigan **Univ./degree:** A.A., Business, Baker College, 1985 **Current organization:** Michael Trucking LLC **Title:** Owner/Office Manager **Type of organization:** Trucking company **Major product:** Car hauler/auto transport **Area of distribution:** National **Expertise:** Operations, office administration **Hob./spts.:** Travel, car shows (1932 Roadster) **SIC code:** 47 **Address:** Michael Trucking LLC, 3360 S. Putnam Rd., Laingsburg, MI 48848 **E-mail:** monica@ispn.cc

MICHALAK, DAVID G.
Industry: Television broadcasting **Born:** December 16, 1949, Milwaukee, Wisconsin **Univ./degree:** A.A.S., Electrical Communication, Milwaukee Institute of Technology, 1970 **Current organization:** WITI Fox 6 **Title:** Senior Broadcast Engineer **Type of organization:** Television station **Major product:** Live TV **Area of distribution:** Wisconsin **Expertise:** 5.2 audio reproduction, electrical, tape and sound engineer **Affiliations:** International Brotherhood of Electrical Workers; Executive Board member and Union Activist, Local 715; Audio Engineering Society; Society of Broadcast Engineers **Hob./spts.:** Cars, sound system design, woodworking **SIC code:** 48 **Address:** WITI Fox 6, 9001 N. Green Bay Rd., Milwaukee, WI 53209 **E-mail:** dmichalak@wi.rr.com **Web address:** www.fox6milwaukee.com

MILLER, KATHRYN E.
Industry: Broadcasting **Born:** December 5, 1941, Fort Wayne, Texas **Univ./degree:** M.A., University of Texas, 1980 **Current organization:** KWTX/KBTX L.P. **Title:** Special Projects Coordinator **Type of organization:** Television **Major product:** Television programming, broadcasting **Area of distribution:** National **Expertise:** FCC, Children's programming, satellite, affiliate relations **Affiliations:** International Executive Guild **SIC code:** 48 **Address:** KWTX/KBTX L.P., P.O. Box 2636, Waco, TX 76702 **E-mail:** kmiller@kwtx.com

MILLER, STEVEN W.
Industry: Municipal water utility **Born:** January 6, 1958, Las Vegas, Nevada **Univ./degree:** Class A Operator **Current organization:** Marion Filter Plant **Title:** Operator Responsibility Charge **Type of organization:** Water plant **Major product:** City water service **Area of distribution:** Marion, North Carolina **Expertise:** Drinking water management; Licensed Class A Operator **Affiliations:** A.W.W.A.; N.W.W.A. **Hob./spts.:** Racing **SIC code:** 49 **Address:** Marion Filter Plant, 801 Old Greenlee Rd., Marion, NC 28752

MILLS, NORMAN
Industry: Communications **Univ./degree:** B.S.E.E., Communications, University of Utah **Current organization:** Colstrip Cable T.V. **Title:** President **Type of organization:** Service provider **Major product:** Cable TV **Area of distribution:** National **Expertise:** Engineering **Affiliations:** A.C.A. **SIC code:** 48 **Address:** P.O. Box 20183, Billings, MT 59102

MISENHEIMER, VIRGIL L.
Industry: Transportation **Born:** May 7, 1956, Salisbury, North Carolina **Univ./degree:** Technical Certification in Automotive, Diesel and welding courses, Nashville Auto Diesel College; Certified to teach in a vocational classroom setting **Current organization:** U.S. Airways **Title:** Production Supervisor **Type of organization:** Airline **Major product:** Air travel **Area of distribution:** International **Expertise:** Engineering and facility maintenance; Special Training in- Hazardous Waste Management, OSHA, Boiler Efficiencies and Compressed Air, Programmable Logic Controllers A/B PLC-3

Hob./spts.: Fishing, hunting, coaching **SIC code:** 45 **Address:** US Airways, CLT M450 P.O. Box 19368, Charlotte, NC 28219-9368 **E-mail:** virgilm@usairways.com

MORROW, LISA M.
Industry: Communications **Born:** September 9, 1967, Syracuse, New York **Current organization:** Galaxy Communications **Title:** Vice President **Type of organization:** Event/promotional marketing **Major product:** Broadcasting, event planning **Area of distribution:** National **Expertise:** Marketing; Certificate from the American Bar Association **Hob./spts.:** Equestrian, coaching and mentoring the Special Olympics **SIC code:** 48 **Address:** Galaxy Communications, 235 Walton St., Syracuse, NY 13202 **E-mail:** lmorrow@galaxycommunications.com

NAJMI, NAJAM A.
Industry: Telecommunications **Born:** April 8, 1953, Karachi, Pakistan **Univ./degree:** B.S., Hamilton University, 1984 **Current organization:** Qwest Communications Corp. **Title:** Lead Technical Project Manager **Type of organization:** Major telecom **Major product:** Telecom, DSL, IP, IT, Local/long distance service **Area of distribution:** International **Expertise:** Engineering, technical support, standards and codes **Honors/awards:** Recognition Award, for Outstanding Service in Security in the Gulf War **Published works:** 1 book, "Cooling Towers", 1986 **Affiliations:** I.P.M.; I.I.E.; N.F.P.A.; R.S.E.S.; A.E.E.; A.S.H.R.E.; A.S.S.E.; I.I.R.; Certified Mediator; Volunteer, Local Bar Association; Notary Public **SIC code:** 48 **Address:** Qwest Communication Corp., 9727 Business Park Dr., Suite H, Sacramento, CA 95827 **E-mail:** najam.najmi@qwest.com

NEUMEISTER, TONI
Industry: Hospitality **Born:** September 21, 1959, Austria **Univ./degree:** Batgleichenberg Culinary School, Austria, 1975 **Current organization:** Crystal Cruises **Title:** Vice President, Food and Beverage Operations **Type of organization:** Cruise line **Major product:** Food, entertainment **Area of distribution:** International **Expertise:** Food and beverage management **Affiliations:** A.C.A. **Hob./spts.:** Jogging **SIC code:** 44 **Address:** Crystal Cruises, 2049 Century Park East, Suite 1400, Los Angeles, CA 90067 **E-mail:** tneumeister@crystalcruises.com

NGUYEN, JOHN H.
Industry: Electric utility **Univ./degree:** B.S., Iowa State University, 1989; M.B.A., Creighton University, 1997 **Current organization:** Omaha Public Power District **Title:** Engineer (Design) **Type of organization:** Power utility **Major product:** Electrical generation, transmission, distribution **Area of distribution:** Nebraska **Expertise:** Engineering consulting of prototypes **Affiliations:** I.E.E.E. **SIC code:** 48 **Address:** Omaha Public Power District, 444 S. 16th St. Mall, Omaha, NE 68102 **E-mail:** jnguyen@oppd.com

NICHOLS, BOBBY B.
Industry: Education **Born:** July 19, 1946, Orangeburg, South Carolina **Univ./degree:** M.S., Communications, S.C. State University, 1972 **Current organization:** Nicwild Communications Inc. (WIIZ-FM) **Title:** CEO, GM **Type of organization:** Radio station **Major product:** Broadcasting **Area of distribution:** South Carolina/Georgia **Expertise:** Marketing **Honors/awards:** Listed in Outstanding Young Men in America, 1980; Male Minority Business Owner of the Year, CSRA Business League, 1999-2000; Business Leader's Award, Big Seven Association, 2001 **Affiliations:** G.B.A.; N.A.B.; South Carolina Broadcasters Association; Alpha Phi Alpha Fraternity, Inc. **Hob./spts.:** Traveling, reading, landscape gardening, basketball **SIC code:** 48 **Address:** Nicwild Communications, Inc. (WIIZ-FM), 8968 Marlboro Ave., Barnwell, SC 29812 **E-mail:** thewiz@wiiz979.com

NOE, KAREN G.
Industry: Utility **Born:** January 13, 1956, Kansas City, Kansas **Univ./degree:** B.S., Arts, Excelsior College, 2002 **Current organization:** Public Service Electric & Gas **Title:** Business Manager - Transmission **Type of organization:** Electric & Gas company **Major product:** Electricity **Area of distribution:** New Jersey **Expertise:** Operations, maintenance **Affiliations:** Association of Quality Control; Toastmasters; 22 years in the Military **Hob./spts.:** Hiking, Biking, outdoor activities **SIC code:** 49 **Address:** Public Service Electric & Gas, 4000 Hadley Rd., South Plainfield, NJ 07080 **E-mail:** karen.noe@pseg.com **Web address:** www.pseg.com

OSTERN, WILHELM L.
Industry: Telecommunications **Born:** New York, New York **Univ./degree:** B.A., German and Communications, Muskingum College, Ohio, 1991; M.Ed., University of Pittsburgh, Pennsylvania, 1995 **Current organization:** WDS Global **Title:** Technical Support Analyst **Major product:** Communications **Area of distribution:** International **Hob./spts.:** Hiking, cycling, outdoor activities **SIC code:** 48 **Address:** 730 Bellevue Ave. East, #403, Seattle, WA 98102 **E-mail:** wlostern@yahoo.com

PAELLMANN, NILS
Industry: Telecommunications **Born:** May 25, 1963, Kiel, Germany **Univ./degree:** Ph.D., Finance, New York University, 1994 **Current organization:** Deutsche Telekom **Title:** Vice President **Type of organization:** Service **Major product:** Fixed and wireless phone services **Area of distribution:** International **Expertise:** Investor relations **Affiliations:** N.I.R.I. **Hob./spts.:** Opera, modern architecture **SIC code:** 48 **Address:** Deutsche Telekom, 280 Park Ave., 26th floor, New York, NY 10017 **E-mail:** nils.paellmann@usa.telekom.de

PAGÁN BEAUCHAMP, CARLOS F.
Industry: Broadcasting **Born:** April 11, 1956, San Juan, Puerto Rico **Univ./degree:** B.A., Washington and Jefferson College, 1978 **Current organization:** Univision Puerto Rico **Title:** General Sales Manager **Major product:** Television, entertainment **Area of distribution:** National **Expertise:** Sales, marketing **Affiliations:** S.M.E.A.; Chamber of Commerce **Hob./spts.:** Family, racing off-shore boats, waterskiing, soccer, volleyball, baseball, mountain biking **SIC code:** 48 **Address:** Univision Puerto Rico, Box 10000, San Juan, PR 00908 **E-mail:** cpagan@univision.net

PARKS, MICHAEL R.
Industry: Telecommunications **Born:** September 20, 1979, Park Ridge, Illinois **Univ./degree:** Provisioning Certificate, Comcast University, 2002 **Current organization:** Comcast Communications Inc. **Title:** Provisioning Specialist **Type of organization:** Cable operator **Major product:** Communications services **Area of distribution:** International **Expertise:** Telephony provision, troubleshooting, team training **Published works:** 2 training manuals **Hob./spts.:** Sports enthusiast, reading **SIC code:** 48 **Address:** Comcast Communications Inc., 1500 McConnor Pkwy., Schaumburg, IL 60173 **E-mail:** mike_parks@cable.comcast.com

PETERSON, JOSEPH F.
Industry: Communications **Born:** Colorado Springs, Colorado **Univ./degree:** Certification in Electronics Technology, Pikes Peak Community College, 1998 **Current organization:** Adelphia **Title:** Maintenance Technician **Type of organization:** M.S.O. **Major product:** Advanced cable TV, high speed internet service **Area of distribution:** National **Expertise:** Fiber optics, coax maintenance, specialty fibers **Affiliations:** C.T.E.; S.C.T.E. **SIC code:** 48 **Address:** Adelphia, 525 Babcock Rd., Colorado Springs, CO 80915 **E-mail:** joe.peterson@adelphia.net

PLASSE, JASON W.
Industry: Communications **Born:** March 9, 1962 Santa Monica, California **Univ./degree:** A.S., Micro Computer Operations and Accounting, Eldorado College, 1990; Lucent Technology, Siecor Corp. Design and Engineering Certificate **Current organization:** Ficom Corp. **Title:** Vice President of Business Development **Type of organization:** Contractor **Major product:** Communications installation **Area of distribution:** International **Expertise:** Engineering **Hob./spts.:** Spending time with his children, racing, fishing, public speaking (Honorary MC for fishing tournament) **SIC code:** 48 **Address:** Ficom Corp., 2280 Micro Place, Escondido, CA 92029 **E-mail:** jplasse@ficom.com **Web address:** www.ficom.com

PLICQUE JR., JACOB A.
Industry: Utilities **Born:** August 16, 1952, New Orleans, Louisiana **Univ./degree:** B.S., Mechanical Engineering, University of New Orleans, 1977; M.B.A., University of Phoenix, 2002 **Current organization:** JEA **Title:** Manager, Project Design **Type of organization:** Municipal utility **Major product:** Electricity, water, sewers, chilled water **Area of distribution:** Jacksonville, Florida **Expertise:** Mechanical engineering **Published works:** Write-ups **Affiliations:** A.S.M.E.; A.S.R.A.E.E. **Hob./spts.:** Chess, photography, prison ministry **SIC code:** 49 **Address:** JEA, 21 W. Church St., 10th floor, Jacksonville, FL 32202 **E-mail:** plicja@jea.com **Web address:** www.jea.com

PRIETO, SALVADOR
Industry: Communications **Born:** December 25, 1971, Mexticacan, Mexico **Current organization:** Lazer Broadcasting Corp. **Title:** Program Director **Type of organization:** Advertising **Major product:** Broadcasting and advertising **Area of distribution:** California **Expertise:** D.J., programming music **Hob./spts.:** Basketball, physical fitness **SIC code:** 48 **Address:** Lazer Broadcasting Corp., 200 S. "A" St., Suite 400, Oxnard, CA 93030 **E-mail:** salvadorprieto@aol.com

PURVIS, SCOTT G.
Industry: Communications **Born:** February 2, 1958, Beaumont, Texas **Univ./degree:** A.S. Technical school, Dallas, Tx, 1977 **Current organization:** WorldCom **Title:** Advisory Engineer **Type of organization:** Communications services **Major product:** Cellular communication, wireless communications **Area of distribution:** National **Expertise:** Patent (U.S. postal-architectural) **Honors/awards:** Smithsonian Award **Published works:** Articles **Hob./spts.:** Numismatics **SIC code:** 48 **Address:** 106 Southern Pine Ct., Arlington, TX 76018 **E-mail:** scott.purvis@wcom.com

RANGEL, LUPE A.
Industry: Utilities **Born:** March 16, 1954, Gallup, New Mexico **Univ./degree:** A.S., Chemistry, University of New Mexico, 1978 **Current organization:** Williams Energy Services **Title:** Director, New Mexico Training Center **Type of organization:** Distribution **Major product:** Natural gas **Area of distribution:** New Mexico **Expertise:** Training, safety - OSHA, EPA, DOT **Affiliations:** A.S.S.E. **Hob./spts.:** Bodybuilding

SIC code: 49 **Address:** Williams Energy Services, 3105 Centenary Ave., Farmington, NM 87402 **E-mail:** lupe.rangel@iwilliams.com

REDMAN SR., GERALD N.
Industry: Water and wastewater **Born:** July 30, 1958, Lander, Wyoming **Current organization:** Northern Arapaho Tribe Utilities **Title:** Director **Type of organization:** Utility **Major product:** Wastewater **Area of distribution:** Wyoming **Expertise:** Engineering, contracting **Hob./spts.:** Hunting, fishing, raising quarter horses **SIC code:** 49 **Address:** P.O. Box 1034, Ft. Washakie, WY 82514 **E-mail:** fredman@northernarapaho.com

RIDER JR., LARRY D.
Industry: Communications **Current organization:** A&L Contractors, Inc. **Title:** President **Type of organization:** Telecommunications provider **Major product:** CATV, high speed Internet **Area of distribution:** Moody, Alabama **Expertise:** Building TV cables , internet modems **Affiliations:** Society of Cable Telecommunications Engineers; Better Business Bureau **SIC code:** 48 **Address:** A&L Contractors, Inc., 3003 Daniel Dr., Moody, AL 35004 **E-mail:** rider3003@aol.com

RIPP, DANIEL J.
Industry: Cable advertising technology **Current organization:** Comcast Cable, Spotlight Division **Title:** Vice President of Operations and Engineering **Type of organization:** Cable TV provider **Major product:** Cable advertising **Area of distribution:** National **Expertise:** Engineering and operations **Affiliations:** S.C.T.E.; C.T.A.M. **SIC code:** 48 **Address:** 1700 Paoli Pike, Malvern, PA 19355 **E-mail:** dan_ripp@cable.comcast.com

RIVERA MENÉNDEZ, RAÚL G.
Industry: Radio **Born:** April 22, 1965, Fajardo, Puerto Rico **Univ./degree:** A.S., Communications, InterAmerican University, 1987; Public and Community Relations Course, Radio, TV, Newswriter, U.S. Army, Ft. Benjamin Harrison, Indiana, 1988; B.A., Mayor Management, InterAmerican University, 1992 **Current organization:** El Yunque Broadcasting Inc., WYQE FM Yunque 93 **Title:** Executive Vice President **Type of organization:** Radio station **Major product:** Music **Area of distribution:** Puerto Rico **Expertise:** Radio, communications, public relations, consultant, radio management, programming production and operations **Honors/awards:** Numerous including, Executive Radio Man of the Year, People Latin Awards, San Juan, PR, 2005; Director of the Year (Radio), Century Music Award, San Juan, PR, 2005; Director of the Year (Radio), Paoli Awards, Rio Grande, PR, 2004; Director of the Year (Radio), Paoli Awards, San Juan, PR, 2003, 2002, 2001, 2000, 1999, 1998, 1997, 1996, 1983; Director of the Year (Radio), Farándula Awards, San Juan, PR, 1999, 1998, 1997, 1996; Director of the Year (Radio), Radio & Music Awards, Los Angeles, CA, 1996 **Affiliations:** Radio Broadcasters of Puerto Rico; Radio Broadcasters of Latinoamerican; Professional Consultant Association, USA; American Management Association International, NY; Activities & Communications Committee for American Society of Cancer, San Juan, PR; Communication Committee Santiago Apostol, Catholic Church, Fajardo, PR **Hob./spts.:** Travel **SIC code:** 48 **Address:** WYQE FM, P.O. Box 9300, Naguabo, PR 00718-9300 **E-mail:** raulgrivera@hotmail.com

ROBERTS, CHRIS B.
Industry: Transportation **Univ./degree:** B.A., University of Arkansas; 1998 **Current organization:** JB Hunt **Title:** Pricing administrator **Type of organization:** Transportation provider **Major product:** Transportation services **Area of distribution:** National **Expertise:** Logistics **Affiliations:** N.S.S.; P.S. **Hob./spts.:** Football, science **SIC code:** 47 **Address:** 511 Evergreen Circle, Lowell, AR 72745 **E-mail:** spacelife@wmconnect.com

ROBLES, JOE T.
Industry: Utilities **Born:** January 4, 1951, Tucson, Arizona **Univ./degree:** M.S., Organizational Management, University of Phoenix, 2000 **Current organization:** Southern California, Edison **Title:** Electrical Supervisor III **Type of organization:** Utility distributor **Major product:** Production of electricity **Area of distribution:** National **Expertise:** Management, electrical instrument test group **Affiliations:** Elks Lodge **Hob./spts.:** Hunting, fishing **SIC code:** 49 **Address:** Southern California, Edison, 655 Bruce Woodbury Dr., Laughlin, NV 89029 **E-mail:** roblesjt@sce.com **Web address:** sce.com

RODRIGUEZ, JOSE ANTONIO
Industry: Freight transportation **Born:** September 13, 1953, Guantanamo Bay, Cuba **Univ./degree:** B.A., University of Miami, 1978 **Current organization:** Federal Express Corp. **Title:** Senior Project Manager **Type of organization:** Distributors **Major product:** Freight forwarding **Area of distribution:** Florida **Expertise:** Architecture, construction management **Honors/awards:** Recognition of Outstanding Achievement, Federal Express **Affiliations:** Project Managers Institute **Hob./spts.:** Stained glass art, sailing, kayaking **SIC code:** 42 **Address:** Federal Express Corp., 5341 N.W. 33rd Ave., Ft. Lauderdale, FL 33309 **E-mail:** jarodriguez@fedex.com

RODRIGUEZ, MARK A.
Industry: Utilities **Born:** February 23, 1955, Albuquerque, New Mexico **Univ./degree:** B.S., Chemistry, New Mexico State University, 1986 **Current organization:** El Paso Electric Co. **Title:** Senior Environmental Scientist **Type of organization:** Electric utility **Major product:** Generation and distribution of electricity **Area of distribution:** International **Expertise:** Environmental (air quality) **Published works:** Co-authored papers **Hob./spts.:** Organic gardening, constructing passive solar adobe homes **SIC code:** 49 **Address:** 5225 Valle Bonita Dr., Las Cruces, NM 88007 **E-mail:** mrodrigl@epelectric.com **Web address:** www.elpasoelectric.com

ROMERO, SERGIO
Industry: Television **Born:** March 3, 1966, El Paso, Texas **Current organization:** Univision Television Network **Title:** Senior Director of Promotions **Type of organization:** Television network **Major product:** Information and entertainment **Area of distribution:** International **Expertise:** On-air promotions **Affiliations:** N.A.T.A.S. **Hob./spts.:** Music **SIC code:** 48 **Address:** Univision Television Network, 9405 N.W. 41st St., Miami, FL 33178 **E-mail:** rome5532@bellsouth.net

ROSEMAN, BEVERLY
Industry: Travel **Born:** February 26, 1963, Pittsburgh, Pennsylvania **Univ./degree:** B.S., Journalism, Broward Community College, 1985 **Current organization:** Oceania Cruises **Title:** Senior Director of Brand Management **Type of organization:** Cruise line **Major product:** Luxury cruises **Area of distribution:** International **Expertise:** Direct mail marketing **Hob./spts.:** Family, mountain hiking, the outdoors, log cabin vacations **SIC code:** 44 **Address:** Oceania Cruises, 8300 N.W. 33rd St., Suite 308, Miami, FL 33122 **E-mail:** broseman@oceaniacruises.com

ROTH, KENNETH E.
Industry: Warehousing/transportation **Born:** July 8, 1944, Seymour, Indiana **Current organization:** DMI Distribution & Transportation **Title:** Corporate Safety Director **Type of organization:** Warehouse and distribution center **Major product:** Warehousing **Area of distribution:** National **Expertise:** Operations **Affiliations:** N.S.C.; I.T.A.; A.T.A. **Hob./spts.:** Travel **SIC code:** 42 **Address:** DMI Distribution & Transportation, 3500 Hamilton Ave., Muncie, IN 47302 **E-mail:** kroth@dmidistribution.com

ROTHLISBERGER, JAMES L.
Industry: Telecommunications **Born:** Oakdale, California **Univ./degree:** A.S., Communications, U.S. Navy **Current organization:** Sprint Nextel **Title:** Senior Equipment Engineer **Type of organization:** Communications **Major product:** Telephones, cell phones **Area of distribution:** International **Expertise:** Installation quality **Affiliations:** Board Member, Telcordia Advisory Committee **Hob./spts.:** Family **SIC code:** 48 **Address:** Sprint Nextel, 5996 Gleason Dr., Dublin, CA 94568 **E-mail:** jim.rothlisberger@sprint.com **Web address:** www.sprint.com

RUNGE, EDWARD F.
Industry: Telecommunications **Born:** September 20, 1949, Lincoln, Nebraska **Univ./degree:** A.A.S., Architecture, Southeast Community College, Nebraska, 1971 **Current organization:** Alltel **Title:** Building Design Engineer/Mechanical Engineer **Type of organization:** Telecommunications provider **Major product:** Wireline and wireless services **Area of distribution:** International **Expertise:** Mechanical engineering, HVAC & plumbing **Honors/awards:** International Who's Who of Professionals; Meritorius Service Medal, Nebraska National Guard, 1988-1997 **Affiliations:** A.S.H.R.A.E.; A.S.P.E. **Hob./spts.:** Biking, home improvements (remodeling, gardening) **SIC code:** 48 **Address:** Alltel, P.O. Box 81309, 1620 "M" St., Lincoln, NE 68501-1309 **E-mail:** ed.runge@alltel.com

RUUD, ARNE CONRAD
Industry: Travel marketing, worldwide tour operators, incentive planners, global conference orchestration **Univ./degree:** Journalism, University of Uppsala, Sweden; Diploma in Public Relations/Business Administration, Los Angeles City College **Current organization:** Travel Marketing Media/HolidayWorld Productions/TMM International Inc. **Title:** Chairman/Executive Producer **Type of organization:** Travel marketing, tours, incentives, conference and convention planners **Major product:** Destination/travel marketing and promotions, tour operations and conferences **Area of distribution:** International **Expertise:** Geography, holiday destinations, lecturing, global tour and convention planning, travel documentary productions for TV, DVD **Honors/awards:** Awards for authorship, production management of HolidayWorld Productions international broadcast series; Numerous awards and citations presented at industry meetings for excellence in destination promotion and/or marketing presented by Governments of Malaysia, Philippines and Singapore; The Coveted Africa and India Trophies for outstanding industry marketing of both destinations at ASTA World Convention, 1969; Best TV Documentary Broadcast by Advertising Club awarded HolidayWorld Production for his TV production of Birmingham, UK, 1995; Currently New York State Chairman for the (national) Business Advisory Council, appointed by Congressional Committee, 2003 **Published works:** Numerous including syndicated broadcast series HolidayWorld of Travel (500 stations), feature, articles in Medico Interamericana, Physicians Radio Network **Hob./spts.:** Sailing, hunting, skiing, moun-

taineering, anthropology **SIC code:** 47 **Address:** 406 Soundview Ave., Mamaroneck, NY 10543

RYPINS, ROBERT M.
Industry: Industrial service **Born:** September 4, 1932, San Francisco, California **Current organization:** R&L Warehouse Distribution Services, Inc. **Title:** Executive Vice President **Type of organization:** Industrial public warehouse **Major product:** Public warehouse, trucking services **Area of distribution:** National **Expertise:** Sales, marketing, management **Affiliations:** International Warehouse Logistics Association **SIC code:** 42 **Address:** R&L Warehouse Distribution Services, Inc., 1490 66th St., Emeryville, CA 94608-1014 **E-mail:** miker@warehousedistribution.com

SAMBERG, LINDA
Industry: Telephony **Born:** January 14, 1951, Indianapolis, Indiana **Current organization:** SBC Communications **Title:** Director **Type of organization:** Communications provider **Major product:** Communications **Area of distribution:** National **Expertise:** Planning, engineering **Published works:** Diversity Magazine; Co-Author of Telecom papers **Hob./spts.:** Gardening, swimming, reading **SIC code:** 48 **Address:** SBC Communications, 220 N. Meridian St., Room 940, Indianapolis, IN 46204 **E-mail:** lsam3120@aol.com

SANDIFER, MICHAEL A.
Industry: Telecommunications **Born:** August 3, 1969, Jacksonville, Florida **Univ./degree:** B.S., Finance, Auburn University, 1993 **Current organization:** Excell Communications Inc. **Title:** Project Director **Type of organization:** Consulting/telecommunications; turnkey service provider for wireless infrastructure **Major product:** Project management, site development, construction **Area of distribution:** Southeast U.S. **Expertise:** Engineering, project management **Affiliations:** N.A.T.E.; Tennessee Wireless Association; Alabama Wireless Association **Hob./spts.:** Spending time with wife and children, golf **SIC code:** 48 **Address:** Excell Communications Inc., 6247 Amber Hills Rd., Trussville, AL 35173

SANFORD, MICHAEL P.
Industry: Communications **Born:** July 28, Greenwood, Mississippi **Current organization:** Cable One Advertising **Title:** Regional Production Manager **Type of organization:** Provider of cable advertising and video production **Major product:** T.V. commercials **Area of distribution:** National **Expertise:** Creating and producing cable T.V. commercials **Hob./spts.:** Fishing, hunting **SIC code:** 48 **Address:** Cable One Advertising, 2247 S. Commerce St., Grenada, MS 38901 **E-mail:** msanford@cableone.net

SCHERER, MIKE
Industry: Wireless communications **Born:** Danville, Indiana, 1964 **Current organization:** JDH Contracting, Inc. **Title:** Wireless Division Manager **Type of organization:** General contractor **Major product:** Cellular site construction **Area of distribution:** National **Expertise:** Project manager/estimator **Affiliations:** N.A.T.E.; F.A.A. **Hob./spts.:** Gold, boating, fishing, hiking **SIC code:** 48 **Address:** JDH Contracting, Inc., 8109 Network Dr., Plainfield, IN 46168 **E-mail:** mscherer@jdhcontracting.com **Web address:** www.jdhcontracting.com

SCHMID-FRAZEE, CAROL A.
Industry: Utilities **Univ./degree:** B.S., Business Administration, University of California, Berkeley, 1978; J.D., U.C.L.A. Law School, 1981 **Current organization:** Southern California Edison Co. **Title:** Senior Attorney **Type of organization:** Electric utility company **Major product:** Electricity **Area of distribution:** Southern California **Expertise:** Regulatory law **Affiliations:** Conference of California Public Utility Counsel **Hob./spts.:** Hiking, reading **SIC code:** 49 **Address:** Southern California Edison Co., 2244 Walnut Grove, Rosemead, CA 91770

SETINA, JOE D.
Industry: Transportation **Born:** March 2, 1980, Salem, Oregon **Current organization:** Joe Tex Inc. **Title:** CEO/President **Type of organization:** Truck transportation company **Major product:** National freight services **Area of distribution:** National **Expertise:** Logistics/brokerage/transportation **Hob./spts.:** Fishing, golf **SIC code:** 41 **Address:** Joe Tex Inc., 619 West Rutherford, Pittsburg, TX 75686 **E-mail:** joe@joetexusa.com **Web address:** www.joetexusa.com

SHAHZAD, MOHAMMAD A.
Industry: Communications **Born:** January 25, 1973, Jehlum, Pakistan **Univ./degree:** B.S.E.E., Virginia State University, 1994; M.B.A., Technology Management, University of Phoenix, 2001; J.D. Candidate, Concord Law School **Current organization:** General Dynamics Network Systems **Title:** Sr. Telecommunications Engineer **Type of organization:** Telecommunications **Major product:** Cisco IP Telephony contracts **Area of distribution:** International **Expertise:** Management of IP Telephony and IP Contact Centers for the Dept. of Commerce; training **Honors/awards:** International Computer Networks ABCD Award **Affiliations:** Call Center Network Group; National Business Management Organization **Hob./spts.:** Football, reading law books, running, volunteer IP telephony **SIC code:** 48 **Address:** 6800 Lamp Post Lane, Alexandria, VA 22306 **E-mail:** mhshahzad@hotmail.com

SHOPTAW JR., ROBERT L.
Industry: Transportation and logistics **Born:** March 13, 1969, Harrison, Arkansas **Univ./degree:** B.S., Communications, University of Arkansas, Fayetteville, 1997 **Current organization:** Proactive Logistics Solutions, Inc. **Title:** President **Type of organization:** Consulting/freight movement **Major product:** Full truckload service **Area of distribution:** National, Canada **Expertise:** Logistics services **Hob./spts.:** Golf, fishing, coaching Little League soccer and basketball **SIC code:** 42 **Address:** Proactive Logistics Solutions, Inc., 1202 N. Mallard Lane, Rogers, AR 72756 **E-mail:** robert@proactivelogisticssolutions.com **Web address:** www.proactivelogisticssolutions.com

SHULTZ, DEBORAH
Industry: Broadband cable **Born:** January 11, 1959, Hammond, Indiana **Univ./degree:** Master Technician Degree, National Cable Television Institute (NCIT); Further studies at Sawyer College **Current organization:** Comcast **Title:** Cable Headend Engineer **Type of organization:** MSO Cable Operator **Major product:** Cable TV, HIS **Area of distribution:** Hammond, Indiana **Expertise:** Head end **Honors/awards:** You Make A Difference Award, 1st quarter 2000 **Affiliations:** Society of Cable Television Engineers **Hob./spts.:** Woodworking, painting **SIC code:** 48 **Address:** 1530 174th Place, Hammond, IN 46324-2858 **E-mail:** deb4wood@comcast.net **Web address:** www.comcast.net

SIMONS, EGLON E.
Industry: Cable television **Univ./degree:** B.A., City College of New York, 1968; M.B.A., Harvard Business School, 1976 **Current organization:** Cablevision Systems Co./Rainbow Advertising Sales Division **Title:** Executive Vice President **Type of organization:** Cable television **Major product:** Cable television sales **Area of distribution:** National **Expertise:** Sales, operations **Affiliations:** National Board of Directors, National Down Syndrome Society **Hob./spts.:** Golf, tennis **SIC code:** 48 **Address:** Cablevision Systems Co., Rainbow Advertising Sales Division, 530 Fifth Ave., New York, NY 10036 **E-mail:** eesimons@rainbow-media.com

SKIDMORE, ROGER R.
Industry: Communications **Born:** May 9, 1972, Pennington Gap, Virginia **Univ./degree:** B.S., 1995; M.S., Computer Engineering, 1997; Ph.D., 2003, Virginia Tech **Current organization:** Wireless Valley Communications Inc. **Title:** President **Type of organization:** Wireless communications/engineering **Major product:** Software engineering applications **Area of distribution:** International **Expertise:** Software engineering, wireless communication systems **Affiliations:** I.E.E.E.; A.C.M. **SIC code:** 48 **Address:** Wireless Valley Communications Inc., 2404 Rutland Dr., Suite 700, Austin, TX 78758 **E-mail:** skid@wirelessvalley.com

SMITH, PAUL B.
Industry: Energy **Born:** October 11, 1956, Tauton, England **Univ./degree:** B.S.C., Marine Engineering, University of South Hampton, England, 1976 **Current organization:** Wartsila Development & Financial Services, Inc. **Title:** Director, Development Services **Type of organization:** Manufacturing/development **Major product:** Power plant development, electrical energy **Area of distribution:** National **Expertise:** Project Developer **Affiliations:** I.M.E. **Hob./spts.:** Cycling **SIC code:** 49 **Address:** Wartsila Development & Financial Services, Inc., 201 Defense Hwy., Suite 100, Annapolis, MD 21401 **E-mail:** paul.smith@wartsila.com

SPANGLER, JUDIE L.
Industry: Aviation **Current organization:** Aerosmith Aviation Inc. **Title:** Controller **Type of organization:** Aviation **Major product:** On demand custom air charter services **Area of distribution:** International **Expertise:** Financial planning, accounting, bookings, customer service **Affiliations:** D.A.R.; Eastern Star **Hob./spts.:** Reading, church, shopping, charity work with youth groups; Antique dealer specializing in rare and hard to find items **SIC code:** 45 **Address:** Aerosmith Aviation Inc., 500 Sally Ride Dr., Concord, CA 94520 **E-mail:** yodster@earthlink.net

STECKER, WILLIAM E.
Industry: Power plant construction **Born:** August 31, 1954, Monterey, California **Univ./degree:** B.S., Lehigh University, 1976 **Current organization:** Calpine Power Corp. **Title:** Technical Advisor **Type of organization:** Power producer **Major product:** Power **Area of distribution:** National **Expertise:** Engineering **Affiliations:** A.S.M.E. **Hob./spts.:** Skiing, hiking, vintage cars **SIC code:** 49 **Address:** Calpine Power Corp., 10808 E. Maplewood Dr., Englewood, CO 80111 **E-mail:** bstecker@calpine.com

STEVENS, SUZANNE E.
Industry: Travel **Born:** August 27, 1937, Milwaukee, Wisconsin **Current organization:** Travel International **Title:** President/Owner **Type of organization:** Travel agency **Major product:** Corporate and leisure travel **Area of distribution:** International **Expertise:** Management, marketing, sales **Affiliations:** Association of International

Travel Agents; American Society of Travel Agents; Kenosha Chamber of Commerce; Business After Five Club **Hob./spts.:** Green Bay Packers, travel, family activities **SIC code:** 47 **Address:** Travel International, 4653 75th St., Kenosha, WI 53142

STONE, DOUGLAS H.
Industry: Electric power generation **Univ./degree:** B.S.M.E., Clemson University, 1987 **Current organization:** Allegheny Energy **Title:** Manager, Business Support **Type of organization:** Electric power generator **Major product:** Electric power **Area of distribution:** Pennsylvania, Maryland, West Virginia **Expertise:** Registered P.E.; restructuring and managing core business processes; developing new generation projects and opportunities through sales and purchases; 13 years experience with large E&C company developing, designing, constructing and managing work associated with new power generation projects **Affiliations:** A.S.M.E. **Hob./spts.:** Coaching, home improvement, travel, sports **SIC code:** 49 **Address:** Allegheny Energy, 4350 Northern Pike, Monroeville, PA 15146 **E-mail:** dstone2@alleghenyenergy.com

STULTZ, DEBBIE
Industry: Communications **Born:** Salem, Virginia **Univ./degree:** A.A., Computer Systems Management, National Business College, 1999 **Current organization:** Cox Communications **Title:** Administrative Assistant **Type of organization:** Telecommunications **Major product:** Telephone, cable, Internet **Area of distribution:** Roanoke, Virginia **Expertise:** Communications **Honors/awards:** Employee of the Year, 2000 and 2001; Employee of the Quarter, 3rd Quarter 2004; Who's Who Among American Junior Colleges 1999, Deans List **Hob./spts.:** Volleyball, softball, Mary Kay Cosmetics **SIC code:** 48 **Address:** Cox Communications, 5400 Fallowater Lane, Roanoke, VA 24018 **E-mail:** debbie.stultz@cox.com **Web address:** www.marykay.com/dstultz1

TANNER, LINDA K.
Industry: Packing/shipping **Univ./degree:** A.S., Business Management and Computers, Rutledge College, 1989 **Current organization:** Pak Mail #136 **Title:** Owner **Type of organization:** Packing and shipping **Major product:** Boxes, shipping services **Area of distribution:** International **Expertise:** Management, packing, crating **SIC code:** 47 **Address:** Pak Mail #136, 5101 Ashley Phosphate Rd., Suite 104, North Charleston, SC 29418 **E-mail:** linda.tanner@knology.net

TAYLOR III, CLYDE S.
Industry: Communications **Univ./degree:** B.A., Marketing, 1975; B.A., Communications, 1975, Bowling Green State University **Current organization:** Taylor Communications **Title:** President **Type of organization:** Marketing and training firm **Major product:** Marketing communications, consulting services **Area of distribution:** International **Expertise:** Marketing, staff development **Published works:** Trade articles **Affiliations:** P.M.A.I.; R.D.C.M.; Rochester Advertising Association **Hob./spts.:** Photography, running, reading **SIC code:** 48 **Address:** Taylor Communications, 56 Kings Lacey Way, Fairport, NY 14450 **E-mail:** cstthree@aol.com

THAKUR, ANTHONY E.
Industry: Telecommunications **Born:** February 3, 1960, Bartica, Guyana **Univ./degree:** B.S.E.E., University of Texas, 1987; M.S., Florida Institute of Technology, 1993 **Current organization:** Time Warner Telecom **Title:** Vice President, Engineering & Technology **Type of organization:** Telecommunications **Major product:** Telecom services **Area of distribution:** Colorado **Expertise:** Engineering, technology, telephony **Affiliations:** I.E.E.E.; I.E.C. **Hob./spts.:** Travel, sports, golf **SIC code:** 48 **Address:** Time Warner Telecom, 10475 Park Meadows Dr., Littleton, CO 80124 **E-mail:** tony.thakur@twtelecom.com

THIEM, CARL W.
Industry: Warehousing/trucking/logistics **Univ./degree:** M.B.A., Harvard University, 1976 **Current organization:** Leicht Transfer & Storage **Title:** President **Type of organization:** Distributors **Major product:** Warehousing and distribution, transportation, cross-dock, supply chain consulting, material handling consulting **Area of distribution:** International **Expertise:** General management **Published works:** Articles **Hob./spts.:** Sports, outdoor activities, reading **SIC code:** 47 **Address:** Leicht Transfer & Storage, 1401 State St., P.O. Box 2447, Green Bay, WI 54306 **E-mail:** carlthiem@leichtgb.com **Web address:** www.leichtgb.com

THIRUPATI, SREE
Industry: Telecommunications **Born:** April 10, 1973, Nellore, India **Univ./degree:** B.A., Mechanical Engineering, Nagarjuna University, 1995; Post Grad Certificate, Computer Applications, 1996 **Current organization:** CenturyTel **Title:** Lead Web Developer **Type of organization:** Communications **Major product:** Corporate web sites **Area of distribution:** International **Expertise:** Web technologies **Affiliations:** C.F. Users Group **Hob./spts.:** Camping, hiking, racquetball, table tennis **SIC code:** 48 **Address:** CenturyTel, 100 CenturyTel Dr., 2TS, Monroe, LA 71203 **E-mail:** t_sam_2000@yahoo.com

THOMAS, JOHN M.
Industry: Communications **Born:** October 22, 1951, Zelienople, Pennsylvania **Current organization:** WICT-FM Radio **Title:** Program Director **Type of organization:** Radio **Major product:** Music/news/information **Area of distribution:** Eastern Ohio, Western Pennsylvania **Expertise:** Music, programming/on-air **Published works:** Music **Affiliations:** Country Music Association **Hob./spts.:** Music collecting, woodworking, baseball **SIC code:** 48 **Address:** WICT-FM Radio, 6874 Strimbu Drive S.E., Brookfield, OH 44403 **E-mail:** jthomas95@yahoo.com

THOMPSON, DONALD W.
Industry: Private ambulance service **Born:** January 3, 1965, Houston, Texas **Current organization:** Elite Care Emergency Medical Service **Title:** CEO **Type of organization:** Emergency medical service/private ambulance **Major product:** Transportation, ambulance **Area of distribution:** Texas **Expertise:** Project management, business development, patient care, transportation of patients from emergency situations **Affiliations:** Houston EMS Council; Texas EMS Association **Hob./spts.:** Golf, bowling, dancing, Baptist Minister **SIC code:** 41 **Address:** Elite Care Emergency Medical Service, 5645 Hillcroft, #501, Houston, TX 77036 **E-mail:** elitecareems@yahoo.com

TIMMER, JOLLY JOE
Industry: Communications **Born:** February 16, 1930, Bethlehem, Pennsylvania **Current organization:** WGPA, Sunny 1100 **Title:** Owner/General Manager **Type of organization:** Radio station **Major product:** Radio broadcasting **Area of distribution:** Bethlehem, Pennsylvania **Expertise:** Administration, program hosting **Affiliations:** N.A.B.; R.A.B.; P.A.B. **Hob./spts.:** Polka music **SIC code:** 48 **Address:** WGPA, Sunny 1100, 528 N. New St., Bethlehem, PA 18018 **E-mail:** joetimmer@jollyjoetimmer.com

TONCICH, STANLEY S.
Industry: Telecommunications **Univ./degree:** Ph.D., Case Western Reserve University, Cleveland **Current organization:** Qualcomm, Inc. **Title:** Ph.D. **Type of organization:** Communications engineering **Major product:** Wireless communications systems **Area of distribution:** International **Expertise:** Corporate R&D (electronics engineering), frequency agile communication systems and radio architectures **Published works:** M.T.T. articles and journals nationally; 29 US patents issued and 9 international patents **Affiliations:** I.E.E.E. **SIC code:** 48 **Address:** 11136 Montaubon Way, San Diego, CA 92131 **E-mail:** stoncich@qualcomm.com

TOVAR, WILLIAM
Industry: Communications/media sales **Born:** October 25, 1974, San Gabriel Valley, Georgia **Current organization:** Time Warner Cable Media Sales **Title:** Coordinator **Type of organization:** Cable network **Major product:** Media sales **Area of distribution:** California and Hawaii **Expertise:** Advertising, computer graphics, art **Hob./spts.:** Oil painting, guitar, computer graphics **SIC code:** 48 **Address:** Time Warner Cable Media Sales, 6021 Katella Ave., Suite 100, Cypress, CA 90630 **E-mail:** william.tovar1@yahoo.com

TUNG, SIMON
Industry: Transportation **Born:** April 26, 1960, Hong Kong, China **Univ./degree:** B.A., Economics, Columbia University **Current organization:** Columbia Logistics, Inc. **Title:** President/Owner **Type of organization:** Transportation **Major product:** Ocean and air movement of cargo **Area of distribution:** International **Expertise:** Logistic solutions, consulting **Affiliations:** M.B.O.C.C.; I.A.T.A.; C.T.P. **Hob./spts.:** Running **SIC code:** 44 **Address:** Columbia Logistics, Inc., 175-11 148th Rd., Jamaica, NY 11434 **E-mail:** simon@columbialogistics.com

URBAN-FLORES, MICHELLE
Industry: Telecommunications **Born:** January 16, 1961, Greenfield, Massachusetts **Univ./degree:** B.S., Business Administration, Kennedy Western University **Current organization:** RCN **Title:** Senior Strategic Sourcing Manager **Type of organization:** Service provider **Major product:** Cable, phone and Internet provider **Area of distribution:** National **Expertise:** Purchasing **Affiliations:** S.C.T.E. **SIC code:** 48 **Address:** RCN, 105 Carnegie Center, Princeton, NJ 08540 **E-mail:** michelle.flores@rcn.net

VANN, DIANA R.
Industry: Transportation **Born:** July 20, 1960, Dayton, Ohio **Current organization:** Country Wide Moving & Storage, Inc. **Title:** President **Type of organization:** Trucking and storage **Major product:** Moving and storage of household goods **Area of distribution:** National, local, intrastate, interstate **Expertise:** Overseeing operations **Affiliations:** Dayton Area Chamber of Commerce; American Moving & Storage Association (AMSA); Ohio Movers Association; Diversity Business. Com (on Top 50 List for the State of Ohio, 2005) **Hob./spts.:** Travel, knitting, crocheting, cooking, gardening, family **SIC code:** 42 **Address:** Country Wide Moving & Storage, Inc., 1737 Stanley Ave., Dayton, OH 45404 **E-mail:** dvann@cwms.net

WALLACE, JOHN K.
Industry: Telecommunications **Born:** November 12, 1949, Salina, Kansas **Univ./degree:** B.S.; M.B.A. pending **Current organization:** Sprint **Title:** Client Support

Analyst **Type of organization:** Telephone service provider **Major product:** Telecommunication services **Area of distribution:** International **Expertise:** Information services, Internet technology **Hob./spts.:** Golf, sports, outdoor activities **SIC code:** 48 **Address:** Sprint, 10151 Deerwood Park Blvd., Jacksonville, FL 32256 **E-mail:** jwalla04@sprintspectrum.com

WALTON, DAVID P.
Industry: Electric utility **Born:** January 12, 1953, Philadelphia, Pennsylvania **Univ./degree:** M.B.A., Lehigh University, 1981 **Current organization:** PPL **Title:** Director of Information Technology **Type of organization:** Utilities **Major product:** Electric generation and delivery **Area of distribution:** Pennsylvania **Expertise:** Information technology **Affiliations:** Board Member, PPL Credit Union; Chairman, Christian Sports; Co-Founder, Push the Rock **Hob./spts.:** Sports, tennis, coaching for 3 teams, nonprofit work, **SIC code:** 49 **Address:** PPL, 2 N. Ninth St., Allentown, PA 18101 **E-mail:** dpwalton@pplweb.com

WARRIOR, WINSTON P.
Industry: Communications **Born:** February 2, Atlanta, Georgia **Univ./degree:** M.B.A., Marketing, University of Miami, Florida, 1996 **Current organization:** Cox Communications, Inc. **Title:** Product Manager, Residential High Speed Internet Services **Type of organization:** Communications and entertainment **Major product:** Cable TV, telephone, high-speed networks **Area of distribution:** National **Expertise:** Marketing **Honors/awards:** Numerous including: 2003 IN DEMAND/Multichannel News / Digital Case Study Award (1st Place), Cox Comm 2003 Crystal Vision Award Winner (1st ever presented at Cox/highest honor at Cox Comm.), 2003 Fox Cable Networks/ Multichannel News and Cable and Television Association for Marketing (CTAM), Marketing Retention Case Study Award (2nd Place), Silver Design of the Times Award, 1 CTAM Gold Mark and 2 Silver Mark Awards **Affiliations:** National Association of Minorities in Cable (NAMIC) Atlanta Chapter President (2003), Vice President (2002); American Marketing Association (AMA) member; Cable and Television Association for Marketing (CTAM) member; Founding Member of Cox Communications Internet Advisory Board; Team Co-captain, Atlanta Lawn and Tennis Association; Kappa Alpha Psi Fraternity, Inc. **Hob./spts.:** Tennis, music **SIC code:** 48 **Address:** Cox Communications, Inc., 1400 Lake Hearn Dr. N.E., Atlanta, GA 30319 **E-mail:** w.warrior@att.net

WARWELL, RONALD A.
Industry: Emergency services **Born:** Brooklyn, New York **Current organization:** U.S. Emergency Medical Service **Title:** Founder **Type of organization:** Nonprofit **Major product:** Ambulance services **Area of distribution:** National **Expertise:** Paramedic **Affiliations:** International Fire Chiefs Association **SIC code:** 41 **Address:** U.S. Emergency Medical Service, 280 Link Rd., Reidsville, NC 27320 **E-mail:** rwarwell@usemergencymedicalservice.org **Web address:** www.usemergencymedicalservice.org

WHITE, RON K.
Industry: Transportation **Born:** September 6, 1968, Birmingham, Alabama **Univ./degree:** University of Montevello, Alabama **Current organization:** Great Rigs Inc. **Title:** Systems Coordinator **Major product:** Auto transportation **Area of distribution:** National **Expertise:** Computer systems engineer **Honors/awards:** Company Recognition Award, 2001 **Affiliations:** N.A.S.P.A. **Hob./spts.:** College football, outdoors, family **SIC code:** 47 **Address:** Great Rigs, Inc., 1751 Varnon Ct., Birmingham, AL 35214 **E-mail:** rbama1@aol.com

WILLER, RICHARD A.
Industry: Utilities **Born:** Evanston, Illinois **Univ./degree:** B.S.C.E., Chicago Technical College, 1970 **Current organization:** Nevada Power Co. **Title:** Engineer IV, Civil **Type of organization:** Fully integrated utility **Major product:** Electricity **Area of distribution:** Nevada **Expertise:** Water supply **Honors/awards:** National Energy Award, 1988; Listed in: Who's Who in Environmental Engineering, 1993; Sterling Who's Who, 1994 **Published works:** "Innovations in Wastewater Aeration" **Affiliations:** A.S.C.E.; A.W.W.A.; A.P.W.A. **Hob./spts.:** Swimming **SIC code:** 49 **Address:** Nevada Power Co., 6226 W. Sahara Ave., Las Vegas, NV 89151-0001 **E-mail:** rwiller@nevp.com

WILLIAMS, A. ALLEN
Industry: Communications **Born:** Lafayette, Indiana **Univ./degree:** Purdue University **Current organization:** Ra-Comm Inc. **Title:** Vice President, Sales and Marketing **Type of organization:** Sales, service **Major product:** 2-way radio communications **Area of distribution:** Indiana **Expertise:** Sales and marketing **Affiliations:** APCO **Hob./spts.:** Hunting, fishing, firearms and hunting safety instruction **SIC code:** 48 **Address:** Ra-Comm Inc., 2682 N. Ninth St. Rd., Lafayette, IN 47904

WINSTEAD, ANDRE L.
Industry: Communications **Born:** June 13, 1970, Wilson, North Carolina **Univ./degree:** B.S., Electrical Engineering; M.S., Industrial Technology, 1999, North Carolina A&T State University **Current organization:** Verizon **Title:** Engineer III **Type of organization:** Communication services provider **Major product:** Telecommunications **Area of distribution:** International **Expertise:** Tier II support and upgrades **Affiliations:** I.E.E.E. **Hob./spts.:** College marching band leader **SIC code:** 48 **Address:** Verizon, 7000 Weston Pkwy., Cary, NC 27513 **E-mail:** andre.winstead@mci.com **Web address:** www.verizonbusiness.com

WOODWARD, MARCIA G.
Industry: Government/food **Born:** April 22, 1956, Jackson, Michigan **Univ./degree:** B.S., Elementary Education, Indiana University, 1978 **Current organization:** U.S.P.S./ Marsh **Title:** RCA/Floral Designer **Type of organization:** Post office/retailer **Major product:** Mail/flowers **Expertise:** Education; Certified in Floral Management **Hob./spts.:** Beadwork, sewing **SIC code:** 43 **Address:** 8239 Plaza Lane, #D, Indianapolis, IN 46268

YATES, STEVEN K.
Industry: Transportation **Born:** March 2, 1948, Altadena, California **Univ./degree:** M.A., University of Northern Colorado, 1977 **Current organization:** Hartsfield Atlanta International Airport **Title:** Aviation Transportation Systems Manager **Type of organization:** Airport **Major product:** Transportation **Area of distribution:** Georgia **Expertise:** Operations, maintenance, program development **Published works:** "Standards" **Affiliations:** A.S.C.E.; I.A.A.P.M.A. **Hob./spts.:** Tennis, skiing, boating, biking **SIC code:** 45 **Address:** 222 Newport Dr., Peachtree City, GA 30269 **E-mail:** steve.yates@atlanta.airport.com

YOUNG, JAMES H.
Industry: Engineering **Born:** February 3, 1960, Queens, New York **Univ./degree:** B.S., Electrical Engineering, New York University, 1982; M.S., Electrical Engineering, MIT, 1984 **Current organization:** Dynamo Power Inc. **Title:** P.E./Senior Engineer **Type of organization:** Contraction **Major product:** Electrical power **Area of distribution:** International **Expertise:** Engineer **Published works:** 6 articles **Affiliations:** I.E.E.E.; E.C.M.; N.E.C.O.N. **Hob./spts.:** Motorcross, surfing **SIC code:** 49 **Address:** Dynamo Power Inc., Engineering Division, 5910 Yucca Dr., Ft. Pierce, FL 34982 **E-mail:** nfpamaster@yahoo.com

ZASTROW, FRANKLIN J.
Industry: Communications **Born:** October 27, 1965, Wausau, Wisconsin **Univ./degree:** A.E., North Central Technical College, 1989 **Current organization:** WRIG Inc. **Title:** Engineer **Type of organization:** Radio station **Major product:** AM and FM broadcast **Area of distribution:** Wisconsin **Expertise:** Engineering **Affiliations:** S.P.E. **Hob./spts.:** Hunting, fishing, photography **SIC code:** 48 **Address:** WRIG Inc., 557 Scott St., Wausau, WI 54403 **E-mail:** frank@mwcradio.com

ZAVALETA, ERNESTO G.
Industry: Travel **Born:** May 20, 1968, Lima, Peru **Univ./degree:** M.D., Universidad Peruana Cayetano Heredia, Peru, 1994 **Current organization:** Vanter Ventures **Title:** M.D. **Type of organization:** Cruiseline **Major product:** Cruises **Area of distribution:** Florida **Expertise:** Internal medicine **Published works:** 5 publications **Affiliations:** A.C.P.; P.C.P. **Hob./spts.:** Soccer, golf, white water rafting **SIC code:** 44 **Address:** Vanter Ventures, 201 Plantation Club Dr., #111, Melbourne, FL 32940 **E-mail:** zpak@hotmail.com

ZELMAN, HENRY R.
Industry: Telecommunications **Born:** January 10, 1956, California **Univ./degree:** B.S., Business Management, University of Redlands, 1997 **Current organization:** Verizon Logistics **Title:** Manager **Type of organization:** Service **Major product:** Metrology services **Area of distribution:** National **Expertise:** Management **Affiliations:** ASQ **Hob./spts.:** Travel, music, sports **SIC code:** 48 **Address:** Verizon Logistics, 2970 Inland Empire Blvd., Ontario, CA 91764 **E-mail:** rick.zelman@verizon.com

Wholesalers

ABRAHAM, ARMIN
Industry: Food **Born:** July 23, 1920, Russia **Current organization:** Hillcrest Food Service **Title:** C.E.O. **Type of organization:** Distributing **Major product:** Food services **Area of distribution:** Cleveland, Ohio **Expertise:** Administration **Hob./spts.:** Religion **SIC code:** 51 **Address:** 2695 E. 40th St., Cleveland, OH 44115 **E-mail:** www.hillcrestfoods.com

ALCEDO, RICHARD
Industry: Candles **Born:** July 25, 1951, Lima, Peru **Univ./degree:** B.S., International Marketing & Logistics, California State University, 1979 **Current organization:** Bright Glow Candle Corp. **Title:** President **Type of organization:** Manufacturing **Major product:** Religious Novena candles **Area of distribution:** International **Expertise:** Marketing, management **Hob./spts.:** The outdoors, gardening **SIC code:** 51 **Address:** Bright Glow Candle Corp., 4820 Everett Ct., Vernon, CA 90058 **E-mail:** bgcc@brightglowcandle.com **Web address:** brightglowcandle.com

BARKER-SMITH, ANNE D.
Industry: Food **Born:** October 28, 1959, Norfolk, Virginia **Univ./degree:** B.S., Food Science Technology, Virginia Tech, 1982 **Current organization:** Pocahontas Foods USA **Title:** Director QA Services **Type of organization:** Food service marketing group **Major product:** Food Service Marketing of the Pocahontas, All Kitchens, Bakery Distributors of America and Buinamici International Brands **Area of distribution:** National **Expertise:** Quality assurance, food safety, technical sales **Published works:** Newsletters **Affiliations:** I.F.T.; Past President, Virginia Food & Beverage Association **Hob./spts.:** Horses and sewing **SIC code:** 51 **Address:** Progressive Group Alliance, 7420 Ranco Rd., Richmond, VA 23228 **E-mail:** abarker-smith@progrouponline.com **Web address:** www.progrouponline.com

BATTAGLINI, SHAUNA
Industry: Healthcare **Born:** September 10, Binghamton, New York **Univ./degree:** A.S., Marketing Management, Broome Community College **Current organization:** Apria Healthcare **Title:** Branch Manager **Type of organization:** Distributing **Major product:** Respiratory care products **Area of distribution:** National **Expertise:** Revenue management **Affiliations:** American Cancer Society; Red Cross **Hob./spts.:** Family activities, skiing, boating, hiking **SIC code:** 50 **Address:** 3016 Yale St., Endwell, NY 13760 **E-mail:** ssbatt@wmconnect.com

BATTERSHELL, ARTHUR J.
Industry: Electronics **Born:** January 21, 1934, Montana **Univ./degree:** B.S., Business Administration, University of Montana **Current organization:** Supreme Lighting Systems **Title:** President **Type of organization:** Distributing **Major product:** Sound and fire alarm systems **Area of distribution:** Montana **Expertise:** Engineering **Affiliations:** N.F.P.A.; I.S.O.E.; N.S.C.A.; American Legion; Elks Club **SIC code:** 50 **Address:** Supreme Lighting Systems, 521 N. Sanders St., Helena, MT 59601-4528

BELLIBONI, RANDY J.
Industry: Material handling **Born:** February 18, 1968, Syracuse, New York **Univ./degree:** B.S., Le Moyne College, 1990 **Current organization:** Pengate Handling Systems of New York **Title:** Sales Manager, New York **Type of organization:** Distributors/manufacturers' reps **Major product:** Raymond forklifts, warehouse design, material handling products **Area of distribution:** National **Expertise:** Warehouse design **Affiliations:** Local Chamber of Commerce **Hob./spts.:** Golf, physical fitness **SIC code:** 50 **Address:** Pengate Handling Systems of New York, 6700 Old Collamer Rd., Suite 109A, East Syracuse, NY 13057 **E-mail:** rbelliboni@pengate.com

BELSON, DANIEL
Industry: Steel **Born:** May 9, 1965, Kalamazoo, Michigan **Current organization:** Allied Crawford **Title:** General Manager **Type of organization:** Private steel service center, distributor **Major product:** Carbon steel products **Area of distribution:** Florida **Expertise:** Sales management **Hob./spts.:** Golf, walking, outdoors, study, investments **SIC code:** 50 **Address:** Allied Crawford, 1500 Fish Hatchery Rd., Lakeland, FL 33801 **E-mail:** dbelson1@tampabay.rr.com

BERNSTEIN, KENNETH S.
Industry: Building products **Born:** February 20, 1962, Somerville, New Jersey **Univ./degree:** M.S., Psychology, American University **Current organization:** Mid-State Lumber Corp. **Title:** Executive Vice President **Type of organization:** Wholesale distribution **Major product:** Lumber, building materials **Area of distribution:** New Jersey **Expertise:** International business **Affiliations:** Phi Sigma Kappa; Jewish Community Center **Hob./spts.:** Physical fitness, golf, travel, reading **SIC code:** 50 **Address:** Mid-State Lumber Corp., 200 Industrial Pkwy., Branchburg, NJ 08876 **E-mail:** kenb@midstatelumber.com **Web address:** www.midstatelumber.com

BLOODGOOD, JEFFREY A.
Industry: Earthmoving equipment/construction **Born:** April 15, 1959, Coventry, Connecticut **Current organization:** Continental Equipment Co., L.P. **Title:** Vice President **Type of organization:** Distributors **Major product:** Komatsu, Goodall, Hamm earthmoving equipment **Area of distribution:** Texas **Expertise:** Product support **Affiliations:** Association of Equipment Management Professionals **Hob./spts.:** Family, sports, running, fishing **SIC code:** 50 **Address:** Continental Equipment Co., L.P., 8505 S. Central Expwy., Dallas, TX 75241 **E-mail:** jbloodgood@thenewcontinental.com **Web address:** www.thenewcontinental.com

BOLTON, PAUL S.
Industry: Clothing and footwear **Born:** March 1944, Longview, Texas **Univ./degree:** B.A., Accounting, Texas Tech, 1966 **Current organization:** Tingley Rubber Corp. **Title:** President **Type of organization:** Distributing **Major product:** Protective clothing and footwear **Area of distribution:** National **Expertise:** Finance/marketing **Hob./spts.:** Golf **SIC code:** 50 **Address:** Tingley Rubber Corp., One Cragwood Rd., South Plainfield, NJ 02080 **E-mail:** pbolton@tingleyrubber.com

BOWEN, JONATHAN E.
Industry: Construction **Born:** January 7, 1970, Indianapolis, Indiana **Univ./degree:** A.A., Computer Science, Grantham College, 1997 **Current organization:** Reese Central Wholesale **Title:** Director, Information Technology **Type of organization:** Distributing **Major product:** Building materials **Area of distribution:** Indiana **Expertise:** Engineering, management **Affiliations:** I.E.E.E. **Hob./spts.:** Golf **SIC code:** 50 **Address:** Reese Central Wholesale, 1155 E. 54th St., Indianapolis, IN 46220 **E-mail:** jbowen@reesewholesale.com **Web address:** www.reesewholesale.com

BOWERS, CHRYSTI ANN
Industry: Healthcare **Born:** May 15, 1963, Baltimore, Maryland **Univ./degree:** B.S., Radiologic Science, York College, 1983 **Current organization:** Mid-Atlantic Imaging Services **Title:** Radiologic Technologist **Type of organization:** Distributing **Major product:** Nuclear medicine cameras **Area of distribution:** National **Expertise:** Sales, marketing, training **Affiliations:** A.S.R.T.; A.R.R.T. **SIC code:** 50 **Address:** Mid-Atlantic Imaging Services, 3515 Santee Ct., Baltimore, MD 21236

BOWMAN, GARY E.
Industry: Aerospace/automotive/OEM **Born:** March 24, 1955, Denver, Colorado **Current organization:** Krayden Inc. **Title:** Sales Manager **Type of organization:** Distributor **Major product:** Adhesives, sealants, potting material, conformal coating **Area of distribution:** National **Expertise:** Management **Affiliations:** S.N.T.A.; S.M.E. **Hob./spts.:** Family, golf, fishing **SIC code:** 51 **Address:** Krayden Inc., 491 E. 124th Ave., Denver, CO 80241 **E-mail:** gbowman@krayden.com

BRADFORD, MARK E.
Industry: Welding supplies/industrial gases **Born:** January 19, 1970, Malvern, Arkansas **Current organization:** PRAXAIR **Title:** Gas and liquid processor **Type of organization:** Distributor **Major product:** Welding supplies **Area of distribution:** Signal Hill, California **Expertise:** Gas and liquid processing **Hob./spts.:** Collecting music **SIC code:** 50 **Address:** PRAXAIR, 2677 Signal Pkwy., Signal Hill, CA 90806

BRAMBILA, ROGER
Industry: Batteries **Born:** December 14, 1954, San Diego, California **Univ./degree:** B.S., Electrical/Mechanical Engineering, San Diego State University, 1977 **Current organization:** North American Battery Co. **Title:** Director of Engineering **Type of organization:** Manufacturing and distribution facility **Major product:** Rechargeable batteries **Area of distribution:** National **Expertise:** Product management, engineering, materials management **Hob./spts.:** Football **SIC code:** 50 **Address:** North American Battery Co., 2155 Paseo de las Americas, Suite 31, San Diego, CA 92154 **E-mail:** roger.brambila@nabcorp.com

BRONSON, CULLEY J.
Industry: Commercial metals **Born:** December 12, 1967, Salt Lake City, Utah **Univ./degree:** A.S., Business Administration, Independence Community College **Current organization:** CMC Recycling Branch 206 **Title:** Operations Manager **Type of organization:** Recycling center **Major product:** Recyclable metals **Area of distribution:** International **Expertise:** Operations, administration **Hob./spts.:** Fishing, rebuilding vintage cars **SIC code:** 50 **Address:** CMC Recycling Branch 206, 501 S. 20th, Independence, KS 67301 **E-mail:** cbronson@cmc-scrap.com **Web address:** www.cmc-scrap.com

BURKE, MICHAEL W.
Industry: HVAC **Born:** April 20, 1965, Linwood, California **Current organization:** Burke Engineering Co. **Title:** CEO **Type of organization:** Wholesale Distributor **Major product:** Equipment controls and accessories **Area of distribution:** National **Expertise:** Sales and marketing **Affiliations:** Western Regional Director and Chair, H.A.R.D.I. **Hob./spts.:** Spending time with his children, coaching, travel **SIC code:** 50 **Address:** Burke Engineering Co., 9700 Factorial Way, South El Monte, CA 91733 **E-mail:** mike.burke@burkehvacr.com

BUTCHKO, ROBERT E.
Industry: Fire alarms systems **Born:** January 7, 1946, Bayonne, New Jersey **Univ./degree:** B.S., Mechanical Engineering, New Jersey Institute of Technology, 1979 **Current organization:** Siemens Building Technologies, Inc. **Title:** Manager, Field Operations **Type of organization:** Manufacturing, system supplier **Major product:** Fire/life safety systems **Area of distribution:** United States & Canada **Expertise:** Engineering **Affiliations:** S.F.P.E.; N.F.P.A.; Member, Technical Committee, National Fire Alarm Code **SIC code:** 50 **Address:** Siemens Building Technologies, Inc., 4711 Innovation Dr., Lincoln, NE 68521 **E-mail:** bob.butchko@siemens.com **Web address:** www.spt.siemens.com/FIS

CAMPBELL, JOHN A.
Industry: Liquid siding **Born:** August 8, 1953, Arlington, Virginia **Current organization:** Procraft of Colorado, LLC **Title:** CEO/Principal **Type of organization:** Distributor, service **Major product:** Liquid siding **Area of distribution:** International **Expertise:** Administration, operations **Affiliations:** Trout Unlimited **Hob./spts.:** Fly-fishing, whitewater rafting **SIC code:** 50 **Address:** Procraft of Colorado, LLC, 4750 S. Santa Fe Circle, #4, Englewood, CO 80110 **E-mail:** procraftco@yahoo.com **Web address:** www.kryton.com

CHURCH, DAVID A.
Industry: Systems automation **Born:** August 21, 1953, Berkeley, California **Univ./degree:** B.S., Electronic Engineering, Canterbury University, 1995; Th.B. & M.S., Theology, Andersonville Baptist Seminary **Current organization:** Omron IDM Controls **Title:** Service Engineer **Type of organization:** Sales and service **Major product:** Motion control components and service **Area of distribution:** International **Expertise:** Automation engineering, integration **Affiliations:** I.E.E.E. **Hob./spts.:** Reading, camping, hiking, scuba diving, church volunteering **SIC code:** 50 **Address:** Omron IDM Controls, 12000 E. Slauson Ave., Santa Fe Springs, CA 90670

COMBS, GARY W.
Industry: HVAC, electrical and industrial supplies **Univ./degree:** B.S., U.S. Military Academy, West Point, 1975 **Current organization:** Noland Company **Title:** Marketing Manager **Type of organization:** Distribution/wholesaler **Major product:** HVAC, plumbing, electrical and industrial supplies **Area of distribution:** Mid-Atlantic, Southeast and South Central U.S. **Expertise:** Marketing **Honors/awards:** Church Elder **Affiliations:** I.M.A.R.K.; A.C.C.A. **Hob./spts.:** Golf, biking, beach walks, home improvements, music/singing, boating **SIC code:** 50 **Address:** 1312 Rylands Rd., Virginia Beach, VA 23455 **E-mail:** gcombs1@cox.net

COSTA JR., LUIS
Industry: Fuel service **Born:** March 31, 1986, Miami, Florida **Current organization:** Costa Oil **Title:** Marine Division Manager **Type of organization:** Distributing **Major product:** Diesel fuel, gasoline, oil **Area of distribution:** Florida **Expertise:** Marina and direct boat fueling, consulting **Affiliations:** Latin Builders Association **Hob./spts.:** Fishing, golf, ping-pong **SIC code:** 51 **Address:** Costa Oil, 9780 NW 115 Way, Medley, FL 33178 **E-mail:** lcosta02@costaoil.com **Web address:** www.costaoil.com

COTTON, BART
Industry: Food service equipment **Current organization:** Restaurant Warehouse **Title:** President **Type of organization:** Distributing **Major product:** Restaurant equipment supplies, complete designing and interior decorating **Area of distribution:** International **Expertise:** Marketing/Food Service Consultant **SIC code:** 50 **Address:** Restaurant Warehouse, 3555 N. Andrews Ave., Oakland Park, FL 33309 **E-mail:** restaurantwarehouse@earthlink.net **Web address:** www.restaurantwarehouse.com

DAUGHTRY, SYLVIA J.
Industry: Wellness products **Born:** November 8, 1934, Columbia, South Carolina **Univ./degree:** A.B., English Education, University of South Carolina, 1957; M.Ed., English Education, University of Georgia, 1976 **Current organization:** NSA International **Title:** Independent Distributor **Type of organization:** Distributor **Major product:** Water filters, air filters, Juice Plus+ **Area of distribution:** International **Expertise:** Consulting **Affiliations:** President, Tucker Woman's Club; Georgia State President, Delta Kappa Gamma Society International; Southeast Regional Director, Journalism Education Association **Hob./spts.:** Reading, watching college sports **SIC code:** 50 **Address:** Sylvia J. Daughtry (Mrs. Joseph B. Brown), 2038 Zelda Dr. N.E., Atlanta, GA 30345-3742 **E-mail:** sdsylviajd@aol.com

DHILLON, KANWAR INDER S.
Industry: Beverages **Born:** August 9, 1980, Chandigarh, India **Univ./degree:** B.B.A., University of Texas at Austin, 2001 **Current organization:** Dhillon Group **Title:** CEO **Type of organization:** Manufacturer/distributor **Major product:** Pepsi-Cola, Seagram's **Area of distribution:** International **Expertise:** General management, finance **Honors/awards:** Texas-Ex Students Association, India Representative, University of Texas **Affiliations:** N.S.C.S.; A.L.D.; P.E.S. **Hob./spts.:** National rifle shooting, tennis, squash, basketball **SIC code:** 51 **Address:** Bugalow 301 Sector 9, Chandigarh, IN 160009 **E-mail:** kanwar.dhillon@dhillon-group.com **Web address:** www.dhillon-group.com

DOBRICK, DAVID M.
Industry: Automotive **Born:** September 21, 1957, Louisville, Kentucky **Univ./degree:** B.S., Industrial Engineering, Western Kentucky University, 1980 **Current organization:** Exiss Acuminum Trailers **Title:** Product Engineering Manager **Type of organization:** Manufacturing **Major product:** Equine & livestock trailers **Area of distribution:** Oklahoma **Expertise:** Engineering **Hob./spts.:** Camping, golf, woodworking **SIC code:** 50 **Address:** Exiss Acuminum Trailers, 900 Exiss Blvd., El Reno, OK 73036 **E-mail:** ddobrick@exiss.net

DORMAN, DAVID E.
Industry: Apparel **Born:** January 14, 1946, Aberdeen, Maryland **Current organization:** Dorman & Co., Inc. **Title:** President **Type of organization:** Global sourcing company **Major product:** Textiles, apparel **Area of distribution:** International **Expertise:** Apparel **Honors/awards:** Mayor of Melissa, Texas; Top 21 Leaders to lead Collin County into the 21st Century **Hob./spts.:** Growing orchards **SIC code:** 51 **Address:** Dorman & Co., Inc., 105 N. Benge St., McKinney, TX 75069 **E-mail:** dedorman1@aol.com

DOUGHTY, LAWRENCE
Industry: Construction **Born:** August 4, 1946, Newburgh, New York **Univ./degree:** B.S., Business/Marketing, State University of New York, 1968 **Current organization:** Capitol Light & Supply Co. **Title:** Vice President, Marketing **Type of organization:** Distributors **Major product:** Electrical supplies and lighting **Area of distribution:** National **Expertise:** Marketing **Hob./spts.:** Boating, fishing **SIC code:** 50 **Address:** Capitol Light & Supply Co., 270 Locust St., Hartford, CT 06114 **E-mail:** ldoughty@clsco.com

DU PONT, BERNARD MALET
Industry: Food and wines/consulting **Born:** May 16, 1964, France **Univ./degree:** Graduate, Hotel and Restaurant Management Program, Université de Pau et des Pays de l'Adour, France, 1982 **Current organization:** Du Pont World Wines & Beverages, Inc. **Title:** CEO/President **Type of organization:** Import/export/distributor **Major product:** Wines and foods **Area of distribution:** International **Expertise:** Marketing, management **Affiliations:** N.R.C.C. **Hob./spts.:** Reading, horseback riding, tennis, golf, travel **SIC code:** 51 **Address:** Du Pont World Wines & Beverages, Inc., 111-32 76 Ave., Suite 5A, Forest Hills, NY 11375 **E-mail:** bernardmdupont@aol.com

ELLIOTT, JOHN E.
Industry: Office products **Born:** May 2, 1948, Fort Worth, Texas **Univ./degree:** B.B.A., Texas Christian University, 1971 **Current organization:** S.P. Richards Co. **Title:** Vice President, Advertising **Type of organization:** Distributing **Major product:** Office products **Area of distribution:** National **Expertise:** Marketing/advertising **Hob./spts.:** Golf, tennis **SIC code:** 50 **Address:** S.P. Richards Co., 6300 Highlands Pkwy., Smyrna, GA 30082 **E-mail:** jelliott@sprich.com

FILIPPELLI, ALDO R.
Industry: Electronics/audio **Born:** July 1, 1966, Melrose Park, Illinois **Univ./degree:** M.B.A., University of Illinois, 1993 **Current organization:** Dynaudio North America **Title:** Vice President/General Manager **Type of organization:** Distributor **Major product:** High performance loud speakers for home and auto **Area of distribution:** United Stated, Canada, Caribbean **Expertise:** Marketing, sales **Hob./spts.:** Hockey, weightlifting, sailing, cars **SIC code:** 50 **Address:** Dynaudio North America, 1144 Tower Lane, Bensenville, IL 60106 **E-mail:** af@dynaudiousa.com

FULSON, FREDDIE L.
Industry: Natural gas **Born:** May 19, 1948, Oklahoma City, Oklahoma **Univ./degree:** Attended 3 years of undergraduate school; Certificate in Philosophy **Current organization:** Nicole Energy Marketing, Inc. **Title:** Founder/President **Type of organization:** Distributing, retail **Major product:** Natural gas **Area of distribution:** Mid-west and east coast **Expertise:** Marketing **Honors/awards:** Ohio Businessman of the Year, 2000 & 2001 **Affiliations:** Ambassador for Dr. Robert H. Shulers Ministry **Hob./spts.:** Football, basketball **SIC code:** 51 **Address:** Nicole Energy Marketing, Inc., 6264 Sunbury Rd., Westerville, OH 43086 **E-mail:** flfulson@nicole-energy.com **Web address:** www.nicole-energy.com

GUALA, PETER J.
Industry: Professional service **Born:** December 12, 1957, Wilmington, Delaware **Univ./degree:** B.S.B.A., Marketing, Manhattan College, 1980 **Current organization:** Corporate Express **Title:** President/Chief Operating Officer (Eastern Region) **Type of organization:** Distributor **Major product:** Office supplies, furniture **Area of distribution:** East coast **Expertise:** Executive management, business to business provider of products and services to corporations **Affiliations:** Board Member, JIT2 **SIC code:** 50 **Address:** 7 Dogwood Ct., Princeton Junction, NJ 08550 **E-mail:** peter.guala@cexp.com

HALE JR., BEN
Industry: Industrial sales **Born:** October 9, 1962, Johnson City, Tennessee **Univ./degree:** East Tennessee State University, 1982 **Current organization:** Dillon Supply **Title:** Operations Manager **Type of organization:** Distributing **Major product:** Industrial and construction supplies and equipment; MRO, safety, materials handling and steel **Area of distribution:** National **Expertise:** Overseeing branch operations, industrial sales and equipment **Affiliations:** Johnson City Emergency Rescue Squad **Hob./spts.:** Fishing, hunting **SIC code:** 50 **Address:** Dillon Supply, 102 Dillon Ct., Gray, TN 37615 **E-mail:** bhale@dillonsupply.com

HARING, THOMAS L.
Industry: Automotive **Current organization:** WAI **Title:** Director of Corporate Quality **Type of organization:** Distributing/manufacturing **Major product:** Automotive supplies and parts **Area of distribution:** International **Expertise:** Quality **Affiliations:** S.Q.E. **SIC code:** 50 **Address:** 801 Jackson St., Birbsboro, PA 19508 **E-mail:** tom_haring@wai-wetherill.com

HOBBS, RICHARD
Industry: Environmental products/Nonprofit agency **Born:** San Antonio, Texas **Univ./degree:** B.A., Political Science, St. Mary's University **Title:** Chaplain/Business Owner/CEO **Type of organization:** Distributing/Nonprofit **Major product:** Air and water purification equipment/Community outreach **Area of distribution:** San Antonio, Texas **Expertise:** Claims resolution; claims consulting and investigation; instructor in the field of insurance, investigation and claims resolutions; leadership and marketing consulting; Police Chaplain for a large International Airport Police Dept. **Affiliations:** American Academy of Experts in Traumatic Stress; Nova-National Organization for Victims Assistance **Hob./spts.:** Reading **SIC code:** 50 **Address:** Eagle Enterprises International, Leadership Marketing Consulting, 8427 Timber Whisper, San Antonio, TX 78250 **E-mail:** hobbsjr@earthlink.net **Web address:** www.ecoquestintl.com/rhobbs

HOLLIS, GARY L.
Industry: Dairy products **Born:** January 25, 1955, Columbus, Mississippi **Current organization:** Luvel Dairy Products, Inc. **Title:** General Sales Manager **Type of organization:** Manufacturer/wholesaler **Major product:** Dairy and frozen dessert products **Area of distribution:** Mississippi, West Alabama, Northeast and Southwest Louisiana **Expertise:** Sales and distribution **Affiliations:** Exchange Club **Hob./spts.:** Golf, children's director with local church **SIC code:** 51 **Address:** Luvel Dairy Products, Inc., 427 Dory St., Jackson, MS 39201 **E-mail:** gthollis@aol.com

HONIGBERG, JOEL D.
Industry: Export/import **Born:** November 17, 1926, St. Louis, Missouri **Univ./degree:** B.S., Chemistry, University of Chicago, 1948; M.A., Chemical Engineering, University of Paris, 1950 **Current organization:** J.D. Honigberg International, Inc. **Title:** President **Type of organization:** Export sales and management **Major product:** Medical devices and other machinery products **Area of distribution:** International **Expertise:** Administration, marketing **Affiliations:** President Emeritus; I.B.C.; I.E.M.C.; I.V.C. **Hob./spts.:** Symphonic music, art museums **SIC code:** 50 **Address:** J.D. Honigberg International, Inc., 85 Revere Dr., Suite D, Northbrook, IL 60062 **E-mail:** jhonigberg@jdintl.com **Web address:** www.jdhintl.com

HOUSE, TODD L.
Industry: Food **Born:** December 16, 1966, Fort Smith, Arkansas **Current organization:** Collier Foods, Inc. **Title:** Associate Manager **Type of organization:** Supplier **Major product:** Provide food and supplies for restaurants **Area of distribution:** Tennessee **Hob./spts.:** Spending time with family, fishing, basketball, baseball **SIC code:** 50 **Address:** Collier Foods, Inc., 3610 Pkwy., Pigeon Forge, TN 37863

JOHNSON, JOE W.
Industry: Sales/marketing **Born:** November 18, 1952, Tennessee **Current organization:** The Johnson Group **Title:** Owner **Type of organization:** Independent Business **Major product:** Gift albums for employees and all occasions **Area of distribution:** National **Expertise:** Sales and marketing **Affiliations:** Chamber of Commerce **Hob./spts.:** Travel, concerts, sight seeing **SIC code:** 50 **Address:** The Johnson Group, 5361 Granny White Pike, Brentwood, TN 37027 **Phone:** (866)277-0372 **Fax:** (615)376-0991 **E-mail:** joenash@bellsouth.net

JOHNSON, MARK W.
Industry: Food processing **Born:** December 2, 1954, Hutchinson, Kansas **Univ./degree:** B.S., Food Science and Management, Kansas State University, 1987 **Current organization:** Dairy Engineering Co. **Title:** Sales Representative **Type of organization:** Engineering and distributing **Major product:** Food grade process equipment-industrial **Area of distribution:** National **Expertise:** Troubleshooting, mechanical **Affiliations:** Dairy Technology Society **Hob./spts.:** Kansas State basketball and football, travel, golf **SIC code:** 50 **Address:** Dairy Engineering Co., 4507 Foothill Dr., Hutchinson, KS 67502 **E-mail:** mcgwb@cox.net

KLEIN, EUGENE M.
Industry: Food **Univ./degree:** B.S., History and Political Science, Clemson University, 1967; M.S., Business, Amber University, 1983 **Current organization:** SYSCO Corp. **Title:** Dept. Manager **Type of organization:** Distributing **Major product:** Food distribution **Area of distribution:** International **Expertise:** Operations and regulatory management **Affiliations:** American Frozen Food Institute; Warehousing Educational and Research Council **Hob./spts.:** Golf, cultivating roses **SIC code:** 51 **Address:** SYSCO Corp., 1390 Enclave Pkwy., Houston, TX 77077 **E-mail:** klein.gene@corp.sysco.com

KOENIG, PETER A.
Industry: Food **Born:** November 10, 1967, Burlington, Wisconsin **Univ./degree:** B.S., Business Administration, University of Wisconsin, Steven's Point, 2000 **Current organization:** Reinhart Food Service, Milwaukee Division **Title:** Director of Purchasing **Type of organization:** Distributing **Major product:** All food service products **Area of distribution:** Northeast U.S. **Expertise:** Merchandising, purchasing, inventory management, presentations, staff training; Director of Purchasing Committee **Hob./spts.:** Golf, football **SIC code:** 51 **Address:** Reinhart Food Service, Milwaukee Division, 9950 S. Reinhart Dr., Oak Creek, WI 53154 **E-mail:** pakoenig@reinhartfoodservice.com

LACKLAND, ALBERT
Industry: Hardware/home improvement **Born:** December 30, 1950, Chicago, Illinois **Univ./degree:** B.S., Chemistry, St. Louis University, 1974 **Current organization:** Black & Decker **Title:** General Manager **Type of organization:** Manufacturing **Major product:** Door locks and faucets **Area of distribution:** International **Expertise:** Packaging development **Published works:** multiple publications **Affiliations:** I.O.P.P. **Hob./spts.:** Golf **SIC code:** 50 **Address:** Black & Decker, 19701 Da Vinci, Foothill Ranch, CA 92610 **E-mail:** al.lackland@bdhhi.com

LANGERUD, MARK K.
Industry: Heavy equipment **Born:** March 9, 1957, Forest City, Iowa **Univ./degree:** B.B.A., Iowa State University, 1978 **Current organization:** YMH-Torrance, Inc. **Title:** General Sales Manager/Mayor of Pleasant Hill, Iowa **Type of organization:** Distributors **Major product:** Heavy equipment **Area of distribution:** Iowa **Expertise:** Sales management **Affiliations:** Current Mayor, Pleasant Hill, Iowa; Past City Councilman, Pleasant Hill, Iowa **Hob./spts.:** Family, playing and teaching golf **SIC code:** 50 **Address:** YMH-Torrance, Inc., 1815 Hull Ave., Des Moines, IA 50313 **E-mail:** langerudm@ymhtorr.com **Web address:** www.ymhtorr.com

LANOUX-LEHR, VIEVIA A.
Industry: Food supplies **Born:** August 9, 1953, Portsmouth, Ohio **Current organization:** Edward Don and Co. **Title:** Sales Consultant **Type of organization:** Distributing **Major product:** Restaurant and food service supplies **Area of distribution:** National **Expertise:** Consulting, sales **Honors/awards:** Edward Don Bell Ringer-9 times, Salesperson of the Year-2 times, Vince Lombardi Award-1 time **Hob./spts.:** Horseback riding, reading, teaching confirmation at church **SIC code:** 50 **Address:** Edward Don and Co., 8680 Shoe Overlook Dr., Fishers, IN 46038 **E-mail:** vievialanoux-lehr@don.com

LASHBROOK, RANDALL B.
Industry: Entertainment **Born:** February 23, 1962, San Diego, California **Univ./degree:** B.S., Information Systems Management, University of Tennessee, 1985 **Current organization:** Warner Bros./Warner Home Video **Title:** Production Manager **Type of organization:** Distributing **Major product:** DVD's, theatrical home video production **Area of distribution:** National **Expertise:** Sourcing, management **Honors/awards:** Team Project Award, 2005 **Hob./spts.:** Auto racing **SIC code:** 50 **Address:** Warner Bros./Warner Home Video, 3400 Riverside Dr., Bldg. 160, Room 6150, Burbank, CA 91522 **E-mail:** randall.lashbrook@warnerbros.com

LEWIS, OSCAR S.
Industry: Water jet pumps for boats **Born:** May 4, 1951, Atlanta, Georgia **Univ./degree:** M.B.A., Finance, Georgia State University, 1976 **Current organization:** Hamilton Jet, Inc. **Title:** Comptroller **Type of organization:** Distributors **Major product:** Water jet pumps for boats **Area of distribution:** International **Expertise:** Finance **Affiliations:** A.B.P.; I.M.A. **Hob./spts.:** Golf, baseball umpire **SIC code:** 50 **Address:** Hamilton Jet, Inc., 1111 N.W. Ballard Way, Seattle, WA 98107 **E-mail:** oscarl@hamiltonjet.com

LIPSACK, LONNIE R.
Industry: Electric motors **Born:** January 25, 1943, Hastings, Nebraska **Current organization:** Hatten Electric Service & Bak-Vol **Title:** Sales Engineer **Type of organization:** Service and distributor **Major product:** Electric motors, gear boxes, pumps **Area of distribution:** International **Expertise:** Engineering and sales **Affiliations:** N.I.C.E.T. **Hob./spts.:** Hunting, fishing, building custom cars **SIC code:** 50 **Address:** Hatten Electric Service & Bak-Vol, 130 S. Hastings Ave., Hastings, NE 68901 **E-mail:** hatten@inebraska.com

LOEBERTMANN, DOUG
Industry: Construction equipment **Born:** May 31, 1966, Shakopee, Minnesota **Univ./degree:** B.S., Mechanical Engineering, University of Minnesota, 1997 **Current organization:** Satellite Industries, Inc. **Title:** Director of Supply **Type of organization:** Distributors **Major product:** Portable restrooms **Area of distribution:** International **Expertise:** Engineering **Hob./spts.:** Fishing, boating, home remodeling **SIC code:** 50 **Address:** Satellite Industries Inc., 2530 Xenium Lane, Minneapolis, MN 55441 **E-mail:** doug1@satelliteco.com

LOVE, JAMES "KELLY"
Industry: Vending machines **Born:** February 10, 1976, Biloxi, Mississippi **Univ./degree:** Religion, University of Mobile, 1994-1997 **Current organization:** Wacky Fun Factory.com Inc. **Title:** President **Type of organization:** Distributing **Major product:** Kinetic vending machines **Area of distribution:** International **Expertise:** Marketing **Honors/awards:** Pat Summerall's Champions of Industry, Discovery Channel, 2002; Honorary Chairman for the business advisory council for the President of the United States of America, 2002-2003 **Hob./spts.:** Football, business development **SIC code:** 50 **Address:** Wacky Fun Factory .com Inc., 4280 Industrial Pkwy., Mobile, AL 36613 **E-mail:** klove@direcway.com

MCMULLIN, GARY D.
Industry: Telecommunications **Born:** April 9, 1937, Kansas City, Missouri **Univ./degree:** B.S., Engineering, University of California at Los Angeles, 1959 **Current organization:** Telmar Distributing Co. **Title:** Executive Vice President **Type of organization:** Testing and distributing company **Major product:** Transmission, distribution and switching circuit cards **Area of distribution:** International **Expertise:** Management consultant, engineer and lecturer **Honors/awards:** Dean's Advisory Board, Elgin Community College; Motorda Science Advisory Board, 1978-79, Department of Navy Fellowships (two); L.A. City Goals Project **Affiliations:** American Society for Quality Control; Certified Quality Engineer **Hob./spts.:** Cosmology, evolution, quantum mechanics, hiking, fishing, opera, classical music **SIC code:** 50 **Address:** Telmar Distributing Co., 16781 Noyes Ave., Irvine, CA 92606 **E-mail:** gary.mcmullin@telmarnt.com **Web address:** www.tlmr.com

MCNUTT, TERRY A.
Industry: Steel **Born:** April 9, 1957, Fort Oglethorpe, Georgia **Univ./degree:** Attended Chattanooga State Technical Community College **Current organization:** Allied Crawford Steel - Lakeland **Title:** Plant Manager **Type of organization:** Distributing **Major product:** Carbon steel **Area of distribution:** International **Expertise:** Warehousing, processing **Affiliations:** Florida Chamber of Commerce **Hob./spts.:** Woodworking, martial arts **SIC code:** 50 **Address:** Allied Crawford Steel - Lakeland, P.O. Box 3977, Lakeland, FL 33802 **E-mail:** mcnutt9113@aol.com

MCSHANE, BRIAN H.
Industry: Office equipment and supplies **Born:** September 19, 1954, Munster, Indiana **Univ./degree:** B.S., Purdue University **Current organization:** McShane's Inc. **Title:** President, CEO **Type of organization:** Wholesale/retail **Major product:** Office equipment- copiers, fax machines, printers **Area of distribution:** Indiana **Expertise:** Management **Hob./spts.:** Community service **SIC code:** 50 **Address:** McShane's Inc., 1844 45th St., Munster, IN 46321 **E-mail:** bmcshane@mcshanes.com

MEIVERS, MICHAEL R.
Industry: Industrial hygiene & pollution monitoring instruments and medical instruments **Univ./degree:** B.S., M.S., Aerospace Engineering; MBA, Georgia State University **Current organization:** MRM International **Title:** Owner **Type of organization:** Distributor **Major product:** Miniature compressors & vacuum pumps **Area of distribution:** International **Expertise:** Marketing & engineering **Affiliations:** Duluth Merchants & Chamber of Commerce **Hob./spts.:** Photography **SIC code:** 50 **Address:** MRM International, 3905 Whitney Place, Duluth, GA 30096 **E-mail:** mike@mrm-international.com

MILLS, TRACY
Industry: Molding/plastics & rubber **Born:** February 15, 1952, Virginia Beach, Virginia **Univ./degree:** B.S., Marketing, Virginia Common Wealth University, 1974 **Current organization:** Volunteer Industrial Products **Title:** Owner **Type of organization:** Distribution **Major product:** Electrical components **Area of distribution:** Southwestern U.S. **Expertise:** Engineering, marketing **Published works:** Article **SIC code:** 50 **Address:** Volunteer Industrial Products, 309 Independence Dr., Jefferson City, TN 37760-3838 **E-mail:** tracy.mills@earthlink.net

MONTEMAYOR, TOMAS E.
Industry: Construction **Born:** March 13, 1953, Williams County, Texas **Current organization:** Transit Mix Concrete & Materials **Title:** Plant Manager **Type of organization:** Distributing **Major product:** Ready mix concrete **Area of distribution:** National **Expertise:** 33 service ready mix concrete **Affiliations:** N.R.M.C.A. **Hob./spts.:** Hunting, fishing, golf **SIC code:** 50 **Address:** Transit Mix Concrete & Materials, 50 Country Rd. 219, Florence, TX 76527-4343 **E-mail:** tomasmontemayor@earthlink.net

MOUZY, MARK
Industry: Agriculture/General Industry/OEM's **Born:** December 17, 1958, Jonesboro, Arkansas **Univ./degree:** Attended 2 years Arkansas State University **Current organization:** Valley View Agri & Supply **Title:** Sales Manager **Type of organization:** Distributor industrial supplies **Major product:** Bearings and power transmission products **Area of distribution:** Arkansas/Louisiana/Mississippi/Missouri **Expertise:** Sales, marketing, application design **Hob./spts.:** Family, A.A.U. basketball coach **SIC code:** 50 **Address:** Valley View Agri & Supply, 8304 Hwy. 49 South, Jonesboro, AR 72404 **E-mail:** mark@valleyviewagri.com **Web address:** www.valleyviewagri.com

NEWMAN, IRWIN J.
Industry: Medical equipment **Born:** May 7, 1948, Brooklyn, New York **Univ./degree:** B.S., Business Administration, Real Estate and Urban Development, Syracuse University, 1970; J.D., University of Florida Law School, 1973 **Current organization:** Life Without Pain LLC **Title:** President and CEO **Type of organization:** Distribution **Major product:** Pain relief medical devices **Area of distribution:** International **Expertise:** Mergers and acquisitions **Affiliations:** Senior Partner, Newman, Pollock & Klein; President and CEO, Jenex Financial Services, Inc.; Economic Development Council of Boca Raton; Children's Home Society; Member, F.C.A. **Hob./spts.:** Reading, golf **SIC code:** 50 **Address:** Life Without Pain LLC, 2400 E. Commercial Blvd., Suite 500, Ft. Lauderdale, FL 33308 **E-mail:** irwin.newman@lifewithoutpain.net **Web address:** www.lifewithoutpain.net

OBESO, MARIO M.
Industry: Electric **Born:** February 18, 1944, Consolación del Sur, Cuba **Current organization:** Tradinter Development Co., Inc. **Title:** President **Type of organization:** Distributing **Major product:** Electrical supplies **Area of distribution:** International **Expertise:** High voltage materials and equipment **Affiliations:** National Association of Electrical Distributors **SIC code:** 50 **Address:** Tradinter Development Co., Inc., 8035 NW 60th St., Miami, FL 33166 **E-mail:** marioobeso@tradinter.net

ORR, SUSAN K.
Industry: Foodservice equipment **Born:** Blount County, Tennessee **Univ./degree:** B.B.A., Alameda University **Current organization:** Strategic Equipment & Supply **Title:** Sales Representative **Type of organization:** Distributor **Major product:** Equipment and smallwares **Area of distribution:** National **Expertise:** Restaurants, healthcare, C-stores **Hob./spts.:** Gardening, motorcycling, crafts **SIC code:** 50 **Address:** Strategic Equipment & Supply, 3011 Industrial Pkwy. East, Knoxville, TN 37921 **E-mail:** sorr@strategicequipment.com **Web address:** www.strategicequipment.com

PENCE, BOB
Industry: Supply and design **Born:** September 7, 1950, Chicago, Illinois **Current organization:** Capital Wholesale Electric **Title:** General Manager **Type of organization:** Distributors **Major product:** Appliances and lighting **Area of distribution:** National **Expertise:** Marketing; Kitchen Design Certificate; National Association of Home Builders Certified Graduate **Affiliations:** N.A.H.B.; National Kitchen and Bath Association **Hob./spts.:** Golf **SIC code:** 50 **Address:** Capital Wholesale Electric, 527 Fairview Dr., Carson City, NV 89701 **E-mail:** bob@cwe.bz **Web address:** www.capitalwholeelectric.com

PETRUCCI, MARY ELAINE
Industry: Pharmaceuticals **Born:** February 17, 1954, Denver, Colorado **Univ./degree:** M.B.A., Boston University, 1992 **Current organization:** Professional Detailing, Inc. **Title:** Sales Representative **Type of organization:** Contract sales organization **Major product:** Pharmaceutical sales **Area of distribution:** National **Expertise:** Sales/consulting **Hob./spts.:** Visiting museums, classical music **SIC code:** 51 **Address:** Professional Detailing, Inc., 10 Mountain View Rd., Upper Saddle River, NJ 07458-9981 **E-mail:** mpetrucci@pdi-inc.com

PHELPS, RONNIE J.
Industry: Oilfield equipment suppliers **Born:** July 5, 1956, Fort Worth, Texas **Univ./degree:** A.A., Business Administration, Terent County College, 1977 **Current organization:** Phelps Consulting, Inc. **Title:** President **Type of organization:** Sales and service **Major product:** Oilfield equipment **Area of distribution:** International

Expertise: Fracturing and cementing equipment **Affiliations:** T.O.G.A.; S.P.E. **Hob./spts.:** Golf **SIC code:** 50 **Address:** 5125 Turtlecreek Ct., Ft. Worth, TX 76116 **E-mail:** ronniepci@aol.com

PIERSON, MARY L.
Industry: Software **Born:** Milwaukee, Wisconsin **Univ./degree:** Attended University of Minnesota for Nursing and Psychology; Certified, N.R.A., S.H.R.M.P.H.R. **Current organization:** ARI Network Services **Title:** Human Resources Manager **Type of organization:** Distributing **Major product:** Software for the catalog industry **Area of distribution:** International **Expertise:** Facility acquisitions, stock options, benefits **Affiliations:** S.H.R.M.; Founder, Mounted Justice **Hob./spts.:** Cowboy Mounted Shooting **SIC code:** 50 **Address:** ARI Network Services, 11425 W. Lake Park Dr., Milwaukee, WI 53224 **E-mail:** pierson@arinet.com **Web address:** www.arinet.com

PILLER, DEBRA L.
Industry: Laser cut stencil **Born:** March 20, 1956, Grant's Pass, Oregon **Current organization:** Integrated Ideas & Technologies, Inc. **Title:** Controller **Type of organization:** Manufacturing **Major product:** Laser cut stencil **Area of distribution:** International **Expertise:** Accounting, human resources **Affiliations:** Chamber of Commerce **Hob./spts.:** Fishing, camping, reading **SIC code:** 50 **Address:** Integrated Ideas & Technologies, Inc., 3896 N. Schreiber Way, Coeur d'Alene, ID 83815-8362 **E-mail:** debbiep@integratedideas.com **Web address:** www.integratedideas.com

POWELL SR., JAMES D.
Industry: Tires **Born:** September 23, 1947, Advance, Missouri **Current organization:** Gateway Tire & Wheel LLC **Title:** President **Type of organization:** Distributing **Major product:** Tires and wheels for golf carts and golf courses **Area of distribution:** National **Expertise:** OE and after market tires **Hob./spts.:** Baseball scouting for the N.Y. Yankees; managing his sports clinic for youngsters **SIC code:** 50 **Address:** Gateway Tire & Wheel LLC, 120 Industrial Dr., Litchfield, IL 62056 **E-mail:** gatewaytire@hotmail.com

REYNOLDS, RAYMOND A.
Industry: Wheelchair lifts **Current organization:** Ricon Corp. **Title:** Product Development Manager **Type of organization:** OEM/manufacturing **Major product:** Wheelchair lifts **Area of distribution:** International **Expertise:** Product design, project management **Hob./spts.:** Scuba diving **SIC code:** 50 **Address:** Ricon Corp., 7900 Nelson Rd., Panorama City, CA 91402 **E-mail:** reymonrey@comcast.net

RUIZ, JUAN C.
Industry: Custom brokers **Born:** April 27, 1972, Hermosillo, Mexico **Univ./degree:** B.A., Business Administration, Institute of Technology, Mexico, 1996 **Current organization:** Ruiz Warehouse, LLC **Title:** Logistics **Type of organization:** Distributing **Major product:** Import/export **Area of distribution:** International **Expertise:** Mexican custom broker **Hob./spts.:** Restoring old cars **SIC code:** 50 **Address:** Ruiz Warehouse, LLC, 447 W. La Quinta Rd., Rio Rico, AZ 85621 **E-mail:** jcrc72@hotmail.com

SALWAN, AYODHIA & PREM
Industry: Asian Food and Spices **Born:** Ayodhia, March 26, 1948, Amritsar, India; Prem (wife), February 9, 1952, Amritsar, India **Current organization:** Salwan Trading, Inc. **Title:** President **Type of organization:** Direct Importer, wholesale, distribution **Major product:** Spices/rice/nuts **Area of distribution:** National/International **Expertise:** Management and operations marketing **Affiliations:** President, Hindu Society of Metropolitan Chicago **Hob./spts.:** Travel **SIC code:** 51 **Address:** Salwan Trading, Inc., 1125 Westover Lane, Schaumburg, IL 60193 **E-mail:** ansalwan@salwantrading.com

SANDERS, WILLIAM E.
Industry: Books **Born:** November 16, 933, Randolph, North Carolina **Univ./degree:** B.A., Political Science, University of North Carolina, 1957 **Current organization:** S&W Distributors, Inc. **Title:** President **Type of organization:** Distributors **Major product:** Books **Area of distribution:** National **Expertise:** Project management, business development, sales, marketing, quality assurance, client relations **Honors/awards:** Kentucky Colonel; Honorary Ambassador of Labor, Commonwealth of Kentucky; Honorary Staff of Lieutenant Governor State of Louisiana; Production awards for forty years as part of American Media; Listed in Marquis Who's Who in America, Marquis Who's Who in the World, Marquis Who's Who in Media & Communications, Marquis Who's Who in Finance Industry **Hob./spts.:** Golf, fishing **SIC code:** 50 **Address:** S&W Distributors, Inc., 2582 Fox Ridge Rd., Asheboro, NC 27205-8910 **E-mail:** swncbooks1@aol.com

SHOENFELT, CATHERINE R.
Industry: Medical **Born:** December 9, 1954, Dallas, Texas **Univ./degree:** B.A., Music Education, University of Texas, 1980 **Current organization:** CRS Medical Sales, Inc. **Title:** President/Owner **Type of organization:** Sales/distributor **Major product:** Lymphedema products, durable medical equipment **Area of distribution:** National **Expertise:** Sales, management **Affiliations:** N.A.F.E. **Hob./spts.:** Reading, travel, jazzercise, needlework **SIC code:** 50 **Address:** CRS Medical Sales, Inc., 18307 Elmdon Drive, Houston, TX 77084 **E-mail:** crs@academicplanet.com

SKOPIK, DAVID A.
Industry: Waterworks **Born:** September 14, 1960, Waco, Texas **Univ./degree:** A.B., 1984 **Current organization:** National Waterworks **Title:** Estimator Coordinator **Type of organization:** Distributing **Major product:** Municipalities water and sewer materials **Area of distribution:** Texas **Expertise:** Project management **SIC code:** 50 **Address:** National Waterworks, 5000 Franklin Ave., Waco, TX 76710

SONIA, GAILYC C.
Industry: Jewelry/diamonds **Univ./degree:** B.A., English, Simmons College, Massachusetts, 1990; J.D., Suffolk University School of Law, 1997 **Current organization:** Hearts On Fire Co., LLC **Title:** General Counsel **Type of organization:** Wholesale/retail **Major product:** Diamonds, jewelry **Area of distribution:** International **Expertise:** Attorney **Affiliations:** A.B.A.; Commonwealth of Massachusetts; Boston Bar Association; Massachusetts Bar Association **SIC code:** 50 **Address:** Hearts on Fire Co., LLC, 99 Summer St., Boston, MA 02110 **E-mail:** gsonia@heartsonfire.com

SOSA, MANUEL O.
Industry: Food **Current organization:** Century Sales **Title:** Assistant Food & Beverage **Type of organization:** Distributing **Major product:** Food and beverages **Area of distribution:** National, international **Expertise:** Marketing **Affiliations:** University of Puerto Rico; Chamber of Commerce **Hob./spts.:** Stamp and coin collecting, music **SIC code:** 51 **Address:** Century Sales, P.O. Box 364552, San Juan, PR 00936-4552

SPONSELLER, BRYON D.
Industry: Concrete **Current organization:** Fourth Street Rock **Title:** Sales Manager **Type of organization:** Distributing **Major product:** Concrete **Area of distribution:** Western U.S. **Expertise:** Sales, marketing, business development **SIC code:** 50 **Address:** Fourth Street Rock, 23918 Cedar Creek Terrace, Moreno Valley, CA 92557 **E-mail:** bsponseller@fourthstreetrock.com

STATON JR., ALBERT H.
Industry: Beverage bottlers **Born:** April 1, 1921, Atlanta, Georgia **Univ./degree:** B.S., Chemical Engineering, Georgia Institute of Technology, 1941 **Current organization:** Panamerican Beverages, Inc. **Title:** Chairman of the Board Emeritus **Type of organization:** Largest soft drink bottler in Latin America; one of the world's largest bottler of soft drink products of the Coca-Cola Co. **Major product:** Coca-Cola and other products of the Coca-Cola Co. **Area of distribution:** Latin America **Expertise:** Top management, operations **Honors/awards:** Bronze Star, Okinawa, World War II; 1 billion dollars in sales; 3 billion dollars in assets with 40,000 employees **Affiliations:** Advisory Board of College of Engineering, Georgia Institute of Technology; New York Stock Exchange (Listed as Panambev) **Hob./spts.:** Music, golf, photography **SIC code:** 51 **Address:** Panamerican Beverages, Inc., 8091 Los Pinos Blvd., Miami, FL 33143--645 **E-mail:** ahsmjs@mediaone.net

STREETER, JAMES E.
Industry: Communications **Born:** October, 6, 1937, Grand Rapids, Michigan **Univ./degree:** Federal Communications License **Current organization:** J.E.S. & Sons, Inc. **Title:** President/Chairman of the Board **Type of organization:** Private Professional Corporation **Major product:** Commercial two way radio sales and services **Area of distribution:** Local **Expertise:** Law enforcement communications **Affiliations:** U.S. Army Military Police, 1955-1959; Indianapolis Chamber of Commerce; U.S. Chamber of Commerce **Hob./spts.:** Fishing, family **SIC code:** 50 **Address:** J.E.S. & Sons, Inc., 817 E. Murry St., Indianapolis, IN 46227 **E-mail:** jstreeter@jesandsons.com

STRICKLAND, WILLIAM C.
Industry: Food **Born:** August 21, 1947, West Point, Georgia **Univ./degree:** M.B.A., University of Wisconsin, 1979 **Current organization:** The Strickland Companies, Inc. **Title:** President **Type of organization:** Retail **Major product:** Food service to weddings, receptions, restaurants **Area of distribution:** Houston, Texas **Expertise:** Education, marketing **Honors/awards:** Outstanding Lecturer **SIC code:** 51 **Address:** The Strickland Companies, Inc., 3415 Glastonbury Dr., Pearland, TX 77581 **E-mail:** wcstrickland1@prodigy.net

TANNER, ANTHONY G.
Industry: Police and military equipment **Born:** October 14, 1949, E. London, South Africa **Univ./degree:** Certificate, 1987; Advanced Certificate, 1988; Road Transportation Engineering Diploma, Rand Afrikaans University, 1989; Business Degree, Academy of Advanced Training (Johannesburg) **Current organization:** Kejo Limited Co. **Title:** President **Type of organization:** Wholesaler/distributor **Major product:** Military vehicles, equipment, body armor, ballistic products **Area of distribution:** International **Expertise:** Entrepreneur **Honors/awards:** Congressional Order of Merit, 2003, National Republican Congressional Committee; Honorary Chair, House of Representatives, State of Florida, 2003 **Published works:** Tampa Business Times Review **Affiliations:** Rhodesian Army Signals Officer, 1967-1980; Delasalle College, South

Africa Alumni Association **Hob./spts.:** Rugby, soccer, cricket, motorcycle touring **SIC code:** 50 **Address:** Kejo Limited Co., 2027 N. Keene Rd., Clearwater, FL 33755 **E-mail:** kejocompany@mindspring.com **Web address:** www.bodyarmorcompany.com

TARASULA, ALEKSANDR
Industry: Sprinklers **Born:** March 2, 1949, Odessa, Russia **Univ./degree:** M.A., Odessa Technical College, 1975 **Current organization:** Reliable Automatic Sprinkler Co. **Title:** Quality Control Technician **Type of organization:** Manufacturing **Major product:** Fire protection **Area of distribution:** International **Expertise:** Technician **Honors/awards:** Bronze Medal for Achievements in Developing Quality Control System, 1985; 5 patents in quality control technology **Published works:** 40 publications including: Journal of Institute of General and Inorganic Chemistry of Sciences of the Ukrainian SSR **Affiliations:** A.S.Q. **Hob./spts.:** Coin collecting, travel **SIC code:** 50 **Address:** Reliable Automatic Sprinkler Co., 525 N. MacQuesten Pkwy., Mount Vernon, NY 10552 **E-mail:** atarasula@reliablesprinkler.com

VALDEZ, SONNY
Industry: Car stereo equipment **Born:** May 19, 1964, Long Beach, California **Univ./degree:** B.B.A., California State University, 1986 **Current organization:** Fujitsu Ten Corp. of America **Title:** Regional Credit Manager **Type of organization:** Manufacturing **Major product:** Car stereo equipment **Area of distribution:** National **Expertise:** Credit and collections **Hob./spts.:** Fishing, travel, playing pool, basketball, softball **SIC code:** 50 **Address:** Fujitsu Ten Corp. of America, 19600 S. Vermont Ave., Torrance, CA 90502 **E-mail:** valdez@lao.ten.fujitsu.com

VALVA, MARK W.
Industry: Tile **Born:** June 27, 1961, New York, New York **Univ./degree:** B.S., Accounting, Long Island University C.W. Post Campus **Current organization:** Cancos Tile Corp. **Title:** Vice President **Type of organization:** Distributor **Major product:** Importers of ceramic tile **Area of distribution:** New York **Expertise:** Management **Hob./spts.:** Surfing **SIC code:** 50 **Address:** Cancos Tile Corp., 1085 Portion Rd., Farmingville, NY 11738 **E-mail:** mvalva@cancos.com **Web address:** www.cancos.com

WHITE, KIM
Industry: Agricultural products **Born:** July 30, 1934, Sacramento, California **Univ./degree:** B.S., Agronomy, University of California, 1957 **Current organization:** Agra Trading **Title:** Owner **Type of organization:** Wholesale marketing **Major product:** Sales of agricultural by-products, sized walnut shell, almond shell, wood chips **Area of distribution:** California, Oregon, Nevada **Expertise:** Sales, overseeing operations **Affiliations:** N.R.A.; Farm Bureau; Alpha Gamma Rho **Hob./spts.:** Fishing, hunting **SIC code:** 51 **Address:** Agra Trading, 60 Independence Circle, Suite 203, Chico, CA 95973 **E-mail:** lori@agratradingonline.com

WHITLEY, WILLIAM D.
Industry: Electrical **Born:** Wilson, North Carolina **Univ./degree:** A.A., Electronics, McDowell Tech **Current organization:** Rexel **Title:** Area Sales Manager **Type of organization:** Distributing **Major product:** Electrical and datacom parts and supplies **Area of distribution:** International **Expertise:** Sales, marketing, engineering **Hob./spts.:** Golf, fishing **SIC code:** 50 **Address:** Rexel, 157 Asheland Ave., Asheville, NC 28801-4045 **E-mail:** dwhitley@rexelusa.com **Web address:** www.rexelusa.com

WILLIAMS, JAY L.
Industry: Grocery distribution **Born:** February 2, 1966, Carlisle, Pennsylvania **Current organization:** ES3, LLC **Title:** Safety Manager, CHCM **Type of organization:** Distributors/TPL **Major product:** Grocery and associated products **Area of distribution:** National **Expertise:** Safety - compliance; Certified Hazard Control Manager; AIB Certified, Sanitation **Affiliations:** Co-chair, Safety Council of Central Pennsylvania **Hob./spts.:** Singing (chorus, barber shop quartet), hunting **SIC code:** 50 **Address:** ES3, LLC, 4875 Susquehanna Trail, York, PA 17402 **E-mail:** jaybarbershopper@earthlink.net

WILLIS, JOHN W.
Industry: Automotive **Born:** May 15, 1943, Seattle, Washington **Univ./degree:** Everett Community College **Current organization:** JEM Distributors **Title:** President **Type of organization:** Distributing **Major product:** Specialty additives (smokeless oil, head gasket sealers) **Area of distribution:** National **Expertise:** Specializes in additives for used cars **Affiliations:** Washington Independent Dealers Association **Hob./spts.:** NASCAR crew chief, Official Yakima Speedway, Monroe's Evergreen Speedway **SIC code:** 51 **Address:** JEM Distributors, P.O. Box 1560, Marysville, WA 98270 **E-mail:** jemdistributors@earthlink.net **Web address:** www.jemdistributors.com

WOJISKI, WARREN
Industry: Food **Current organization:** Delmonte Fresh Produce **Title:** Director of Operations **Type of organization:** Distributing **Major product:** Fresh produce **Area of distribution:** International **Expertise:** Leadership, problem solving **Affiliations:** Chair, Barish Financial Council **Hob./spts.:** Ashing, reading, stamp collecting **SIC code:** 51 **Address:** Delmonte Fresh Produce, 1400 Parker St., Dallas, TX 75222 **E-mail:** wwojiski@verizon.net

WOODWARD, DANIEL K.
Industry: Fireplaces **Born:** May 8, 1955, Cedar Rapids, Iowa **Univ./degree:** B.S., Hyles Anderson College, 1985 **Current organization:** Hearth Technologies **Title:** RCI/Flow Manager **Type of organization:** Manufacturing **Major product:** Fireplaces **Area of distribution:** National **Expertise:** Lean consulting **Affiliations:** S.M.E. **SIC code:** 50 **Address:** Hearth Technologies, 1915 W. Saunders St., Mount Pleasant, IA 52641 **E-mail:** woodward@hearthtech.com **Web address:** www.hearthtech.com

YOUNGBLOOD, ADAM
Industry: Truck equipment **Univ./degree:** B.A., U.I.V., 2004 **Current organization:** The Mouat Company **Title:** Warehouse Manager **Type of organization:** Wholesale distributing **Major product:** Lift truck parts **Area of distribution:** National **Expertise:** Numbers/record keeping **SIC code:** 50 **Address:** The Mouat Company, 2923 Commerce Blvd., Irondale, AL 35210 **E-mail:** adamyoungblood@yahoo.com

Retailers

ABBOTT, KEVIN B.
Industry: Food **Born:** April 2, 1973, Long Valley, New Jersey **Univ./degree:** B.A., English, Film, Theatre and Hotel Restaurant Management **Current organization:** Joe's Public LLC/Joe's Pub **Title:** General Manager **Type of organization:** Restaurant/bar/performance venue **Major product:** Food, liquor and entertainment **Area of distribution:** New York **Expertise:** General management **Hob./spts.:** Music, theatre **SIC code:** 58 **Address:** Joe's Pub, 425 Lafayette St., New York, NY 10003 **E-mail:** kevin@joespub.com

ADAMS, VICKI
Industry: Outdoor sporting **Current organization:** Sound Bikes & Kayaks **Title:** President **Type of organization:** Retail **Major product:** Bicycles, kayaks **Area of distribution:** National **Expertise:** Sales, rentals, clinics **Affiliations:** OPP; Port Angeles Chamber of Commerce; Kiwanis Club **SIC code:** 59 **Address:** Sound Bikes & Kayaks, 120 E. Front St., Port Angeles, WA 98362 **E-mail:** vicki@soundbikeskayaks.com **Web address:** www.soundbikeskayaks.com

AGEE, JACQUELINE R.
Industry: Food **Born:** July 7, 1967, Wilmington, Delaware **Current organization:** Wendy's **Title:** General Manager **Type of organization:** Restaurant **Major product:** Food services **Area of distribution:** Hammonton, New Jersey **Expertise:** Customer service **Hob./spts.:** Football, church **SIC code:** 58 **Address:** Wendy's, 65 S. Whitehorse Pike, Hammonton, NJ 08037 **E-mail:** jacragee@netzero.net

ALBERINI, CARLOS E.
Industry: Fashion **Born:** July 15, 1955, Cordoba, Argentina **Univ./degree:** B.A., 1977; M.B.A., 1978, University of Buenos Aires **Current organization:** Guess? Inc. **Title:** President, C.O.O. **Type of organization:** Retail **Major product:** Apparel and accessories **Area of distribution:** International **Expertise:** Administration, operations **Affiliations:** A.I. C.P.A.; P.I.C.P.A.; Member, Board of Directors, Guess? Inc. **Hob./spts.:** Golf **SIC code:** 56 **Address:** 17647 Belinda St., Encino, CA 91316 **E-mail:** carloal@guess.com

ALI, AHMAD A.
Industry: Automotive **Born:** December 28, 1977, Kuwait **Current organization:** Cerritos Nissan **Title:** Finance Director **Type of organization:** Automobile firm **Major product:** Automobile loans/sales **Area of distribution:** Laguna Hills, California **Expertise:** Marketing, finance **Hob./spts.:** Golf, basketball **SIC code:** 55 **Address:** Cerritos Nissan, 23411 Summerfield, #19-C, Laguna Hills, CA 92656 **E-mail:** thewizofozzz@aol.com

ALLARDICE, KEVIN P.
Industry: Restaurants **Born:** February 26, 1963, Danvers, Massachusetts **Current organization:** The Bloomin' Apple/T.S.S.O. North, Inc. **Title:** President **Type of organization:** Casual dining restaurants **Major product:** Neighborhood dining and beverages **Area of distribution:** Missouri, Illinois, Wisconsin, Iowa **Expertise:** Management/operations (16 restaurants) **Honors/awards:** Customer Satisfaction Award, Applebee's International, 2001 **Affiliations:** Boy Scouts of America **Hob./spts.:** Soccer coach, softball, running **SIC code:** 58 **Address:** The Bloomin' Apple/T.S.S.O. North, Inc., 1303 Ben Sawyer Blvd., Suite #10, Mount Pleasant, SC 29464 **E-mail:** kallardice@bloominapple.com

ALLEN, DAVID PAUL
Industry: Restaurant **Univ./degree:** B.S., Human Biology, University of Wisconsin, 1997 **Current organization:** Pizzeria Uno West **Title:** General Manager **Type of organization:** Restaurant/retailer **Major product:** Food service **Expertise:** Management and marketing **Affiliations:** Nightclub & Bar Association; National Association of Sports Officials **SIC code:** 58 **Address:** 5001 Sheboygan Ave., #307, Madison, WI 53705-2809 **E-mail:** davidallen@sbcglobal.net

ALLEN, SARAH E.
Industry: Restaurant **Born:** October 19, 1975, Huntington, West Virginia **Current organization:** Restaurant Management Group **Title:** Manager **Type of organization:** Fast food restaurant (Hardee's)/retail **Major product:** Fast food **Area of distribution:** Rainelle, West Virginia **Expertise:** Training **Hob./spts.:** Family, reading **SIC code:** 58 **Address:** Restaurant Management Group, 208 Kanawha, Rainelle, WV 25962 **E-mail:** sarahallen@charter.net

ANTONIOU, TONY
Industry: Restaurant **Born:** August 25, 1970, Jersey City, New Jersey **Univ./degree:** B.S., Business Management, Farleigh Dickinson University, 1992 **Current organization:** Hanratty's Restaurant **Title:** General Manager **Type of organization:** Full service restaurant **Major product:** Food and beverage service **Area of distribution:** New York, New York **Expertise:** Management **Hob./spts.:** Travel **SIC code:** 58 **Address:** Hanratty's Restaurant, 1410 Madison Ave., New York, NY 10029

ARMSTRONG, MICHAEL M.
Industry: Restaurant **Born:** April 1, 1958, Houston, Texas **Current organization:** Truluck's Restaurant Group **Title:** Partner **Type of organization:** Restaurant **Major product:** Food **Area of distribution:** Houston, Texas **Expertise:** Partner **Affiliations:** Nonprofit H.G.A.; N.R.A.; H.R.A.; T.R.A. **SIC code:** 58 **Address:** Truluck's Restaurant Group, 5919 Westheimer, Houston, TX 77057 **E-mail:** marmstrong@trulucks.com

ATENCIO, DWAYNE "ROCKY"
Industry: Automotive **Born:** December 9, 1971, Albuquerque, New Mexico **Univ./degree:** Attended Eastern New Mexico University and University of New Mexico **Current organization:** Carter County Dodge Chrysler Jeep **Title:** General Manager/Owner **Type of organization:** Retailer **Major product:** Automobiles (used and new) **Area of distribution:** National **Expertise:** Management **Hob./spts.:** Coaching sports (basketball, football, baseball), skiing **SIC code:** 55 **Address:** Carter County Dodge Chrysler Jeep, 3600 W. Broadway St., Ardmore, OK 73401

AUDDINO, MARCO
Industry: Food **Born:** September 16, 1977, Columbus, Ohio **Current organization:** Auddino's Italian Bakery **Title:** Production Manager **Type of organization:** Bakery **Major product:** Bread, baked goods **Area of distribution:** Columbus, Ohio **Expertise:** Mechanical repair **Hob./spts.:** Fishing, motor cross **SIC code:** 54 **Address:** Auddino's Italian Bakery, 1490 Clara St., Columbus, OH 43211 **E-mail:** bkrson3@aol.com

BAKER, WILLIAM
Industry: Remodeling **Born:** July 15, 1966, Hamilton County, Ohio **Current organization:** Cincinnati Kitchen & Bath **Title:** Vice President **Type of organization:** Retail **Major product:** Kitchen, bath and plumbing products, cabinets **Area of distribution:** Ohio **Expertise:** Management **Affiliations:** B.B.B.; Remodeling King; Impact Management **Hob./spts.:** Travel **SIC code:** 59 **Address:** Cincinnati Kitchen & Bath, 11154 Luschek Dr., Cincinnati, OH 45241 **E-mail:** cintikitchenandbath@fuse.net

BANTAU, RAINER
Industry: Food **Current organization:** Rovin Inc. dba Babe's Chicken Dinner House **Title:** General Manager **Type of organization:** Restaurant **Major product:** Home cooked food **Area of distribution:** Texas **Expertise:** Management **SIC code:** 58 **Address:** 13632 Cherokee Ranch Rd., Roanoke, TX 76262 **E-mail:** rainier@lscom.net

BARNETT, JOSHUA J.
Industry: Food **Current organization:** Casa Ole **Title:** General Manager **Type of organization:** Restaurant **Major product:** Food **Area of distribution:** Texas **Expertise:** Management, daily operations, human resources **Hob./spts.:** Fishing, hunting, racehorses **SIC code:** 58 **Address:** Casa Ole, 2730 E. Hwy. 190, Copperas Cove, TX 76522 **E-mail:** casaole51gm@hotmail.com

BENDTSEN JR., BENDT L.
Industry: Food **Born:** January 13, 1956, Racine, Wisconsin **Current organization:** Bendtsen Bakery Inc. **Title:** President **Type of organization:** Third generation family owned bakery **Major product:** Handmade Kringles and bakery products **Area of distribution:** National **Expertise:** Daily operations oversight, baking, management **Affiliations:** Appeared on the Food Network, TV specials, Discover Wisconsin and the Today Show **Hob./spts.:** Golf, bowling, fishing, trap shooting, hunting, travel **SIC code:** 54 **Address:** Bendtsen Bakery Inc., 3200 Washington Ave., Racine, WI 53405 **Web address:** www.bendtsensbakery.com

BESH, JOHN P.
Industry: Food **Born:** May 14, 1968, Mississippi **Univ./degree:** Culinary School of America, 1991 **Current organization:** Restaurant August & Besh Steakhouse **Title:** Executive Chef **Type of organization:** Fine dining restaurant **Major product:** Contemporary French cuisine **Area of distribution:** New Orleans, Louisiana **Expertise:** Culinary arts **Published works:** TV appearance on the Today Show and Food Network **Affiliations:** A.L.D. Foundation **Hob./spts.:** Hunting, fishing, water sports **SIC code:** 58 **Address:** Restaurant August & Besh Steakhouse, 301 Tchoupitoulas St., New Orleans, LA 70130 **E-mail:** johnb@rest-august.com **Web address:** www.restaurantaugust.com

BEYER, MARY A.
Industry: Home furnishings **Born:** July 15, 1941, Atlantic City, New Jersey **Univ./degree:** M.S., Drexel University, 1978 **Current organization:** Consignment Galleries **Title:** Owner **Type of organization:** Gallery/retail **Major product:** High-end home furnishings, artwork **Area of distribution:** Wayne, Pennsylvania **Expertise:** Service to the community **Hob./spts.:** Dragonboat racing, intellectual reading, walking, modified hiking, kayaking **SIC code:** 57 **Address:** Consignment Galleries, 163 W. Lancaster Ave., Wayne, PA 19087

BIAGAS, LILLIE B.
Industry: Automotive **Born:** November 4, 1949, Lake Charles, Louisiana **Current organization:** Fairway Automotive Group, Inc. **Title:** President/CEO **Type of organization:** Retailer **Major product:** Selling and servicing cars and trucks **Area of distribution:** Jenkintown, Pennsylvania **Expertise:** Overseeing company **Published works:** Articles **Affiliations:** G.M.M.D.A. **Hob./spts.:** Golf **SIC code:** 55 **Address:** Fairway Automotive Group, Inc., 1750 The Fairway, Jenkintown, PA 19046-1606 **E-mail:** edb1024@aol.com **Web address:** www.fairwayautogroup.com

BIANCHI, JAMES V.
Industry: Food **Born:** November 21, 1963, New York **Current organization:** Anthony's Restaurant **Title:** Owner **Type of organization:** Restaurant **Major product:** Upscale fine Italian dining **Area of distribution:** New York **Expertise:** Chef, management **Hob./spts.:** Family, tropical fish, charity work **SIC code:** 58 **Address:** Anthony's Restaurant, 222-02 Union Tpke., Bayside, NY 11364 **E-mail:** jbianchi1@nyc.rr.com **Web address:** www.bellabianchis.com

BILL, JOHN J.
Industry: Electronics **Born:** May 14, 1948, New York, New York **Univ./degree:** M.AD, Pan American Arts School, 1969 **Current organization:** Electronics Expo **Title:** Advertising Manager **Type of organization:** Retail **Major product:** Electronics **Area of distribution:** New Jersey **Expertise:** Marketing, advertising **Affiliations:** New Jersey Advertising Club **Hob./spts.:** Motorcycling **SIC code:** 59 **Address:** Electronics Expo, 275 State Rt. 10 East, Succasunna, NJ 07876 **E-mail:** john @electronics-expo.com

BLACKSTOCK, JAMES F.
Industry: Restaurants **Univ./degree:** J.D., University of Southern California, 1976 **Current organization:** CBRL Group, Inc. **Title:** Sr. V.P./General Counsel **Type of organization:** Restaurant chain **Major product:** Family dining/casual dining **Area of distribution:** National **Expertise:** Business, real estate & securities law **Affiliations:** A.B.A., Tour of Roses **Hob./spts.:** Horseback riding, sailing, drawing, painting **SIC code:** 58 **Address:** 533 Turtle Creek Dr., Brentwood, TN 37027 **E-mail:** jim.blackstock@cbrlgroup.com

BOHART, JAMES G.
Industry: Sailboats **Born:** May 9, 1954, New Rochelle, New York **Univ./degree:** A.D., Chemistry, Santa Fe Community College, 1976 **Current organization:** Sailboats, Inc. **Title:** Vice President, General Manager **Type of organization:** Dealership **Major product:** Beneteau sailboats **Area of distribution:** International **Expertise:** Management **Affiliations:** National Marine Manufacturers Association; Southern California Marine Association **Hob./spts.:** Sailing, golf, target shooting **SIC code:** 55 **Address:** Sailboats, Inc., 13505 Bali Way, Marina del Rey, CA 90292 **E-mail:** jbohart@msn.com

BOHLMAN, BARBARA ANN
Industry: National retail florists **Born:** February 21, 1938, Niagara Falls, New York **Univ./degree:** B.S., Science/Nursing, University of Buffalo, 1959; M.B.A., University of Pennsylvania, 1977 **Current organization:** Gerald Stevens, Inc. **Title:** Director of Human Resources-Compensation & Benefits **Type of organization:** Retail florists **Major product:** Flowers **Area of distribution:** National **Expertise:** Consulting, compensation, benefits **Affiliations:** I.F.E.B.P. **Hob./spts.:** Golf **SIC code:** 59 **Address:** Gerald Stevens, Inc., 1800 Eller Dr., Suite 300, Ft. Lauderdale, FL 33433 **E-mail:** barbara.bohlman@geraldstevens.com

BOJORQUEZ, SHELLY M.
Industry: Food **Univ./degree:** B.A., Business, California State University; Culinary Arts, Los Angeles Trade Technical College **Current organization:** 555 E. Steakhouse **Title:** Executive Chef **Type of organization:** Restaurant **Major product:** Fine dining, prime steakhouse **Area of distribution:** California **Expertise:** Steak and seafood **Published works:** Cable shows and networking programs **SIC code:** 58 **Address:** 2609 E. Third St., Long Beach, CA 90814 **E-mail:** sbojorquez@kingsseafood.com

BOLOGNA, JAMES P.
Industry: Food **Born:** October 30, 1973, Grosse Pointe, Michigan **Current organization:** Unique Restaurant Corp. **Title:** Executive Chef **Type of organization:** Restaurant and catering **Major product:** Upscale dining **Area of distribution:** Michigan **Expertise:** Upscale Michigan cuisine, consulting, staff management **Published works:** Published several times including the Metro Times and Detroit News; has appeared on numerous televisions shows **Affiliations:** A.C.F. **Hob./spts.:** Rock climbing, waterskiing, golf, hockey, snow skiing **SIC code:** 58 **Address:** Unique Restaurant Corp., 30100 Telegraph Rd., Bingham Farms, MI 48025

BOOHER, DAN
Industry: Office supplies **Born:** June 29, 1958, Oakland, California **Univ./degree:** M.S., Civil Engineering, University of Missouri at Rolla, 1981 **Current organization:** Office Depot **Title:** V.P. Design & Construction **Type of organization:** Retail **Major product:** Office products and services **Area of distribution:** International **Expertise:** Real estate development **Affiliations:** I.C.S.C.; Board Member, SPECS **Hob./spts.:** Scuba diving **SIC code:** 59 **Address:** Office Depot, 2200 Old Germantown Rd., Delray Beach, FL 33445 **E-mail:** dbooher@officedepot.com

BORDERS, RUSSELL
Industry: Hospitality **Current organization:** Western Omelette Restaurant **Title:** CFO/Partner/Manager **Type of organization:** Restaurant **Major product:** Food **Area of distribution:** National **Expertise:** All day to day operations of business - payroll, accounts payable; public speaking, lecturing and consulting **SIC code:** 58 **Address:** Western Omelette Restaurant, 16 S. Walnut St., Colorado Springs, CO 80905 **E-mail:** russellborders@email.com

BROADWELL, WAYNE
Industry: Food **Born:** October 6, 1952, Greensboro, North Carolina **Current organization:** M Crowd/Restaurant Life **Title:** Director of Public Relations **Type of organization:** Restaurant **Major product:** Food/beverage **Area of distribution:** Dallas, Texas **Expertise:** Restaurant consulting **Hob./spts.:** Reading, travel **SIC code:** 58 **Address:** M Crowd/Restaurant Life, 4122 Bowser Ave., Unit C, Dallas, TX 75219 **E-mail:** waynebroadwell@sbcglobal.net

BROWN, FRANK E.
Industry: Personal protection equipment **Univ./degree:** B.A., Business, Wichita State University **Current organization:** Today's Security dba Today's Upper Edge **Title:** President, Owner **Type of organization:** Retail **Major product:** Electronic surveillance, stun guns, pepper spray **Area of distribution:** Colorado **Expertise:** Sales, administration, presentation **SIC code:** 59 **Address:** Today's Security dba Today's Upper Edge, 5433 W. 88th Ave., Space 4C, Westminster, CO 80031 **E-mail:** fbrown221@aol.com

BURNETT, TERRY K.
Industry: Retail **Born:** October 31, 1957, Grenada, Mississippi **Current organization:** Satellite Source, Inc. **Title:** President **Type of organization:** Retail sales and service **Major product:** Satellite sales and installation **Area of distribution:** Midwest **Expertise:** Marketing and sales, operations **Affiliations:** I.E.E.E.; Satellite Broadcasting Communication Organization; Chamber of Commerce, Kentucky **Hob./spts.:** Fishing, college football and basketball **SIC code:** 59 **Address:** Satellite Source, Inc., 7412 Preston Hwy., Louisville, KY 40219 **E-mail:** terry@thesatellitestore.com **Web address:** www.thesatellitestore.com

BUSH, MILTON H.
Industry: Recreational vehicles **Born:** November 27, 1927, Bendon, Michigan **Univ./degree:** B.S., Business, Trevor City College, 1946 **Current organization:** Leisure Time RV **Title:** Manager **Type of organization:** Retail **Major product:** Recreational vehicle sales and service **Area of distribution:** Michigan **Expertise:** RV's, spiritual church advisor **Affiliations:** Odd Pillars Organization **Hob./spts.:** Theatre, national music camp **SIC code:** 55 **Address:** Leisure Time RV, 2859 Benzie Hwy., Benzonia, MI 49616 **E-mail:** motsale1@yahoo.com

BUTZ, WENDY E.
Industry: Food **Univ./degree:** B.S., Psychology, Boise State University **Current organization:** Chester's Steakhouse **Title:** General Manager **Type of organization:** Restaurant **Major product:** Food **Area of distribution:** Wilmington, North Carolina **Expertise:** Operations **Published works:** Articles in wine magazine **SIC code:** 58 **Address:** Chester's Steakhouse, 1900 Eastwood Rd., Suite 2, Wilmington, NC 28403 **E-mail:** wendybutz@yahoo.com

CABONILAS, FRANKLIN J.
Industry: Pharmacy Benefits Management **Univ./degree:** B.S., New Jersey Institute of Technology, 1976 **Current organization:** Medco Health Solutions, Inc. **Title:** Manager, Reliability Engineering **Type of organization:** Mail Service Pharmacy **Major product:** Pharmaceuticals **Area of distribution:** National **Expertise:** Engineering **Published works:** Critical infrastructure and preventive maintenance protocols **Hob./spts.:** Baseball, basketball, football, fishing, skiing **SIC code:** 59 **Address:** 23 Jonquil Circle, Fords, NJ 08863 **E-mail:** franklin_cabonilas@medcohealth.com **Web address:** www.medcohealth.com

CALA, JEFF S.
Industry: Restaurant **Born:** November 19, 1970, Rochester, New York **Current organization:** Alchemy Cafe & Bistro/Cala's Restaurant **Title:** Chef/Owner **Type of organization:** Restaurant **Major product:** Food and beverage **Area of distribution:** Gloucester, Massachusetts **Expertise:** Eclectic cuisine **Affiliations:** A.C.F. **Hob./spts.:** Family, hiking, travel, baseball, music, swimming **SIC code:** 58 **Address:** Alchemy Cafe & Bistro/Cala's Restaurant, 3 Duncan St., Gloucester, MA 01930

CANCEL, SHARON M.
Industry: Medical sales **Born:** May 3, 1956, Brooklyn, New York **Univ./degree:** B.S., Temple University, 1978 **Current organization:** Philips Medical Systems **Title:** Sales Executive **Type of organization:** Medical equipment sales **Major product:** Medical equipment **Area of distribution:** National **Expertise:** Medical sales **Published works:** Article in Black Entrepreneurs Magazine, March, 2002 **Affiliations:** A.A.R.T.; American Motorcycle Association **Hob./spts.:** Motorcycling (28 yrs), martial arts **SIC code:** 59 **Address:** 117-49 225th St., Cambria Heights, NY 11411 **E-mail:** 2x750cc@netzero.com

CARPENTER, BONNIE
Industry: Restaurant and lounge **Born:** January 31, 1951, Hampton, Iowa **Univ./degree:** ICS Degree, Administration, 1982 **Current organization:** Carpenter Enterprises Inc. (dba Lapine Inn, Restaurant & Lounge) **Title:** Owner **Type of organization:** Restaurant **Major product:** Food and alcohol **Area of distribution:** Oregon **Expertise:** Business administration **Affiliations:** A.B.W.A.; S.C.O.O.T.R.; Lapine Chamber of Commerce **Hob./spts.:** Billiards, reading **SIC code:** 58 **Address:** Carpenter Enterprise Inc. (dba Lapine Inn, Restaurant & Lounge), 51490 Hwy. 97, P.O. Box 498, Lapine, OR 97739 **E-mail:** bonralf@aol.com

CARROLL, RHONDA L.
Industry: Mobile homes **Born:** October 1, 1965, Lake City, Florida **Current organization:** R. Carroll DBA Corbett's Mobile Home Supplies of Lake City **Title:** Owner **Type of organization:** Retail **Major product:** Mobile home supplies **Area of distribution:** Florida **Expertise:** Sales and service of sheds, trailers, carports, screen rooms **Hob./spts.:** NASCAR **SIC code:** 52 **Address:** R. Carroll DBA Corbett's Mobile Home Supplies of Lake City, 7232 59th Dr., Live Oak, FL 32060

CASTELLOTTI, LISA
Industry: Hospitality **Current organization:** John's Restaurant **Title:** President **Type of organization:** Restaurant **Major product:** Food, pizza **Area of distribution:** New York, New York **Expertise:** Management **SIC code:** 58 **Address:** John's Restaurant, 260 W. 44th St., New York, NY 10036 **E-mail:** johnspizzeriany@aol.com

CASTELLOTTI, MADELINE
Industry: Hospitality **Type of organization:** Restaurant **Major product:** Food, pizza **SIC code:** 58 **Address:** John's Restaurant, 260 W. 44th St., New York, NY 10036

CELLUPICA, RENATO
Industry: Food **Born:** March 6, 1949 **Univ./degree:** B.S., Business Administration, University of Albany, 1971 **Current organization:** Golub Corp. **Title:** Vice President, Distribution **Type of organization:** Supermarket/retail **Major product:** Food **Area of distribution:** National **Expertise:** Distribution, logistics, supply chain management, warehousing, transportation, business development, team leadership; Public Speaker and Lecturer at seminars and conferences pertaining to the food industry **Affiliations:** A.T.A.; F.M.I., N.P.T.C. **Hob./spts.:** Golf, the arts, music, physical fitness **SIC code:** 54 **Address:** 501 Duanesburg Rd., Schenectady, NY 12306 **E-mail:** roncellupica@pricechopper.com

CHASE, SUZANN K.
Industry: Animal specialty services **Current organization:** Tropical Imports Unlimited **Title:** Owner **Type of organization:** Retail **Major product:** Tropical and pond fish, reptiles, birds, ferrets **Area of distribution:** National **Expertise:** Supervising all operations and all aspects of management **SIC code:** 59 **Address:** Tropical Imports Unlimited, 4100 S. 6th St., Klamath Falls, OR 97603 **E-mail:** smcritters4@yahoo.com

CHERAMIE, LEVITA C.
Industry: Food **Born:** November 29, 1943, Grand Isle, Louisiana **Current organization:** Cigar's Cajun Cuisine/Marina Motel **Title:** Owner **Type of organization:** Retailer **Major product:** Seafood **Area of distribution:** International **Expertise:** Cooking **Honors/awards:** Small Business of the Year Award, 1998; National Leadership Award, Washington, D.C. **Affiliations:** Grand Isle Chamber of Commerce **Hob./spts.:** Reading, swimming, cooking **SIC code:** 54 **Address:** Cigar's Cajun Cuisine, Marina Motel, 1119 Hwy. 1 South, Grand Isle, LA 70358

CHIN, ANGY C.
Industry: Restaurant franchise **Born:** August 18, 1969, Singapore **Univ./degree:** B.S., University of Kansas, 1993; M.B.A., University of Chicago, 1995 **Current organization:** Yum! Brands Inc. **Title:** Multibrand Finance Manager **Type of organization:** Quick service restaurants **Major product:** Food **Area of distribution:** International **Expertise:** Finance **Honors/awards:** Graduated with Highest Honors and Distinction with Honors Thesis on International Marketing Ethics, University of Kansas **Affiliations:** I.M.A. **Hob./spts.:** Golf, gardening, dogs, international travel **SIC code:** 58 **Address:** Yum! Brands Inc., 1900 Colonel Sanders Lane, Louisville, KY 40213 **E-mail:** angy.chin@yum.com

CIVALE, CATHLEEN
Industry: Handbags/accessories **Born:** April 5, 1948, New York, New York **Univ./degree:** A.A., Fashion Institute of Technology **Current organization:** LeSportsac **Title:** Senior Vice President Sales **Type of organization:** Retailer/manufacturing **Major product:** Rip stop nylon handbags **Area of distribution:** International **Expertise:** Sales **Hob./spts.:** Yoga, reading, sailing, adventure vacations, charity work **SIC code:** 56 **Address:** LeSportsac, 358 Fifth Ave., Eighth floor, New York, NY 10001 **E-mail:** ccivale@lesportsac.com

CLAYTON, WILLIAM A.
Industry: Flags **Born:** August 13, 1971, Denver, Colorado **Current organization:** Heads Flags Inc. **Title:** Owner **Type of organization:** Retail/manufacturing **Major product:** Flags, flagpoles, banners **Area of distribution:** National **Expertise:** Flags and banners **Affiliations:** Denver Chamber of Commerce **Hob./spts.:** Fishing **SIC code:** 59 **Address:** Heads Flags Inc., 381 S. Henderson Blvd., Tampa, FL 33629 **E-mail:** headsflags@tampdsl.net **Web address:** www.headsflags.net

COBLE, BEVERLY
Industry: Hospitality **Born:** June 20, 1950, Carlsbad, New Mexico **Current organization:** Memories Restaurant **Title:** Owner **Type of organization:** Restaurant **Major product:** Fine dining **Area of distribution:** New Mexico **Expertise:** All phases of restaurant management; culinary arts; administration **Affiliations:** New Mexico Restaurant Association; Alamogordo Chamber of Commerce; Honorary Member, Business Advisory Council (for the President of U.S.) **Hob./spts.:** Family, grandchildren, collecting antiques, eggs, angels **SIC code:** 58 **Address:** Memories Restaurant, 1223 New York Ave., Alamogordo, NM 88310 **E-mail:** memories@zianet.com **Web address:** www.zianet.com/memories

COLLINS, TEDDIE RAE
Industry: Florist/interior design **Born:** December 23, 1951, Stillwater, Oklahoma **Current organization:** Flowers by Teddie Rae, Inc. **Title:** Proprietor, Advanced Master Florist **Type of organization:** Retail florist **Major product:** Flowers, gifts, décor **Area of distribution:** National **Expertise:** Floral design **Affiliations:** O.F.A.; Ozark Florist Association **Hob./spts.:** Antiquing, dogs (Miniature Schnauzers) **SIC code:** 59 **Address:** Flowers by Teddie Rae, Inc., 405 N.E. 1st St., Pryor, OK 74361 **E-mail:** teddierae@sstelco.com

CONDE, BINTOU
Industry: Precious stones **Born:** June 24, 1957, Kindia **Current organization:** HRD - Antwerp World Diamond Center/Guinea Embassy **Title:** Economic Counselor **Type of organization:** Gemological organization **Major product:** Diamonds **Area of distribution:** International **Expertise:** Gemologist-Diamond Appraiser **Hob./spts.:** Badminton **SIC code:** 59 **Address:** Guinea Embassy, 2112 Leroy Place N.W., Washington, DC 20008 **E-mail:** bintouco@hotmail.com

CONTRISCIANI, ALFONSO A.
Industry: Food, beverage and entertainment **Born:** July 16, 1959, Lancedown, Pennsylvania **Univ./degree:** B.A., Johnson & Wales University, Rhode Island, 1996 **Current organization:** Kahunaville Restaurant Group **Title:** Vice President, Culinary Operations **Type of organization:** Chain restaurants **Major product:** Hospitality **Area of distribution:** Delaware **Expertise:** Food and beverage **Honors/awards:** Culinary of the Year, 2000, Delaware Valley Chef Organization **Published works:** "My Favorite Herb", The Best of Food & Wine, 1999 **Affiliations:** A.C.F.; World Master Chef Society of London **Hob./spts.:** Art, drawing, painting, golf **SIC code:** 58 **Address:** Kahunaville Restaurant Group, 500 S. Madison St., Wilmington, DE 19801 **E-mail:** alfonse@kahunaville.com

CORANTE, LEON
Industry: Food **Born:** December 26, 1945, Lima, Peru **Univ./degree:** B.S., Accounting, Dominguez Hills University, 1989 **Current organization:** Hamada of Japan **Title:** Vice President, Administration **Type of organization:** Restaurant **Major product:** Japanese cuisine **Area of distribution:** Nevada **Expertise:** Administration **Hob./spts.:** Electronics, auto racing **SIC code:** 58 **Address:** Hamada of Japan, 3900 Paradise Rd., Suite 233, Las Vegas, NV 89109 **E-mail:** len@hamadaofjapan.com **Web address:** www.hamadaofjapan.com

CORWINE, BETTY
Industry: Arts, crafts, seasonal **Born:** December 26, 1939, Brooklyn, New York **Univ./degree:** A.S., X-Ray Technology, U.S. Army **Current organization:** Santa's Lane **Title:** Owner **Type of organization:** Retail **Major product:** Quilts, lighted lawn decorations, all holiday goods **Area of distribution:** International **Expertise:** Quilting **Affiliations:** Tree City Quilters; donates quilts to hospices and children's cancer centers **Hob./spts.:** Quilting, crochet, knitting, family **SIC code:** 57 **Address:** Santa's Lane, 3499 N.W. 97th Blvd., #8, Gainesville, FL 32606 **E-mail:** betty@santaslane.com **Web address:** www.santaslane.com

COX, PEGGY J.
Industry: Pharmacy **Born:** April 30, 1967, St. Clair, Missouri **Univ./degree:** RPh., St. Louis College of Pharmacy, 1990 **Current organization:** The Medicine Shop **Title:** RPh. **Type of organization:** Pharmacy **Major product:** Prescription dispensing **Area of distribution:** Missouri **Expertise:** Pharmacy **Affiliations:** Monthly radio program on KLPW 1250AM **Hob./spts.:** Family **SIC code:** 59 **Address:** The Medicine Shop, P.O. Box 248, St. Clair, MO 63077 **E-mail:** pjcrph@hotmail.com

CRAIG, SHERRY
Industry: Signs **Univ./degree:** B.A., University of Texas, 1981 **Current organization:** A-Okay Signs & Graphics **Title:** Owner **Type of organization:** Retail store **Major product:** Signs, design **Area of distribution:** Austin, Texas **Expertise:** Non electric signs **Affiliations:** Better Business Bureau **SIC code:** 59 **Address:** A-Okay Signs & Graphics, 1015 Reinli St., Austin, TX 78723 **E-mail:** aokaysigns@peoplepc.com

CUCE, MUSTAFA
Industry: Food **Born:** August 1, 1979, Turkey **Current organization:** Sunrise Family Restaurant **Title:** Owner **Type of organization:** Restaurant/retail **Major product:** Family style food **Area of distribution:** Onley, Virginia **Expertise:** American cuisine **Hob./spts.:** Work **SIC code:** 58 **Address:** Sunrise Family Restaurant, 25345 Lankford Hwy., Onley, VA 23148 **E-mail:** cuce1979@yahoo.com

DAGNOGO, AMBERLY A.
Industry: Direct marketing/law **Born:** July 17, 1970, Jonesboro, Arkansas **Univ./degree:** B.A., Finance and Accounting, Stephens College, 1995; M.A., Accounting, University of Indianapolis, 1998; J.D., Indiana University, 2002 **Current organization:** Redcats USA **Title:** General Counsel/Privacy Officer/Risk Manager **Type of organization:** Retail, multi-channel **Major product:** Catalog distribution (US Division of La Redoute Catalogs) **Area of distribution:** International **Expertise:** Management of legal division, national presentation of privacy **Affiliations:** Founder, Creative Arts Legal League; Founder, President, Redcats, Audit Committee; Indiana Bar Association; American Bar Association **Hob./spts.:** Travel, learning French **SIC code:** 59 **Address:** Redcats USA, 2300 Southeastern Ave., Indianapolis, IN 46201 **E-mail:** amberly.dagnogo@redcatsusa.com **Web address:** www.redcatsusa.com

DANIELS, EVELYN M.
Industry: Food **Univ./degree:** Certification in Secretarial Science **Current organization:** Domino's Pizza **Title:** Franchisee **Type of organization:** Restaurant/retail **Major product:** Thin crust, deep dish and hand tossed pizzas **Area of distribution:** Local **Expertise:** Oversight of daily operations; Certification in Secretarial Science **Affiliations:** Treasurer of Downtown Development; Chamber of Commerce; Treasurer of Rawlins Community Association; Rawlins Lyons Club **SIC code:** 58 **Address:** Domino's Pizza, 312 W. Cedar St., Rawlins, WY 82301 **E-mail:** dominos@wyoming.com

DANZI, CRISTOF S.
Industry: Food **Born:** July 24, 1958, Italy **Univ./degree:** Interior Design, Inst. Egrate, Milan, Italy **Current organization:** McGregor Café, Inc. **Title:** Owner **Type of organization:** Restaurant **Major product:** Italian cuisine **Area of distribution:** Fort Myers, Florida **Expertise:** Italian culinary arts **Hob./spts.:** Family **SIC code:** 58 **Address:** McGregor Café, Inc., 4305 McGregor Blvd., Ft. Myers, FL 33901

DAPONTE III, GEORGE ARTHUR
Industry: Food **Born:** May 6, 1965, Providence, Rhode Island **Univ./degree:** Apprentice Program, Sheraton International, Orlando **Current organization:** MMI Mississippi Catering **Title:** Executive Kosher Chef **Type of organization:** Restaurant/residential dining **Major product:** Food service **Area of distribution:** Orlando, Florida **Expertise:** Kosher food; Certified Food Safety Management **Hob./spts.:** Collector of art and ancient artifacts **SIC code:** 58 **Address:** MMI Mississippi Catering, 515 S. Delaney Ave., Orlando, FL 32801 **E-mail:** gdaponte1@netzero.com

DASILVA, ANTONIO M.
Industry: Food **Born:** June 14, Portugal **Current organization:** Silma Inc. dba Rocco Restaurant **Title:** President **Type of organization:** Restaurant **Major product:** Fine upscale Italian food and wine; hosting corporate parties and weddings **Area of distribution:** New York **Expertise:** Chef **Hob./spts.:** Football, baseball, reading **SIC code:** 58 **Address:** Silma Inc. (dba Rocco Restaurant), 181 Thompson St., New York, NY 10012 **E-mail:** roccorestaurant@msn.com **Web address:** www.roccorestaurant.com

DAVIS, REGINA
Industry: Food **Born:** August 18, 1969, Alliance, Ohio **Univ./degree:** A.S., Human Services and Corrections, Hocking College, 1991 **Current organization:** McDonalds Restaurants of Ohio **Title:** Store Manager **Type of organization:** Fast food restaurant **Major product:** Fast food services **Area of distribution:** Ohio **Expertise:** Management **Affiliations:** M.A.D.D. **Hob./spts.:** Spending time with family, reading **SIC code:** 58 **Address:** McDonalds Restaurants of Ohio, 825 N. Main St., Orrville, OH 44667 **E-mail:** 01boobear@aol.com

DAWSON, STEPHEN M.
Industry: Food **Born:** November 29, 1957, Hartford, Connecticut **Univ./degree:** B.S., Environmental Science, Southern Connecticut State University, 1982 **Current organization:** Culin Art, Inc. **Title:** Senior Director of Corporate Sales **Type of organization:** Food management service (privately held) **Major product:** Onsite dining services **Area of distribution:** NY, NJ, CT, MA, PA, WV **Expertise:** Overseeing sales **Affiliations:** Society Food Management **Hob./spts.:** Family, basketball, skiing, golf **SIC code:** 58 **Address:** Culin Art, Inc., 1979 Marcus Ave., Lake Success, NY 11042 **E-mail:** sdawson@culinartinc.com **Web address:** www.culinartinc.com

DEFLIPPO, GERALD R.
Industry: Food **Born:** November 6, 1939, Newark, New York **Univ./degree:** A.A., Culinary Arts, N.C.C.C., 1979 **Current organization:** DeFlippo's Restaurant **Title:** Owner **Type of organization:** Restaurant/retailer **Major product:** Food **Area of distribution:** New York **Expertise:** Management **Honors/awards:** Republican of the Year Award **Affiliations:** Niagara Chamber of Commerce; Past President, Optimists Club; President, Lockport Business Association **Hob./spts.:** Collecting sports memorabilia **SIC code:** 58 **Address:** DeFlippo's Restaurant, 326 West Ave., Lockport, NY 14094 **E-mail:** jerryd@vplp.net **Web address:** www.deflippos.com

DEPABLOS, IBEL CHELY
Industry: Perfumes **Born:** April 5, 1950, Caracas, Venezuela **Univ./degree:** B.S., Arts Administration, New York University, 1992 **Current organization:** Annick Goutal Parfum at Bloomingdale's 59th St. **Title:** Manager **Type of organization:** Retail, marketing parfum **Major product:** Parfumerie, artistry **Area of distribution:** International **Expertise:** Administration, marketing, sales **Honors/awards:** Best Bloomingdale's Manager, Spring 2001 **Affiliations:** Bolivarian Society; Venezuelan-American Cultural Association; Founder, Aid for AIDS **Hob./spts.:** Swimming, travel, philanthropy, theatre, arts **SIC code:** 59 **Address:** Annick Goutal Parfum at Bloomingdale's 59th St., 600 Madison Ave., 24th floor, New York, NY 10019 **E-mail:** chelyd@aol.com **Web address:** www.chelydepablos.com

DEVANE II, EDWARD A.
Industry: Automotive **Born:** March 6, 1965, San Antonio, Texas **Univ./degree:** Attended University of Texas at San Antonio **Current organization:** Benson Enterprises dba Ingram Park Auto Center **Title:** President/COO **Type of organization:** Retailer **Major product:** Chrysler, Jeep, Nissan, Mazda and GM auto sales **Area of distribution:** Texas **Expertise:** Management **Affiliations:** N.A.D.A. **Hob./spts.:** Golf **SIC code:** 55 **Address:** Benson Enterprises dba Ingram Park Auto Center, 7000 N.W. Loop 410, San Antonio, TX 78238 **E-mail:** edevane@benson-enterprises.com

DUFFY, SHELLY R.
Industry: Food **Born:** July 25, 1964, Marshalltown, Iowa **Univ./degree:** A.S., Nursing, Marshall Community College, 1986; A.S., Theology (Mission & Counseling), Faith Baptist Bible College, 1991 **Current organization:** FBBC&TS Dining and Conference Services **Title:** Dining Services Manager **Type of organization:** College food service **Major product:** Food service/catering **Area of distribution:** Ankeny, Iowa **Expertise:** Food management **Affiliations:** N.A.C.U.F.S; Board Member, Education Committee for IA, NE, MO & NRA **Hob./spts.:** Camping, reading, Member, Campus Baptist Church of Iowa **SIC code:** 58 **Address:** FBBC&TS Dining and Conference Services, 1900 N.W. Fourth St., Ankeny, IA 50021 **E-mail:** duffys@faith.edu **Web address:** www.dining@faith.edu

DURFORT, DANIEL G.
Industry: Restaurant **Born:** November 23, 1952, Tours, France **Univ./degree:** Culinary School, 1970 **Current organization:** La Parisienne Restaurant **Title:** Executive Chef **Type of organization:** Restaurant **Major product:** French dining **Area of distribution:** California **Expertise:** Upscale fine dining **Published works:** T.V. appearances **Hob./spts.:** Cooking, wines **SIC code:** 58 **Address:** 612 W. Foothill Blvd., #A, Monrovia, CA 91016 **E-mail:** durfort@starchefs.com

EHRENBECK, JOHN E.
Industry: Restaurants **Born:** December 17, 1965, Morristown, New Jersey **Univ./degree:** Culinary Institute of America **Current organization:** Growth Restaurants Inc. **Title:** Executive Chef **Type of organization:** Restaurants/retail **Major product:** Food and beverage **Area of distribution:** New Jersey **Expertise:** Culinary arts, ordering, specials **Hob./spts.:** Off-premise catering, skiing, hockey **SIC code:** 58 **Address:** Growth Restaurants Inc., 55 S. Finley Ave, Basking Ridge, NJ 07920 **E-mail:** chefjohn@growthrestaurants.com

ELLIS, CHRISTOPHER J.
Industry: Hospitality **Born:** June 7, 1973, Baltimore, Maryland **Univ./degree:** Culinary Arts, Baltimore International College, 1995 **Current organization:** An Poitin Stil **Title:** Executive Chef **Type of organization:** Restaurant **Major product:** Food, wine **Area of distribution:** Timonium, Maryland **Expertise:** Chef **Affiliations:** Junior Member, A.C.F. **Hob./spts.:** Building computers, playing soccer **SIC code:** 58

Address: An Poitin Stil, 2323 York Rd., Timonium, MD 21093 **E-mail:** chefla1@aol.com

FASULLO JR., PHILIP A.
Industry: Food **Born:** August 28, 1943, New Orleans, Louisiana **Univ./degree:** Business Management, Southeastern Louisiana University **Current organization:** P.A.F. Inc. dba Fasullo's Piggly Wiggly **Title:** President/Owner **Type of organization:** Franchise retail store **Major product:** Groceries **Area of distribution:** New Orleans **Expertise:** Management **Honors/awards:** Piggly Wiggly Spirit Award, Affiliated Foods, 2005 **Published works:** Articles in "New Orleans Times-Picayune" on family history **Affiliations:** Louisiana Grocers Association; Past Member, Board of Directors, Louisiana Grocers Coop **Hob./spts.:** Fishing, golf, cruise travel **SIC code:** 54 **Address:** P.A.F. Inc. dba Fasullo's Piggly Wiggly, 909 West Bank Expwy., Westwego, LA 70094 **E-mail:** philjr@faspigwig2.nocoxmail.com

FERREE, NORMA C.
Industry: Food **Born:** April 23, 1934, Philadelphia, Pennsylvania **Current organization:** Auntie Anne's, Inc. **Title:** Store Manager **Type of organization:** Retail chain store **Major product:** Hand rolled pretzels **Area of distribution:** National **Expertise:** Training and administration of staff **Hob./spts.:** Reading, crossword puzzles, watching football and basketball games **SIC code:** 54 **Address:** Auntie Anne's, Inc., 2801 E. Market St., York, PA 17402 **E-mail:** norma@blazenet.net

FILIPCIK, STEFAN
Industry: Hospitality **Born:** May 12, 1953, Czech Republic **Univ./degree:** B.A., Hospitality, The Hotel School, 1971 **Current organization:** Schroeder's **Title:** Owner, Head Chef **Type of organization:** Restaurant/retail **Major product:** Authentic Bavarian cuisine **Area of distribution:** San Francisco, California **Expertise:** European, German, Seafood cuisine **Hob./spts.:** Tennis, travel **SIC code:** 58 **Address:** Schroeder's, 240 Front St., San Francisco, CA 94111 **E-mail:** filipcik@aol.com **Web address:** www.schroederssf.com

FLORES FIGUEROA, REY F.
Industry: Medical equipment **Born:** September 11, 1968, Caguas, Puerto Rico **Univ./degree:** B.S., Accounting, Inter-American University, San Juan, Puerto Rico, 1992 **Current organization:** P.K. Industries, Corp./Medics **Title:** Comptroller **Type of organization:** Distributors **Major product:** Sales, rental of medical equipment **Area of distribution:** National **Expertise:** Finance, accounting **Hob./spts.:** Travel, computers **SIC code:** 59 **Address:** P.K. Industries, Corp./Medics, 3 Ave. Ruiz Soler, Bayamón, PR 00959 **E-mail:** florescostas9@hotmail.com

FOSTER, MATTHEW
Industry: Food **Born:** March 19, 1960, Donney, California **Univ./degree:** Attended Calpoly Pomona College **Current organization:** CSI/Chevron **Title:** Manager **Type of organization:** Retail **Major product:** Gasoline, food products **Area of distribution:** Riverside, California **Expertise:** Management **Affiliations:** P.G.A. **Hob./spts.:** Golf, pool, camping **SIC code:** 55 **Address:** 1325 E. Citrus Ave., #6H, Redlands, CA 92374

FOSTER, MICHAEL W.
Industry: Food **Born:** August 28, 1964, Champaign, Illinois **Univ./degree:** A. S., Management and Business, Chaffey College **Current organization:** Wingstop Restaurants, Inc. **Title:** Vice President **Type of organization:** Restaurant franchise **Major product:** Buffalo style chicken wings **Area of distribution:** National **Expertise:** Training, human resources, business development, quality control, operations, management, program design and implementation, budget forecasting **Published works:** 1 article, The Franchise Times, 2003 **Affiliations:** I.F.A. **Hob./spts.:** Ballroom and Latin dancing/performing, is an Avian Behaviorist **SIC code:** 58 **Address:** Wingstop Restaurants, Inc., 1234 Northwest Hwy., Garland, TX 75041 **E-mail:** michael@wingstop.com

FOULKES, DALE
Industry: Corporate food service **Born:** August 11, 1960, Spring Valley, New York **Univ./degree:** A.S., Business, Rockland Community College, 1992 **Current organization:** Sodexho at Covington & Burling **Title:** General Manager **Major product:** Food service **Area of distribution:** Washington, D.C. **Expertise:** Management **Hob./spts.:** Bass fishing, music **SIC code:** 59 **Address:** Sodexho at Covington & Burling, 1201 Pennsylvania Ave. N.W., Washington, DC 20004

FRICK, RICHARD DEAN
Industry: Automotive **Born:** May 23, 1940, Tucson, Arizona **Univ./degree:** B.S., Transportation and Public Utility, University of Arizona, 1962 **Current organization:** American Honda Motor Co., Inc. **Title:** Manger, Automobile Logistics **Type of organization:** Distributor **Major product:** Automobiles, motorcycles, power equipment **Area of distribution:** International **Expertise:** Logistics, transportation of automobiles globally; speaking tours (18 years) **Hob./spts.:** Golf **SIC code:** 55 **Address:** American Honda Motor Co., Inc., 1919 Torrance Blvd., MS 100-3W-5D, Torrance, CA 90501-2746 **E-mail:** richard_frick@ahm.honda.com

FRIEL, JOSEPH C.
Industry: Hotel/casino **Univ./degree:** A.A., Hotel/Restaurant Management, Brooklyn New York Tech **Current organization:** Beau Rivage Resort & Casino **Title:** Executive Chef **Type of organization:** Hotel/casino **Major product:** Food service/lodging/casino **Area of distribution:** Biloxi, Mississippi **Expertise:** Large food production **Published works:** Newspaper articles, TV appearances **Affiliations:** New York Chefs' Association **SIC code:** 58 **Address:** Beau Rivage Resort & Casino, 875 Beach Blvd., Biloxi, MS 39530 **E-mail:** jfriel@beaurivage.com

FROIO, TONI
Industry: Restaurant **Born:** May 5, 1940, Chiaravalle Centrale, Italy **Current organization:** I Cavallini **Title:** Executive Chef **Type of organization:** Restaurant **Major product:** Fine Italian cuisine **Area of distribution:** New Jersey **Expertise:** Modern Italian, homemade pasta and desserts **Hob./spts.:** Travel **SIC code:** 58 **Address:** 26 Crooked Stick Rd., Jackson, NJ 08527

GALLAGHER, THOMAS J.
Industry: Pharmacy **Born:** January 19, 1976, Philadelphia, Pennsylvania **Univ./degree:** B.Pharm., Ferris University **Current organization:** Kmart Pharmacy **Title:** Pharmacist **Type of organization:** Retail **Major product:** Prescription and OTC medication **Area of distribution:** National **Expertise:** Counseling **Hob./spts.:** Drawing, golf, reading **SIC code:** 59 **Address:** Kmart Pharmacy, 1145 N. Belsay Rd., Burton, MI 48509 **E-mail:** gallagher.23@msn.com

GARDNER, LARRY D.
Industry: Toys **Born:** September 15, 1954 **Current organization:** Toys "R" Us, International Division **Title:** Vice President, International Division **Type of organization:** Retail **Major product:** Children's toys, electronics, baby products **Area of distribution:** International **Expertise:** Operations, franchising **Hob./spts.:** Vintage automobile racing **SIC code:** 59 **Address:** Toys "R" Us, International Division, 1 Geoffrey Way, Wayne, NJ 07470 **E-mail:** gardnerl@toysrus.com

GARRETT, DAVE L.
Industry: Automotive **Title:** Sales Manager **Type of organization:** Retail **Major product:** NAPA auto parts **Expertise:** Sales **SIC code:** 55 **Address:** Girard Auto Supply, 716 W. Walnut, Girard, KS 66743 **E-mail:** napa_dave55@hotmail.com

GAYLE, CHRIS
Industry: Food **Born:** May 1, 1975, Snyder, Texas **Univ./degree:** B.S., Food & Beverage Management, New England Culinary Institute, 2001 **Current organization:** Pallino Pastaria **Title:** Restaurant General Manager **Type of organization:** Restaurant **Major product:** Casual dining **Area of distribution:** Washington **Expertise:** Management/operations **Hob./spts.:** Golfing, outdoor tennis **SIC code:** 58 **Address:** 12221 100th Ave. N.E., #101, Kirkland, WA 98034 **E-mail:** chrisgayle3@aol.com

GIANNINI, ROSSANO
Industry: Food **Born:** November 4, 1959, Italy **Univ./degree:** B.A., 1979; Master of Culinary Arts, Italy, 1981 **Current organization:** Lanterna Tuscan Bistro **Title:** Executive Chef/Owner **Type of organization:** Restaurant **Major product:** Food service **Area of distribution:** National **Expertise:** Culinary arts; Publisher, Cucinarte Magazine **Affiliations:** A.C.F.; F.I.C., Italy; President, Federation of Italian Chefs of America **Hob./spts.:** Tennis, chess, soccer **SIC code:** 58 **Address:** Lanterna Tuscan Bistro, 3 S. Broadway, Nyack, NY 10960 **E-mail:** rossano@lanternausa.com **Web address:** www.lanternausa.com

GIESE, ROBERT L.
Industry: Automotive **Born:** September 15, 1943, California **Current organization:** Toyota Racing Development **Title:** Manager **Type of organization:** Distributing **Major product:** Automotive performance parts **Area of distribution:** National **Expertise:** Product development **Honors/awards:** Race Car featured on 3 magazine covers **Published works:** Numerous magazine articles **Hob./spts.:** Motorcycle riding, skeet shooting, waterskiing, wakeboarding **SIC code:** 55 **Address:** Toyota Racing Development, 1382 Valencia Ave., Tustin, CA 92780 **E-mail:** bob_giese@toyota.com

GILLMAN, PETER MICHAEL
Industry: Food/restaurant **Born:** August 8, 1964, Grenock, Scotland **Univ./degree:** B.A., Education, Toledo University, 1988 **Current organization:** Gillman Enterprises, Inc. **Title:** President **Type of organization:** Restaurant **Major product:** Food and beverage **Area of distribution:** Humacao, Puerto Rico **Expertise:** Food and beverage **Affiliations:** N.B.A. **Hob./spts.:** Tennis **SIC code:** 58 **Address:** Gillman Enterprises, Inc., 295 Palmas Inn Way, Box 248, Humacao, PR 00791 **E-mail:** mango@caribe.net

GONZALEZ LANDIN, JAVIER
Industry: Networks/security/software **Born:** December 3, 1972, Mexico City, Mexico **Univ./degree:** B.S., La Salle University, 1997 **Current organization:** Cyber-Systems **Title:** President **Type of organization:** Retail **Major product:** Networks/security/software **Area of distribution:** Puerto Rico **Expertise:** Cybernetic engineering, consulting

Published works: 1 book **Hob./spts.:** Family, reading, science, artificial intelligence, cycling, water sports and rappelling **SIC code:** 59 **Address:** Cyber-Systems, P.O. Box 192023, San Juan, PR 00919-2023 **E-mail:** jlandin@mexico.com

GREEN, LYNN C.
Industry: Healthcare apparel **Born:** Baltimore, Maryland; Maiden name: Passen **Children:** Tami Hines, Jill Green, Michelle Green-Carrillo, Richard Green, Ryan Green **Current organization:** Mind Body & Spirit Oncology Apparel (the only "Complete" Oncology Apparel store in the state of Nevada)/ Mind Body & Spirit Foundation **Title:** President/CEO **Type of organization:** Apparel/ Nonprofit **Major product:** Apparel for cancer patients/ Nonprofit that deals with cancer, but also working to put Sports and Music Education back into the school system as it is very important for the students to participate in these activities **Area of distribution:** Nevada **Expertise:** Marketing **Affiliations:** Sits on Board of Directors for Helping Hands of Vegas Valley; Bridges Counseling; Women's Chamber of Commerce **Career accomplishments:** American Cancer Society Advocate, Breast Cancer Coalition of Nevada-Legislative Chair, National Breast Cancer Coalition-Team Leader and Advocate, Sits on Business Advisory Board for a Congressional Committee in D.C. as an Honorary Co-Chairman for the State of Nevada, received National Business Woman of the Year Award from Congress from the State of Nevada, received Woman of the Year Award from the American Biographical Institute, on Honor Roll in D.C. and a Gold Medal Award from Congress **Hob./spts.:** Music, the arts, bowling, tennis, learning to play golf **SIC code:** 56 **Address:** Mind Body & Spirit Foundation, 9165 W. Desert Inn Rd., Bldg. N207, Las Vegas, NV 89117 **Phone:** (702)591-0492 **Fax:** (702)731-6388 **E-mail:** reds_89117@yahoo.com

HALL, HEIDEMARIE
Industry: Consumer goods **Born:** September 11, 1958, Oldenburg, Germany **Univ./degree:** B.A., Nursing, Weber State University, 1992 **Current organization:** Maternal Instincts **Title:** President, RN, BSN, IBCLC, CMF Certifications **Type of organization:** Retail **Major product:** Breast pumps sales and rentals, bras **Area of distribution:** National **Expertise:** Lactation **Honors/awards:** Member, Nu Nu Chapter of Sigma Theta Tau International Honor Society of Nursing, 1992; Member, Phi Kappa Phi, 1989; National Deans List 1986; Honor Member of Regents of the Nightingale Society **Hob./spts.:** Horseback riding **SIC code:** 59 **Address:** Maternal Instincts, 676 E. Union Sq., Sandy, UT 84070 **E-mail:** heidi@themomshop.com **Web address:** www.themomshop.com

HAMBLIN, DALE P.
Industry: Food **Born:** March 17, 1949, Plymouth, Massachusetts **Current organization:** Desert Subway **Title:** Manager **Type of organization:** Restaurant/retail **Major product:** Sandwiches, salads and wraps **Area of distribution:** Sedona, Arizona **Expertise:** Food preparation and distribution **SIC code:** 58 **Address:** 50 Cruz Cr., Cottonwood, AZ 86326 **Web address:** www.desertsubway.com

HAMPTON, MARK A.
Industry: Food **Univ./degree:** M.S., Business, Columbus University, 2000 **Current organization:** VICORP Restaurants, Inc. **Title:** V.P., Purchasing & Distribution **Type of organization:** Restaurant company **Major product:** Food, family dining **Area of distribution:** National **Expertise:** Negotiations **Affiliations:** Treasurer and Board Member, Food Services and Procurement, I.S.M. **Hob./spts.:** Game-sport fishing, sailing **SIC code:** 58 **Address:** VICORP Restaurants, Inc., 400 W. 48th Ave., Denver, CO 80216 **E-mail:** mark.hampton@vicorpinc.com

HARPER, CHRIS
Industry: Automotive **Born:** April 24, 1967, Goldsboro, North Carolina **Current organization:** Cox Chrysler, Jeep, Dodge **Title:** Business Manager **Type of organization:** Auto dealership **Major product:** Auto sales **Area of distribution:** North Carolina **Expertise:** Financial services **Affiliations:** B.M.A. **Hob./spts.:** Hiking, nature, wildlife advocate **SIC code:** 55 **Address:** 2132 Beekman Place, Wilson, NC 27896 **E-mail:** c_crazybear@yahoo.com

HARVELL, DONA MARIE
Industry: Convenience store **Born:** May 6, 1950, Dallas, Texas **Univ./degree:** B.S., Mathematics, University of Texas at Arlington, 1992 **Current organization:** 7-11 Inc. **Title:** Gasoline Pricing Analyst **Type of organization:** Retailer **Major product:** Food, merchandise, gasoline **Area of distribution:** Northeastern U.S. **Expertise:** Analyzing, strategizing, pricing **Hob./spts.:** Horse racing, family genealogy, needlecraft, reading, gardening **SIC code:** 54 **Address:** 7-11 Inc., 2711 N. Haskell Ave., Dallas, TX 75204 **E-mail:** dharve01@7-11.com

HEARNS, ELDENE L.
Industry: Flooring **Born:** December 18, 1931, Detroit, Michigan **Current organization:** Great Lakes Carpet & Tile Inc. **Title:** CEO **Type of organization:** Retail **Major product:** Floor coverings **Area of distribution:** Lady Lake, Florida **Expertise:** Tile, carpet **Affiliations:** Alpha Phi **Hob./spts.:** Scrapbooking, painting china **SIC code:** 57 **Address:** Great Lakes Carpet & Tile Inc., 13553 US 441, Lady Lake, FL 32159 **E-mail:** verniegoblue@hotmail.com **Web address:** www.greatlakescarpet.com

HEATH, DAVID J.
Industry: Automotive **Born:** May 16, 1954, Meadville, Pennsylvania **Univ./degree:** B.S., Eastern Michigan, 1980; M.S., California State, Long Beach, 1984 **Current organization:** American Honda Motor Co. **Title:** Senior Manager Sales Communication **Type of organization:** Distributors **Major product:** Honda and Acura automobiles **Area of distribution:** National **Expertise:** Sales and marketing **Affiliations:** S.A.E.; A.S.T.D. **Hob./spts.:** Sailing, boats, cars, youth activities **SIC code:** 55 **Address:** American Honda Motor Co., 1919 Torrance Blvd., Torrance, CA 90501 **E-mail:** david_heath@ahm.honda.com

HECK, RHONDA J.
Industry: Food **Born:** May 9, 1954, Reading, Pennsylvania **Univ./degree:** B.A., Psychology, Kutztown University, Pennsylvania, 1977 **Current organization:** Silver Creek Country Club **Title:** General Manager/Function Coordinator **Type of organization:** Banquet facility, golf course **Major product:** Banquet services, catering **Area of distribution:** Allentown, Pennsylvania **Expertise:** Food service, catering, functions **Affiliations:** C.O.C., Allentown **Hob./spts.:** Golf, fishing, theatre, music, football **SIC code:** 58 **Address:** Masters at Shepherd Hills, 1160 S. Krocks Rd., Wescosville-Allentown, PA 18106 **E-mail:** golfclub51@aol.com

HENKEL, MARK R.
Industry: Restaurant **Born:** June 14, 1969, Denison, Iowa **Current organization:** Hy-Vee Food Stores **Title:** Manager **Type of organization:** Restaurant **Major product:** Restaurant catering **Area of distribution:** National **Expertise:** Food and entertainment **Hob./spts.:** Volunteer firefighter. Music, darts **SIC code:** 58 **Address:** Hy-Vee Food Stores, 1426 Broadway, Denison, IA 51442 **E-mail:** henkel@schallertel.net

HERRERA, VICTOR E.
Industry: Furniture **Born:** July 8, 1955, Arequipa, Peru **Current organization:** Family Furniture **Title:** Store Manager **Type of organization:** Retailer **Major product:** Home furnishings **Area of distribution:** Rockville, Maryland **Expertise:** General management and operations **Hob./spts.:** Community volunteering **SIC code:** 57 **Address:** 14105 Park Vale Rd., Rockville, MD 20853

HOFFMAN, RONALD J.
Industry: Recreational vehicles **Born:** October 18, 1950, Northville, Michigan **Univ./degree:** M.A., Business, Scarsdale University, 2004 **Current organization:** RV CITY, Inc. **Title:** President **Type of organization:** Dealership **Major product:** Recreational vehicles **Area of distribution:** National **Expertise:** RV sales, finance **Affiliations:** Huachuca Chamber of Commerce; Better Business Bureau **Hob./spts.:** Movies **SIC code:** 55 **Address:** RV CITY, Inc., 2095 N. Hwy. 90, Huachuca, AZ 85616 **E-mail:** ron@rvcity.net **Web address:** www.rvcity.net

HOLMES, MARLON U.
Industry: Automotive **Born:** March 24, 1969, Lexington, North Carolina **Univ./degree:** B.S., Mass Communications, East Tennessee State University, 1991 **Current organization:** Plaza Ford Lincoln Mercury **Title:** Financial Services Manager **Type of organization:** Retail **Major product:** Motor vehicles **Area of distribution:** Lexington, North Carolina **Expertise:** Financial services, appraisals **Hob./spts.:** Golf **SIC code:** 55 **Address:** Plaza Ford Lincoln Mercury, 98 New Hwy. 64 West, Lexington, NC 27295 **E-mail:** tkmholmes@lexcominc.net

HOLTHUES, MISTY D.
Industry: Telecommunications **Born:** May 2, 1975, Thermopolis, Wyoming **Univ./degree:** B.S., Accounting and Financial Management, University of Wyoming **Current organization:** Extreme Integration **Title:** Controller **Type of organization:** Retailer **Major product:** Converged networks: voice/video/data **Area of distribution:** National **Expertise:** Accounting **Affiliations:** A.M.A. **Hob./spts.:** Scrap booking, continuing education, movies **SIC code:** 59 **Address:** Extreme Integration, 668 N. 44th St., Suite 236, Phoenix, AZ 85008 **E-mail:** mholthues@extremintegration.net **Web address:** www.extremintegration.net

HORVATINOVICH JR., JOHN S.
Industry: Food **Born:** May 1, 1979, Hastings, Michigan **Univ./degree:** A.A., Colorado Institute of Art; Culinary School of Arts, 1998 **Current organization:** Carrabba's Italian Grill **Title:** Proprietor **Type of organization:** Restaurant **Major product:** Food and beverage **Area of distribution:** Omaha, Nebraska **Affiliations:** Omaha Chamber of Commerce **Hob./spts.:** Basketball, football, restaurant magazines **SIC code:** 58 **Address:** Carrabba's Italian Grill, 14520 W. Maple Rd., Omaha, NE 68116 **E-mail:** omaha@carrabbas.com

HU, TONY
Industry: Restaurant **Born:** August 25, 1967, Sze Chuan, China **Univ./degree:** M.A., Culinary Institute, Sze Chuan, China, 1989 **Current organization:** Lao Sze Chuan,

Inc., (Also located at 1520 West Taylor St., Chicago, IL and 500 E. Ogden Ave., Wesemont, IL,) **Title:** President **Type of organization:** Chinese restaurant **Major product:** Traditional and very popular Chinese food **Area of distribution:** Chicago **Expertise:** Traditional and popular Chinese dishes from China **Honors/awards:** American Hall of Fame, 2002; Write-ups in the Chicago Tribune regarding his restaurants and many television interviews **Published works:** Recipes, China Star Newspaper; Cooking show, Channel 13 **Hob./spts.:** All sports **SIC code:** 58 **Address:** Lao Sze Chuan, Inc., 2172 S. Archer Ave., Chicago, IL 60616 **E-mail:** tonygourmet@yahoo.com

HUNSICKER, TEENA
Industry: Healthcare **Title:** Manager **Type of organization:** Medical equipment supplier **Major product:** Medical equipment/supplies **Expertise:** Mastectomy fitter **SIC code:** 59 **Address:** Nazareth Medical Equipment, 19 S. Broad St., Nazareth, PA 18064 **E-mail:** nazmed@ptd.net

HUTCHISON, LOYAL D.
Industry: Pharmacies **Univ./degree:** B.S., Pharmacy, University of Pacific School of Pharmacy, 1966 **Current organization:** Hutchison Pharmacies, Inc., d/b/a Fifth Street Pharmacy **Title:** Pharmacist/President **Type of organization:** Retail pharmacy **Major product:** Prescriptions **Area of distribution:** California **Expertise:** Patient consultation, prescriptions **Affiliations:** Fellow, American College of Apothecaries; American Pharmaceutical Association; California Pharmaceutical Association; National Community Pharmacists Association; Pacific Pharmacy Alumni Association **Hob./spts.:** Gardening, backpacking **SIC code:** 59 **Address:** Hutchison Pharmacies, Inc., d/b/a Fifth Street Pharmacy, P.O. Box 1737, Stockton, CA 95201 **E-mail:** fstpharm@sbcglobal.net **Web address:** www.mygnp.com

HUTTON, CHRISTOPHER
Industry: Automotive **Born:** September 29, 1968, Auburn, Indiana **Current organization:** United Auto Group **Title:** General Manager **Type of organization:** Retail sales, service and parts **Major product:** New Toyota vehicles, used and pre-owned **Area of distribution:** National **Expertise:** Operations, management; Dealership Management Certification **Hob./spts.:** Artist - pastels and airbrush, basketball **SIC code:** 55 **Address:** United Auto Group, 1765 S. Telegraph Rd., Bloomfield Hills, MI 48302 **E-mail:** chutton@unitedauto.com

IGLESIAS, MERCY
Industry: Food **Born:** January 19, 1963, Miami, Florida **Univ./degree:** A.A., Business, Miami Dade Community College, 1984 **Current organization:** The Capital Grille **Title:** Sales and Marketing **Type of organization:** Restaurant **Major product:** Food and beverage **Area of distribution:** Miami, Florida **Expertise:** Public relations **Affiliations:** Chamber of Commerce; Downtown Development Authority **Hob./spts.:** Reading, dancing, attending her kid's baseball games **SIC code:** 58 **Address:** The Capital Grille, 444 Brickell Ave., Miami, FL 33131

IRWIN, MARK L.
Industry: Office equipment **Born:** March 22, 1964, San Jose, California **Univ./degree:** A.S., Computer Information Systems, Phillips University, 1995 **Current organization:** Rabbit Office Automation **Title:** Vice President **Type of organization:** Retail **Major product:** Networked office products **Area of distribution:** National **Expertise:** Engineering, overseeing technology with internal operations **Published works:** Photographs published in newspapers **Affiliations:** Copier Dealers Association **Hob./spts.:** Kayaking, photography, fly-fishing **SIC code:** 59 **Address:** Rabbit Office Automation, 904 Weddell Ct., Sunnyvale, CA 94089 **E-mail:** marki@rabbitoa.com **Web address:** www.rabbitoa.com

JACKSON, DOUG
Industry: Food **Born:** June 18, 1978, Hickory, North Carolina **Univ./degree:** A.S., Hotel/Restaurant Management, St. Mary's College, Minnesota **Current organization:** Pizza Hut-Daland Corp. **Title:** General Manager **Type of organization:** Restaurant **Major product:** Food and beverage **Area of distribution:** Dahlonega, Georgia **Expertise:** Management **Hob./spts.:** Kayaking, home improvements **SIC code:** 58 **Address:** Pizza Hut-Daland Corp., 63 J Mountain Dr., P.O. Box 426, Dahlonega, GA 30533 **E-mail:** dj1919@hotmail.com

JACOBS, TODD E.
Industry: Food **Born:** September 8, 1963, Franklin Square, New York **Univ./degree:** Diploma, The French Culinary Institute, 1986; Muhlenberg College for Natural Sciences **Current organization:** Tierra Mar Restaurant, Atlantica Catering **Title:** CEO & Executive Chef **Type of organization:** Ballroom restaurant and catering **Major product:** French cuisine **Area of distribution:** New York **Expertise:** Management **Honors/awards:** DiRona Award, American Hotel, Sag Harbor **Published works:** Catering menus **Affiliations:** Board of Directors, Peconic Bay Keeper; Slow Food; Northeastern Organic Farmers Association **Hob./spts.:** Surfing, cooking, hiking **SIC code:** 58 **Address:** Tierra Mar Restaurant, Atlantica Catering, 231 Dune Rd., Westhampton Beach, NY 11978 **E-mail:** todd@tierramar.com **Web address:** www.ontheatlantic.con

JAKUBOVIC, VALDET
Industry: Food and hospitality **Born:** December 5, 1960, Bosnia **Univ./degree:** Culinary Academy, Yugoslavia, 1982 **Current organization:** Hotel Mariani's Inn & Restaurant **Title:** Certified Executive Chef **Type of organization:** Hotel **Major product:** Fine meals, hospitality **Area of distribution:** International kitchen **Expertise:** International cooking; Certified, A.C.F.; Certified, Food Protection Management **Honors/awards:** Hilton Priority One Certification **Published works:** 1 book, "National Ice Carving" **Hob./spts.:** Playing piano and guitar **SIC code:** 58 **Address:** Hotel Mariani's Inn & Restaurant, 2500 El Camino Real, Santa Clara, CA 95051 **Web address:** ww.marianis.com

JELINEK, FLORENCE L.
Industry: Food **Born:** March 21, 1921, Sidney, Nebraska **Current organization:** Dude's Steak House/The Brandin Iron Bar & Lounge, Inc. **Title:** President **Type of organization:** Restaurant & Lounge **Major product:** "Family owned" food and beverage service **Area of distribution:** Sidney, Nebraska **Expertise:** Restauranteur **Honors/awards:** Business Hall of Fame **Hob./spts.:** Reading, travel, grandchildren **SIC code:** 58 **Address:** Dude's Steak House/The Brandin Iron Bar & Lounge, Inc., 2124-2130 Illinois St., Sidney, NE 69162

JINNAH, KHALIL K.
Industry: Wireless communications **Born:** July 21, 1970, Pakistan **Univ./degree:** B.B.A., University of Houston, Texas, 1996 **Current organization:** Prime Communications **Title:** Vice President of Operations **Type of organization:** Retailer **Major product:** Wireless cell phones **Area of distribution:** Texas **Expertise:** Management, information systems, purchasing, distribution **Affiliations:** A.I.C.P. **Hob./spts.:** Volunteering, community/faith services **SIC code:** 59 **Address:** Prime Communications, 12705 S. Kirkwood Dr., #215, Stafford, TX 77477 **E-mail:** kjinnah@primecomms.com **Web address:** www.primecomms.com

JOHNSON, J. KEN
Industry: Pharmacy **Born:** October 2, 1958, San Jose, California **Univ./degree:** B.S., Pharmacy, Oregon State University, 1994; Pre-Med course, Zoology, Brigham Young University, 1994 **Current organization:** Jacksonville Pharmacy, LLC **Title:** Founder/Owner **Type of organization:** Pharmacy **Major product:** Pharmaceuticals and healthcare products **Area of distribution:** Jacksonville, Oregon **Expertise:** Administration/management **Honors/awards:** Golden Key Honor Society, Brigham Young University **Affiliations:** Former Military Intelligence Morse Code Interceptor, U.S. Army; President, Church of Jesus Christ of Latter Day Saints; National Community Pharmaceutical Association; Oregon State Pharmaceutical Association; Rotary Club, Jacksonville **Hob./spts.:** Family, riding quads **SIC code:** 59 **Address:** Jacksonville Pharmacy, LLC, 725 N. 5th St., Suite 100, Jacksonville, OR 97530 **E-mail:** jkenRPh@jacksonvillepharmacy.com **Web address:** www.jacksonvillepharmacy.com

KAIB, TODD L.
Industry: Bicycles **Born:** April 13, 1965, Pittsburgh, Pennsylvania **Univ./degree:** B.B.A., Kennesaw State University, 1993 **Current organization:** Roswell Bicycles, Inc. **Title:** President **Type of organization:** Retail **Major product:** Bicycles **Area of distribution:** Georgia **Expertise:** Operations, management, sales; retail; Advocate for bike lanes, greenways, trail systems **Honors/awards:** 2006 National Geographic Adventure's Top Retailer Award; Bicycle Retailer and Industry News Top 100 Retailer Award, 1999-2006; 2006 League of American Wheelmen Bike Friendly City Award; past competitive cyclist and Georgia State Road Champion, 1983; On the cover of Independent Business Magazine, May/June 1995 **Affiliations:** National Geographic Adventure's Retail Advisory Board; Board Member, City of Roswell Traffic Advisory Board; Board Member, Bike Roswell; Board Member National Bicycle Dealers Association **Hob./spts.:** Bicycling, collecting and restoring 50's and 60's muscle cars **SIC code:** 59 **Address:** Roswell Bicycles, Inc., 670 Houze Way, Roswell, GA 30076 **E-mail:** rbi@charter.net **Web address:** www.roswellbicycles.com

KANOUJIA, ALKA
Industry: Food **Born:** August 25, 1965, Delhi, India **Univ./degree:** B.A., English, University of Delhi - Maranda House, 1981 **Current organization:** India House Restaurant **Title:** Manager **Type of organization:** Restaurant **Major product:** Food and beverage **Area of distribution:** Northampton, Massachusetts **Expertise:** Customer services, hospitality, cooking **Hob./spts.:** Cooking lessons, listening to music **SIC code:** 58 **Address:** India House Restaurant, 45 State St., Northampton, MA 01060 **Web address:** www.indiahousenorthhampton.com

KARSOK, ALBERT J.
Industry: Golf club/food **Born:** May 13, 1961, Abilene, Texas **Univ./degree:** B.S., Finance, University of Nevada at Reno, 1985 **Current organization:** Loeb Enterprises, Red Hawk Golf Club **Title:** Director of Food & Beverage **Type of organization:** Golf club/restaurant **Major product:** Golf, food **Area of distribution:** Nevada **Expertise:** Restaurant management **Published works:** Articles in Nevada Gazette **Hob./spts.:** Golf, snow skiing, water skiing, trout fishing **SIC code:** 58 **Address:** Loeb Enterprises,

Red Hawk Golf Club, 6590 N. Wingfield Pkwy., Sparks, NV 89436 **E-mail:** akarsok@wingfieldsprings.com

KATHMAN, MARK R
Industry: Food service **Born:** June 9, 1976, Cincinnati, Ohio **Univ./degree:** B.A., Communications, University of Cincinnati, 2000 **Current organization:** Sodexho c/o The Cincinnati Zoo **Title:** General Manager of Food Service **Type of organization:** Corporate food service at the zoo **Major product:** High volume concessions/catering **Area of distribution:** National **Expertise:** Management, purchasing, inventory, shipping **Affiliations:** LaSalle Business Association **Hob./spts.:** Physical fitness, running, basketball **SIC code:** 58 **Address:** Sodexho c/o The Cincinnati Zoo, 3400 Vine St., Cincinnati, OH 45220 **E-mail:** mark.kathman@cincinnatizoo.org **Web address:** www.cincinnatizoo.org

KATZ, MINDY S.
Industry: Direct sales **Current organization:** Princess House **Title:** Director of Product Development & Merchandising **Type of organization:** Direct sales **Major product:** Home goods **Area of distribution:** International **Expertise:** Marketing and product development, international merchandising **Affiliations:** D.S.A. **SIC code:** 57 **Address:** Princess House, 198 Laurel Ave., Providence, RI 02906 **E-mail:** mskat22@aol.com

KHARTAMI, KHALID
Industry: Food **Born:** January 29, 1968, Casablanca, Morocco **Univ./degree:** B.S., Linguistics, Hassan University, Morocco, 1991 **Current organization:** Ben Inc. **Title:** Owner **Type of organization:** Restaurant business and investments **Major product:** Food **Area of distribution:** Washington, D.C. **Expertise:** Management **Hob./spts.:** Reading, travel **SIC code:** 58 **Address:** Ben Inc., 1714 Connecticut Ave. N.W., Washington, DC 20009

KING, RONALD R.
Industry: Communications **Born:** July 18, 1944, Tacoma Washington **Univ./degree:** B.A., Washington State University, 1967 **Current organization:** New Northwest Broadcasters **Title:** National Sales Director **Type of organization:** Radio station **Major product:** Radio broadcasting **Area of distribution:** National **Expertise:** radio sales **Hob./spts.:** Golf **SIC code:** 59 **Address:** New Northwest Broadcasters, 320 Stanley Blvd., Yakima, WA 98902 **E-mail:** radiogolfr@aol.com

KING, THERESA A.
Industry: Food/beverage **Born:** Prince Frederick, Maryland **Univ./degree:** M.S., Computer Science, University of Maryland **Current organization:** Beach Cove Restaurant & Lounge **Title:** Co-Owner **Type of organization:** Restaurant & lounge **Major product:** Fresh steaks and seafood **Area of distribution:** Calvert County/Anne Arundel County, Maryland **Expertise:** Management/system integration **Honors/awards:** Communicator Award, 1996; Telly Award, 1996 **Affiliations:** Restaurant Association **Hob./spts.:** Diving, boating **SIC code:** 58 **Address:** Beach Cove Restaurant & Lounge, 8416 Bayside Rd., Box 835, Chesapeake Beach, MD 20732 **E-mail:** taking10@earthlink.net

KRANITZ, MORT K.
Industry: Automotive **Born:** February 10, 1926, St. Joseph, Missouri **Current organization:** Kranitz Automotive Group, Inc. **Title:** President **Type of organization:** Automotive dealer **Major product:** Retail, wholesale, cars and trucks **Area of distribution:** Tucson, Arizona **Expertise:** Pricing, financing, leasing, knowledge **Honors/awards:** Lifetime Achievement Award, American Cancer Society, 2006 **Affiliations:** American Cancer Society; Founder, Tucson Celebrity Tennis Classics **Hob./spts.:** Tennis **SIC code:** 55 **Address:** Kranitz Automotive Group, Inc., 5726 E. 22nd St., Tucson, AZ 85711 **E-mail:** kranitzautomotiv@qwest.net

KURAHASHI, YOSHIJI
Industry: Semiconductors **Born:** January 26, 1939, Toyota, Japan **Univ./degree:** M.S., Electrical Engineering and Computer Science, University of California, Berkeley **Current organization:** Design Center, ROHM Electronics USA **Title:** President **Type of organization:** Retail **Major product:** Design and development services, semiconductors **Area of distribution:** National **Expertise:** Engineering, management **Affiliations:** I.E.E.E.; N.T.A. **Hob./spts.:** Golf, teaching English **SIC code:** 59 **Address:** Design Center, ROHM Electronics USA, 10145 Pacific Heights Blvd., Suite 1000, San Diego, CA 92121 **E-mail:** yoshi_k@rohm.com

LABROSCIANO, ANTHONY F.
Industry: Food **Born:** February 26, 1971, White Plains, New York **Current organization:** Firehouse Deli **Title:** President **Type of organization:** Deli **Major product:** Food **Area of distribution:** Connecticut **Expertise:** Deli and catering, management **Hob./spts.:** Golf, basketball **SIC code:** 58 **Address:** Firehouse Deli, 265 Mill St., Byram, CT 06830 **E-mail:** anthonyfirehouse@aol.com **Web address:** www.firehsedeli.com

LACEY, EDWARD PATRICK
Industry: Auto **Born:** March 17, 1956, Flint, Michigan **Univ./degree:** A.A., Business Management, Northwood University, 1977 **Current organization:** Gateway Ford **Title:** Owner/LLC **Type of organization:** Auto retail **Major product:** Ford cars and trucks service/parts **Area of distribution:** Michigan **Expertise:** Marketing **Published works:** Published column, write-ups **Affiliations:** Member, Board of Directors, Templin Lake Property Owners' Association **Hob./spts.:** Family, golf, Harley Davidson motorcycles **SIC code:** 55 **Address:** Gateway Ford, 70135 S. Centerville, Sturgis, MI 49091 **E-mail:** eplacey17@netscape.net

LACONA, BERNADETTE J.
Industry: Food **Born:** August 6, 1958, Des Moines, Iowa **Univ./degree:** M.S., Law, Drake University, 1982 **Current organization:** Noah's Ark Restaurant **Title:** Owner/Secretary/Treasurer **Type of organization:** Restaurant **Major product:** Italian food **Area of distribution:** Des Moines, Iowa **Expertise:** Culinary arts **Affiliations:** Cooking Club of America; Wine Club of America **Hob./spts.:** Stock market **SIC code:** 58 **Address:** Noah's Ark Restaurant, 2400 Ingersoll Ave., Des Moines, IA 50312 **E-mail:** einrebel1@msn.com

LAM, JANNY
Industry: Food/restaurant **Univ./degree:** IHMES International Hotel School **Current organization:** Chengdu Chinese Restaurant **Title:** Manager/Owner **Type of organization:** Restaurant **Major product:** Chinese food/take out **Area of distribution:** West Hartford, Connecticut **Expertise:** Culinary arts **Hob./spts.:** Travel; actively involved in housing development and renovations in the Norwich, Connecticut area **SIC code:** 58 **Address:** 179 Park Rd., West Hartford, CT 06107

LAMENSDORF, LOUISE D.
Industry: Food **Born:** January 16, 1937, Louisiana **Univ./degree:** B.S., Business Administration, Tulane University, 1960; CCP, 1988 **Current organization:** Bistro Louise Restaurant **Title:** Executive Chef/Owner **Type of organization:** Restaurant **Major product:** French food **Area of distribution:** Fort Worth, Texas **Expertise:** Chef, management **Honors/awards:** Zagat Award **Affiliations:** International Association of Culinary Professionals **Hob./spts.:** Music, opera, travel, skiing **SIC code:** 58 **Address:** Bistro Louise Restaurant, 2900 S. Hulen, Suite 40, Ft. Worth, TX 76109 **E-mail:** bistrolouise@hotmail.com

LANDRUM, ROGER
Industry: Glass **Born:** April 30, 1967, Oak Ridge, Tennessee **Current organization:** Cool Shades Window Tinting & Auto Accessories **Title:** President **Type of organization:** Commercial and residential glass sales and service **Major product:** Window tinting **Area of distribution:** Livingston, Texas **Expertise:** Glass tinting **Hob./spts.:** Fishing, hunting **SIC code:** 52 **Address:** Cool Shades Window Tinting & Auto Accessories, 840 W. Church St., Livingston, TX 77351

LANO, CHRISTOPHER T.
Industry: Food **Born:** October 31, 1976, Manhasset, New York **Univ./degree:** B.A., Culinary Arts, The New York Restaurant School, 1995 **Current organization:** Tre Scalini Restaurant **Title:** Co-Owner, Executive Chef **Type of organization:** Restaurant **Major product:** Food **Area of distribution:** Long Island, New York **Expertise:** Culinary arts **Honors/awards:** Named "Best New Italian Restaurant" by Best of Long Island Restaurants Magazine; Review from Joan Reminick, Newsday, "Great Restaurants of Long Island" **Hob./spts.:** Golf, charity work **SIC code:** 58 **Address:** Tre Scalini Restaurant, 1870 E. Jericho Tpke., Huntington, NY 11743 **E-mail:** chef1031@aol.com

LAROW, JOY I.
Industry: Jewelry **Born:** April 23, 1938, Stanmore, Middlesex, England **Univ./degree:** Attendedn St. Martins College of Art and Design, England **Current organization:** Whistle Stop Gift Shop **Title:** Owner **Type of organization:** Retail **Major product:** Gifts, fine jewelry **Area of distribution:** Bradenton - Sarasota, Florida **Expertise:** Sales **Hob./spts.:** Tennis **SIC code:** 59 **Address:** Whistle Stop Gift Shop, 3234 East Bay Dr., Holmes Beach, FL 34217

LAWRENCE, KERRY J.
Industry: Food **Born:** January 17, 1974, New Orleans, Louisiana **Univ./degree:** B.S., Business, University of New Orleans, 1993 **Current organization:** Chartwells School Dining **Title:** Director of Dining Services **Type of organization:** Professional food contract service **Major product:** Food service management **Area of distribution:** International **Expertise:** District Manager/Coordinator **Hob./spts.:** Boating, fishing, hunting **SIC code:** 58 **Address:** Chartwells School Dining, 160 St. Peters St., Biloxi, MS 39530 **E-mail:** kerry.lawrence@exch.compass_usa.com

LEANARDI, JOHN MICHAEL
Industry: Automotive **Born:** June 18, 1954, Chicago, Illinois **Univ./degree:** B.S., Psychology, University of Illinois, 1974 **Current organization:** Patrick Auto Group **Title:** General Manager **Type of organization:** Automotive dealership **Major product:** New

car sales **Area of distribution:** Illinois **Expertise:** Marketing, management **Hob./spts.:** Boating **SIC code:** 55 **Address:** Patrick Auto Group, 526 Mall Dr., Schaumburg, IL 60173

LEE, BOON
Industry: Restaurant **Current organization:** Hunan Legend Restaurant **Title:** Manager **Type of organization:** Restaurant/retail **Major product:** Food service **Expertise:** Customer service **SIC code:** 58 **Address:** Leeha Enterprise (Hunan Legend Restaurant), 4725 Dorsey Hall Dr., Suite D, Ellicott City, MD 21042 **Web address:** www.hunanlegend.com

LEE, TAMMIE
Industry: Restaurant **Born:** November, 11, 1958, Taiping, Malaysia **Current organization:** Leeha Enterprise (Hunan Legend Restaurant) **Title:** Manager **Type of organization:** Restaurant/retail **Major product:** Food service **Area of distribution:** Ellicott City, Maryland **Expertise:** Customer service **Affiliations:** Chamber of Commerce **SIC code:** 58 **Address:** Leeha Enterprise (Hunan Legend Restaurant), 4725 Dorsey Hall Dr., Suite D, Ellicott City, MD 21042 **E-mail:** jennifer6621@aol.com **Web address:** www.hunanlegend.com

LESCAULT, ALICE W.
Industry: Clothing **Born:** January 22, 1955, Glenridge, New Jersey **Univ./degree:** B.A., Music Education, Virginia Commonwealth University, 1976 **Current organization:** Bear Hugs, Inc. **Title:** President **Type of organization:** Retailer/manufacturing **Major product:** Uniforms / scrubs **Area of distribution:** Virginia **Expertise:** Human resources **Honors/awards:** Senior Professional Human Resources, notary public **Affiliations:** SHRM; EMA; Hampton Roads Chamber of Commerce; Arthritis Foundation; member, Notary Law Institute; member, American Sewing Guild **Hob./spts.:** Watching football, counter cross-stitch needlework, reading **SIC code:** 56 **Address:** Bear Hugs, Inc., 2232 Virginia Beach Blvd., Suite 101, Virginia Beach, VA 23454 **E-mail:** nothyme@msn.com

LIAO, CHUN (SLY) H.
Industry: Hospitality **Born:** January 15, 1964, Calcutta, India **Univ./degree:** B.A., Accounting, Saint Xavier College, 1984 **Current organization:** Sequoia (Ark Restaurant Corp.) **Title:** Regional Director **Type of organization:** Restaurant **Major product:** Food service **Area of distribution:** National **Expertise:** Menu planning, execution, concept **Hob./spts.:** Motorcycling, painting **SIC code:** 58 **Address:** Sequoia (Ark Restaurant Corp.), 3000 K St., Washington, DC 20007 **E-mail:** slyliao@aol.com **Web address:** www.arkrestaurant.com

LISTER, DAVID WAYNE
Industry: Food **Current organization:** Fausto's Chicken and Seafood Restaurant **Title:** Manager **Type of organization:** Restaurant **Major product:** Fried chicken and seafood **Area of distribution:** Center, Texas **Expertise:** Cajun cooking Texas style **Affiliations:** N.H.S.; T.H.H.S. **SIC code:** 58 **Address:** Fausto's Chicken and Seafood Restaurant, 714 Shelbyville St., Center, TX 75935

LOCICERO, DUKE E.
Industry: Food **Born:** March 21, 1961, New Orleans, Louisiana **Current organization:** Café Giovanni **Title:** Executive Chef and Manager **Type of organization:** Restaurant **Major product:** Food **Area of distribution:** New Orleans, Louisiana **Expertise:** Management **Honors/awards:** Chef of the Year Award, presented by ACF, 1999; Under 40 Major Young Business Leaders; Chef of the Year Award, presented by American Tasting Institute, 2000 **Published works:** 100 recipes **Affiliations:** A.C.F.; A.C.A.; Founder and President, U.D.A.; C.E.O., Chef Duke's Foundation **Hob./spts.:** Family **SIC code:** 58 **Address:** Café Giovanni, 117 Decatur Rue, New Orleans, LA 70130 **Web address:** www.digforum.com; www.chefduke.com; www.cafegiovan

LOGSDON, MARY VAIL
Industry: Piano **Born:** February 26, 1949, Madison, Wisconsin **Univ./degree:** B.S., With Honors, Music Education and instrumental Music, Indiana State University, 1971 **Current organization:** Henderson Music Co., Inc. **Title:** Manager, Lexington Location **Type of organization:** Retail **Major product:** Yamaha, acoustic and digital pianos **Area of distribution:** Kentucky **Expertise:** Sales management; marketing to universities and churches; piano presentations **Honors/awards:** Yamaha's Touchtone Award for Outstanding Sales Performance, 1998 through 2006 **Affiliations:** National Federation of Music Teachers **SIC code:** 57 **Address:** Henderson Music Co., Inc., 1301 Winchester Rd., Suite 255, Lexington, KY 40505 **E-mail:** mpoppins50@yahoo.com **Web address:** www.hendersonmusic.com

LOPERGOLO, VALENTINO
Industry: Construction **Born:** October 18, 1966, Miglionico, Italy **Current organization:** Masterpiece Tile & Marble Corp. **Title:** President **Type of organization:** Retail **Major product:** Marble, mosaic, ceramic tile **Area of distribution:** New Rochelle, New York **Expertise:** Installation and design **Affiliations:** C.T.N.A.; New Rochelle Chamber of Commerce; New Rochelle Better Business Bureau **Hob./spts.:** Bicycling, soccer **SIC code:** 52 **Address:** Masterpiece Tile & Marble Corp., 255 Main St., New Rochelle, NY 10801 **E-mail:** v.lopergolo@att.net

LUNDY, BRENDA M.
Industry: Windows **Born:** May 10, 1956, Boise, Idaho **Current organization:** Kinro **Title:** Human Resources/Safety Chairman **Type of organization:** Manufacturing **Major product:** Vinyl windows **Area of distribution:** National **Expertise:** Accounting, public relations, human resources, safety, shipping/receiving **Affiliations:** Former Member, Women in Business; Women in Construction; Teamsters Union **Hob./spts.:** Water skiing, camping, softball **SIC code:** 52 **Address:** Kinro, 944 No. Kings Rd., Nampa, ID 83687 **E-mail:** blundy@kinro.net **Web address:** www.kinro.net

LYNN, SUSAN G.
Industry: Consumer goods **Born:** August 3, 1954, Philadelphia, Pennsylvania **Univ./degree:** B.A., Villanova University, 1976 **Current organization:** What a Girl Wants & a guy needs **Title:** President/Owner **Type of organization:** Boutique shop **Major product:** Fine chocolate, gifts, designer clothing for men and women **Area of distribution:** Philadelphia, Pennsylvania **Expertise:** Marketing **Affiliations:** M.A.B.A.; M.A.F.F.; S.B.N.; E.M.A.N.; W.M.A.N. **SIC code:** 53 **Address:** What a Girl Wants & a guy needs, 7125 Germantown Ave., Philadelphia, PA 19119 **E-mail:** inmtairy@hotmail.com **Web address:** www.inmtairy.com

MACKIN, ROBERT L.
Industry: Fire/safety **Current organization:** Paladin Corp. **Title:** President/Owner **Type of organization:** Retail **Major product:** Fire extinguishers **Expertise:** Sales **SIC code:** 59 **Address:** Paladin Corporation, 800 W. Sixth St., Lorain, OH 44052

MADERO, HERNANDO
Industry: Food **Born:** June 18, 1939, Norman, Oklahoma **Univ./degree:** M.S., Operations Research, Georgetown University, 1964 **Current organization:** Bistro Du Vin **Title:** President **Type of organization:** Restaurant **Major product:** Food service **Area of distribution:** Virginia **Expertise:** Finance, operations **Hob./spts.:** Wine collecting **SIC code:** 58 **Address:** Bistro Du Vin/Le Relais Restaurant, 1025 - I Seneca Rd., Great Falls, VA 22066 **E-mail:** lerelaisrest@aol.com

MANGRUM, RICKEY E.
Industry: Furniture **Born:** September 16, 1959, Franklin, Tennessee **Univ./degree:** Bachelor of Business Administration, Middle Tennessee State University, 1981 **Current organization:** Sprintz Furniture Showroom Inc. **Title:** Controller **Type of organization:** Retailer **Major product:** Middle and high end furniture **Area of distribution:** Tennessee **Expertise:** Accounting; CPA **Hob./spts.:** Photography, hiking, boating, cycling **SIC code:** 57 **Address:** Sprintz Furniture Showroom Inc., 6205 Cockrill Bend Circle, Nashville, TN 37209 **E-mail:** rmangrum@sprintz.com

MCCABE, SANDRA
Industry: Equipment/tool rentals **Current organization:** McCabe Brothers Inc. **Title:** President/Co-owner **Type of organization:** Retail **Major product:** Full service tool rental **Area of distribution:** Within 75 mile radius of Champaign, Illinois **Expertise:** Executive management, finance **Affiliations:** American Rental Association; National Federation of Independent Businesses; Chamber of Commerce; U.S. Chamber of Commerce; Cornbelt Rental Association; A.R.A. of Illinois **Hob./spts.:** Family, bowling **SIC code:** 52 **Address:** McCabe Brothers Inc., P.O. Box 562, Champaign, IL 61824 **E-mail:** sandramccabe@netzero.net **Web address:** www.mcequiprental.com

MCMAHON, PACHARIN "TOY"
Industry: Fishing supplies **Born:** June 27, 1957, Bangkok, Thailand **Univ./degree:** B.A., 1981; M.A., 1983, Business Administration, University of Portland **Current organization:** The Guide Shop **Title:** General Manager **Type of organization:** Shop/Restaurant **Major product:** Bait and tackle, G Loomis rods, reels, gear, clothing, gifts **Area of distribution:** Tillamook, Oregon **Expertise:** Management of shop and restaurant, training **Hob./spts.:** Tennis, soccer **SIC code:** 59 **Address:** The Guide Shop, 12140 Wilson River Hwy., Tillamook, OR 97141 **E-mail:** guide@pacifier.com **Web address:** www.guideshop.com

MCNEELY, WAYNE E.
Industry: Consumer goods **Born:** Douglas, Nebraska **Univ./degree:** M.S., Petroleum Engineering, Colorado School of Mines, 1951 **Current organization:** Yellowstone General Stores **Title:** Store Manager **Type of organization:** Retail **Major product:** Food, souvenirs, personal service **Area of distribution:** Yellowstone Park, Wyoming **Expertise:** Personnel management **Affiliations:** Society of Petroleum Engineers; American Petroleum Institute **Hob./spts.:** Coin collecting, travel **SIC code:** 53 **Address:** Yellowstone General Stores, Old Faithful Upper Store YGS 301, Yellowstone, WY 82190 **E-mail:** waynemcn@aol.com

MIANO, EDWARD J.
Industry: Restaurants/hospitality **Current organization:** Cafe Ponte **Title:** General Manager **Type of organization:** Restaurant/retail **Major product:** Fine continental

dining, lunch and dinner **Area of distribution:** Clearwater, Florida **Expertise:** Management, operations, service **SIC code:** 58 **Address:** Cafe Ponte, 13505 Icot Blvd., #214, Clearwater, FL 33760 **E-mail:** cafeponte@verizon.net

MINETOS, JERRY
Industry: Food **Born:** February 24, 1958, Greece **Univ./degree:** Master Chef, 1972 **Current organization:** Robola Restaurant, Inc. **Title:** Chef/Manager **Type of organization:** Restaurant **Major product:** Food **Area of distribution:** New York **Expertise:** Culinary arts, management **Hob./spts.:** Scuba diving **SIC code:** 58 **Address:** 2 Vernon Place, 4C, Yonkers, NY 10704

MITCHELL, NANCE
Industry: Cosmetic consultation **Univ./degree:** B.S., Chemistry; M.S., Art History **Current organization:** Nance Mitchell Co., Inc. **Title:** President/Founder **Type of organization:** Retailer **Major product:** Skin care **Area of distribution:** International **Expertise:** Marketing, lecturing, writing **Published works:** 1 book, "Skin Sense" **Hob./spts.:** Reading, needlepoint, skiing, walking **SIC code:** 59 **Address:** Nance Mitchell Co., Inc., P.O. Box 5335, Beverly Hills, CA 90209 **E-mail:** nance@nancemitchell.com **Web address:** www.nancemitchell.com

MOSER, ELMO H.
Industry: Restaurant **Born:** November 9, 1932, Switzerland **Univ./degree:** Culinary School, Switzerland **Current organization:** Sovereign Restaurant **Title:** Owner/Executive Chef **Type of organization:** Restaurant/banquet facility **Major product:** French continental food/wines **Area of distribution:** Gainesville, Florida **Expertise:** Culinary arts **Hob./spts.:** Harley riding **SIC code:** 58 **Address:** Sovereign Restaurant, 12 S.E. 2nd Avenue, Gainesville, FL 32601

NEIDLINGER, BILLIE JO
Industry: Entertainment **Born:** October 11, 1965, Anchorage, Alaska **Current organization:** The Garden of Eden **Title:** Director of Special Events **Type of organization:** Nightclub **Major product:** Special events venue; catering; entertainment; hosts Oscar, Emmy and Grammy after-award parties **Area of distribution:** National **Expertise:** Sales, marketing **Published works:** Worked with Tony Robbins and Deepak Chopra **Affiliations:** Meeting Professionals International; Executive Board, Children's Inc.; Hollywood Chamber of Commerce; International Special Events Society **Hob./spts.:** Tennis, physical fitness **SIC code:** 58 **Address:** The Garden of Eden, 7080 Hollywood Blvd., Suite 307, Hollywood, CA 90028 **E-mail:** billiejo@gardenofedenla.com **Web address:** www.gardenofedenla.com

NETZNIK, ERIC J.
Industry: Home improvement **Born:** April 2, 1955, Springfield, Illinois **Univ./degree:** A.S., Technical Engineering, Lincoln Technical School **Current organization:** Lowe's Home Improvement, Inc. **Title:** Customer Service Associate of Electrical Department **Type of organization:** Retail/manufacturing **Major product:** Home improvement goods and services **Area of distribution:** Indiana **Expertise:** Engineering, marketing, tool and die making **Affiliations:** Hoosier Environmental Council **Hob./spts.:** Playing guitar **SIC code:** 52 **Address:** Lowe's Home Improvement, Inc., 8801 E. 25th St., Indianapolis, IN 46229 **Web address:** www.lowes.com

NUCCIO, MICHAEL J.
Industry: Food **Born:** July 22, 1971, Chicago, Illinois **Current organization:** Jamba Juice **Title:** General Manager **Type of organization:** Retail **Major product:** Food service, blended beverages **Area of distribution:** Illinois **Expertise:** Restaurant management, personal development **Hob./spts.:** Baseball, motorcycles, martial arts **SIC code:** 58 **Address:** Jamba Juice, 1468 Oxford St., Carol Stream, IL 60188 **E-mail:** mnuccio@jambajuice.com **Web address:** www.jambajuice.com

ORTIZ, JAIME
Industry: Automotive **Born:** November 16, 1949, Colombia **Current organization:** La Fiesta Auto Sales **Title:** Manager **Type of organization:** Car dealership **Major product:** Car sales **Area of distribution:** Houston, Texas **Expertise:** Customer service **Hob./spts.:** Cars, soccer, tennis **SIC code:** 55 **Address:** 1210 El Camino Village Dr., #3701, Houston, TX 77058 **E-mail:** ccortiz@hotmail.com

OTTE, DONNA JEAN
Industry: Food **Born:** November 11, 1955, Lincoln, Nebraska **Current organization:** DJ's Bar & Grill **Title:** Owner **Type of organization:** Restaurant/bar **Major product:** Fine American and Mexican cuisine, wine and spirits **Area of distribution:** Staplehurst, Nebraska **Expertise:** Business management and culinary arts **Hob./spts.:** Family, grandchildren, walking, art **SIC code:** 58 **Address:** DJ's Bar & Grill, 330 A. St., P.O. Box 194, Staplehurst, NE 68439

PALMER, TED D.
Industry: Logistics-retail **Born:** June 2, 1963, Campton, Kentucky **Univ./degree:** B.S., Engineering, University of Cincinnati, 1982 **Current organization:** Federated Dept. Stores **Title:** V.P. **Type of organization:** Retailer **Major product:** Home furnishings **Area of distribution:** National **Expertise:** Distribution and operations **Published works:** Furniture Today; Tampa Tribute; Dayton Herald **Hob./spts.:** Weightlifting, tennis **SIC code:** 57 **Address:** Federated Dept. Stores, 7100 N.W. 32nd Ave., Miami, FL 33023 **E-mail:** tpalmer@fds.com

PECKHAM, TONY D.
Industry: Automotive **Born:** May 24, 1967, Dallas, Texas **Current organization:** Aable Used Cars **Title:** Sales **Type of organization:** Used car dealership **Major product:** Car sales and service **Area of distribution:** Colorado **Expertise:** Sales management **Honors/awards:** GM Award of Excellence, Top 500 in Sales **Hob./spts.:** Building cars **SIC code:** 55 **Address:** Aable Used Cars, 2014 Edmonds St., Brush, CO 80723 **E-mail:** tpeckhm@aol.com

PESUSICH, SIMON I.
Industry: Food **Born:** October 8, 1946, Croatia, Yugoslavia **Current organization:** Main Street Ventures **Title:** Executive Corporate Chef **Type of organization:** Restaurant **Major product:** Service and food **Area of distribution:** National **Expertise:** Cuisine, all phases of establishing and managing restaurants **Affiliations:** N.R.A.; M.R.A. **Hob./spts.:** Golf, reading **SIC code:** 58 **Address:** Main Street Ventures, 605 S. Main, Suite 2, Ann Arbor, MI 48104 **E-mail:** spesusich@mventures.net

PETTY, RICHARD A.
Industry: Restaurant **Born:** June 28, 1954, Detroit, Michigan **Univ./degree:** A.A., California Culinary Academy, San Francisco, 1994 **Current organization:** Reign Restaurant **Title:** Executive Chef **Type of organization:** Restaurant **Major product:** Food **Area of distribution:** Beverly Hills, California **Expertise:** Contemporary southern cuisine, French/African/Asian cuisine **Affiliations:** James Baird Foundation; Chef de Cuisine of Los Angeles **Hob./spts.:** Chess, cycling **SIC code:** 58 **Address:** Reign Restaurant, 180 N. Robertson Blvd., Beverly Hills, CA 90211 **E-mail:** okragr@packbell.net

PHIPPS, WILLIAM R.
Industry: Footwear **Born:** January 18, 1950, Butler, Pennsylvania **Univ./degree:** B.S., Business Administration, Montreat College, North Carolina, 1996 **Current organization:** Rackroom Shoes, Inc. **Title:** DC Planning & Logistics Manager **Type of organization:** Retail **Major product:** Footwear **Area of distribution:** International **Expertise:** Logistics, inbound merchandise, internal software **Affiliations:** American Management Association **SIC code:** 56 **Address:** Rackroom Shoes, Inc., 8310 Technology Dr., Charlotte, NC 28262 **E-mail:** rphipps@rackroom.com

PLATA, ALEX A.
Industry: Food service **Born:** April 7, 1969, Puerto Rico **Univ./degree:** Attended California Culinary Institute **Current organization:** Circa 21 Playhouse **Title:** Executive Chef **Type of organization:** Dinner playhouse **Major product:** Food, entertainment, comedy **Area of distribution:** Rock Island, Illinois **Expertise:** Executive gourmet cooking **Published works:** Write ups **SIC code:** 58 **Address:** Circa 21 Playhouse, 1828 Third Ave., Rock Island, IL 61201

POWERS, ROBIN K.
Industry: Construction **Born:** April 3, 1963, Manassas, Virginia **Current organization:** Ritchie's Millwork **Title:** Manager **Type of organization:** Retail **Major product:** Custom mouldings **Area of distribution:** Midland, Virginia **Expertise:** Business management **Hob./spts.:** Cake decorating **SIC code:** 52 **Address:** Ritchie's Millwork, 10305 Oakridge Lane, Midland, VA 22728 **E-mail:** richieslumber@aol.com

PRENTICE, MATTHEW
Industry: Food **Univ./degree:** Attended Culinary Institute of America **Current organization:** Matt Prentice Restaurant Group **Title:** C.E.O. **Type of organization:** Restaurant/retail **Major product:** Multi-unit food concepts, catering **Area of distribution:** Bingham Farms, Michigan **Expertise:** Culinary arts, supervising and organizing rescue mission for children's charity **Affiliations:** Board of Directors, Variety, the Children's Charity **Hob./spts.:** Skiing, golf **SIC code:** 58 **Address:** Matt Prentice Restaurant Group, 30100 Telegraph St., #251, Bingham Farms, MI 48025 **E-mail:** mattp@mattprenticerg.com **Web address:** www.mattprenticerg.com

PROKOS, ERNEST O.
Industry: Food **Born:** June 21, 1942, Athens, Greece **Univ./degree:** Diploma, Culinary School, France; Attended Cordon Blue School, Paris **Current organization:** Bayou Grill **Title:** Owner/Chef **Type of organization:** Restaurant **Major product:** Cajun and Mediterranean food **Area of distribution:** Belleville, Michigan **Expertise:** Chef/management; Certified Executive Chef, Certified Food and Beverage Executive **Honors/awards:** 9 Gold Medals for Culinary Jr. Olympics; Grand Prize Winner, Kraft Foods Nationwide Recipe Contest, 1976 & 1977; Awarded 7 Gold Medals at the Indianapolis Culinary Arts Show for his displays, 1980; Grand Prize Winner, Kentucky Chefs deCuisine Contest, 1981; Honored as one of America's Outstanding Chefs by Chefs in America, The National Registry, 1988; has also won numerous awards for his ice-food carvings and sculptures **Published works:** Multiple articles **Affiliations:**

A.C.F.; F.B.E.A.; Member, Chefs Association of the Pacific Coast **Hob./spts.:** Chess, karate **SIC code:** 58 **Address:** Bayou Grill, 404 Main St., Belleville, MI 48111-2648 **E-mail:** bayougrill@sbcglobal.net

PROPHETER-CAMPER, WILLENA E.
Industry: Stoves **Born:** August 9, 1941, Jamestown, New York **Current organization:** Cornerstone Stoves & Accessories **Title:** Owner **Type of organization:** Retail **Major product:** Coal, wood, gas, electric stoves **Area of distribution:** Falconer, New York **Expertise:** Sales, marketing **Affiliations:** National Small Business Foundation; Falconer, New York Better Business Bureau **Hob./spts.:** Birds **SIC code:** 57 **Address:** Cornerstone Stoves & Accessories, 1555 Rte. 394, Falconer, NY 14733 **E-mail:** pelletqueen@alltel.net **Web address:** www.cornerstonesandaccessories.com

RAVAL, JEFF-MARTIN C.
Industry: Food **Born:** January 15, 1974, Jamaica, New York **Univ./degree:** B.S., Mechanical Engineering, University of Houston **Current organization:** Brinker International/Chili's **Title:** Manager **Type of organization:** Corporate restaurant chain **Major product:** Food service **Area of distribution:** National **Expertise:** Management, marketing, service **Hob./spts.:** Sports, billiards, gaming (casino) **SIC code:** 58 **Address:** Brinker International/Chili's, 10101 S. Post Oak, Houston, TX 77091 **E-mail:** eggroll-raval@sbc.net **Web address:** www.chili's.com

REIGER, DANIEL H.
Industry: Fine dining **Born:** December 26, 1950, Cleveland, Ohio **Univ./degree:** Business Administration, Cleveland State University, 1978 **Current organization:** Sammy's Metropolitan Ballroom/Restaurant **Title:** General Manager **Type of organization:** Restaurant **Major product:** Food and beverage **Area of distribution:** Cleveland, Ohio **Expertise:** Catering to fine dining patrons **Honors/awards:** Employee of the Month; Catholic War Veterans Americanism Award **SIC code:** 58 **Address:** Sammy's Metropolitan Ballroom/Restaurant, 925 Euclid Ave., Suite 2100, Cleveland, OH 44115 **E-mail:** dannyr@sammys.com

RHODES, BENJAMIN
Industry: Food **Born:** June 21, 1968, Wilmington, Ohio **Univ./degree:** A.A., Snead State College **Current organization:** Avado Brands/Don Pablo's Mexican Kitchen **Title:** Assistant General Manager **Type of organization:** Restaurant **Major product:** Mexican food **Area of distribution:** National **Expertise:** Training **Affiliations:** C.H.A.R.T. **Hob./spts.:** Tennis **SIC code:** 58 **Address:** Avado Brands/Don Pablo's Mexican Kitchen, 705 Kemper Commons Circle, Springdale, OH 45246 **E-mail:** benjaminrhodes2003@yahoo.com

RICHARDSON, CARL W.
Industry: Automotive **Born:** November 26, 1937, Ontario, Canada **Univ./degree:** A.S., Industrial Management, Fanshawe College, 1968 **Current organization:** Kenmar Corp. **Title:** Quality Consultant **Type of organization:** Manufacturer's representative for automotive suppliers **Major product:** Consulting, sales, marketing **Area of distribution:** International **Expertise:** Marketing, engineering, consulting - Quality Management System; Certified Lead Auditor, 1509001:2000 by International Register of Certified Auditors; Assisted organizations in obtaining registration to 1509001; 18014001; ISO 1TS16949 and OHSAS 18001 **Affiliations:** A.S.Q.C. **Hob./spts.:** Golf **SIC code:** 55 **Address:** Kenmar Corp., 17515 W. 9 Mile Rd., Southfield, MI 48075

ROTMAN, DAVID J.
Industry: Hospitality **Univ./degree:** B.S., Communications/Sociology, Texas Christian University **Current organization:** Cafe Aspen Inc. **Title:** Owner/General Manager **Type of organization:** Restaurant/bar **Major product:** Food, beverage, catering **Area of distribution:** Fort Worth, Texas **Expertise:** Management **Affiliations:** Texas Restaurant Association; Big Brothers Big Sisters; YMCA **Hob./spts.:** Weight training, motorcycling, boating **SIC code:** 58 **Address:** Cafe Aspen Inc., 6103 Camp Bowie Blvd., Ft. Worth, TX 76116

RUTTER, ALAN D.
Industry: Restaurant **Born:** July 22, 1958, Pottsville, Pennsylvania **Univ./degree:** A.A., Culinary Arts, Culinary Institute of America **Current organization:** Chef Alan's American Bistro **Title:** President **Type of organization:** Restaurant **Major product:** Food and liquor **Area of distribution:** Reading, Pennsylvania **Expertise:** Chef **Affiliations:** Restaurant Association **Hob./spts.:** Politics, skiing, stock investments **SIC code:** 58 **Address:** Chef Alan's American Bistro, 3050 N. Fifth St. Hwy, Reading, PA 19605 **E-mail:** arrr39@aol.com **Web address:** www.cheflans.com

SAGERT, DUANE
Industry: Fire and safety **Current organization:** Romco Fire & Safety **Title:** President **Type of organization:** Retail **Major product:** Fire extinguishers **Expertise:** Office sales **SIC code:** 59 **Address:** Romco Fire & Safety, 800 West Sixth St., Lorain, OH 44052

SAITO, MADAME
Industry: Food **Born:** January 24, 1950, Kobe, Japan **Univ./degree:** B.A., Domestic Sciences, Tokyo University, 1975 **Current organization:** Le Champignon de Tokio Restaurant **Title:** Owner **Type of organization:** Restaurant/retail **Major product:** Japanese cuisine **Area of distribution:** Philadelphia, Pennsylvania **Expertise:** Sushi Instructor **Affiliations:** Japanese-American Society **Hob./spts.:** Dancing, sushi making **SIC code:** 58 **Address:** Le Champignon de Tokio Restaurant, 122-124 Lombard St., Philadelphia, PA 19147 **Web address:** www.lechampignon-tokio.com

SALOUS, MIKE S.
Industry: Food **Born:** February 1, 1969, Kuwait **Univ./degree:** Business Management, Midwestern State University, 1991 **Current organization:** IHOP Restaurant **Title:** Franchisee **Type of organization:** Restaurant **Major product:** Family Dining **Area of distribution:** Oklahoma **Expertise:** Management **Affiliations:** National Restaurant Association **Hob./spts.:** Soccer **SIC code:** 58 **Address:** IHOP Restaurant, 5929 N. May Ave., Suite 204, Oklahoma City, OK 73112 **E-mail:** msal30@yahoo.com

SCALA JR., GERARDO
Industry: Restaurant **Born:** December 7, 1970, Springfield, Massachusetts **Current organization:** Caffeine's Downtown, Art-é-pasta, Shadow Lounge **Title:** President/Owner **Type of organization:** Restaurant/lounge **Major product:** Various foods **Area of distribution:** Springfield, Massachusetts **Expertise:** Concept development, marketing, management **Affiliations:** N.R.A.; M.A.R.A. **Hob./spts.:** Golf, Formula One Auto Racing **SIC code:** 58 **Address:** Caffeine's Downtown, 254 Worthington St., Suite 207, Springfield, MA 01103 **E-mail:** gscalajr@aol.com **Web address:** www.caffeinesdowntown.com

SCHILLINGER, JEAN YVES
Industry: Restaurant **Born:** March 23, 1963, Colmar, France **Current organization:** Olica Restaurant **Title:** Co-Owner **Type of organization:** Restaurant **Major product:** Food, beverage **Area of distribution:** New York, New York **Expertise:** Chef **Hob./spts.:** Golf, skiing **SIC code:** 58 **Address:** Olica Restaurant, 145 E. 50th St., New York, NY 10022

SCHLEICHER, CORY
Industry: Food **Born:** October 30, 1969, Portsmouth, Virginia **Univ./degree:** B.S., Culinary Arts, Newberry Culinary College, 1994 **Current organization:** Port O' Call Restaurant & Saloon **Title:** Executive Chef **Type of organization:** Restaurant **Major product:** Food service **Area of distribution:** North Carolina **Expertise:** Sautiér **Affiliations:** A.C.I. **Hob./spts.:** Swimming, diving, cooking **SIC code:** 58 **Address:** Port O' Call Restaurant & Saloon, 504 S. Virginia Dare Trail, Kill Devil Hills, NC 27948 **E-mail:** caschef@earthlink.com **Web address:** www.pockitchen.agnet.com

SCORDO, MICHELE A.
Industry: Food **Born:** August 12, 1963, New York **Univ./degree:** A.S., Restaurant and Hotel Management, Nassau Community College, 1983 **Current organization:** Gebhardt's Restaurant **Title:** Manager **Type of organization:** Restaurant **Major product:** Food and beverage **Area of distribution:** New York **Expertise:** Management **Published works:** local papers **SIC code:** 58 **Address:** Gebhardt's Restaurant, 230 Jericho Tpke., Floral Park, NY 11040

SCOTT, MARK
Industry: Food **Born:** May 1, 1968, Newark, New Jersey **Current organization:** The Copper Bottom Restaurant **Title:** Owner/President **Type of organization:** Restaurant/retail **Major product:** Contemporary Conitental Cuisine **Area of distribution:** Florida, New York **Expertise:** Management, service **Honors/awards:** Gold Record Award (RIAA Certified); Ampex Golden Reel Award; Best Concert Tour '91, Metal Edge Magazine; NAJE Special Citation for Outstanding Musicianship; **Published works:** 2 major label recording releases - MCA Records: "Trixter" and "Hear"; 1 independent recording release - Backstreet Records: "Undercovers" **Affiliations:** Former Drummer, Rock Band "Trixter"; International Association of Amusement Parks and Attractions; American Bus Association; National Tour Association; N.J. Recreation and Park Association; N,Y, State Recreation and Park Society; Westchester County Chamber of Commerce; Greater Paramus Chamber of Commerce; New Rochelle Chamber of Commerce; Rockland Business Association; Co-chair, RBA's Hospitality and Tourism Alliance **Hob./spts.:** Time with family **SIC code:** 58 **Address:** The Copper Bottom Restaurant, 162 North Main St., Florida, NY 10921 **E-mail:** info@thecopperbottom.com **Web address:** www.thecopperbottom.com

SEDIGH, BEHROUZ
Industry: Food **Univ./degree:** M.S., Business Management, University of Tehran, Iran, 1978 **Current organization:** BSD Bar & Grill **Title:** President **Type of organization:** Restaurant **Major product:** Food (Italian continental cuisine), beverages **Area of distribution:** Manhattan Beach, California **Expertise:** Marketing **Affiliations:** H.M.A.; N.C.A. **SIC code:** 58 **Address:** BSD Bar & Grill, 1019 Manhattan Beach Blvd., Manhattan Beach, CA 90266 **E-mail:** behrouzsedigh@aol.com

SHEEN, ED C.
Industry: Construction materials **Born:** October 9, 1942, Kearney, Nebraska **Univ./degree:** B.Ed., University of Nebraska at Kearney, 1966 **Current organization:** Minden Lumber & Concrete **Title:** Manager/Owner **Type of organization:** Retail home center **Major product:** Lumber, hardware, ready mix **Area of distribution:** Minden, Nebraska **Expertise:** Administration, service **Affiliations:** Ready Mix and Nebraska Lumber Dealers Association **Hob./spts.:** Motorcycles, building street riders, gardening **SIC code:** 52 **Address:** Minden Lumber & Concrete, 247 N. Colorado Ave., Minden, NE 68959 **E-mail:** mlc2157@yahoo.com

SHOBOLA, KENNETH O.
Industry: Pharmacy **Univ./degree:** M.S., Pharmacy, University of Sunderland, 1985 **Current organization:** Ken Drugs, Inc. **Title:** President **Type of organization:** Pharmacy **Major product:** Pharmaceuticals, prescription and OTC drugs **Area of distribution:** Tampa, Florida **Expertise:** Management, daily operations **Affiliations:** American Pharmacy Association; Florida Board of Pharmacy; Florida Pharmacy Association **SIC code:** 59 **Address:** Ken Drugs, Inc., 4730 N. Habana Ave., Suite 101, Tampa, FL 33614

SHORT, TRENT
Industry: Automotive **Title:** General Sales Manager **Type of organization:** Retail **Major product:** Automotive sales **Expertise:** Management **SIC code:** 55 **Address:** Tim Short Chrysler, 270 Fitzgilbert Rd., Hazard, KY 41701 **E-mail:** trent2224@yahoo.com

SINGH, NONA
Industry: Food **Born:** May 4, 1981, India **Univ./degree:** B.A., American River College, 2005 **Current organization:** Carrows **Title:** Associate Manager **Type of organization:** Restaurant **Major product:** Food services **Area of distribution:** California **Expertise:** Management **Hob./spts.:** Surfing, driving **SIC code:** 58 **Address:** 204 San Carlos Way, Stockton, CA 95207

SIRAGUSA, GAETANO
Industry: Hospitality **Title:** Owner **Type of organization:** Restaurant **Major product:** Italian cuisine and wine **Expertise:** Management, chef **SIC code:** 58 **Address:** Gaetano Ristorante Italiano, 323 N.E. St., Grants Pass, OR 97526 **E-mail:** gaetanosiragusa@yahoo.com

SMITH, MARSHALL J.
Industry: Hospitality **Born:** February 3, 1955, Tulsa, Oklahoma **Current organization:** Hamilton House Restaurant **Title:** Executive Chef, Manager **Type of organization:** Restaurant **Major product:** Food, beverage service **Area of distribution:** Arkansas **Expertise:** Culinary arts and management **Published works:** Articles about him **SIC code:** 58 **Address:** Hamilton House Restaurant, 130 Van Lyell Terrace, Hot Springs, AR 71913 **Web address:** www.hamiltonhouserestaurant.com

SMITH JR., B. FRANKLIN
Industry: Oil and gasoline **Born:** December 30, 1948, Welcome, North Carolina **Univ./degree:** Attended Mars Hill College (2 years) **Current organization:** Ripple Oil Co., Inc. **Title:** Vice President/Treasurer **Type of organization:** Fuel dealer/distributor (Exxon Mobil Products) **Major product:** Gas, diesel, fuel oil, kerosene **Area of distribution:** Welcome, North Carolina **Expertise:** Exxon Mobil Products, sales, general management, administration, credit manager; 6 Convenience stores and 2 service stations owned by Ripple Oil Co., Inc. **Honors/awards:** Most Outstanding Band Award; Member, Strathmore's Who's Who **Affiliations:** North Carolina Petroleum Marketers Association **Hob./spts.:** Boating, reading, movies **SIC code:** 59 **Address:** Ripple Oil Co., Inc., 6178 Old Hwy. 52, P.O. Box 59, Welcome, NC 27374 **E-mail:** RippleOilco@triadbiz.rr.com

SOUTER, JEFFREY A.
Industry: Food/hospitality **Born:** July 15, 1962, Beverly, Massachusetts **Univ./degree:** A.S., Culinary Arts, Johnson & Wales University, 1982 **Current organization:** K.A.S. Rest Corp., dba Capt'n Nicks Restaurant **Title:** President **Type of organization:** Full service restaurant **Major product:** Food and spirit **Area of distribution:** Maine **Expertise:** Chef **Affiliations:** Chamber of Commerce **Hob./spts.:** Motorcycle enthusiast, the outdoors, water sports, cooking **SIC code:** 58 **Address:** K.A.S. Rest Corp., dba Capt'n Nicks Restaurant, 724 Main St., P.O. Box 1734, Oqunquit, ME 03907 **E-mail:** captnicks@qui.net

SPENCER, WAYNE R.
Industry: Food **Born:** August 15, 1959, Paw Paw, Michigan **Univ./degree:** Lake Michigan College **Current organization:** New Green Briar Restaurant Lounge **Title:** General Manager/Partner **Type of organization:** Restaurant **Major product:** Food and beverage **Area of distribution:** Moline, Illinois **Expertise:** Management **Affiliations:** Quad City Chamber of Commerce **Hob./spts.:** Golf, NASCAR **SIC code:** 58 **Address:** New Green Briar Restaurant Lounge, 4506 27th St., Moline, IL 61265

STARRETT, MARK D.
Industry: Food **Born:** May 14, 1971, Fitchburg, Massachusetts **Univ./degree:** A.S., Culinary Arts, New England Culinary Institute, 1993 **Current organization:** Mark's Monadnock Mountain View Restaurant **Title:** Owner/Chef **Type of organization:** Restaurant **Major product:** Food, beverage **Area of distribution:** Troy, New Hampshire **Expertise:** Food preparation **Hob./spts.:** Fishing, skiing, hiking **SIC code:** 58 **Address:** Mark's Monadnock, Mountain View Restaurant, 7 Marlborough Rd., Troy, NH 03465 **E-mail:** mark@mmvrestaurant.com **Web address:** www.marksmmvrestaurant.com

STROUSE, ARNOLD
Industry: Glass **Current organization:** A. Strouse & Son Glass Inc. **Title:** President **Type of organization:** Retail **Major product:** Residential and commercial glass **Area of distribution:** Seaside, California **Expertise:** Service residential and commercial glass sales **Affiliations:** Navy League **Hob./spts.:** Skydiving **SIC code:** 52 **Address:** A. Strouse & Son Glass Inc., 1333 Fremont Blvd., Seaside, CA 93955

SUH, JI Y.
Industry: Automotive **Born:** March 26, 1952, Seoul, Korea **Univ./degree:** B.S., Biology, University of California, Los Angeles **Current organization:** Vermont Chevrolet Buick **Title:** Owner/General Manager **Type of organization:** Automobile dealership **Major product:** Automobile retail sales, service, parts **Area of distribution:** California **Expertise:** Business administration, sales, marketing **Hob./spts.:** Harley Davidson's, golf, bonsai, gardening **SIC code:** 55 **Address:** Vermont Chevrolet Buick, 444 S. Vermont Ave., Los Angeles, CA 90020 **E-mail:** jisuh@vchevy.com **Web address:** www.vchevy.com

SWANSON II, ROBERT L.
Industry: Construction **Born:** October 22, 1954, Encino, California **Current organization:** Quality Windows & Doors **Title:** Owner **Type of organization:** Retail **Major product:** Windows and doors **Area of distribution:** Van Nuys, California **Expertise:** Custom window and door installation **Affiliations:** N.C.C.; Better Business Bureau **Hob./spts.:** Hot rods, off roading **SIC code:** 52 **Address:** Quality Windows & Doors, 7824 Balboa Blvd., Van Nuys, CA 91406

TAGLIASACCHI, ACHILLE "JACK"
Industry: Food **Born:** July 13, 1930, Parma, Italy **Univ./degree:** Attended Instituto Macedonio Melloni for Business Studies **Current organization:** Il Capuccino Inc. **Title:** President/Owner **Type of organization:** Restaurant/retail **Major product:** Fine Italian cuisine **Area of distribution:** New York **Expertise:** 50 years experience in the restaurant business; financial administration and management **Honors/awards:** Culinary Award of Excellence, Suffolk County Community College, 2000 **Affiliations:** Sag Harbor Chamber of Commerce; Past President, former Vice President, East Hampton Chamber of Commerce; New York Restaurant Association **Hob./spts.:** Golf, painting, travel **SIC code:** 58 **Address:** Il Capuccino Inc., P.O. Box 1438, Sag Harbor, NY 11963 **E-mail:** ataglias@aol.com **Web address:** www.ilcapuccino.com

TAIT, DON A.
Industry: Equipment dealer **Current organization:** Robinson Equipment Co., Inc. **Title:** Sales Representative **Type of organization:** Equipment dealership **Major product:** Tractors, back hoes, forklifts, mowers **Area of distribution:** Florida **Expertise:** Sales, marketing **Affiliations:** Eagles Legion; Everglades Golf Course **Hob./spts.:** Fishing, boating, camping, travel **SIC code:** 52 **Address:** Robinson Equipment Co., Inc., P.O. Box 12, Titusville, FL 32781 **E-mail:** dtait@hotmail.com

TANG, KIMMY
Industry: Food **Born:** April 2, 1965, Ho Chi Minh City, Viet Nam **Current organization:** Michelia Restaurant **Title:** Chef **Type of organization:** Restaurant **Major product:** Food, beverage **Area of distribution:** Los Angeles, California **Expertise:** Culinary arts **Hob./spts.:** Menu preparation, planning, vendor relations **SIC code:** 58 **Address:** Michelia Restaurant, 8738 W. Third St., Los Angeles, CA 90048 **E-mail:** kimmytang@msn.com

TARSOVICH, MARGARET VIOLA
Industry: Healthcare **Born:** July 5, 1945, New York, New York **Univ./degree:** Attended City College of New York, Baruch Administration School **Current organization:** Accutone Hearing Aid Center **Title:** Board Certified Hearing Instrument Specialist **Type of organization:** Retail **Major product:** Hearing aids and A.L.D.S. **Area of distribution:** Pennsylvania **Expertise:** Hearing tests, advisement on hearing aids **Affiliations:** National Hearing Aid Society; Pennsylvania Hearing Aid Association **Hob./spts.:** Swimming, ventriloquism, gardening (flowers and vegetables) **SIC code:** 59 **Address:** Accutone Hearing Aid Center, 532 Goucher St., Johnstown, PA 15905 **E-mail:** jkraft168@aol.com

THARP, DAVID M.
Industry: Healthcare/pharmacy **Born:** November 22, 1948, Nashville, Tennessee **Univ./degree:** B.S., Pharmacy, University of Georgia, 1972 **Current organization:** CVS Drugs **Title:** Pharmacist **Type of organization:** Pharmacy **Major product:**

Pharmacy services **Area of distribution:** National **Affiliations:** Florida Pharmacy Association; A.P.H.A. **Hob./spts.:** Off-road motorcycle racing **SIC code:** 59 **Address:** 1611 Redwood Dr., Tallahassee, FL 32301-2731

THIBAULT, DANIEL
Industry: Xerox solutions **Born:** February 26, 1979, Torrington, Connecticut **Current organization:** WorkCenter, Inc. **Title:** Sales Manage, Xerox Division **Type of organization:** Business sales and consulting **Major product:** Xerox solutions and steel case products **Area of distribution:** Connecticut **Expertise:** Sales and consulting **Honors/awards:** VICA Award; Citizenship Award from the Connecticut State Governor **Hob./spts.:** Political debates, tennis, volleyball, golf, literature, theatre, opera **SIC code:** 59 **Address:** WorkCenter, Inc., 33 East Main St., Torrington, CT 06790 **E-mail:** dan@workcenterinc.net **Web address:** www.workcenterinc.net

THOMAS, LISA E.
Industry: Healthcare equipment **Born:** September 15, 1965, Birmingham, Alabama **Current organization:** Medsouth Inc. **Title:** Regional Manager **Type of organization:** Retail **Major product:** Home health equipment and durable medical supplies **Area of distribution:** Alabama **Expertise:** Management, billing **Affiliations:** Birmingham Lions Club **Hob./spts.:** Family activities, reading **SIC code:** 59 **Address:** Medsouth Inc., 450 Tenth Ave. South, Birmingham, AL 35205 **E-mail:** lthomas@medsouthinc.net

TOLEDO, LIZA
Industry: Clothing **Current organization:** Guess **Title:** Store Manager **Type of organization:** Retail **Major product:** Apparel **Area of distribution:** International **Expertise:** Training management **SIC code:** 56 **Address:** Guess, 7517 N. Kendall Dr., #12707, Miami, FL 33156 **E-mail:** lizatoledo@hotmail.com

TRIGG, J. TRACY
Industry: Recreation **Born:** February 15, 1921, Corydon, Kentucky **Univ./degree:** B.S., Agriculture, University of Kentucky, 1949 **Current organization:** Tracy's R.V., Inc. **Title:** President **Type of organization:** Retail and service **Major product:** Recreational vehicles **Area of distribution:** South Carolina **Expertise:** Management and sales **Hob./spts.:** Sunday school teacher, reading, travel **SIC code:** 55 **Address:** 940 Gold Hill Rd., Ft. Mill, SC 29708

TRUPO, SALVATORE A.
Industry: Food **Born:** February 11, 1966, Brooklyn, New York **Univ./degree:** A.A., Hotel and Restaurant Management, Edison Community College, 1993 **Current organization:** Applebee's (Florida Apple West) **Title:** General Manager **Type of organization:** Casual dining restaurant **Major product:** Food and beverage **Area of distribution:** Cape Coral, Florida **Expertise:** Managing employees, costs, marketing **Affiliations:** Served in U.S. Army, Communications Specialist **Hob./spts.:** Golf, soccer **SIC code:** 58 **Address:** 827 N.E. 11th Terrace, Cape Coral, FL 33909 **E-mail:** saltrupo@swfla.rr.com

TSANG, CHRISTINA YEELEE
Industry: Hospitality **Born:** China **Univ./degree:** M.Div., Beacon University **Current organization:** Christina's Empress of China **Title:** President/Owner **Type of organization:** Restaurant **Major product:** Fine oriental cuisine **Area of distribution:** Louisiana **Expertise:** Administration, management **Affiliations:** Louisiana Restaurant Association **Hob./spts.:** Ministry and missionary work **SIC code:** 58 **Address:** 24 Magnolia Trace Dr., Harvey, LA 70058

VENTURO, SHANNON L.
Industry: Restaurant **Born:** March 8, 1966, Yuma, Arizona **Univ./degree:** A.B.A., Arizona Western College **Current organization:** The Cheesecake Factory **Title:** General Manager **Type of organization:** Restaurant **Major product:** Upscale casual dining **Area of distribution:** National **Expertise:** Management **Affiliations:** A.C.F.; Kiwanis Club **Hob./spts.:** Cooking Italian food **SIC code:** 58 **Address:** The Cheesecake Factory, 4400 Ashford Dunwoody Rd., Atlanta, GA 30346 **E-mail:** slventuro@yahoo.com

VIERS, JOHN T.
Industry: Plastic valves and fittings **Born:** December 30, 1942, Cleveland, Ohio **Current organization:** VPE, Inc. **Title:** U.S. Sales and Marketing Manager **Type of organization:** Retail **Major product:** Plastic valves and fittings for swimming pools **Area of distribution:** National **Expertise:** Sales and marketing **Hob./spts.:** Golf, jogging, biking, Country Western dancing **SIC code:** 52 **Address:** VPE, Inc., 372 Saint Julian Place, North Augusta, SC 29860 **E-mail:** jtvvpeinc@aol.com

WALKER, CLAYTON D.
Industry: Restaurant/hospitality **Born:** March 3, 1969, Los Angeles, California **Univ./degree:** B.A., Brown University, 1992 **Current organization:** The Emerald Planet **Title:** Founder/CEO **Type of organization:** Restaurant/retail **Major product:** Food service, sandwiches **Area of distribution:** New York **Expertise:** Marketing **Affiliations:** National Restaurant Association **Hob./spts.:** Skiing, surfing **SIC code:** 58 **Address:** The Emerald Planet, 2 Great Jones St., New York, NY 10012 **E-mail:** eplanet@inch.com

WALL, STEVEN L.
Industry: Automotive **Born:** June 3, 1960, Mountain Lake, Minnesota **Univ./degree:** M.S., Mechanical Engineering, University of Michigan, 1994 **Current organization:** Visteon Corp. **Title:** Product Design Engineer/FE Analyst **Type of organization:** Auto supplier **Major product:** Automobile components **Area of distribution:** International **Expertise:** Finite element analysis **Published works:** Article **Hob./spts.:** Coin collecting, homebuilding, model building **SIC code:** 55 **Address:** 2101 E. Williams Circle, Westland, MI 48186 **E-mail:** swall@visteon.com

WALLACE, ERNEST P.
Industry: Fire equipment **Born:** April 2, 1941 **Current organization:** Shipman's Fire Equipment Co., Inc. **Title:** CEO, Owner **Type of organization:** Retail **Major product:** Fire protection equipment and clothing **Area of distribution:** National **Expertise:** Director of finance **Affiliations:** N.E.F.C.; N.F.P.A.; N.A.F.E.D. **Hob./spts.:** Golf **SIC code:** 59 **Address:** Shipman's Fire Equipment Co., Inc., 172 Cross Rd., Waterford, CT 06385 **E-mail:** info@shipmans.com **Web address:** www.shipmans.com

WARNER, MICHAEL D.
Industry: Food **Born:** October 15, 1948, Wichita, Kansas **Univ./degree:** Tarrant County Junior College, 1981 **Current organization:** El Fenix Corp. **Title:** Safety Coordinator **Type of organization:** Retail/restaurant **Major product:** Tex-Mex ethnic foods **Area of distribution:** Texas **Expertise:** Safety, quality **Affiliations:** American Society for Quality **Hob./spts.:** Astronomy, camping, radio-controlled modeling **SIC code:** 54 **Address:** El Fenix Corp., 11075 Harry Hines Blvd., Dallas, TX 75209 **E-mail:** mwarner1815@ont.com

WATERS, CATHERINE E.
Industry: Floor covering **Born:** January 25, 1967, Atlanta Georgia **Univ./degree:** B.A., University of Maryland, 1986 **Current organization:** Antique Heart Pine Flooring **Title:** Accounts Manager **Type of organization:** Retail **Major product:** Specialty wood sales, installation and finishing **Area of distribution:** Blythewood, South Carolina **Expertise:** Records management **Affiliations:** I.I.M.C.; M.M.C.A. **Hob./spts.:** Cooking **SIC code:** 57 **Address:** Antique Heart Pine Flooring, 424 Blythewood Rd., Blythewood, SC 29016-9517 **E-mail:** antiqueheartpine@att.net

WEAVER, LAURIE A.
Industry: Food **Born:** April 24, 1961, Slatington, Pennsylvania **Current organization:** Pizza Hut **Title:** Restaurant General Manager **Type of organization:** Restaurant **Major product:** Pizza, food **Area of distribution:** Walnutport, Pennsylvania **Expertise:** Supervising daily operations **Honors/awards:** Manager of the Year, QSM, LLC, 2004 **Hob./spts.:** Computers **SIC code:** 58 **Address:** Pizza Hut, 350 Best Ave., Walnutport, PA 18088 **E-mail:** mrslauriepizza@yahoo.com

WHEELER, MICHAEL S.
Industry: Hearing aids **Born:** February 1, 1963, Seminole, Florida **Univ./degree:** B.C.-H.I.S. **Current organization:** Audibel Hearing Aid Center **Title:** President **Type of organization:** Retail **Major product:** Digital hearing aids **Area of distribution:** Seminole, Florida **Expertise:** Audiometric testing and fitting of hearing instruments; Hearing aid science (Board Certified) **Affiliations:** N.H.A.S.; F.H.A.S. **Hob./spts.:** Motocross, physical fitness, boating **SIC code:** 59 **Address:** Audibel Hearing Aid Center, 10720 Park Blvd., Suite A, Seminole, FL 33772 **E-mail:** audibel@verizon.net

WHITTAKER, BRIAN F.
Industry: Restaurant development **Born:** April 21, 1965, Kansas City, Missouri **Univ./degree:** B.B.A., Economics, University of Missouri at Kansas City, 1989 **Current organization:** FPS Restaurant Group, LLC **Title:** Owner/CEO **Type of organization:** Development **Major product:** Restaurants **Area of distribution:** Missouri **Expertise:** Administration, marketing, business strategy **Affiliations:** Board Member, Kansas City Restaurant Association; National Restaurant Association **Hob./spts.:** Family, fishing, hunting **SIC code:** 58 **Address:** FPS Restaurant Group, L.L.C., 1235 W. 69th St., Kansas City, MO 64113 **E-mail:** dbwhitt@sbcglobal.net

WIEMERS, MIKE W.
Industry: Restaurant **Born:** November 1, 1961, Moline, Illinois **Current organization:** Huddle House Inc. **Title:** Vice President, Training **Type of organization:** Retail **Major product:** Franchised restaurants **Area of distribution:** National **Expertise:** Training **Affiliations:** I.F.A. Charter **Hob./spts.:** Hiking, boating **SIC code:** 58 **Address:** Huddle House Inc., 2969 E. Ponce de Leon Ave., Decatur, GA 30030 **E-mail:** mwiemers@huddlehouse.com **Web address:** www.huddlehouse.com

WIGGS III, WILLIAM L.
Industry: Healthcare **Born:** April 11, 1040, Pinehurst, North Carolina **Univ./degree:** B.A., History, University of North Carolina, 1961; A.A.S., Ophthalmic Dispensing, Erie Community College **Current organization:** WL Wiggs Opticians Inc. **Title:**

President/Optician **Type of organization:** Optical care, retail **Major product:** Eye care, eye wear **Area of distribution:** New York, North Carolina **Expertise:** Optical care, management **Affiliations:** National Academy of Opticianry; Rocky Point Lion's Club **Hob./spts.:** Golf, community involvement **SIC code:** 59 **Address:** WL Wiggs Opticians Inc., 125 Main St., Stony Brook, NY 11790 **E-mail:** wlwoptl@optonline.net

WILLIAMS, MARY J.
Industry: Food **Born:** August 26, 1942, Hartwell, Georgia **Current organization:** Kentucky Fried Chicken **Title:** Assistant Manager **Type of organization:** Restaurant/retail **Major product:** Food (chicken) and beverage **Area of distribution:** Georgia **Expertise:** Management **Hob./spts.:** Travel **SIC code:** 58 **Address:** Kentucky Fried Chicken, 509 S. Big A Rd., Toccoa, GA 30577 **E-mail:** pmtd2004@yahoo.com

WILSON, DOUGLAS M.
Industry: Food and service **Born:** May 21, 1947, Greenville, South Carolina **Current organization:** Thomas and King, Inc. **Title:** Partner **Type of organization:** Retailer/restaurant **Major product:** Food and service **Area of distribution:** National **Expertise:** Real estate development, specializing in the food service industries, site acquisitions, business development, finance **Affiliations:** Rotary; Greenville Country Club; Greenville First Baptist Church **Hob./spts.:** Hunting, fishing, collecting Harley Davidson's **SIC code:** 58 **Address:** Thomas and King, Inc., 164 Milestone Way, Greenville, SC 29615 **E-mail:** dwilson@tandk.com

WILSON, EUGENE A.
Industry: Restaurant/fine dining **Born:** October 17, 1965, Dublin, Ireland **Current organization:** Magee Mahon Café, Inc. **Title:** Manager **Type of organization:** Café/retail **Major product:** Food and beverage **Expertise:** Cost accounting, management; Certified, Sales Planning & Management **Hob./spts.:** Soccer **SIC code:** 58 **Address:** Magee Mahon Café, Inc., 58 W. 48th St., New York, NY 10036

WINN, JAN
Industry: Food **Born:** November 2, 1954, Springfield, Massachusetts **Univ./degree:** B.A., Western New England University, 1976 **Current organization:** Big Y Foods, Inc. **Title:** Director of HAOC/GM **Type of organization:** Retail **Major product:** Food, health and beauty care, prescriptions **Area of distribution:** Massachusetts **Expertise:** Sales, marketing **Hob./spts.:** Music, gardening, physical fitness, the beach, her dogs **SIC code:** 54 **Address:** Big Y Foods, Inc., 2145 Roosevelt Ave., Springfield, MA 01102 **E-mail:** winn@bigy.com **Web address:** www.bigy.com

WOODARD, CARL G.
Industry: Healthcare **Born:** March 15, 1950, Cullman, Alabama **Current organization:** NIKKEN **Title:** Consultant **Type of organization:** Distributor **Major product:** Alternative health products, nutritional supplements, body healing aids **Area of distribution:** International **Expertise:** Marketing **Hob./spts.:** Poetry, woodworking **SIC code:** 59 **Address:** NIKKEN, 1541 Country Rd., #702, Cullman, AL 35058 **E-mail:** 781247800@5pillars.com

WRIGHT, ANDREW S.
Industry: Restaurants/retail **Born:** March 22, 1960, Cheraw, South Carolina **Current organization:** Iron Skillet Restaurant **Title:** General Manager **Type of organization:** Restaurant/truck stopping center **Major product:** Country cooking **Area of distribution:** National **Expertise:** Troubleshooting at other locations; Certified, Advanced Management, Pizza Hut and Iron Skillet **Hob./spts.:** Building cars, car shows, church **SIC code:** 58 **Address:** Iron Skillet Restaurant, 3001 T.V. Rd., Florence, SC 29501 **E-mail:** hsvscflis@aol.com

WRIGHT, TAMIKA L.
Industry: Pharmacy **Univ./degree:** B.S., Pharmacology, University of North Carolina, Chapel Hill, 1994 **Current organization:** Wright's Pharmacy **Title:** Owner/Pharmacist **Type of organization:** Pharmacy/retailer **Major product:** Prescriptions, over the counter merchandise, home medical equipment **Area of distribution:** Greensboro, North Carolina **Expertise:** Pharmacology **Hob./spts.:** Writing poetry and short stories, singing, piano **SIC code:** 59 **Address:** Wright's Pharmacy, 709 E. Market St., Suite 100, Greensboro, NC 27401 **E-mail:** wrig4710@bellsouth.net

YOO, YOUNG N.
Industry: Telecommunications **Born:** October 14, 1969, Seoul, South Korea **Univ./degree:** B.S., Seoul, South Korea **Current organization:** Wide Cellular **Title:** President **Type of organization:** Retailer **Major product:** Cellular phones **Area of distribution:** Dallas, Texas **Expertise:** Retail/wholesale **Hob./spts.:** Fishing, basketball **SIC code:** 59 **Address:** Wide Cellular, 4438 Maple Ave., Dallas, TX 75219 **E-mail:** dave@widecellular.com **Web address:** www.widecellular.com

YOUSEFZADEH, BENYAMIN
Industry: Restaurant **Born:** July 1, 1971, Iran **Current organization:** Benny's Steak & Seafood **Title:** Owner **Type of organization:** Restaurant **Major product:** Steaks, seafood, sushi **Area of distribution:** Jacksonville, Florida **Expertise:** Chef, management **Hob./spts.:** Golf, football **SIC code:** 58 **Address:** Benny's Steak & Seafood, 2 Independent Dr., Suite 75, Jacksonville, FL 32202 **E-mail:** bennys@bellsouth.net

ZAPATA, LIONEL A.
Industry: Engineering **Born:** July 1, 1973, Managua, Nicaragua **Univ./degree:** B.S.C.E., Florida International University, 1999 **Current organization:** Rinker Materials **Title:** Pavement Design Engineer **Type of organization:** Building material distributor **Major product:** Cement, aggregate, ready-mix concrete, concrete pipe **Area of distribution:** Florida **Expertise:** Concrete, pavement, technical support and design **Affiliations:** A.S.C.E.; N.S.P.E.; A.C.I.; N.R.M.C.A.; Florida Engineering Society **Hob./spts.:** Active member of the First Hispanic Baptist Church **SIC code:** 52 **Address:** Rinker Materials, 29 S.W. 33rd St., Ft. Lauderdale, FL 33315 **E-mail:** lzapata@rinker.com **Web address:** www.rinker.com

ZAREEN-RAUF, AHAMED S.
Industry: Restaurant **Born:** August 9, 1977, Colombo, Sri Lanka **Current organization:** Cloverleaf Tavern **Title:** Manager **Type of organization:** Food tavern, retailer **Major product:** Steaks, burgers, fish **Area of distribution:** New Jersey **Expertise:** Management **Hob./spts.:** Soccer, gym **SIC code:** 58 **Address:** 348 Bloomfield Ave., Apt. 9, Caldwell, NJ 07006 **E-mail:** shafraz@email.com

ZONNEVELD, JOHN FRANCISCUS
Industry: Silver **Born:** February 24, 1937, Leiden, Netherlands **Current organization:** LJ Lewis Silver Co. **Title:** Master Silver Engraver/President **Type of organization:** Retail sales **Major product:** Silver sales and engraving **Area of distribution:** International **Expertise:** Hand engraving of silver pieces **Hob./spts.:** Skiing, painting, soccer, photography, volleyball **SIC code:** 59 **Address:** LJ Lewis Silver Co., 164 W. Wieuca Rd., #6 NW, Atlanta, GA 30342 **E-mail:** ljlewissilver@earthlink.net

ZUMBO, JAMES N.
[illegible], Pennsylvania [illegible] **Current organization:** [illegible] **of organization:** [illegible] **Major product:** [illegible] **Area of distribution:** Pittsburgh [illegible]truction, A.S.E. [illegible] Certified; GM [illegible] excursion trains, [illegible] 15236 **E-mail:** [illegible]

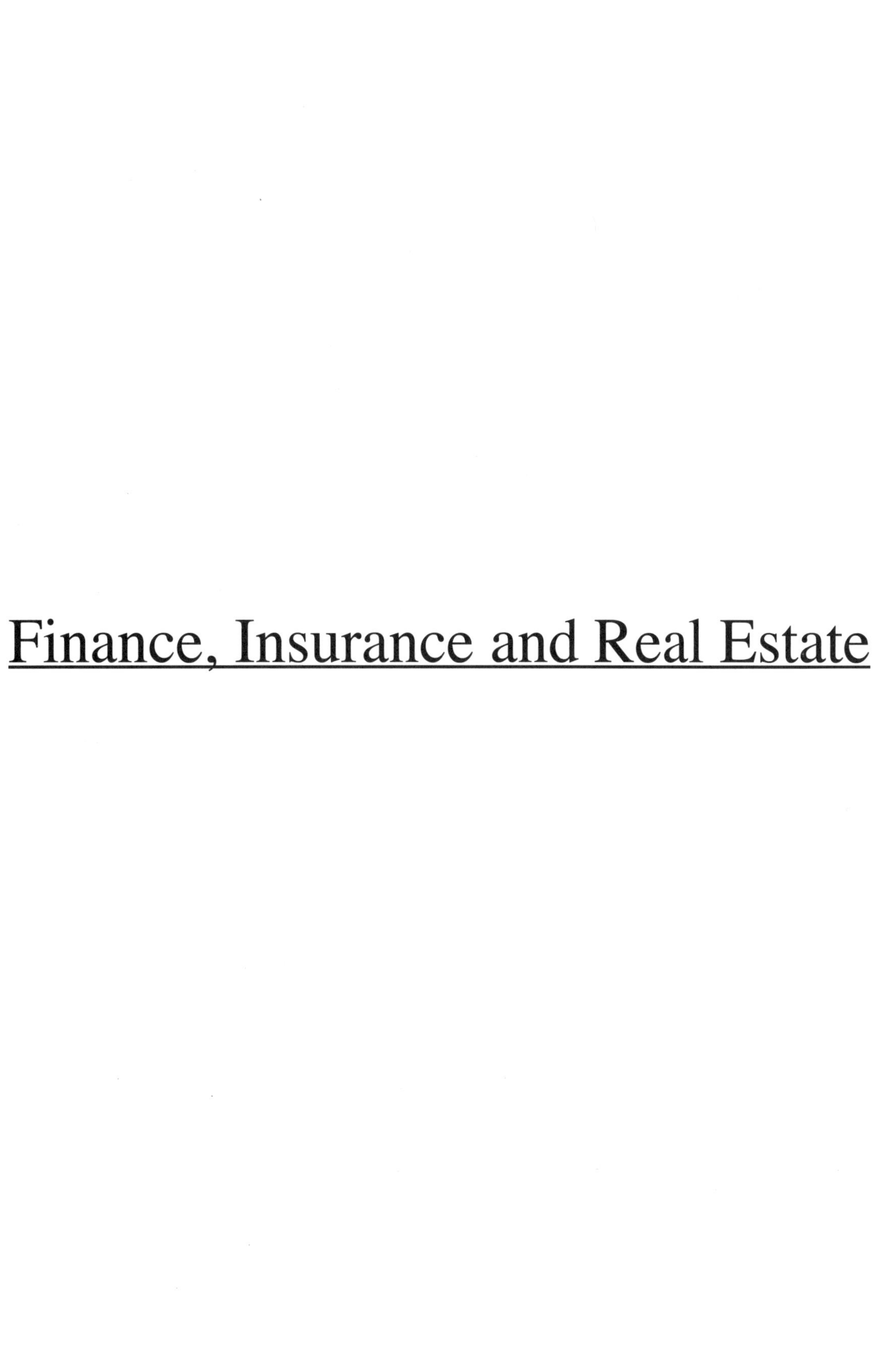

Finance, Insurance and Real Estate

AARDSMA, RICHARD J.
Industry: Insurance **Born:** May 1, 1958, Harvey, Illinois **Univ./degree:** A.S., Business Administration, South Suburban Community College, 1979 **Current organization:** Professional Insurance Services **Title:** President **Type of organization:** Insurance agency **Major product:** Insurance **Area of distribution:** Indiana **Expertise:** Lecturing, risk management, church insurance; Certified Insurance Consultant **Honors/awards:** Million Dollar Award, West Bend Mutual Insurance, 2002; Partners in Excellence Award; Dedicated Service Award, Illiana Christian Athletic Association, 1987 **Affiliations:** Christian Businessmen's Committee **Hob./spts.:** Reading, writing, woodworking **SIC code:** 64 **Address:** Professional Insurance Services, 425 Joliet St., Suite 323, Dyer, IN 46311 **E-mail:** raardsma@pro-ins.com **Web address:** www.pro-ins.com

ALMANZAR, JOSE L.
Industry: Real Estate **Born:** January 16, 1957, Santo Domingo, Dominican Republic **Univ./degree:** M.A., Management, Instituto Tecnológico de Santo Domingo (INTEC), 1989 **Current organization:** Realty Properties **Title:** Real Estate Broker **Type of organization:** Realty **Major product:** Realty services **Area of distribution:** Miami, Florida **Expertise:** Real estate financial advisor, investments **Affiliations:** National Association of Realtors; Florida Association of Realtors **Hob./spts.:** Golf **SIC code:** 65 **Address:** Realty Properties, 11236 SW 137th Ave., Miami, FL 33186 **E-mail:** jose@myrealtyproperties.com **Web address:** www.josealmanzar.com

ALVINE, ROBERT
Industry: Finance and general industrial **Born:** August 25, 1938, Newark, New Jersey **Univ./degree:** B.A., Chemistry/Chemical Engineering, Rutgers University; Graduate Program, Marketing, Syracuse University; P.M.D., Harvard Business School **Current organization:** i-Ten Management Corp. **Title:** Chairman/CEO/President **Type of organization:** Investments **Major product:** Private equity investments, mergers and acquisitions **Area of distribution:** Connecticut, New York, Massachusetts **Expertise:** General management, mergers and acquisitions, investment decisions **Honors/awards:** Honorary Doctorate of Human Letters, University of New Haven; "Outstanding Achievement in Business and Distinguished Leadership" Award; "Proclamation for Supreme Achievement in the International Community" **Affiliations:** Chair, Board, University of New Haven; Board Member, The Jackson Laboratory; Board Member, EDO Corp.; Board Member, Long Wharf Theater **Hob./spts.:** Reading, gardening, education, travel, wildlife, art **SIC code:** 67 **Address:** i-Ten Management Corp., 55 N. Racebrook Rd., Woodbridge, CT 06525

AMATO, DAWN
Industry: Financial **Born:** March 10, 1965, Port Jervis, New York **Current organization:** Kolmar NY Employees FCU **Title:** Administrator **Type of organization:** Credit union **Major product:** Retail financial services **Area of distribution:** Port Jervis, New York **Expertise:** Finances **Affiliations:** Auxiliary Vice President Firewoman; Methodist Church **Hob./spts.:** Baseball with children **SIC code:** 60 **Address:** Kolmar NY Employees FCU, Box 1111 King St., Port Jervis, NY 12771 **E-mail:** damato.cu@frontier.net

ANAND, SHIV
Industry: Real estate **Born:** November 24, 1965, Dix Hills, New York **Univ./degree:** B.S., Accounting, Hofstra University, 1985; M.S., Taxation, Adelphi University, 1986 **Current organization:** Nationwide Court Services, Inc. **Title:** President/CEO **Major product:** Title insurance **Area of distribution:** National **Affiliations:** A.I.C.P.A.; Long Island Association; New York State Land & Title Association **SIC code:** 65 **Address:** Nationwide Court Services, Inc., 4250 Veterans Memorial Hwy., Suite 4000, West Wing, Holbrook, NY 11741

ANDREWS, DEANNE D.
Industry: Insurance **Born:** November 6, 1964, Burlington, North Carolina **Current organization:** Blue Cross Blue Shield, North Carolina **Title:** Case Management Team Leader **Type of organization:** Health insurance company **Major product:** Health insurance **Area of distribution:** North Carolina **Expertise:** Medical Care Provider/Insured Liaison; member education **Affiliations:** C.M.S.A. **Hob./spts.:** Horseback riding **SIC code:** 63 **Address:** Blue Cross Blue Shield, North Carolina, P.O. Box 2291, Durham, NC 27702 **E-mail:** deandrew@bellsouth.net

ANTONOV, IVO A.
Industry: Finance, banking **Born:** August 14, 1966, Bulgaria **Univ./degree:** M.S., Computer Science, Technical University, Bulgaria, 1992; M.B.A., Cypress International Institute of Management, 1993 **Current organization:** Moody's KMV **Title:** Vice President, Project Manager **Type of organization:** Financial service company **Major product:** Credit risk management services **Area of distribution:** US, Canada **Expertise:** Credit default models **Hob./spts.:** Music, travel **SIC code:** 61 **Address:** Moody's KMV, 99 Church St., New York, NY 10007 **E-mail:** ivo.antonov@moodys.com

ANZALONE, JONO A.
Industry: Finance **Born:** November 4, 1978, Omaha, Nebraska **Univ./degree:** B.S., Political Science, Creighton University, 2002; M.S., Economics, University of Nebraska, 2003 **Current organization:** Charles Schwab & Co. **Title:** Financial Consultant **Type of organization:** Financial firm **Major product:** Financial services and products **Area of distribution:** National **Expertise:** Financial consulting **Affiliations:** A.P.S.A.; Midwest Economics Association; Democratic National Party **Hob./spts.:** Running, travel **SIC code:** 67 **Address:** Charles Schwab & Co., 3555 Leavenworth St., Omaha, NE 68105-1907 **E-mail:** jnanzalone@aol.com

ARRINGTON, DARRELL K.
Industry: Insurance **Born:** March 21, 1960, Alexandria, Louisiana **Univ./degree:** A.S., Career College, 1988 **Current organization:** Woodmen of the World/Omaha Woodmen Life Insurance Society **Title:** Field Representative **Type of organization:** Insurance company **Major product:** Insurance **Area of distribution:** Louisiana **Expertise:** Estate management **Hob./spts.:** Bass fishing **SIC code:** 63 **Address:** Woodmen of the World/Omaha Woodmen Life Insurance Society, 190 Burma Rd., Ball, LA 71405 **E-mail:** dkarrington@bellsouth.net

AUDITORE, FRANK C.
Industry: Financial **Born:** February 7, 1961, Boston, Massachusetts **Univ./degree:** B.S., Financial Management; B.A., Communications, Stonehill College, 1982 **Current organization:** L&M Securities Co., Inc. **Title:** President **Type of organization:** Brokerage firm **Major product:** Financial services **Area of distribution:** Walpole, Massachusetts **Expertise:** 401K's, stock transactions, office management **Affiliations:** Notary Public **Hob./spts.:** Golf **SIC code:** 62 **Address:** L&M Securities Co., Inc., 969 Main St., Suite 206, Walpole, MA 02081 **E-mail:** fauditore@lmsec.com

BAILEY, LIZA
Industry: Investment banking **Born:** February 24, 1954, Paterson, New Jersey **Univ./degree:** B.A., Economics, Georgetown University, 1974 **Current organization:** Credit Suisse First Boston **Title:** Managing Director **Type of organization:** Banking firm **Major product:** Financial advisory **Area of distribution:** International **Expertise:** Consumer products **SIC code:** 62 **Address:** Credit Suisse First Boston, 11 Madison Ave., New York, NY 10010 **E-mail:** liza.bailey@csfb.com **Web address:** www.csfb.com

BAKER, JAMES COLEMAN
Industry: Financial **Born:** June 27, 1957, Evanston, Illinois **Univ./degree:** J.D., Harvard University; LL.M., Taxation, New York University **Current organization:** Neuberger Berman **Title:** Managing Director **Type of organization:** Brokerage, asset manager **Major product:** Investment management **Area of distribution:** National **Expertise:** Portfolio manager **Affiliations:** A.B.A.; Harvard Club **Hob./spts.:** Piano, bicycling **SIC code:** 64 **Address:** Neuberger Berman, 605 Third Ave., New York, NY 10158 **E-mail:** jbaker@nb.com

BALDWIN, DONNA A.
Industry: Real Estate **Born:** September 4, 1960, Defiance, Ohio **Univ./degree:** B.S., Davis Business College **Current organization:** Real Living/Baldwin Realty **Title:** Broker/Owner **Type of organization:** Real estate (LLC) **Major product:** Listing and selling of real estate **Area of distribution:** Ohio **Expertise:** Real estate **Honors/awards:** GRI/ABR/Million Dollar Sales Club 1997 to present **Affiliations:** ZONTA; Northwestern Ohio Board of Realtors; Chamber of Commerce **SIC code:** 65 **Address:** Real Living/Baldwin Realty, 319 E. Second, Defiance, OH 43512 **E-mail:** donna.baldwin@realliving.com

BARAKAT, MUNIR V.
Industry: Financial services **Univ./degree:** M.B.A., Pace University, 1981 **Current organization:** WAFRA Investment Advisory Group, Inc. **Title:** Managing Director **Type of organization:** Institutional money management **Major product:** Investment banking **Area of distribution:** International **Expertise:** Business and product development **Published works:** Co-author, Harvard Paper **Affiliations:** Director, Arab Bankers Association of the Northeast **SIC code:** 60 **Address:** WAFRA Investment Advisory Group, Inc., 345 Park Ave., Armonk, NY 10504 **E-mail:** m.barakat@wafra.com

BARRETT, DELLA T.
Industry: Real Estate **Univ./degree:** North Lake Community College **Current organization:** Watson Realty Corp. **Title:** Realtor **Type of organization:** Realty **Major product:** New homes, re-sales, commercial, land **Area of distribution:** Florida **Expertise:** Sales **Affiliations:** Women's Council of Realtors; Chamber of Commerce **Hob./spts.:** International travel, baking, sky-diving, gardening **SIC code:** 65 **Address:** Watson Realty Corp., 1390 Hancock, Clermont, FL 34711 **E-mail:** dbarrett4@cfl.rr.com

BATISTE, DESIREE
Industry: Financial **Born:** September 7, 1950, Houston, Texas **Current organization:** 1st Discount Brokerage Inc. **Title:** Financial Advisor **Type of organization:** Brokerage firm **Major product:** Financial planning, securities and insurance **Area of distribu-**

tion: National **Expertise:** Tax sheltering, college funding, insurance planning **Hob./spts.:** Swimming, diving, snow skiing, running, ballet **SIC code:** 62 **Address:** 1st Discount Brokerage Inc., 3311 Richmond Ave., Suite 150, Houston, TX 77098 **E-mail:** dbatiste@1dbdirect.com

BAUER-GOLDSMITH, TINA B.
Industry: Finance **Born:** April 5, 1952, Brooklyn, New York **Univ./degree:** B.A., Sociology/Psychology, Minor in Public Relations, University of Miami, 1993; M.S., Marriage and Family Therapy, Specialty in Medical Therapy and Hypnotherapy, Nova Southeastern University, 1996 **Current organization:** Mortgage Loan Specialists, Inc. **Title:** Mortgage Banker **Type of organization:** Loan processing specialists **Major product:** Mortgage loans **Area of distribution:** National **Expertise:** Psychotherapy/public relations/Professor for Critical Argumentative Discourse/Professor for Sociology & Social Problems **Honors/awards:** Golden Key National Honor Society **Affiliations:** Society of Teachers of Family Medicine; Mortgage Bankers Association **Hob./spts.:** Horseback riding, needlecraft, physical fitness, theatre, ballet, ballroom dancing **SIC code:** 61 **Address:** Mortgage Loan Specialists, Inc., 750 Broad St., Shrewsbury, NJ 07702 **E-mail:** tbauer@mlsloan.com

BAY, JOANN R.
Industry: Finance **Born:** September 29, 1926, Williamsport, Pennsylvania **Univ./degree:** B.A., English/Psychology, Bucknell University, 1948 **Current organization:** J.R. Bay Associates **Title:** Owner **Type of organization:** Financial planners **Major product:** Financial advice, "fee only" planner **Area of distribution:** National-largely eastern U.S. **Expertise:** Comprehensive personal financial planning, individual counseling and group seminars; Certified Financial Planner (CFP); Registered Investment Advisor (RIA) with Pennsylvania Securities Commission; has been active for many years as a public speaker on personal financial planning for many professional and community groups; Expert Witness in Court involving trust investments **Honors/awards:** Named as one of the 200 best financial advisors in the U.S. by Money Magazine in 1987; listed in National Registry of Who's Who at the Library of Congress in Washington, DC and in Strathmore's Who's Who and Who's Who of American Women **Affiliations:** National and local Chapter membership in the Financial Planning Association as a Licensed Practitioner; Former Board of Directors, Delaware Valley Chapter of the I.A.F.P., Former Member of Philadelphia County Estate Planning Association and Delaware County Estate Planning Association; Former Member, Women in Transition; Former Chairman of Investment Committee of the Community Y Foundation Board of Trustees **Hob./spts.:** Playing piano; Supporter of Kimmel Center for the Performing Arts and Philadelphia Art Museum **SIC code:** 62 **Address:** J.R. Bay Associates, 5022 Sylvia Rd., Drexel Hill, PA 19026 **E-mail:** jb92926@rcn.com

BECK, GARY L.
Industry: Insurance **Born:** June 20, 1952, McAlester, Oklahoma **Univ./degree:** Community College of the Air Force **Current organization:** CompSource Oklahoma **Title:** Information Systems Network Management **Type of organization:** State insurance agency **Major product:** Workers compensation **Area of distribution:** Oklahoma **Expertise:** Multi-layered Cisco Networks; Microsoft Networks/Servers/Desktops; Network Security **Honors/awards:** United States Air Force Commendation Medal for Act of Courage, Honduras, March 31, 1990; Compsource Oklahoma Customer Service Award, 2005 **Affiliations:** I.E.E.E.; Oklahoma Cyber Security Alliance; Veterans of Foreign Wars; U.S. Air Force (Retired); National Republican Party **Hob./spts.:** Home improvement, travel, electronics, sporting events **SIC code:** 63 **Address:** CompSource Oklahoma, 1901 N. Walnut, Oklahoma City, OK 73105 **E-mail:** gary_b@compsourceok.com

BENGEL, JENNIFER G.
Industry: Financial **Univ./degree:** Paralegal Degree, Executive Secretarial School, 1993; A.A., Business Management, Richland College, 1998 **Current organization:** Legg Mason Wood Walker **Title:** Assistant **Type of organization:** Brokerage firm **Major product:** Institutional equity sales **Area of distribution:** National **Expertise:** Administration **SIC code:** 62 **Address:** Legg Mason Wood Walker, 2100 McKinney Ave., Suite 1950, Dallas, TX 75201 **E-mail:** jgbengel@leggmason.com

BERRY, SARAH GARFIELD
Industry: Financial **Born:** June 29, 1951, Hartford, Connecticut **Univ./degree:** B.A., Bennington College, Vermont, 1973 **Current organization:** AG Edwards & Sons, Inc. **Title:** Vice President/Branch Manager **Type of organization:** N.Y.S.E. firm/investment firm **Major product:** Investments **Area of distribution:** National **Expertise:** Portfolio and investment management **Affiliations:** Board Member, Bancroft School; University of Massachusetts Memorial Healthcare System; President & Board Member, Worcester Art Museum **Hob./spts.:** Reading, cooking, sailing, dogs **SIC code:** 67 **Address:** AG Edwards & Sons, Inc., One Boston Place, Suite 3500, Boston, MA 02108 **Web address:** www.agedwards.com

BIVINS, MARTHA G.
Industry: Insurance **Born:** August 8, 1949, Florence, South Carolina **Univ./degree:** B.S., Education, Winthrop College, 1970; M.Ed., Clemson University, 1975 **Current organization:** AFLAC **Title:** Benefits Specialist **Type of organization:** Insurance sales and service **Major product:** Supplemental insurance **Area of distribution:** Shelby, North Carolina **Expertise:** Payroll accounts, benefits for businesses **Affiliations:** National Association of Professional Agents; Cleveland County Chamber of Commerce **Hob./spts.:** Music, reading **SIC code:** 64 **Address:** AFLAC, 1455 E. Marion St., Suite D, Shelby, NC 28150 **E-mail:** bivinsmg@aol.com

BOCKHOLD, HAROLD J.
Industry: Real Estate **Born:** January 5, 1926, Chicago, Illinois **Current organization:** Freedom of Choice Realty **Title:** CEO **Type of organization:** Realty **Major product:** Real estate **Area of distribution:** Florida **Expertise:** Real estate associate consulting; Licensed in real estate, mortgage banking, electrical and general contracting **Honors/awards:** International Real Estate Hall of Fame **Affiliations:** American Legion; S. Florida Lic. Trainer; Mayor Retired, City of Parkland, Florida, 1972-1978; President, Historical Society of Parkland, Florida; Served at Pleasure of Leroy Collins, Governor Retired, State of Florida **Hob./spts.:** Thoroughbred horses **SIC code:** 65 **Address:** Freedom of Choice Realty, 7373 82nd Terrace, Parkland, FL 33067 **E-mail:** fcr25@bellsouth.net **Web address:** www.fcr25.com

BONHEIMER, DICK
Industry: Real estate **Born:** October 26, 1943, Canton, Ohio **Current organization:** Murexproperties **Title:** Accredited Community Manager **Type of organization:** Realtor **Major product:** New homes, resale of homes, tenants rights **Area of distribution:** National **Expertise:** Property management **Affiliations:** Oregon Manufactured Housing Association; Manufactured Housing Industry **Hob./spts.:** Golf, reading **SIC code:** 65 **Address:** Murexproperties, 10 E. South Stage Rd., Medford, OR 97501 **E-mail:** rbonheimer@murexproperties.com **Web address:** www.murexproperties.com

BONTEMPO, TONY L.
Industry: Real Estate **Born:** June 17, 1970, San Gabriel, California **Univ./degree:** A.S., Accounting, Highline College **Current organization:** Sound Side Homes **Title:** Real Estate Associate **Type of organization:** Real estate brokerage **Major product:** Buying and selling real estate property **Area of distribution:** Washington **Expertise:** Residential/condo real estate **Affiliations:** N.W.L.M.S.; C.B.A. **Hob./spts.:** Meteorology, sports, reading, travel **SIC code:** 65 **Address:** Sound Side Homes, 22015 Marine View Dr. S., Des Moines, WA 98198 **E-mail:** tlbdana812@yahoo.com **Web address:** www.mls.com

BOREING, DONNA L.
Industry: Insurance **Univ./degree:** B.S., Business Administration, University of Phoenix, 1997 **Current organization:** Wellpoint Blue Cross and Blue Shield **Title:** Vice President, Operations **Type of organization:** Insurance company **Major product:** Health, dental, vision, life insurance products **Area of distribution:** National **Expertise:** Operations **Affiliations:** Denver Women's Chamber of Commerce **SIC code:** 63 **Address:** Well Point BC/BS, 700 Broadway, Mail Code #EX0359, Denver, CO 80273 **E-mail:** donna.moreing@anthem.com

BOROZAN, BORIS ALEXANDAR
Industry: Finance **Born:** May 21, 1948, Belgrade, Yugoslavia **Univ./degree:** B.S., Belgrade University; M.S., Columbia University; M.B.A., Wharton School of Business, Pennsylvania, 1981 **Current organization:** HSBC Securities (USA) Inc. **Title:** Managing Director **Type of organization:** Bank **Major product:** Investment banking, fixed income **Area of distribution:** International **Expertise:** Financial/Economic Expert **Honors/awards:** Mortgage Banker of the Year **Hob./spts.:** Sailing, mountain climbing, skiing, speaks several languages **SIC code:** 60 **Address:** HSBC Securities (USA) Inc., 452 Fifth Ave., Tenth floor, New York, NY 10018 **E-mail:** boris.borozan@ushsbc.com

BOSCH, ASHLEY P.
Industry: Real estate **Born:** May 3, 1971, Coral Gables, Florida **Univ./degree:** B.A., Marketing/International Affairs, Florida State University; J.D., Florida State University School of Law, 1997 **Current organization:** BLOK Development Group, LLC **Title:** Managing Member **Type of organization:** Private development, design/build **Major product:** Residential and mixed use products **Area of distribution:** South Florida **Expertise:** Finance, legal, acquisition, disposition and construction **Honors/awards:** Developer of the Year, 2000-01; Developer of the Related Group of Florida **Affiliations:** The Builders Association of South Florida; The Latin Builders Association **Hob./spts.:** Golf, bottom fishing, spectator sports **SIC code:** 65 **Address:** BLOK Development Group, LLC, 2655 S. LeJeune Rd., Suite 409, Coral Gables, FL 33134 **E-mail:** abosch@blokgroup.com

BRADFORD, LANCE K.
Industry: Financial **Born:** Klamath Falls, Oregon **Univ./degree:** B.S., Accounting, University of Nevada, 1988 **Current organization:** Vestin Group **Title:** President **Type of organization:** Mortgage company **Major product:** Commercial mortgage lending **Area of distribution:** Nevada **Expertise:** Certified Public Accountant **Affiliations:** Y.P.O.; A.I.C.P.A.; Nevada Society of CPAs **Hob./spts.:** Family, golf **SIC code:** 61

Address: Vestin Group, 3441 S. Eastern Ave., Las Vegas, NV 89109 **E-mail:** lanceb@vestingroup.com

BRAY, DONALD J.
Industry: Real estate **Title:** President **Type of organization:** Title insurance agency **Major product:** Title insurance **Expertise:** Title insurance, real estate closings **SIC code:** 65 **Address:** Investors Real Estate Services, 214 W. Hartford St., Milford, PA 18337 **E-mail:** iamilfd@ptd.net

BRINZAN, VADIM
Industry: Financial **Born:** December 23, 1971, Moldova **Univ./degree:** M.B.A., Harvard Business School, 2001 **Current organization:** Merrill Lynch & Co. **Title:** Vice President **Type of organization:** Investment banking **Major product:** Principal investing **Area of distribution:** International **Expertise:** Investment management **Hob./spts.:** History, judo **SIC code:** 62 **Address:** Merrill Lynch & Co., 4 World Financial Center, New York, NY 10080 **E-mail:** vbrinzan@hotmail.com

BROWN, DEBRA L.
Industry: Real estate **Born:** October 21, 1962, Tampa, Florida **Univ./degree:** A.S., Banking, Finance, South Florida Community College, 1993 **Current organization:** A.D. Mortgage Loan Specialist, Inc. **Title:** Owner **Type of organization:** Broker **Major product:** Financing for residential and commercial properties **Area of distribution:** Port Charlotte, Florida **Expertise:** Financing **Affiliations:** Women's Realtor Council; Port Charlotte and Tampa Chamber of Commerce **Hob./spts.:** Swimming, camping, horseback riding **SIC code:** 64 **Address:** A.D. Mortgage Loan Specialist, Inc., 20020 Veterans Blvd., #14, Port Charlotte, FL 33954 **E-mail:** admortgage@earthlink.net

BRUENING, KEVIN L.
Industry: Financial **Born:** February 24, 1971, Tokyo, Japan **Univ./degree:** B.S., Economic History, University of Maryland **Current organization:** Wachovia Securities **Title:** Investment Advisor **Type of organization:** Financial firm **Major product:** Financial services **Area of distribution:** National **Expertise:** Asset allocation **Published works:** "Christmas in April" **Affiliations:** A.S.C.P.A.; University of Maryland Alumni Association; Laurel Citizens Police Academy **Hob./spts.:** Golf **SIC code:** 67 **Address:** Wachovia Securities, 10500 Little Patuxent Pkwy., Columbia, MD 21044 **E-mail:** kevin_bruening@prusec.com

BRUN, JANE M.
Industry: Insurance/Risk Management **Born:** April 14, 1956, Brooklyn, New York **Univ./degree:** B.A., Communications/Educational Psychology, St. John's University, 1978 **Current organization:** Acordia Mountain West **Title:** Vice President **Type of organization:** Insurance and brokerage firm **Major product:** Commercial property and casualty insurance consulting **Area of distribution:** International **Expertise:** Domestic and international insurance needs **SIC code:** 64 **Address:** Acordia Mountain West, 5755 Mark Dabling Blvd., #300, Colorado Springs, CO 80919 **E-mail:** jane_brun@acordia.com

BUCKLEY, JOSHUA D.
Industry: Financial **Born:** October 24, 1978, Cleveland, Ohio **Univ./degree:** B.S., Mechanical Engineering, Johns Hopkins University, 2001 **Current organization:** American Home Mortgage **Title:** Secondary Market Trader **Type of organization:** Mortgage bank **Major product:** Mortgage products **Area of distribution:** New York **Expertise:** Mortgage trading **Affiliations:** A.S.M.E. **Hob./spts.:** International music, playing soccer, travel **SIC code:** 67 **Address:** American Home Mortgage, 12 E. 49th St., 29th Floor, New York, NY 10017 **E-mail:** jbuckley@jhu.edu

BYRD, CARUTH C.
Industry: Real Estate/ Entertainment **Univ./degree:** General Animal Science **Current organization:** Caruth C. Byrd Enterprises **Title:** President **Type of organization:** Real estate development/movie production/professional musician **Major product:** Commercial and residential real estate development/financing motion pictures, television commercial productions **Area of distribution:** National **Expertise:** Business, land development, motion picture and TV production, music **Affiliations:** Founder, Caruth C. Byrd Wildlife Foundation **Hob./spts.:** Fishing, professional musician, playing the piano **SIC code:** 65 **Address:** Caruth C. Byrd Enterprises, 2611 Westgrove Drive, Suite 105, Carrolton, TX 75006

BYRD, DONALD G.
Industry: Real estate **Born:** September 21, 1925, Muncie, Indiana **Univ./degree:** B.A., Psychology, University of Arizona, 1950 **Current organization:** Wawasee Real Estate Development, LLC **Title:** Owner/President **Type of organization:** Real estate **Major product:** Development and sales of lots, lake fronts and lake access **Area of distribution:** Syracuse, Indiana **Expertise:** Administration and sales **Hob./spts.:** Golf - Life Member, Professional Golf Association of America **SIC code:** 65 **Address:** Wawasee Real Estate Development, LLC, 8241 E. Constitution Dr., Syracuse, IN 46567-7307

CALVIN, WALTER C.
Industry: Financial **Born:** February 3, 1931, Decatur, Illinois **Current organization:** Greater Galilee Baptist Credit Union **Title:** Board Chairman **Type of organization:** Credit union **Major product:** Banking services, loans; helping church members and senior citizens with getting loans **Area of distribution:** Wisconsin **Expertise:** Banking, operations **Affiliations:** Past Member, Boys Club; Past Scout Master, Troop 39 **Hob./spts.:** Stamp collecting **SIC code:** 61 **Address:** Greater Galilee Baptist Credit Union, 2432 N. Teutonia Ave., Milwaukee, WI 53206

CARROLL JR., CHARLES V.
Industry: Finance **Born:** November 18, 1939, High Point, North Carolina **Univ./degree:** M.A., Finance, Wake Forest University, 1963 **Current organization:** Harris Private Bank **Title:** President/Senior Trust Officer **Type of organization:** Bank **Major product:** Financial services **Area of distribution:** Naples, Florida **Expertise:** Trusts and investments **Affiliations:** F.C.C.; A.H.A.; G.S.P.H., U.A.C.; Naples Chamber of Commerce **Hob./spts.:** Tennis, golf, theatre **SIC code:** 60 **Address:** Harris Private Bank, 4040 Gulf Shore Blvd., Naples, FL 34103 **E-mail:** charles.carroll@harrisbank.com **Web address:** www.harrisbank.com

CASAZZA, RALPH A.
Industry: Real estate **Current organization:** Shopper's Square, Tore Ltd., R&E Development **Title:** President, CEO **Type of organization:** Realtor **Major product:** Malls, national chain stores **Area of distribution:** National **Expertise:** Real estate development and acquisition **Affiliations:** A.I.A.; I.C.S.S. **Hob./spts.:** Golf **SIC code:** 65 **Address:** Shopper's Square, Tore Ltd., R&E Development, 370 Casazza Dr., Reno, NV 89502 **Phone:** (775)323-0430 **Fax:** (775)323-6824 **E-mail:** shopperssquare@sbcglobal.net

CASWELL, LINDA K.
Industry: Insurance **Born:** Canton, Ohio **Current organization:** Golden Horizons Insurance Agency, Inc. **Title:** President **Type of organization:** Insurance agency **Major product:** LTC coverage, Medi Gap, annuities **Area of distribution:** Canton, Ohio **Expertise:** Retirement planning, insurance investments **Published works:** Who's Who **Affiliations:** A.F.A. **Hob./spts.:** Animals, playing cards **SIC code:** 64 **Address:** Golden Horizons Insurance Agency, Inc., 5874 Fulton Rd. N.W., Canton, OH 44718 **E-mail:** mslritzy@aol.com

CHAPMAN, JUDY K.
Industry: Real Estate **Born:** October 20, 1948, Tilden, Nebraska **Current organization:** Benchmark Realty **Title:** President/Owner **Type of organization:** Real estate broker **Major product:** Real estate sales and property management **Area of distribution:** National **Expertise:** Residential, commercial, property management **Affiliations:** Multimillion Dollar Club; Springfield Board of Realtors; National Agency of Realtors; Notary Public **Hob./spts.:** Gardening, reading, the outdoors **SIC code:** 65 **Address:** Benchmark Realty, 3767 N. Glenstone, Springfield, MO 65803 **E-mail:** benchmark-realty@axs.net

CHARLES, TERRI A.
Industry: Insurance/beauty **Title:** Commercial Policy Technician **Type of organization:** Insurance/cosmetics **Major product:** Insurance/beauty products **Expertise:** Underwriting/beauty consultant **SIC code:** 64 **Address:** Creative Underwriters Corp./Avon, 3066 Sugar Maple Court, Carmel, IN 46033 **E-mail:** dancngtc@indy.rr.com

CHEN, NING
Industry: Finance **Born:** February 28, 1977, Nanyang, China **Univ./degree:** Ph.D., Finance, University of California at Berkeley **Current organization:** Lehman Brothers **Title:** Financial Analyst **Type of organization:** Investment company **Major product:** Money management **Area of distribution:** International **Expertise:** Global financial analysis **Affiliations:** Chinese Finance Association; Co-Founder, Berkeley China Review **Hob./spts.:** Golf, basketball, auto racing **SIC code:** 67 **Address:** Lehman Brothers, 745 7th Ave., 14th floor, New York, NY 10019 **E-mail:** ningchen.cal@gmail.com

CHRISTENSEN, MICHELLE L.
Industry: Financial **Born:** June 7, 1975, Fairfax, Virginia **Univ./degree:** B.A., Dance, Brigham Young University, 2000; J.D., Thomas Jefferson School of Law, 2003 **Current organization:** Transportation Alliance Bank Inc. **Title:** Assistant General Counsel **Type of organization:** Banking for the transportation and hospitality industries **Major product:** Banking and finance law **Area of distribution:** National **Expertise:** Corporate contracts and litigation management **Honors/awards:** Top 50 Attorneys in Utah, 2005 **Affiliations:** Utah State Bar; Board Member, Utah Humane Society; A.B.A.; A.T.L.A. **Hob./spts.:** Dance, humanitarian causes, golf **SIC code:** 60 **Address:** Transportation Alliance Bank Inc., 4185 Harrison Blvd., Suite 200, Ogden, UT 84403 **E-mail:** michelle.christensen@tabbank.com

CLINKENBEARD, DOUGLAS E.
Industry: Real estate **Univ./degree:** Attended McKendree College **Current organization:** Re/Max Executive Group, Inc./Superior Homes Inc. **Title:** Broker/Owner, President **Type of organization:** Real estate/construction **Major product:** Residential, commercial, land, multifamily sales/residential **Area of distribution:** Central Kentucky **Expertise:** Certified Residential Specialist; Graduate Realtors Institute **Honors/awards:** Re/Max Chairman's Club, 2004, 2005; Re/Max Hall of Fame; Re/Max Platinum Club, 2000-03 **Affiliations:** National Association of Realtors **SIC code:** 65 **Address:** Re/Max Executive Group, Inc., 2110 N. Dixie Hwy., Elizabethtown, KY 42701 **E-mail:** douglas@clickenbeardteam.com **Web address:** www.kyhomesales.com

COATANLEM, YANN
Industry: Financial **Born:** June 19, 1969, Reims, France **Univ./degree:** M.S., International Finance, HEC, France, 1994; M.S., Applied Mathematics, ENSIMAG, France, 1992 **Current organization:** Salomon Smith Barney **Title:** Director **Type of organization:** Investment bank **Major product:** Fixed income derivatives **Area of distribution:** International **Expertise:** Quantitative research **Affiliations:** The University Club **Hob./spts.:** Music, literature, the arts, food and travel **SIC code:** 62 **Address:** Salomon Smith Barney, 400 Chambers St. #5D, New York, NY 10282 **E-mail:** yann.coatanlem@citigroup.com

COHEN, GARY N.
Industry: Finance/investment **Born:** July 19, 1957, Rochester, New York **Univ./degree:** J.D., State University of New York at Buffalo, 1981; M.B.A., Northwestern University, 1983 **Current organization:** eAdvisor **Title:** Vice President **Type of organization:** Internet application service provider **Major product:** Web-based financial and investment advice **Area of distribution:** National **Expertise:** Personal financial planning, tax law **Published works:** Tax Planner Magazine; Ernst & Young: Financial Planning Report, Guide to the New Tax Law, Tax Guide **Affiliations:** American Bar Association; Investment Management Consultant Association **Hob./spts.:** Tennis, history and archeology **SIC code:** 62 **Address:** eAdvisor, 2013 Winsted Way, Marietta, GA 30062 **E-mail:** gary.cohen@ey.com

COHEN, MATTHEW J.
Industry: Financial services **Born:** March 1, 1967, Manchester, New Hampshire **Univ./degree:** M.B.A., Finance, Boston University, 1996 **Current organization:** Acadian Asset Management **Title:** Senior Vice President **Type of organization:** Investment management firm **Major product:** Management of global equity assets **Area of distribution:** National **Expertise:** International equities, equity evaluation technology **Affiliations:** B.S.A.S.; A.I.M.R.; S.Q.A. **Hob./spts.:** Photography, basketball **SIC code:** 67 **Address:** Acadian Asset Management, 10 Post Office Sq., Eighth floor, Boston, MA 02109 **E-mail:** mcohen@acadian-asset.com

COHN, FERN S.
Industry: Real Estate **Born:** January 27, 1931, Bronx, New York **Current organization:** Fern Cohn Realty **Title:** Owner **Type of organization:** Realty **Major product:** Real estate sales **Area of distribution:** National **Expertise:** City/state grants to low income people **Affiliations:** Georgia Association of Realtors; Alabama Association of Realtors; Hadassah **Hob./spts.:** Art **SIC code:** 65 **Address:** Fern Cohn Realty, 738 Second Ave., Columbus, GA 31901 **E-mail:** ferncohnrealty@mindspring.com **Web address:** www.ferncohnrealty.com

COLE, GEORGE W.
Industry: Real Estate **Born:** February 28, 1951, Hudson, New York **Univ./degree:** A.A., Business, Ulster County Community College, 1971 **Current organization:** George Cole Auctions & Realty, Inc. **Title:** President **Type of organization:** Realty **Major product:** Real estate appraisal liquidation **Area of distribution:** National **Expertise:** Estate liquidations **Affiliations:** New York State Realtors Association; National Auctioneers Association; New York State Auctioneers Association **SIC code:** 65 **Address:** George Cole Auctions & Realty, Inc., 7578 N. Broadway, Red Hook, NY 12571 **E-mail:** georgecole@georgecoleauctions.com **Web address:** www.georgecoleauctions.com

COMPTON, AARON
Industry: Financial **Univ./degree:** B.S., Management/Ethics, Mid-America Bible College **Current organization:** Third Age Group **Title:** President **Type of organization:** Holding company **Major product:** Media buying service and misc. business interests **Area of distribution:** National **Expertise:** Business development **Affiliations:** Chairman, Public Relations Committee, Oklahoma Pedorthic Association **Hob./spts.:** Outdoor activities, church elder **SIC code:** 67 **Address:** Third Age Group, P.O. Box 6975, More, OK 73153 **E-mail:** thirdagefeet@aol.com

CONLIN, JAMES
Industry: Financial **Born:** July 1967, Morristown, New Jersey **Univ./degree:** B.A., Finance, Lehigh University, 1992 **Current organization:** Kabrik Trading LLC **Title:** President **Type of organization:** Broker/dealer **Major product:** US Equity Executions **Area of distribution:** New York, New York **Expertise:** NYSE Floor Member **Hob./spts.:** Skiing, golf, fishing **SIC code:** 62 **Address:** Kabrik Trading LLC, 11 Broadway, Suite 814, New York, NY 10004 **E-mail:** jconlin@kabrik.com **Web address:** www.kabrik.com

CONNORS, CHARLES M.
Industry: Real estate **Born:** April 24, 1964, Cambridge, Massachusetts **Current organization:** Toll Brothers Inc. **Title:** Assistant Vice President **Type of organization:** Real estate agency **Major product:** Single and multi-family homes **Area of distribution:** New England **Expertise:** Operations **Hob./spts.:** Family, golf, coaching youth sports - hockey **SIC code:** 65 **Address:** Toll Brothers Inc., 83 Cedar St., Milford, MA 01757 **E-mail:** cconnors@tollbrothersinc.com

CONTI, KRISTEN D.
Industry: Real estate **Born:** January 1, 1965, Westerly, Rhode Island **Univ./degree:** B.A., Rhode Island University, 1990 **Current organization:** Salefish Realty Inc. **Title:** President/Founder/Owner **Type of organization:** Realtor **Major product:** Real estate sales and service **Area of distribution:** International **Expertise:** Waterfront property, commercial property, new home construction, second and vacation homes **Honors/awards:** Realtor Rookie of the Year **Affiliations:** Women's Council of Realtors; National Association for Female Executives; Realtors Association of the Palm Beaches, National Association of Realtors, Florida Association of Realtors **Hob./spts.:** Boating, snorkeling, golf, worldwide travel, wine-tasting **SIC code:** 65 **Address:** Salefish Realty Inc., 1499 S. McCall Rd., Suite A, Englewood, FL 34223 **E-mail:** kristen@kristenconti.com **Web address:** www.salefishrealty.com

COOK, GUY
Industry: Real Estate **Born:** April 1, 1931, Pocatello, Idaho **Univ./degree:** M.B.A., University of Utah, 1969 **Current organization:** Nexia Holdings Inc. **Title:** Controller, CPA **Type of organization:** Holding corporation **Major product:** Real estate, fashion, design **Area of distribution:** National **Expertise:** Accounting, finance **Affiliations:** Former Member, A.I.C.P.A.; C.S.C.P.A.; F.A.S.B. **Hob./spts.:** Tennis, skiing, basketball, football **SIC code:** 67 **Address:** Nexia Holdings Inc., 59 West 100 South, Salt Lake City, UT 84101 **E-mail:** guy@nexiaholdings.com

COON, FRANK D.
Industry: Real estate **Born:** March 26, 1944, Auburn, New York **Current organization:** Carefree Realty, Inc. **Title:** President/Owner **Type of organization:** Real estate brokerage **Major product:** Sales of residential and commercial properties **Area of distribution:** Sarasota and Bradenton, Florida **Expertise:** Management **Affiliations:** N.A.R.; F.A.R; N.M.B.A.; F.M.B.A **Hob./spts.:** Travel **SIC code:** 65 **Address:** Carefree Realty, Inc., 3605 57th Ave. Dr. West, Bradenton, FL 34210 **E-mail:** frankc@carefreerealtyfl.us **Web address:** www.carefreerealty.us

COYLE, JOHN C.
Industry: Insurance and Financial Services **Born:** October 17, 1962 **Univ./degree:** Life Underwriters Training Council Fellow, Graduate, The American College, 1993 **Current organization:** State Farm Insurance Companies, Address: 4012 Preston Rd., Suite 200, Plano, TX 75093 **Title:** Sr. Account Representative **Type of organization:** Insurance and Financial Services **Major product:** Insurance - Life, Health, Automobile, Home and Banking **Area of distribution:** Texas **Expertise:** Business and Personal Insurance and Financial Planning **Hob./spts.:** Music-guitar and keyboards; Texas Motor Speedway-NASCAR and IRL racing; Charities-Speedway Children's Charities, The Victory Junction gang camp **SIC code:** 63 **Address:** John C, Coyle, LUTCF, 2713 Thomdale Circle, Plano, TX 75074 **Phone:** (972)758-1111 **Fax:** (972)758-1440 **E-mail:** jccoyle@comcast.net

CROSLAND, DAVID P.
Industry: Private equity **Born:** January 1, 1959, New Orleans, Louisiana **Univ./degree:** M.A., Business, Harvard University, 1988 **Current organization:** Crescent Capital Investments, Inc. **Title:** President **Type of organization:** Investment firm **Major product:** Buy-outs **Area of distribution:** International **Expertise:** Investment banking **Hob./spts.:** Classical music, golf **SIC code:** 67 **Address:** Crescent Capital Investments, Inc., 75 Fourteenth St., 24th floor, Atlanta, GA 30309 **E-mail:** dcrosland@crescentcapital.com

DAHLBERG, DAVID F.
Industry: Financial services **Born:** December 13, 1957, Garrison, North Dakota **Univ./degree:** B.A., Biochemistry, Northwestern University, 1980 **Current organization:** Clipper Trading Associates, LLC **Title:** Managing Director **Type of organization:** Hedge fund advisor **Major product:** Hedge fund management **Area of distribution:** International **Expertise:** U.S. Treasury fixed income trading **Hob./spts.:** Sky diving, downhill skiing, Tae-Kwon-Do **SIC code:** 62 **Address:** Clipper Trading Associates, LLC, 1501 Broadway, #2302, New York, NY 10036

DAVIDSON, STEPHANIE J.
Industry: Financial **Born:** October 5, 1976, El Paso, Texas **Univ./degree:** B.A., Wayland Baptist University, 1999 **Current organization:** New York Life **Title:** Agent **Type of organization:** Mutual insurance company **Major product:** Investments - life insurance, annuities **Area of distribution:** El Paso, Texas **Hob./spts.:** Spending time with her family, piano, music (performing) **SIC code:** 64 **Address:** New York Life, 201 E. Main St., Suite 600, El Paso, TX 79901 **E-mail:** spaselk@yahoo.com

DE ANGELIS, ROSE C.
Industry: Construction **Born:** October 4, Queens, New York **Univ./degree:** B.A., Marketing; B.S., Psychology **Current organization:** Quantum Development Bahamas **Title:** Director **Type of organization:** Real Estate **Major product:** Construction and site development services specializing in pizza restaurants and ice cream parlors **Area of distribution:** International **Expertise:** Marketing, business development, site acquisitions, sales, project management and client relations **Hob./spts.:** Community service (helping children with drug addiction), music, cats, travel **SIC code:** 65 **Address:** Quantum Development Bahamas, 1034 Russell Dr., Highland Beach, FL 33487-4230 **E-mail:** rosede@adelphia.net

DEAN III, HARRY E.
Industry: Finance **Born:** October 21, 1968, Clarksburg, West Virginia **Univ./degree:** A.A., West Virginia University, 1990 **Current organization:** George Mason Mortgage, LLC **Title:** Executive Vice President **Type of organization:** Financial services **Major product:** Mortgage banking **Area of distribution:** Virginia **Expertise:** Sales **Honors/awards:** #1 Producer since 1997 **Affiliations:** M.B.A. Northern Virginia Builders Association **Hob./spts.:** Golf, travel, family **SIC code:** 60 **Address:** George Mason Mortgage, LLC, 4035 Ridge Top Rd., Fairfax, VA 22030 **E-mail:** edean@gmmc.com **Web address:** www.gmmc.com/eddean

DEASY, JACQUELINE H.
Industry: Finance **Born:** October 17, 1959, Rotterdam, The Netherlands **Univ./degree:** M.A., Business Policy Studies, SUNY Empire State College, 2000 **Current organization:** CGU Life Insurance Co. of New York **Title:** Supervisor, Customer Service **Type of organization:** Insurance company **Major product:** Life insurance and annuities **Area of distribution:** International **Expertise:** Management **Affiliations:** A.A.U.W.; Leadership Niagara **Hob./spts.:** Reading, walking **SIC code:** 64 **Address:** CGU Life Insurance Co. of New York, 100 Corporate Pkwy., Suite 300, Buffalo, NY 14226 **E-mail:** deiseach1058@juno.com

DENOOY, DEBORAH J.
Industry: Finance **Born:** March 2, 1949, Washington, D.C. **Univ./degree:** B.F.A., Lake Forest College, 1972 **Current organization:** Morgan Stanley **Title:** Sr. Vice President/F.P.A./Financial Advisor **Type of organization:** Personal finances **Major product:** Financial services **Area of distribution:** International **Expertise:** Financial advise, administration **Published works:** Newsletter **Affiliations:** F.P.A.; Financial Women's Association **Hob./spts.:** Family, reading, swimming, sports **SIC code:** 62 **Address:** Morgan Stanley, 1775 Eye St. N.W., Washington, DC 20006 **E-mail:** deborah.denooy@morganstanley.com

DICKEY, JOSEPH F.
Industry: Financial **Born:** April 1, 1934, Orange County, North Carolina **Univ./degree:** B.S., Animal Science, 1956; M.S., Reproductive Physiology and Endocrinology, 1962, North Carolina State University; Ph.D., Reproductive Physiology and Endocrinology, 1965, Clemson University **Current organization:** World Financial Group **Title:** Marketing Director **Type of organization:** Financial services **Major product:** Mutual funds, annuities, insurance **Area of distribution:** South Carolina **Expertise:** Marketing to seniors, securities, mutual funds, insurance, estate planning; Certified Worksite Instructor **Affiliations:** N.I.C.E.P.; C.S.A. **SIC code:** 62 **Address:** World Financial Group, 218 Hunter Ave., Clemson, SC 29631 **E-mail:** jfdickey@bellsouth.net **Web address:** www.jdickey.wsgnet.com

DICKINSON, ROBERT M.
Industry: Financial **Born:** June 15, 1932, Columbus, Ohio **Univ./degree:** A.B., 1954; M.B.A., 1960, Harvard Business School **Current organization:** Ameriprise Financial Services, Inc. **Title:** Financial Advisor **Type of organization:** Financial services **Major product:** Financial planning, investments, insurance, annuities, certificates **Area of distribution:** National **Affiliations:** Financial Planning Association; Reserve Officers Association; Military Officers Association of America; Colonel (Retired), U.S. Army **Hob./spts.:** Painting, golf **SIC code:** 62 **Address:** Ameriprise Financial Services, Inc., 209 Tabor St., Punta Gorda, FL 33950 **E-mail:** pgefa@aol.com

DITARANTO, RICHARD M.
Industry: Financial **Born:** February 11, 1968, Paterson, New Jersey **Current organization:** Retirement Investment Services **Title:** President **Type of organization:** Consultant **Major product:** Retirement services **Area of distribution:** New Jersey **Expertise:** Retirement planning **Hob./spts.:** Golf, family **SIC code:** 62 **Address:** Retirement Investment Services, 30 Two Bridges Rd., Suite 205, Fairfield, NJ 07004

DONOVAN, SALLYANNE
Industry: Insurance/law **Born:** February 5, 1954, Philadelphia, Pennsylvania **Univ./degree:** B.S., LaSalle University, 1975; J.D., Cum Laude, Widener School of Law, 1994 **Current organization:** Harleysville Insurance Co. **Title:** Vice President & Director of Property/Casualty Claims **Type of organization:** P&C insurance company **Major product:** Insurance **Area of distribution:** National **Expertise:** Insurance/legal **Honors/awards:** Certificate of Achievement in Advanced Insurance; The American Jurisprudence Award in Insurance Law **Published works:** "Networking Among the Mutuals" **Affiliations:** Pennsylvania Bar Association; New Jersey Bar Association; Pennsylvania Defense Institute; Montgomery Bar Association; Pennsylvania Trial Lawyers Association **Hob./spts.:** Golf, theatre, reading **SIC code:** 63 **Address:** Harleysville Insurance Co., 355 Maple Ave., Harleysville, PA 19438 **E-mail:** sdonovan@harleysvillegroup.com **Web address:** www.harleysvillegroup.com

DOUBEK, CHRISTOPHER R.
Industry: Finance **Born:** March 9, 1962 **Current organization:** Terra Nova Trading L.L.C. **Title:** President/Co-Owner **Type of organization:** Brokerage firm **Major product:** Financial services **Area of distribution:** International **Expertise:** Financial market **Published works:** Chicago Sun Times **Affiliations:** N.A.S.D. **Hob./spts.:** Sailing **SIC code:** 62 **Address:** Terra Nova Trading L.L.C., 100 S. Wacker Dr., Suite 1550, Chicago, IL 60606 **E-mail:** c.doubek@terranovatrading.com **Web address:** www.terranovatrading.com

DOUGHERTY, PATRICK E.
Industry: Real Estate **Current organization:** TimeShares United Inc. **Title:** Founder **Type of organization:** Time share brokerage **Major product:** Vacation properties **Area of distribution:** International **Expertise:** Marketing and advertising vacation properties **Honors/awards:** Congressional Medal Business Award **Affiliations:** B.A.C. **Hob./spts.:** Tampa Bay Thunder Lacrosse team **SIC code:** 65 **Address:** TimeShares United Inc., 2643 Gulf to Bay Blvd., Suite 1560-405, Clearwater, FL 33759 **E-mail:** patrick@timesharesunited.com **Web address:** www.timesharesunited.com

DOW, J. MICHAEL
Industry: Real estate **Born:** October 9, 1947, Glasgow, Scotland, U.K. **Univ./degree:** University of the West of England, 1969 **Current organization:** CRESA Partners **Title:** President **Type of organization:** Real estate broker **Major product:** Corporate real estate services **Area of distribution:** International **Expertise:** Commercial office space **Honors/awards:** Member, The Royal Institute of Chartered Surveyors; Site Selection Award to CRESA Partners, 2001-2005 **Affiliations:** The Urban Land Institute; Founding member, CORENET, European Chapter **Hob./spts.:** Golf, downhill skiing, badminton, theatre **SIC code:** 65 **Address:** CRESA Partners, 100 Park Ave., 24th floor, New York, NY 10017 **E-mail:** mdow@cresapartners.com **Web address:** www.cresapartners.com

DRAKE, BRIAN N.
Industry: Financial services **Born:** March 17, 1941, Teaneck, New Jersey **Univ./degree:** B.A., General Studies, University of Nebraska, 1972 **Current organization:** Drake, Saunders & Diwinsky, Ltd. **Title:** President/Certified Senior Advisor (CSA) **Type of organization:** Financial **Major product:** Pre-retirement and retirement planning for seniors **Area of distribution:** National **Expertise:** Advising seniors about investing **Affiliations:** S.S.M.P.; S.C.S.A.; F.P.A.; N.C.A.; A.A.R.P. **Hob./spts.:** Reading, golf, boating **SIC code:** 62 **Address:** Drake, Saunders & Diwinsky, Ltd., P.O. Box 489, South Orleans, MA 02662 **E-mail:** senioradvisor@email.com

DREW, RANDAL H.
Industry: Financial **Univ./degree:** B.S., Finance and Accounting, Florida State University J.D., University of Florida, 1984 **Current organization:** V3 Capital Strategies, LLC **Title:** President & CEO **Type of organization:** Financial consulting, investment firm **Major product:** Investment banking **Area of distribution:** International **Expertise:** Management **Affiliations:** T.M.A. **Hob./spts.:** Woodworking **SIC code:** 67 **Address:** V3 Capital Strategies, LLC, 17 State St., 8th floor, New York, NY 10004 **E-mail:** rhdrew@v3capital.com

DUMLER, JAMES M.
Industry: Financial **Born:** July 8, 1960, Denver, Colorado **Univ./degree:** M.B.A., Duke University, 1989 **Current organization:** Republic Financial Corp. **Title:** Managing Director **Type of organization:** Financial **Major product:** Private Equity, Special Assets, Structured Finance; Industries: Energy, Chemicals, Polymers, Packaging, Animal Nutrition, Distribution, Agriculture **Area of distribution:** International **Expertise:** Finance, general management, turnarounds **Published works:** Article **Affiliations:** Turnaround Management Association; Rocky Mountain Venture Club **Hob./spts.:** Flyfishing **SIC code:** 62 **Address:** 7126 S. Oneida Circle, Centennial, CO 80112 **E-mail:** jd7626@aol.com

DUNKELMAN, DAVID M.
Industry: Real estate **Born:** March 3, 1977, Voorhees, New Jersey **Univ./degree:** B.S., Criminology, Rutgers University **Current organization:** Colliers L&A **Title:**

Sr. Associate **Type of organization:** Full service commercial real estate firm **Major product:** Retail, office and industrial sales and leasing, investments sales, appraisal, property management, construction, finance and asset management **Area of distribution:** Pennsylvania **Expertise:** Retailers and landlords **Affiliations:** I.C.S.C.; Tri-State Realtors Commercial Alliance **Hob./spts.:** Sports, movies, biography **SIC code:** 65 **Address:** Colliers L&A, 399 Market St., 3rd floor, Philadelphia, PA 19106 **E-mail:** david.dunkelman@colliers.com

DURDEN, LLEWELLYN GARVIN
Industry: Real estate **Current organization:** Point South Realty Group Inc. **Title:** President, Broker **Type of organization:** Brokerage **Major product:** Real estate sales and investments **Area of distribution:** South Carolina **Expertise:** Residential, commercial, industrial, land, business properties **Honors/awards:** Circle of Excellence, 1989-1992 **Affiliations:** Aiken Chamber of Commerce **SIC code:** 65 **Address:** Point South Realty Group Inc., 948 Dougherty Rd, Aiken, SC 29803 **E-mail:** pointstrealty@bellsouth.net

EMERY, BARBARA L.
Industry: Financial **Born:** May 14, 1952, Ithaca, New York **Current organization:** Tompkins Employees Federal Credit Union **Title:** Manager **Type of organization:** Lending institution **Major product:** Loans **Area of distribution:** Ithaca, New York **Expertise:** Personal, automobile, home improvement loans **Affiliations:** Ithaca Chamber of Commerce **Hob./spts.:** Boy Scouts of America, crafting **SIC code:** 61 **Address:** Tompkins Employees Federal Credit Union, 322 W. State St., Ithaca, NY 14850 **E-mail:** tefcu@tefcu.com **Web address:** www.tefcu.com

EVANS, GINNY A.
Industry: Title insurance **Born:** September 29, 1940, Bunkie, Louisiana **Current organization:** First American Title Insurance Co. **Title:** Louisiana State Marketing Director **Type of organization:** Underwriter **Major product:** Title insurance **Area of distribution:** National **Expertise:** All areas of title insurance **Hob./spts.:** Singing, painting **SIC code:** 63 **Address:** First American Title Ins. Co., 101 Hartford Circle, West Monroe, LA 71291 **E-mail:** gevans@firstam.com

EXCELL, ALTHEA KAY
Industry: Financial **Univ./degree:** B.A., Tourism, University of Montego Bay, Jamaica **Current organization:** Dell Mortgage Financial Co. **Title:** President **Type of organization:** Finance company **Major product:** Financial lending, mortgages **Area of distribution:** Florida **Expertise:** Refinancing, first time mortgages **SIC code:** 61 **Address:** Dell Mortgage Financial Co., 55275 S. University Dr., Davie, FL 33328 **E-mail:** kxl@delmortgage.net

FALISI, MARIA C.
Industry: Financial/Real Estate **Born:** June 21, 1960, San Juan, Puerto Rico **Univ./degree:** B.A., Business, Pace University, 1984 **Current organization:** Republic Home Mortgage Corp./Republic Home Realty Corp. **Title:** President **Type of organization:** Mortgage company/Real estate broker **Major product:** Mortgages/real estate sales **Area of distribution:** Brooklyn, New York **Expertise:** Mortgage and real estate broker **Affiliations:** National Association of Mortgage Brokers; New York Association of Mortgage Brokers; Yoli Cancer Foundation **Hob./spts.:** Golf **SIC code:** 61 **Address:** Republic Home Mortgage Corp./Republic Home Realty Corp., 190 N. Tenth St., Brooklyn, NY 11211 **E-mail:** republichome1@aol.com **Web address:** www.therepublicsgroup.com

FARASY, THOMAS M.
Industry: Real estate **Univ./degree:** B.S., Business Administration, St. Louis University, 1967 **Current organization:** Mid-City Financial Corp. **Title:** President/CEO **Type of organization:** Real estate developer **Major product:** Real estate **Area of distribution:** Maryland **Expertise:** Apartment and single family homes; teaches Real Estate Principals and Investments at The American University Graduate School **Affiliations:** N.A.H.B.; U.L.I.; M.N.C.B.I.A.; Victory Housing; Mother Dear's Community Center **Hob./spts.:** Family, jogging, collecting antique trains **SIC code:** 65 **Address:** Mid-City Financial Corp., 8403 Colesville Rd., Suite 400, Silver Spring, MD 20910 **E-mail:** tomf@midcityfinancial.com **Web address:** www.midcityfinancial.com

FELT, ALLEN R.
Industry: Real estate **Current organization:** Ideal Suburban Homes Inc. **Title:** Vice President **Type of organization:** New home construction **Major product:** Sales and construction of new homes **Area of distribution:** Indiana **Expertise:** Sales and new home construction **Honors/awards:** Realtor of the Year **Affiliations:** President, Adam J. Wells Board of Realtors; Chair; Allen County Indian Farm Bureau Policy **SIC code:** 65 **Address:** Ideal Suburban Homes Inc., 522 S. 13th St., Box 549, Decatur, IN 46733 **E-mail:** allenfelt@ideal.com

FISHER, ROBERT W.
Industry: Financial **Born:** September 17, 1952, Springfield, Ohio **Univ./degree:** M.B.A., University of Toledo, 1975 **Current organization:** Morgan Stanley **Title:** Financial Advisor/Retirement Planning Specialist **Type of organization:** Financial advisory corporation **Major product:** Financial planning/investments **Area of distribution:** National **Expertise:** Retirement planning **Affiliations:** American Institute of Certified Public Accountants; Wisconsin Institute of Certified Public Accountants **Hob./spts.:** College football **SIC code:** 62 **Address:** Morgan Stanley, 4545 W. College Ave., Appleton, WI 54914 **E-mail:** rfisher2@new.rr.com

FOLEY, DANIEL PATRICK
Industry: Financial **Born:** December 17, 1976, Pasadena, California **Univ./degree:** B.S., Economics, University of Utah, 2000 **Current organization:** Fulcrum Global Partners **Title:** Associate Analyst **Type of organization:** Independent research-equities **Major product:** Equity research **Area of distribution:** National **Expertise:** Regional banks **Affiliations:** New York Society of Security Analysts **Hob./spts.:** Biking **SIC code:** 67 **Address:** Fulcrum Global Partners, 535 Madison Ave., 8th floor, New York, NY 10006 **E-mail:** dfoley@fulcrumgp.com **Web address:** www.fulcrumgp.com

FONTI, ROBERT G.
Industry: Realty **Univ./degree:** M.A., St. John's University, 1985 **Current organization:** Vincent James Management Co., Inc. **Title:** President **Type of organization:** Real estate **Major product:** Consulting/management **Area of distribution:** National **Expertise:** Real estate **Published works:** Articles **Affiliations:** Huntington Housing Authority; Board Member, Respect for Law Alliance, Inc. **SIC code:** 65 **Address:** Vincent James Management Co., Inc., 31 E. 32nd St., 12th floor, New York, NY 10016 **E-mail:** vjmco@hotmail.com

FORESPRING, JOHN A.
Industry: Insurance **Current organization:** State Farm Independent Agency **Title:** LUTCF Agent **Type of organization:** Insurance agency **Major product:** All lines of insurance **Area of distribution:** National **Expertise:** Life, homeowners and auto insurance **Affiliations:** R.E.S.A.; Y.M.B.A. **Hob./spts.:** Car racing **SIC code:** 64 **Address:** State Farm Independent Agency, 1405 Harrison Ave. N.W., Suite 203, Olympia, WA 98502 **E-mail:** john.forespring.b7tl@statefarm.com

FOX, JONATHAN A.
Industry: Finance **Born:** January 4, 1958, Boston, Massachusetts **Univ./degree:** M.B.A., Harvard University, 1985 **Current organization:** Westley Capital, LLC **Title:** President **Type of organization:** Investment management **Major product:** Private investment funds **Area of distribution:** International **Expertise:** Vulpin fund, alopex fund and hedge fund **Hob./spts.:** Golf, skiing, theatre **SIC code:** 67 **Address:** Westley Capital, LLC, 40 Grove St., Wellesley, MA 02482 **E-mail:** foxjunk@yahoo.com

FRANCO, LYNN H.
Industry: Title insurance **Born:** August 15, 1946, Freeport, New York **Univ./degree:** A.S., Business, Suffolk Community College **Current organization:** Maximus Title, LLC **Title:** Vice President/Title Officer **Type of organization:** Title agency **Major product:** Title insurance **Area of distribution:** New York **Expertise:** Managing clearance officer of title agency; lecturing **Honors/awards:** Honored by Huntington Chamber of Commerce for Volunteerism; "Woman of Distinction", Soroptimist International **Affiliations:** Former Owner/Operator, Abstract Reports, Ltd.; Past President, Treasurer and Board Member, Soroptimist International; Member, President's Counsel, Long Island Women's Agenda; Past Vice President, L.E.T.I.P. **Hob./spts.:** Physical fitness, reading, gourmet cooking, travel **SIC code:** 64 **Address:** Maximus Title, LLC, 780 New York Ave., Suite 2, Huntington, NY 11743 **E-mail:** lhfranco@maximustitle.com

FRANKS, DOUGLAS
Industry: Real estate **Current organization:** Douglas Franks Realty **Title:** Owner/Broker **Type of organization:** Realty **Major product:** Residential real estate **Area of distribution:** Staten Island, New York **Expertise:** Facilitating the purchase and sale of homes **SIC code:** 65 **Address:** Douglas Franks Realty, 770 Castleton Ave., Staten Island, NY 10310 **E-mail:** dfhomes@aol.com **Web address:** www.douglasfranks.com

FRANTZ, HARRY F.
Industry: Real estate **Born:** September 22, 1924, South Buffalo Township, Pennsylvania **Current organization:** Howard Hanna Valley Realty **Title:** Owner/Broker **Type of organization:** Realty **Major product:** Real estate sales **Area of distribution:** Freeport, Pennsylvania **Expertise:** Commercial and residential real estate, insurance, appraisals **Affiliations:** National Association of Realtors; Pennsylvania Association of Realtors **SIC code:** 65 **Address:** Howard Hanna Valley Realty, 996 Freeport Rd., Freeport, PA 16229 **E-mail:** harryf01@alltel.net

FRIEND, MICHAEL S.
Industry: Real estate **Born:** August 11, 1960, Philadelphia, Pennsylvania **Current organization:** Remi Developers **Title:** President **Type of organization:** Real estate development **Major product:** Construction, design of high-end residential single family homes **Area of distribution:** Florida **Expertise:** Marketing, design, finance, construction, sales **Affiliations:** National Builders Association; Vice President, Chamber of Commerce for Lighthouse Point **Hob./spts.:** Boating **SIC code:** 65 **Address:** Remi

Developers, 1819 N.E. 25th St., Lighthouse Point, FL 33064 **E-mail:** lil@remidevelopers.com **Web address:** www.remidevelopers.com

FUENTES PUJOLS, MARIA M.
Industry: Financial **Born:** October 25, 1955, Ponce, Puerto Rico **Univ./degree:** M.A., Finance, 1979; M.A., Management, 1981, University of Arizona **Current organization:** Self-employed **Title:** Consultant **Type of organization:** Consulting **Major product:** Banking transactions, contracts, banking projects **Area of distribution:** Puerto Rico **Expertise:** Banking, finance **Affiliations:** American Association of Financial Professionals **Hob./spts.:** Classical music, dancing, jogging **SIC code:** 60 **Address:** Colinas Monte Carlo, 34th St. C7, San Juan, PR 00936

FULK, GARY R.
Industry: Financial **Univ./degree:** B.S., Indiana University, 1964 **Current organization:** Fulk Financial Corp. **Title:** CEO **Type of organization:** Investment firm **Major product:** Investment services **Area of distribution:** National, international **Expertise:** Management **SIC code:** 67 **Address:** Fulk Financial Corp., 800 W. 47th St., Suite 610, Kansas City, MO 64112 **E-mail:** garyf@fulkfinancial.com **Web address:** www.fulkfinancial.com

FURMAN, MARK
Industry: Finance **Univ./degree:** B.A., Economics, 1975, John Jay College CUNY **Current organization:** Materetsky Financial Group **Title:** Partner **Type of organization:** Independent financial planning company specializing in complete retirement management **Major product:** Financial planning **Area of distribution:** Florida and New York **Expertise:** Fixed income planning, income distribution planning, long term care planning **Affiliations:** Financial Planning Association; Financial Services Institute; Society of Certified Senior Advisors **Hob./spts.:** ASA umpire, golf **SIC code:** 62 **Address:** Materetsky Financial Group, 50 Charles Lindbergh Blvd., Suite 400, Uniondale, NY 11553 **E-mail:** mark@materetsky.com **Web address:** www.materetsky.com

GALIETI, CAM A.
Industry: Insurance **Born:** August 9, 1923, Alliance, Ohio **Current organization:** State Farm Insurance **Title:** Agent **Type of organization:** Insurance company **Major product:** General insurance **Area of distribution:** California **Expertise:** Auto, fire, life, home insurance **Hob./spts.:** Physical fitness **SIC code:** 63 **Address:** State Farm Insurance, 18127 Parthenia St., Northridge, CA 91325

GAMINO JR., MIGUEL A.
Industry: Insurance **Born:** May 21, 1976, Yuma, Arizona **Univ./degree:** B.B.A., Accounting/Computer Information Systems, University of Texas, El Paso, 1999 **Current organization:** JDW Insurance **Title:** Vice President/CIO/Controller **Type of organization:** Sales agency **Major product:** Risk management services, insurance **Area of distribution:** National **Expertise:** Accounting, technology **Affiliations:** Founder, A.I.T.P. **Hob./spts.:** Auto racing **SIC code:** 64 **Address:** JDW Insurance, 415 E. Yandell, El Paso, TX 79902 **E-mail:** mgamino@jdw-insurance.com

GARCIA, J. RAFAEL
Industry: Insurance **Born:** June 28, 1951, Nicaragua **Univ./degree:** B.A., 1980, Mexico **Current organization:** Universe Insurance **Title:** President **Type of organization:** Insurance agency **Major product:** Automobile insurance **Area of distribution:** Miami, Florida **Expertise:** General lines agent **Affiliations:** L.A.A. **Hob./spts.:** Baseball, swimming **SIC code:** 64 **Address:** Universe Insurance, 1563 NW 27th Ave., Miami, FL 33125 **E-mail:** universe_insurance@yahoo.com

GARY, LINDA A.
Industry: Real Estate **Born:** April 11, 1950, Pittsburg, Pennsylvania **Current organization:** Linda A. Gary R.E. Inc. **Title:** President/Broker **Type of organization:** Real estate broker **Major product:** Residential and commercial real estate **Area of distribution:** National **Expertise:** Homes, condos, commercial sales and/or rentals **Affiliations:** N.A.R.; R.B.R.; P.B.B.R.; Chamber of Commerce **Hob./spts.:** Walking **SIC code:** 65 **Address:** Linda A. Gary R.E. Inc., 420 S. County Rd., Palm Beach, FL 33480 **E-mail:** lagre205@aol.com **Web address:** www.lindaagary.com

GELLER, JOSEPH J.
Industry: Investment services **Born:** November 20, 1951, Chicago, Illinois **Univ./degree:** University of Wisconsin at Madison **Current organization:** U.S. Bank **Title:** Application Consultant **Type of organization:** Holding company **Major product:** Software applications **Area of distribution:** National **Expertise:** Design systems, data warehousing and logistics, analyzing systems, technical documentation **Hob./spts.:** Amateur photography, playing the guitar and piano **SIC code:** 67 **Address:** S69W14090 Tess Corner Dr., Muskego, WI 53150 **E-mail:** joejvg@wi.rr.com

GODDARD, GABRIEL L.
Industry: Insurance **Born:** July 22, 1972, Cincinnati, Ohio **Current organization:** Cincinnati Insurance Co. **Title:** Staff Counsel **Type of organization:** Insurance company **Major product:** Insurance **Area of distribution:** Ohio **Expertise:** Insurance coverage and contracts **Affiliations:** Ohio State Bar Association; Columbus Bar Association; Defense Research Institute **Hob./spts.:** Music, golf **SIC code:** 63 **Address:** Cincinnati Insurance Co., 6200 S. Gilmore Rd., Fairfield, OH 45014 **E-mail:** gabe_goddard@staffdefense.com

GODSY, J. MARCUS
Industry: Financial services **Born:** December 22, 1955, Oklahoma City, Oklahoma **Univ./degree:** B.A., University of Oklahoma,1978 **Current organization:** Bank One, Oklahoma **Title:** Senior Vice President **Type of organization:** Financial Institution **Major product:** Commercial real estate **Area of distribution:** National **Expertise:** Commercial real estate manager **Affiliations:** Member, Board of Directors, Leadership Oklahoma City; Associate Member, Oklahoma City Chamber of Commerce; Associate Member, Central Oklahoma Homebuilders Association; Commercial Real Estate Council; Edmond Economic Development Council **Hob./spts.:** Coaching baseball and basketball **SIC code:** 61 **Address:** Bank One, Oklahoma, 1200 N.W. 63rd St., Suite 400, Oklahoma City, OK 73116 **E-mail:** marcus_godsy@bankone.com

GOGLIETTINO, JOHN C.
Industry: Finance **Born:** Danbury, Connecticut **Univ./degree:** B.A., Western Connecticut State University, 1975 **Current organization:** John C. Gogliettino - Insurance Broker **Title:** Owner **Type of organization:** Marketing/brokerage firm **Major product:** Insurance **Area of distribution:** Danbury, Connecticut **Expertise:** Life insurance, health insurance, disability and long term care **Affiliations:** NAIFA; NAHU; Society of Financial Service Professionals **Hob./spts.:** Stamp collecting, coin collecting **SIC code:** 64 **Address:** John C. Gogliettino - Insurance Broker - Designations RHU; IUTCF; RFBC, 129 Lake Place, Danbury, CT 06810 **Phone:** (203)792-3629 **Fax:** (203)748-3602 **E-mail:** jcgogliettino@aol.com

GRAF, T. MICHAEL
Industry: Finance **Univ./degree:** M.S., Business Administration, Harvard Business School, 1962 **Current organization:** Bjurman, Barry & Associates, Inc. **Title:** Senior V.P. **Type of organization:** Investment counseling **Major product:** Portfolio management **Area of distribution:** National **Expertise:** Marketing **Affiliations:** A.I.M.R.; L.A.F.A.S. **SIC code:** 67 **Address:** Bjurman, Barry & Associates, Inc., 10100 Santa Monica Blvd., Suite 1200, Los Angeles, CA 90067 **E-mail:** tmgraf@bjurman.com

GREEN, ERNEST G.
Industry: Financial **Born:** September 22, 1941, Little Rock, Arkansas **Univ./degree:** M.A., Sociology, Michigan State University, 1964 **Current organization:** Lehman Bros. **Title:** Managing Director **Type of organization:** Investment banking **Major product:** Financial services **Area of distribution:** International **Expertise:** Public finance **Affiliations:** N.A.S.P.; Council on Foreign Relations **SIC code:** 67 **Address:** Lehman Bros., 800 Connecticut Ave. N.W., Washington, DC 20006 **E-mail:** egreen@lehman.com

GREEN, MARGO
Industry: Real estate **Born:** July 10, Binghamton, New York **Univ./degree:** Attended Syracuse University for Business; Attended Tulane University for Paralegal Studies **Current organization:** Century 21 Marie K. Butler, R.E. **Title:** Broker/Owner **Type of organization:** Brokerage **Major product:** Real estate sales **Area of distribution:** Northern New Jersey, **Expertise:** Residential and commercial sales, commercial property **Honors/awards:** Million Dollar Producer; Agent Awards **Affiliations:** National Association of Realtors; New Jersey Association of Realtors; Professional Standards Committee, The Real Source Board of Realtors (Professional Standards Committee **Hob./spts.:** Reading, physical fitness, travel **SIC code:** 65 **Address:** Century 21 Marie K. Butler, R.E., 30 Kinderkamack Rd., Oradell, NJ 07646 **E-mail:** c21mah@aol.com

GRISWOLD, ROBERT M.
Industry: Financial **Born:** Montclair, New Jersey **Univ./degree:** B.S., Engineering, Cornell University; M.B.A., Houston Baptist University; Ph.D., Finance, Madison University **Current organization:** General Financial Services **Title:** President **Type of organization:** Financial firm **Major product:** Consulting **Area of distribution:** National **Expertise:** Finance **Honors/awards:** Sigma Beta Delta, National Honor Society **Published works:** 6 articles **Affiliations:** F.P.A.; N.A.T.P.; N.S.P.S.; A.I.T.S.; A.C.H.E.; H.F.M.A. **Hob./spts.:** Golf, sailing, swimming, jogging **SIC code:** 67 **Address:** General Financial Services, 9898 Bissonnet St. #250, Houston, TX 77036 **E-mail:** rmgriswold@aol.com **Web address:** www.goodplanner.org

GROPPE, PAULA
Industry: Real estate **Born:** February 24, Alexandria, Louisiana **Univ./degree:** Attended Murray State University, Kentucky **Current organization:** Century 21 Solid Gold Realty, Inc. **Title:** President/Broker **Type of organization:** Real estate office **Major product:** Servicing buyers and sellers **Area of distribution:** Central New Jersey **Expertise:** New home construction, administration, sales **Honors/awards:** Member, Million Dollar Club, 1972-85; Broker of Record, 1985 **Affiliations:** Buck Township Chamber of Commerce; Century 21 Broker's Council **Hob./spts.:** Riding

horseback, skiing **SIC code:** 65 **Address:** Century 21 Solid Gold Realty, Inc., 721 Brick Blvd., Brick, NJ 08723 **E-mail:** gold721@aol.com

GULLETT, NIKKI S.
Industry: Insurance **Born:** October 7, 1971, Orange City, California **Current organization:** Title America of Jacksonville **Title:** President, Owner **Type of organization:** Real estate title company **Major product:** Title insurance **Area of distribution:** Jacksonville, Florida **Expertise:** Closing services **Honors/awards:** #1 Florida Agent 4 Years in a Row, United General Title Insurance Co. **Affiliations:** W.C.R.; N.E.F.A.R.; Jacksonville Chamber of Commerce **Hob./spts.:** Travel, race cars, interior decorating **SIC code:** 64 **Address:** Title America of Jacksonville, 10448 Old St. Augustine Rd., Jacksonville, FL 32257 **E-mail:** nikki@titleamerica.us **Web address:** www.titleamerica.us

HADLEY, NEIFA ELDEICA
Industry: Healthcare/insurance **Univ./degree:** M.S.N., St. Peter's College, 2004 **Current organization:** Horizon Blue Cross Blue Shield of New Jersey **Title:** Hospital Oversight Nurse **Type of organization:** Insurance company **Major product:** Medical insurance **Area of distribution:** National **Expertise:** Hospitalist oversight nurse - program development **Affiliations:** C.M.S.A.; Hospitalist Org. **Hob./spts.:** Reading, travel, cooking **SIC code:** 63 **Address:** 95 Clendenny Ave., Jersey City, NJ 07304 **E-mail:** neifa_hadley@horizonblue.com

HAKALA, THOMAS J.
Industry: Financial **Born:** July 6, 1948, Bayonne, New Jersey **Univ./degree:** A.B., Georgetown University, 1970; J.D., St. John's University School of Law, 1975 **Current organization:** Wilmington Trust Co. **Title:** Managing Director **Type of organization:** Bank/trust company **Major product:** Financial services **Area of distribution:** National **Expertise:** Accounting, estate planning, tax planning, business development, corporate management; Certified Public Accountant **Published works:** Articles **Affiliations:** A.I.C.P.A.; State Planning Council of New York City; New York State Society of Certified Public Accountants **Hob./spts.:** Fishing, golf, jogging, swimming **SIC code:** 60 **Address:** Wilmington Trust Co., 520 Madison Ave., New York, NY 10022 **E-mail:** thakala@wilmingtontrust.com **Web address:** www.wilmingtontrust.com

HAMECS, ROBERT T.
Industry: Finance **Born:** August 10, 1947, Hazleton, Pennsylvania **Univ./degree:** M.B.A., Fordham University, 1972 **Current organization:** Clinton Group **Title:** Portfolio Manager **Major product:** Financial trading **Area of distribution:** International **Expertise:** Trading **Affiliations:** N.Y.A.C.; Upper Ridgewood Tennis Club **SIC code:** 67 **Address:** Clinton Group, 55 Water St., New York, NY 10005 **E-mail:** hamecr@cncdsl.com

HAMPTON, HEATH H.
Industry: Finance **Born:** May 24, 1968, Pratt, Kansas **Univ./degree:** A.A., Business, Wichita State University; B.P.A., Washburn University-1994 **Current organization:** New England Financial **Title:** Managing Associate **Type of organization:** Financial **Major product:** Financial services/products **Area of distribution:** International **Expertise:** Marketing/recruiting **Affiliations:** P.A.A.K. **Hob./spts.:** Fishing, golf **SIC code:** 60 **Address:** New England Financial, P.O. Box 8820, Topeka, KS 66608 **E-mail:** hhampton@kscable.com

HARBERS, RONALD R.
Industry: Real estate **Born:** May 4, 1952, Dallas, Texas **Current organization:** M.S.D.W. Thanksgiving Tower Project, LP **Title:** RPA, FMA **Expertise:** Engineering **Affiliations:** B.O.M.A. **Hob./spts.:** Bird watching, water gardening **SIC code:** 65 **Address:** MSDW Thanksgiving Tower Project, LP, 1601 Elm St., Suite 325, Dallas, TX 75201 **E-mail:** rharbers@macfarlan.com

HARMS, LARRY D.
Industry: Finance **Born:** October 6, 1943, Pontiac, Michigan **Univ./degree:** B.B.A., Finance, University of Michigan, 1974 **Current organization:** Financial Consulting Services **Title:** Financial Planner **Type of organization:** Financial services **Major product:** Fee only financial planning **Area of distribution:** New Orleans, Louisiana **Expertise:** Asset management **Affiliations:** F.P.A.; R.N.C.; Pacoderm Society **Hob./spts.:** Golf, politics **SIC code:** 62 **Address:** 70 English Turn Dr., New Orleans, LA 70131 **E-mail:** ldharms@bellsouth.net

HARRIS, KEITH P.
Industry: Insurance **Born:** July 28, 1961, St. Louis, Missouri **Univ./degree:** B.A., University of Hawaii, 1986 **Current organization:** OFAM Adjusters, Inc. **Title:** President **Type of organization:** Independent adjusters **Major product:** Adjusting and surveying **Area of distribution:** International **Expertise:** Cranes and heavy equipment **Hob./spts.:** Camping, hiking, boating, martial arts, hunting **SIC code:** 64 **Address:** OFAM Adjusters, Inc., 2375 E. Tropicana Ave., Suite 157, Las Vegas, NV 89119 **E-mail:** keith@ofamadjuster.com

HARVEY, LEE G.
Industry: Real Estate **Born:** April 15, 1927, Candler, North Carolina **Univ./degree:** A.A. with Honors, Law, Southwestern College, 1992 **Current organization:** A United Professional Corp. DBA Professional Real Estate Management **Title:** President **Type of organization:** Property management **Major product:** Apartments, shopping centers, condo associations, condo-conversions **Area of distribution:** California **Expertise:** Entrepreneur in property management, general contractor, electrical contractor, landscaping contractor **Honors/awards:** Woman of the Year, San Diego Apartment Association, 1994 **Affiliations:** Past Founding Board Member, California Association of Community Managers; Community Institute Association; President, Highland Avenue Renovation Project **Hob./spts.:** Quilt making **SIC code:** 65 **Address:** A United Professional Corp. DBA Professional Real Estate Management, 4305 Gesner St., Suite 340, San Diego, CA 92117 **E-mail:** lee@propmgr.us

HATFIELD, JEFFREY W.
Industry: Real estate **Born:** December 18, 1968, Lawrence, Kansas **Univ./degree:** B.S., Political Science, University of Kansas, 1991 **Current organization:** Larry A. Hatfield Appraisals L.C. **Type of organization:** Real estate appraiser **Major product:** Carwashes, apartments, commercial buildings, single family investments **Area of distribution:** Kansas **Expertise:** Consulting, investments, expert witness **Affiliations:** I.F.A.; Douglas County Big Brothers/Big Sisters Program **SIC code:** 65 **Address:** Larry A. Hatfield Appraisals L.C., 3120 Mesa Way, Suite A, Lawrence, KS 66049 **E-mail:** jeffhatfield@sunflower.com **Web address:** www.hatfieldappraisals.com

HELGREN, BARBARA M.
Industry: Real estate **Born:** November 10, Elmhurst, New York **Univ./degree:** B.S., Morrison University, Nevada **Current organization:** The Equity Group **Title:** President **Type of organization:** Commercial real estate **Major product:** Full service asset management and leasing **Area of distribution:** Nevada **Expertise:** Commercial real estate management and leasing; Certified Property Manager with the Institute of Real Estate Management **Honors/awards:** 2001 Community Achievement Award, Las Vegas Chamber of Commerce; Woman of Distinction Award, National Association of Women Business Owners, 2002; Recipient of the first Sandy Thompson Award for her meritorious service with CIA; Member of the Year 2000, N.C.R.E.W. **Published works:** Write-ups **Affiliations:** Founding Member & Past President, B.O.M.A. (Building Owners and Managers Association); Charter Member, N.C.R.E.W. (Nevada Commercial Real Estate Women); Board Member, Community Counseling Center; Team Leader for United Way's Program Selection Committee; PAYBAC, YES, Inc. Junior Achievement and Child Haven **Hob./spts.:** Family, hiking, running, gourmet cooking **SIC code:** 65 **Address:** The Equity Group, 2500 W. Sahara, Suite 211, Las Vegas, NV 89102 **E-mail:** bhelgren@theequitylb.com

HENDERSON, KAY
Industry: Real Estate **Title:** Licensed Real Estate Broker **Type of organization:** Realty **Major product:** Real estate sales **Expertise:** Managing broker **SIC code:** 65 **Address:** Worthington Realty, Inc., 17901 Summerlin Rd., Suite D, Ft. Myers, FL 33908 **E-mail:** khenderson@worthington-realty.com

HENRY, GEORGE M.
Industry: Financial services **Born:** July 23, 1951, Alexandria, Alabama **Univ./degree:** B.S., Accounting, University of Alabama, 1974 **Current organization:** Stone & Youngberg, LLC **Title:** Municipal Research Director **Type of organization:** Private investment firm **Major product:** Fixed income investments **Area of distribution:** National **Expertise:** Investment analysis **Affiliations:** N.F.M.A.; C.S.M.A. **SIC code:** 67 **Address:** Stone & Youngberg, LLC, 50 California St., 35th floor, San Francisco, CA 94111 **E-mail:** GMHen1@aol.com

HOCKENBROUGH, DAN
Industry: Financial **Univ./degree:** B.S., Finance, B.S., Accounting, Northern Texas State University, 1982; M.S., Taxation, Texas A&M University, 1989 **Current organization:** Self-employed **Title:** Financial Advisor **Area of distribution:** International **Expertise:** Management **Affiliations:** Texas Society of CPAs (TSCPA); American Institute of Certified Public Accountants (AICPA) **Hob./spts.:** Family, sports **SIC code:** 67 **Address:** 2420 Bowie Lane, Grapevine, TX 76051 **E-mail:** danh@mcstay.com

HOFFMEISTER, JESSICA L.
Industry: Financial **Born:** April 22, 1983, Spokane, Washington **Current organization:** Goldman Sachs **Title:** Site Manager **Type of organization:** Investment banking **Major product:** Financial products **Area of distribution:** International **Expertise:** Management **Honors/awards:** National Leadership Award, 2002; Business Woman of the Year, 2002 **Affiliations:** Muscular Dystrophy Association; Habitat for the Humanities **Hob./spts.:** Physical fitness, music, reading, car racing **SIC code:** 62 **Address:** Goldman Sachs, 719 Second Ave., Suite 1300, Seattle, WA 98104 **E-mail:** jessica.hoffmeister@gs.com

HOKETT, TERRY D.
Industry: Property management **Title:** Manager **Major product:** Property management **SIC code:** 65 **Address:** Advanced Property Management, 2960 W. Orange Ave., #9, Anaheim, CA 92804 **E-mail:** terryhokett0711@yahoo.com **Web address:** www.advancedmgt.com

HOLST, RACHEL M.
Industry: Financial **Born:** Osceola, Iowa **Univ./degree:** B.S., Business, Upper Iowa University **Current organization:** Wells Fargo Home Mortgage **Title:** Vice President **Type of organization:** Mortgage company **Major product:** Home mortgages **Area of distribution:** National **Expertise:** Corporate real estate and facilities services **Affiliations:** M.C.R., 1999; S.L.C.R., 2004 (Certifications through CoreNet) **Hob./spts.:** Gourmet cooking, travel **SIC code:** 61 **Address:** Wells Fargo Home Mortgage, 1 Home Campus, X2401-057, Des Moines, IA 50328-0001 **E-mail:** rachel.holst@wellsfargo.com

HOOPER, WILLIAM F.
Industry: Insurance **Born:** July 29, 1920, Oakland, California **Univ./degree:** B.A., Stanford University, 1948 **Current organization:** Student Insurance **Title:** President **Type of organization:** Insurance **Major product:** Accident and health insurance for students **Area of distribution:** Los Angeles, California **Expertise:** Accident and health coverage **Published works:** Legislation Protecting Athletes' Rights **Affiliations:** Rotary, Stanford Alumni; National Championship Basketball Team, 1942, Stanford University (only living member) **Hob./spts.:** Golf **SIC code:** 63 **Address:** Student Insurance, 11661 San Vicente Blvd., Los Angeles, CA 90049

HORSEY, WADE H.
Industry: Finance **Born:** February 16, 1944, Baltimore, Maryland **Univ./degree:** M.B.A., Harvard University, 1974 **Current organization:** Horsey & Co., LLC **Title:** President **Type of organization:** Brokerage firm **Major product:** Investments **Area of distribution:** National **Expertise:** Stock market; Certified financial advisor **Hob./spts.:** Lacrosse **SIC code:** 67 **Address:** Horsey & Co., LLC, 30 Tower Lane, Avon, CT 06001

HUGHES, BRADFORD J.
Industry: Finance **Born:** January 13, 1976, Arlington Heights, Illinois **Univ./degree:** B.S.E.E., University of Illinois, 1998; M.B.A., Finance and Marketing, University of Chicago, 2003 **Current organization:** Lehman Brothers **Title:** M.B.A. **Type of organization:** Financial advisement, planning, brokerage firm **Major product:** Financial services **Area of distribution:** International **Expertise:** Finance **Affiliations:** C.F.A. **Hob./spts.:** Golf, racquetball **SIC code:** 67 **Address:** 2671 N. Lincoln #4S, Chicago, IL 60614 **E-mail:** bhughes@mail.com

HURTADO, JON R.
Industry: Financial **Born:** Detroit, Michigan **Univ./degree:** B.A., Business, University of Michigan **Current organization:** Elite Financial Design, LLC **Title:** President/CEO **Type of organization:** Financial design company **Major product:** Wealth accumulation investments, insurance, asset accumulation, recruiting and marketing strategies **Area of distribution:** National **Expertise:** Wealth accumulation, insurance investment, asset accumulation, recruitments, advertising, marketing and strategies **Honors/awards:** Businessman of the Year, House Leadership Committee, 2006; Michigan Businessman of the Year, National Congressional Committee, 2005; National Congressional Committee Leadership Award, 2005; GAMA Leadership and Management Award, 2005 and 2006; Top Partner Award, New York Life, 2003; Top Recruitment Award, New York Life, 2003; Member, National Register's Who's Who for Business Executives; BIA Spike Award for Management and Recruiting Achievement, 2000 **Affiliations:** G.A.M.A.; B.I.A, **Career accomplishments:** Created a number of successful companies. Elite Financial began operations in November of 2003. By mid 2004 had become a multi-million dollar financial services enterprise. Has worked successfully to put together a team to make initial public offerings. Has managed over $100 million of revenue generated from major companies with 2500 employees. **Hob./spts.:** 3 time World Bench Press Champion; 3 time World Power Lifting Champion **SIC code:** 67 **Address:** Elite Financial Design, LLC, 30100 Telegraph Rd., Suite 480, Bingham Farms, MI 48025 **E-mail:** jonhurtado394@msn.com

JACOBY, SARA T.
Industry: Financial **Born:** September 10, 1964, Huntington, Pennsylvania **Univ./degree:** B.S., Finance, Shippensburg University, 1986 **Current organization:** Morgan Stanley **Title:** C.F.P./Financial Advisor **Type of organization:** Investment bank **Major product:** Investments and financial planning **Area of distribution:** International **Expertise:** Financial consulting, investment planning, strategic analysis, administrative management, business development, sales, marketing **Honors/awards:** Speaker at investment seminars **Affiliations:** Financial Planning Association (FPA); Baltimore Estate Planning Council; Chesapeake Planned Giving Council **Hob./spts.:** Golf, gardening, church activities, youth enrichment, community service work **SIC code:** 62 **Address:** Morgan Stanley, 10751 Falls Rd., Suite 302, Lutherville, MD 21093 **E-mail:** sara.jacoby@morganstanley.com

JOHNSON, DOROTHY
Industry: Financial **Born:** January 21, 1950, Rochester, New York **Univ./degree:** B.A., Business, West Georgia University, 1974 **Current organization:** AIG/Royal Alliance Assoc. **Title:** Eastern Regional Manager **Type of organization:** Securities/brokerage **Major product:** Money management **Area of distribution:** National **Expertise:** Compliance **Affiliations:** N.A.S.D. Arbitrator; Association of Insurance Compliance Professionals **Hob./spts.:** Photography, hiking, children's rights **SIC code:** 62 **Address:** AIG/Royal Alliance Assoc., 13720 Cypress Terrace Circle, Suite 301, Ft. Myers, FL 33907 **E-mail:** compliance2@aol.com

JOHNSON, KEVIN J.
Industry: Financial services **Born:** July 14, 1954, Buffalo, New York **Univ./degree:** A.S., Criminal Justice, Hudson Valley College, 1974 **Current organization:** New York Long Term Care Brokers Ltd. **Title:** President **Type of organization:** Insurance **Major product:** Long term care insurance **Area of distribution:** National **Expertise:** Sales, marketing, management **Affiliations:** Board Member, A.A.L.T.C.I.; A.H.I.A.; S.F.P.; N.A.I.I.A.; N.A.H.U. **Hob./spts.:** Harley bikes, skiing, boating, mountain biking **SIC code:** 64 **Address:** New York Long Term Care Brokers Ltd., 11 Halfmoon Executive Park, Clifton Park, NY 12065-5631 **E-mail:** k-johnson@nyltcb.com

JOHNSON, TERESA H.
Industry: Financial **Born:** Great Falls, Montana **Univ./degree:** B.A., Sociology, University of Pennsylvania; J.D., Vanderbilt University **Current organization:** Money Gram International Inc. **Title:** Executive Vice President and General Counsel **Type of organization:** Financial services **Major product:** Worldwide money transfer **Area of distribution:** International **Expertise:** General legal counsel **Honors/awards:** Women Changemaker Award, 2005 **Affiliations:** Association of Corporate Counsel, Minnesota State Bar Association; Pennsylvania Bar Association; Tennessee Bar Association; American Bar Association, Minnesota Chapter; American Society of Corporate Secretaries; Board of Directors & V.P. of Minnesota Chapter of Association of Corporate Counsel **Hob./spts.:** Golf **SIC code:** 61 **Address:** Money Gram International Inc., 1550 Utica Ave. South, Minneapolis, MN 55416

JONES, THOMAS A.
Industry: Real estate **Born:** February 18, 1935, Newark, New Jersey **Current organization:** Tom Jones Agency **Title:** Owner **Type of organization:** Real estate and appraisals **Major product:** Sales and service **Area of distribution:** Market area: Warren Co., NJ & Northampton Co., PA **Expertise:** Sales of residential & commercial properties and residential appraisals **Affiliations:** N.A.R.; N.J.A.R.; Warren Co., NJ & Northampton Co., PA Board of Realtors **Hob./spts.:** Singing and playing guitar **SIC code:** 65 **Address:** Tom Jones Agency, 406 Rte. #57, Phillipsburg, NJ 08865 **E-mail:** tomjones@fast.net

JUSTICE, EDDY A.
Industry: Financial **Born:** March 10, 1973, Rawlins, Wyoming **Univ./degree:** B.S., Business Administration, John Brown University, 1995 **Current organization:** State Farm Insurance **Title:** Owner/Agent **Type of organization:** Insurance agency **Major product:** Insurance, investments, banking services **Area of distribution:** Poplar Bluff, Missouri **Expertise:** Insurance, financial planning **Affiliations:** Poplar Bluff Lions Club; Greater Poplar Bluff Chamber of Commerce **Hob./spts.:** Baseball **SIC code:** 64 **Address:** Eddy Justice State Farm Insurance Agency, 204 Ferguson, Poplar Bluff, MO 63901 **E-mail:** eddy@eddyjustice.com **Web address:** www.eddyjustice.com

KADZOMBE, WASHINGTON D.
Industry: Financial services **Born:** July 3, 1961, Zimbabwe **Univ./degree:** B.S., Accounting, DeVry University, 1999; M.B.A., Global Management, University of Phoenix, 2003 **Current organization:** Micro Loan One, LLC **Title:** Proprietor **Type of organization:** Loan office **Major product:** Micro loans **Area of distribution:** California **Expertise:** Accounting, consulting **Honors/awards:** N.R.C.C. Businessman of the Year, 2003 **Published works:** 12 newspaper statements **Affiliations:** Board Member, I.M.A.; Business Advisory Council for Republican National Committee **Hob./spts.:** Scuba diving, karate, meditation **SIC code:** 61 **Address:** Micro Loan One LLC, 276 W. Highland Ave., San Bernardino, CA 92405 **E-mail:** instantcash@att.net

KAMEROW, NORMAN W.
Industry: Financial **Univ./degree:** M.S., Financial Service, American College, Pennsylvania, 1984 **Current organization:** Capital Financial Group **Title:** Chairman/Founder **Type of organization:** Independent broker/dealer **Major product:** Financial services **Area of distribution:** National **Expertise:** Personal and business financial planning **Affiliations:** A.S.F.C.; Million Dollar Round Table **Hob./spts.:** Family, tennis, opera **SIC code:** 67 **Address:** Capital Financial Group, 11140 Rockville Pike, 4th floor, Rockville, MD 20852 **E-mail:** nkamerow@cfginc.com **Web address:** www.cfginc.com

KARP, JEROME J.
Industry: Real Estate **Born:** November 5, 1938, Jerusalem **Univ./degree:** Penn State, Industrial Engineering, 1960; M.B.A., Wharton, 1962 **Current organization:**

Southblock, LLC **Title:** Consultant **Type of organization:** Real estate developer **Major product:** Real estate development **Area of distribution:** National **Expertise:** Multi-family, commercial and mixed use development **Hob./spts.:** Travel, swimming, photography, tennis, politics, interior design **SIC code:** 65 **Address:** Southblock, LLC, 828 S. Wabash, Chicago, IL 60605 **E-mail:** joram@southblock.com **Web address:** www.southblock.com

KAUCHAK, JOHN J.
Industry: Banking **Born:** August 10, 1953, Elizabeth, New Jersey **Univ./degree:** B.A., Accounting, King College, 1978 **Current organization:** Unity Bank **Title:** COO/ EVP - Administration **Type of organization:** Bank **Major product:** Financial services **Area of distribution:** Hunterson - Somerset - Union Counties **Expertise:** Operations, information technology, branch, loan servicing **Hob./spts.:** Photography, swimming **SIC code:** 60 **Address:** Unity Bank, 64 Old Highway 22, Clinton, NJ 08809 **E-mail:** john.kauchak@unitybank.com

KAYELLO, SAMMY
Industry: Financial **Univ./degree:** B.S.C.E., University of South Carolina, 1978; M.B.A., Duke University, 1985; Ph.D. Candidate, Duke University **Current organization:** Morgan Stanley **Title:** Managing Director for a European Location **Type of organization:** Investment bank **Major product:** Financial services **Area of distribution:** International **SIC code:** 62 **Address:** Morgan Stanley, 1585 Broadway, New York, NY 10036 **E-mail:** sammy.kayello@morganstanley.com

KELLER, DAVID C.
Industry: Insurance **Born:** July 17, 1952, Philadelphia, Pennsylvania **Univ./degree:** B.S., Business Administration, St. Joseph's University, Philadelphia, Pennsylvania, 1975; Certification, Sales and Marketing Management, University of Pennsylvania Wharton School, 1991 **Current organization:** Berkley Mid-Atlantic Group **Title:** Vice President, Sales and Marketing **Type of organization:** Insurance company **Major product:** Commercial lines P & C (small and middle market) **Area of distribution:** Virginia **Expertise:** Marketing **Hob./spts.:** Family, model trains **SIC code:** 63 **Address:** Berkley Mid-Atlantic Group, 4820 Lake Brook Dr., Glen Allen, VA 23060 **E-mail:** dkeller@wrbmag.com

KELLEY, PAUL E.
Industry: Residential real estate **Born:** July 3, 1939, Portland, Oregon **Univ./degree:** M.S., Computer Science, American University, Washington D.C., 1989 **Current organization:** RE/MAX Affiliates **Title:** Broker **Type of organization:** Real estate brokerage **Major product:** Real estate **Area of distribution:** International **Expertise:** Buyer representation; 20 yr. Air Force veteran **Published works:** Article, "Common Wealth", Real Estate Magazine **Affiliations:** N.A.R.; C.R.S.; C.R.B.; A.B.R. **Hob./spts.:** Photography **SIC code:** 64 **Address:** RE/MAX Affiliates, 6084A Franconia Rd., Alexandria, VA 22310 **E-mail:** vet1nam@pkelley.com **Web address:** www.pkelley.com

KEMP, TERRY LEON
Industry: Mortgage banking **Born:** January 29, 1954, Knoxville, Tennessee **Univ./degree:** A.B., Government and Economics, Oberlin College, 1978; M.P.M., Carnegie Mellon University, 1985 **Current organization:** Citizens Trust Bank Mortgage Services, Inc. **Title:** President/CEO **Type of organization:** Regional community bank **Major product:** Residential/commercial mortgages **Area of distribution:** Georgia **Expertise:** Marketing, finance **Affiliations:** Mortgage Expert, Board Member, Fanny Mae Public Housing **Hob./spts.:** Swimming, reading, weightlifting **SIC code:** 60 **Address:** Citizens Trust Bank Mortgage Services, Inc., 5240 B Panola Industrial Blvd., Decatur, GA 30035 **E-mail:** terry.kemp@ctbmsi.com **Web address:** www.ctbmsi.com

KETTERMAN, KEITH A.
Industry: Financial services **Born:** November 2, 1943, Seymour, Indiana **Univ./degree:** B.S., Business Administration, University of Trevecca, Tennessee, 1970 **Current organization:** National Bank of Tennessee & NBN Corp. **Title:** President/ Chief Executive Officer/Vice Chairman **Type of organization:** Commercial bank **Major product:** Banking **Area of distribution:** National **Expertise:** Manages a $260 million financial organization that includes two banks and deals with lending and financial products **Published works:** Write-ups **Affiliations:** Elected Chairman of Tennessee Bankers Association (June 2003); American Red Cross; Kiwanis; Chamber of Commerce; Economic Development Commission; Educational Foundation; School Board **Hob./spts.:** Sports, collectibles, golf **SIC code:** 60 **Address:** National Bank of Tennessee & NBN Corp., 262 E. Broadway, Newport, TN 37821 **E-mail:** ketterman@nbotbank.com **Web address:** www.nbotbank.com

KHAN, MOHAMED
Industry: Financial **Type of organization:** Credit institution **SIC code:** 61 **Address:** Americlean Express, Inc., 1199 N.E. 1st Ave., Florida City, FL 33034

KINSEY, ARDDA L.
Industry: Real Estate **Born:** May 23, 1941, Cincinnati, Ohio **Univ./degree:** Attended Mount San Antonio College **Current organization:** Crestview Realty **Title:** Broker/ Owner **Type of organization:** Real estate agency **Major product:** Real estate **Area of distribution:** Northwestern Arizona **Expertise:** Relocation, commercial, administration, property investments **Honors/awards:** Million Dollar Club Member, Multiple Listing Service **Affiliations:** Republican Women's League; National Republican Congressional Committee **Hob./spts.:** Playing darts, crafts, swimming, gardening **SIC code:** 65 **Address:** Crestview Realty, 1912 E. Andy Devine Ave., Kingman, AZ 86401 **E-mail:** ardda@crestviewrealty.us **Web address:** www.crestviewrealty.us

KNAPP, KEVIN C.
Industry: Real estate **Born:** July 11, 1974, Chicago, Illinois **Univ./degree:** A.S., Electronic Engineering, DeVry Institute, 1999 **Current organization:** Keller Williams Realty **Title:** Realtor **Type of organization:** Real estate firm **Major product:** Properties **Area of distribution:** Illinois **Expertise:** Sales **Hob./spts.:** Building computers, servers and race cars **SIC code:** 65 **Address:** Keller Williams Realty, 1271 Rickert Dr., Suite 111, Naperville, IL 60544 **E-mail:** kknapp23@attbi.com

KODATT, CHARLIE A.
Industry: Real estate development **Born:** October 12, 1976, Santa Barbara, California **Univ./degree:** B.B.A., Finance; B.B.A., Banking, University of Mississippi, 2000 **Current organization:** Kodatt Group, LLC **Title:** President **Type of organization:** Real estate development and investment firm **Major product:** Shopping centers, multi-family homes, master-planned communities; investment services **Area of distribution:** National **Expertise:** Real estate and investment strategy, urban development, REIT's **Published works:** 2 articles **Affiliations:** U.L.I.; N.A.I.O.P. **Hob./spts.:** Golf, community and charitable volunteering **SIC code:** 65 **Address:** Kodatt Group, LLC, 3928 Baymeadows Rd., Jacksonville, FL 32217 **E-mail:** charlie@kodattgroup.com **Web address:** www.kodattgroup.com

KOEHLER, SCOTT
Industry: Security **Born:** November 28, 1953 **Univ./degree:** B.S., General Engineering, U.S. Military Academy, 1976; M.A., International Relations, University of Southern California, 1980; M.S., Educational Leadership, Troy State University, 1994 **Current organization:** Frost National Bank **Title:** Vice President-Security Manager **Type of organization:** Bank **Major product:** Financial services **Area of distribution:** Texas **Expertise:** Security services **Honors/awards:** Board Certified in Security Management: ASIS Certified Protection Professional (CPP) **Affiliations:** American Society of Industrial Security (ASIS); Professional Association of Diving Instructors (PADI) **Hob./spts.:** Scuba diving, sailing, swimming, running **SIC code:** 60 **Address:** Frost National Bank, 100 W. Houston St., Suite 1102, San Antonio, TX 78296 **E-mail:** scott.koehler@frostbank.com

LAGASSE, JAMES R.
Industry: Financial **Born:** February 1, 1969, Augusta, Maine **Univ./degree:** Computer Information Systems, Thomas College, 1990 **Current organization:** Kennebec Savings Bank **Title:** Chief Technology Officer and Vice President **Type of organization:** Financial institution **Major product:** Deposits and loans **Area of distribution:** Augusta, Maine **Expertise:** Information technology **Affiliations:** OSI Technical Users Group; Chairman, Technology Committee; Maine Children's Alliance **SIC code:** 60 **Address:** Kennebec Savings Bank, 150 State St., Augusta, ME 04330 **E-mail:** jlagasse@kennebecsavings.com **Web address:** www.kennebecsavings.com

LAM, ROBERT Q.
Industry: Financial **Univ./degree:** D.B.A.; J.D. **Current organization:** The Millennium International Group, LLC **Title:** Chief Executive Officer **Type of organization:** Consulting, financial services **Major product:** Consulting, financial, hospitality **Area of distribution:** International **Expertise:** Investment banking, operations **SIC code:** 67 **Address:** The Millennium International Group, LLC, 19925 Stevens Creek Blvd., Suite 126, Cupertino, CA 95014 **E-mail:** drlam@millenniumig.com **Web address:** www.millenniumig.com

LANG, RAYMOND B.
Industry: Investment banking **Born:** February 6, 1959, Mineola, New York **Univ./degree:** J.D., New York Law School, 1984 **Current organization:** BNY Capital Markets, Inc. (subsidiary of The Bank of New York Co.) **Title:** Managing Director **Type of organization:** Bank **Major product:** Equity financing **Area of distribution:** International **Expertise:** Corporate finance **Honors/awards:** Elizabeth Ann Seaton Award **Affiliations:** N.Y.B.A.; Life Member, Republican National Committee **Hob./spts.:** CYO coaching, basketball, golf, religious education **SIC code:** 67 **Address:** BNY Capital Markets, Inc., 32 Old Slip, New York, NY 10286 **E-mail:** blang@bankofny.com

LANGHOFER, GAYLIN J.
Industry: Real estate **Born:** May 25, 1952, Duncan, Oklahoma **Univ./degree:** Elementary Education, Cameron State University **Current organization:** Ritchie Associates

Inc. **Title:** Realtor New Home Specialist **Type of organization:** Builder/developer **Major product:** Sales and design for residential construction **Area of distribution:** Kansas **Expertise:** Marketing design of new construction **Affiliations:** National Board of Realtors; Wichita Builders Association; Lambda Tau Delta; Kansas Board of Realtors **Hob./spts.:** Scrapbooking, boating, reading, floral arrangements **SIC code:** 65 **Address:** Ritchie Associates Inc., 8100 E. 22nd St., Bldg. 1000, Wichita, KS 67226 **E-mail:** gaylin@ritchieassociates.com **Web address:** www.ritchieassociates.com

LAWRENCE, DAVID
Industry: Real Estate **Born:** January, 1, 1964, Norwich, Connecticut **Univ./degree:** B.S., Accounting, Midwestern State University **Current organization:** Texas Home Realty/Texans Commercial Realty **Title:** Broker/Owner **Type of organization:** Real Estate **Major product:** Real estate books/publications **Area of distribution:** National **Expertise:** Residential, commercial realty **Published works:** "For Sale By Owner", "Real Estate Blues", "Home Buyers Guide to Real Estate" **Affiliations:** N.A.R.; T.A.R.; C.C.A.R.; Metro Tech, San Antonio Association of Realtors; Houston Board of Realtors **Hob./spts.:** Martial arts, (Tae Kwan Do), computers, family activities **SIC code:** 65 **Address:** Texas Home Realty/Texans Commercial Realty, 3025 Laguna, Plano, TX 75023 **E-mail:** dave@texanshomerealty.com **Web address:** www.texanshomerealty.com

LAYNE, ANDREW P.
Industry: Real Estate **Born:** October 22, 1973, Sarasota, Florida **Univ./degree:** B.A., Liberal Arts, University of Toledo **Current organization:** Anchor Appraisals, Inc. **Title:** President/Owner **Type of organization:** Appraisal firm **Major product:** Real estate appraisal services **Area of distribution:** Florida **Expertise:** Residential appraisals **Affiliations:** U.S.A.P.P.; A.O.P.A.; Appraisal Institute; Independent Appraisers **Hob./spts.:** Airplane pilot **SIC code:** 65 **Address:** Anchor Appraisals, Inc., 400 E. Airport Ave., Venice, FL 34285 **E-mail:** andrew@anchorappraisalsinc.com **Web address:** www.anchorappraisalsinc.com

LE, TINA T.
Industry: Insurance **Born:** July 24, 1973, Vietnam **Current organization:** Tina T. Le Insurance Agency **Title:** President **Type of organization:** Insurance agency **Major product:** Insurance services **Area of distribution:** Houston, Texas **Expertise:** Auto, home, health, life, commercial, tax advisory **Hob./spts.:** Music **SIC code:** 64 **Address:** Tina T. Le Insurance Agency, 6918 Corporate Dr., Suite A15, Houston, TX 77036 **E-mail:** hebui@farmersagent.com

LEBLANC, BETTY
Industry: Real Estate **Born:** March 10, 1944, Abbeville, Louisiana **Current organization:** Betty LeBlanc Realty Inc. **Title:** Owner/Broker **Type of organization:** Realty **Major product:** Real estate **Area of distribution:** National **Expertise:** Residential, land, pasture, county property **Hob./spts.:** Gardening, fish pond, camping **SIC code:** 65 **Address:** Betty LeBlanc Realty Inc., 107 S. Louisiana Ave., Abbeville, LA 70510 **E-mail:** bettyleb@bettyleblanc.com **Web address:** www.bettyleblanc.com

LEE, STEPHEN B.
Industry: Land development **Born:** March 6, 1937, Brooklyn, New York **Univ./degree:** A.S., Business Administration, St. Petersburg Jr. College, 1976 **Current organization:** Clayton Property Development, LLC **Title:** Partner **Type of organization:** Property development/management firm **Major product:** Shopping centers **Area of distribution:** New Jersey **Expertise:** Commercial property **Affiliations:** A.O.P.A.; Experimental Aircraft Association **Hob./spts.:** Aircraft building and flying, bowling, boating, travel **SIC code:** 65 **Address:** 11314 Portsmouth St., Spring Hill, FL 34609

LENTINI, DOMENICO JOSEPH
Industry: Real estate **Born:** October 13, 1949, Washington, D.C. **Current organization:** Marian Properties, LLC **Title:** Vice President **Type of organization:** Real Estate Broker **Major product:** Family owned real estate services **Area of distribution:** North Potomac, Maryland **Expertise:** Real estate **SIC code:** 65 **Address:** Marian Properties, LLC, 12605 High Meadow Rd., North Potomac, MD 20878

LINDQUIST, ANDERS R.
Industry: Financial **Born:** August 3, 1954, Boras, Sweden **Univ./degree:** B.A., Languages, Institute Diavot, Switzerland, 1977 **Title:** President **Type of organization:** Investment banking/brokerage **Major product:** Scandinavian equities **Area of distribution:** International **Expertise:** Administration, equity sales **Affiliations:** I.S.M.A. **Hob./spts.:** Golf, tennis, sailing **SIC code:** 62 **Address:** Nordic Partners, 488 Madison Ave., 17th floor, New York, NY 10022 **E-mail:** al@nordic-partners.com

LLINAS-FLORENTINO, LARISSA
Industry: Real estate **Born:** April 26, 1969, Mexico City **Univ./degree:** B.A., Economics, Poncincia University, 1992; M.S., Arthur D. Little School, 1996 **Current organization:** Gestion y Servicios Empresariales,SA **Title:** Executive Vice President **Type of organization:** Business services **Major product:** Brokerage **Area of distribution:** International **Expertise:** Marketing, sales, negotiation **Affiliations:** Real Estate Association of the Dominican Republic **Hob./spts.:** Racquetball, wine connoisseur **SIC code:** 65 **Address:** Gestion Y Servicios Empresariales, SA, 10411 N.W. 28th St., Suite C-104, Miami, FL 33172 **E-mail:** llinaslf@aol.com

LOMBARDY, ROSEMARY
Industry: Finance **Born:** August 19, 1955, Amityville, New York **Univ./degree:** B.A. With Honors, Spanish/Latin American Studies, University of Florida, 1976 **Current organization:** UBS Paine Webber **Title:** Senior Vice President - Investments **Type of organization:** Financial services **Major product:** Investments **Area of distribution:** International **Expertise:** Financial planning and investment management **Affiliations:** Past Member, Exchange Club of Murfreesboro **Hob./spts.:** Family, reading **SIC code:** 67 **Address:** UBS Paine Webber, 3102 W. End Ave., Suite 500, Nashville, TN 37203 **E-mail:** rosemary.lombardy@ubspw.com **Web address:** www.ubspw.com

LONG, ARCHIE L.
Industry: Commercial leasing, construction **Current organization:** Long-Middendorf Corp. **Title:** Facilities Manager **Type of organization:** Real estate **Major product:** Real estate, construction **Area of distribution:** National **Expertise:** Licensed General Contractor; security, fire and safety systems, organizational planning, team leadership, program design and implementation, plumbing, heavy equipment operations **Hob./spts.:** Photography, computers, sports **SIC code:** 65 **Address:** Long-Middendorf Corp., 3200 S. Sheffield Ave., Hammond, IN 46327 **E-mail:** prof-gizmo1@msn.com

LUTZ, GARY JAMES
Industry: Insurance **Born:** November 29, 1954, New York, New York **Univ./degree:** M.A., State University of New York, 1983 **Current organization:** AIG **Title:** Vice President **Type of organization:** Insurance Company/stock corp. **Major product:** Environmental insurance **Area of distribution:** National **Expertise:** Marketing, underwriting, licensed CPA, Unlimited Master Mariner (captain's license) **Affiliations:** P.I.M.A. **Hob./spts.:** Golf, tennis, bike riding **SIC code:** 64 **Address:** AIG, 777 S. Figueroa St., Los Angeles, CA 90017 **E-mail:** gary.lutz@aig.com

MA, JOHN
Industry: Real estate **Born:** September 7, 1944, Canton, China **Univ./degree:** Attended C.W. Post College, Long Island University **Current organization:** Century 21 Milestone Realty **Title:** CEO/Broker **Type of organization:** Real estate broker **Major product:** Residential and commercial real estate sales **Area of distribution:** Flushing, New York **Expertise:** Sales **Hob./spts.:** Tennis **SIC code:** 65 **Address:** Century 21 Milestone Realty, 135-14 Northern Blvd., Flushing, NY 11354 **E-mail:** jm@century21.com **Web address:** www.century21.com

MALONE, THERESA C.
Industry: Insurance **Born:** March 23, 1959, Phoenix, Arizona **Current organization:** TCM Auto & Home Ins., Inc. **Title:** President **Type of organization:** Agency **Major product:** Personal and auto insurance **Area of distribution:** Phoenix, Arizona **Expertise:** Auto, home, commercial insurance and bonds **Affiliations:** A.I.A.A. **Hob./spts.:** Fundraising **SIC code:** 64 **Address:** TCM Auto & Home Ins., Inc., 1309 W. McDowell Rd., Phoenix, AZ 85007 **E-mail:** tcmauto@hotmail.com **Web address:** www.tcminsurance.com

MALONEY, JOHN E.
Industry: Financial **Born:** August 21, 1953, Malden, Massachusetts **Univ./degree:** M.B.A., Columbia University, 1978 **Current organization:** M&R Capital Management Inc. **Title:** President **Type of organization:** Investment/value manager **Major product:** Investment management **Area of distribution:** National **Expertise:** Money management, stocks, equities **Hob./spts.:** Weightlifting, theatre **SIC code:** 62 **Address:** M&R Capital Management Inc., 40 Fulton St., 21st floor, New York, NY 10038 **E-mail:** jmaloney@mrcapco.com **Web address:** www.mrcapco.com

MANGANIELLO, FILOMENA M.
Industry: Financial services **Born:** October 12, 1955, Salerno, Italy **Univ./degree:** B.A., Mercy College, 1996 **Current organization:** First Union National Bank **Title:** Senior Financial Specialist **Type of organization:** Bank/financial consumer services **Major product:** Financial advice services **Area of distribution:** Croton on the Hudson, New York **Expertise:** Total financial reviews, banking, lending, brokerage, personal and commercial **Honors/awards:** Medallion Club Award, Top Loan Officer **Affiliations:** Business Network International **Hob./spts.:** Travel **SIC code:** 60 **Address:** First Union National Bank, 50 Maple St., Croton-on-Hudson, NY 10520 **E-mail:** filommf@aol.com

MARINO-GURGANUS, MARIA
Industry: Abstracting **Born:** March 19, 1952, Morehead City, North Carolina **Current organization:** Coastal Abstracting Inc. **Title:** President **Type of organization:** Title abstract office **Major product:** Title searches and closings **Area of distribution:** National **Expertise:** Document retrievals, full title searches **Affiliations:** P.A.N.C. **Hob./spts.:** Swimming **SIC code:** 65 **Address:** Coastal Abstracting Inc., 738 Court St., Jacksonville, NC 28540 **E-mail:** coastalabst@earthlink.net

MARTIN, JERRY L.

Industry: Real estate **Born:** June 27, 1951, Philadelphia, Pennsylvania **Univ./degree:** Attended Annapolis, Engineering and Realty Designations, ABR, CRB, CRS, GRI, **Current organization:** RE/MAX Northwest Realtors **Title:** Broker/Owner **Type of organization:** Real estate brokerage **Major product:** Professional realtor services **Area of distribution:** Washington **Expertise:** Residential, management, marketing, expert witness **Honors/awards:** 100% Club, 2005; Recruiter of the Year, 2002 **Published works:** Real estate article in Planet Guru **Affiliations:** Seattle-Kings County Association of Realtors; Board of Realtors 2000-2006 **Hob./spts.:** Basketball, skiing, waterskiing, fishing **SIC code:** 65 **Address:** RE/MAX Northwest Realtors, 11250 Kirkland Way, Suite 200, Kirkland, WA 98033 **E-mail:** jerrym@remax.net **Web address:** www.seattlelifestyles.com

MATERETSKY, HOWARD

Industry: Financial services **Born:** September 14, 1942, Brooklyn, New York **Univ./degree:** B.S., Long Island University, 1965 **Current organization:** Integrated Financial Designs, Inc. **Title:** Certified Senior Advisor **Type of organization:** Financial services limited to people of retirement age **Major product:** Retirement advice, dedication to helping retirees secure income flow they need while helping to assure they will not run out of money **Area of distribution:** National **Expertise:** Retirement management **Affiliations:** Society of Certified Senior Advisors; B.B.B.; National Association of Security Dealers **SIC code:** 62 **Address:** Integrated Financial Designs, Inc., 1325 S. Congress Ave., Suite 200, Boynton Beach, FL 33426 **E-mail:** ifshoward@aol.com

MATERETSKY, IRA S.

Industry: Financial Services **Born:** December 9, 1966, Brooklyn, New York **Univ./degree:** Rutgers University **Current organization:** Integrated Financial Designs, Inc. **Title:** Financial Advisor **Type of organization:** Financial consulting **Major product:** All investment and Insurance products **Area of distribution:** National **Expertise:** Educating, advising, financial planning for retirees **Hob./spts.:** Family, music, golf and all sports **SIC code:** 62 **Address:** Integrated Financial Designs, Inc., 1325 S. Congress Ave. #200, Boynton Beach, FL 33426 **E-mail:** ifdira@aol.com

MAXWELL, SUSAN B.

Industry: Real Estate **Born:** April 29, 1949, Grand Rapids, Michigan **Univ./degree:** B.S., Health Education, Northern Michigan University, 1969 **Current organization:** Edward Rose & Sons **Title:** Resident Manager **Type of organization:** Property management, apartment communities **Major product:** Multi-housing **Area of distribution:** Walker, Michigan **Expertise:** Multi-housing management **Hob./spts.:** Travel, auto racing **SIC code:** 65 **Address:** Edward Rose & Sons, 545 Hampton Lane N.W., Walker, MI 49534

MAZUMDAR, MANU

Industry: Financial **Univ./degree:** M.B.A., Westchester University, Pennsylvania, 1990 **Current organization:** Mass Mutual Financial Group **Title:** Second Vice President **Type of organization:** Financial services **Major product:** Defined benefits, investment services, defined contribution **Area of distribution:** National **Expertise:** Executive management **Honors/awards:** International Who's Who **Published works:** Articles **Affiliations:** M.L.K.C.C. **SIC code:** 62 **Address:** Mass Mutual Financial Group, 1295 State St., Mail Stop N347, Springfield, MA 01111 **E-mail:** mmazumdar@massmutual.com

MCCARTY, WILLIAM

Industry: Insurance **Born:** October 6, 1952, Guthrie Center, Iowa **Univ./degree:** B.S., Business Administration, Northwest Missouri State University, 1976 **Current organization:** Brokers International Ltd. **Title:** President **Type of organization:** Insurance marketing company **Major product:** Annuity sales, marketing services **Area of distribution:** National **Expertise:** Management **Affiliations:** National Association of Independent Life Brokerage Agencies **Hob./spts.:** Golf, horseback riding, piloting airplanes **SIC code:** 64 **Address:** Brokers International Ltd., 1200 E. Main St., Panora, IA 50216

MCCORMICK, JOHN G.

Industry: Financial **Born:** September 26, 1965, Meadow Brook, Pennsylvania **Univ./degree:** B.A., American Government, Georgetown University; J.D., Temple University, 1990 **Current organization:** Axa Advisors, LLC **Title:** Financial Consultant **Type of organization:** Investment firm **Major product:** Insurance, retirement planning, estate planning, employee benefits **Area of distribution:** New Jersey **Expertise:** Financial planning **Affiliations:** S.F.S.P.; P.B.A.; Philadelphia Bar Association, Probate & Trust Section; Camden County Probate and Trust Commission **Hob./spts.:** History, music **SIC code:** 67 **Address:** Axa Advisors, LLC, 9 E. Stow Rd., Suite A, Marlton, NJ 08053 **E-mail:** john.mccormick@axa-advisors.com

MCLAUGHLIN, JAMES R.

Industry: Finance **Born:** October 22, 1940, Juniata County, Pennsylvania **Current organization:** The First National Bank of Mifflintown **Title:** Chairman, President and C.E.O. **Type of organization:** Community bank **Major product:** Financial services **Area of distribution:** Juniata and Perry Counties, Pennsylvania **Affiliations:** Chairman, First Community Financial Corp.; Chairman, First Monetary Mutual, Ltd.; Board of Directors, Capital Blue Cross; President, DeLauter Youth Center; Past Chairman, Mifflintown Rotary Club; Past Chairman, Pennsylvania Association of Community Bankers (PACB); Past Chairman, United Way of Mifflin-Juniata **Hob./spts.:** Hunting, baseball, football **SIC code:** 60 **Address:** The First National Bank of Mifflintown, 2 N. Main St., P.O. Box 96, Mifflintown, PA 17059 **E-mail:** jrmclaughlin@fnbmifflintown.com **Web address:** www.fnbmifflintown.com

MCMURRAN JR., RICHARD EPES

Industry: Real estate **Born:** November 2, 1956, Newport News, Virginia **Univ./degree:** B.A., Political Science and History, Emory University, Georgia, 1978 **Current organization:** Barker & Associates, Inc. **Title:** Senior Real Estate Appraiser **Type of organization:** Real estate firm **Major product:** Real estate appraisals **Area of distribution:** Virginia **Expertise:** Residential real estate appraisals; Certified SRA, Appraisal Institute, 1993; Certified Real Estate Appraiser License, Virginia, 1993; HUD/FHA approved, 1994 **Affiliations:** Board of Directors, Hampton Roads Chapter, Appraisal Institute; Smithsonian Institute; National Trust **Hob./spts.:** Tennis, running, photography **SIC code:** 65 **Address:** Barker & Associates Inc., 709 Middle Ground Blvd., A101, Newport News, VA 23606-4548 **E-mail:** epes@webtv.com

MCSPADDEN, DAVID

Industry: Financial **Univ./degree:** A.A.S., Applied Accounting, Ivy Technical State College, 1998 **Current organization:** Indiana Members Credit Union **Title:** Network Administrator **Type of organization:** Credit union **Major product:** Financial services **Area of distribution:** Indianapolis, Indiana **Expertise:** Monitoring and maintaining networks, file servers, work stations, internal and external security; Microsoft Certified professional **Affiliations:** Treasurer, Student Activity Council, Kelly School of Business **SIC code:** 60 **Address:** Indiana Members Credit Union, 5103 Madison Ave., Indianapolis, IN 46227 **E-mail:** davidm@imcu.com

MEAKEM, CAROLYN S.

Industry: Financial services **Born:** January 11, 1936, Columbus, Ohio **Univ./degree:** M.S., University of Maryland, 1970 **Current organization:** Legg Mason **Title:** C.F.P./Sr. Vice President of Investments **Type of organization:** Brokerage/financial services firm **Major product:** Money management **Area of distribution:** National **Expertise:** Financial education, advice, planning and retirement projections **Affiliations:** Financial Planners Association **Hob./spts.:** Skiing, reading, walking on the beach **SIC code:** 64 **Address:** 10215 Gainsborough Rd., Potomac, MD 20854 **E-mail:** csmeakem@leggmason.com

MESHENBERG, MILANA

Industry: Title insurance **Born:** November 2, 1970, Kiev, Ukraine **Univ./degree:** J.D., University of Miami **Current organization:** Milana Meshenberg, P.A. **Title:** Attorney **Type of organization:** Title insurance agency **Major product:** Title insurance **Area of distribution:** Florida **Expertise:** Title insurance **Affiliations:** New York State Bar Association; The Florida Bar, American Bar Association **SIC code:** 65 **Address:** Milana Meshenberg, P.A., 6237 N.W. 74th Terrace, Parkland, FL 33067 **E-mail:** mmpa@bellsouth.net

METZ, MARILYN J.

Industry: Financial **Born:** November 10, 1949, Denver, Colorado **Univ./degree:** B.A., Business Administration, Colorado State University, 1978 **Current organization:** Wells Fargo **Title:** Regional Private Banking Manager **Type of organization:** Bank **Major product:** Banking, financial services, investments **Area of distribution:** National **Expertise:** Financial advisor, credit **Hob./spts.:** Golf, travel **SIC code:** 60 **Address:** Wells Fargo, 205 108th Ave. N.E., Suite 600, Bellevue, WA 98004 **E-mail:** metzma@wellsfargo **Web address:** www.wellsfargo.com

MICHIE, ROBERT A.

Industry: Real estate **Current organization:** Prudential St. George Realty **Title:** Principal Broker **Type of organization:** Real estate firm **Major product:** Residential sales **Area of distribution:** St. George, Utah **Expertise:** Residential sales **Affiliations:** GRI Designation; ABR Designation; C.C.S.S. **SIC code:** 65 **Address:** Prudential St. George Realty, 619 S. Bluff St., Tower 2, Suite 1A, St. George, UT 84770 **E-mail:** prudentialstgeorge@infowest.com

MILLER, DIANE F.

Industry: Finance **Born:** July 27, 1955, Boston, Massachusetts **Univ./degree:** B.A., Mathematics, Boston University, 1978 **Current organization:** Miller Financial Planning **Title:** CFP **Type of organization:** Financial services **Major product:** Investments, mutual funds, retirement planning **Area of distribution:** Massachusetts **Expertise:** Financial planning **Affiliations:** Financial Planning Association **Hob./spts.:** Scuba diving, reading **SIC code:** 67 **Address:** Miller Financial Planning, 73 Gore St., Cambridge, MA 02141 **E-mail:** dfmdfm@aol.com

MILLIGAN, BILL
Industry: Financial **Univ./degree:** B.S., Finance, S.M.U., 1966 **Current organization:** FTN Financial (First Tennessee Bank) **Title:** Senior Vice President **Type of organization:** Investment bank **Major product:** Securities **Area of distribution:** National **Expertise:** Investment banking **SIC code:** 60 **Address:** FTN Financial (First Tennessee Bank), 845 Crossover Lane, Suite 150, Memphis, TN 38117

MOHLER, SANDRA L.
Industry: Financial **Born:** October 28, 1965, Reading, Pennsylvania **Univ./degree:** B.A., Psychology, Communications, Lebanon Valley College, 1987 **Current organization:** Ira G. Mohler & Son, Inc. **Title:** President **Type of organization:** Insurance agency **Major product:** Insurance and financial instruments **Area of distribution:** Shillington, Pennsylvania **Expertise:** Business and personal insurance **Affiliations:** National Association of Insurance and Financial Advisors; Insurance Agent and Brokers Association **Hob./spts.:** Animals (part time veterinarian technician) **SIC code:** 64 **Address:** Ira G. Mohler & Son, Inc., 20 W. Lancaster Ave., Shillington, PA 19607 **E-mail:** sandy@mohlerinsurance.com **Web address:** www.mohlerinsurance.com

MOON, PHILIP M.
Industry: Real estate **Born:** Muscatine, Iowa **Univ./degree:** B.A., Music Education, North Texas State University, 1973 **Current organization:** Moon & Associates **Title:** Real Estate Appraiser **Type of organization:** Appraiser **Major product:** Property appraisals **Area of distribution:** Louisiana **Expertise:** Commercial and residential real estate appraisals **Affiliations:** Appraisal Institute; Louisiana Real Estate Association **Hob./spts.:** Skiing, travel, racquetball **SIC code:** 65 **Address:** Moon & Assoc., 912 E. 70th, Shreveport, LA 71106 **E-mail:** moonmai@bellsouth.net

MOREAU, ANDREA L.
Industry: Finance **Born:** December 23, 1945, Pittsburgh, Pennsylvania **Univ./degree:** Attended Institute for Financial Education, Chicago, 1980 **Current organization:** M&T Bank **Title:** Vice President, Branch Manager **Type of organization:** Bank **Major product:** Loans, savings/checking accounts, investments **Area of distribution:** North Tonawanda, New York **Expertise:** All areas of banking **Affiliations:** Zonta International; Lumber City Economic Development Corp.; Grand Island Chamber of Commerce **Hob./spts.:** Golf **SIC code:** 60 **Address:** M&T Bank, 1007 Payne Ave., North Tonawanda, NY 14120 **E-mail:** andrealmoreau@mandtbank.com **Web address:** www.mandtbank.com

MORGAN, REBECCA ANN
Industry: Financial **Born:** December 15, 1952, Hayti, Missouri **Current organization:** American Cash Advance, Inc. **Title:** Manager **Type of organization:** Loan service company **Major product:** Car title loans, prepaid home phone services, cellular services **Area of distribution:** Missouri **Expertise:** Cash advances, Notary Public **Hob./spts.:** Arts and crafts **SIC code:** 61 **Address:** American Cash Advance, Inc., 313 Ward Ave., Caruthersville, MO 63830 **E-mail:** rmorgan1971@hotmail.com

MOSS, MICHAEL A.
Industry: Commercial real estate **Born:** August 8, 1968, Huntington Valley, Pennsylvania **Univ./degree:** J.D., Widener University School of Law **Current organization:** Kramont Realty Trust **Title:** Vice President, Director of Leasing **Type of organization:** Real estate **Major product:** Shopping centers **Area of distribution:** Pennsylvania **Expertise:** Leasing of 94 properties **Affiliations:** I.C.S.C. **Hob./spts.:** Sports, physical fitness **SIC code:** 65 **Address:** Kramont Realty Trust, 580 W. Germantown Pike, Suite 200, Plymouth Meeting, PA 19462 **E-mail:** mmoss@kramont.com

MURPHY, DWAYNE P.
Industry: Financial **Univ./degree:** Midland College **Current organization:** Ameriprise Inc. **Title:** Financial Advisor **Type of organization:** Financial planning **Major product:** Financial services **Area of distribution:** National **Expertise:** Securities and insurance **Honors/awards:** Master Millionaires Club **Affiliations:** Toastmasters **SIC code:** 62 **Address:** Ameriprise Inc., 2011 S. 181st Circle, Omaha, NE 68130 **E-mail:** dpmurphy36@hotmail.com

MURPHY, KELLY R.
Industry: Insurance **Born:** April 23, 1974, Ponca City, Oklahoma **Univ./degree:** B.S., Public Relations, Oklahoma State University, 1997 **Current organization:** Larry Murphy Insurance Agency, Inc. **Title:** Producer, New Business **Type of organization:** Insurance agency **Major product:** Insurance services **Area of distribution:** Oklahoma **Expertise:** Commercial insurance **Affiliations:** Independent Insurance Agents of Oklahoma; National Association of Professional Insurance Agents **Hob./spts.:** Golf **SIC code:** 64 **Address:** Larry Murphy Insurance Agency, Inc., 400 E. Central St., Suite 303, Ponca City, OK 74601 **E-mail:** kelly@larrymurphyinsurance.com **Web address:** www.larrymurphyinsurance.com

MURRIL, RENEE
Industry: Financial **Born:** March 6, 1953 **Current organization:** National City Bank **Title:** Assistant Vice President **Type of organization:** Bank **Major product:** Financial services **Area of distribution:** Detroit, Michigan **Expertise:** Training, sales, staffing **Affiliations:** I.B.B.; J.E.B.A.; Advisory Board, Salvation Army **Hob./spts.:** Youth ministry **SIC code:** 60 **Address:** National City Bank, 13230 E. Jefferson Ave., Detroit, MI 48215 **E-mail:** renee.murril@nationalcity.com

NAYAK, RAJESH A.
Industry: Financial **Born:** June 30, 1970, Bombay, India **Univ./degree:** B.S., Electrical Engineering; M.A., Electrical Engineering, Indian Institute of Science, 1994 **Current organization:** Cendant Mortgage **Title:** Senior Database Administrator **Type of organization:** Mortgage company **Major product:** Mortgage products (home loans) **Area of distribution:** National **Expertise:** Computer technology - databases **Affiliations:** I.S.U.G. **Hob./spts.:** History, science, shuttle badminton, ping pong, swimming **SIC code:** 61 **Address:** Cendant Mortgage, 228 Strawbridge Dr., Moorestown, NJ 08057 **E-mail:** rajesh.nayak@mortgagefamily.com **Web address:** www.cendantmortgage.com

NICHOLS, JEFF
Industry: Financial services **Born:** July 18, 1967, Rock Hill, South Carolina **Univ./degree:** B.A., Journalism, University of South Carolina, 1990 **Current organization:** BB&T Corp. **Title:** Vice President **Type of organization:** Financial holding company **Major product:** Financial services **Area of distribution:** National **Expertise:** Public Relations **Honors/awards:** Numerous corporate/newspaper writing awards **Published works:** Co-author, 1 book "Building on our Values: A History of BB&T Corporation", 1999 **Hob./spts.:** Weightlifting, running, reading **SIC code:** 67 **Address:** BB&T Corp., 1100 Reynolds Blvd., 3rd floor, Winston-Salem, NC 27105 **E-mail:** jjnichols@bbandt.com

NICHOLS, LAURA
Industry: Real estate **Univ./degree:** Attended University of Maryland for Marketing **Current organization:** Landmark Resources, LLC **Title:** Owner/President **Type of organization:** Real estate **Major product:** Residential, some commercial **Area of distribution:** South Carolina **Expertise:** Sales, Rentals, Homeowners Association Management **Affiliations:** Secretary/Treasurer, Multiple Listing Service **SIC code:** 65 **Address:** Landmark Resources, LLC, 1516 Richland St., Columbia, SC 29201 **E-mail:** lnichols@landmarkresources.biz **Web address:** www.landmarkresources.biz

NOBLE, DAVID J.
Industry: Insurance **Current organization:** American Equity Life Insurance Co. **SIC code:** 63 **Address:** American Equity Life Insurance Co., 5000 Westown Pkwy., Suite 440, West Des Moines, IA 50266 **E-mail:** dnoble@american-equity.com

OLSEN, WENDELL C.
Industry: Banking **Born:** April 30, 1926 **Univ./degree:** Attended Oregon State University **Current organization:** Investment Banking/ Securities Dealing **Title:** President **Type of organization:** Securities **Major product:** Investments **Area of distribution:** International **Expertise:** Dealing **Affiliations:** The Oxford Club; WW II Veteran; Korean War Reserves **Hob./spts.:** Fishing, baseball **SIC code:** 62 **Address:** Investment Banking/ Securities Dealing, 494 N.W. 22nd Ave., Canby, OR 97013-2201

O'MALLEY, MICHAEL J.
Industry: Banking and brokerage **Born:** January 27, 1937, Limerick City, Ireland **Univ./degree:** A.S., Data Processing, Fordham University, 1974 **Current organization:** Chase of North America **Title:** SVP, Finance/Consultant **Type of organization:** Bank **Major product:** Data processing (IBM equipment) **Area of distribution:** New York **Expertise:** Development of banking and financial applications **Published works:** Several articles **Affiliations:** Professional Programmers **Hob./spts.:** Travel, sports, computer programming **SIC code:** 60 **Address:** 492 Ocean Ave., Central Islip, NY 11722 **E-mail:** mikeomalley2003@yahoo.com

O'MALLEY, WILLIAM E.
Industry: Finance **Univ./degree:** B.A., University of Virginia, 1951 **Current organization:** East West Securities Co. **Title:** Owner **Type of organization:** Advisory firm **Major product:** Investment advice **Area of distribution:** Latham, New York **Expertise:** Investments **SIC code:** 67 **Address:** East West Securities Co., 12 Avis Dr., Latham, NY 12110 **E-mail:** w.e.omalley@att.net

PALLAGHY, CHABA M.
Industry: Real estate **Born:** September 23, 1932, White Colony, Hungary **Univ./degree:** M.A., Economics, University of Hungary **Current organization:** C.M. Pallaghy Inc., Real Estate **Title:** President/Broker **Type of organization:** Real estate **Major product:** Residential and commercial appraisal service **Area of distribution:** Pennsylvania, New York and New Jersey **Expertise:** Marketing **Honors/awards:** Bronze and Gold Medal Fencer **Affiliations:** C.P.R; B.G.S.M.R. **Hob./spts.:** Saber fencing **SIC code:** 64 **Address:** C.M. Pallaghy Inc., Real Estate, 1036 Pennsylvania Ave., Matamoras, PA 18336 **E-mail:** cmpallaghy@optonline.net

PEARSALL, JOHN D.
Industry: Financial **Born:** August 23, 1955, Mount Pleasant, Michigan **Univ./degree:** B.A., Business Management and Hotel/Restaurant Management, Central Michigan University, 1979 **Current organization:** Flagstar Bank **Title:** Vice President of Sales **Type of organization:** Bank **Major product:** Financial services **Area of distribution:** National **Expertise:** Native American lending **Affiliations:** Board of Realtors; Homebuilders Association **Hob./spts.:** Golf, travel **SIC code:** 60 **Address:** Flagstar Bank, 1222 S. Mission, Suite A, Mount Pleasant, MI 48858 **E-mail:** john.pearsall@flagstar.com **Web address:** www.flagstar.com

PETROW, CHRISTOPHER G.
Industry: Financial **Born:** July 25, 1954, Boston, Massachusetts **Univ./degree:** B.S., Physiological Psychology, Vassar College, 1978; M.B.A., Boston University, 1985 **Current organization:** Morgan Stanley **Title:** Managing Director, Strategist **Type of organization:** Investment bank **Major product:** Investments **Area of distribution:** International **Expertise:** Asset allocation, investment strategy **Hob./spts.:** Sports, bird watching, classical music **SIC code:** 62 **Address:** Morgan Stanley, 1221 Avenue of the Americas, New York, NY 10020 **E-mail:** christopher.petrow@morganstanley.com **Web address:** www.morganstanley.com

PHILLIPS, DANIEL A.
Industry: Financial services **Born:** February 24, 1938, Boston, Massachusetts **Univ./degree:** A,B., Cum Laude, History, Harvard University, 1960; M.B.A., Harvard Business School, 1963 **Title:** Chairman (Retired 2003), Fiduciary Trust Co. **Type of organization:** Trust company **Major product:** Personal investments **Area of distribution:** National **Expertise:** Management, personal and institutional investments **Honors/awards:** Recipient of Harvard Alumni Association Award 1995; Grand Medal of Reims 1998, Regional Champagne-Ardenne Medal 1998 and Legion of Honor-Chevalier 2002 from American Memorial Hospital in Reims, France; French Legion of Honor 2003 **Affiliations:** Boston Economic Club; Board of Directors, former Vice Chairman of the Board, United Way of Massachusetts; Treasurer 1998-present, former President 1988-98, American Committee of the American Memorial Hospital, Reims, France; Director, Alliance for Children and Families; Advisory Board, CEO's for Fundamental Change in Education; Board of Directors, Families International Inc.; Treasurer and Director, Grimes-King Foundation for the Elderly Inc. **Hob./spts.:** Gardening, hiking, travel **SIC code:** 62 **Address:** Fiduciary Trust Co., 175 Federal St., Boston, MA 02110 **E-mail:** danp@fiduciary-trust.com **Web address:** www.fiduciary-trust.com

PIZARRO-GARCÍA, CARLOS JOR-EL
Industry: Real estate **Univ./degree:** A.S., Business Administration, Banking Finance, 1982; B.S., Business Administration, Minor in Finance, 1997, University of Puerto Rico **Current organization:** Alberto Hernández Real Estate, Inc. **Title:** Operations Manager, Rid Piedras Office **Type of organization:** Real Estate Broker **Major product:** Real Estate and Field Services **Area of distribution:** Puerto Rico **Expertise:** Residential, new development, re-sale **Affiliations:** National Center for Housing Professional Management; Society of Field Inspectors-SOFI Field Services Industry **Hob./spts.:** Travel, sports, bicycling **SIC code:** 65 **Address:** Alberto Hernández Real Estate, Inc., #714 65th Infantry Ave., Edif. Norte, Suite 105, San Juan, PR 00924 **E-mail:** gatgetpr@coqui.net

PORTER, RUSSELL F.
Industry: Insurance coverages/financial investments **Born:** July 13, 1955, Los Angeles, California **Current organization:** Porter Insurance Services **Title:** Proprietor **Type of organization:** Insurance sales **Major product:** Health, auto, home,motorhome, boat, motorcycle, ATV's, personal umbrella and medical insurance **Area of distribution:** Shasta County, California **Expertise:** Senior insurance protection **Honors/awards:** Recognition and Production Awards from Mutual of Omaha, Allstate, Ohio Capital American & Western Workers Association **Published works:** Advice articles published in The Consolidated Press, The Ridge Writer and East Valley Times, The Record Searchlight Newspapers, author of several newsletters **Affiliations:** Chamber of Commerce Honey Bee Festival; American Cancer Society; Senior Coalition helper; Jehovah's Witnesses **Hob./spts.:** Jigsaw puzzles, non hunting archery, fishing **SIC code:** 64 **Address:** Porter Insurance Services, 9485 Deschutes Ave., Suite E, Palo Cedro, CA 96073 **Phone:** (530)547-1131 **Fax:** (530)547-1201 **E-mail:** rporterl@farmersagent.com

POTTER, KATHLEEN A.
Industry: Financial **Current organization:** M&I Bank FSB **Title:** Vice President **Type of organization:** Bank **Major product:** Retail and commercial banking **Area of distribution:** Las Vegas, Nevada **Expertise:** Customer service **Affiliations:** International Association of Financial Crimes Investigators; Las Vegas Chamber of Commerce **SIC code:** 60 **Address:** M&I Bank FSB, 3993 Howard Hughes Pkwy, #100, Las Vegas, NV 89169 **E-mail:** kathleen.potter@micorp.com **Web address:** www.mibank.com

PRANGE, MARILYN J.
Industry: Real estate **Born:** November 19, 1935, Gary, Indiana **Current organization:** Lake County Realty Inc. **Title:** Secretary, Treasurer/Owner **Type of organization:** Real estate developer/contractor **Major product:** Residential and light commercial building and development **Area of distribution:** Indiana **Expertise:** Corporate finance, real estate **Hob./spts.:** Playing sweepstakes **SIC code:** 65 **Address:** 310 Nichols St., Lowell, IN 46356 **E-mail:** mjprange@sbcglobal.net

PROFACI, DOMINICK P.
Industry: Financial **Born:** May 5, 1967, Newburgh, New York **Univ./degree:** M.S., Environmental Engineering, Manhattan College, 1995 **Current organization:** Edward Jones **Title:** Investment Representative **Type of organization:** Investment - partnership **Major product:** Investments **Area of distribution:** International **Expertise:** Retirement planning **SIC code:** 67 **Address:** Edward Jones, 4246 Albany Post Rd., Hyde Park, NY 12538

PROFACI, JOSEPH EMANUEL
Industry: Financial **Born:** June 20, 1960, Newburgh, New York **Univ./degree:** B.S., St. John's University, 1981 **Current organization:** Edward Jones **Title:** Investment Representative **Type of organization:** Partnership **Major product:** Investments **Area of distribution:** International **Expertise:** Retirement planning **Hob./spts.:** Gardening, reading, water sports, boating **SIC code:** 67 **Address:** Edward Jones, 297 S. Plank Rd., Newburgh, NY 12550 **E-mail:** jeprofaci@earthlink.net

QUAN, MARLON M.
Industry: Financial **Univ./degree:** B.S., New York University, 1977 **Current organization:** Acorn Capital Group **Title:** President **Type of organization:** Financial institution **Major product:** Financial services **Area of distribution:** National **Expertise:** Asset-based lending (commercial) **Honors/awards:** Top 50 Businessmen, Asian American Business Development Center, 2002 **SIC code:** 67 **Address:** Acorn Capital Group, 2 Greenwich Office Park, Greenwich, CT 06831 **E-mail:** mquan@acorncap.com

RAMIREZ, LINDA E.
Industry: Insurance/financial **Born:** February 5, Fajardo, Puerto Rico **Univ./degree:** M. S., Marketing, Turabo College, Puerto Rico **Current organization:** Cuna Mutual **Title:** Account Relationship Manager **Type of organization:** Insurance company **Major product:** Insurance coverage **Area of distribution:** Puerto Rico **Expertise:** Sales, customer service, teaching **Honors/awards:** Teacher of the Year Award, 1987 **Hob./spts.:** Her children, singing, golf, former Girl Scout leader and basketball coach **SIC code:** 63 **Address:** Cuna Mutual, 239 Arterial Hostos Ave., Capital Bldg. #1, Suite 10-04, San Juan, PR 00918-1476 **E-mail:** lramirezl@yahoo.com

RATFIELD, PAMELA
Industry: Real estate **Born:** March 6, 1967, Germany **Univ./degree:** Real Estate degree **Current organization:** Ratfield Real Estate, LLC **Title:** Broker/Owner **Type of organization:** Real estate brokerage **Major product:** Real estate sales **Area of distribution:** Texas **Expertise:** Residential and land sales **Honors/awards:** Nominated Top Producer for the past 3 years, Austin, Texas **Hob./spts.:** Helping people, animals **SIC code:** 65 **Address:** Ratfield Real Estate, LLC, 6400 Lohman Ford, Lago Vista, TX 78645 **E-mail:** pratfield@austin.rr.com

RESNICK, RALPH
Industry: Real Estate **Born:** February 13, 1929, Akron, Ohio **Univ./degree:** University of Miami, 1953 **Current organization:** New York Life Insurance Co. **Title:** Agent **Type of organization:** Insurance company **Major product:** Life insurance, pensions, annuities **Area of distribution:** National **Expertise:** Life insurance, pensions **Affiliations:** Charter Life Underwriters **Hob./spts.:** Selling real estate **SIC code:** 64 **Address:** New York Life Insurance Co., 1450 N.W. 175th St., Miami Gardens, FL 33169-4661 **E-mail:** rresnick@ft.newyorklife.com

RHOTEN, ALEX
Industry: Real Estate **Born:** November 30, 1961, Salem Oregon **Current organization:** Coldwell Banker Commercial Mountain West Real Estate **Title:** Principal Broker **Type of organization:** Real Estate agency **Major product:** Commercial real estate, sales, maintenance **Area of distribution:** Oregon **Expertise:** Industrial investment and development **Honors/awards:** No. 11 in Worldwide Sales, Coldwell Banker Commercial Real Estate, 2005 **Affiliations:** National Association of Realtors; C.C.I.M. **Hob./spts.:** Golf, fishing, hunting, snowboarding, international travel **SIC code:** 65 **Address:** Coldwell Banker Commercial Mountain West Real Estate, 698 12th St. S.E., Suite 100, Salem, OR 97301 **E-mail:** arhoten@cbcre.com **Web address:** www.cbcre.com

RINEHART, WAYNE
Industry: Real Estate **Born:** October 21, 1955, Miami, Florida **Current organization:** Costa Realtors Corp. **Title:** Partner **Type of organization:** Real estate broker **Major product:** Real estate sales **Area of distribution:** Florida **Expertise:** Sales and management of commercial properties **Affiliations:** Northwest Dade Association of Realtors; The Miami-Dade County Planning Advisory Board **Hob./spts.:** Golf **SIC code:** 65 **Address:** Costa Realtors Corp., 14160 N.W. 77th Ct., Suite 32, Miami Lakes, FL 33016 **E-mail:** wayner@costarealty.com **Web address:** www.costarealty.com

ROBERTS, LEIGH G.
Industry: Real Estate **Univ./degree:** B.A., Early Childhood Education, Texas Woman's University, 1979 **Current organization:** Leigh Glendenning Real Estate, Inc. **Title:** Owner, Broker **Type of organization:** Brokerage **Major product:** Real estate sales **Area of distribution:** Texas **Expertise:** Commercial real estate, land development, residential, acquisition **Affiliations:** Celina Chamber of Commerce; Celina Heritage Association; Celina Economic Development **Hob./spts.:** Reading **SIC code:** 65 **Address:** Leigh Glendenning Real Estate, Inc., P.O. Box 668, Celina, TX 75009 **E-mail:** leighreal@msn.com

ROGERS, MATTHEW F.
Industry: Real estate **Univ./degree:** B.S., Biology, University of Michigan, 2001 **Current organization:** Brush & Co. LLC **Title:** Partner; Acting Food & Beverage Manager, 5 Star & 5 Diamond restaurant **Type of organization:** Investment group **Major product:** Purchasing and sales **Expertise:** Sales and purchasing **Published works:** Science Journal **Affiliations:** National Philosophers Society **SIC code:** 65 **Address:** Brush & Co. LLC, 14250 North Rd., Fenton, MI 48430 **E-mail:** classycomposure@hotmail.com

ROMEO, WILLIAM V.
Industry: Financial **Univ./degree:** B.A., University of Hawaii, 1978 **Current organization:** R&R Financial Planners, Inc. **Title:** C.F.P./C.E.O. **Type of organization:** Financial **Major product:** Financial planning services and products **Area of distribution:** National **Expertise:** Estate planning, retirement planning; C.F.P., Adelphi University, 1984 **Affiliations:** F.P.A. **SIC code:** 62 **Address:** R&R Financial Planners, Inc., 1802 Hempstead Tpke., East Meadow, NY 11554 **E-mail:** bill@rnrsecurities.com

ROSZ, HEIDI ANN
Industry: Medical insurance **Born:** March 1, 1955, Michigan **Univ./degree:** M.B.A., University of Miami, Florida **Current organization:** Liberty Mutual Insurance Group/Boston **Title:** Medical Consultant/Contract Negotiator **Type of organization:** Insurance agency **Major product:** Managed care products **Area of distribution:** National **Expertise:** Registered Nurse, contract negotiator, managed healthcare **Affiliations:** A.C.H.C.E.; C.C.M.; C.I.R.S.; S.D.A.F. **Hob./spts.:** Long distance writing, sailing, golfing **SIC code:** 63 **Address:** Liberty Mutual Insurance Group/Boston, 3601 Thomas St., Hollywood, FL 33021-3612

ROTHWELL, D. HUNTER
Industry: Financial **Born:** February 10, 1974, Charlottesville, Virginia **Univ./degree:** B.S., Business/Economics, High Point University, 1996 **Current organization:** UBS Financial Services Inc. **Title:** Accounting Vice President **Type of organization:** Financial services **Major product:** Managed money, securities-based lending, trust, insurance **Area of distribution:** National **Expertise:** Wealth management **Affiliations:** C.I.C.; Y.M.C.A.; United Way **Hob./spts.:** Deep sea fishing, mountain biking, music **SIC code:** 62 **Address:** UBS Financial Services Inc., 401 S. Tryon St., Suite 2500, Charlotte, NC 28202 **E-mail:** hunter.rothwell@ubs.com

ROWLAND III, SHERWOOD L. "SKIP"
Industry: Insurance **Born:** April 8, 1965, Waterbury, Connecticut **Current organization:** Martin & Rowland, Inc. **Title:** President/CEO **Type of organization:** Independent insurance agency **Major product:** Property, casualty, life and health sales **Area of distribution:** Connecticut **Expertise:** Marketing, sales **Affiliations:** P.I.A. **Hob./spts.:** Playing the guitar, boating **SIC code:** 64 **Address:** Martin & Rowland, Inc., 951 Chase Pkwy., Waterbury, CT 06722 **E-mail:** slrow1@aol.com

RUSSELL, KATHRYN E.
Industry: Construction/real estate **Born:** February 12, 1958, Knoxville, Tennessee **Current organization:** One Stop Realty, Hendersonville/Murray, Russell & Assoc. **Title:** ARB, GRI, Broker, Real Estate Sales, Relocation/Partner, Vice-President Marketing, Sales & Planning **Type of organization:** Real estate sales, relocation/general contractor (residential/commercial); **Major product:** Homes, apartments, offices **Area of distribution:** Tennessee **Expertise:** Sales, marketing, finance; Tennessee Licensed Real Estate Broker, Tennessee Licensed Contractor-Residential/Commercial **Honors/awards:** Sales Award of Excellence, Sumner Assoc. of Realtors, Greater Nashville Assoc. of Realtors; Past & Current President, "Key to the City Club of Hendersonville"; Past President, Parent Teacher Organization **Affiliations:** National Association of Realtors; National Home Builders Association; Tennessee Association of Realtors; Sumner Association of Realtors **Hob./spts.:** Travel, swimming, boating **SIC code:** 65 **Address:** Murray, Russell & Assoc., 116 Secretariat Place, Hendersonville, TN 37075 **E-mail:** kaysellshomes@yahoo.com

RUSSELL, R. WAYNE
Industry: Financial **Born:** March 15, 1955, Lafayette, Georgia **Univ./degree:** B.A., Banking/Finance, University of Georgia, 1987 **Current organization:** Georgia Community Bank **Title:** President/CEO **Type of organization:** Retail banking **Major product:** Banking **Area of distribution:** Dalton, Georgia **Expertise:** Marketing, commercial lending **Affiliations:** G.B.A. **Hob./spts.:** Family, golf **SIC code:** 60 **Address:** Georgia Community Bank, 111 N. Tentz St., Dalton, GA 30722 **E-mail:** wrussell@georgiacommunitybank.com

SANCHEZ, GRACIELA A.
Industry: Real estate **Current organization:** Star Realty Inc./AAA Financial Solutions DBA American Freedom Group Inc. **Title:** Owner, Broker **Type of organization:** Realtor/Mortgage brokerage **Major product:** Full service realty and mortgage brokerages **Area of distribution:** Washington/California, Washington, Idaho **Expertise:** Business development, residential and commercial investment property, open to property management, bi-lingual; Real Estate licensing, 1993, Real Estate Broker, 1997, Mortgage Broker, 2005 **SIC code:** 65 **Address:** Star Realty Inc./AAA Financial Solutions DBA American, Freedom Group Inc., 151 Division St., Grandview, WA 98930-1355 **E-mail:** qwicmortgages@yahoo.com **Web address:** www.starrealtyinc.net

SAVARD, PAULA K.
Industry: Real Estate **Born:** December 15, 1943, Albany, New York **Univ./degree:** Certified Residential Specialist, Realtors National Marketing Group **Current organization:** Paula K. Aberman Assoc. Inc. **Title:** President/Treasurer **Type of organization:** Brokerage **Major product:** Real estate sales **Area of distribution:** Boston, Massachusetts **Expertise:** 38 years as a Licensed Realtor, residential specialist **Honors/awards:** Top 50 Educators in the U.S., 1993 **Published works:** Articles for real estate journals **Affiliations:** National Board of Realtors; Massachusetts Board of Realtors; Past President & Chair, Investment Committee **Hob./spts.:** Sailing, piloting her private plane, reading **SIC code:** 65 **Address:** Paula K. Aberman Assoc. Inc., 2086 Main St., Lancaster, MA 01523 **E-mail:** psavard@realtor.com **Web address:** www.realtor.com

SCARPITTI, VICKY H.
Industry: Finance/insurance **Univ./degree:** B.A., Ohio State University, 1987 **Current organization:** Nationwide Financial **Title:** Marketing Manager **Type of organization:** Insurance company **Major product:** Life insurance and annuities **Area of distribution:** National **Expertise:** Actuary, marketing **Affiliations:** M.A.A.A.; A.S.A. **SIC code:** 64 **Address:** Nationwide Financial, 1 Nationwide Plaza, 3-21-05, Columbus, OH 43215 **E-mail:** scarpiv@nationwide.com

SCHIMMING, VICTOR M.
Industry: Financial **Title:** CFP®/Registered Principal **Type of organization:** Financial service broker/dealer **Major product:** Financial planning/investment advisory services **Expertise:** Financial Planning/Investment Advisor **SIC code:** 62 **Address:** FSC Securities Corp., 6211 E. Peach Tree Lane, Wichita, KS 67218 **E-mail:** aschimming@fscadvisor.com

SCHUMACHER, WILLIAM S.
Industry: Financial services **Born:** January 13, 1947, New York, New York **Univ./degree:** B.A., History, Rutgers University, 1973; Certified Investment Management Analyst, Wharton School of Business, 1997 **Current organization:** Smith Barney **Title:** First Vice President, Divisional Sales Director **Type of organization:** Broker dealer **Major product:** Private equity **Area of distribution:** International **Expertise:** Investment management analysis/sales **Affiliations:** Investment Management Consultants Association; Association of Professional Investment Consultants **Hob./spts.:** Boating **SIC code:** 64 **Address:** Smith Barney, 18167 N. US Hwy. 19, Pinellas Park, FL 33781 **E-mail:** wschum007@aol.com

SCULLION, EDWARD
Industry: Real estate **Born:** May 9, 1978, Point Pleasant, New Jersey **Univ./degree:** B.S., Environmental Sciences, University of North Carolina at Wilmington, 2000 **Current organization:** Diane Turton, Realtors **Title:** Sales Associate **Type of organization:** Real estate **Major product:** Full service-residential, commercial, land **Area of distribution:** Ocean Grove, New Jersey, Monmouth and Ocean Counties **Expertise:** Customer service, market understanding; Turton Training; B.E.S.T.T. Training **Affiliations:** RELO (Relocation Network); National Association of Realtors **Hob./spts.:** World travel, surfing, running **SIC code:** 65 **Address:** Diane Turton, Realtors, 45 Main Ave., Ocean Grove, NJ 07756 **E-mail:** escullion@dianeturton.com **Web address:** www.dianeturton.com

SCULLY, MICHAEL W.
Industry: Finance **Born:** September 11, 1964, New York, New York **Univ./degree:** B.B.A., Public Accounting, Iona College, 1986 **Current organization:** Peak Financial Management Co. **Title:** President **Type of organization:** Financial management company **Major product:** Financial services **Area of distribution:** National **Expertise:** Financial advice, client management **Affiliations:** N.A.T.P.; N.S.T.P.; N.A.A.; I.A.F.P **Hob./spts.:** Family, golf **SIC code:** 67 **Address:** Peak Financial Management Co., 800 Summer St., Stamford, CT 06901 **E-mail:** pfmco@msn.com

SETLIFF, ELAINE FUQUA
Industry: Real Estate **Born:** February 1, 1963, Pineville, Louisiana **Univ./degree:** Attended Louisiana College for Business and Accounting **Current organization:**

Louisiana Lagniappe Realty **Title:** Broker/Owner **Type of organization:** Realty **Major product:** Listing and selling of all types of real estate **Area of distribution:** Central Louisiana **Expertise:** Development of residential subdivisions and town homes; public speaking on industry changes **Honors/awards:** Realtor of the Year for Central Louisiana, 2004 **Affiliations:** Central Louisiana Board of Realtors; Board Member, Central Louisiana YMCA; Christian talk show host **Hob./spts.:** Fishing, physical fitness, travel **SIC code:** 65 **Address:** Louisiana Lagniappe Realty, 812 Versailles Blvd, Suite B, Alexandria, LA 71303 **E-mail:** elaine@louisianalagniapperealty.com **Web address:** www.louisianalagniapperealty.com

SHAH, PRAKASH A.
Industry: Finance/real estate **Univ./degree:** M.A., Stevens University, 1969 **Current organization:** First Growth Mortgage & Realty Group, LLC **Title:** Chairman/CEO **Type of organization:** Mortgage banker, commercial realty, title insurance agency **Major product:** Mortgages, title insurance, hotel realty **Area of distribution:** National **Expertise:** Management, entrepreneurs, hotel owners **Affiliations:** President, Indo-American Chamber of Commerce in New York; Member, Board of Directors, "Just Say No"; Chair, NJDA; Member, Board of Directors, Southern Africa Enterprises Developing Fund **SIC code:** 61 **Address:** First Growth Mortgage & Realty Group, LLC, First Growth Plaza, 33 Second St., Raritan, NJ 08869 **E-mail:** firstgrwth@aol.com **Web address:** www.firstgrowthgroupinc.com

SHARP, ROYCE
Industry: Financial **Univ./degree:** B.B.A., University of Alabama, 1993 **Current organization:** Community Home Lending **Title:** Mortgage Loan Officer **Type of organization:** Mortgage brokers **Major product:** Mortgage loans **Area of distribution:** Birmingham, Alabama **Hob./spts.:** Pittsburgh Steelers football **SIC code:** 61 **Address:** 1512 Center Point Pkwy., Birmingham, AL 35215

SHELLEY, MALINDA
Industry: Real Estate **Born:** April 23, LaGrange, Georgia **Current organization:** Keller Williams Realty **Title:** Broker Associate **Type of organization:** Real estate **Major product:** Real estate sales **Area of distribution:** National **Expertise:** Sales; Broker Associate **Affiliations:** N.A.R.; G.A.R. **Hob./spts.:** Piano, African gray parrots, pool, travel **SIC code:** 65 **Address:** Century 21 Southern Crescent, 635 North Glynn St., Fayetteville, GA 30214 **E-mail:** malindashelley@bellsouth.net

SLATER, WANDA W.
Industry: Real estate **Born:** February 18, 1927 **Current organization:** Slater Rentals **Title:** Owner/Manager **Major product:** Rental property **Area of distribution:** Hebron, Ohio **Expertise:** Owning, managing rental property **Honors/awards:** Listed in, Marquis Who's Who of American Women, Who's Who in Society, the International Directory of Distinguished Leadership as a Volunteer; Ohio State Senate and House of Representatives Award for Outstanding Achievement; Recognition Award, Creative Living; Appreciation Award, CARE **Published works:** Editor, OFWC "Buckeye" Magazine (Retired) **Affiliations:** Notary Public, State of Ohio (Ret, 1997); past President, Ohio Federation of Women's Clubs; past Worthy Matron, Clyde Chapter and Hebron Chapter, Order of the Eastern Stars **Hob./spts.:** Volunteer in her community **SIC code:** 65 **Address:** Slater Rentals, 36 Worth Dr. S.E., Hebron, OH 43025-9760 **E-mail:** cardinal218@avolve.net

SLAVENT, MARIAN L.
Industry: Real estate **Born:** October 16, 1925, New Orleans, Louisiana **Current organization:** D.B. Real Estate, Inc. **Title:** Realtor **Type of organization:** Real estate **Major product:** Residential and commercial properties **Area of distribution:** Monroe, Louisiana **Expertise:** Real estate sales **Honors/awards:** Realtor Associate of the Year, State of Louisiana; Local Realtor of the Year; Most Transactions Award Ruby Pin, 3 years **Affiliations:** Catholic Daughters of America; Quoto Club; Northern Board of Realtors National Realtors and State; American Business Women's Association; Ladies Birthday Club; Players Investment Co. **Hob./spts.:** Travel, tours **SIC code:** 65 **Address:** D.B. Real Estate, Inc., 2703 Indian Mound Blvd., Monroe, LA 71201

SMITH, KEVIN E.
Industry: Financial **Born:** November 29, 1962, Columbus, Ohio **Univ./degree:** B.S., Sales and Marketing, University of Rio Grande, 1986 **Current organization:** Market Force **Title:** President **Type of organization:** Wealth management **Major product:** Business development services for wealth management advisors **Area of distribution:** Ohio **Expertise:** Marketing, business development services **Affiliations:** S.R.S.P. **Hob./spts.:** Golf, hunting, fishing **SIC code:** 62 **Address:** Market Force, 545 Metro Place South, Suite 100, Dublin, OH 43017 **E-mail:** kevinsmith@marketforce.com **Web address:** www.marketforce.com

SMITH, NANCY K.
Industry: Real estate **Born:** January 11, 1963, Dubuque, Iowa **Univ./degree:** B.A., Social Work, Loras College, 1985 **Current organization:** First Weber Group **Title:** Broker Associate/Office Manager **Type of organization:** Real estate **Major product:** Marketing and selling real estate **Area of distribution:** Wisconsin **Expertise:** New construction, resale, condos **Hob./spts.:** Reading, walking **SIC code:** 65 **Address:** First Weber Group, 1102 Bequette St., Dodgeville, WI 53533 **E-mail:** smithnk@firstweber.com **Web address:** www.firstweber.com

SMITH-PINKDON, ALECIA
Industry: Real Estate **Born:** August 12, 1956, Chicago, Illinois **Univ./degree:** B.A., University of Illinois **Current organization:** Habitat Company, LLC **Title:** Property Manager **Type of organization:** Real estate **Major product:** Real estate sales **Area of distribution:** Chicago, Illinois **Expertise:** Certified property manager, real estate broker **Affiliations:** I.R.E.M.; N.A.R.; A.B.O.M.A.; C.A.R. **Hob./spts.:** Singing, cycling, volleyball **SIC code:** 65 **Address:** Habitat Company LLC, 2001 South Michigan Ave., Chicago, IL 60616 **E-mail:** asmith@habitat.com **Web address:** www.habitat.com

SODEN, GEORGE A.
Industry: Real estate **Univ./degree:** M.B.A., University of Dublin, Ireland **Current organization:** Coldwell Banker **Title:** Real Estate Broker/Sales Associate **Type of organization:** Realtor **Major product:** Residential homes and commercial **Area of distribution:** Mendham, Harding, Morristown, Chester, Bernardsville and Bedminster, New Jersey **Expertise:** Listing and selling real estate **Affiliations:** N.C.J.A.R.; C.B.A. **Hob./spts.:** Golf, lacrosse, soccer **SIC code:** 65 **Address:** Coldwell Banker, 21 E. Main St., Mendham, NJ 07945 **E-mail:** georgesoden@yahoo.com

SPRAGUE, A. JEANNE
Industry: Real estate **Born:** February 18, 1935, Jackson, Michigan **Univ./degree:** B.S., Business, Colorado State University, 1965 **Current organization:** The Group, Inc. Realtors **Title:** Broker Associate/Partner **Type of organization:** Real estate **Major product:** Commercial and residential sales **Area of distribution:** Colorado **Expertise:** Marketing **Honors/awards:** First Woman President, Chamber of Commerce **Published works:** Write-up **Affiliations:** Colorado Association of Realtors; National Association of Realtors; St. Luke's Episcopalian Church **Hob./spts.:** Bridge, hunting **SIC code:** 65 **Address:** The Group, Inc. Realtors, 401 W. Mulberry St., Ft. Collins, CO 80521 **E-mail:** sprague@frii.com **Web address:** www.ftcollins.comtq2

STABENFELDT, JOHN I.
Industry: Insurance **Born:** May 25, 1941, Republic, Washington **Univ./degree:** B.A., Eastern University, 1964 **Current organization:** Farmers Insurance **Title:** Agent **Type of organization:** Insurance agency **Major product:** All lines of insurance **Area of distribution:** Republic, Washington **Expertise:** Farm insurance **Affiliations:** T.R.A.; C.A. **Hob./spts.:** Riding horses, fishing, hunting **SIC code:** 64 **Address:** Farmers Insurance, 56 N. Clark, Republic, WA 99166 **E-mail:** jstabenfeldt@farmersagent.com

STACK, SHERI L.
Industry: Financial **Born:** June 10, 1967, St. Charles, Missouri **Univ./degree:** B.S., Accounting, Evangel University **Current organization:** Stack Financial Services **Title:** Owner/Enrolled Agent **Type of organization:** Financial consulting firm **Major product:** Mutual funds annuities **Area of distribution:** Missouri **Expertise:** Tax preparation, tax planning accounting and investments **Hob./spts.:** Swimming, tennis, reading **SIC code:** 62 **Address:** Stack Financial Services, 123 W. Fourth St., Salem, MO 65560 **E-mail:** sheristack@earthlink.net

STEINBERG, ALAN
Industry: Real Estate **Born:** May 13, 1953, New York, New York **Univ./degree:** B.A., Rider University, 1975 **Current organization:** Newmark Knight Frank **Title:** Asset Manager **Type of organization:** Commercial real estate broker **Major product:** Office space and buildings **Area of distribution:** New York, New York **Expertise:** Leasing, management **Affiliations:** N.Y.B.O.R. **Hob./spts.:** Physical fitness, travel, music **SIC code:** 65 **Address:** Newmark Knight Frank, 594 Broadway, New York, NY 10012 **E-mail:** asteinberg@newmarkkf.com

STINNETT, TERRANCE L.
Industry: Bank **Born:** July 22, 1940, Oakland, California **Spouse:** Annette Taub **Married:** June 29, 1991 **Univ./degree:** B.S., Stanford University, 1962; J.D., Magna Cum Laude, Santa Clara University, 1969 **Current organization:** Fremont Bank **Title:** General Counsel **Type of organization:** Bank **Major product:** Banking services **Area of distribution:** California **Area of practice:** Bankruptcy law, business reorganizations **Expertise:** Bankruptcy law, business reorganizations **Honors/awards:** "Super Lawyer", Northern California, 2006; Listed in: Marquis Who's Who in America, 2000; Marquis Who's Who in American Law, 2000; Continental Who's Who, 2007; "AV" rated, Martindale-Hubbell **Affiliations:** American Bar Association; San Francisco Bar Association; State Bar of California; Former Director, Bay Area Bankruptcy Forum; Board of Visitors, Santa Clara University School of Law, 1998 to present; Director, Fremont Bank and Fremont Bancorporation, 1990 to present **Career accomplishments:** Bench Bar Liaison Committee for the United States Bankruptcy Courts for the Northern District of California (Member 1995-97) (Chairman 1997) **Hob./spts.:** Golf, race car driving, baking **SIC code:** 60 **Address:** Goldberg, Stinnett, Meyers & Davis, A Professional Corp, 44 Montgomery St., Suite 2900, San Francisco, CA 94104

Phone: (510)505-5251 **Fax:** (510)795-5715 **E-mail:** terrance.stinnett@fremont bank.com **Web address:** www.fremontbank.com

SURBER, RICHARD D.
Industry: Real Estate **Born:** March 24, 1973, St. Petersburg, Florida **Univ./degree:** J.D., University of Utah, 1998 **Current organization:** Nexia Holdings Inc. **Title:** CA Attorney **Type of organization:** Real estate holding company **Major product:** Real estate/fashion/design **Area of distribution:** National **Expertise:** Asset holdings **Affiliations:** C.B.A. **Hob./spts.:** Racquetball, scuba diving, marathons **SIC code:** 67 **Address:** Nexia Holdings Inc., 59 West 100 South, Salt Lake City, UT 84101 **E-mail:** richardsurber@nexiaholdings.com **Web address:** www.nexiaholdings.com

TASSONE, GREGORY J.
Industry: Real estate **Born:** April 9, 1962, Cincinnati, Ohio **Univ./degree:** J.D., University of Toledo, 1988 **Current organization:** Coldwell Banker, West Shell **Title:** Sales Associate, Previews Property Specialist **Type of organization:** Real estate **Major product:** Real estate sales, law **Area of distribution:** National **Expertise:** Real estate sales and law **Published works:** Articles **Affiliations:** Ohio State Bar Association; Cincinnati Bar Association; National Association of Realtors; Ohio Association of Realtors **Hob./spts.:** Family, sports, music, teaching Sunday school **SIC code:** 65 **Address:** Coldwell Banker, West Shell, 9600 Montgomery Rd., Cincinnati, OH 45242 **E-mail:** gtassone@gregtassone.com **Web address:** www.gregtassone.com

TAYLOR, LESLIE G.
Industry: Financial **Born:** October 8, London, England **Univ./degree:** M.B.A., University of Buffalo, 1952 **Current organization:** Leslie G. Taylor & Co. **Title:** President/Owner **Type of organization:** Financial services **Major product:** Mergers and acquisitions **Area of distribution:** International **Expertise:** Management and M&A **Affiliations:** S.A.E. **SIC code:** 67 **Address:** Leslie G. Taylor & Co., 274 Castle Creek Rd., Grants Pass, OR 97526 **E-mail:** lgtaylor@terragon.com

THOMSON, KATINA
Industry: Real estate **Univ./degree:** Attended University of Laramie, Paralegal School **Current organization:** ERA Beartooth Realty, LLC **Title:** Broker/Owner **Type of organization:** Real estate office **Major product:** Real estate sales **Area of distribution:** International **Expertise:** Residential, recreational **Affiliations:** W.A.R.; N.A.R.; Park County Board **Hob./spts.:** Golf, hiking, charitable work, mentoring **SIC code:** 65 **Address:** ERA Beartooth Realty, LLC, 1301 Sheridan Ave., Cody, WY 82414 **E-mail:** thomsont@wavecom.net

THUR, SHARYN MARIE
Industry: Real Estate **Born:** November 1, 1961, Garfield Heights, Ohio **Univ./degree:** B.A., Business, University of Maryland, 1983 **Current organization:** Ronus Properties **Title:** V.P., Regional Director of Leasing **Type of organization:** Commericial real estate **Major product:** Leasing, tenant representation **Area of distribution:** National **Expertise:** Retail leasing **Published works:** Write-ups, articles **Affiliations:** International Council of Shopping Centers; C.C.I.M. **Hob./spts.:** Travel, golf **SIC code:** 65 **Address:** Ronus Properties, 8260 Greensboro Dr., Suite 275, McLean, VA 22102 **E-mail:** retailsites@sharythur.com **Web address:** www.sharythur.com

TOMANEK, THOMAS J.
Industry: Real estate **Born:** January 5, 1931, Hodonin, Czech Republic **Univ./degree:** Ph.D., Charles University, Prague, Czech Republic, 1955 **Current organization:** T.I.C. Tomanek International Co. **Title:** Owner/President **Type of organization:** Real estate developer **Major product:** Apartment buildings **Area of distribution:** International **Expertise:** Developer, owner, manager **Honors/awards:** "Best Affordable Housing Project" Award for Scabreeze Apartments (184 units), City of Vallejo, California, 1986 **Published works:** 9 articles **Affiliations:** California State University, Retired Faculty **Hob./spts.:** Reading, various sports, skiing, swimming, diving **SIC code:** 65 **Address:** T.I.C. Tomanek International Co., 26601 Durham Way, Hayward, CA 94542

TORBETT, JANICE G.
Industry: Financial **Born:** June 8, 1950, Weathers, Arkansas **Univ./degree:** Trust Degree, Southwestern Graduate School of Banking at Southern Methodist University, 1983; B.A., Finance and Banking, University of Arkansas, 1990 **Current organization:** The Bank of Fayetteville N.A. **Title:** Senior Vice President and Trust Dept. Manager **Type of organization:** Bank **Major product:** Financial services **Area of distribution:** Fayetteville, Arkansas **Expertise:** Trust management, administration **Affiliations:** C.R.S.P.; American Bankers Association **Hob./spts.:** Needlework, hiking **SIC code:** 60 **Address:** The Bank of Fayetteville N.A., Trust Dept., 1 S. Block St., Fayetteville, AR 72701 **E-mail:** jtorbett@mail.bof.com

TOWNSEND, CURTIS O.
Industry: Finance **Born:** March 6, 1946, New Jersey **Univ./degree:** B.A., Seton Hall University; M.B.A., New York University, 1959 **Current organization:** Tiffany Capital Advisors, Inc. **Title:** President/CIO **Type of organization:** Registered investment advisor **Major product:** Mid-cap growth domestic equities **Area of distribution:** International **Expertise:** Investment management **Honors/awards:** Baseball Scholarship, Seton Hall University **Published works:** Write-ups **Affiliations:** N.A.A.P.; 100 Men in Philadelphia; Certifications, N.E.S.D., N.Y.S.C. **Hob./spts.:** Baseball, reading, interfacing, travel **SIC code:** 67 **Address:** Tiffany Capital Advisors, Inc., 2300 Computer Ave., Suite C13, Willow Grove, PA 19090 **E-mail:** curt@tiffanycapital.com **Web address:** www.tiffanycapital.com

TRIANO, ANGELA M.
Industry: Financial **Born:** April 10, 1970, Dallas, Texas **Univ./degree:** B.A., Communications, Saint Mary's College, Notre Dame, 1993 **Current organization:** HLR Federal Credit Union **Title:** Vice President, Marketing **Type of organization:** Credit union (not-for-profit) **Major product:** Full financial services (savings, loans, investments) **Area of distribution:** National **Expertise:** Marketing **Affiliations:** M.A.C.; C.U.E.S.; C.U.N.A. **Hob./spts.:** Family **SIC code:** 60 **Address:** HLR Federal Credit Union, 536 Washington Ave., Nutley, NJ 07110 **E-mail:** angela.triano@hlrfcu.org

TRUITT, DONALD E.
Industry: Real estate **Born:** November 15, 1929, Kirksville, Missouri **Univ./degree:** M.S., University of Missouri **Current organization:** Chartwell Associates **Title:** President **Type of organization:** Commercial real estate broker **Major product:** Sales and management of commercial real estate **Area of distribution:** Illinois **Expertise:** Real estate sales and management **Hob./spts.:** National ski patrol; Emergency medical technician **SIC code:** 65 **Address:** Chartwell Associates, 321 E. Hillside Ave., Barrington, IL 60010

TRUITT, SUZANNE
Industry: Real estate **Born:** August 20, 1943, Lewes, Delaware **Univ./degree:** A.A., Business/Accounting, Goldey-Beacom College **Current organization:** Century 21/Mann Moore Assoc. Inc. **Title:** Broker **Type of organization:** Real estate **Major product:** Residential real estate **Area of distribution:** Rehoboth Beach, Delaware **Expertise:** Brokerage/sales; Licensed Broker in Maryland, Delaware, Pennsylvania **Affiliations:** A.B.R.; C.R.B.; C.R.S.; G.R.I.; W.C.R. **Hob./spts.:** Golf, reading, beaches **SIC code:** 65 **Address:** Century 21/Mann Moore Assoc. Inc., 8 Sheffield Rd., RBCC, Rehoboth Beach, DE 19971-1400 **E-mail:** suetruitt@dmv.com

TSAI HUANG, AGNES L.
Industry: Real estate **Born:** October 20, 1937, Taiwan **Univ./degree:** B.S., University of Pennsylvania, 1955 **Current organization:** Century 21 **Title:** Real Estate Broker **Type of organization:** Real estate brokerage **Major product:** Houses, land **Area of distribution:** California **Hob./spts.:** Reading **SIC code:** 65 **Address:** 14481 Maplewood St., Poway, CA 92064

UFERT, DEBORAH A.
Industry: Financial **Current organization:** National City Bank **Title:** Bank Manager **Type of organization:** Bank **Major product:** Banking services **Area of distribution:** Bloomington, Illinois **Expertise:** Management **Affiliations:** Twin City Professional Group; Rotary Club **Hob./spts.:** Family, camping, canoeing, community events **SIC code:** 60 **Address:** National City Bank, 1332 E. Empire, Bloomington, IL 61701 **E-mail:** daufert@aol.com

URBANSKI, LEO A.
Industry: Real estate **Born:** September 27, 1940, Pennsylvania **Univ./degree:** B.S., 1985; M.B.A., 1990, Hamilton University **Current organization:** Hamilton Business Services, Inc. **Title:** President **Type of organization:** Builders and developers **Major product:** Residential and commercial development **Area of distribution:** National **Expertise:** Marketing/management/business consulting **Affiliations:** Chamber of Commerce; Better Business Bureau; American Consultants League **SIC code:** 65 **Address:** Hamilton Business Services, 859 Washington St., Suite 211, Red Buff, CA 96080 **E-mail:** celeb@tehama.net

VAALER, DAVID
Industry: Insurance **Born:** February 6, 1930 **Univ./degree:** J.D., University of North Dakota, 1957 **Current organization:** Vaaler Insurance, Inc. **Title:** C.E.O. **Type of organization:** Insurance services company **Major product:** Special insurance programs **Area of distribution:** National **Expertise:** Health facilities **Hob./spts.:** Travel, golf **SIC code:** 64 **Address:** Vaaler Insurance, Inc., 2701 Columbia Rd., Grand Forks, ND 58201 **E-mail:** dave@vaaler.com

VARUD, GUY
Industry: Financial **Born:** January 26, 1942, North Dakota **Univ./degree:** B.S., Business, University of Sioux Falls, 1965 **Current organization:** Varud & Associates Financial **Title:** President **Type of organization:** Financial advisory firm **Major product:** Financial services **Area of distribution:** South Dakota **Expertise:** Harry Dent Master Certified Advisor, Investments, Seminars **Hob./spts.:** Boating **SIC code:** 62 **Address:** Varud & Associates Financial, 2105 W. 18th St., Sioux Falls, SD 57105 **E-mail:** GVARUD@planmembersec.com **Web address:** www.planmembersec.com

VENVERTLOH, BERNARD J.
Industry: Financial **Title:** Accounting Officer **Type of organization:** Bank **Major product:** Financial and banking services **Expertise:** Accounting **SIC code:** 60 **Address:** Mercantile Trust & Savings Bank, 440 Maine St., Quincy, IL 62301

WAITT, CHERYL S.
Industry: Real estate **Born:** April 9, 1964, Winchester, Massachusetts **Current organization:** Fine Homes by Beaulieu LLC **Title:** Manager **Type of organization:** Real estate firm **Major product:** Real estate development/new construction **Area of distribution:** New Hampshire **Expertise:** Land development, new construction **Affiliations:** National Association of Realtors; New Hampshire Association of Realtors **Hob./spts.:** Family, showing horses, motorcycling **SIC code:** 65 **Address:** Fine Homes by Beaulieu LLC, 2 Chester Rd., Suite 302, Derry, NH 03038 **E-mail:** homesofnh@aol.com

WALTON III, BILL J.
Industry: Land development **Born:** December 23, 1973, Flagstaff, Arizona **Current organization:** Golden Crest Development Inc. **Title:** President **Type of organization:** Land development and construction services **Major product:** Buildable lots, small construction **Area of distribution:** Oregon **Expertise:** Management, operations **Affiliations:** Better Business Bureau **Hob./spts.:** Sky diving, travel **SIC code:** 65 **Address:** Golden Crest Development Inc., 477 N.E. Greenwood Ave., Suite A, Bend, OR 97701 **E-mail:** bjwalton3@yahoo.com

WARD, MICHAEL HYGH
Industry: Real estate/construction **Born:** May 1, 1958, Austin, Texas **Univ./degree:** J.D., University of Texas School of Law, 1990 **Current organization:** H.J. Russell & Co. **Title:** General Counsel **Type of organization:** Construction, real estate company **Major product:** Construction, real estate development, property management **Area of distribution:** National **Expertise:** Real estate law, corporate, finance, tax and construction law **Published works:** Article in GC South, May, 2003 **Affiliations:** A.I.C.P.A.; Atlanta Bar Association; Board Member, Atlanta Bar Association, Construction Law Section **Hob./spts.:** Family, piano, football, basketball **SIC code:** 65 **Address:** H.J. Russell & Co., 504 Fair St., S.W., Atlanta, GA 30313 **E-mail:** mward@hjrussell.com **Web address:** www.hjrussell.com

WETTERNACH, EDNA P.
Industry: Real estate **Born:** June 22, 1920, Webb, Iowa **Univ./degree:** B.A., Cedar Falls, Iowa Teachers College; B.A., Business Management & Accounting **Current organization:** The Dowling Apartment Building **Title:** Owner/Manager **Type of organization:** Real estate management **Major product:** Rentals **Area of distribution:** Madison, Wisconsin **Expertise:** Project management **Honors/awards:** Received national honors for being the "Top Salesperson Worldwide for a Month", Niagara Therapeutic Co., 1972; Preservation Award Winner, Madison Trust for Historic Preservation, 2003 (for long term care of the historic Dowling Apartments); listed in National Register's Who's Who in Executives and Professionals; nominated by the Governing Board of Editors of the American Biographical Institute for inclusion in the Tenth Commemorative Edition of 2,000 Notable American Women; the Dowling Apartment Building is listed with the State and National Historical Society (it is over 80 years old) **Affiliations:** Daughters of the Nile; Daughters of the American Revolution **Hob./spts.:** Dancing, aerobics, travel, reading, fishing **SIC code:** 65 **Address:** \, 445 W. Wilson, Madison, WI 53703

WILLIAMS-BLACKWELL, TAMMY M.
Industry: Financial **Born:** December 9, 1967, Winston-Salem, North Carolina **Univ./degree:** B.S., Criminal Justice, University of North Carolina, 1989; Realty Institute, 2005 **Current organization:** Weichert Realtors **Title:** Broker **Type of organization:** Real estate broker **Major product:** Real estate **Area of distribution:** National **Expertise:** High-end residential home sales **Honors/awards:** Rookie of the Year Awards, 2002; NJAR Circle of Excellence Award Bronze Level, 2003, 2005; Weichert Realtors Million Dollar Sales & Marketing Award. 2002-2005; Top Producer of the Year Award, Upper Montclair Office, 2002-2005 **Affiliations:** W.O.A.H.O.; National Association of Realtors; Garden State Multiple Listing System; New Jersey Association of Realtors; Alpha Kappa Alpha Sorority Inc.; Jack & Jill of America **Hob./spts.:** Outdoor activities, running, reading, biking **SIC code:** 65 **Address:** Weichert Realtors, 272 Bellevue Ave., Montclair, NJ 24043 **E-mail:** twmsblackwell@comcast.net

WILSON, PAUL
Industry: Financial **Born:** November 18, 1965, Baltimore, Maryland **Univ./degree:** A.A., Business **Current organization:** J.P. Morgan Chase **Title:** Loan Originator **Type of organization:** Mortgage lender **Major product:** Mortgage loans **Area of distribution:** National **Expertise:** Origination **SIC code:** 62 **Address:** JP Morgan Chase, 100 West Rd., Suite 220, Towson, MD 21204 **E-mail:** mortgagelender2@aol.com

WILSON, RONALD J.
Industry: Insurance **Born:** October 19, 1939, Wyandotte, Michigan **Univ./degree:** American College-CLU; ChFC, Honorary DBM-Indiana Western University, 1990 **Current organization:** R.J. Wilson & Associates Ltd. **Title:** President **Type of organization:** MGU & Reinsurance **Major product:** Special insurance **Area of distribution:** United States and Canada **Expertise:** Railroads **Published works:** 2 books, 15 articles **Affiliations:** N.A.P.S.L.O.; P.I.A.; S.I.A.; Society of Financial Service Professionals **Hob./spts.:** Rare books, history, genealogy **SIC code:** 64 **Address:** 828 Federal Hill Rd., Street, MD 21154 **E-mail:** rwilson@rjwltd.com

WINES JR., PRESTON L.
Industry: Finance **Born:** August 1, 1961, Middletown, Ohio **Univ./degree:** B.A. Summa Cum Laude, Pastoral Ministries, Southeastern College, 1987; M.A. With Honors, Bible Studies, Assemblies of God Theological Seminary, 1994; M.B.A. Candidate **Current organization:** Edward Jones Investments **Title:** Investment Representative **Type of organization:** Investment and financial consulting **Major product:** Personalized investment and financial consulting **Area of distribution:** International **Expertise:** I.R.A.'s, mutual funds; Accredited Asset Management Specialist; Lectures locally at colleges and universities on investment principals and workshops **Honors/awards:** Extra Mile Recipient, Edward Jones, 2004 **Affiliations:** The New IR Support Specialist, Edward Jones **Hob./spts.:** Antiques, farming **SIC code:** 62 **Address:** Edward Jones Investments, 1308 Devil's Reach Rd., #301, Woodbridge, VA 22192 **E-mail:** prestonwinesjr@aol.com **Web address:** www.edwardjones.com

WINGERT, KEVIN R.
Industry: Financial **Born:** November 20, 1957, Sioux City, Iowa **Univ./degree:** B.A., Public Administration, Drake University, 1979 **Current organization:** American Equity Investment Life Insurance Co. **Title:** President **Type of organization:** Insurance company, underwriter **Major product:** Fixed and equity indexed annuities **Area of distribution:** National **Expertise:** Marketing and operations **Affiliations:** C.L.U.; C.H.F.C. **Hob./spts.:** Spending time with his children **SIC code:** 63 **Address:** American Equity Investment Life Insurance Co., 5000 Westown Pkwy., Suite 440, West Des Moines, IA 50266 **E-mail:** kwingert@americanequity.com

WOOD, RICHARD R.
Industry: Real estate **Born:** November 8, 1922, Salem, Massachusetts **Univ./degree:** B.S., 1943; M.B.A., Science, Harvard University **Current organization:** Renwood Properties, Inc. **Title:** President **Type of organization:** Real estate brokerage **Major product:** Ownership and management of Government subsidized low income housing **Area of distribution:** National **Expertise:** Finance **Honors/awards:** Candidate, US House of Representatives **Affiliations:** M.R.E.I.T.; Director, G.B.R.B.; District President, R.E.S.S.I.; N.L.H.A.; C.R.H.D.; I.C.S.C.; C.R.B. **Hob./spts.:** Tennis, ski racing **SIC code:** 65 **Address:** Renwood Properties, Inc., 875 Massachusetts Ave., Cambridge, MA 02139 **E-mail:** renwoodprops@aol.com

WOODARD JR., EDWARD J.
Industry: Financial **Born:** March 9, 1943, Portsmouth, Virginia **Univ./degree:** B.S., Chemistry, Old Dominion University **Current organization:** Bank of the Commonwealth **Title:** Chairman of the Board/President & CEO **Type of organization:** Bank **Major product:** Commercial banking **Area of distribution:** Virginia **Expertise:** Financial consulting, marketing **Published works:** Magazine articles **Affiliations:** American Bankers Association; Virginia Bankers Association; President, Tidewater Business Division Association; Norfolk Chamber of Commerce **Hob./spts.:** Family, church **SIC code:** 60 **Address:** Bank of the Commonwealth, 403 Boush St., Norfolk, VA 23510 **E-mail:** ewoodard@bocmail.net

WORDEN, MODINA
Industry: Real Estate **Born:** March 15 **Univ./degree:** B.S., Business, San Jose State College, 1940 **Current organization:** Anchor Real Estate **Title:** Principal Broker **Type of organization:** Real estate firm **Major product:** Residential and commercial properties **Area of distribution:** Southwestern Oregon **Expertise:** Certified Real Estate Broker; Management Accredited Buyer Representative **Affiliations:** National Association of Realtors; Bandon Chamber of Commerce **SIC code:** 65 **Address:** Anchor Real Estate, Hwy. 101 and 11th St., P.O. Box 1252, Bandon-by-the-Sea, OR 97411-1252 **E-mail:** anchorre@harborside.com **Web address:** www.anchorrealestatebandon.com

WORRALL, JONATHAN H.
Industry: Financial information services **Born:** Manchester, England **Current organization:** Mergent, Inc. **Title:** CEO **Type of organization:** Financial information distributor **Major product:** Business and financial information **Area of distribution:**

International **Expertise:** Financial business development **Affiliations:** Chamber of Commerce **Hob./spts.:** Rugby, sailing **SIC code:** 62 **Address:** Mergent, Inc., 5250 77 Center Dr., Charlotte, NC 28217 **E-mail:** jonathan.worrall@mergent.com

WRIGHT JR., ALTON A.
Industry: Insurance **Univ./degree:** B.S., Health Administration, Pennsylvania State University **Current organization:** Keystone Health Plan Central **Title:** Account Executive **Type of organization:** Health insurance company **Major product:** Health insurance **Area of distribution:** Pennsylvania **Expertise:** Sales and marketing **Honors/awards:** KHP Central Awards (named Rep of the Month 9 times) **Affiliations:** M.H.P. Designation from H.I.A.A.; N.A.A.C.P.; Member, Board of Directors, Harrisburg Young Professionals; Chair, Political Action Committee; Highmark Golf League; Lambda Chi Alpha; Leadership Development Institute; American Heart Association Jail Bail **Hob./spts.:** Sports, cigar collecting **SIC code:** 63 **Address:** Keystone Health Plan Central, 300 Corporate Center Dr., Camp Hill, PA 17011 **E-mail:** alton.wright@khpc.com **Web address:** www.khpc.com

YANG, CHOR JAY
Industry: Independent financial **Univ./degree:** B.A., Metropolitan State University **Current organization:** Great American Mortgage **Title:** President **Type of organization:** Mortgage banking **Major product:** Home loans **Area of distribution:** International **Expertise:** Loans **Hob./spts.:** Soccer, golf, bowling **SIC code:** 61 **Address:** Great American Mortgage, 500 Grotto St. North, Suite 3, St. Paul, MN 55104 **E-mail:** jayyang75@yahoo.com

YAWN, WILLIAM MARK
Industry: Financial **Born:** August 30, 1955, Augusta, Georgia **Univ./degree:** B.A., Florida State University, 1977 **Current organization:** Regions Morgan Keegan Trust Co. FSB **Title:** Senior Vice President **Type of organization:** Trust company **Major product:** Investment, foundation, multigenerational **Area of distribution:** Tennessee **Expertise:** Wealth management consulting **Published works:** 10 articles **Affiliations:** I.M.C.A.; A.I.M.R. **Hob./spts.:** Family, golf, travel, sports dad **SIC code:** 61 **Address:** Regions Morgan Keegan Trust Co. FSB, 150 Fourth Ave. North, Suite 1500, Nashville, TN 37219 **E-mail:** mark.yawn@regions.com **Web address:** www.thesafergroup.mkadvisor.com

YIP, BENNY C.
Industry: Finance **Born:** June 4, 1974, Hong Kong **Univ./degree:** M.B.A., New York University, 2001 **Current organization:** Guardian Life Insurance Co. **Title:** Equity Trader **Type of organization:** Insurance company **Major product:** Financial services, mutual funds **Area of distribution:** National **Expertise:** U.S. equity trading **Honors/awards:** International Honor Society in Economics; National Scholastic Honor Society in Business **Affiliations:** Beta Gamma Sigma; Omicron Delta Epsilon **Hob./spts.:** Golf, motorcycle riding, wine tasting, sports **SIC code:** 64 **Address:** Guardian Life Insurance Co., 7 Hanover Sq., H-20A, New York, NY 10004 **E-mail:** benny_yip@glic.com

YOUNG, STEPHEN C.
Industry: Finance **Univ./degree:** B.S., University of Vermont, 1991 **Current organization:** The CIT Group **Title:** Senior Vice President **Type of organization:** Commercial finance **Major product:** Inventory finance - marine and RV **Area of distribution:** National **Expertise:** Operations **Affiliations:** Commercial Finance Association; American Management Association **SIC code:** 64 **Address:** The CIT Group-Inventory Finance, 9900 W. 109th St., Suite 400, Overland Park, KS 66210 **E-mail:** steve.young@cit.com

ZACHARY, STEVEN W.
Industry: Financial **Born:** April 24, 1958, St. Paul, Minnesota **Univ./degree:** J.D., University of Minnesota, 1984 **Current organization:** Conseco Finance **Title:** Attorney **Type of organization:** Bank **Major product:** Financial services, insurance, banking **Area of distribution:** National **Expertise:** Labor, employment law **Published works:** 1 article **Affiliations:** Minnesota State Bar Association; State Bar of Arizona; Conference on Consumer Finance Law **Hob./spts.:** Volunteer work with church, sports **SIC code:** 60 **Address:** Conseco Finance, 332 Minnesota St., Suite 600, St. Paul, MN 55101 **E-mail:** attyz@attbi.com

ZAMORA, CHRISTOPHER R.
Industry: Financial **Born:** June 17, 1949, Boulder, Colorado **Univ./degree:** M.B.A. **Current organization:** Deloitte **Title:** Director **Type of organization:** Financial consulting firm **Major product:** Tax and business consulting **Area of distribution:** National **Expertise:** Tax consulting for major utilities **SIC code:** 62 **Address:** Deloitte, 555 17th St., Suite 3600, Denver, CO 80202-3907 **E-mail:** czamora@deloitte.com

ZIRPOLO, MARIA J.
Industry: Insurance **Current organization:** Zirpolo Insurance and Travel **Title:** Insurance Broker/Travel Agent **Type of organization:** Insurance Company/Travel Agency **Major product:** Insurance and travel services **Area of distribution:** Local **Expertise:** Insurance, travel **Affiliations:** Latin American Travel Association **SIC code:** 64 **Address:** Zirpolo Insurance & Travel, 20 Church St., Paterson, NJ 07505 **E-mail:** mzirpolo@hotmail.com

ZSCHERING, ROBERT E.
Industry: Real estate development **Born:** September 2, 1945, Detroit, Michigan **Univ./degree:** B.S., Education, Concordia College, 1969 **Current organization:** Schostak Brothers & Co., Inc. **Title:** Vice President, Development **Type of organization:** Real estate development **Major product:** Development and management of commercial, retail and residential real estate **Area of distribution:** National **Expertise:** Development of new properties, re-development of old properties **Hob./spts.:** Classic and muscle cars, fishing, family **SIC code:** 65 **Address:** Schostak Brothers & Co., Inc., 25800 Northwestern Hwy., Suite 750, Southfield, MI 48075 **E-mail:** zschering@schostak.com **Web address:** www.schostak.com

Services

ABBAOUI, JALIL
Industry: Hospitality **Born:** January 30, 1965, Casablanca, Morocco **Univ./degree:** B.S., Engineering Management, Chelsea University, London, United Kingdom **Current organization:** Sandals Resort International **Title:** Director of Engineering **Type of organization:** Hotel/resort **Major product:** Lodging, food, entertainment **Area of distribution:** International **Expertise:** Engineering, maintenance **Affiliations:** A.E.E.; Bahamas Society of Engineers; Instructor, Educational Institute from American Hotel & Lodging Association, Orlando, Florida; President/ Director, EMTS Ltd., an energy management company in the Bahamas **Hob./spts.:** Private pilot, windsurfing **SIC code:** 70 **Address:** Sandals Resort International, 4950 S.W. 72nd Ave., Suite 201, Miami, FL 33155 **E-mail:** jalil@coralwave.com

AGUILAR, VICTOR A.
Industry: Technology **Born:** August 27, 1969, Juana Diaz, Puerto Rico **Univ./degree:** B.S., Industrial Engineering, University of Massachusetts, 1991 **Current organization:** GE Consumer Products **Title:** Plant Manager **Type of organization:** Supplier **Major product:** Providing innovative product and service solutions for commercial, industrial, residential and utility applications **Area of distribution:** Humacao, Puerto Rico **Expertise:** Plant/materials management **Affiliations:** N.S.I.E.; N.S.E. **Hob./spts.:** Family - spending time with his 2 children, golf, baseball **SIC code:** 73 **Address:** 68 Palmeres St., Palmas Reales, Humacao, PR 00791 **E-mail:** victor.aguilar@ge.com

ALBERTS, ADAM
Industry: Personal services **Current organization:** Badvantage **Title:** Relationship Expert **Type of organization:** Dating and relationship services company **Major product:** Dating and social dynamic services **Area of distribution:** National **Expertise:** Dating, relationships and social atmospheres **Hob./spts.:** Baseball, football **SIC code:** 72 **Address:** Badvantage, 111 Market St., Suite 413, Saugerties, NY 12477 **E-mail:** baddvantage@aol.com

ALDRIDGE, ARVIL
Industry: Pest control **Title:** Owner **Type of organization:** Extermination company **Major product:** Pest control services **SIC code:** 73 **Address:** Miami Valley Pest Control Services, Inc., 21 W. Main St., New Lebanon, OH 45345

ALFANO, DIANE E.
Industry: Financial **Born:** January 31, 1956, Hartford, Connecticut **Univ./degree:** B.A., Political Science and French, Tufts University, 1978 **Current organization:** Institutional Investor **Title:** Managing Director **Type of organization:** Financial communications company **Major product:** Magazines, newsletters, conferences, journals **Area of distribution:** International **Expertise:** Sales, management **Honors/awards:** First woman appointed to Board of Directors, 2000 **Hob./spts.:** Sailing, skiing, ballet, opera, fluent in French and Italian **SIC code:** 73 **Address:** Institutional Investor, 225 Park Ave. South, 7th floor, New York, NY 10003 **E-mail:** dalfano@iiconferences.com **Web address:** www.institutionalinvestor.com

AL-FAQIH, FADEY WAJIH
Industry: Hotel/hospitality **Born:** August 13, 1954, Beirut, Lebanon **Univ./degree:** A.A., Honor Roll/Deans List, Physical Education, Montgomery College, 1982; Certificate in Advanced Management Techniques/F&B Operations/Front Office & Back of House Operations/Restaurant & Hotel Law, International Hotel/Restaurant Institute (top 3%), 1984 **Current organization:** Hilton Springfield **Title:** Food and Beverage Director/Banquet Director **Type of organization:** Full service hotel **Major product:** Lodging, event and meeting space, food and beverage **Area of distribution:** International **Expertise:** Customer satisfaction, weddings of all cultures, above average personal skills and major events **Honors/awards:** Outstanding Manager of 1st and 3rd Quarters, 2002; Awarded Appreciation Certificate for Outstanding Service from the U.S. Army Criminal Investigative Command, 2003; Awarded the Outstanding Spirit of Hospitality Award, 2003; Received Outstanding Supervisor & Skill Builders Award, 2003; Over 500 Letters of Appreciation received **Hob./spts.:** Family, yard work, swimming, the beach **SIC code:** 70 **Address:** Hilton Springfield, 6550 Loisdale Rd., Springfield, VA 22150 **E-mail:** fadey_al-faqih@hilton.com **Web address:** www.hilton.com

ALICEA JR., JOSÉ L.
Industry: Business services **Born:** June 2, 1968, Paterson, New Jersey **Current organization:** Microsoft Corp. **Title:** Support Professional **Type of organization:** Information technology **Major product:** Software support **Area of distribution:** International **Expertise:** Corporate e-mail administration **Affiliations:** Certified, M.C.S.E.; M.C.S.A. **Hob./spts.:** Softball, weightlifting, golf **SIC code:** 73 **Address:** Microsoft Corp., 8055 Microsoft Way, Charlotte, NC 28273 **E-mail:** aliceajose@hotmail.com

ALVAREZ, JOSE FABIAN
Industry: Technology **Born:** November 15, 1974, Jersey City, New Jersey **Univ./degree:** U.S. Amy Signal School, 1992; GTE Resident School, 1992; Kean University, 1993; Aviation & Electronic School of America, 1999; National Technology Transfer Institute, 2002; Red Rock College, 2003 **Current organization:** Comp Depot L.L.C./ Verizon Co. **Title:** President/CEO, Facilities & Fiber Optic Technician **Type of organization:** Network computers/communications **Major product:** Semiconductors/ computer hardware **Area of distribution:** International **Expertise:** Electrical technology, computer science, fiber optic technology, data cabling **Honors/awards:** Magna Cum Laude, Aviation & Electronics School of America; Magna Cum Laude, National Technology Transfer Institute; Lifetime Member of Strathmore's Who's Who; 3 U.S. Army Achievements Medals; Certificate of Achievement in Satellite Communications **Affiliations:** Fiber Optic Association; U.S. Army Signal Corps; Veterans of Foreign Wars; American Legion; International Brotherhood of Electrical Workers **Hob./spts.:** Tutoring mathematics, flying, tennis, boating, motorcycling **SIC code:** 73 **Address:** 16 Marshall St. #7-U, Irvington, NJ 07111 **E-mail:** alvarezj93@aol.com

ALVORD, VICKI B.
Industry: Software **Born:** April 21, 1947, Georgetown, Texas **Current organization:** COOP Systems **Title:** C.O.O. **Type of organization:** Business continuity planning **Major product:** BCP software and services **Area of distribution:** International **Expertise:** Management; Certified, Disaster Recovery **Affiliations:** 2nd Vice President of the Virginia Federation of Republican Women; Association of Continuity Planners; International Association of Business Continuity Planners **SIC code:** 73 **Address:** COOP Systems, 607 Herndon Pkwy, Suite 108, Herndon, VA 20170 **E-mail:** vickialvord@coop-systems.com

ANDERSON, BRUCE
Industry: Technology **Born:** October 16, 1962, Springfield, Massachusetts **Univ./degree:** B.S.E.E., Western New England College, 1984 **Current organization:** INVIDI Technologies Corp. **Title:** COO & CTO **Type of organization:** Media solutions company **Major product:** Digital TV audience targeting **Area of distribution:** National **Expertise:** Digital TV systems integration **Affiliations:** I.E.E.E.; A.C.F.; S.M.P.T.E. **Hob./spts.:** Music, football **SIC code:** 73 **Address:** INVIDI Technologies Corp., 750 College Rd. East, Suite 175, Princeton, NJ 08540-6449 **E-mail:** bruce.anderson@invidi.com **Web address:** www.invidi.com

ARLOTTA, BOB
Industry: Automotive **Born:** June 6, 1963, Kearny, New Jersey **Univ./degree:** Lincoln Technical Institute **Current organization:** Long Hill Auto Service Inc. **Title:** President/ Owner **Type of organization:** Auto repair shop **Major product:** Automobile service **Area of distribution:** Millington, New Jersey **Expertise:** Management and operations **Affiliations:** National Federation of Independent Business; A.S.E.; B.B.B. **Hob./spts.:** Showing cars at auto shows **SIC code:** 75 **Address:** Long Hill Auto Service Inc., 1905 Long Hill Rd., Millington, NJ 07946 **E-mail:** barl6663@aol.com **Web address:** www.longhillauto.com

ARNOLD, BRIGITTE A.
Industry: System service provider **Current organization:** Computer Sciences Corp. **Title:** Director, Business Development **Type of organization:** Software developer **Major product:** Software **Area of distribution:** National **Expertise:** Marketing/ logistics **Hob./spts.:** Advocate for the disabled, travel, reading **SIC code:** 73 **Address:** Computer Sciences Corp., 3 N. Overcash Ave., Chambersburg, PA 17201 **E-mail:** jbarnold@mindspring.com

ASHMORE, NANCY
Industry: Personal services **Born:** December 31, 1951, Pennsylvania **Current organization:** Artisan's Salon & Day Spa **Title:** Owner/Partner **Type of organization:** Salon/ Day Spa **Major product:** Hair care, facials, body treatments **Area of distribution:** Emmaus, Pennsylvania **Expertise:** Hairstyling, management, marketing **Affiliations:** Lehigh Valley Chamber of Commerce; Le Tip **Hob./spts.:** Avid skier **SIC code:** 72 **Address:** Artisan's Salon & Day Spa, 413 Chestnut St., Emmaus, PA 18049 **E-mail:** artisansds@fast.net **Web address:** www.artisansdayspa.com

ATKINSON, ROSS C.
Industry: Technology **Born:** July 4, 1968, Fond du Lac, Wisconsin **Univ./degree:** B.S., Marketing, Real Estate, Urban Development, University of Wisconsin at Milwaukee, 1990 **Current organization:** Outtask, Inc. **Title:** EVP, CMO **Type of organization:** Software **Major product:** Software **Area of distribution:** International **Expertise:** Marketing **Affiliations:** S.H.R.M.; National Business Travelers Association **Hob./spts.:** Family, gardening **SIC code:** 73 **Address:** Outtask, Inc., 209 Madison St., Suite 400, Alexandria, VA 22314 **E-mail:** ratkinson@outtask.com

AUERBACH, ROBERT F.
Industry: Hospitality **Univ./degree:** A.A., Hospitality Management, Johnson & Wales University, 1990; B.A., Hospitality Management, F.I.U., 1993 **Current organization:** Innkeepers Hospitality **Title:** Director of Purchasing **Type of organization:** Hotel **Major product:** Lodging, food and beverage **Area of distribution:** National **Expertise:** Purchasing - capital and operations **Affiliations:** American Hotel & Lodging Association **SIC code:** 70 **Address:** Innkeepers Hospitality, 306 Royal Poinciana Plaza, Palm Beach, FL 33480 **E-mail:** rauerbach@ih-corp.com

BAILEY, DEBORAH A.
Industry: Advertising **Univ./degree:** B.A., Lackawanna College, 2004 **Current organization:** Bailey Design & Advertising **Title:** Owner **Type of organization:** Advertising agency **Major product:** Advertising **Area of distribution:** Pennsylvania tri-state area **Expertise:** Marketing **Honors/awards:** Two Communicator Award of Distinction, 2002; Nominee, Award for Woman Entrepreneur from the University of Scranton, 2004 **Affiliations:** Member, Pennsylvania Society; Publisher, Connections Magazine; Better Business Bureau **Hob./spts.:** Painting, photography **SIC code:** 73 **Address:** Bailey Design & Advertising, 18 Collan Park, Suite C&D, Honesdale, PA 18431 **E-mail:** baileyd@ptd.net **Web address:** www.connections-magazine.com

BAILEY, SUSAN E.
Industry: Human Resources **Univ./degree:** A.S.N., South Ohio College, 1987 **Current organization:** ASD Staffing **Title:** President **Type of organization:** Staffing agency **Major product:** Temporary staffing **Area of distribution:** Fairfield, Ohio **Expertise:** Staffing services to major corporations **Hob./spts.:** Equestrian (owns thoroughbreds) **SIC code:** 73 **Address:** ASD Staffing, 6600 Dixie Hwy., Suite W, Fairfield, OH 45014 **E-mail:** susanbailey@asdstaffing.com

BALLARD, REXFORD E.
Industry: Information systems/computers **Born:** December 27, 1955, Denver, Colorado **Univ./degree:** B.A., Performing Arts Management, Loretto Heights College (now part of Regis University), 160 CEU's-Landmark Education Leadership, Communications and Wisdom Programs **Current organization:** IBM **Title:** Enterprise IT Architect, Business Innovation Systems **Major product:** Commercialization of emerging technology, enterprise integration, business to business integration **Area of distribution:** Global **Expertise:** Introducing new technology to the public in ways that create new economic opportunity since 1974. This includes CB radios, VCR's, PC's, Information Services, Internet, Open Source and Linux **Honors/awards:** 3 Bravo Zulu Awards at Federal Express, Team awarded Malcolm Baldridge Award **Published works:** Roughly 3000 articles on the commercialization of the Internet, over 7000 articles on the commercialization of Linux and Open Source technology **Affiliations:** Landmark Education, Linux Advocacy groups, International Executive Guild, Online Newspapers, Online Publishers **SIC code:** 73 **Address:** IBM, 491 Valley Rd., Gillette, NJ 07933-2111 **E-mail:** r.eballard@usa.net **Web address:** www.open4success.com

BANDAK, MIKE
Industry: Language **Born:** December 29, 1970 **Univ./degree:** University of Virginia, 1993; C.I.S., Business Management, University of Houston, 1997 **Current organization:** Sharper Translation Services, Inc. **Title:** Owner/President **Type of organization:** Multilingual services **Major product:** Translation, interpretation and recruitment **Area of distribution:** International **Expertise:** Linguistics, translation **Hob./spts.:** Writing poetry, business consulting **SIC code:** 73 **Address:** Sharper Translation Services, Inc., 10700 Richmond Ave., Suite 100, Houston, TX 77042 **E-mail:** mike@sharpertranslation.com

BARNES, MITCHELL
Industry: Beauty/cosmetics **Born:** Nortonville, Kentucky **Current organization:** Carter Barnes Inc. **Title:** Vice President/Co-Owner **Type of organization:** Beauty salon and spa/retailer **Major product:** Health and beauty services/cosmetics **Area of distribution:** National **Expertise:** Beauty and cosmetic services **SIC code:** 72 **Address:** Carter Barnes Inc., Phipps Plaza Bldg., 3500 Peachtree Rd. N.E., Atlanta, GA 30326 **E-mail:** mitchell@carterbarnes.com **Web address:** www.mitchell@carterbarnes.com

BARNES, PHILLIP Q.
Industry: Security **Born:** October 8, 1977, Arlington, Illinois **Current organization:** Alarm Security, Inc. **Title:** Operations Manager **Type of organization:** Security services **Major product:** Service, installation **Area of distribution:** Illinois **Expertise:** Operations, engineering **Affiliations:** N.F.P.A. **SIC code:** 73 **Address:** Alarm Security, Inc., 1245 Forest Ave., Unit 12, Des Plaines, IL 60018 **E-mail:** phil@alarmsec.com

BARO, NATALIE
Industry: Marketing/Advertising/Consulting **Born:** March 25, 1965, Queens, New York **Univ./degree:** Advertising and Design, Art Institute of Fort Lauderdale **Current organization:** Michelsen Advertising **Title:** President **Type of organization:** Advertising Agency **Major product:** Media buying and planning **Area of distribution:** National **Expertise:** Advertising/Creative Marketing Specialist **Affiliations:** American Marketing Association; Miami Chamber of Commerce; Advertising Associates; Greater Miami Chamber of Commerce **Hob./spts.:** Travel, skiing, rafting, boating and going to the beach **SIC code:** 73 **Address:** Michelsen Advertising, 9590 NW 25th Street, Miamai, FL 33172 **E-mail:** nbaro@michelsenadvertising.com **Web address:** www.michelsenadvertising.com

BARRACO, CAROLE
Industry: Electrolysis **Current organization:** Advanced Electrolysis of Suffolk; 2nd location: 1641 Deer Park Ave., Suite B, Deer Park, New York 11729 **Title:** Owner **Type of organization:** Private practice **Major product:** Permanent hair removal **Area of distribution:** New York **Expertise:** Electrolysis techniques, intradermal cosmetology, photo rejuvenation **Hob./spts.:** Piano, artwork, painting, drawing, waterskiing, golf **SIC code:** 72 **Address:** Advanced Electrolysis of Suffolk, 28 N. Country Rd., Suite 101, Mount Sinai, NY 11766

BARTUCCA, MARA J.
Industry: Public relations **Born:** November 1, 1965, Cleveland, Ohio **Univ./degree:** B.A., Communications, Stephen F. Austin State University, 1987 **Current organization:** Emerge Public Relations **Title:** Owner **Type of organization:** Public relations firm **Major product:** Enterprise software **Area of distribution:** National **Expertise:** Executive coaching, strategy, media opportunities, lecturer at conferences and universities **Honors/awards:** National Leadership Award presented by Massachusetts Congressman John DeLay, 2003 **Published works:** 6 articles **Affiliations:** Advisory Board Member of Northeast Chapter, Public Relations Society of America; Advisory Sponsor, MIT Enterprise Forum **SIC code:** 73 **Address:** Emerge Public Relations, 1 Pleasant St., Suite 8, Cohasset, MA 02025

BAST, JOY
Industry: Hospitality **Born:** July 4, 1972, Silver Spring, Maryland **Univ./degree:** Attended University of West Virginia and University of Connecticut for Restaurant Management **Current organization:** Hyatt Hotels & Resorts **Title:** Revenue Manager **Type of organization:** Hotel **Major product:** Lodging, food and beverage **Area of distribution:** Boston, Massachusetts **Expertise:** Revenue management **Affiliations:** Special Olympics **Hob./spts.:** Plays softball, watches sports **SIC code:** 70 **Address:** Hyatt Hotels & Resorts, 1 Ave de Lafayette, Boston, MA 02111

BEASLEY, O.C.
Industry: Security **Born:** Birmingham, Alabama **Univ./degree:** M.Ed., University of Alabama, Birmingham **Current organization:** Pinson Valley Security Inc. **Title:** President **Type of organization:** Security firm **Major product:** Security services, personal protection **Area of distribution:** Alabama **Expertise:** Marketing, security, business management **Affiliations:** V.F.W.; Birmingham Fraternal Club of Dancing; Elks Club **Hob./spts.:** Dancing **SIC code:** 73 **Address:** Pinson Valley Security Inc., 1324 Main St., Birmingham, AL 35217

BERMAN, JERRY L.
Industry: Real Estate **Born:** August 28, 1937, Philadelphia, Pennsylvania **Univ./degree:** B.A., Business, Pierce Business College, 1962 **Current organization:** Jerry L. Berman Appraisers, Inc. **Title:** Certified Real Estate Appraisers, Inc. **Type of organization:** Appraisal firm **Major product:** Real estate appraisals **Area of distribution:** Bucks County, Pennsylvania **Expertise:** Brokering since 1959, investments, residential and commercial properties; Certified Real Estate Appraiser **Affiliations:** National Association of Real Estate Appraisers **Hob./spts.:** Tennis, travel, theatre **SIC code:** 73 **Address:** Jerry L. Berman Appraisers, Inc., 704 Willow St., Southampton, PA 18966-3430 **E-mail:** jerry1@voicenet.com **Web address:** www.jerrybermanappraisers.com

BERNET, HANSPETER
Industry: Hospitality **Born:** July 29, 1949, Switzerland **Univ./degree:** Certified Chef, Palace Hotel Culinary Program, Switzerland, 1967 **Current organization:** Crowne Plaza, Cincinnati **Title:** Executive Chef **Type of organization:** Hotel **Major product:** Hospitality **Area of distribution:** Ohio **Expertise:** Culinary arts **Hob./spts.:** Soccer, baseball **SIC code:** 70 **Address:** Crowne Plaza, 15 W. Sixth St., Cincinnati, OH 45202 **E-mail:** cplazacin@aol.com

BEROS, JODIE LEE
Industry: Hospitality **Born:** May 15, 1972, Goulbrun, Australia **Univ./degree:** Certificate, Ryde Technical College, Sydney, Australia **Current organization:** Deer Valley Resort **Title:** Snowpark & Empire Lodges Executive Chef **Type of organization:** Ski resort **Major product:** Food, beverage, lodging, skiing **Area of distribution:** Park City, Utah **Expertise:** Cooking, guest services **Affiliations:** Utah Restaurant Association **Hob./spts.:** Hiking, swimming, skiing, cooking, reading **SIC code:** 70 **Address:** Deer Valley Resort, 2500 Deer Valley Dr. South, P.O. Box 889, Park City, UT 84060 **E-mail:** jberos@deervalley.com

BERRY, CHARLENE HELEN

Industry: Entertainment **Born:** January 4, 1947, Highland Park, Michigan **Univ./degree:** B.S.E., 1968; M.A., 1970; M.S.L.S., 1974, W.S.U., MI; CMT, 1998 EMF; D.Min, U.S.C.; Diplomate, Specs Howard, 1992; Diplomate, I.M.I., 1997; D. Min. (Honorary), Destiny Christian University, 2008 **Current organization:** Dulcimer Evente **Title:** Chief Executive Officer/Owner **Type of organization:** Music **Major product:** Live and pre-recorded music (tapes and CD's) **Area of distribution:** National **Expertise:** Special music for special people, original compositions, improvisations; Endorsed Artist, Christian Music Presenters **Honors/awards:** Listed in, Who's Who Worldwide Global Registry; World Who's Who of Women; Dictionary of Int'l Biographies; Int'l Who's Who of Intellectuals; Who's Who in the World; Who's Who in the Midwest; Who's Who in America; 2000 Notable American Women; Most Admired Men & Women of the Year; Int'l Directory of Distinguished Leadership; Int'l Who's Who of Professional and Business Women; Michigan Touring Arts Directory; 20th Century Award of Achievement; Int'l Order of Merit; Star of the Stars Music Award, 2006; Silver Medal Winner, Christian Music Connection, 2006; Businesswoman of the Year, 2003, 2004; Ronald Reagan Award, 2004 **Published works:** Dulcimer Delights, v.1, 1991; Marches, Waltzes, Free Composition and Solo Symphony, v.2, 1993; Hammering the Hammer Dulcimer, video, 1994 **Affiliations:** B.P.W.; A.A.U.W.; American Federation of Musicians; American Guild of Organists; Gospel Music Association; Fellow, American Biological Institute; Life Fellow, International Biological Association; Deputy Governor American Biog. Inst. Res. Association **Career accomplishments:** Leader in the current revival of the hammer dulcimer and the development of hammering techniques, performance and practice **Hob./spts.:** Landscape painting, photography **SIC code:** 79 **Address:** Dulcimer Evente, 49614 Oak Street, Plymouth, MI 48170 **E-mail:** cberry@dulcimerworld.com **Web address:** www.dulcimerworld.com

BHATT, JIGNESH C.

Industry: Data/payroll processing **Born:** November 22, 1963, Navsari, India **Univ./degree:** Bachelor of Physics in Electronics, St. Xavier's University, India, 1997 **Current organization:** ADP Inc. **Title:** Manager, Internet Implementation **Type of organization:** Software **Major product:** Payroll and human resources services **Area of distribution:** International **Expertise:** IT Infrastructure, Internet and CRM **Hob./spts.:** Reading, travel, model airplanes, his children **SIC code:** 73 **Address:** ADP Inc., 15 Waterview Blvd., Parsippany, NJ 07054 **E-mail:** jignesh_bhatt@adp.com

BINKLEY, TAMA S.

Industry: Electrolysis **Born:** Elyria, Ohio **Univ./degree:** Ohio Institute of Electrology, 1998 **Current organization:** Tama S. Binkley CT, LE, Electrolysis **Title:** Owner **Type of organization:** Solo practice **Major product:** Permanent hair removal **Area of distribution:** Vermilion, Ohio **Expertise:** Certified Electrolysis **Hob./spts.:** Family **SIC code:** 72 **Address:** Tama S. Binkley CT, LE, Electrolysis, 3409 Liberty Ave., Suite 202, Vermilion, OH 44089

BOFILL, PETER

Industry: Recreation **Current organization:** RNT Sports Corp. **Title:** President/Owner **Type of organization:** Paintball field **Major product:** Entertainment **Area of distribution:** National **Expertise:** Management; Exporting goods internationally **Affiliations:** Greater Miami Chamber of Commerce **SIC code:** 79 **Address:** RNT Sports Corp., 13200 N.W. 43rd Ave., Opa-Locka, FL 33054 **E-mail:** info@ruffntuff-paintball.com **Web address:** www.rntpaintball.com

BOISDRON, LAURENT J.

Industry: Hospitality **Born:** August 19, 1971, Nantes, France **Univ./degree:** Food and Beverage Degrees, Bougainville Catering School, Nantes, France, 1989; Branly Catering School, La Roche Sur Yon, France, 1991 **Current organization:** Hotel Sofitel Water Tower **Title:** Director of Food and Beverage **Type of organization:** Hotel **Major product:** Lodging, food and beverage **Area of distribution:** Illinois **Expertise:** Food and beverage operations, management **Hob./spts.:** Passion for Spain, arts (opera, baroque music), photography, travel, oenology **SIC code:** 70 **Address:** Hotel Sofitel Water Tower, 20 E. Chestnut St.-Downtown, Chicago, IL 60611 **E-mail:** lboisdron@hotmail.com

BOISSONNADE, AUGUSTE C.

Industry: Consulting **Born:** January 19, 1953, Paris, France **Univ./degree:** Ph.D., Civil Engineering, Stanford University, 1984 **Current organization:** Risk Management Solutions **Title:** Vice President/Principal Scientist **Type of organization:** Information/financial services **Major product:** Software **Area of distribution:** International **Expertise:** Engineering **Affiliations:** A.S.C.E.; A.M.S. **SIC code:** 73 **Address:** Risk Management Solutions, 7015 Gateway Blvd., Newark, CA 94560-1011 **E-mail:** augusteb@rms.com

BOND, DEREK S.

Industry: Entertainment **Univ./degree:** B.S., Business Administration, University of Southern California, 1990 **Current organization:** Telemundo Network **Title:** Senior Vice President, Telemundo Studios **Type of organization:** Television entertainment **Major product:** Film and TV programming **Expertise:** Production **SIC code:** 79 **Address:** Telemundo Network, 2290 W. Eighth Ave., Hialeah, FL 33010 **E-mail:** dsbond@telemundo.com **Web address:** www.telemundo.com

BORDAN, CLAY W.

Industry: Hospitality **Born:** March 20, 1968, Hartford, Connecticut **Current organization:** American Property Management Corp. **Title:** Corporate Executive Chef **Type of organization:** Property management corporation **Major product:** Hotels/resorts/restaurants **Area of distribution:** National **Expertise:** Corporate Executive Chef **Published works:** Articles **Hob./spts.:** Surfing **SIC code:** 70 **Address:** American Property Management Corp., 8910 University Center Lane, Suite 500, San Diego, CA 92122 **E-mail:** cbordan@apmc.net

BOYD, HARRY J.

Industry: Hospitality **Born:** May 1, 1948, Lexington, Mississippi **Current organization:** Holiday Inn at South County **Title:** Executive Chef **Type of organization:** Hotel **Major product:** Lodging, food and beverage **Area of distribution:** Missouri **Expertise:** Preparing food for groups of 25-1500 people **Affiliations:** Chefs of America **Hob./spts.:** Fishing **SIC code:** 70 **Address:** 3425 Connecticut St., St. Louis, MO 63118 **E-mail:** jewellb1225@aol.com

BOYD, VENETIA R.

Industry: Interior design **Born:** September 29, 1958, Riverhead, New York **Univ./degree:** B.S., Mental Health Technology, Morgan State University **Current organization:** Décor & You **Title:** Owner **Type of organization:** Full service décor **Major product:** Residential and commercial interiors **Area of distribution:** National **Expertise:** Decoration and design **Published works:** Howard County Women's Journal **Affiliations:** T.I.P. International; H.B.A.M.; N.A.H.B. **Hob./spts.:** Photography, seamstress, drawing, painting **SIC code:** 73 **Address:** Décor & You, P.O. Box 734, Clarksville, MD 21029 **E-mail:** vboyd@decorandyou.com **Web address:** www.decorandyou.com/vboyd

BRACKER, RICHARD

Industry: Business marketing, public relations and market research **Univ./degree:** B.A., Editorial Journalism, Ohio State University, Columbus **Current organization:** Bracker Communications **Title:** President **Type of organization:** Marketing communications **Major product:** Marketing communications, public relations, advertising and market research **Area of distribution:** International **Expertise:** Marketing support and writing **Honors/awards:** Invited and served as EFFIE Awards Judge, New York Marketing Association; 1st Place Award for company publications, Direct Marketing Association **Published works:** Area Development; Sales & Marketing Ideas; Resort Management & Operations; Earthmover & Civil Contractor; National Golfer; Plan & Print Magazines. Take Note, Atlanta (GA) Symphony newsletter; Editor-in-Chief, United States Gypsum Co. **Affiliations:** Cleveland, Ohio Advertising Club; Lifetime Member, Sigma Delta Chi **Hob./spts.:** Golf, tennis **SIC code:** 73 **Address:** Bracker Communications, 6450 Industrial Way, Suite #115, Alpharetta, GA 30004 **E-mail:** rbracker@bellsouth.net

BRENNAN, JOHN

Industry: Food service **Born:** June 4, 1946, Liverpool, England **Univ./degree:** A.S., Food Service, Nautical Catering College, Liverpool England, 1962 **Current organization:** Inn on the River/Days Inn River View **Title:** Executive Chef **Type of organization:** Hotel **Major product:** Food, beverages. lodging **Area of distribution:** New York **Expertise:** Culinary arts, banquets for 1250 persons **Honors/awards:** Chef of the Year, 1985 **Published works:** Journals **Affiliations:** Past President, Chef Association **SIC code:** 70 **Address:** Inn on the River/Days Inn River View, 701 & 401 Buffalo Ave., Niagara Falls, NY 14304

BROWN, PATRICIA A.

Industry: Hospitality **Born:** Galveston, Texas **Univ./degree:** Attended, Sam Houston State Teacher's College **Current organization:** Caesars Palace **Title:** Office Manager, F & B Division **Type of organization:** Resort/casino **Major product:** Gaming, hotel rooms, restaurants **Area of distribution:** Nevada **Expertise:** Food and beverage **Affiliations:** I.A.A.P.; National Notary Association **Hob./spts.:** Gardening, reading **SIC code:** 70 **Address:** Caesars Palace, 3570 Las Vegas Blvd. South, Las Vegas, NV 89109 **E-mail:** brownpat@parkplace.com

BROWN, ROMERO
Industry: Hospitality **Univ./degree:** B.A., Oklahoma University, 1982 **Current organization:** Navajoland Days Inn & Denny's **Title:** President/Owner **Type of organization:** Hotel, restaurant **Major product:** Lodging, food and guest services **Area of distribution:** St. Michaels, Arizona **Expertise:** Administration **Affiliations:** N.Y.R.; H.A.; Navajo Reservation **Hob./spts.:** Coaching baseball, fishing, golf **SIC code:** 70 **Address:** Navajoland Days Inn & Denny's, 392 West Hwy. 264, St. Michaels, AZ 86511 **E-mail:** navajolanddaysinn@citibank.net

BUCCAT, ROMEO C.
Industry: Security/fire/access **Born:** March 18, 1966, Guam **Current organization:** Pacific Security Alarm Inc. **Title:** Technical Division Supervisor **Type of organization:** Retail, installation **Major product:** Security systems **Area of distribution:** Guam **Expertise:** Technical support **Affiliations:** N.A.A.A. **Hob./spts.:** Bowling **SIC code:** 73 **Address:** Pacific Security Alarm, Inc., 1406 N. Marine Dr., Suite 201, Tamuning, GU 96913 **E-mail:** rcbuccat@yahoo.com

BUCCI, VINCENT A.
Industry: Hospitality **Born:** November 1, 1960, New York **Univ./degree:** A.A., Accounting, Pierce College, 1980 **Current organization:** Horizon Hotels Ltd. **Title:** Vice President Food & Beverage **Type of organization:** Hotels, resorts **Major product:** Food, beverage, lodging **Area of distribution:** National **Expertise:** Food & beverage (Certified, 1990) **Published works:** Write-ups **Affiliations:** N.J.R.A.; American Hotel Management **Hob./spts.:** Golf **SIC code:** 70 **Address:** Horizon Hotels Ltd., 16 Christopher Way, Eatontown, NJ 07724 **E-mail:** vbucci@horizonhotels.com **Web address:** www.horizonhotels.com

CANDIANO, BETTY J.
Industry: Research/credit and background checks **Born:** February 29, 1936, Gary, Indiana **Univ./degree:** L.P.N., Ivy Tech College **Current organization:** P&B Research **Title:** L.P.N. **Type of organization:** Data processing **Major product:** Collect court reports and research reports for credit bureau/background checks for people applying for jobs **Area of distribution:** Indiana **Expertise:** Rehab/wound care **Affiliations:** Indiana State Nurses Association **Hob./spts.:** Crochet, painting **SIC code:** 73 **Address:** P&B Research, 741 Westerfield Rd., Hebron, IN 46341 **E-mail:** bettyboo@netnitco.net

CANERI, EDOARDO
Industry: Hotel **Born:** January 10, 1948, Parma, Italy **Univ./degree:** "Ospitalita", Varano, Italy, Studied Culinary Arts in Italy, Paris, France and London, England **Current organization:** 6 Continents, Crowne Plaza Union Square **Title:** Food and Beverage Director **Type of organization:** Hotel **Major product:** Lodging **Area of distribution:** International **Expertise:** Mediterranean cuisine **Honors/awards:** America's Tasting Award, 2000-1 **Affiliations:** A.T.A.; C.C.A. **Hob./spts.:** Semi-pro Soccer, languages (speaks French, Italian, English and Spanish) **SIC code:** 70 **Address:** 6 Continents, Crowne Plaza Union Square, , 480 Sutter St., San Francisco, CA 94108 **E-mail:** ecaneri@bristolhotels.com

CARTER, CAREY K.
Industry: Beauty and cosmetics **Current organization:** Carter Barnes Inc. **Title:** President **Type of organization:** Beauty salon and spa/retailer **Major product:** Health and beauty services/cosmetics **Area of distribution:** National **Expertise:** Beauty and cosmetic services **Hob./spts.:** Landscaping **SIC code:** 72 **Address:** Carter Barnes Inc., Phipps Plaza Bldg., 3500 Peachtree Rd. N.E., Atlanta, GA 30326 **E-mail:** carey@carterbarnes.com **Web address:** www.carterbarnes.com

CASTELLO, OTIS ST.
Industry: Hospitality/Food **Born:** January 14, 1968, Georgetown, Washington, D.C. **Univ./degree:** Georgetown Culinary School **Current organization:** Millennium Hotel, UN Plaza, New York **Title:** Banquet Chef **Type of organization:** Hotel group **Major product:** Banquets, catering, lodging **Area of distribution:** New York **Expertise:** Specialty Chef **Affiliations:** American Culinary Federation **Hob./spts.:** Basketball, soccer, billiards, table tennis **SIC code:** 70 **Address:** 2216 Aqueduct Ave., Bronx, NY 10453 **E-mail:** pocastell@aol.com

CATANIA, RICHARD V.
Industry: Hotel/restaurant **Univ./degree:** B.S., Merrimack College, 1979 **Current organization:** Dan'l Webster / Hearth 'n Kettle Management Group **Title:** Vice President & Corporate Chef **Type of organization:** Hotel/restaurant **Major product:** Lodging, food and wine **Area of distribution:** Massachusetts **Expertise:** Wine **Affiliations:** Cape Cod Chamber of Commerce; Hook Fisherman's Association **Hob./spts.:** Skiing, golf **SIC code:** 70 **Address:** Dan'l Webster / Hearth 'n Kettle Management Group, 141 Falmouth Rd., Hyannis, MA 02601

CAUDLE SR., OTTIS E.
Industry: Hospitality **Born:** February 1, 1949, Illinois **Current organization:** Crown Plaza **Title:** Purchasing Manager/Executive Chef **Type of organization:** Hotel/restaurant **Major product:** Lodging, food **Area of distribution:** Illinois **Expertise:** Purchasing and control of supplies, restaurant management, training **Affiliations:** Vietnam Veteran with eight years of service, U.S. Air Force **Hob./spts.:** Golf, fishing, home renovations, fine dining **SIC code:** 70 **Address:** 501 S. Wesley, Springfield, IL 62703

CHOTA, GJON
Industry: Security **Born:** February 20, 1957, Montenegro, Yugoslavia **Univ./degree:** B.S., Law, University of Titogradin, Yugoslavia **Current organization:** Universal Lock Service Co., Inc. **Title:** President **Type of organization:** Lock and door services **Major product:** Locks, doors, alarms, intercoms **Area of distribution:** Bronx, New York **Expertise:** Management **Affiliations:** Albanian American Academy of Science and Art; Board Member, I.N.H.A. **Hob./spts.:** Flying, travel, airplane building **SIC code:** 73 **Address:** Universal Lock Service Co., Inc., 603 Crescent Ave., Bronx, NY 10458

CLARK BARTLETT, MARY
Industry: Food **Born:** New York, New York **Current organization:** Epicurean Group **Title:** CEO/President **Type of organization:** Food service contractor **Major product:** Fresh natural and organic foods **Area of distribution:** California **Expertise:** Corporate and education clients, administration, growth, sales **Affiliations:** Los Altos Chamber of Commerce; Marin County Chamber of Commerce **Hob./spts.:** Rose gardening, hiking, physical fitness **SIC code:** 73 **Address:** Epicurean Group, 111 Main St., Suite 3, Los Altos, CA 94022 **Web address:** www.epicurean-group.com

COELHO, SANDRA S.
Industry: Consulting/education **Univ./degree:** B.S., 1962; M.S., 1968, Central Connecticut State University; 6 Year Degree, Teaching Curriculum, University of Connecticut, 1981 **Current organization:** Coelho Enterprises **Title:** President **Type of organization:** Private consultant **Major product:** Consulting: education, training, technology, professional development, computers **Area of distribution:** Connecticut **Expertise:** Training, math, computer training, networks **Published works:** 1 article **Affiliations:** ATOMIC; Phi Delta Kappa **SIC code:** 73 **Address:** Coelho Enterprises, 50 Smalley Rd., Windsor Locks, CT 06096 **E-mail:** sandrac101@aol.com

COLEMAN, SEABORN L.
Industry: Aerospace **Born:** December 27, 1941, Atlanta, Georgia **Current organization:** Griffin Services **Title:** Special Purpose Maintenance Technician **Type of organization:** Facility management/operations engineers **Major product:** Transportation services, fleet management **Area of distribution:** International **Expertise:** Heavy mobile equipment maintenance **Hob./spts.:** Airplane pilot **SIC code:** 73 **Address:** Griffin Services, 926 Industrial Dr., Bldg. 516, Marietta, GA 30069 **E-mail:** seaborn.coleman@dobbins.af.mil

COLLARD, CLINT B.
Industry: Pest control **Born:** October 17, 1958, Glendale, California **Current organization:** Terminix **Title:** Pest and Termite Control Specialist **Type of organization:** Extermination services **Major product:** Termite control **Area of distribution:** National **Expertise:** Outside sales, pest control **Affiliations:** Springfield COFC; Springfield Better Business Bureau **Hob./spts.:** Hunting, fishing, church **SIC code:** 73 **Address:** Terminix, 3048 S. Clifton, Springfield, MO 65804 **E-mail:** collardpatch@centurytel.net

COLLINS SR., JOHN J.
Industry: Funeral service **Born:** June 15, 1923, Blossburg, Pennsylvania **Univ./degree:** B.S., Mortuary Science, New York University School of Mortuary Science, 1948 **Current organization:** Collins - Olney Funeral Home **Title:** Supervisor **Type of organization:** Funeral home **Major product:** Funerals **Area of distribution:** Galeton, Pennsylvania **Expertise:** General service **Affiliations:** N.F.D.; P.F.D.; P.C.F.D.; N.H.S.; P.H.S.; Smithsonian Institute **Hob./spts.:** Golf, travel. community service **SIC code:** 72 **Address:** Collins - Olney Funeral Home, 14 West St., Galeton, PA 16922

COOK, VIRGINIA L.
Industry: Hospitality/entertainment **Born:** February 24, 1928, Carlsbad, New Mexico **Current organization:** New Frontier Hotel & Casino **Title:** Pit Clerk **Type of organization:** Hotel/casino **Major product:** Hotel services, recreational activities **Area of distribution:** Nevada **Expertise:** Input ratings into casino system **Affiliations:** University of Nevada; University of Oregon **Hob./spts.:** Scrapebooking, photography **SIC code:** 70 **Address:** 3757 Fairlawn Ave., Las Vegas, NV 89121

COONEY, STEPHEN W.
Industry: Food **Born:** September 19, 1962, Gloucester, Massachusetts **Univ./degree:** A.A., Culinary Arts, Culinary Institute of America, 1983 **Current organization:** Sodexho **Title:** Regional Executive Chef, Senior Manager of Culinary Development **Type of organization:** Service outsourcing **Major product:** Food service operations, grounds maintenance, facilities management **Area of distribution:** International **Expertise:** K-12 schools food service **Honors/awards:** Augie Award, Culinary Institute of America, 1996; Award of Excellence, Sodexho USA, 1998 **Affiliations:** American

Culinary Federation (ACF); Founding Member, Sodexho's Chef's Association **Hob./spts.:** Kayaking, reading, cooking, the beach **SIC code:** 73 **Address:** Sodexho, 17 Algonquin Rd., New Britain, PA 18901 **E-mail:** stephen.cooney@sodexhousa.com

COOPER, MITCHELL C.
Industry: Hospitality **Born:** October 23, 1969, Baltimore, Maryland **Univ./degree:** A.A., Hospitality/Restaurant Culinary, Baltimore International Culinary College **Current organization:** Marriott International Hotels & Resort **Title:** Executive Chef **Type of organization:** Hotel **Major product:** Lodging, food and beverage **Expertise:** Culinary arts, menu planning, banquets, catering **Honors/awards:** Award of Culinary Excellence, 2001 **Hob./spts.:** Golf, travel **SIC code:** 70 **Address:** Marriott International Hotels & Resort, 110 S. Eutaw St., Baltimore, MD 21201 **E-mail:** mitch.cooper@marriott.com

COOPER-BROSKI, ELISA B.
Industry: Advertising/healthcare **Born:** August 1958, Summit, New Jersey **Univ./degree:** B.A., Visual Communications and Art Education/Remedial Reading K-12 grade, Kean College of New Jersey, 1979 **Current organization:** Bruce Leeb & Company **Title:** President **Type of organization:** Advertising agency **Major product:** Marketing of pharmaceutical products and medical devices **Area of distribution:** National/International **Expertise:** Pharmaceutical advertising; marketing support; Business Development Specialist **Affiliations:** Healthcare Businesswomen's Association (HBA); Healthcare Marketing Council (HMC); Dionysian Society; Outdoors Club of New Jersey **Hob./spts.:** Gourmet cooking, wine tasting, hiking, biking, Yoga **SIC code:** 73 **Address:** Bruce Leeb & Company, 17-17 Route 208 North, Fair Lawn, NJ 07410 **E-mail:** ebroski@blc1.com **Web address:** www.blc1.com

CORCORAN, ROBERT D.
Industry: Resort **Born:** December 10, 1965, Chicago, Illinois **Current organization:** Keystone Ski Resort **Title:** Lift Mechanic **Type of organization:** Ski resort **Major product:** Skiing, snowboarding **Area of distribution:** Colorado **Expertise:** Lift operations, engineering, maintenance and organization planning **Hob./spts.:** Travel, hiking, camping, 4 wheeling, coin collecting **SIC code:** 70 **Address:** P.O. Box 4614, Dillon, CO 80435 **E-mail:** corcoran@aol.com

CROWDER, TED
Industry: Entertainment **Born:** November 4, 1964, Marietta, Georgia **Univ./degree:** A.S., Chattahoochee Technical Institute **Current organization:** Atlanta Bands & DJ's **Title:** President **Type of organization:** Entertainment company **Major product:** Entertainers, DJ's **Area of distribution:** Georgia **Expertise:** DJ & planner **Affiliations:** President, Georgia Mobile DJ Association; Board of Directors, N.A.C.E.; I.S.E.S.; A.C.P.W.C. **Hob./spts.:** Guitar, mountain biking **SIC code:** 79 **Address:** Atlanta Bands & DJ's, 1045 Grimes Bridge Rd., Roswell, GA 30075

CRUM, FRANK J.
Industry: Telecommunications **Born:** January 16, 1973, Tampa, Florida **Univ./degree:** B.S., Telecommunications, University of Florida, 1995 **Current organization:** City of Tampa Television **Title:** Producer/Director **Type of organization:** City government **Major product:** Cable programming **Area of distribution:** Florida **Expertise:** Television producer **Affiliations:** Media Professional of Florida, Inc.; Tampa Bay Association of Black Communicators **Hob./spts.:** Watching movies **SIC code:** 79 **Address:** City of Tampa Television, 202 W. Seventh Ave., Tampa, FL 33612 **E-mail:** frank.crum@tampagov.net

DALGADO, RONNIE L.
Industry: Hospitality **Born:** November 2, 1964, Kenya **Univ./degree:** B.S., Psychology and Economics, Bombay University, 1984; Diplomate, Hotel Administration, Sophia Polytechnic, 1987 **Current organization:** Doubletree Hotel **Title:** Director of Food and Beverage **Type of organization:** Hotel **Major product:** Lodging, food and beverage **Area of distribution:** Santa Ana, California **Expertise:** Food and beverage operations, budgeting, marketing **Hob./spts.:** Golf, reading **SIC code:** 70 **Address:** Doubletree Hotel, 201 E. MacArthur Blvd., Santa Ana, CA 92707 **E-mail:** rdalgado@doubletreeocairport.com **Web address:** www.doubletreeocairport.com

DALUZ, JOSEPH
Industry: Software **Born:** January 1, 1949, Vienna, Austria **Univ./degree:** M.B.A., College of St. Elizabeth, New Jersey **Current organization:** Computer Horizons Corp. **Title:** Vice President/CIO **Type of organization:** Services provider **Major product:** Software **Area of distribution:** International **Expertise:** Management **Published works:** Articles **Affiliations:** A.C.M.; I.E.E.E. **Hob./spts.:** Chess, tennis, golf, Tai Chi **SIC code:** 73 **Address:** Computer Horizons Corp., 49 Old Bloomfield Ave., Mountain Lakes, NJ 07046 **E-mail:** jdaluz@computerhorizons.com

D'AMORE, DEIRDRE R.
Industry: Mail services **Born:** November 7, 1964, Florida **Univ./degree:** Attended UNLVN; UNR, Business **Current organization:** Mailbox Express **Title:** Owner **Type of organization:** Shipping and postal services **Major product:** Mail boxes, notary, packaging, shipping **Area of distribution:** International **Expertise:** Business, entrepreneurialism **Hob./spts.:** All sports **SIC code:** 73 **Address:** Mailbox Express, 3172 N. Rainbow Blvd., Las Vegas, NV 89108 **E-mail:** mailbox.express@earthlink.net

DANA, RICHARD H.
Industry: Hospitality **Born:** November 22, 1944, Norwood, Massachusetts **Current organization:** Four Points Sheraton **Title:** Property Operations Manager **Type of organization:** Hotel/conference center **Major product:** Food, beverage, lodging **Area of distribution:** International **Expertise:** Property management **Affiliations:** N.F.P.A. **Hob./spts.:** Hunting, fishing, camping, boating **SIC code:** 70 **Address:** Four Points Sheraton, 1125 Boston-Providence Tpke., Norwood, MA 02062 **E-mail:** richard.dana@hobbsbrook.com

DAVIS, ESIN D.
Industry: Hospitality **Born:** October 26, 1946, Athens, Greece **Univ./degree:** B.S., Psychology, Ankara University, Turkey, 1974 **Current organization:** Coral Hospitality **Title:** Sales and Marketing Director **Type of organization:** Hotel **Major product:** Hotel accommodations **Area of distribution:** International **Expertise:** Sales, marketing, operations revenue management, staff training **Affiliations:** American Marketing Association; H.S.A.M International **Hob./spts.:** Bicycling, jogging, swimming **SIC code:** 70 **Address:** Coral Hospitality, 9793 Arbor Oaks Lane, #204, Boca Raton, FL 33428 **E-mail:** esindavis@aol.com

D'AYON, TERRI
Industry: Hospitality **Born:** February 14, 1957, Sacramento, California **Univ./degree:** A.S., American River College, 1977 **Current organization:** The Stanford Court, A Renaissance Hotel **Title:** Director of Hotel Sales **Type of organization:** Hotel **Major product:** Hotel accommodations, corporate meetings **Area of distribution:** International **Expertise:** Sales, marketing **Affiliations:** P.C.M.A.; Insurance Conference Planners Association **SIC code:** 70 **Address:** The Stanford Court, A Renaissance Hotel, 905 California St. Atop Nob Hill, San Francisco, CA 94108 **E-mail:** terridayon@stanfordcourt.net

DE SOUSA, GEOFFREY W.
Industry: Interior Design **Univ./degree:** B.A., Art History, University of Massachusetts **Current organization:** De Sousa Hughes, LLC **Title:** President **Type of organization:** Interior design firm/trade showroom **Major product:** Interior design; furniture, textiles, lighting, art and accessories **Area of distribution:** National **Expertise:** Residential interior design **Published works:** 20 articles **Affiliations:** New York School of Interior Design **SIC code:** 73 **Address:** DeSousa Hughes, LLC, 2 Henry Adams St., #220-290, San Francisco, CA 94103 **Web address:** www.desousahughes.com

DESAI, MRUGAN H.
Industry: IT Consulting **Born:** March 24, 1968, Bardoli, India **Univ./degree:** B.S., Computer Science, Lock Haven University, 1990; M.S., Telecomputing Engineering, University of Oklahoma, 2002 **Current organization:** I.B.M. **Title:** Advisory IT Consultant - Enterprise Resource Planning **Type of organization:** Business transformation **Major product:** Software, energy, ERP **Area of distribution:** National **Expertise:** Enterprise resource planning - implementation and processes **Affiliations:** Associate Member, I.E.E.E. **Hob./spts.:** Photography, gardening, golf, travel **SIC code:** 73 **Address:** 7933 S. 92 E. Place, Tulsa, OK 74133 **E-mail:** mrugan@mrugan.com

DEVESA, SERGE
Industry: Hospitality **Current organization:** Hotel Sositel **Title:** Executive Chef **Type of organization:** Hotel **Major product:** Hotel accommodations, fine cooking **Area of distribution:** Bloomington, Minnesota **Expertise:** Supervision of staff and 2 restaurants, catering, banquets **Affiliations:** Chaine des Rotisseurs **SIC code:** 70 **Address:** Hotel Sositel, 5601 W. 78th St., Bloomington, MN 55439 **E-mail:** sergedevesa@yahoo.com

DIGLIO III, JOHN J.
Industry: Automotive **Current organization:** Digger's Harley Service, LLC **Title:** Owner **Type of organization:** Motorcycle repair, service and sales **Major product:** Harley Davidson service, building, repair, parts **Area of distribution:** Connecticut **Expertise:** Motorcycle service, repair and customization **SIC code:** 75 **Address:** Digger's Harley Service, LLC, 1065 Middletown Ave., Northford, CT 06472 **E-mail:** diggers9899@sbcglobal.net

DINSMORE, MICHAEL P.
Industry: High technology **Born:** December 11, 1965, Longmont, Colorado **Univ./degree:** A.S., Chemistry, Front Range Community College; B.A., Chemistry, University of Colorado at Boulder, 1999 **Current organization:** Seagate Technology LLC **Title:** Senior Material Science Advisor **Type of organization:** Research and development **Major product:** Storage data **Area of distribution:** International **Expertise:** Physical and organic chemistry, analytical analysis **Honors/awards:** 4 patents **Published works:** American Science Magazine journals **Hob./spts.:** Hockey, mountain biking

SIC code: 73 **Address:** Seagate Technology LLC, 389 Disc Dr., Longmont, CO 80503 **E-mail:** mike.dinsmore@seagate.com

DIVITO, JEFFREY C.
Industry: Casinos **Univ./degree:** B.A., Fairleigh Dickinson University, New Jersey, 1976 **Current organization:** Station Casinos Inc. **Title:** Corporate Vice President of Food and Beverage **Type of organization:** Casinos (13 in Las Vegas) **Major product:** Gaming and entertainment **Area of distribution:** Las Vegas, Nevada **Expertise:** Food and beverage concepts and operations **Hob./spts.:** Boating, horseback riding, waterskiing **SIC code:** 79 **Address:** Station Casinos Inc., 2800 S. Rancho Dr., Las Vegas, NV 89102 **E-mail:** jeff.divito@stationcasinos.com

DOBBS, RODNEY W.
Industry: Security and communication integration **Born:** July 27, 1974, Oklahoma City, Oklahoma **Current organization:** Central Systems Communications & Security Inc. **Title:** Vice President of Sales & Operations **Type of organization:** Retail services **Major product:** Security and communication integration **Area of distribution:** Oklahoma **Expertise:** Sales, marketing, technical advisor **Affiliations:** N.R.A.; National Burglar and Fire Alarm Association; Oklahoma Burglar and Fire Alarm Association; National Arbor Day Foundation **Hob./spts.:** Skydiving, scuba diving, football, hiking, rafting, hunting, fishing, outdoor activities **SIC code:** 73 **Address:** Central Systems Communications & Security Inc., 1937 S. May Ave., Oklahoma City, OK 73173 **E-mail:** rodneydobbs@centralsystemsonline.com

DONIGER, WALTER
Industry: Entertainment **Born:** July 1, 1917, New York, New York **Univ./degree:** B.A., Business, Howard University; Physics, Duke University **Current organization:** Bettina Productions, Ltd. **Title:** President **Type of organization:** Film/TV production **Major product:** Movies, TV programming **Area of distribution:** International **Expertise:** Producing, writing, directing **Honors/awards:** Golden Globe Nominee, 1977 **Affiliations:** Directors Guild of America; Writers Guild of America; Academy of Motion Picture Arts & Sciences **Hob./spts.:** Boating, sports, reading **SIC code:** 79 **Address:** Bettina Productions, Ltd., 624 S. June St., Los Angeles, CA 90005 **E-mail:** wdoniger@aol.com

DONTJE, M. ADRIANA
Industry: Advertising **Born:** February 25, 1964, San Diego, California **Univ./degree:** B.A., Marketing, Patricia Stevens Fashion College, 1986 **Current organization:** International Media Services **Title:** Sole Proprietor **Type of organization:** Marketing/public relations/advertising **Major product:** Television/radio media buying, specializing in cable buying **Area of distribution:** National **Expertise:** Marketing in Hispanic media **Affiliations:** North County Latinas Association; Breast Cancer Society **Hob./spts.:** Travel, fine wine **SIC code:** 73 **Address:** International Media Services, 1104 Camino del Mar, Suite 4, Del Mar, CA 92014 **E-mail:** adriana@intlmediaservices.com

DRAGHICI, ADRIAN
Industry: Internet technology **Univ./degree:** B.S., Robotics, 1998; M.S., Product Design, 2005, Politehnica University, Bucharest, Romania **Current organization:** Breece Hill L.L.C. **Title:** Mechanical Engineer **Type of organization:** IT manufacturing/engineering **Major product:** Tape automation **Area of distribution:** International **Expertise:** IT mechanical engineering **Affiliations:** Romanian Engineering Association **SIC code:** 73 **Address:** 1603 Cottonwood Dr., #E, Louisville, CO 80027 **E-mail:** adraghici@hotmail.com

DREW, PAUL S.
Industry: Hospitality **Univ./degree:** City and Guilds of London Institute, 1975; Executive Chef Certification, American Culinary Federation, 2001 **Current organization:** Sands Casino & Hotel **Title:** Executive Chef, CEC **Type of organization:** Casino and hotel **Major product:** Lodging, food and beverage, entertainment **Area of distribution:** Atlantic City, New Jersey **Expertise:** Executive Chef **Honors/awards:** Chef of the Year Award, Professional Chefs Association, South New Jersey Chapter, 2003; Professionalism Award, South New Jersey Chapter, 2001; ACF Bronze Medal, International Dishes, 1986 **Published works:** Gourmet magazine articles **Affiliations:** A.C.F. **SIC code:** 70 **Address:** Sands Casino & Hotel, Indiana Ave. & Brighton Park, Atlantic City, NJ 08401-6870 **E-mail:** pdrew@sandsac.com

DUMAS, VERONICA G.
Industry: Hospitality **Current organization:** Holiday Inn Tinton Falls **Title:** Director of Sales **Type of organization:** Hotel **Major product:** Lodging, food and beverage **Area of distribution:** International **Expertise:** Sales, marketing, advertising **Affiliations:** S.G.T.P.; E.M.A.C.G.; S.R.T.C. **Hob./spts.:** Bowling, ice-skating, cooking, decorating **SIC code:** 70 **Address:** Holiday Inn Tinton Falls, 700 Hope Rd., Tinton Falls, NJ 07724 **E-mail:** vdumas@ahmco.net

DUNN, JOHN T.
Industry: Security **Born:** January 10, 1947, Sommerville, New Jersey **Univ./degree:** B.A., American History, Temple University, Pennsylvania, 1970 **Current organization:** Glasco Security Corp. **Title:** President **Type of organization:** Security **Major product:** Locksmith, safe, alarm, access control **Area of distribution:** Pennsylvania **Expertise:** Master key systems **Honors/awards:** Business Man of the Year, NRCC, 2003 **Published works:** 3 articles in trade journals, Keynotes **Affiliations:** Past Chairman & Current Secretary, Pennsylvania State Chapter, A.L.O.A.; Founding Member & Board Emeritus, Diversified Investor Group **Hob./spts.:** Jazz music, saxophone, clarinet, travel, reading, martial arts **SIC code:** 73 **Address:** Glasco Security Corp., 5553 Morris St., Philadelphia, PA 19144-3806

EHRLER, MARC J.G.
Industry: Hospitality **Born:** September 20, 1958, French Riviera, France **Univ./degree:** French Culinary Academy **Current organization:** Loews Miami Beach Hotel **Title:** Executive Chef **Type of organization:** Hotel **Major product:** Convention hotel **Area of distribution:** National **Expertise:** Culinary arts (Available for seminars/speaker & demos) **Affiliations:** Master Chefs of France; French Culinary Academy **Hob./spts.:** Mountain biking, windsurfing **SIC code:** 70 **Address:** Loews Miami Beach Hotel, 1601 Collins Ave., Miami Beach, FL 33139 **E-mail:** mehrler@loews.com

ELIAS, ADIL R.
Industry: Property development investment **Born:** September 20, 1952, Sudan, Africa **Univ./degree:** Ph.D., Medical Engineering, London University, 1976 **Current organization:** Ronical International **Title:** Dr. **Type of organization:** Property development/restaurants **Major product:** Property/restaurants **Area of distribution:** International **Expertise:** Business, marketing **Affiliations:** B.I.M.; C.E.N.G. **Hob./spts.:** Swimming, golf, travel **SIC code:** 73 **Address:** Ronical International, 7500 I Drive, Orlando, FL 32819

ENCISO, ALYCIA D.
Industry: Interior design **Born:** San Bernardino, California **Univ./degree:** Interior Design, UCLA, 1983 **Current organization:** Alycia Enciso & Associates **Title:** President **Type of organization:** Interior design firm **Major product:** Design services **Area of distribution:** National **Expertise:** Space planning, decoration **Published works:** Write-up **Affiliations:** Chair, Los Angeles Cultural Design; Chair, 33rd Congress of Student Arts **Hob./spts.:** Travel, photography, art collector **SIC code:** 73 **Address:** Alycia Enciso & Associates, 8861 Alden Dr., Los Angeles, CA 90048 **E-mail:** aeadesign@worldnet.att.net **Web address:** www.alyciaenciso.com

ESTEVEZ, JASON
Industry: Locks and safes **Born:** February 18, 1978, Miami, Florida **Current organization:** A-Able Locksmiths **Title:** President **Type of organization:** Locksmith **Major product:** Locks and safes **Area of distribution:** Florida **Expertise:** High security locks, safes **Hob./spts.:** Boating **SIC code:** 76 **Address:** A-Able Locksmiths, 8783 SW 134th St., Miami, FL 33176 **E-mail:** security@aablelocksmith.com

EVANS, WEBB D.
Industry: Food/beverage **Born:** December 29,1933, Salt Lake City Utah **Univ./degree:** B.A., Nutrition & Food Management, University of Utah, 1961 **Current organization:** Apache Gold Casino Resort **Title:** Food & Beverage Director **Type of organization:** Casino **Major product:** Food service (grill, buffet, conventions, snack bars), consulting **Area of distribution:** Arizona **Expertise:** Culinary arts, management **Honors/awards:** National Presidential Citation, 1994; Chapter President of the Year, Western Region, 1992; Chapter Chef of the Year, 1990 **Published works:** 1 article **Affiliations:** A.C.F.; Past President, Local Chapters of A.C.F. **Hob./spts.:** Photography, cooking **SIC code:** 70 **Address:** Apache Gold Casino Resort, P.O. Box 1210, San Carlos, AZ 85550 **E-mail:** wevans@cableone.net

EVANS, WILLIAM F.
Industry: Software **Born:** December 22, 1957, Hamilton, Ohio **Univ./degree:** B.S., Magna Cum Laude, Chemistry, Rose Hulman Institute of Technology, 1980 **Current organization:** J.D. Edwards & Co. **Title:** Security/OPS Architect **Type of organization:** Manufacturing **Major product:** Enterprise software/consulting **Area of distribution:** National **Expertise:** E-business architecture specialist, process design, LIMS **Affiliations:** F.A.I.C.; A.C.S. **Hob./spts.:** Chess, stamp collecting **SIC code:** 73 **Address:** J.D. Edwards & Co., One Technology Way, Denver, CO 80237 **E-mail:** wiliam_evans@jdedwards.com

FADEN, LEE J.
Industry: Expert referral service **Born:** December 18, 1953, Philadelphia, Pennsylvania **Univ./degree:** M.B.A., Temple University, Pennsylvania, 1979 **Current organization:** Technical Advisory Service, Inc. **Title:** CO-CEO **Type of organization:** Oldest and largest provider of technical experts **Major product:** Technical and scientific experts and consultants **Area of distribution:** International **Expertise:** Corporate management **Affiliations:** American Management Association; American Financial Association

Hob./spts.: Scouting, biking **SIC code:** 73 **Address:** Technical Advisory Service, Inc., 1166 DeKalb Pike, Blue Bell, PA 19422-1853 **E-mail:** lfaden@tasanet.com

FARTHING, ROY KEVIN
Industry: Transportation **Born:** April 17, 1958, Indiana **Current organization:** Waffco Inc. **Title:** Vice President **Type of organization:** Towing company **Major product:** Towing and recovery of vehicles **Area of distribution:** Indiana **Expertise:** Heavy duty towing **Affiliations:** Indiana Towing and Recovery Association **Hob./spts.:** Boating **SIC code:** 75 **Address:** Waffco Inc., 2350 Pike St., Lake Station, IN 46405 **E-mail:** waffco08@aol.com **Web address:** www.waffco.net

FEDORCHUK, PETER D.
Industry: Hospitality **Born:** November 29, 1967, Royal Oak, Michigan **Univ./degree:** C.H.A., American Hotel and Motel Association **Current organization:** Best Western Sterling Inn **Title:** Hotel Manager **Type of organization:** Hotel **Major product:** Lodging, banquets, conventions, indoor water park **Area of distribution:** International **Expertise:** Management, operations **Hob./spts.:** Hunting, golf, family activities **SIC code:** 70 **Address:** Best Western Sterling Inn, 34911 Van Dyke Ave., Sterling Heights, MI 48312-4662 **E-mail:** petef@sterlinginn.com

FERGUSON, WENDELL
Industry: Entertainment **Born:** May 6, 1954, Washington, Georgia **Univ./degree:** Alpena Community College **Current organization:** Ferguson's Entertainment **Title:** Educator/Producer/Author/Entertainer **Type of organization:** Private enterprise, producer, consultant **Major product:** Producing artists for recording, acting, modeling, CD's, DVD's, albums **Area of distribution:** International **Expertise:** Writer, creator, inventor **Affiliations:** J.D. Sims & Berdell Park Recreation **Hob./spts.:** Music, writing, inventing **SIC code:** 79 **Address:** 3072 Washington Blvd., #L-7, East Point, GA 30344 **E-mail:** dellthangs@bellsouth.net

FERNANDEZ, IVAN
Industry: Entertainment **Born:** March 25, 1942, Havana, Cuba **Univ./degree:** Attended Universidad Masónica and Aurora College for Business/Accounting **Current organization:** Aragon Entertainment Center/Aragon Ballroom **Title:** President **Type of organization:** Concert/dance hall **Major product:** Festivals, concerts, sporting events **Area of distribution:** International **Expertise:** Production, entertainment booking **Honors/awards:** Man of the Year, Illinois Spanish Chamber of Commerce, 2005; Businessman of the Year, St. Augustine College, 2006 **Affiliations:** Established The Alamo, 1983; Vice President, Promotoras Bonitos **Hob./spts.:** Entertainment, theatre, travel, baseball **SIC code:** 79 **Address:** Aragon Entertainment Center/Aragon Ballroom, 1106 W. Lawrence Ave., Chicago, IL 60640 **E-mail:** ifernandez@aragon.com **Web address:** www.aragon.com

FEST, THEODORE J.
Industry: Merchandising (Consulting) **Born:** April 11, 1950, San Antonio, Texas **Univ./degree:** B.S., Software Engineering, University of Phoenix, 1993 **Current organization:** TMS Service Corp. **Title:** V.P., Info Systems **Type of organization:** Distributor/manufacturing **Major product:** Software, hardware, LAN, WAN **Area of distribution:** National **Expertise:** Microsoft/Citrix servers **Hob./spts.:** Golf, boating **SIC code:** 73 **Address:** TMS Service Corp., 6205 S. 231st St., Kent, WA 98032 **E-mail:** ted@tmssupply.com

FINN, DENNIS J.
Industry: Records management **Born:** Cleveland, Ohio **Univ./degree:** A.A., Management, University of Texas at Arlington **Current organization:** The Houston File Room, Inc. **Title:** President **Type of organization:** Commercial record management center **Major product:** Filing, record keeping **Area of distribution:** Texas **Expertise:** Administration, management **Affiliations:** Diplomat, South Montgomery Chamber of Commerce **Hob./spts.:** Family **SIC code:** 73 **Address:** The Houston File Room, Inc., 4747 RFD Suite 180207, The Woodlands, TX 77381 **E-mail:** betfinn@earthlink.net **Web address:** www.houstonfileroom.com

FIREBAUGH IV, ALBERT MATHIS
Industry: Hospitality **Born:** San Diego, California **Current organization:** Best Western Florida City **Title:** General Manager/Controller **Type of organization:** Hotel/resort **Major product:** Hotel accommodations **Area of distribution:** National **Expertise:** Hotel operations, organizational leadership, project management **Honors/awards:** Golden Pineapple Award by Super 8 Motels, Outstanding Leader in the Industry **Hob./spts.:** Family, music, boating, outdoor activities **SIC code:** 70 **Address:** Best Western Florida City, 411 S. Krome Ave., Florida City, FL 33034 **E-mail:** amf4@dsli.com

FISHER, RICHARD S.
Industry: Hospitality **Univ./degree:** Pennsylvania Culinary Institute, 1992 **Current organization:** Mystic Lake Casino Hotel **Title:** Executive Chef **Type of organization:** Casino/hotel/resort **Major product:** Lodging, food and beverage, gaming **Area of distribution:** Minnesota **Expertise:** Certified Executive Chef, American Culinary Federation; regional American cuisine **Affiliations:** I.A.C.T.; World Master Chefs Association; James Beard Society **Hob./spts.:** Music, skiing **SIC code:** 70 **Address:** Mystic Lake Casino Hotel, 2400 Mystic Lake Blvd., Prior Lake, MN 55372 **E-mail:** richardchef@hotmail.com

FITZGERALD, KATHLEEN A.
Industry: Hospitality **Born:** Middlesex, England **Univ./degree:** B.S., Psychology, University of Southern Mississippi **Current organization:** Beau Rivage Resort & Casino **Title:** Division Training Manager **Type of organization:** Resort and casino **Major product:** Gaming, food, beverage, guest services **Area of distribution:** Mississippi **Expertise:** Training, human resources **Published works:** 1 training article **Affiliations:** American Society for Training & Development **Hob./spts.:** Aerobics **SIC code:** 70 **Address:** Beau Rivage Resort & Casino, 875 Beach Blvd., Biloxi, MS 39530 **E-mail:** kfitzgerald@beaurivage.com

FOSTER, KENNETH WILLIAM
Industry: Entertainment **Born:** December 16, 1964, Bronx, New York **Univ./degree:** Audio Engineering, Minor in Music, City University of New York **Current organization:** Mad Bunch Entertainment LLC **Title:** CEO/President **Type of organization:** Music production and development **Major product:** Music **Area of distribution:** New York **Expertise:** Producing, studio engineering **Hob./spts.:** Computers **SIC code:** 79 **Address:** Mad Bunch Entertainment LLC, 1075 University Ave., Suite 2F, Bronx, NY 10452 **E-mail:** lbo@msn.com

FRANGOS, SPIRO
Industry: Hospitality **Born:** January 29, 1976, Queens, New York **Univ./degree:** A.A., Hospitality, Hotel Restaurant Management, New York Restaurant School **Current organization:** Sheraton Meadowlands **Title:** Sr. Food & Beverage Manager **Type of organization:** Hotel/resort **Major product:** Food, beverage and lodging **Area of distribution:** National **Expertise:** Food and beverage/business consulting **Hob./spts.:** Baseball **SIC code:** 70 **Address:** Sheraton Meadowlands, 2 Meadowlands Plaza, East Rutherford, NJ 07073 **E-mail:** spiro.frangos@sheraton.com

FRANZOI, JOHN C.
Industry: Gaming **Born:** Providence, Rhode Island **Univ./degree:** State of Nevada, General Contractor's License **Current organization:** Riviera Hotel & Casino **Title:** Vice President, Construction **Type of organization:** Hotel and casino **Major product:** Lodging, food and beverage, entertainment, gaming, conventions **Area of distribution:** International **Expertise:** Construction, engineering, project management, strategic planning **Hob./spts.:** Golf, fishing, hunting **SIC code:** 70 **Address:** Riviera Hotel & Casino, 2901 Las Vegas Blvd. South, Las Vegas, NV 89109 **E-mail:** cfranzoi@theriviera.com

GABOS, MATTHEW ANTHONY
Industry: Hospitality **Born:** May 7, 1969, Long Island, New York **Univ./degree:** A.A., Scottsdale Community College **Current organization:** Pebble Beach Company **Title:** Director of Banquets **Type of organization:** Resort **Major product:** Hospitality **Area of distribution:** Pebble Beach, California **Expertise:** Food, beverage **Hob./spts.:** Golf, skiing **SIC code:** 70 **Address:** Pebble Beach Company, 1700 17 Mile Dr., Pebble Beach, CA 93923 **E-mail:** gabosm@pebblebeach.com

GAFFNEY III, JEREMIAH C.
Industry: Mortuary **Born:** May 12, 1958, Bronx, New York **Univ./degree:** M.A., Morehouse College; Ph.D., Oxford University **Current organization:** Jeremiah C. Gaffney's Funeral Home Inc. **Title:** Ph.D./Director **Type of organization:** Funeral home **Major product:** Funeral services **Area of distribution:** International **Expertise:** Mortuary science **Affiliations:** N.F.D.M.A.; N.F.D.A.; Morehouse College Alumni Association **Hob./spts.:** Golf, swimming, reading, lecturing **SIC code:** 72 **Address:** Jeremiah C. Gaffney's Funeral Home Inc., 92 Wahl Ave., Inwood, NY 11096 **E-mail:** gaffhome@earthlink.net **Web address:** www.jcgaffney.com

GAMBOA, ROGER
Industry: Hospitality **Current organization:** Pacific Palms Conference Resort **Title:** Executive Chef **Type of organization:** Hotel, resort **Major product:** Hotel accommodations, catering **Area of distribution:** International **Expertise:** Culinary **Affiliations:** A.C.F. **SIC code:** 70 **Address:** Pacific Palms Conference Center, 1 Industry Hills Pkwy., Industry Hills, CA 91744 **E-mail:** rgamboa@pacificpalmsresort.com

GARVIN, JOHNNYRAY
Industry: Automotive Consulting **Univ./degree:** B.A., Business Administration, Adams State College, 1981 **Current organization:** The Smart Shopper Solution Inc., Company of GEI **Title:** President/CEO **Type of organization:** Dealership (leasing and financing co.) **Major product:** Any make, any model, new or used cars **Area of distribution:** National **Expertise:** Management, marketing **Honors/awards:** Bergen County Small Business Entrepreneur Award, 2002; All American Football VCAA Division II **Published works:** National Register 2000-2002, Who's Who **Affiliations:** Teaneck Chamber of Commerce; New Jersey Business Industry Association **SIC code:** 73 **Address:** The Smart Shopper Solution Inc., 319 Queen Anne Rd., Teaneck, NJ

07666 **Phone:** (201)928-4000 **Fax:** (201)928-2000 **E-mail:** smartshoppersolution@yahoo.com

GARY, LEE W.

Industry: Promotions/sales of John Gary's music **Born:** January 31, 1933, Dallas, Texas **Univ./degree:** B.A., Theatre Arts, University of North Texas, 1954 **Current organization:** John Gary International Fan Club/Briarwood Management **Title:** President **Type of organization:** Non-profit educational **Major product:** Promotions for John Gary's music, RCA recording artist, CDs, tapes, newsletters **Area of distribution:** International **Expertise:** Marketing **Published works:** Shows, newsletters; John Gary, author "Fragment of Time", 1971; "Lights, Camera, Action" **Affiliations:** Board Member, M.E.S.A.; Richardson Symphony Board **Hob./spts.:** Art **SIC code:** 79 **Address:** John Gary International Fan Club, Seven Briarwood Circle, Richardson, TX 75080 **E-mail:** leegary@webtv.net **Web address:** www.johngary.com

GAUTHIER, DAVID M.

Industry: Hospitality **Born:** March 2, 1962, Bonmar, Pennsylvania **Univ./degree:** B.S., Journalism, Texas Christian University **Current organization:** Hyatt Regency Denver at Colorado Convention Center **Title:** Director of Sales and Marketing **Type of organization:** Hotel **Major product:** Hotel accommodations **Area of distribution:** National **Expertise:** Sales, marketing, business travel **Hob./spts.:** His children's sports, home improvements **SIC code:** 70 **Address:** Hyatt Regency Denver at Colorado Convention Center, 555 17th St., Suite 300, Denver, CO 80202 **E-mail:** dgauthie@denrdpo.hyatt.com

GEAR JR., ROBERT B.

Industry: Consulting **Born:** February 18, 1933, Chicago, Illinois **Univ./degree:** B.S.E.E., Purdue University **Current organization:** Underground Systems, Inc. **Title:** Vice President **Type of organization:** Consulting firm **Major product:** Electrical power **Area of distribution:** National **Expertise:** Engineering, underground cables **Published works:** Published over 25 technical papers **Affiliations:** Member, Institute of Electronic & Electrical Engineers **Hob./spts.:** Stamp collecting, photography, football **SIC code:** 73 **Address:** Underground Systems, Inc., 830 South Monroe Street, Hinsdale, IL 60521

GEWONT, MARGARET

Industry: Hospitality **Born:** January 18, 1954, Zakopane, Poland **Spouse:** Eugene Tokarczyk **Married:** July 26, 1979, City Hall, Zakopane, Poland; July 29, 1979, church, Witów, Poland **Children:** Sgt. Andrew Peter Andrew, USMC, October 12, 1979; Katherine Marie Tokarczyk, March 10, 1984 **Univ./degree:** M.S., Jagiellonian University, Kraków, Poland; M.S., DeKalb University, Kennedy Western University; Richard Daley College **Current organization:** Fitzgerald's Motel **Title:** General Manager **Type of organization:** High-end motel **Major product:** Hotel accommodations **Area of distribution:** Wisconsin Dells, Wisconsin **Expertise:** Daily operations oversight **Affiliations:** Catholic Church **Hob./spts.:** Reading, hiking, biking, skiing **SIC code:** 70 **Address:** Fitzgerald's Motel, 530 Broadway, Wisconsin Dells, WI 53965-1500 **Web address:** www.fitzgeraldsmotel.com

GHAFARI, THERESA G.

Industry: Staffing **Born:** November 22, 1953, Lebanon **Current organization:** G-Tech Professional Staffing, Inc. **Title:** President/COO **Type of organization:** Staffing **Major product:** Staffing services to the automotive and construction industries **Area of distribution:** National **Expertise:** Operations, management **Affiliations:** N.T.S.A. **Hob./spts.:** Church, reading, swimming **SIC code:** 73 **Address:** G-TECH Professional Staffing, Inc., 17101 Michigan Ave., Dearborn, MI 48126 **E-mail:** tgghafari@gogtech.com

GILDAWIE, CLIFF R.

Industry: Auto repair **Born:** January 14, 1943, Jersey City, New Jersey **Current organization:** Seville Auto Body **Title:** Owner/CEO **Type of organization:** Auto repair shop **Major product:** Auto body repair and painting **Area of distribution:** Perth Amboy, New Jersey **Expertise:** Collision repair and painting **Affiliations:** American Legion **Hob./spts.:** Golf, cars **SIC code:** 75 **Address:** Seville Auto Body, 488 Fayette St., Perth Amboy, NJ 08861 **E-mail:** gildaw7@aol.com

GIZZO, CHRISTOPHER R

Industry: Catering **Univ./degree:** B.S., Elizabeth Seton University, 1992 **Current organization:** Surf Club **Title:** General Manager **Type of organization:** Banquet facility/beach club **Major product:** Gourmet food and decorating theme events **Area of distribution:** New Rochelle, New York **Expertise:** Customized events **SIC code:** 79 **Address:** Surf Club, 280 Davenport Ave., New Rochelle, NY 10805 **Web address:** www.surfclubofnewrochelle.com

GLOVER, LARRY E.

Industry: Advertising **Born:** March 4, 1950, Stuart, Florida **Univ./degree:** M.A., Marketing, Hampton University, 1976 **Current organization:** Muse, Cordero, Chen & Partners **Title:** Senior Vice President, Director of Account Services **Type of organization:** Advertising agency **Major product:** Consumer products advertising **Area of distribution:** International **Expertise:** Marketing **Affiliations:** Board Member, American Marketing Association; Executive Advisor, National Association of Marketing Developers **Hob./spts.:** Golf, sports enthusiast **SIC code:** 73 **Address:** Muse, Cordero, Chen & Partners, 210 E. 52nd St., New York, NY 10022 **E-mail:** larry@musecordero.com

GOFF, JEANETTE

Industry: Personal services **Born:** September 21, 1950, Bloomfield, New Jersey **Univ./degree:** Barber's Diploma and License, R.S. Hair Care Institute, 1978 **Current organization:** Artisan's Salon and Day Spa **Title:** Owner/Partner **Type of organization:** Salon/Day Spa **Major product:** Hair care, facials, body treatments **Area of distribution:** Emmaus, Pennsylvania **Expertise:** Hairstyling, management, marketing **Affiliations:** Lehigh Valley Chamber of Commerce; Le Tip **Hob./spts.:** Music, (church worship leader), travel, physical fitness **SIC code:** 72 **Address:** Artisan's Salon and Day Spa, 413 Chestnut St., Emmaus, PA 18049 **E-mail:** artisansds@fast.net **Web address:** www.artisansdayspa.com

GOLDBERG, WAYNE B.

Industry: Hotel **Born:** May 10, 1960. Louisville, Kentucky **Univ./degree:** B.A., University of Louisville, 1986 **Current organization:** La Quinta, Corp. **Title:** Senior Vice President, Operations **Type of organization:** Hotel **Major product:** Lodging, food and beverages **Area of distribution:** National **Expertise:** Operations **Affiliations:** D.S.L.; L.D.P.; A.B.S. **Hob./spts.:** Family **SIC code:** 70 **Address:** La Quinta Corp., 909 Hidden Ridge, Suite 600, Irving, TX 75038 **E-mail:** wayne.goldberg@laquinta.com **Web address:** www.laquinta.com

GONZALEZ, JOSE A.

Industry: HVAC **Born:** September 22, 1949, Mexico City, Mexico **Current organization:** JAG Cool Systems, Co. **Title:** President **Type of organization:** Repair/retail **Major product:** Residential and commercial HVAC installations, repairs and retail service **Area of distribution:** Florida **Expertise:** Marketing, business development, administration; E.P.A. Licensed **Hob./spts.:** Reading, travel **SIC code:** 76 **Address:** JAG Cool Systems, Co., 929 N.E. 78th St., Miami, FL 33138 **E-mail:** cooljag929@yahoo.com

GONZALEZ JR., ALEJANDRO

Industry: Self improvement **Born:** May 13, 1935, Laredo, Texas **Univ./degree:** B.B.A., Laredo State University, 1984 **Current organization:** Silva Ultra Mind Systems **Title:** Director/Sr. V.P./ Manager **Type of organization:** Training course with meditation **Major product:** Instruction in problem solving **Area of distribution:** International **Expertise:** Course administration **Honors/awards:** Meritorious Service Award **Published works:** CD's, books, manuals **Affiliations:** U.S. Air Force (Retired Sr. Master Sgt., 1976); Laredo Chamber of Commerce **Hob./spts.:** Travel, swimming **SIC code:** 72 **Address:** Silva Ultra Mind Systems, 6017 McPherson Rd., Suite C, Laredo, TX 78041 **E-mail:** alex@silvaultramind.net **Web address:** www.silvaultramind.net and www.silvahealing.com

GOONER, RANDY

Industry: Automotive **Born:** May 28, 1951, Lewis, Delaware **Univ./degree:** A.A., Psychology, Del-Tech Community College; 1974 **Current organization:** 4 N Car, Inc. **Title:** President **Type of organization:** Automotive Services **Major product:** Specialized Honda/Toyota repair sales **Area of distribution:** Georgetown, Delaware **Expertise:** Managing, consulting **Affiliations:** U.S. Army, 193rd Infantry **Hob./spts.:** Snowmobiling **SIC code:** 75 **Address:** 4 N CAR, Inc., 20185 DuPont Blvd., Georgetown, DE 19947 **E-mail:** g4ncar@aol.com

GORNEY, JANE E.

Industry: Hospitality **Born:** August 8, 1953, Los Angeles, California **Univ./degree:** Attended Ohio State University **Current organization:** Bon Management Group, Inc. **Title:** President **Type of organization:** Professional service **Major product:** Hotel management **Area of distribution:** National **Expertise:** Overseeing all aspects of hotel operations; Certified Hotel Administrator **Affiliations:** California State EAC; American Cancer Society **Hob./spts.:** Daughter, basketball, reading **SIC code:** 73 **Address:** Bon Management Group, Inc., 4500 E. Thousand Oaks Blvd., #104, Westlake Village, CA

91362 **E-mail:** jgorney@bonmanagement.com **Web address:** www.bonmanagement.com

GOUNDEN, PREGA M.
Industry: Motels **Born:** November 5, 1950 **Current organization:** Alpha Omega Lodging Corp. **Title:** CEO, President **Type of organization:** Motels **Major product:** Lodging, food and beverage **Area of distribution:** International **Expertise:** Daily operations, management, hospitality **Honors/awards:** Business Man of the Year, 2005 **Affiliations:** Bristol Lions Club **Hob./spts.:** Tennis, table tennis **SIC code:** 70 **Address:** Alpha Omega Lodging Corp., 620 Green Valley Dr., Dandridge, TN 37725

GRANIELA, KEVIN J.
Industry: Health and beauty **Born:** Key West, Florida **Univ./degree:** B.S., Electronic Engineering, Community College of the Air Force; M.S., Astrophysics, 1994; Ph.D., Astrophysics, 2006, Oklahoma University; Ph.D., Astronomy, 2006; Ph.D., Physics, 2006, Canterbury University, United Kingdom **Current organization:** Petals..A Day Spa **Title:** Owner **Type of organization:** Spa **Major product:** Body treatments, facials, manicures and pedicures, massages, waxing **Area of distribution:** Key West, Florida **Expertise:** Daily operations oversight, management **Hob./spts.:** Billiards, art, hunting, fishing **SIC code:** 72 **Address:** Petals..A Day Spa, 3845 Seaside Dr., Suite 102, Key West, FL 33040 **E-mail:** petalsadayspa@bellsouth.net

GRAVES, ANGELICA LEE
Industry: Recording/production/promotion **Born:** October 19, 1977, Chicago, Illinois **Univ./degree:** M.S., Business Management **Current organization:** W' Nice Records Inc. **Title:** Director **Type of organization:** Recording company **Major product:** Production/promotion **Area of distribution:** National **Expertise:** Production, promotion, legal counseling **Affiliations:** S.I.S.E. **Hob./spts.:** Motorcycles **SIC code:** 73 **Address:** 2222 S. McKinley St., #B, Casper, WY 82601

GREENBERGER, RAYMOND STUART
Industry: Security services **Born:** July 3, 1945, New York, New York **Univ./degree:** B.A., Accounting, Queens College, 1967 **Current organization:** AFA Protective Systems, Inc. **Title:** Treasurer & CFO **Type of organization:** Security service corp. **Major product:** Fire and security services **Area of distribution:** National **Expertise:** Finance and administration **Affiliations:** A.I.C.P.A.; N.Y.S.C.P.A. **Hob./spts.:** Family, golf, reading, tennis **SIC code:** 73 **Address:** AFA Protective Systems, Inc., 155 Michael Dr., Syosset, NY 11791 **E-mail:** rgreenberger@afap.com **Web address:** www.afaprotectivesystems.com

GREGORY, RICHARD C.
Industry: Human resources **Born:** January 22, 1948, Indiana **Current organization:** Allstates Employer Services, Inc. **Title:** President **Type of organization:** Professional employer organization **Major product:** Human resource management **Area of distribution:** National **Expertise:** Human resource outsourcing **Honors/awards:** Corporate sponsor for NASCAR **Affiliations:** N.A.P.E.O.L.; F.A.P.E.O.L. **Hob./spts.:** Golf, fishing, racing **SIC code:** 73 **Address:** Allstates Employer Services, Inc., 6400 North "W" St., Pensacola, FL 32505 **Phone:** (850)477-4449 **E-mail:** marketing@aeshr.com **Web address:** www.aeshr.com

GUTHRIE, JOHN A.
Industry: Amusement/recreation **Born:** July 13, 1958, Los Angeles, California **Current organization:** G&G Amusement, Inc. **Title:** CEO **Type of organization:** Operator **Major product:** Juke box/games/pool tables **Area of distribution:** Southern California **Expertise:** Operations, management **Affiliations:** C.A.D.O.; A.M.O.A. **Hob./spts.:** Motorcycling **SIC code:** 79 **Address:** G&G Amusement, Inc., 6415 Canning St., Commerce, CA 90040 **E-mail:** jaguthrie@ggamuseco.com

GUTHRIE, LUTHER N.
Industry: Automotive **Born:** January 3, 1928, Townley, Alabama **Current organization:** Luke's Auto Body Repair **Title:** President **Type of organization:** Automotive repair **Major product:** Auto mechanics/repair **Area of distribution:** Haverstraw, New York **Expertise:** Auto body collision/repair **Hob./spts.:** Camping **SIC code:** 75 **Address:** Luke's Auto Body Repair, 22 Maple Ave., Haverstraw, NY 10927 **E-mail:** kevinthebodyman@aol.com

HAARBAUER, BARBARA E.
Industry: Recreation/RV sites **Born:** January 21, 1951, Toledo, Ohio **Univ./degree:** B.S., Business and Marketing, University of Toledo, 1972 **Current organization:** Twin Oaks RV Park **Title:** Owner/Operator **Type of organization:** RV Park **Major product:** Supplying RV sites to customers **Area of distribution:** National **Expertise:** Management **Affiliations:** Perry Chamber of Commerce, Georgia **Hob./spts.:** Family, horseback riding, all-terrain vehicles **SIC code:** 70 **Address:** Twin Oaks RV Park, 305 Hwy 26 East, Elko, GA 31025

HALL, JOHN A.
Industry: Health/fitness **Born:** December 20, 1964, Chicago, Illinois **Univ./degree:** B.S., Southern Illinois University, 1987; Pharm. D., University of Illinois, 1998 **Current organization:** John Hall Studios **Title:** Personal Trainer/Owner **Type of organization:** Personal training studio **Major product:** Training **Area of distribution:** Chicago, Illinois **Expertise:** Training for prevention of illness and injury **Affiliations:** N.S.C.A. **Hob./spts.:** Basketball, photography **SIC code:** 72 **Address:** John Hall Studios, 1658 N. Milwaukee, Suite 444, Chicago, IL 60647 **E-mail:** jh1629@sbcglobal.net

HAMPTON, ALEXA
Industry: Interior Design **Born:** April 24, 1971 **Univ./degree:** B.A., Literature, History, Brown Univ., 1993; studied Fine Arts at The Institute for the Study of Classical Architecture & the Rhode Island School of Design; Graduate work at New York Univ. Institute of Fine Arts in Florence, Italy & NY **Current organization:** Mark Hampton, LLC **Title:** CEO **Type of organization:** Design firm **Major product:** Home design and furnishings **Area of distribution:** International **Expertise:** Domestic and international projects, high-end apartments and large residences, private airplanes and yachts **Honors/awards:** Numerous including- AD 100, Architectural Digest's directory of world's best 100 designers and architects, 2002, 2003, 2004; America's Best 100 Designers, House Beautiful; 100 Best Architects and Decorators, New York Magazine, 2002; hailed in the Fall 2000 issue of Home Design section of the New York Times **Published works:** House design featured on the cover of the December 1999 issue of Architectural Digest; has had work featured in Architectural Design and House Beautiful; The Alexa Hampton Furniture Collection; designed a line of woven fabrics for Kravet Fabrics Inc. **Affiliations:** Continuing cast member of PBS's This Old House; selected by the Trowbridge House Foundation to be the interior designer for Trowbridge House, the new official Guest House for Former Presidents of the U.S. **SIC code:** 73 **Address:** Mark Hampton, LLC, 654 Madison Ave., 21st floor, New York, NY 10021 **Web address:** www.markhampton.com

HANHART, CLAUDE
Industry: GIS mapping/transportation **Univ./degree:** M.S., Archeology, University of Berne, Switzerland, 2001; M.S., Geography, G.I.S., University of Minnesota, 2003 **Current organization:** NAVTEQ North America, LLC **Title:** Systems Engineer **Type of organization:** Private sector **Major product:** NAVSTREETS database **Area of distribution:** National **Expertise:** Geographic information systems (GIS) **Affiliations:** A.A.G.: I.L.G.S.A. **SIC code:** 73 **Address:** 70 West Huron St., #1508, Chicago, IL 60610 **E-mail:** claude_hanhart@yahoo.com

HARGETT III, NATHANIEL E.
Industry: Funeral **Born:** March 8, 1978, Greensboro, North Carolina **Current organization:** Hargett Funeral Service **Title:** President/CEO **Type of organization:** Funeral home **Major product:** Funeral services **Area of distribution:** Greensboro, North Carolina **Expertise:** Funeral Director **Affiliations:** Rotary International; N.F.I.B.; Greensboro Chamber of Commerce **Hob./spts.:** Golf **SIC code:** 73 **Address:** Hargett Funeral Service, 905 E. Market St., Greensboro, NC 27401 **E-mail:** hargettfuneralne@bellsouth.net

HARRIS, DEVAUGHN J.
Industry: Metals **Born:** October 14, 1943, Ty Ty, Georgia **Univ./degree:** B.S., Metals Technology, University of Georgia, 1973 **Current organization:** Tifton Machine Works Inc. **Title:** General Manager **Type of organization:** Welding/machine shop **Major product:** Custom welding/machine repair **Area of distribution:** International **Expertise:** Metals technology **Affiliations:** A.W.S. **Hob./spts.:** Riding motorcycles **SIC code:** 76 **Address:** Tifton Machine Works Inc., US Hwy. 319N, P.O. Box 731, Tifton, GA 31793 **E-mail:** tmwi@friendlycity.net

HARVELL, PAUL
Industry: Software and applications **Born:** January 5, 1968, Nottingham, United Kingdom **Univ./degree:** B.S., Nottingham Polytechnic University, 1989 **Current organization:** Cadtek USA Inc. **Title:** Technical Director **Type of organization:** Software sales, support **Major product:** Electrical engineering applications **Area of distribution:** United States, United Kingdom **Expertise:** Engineering **Hob./spts.:** Soccer, golf **SIC code:** 73 **Address:** Cadtek USA Inc., 25 N. Sixth St., Stroudsburg, PA 18360 **E-mail:** paul.harvell@cadtek.com **Web address:** www.cadtek.com

HASSAN, ABRAHAM F.
Industry: Janitorial services **Born:** July 26, 1954, Jamaica **Univ./degree:** B.A., Journalism, Southern Illinois University, 1986 **Current organization:** H&M Janitorial Services **Title:** Owner **Type of organization:** Janitorial **Major product:** Commercial and industrial janitorial services **Area of distribution:** Illinois **Expertise:** Management, operations **Affiliations:** Building Contractors Association **Hob./spts.:** Football, basketball, baseball **SIC code:** 73 **Address:** H&M Janitorial Services, 802 Morton Ave., Edwardsville, IL 62025 **E-mail:** abe1261@hmjan.com

HAVLIK, JOE J.
Industry: Computers **Born:** November 26, 1955, Alexandria, Egypt **Univ./degree:** M.S., Business, Coe College, 1979 **Current organization:** Advanced Tech Enterprises, Inc. **Title:** President **Type of organization:** Computers **Major product:** Computer service, sales **Area of distribution:** National **Expertise:** Management **Affiliations:** Legal Connection; CEO Networks **Hob./spts.:** Golf **SIC code:** 73 **Address:** Advanced Tech Enterprises, Inc., 2014 Platinum St., P.O. Box 551475, Garland, TX 75042 **E-mail:** ate@ate.net

HEIM, JEAN-MARC
Industry: Hospitality **Born:** April 9, 1957, Obernai, France **Univ./degree:** Culinary Apprenticeship, Ecole A'Hotellerie Et De Tourisme, France, 1971 **Current organization:** Hapuna Beach Prince Hotel **Title:** Restaurant Chef **Type of organization:** Hotel/resort **Major product:** Pacific Rim cuisine **Area of distribution:** Hawaii **Expertise:** Culinary arts **Honors/awards:** Culinary Competition Award; French National Trade Expo **Affiliations:** Officer Chef Rôtisseur, Chaine des Rôtisseurs, since 1992 **Hob./spts.:** Canoeing, Judo **SIC code:** 70 **Address:** Hapuna Beach Prince Hotel, P.O. Box 384913, Waikoloa, HI 96738 **E-mail:** threeofus@hawaii.rr.com

HELSTROM, CHARLES E.
Industry: Security and Law Enforcement Consultant **Born:** March 17, 1935, St. John, New Brunswick, Canada **Univ./degree:** Police Science, University of Hawaii, 1968 **Current organization:** Currently retired **Type of organization:** Security and law enforcement **Major product:** Investigator **Area of distribution:** Pacific region, Republic of the Marshall Islands, Federated States of Micronesia (Pohnpei, Chuuk, Yap, Kosrae), Republic of Palau, U.S. Commonwealth of the Northern Mariana Islands, formerly known as the Trust Territory of the Pacific Islands (TTPI) **Expertise:** Legal investigator (over 25 years overseas) **Affiliations:** International Association of Chiefs of Police (IACP); International Narcotic Enforcement Officers Association (INEOA); Disabled American Veterans (DAV); American Legion **Hob./spts.:** Bowling, golf, tennis, NASCAR racing, football **SIC code:** 73 **Address:** The Wackenhut Corp., 4110 Donovan Way, North Las Vegas, NV 89030-7512 **E-mail:** helstromce@amvets.us

HERGER, ERHARD HARDY
Industry: Engineering **Born:** February 10, 1935, Urnerboden-Uri, Switzerland **Univ./degree:** B.S., Electrical Engineering, 1962; M.S., Electrical Engineering, 1966; M.S.; B.S., 1995; M.S., 1997 **Current organization:** Squaw Valley Ski Corp. **Title:** Electrical Engineer **Type of organization:** Ski resort **Major product:** Electrical engineering, repairs of heat pumps, lifts and trams **Area of distribution:** National **Expertise:** Design engineering; specialist in alternative energy, has installed 19 cost reducing solar energy systems worldwide **Affiliations:** Assistant Professor, San Diego Bible College **Hob./spts.:** Skiing, hiking, travel, rocket building **SIC code:** 70 **Address:** Squaw Valley Ski Corp., 1960 Squaw Valley Rd., Olympic Valley, CA 96146

HERMAN, SHMUEL A.
Industry: Locksmith **Born:** January 7, 1969, Philadelphia, Pennsylvania **Univ./degree:** B.S., Security, Hebrew University, 1995 **Current organization:** SH Rescue & Protection **Title:** Locksmith **Type of organization:** Locks and security **Area of distribution:** New Jersey **Expertise:** Locks **Affiliations:** Vice President, New York Association of In-House Locksmiths; American Locksmith Organization; National Institute of Locksmiths **SIC code:** 76 **Address:** SH Rescue & Protection, 196 Lindbergh Blvd., Teaneck, NJ 07666 **E-mail:** shmuel@locksmith.org

HERNANDEZ-ORMONDE, REBECCA
Industry: Entertainment **Born:** January 31, 1967 **Current organization:** Disney Consumer Products **Title:** Senior Designer **Type of organization:** Movie studio **Major product:** Motion pictures **Area of distribution:** National/international **Expertise:** Packaging design/graphic design for products **Affiliations:** Graphic Artists Guild, Los Angeles Chapter **Hob./spts.:** Volunteer work, youth work **SIC code:** 78 **Address:** 4231 Blanchard St., Los Angeles, CA 90063 **E-mail:** reormonde@hotmail.com

HODGE, BRENDA L.
Industry: Technology **Born:** November 29, 1963, North Carolina **Univ./degree:** B.S., Computer Science & Math, Vanderbilt University, 1985 **Current organization:** SAS Institute Inc. **Title:** Senior Director, SAS Americas Marketing & Support **Type of organization:** Software Development **Major product:** Software and services **Area of distribution:** International **Expertise:** Marketing **Affiliations:** Past Member, Conference Board, Marketing Leadership Council **Hob./spts.:** Gardening, bicycling **SIC code:** 73 **Address:** SAS Institute Inc., SAS Campus Dr., Cary, NC 27513 **E-mail:** brenda.hodge@sas.com **Web address:** www.sas.com

HOEFER, TAMMY M.
Industry: Cleaning services **Born:** December 11, 1959, Detroit, Michigan **Univ./degree:** B.S., Wayne State University, Michigan, 2001 **Current organization:** Spot Catchers **Title:** CEO/Owner **Type of organization:** Commercial/construction/industrial cleaning **Major product:** Cleaning services **Area of distribution:** Michigan **Expertise:** Cleaning, management **Affiliations:** Women's Association of Wayne State **Hob./spts.:** Family, camping, hiking, arts & crafts, attending her children's sports events, outdoor activities **SIC code:** 73 **Address:** Spot Catchers, 2002 Mayer Rd., Kimball Township, MI 48074 **E-mail:** wtttcth@aol.com

HOLBROOK, D. SCOTT
Industry: Healthcare/technology **Born:** June 29, 1972, Norton, Virginia **Univ./degree:** B.S., Nuclear Medical Technology, Wheeling Jesuit University, 1996 **Current organization:** PETNET Pharmaceuticals **Title:** Territory Manager **Type of organization:** Technology, R&D **Major product:** Provider of molecular tracers for PET imaging **Area of distribution:** National **Expertise:** Consultation services, imaging, negotiations **Affiliations:** A.R.R.T.; Society of Nuclear Medicine **Hob./spts.:** Cycling, guitar, hiking **SIC code:** 73 **Address:** 11515 Frederick Rd., Coeburn, VA 24230 **E-mail:** dshcrh1@verizon.net

HOLLOWAY, MITCHELL L.
Industry: Hospitality **Born:** May 5, 1966, Cleveland, Tennessee **Current organization:** Fitzgeralds Casino & Hotel **Title:** Director of Hotel Operations **Type of organization:** Resort/hotel **Major product:** Casino and hotel **Area of distribution:** Las Vegas, Nevada **Expertise:** Hotel operations and sales **Affiliations:** M.P.I. **Hob./spts.:** Golf **SIC code:** 70 **Address:** Fitzgeralds Casino & Hotel, 301 Fremont St., Las Vegas, NV 89101 **E-mail:** mholloway@fitzgeraldslasvegas.com

HOOD, BRUCE W.
Industry: Automotive **Born:** September 9, 1966, Missoula, Montana **Univ./degree:** A.S., Business, Green River Community College, 1986 **Current organization:** Central Collision **Title:** President **Type of organization:** Service and repair shop **Major product:** Automotive service and repair **Area of distribution:** Washington **Expertise:** Fiberglass repairs, cars, boats, RV's, motorcycles **Affiliations:** Autobody Craftsman Organization; Marine Trade Association **Hob./spts.:** Boating **SIC code:** 75 **Address:** Central Collision, 821 Central Ave. South, Kent, WA 98032 **E-mail:** centralcollisionmc@hotmail.com

HOWARD, BETH S.
Industry: Food and beverage/private clubs **Born:** February 28, 1963, Belmond, Iowa **Univ./degree:** B.A., Food, Nutrition and Business, University of North Iowa, 1985 **Current organization:** Vail Resorts-Beaver Creek Mountain Dining & Clubs **Title:** Director **Type of organization:** Luxury resort **Major product:** Skiing **Area of distribution:** International **Expertise:** Resort operations **Affiliations:** Colorado Restaurant Association **Hob./spts.:** Skiing, snowshoeing, golf **SIC code:** 70 **Address:** Vail Resorts, P.O. Box 915, Avon, CO 81620 **E-mail:** bethh@vailresorts.com

HOWARD, CONNIE C.
Industry: Racing **Born:** September 27, 1954, Michigan City, Indiana **Univ./degree:** B.A., Political Science; B.A., Admin, of Justice, Southern Illinois University **Current organization:** NASCAR - ARCA Series **Title:** Manager of Promotions for racer Shelby Howard **Type of organization:** Racing **Major product:** Professional auto racing **Area of distribution:** National **Hob./spts.:** Photography **SIC code:** 79 **Address:** 420 Jaynes Circle, Greenwood, IN 46142 **E-mail:** senatorch@aol.com

HOWE, TODD C.
Industry: Hospitality **Born:** August 16, 1966, Norwalk, Connecticut **Univ./degree:** B.A., Business, Western Connecticut State university, 1989 **Current organization:** Four Points Sheraton Hotel **Title:** Director of Sales **Type of organization:** Hotel **Major product:** Lodging, food, entertainment **Area of distribution:** National **Expertise:** Sales, management **Hob./spts.:** Golf, tennis **SIC code:** 70 **Address:** Four Points Sheraton Hotel, 426 Main Ave., Norwalk, CT 06851 **E-mail:** thowe@whghotels.com

HOWITZ, CARSTEN F.
Industry: Software **Born:** February 3, 1965, Copenhagen, Denmark **Univ./degree:** B.S., Business; B.S. Computer Science, The Technical University of Denmark, 1992 **Current organization:** SimCrest, Inc. **Title:** President **Type of organization:** Computer services company **Major product:** Software development **Area of distribution:** International **Expertise:** Microsoft business solutions **Hob./spts.:** Running **SIC code:** 73 **Address:** SimCrest, Inc., 1202 Richardson Dr., Suite 300, Richardson, TX 75080 **E-mail:** howitz@simcrest.com **Web address:** www.simcrest.com

HUCKABY II, CARL L.
Industry: Hospitality **Born:** July 15, 1976, Beech Grove, Indiana **Current organization:** Nordstrom's, The Grille **Title:** Kitchen Manager/Executive Chef **Type of organization:** Full service restaurant **Major product:** Food, beverage, retail **Area of distribution:** Indianapolis, Indiana **Expertise:** Culinary arts/restaurant manager **Published works:** Recipes **Affiliations:** I.A.C.P.; A.C.F. **Hob./spts.:** NASCAR, football **SIC code:** 70 **Address:** Nordstrom's, The Grill, 130 S. Meridian St., Indianapolis, IN 46142 **E-mail:** carl.huckabyii@ameritech.net

HUGHES, ALEXANDRA O.

Industry: Entertainment **Born:** January 30, 1957, New York, New York **Univ./degree:** B.F.A., Bennington College, 1973; B.M.F.A., The Julliard School of Music, 1978; M.A., The Julliard School of Music, 1979 **Current organization:** Self employed **Title:** Opera Singer, Artistic Liaison to the Nuage France Foundation (www.nuage-france.org) **Major product:** Opera, recital and orchestral engagements, crossover popular events, recordings **Area of distribution:** International **Expertise:** Mezzo soprano **Honors/awards:** Acclaimed by critics worldwide for her performances in "Tristan und Isolde" (Brangaene), Honolulu Star Bulletin, Opera, Opera News; "Das Rheingold" (Fricka), Seattle Post Intelligencer, Seattle Times, Opera, London Observer; "Werther" (Charlotte), Opernwelt, Das Orchester, Sudkurier; "Hansel und Gretal" (Hansel), Opera, Seattle Post Intelligencer; "Der Rosenkavalier" (Octavian), Opera, Montreal Gazette, The Suburban; "Ariadne auf Naxos" (Komponist), Badische Zeitung, Basler Zeitung, Sudkurier, Sudwest Presse; "Carmen" (Carmen), Openwelt, Seattle Gay News; "Samson and Dalila" (Dalila), Fyns Stiffende Odense; "The Turn of the Screw" (Mrs. Grose), The New York Times, The Philadelphia Enquirer, Opera News, New York Magazine; Performing venues worldwide include Carnegie Hall, San Francisco Opera, Seattle Opera Co., New York City Opera Co., Canadian Opera Co., Montreal Opera, Live from Town Hall with Garrison Keillor, Cabrillo Festival, St. Paul Chamber Orchestra, New Orleans Opera, Opera Omaha, Detroit Opera, Pierpont Morgan Library, Hyde Collection, Brooklyn Bargemusic Series, Philadelphia Museum of Art, Grand Theatre Geneva, Opera de Marseille, Giverny, Basle Opera Switzerland, American Choral Society Soloist in Paris, Finnish National Opera, Odense Symphony Orchestra as well as the Aspen Music Festival and Cologne Philharmonic Orchestra **Published works:** Recordings: Finnish National Opera, Richard Wagner, "Die Walküre, Act II, Scene II"; "You Must Remember This From Gershwin to Lerner and Lowe"; "Alexandra Hughes, Monteverdi Excerpts"; "Alexandra Hughes, Mezzo Soprano"; "Alexandra Hughes, American Music in the time of Thomas Eakins"; "Alexandra Hughes, Italian Arias & Duets" **Hob./spts.:** Physical fitness, the outdoors, sailing, painting; fluent in English, French and German **SIC code:** 79 **Address:** 11 E. 80th St., #2A, New York, NY 10021 **E-mail:** alexamezza@aol.com **Web address:** www.alexandrahughes.com

HUNT, CAROLINE V.

Industry: Hospitality **Born:** September 30, 1965, Gweru, Zimbabwe **Current organization:** Raffles International Hotels & Resorts **Title:** Director, Global Sales - The Americas **Type of organization:** Hotels **Major product:** Hospitality for business and leisure travel **Area of distribution:** International **Expertise:** Global sales and marketing to corporations **Affiliations:** A.C.T.E.; N.B.T.E. **Hob./spts.:** Tennis **SIC code:** 70 **Address:** Raffles International Hotels & Resorts, 440 Park Ave., 6th floor, New York, NY 10022 **E-mail:** caroline.hunt@raffles.com

HURLEY, JAMES J.

Industry: Automotive **Born:** February 25, 1963, Jersey City, New Jersey **Current organization:** Village Car Care **Title:** Owner **Type of organization:** Automotive mechanics/repair shop **Major product:** Automotive services **Area of distribution:** Arizona **Expertise:** Auto repair **Affiliations:** A.S.A.; A.S.E. Certified **Hob./spts.:** 4-wheeling **SIC code:** 75 **Address:** Village Car Care, 6416 Hwy. 179, Sedona, AZ 86351 **E-mail:** villagecarcare@esedona.net

HUTCHINSON, JIM

Industry: Internet services **Born:** August 4, 1957, St. Paul, Minnesota **Univ./degree:** Continuing education courses **Current organization:** Website Managers, LLC **Title:** Website Manager **Type of organization:** Internet services **Major product:** Website hosting **Area of distribution:** International **Expertise:** Database management **Honors/awards:** Listed in Strathmore's Who's Who; Presidential Award, Freedom for Closure Prevention Services **Affiliations:** Better Business Bureau **Hob./spts.:** Billiards **SIC code:** 73 **Address:** Website Managers, LLC, 3510 N. Ninth St., Suite 92, Carter Lake, IA 51510 **E-mail:** jim@websitemanagers.net

INGRAM, THURSTON PATRICK

Industry: Business services **Born:** June 8, 1952, Parkersburg, West Virginia **Univ./degree:** B.A., 2004; M.B.A. Candidate, Kennedy-Western University **Current organization:** Ingrams Cleaning Service **Title:** Owner **Type of organization:** Janitorial services and consulting **Major product:** Commercial cleaning **Area of distribution:** Pennsylvania **Expertise:** Consulting, sales **Affiliations:** Lions Club; Spokesman Club; LifeNets **Hob./spts.:** Coin collecting, fishing **SIC code:** 73 **Address:** Ingrams Cleaning Service, 5111 First St., McKeesport, PA 15132 **E-mail:** t.ingram@comcast.com

ITZHAKI, TAL

Industry: Hospitality **Born:** April 19, 1974, Tel-Aviv, Israel **Univ./degree:** B.S., Hotel, Restaurant Institutional Management, Johnson & Wales University, 2000 **Current organization:** Hilton Short Hills **Title:** Beverage Manager **Type of organization:** Hotel **Major product:** Lodging, food and beverages **Area of distribution:** Short Hills, New Jersey **Expertise:** Management **SIC code:** 70 **Address:** Hilton Short Hills, 41 JFK Pkwy., Short Hills, NJ 07078 **E-mail:** tal_itzhaki@hilton.com

JACOBUS, GERALD W.

Industry: Automotive **Born:** December 18, 1936 **Current organization:** Jacobus Car Star, Inc. **Title:** Owner/Partner **Type of organization:** Auto body service **Major product:** Collision repair and paint **Area of distribution:** National **Expertise:** All phases of auto body repair **Affiliations:** American Legion (30 year member) **Hob./spts.:** Trains, travel **SIC code:** 75 **Address:** Jacobus Car Star, Inc., 6710 N.E. St. Johns Rd., Vancouver, WA 98661 **E-mail:** carstar-jacobus@integraonline.com

JACOBY JR., NEIL H.

Industry: Estate management **Born:** October 20, 1940, Chicago, Illinois **Univ./degree:** B.A., Astronomy, 1965; M.S., Engineering, 1969; Post M.S. Studies, Mathematical Economics, Optimization Theory, Statistics, 1970-72, University of California at Los Angeles **Current organization:** Self-employed **Title:** Property and Investment Manager **Type of organization:** Estate management **Major product:** Maintenance and management of family estate and investments, astrodynamics problem solving **Area of distribution:** Los Angeles, CA **Expertise:** Management, engineering, astrodynamics **Honors/awards:** Alpha Gamma Sigma (Junior College Honor Society) **Published works:** Numerous including, "Generation of Prag Satellite Lifetime Model Coefficients for Selected Sets of Restraints," System Development Corporation, 1980; Co-author "Preliminary Orbit Determination Method Having No Co-Planar Singularity, "Celestial Mechanics, 1977; Co-author, "Technical Memorandum on the Deep Space Surveillance Satellite," Computer Science Corporation, 1975 **Affiliations:** Sr. Member, A.A.S.; A.I.A.A.; American Association for the Advancement of Science; New York Academy of Sciences; Board of Directors, Homeowners of South Westwood, Inc.; Member, International Biographical Association; Marquis Who's Who **Hob./spts.:** Swimming, surfing, jogging, physical fitness **SIC code:** 73 **Address:** 1434 Midvale Ave., Los Angeles, CA 90024 **E-mail:** neiljacoby@yahoo.com **Web address:** www.geocities.com/researchtriangle/facility/2435

JENS, JAMES C.

Industry: Hotel **Born:** September 30, 1976, Sheboygan, Wisconsin **Univ./degree:** A.S., Culinary Arts, Fox Valley Technical College, 1997 **Current organization:** Hilton Madison Monona Terrace **Title:** Executive Chef **Type of organization:** Hospitality **Major product:** Food & beverage **Area of distribution:** Wisconsin **Expertise:** Cooking, menu creation **Published works:** Article, Wisconsin Trails Magazine **Affiliations:** 4-H **Hob./spts.:** Golf, mountain biking, home restoration **SIC code:** 70 **Address:** Hilton Madison Monona Terrace, 9 E. Wilson St., Madison, WI 53703 **E-mail:** jamesjens@hiltonmadison.com **Web address:** www.capitalchophouse.com

JOANNIDES, NICKOLAS S.

Industry: Hospitality **Born:** August 10, 1975, Rock Island, Illinois **Univ./degree:** A.S., Hotel & Restaurant Management, William Penn College, 1995 **Current organization:** Six Continents Hotels dba Holiday Inn Anaheim Resort **Title:** General Manager **Type of organization:** Hotel **Major product:** Hospitality **Area of distribution:** National **Expertise:** Operations/general management **Affiliations:** A.H.L.A.; Vice President, Albuquerque Innkeepers Association, 2000-2001; Former Member, Anaheim Chamber of Commerce **Hob./spts.:** College basketball, fitness, travel **SIC code:** 70 **Address:** Six Continents Hotels dba Holiday Inn Anaheim Resort, 1915 S. Manchester Ave., Anaheim, CA 92802 **E-mail:** nick.joannides@gc.com

JOHNSON, ARNA L.

Industry: Photography **Born:** February 6, 1958, Honolulu, Hawaii **Univ./degree:** B.A., Brooks Institute of Photography, 1980 **Current organization:** Arna Photography, Inc. **Title:** President **Type of organization:** Professional photography **Major product:** Photography and fine art for weddings, commercial and editorial **Area of**

distribution: National **Expertise:** Photography, weddings, purchasing and hanging of fine art **Affiliations:** Professional Photographers of America; Better Business Bureau of Hawaii **Hob./spts.:** Music, guitar, ukulele, cooking, gardening **SIC code:** 72 **Address:** Arna Photography, Inc., 614 B Kaha St., Kailua, HI 96734 **E-mail:** arna@arnaphoto.com **Web address:** www.arnaphoto.com

JOHNSON, OBIE J.E.
Industry: Defense **Born:** May 26, 1962, Saint Petersburg, Florida **Univ./degree:** M.S., Electrical Engineering, University of South Florida, 1986 **Current organization:** Intelligent System and Solution Services **Title:** President **Type of organization:** Design **Major product:** Radios, satellites **Area of distribution:** National **Expertise:** Engineering **Published works:** Articles **Affiliations:** I.E.E.E. **Hob./spts.:** Race cars, motorcycles, scuba diving **SIC code:** 73 **Address:** Intelligent System and Solution Services, 536 20th Ave., Indian Rocks Beach, FL 33785 **E-mail:** obieone@tampabay.rr.com

JONES, DARRYL N.
Industry: Music **Born:** December 11, 1961, Chicago, Illinois **Univ./degree:** Honorary Doctorate, American Conservatory of Music, Illinois **Current organization:** Les Munch, Inc. **Title:** Musician/Composer **Type of organization:** Music composition **Major product:** Music **Area of distribution:** International **Expertise:** Bass guitar for Sting, Miles Davis, Madonna, Rolling Stones **Published works:** Musical compositions **Affiliations:** American Federation of Music **Hob./spts.:** Reading, boxing fan **SIC code:** 79 **Address:** Les Munch, Inc., 8224 S. Lafayette Ave., Chicago, IL 60620 **E-mail:** losound@aol.com

KAHLHAMER, DANA K.
Industry: Hospitality **Born:** June 1, 1972, Little Falls, Minnesota **Univ./degree:** B.S., Hotel and Restaurant Management, Moorhead State University, Moorhead, Minnesota, 1994 **Current organization:** The Vintage Hotel **Title:** Sales Manager **Type of organization:** Full service hotel **Major product:** Food, lodging, conference facilities **Area of distribution:** Colorado, Domestic and International **Expertise:** Group sales and service for groups ranging from International to SMERF **Honors/awards:** Mary Mitchell Award, Sales Director of the Year, awarded by Colorado Hotel & Lodging Association, 2004 **Hob./spts.:** Skiing, hiking, mountain biking **SIC code:** 70 **Address:** The Vintage Hotel, 100 Winter Park Dr., Winter Park, CO 80482 **E-mail:** sales@vintagehotel.com **Web address:** www.vintagehotel.com

KAMASH, M.A.
Industry: Biotechnology **Born:** March 28, 1947, Alexandria, Virginia **Univ./degree:** Ph.D., Wayne State University, 1978 **Current organization:** Kamox Universal **Title:** President **Type of organization:** Manufacturing **Major product:** Bio-technology **Area of distribution:** International **Expertise:** International business **Honors/awards:** Ford Foundation Award; Devilage Foundation Award **Affiliations:** A.P.S.; Andrology Society **Hob./spts.:** Tennis, chess **SIC code:** 73 **Address:** Kamox Universal, 2135 W. Fairview Ave., Montgomery, AL 36108 **E-mail:** kamoxuniv@aol.com

KAMEL, ANTOINE M.
Industry: Hospitality **Univ./degree:** B.S., Hotel Management, **Current organization:** API Hotels **Title:** Chairman **Type of organization:** Worldwide hotel reservations **Major product:** Hotel accommodations for airline crews, corporations and individuals **Area of distribution:** International **Expertise:** Hospitality, business management **Hob./spts.:** Tennis, swimming, golf **SIC code:** 70 **Address:** API Hotels, 4240 Merrick Rd., Massapequa, NY 11758 **E-mail:** tkamel@apihotels.com **Web address:** www.apihotels.com

KAUFFMANN, ROBERT F.
Industry: Defense/software **Born:** December 13, 1963, Willingboro, New Jersey **Univ./degree:** B.A., Rutgers University, 1987 **Current organization:** Computer Sciences Corp. **Title:** Software Engineer/Film Maker **Type of organization:** Defense contractor **Major product:** Software **Area of distribution:** National **Expertise:** Software engineering **Honors/awards:** Worldfest Houston 2004, Gold Award, Traditional Animation; Da Vinci Film Festival, Best Animation, July 2001; Columbus International Film Festival 2000, Honorable Mention; Twin Rivers Film Festival, 3rd Place-Animation, Oct. 2000; Rochester Film Festival, Certificate of Merit, May 2000; PWCC 99th Annual, Benton Spruance Award for Prints, Jan. 2000; Filmography (films produced): "Food Chain Inversion", produced award-winning animated film, 2004; "Osama Bin Lobster", produced animated film, 2002; "Masque of Ollock", produced award-winning animated film, 1999; "Animated Shorts", produced award-winning animated film, 1995 **Published works:** "The Mask of Ollock", Arx Publishing, 2002; "Implementing Trigonometric Splines", Dr. Dobbs Journal, May 1997 **Affiliations:** International Animated Film Society (ASIFA); IEEE Computer Society; American Academy of Poets **Hob./spts.:** Karate, poetry **SIC code:** 73 **Address:** 2401 Arden Rd., Cinnaminson, NJ 08077 **E-mail:** rkauffma@csc.com **Web address:** www.arxpub.com/kauffmannart.html

KENYON, MELVIN E.
Industry: Open-wheel racing **Born:** April 15, 1933, Illinois **Current organization:** 3K Racing Ent. Inc. **Title:** Co-Owner/Race Car Driver **Type of organization:** Manufacturing/maintenance of race cars **Major product:** Open-wheel race cars **Area of distribution:** International **Expertise:** Inspirational speeches, open wheel race car driving **Honors/awards:** National and International Motor Sports Hall of Fame, 2003 **Published works:** Books, "Hand for the Wheel" and "Burned to Life" **Affiliations:** U.S. Auto Club **Hob./spts.:** Race cars **SIC code:** 75 **Address:** 3K Racing Ent. Inc., 2685 S. 25W., Lebanon, IN 46052 **E-mail:** jodi1733@cs.com

KHAN, GENGHIS A.
Industry: Cleaning service **Born:** August 20, 1971 **Univ./degree:** A.A., Robert Morgan Vocational Technical Institute, 1992 **Current organization:** Americlean Express Inc. **Title:** Owner **Type of organization:** Dry cleaner **Major product:** Solvent-free dry cleaning **Area of distribution:** Florida **Expertise:** Management **Affiliations:** International Fabric Care Institute; Rotary International, Homestead, Florida **Hob./spts.:** Family, movies, car racing **SIC code:** 72 **Address:** Americlean Express Inc., 1199 N.E. First Ave., Florida City, FL 33034 **E-mail:** floridacleaner@yahoo.com

KIRK, WILLIAM A.
Industry: Hospitality **Born:** January 26, 1949, Tyenmouth, England **Current organization:** Northstar Hospitality LLC **Title:** Director of Operations **Type of organization:** Hotel management company **Major product:** Hotels **Area of distribution:** Kentucky **Expertise:** Hotel operations, Certified Hotel Administrator **Affiliations:** American Hotel and Lodging Association **Hob./spts.:** Coaching soccer, playing guitar, music, golf **SIC code:** 70 **Address:** Northstar Hospitality LLC, 3620 Walden Dr., Suite 200, Lexington, KY 40517 **E-mail:** billkirk@northstarhospitality.com **Web address:** www.northstarhospitality.com

KISS, JOSEPH A.
Industry: Entertainment **Born:** February 28, 1934, Windsor, Ontario, Canada **Univ./degree:** B.E.E., University of Detroit, Michigan, 1959 **Title:** Engineer (Retired) **Type of organization:** Post production **Major product:** TV commercials and shows **Area of distribution:** New York, New York **Expertise:** Engineering **Affiliations:** I.E.E.E. **Career accomplishments:** Designed Blanking Analyzer, Color Corrector; Manufactured, designed and built numerous small items for work **Hob./spts.:** Photography, computers, 2 St. Bernards **SIC code:** 79 **Address:** 65 Moraine Rd., Morris Plains, NJ 07950-2752 **E-mail:** jkiss33@msn.com

KISSANE, SHARON F.
Industry: Public relations **Born:** July 2, 1940, Chicago, Illinois **Univ./degree:** B.S., English & Speech, DePaul University; M.S., Northwestern University; Ph.D., Education and Curriculum Supervision, Loyola University, Illinois **Current organization:** Kissane Communications, Ltd. **Title:** President **Type of organization:** Public relations firm **Major product:** Public relations services, specialized writing **Area of distribution:** National **Expertise:** Marketing and public relations **Affiliations:** Midwest Society of Professional Consultants; Board of Directors, Barrington Area United **Hob./spts.:** Sports, reading, art, painting **SIC code:** 73 **Address:** Kissane Communications, Ltd., P.O. Box 1300, Barrington, IL 60011

KNOX, ELIZABETH M.
Industry: Special events sales, design and coordination **Univ./degree:** B.A., University of Arkansas, 1980 **Current organization:** The Century Club **Title:** Director of Special Events **Type of organization:** Supper club, nightclub, special events venue **Major product:** Special events sales and production including concept and design **Area of distribution:** National **Expertise:** Full service event development including corporate, social and entertainment industry events **Published works:** L.A. Times; Variety; Hollywood Reporter **Affiliations:** L.A. Chamber of Commerce; L.A. Convention and Visitors Bureau; Century City Chamber of Commerce **SIC code:** 79 **Address:** The Century Club, 10131 Constellation Blvd., Los Angeles, CA 90067 **E-mail:** lizknox@earthlink.net

KOZYRKOV, VADIM
Industry: Information technology **Born:** October 23, 1964, Moldova, Russia **Univ./degree:** Ph.D., M.B.A., B.A.,Technical University, Port Elizabeth, South Africa; B.S., M.S., Physics, Moscow University **Current organization:** GVW Services **Title:** Partner, IT Services **Type of organization:** IT **Major product:** All IT related services **Area of distribution:** International **Expertise:** System architecture and problem solving **SIC code:** 73 **Address:** GVW Services, 940 S. State 32, Union City, IN 47390 **E-mail:** vkozyrdov@hvwholdings.com **Web address:** www.gvwservices.com

KPODZO, ELIAS B.
Industry: CDMA and GSM/EDGE Mobile Wireless Systems Research and Products Development **Born:** July 14, 1942, Ghana, West Africa **Univ./degree:** Ph.D., Technical University of Braunschweig, Germany, 1981 **Current organization:** Tyco Electronics, M/A-COM Inc. **Title:** Staff Principal Engineer **Type of organization:** Systems Engineering, WiNova **Major product:** Digital Polar Transmitter **Area of distribution:**

International **Expertise:** RF Design, Microwave and Millimeter-Wave Systems and Hardware Design Engineering, Wireless Products Research and Development, HD Radio Digital Technology (IBOC) **Honors/awards:** 2 patents, graduate research grants from the German Research Foundation 1977-82, research grants from the U.S. Air Force 1982-85, BNR (Nortel) Award for contributions to the Initial SONET Radio 4/40 Project in Bell Ontario **Published works:** 31 articles and published works reprinted in 2 books **Affiliations:** Senior Member, I.E.E.E.; Member of International Who's Who of Professionals 2001 **Hob./spts.:** Tennis, jogging, reading, travel **SIC code:** 73 **Address:** Tyco Electronics, M/A-COM Inc., Patriots Plaza - 60 Columbia Rd,, Morristown, NJ 07960 **E-mail:** kpodzoe@tycoelectronics.com **Web address:** www.macom.com

KRAMER, ALLEN LEE

Industry: Hospitality **Born:** September 20, 1958, Gettysburg, Pennsylvania **Univ./degree:** Music, Northeastern Christian Junior College **Current organization:** Holiday Inn **Title:** Food and Beverage Manager **Type of organization:** Hotel Chain **Major product:** Food, beverage and lodging **Area of distribution:** International **Expertise:** Food and beverage management **Honors/awards:** Sheridan Valley Forge Manager of the Month **Published works:** Write-up, King of Prussia Newspaper **Affiliations:** Rotary Club; Church of Christ **Hob./spts.:** Softball, football, swimming, tennis **SIC code:** 70 **Address:** Holiday Inn, 943 S. High St., West Chester, PA 19382

KRUEGER, RONALD P.

Industry: Theatres/entertainment **Born:** October 19, 1940, St. Louis, Missouri **Univ./degree:** B.S., Accounting, Westminster College, 1961 **Current organization:** Wehrenberg Theatres Inc. **Title:** CEO/President **Type of organization:** Movie theater **Major product:** First run movies **Area of distribution:** Missouri, Iowa, Illinois, Minnesota **Expertise:** Administration, marketing, site development, historical and promotional lecturing **Published works:** 1 book **Affiliations:** Y.P.O., Past Potentate, 33rd Scottish Rite, Moolah Shrine; Past Knight Commander, York Rite; Past Chair, Salvation Army Advisory Board; Board Member, National Association of Theatre Owners **Hob./spts.:** Big game hunting, antique cars, fishing **SIC code:** 79 **Address:** Wehrenberg Theatres Inc., 12800 Manchester Rd., St. Louis, MO 63131 **E-mail:** ronaldkreuger@wehrenberg.com **Web address:** www.wehrenbergtheatres.com

KRUSE, DANIEL

Industry: Auctions **Born:** March 16, 1950, Angola, Indiana **Univ./degree:** Indiana University **Current organization:** Kruse Asset Management , Inc./Superior Asset Management, Inc. **Title:** President/CEO **Type of organization:** Appraisal, sale and auction group **Major product:** Appraisals, auctions, equipment sales **Area of distribution:** International **Expertise:** Auctions **Affiliations:** National Auctioneers Association; Texas Auctioneers Association **Hob./spts.:** Racing, fine dining **SIC code:** 73 **Address:** Kruse Asset Management , Inc., Superior Asset Management, Inc., 11202 Disco, San Antonio, TX 78216 **E-mail:** dankruse@kruseasset.com **Web address:** www.kruseasset.com

KUGHN, BARRY J.

Industry: Mortuary **Born:** February 6, 1953, Hayti, Missouri **Univ./degree:** A.S., Mortuary Science, Jefferson State Community College, 1973 **Current organization:** Brown & Kughn Memory Chapel **Title:** Funeral Director, Vice President **Type of organization:** Funeral home **Major product:** Funeral services **Area of distribution:** Alabama **Expertise:** Mortician **Affiliations:** Alabama Funeral Directors Association; Southern Funeral Directors Association; National Funeral Directors Association; Kiwanis Club **Hob./spts.:** Writing **SIC code:** 72 **Address:** 711 Keith Ave., Anniston, AL 36207 **E-mail:** bjkughn@hotmail.com

LALLI, JOHN M.

Industry: Broadcasting/entertainment **Born:** March 31, 1942, Mt. Vernon, New York **Spouse:** D. Leigh Lalli **Children:** John M. Lalli Jr., 34; James T. Lalli, 33; Martin K. Lalli, 31; Kirsten G. Lalli, 12; Scott M. Lalli, 10 **Univ./degree:** B.A., Cum Laude, Economics and Management Sciences, University of Notre Dame, Indiana; Post-graduate studies, Computer Science, University of Notre Dame and Pace University, New York **Current organization:** Infocrossing Inc. **Title:** Senior Vice-President, Strategic Services **Type of organization:** IT Outsourcing Services Provider **Major product:** IT Infrastructure Support Services **Area of distribution:** International **Expertise:** Information technology, media/entertainment **Honors/awards:** Who's Who in Colleges and Universities (1964); Decorated Vietnam Veteran, US Army Intelligence; Invited by the White House as subject matter expert technology consultant (Carter Administration) to join 'White House Committee on Technology'; American Management Association Philosophy of Education and Services Award; DeSeversky Institute CBS School of Management Award for Leadership; Appointed Honorary Chairman and Speaker, Blessed Sacrament High School Alumni Association; Appointed to Board of Trustees and Executive Finance Committee, Meadowlands Hospital Medical Center, Liberty Health System (2002 - present) **Published works:** Articles in several trade journals, **Affiliations:** American Association of Blood Banks **Career accomplishments:** Significant P&L responsibility for sales and marketing, analysis, proposal development and delivery of services for new outsourcing business designed to leverage resources to maximize profits; developed and installed disaster recovery plans for all computing platforms company-wide; delivered information processing contract services resulting in $7 million repeat annual revenue; significant intrapreneurial accomplishment in application development increasing services and value-adds to both advertisers and viewers; specific range from interactive voice response and on-line services applications to direct marketing and advertising campaigns utilizing interactive new media products; negotiated major long term voice and data contracts with MCI and ATT resulting in $3 million average annual savings over 6 years **Hob./spts.:** Golf, family **SIC code:** 79 **Address:** Infocrossing Inc., 2 Christie Heights St., 2nd floor, Leonia, NJ 07605 **E-mail:** jlalli@infocrossing.com **Web address:** www.infocrossing.com

LANDRY-ANDREWS, COREY

Industry: Medical imaging technology **Univ./degree:** Certified, Radiology, Lafayette General Medical Center School of Health Sciences, 1988 **Current organization:** GE Medical Systems Information Technologies **Title:** RT **Type of organization:** Information technology **Major product:** Medical imaging software and hardware **Area of distribution:** International **Expertise:** E-learning development, training **Affiliations:** A.S.R.T., L.S.R.T. **Hob./spts.:** Gardening, tennis, running, family, cooking **SIC code:** 73 **Address:** 103 Ellerslie Ct., Lafayette, LA 70503 **E-mail:** corey.landryandrews@med.ge.com **Web address:** www.gehealthcare.com/

LARRACUENTE-OCASIO, MARIA C.

Industry: Hospitality **Born:** May 2, 1963, Mayaguez, Puerto Rico **Univ./degree:** A.S., Assistant Administration, American Business Institute, Philadelphia, Pennsylvania **Current organization:** Hyatt Dorado Beach Resort & Country Club **Title:** Convention & Catering Manager **Type of organization:** Hotel **Major product:** Lodging **Area of distribution:** International **Expertise:** Conventions and catering **Honors/awards:** Hyatt Dorado Beach Resort & Country Club, Manager of the Month, December, 1996; Manager of the Year, 1996; Manager of the Month, February, 2002 **Hob./spts.:** Family activities **SIC code:** 70 **Address:** Hyatt Dorado Beach Resort & Country Club, Route 693, Dorado, PR 00646 **E-mail:** mocasio@doradpo.hyatt.com

LASATER, THAD E.

Industry: Recreation **Born:** June 23, 1971, Borger, Texas **Univ./degree:** Attended, Business Administration, Panhandle State University **Current organization:** Borger Country Club **Title:** General Manager/Head Golf Professional **Type of organization:** Country club **Major product:** Golf, tennis, swimming, dining **Area of distribution:** Borger, Texas **Expertise:** Golf operations **Affiliations:** Ducks Unlimited; Professional Golfers' Association of America **Hob./spts.:** Hunting, fishing **SIC code:** 79 **Address:** Borger Country Club, 599 Broadmoor, Borger, TX 79007 **E-mail:** no3putts@pga.com

LAWLER, MARITA A.

Industry: Consulting **Born:** July 14, 1947, Albany, California **Univ./degree:** B.S., Human Services, Thomas Edison State College, 1998; M.S., Capella University, 2000 **Current organization:** Lawler Consulting **Title:** Addiction Therapist/Consultant **Type of organization:** Consulting, individual therapeutic practice **Major product:** Individual, group and family therapy **Area of distribution:** National **Expertise:** Addiction, mental health, forensics **Published works:** Published poet; has written, designed and implemented state and non-profit counseling and education programs **Hob./spts.:** Camping, fishing, hiking, music, her two children, life long learning **SIC code:** 73 **Address:** Lawler Consulting, 1150 S. Colony Way, Suite 3 PMB352, Palmer, AK 99645 **E-mail:** marita.ms@healingwell.com **Web address:** www.marita.ms.healingwell.com

LEE, MORRIS R.

Industry: Employment/aviation **Born:** Tuscaloosa, Alabama **Univ./degree:** M.S., Economics, Queens College, New York, 1971 **Current organization:** Council for Airport Opportunity **Title:** Executive Director **Type of organization:** Employment agency **Major product:** Employment for minorities in the airport industry **Area of distribution:** New York City and New Jersey **Expertise:** Finding suitable candidates for airline jobs **Affiliations:** Phi Beta Sigma **Hob./spts.:** Golf, baseball **SIC code:** 73 **Address:** Council for Airport Opportunity, Inc., 90-04 161st St., Jamaica, NY 11432 **E-mail:** caony@earthlink.net

LEEPER, HERBERT

Industry: Automotive **Born:** April 22, 1949, Neptune, New Jersey **Current organization:** North End Auto Repair **Title:** Owner **Type of organization:** Repair and towing

Major product: Car and light truck repair **Area of distribution:** Wichita, Kansas **Expertise:** Car/truck repair and towing **Affiliations:** N.F.B.; B.B.B. **Hob./spts.:** Motocross racing **SIC code:** 75 **Address:** North End Auto Repair, 725 W. 61st St. North, Wichita, KS 67204 **E-mail:** hleeper@cox.net

LEHMAN, HYLA BEROEN
Industry: Performing arts/education **Born:** Story City, Iowa **Univ./degree:** B.A., M.A., Theatre Arts Education, Drake University **Current organization:** Dance Theatre of the Hemispheres **Title:** Director (Retired) **Type of organization:** Theatre and dance **Major product:** Performing, teaching, directing **Area of distribution:** National **Expertise:** Theatre and dance performance **Honors/awards:** Outstanding Woman of the 20th Century; Woman of the Year, 1996; Hall of Fame, American Biographical Institute **Published works:** Write-ups **Affiliations:** Chair, Reagents Waldorf University; President, American Association of University Women; International Who's Who for Intelligence **Hob./spts.:** Theatre, arts, music, reading, dance **SIC code:** 79 **Address:** Francis Holmund Living, 750 S. Laposada Circle, Suite 34, Green Valley, AZ 85614

LEO, WILLIAM T.
Industry: Information Technology **Born:** November 22, 1963, Brooklyn, New York **Current organization:** Oliver Wyman - Delta Organization & Leadership **Title:** C.I.O. **Type of organization:** Consulting firm **Major product:** Professional services **Area of distribution:** International **Expertise:** Technology/IT management **Affiliations:** A.M.A.; American College of Forensic Examiners Institute; Computer Security Institute; Ferris Research Board; Council of Communications Advisors; IDC Enterprise Panel; IDC; Corporate Computer Council; NASPA; PMI; Infrared WSTA; IEEE Society; Information Systems Audit and Control Association; Association of Information Technology Professionals **Hob./spts.:** Golf, reading, fishing **SIC code:** 73 **Address:** Oliver Wyman - Delta Organization & Leadership, 1166 Avenue of the Americas, 40th floor, New York, NY 10036 **E-mail:** bill.leo@oliverwyman.com **Web address:** www.oliverwyman.com

LEONE, RICHARD A.
Industry: Entertainment **Born:** September 25, 1937, Tampa, Florida **Univ./degree:** B.A., Radio TV Film (Communications), University of Miami, 1959 **Current organization:** Network Voice Promos, Inc. **Title:** President **Type of organization:** Communications **Major product:** Radio and television program producer of "Entertainment Spotlight" a movie review radio program on the web and Entertainment Spotlight, T.V., a film review show on Miami Dade cable TV channel 29; Also produces voice-overs for TV and radio nationally **Area of distribution:** Florida **Expertise:** Recently retired from WSVN, Miami after 27 years as Staff Announcer, Weatherman and Children's Show Host of the "Sunday Funnies"; he has been dancing and performing as a radio and television personality since age 10 (when he started on ABC Radio as child-emcee host of "Tom Thumb Follies" and "Young Americans Club" in 1948); he has also appeared in many musical comedy productions **Published works:** "Caught On The Runway", Postscript to September 11th **Affiliations:** Operations, Producer and TV Station Announcer for WLRN-TV PBS, Miami; Suncoast Chapter, National Academy of Television Arts and Sciences; Miami International Press Club **Hob./spts.:** Entertainer-singer, dancer, professional actor **SIC code:** 79 **Address:** Network Voice Promos, Inc., 7751 N.E. Bayshore Court, # 2D, Miami, FL 33138 **Phone:** (305)756-7408 **Fax:** (305)756-7408 **E-mail:** n_v_p@bellsouth.net **Web address:** www.entertainment-spotlight.com

LESPERANCE, JESSE P.
Industry: Hospitality **Born:** May 29, 1977, Sanford, Maine **Univ./degree:** B.A., Computer Science, Arizona State University, 1977 **Current organization:** Super 8 Motel **Title:** Manager **Type of organization:** Hotel **Major product:** Lodging, food and beverage **Area of distribution:** Lewiston, Maine **Expertise:** Hotel management **Hob./spts.:** Martial arts **SIC code:** 70 **Address:** Super 8 Motel, 1440 Lisbon St., Lewiston, ME 04240 **E-mail:** jnjwebder@yahoo.com

LEWIS, JETTYE T.
Industry: Food service management **Born:** January 28, 1963, Goldsboro, North Carolina **Univ./degree:** B.S., Business Administration, Atlantic Christian College, North Carolina, 1985; M.A., Methods of Management/Human Resources, Webster University, South Carolina, 1998 **Current organization:** HDS Services **Title:** Program Support Specialist **Type of organization:** Food service/hospitality management/consulting **Major product:** Provide management services to hospitals, nursing homes, retirement homes, clubs and resorts, schools and colleges **Area of distribution:** Michigan **Expertise:** Management/consulting **Hob./spts.:** Bowling, reading **SIC code:** 73 **Address:** HDS Services, 39395 W. 12 Mile Rd., Suite 101, Farmington Hills, MI 48331 **E-mail:** jettye@bellsouth.net

LEWIS, KELLY J.
Industry: Hospitality **Current organization:** Daufauskie Island Club Resort & Breathe Spa **Title:** General Manager **Type of organization:** Resort and spa **Major product:** Hotel accommodations, golf, tennis, spa **Area of distribution:** South Carolina **Expertise:** Daily operations, financing **Affiliations:** Chamber of Commerce **Hob./spts.:** Golf **SIC code:** 70 **Address:** Daufuskie Island Resort & Breathe Spa, 421 Squire Pope Rd., Hilton Head Island, SC 29926 **E-mail:** klewis@daufuskieresort.com **Web address:** www.daufauskieresort.com

LEWIS, ROBERT W.A.
Industry: Hospitality **Born:** January 21, 1962, St. Louis, Missouri **Current organization:** Holiday Inn Southwest/Viking **Title:** Purchasing Manager **Type of organization:** Hotel **Major product:** Lodging/food **Area of distribution:** Missouri **Expertise:** Purchasing food and beverage, inventory, receiving **Hob./spts.:** Family **SIC code:** 70 **Address:** Holiday Inn Southwest/Viking, 10709 Watson Rd., St. Louis, MO 63127 **E-mail:** bob.lewis@holidayinnviking.com

LIEBE, RINA E.
Industry: Hospitality **Univ./degree:** A.S., Art, Illinois Valley Community College **Current organization:** Starved Rock Lodge & Conference Center **Title:** Manager **Type of organization:** Lodge **Major product:** Lodging, food, conference center **Area of distribution:** Illinois **Expertise:** Communications, employee relations **Published works:** Article **SIC code:** 70 **Address:** Starved Rock Lodge & Conference Center, Rte 71 & 178 Box 570, Utica, IL 61329 **E-mail:** onlyrina@insightbb.com

LIGGETT, TWILA C.
Industry: Television **Born:** March 25, 1944, Pipestone, Minnesota **Univ./degree:** B.A., Secondary and Music Education, Union College, Lincoln, Nebraska; M.A., Elementary Education; Ph.D., Administration Curriculum & Instruction University of Nebraska, 1977 **Current organization:** Marymount Manhattan College **Title:** Professor/Teacher **Type of organization:** Four year liberal arts college **Major product:** Education/literacy **Expertise:** Educational design, literacy **Honors/awards:** 24 Emmys; 120 Emmy nominations; American Educational Research Award, 1979; Honored by the International Reading Association for exceptional contributions to worldwide literacy, 1992 **Published works:** The Reading Rainbow Guide to Children's Books: The 101 Best Titles; The Whole Person Book: Toward Self-Discovery and Life Options; Chapters for Family Literacy: Connections in School and Communities, 1995; A Handbook for Literacy Educators: Research on Teaching the Communicative and Visual Arts, 1998 **Affiliations:** National Academy of Arts and Sciences; International Reading Association **Career accomplishments:** As executive producer for Reading Rainbow, the show has won over 150 awards including the Prix Jenesse, 1992, The Peabody, 1993 and 13 National Emmys; As primary fundraiser for Reading Rainbow, has secured over $40 million in underwriting from foundations and corporations including The Kellogg Company, B. Dalton Booksellers, Barnes and Noble, Carnegie Foundation and the National Science Foundation **Hob./spts.:** Windsurfing, reading, boating, race walking **SIC code:** 79 **Address:** Lancit Media Entertainment, Ltd., 555 W. 57th St., 11th floor, New York, NY 10021 **E-mail:** rainbow1@aol.com

LIND, ARPAD Z.
Industry: Stamping/assemblies **Univ./degree:** A.S., Mechanical Engineering, Wentworth College, 1966 **Current organization:** Brainin Advance Ind. **Title:** Prototype Manager **Type of organization:** Manufacturing **Major product:** Precision stamping, welded contact assemblies, rivet lay assemblies and brazed assemblies **Area of distribution:** National **Expertise:** Engineering, tooling **Hob./spts.:** Fishing, photography **SIC code:** 76 **Address:** Brainin Advance Ind., 48 Frank Mossberg Dr., Attleboro, MA 02703 **E-mail:** alind@brainin.com

LINDEN, HAROLD A.
Industry: Interior design/consulting **Born:** May 25, 1941, Brooklyn, New York **Univ./degree:** B.A., Art, 1964; M.A., Interior Design, 1967, City University of New York **Current organization:** Mobili Internationale, Inc. **Title:** President **Type of organization:** Retailer **Major product:** Consultation, space planning, purchasing **Area of distribution:** East coast from Massachusetts to Florida **Expertise:** Design director for commercial and residential projects **Honors/awards:** ` **Published works:** "The furniture design of Ludwig Mies Van der Rohe and their influence on subsequent designers" **Hob./spts.:** Tennis, jazz music **SIC code:** 73 **Address:** Mobili Internationale, Inc., Matamoras Post Office, P.O. Box 60, Matamoras, PA 18336 **E-mail:** hal525linden@yahoo.com

LINDNER, PERRI L.
Industry: Beauty/cosmetics **Born:** Sydney, Australia **Current organization:** Carter Barnes Inc. **Title:** Co-owner/Secretary/Treasurer **Type of organization:** Beauty salon and spa/retailer **Major product:** Health and beauty services/cosmetics **Area of distribution:** National **Expertise:** Marketing, operations, staff training and motivation **Honors/awards:** Top Colorist, "Allure" Magazine, 2002; Olympic Torch Bearer for Athens, Greece, 2004 **Affiliations:** Cosmetology Association of Georgia **Hob./spts.:** Running **SIC code:** 72 **Address:** Carter Barnes Inc., Phipps Plaza Bldg., 3500 Peachtree Rd. N.E., Atlanta, GA 30326 **E-mail:** perri@carterbarnes.com

LOOMOS, MELANIE D.
Industry: Software **Born:** March 27, 1968, Chicago, Illinois **Current organization:** Ergosoft, Inc. & Butpillow, Inc. **Title:** Founder/President **Type of organization:** Inventing/manufacturing **Major product:** Software/cushions **Area of distribution:** National **Expertise:** Administration, marketing, inventing **Honors/awards:** 2 patents **SIC code:** 73 **Address:** Ergosoft, Inc. & Butpillow, Inc., 15403 S.W. 142nd Ave., Miami, FL 33177

LOWE, JOHN F.
Industry: Hospitality **Born:** April 15, 1966, Philadelphia, Pennsylvania **Univ./degree:** A.A., English, **Current organization:** Hilton Wilmington/Christiana **Title:** Director of Food & Beverage **Type of organization:** Hotel **Major product:** Lodging, banquets & restaurants **Area of distribution:** National **Expertise:** Food & beverage **Affiliations:** A.H.L.A.; N.R.A.; Rotary Club **Hob./spts.:** Reading, writing **SIC code:** 70 **Address:** Hilton Wilmington/Christiana, 100 Continental Dr., Newark, DE 19713 **E-mail:** jlowe@chrishil.meyerjabara.com

LUCIA, ROCCO P.
Industry: Hospitality **Born:** Asbury Park, New Jersey **Univ./degree:** B.S., Computer Science, Devry Technical Institute **Current organization:** B.R. Guest, Inc. **Title:** Corporate Director of IT **Type of organization:** Hotels and restaurants **Major product:** Hospitality and all guest services **Area of distribution:** National **Expertise:** Technology **Published works:** Several articles for Hospitality Technology Magazine **Affiliations:** Board Member, Advisory Board of Hospitality Technology Magazine **Hob./spts.:** Professional drummer, golf **SIC code:** 70 **Address:** B.R. Guest, Inc., 206 Spring St., New York, NY 10012 **E-mail:** rlucia@brguestinc.com

LUTZ, DALE R.
Industry: Computer hardware/software **Born:** St. Louis, Missouri **Current organization:** Hewlett-Packard **Title:** Computer Environment Specialist **Type of organization:** Business services **Major product:** Hardware, software, consulting **Area of distribution:** National **Expertise:** Computer room environment consultant **Affiliations:** Association of Energy Engineers **Hob./spts.:** Reading **SIC code:** 73 **Address:** Hewlett-Packard, 721 Emerson Rd., St. Louis, MO 63141 **E-mail:** dale.lutz@hp.com

LUU, LILLIAN
Industry: Hospitality **Born:** August 28, 1969, China **Univ./degree:** B.S., Business Administration/Accounting, St. Mary's College, California, 1991 **Current organization:** Sunterra Financial Services **Title:** Director of Finance **Type of organization:** Hotel **Major product:** Mortgage receivable **Area of distribution:** National **Expertise:** Finance, accounting **Affiliations:** A.I.C.P.A. **Hob./spts.:** Hiking **SIC code:** 70 **Address:** Sunterra Financial Services, 9921 Covington Cross Dr., Suite 105, Las Vegas, NV 89144 **E-mail:** lluu@sunterra.com

MACONI, KATHLEEN
Industry: Beauty and wellness **Born:** May 8, 1962, Denville, New Jersey **Current organization:** Elysium Salon and Spas **Title:** Owner/Master Stylist **Type of organization:** Salon and spas **Major product:** Hair styling and spa services **Area of distribution:** Lincoln Park, New Jersey/Montville, New Jersey **Expertise:** Hair design, color and product knowledge **Affiliations:** T.S.A. **Hob./spts.:** Boating, travel, education **SIC code:** 72 **Address:** Elysium Salon and Spas, 2 Changebridge Rd., Montville, NJ 07045, 183 Main St., Lincoln Park, NJ 07035 **E-mail:** elysiumsalonspa@verizon.net **Web address:** www.elysiumsalonspa.com

MADDEN, MICHAEL H.
Industry: Hospitality **Univ./degree:** A.A., Culinary Institute of America, 1974 **Current organization:** Embassy Suites Hotel **Title:** Executive Chef **Type of organization:** Hotel **Major product:** Food, beverage and lodging **Area of distribution:** International **Expertise:** Food art creation **Published works:** Publications **SIC code:** 70 **Address:** Embassy Suites Hotel, 654 S. College Ave., Newark, DE 19713 **E-mail:** michael_madden@hilton.com

MAHADEO, EDWARD
Industry: Entertainment **Born:** December 29, 1977, Guyana, South America **Univ./degree:** B.S., Business Administration and Information Technology, University of Phoenix, 2005 **Current organization:** TeleVest Daytime Programs **Title:** Information Technology Manager **Type of organization:** Entertainment production **Major product:** Daytime television programming production **Area of distribution:** New York **Expertise:** Administration **Affiliations:** N.A.T.A.S. **Hob./spts.:** Bodybuilding, football **SIC code:** 79 **Address:** TeleVest Daytime Programs, 825 Eighth Ave., 35th floor, New York, NY 10019 **E-mail:** edward.mahadeo@televest.com

MAISON-LUISI, ONITA A.
Industry: Cosmetology **Born:** February, 11, 1962, London, England **Univ./degree:** Associates Degree in Fashion, Barnfield College, England, 1980; Graduate, London College of Beauty Therapy, 1982 **Current organization:** CHiPS, Salon & Hair Spa **Title:** Owner **Type of organization:** Hair Salon and Spa **Major product:** Hair straightening and coloring **Area of distribution:** National **Expertise:** Professional consulting, educator for Paul Mitchell; Hair colorist (Board Certified, American Board of Hair Colorists) **Honors/awards:** Outstanding Service Award in Educational Excellence, Emiliani Enterprises, 2005 **Published works:** 1 book in progress **Affiliations:** National Cosmetology Association ; The Salon Association; givemeservice.com **Hob./spts.:** Ballroom dancing, travel **SIC code:** 73 **Address:** CHiPS, Salon & Hair Spa, 8 South Main St., Marlboro, NJ 07746 **E-mail:** onitaluisi@optonline.net **Web address:** www.chipssalonandspa.com

MAJDALANY, MICHAEL
Industry: Association management **Born:** May 26, 1954, San Francisco, California **Univ./degree:** B.S.E., State University of New York; M.B.A., Stanford University; M.S., Engineering, Massachusetts Institute of Technology **Current organization:** LoBue and Majdalany Management Group **Title:** Vice President/COO **Type of organization:** Service provider **Major product:** Management and consulting services, catering to trade associations and nonprofit groups **Area of distribution:** International **Expertise:** Governance, board management, administration, sales, marketing and business development; frequent lecturer and public speaker on a national level **Affiliations:** A.S.A.E. **Hob./spts.:** Motor sports, charity donations to academic institutions **SIC code:** 73 **Address:** LoBue and Majdalany Management Group, 572B Ruger St., #29920, San Francisco, CA 94129 **E-mail:** majdalany@lm-mgmt.com **Web address:** www.lm-mgmt.com

MANCUSO, LOU
Industry: Weight loss/nutrition **Born:** March 28, 1941, Yonkers, New York **Univ./degree:** B.S., Business Administration, Fordham University, 1963 **Current organization:** Jenny Craig, Inc. **Title:** Vice President, Development **Type of organization:** Weight management service company **Major product:** Nutrition, weight loss **Area of distribution:** National **Expertise:** Development, construction, real estate **Affiliations:** International Council of Shopping Centers **SIC code:** 72 **Address:** Jenny Craig, Inc., 5770 Fleet St., Carlsbad, CA 92008 **E-mail:** lmancuso@jennycraig.com **Web address:** www.jennycraig.com

MAPLES, STEPHEN E.
Industry: Creative consulting **Born:** Greenville, Mississippi **Univ./degree:** B.A., Magna Cum Laude, Visual Design and Communication, Southern Arkansas University; Further studies in Intellectual Property Law at Widener University School of Law and University of Victoria, British Columbia **Current organization:** moreTree, LLC **Title:** Founder, Author, Developer and Sole Managing Member **Type of organization:** Online creative market planning system and design consultancy **Major product:** Offers start-up entrepreneurs and existing business owners an insightful new approach that helps them redefine themselves, their ideas, their offerings, their corporate identity and their market position to cultivate market life and devotion for their business planning and marketing efforts, all from the convenience of their own computer by accessing www.moretree.com; also provides one-on-one creative counseling and design services on a freelance basis **Area of distribution:** Pennsylvania **Expertise:** Marketing systems, creative promotions and design **Honors/awards:** Alpha Chi National Honor Society **Published works:** The Online moreTree Market Planning Guide **Affiliations:** Pennsylvania Young Professionals Association (Harrisburg Chapter); Phi Alpha Delta Law Society; American Bar Association; A.T.L.A. **Hob./spts.:** Play violin and guitar, painting, reading, travel, volleyball **SIC code:** 73 **Address:** moreTree, LLC, 3152 Sycamore St., P.O. Box 4315, Harrisburg, PA 17111 **Phone:** (717)561-1491 **Fax:** (717)561-1492 **E-mail:** semaples@hotmail.com **Web address:** www.moretree.com

MARKS, H. LEE
Industry: Business services/building materials **Born:** April 26, 1971, Homestead, Florida **Univ./degree:** B.S., Computer Information Science, Virginia Technical Institute, 1993 **Current organization:** Activant Solutions Inc. **Title:** R&D Project Leader **Type of organization:** Total solution provider **Major product:** Enterprise resource planning software systems **Area of distribution:** International **Expertise:** New product development engineering, installation consultant **Affiliations:** Association for Computing Machinery; Technical Panel Member, I.E.E.E. **Hob./spts.:** Football, computers, motorcycle touring **SIC code:** 73 **Address:** Activant Solutions Inc., 5 Independence Pt., Greenville, SC 29615 **E-mail:** lee.marks@activant.com **Web address:** www.activant.com

MARKUSON, GLORIA CROWLEY
Industry: Law **Born:** September 12, Manhattan, New York **Univ./degree:** J.D. Fordham University School of Law **Current organization:** Gloria Crowley Markuson, Attorney at Law **Title:** Attorney at Law **Type of organization:** Law firm **Major product:** Legal services **Area of distribution:** National **Expertise:** Wills, estates, trusts **Honors/awards:** First Woman President of Westchester County Bar Association **Published works:** 300+ volumes and revisions in print **Affiliations:** Life Fellow, New York State Bar Foundation; Life Fellow, American Bar Foundation; A.B.A. **Hob./spts.:** Designing clothes and hats, gourmet cooking, charitable work, entertaining **SIC code:** 71 **Address:** Gloria Crowley Markuson, Attorney at Law, 185 Summerfield St., Scarsdale, NY 10583

MARRAPODI, GREGG
Industry: Automotive/Real Estate **Born:** May 3, 1952, Brooklyn, New York **Current organization:** Automobilia Inc/King Street Ent. Inc. **Title:** President **Type of organization:** Auto repair facility/real estate holdings **Major product:** Auto repair/real estate investments **Area of distribution:** Florida **Expertise:** Auto repair **Affiliations:** Port Charlotte Chamber of Commerce; Rotary Club; B.B.B.; Boys and Girls Club of America; Punta Gorda Chamber of Commerce; Charlotte Technical Advisory Board; Sponsoring Member, IATN; A.S.E., Master Technician Heavy Trucks, Automobiles; Dept. of Education, School Bus Repair, Alternate Fuels and Propane Repair **Hob./spts.:** Sailing, scuba diving **SIC code:** 75 **Address:** Automobilia Inc/King Street Ent. Inc., 15121 Gulistan Ave., Port Charlotte, FL 33953 **E-mail:** gmarrapodi@earthlink.net

MARSHALL, WAYNE
Industry: Energy services **Born:** June 29, 1962, Western Salem, North Carolina **Univ./degree:** B.S.E., University of North Carolina, Charlotte, 1984 **Current organization:** Ameresco **Title:** Vice President, U.S. Sales **Type of organization:** Energy services **Major product:** Energy demand side projects **Area of distribution:** National **Expertise:** Sales and marketing **Honors/awards:** Young Engineer of the Year, N.S.P.E., 1995 **Published works:** A.A.T.C.C. Journal **Affiliations:** Professional Engineers of North Carolina **Hob./spts.:** Golf, baseball, football, basketball **SIC code:** 73 **Address:** Ameresco, 128 S. Tryon St., Suite 2200, Charlotte, NC 28202 **E-mail:** mars9206@bellsouth.net **Web address:** www.ameresco.com

MARTIN, CHARLAINE
Industry: Sound productions **Born:** July 25, 1953 **Univ./degree:** B.S., Education, Central Michigan University, 1975 **Current organization:** Sound Images, Inc. **Title:** Vice President **Type of organization:** Custom audio solutions company **Major product:** Sound communications, recordings **Area of distribution:** National **Expertise:** Marketing operations **Affiliations:** Advertising Club of Cincinnati **Hob./spts.:** Theatre **SIC code:** 73 **Address:** Sound Images, Inc., 602 Main St., Suite 222, Cincinnati, OH 45202 **E-mail:** charlie@soundimages.com **Web address:** www.soundimages.com

MARTIN, DWAYNE A.
Industry: Hospitality **Born:** September 4, 1964, Oakland, California **Univ./degree:** A.A., Accounting and Purchasing **Current organization:** Hilton Hotels **Title:** Food & Beverage Buyer **Type of organization:** Hotels **Major product:** Lodging, food and beverages **Area of distribution:** San Francisco, California **Expertise:** Purchasing/accounting **Hob./spts.:** Golf, bowling **SIC code:** 70 **Address:** Hilton Hotels, 333 O'Farrell St., San Francisco, CA 94102 **E-mail:** dwayne_a_martin@hilton.com

MARTINCEVIC, LESLIE J.
Industry: Project Management, Software Development and Implementation, Supply Management **Born:** February 17, 1959, Zambia **Univ./degree:** Cape Town Technical University, 1983 NDE (Electrical Engineering), 1984 NHDE (Electrical Engineering) **Current organization:** Paragon Solutions Inc. **Title:** Partner **Type of organization:** Consulting to Process Industries **Major product:** Project Management, Software and IT Consulting **Area of distribution:** International **Expertise:** Project Management, Software Development and Implementation, Supply Chain **Published works:** "Requiem for the EOQ", Journal and Proceedings of the South African Institute of Industrial Engineers (SAIIE); "Twelve Reasons Why Your Implementation Might Fail and What You Can Do About It", Journal and Proceedings of the South African Institute of Industrial Engineers (SAIIE); "Start Talking and Get Back to Work", Insight Magazine, The Journal to the EAM Industry **Hob./spts.:** Warhammer enthusiast **SIC code:** 73 **Address:** Paragon Solutions Inc., 620 N. Hollywood Way, Suite 311, Burbank, CA 91505 **E-mail:** lmartincevic@team-paragon.com

MATOCINOS, NONITO B.
Industry: Hospitality **Born:** February 23, 1947, Albay, Philippines **Current organization:** Woodfin Suites & Hotel **Title:** Executive Chef/Director of Food & Beverage **Type of organization:** Hotel **Major product:** Lodging **Area of distribution:** Emeryville, California **Expertise:** Culinary arts, customer service **Affiliations:** T.A.G.A.S. Internationale **Hob./spts.:** Swimming **SIC code:** 70 **Address:** Woodfin Suites & Hotel, 5800 Shellmound St., Emeryville, CA 94608 **E-mail:** nitom@msu.com

MAULDEN, JEFF T.
Industry: Advertising **Born:** March 25, 1974, Kennewick, Washington **Univ./degree:** B.A., Communication Advertising Broadcasting, Washington State University **Current organization:** Kaiser Marketing **Title:** Vice President; Account Director **Type of organization:** Full service advertising agency **Major product:** Marketing materials **Area of distribution:** National **Expertise:** Travel and leisure marketing **Hob./spts.:** Golf, art, friends, wine **SIC code:** 73 **Address:** Kaiser Marketing, 1631 Pontius Ave., Los Angeles, CA 90025

MAURER, JEFFREY L.
Industry: Hospitality **Born:** May 30, 1970, Zanesville, Ohio **Current organization:** Red Roof Inn Accor **Title:** General Manager **Type of organization:** Hotel **Major product:** Lodging **Area of distribution:** Poland, Ohio **Expertise:** Operations, human resources, sales **Honors/awards:** Board Member, Mahoning County Convention and Visitor's Bureau; District Sales Award, 2003; Quality Award, 2003 **Affiliations:** Vice Chairman, Mahoning County Lodging Council **Hob./spts.:** Horseback riding **SIC code:** 70 **Address:** Red Roof Inn Accor, 1015 S. Tiffany, Poland, OH 44514 **E-mail:** i0253@redroof.com

MAYO, LINDA J.
Industry: Healthcare **Born:** January 13, 1952, Oakland, California **Univ./degree:** Electrology, Citrus College, 1983; B.A. Candidate, Psychology/Child Development, Merced College **Current organization:** Beauty & Health Enhancements **Title:** Electrologist/Herbalist **Type of organization:** Private practice **Major product:** Beauty and health services **Area of distribution:** California **Expertise:** Hair removal (Certified Registered Electrologist), herbalism, consulting; Certified Technician, Quantitative Fluid Analyzer **Honors/awards:** Development awards for recruiting and training in health business **Affiliations:** A.E.A.; E.A.C.A. **Hob./spts.:** Music, travel **SIC code:** 73 **Address:** Beauty & Health Enhancements, 6 W. Main St., Merced, CA 95340

MAZZONI, RICHARD D.
Industry: Automotive **Born:** June 1, 1959, Brooklyn, New York **Current organization:** Midas Auto Service Experts **Title:** Owner **Type of organization:** Auto repair shop **Major product:** Auto mechanics/repair **Area of distribution:** Brooklyn, New York **Expertise:** Auto repair **Affiliations:** Motorist Assurance Program **Hob./spts.:** Baseball **SIC code:** 75 **Address:** Midas Auto Service Experts, 801 Fourth Ave., Brooklyn, NY 11232 **E-mail:** lamazinc@aol.com **Web address:** www.midas.com

MCCABE, MAURICE
Industry: Television production **Univ./degree:** B.A., Communication, Art Institute of Pennsylvania, 2003 **Current organization:** Riptide Entertainment LLC **Title:** Executive Producer/Founder **Type of organization:** Television production **Major product:** Commercials/television shows **Area of distribution:** National **Expertise:** Client presentation, finance and business, staff management, directing, editing **SIC code:** 78 **Address:** Riptide Entertainment LLC, 317 Seaman Ave., Beachwood, NJ 08722 **E-mail:** reece@riptideentertainment.com

MCCURDY, PAMELA S.
Industry: Hospitality **Born:** April 10, 1954, Rome, New York **Univ./degree:** Ph.D., Hotel Management, University of Maryland, 1988 **Current organization:** Tours, Lodging & Conferences, Inc. **Title:** CEO **Type of organization:** Event and conference planning **Major product:** Meetings, events, conferences **Area of distribution:** National **Expertise:** Meeting planning for corporations; management **Affiliations:** Humanitarian Foundation, ISO 9000 Certified Company **Hob./spts.:** Reading, sewing, volunteer work **SIC code:** 73 **Address:** Tours, Lodging & Conferences, Inc., 5801 Allentown Rd., #302, Camp Springs, MD 20746 **E-mail:** pmccu95278@aol.com

MCDADE, HUGH
Industry: Pest control **Born:** July 29, 1942, Scotland **Univ./degree:** A.S., Business, Suffolk County Community College, 1978 **Current organization:** Bugfree Inc. DBA A-Vanish Pest Control **Title:** President **Type of organization:** Exterminator **Major product:** Pest control **Area of distribution:** Florida **Expertise:** Pest control, lawns, termites, fumigation **Affiliations:** B.B.B.; Florida Pest Management Association **Hob./spts.:** Golf, fishing **SIC code:** 73 **Address:** Bugfree Inc. DBA A-Vanish Pest Control, 12172 S.W. 131 Ave., Miami, FL 33186 **E-mail:** avanish@bellsouth.net **Web address:** www.avanishpestcontrol.com

MCFARLAND, GENE
Industry: Oil **Born:** March 20, 1970, Wichita, Kansas **Current organization:** Frank's Westates Services Inc. **Title:** President **Type of organization:** Contractor, leaser **Major product:** Oil field services and equipment rentals **Area of distribution:** Utah **Expertise:** Management, operations **Hob./spts.:** Fishing **SIC code:** 73 **Address:** Frank's Westates Services Inc., 1304 S. 1200 East, Vernal, UT 84078 **E-mail:** westates@ubtanet.com

MCFARLAND, MIKE
Industry: Hospitality **Born:** May 7, 1954, Dayton, Ohio **Univ./degree:** B.S., Hospitality, Purdue University, 1992 **Current organization:** Palm Island Resort **Title:** President **Type of organization:** Resort **Major product:** Full resort accommodations **Area of distribution:** Florida **Expertise:** Resort management **Affiliations:** Florida Hotel/Motel Association **Hob./spts.:** Golf **SIC code:** 70 **Address:** Palm Island Resort, 7092 Placida Rd., Cape Haze, FL 33946 **E-mail:** mmcfarland@palmisland.com

MEADATH, THOMAS W.
Industry: Business services **Univ./degree:** B.S., Natural Science, George Williams College, 1980 **Current organization:** Superior Online Solutions, Inc. **Title:** President **Type of organization:** Value added reseller **Major product:** Custom website design, secure hosting **Area of distribution:** Illinois **Expertise:** Personal training for website upkeep, setting up business networks **Affiliations:** I.W.M.A.; Chamber of Commerce; Small Business Development Committee **SIC code:** 73 **Address:** Superior Online Solutions, Inc., P.O. Box 3188, St. Charles, IL 60174-9096 **E-mail:** thomas@superioronlinesolutions.com **Web address:** www.superioronlinesolutions.com

MEDINA, NELSON
Industry: Automotive design **Born:** April 1, 1953 **Current organization:** N. Medina Co., Inc. **Title:** Owner **Type of organization:** Manufacturing **Major product:** Auto ornamentation **Area of distribution:** National **Expertise:** Pinstriping, artist, design **SIC code:** 75 **Address:** N. Medina Co., Inc., P.O. Box 715, Lake Grove, NY 11755 **E-mail:** medinart@aol.com

MEGARGLE, ROBERT J.
Industry: Food service & gaming **Born:** August 21, 1954, Grosse Pointe, Michigan **Univ./degree:** B.A., Wayne State University, Detroit, Michigan **Current organization:** Isle of Capri Casinos, Inc. **Title:** Senior Director of Food, Beverage & Hotel Operations **Type of organization:** Casino group **Major product:** Hospitality, entertainment **Area of distribution:** National **Expertise:** Operations management **Affiliations:** N.R.A.; M.R.A. **Hob./spts.:** Golf, fishing **SIC code:** 79 **Address:** Isle of Capri Casinos, Inc., 1641 Popps Ferry Rd., Suite B-1, Biloxi, MS 39532 **E-mail:** bob_megargle@islecorp.com

MELE, CRAIG R.
Industry: Security/electronic systems **Born:** April 23, 1976, New York **Univ./degree:** B.S., Psychology, State University of New York College at Oneonta, 1999 **Current organization:** All Action Communication **Title:** President **Type of organization:** Security service **Major product:** Security and entertainment systems **Area of distribution:** Long Island, New York **Expertise:** Electronic systems integration, customer relations **SIC code:** 73 **Address:** All Action Communication, 25 Horton Dr., Huntington Station, NY 11746 **E-mail:** getboris@aol.com

MENENDEZ, JOAQUIN
Industry: Hospitality **Born:** May 14, 1970, Spain **Univ./degree:** A.O.S., Food and Beverage Management, Latin American Culinary Institute; B.A., New England Culinary Institute; M.B.A., University of Phoenix **Current organization:** The Gold Miner's Daughter Lodge **Title:** Executive Chief **Type of organization:** Ski resort/lodge **Major product:** Lodging, resort services, food, retail, skiing **Area of distribution:** Alta, Utah **Expertise:** Food and beverages management **Hob./spts.:** Skiing, hiking, tennis **SIC code:** 70 **Address:** The Gold Miner's Daughter Lodge, P.O. Box 8055, Alta, UT 84092-8055 **E-mail:** 2jomzbela@msn.com

MESA, HECTOR A.
Industry: Maintenance **Born:** June 30, 1970, Bogotá, Colombia **Current organization:** Niagara Cleaning Services, Inc. **Title:** President **Type of organization:** Cleaning service **Major product:** Janitorial/floor specialist **Area of distribution:** Florida **Expertise:** Janitorial, maintenance, arenas **Hob./spts.:** Television, theatre **SIC code:** 73 **Address:** Niagara Cleaning Services Inc., 8181 N.W. 36th St., Suite 8A, Miami, FL 33166 **E-mail:** ncsdoral@bellsouth.net **Web address:** www.niagaracleaning.com

MEYER, TODD
Industry: Computer hardware/software **Born:** January 26, 1964, Iowa **Current organization:** TTI, Inc. **Title:** President **Type of organization:** Systems integration **Major product:** Consulting engineering **Area of distribution:** International **Expertise:** Systems engineering **SIC code:** 73 **Address:** TTI, Inc., 805 Buddy Holly Place, Clear Lake, IA 50428 **E-mail:** todd@ttiinc.net

MILELLI, GINO R.
Industry: Automotive **Current organization:** TRM Transmissions Inc. **Title:** Owner/Manager **Type of organization:** Repair center **Major product:** Repair/rebuilt auto transmissions **Area of distribution:** New Jersey **Expertise:** Hydraulics, transmissions **SIC code:** 75 **Address:** TRM Transmissions Inc., 3 Mount Kemble Ave., Morristown, NJ 07960

MILES-CHRISTY, MELISSA S.
Industry: Pharmaceutical/Healthcare **Born:** 1968 **Univ./degree:** M.L.T., J. Sargeant Reynolds Community College; B.S. Candidate, Healthcare Management, Bellevue University **Current organization:** Managed Health Care Associates, Inc. **Title:** Personal Account Representative/Medical Technologist **Type of organization:** Group purchasing organization **Major product:** Competitive contract purchasing services to LTC, Home Health/Home Infusion and alternate site facilities on everything from pharmaceuticals and medical supplies to capital equipment and food; provides a variety of services to pharmaceutical manufacturers including contract administration, marketing and continuing education **Area of distribution:** National **Expertise:** Account management, research, technical support, customer service, laboratory testing **Honors/awards:** Appointed to Congressman Eric Cantor's Advisory Council, 2004 **Affiliations:** American Society of Clinical Pathologists **Hob./spts.:** Community and political involvement, sports **SIC code:** 73 **Address:** Managed Health Care Associates, Inc., PO Box 4775, Midlothian, VA 23112 **E-mail:** critterville95@comcast.net

MILLER, HAROLD "BUD" K.
Industry: Entertainment **Born:** June 7, 1926, Healdsburg, California **Current organization:** Creative Artists Center **Title:** President **Type of organization:** Entertainment, non-profit **Major product:** New artists **Area of distribution:** Weed, California **Expertise:** Booking and assisting new artists **Hob./spts.:** Music **SIC code:** 79 **Address:** Creative Artists Center, 3510 Eddy Creek Rd., P.O. Box 460, Weed, CA 96094 **E-mail:** bdmiller@jps.net

MILLER, LAURA A.
Industry: Mystery shopping **Univ./degree:** B.A., McDaniel College, 1990 **Current organization:** Satisfaction Services **Title:** Managing Partner **Major product:** Online, telephone, in person audits **Area of distribution:** National **Expertise:** Hospitality, restaurant, tourism, business services **Affiliations:** National Restaurant Association; Greater Fort Lauderdale Hospitality Association **SIC code:** 73 **Address:** Satisfaction Services, 19015 Highstream Dr., Germantown, MD 20874 **E-mail:** lmiller@satisfactionservicesinc.com

MILLER, ROBERT A.
Industry: Hospitality/food service **Born:** March 23, 1956, Aberdeen, Washington **Current organization:** Oyster Bay Inn **Title:** Chef **Type of organization:** Inn **Major product:** Food, beverage, lodging **Area of distribution:** Bremerton, Washington **Expertise:** Culinology **Affiliations:** Gourmet Dining Society of North America **Hob./spts.:** The outdoors **SIC code:** 70 **Address:** Oyster Bay Inn, 4412 Kitsap Way, Bremerton, WA 98312

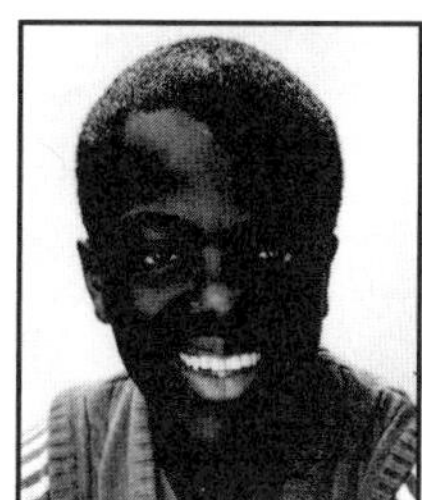

MILLER, SELWYN EMERSON
Industry: Entertainment **Born:** January 5, 1960, Berkeley, California **Current organization:** Selwyn Emerson Miller, Professional Actor **Title:** Actor **Type of organization:** Entertainment **Major product:** Television: Blink 182 Dancer, "MTV Music Video Awards", Radio City Music Hall; Bodyguard, "Dennis Rodham TV.com Launch Party", Live Television; Prince Selwyn, "Rollerjam", TNN; Twenty, "Comic View", BET; Chris, "The Imitation of Chris", A&E Network; Ewok," Ewoks: The Battle for Endor", Cable-TV; Motion Pictures: Hot Traxx DJ, "Boogie Nights", New Line Cinema; Lawn Jockey, "Jekyll and Hyde-Together Again", Paramount; Music Videos: Leprechaun, Bloodhound Gang, MTV; Dancers' Assistant, Smashing Pumpkins, MTV; Waiter, Janet Jackson, MTV; Album Cover Model, Beatnik Beatch, MTV; Theatre: Nano, "Volpone", Berkeley Repertory; Bilbo Baggins, "The Hobbit", Albany Theatre; Touring: Bodyguard, Offspring-North American Tour, Columbia Records **Area of distribution:** National **Expertise:** Performer, artist, outstanding dancer, swimmer, wrestler, juggler **Honors/awards:** Biographee, 3rd edition, Marquis Who's Who in Entertainment; BRICK, Berkeley Repertory Theatre Courtyard (generated over 1/6 of a million dollars for Berkeley Repertory Theatre) **Affiliations:** Screen Actors Guild; Actors Equity Association; American Federation of TV and Radio Artists **Hob./spts.:** Swimming, tennis, football **SIC code:** 79 **Address:** 505 Coventry Rd., Kensington, CA 94707 **E-mail:** 18186365770@mycingular.com

MIRANDA JR., ARMINDO
Industry: Information technology **Born:** November 17, 1966, New York, New York **Univ./degree:** A.A., Applied Computer Science, Westchester Business Institute, 2001 **Current organization:** Vestals, Inc. **Title:** Information Technologist **Type of**

SERVICES

organization: Publishing **Major product:** Web site services **Area of distribution:** New York **Expertise:** Management of information system, information technology **Honors/awards:** Regents Scholarship, Math & Science, Lavelle School **SIC code:** 73 **Address:** Vestals, Inc., 18 E. 41st St., Second floor, New York, NY 10017 **E-mail:** novastrm@concentrice.net

MITCHELL, KEVIN E.
Industry: Hospitality **Born:** June 11, 1970, Rahway, New Jersey **Univ./degree:** A.O.S., Culinary Arts; B.B.S., Culinary Arts Management, Culinary Institute of America **Current organization:** Westin Detroit Metropolitan Hotel, Dema Restaurant **Title:** Chef de Cuisine/Executive Sous Chef **Type of organization:** Hotel/restaurant **Major product:** Asian restaurant, room service, banquets **Area of distribution:** International **Expertise:** Menu development, contemporary Southern cuisine **Hob./spts.:** Spectator sports, reading, writing **SIC code:** 70 **Address:** Westin Detroit Metropolitan Hotel, Dema Restaurant, 2501 Worldgateway Place, Detroit, MI 48242 **E-mail:** kevin.mitchell@westin.com

MITTENDORF, JANET
Industry: Skin care **Born:** April 23, 1933, Chicago, Illinois **Univ./degree:** Skin Care Diploma, Westminster Community College, 1980 **Current organization:** Janet Mittendorf's Skin Care Plus, Inc. **Title:** CEO & President **Type of organization:** Salon and spa **Major product:** Skin care **Area of distribution:** Florida **Expertise:** Certified Paramedical Esthetician; skin care consulting, speaking, radio interviews, seminars **Honors/awards:** Nominated Woman of the Year, St. Petersburg Chamber of Commerce, 2003 **Published works:** Numerous articles on skin care and hair **Affiliations:** Past President, Toastmasters; Allied Medical Health St. Petersburg Chamber of Commerce **Hob./spts.:** Golf, swimming, cruises, travel **SIC code:** 72 **Address:** 8850 Fourth St. North, St. Petersburg, FL 33702 **E-mail:** janetm@verizon.net **Web address:** www.janetmittendorf.com

MOOSIC, MARK M.
Industry: Hospitality/lodging **Born:** December 21, 1959, Harrisburg, Pennsylvania **Current organization:** Memphis Marriot East/Interstate Hotels **Title:** General Manager **Type of organization:** Hotel **Major product:** Lodging/food and beverage **Area of distribution:** International **Expertise:** Hospitality, asset management, food and beverage **Affiliations:** Memphis Chamber of Commerce **Hob./spts.:** Paintball, skiing **SIC code:** 70 **Address:** Memphis Marriott East/Interstate Hotels, 2625 Thousand Oaks Blvd., Memphis, TN 38118 **E-mail:** mmoosic@aol.com

MORFORD, VIVIAN W.
Industry: Hospitality **Born:** June 27, 1943, Aronton, Ohio **Univ./degree:** Executive Secretarial Degree, Bliss Commercial College, 1964; Marshall University, currently enrolled **Current organization:** Radisson Hotel **Title:** Banquet and Catering Manager **Type of organization:** Hotel **Major product:** Food, beverage and lodging **Area of distribution:** West Virginia, Kentucky, Ohio **Expertise:** Sales, service **Honors/awards:** Employee of the Year, 1994; Best in the Tri-State, Bridal Consultant, 1997-2001 **Published works:** Poems **Affiliations:** Cabell County Medical Alliance; Volunteer, Cabell Huntington Hospital; United Way Loaned Executive; Judge, Lawrence County Election Board; First Church of Nazarene **Hob./spts.:** Hunting, fishing, swimming, raising/breeding dogs (Black Labrador Retrievers) **SIC code:** 70 **Address:** Radisson Hotel, 392 Township Rd., 1202, Chesapeake, OH 45619 **E-mail:** xpensv@aol.com

MOSLEHI, MEHRDAD M.
Industry: Semiconductors/on-line education **Born:** 1959, Tehran, Iran **Univ./degree:** M.S., Electrical Engineering, 1983; Ph.D., Electrical Engineering, 1986, Stanford University **Current organization:** SemiZone Inc. **Title:** Founder/Chairman/CEO **Type of organization:** Training/education **Major product:** Semiconductor education and training, largest array of online courses and programs for the semiconductor and related industries **Area of distribution:** International **Expertise:** Semiconductors and micro electronics **Published works:** 120+ issued patents; 100+ articles **Affiliations:** Senior Member, I.E.E.E.; S.P.I.E.; A.V.S.; American Physical Society; Electrochemical Society **Hob./spts.:** Family, travel, reading **SIC code:** 73 **Address:** SemiZone Inc., 236 Stanford Ave., #443, Palo Alto, CA 94306 **E-mail:** moslehi@semizone.com **Web address:** www.semizone.com

MUMPOWER, TOM M.
Industry: Hospitality **Current organization:** Sonnenalp Resort of Vail **Title:** Purchasing Assistant **Type of organization:** Hotel/resort **Major product:** Lodging, food and beverage **Area of distribution:** Vail, Colorado **Expertise:** Purchasing, problem solving **SIC code:** 70 **Address:** Sonnenalp Resort of Vail, 20 Vail Rd., Vail, CO 81657 **E-mail:** tmumpower@sonnenalp.com

MUNJAL, GOBIND P.
Industry: Hospitality/hotels **Born:** October 10, 1944, India **Univ./degree:** New York University; C.P.A., 1982 **Current organization:** TAJ Hotels, Resorts and Palaces **Title:** Sr. Vice President, Development and Finance **Type of organization:** A major hotel group **Major product:** Hotel operations and management **Area of distribution:** North America **Expertise:** Hotel development and finance **Honors/awards:** Certified Hotel Administrator **Affiliations:** Hospitality Finance and Technology Professionals; Asian American Hotel Owners Association **Hob./spts.:** Travel, reading, deal structuring and acquiring more knowledge **SIC code:** 70 **Address:** TAJ Hotels, Resorts and Palaces, International Division Executive Offices, 13-34 139th St., Flushing, NY 11357 **E-mail:** gpmunjal@aol.com

MUNNEKE, LLOYD
Industry: Environmental **Born:** August 3, 1939, Geddes, South Dakota **Univ./degree:** B.A., English, History, Augustana College, 1964; M.A., Workshop Administration, University of Wisconsin at Madison, 1967 **Current organization:** Professional House Doctors/P&K Extermination **Title:** Owner **Type of organization:** Air quality and extermination service company **Major product:** Radon gas removal, termite removal **Area of distribution:** Iowa **Expertise:** Air quality mitigation, community involvement **Published works:** 1 chapter in "The Guardianships of Handicapped People" **Affiliations:** Board of Industry, South Dakota State Penitentiary; Rock Valley Chamber of Commerce; Title XX Advisory Committee, State of Iowa; Title XIX Advisory Committee, State of Iowa; Vocational Advisory Committee, Governor's Appointment, Sate of Iowa; Past President, Iowa Association of Rehabilitation Facilities **Hob./spts.:** Woodworking, oil painting **SIC code:** 73 **Address:** Professional House Doctors/P&K Extermination, 910 Greenway Dr., Rock Valley, IA 51247

MURPHY, NICHOLAS E.
Industry: Software **Born:** November 30, 1967, Seattle, Washington **Univ./degree:** B.A., Theatre Arts, Gonzaga University; Certified M.C.S.E., Knowledge Alliance School, 1999 **Current organization:** Tritech Software Systems **Title:** System Integration Engineer **Type of organization:** Software development **Major product:** 911 software, dispatch software **Area of distribution:** International **Expertise:** Systems integration engineering, installation **Hob./spts.:** Mountain biking, hiking **SIC code:** 73 **Address:** Tritech Software Systems, 9860 Mesa Rim Rd., San Diego, CA 92121 **E-mail:** nicholas.murphy@tritech.com

MURRAY, ANTHONY
Industry: Food and nutrition services **Born:** October 31, 1963, Queens, New York **Univ./degree:** A.S., Computer Programming, Staten Island Community College, New York, 1985; B.B.A. Candidate, Avery University **Current organization:** Morrison Management Specialists (National Rehabilitation Hospital) **Title:** Food and Nutrition Services Director **Type of organization:** Service **Major product:** Providing food, nutrition and dining services to healthcare industry **Area of distribution:** International **Expertise:** Nutritional and culinary services **Honors/awards:** Served in Active Duty, U.S. Navy, 1968-2002; U.S. Navy Reserves, 2002-03 **Hob./spts.:** Karate, jiu-jitsu (black belt), handball, golf **SIC code:** 73 **Address:** Morrison Management Specialists (National Rehabilitation Hospital), Attn: Food Services, 102 Irving St. N.W., Washington, DC 20010 **E-mail:** anthony.murray@medstar.net

NAGLE, GLORIA J.
Industry: Fundraising **Born:** August 4, 1923, Brooklyn, New York **Univ./degree:** New York University **Current organization:** Na'Amat, USA L.A. Council **Title:** President **Major product:** Fundraising **Area of distribution:** International **Expertise:** Management **Affiliations:** The Jewish Labor Committee; Ameinu, Institute of Jewish Education **Hob./spts.:** Sports **SIC code:** 73 **Address:** Na'Amat, USA L.A. Council, 8339 W. Third St., Los Angeles, CA 90048

NAKAMOTO, GARY
Industry: Information technology **Born:** March 14, 1964, Sacramento, California **Univ./degree:** B.S., Ohio University, 1988 **Current organization:** Base Technologies, Inc. **Title:** CEO **Type of organization:** Technology **Major product:** Information technology services, integration, programming, solutions **Area of distribution:** International **Expertise:** Business development, marketing, business operations **Affiliations:** Board Member, Northern Virginia Technology Council; CEO, RoundTable **Hob./spts.:** History, politics, the outdoors **SIC code:** 73 **Address:** Base Technologies, Inc., 1749 Old Meadow Rd., Suite 500, McLean, VA 22102 **E-mail:** gnakamoto@basetech.com

NASH, JIM
Industry: Surveying **Born:** January 21, 1960, Bristol, United Kingdom **Univ./degree:** B.S.E.E., University of the West of England, United Kingdom, 1980 **Current organization:** In Depth Surveys, Inc. **Title:** President **Type of organization:** Surveying services **Major product:** Hydrographic surveys **Area of distribution:** International **Expertise:** Oil exploration **Affiliations:** S.E.G.; Hydrographic Society of America, Houston Chapter **SIC code:** 73 **Address:** In Depth Surveys, Inc., 3776 Green Briar Dr., Stafford, TX 77477 **E-mail:** jnash@indepth-surveys.com **Web address:** www.indepth-surveys.com

NEES, MARK H.
Industry: Security **Univ./degree:** Microsoft Certification, University of Texas **Current organization:** TotalCom Management Inc. **Title:** Security Manager **Type of organization:** Property Protection **Major product:** Fire, security, CCTV, access control **Area of**

distribution: Texas **Expertise:** Business security **Affiliations:** N.F.P.A.; South Texas Alarm Association; National Burglar and Fire Alarm Association **Hob./spts.:** Hunting **SIC code:** 73 **Address:** TotalCom Management Inc., 12018 Warfield St., San Antonio, TX 78216 **E-mail:** mark@totalcom-inc.com

NEEVES, PHILLIP W.
Industry: Business services **Univ./degree:** B.A., Business Administration-CPM Designation **Current organization:** Energy Billing Systems **Title:** Executive V.P. **Type of organization:** Billing services **Major product:** Energy billing for multi-family housing **Area of distribution:** National **Expertise:** Marketing, engineering **Published works:** Articles in Multi-Family News and executive trade journals **Affiliations:** Member, Board of Directors, N.S.U.A.A. **Hob./spts.:** Family, golf **SIC code:** 73 **Address:** Energy Billing Systems, 2150 Lelaray St., Colorado Springs, CO 80909-2808 **E-mail:** neeves@ebssystems.com

NEUBERT, BOBBIE J.
Industry: Information technology/3D computer modeling **Born:** December 17, 1952, Houston, Texas **Univ./degree:** B.S., Industrial Engineering, Purdue University, 1975 **Current organization:** Real Earth Models **Title:** Founder/CEO **Type of organization:** Consulting/manufacturing **Major product:** "3D" photo realistic models for oil companies, insurance companies and attorneys **Area of distribution:** International **Expertise:** Finance, accounting, oil exploration, computer modeling **Hob./spts.:** Scuba diving, rocketry, pyrotechnics **SIC code:** 73 **Address:** Real Earth Models, 4100 McEwen Rd., Suite 240, Dallas, TX 75244-5184 **E-mail:** bobbien@realearthmodels.com

NICKLE, NANCY A.
Industry: Entertainment **Born:** December 27, 1950, Long Beach, California **Univ./degree:** Business Administration, Sacramento City College, California **Current organization:** Catz Go Round Records, LLC **Title:** President/CEO **Type of organization:** Indie Record Label **Major product:** Music/CD's/Music artists **Area of distribution:** International **Expertise:** Independent artists, P&L, contracts, marketing **Affiliations:** N.A.R.M.; Homeward Bound Golden Retriever Rescue **Hob./spts.:** Gardening **SIC code:** 79 **Address:** Catz Go Round Records, LLC, 1730 Baines Ave., Sacramento, CA 95835

OAKES JR., LEONARD
Industry: Gaming/hospitality **Born:** August 8, 1966, Cortland, New York **Current organization:** Mohawk Bingo Palace Class II Casino **Title:** General Manager **Type of organization:** Tribally owned and operated gaming facility **Major product:** Gaming machines and Bingo **Area of distribution:** Akwesasne, New York **Expertise:** Management, daily operations, compliance, guest service; 13+ years in the gaming industry both Class III as well as Class II; Held Directorships on Table Games, Food & Beverage and Compliance departments at Akwesasne Mohawk Casino **Affiliations:** Morrisville Community College; Devry Institute of Technology, Toronto, Ontario; Board President Akwesasne Boys & Girls Club of America; Independent Distributor for Reliv Inc. (Master Affiliate level) **SIC code:** 79 **Address:** Mohawk Bingo Palace Class II Casino, 202 State Rt. 37, Akwesasne, NY 13655 **E-mail:** loakes@mohawkpalace.com

ODEN, ERIC JAMES
Industry: Hospitality, food/video productions, voice over **Univ./degree:** B.A., Columbia University, 1996; Graduate, Cooking and Hospitality Institute of Chicago, 2000 **Current organization:** Fairmont Hotel (Garde Manger)/Banquet Chef **Title:** Chef/Ethnic Cooking Consultant **Type of organization:** Hotel/independent vendor **Major product:** Cultural cuisine **Area of distribution:** Illinois **Expertise:** Ethnic cuisine; Certified in Professional Baking and Cooking, 1999 and 2000; Certified Sanitation License **Affiliations:** American Culinary Federation; Society of Motion Pictures and TV Engineers, 1991; Cooking Hospitality Institute of Chicago; National Geographic Society (since 1988) **Hob./spts.:** Video production, charity work with blind and deaf organizations, literary collector (comics) **SIC code:** 70 **Address:** Cultural Expressions, 10848 S. Parnell St., Chicago, IL 60628

OHLENBUSCH, BRIAN L.
Industry: Cranes **Born:** April 14, 1962, Escondido, California **Current organization:** Alamo Crane Service **Title:** Crane Operator **Type of organization:** Service-field work **Major product:** Crane rental service **Area of distribution:** Regional **Expertise:** Sales, certified crane operator **Hob./spts.:** Hunting, family **SIC code:** 75 **Address:** Alamo Crane Service, 346 Paisano St., New Braunfels, TX 78130 **E-mail:** bomo346@aol.com

OPP, WREATH MARIE
Industry: Hospitality **Univ./degree:** Business, North State Business College **Current organization:** La Quinta/American Canyon Hotel Investors **Title:** Corporate Regional Manager **Type of organization:** Hotel **Major product:** Hotel accommodations **Area of distribution:** California **Expertise:** Marketing, sales, management **SIC code:** 70 **Address:** La Quinta/American Canyon Hotel Investors, 8465 Enterprise Way, Oakland, CA 94621 **E-mail:** napavalley1hotel@sbcglobal.net

OSEGUERA, RAMIRO LOPEZ
Industry: Telecommunications **Born:** May 27, 1963, Michoacán, Mexico **Univ./degree:** Licenciado en Administracion Area Computacion, Business Administration, Iteso University; B.S., Telecommunications, Roosevelt University, 1999 **Current organization:** AT&T **Title:** Deployment Manager **Type of organization:** Technology **Major product:** Computer technology and telephony **Area of distribution:** National **Expertise:** Computer telecommunications **Hob./spts.:** Electronic projects, movies **SIC code:** 73 **Address:** AT&T, 3816 Morton Ave., Brookfield, IL 60513-1527 **E-mail:** paxacu@prodigy.net

PABON, ANGEL L.
Industry: Internet search advertising **Born:** March 29, 1973, Brooklyn, New York **Current organization:** Adorigin Corp. **Title:** CEO **Type of organization:** Internet advertising **Major product:** Keyword listing, pay-per-click; advertising **Area of distribution:** International **Expertise:** Marketing, sales, biz development **Hob./spts.:** Radio control cars, football, baseball **SIC code:** 73 **Address:** Adorigin Corp., 4223 First Ave., 4th floor, New York, NY 11232

PACE SR., JERRY L.
Industry: Repair services **Born:** August 2, 1952, Danville, Virginia **Univ./degree:** Refrigeration Technology Degree, Barton Community College, 1997 **Current organization:** Robersonville Refrigeration Co. **Title:** Owner **Type of organization:** Service and repair **Major product:** Refrigeration repair service (commercial and industrial) **Area of distribution:** North Carolina **Affiliations:** I.I.A.R. **SIC code:** 76 **Address:** Robersonville Refrigeration Co., 804 Academy St., Robersonville, NC 27871

PALOMINO, ANGELA J.
Industry: Hospitality **Born:** April 7, 1947, Kingston, Jamaica **Univ./degree:** St. Andrews University, London, 1964 **Current organization:** Mainstay Suites **Title:** General Manager **Type of organization:** Hotel **Major product:** Hotel accommodations **Area of distribution:** South Carolina **Expertise:** Operations, troubleshooting, many hospitality related courses **Honors/awards:** Senior Cambridge Certificate **Hob./spts.:** Tennis (former competitive player), playing cards, crossword puzzles **SIC code:** 70 **Address:** Mainstay Suites, 2671 Dry Pocket Rd., Greer, SC 29650-4543 **E-mail:** a.palomino@concordhotels.com

PASQUALE, STEPHEN
Industry: Information Technology **Born:** June 1, 1957, Jersey City, New Jersey **Univ./degree:** A.A., Jersey City State University, 1977 **Current organization:** IBM **Title:** Senior Delivery Executive **Type of organization:** Software & applications development **Major product:** Consulting services, application development **Area of distribution:** International **Expertise:** Information technology, sales and service **Affiliations:** P.M.I. **Hob./spts.:** Fishing, photography, outdoor activities, hiking **SIC code:** 73 **Address:** IBM, 203 Boiling Springs Ave., East Rutherford, NJ 07073

PATEL, BHAILAL (BOB) L.
Industry: Hospitality **Born:** July 2, 1947, Virol, India **Univ./degree:** M.S., Biochemistry, University of Scranton, Pennsylvania **Current organization:** New Falls Motel **Title:** President **Type of organization:** Motel **Major product:** Lodging **Area of distribution:** Pennsylvania **Expertise:** Management, development **Hob./spts.:** Travel, cricket, swimming **SIC code:** 70 **Address:** New Falls Motel, 201 Lincoln Hwy., Fairless Hills, PA 19030

PATEL, SHASHIKANT G.
Industry: Hospitality **Born:** January 4, 1947, Africa **Univ./degree:** M.B.A., Lincoln Law School, 1974 **Current organization:** Clarion Hotel **Title:** Owner **Type of organization:** Hotel **Major product:** Guest accommodations and services **Area of distribution:** Monterey, California **Expertise:** Real estate investments, operations management **Affiliations:** American Hotel & Lodging Association; Monterey Chamber of Commerce; Better Business Bureau **Hob./spts.:** Sports **SIC code:** 70 **Address:** Clarion Hotel, 1036 Munras Ave., Monterey, CA 93940 **E-mail:** info@clarionhotel-monterey.com **Web address:** www.clarionhotelmonterey.com

PATRICK, GAIL A.
Industry: Photography **Born:** September 23, 1965, Dixon, Tennessee **Univ./degree:** A.A., Candidate, Nashville State Community College **Current organization:** Gail A. Patrick, Photographer **Title:** Photographer **Type of organization:** Photography studio **Major product:** Portraits, animals, weddings, landscape **Area of distribution:** International **Affiliations:** N.A.P.P.; Phi Beta Kappa; International Photographers Association **Hob./spts.:** Reading, riding horseback, movies **SIC code:** 72 **Address:** Gail A. Patrick, Photographer, 104 Guy Barnett Dr., Waverly, TN 37185 **E-mail:** gailptrck@aol.com

PATTERSON, NENA R.
Industry: Business services **Born:** November 22, 1960, Chicago, Illinois **Current organization:** Independent Contractors & Resources **Title:** President **Type of organization:** Staffing agency **Major product:** Real estate, healthcare, investments **Area of distribution:** Illinois **Expertise:** Nurse staffing, marketing and healthcare;

SERVICES

Radiographer **Hob./spts.:** Travel, real estate, interior design **SIC code:** 73 **Address:** Independent Contractors & Resources, 980 N. Michigan Ave., Suite 1400, Chicago, IL 60610 **E-mail:** nicrjobs@aol.com

PAULRAJ, NAOMI C.
Industry: Hospitality **Univ./degree:** B.S., Business Management, University of Maryland, 1987 **Current organization:** Marriott International **Title:** Director **Type of organization:** Hotel **Major product:** Lodging, food and beverage **Area of distribution:** International **Expertise:** Business management **Affiliations:** National Association of Women in Hospitality; International Association of Hotel Administrators **Hob./spts.:** Dining, travel, the arts, theatre **SIC code:** 70 **Address:** Marriott International, 1 Marriott Dr., Washington, DC 20058 **E-mail:** naomi.paulraj@marriott.com

PEDRO, JAMES M.
Industry: Hospitality **Born:** June 1, 1962, Pendleton, Oregon **Univ./degree:** Hotel & Restaurant Management Program, San Francisco City College **Current organization:** Fairmont Hotel **Title:** Executive Chef **Type of organization:** Hotel/restaurant **Major product:** Lodging, food and beverage **Area of distribution:** San Francisco, California **Expertise:** International cuisine **Affiliations:** National Chef Board, American Chef Institute **Hob./spts.:** Billiards, snow and waterskiing, swimming, computers **SIC code:** 70 **Address:** Fairmont Hotel, 950 Mason St., San Francisco, CA 94108 **E-mail:** james.pedro@fairmont.com **Web address:** www.fairmont.com

PEÑA, DALIA
Industry: Hospitality **Born:** Corpus Christi, Texas **Current organization:** Boardwalk Inn - Kemah **Title:** General Manager **Type of organization:** Hotel, restaurant **Major product:** Lodging, food and beverages **Area of distribution:** Kemah, Texas **Expertise:** Management, providing quality service **Affiliations:** American Hotel & Lodging Association **Hob./spts.:** Golf **SIC code:** 70 **Address:** Boardwalk Inn - Kemah, #8 Waterfront, Kemah, TX 77565 **E-mail:** daliap1611@yahoo.com

PEÑA, JUAN JOSÉ
Industry: Interpretation and translation **Born:** December 13, 1945, Hagerman, New Mexico **Univ./degree:** B.A., 1968; M.A., Spanish Literature and History, 1972; Ph.D., Spanish Literature and History, 1981, New Mexico Highlands University **Current organization:** Peña's Certified Interpreting & Translation Services **Title:** Certified Court Interpreter **Type of organization:** Interpretation and translation service **Major product:** Legal, technical and professional translation, literary **Area of distribution:** International **Expertise:** Legal, technical and professional interpreting and translating terminology **Honors/awards:** Numerous including, City of Albuquerque Human Rights Board Human Rights Award; International Who's Who of Contemporary Achievement, 3rd Edition, American Biographical Institute; Profile of Courage Award, Vietnam Veterans of America, NM State Council; Men of Achievement, 16th Edition, 15th Edition; International Biographical Centre, England; Marquis Who's Who in the World, Who's Who in America, Who's Who in the West, Who's Who in American Politics; Numerous awards, U.S. Army, 1969-70 **Published works:** Many articles, poetry, artwork; short stories-"Los Bandidos" 1986, "El Tesoro de Juan Bernal" 1986, "La Catina" 1987, "El Martirio de Sóstenes Archibeque 1992; works in progress-"Memorias de mi Barrio" autobiography, "Hombres de Piedra" historical novel, "Memorias de Vietnam", "The Chicano Movement in New Mexico" **Affiliations:** Numerous including, National Association for Judiciary Interpreters; New Mexico Translators and Interpreters Association; Executive Board, New Mexico Land Grant Forum; 2001 New Mexico Dept. of Education Textbook Review Commission; 35th Infantry Brigade Association; 2001 Barelas Community Development Corporation Representative to the Historic Neighborhoods Alliance; Board of Directors, Explora Children's Museum; National Secretary, American GI Forum of the U.S. **Hob./spts.:** Civil rights activist, civil rights issues, swimming, camping, hiking, travel **SIC code:** 73 **Address:** Pena's Certified Interpreting and Translation Service, 1115 9th Street S.W., Albuquerque, NM 87102-4027 **Phone:** (505)242-8085 **Fax:** (505)764-8527 **E-mail:** jpena.71@comcast.net

PETERSON, RONNIE
Industry: Business services/printing **Born:** April 25, 1965, Nissequoque, New York **Univ./degree:** Attended Wilson Tech for Lithography **Current organization:** The Print Network **Title:** Sales Manager **Type of organization:** Printer **Major product:** Commercial printing **Area of distribution:** National **Expertise:** Production printing **Affiliations:** Torrance Chamber of Commerce; South Bay Police & Fire Committee **Hob./spts.:** Golf, waterspouts **SIC code:** 73 **Address:** The Print Network, 3621 Torrance Blvd., Torrance, CA 90503 **E-mail:** ronniep@theprintnetwork.com **Web address:** www.theprintnetwork.com

PETTIT, RICHARD K.
Industry: Business services **Born:** September 3, 1953, Columbia, South Carolina **Univ./degree:** B.A., Liberal Arts, University of South Carolina, 1974 **Current organization:** Multi-Media Services, Inc. **Title:** Project Manager & Coordinator **Type of organization:** Reseller **Major product:** Corporate-educational audio visual **Area of distribution:** South Carolina **Expertise:** Management, coordination **Hob./spts.:** Boating, waterskiing, wake boarding **SIC code:** 73 **Address:** Multi-Media Services, Inc., 1029 Thousand Oaks Blvd., Greenville, SC 29607 **E-mail:** richardp@mmsav.com

PHILLIPS, MICHAEL J.
Industry: Hospitality **Born:** December 23, 1955, Inglewood, California **Current organization:** Inn at Otter Crest **Title:** General Manager **Type of organization:** Resort/management company **Major product:** Food, beverage, lodging, entertainment **Area of distribution:** Otter Rock, Oregon **Expertise:** Resort management/consulting; Licensed in Real Estate, Utah **Affiliations:** President, Central Oregon Coast Association **Hob./spts.:** Flying, golf, water sports, reading, travel **SIC code:** 70 **Address:** Inn at Otter Crest, 301 Otter Crest Loop, Otter Rock, OR 97369 **E-mail:** mphillips@innatottercrest.com **Web address:** www.condominiumresortmanagement.com

PIASECKI, BRIAN L.
Industry: Entertainment **Born:** December 13, 1970, Toledo, Ohio **Current organization:** Walt Disney World **Title:** Chef **Type of organization:** Amusement park **Major product:** Entertainment/hospitality **Area of distribution:** Lake Buena Vista, Florida **Expertise:** Culinary arts, Certified from A.C.F. at Walt Disney World, 1994 **Honors/awards:** Partners in Excellence Award, Walt Disney World, 1997 **Affiliations:** A.C.F.; N.R.A.; Wine Educators Society **Hob./spts.:** Reading **SIC code:** 79 **Address:** Walt Disney World, 1610 North Ave. of the Stars, Lake Buena Vista, FL 32830 **E-mail:** brian.piasecki@disney.com

PONAMAN, ALBERT L.
Industry: Executive search consultants **Born:** May 16, 1931, Brooklyn, New York **Current organization:** Al Ponaman Co. **Title:** Owner/Manager **Type of organization:** Executive search firm for the banking industry **Major product:** Placement of officer level banking professionals **Area of distribution:** California **Expertise:** Management, operations, recruiting **Affiliations:** Former Charter Member, M.A.E.R.; Member, California Staffing Professionals **SIC code:** 73 **Address:** Al Ponaman Co., 10041-5 Larwin Ave., Chatsworth, CA 91311-7406 **E-mail:** info@banking-careers.com

PORTILLO MAZAL, DIEGO
Industry: Economics **Born:** January 22, 1974, Buenos Aires, Argentina **Univ./degree:** B.S., International Economics, Finance **Current organization:** DRI-WEFA **Title:** Senior Analyst **Area of distribution:** International **Expertise:** Economist **Hob./spts.:** Reading, travel **SIC code:** 73 **Address:** DRI-WEFA, 24 Hartwell Ave., Lexington, MA 02421 **E-mail:** diegoportillo@dri-wefa.com

POSTLE, BRIAN L.
Industry: Hospitality **Born:** January 14, 1968, Mobile, Alabama **Univ./degree:** B.S., Sales and Marketing, University of South Alabama, 1991 **Current organization:** Marriott Frenchman's Reef & Morning Star Beach Resort **Title:** Director of Sales **Type of organization:** Resort and hotel **Major product:** Hotel accommodations **Area of distribution:** National **Expertise:** Sales and marketing, administration, training **Affiliations:** Board Member, The Ad Club; St. Thomas Chamber of Commerce **SIC code:** 70 **Address:** Marriott Frenchman's Reef & Morning Star Beach Resort, P.O. Box 7100, #5 Est. Bakkeroe, St. Thomas, VI 00801 **E-mail:** brian.postle@marriotthotels.com **Web address:** www.marriottfrenchmansreef.com

PRATHER, BEVERLY L.
Industry: Hospitality **Born:** December 27, San Bernardino, California **Univ./degree:** Real Estate Principles, San Bernardino Valley College **Current organization:** Sam's Town Hotel & Gambling Hall **Title:** Sales Manager **Type of organization:** Hotel/casino **Major product:** Lodging, food and beverage/gaming **Area of distribution:** National **Expertise:** Sales, marketing **Honors/awards:** State of Nevada Tourism Development Award; Las Vegas Chamber of Commerce Customer Service Excellence Award **Affiliations:** President, Boulder Strip Association; Las Vegas Territory; Hospitality Sales and Marketing Association International **Hob./spts.:** Fishing, the outdoors **SIC code:** 70 **Address:** Sam's Town Hotel & Gambling Hall, 5111 Boulder Hwy., Las Vegas, NV 89122 **E-mail:** beverlyprather@boydgaming.com **Web address:** www.samstownlv.com

PRATT, ANDY N.
Industry: Engineering **Born:** January 31, 1941, Dallas ,Texas **Current organization:** Unique Digital, Inc. **Title:** Founder/President/Owner **Type of organization:** Integrator **Major product:** Computing infrastructure **Area of distribution:** International **Expertise:** Engineering **Affiliations:** S.E.G. **Hob./spts.:** Work **SIC code:** 73 **Address:** Unique Digital, Inc., 10595 Westoffice Dr., Houston, TX 77042 **E-mail:** apratt@uniquedigital.com

PRINS, RONALD J.
Industry: Transportation **Born:** May 26, 1968, Worthington, Minnesota **Univ./degree:** A.S., Diesel Mechanics, Alexandria Technical Institute, 1988 **Current organization:** Ron's Repair **Title:** Owner **Type of organization:** Repair shop **Major product:** Diesel repair, engines, transmissions **Area of distribution:** National **Expertise:** Over-the-road repairs, A.S.E. Certified; Certified by Dept. of Transportation, Minnesota **Affiliations:**

Chamber of Commerce **Hob./spts.:** Race car driving **SIC code:** 75 **Address:** Ron's Repair, 2385 Hwy. 60, Worthington, MN 56187 **E-mail:** ronsrepair@iw.net

PRUNES, LOUIS
Industry: Cleaning **Born:** November 17, 1953, Mexico City, Mexico **Current organization:** A-mazing Chem-Dry **Title:** President/Owner **Type of organization:** Cleaning franchise **Major product:** Carbonated cleaner **Area of distribution:** Houston, Texas **Expertise:** Carpet and upholstery cleaning **Affiliations:** I.I.C.R.C.; B.B.B. **Hob./spts.:** Golf, sports, Harley Davidson motorcycles **SIC code:** 72 **Address:** A-mazing Chem-Dry, 15255 Gulf Fwy., Suite 138-A, Houston, TX 77034 **E-mail:** amazingchemdry@sbcglobal.net **Web address:** www.amazingchemdry.com

PUERTO, AILEEN M.
Industry: Hospitality **Born:** May 17, 1968, New York, New York **Current organization:** Hyatt Dorado Beach Resort & Country Club **Title:** Convention & Catering Manager **Type of organization:** Hotel **Major product:** Food, beverages, lodging, catering **Area of distribution:** International **Expertise:** Hotel management, event planning **Hob./spts.:** Nature walks, the beach, reading **SIC code:** 70 **Address:** Hyatt Dorado Beach Resort & Country Club, Route 693, Dorado, PR 00646

PURYEAR, COLLEEN M.
Industry: Employment **Born:** February 4, 1964, Roseburg, Oregon **Current organization:** Cardinal Services, Inc. **Title:** Branch Manager/Director of Corporate Recruitment **Type of organization:** Employment service **Major product:** Human resources **Area of distribution:** Roseburg, Oregon **Expertise:** Human relations, policies and procedures, overseeing operations **Affiliations:** Chair of Membership Committee, Chamber of Commerce; Douglas Timber Operators; Community Chair, Community Regional Workforce **SIC code:** 73 **Address:** Cardinal Services, Inc., 250 N.E. Garden Valley Blvd., #17, Roseburg, OR 97470 **E-mail:** colleen@cardinal-services.com

RACELA, BEN P.
Industry: Business services/gaming **Born:** January 7, 1965, Agana, Guam **Univ./degree:** A.A., Heald College **Current organization:** The Gillmann Group **Title:** Vice President, Operations **Type of organization:** Developer/consulting **Major product:** Slot operations, poker, roulette, craps, black jack **Area of distribution:** Albuquerque, New Mexico **Expertise:** Management **Hob./spts.:** Reading, rollerblading, mountain biking **SIC code:** 73 **Address:** The Gillmann Group, 8110 Camino Del Venado N.W., Albuquerque, NM 87120 **E-mail:** ben@thegillmanngroup.com

RADKE, MICHAEL PATRICK
Industry: Parking facilities **Born:** April 17, 1971, St. Joseph, Michigan **Univ./degree:** A.A., General Studies, Holy Cross College, 1993 **Current organization:** AMPCO System Parking **Title:** Operation Manager **Type of organization:** Parking facility management **Major product:** Valet parking **Area of distribution:** National **Expertise:** Marketing, sales, management **Honors/awards:** All-Star Service Award, 2003 **Hob./spts.:** American Amateur Golf Tour **SIC code:** 73 **Address:** AMPCO System Parking, 1459 Hamilton Ave., Cleveland, OH 44114 **E-mail:** mradke@abm.com

RAHMAN, MOMEN M.
Industry: Hospitality **Univ./degree:** M.S., Physics, Bangladesh, 1989 M.A., Business Administration, Penn State University, 1991; M.S., Transportation Management, SUNY, 1996 **Current organization:** Star Motel **Title:** President/Owner **Type of organization:** Motel **Major product:** Guest accommodations **Area of distribution:** International **Expertise:** Business management, marketing, sales **Honors/awards:** Beautification Award, Cave City Council, 2005 **Affiliations:** Cave City Chamber of Commerce; Western Kentucky Salvation Army **Hob./spts.:** Fishing, gardening **SIC code:** 70 **Address:** Star Motel, 908 South Dixie Hwy., Cave City, KY 42127 **E-mail:** 1mmrahman@comcast.net

REEVES, JOHN E.
Industry: Hospitality **Born:** November 14, 1965, Mishawaka, Indiana **Univ./degree:** B.S., Business Administration, Georgia State University, 1992 **Current organization:** Ocean Properties **Title:** Food & Beverage Director **Type of organization:** Hotel **Major product:** Food, beverage, lodging **Area of distribution:** International **Expertise:** Food and beverage, events coordination **Hob./spts.:** Softball, baseball, scuba diving, coaching City League, 1994-96 **SIC code:** 70 **Address:** 2929 Fogarty Ave., Key West, FL 33040 **E-mail:** hiltonreeves@yahoo.com

REINACH, DEBORAH B.
Industry: Advertising/public relations **Born:** April 6, 1955, Shreveport, Louisiana **Current organization:** The Reinach Advertising Agency **Title:** Owner **Type of organization:** Advertising, press and public relations firm **Major product:** Project development, public relations, media planning and buying **Area of distribution:** Tennessee **Expertise:** Marketing, editing **Hob./spts.:** Running **SIC code:** 73 **Address:** The Reinach Advertising Agency, 1910 Madison Ave., #724, Memphis, TN 38104 **E-mail:** rreinac1@midsouth.rr.com

REINBOLD, GUY R.
Industry: Hospitality **Born:** November 8, 1956, Bryn Mawr, Pennsylvania **Univ./degree:** A.A., Occupational Services, Culinary Institute of America, 1976 **Current organization:** Baltimore Marriott Waterfront Hotel **Title:** Director, Food & Beverage **Type of organization:** Hotel **Major product:** Lodging, food and beverage **Area of distribution:** Maryland **Expertise:** Culinary department operations and coordination **Affiliations:** American Culinary Federation; Board Member, Maryland Hospitality Education Foundation **Hob./spts.:** Golf, gardening **SIC code:** 70 **Address:** 4759 Ilkley Moor Lane, Ellicott City, MD 21043 **E-mail:** greinbold56@yahoo.com

REIS, GLENN V.
Industry: Software technology **Born:** November 29, 1953, Weymouth, Massachusetts **Univ./degree:** B.A., Business Administration and Marketing, Marietta College, Ohio, 1977 **Current organization:** Engineous Software, Inc. **Title:** Vice President, Business Development **Type of organization:** Software development **Major product:** Engineering, design integration framework **Area of distribution:** International **Expertise:** Engineering **Affiliations:** S.A.E.; A.S.M.E. **Hob./spts.:** Golf, acoustic guitar, literature, reading **SIC code:** 73 **Address:** Engineous Software, Inc., 2000 Centre Green Way, Cary, NC 27513-5756 **E-mail:** reis@engineous.com **Web address:** www.engineous.com

RHOADES, CHRISTOPHER
Industry: Food **Born:** June 29, 1971, Tyrone, Pennsylvania **Univ./degree:** B.S., Hotel and Restaurant Institutional Management, Pennsylvania State University, 1996 **Current organization:** Sodexho Campus Services **Title:** Unit Manager **Type of organization:** Contract management **Major product:** Dining services **Area of distribution:** Plattsburgh, New York **Expertise:** Marketing **Hob./spts.:** Football, music, drawing **SIC code:** 73 **Address:** Sodexho Campus Services, Clinton Dining Hall, 101 Broad St., Plattsburgh, NY 12901 **E-mail:** cheetah12901@yahoo.com

RHODES, KRISTINE R.
Industry: Advertising/communications **Born:** May 19, 1965, St. Paul, Minnesota **Univ./degree:** B.A., Communications, Southern Methodist University **Current organization:** BSA Advertising **Title:** Vice President **Type of organization:** Advertising and interactive production **Major product:** Advertising/creative/interactive **Area of distribution:** International **Expertise:** Client service, management, director **Honors/awards:** Mother & Daughter listed in Who's Who **Affiliations:** D.H.R.; E.M.A. **Hob./spts.:** Reading, fishing, camping **SIC code:** 73 **Address:** 4624 Bretton Bay Lane, Dallas, TX 75287 **E-mail:** krhodes@bsa.com **Web address:** www.bsa.com

RICHARDS, LLOYD P.
Industry: Engineering **Born:** April 8, 1960, Radford, Virginia **Univ./degree:** B.S., Engineering Technology, Trinity University, 2003 **Current organization:** MCDean/CIM Automation Systems **Title:** Automation Controls Engineer **Type of organization:** System integrator **Major product:** High performance web handling systems, automation controls, Rockwell, Siemens, Square D **Area of distribution:** Virginia **Expertise:** Winders **Hob./spts.:** Hunting, fishing, camping **SIC code:** 73 **Address:** MCDean/CIM Automation Systems, 1731 Bishop Rd., Blacksburg, VA 24060 **E-mail:** llrichards@adelphia.net

RICHARDSON, EUGENE N.
Industry: Transportation **Born:** November 26, 1950, Wichita, Kansas **Current organization:** Arrow Wrecker Services, Inc. **Title:** President **Type of organization:** Towing company **Major product:** Vehicle towing and recovery **Area of distribution:** Kansas **Expertise:** Law enforcement vehicle impounds **Affiliations:** His church **Hob./spts.:** Fishing **SIC code:** 75 **Address:** 1610 Haskell St., Wichita, KS 67213 **E-mail:** gene@arrowtow.com **Web address:** www.arrowtow.com

RICHMOND, TIMOTHY A.
Industry: Hospitality **Born:** October 13, 1961, Sanford, North Carolina **Univ./degree:** Business Management, American Business & Fashion Institute **Current organization:** The John Randall House **Title:** Co-Owner **Type of organization:** Bed and breakfast **Major product:** Hospitality **Expertise:** Food, guest relations **Hob./spts.:** Sports, art, dancing, cooking **SIC code:** 70 **Address:** The John Randall House, 140 Bradford St., Unit 1, Provincetown, MA 02657 **E-mail:** johnrandallhouse@aol.com **Web address:** www.johnrandallhouse.com

RICKARDS, JIM
Industry: Hospitality **Univ./degree:** B.A., Business Administration/Management, Auburn University **Current organization:** Courtyard by Marriott **Title:** General Manager **Type of organization:** Hotel **Major product:** Hotel accommodations, food and beverage **Area of distribution:** Oklahoma **Expertise:** Management, operations **Affiliations:** Board of Directors, O.H.A.L.A. **Hob./spts.:** Family, golf, water sports, landscaping **SIC code:** 70 **Address:** Courtyard by Marriott, 2 W. Reno Ave., Oklahoma City, OK 73102 **E-mail:** jim.rickards@jqh.com

RICOTTA, ANTHONY G.
Industry: Entertainment **Born:** September 9, 1959, New York, New York **Univ./degree:** B.A., Wagner College, New York, 1981 **Current organization:** Cirque du Soleil at Bellagio **Title:** Operations Production Manager **Type of organization:** Entertainment company **Major product:** Live theatrical production **Area of distribution:** International **Expertise:** Technical supervision **Affiliations:** I.A.T.S.E. **Hob./spts.:** Golf, scuba diving, woodworking **SIC code:** 79 **Address:** Cirque du Soleil "O" at Bellagio, 3600 Las Vegas Blvd. South, Las Vegas, NV 89109 **E-mail:** tony.ricotta@cirquedusoleil.com **Web address:** www.cirquedusoleil.com

RIZZO, CHAD
Industry: Promotional products **Born:** November 3, 1975, Gowanda, New York **Current organization:** X-press Screen Printing & Embroidery, Inc. **Title:** President **Type of organization:** Printing, embroidery **Major product:** Wearables **Area of distribution:** National **Expertise:** Marketing, sales, management **Affiliations:** Rotary Club; Fredonia Chamber of Commerce **Hob./spts.:** Family, motorcycling, golf **SIC code:** 73 **Address:** X-press Screen Printing & Embroidery, Inc., 15 Water St., Fredonia, NY 14063 **E-mail:** crizzo@xpresspromosolutions.com **Web address:** www.xpresspromosolutions.com

ROANE, COURTNEY R.
Industry: Hospitality **Born:** July 30, 1964, Charlottesville, Virginia **Univ./degree:** B.A., Piedmont College **Current organization:** Wyndham Hotels **Title:** Director of Food and Beverage **Type of organization:** Hotel **Major product:** Hotel accommodations **Area of distribution:** Baltimore, Maryland **Expertise:** Food, beverage, culinary, guest services **Hob./spts.:** Golf, NASCAR **SIC code:** 70 **Address:** Wyndham Hotels, 101 W. Fayette St., Baltimore, MD 21201 **E-mail:** croane@wyndham.com

ROBBIO JR., ANTHONY J.
Industry: Security services **Born:** April 8, 1936, West Warwick, Rhode Island **Spouse:** Anne Murphy **Married:** July 21, 1963 **Children:** Karen, 32; Anthony III, 28; Kimberly, 25 **Univ./degree:** M.S.; Ph.D., Security Administration, Northwestern University, 1986; Professional Certificate in Law Enforcement & Criminal Justice, 1990 **Current organization:** AAA Enterprises, Inc., d/b/a AAA Security Task Force Inc. **Title:** President **Type of organization:** Protection services **Major product:** Armed and unarmed guards, installation of diversified alarm systems **Area of distribution:** New England **Expertise:** Protection of life and property, corporate management and operations; licensed Private Detective - State of Rhode Island **Honors/awards:** The John Edgar Hoover Memorial Gold Medal for Distinguished Public Service; The American Police Hall of Fame Commemorative Legion of Honor Medal; Listed: Who's Who in Rhode Island, 1990; Who's Who in American Law Enforcement - 6th edition; Who's Who International, 1994 **Published works:** Public speaking, teaching **Affiliations:** Cranston Community Action Program; Retired Chief Warrant Officer, U.S. Army Reserve; Community Organization for Drug Abuse Control; National Alarm Association of America ; The American Society for Industrial Security; National Association of Chiefs of Police; Reserve Officers Association of the United States; Training Officer, Providence Police Department; Constable with Power, Superior, District & Family Courts; National Association of Professional Process Servers; Rhode Island Security & Detective Association; R.I.R.A.; N.R.A.A.; Chairman of the Board, Better Business Bureau; National Committee for the Employer Support of the Guard & Reserve; Southern New England Security Alliance; The National Association of Private Security Industries; Special Agent, International Intelligence & Organized Crime Investigators Association **Hob./spts.:** Camping, stamp collecting **SIC code:** 73 **Address:** AAA Enterprises, Inc., dba AAA Security Task Force Inc., 117 Beacon St., P.O. Box 3579, Cranston, RI 02910 **E-mail:** arj117@aol.com

ROBERTS, ROBIN C.
Industry: Notary public **Born:** August 18, 1941, Norfolk, Virginia **Univ./degree:** B.S.E.E., 1980; M.S., Physics, 1991; Ph.D., Business Administration, 2003, Rochelle University **Current organization:** Allthings Notary **Title:** Certified Signing Agent **Type of organization:** Notary **Major product:** Document signing and notarization **Area of distribution:** San Francisco, California **Expertise:** Signing agent, entrepreneur **Honors/awards:** 100+ technical manuals, novels including "Backdrop.Net; Scenery & Props" **Affiliations:** National Notary Association; U.S. Navy, 1957-1966 **Hob./spts.:** Painting, writing, jogging, inventor, clothing designer, dog breeder **SIC code:** 73 **Address:** Allthings Notary, 2218-A Wyandotte St., Mountain View, CA 94043 **E-mail:** robin@allthingsnotary.com **Web address:** www.allthingsnotary.com

ROBINSON, KENNETH L.
Industry: Insurance **Born:** September 20, 1944, Carrollton, Georgia **Current organization:** Coastal Marketing **Title:** President **Type of organization:** Marketing **Major product:** Life and health insurance **Area of distribution:** Georgia, Mississippi and Alabama **Expertise:** Marketing and development **Honors/awards:** Master Manager Award, 1975-77; President's Advisory Council, 1985-87; President's Club, 1987; Listed in Who's Who in the South & S.E., 1991; President, National Security's All Star Conference, 2002 **Hob./spts.:** Sailing, golf **SIC code:** 73 **Address:** Coastal Marketing, 3364 W. Mildred St., Mobile, AL 36605 **E-mail:** coastalmktng@aol.com

ROCAMONTES, RICHARD R.
Industry: Elevators **Born:** January 12, 1963, San Antonio, Texas **Univ./degree:** B.S., Electrical Engineering, Old Dominion University **Current organization:** York United Soccer Club **Title:** Coach **Type of organization:** Soccer club **Major product:** Soccer skill training and education **Area of distribution:** York County, Pennsylvania **Expertise:** Coaching soccer **Honors/awards:** Expeditionary Medal, Lebanon Peacekeeping Crisis, U.S. Navy, 1983 **Affiliations:** West York Soccer Club; Manufacturing Engineering Manager, Schindler Elevator Corporation **Hob./spts.:** Golf **SIC code:** 79 **Address:** Schindler Elevator Corp., 1200 Biglerville Rd., Gettysburg, PA 17325 **E-mail:** coachrock1@aol.com **Web address:** www.schindler.com

ROCHE, KEVIN J.
Industry: Engineering management **Born:** August 16, 1957, Pocatello, Idaho **Current organization:** Engine Masters **Title:** Administrative Director **Type of organization:** Engineering management **Major product:** Cryptographic database infrastructures; GSA-FAR FCA coordination of public awareness services for the private sector **Area of distribution:** International **Expertise:** Policy preface services for secure government and private communications standards **Affiliations:** U.S. Geological Survey; IBM WebSphere World Partners **Hob./spts.:** Drag racing, rebuilding engines **SIC code:** 73 **Address:** 364 Upland Blvd., Las Vegas, NV 89107 **E-mail:** ufos508universe@worldnet.att.net

ROCK, JOSHUA DAVID
Industry: Hospitality **Born:** November 4, 1976, Waynesboro, Pennsylvania **Current organization:** Hampshire Hospitality Group @ Clarion Hotel & Conference Center **Title:** Head Chef **Type of organization:** Hotel and restaurant/banquet facility **Major product:** Hotel services, food **Area of distribution:** Massachusetts **Expertise:** Culinary arts **Hob./spts.:** Biking, frisbee, hiking **SIC code:** 70 **Address:** 22 Rampart Ct., Holyoke, MA 01040 **E-mail:** jdrock1976@yahoo.com

ROEBUCK, SONETTE S.
Industry: Facility/business services **Univ./degree:** B.S., Public Health Administration, Rutgers University, New Jersey, 1993 **Current organization:** Aramark Corp. **Title:** Manager, Safety and Loss Prevention **Major product:** Facility/management services for large institutions **Area of distribution:** International **Expertise:** Safety/public health **Affiliations:** National Association for Fire Prevention **Hob./spts.:** Reading **SIC code:** 73 **Address:** Aramark Corp., 3243 N. 38th St., Unit #5, Phoenix, AZ 85018 **E-mail:** roebuck-sonette@aramark.com

ROTH, LORI ANN
Industry: Education **Born:** May 30, 1963, Twentynine Palms, California **Univ./degree:** Ph.D., Virginia Polytechnic Institute, 2003 **Current organization:** SBS, Inc. **Title:** Ph.D. **Type of organization:** I.T. **Major product:** Adult education **Area of distribution:** Virginia **Expertise:** Curriculum development **Affiliations:** N.A.F.E.; N.S.T.D. **Hob./spts.:** Weightlifting, walking, reading **SIC code:** 73 **Address:** 7752 Northedge Ct., Springfield, VA 22153

RUBINO, ANTHONY R.
Industry: Advertising/public relations **Born:** April 4, 1964, Paterson, New Jersey **Univ./degree:** B.S., Business Administration, Seton Hall University, New Jersey, 1986 **Current organization:** Rowland Worldwide **Title:** Senior Vice President/Controller **Type of organization:** Integrated marketing **Major product:** Advertising, public relations **Area of distribution:** International **Expertise:** Finance, operations, administration; Certified Public Accountant **Honors/awards:** National Instructor of the Year Award **Affiliations:** New Jersey Society of Certified Public Accountants; Fundraiser, Boomer Esiason Association; Fundraiser, American Cancer Society; Fundraiser, Jimmy Fund **Hob./spts.:** Football **SIC code:** 73 **Address:** Rowland Worldwide, 52 Mary Ave., West Patterson, NJ 07424 **E-mail:** arubino@rowland.com **Web address:** www.rowland.com

RUIZ JR., JESSE REY
Industry: Technology **Born:** December 25, 1971, Los Angeles, California **Current organization:** IKON Office Solutions, LLC **Title:** Sales Professional **Type of organization:** Document solutions/EDM **Major product:** Ricoh, Canon, HP, Konica/Minolta **Area of distribution:** National **Expertise:** National accounts **Hob./spts.:** Softball, boating **SIC code:** 73 **Address:** IKON Office Solutions, 16715 Von Karman Ave., Irvine, CA 92606 **E-mail:** reyreyruiz@yahoo.com **Web address:** www.ikon.com

RUSSELL, ROB
Industry: Hospitality **Born:** June 17, 1958, Bay Shore, New York **Univ./degree:** B.A., Fine Arts, 1980 **Current organization:** The Colony Hotel **Title:** Entertainment Director **Type of organization:** Legendary hotel with famous cabaret room **Major product:** Lodging, food **Area of distribution:** Florida **Honors/awards:** Employee of the Year Best of the Best, 2000 **Affiliations:** President & Founder, Mercer Park Neighborhood Association; Chamber of Commerce **Hob./spts.:** Tennis, champion swimmer, reading **SIC code:** 70 **Address:** The Colony Hotel, 155 Hammon Ave., Palm

Beach, FL 33480 **E-mail:** robrussell@thecolonypalmbeach.com **Web address:** www.thecolonypalmbeach.com

RUSSO, MARK S.
Industry: Martial arts **Born:** August 3, 1957, Miami, Florida **Univ./degree:** M.B.A., University of South Florida, 1993 **Current organization:** Quest Martial Arts **Title:** Shidoshi/President **Type of organization:** Martial arts school **Major product:** To Shin Do instruction, practical self-defense **Area of distribution:** National **Expertise:** Instruction **Affiliations:** Warrior Knights of the Blade; Screen Actors Guild **Hob./spts.:** Hiking, mountain climbing, gardening **SIC code:** 79 **Address:** Quest Martial Arts, 15049 Bruce B. Downs Blvd., Tampa, FL 33647 **E-mail:** info@tampaquestma.com

RYAN, DORIS IRVIN
Industry: Funeral services **Born:** Wytheville, Virginia **Univ./degree:** Virginia Funeral Directors License, 1974 **Current organization:** Ryan Funeral Home **Title:** Director/Owner **Type of organization:** Full service funeral home **Major product:** Pre-arranged, pre-need and monuments **Area of distribution:** Virginia **Expertise:** Overseeing all aspects of company, performing over 100 services per year **Affiliations:** Founding Member, Chamber of Commerce; Virginia Funeral Directors Association; National Funeral Directors Association; Charter Member, Greene County Rescue Squad; Former Chairman, Greene County Heart Association **SIC code:** 72 **Address:** Ryan Funeral Home, P.O. Box 33, Route 33, Quinque, VA 22965

SALEEM, MAJOR M.
Industry: Security **Univ./degree:** M.B.A., Business Management, Parkwood University, 2004 **Current organization:** Virginia Surveillance Force **Title:** Public Relations Manager **Type of organization:** Security firm **Major product:** Security guard and patrol services **Area of distribution:** National **Expertise:** Security services, management, administration **Affiliations:** Law Enforcement Alliance of America **Hob./spts.:** Family activities **SIC code:** 73 **Address:** Virginia Surveillance Force, 7544 Diplomat Dr., Suite 101, Manassas, VA 20109 **E-mail:** info@vsfprotection.com **Web address:** www.vsfprotection.com

SANDERS, TIMOTHY
Industry: Golf **Born:** Sumter, South Carolina **Current organization:** Forest Park Golf Course **Title:** Head Golf Professional **Type of organization:** Municipal golf course **Major product:** Golf and golf instruction for general public **Area of distribution:** Baltimore, Maryland **Expertise:** Management, golf instruction **Affiliations:** Gwen Oaks Woodlawn Optimus Club; Calvary Baptist Church **Hob./spts.:** Bowling, freshwater fishing **SIC code:** 79 **Address:** Forest Park Golf Course, 2900 Hillsdale Rd., Baltimore, MD 21207 **E-mail:** tsanders@pga.com

SANTOS, NEOFITO T.
Industry: Hospitality **Born:** January 20, 1945, Pampanga, Philippines **Univ./degree:** A.B., Political Science, Holy Angel College, Philippines; Computer Programming. MTI Business Colleges, San Jose, CA; Business Admin./Date Processing and Hotel-Motel Mgmt., Monterey Peninsula College, CA; Food Cost Control, University of Las Vegas-Nevada **Current organization:** Portola Plaza Hotel @ Monterey Bay **Title:** Purchasing Director **Type of organization:** Hotel and resort **Major product:** Lodging, food and beverage **Area of distribution:** Monterey, California **Expertise:** Purchasing, F&B, cost control, security **Honors/awards:** Masonic: Jr. Deacon, Central Coast Counties #213, Allied Masonic Degrees; Past Commander, Watsonville Commandery #22 Knights Templar of CA; Illustrious Master, Santa Cruz Council #17, Cryptic Masons of CA; King, Salinas Chapter #59, Royal Arch Masons of CA; Cross of Honor, Order of DeMolay; Hiram Award **Affiliations:** Masonic: Past Master, Monterey Masonic Lodge #217 F&AM; Past President, Central California Pastmaster's Association; Pharos, 9th degree Team, Monterey Peninsula Scottish Rite Club; Jr. Warden, 18th degree Team, Monterey Peninsula Scottish Rite Club; Flag Bearer, Monterey Peninsula #68, OES; Advisory Council Member, Monterey Peninsula Chapter Order of DeMolay; Past President, Monterey County Scottish Rite Club; Member, Islam Temple, AAONMS of San Mateo, CA; Past Director, Monterey Amigo Marching Unit; Past President, Monterey Peninsula Shrine Club; Past Potentate's Aide (Potentate-Paul Stevens) **Hob./spts.:** Reading, church **SIC code:** 70 **Address:** Portola Plaza Hotel @ Monterey Bay, 2 Portola Plaza, Monterey, CA 93940-2419 **E-mail:** neofitosantos@hotmail.com

SAX, STERLING
Industry: Music **Born:** August 27, 1947, Port Jefferson, New York **Univ./degree:** B.S., Stony Brook University, 1974 **Current organization:** Sterling Sax Music Co. **Title:** Owner **Type of organization:** Contracting **Major product:** Digital recording **Area of distribution:** National **Expertise:** Weddings, events, entertainment **Hob./spts.:** Detailing cars **SIC code:** 79 **Address:** Sterling Sax Music Co., 16 Littleworth Lane, Sea Cliff, NY 11579-1813 **E-mail:** sterlingsax47@yahoo.com

SCHEMBRI-SANT, IAN
Industry: Hospitality **Born:** December 25, 1968, Malta **Univ./degree:** B.B.A. with Honors, University of Malta, 1987; M.B.A., Cambridge University, 1989 **Current organization:** Starz Resorts **Title:** President/CEO **Type of organization:** Resort hotels **Major product:** Hospitality **Area of distribution:** International **Expertise:** Management, creative concepts, marketing; lecturing on tourism investments **Affiliations:** H.C.I.M.A. **Hob./spts.:** Soccer, Formula 1 racing **SIC code:** 70 **Address:** Starz Resorts, EPS D310, P.O. Box 025548, Miami, FL 33102 **E-mail:** ian@starzresorts.com **Web address:** www.starzresorts.com

SCHERBAKOV, EFIM
Industry: Professional service **Univ./degree:** A.S., Massage Therapy, Ohio College of Massage Therapy **Current organization:** TheraTouch, Ltd. **Title:** Owner **Major product:** Wellness programs, worker's compensation, massotherapy **Area of distribution:** Akron, Ohio **Expertise:** Massotherapy **Affiliations:** A.B.M.P. **SIC code:** 73 **Address:** TheraTouch, Ltd., 135 Brookrun Dr., Akron, OH 44321 **Web address:** wellness@theratouch.com

SCHILLING, PETER M.
Industry: Biotechnology **Univ./degree:** B.S.M.E., University of Notre Dame, 1991; M.S., Biomedical Engineering, University of Texas at Arlington, 1996 **Current organization:** Genaissance Pharmaceuticals **Title:** Software Engineer **Type of organization:** Biotechnology services **Major product:** Pharmacogenomics **Area of distribution:** National **Expertise:** Engineering **Hob./spts.:** Soccer, hiking **SIC code:** 73 **Address:** 7 Kaye Plaza, Apt. F11, Hamden, CT 06514 **E-mail:** pschilling91@netscape.net

SCOTT, NEIL D.
Industry: Reprographics **Born:** December 17, 1953, Brooklyn, New York **Univ./degree:** B.A., Psychology, C.U.N.Y. **Current organization:** BPI Reprographics, LLP **Title:** V.P., Information Services **Type of organization:** Retailer **Major product:** Digital output/E-commerce **Area of distribution:** International **Expertise:** Information Technology **Affiliations:** N.A.A.C.P.; B.D.P.A.; M.S.D.N. **Hob./spts.:** Cooking **SIC code:** 73 **Address:** BPI Reprographics, LLP, 79 Fifth Ave., New York, NY 10003 **E-mail:** nscott@bpirepro.com

SEGGIE, DIANA
Industry: Art/sports **Born:** July 29, 1940, Rhodesia/Zimbabwe **Univ./degree:** Tennis, Van der Meer Tennis University to Professional Tennis Registry, Hilton Head Island, South Carolina, 1983 **Current organization:** Self employed Tennis Teaching Pro **Title:** Professional Tennis Coach, Artist **Type of organization:** International Professional Tennis Registry **Major product:** Tennis **Area of distribution:** International **Expertise:** National Tester for Professional Tennis Registry; Has worked in every part of the game of tennis plus Wheelchair Tennis Special Olympics; Volunteered for elementary schools when children have done good work and can then take free tennis lessons as a reward **Honors/awards:** Won Ladies' Doubles 55's at PTR International Championships, 2003; Won Ladies' Doubles 45's PTR International Championships, 1997; Merit Achievement Program - 4A- (Professional Tennis Registry); Started "CONDO" Tennis on Hutchinson Island, Jensen Beach Florida, in conjunction with the American Tennis Industry; Taught "Play Tennis America", Florida; Taught Special Olympics, last 4 years; National Tennis Team Selector at Senior and Junior Levels in Africa; Professional Tennis Registry Volunteer of the Year **Published works:** Articles in magazines, books, newspapers in Rhodesia, Zimbabwe, South Africa, Zambia, USA **Affiliations:** United States Tennis Association; South African Tennis Association; Professional Tennis Registry USA; Lawn Tennis Association-England; South Carolina Tennis Association **Hob./spts.:** Sports, music, reading, travel **SIC code:** 79 **Address:** 28 Bailey Lane, Bluffton, SC 29909 **E-mail:** Mdseggie@aol.com

SEPPALA, TERENCE A.
Industry: Hospitality **Born:** Hibbing, Minnesota **Univ./degree:** B.A., Business Management, Hamline University, 1992 **Current organization:** Four Points by Sheraton Minneapolis **Title:** Director of Operations **Type of organization:** Hotel **Major product:** Lodging, food and beverage **Area of distribution:** International **Expertise:** Hotel management, IT management, organizational leadership, project management, mentoring, career development of subordinates, financial planning, budgeting, forecasting, fundraising for nonprofit organizations, event planning **Affiliations:** Member, Pontiac Oakland Club International **Hob./spts.:** Playing trumpet in a 20-piece Band, classic car restoration, home improvements, reading (mystery thrillers), travel **SIC code:** 70 **Address:** Four Points by Sheraton Minneapolis, 1330 Industrial Blvd., Minneapolis, MN 55413 **E-mail:** terry.seppala@fourpoints.com

SHADE, HENRY E.
Industry: Pipelines and sewer systems **Born:** August 11, 1929, Dillingham, Alaska **Current organization:** Bristol Bay Area Health Corporation **Title:** Remote Maintenance Worker **Type of organization:** Environmental health through hospital **Major product:** Clean water/sewage disposal **Area of distribution:** Alaska **Expertise:** Maintenance **Hob./spts.:** Flying airplanes **SIC code:** 73 **Address:** 4780 Shannon Lake Rd., P.O. Box 2, Dillingham, AK 99576 **E-mail:** henrys@nushdel.com

SHAH, DILIPKUMAR
Industry: Hospitality **Current organization:** Rory at Highland Lake LLL/Holiday Inn **Title:** General Manager **Type of organization:** Hotel **Major product:** Hospitality

SERVICES

Area of distribution: Local **Expertise:** Marketing **Affiliations:** Lions Club **SIC code:** 70 **Address:** Rory at Highland Lake LLL/Holiday Inn, 200 E. Lake St., Winsted, CT 06098 **E-mail:** shah3850@aol.com

SHAHIN, AMY B.
Industry: Hospitality **Born:** January 26, 1974, Minneapolis, Minnesota **Univ./degree:** B.A., University of Wisconsin, 1996 **Current organization:** Park Plaza **Title:** Director of Sales **Type of organization:** Hotel **Major product:** Hotel accommodations **Area of distribution:** National **Expertise:** Sales and marketing **Honors/awards:** Manager of the Quarter, 1998; Manager of the Year, 1998; Outstanding National Sales Leads, 2000 **Affiliations:** N.C.B.T.A., Membership Committee 1998-99, Special Events Committee, 1998-2004, Board of Directors 2005, Education Day, 2005-06 **Hob./spts.:** Travel **SIC code:** 70 **Address:** Park Plaza, 4460 W. 78th St. Circle, Bloomington, MN 55435 **E-mail:** amy.shahin@parkplaza.com **Web address:** www.parkplaza.com/bloomingtonmn

SHAKERIAN, BRUCE
Industry: Hotel **Univ./degree:** B.A., Business, Iran University; A.S., Hospitality and Management, ICS, Priority One Management training with Hilton, Inc. **Current organization:** Best Hotel & Suites **Title:** General Manager/DOS **Type of organization:** Hotel **Major product:** Lodging **Area of distribution:** National **Expertise:** Marketing **Hob./spts.:** Poker, gardening **SIC code:** 70 **Address:** Best Hotel & Suites, 117 S. Watson Rd., Arlington, TX 76010 **E-mail:** bruceshakerian@sbcglobal.net **Web address:** www.besthotelandsuites.net

SHALEVICH, LILIYA
Industry: Media/entertainment **Born:** September 23, 1956, Russia **Univ./degree:** M.S., Computer Science, Taganrog Radio Technological University, Russia, 1992 **Current organization:** Paramount Advertiser Services/Paramount Pictures **Title:** Project Manager **Type of organization:** Advertising sales **Major product:** Television commercial airtime **Area of distribution:** International **Expertise:** Computer programming **Hob./spts.:** Spending time with her kids, travel, reading **SIC code:** 70 **Address:** 2656 E. 27th St., Brooklyn, NY 11235 **E-mail:** liliya_shalevich@paramount.com

SICILIANO, GAETANO
Industry: Software **Born:** May 15, 1958, Brooklyn, New York **Univ./degree:** Attended, Stevens Institute of Technology, Computer Science **Current organization:** Tingley Systems, Inc. **Title:** Director of Network Services **Type of organization:** Manufacturing **Major product:** Software **Area of distribution:** International **Expertise:** Engineering; IBM Certified Specialist AIX; AT&T IP Certified **Hob./spts.:** Photography, woodworking **SIC code:** 73 **Address:** Tingley Systems, Inc., 31722 State Rd. 52, San Antonio, FL 33576 **E-mail:** guy@tingley.net **Web address:** www.tingley.net

SIEGEL, BARRY D.
Industry: Professional services **Born:** November 9, 1942, New York, New York **Spouse:** Barbara (Bobbie) Siegel, maiden name Stasko **Children:** Debbie Psifidis, Niki Warren **Univ./degree:** B.S., Business Management, Fairleigh Dickinson University, 1964 **Current organization:** Recruitment Enhancement Services **Title:** President **Type of organization:** Provider of solutions for staffing functions **Major product:** Recruitment Process Outsourcing **Area of distribution:** National **Expertise:** Recruitment marketing, recruiting, hiring process re-engineering, staffing technology **Honors/awards:** Recognized as 'Inventor of Recruitment Process Outsourcing', 'One of the 100 Superstars of Human Resource Outsourcing', HRO Today Magazine **Published works:** "The Keys to Successful Recruiting and Staffing", published by Weddle's, www.weddles.com, ISBN: 1-928734-17-0. Book is about making smart investments in talent acquisition. He has drawn on his 30+ years of experience to craft a roadmap for organizations that realize the importance of preparing now for the competition they will face for top talent in the future. Those that follow his advice will be well positioned to compete for the best talent and, as a consequence, better able to implement brands with power and distinction. He has also written a white paper entitled "The Business Case for Recruitment Process Outsourcing", available at www.resjobs.com **Affiliations:** S.H.R.M. **Career accomplishments:** Joined Bernard Hodes Group in 1971 as an Account Executive and progressed to Account Supervisor, Creative Director, Branch Manager, Regional Manager, Vice President, Senior Vice President, Executive Vice President and President of Interactive and Staffing Solutions. He still holds the last title at Bernard Hodes Group, along with serving as President of Recruitment Enhancement Services **Hob./spts.:** Music, tennis **SIC code:** 73 **Address:** Recruitment Enhancement Services, 7676 Hillmont, Houston, TX 77040 **E-mail:** bsiegel@resjobs.com

SIFFORD, WM. MORGAN
Industry: Funeral service **Born:** June 23, 1960 **Univ./degree:** A.S., Mortuary **Current organization:** Morgan Sifford Funeral Home **Title:** Funeral Director, Coroner **Type of organization:** Funeral home **Major product:** Funeral services **Area of distribution:** Puxico, Missouri **Expertise:** Funeral services, law enforcement autopsies, communicating with people **Hob./spts.:** Basketball, baseball, horses **SIC code:** 72 **Address:** Morgan Sifford Funeral Home, P.O. Box 284, Puxico, MO 63960 **E-mail:** morgansifford@semo.net

SIMMA, LARRY S.
Industry: Billing Servies **Born:** December 6, 1948, Tulsa, Oklahoma **Univ./degree:** BBA, Accounting, University of New Mexico, 1977 **Current organization:** BRG-Specialty Physician's Billing, Inc. **Title:** President/CEO **Type of organization:** Specialty physician's billing **Major product:** Consulting, management and billing services **Area of distribution:** Alabama **Expertise:** Accounting, CPA **Honors/awards:** multiple awards **Affiliations:** Alabama Society of CPA's; Louisiana Society of CPA's; New Mexico Society of CPA's; Medical Group Management Association; Radiology Business Managers Association **Hob./spts.:** Fishing, boating, sports **SIC code:** 73 **Address:** BRG-Specialty Physician's Billing, Inc., 2000A Southbridge Pkwy., Suite 300, Birmingham, AL 35209 **E-mail:** larrysimma@brg-spb.com **Web address:** www.brg-spb.com

SIMONSON, RICK L.
Industry: Illustration/graphic design **Born:** August 1, 1973, Minnesota **Univ./degree:** M.S., University of Nebraska, 1999 **Current organization:** R.L. Simonson Studios **Title:** Scientific Illustrator **Type of organization:** Illustration/design studio **Major product:** Illustration services **Area of distribution:** National **Expertise:** Scientific illustrations **Affiliations:** G.N.S.I.; N.A.P.P. **Hob./spts.:** Biking **SIC code:** 73 **Address:** R.L. Simonson Studios, 4010 Ave. R., #G8, Kearney, NE 68847 **E-mail:** rlsimonson@mac.com

SIMS JR., PETE
Industry: Funerals **Born:** May 11, 1924, El Dorado, Arkansas **Univ./degree:** B.S., Funeral Services, Gupton-Jones College of Mortuary Science, Atlanta, 1950 **Current organization:** Sims Mortuary, Inc. **Title:** President **Type of organization:** Mortuary **Major product:** Funeral services **Area of distribution:** El Dorado, Arkansas **Expertise:** Customer service, insurance, consultations **Affiliations:** National Funeral Directors & Morticians Association **Hob./spts.:** Basketball **SIC code:** 72 **Address:** Sims Mortuary, Inc., 432 Liberty St., El Dorado, AR 71730 **E-mail:** psims@cox-internet.com

SINHA, VIKAS
Industry: Information Technology **Born:** September 20, 1967, India **Univ./degree:** B.Tech., Sri Venkateswara University, India, 1988; M.S., Engineering, Florida Atlantic University, 1991; Doctoral Research, Dept. of Ocean Engineering, Florida Atlantic University, 1991-94; KMI, Kellogg School of Management. Northwestern University, 2003 **Current organization:** SPSS Inc. **Title:** Director, R&D **Type of organization:** Research and Software Development **Major product:** Predictive analytics, statistics, market research applications **Area of distribution:** International **Expertise:** Research and development, project management, process management, software development life cycle and methodologies, software localization and internationalization, software digital rights management **Honors/awards:** Gold Medal for Academic Excellence in the Undergraduate Engineering Program, 1988; Listed in Who's Who Amount Students in American Universities and Colleges, 1993-94; Awarded K-PIN for Outstanding Performance and Customer Satisfaction, 1995; Nominated to Keane's Authors Club, 1995; Award for Excellence, SPSS, 1997, 1998 **Published works:** Over a dozen publications and presentations at national and international conferences **Affiliations:** Member, The IndUS Entrepreneurs; Member, Project Management Institute; Member, Association for Computing Machinery **Hob./spts.:** Travel, music **SIC code:** 73 **Address:** 2309 Glengary Court, Schaumburg, IL 60194 **E-mail:** vsinha-exed@kellogg.northwestern.edu

SMITH, MARTIN J.
Industry: Aerospace/semiconductors **Born:** August 15, 1963, Baldwin Park, California **Univ./degree:** A.S., Business, Cerritos College, California **Current organization:** Astro Pak Corp. **Title:** Quality Assurance Manager **Type of organization:** Precision cleaning and passivation contractor **Major product:** Cleaning of high purity gas and fluid systems **Area of distribution:** International **Expertise:** Quality assurance, meeting specifications **Affiliations:** A.S.Q. **Hob./spts.:** Softball. movies, video games **SIC code:** 73 **Address:** Astro Pak Corp., 12201 Pangborn Ave., Downey, CA 90241 **E-mail:** msmith@astropak.com **Web address:** www.astropak.com

SNYDER, BRUCE G.
Industry: Hospitality **Born:** July 23, 1960, Elkhart, Indiana **Current organization:** Marriott **Title:** Executive Chef **Type of organization:** Hotel **Major product:** Hotel accommodations, 2 restaurants and bar **Area of distribution:** National **Expertise:** Executive Chef **Hob./spts.:** Woodworking, ice sculpture, outdoor activities **SIC code:** 70 **Address:** Marriott, 6580 Fannin St., Houston, TX 77030 **E-mail:** lsnyderb@sbcglobal.net

SODHA, JENNIFER N.
Industry: Computers/IT **Born:** January 6, 1977, Syracuse, New York **Univ./degree:** M.S., Pace University, 2001 **Current organization:** IBM **Title:** Business Analyst **Type of organization:** Services - web hosting **Major product:** Hardware, services, web hosting **Area of distribution:** International **Expertise:** IT/business **Affiliations:**

A.C.E. **Hob./spts.:** Opera, theatre, hiking, biking, travel **SIC code:** 73 **Address:** IBM, 299-300 Long Meadow Rd., Sterling Forest, NY 10970 **E-mail:** jnsodha@us.ibm.com

SORENSEN, GLENN T.
Industry: Technology consulting **Born:** May 8, 1951, Brooklyn, New York **Current organization:** Commworks A 3Com Co. **Title:** Vice President **Type of organization:** Network consulting firm **Major product:** Consultation/adaptation **Area of distribution:** International **Expertise:** Information analysis **Hob./spts.:** Golf, landscaping, white water canoeing **SIC code:** 73 **Address:** Commworks A 3Com Co., 100 Davidson Ave., Suite 200, Somerset, NJ 08873 **E-mail:** glenn-sorensen@3com.com

SOROCA, ADAM L.
Industry: E-commerce **Univ./degree:** B.A., Economics, Middlebury College, 1994 **Current organization:** Terra Lycos **Title:** General Manager Search **Type of organization:** Internet provider **Major product:** Internet provider, online products and services **Area of distribution:** International **Expertise:** Search - marketing **Affiliations:** American Marketing Association **Hob./spts.:** Skiing, tennis, jazz music **SIC code:** 73 **Address:** Terra Lycos, 100 Fifth Ave., Waltham, MA 02451 **E-mail:** adam.soroca@corp.terralycos.com **Web address:** www.lycos.com

SPALAZZI, LINDA
Industry: Video/film production **Born:** June 15, 1947, New Albany, Indiana **Univ./degree:** B.A., Radio and Television, Indiana University, 1969 **Current organization:** Bright Light Visual Communications **Title:** CEO **Type of organization:** Visual communications **Major product:** Commercials, corporate work, documentaries **Area of distribution:** International **Expertise:** Producer/director **Affiliations:** Women in Communications; National Association of Broadcasters **Hob./spts.:** Football **SIC code:** 78 **Address:** Bright Light Visual Communications, 602 Main St., Suite 810, Cincinnati, OH 45202 **E-mail:** linda@brightlightusa.com **Web address:** www.brightlightusa.com

SPENCER, CHRISTINE G.
Industry: Hospitality **Univ./degree:** Julliard School of Music, VOI.AN., 1952 **Current organization:** Renaissance Hotel **Title:** Chief Concierge **Type of organization:** Hotel **Major product:** Full hotel accommodations **Area of distribution:** New York **Expertise:** Providing service to professional and leisure guests **Hob./spts.:** Acting, travel, music, singing, mentoring **SIC code:** 70 **Address:** Renaissance Hotel, 714 Seventh Ave., New York, NY 10036 **E-mail:** chefmomz1@aol.com

SPRITE, ANDREW J.
Industry: Hospitality **Born:** June 26, 1974, Grand Rapids, Michigan **Univ./degree:** A.S., Culinary Arts, Grand Rapids Community College **Current organization:** Grand Haven Waterfront Holiday Inn **Title:** Executive Chef **Type of organization:** Hotel **Major product:** Hospitality, food **Area of distribution:** National **Expertise:** Food, menu development, ordering **Hob./spts.:** Family **SIC code:** 70 **Address:** Grand Haven Waterfront Holiday Inn, 940 W. Savidge St., Spring Lake, MI 49456 **E-mail:** asprite@higrandhaven.com

STAHLHUTH, GAYLE
Industry: Entertainment/Arts **Born:** August 11, Indianapolis, Indiana **Spouse:** Lee O'Connor **Married:** November 8, 1981 **Univ./degree:** B.A., Theatre, University of Indianapolis, 1972 **Current organization:** East Lynne Theater Co. **Title:** Artistic Director **Type of organization:** Equity professional theatre company **Major product:** Plays (early American playwrights and adaptations about America's theatrical heritage) **Area of distribution:** National **Expertise:** Acting, playwriting, directing, producing **Honors/awards:** Applause Award, New Jersey Theatre Alliance, 1998; Grants: New York State Foundation for Arts; Utah Arts Council; Mid-Atlantic Arts Foundation; New Jersey Humanities Council **Published works:** Play, "Beast in the Jungle"; Article (Backstage), "The Leach Diaries: The First Four Years" **Affiliations:** Actors Equity Association; Screen Actors Guild; American Federation of TV and Radio Artists; Active Member, Dramatists Guild **Career accomplishments:** For her work as an actor, playwright and director, listed among 200 artists of varied disciplines in the National Endowment for the Arts "Directory of Community Artists"; Commissions from Pennsylvania Stage Company and Theatre Works/USA; Perform off-Broadway, regional theatre, film and TV; One-person shows throughout the country **Hob./spts.:** Bicycling, swimming, fishing, model trains **SIC code:** 79 **Address:** East Lynne Theater Co., 121 Fourth Ave., West Cape May, NJ 10016 **E-mail:** gaylestahl@aol.com **Web address:** www.eastlynnetheater.org

STALNAKER, MARTY N.
Industry: Resorts **Current organization:** Vail Resorts **Title:** Maintenance Apprentice **Type of organization:** Ski resort **Major product:** Skiing, recreation **Area of distribution:** Vail, Colorado **Expertise:** Maintenance **Hob./spts.:** Motorcycle racing **SIC code:** 70 **Address:** Vail Resorts, 862 S. Frontage Rd., Vail, CO 81658 **E-mail:** thumperz@hotmail.com

STARK, RAYMOND E.
Industry: Beauty salon **Born:** February 8, 1966, Dallas, Texas **Univ./degree:** M.A., Hairdressing, Germany **Current organization:** Raymond Stark Salon Inc. **Title:** President **Type of organization:** Hair salon **Major product:** Beauty, hair styling services **Area of distribution:** Dallas, Texas **Expertise:** Coloring, management **Affiliations:** T.S.A., Professional Beauty Association **Hob./spts.:** Travel **SIC code:** 72 **Address:** Raymond Stark Salon Inc., 5290 Beltline Rd., Suite 152, Dallas, TX 75240 **E-mail:** raystark@swbell.net **Web address:** www.raymondstarksalon.com/

STEBBINS, JOY E.
Industry: Music **Born:** October 12, 1948, Allentown, Pennsylvania **Univ./degree:** Dr. Homer Nearing's School of Music, 1966; Attended Lindenwood College, St. Louis, Missouri **Current organization:** Pike County Choral Society **Title:** Co-Director **Type of organization:** Choral society **Major product:** Classical concerts **Area of distribution:** Pennsylvania **Expertise:** Piano, concerts, organ lessons **Honors/awards:** Selected as "Outstanding Young Woman of America", 1982 **Published works:** Music compositions; "This is the Advent of our God" and "Will We Have Tomorrow?", published by Worldwide Music, Florida; Original piano composition "Oceans" introduced at the Allentown Art Museum, 1978 **Affiliations:** Organist for St. Marks Lutheran Church, Lackawaxen, Pennsylvania; Director of the Annual Music Fest Choir in Pike County, Pennsylvania **Hob./spts.:** Music, grandchildren, travel, working with children (especially those with disabilities) **SIC code:** 79 **Address:** Pike County Choral Society, Rte. 209, Milford, PA 18337 **E-mail:** joypecks@msn.com

STEFFAN-TEETER, LOIS
Industry: Staffing **Current organization:** Allied Employment Svcs. Inc. **Title:** CEO **Type of organization:** Staff support company **Major product:** Employment services **Area of distribution:** National **Expertise:** Employment of support staff through upper level management **Published works:** Who's Who in Executive and Professionals, 1994-95 **Affiliations:** N.F.I.B.; Bay County Chamber of Commerce; Florida Sheriff's Association **Hob./spts.:** Fishing, writing **SIC code:** 73 **Address:** Allied Employment Svcs. Inc., 119 West 23rd St., Panama City, FL 32405 **Web address:** www.alliedemploymentservicesinc.com

STEPHENSON, RICHARD D.
Industry: Electrical utility **Born:** June 6, 1951, Birmingham, Alabama **Univ./degree:** B.S., Summa Cum Laude, Chemical Engineering, Christian Brothers University, Tennessee, 1973; M.B.A., San Diego State University, 1980 **Current organization:** Edison International **Title:** Manager of IT, Application & Technology Support **Type of organization:** Information technology **Major product:** Business process software **Area of distribution:** International **Expertise:** Computer applications **Affiliations:** US Navy, 1974-80 **Hob./spts.:** Golf, tennis **SIC code:** 73 **Address:** Edison International, 123 Little Oaks Rd., Encinitas, CA 92024 **E-mail:** richstep51@gmail.com

STUBBS, JACK R.
Industry: Hospitality **Born:** February 22, 1956, Bahamas **Univ./degree:** B.A., History, Art, College of the Bahamas; Attended Johnson & Wales, Culinary Arts **Current organization:** Hyatt Regency Bethesda **Title:** Executive Chef **Type of organization:** Hotel and banquet hall **Major product:** Hospitality and fine dining **Area of distribution:** Maryland **Expertise:** Management of kitchen staff and banquet hall **Hob./spts.:** Playing piano, creating art **SIC code:** 70 **Address:** Hyatt Regency Bethesda, Wisconsin Ave., Bethesda, MD 20814 **E-mail:** jstubb@bethepo.hyatt.com

STYLES, TINA N.
Industry: Personal services **Univ./degree:** A.S., Cosmetology, Western Piedmont Community College **Current organization:** Tina's Shop And Tan **Title:** Owner, Operator **Type of organization:** Tanning salon, retail boutique **Major product:** Tanning services, handmade gift baskets and candles **Area of distribution:** National **Expertise:** Cosmetology, web site builder, consultant **SIC code:** 72 **Address:** Tina's Shop And Tan, 117 W. Union St., Morganton, NC 28655 **E-mail:** affiliatemama@aol.com

SULLIVAN, WILLIAM H.
Industry: Transportation **Born:** December 1, 1948, Butte, Montana **Current organization:** Liberty Towing Inc. **Title:** President **Type of organization:** Transportation company **Major product:** Transportation services, towing **Area of distribution:** University Place, Washington **Expertise:** Towing **Affiliations:** Washington Tow and Recovery Association **Hob./spts.:** Hunting, fishing, boating, rebuilding muscle cars **SIC code:** 75 **Address:** Liberty Towing Inc., 2912 69th Ave. West, Bldg. B, University Place, WA 98466 **E-mail:** libertytowing@sprynet.com

SUMPTER, JOYCLAN E.
Industry: Cable television **Born:** February 8, 1962, Evergreen, Alabama **Univ./degree:** B.S., Accounting, University of Alabama, 1986 **Current organization:** The Weather Channel **Title:** Director, Affiliate Operations **Type of organization:** Cable television network **Major product:** Cable television programming **Area of distribution:** National **Expertise:** Accounting, operations, information technology **Affiliations:** W.I.C.T.; C.T.A.M. **Hob./spts.:** Biking, outdoor sports **SIC code:** 79 **Address:**

The Weather Channel, 300 Interstate North Pkwy., S.E., MS-730, Atlanta, GA 30339 **E-mail:** jsumpter@weather.com

TACCOLINI, DAVID G.
Industry: Residential services **Born:** May 18, 1965, Marquette, Michigan **Univ./degree:** University of Michigan, 1987 **Current organization:** Service Brands International **Title:** C.F.O. **Type of organization:** Franchise **Major product:** Home services franchises **Area of distribution:** International **Expertise:** Finance, human resources, tax **Published works:** 1 newspaper article **Affiliations:** A.I.C.P.A.; M.A.C.P.A. **Hob./spts.:** Family, sports dad **SIC code:** 73 **Address:** Service Brands International, 3948 Ranchero Dr., Ann Arbor, MI 48108 **E-mail:** dtaccpa@rc.net

TALLAU, KIM I.
Industry: Photography **Univ./degree:** B.A., Marketing, Psychology, Fairleigh Dickinson University **Current organization:** Innovative Images, LLC **Title:** Owner **Type of organization:** Photography studio **Major product:** Photography services **Area of distribution:** New Jersey **Expertise:** Weddings, portraits, restorations **Honors/awards:** New Jersey Businesswoman of the Year, 2005 **Affiliations:** Sussex Business Advisory Council **Hob./spts.:** Figure skating, family activities **SIC code:** 72 **Address:** Innovative Images, LLC, 6 Stone Ridge Rd., Sussex, NJ 07461 **E-mail:** kim@innovativeimages.net

TAYLOR, DAVID G.
Industry: Construction management **Born:** September 29, 1949, La Porte, Indiana **Current organization:** AMEC **Title:** MEP Senior Project Manager **Type of organization:** Construction **Major product:** Management **Area of distribution:** International **Expertise:** Mechanical/PLBG/Electrical/Fire Protection **Affiliations:** Indiana Chapter, P.H.C.C. **Hob./spts.:** Golf, boating **SIC code:** 73 **Address:** AMEC, 6600 N. Andrews Ave., Suite 590, Ft. Lauderdale, FL 33309 **E-mail:** david.g.taylor@amec.com

TENBRAAK, RICHARD C.
Industry: Hospitality **Title:** Director of Marketing **Type of organization:** Hotel **Major product:** Lodging, food and beverages **Expertise:** Marketing **SIC code:** 70 **Address:** Manor Vail Resort, 595 E. Vail Valley Dr., Vail, CO 81657 **E-mail:** rtenbraak@manorvail.com

TERRISSE, SOPHIE ANN
Industry: Marketing **Born:** January 3, 1967, Paris, France **Univ./degree:** Law Degree, Paris Assay-la-Sorbonne **Current organization:** STC Associates Inc. **Title:** CEO **Type of organization:** Agency **Major product:** Consumer, hi-tech and luxury marketing **Area of distribution:** International **Expertise:** Branding and corporate renewal **Published works:** Articles in trade magazines **Hob./spts.:** Counselor at Camp Happy Days for kids with cancer **SIC code:** 73 **Address:** STC Associates Inc., 224 Fifth Ave., New York, NY 10001 **E-mail:** sophie@stcassociates.com **Web address:** www.stcassociates.com

THOMAS, SHAUN M.
Industry: Media/communications **Current organization:** Agape Media Design **Title:** Owner/Designer **Type of organization:** Media solutions for nonprofit or small businesses **Major product:** Websites and DVD/CD materials **Area of distribution:** Alabama **Expertise:** Design **SIC code:** 73 **Address:** Agape Media Design, P.O. Box 3353, Montgomery, AL 36109 **E-mail:** shaun@agapemediadesign.com **Web address:** www.agapemediadesign.com

THORNE, VICTOR M.
Industry: Technology **Born:** June 14, 1974, Newark, Ohio **Univ./degree:** B.A., Anthropology, Harvard University, 1996 **Current organization:** EFS Network, Inc. **Title:** Co-Founder/Business Development Manager **Type of organization:** Technology provider **Major product:** Food service supply chain technology services **Area of distribution:** International **Expertise:** Sales, business development **Hob./spts.:** Golf, travel **SIC code:** 73 **Address:** 1627 Ridge Ave. Unit 16 #2, Evanston, IL 60201 **E-mail:** victor.thorne@efsnetwork.com

TIETJENS, JOSEPH R.
Industry: Water treatment **Born:** April 12, 1972, Kankakee, Illinois **Univ./degree:** M.S., Mechanical Engineering, I.I.T., 2003 **Current organization:** GE Betz **Title:** Account Representative **Major product:** Water treatment chemicals **Area of distribution:** Illinois **Expertise:** Technical sales and service; engineering **Affiliations:** A.S.M.E.; A.S.M. **Hob./spts.:** Aviation, scuba diving **SIC code:** 73 **Address:** 377 Ashley Ave., Bourbonnais, IL 60914 **E-mail:** joseph.tietjens@gesm.ge.com

TOKARCZYK, EUGENE J.
Industry: Hospitality **Born:** March 1, 1950, Jablonka, Poland **Univ./degree:** M.S., Jagiellonian University, Poland **Current organization:** Fitzgerald's Motel **Title:** Manager **Type of organization:** High-end motel **Major product:** Hotel accommodations **Area of distribution:** Wisconsin Dells, Wisconsin **Expertise:** Daily operations oversight **Affiliations:** Catholic Church **Hob./spts.:** Hiking, reading **SIC code:** 70 **Address:** Fitzgerald's Motel, 530 Broadway, Wisconsin Dells, WI 53965-1550

TOLBERT, SAMUEL L.
Industry: Funeral service **Born:** March 28, 1947, Clarkesville, Georgia **Univ./degree:** Ph.D., Notorian College of Philosophy, 1975 **Current organization:** Hillside Memorial Chapel & Gardens **Title:** CEO, President **Type of organization:** Funeral home and gardens **Major product:** Funeral and cemetery services **Area of distribution:** Clarkesville, Georgia **Expertise:** Funeral Director **Honors/awards:** Mayor of Clarkesville, 20 years **Affiliations:** I.F.D.G. **Hob./spts.:** Collecting antiques **SIC code:** 72 **Address:** Hillside Memorial Chapel & Gardens, 123 N. Laurel, Clarkesville, GA 30523 **E-mail:** hillsidememorialchapel@alltel.net

TOROMAN, GORAN
Industry: Computer hardware/software **Born:** August 6, 1953, Karlovac, Croatia **Univ./degree:** B.S., Computer Science **Current organization:** Delphi Displays Systems **Title:** Lead Engineer **Type of organization:** Manufacturing **Major product:** Custom computers and software **Area of distribution:** International **Expertise:** Engineering, quality **Hob./spts.:** Tennis **SIC code:** 73 **Address:** 8362 Munster Dr., Huntington Beach, CA 92646-5029 **E-mail:** gtoroman@delphidisplay.com

TOUHY, TIM
Industry: Public relations **Born:** August 18, 1968, Chicago, Illinois **Univ./degree:** B.A., Communications, Loyola University, Illinois, 1990 **Current organization:** Hill & Knowlton, Inc. **Title:** Vice President **Type of organization:** Public relations firm **Major product:** Public relations **Area of distribution:** International **Expertise:** Communications, crisis counseling, government, labor, media **Affiliations:** P.R.S.A.; Board Member, Norbic; Member, Marketing Committee, Juvenile Diabetes Research Foundation, Chicago Chapter; Former Deputy Press Secretary, Cook County States Attorneys' Office, 1990-97; Former Assistant Press Secretary for Former Illinois Governor Jim Edgar, 1998-99 **Hob./spts.:** Volleyball, playing guitar **SIC code:** 73 **Address:** Hill & Knowlton, Inc., 900 N. Michigan Ave., Suite 2100, Chicago, IL 60657 **E-mail:** tim.touhy@hillandknowlton.com **Web address:** www.hillandknowlton.com

TRUDEAU, JOHN D.
Industry: Hospitality **Born:** June 18, 1971, Illinois **Univ./degree:** B.S., Organization Leadership & Supervision, Purdue University, 1993; A.S., Culinary Art, Johnson & Wales University, 1998 **Current organization:** Mystic Marriott Hotel & Spa **Title:** Executive Chef **Type of organization:** Hotel **Major product:** Lodging, food & beverage **Area of distribution:** Connecticut **Expertise:** Culinary operations **Hob./spts.:** Golf **SIC code:** 70 **Address:** Mystic Marriott Hotel & Spa, 625 North Rd. Rte. 117, Groton, CT 06340 **E-mail:** jtrudeau@whghotels.com

TUGWELL, ANDREW
Industry: Staffing **Univ./degree:** M.B.A., 1991 **Current organization:** Link Staffing Services **Title:** President **Type of organization:** Staffing company **Major product:** Employment services **Area of distribution:** Shenandoah, Texas **Expertise:** Industrial temporary staffing; Certified C.F.E. **Hob./spts.:** RC airplanes (20 years in aviation) **SIC code:** 73 **Address:** Link Staffing Services, 29801 IH 45N, #102, Shenandoah, TX 77381 **E-mail:** andrew@linkstaffing.com **Web address:** www.linkstaffing.com

TUNIEWICZ, ROBERT M.
Industry: Electrical power **Born:** August 11, 1949, New York **Univ./degree:** B.S., Stevens Institute of Technology/New York Institute of Technology, 1971 **Current organization:** Tri-Tech Sales Associates, Inc./ACD, Inc. **Title:** President **Type of organization:** Manufacturing representative/manufacturer **Major product:** Sales representative/electrical manufacturing and manufacturer of switch and pump control products **Area of distribution:** National and international **Expertise:** Sales, marketing, manufacturing **Published works:** 3 patents, #'s 6,753,485; 6,791,039; 6,827,230; Articles in Power Magazine **Affiliations:** I.E.E.E.; N.E.M.R.A. **Hob./spts.:** Golf, skiing **SIC code:** 73 **Address:** Tri-Tech Sales Associates, Inc., 29 Crystal Brook Hollow Rd., Mount Sinai, NY 11766 **E-mail:** rtuniewicz@tri-techsales.com/bob@acdproducts.com **Web address:** www.tri-techsales.com

VAN AKIN, WAYNE D.
Industry: Hospitality **Born:** July 11, 1963, South Carolina **Univ./degree:** A.S., California School of culinary Arts **Current organization:** Sheraton Meadowlands **Title:** Executive Chef **Type of organization:** Hotel **Major product:** Food, beverage, lodging **Area of distribution:** New Jersey **Expertise:** Executive chef **Hob./spts.:** Family, mountain biking, hiking, tennis **SIC code:** 70 **Address:** Sheraton Meadowlands, 2 Meadowlands Plaza, East Rutherford, NJ 07073 **E-mail:** wayne.vanakin@sheraton.com

VANCE, EVELYN R.
Industry: Financial **Born:** July 10, Mannington, West Virginia **Univ./degree:** B.A., Home Economics, Ohio State University, 1944; Dietetics Certification, Barnes Hospital **Current organization:** Vance Tax Service **Title:** Owner **Type of organization:** Tax

services **Major product:** Tax preparation **Area of distribution:** Colorado **Expertise:** Taxes - corporate, partnerships, individual **Honors/awards:** Elected City Councilwoman in Nebraska **Affiliations:** American Dietetic Association **Hob./spts.:** Travel, bowling **SIC code:** 73 **Address:** Vance Tax Service, 3870 Bunk House Dr., Colorado Springs, CO 80917 **E-mail:** apache7@gbronline.com

VENTURINI, MICHAEL T.
Industry: General construction **Univ./degree:** B.S., Engineering, City College **Current organization:** Chick Relocation Services **Title:** Vice President **Type of organization:** Packaging **Major product:** Special construction and plant relocation in food and beverage, automotive **Area of distribution:** National **Expertise:** Construction, relocation **SIC code:** 73 **Address:** Chick Relocation Services, 14220 Northbrook Dr., #500, San Antonio, TX 78232

WADDELL, JEFFERY A.
Industry: Hospitality **Born:** September 11, 1964, Pendelton, Oregon **Current organization:** Starwood Hotels-Sheraton Suites San Diego **Title:** Executive Chef **Type of organization:** Hotel **Major product:** Food, beverage, lodging **Area of distribution:** National **Expertise:** French/American cuisine **Affiliations:** A.C.F.; American Legion **Hob./spts.:** Golf **SIC code:** 70 **Address:** Starwood Hotels-Sheraton Suites San Diego, 701 A. St., San Diego, CA 92101 **E-mail:** chefwaddell@cox.net

WAGONER, DONALD G.
Industry: Computers, telecommunication **Born:** September 25, 1946, Kansas **Spouse:** Michele Aroele **Married:** 1981 **Children:** David. 23; Kevin, 19; Hannah, 16 **Univ./degree:** B.S.E.E., University of Illinois, 1972 **Current organization:** Semi retired consultant, IT **Title:** Technology Consultant **Major product:** Disaster backup and recovery, Global ATM/Frame Relay Network, security **Expertise:** Capacity planning, AI, programming, security, backup, Data Mining, very large network architecture and design **Honors/awards:** Listed in Strathmore's Who's Who **Affiliations:** I.E.E.E.; Tau Beta Pi; Eta Kappa Nu **Career accomplishments:** Built largest IDNX/Timeplex network; Designed and built IBM disaster backup business; Built IBM network that saved IBM $700 million a year; Designed Global network that became the AT&T Frame Relay/ATM Global Internet **Hob./spts.:** tennis, karate, classical guitar **SIC code:** 73 **Address:** Technology Consultant, 531 Buckthorn Way, Louisville, CO 80027 **E-mail:** dgwagoner@msn.com

WARD, KEVIN M.
Univ./degree: University of Salford, 1990 **Current organization:** Self-employed **Title:** Owner **Type of organization:** Sole proprietorship **Major product:** Translated text **Area of distribution:** International **Expertise:** Language services **Affiliations:** A.T.A. **SIC code:** 73 **Address:** 4443 Mountain Rd., Pasadena, MD 21122 **E-mail:** khml09@aol.com

WASHINGTON, JAMES M.
Industry: Automotive **Current organization:** Meineke Car Care Center **Title:** Owner **Type of organization:** Full service mechanical repair shop **Major product:** Car maintenance **Area of distribution:** Local **Expertise:** A.S.E. Certified, brakes and diagnostic work **SIC code:** 75 **Address:** Meineke Car Center, 7700-E Backlick Rd., Springfield, VA 22150 **E-mail:** shop.916@mail.meineke.net

WEBBER, ERIC T.
Industry: Advertising **Born:** February 12, 1960, McConnell Air Force Base, Kansas **Univ./degree:** B.S., Advertising, University of Texas **Current organization:** GSD&M **Title:** Vice President/Marketing Director **Type of organization:** Advertising agency **Major product:** Advertising **Area of distribution:** National **Expertise:** Marketing, public relations **Affiliations:** Peace Council; American Association of Advertising Agencies **Hob./spts.:** Family, soccer, golf, travel **SIC code:** 73 **Address:** GSD & M, 828 W. Sixth St., Austin, TX 78763 **E-mail:** eric_webber@gsdm.com

WEEDEN, RICHARD J.
Industry: Government/Information technology **Born:** December 26, 1971, Washington, D.C. **Current organization:** General Services Administration **Title:** Computer Specialist **Type of organization:** Business services for the federal government **Major product:** IT support **Area of distribution:** Washington, D.C. **Expertise:** Computers **Hob./spts.:** Gymnastics, outdoor activities, fishing **SIC code:** 73 **Address:** General Services Administration, 1800 F St. N.W., Room 4221, Washington, DC 20405 **E-mail:** richard.weeden@gsa.gov

WENTZEL, NANCY A.
Industry: Screen-printing/embroidery **Born:** February 1, 1952, Lewisburg, Pennsylvania **Current organization:** Sew Creature **Title:** Owner **Type of organization:** Screen-printing and embroidery exporters **Major product:** Screen-printing and embroidery products **Area of distribution:** International **Hob./spts.:** Quilting, swimming, embroidery **SIC code:** 73 **Address:** Sew Creature, RR1 Box 96, Winfield, PA 17889

WHITEHEAD, EDWARD ALBERT
Industry: Computer software **Born:** February 8, 1949, Corning, New York **Univ./degree:** A.S., 1973; B.S., Administration, 1999 **Current organization:** BMC Software Inc. **Title:** Lead Technical Support Analyst **Type of organization:** Manufacturing **Major product:** Software, technical support **Area of distribution:** International **Expertise:** Data processing management, technical support, strategic planning, information systems programming, client relations **Affiliations:** Served in U.S. Army for 3 years, stationed in Germany and Korea **Hob./spts.:** Politics, sports **SIC code:** 73 **Address:** BMC Software Inc., 2101 City West Blvd., Houston, TX 77042 **E-mail:** ed_whitehead@bmc.com

WILDER, DONALD E.
Industry: Telecommunications **Born:** December 22, 1955, El Paso, Texas **Spouse:** Barbara A. **Married:** April 20, 1985 **Children:** Michael, 10; John, 8 **Univ./degree:** B.S., Computer Science, University of Maryland, 1989 **Current organization:** XIF Communications **Title:** Director of Engineering **Type of organization:** OEM/VAR **Major product:** Internet services **Area of distribution:** International **Expertise:** Engineering **Affiliations:** Institute of Electrical and Electronics Engineers **Career accomplishments:** Designed and installed 6000 node switched network; designed and installed network for Terrashare.com **Hob./spts.:** Building networks **SIC code:** 73 **Address:** 14917 Carlbern Dr., Centreville, VA 20120-1510 **E-mail:** don@thewilders.org

WILLIAMS, JASON B.
Industry: Marketing **Univ./degree:** B.S., University of Wisconsin, 1996 **Current organization:** Findwhat.com **Title:** SVP/GM Merchant Services **Type of organization:** Marketing services, software **Major product:** Internet marketing **Area of distribution:** International **Expertise:** Business strategy, patent law **Hob./spts.:** Tennis, boating, water skiing **SIC code:** 73 **Address:** Findwhat.com, 5220 Summerlin Commons Blvd., Suite 500, Ft. Myers, FL 33907 **E-mail:** jasonw@findwhat.com **Web address:** www.findwhat.com

WINFIELD, JOHN G.
Industry: Hospitality **Univ./degree:** B.S., Strategic Management, Pepperdine University **Current organization:** Pebble Beach Co. **Title:** Beverage Manager for The Lodge at Pebble Beach **Type of organization:** Golf resort **Major product:** Hotel accommodations, food and beverage, entertainment **Area of distribution:** Pebble Beach, California **Expertise:** Beverage service **SIC code:** 70 **Address:** Pebble Beach Co., 1700 17 Mile Dr., Pebble Beach, CA 93953 **E-mail:** winfield@pebblebeach.com **Web address:** www.pebblebeach.com

WOLFE, BEATRICE
Industry: Hospitality **Born:** November 11, 1955, Caledonia, Mississippi **Current organization:** Master Hosts Inns & Suites **Title:** Sales Manager **Type of organization:** Hotel/motel/restaurant/lounge **Major product:** Lodging, food and beverage **Area of distribution:** Mississippi **Expertise:** Marketing **Affiliations:** American Businesswomen's Association; Columbus Link Ambassador Committee **Hob./spts.:** Sewing, reading, dancing, travel **SIC code:** 70 **Address:** Master Hosts Inns & Suites, 506 Hwy. 45N, Columbus, MS 39701 **E-mail:** beatricewolfe@bellsouth.net

WONG, ERIC
Industry: Entertainment/music **Born:** February 17, 1976, New York, New York **Univ./degree:** B.A. with Honors, Communications, New York University, 1998 **Current organization:** The Island Def Jam Music Group **Title:** Vice President, Marketing **Type of organization:** Record label **Major product:** Music from Rap, Hip Hop Rock, R&B **Area of distribution:** International **Expertise:** Marketing, management, develops and implements plans for the artists **Affiliations:** N.A.R.A.S. **SIC code:** 73 **Address:** The Island Def Jam Music Group, 825 Eighth Ave., 28th floor, New York, NY 10019 **E-mail:** eric.wong@umusic.com **Web address:** www.islandrecords.com

WOOTEN, HOLLIS DARWIN
Industry: Environment **Born:** September 29, 1939, South Pittsburgh, Tennessee **Univ./degree:** B.S.E., University of Tennessee, 1975 **Current organization:** Bechtel Jacobs Co. LLC **Title:** Senior Construction Engineer **Type of organization:** Field services **Major product:** Environmental clean up **Area of distribution:** Oak Ridge, Tennessee **Expertise:** Engineering **Published works:** College pamphlets **Affiliations:** T.S.P.E.;

A.S.H.R.A.E. **Hob./spts.:** Hunting **SIC code:** 73 **Address:** Bechtel Jacobs Co. LLC, P.O. Box 4699, Oak Ridge, TN 37831-4699 **E-mail:** wootenhd@bechteljacobs.org

WRIGHT, WILLIAM D.

Industry: Inventory **Born:** November 20, 1933, Nashville, Tennessee **Current organization:** GOHS Inventory Service, Inc. **Title:** President/Owner **Type of organization:** Inventory company **Major product:** Inventory accounting **Area of distribution:** Michigan **Expertise:** Retail and wholesale accounting **Affiliations:** B.B.B.; V.F.W.; National Association of Inventory; National Federation of Small Businesses **Hob./spts.:** Bowling, golf **SIC code:** 73 **Address:** GOHS Inventory Service, Inc., 24293 Telegraph Rd., Suite 224, Southfield, MI 48034

XIE, MENG

Industry: Hospitality **Born:** August 3, 1978 **Univ./degree:** B.S., Hotel Management, Switzerland **Current organization:** Boar's Head Inn Resort **Title:** Assistant Manager **Type of organization:** Resort hotel **Major product:** Hotel accommodations, catering, golf course **Area of distribution:** National **Expertise:** Hotel management **Hob./spts.:** Dancing **SIC code:** 70 **Address:** 2633 Barracks Rd., #C, Charlottesville, VA 22903

YADAV, RAMPAL S.

Industry: Hotel **Current organization:** Best Western Executive Inn **Title:** Owner **Type of organization:** Hotel **Major product:** Hotel accommodations, trade show promotions, jewelry import and sales **Area of distribution:** International **Expertise:** Manufacturing, marketing **Hob./spts.:** Mentoring **SIC code:** 70 **Address:** Best Western Executive Inn, 333 W. Drachman St., Tucson, AZ 85705 **E-mail:** bwinns@yahoo.com

YERGER, CRAIG R.

Industry: Hotel **Born:** October 28, 1976, Lewisburg, Pennsylvania **Univ./degree:** A.S., Hotel and Restaurant Management **Current organization:** Genetti Hotel and Convention Center **Title:** Executive Chef **Type of organization:** Hotel/convention center **Major product:** Food, entertainment, hospitality **Area of distribution:** Pennsylvania **Expertise:** Banquet food and ala carte cooking **Honors/awards:** 2001 Award Winner for the #1 Chili in Pennsylvania **Affiliations:** A.C.F. **Hob./spts.:** Golf, hunting, sports **SIC code:** 70 **Address:** Genetti Hotel and Convention Center, 200 W. Fourth St., Williamsport, PA 17701

YOUNG, BENJAMIN H.

Industry: Hospitality **Born:** January 12, 1966, Springfield, Massachusetts **Current organization:** Carlson Corporation/Radisson Plaza Warwick **Title:** Executive Chef/ Food and Beverage Director **Type of organization:** Hotel **Major product:** Hotel accommodations **Area of distribution:** Pennsylvania **Expertise:** Administration of all food and beverage services **Affiliations:** A.C.F.; Chefs 'N' Kids **Hob./spts.:** Basketball, football, archery **SIC code:** 70 **Address:** Radisson Plaza Warwick, 1701 Locust St., Philadelphia, PA 19103 **E-mail:** ben.young@radisson.com

YUSZA III, JOHN WALTER

Industry: Security alarm systems **Born:** September 9, 1966, Meriden, Connecticut **Univ./degree:** A.A., Electrical Engineering, Greater New Haven Technical College, 1986 **Current organization:** Monitor Controls, Inc. **Title:** Vice President **Type of organization:** Sales, service, monitoring services **Major product:** Security alarm services **Area of distribution:** Southern New England **Expertise:** Sales, design and engineering **Affiliations:** National Burglar and Fire Alarm Association **SIC code:** 73 **Address:** Monitor Controls, Inc., 178 Center St., Wallingford, CT 06492 **E-mail:** jyusza3@monitorcontrols.com **Web address:** www.monitorcontrols.com

ZOUARI, ABDEL

Industry: Hospitality **Born:** April 20, 1950, Sfax, Tunisia **Univ./degree:** M.Ed., French Institute of Sports, France, 1974; C.H.A., Educational Hospitality Management Diploma, 2000 **Current organization:** Wyndham Sugar Bay Resort **Title:** General Manager **Type of organization:** Hotel/resort **Major product:** Lodging, food and beverage, entertainment **Area of distribution:** International **Expertise:** Hospitality, management **Affiliations:** Chairman, Education and Training Committee, St. Thomas Hotel Association **Hob./spts.:** Soccer, gourmet cooking **SIC code:** 70 **Address:** Wyndham Sugar Bay Resort, 6500 Smith Bay, St. Thomas, VI 00802 **E-mail:** azouari@wyndham.com

ZOUHBI, HUSSAIN

Industry: Hospitality **Born:** March 13, 1974, Vienna, Austria **Univ./degree:** B.S., Hotel Management **Current organization:** The Weston South Coast Plaza **Title:** Executive Chef **Type of organization:** Hotel **Major product:** Lodging, banquets, parties **Area of distribution:** International **Expertise:** Culinary arts, food service management **Hob./spts.:** Information technology **SIC code:** 70 **Address:** The Weston South Coast Plaza, 686 Anton Blvd., Costa Mesa, CA 92626 **E-mail:** hussain.zouhbi@westin.com

Medical

ABADIR, MICHELLE C.
Industry: Healthcare **Born:** November 16, 1963, New York, New York **Univ./degree:** M.D., State University of New York Downstate, 1990 **Current organization:** Abadir Associates, M.D., P.C. **Title:** M.D. **Type of organization:** Private practice **Major product:** Patient care, dermatologic surgery **Area of distribution:** Rye Brook, New York **Area of Practice:** Dermatology **Published works:** 3 articles **Affiliations:** A.M.A.; A.A.D.; A.S.D.S. **Hob./spts.:** Golf, sailing, skiing **SIC code:** 80 **Address:** Abadir Associates, M.D., P.C., 90 S. Ridge St., Rye Brook, NY 10573 **E-mail:** mabadir@optonline.net

ABBAS, ISMETH SUFI
Industry: Healthcare **Born:** January 21, 1968 **Univ./degree:** M.D., PSC Institute of Medical Science and Research, 1992 **Current organization:** Southeast Missouri Hospital **Title:** M.D. **Type of organization:** Hospital **Major product:** Patient care **Area of Practice:** Internal medicine/hospitalist **Affiliations:** A.C.P.; Mensa **Hob./spts.:** Adventure sports, flying airplanes **SIC code:** 80 **Address:** Southeast Missouri Hospital, 1701 Lacey St., Cape Girardeau, MO 63701 **E-mail:** rsabbas898@pol.net

ABBOTT, PHYLLIS
Industry: Healthcare **Born:** May 22, 1948, Flint, Michigan **Univ./degree:** R.N., Registered Nurse, University of Flint, 1981; B.A.S., Bachelor of Applied Science, Siena Heights University, 1989; M.B.A., University of Phoenix, 1996 **Current organization:** St. Mark's Hospital **Title:** Director of Surgical Services **Type of organization:** Hospital **Major product:** Patient care **Area of distribution:** Salt Lake City, Utah **Area of Practice:** Surgical services **Honors/awards:** Excellence in Job Performance Standards from Scripps Hospital, 1995 **Published works:** "Surgical Services Management", 1997 **Affiliations:** A.O.R.N.; N.A.O.N. **Hob./spts.:** Golf **SIC code:** 80 **Address:** St. Mark's Hospital, 1200 E. 3900 S., Salt Lake City, UT 84124 **E-mail:** Phyllis.Abbott@Mountainstarhealth.com

ABBY, DIANE
Industry: Healthcare **Born:** January 11, 1954, Detroit, Michigan **Univ./degree:** D.O., Michigan State University, 1987 **Current organization:** Abby & Izima D.O., P.C. **Title:** D.O. **Type of organization:** Private practice **Major product:** Patient care **Area of distribution:** Jackson, Michigan **Area of Practice:** Internist **Affiliations:** A.O.A.; A.M.A.; A.C.F.P. **Hob./spts.:** Helping the elderly and the homeless **SIC code:** 80 **Address:** Abby & Izima D.O., P.C., 766 W. Michigan Ave., Suite F, Jackson, MI 49201 **E-mail:** bendiane@earthlink.net

ABELA, GEORGE S.
Industry: Medical **Born:** January 1, 1950, Tripoli, Lebanon **Univ./degree:** M.Sc., Pharmacology, 1974; M.D., 1976, American University of Beirut; M.B.A., Michigan State University, 1998 **Current organization:** Michigan State University **Title:** M.D./Chief of Cardiology, Dept. of Medicine **Type of organization:** University **Major product:** Healthcare, education **Area of distribution:** International **Area of Practice:** Professor of international lecturing; Director of training program; Plaque rupture and thrombosis; Lasers in cardiovascular medicine **Honors/awards:** Alpha Omega Alpha Honor Society, 2002 **Published works:** 60+ articles, 100+ abstracts, 150+ national and international presentations, 40+ book chapters and 30+ review articles; 9 edited textbooks, most recent "Myocardial Revascularization: Novel Percutaneous Approaches", John Wiley & Sons Inc., New York, NY, 2001; "Peripheral Vascular Disease: Diagnostic and Therapeutic Approaches", Lippincott Publisher Inc., New York, NY, 2004; 19 cardiac device patents **Affiliations:** Fellow, A.H. A.; Fellow, American College of Cardiology; Fellow, American Society for Laser Medicine & Surgery **Hob./spts.:** Painting, international travel **SIC code:** 80 **Address:** Michigan State University, B-208 Clinical Center, East Lansing, MI 48824 **E-mail:** george.abela@ht.msu.edu

ABORDO, MELECIO GUANCO
Industry: Healthcare **Born:** July 24, 1965, Caloocan, Philippines **Univ./degree:** M.D., University of Philippines, 1991 **Current organization:** Family Medical Specialty Clinic **Title:** M.D. **Type of organization:** Private medical practice **Major product:** Patient care **Area of distribution:** Kentucky **Area of Practice:** Cardiology **Published works:** 6 research articles **Affiliations:** American College of Physicians **Hob./spts.:** Basketball, cycling, fishing **SIC code:** 80 **Address:** Family Medical Specialty Clinic, 1550 Hwy. 15 South, Jackson, KY 41339 **E-mail:** melabordo@bellsouth.net

ABRAHAM, TERRI
Industry: Healthcare **Spouse:** Bryan Wilson **Married:** November 3, 2001 **Univ./degree:** M.S.N., Case Western Reserve University, Frances P. Bolton School of Nursing, 1985; M.B.A., University of Miami, 1997; Certification, Healthcare Administration, University of Miami, 1997 **Current organization:** Lancaster Regional Medical Center **Title:** Director, Surgical Services and Robotics Coordinator **Type of organization:** Hospital **Major product:** Patient care **Area of distribution:** Pennsylvania **Area of Practice:** Critical care, operating room, hospital administration **Honors/awards:** Louise Mellen Scholar Critical Care Nursing **Affiliations:** A.O.R.N. **Career accomplishments:** Outstanding Operating Room Director, Mid-Atlantic Division, HCA; Major program development of operating rooms and open heart surgery programs; Developed GI/Endo and Special Procedures Lab utilizing a Point-Of-Care Approach; Redesigned hospital-wide healthcare delivery system; Designed and implemented a Robotics Program for a variety of surgical specialties **Hob./spts.:** Dancing, reading, weightlifting, bodybuilding **SIC code:** 80 **Address:** Lancaster Regional Medical Center, 250 College Ave., Lancaster, PA 17603 **E-mail:** TrrAbraham@aol.com

ABRAMSON, GADY
Industry: Healthcare **Born:** April 7, 1970, Israel **Univ./degree:** D.C., Life University **Current organization:** Gady Abramson, D.C. **Title:** D.C. **Type of organization:** Private practice **Major product:** Chiropractic care/Neuro-Physiological Pain Profiler assessments **Area of distribution:** Hollywood, Florida **Area of Practice:** Chiropractic **Published works:** Posture analysis program: www.postureit.com **Affiliations:** Neuro-Autonomic Testing Services, Inc. **Hob./spts.:** Inventor: Neuro-Physiological Pain Profiler (NPP) www.paintronic.com; www.neuroautonomic.com **SIC code:** 80 **Address:** Gady Abramson, D.C., 450 N. Park Rd., #200, Hollywood, FL 33021 **E-mail:** gady@abramschiropractic.com **Web address:** www.abramsonchiropractic.com

ABUDAYEH, NABIL K.
Industry: Healthcare **Univ./degree:** B.S., San Francisco State University, 1981; M.D., Chicago University Medical School, 1985 **Current organization:** Nabil K. Abudayek M.D. **Title:** M.D., F.A.C.C. **Type of organization:** Private medical practice **Major product:** Patient care **Area of distribution:** California **Area of Practice:** Cardiology **Published works:** Articles **Affiliations:** F.A.C.C.; A.C.C.M.A. **SIC code:** 80 **Address:** Nabil K. Abudayek M.D., 20126 Stanton Ave., Suite 201, Gastro Valley, CA 94546 **E-mail:** drnka@aol.com

ABUHOULI, AWAD H.
Industry: Medical **Born:** August 19, 1940, Cairo, Egypt **Univ./degree:** M.D., Ainshans University, Cairo, Egypt **Current organization:** University of Illinois at Urbana-Champaign **Title:** MD, MRCP, MACP, Attending Physician **Type of organization:** University medical center **Major product:** Medical education, services **Area of distribution:** National **Area of Practice:** Internal medicine/diabetes **Affiliations:** A.M.A. **Hob./spts.:** Gardening, walking **SIC code:** 80 **Address:** 802 N. Cedarridge Ct., Mahomet, IL 61853-8980 **E-mail:** aabuhoul@yahoo.com

ACKERMAN, CHERYL D.
Industry: Healthcare **Born:** December 7, 1958, Jersey City, New Jersey **Univ./degree:** M.D., Downstate Medical Center, 1986 **Current organization:** Cheryl D. Ackerman, M.D. **Title:** Dermatologist **Type of organization:** Private practice **Major product:** Skin care **Area of distribution:** Glen Ridge, New Jersey **Area of Practice:** Dermatology **Honors/awards:** UpJohns Young Investigator Award, 1991 **Published works:** "Dermatology in General Medicine", Chapter 118, IV edition, 1992 **Affiliations:** F.A.A.D.; F.A.C.P.; New Jersey Medical Association; Women's Dermatologic Society **Hob./spts.:** Dancing, cooking, travel, family, all sports **SIC code:** 80 **Address:** Cheryl D. Ackerman, M.D., 368 Ridgewood Ave., Glen Ridge, NJ 07028 **E-mail:** dermdoc368@aol.com

ACOSTA, ALEJANDRO
Industry: Healthcare **Born:** July 12, 1956, New York, New York **Univ./degree:** M.D., University of Puerto Rico School of Medicine, 1982 **Current organization:** Dr. Alejandro Acosta Office **Title:** M.D. **Type of organization:** Private practice **Major product:** Ophthalmology **Area of distribution:** Puerto Rico **Area of Practice:** Cataracts, glaucoma, eye surgery, diabetic eye problems **Affiliations:** Diplomate, A.B.O., N.B.M.E.; F.A.A.O. **Hob./spts.:** Fishing **SIC code:** 80 **Address:** Dr. Alejandro Acosta Office, Calle Luna Esq., Calle Salud #139, San Germán, PR 00623 **E-mail:** alenid@aol.com

ADAMS, BARBARA J.
Industry: Healthcare **Born:** November 7, 1951, Ypsilanti, Michigan **Univ./degree:** C.S.T., St. Joseph Mercy Hospital **Title:** Certified Surgical Technologist **Type of organization:** Healthcare **Major product:** Medical services **Area of distribution:** National **Area of Practice:** Surgical preparation, teaching and mentoring **Honors/awards:** Received the first Association of Surgical Technologists Public Relations Award, 1984 **Affiliations:** Vascular Association; Associates of Michigan Christian College; BOD/Secretary BOD, Michigan Christian College; American Red Cross; National Girl Scout Council; BOD, Huron Valley Girl Scout Council; National Association of Surgical Technologists, Inc.; AST: National Level-Education Representative; Regional Level-President, Secretary, Reg. 5; Local Level-President, Secretary, Treasurer, Chapter 10-Michigan; Instructor CPR/First Aid-American Heart/American Red Cross; Member/Teacher, Broadway Church of Christ, Paducah, Kentucky **Hob./spts.:** Family, cooking, teaching Bible School **SIC code:** 80 **Address:** 37 Tyler Lane, Metropolis, IL 62960 **E-mail:** barbara.adams@bhsi.com

ADAMS, R. DOUGLAS
Industry: Healthcare **Born:** October 14, 1961, Berlin, Germany **Univ./degree:** M.D., University of Illinois, 1988 **Current organization:** Owensboro Cardiovascular & Thoracic Surgeons **Title:** Surgeon **Type of organization:** Group practice **Major product:**

Patient care **Area of distribution:** National **Area of Practice:** Cardiovascular surgery **Published works:** 1 book **Affiliations:** S.T.S.; A.C.S.; A.C.P.; K.M.A.; A.S.A.C. **Hob./spts.:** Writing, tennis **SIC code:** 80 **Address:** Owensboro Cardiovascular & Thoracic Surgeons, 1000 Breckenridge St., #404, Owensboro, KY 42303 **E-mail:** rdadams@ocvtsurg.com

ADEN, LESLIE BRANNON
Industry: Healthcare **Born:** December 12, 1969, Jackson, Mississippi **Univ./degree:** M.D., Tulane University, 1996 **Current organization:** Mississippi Vision Correction Center, PLLC **Title:** M.D. **Type of organization:** Private practice **Major product:** Ophthalmology **Area of distribution:** Mississippi **Area of Practice:** Cataract and refractive surgery **Affiliations:** A.M.A.; A.A.O.; A.S.C.R.S. **Hob./spts.:** Literature, distance running, travel **SIC code:** 80 **Address:** Mississippi Vision Correction Center, PLLC, 1421 N. State St., Suite 501, Jackson, MS 39202 **E-mail:** mvcc@jam.rr.com

ADEOYE, MARTINS
Industry: Healthcare **Univ./degree:** M.D., University of Ibadan, Nigeria **Current organization:** Orland Family Institute/Martins Adeoye, LLC **Title:** M.D. **Type of organization:** Behavioral medicine clinic **Major product:** Patient care, mental health services **Area of distribution:** Orland Park, Illinois **Area of Practice:** Adult psychiatry/child and adolescent psychiatry **Affiliations:** A.P.A.; A.M.A.; American Academy of Child and Adolescent Psychiatry **Hob./spts.:** Basketball, soccer, basketball **SIC code:** 80 **Address:** Orland Family Institute/Martins Adeoye, LLC, 15030 South Ravinia Ave., Suite 30, Orland Park, IL 60462 **E-mail:** madeoye@hotmail.com

ADER, CARLOTA HUFANA
Industry: Healthcare **Univ./degree:** B.A., Medical Technology, Manila Central University, Philippines, 1969 **Current organization:** Waianae Coast Comprehensive Health Center **Title:** Senior Medical Technologist/Coagulation Supervisor **Type of organization:** Private laboratory **Major product:** Laboratory medicine **Area of distribution:** National **Area of Practice:** Blood bank, hematology, coagulation, tutoring and training medical personnel **Honors/awards:** One of 100 of Philippine Ancestry "Achievement Contribution", 2006 **Affiliations:** American Society for Clinical Laboratory Science; National Credentialing Agency for Laboratory Personnel **Hob./spts.:** Reading, bowling, golf **SIC code: 80 Address:** Waianae Coast Comprehensive Health Center, 86-260 Farrington Hwy., Waianae, HI 97692-3128 **E-mail:** atecarla@aol.com

ADKINSON, CHARLOTTE L.
Industry: Healthcare **Univ./degree:** B.S.N., Georgia Southwestern University **Current organization:** Surgical Center for Excellence **Title:** R.N. Administrator **Type of organization:** Ambulatory surgery center **Major product:** Outpatient surgery **Area of distribution:** Florida **Area of Practice:** ENT and plastic surgery, staff development **Affiliations:** A.N.A.; A.O.R.N.; A.P.I.C.; Charlotte A.A.A.H.C. **Hob./spts.:** Gardening, tag sales, antique shows, sporting events **SIC code:** 80 **Address:** Surgical Center for Excellence, 202 Doctors Dr., Panama City, FL 32405 **E-mail:** charlotte@surgicalcenterpc.com

ADLER, PHILIP
Industry: Healthcare **Born:** February 18, 1927, Hartford, Connecticut **Univ./degree:** B.S., Political Science, University of Vermont, 1949; M.D., University of Vermont School of Medicine, 1953 **Current organization:** Health Point Medical Group **Title:** M.D. **Type of organization:** Group practice **Major product:** Patient care **Area of distribution:** Florida **Area of Practice:** Pediatrics, Allergy and Immunology **Honors/awards:** Listed in "The Best Doctors in America", 3rd and 4th editions; First Pediatric Physician of the Year, awarded by Tampa Children's Hospital at St. Josephs, Tampa, Florida, March 2000 **Published works:** 14 articles (peer-reviewed), 1 book chapter **Affiliations:** F.A.A.P.; American Medical Association; Florida Medical Association; Florida Pediatric Society; served in active duty, U.S. Army 1945-47 **Hob./spts.:** Travel **SIC code:** 80 **Address:** Health Point Medical Group, 10909 W. Linebaugh Ave., Suite 100, Tampa, FL 33626

AFTAB, MUHAMMAD
Industry: Healthcare **Born:** October 11, 1975, Bahaar, Pakistan **Univ./degree:** M.D., King Edward's Medical College, 1999 **Current organization:** Long Island Jewish Medical Center **Title:** M.D. **Type of organization:** Medical center **Major product:** Patient care **Area of distribution:** National **Area of Practice:** Colon cancer surgery **Affiliations:** A.A.C.R.; A.G.A.; A.S.A.S. **SIC code:** 80 **Address:** Long Island Jewish Medical Center, 306 Community Dr., #5K, Manhasset, NY 11030 **E-mail:** erasta75@aol.com

AGAMASU, JACOB K.
Industry: Healthcare **Born:** October 20, 1962, Accra, Ghana **Univ./degree:** M.D., Semmelweis University, Budapest, Hungary; Residency, GWUMC - Providence Hospital, Washington, D.C. **Current organization:** Cardiology Care Center **Title:** M.D. **Type of organization:** Private practice in cardiology **Major product:** Patient care **Area of distribution:** Florida **Area of Practice:** Interventional cardiology **Honors/awards:** Fellowship, University of Kentucky at Lexington **Published works:** 3 articles **Affiliations:** A.C.C.; A.M.A.; A.C.I.P.; A.S.I.M. **Hob./spts.:** Family, reading **SIC code:** 80 **Address:** Cardiology Care Center, 515 W. State Rd., #434, Suite 301, Longwood, FL 32750

AGARWAL, SUDHIR K.
Industry: Healthcare **Born:** October 13, 1956, India **Univ./degree:** M.D., SMS Medical College, India, 1983 **Current organization:** Sudhir K. Agarwal, M.D. **Title:** M.D. **Type of organization:** Private practice **Major product:** Patient care **Area of distribution:** New Jersey **Area of Practice:** Gastroenterology **Published works:** Articles **Affiliations:** A.G.A.; A.S.G.E. **SIC code:** 80 **Address:** Sudhir K. Agarwal, M.D., 15 Commerce Blvd. #202, Succasunna, NJ 07876

AGHA, TASNEEM K.
Industry: Healthcare **Born:** February 12, 1962, Karachi, Pakistan **Univ./degree:** M.D., University of Karachi, Pakistan, 1994 **Current organization:** Greater Dallas Anesthesia and Pain Management **Title:** President/M.D. **Type of organization:** Outpatient facility **Major product:** Anesthesia and pain management **Area of distribution:** International **Area of Practice:** Chief Anesthesiologist **Honors/awards:** Outstanding Student Award; Chief Resident **Affiliations:** A.S.A.; T.M.A. **Hob./spts.:** Social work, youth group, swimming, table tennis, travel **SIC code:** 80 **Address:** Greater Dallas Anesthesia and Pain Management, 105 No. Stemmons, Sanger, TX 76266 **E-mail:** sa70015@aol.com

AGNANT, GUIRLAINE L.
Industry: Healthcare **Born:** September 20, 1954, Port Au Prince, Haiti **Univ./degree:** M.D., University of Guadalajara, Mexico, 1981 **Current organization:** Guirlaine Agnant, M.D., P.C. **Title:** M.D. **Type of organization:** Private practice **Major product:** Patient care **Area of distribution:** National **Area of Practice:** Ob/Gyn **Affiliations:** N.M.A.; W.M.A.; W.O.B.G.Y.N Society **SIC code:** 80 **Address:** Guirlaine Agnant, M.D., P.C., 100 Stevens Ave., Suite 601, Mount Vernon, NY 10550

AGODOA, LAWRENCE
Industry: Healthcare **Born:** July 28, 1943 **Univ./degree:** M.D., Cornell University, 1971 **Current organization:** National Institute of Health **Title:** M.D. **Type of organization:** Health institute **Major product:** Patient care **Area of distribution:** International **Area of Practice:** Nephrology **Affiliations:** N.A.A.; N.S.N.; A.S.N. **SIC code:** 80 **Address:** National Institute of Health, 9000 Rockville Pike, Bethesda, MD 20892

AGRAWAL, MANOJ K.
Industry: Healthcare **Born:** November 9, 1970, India **Univ./degree:** M.D. **Current organization:** T.M. Jain, M.D., Inc. **Title:** M.D. **Type of organization:** Group practice **Major product:** Patient care **Area of distribution:** Ohio **Area of Practice:** Cardiology **SIC code:** 80 **Address:** T.M. Jain, M.D., Inc., 970 E. Washington St., Medina, OH 44256 **E-mail:** mkagrawal_ny@hotmail.com

AGUAYO, FRED
Industry: Healthcare **Born:** May 9, 1917, El Paso, Texas **Univ./degree:** D.C., Parker College of Chiropractic, 1996 **Current organization:** Southwest Chiropractic **Title:** Chiropractor **Type of organization:** Private practice **Major product:** Patient care **Area of distribution:** International **Area of Practice:** Chiropractic wellness and rehabilitation **Affiliations:** Texas Chiropractic Association; Hispanic Chamber of Commerce **Hob./spts.:** Basketball, chess, travel **SIC code:** 80 **Address:** Southwest Chiropractic, 1030 N. Zaragoza Rd., Suite O, El Paso, TX 79907 **E-mail:** aguayo13@msn.com

AGUILLARD, LESLIE A.
Industry: Healthcare/art **Born:** May 11, 1946, Independence, Louisiana **Univ./degree:** B.A., Art Education, Illinois State University; R.N., Community College of Denver, 1990 **Current organization:** Artemis Healing & Fine Arts **Title:** C.R.R.N/Director/Therapist/ Reiki Master **Type of organization:** Art studio, alternative healing therapies **Major product:** Fine art and healing **Area of distribution:** National **Area of Practice:** Reiki Master - teaching/Artist and sculptress **Published works:** Articles, poems, short stories **Affiliations:** The Women's Caucus for the Arts; Association for Research and Enlightenment; Rocky Mountain Poison & Drug Center **SIC code:** 80 **Address:** Artemis Healing & Fine Arts, P.O. Box 40435, Denver, CO 80204 **E-mail:** lesliereiki@msn.com **Web address:** www.prosperity.com/leslie

AGUSALA, MADHAVA
Industry: Healthcare **Born:** January 9, 1955, India **Univ./degree:** M.D., Osmania Medical College, India, 1978 **Current organization:** Madhava Agusala, M.D. P.A., Cardiologist, Internal Medicine **Title:** M.D. **Type of organization:** Private practice **Major product:** Patient care **Area of distribution:** Texas **Area of Practice:** Cardiology, internal medicine **Affiliations:** A.M.A.; Texas State Medical Association **SIC code:** 80 **Address:** Madhava Agusala, M.D. P.A., Cardiologist, Internal Medicine, 318 N. Alleghaney Ave., Suite 402, Odessa, TX 79761

AHMAD, IMTIAZ
Industry: Healthcare **Born:** July 18, 1941, Sialkot, Pakistan **Univ./degree:** M.D., King Edward Medical College, 1962; Board Certification, Thoracic and Cardiac Surgery, American Board of Thoracic Surgery **Current organization:** Cardiothoracic & Vascular Associates **Title:** M.D. **Type of organization:** Medical facility **Major product:** Vascular surgery, vein care **Area of distribution:** Trenton, New Jersey **Area of Practice:** Cardiovascular & thoracic surgery, venous disease **Honors/awards:** The Hamiltonian Award, 1986 **Affiliations:** A.M.A.; A.C.S.; Royal College of Surgeons at Edenburg, England; Northeast Academy of Martial Arts; American Martial Arts & Healing Association **Hob./spts.:** Tennis, photography, martial arts - Black Belt Certification August 3, 2001 **SIC code:** 80 **Address:** Cardiothoracic & Vascular Associates, 1760 Whitehorse Hamilton Square Rd., Trenton, NJ 08690 **E-mail:** iamdpa@voicenet.com **Web address:** www.cvtc.net

AHMAD, MAHNAZ
Industry: Healthcare **Univ./degree:** M.B.B.S., Bangladesh, 1992 **Current organization:** The Brooklyn Hospital Center **Title:** M.D. **Type of organization:** Hospital **Major product:** Patient care **Area of distribution:** New York **Area of Practice:** Geriatrics **SIC code:** 80 **Address:** The Brooklyn Hospital Center, 121 Dekalb Ave., Brooklyn, NY 11201

AHMED, NADEEM
Industry: Healthcare **Born:** August 4, 1961, Lahore, Pakistan **Univ./degree:** M.D., Ross University, 1985 **Current organization:** Midwest Pulmonary & Critical Care **Title:** M.D./Clinical Assistant Professor, Kirksville College of Osteopathic Medicine **Type of organization:** Private practice **Major product:** Patient care **Area of distribution:** St. Louis, Missouri **Area of Practice:** Pulmonary and critical care **Published works:** American Review of Respiratory Disease **Affiliations:** A.C.C.P.; A.T.S.; S.C.C.M. **Hob./spts.:** Photography, tennis, racquetball **SIC code:** 80 **Address:** Midwest Pulmonary & Critical Care, 6125 Clayton Ave., #119, St. Louis, MO 63139 **E-mail:** lahoridoc@yahoo.com

AKE, CATHERINE S.
Industry: Mental healthcare/social service **Born:** August 12, 1952, San Marcos, Texas **Univ./degree:** B.A., Social Work, Auburn University, 1975; M.S., Social Work, University of Georgia, 1981 **Current organization:** New Beginnings **Title:** Executive Director **Type of organization:** Mental health center **Major product:** Counseling, adoption supervision, visitations **Area of distribution:** Florida **Area of Practice:** Administration, mental health counseling **Affiliations:** National Association of Social Workers; American Counseling Association **Hob./spts.:** Raising Pomeranians **SIC code:** 80 **Address:** New Beginnings, 310 E. 11th St., Panama City, FL 32401 **E-mail:** newbeginnings@knology.com **Web address:** www.nasw.com

AKINDURO, OLUSINA M.
Industry: Healthcare **Born:** May 2, 1962, Ondo, Nigeria **Univ./degree:** M.D., Ibadan University, Nigeria, 1984 **Current organization:** Lyster Army Hospital **Title:** M.D. **Type of organization:** Hospital **Major product:** Patient care **Area of distribution:** Alabama **Area of Practice:** Internal medicine **Published works:** British Medical Journal, 2 articles **Affiliations:** A.M.A.; A.P.P.A. **Hob./spts.:** Paintball, table tennis **SIC code:** 80 **Address:** Lyster Army Hospital, 301 Andrews Ave., Building 301, Ft. Rucker, AL 36362 **E-mail:** oakinduro@hotmail.com

AKULA, SHIVA K.
Industry: Healthcare **Born:** March 4, 1956, India **Univ./degree:** M.B.B.S., Osomania University, 1979 **Current organization:** VA Medical Center **Title:** M.D. **Type of organization:** Hospital **Major product:** Patient care **Area of distribution:** New Orleans, Louisiana **Area of Practice:** Infectious disease, medicine, hospice **Published works:** Book chapter, "Oral Aids" **Affiliations:** Chair, Canon Health Care Co.; President, Akula Family Foundation **SIC code:** 80 **Address:** 2029 S. Carrollton, New Orleans, LA 70118 **E-mail:** akulashiva@yahoo.com

ALAR, NASIR G.
Industry: Healthcare **Born:** May 5, 1951, Kenya, Africa **Univ./degree:** M.D., Glasgow University, Scotland, 1976 **Current organization:** Nasir Alar, M.D., P.A. **Title:** M.D. **Type of organization:** Private practice **Major product:** Patient care **Area of distribution:** Orlando, Florida **Area of Practice:** Gastroenterology **Affiliations:** A.C.G.; A.M.A.; A.G.A. **Hob./spts.:** Soccer, basketball **SIC code:** 80 **Address:** 9430 Turkey Lake Rd., Suite 110, Orlando, FL 32819 **E-mail:** nalari@aol.com

ALATKAR SHARATHKUMAR, ANJALI
Industry: Medical **Born:** March 7, 1964, Sholapur, India **Univ./degree:** M.D.; Fellowship, Hematology and Oncology, University of Toronto, Canada, 1999 **Current organization:** University of Michigan at Ann Arbor **Title:** M.D. **Type of organization:** University hospital **Major product:** Patient care, pediatrics **Area of distribution:** Michigan **Area of Practice:** Hematology, oncology, pediatric coagulation disorders **Affiliations:** American Society of Hematology **Hob./spts.:** Classical music **SIC code:** 80 **Address:** University of Michigan at Ann Arbor, 1500 E. Medical Center Dr., Ann Arbor, MI 48109 **E-mail:** aalatkar@umich.edu

AL-BATAINEH, MOHAMMAD A.
Industry: Medical **Born:** December 1, 1968, Jordan **Univ./degree:** M.D., Jordan University of Science & Technology, 1992 **Current organization:** Louisiana State University, Section of Cardiology **Title:** M.D. **Type of organization:** University hospital **Major product:** Medical services **Area of distribution:** International **Area of Practice:** Cardiology, cardiac pacemakers and cardiac electrophysiology **Published works:** 10 articles **Affiliations:** F.A.C.C.; N.A.S.P.E. **Hob./spts.:** Family **SIC code:** 80 **Address:** Louisiana State University, Section of Cardiology, 1542 Tulane Ave., B23M-3, Room 436A, New Orleans, LA 70112 **E-mail:** alujane@msn.com

ALEXANDER, JANICE H.
Industry: Healthcare **Born:** June 24, 1949, Detroit, Michigan **Univ./degree:** B.S.N., Wayne State University, 1971; M.D., Wayne State Medical School, 1979; Fellowship, Ob/Gyn, Providence Hospital, Michigan **Current organization:** Mayo Health/Marquette University **Title:** M.D. **Type of organization:** Hospital/private practice **Major product:** Medical services **Area of distribution:** International **Area of Practice:** Ob/Gyn, family medicine **Honors/awards:** Wisconsin Women's Champion in Women's Health, 2004/2005 **Affiliations:** A.M.A.; F.A.C.O.G.; A.A.G.L.; S.L.F.; A.I.U.M.; American Red Cross; Wisconsin Women's Health **SIC code:** 80 **Address:** 464 S. St. Joseph Ave., Arcadia, WI 54612 **E-mail:** janobgyn@naspa.net

ALEXANDER, ONNIE S.
Industry: Healthcare **Title:** A.C.R.N. **Type of organization:** Nonprofit **Major product:** Home services to individuals with AIDS/HIV **Area of Practice:** AIDS certified RN case manager **SIC code:** 80 **Address:** Community Care HIV/AIDS Project, 14644B Lakeshore Dr., Clearlake, CA 95422 **E-mail:** venusdimilo@adelphia.net

ALEXANDRE SR., JEAN C.
Industry: Healthcare **Born:** June, 6, 1942, Port-au-Prince, Haiti **Univ./degree:** M.D., State University of Haiti **Current organization:** The Center For Women **Title:** M.D. **Type of organization:** Private Practice **Major product:** Women's healthcare **Area of distribution:** Melrose Park, Illinois **Area of Practice:** Medical Ob/Gyn **Honors/awards:** Past Ambassador of U.S. to Haiti (speaker at the UN) **Published works:** Co-authored several research articles **Affiliations:** Fellow, American College of Obstetricians and Gynecologists; American College of Surgeons; Assistant Professor, Loyola University Medical School **SIC code:** 80 **Address:** The Center for Women, 1419 W. Lake St., Suite B, Melrose Park, IL 60160 **E-mail:** perfrancois2004@yahoo.com

ALEXANDRESCU, RODICA S.
Industry: Healthcare **Born:** December 21, 1938, Bucharest, Romania **Univ./degree:** M.D., University of Bucharest, 1961; Ph.D., Cardiology, New York Medical College **Current organization:** Metropolitan Hospital **Title:** Chief of Rehabilitation/Associate Professor at New York Medical College **Type of organization:** Hospital **Major product:** Patient care **Area of distribution:** New York **Area of Practice:** General rehabilitation medicine, cardiac rehabilitation, electrodiagnostic studies, clinical instruction, pain management (Board Certified), physical and medical rehabilitation (Board Certified) **Affiliations:** American Academy of Pain Management **Hob./spts.:** Gymnastics, painting, studying languages **SIC code:** 80 **Address:** Metropolitan Hospital, 1901 1st Ave., New York, NY 10029 **E-mail:** ralexandrescu@nyc.rr.com

ALFANO, FRANK D.
Industry: Healthcare **Born:** September 27, 1951, Stamford, Connecticut **Univ./degree:** B.S., Physics, Fordham University, 1973; M.D., Columbia School of Medicine, 1978 **Current organization:** Medical Oncology-Hematology **Title:** M.D. **Type of organization:** Group practice **Major product:** Medical therapy and research **Area of distribution:** Connecticut **Area of Practice:** Theoretical biology, mathematical, analysis of oncogenes **Published works:** Author/Co-Author of articles in medical journals including "A stochastic model of oncogene expression and the relevance of this model to cancer therapy" and "Selective elimination of fibroblasts from cultures of normal human melanocytes" **Affiliations:** W.M.A.; L.C.M.A., F.A.C.O. **Hob./spts.:** Tennis, reading, biking **SIC code:** 80 **Address:** Medical Oncology-Hematology, 1075 Chase Pkwy., Waterbury, CT 06830 **E-mail:** fralfano@aol.com

ALFRED, KARL S.
Industry: Healthcare **Born:** Norway **Spouse:** Mollie Bombach **Married:** 1951 **Children:** Peter, 62; Richard, 63, Step-daughter, Patricia Alleman, 66 (6 grandchildren and 3 great-grandchildren) **Univ./degree:** 5AB, University of Virginia, Pre-Med, 1938; M.D., Downstate Medical Center (SUNY), Brooklyn, New York, 1942; Internship, Mountainside Hospital, Montclair, New Jersey; Residency, University Hospitals, Cleveland **Current organization:** Karl S. Alfred, M.D., L.F.A.C.S. **Title:** M.D./ Life Fellow, American College of Surgeons (Retired) **Type of organization:** Private practice **Major product:** Patient care, medical consultation, medical meetings **Area of distribution:** International **Area of Practice:** Orthopaedic surgery consulting, lecturing **Honors/awards:** Lectureship in his Honor and Teacher of the Year, Cleveland Clinic Orthopaedic Department (3 times); Special Honors Award for Many Years of Service with Distinction, Cleveland Academy of Medicine, 1989; Charles Hudson Award for Distinguished Service, 1994; Presented with a plaque in recognition for all the contributions to the Dept. of Orthopaedic Surgery in the capacity of Affiliate Faculty, the Cleveland Clinic Education Foundation, 1960-88; Honors for many years of distinguished service to St. Vincent Charity Hospital, its patients and to the mission of the hospital, St. Vincent Charity Hospital's Society of St. Luke, 2004; Edward F. Myers Award as Outstanding Hospital Trustee, Center for Health Affairs **Published works:** 5 publications to journals, 7 exhibits and lectures delivered nationally and internationally **Affiliations:** Lt. Commander, US Navy Medical Corps., American Medical Association; Life Fellow, American College of Surgeons; Fellow, American Academy of Orthopaedic Surgeons; Clinical Orthopaedic Society; Mid-America Orthopedic Society; International College of Surgeons; Norwegian American Orthopedic Society; Professor, Cleveland Clinic; Member, Board of Directors, Cleveland Academy of Medicine (8 years); Cleveland Orthopedic Society **Hob./spts.:** Travel, sports, swimming, walking **SIC code:** 80 **Address:** 20 Brandywood Dr., Pepper Pike, OH 44124

ALHADHERI, SHABIB A.
Industry: Healthcare **Born:** April 25, Yemen **Univ./degree:** M.B.B.S., King Saud University, Saudi Arabia, 1992 **Current organization:** Children's Heart Institute **Title:** M.D. **Type of organization:** Group practice **Major product:** Patient care **Area of distribution:** International **Area of practice:** Pediatric cardiology **Area of Practice:** Pediatric cardiology **Honors/awards:** Teacher of the Year, Upstate Medical University, 1998-2000; Physician's Recognition Award, American Medical Association, 2000-2003 **Published works:** Doctor's Ethics, 1992 Ed.; Alcohol and Diseases, 1993 Ed.; Towards Understanding Sleep Theories, 1997 Ed.; **Affiliations:** F.A.A.P; A.C.C.; A.H.A.; S.O.P.E.; A.M.A. **Hob./spts.:** Traveling with family, camping, reading **SIC code:** 80 **Address:** Children's Heart Institute, 9550 Surveyor Ct., Manassas, VA 20110 **E-mail:** alhadhes@upstate.edu **Web address:** www.childrenheartinstitute.org

ALKHALILI, ADNAN R.
Industry: Healthcare **Born:** March 28, 1966, Nablus, Jordan **Univ./degree:** M.D., College of Medicine at Jordan University, 1990 **Current organization:** Marquette General Health System **Title:** M.D. **Type of organization:** Hospital **Major product:** Patient care **Area of Practice:** Internal medicine, oncology, medical liaison **Published works:** 6 articles **Affiliations:** A.S.C.O.; A.M.A. **Hob./spts.:** Soccer, swimming **SIC code:** 80 **Address:** Marquette General Health System, 510 Ashmun St., Sault Sainte Marie, MI 49783 **E-mail:** adkhalili@pol.net

ALLAHRAKHA, MOHAMMED F.
Industry: Healthcare **Born:** January 12, 1975, Karachi, Pakistan **Univ./degree:** M.D., American University of the Caribbean, 1997 **Current organization:** Trinity Medical Center **Title:** M.D. **Type of organization:** Hospital **Major product:** Medical services **Area of distribution:** International **Area of Practice:** Family practice **Hob./spts.:** Computers, home remodeling **SIC code:** 80 **Address:** Trinity Medical Center, 104 W. 18th Ave., Coal Valley, IL 61240 **E-mail:** mferoza@pol.net

ALLEGRA II, EDWARD C.
Industry: Healthcare **Born:** February 17, 1962, Red Bank, New Jersey **Univ./degree:** M.D., Universidad Autonoma de Guadalajara, 1988 **Title:** M.D. **Type of organization:** Private practice **Major product:** Patient care **Area of distribution:** National **Area of Practice:** Arthritis, rheumatology **Affiliations:** N.J.M.S.; A.C.R. **Hob./spts.:** Golf **SIC code:** 80 **Address:** 282 Broad St., Red Bank, NJ 07701

ALLEN, BRENDA O.
Industry: Healthcare **Born:** November 24, 1949, Fort Worth, Texas **Current organization:** Tarrant County Infectious Disease Associates **Title:** Business Manager **Type of organization:** Private practice **Major product:** Patient care **Area of distribution:** Texas **Area of Practice:** Administration **Published works:** Policy and procedures **Affiliations:** M.M.M.A.; A.C.E.M.P.E.; Certified, M.O.M. **Hob./spts.:** Grandchildren, yard work, crocheting **SIC code:** 80 **Address:** Tarrant County Infectious Disease Associates, Daniel Barbaro, M.D., 1125 College Ave., Ft. Worth, TX 76104 **E-mail:** brenda@tarrantcountyinfectiousdisease.com **Web address:** www.tarrantcountyinfectiousdisease.com

ALLEN, GEORGE D.
Industry: Medical **Born:** July 24, 1952, Trinidad, West Indies **Univ./degree:** Ph.D., Kenniston University, 1998 **Current organization:** Downstate Medical Center **Title:** Director, Infection Control **Type of organization:** University hospital **Major product:** Patient care, medical education **Area of distribution:** Brooklyn, New York **Area of Practice:** Epidemiology, infection control **Honors/awards:** Barduti, 2001 **Affiliations:** Association for Professionals in Infection Control & Epidemiology **Hob./spts.:** Reading, stamp collecting **SIC code:** 80 **Address:** Downstate Medical Center, 450 Clarkson Ave., Box 1187, Brooklyn, NY 11203 **E-mail:** allen_g1@yahoo.com

ALLEN, KA RÉN A.
Industry: Healthcare **Born:** Philadelphia, Pennsylvania **Univ./degree:** R.N., B.S.N., Widener University **Current organization:** Temple Northeastern Hospital **Title:** R.N. **Type of organization:** Hospital **Major product:** Patient care **Area of distribution:** Philadelphia, Pennsylvania **Area of Practice:** Surgical nursing, acute care **Affiliations:** A.N.A.; Hispanic Nursing Society **Hob./spts.:** Nursing research, applied nursing **SIC code:** 80 **Address:** Temple Northeastern Hospital, 2100 E. Allegheny Ave., Philadelphia, PA 19134 **E-mail:** kammi_bsn@rn.com

ALLISON, STACY L.
Industry: Healthcare **Born:** August 23, 1964, Belleville, Illinois **Univ./degree:** B.S., Biology, 1986; B.S., Medical Technology, 1987, Pittsburgh State University **Current organization:** Bradley Memorial Hospital **Title:** Medical Technologist/Laboratory Manager **Type of organization:** Hospital **Major product:** Patient care **Area of distribution:** Georgia **Area of Practice:** Medical technology **Affiliations:** A.S.C.P. **Hob./spts.:** Volleyball, softball, gardening **SIC code:** 80 **Address:** Bradley Memorial Hospital, 230 S. Chambliss Ave., Cleveland, TN 37311 **E-mail:** sallison@chs.net

ALMASALMEH, NASER
Industry: Healthcare **Born:** August 12, 1964, Deraa, Syria **Univ./degree:** M.D., Damascus University, Syria **Current organization:** Elite Medical **Title:** M.D. **Type of organization:** Medical practice **Major product:** Patient care **Area of distribution:** Illinois **Area of Practice:** Internal medicine **Affiliations:** A.M.A.; A.C.P. **Hob./spts.:** Music, weightlifting, fishing, reading, chess, skiing **SIC code:** 80 **Address:** Elite Medical, 620 E. Third St., #200, Alton, IL 62002

ALMEIDA, JOSE I.
Industry: Healthcare **Born:** December 12, 1963, Kansas City, Missouri **Univ./degree:** Attended Loyola University, Biology, 1981-83; B.S., Biology, University of South Florida, 1987; M.D., University of South Florida College of Medicine, 1991 **Current organization:** Miami Vein Center **Title:** M.D./Vascular Surgeon **Type of organization:** Private practice **Major product:** Endovenous laser treatment, varicose veins, vein disease, spider veins, laser ablation, radiofrequency ablation, sclerotherapy, phlebology **Area of distribution:** Florida **Area of Practice:** Venous disease **Honors/awards:** Beta Beta Beta Honorary Biological Society, 1982; Alpha Epsilon Delta Premedical Honor Society, 1984-1987; Most Outstanding Surgical Student, USFCOM, 1991; America's Top Surgeons, Consumers Research Council of America, 2002-03, 2004-05, 2006; Listed in Strathmore's Who's Who, 2004-05 **Published works:** Numerous publications including: Almeida JI, Colombo JA. In vitro of neural cell aggregates; effects on attachment and growth. Anat Rec 1987;218:8A; Almeida JI, Liem TK, Silver D. Heparin-bonded grafts induce platelet aggregation in the presence of heparin-associated antiplatelet antibodies. J Vasc Surg 1998;Vol27(5):896-901; Almeida JI, RFA versus laser ablation of the saphenous vein. Endovascular Today. 2004;Vol3(10)Supp:15-19 **Affiliations:** Society For Vascular Surgery; American College of Surgeons; American Venous Forum; International Society for Vascular Surgery; American College of Phlebology; Florida Medical Society; Jackson Surgical Society; American Registry for Diagnostic Medical Sonography **Hob./spts.:** Black Belt in Karate, body building, skiing **SIC code:** 80 **Address:** Miami Vein Center, L.L.C., 1501 South Miami Ave., Miami, FL 33129 **E-mail:** almeida_ji@hotmail.com **Web address:** www.miamiveincenter.com

ALMEYDA, ELIZABETH A.
Industry: Healthcare **Born:** September 2, 1952, New York, New York **Univ./degree:** B.S. 1974; M.D., 1978, University of Rochester, New York **Current organization:** Elizabeth A. Almeyda, M.D. **Title:** M.D. **Type of organization:** Private medical practice **Major product:** Plastic and reconstructive surgery **Area of distribution:**

New York **Area of Practice:** Plastic reconstructive surgery **Affiliations:** American Medical Association; New York State Medical Society; American Society of Plastic and Reconstructive Surgery **Hob./spts.:** Skiing, golf **SIC code:** 80 **Address:** Elizabeth A. Almeyda, M.D., 75 Central Park W., New York, NY 10023

ALMOND, KELLY B.
Industry: Healthcare **Univ./degree:** B.S., Biology, Appalachian State University, North Carolina, 1985; M.S., Biochemistry, University of North Carolina, Greensboro, 1988 **Current organization:** Stanly Regional Medical Center **Title:** Manager, Pathology and Laboratory Services **Type of organization:** Medical center **Major product:** Patient care **Area of distribution:** North Carolina **Area of Practice:** Medical Technologist MT(ASCP) **Affiliations:** Southeastern Association for Clinical Microbiologists; Habitat for Humanity; Healing Touch **Hob./spts.:** Community theatre, church, choir **SIC code:** 80 **Address:** Stanly Regional Medical Center, 301 Yadkin St., Albemarle, NC 28001 **E-mail:** kelly.almond@stanly.org

AL-MUBARAK, NADIM
Industry: Medical **Born:** February 18, 1962, Saudi Arabia **Univ./degree:** M.D., University of Vienna School of Medicine, 1987 **Current organization:** University Hospitals of Cleveland **Title:** M.D. **Type of organization:** University hospital **Major product:** Medical services **Area of Practice:** Interventional cardiology **Published works:** 30+ articles, 1 book **Affiliations:** American College of Cardiology; American Heart Association **Hob./spts.:** Reading, writing, horseback riding, swimming **SIC code:** 80 **Address:** 205-25 Center Ridge Rd., Room 400, Rocky River, OH 44116 **E-mail:** nalmubarak@aol.com

ALSOKARY, ZIAD
Industry: Medical **Univ./degree:** M.S.N., San Francisco University, 2003 **Current organization:** Society of Critical Care Medicine **Title:** Clinical Nurse Specialist in Critical Care **Type of organization:** University hospital **Major product:** Patient care **Area of distribution:** Mountain View, California **Area of Practice:** Critical care medicine **Affiliations:** American Association of Critical Care Nurses **Hob./spts.:** Soccer, scuba diving instructor, underwater photography **SIC code:** 80 **Address:** 1050 Crestview Dr., #315, Mountain View, CA 94040 **E-mail:** alsokary@yahoo.com

ALSTON, CHERYL A.
Industry: Healthcare **Born:** June 24, 1946, Joliet, Illinois **Univ./degree:** M.A., Psychology, University of North Colorado, 1984 **Current organization:** Family Management Services, Inc. **Title:** President, CEO **Type of organization:** Family management service **Major product:** Case management, home care **Area of distribution:** National **Area of Practice:** Psychology, counseling **Affiliations:** N.A.P.G.C.M.; N.G.A.; V.G.A.; V.A.H.C. **Hob./spts.:** Yacht captain, poetry **SIC code:** 80 **Address:** Family Management Services, Inc., 10306 Eaton Pl., Suite 250, Fairfax, VA 22030 **E-mail:** calstonoffms@verizon.net **Web address:** www.familymgmt.com

ALVA, CATHERINE M.
Industry: Healthcare **Born:** February 17, 1960, Detroit, Michigan **Univ./degree:** B.S., Medical Technology, Western Michigan University, 1982 **Current organization:** Wellington Regional Medical Center **Title:** Medical Technologist **Type of organization:** Hospital **Major product:** Patient care **Area of distribution:** Florida **Area of Practice:** Microbiology supervisor, hospital laboratory services **Affiliations:** A.S.C.P. **Hob./spts.:** Soccer, softball **SIC code:** 80 **Address:** 191 Martin Circle, Royal Palm Beach, FL 33411

ALVARADO, STEPHEN P.
Industry: Healthcare **Born:** December 28, 1966, Sayre, Pennsylvania **Univ./degree:** M.D., State University of New York, Stony Brook, 1997 **Current organization:** Branch Pediatrics **Title:** M.D. **Type of organization:** Private practice **Major product:** Children's healthcare **Area of distribution:** Long Island, New York **Area of Practice:** Pediatrics **Published works:** Multiple publications **Affiliations:** F.A.A.P.; New York State Medical Society; Suffolk County Pediatric Society **SIC code:** 80 **Address:** Branch Pediatrics, 300 E. Main St., Suite 5, Smithtown, NY 11787 **E-mail:** p.brnped@optonline.net

ALVERSON, ELIZABETH A.
Industry: Healthcare **Born:** May 23, 1950, Oelwein Iowa **Univ./degree:** B.S., Chemistry, Upper Iowa College, 1972; B.S., Medical Technology, 1973 **Current organization:** Mercy Medical Center - North Iowa **Title:** Laboratory Supervisor **Type of organization:** Hospital **Major product:** Patient care **Area of distribution:** National **Area of Practice:** Clinical laboratory services, clinical chemistry **Affiliations:** American Society for Clinical Laboratory Science **Hob./spts.:** Reading, genealogy **SIC code:** 80 **Address:** Mercy Medical Center - North Iowa, 1000 4th St. SW, Mason City, IA 50401 **E-mail:** alversob@mercyhealth.com

ALWANI, ABDULLA
Industry: Healthcare **Univ./degree:** M.D., Damascus University Hospital, Syria 1979: SUNY Downstate New York Medical School, 1986 **Current organization:** Bay Ridge Pediatrics and Adolescents Office P.C. **Title:** M.D. **Type of organization:** Medical center **Major product:** Patient care **Area of distribution:** Brooklyn, New York **Area of Practice:** Pediatrics **Affiliations:** Kings County Medical Society; Fellow, American Academy of Pediatrics **Hob./spts.:** Reading, golf **SIC code:** 80 **Address:** Bay Ridge Pediatrics & Adolescents Office P.C., 217 73rd St., Brooklyn, NY 11209 **E-mail:** aalwanimd@aol.com

ALWAWI, MOUSA
Industry: Healthcare **Born:** December 5, 1967, Jordan **Univ./degree:** M.D., Faculty Medical University of Jordan, 1992 **Current organization:** Comprehensive Care Medical Offices **Title:** M.D. **Type of organization:** Clinic/hospital **Major product:** Patient care **Area of distribution:** Georgia **Area of Practice:** Internal medicine **Published works:** 1 peer reviewed article **Affiliations:** A.C.P.; A.S.I.M. **SIC code:** 80 **Address:** Comprehensive Care Medical Offices, 115 Tom Chapman Blvd., Suite 1006, Warner Robins, GA 31088 **E-mail:** malwawi@aol.com **Web address:** www.myhealth.com\maher-abdulla

ALZAGHRINI, GHASSAN J.
Industry: Healthcare **Born:** April 12, 1968, Lebanon **Univ./degree:** B.S., Biology, American University, 1988; M.D., American University School of Medicine, 1992 **Current organization:** Hillcroft Medical Clinic **Title:** MD/FACC **Type of organization:** Clinic **Major product:** Patient care **Area of distribution:** Texas **Area of Practice:** Cardiology **Published works:** Abstracts **Affiliations:** F.A.C.C.; Harris County Medical Society **SIC code:** 80 **Address:** Hillcroft Medical Clinic, 2500 Fondren Rd., Suite 270, Houston, TX 77063

AMARCHAND, LINGAPPA
Industry: Healthcare **Born:** April 5, 1956, Bangalore, India **Univ./degree:** M.D., India, 1980 **Current organization:** Lingappa Amarchand, M.D. **Title:** M.D. **Type of organization:** Private practice **Major product:** Patient care **Area of distribution:** Brookville, Florida **Area of Practice:** Cardiology **Published works:** Articles **Affiliations:** A.M.A.; American College of Physicians **Hob./spts.:** Tennis, golf **SIC code:** 80 **Address:** Lingappa Amarchand, M.D., 750 DeSoto Ave., Brooksville, FL 34601

AMLER, DAVID H.
Industry: Healthcare **Born:** November 4, 1943, New York, New York **Univ./degree:** M.D., State University of New York, Buffalo **Current organization:** Chester Pediatrics **Title:** M.D. **Type of organization:** Private practice **Major product:** Patient care **Area of distribution:** White Plains, New York **Area of Practice:** General pediatrics **Affiliations:** A.A.P.; A.M.A. **Hob./spts.:** Golf, skiing **SIC code:** 80 **Address:** Chester Pediatrics, 15 North Broadway, White Plains, NY 10601

ANCONA, KEITH G.
Industry: Healthcare **Born:** January 5, 1973, Brooklyn, New York **Univ./degree:** M.D., Rush University, 1998 **Current organization:** Branch Pediatrics **Title:** M.D. **Type of organization:** Private practice **Major product:** Children's healthcare **Area of distribution:** Long Island, New York **Area of Practice:** Pediatrics **Published works:** 2 articles **Affiliations:** A.A.P.; Suffolk County Medical Society **Hob./spts.:** Skiing **SIC code:** 80 **Address:** Branch Pediatrics, 300 E. Main St., Suite 5, Smithtown, NY 11787 **E-mail:** brnchped@optonline.net

ANCONA, RICHARD C.
Industry: Healthcare **Born:** M.D., University of Bonn, Germany, 1975 **Univ./degree:** December 21, 1946, Brooklyn, New York **Current organization:** Branch Pediatrics/SUNY at Stony Brook **Title:** M.D./Clinical Assistant Professor **Type of organization:** Private practice/university **Major product:** Patient care/higher education **Area of distribution:** New York **Area of Practice:** Pediatrics **Published works:** Multiple publications **Affiliations:** A.A.P.; Suffolk County Medical Society; New York Academy of Sciences **Hob./spts.:** Hockey, skiing, boating **SIC code:** 80 **Address:** Branch Pediatrics, 300 E. Main St., Suite 5, Smithtown, NY 11787 **E-mail:** brnped@optonline.net

ANDERSON, BEVERLY C.
Industry: Healthcare **Univ./degree:** B.S., Nebraska Wesleyan University, 1973; R.N. Diploma, Bryan Memorial Hospital School of Nursing **Current organization:** Asera Care Hospice **Title:** Director of Clinical Operations **Type of organization:** Home healthcare/hospice **Major product:** End of life care for family and patient **Area of distribution:** Nebraska **Area of Practice:** Medical/nursing **Affiliations:** UM Church **Hob./spts.:** Board Member of local church, crafts, gardening, music **SIC code:** 80 **Address:** Asera Care Hospice, 1909 Vicki Lane, Norfolk, NE 68701 **E-mail:** beliveau@stanton.net

ANDERSON, CYNTHIA W.
Industry: Healthcare **Univ./degree:** M.S.N., Medical University of South Carolina, 1988; N.P., University of South Carolina, 1994 **Current organization:** Charleston Neurosurgical Associates, LLC **Title:** RN, ACNP, CNRN **Type of organization:** Private neurosurgical practice **Area of distribution:** South Carolina **Area of Practice:**

Neurosurgery **Affiliations:** A.N.A.; A.A.N.S.; A.A.N.N. **Hob./spts.:** Softball, physical fitness **SIC code:** 80 **Address:** Charleston Neurosurgical Associates, LLC, 9275-B Medical Plaza Dr., Charleston, SC 29406 **E-mail:** caneuron@aol.com

ANDERSON, DAVID JAY
Industry: Healthcare/medical research **Born:** May 21, 1957, New York, New York **Univ./degree:** M.D., University of Texas at Galveston, 1985 **Current organization:** Stony Brook University School of Medicine **Title:** M.D. **Type of organization:** Medical school **Major product:** Patient care, research, education, natural product development and evaluation, claims maximization **Area of distribution:** International **Area of Practice:** Claims substantiation, alternatives to animal testing, internal medicine, pulmonary medicine, natural medicine **Published works:** Medical journals **Affiliations:** American Medical Association **SIC code:** 80 **Address:** 26 Bunny Lane, East Setauket, NY 11733 **E-mail:** dja@netzero.com

ANDERSON, JOHN A.
Industry: Healthcare **Born:** February 22, 1949, Orlando, Florida **Univ./degree:** D.D.S., Emory University, 1975 **Current organization:** Daytona Denture Center **Title:** D.D.S., M.S. **Type of organization:** Private practice, 3 offices **Major product:** Prosthodontist **Area of distribution:** Daytona Beach, Florida **Area of Practice:** Removable prosthodontics, implants **Affiliations:** American Dental Association; American College of Prosthodontics; Florida Association of Prosthodontics **Hob./spts.:** Automobiles, muscle cars, fast cars **SIC code:** 80 **Address:** Daytona Denture Center, 1516 S. Nova Blvd., Daytona Beach, FL 32114 **E-mail:** jasmar3002@hotmail.com **Web address:** www.daytonadental.com

ANDERSON, LANETTA L.
Industry: Healthcare **Univ./degree:** B.S., Chemistry/Biology, Lake Forest University, 1988; M.D., Johns Hopkins University Medical School, 1992 **Current organization:** Women's Physician Group **Title:** M.D. **Type of organization:** Group practice **Major product:** Patient care **Area of distribution:** Tennessee **Area of Practice:** Ob/Gyn **Affiliations:** A.M.A.; Tennessee Medical Association **SIC code:** 80 **Address:** Women's Physician Group, 1469 Poplar Ave., Memphis, TN 38104

ANDREWS, DIANE
Industry: Healthcare **Born:** Baton Rouge, Louisiana **Univ./degree:** M.B.A., University of Phoenix, Arizona, 2000 **Current organization:** Home Health Solutions Home Care, Inc. **Title:** Owner/Administrator **Type of organization:** In-home medical provider **Major product:** Home healthcare services **Area of distribution:** Louisiana **Area of Practice:** Operations, management, administrator **Published works:** Motivational calendar, "Gumbo for the Heart" **Affiliations:** National Black MBA Association **Hob./spts.:** Flower arrangements **SIC code:** 80 **Address:** Home Health Solutions Home Care, Inc., 3875 Florida Blvd., Baton Rouge, LA 70806 **E-mail:** hsihhcare@aol.com

ANDREWS, GRAN L.
Industry: Healthcare **Born:** September 2, 1977, Franklin, Louisiana **Univ./degree:** A.A., Applied Sciences/Radiologic Technology, 1997, Copiah-Lincoln Community College; Certificate of Nuclear Medicine Technology, University Medical Center of Jackson, MS, 1998 **Current organization:** Acadiana Oncologic Imaging **Title:** Chief Nuclear Medicine Technologist **Type of organization:** Imaging center **Major product:** Imaging **Area of Practice:** Nuclear Medicine/PET scans **Affiliations:** Society of Nuclear Medicine; Academy of Molecular Imaging; American Society of Radiologic Technologists; Nuclear Medicine Technology Certificate Board **Hob./spts.:** Fishing, hunting, golf **SIC code:** 80 **Address:** 103 Ellerslie Ct., Lafayette, LA 70503 **E-mail:** gacand@yahoo.com

ANDREWS, RICHARD V.
Industry: Healthcare **Born:** July 20, 1949, Tacoma, Washington **Univ./degree:** M.D., University of Iowa, 1976 **Current organization:** RaNeurological **Title:** Physician **Type of organization:** Private practice **Major product:** Patient care **Area of distribution:** Omaha. Nebraska **Area of Practice:** Neurology **Affiliations:** A.M.A.; N.E.S.; A.C.N.S.; F.P.A. **Hob./spts.:** Flying (pilot) **SIC code:** 80 **Address:** RaNeurological, 11930 Arbor St., Suite 200, Omaha, NE 68144 **E-mail:** rneuro@aol.com

ANDREWS, ROXANNE R.
Industry: Healthcare **Born:** May 12, 1951, Dover-Foxcraft, Maine **Current organization:** Branches Home Care **Title:** Director **Type of organization:** Home health companion agency **Major product:** Services for the elderly **Area of distribution:** Maine **Area of Practice:** Home healthcare, administration, companionship, errands **Hob./spts.:** Travel, reading **SIC code:** 80 **Address:** Branches Home Care, 15 Parsons Rd., Westport Island, ME 04578 **E-mail:** branchesathome@msn.com **Web address:** www.brancheshomecare.org

ANDRONE, ANA SILVIA
Industry: Medical **Born:** November 23, 1969, Bucharest, Romania **Univ./degree:** M.D., Carol Davila School of Medicine, Bucharest, Romania, 1994 **Current organization:** Yale University, American Heart Association **Title:** M.D. **Type of organization:** University hospital **Major product:** Research, medical education, patient care **Area of distribution:** International **Area of Practice:** Heart failure, transplantation, internal medicine **Published works:** 2 reference journals (7 pending), 10 abstracts/conference papers **Affiliations:** F.A.C.P.; A.H.A.; A.M.A. **Hob./spts.:** Tennis, swimming **SIC code:** 80 **Address:** 1083 Astor Ave, Bronx, NY 10469 **E-mail:** silviuta@hotmail.com

ANGELATS, JUAN
Industry: Medical **Born:** September 7, 1941, Peru **Univ./degree:** M.D., San Marcos University Medical School, Peru, 1967 **Current organization:** Loyola University **Title:** M.D., Professor and Chief of Plastic Surgery **Type of organization:** University/hospital **Major product:** Medical services **Area of distribution:** Illinois **Area of Practice:** Plastic surgery, administration, teaching, research **Published works:** 21 publications including, Co-author, "Modified Autogenous Latissimus Breast Reconstruction and the Box Top Nipple", Plastic & Reconstructive Surgery 106(4):763-768, Sept. 2000; "Skin-Sparing Mastectomy with Sentinel Lymph Node Dissection: Less is More", Archives of Surgery 136:1069-1075, Sept. 2001; "Incidence of Intercostobrachial Nerve Injury After Transaxillary Breast Augmentation", Aesthetic Surgery Journal 22(1):26-32, 2002; Co-Author, A Full Nasal Skin Rotation Flap for Closure of Soft Tissue Defects in the Lower One-Third of the Nose, Plastic & Reconstructive Surgery 98(1):163-66, July 1996 **Affiliations:** A.C.S.; A.S.P.S. **SIC code:** 80 **Address:** Loyola University, Division of Plastic Surgery, 2160 S. First Ave., Maywood, IL 60153 **E-mail:** jangela@lumc.edu

ANSA, EVELYN M.
Industry: Medical **Born:** April 27, 1964, Accra, Ghana **Univ./degree:** M.B.; Ch.B.; B.Sc.; University of Science & Technology, Kumasi, Ghana **Current organization:** Williamsburg Regional Hospital **Title:** M.D. **Type of organization:** Community hospital **Major product:** Medical services **Area of distribution:** International **Area of Practice:** Obstetric anesthesia **Affiliations:** A.S.A.; S.O.A.P.; N.Y.S.S.A. **Hob./spts.:** Music, basketball **SIC code:** 80 **Address:** Albany Medical Center, 12 Heritage Ct., Kingston, NY 12401 **E-mail:** asare@aol.com

ANSARA, MAHA F.
Industry: Healthcare **Born:** April 18, 1959, Egypt **Univ./degree:** M.D., Islet Cell Transplant, Ainshams University, Egypt and Washington University, 1994 **Current organization:** Regency Endocrinology and Diabetes **Title:** Doctor **Type of organization:** Private practice **Major product:** Endocrinology **Area of distribution:** Florida **Area of Practice:** Endocrinology, diabetes **Published works:** 25+ papers and articles **Affiliations:** A.M.A.; American Diabetes Association **Hob./spts.:** Basketball, swimming, singing **SIC code:** 80 **Address:** 4106 W. Lake Mary Blvd., Suite 325, Lake Mary, FL 32766

ANSINGKAR, KAMLESH G.
Industry: Education **Born:** June 12, 1964, India **Univ./degree:** M.D., Government Medical College, Nagpur, India, (Affiliated to Nagpur University) 1987; M.S., Health Informatics, University of Alabama at Birmingham, 2002 **Current organization:** Creighton University **Title:** Manager/M.D. **Type of organization:** University **Major product:** Higher education **Area of distribution:** Nebraska **Published works:** 13 publications **Affiliations:** International Society of Cardiovascular Ultrasound; Healthcare Information and Management Systems Society; American Health Information Management Association; Association of Otlaryngologists of India (Vidarbha Branch) **Hob./spts.:** Family, reading **SIC code:** 80 **Address:** 19302 N St., Omaha, NE 68135 **E-mail:** kansingkar@yahoo.com

ANTHONY, KRISTEN D.
Industry: Healthcare **Born:** January 22, 1970, St. Louis, Missouri **Current organization:** Bethesda Health Group **Title:** R.N., Nurse Manager **Type of organization:** Nursing home **Major product:** Patient care **Area of distribution:** Missouri **Area of Practice:** Medicare, transitional care, administration **Affiliations:** A.A.N.A.C. **Hob./spts.:** Gardening, soccer **SIC code:** 80 **Address:** Bethesda Health Group, 322 Old State Rd., Division 200, Ellisville, MO 63021 **E-mail:** kdanthony@bethesdahealthgroup.org

ANZOLA JR., JOSEPH R.
Industry: Healthcare **Born:** May 28, 1957, Ft. Monmouth, New Jersey **Univ./degree:** A.S., Radiology, Santa Rosa Junior College, 1995 **Current organization:** Sutter Medical Center of Santa Rosa **Title:** R.T. (R)(CT) A.R.R.T. (CRT)(LRT) **Type of organization:** Hospital **Major product:** Patient care **Area of distribution:** California **Area of Practice:** Lead Technologist, diagnostic imaging (X-ray, MRI) **Honors/awards:** Deans High Honors; Sixth U.S. Army Commanders Volunteer Service Award; Board Member, SEIU Local 702; Union Steward, SEIU Local 707 **Affiliations:** A.R.R.T.; A.S.R.T.; C.S.R.T., Former President, North Bay Radiographers **SIC code:** 80 **Address:** Sutter Medical Center of Santa Rosa, 3325 Chanate Rd., Santa Rosa, CA 95404 **E-mail:** x-rayjoe@comcast.net

APFELDORF, WILLIAM J.
Industry: Medical **Born:** October 27, 1959, New York, New York **Univ./degree:** B.S.; M.S., Yale University; M.D.; Ph.D., Yale University School of Medicine **Current organization:** University of New Mexico School of Medicine **Title:** Associate Professor of Psychiatry **Type of organization:** University, hospital **Major product:** Patient care, medical education **Area of distribution:** New Mexico **Area of Practice:** Geriatric psychiatry **Affiliations:** A.M.A.; A.P.A. **SIC code:** 80 **Address:** University of New Mexico School of Medicine, 1 U.N.M. Place, NE MSC09 5030, Albuquerque, NM 87131 **E-mail:** wapfeldorf@salud.unm.edu

APPELL, RODNEY A.
Industry: Medical **Born:** February 23, 1947, Philadelphia, Pennsylvania **Univ./degree:** M.D., Jefferson Medical College, 1973 **Current organization:** Baylor College of Medicine **Title:** M.D. **Type of organization:** Medical college **Major product:** Patient care, medical education, research **Area of distribution:** National **Area of Practice:** Urology (specializing in females) **Published works:** 200+ publications **Affiliations:** A.U.A.; I.C.S.; President, S.U.F.U. **Hob./spts.:** Spectator sports, travel **SIC code:** 80 **Address:** Baylor College of Medicine, 5211 Aspen St., Bellaire, TX 77401 **E-mail:** rappell@bcm.tmc.edu

APPLEGATE, STEPHEN M.
Industry: Healthcare **Born:** April 27, 1961, Versailles, Kentucky **Univ./degree:** B.S., Psychology/Bible Studies, Asbury College,1983; M.S., Counseling/Psychology, University of Kentucky, 1986 **Current organization:** Bluegrass Regional Mental Health-Mental Retardation Board, Inc. **Title:** Children's Regional Program Director **Type of organization:** Nonprofit mental health center **Major product:** Mental health treatment services **Area of distribution:** National **Area of Practice:** Counseling, psychology **Affiliations:** Past member, Kentucky Psychological Association **Hob./spts.:** All sports, theatre, church activities **SIC code:** 80 **Address:** Bluegrass Regional Mental Health &, Mental Retardation Board Inc., P.O. Box 11428, Lexington, KY 40575 **E-mail:** smapplegat@bluegrass.org **Web address:** www.bluegrass.org

ARAIN, SHAKOOR A.
Industry: Healthcare **Univ./degree:** M.D., Chanaka Medical College, Pakistan, 1979; Diploma, Cardiology, Univ. of London, UK, 1988; M.R.C.P., Royal College of Physicians, UK, 1990; Residency, WSU School of Medicine, 1990-93; Fellowship Cardiology, Yale Univ./Norwalk Hospital, 1993-96 **Current organization:** Treasure Coast Cardiology **Title:** M.D. **Type of organization:** Private practice **Major product:** Patient care **Area of distribution:** Florida **Area of Practice:** Cardiology **Honors/awards:** Chief Resident Teaching Award **Published works:** 1 article **Affiliations:** A.M.A.; A.C.P.; A.C.N.M.; F.A.C.C.; N.A.S.P.E. **Hob./spts.:** Golf **SIC code:** 80 **Address:** Treasure Coast Cardiology, 1600-B S.W. 2nd Ave., Okeechobee, FL 34974

ARES, NEFTALI ORTIZ
Industry: Healthcare **Born:** March 11, 1949, Naguabo, Puerto Rico **Univ./degree:** M.D., University of Automata, Dominican Republic **Current organization:** Consultorio Medico Familiar **Title:** M.D. **Type of organization:** Private medical practice **Major product:** Patient care **Area of distribution:** Naguabo, Puerto Rico **Area of Practice:** General practice **Affiliations:** American Medical Association; Medical Association of Puerto Rico **Hob./spts.:** Lecturing, faith in God, medical lectures **SIC code:** 80 **Address:** Consultorio Medico Familiar, Carretera 31, Kilometro 9.8, Barrio Rio Blanco, Naguabo, PR 00744-0294

ARGUETA, MIGUEL A.
Industry: Healthcare **Born:** December 8, 1963, Honduras **Univ./degree:** D.O., Nova Southeastern University, 1996 **Current organization:** Around the Clock Medical Center **Title:** D.O. **Type of organization:** Medical center **Major product:** Patient care **Area of distribution:** Florida **Area of Practice:** Family medicine **Honors/awards:** Dean's List, Post Graduate **Affiliations:** A.M.A.; A.O.A. **Hob./spts.:** The Internet **SIC code:** 80 **Address:** Around the Clock Medical Center, 2050 N.E. 163rd St., North Miami Beach, FL 33162 **E-mail:** margueta@pol.net

ARIAS, MAYDA
Industry: Healthcare **Born:** March 2, 1964, Santiago, Cuba **Univ./degree:** M.D., University of Miami, 1989 **Current organization:** Southeast Florida Hematology/Oncology **Title:** M.D. **Type of organization:** Hospital **Major product:** Patient care **Area of distribution:** Fort Lauderdale, Florida **Area of Practice:** Hematology/oncology **Affiliations:** A.M.A.; A.C.P.; A.M.S.; A.S.C.O. **Hob./spts.:** Reading, sailing, travel **SIC code:** 80 **Address:** Southeast Florida Hematology/Oncology, 5700 N. Federal Hwy., #5, Ft. Lauderdale, FL 33308

ARMASHI, HUSSAM
Industry: Healthcare **Born:** April 19, 1947, Damascus, Syria **Univ./degree:** M.D., Cairo, Egypt **Current organization:** Active Pain Control Center **Title:** M.D. **Type of organization:** Medical practice **Major product:** Patient care **Area of distribution:** Florida **Area of Practice:** Pain management; Board Certified, Anesthesiologist **Affiliations:** A.S.A.; A.A.P.M. **SIC code:** 80 **Address:** Active Pain Control Center, 12228 Cortez Blvd., Brooksville, FL 34613 **E-mail:** armashi@hotmail.com

ARMINIO, THOMAS A.
Industry: Healthcare **Born:** April 8, 1929, Ossining, New York **Univ./degree:** B.S., St. Bonaventure University, 1952; M.D., Dalhousie University, 1959 **Current organization:** Thomas A. Arminio, M.D. **Title:** M.D. **Type of organization:** Private practice **Major product:** Patient care **Area of distribution:** Ossining, New York **Area of Practice:** Family practice/sports medicine; Head School Physician; Police/Fire Surgeon, Village of Ossining **Honors/awards:** Recognition Award from the Fire Department of Ossining, Member of Athlete Hall of Fame **Affiliations:** Diplomate, A.A.F.P.; A.M.D.A.; A.A.G.P.; Lt. Col., U.S. Army Reserve Medical College **Hob./spts.:** Golf, all sports **SIC code:** 80 **Address:** Thomas A. Arminio, M.D., Park Prof. Bldg., 100 S. Highland Ave., Ossining, NY 10562 **E-mail:** dr.armino@ipninet.com

ARMSTRONG, WILLIAM R.
Industry: Healthcare **Univ./degree:** M.D., University of Michigan, 1969 **Current organization:** Lexington Medical Center **Title:** M.D. **Type of organization:** Medical center **Major product:** Patient care **Area of distribution:** West Columbia, South Carolina **Area of Practice:** Pathology, hematopathology, coagulation, teaching forensic medicine **Affiliations:** A.M.A; Clinical Professor of Pathology, University of South Carolina; South Carolina Medical Association; American Society of Clinical Pathologists; Columbia Medical Society; College of American Pathologists; American Society of Hematology; International Society for Laboratory Hematology; International Society on Thrombosis and Hemostasis; International Academy of Clinical and Applied Thrombosis/Hemostasis **Hob./spts.:** Music, metal sculpture, furniture refinishing **SIC code:** 80 **Address:** Lexington Medical Center, 2720 Sunset Blvd., West Columbia, SC 29169 **E-mail:** wrarmstrong@lexhealth.org

ARNOLD JR., WILLIAM P.
Industry: Healthcare **Born:** May 10, 1922, Waterbury, Connecticut **Univ./degree:** M.D., Columbia College of Physicians and Surgeons, 1946 **Current organization:** William P. Arnold, Jr., M.D. (Retired) **Title:** M.D. **Type of organization:** Private practice **Major product:** Internal medicine **Area of distribution:** Middlebury, Connecticut **Area of practice:** Internal medicine **Area of Practice:** Internal medicine **Published works:** 2 articles **Affiliations:** A.M.A.; American College of Physicians **Hob./spts.:** Walking, rodeo **SIC code:** 80 **Address:** 142 White Deer Rock Rd., Middlebury, CT 06762

AROESTY, JEFFREY H.
Industry: Healthcare **Born:** April 8, 1963, Brooklyn, New York **Univ./degree:** M.D., SUNY Downstate Medical Center, Brooklyn, 1988 **Current organization:** Jeffrey H. Aroesty M.D., P.C. **Title:** M.D. **Type of organization:** Medical practice **Major product:** Patient care **Area of distribution:** New Jersey **Area of Practice:** Otolaryngology/head & neck surgery **Affiliations:** F.A.C.S.; A.M.A.; A.C.S.; Medical Society State of New Jersey **Hob./spts.:** Skiing, running, swimming, bike riding **SIC code:** 80 **Address:** Jeffrey H. Aroesty M.D., P.C., 195 Rt. 46, Suite 204, Mine Hill, NJ 07803 **E-mail:** patty.jha@verizon.net

ARREY-MENSAH, ANNIE A.
Industry: Healthcare **Born:** Cameroon **Univ./degree:** M.D., University of Ibadan, Nigeria **Title:** M.D. **Type of organization:** Medical center **Major product:** Patient care **Area of distribution:** Michigan **Area of Practice:** Pediatrics **Affiliations:** A.M.A., American Association of Pediatricians **Hob./spts.:** Tennis, golf, singing, dancing, cooking, home decorating **SIC code:** 80 **Address:** 23749 Riverside Dr., Southfield, MI 48034 **E-mail:** aaarrey@yahoo.com

ARROYO-FLORES, MIGNA
Industry: Healthcare **Born:** July 13, 1956, Caguas, Puerto Rico **Univ./degree:** M.D., University of San Pedro, Santo Domingo, 1985 **Current organization:** Migna Arroyo-Flores, M.D. **Title:** Pediatrician **Type of organization:** Private practice **Major product:** Children's healthcare **Area of distribution:** Guagnaho, Puerto Rico **Area of Practice:** Pediatrics **Affiliations:** A.M.A.; Puerto Rico College of Surgeons; Puerto Rico Medical Association; Knights of Columbus; American Legion **Hob./spts.:** Calligraphy, folklore dancing for 15 years, sewing, knitting **SIC code:** 80 **Address:** 46 Topacio St., Villa Blanca, Caguas, PR 00725-1937 **E-mail:** drarroyo@prtc.net

ARTIN, KAMAL HAYDARI
Industry: Medical **Born:** September 25, 1959, Kermanshan, Iran **Univ./degree:** M.D., University of Zurich, Switzerland, 1995 **Current organization:** Johns Hopkins University **Title:** M.D. **Type of organization:** University hospital **Major product:** Patient care, medical education **Area of distribution:** Maryland **Area of Practice:** Psychiatry **Published works:** Co-author, 2 papers **Affiliations:** A.M.A.; A.P.A. **Hob./spts.:** Family, travel, camping **SIC code:** 80 **Address:** Johns Hopkins University, 600 N. Wolfe St., Meyer-131, Baltimore, MD 21287 **E-mail:** kartin@jhmi.ed

ARVIDSON, EBBE C.
Industry: Healthcare **Born:** April 20, 1956, Oklahoma **Univ./degree:** A.A.S., Biological Technology, North County Community College, 1978 **Current organization:** Western Maryland Hospital Center **Title:** PHLT3 **Type of organization:** Hospital **Major product:** Patient care **Area of distribution:** Maryland **Area of Practice:** General **Hob./spts.:** Softball, stamp and coin collecting, computers, choir **SIC code:** 80 **Address:** Western Maryland Hospital Center, 1500 Pennsylvania Ave., Hagerstown, MD 21742 **E-mail:** arvid3256@aol.com

ARYA, BASANT
Industry: Healthcare **Born:** February 8, 1973, India **Univ./degree:** M.D., Madras Medical College, India, 1996; M.R.C.P., United Kingdom, 2000; Diploma in Geriatrics, Royal College of Physicians, United Kingdom **Current organization:** Medical College of Wisconsin **Title:** M.D., M.R.C.P. (U.K.), Dip Geriatrics (U.K.) **Type of organization:** Medical college **Major product:** Healthcare services, medical education **Area of distribution:** International **Area of Practice:** Internal Medicine & Cardiology **Honors/awards:** Best Regional Resident Presentation and Best Resident Vignette Award, Midwest Society of General Internal Medicine regional meeting, Chicago, IL, 2004 **Published works:** Co-Authored, Myocardial Infarction: A Rare Complication of Dothiepin Overdose, International Journal of Cardiology, 2004 Sep;96(3):493-4; Co-Author, Myxomatous Meningeal Tumor: A Case of "Metastatic" Cardiac Myxoma, International Journal of Cardiology, 2004 Sep;96(3):471-3; Co-Author, Rhodococcus Equii Pneumonia in a Transplant Patient: Case Report and Review of Literature, Clinical Transplantation 2004:18:748-752 **Affiliations:** Member, Royal College of Physicians, U.K.; Associate Member, American College of Physicians; Associate Member, Society of General Internal Medicine **Hob./spts.:** Cricket **SIC code:** 80 **Address:** Medical College of Wisconsin, 8700 W. Watertown Plank Rd., Milwaukee, WI 53226 **E-mail:** barya@mcw.edu

ARZUMANOVA, KARINA G.
Industry: Healthcare **Born:** February 7, 1956, Soviet Union **Univ./degree:** M.D., Azerbaijan State Medical Institute, Soviet Union, 1980 **Current organization:** Karina G. Arzumanova, M.D. **Title:** M.D. **Type of organization:** Private practice **Major product:** Patient care **Area of distribution:** San Francisco, California **Area of Practice:** Internal medicine, primary care **Affiliations:** A.M.A.; A.I.M.B. **Hob./spts.:** Art **SIC code:** 80 **Address:** Karina G. Arzumanova, M.D., 2299 Post St., Suite203, San Francisco, CA 94115 **E-mail:** zummd@aol.com

ASCIUTO, THOMAS
Industry: Healthcare **Born:** May 23, 1963, New York, New York **Univ./degree:** B.A.; M.D., 1989, Universidad del Salvador, Argentina **Current organization:** Memorial Pulmonary & Sleep Consultants **Title:** M.D. **Type of organization:** Group practice **Major product:** Patient care **Area of distribution:** California **Area of Practice:** Pulmonary and critical care medicine **Published works:** 1 article **Affiliations:** F.A.C.C.P.; American Thoracic Society **Hob./spts.:** Soccer **SIC code:** 80 **Address:** Memorial Pulmonary & Sleep Consultants, 701 E. 28th St., Suite 318, Long Beach, CA 90806

ASFAW, ZERGABACHEW
Industry: Healthcare **Born:** September 10, 1950, Ethiopia **Univ./degree:** M.D., Addis Ababa University, 1989 **Current organization:** A-Z Medical Services **Title:** M.D. **Type of organization:** Medical practice **Major product:** Patient care **Area of distribution:** New York **Area of Practice:** Internal medicine, geriatrics **Affiliations:** A.G.S.; A.C.P.-A.S.I.M.; A.M.A. **Hob./spts.:** Photography, tennis, travel **SIC code:** 80 **Address:** A-Z Medical Services, 3965 Sedgewick Ave., Bronx, NY 10463 **E-mail:** zasfaw@aol.com

ATANASOSKI-MCCORMACK, VIOLETA
Industry: Healthcare **Born:** August 19, 1956, Macedonia **Univ./degree:** M.D., University of Yugoslavia, 1981; Residency, University of Nevada; Fellow, University of Miami **Current organization:** Cardiology Associates of Fort Lauderdale, P.A. **Title:** M.D. **Type of organization:** Group medical practice **Major product:** Cardiology **Area of distribution:** Fort Lauderdale, Florida **Area of Practice:** Cardiovascular disease **Honors/awards:** Fellowship of the Year Award **Affiliations:** American College of Cardiology; American College of Physicians **Hob./spts.:** Skiing **SIC code:** 80 **Address:** Cardiology Associates of Fort Lauderdale, P.A., 1880 E. Commercial Blvd., Ft. Lauderdale, FL 33308 **Web address:** www.cardiologyassociates.com

ATILANO, LEON
Industry: Dentistry **Univ./degree:** D.M.D., University of Puerto Rico, 1974; Residency, University of Puerto Rico School of Dentistry **Current organization:** Oral & Maxillofacial Surgery Center **Title:** Partner **Type of organization:** Private practice **Major product:** Oral and maxillofacial surgery **Area of distribution:** Puerto Rico **Area of Practice:** Cosmetic facial dentistry surgery **Affiliations:** A.D.A.; A.C.C.C.; P.S.O.M.F.S.; A.B.O.M.F.S.; P.R.S.O.M.F.S. **SIC code:** 80 **Address:** Leon Atilano, DMD, Oral & Maxillofacial Surgery Center, Concordia Shopping Center, Rio Piedras, PR 00923 **E-mail:** maxilo@prtx.net

ATKINS, JAMES S.
Industry: Healthcare **Born:** May 1, 1954, Jacksonville, Florida **Univ./degree:** B.S., Biology, Stetson University, 1976; M.D., University of Florida, 1980 **Current organization:** Florida Ear & Balance Center **Title:** M.D. **Type of organization:** Medical practice **Major product:** Patient care **Area of distribution:** Florida **Area of Practice:** Otolaryngology, neurology **Published works:** 4 articles **Affiliations:** American Academy of Otolaryngology; American Neurology Society **Hob./spts.:** Boating, tennis **SIC code:** 80 **Address:** Florida Ear & Balance Center, 400 Celebration Place, Suite A-360, Celebration, FL 34747 **E-mail:** flear@atlantic.net

AUGOUSTIDES, JOHN G.T.
Industry: Medical **Born:** May 31, 1967, Capetown, South Africa **Univ./degree:** M.D., University of Capetown, South Africa, 1990 **Current organization:** Hospital of the University of Pennsylvania **Title:** M.D. **Type of organization:** University/hospital **Major product:** Medical services **Area of distribution:** International **Area of Practice:** Cardiothoracic anesthesia **Published works:** 9 Peer Reviewed Research Publications including, co-author, "An Unusual Cause of Confusion in the Electrophysiology Laboratory", J.Cardiothor.Vasc.Anesth., 16(3): 351-353, 2002; "The Use of Intraoperative Echocardiography During Insertion of Ventricular Assist Devices", J.Cardiothor.Vasc.Anesth., 17(1): 113-120, 2003; "Acute Effects of Intravenous Amiodarone Loading in Cardiac Surgical Patients", Am.Thor.Surg. 76:535-41, 2003; 26 Abstracts, 16 Editorials, Reviews, Chapters; 6 Alternative Media; Guest Reviewer for Anesthesia and Analgesia and Anesthesiology **Affiliations:** A.S.A.; S.C.A.; American Heart Association; American Society of Echocardiography; International Anesthesia Research Society; European Society of Anesthesiologists **Hob./spts.:** Golf, swimming, tennis **SIC code:** 80 **Address:** Hospital of the University of Pennsylvania, Dept. of Anesthesia, 3400 Spruce St., Philadelphia, PA 19104-4283 **E-mail:** yiandoc@hotmail.com

AUGSPURGER, RICHARD R.
Industry: Healthcare **Born:** October 23, 1947, Columbus, Ohio **Univ./degree:** M.D., Ohio State University, 1973 **Current organization:** Western Urologic Associates, PC **Title:** President/Medical Director **Type of organization:** Private group practice **Major product:** Urologic medicine **Area of distribution:** Wheat Ridge, Colorado **Area of Practice:** Urology **Published works:** Articles, 6 book chapters **Affiliations:** A.U.A. **Hob./spts.:** Skiing **SIC code:** 80 **Address:** Western Urologic Associates, PC, 3555 Lutheran Pkwy., Wheat Ridge, CO 80033 **E-mail:** augsrich@aol.com **Web address:** www.westernurologic.com

AULTMAN, WILLIAM A.
Industry: Healthcare **Born:** November 22, 1954, Albany, Georgia **Univ./degree:** M.D., Medical College of Georgia, 1982 **Current organization:** Ob-Gyn Associates of Albany, P.C. **Title:** M.D. **Type of organization:** Medical practice **Major product:** Women's healthcare **Area of distribution:** Albany, Georgia **Area of Practice:** Obstetrics, gynecology **Affiliations:** F.A.C.O.G.; Medical Association of Georgia; Georgia Ob-Gyn Society; Dougherty County Medical Society **Hob./spts.:** Hunting, fishing, golf, travel **SIC code:** 80 **Address:** Ob-Gyn Associates of Albany, P.C., 2701 Merdyth Dr., Albany, GA 31701

AVULA, SATYANARAYAN
Industry: Healthcare **Born:** January 1, 1947, India **Univ./degree:** M.D., Katiya Medical College, India, 1972 **Current organization:** Satyanarayan Avula, M.D., F.A.C.C. **Title:** M.D., F.A.C.C./Associate Professor **Type of organization:** Private practice **Major product:** Patient care **Area of distribution:** Staten Island, New York **Area of Practice:** Cardiology **Honors/awards:** Who's Who in America **Affiliations:** Fellow, American College of Cardiology **Hob./spts.:** Racquetball, golf, tennis, music, theater **SIC code:** 80 **Address:** Satyanarayan Avula, M.D., F.A.C.C., 1285 Richmond Ave., Staten Island, NY 10314 **E-mail:** saty0816@aol.com

AWAD, ERIC A.
Industry: Healthcare **Born:** Damascus, Syria **Univ./degree:** M.D., University of Damascus, 1986 **Current organization:** Eric A. Awad, M.D., L.L.C. **Title:** M.D. **Type of organization:** Private practice **Major product:** Patient care **Area of distribution:** Atlanta, Georgia **Area of Practice:** Neurology **Affiliations:** A.M.A.; A.A.N.; A.H.S. **Hob./spts.:** Painting, playing polo, photography **SIC code:** 80 **Address:** Eric A. Awad, M.D., L.L.C., 1938 Peachtree Rd. N.W., Suite 412, Atlanta, GA 30309 **Web address:** www.cerebrex.neurohub.net

AYERS, ERIC WYNTON
Industry: Medical **Born:** February 21, 1962, Detroit, Michigan **Univ./degree:** M.D., Internal Medicine/Pediatrics, Wayne State University **Current organization:** Wayne State University School of Medicine **Title:** M.D., Residency Program Director **Type of organization:** University clinic **Major product:** Teaching, residency program **Area of distribution:** National **Area of Practice:** Internal medicine, pediatrics **Honors/awards:** Outstanding Citizen, City Counsel of Detroit; Alpha Omega Alpha; Recognized Outstanding Teacher in Medical School, 1997, 2001 **Published works:** Articles **Hob./spts.:** Running, weight lifting, nature **SIC code:** 80 **Address:** Wayne

State University School of Medicine, 5C UHC 4201 St. Antoine, Detroit, MI 48201 **E-mail:** eayers@intmed.wayne.edu

AYINLA, RAJI M.
Industry: Healthcare **Univ./degree:** M.D., Poland **Current organization:** Concourse Medical Office, PC **Title:** M.D., F.C.C.P. **Type of organization:** Medical practice **Major product:** Patient care **Area of distribution:** Bronx, New York **Area of Practice:** Lung diseases, asthma, chronic coughs, sleep disorder **Affiliations:** F.C.C.P.; S.C.C.M.; A.M.A.; A.C.P.; American Thoracic Society **SIC code:** 80 **Address:** Concourse Medical Office, PC, 3131 Grand Concourse, Suite 1B, Bronx, NY 10468 **E-mail:** raji.ayinla@ngsc.org

AYOUB, MICHAEL
Industry: Healthcare **Univ./degree:** D.D.S., Columbia University, 1997 **Current organization:** The Dental Way **Title:** D.D.S. **Type of organization:** Private practice **Major product:** Dental care **Area of distribution:** New Jersey **Area of Practice:** Orthodontics **Affiliations:** A.D.A.; A.A.O.; N.J.D.A. **SIC code:** 80 **Address:** The Dental Way, 155 S. Washington Ave., Bergenfield, NJ 07621 **E-mail:** mayoub2@aol.com

AYUSO, JESÚS M.
Industry: Healthcare **Born:** November, 1935, Carolina, Puerto Rico **Univ./degree:** B.S., University of Puerto Rico M.D., Salamanca Medical School, 1966 **Current organization:** Jesús M. Ayuso, M.D. **Title:** M.D. **Type of organization:** Private practice **Major product:** Patient care **Area of distribution:** Carolina, Puerto Rico **Area of Practice:** Family healthcare **Published works:** 2 books (non-medical) **Affiliations:** A.M.A.; P.A.M.A.; I.A.P. **SIC code:** 80 **Address:** Jesús M. Ayuso, M.D., Professional Medical Office, Muñoz Rivera 204, Carolina, PR 00986

AYYAR, RAJI
Industry: Healthcare **Born:** November 13, 1949, Kumba Konam, India **Univ./degree:** B.S., Zoology, Izabel Thobern College, 1967; M.D., King George School of Medicine, India, 1972; **Current organization:** Kaiser Permanente **Title:** M.D. **Type of organization:** Hospital **Major product:** Medical care **Area of distribution:** Santa Clara, California **Area of Practice:** Oncology, hematology **Affiliations:** A.S.H.; A.S.C.O. **Hob./spts.:** Reading, yoga **SIC code:** 80 **Address:** Kaiser Permanente, 900 Kiely Blvd., Santa Clara, CA 95051 **E-mail:** raji.ayyar@kp.org

BABBITT, MARK A.
Industry: Healthcare **Born:** February 8, 1970, Santa Monica, California **Univ./degree:** D.D.S., Creighton University, 1996 **Current organization:** Mark A. Babbitt, D.D.S. **Title:** D.D.S. **Type of organization:** Private dental practice **Major product:** Dental care **Area of distribution:** Ventura, California **Area of Practice:** Family dentistry, cosmetic dentistry **Affiliations:** A.D.A.; C.D.A.; A.G.D. **SIC code:** 80 **Address:** Mark A. Babbitt, D.D.S., 2901 Loma Vista Rd., Ventura, CA 93003 **E-mail:** babbittdds@sbcglobal.net

BABIAK, RYAN
Industry: Healthcare **Born:** November 19, 1948, Brooklyn, New York **Univ./degree:** B.S., Telecommunications, Almeda College, 2003 **Current organization:** Coram, Inc. **Title:** Director, MIS Telecom-Datacom **Type of organization:** Medical **Major product:** Home healthcare **Area of distribution:** National **Area of Practice:** Telecommunications technology, voice and data **Affiliations:** Notary Public **Hob./spts.:** Baseball, photography, golf **SIC code:** 80 **Address:** Coram, Inc., 11 H Commerce Way, Totowa, NJ 07512 **E-mail:** rbabiak@coramhc.com **Web address:** www.coramhc.com

BABU, LEKHA
Industry: Healthcare **Born:** February 8, 1957, India **Univ./degree:** M.D., Kottayam Medical College, India, 1984 **Current organization:** Suburban Heights Medical Center, S.C. **Title:** M.D. **Type of organization:** Medical center **Major product:** Patient care **Area of distribution:** Chicago Heights, Illinois **Area of Practice:** Oncology **Published works:** Multiple abstracts **Affiliations:** A.S.C.O. **Hob./spts.:** Music, reading **SIC code:** 80 **Address:** Suburban Heights Medical Center, S.C., 333 Dixie Hwy., Chicago Heights, IL 60411 **E-mail:** lsbabu4@yahoo.com

BACHTEL, MICHELLE D.
Industry: Healthcare **Born:** March 11, 1965, St. Louis, Missouri **Univ./degree:** B.S., Biology/Psychology, Indiana University at Bloomington, 1987; M.D., University of Missouri School of Medicine at Columbia, 1991 **Current organization:** Tallahassee Cardiology Associates **Title:** M.D., F.A.C.C. **Type of organization:** Private practice **Major product:** Patient care **Area of distribution:** Florida **Area of Practice:** Cardiology **Published works:** Write-ups **Affiliations:** F.A.C.C.; American Heart Association **SIC code:** 80 **Address:** Tallahassee Cardiology Associates, 2626 Care Dr., Suite 100, Tallahassee, FL 32308

BACIC, MIMA
Industry: Healthcare **Born:** May 21, 1951, Puracic, Yugoslavia **Univ./degree:** M.D., University of Sarajevo, Bosnia, 1976; Ph.D., Military Medical Academy, Belgrade, Yugoslavia, 1986 **Current organization:** Mercy General Health Partners **Title:** M.D., Ph.D., Assistant Clinical Professor, Michigan State University **Type of organization:** Hospital **Major product:** Patient care **Area of distribution:** Muskegon, Ottawa and Oceana Counties **Area of Practice:** Internal medicine, angiogenesis **Honors/awards:** Best Medical American Chest Physician, 2003 **Published works:** Multiple publications **Affiliations:** A.M.A.; A.C.P. **Hob./spts.:** Reading, theatre, museums, classical music, ballroom dancing, travel, skiing **SIC code:** 80 **Address:** Mercy General Health Partners, 1500 E. Sherman Blvd., Muskegon, MI 49443 **E-mail:** mimib@prodigy.net

BADAR, JEHANGIR
Industry: Medical **Born:** April 1, 1972, Lahore, Pakistan **Univ./degree:** M.D., Punjab University, Pakistan **Current organization:** Brigham & Women's Hospital/Harvard School of Medicine **Title:** Fellow, Surgical Critical Care **Type of organization:** Hospital/university **Major product:** Patient care/medical education **Area of distribution:** National **Area of Practice:** Surgery and Surgical Intensivist **Hob./spts.:** Cricket, reading, hiking **SIC code:** 80 **Address:** 75 Francis St., 7C-48, Boston, MA 02115 **E-mail:** badarmd@hotmail.com

BADER, FAYEZ A.
Industry: Healthcare **Univ./degree:** M.D., Free University of Berlin, 1998 **Current organization:** Downstate Medical Center **Title:** M.D. **Type of organization:** Hospital **Major product:** Patient care **Area of distribution:** New York **Area of Practice:** Pulmonary and critical care **Affiliations:** A.M.A.; Medical Society of the State of New York; American College of Physicians **SIC code:** 80 **Address:** 333 McDonald Ave., #7L, Brooklyn, NY 11218 **E-mail:** baderdoc@yahoo.com

BAGHAL, TAREQ ADNAN
Industry: Healthcare **Born:** November 23, 1970, Amman, Jordan **Univ./degree:** M.D., St. George's School of Medicine, 1999 **Current organization:** St. Joseph's Regional Medical Center **Title:** M.D. **Type of organization:** Hospital **Major product:** Patient care **Area of distribution:** New Jersey **Area of Practice:** Internal medicine **Affiliations:** A.M.A. **SIC code:** 80 **Address:** St. Joseph's Regional Medical Center, 61 E. Harwood Terrace, Palisades Park, NJ 07650 **E-mail:** drtbaghal@aol.com

BAIER, RONALD JOHN
Industry: Medical **Born:** December 29, 1956, Winnipeg, Manitoba **Univ./degree:** M.D., University of Manitoba, 1981 **Current organization:** LSUHSC **Title:** M.D. **Type of organization:** University hospital **Major product:** Patient care, medical education **Area of distribution:** Shreveport, Lousiana **Area of Practice:** Neonatal/perinatal medicine **Published works:** 15 medical articles **Affiliations:** S.S.P.R.; S.P.R.; A.A.S.; A.S.M. **Hob./spts.:** Classical music (playing and listening) **SIC code:** 80 **Address:** LSUHSC, 1501 Kings Hwy., Shreveport, LA 71130 **E-mail:** jbaier@lsuhsc.edu

BAILEY, JOHN ALAN
Industry: Healthcare **Born:** August 15, 1965, Appomattox, Virginia **Univ./degree:** A.A.S., Radiologic Technology, 1986; B.S., Radiologic Science, 1988, MCVCU **Current organization:** Bon Secours, St. Mary's Hospital **Title:** Administrative Director of Medical Diagnostics **Type of organization:** Hospital **Major product:** Patient care **Area of distribution:** National **Area of Practice:** Diagnostic imaging, radiological administration, D.I.S. **Affiliations:** C.R.A. with A.H.R.A.; A.R.R. **Hob./spts.:** Martial arts, motorcycles, family **SIC code:** 80 **Address:** 9110 Rouzie Ct., Mechanicsville, VA 23116 **E-mail:** alan_bailey@bshsi.com **Web address:** www.bshsi.com

BAKAY, ROY A. E.
Industry: Medical **Born:** March 5, 1949, Chicago, Illinois **Univ./degree:** M.D., Northwestern University, 1975 **Current organization:** Rush-Presbyterian-St. Luke's Medical Center **Title:** Professor, Vice Chairman **Type of organization:** University medical center **Major product:** Patient services, medical education **Area of distribution:** Illinois **Area of Practice:** Neurosurgery **Published works:** 100+ articles, 50+ book chapters, 3 books **Affiliations:** A.M.A.; American Association of Neurological Surgeons; Society for Neuroscience **Hob./spts.:** Outdoors, fishing, hiking **SIC code:** 80 **Address:** Rush-Presbyterian-St. Luke's Medical Center, 1725 W. Harrison St., Suite 970, Chicago, IL 60612 **E-mail:** rbakay@cinn.org **Web address:** www.cinn.org

BAKDOUD, ZUHAIR M.
Industry: Healthcare **Born:** August 14, 1936, Freetown, Sierra Leone **Univ./degree:** M.D., University of Arkansas, 1970 **Current organization:** Washington Regional Medical Center **Title:** Neonatologist (Board Certified) **Type of organization:** Medical center **Major product:** Patient care **Area of distribution:** Arkansas **Area of Practice:** Obstetrics, gynecology **Hob./spts.:** Playing piano, jogging **SIC code:** 80 **Address:** Washington Regional Medical Center, 1630 Timbercrest Ave., Fayetteville, AR 72704 **E-mail:** zbak36@aol.com

BAKER, AZZAM A.
Industry: Healthcare **Born:** March 26, 1948, Jordan **Univ./degree:** M.D., Cairo University, Egypt; Postgraduate Training - UMDNJ **Current organization:** Riverside

Pediatric Group **Title:** M.D., President, Director of Pediatrics Department, Meadowlands Hospital Medical Center **Type of organization:** Private medical practice **Major product:** Patient care **Area of distribution:** Hudson and Bergen Counties, New Jersey **Area of Practice:** Pediatrics **Affiliations:** Hackensack University Medical Center; Meadowlands Hospital Medical Center; Christ Hospital; St. Mary Hospital; Palisades Medical Center; St. Joseph's Hospital; Holy Name Hospital; American Academy of Pediatrics; New Jersey Society of Pediatricians; Physicians for Peace **Hob./spts.:** N.B.A. basketball, volunteers pediatric care in the inner cities and overseas **SIC code:** 80 **Address:** Riverside Pediatric Group, 714 Tenth St., Secaucus, NJ 07094

BAKER, BOBBY W.
Industry: Healthcare **Born:** August 29, 1947, Hamilton, Texas **Univ./degree:** B.B.A., Management, University of Houston, 1975; M.S. Candidate, Hospital Administration, Kennedy West University **Current organization:** Eastern New Mexico Medical Center **Title:** Director of Materials Management Services **Type of organization:** Hospital **Major product:** Patient care **Area of distribution:** Roswell, New Mexico **Area of Practice:** Inventory control **Honors/awards:** Served in active duty, U.S. Navy, 1967-70 **Affiliations:** A.H.A.; A.H.R.M.M. **Hob./spts.:** Skiing, jogging, biking, outdoor activities **SIC code:** 80 **Address:** Eastern New Mexico Medical Center, 405 W. Country Club Rd., Roswell, NM 88201 **E-mail:** bobby_baker@chs.net **Web address:** www.enmmc.com

BAKER, ELIZABETH A.
Industry: Healthcare **Born:** December 15, 1963, San Juan, Puerto Rico **Univ./degree:** M.D., Columbia University of Physicians and Surgeons, 1989 **Current organization:** The Physical Medicine & Rehab Center **Title:** M.D. **Type of organization:** Private medical practice **Major product:** Patient care **Area of distribution:** Englewood, New Jersey **Area of Practice:** Physical medicine, rehabilitation, pain management **Published works:** Magazine articles **Affiliations:** A.A.P.M.R.; A.M.A.; A.A.E.M. **Hob./spts.:** Dancing, spending time with her children, theater **SIC code:** 80 **Address:** The Physical Medicine & Rehab Center, 15 Engle St., Suite 205, Englewood, NJ 07631

BAKRY, MOHAMED B.
Industry: Healthcare **Born:** December 28, 1967, Egypt **Univ./degree:** M.D., 1991; M.S., Chest Diseases, 1996, Ain Shams University **Current organization:** Memorial Sloan Kettering Hospital **Title:** M.D. **Type of organization:** Hospital **Major product:** Patient care **Area of Practice:** Pulmonology/internal medicine **Honors/awards:** 1 patent pending, pleural biopsy **Affiliations:** A.C.C.P.; A.C.P. **Hob./spts.:** Computer technology **SIC code:** 80 **Address:** 1233 York Ave., Apt 90, New York, NY 10021 **E-mail:** mbakry@nyc.rr.com

BAKSHI, KALIND R.
Industry: Healthcare **Born:** December 9, 1946, Bombay, India **Univ./degree:** M.D., Seth Gordhandas Sunderdas Medical College, 1967 **Current organization:** N.E. Phila. Vascular Surgeons, P.C. **Title:** M.D./Assistant Professor, Medical College of Pennsylvania **Type of organization:** Group Practice **Major product:** Ptient care **Area of distribution:** Bensalem, Pennsylvania **Area of Practice:** Vascular surgery **Affiliations:** A.C.S.; Eastern Vascular Society **SIC code:** 80 **Address:** N.E. Phila. Vascular Surgeons, P.C., 2742 Knights Rd., Bensalem, PA 19020 **E-mail:** kbakshi@aol.com

BAKSHI, PARAG A.
Industry: Healthcare **Univ./degree:** M.D., Medical College of New York, 1985 **Current organization:** Internal Medicine Association **Title:** M.D. **Type of organization:** Healthcare facility **Major product:** Patient care **Area of distribution:** Wilmington, Delaware **Area of Practice:** Internal medicine **Affiliations:** A.C.P.; A.M.A. **Hob./spts.:** Hunting, tennis, saxophone **SIC code:** 80 **Address:** Internal Medicine Association, 3105 Limestone Rd., Suite 301, Wilmington, DE 49808

BALACHANDRA, THALERNG
Industry: Healthcare **Born:** April 1, 1935, Thailand **Univ./degree:** M.D., Mahidol University, Thailand, 1960 **Current organization:** Veterans' Affairs Medical Center **Title:** Chief of Nuclear Medicine **Type of organization:** Medical center **Major product:** Patient care **Area of distribution:** North Chicago, Illinois **Area of Practice:** Nuclear medicine **Affiliations:** Chicago Medical School **Hob./spts.:** Classical music **SIC code:** 80 **Address:** Veterans' Affairs Medical Center, 3001 Green Bay Rd., North Chicago, IL 60064-3048 **E-mail:** balachandra.thalerngmd@n.chicago.med.va.gov

BALDWIN, CARROLL E.
Industry: Healthcare **Born:** July 30, 1950, Grundy, Virginia **Univ./degree:** A.S., Accounting, 1985; A.S., Applied Science, Southwest Virginia Community College, 1997 **Current organization:** Buchanan General Hospital **Title:** Radiation Safety Officer, CNMT, RT(R) **Type of organization:** Hospital **Major product:** Patient care **Area of distribution:** Grundy, Virginia **Area of Practice:** Radiologic technology, nuclear medicine **Honors/awards:** Outstanding Radiology Student, Southwest Virginia Community College Hall of Fame **Affiliations:** N.M.S.; A.S.R.T. **Hob./spts.:** Playing piano, gardening, outdoor activities, physical fitness **SIC code:** 80 **Address:** Buchanan General Hospital, Nuclear Medicine Dept., Rt. 5 Box 20, Grundy, VA 24614 **E-mail:** cb8196@yahoo.com

BALFOUR, GUILLERMO A.
Industry: Medical **Born:** October 14, 1937, Argentina **Univ./degree:** B.A., Quilmis University, Argentina, 1953; M.D., Buenos Aires University School of Medicine, 1959 **Current organization:** Guillermo A. Balfour, M.D./Georgetown University **Title:** M.D./Clinical Professor of Pediatrics **Type of organization:** Private practice/university **Major product:** Patient care/higher education **Area of distribution:** Washington D.C. **Area of Practice:** Pediatrics, clinical office laboratory research, teaching **Published works:** 6 articles, 1 book **Affiliations:** Past President, Georgetown Faculty; Past President, A.A.P. **Hob./spts.:** Opera, theatre, golf **SIC code:** 80 **Address:** Guillermo A. Balfour, M.D./Georgetown University, 3301 New Mexico Ave. N.W., Suite 238, Washington, DC 20016

BALIS, ULYSSES J.
Industry: Medical **Univ./degree:** M.D., University of South Florida, 1991 **Current organization:** Massachusetts General Hospital & Harvard Medical School **Title:** M.D., Chief of Pathology, Center for Engineering & Medicine **Type of organization:** Hospital/medical school **Major product:** Patient care/medical education **Area of distribution:** International **Area of Practice:** Micro-fabricated rare cell isolation modules; bio artificial tissue engineering; advanced digital imaging **Affiliations:** I.E.E.E.; A.M.A.; College of American Pathologists; Massachusetts Medical Association **SIC code:** 80 **Address:** Massachusetts General Hospital & Harvard Medical School, 55 Fruit St., Boston, MA 02114 **E-mail:** balis@helix.mgh.harvard.edu

BALLEM, RAO V.
Industry: Healthcare **Univ./degree:** M.D., Andhra University, India, 1970 **Current organization:** Breast Care Center of New Jersey **Title:** M.D. **Type of organization:** Medical practice **Major product:** Patient care **Area of distribution:** New Jersey **Area of Practice:** Breast surgery **Affiliations:** A.M.A.; American College of Surgeons **SIC code:** 80 **Address:** Breast Care Center of New Jersey, 230 Sherman Ave., Glen Ridge, NJ 07028 **E-mail:** ruballem@hotmail.com

BALSAM, RICHARD F.
Industry: Healthcare **Born:** March 8, 1938, Port Chester, New York **Univ./degree:** B.S., Union University, 1959; M.D., Albany State University School of Medicine, 1964 **Current organization:** Community Care Physicians **Title:** M.D. **Type of organization:** Group medical practice **Major product:** Patient care **Area of distribution:** Albany, New York **Area of Practice:** Cardiology **Affiliations:** Founder & Former President, Cardiology Society of Upstate New York; A.C.C.; A.C.P.-A.S.I.M.; A.H.A. **Hob./spts.:** Golf, tennis, swimming, music **SIC code:** 80 **Address:** Community Care Physicians, 1365 Washington Ave., Suite 100, Albany, NY 12206

BAMAN, AJAY
Industry: Healthcare **Univ./degree:** D.D.S., New York University **Current organization:** Ajay Baman, D.D.S. **Title:** D.D.S. **Type of organization:** Dental practice **Major product:** General dentistry **Area of distribution:** West Nyack, New York **Area of Practice:** Dentistry **Affiliations:** A.D.A.; New York State Dental Society; Bronx Dental Association; 9th District Dental Society; Indian Association **SIC code:** 80 **Address:** Ajay Baman, DDS, 2 Strawtown Rd., West Nyack, NY 10994 **E-mail:** ajbaman@optonline.net

BANAS JR., JOHN S.
Industry: Healthcare **Born:** October 19, 1937, Springfield, Massachusetts **Univ./degree:** M.D., Tufts University School of Medicine, Massachusetts, 1963 **Current organization:** Morristown Memorial Hospital **Title:** M.D. **Type of organization:** Hospital **Major product:** Patient care **Area of distribution:** National **Area of Practice:** Cardiovascular medicine **Honors/awards:** Outstanding Research, Cardiovascular Program Development **Published works:** 100 papers, abstracts and book chapters **Affiliations:** Fellow, American College of Cardiology; Fellow, American College of Physicians; Fellow, American College of Chest Physicians; American Medical Association, Endowed Chair, Dorothy and Lloyd Huck; Faculty, Columbia University, New York; Professor of Clinical Medicine, College of Physicians and Surgeons; President, Cardiovascular Health Consultants Inc. **Hob./spts.:** Scuba diving, tennis, classical music **SIC code:** 80 **Address:** Morristown Memorial Hospital, 100 Madison Ave., Morristown, NJ 07962-1956 **E-mail:** john.banas@ahsys.org

BANGARA, SURESH C.
Industry: Medical **Born:** November 5, 1948, Madras, India **Univ./degree:** M.D., University of Guadalajara, Mexico, 1981 **Current organization:** Integrated Healthcare Partners, University of Southern California Keck School of Medicine **Title:** M.D. **Type of organization:** University hospital **Major product:** Medical services **Area of distribution:** National **Area of Practice:** Teaching, clinical service, research, software and healthcare design **Published works:** Manuals and guidelines about mental health and substance abuse **Affiliations:** A.M.A.; A.P.A. **Hob./spts.:** Professional tennis, music,

reading **SIC code:** 80 **Address:** 1731 La Cresta Dr., Pasadena, CA 91103 **E-mail:** surbang@aol.com

BANKS, ROBIN D.
Industry: Medical **Born:** March 25, 1954, Chicago, Illinois **Univ./degree:** M.S., Governors State University, 1995 **Current organization:** University of Illinois Hospital **Title:** Assistant Head Nurse **Type of organization:** Hospital **Major product:** Patient care **Area of distribution:** Illinois **Area of Practice:** Obstetric nursing **Affiliations:** A.N.A.; A.D.A.; P.N.A.; President, Sigma Theta Tau; Board of Directors, GSU Alumni Association **Hob./spts.:** Swimming, tennis **SIC code:** 80 **Address:** University of Illinois Hospital, 1740 W. Taylor, Chicago, IL 60612 **E-mail:** rfulton@uic.edu

BARBATI, ALFONSO J.
Industry: Healthcare **Born:** April 1, 1958, Ellwood City, Pennsylvania **Univ./degree:** D.O., Philadelphia College of Osteopathic Medicine, 1984 **Current organization:** Southwest Gastroenterology Assoc. **Title:** D.O. **Type of organization:** Medical practice **Major product:** Patient care **Area of distribution:** Clairton, Pennsylvania **Area of Practice:** Gastroenterology, internal medicine **Affiliations:** A.O.A.; A.S.G.E.; F.A.C.O.I. **Hob./spts.:** Reading, theatre **SIC code:** 80 **Address:** Southwest Gastroenterology Assoc., 1200 Brook Lane, Suite 260, Clairton, PA 15025

BARIBEAU, YVON RAOUL
Industry: Healthcare **Born:** April 4, 1956, Montreal, Canada **Univ./degree:** M.D., University of Montreal, 1981 **Current organization:** Cardiothoracic Surgical Associates, P.A. **Title:** M.D. **Type of organization:** Private practice **Major product:** Patient care **Area of distribution:** National **Area of Practice:** Vascular and Thoracic Surgery (Board Certified), stroke prevention in cardiac surgery **Published works:** 5+ book chapters, 28 articles **Affiliations:** Fellow, A.C.S.; S.T.S.; International Society of Cardiovascular Surgeons; The Canadian Society for Vascular Surgery; The Eastern Vascular Society; The New England Society for Vascular Surgery **Hob./spts.:** Charity work, hockey, tennis, skiing **SIC code:** 80 **Address:** Cardiothoracic Surgical Associates, P.A., Catholic Medical Center, 100 McGregor St., Manchester, NH 03102 **E-mail:** baribeau@nhheart.com **Web address:** www.nhheart.com

BARKIN, RONALD J.
Industry: Healthcare **Born:** July 13, 1961, Nyack, New York **Univ./degree:** M.D., New York University **Current organization:** Gastroenterology & Hepatology Associates **Title:** M.D. **Type of organization:** Medical practice **Major product:** Patient care **Area of distribution:** Alexandria, Virginia **Area of Practice:** Gastroenterology **Affiliations:** A.G.A.; A.S.G.E.; A.C.P; Crones & Coalites Foundation **Hob./spts.:** Scuba diving **SIC code:** 80 **Address:** Gastroenterology & Hepatology Associates, 4660 Kenmore Ave., Suite 810, Alexandria, VA 22304

BARNETT, JAMES E.
Industry: Healthcare **Born:** November 2, 1926, Marietta, South Carolina **Univ./degree:** M.D., University of South Carolina, 1954 **Current organization:** Greenville Memorial Hospital **Title:** M.D. **Type of organization:** Medical practice **Major product:** Patient care **Area of distribution:** Travelers Rest, South Carolina **Area of Practice:** Family medicine **SIC code:** 80 **Address:** Greenville Memorial Hospital, Nine McElhaney Rd., Travelers Rest, SC 29690

BARQUIST, ERIK S.
Industry: Healthcare **Born:** 1960, Santa Barbara, California **Univ./degree:** M.D., 1987; Residency and Surgical Internship, University of California, San Francisco **Current organization:** University of Miami, Jackson Memorial Medical Center **Title:** Director, Trauma & Critical Care Fellowship Program **Type of organization:** University hospital **Major product:** Patient care **Area of distribution:** National **Area of Practice:** Surgical infection, critical illness, multiple organ dysfunction; Surgery (Board Certified) **Published works:** 26 peer reviewed articles and abstracts **Affiliations:** Fellow, American College of Surgeons; Fellow, American College of Critical Care Medicine; American Association for the Surgery of Trauma **Hob./spts.:** Scuba diving, bicycling, dog lover **SIC code:** 80 **Address:** University of Miami, Jackson Memorial Medical Center, Dept. of Surgery, Suite 100, 9380 SW 150th St., Miami, FL 33176 **E-mail:** ebarquis@med.miami.edu

BARR, LORI LEE
Industry: Healthcare **Born:** May 18, 1961, Portsmouth, Virginia **Univ./degree:** M.D., LSU School of Medicine, 1984 **Current organization:** Austin Radiological Association **Title:** M.D., F.A.C.R. **Type of organization:** Private practice **Major product:** Pediatric radiology **Area of distribution:** National **Area of Practice:** Pediatric radiology **Published works:** Articles, books **Affiliations:** American College of Radiology; American Institute of Ultrasound in Medicine **Hob./spts.:** Snorkeling, travel, reading **SIC code:** 80 **Address:** Austin Radiological Association, 6101 W. Courtyard Blvd., Bldg. 5, Austin, TX 78730-5033 **E-mail:** llbarr@austin.rr.com **Web address:** www.ausrad.com

BARRELL, NAN M.
Industry: Healthcare **Born:** September 8, 1953, Salem, Massachusetts **Univ./degree:** B.S., Psychology, 1976; M.A, Community Counseling, Towson State University, 1981 **Title:** Counselor **Major product:** Mental healthcare, prevention of child abuse and neglect **Area of distribution:** Connecticut **Area of Practice:** Counseling, child abuse, parent groups and adolescents **Published works:** Assisted in development of a workbook to be used in conjunction with psychological testing by Anne Anastas **Affiliations:** Certified Domestic Violence Counselor; Licensed Professional Counselor; Diplomate of the American Psychotherapy Association; Certified Sports Counselor; National Board of Forensic Counseling **Hob./spts.:** Crafts, computer graphics **SIC code:** 80 **Address:** 24 Greenway St., Hamden, CT 06517 **E-mail:** nbarrell@aol.com

BARRETT, JENETTE M.
Industry: Healthcare **Born:** April 30, 1960, Salem, Ohio **Univ./degree:** A.S., Kent State University, Ohio, 1989 **Current organization:** Employed by various medical staffing agencies **Title:** Multi-Modality Technologist/Independent Contractor **Type of organization:** Medical staffing specialists **Major product:** Multi-modality technology **Area of distribution:** National traveler **Area of Practice:** Mammography; Radiologic Technologist, cat scan **Honors/awards:** Student Essay Award For CT-sialography, Ohio, 1988 **Published works:** Paper, CT-saliography **Affiliations:** National Breast Cancer Foundation; Noah's Lost Ark Animal Sanctuary **Hob./spts.:** Travel, hiking, hunting, fishing **SIC code:** 80 **Address:** 7026 Woodley Lane, Falls Church, VA 22042 **E-mail:** jenbar420@aol.com

BARRETT, LEONARD O.
Industry: Healthcare **Born:** April 13, 1950, Jamaica, West Indies **Univ./degree:** B.S., Iona College, New York, 1978; M.D., SUNY Brooklyn, 1983 **Current organization:** Nassau County Medical Center, Dept. of Surgery **Title:** Chief Thoracic Surgeon/Director, Surgical Critical Care/Acting Medical Director **Type of organization:** Hospital **Major product:** Medical, surgical services **Area of distribution:** New York **Area of Practice:** Cardiothoracic and vascular surgery, critical care **Affiliations:** Fellow, American College of Surgeons; American Society of Critical Care Medicine; The Society of Thoracic Surgeons **Hob./spts.:** Community services (urban renewal), jogging, bowling, reading **SIC code:** 80 **Address:** Nassau County Medical Center, Dept. of Surgery, 2201 Hempstead Tpke., East Meadow, NY 11554 **E-mail:** lbarrett@ncmc.edu **Web address:** www.ncmc.edu

BARTON, CYRIL HENRY
Industry: Medical **Born:** July 20, 1945, Wilshire, England **Univ./degree:** M.D., University of Colorado, 1972 **Current organization:** UCI Medical Center - Nephrology Division **Title:** M.D./Associate Professor/Co-Chair, Dept. of Nephrology **Type of organization:** University hospital **Major product:** Patient care, medical education **Area of distribution:** Orange, California **Area of Practice:** Nephrology, kidney specialist **Hob./spts.:** Reading **SIC code:** 80 **Address:** UCI Medical Center - Nephrology Division, 101 City Dr. South, Building 53, Room 125, Orange, CA 92868 **E-mail:** chbarton@uci.edu

BARTON, LESLI A.
Industry: Healthcare **Born:** December 2, 1977, Crawfordsville, Indiana, 47933 **Univ./degree:** A.A., Occupational Medicine, Ivy Tech State College, 2001 **Current organization:** Athens Medical Group **Title:** RN, COHN **Type of organization:** Medical facility - physician's office **Major product:** Patient care **Area of Practice:** Certified, Council for Accreditation in Occupational Hearing Conservation; Certified Occupational Health Nurse, 2003 **Affiliations:** A.A.O.H.N.; A.B.O.H.N. **Hob./spts.:** Softball **SIC code:** 80 **Address:** Athens Medical Group, 1702 Lafayette Rd., Crawfordsville, IN 47933 **E-mail:** occmed@athensmed.org **Web address:** www.athensmed.org

BASCEANU, LIANA
Industry: Dentistry **Born:** January 30, 1962, Romania **Univ./degree:** B.S., Biochemistry, Hofstra University; D.D.S., New York University **Current organization:** Bergen Periodontics Associates, LLC **Title:** Owner **Type of organization:** Dental office **Major product:** Periodontal treatment (surgical and non-surgical) and placement of dental implants; Advanced bone and gum tissue grafting **Area of distribution:** New Jersey **Area of Practice:** Comprehensive diagnosis and treatment planning to restore oral health and retain patient's dentition; Treatment of temporo-mandibular dysfunction and oral medicine; State of the art, highly efficient and comfortable office, offering digital radiography, perioscopy, computerized patient education tools using the latest, most predictable regenerative materials and surgical and non-surgical techniques; Philosophy is to deliver the highest quality patient-centered care while minimizing patient anxiety and discomfort **Affiliations:** American Academy of Periodontology; Academy of Osseointegration; Northeast Society of Periodontists; New Jersey Society of Periodontists; New Jersey Dental Association; Bergen County Dental Society, Board of Trustees; Pascach Valley Study Club, President; Girl Scouts of America, Troop Leader **Hob./spts.:** Ballroom dancing, art collecting, coaching sports **SIC code:** 80 **Address:** Bergen Periodontics Associates, LLC, 333 Old Hook Rd., Suite 104, Westwood, NJ 07675 **E-mail:** drlianabasceanu@aol.com

BASILIO, CARLOS M.
Industry: Medicine **Born:** April 10, 1931, Chile **Univ./degree:** M.D., University of Chile **Current organization:** University of Puerto Rico School of Medicine **Title:** M.D., Professor **Type of organization:** University **Major product:** Higher education, research **Area of distribution:** San Juan, Puerto Rico **Area of Practice:** Medicine, science, molecular biology, transcription of genetic information **Published works:** 60+ publications **Affiliations:** F.A.I.C.; A.A.A.S. **Hob./spts.:** Music, playing guitar, reading **SIC code:** 80 **Address:** University of Puerto Rico School of Medicine, G.P.O. Box 5067, San Juan, PR 00936 **E-mail:** cbasilio@rcm.upr.edu

BASSA RAMIREZ, RAMON A.
Industry: Healthcare **Born:** March 28, 1959, Dominican Republic **Univ./degree:** M.D., University of Central Del Este **Current organization:** Ramon A. Bassa, M.D. **Title:** M.D. **Type of organization:** Private practice **Major product:** Patient care **Area of distribution:** Bayamon, Puerto Rico **Area of Practice:** Internal medicine **Affiliations:** Puerto Rico Medical Association **SIC code:** 80 **Address:** Ramon A. Bassa M.D., Torre San Pablo, Suite 803-B, Bayamón, PR 00959 **E-mail:** anasig@hotmail.com

BASSILY-MARCUS, ADEL
Industry: Healthcare **Born:** July 3, 1967, Cairo, Egypt **Univ./degree:** M.D., Ain Shams University, Egypt **Current organization:** Mount Sinai Medical Center **Title:** M.D. **Type of organization:** Hospital **Major product:** Patient care **Area of distribution:** New York, New York **Area of Practice:** Critical care medicine **Affiliations:** A.C.P.; A.S.I.M.; A.M.A.; S.C.C.M.; M.C.C.P.; M.M.S. **Hob./spts.:** Swimming, travel, chess, museums **SIC code:** 80 **Address:** Mount Sinai Medical Center, 1 Gustave Levy Place, New York, NY 10029 **E-mail:** adel777@bigfoot.com

BATTLE, RUTH
Industry: Healthcare **Born:** Georgia **Univ./degree:** B.S.N., Medgar Evers University, New York **Current organization:** Homes Regional Medical Center **Title:** R.N., C.B.S.N. **Type of organization:** Hospital **Major product:** Patient services **Area of distribution:** Florida **Area of Practice:** Level 2 trauma **Affiliations:** N.A.A.C.P.; American Association of University Women; Ambassador, People to People; Board Member, Mount Morriah Advisory Baptist Church **Hob./spts.:** Playing the organ, travel **SIC code:** 80 **Address:** Homes Regional Medical Center, 1350 S. Hickory St., Melbourne, FL 32901 **E-mail:** ruth728428@aol.com

BAUER, J. CHRISTOPHER
Industry: Healthcare **Born:** May 5, 1971, Albany, Missouri **Univ./degree:** M.D., University of Missouri at Columbia, 1997 **Current organization:** North Missouri Family Health Center **Title:** M.D. **Type of organization:** Private medical clinic **Major product:** Patient care, emergency room hospital services **Area of distribution:** Missouri **Area of Practice:** Internal medicine, pediatrics **Published works:** 1 article **Affiliations:** A.C.P.; A.M.A.; American Association of Pediatrics **Hob./spts.:** Motorcycles, family **SIC code:** 80 **Address:** North Missouri Family Health Center, 2703 Miller St., Bethany, MO 64424 **E-mail:** cbauer@grm.net

BAUER, JOEL J.
Industry: Healthcare **Born:** August 16, 1942, New York, New York **Univ./degree:** M.D., New York University **Current organization:** Mt. Sinai Medical Center **Title:** M.D. **Type of organization:** Medical center **Major product:** Patient care **Area of distribution:** International **Area of Practice:** Surgery **Published works:** 2 books, several chapters, 100+ journal articles **Affiliations:** A.C.S.; A.S.C.R.S.; S.S.E.T.; A.C.G.; N.Y.A.S.; N.Y.S.S. **Hob./spts.:** Golf, skiing, biking, gardening **SIC code:** 80 **Address:** Mt. Sinai Medical Center, 25 E. 69th St., New York, NY 10021

BAXTER, ELIZABETH A.
Industry: Healthcare **Born:** May 24, 1953, Dearborn, Michigan **Univ./degree:** Vanderbilt University **Current organization:** Dr. Elizabeth A. Baxter **Title:** President **Type of organization:** Medical advocacy services **Major product:** Psychiatry, lectures **Area of distribution:** International **Area of Practice:** Addictions, disabilities **Published works:** "The Gift of Depression" **Affiliations:** A.P.A.; Tennessee Women's Medical Association **Hob./spts.:** Cooking, knitting, writing, travel **SIC code:** 80 **Address:** Dr. Elizabeth A. Baxter, 2300 21st Ave., South, Suite 303, Nashville, TN 37212 **E-mail:** bethbaxter@earthlink.net

BEALS, CAROL A.
Industry: Healthcare **Married:** Widowed **Children:** 2 children, 5 step-children, 18 grandchildren **Univ./degree:** RN, Harrisburg Poly Clinic, PA, 1963; BS RN, MSU, 1972; Graduate, MSU College of Human Medicine, 1976; Internal Medicine Residency-MSU, 1979; Subspecialty-U of M Fellowship in Rheumatology, 1981; Certification in Bone Mineral Densitometry, 2001 **Current organization:** Beals Institute, P.C. **Title:** Chief Executive Officer **Type of organization:** Private practice **Major product:** Medical services **Area of distribution:** Lansing, Michigan **Area of Practice:** Osteoporosis, arthritis, autoimmune diseases **Honors/awards:** Governor's Award; Best Doctor in America; Outstanding Alumni, MSU; Outstanding Women of the Year 2002; Best Doctor 2000, 2002; Numerous other awards and honors throughout 1981 to 2004 **Published works:** Numerous including, Co-author, "Measurement of exercise tolerance in patients with rheumatoid arthritis and osteoarthritis", Journal of Rheumatology, 12(3): 458-61, Jun. 1985; Author, "Link probed between low CD4 T-lymphocyte counts and P. Carini", Rheumatology News, vol. 21, Nov. 4, 1993, Apr. Presented at International Conference in Tel Aviv, Israel; Author, "Fibromyalgia Network" and several other articles published in journals and published talks **Affiliations:** American Medical Association; American College of Rheumatology; American College of Physicians; I.C.C.; Board Member (for 10 years), Michigan Arthritis Foundation; Board Member (1 year), National Scleroderma Foundation; Board Member (9 years), Sparrow Hospital Development Board; Current Board Member, Lansing Symphony Orchestra; Member, Hadassah; U of M Alumni Association; MSU Alumni Association; National Osteoporosis Foundation **Career accomplishments:** Integrated and comprehensive approach to the medical treatment of arthritis, autoimmune diseases and osteoporosis for 23 years; Leader in the field of osteoporosis starting in 1989 and have done greater than 25,000 Bone Mineral Density Tests; Osteoporosis Clinic for testing, prevention and treatment of osteopenia to severe osteoporosis; Infusion service for state of the art biologic medications for inflammatory arthritis and intravenous treatment for osteoporosis; Holistic approach to medical treatment emphasizing the mind-body-spiritual connection and education of the patient service provided to 12,000 patient visits per year **Hob./spts.:** Traveled to 15 foreign countries, eclectic art collection of American-Indian pottery, blown glass from Venice and U.S., paintings from multiple countries and artists, Oriental rugs, Israeli sculptures, amateur photographer, lover of music and theatre **SIC code:** 80 **Address:** Beals Institute. P.C., 4333 W. Saint Joseph Hwy., Lansing, MI 48917 **E-mail:** BealsFarm@msn.com

BEAR, DAVID M.
Industry: Healthcare **Born:** March 14, 1943, Akron, Ohio **Univ./degree:** M.D., Harvard Medical School **Current organization:** Acadia Hospital **Title:** M.D./Psychiatrist **Type of organization:** Hospital **Major product:** Patient care **Area of distribution:** Maine **Area of Practice:** Psychiatry, use of telemedicine **Affiliations:** Professor of Psychiatry, University of Massachusetts Medical Center **Hob./spts.:** Music, philosophy **SIC code:** 80 **Address:** Acadia Hospital, 268 Stillwater Ave., Bangor, ME 04402 **E-mail:** dbear@emh.org

BEARD, MARY K.
Industry: Healthcare **Univ./degree:** B.S., Central Missouri State University; M.D., University of Arkansas School of Medicine, 1965 **Current organization:** Avenues Women Center **Title:** M.D., F.A.C.O.G. **Type of organization:** Women's health center **Major product:** Patient care **Area of distribution:** Utah **Area of Practice:** Board Certified, OB-GYN **Affiliations:** F.A.C.O.G. **SIC code:** 80 **Address:** Avenues Women Center, 455 E. South Temple, Salt Lake City, UT 84111 **E-mail:** drmarybeard@west.net

BEAUBOEUF, ALPHONSE L.A.
Industry: Healthcare **Born:** Haiti **Univ./degree:** M.D., University of Medicine, Haiti **Current organization:** Medical Practice of Alphonse Beauboeuf, M.D. **Title:** M.D. **Type of organization:** Private practice **Major product:** Patient care **Area of distribution:** St. Louis, Missouri **Area of Practice:** Internal medicine **Affiliations:** A.S.I.M.; Haitian Medical Association **Hob./spts.:** Music **SIC code:** 80 **Address:** Medical Practice of Alphonse Beauboeuf, M.D., 2415 N. Kingshighway Blvd., St. Louis, MO 63113

BEAUDUY, AUDREY B.
Industry: Medical **Born:** January 10, 1953, Chicago, Illinois **Univ./degree:** B.S.N., Chicago State University, 1995 **Current organization:** University of Illinois Hospital **Title:** R.N. **Type of organization:** University hospital **Major product:** Medical services **Area of distribution:** Illinois **Area of Practice:** Women's healthcare **Published works:** 1 article **Affiliations:** A.N.A.; Sigma Beta Tau **Hob./spts.:** Sewing, reading **SIC code:** 80 **Address:** University of Illinois Hospital, 1740 W. Taylor, Chicago, IL 60612 **E-mail:** abeauduy@uic.edu **Web address:** www.uic.edu

BECKEMEYER, SHAWN D.
Industry: Healthcare **Born:** May 11, 1970, Belleville, Illinois **Univ./degree:** M.D., South Illinois School of Medicine, 1995 **Current organization:** Coulterville Medical Clinic **Title:** M.D. **Type of organization:** Hospital owned medical clinic **Major product:** Patient care **Area of distribution:** Coulterville, Illinois **Area of Practice:** Family medicine **Honors/awards:** Girl Scout Gold Award; Chief Resident, Residency Research Award **Affiliations:** A.M.A.; A.A.F.P.; A.M.W.A.; Junior Chamber Girl Scouts of U.S.A. **Hob./spts.:** Horseback riding, sailing, scuba diving, Girl Scouts **SIC code:** 80 **Address:** Coulterville Medical Clinic, 203 E. Grant, Coulterville, IL 62237

BECKWITH, MARY KRISTINE
Industry: Healthcare **Born:** December 8, 1955, Cherokee, Iowa **Univ./degree:** M.D., University of Iowa, 1982 **Current organization:** Clearvista Women's Care **Title:** M.D. **Type of organization:** Group practice **Major product:** Patient care **Area of distribution:** Indiana **Area of Practice:** Obstetrics/gynecology **Honors/awards:** Chief Resident Art of the Medicine Award, 1986; Chairman of the Dept. OBGYN

Resident **Affiliations:** A.C.O.G.; A.M.S.U. **Hob./spts.:** Ballet **SIC code:** 80 **Address:** Clearvista Women's Care, 8040 Clearvista Pkwy., Suite 490, Indianapolis, IN 46256

BEDARD, JOEL
Industry: Healthcare **Born:** June 27, 1953, Haiti **Univ./degree:** M.D., Universidad Autonoma de Guadalajara School of Medicine, 1976 **Current organization:** Eben-Ezer Medical Associates **Title:** M.D. **Type of organization:** Medical office **Major product:** Patient care/psychiatry **Area of distribution:** Hempstead, New York **Area of Practice:** Psychiatry; Board Certified, American Psychiatric Association, American Neurological Association and Oral Board of Examiners, Part II **Affiliations:** American Psychiatric Association; American Neurological Association **SIC code:** 80 **Address:** 275 Jerusalem Ave., Hempstead, NY 11550

BEENKEN, SAMUEL W.
Industry: Medical **Born:** November 7, 1951, Sioux Falls, South Dakota **Univ./degree:** M.D., University of Manitoba School of Medicine, Canada, 1975 **Current organization:** University of Alabama at Birmingham **Title:** M.D. **Type of organization:** University/hospital **Major product:** Surgery, medical education, translational research **Area of distribution:** Alabama **Area of Practice:** Cancer surgery, cancer prevention **Honors/awards:** Professor of Surgery; Best Doctors in America **Published works:** 50 articles, book chapters **Affiliations:** A.A.E.S.; A.H.N.S.; S.S.O.; A.A.C.R.; A.S.C.O. **Hob./spts.:** Golf, hunting, reading **SIC code:** 80 **Address:** The University of Alabama at Birmingham, WTI 620, 1530 Third Ave. South, Birmingham, AL 35294--330 **E-mail:** samuel.beenken@ccc.uab.edu **Web address:** www.uab.edu/surgonc/

BEHZADI, HAMID N.
Industry: Healthcare **Born:** Iran, Hashtpar **Univ./degree:** M.D., Spartan Health Sciences University, 1987/Post Graduate, SUNY-KCHC, 1998 **Current organization:** Hamid N. Behzadi, M.D., F.C.C.P. **Title:** M.D., F.C.C.P. **Type of organization:** Private practice with academic involvement **Major product:** Patient care, education **Area of distribution:** New York **Area of Practice:** Internal medicine, pulmonary disease, critical care medicine, emergency medicine **Affiliations:** A.M.A.; A.T.S.; A.C.C.P.; N.Y.S.T.S.; S.C.C.M.; A.C.P.; St. Luke's/Roosevelt University Hospitals of Columbia; University College of Physicians and Surgeons **Hob./spts.:** Tennis, racquetball, soccer **SIC code:** 80 **Address:** Hamid N. Behzadi, M.D., F.C.C.P., 25 Central Park West, Suite 1M, New York, NY 10023 **Phone:** (212)307-0487 **Fax:** (212)307-0734 **E-mail:** hamidmahdis@aol.com

BELIZAIRE, DELORES
Industry: Healthcare **Born:** September 20, 1938, Brooklyn, New York **Univ./degree:** A.A.S., Queensboro Community College; B.S., Theology, Evangelical Worldwide Institute of Biblical Studies, 1995 **Current organization:** Waterview Nursing Care Center **Title:** Director of Nursing Services **Type of organization:** Nursing home **Major product:** Providing and directing resident care **Area of distribution:** National **Area of Practice:** Nursing **Affiliations:** Vice President, Vision From the Heart Ministries; member and Chair, Nursing Administration, American College of Health Care Administrators **Hob./spts.:** Church activities, singing in the choir, volleyball, **SIC code:** 80 **Address:** Waterview Nursing Care Center, 119-15 27th Ave., Flushing, NY 11354 **E-mail:** delo920@aol.com

BELLISTRI, STEVEN V.
Industry: Healthcare **Born:** May 19, 1953, Baltimore, Maryland **Univ./degree:** B.S., Loyola College, Baltimore, Maryland, 1975 **Current organization:** The Memorial Hospital of Salem County (CHS) **Title:** Director of Laboratory Services **Type of organization:** Hospital **Major product:** Patient care, clinical laboratory services **Area of distribution:** Southern New Jersey **Area of Practice:** Medical technology **Honors/awards:** International Who's Who, President's Award, Baxter Healthcare, Six Sigma, Green Belt **Affiliations:** A.S.C.P.; A.A.C.C.; C.L.M.A. **Hob./spts.:** Fly-fishing, the outdoors **SIC code:** 80 **Address:** The Memorial Hospital of Salem County, 310 Woodstown Rd., Salem, NJ 08079 **E-mail:** steve_bellistri@chs.net

BELLO, SANDRA M.
Industry: Healthcare **Univ./degree:** M.D., Michigan State University, 1992; Fellowship, University of Southern California, 1999 **Current organization:** West Texas Reproductive Center **Title:** M.D. **Type of organization:** Private practice **Major product:** Health services **Area of distribution:** Odessa, Texas **Area of Practice:** Reproductive endocrinology, hormonal endocrinology **Affiliations:** American Society for Reproductive Medicine **Hob./spts.:** Gardening, running, physical fitness **SIC code:** 80 **Address:** West Texas Reproductive Center, 703 W. Hancock, Odessa, TX 79761 **E-mail:** sbello@westtexasreproductive.com **Web address:** www.westtexasreproductive.com

BELLO, VIOLETA F.
Industry: Healthcare **Born:** June 27, 1957, Santo Domingo, Dominican Republic **Univ./degree:** M.D., Dominican Republic, 1983 **Current organization:** Permian Pediatrics **Title:** Pediatrician **Type of organization:** Private practice **Major product:** Children's healthcare **Area of distribution:** Odessa, Texas **Area of Practice:** Pediatrics **Affiliations:** A.M.A.; A.A.P. **Hob./spts.:** Family activities **SIC code:** 80 **Address:** Permian Pediatrics, 303 E. 7th St., Odessa, TX 79761 **E-mail:** permianped@sbcglobal.net

BELMONT, JOANN
Industry: Healthcare **Born:** July 3, 1960, Brooklyn, New York **Univ./degree:** B.S.N., State University of New York, New Paltz, 1980 **Current organization:** St. Barnabas Medical Center **Title:** RN, Administrative Director **Type of organization:** Hospital **Major product:** Patient care **Area of distribution:** New Jersey **Area of Practice:** Case management, **Affiliations:** N.A.H.C.Q.; American Society for Quality **SIC code:** 80 **Address:** St. Barnabas Medical Center, East Wing, Suite 505, Livingston, NJ 07039 **E-mail:** bjoa5@aol.com

BELMONTE, EDGAR C.
Industry: Medical **Born:** October 25, 1940, Santa Cruz, Bolivia **Univ./degree:** M.D., San Andres School of Medicine, 1969 **Current organization:** St. Luke's Memorial Hospital **Title:** M.D./Associate Professor, Ponce Medical School **Type of organization:** Hospital/University **Major product:** Patient care/medical education **Area of distribution:** Puerto Rico **Area of Practice:** Pathology **Affiliations:** American Society of Clinical Pathologists; American College of Pathology **Hob./spts.:** Snorkeling, bird watching **SIC code:** 80 **Address:** P.O. Box 801024, Coto Laurel, PR 00780-1024

BELTON, RUBY L.
Industry: Healthcare **Born:** August 21, 1946, Crystal Springs, Mississippi **Univ./degree:** M.D., University of Rochester School of Medicine and Dentistry, 1972 **Current organization:** Rochester Radiology Associates **Title:** M.D. **Type of organization:** Hospital and private practice **Major product:** Radiology and healthcare **Area of distribution:** Rochester, New York **Area of Practice:** Abdominal ultrasound, gastrointestinal radiology, body computed tomography, mammography including interventional breast and breast ultrasound **Honors/awards:** First African-American Director of Mammography and Interventional Breast Division, past Chief of Body Computer Tomography, past Chief of Abdominal Ultrasound, Rochester General Hospital **Published works:** 1 article, "Congenital absence of the left lobe of the liver: A Radiologic Diagnosis", August, 1982 **Affiliations:** A.C.R.; Post-Baccalaureate Macy Foundation Fellow: Haverford College and Oberlin College; Mount Olivet Baptist Church **Hob./spts.:** Family, work, religion, **SIC code:** 80 **Address:** Rochester Radiology Associates, Rochester General Hospital, 1425 Portland Ave., Rochester, NY 14621

BELTZ, HOMER F.
Industry: Healthcare **Born:** April 21, 1944, Detroit. Michigan **Univ./degree:** M.D., University of Michigan, 1970 **Current organization:** Northwest Radiology Network, P.C. **Title:** M.D./President/CEO **Type of organization:** Medical group **Major product:** Professional radiology **Area of distribution:** Indianapolis, Indiana **Area of Practice:** Radiology **Published works:** Articles **Affiliations:** A.M.A.; A.C.R.; R.S.N.A. **Hob./spts.:** Golf, horses **SIC code:** 80 **Address:** Northwest Radiology Network, P.C., 5756 W. 71st St., Indianapolis, IN 46278 **E-mail:** nierlino@aol.com

BENAVIDES, MOSES BENAIAH
Industry: Medical **Born:** December 29, 1960, Crystal City, Texas **Univ./degree:** M.D., Meharry Medical College, Tennessee, 1999 **Current organization:** University Family Physicians **Title:** M.D. **Type of organization:** University medical center **Major product:** Patient care, medical education **Area of distribution:** Knoxville, Tennessee **Area of Practice:** Family medicine **Affiliations:** A.M.A.; Christian Medical & Dental Association **Hob./spts.:** Travel, recreational flying, billiards, cooking, motorcycling, jet skiing, waterspouts, mountain biking, repairing engines and computers **SIC code:** 80 **Address:** University Family Physicians, 1924 Alcoa Hwy., Knoxville, TN 37920 **E-mail:** mosesbenavides@msn.com

BENEDICT, H.E. ORLANDO I.
Industry: Healthcare, consultation in geriatrics **Born:** October 2, 1958, San Juan, Puerto Rico, U.S.A. **Univ./degree:** M.D., U.S.A., 1983 **Current organization:** Dr. Benedict & Associates **Title:** President **Type of organization:** Private practice **Major product:** Medical care and teaching **Area of distribution:** National **Area of Practice:** Geriatrics and Medicine (Board Certified), consulting in Genesis Health Systems **Published works:** Michigan State University School of Medicine, Research and others **Affiliations:** M.S.M.S.; A.M.S.U.S.; Genesee County Medical Society; G.C.M.S.; O.St. L. J. **Hob./spts.:** Heraldry, racquetball, British squash **SIC code:** 80 **Address:** Viscount of Mericourt, 8392 Holly Rd., Grand Blanc, MI 48439 **E-mail:** oibenedict@aol.com

BENFORD, MARTHA K.
Industry: Healthcare **Born:** Covington, Alabama **Univ./degree:** B.S., Nursing, University of St. Francis **Current organization:** Health Benefits Pain Management Service **Title:** R.N., Director of Nursing **Type of organization:** Clinic **Major product:** Patient care **Area of distribution:** Chicago, Illinois **Area of Practice:** Pain management **Affiliations:** American Society for Pain Management Nursing; Honorable Discharge, U.S. Army Nurse Corp **Hob./spts.:** Beading, painting, classical music **SIC code:** 80

Address: Health Benefits Pain Management Service, 25 E. Washington, Suite 1329, Chicago, IL 60602 **E-mail:** benfordrn@sbcglobal.net

BENITEZ, WANDA I.
Industry: Healthcare **Born:** May 15, 1952, Ponce, Puerto Rico **Univ./degree:** B.S., Cum Laude, Biology, University of Puerto Rico at Mayaguez, 1975; M.D., University of Puerto Rico, School of Medicine, 1979 **Current organization:** Concepcion Hospital **Title:** Diagnostic Radiologist/Neuroradiologist **Type of organization:** Hospital **Major product:** Neuroradiology diagnostic services **Area of distribution:** San German, Puerto Rico **Area of Practice:** Neuroradiology **Honors/awards:** One of Tenth Distinguished Woman Doctor in Western Puerto Rico, November, 1996, A.M.D.O., Mayaguez, Puerto Rico; Distinguished President of Social Activities Committee of Puerto Rico Medical and Surgeon College, June, 1997, Mayaguez, Puerto Rico; Most Enthusiasm and Distinguished President of A.M.D.O., November, 1997, Mayaguez, Puerto Rico; Distinguished President, Credential Committee of San Antonio Hospital, November, 1999, Mayaguez, Puerto Rico **Published works:** Co-Author, "Craniopharyngioma presenting as a Nasopharyngeal Mass: Ct and MRI findings", J. Comp Assist Tomong, 12: 1068-1071, 1988; Co-Author, "MRI findings in Childhood Ganglioglioma: Correlation with CT and Histology", J. Comp Assist Tomong, 14: 712-716, 1990; several abstracts, presentations and T.V. presentations **Affiliations:** American College of Radiology; Senior Member, American Society of Neuroradiology; American Society of Head and Neck Radiology; Radiology Society of North America; American Medical Association; PR Chapter, Western Region, American Medical Association; Puerto Rico Radiologist Society; Society of Diagnostic Medical Sonographers; Puerto Rico Medical and Surgeons College **SIC code:** 80 **Address:** Concepcion Hospital, P.O. Box 285, San Germán, PR 00683

BENJAMIN, ARTHUR B.
Industry: Healthcare **Born:** November 30, 1948, New York, New York **Univ./degree:** D.D.S., New York University **Current organization:** Arthur Benjamin, DDS **Title:** D.D.S. **Type of organization:** Private practice **Major product:** Dental services **Area of distribution:** New York, New York **Area of Practice:** Prosthodontics, implant restoration, cosmetics **Affiliations:** A.D.A., O.K.U. **Hob./spts.:** Physical fitness, biking, travel **SIC code:** 80 **Address:** Arthur Benjamin, DDS, 121 E. 60th St., New York, NY 10022

BENNETT, MICHAEL
Industry: Healthcare **Born:** February 11, 1936, Goose Creek, Texas **Univ./degree:** M.D., Baylor University, 1961 **Current organization:** University of Texas Southwestern Medical Center **Title:** Professor **Type of organization:** University hospital **Major product:** Medical services, research **Area of distribution:** International **Area of Practice:** Pathology, immunology research **Honors/awards:** Best Cancer Research Program **Published works:** 200 articles **Affiliations:** A.E.I.; I.S.E.H. **Hob./spts.:** Mystery novels **SIC code:** 80 **Address:** University of Texas, Southwestern Medical Center, 5323 Harry Hines Blvd., Dallas, TX 75390-9072 **E-mail:** michael.bennett@utsouthwestern.edu

BENSON, WENDY K.
Industry: Healthcare **Born:** February 4, 1966, Salinas, California **Univ./degree:** B.S., Chemistry, University of Washington, 1989 **Current organization:** Roche Molecular Diagnostics **Title:** Commercial business development **Type of organization:** Product Supplier **Major product:** Diagnostics **Area of distribution:** International **Area of Practice:** Marketing, Business Development, Asia-Pacific **Affiliations:** A.A.B.B. **Hob./spts.:** Scuba diving, swimming, bicycling **SIC code:** 80 **Address:** Roche Molecular Diagnostics, 4300 Hacienda Dr., Pleasanton, CA 94588 **E-mail:** wendy.benson@roche.com **Web address:** www.roche.com

BENTLIF, PHILIP SIDNEY
Industry: Healthcare **Born:** March 20, 1932, St. Saviour, Jersey, Channel Isles **Univ./degree:** M.D., Cambridge University, 1956 **Current organization:** Medical Clinic of Houston, LLP **Title:** M.D. **Type of organization:** Medical group **Major product:** Clinical practice and teaching **Area of distribution:** Houston, Texas **Area of Practice:** Gastroenterology-inflammatory bowel disease **Published works:** 30+ publications **Affiliations:** Fellow, American College of Physicians; American College of Gastroenterology; American Gastroenterological Association **Hob./spts.:** Theatre, eco travel, Australian Aboriginal art, swimming **SIC code:** 80 **Address:** Medical Clinic of Houston, LLP, 6624 Fannin St., Suite 1700, Houston, TX 77030 **E-mail:** pbentlif@aol.com

BENTON, ARLENE
Industry: Healthcare **Born:** December 25, 1948, St. Cloud, Minnesota **Current organization:** Norwood Healthcare **Title:** Nurse **Type of organization:** Psychiatric Hospital **Major product:** Patient care **Area of distribution:** Marshfield, Wisconsin **Area of Practice:** Psychiatric nursing **Affiliations:** A.N.A. **Hob./spts.:** Needlework, horseback riding **SIC code:** 80 **Address:** Norwood Healthcare, 1600 N. Chestnut Ave., Marshfield, WI 54449 **E-mail:** abinhome@aol.com

BERCOW, NEIL R.
Industry: Healthcare **Born:** September 20, 1959, Elizabeth, New Jersey **Univ./degree:** M.D., St. George's University School of Medicine, 1985 **Current organization:** Cardiothoracic Surgery, PC **Title:** M.D. **Type of organization:** Private practice **Major product:** Patient care **Area of distribution:** Roslyn, New York **Area of Practice:** Heart surgery **Honors/awards:** Top Doctor, New York Metropolitan Area **Affiliations:** S.T.S.; American College of Surgeons **Hob./spts.:** Skiing, sailboat racing **SIC code:** 80 **Address:** Cardiothoracic Surgery, PC, 100 Port Washington Blvd., Roslyn, NY 11576 **E-mail:** nbercow@ctsurg.com

BERG, VIOLA GRUYS
Industry: Healthcare **Born:** July 27, 1914, Annandale, Minnesota **Univ./degree:** B.A., Education, Sociology, University of California at Sacramento, 1953; M.A., Education, Psychology and School Administration, University of California at Long Beach, 1965 **Current organization:** Berg Educational Assistance **Title:** Speech, Language Pathologist/Educational Psychologist **Type of organization:** Hospital/private practice **Major product:** Educational/personal development **Area of distribution:** California **Area of Practice:** Licensed Speech Pathologist, State of Washington; General administration, pupils' personnel service, psychology and supervision **Affiliations:** American Speech-Language-Hearing Association; National Association of School Psychologists; National Education Association; California Teachers' Association; California Speech-Language-Hearing Association; Washington Speech & Hearing Association; Washington State Association of School Psychologists **Hob./spts.:** Travel, sports, politics, art **SIC code:** 80 **Address:** Berg Educational Assistance, 150 Sky Valley Drive, #338, Reno, NV 89503

BERGER, GARY G.
Industry: Healthcare **Born:** October 23, 1957, Philadelphia, Pennsylvania **Univ./degree:** D.O., Philadelphia College of Osteopathic Medicine **Current organization:** Gary G. Berger, D.O. **Title:** D.O. **Type of organization:** Private practice **Major product:** Patient care **Area of distribution:** Overland Park, Kansas **Area of Practice:** Physical medicine and rehabilitation **Affiliations:** American Academy of Physical Medicine and Rehabilitation **Hob./spts.:** Collector of Disney memorabilia, stamp collecting, running **SIC code:** 80 **Address:** Gary G. Berger, D.O., 5701 W. 119th St., Suite 116, Overland Park, KS 66209

BERGSTEIN, MICHAEL
Industry: Healthcare **Born:** January 28, 1958 **Univ./degree:** M.D., University of Buffalo, 1980 **Current organization:** ENT: Allergy Associates **Title:** M.D. **Type of organization:** Private practice **Major product:** Patient care **Area of distribution:** New York **Area of Practice:** Ear, nose and throat/facial plastic and reconstructive surgery **Honors/awards:** Phi Beta Kappa; "Best Doctors", New York Magazine **Affiliations:** Phelps Memorial Hospital; Hudson Valley Hospital; Northern Westchester Hospital **SIC code:** 80 **Address:** 358 N. Broadway, Sleepy Hollow, NY 10591

BERKELHAMMER, CHARLES
Industry: Healthcare **Born:** Septmember 10, 1956, Canada **Univ./degree:** B.S.V., University of Toronto; M.D., University of Toronto Medical School, 1980 **Current organization:** Southwest Center for Gastroenterology **Title:** M.D., F.A.C.G. **Type of organization:** Medical clinic **Major product:** Gastroenterology **Area of distribution:** Illinois **Area of Practice:** Gastroenterology **Published works:** 32 articles **Affiliations:** F.A.C.G.; A.G.A.; A.S.G.E. **SIC code:** 80 **Address:** Southwest Center for Gastroenterology, 9921 Southwest Hwy., Oak Lawn, IL 60453 **E-mail:** charlesberkel@aol.com

BERKOWITZ, KEVIN D.
Industry: Healthcare **Born:** March 18, 1971, Patchogue, New York **Univ./degree:** D.P.M., Barry University, 1997 **Current organization:** Foot and ankle specialists of Miami Beach **Title:** Physician/Podiatrist **Type of organization:** Private practice **Major product:** Patient care **Area of distribution:** International **Area of Practice:** Foot and ankle surgery/wound healing **Affiliations:** American Podiatric Medical Association; American College of Foot and Ankle Surgeons **Hob./spts.:** Teaching, literature, water sports **SIC code:** 80 **Address:** Foot & Ankle Specialists of Miami Beach, 420 Lincoln Rd., Suite 2C, Miami Beach, FL 33139 **E-mail:** carmelberko@yahoo.com

BERMEL, JOSEPHINE A.
Industry: Healthcare **Born:** September 24, 1937, Kansas City, Missouri **Univ./degree:** Attended Metropolitan Junior College **Current organization:** Colon & Rectal Surgeons of Kansas City **Title:** Administrator **Type of organization:** Private medical practice **Major product:** Colon and rectal surgery **Area of distribution:** National **Area of Practice:** Administration **Affiliations:** A.C.M.P.E.; M.M.A.; M.G.M.A. Missouri & Northland Medical Managers Association; Greater Kansas City Medical Managers Association **Hob./spts.:** Swimming, golf **SIC code:** 80 **Address:** Colon & Rectal Surgeons of Kansas City, 8901 W. 74th St., Suite 149, Shawnee Mission, KS 66204

BERNARD, CORINE G.
Industry: Healthcare **Born:** June 14, 1962, Belgium **Univ./degree:** B.S., Healthcare Administration **Current organization:** Villa Siena **Title:** Executive Director **Type**

of organization: Nursing home **Major product:** Healthcare for the elderly **Area of distribution:** California **Area of Practice:** Management, operations quality **Hob./spts.:** Baseball **SIC code:** 80 **Address:** Villa Siena, 1855 Miramonte Ave., Mountain View, CA 94040 **E-mail:** vsiena@pacbell.net

BERNARD, GARY C.
Industry: Healthcare **Univ./degree:** M.D., Meharry Medical College, Nashville, Tennessee, 1992 **Current organization:** Pointe Medical Services, Inc. **Title:** M.D., President **Type of organization:** Medical office **Major product:** Patient care **Area of distribution:** Orange Park, Florida **Area of Practice:** Board Certified, Internal Medicine **Affiliations:** A.A.P.M.; A.M.A.; C.C.M.S.; A.C.P.-A.S.I.M., F.M.A. **SIC code:** 80 **Address:** Pointe Medical Services, Inc., 1996 Kingsley Ave., Orange Park, FL 32073 **E-mail:** gbernard@pointemed.com

BERROYA, RENATO B.
Industry: Healthcare **Univ./degree:** M.D., University of Santo Tomas, Philippines **Current organization:** Long Island Surgical **Title:** M.D./Chief, Vascular Surgery Dept. **Type of organization:** Private practice **Major product:** Patient care **Area of distribution:** National **Area of Practice:** Vascular surgery, corrated arteries, aneurisms **Published works:** Numerous journal articles **Affiliations:** F.A.C.S.; F.A.M.A.; F.C.V.S.; Chief, Vascular Surgery Dept., St. Francis Hospital **SIC code:** 80 **Address:** Long Island Surgical, 639 Port Washington Blvd., Port Washington, NY 11050 **E-mail:** lissvasc@aol.com

BERTILSON, SHEILA J.
Industry: Medical **Born:** May 23, 1957, Minneapolis, Minnesota **Univ./degree:** B.S., Medical Technology, Morehead State University, 1980 **Current organization:** Madelia Community Hospital **Title:** Lab/Radiology Manager **Type of organization:** Hospital **Major product:** Patient care, radiology services **Area of distribution:** Minnesota **Area of Practice:** Administration of lab and radiology departments **Affiliations:** A.S.C.P. **Hob./spts.:** Family activities, movies, real estate **SIC code:** 80 **Address:** Madelia Community Hospital, 121 Drew Ave. S.E., Madelia, MN 56062 **E-mail:** sheilabertilson@yahoo.com

BESSER, GARY STEVEN
Industry: Healthcare **Born:** March 20, 1954, New York, New York **Univ./degree:** B.S., Biochemical Engineering, MIT, 1976; M.D., SUNY School of Medicine, 1982 **Current organization:** Ob/Gyn Associates **Title:** M.D. **Type of organization:** Private practice **Major product:** Patient care **Area of distribution:** Connecticut **Area of Practice:** Ob/Gyn **Published works:** 8 articles **Affiliations:** F.A.C.O.G.; A.A.G.L. **Hob./spts.:** Skiing, golf **SIC code:** 80 **Address:** Ob/Gyn Associates, 190 W. Broad St., Suite 401G, Whittingham Pavilion, Stamford, CT 06902 **E-mail:** gsbesser@aol.com

BETHEA, WILLIAM M.
Industry: Healthcare **Born:** November 10, 1945, Albany, Georgia **Univ./degree:** M.D., Medical College of Georgia, 1971 **Current organization:** Sentara Executive Evaluation Center **Title:** M.D. **Type of organization:** Medical practice **Major product:** Preventative physical examinations **Area of distribution:** Norfolk, Virginia **Area of Practice:** Internal medicine **Affiliations:** F.A.C.P.; American Board of Internal Medicine **SIC code:** 80 **Address:** Sentara Executive Evaluation Center, 900 Wainwright Bldg., Norfolk, VA 23510 **Phone:** (757)668-1870 **Fax:** (757)625-6062 **Web address:** www.eecva.com

BEUCHERT, PHILIP
Industry: Radiology **Born:** March 8, 1968, Yonkers, New York **Univ./degree:** M.D., Radiology, Albany Medical College, 1994 **Current organization:** BAB Radiology **Title:** Physician/Radiologist **Type of organization:** Radiology center **Major product:** Radiology **Area of distribution:** Long Island, New York **Area of Practice:** Body imaging, PET scanning **Published works:** Articles **Affiliations:** New York Medical Association; American College of Therapeutic Radiology; Radiologic Society of North America; American Roentgen Ray Society; American College of Radiology **SIC code:** 80 **Address:** BAB Radiology, 175 E. Main St., Huntington, NY 11743

BEYTH, REBECCA J.
Industry: Medical **Born:** February 5, 1960, Sharon, Pennsylvania **Univ./degree:** B.S., Biology/Psychology, Case Western Reserve University, 1982; M.D., Jefferson Medical College, 1987; M.S., Biostatistics, University of Michigan, Ann Arbor, 1999 **Current organization:** Baylor College of Medicine & Houston VAMC **Title:** MD, MS **Type of organization:** Medical college **Major product:** Medical services **Area of distribution:** Texas **Area of Practice:** Thromboembolic disorders **Affiliations:** A.C.P.; A.C.C.P.; A.G.S.; Society of General Internal Medicine **Hob./spts.:** Gardening, swimming **SIC code:** 80 **Address:** Baylor College of Medicine & Houston VAMC, HVAMC (152), 2002 Holcombe Blvd., Houston, TX 77030 **E-mail:** rbeyth@bcm.tmc.edu

BHALLA, RITU
Industry: Medical **Born:** Kanpur, India **Univ./degree:** M.D., GSVM Medical College, Kanpur, India, 1993; Diplomate of American Board of Pathology (in combined APCP),; Diplomate of American Board of Pathology (in Cytopathology) **Current organization:** Hartford Hospital **Title:** M.D. **Type of organization:** Academic hospital/university **Major product:** Patient care, medical education **Area of distribution:** Hartford, Connecticut **Area of Practice:** Cytopathology, surgical pathology **Affiliations:** A.M.A.; American Society of Cytopathology; College of American Pathologists; United States and Canadian Academy of Pathology; American Society of Clinical Pathologists; Ohio Society of Pathologists **Hob./spts.:** Swimming, painting, travel **SIC code:** 80 **Address:** Hartford Hospital, 80 Seymour St., Hartford, CT 06102 **E-mail:** rbhalla13@yahoo.com

BHARUCHA, ASHOK J.
Industry: Medical **Born:** May 9, 1967, Avidha, India **Univ./degree:** B.A., Chemistry and German, Bucknell University; M.D., Penn State College of Medicine; Residency, Adult Psychiatry, Harvard Medical School (McLean Hospital); Fellowship in Geriatric Psychiatry, University of Washington School of Medicine **Current organization:** Western Psychiatric Institute and Clinic, University of Pittsburgh Medical School **Title:** M.D. **Type of organization:** Academic medical center **Major product:** Patient care, medical education, clinical research **Area of distribution:** Pennsylvania **Area of Practice:** Adult and geriatric psychiatry, clinical research **Honors/awards:** Outstanding Achievement in Advanced German, Middlebury College, 1995; Fellow, American Psychoanalytic Association, 1996-97; Teacher of the Year Award, Western Psychiatric Institute and Clinic, 2002; AMSIP Award for Psychiatric Education, University of Pittsburgh School of Medicine, 2002; AcademiKey's Who's Who in Medical Science, 2005; Strathmore's Who's Who, 2005; Marquis Who's Who, 2005; Strathmore's Who's Who Professional of the Year in Psychiatry Education, 2006 **Published works:** Bharucha AJ, Pearlman RA, Back AL, Gordon J, Starks H, Hsu C, The pursuit of physician-assisted suicide: role of psychiatric factors. J Palliat Med 2003;6:873-884; Bharucha AJ, Pandv R, Shen C, Dodge HH, Ganguli M. Predictors of nursing facility admission: a 12 year epidemiological study in the USA. J Am Geriatr Soc 2004;52:434-439; Bharucha AJ, Barnard D, London AJ, Wactlar H. Dew MA, Reynolds CF. Ethical considerations in the conduct of electronic surveillance research. J Law Med Ethics 2006;34(3):611-619 **Affiliations:** American Psychiatric Association; American Association for Geriatric Psychiatry; American Geriatrics Society; American Medical Directors Association; American Neuropsychiatric Association; International Psychogeriatric Association **Career accomplishments:** Principal Investigator or Co-Principal Investigator on several grants from the National Institute on Aging and the National Science Foundation **Hob./spts.:** Tennis **SIC code:** 80 **Address:** University of Pittsburgh, 5030 Fifth Ave. 315, Pittsburgh, PA 15232 **E-mail:** abharucha@comcast.net

BHAVNANI, VINOD D.
Industry: Healthcare **Born:** June 2, 1963, Bombay, India **Univ./degree:** M.D. **Current organization:** Glaucoma & Cataract Eye Institute, Inc. **Title:** Ophthalmologist **Type of organization:** Medical office **Major product:** Ophthalmology **Area of distribution:** Florida **Area of Practice:** Treatment of cataracts and glaucoma **Hob./spts.:** Boating, running, reading **SIC code:** 80 **Address:** Glaucoma & Cataract Eye Institute, Inc., 9371-15 Cypress Lake Dr., Ft. Myers, FL 33919 **E-mail:** glaucomasurgeon@aol.com

BIANCHINI, DEBORAH LYNN
Industry: Healthcare **Born:** October 26, 1954, Philadelphia, Pennsylvania **Univ./degree:** B.A., Allied Health, Widener University, 2000 **Current organization:** Virtua Memorial Hospital **Title:** Lead Diagnostic Technologist/Mammographer **Type of organization:** Hospital **Major product:** Patient care **Area of distribution:** Mt. Laurel, New Jersey **Area of Practice:** Mammography **Affiliations:** American Society of Radiologic Technologists **Hob./spts.:** Bowling **SIC code:** 80 **Address:** Virtua Memorial Hospital, 175 Madison Ave., Mount Holly, NJ 08660 **E-mail:** debbimamm@aol.com

BICE, JAMES B.
Industry: Healthcare **Born:** September 16, 1963, DesMoines, Iowa **Univ./degree:** D.O., University of Osteopathic Health Sciences, 1990 **Current organization:** Mercy Indianola Medical Clinic **Title:** D.O. **Type of organization:** Private clinic **Major product:** Medical care services **Area of distribution:** Indianola, Iowa **Area of Practice:** Family practice **Affiliations:** A.C.S.M.; Fellow, A.A.F.P. **Hob./spts.:** Golf, running, bicycling **SIC code:** 80 **Address:** Mercy Indianola Medical Clinic, 108 N. Jefferson, Indianola, IA 50125

BICKNELL, TRACY L.
Industry: Healthcare **Born:** April 3, 1973, Camp Springs, Maryland **Univ./degree:** A.A., College of Southern Maryland, 1996 **Current organization:** Calvert County Nursing Center **Title:** R.N. **Type of organization:** Nursing home **Major product:** Patient care **Area of distribution:** Maryland **Area of Practice:** Geriatrics **Affiliations:** American Nurses Association; Maryland Nurses Association **Hob./spts.:** Fishing **SIC code:** 80 **Address:** Calvert County Nursing Center, 85 Hospital Rd., Prince Frederick, MD 20678 **E-mail:** tbicknell@ccncmd.org

BIDANI, RAKESH
Industry: Medical **Born:** June 8, 1962, New Delhi, Indiana **Univ./degree:** M.D., Maulama Azad Medical School, 1985 **Current organization:** State University of New

York at Buffalo, ECMC **Title:** M.D. **Type of organization:** University/medical center **Major product:** Medical services **Area of distribution:** New York **Area of Practice:** Internal medicine **Honors/awards:** National Talent Search Scholarship from the Government of India, 1980; Teaching Recognition Award, University of Buffalo, 1999; Teaching Recognition Award, Department of Medicine, University of Buffalo, 2001 **Published works:** Journal, Allergy and Immunology; Journal, Association of Physicians of India **Affiliations:** A.C.P.; A.S.I.M. **SIC code:** 80 **Address:** State University of New York at Buffalo, ECMC, 462 Grider St., Buffalo, NY 14215

BIDDLE, SANDRA S.
Industry: Healthcare **Born:** December 6, 1946, South Bend, Indiana **Univ./degree:** Master in Public Administration and Finance, Indiana University, 1992 **Current organization:** Centennial Healthcare/Caroll Woods Health & Rehabilitation Center **Title:** Administrator **Type of organization:** Nursing center **Major product:** Patient long term care/Rehab-to-home **Area of distribution:** South Bend, Indiana **Area of Practice:** Employee relations **Affiliations:** National Honor Society for Public Administrators; National Association for Female Executives **Hob./spts.:** Reading **SIC code:** 80 **Address:** 930 Beale St., South Bend, IN 46616 **E-mail:** sandy1ems@earthlink.net

BIEREMA, CHARLENE M.
Industry: Healthcare **Born:** September 11, 1951, Yankton, South Dakota **Univ./degree:** B.S.N., Mt. Marty College, South Dakota, 1972; M.S.N., Texas Women's University, 1980 **Current organization:** Bethel Lutheran Home **Title:** Director, Nursing Service **Type of organization:** Long-term healthcare **Major product:** Patient care **Area of distribution:** North Dakota **Area of Practice:** Administration, teaching **Published works:** 1 article-History of South Dakota C-EARP **Affiliations:** American Nursing Association; Nurses Administration of Long-Term Healthcare; American Healthcare Association **Hob./spts.:** Sewing, fishing, gardening **SIC code:** 80 **Address:** 405 15th Ave. West, Williston, ND 58801 **E-mail:** cbierema@ruggedwest.com

BIERNAT, BOZENA J.
Industry: Healthcare **Born:** October 14, 1961, Warsaw, Poland **Univ./degree:** M.D., Medical Academy of Warsaw, Poland, 1986 **Current organization:** Bellin Health Family Medical Centers **Title:** M.D. **Type of organization:** Hospital **Major product:** Patient care **Area of distribution:** Eads, Colorado **Area of Practice:** Family medicine **Affiliations:** American Physicians Organization **Hob./spts.:** Reading, classical music, travel **SIC code:** 80 **Address:** Bellin Health Family Medical Centers, 555 Red Bird Circle, Green Bay, WI 54301

BIERSAY, GWENDOLYN M.
Industry: Healthcare **Born:** November 17, 1945, Jamaica, West Indies **Current organization:** Claridge House Nursing & Rehab Center **Title:** Assistant Director of Nursing **Type of organization:** Nursing and rehabilitation center **Major product:** Long-term healthcare, rehabilitation **Area of distribution:** North Miami, Florida **Area of Practice:** Administration, staff education risk management **Affiliations:** F.A.D.O.N.A. **Hob./spts.:** Reading, gardening **SIC code:** 80 **Address:** Claridge House Nursing & Rehab Center, 13900 N.E. Third Ct., North Miami, FL 33161 **E-mail:** gbiersay@aol.com

BIRD, STEPHANIE C.
Industry: Medical **Born:** July 11, 1954, Washington, D.C. **Univ./degree:** B.S., Biology, Harvard University, 1977; M.D., Tufts University School of Medicine, 1983 **Current organization:** Harvard Medical School/Brigham & Women's Hospital , Women's Health Center **Title:** M.D. **Type of organization:** University hospital **Major product:** Medical services **Area of distribution:** Massachusetts **Area of Practice:** OB/GYN, medical education **Published works:** 3 journal articles **Affiliations:** F.A.C.O.G. **Hob./spts.:** Skiing, wind surfing, cooking **SIC code:** 80 **Address:** Harvard Medical School, Brigham & Women's Hospital, Women's Health Center, 45 Francis St., Boston, MA 02115 **E-mail:** sbird@partners.org

BITTING, KEVIN NOEL
Industry: Healthcare **Born:** December 18, 1957, Kenmore, New York **Univ./degree:** B.A., Psychology, Villanova University, 1980; Degree in Prosthetics, Northwestern University, 1989 **Current organization:** Cranial Therapies, Inc. **Title:** Chief, Pediatric Craniofacial Orthotist **Type of organization:** Pediatric practice **Major product:** Cranial orthoses **Area of distribution:** Southern California **Area of Practice:** Infant cranial remodeling; Board of Orthotist Certification, 1995 **Honors/awards:** Marquis Who's Who: Who's Who in Medicine & Health, 5th Edition, 2004-05; Who's Who in the West, 27th and 28th Editions, 2000-01, 2002-03; Who's Who in America, 55th, 56th 57th and 58th Editions, 2001-04; Who's Who in the World, 17th, 19th and 21st Editions, 2000-04; Who's Who in Science and Engineering, 7th and 8th Editions, 2003-06; The International Biographical Centre-Cambridge, England: Dictionary of International Biography; Medicine-28th, 29th and 30th Editions, 2000-02; Who's Who in the 21st Century, 1st and 2nd Editions, 2002-03; The American Biographical Institute: Research Board of Advisors, 2000 **Affiliations:** International Association of Orthotics and Prosthetics (IAOP); American Orthotic Prosthetic Association (AOPA) **Hob./spts.:** Alpine skiing, physical fitness, swimming, computers, art **SIC code:** 80 **Address:** Cranial Therapies, Inc., 4444 Lankershim Blvd., Suite 108, Toluca Lake, CA 91602 **E-mail:** cranialtherapies@linkline.com

BLACKMON, LAWRENCE B.
Industry: Healthcare **Born:** December 23, 1957, Memphis, Tennessee **Univ./degree:** D.D.S., Meharry Medical College, School of Dentistry, 1983 **Current organization:** Lawrence B. Blackmon, D.D.S., Inc. **Title:** Dentist **Type of organization:** Private practice **Major product:** Patient care **Area of distribution:** Moreno Valley, Rancho Mirage, California **Area of Practice:** Restorative dentistry **Honors/awards:** Commendation, Meritorious Medal Awards, U.S. Air Force Dental Corp, 1983 **Affiliations:** A.D.A.; C.D.A.; Tri-County Dental Society **Hob./spts.:** Golf **SIC code:** 80 **Address:** Lawrence B. Blackmon, D.D.S., Inc., 12818 Heacock St., #C-3, Moreno Valley, CA 92553 **Web address:** www.blackmondds.com

BLACKMON, MICHAEL G.
Industry: Healthcare **Born:** December 18, 1961, Bremerton, Washington **Univ./degree:** A.S., Electronics, Gateway Technical College; B.S., Business Management, Cardinal Stritch University **Current organization:** All Saints Healthcare **Title:** Project Manager **Type of organization:** Hospitals/clinics **Major product:** Patient care **Area of distribution:** Wisconsin **Area of Practice:** Information technology, electronics, project management, strategic analysis, business development, program design and implementation, plant operations, building management **Affiliations:** Project Management Institute; National Fire Protection Agency **Hob./spts.:** Street rods **SIC code:** 80 **Address:** All Saints Healthcare, 3801 Spring St., Racine, WI 53405 **E-mail:** im1mgb@hotmail.com

BLAIR, ANGELA F.
Industry: Healthcare **Born:** January 9, 1972, Paintsville, Kentucky **Univ./degree:** A.S., Moorhead State University, 1993; C.T., M.R.I. Certification, Kettering College, 1993 **Current organization:** Proscan Imaging/Nicholasville Rd. MRI **Title:** Assistant Manager **Type of organization:** Imaging center **Major product:** Medical imaging services (MRI, CAT Scans) **Area of distribution:** Lexington, Kentucky **Area of Practice:** C.T., M.R.I. **Affiliations:** A.S.R.T.; A.R.R.T. **SIC code:** 80 **Address:** Proscan Imaging, Nicholasville Rd. MRI, 2463 Nicholasville Rd., Lexington, KY 40503 **E-mail:** ablair@proscan.com **Web address:** www.proscan.com

BLAIR, CHARLES E.
Industry: Healthcare **Born:** January 25, 1952, Bellefontaine, Ohio **Univ./degree:** A.S., Laboratory Medicine, Clark State University, Springfield, Ohio, 1976 **Current organization:** Mary Rutan Hospital **Title:** Chemistry Coordinator **Type of organization:** Hospital **Major product:** Patient care **Area of distribution:** Ohio **Area of Practice:** Clinical chemistry, laboratory health services **Affiliations:** Registration for Clinical Laboratory **Hob./spts.:** Golf, hiking, laboratory medicine, science, travel **SIC code:** 80 **Address:** Mary Rutan Hospital, 205 Palmer Ave., Bellefontaine, OH 43311 **E-mail:** eblair52@yahoo.com

BLAIR, DENNIS A.
Industry: Dentistry **Born:** June 1, 1951, Binghamton, New York **Univ./degree:** D.D.S., University of Buffalo, 1977 **Current organization:** Dennis A. Blair, D.D.S. **Title:** Dentist **Type of organization:** Private practice **Major product:** Dental care **Area of distribution:** Orchard Park, New York **Area of Practice:** Restorative and aesthetic dentistry **Affiliations:** 8th District Dental Society; Academy of Cosmetic Dentistry; Academy of Sports Dentistry; Member, Chicago Dental Society; American Dental Association (ADA) **SIC code:** 80 **Address:** Dennis A. Blair, D.D.S., 6548 E. Quaker St., Orchard Park, NY 14127 **E-mail:** dblair5085@aol.com

BLAIR, DONNA A.
Industry: Healthcare **Born:** June 10, 1954, North Adams, Massachusetts **Current organization:** North Adams Regional Hospital **Title:** Specialty Technologist **Type of organization:** Hospital **Major product:** Patient care **Area of distribution:** Massachusetts **Area of Practice:** CT, radiology, ultrasound **Published works:** Article **Hob./spts.:** Watercolor painting, gardening **SIC code:** 80 **Address:** North Adams Regional Hospital, Hospital Ave., North Adams, MA 01247

BLAIVAS, MILA
Industry: Medical **Born:** August 6, 1936, Moscow, Russia **Univ./degree:** M.D., 2nd Moscow Medical School, 1961; Ph.D., Brain Institute, USSR Academy of Medicine, 1968 **Current organization:** University of Michigan **Title:** M.D./Associate Professor **Type of organization:** University, medical school **Major product:** Medical services **Area of distribution:** National **Area of Practice:** Neuropathology, muscle, nerve and brain diseases **Honors/awards:** Top 100 Physicians, University of Michigan, Pathology **Published works:** 90+ publications **Affiliations:** C.A.P.; W.M.A.; A.A.S.; A.A.N.P.; A.A.N.; P.N.S. **Hob./spts.:** Reading, dancing **SIC code:** 80 **Address:** University of Michigan, Pathology Dept., 1301 Catherine St. MSI, Ann Arbor, MI 48109-0602 **E-mail:** blaivas@umich.edu

BLANCHETTE, DENNIS A.
Industry: Healthcare **Univ./degree:** M.D., Hahnemann School of Medicine, Pennsylvania **Current organization:** Dennis A. Blanchette M.D., P.C. **Title:** M.D. **Type of organization:** Private practice **Major product:** Patient care **Area of distribution:** New York **Area of Practice:** Ob/Gyn **Affiliations:** F.A.C.O.G. **SIC code:** 80 **Address:** Dennis A. Blanchette M.D., P.C., 148 Pierport St., Brooklyn, NY 11201

BLAUGRUND, MARVIN L.
Industry: Healthcare **Born:** July 27, 1944, Albuquerque, New Mexico **Univ./degree:** D.D.S., Baylor College **Current organization:** Marvin L. Blaugrund D.D.S., P.A. **Title:** Owner/D.D.S. **Type of organization:** Private practice **Major product:** Dentistry **Area of distribution:** Albuquerque, New Mexico **Area of Practice:** General dentistry **Affiliations:** A.D.A., A.M.A. **Hob./spts.:** Golf **SIC code:** 80 **Address:** Marvin L. Blaugrund D.D.S., P.A., 1101 Medical Arts Ave. N.E., Albuquerque, NM 87102 **E-mail:** mlb727@aol.com

BLESSITT, KRISTI L.
Industry: Medical **Born:** January 14, 1973, Greenville, Mississippi **Univ./degree:** M.D., University of Mississippi, 2000 **Current organization:** University of Mississippi Medical Center **Title:** M.D. **Type of organization:** University hospital **Major product:** Medical services **Area of distribution:** Jackson, Mississippi **Area of Practice:** Obstetrics, gynecology **Affiliations:** A.M.A.; A.C.O.G. **Hob./spts.:** Watercolors, waterskiing **SIC code:** 80 **Address:** University of Mississippi Medical Center, 2500 N. State St., Jackson, MS 39202

BLOMMEL, GREGORY G.
Industry: Healthcare **Born:** March 5, 1960, Wisconsin **Univ./degree:** M.D., Medical College of Wisconsin, 1985 **Current organization:** West Bend Clinic **Title:** President, M.D. **Type of organization:** Multi-specialty clinic **Major product:** Patient care **Area of distribution:** West Bend, Wisconsin **Area of Practice:** Medical management, internal medicine **Affiliations:** A.M.A.; A.C.P.; A.S.E.; A.C.P.E. **Hob./spts.:** Racquetball **SIC code:** 80 **Address:** West Bend Clinic, 1700 W. Paradise Dr., West Bend, WI 53095 **E-mail:** gblommel@wbclinic.com

BLOOM, ELIZABETH S.
Industry: Medical **Born:** October 25, 1966, Seattle, Washington **Univ./degree:** M.D., Northwestern, 1990 **Current organization:** University of Texas, M.D. Anderson Cancer Center, Radiation Treatment Center at Bellaire **Title:** M.D., Assistant Professor **Type of organization:** University, satellite of medical center **Major product:** Medical services **Area of distribution:** Texas **Area of Practice:** Radiation oncology **Affiliations:** A.M.A.; A.S.T.R.O.; A.C.R.O.; A.C.R.; A.S.C.O.; A.A.W.R.; T.R.S.; Harris County Medical Society; The University of Texas M.D. Anderson Associates; The Gilbert H. Fletcher Society **Hob./spts.:** Swimming, speed walking biking **SIC code:** 80 **Address:** University of Texas, M.D. Anderson Cancer Center, Radiation Treatment Center at Bellaire, 6602 Mapleridge St., Houston, TX 77081 **E-mail:** ebloom@mdanderson.org

BLOOMBERG, SANFORD
Industry: Healthcare **Title:** M.D. **Type of organization:** Private practice **Major product:** Patient care **Area of Practice:** Psychiatry **SIC code:** 80 **Address:** Sanford Bloomberg, M.D., 112 Washington Ave., Northampton, MA 01060 **E-mail:** sanford.bloomberg@verizon.net

BOCCUZZI, LORENZO
Industry: Healthcare **Born:** 1962, Naperville, Illinois **Univ./degree:** D.O., Des Moines University College of Osteopathic Medicine and Surgery, 1989 **Current organization:** Genesis Medical Center **Title:** D.O./F.A.A.P./F.A.C.O.P. **Type of organization:** Hospital **Major product:** Patient care **Area of distribution:** Davenport, Iowa **Area of Practice:** Internal medicine, pediatrics **Honors/awards:** America's Top Pediatricians, 2002-2003; National Registry of Who's Who, 2001; Scholastic All-American Award Collegiate; Who's Who in American Colleges and Universities **Affiliations:** A.M.A.; A.O.A.; A.C.O.P.; I.M.S.; A.C.P.; A.A.P.; S.C.M.S. **Hob./spts.:** Pilot, skiing, oil painting, sketching, photography **SIC code:** 80 **Address:** Genesis Medical Center - Acute Care Clinics, 1520 W. 53rd St., Suite 2, Davenport, IA 52806 **E-mail:** boccuzzil@genesishealth.com

BODDAPATI, MANORANJAN
Industry: Healthcare **Born:** June 3, 1973, India **Univ./degree:** M.D., India, 1996 **Current organization:** Overton Brooks VA Medical Center **Title:** M.D. **Type of organization:** Hospital **Major product:** Patient care **Area of distribution:** Louisiana **Area of Practice:** Hematology and medical oncology **Affiliations:** A.C.P.; A.S.H.; A.S.C.O.; A.S.B.M.T.; A.A.A.S. **Hob./spts.:** Rollerblading, bicycling **SIC code:** 80 **Address:** 1333 Coates Bluff Dr., #523, Shreveport, LA 71104 **E-mail:** boddapatim@yahoo.com

BODOUTCHIAN, ANI A.
Industry: Healthcare **Born:** July 8, 1963, Plovdiv, Bulgaria **Univ./degree:** M.D., Autonomous University of Guadalajara, Mexico **Current organization:** Nassau Suffolk Medical Practice **Title:** M.D. **Type of organization:** Medical practice **Major product:** Patient care **Area of distribution:** New York **Area of Practice:** Family medicine **Affiliations:** A.A.F.P. **Hob./spts.:** Music, travel, physical fitness **SIC code:** 80 **Address:** Nassau Suffolk Medical Practice, 120 Rt. 109, West Babylon, NY 11704

BOLING, EUGENE P.
Industry: Healthcare **Born:** November 13, 1950, Oakland, California **Univ./degree:** M.D., UCLA School of Medicine, 1976; John Hopkins University, Rheumatology, 1983 **Current organization:** Inland Rheumatology & Osteoporosis Medical Group **Title:** M.D. **Type of organization:** Private practice **Major product:** Patient care **Area of distribution:** International **Area of Practice:** Rheumatology, internal medicine (Board Certified) **Published works:** 7 peer reviewed journal articles **Affiliations:** F.A.C.P.; F.A.C.R.; Advisory Board Member, Proctor & Gamble, Advents, Lilly, Merck Pharmaceutical Co. **Hob./spts.:** Skiing, driving his 1959 Austin Healey **SIC code:** 80 **Address:** Inland Rheumatology & Osteoporosis Medical Group, 8283 Grove Ave., Suite 203, Rancho Cucamonga, CA 91730 **E-mail:** eboling@bolingclinical.com

BOLTON, MARY BETH
Industry: Healthcare **Born:** Detroit, Michigan **Univ./degree:** M.D., University of California, San Francisco, 1981 **Current organization:** Health Alliance Plan **Title:** Senior Vice President/Chief Medical Officer **Type of organization:** Nonprofit HMO **Major product:** Health insurance **Area of distribution:** National **Area of Practice:** Internal medicine, design and development of care management and quality programs, asthma education, residency education **Affiliations:** Board Member, Hospice of Michigan & St. John's Health System; Active Senior Staff Physician, Henry Ford Medical Group **Hob./spts.:** Spending time with family, yoga, gardening **SIC code:** 80 **Address:** Health Alliance Plan, 2850 W. Grand Blvd., Detroit, MI 48202 **E-mail:** mbolton@hap.org

BONKOVSKY, HERBERT L.
Industry: Medical **Born:** December 29, 1941, Cleveland, Ohio **Univ./degree:** M.D., Western Reserve University School of Medicine, 1967 **Current organization:** University of Connecticut School of Medicine **Title:** Director, Office of Clinical Research **Type of organization:** Academic medical center **Major product:** Medical services, biomedical research **Area of distribution:** International **Area of Practice:** Gastroenterology, hepatology **Published works:** Numerous abstracts, reports, letters, papers, book chapters and books, including: Herbert L. Bonkovsky and Graham F. Barnard. "The hepatic porphyrias." In L. Brandt (ed). Clinical Practice of Gastroenterology. Current Medicine, Philadelphia, 1998, pp. 947-960; Herbert L. Bonkovsky, Richard W. Lambrecht and Ying Shan. Iron as a co-morbid factor in non-hemochromatotic liver disease. Alcohol 30: 137-144, 2003; Herbert L. Bonkovsky, Riad Azar, Steven Bird, Gyongyi Szabo and Barbara Banner. Severe cholestatic hepatitis caused by thiazolidinediones - risks associated with substituting rosiglitazone for troglitazone. Dig. Dis & Sci. 47: 1632-1637, 2202; "Hepatic manifestations of systemic disease", Editor's preface to a vol. of Clinics in Liver Disease of the same name. Clinics in Liver Disease 6: 1-2, 2002 **Affiliations:** F.A.C.G.; F.A.C.P.; A.A.S.L.D.; A.G.A.; European Association for the Study of the Liver; International Association for the Study of the Liver; American Society for Clinical Investigation; Association of American Physicians; American Federation for Medical Research **Hob./spts.:** Hiking, gardening, tennis **SIC code:** 80 **Address:** MC-III, UCHC, 263 Farmington Ave., Farmington, CT 06030-1111 **E-mail:** bonkovsky@uchc.edu

BONOMO, EDWARD C.
Industry: Healthcare **Born:** May 13, 1944, Newark, New Jersey **Univ./degree:** D.D.S., West Virginia University School of Dentistry, 1970 **Current organization:** Edward C. Bonomo, DDS, PA dba Carolina Denture Center **Title:** D.D.S. **Type of organization:** Free standing clinic **Major product:** All dental services **Area of distribution:** North Carolina **Area of Practice:** Geriatric dentistry **Affiliations:** American Dental Association **Hob./spts.:** Golf, skiing, grandchildren **SIC code:** 80 **Address:** Edward C. Bonomo, DDS, PA dba Carolina Denture Center, 400 Westinghouse Blvd., Charlotte, NC 28273

BOOKER, KARLA LORRAINE
Industry: Healthcare **Born:** March 21, 1963, Washington D.C. **Univ./degree:** M.D., Meharry Medical College, 1989 **Current organization:** Consolidated OB/GYN **Title:** M.D./Associate **Type of organization:** Private Practice **Major product:** Teen issues, menopause, laparoscopic surgery **Area of distribution:** Lilburn, Georgia **Area of Practice:** Obstetrics and gynecology **Affiliations:** F.A.C.O.G.; D.A.B.O.G.; N.M.A. **Hob./spts.:** Family, jazz, weightlifting **SIC code:** 80 **Address:** Consolidated OB/GYN, 4201 Rainbow Dr., Decatur, GA 30034 **E-mail:** ladydoc321@aol.com

BOONE, TIMOTHY B.
Industry: Healthcare **Born:** February 7, 1955, Dallas, Texas **Univ./degree:** M.D., Ph.D., University of Texas Medical School at Houston, 1985 **Current organization:** Baylor College of Medicine **Title:** M.D., Ph.D. **Type of organization:** Medical school **Major product:** Patient care **Area of distribution:** Texas **Area of Practice:** Urology **Affiliations:** The Methodist Hospital, VA Medical Center-Spinal Cord Injury Unit

Hob./spts.: Sailing, Photography **SIC code:** 80 **Address:** Baylor College of Medicine, 6560 Fannin, #2100, Houston, TX 77030 **E-mail:** tboone@www.urol.bcm.tmc.edu

BORCHERDING, HARLAN J.
Industry: Healthcare **Born:** August 16, 1939, New Hampton, Iowa **Univ./degree:** D.O., Kansas City University of Medical and Biological Sciences, 1965 **Current organization:** Integra Medical Clinic **Title:** D.O. **Type of organization:** Clinic **Major product:** Patient care **Area of distribution:** The Woodlands, Texas **Area of Practice:** Pain management **Affiliations:** Fellow, American Academy of Disability Evaluating Physicians; Diplomate, American Academy of Pain Management; Texas Osteopathic Medical Association; Houston Osteopathic Medical Association **Hob./spts.:** Golf, reading, travel **SIC code:** 80 **Address:** Integra Medical Clinic, 3074 College Park Dr., The Woodlands, TX 77384 **E-mail:** drhjbdo@aol.com

BORER, JEFFREY S.
Industry: Medical **Born:** January 22, 1945, DeLand, Florida **Univ./degree:** B.A., Government, Harvard University, 1965; M.D., Cornell University Medical College, 1969; Fellowship, Clinical Medicine, Massachusetts General Hospital, Harvard University, 1969-71 **Current organization:** Weill Medical College of Cornell University **Title:** Chief, Division of Cardiovascular Pathophysiology **Type of organization:** University medical center **Major product:** Biomedical research, medical services, medical education **Area of distribution:** New York **Area of Practice:** Cardiovascular medicine and research; Gladys and Roland Harriman Professor of Cardiovascular Medicine **Affiliations:** A.C.C.; A.H.A.; A.S.C.I.; Director, Howard Gilman Institute for Valvular Heart Diseases **Hob./spts.:** Ancient Greek history, Chinese calligraphy **SIC code:** 80 **Address:** Weill Medical College of Cornell University, 47 E. 88th St., New York, NY 10128-1142 **E-mail:** canadaD45@aol.com **Web address:** www.gilmanheartvalve.org

BORGHEI, PEYMAN
Industry: Healthcare **Title:** M.D. **Type of organization:** Medical center **Major product:** Patient care **Area of Practice:** Musculoskeletal research **SIC code:** 80 **Address:** University of California, Irvine Medical Center, Dept. of Radiology, 101 City Dr., Orange, CA 92868

BORIO, EDWARD A.
Industry: Healthcare **Born:** May 11, 1955, Charleston, South Carolina **Univ./degree:** D.D.S., University of Detroit **Current organization:** Edward A. Borio, D.D.S. **Title:** D.D.S. **Type of organization:** Dental practice **Major product:** Dental care **Area of distribution:** Michigan **Area of Practice:** Restorative and cosmetic dentistry **Affiliations:** A.D.A.; Michigan Dental Association; Academy of General Dentistry; Frances B. Vedder Crown & Bridge Society **Hob./spts.:** Skiing, golf, tennis, running **SIC code:** 80 **Address:** Edward A. Borio, D.D.S., 50 W. Big Beaver Rd., Suite 100B, Bloomfield, MI 48304

BORISENKO, SLAVA
Industry: Healthcare **Born:** September, 5, 1961 **Univ./degree:** D.C., 2006 **Current organization:** N.W. Spinal Rehabilitation Clinic, P.S. **Title:** Chiropractor **Type of organization:** Clinic **Major product:** Pettibon System - spine restoration without surgery **Area of distribution:** Washington **Area of Practice:** Pettibon System, spine restoration, spine discs and disc bulge restoration **SIC code:** 80 **Address:** NW Spinal Rehabilitation Clinic, P.S., 10024 SE 240th St., S119, Kent, WA 98031 **E-mail:** nwsrc@quest.net

BORUM, KENNETH S.
Industry: Healthcare **Born:** December 28, 1963, Athens, Tennessee **Univ./degree:** B.S., Healthcare Management, Southern Illinois University **Current organization:** Borum Healthcare **Title:** President, C.E.O. **Type of organization:** Nursing home **Major product:** Health and rehabilitation **Area of distribution:** North Carolina **Area of Practice:** Supervising daily operations **Affiliations:** N.C.H.F.A.; A.H.C.A.; Kiwanis; American College of Healthcare Administrators **Hob./spts.:** Boating, golf **SIC code:** 80 **Address:** Borum Healthcare, 211 Milton Brown Heirs Rd., Boone, NC 28607 **E-mail:** scottborum@borumhealthcare.com **Web address:** www.glenbridge.org

BOSCH-RAMIREZ, MARCIAL V.
Industry: Healthcare **Born:** February 24, 1947, Ponce, Puerto Rico **Spouse:** Mercedes Bosch **Married:** May 26, 1967 **Children:** Victor A., 35; Rita C., 32; Damaris, 26; Grandchildren: David, Evelyn, Jhewell, Nickaella, Elena, Ramon, Andrea **Univ./degree:** M.D., Universidad Central Del Este, Dominican Republic; Anesthesiologist, Puerto Rico School of Medicine **Current organization:** Pavia Anesthesia P.S.C. **Title:** M.D. **Type of organization:** Hospital **Major product:** Patient care **Area of distribution:** Puerto Rico **Area of Practice:** Anesthesiology **Affiliations:** A.M.A.; Puerto Rico Medical Association **Hob./spts.:** Art collecting, hunting, skeet shooting, Paso Fino horses, motorcycling **SIC code:** 80 **Address:** Luna St., #255, 2nd floor, Old San Juan, PR 00901

BOSHES, ROGER A.
Industry: Medical **Born:** December 23, 1939, Chicago, Illinois **Univ./degree:** B.A., American Literature and English, Haverford College, 1961; M.D., Yale Medical School, 1976; Ph.D., Molecular Biology, University of Chicago, 1968 **Current organization:** John C. Corrigan Mental Health Center/Harvard Medical School **Title:** Professor of Psychiatry/Associate Medical Director of Crisis Services **Type of organization:** Mental health center/ University medical school **Major product:** Mental healthcare, education, research **Area of distribution:** National **Area of Practice:** Psychiatry, psychopharmacology, research in schizophrenia and genetics; Psychiatry and Neurology (Board Certified) **Published works:** 50 articles, 4 book chapters **Affiliations:** Physicians for Social Responsibility; Massachusetts Psychiatric Association; American Psychiatric Association **Hob./spts.:** Tennis, skiing, Chicago Bears, dogs **SIC code:** 80 **Address:** John C. Corrigan Mental Health Center/, Harvard Medical School, 49 Hillside St., Fall River, MA 02720 **E-mail:** roger.boshes@dmh.state.ma.us

BOTTA, JOSEPH
Industry: Healthcare **Born:** July 21, 1970, Brooklyn, New York **Univ./degree:** B.S., Psychology/Biology, Hamilton College, 1992; M.D., University of Tel Aviv School of Medicine, Israel, 1997 **Current organization:** Day Kimball Hospital **Title:** M.D. **Type of organization:** Hospital **Major product:** Patient care **Area of distribution:** Connecticut **Area of Practice:** Geriatrics, internal medicine **Affiliations:** A.C.P.-A.S.I.M.; A.M.A.; A.G.S. **Hob./spts.:** Tropical fish, skiing **SIC code:** 80 **Address:** Day Kimball Hospital, 320 Pomfret St., Putnam, CT 06260

BOUCHER, LISA FRANCES
Industry: Healthcare **Born:** April 5, 1959, Lowell, Massachusetts **Univ./degree:** A.S.N., Northern Essex Community College, Massachusetts, 1994; B.S.N., Rivier College, Nashua, New Hampshire, 2003 **Current organization:** Souhegan Home & Hospice Care **Title:** Performance Improvement Coordinator **Type of organization:** Home and hospice care service **Major product:** Patient care, home care **Area of distribution:** Southern New Hampshire and Northern Massachusetts **Area of Practice:** Performance improvement, quality assurance, utilization review, staff development, Registered Nurse **Honors/awards:** Magna Cum Laude, Academic Honors, Nursing Honors **Affiliations:** Nursing Honors Society; Rivier College Alumni **Hob./spts.:** Needlework, gardening, swimming, physical fitness, drawing **SIC code:** 80 **Address:** Souhegan Home & Hospice Care, 24 North River Road, Milford, NH 03055 **E-mail:** lboucher@sjh-nh.org **Web address:** www.souheganhhc.com

BOURGEOIS, CLARENCE F.
Industry: Healthcare **Born:** May 7, 1970, Jefferson, Louisiana **Univ./degree:** Attended, Universal Technical School and River Parish Technical Institute, Air Conditioning Technology **Current organization:** St. James Parish Hospital **Title:** Maintenance Manager, Director **Type of organization:** Hospital **Major product:** Patient care **Area of distribution:** Louisiana **Area of Practice:** Maintenance engineering **Honors/awards:** Employee of the Year, 2001 **Hob./spts.:** Fishing, football **SIC code:** 80 **Address:** St. James Parish Hospital, 2471 Louisiana Ave., Lutcher, LA 70071

BOWERS, PAULA J.
Industry: Healthcare **Born:** July 10, 1956, Allendale, South Carolina **Univ./degree:** M.S.N., Healthcare Administration, Texas Woman's University, 2001 **Current organization:** Memorial Hermann Southeast Hospital **Title:** Director of Acute Care Services **Type of organization:** Non-profit healthcare facility hospital **Major product:** Patient care **Area of distribution:** Houston, Texas **Area of Practice:** Nurse administrator **Published works:** Poster **Affiliations:** A.O.N.E.; H.O.N.E.; Home Nursing Society **Hob./spts.:** Antique shopping, home decorating **SIC code:** 80 **Address:** 11800 Astoria Blvd., Houston, TX 77089 **E-mail:** paula_bowers@mhhs.org

BOWMAN, MELISA A.
Industry: Healthcare **Born:** October 9, 1958, Springfield, Missouri **Univ./degree:** A.S., Nursing, Missouri Southern State College, 1978 **Title:** R.N. **Type of organization:** Healthcare **Major product:** Patient care **Area of distribution:** Missouri **Area of Practice:** Geriatrics **Honors/awards:** Who's Who in American Nursing; Who's Who Registry of Rising Young Americans; American Biographical Institute-Woman of the Year; American Biographical Institute-Research Board of Advisors; American Biographical Institute-Most Admired Woman of the Decade; Who's Who of American Woman **Hob./spts.:** Fishing, camping, horses **SIC code:** 80 **Address:** 221 West College, Aurora, MO 65605 **E-mail:** mteague@mo-net.com

BOYLAN ALFORD, NANCY
Industry: Healthcare **Born:** October 12, 1941, Portsmouth, Virginia **Univ./degree:** Psy.D., Florida Institute of Technology, 1985 **Current organization:** Carriage House Psychological Associates, PLLC **Title:** Dr. **Type of organization:** Patient care **Major product:** Psychological services **Area of distribution:** National **Area of Practice:** Clinical psychology, trauma victims **Affiliations:** American Psychological Association **SIC code:** 80 **Address:** Carriage House Psychological Associates, PLLC, 600 Jackson St., Suite B, Roanoke Rapids, NC 27870 **E-mail:** nalford191@aol.com

BRADLEY, ANN MARIE
Industry: Healthcare **Born:** January 19, 1953, Duluth, Minnesota **Univ./degree:** B.A., Nursing **Current organization:** North Country Home Care & Hospice **Title:** R.N./ Intake Coordinator **Type of organization:** Hospital home care hospice **Major product:** Home healthcare **Area of distribution:** Bemidji, Minnesota **Area of Practice:** Nursing therapy (PT, OT, HCA) **Hob./spts.:** Outdoor activities, reading, bird watching **SIC code:** 80 **Address:** North Country Home Care & Hospice, 3525 Pine Ridge Ave. N.W., Bemidji, MN 56601

BRANDOW, STEPHEN J.
Industry: Healthcare/ministry **Born:** December 25, 1960, Olean, New York **Univ./ degree:** B.A., General Studies, 1983; B.A., Social Work, 1985, Northwestern State University, Louisiana; M.Div., 1996, Notre Dame Seminary **Current organization:** Immaculate Heart of Mary/VA Medical Center of Alexandria **Title:** Reverend/Staff Chaplain **Type of organization:** Hospital/religion **Major product:** Patient care/religion **Area of distribution:** Louisiana **Area of Practice:** Chaplaincy **Honors/awards:** Whitney Young Service Award, BSA, 2001; Bronze Pelican, Catholic Commission on Scouting, 2003; St. George Award, Catholic Commission on Scouting, 2004 **Published works:** 30 articles **Affiliations:** N.A.C.C.; N.V.C.A.; N.C.V.A.C.C.; L.L.A.; Board of Directors, Attakapas Council, BSA, 2002; Vice President for Relationships, Attakapas Council, BSA, 2002; Community Advisory Board, Quachita Valley Council, BSA; Board of Directors, 2003-04, Louisiana Purchase Council; Board of Directors, Family Council Agency, 2001; Board of Directors, Bolton Ave Lions; Lifetime Member, National Eagle Scout Association; National Catholic Council for Scouting **Hob./spts.:** Yoga, reading **SIC code:** 80 **Address:** Immaculate Heart of Mary/VA Medical Center of Alexandria, 1220 Tioga Rd., Pineville, LA 71360 **E-mail:** sbran62261@aol.com

BRANOVAN, DANIEL I.
Industry: Healthcare **Born:** Kaliningrad, Russia **Univ./degree:** M.D., Stanford University, 1992 **Current organization:** New York Eye and Ear Infirmary **Title:** Director, Thyroid Center/Director, Resident Training/Associate Professor, Sinus Surgery **Type of organization:** Eye and ear infirmary **Major product:** Patient care **Area of distribution:** International **Area of Practice:** Surgery-endoscopic sinus/thyroid **Honors/ awards:** New York Magazine, Best Doctor of Minimum Invasive Sinus Surgery; Best Doctor in New York **Published works:** Book chapters **SIC code:** 80 **Address:** New York Eye and Ear Infirmary, 310 E. 14th St., New York, NY 10003 **E-mail:** dbranovan@nyee.edu

BRAUN, DIANA R.
Industry: Healthcare **Born:** April 20, 1963, Asmara, Ethiopia **Univ./degree:** B.S., Healthcare Administration, University of New Hampshire, 2001 **Current organization:** Braun Consulting, Inc. **Title:** Executive Director **Type of organization:** Women's healthcare center **Major product:** Health services **Area of distribution:** National **Area of Practice:** Healthcare administration **Affiliations:** American College of Healthcare Executives; National Network of Abortion Funds **Hob./spts.:** Golf, collecting antiques **SIC code:** 80 **Address:** Braun Consulting, Inc., 8513 Hempton Cross Dr., Wake Forest, NC 27587 **E-mail:** dianaspc@rcn.com

BRAUN, NOHL A.
Industry: Healthcare **Univ./degree:** M.D., Marshall School of Medicine, 1993 **Current organization:** Process Strategies Institute Affiliated with Highland Behavioral Health Svcs. **Title:** M.D. **Type of organization:** Hospital **Major product:** Patient care **Area of distribution:** West Virginia **Area of Practice:** Child psychiatry, admissions, telepsychiatry **Affiliations:** A.M.A.; American Psychiatric Association; American Academy of Child and Adolescent Psychiatry; Kanawha Medical Society **SIC code:** 80 **Address:** Process Strategies Institute, Affiliated with Highland Behavioral Health Svcs., 1418A MacCorkle Ave., South Charleston, WV 25303

BRAVER, JOEL K.
Industry: Healthcare **Born:** July 8, 1962, Bridgeport, Connecticut **Univ./degree:** M.D., Robert Wood Johnson Medical School, 1991 **Current organization:** Associated Radiologists, P.A. **Title:** Associate Director **Type of organization:** Medical group **Major product:** Radiology, oncology **Area of distribution:** Warren, New Jersey **Area of Practice:** Radiation oncology **Affiliations:** A.S.T.R.O.; American Cancer Society **Hob./spts.:** Tennis, running **SIC code:** 80 **Address:** Associated Radiologists, P.A., 16 Mountain Blvd., Warren, NJ 07059

BREWER, LISA K.
Industry: Healthcare **Title:** Medical Technologist **Type of organization:** Hospital **Major product:** Patient care **Area of Practice:** Medical technology **SIC code:** 80 **Address:** Baptist Memorial Hospital, 2520 Fifth St. North, Columbus, MS 39701 **E-mail:** mbrewer6824@yahoo.com

BRICKER, DONALD L.
Industry: Healthcare **Born:** January 7, 1935, Denver, Colorado **Univ./degree:** B.S., Colorado State University, 1956; M.D., Cornell University College of Medicine, 1959; Internship, New York Hospital; Residency, New York Hospital and Baylor University Affiliated Hospitals **Current organization:** Covenant Cardiovascular Surgery **Title:** M.D./Director of Surgical Services **Type of organization:** Hospital **Major product:** Cardiovascular surgery **Area of distribution:** International **Area of Practice:** Cardiac and Peripheral Vascular Surgery; Certifications: American Board of Surgery (special qualifications in General Vascular Surgery), American Board of Thoracic Surgery **Honors/awards:** Award Winning Exhibits: 1st Place 1965, 1st Place 1969, 2nd Place 1970; Award Winning Presentations: Houston Surgical Society Award for Best Scientific Papers 1962, President's Award for Best Scientific Paper, Southern Thoracic Surgical Association 1973 **Published works:** 60 articles; Films: "Management of the Crushed Chest" (471-10) **Affiliations:** Numerous including: Fellow, American College of Surgeons; Fellow, American College of Chest Physicians; Fellow, American College of Cardiology; Fellow, American Association for the Surgery of Trauma; Fellow, Texas Surgical Society; Fellow, American Association for Thoracic Surgery; Fellow, Council on Cardiovascular Surgery, American Heart Association; Hospital Affiliations: Active Staff, Covenant Medical Center (formerly Methodist Hospital), Lubbock TX; Active Staff, Covenant Medical Center Lakeside (formerly St. Mary of the Plains Hospital), Lubbock TX; Courtesy Staff, University Medical Center, Lubbock, TX **Hob./spts.:** Big-game hunting, fishing, photography **SIC code:** 80 **Address:** Covenant Cardiovascular Surgery, 3514 21st St., Lubbock, TX 79410 **E-mail:** sbricker1@earthlink.net **Web address:** www.covenant.com

BRIGHT, ROBERT K.
Industry: Medical **Born:** February 7, 1964, Idaho Falls, Idaho **Univ./degree:** Ph.D., University of Texas for Health and Science, 1994 **Current organization:** Texas Tech University Hospital Science Center **Title:** Associate Professor **Type of organization:** University, medical school **Major product:** Patient care, medical education **Area of distribution:** National **Area of Practice:** Cancer research, cancer vaccine development **Published works:** 32 articles, 32 abstracts, 1 book chapter **Affiliations:** A.A.C.R.; A.A.A.S.; A.A.I. **Hob./spts.:** Golf, weight lifting, playing guitar, singing country music **SIC code:** 80 **Address:** Texas Tech University Hospital Science Center, Dept. of Microbiology & Immunology, 369 Fourth Street, Stop 6591, Lubbock, TX 79430 **E-mail:** robert.bright@ttuhsc.edu

BRION, LUC P.
Industry: Medical **Born:** April 30, 1953, Brussels, Belgium **Univ./degree:** M.D., Université Libre de Bruxelles, Belgium, 1976 **Current organization:** Albert Einstein College of Medicine, Children's Hospital at Montefiore Weiler Hospital **Title:** M.D. **Type of organization:** Hospital, medical school **Major product:** Children's healthcare, medical education **Area of distribution:** New York **Area of Practice:** Neonatal - Perinatal Medicine **Published works:** 50+ publications **Affiliations:** A.A.P.; S.P.R.; A.M.A.; E.S.P.R.; A.S.N.; A.P.S.; A.S.P.M. **Hob./spts.:** Travel **SIC code:** 80 **Address:** Albert Einstein College of Medicine, Children's Hospital at Montefiore Weiler Hospital, 1825 Eastchester Rd., Room 725, Bronx, NY 10461 **E-mail:** brionlp@aol.com

BROADHEAD, RICHARD
Industry: Healthcare **Born:** April 3, 1948, New Eagle, Pennsylvania **Univ./degree:** M.D., University of Pittsburgh, 1974 **Current organization:** Polk Center **Title:** M.D., Medical Director **Type of organization:** Medical center **Major product:** Healthcare for the mentally handicapped **Area of distribution:** Pennsylvania **Area of Practice:** Internal medicine/geriatrics **Affiliations:** Pittsburgh Medical Society **Hob./spts.:** Coaching archery **SIC code:** 80 **Address:** P.O. Box 137, Polk, PA 16342 **E-mail:** rbmudder@alltel.net

BROCK, LORI L.
Industry: Healthcare **Born:** March 15, 1958, Vinton, Iowa **Univ./degree:** A.A., Accounting, Hawkeye Community College, 1979 **Current organization:** Iowa City Family Practice Clinic **Title:** Office Manager **Type of organization:** Medical clinic **Major product:** Patient care **Area of distribution:** Iowa **Area of Practice:** Acounting/ administration **Published works:** In-house manual of policies and procedures **Affiliations:** American Association of Healthcare Administrative Management; Medical Association of Managers **Hob./spts.:** Swimming, tennis, golf, cooking **SIC code:** 80 **Address:** Iowa City Family Practice Clinic, 269 N. First Avenue, Iowa City, IA 52245 **E-mail:** lori.brock@mercyic.org

BROCKENFELT, DENISE J.
Industry: Healthcare **Born:** September 7, 1957, Camden, New Jersey **Current organization:** Emory Healthcare **Title:** MRI Supervisor **Type of organization:** Hospital **Major product:** Patient care **Area of distribution:** Georgia **Area of Practice:** MRI technology **Affiliations:** A.R.R.T.; A.S.R.T.; S.M.E.T. **Hob./spts.:** Hiking, travel, theatre, music **SIC code:** 80 **Address:** 2936 Castle Dr., Lawrenceville, GA 30044 **E-mail:** denise_brockenfelt@emoryhealthcare.net

BROEKER, CATHÉ B.
Industry: Healthcare **Univ./degree:** R.N., McQueen Gibbs Willis School of Nursing, Maryland **Current organization:** Seven Hills Surgery Center **Title:** O.R. Manager **Type of organization:** Free standing surgery center **Major product:** Ambulatory surgery **Area of distribution:** Henderson, Nevada **Area of Practice:** Operating Room

Registered Nurse, staff management **Affiliations:** Association of Operating Room Nurses **Hob./spts.:** Skiing, walking, her Newfoundland and Lab dogs **SIC code:** 80 **Address:** Seven Hills Surgery Center, 876 Seven Hills Dr., Henderson, NV 89052 **E-mail:** cbroeker@cox.net

BROWN, ALAN STEVEN
Industry: Healthcare **Born:** December 17, 1954, Chicago, Illinois **Univ./degree:** M.D., Loyola University Medical School, 1980 **Current organization:** Midwest Heart Specialists **Title:** M.D. **Type of organization:** Group practice **Major product:** Cardiovascular medicine **Area of distribution:** International **Area of Practice:** Interventional and preventative cardiology **Published works:** Book chapter, articles, co-editor of 1 book **Affiliations:** Illinois Chapter, American College of Cardiology; Board of Governor, American College of Cardiology **SIC code:** 80 **Address:** Midwest Heart Specialists, 120 Spalding, Suite 206, Naperville, IL 60540 **E-mail:** abrown@midwestheart.com

BROWN, BRENDA L.
Industry: Healthcare **Univ./degree:** A.S., Medical Laboratory Technology, Barton County Community College, 2003 **Current organization:** Lab Corp at Winfield Medical Arts **Title:** Lab Supervisor **Type of organization:** Clinical laboratory **Major product:** Laboratory tests and patient care **Area of distribution:** Winfield, Kansas **Area of Practice:** Lab supervision, oversight of all testing and lab findings **Affiliations:** American Society for Clinical Pathologists **SIC code:** 80 **Address:** 514 Alexander St., Winfield, KS 67156 **E-mail:** brendabrown@cox.net

BROWN, CYNTHIA L.
Industry: Healthcare **Born:** September 2, 1953, Pittsburg, Texas **Univ./degree:** A.S., Nursing, Northeast Texas Community College, 1994; B.S.N. Candidate, University of Texas at Arlington **Current organization:** Titus Regional Medical Center **Title:** RN/Nurse Director **Type of organization:** Hospital **Major product:** Patient care **Area of distribution:** Mt. Pleasant, Texas **Area of Practice:** Nursing **Honors/awards:** Outstanding Alumni , Northeast Texas Community College, 1999; Listed in Strathmore's Who's Who, 2002-2003 **Affiliations:** N.A.A.C.P.; St. Butler CMA: Vice President, Missionary Society of St. Butler; District Usher Association; CMF Usher Association **Hob./spts.:** Sewing, walking **SIC code:** 80 **Address:** Titus Regional Medical Center, 200 N. Jefferson, Mount Pleasant, TX 75455 **E-mail:** browncynthial@hotmail.com

BROWN, DAVID S.
Industry: Healthcare **Born:** March 24, 1959 **Univ./degree:** M.D., Temple University, 1987 **Current organization:** David S. Brown & Associates, P.A. **Title:** M.D. **Type of organization:** Outpatient clinic **Major product:** Patient care **Area of distribution:** Aventura, Florida **Area of Practice:** Internal medicine, hyperbaric medicine **Affiliations:** American Board of Internal Medicine; Southern Medical Association **Hob./spts.:** Music, racquetball, tennis, basketball, home improvement **SIC code:** 80 **Address:** David S. Brown & Associates, P.A., 20450 W. Dixie Hwy., Aventura, FL 33180 **E-mail:** brownassocb@aol.com

BROWN, DEBRA MARIE
Industry: Healthcare **Born:** June 17, 1957, Little Rock, Arkansas **Univ./degree:** M.D., University of Arizona, 1982 **Current organization:** LabCorp of America **Title:** M.D. **Type of organization:** Private laboratory **Major product:** Laboratory testing **Area of distribution:** National **Area of Practice:** Pathology **Affiliations:** C.A.P.; A.S.C.P. **Hob./spts.:** Travel **SIC code:** 80 **Address:** LabCorp of America, 4500 Conaem Dr., Louisville, KY 40213 **E-mail:** brownd3@labcorp.com

BROWN, DELORISE
Industry: Healthcare **Born:** April 10, 1948, Red Banks, Mississippi **Univ./degree:** B.S., Chemistry, Wichita State University, 1970; M.D., University of Kansas School of Medicine, 1974 **Current organization:** Brown Medical Center **Title:** M.D. **Type of organization:** Medical center **Major product:** Patient care **Area of distribution:** Cleveland, Ohio **Area of Practice:** Internal medicine, endocrinology **Published works:** 3 articles **Hob./spts.:** Skiing, reading, golf **SIC code:** 80 **Address:** Brown Medical Center, 1831 Forest Hills, #105, Cleveland, OH 44112 **E-mail:** delorise.brown@sbcglobal.net

BROWN, FRANCIS N.
Industry: Healthcare **Born:** April 7, 1942, Johnstown, Pennsylvania **Univ./degree:** D.D.S., University of Maryland, 1968 **Current organization:** Family Dental Associates **Title:** D.D.S. **Type of organization:** Private practice **Major product:** Dental care **Area of distribution:** Frederick, Maryland **Area of Practice:** General practitioner **Affiliations:** American Dental Association; Frederick City Dental Society; Maryland State Dental Association **Hob./spts.:** Antique cars, muscle cars, woodworking. sports **SIC code:** 80 **Address:** Family Dental Associates, 504B W. Patrick St., Frederick, MD 21701

BROWN, HENRIETTA W.
Industry: Healthcare **Born:** Mobile, Alabama **Univ./degree:** B.S.N., M.S.N., University of South Alabama **Current organization:** USA Knollwood Hospital **Title:** Nurse Manager, ICU/Acting Assistant Administrator **Type of organization:** Hospital **Major product:** Patient care **Area of distribution:** Alabama **Area of Practice:** Administration **Affiliations:** A.N.A.; A-1; National Nursing Honor Society **Hob./spts.:** Water sports, football, church activities **SIC code:** 80 **Address:** USA Knollwood Hospital, 5600 Girby Rd., Mobile, AL 36693 **E-mail:** hbrown@usouthal.edu

BROWN, MELISSA M.
Industry: Healthcare **Born:** October 11, 1950, Memphis, Tennessee **Univ./degree:** M.A., Nursing, Emory University, Georgia **Current organization:** Center for Value Based Medicine **Title:** M.N./M.D./M.B.A. **Type of organization:** Private ophthalmology practice/research center **Major product:** Patient care, economic research **Area of distribution:** International **Area of Practice:** Ophthalmology **Affiliations:** American Academy of Ophthalmology; Pennsylvania Medical Society; Montgomery County Medical Society **Hob./spts.:** Biking **SIC code:** 80 **Address:** Melissa M. Brown, M.D., PC, 1109 Bethlehem Pike, Suite 210, Flourtown, PA 19031

BROWN, MICHAELE L.
Industry: Healthcare **Born:** December 25, 1965, New Orleans, Louisiana **Univ./degree:** B.S., Chemistry, Xavier University, 1987; M.D., Louisiana State University, 1991 **Current organization:** Michaele L. Brown, MD, LLC **Title:** Physician **Type of organization:** Private practice **Major product:** Patient care **Area of distribution:** Louisiana **Area of Practice:** Internal medicine **Published works:** 5 articles **Affiliations:** New Orleans Parish Medical Society; National Association for Female Executives **Hob./spts.:** Family, reading **SIC code:** 80 **Address:** 4400 General Meyer Ave., Suite 404, New Orleans, LA 70131 **E-mail:** mlbmd@networktel.net

BROWNELL, JANELLE NELSON
Industry: Healthcare **Born:** August 19, 1974, Conrad, Montana **Univ./degree:** A.D.N., Miles Community College, 1995 **Current organization:** Marias Medical Center **Title:** Manager, Operating Room, Emergency Room, Obstetrics/Registered Nurse **Type of organization:** Hospital rural **Major product:** Patient care **Area of Practice:** Operating room and ER and management healthcare provider and community CPR and first aid instruction, staff education and development, quality control provision of healthcare **Affiliations:** Association of Operating Room Nurses; American Heart Association; Director, Marias Medical Center Health and Wellness Committee **SIC code:** 80 **Address:** Marias Medical Center, 640 Park Ave., Shelby, MT 59474 **E-mail:** janellenbrownell@yahoo.com

BRUNNGRABER, LEE
Industry: Education **Born:** June 8, 1954, Dumont, New Jersey **Univ./degree:** M. S., Psychiatric Mental Health Nursing, University of Colorado **Current organization:** Cabrillo College **Title:** Nursing Instructor **Type of organization:** Junior College **Major product:** Nursing education **Area of distribution:** California **Area of Practice:** Nursing education **Affiliations:** A.N.A. **Hob./spts.:** Skiing, rollerblading, snorkeling, theatre, dance **SIC code:** 80 **Address:** Cabrillo College, 6500 Hotel Ave., Aptos, CA 95020 **E-mail:** rlkt4@pacbell.net

BRUNO, DANTE S.
Industry: Healthcare **Born:** October 2, 1942, Marikina, Philippines **Univ./degree:** M.D., Far Eastern University Institute of Medicine, Philippines **Current organization:** Emergicare of South Boston, VA Inc. **Title:** M.D. **Type of organization:** Medical clinic **Major product:** Patient care **Area of distribution:** Virginia **Area of Practice:** General medical services **Affiliations:** A.M.S.; M.S.V.; H.P.A. **Hob./spts.:** Tennis, golf, hunting **SIC code:** 80 **Address:** Emergicare of South Boston, VA Inc., 1020 Bill Tuck Hwy., Suite 900, South Boston, VA 24592 **E-mail:** emergicare@pure.net

BRYK, LEOKADIA M.
Industry: Healthcare **Born:** October 1, 1949, Freiberg, West Germany **Univ./degree:** B.S.N., University of South Florida, Tampa, 1995 **Current organization:** St. Joseph Hospital **Title:** Clinical Resource Expert (RN) **Type of organization:** Hospital **Major product:** Patient care **Area of distribution:** Tampa, Florida **Area of Practice:** Certified in Psychiatric Nursing **Published works:** 1 article **Affiliations:** Florida Nurses Association; American Nurses Association **Hob./spts.:** Spending time with friends, reading, travel, church activities **SIC code:** 80 **Address:** St. Joseph Hospital, 3001 W. Martin Luther King Blvd., Tampa, FL 33607 **E-mail:** wisslerlorenz@msn.com

BUCHIGNANI JR., JOHN S.
Industry: Healthcare **Born:** July 30, 1941, Memphis, Tennessee **Univ./degree:** B.S., With Honors, 1962; M.D., With Honors, 1965, University of Tennessee **Current organization:** MID-South Imaging & Therapeutics P.C. **Title:** Associate Radiologist **Type of organization:** Radiology group **Major product:** Radiologic services **Area of distribution:** Memphis, Tennessee **Area of Practice:** Nuclear medicine radiology **Honors/awards:** The Best Doctors in America: Midwest Region, 1996-97 and 1998-99 **Published works:** Co-author, "Colitis Cystica Profunda", Radiology, 96:447-452, 1970;

"Subtraction Sialography: An Improved and Simplified Technique" Oral Surgery, Oral Medicine and Oral Pathology, 31:828-830, 1971; "Changes in Latent Image of X-Ray Film", Year Book of Diagnostic Radiology, 1975 **Affiliations:** Tennessee Medical Association; Society of Nuclear Medicine; American Medical Association **Hob./spts.:** Hunting, fishing **SIC code:** 80 **Address:** MID-South Imaging & Therapeutics P.C., 6305 Humphrey's Blvd., Suite 205, Memphis, TN 38120 **E-mail:** www.msit.com

BUFALINO, VINCENT J.
Industry: Healthcare **Born:** May 29, 1952, Chicago, Illinois **Univ./degree:** B.S., Biology, 1974; M.D., 1979, Loyola University **Current organization:** Midwest Heart Specialists **Title:** M.D./ President/C.E.O./Medical Director **Type of organization:** Private practice/hospital/healthcare foundation **Major product:** Patient care **Area of distribution:** International **Area of Practice:** Preventative cardiology, administration, development **Affiliations:** F.A.C.C.; F.A.C.P.; F.A.C.C.P.; Board of Directors, American Heart Association; Chairman and Founder, Midwest Heart Foundation **Hob./spts.:** Fishing, hunting, golf, triathlon, bicycling **SIC code:** 80 **Address:** Midwest Heart Specialists, 801 South Washington, 4th floor, Naperville, IL 60540 **E-mail:** vbufalino@midwestheart.com **Web address:** www.midwestheart.com

BUHRDORF, CHRISTINE R.
Industry: Healthcare **Born:** May 28, 1959, Laramie, Wyoming **Univ./degree:** A.S., Radiologic Technology, Laramie Community College **Current organization:** Memorial Hospital **Title:** R.T. (R)(MR) **Type of organization:** Hospital **Major product:** Patient care, medical imaging **Area of distribution:** Colorado **Area of Practice:** Magnetic resonance imaging **Affiliations:** A.S.R.T.; S.M.R.T.; A.R.R.T. **Hob./spts.:** Hiking, reading, skiing, furniture refinishing **SIC code:** 80 **Address:** Memorial Hospital, 1400 E. Boulder Hwy., Colorado Springs, CO 80909 **E-mail:** chrisbuhrdorf@yahoo.com

BUIKEMA, DANIEL R.
Industry: Healthcare **Born:** October 7, 195, Hammond, Indiana **Current organization:** Patient Advocate Home Care **Title:** C.O.O., Director **Type of organization:** Healthcare **Major product:** Medical services **Area of distribution:** Indiana **Area of Practice:** Sleep disorders, diagnostics, durable medical equipment; Runs 2 other companies, Regional Sleep Labs and Illiana Institute of Sleep Disorder **Hob./spts.:** Sports, boating **SIC code:** 80 **Address:** Patient Advocate Home Care, 521 E. 86th Ave., Suite H, Merrillville, IN 46410 **E-mail:** drbuikema@hotmail.com

BUKHOLTS, BENJAMIN
Industry: Mental healthcare **Born:** May 13, 1948, Nezhin, Ukraine **Univ./degree:** M.D., Kiev Medical Institute, 1973 **Current organization:** Benjamin Bukholts, M.D. **Title:** Psychiatrist **Type of organization:** Private practice **Major product:** Patient care **Area of distribution:** National **Area of Practice:** Psychiatry, fluent in several languages - Russian, Ukraine, Polish, Yiddish, English **Affiliations:** A.P.A.; A.M.A.; New York Medical Society **Hob./spts.:** Theatre, museums **SIC code:** 80 **Address:** Benjamin Bukholts, M.D., 323 E. 17th St., New York, NY 10003

BULLEN, AMY R.
Industry: Healthcare **Born:** December 15, 1973, Framingham, Massachusetts **Univ./degree:** M.M.; M.H.A., Cambridge College, 2001 **Current organization:** Healthsouth Diagnostic Centers **Title:** Regional Director **Type of organization:** Healthcare, free-standing centers **Major product:** Diagnostic imaging **Area of distribution:** Massachusetts **Area of Practice:** Management, CQI, administrative **Published works:** Article **Affiliations:** A.S.R.T.; A.R.R.T. **Hob./spts.:** Running, painting, reading on an educational level **SIC code:** 80 **Address:** 148 Chauncy St., #1, Mansfield, MA 02048 **E-mail:** bullenar@netscape.net

BUMB, STEVEN W.
Industry: Healthcare **Born:** November 8, 1963, Columbus, Ohio **Univ./degree:** M.D., Medical College of Ohio, 1991 **Current organization:** Gerber Memorial Health Services **Title:** M.D. **Type of organization:** Medical practice **Major product:** Internal medicine, pediatrics **Area of distribution:** Michigan **Area of Practice:** Diabetes care **Affiliations:** A.M.A.; A.S.A.M.; F.A.A.P. **Hob./spts.:** Fishing **SIC code:** 80 **Address:** 3917 South Croswell Ave., Fremont, MI 49412

BURCHFIELD, SHAWN M.
Industry: Healthcare **Born:** Morristown, Tennessee **Univ./degree:** B.S., Microbiology; A.S., Medical Lab Technology, East Tennessee State University **Current organization:** Hamblen Healthcare System **Title:** Lead Tech **Type of organization:** Hospital **Major product:** Patient care **Area of distribution:** Morristown, Tennessee **Area of Practice:** Microbiology, laboratory testing **Affiliations:** A.S.C.P.; American Microbiology Society **Hob./spts.:** Reading, cooking, UT football **SIC code:** 80 **Address:** Morristown-Hamblen Healthcare System, 908 W. 4th North St., Morristown, TN 37814 **E-mail:** sburchfield@mhhs1.org

BURKART, DAVID JOSEPH
Industry: Healthcare **Born:** October 13, 1967, McAlester, Oklahoma **Univ./degree:** M.D., University of Missouri-Kansas City, 1991 **Current organization:** Alliance Radiology, P.A. **Title:** M.D. **Type of organization:** Medical practice **Major product:** Patient care **Area of distribution:** Kansas **Area of Practice:** Interventional radiology **Published works:** 12 journal articles, 50 abstracts **Affiliations:** A.M.A.; A.C.R.; R.S.N.A.; S.I.R. **Hob./spts.:** Family **SIC code:** 80 **Address:** Alliance Radiology, P.A., 9212 Nieman Rd., Overland Park, KS 66214 **E-mail:** dburkart@kc.rr.com

BUROV, ELLEN A.
Industry: Healthcare **Born:** August 26, 1960, Moscow, Russia **Univ./degree:** M.D., Moscow School of Medicine and Dentistry, Russia, 1983 **Current organization:** Ellen A. Burov, M.D./Albert Einstein College of Medicine **Title:** Clinical Assistant Professor **Type of organization:** Private practice **Major product:** Patient care/education **Area of distribution:** New York **Area of Practice:** General and cosmetic dermatology **Honors/awards:** Certificate of Appreciation, Pennsylvania Academy of Dermatology **Published works:** Authored and co-authored: "Morpheaform sarcoidosis. Report of 3 cases", 1998; "Oncocerciasis presenting with lower extremity, hypopigmented macules, 2000; "Comparative analysis of immunologic responses in children with scleroderma", 1987; "Clinical presentations of genital lichen sclerosus in children", 1988; "Sex hormones and gonadotropins in girls with genital lichen sclerosus" in Pathogenesis and Treatment of Pediatric Dermatoses, 1988; "New therapy of lichen sclerosus in children with 5% parmidine ointment", 1988; "Connective tissue nevi in children", 1993 **Affiliations:** American Academy of Dermatology; Greater New York Dermatologic Society **Hob./spts.:** Skiing **SIC code:** 80 **Address:** Ellen A. Burov, M.D., 1317 Third Ave., 9th floor, New York, NY 10021 **E-mail:** e_burov@yahoo.com

BURREI, CHRISTOPHER N.
Industry: Healthcare **Born:** November 10, 1966 **Univ./degree:** B.S., Biology, Ithaca College, 1988; D.O., New York College of Osteopathic Medicine, 1992; Internship, St. Barnabas, New York; Residency, Nassau University Medical Center **Current organization:** Long Island Physical Medicine & Rehab Assoc. **Title:** Doctor of Osteopathic Medicine **Type of organization:** Private practice **Major product:** Patient care **Area of distribution:** New York **Area of Practice:** Physical medicine and rehabilitation, testing, pain medicine and treatment; **Affiliations:** American Medical Association; American Association of Neuromuscular and Electrodiagnostic Medicine; New York State Medical Society; Nassau County Medical Society; Workers Compensation Committee **SIC code:** 80 **Address:** Long Island Physical Medicine & Rehab Assoc., 2920 Hempstead Tpke., Levittown, NY 11756 **E-mail:** burrei@LIPMR.com

BUSHNICK, PHILIP N.
Industry: Healthcare **Born:** Chicago, Illinois **Univ./degree:** M.D., University of Illinois at Chicago, 1978 **Current organization:** Cosmetic & Plastic Surgery Associates **Title:** M.D./Owner **Type of organization:** Medical practice **Major product:** Plastic surgery **Area of distribution:** Hoffman Estates, Illinois **Area of Practice:** Cosmetic and plastic surgery **Affiliations:** A.S.P.S.; F.A.C.S. **Hob./spts.:** Skiing, boating **SIC code:** 80 **Address:** Cosmetic & Plastic Surgery Associates, 1585 Barrington Rd., Suite 504, Hoffman Estates, IL 60194 **E-mail:** pbushnickmd@aol.com

BUTKA, PATRICIA CATHERINE
Industry: Healthcare **Univ./degree:** B.S.N., Downstate Medical Center **Current organization:** Patient Care, Inc. **Title:** Senior Field Nurse Supervisor/Registered Nurse/Certified Community Health Nurse **Type of organization:** Home healthcare **Major product:** Patient care, nursing (accredited by joint commission) **Area of distribution:** Elmhurst, New York **Area of Practice:** Home healthcare **Affiliations:** F.N.G.S.; Executive Vice President, Yoga Foundation **SIC code:** 80 **Address:** 90-48 51th Ave., Elmhurst, NY 11373

BUTLER, NANCY
Industry: Healthcare **Born:** April 23, 1958, Fayette, Mississippi **Univ./degree:** A.A.S., Hinds Junior College, B.S.N., Alcorn State University, 1992 **Current organization:** Promise Health Care **Title:** R.N. **Type of organization:** Hospital **Major product:** Patient care **Area of distribution:** Mississippi **Area of Practice:** Healthcare management **Affiliations:** Mississippi Nurses Association; American Nurses Association; Alcorn State University Alumni Association **Hob./spts.:** Crossword puzzles **SIC code:** 80 **Address:** 111 Colonial Dr., Vicksburg, MS 39180 **E-mail:** nanrn17@bellsouth.net

BUTLER-SUMNER, SUSAN M.
Industry: Healthcare **Born:** September 27, 1954, Chattanooga, Tennessee **Univ./degree:** M.D., Medical College of Georgia, 1982 **Current organization:** Cave Spring Medical Center **Title:** M.D. **Type of organization:** Solo practice **Major product:** Patient care **Area of distribution:** Georgia **Area of Practice:** Family practice **Honors/awards:** The Georgia Disability Employment Committee, 1988 & 1999; speaker for Wyeth/Aventis/Glasco **Affiliations:** A.A.P.S.; A.A.F.P. **Hob./spts.:** Snorkeling **SIC code:** 80 **Address:** Cave Spring Medical Center, 28 Rone Rd., Cave Spring, GA 30124 **E-mail:** rpsumner@aol.com

BUTT, MOHAMMAD
Industry: Healthcare **Born:** February 19, 1964, Pakistan **Univ./degree:** M.D., King Edward Medical College, Lahore, Pakistan **Current organization:** Shorefront Jewish Geriatric Center, N.Y. **Title:** M.D. **Type of organization:** Nursing home **Major product:** Patient care, long term care **Area of distribution:** New York **Area of Practice:** Internal medicine, geriatric medicine **Honors/awards:** V.A. Medical Center 100 Hours Award of the Year 1994; Physicians Recognition Award by Johns Hopkins University School of Medicine; Physicians Recognition Award by Medicom Worldwide, Inc.; Physicians Recognition Award of American Medical Association; Physicians Recognition Award by American Geriatrics Society; Physicians Recognition Award by Institute for Continuing Healthcare Education **Published works:** Numerous research studies including: "Treatment of Urinary Tract Infection Verses Colonization"; "Underutilization of Aspirin in Patients with Coronary Artery Disease and Cerebrovascular Accidents"; "Role of Megestrol As An Appetite Stimulant in the Elderly Population"; Numerous presentations including: "Pressure Sore Prevention and Treatment Protocols"; "Core Topics in Geriatric Medicine"; "Principles of Management of Delirium in Elderly Population" **Affiliations:** Diplomate in Internal Medicine and Diplomate in Geriatric Medicine by American Board of Internal Medicine (ABIM); Healthcare provider of American Heart Association (AHA); Resident Member, American Society of Internal Medicine; Member, Association of Pakistani Physicians of North America (APPNA); Member, Pakistan Medical and Dental Council (PMDC) **Hob./spts.:** Music, coin and stamp collecting, travel **SIC code:** 80 **Address:** Shorefront Jewish Geriatric Center, 3015 W. 29th St., Brooklyn, NY 11224 **E-mail:** zamanbutt@hotmail.com

BUTTS, DONALD H.
Industry: Healthcare **Born:** July 9, 1938, Winona, Mississippi **Univ./degree:** M.D., University of Mississippi School of Medicine, 1980 **Current organization:** Donald H. Butts, M.D., P.A. **Title:** M.D. **Type of organization:** Private practice **Major product:** Medical services/consulting **Area of distribution:** Jackson, Mississippi **Area of Practice:** Neurology **Affiliations:** A.M.A.; M.S.M.A. **Hob./spts.:** Reading **SIC code:** 80 **Address:** Donald H. Butts, M.D., P.A., 1920 Chadwick Dr., #109, Jackson, MS 39204 **E-mail:** dhbutts@yahoo.com

BYNES JR., FRANK H.
Industry: Healthcare **Born:** December 3, 1950, Savannah, Georgia **Univ./degree:** B.S., Biology, Savannah State University, 1972; M.D., Meharry Medical College, Tennessee, 1977; General Surgery Residency, Staten Island Hospital, 1978-82; Internal Medicine Residency, New York University Downtown Hospital, 1983-86 **Current organization:** Frank H. Bynes, Jr. MD PC **Title:** M.D. **Type of organization:** Private medical practice **Major product:** Patient care **Area of distribution:** Georgia **Area of Practice:** Internal medicine; Licensed in NY, GA, AL, SC; Certified in Advanced Trauma Life Support and Pediatric Life Support **Affiliations:** American Medical Association; New York Academy of Social Sciences; American College of Physicians; American Association for the Advancement of Science; Association of Military Surgeons of the United States; South Atlantic Medical Association **Hob./spts.:** Chess, gardening, dog shows **SIC code:** 80 **Address:** Frank H. Bynes, Jr. MD PC, 703 Noble Oaks Dr., Savannah, GA 31406 **E-mail:** fbynesjr@aol.com

CABALLERO, BARUCH O.
Industry: Healthcare **Born:** May 2, 1954, Spain **Univ./degree:** M.D., Santander School of Medicine, Spain, 1981 **Current organization:** Baruch O. Caballero, MD, FACC **Title:** M.D. **Type of organization:** Private practice **Major product:** Patient care **Area of distribution:** Puerto Rico **Area of Practice:** Cardiology **Honors/awards:** Healthcare communicator for television and radio **Published works:** Conference papers **Affiliations:** Assistant Professor, Puerto Rico School of Medicine **Hob./spts.:** Family **SIC code:** 80 **Address:** Urb La Vista, F-9, San Juan, PR 00924 **E-mail:** enlil_imanol@hotmail.com

CABAN, VIVIANA T.
Industry: Medical **Born:** February 20, 1973, San Juan, Puerto Rico **Univ./degree:** M.D., Ponce School of Medicine, 1999 **Current organization:** Rush-Presbyterian St. Luke's Medical Center **Title:** M.D. **Type of organization:** University hospital **Major product:** Medical services **Area of distribution:** Illinois **Area of Practice:** Internal medicine **Honors/awards:** Chief Resident **Published works:** 1 article for A.C.G.I. **Affiliations:** A.M.A.; A.C.P. **Hob./spts.:** Dancing, swimming **SIC code:** 80 **Address:** 1133 N. Dearborn, #2401, Chicago, IL 60610 **E-mail:** vivcaban@yahoo.com

CABRERA, FRANCESCO
Industry: Medical **Born:** August 24, 1958, Cuba **Univ./degree:** B.S., Microbiology; B.A., Psychology, University of Florida, 1986; M.D., University of Miami School of Medicine, 1990 **Current organization:** ERMD, Inc. **Title:** M.D. **Type of organization:** Private practice **Major product:** Patient care **Area of distribution:** Miami, Florida **Area of Practice:** Internal medicine **Published works:** Article **Affiliations:** Florida Medical Association; Dade County Medical Association **Hob./spts.:** Sports, golf, fishing **SIC code:** 80 **Address:** ERMD, Inc., 11880 Bird Rd., Suite 405, Miami, FL 33175 **E-mail:** ermdinc@bellsouth.net

CABRERA, LEOPOLDO A.
Industry: Healthcare **Born:** October 30, 1958, Manila, Philippines **Univ./degree:** M.D., Far Eastern University, Philippines, 1982 **Current organization:** Covenant Family Healthcare Center **Title:** M.D. **Type of organization:** Medical practice **Major product:** Patient care **Area of distribution:** Texas **Area of Practice:** Pediatrics **Published works:** Multiple publications **Affiliations:** A.M.A.; F.A.C.P.; P.C.C.P.; Texas Medical Association **Hob./spts.:** Piano, basketball **SIC code:** 80 **Address:** Covenant Family Healthcare Center, 6502 Slide Rd., Lubbock, TX 79424 **E-mail:** cabsmd@aol.com

CABRERA, MARIA R.
Industry: Medical **Born:** June 18, 1954, Miami, Florida **Univ./degree:** B.S., Health Management, University of Miami **Current organization:** University of Miami Hospital/Clinics, Sylvester Center **Title:** Manager of Perioperative Services **Type of organization:** University hospital **Major product:** Patient care **Area of distribution:** Florida **Area of Practice:** Perioperative care **Affiliations:** A.O.R.N.; H.N.A.; A.P.M.A.; F.N.A.; A.N.N.A.; S.G.N. **Hob./spts.:** Cooking, crafts **SIC code:** 80 **Address:** UM Sylvester Comprehensive Cancer Center, 1475 N.W. 12th Ave., Miami, FL 33136 **E-mail:** mcabrera@med.miami.edu

CABRERA, MIGUEL F.
Industry: Healthcare **Born:** September 13, 1949, Cascas, Peru **Univ./degree:** B.S., Biology, 1968; M.D., National University of Trujillo **Current organization:** Greater Lawrence Family Health Center **Title:** M.D./Director, Woodmill Nursing Home **Type of organization:** Community health center **Major product:** Patient care **Area of distribution:** International **Area of Practice:** Internal medicine, primary care, fluent in Spanish, Portuguese, English and French **Honors/awards:** GLFHC, 10 Years of Excellence Award, 2006; Honored for Outstanding Service at Woodmill Nursing Home, 2006 **Affiliations:** American College of Physicians; Massachusetts Medical Society; American Medical Director's Association **Hob./spts.:** Reading, swimming, missionary work **SIC code:** 80 **Address:** Greater Lawrence Family Health Center, 73D Winthrop Ave. (Plaza 114), Lawrence, MA 01843 **E-mail:** mcabrera@glfhc.org

CAI, JUNE
Industry: Medical **Born:** China **Univ./degree:** M.D., Shanghai Railway Medical College **Current organization:** The Miriam Hospital, Brown University School of Medicine, Dept. of Psychiatry **Title:** Director, Consultation-Liaison Psychiatry Services/Assistant Professor in Psychiatry & Human Behavior **Type of organization:** University Hospital **Major product:** Mental healthcare, medical education, research **Area of distribution:** Rhode Island **Area of Practice:** Psychiatry, psychosomatic medicine, administration **Honors/awards:** William Webb Fellowship Award; Seymour Kety Fellowship Award; American Psychosomatic Association Fellowship; A.M.A. Physician Recognition Award, 2001-02 **Published works:** 2 journals **Affiliations:** A.P.A.; A.P.M.; Endocrine Society; American Diabetic Association; American Chinese Medical Society **Hob./spts.:** Travel, swimming, reading **SIC code:** 80 **Address:** 10101 Grosvenor Place, Apt. 1001, North Bethesda, MD 20852 **E-mail:** junecai@brown.edu

CALAWAY, ALBERT C.
Industry: Healthcare **Born:** July 4, 1933, New Richmond, Ohio **Univ./degree:** D.D.S., Ohio State University, 1957 **Current organization:** Dedicated Dentistry **Title:** Dentist **Type of organization:** Private practice **Major product:** Cosmetic and restorative dentistry **Area of distribution:** National **Area of Practice:** Family dentistry **Affiliations:** Oral Dynamics; L.D. Pankey Institute for Advanced Dentistry **Hob./spts.:** Basketball, bowling, skiing **SIC code:** 80 **Address:** Dedicated Dentistry, 4708 Bradley Blvd., Chevy Chase, MD 20815 **E-mail:** acalaway@netzero.net

CALDWELL, SHAWN M.
Industry: Healthcare **Univ./degree:** D.C., Life Chiropractic College, 1987 **Current organization:** Caldwell Chiropractic Center **Title:** Doctor of Chiropractic **Type of organization:** Private practice **Major product:** Patient care **Area of distribution:** Wheat Ridge, Colorado **Area of Practice:** Chiropractic medicine, teaching post graduate studies; Doctor for Denver Broncos and Colorado Rockies **Affiliations:** C.I.P.A.S.; Pro-football Chiropractic Society **SIC code:** 80 **Address:** Caldwell Chiropractic Center, 3490 Youngfield St., Suite B, Wheat Ridge, CO 80033

CAMOENS, REENA M.
Industry: Mental healthcare **Born:** January 1, 1954, India **Univ./degree:** B.S., Math/Physics/Chemistry, University of Kerala, India, 1971; M.D., Meharry Medical College, Tennessee, 1993 **Current organization:** Family Psych Services/Comprehensive Care Center/Preferred Alternatives **Title:** Medical Director **Type of organization:** Private practice/group practice/public health clinic **Major product:** Patient care **Area of distribution:** Tennessee **Area of Practice:** Psychiatry **Affiliations:** A.P.A.; A.M.A.; Tennessee State Medical Association; Southern Medical Association **Hob./spts.:** Family, physical fitness, community volunteering **SIC code:** 80 **Address:** Family Psych Services, 2021 21st Ave. South, Suite B-107, Nashville, TN 37212 **E-mail:** rcamoens@hotmail.com

CAMPOS, MARIA H.
Industry: Healthcare **Univ./degree:** B.S., Physical Therapy, Kean University, UMDNJ, 1998 **Current organization:** St. Barnabas Medical Center **Title:** Senior Cardiopulmonary Physical Therapist **Type of organization:** Medical center/hospital **Major product:** Patient care **Area of distribution:** New Jersey **Area of Practice:** Cardiac Physical Therapy; Certified Clinical Instructor **Affiliations:** American Physical Therapy Association **Hob./spts.:** Tennis, hiking, travel, bicycling **SIC code:** 80 **Address:** St. Barnabas Medical Center, 95 Old Short Hill Rd., Livingston, NJ 07039 **E-mail:** mhc15@earthlink.net

CAMUÑAS-CÓRDOVA, JOSÉ F.
Industry: Medical **Born:** March 31, 1961, Fajardo, Puerto Rico **Univ./degree:** B.S., Biology, University of Puerto Rico, Rio Piedras Campus at San Juan, 1987; M.D., University of Puerto Rico School of Medicine, Medical Sciences Campus at San Juan, Puerto Rico, 1990 **Current organization:** University of Puerto Rico School of Medicine, Family Practice Dept. **Title:** M.D. **Type of organization:** University **Major product:** Medical services **Area of distribution:** National **Area of Practice:** Family medicine, sports medicine **Honors/awards:** Team Physician, Member of the Medical Delegation, Puerto Rico Olympic Team, 2000 Olympic Games at Sydney, Australia; XVI Cetroamerican & Caribbean Games, Mexico City, Mexico, 1990; Team Physician, Member of the Medical Delegation, Puerto Rico Olympic Team, XI Pan American Games, Havana, Cuba, 1991; Team Physician Member of the Medical Delegation, Puerto Rico Olympic Team, XVII Centroamerican & Caribbean Games, Ponce, Puerto Rico, 1993; Team Physician Member of the Medical Delegation, Puerto Rico Olympic Team, XII Pan American Games, Mar del Plata, Argentina, 1995; XVIII Centroamerican and Caribbean Games, Maracaibo, Venezuela **Affiliations:** A.A.F.P.; Puerto Rico Sports Medicine Federation; American College of Sports Medicine **Hob./spts.:** Family, biking, physical fitness **SIC code:** 80 **Address:** University of Puerto Rico School of Medicine, Family Practice Dept., FO-2 Marginal Esq, Calle 5, Ext. Villamar, Isla Verde, Carolina, PR 00979 **E-mail:** jcamunas@coqui.net

CANCELLIERI, RUSSELL P.
Industry: Healthcare **Born:** January 15, 1948, Southampton, New York **Univ./degree:** M.D., Georgetown University, 1974 **Current organization:** Russell P. Cancellieri M.D. **Title:** M.D. **Type of organization:** Private medical practice **Major product:** Patient care **Area of distribution:** Long Island, New York **Area of Practice:** Allergy and immunology **Affiliations:** F.A.A.A.A.I. **SIC code:** 80 **Address:** Russell P. Cancellieri M.D., 596 Hampton Rd., Southampton, NY 11968

CANNON, GERALDINE P.
Industry: Healthcare **Born:** June 7, 1946, Bronx, New York **Univ./degree:** R.N., California Hospital Medical Center School of Nursing, 1967 **Current organization:** Davita Dialysis Center of Vacaville **Title:** R.N./Certified Nephrology Nurse/ Administrator **Type of organization:** Dialysis center **Major product:** Patient care **Area of distribution:** Vacaville, California **Area of Practice:** Nursing, nephrology specialist, acute care **Honors/awards:** Outstanding Performance Award, Davita, 2002; St. Joseph's Hospital Health System Award of Excellence, 1999 **Affiliations:** Treasurer of the East Bay (Chapte. 519), A.N.N.A. **Hob./spts.:** Music, playing piano, singing **SIC code:** 80 **Address:** Davita Dialysis Center of Vacaville, 1241 Alamo Dr., Suite 7, Vacaville, CA 95687 **E-mail:** gcannon@davita.com **Web address:** www.davita.com

CANNON-SMITH, GERRI A.
Industry: Healthcare **Born:** Brandon, Mississippi **Univ./degree:** B.S., Howard University; M.D., University of Mississippi Medical Center, 1979; M.P.H., University of California at Berkley, 1985 **Current organization:** Family Health Care Clinic **Title:** M.D., M.P.H. (QI Coordinator) **Type of organization:** Community health clinic **Major product:** Patient care **Area of distribution:** Brandon, Mississippi **Area of Practice:** Pediatrics, public health **Affiliations:** N.M.A.; A.A.P.; A.P.H.A.; Mississippi Chapter of A.A.P.; Chair, Public Health Committee; Assistant Clinical Professor - University of Tennessee, Jackson State University School of Public Health, University of Mississippi Medical School (Dept. of Pediatrics) **Hob./spts.:** Reading, art, crafts, stained glass, health education, program development **SIC code:** 80 **Address:** Pediatric Consultant, P.O. Box 1385, Brandon, MS 39043

CANO, CARINA
Industry: Healthcare **Born:** August 9, 1978, Chicago, Illinois **Univ./degree:** A.S., San Jacinto University; B.S. Candidate, Radiology, M.S.U. **Current organization:** River Oaks Imaging & Diagnostics **Title:** Lead Mammographer **Type of organization:** Medical clinic **Major product:** Diagnostic imaging services **Area of distribution:** Texas **Area of Practice:** Mammography **Hob./spts.:** Jogging, softball **SIC code:** 80 **Address:** River Oaks Imaging & Diagnostics, 3620 Spencer Hwy., Pasadena, TX 77503 **E-mail:** carico9@yahoo.com

CANTER, DIANA M.
Industry: Healthcare **Born:** Buenos Aires, Argentina **Univ./degree:** D.D.S., University of Southern California, 1974 **Current organization:** Diana Maler Canter, DDS **Title:** D.D.S. **Type of organization:** Private dental practice **Major product:** Dental health services **Area of distribution:** Orange, Los Angeles and San Diego Counties, California **Area of Practice:** Family, general dentistry and cosmetics **Affiliations:** American Dental Association; Orange County Dental Society; California Dental Association; OKU Honorary Dental Society **Hob./spts.:** Opera, concerts, theatre, gardening **SIC code:** 80 **Address:** Diana Maler Canter, DDS, 1781 W. Romneya Dr., #H, Anaheim, CA 92801

CARABELLO, BLASE A.
Industry: Medical **Born:** August 5, 1947, Reading, Pennsylvania **Univ./degree:** M.D., Temple University, 1973; Internship & Residency, Massachusetts General Hospital, Boston; Fellowship, Cardiology, Birmingham Hospital **Current organization:** Houston VA Medical Center/Baylor College of Medicine **Title:** M.D./Professor of Medicine **Type of organization:** Medical center/university **Major product:** Medical services **Area of distribution:** Texas **Published works:** 200 articles, book chapters **Affiliations:** A.H.A.; American Society for Clinical Investigation; Association of University Cardiologists **Hob./spts.:** Food and wine **SIC code:** 80 **Address:** Houston VA Medical Center/Baylor College of Medicine, 2002 Holcombe Blvd., Houston, TX 77030 **E-mail:** blaseanthony.carabello@med.va.gov

CARBONE, JOANNE H.
Industry: Healthcare **Born:** August 22, 1942, Providence, Rhode Island **Univ./degree:** M.Ed., Cambridge College, Harvard University, 1982 **Current organization:** Beverly Enterprises, Greycliff at Cape Ann **Title:** Executive Director **Type of organization:** Nursing home **Major product:** Short and long term skilled nursing and rehabilitation care **Area of distribution:** National **Area of Practice:** Administration **Affiliations:** A.C.H.C.E.; A.H.C.A. **Hob./spts.:** Airplane pilot, sailing, golf **SIC code:** 80 **Address:** Beverly Enterprises, Greycliff at Cape Ann, 272 Washington St., Gloucester, MA 01930 **E-mail:** joanne_carbone@beverlycares.com

CARCAMO, RAFAEL
Industry: Healthcare **Born:** August 15, 1967, Nicaragua **Univ./degree:** M.D., National University School of Medicine, Nicaragua, 1992 **Current organization:** San Rafael Community Medical Clinic **Title:** M.D. **Type of organization:** Medical clinic **Major product:** Patient care **Area of distribution:** California **Area of Practice:** Family practice **Affiliations:** A.A.F.P.; A.M.A. **SIC code:** 80 **Address:** San Rafael Community Medical Clinic, 647 E. Arrow Hwy., Azusa, CA 91702 **E-mail:** drcarcamo@aol.com

CAREY, JUDITH A. (FARNSWORTH/REYNOLDS)
Industry: Healthcare **Born:** February 2, 1942, Denver, Colorado **Current organization:** Radiology Imaging **Title:** Mammographer Specialist **Type of organization:** Private practice **Major product:** Diagnostic imaging services **Area of distribution:** Denver, Colorado **Area of Practice:** Mammography, quality control, patient liaison **Affiliations:** A.R.R.T.; A.S.R.T. **Hob./spts.:** Photography, baking **SIC code:** 80 **Address:** Radiology Imaging, 2572 W. 107th Place, Westminster, CO 80234 **E-mail:** strawberryannie@usa.com

CARMICHAEL, BENJAMIN M.
Industry: Healthcare **Born:** July 15, 1939, Atlanta, Georgia **Univ./degree:** B.S., Psychology, Emory University, 1961; M.D., Emory University, 1965; Internship, Walter Reed Army Medical Center; Residency, Internal Medicine, Walter Reed Army Medical Center; Fellowship, Cardiology, Brook Army Medical Center (1969-1971) **Current organization:** Hattiesburg Clinic **Title:** M.D. **Type of organization:** Large group practice clinic **Major product:** Patient care **Area of Practice:** Cardiology: Director of Nuclear Cardiology; Internal Medicine and Cardiovascular Diseases (Board Certified) **Honors/awards:** Recipient, Hattiesburg "Hub Award", 1986; Recipient, "Friend of the University of Southern Mississippi", 2000 **Affiliations:** A.C.P.; A.C.C.; American Heart Association; Mississippi Medical Association; Southern Mississippi Medical Association; Southern Medical Association; President, University of Southern Mississippi Foundation, 2000-2001; Member (Sec.) Board of Trustees **Hob./spts.:** Music, playing piano and the organ **SIC code:** 80 **Address:** Hattiesburg Clinic, 415 S. 28th Ave., Hattiesburg, MS 39401 **E-mail:** bmcshc@aol.com

CARMUSCIANO, VINCENT
Industry: Healthcare **Born:** February 7, 1954, Brooklyn, New York **Univ./degree:** M.D., University of Rome, Italy, 1983 **Current organization:** Vincent Carmusciano M.D., P.C. **Title:** M.D. **Type of organization:** Private practice **Major product:** Patient care **Area of distribution:** New York **Area of Practice:** Internal medicine **Affiliations:** A.C.P.; Medical Society of the State of New York **Hob./spts.:** Sports, coaching basketball, movies, theatre, music **SIC code:** 80 **Address:** Vincent Carmusciano M.D., P.C., 560 Bay Ridge Pkwy., Brooklyn, NY 11209

CARRAO, VINCENT
Industry: Healthcare **Born:** June 22, 1967, Queens, New York **Univ./degree:** B.S., Economics, New York University, 1989; D.D.S, Columbia University, 1993; M.D., Columbia University School of Medicine, 1996 **Current organization:** Vincent Carrao, DDS, MD, Oral & Maxillofacial Surgery **Title:** D.D.S.; M.D. **Type of organization:** Private practice **Major product:** Oral and maxillofacial surgery **Area of distribu-**

tion: New York **Area of Practice:** Oral and maxillofacial surgery **Published works:** 3 articles in Columbia Medical Journal **Affiliations:** A.M.A.; A.D.A. **Hob./spts.:** Family **SIC code:** 80 **Address:** Vincent Carrao, DDS, MD, New York Presbyterian Hospital, 630 W. 168th St., New York, NY 10032

CARRION, CARLOS A.
Industry: Healthcare **Born:** June 7, 1950, Puerto Rico **Univ./degree:** M.D., University of Santa Diego de Compostela, Spain, 1977 **Current organization:** G.U.M.E.T. **Title:** M.D. **Type of organization:** Medicine provider services in a reform model **Major product:** Patient care **Area of distribution:** Puerto Rico **Area of Practice:** General physician **Affiliations:** Medical College of Puerto Rico **Hob./spts.:** Reading, swimming, cockfights **SIC code:** 80 **Address:** P.O. Box 68, Yabucoa, PR 00767

CARRO PAGÁN, CARLOS J.
Industry: Healthcare **Born:** Puerto Rico **Univ./degree:** M.D., University of Santo Domingo, 1978; Cardiology Degree, Ponce School of Medicine, 1986 **Current organization:** Advanced Cardiology Center **Title:** Cardiologist **Type of organization:** Medical office **Major product:** Patient care **Area of distribution:** Puerto Rico **Area of Practice:** Cardiology, internal medicine **Published works:** 6 articles **Affiliations:** A.M.A.; Puerto Rico Board of Physicians **Hob./spts.:** Golf, fishing **SIC code:** 80 **Address:** Advanced Cardiology Center, P.O. Box 331788, Ponce, PR 00733-1788 **E-mail:** carropagancarlosj@prtc.net

CARROLL, M. GAIL
Industry: Healthcare **Born:** October 1, 1952, Springfield, Missouri **Univ./degree:** B.S.N., Drury University, 1995 **Current organization:** Cox Health **Title:** Staff Nurse **Type of organization:** Hospital **Major product:** Patient care **Area of distribution:** Missouri **Area of Practice:** Emergency nursing **Affiliations:** E.N.A. **Hob./spts.:** Boating, crafts **SIC code:** 80 **Address:** Cox Health, Emergency Dept., 1423 N. Jefferson Ave., Springfield, MO 65802

CART, PAULINE H.
Industry: Health educator **Born:** November 3, 1914, Jamestown, Kentucky **Univ./degree:** B.A., Berea College, Kentucky; M.A., University of Michigan; N.D., Ph.D., Institute of Natural Health Sciences **Current organization:** General Health Needs Inc. **Title:** N.D., Ph.D., Professor **Type of organization:** Health needs provider **Major product:** Education, nutritional supplements, counseling **Area of distribution:** Ann Arbor, Michigan **Area of Practice:** Education **Honors/awards:** Marquis Who's Who: Women Educators of the U.S.A., Women of the World; Georgetown Works Award **Affiliations:** A.A.E.A.; N.H.F.; M.E.A.; N.E.A.; I.M.A.; C.M.T.A. **Hob./spts.:** Lectures, poetry, travel **SIC code:** 80 **Address:** 2564 Hawks Ave., Ann Arbor, MI 48108 **E-mail:** cchr80Ayahoo.com

CARTER, ZONDRA
Industry: Medical **Born:** New York, New York **Univ./degree:** B.S., Biology, C.C.N.Y., 1972 **Current organization:** St. Vincent's Hospital - Manhattan **Title:** Hematology Supervisor **Type of organization:** Teaching hospital **Major product:** Patient care, medical education **Area of distribution:** New York, New York **Area of Practice:** Administration **Hob./spts.:** Reading, church **SIC code:** 80 **Address:** St. Vincent's Hospital - Manhattan, 170 W. 12th St., New York, NY 10011 **E-mail:** zon44@aol.com

CASSELL, LAUREN S.
Industry: Healthcare **Title:** M.D. **Type of organization:** Private practice **Major product:** Patient care **Area of Practice:** Breast surgery **SIC code:** 80 **Address:** Lauren Cassell, M.D., 114a E. 78th St., New York, NY 10021

CASTANIAS, ALECIA KOCH
Industry: Healthcare **Born:** December 19, 1968, Greenfield, Ohio **Univ./degree:** B.A., Mass Communications, Miami University, 2003 **Current organization:** Otterbein Retirement Living Community **Title:** Director of Marketing **Type of organization:** Continuing care retirement community **Major product:** Long-term healthcare **Area of distribution:** Ohio **Area of Practice:** Marketing **Affiliations:** Lebanon Chamber of Commerce; Business and Professional Women **Hob./spts.:** Arts, theatre, scuba diving **SIC code:** 80 **Address:** Otterbein Retirement Living Community, 585 N. State Rt. 741, Lebanon, OH 45036 **E-mail:** acastanias@otterbein.org **Web address:** www.otterbein.org

CASTELLANI, SAM U.
Industry: Healthcare **Born:** September 14, 1941, Lansing, Michigan **Univ./degree:** M.D., Wayne State University, 1969 **Current organization:** Spina Health Center **Title:** M.D. **Type of organization:** Private practice **Major product:** Patient care **Area of distribution:** Madison, Tennessee **Area of Practice:** Psychiatry **Hob./spts.:** Classical guitar **SIC code:** 80 **Address:** Spina Health Center, 500 Lentz Dr., Suite 90B, Madison, TN 37115 **E-mail:** samcastellani@msn.com

CASTELLANO, MICHAEL LEO
Industry: Healthcare **Born:** February 25, 1961 **Univ./degree:** B.S., Biology/Chemistry, Union College, 1983; M.D., New York University Medical College, 1987 **Current organization:** Michael Leo Castellano MD, FACS **Title:** MD, FACS **Type of organization:** Private practice **Major product:** Patient care **Area of distribution:** New York **Area of Practice:** General surgery **Published works:** Article **Affiliations:** F.A.C.S. **SIC code:** 80 **Address:** Michael Leo Castellano MD, FACS, 145 E. 16th St., Ground Fl., New York, NY 10003

CASTELLUCCI, DEBORAH S.
Industry: Healthcare **Born:** New York, New York **Univ./degree:** B.S.N., Villanova University; M.A., Public Administration, James Madison University **Current organization:** Morristown Memorial Hospital **Title:** Clinical Nurse Specialist **Type of organization:** Hospital **Major product:** Patient care **Area of distribution:** Morristown, New Jersey **Area of Practice:** Medical cardiology **Affiliations:** A.A.C.N. **Hob./spts.:** Golf, skiing, cooking **SIC code:** 80 **Address:** Morristown Memorial Hospital, 100 Madison Ave., Morristown, NJ 07930 **E-mail:** dsc78@msn.com

CASTELLVI, ANTONIO E.
Industry: Healthcare **Born:** November 14, 1952, Havana, Cuba **Univ./degree:** M.D., Zaragoza Medical School, Spain, 1976; Fellowship, Spinal Surgery, University of Rochester, New York, 1981; Diplomate, American Board of Orthopaedic Surgeons, 1982 **Current organization:** Florida Orthopaedic Institute **Title:** Physician **Type of organization:** Private practice **Major product:** Orthopaedic surgery **Area of distribution:** International **Area of Practice:** Scoliosis, motion preservation techniques, lumbar degeneration, cervical, thoracic and general pathology, adult degeneration deformities **Honors/awards:** Matricula de Honor Pharmacology and General Pathology, 1973: Peer elected for inclusion, Best Doctors in America, 1998-99 and 2005-06; America's Top Surgeons, Consumer Research Council, 2003 and 2006; Bay Area, Best Doctors, Tampa Bay, Florida, 2006 **Published works:** 83 articles, 9 poster presentations, 4 videos **Affiliations:** F.A.A.O.S.; N.A.S.S.; E.D.A.; A.M.A.; F.O.S.; Cuban Medical Association; Florida Medical Association; Southern Orthopaedic Society; Hillsborough County Medical Association; North American Spine Society; Eastern Orthopaedic Society; Sisyphean Spinal Society; Spine Arthroplasty; Director, Spine Fellowship, Florida Orthopaedic Institute, 2004 - present **Hob./spts.:** Fishing, boating, hunting **SIC code:** 80 **Address:** Florida Orthopaedic Institute, 13020 Telecom Pkwy. N., Temple Terrace, Fl 33637-0, 2727 Martin Luther King Jr. Blvd., Suite 630, Tampa, FL 33607 **E-mail:** acastellvi@floridaortho.com

CASTIGLIONE, CHARLES L.
Industry: Healthcare **Born:** February 9, 1956, New Haven, Connecticut **Univ./degree:** B.S., Yale University, 1977; M.D., Columbia University School of Medicine, 1981 **Current organization:** Connecticut Surgical Group **Title:** M.D. **Type of organization:** Multispecialty surgical group **Major product:** Patient care **Area of distribution:** Connecticut **Area of Practice:** Pediatrics, cosmetic surgery (breast surgery) **Affiliations:** F.A.C.S.; A.S.P.S. **Hob./spts.:** Running, baseball, music **SIC code:** 80 **Address:** Connecticut Surgical Group, 85 Seymour St., Suite 401, Hartford, CT 06106

CASTOR JR., C. WILLIAM
Industry: Medical **Born:** October 9, 1925, Ferndale, Michigan **Univ./degree:** M.D., University of Michigan at Ann Arbor, 1951 **Current organization:** University of Michigan **Title:** Professor of Medicine and Rheumatology Emeritus (Retired) **Type of organization:** University/hospital **Major product:** Education, research, patient care **Area of distribution:** International **Area of Practice:** Rheumatology and internal medicine **Honors/awards:** Served in active duty during WWII, U.S. Army Medical Corp. **Published works:** 101 articles **Affiliations:** F.A.C.P.; Honorary Member, The Australian Rheumatism Association; Founding Fellow, American Rheumatism Association; Alpha Omega Alpha **Hob./spts.:** Woodworking **SIC code:** 80 **Address:** 2217 Independence Blvd., Ann Arbor, MI 48104

CASTRO, GLORIA E.
Industry: Healthcare **Univ./degree:** M.D., University Medical School of Puerto Rico, 1979 **Current organization:** Phoenix Indian Medical Center **Title:** M.D. **Type of organization:** Medical center/federal government - DHH/IHS **Major product:** Patient care **Area of distribution:** National **Area of Practice:** Pathology, clinical laboratory sciences, management **Affiliations:** Fellow, College of American Pathologists; American Society for Clinical Pathology; Arizona Pathology Society; Founder, Arizona Latin-American Medical Association **SIC code:** 80 **Address:** Phoenix Indian Medical Center, 4212 North 16th St., Phoenix, AZ 85016 **E-mail:** gloria.castro@ihs.gov

CAUSER, BRENDA L.
Industry: Healthcare **Born:** December 1, 1969, Altoona, Pennsylvania **Univ./degree:** L.P.N., Altoona Vocational Technical School, 1985 **Current organization:** Morans Home **Title:** Personal Care Administrator/LPN **Type of organization:** Healthcare facility **Major product:** Long term patient care **Area of distribution:** Pennsylvania **Area of Practice:** Personal care administration, geriatrics **Affiliations:** N.A.P.C.H.A.A.;

Medical Reserve Care **SIC code:** 80 **Address:** Morans Home, 402 Maple Ave., Bellwood, PA 16617 **E-mail:** brendanick2@aol.com

CAVALIERE, LUDOVICO F. R.
Industry: Medical **Born:** June 1, 1954, San Francisco, California **Univ./degree:** M.D., University of Bologna, Italy, 1985 **Current organization:** New York Medical College, Division of Rheumatic Diseases **Title:** M.D., Director of Rheumatology Fellowship Training Program since 1998 **Type of organization:** Medical school **Major product:** Healthcare and education **Area of distribution:** Valhalla, New York **Area of Practice:** Rheumatology **Honors/awards:** Fellowship Status at ACP, 2000; Top Doctors, New York Metropolitan Area; Strathmore Who's Who **Published works:** Journal of Infectious Diseases **Affiliations:** A.C.P.; A.C.R.; A.M.A. **Hob./spts.:** Family **SIC code:** 80 **Address:** New York Medical College, Division of Rheumatic Diseases, Munger Pavilion G73, Valhalla, NY 10595 **E-mail:** frank_cavaliere@nymc.edu

CEBELENSKI, ROSANNE M.
Industry: Healthcare **Born:** January 23, 1962, Flushing, New York **Univ./degree:** B.S., Biology, City University of New York, 1987; M.D., 1994 **Current organization:** Roseanne M. Cebelenski, D.O., P.C. **Title:** D.O. **Type of organization:** Private medical practice **Major product:** Patient care **Area of distribution:** New York **Area of Practice:** Family medicine **Affiliations:** F.A.C.O.P.; A.O.A. **Hob./spts.:** Dog breeding (Pomeranians), dogs shows, champions **SIC code:** 80 **Address:** Rosanne M. Cebelenski, D.O., P.C., 1644 Deer Park Ave., Deer Park, NY 11729

CERNIK, CHRISTINE C.
Industry: Healthcare **Born:** February 29, 1956, Scott Air Force Base, Illinois **Univ./degree:** M.D., Rush Medical College, 1987 **Current organization:** Ste. Genevieve County Memorial Hospital **Title:** M.D., Chief of Surgery/Chief of Staff **Type of organization:** Hospital **Major product:** Patient care **Area of distribution:** Ste. Genevieve, Missouri **Area of Practice:** Maternal, Ob/Gyn **Affiliations:** Fellow, American College of Obstetricians and Gynecologists; Missouri Medical Association; Society of Laparoendoscopic Surgeons **SIC code:** 80 **Address:** Ste. Genevieve County Memorial Hospital, 990 Park Dr., Ste. Genevieve, MO 63670 **E-mail:** cernik@sbcglobal.net

CHAAR, BASSEM T.
Industry: Healthcare **Born:** May 18, 1973, Beirut, Lebanon **Univ./degree:** B.S., Biology, 1994; M.D., 1998, American University of Beirut **Current organization:** Bothwell Regional Health Center **Title:** Staff Hematologist/Oncologist **Type of organization:** Hospital **Major product:** Patient care **Area of distribution:** Sedalia, Missouri **Area of Practice:** Internal Medicine (Board Certified); Hematology, oncology **Honors/awards:** Chief Resident, St. Louis University **Published works:** Several articles **Affiliations:** American Society of Internal Medicine; American Society of Clinical Oncology; American Medical Association; American Society of Hematology **Hob./spts.:** Swimming, jogging **SIC code:** 80 **Address:** Bothwell Regional Health Center, 601 E. 14th St., Sedalia, MO 65301 **E-mail:** chaarbt@iland.net

CHABRIA, SHIVEN B.
Industry: Medical **Born:** December 19, 1973, Bombay, India **Univ./degree:** M.B.B.S., University of Pune, India, 1997; Residency, Internal Medicine, Lincoln Medical Center, Bronx, New York, 2004 **Current organization:** Waterbury Hospital/Yale Medical School **Title:** M.D./Clinical Instructor, Internal Medicine, Yale Hospital **Type of organization:** Hospital/medical school **Major product:** Patient care, medical education **Area of distribution:** Connecticut **Area of Practice:** Hospital medicine **Affiliations:** A.C.P.; A.M.A.; S.H.M. **Hob./spts.:** Guitar, piano, calligraphy, building computers **SIC code:** 80 **Address:** 2600 Park Ave., #9N, Bridgeport, CT 06604 **E-mail:** shivenchabria@yahoo.com

CHACHKO, FAINA
Industry: Healthcare **Born:** April 7, 1949, Odessa, Ukraine **Univ./degree:** M.D., Kishinev State Medical Institute-1972 **Current organization:** Faina Chachko, M.D. **Title:** M.D. **Type of organization:** Psychiatric office **Major product:** Patient care **Area of distribution:** New York, New Jersey **Area of Practice:** Psychiatry **Affiliations:** A.M.A.; A.P.A.; American Academy of Child and Adolescent Psychiatry **Hob./spts.:** Art, music **SIC code:** 80 **Address:** Faina Chachko, M.D., 305 E. 55th St., Suite 203, New York, NY 10022 **Phone:** (212)759-5550 **Fax:** (212)759-9788

CHADHA, MANJEET
Industry: Healthcare **Univ./degree:** M.D., Government Medical College, Amritsar, India, 1979 **Current organization:** Beth Israel Medical Center, Dept. of Radiation Oncology **Title:** Associate Chairman, Radiation Oncology **Type of organization:** Hospital **Major product:** Medical services, radiation oncology **Area of distribution:** New York **Area of Practice:** Radiology oncology, breast and gynecologic malignancies, treatment of lymphoma, external beam therapy and brachytherapy **Honors/awards:** American Board of Radiology, 1985 **Affiliations:** American College of Radiology; American Society of Therapeutic Radiology and Oncology; American Society of Clinical Oncology; St. Luke's-Roosevelt Hospital Center; New York Eye & Ear Center **SIC code:** 80 **Address:** Beth Israel Medical Center, Dept. of Radiation Oncology, 10 Union Square East, New York, NY 10003 **E-mail:** mchadha@bethisraelny.org

CHAE, HEECHIN
Industry: Healthcare **Born:** February 8, 1967, Seoul, Korea **Univ./degree:** B.S., Psychology, University of Virginia, 1990; M.D., Medical College of Virginia, 1994 **Current organization:** Spaulding Rehabilitation Hospital **Title:** M.D. **Type of organization:** Hospital **Major product:** Patient care **Area of distribution:** Massachusetts **Area of Practice:** Physical medicine and rehabilitation **Published works:** 5 articles, 1 book chapter **Affiliations:** A.A.P.M.R. **SIC code:** 80 **Address:** Spaulding Rehabilitation Hospital, 125 Nashua St., Boston, MA 02114 **E-mail:** hchae@partners.org **Web address:** www.partners.org

CHAMPEAUX, ROSALIE MARIE L.
Industry: Healthcare **Title:** Director **Type of organization:** Hospital **Major product:** Patient care **Area of Practice:** Registered nurse **SIC code:** 80 **Address:** Children's Miracle Network of, Christus St. Patrick Hospital, 1614 Watkins St., Lake Charles, LA 70601

CHAMSUDDIN, ABBAS AFIF
Industry: Medical **Born:** Beirut, Lebanon **Univ./degree:** M.D., American University of Beirut, 1991 **Current organization:** University of Tennessee **Title:** M.D. **Type of organization:** University hospital **Major product:** Medical services **Area of distribution:** Memphis, Tennessee **Area of Practice:** Interventional radiology **Honors/awards:** American Medical Association Physician Recognition Award **Published works:** 1 book, "Stent-Grafts: Clinical Approach" **Affiliations:** Society of Cardiovascular and Interventional Radiology; American College of Radiology; Radiological Society of North America **Hob./spts.:** Horseback riding, swimming **SIC code:** 80 **Address:** University of Tennessee, 800 Madison Ave., Memphis, TN 38163 **E-mail:** achamsuddin@utmem.edu

CHAN, ALBERT W.
Industry: Healthcare **Born:** June 10, 1969, Hong Kong **Univ./degree:** M.D., University of Toronto School of Medicine, Canada, 1994 **Current organization:** Ochsner Clinic Foundation **Title:** M.D., Principal Investigator **Type of organization:** Hospital **Major product:** Cardiac healthcare, research, education **Area of distribution:** International **Area of Practice:** Interventional cardiology, internal medicine **Published works:** 40 articles, 7 book chapters **Affiliations:** F.A.C.C.; F.R.C.P. (Canada); A.M.A.; A.H.A. **SIC code:** 80 **Address:** Ochsner Clinic Foundation, 1514 Jefferson Hwy., New Orleans, LA 70121 **E-mail:** achan@ochsner.org **Web address:** www.ochsner.org

CHANDA, RANJAN
Industry: Healthcare **Born:** December 16, 1976, India **Univ./degree:** M.D., All-India University, 2000; M.P.H., University of Buffalo, 2005 **Current organization:** Lonestar Internal Medicine Assoc. **Title:** M.D., M.P.H. **Type of organization:** Group practice **Major product:** Patient care **Area of distribution:** Richardson, Texas **Area of Practice:** Internal medicine **Affiliations:** A.M.A.; A.P.H.A.; T.M.I. **Hob./spts.:** History, reading, basketball **SIC code:** 80 **Address:** Lonestar Internal Medicine Assoc., 3146 Maple Leaf lane, Richardson, TX 75082 **E-mail:** ranjanchanda@hotmail.com

CHANDLER-ROBLEDO, JEAN
Industry: Healthcare **Born:** October 22, 1947, Paducah, Kentucky **Univ./degree:** B.S., Healthcare Administration, Chapman University, 2000 **Current organization:** Vitas Hospice **Title:** R.N. **Type of organization:** Hospice **Major product:** End of life care **Area of distribution:** California **Area of Practice:** Management; Certified Case Manager, 1995 **Hob./spts.:** Reading, crossword puzzles **SIC code:** 80 **Address:** Vitas Hospice, 9655 Grant Ave., Suite 300, San Diego, CA 92123 **E-mail:** jeanrobledo@yahoo.com

CHANDOK, DINESH
Industry: Medical **Born:** March 12, 1969, Saharanpur, India **Univ./degree:** M.B.B.S., Government Medical College, Nagpur, India, 1995; Fellowship, Cardiology, 2006; Candidate for Fellowship, Interventional Cardiology, University of Massachusetts, 2007 **Current organization:** University of Massachusetts Medical School **Title:** M.D. **Type of organization:** Medical center/medical school **Major product:** Patient care, medical education **Area of distribution:** International **Area of Practice:** Echo cardiography **Affiliations:** A.M.A.; S.C.A.I.; A.C.C. **Hob./spts.:** Computers, travel, golf **SIC code:** 80 **Address:** University of Mass. Medical School, 55 Lake Ave., Worcester, MA 01655 **E-mail:** dchandok@msn.com

CHANDRA, SUBANI
Industry: Healthcare **Univ./degree:** M.D., India, 2002 **Current organization:** Long Island Jewish Medical Center **Title:** M.D. **Type of organization:** Hospital **Major product:** Patient care **Area of distribution:** Bellerose, New York **Area of Practice:** General healthcare, internal medicine **Affiliations:** A.M.A., M.S.N.Y., A.C.P., A.C.C.P., A.D.S. **SIC code:** 80 **Address:** Long Island Jewish Medical Center, 246-15A Union Tpke., Bellerose, NY 11426 **E-mail:** subani@chandra.gmail.com

CHANE, MAJED
Industry: Medical **Born:** July 28, 1971, Damascus, Syria **Univ./degree:** M.D., Damascus University, Syria, 1994 **Current organization:** University of Southern California **Title:** M.D. **Type of organization:** University hospital **Major product:** Patient care, medical education **Area of distribution:** International **Area of Practice:** Internal medicine, cardiology **Published works:** New in Pediatrics, Graduation Thesis, Damascus University Press 1994; Chane M., Richeh R., Bradycardia: diagnosis and treatment. Medical Arab Journal 2000; 145:p. 36-40; Sadun A, Chane M., Sadaati M., Ocular motility problems associated with sumatriptan administration. Annals of Ophthalmology 2001 (33): P231-232 **Affiliations:** A.C.P - A.S.I.M.; A.C.C. **Hob./spts.:** Ping pong **SIC code:** 80 **Address:** University of Southern California, 1340 S. Beverly Glen Blvd., Unit 101, Los Angeles, CA 90024

CHANG, JOE YUJIAO
Industry: Medical **Born:** China **Univ./degree:** M.D., Shanghai, 1995; Ph.D., Anderson Cancer Center, 1997 **Current organization:** M.D. Anderson Cancer Center **Title:** M.D., Ph.D. **Type of organization:** University/medical center **Major product:** Medical services **Area of distribution:** Texas **Area of Practice:** Radiation oncology **Affiliations:** A.S.T.R.O.; A.S.C.O.; R.S.N.A. **Hob./spts.:** Fishing, jogging, music, travel **SIC code:** 80 **Address:** M.D. Anderson Cancer Center, 1515 Holcombe Blvd., Houston, TX 77030 **E-mail:** joeyujiaochang@yahoo.com

CHANG, KAY W.
Industry: Medical **Born:** June 3, 1968, Bellflower, California **Univ./degree:** M.D., Brown University, 1992 **Current organization:** Stanford University **Title:** M.D. **Type of organization:** University **Major product:** Pediatric healthcare **Area of distribution:** International **Area of Practice:** Pediatric otolaryngology **Affiliations:** A.A.O.H.N.S.; A.S.P.O.; S.E.N.T.A.C.; C.O.G **Hob./spts.:** Salsa dancing, mountain biking **SIC code:** 80 **Address:** Stanford University, 801 Welch Rd., Stanford, CA 94305 **E-mail:** kaychang@yahoo.com **Web address:** www.med.stanford.edu/profiles/kay_chang

CHANG, VICTOR T.
Industry: Healthcare **Born:** November 28, 1956, New York, New York **Univ./degree:** M.D., New York University, 1983 **Current organization:** VA New Jersey Health Care System/UMDNJ **Title:** M.D. **Type of organization:** University hospital **Major product:** Hematology, oncology, palliative medicine **Area of distribution:** East Orange, New Jersey **Area of Practice:** Clinical research **Published works:** Published in a journal called Cancer **Affiliations:** American Society of Hematology; A.S.C.O.; A.P.S. **Hob./spts.:** History, music **SIC code:** 80 **Address:** VA New Jersey Health Care System/UMDNJ, 385 Tremont Ave., East Orange, NJ 07018 **E-mail:** chang.victor_t@east-orange.va.gov

CHAPA, HECTOR O.
Industry: Healthcare **Univ./degree:** M.D., Texas Southwestern University, 1996 **Current organization:** Woman's Specialty Center **Title:** M.D. **Type of organization:** Private practice **Major product:** Women's healthcare **Area of distribution:** Texas **Area of Practice:** Ob/Gyn, infertility **Affiliations:** A.M.A. **SIC code:** 80 **Address:** Woman's Specialty Center, 221 W. Colorado Blvd., #425, Dallas, TX 75208 **E-mail:** chapamd@aol.com

CHAPLES, SHARON (TAPLETT)
Industry: Healthcare **Born:** March 7, 1953, Sioux Falls, South Dakota **Univ./degree:** M.S. Business, City College/University of Seattle, 1981 **Current organization:** VA Hospital **Title:** Industrial Hygienist, R.P.I.H. **Type of organization:** Hospital **Major product:** Employee Occupational Health and Safety **Area of distribution:** National **Area of Practice:** Industrial Hygienist **Honors/awards:** Captain, Army Reserve, Meritorious Service Medal **Affiliations:** American Conference of Government Industrial Hygienists; Association of Professional Industrial Hygienists **Hob./spts.:** Golfing, woodworking, gardening **SIC code:** 80 **Address:** VA Hospital, 2501 W. 22nd St., Sioux Falls, SD 57105 **E-mail:** sharon.chaples@med.va.gov

CHARNLEY, KIM R.
Industry: Healthcare **Univ./degree:** B.S., Central Michigan University, 1980 **Current organization:** Davison Dental Laboratory, Inc. **Title:** President **Type of organization:** Dental laboratory **Major product:** Dentures, partials, crowns, cosmetic **Area of distribution:** National **Area of Practice:** 33 years dental technician experience **Affiliations:** N.A.D.L.; M.A.C.D.L.; M.B.A. **SIC code:** 80 **Address:** Davison Dental Laboratory, Inc., 6318 Taylor Dr., Flint, MI 48507 **E-mail:** laserlab2@hotmail.com

CHATTERJEE, SUBROTO B.
Industry: Medical **Univ./degree:** Ph.D., University of Toronto, 1972 **Current organization:** Johns Hopkins University School of Medicine **Title:** Professor/Director **Type of organization:** University hospital **Major product:** Patient care, medical education **Area of distribution:** International **Area of Practice:** Biology **Affiliations:** A.A.A.S. **SIC code:** 80 **Address:** Johns Hopkins University School of Medicine, 550 N. Broadway, Suite 312, Baltimore, MD 21205 **E-mail:** schatte2@jhmi.edu

CHECK, JEROME H.
Industry: Medical **Born:** May 11, 1946, Philadelphia, Pennsylvania **Univ./degree:** M.D., Ph.D., 1974 **Current organization:** Cooper Hospital, University Medical Center **Title:** M.D., Ph.D. **Type of organization:** University hospital **Major product:** Patient care, medical education **Area of distribution:** International **Area of Practice:** Reproductive endocrinology **Honors/awards:** 25 Year Achievement Award **Published works:** 450 articles **Affiliations:** S.A.R.T.; American Society of Reproductive Medicine **Hob./spts.:** Racquetball **SIC code:** 80 **Address:** Cooper Hospital, University Medical Center, 8002 E. Greentree Commons, Marlton, NJ 08053 **E-mail:** dcheck@op.net

CHEEMA, IMRAN Q.
Industry: Healthcare **Born:** October 1, 1968, Pakistan **Univ./degree:** M.D., Pakistan King Edward Medical College, 1993; M.P.H., University of Illinois, 1999 **Current organization:** Ellett Memorial Hospital **Title:** M.D./M.P.H. **Type of organization:** Hospital **Major product:** Patient care **Area of distribution:** Appleton City, Missouri **Area of Practice:** Internal medicine, occupational medicine **Affiliations:** A.C.P.; A.C.C.P.; American Thoracic Society; American Public Health Association; American College of Occupational & Environmental Health **Hob./spts.:** Fishing, football **SIC code:** 80 **Address:** Ellett Memorial Hospital, 610 N. Ohio St., Appleton City, MO 64724 **E-mail:** iqcheema@hotmail.com

CHEN, CLARENCE L.
Industry: Psychiatry **Born:** May 15, 1949, Chicago, Illinois **Univ./degree:** B.A., Oberlin College, 1970; M.S., Columbia University, 1974; M.D., Columbia University, 1978 **Current organization:** Gracie Square Hospital **Title:** Director of Dual Diagnosis Psychiatry **Type of organization:** Hospital **Major product:** Psychiatric treatment **Area of distribution:** New York, New York **Area of Practice:** Psychotherapy, psychoanalysis, psychopharmacology **Honors/awards:** Phi Beta Kappa, Sigma Xi (honorary science achievement society), graduation Magna Cum Laude with High Honors in Psychology from Oberlin College, 1970; Dean's Summer Research Fellowship, Columbia University College of Physicians and Surgeons, 1975; Resident Research Award, new York County American Psychiatric Association, 1980; Awarded Minority Fellowship in Psychiatry, National Institute of Mental Health, 1981; Honored Member, Strathmore's Who's Who 2001-2002; Certificate in Psychoanalysis, William Alanson White Institute, 2002; Named among "America's Psychiatrists" by the Consumer's Research Council of America, 2002 **Published works:** Chen. C.L., "The Need for Dual Diagnosis Treatment", The Recovery Link, Vol. 1. Issue 10, p. 14, 1995; Chen, C.L., "Culture Versus Biology", International Psychiatrists Forum, Vol. 3, Number 1, pp2-3, April, 1988; Chen, C.L. "A Look to Psychiatry's Past" (book review) Contemporary Psychiatry, Vol. 6, No. 1 pp. 32-34, March 1987; Chen, C.L. (contributing author) Self-Assessment of Current Knowledge in Psychiatry, fifth edition, Richard J. Frances, editor, Medical Examination Publishing Co., 1985 **Affiliations:** William A. White Psychoanalytic Institute Clinic; American Psychiatric Association **Hob./spts.:** Basketball, science fiction **SIC code:** 80 **Address:** Gracie Square Hospital, 420 E. 76th St., New York, NY 10021 **Phone:** (212)988-4400 **Fax:** (212)434-5373 **E-mail:** cchenmd@aol.com

CHEN, FRANKLIN
Industry: Healthcare **Born:** August 7, 1964, New York, New York **Univ./degree:** B.S., Magna Cum Laude, Neuroscience, Brown University, 1986; M.D., Johns Hopkins Medical School, 1990 **Current organization:** Edison-Metuchen Orthopedic Group **Title:** M.D. **Type of organization:** Group practice **Major product:** Patient care **Area of distribution:** New Jersey **Area of Practice:** Hand surgery **Honors/awards:** Sigma Xi Society Award, 1986, Honors with Distinction, 1986, Brown University; Physician's Recognition Award, American Medical Association, 2000 **Published works:** Numerous publications, including; Co-Author, "Key Techniques in Orthopaedic Surgery", New York, Thieme Medical and Scientific Publishers, 2001; "Scaphoid nonunion", Current Opinions in Orthopaedics, 7:24-30, 1996; "The operative treatment of peroneal nerve palsy", Bone & Joint Surg, 78-A:863-870, 1996 **Affiliations:** A.S.S.H.; A.A.O.S.; N.J.O.S. **SIC code:** 80 **Address:** Edison-Metuchen Orthopedic Group, 10 Parsonage Rd., Suite 500, Edison, NJ 08837

CHEN, LEI
Industry: Healthcare **Born:** November 1, 1962, Guangzhou, China **Current organization:** St. Mary's Women's Healthcare, P.C. **Title:** M.D. **Type of organization:** Medical practice **Major product:** Women's healthcare **Area of distribution:** St. Mary's Pennsylvania **Area of Practice:** Ob/Gyn **Affiliations:** A.C.O.G.; A.M.A.; A.A.G.L. **Hob./spts.:** Fishing, hunting **SIC code:** 80 **Address:** Saint Mary's Women's Healthcare, P.C., 761 Johnsonburg Rd., Suite 340, St. Marys, PA 15857

CHEN, TIAN DAVID
Industry: Healthcare **Born:** September 18, 1959, Hong Zhou, China **Univ./degree:** M.D., Zhetiang China Medical University, 1984; Ph.D., Michigan State University, 1990 **Current organization:** Henry Ford Hospital **Title:** Systems Administrator **Type of organization:** Hospital **Major product:** Patient care **Area of distribution:** Michigan **Area of Practice:** Bioinformatics **Published works:** Journals **Affiliations:** A.C.P.A.; N.B.I. **Hob./spts.:** Coin collecting, golf, fishing **SIC code:** 80 **Address:**

Henry Ford Hospital, Pathology Dept., 2799 W. Grand Blvd., Detroit, MI 48202 **E-mail:** dchen1@hfhs.org

CHERUKURI, VIJAYA L.
Industry: Healthcare **Born:** June 1, 1965, Vijayawada, India **Univ./degree:** M.D., Long Island College Hospital, 1998 **Current organization:** Premier Healthcare **Title:** M.D., President **Type of organization:** Healthcare **Major product:** Patient care **Area of distribution:** Florida **Area of Practice:** Internal medicine, geriatrics **Affiliations:** A.M.A. **Hob./spts.:** Physical fitness, surfing the Internet, stock market **SIC code:** 80 **Address:** Premier Health Care, 218 Pasadena Ave. South, Suite 2C, St. Petersburg, FL 33707 **E-mail:** jayache2@aol.com

CHESIN, CAROLE M.
Industry: Healthcare **Univ./degree:** B.S., Education, Slippery Rock University, Pennsylvania, 1972; M.D., University of Pennsylvania, 1978 **Current organization:** Magee Women Care Associates of UPMC **Title:** M.D. **Type of organization:** Private medical practice **Major product:** Women's healthcare **Area of distribution:** Pennsylvania **Area of Practice:** Ob/Gyn **Affiliations:** A.M.A.; Pennsylvania Medical Society; American Board of Obstetrics and Gynecology **SIC code:** 80 **Address:** Magee Women Care Associates of UPMC, 9104 Babcock Blvd., Suite 6107, Pittsburgh, PA 15237 **E-mail:** mendhimon@aol.com

CHETTA, SERENA A.
Industry: Healthcare **Univ./degree:** M.S., Nursing, Hunter College, New York, 1975 **Current organization:** VITAS Healthcare Corp. **Title:** Patient Care Administrator **Type of organization:** Hospice **Major product:** Patient care **Area of distribution:** National **Area of Practice:** Nursing administration **Affiliations:** Board Certified, Nursing Administrator; Naval Reserve Association; Sigma Theta Tau; Nurse Corps Naval Reserve, Rank Commander **SIC code:** 80 **Address:** VITAS Healthcare Corp., 12515 N. Kendall Dr., Miramar, FL 33186 **E-mail:** serena.chetta@vitas.com

CHIAPCO, OLIVER ROCES
Industry: Healthcare **Born:** September 6, 1969, Manila, Philippines **Univ./degree:** M.D., De La Salle University College of Medicine, Philippines, 1994 **Current organization:** Medical Specialists **Title:** M.D. **Type of organization:** Private practice **Major product:** Children's healthcare **Area of distribution:** St. Augustine, Florida **Area of Practice:** Pediatrics **Published works:** Malignant Large Cell Lymphoma presenting as Musculoskeletal Syndrome, International Pediatrics, Volume 16, No. 1 **Affiliations:** A.M.A.; A.A.P. **Hob./spts.:** Guitar, martial arts **SIC code:** 80 **Address:** Medical Specialists, 240 S. Park Circle East, St. Augustine, FL 32086 **E-mail:** ochiapco@juno.com

CHIN, JEAN M.
Industry: Healthcare **Born:** October 5, 1950, Kingston, Jamaica **Children:** Kerrie, 25; Germane, 20 **Univ./degree:** M.D., Columbia University, 1976 **Current organization:** Jean M. Chin, M.D. **Title:** M.D. **Type of organization:** Private practice **Major product:** Gynecology **Area of distribution:** New York, New York **Area of practice:** Menopause **Area of Practice:** Menopause **Affiliations:** Fellow, American College of Obstetricians and Gynecologists; New York State Medical Society; Alpha Omega Alpha **SIC code:** 80 **Address:** Jean M. Chin, M.D., 785 Park Ave., New York, NY 10021

CHINTAPALLI, HARISH C.
Industry: Healthcare **Born:** October 14, 1970, Guntur, India **Univ./degree:** D.O., University of North Texas Health Science Center, 1997 **Current organization:** University of Texas Health Science Center, San Antonio **Title:** Neroradiology Fellow **Type of organization:** Hospital **Major product:** Diagnostic imaging **Area of distribution:** Texas **Area of Practice:** Neuroradiology **Honors/awards:** Chief Resident, 2001-02; Outstanding College Students of America 1992; Outstanding High School Students of America, 1988 **Published works:** Papers, scientific enhibits **Affiliations:** A.M.A.; T.M.A.; A.O.A.; T.O.M.A.; A.C.R.; A.O.C.R. **Hob./spts.:** Sports, movies, music **SIC code:** 80 **Address:** 5600 Babcock Rd., Apt. 3205, San Antonio, TX 78240 **E-mail:** dochcc21@sbcglobal.net

CHIU, YANEK S.Y.
Industry: Healthcare **Born:** June 29, 1945, Hong Kong **Univ./degree:** M.D., Boston University, 1971 **Title:** M.D. **Type of organization:** Private practice **Major product:** Patient care **Area of distribution:** National **Area of Practice:** Colon and rectal surgery **Published works:** Multiple book chapters **Affiliations:** F.A.C.S.; V.P., A.S.C.R.S. **Hob./spts.:** Music **SIC code:** 80 **Address:** 3838 California St., Suite 616, San Francisco, CA 94118 **E-mail:** sfsurgical@aol.com

CHOATE-HEFLIN, PATRICIA L.
Industry: Healthcare **Univ./degree:** B.S., Austin Peay State University, Clarksville, Tennessee, 1977; A.S., Nashville State Technical Institute, Nashville, Tennessee, 1979 **Current organization:** Dept. of Pathology, Blanchfield Army Community Hospital **Title:** Chemistry Supervisor **Type of organization:** Army hospital **Major product:** Patient care **Area of distribution:** Kentucky **Area of Practice:** Chemistry, Urinalysis **Honors/awards:** Civilian Employee of the Year Professional Category Post Level **Affiliations:** A.S.C.L.S., Cap Inspector **Hob./spts.:** Gardening **SIC code:** 80 **Address:** Dept. of Pathology, Blanchfield Army Community Hospital, 650 Joel Dr., Ft. Campbell, KY 42223-5349 **E-mail:** patricia.choate-heflin@se.amedd.army.mil

CHOUFANI, ELIE
Industry: Healthcare **Born:** February 5, 1962, Beirut, Lebanon **Univ./degree:** M.D., St. Joseph University Medical School, 1989 **Current organization:** Parker Hill Oncology-Hematology **Title:** M.D. **Type of organization:** Private medical practice **Major product:** Patient care **Area of distribution:** East coast **Area of Practice:** Internal medicine, cancer care, blood diseases, metabolic diseases, bone marrow transplantation **Affiliations:** Massachusetts Medical Society; American Society of Clinical Oncology; American Society of Hematology **Hob./spts.:** Tennis, basketball **SIC code:** 80 **Address:** 2000 Commonwealth Ave., #708, Brighton, MA 02135 **E-mail:** echoufani@pol.net

CHOWHAN, ANIKA
Industry: Healthcare **Born:** January 6, 1970, Pakistan **Univ./degree:** M.D., Baylor College, 1996 **Current organization:** Old Towne Pediatrics **Title:** M.D. **Type of organization:** Private practice **Major product:** Child health services **Area of distribution:** Manassas, Virginia **Area of Practice:** Pediatrics **Affiliations:** A.A.P.; V.M.S. **Hob./spts.:** Foreign films, hiking, multi languages **SIC code:** 80 **Address:** Olde Towne Pediatrics, 9324 West St., Suite 101, Manassas, VA 20110 **E-mail:** anikachowhan@comcast.net **Web address:** www.oldetownepeds.com

CHOY, EUGENE
Industry: Healthcare **Born:** January 28, 1939, Isleton, California **Univ./degree:** B.S., Pre-Dental, University of Nevada, Reno, 1960; D.D.S., Northwestern University School of Dentistry, 1963; M.S.D., University of Washington School of Dentistry, 1976; Residency in Maxillofacial Prosthetics, University of Alabama at Birmingham **Current organization:** Eugene Choy, DDS, MSD **Title:** Master of Dentistry **Type of organization:** Private practice **Major product:** Prosthodontics - removeable **Area of distribution:** Puyallup, Washington **Area of Practice:** Cosmetic dentistry, dentures, implants, general dentistry **Published works:** 5+ articles **Affiliations:** Fellow, American Academy of Maxillofacial Prosthetics; Fellow, Pacific Coast Society of Prosthodontists; Pierre Fouchard Academy **Hob./spts.:** Reading, follows his Alma Mater sports teams, travel, photogrpahy, gardening **SIC code:** 80 **Address:** Eugene Choy, DDS, MSD, 1410 Meridian South, Suite B, Puyallup, WA 98371

CHRISTIAENS, PHYLLIS CHARLENE
Industry: Healthcare **Born:** August 23, 1954, Conrad, Montana **Univ./degree:** M.N., Montana State University, 1991 **Current organization:** Benefis Healthcare **Title:** Clinical Standards Coordinator **Type of organization:** Hospital **Major product:** Patient care **Area of distribution:** Montana **Area of Practice:** Clinical Nurse Specialist; Med-surg, pain management, diabetes **Affiliations:** A.A.D.E.; Pain Management Society; Intravenous Nurses Society **Hob./spts.:** Crafts, reading **SIC code:** 80 **Address:** Benefis Healthcare, 1101 26th St. South, Great Falls, MT 59401 **E-mail:** chriphyc@benefis.org

CHRUSZ, MARK E.
Industry: Healthcare **Born:** January 28, 1952, Cambridge, Massachusetts **Univ./degree:** D.D.S., Loyola Medical College, 1980 **Current organization:** Dr. Mark E. Chrusz **Title:** D.D.S. **Type of organization:** Private practice **Major product:** Dental care **Area of distribution:** Rochester, New Hampshire **Area of Practice:** General sports dentistry **Affiliations:** F.I.A.S.D.; F.A.G.D.; A.D.A. **Hob./spts.:** Marathon running, triathlons **SIC code:** 80 **Address:** Dr. Mark E. Chrusz, 23 Meadowbrook Village, Rochester, NH 03867 **E-mail:** mectrimk@aol.com

CHUTANI, SURENDRA K.
Industry: Medical **Born:** June 3, 1953, India **Univ./degree:** M.D., D.M., Institute of Medical Education and Research, 1986 **Current organization:** Brookdale University Medical Center and Hospital **Title:** D.M. **Type of organization:** University hospital **Major product:** Medical services **Area of distribution:** Brooklyn, New York **Area of Practice:** Cardiology **Published works:** 40+ articles **Affiliations:** A.M.A.; American Heart Association; Cardiology Society of India; American College of Physicians **Hob./spts.:** Lecturing, debating **SIC code:** 80 **Address:** 660 E. 98th St., Apt 11E, Brooklyn, NY 11236 **E-mail:** chutanisk1@rediffmail.com

CHYU, AUGUSTIN I.
Industry: Healthcare **Born:** January 18, 1925, Seoul, Korea **Univ./degree:** M.D., Seoul National University College of Medicine, 1950 **Current organization:** Maryland State Medical Society **Title:** M.D., M.P.H., Dr.Med.Sci. **Type of organization:** Veterans Affairs Hospital **Major product:** Patient care **Area of distribution:** Maryland **Area of Practice:** Internal medicine **Honors/awards:** Emeritus Member, Med Chi **Published works:** Korean Journal of Medicine; books, "My Journey Around the World", 1992; "Seventy Years of Upheavals", 1995; "Medical Parasitology", 1967, second edition, 1969 **Affiliations:** Member, Med Chi; Academic Dean, Catholic Medical College

Hob./spts.: Golf **SIC code:** 80 **Address:** 5812 Wyndham Circle, #205, Columbia, MD 21044 **E-mail:** aichyu@aol.com

CIOCCA, ROCCO G.
Industry: Medical **Born:** April 12, 1960, Utica, New York **Univ./degree:** B.S., Biochemistry, Bowdoin College, 1982; M.D., New York University, 1986 **Current organization:** Robert Woods Johnson Medical School **Title:** M.D. **Type of organization:** University hospital **Major product:** Patient care, medical education **Area of distribution:** New Jersey **Area of Practice:** Vascular surgery **Published works:** 30+articles, book chapters **Affiliations:** F.A.C.S., American Association of Vascular Surgeons **SIC code:** 80 **Address:** Robert Woods Johnson Medical School, Dept. of Vascular Surgery, 1 Robert Wood Johnson Place, MEB541, New Brunswick, NJ 08901

CIRESI, KEVIN F.
Industry: Healthcare **Univ./degree:** M.D., University of Minnesota, 1986 **Current organization:** Kevin F. Ciresi, M.D. **Title:** M.D. **Type of organization:** Private practice **Major product:** Patient care **Area of distribution:** San Ramon, California **Area of Practice:** Plastic, cosmetic and reconstructive surgery **Affiliations:** F.A.C.S.; F.I.C.S.; A.S.P.S.; A.B.P.S. **SIC code:** 80 **Address:** Kevin F. Ciresi, MD, 5201 Norris Canyon Rd., Suite 110, San Ramon, CA 94583 **E-mail:** abito@drciresi.com **Web address:** www.drciresi.com

CLAAR, MARLENE G.
Industry: Healthcare **Born:** Sturgis, Michigan **Univ./degree:** A.A. and A.B., Glen Oak Community College, 1981; A.D.N., Kellogg College, 1987; B.S.N., Western Michigan University, 2003 **Current organization:** Three Rivers Health **Title:** R.N., Patient Safety Officer/Director of Safety **Type of organization:** Hospital **Major product:** Medical services **Area of distribution:** Three Rivers, Michigan **Area of Practice:** Safety **Affiliations:** Michigan Nurses Association; Michigan Organization of Nurse Executives; American Organization of Nurse Executives; 5th District Medical Response Coalition of Michigan; Michigan Health & Safety Coalition; Lillian Wald Nursing Honor Society **Hob./spts.:** Photography, playing the violin **SIC code:** 80 **Address:** Three Rivers Health, 701 S. Health Pkwy., Three Rivers, MI 49093 **E-mail:** mclaar@threerivershealth.org **Web address:** www.threerivershealth.org

CLAIRMONT, GEORGE J.
Industry: Healthcare **Born:** July 26, 1954 **Univ./degree:** M.D., Tufts University School of Medicine, 1982 **Current organization:** Compass Medical, P.C. **Title:** President **Type of organization:** Medical corporation/multispecialty practice **Major product:** Primary/multispecialty care **Area of distribution:** Brockton, Massachusetts **Area of Practice:** Primary care medicine **Honors/awards:** Nesson Award for Innovation in Diabetes Research, 2001 **Affiliations:** Massachusetts Medical Society; American Medical Association; Partner Health Care System; Medical Group Management Association; Trustee, Partners Community Health Care **Hob./spts.:** Travel, skiing **SIC code:** 80 **Address:** Compass Medical, P.C., 500 Belmont St., Suite 150, Brockton, MA 02301 **E-mail:** gclairmont@pchi.partners.org

CLAPHAN, CHERYL J.
Industry: Healthcare **Born:** November 7, 1954, Great Bend, Kansas **Univ./degree:** A.A.S., Radiology, Hutchinson Community College, Kansas, 1988; Graduate of the MRI Certificate Program at St. Francis Regional Medical Center, Kansas, 1988 **Current organization:** Bon Secour Venice Hospital **Title:** Supervisor MRI **Type of organization:** Hospital **Major product:** Patient care/medical testing **Area of distribution:** Venice, Florida **Area of Practice:** Administration and operations, staffing, troubleshooting **Affiliations:** A.R.R.T.; Kansas MRI Society **Hob./spts.:** Reading, golf, swimming **SIC code:** 80 **Address:** Bon Secour Venice Hospital, 540 The Rialto, Venice, FL 34285 **E-mail:** mque8947@aol.com

CLARK, JAY D.
Industry: Healthcare **Born:** July 17, 1946, Los Angeles, California **Univ./degree:** M.D., Autonomous University of Guadalajara, Mexico, 1974 **Current organization:** Cataract & Lasik Center of Utah **Title:** M.D. **Type of organization:** Ophthalmic ambulatory surgical center **Major product:** Patient care **Area of distribution:** Utah **Area of Practice:** Cataract and laser vision surgery **Honors/awards:** First Medicare Certified Ophthalmic Ambulatory Surgical Center in Utah **Affiliations:** American Academy of Ophthamology; International Society of Refractive Surgery **Hob./spts.:** Scuba diving, opera **SIC code:** 80 **Address:** Cataract & Lasik Center of Utah, 175 N. 400 West, Orem, UT 84057 **E-mail:** lasikjay@earthlink.net

CLARK, ROBERT W.
Industry: Healthcare **Born:** June 17, 1951, Sharon, Pennsylvania **Univ./degree:** R.N., St. Elizabeth Hospital Medical Center School of Nursing, 1992 **Current organization:** Trumbull Memorial Hospital - Forum Health **Title:** R.N. **Type of organization:** Hospital **Major product:** Acute care **Area of distribution:** Warren, Ohio **Area of Practice:** Behavioral health **Published works:** Poetry and short stories **Hob./spts.:** NASCAR, sporting activities, writing poetry and short stories, reading **SIC code:** 80 **Address:** Trumbull Memorial Hospital - Forum Health, 1350 E. Market St., Warren, OH 44482 **E-mail:** jc8bc@yahoo.com

CLARKE, KAREN A.
Industry: Healthcare **Born:** January 21, 1969, Freeport, Bahamas **Univ./degree:** M.D., New York Medical College, 1996 **Current organization:** Catskill Regional Medical Center **Title:** Physician **Type of organization:** Hospital **Major product:** Patient care **Area of distribution:** Harris, New York **Area of Practice:** Internal medicine **Published works:** Article **Affiliations:** A.C.P.-A.I.S.M. **Hob./spts.:** Travel **SIC code:** 80 **Address:** Catskill Regional Medical Center, 68 Harris Rd., Harris, NY 12742-5030

CLAYCOMB, STEPHEN H.
Industry: Healthcare **Born:** October 4, 1961, Pine Bluff, Arkansas **Univ./degree:** M.D., University of Arkansas **Current organization:** Middle Tennessee Pediatrics & Adolescent Medicine, PC **Title:** M.D., President **Type of organization:** Pediatric health care practice **Major product:** Patient care **Area of distribution:** Lebanon, Tennessee **Area of Practice:** Pediatrics **Published works:** 1 article **Affiliations:** A.M.A; A.A.P; T.M.A **Hob./spts.:** Swimming and coaching swimming **SIC code:** 80 **Address:** Middle Tennessee Pediatrics and Adolescent Medicine, PC, 1405 Baddour Pkwy., Suite 101, Lebanon, TN 37087 **E-mail:** shclaycomb@msn.com

CLEMENS, CHARLENE K.
Industry: Healthcare **Born:** April 9, 1947, Potsdam, Pennsylvania **Current organization:** Maine Coast Memorial Hospital/Breast Clinic **Title:** Supervisor of Breast Clinic/RTRM **Type of organization:** Hospital/clinic **Major product:** Patient care, information center about mammography and breast disease **Area of distribution:** Maine **Area of Practice:** Certified, radiology and mammography **Affiliations:** A.S.R.T.; S.M.R.T. **Hob./spts.:** Snow mobiling, breeding and raising boxers **SIC code:** 80 **Address:** Maine Coast Memorial Hospital, Breast Clinic, 50 Union St., Ellsworth, ME 04609

CLEMENTS, TRICIA C.
Industry: Healthcare **Born:** June 23, 1958, Illinois **Univ./degree:** RT(R), Henry Ford Hospital, Detroit, 1990 **Current organization:** Desert Springs Hospital **Title:** Mammography Coordinator **Type of organization:** Hospital **Major product:** Patient care **Area of distribution:** Nevada **Area of Practice:** Certified Radiologist; mammography and trauma, program management and protocol **Honors/awards:** Radio Commercial Writing Award, 1971 **Published works:** Article **Affiliations:** A.R.R.T.; A.S.R.T.; Hospital Service Excellence Committee; Senior Dimensions Program Educator **Hob./spts.:** Scuba diving, reading, travel **SIC code:** 80 **Address:** Desert Springs Hospital, 2075 E. Flamingo Rd., Las Vegas, NV 89119 **E-mail:** tricia.clements@uhsinc.com

COHEN, CHARMIAN D.
Industry: Healthcare **Born:** Capetown, South Africa **Univ./degree:** M.D., University of Capetown, 1977 **Current organization:** Charmian D. Cohen, M.D. **Title:** M.D. **Type of organization:** Private practice **Major product:** Patient care **Area of distribution:** Bronx, New York **Area of Practice:** Diabetes specialist **Affiliations:** F.A.C.P.; A.D.A.; F.A.C.E.; Medical Society State of New York **Hob./spts.:** Tennis **SIC code:** 80 **Address:** Charmian D. Cohen, M.D., 1200 Waters Place, Suite M105, Bronx, NY 10461

COLAIANNIA, LOUIS M.
Industry: Healthcare **Univ./degree:** D.D.S., University of Colorado, 1980 **Current organization:** Mountain Home Health Care, Inc. **Title:** D.D.S. **Type of organization:** Private practices **Major product:** Home health services **Area of distribution:** Lakewood, Colorado **Area of Practice:** Dentistry **Hob./spts.:** Music composer **SIC code:** 80 **Address:** Mountain Home Health Care, Inc., 1300 Carr St., Lakewood, CO 80214 **E-mail:** drlou@concentric.net

COLAIUTA, ELIZABETH A.
Industry: Medical **Born:** August 7, 1959, Wilmington, Delaware **Univ./degree:** M.D., American University of the Caribbean, 1991 **Current organization:** St. Clair Vascular Associates, P.C. **Title:** M.D. **Type of organization:** Medical practice **Major product:** Patient care **Area of distribution:** Mount Clemens, Michigan **Area of Practice:** Vascular surgery **Honors/awards:** Jack Pheiffer Award **Published works:** Journal of Cardio-Thoracic Surgery **Affiliations:** A.M.A.; Detroit Academy of Surgery; Detroit Surgical Association; Michigan Vascular Society **Hob./spts.:** Equestrian **SIC code:** 80 **Address:** St. Clair Vascular Associates, P.C., 1030 Harrington, Suite 103, Mount Clemens, MI 48043 **E-mail:** colaiutae@stclairvascular.com

COLCOLOUGH, HARRY L.
Industry: Healthcare **Born:** July 21, 1937, Charleston, South Carolina **Univ./degree:** B.S., Biology, Loyola University, 1960; M.D., Tulane University, 1963 **Current organization:** Methodist Primary Care Associates **Title:** M.D., Director **Type of organization:** Primary care **Major product:** Patient care, medical missionary work **Area of distribution:** New Orleans, Louisiana **Area of Practice:** Internal medicine **Published works:** 30 publications **Affiliations:** Fellow, American College of Physicians; American Medical Association; Louisiana State Medical Society; Orleans Parish

Medical Society; American Academy of General Physicians; Academy International Medical Studies; Catholic Medical Assoc. **Hob./spts.:** Automobile mechanics, family, travel, medical missionary services **SIC code:** 80 **Address:** Methodist Primary Care Associates, 5646 Read Blvd., #317, New Orleans, LA 70127 **E-mail:** cetro98@aol.com

COLE, ARTHUR NEIL
Industry: Healthcare **Univ./degree:** M.D., Howard University, 1981 **Current organization:** Arthur Neil Cole, M.D., Inc. **Title:** M.D., F.A.C.S. **Type of organization:** Private practice **Major product:** Patient care **Area of distribution:** Ohio **Area of Practice:** Neurosurgery **Affiliations:** F.A.C.S.; A.A.N.S.; N.A.S.S.; A.M.A.; Ohio Medical Association **SIC code:** 80 **Address:** Arthur Neil Cole, M.D., Inc., 2200 N. Limestone St., Suite 100, Springfield, OH 45503

COLE, DONAS H.
Industry: Healthcare **Born:** August 21, 1968, Sherman, Texas **Univ./degree:** B.A., Business Administration, Texas A&M University, 2001 **Current organization:** North Central Medical Center - Senior Health Center **Title:** Operations Director **Type of organization:** Hospital **Major product:** Senior health **Area of distribution:** Texas **Area of Practice:** Management **Honors/awards:** N.R.C.C. Award, 2002 **Affiliations:** Alpha Chi, Alpha Sigma Lambda National Honorary Society **SIC code:** 80 **Address:** 1212 Cedar Rd., Sherman, TX 75090 **E-mail:** cdonas@hotmail.com

COLE, JAMES K.
Industry: Healthcare **Born:** November 12, 1962, Bristol, Tennessee **Univ./degree:** B.E., Electrical Engineering, Vanderbilt University, 1989; M.D., East Tennessee University, College of Medicine, 1994 **Current organization:** Midwest Orthopedic Surgery **Title:** M.D. **Type of organization:** Medical practice **Major product:** Patient care **Area of distribution:** Missouri **Area of Practice:** Spinal surgery **Honors/awards:** Thomas G. Arnold Prize: Biomedical Research, Vanderbuilt University, 1989; Tau Beta Pi: Engineering, University of Tennessee, 1988; Phi Eta Sigma: Engineering, University of Tennessee, 1984 **Published works:** Book Chapters; Co-author, Focal Mercury Toxicity. J Hand Surg (AM), 1994 July, 19(4):602-3; Radiographic Analysis of Femoral Tunnel Position in Anterior Criciate Ligament Reconstruction. American Journal of Knee Surgery 2000, 13. No. 4: 218-222 **Affiliations:** A.M.A.; A.A.C.O.P.; M.S.M.O. **Hob./spts.:** Computer programming, wood working, bike racing **SIC code:** 80 **Address:** Midwest Orthopedic Surgery, 3105 McClelland Blvd., Joplin, MO 64804 **Web address:** www.moidocs.com

COLE, PAMELA L.
Industry: Healthcare **Born:** October 19, 1958, Chicago, Illinois **Univ./degree:** R.T., Cook County Hospital, 1982 **Current organization:** LaGrange Hospital **Title:** R.T. (R) (M) (C.T.) **Type of organization:** Hospital **Major product:** Radiological technology science, X-rays **Area of distribution:** LaGrange, Illinois/Chicago, Illinois/Northwest Indiana **Area of Practice:** Mammography, Computer Technology, Sonography **Hob./spts.:** Knitting, crocheting, reading **SIC code:** 80 **Address:** LaGrange Hospital, 5101 Willowspring Rd., LaGrange, IL 60525

COLE, SOLON R.
Industry: Medical **Born:** September 18, 1937, McComb, Mississippi **Univ./degree:** M.D., Tulane University, 1962; Internship, St. Vincent's Hospital; Residency, Boston City Hospital; Fellow, Harvard University **Current organization:** University of Connecticut Medical School **Title:** M.D./Professor/Legal Consultant **Type of organization:** University **Major product:** Patient care, medical education **Area of distribution:** International **Area of practice:** Pathology, occupational lung disease, legal work, court testimony **Area of Practice:** Pathology, occupational lung disease, legal work, court testimony **Honors/awards:** Guide to 'Top Doctors in America', 2001 & 2002; Top Legal Testimony Doctor in America; England, Top History Authority; Received the International Scientist of the Year Award from the International Medical Society, 2004 **Published works:** 100+ articles, 5 books (pathology), 4 history books **Affiliations:** F.I.A.P.; F.C.A.P. **Hob./spts.:** Gardening, history writing **SIC code:** 80 **Address:** The Bushnell Tower, 1 Gold St., Suite 23E, Hartford, CT 06103 **E-mail:** solonc@snet.net

COLEMAN, ANNE LOUISE
Industry: Medical **Born:** Richmond, Virginia **Univ./degree:** M.D., Medical College of Virginia, 1984; Ph.D., UCLA, 1997 **Current organization:** Jules Stein Eye Institute **Title:** M.D., Ph.D. **Type of organization:** University **Major product:** Eye care **Area of distribution:** International **Area of Practice:** Ophthalmology **Honors/awards:** A.O.A., Honor Award **Affiliations:** A.G.S.; A.A.O. **Hob./spts.:** Hiking **SIC code:** 80 **Address:** Jules Stein Eye Institute, 100 Stein Plaza 2-118, Los Angeles, CA 90095 **E-mail:** colemana@ucla.edu

COLLINS, PATRICIA L.
Industry: Healthcare **Born:** December 14, 1954, Denison, Iowa **Univ./degree:** A.A., Nursing, Marshall Town Community College **Current organization:** Mercy Medical Center **Title:** R.N. **Type of organization:** Hospital **Major product:** Patient care **Area of distribution:** Iowa **Area of Practice:** Critical care nursing/education **Hob./spts.:** Crochet, stained glass, entrepreneur (candle business) **SIC code:** 80 **Address:** 1858 105th St., Union, IA 50258 **E-mail:** collins@netins.net

COLLINS, SHIRLEY A.
Industry: Healthcare **Born:** July 9, 1948, Cameron, Texas **Univ./degree:** MSN, University of Oklahoma, 1987 **Current organization:** Central Texas Veterans Health Care System **Title:** Nurse Recruiter **Type of organization:** Federal hospital **Major product:** Patient care **Area of distribution:** National **Area of Practice:** Recruiting **Affiliations:** Sigma Theta Tau, V.A.N.R.A., A.N.A., A.N.H.C.R **Hob./spts.:** Gardening **SIC code:** 80 **Address:** Central Texas Veterans Health Care System, 1901 Veterans Memorial Dr., Temple, TX 76504 **E-mail:** shirley.collins@med.va.gov

COLÓN, MARIBEL GARCÍA
Industry: Healthcare **Born:** January 16, 1966, San Juan, Puerto Rico **Univ./degree:** M.D., University of Puerto Rico **Current organization:** San Jorge Medical Specialties **Title:** M.D. **Type of organization:** Medical practice **Major product:** Patient care **Area of distribution:** San Juan, Puerto Rico **Area of Practice:** Pediatric hematology and oncology **Affiliations:** A.A.P.; A.A.P., Puerto Rico Chapter; Puerto Rico Hematology Society **Hob./spts.:** Has a radio program of Catholic music, working with choirs and youth groups **SIC code:** 80 **Address:** San Jorge Medical Specialties, 258 San Jorge St., Suite 504, San Juan, PR 00912 **E-mail:** mgarcia@coqui.net

COLON-MOLERO, ANGEL L.
Industry: Healthcare **Born:** June 13, 1961, Rio Piedras, Puerto Rico **Univ./degree:** M.D., Universidad Católica Madre y Maestra,1986 **Current organization:** Dept. of Veterans **Title:** M.D. Internal Medicine, Diving & Hyperbaric Medicine **Type of organization:** Hospital/clinic **Major product:** Patient care; Patient and Family Educator **Area of distribution:** San Juan, Puerto Rico **Area of Practice:** Internal medicine, diving and hyperbaric medicine, diving instruction for the handicapped **Published works:** 2 publications **Affiliations:** American College of Physicians; Professional Association of Diving Instructors (PADI); Undersea & Hyperbaric Medicine Society; Center of Excellence for Women's Health, University of Puerto Rico; Instructor, Medical Science Campus, University of Puerto Rico; Puerto Rico College of Physicians; Handicapped Scuba Association; United States Power Sqaudron **Hob./spts.:** Diving, boating, shooting **SIC code:** 80 **Address:** Torricllas G12, Colinas, Metropolitanos, Guaynabo, PR 00969 **E-mail:** colon_molero@hotmail.com

COLUCCI, RANDALL A.
Industry: Healthcare **Univ./degree:** D.O., Ohio University School of Osteopathic Medicine, 1998; M.P.H., Environmental Toxicology, University of South Florida; M.S., Medical Biology, Long Island University - C.W. Post Campus **Current organization:** Ohio Health **Title:** Physician **Type of organization:** Private practice **Major product:** Patient care **Area of distribution:** Ohio **Area of Practice:** Family medicine **Published works:** 6+ articles **Affiliations:** A.O.A.; A.M.A.; A.C.P.M. **SIC code:** 80 **Address:** Ohio Health, 2030 Stringtown Rd., Grove City, OH 43123 **E-mail:** rcolucci@columbus.rr.com

COMPTON, AUDREY
Industry: Healthcare **Born:** May 24, 1953, Fort Benning, Georgia **Univ./degree:** M.D., Tufts University **Current organization:** Holy Name Hospital **Title:** M.D. **Type of organization:** Hospital **Major product:** Patient care **Area of distribution:** New Jersey **Area of Practice:** Director of Outcomes Management **Affiliations:** A.M.A.; A.A.M.E.P. **Hob./spts.:** Church, running, sports **SIC code:** 80 **Address:** Holy Name Hospital, 718 Teaneck Rd., Teaneck, NJ 07666 **E-mail:** ccm2@eudoramail.com

CONFIDENT, LUDNER
Industry: Healthcare **Born:** March 24, 1949, Haiti **Univ./degree:** M.D., Faculte de Medecine et de Pharmaci d'Haiti, 1973 **Current organization:** Bayfront Anesthesia Services **Title:** M.D. **Type of organization:** Medical services **Major product:** Anesthesia for surgical services **Area of distribution:** Florida **Area of Practice:** Anesthesiology **Affiliations:** A.S.A.; F.S.A. **Hob./spts.:** Visual art, tennis, golf, swimming, soccer **SIC code:** 80 **Address:** 1416 72nd Ave. N.E., St. Petersburg, FL 33702 **E-mail:** lconfident@aol.com

CONLEY, ELIZABETH J.
Industry: Healthcare **Born:** September 2, 1947, Monett, Missouri **Univ./degree:** D.O., Kirksville College of Osteopathic Medicine, 1979 **Current organization:** Correctional Medical Services **Title:** D.O. **Type of organization:** Corporation **Major product:** Correctional medical services **Area of distribution:** National **Area of Practice:** Family medicine **Honors/awards:** Medical Director of the Year 2000 **Affiliations:** American Osteopathic College of Family Physicians; American Association of Osteopathic Physicians **SIC code:** 80 **Address:** Correctional Medical Services, 3702 W. Truman Blvd., Suite 104, Jefferson City, MO 65109 **E-mail:** econley@spectrumhealth.com

CONROW, CRAIG
Industry: Healthcare **Born:** March 7, 1964 **Univ./degree:** D.D.S., University of Pacific, 1990 **Current organization:** Craig Conrow, DDS **Title:** Board Certified

Prosthodontist **Type of organization:** Private practice **Major product:** Dentistry **Area of distribution:** Palm Desert, California **Area of Practice:** Cosmetic, restorative and implant dentistry **Affiliations:** A.O.I.; F.A.C.P.; A.A.C.D.; C.D.A. **Hob./spts.:** Water skiing **SIC code:** 80 **Address:** Craig Conrow, DDS, 73993 Hwy. 111, Suite 200, Palm Desert, CA 92260 **E-mail:** craigconrowdds@earthlink.net **Web address:** www.palmdesertdentist.com

CONSTANTINOU, CHRISTODOULOS
Industry: Healthcare **Born:** November 1, 1943, Nicosia, Cyprus **Univ./degree:** PhD, Medical Physics, London University, 1978 **Current organization:** B.O. Cyprus Oncology Center & CNC **Title:** Ph.D./DABR/DABMP/Director of Medical Physics Dept. **Type of organization:** Hospital **Major product:** Radiation physics services, design and production of tissue equivalent materials **Area of distribution:** National **Area of Practice:** Applications of physics in medicine **Published works:** British Journal of Radiology, Medical Physics Journal, Protocol & Procedures for Quality Assurance of Linear Acceleration **Affiliations:** A.C.M.P.; B.S.R.; American Association of Physicists in Medicine **Hob./spts.:** Swimming, music **SIC code:** 80 **Address:** Faculty, Harvard University, School of Medicine, 2 Woodledge Lane, North Easton, MA 02356 **E-mail:** chris.constantinou@bococ.org

COOK, DONALD E.
Industry: Healthcare **Born:** March 24, 1928, Pittsburgh, Pennsylvania **Univ./degree:** B.A., Chemistry, Colorado College, 1952; M.D., University of Colorado, 1955 **Current organization:** Monfort Children's Clinic **Title:** M.D./Founder/Owner **Type of organization:** Community health center **Major product:** Pediatric care **Area of distribution:** Greeley, Colorado **Area of Practice:** Primary pediatric care **Affiliations:** American Academy of Pediatrics **Hob./spts.:** Family - spending time with his children and grandchildren, fishing, hunting, gardening, music **SIC code:** 80 **Address:** Monfort Children's Clinic, 100 N. Eleventh Ave., Greeley, CO 80631 **E-mail:** dcook@aap.org

COOK, PATRICA SMITH
Industry: Healthcare **Born:** New Orleans, Louisiana **Univ./degree:** M.D., Louisiana State University, 1960 **Current organization:** Patricia Smith Cook, M.D., A.P.M.C. **Title:** M.D. **Type of organization:** Private practice **Major product:** Patient care **Area of distribution:** National **Area of Practice:** Neurology **Affiliations:** A.M.A.; American Academy of Neurology; American Epilepsy Society **Hob./spts.:** Figure skating, art **SIC code:** 80 **Address:** Patricia Smith Cook, M.D., A.P.M.C., 110 Veterans Memorial Blvd., Suite 105, Metairie, LA 70005 **Web address:** www.patriciacookmd.com

COOPER, CAROL L.
Industry: Healthcare **Born:** November 2, 1955, Torrance, California **Univ./degree:** M.D., 1987; Ph.D., 1988, Case Western Reserve **Current organization:** Mid Michigan Cardiology **Title:** M.D., Ph.D. **Type of organization:** Private physician's office **Major product:** Patient care **Area of distribution:** Midland, Michigan **Area of Practice:** Ophthalmology **Affiliations:** F.A.A.O.; A.S.C.R.S. **Hob./spts.:** Family **SIC code:** 80 **Address:** Mid Michigan Cardiology, 4007 Orchard Dr., Suite 3003, Midland, MI 48640 **E-mail:** mmcardiology@msms.org

COOPERMAN, ARTHUR
Industry: Healthcare **Born:** March 1, 1956, New York, New York **Univ./degree:** M.D., University of Pittsburgh, 1981 **Current organization:** Winthrop University Hospital **Title:** Chief, Cardiac Anesthesiologist **Type of organization:** Hospital **Major product:** Patient care **Area of distribution:** New York **Area of Practice:** Anesthesia, consulting **Published works:** Article - "Brain Research", abstracts **Affiliations:** A.M.A.; American Society of Anesthesiologists **Hob./spts.:** Skiing, tennis **SIC code:** 80 **Address:** Winthrop University Hospital, 259 First St., Mineola, NY 11501 **E-mail:** coopcoopkc@aol.com

CORDON-CARDO, CARLOS
Industry: Healthcare **Univ./degree:** M.D., University of Barcelona, Spain, 1980; Ph.D., Cornell University, 1985 **Current organization:** Memorial Sloan Kettering Cancer Center **Title:** M.D., Ph.D. **Type of organization:** University hospital **Major product:** Patient care, Cancer care **Area of distribution:** New York **Area of Practice:** Pathology **Published works:** 250+ publications **Affiliations:** American Society for Cancer Research; International Union Against Cancer **SIC code:** 80 **Address:** Memorial Sloan Kettering Cancer Center, 1275 York Ave., New York, NY 10021 **E-mail:** cordon.c@mskcc.org

CORMAN, LOURDES C.
Industry: Healthcare **Born:** December 29, 1944, Havana, Cuba **Univ./degree:** M.D., Women's Medical College, Pennsylvania, 1970 **Current organization:** University of Alabama School of Medicine, Huntsville Campus, Internal Medicine Program **Title:** M.D./Professor/Chief, Internal Medicine Group **Type of organization:** Medical college **Major product:** Patient care, medical education **Area of distribution:** Alabama **Area of Practice:** Medical care, geriatrics, rheumatology, clinical care, teaching **Affiliations:** Fellow, American College of Physicians; American Society of Internal Medicine; American College of Rheumatology **Hob./spts.:** Reading, needlepoint **SIC code:** 80 **Address:** University of Alabama School of Medicine, Huntsville Campus, 109 Governor's Dr. S.W., 213 Clinical Sciences Center, Huntsville, AL 35801

CORYLLOS, ELIZABETH V.
Industry: Medical **Born:** July 3, 1929, Manhattan, New York **Univ./degree:** B.A., Chemistry, Barnard University; M.D., Cornell Weill Medical School **Current organization:** Winthrop University Hospital **Title:** M.D./Emeritus Chief of Pediatric Surgeon **Type of organization:** University hospital **Major product:** Medical services **Area of distribution:** International **Area of Practice:** General surgery, lactation consulting, state faculty ATLS, teaching medical students, nurses and residents **Honors/awards:** Lifetime Achievement Award, Winthrop University Hospital/Division of Pediatrics; Woman of the Year, Glen Head Lyons Club, 1975 **Published works:** Book chapters, articles and abstracts **Affiliations:** A.M.A.; American Academy of Pediatrics; National Center on Breast Feeding; American Trauma Society; Nassau County Medical Society; Injury Prevention Committee; New York State Medical Society; Past President, Hellenic Medical Society; Associate Professor of Surgery, SUNY at Stonybrook **Hob./spts.:** Family, farming, gardening, horseback riding, outdoor activities, travel, theatre **SIC code:** 80 **Address:** 8 Jaegger Dr., Glen Head, NY 11545 **E-mail:** eisforme@aol.com

COSTA, DENNIS JAMES
Industry: Healthcare **Born:** October 7, 1950, Milwaukee, Wisconsin **Univ./degree:** M.D., Medical College of Wisconsin, 1984 **Current organization:** Lake Vista Cancer Center **Title:** M.D. **Type of organization:** Cancer center **Major product:** Patient care **Area of distribution:** Lewisville, Texas **Area of Practice:** Hematology, oncology **Published works:** Articles, abstracts **Affiliations:** A.S.C.O.; A.S.H.; American College of Physicians **SIC code:** 80 **Address:** Lake Vista Cancer Center, 2790 Lake Vista Dr., Lewisville, TX 75067

COTELINGAM, JAMES D.
Industry: Medicine **Born:** December 26, 1941, Mysore City, India **Univ./degree:** Intermediate Science, Ewing Christian College, Allahabad, India, 1959; M.B.B.S., 1966; M.D., Path., 1972 Christian Medical College (Punjab University), Ludhiana, India; Diplomate, American Board of Pathology (Hematology), 1984 **Current organization:** Louisiana State University Health Sciences Center **Title:** Director, Clinical Laboratories **Type of organization:** University hospital **Major product:** Patient care, medical education, research **Area of distribution:** International **Area of Practice:** Pathology; (Anatomic Pathology, Clinical Pathology, Hematopathology) Board Certified; FLEX Certification, 1974 **Honors/awards:** Navy Commendation Medal for Meritorious Service, 1977-1981; Lead Surgical Pathologist to President Ronald Reagan, Vice-President George Bush Sr., Members of Congress, Supreme Court and Foreign Dignitaries; National Defense Ribbon, U. S. Navy, 1991; Listed in Marquis Who's Who in the East and America; Who's Who Worldwide; Outstanding Service Medal, Uniformed Services University of the Health Sciences, Bethesda, Maryland, 1981-1977; Listed in "Guide to America's Top Physicians" **Affiliations:** College of American Pathologists; American Society of Clinical Pathologists; U.S. - Canadian Academy of Pathology; Association of Military Surgeons of the U.S.; New York Academy of Sciences; Indian Medical Association; Hope Foundation; International Society for Laboratory Hematology; Society for Hematopathology ; European Association for Hematopathology **Hob./spts.:** Music, reading, walking **SIC code:** 80 **Address:** Louisiana State University Health Sciences Center, 1501 Kings Hwy., Shreveport, LA 71130 **E-mail:** jcotel@lsuhsc.edu

COUTURIER, GEORG
Industry: Medical **Born:** March 11, 1965, Zweibrücken, Germany **Univ./degree:** M.D., Medical-Faculty at University of Saarland in Homburg, 1991 **Current organization:** Phillips Ambulatory Care, Beth Israel Medical Center/Albert Einstein College of Medicine **Type of organization:** Hospital/college of medicine **Major product:** Medical services **Area of distribution:** International **Area of Practice:** Cardiology, internal medicine **Published works:** 5 articles, 8 abstracts **Affiliations:** A.C.C.; A.C.P.; A.S.I.M.; D.A.B.I.M. **Hob./spts.:** Boating, skiing **SIC code:** 80 **Address:** 3755 Oleta Place, Seaford, NY 11783 **E-mail:** gcouturi@chpnet.org

COVER, PHILLIP J.
Industry: Healthcare **Born:** Illinois **Univ./degree:** M.D., University of Illinois, 1983 **Current organization:** Samaritan Regional Health Systems **Title:** M.D. **Type of organization:** Hospital **Major product:** Patient care **Area of distribution:** Ashland, Ohio **Area of Practice:** Emergency medicine **Affiliations:** A.C.P.; A.C.E.P. **Hob./spts.:** Computers, electronics **SIC code:** 80 **Address:** Samaritan Regional Health Systems, 1025 Center St,, Ashland, OH 44805 **E-mail:** oheddoc@hotmail.com

COWAN, HONEY
Industry: Mental healthcare **Born:** October 29, 1939 **Univ./degree:** R.N., 1959; M.A., Clinical Counseling, California State University, 1983 **Current organization:** Riding High Equestrian Program **Title:** Executive Director **Type of organization:** Mental health program **Major product:** Patient mental healthcare **Area of distribution:** California **Area of Practice:** Animal facilitator psychotherapy **Honors/awards:** Scholar-

ship Nsg. Graduation, Diplomate, American Psychotherapy Association **Affiliations:** North American Riding for the Handicapped Association; Equine Assisted Growth and Learning Association; California Association of Marriage and Family Therapists **Hob./spts.:** Horses, horseback riding **SIC code:** 80 **Address:** Riding High Equestrian Program, 11685 Lorenson Rd., Auburn, CA 95602 **E-mail:** ridinghieq@aol.com **Web address:** www.ridinghighprogram.org

COWAN, KAREN SISTRUNK
Industry: Healthcare **Born:** February 27, St. Louis, Missouri **Univ./degree:** B.A., Biology, University of Missouri, St. Louis, 1983; M.D., University of Missouri, Columbia, School of Medicine, 1988 **Current organization:** Metropolitan St. Louis Psychiatric Center **Title:** M.D., Attending Physician **Type of organization:** State hospital **Major product:** Biologic psychiatry **Area of distribution:** Missouri **Area of Practice:** Psychiatry and epidemiology **Affiliations:** American Psychiatric Association; American Medical Association **Hob./spts.:** Swimming, writing, travel, theatre, music **SIC code:** 80 **Address:** Metropolitan St. Louis Psychiatric Center, 5351 Delmar Blvd., St. Louis, MO 63112 **E-mail:** ksistrunkcowanmd@netscape.net

COX, CHARLES E.
Industry: Medical **Born:** November 25, 1947, St. George, Utah **Univ./degree:** M.D., University of Utah, 1975 **Current organization:** University of South Florida **Title:** Professor of Surgery **Type of organization:** University hospital **Major product:** Cancer care, medical education **Area of distribution:** International **Area of Practice:** Surgical oncology of the breast **Affiliations:** American College of Surgeons; Southern Surgical Association **Hob./spts.:** Hunting, fishing, backpacking **SIC code:** 80 **Address:** University of South Florida, 12902 Magnolia Dr., #3157, Tampa, FL 33612 **E-mail:** coxce@moffitt.usf.edu

COYLE, GREGORY A.
Industry: Healthcare **Born:** September 4, 1968, Milford, Connecticut **Univ./degree:** B.S.N., Sacred Heart University; B.A., Business Health Administration, Yale University **Current organization:** Sigma Theta Tau, Mu Delta **Title:** R.N.C., Behavior Health Clinical Specialist **Type of organization:** Forensic home care agency **Major product:** Forensic home care **Area of distribution:** Ansonia, Connecticut **Area of Practice:** Forensic nursing; Certified Nutritionalist **Affiliations:** V.F.W.; American Legion; U.S. Ranger Battalion; Persian Gulf War Veterans Society **Hob./spts.:** Physical fitness, hiking **SIC code:** 80 **Address:** Sigma Theta Tau, Mu Delta, 48 Berkshire Rd., Ansonia, CT 06401 **E-mail:** coy1234@msn.com

CRABTREE, STEPHEN A.
Industry: Healthcare **Born:** December 23, 1963, Oklahoma City, Oklahoma **Univ./degree:** D.O., Oklahoma College of Osteopathic Medicine **Current organization:** Integris Baptist Medical Center **Title:** D.O. **Type of organization:** Hospital **Major product:** Patient care **Area of distribution:** Oklahoma **Area of Practice:** Emergency medicine, acute care medicine **Affiliations:** American College of Osteopathic Medicine **Hob./spts.:** Bow hunting, scuba diving, woodworking **SIC code:** 80 **Address:** 7401 N.E. 95th St., Oklahoma City, OK 73151 **E-mail:** scrab@direway.com

CRAIG, CHARLES P.
Industry: Healthcare **Univ./degree:** M.D., University of Pittsburgh, 1961 **Current organization:** St. Joseph Mercy Health System **Title:** M.D. **Type of organization:** Hospital **Major product:** Patient care, education **Area of distribution:** National **Area of Practice:** Infectious diseases **Published works:** 75 scientific publications, 3 textbooks **Affiliations:** F.A.C.P.; F.I.D.S.A.; F.C.C.P.; A.P.I.C.; A.S.M.; A.M.A.; M.S.M.S **Hob./spts.:** Travel **SIC code:** 80 **Address:** St. Joseph Mercy Health System, 4870 Clark Rd., #204, Ypsilanti, MI 48197 **E-mail:** chiefchas@pol.net

CRAIG, JUDY ANE
Industry: Healthcare **Univ./degree:** B.S., Medical Technology, University of Massachusetts, 1995 **Current organization:** Caritas Norwood Hospital **Title:** Hematology Section Supervisor **Type of organization:** Hospital **Major product:** Patient care **Area of distribution:** Massachusetts **Area of Practice:** Overseeing daily operations of lab **SIC code:** 80 **Address:** Caritas Norwood Hospital, 800 Washington St., Norwood, MA 02062 **E-mail:** judyane_craig@cchcs.org

CRAIGG, GERALD B.R.
Industry: Healthcare **Born:** August 24, 1963, West Indics **Univ./degree:** M.D., Loma Linda University **Current organization:** Good Shepherd Medical Group **Title:** M.D. **Type of organization:** Hospital based medical practice **Major product:** Patient care **Area of distribution:** Oregon **Area of Practice:** Internal medicine **Affiliations:** A.C.P.; A.M.A. **Hob./spts.:** Basketball, soccer, racquetball **SIC code:** 80 **Address:** Good Shepherd Medical Group, 600 N.W. 11th, #E-37, Hermiston, OR 97838

CRAIGHEAD JR., CLAUDE CLAIBORNE
Industry: Healthcare **Born:** August 30, 1919, Shreveport, Louisiana **Univ./degree:** M.D., Louisiana State University, 1939 **Current organization:** Louisiana State University School of Medicine **Title:** Professor of Surgery **Type of organization:** Hospital **Major product:** Patient care, surgery **Area of distribution:** New Orleans, Louisiana **Area of Practice:** Thoracic surgery **Published works:** 100 articles **Affiliations:** Southern Surgical; American College of Surgeons; Orleans Parrish Medical Society **SIC code:** 80 **Address:** Louisiana State University School of Medicine, 1542 Tulane Ave., New Orleans, LA 70012

CRAIN, FRANCES UTTERBACK
Industry: Healthcare **Born:** December 28, 1914, Crawfordsville, Indiana **Spouse:** James W. Crain (Deceased) **Married:** September 13, 1937 **Children:** James Michael Crain, May 9, 1942; Patrick Desmond Crain, July 23, 1943 **Univ./degree:** B.A., Nutrition, University of Illinois, 1935 **Current organization:** Shelby County, Oakville Healthcare Center **Title:** Dietitian (Retired) **Type of organization:** Healthcare center **Major product:** Healthcare, nutrition **Area of distribution:** Memphis, Tennessee **Area of Practice:** Nutrition **Honors/awards:** 1955 Memphis Career Woman of the Year; 1976 Tennessee Outstanding Dietitian; 1977 Tennessee Outstanding Dietician; Salvation Army Certificate of Appreciation; 2003 Frances Crain Book Fund established by Memphis area Nutrition Council & Memphis District Dietetic Assoc. **Published works:** Book, "Of Weeds and Views", 2000; "To Your Taste - Butter", National Dairy Council, 1958; Weekly food feature article for The Commercial Appeal, Memphis, TN, 1952-61 **Affiliations:** Numerous including: President, Memphis District Dietetic Association, 1949-50; President, Tennessee Dietetic Association; District Governor Quota Club International; President Shelby County Retirees Organization, 1987-89 **Career accomplishments:** Employed by Shelby County in 1969. Thereafter, her time was split between Shelby County Hospital and Shelby County Penal Farm. After becoming full time at Shelby County Hospital, she was retained on a consulting basis at Shelby County Penal Farm until retirement in 1980. **Hob./spts.:** Scrabble, home maintenance **SIC code:** 80 **Address:** 255 N. Avalon St., Memphis, TN 38112-5101 **E-mail:** fran255@aol.com

CRAINE, PATRICIA
Industry: Healthcare **Univ./degree:** B.A., Education, San Jose State University, 1967; Graduate Studies, Elementary Education, Wayne State University, 1968; M.A. with High Honors, Counseling/Psychology, National University, 1986 **Current organization:** Patricia Craine, M.A., L.M.F.T., D.A.P.A., C.R.S. **Title:** M.A., L.M.F.T. **Type of organization:** Private practice **Major product:** Psychotherapy **Area of distribution:** National **Area of Practice:** Women's issues, coaching, couple therapy, positive problem solving; Certified Relationship Specialist **Honors/awards:** Numerous awards for community service **Published works:** Wendy's Club (ISBN# 1425960472) **Affiliations:** C.A.M.F.T.; Diplomate, A.P.A.; N.B.A.E., National Board of Cognitive Behavioral Therapists; California Board of Addiction Examiners; American Holistic Association; American Association of Christian Counselors; Board of Guide Dogs of the Desert; Board, Animal Samaritans; Board, Habitat for Humanity; Dusty Wings; National Chair, Delta Gamma **Hob./spts.:** Guide Dogs, gardening, community fundraising **SIC code:** 80 **Address:** 2150 Tahquitz Way, Suite #3, Palm Springs, CA 92262 **E-mail:** pbcraine@aol.com

CRAWFORD, ALICIA P.
Industry: Healthcare **Born:** March 25 **Univ./degree:** M.D., University of Illinois, 1980 **Current organization:** Family Practice Center **Title:** M.D. **Type of organization:** Medical practice **Major product:** Patient care **Area of distribution:** National **Area of Practice:** Family practice, internal medicine **Affiliations:** American Medical Association; National Medical Association **Hob./spts.:** Watercolor painting, horseback riding, skating, poetry **SIC code:** 80 **Address:** Family Practice Center, 111 W. Main St., Du Quoin, IL 62832 **E-mail:** docali@netscape.net

CRAWFORD, MONA A.
Industry: Medical **Born:** June 26, 1953, Tripoli, Lebanon **Univ./degree:** B.S., Cytology, Saint Elie **Current organization:** St. Peter's University Hospital **Title:** Anatomic Pathology Supervisor **Type of organization:** University hospital **Major product:** Patient care, medical education **Area of distribution:** New Jersey **Area of Practice:** Pathology, cytology **Affiliations:** A.S.C **Hob./spts.:** Skiing **SIC code:** 80 **Address:** St. Peter's University Hospital, 254 Easton Ave., New Brunswick, NJ 08901 **E-mail:** mcrawford@saintpetersuh.com

CREASY, JEFF L.

Industry: Healthcare/education **Born:** November 14, 1954, Vestal, New York **Univ./degree:** B.S., Michigan State University, 1976; M.D., University of North Carolina at Chapel Hill, 1980 **Current organization:** Vanderbilt University, Dept. of Radiology **Title:** M.D./Associate Professor **Type of organization:** University hospital **Major product:** Medical care, teaching **Area of distribution:** Tennessee **Area of Practice:** Neuroradiology **Affiliations:** A.S.N.R.; R.S.N.A.; A.R.S. **Hob./spts.:** Photography **SIC code:** 80 **Address:** Vanderbilt University, Dept. of Radiology, 21st & Garland, Nashville, TN 37232

CREAVEN, PATRICK J.

Industry: Healthcare **Born:** January 31, 1933, London, England **Univ./degree:** M.B.B.S (M.D.), 1956; Ph.D., Biochemistry, 1964, University of London, England **Current organization:** Roswell Park Cancer Institute **Title:** Director, Phase I Program **Type of organization:** Hospital **Major product:** Patient care **Area of distribution:** New York **Area of Practice:** Cancer research **Published works:** 2 books, 3 book chapters, 193 abstracts **Affiliations:** A.A.C.R.; A.S.C.O.; F.C.P.; F.R.S.H. **SIC code:** 80 **Address:** Roswell Park Cancer Institute, Dept. of Medicine, Elm & Carlton Streets, Buffalo, NY 14263 **E-mail:** patrick.creaven@roswellpark.org

CRESPO, CARMELO A.

Industry: Healthcare **Born:** January 7, 1945, Puerto Rico **Univ./degree:** M.D., University of Autonomous, Dominican Republic, 1975 **Current organization:** Dr. Crespo Medical Office **Title:** M.D. **Type of organization:** Solo practice **Major product:** Patient care **Area of distribution:** Dorado, Puerto Rico **Area of Practice:** Emergency medicine **Affiliations:** Puerto Rico Medical Association **Hob./spts.:** Golf **SIC code:** 80 **Address:** Dr. Crespo Medical Office, 338 Mendez Vigo St., Dorado, PR 00646-0687 **E-mail:** drcrespo@coqui.net

CRISWELL, BETH M.

Industry: Healthcare **Born:** September 27, 1954, Ithaca, New York **Univ./degree:** A.S.N., Cayuga County Community College, 1977 **Current organization:** Tsali Care Center **Title:** Director of Nursing **Type of organization:** Long-term healthcare facility **Major product:** Patient care **Area of distribution:** North Carolina **Area of Practice:** Wound care, IV therapy, chemotherapy, preceptor **Honors/awards:** Clinical Excellence Award, STAR Award for Employee Excellence; Perfect Score-Telemetry **Affiliations:** North Carolina Health Care Facilities Association; Oncology Nursing Society **Hob./spts.:** Cross-stitching, reading, hiking **SIC code:** 80 **Address:** Tsali Care Center, 55 Echota Church Rd., Cherokee, NC 28719 **E-mail:** bcriswell@nc-cherokee.com

CROHN, MICHAEL H.

Industry: Healthcare **Born:** June 7, 1954, Brooklyn, New York **Univ./degree:** D.C., Life Chiropractic College, 1983 **Current organization:** Glendale Family Chiropractic **Title:** D.C. **Type of organization:** Private practice **Major product:** Patient care **Area of distribution:** Glendale, New York **Area of Practice:** Chiropractics **Affiliations:** New York Chiropractic Council; Glendale Kiwanis Council **Hob./spts.:** Whitewater rafting, skiing **SIC code:** 80 **Address:** Glendale Family Chiropractic, 68-15 Myrtle Ave., Glendale, NY 11385 **E-mail:** spinedr@mindspring.com

CROPP, GERD J.

Industry: Medical **Born:** July 2, 1930, Delmenhorst, Germany **Univ./degree:** M.D., Cum Laude, 1958; Ph.D., 1965, University of Western Ontario **Current organization:** University of California, San Francisco **Title:** Professor Emeritus **Type of organization:** University hospital **Major product:** Patient care, medical education **Area of distribution:** International **Area of Practice:** Pediatric pulmonology **Honors/awards:** NIH Research Career Development Award; Recipient of Purkinje Medal **Affiliations:** A.T.S.; E.R.S.; A.P.S.; A.A.P.; A.C.C.P. **Hob./spts.:** Outdoor activities **SIC code:** 80 **Address:** 70 Buena Vista Terrace, San Francisco, CA 94117 **E-mail:** croppgj@msn.com

CROSS, MYRA DIANE

Industry: Healthcare **Born:** Albany, Kentucky **Univ./degree:** M.S., Public Health, Tulane University **Current organization:** Clinton County Hospital **Title:** Director, Surgical Services; R.N. **Type of organization:** Hospital **Major product:** Patient care **Area of distribution:** Kentucky **Area of Practice:** Operating room **Affiliations:** A.O.R.M.; military duty during Desert Storm **Hob./spts.:** Crafts, gardening, travel **SIC code:** 80 **Address:** Clinton County Hospital, 723 Burkesville Rd., Albany, KY 42602 **E-mail:** di51c@earthlink.net

CROW, JUDSON L.

Industry: Healthcare **Born:** April 16, 1936, Brinkley, Arkansas **Univ./degree:** M.D., University of Arkansas, 1961 **Current organization:** Red River Plastic Surgery Clinic **Title:** M.D. **Type of organization:** Medical clinic **Major product:** Patient care **Area of distribution:** East Grand Forks, Minnesota **Area of Practice:** Plastic/cosmetic surgery **Affiliations:** Diplomate, American Board of Surgery; Fellow, American College of Surgeons; American Society for Aesthetic Plastic Surgery; American Society of Plastic Surgery **Hob./spts.:** Jazz, guitar, gardening **SIC code:** 80 **Address:** Red River Plastic Surgery Clinic, 1428 Central Ave. N.E., East Grand Forks, MN 56721 **E-mail:** jcrow@riverviewhealth.org

CRUIKSHANK, STEPHEN H.

Industry: Healthcare **Born:** December 4, 1950, Parksburg, West Virginia **Spouse:** Britt-Marie **Married:** June 13, 1998 **Univ./degree:** M.D., Wake Forest University, 1976; J.D., Northwestern International University, 2002 **Current organization:** Miami University **Title:** M.D./Director, OB-GYN **Type of organization:** Research center/hospital **Major product:** Women's healthcare **Area of distribution:** Cincinnati, Ohio **Area of Practice:** Urogynecology and reconstructive pelvic surgery **Published works:** 70+ publications **Affiliations:** F.A.C.O.G.; F.A.C.S.; C.A.O.G.; S.G.S. **Hob./spts.:** Physical fitness, hunting, fishing **SIC code:** 80 **Address:** 884 River Forest Dr., Maineville, OH 45039 **E-mail:** shcbmc@aol.com

CRUTCHFIELD, SUSAN R.

Industry: Medical/education **Univ./degree:** Ph.D., University of Birmingham, England **Current organization:** U.C.S.D. Medical Center **Title:** Ph.D. **Type of organization:** University hospital **Major product:** Medical services and research **Area of distribution:** National **Area of Practice:** Neutophysiologist, Clinical and Research **Affiliations:** A.R.V.O.; I.C.S.E.V. **SIC code:** 80 **Address:** 1710 Upper Canyon Rd., Santa Fe, NM 87501 **E-mail:** scrutchfield@ucsd.edu

DACOSTA, GASTON F.

Industry: Healthcare **Born:** December 1, 1955, Jamaica, West Indies **Univ./degree:** Ph.D., Biochemiostry, State University of New York at Buffalo, 1982; M.D., University of Medicine and Dentistry of New York, 1989 **Current organization:** Women First Obstetrics & Gynecology **Title:** M.D./Ph.D./F.A.C.O,G. **Type of organization:** Private practice **Major product:** Ob/Gyn **Area of distribution:** Carthage, New York **Area of Practice:** Medicine **Published works:** Articles **Affiliations:** F.A.C.O.G. **Hob./spts.:** Water sports **SIC code:** 80 **Address:** Women First Obstetrics & Gynecology, 36381 NYS Route 26, Carthage, NY 13619 **E-mail:** gastondacosta@hotmail.com

D'AGOSTINO, RONALD D.

Industry: Healthcare **Born:** November 23, 1958, Brooklyn, New York **Univ./degree:** B.S., Biology, Boston College, 1980; M.D., New York Medical College, 1985 **Current organization:** Long Island Cardiovascular Consultants **Title:** M.D./F.A.C.C./F.A.C.P. **Type of organization:** Group practice **Major product:** Patient care **Area of distribution:** New York **Area of Practice:** Cardiology - vascular **Published works:** 6 articles **SIC code:** 80 **Address:** Long Island Cardiovascular Consultants, 1129 Northern Blvd., Suite 408, Manhasset, NY 11030

DAHAN, MICHAEL H.

Industry: Medical **Born:** October 12, 1970, Montreal, Canada **Univ./degree:** M.D., SUNY Stony Brook, 1996 **Current organization:** University of California at San Diego **Title:** M.D. **Type of organization:** University hospital **Major product:** Medical services **Area of distribution:** California **Area of Practice:** Reproductive endocrinology, Polycystic Ovary Syndrome **Affiliations:** A.S.R.M.; S.R.E.I. **Hob./spts.:** Restoring antiques **SIC code:** 80 **Address:** University of California at San Diego, 9500 Gilman Dr. (0633), La Jolla, CA 92122 **E-mail:** dahanhaim@hotmail.com@ucsd.edu

DALE, CAROLINE G.

Industry: Healthcare **Univ./degree:** B.S., Biology/Chemistry, Converse College; M.D., Medical University of South Carolina, 1989 **Title:** M.D. **Type of organization:** Private medical practice **Major product:** Patient care **Area of distribution:** Maryland **Area of Practice:** Internal medicine **Affiliations:** American College of Physicians; American Medical Association **Hob./spts.:** Family, horseback riding, running, gardening **SIC code:** 80 **Address:** 23214 Galloway Place, Hollywood, MD 20636 **E-mail:** drothfield@aol.com

DAMERAU, MARK T.

Industry: Healthcare **Born:** November 8, 1961, Buffalo, New York **Univ./degree:** D.M.D., University of Florida, 1989 **Current organization:** Dr. Mark Damerau **Title:** D.M.D. **Type of organization:** Private practice **Major product:** Patient care **Area of distribution:** National **Area of Practice:** Reconstructive and cosmetic dentistry **Affiliations:** A.A.C.O.; A.D.A.; A.O.D. **Hob./spts.:** Ice hockey, weight training, scuba diving **SIC code:** 80 **Address:** Dr. Mark Damerau, 400 Village Square Crossing, Suite 1, Palm Beach Gardens, FL 33410 **E-mail:** bigsmile@runbox.com

DAMIANO, ANGELA

Industry: Healthcare **Born:** January 28, 1963, Italy **Univ./degree:** B.S., Chemistry, New York University, 1987; M.D., Albert Einstein School of Medicine, 1991 **Current organization:** ENT Faculty Practice **Title:** M.D./F.A.C.S. **Type of organization:** Group practice **Major product:** Patient care **Area of distribution:** New York **Area of Practice:** Otolaryngology, head and neck surgery **Published works:** 10-12 articles **Affiliations:** F.A.C.S.; A.M.A. **SIC code:** 80 **Address:** ENT Faculty Practice, 1055 Saw Mill River Rd., Ardsley, NY 10502

D'AMICO, RICHARD A.
Industry: Healthcare **Born:** May 2, 1951, New York, New York **Univ./degree:** M.D., New York University School of Medicine, 1976 **Current organization:** Richard A. D'Amico, M.D. **Title:** M.D. **Type of organization:** Private practice **Major product:** Plastic surgery **Area of distribution:** Englewood, New Jersey **Area of Practice:** Cosmetic and reconstructive surgery **Honors/awards:** Spokesperson for American Society of Plastic Surgeons **Published works:** "Cancer of the Skin," chapter in Management of the Patient with Cancer, W.B. Saunders, 3rd Ed. (co-author with N.E. Hugo), 1986; "Regulatory Issues in Ultrasonic Lipoplasty," Chapter in Plastic Surgery Clinics of North America, in press **Affiliations:** Assistant Clinical Professor, Mt. Sinai Hospital; Chief of Plastic Surgery, Englewood Hospital and Medical Center; Past President, New Jersey Society of Plastic Surgeons; Chairman, Breast Implant Task Force A.P.S.; Vice President and Board of Directors, American Society of Plastic Surgeons **Hob./spts.:** Tennis, skiing, overseas volunteer plastic surgery **SIC code:** 80 **Address:** Richard A. D'Amico, M.D., 180 N. Dean St., Suite 3N, Englewood, NJ 07631

DANIEL, MARTHA PEASLEE
Industry: Healthcare **Born:** February 1, 1952, Stillwater, Minnesota **Univ./degree:** B.S., Nursing, College of St. Catherine, Minnesota; Certificate in Public Health **Current organization:** RN Specializing in LTC, Geriatric Health Services **Title:** R.N., Consultant **Type of organization:** Private consulting, RCFE, Long Term Care, Retirement communities **Major product:** Assisted living, health services coordination **Area of distribution:** Santa Barbara, California **Area of Practice:** Coordination, health services and advocacy **Affiliations:** Association of California Nurse Leaders; Sigma Theta Tau **Hob./spts.:** Family activities, swimming, dogs, reading **SIC code:** 80 **Address:** RN Specializing in LTC,, Geriatric Health Services, Santa Barbara, CA 93111 **E-mail:** marthadaniel@cox.net

DANRAD, RAMAN
Industry: Medical **Born:** Delhi, India **Univ./degree:** M.B.B.S., University of Delhi, India, 1992; Fellowship, Abdominal Imaging, Emory University, 2005; Fellowship, M.R. Imaging, University of Massachusetts, 2006 **Current organization:** University of Massachusetts Memorial Medical Center **Title:** M.D. **Type of organization:** Medical center/medical school **Major product:** Patient care, medical education **Area of distribution:** National **Area of Practice:** Radiology, MR imaging **Affiliations:** A.C.R.; A.R.R.S.; R.S.N.A. **Hob./spts.:** Camping, the outdoors **SIC code:** 80 **Address:** 115 John Olds Dr., #106, Manchester, CT 06040 **E-mail:** rdanrad@gmail.com

DAO, LIANA T.
Industry: Healthcare **Born:** November 19, 1972, New York, New York **Univ./degree:** M.D., Ross University, 2000 **Current organization:** William F. Ryan Community Center **Title:** M.D. **Type of organization:** Outpatient clinic **Major product:** Patient care **Area of distribution:** New York, New York **Area of Practice:** Family practice **Affiliations:** A.M.A; American Academy of Family Physicians; American Board of Family Medicine **Hob./spts.:** Tennis, skiing, travel **SIC code:** 80 **Address:** William F. Ryan Center, 110 W. 97th St., New York, NY 10025 **E-mail:** lianedao@gmail.com

DAPAAH, VICTORIA A.
Industry: Healthcare **Born:** December 27, 1954, Ghana, South Africa **Univ./degree:** R.N., **Current organization:** Riverdale Nursing Home **Title:** Director of Nursing **Type of organization:** Nursing home **Major product:** Patient care **Area of distribution:** Bronx, New York **Area of Practice:** Sub-acute rehabilitation, Alzheimer's Disease, schizophrenia, long-term care, administration, team building **Hob./spts.:** Community service **SIC code:** 80 **Address:** Riverdale Nursing Home, 641 W. 230th St., Bronx, NY 10463

DAR, QUTUBUDDIN KARAMAT
Industry: Healthcare **Born:** July 7, 1963, Karachi, Pakistan **Univ./degree:** M.D., Dow Medical College, Karachi, Pakistan, 1989 **Current organization:** Qutubuddin Karamat Dar, M.D. **Title:** M.D. **Type of organization:** Solo practice **Major product:** Patient care **Area of distribution:** New York **Area of Practice:** Internal medicine/ pulmonary medicine; Board Certified, Chest Medicine; Board Certified, Internal Medicine **Affiliations:** American Thoracic Society **Hob./spts.:** Baseball **SIC code:** 80 **Address:** Qutubuddin Karamat Dar, M.D., 400 N. Main St., Warsaw, NY 14569 **E-mail:** qutubuddindar@msn.com

DAREVSKAYA, LILYA
Industry: Healthcare **Born:** April 23, 1959, Russia **Univ./degree:** D.O., New York College of Osteopathic Medicine, 1995 **Current organization:** L. Darevskaya Pediatric Center **Title:** D.O. **Type of organization:** Private medical practice **Major product:** Children's healthcare **Area of distribution:** National **Area of Practice:** Pediatrics **Affiliations:** A.O.A.; American Academy of Pediatrics **Hob./spts.:** Travel **SIC code:** 80 **Address:** L. Darevskaya Pediatric Center, 7819 19th Ave., Brooklyn, NY 11214

DARLING, RAYMON E.
Industry: Healthcare **Born:** September 7, 1954, Shawnee, Oklahoma **Univ./degree:** M.D., University of Iowa, 1980 **Current organization:** Affinity Medical Group, Dept. of Ob/Gyn **Title:** M.D. **Type of organization:** Multi-specialty clinic **Major product:** Healthcare **Area of distribution:** Wisconsin **Area of Practice:** Obstetrics and gynecology, advanced operative endoscopy and infertility **Affiliations:** A.C.O.G.; A.S.R.M.; A.A.G.L. **Hob./spts.:** Golf, skiing **SIC code:** 80 **Address:** Affinity Medical Group, Dept. of Ob/Gyn, 1531 S. Madison St., Suite 350, Appleton, WI 54915 **E-mail:** imbue@athenet.net

DAS, SURESH S.
Industry: Healthcare **Born:** March 9, 1953, Mysore, India **Univ./degree:** B.S., University of Mysore, 1976; A.A., 1980; B.S., 1981, Eastern Kentucky University; M.D., University of Santiago, 1987 **Current organization:** Spring View Hospital **Title:** Director of Laboratory and Cardiopulmonary/RT **Type of organization:** Hospital **Major product:** Patient care **Area of distribution:** Kentucky **Area of Practice:** Direct and manage: Clinical laboratory and cardiopulmonary / respiratory therapy **Honors/awards:** Mercy Award, Life Point Corp., 2006 **Affiliations:** American Society of Clinical Pathologists; American Medical Technologists; Clinical Laboratory Management Association; Boy Scouts of America **Hob./spts.:** Scout Master since 1955, time with family, travel, sports **SIC code:** 80 **Address:** Spring View Hospital, 320 Loretto Rd., Lebanon, KY 40033 **E-mail:** suresh.das@lpnt.net

DASGUPTA, INDRANIL
Industry: Medical **Born:** May 24, 1960, Barielly, India **Univ./degree:** B.A., Philosophy, Duke University, 1982; M.P.H., Loma Linda University, 1987; M.B.A., Finance, George Washington University, 1989; M.D., St. George's University, Grenada, 1994 **Current organization:** Thomas Jefferson University Hospital/Jefferson Medical College **Title:** M.D./M.B.A./M.P.H./Assistant Professor of Medicine **Type of organization:** University medical center **Major product:** Patient care **Area of distribution:** Philadelphia, Pennsylvania **Area of Practice:** Cardiovascular diseases **Affiliations:** American Heart Association; New York Academy of Science; New Jersey Medical Society; Pennsylvania Medical Society; American Medical Association; American College of Physicians **Hob./spts.:** Soccer, travel **SIC code:** 80 **Address:** Thomas Jefferson University Hospital/Jefferson Medical College, 2528 Tigani Dr., Wilmington, DE 19808

DAVID, DANIELLA
Industry: Medical **Born:** December 28, 1958, Bucharest, Romania **Univ./degree:** M.D. **Current organization:** University of Miami/Veterans' Affairs Medical Center **Title:** M.D./Associate Professor **Type of organization:** Medical school/veteran's medical center **Major product:** Medical education/healthcare for veterans and military patients **Area of distribution:** Miami, Florida **Area of Practice:** Psychiatry, anxiety, post traumatic stress disorder **Hob./spts.:** Reading, travel **SIC code:** 80 **Address:** University of Miami/ Veterans' Affairs Medical Center, 1201 N.W. 16th St., 116A12, Room B524, Miami, FL 33125 **E-mail:** daniella.david@med.va.gov

DAVID, NASIM S.
Industry: Healthcare **Born:** October 20, 1954, Dominican Republic **Univ./degree:** M.D., Autonomic University, Santo Domingo, 1980 **Current organization:** Private Pediatric Practice **Title:** M.D. **Type of organization:** Private medical practice **Major product:** Patient care **Area of distribution:** Arecibo, Puerto Rico **Area of Practice:** Pediatrics **Honors/awards:** Cum Laden **Affiliations:** American College of Physicians, Puerto Rico College of Physicians **Hob./spts.:** Tennis, swimming **SIC code:** 80 **Address:** Private Pediatric Practice, 107B Calle Rodriquez Irizarry, Arecibo, PR 00612

DAVIS, JOHN R.
Industry: Healthcare **Born:** August 7, 1925, Nephi, Utah **Univ./degree:** D.M.D., University of Oregon, 1949; Orthodontic Specialty, University of Washington, 1957 **Current organization:** John R. Davis, D.M.D. **Title:** D.M.D./ F.I.C.D. **Type of organization:** Private orthodontic practice **Major product:** Orthodontics **Area of distribution:** Pocatello, Idaho **Area of Practice:** Orthodontics **Affiliations:** Fellow, International College of Dentists; A.A.O.; A.D.A.; R.M.S.O.; I.S.O.; Rotary Club **Hob./spts.:** Family, automobiles, building kit cars, woodwork **SIC code:** 80 **Address:** 115 S. 15th Ave., Suite F, Pocatello, ID 83201 **E-mail:** docdavis@ida.net

DAVIS, KENNETH D.
Industry: Healthcare **Born:** April 6, 1933 Rochester, New York **Univ./degree:** M.D., New York Medical College, 1958 **Current organization:** Kenneth D. Davis, M.D. **Title:** M.D. **Type of organization:** Private practice **Major product:** Patient care **Area of distribution:** Evansville, Indiana **Area of Practice:** Orthopedic surgery, laser surgery **Affiliations:** A.C.S.M.; M.L.S.; A.S.L.M.S, I.M.A. **Hob./spts.:** Work **SIC code:** 80 **Address:** Kenneth D. Davis, M.D., 801 St. Marys Dr., Suite 007, Evansville, IN 47714 **E-mail:** kdd263@aol.com

DAVIS, MICHAEL J.
Industry: Healthcare **Born:** May 2, 1976, Dallas, Texas **Univ./degree:** M.S., Healthcare Administration, University of Kansas, 2001 **Current organization:** Yakima Regional Medical Heart Center **Title:** Chief Operating Officer **Type of organization:**

Medical center **Major product:** Patient care **Area of distribution:** Washington **Area of Practice:** Operations **Affiliations:** Rotary International; Board Member, Make-A-Wish Foundation; Special Olympics **Hob./spts.:** Tennis, golf **SIC code:** 80 **Address:** HMA, Inc.: Yakima Regional Medical & Heart Center, 110 S. Ninth Ave., Yakima, WA 98901 **E-mail:** michael.davis@yakima.hma-corp.com

DAWSON, ANGELA K.
Industry: Healthcare **Born:** October 11, 1964, Charleston, West Virginia **Univ./degree:** M.D., Mercer University School of Medicine, 1992 **Current organization:** Horbin Clinic **Title:** M.D. **Type of organization:** Multi specialty medical clinic **Major product:** Patient care **Area of distribution:** Georgia **Area of Practice:** Child & adolescent psychiatry **Affiliations:** A.M.A.; A.P.A. **Hob./spts.:** Dancing, hiking, oil painting, creative writing **SIC code:** 80 **Address:** Horbin Clinic, 540 Redman Rd., Rome, GA 30165 **Web address:** www.horbinclinic.com

DE JESÚS, MARITZA VEGA
Industry: Healthcare **Born:** March 3, 1962, Puerto Rico **Univ./degree:** M.S.N., University of Puerto Rico, 1985; MBA/HCM, University of Phoenix, 2004 **Current organization:** San Juan Health Dept. **Title:** Executive Nurse Director **Type of organization:** Healthcare **Major product:** Direct patient care **Area of distribution:** Puerto Rico **Area of Practice:** Supervision, nursing, coordinating quality control and epidemiology services **Affiliations:** Professional College of Nursing; Society of Healthcare Administration; American College of Healthcare Executives **Hob./spts.:** Walking, music, study **SIC code:** 80 **Address:** P.O. Box 810202, Carolina, PR 00981-0202 **E-mail:** mmperozavega@aol.com

DE LA CRUZ, FRANKLIN O.
Industry: Healthcare **Born:** May 16, 1958, San Francisco de Macoris, Dominican Republic **Univ./degree:** M.D., Cetec University, 1982 **Current organization:** Bardstown Women's Center **Title:** M.D. **Type of organization:** Hospital **Major product:** Patient care **Area of distribution:** Bardstown, Kentucky **Area of Practice:** Obstetrics/gynecology **Affiliations:** American College of Obstetrics and Gynecology; Kentucky Medical Association **Hob./spts.:** Fishing, golf, swimming **SIC code:** 80 **Address:** Bardstown Women's Center, 201 S. Fifth St., Suite 9, Bardstown, KY 40004 **E-mail:** fdelacruz@prodigy.net

DE LEON, ARTURO J.
Industry: Medical **Univ./degree:** M.D., Far Eastern University, Philippines, 1961 **Current organization:** Carolina Medical Mission **Title:** M.D./Co-founder **Type of organization:** Medical mission to the indigent Philipinos **Major product:** Healthcare **Area of distribution:** International **Area of Practice:** Family medicine **Affiliations:** American Board of Family Practice; American Disability Board **SIC code:** 80 **Address:** Carolina Medical Mission, 2903 Adrian Ct., Raleigh, NC 27604 **E-mail:** ardelen@nc.rr.us **Web address:** www.carolinamedicalmission.com

DEAN, DIANA S.
Industry: Healthcare **Born:** June 17, 1969, Quincy, Illinois **Univ./degree:** M.D., University of Alabama School of Medicine, 1995 **Current organization:** Mayo Clinic Endocrinology Dept. **Title:** Senior Associate Consultant **Type of organization:** Clinic **Major product:** Patient care **Area of distribution:** International **Area of Practice:** Ultrasound guided fine needle aspiration of thyroid nodules **Affiliations:** A.M.A.; A.A.C.E.; A.T.A.; A.C.T.; Endocrine Society **Hob./spts.:** Family activities **SIC code:** 80 **Address:** Mayo Clinic Endocrinology Dept., 200 First St. S.W., West 18, Rochester, MN 55905 **E-mail:** dean.diana@mayo.edu **Web address:** www.mayo.edu

DEANGELIS, DAVID A.
Industry: Healthcare **Born:** August 30, 1963, Charleston, South Carolina **Univ./degree:** M.D., Southern Illinois University, 1991 **Current organization:** Dean Medical Center **Title:** M.D. **Type of organization:** Medical center **Major product:** Patient care **Area of distribution:** Madison, Wisconsin **Area of Practice:** General and vascular surgery **Published works:** Multiple articles **Affiliations:** A.M.A.; A.C.S.; S.A.G.E.S. **Hob./spts.:** Windsurfing, scuba diving **SIC code:** 80 **Address:** Dean Medical Center, 1313 Fish Hatchery Rd., Madison, WI 53715 **E-mail:** shawn1dave@aol.com

DEARDORFF, KATHLEEN U.
Industry: Maternal/child nursing **Born:** June 26, 1944, Chicago, Illinois **Univ./degree:** M.S.N., University of Pennsylvania **Current organization:** The University of Texas at Tyler, Dept. of Nursing Education **Title:** Senior Lecturer **Type of organization:** University **Major product:** Education of nursing students **Area of distribution:** Tyler, Texas **Area of Practice:** Nursing, maternal child health **Affiliations:** American Association of University Women; International Association for Human Caring; Sigma Theta Tau; Nurses' Christian Fellowship **Hob./spts.:** Horses, water sports, gardening **SIC code:** 80 **Address:** The University of Texas at Tyler, College of Nursing, 3900 University Blvd., Tyler, TX 75799 **E-mail:** kdeardor@mail.uttyl.edu

DECCO, MARK L.
Industry: Healthcare **Born:** September 11, 1966, Butte, Montana **Univ./degree:** B.S., Biomedical Sciences, Montana State University, 1988; M.D., University of Washington School of Medicine, 1992 **Current organization:** Grosse Point Allergy & Asthma Center **Title:** M.D. **Type of organization:** Group practice **Major product:** Patient care **Area of distribution:** Michigan **Area of Practice:** Allergy, asthma **Published works:** 4 articles **Affiliations:** American Academy of Allergy, Asthma and Immunology; American College of Allergy, Asthma and Immunology **Hob./spts.:** Family, backpacking, photography **SIC code:** 80 **Address:** Grosse Point Allergy & Asthma Center, 21300 Kelly Rd., East Pointe, MI 48021 **E-mail:** mcd911@yahoo.com

DEGROOT, MELANIE D.
Industry: Healthcare **Born:** April 22, 1961. Danville, Illinois **Univ./degree:** M.D., Chicago Medical School, 1987 **Current organization:** Coventry Pediatrics **Title:** M.D. **Type of organization:** Group practice **Major product:** Children's healthcare **Area of distribution:** Pottstown, Pennsylvania **Area of Practice:** Pediatrics **Affiliations:** F.A.A.P. **Hob./spts.:** Cooking **SIC code:** 80 **Address:** Coventry Pediatrics, 1610 Medical Dr., Suite 105, Pottstown, PA 19464

DEGUZMAN, ANTHONY A.
Industry: Healthcare **Born:** June 1, 1960, Jamaica, New York **Univ./degree:** M.D., University of Miami, 1990 **Current organization:** Primary Care **Title:** M.D. **Type of organization:** Clinic **Major product:** Patient care **Area of distribution:** Kentucky **Area of Practice:** Family practice and internal medicine **Published works:** Methods in Enzymology **Affiliations:** K.M.K.; A.M.A.; Ambulatory Care Association **Hob./spts.:** Golf, football, basketball **SIC code:** 80 **Address:** Primary Care, 309 Broadway St., #1, Paintsville, KY 41240

DEIF, ATEF A.
Industry: Healthcare **Born:** August 22, 1945, Cairo, Egypt **Univ./degree:** B.S., Chemistry, Geology, 1965; M.S., Chemistry, 1970, Ain-Shams University, Cairo, Egypt **Current organization:** Sullivan County Memorial Hospital **Title:** Laboratory Manager **Type of organization:** Hospital **Major product:** Patient care **Area of distribution:** National **Area of Practice:** Clinical laboratory management **Affiliations:** A.S.C.P., A.C.S., Agency for Healthcare Administrators **Hob./spts.:** History, religion, reading, sailing, fishing **SIC code:** 80 **Address:** Sullivan County Memorial Hospital, 630 W. Third St., Milan, MO 63556

DELA CRUZ, FANNY A.
Industry: Healthcare **Born:** August 20, 1943, Philippines **Univ./degree:** M.D., University of the Philippines, 1981 **Current organization:** West Bloomfield Plastic Surgery Center **Title:** M.D. **Type of organization:** Private practice **Major product:** Plastic surgery **Area of distribution:** National **Area of Practice:** Plastic and reconstructive surgery, hand surgery **Affiliations:** Association of Women Surgeons; American Society of Plastic Surgeons; American Society for Reconstructive Microsurgery Surgery; American Association for Hand Surgery; American Association of Aesthetic Medicine and Surgery; Medical Missions Foundation **Hob./spts.:** Painting, playing the organ, hiking, foreign languages **SIC code:** 80 **Address:** West Bloomfield Plastic Surgery Center, 7091 Orchard Lake Rd., West Bloomfield, MI 48322 **Web address:** www.westbloomfieldplasticsurgerycenter.com

DELACRUZ, FREDY E.
Industry: Healthcare **Univ./degree:** M.D., Guantamo, Mexico, 1972 **Current organization:** Omni Healthcare **Title:** M.D. **Type of organization:** Private practice **Major product:** Patient care **Area of distribution:** Florida **Area of Practice:** Urology **Affiliations:** Fellow, American Urology Association **SIC code:** 80 **Address:** Omni Healthcare, 1421 Malabar Rd. N.E., #205, Palm Bay, FL 32907 **E-mail:** fredy862@pc.com

DELGADO, HECTOR M.
Industry: Healthcare **Born:** July 7, 1963, Havana, Cuba **Univ./degree:** D.O., Nova Southeastern, 1990 **Current organization:** Kendall Family Medical Center **Title:** D.O. **Type of organization:** Medical center **Major product:** Patient care **Area of distribution:** Miami, Florida **Area of Practice:** Preventive primary care **Affiliations:** Diplomate, A.M.A.; A.O.A. **SIC code:** 80 **Address:** Kendall Family Medical Center, 8740 N. Kendall Dr., #101, Miami, FL 33176 **E-mail:** dvhmd8740@hotmail.com

DELIA, APRIL C.
Industry: Healthcare **Born:** June 14, 1966, Brooklyn, New York **Univ./degree:** B.S.N., Adelphi University, 1997 **Current organization:** St. Charles Hospital **Title:** RN, BSN, ONC, ANCC **Type of organization:** Hospital **Major product:** Patient care **Area of distribution:** New York **Area of Practice:** General surgery, orthopaedics, Ob/Gyn, plastics **Affiliations:** N.A.O.N. **Hob./spts.:** Raising beta fish, the beach, dancing, coin collecting **SIC code:** 80 **Address:** 29 Rosedale Rd., Sound Beach, NY 11789

DELLORUSSO, ANA MARIA
Industry: Healthcare **Born:** December 26, 1962, Havana, Cuba **Univ./degree:** M.D., State University of New York Health Science Center at Syracuse, 1989 **Current organization:** Park Pediatrics, LLP **Title:** M.D. **Type of organization:** Medical practice **Major product:** Patient care **Area of distribution:** Long Island, New York **Area of Practice:** Pediatrics **Affiliations:** A.A.P. **Hob./spts.:** Running, reading, sports **SIC code:** 80 **Address:** Park Pediatrics, LLP, 271 Jericho Tpke., Floral Park, NY 11001 **E-mail:** joeana@aol.com

DELPASSAND, EBRAHIM S.
Industry: Medical **Born:** 1957 Tehran, Iran **Univ./degree:** M.D., Tehran School of Medicine, 1981 **Current organization:** UT MD Anderson Cancer Center **Title:** M.D., Associate Professor, Section Chief **Type of organization:** University hospital **Major product:** Medical services **Area of distribution:** Texas **Area of Practice:** Neuclear medicine, therapeutic, diagnostic, cancer research **Published works:** 50+ articles, chapters **Affiliations:** A.M.A., Board Certified; Society of Nuclear Medicine **SIC code:** 80 **Address:** UT MD Anderson Cancer Center, 1515 Holcombe Blvd., Box 83, Houston, TX 77030 **E-mail:** edelpassand@di.mdacc.tmc.edu

DESAI, MEGHNA R.
Industry: Healthcare **Born:** January 24, 1974, Nagpur, India **Univ./degree:** M.B.B.S., Mahatma Gandhi Mission Medical College, 1997 **Current organization:** Northern Maine Medical Center **Title:** M.D./Attending Physician **Type of organization:** Medical center, nonprofit **Major product:** Medical services **Area of distribution:** Northern Maine **Area of Practice:** Board Certified in Internal Medicine, Hematology and Medical Oncology **Honors/awards:** Awarded Fellowship in Hematology and Medical Oncology, North Shore University Hospital, NYU School of Medicine **Published works:** Unusual Presentations of prostate Adenocarcinoma: Lymph node metastases. Meghna Desai, M.D., Aamir Awan, M.D., Ibrahim Hitti, M.D., Parthas Narasimhan, M.D., Elizabeth McDonald, M.D., Hospital Physician. March 2002 vol 38, number 343-48 (Published in the Hospital Physician); Role of Low dose Heparin, Ursodiol and Glutamine in preventing Venooclussive disease of the liver in adults undergoing Stem cell transplantation. Meghna Desai, M.D., Edwin Mcreary, M.D., Ruthee Bayer, M.D., Abstract and poster presentation in the 2004 tandem BMT meeting (Accepted as an abstract publication in the Biology of Blood and Marrow Transplantation) **Affiliations:** A.M.A.; A.C.P.; A.S.C.O.; A.S.H.; Drug Enforcement Administration (DEA) License, U.S. Dept. of Justice **Hob./spts.:** Hiking, photography, reading, cooking **SIC code:** 80 **Address:** Northern Maine Medical Center, 11 Pearl St., Ft. Kent, ME 04743 **E-mail:** desaimeghna@hotmail.com

DESAI, RAVI V.
Industry: Healthcare **Univ./degree:** M.B.B.S., Karnataka University, India, 1997; Fellowship, Critical Care, Mount Sinai, 2007 **Current organization:** Mt. Sinai Hospital **Title:** M.D. **Type of organization:** Medical center/medical school **Major product:** Patient care, medical education **Area of distribution:** International **Area of Practice:** Critical Care Medicine; Ultrasound and Critical Care **Affiliations:** S.C.C.M.; A.C.C.P.; A.C.P **SIC code:** 80 **Address:** 616 Onderdonk Ave., #2L, Ridgewood, NY 11385 **E-mail:** ravivdesai@yahoo.com

DEVITO, ROBERT A.
Industry: Healthcare **Born:** July, 19, 1935, Portsmouth, New Hampshire **Univ./degree:** M.D., Loyola University, 1961 **Current organization:** Carl Pfeiffer Treatment Center **Title:** Sr. Consulting Psychiatrist **Type of organization:** Treatment center **Major product:** Biochemical analysis of nutrients; nutrient treatment on outpatient basis **Area of distribution:** International **Area of Practice:** Consultation with staff on clinical, research and administrative matters **Honors/awards:** Psychiatrist of the Year by the National Alliance for the Mentally Ill, Illinois Branch, 1998; Received an Air Force Commendation Medal for Designer and program architect of the First Community Mental Health Center in the U.S. Air Force, at Sheppard Air Force Base in Wichita Falls, Texas; Received the special honor of having the Madden Mental Health Center auditorium named after him for his administrative and educational accomplishments during nearly 8 years that he served as the facility superintendent; Received a special commendation by the Illinois Senate and House of Representatives, for his outstanding leadership as a cabinet officer in the Thompson administration **Published works:** 25 journal articles, edited a book **Affiliations:** A.P.A.; I.P.S. **Hob./spts.:** Tennis, hiking, baseball and basketball statistics, cardiovascular and cybex weight workouts **SIC code:** 80 **Address:** Carl Pfeiffer Treatment Center, 1804 Centre Point Circle, Suite 102, Naperville, IL 60563

DEWBERRY, ANGIE GLASGOW
Industry: Healthcare **Born:** December 15, 1953 Russellville, Alabama **Univ./degree:** B.S., Marketing/Management, University of North Alabama, 1976 **Current organization:** William Wellborn, M.D. **Title:** Office Manager **Type of organization:** Private practice **Major product:** Patient care **Area of distribution:** Southeast United States **Area of Practice:** Marketing, management **Affiliations:** Former President, M.G.M.A. of Alabama **Hob./spts.:** Family, tennis, reading **SIC code:** 80 **Address:** William Wellborn, M.D., 211N. Atlanta Ave., Sheffield, AL 35660 **E-mail:** agdewberry@aol.com

DHILLON, SAMJOT
Industry: Healthcare **Univ./degree:** M.D., All India Institute of Medical Science, New Delhi, India **Current organization:** LRG Healthcare **Title:** Chief of Pulmonary & Critical Care Medicine **Type of organization:** Hospital **Major product:** Patient care **Area of distribution:** National **Area of Practice:** Pulmonary and critical care medicine, treatment of sleep apnea, asthma **SIC code:** 80 **Address:** 108 Hickory Stick Lane, Laconia, NH 03246

DHINGRA, HEMANT
Industry: Medical **Born:** August, 1968 Jalandhar, India **Univ./degree:** M.B.B.S., Government Medical College, Amritsar, India 1992; M.D., Mount Sinai School of Medicine, 2003 **Current organization:** University of New Mexico Health Science Center **Title:** Assistant Professor/Director of Nephrology **Type of organization:** Teaching hospital **Major product:** Patient care and medical education **Area of distribution:** National **Area of Practice:** Nephrology, dialysis, pre-ESRD care **Honors/awards:** Chief Resident and Best Resident of the Year, Mount Sinai, 2001 **Published works:** 26 articles on Internal Medicine and Nephrology **Affiliations:** Fellow, American College of Physicians; American Society of Nephrology; American Association of Physicians of Indian Origin; Medical Director, Dialysis Unit, Plains Regional Medical Center **Hob./spts.:** Lawn tennis, squash, billiards **SIC code:** 80 **Address:** University of New Mexico, Health Science Center, Albuquerque, NM 87131 **E-mail:** dhi68@gmail.com

DHIR, GUNJAN
Industry: Healthcare **Born:** September 26, 1978, India **Univ./degree:** M.A., Dentistry, Marquette Medical College, 2005 **Current organization:** Tufts Dental School **Title:** Assistant Professor **Type of organization:** College **Major product:** Dentistry education **Area of distribution:** Boston, Massachusetts **Area of Practice:** Prosthodontics **Affiliations:** A.C.O.; A.A.I.D.; A.C.S. **Hob./spts.:** Water sports, piloting air craft **SIC code:** 80 **Address:** 9603 E. Fourth Ave., #A, Spokane Valley, WA 99206 **E-mail:** gunjandhir@yahoo.co.in

DI GIANFILIPPO, ANTHONY
Industry: Healthcare **Born:** February 15, 1957, Chicago, Illinois **Univ./degree:** B.S., Psychology, Northwestern University, 1979; M.D., University of Illinois, 1983 **Current organization:** West Suburban Neurosurgical Associates **Title:** M.D. **Type of organization:** Group practice **Major product:** Patient care **Area of distribution:** Illinois **Area of Practice:** Neurosurgery **Affiliations:** A.A.N.S.; Congress of Neuro Surgeons **SIC code:** 80 **Address:** West Suburban Neurosurgical Associates, 20 E. Ogden Ave., Hinsdale, IL 60521

DI MAURO, CYNTHIA L.
Industry: Healthcare **Born:** Elizabeth, New Jersey **Univ./degree:** Pre-Med, Pennsylvania State University; M.D., American University of the Caribbean School of Medicine, 1982 **Current organization:** Western PA Rehab Associates, LTD **Title:** M.D. **Type of organization:** Private practice **Major product:** Healthcare services **Area of distribution:** McMurray, Pennsylvania **Area of Practice:** Supervise operations, physical medicine and rehabilitation **Affiliations:** A.M.A; American Association of Electrodiagnostic Medicine; Pennsylvania Medical Society; American Academy of Physical Medicine and Rehabilitation; Pennsylvania Academy of Physical Medicine and Rehabilitation **Hob./spts.:** Skiing, travel **SIC code:** 80 **Address:** Western PA Rehab Associates, LTD, 6000 Waterdam Plaza Dr., Suite 260, McMurray, PA 15317 **E-mail:** wpramd@yahoo.com

DIB, JOE E.
Industry: Healthcare **Born:** July 16, 1969, Beirut, Lebanon **Univ./degree:** B.S., Chemistry, City University of New York at Brooklyn, 1990; M.D., State University of New York Downstate, 1994 **Current organization:** Emergency Medical Associates **Title:** M.D. **Type of organization:** Hospital **Major product:** Patient care **Area of distribution:** New York **Area of Practice:** Emergency medicine, internal medicine **Published works:** Article **Affiliations:** F.A.C.P.; F.A.C.E.P.; A.M.A.; New Jersey State Medical Association **SIC code:** 80 **Address:** Emergency Medical Associates, 651 W. Mount Pleasant Ave., Livingston, NJ 07039 **E-mail:** joeedib@msn.com **Web address:** www.ema.com

DIDIER, CHERI D.
Industry: Healthcare **Born:** May 25, 1956, Spokane, Washington **Current organization:** Rockwood Clinic PS **Title:** Purchasing Manager **Type of organization:** Clinic/surgery center **Major product:** Patient care, surgical services **Area of distribution:** Spokane, Washington **Area of Practice:** Management **Affiliations:** M.G.M.A. **Hob./spts.:** Reading, hiking, walking, outdoor activities, bowling **SIC code:** 80 **Address:** Rockwood Clinic PS, Purchasing Dept., 400 E. Fifth Ave., Spokane, WA 99202 **E-mail:** cdidier@rockwoodclinic.com **Web address:** www.rockwoodclinic.com

DIDRIKSON, LYNNE M.
Industry: Healthcare **Born:** December 15, 1954, Mason City, Iowa **Univ./degree:** M.D., University of Minnesota, 1982 **Current organization:** Altru Clinic **Title:** M.D. **Type of organization:** Clinic **Major product:** Patient care **Area of distribution:**

Minnesota **Area of Practice:** Family practice, women's healthcare, pediatrics **Published works:** Articles **Affiliations:** A.M.A.; A.A.F.P. **Hob./spts.:** Quilting, reading **SIC code:** 80 **Address:** Altru Clinic, 711 Delmore Dr., Roseau, MN 56751 **E-mail:** ldidrikson@altru.org

DIEZ, JOSE G.
Industry: Medical **Born:** November 14, 1966, Bogota, Colombia **Univ./degree:** M.D., Javeriana University, Colombia, 1989 **Current organization:** Tulane University Health Sciences Center **Title:** M.D., F.A.C.C., F.S.C.A.I. **Type of organization:** University hospital **Major product:** Advanced interventional coronary and peripheral procedures **Area of distribution:** National **Area of Practice:** Interventional Cardiology **Honors/awards:** Chief Resident, Javeriana University; Chief Fellow, Texas Heart Institute; AHA/ACC Educational Awards **Published works:** Articles, book chapters **Affiliations:** F.A.C.C.; A.H.A.; S.C.A.I. **SIC code:** 80 **Address:** Tulane University Health Sciences Center, 1430 Tulane Ave., SL-48, New Orleans, LA 70112 **E-mail:** jdiez@tulane.edu

DIFRANCESCO, EILEEN
Industry: Healthcare **Univ./degree:** M.D. **Area of distribution:** National **SIC code:** 80 **Address:** 11 East 66th St., New York, NY 10021 **E-mail:** edifran@msn.com

DIGEROLAMO, ALBERT
Industry: Healthcare **Born:** April 25, 1952, Hammonton, New Jersey **Univ./degree:** M.D., Jefferson Medical College, 1982 **Current organization:** Family Medicine Associates **Title:** M.D. **Type of organization:** Private practice **Major product:** Patient care **Area of distribution:** Maryland **Area of Practice:** Family practice **Affiliations:** A.A.F.P.; Maryland Academy of Family Physicians; St. Joseph's Hospital, Baltimore, Maryland **Hob./spts.:** Weight training, bicycling **SIC code:** 80 **Address:** Family Medicine Associates, 35 E. Padonia Rd., Timonium, MD 21093 **E-mail:** gerolamo@webtv.net

DIKANSKY, YURY
Industry: Dentistry **Born:** August 14, 1945, Ukraine **Univ./degree:** D.D.S., New York University Dental School, 1969 **Current organization:** Yury Dikansky, D.D.S. **Title:** D.D.S. **Type of organization:** Dental office **Major product:** Dental services **Area of distribution:** Brooklyn, New York **Area of Practice:** General and cosmetic dentistry **Honors/awards:** America's Top Dentists 2003-2004; listed as a member in The National Register's Who's Who in Executives and Professionals, 2004-2005 edition; Best Doctor's 2004, Better Living Magazine **Hob./spts.:** Ping pong, tennis **SIC code:** 80 **Address:** Yury Dikansky, D.D.S., 7712 Bay Pkwy., Brooklyn, NY 11214 **E-mail:** ydikansky@yahoo.com

DILLARD, DEANNE
Industry: Healthcare **Born:** Garden City, Kansas **Univ./degree:** A.S., Nursing, Amarillo College **Current organization:** Accolade Healthcare **Major product:** Patient care **Area of distribution:** Amarillo, Texas **Hob./spts.:** Family, beauty consulting **SIC code:** 80 **Address:** Accolade Healthcare, 6300 540 West, Suite 2210, Amarillo, TX 79106 **E-mail:** dillard@kindstar.net

DIMANCESCU, MIHAI D.
Industry: Healthcare **Born:** March 2, 1940, Maidenhead, England **Univ./degree:** M.D., University of Toulouse, France, 1969 **Current organization:** Neurological Surgery, P.C.; 2nd address, 520 Franklin Ave., Garden City, NY 11530 **Title:** M.D. **Type of organization:** Medical practice/hospital **Major product:** Medical service **Area of distribution:** Freeport, New York **Area of Practice:** Board Certified, Neurosurgery **Published works:** Articles **Affiliations:** American Association of Neurological Surgery **Hob./spts.:** Old home restoration, travel **SIC code:** 80 **Address:** Neurological Surgery, P.C., 88 S. Bergen Place, Freeport, NY 11520 **E-mail:** neurofree@aol.com

DIMAURO, SALVATORE
Industry: Medical **Born:** November 14, 1939, Italy **Univ./degree:** M.D., University Padova, Italy, 1957 **Current organization:** Columbia University **Title:** M.D./Professor **Type of organization:** University hospital **Major product:** Medical services **Area of distribution:** International **Area of Practice:** Neurology **Honors/awards:** Lucy G. Moses Professor **Published works:** 600+ articles, book chapters **Affiliations:** Institute of Medicine; American Academy of Sciences **Hob./spts.:** Languages **SIC code:** 80 **Address:** Columbia University, College of Physicians & Surgeons, 630 W. 168th St., New York, NY 10032 **E-mail:** sd@columbia.edu **Web address:** www.columbia.edu

DIMICCO, ROBERT K.
Industry: Healthcare **Born:** April 30, 1955, Cranston, Rhode Island **Univ./degree:** A.S., Culinary Arts, Johnson & Wales University, 1972; A.S., Dietary Management & Nutrition, Community College of Rhode Island, 1985 **Current organization:** Montserrat of Beverly **Title:** Director of Nutritional Services **Type of organization:** Rehab and nursing center **Major product:** Patient nutrition/care **Area of distribution:** Beverly, Massachusetts **Area of Practice:** Administration, nutrition, dietary needs for the elderly **Published works:** Recipes **Hob./spts.:** Golf, Composer of music **SIC code:** 80 **Address:** 202 Lewis St., Lynn, MA 01902

DINCES, ELIZABETH A.
Industry: Medical **Born:** October 30, 1965, New York, New York **Univ./degree:** M.D., Albert Einstein University, 1991 **Current organization:** Montefiore Medical Center **Title:** M.D. **Type of organization:** University hospital **Major product:** Medical services **Area of distribution:** National **Area of Practice:** Otology, neurotology, surgery for hearing loss, skull base tumors and facial nerve disorders **Affiliations:** American Academy of Otolaryngology/Head and Neck Surgery; American Neurotology Society; Association for Research in Otolaryngology **Hob./spts.:** Sailing, scuba diving, skiing **SIC code:** 80 **Address:** Montefiore Medical Center, 3400 Bainbridge Ave., Third floor, Bronx, NY 10467 **E-mail:** edinces@montefiore.org

DIONYSIAN, EMIL
Industry: Healthcare **Univ./degree:** M.D., Chicago Medical School **Current organization:** Harbor McArthur Medical Office, Kaiser Permanente **Title:** M.D. **Type of organization:** Medical office **Major product:** Patient care **Area of distribution:** California **Area of Practice:** Orthopaedic surgery, hand surgery **Published works:** JHS, May 2000; JHS, May 2005 **Affiliations:** A.S.S.H.; B.E.S.; C.M.A.; A.A.O.S.; N.Y.A.S. **Hob./spts.:** Yoga, meditation **SIC code:** 80 **Address:** Harbor McArthur Medical Office, Orthopaedic Surgery, 3401 S. Harbor Blvd., Santa Ana, CA 92704

DISSIN, JONATHAN
Industry: Healthcare **Born:** August 4, 1948, Philadelphia, Pennsylvania **Univ./degree:** M.D., St. George's University; Residency, University of Vermont; Fellowship, Massachusetts General Hospital **Current organization:** Albert Einstein Medical Center **Title:** M.D. **Type of organization:** Tertiary care hospital **Major product:** Patient care **Area of distribution:** Pennsylvania **Area of Practice:** Neurology **Affiliations:** A.A.N.; American Heart Association; Society for Neuroscience **Hob./spts.:** Scuba diving, gourmet cooking **SIC code:** 80 **Address:** Albert Einstein Medical Center, Neurology Dept., 5501 Old York Rd., Philadelphia, PA 19141 **E-mail:** dissinj@einstein.edu

DOGRA, VIKRAM S.
Industry: Medical **Born:** January 27, 1953, India **Univ./degree:** M.D., Jawaharlal Lal Institute of Post Graduate Medical Education and Research, India, 1977; M.D., Yale University School of Medicine, 1995 **Current organization:** University Hospitals of Cleveland **Title:** M.D. **Type of organization:** University hospital **Major product:** Patient care/education **Area of distribution:** Ohio **Area of Practice:** Radiology, ultrasound and cross sectional imaging **Affiliations:** Radiological Society of North America **Hob./spts.:** Golf, music **SIC code:** 80 **Address:** University Hospitals of Cleveland, 11100 Euclid Ave., Cleveland, OH 44106 **E-mail:** dogra@uhrad.com

DOLLAR, DEBBIE N.
Industry: Healthcare **Born:** October 9, 1950, Albany, Georgia **Current organization:** Nacogdoches Neurosurgery, P.A. **Title:** Administrator **Type of organization:** Medical practice **Major product:** Patient care **Area of distribution:** Texas **Area of Practice:** Administration **Hob./spts.:** Spending time with her grandchildren and family **SIC code:** 80 **Address:** Nacogdoches Neurosurgery, P.A., 617 Russell Blvd., Nacogdoches, TX 75965 **E-mail:** debbied@txucom.net

DOMANTAY, PHILLIP A.
Industry: Healthcare **Born:** March 24, 1979, San Jose, California **Univ./degree:** B.S., Hotel and Restaurant Management, University of Baguio, Philippines, 2000 **Current organization:** Sunrise Senior Living **Title:** Dining Services Director **Type of organization:** Senior facility **Major product:** Elder care **Area of distribution:** National **Area of Practice:** Culinary arts; Certified Hospitality Supervisor; Certified Hospitality Professional; Certified Food Safety Manager **Honors/awards:** Trainer of the Year, American Hospitality Academy, 2003 **Affiliations:** American Hotel and Lodging Association; American Hospitality Academy **Hob./spts.:** Golf, cooking, travel **SIC code:** 80 **Address:** Sunrise Senior Living, 4855 San Felipe Rd., San Jose, CA 95135 **E-mail:** phillipdomantay@aol.com **Web address:** www.sunriseseniorliving.com

DOMINGUEZ, CARLOS E.
Industry: Healthcare **Born:** October 2, 1954, Ponce, Puerto Rico **Univ./degree:** M.D. **Current organization:** Jacajuax Healthcare Group, Inc. **Title:** M.D. **Type of organization:** Medical practice **Major product:** Patient care **Area of distribution:** Juana Diaz, Puerto Rico **Area of Practice:** HIV Specialist **Published works:** Multiple publications **Affiliations:** American Academy of HIV Medicine **Hob./spts.:** Golf **SIC code:** 80 **Address:** Jacajuax Healthcare Group, Inc., Calle Las Flores 168-A, Juana Diaz, PR 00795 **E-mail:** dominguezcmd@aol.com

DONOHOE, JEFFREY M.
Industry: Medical **Univ./degree:** M.D., New York Medical College, 1997 **Current organization:** Children's Medical Center **Title:** M.D. **Type of organization:** University/hospital **Major product:** Patient care, medical education **Area of distribution:** Georgia **Area of Practice:** Pediatric urology **SIC code:** 80 **Address:** Children's

Medical Center, BT 5726, 1446 Harper St., Augusta, GA 30907 **E-mail:** jdonohoe@mcg.edu

DOOLEY, WILLIAM C.
Industry: Medical **Born:** September 6, 1956 **Univ./degree:** B.S. with Honors, Stanford University, 1978; M.D., Vanderbilt University, 1982 **Current organization:** University of Oklahoma **Title:** M.D./Professor of Surgical Oncology **Type of organization:** University **Major product:** Patient care, medical education **Area of distribution:** Oklahoma City, Oklahoma **Area of Practice:** Surgical oncology **Affiliations:** Fellow, American College of Surgeons; American Society of Clinical Oncology; Association for Academic Surgery **Hob./spts.:** Fly-fishing, horseback riding **SIC code:** 80 **Address:** University of Oklahoma, 920 S L Young Blvd., Oklahoma City, OK 73104 **E-mail:** william-dooley@ouhsc.edu

DOPPELT, CELA
Industry: Healthcare **Born:** July, 1952, Kansas City, Missouri **Univ./degree:** M.D., University of Missouri, 1979 **Current organization:** Wellesley Women's Care **Title:** M.D. **Type of organization:** Women's health facility **Major product:** Obstetrics, gynecology, infertility care **Area of distribution:** Wellesley, Massachusetts **Area of Practice:** Menopause management **Affiliations:** A.M.W.A.; M.M.S. **Hob./spts.:** Cooking, films **SIC code:** 80 **Address:** Wellesley Women's Care, 204 Worcester Rd., Wellesley, MA 02481

DORMANS, JOHN P.
Industry: Medical **Born:** January 13, 1957, Wayne, Indiana **Univ./degree:** M.D., Indiana University, 1983 **Current organization:** Children's Hospital of Philadelphia, The University of Pennsylvania **Title:** Chief of Orthopaedic Surgery, Professor of Orthopaedic Surgery, The University of Pennsylvania School of Medicine **Type of organization:** University hospital - children's hospital **Major product:** Medical services, teaching, research **Area of distribution:** Philadelphia, Pennsylvania **Area of Practice:** Orthopaedic surgery (pediatric) **Honors/awards:** President of Medical Staff, The Children's Hospital of Philadelphia, 1999-2001; Orthopaedics Overseas Leadership Award, 2002; Nicholson Award for Teaching, 1993; Kashiwagi-Juzuki Traveling Fellow, A.A.O.S., 1996 **Published works:** 140+ papers, 50+ chapters, 4 books **Affiliations:** F.A.A.O.S.; P.O.S.N.A.; S.R.S.; A.B.O.S.; A.O.A.; M.S.T.S.; S.I.C.O.T.; D.O. **Hob./spts.:** Family, travel, painting, reading **SIC code:** 80 **Address:** Children's Hospital of Philadelphia, 34th St. & Civic Center Blvd., Philadelphia, PA 19104-4399 **E-mail:** dormans@email.chop.edu

DOSKOW, JEFFREY B.
Industry: Healthcare **Current organization:** Suburban Heart Group, P.A. **Title:** M.D. **Type of organization:** Group practice **Major product:** Patient care **Area of distribution:** New Jersey **Area of Practice:** Cardiology **SIC code:** 80 **Address:** Suburban Heart Group, P.A., 2333 Morris Ave., Suite D-1, Union, NJ 07083

DOTSON, SUSAN L.
Industry: Healthcare **Born:** February 2, 1958, Tucson, Arizona **Univ./degree:** R.N., Mount Carmel School of Nursing, 1979; Certificate, Georgetown University Healthcare Leadership Institute, 2003; B.S. Candidate, North Carolina A&T State University School of Nursing **Current organization:** Moses Cone Health System, Wesley Long Community Hospital **Title:** Director of Operative Services **Type of organization:** Hospital **Major product:** Patient care **Area of distribution:** Greensboro, North Carolina **Area of Practice:** Operative services **Honors/awards:** Member, Golden Key International Honour Society **Affiliations:** A.O.R.N.; Phi Kappa Phi **Hob./spts.:** Spending time with family, the outdoors, reading **SIC code:** 80 **Address:** Moses Cone Health System, Wesley Long Community Hospital, 501 North Elam Ave., Greensboro, NC 27403-1199 **E-mail:** sue.dotson@mosescone.com **Web address:** www.mosescone.com

DOUGHERTY, ERICKA W.
Industry: Healthcare **Born:** September 12, 1979, San Antonio, Texas **Univ./degree:** National Certification for Massage Therapy, L'Oreal Academy and Esthetician at Loraine's Academy **Current organization:** Ericka W. Dougherty LLC **Title:** Founder/Owner **Type of organization:** Health spa **Major product:** Total body & mind rehabilitation **Area of distribution:** Clearwater, Florida **Area of Practice:** Therapeutic massage and skincare **Published works:** Poems and articles **Affiliations:** NCBTMB; ABMP; NPI **Hob./spts.:** Writing, reading, golf, canoeing, volunteer work **SIC code:** 80 **Address:** Ericka W. Dougherty Spa, 600 Lakeview Road, Suite E, Clearwater, FL 33756 **E-mail:** erickawdougherty@zoomshare.com

DOUGHERTY, LORALEE
Industry: Healthcare **Born:** November 30, 1949, Teaneck, New Jersey **Univ./degree:** B.S.N., Monmouth University, 1999 **Current organization:** Optimum Health Care **Title:** Doctor of Naturology **Type of organization:** Visiting nurse association **Major product:** Patient care **Area of distribution:** New Jersey **Area of Practice:** Holistic Health Practitioner **Hob./spts.:** Golf, kayaking **SIC code:** 80 **Address:** Optimum Health Care, 3 Beverout Place, Atlantic Highlands, NJ 07716 **E-mail:** loralee@monmouth.com

DOUGLAS, DEBRA A.
Industry: Healthcare **Born:** January 30, 1955, Wisconsin **Univ./degree:** M.S., Nursing, Anna Maria College, 1990 **Current organization:** Roger Williams Medical Center **Title:** M.S.N., R.N., C.N.A. **Type of organization:** Hospital **Major product:** Patient care **Area of distribution:** Rhode Island **Area of Practice:** Nursing- administration/education **Published works:** Articles **Affiliations:** A.C.M., American Heart Association **Hob./spts.:** Swimming, golf **SIC code:** 80 **Address:** Roger Williams Medical Center, 185 Chalkstone Ave., Providence, RI 02908 **E-mail:** dadoug@msn.com

DOYLE, SHEILA MARIE
Industry: Healthcare **Born:** July 12, 1958, St. Louis, Missouri **Current organization:** St. Joseph Health Center **Title:** Cancer Registry Coordinator **Type of organization:** Hospital **Major product:** Patient care **Area of distribution:** St. Charles, Missouri **Area of Practice:** Cancer registry/oncology; RHIT Certified, Tumor Register **Affiliations:** A.H.I.M.A.; N.C.R.A.; M.O.S.T.R.A. **Hob./spts.:** Fishing, reading, Cocker Spaniels, home decorating, arts and crafts **SIC code:** 80 **Address:** St. Joseph Health Center, 300 First Capitol Dr., St. Charles, MO 63301 **E-mail:** sheila_m_doyle@ssmhc.com

DRISCOLL, DAVID L.
Industry: Healthcare **Born:** August 3, 1954, Storm Lake, Iowa **Univ./degree:** D.C., Logan University, 1978 **Current organization:** David L. Driscoll, D.C. **Title:** Doctor of Chiropractic **Type of organization:** Private practice **Major product:** Patient care **Area of distribution:** Colorado Springs, Colorado **Area of Practice:** Acupuncture, chiropractic **Affiliations:** F.I.B.C.A.; A.C.A.; C.C.A.; E.P.C.C.A. **Hob./spts.:** Fishing, hiking, reading, golf **SIC code:** 80 **Address:** David L. Driscoll, D.C., 1819 W. Colorado Ave., Colorado Springs, CO 80904 **E-mail:** driscollbct@aol.com

DUAN, DAYUE
Industry: Medical/cardiovascular **Born:** October 9, 1958, China **Univ./degree:** M.S., Sun Yat-Sen University of Medical Sciences, 1987; M.D., Hunan Medical University, 1982; Ph.D., McGill University, 1996 **Current organization:** University of Nevada School of Medicine **Title:** M.D./Ph.D./Associate Professor **Type of organization:** University **Major product:** Patient care, medical education and research **Area of distribution:** Reno, Nevada **Area of Practice:** Pharmacology, cardiology, functional genomics **Honors/awards:** Grantee, A.H.A., 1999; N.I.H., 2000 **Published works:** 30 articles in professional journals **Affiliations:** A.A.A.S.; A.H.A.; I.S.H.R.; A.P.S.; FB?; Biophysics Society **Hob./spts.:** Golf, tennis, basketball **SIC code:** 80 **Address:** University of Nevada School of Medicine, Dept. of Pharmacology MS 318, Reno, NV 89557 **E-mail:** dduan@med.unr.edu

DUBLIN, TREVOR J.A.
Industry: Healthcare **Title:** Administrator **Type of organization:** Nursing and residential center **Major product:** Long term care **Area of Practice:** Administration **SIC code:** 80 **Address:** Maple Glen Center, 12-15 Saddle River Dr., Fairlawn, NJ 07410 **E-mail:** trevor.dublin@genisishcc.com **Web address:** www.genesishcc.com

DUDRICK, STANLEY J.
Industry: Medical **Born:** April 9, 1935, Pennsylvania **Univ./degree:** M.D., University of Pennsylvania School of Medicine, 1961 **Current organization:** Bridgeport Hospital - Yale New Haven Health **Title:** M.D./Chair, Dept. of Surgery **Type of organization:** University hospital **Major product:** Patient care, medical education **Area of distribution:** Bridgeport, Connecticut **Area of Practice:** Gastroenterology, oncology **Published works:** Multiple publications **Affiliations:** F.A.C.S.; A.S.A.; S.U.S. **Hob./spts.:** Sailing, hiking, skiing **SIC code:** 80 **Address:** Bridgeport Hospital - Yale New Haven Health, 267 Grant St., Bridgeport, CT 06610 **E-mail:** psdudr@bpthosp.org

DUNHAM, GLYNIS D.
Industry: Healthcare **Born:** August 5, 1975, Newport, Arkansas **Univ./degree:** A.A.S., Med. Lab Technology, Arkansas State University, 1996 **Current organization:** Harris Hospital **Title:** Laboratory Director **Type of organization:** Hospital/laboratory **Major product:** Patient care, lab science **Area of distribution:** Newport, Arkansas **Area of Practice:** Laboratory science, microbiology, chemistry, hematology, management **Affiliations:** American Society of Clinical Pathologists; Hospital Patient Safety Committee **Hob./spts.:** Interior decorating, crafts (floral design) **SIC code:** 80 **Address:** Harris Hospital, 1205 McLain St., Newport, AR 72112 **E-mail:** glynis_dunham@chs.net

DUNN, RICHARD B.
Industry: Healthcare **Born:** June 7, 1954, Brooklyn, New York **Univ./degree:** B.S., with Honors, Biology, Franklin & Marshall College, 1976; M.S., Head and Neck Cancer, Roswell Park Memorial Institute; D.D.S., New York University College of Dentistry, 1980 **Current organization:** Chemung Family Dental Center **Title:** President **Type of organization:** Private practice **Major product:** Patient care **Area of distribution:** New York **Area of Practice:** Esthetic dentistry, implants, cerac system **Honors/**

awards: Pierre Fouche Dental Honor Society **Affiliations:** American Dental Association, 6th District; New York State Dental Association; Co-Chair, District Malpractice Claims Committee; BOCES, Dental Advisory Board **Hob./spts.:** Skiing, sailing, travel **SIC code:** 80 **Address:** Chemung Family Dental Center, 1007 Broadway, Elmira, NY 14904 **E-mail:** rdunn@stny.rr.com

DURST, JULIE A.
Industry: Healthcare **Born:** January 4, 1956, John Day, Oregon **Univ./degree:** R.N., Linn-Benton Community College **Current organization:** Avamere-Lebanon Rehab & Specialty Care **Title:** R.N., Director of Nursing **Type of organization:** Nursing home **Major product:** Elder care **Area of distribution:** Oregon **Area of Practice:** Alzheimer's nursing, gerontology **Affiliations:** Oregon Healthcare Association **Hob./spts.:** Music, painting, writing romance novels **SIC code:** 80 **Address:** Avamere-Lebanon Rehab & Specialty Care, 350 S. Eighth, Lebanon, OR 97355 **E-mail:** john.durst@worldnet.att.net

DUVVURI, SRINIVAS
Industry: Healthcare **Born:** August 27, 1960, Visakhapatnam, India **Univ./degree:** M.D., University of West Indies, Jamaica, 1984 **Current organization:** Swamy & Ariton Cardiology Associates **Title:** M.D. **Type of organization:** Cardiology practice **Major product:** Cardiology **Area of distribution:** Staten Island and Manhattan, New York **Area of Practice:** Interventional cardiology **Affiliations:** Fellow, American College of Cardiology; America Heart Association **Hob./spts.:** Tennis, swimming **SIC code:** 80 **Address:** Swamy & Ariton Cardiology Associates, 1366 Victory Blvd., Suite B, Staten Island, NY 10301 **E-mail:** sriniduv@aol.com

DYNSKI, MARGUERITE
Industry: Healthcare **Born:** March 23, 1947, Rochester, New York **Univ./degree:** M.D., SUNY Buffalo, 1975 **Current organization:** Rochester General Hospital **Title:** M.D., Sister of Saint Joseph **Type of organization:** Hospital **Major product:** Patient care, surgery **Area of distribution:** Rochester, New York **Area of Practice:** Breast surgery **Honors/awards:** Certificate of Achievement, Rochester Academy of Medicine, 2001; Diploma in Tropical Medicine & Hygiene, University of Liverpool, England, 1975 **Affiliations:** Past President, The Association of Sister, Brother & Priest Physicians; Association of Women Surgeons; Fellow, American College of Surgeons, 2000; A.M.A.; Medical Society of the State of New York; Rochester Academy of Medicine; Rochester Surgical Society; Monroe County Medical Society; Sisters of St. Joseph (Roman Catholic Nun) **Hob./spts.:** Traveling (visiting family in Poland), golf, reading, singing, playing accordion **SIC code:** 80 **Address:** Rochester General Hospital, 1445 Portland Ave., Suite 301, Rochester, NY 14621

DZAMASHVILI, KONSTANTIN
Industry: Healthcare **Born:** May 17, 1951, Republic of Georgia **Univ./degree:** M.D.; M.Sc., Tbilisi Medical School, 1973; Tbilisi State University 1981 **Current organization:** Neuromed **Title:** M.D., Ph.D. **Type of organization:** Hospital **Major product:** Patient care **Area of distribution:** De Page County, Illinois **Area of Practice:** Neurology **Honors/awards:** Board Certified, A.B.P.N. **Published works:** Journal of Cephalalgia **Affiliations:** A.M.A.; A.A.N. **Hob./spts.:** Jogging **SIC code:** 80 **Address:** Dr. Konstantin Dzamashvili, Neuromed - 3 South, 517 Winfield Rd., Warrenville, IL 60555 **E-mail:** kotiko@telocity.com

ECHEVARRIA, EDGAR
Industry: Dentistry **Born:** April 20, 1951, San Juan, Puerto Rico **Univ./degree:** D.M.D., University of Puerto Rico School of Dentistry, 1976 **Current organization:** Oral & Maxillofacial Surgery Center **Title:** D.M.D., Professor **Type of organization:** Private practice **Major product:** Oral & maxillofacial surgery **Area of distribution:** Puerto Rico **Area of Practice:** Restorative and cosmetic surgery of the face **Published works:** 4 journal articles, 1 book (Dental Guide) **Affiliations:** Puerto Rico Society of Dentistry; American Academy of Cosmetic Surgery **Hob./spts.:** Music, playing drums **SIC code:** 80 **Address:** Oral & Maxillofacial Surgery Center, Concordia Shopping Center, 65th Infantry Ave., Suite 208, San Juan, PR 00926 **E-mail:** maxilo@prtc.net

EDWARDS, BETTY J.
Industry: Healthcare **Born:** December 15, 1950, Houston, Texas **Univ./degree:** M.D., University of Texas, Medical Branch, Galveston, 1976 **Current organization:** Betty J. Edwards, M.D. **Title:** M.D. **Type of organization:** Private practice **Major product:** Women's healthcare **Area of distribution:** Houston, Texas **Area of Practice:** Ob/Gyn **Affiliations:** F.A.C.O.G. **SIC code:** 80 **Address:** Betty J. Edwards, M.D., 17070 Red Oak Dr., Suite 405, Houston, TX 77090

EDWARDS, FRANKLIN G.
Industry: Medical **Born:** November 13, 1954, Kingston, Jamaica **Univ./degree:** M.D., University of Western Jamaica, 1981 **Current organization:** SUNY Downstate University Hospital **Title:** M.D. **Type of organization:** University hospital **Major product:** Patient care, medical education **Area of distribution:** Brooklyn, New York **Area of Practice:** Family practice **Published works:** Multiple publications **Affiliations:** A.A.F.P. **Hob./spts.:** Tennis, jogging, soccer **SIC code:** 80 **Address:** SUNY Downstate University Hospital, 450 Clarkson Ave., Brooklyn, NY 11203

EFFENDI, ABDUL R.
Industry: Healthcare **Born:** June 11, 1965, Syria **Univ./degree:** M.D., Magna Cum Laude, Aleppo University, Syria, 1989 **Current organization:** Abdul R. Effendi, M.D. P.C. **Title:** M.D. **Type of organization:** Private practice **Major product:** Patient care **Area of distribution:** Troy, Michigan **Area of Practice:** Nephrology **Affiliations:** American Society of Nephrology; Michigan State Medical Society; Board Member, International Association of Organ Donation; Wayne County Medical Society **SIC code:** 80 **Address:** Abdul R. Effendi, M.D. P.C., 2546 Haverford Dr., Troy, MI 48098 **E-mail:** areffendi@yahoo.com

EGWELE, RICHARD A.
Industry: Healthcare **Born:** December 29, 1947, Nigeria **Univ./degree:** M.D., Universidad de Navarra, 1973 **Current organization:** Exchange Medical Center **Title:** M.D. **Type of organization:** Medical facility **Major product:** Patient care **Area of distribution:** Chicago, Illinois **Area of Practice:** Orthopaedic surgery **Affiliations:** F.A.A.O.S.; N.M.A.; I.O.S. **Hob./spts.:** Golf **SIC code:** 80 **Address:** Exchange Medical Center, 9135 S. Exchange Ave., Chicago, IL 60617 **E-mail:** regwele@yahoo.com

EHRLICH, PAUL M.
Industry: Healthcare **Born:** June 8, 1944, New York, New York **Univ./degree:** B.A., Art History, Columbia University, 1966; M.D., New York University, 1970; Diplomate, American Boards of Pediatrics and Allergy and Immunology **Current organization:** Allergy & Asthma Associates of Murray Hill **Title:** M.D. **Type of organization:** Group practice **Major product:** Patient care **Area of distribution:** New York **Area of Practice:** Allergies and asthma; Trained at Bellevue Hospital in Pediatrics, Walter Reed Army Medical Center and NYU Medical Center **Honors/awards:** Listed, Best Doctors in Allergy for 1998, 1999, 2000; Profiled by Biography Magazine **Published works:** Numerous articles published in national and international professional journals; Book, "What Your Doctor May Not Tell You About Your Children's Allergies and Asthma" **Affiliations:** American Academy of Allergy, Asthma and Immunology; American Academy of Pediatrics; Beth Israel Medical Center; NYU Medical Center **Hob./spts.:** Art history, reading **SIC code:** 80 **Address:** Allergy & Asthma Associates of Murray Hill, 35 E. 35th St., New York, NY 10016 **E-mail:** drpaulehrlich@aol.com **Web address:** www.allergy-asthma-associates.com/

EIKE, THELMA L.
Industry: Healthcare **Born:** March 13, 1930, Woodward, Oklahoma **Univ./degree:** B.S., Education, 1977; M.S., Guidance, Counseling, Psychology, 1985, Northwest Oklahoma State University **Current organization:** Thelma L. Eike, Therapist, Counselor **Title:** Licensed Therapist and Counselor **Type of organization:** Private practice **Major product:** Therapy, counseling **Area of distribution:** Oklahoma **Area of Practice:** Family and marital therapy, pathology counseling **Hob./spts.:** Sports, church, volunteering, teaching, sewing **SIC code:** 80 **Address:** Rt. 1, Box 80, Fargo, OK 73840-9726

EISEN, RICHARD N.
Industry: Medical **Born:** May 17, 1958, Freeport, New York **Univ./degree:** M.D., SUNY Downstate, 1984 **Current organization:** Greenwich Hospital/Yale University **Title:** Associate Attending Pathologist/Clinical Assistant Professor **Type of organization:** Hospital/university **Major product:** Medical services **Area of distribution:** Greenwich, Connecticut **Area of Practice:** Surgical pathology, immunohistochemistry **Honors/awards:** Member, Alpha Omega Alpha; Phi Beta Kappa **Published works:** Articles, book chapters **Affiliations:** U.S.C.A.P. **Hob./spts.:** Bike riding **SIC code:** 80 **Address:** Greenwich Hospital/Yale University, Dept. of Pathology, 5 Perryridge Rd., Greenwich, CT 06830 **E-mail:** richarde@greenhosp.org **Web address:** www.greenhosp/org

EISENBERG, HARVEY
Industry: Healthcare **Current organization:** Harvey Eisenberg, M.D. **Title:** President **Type of organization:** Private practice **Major product:** Body scanning, radiology **Area of distribution:** International **Area of Practice:** Body scanning, radiology, inventions **Affiliations:** C.T.C. **SIC code:** 80 **Address:** 12 Corporate Plaza Dr., Suite 120, Suite 120, CA 92660 **E-mail:** hceisenberg@healthview.com

EL-ATTRACHE, SELIM F.
Industry: Healthcare **Born:** July 25, 1928, As Suwayda, Syria **Univ./degree:** M.D., University of Lyon **Current organization:** Selim El-Attrache, M.D., F.A.C.S. **Title:** Physician **Type of organization:** Rehabilitation center **Major product:** Treatment for orthopaedic disability, sports medicine **Area of distribution:** International **Area of practice:** Surgical pathology, forensic medicine, orthopaedics, rehabilitation **Area of Practice:** Surgical pathology, forensic medicine, orthopaedics, rehabilitation **Honors/awards:** Congressional Medal of Honor **Affiliations:** F.A.C.S.; A.B.O.S.; American Academy of Orthopaedic Surgeons; American Medical Association; Pennsylvania Medical Society; Westmoreland County Medical Society; Interstate Orthopaedic

Society; Eastern Orthopaedic Association, Inc.; Pittsburgh Arthritis Foundation; Pittsburgh Rheumatism Association; American Back Society; American College of Sports Medicine; American Orthopaedic Foot and Ankle Society; American College of Forensic Examiners; American Academy of Pain Management; American College of International Physicians; American Druze Society; International Intradiscal Therapy Society, Inc.; National Arab American Medical Association; Pedorthic Footwear Association; Spine Arthroplasty Society; American Academy of Thermology **SIC code:** 80 **Address:** Selim El-Attrache, M.D., F.A.C.S., 606 S. Church St., Mount Pleasant, PA 15666 **E-mail:** docselim@aol.com

ELDRIDGE, JOEL GLEN
Industry: Healthcare **Born:** July 21, 1961, Winnsboro, Louisiana **Univ./degree:** B.S., Northeast Louisiana University, 1983; M.D. Kirksville School of Osteopathic Medicine, 1987 **Current organization:** Franklin Medical Center, Emergency Dept. **Title:** D.O. **Type of organization:** Hospital **Major product:** Patient care, ambulance service **Area of distribution:** Louisiana **Area of Practice:** Emergency medicine **Published works:** Local newspaper articles **Affiliations:** A.O.A.; A.M.A., President, Northeast Ambulance Service **SIC code:** 80 **Address:** Franklin Medical Center, Emergency Dept., 2106 Long Rd., Winnsboro, LA 71295

ELEUTERIUS, NANCY L.
Industry: Healthcare **Born:** August 19, 1943, Biloxi, Mississippi **Univ./degree:** Attended Virginia Wesleyn **Current organization:** Sentara Mental Health Management **Title:** President/CEO **Type of organization:** Managed care behavioral health **Major product:** Insurance **Area of distribution:** Virginia **Area of Practice:** Behavioral healthcare **Honors/awards:** Women of the Year Award **Published works:** Articles **Affiliations:** Virginia Hospital Association **Hob./spts.:** Theatre, music **SIC code:** 80 **Address:** Sentara Mental Health Management, 4417 Corporation Lane, Suite 250, Virginia Beach, VA 23462 **E-mail:** nleleute@sentara.com

EL-GABALAWY, MOHAMED
Industry: Healthcare **Born:** April 22, 1954, Cairo, Egypt **Univ./degree:** M.D., Cairo University, 1978 **Current organization:** Mohamed El-Gabalawy M.D. **Title:** M.D./Staff Psychiatrist **Type of organization:** Private practice **Major product:** Psychiatry **Area of distribution:** California **Area of Practice:** Psychiatry and addiction **Affiliations:** A.S.A.M.; California Psychiatric Association; American Psychiatric Association; Medical Director, Huntington Memorial Hospital **Hob./spts.:** Travel **SIC code:** 80 **Address:** Mohamed El-Gabalawy M.D., 1111 S. Arroyo Pkwy., #415, Pasadena, CA 91105 **E-mail:** elgabalawy@earthlink.net

ELIE, JACQUELINE
Industry: Healthcare **Current organization:** Long Island Health & Safety Collection Inc. **Title:** President **Type of organization:** Drug and alcohol testing facility **Major product:** Promoting a drug and alcohol free workplace **Area of Practice:** Workplace testing **SIC code:** 80 **Address:** Long Island Health & Safety Collection Inc., 33 Front St., Suite 206, Hempstead, NY 11550-3601 **E-mail:** lihsafetycollectioninc@yahoo.com

ELLINGTON, OWEN B.
Industry: Healthcare/Law **Born:** November 22, 1946, Harrisburg, Pennsylvania **Univ./degree:** M.D., Penn State University Hershey Medical Center; J.D., Concord School of Law **Current organization:** Amerigroup Corporation **Title:** Vice President and Medical Director **Type of organization:** HMO **Area of distribution:** National **Area of Practice:** Internal medicine, hematology-oncology **Published works:** Numerous, including; (co-author) "Plasmapheresis with Antiplatelet Antibody", 1983; "Marrow Transplantation in Acute Leukemia", New England Journal of Medicine, 302:1041-1046, May 8, 1980; "Non-Tropical Spruce and B12 Deficiency", European Journal of Neurology, 16:11-15, 1977 **Affiliations:** National Medical Society; American Society of Internal Medicine; American College of Physician Executives; American Society of Hematology and Oncology **Hob./spts.:** Professional saxophone player **SIC code:** 80 **Address:** Amerigroup Corporation, 6700 West Loop South, #200, Houston, TX 77006 **E-mail:** oellington@houston.rr.com

ELLIOTT, ROBERT N.
Industry: Healthcare **Born:** July 30, 1975, Louisville, Kentucky **Univ./degree:** B.A., Chemistry/Biology, Indiana University; M.D., Indiana University School of Medicine, 1997 **Current organization:** St. Vincent Hospital **Title:** M.D. **Type of organization:** Hospital **Major product:** Patient care, medical education **Area of Practice:** Internal medicine **Affiliations:** A.C.P.; A.M.A. **Hob./spts.:** Softball, strength training, family **SIC code:** 80 **Address:** St. Vincent Hospital, Medical Education Dept., 2001 W. 86th St., Indianapolis, IN 46240 **E-mail:** drelliott20@hotmail.com

ELLIS, ANNE G.
Industry: Medical **Born:** October 10, 1953, Grenada **Univ./degree:** M.S.N., SUNY Downstate **Current organization:** Downstate Medical Center **Title:** Assistant Director of Nursing **Type of organization:** Hospital **Major product:** Patient care **Area of distribution:** Brooklyn, New York **Area of Practice:** Clinical Educator **Affiliations:** Society of Critical-Care Nurses; National Association for Staff Development; Brooklyn Association of Critical-Care Nurses; American Association of Critical-Care Nurses **Hob./spts.:** Reading, travel, music, yoga, athletics **SIC code:** 80 **Address:** 66 Rutland Rd., Brooklyn, NY 11225 **E-mail:** anne.ellis@downstate.edu

ELLIS, GEORGE L.
Industry: Healthcare **Born:** August 22, 1951, Upland, Pennsylvania **Univ./degree:** M.D., University of Pennsylvania, 1979 **Current organization:** Robert Packer Hospital **Title:** Chairman, Dept. of Emergency Medicine **Type of organization:** Hospital **Major product:** Patient care **Area of distribution:** National **Area of Practice:** Emergency medicine **Published works:** 1 book, 20 articles/chapters **Affiliations:** American college of Emergency Physicians **SIC code:** 80 **Address:** Robert Packer Hospital, 1 Guthrie Square, Sayre, PA 18840 **E-mail:** gellis@inet.guthrie.org

ELLIS, GERALD A.
Industry: Medical **Univ./degree:** M.B.A., Lawrence University, California, 1990 **Current organization:** Loma Linda University Medical Center **Title:** Senior Vice President **Type of organization:** University hospital **Major product:** Medical services **Area of distribution:** National **Area of Practice:** Hospital administration **Published works:** 1 chapter, 5 articles, 2 abstracts **Affiliations:** A.C.H.E. **SIC code:** 80 **Address:** Loma Linda University Medical Center, 11234 Anderson St., Loma Linda, CA 92354 **E-mail:** gellis@ahs.llumc.edu

EL-MANSOURY, JEYLAN
Industry: Healthcare **Born:** March 15, 1950, Alexandria, Egypt **Univ./degree:** M.D., 1974; Ph.D., 1978, Alexandria University School of Medicine **Current organization:** Jeylan El-Mansoury, M.D., Ph.D. **Title:** M.D., Ph.D. **Type of organization:** Private practice **Major product:** Medical services, patient consultation **Area of distribution:** Pennsylvania **Area of Practice:** Ophthalmology **Published works:** 7 articles **Affiliations:** A.M.A.; A.A.O. **SIC code:** 80 **Address:** Jeylan El-Mansoury, M.D., Ph.D., The Pavilion, 261 Old York Rd., Suite 520, Jenkintown, PA 19046

ELWELL, GLORIA
Industry: Healthcare **Born:** August 25, 1959, Tampa, Florida **Univ./degree:** Ph.D., Sexology, Maimonides University, 2002 **Current organization:** Meridian Counseling Center, Inc. **Title:** Psychotherapist **Type of organization:** Private practice **Major product:** Counseling, psychotherapy, hypnotherapy **Area of distribution:** Florida **Area of Practice:** Trauma, anxiety, depression **Affiliations:** A.A.M.F.T.; I.A.A.C.H.; A.T.R.T.R. **Hob./spts.:** Fishing, biking **SIC code:** 80 **Address:** Meridian Counseling Center, Inc., 38052 Meridian Ave., Dade City, FL 33526 **E-mail:** meridian352@earthlink.net **Web address:** www.meridiancounselingcenter.net

ELZEY, MARY K.
Industry: Healthcare **Born:** March 5, 1928, Denton, Maryland **Univ./degree:** R.N., 3 year Nursing Program, Easton Memorial Hospital, 1951; Completed summer school course on Alcohol Studies, Rutgers University, New Jersey **Title:** Clinical Psychiatric Nurse (Retired), Eastern Shore State Hospital Center **Type of organization:** Psychiatric hospital **Major product:** Mental health services **Area of distribution:** Maryland **Area of Practice:** Psychiatry, nursing; Was liaison person from E.S.H.C., organized a treatment aftercare program for the mentally ill in Talbot and Caroline counties giving the community health nurses support; Taught Sunday school for the mentally ill; Taught a grief counseling course at her church; Assisted in the opening of a new psychiatric hospital in Chestertown, Maryland **Affiliations:** Patient Service Chairperson, American Cancer Society (5 years); **Hob./spts.:** Gardening, walking, church, singing, sewing, crocheting **SIC code:** 80 **Address:** 309 Nathans Ave., Cambridge, MD 21613-2501

EMANUELE, SUSAN S.
Industry: Healthcare **Born:** June 28, 1957, Brooklyn, New York **Univ./degree:** B.S., Chemistry, Wagner College, New York; M.D., St. George's School of Medicine, Grenada, 1987 **Current organization:** Twin Forks Hematology Oncology **Title:** M.D. **Type of organization:** Private practice **Major product:** Patient care **Area of distribution:** New York **Area of Practice:** Hematology, oncology **Affiliations:** A.S.C.O.; A.S. Hematology; Medical Society of Suffolk County **SIC code:** 80 **Address:** Twin Forks Hematology Oncology, 36 Osprey Ave., Riverhead, NY 11901

ENGLISH III, JOSEPH M.
Industry: Healthcare **Born:** January 3, 1943, Philadelphia, Pennsylvania **Univ./degree:** M.D., Georgetown University, 1968 **Current organization:** Joseph M. English III, M.D. **Title:** M.D. **Type of organization:** Private practice **Major product:** Patient care **Area of distribution:** Bethesda, Maryland **Area of Practice:** Pediatrics **Affiliations:** Alpha Omega Alpha; Maryland Medical Society; Montgomery County Medical Society **Hob./spts.:** Golf **SIC code:** 80 **Address:** Joseph M. English III, M.D., 5301 Westbard Circle, #4, Bethesda, MD 20816

ERDAIDE, ELVIRA E.
Industry: Healthcare **Born:** January 26, 1958, Colombia **Current organization:** N.D. Ruble, M.D. **Title:** Radiologic Technologist/Mammographer **Type of organization:**

Private practice **Major product:** Patient care **Area of distribution:** Astoria, New York **Area of Practice:** Mammography, bone scans, x-rays **Affiliations:** A.R.R.T.; A.S.R.T. **Hob./spts.:** The arts, sewing, cooking **SIC code:** 80 **Address:** 107-39 Inwood St., 2nd floor, Jamaica, NY 11435

ERIKSON, KAREN S.
Industry: Healthcare **Born:** September 11, 1953, Columbia, South Carolina **Univ./degree:** University of South Carolina, 1997-1973; Medical Manager Certification in 1991 from Professional Association of Healthcare Office Manager (PAHCOM) **Current organization:** Columbia Gastroenterology Associates **Title:** Practice Administrator **Type of organization:** Group practice **Major product:** Patient care **Area of distribution:** South Carolina **Area of Practice:** Practice management, medical administration, medical consulting and training/teaching Medical Administrative Office Assistant courses **Affiliations:** Professional Association of Healthcare Office Managers, Area Representative for Columbia, South Carolina; South Carolina Medical Managers Association for Columbia and Lexington Chapters; Medical Group Management Association; North Carolina/South Carolina GI Administrators Group **Hob./spts.:** Shopping, swimming, teaching, travel, spending time with grandson (Layne) **SIC code:** 80 **Address:** 548 Cold Stream Dr., Columbia, SC 29212 **E-mail:** karenerikson@aol.com

ERLENMEYER-KIMLING, L.
Industry: Healthcare **Born:** April 18, 1932, Princeton, New Jersey **Univ./degree:** Ph.D., Columbia University, 1961 **Current organization:** NYS Psychiatric Institute **Title:** Chief, Dept. of Medical Genetics **Type of organization:** Hospital **Major product:** Psychiatry, education, research **Area of distribution:** National **Area of Practice:** Research genetics of mental disorders **Published works:** 150+ published works **Affiliations:** A.P.A.; A.P.S.; A.S.H.G. **Hob./spts.:** Animal protection **SIC code:** 80 **Address:** NYS Psychiatric Institute, 1051 Riverside Dr., Mail Unit #6, New York, NY 10032 **E-mail:** le4@columbia.edu

ERLICHMAN, MICHAEL C.
Industry: Healthcare **Born:** June 28, 1946, Bronx, New York **Univ./degree:** B.S., Biology, Farleigh Dickenson University, 1968; D.D.S., New York University School of Dentistry, 1973 **Current organization:** Michael C. Erlichman, D.D.S. **Title:** Oral Surgeon/Associate Professor, Seton Hall School of Graduate Medicine **Type of organization:** Private practice/Graduate dental school **Major product:** Patient care/Education **Area of distribution:** New Jersey **Area of Practice:** Oral and maxillofacial surgery **Honors/awards:** Diplomate, American Board of Oral and Maxillofacial Surgery **Published works:** 6+ articles **Affiliations:** Attending Surgeon, St. Joseph's Mountainside Hospital, New Jersey; Fellow, American College of Dentists; Chief Resident, Oral and Maxillofacial Surgery, Montefiore Hospital, 1976 **Hob./spts.:** Cooking, physical fitness **SIC code:** 80 **Address:** Michael C. Erlichman, D.D.S., 50 E. Main St., Little Falls, NJ 07424 **E-mail:** drmce@msn.com

ERNEST, PAUL H.
Industry: Healthcare **Born:** December 21, 1947, Toledo, Ohio **Univ./degree:** M.D., Wayne State University School of Medicine, 1973 **Current organization:** TLC Eye Care of Michigan **Title:** M.D. **Type of organization:** Ophthalmology practice **Major product:** Ophthalmology **Area of distribution:** Michigan **Area of Practice:** Cataract and refractive surgery **Affiliations:** A.A.O.; A.S.C.R.S.; A.B.E.S. **Hob./spts.:** Collecting antique furniture and clocks, golf, travel **SIC code:** 80 **Address:** TLC Eye Care of Michigan, 1116 W. Ganson, Jackson, MI 49202 **E-mail:** paul.ernest@tlcvision.com **Web address:** www.tlcvision.com

ESCARO, DANILO U.
Industry: Healthcare **Born:** December 31, 1940, Tiaong-Quezon, Philippines **Univ./degree:** M.D., University of Santo Tomas, Manila, Philippines, 1963 **Current organization:** York Hospital, Dept. of Pathology **Title:** M.D, **Type of organization:** Hospital **Major product:** Medical laboratory services **Area of distribution:** York, Pennsylvania **Area of Practice:** Pathology **Published works:** 1 article **Affiliations:** Fellow, C.A.P.; Fellow, A.A.C.S.; Fellow, M.C.P.; Fellow, I.A.P.; P.S.P.; N.J.S.P.; A.M.A.; P.M.S.; A.C.M.; A.F.P.C.C.; P.A.B.B.; F.S.M.B.; I.S.B.P.; N.K.F.; Rotary International **Hob./spts.:** Golf, classic guitar **SIC code:** 80 **Address:** York Hospital, Dept. of Pathology, 1001 S. George St., York, PA 17405 **E-mail:** descaro@wellspan.org **Web address:** www.wellspan.org

ESERNIO-JENSSEN, DEBRA D.
Industry: Healthcare **Born:** February 28, 1956, Queens, New York **Univ./degree:** B.S., Biology, SUNY Binghamton, 1978; M.D., University of Rochester School of Medicine, 1982 **Current organization:** Schneider Children's Hospital **Title:** M.D. **Type of organization:** Children's hospital **Major product:** Patient care **Area of distribution:** New York **Area of Practice:** Child abuse **Published works:** 15 articles, 2 chapters **Affiliations:** A.A.P.; A.P.S. **Hob./spts.:** Family, golf, kickboxing **SIC code:** 80 **Address:** Schneider Children's Hospital, 410 Lakeville Rd., Suite 108, New Hyde Park, NY 11042 **E-mail:** dejenssen@aol.com

ESTAFAN, MAGED MAHER
Industry: Healthcare **Born:** August 27, 1955 **Univ./degree:** M.D., Cairo University, Egypt, 1981 **Current organization:** Human Services Center **Title:** M.D. **Type of organization:** Hospital **Major product:** Mental healthcare **Area of distribution:** South Dakota **Area of Practice:** Psychiatry **Published works:** Articles **Affiliations:** A.M.A., A.P.A. **Hob./spts.:** Reading, tennis **SIC code:** 80 **Address:** Human Services Center, 3515 Broadway, Yankton, SD 57079 **E-mail:** mestafan2002@yahoo.com

ESTRADA, ADAHLI
Industry: Healthcare **Born:** April 13, 1965, San Juan, Puerto Rico **Univ./degree:** M.D., University of Puerto Rico, 1990 **Current organization:** East Alabama Arthritis Center **Title:** M.D. **Type of organization:** Medical clinic **Major product:** Patient care, rheumatology, treatment of rheumatic diseases **Area of distribution:** Puerto Rico **Area of Practice:** Subspecialty - rheumatology **Affiliations:** M.A.S.A.; American College of Rheumatology **Hob./spts.:** Tennis, aerobic fitness, reading, travel, birdwatching **SIC code:** 80 **Address:** East Alabama Arthritis Center, 1536 Professional Pkwy., Auburn, AL 36830 **E-mail:** aestrada@mindspring.com

EVANS, ERIN
Industry: Healthcare **Born:** April 6, 1962, Ridgewood, New Jersey **Univ./degree:** D.D.S., Indiana University School of Dentistry, 1990 **Current organization:** Dr. Erin Evans **Title:** Dentist **Type of organization:** Private practice **Major product:** Dental care **Area of distribution:** Lafayette, Indiana **Area of Practice:** Dental implants, cosmetics and restorative, ICOI Mastership **Affiliations:** A.D.A.; I.C.O.I. **Hob./spts.:** Golf, reading **SIC code:** 80 **Address:** Dr. Erin Evans, 1721 S. Ninth St., Lafayette, IN 47905-2128 **E-mail:** eevansdds@juno.com

EXELBERT, LOIS L.
Industry: Healthcare **Born:** November 12, 1948, Brooklyn, New York **Univ./degree:** M.S., Florida International University, 1982 **Current organization:** Baptist Hospital of Miami **Title:** Administrative Director Diabetes Care Center **Type of organization:** Hospital **Major product:** Patient care **Area of distribution:** International **Area of Practice:** Health education **Honors/awards:** Board Certified **Affiliations:** A.D.A.; A.D.E. **Hob./spts.:** Writing poetry, needlepoint, yoga **SIC code:** 80 **Address:** Baptist Hospital of Miami, 8940 N. Kendall Dr., Miami, FL 33143 **E-mail:** loise@bhssf.org

EYZAGUIRRE, EDUARDO
Industry: Medical **Born:** February 7, 1961, Buenos Aires, Argentina **Univ./degree:** M.D., Cayetano Heredia University, 1997 **Current organization:** University of Texas Medical Branch **Title:** Assistant Professor, M.D. **Type of organization:** University **Major product:** Patient care, medical education **Area of distribution:** International **Area of Practice:** Pathology **Published works:** 18 articles, book chapters **Hob./spts.:** Nature photography, Tae Kwon-Do (Red Belt) **SIC code:** 80 **Address:** University of Texas Medical Branch, 301 University Blvd., John Sealy Annex, Room 2.190, Galveston, TX 77555-0588 **E-mail:** ejeyzagu@utmb.edu

FALAIYE, VICTOR O.
Industry: Healthcare **Born:** May 29, 1954, Nigeria **Univ./degree:** B.D.S., University of Lagos, Nigeria; M.S.; Ph.D., University of Manchester, U.K.; D.M.D., University of Pennsylvania School of Dental Medicine **Current organization:** Family Dentistry **Title:** D.M.D. **Type of organization:** Dental office **Major product:** General dentistry **Area of distribution:** Lorton, Virginia **Area of Practice:** Dental surgery **Affiliations:** Fellow, International College of Oral Implantology; A.D.A.; Virginia Dental Society; Virginia Dental Association; Academy of Dentistry **Hob./spts.:** Athletics, tennis **SIC code:** 80 **Address:** Family Dentistry, 9502 Richmond Hwy., Lorton, VA 22079

FARMER, ALVA R.
Industry: Healthcare **Born:** July 1, 1944, Clearwater, Florida **Univ./degree:** HTASCP, Medical College of Georgia, 1969 **Current organization:** Veterans Administration Medical Center **Title:** Histopathology Technician **Type of organization:** Veterans' hospital **Major product:** Medical care for veterans and their families **Area of distribution:** North Carolina **Area of Practice:** Pathology **Affiliations:** American Society of Clinical Pathologists **Hob./spts.:** Crafting jewelry, reading, travel **SIC code:** 80 **Address:** Veterans Administration Medical Center, 1100 Tunnel Rd., Asheville, NC 28805-2043

FARNER, ROBERT LEWIS
Industry: Healthcare **Born:** February 4, 1930, Streator, Illinois **Univ./degree:** Pre-med., Wartburg College, Waverly, Iowa; M. D., University of Illinois College of Medicine, 1955; Intern: Illinois Central Chicago Hospital; USAF School of Aviation Medicine with service in Goose Bay, Labrador and Thule Greenland **Title:** M.D. (Retired) **Type of organization:** Solo practice in Family Medicine **Major product:** Patient care **Area of distribution:** International **Area of Practice:** Family Medicine and Surgery **Affiliations:** A.M.A.; A.A.F.P.; Illinois State Medical Society; LaSalle County Medical Society; American Academy of Family Practice; American Lutheran Church **Hob./spts.:** Antiquing, American pattern glass, rollerblading, travel, visiting family in Spokane, WA, Houston, TX, CA, CO, Holeman, WI, Englewood, FL and

Apache Junction; playing the piano and organ **SIC code:** 80 **Address:** 403 W. Santa Fe Ave., Toluca, IL 61369 **E-mail:** dtdt@maxiis.com

FARO, JOAN C.
Industry: Healthcare **Univ./degree:** M.D., SUNY Stony Brook, 1982 **Current organization:** The John T. Mather Memorial Hospital **Title:** Vice President of Clinical Affairs **Type of organization:** Hospital **Major product:** Patient care **Area of distribution:** Port Jefferson, New York **Area of Practice:** Internal medicine/administration **Affiliations:** F.A.C.P.; Internal Medicine (Board Certified) **Hob./spts.:** Bodybuilding, snowboarding **SIC code:** 80 **Address:** The John T. Mather Memorial Hospital, 75 North Country Rd., Port Jefferson, NY 11777 **E-mail:** jfaro@matherhospital.org

FARRELL, JULIE ANN
Industry: Healthcare **Born:** May 30, 1953, Cincinnati, Ohio **Children:** Charles M. Williams, 22; Elizabeth A. Williams, 20; Michael F. Williams, 19 **Univ./degree:** B.S., Magna Cum Laude, Xavier University, Ohio, 1975; M.D., University of Cincinnati Medical School, Ohio, 1979; Residency, Diagnostic Radiology, University of Cincinnati Medical Center, Ohio, 1979-83 **Current organization:** Brown County General Hospital-Diagnostic Imaging/Alliance Primary Care of Crestview, Kentucky **Title:** Chief of Radiology/Director of Mammography **Type of organization:** Hospital **Major product:** Medical services/radiology **Area of distribution:** National **Area of Practice:** Radiology (Board Certified since 1983) **Published works:** "Perforated Carcinoma of Transverse Colon Presenting as Supra Renal Mass: The CT Appearance", Journal of Computer Tomography, 1981, Vol. 5, pg. 55-58 **Affiliations:** Alpha Omega Alpha National Medical Honor Society; American Medical Association; National Board of Radiology; Ohio Medical Association; Cincinnati Radiological Society; Brown County Medical Society; Life Member, Kingston's National Registry of Who's Who; National Leadership Award-Honorary Co-Chair, Physicians' Advisory Board **Career accomplishments:** Vice President, Brown County General Hospital Medical Staff, 1994-96; President, Brown County General Hospital Medical Staff, 1996-98 **Hob./spts.:** Tennis, swimming, reading, show horses **SIC code:** 80 **Address:** Brown County General Hospital-Diagnostic Imaging, 425 Home St., Georgetown, OH 45121 **E-mail:** julieann_farrell@yahoo.com **Web address:** www.browncountygeneralhospital.org

FAS, NORBERTO
Industry: Healthcare **Univ./degree:** M.D., University of Puerto Rico, 1992 **Current organization:** Atlanta VA Medical Center **Title:** Senior Medical Adviser **Type of organization:** Employee health clinic **Major product:** Patient care **Area of distribution:** Georgia **Area of Practice:** Internal medicine **Affiliations:** A.C.P.-A.S.I.M.; A.C.P.E. **SIC code:** 80 **Address:** Atlanta VA Medical Center, 5035 Ashurst Dr., Roswell, GA 30075 **E-mail:** norberto.fas@med.va.gov

FAUST, THOMAS W.
Industry: Medical **Born:** August 8, 1956, Flint, Michigan **Univ./degree:** M.D., University of Tennessee, 1983 **Current organization:** The University of Pennsylvania Health System **Title:** M.D. **Type of organization:** University/hospital **Major product:** Medical services **Area of distribution:** Pennsylvania **Area of Practice:** Hepatology and liver transplantation **Published works:** Numerous publications including; Co-Author, "Budd-Chiari Syndrome" In Diseases of the Liver Eighth Ed. Eds., Lippincott-Raven, Philadelphia, 1999, 1207-1213; Author, "Recurrent Disease of Presumed Autoimmune Origin" In Transplantation of the Liver. 3rd Ed. Lippincott Williams and Williams, Philadelphia, 2001, 371-383; :Update on Primary Sclerosing Cholangitis" Syllabus for CCFA symposium: Expert Testimony in Inflammatory Bowel Disease 2001 and Beyond **Affiliations:** F.A.C.P.; F.A.C.G.; A.G.A.; A.S.T.; A.A.S.L.D.; International Liver Transplant Society **Hob./spts.:** Family, biking, running, skiing, tennis **SIC code:** 80 **Address:** The University of Pennsylvania Health System, 3400 Spruce St., Philadelphia, PA 19104 **E-mail:** thomas.faust@uphs.upenn.edu

FECHTER, JANET M.
Industry: Healthcare **Born:** October 15, 1969, West Bend, Wisconsin **Univ./degree:** B.S., Biology, University of Wisconsin at Milwaukee, 1992; M.S., Endocrinology Reproductive Physiology, University of Wisconsin at Madison, 2000; M.D., St. George's University, Grenada, 2000 **Current organization:** Mercy Health Care System **Title:** M.D. **Type of organization:** Community hospital **Major product:** Medical services **Area of distribution:** Janesville, Wisconsin **Area of Practice:** Patient care **Honors/awards:** "Woman of the Year", 2000, "Humanitarian Award", 2001-2002, Mercy Health System Family Practice Residency Program **Published works:** Co-author, "Excision and disassembly of sperm tail microtubules during sea urchin fertilization: requirements for microtubule dynamics", Cell Motil Cytoskeleton 1996;35(4):281-8 **Affiliations:** A.A.F.P.; A.M.A.; B.L.S.; A.C.L.S.; N.A.L.S.; American Academy of Family Physicians **Hob./spts.:** Running, softball, reading, triathlon, biathlon, volleyball, racquetball **SIC code:** 80 **Address:** Mercy Health Care System, 709 N. Wuthering Hills, Janesville, WI 53546 **E-mail:** mrrbtj6@msn.com

FEIN, LESLEY A.
Industry: Healthcare **Born:** August 24, 1953, Johannesburg, South Africa **Univ./degree:** MPH, Columbia University, 1979; M.D., George Washington University, 1981 **Current organization:** Lesley A. Fein, M.D., MPH **Title:** MD, MPH **Type of organization:** Private practice **Major product:** Patient care **Area of distribution:** National **Area of Practice:** Rheumatology, Lyme Disease, Chronic Fatigue Syndrome **Affiliations:** Lyme Disease Foundation; Medical Director, Lyme Disease Society; Lyme Disease Caucus **Hob./spts.:** Tennis, skiing **SIC code:** 80 **Address:** 1099 Bloomfield Ave., West Caldwell, NJ 07006

FEIN, SIDNEY
Industry: Healthcare **Born:** February 4, 1940, Brooklyn, New York **Univ./degree:** B.A., Biological Sciences, Brooklyn College, 1969; M.S., Health, City College of New York, 1978; M.D., Universidad De Cetec Medical School, Santo Domingo, D.R., 1982 **Current organization:** New York Methodist Hospital **Title:** M.D. **Type of organization:** Hospital **Major product:** Medical services **Area of distribution:** New York **Area of Practice:** Child and adult psychiatry, Instructor of SUNY Downstate and NYCOM medical students in Mental Status and Psychopharmacology (1990-98), Assistant Clinical Professor SUNY Downstate (1991-present) **Published works:** 17 publications including "Treatment of Drug Refractory Schizophrenia", Psychiatry Annals, 27(4), 4/98; "Combination Treatment Strategies in Resistant Anxiety Disorders", Primary Psychiatry, p. 52-56, 3/96 **Affiliations:** National Speaker for Janssen Pharmaceutica and Eli Lilly; 6 APA Presentations in the past 11 years **Hob./spts.:** Basketball, collecting art, writing, public speaking **SIC code:** 80 **Address:** 115 Prospect Park West, Brooklyn, NY 11215

FEINBERG, LILIA E.
Industry: Healthcare **Born:** April 23, 1962, Enakievo, Ukraine **Univ./degree:** M.D., Second Moscow Medical Institute, 1986 **Current organization:** Carney Hospital **Title:** M.D. **Type of organization:** Hospital **Major product:** Patient care **Area of distribution:** Massachusetts **Area of Practice:** Psychiatry **Affiliations:** A.P.A. **Hob./spts.:** Studying people **SIC code:** 80 **Address:** Carney Hospital, 2100 Dorchester Ave., Dorchester, MA 02124 **E-mail:** liliafein@attbi.com

FEINSTEIN, LAINA
Industry: Healthcare **Univ./degree:** M.D., Odessa Medical School, 1983 **Current organization:** University Center for Internal Medicine **Title:** M.D. **Type of organization:** Private internal medicine, cardiology and medical acupuncture office **Major product:** Patient care, stress tests, nuclear studies, ultrasound **Area of distribution:** Farmington Hills, Michigan **Area of Practice:** Meridian Regulatory Acupuncture **Affiliations:** A.M.A.; A.C.P.; M.R.A. Association; Oakland Medical Association **Hob./spts.:** Dancing, playing piano, reading **SIC code:** 80 **Address:** Laina Feinstein, M.D., 29355 Northwestern Hwy. 210, Southfield, MI 48034-1053

FELICIANO, CALEB E.
Industry: Medical **Born:** November 26, 1974, Mayagüez, Puerto Rico **Univ./degree:** M.D., University of Puerto Rico, 2001 **Current organization:** University of Puerto Rico, School of Medicine **Title:** M.D. **Type of organization:** University hospital **Major product:** Patient care, medical education **Area of distribution:** San Juan, Puerto Rico **Area of Practice:** Neurosurgery **Published works:** "The Association of 4-(N,N-dimethylamino)benzonitrile and ß-Cyclodextrin in dimenthyl sulfoxide and N,N-dimethylformamide"; "A kinetic Approach for the Determination of Host-Guest Binding Constants" **Affiliations:** A.M.A.; Alpha Omega Alpha; Honor Medical Society **Hob./spts.:** Table tennis, tennis, physical fitness, scuba diving **SIC code:** 80 **Address:** University of Puerto Rico, School of Medicine, P.O. Box 372230, Cayey, PR 00737 **E-mail:** caleb@adam.uprr.pr

FENNESSY, CHERYL L.
Industry: Healthcare **Born:** November 13, 1954, Rochester, New York **Univ./degree:** A.S.N., Excelsior College (formerly Regents College) **Current organization:** Lifetime Health Medical Group **Title:** R.N. **Type of organization:** Medical office **Major product:** Patient care **Area of distribution:** Rochester, New York **Area of Practice:** Pediatric nursing **Hob./spts.:** Reading, crossword puzzles, needlework **SIC code:** 80 **Address:** Lifetime Health Medical Group, 800 Carter St., Rochester, NY 14621 **E-mail:** clfennessy@aol.com

FERNANDEZ, JACQUELINE A.
Industry: Healthcare **Born:** November 12, 1962, Dominican Republic **Univ./degree:** B.S., Biology, New York University, 1984; M.D., Hahnemann University Medical School, 1991 **Current organization:** Union Internal Medicine **Title:** M.D. **Type of organization:** Private practice **Major product:** Patient care **Area of distribution:** International **Area of Practice:** Internal medicine (Board Certified) adolescents to geriatrics, teaching residents **Affiliations:** A.M.A.; Medical Director, Iglesia Misión Cristiana; American College of Physicians; Attending Physician, Overlook Hospital **Hob./spts.:** Missionary work in South America, church involvement, playing classical piano **SIC code:** 80 **Address:** Union Internal Medicine, 2027 Morris Ave., Union, NJ 07083 **E-mail:** pri112191@aol.com

FERNANDEZ-GOMEZ, GLORIA
Industry: Healthcare **Born:** June 14, 1941, Manila, Philippines **Univ./degree:** M.D., Philippines, 1968 **Current organization:** East Mississippi State Hospital **Title:** Physician **Type of organization:** Hospital **Major product:** Patient care **Area of distribution:** National **Area of Practice:** Pediatrics **Affiliations:** A.P.P.M.A. **Hob./spts.:** Gardening, reading **SIC code:** 80 **Address:** East Mississippi State Hospital, 4555 Highland Park Dr., Meridian, MS 39307

FIKS, EVA N.
Industry: Healthcare **Born:** December 12, 1929, Ukraine **Univ./degree:** M.D., Odessa Institute, 1953 **Current organization:** Westlake Hospital **Title:** M.D. **Type of organization:** Hospital **Major product:** Patient care **Area of distribution:** Illinois **Area of Practice:** Physical medicine **Affiliations:** A.M.A.; Chicago Medical Society **Hob./spts.:** Swimming, reading, travel **SIC code:** 80 **Address:** Westlake Hospital, 1225 Lake St., Melrose Park, IL 60160

FINK, RICHARD A.
Industry: Dental healthcare **Born:** January 23, 1948, Buffalo, New York **Spouse:** Sandra Fink **Children:** Laurie Fraser, Jeff Fink **Univ./degree:** B.A., SUNY Buffalo, 1970; D.D.S., Meharry Dental School, 1974; Certificate of Periodontics, College of Medicine and Dentistry of New Jersey, 1976 **Current organization:** Richard A. Fink, D.D.S. **Title:** D.D.S. **Type of organization:** Private practice **Major product:** Periodontics - bone grafting, implants **Area of distribution:** New Mexico **Area of Practice:** Periodontal surgery **Honors/awards:** Inducted into the Pierre Fouchard Academy, 2005; Inducted into the International College of Dentists, 2005; **Published works:** "Effect of Topical Folic Acid on Gingival Health", Vogel, Fink, Schneider, Frank and Baker, Journal of Periodontics 47 Page 667- 1976; "Effect of Topical Folic Acid on Gingival Health", Journal of Oral Medicine 33 Page 20- 1978 **Affiliations:** President, Alpha Omega Dental Fraternity, 1981-82 and 2006; President, Niagara County Dental Society, 1997; President, Eighth District Dental Society, 2005; Chair, Strategic Planning Committee of the Eighth District Dental Society, 2003; Chair, Budget, Audit and Finance Committee of the Eighth District Dental Society, 2004; A.D.A. Delegate, 2003-05: Sandia Pueblo (provides periodontal services to the Indian Nation **Hob./spts.:** Golf, scuba diving, divemaster (PADI), skiing **SIC code:** 80 **Address:** Richard A. Fink, D.D.S., 1594 Sara Rd., Rio Rancho, NM 87124 **E-mail:** rafink58@msn.com

FISHER, BARBARA ANN
Industry: Healthcare **Born:** March 27, 1952, Philadelphia, Pennsylvania **Univ./degree:** B.S.N., Excelsior College, 1990; M.S., Healthcare Administration, Capitol University, 2003 **Current organization:** Kaiser Permanente **Title:** Clinic Supervisor **Type of organization:** Hospital **Major product:** Patient care **Area of distribution:** National **Area of Practice:** Healthcare administration **Hob./spts.:** Swimming, reading, cooking **SIC code:** 80 **Address:** Kaiser Permanente, 910 Wainee St., Lahaina, HI 96761 **E-mail:** barbarafisher@kp.org **Web address:** www.kp.org

FISHER, MARLON G.
Industry: Medical **Born:** April 4, 1975, Berwyn, Illinois **Univ./degree:** M.D., Meharry Medical College, 2001 **Current organization:** Howard University Hospital **Title:** M.D. **Type of organization:** University hospital **Major product:** Medical services **Area of distribution:** Washington, D.C. **Area of Practice:** Emergency medicine **Affiliations:** E.M.R.A.; S.E.A.M.; A.M.A. **Hob./spts.:** Travel, weight training, sports cars **SIC code:** 80 **Address:** 4333 Third St. N.W., Washington, DC 20011 **E-mail:** bigfish35@hotmail.com

FISHER, STANLEY E.
Industry: Medical **Born:** May 23, 1944, Saginaw, Michigan **Univ./degree:** M.D., Johns Hopkins University, 1969 **Current organization:** SUNY Downstate Medical Center **Title:** M.D. **Type of organization:** University hospital **Major product:** Medical services **Area of distribution:** National **Area of Practice:** Pediatric gastroenterology **Published works:** 100+ articles and journals **Affiliations:** Society for Pediatric Research; American Pediatric Society; North American Society of Pediatric Enterology, Hepatology and Nutrition; American Gastroenterology Association **SIC code:** 80 **Address:** SUNY Downstate Medical Center, 450 Clarkson Ave., Box 49, Brooklyn, NY 11203 **E-mail:** sfisher@downstate.edu

FISHMAN, JOSEPH H.
Industry: Healthcare **Born:** March 2, 1942, Louisville, Kentucky **Univ./degree:** M.D., University of Louisville, 1968 **Current organization:** Clearwater Center for Cosmetic Surgery **Title:** M.D. **Type of organization:** Medical practice **Major product:** Plastic surgery **Area of distribution:** Clearwater, Florida **Area of Practice:** Facial cosmetic surgery **Affiliations:** American Society of Plastic Surgeons **SIC code:** 80 **Address:** Clearwater Center for Cosmetic Surgery, 609 Lakeview Rd., Clearwater, FL 33756

FITZGERALD JR., ROBERT H.
Industry: Healthcare **Born:** August 25, 1942, Denver, Colorado **Univ./degree:** M.D., University of Kansas, 1967 **Current organization:** Upper Peninsula Orthopaedic Surgery **Title:** M.D. **Type of organization:** Private practice **Major product:** Reconstructive musculoskeletal surgery **Area of distribution:** Upper Peninsula, Michigan **Area of Practice:** Orthopaedic surgery **Honors/awards:** ABC Traveling Fellow; Charnley Award for Original Research of the Hip **Published works:** 4 textbooks including recently published "Orthopedics"; Author/co-author 200 published manuscripts **Affiliations:** A.O.A.; F.A.A.O.S.; I.H.S.; A.H.S.; President, American Hip Society, 1994 **SIC code:** 80 **Address:** Upper Peninsula Orthopaedic Surgery, 97 S. Fourth St., Ishpeming, MI 49849 **E-mail:** drfitzgerald@bellmemorial.org

FLANIGAN, LYNN F.
Industry: Behavioral healthcare **Born:** March 15, 1952, Brooklyn, New York **Univ./degree:** B.S.N., Hartwick University, 1975; M.S.W., University of Maryland, 1981 **Current organization:** Sheppard Pratt Health System **Title:** Regional Director, General Hospital Services **Type of organization:** Hospitals, schools and ambulatory services **Major product:** Psychiatric and school education services **Area of distribution:** Maryland **Area of Practice:** Regulatory compliance and operations **Hob./spts.:** Special Olympics, sailing, family **SIC code:** 80 **Address:** Sheppard Pratt Health System, 6501 N. Charles St., Towson, MD 21285-6815 **E-mail:** lflanigan@sheppardpratt.org **Web address:** www.sheppardpratt.org

FLASTER, RONALD D.
Industry: Healthcare **Born:** January 4, 1957, New York, New York **Univ./degree:** M.D., U.C.E., Dominican Republic, 1983 **Current organization:** Northwest Medical Center **Title:** M.D. **Type of organization:** Hospital **Major product:** Patient care **Area of distribution:** Wellington, Florida **Area of Practice:** Pediatric emergency room; Pediatrics (Board Certified) **Affiliations:** Fellow, American Academy of Pediatrics **Hob./spts.:** Music **SIC code:** 80 **Address:** Northwest Medical Center, 9866 Scribner Lane, Wellington, FL 33414 **E-mail:** bwig19866@bellsouth.net

FLEISCHER, LESLIE R.
Industry: Healthcare **Born:** April 13, 1948, Washington DC **Univ./degree:** M.D., Creighton University, 1975 **Current organization:** White Wilson Medical Center **Title:** M.D. **Type of organization:** Medical clinic **Major product:** Patient care **Area of distribution:** Fort Walton Beach, Florida **Area of Practice:** Cardiology **Affiliations:** F.A.C.C.; F.A.C.P.; F.S.C.I.; Mensa **Hob./spts.:** Music, fishing **SIC code:** 80 **Address:** White Wilson Medical Center, 1005 Mar-Walt Dr., Ft. Walton Beach, FL 32547 **E-mail:** lfleischer@white-wilson.com

FLEMING, FLORENCE RUTH
Industry: Medical **Born:** St. Paul, Minnesota **Univ./degree:** D.S.W., Philosophical Foundation, Rutgers University, 1978 **Current organization:** Mt. Sinai Medical Center **Title:** Protestant Chaplain/Instructor and Counselor of Clinical & Pastoral Education **Type of organization:** Hospital/Chaplaincy **Major product:** Patient care **Area of practice:** Trainer: Clinical Pastoral Education **Area of Practice:** Trainer: Clinical Pastoral Education **Affiliations:** United Methodist Church; Republican National Committee; Tri State Group of Counselors **Hob./spts.:** Cooking, opera, piano **SIC code:** 80 **Address:** 1270 Museum Mile, 6T, New York, NY 10029 **E-mail:** fruthf@aol.com

FLENNIKEN, ERIC T.
Industry: Healthcare **Born:** February 11, 1965, Longview, Texas **Univ./degree:** A.A.S. with Honors, Radiography, 1999; Diploma with Honors, Computed Technology and Magnetic Resonance Imaging Technology, 2000, Caldwell Community College and Technical Institute; A.A. with Honors, Catawba Valley Community College, 2003; B.S. Candidate **Current organization:** Catawba Valley Medical Center **Title:** Radiologic Technologist RT-(R)(CT)(MR) **Type of organization:** Hospital **Major product:** Diagnostic imaging **Area of distribution:** North Carolina **Area of Practice:** Magnetic resonance imaging **Honors/awards:** Good Conduct Ribbon and Medal, U.S. Navy; Navy Unit Citation; Coast Guard Meritorious Unit Citation; Expeditionary Ribbon and Medal; Battle "E" (Efficiency) Ribbon; Sea Service Ribbon; Listed in 2005 Strathmore's Who's Who; Member, Phi Theta Kappa; Listed in 2003-04 edition of The National Dean's List **Published works:** "Thoracic Outlet Syndrome: A Real Pain in the Neck and More", Advance for Imaging and Radiation Therapy Professionals, Vol. 14 No. 24; "CT: a Slice of Imaging History", Advance for Imaging and Radiation Therapy Professionals, Vol. 15, No. 10 **Affiliations:** A.R.R.T., A.S.R.T. **Hob./spts.:** Deep sea fishing **SIC code:** 80 **Address:** 1910 20th Ave. Dr. N.E., #39, Hickory, NC 28601 **E-mail:** eflenniken@earthlink.net

FLETCHER, MARK H.
Industry: Healthcare **Born:** December 24, 1961, Gadsden, Alabama **Univ./degree:** M.D., University of Alabama School of Medicine, Birmingham, 1988 **Current organization:** Tupelo Neurology Clinic **Title:** Neurologist **Type of organization:** Group practice **Major product:** Patient care **Area of distribution:** Mississippi **Area of Practice:** Neurology, botox applications **Affiliations:** A.M.A.; American Academy of Neurology; American College of Physician Executives; Mississippi State Medical Association; North Mississippi Medical Society **Hob./spts.:** Music, reading **SIC code:** 80 **Address:** Tupelo Neurology Clinic, 609 Brunson Dr., Tupelo, MS 38801 **E-mail:** mfletcher@nmhs.net

FLETCHER, SHEILA
Industry: Healthcare **Born:** December 22, 1955, Yazoo City, Mississippi **Univ./degree:** L.P.N., Hinds Jr. College, 1979; A.S., Nursing, Wallace Community College, 1988 **Current organization:** Kindred Hospital of Tarrant County **Title:** R.N. **Type of organization:** Hospital **Major product:** Patient care, rehab **Area of distribution:** Texas **Area of Practice:** Nursing, infection control, geriatrics, pediatrics, emergency rescue (EMTP), trauma nursing, mobile intensive care, life care transport, nursing supervision **Affiliations:** A.P.I.C.; M.A.S.T. Council **Hob./spts.:** Reading, sewing, active in the community teaching CPR **SIC code:** 80 **Address:** Kindred Hospital of Tarrant County, 1000 N. Cooper St., Arlington, TX 76011 **E-mail:** s.fletcher@comcast.net

FLEURY, AMY B.
Industry: Healthcare **Born:** June 28, 1966, Northampton, Massachusetts **Univ./degree:** B.S.N., Elms College, 1988 **Current organization:** Cooley Dickinson Hospital **Title:** RN **Type of organization:** Hospital **Major product:** Charge nurse, patient care area **Area of distribution:** Williamsburg, Massachusetts **Area of Practice:** Medical-surgical nurse, oncology **Affiliations:** M.N.A. **Hob./spts.:** Playing guitar, horseback riding **SIC code:** 80 **Address:** Cooley Dickinson Hospital, 30 Locust St., Northampton, MA 10160 **E-mail:** amy_fleury@cooley-dickinson.org

FLEYSH, KLARA
Industry: Healthcare **Born:** February 27, 1952, St. Petersburg, Russia **Univ./degree:** M.D., Medical School in St. Petersburg, 1974; D.D.S., Marquette University School of Dentistry, 1996 **Current organization:** Family Dentistry **Title:** D.D.S. **Type of organization:** Dental office **Major product:** Dental services **Area of distribution:** Milwaukee, Wisconsin **Area of Practice:** General and cosmetic dentistry **Affiliations:** American Dental Association; Wisconsin Dental Association **Hob./spts.:** Music **SIC code:** 80 **Address:** Family Dentistry, 1714 E. Capitol Dr., Milwaukee, WI 53211 **E-mail:** fleyshdds@yahoo.com

FLOWERS, PATRICIA L.
Industry: Healthcare **Born:** March 1, 1952, Opelousas, Louisiana **Univ./degree:** B.S.N., Northwestern State University, 2000 **Current organization:** Winn Parish Medical Center **Title:** Chief Nursing Officer **Type of organization:** Hospital **Major product:** Patient care **Area of distribution:** Winnfield, Louisiana **Area of Practice:** Nursing; R.N. **Affiliations:** Louisiana Organization of Nurse Executives **Hob./spts.:** Gardening, reading **SIC code:** 80 **Address:** Winn Parish Medical Center, 301 W. Boundary St., Winnfield, LA 71483 **E-mail:** patricia.flowers@hcahealthcare.com

FLYNN, MARYIRENE ILCHERT
Industry: Healthcare **Born:** February 16, 1959, Astoria, New York **Univ./degree:** M.D., Albert Einstein College of Medicine of Yeshiva University, Bronx, New York, 1986 **Current organization:** Staten Island Orthopedics & Sports Medicine **Title:** M.D. **Type of organization:** Orthopedic surgery practice **Major product:** Medical services **Area of distribution:** Staten Island, New York **Area of Practice:** Sports medicine **Published works:** Co-author of book **Affiliations:** A.A.O.S. **Hob./spts.:** Family, coaching basketball **SIC code:** 80 **Address:** Staten Island Orthopedics & Sports Medicine, 1551 Richmond Rd., Staten Island, NY 10304

FONTES, PAULO A.
Industry: Medical **Born:** January 20, 1962, Brazil **Univ./degree:** M.D., Sao Paulo State University, 1985 **Current organization:** Thomas E. Stazl Transplantation Institute **Title:** Co-Director, Liver Transplantation **Type of organization:** University hospital **Major product:** Transplants **Area of distribution:** International **Area of Practice:** Liver transplantation **Affiliations:** American College of Surgeons, American Society of Transplantation **Hob./spts.:** Sailing, surfing **SIC code:** 80 **Address:** Thomas E. Stazl Transplantation Institute, UPMC Montefiore, 7 South, Pittsburgh, PA 15213-2582 **E-mail:** fontesp@upmc.edu

FORBES, HUGH P.
Industry: Healthcare **Univ./degree:** M.D., University of Medicine and Dentistry of New Jersey, 1990 **Current organization:** Women First Obstetrics & Gynecology **Title:** M.D./President **Type of organization:** Private practice **Major product:** Obstetrics and gynecology **Area of distribution:** Carthage, New York **Area of Practice:** Medicine, women's healthcare **Honors/awards:** Director of Ob/Gyn Dept., re-elected for third term **Published works:** Newsletter **Affiliations:** A.M.A.; F.A.C.O.G.; A.I.U. **Hob./spts.:** Spending time with family, singing **SIC code:** 80 **Address:** Women First Obstetrics & Gynecology, PC, P.O. Box 270, Carthage, NY 13619

FORBES, SARAH E.
Industry: Healthcare **Born:** May 4, 1928, Currituck, North Carolina **Univ./degree:** B.A., University of Rochester; M.D., Medical College of Virginia, 1954 **Current organization:** Women's Complete Health Care/Forbes Enterprises **Title:** M.D. **Type of organization:** Private practice **Major product:** Ob/Diag., Gynecology, complete female healthcare, primary care and geriatrics **Area of distribution:** Newport News, Virginia **Area of practice:** Obstetrics, gynecology, entrepreneurial services **Area of Practice:** Obstetric consults, gynecology **Honors/awards:** The Medallion Award, The Boys and Girls Club; American Medical Association Physician Recognition Award; The YWCA Twin Award Tribute to Women in Business and Industry; Woman of the Year for the Peninsula Award; The Forty Year S.P.C.A. Presidential Award **Affiliations:** F.A.C.O.G.; A.M.A.; Medical Society of Virginia; Newport News Medical Society; President, Virginia Peninsula Boys & Girls Club **Career accomplishments:** Owner of Windmill Point Restaurant & Rentals on the Ocean Cottages, Nags Head, North Carolina, SEBROF Corporation Construction Co., Mary B. Forbes Land Corporation, Newport News, Virginia **Hob./spts.:** Philanthropy, sailing, nature lover **SIC code:** 80 **Address:** Women's Complete Health Care/Forbes Enterprises, 12420 Warwick Blvd., Bldg. #5, Newport News, VA 23606 **E-mail:** sforbes@visi.net **Web address:** www.rentalsontheocean.com or www.windmillrestauran

FORD, JOHN CONNELL
Industry: Healthcare/dentistry **Born:** May 16, 1953, Evanston, Illinois **Univ./degree:** B.A., Biology, Brown University, 1975; D.M.D., University of Pennsylvania School of Dental Medicine, 1982; M.S. & Certificate in Orthodontics, Northwestern University Dental School, 1984 **Current organization:** Ford Orthodontics, Ltd. **Title:** Orthodontist **Type of organization:** Private practice **Major product:** Orthodontics **Area of distribution:** National **Area of Practice:** Orthodontics and dentofacial orthopedics **Honors/awards:** Service Award, Northwestern University Alumni Association; Diplomate, American Board of Orthodontics **Affiliations:** Fellow, World Federation of Orthodontists; Fellow, International College of Dentists; Fellow, American College of Dentists; American Dental Association; Chicago Dental Society; American Association of Orthodontists; Midwest Society of Orthodontists; Illinois Society of Orthodontists **Hob./spts.:** Family, children **SIC code:** 80 **Address:** Ford Orthodontics, Ltd., 585 Lincoln Ave., Winnetka, IL 60093 **E-mail:** jcfortho@aol.com

FORMAN, ROBERT
Industry: Medical **Univ./degree:** M. D., University of Cape Town, 1962; Cardiology training, Brigham Hospital **Current organization:** Albert Einstein College Hospital, Montefiore Medical Center **Title:** M.D./Professor of Medicine **Type of organization:** University hospital/private practice **Major product:** Medical services **Area of distribution:** International **Area of Practice:** Cardiology/training at Brigham Hospital, Boston, Massachusetts **Honors/awards:** Studied with Dr. Christian Barnard **Affiliations:** Director, CCU **SIC code:** 80 **Address:** Albert Einstein College Hospital, Montefiore Medical Center, 1825 Eastchester Rd., Bronx, NY 10583 **E-mail:** rforman@montefiore.org

FORMICA, PALMA E.
Industry: Healthcare **Born:** June 14, 1928, Windber, Pennsylvania **Univ./degree:** M.D., University of Rome, Italy, 1953 **Current organization:** Saint Peter's University Hospital **Title:** Chair, Dept. of Family Practice **Type of organization:** Hospital **Major product:** Patient care **Area of distribution:** National **Area of practice:** Family practitioner **Area of Practice:** Family practitioner **Honors/awards:** Honorary Degree, Seton Hall University, 1998 **Affiliations:** F.A.A.F.P.; Past Trustee, A.M.A.; Past President, Medical Society of New Jersey; President, Medical/Dental Staff, St. Peter's Medical Center **Hob./spts.:** Writing, public speaking, painting **SIC code:** 80 **Address:** Saint Peter's University Hospital, Dept. of Family Practice, 254 Easton Ave., New Brunswick, NJ 08903 **E-mail:** pformica@saintpetersuh.com **Web address:** www.saintpetersuh.com

FORTE, RICHARD
Industry: Healthcare **Born:** December 28, 1963, Brooklyn, New York **Current organization:** North Shore Hematology Oncology, PLLC **Title:** M.D. **Type of organization:** Group practice **Major product:** Patient care **Area of distribution:** Manhasset, New York **Area of Practice:** Hematology, oncology, internal medicine **Affiliations:** A.S.H.; A.S.C.O.; New York State Medical Society **Hob./spts.:** Family **SIC code:** 80

Address: North Shore Hematology Oncology, PLLC, 1201 Northern Blvd., Manhasset, NY 11030 **E-mail:** nsheonc@optonline.net

FOSKETT, JONATHAN W.
Industry: Healthcare **Born:** March 9, 1972, Dayton, Ohio **Univ./degree:** B.S., Medical Technology, Northern Illinois University, 1995; M.S., Health Science Administration, University of St. Francis, 2006 **Current organization:** Silver Cross Hospital **Title:** Lab Manager, MT(ASCP) **Type of organization:** Hospital **Major product:** Patient care **Area of distribution:** Illinois **Area of Practice:** Informatics, auto-validation process, lab management **Published works:** 1 article **Affiliations:** A.S.C.P.; C.L.M.A. **SIC code:** 80 **Address:** Silver Cross Hospital, 1200 Maple Rd., Joliet, IL 60432 **E-mail:** jfoskett@silvercross.org **Web address:** www.silvercross.org

FOSSUM, GREGORY T.
Industry: Healthcare **Born:** January 29, 1956, Milwaukee, Wisconsin **Univ./degree:** M.D., University of Wisconsin, 1982 **Current organization:** Thomas Jefferson University **Title:** Director of Reproductive Endocrinology **Type of organization:** University **Major product:** Patient care **Area of distribution:** Philadelphia, Pennsylvania **Area of Practice:** Reproductive endocrinology, infertility **Published works:** Multiple publications **Affiliations:** A.S.R.M.; F.A.C.O.G.; Society of Reproductive Endocrinology **Hob./spts.:** Fishing **SIC code:** 80 **Address:** Thomas Jefferson University, 834 Chestnut St., Suite 400, Philadelphia, PA 19107 **E-mail:** gregoryfossum@mail.tju.edu

FOULKS, GARY N.
Industry: Medical **Born:** June 7, 1944, Salt Lake City, Utah **Univ./degree:** M.D., Columbia College of Physicians and Surgeons **Current organization:** University of Louisville **Title:** M.D. **Type of organization:** University **Major product:** Higher education, patient care **Area of distribution:** International **Area of Practice:** Ophthalmology **Affiliations:** American Academy of Ophthalmology; Cornea Society; Tear Film and Ocular Surface Society **Hob./spts.:** Fly-fishing **SIC code:** 80 **Address:** University of Louisville, 301 E. Muhammad Ali Blvd., Louisville, KY 40202 **E-mail:** gnfoul01@louisville.edu

FOURNIER, JOSEPH N.
Industry: Healthcare **Univ./degree:** Physical Therapy, University of New England **Current organization:** Maine General Health **Title:** Physical Therapist **Type of organization:** Multi-site hospital **Major product:** Patient care, rehabilitation **Area of distribution:** Maine **Area of Practice:** Orthopedic, neurological, chronic pain management **Published works:** Educational publications **Affiliations:** A.P.T.A. **Hob./spts.:** Amateur weightlifting coach, Capital City Pistol & Rifle Club **SIC code:** 80 **Address:** Maine General Medical Ctr., Physical Therapy Outpatient Center (Seton Unit), Waterville Campus 30 Chase Ave., Waterville, ME 04901 **E-mail:** joseph.fournier@mainegeneral.org

FOWLER, CARL D.
Industry: Healthcare **Born:** June 17, 1952, Detroit, Michigan **Univ./degree:** B.S., Biology, University of Michigan; M.D., Wayne State University School of Medicine, 1981 **Current organization:** Northwest Industrial & Medical Clinic, P.C. **Title:** M.D. **Type of organization:** Multi-specialty group practice **Major product:** Patient care **Area of distribution:** Detroit, Michigan **Area of Practice:** Family practice, internal medicine, general surgery **Affiliations:** A.A.F.P.; A.C.P.-A.S.I.M.; Surgical Committee, Northeast Community Hospital **Hob./spts.:** Family, swimming, church **SIC code:** 80 **Address:** Northwest Industrial & Medical Clinic, P.C., 9600 Dexter Ave., Detroit, MI 48206 **E-mail:** fowlerc3@comcast.net

FOY, ROBIN L.
Industry: Healthcare **Born:** September 22, 1961, Syracuse, New York **Univ./degree:** A.A.S., Medical Technology, Parkersburg Community College **Current organization:** Cape Fear Hospital **Title:** Hematology Lead Tech **Type of organization:** Orthopaedic hospital **Major product:** Patient care **Area of distribution:** North Carolina **Area of Practice:** Laboratory technology, hematology management, quality control, procedure manuals **Affiliations:** American Society for Clinical Pathology **Hob./spts.:** Community involvement, working with children **SIC code:** 80 **Address:** Cape Fear Hospital, 5301 Wrightsville Ave., Wilmington, NC 28403 **E-mail:** robin.foy@nhhn.org

FOYOUZI, NASTARAN
Industry: Medical **Born:** July 3, 1967, Tehran, Iran **Univ./degree:** M.D., Shahid Beheshti Medical University, Tehran, Iran, 1992; Research Fellowship, Infertility/High Risk Pregnancy, 2005; Resident, Ob/Gyn, Yale University **Current organization:** Yale University Hospital **Title:** M.D. **Type of organization:** University hospital **Major product:** Patient care, medical education **Area of distribution:** International **Area of Practice:** Ob/Gyn, high risk pregnancy, infertility **Honors/awards:** Outstanding Contribution, American Society for Reproductive Endocrinology and Infertility, 2004, travel grant provided to SGI from NIH, NICHD, 2005 **Affiliations:** A.C.O.G; A.I.U.M. **Hob./spts.:** Yoga, meditation, reading **SIC code:** 80 **Address:** 100 York St., #6G, New Haven, CT 06511 **E-mail:** nastaran.foyouzi@yale.edu

FRAGEN, RONALD A.
Industry: Healthcare **Born:** February 17, 1940, Indiana **Univ./degree:** M.D., Indiana University, 1964 **Current organization:** Fragen Cosmetic Surgery Center **Title:** M.D. **Type of organization:** Private practice **Major product:** Patient care **Area of distribution:** California **Area of Practice:** Cosmetic surgery **Affiliations:** A.B.O.; A.S.C.B.S.; Board of Directors, American Board of Cosmetic Surgery; Board of Directors, American Academy of Cosmetic Surgery **Hob./spts.:** Skiing, scuba diving, tennis **SIC code:** 80 **Address:** Fragen Cosmetic Surgery Center, 1900 East Tahquitz Canyon Way, Palm Springs, CA 92262

FRAKER, DOUGLAS L.
Industry: Medical **Born:** December 15, 1956, Waverly, Iowa **Univ./degree:** M.D., Harvard Medical School, 1983 **Current organization:** University of Pennsylvania **Title:** Chief, Division of Surgical Oncology **Type of organization:** University hospital **Major product:** Patient care, medical education **Area of distribution:** National **Area of Practice:** Surgical oncology **Published works:** 55 book chapters, 150 articles **Affiliations:** F.A.C.S.; A.S.A.; A.A.C.R.; S.S.O **Hob./spts.:** Golf **SIC code:** 80 **Address:** University of Pennsylvania, Dept. of Surgery, 3400 Spruce St., Philadelphia, PA 19104 **E-mail:** fraker@mail.med.upenn.edu

FRANCALANCIA, NICOLA A.
Industry: Healthcare **Born:** November 3, 1956, Toro, Italy **Univ./degree:** M.D., Johns Hopkins University, 1988 **Current organization:** Brody School of Medicine at ECU **Title:** M.D., F.A.C.S. **Type of organization:** University Medical Center **Major product:** Patient care **Area of distribution:** National **Area of Practice:** Thoracic surgery (heart, lungs, chest) **Published works:** Articles, book chapters **Affiliations:** A.C.S.; A.H.A. **Hob./spts.:** Skiing **SIC code:** 80 **Address:** Brody School of Medicine at ECU, Dept. of Surgery, 600 Moye Ave., Greenville, NC 27858 **E-mail:** francalancia@md.ecu.edu

FRANCIS, MARION DAVID
Industry: Medical consulting **Univ./degree:** Ph.D., Biology, University of Iowa, 1953 **Title:** Ph.D./consultant **Type of organization:** Independent consultant **Major product:** Medical, pathology and pharmaceutical consulting **Area of distribution:** International **Area of Practice:** Bone and physiology - therapeutics, biochemistry, expert witness **Published works:** 140 publications **Affiliations:** American Chemical Society **Hob./spts.:** Tennis, golf **SIC code:** 80 **Address:** Marion D. Francis, Ph.D., 23 Diplomat Dr., Cincinnati, OH 45215 **E-mail:** mfrancis3@cinci.rr.com

FRANCIS, THOMAS A.
Industry: Healthcare **Born:** April 14, 1959, Granite City, Illinois **Univ./degree:** M.D., Southern Illinois University, 1986 **Current organization:** Scottsdale Healthcare, Family Care **Title:** M.D. **Type of organization:** Private practice **Major product:** Patient care **Area of distribution:** Scottsdale, Arizona **Area of Practice:** Family practice **Affiliations:** American Academy of Family Physicians; Arizona Academy of Physicians **Hob./spts.:** Hiking, camping, hunting, raising bonsai, walking **SIC code:** 80 **Address:** Thomas A. Francis, M.D., 9641 N. 83rd Way, Scottsdale, AZ 85258

FRANCO, MARIA E.
Industry: Healthcare **Born:** April 9, 1963, Bogota, Colombia **Univ./degree:** M.D., University of El Rosario for Medicine, 1987; Residency, Hahmman University, Pediatrics; Pulmonology Fellowship, Temple University **Current organization:** Miami Children's Hospital **Title:** M.D. **Type of organization:** Hospital **Major product:** Children's healthcare **Area of distribution:** International **Area of Practice:** Pediatric pulmonology **Published works:** Articles **Affiliations:** A.T.S.; A.M.A. **Hob./spts.:** Volunteering, children **SIC code:** 80 **Address:** Miami Children's Hospital, Medical Office Bldg., 3200 S.W. 60th Ct., Suite 203, Miami, FL 33155-4076 **E-mail:** maria.franco@mch.com

FRAYNE, CHRISTINA M.
Industry: Healthcare **Born:** February 3, 1956, Binghamton, New York **Univ./degree:** B.S., Medical College of Georgia, 2002 **Current organization:** Eisenhower Army Medical Center **Title:** B.S., R.T. (M)(QM), Mammographer **Type of organization:** Hospital **Major product:** Patient care **Area of distribution:** Georgia **Area of Practice:** Mammography **Affiliations:** A.S.R.T.; A.R.R.T. **Hob./spts.:** Walking, the outdoors **SIC code:** 80 **Address:** 4716 Mill Pond Ct., Grovetown, GA 30813 **E-mail:** cmfrayne@yahoo.com

FRAZEE, DANIEL C.
Industry: Healthcare **Univ./degree:** R.N., St. Vincent's School of Nursing, Iowa, 16971 **Current organization:** Aurora Medical Center **Title:** R.N., B.L.S., A.C.L.S. **Type of organization:** Hospital **Major product:** Patient care **Area of distribution:** Illinois **Area of Practice:** Pain management **Affiliations:** A.O.R.N.; F.R.A.; M.O.A.; Lt. Commander, US Navy (27 years) **Hob./spts.:** Fishing, reading **SIC code:** 80 **Address:** 2013 Kedron Blvd., Zion, IL 60099 **E-mail:** dfrazee290@aol.com

FREY, BARBARA R.
Industry: Mental health **Born:** September 16, 1947, Cedar Falls, Iowa **Univ./degree:** M.S.W., University of Iowa, 1998 **Current organization:** Associates for Psychological & Therapy Services **Title:** L.I.S.W. Therapist **Type of organization:** Mental health services **Major product:** Patient care **Area of distribution:** International **Area of Practice:** Family, individual, couples, child therapy **Affiliations:** N.A.S.W. **Hob./spts.:** Sewing, quilting, community service, gardening **SIC code:** 80 **Address:** Associates for Psychological & Therapy Services, 1551 Indian Hills Dr., Suite 221, Sioux City, IA 51104-1857 **E-mail:** brfrey@ncn.net

FREY, R. TERRELL
Industry: Healthcare **Born:** February 26, 1947, Cincinnati, Ohio **Univ./degree:** B.S., Summa Cum Laude, Xavier University, 1969; M.D., University of Cincinnati, 1973 **Current organization:** Medical X-Ray Inc. **Title:** M.D. **Type of organization:** Single specialty medical practice **Major product:** Diagnostic imaging **Area of distribution:** Cincinnati, Ohio **Area of Practice:** Diagnostic radiology **Honors/awards:** Awarded Silver Medal of the Ohio State Radiological Society **Published works:** Articles **Affiliations:** A.M.A.; R.S.N.A.; A.C.R. **Hob./spts.:** Golf **SIC code:** 80 **Address:** Medical X-Ray Inc., 375 Dixmyth Ave., Cincinnati, OH 45220

FREYLE, JAIME
Industry: Healthcare **Born:** September 9, 1968 Bogota, Colombia **Univ./degree:** M.D., Colegio Mayor del Rosario, Colombia 1993 **Current organization:** Maimonides Medical Center **Title:** M.D. **Type of organization:** Medical center **Major product:** Patient care **Area of distribution:** New York **Area of Practice:** Urology **Published works:** 3 Articles **Affiliations:** A.U.A.; A.M.A. **Hob./spts.:** All sports **SIC code:** 80 **Address:** 8801 Shore Pkwy., Apt. 2 H.S., Brooklyn, NY 11209 **E-mail:** jfreyle@hotmail.com

FRIEDLANDER, MILES
Industry: Medical **Born:** April 29, 1935, Washington, Pennsylvania **Univ./degree:** M.D., Louisiana State University, 1959 **Current organization:** Tulane University, Dept. of Ophthalmology **Title:** M.D. **Type of organization:** University **Major product:** Higher education, patient care **Area of distribution:** National **Area of Practice:** Ophthalmology, refractive eye surgery **Affiliations:** American Academy of Ophthalmology; International Society of Refractive Surgery **Hob./spts.:** Digital photography **SIC code:** 80 **Address:** 136 Bellaire Dr., New Orleans, LA 70124 **E-mail:** milesf@tulane.edu

FRIEDMAN, RENAY M.
Industry: Healthcare **Univ./degree:** D.C., Logan College of Chiropractic **Current organization:** Friedman Chiropractic **Title:** D.C. **Type of organization:** Medical practice **Major product:** Chiropractic patient care **Area of distribution:** Freehold, New Jersey **Area of Practice:** Family practice **Affiliations:** A.C.A.; Lions Club **SIC code:** 80 **Address:** Friedman Chiropractic, 80 Scenic Dr., #4, Freehold, NJ 07728

FRONTELA, ODALYS P.
Industry: Healthcare **Born:** October 12, 1959, Cuba **Children:** Hamlet Sanchez, 15 **Univ./degree:** M.D., University of Costa Rica, 1988 **Current organization:** Miami Dade Health & Rehabilitation Services, Inc. **Title:** M.D., F.A.C.P. **Type of organization:** Hospital/clinic **Major product:** Patient care **Area of distribution:** Florida **Area of practice:** Internal medicine **Area of Practice:** Internal medicine **Affiliations:** F.M.A.-P.A.C.H.A.; A.C.P.-A.S.I.M.; A.C.P.E.; A.M.A.; A.M.P.A.C.; Diplomate, American Board of Internal Medicine **Hob./spts.:** Family, travel, sports **SIC code:** 80 **Address:** Miami Dade Health & Rehabilitation Services, Inc., 3233 Palm Ave., Hialeah, FL 33012 **Phone:** (305)826-0660 **Fax:** (305)825-0245 **E-mail:** ofrontela@aol.com

FUENTES, HENRY J.
Industry: Healthcare **Univ./degree:** M.D., Universidad de Cartagena, Colombia, 1982 **Current organization:** Parkview Orthopedics **Title:** M.D. **Type of organization:** Orthopedic Group **Major product:** Patient care **Area of distribution:** Illinois **Area of Practice:** Orthopedic surgery, sports medicine **Affiliations:** F.A.A.O.S.; I.S.O.S. **SIC code:** 80 **Address:** Parkview Orthopedics, 7600 College Dr., Palos Hts., IL 60463 **E-mail:** hankgt75@aol.com

FUKUDA, MICHIKO N.
Industry: Research/bio-chemistry **Born:** November 12, 1945, Tokyo, Japan **Univ./degree:** B.S., Education, University of Tokyo, 1968; M.S., 1970; Ph.D., Biochemistry, University of Tokyo, 1980 **Current organization:** The Burnham Institute **Title:** Professor **Type of organization:** Non-profit private research institute **Major product:** Research **Area of distribution:** International **Area of Practice:** Molecular biology, carbohydrate chemistry **Published works:** 70+ articles, 10 chapters **Affiliations:** Society of Biological Chemists; Society for Cell Biology **Hob./spts.:** Family **SIC code:** 80 **Address:** The Burnham Institute, 10901 N. Torrey Pines Rd., La Jolla, CA 92037 **E-mail:** michiko@burnham-inst.org **Web address:** www.burnham-inst.org

FULLAGAR, CHRISTOPHER JASON
Industry: Healthcare **Born:** December 26, 1974 **Univ./degree:** M.D., Jefferson Medical School, Pennsylvania, 1999 **Current organization:** SUNY Upstate Medical University **Title:** M.D. **Type of organization:** University hospital **Major product:** Medicine **Area of distribution:** Gillette, New Jersey **Area of Practice:** Emergency **Affiliations:** American Medical Association; A.E.T.N.A. **Hob./spts.:** Figure skating, First-Aid Teacher, Red Cross **SIC code:** 80 **Address:** 425 New Vernon Rd., Gillette, NJ 07933 **E-mail:** cjfoo1@jefferson.edu

FULLER, BRENDA R.
Industry: Healthcare **Born:** March 1, 1953, Washington, D.C. **Univ./degree:** B.S., Social Work, University of Washington, D.C. **Current organization:** St. Elizabeth's Hospital **Title:** Deputy Chief of Facilities & Support Operations **Type of organization:** Hospital **Major product:** Patient care **Area of distribution:** Washington, D.C. **Area of Practice:** Management of non-clinical staff of 250 **Affiliations:** National Mental Health Association; Maryland State Mental Health Association **Hob./spts.:** Bowling, volunteer work, tutoring children in reading and math **SIC code:** 80 **Address:** St. Elizabeth's Hospital, Behavioral Studies Bldg., Room 142, 2700 MLK Jr. S.E., Washington, DC 20032 **E-mail:** brendafuller@dc.gov

FURMAN, MIGNON
Industry: Education/Dance **Born:** March 11, Cape Town, South Africa **Univ./degree:** University of Cape Town **Current organization:** American Academy of Ballet **Title:** Director **Type of organization:** Dance academy **Major product:** Summer program for students, program for ballet teachers **Area of distribution:** International **Area of Practice:** Ballet teacher and choreographer/administrator **Affiliations:** Unity **Hob./spts.:** Stamp collecting, travel, ballet choreography, collecting Wedgwood **SIC code:** 80 **Address:** American Academy of Ballet, 250 W. 90th St., Suite 3A, New York, NY 10024 **E-mail:** mignonfurman@aol.com **Web address:** www.ameracademyofballet.com

GABEY, MARTHE A.
Industry: Healthcare **Born:** February 7, 1961, Teaneck, New Jersey **Univ./degree:** M.D., Medical College of Virginia, 1988 **Current organization:** Capital District Plastic Surgery Associates **Title:** M.D. **Type of organization:** Private practice **Major product:** Cosmetic and reconstructive surgery **Area of distribution:** Troy, New York **Area of Practice:** Plastic surgery **Affiliations:** American Society of Plastic Surgeons **SIC code:** 80 **Address:** Capital District Plastic Surgery, 147 Hoosick St., Suite G, Troy, NY 12180 **E-mail:** mgabey@nycap.rr.com

GACHAW, GABRA
Industry: Healthcare **Born:** September 11, 1954, Indianapolis, Indiana **Univ./degree:** B.S., Biology, Indiana University, 1976; M.D., Indiana University School of Medicine, 1985 **Current organization:** Interact, L.L.C./Hendricus Community Hospital **Title:** Psychiatrist/CEO/Medical Director **Type of organization:** Medical clinic/hospital **Major product:** Consulting/patient care **Area of distribution:** Indiana **Area of Practice:** Inpatient and forensic consultation/psychiatry **Affiliations:** A.P.A.; A.M.A.; Indiana Medical Association **Hob./spts.:** Photography, computers, music, reading, theatre **SIC code:** 80 **Address:** Interact, L.L.C., 258 Meadow Dr., Danville, IN 46122 **E-mail:** gachaw@aol.com

GADEA-MORA, CARLOS
Industry: Healthcare **Born:** May 3, 1937, San Juan, Puerto Rico **Univ./degree:** M.D., Universidad de Salamanca, Spain, 1967; M.P.H.; University of Puerto Rico, School of Medicine, 1989 **Current organization:** Latin American Center for Sexually Transmitted Diseases **Title:** Executive Director **Type of organization:** Medical center **Major product:** Patient care **Area of distribution:** National **Area of Practice:** Sexually transmitted diseases **Published works:** Multiple publications **Affiliations:** Puerto Rico Medical Association; Puerto Rico College of Physicians and Surgeons; HIV Treaters Association; National Coalition of S.T.D. Directors (N.C.S.D.) **Hob./spts.:** Classical music. Opera **SIC code:** 80 **Address:** Latin American Center for Sexually Transmitted Diseases, P.O. Box 70184, San Juan, PR 00936 **E-mail:** c.gadea@salud.gov.pr

GAFFNEY, THERESA A.
Industry: Healthcare **Univ./degree:** B.S.N., Medical College of Virginia, 1984; M.P.H., Virginia Technology University, 1997 **Current organization:** American Academy of

MEDICAL

Nursing **Title:** R.N., Executive Director **Type of organization:** Professional nursing association **Major product:** Patient care **Area of distribution:** National **Area of Practice:** Nursing administration **Published works:** 1 article, 1 chapter **Affiliations:** A.S.P.A.; A.S.A. Executive **SIC code:** 80 **Address:** American Academy of Nursing, 600 Maryland Ave. SW, Washington, DC 20024 **E-mail:** tgaffney@ana.org **Web address:** www.ana.org

GALLARDO, ANTONIO JOSE
Industry: Healthcare **Born:** November 28, 1948, San Juan, Puerto Rico **Univ./degree:** M.D., Universidad Central del Este, Dominican Republic, 1980 **Current organization:** Darlington Gynecological Services **Title:** M.D. **Type of organization:** Private practice **Major product:** Women's healthcare **Area of distribution:** Rio Piedras, Puerto Rico **Area of Practice:** Gynecology, family planninf **Affiliations:** Puerto Rico Medical Association **Hob./spts.:** Reading **SIC code:** 80 **Address:** Darlington Gynecological Services, Darlington Building, Suite 5, Munoz Rivera 1007 Ave., Rio Piedras, PR 00925-2717

GALLARDO-MÉNDEZ, RAFAEL A.
Industry: Healthcare/eyecare **Born:** October 30, 1951, San Juan, Puerto Rico **Univ./degree:** M.D., Universidad Autonoma, Santo Domingo, 1977 **Current organization:** Rafael Gallardo M.D. & Associates **Title:** M.D. **Type of organization:** Private practice **Major product:** Ophthalmology **Area of distribution:** Puerto Rico **Area of Practice:** Eye physician and surgeon **Affiliations:** American Academy of Ophthalmology; Puerto Rico Ophthalmology Society **SIC code:** 80 **Address:** Rafael Gallardo M.D. & Associates, 1449 Americo Salas St., Suite 203, San Juan, PR 00909 **E-mail:** gallardor@tld.net

GALLO, RICHARD A.
Industry: Healthcare **Born:** March 7, 1953, Milwaukee, Wisconsin, 1978 **Univ./degree:** M.D., Medical College of Wisconsin **Current organization:** Anesthesia Associates of Northeast Alabama, P.A. **Title:** M.D./Anesthesiologist **Type of organization:** Private practice **Major product:** Patient care **Area of distribution:** Alabama **Area of Practice:** Anesthesia **Affiliations:** A.M.A.; American Society of Anesthesiologists; Diplomate, American Board of Anesthesiology; Alabama State Society of Anesthesiologists; Physicians Who Care, Etowah County **Hob./spts.:** Travel, skiing, chess, sporting events **SIC code:** 80 **Address:** Anesthesia Associates of Northeast Alabama, P.A., P.O. Box 8305, Gadsden, AL 35902 **E-mail:** badgerman@cybrtyme.com

GALTON, BARRY B.
Industry: Healthcare **Born:** April 24, 1932, New York, New York **Univ./degree:** M.D., Columbia University College of Physicians and Surgeons, 1958 **Current organization:** Internal Medicine Associates of North Jersey **Title:** M.D., F.A.C.P., F.A.C.C. **Type of organization:** Private practice **Major product:** Patient care **Area of distribution:** Wayne, New Jersey **Area of Practice:** Internal medicine **Affiliations:** President, YM-YWHA of New Jersey, 2003 to present **Hob./spts.:** Travel, cross country skiing, squash **SIC code:** 80 **Address:** Internal Medicine Associates of North Jersey, 1777 Hamburg Turnpike, Suite 302, Wayne, NJ 07470 **Phone:** (973)831-9222 **Fax:** (973)831-1460 **E-mail:** bbgmdsquash.com@aol

GAMBARIN, BORIS
Industry: Healthcare **Born:** December 13, 1945, Volchov, Russia **Univ./degree:** M.D., Uzbekistan (Soviet Union); Ph.D., 1975; Ph.D., 1982, Tashkent Medical Institute **Current organization:** New York Methodist Hospital **Title:** MD, Internal Medicine **Type of organization:** Hospital **Major product:** Patient care **Area of distribution:** New York **Area of Practice:** Internal medicine **Published works:** 150+ articles; 4 books **Affiliations:** Fellow, A.C.P. **Hob./spts.:** Basketball, swimming, travel **SIC code:** 80 **Address:** New York Methodist Hospital, 506 Sixth Street, Brooklyn, NY 11215 **E-mail:** drgamb@aol.com

GAMELLI, RICHARD L.
Industry: Medical **Born:** January 18, 1949, West Springfield, Massachusetts **Univ./degree:** M.D., University of Vermont, 1974 **Current organization:** Loyola University Medical Center **Title:** Chair, Dept. of Surgery/Professor **Type of organization:** Academic/medical institution **Major product:** Medical services **Area of distribution:** Illinois **Area of Practice:** Surgery, burns, trauma, critical care **Affiliations:** A.S.A., A.A.S.T., S.U.S., A.C.S. **Hob./spts.:** Gardening, cycling **SIC code:** 80 **Address:** Loyola University Medical Center, Dept. of Surgery, 2160 S. First Ave. EMS Bldg. 110, Maywood, IL 60153 **E-mail:** rgamell@lumc.edu

GANDHI, VIJAY K.
Industry: Healthcare **Born:** Kathlal, Guj., India **Univ./degree:** M.D., Baroda Medical College, India, 1980 **Current organization:** Vijay K. Gandhi, M.D. **Title:** M.D. **Type of organization:** Private practice **Major product:** Patient care **Area of distribution:** New Jersey **Area of Practice:** Hematology/oncology **Published works:** Presentation at A.S.C.O., "Role of Highdose Methotrexate in Malignant Astrocytoma" **Affiliations:** New Jersey Medical Society; American Society of Clinical Oncology; Diplomat, American Board of Internal Medicine in Medical Oncology, Internal Medicine; past president, Cape May Unit of American Cancer Society; Chief, Division of Hem/Oncology, Burdette Memorial Hospital since 1991 **SIC code:** 80 **Address:** Vijay K. Gandhi, M.D., 301 Stoneharbor Blvd., Unit C, Cape May Court, NJ 08210 **E-mail:** vkg@bellatlantic.net

GARCIA, HERMES R.
Industry: Healthcare **Born:** March 7, 1951, New York, New York **Univ./degree:** M.D., San Juan Baltista Medical School, 1980 **Current organization:** Latin American Center for Sexually Transmitted Diseases **Title:** M.D., Medical Director **Type of organization:** Medical center **Major product:** Patient care, research **Area of distribution:** National **Area of Practice:** Public health, transmitted diseases **Published works:** Multiple publications **Affiliations:** A.M.A.; Puerto Rico Medical Association **Hob./spts.:** Golf, guitar **SIC code:** 80 **Address:** Latin American Center for Sexually Transmitted Diseases, P.O. Box 70184, San Juan, PR 00936

GARCIA, MARCO A.
Industry: Healthcare **Born:** September 30, 1966, Havana, Cuba **Univ./degree:** M.D., Havana, Cuba, 1990 **Current organization:** Marco A. Garcia, M.D. **Title:** M.D. **Type of organization:** Private medical practice **Major product:** Patient care **Area of distribution:** New York **Area of Practice:** Internal medicine **Affiliations:** A.M.A. **SIC code:** 80 **Address:** Marco A. Garcia, M.D., 93-19 Roosevelt Ave., Jackson Heights, NY 11372 **E-mail:** garciamdnyc@aol.com

GARCIA, MARIA-TERESA
Industry: Dentistry **Univ./degree:** D.D.S., University of San Antonio, 1987 **Current organization:** Bright Dental **Title:** D.D.S. **Type of organization:** Private dental practice **Major product:** Patient care **Area of distribution:** Houston, Texas **Area of Practice:** General dentistry **Affiliations:** American Dental Association; Texas Dental Association; Orthodontist Association **Hob./spts.:** Interior design, mission work in Mexico **SIC code:** 80 **Address:** Bright Dental, 909 Dairy Ashford St., Houston, TX 77079

GARCIA BARRETO, LUIS A.
Industry: Healthcare **Born:** September 24, 1964, Arecibo, Puerto Rico **Univ./degree:** M.D., Ponce School of Medicine, 1990 **Current organization:** Luis A. Garcia Barreto, M.D. **Title:** M.D. **Type of organization:** Private practice/sleep laboratory **Major product:** Patient care **Area of distribution:** Puerto Rico **Area of Practice:** Pulmonary disease/sleep disorders **Affiliations:** F.A.C.C.F.; A.P.S. **Hob./spts.:** Tennis, skiing, basketball **SIC code:** 80 **Address:** Santa Maria Medical Building, Suite 126, Ponce, PR 00717-1105 **E-mail:** garbarrt@caribe.net

GARDNER, MARY FRANCES
Industry: Healthcare **Born:** May 22, 1940, Houston, Texas **Univ./degree:** M.D., Tulane University Affiliated Hospital, 1981 **Current organization:** Mary Gardner, M.D. **Title:** M.D. **Type of organization:** Private practice **Major product:** Patient care **Area of distribution:** New Orleans, Louisiana **Area of Practice:** Ob/Gyn **Affiliations:** L.S.M.S.; Fellow, O.B.G.Y.N.; Jefferson Parish Medical Society; Zonta International **SIC code:** 80 **Address:** Mary Gardner, M.D., 927 Broadway St., New Orleans, LA 70118 **E-mail:** mfgardnermd@aol.com

GARIMELLA, SATYA V.
Industry: Healthcare **Born:** March 26, 1967, Hyderabad, India **Univ./degree:** M.B.B.S., Osmani Medical College, India, 1990 **Current organization:** Mountain Comprehensive Health Corp. **Title:** M.D. **Type of organization:** Multispecialty clinic **Major product:** Patient services **Area of distribution:** Kentucky **Area of Practice:** Cardiology, electrophysiology **Affiliations:** F.A.C.C.; N.A.S.P.E. **Hob./spts.:** Tennis, poetry, singing **SIC code:** 80 **Address:** Mountain Comprehensive Health Corp., 226 Medical Plaza Lane, Whitesburg, KY 41858 **E-mail:** satyagarimella@hotmail.com

GARINO, JONATHAN P.
Industry: Medical **Born:** May 31, 1962, Hackensack, New Jersey **Univ./degree:** B.S., Biology, Georgetown University, 1984; M.D., Georgetown University School of Medicine, 1988 **Current organization:** University of Pennsylvania, Dept. Of Orthopedic Surgery **Title:** M.D. **Type of organization:** University hospital **Major product:** Joint replacements **Area of distribution:** Pennsylvania, New Jersey, Delaware **Area of Practice:** Orthopedic surgery **Published works:** 40+ articles, 8 chapters, 2 books edited **Affiliations:** A.M.A.; A.A.O.S. **Hob./spts.:** Family, sports, model trains **SIC code:** 80 **Address:** University of Pennsylvania, Dept. Of Orthopedic Surgery, 3400 Spruce St., Philadelphia, PA 19104 **E-mail:** jonathan.garino@uphs.upenn.edu **Web address:** www.dr-garino.yourmd.com

GARRIDO, ANGELO
Industry: Healthcare **Born:** January 4, 1956, Long Island, New York **Univ./degree:** MD, University of Chicago Health Sciences Medical School, 1986 **Current organization:** University Plaza Obstetrics & Gynecology, LLP **Title:** MD **Type of organization:** Medical practice **Major product:** Patient care **Area of distribution:** Long Island, New York **Area of Practice:** Ob/Gyn **Affiliations:** A.C.O.G.; Nassau

County Ob/Gyn Society; New York Medical Society **Hob./spts.:** Family **SIC code:** 80 **Address:** University Plaza Obstetrics & Gynecology, LLP, 877 Stewart Ave., Suite 7, Garden City, NY 11530

GASIEWICZ, THOMAS A.
Industry: Medical **Born:** June 14, 1950, Buffalo, New York **Univ./degree:** Ph.D., Toxicology, University of Rochester, 1977 **Current organization:** University of Rochester Medical Center **Title:** Chairman, Department of Environmental Medicine **Type of organization:** University medical center **Major product:** Medical services **Area of distribution:** International **Area of Practice:** Molecular toxicology **Affiliations:** A.A.A.S; Society of Toxicology; american Society for Biochemistry and Molecular Biology **Hob./spts.:** His kids, golf, backpacking, travel, home renovations **SIC code:** 80 **Address:** University of Rochester Medical Center, 575 Elmwood Ave., Box EHSC, Rochester, NY 14642 **E-mail:** tom_gasiewicz@urmc.rochester.edu

GASPER, STEVE P.
Industry: Healthcare **Born:** March 16, 1975, Los Angeles, California **Univ./degree:** B.S., Business Management, University of Southern California, 1997 **Current organization:** Catholic Healthcare West **Title:** Learning & Organizational Development Coordinator **Type of organization:** Hospital **Major product:** Patient care **Area of distribution:** California **Affiliations:** I.S.M. **Hob./spts.:** Reading, skiing, boating, basketball, football **SIC code:** 80 **Address:** Catholic Healthcare West, 251 S. Lake Ave., 7th floor, Pasadena, CA 91101

GATES-BELLER, CHERYL K.
Industry: Healthcare **Born:** April 8, 1944, Chillicothe, Ohio **Univ./degree:** Diploma, Riverside-White Cross School of Nursing, Columbus, OH, 1965; B.S., Management of Nursing Services. College of Mount St. Joseph, Cincinnati, OH, 1995; Legal Nurse Consulting, Kaplan College, Boca Raton, FL; Medical Consulting Network, Columbus, OH **Current organization:** Self-employed independent healthcare provider **Title:** Clinician, IV Specialist, Case Management, Supervisor American Nursing Care, Columbus, OH **Type of organization:** Independent healthcare provider **Major product:** Nursing care **Area of distribution:** Central Ohio **Area of Practice:** ANCC Medical-Surgical Certification, Chemo Certification **Affiliations:** American Nursing Association; Ohio Nursing Association; Cross Alumni Association; College of Mount St. Joseph Association and Business Alumni-Honorary **Hob./spts.:** Physical fitness, reading **SIC code:** 80 **Address:** Cheryl K. Gates-Beller, BSMNS, RN, C, Independent Healthcare Provider, 609 Gender Rd., Canal Winchester, OH 43110 **E-mail:** ckbeller@bright.net

GATTI, MARGARET C.
Industry: Healthcare **Born:** February 21, 1956, Washington, D.C. **Univ./degree:** M.S.N., Nursing, Wilmington College, Ohio, 1999 **Current organization:** Healthcare Assoc. **Title:** CSRN/MSN/FNP-C **Type of organization:** Healthcare systems, hospital **Major product:** Patient care, medical services **Area of distribution:** Millsboro, Delaware **Area of Practice:** Family Nurse Practitioner, Occupational Health **Affiliations:** American Academy of Nurse Practitioners **Hob./spts.:** Travel, photography, swimming **SIC code:** 80 **Address:** Healthcare Assoc., 232 Mitchell St., Suite 301, Millsboro, DE 19966 **E-mail:** peggygatti@mchsi.com

GAU-KRUEGER, SUSAN M.
Industry: Healthcare **Born:** March 2, 1952, Wausau, Wisconsin **Univ./degree:** M.S.W., University of Iowa, 1982 **Current organization:** Alliance Counseling Professionals/Melonas Counseling **Title:** Licensed Clinical Social Worker **Type of organization:** Mental health clinic **Major product:** Mental health treatment **Area of distribution:** Wausau, Wisconsin **Area of Practice:** Children, disabilities, family counseling **Affiliations:** N.A.S.W. **Hob./spts.:** Sewing, baking, biking, gardening **SIC code:** 80 **Address:** Alliance Counseling Professionals/Melonas Counseling, 2600 Stewart Ave., Wausau, WI 54401

GAVRILESCU, TUDOR H.
Industry: Healthcare **Univ./degree:** M.D., Romania, 1967; Ph.D., Romania, 1982 **Current organization:** SUNY Downstate Medical Center, Brooklyn, New York **Title:** M.D., Ph.D., F.A.C.O.G., Clinical Associate Professor, Director of Gynecology **Type of organization:** University hospital and faculty, private practice **Major product:** Women's healthcare **Area of distribution:** Long Island, New York **Area of practice:** Obstetrics/Gynecology (Board Certified), gynecologic surgery, vaginal surgery, laparoscopic surgery **Area of Practice:** Obstetrics/Gynecology (Board Certified), gynecologic surgery, vaginal surgery, laparoscopic surgery **Published works:** Articles **Affiliations:** A.C.O.G; American Society of Laparoscopic Surgeons **Hob./spts.:** Tennis, gardening **SIC code:** 80 **Address:** SUNY Downstate Medical Center, 450 Clarkson Ave., Box 24, Brooklyn, NY 11203 **E-mail:** tudororia@hotmail.com

MEDICAL

GAWNE, ANNE CARRINGTON
Industry: Medical **Born:** June 1, 1957, Pasadena, California **Univ./degree:** M.D., Uniformed Services University of the Health Sciences, 1984 **Current organization:** Roosevelt Warm Springs Institute for Rehabilitation **Title:** M.D./Director, Post-Polio Clinic **Type of organization:** Rehabilitation hospital **Major product:** Multidisciplinary Post-Polio evaluation **Area of distribution:** Warm Springs, Georgia **Area of Practice:** Board Certified PM&R EMG **Honors/awards:** Grant Recipient for Research & Enrichment Program **Published works:** Editor: "The State of the Art Reviews in Physical Medicine Rehabilitation"; Archives of Physical Medicine & Rehabilitation; Annuls of the N.Y. Academy of Science; Books: "Managing Post Polio"; "Post Polio Syndrome" **Affiliations:** A.A.E.M.; A.A.P.M.R.; A.C.R.M. **Hob./spts.:** Winter ski patrol P.A., golf, gardening **SIC code:** 80 **Address:** Roosevelt Warm Springs Institute for Rehabilitation, 6135 Roosevelt Hwy., Warm Springs, GA 31830 **E-mail:** acgawne@dol.state.ga.us

GAYLORD, ALBERT E.
Industry: Healthcare **Born:** July 24, 1946, Akron, Ohio **Univ./degree:** B.S., Zoology and Pre-Veterinary Medicine, Ohio State University, 1969 **Current organization:** Deaconess Medical Center **Title:** Laboratory Administrative Director **Type of organization:** Acute care hospital **Major product:** Patient care **Area of distribution:** Spokane, Washington **Area of Practice:** Clinical laboratory sciences **Affiliations:** Clinical Laboratory Management Association; American Society for Clinical Pathology **Hob./spts.:** Reading, stained glass **SIC code:** 80 **Address:** Deaconess Medical Center, 800 W. 5th Ave., Spokane, WA 99204 **E-mail:** gaylora@empirehealth.org

GEBHART, RONALD J.
Industry: Healthcare **Born:** April 10, 1945, Fort Worth, Texas **Univ./degree:** M.D., Medical College of Virginia, 1972 **Current organization:** VA Salt Lake City Healthcare System **Title:** Chief of Staff **Type of organization:** Hospital and clinics **Major product:** Patient care **Area of distribution:** National **Area of Practice:** Internal medicine and infectious diseases **Published works:** Multiple publications **Affiliations:** F.A.C.P.; A.M.A.; I.D.S.A.; S.G.I.M.; Utah Medical Society **Hob./spts.:** Scuba diving, skiing **SIC code:** 80 **Address:** VA Salt Lake City (11 VAMC), 500 Foothill Dr., Salt Lake City, UT 84148 **E-mail:** ronald.gebhart@med.va.gov

GEISER, JOHN F.
Industry: Healthcare **Born:** August 2, 1961, Springfield, Illinois **Univ./degree:** M.D., University of Illinois, 1990 **Current organization:** A.A.M. **Title:** M.D. **Type of organization:** Medical practice **Major product:** Patient care **Area of distribution:** Medford, Oregon **Area of Practice:** Anesthesiology and cardiovascular anesthesiology **Published works:** Articles **Affiliations:** American Society of Anesthesiologists; Society of Cardiovascular Anesthesiology **Hob./spts.:** Running, surfing, skiing, mountain biking **SIC code:** 80 **Address:** A.A.M., 2620-H E. Barnett Rd., Medford, OR 97504-8550

GELMAN, MARTIN L.
Industry: Healthcare **Born:** November 3, 1943 Chicago, Illinois **Univ./degree:** M.D., Indiana University, 1968 **Current organization:** Greater Boston Medical Associates **Title:** M.D. **Type of organization:** Private practice **Major product:** Patient care **Area of distribution:** Massachusetts **Area of Practice:** Internal medicine, nephrology, hypertension **Published works:** 26 Publications **Affiliations:** A.S.N.; A.C.P.; A.S.A.I.O.; A.M.A. **Hob./spts.:** Golf, skiing **SIC code:** 80 **Address:** Greater Boston Medical Associates, 747 Cambridge St., Brighton, MA 02135 **E-mail:** gelman85@aol.com

GEMLICK, BRETT F.
Industry: Healthcare **Born:** March 14, 1969, Cleveland, Ohio **Univ./degree:** M.D., Ohio State University, 1995 **Current organization:** Orthopaedics Northeast **Title:** Orthopaedic Surgeon/M.D. **Type of organization:** Medical practice **Major product:** Orthopaedic surgery **Area of distribution:** Indiana **Area of Practice:** Orthopaedic surgery **Honors/awards:** Outstanding Orthopaedic Resident Award; The Rohn Polanc Award, 2000; Sigma Cum Laude **Published works:** Book chapter, "Osteonecrosis", 1998 **Affiliations:** A.O.A.; Fort Wayne Orthopaedic Society **Hob./spts.:** Family, running **SIC code:** 80 **Address:** 13021 Cavendish Ct., Ft. Wayne, IN 46845 **E-mail:** bgemlick@aol.com

GEMMA, RICK A.
Industry: Healthcare **Born:** February 1, 1972, Warrensville, Ohio **Univ./degree:** D.O., Lake Erie College of Osteopathic Medicine, 1998 **Current organization:** South Pointe Hospital **Title:** D.O. **Type of organization:** Hospital **Major product:** Patient care **Area of distribution:** Ohio **Area of Practice:** General surgery **Affiliations:** A.A.O.S.; A.O.A.; O.O.A. **SIC code:** 80 **Address:** South Pointe Hospital, 4110 Warrensville Center Rd., Solon, OH 44122 **E-mail:** rickgem@aol.com

GENDY, SALWA
Industry: Healthcare **Born:** Cairo, Egypt **Univ./degree:** B.S., Chemistry, Cairo University, M.S., Chemistry, Queens College **Current organization:** Lincoln Medical Center **Title:** Associate Chemist II; Quality Control/Quality Assurance Coordinator **Type of organization:** Medical center **Major product:** Patient care **Area of distribution:** Bronx, New York **Area of Practice:** Quality control **Affiliations:** CAP Inspector **Hob./spts.:** Cooking **SIC code:** 80 **Address:** Lincoln Medical Center, 234 E. 149th St., 2C2 Room 434, Bronx, NY 10451 **E-mail:** salwa.gendy@yahoo.com

GEORGE, ROSHNY A.
Industry: Medical **Born:** July 28, 1973, Kerala, India **Univ./degree:** M.D., Christian Medical College, Vellore, India **Current organization:** New York Medical College **Title:** M.D. **Type of organization:** University hospital **Major product:** Medical services **Area of distribution:** New York **Area of Practice:** Internal medicine **Published works:** Abstracts at national meetings **Affiliations:** A.C.P.; A.M.A.; B.C.M.S.; A.A.P.I.; I.M.A.; M.S.S.N.Y. **Hob./spts.:** Music, baseball, reading, basketball **SIC code:** 80 **Address:** New York Medical College, 600 E. 233rd St., Bronx, NY 10466 **E-mail:** roshnygeorge@yahoo.com

GEORGE, TIMOTHY M.
Industry: Medical **Born:** October 17, 1960, Brooklyn, New York **Univ./degree:** M.D., New York University, 1986 **Current organization:** Duke University Medical Center **Title:** M.D. **Type of organization:** University medical center **Major product:** Medical services **Area of distribution:** National **Area of Practice:** Pediatric neurosurgery **Honors/awards:** Mayfield Award **Published works:** Journals, book chapters **Affiliations:** Congress of Neurosurgical Surgeons; Joint Section of Pediatric Neurosurgical Surgeons **Hob./spts.:** Basketball, music, church activities **SIC code:** 80 **Address:** Duke University Medical Center, Box 3272, Durham, NC 22710 **E-mail:** georg017@mc.duke.edu

GEORGESON, PAMELA A.
Industry: Healthcare **Born:** December 2, Chesterfield, Michigan **Univ./degree:** D.O., Chicago College of Osteopathic Medicine, 1983 **Current organization:** Kenwood Allergy and Asthma Center **Title:** Physician **Type of organization:** Private allergy practice **Major product:** Patient care **Area of distribution:** Chesterfield Township and metropolitan Detroit, Michigan **Area of Practice:** Allergist **Affiliations:** American Academy of Allergy, Asthma and Immunology; American College of Allergy, Asthma and Immunology; American Osteopathic Association **Hob./spts.:** Singing, skiing, travel **SIC code:** 80 **Address:** Kenwood Allergy & Asthma Center, 30170 Twenty Three Mile Rd., Chesterfield Township, MI 48047 **Phone:** (586)949-5900 **Fax:** (586)949-5922 **Web address:** www.kenwoodallergy.com

GERA, SURENDRA N.
Industry: Healthcare **Univ./degree:** M.D., New Delhi, India, 1962 **Current organization:** Surendra N. Gera, M.D. **Title:** M.D. **Type of organization:** Private practice **Major product:** Patient care **Area of distribution:** Grand Prairie, Texas **Area of Practice:** Psychiatry **Affiliations:** A.M.A.; Texas Medical Association **SIC code:** 80 **Address:** Surendra N. Gera, M.D., 2100 Hwy. 360 N., Suite 507A, Grand Prairie, TX 75050

GERARDO, DANNY R.
Industry: Healthcare **Born:** El Paso, Texas **Univ./degree:** A.S., Respiratory Care, California College of Health Sciences, 1992; B.S., Business Administration, University of Phoenix, 2002; M.B.A., University of Texas, El Paso, 2004 **Current organization:** Las Palmas Medical Center **Title:** Director, Respiratory Services **Type of organization:** Hospital (medical center) **Major product:** Patient care (respiratory therapy, hyperbaric medicine, EMG, EEG, EKG) **Area of distribution:** El Paso, Texas **Area of Practice:** Respiratory services **Affiliations:** Texas Society for Respiratory Care **Hob./spts.:** Family, martial arts, collecting comic books **SIC code:** 80 **Address:** Las Palmas Medical Center, 1801 N. Oregon St., El Paso, TX 79902 **E-mail:** danny.gerardo@laspalmashealth.com

GERMAN, VICTOR F.
Industry: Healthcare **Born:** November 17, 1936, Coffeeville, Kansas **Univ./degree:** Ph.D., University of Illinois, 1963; M.D., University of Chicago, 1975 **Current organization:** University of Texas Health Science Center at San Antonio **Title:** M.D., Ph.D., Head of Community Pediatric Program **Type of organization:** University hospital **Major product:** Clinical/teaching **Area of distribution:** San Antonio, Texas **Area of Practice:** Pediatric pulmonology **Affiliations:** A.A.P.; A.F.S. **Hob./spts.:** Travel, history **SIC code:** 80 **Address:** The University of Texas Health Science Center at San Antonio, Dept. of Pediatrics-MSC 7818, 7703 Floyd Curl Dr., San Antonio, TX 78229-3900 **E-mail:** german@uthscsa.edu

GETER, RODNEY K.
Industry: Healthcare **Born:** November 13, 1946, Baton Rouge, Louisiana **Univ./degree:** M.D., University of Missouri, Columbia, 1979 **Current organization:** St. John's Health System **Title:** M.D. **Type of organization:** Multispecialty clinic **Major product:** Patient care **Area of distribution:** Missouri **Area of Practice:** Plastic surgery **Affiliations:** A.S.P.R.S; Missouri State Medical Society; Green County Medical Society **Hob./spts.:** Keyboard player in a 17 piece band, backpacking, fishing **SIC code:** 80 **Address:** St. John's Health System, 3231 South National, Springfield, MO 65807

GETTINGER, SHAREN A.
Industry: Healthcare **Born:** April 7, 1947, Ste. Genevieve, Missouri **Current organization:** Ste. Genevieve County Memorial Hospital **Title:** Nurse Manager **Type of organization:** Hospital **Major product:** Patient care **Area of distribution:** Ste. Genevieve, Missouri **Area of Practice:** Maternity patients and newborns **Affiliations:** A1; American College of Obstetricians and Gynecologists; American Nurses Association **Hob./spts.:** Quilting, reading, travel **SIC code:** 80 **Address:** St. Genevieve County Memorial Hospital, Hwys. 61 & 32, P.O. Box 468, Ste. Genevieve, MO 63670 **E-mail:** sgettinger@stegenevievehospital.org

GETTINGER-ROTTLER, MARIA
Industry: Healthcare **Born:** January 25, 1975, Ste. Genevieve, Missouri **Univ./degree:** B.S., Maryville University, 1998 **Current organization:** Mid America Rehab **Title:** Physical Therapist **Type of organization:** Clinic **Major product:** Physical therapy - inpatient, outpatient, home health care, nursing home care **Area of distribution:** Missouri **Area of Practice:** Women's health, physical therapy; APTA credentialed clinical instructor **Honors/awards:** Outstanding Clinical Instructor, St. Louis University **Affiliations:** American Physical Therapists Association; Missouri Physical Therapists Association **Hob./spts.:** Sports, quilting, gardening **SIC code:** 80 **Address:** Mid America Rehab, Hwy. 32 & 61, Ste. Genevieve, MO 63670 **E-mail:** ptgettinger@hotmail.com

GHAVAMIAN, REZA
Industry: Medical **Univ./degree:** M.D., Boston University **Current organization:** Montefiore Medical Center **Title:** M.D. **Type of organization:** University hospital **Major product:** Patient care **Area of distribution:** Bronx, New York **Area of Practice:** Urologic oncology **Affiliations:** A.U.A.; Society for Urological Oncology; New York Urologic Society **Hob./spts.:** Soccer **SIC code:** 80 **Address:** Montefiore Medical Center, 3400 Bainbridge Ave., Bronx, NY 10467 **E-mail:** rghavami@montefiore.org

GIANSIRACUSA, DAVID F.
Industry: Medical **Born:** June 17, 1949, Boston, Massachusetts **Univ./degree:** M.D., University of California School of Medicine of San Francisco, 1975 **Current organization:** University of Massachusetts Medical School, U. Mass. Memorial Healthcare **Title:** M.D. **Type of organization:** Academic medical center **Major product:** Patient care, medical education **Area of distribution:** Worcester, Massachusetts **Area of Practice:** Internal medicine, rheumatology **Honors/awards:** Outstanding Teacher **Hob./spts.:** Photography **SIC code:** 80 **Address:** University of Massachusetts Medical School, U. Mass. Memorial Healthcare, 55 Lake Ave. North, Worcester, MA 01655 **E-mail:** giansird@ummhc.org

GIBBS, JOHN F.
Industry: Healthcare **Born:** November 8, 1958, San Francisco, California **Univ./degree:** M.D., University of California at San Diego, 1985 **Current organization:** Roswell Park Cancer Institute **Title:** Chief, GI Surgical Oncology **Type of organization:** Academic fertility cancer center **Major product:** Patient care **Area of distribution:** International **Area of Practice:** Pancreas and liver surgery **Affiliations:** Association for Academic Surgery; Society of Surgical Oncology **Hob./spts.:** Tennis **SIC code:** 80 **Address:** Roswell Park Cancer Institute, Elm & Carlton Sts., Buffalo, NY 14263 **E-mail:** johngibbs@roswellpark.org

GIBSON, FANNIE A.
Industry: Healthcare **Born:** May 27, 1931, Lane, South Carolina **Univ./degree:** R.N., New York University (through Kingsborough Community College), 1975 **Current organization:** Kingstree Nursing Facility **Title:** R.N., Supervisor N.D. **Type of organization:** Nursing facility **Major product:** Patient care **Area of distribution:** Kingstree, South Carolina **Area of Practice:** Nursing, Nurse Supervisor **Honors/awards:** McNair Nursing Facility Outstanding Service Award, 2001; Bethel AME Church, 2nd Oldest Sunday School Supportive Member Award, 1996; Kingstree Elementary School Outstanding Service Award, 1989; Town of Kingstree Housing Authority Board of Commissioners, Many Years of Service Award, 1997; Kingstree Elementary School Voluntary Service Rendered to the Special Olympic Award, 1997; Many Years of Service to Bethel AME Church Health Fair RN Award, 1997; Dedicated Service to Liberty Work Chapter #171 Order of the Eastern Star (OES) Award, 2001 (many more) **Affiliations:** N.N.A.; S.C.N.A.; N.C.W.W.; Bethel AME; W.M.S.; N.A.A.C.P.; O.E.S. **Hob./spts.:** Spending quality leisure time with family, discussing the Bible, reading to great grandchildren, gardening, travel, stamp collecting, canning, photography **SIC code:** 80 **Address:** 730 St. John St., Kingstree, SC 29556

GIBSON, PATRIC L.
Industry: Healthcare **Univ./degree:** M.A., San Francisco State University, 1981 **Current organization:** Franklin Square Hospital Center **Title:** Administrative Director, Laboratory Services **Type of organization:** Hospital **Major product:** Patient care, laboratory services **Area of distribution:** Maryland **Area of Practice:** Pathology, administration, business development **Affiliations:** A.S.C.P. **SIC code:** 80 **Address:** Franklin Square Hospital Center, , 9000 Franklin Square Dr., Baltimore, MD 21237 **E-mail:** patric.gibson@medstar.net

GILBERT III, THOMAS J.
Industry: Healthcare **Born:** July 12, 1955, Baltimore, Maryland **Univ./degree:** D.O., Kirksville College, 1989 **Current organization:** Washington County Emergency Medicine Physicians, LLC **Title:** D.O., CHM Emergency Dept. **Type of organization:** Hospital **Major product:** Emergency patient care **Area of distribution:** Hagerstown, Maryland **Area of Practice:** Emergency medicine **Affiliations:** F.A.C.E.P.; A.M.S.U.S. **Hob./spts.:** Football, baseball **SIC code:** 80 **Address:** Washington County Emergency Medicine Physicians, LLC, 251 E. Antietam St., Hagerstown, MD 21740 **E-mail:** gilbertdofacep@earthlink.net

GILBERT-BARNESS, ENID
Industry: Medical **Univ./degree:** M.B.B.S., 1950; M.D., 1983, University of Sydney, Australia; Honorary D.Sci, 1999; Honorary M.D., 1999, University of Wisconsin **Current organization:** University of South Florida, Tampa General Hospital **Title:** Professor **Type of organization:** University hospital **Major product:** Patient care, medical education **Area of distribution:** Florida **Area of Practice:** Pediatric pathology **Affiliations:** American Society for Pediatric Pathology **Hob./spts.:** Writing, reading, travel, theatre **SIC code:** 80 **Address:** University of South Florida, Tampa General Hospital, 2 Columbus Ave., Tampa, FL 33601 **E-mail:** egilbert@tgh.org

GILHORN, JOHN G.
Industry: Healthcare **Born:** May 7, 1941, Philadelphia, Pennsylvania **Univ./degree:** D.M.D., University of Pennsylvania, 1967 **Current organization:** Dr. John G. Gilhorn, Orthodontist P.C. **Title:** President **Type of organization:** Private practice **Major product:** Complete orthodontic treatment **Area of distribution:** Doylestown, Pennsylvania **Area of Practice:** Orthodontics **Affiliations:** A.A.O.; A.S.O.; P.S.O.; G.P.S.O.; A.D.A. **Hob./spts.:** Golf **SIC code:** 80 **Address:** Dr. John G. Gilhorn, Orthodontist P.C., 86 N. Clinton St., Doylestown, PA 18901 **E-mail:** gilhornortho@msn.com

GILMORE, GIBSON THOMAS
Industry: Engineering **Born:** January 10, 1975, Indianapolis, Indiana **Univ./degree:** B.S., Mechanical Engineering, Purdue University, 1997 **Current organization:** Keyence Corporation **Title:** Engineer **Type of organization:** Manufacturing **Major product:** Automation **Area of distribution:** International **Area of Practice:** Engineering **Affiliations:** Mensa **Hob./spts.:** Scuba diving, golf **SIC code:** 80 **Address:** Keyence Corporation, 1051 Perimeter Dr., Suite 650, Schaumburg, IL 60173 **E-mail:** gibgilmore@aol.com

GILMORE, SANDRA A.
Industry: Healthcare **Born:** September 15, 1935, New York, New York **Univ./degree:** M.D., State University of New York at Town State, 1960 **Current organization:** Newton-Wellesley Hospital **Title:** M.D. **Type of organization:** Private practice **Major product:** Patient care **Area of distribution:** Newton, Massachusetts **Area of Practice:** Primary care **Affiliations:** A.M.A.; American Women's Medical Association **Hob./spts.:** Tennis, golf, swimming **SIC code:** 80 **Address:** Newton-Wellesley Hospital, 2000 Washington St., Newton, MA 02462 **E-mail:** md.gils@nwtt.org

GIOSCIA, MICHAEL F.
Industry: Healthcare **Born:** January 14, 1960, Long Island, New York **Univ./degree:** M.D., SUNY Downstate Medical Center, Brooklyn, New York, 1986 **Current organization:** Michael F. Gioscia, M.D., F.A.C.S. **Title:** M.D., F.A.C.S. **Type of organization:** Private practice **Major product:** Laparoscopic surgery, minimally invasive vascular surgery **Area of distribution:** White Plains, New York; Tarrytown, New York; New York, New York **Area of Practice:** Minimally invasive techniques for Venous disease and Intra-abdominal disorders **Published works:** Multiple publications including "Minimally Invasive Abdominal Surgery" (Textbook); Numerous journal articles **Affiliations:** SAGES; Westchester Surgical Society; New York Surgical Society; New York Minimally Invasive Surgical Society **Hob./spts.:** Skiing, surfing, fishing, skeet shooting, flying **SIC code:** 80 **Address:** Michael F. Gioscia, M.D., F.A.C.S., 311 North St., White Plains, NY 10605

GIROUX, JOHN H.
Industry: Healthcare **Born:** June 8, 1959, Akron, Ohio **Univ./degree:** M.D., Chicago School of Medicine, 1985 **Current organization:** Homer Glen Pediatrics **Title:** M.D. **Type of organization:** Private practice **Major product:** Patient care **Area of distribution:** Homer Glen, Illinois **Area of Practice:** Pediatrics **Honors/awards:** Alpha Omega Alpha; Chicago's Best Doctors, 2000 **Affiliations:** A.M.A.; A.A.P.; A.B.P. **Hob./spts.:** Boating **SIC code:** 80 **Address:** Homer Glen Pediatrics, 12701 W. 143rd St., Homer Glen, IL 60441 **E-mail:** johngiroux@worldnet.att.net

GIUSTRA, LAUREN A.
Industry: Healthcare **Born:** September 4, 1966, Brooklyn, New York **Univ./degree:** M.D., State University of New York Downstate Medical Center, 1992 **Current organization:** Mohawk Valley Women's Health Associates **Title:** M.D. **Type of organization:** Group practice **Major product:** Patient care **Area of distribution:** Rome, New York **Area of Practice:** Obstetrics, gynecology **Affiliations:** A.M.A.; American College of Obstetrics and Gynecology **SIC code:** 80 **Address:** Mohawk Valley Women's Health Associates, 107 E. Chestnut St., Rome, NY 13440

GIZZO-WAITLEY, GAIL
Industry: Healthcare **Born:** November 22, 1961, Chicago, Illinois **Univ./degree:** M.D., Rush Medical College, 1991 **Current organization:** Westside Medical Associates, Ltd. **Title:** M.D. **Type of organization:** Hospital **Major product:** Patient care **Area of distribution:** National **Area of Practice:** Internal medicine **Affiliations:** A.M.A.; I.S.M.S.; N.H.A. **Hob./spts.:** Physical fitness, swimming **SIC code:** 80 **Address:** Westside Medical Associates, Ltd., Highland Medical Center, 2340 Highland Ave., Suite 210, Lombard, IL 60148 **E-mail:** gwaitley@msn.com

GLATZ, F. ROBERT
Industry: Healthcare **Born:** December 2, 1970, North Carolina **Univ./degree:** M.D., Lake Forest University **Current organization:** Valley Ear, Nose & Throat **Title:** Pediatrician **Type of organization:** Private group practice **Major product:** Patient care **Area of distribution:** National **Area of Practice:** Pediatric otolaryngology **Affiliations:** A.C.P.R.C.; A.S.L.A.; A.A.O.; A.L.S. **Hob./spts.:** Kite boarding **SIC code:** 80 **Address:** Valley Ear, Nose & Throat, 2101 South Cynthia, McAllen, TX 78503 **E-mail:** bobglatz@rgv.rr.com

GLIEDMAN, PAUL R.
Industry: Healthcare **Born:** Manhattan, New York **Univ./degree:** M.D., Columbia University, 1983 **Current organization:** St. Lukes Roosevelt Hospital **Title:** M.D./ Director of Radiation Oncology **Type of organization:** Hospital **Major product:** Patient care **Area of distribution:** New York **Area of Practice:** Radiation oncology **Published works:** Articles, chapters **Affiliations:** A.S.T.R.O., A.S.C.O. **SIC code:** 80 **Address:** St. Lukes Roosevelt Hospital, Dept. of Radiation Oncology, 1000 Tenth Ave., New York, NY 10019 **E-mail:** pgliedman@chpnet.org

GOEL, NAVEEN
Industry: Medical **Born:** August 20, 1971, New Delhi, India **Univ./degree:** M.B.B.S., Government Medical College, Baroda, Gujarat, India, 1995 **Current organization:** Long Island College Hospital/Kidney Urology Foundation of America **Title:** M.D. **Type of organization:** Teaching hospital **Major product:** Patient care, research, medical education **Area of distribution:** New York **Area of Practice:** Internal medicine, nephrology **Honors/awards:** Clinical and Research Fellowship awarded from Kidney and Urology Foundation of America; Certificate of Achievement awarded from Kidney and Urology Foundation of America, 2003 **Published works:** 2 articles, co-authored 2 book chapters, 3 abstracts **Affiliations:** A.S.N.; A.M.A.; N.K.F.; P.C.S.; I.S.P.D.; R.P.A.; A.S.P.I.O. **Hob./spts.:** Family, skiing, tennis **SIC code:** 80 **Address:** Long Island College Hospital, Kidney & Urology Foundation of America, 339 Hicks St., Box 48, Brooklyn, NY 11201 **E-mail:** drnav5487@pol.net

GOGU, SUDHIR R.
Industry: Healthcare **Born:** December 1, 1955, Hyderabad, India **Univ./degree:** D.O., University of Osteopathic Medicine and Surgery, Des Moines University, IA, 1997 **Current organization:** Urgent Clinic **Title:** D.O., Ph.D. **Type of organization:** Medical clinic **Major product:** Patient care **Area of distribution:** Texas **Area of Practice:** Family medicine **Affiliations:** Texas Osteopathic Medical Association; American

Osteopathic Association **Hob./spts.:** Golf **SIC code:** 80 **Address:** 15930 Tall Heights, San Antonio, TX 78255 **E-mail:** sgogu@sphpo.org

GOJKOVICH, DUSAN
Industry: Healthcare **Born:** August 25, 1935, Berovo, Macedonia **Univ./degree:** M.D., University of Lubljana, Slovenia, 1960 **Current organization:** Associated Psychiatrists **Title:** M.D. **Type of organization:** Medical practice **Major product:** Patient care **Area of distribution:** Kankakee, Illinois **Area of Practice:** General psychiatry **Affiliations:** A.M.A.; A.P.A. **Hob./spts.:** Skiing **SIC code:** 80 **Address:** Associated Psychiatrists, 500 N. Wall St., Suite 200, Kankakee, IL 60901

GOLDENBERG, ALEC S.
Industry: Healthcare **Born:** April 2, 1954, New York, New York **Univ./degree:** M.D., Johns Hopkins University, 1980 **Current organization:** Alec S. Goldenberg, M.D. **Title:** M.D. **Type of organization:** Private practice **Major product:** Patient care **Area of distribution:** National **Area of Practice:** Hematology, oncology **Published works:** Articles, journals **Affiliations:** American Society of Clinical Oncology; American Society of Hematology; New York University Medical School **Hob./spts.:** Sailing **SIC code:** 80 **Address:** Alec S. Goldenberg, M.D., 157 E. 32nd St., New York, NY 10016 **E-mail:** alecgoldus@yahoo.com

GOLDMAN, STANFORD M.
Industry: Medical **Born:** November 28, 1940, Salt Lake City, Utah **Univ./degree:** M.D., Albert Einstein Medical School, 1965 **Current organization:** University of Texas School of Medicine, Dept. of Radiology **Title:** Radiology Professor **Type of organization:** University **Major product:** Patient care, medical education **Area of distribution:** Texas **Area of Practice:** Radiology, education, emergency medicine, uroradiology **Published works:** 140 articles, book chapters, edited 3 books **Affiliations:** A.U.A.; T.M.A.; H.M.A.; H.R.A., R.S.N.A.; A.S.E.R.; A.R.R.S.; Adjunct Professor, Baylor University School of Medicine; Professor, M.D. Anderson Cancer Center **Hob./spts.:** Swimming, travel, music **SIC code:** 80 **Address:** University of Texas School of Medicine, Dept. of Radiology, 6431 Fannin MSB 2.100, Houston, TX 77030 **E-mail:** stanford.m.goldman @uth.tmc.edu

GOLDSTEIN, DANIEL J.
Industry: Healthcare **Born:** August 26, 1965, New York, New York **Univ./degree:** M.D., Mount Sinai School of Medicine, 1991 **Current organization:** St. Barnabas Health Care System **Title:** M.D. **Type of organization:** Hospital **Major product:** Patient care **Area of distribution:** New York **Area of Practice:** Cardiothoracic surgery **Affiliations:** A.H.A.; A.C.S.; A.C.C.; Healing the Children **Hob./spts.:** Magic, soccer **SIC code:** 80 **Address:** 500 W. End Ave., Apt. 1B, New York, NY 10024 **E-mail:** dgoldstein@sbhcs.com

GOMEZ, JESSICA L.
Industry: Healthcare **Born:** December 14, 1951, Salt Lake City, Utah **Univ./degree:** M.B.A., Healthcare Management, University of Phoenix **Current organization:** Memorial Hospital Los Banos **Title:** RN, BSN, MBA/HCM **Type of organization:** Hospital **Major product:** Patient care, community education **Area of distribution:** Los Banos, California **Area of Practice:** Diabetes **Honors/awards:** Women Helping Women Award, Soroptimist International **Affiliations:** American Association of Diabetes Educators; American Diabetes Association **Hob./spts.:** Crocheting, fishing camping, travel, sightseeing **SIC code:** 80 **Address:** Memorial Hospital Los Banos, 520 W. I St., Los Banos, CA 93635 **E-mail:** gomezjl@sutterhealth.org

GOMEZ-ALBA, JOSE R.
Industry: Healthcare **Born:** August 11, 1949, Moca, Dominican Republic **Univ./degree:** M.D., Autonomous University of Santo Domingo, 1976 **Current organization:** Jose R. Gomez-Alba, M.D. **Title:** Psychiatrist **Type of organization:** Private practice/hospital affiliation **Major product:** Psychiatry **Area of distribution:** International **Area of Practice:** Psychiatry **Honors/awards:** Honored, second year resident as Psychiatrist, 1988 **Affiliations:** A.A.F.P.; A.P.A.; A.M.A. **Hob./spts.:** Collecting Jewish-Egyptian art **SIC code:** 80 **Address:** Jose R. Gomez-Alba, M.D., Pravia St. 30-12, V. Asturias, Carolina, PR 00983 **E-mail:** josex@coqui.net

GONSOULIN, BILL
Industry: Healthcare **Born:** Loreauville, Louisiana, October 31, 1972 **Univ./degree:** B.S., Clinical Lab Sciences, Northeastern Louisiana University, 1995 **Current organization:** Our Lady of Lourdes Regional Medical Center **Title:** Microbiology Supervisor/Adjunct Professor **Type of organization:** Hospital, lab **Major product:** Patient care/medical microbiology **Area of distribution:** Louisiana **Area of Practice:** Clinical microbiology **Affiliations:** A.S.M.B.; S.W.A.C.M. **SIC code:** 80 **Address:** Our Lady of Lourdes Regional Medical Center, 213.2 Main St., P.O.B. 126, Loreauville, LA 70552 **E-mail:** bacterjude@cox.net

GONZALES, JORGE M.
Industry: Healthcare **Univ./degree:** M.D., Universidad de San Marco Medical School, Lima, Peru, 1962 **Current organization:** Jorge M. Gonzales, M.D., F.A.C.S. **Title:** M.D. **Type of organization:** Private practice **Major product:** Patient care **Area of distribution:** New Jersey **Area of Practice:** Urology (Board Certified) **Affiliations:** F.A.C.S.; A.M.A.; A.B.U. **SIC code:** 80 **Address:** 102 S. East Ave., P.O. Box 1323, Vineland, NJ 08362

GONZALEZ, ANGELA
Industry: Healthcare **Born:** January 6, 1958, New York, New York **Univ./degree:** M.D., University of Puerto Rico School of Medicine, 1983 **Current organization:** Angela Gonzalez, M.D., P.A. **Title:** M.D. **Type of organization:** Private practice **Major product:** Patient care **Area of distribution:** Florida **Area of Practice:** Internal medicine **Affiliations:** F.A.C.P.; Alpha Omega Alpha **SIC code:** 80 **Address:** Angela Gonzalez, M.D., P.A., 13322 S.W. 128th St., Miami, FL 33186 **E-mail:** agonz0106@aol.com

GONZALEZ, EVELYN
Industry: Healthcare **Born:** January 15, 1952, New York, New York **Univ./degree:** M.D., University of Puerto Rico School of Medicine, 1978 **Current organization:** Evelyn Gonzalez M.D. **Title:** M.D. **Type of organization:** Medical practice **Major product:** Patient care **Area of distribution:** Puerto Rico **Area of Practice:** Child neurology **Affiliations:** A.A.N.; Puerto Rico Academy of Neurology **Hob./spts.:** Fashion design **SIC code:** 80 **Address:** Urb El Senorial, 2060 Calle G. Maranon, San Juan, PR 00926

GONZALEZ, MIRIAM A.
Industry: Healthcare **Born:** March 3, 1964, Cuba **Univ./degree:** B.S., Health Management, Touro College, New York **Current organization:** St. Barnabas Medical Center **Title:** Assistant Vice President, Patient Management Services Compliance **Type of organization:** Hospital **Major product:** Patient care **Area of distribution:** New Jersey **Area of Practice:** Patient services, administration **Affiliations:** A.S.R.A.M.; Healthcare Compliance Association **Hob./spts.:** Family, horseback riding **SIC code:** 80 **Address:** St. Barnabas Medical Center, 94 Old Short Hills Rd., Livingston, NJ 07039 **E-mail:** migonzalez@sch.cs.com **Web address:** www.schcs.com

GONZALEZ, MODESTO
Industry: Healthcare **Born:** September 6, 1948, Arecibo, Puerto Rico **Univ./degree:** M.D., University of Zaragoza, Spain, 1976 **Current organization:** Centro Neumologico de Puerto Rico **Title:** M.D., Senior Partner **Type of organization:** Group medical practice **Major product:** Patient care, pulmonary medicine and critical care **Area of distribution:** Puerto Rico **Published works:** Articles **Affiliations:** A.C.P.; A.M.A.; A.C.C.P.; E.S.R.D. **Hob./spts.:** Golf, reading, photography **SIC code:** 80 **Address:** Centro Neumologico de Puerto Rico, Torre Medica Auxilio Mutuo, Ponce de Leon #735, Suite 716, San Juan, PR 00917 **E-mail:** mfgonza@attglobal.net

GONZALEZ, ORLANDO
Industry: Healthcare **Born:** March 28, 1967, Bayamon, Puerto Rico **Univ./degree:** M.D., University of Puerto Rico Medical School, 1993 **Current organization:** Clinica Oftalmica **Title:** M.D./Assistant Chief of Ophthalmology **Type of organization:** Medical university, private practice **Major product:** Eye care **Area of distribution:** Aibonito, Puerto Rico **Area of Practice:** Ophthalmology **Affiliations:** A.A.O.; F.A.B.O.; P.R.S.O. **Hob./spts.:** Computers **SIC code:** 80 **Address:** Clinica Oftalmica, P.O. Box 455, Aibonito, PR 00705

GONZALEZ, RAFAEL ANGEL
Industry: Healthcare **Born:** October 21, 1948, San Juan, Puerto Rico **Univ./degree:** M.D., Universidad Autonoma, Guadalajara, Mexico, 1976 **Current organization:** Ashford Presbyterian Hospital **Title:** M.D. **Type of organization:** Hospital **Major product:** Patient care **Area of distribution:** San Juan, Puerto Rico **Area of Practice:** Emergency medicine **Affiliations:** A.C.E.P.; Puerto Rico College of Physicians and Surgeons; Puerto Rico Emergency Medical Faculty; Corp. State Insurance Fund **Hob./spts.:** Cycling, swimming **SIC code:** 80 **Address:** Dr. Rafael A. Gonzales, M.D., P.O. Box 361057, San Juan, PR 00936

GONZÁLEZ, BERNARDO A.
Industry: Healthcare **Born:** October 22, 1964, Arecibo, Puerto Rico **Univ./degree:** M.D., Autonomous University, Guadalajara, 1990 **Current organization:** Saint Michael Medical Services **Title:** M.D. **Type of organization:** Medical services **Major product:** Patient care **Area of distribution:** Puerto Rico **Area of Practice:** General surgery **Affiliations:** Puerto Rico Medical Society **Hob./spts.:** Sailing **SIC code:** 80 **Address:** Saint Michael Medical Services, P.O. Box 1729, Vega Baja, PR 00694 **E-mail:** Bernar2@yahoo.com

GONZALEZ-DUEÑAS, ANDREA
Industry: Healthcare **Born:** December 17, 1951, Havana, Cuba **Univ./degree:** M.D., San Juan Bautista, Caguas, Puerto Rico, 1984 **Current organization:** Andrea Gonzalez-Dueñas, M.D. **Title:** M.D. **Type of organization:** Private practice **Major product:** Patient care **Area of distribution:** Condado, Puerto Rico **Area of Practice:** Psychiatry **SIC code:** 80 **Address:** Andrea Gonzalez-Dueñas, M.D., Calle Taft 179, Office 2C, Condado, PR 00910

GOODKIN, KARL
Industry: Medical **Born:** November 18, 1954, Brooklyn, New York **Univ./degree:** M.D., 1982; Ph.D., 1983, University of Miami **Current organization:** University of Miami School of Medicine **Title:** Professor **Type of organization:** University **Major product:** Research, education **Area of distribution:** International **Area of Practice:** Neuropsychiatry, full time AIDS research **Affiliations:** American Society of Microbiology; American Medical Association **Hob./spts.:** Weight training **SIC code:** 80 **Address:** University of Miami School of Medicine, 1400 N.W. Tenth Ave., #803-A, Miami, FL 33136 **E-mail:** kgoodkin@med.miami.edu

GOODLOW, LISA M.
Industry: Healthcare **Born:** December 7, 1956, Cleveland, Ohio **Univ./degree:** B.S.N.; B.A., Psychology, Capital University, 1979; M.S. Candidate, Healthcare Administration, Cleveland State University **Current organization:** Home Health & Hospice Services of Southwest General **Title:** Administrator **Type of organization:** Hospital **Major product:** Patient care **Area of distribution:** Ohio **Area of Practice:** Nursing administration, hospice care, training, presentations **Affiliations:** National Association for Home Care; National Association of Palliative Care; Ohio Council for Home Care **Hob./spts.:** Reading, sewing, needlework, travel **SIC code:** 80 **Address:** Home Health & Hospice Services of Southwest General, 17951 Jefferson Park Blvd., Middleburg Heights, OH 44130 **E-mail:** lgoodlow@swgeneral.com **Web address:** www.swgeneral.com

GOODWIN, ROBIN R.
Industry: Healthcare **Born:** December 22, 1961, Monterrey, California **Univ./degree:** B.S., Biology, Cameron University **Current organization:** USPHS Indian Hospital **Title:** Lieutenant Commander, Commission Corps **Type of organization:** Hospital **Major product:** Patient care **Area of distribution:** Oklahoma **Area of Practice:** Medical Technologist; Hematology Supervisor **Affiliations:** American Society of Clinical Pathologists; Coach, Walters Summer League; A.S.A. Fast-Pitch Softball **Hob./spts.:** Crappie fishing, golf, collecting arrowheads **SIC code:** 80 **Address:** USPHS Indian Hospital, 1515 N.E. Lawrie Tatum Rd., Lawton, OK 73507-3002 **E-mail:** robin.goodwin@ihs.gov **Web address:** www.ihs.gov

GOORAY, DAVID A.
Industry: Healthcare **Born:** June 29, 1949, Essequibo, Guyana **Univ./degree:** M.D., Howard University **Current organization:** Dr. David Gooray, M.D., P.A. **Title:** President/Owner/M.D. **Type of organization:** Private practice **Major product:** Patient care **Area of distribution:** Largo, Maryland **Area of Practice:** Cardiology **Honors/awards:** Outstanding Teacher in Medicine, 2000-2006 **Affiliations:** American Medical Association **Hob./spts.:** Football, ping pong, soccer **SIC code:** 80 **Address:** Dr. David Gooray, M.D., P.A., 1450 Mercantile Lane, Suite 217, Largo, MD 20774 **E-mail:** dag629@aol.com

GORCHYNSKI, JULIE A.
Industry: Medical **Born:** January 4, 1961, Canada **Univ./degree:** M.Sc., California State University, Northridge, 1987; M.D., Creighton University, 1991 **Current organization:** University of California at Irvine Medical Center **Title:** M.D., Assistant Clinical Professor **Type of organization:** University hospital **Major product:** Medical services **Area of distribution:** National **Area of Practice:** Emergency medicine **Published works:** Multiple publications **Affiliations:** A.M.A.; A.C.E.P.; A.A.E.M. **Hob./spts.:** Surfing **SIC code:** 80 **Address:** University of California at Irvine Medical Center, 101 The City Dr., Orange, CA 92868 **E-mail:** jgorchyn@uci.edu

GORE, JOEL M.
Industry: Medical **Born:** March 30, 1949, Boston, Massachusetts **Univ./degree:** M.D., University of Calgary, Alberta, Canada **Current organization:** University of Massachusetts Memorial Medical Center **Title:** M.D., F.A.C.C., F.A.H.A., F.C.C.P. **Type of organization:** Hospital, university **Major product:** Medical services **Area of distribution:** National **Area of Practice:** Cardiology **Published works:** 175 + journal articles, 200 + abstracts, 3 books **Affiliations:** ACC, AHA, MMS, ACCP **Hob./spts.:** Physical fitness, biking, golf **SIC code:** 80 **Address:** University of Massachusetts Memorial Medical Center, 55 Lake Ave. North, Worcester, MA 01655 **E-mail:** gorej@ummhc.org

GORMAN, STEVEN P.
Industry: Healthcare **Born:** April 22, 1963, Long Beach, California **Univ./degree:** B.S., Biology, Humboldt University, 1986; M.D., Creighton University School of Medicine, 1992 **Current organization:** Steven P. Gorman, M.D. **Title:** M.D. **Type of organization:** Private medical office **Major product:** Patient care **Area of distribution:** La Quinta, California **Area of Practice:** Internal medicine **Affiliations:** A.C.P.; A.M.A. **Hob./spts.:** Family, reading, skiing, softball, woodworking, golf **SIC code:** 80 **Address:** Steven P. Gorman, M.D., 78150 Calle Tampico, Suite 100, La Quinta, CA 92253 **E-mail:** dsrtdoc@aol.com

GOROSPE, LUIS V.
Industry: Healthcare **Born:** September 11, 1940, Manila, Philippines **Univ./degree:** A.A., 1962; M.D., 1966, Central Manila Medical College, Philippines **Current organization:** Center for Surgical Weight Control **Title:** M.D. **Type of organization:** Specialty clinic **Major product:** Outstanding patient care **Area of distribution:** International **Area of Practice:** Bariatric surgery **Honors/awards:** Inducted into the U.S. Martial Arts Hall of Fame, 2000, as Master Instructor **Affiliations:** F.A.C.S.; A.S.B.S.; A.S.G.G.; A.M.A.; Tulsa, Oklahoma Surgical Society; Assistant Clinical Professor of General Surgery, Oklahoma University **Hob./spts.:** Martial arts (Judo and Jujitsu), travel **SIC code:** 80 **Address:** Center for Surgical Weight Control, 8803 S. 101 E. Ave., Tulsa, OK 74133 **Web address:** www.centerforsurgicalweightloss.com

GORUM II, W. JAY
Industry: Medical **Born:** August 6, 1967, San Jose, California **Univ./degree:** B.S., Howard University, Chemical Engineering, 1991; M.D., Hahnemann University, 1997 **Title:** M.D. **Type of organization:** Medical university **Major product:** Patient care, medical education **Area of distribution:** Pennsylvania **Area of Practice:** Orthopedics **Published works:** Co-author, "Sports Injury in Field Hockey" and "Flexior Tendon Injury" **Affiliations:** A.A.O.S. **Hob./spts.:** Spending time with family, biking, swimming, running **SIC code:** 80 **Address:** 328 Wellesley Rd., Philadelphia, PA 19119 **E-mail:** jgorum@drexel.edu

GOSLEE, LEONARD T.
Industry: Healthcare **Univ./degree:** M.D., Meharry Medical College, 1958 **Current organization:** Queens L.I. Medical Group **Title:** M.D. **Type of organization:** Medical practice **Major product:** Children's healthcare **Area of distribution:** National **Area of Practice:** Pediatrics **Affiliations:** A.M.A.; Q.M.S.; N.M.S. **Hob./spts.:** Swimming **SIC code:** 80 **Address:** Queens L.I. Medical Group, 112-18 Springfield Blvd., Queens Village, NY 11429

GOULD, RICHARD
Industry: Healthcare **Born:** Rahway, New Jersey **Univ./degree:** A.S., Medical Administration, H.C.C. Community College, 1970 **Current organization:** Watson Clinic LLP **Title:** Radiology Clinical Director **Type of organization:** Private group practice **Major product:** Patient care **Area of distribution:** Lakeland, Florida **Area of Practice:** Supervising operations, radiology administration **Affiliations:** American Society of Clinical Radiologists **Hob./spts.:** Ski Instructor, sailing **SIC code:** 80 **Address:** Watson Clinic LLP, 1600 Lakeland Hills Blvd., Lakeland, FL 33805 **E-mail:** rgould@watsonclinic.com

GOZON, BENJAMIN S.
Industry: Healthcare **Born:** October 19, 1965, Manila, Philippines **Univ./degree:** M.D., University of Philippines College of Medicine, 1992 **Current organization:** Capitol Rehabilitation Clinic **Title:** M.D. **Type of organization:** Medical clinic **Major product:** Patient care **Area of distribution:** Milwaukee, Wisconsin **Area of Practice:** Rehabilitation medicine/electro diagnostics **Published works:** 2 publications **Affiliations:** A.M.A.; A.A.P.M.R.; A.A.E.M.; P.A.S.S.O.R. **Hob./spts.:** Golf **SIC code:** 80 **Address:** Benjamin S. Gozon, MD, S.C., 7220 W. Capitol Dr., Milwaukee, WI 53216 **Phone:** (414)464-4888 **Fax:** (414)464-1850 **E-mail:** bengozon@aol.com

GRAMPSAS, SAMUEL A.
Industry: Healthcare **Born:** January 26, 1968, Denver, Colorado **Univ./degree:** B.S., Molecular Biology, University of Colorado, Boulder, 1990; M.D., University of Colorado Health Sciences Center, 1995 **Current organization:** UroHealth Institute **Title:** Urologist/ Director of Urology **Type of organization:** Private group practice/hospital **Major product:** Patient care **Area of distribution:** Illinois **Area of Practice:** Urologic surgery, focus on female urology, laparoscopic surgery; Urology (Board Certified) **Published works:** 12+ articles **Affiliations:** Fellow, American College of Surgeons; American Urological Association; Board of Directors, Illinois Urological Society **Hob./spts.:** Family life, music, playing guitar, golf **SIC code:** 80 **Address:** UroHealth Institute, 2005 Jacobssen Dr., Suite A, Normal, IL 61761 **E-mail:** grampsas@msn.com **Web address:** www.urologicsurgeryassociates.com

GRANT, RICHARD EDWARD
Industry: Healthcare **Born:** March 16, 1949, Gary, Indiana **Univ./degree:** B.S., Biology, Stanford University, 1971; M.D., Howard University School of Medicine, 1976 **Current organization:** Grant Orthopaedic, Bone & Joint Surgeons **Title:** M.D. **Type of organization:** Orthopaedic medical group **Major product:** Total joint replacement **Area of distribution:** Washington, D.C. **Area of Practice:** Orthopaedics **Published works:** 30 articles, book chapter **Affiliations:** American Board of Orthopaedic Surgeons; Association of Bone and Joint Surgeons **Hob./spts.:** Family, sports, jazz, literature **SIC code:** 80 **Address:** Grant Orthopaedic, Bone & Joint Surgeons, 1160 Varnum St. N.E., #104 Depaul Professional Building, Washington, DC 20017

GRASSO III, MICHAEL
Industry: Healthcare **Born:** May 31, 1961, Philadelphia, Pennsylvania **Univ./degree:** M.D., Thomas Jefferson University, Pennsylvania, 1986 **Current organization:** Saint Vincents Medical Center **Title:** Chair, Dept. of Urology/Tenure Professor; Assistant Professor, Urology, New York University **Type of organization:** Hospital **Major product:** Minimally invasive urology **Area of distribution:** New York, New York **Area of Practice:** Urology, kidney stone disease, developed complex urologic endoscopy **Honors/awards:** Professorship, Vice Chair, New York Medical College; Designated University Scholar, University of Pittsburgh, 1982; Paul D. Zimskind Memorial Prize in Urology, Thomas Jefferson School of Medicine, 1986; Hyman Menduke Prize in Basic Science Research, Thomas Jefferson School of Medicine, 1986; 1st Prize Video Production, Video Urology Times Sixth World Congress of Video Urology, 1994; New York Magazine's Best Doctors 2001/2002 **Published works:** 1 book, "Color Atlas of Endo Eurology"; 70+ publications; Journal of Urology; Journal of Endo Urology Society **Affiliations:** A.U.A.; A.B.U.; L.E.S.; Board Member, A.L.S.; Endo Urology Society **Hob./spts.:** Photography **SIC code:** 80 **Address:** Saint Vincents Medical Center, 170 W. 12th St., Cronin 205, New York, NY 10011 **E-mail:** mgrasso3@earthlink.net

GRAUR, OCTAVIA B.
Industry: Healthcare **Born:** March 23, 1961, Timisoara, Romania **Univ./degree:** M.D., General Medicine,1985; Ph.D., Microbiology, 1996, University of Medicine, Timisoara, Romania **Current organization:** Westshore Pathology Services **Title:** M.D., Ph.D., F.C.A.P. **Type of organization:** Hospital **Major product:** Patient care **Area of distribution:** Michigan **Area of Practice:** Pathology **Affiliations:** U.S.C.A.P.; A.M.A.; American Society of Clinical Pathologists; College of American Pathologists **SIC code:** 80 **Address:** Westshore Pathology Services, 1774 Peck St., Muskegon, MI 49441 **E-mail:** ograur@hackley-health.org

GRAY, NAWANA MIESA
Industry: Healthcare **Born:** April 21, 1972, San Francisco, California **Current organization:** Peebles Assisted Living Services Inc. **Title:** CEO/Administrator **Type of organization:** Non-profit residential care facility **Major product:** Assisted living for the elderly and disabled **Area of distribution:** Stockton, California (San Joaquin County) **Area of Practice:** Business, grant writing/communication **Hob./spts.:** Grant writing, yoga, walking, shopping **SIC code:** 80 **Address:** Peebles Assisted Living Services Inc., 404 N. Broadway, Stockton, CA 95205

GRAZIANO, DONNA M.
Industry: Healthcare **Born:** January 21, 1956, Milton, Massachusetts **Current organization:** New Bedford Medical Associates **Title:** R.T. ®(M)(CT)(Qm)(ARRT) **Type of organization:** Medical center **Major product:** Patient care **Area of distribution:** Massachusetts **Area of Practice:** CT scan, diagnostic radiology, mammography **Affiliations:** A.R.R.T.; A.S.R.T. **Hob./spts.:** Golf, music **SIC code:** 80 **Address:** New Bedford Medical Associates, 53 Marion Rd., Wareham, MA 02571

GREENBERG, MARTIN J.
Industry: Healthcare **Born:** July 23, 1951, New York, New York **Univ./degree:** B.S., Brooklyn College, 1973; M.D., Loyola University Stritch School of Medicine, 1976 **Current organization:** Spine and Orthopaedic Surgery Center **Title:** M.D. **Type of organization:** Private practice/medical center **Major product:** Patient care **Area of distribution:** Illinois **Area of Practice:** Orthopaedic surgery/emergency medicine **Honors/awards:** Certificate of Appreciation ITOA Field Training Exercise TEMS Organizer, 1999 & 2000; Certificate of Appreciation ITOA TEMS Sessions, 1999 & 2000 ITOA Training Conference; Physician Recognition Award, American Medical Association, 1981-present **Published works:** "Fracture Dislocations of the Tarsal Navicular", Orthopaedics, Volume 3-3, Page 254-255, March, 1980; Medical Hazards of Drug Related Missions, ITOA News Magazine, Summer 1999; Dealing with the Threat of Biological Weapons, ITOA News Magazine, Fall 2000; Presentations include: "Functional Anatomy of the Hand", presented at The Illinois Association of Occupational Therapists Annual Meeting, 1979; "Total Joint Arthroplasty Current Status", presented at Chicago Center Hospital, 1985; Domestic Preparedness-Nuclear and Conventional Weapons, IMERT (Illinois Mobile Emergency Response Team) presentation 8/14/00 **Affiliations:** Fellow, American Academy of Orthopaedic Surgeons; Fellow, American College of Surgeons; Fellow, International College of Surgeons; Fellow, Mid-America Orthopaedic Association; Fellow, American Association for Hand Surgery; International Tactical Emergency Medicine Support Association, Category 1 Active Member; Illinois Tactical Officers Association, Category 1 Active Member; National Tactical Officer's Association, Category 2 Active Member; Chicago Orthopaedic Society; Illinois Orthopaedic Society; Our Lady of Resurrection Medical Center, Chicago, Illinois; Illinois Masonic Medical Center, Chicago, Illinois **Hob./spts.:** Martial arts **SIC code:** 80 **Address:** Spine and Orthopaedic Surgery Center, 3000 N. Halsted St., Suite 611, Chicago, IL 60657 **E-mail:** tacmed1@aol.com

GREENBERGER, ANDREW J.
Industry: Dentistry **Born:** March 3, 1960, New York, New York **Univ./degree:** Post Graduate Certification, Periodontics, University of Pittsburgh, 1988 **Current organization:** Periodontics and Implantology Associates, P.C. **Title:** D.M.D. **Type of organization:** Dental office **Major product:** Periodontology **Area of distribution:** West Orange, New Jersey **Area of Practice:** Periodontics **Affiliations:** A.D.A.; A.A.P.; N.E.S.P.; N.J.D.A. **Hob./spts.:** Insurance consulting **SIC code:** 80 **Address:** Periodontics and Implantology Associates, P.C., 97 Northfield Ave., West Orange, NJ 07052

GREENE, VYBERT P.
Industry: Medical **Born:** May 25, South Africa **Univ./degree:** B.S., Chemistry, Howard University, 1971; M.D., George Washington University School of Medicine, 1979 **Current organization:** Michael Reese Hospital/University of Illinois **Title:** M.D./ Director OB/GYN Student & Residency Program/Director of Ambulatory Care Services **Type of organization:** Hospital/university **Major product:** Patient care, medical education **Area of distribution:** Illinois **Area of Practice:** OB/GYN, general practice, teaching **Affiliations:** F.A.C.O.G.; A.I.S. **SIC code:** 80 **Address:** 63 Silo Ridge Rd. South, Orland Park, IL 60467

GREGORY, CHARLEY S.
Industry: Healthcare **Born:** May 23, 1945, Tacoma Park, Maryland **Univ./degree:** R.T., Baptist Medical Center, 1971 **Current organization:** John Peter Smith Hospital **Title:** R.T.(R) (CU) (ARRT) **Type of organization:** Hospital **Major product:** Patient care **Area of distribution:** Texas **Area of Practice:** Vascular - interventional exams **Honors/awards:** Navy - Rank (E5) 2nd Class Hospital Corpsman **Affiliations:** F.W.S.R.T.; A.V.I.R.; A.S.R.T.; T.X.R.T.; C.M.R.T.; Life Member, H.O.G.; National Vice President, Disciples Motorcycle Ministry **Hob./spts.:** Riding Harley motorcycles **SIC code:** 80 **Address:** 2913 Woodlark Dr., Ft. Worth, TX 76123 **E-mail:** c4bj@msn.com

GREGORY, IRVIN T.
Industry: Healthcare **Born:** February 18, 1938, Alexandria, Louisiana **Univ./degree:** B.S., Management, University of Louisiana, 1960 **Current organization:** Health Group Partners, LLC **Title:** President & CEO **Type of organization:** Healthcare investment partnership **Major product:** Ownership and management of acute care hospitals **Area of distribution:** Texas **Area of Practice:** Administration **Hob./spts.:** Travel, golf **SIC code:** 80 **Address:** Health Group Partners, LLC, 17101 Kuykendahl Rd., Suite 230, Houston, TX 77068 **E-mail:** g77gregory@hotmail.com

GREGORY, RICHARD E.
Industry: Healthcare **Born:** October 13, 1942, Glen Falls, New York **Univ./degree:** B.S., Political Science, University of Maryland, 1964 **Current organization:** Women's Complete Healthcare/Forbes Enterprises **Title:** CEO **Type of organization:** Medical practice **Major product:** Patient care, entrepreneurial services **Area of distribution:** Newport News, Virginia **Area of Practice:** Operations, management **Affiliations:** U.S. Airforce Retired Officers Association; American Guild Patients Account Manager **Hob./spts.:** Snowskiing **SIC code:** 80 **Address:** Women's Complete Healthcare/Forbes Enterprises, 12420 Warwick Blvd., Newport News, VA 23606 **E-mail:** s.forbesvisa.net

GREGORY, RICHARD O.
Industry: Healthcare **Born:** May 19, 1940, Indiana **Univ./degree:** M.D., Indiana University School of Medicine, 1971 **Current organization:** Institute of Aesthetic Surgery **Title:** M.D. **Type of organization:** Private practice **Major product:** Cosmetic surgery, aesthetician services, laser hair removal, vein treatment **Area of distribution:** Florida **Area of Practice:** Facial laser surgery, facial plastic surgery (all procedures) **Published works:** Book chapters **Affiliations:** A.A.P.S.; A.S.A.P.S.; General Secretary, A.S.L.M.S. **Hob./spts.:** Cooking, gardening **SIC code:** 80 **Address:** Celebration Institute of Aesthetic Surgery, 400 Celebration Place, Suite A-310, Celebration, FL 34747 **E-mail:** info@drgregory.com

GRESLA, JANIENE F.
Industry: Healthcare **Born:** 1969, Somerset, New Jersey **Univ./degree:** B.S., Chemistry, Miami University, 1969; D.D.S., Ohio State University, 1995 **Current organization:** Janiene F. Gresla D.D.S., P.C. **Title:** D.D.S. **Type of organization:** Dental practice **Major product:** Patient care **Area of distribution:** Burlington, Massachusetts **Area of Practice:** General dentistry **Affiliations:** Massachusetts Dental Society; American Academy of General Dentistry **Hob./spts.:** Travel, scuba diving, sailing **SIC code:** 80 **Address:** Janiene F. Gresla D.D.S., P.C., 120 Cambridge St., Burlington, MA 01803 **E-mail:** jgresla.dds@verizon.net **Web address:** www.burlingtondental.com

GRIFFITH, NANCY J.
Industry: Healthcare **Born:** September 17, 1950, Lubbock, Texas **Univ./degree:** R.N., Amarillo College **Current organization:** Covenant Medical Center **Title:** R.N. **Type of organization:** Hospital **Major product:** Patient care **Area of distribution:** Texas **Area of Practice:** Pediatrics case management **Hob./spts.:** Reading, walking **SIC code:** 80 **Address:** 2302 92nd St., Lubbock, TX 79423 **E-mail:** g.d.griffith@worldnet.att.net

GRIGGS, JESSICA R.
Industry: Healthcare **Born:** July 27, 1972, Warren, Ohio **Univ./degree:** D.O., Ohio University College of Osteopathic Medicine, 1998 **Current organization:** Family Care Center of Lorain **Title:** D.O. **Type of organization:** Medical center **Major product:** Patient care **Area of distribution:** Ohio **Area of Practice:** Family medicine **Honors/awards:** Sigma Gamma Rho **Affiliations:** A.O.A.; A.A.O.; A.A.F.P.; A.C.O.F.P. **SIC code:** 80 **Address:** Family Care Center of Lorain, 1800 Livingston Ave., Lorain, OH 44052 **E-mail:** docgriggs@yahoo.com

GROTHAUS, MATTHEW CHRISTIAN
Industry: Healthcare **Born:** August 2, 1968, Columbus, Ohio **Univ./degree:** M.S., 1995; M.D., 2001, Medical College of Ohio **Current organization:** Medical College of Ohio **Title:** M.D. **Type of organization:** University hospital **Major product:** Medical services **Area of distribution:** Toledo, Ohio **Area of Practice:** Orthopaedic surgery **Honors/awards:** The Vernon Volland Memorial Scholarship, 1999 **Published works:** "Vaccine" **Affiliations:** A.M.A.; Alpha Omega Alpha **Hob./spts.:** Past professional baseball player (Australia's "Manley Whales" & "The Sidney Waves") **SIC code:** 80 **Address:** Medical College of Ohio, 3000 Arlington Ave., Toledo, OH 43614 **E-mail:** mgrothaus@mco.edu

GUERRA, ALDO
Industry: Healthcare **Univ./degree:** B.S., Biology, University of California at San Diego, 1992; M.D., University of California at San Diego Medical School, 1996; Fellowship, Plastic Reconstructive Surgery, Louisiana State University, 2002 **Current organization:** Aesthetic Surgical Associates **Title:** M.D., F.A.C.S. **Type of organization:** Private practice **Major product:** Plastic surgery **Area of distribution:** L.A., A.L. **Area of Practice:** Cosmetic and reconstructive plastic surgery **Honors/awards:** James Barrett Brown Award, American Association of Plastic Surgery, 2005; Physicians Recognition Award, American Medical Association **Published works:** "Cosmetic Surgery", "Astetikos" **Affiliations:** A.M.A.; American Society of Plastic Surgeons; Louisiana Society of Plastic Surgeons; Southeastern Society of Plastic Surgeons; American College of Surgeons; Louisiana Hispanic Medical Association **SIC code:** 80 **Address:** Aesthetic Surgical Associates, 3601 Houma Blvd. Suite 300, Metairie, LA 70003 **E-mail:** drguerra@gmail.com **Web address:** www.guerrmd.com

GUERRA, JIM J.
Industry: Healthcare **Born:** June 25, 1956, Cincinnati, Ohio **Univ./degree:** B.S., Biology, Notre Dame University; M.D., University of Monterrey School of Medicine, Mexico, 1985 **Current organization:** West Texas Internal Medicine Clinic P.A. **Title:** M.D. **Type of organization:** Clinic/private practice **Major product:** Patient care **Area of distribution:** Texas **Area of Practice:** Internal and geriatric medicine (Board Certified) **Affiliations:** American Board of Hospital Medicine; American College of Ethical Physicians; American College of Physicians; American Board of Internal Medicine; American Medical Association **Hob./spts.:** Family, hiking, backpacking, fishing, boating **SIC code:** 80 **Address:** West Texas Internal Medicine Clinic P.A., 7100 Oakmont Blvd., Suite 105, Ft. Worth, TX 76132 **E-mail:** p.guerra14@hotmail.com

GUGGINO, GIACOMO S.
Industry: Healthcare **Born:** April 7, 1940, Tampa, Florida **Univ./degree:** University of Miami, 1966 **Current organization:** Guggino Family Eye Center **Title:** President/CEO **Type of organization:** Eye care center **Major product:** Lasik surgery, strabismus, ophthalmology **Area of distribution:** Tampa, Florida **Area of Practice:** Ophthalmology, adult strabismus **Affiliations:** F.A.C.S.; F.L.M.A.; F.A.A.O. **Hob./spts.:** Cooking, photography, fishing **SIC code:** 80 **Address:** Guggino Family Eye Center, 3115 W. Swann Ave., Tampa, FL 33609 **E-mail:** gugginoeye@verizon.net **Web address:** www.gugginoeye.com

GUIDA, ANTHONY A.
Industry: Healthcare **Born:** February 12, 1953, New Rochelle, New York **Univ./degree:** B.S., Biology, Fordham University, 1975; M.D., SUNY Medical School at Syracuse, 1979 **Current organization:** Guida & Savino LLP **Title:** M.D. **Type of organization:** Private practice **Major product:** Patient care **Area of distribution:** New York **Area of Practice:** Family practice **Published works:** Write-ups **Affiliations:** A.A.F.P.; Director and Board Member, Family Practice, Good Samaritan Hospital **SIC code:** 80 **Address:** Guida & Savino LLP, 373 Sunrise Hwy., West Babylon, NY 11704

GUILBAUD, SERGEO
Industry: Medical **Born:** January 12, 1960, Port-au-Prince, Haiti **Univ./degree:** B.A., Old Dominion University, 1993; M.A. Candidate, Columbia University **Current organization:** Long Island College Hospital **Title:** Education Director **Type of organization:** Hospital **Major product:** Medical services and education **Area of distribution:** National **Area of Practice:** Radiologic sciences **Affiliations:** A.S.R.T.; N.Y.E.S.R.T.; A.E.R.T. **Hob./spts.:** Motorcycling **SIC code:** 80 **Address:** Long Island College Hospital, 340 Court St., Brooklyn, NY 11231 **E-mail:** sguilbau@chpnet.org

GUINNIP, PAULA F.
Industry: Healthcare **Born:** October 18, 1966, Syracuse, New York **Univ./degree:** M.D., Georgetown University, 1992 **Current organization:** Cardiothoracic Surgical Assoc. **Title:** Cardiac Surgeon **Type of organization:** Group medical practice **Major product:** Patient care **Area of distribution:** Marion, Illinois **Area of Practice:** Cardiothoracic surgery **Affiliations:** F.A.S.; F.A.C.P.; A.H.A.; I.M.S.; W.C.M.S.; A.W.P.S. **Hob./spts.:** Karate, yoga, weight training, her children **SIC code:** 80 **Address:** Cardiothoracic Surgical Assoc., 6241 Wards Mill Rd., Marion, IL 62959-6159 **E-mail:** pguinnip@earthlink.net

GULATI, ANKUSH
Industry: Medical **Born:** December 31, 1972, Ahmedabad, India **Univ./degree:** M.D., Gandhi Medical College, India, 1989-95; L.I. College Hospital University, 2002 **Current organization:** L.I. College Hospital **Title:** M.D. **Type of organization:** Medical college **Major product:** Medical services **Area of distribution:** New York **Area of Practice:** Kidney transplant, nephrology **Published works:** 2 articles, 1 book in progress, web site www.pdxmd.com **Affiliations:** I.P.A.; A.S.N.; A.M.A. **Hob./spts.:** Golf, travel **SIC code:** 80 **Address:** 209 Augusta Circle, Mount Laurel, NJ 08054

GUPTA, AKSHAY
Industry: Medicine **Born:** July 22, 1979, India **Univ./degree:** M.D., Albany Institute of Science, 2002 **Current organization:** University of Pittsburgh **Title:** Physician **Type of organization:** University **Major product:** Patient care, medical education **Area of distribution:** National **Area of Practice:** Internal medicine **Affiliations:** A.S.A.; Sigma Phi; A.C.P.; A.M.A. **Hob./spts.:** Football **SIC code:** 80 **Address:** University of Pittsburgh, 7070 Forward Ave., #703, Pittsburgh, PA 15217 **E-mail:** guptaa30@upmc.edu

GUPTA, ANJAN
Industry: Healthcare **Born:** December 20, 1966, Calcutta, India **Univ./degree:** M.D., University of Calcutta School of Medicine, 1990 **Current organization:** Heart Care Associates **Title:** M.D. **Type of organization:** Group practice **Major product:** Patient care **Area of distribution:** Wisconsin **Area of Practice:** Cardiology **Affiliations:** F.A.C.C.; A.C.P. **Hob./spts.:** Computers, web design, travel **SIC code:** 80 **Address:** Heart Care Associates, 2801W. Kinnickinnic River Pkwy., Suite 777, Milwaukee, WI 53215 **E-mail:** agupta@hrtcare.com

GUPTA, PADMA
Industry: Healthcare **Born:** May 16, 1951, Kota, India **Univ./degree:** M.D., Seth Gordhandas Sunderdas Medical College, Mumbai, India,1974 **Current organization:** Padma Gupta, MD, PA **Title:** M.D. **Type of organization:** Private practice **Major product:** Patient care **Area of distribution:** Miami, Florida **Area of Practice:** Pediatrics **Affiliations:** American Academy of Pediatricians; Greater Miami Pediatric Society **Hob./spts.:** Travel, music **SIC code:** 80 **Address:** Padma Gupta, MD, PA, 13500 SW 88th St., Suite 181, Miami, FL 33186 **E-mail:** pg272001@yahoo.com

GUTIERREZ, SYLVIA
Industry: Medical **Born:** December 31, 1970, Cayey, Puerto Rico **Univ./degree:** M.D., Ponce School of Medicine, 2000 **Current organization:** University of Puerto Rico, Medical Sciences Campus **Title:** M.D. **Type of organization:** University hospital **Major product:** Medical services, research **Area of distribution:** Ponce, Puerto Rico **Area of Practice:** Pathology **Honors/awards:** Americo Serra Award, Biology Award **Affiliations:** A.M.P.R.; A.M.A. **Hob./spts.:** Volleyball, dancing, writing **SIC code:** 80 **Address:** Estancias del Golf #566, Ponce, PR 00731 **E-mail:** donpaleto@hotmail.com

GUTIÉRREZ CAMACHO, JORGE H.
Industry: Healthcare **Born:** April 6, 1935, Ponce, Puerto Rico **Univ./degree:** B.A., Chemistry/Biology, Catholic University, Puerto Rico, 1956; M.D., Santiago Compostela, Spain, 1962 **Current organization:** Jorge H. Gutiérrez Camacho, MD **Title:** Medical Doctor **Type of organization:** Private practice (1966 up to present); Former Attending Physician in Medicine and Chief Renal Diseases, Ponce District Hospital (1966-1980) Clinical Assistant Professor Ponce School of Medicine (1980-1995); Instructor in Medicine, P.R. School of Medicine (1970-1980) Sub-director National Medical Care Ponce Hemodialysis Center (1976-1995); Captain, M.C. P.R. National Guard (1965-1971) **Major product:** Patient care **Area of distribution:** Puerto Rico **Area of Practice:** Internal Medicine and Nephrology **Published works:** Psychological, Philosophical, Medical and Social Implications of Hemodialysis and Kidney Transplants. Experience at the Ponce District Hospital (1974); Renal Transplant in Southern P.R. (1976); Goodpasture's Syndrome at Ponce District Hospital (1975); The first 14 Kidney Transplant in Centroamerica (1995); Renal Diseases and Impli-

cations (1996)+ **Affiliations:** Puerto Rico Medical Association; American Medical Association; Southern Medical Association; Nephrology Section P.R.; Renal Physician Association; National Kidney Foundation, Inc. **Hob./spts.:** History of Baseball **SIC code:** 80 **Address:** Jorge H. Gutiérrez Camacho, MD, P.O. Box 330003, Ponce, PR 00733-0003

GUZMAN, ELISCER
Industry: Healthcare **Born:** 1950, Tenares, Dominican Republic **Univ./degree:** M.D., Pedro Henriquez Urena University, Dominican Republic, 1976 **Current organization:** Cardiology Unlimited, PC **Title:** M.D., F.A.C.C. **Type of organization:** Hospital/private medical practice **Major product:** Patient care **Area of distribution:** New York **Area of practice:** Cardiovascular medicine **Area of Practice:** Cardiovascular medicine **Published works:** Numerous including: "Tosades de Pointes Induced by Erythromycin and Terfe", The American Journal of Emergency Medicine, vol. 12, Nov. 6, '94; p. 636-638; Relationship of Cardiac Involvement to the Severity of Acquired Immune Deficiency Syndrome, ACCP, 1995; Contributing Role of Risk Factors Alone and in Combination to Angiographically Proven Coronary Artery Disease, ACCP, 1995; "Repolarization Abnormalities with Chronic Renal Failure Requiring Dialysis", American Federation for Medical Research, 1997; "Efficacy and Repolarization Abnormalities with Antihypertensive Drugs", Journal of Investigative Medicine, (Biomedicine), 1997 **Affiliations:** Fellow, American College of Cardiology; Member, American College of Physicians; Member, New York Academy of Science **Hob./spts.:** Tennis **SIC code:** 80 **Address:** Eliscer Guzman, M.D., 286 Fort Washington Ave., Suite 1B, New York, NY 10031 **E-mail:** eliscer@hotmail.com

GWYNN, VIOLA M.
Industry: Healthcare **Born:** September 21, 1952, Detroit, Michigan **Univ./degree:** A.S., Wayne County Community College, 1984 **Current organization:** New Light Nursing Home **Title:** R.N., A.D.S.N., Director of Nursing, Certified Registered Nurse Assessment Coordinator **Type of organization:** Nursing home **Major product:** Long-term patient care **Area of distribution:** Michigan **Area of Practice:** Geriatric nursing; Manager of Nursing Services **Honors/awards:** Who's Who in American Nursing, 1990-91; Strathmore's Who's Who, 2004-2005 **Affiliations:** N.A.A.C.P. **Hob./spts.:** Gardening, sewing, puzzles, basketball **SIC code:** 80 **Address:** New Light Nursing Home, 9500 Grand River Ave., Detroit, MI 48204 **E-mail:** jvgwynn@comcast.net

HAAS, CHARLES D.
Industry: Healthcare **Title:** D.M.D., F.R.S.H. **Type of organization:** Private practice **Major product:** Dental services **Area of Practice:** Patient dental care **SIC code:** 80 **Address:** Charles D. Haas, D.M.D., F.R.S.H., 1688 Meridian Ave., Miami Beach, FL 33139

HABAL, MUTAZ B.
Industry: Healthcare **Born:** April 27, 1938, Beirut, Lebanon **Univ./degree:** M.D., American University of Beirut **Current organization:** Tampa Bay Craniofacial Center **Title:** M.D., F.R.C.S. **Type of organization:** Multi-specialty medical office **Major product:** Patient care **Area of distribution:** Tampa, Florida **Area of Practice:** Plastic surgery, global lecturer on facial reconstruction **Affiliations:** Fellow, Royal College of Surgeons; American College of Surgeons; International College of Surgeons; American Association of Pediatric Plastic Surgeons; American Society of Plastic Surgeons; American Association of Plastic Surgeons **Hob./spts.:** Kite surfing, windsurfing, off roading **SIC code:** 80 **Address:** Tampa Bay Craniofacial Center, 801 W. Martin Luther King Blvd., Tampa, FL 33603 **E-mail:** mbhabal@gte.net

HABIB, MARCELLE GUERGUES
Industry: Healthcare Provider **Univ./degree:** M.B.B.ch, Doctor of Medicine, Faculty of Medicine, Ain Shams Univ., Egypt, '80; Post Grad. Training & Fellowships: Faculty of Medicine, Louis Pasteur Univ., France, 1982-88: Diplomas-Gastroenterology, Tropical & Infectious Pathology & Clinical Ultrasound **Current organization:** Pediatrics Rainbow, Marcelle G. Habib, M.D., P.A. **Title:** M.D., F.A.A.P., Diplomat of the American Board of Pediatrics/Clinical Assistant Professor with USF Pediatrics Department **Type of organization:** Doctors office **Major product:** Healthcare **Area of distribution:** Palm Harbor, Florida **Area of Practice:** Pediatrics (Board Certified), fluent Arabic, French, English, Spanish **Honors/awards:** Award for service to the poor "La Clinica Guadalupana", Clearwater, Florida, 1999; Award for service of the Community Health Center of Pinellas: for 5 years; Pediatrician of the Year, 1997; Award for service as Faculty Preceptor with the University of South Florida since 1996 **Affiliations:** Fellow, American Academy of Pediatrics; American Board of Pediatrics; Pediatrics Services of Florida; University of South Florida; All Children's Hospital, St. Petersburg, Florida **SIC code:** 80 **Address:** Pediatrics Rainbow, Marcelle G. Habib, M.D., P.A., 34068 US Hwy. 19 North, Palm Harbor, FL 34684 **E-mail:** mhabib88@msn.com

HABIB, MOKSEDUL
Industry: Healthcare **Born:** December 31, 1957, Rangpur **Univ./degree:** M.D., Rangpur Medical School **Current organization:** The Heart Center **Title:** M.D. **Type of organization:** Private medical practice **Major product:** Patient care **Area of distribution:** California **Area of Practice:** Internal medicine, cardiology **Affiliations:** F.A.C.C. **Hob./spts.:** Skiing, gardening **SIC code:** 80 **Address:** The Heart Center, 525 34th St., Bakersfield, CA 93301 **E-mail:** moksedulhabib@yahoo.com

HABWE, VIOLET Q.
Industry: Healthcare **Born:** September 12, 1953, Nairobi, Kenya **Univ./degree:** M.D., Howard University, 1981 **Current organization:** Washington Nephrology Associates **Title:** M.D. **Type of organization:** Medical group **Major product:** Patient care **Area of distribution:** Washington, D.C. **Area of Practice:** Nephrology, kidney disease **Affiliations:** American Society of Nephrology **Hob./spts.:** Golf, tennis, swimming, reading, hiking, water sports, sailing **SIC code:** 80 **Address:** Washington Nephrology Associates, 730 24th St. N.W., #17, Washington, DC 20037

HACKLER, MICHAEL T.
Industry: Healthcare **Univ./degree:** B.S., Louisiana State University at Baton Rouge, Chemical Engineering, 1970; M.D., Louisiana State University School of Medicine, 1977 **Current organization:** CVT Surgical Center **Title:** M.D. **Type of organization:** Group practice **Major product:** Surgery for heart, lung and blood vessel diseases **Area of distribution:** Louisiana **Area of Practice:** Surgery **Published works:** 5 publications **Affiliations:** American Heart Association; American Medical Association; Society of Thoracic Surgeons; American Board of Thoracic Surgeons; Society of General Surgeons, Louisiana State Medical Society **Hob./spts.:** Gardening, excercise, boating, autos **SIC code:** 80 **Address:** CVT Surgical Center, 7777 Hennessy Blvd., Suite 108, Baton Rouge, LA 70808 **E-mail:** michaelthackler@yahoo.com **Web address:** cvtsc.com/doctor4.htm

HADDAD, PHILIP A.
Industry: Healthcare/education **Born:** April 17, 1970, Baabda, Lebanon **Univ./degree:** M.D., American University of Beirut, 1995 **Current organization:** VA Medical Center/Louisiana State University **Title:** M.D./Assistant Professor **Type of organization:** Hospital/university **Major product:** Medical services/higher education **Area of distribution:** National **Area of Practice:** Internal Medicine, Hematology and Oncology (Board Certified) **Published works:** Book chapter, 10 articles, several abstracts **Affiliations:** Fellow, American College of Physicians; Fellow, American College of Chest Physicians; American Society of Hematology; American Society of Breast Diseases **Hob./spts.:** Playing classical piano, fencing **SIC code:** 80 **Address:** 1333 Coates Bluff Dr.,#424, Shreveport, LA 71104 **E-mail:** haddad8838@msn.com

HADDAD, SAMI C.
Industry: Healthcare **Born:** May 3, 1926, Beirut, Lebanon **Univ./degree:** M.D., St. Joseph's University School of Medicine, 1951 **Current organization:** River City Medical Group **Title:** M.D./Medical Director **Type of organization:** Independent medical practice **Major product:** Medical services, patient care **Area of distribution:** Sacramento, California **Area of Practice:** Abdominal surgery, trauma care **Affiliations:** A.C.S.; A.M.A.; California Medical Association **Hob./spts.:** Fishing, tennis **SIC code:** 80 **Address:** River City Medical Group, 3 Park Center Dr., Sacramento, CA 95825 **E-mail:** shaddad@rcmg.com

HAG, SHEHLA A.
Industry: Healthcare **Current organization:** The Snellville Clinic, PC **Title:** Manager **Type of organization:** Medical clinic **Major product:** Patient care **Area of distribution:** Georgia **Area of Practice:** Management **Hob./spts.:** Painting, decorating, designing **SIC code:** 80 **Address:** The Snellville Clinic, PC, 2351 Henry Clower Blvd., Suite B, Snellville, GA 30078 **E-mail:** shehlahag@bellsouth.net

HAGGERTY, BEVERLY S.
Industry: Healthcare **Born:** Canton, Illinois **Univ./degree:** A.S., Nursing; R.N., Spoon River College **Current organization:** Avon Nursing Home **Title:** R.N./D.O.N. **Type of organization:** ICF nursing facility **Major product:** Patient care **Area of distribution:** Avon, Illinois **Area of Practice:** Management **Affiliations:** A.N.A. **SIC code:** 80 **Address:** Avon Nursing Home, 1790 23rd Ave., Avon, IL 61415 **E-mail:** bessie@fambid.com

HAGGERTY, STEPHEN P.
Industry: Healthcare **Born:** February 3, 1967, Kansas City, Missouri **Univ./degree:** M.D., University of Missouri School of Medicine, 1993 **Current organization:** Consultants in General Surgery, S.C. **Title:** M.D./Surgeon **Type of organization:** Private practice **Major product:** Patient care **Area of distribution:** Highland Park, Illinois **Area of Practice:** General surgery specialist **Published works:** 2 book chapters, 3 papers, 1 abstract **Affiliations:** F.A.C.S.; S.A.G.E.S.; A.S.G.S.; A.H.S. **Hob./spts.:** Golf, travel, gourmet cooking, wine **SIC code:** 80 **Address:** Consultants in General Surgery, S.C., 750 Homewood Ave., #320, Highland Park, IL 60035 **E-mail:** shaggert@pol.net

HAKKARAINEN, GLORIA C.
Industry: Healthcare **Born:** June 5, 1967, Stoneham, Massachusetts **Univ./degree:** M.D., Albany Medical College, 1995 **Current organization:** Palm Beach Obstetrics & Gynecology **Title:** M.D. **Type of organization:** Medical practice **Major product:**

Patient care **Area of distribution:** West Palm Beach, Florida **Area of Practice:** OB/GYN **Affiliations:** Diplomate, American College of Obstetrics and Gynecology; Palm Beach County Medical Society **Hob./spts.:** Violinist **SIC code:** 80 **Address:** Palm Beach Obstetrics & Gynecology, 2051 45th St., Suite 207, West Palm Beach, FL 33407 **E-mail:** ghakk@adelphia.net

HALKIAS, JOHN B.
Industry: Medical **Born:** January 15, 1955, New York, New York **Univ./degree:** M.D., Aristotelian University School of Medicine, Greece, 1982 **Current organization:** John B. Halkias, M.D., F.A.A.P. **Title:** M.D./Assistant Professor of Psychiatry, New York Medical College **Type of organization:** Private practice, Medical Director, Queens AIDS Centers of New York, Psychiatric Consultant at The Children's Village **Major product:** Patient care **Area of distribution:** New York **Area of Practice:** Child, adolescent and adult psychiatry, couples, marital and parent therapy **Affiliations:** A.P.A.; American Academy of Psychoanalysts; Hellenic Medical Association **Hob./spts.:** Collecting sports memorabilia, coins, physical fitness, swimming **SIC code:** 80 **Address:** 31-28 41st St., Astoria, NY 11103

HALUM JR., RAMON G.
Industry: Healthcare **Born:** November 14, 1931, Philippines **Univ./degree:** M.D., University of Santo Tomas, 1958 **Current organization:** R.G. Halum, Jr., M.D. Urology Inc. **Title:** M.D. **Type of organization:** Private practice **Major product:** Patient care **Area of distribution:** National **Area of Practice:** Urology **Affiliations:** A.M.A.; American Association of Clinical Urologists; International Society for Sexual Medicine **Hob./spts.:** Tennis, basketball, Chicago Bears fan **SIC code:** 80 **Address:** R.G. Halum, Jr., M.D. Urology Inc., 800 MacArthur Blvd., Suite 1, Munster, IN 46321

HAMAL, REKHA
Industry: Healthcare **Univ./degree:** M.D., University of Maryland, 1998 **Current organization:** Planned Parenthood of Greater Northern New Jersey **Title:** M.D. **Type of organization:** Healthcare facility **Major product:** Women's healthcare **Area of distribution:** National **Area of Practice:** Family practice **Affiliations:** A.F.P.; A.M.A. **SIC code:** 80 **Address:** 219 Springfield Ave., Summit, NJ 07901 **E-mail:** khunu@aol.com

HAMID, MAHMOUD R.
Industry: Healthcare **Born:** October 16, 1933, Cairo, Egypt **Univ./degree:** M.D. (M.B.B.C.H.), Cairo University School of Medicine, 1959 **Current organization:** Steinway Family Health Center/Staten Island Medical Group **Title:** M.D., F.R.C.S. **Type of organization:** Private medical office/medical group **Major product:** Patient care/emergency services **Area of distribution:** New York **Area of Practice:** General practice/ambulatory care **Honors/awards:** Royal College of Surgeons, Edinburg, England **Affiliations:** F.R.C.S.; A.A.A.M.; A.A.P.S.; New York Heart Association **Hob./spts.:** Playing soccer **SIC code:** 80 **Address:** Steinway Family Health Center, 25-92 Steinway St., Astoria, NY 11103 **E-mail:** mrhamidmd@aol.com

HAMILTON, PATRICIA A.
Industry: Healthcare **Born:** July 3, 1963, Owensboro, Kentucky **Univ./degree:** B.S., Biology/Medical Technology, Brescia College, 1985 **Current organization:** Owensboro Medical Health System **Title:** Quality Specialist/Medical Technologist (ASCP) **Type of organization:** Hospital **Major product:** Patient care **Area of distribution:** Kentucky **Area of Practice:** Quality control, quality assurance, medical technology, instrument maintenance **Affiliations:** American Society of Clinical Pathologists **Hob./spts.:** Softball **SIC code:** 80 **Address:** Owensboro Medical Health System, 811 E. Parish Ave., Owensboro, KY 42303 **E-mail:** phamilton@omhs.org

HAMM, LESA S.
Industry: Healthcare **Born:** March 2, 1965, Amory, Mississippi **Univ./degree:** A.A.S., Wallace State Community College, 1992 **Current organization:** Northwest Medical Center **Title:** Director of Cardiopulmonary Services **Type of organization:** Hospital **Major product:** Patient care **Area of distribution:** Alabama **Area of Practice:** Respiratory therapy; Certified Life Support and Advanced Pediatric Life Support Instructor **Affiliations:** M.B.R.C.; A.A.R.C.; A.S.R.C. **Hob./spts.:** Family, antique shopping, reading **SIC code:** 80 **Address:** Northwest Medical Center, P.O. Box 130, Winfield, AL 35594 **E-mail:** lesa.hamm@lpnt.net

HAMMER, GRETCHEN DAVIS
Industry: Mental health **Born:** April 13, 1934, Lynn, Massachusetts **Univ./degree:** M.Ed., Counseling and Teaching, Lyndon State College, Vermont, 1985 **Current organization:** Gretchen D. Hammer, M.Ed. **Title:** Psychotherapist **Type of organization:** Social services, private practice **Major product:** Mental health, adolescents, child custody issues **Area of distribution:** Vermont **Area of Practice:** Psychotherapist **Affiliations:** Vermont Mental Health; A.C.A. **Hob./spts.:** Quilting, swimming **SIC code:** 80 **Address:** Gretchen Davis Hammer, M.Ed., 242 Eastern Ave., St. Johnsbury, VT 05819 **E-mail:** gdh777@yahoo.com

HAMMOND, KAREN C.
Industry: Healthcare **Born:** September 8, 1943, Glen Cove, New York **Current organization:** North Shore University Hospital **Title:** Radiologic Technologist/General X-Ray and Mammography **Type of organization:** Hospital **Major product:** Patient care **Area of distribution:** New York **Area of practice:** Certified X-ray Technologist, mammograms **Area of Practice:** Certified X-ray Technologist, mammograms **Affiliations:** A.S.R.T.; A.R.R.T.; New York State Radiologic Technology Society; Nassau/Suffolk Radiologic Technology Society **Hob./spts.:** Crafts, silk floral arranging, 15 grandchildren **SIC code:** 80 **Address:** 30 Horton Dr., South Huntington, NY 11740

HAMMONDS, LULA
Industry: Healthcare **Univ./degree:** R.T., Howard University/Freedmen's Hospital School of Radiologic Technology, 1968; B.S., Teaching Technology, Washington Technical Institute, 1974; M.Ed. Adult Continuing Education, Howard University Graduate School, 1976 **Current organization:** Howard University Hospital, Dept. of Radiology Technology **Title:** Special Procedures CAT Scan and Assistant Professor **Type of organization:** Hospital **Major product:** Patient care **Area of distribution:** Washington D.C. **Area of Practice:** Board Certified in: Radiologic Technology, Mammography, Cardio Vascular - Interventional Radiology, Computerized Axial Tomography **Honors/awards:** The Outstanding Technologist Award; The Charles H. Kelley's Award for Outstanding Scholastic Achievement; The Mallinckrodt's Outstanding Student's Award; Outstanding Service Award, Radio Club Present, 1980-1982 **Affiliations:** A.S.R.T.; A.R.D.M.S.; A.V.I.R.; D.C, Society of Radiologic Technologists; Phi Delta Kappa, Sorority; Teaches at Howard University; Advisory Board Member, Troop 501 Boy Scouts, Cadets and Seniors; Troop Leader 1845 Girl Scouts; President, Way of the Cross Church Radio Club, 1980-82; Pastor's AID President, 1992 to the present; Student, W.L. Bonner College, Columbia, South Carolina; Student, Capital Bible Seminary, Lanham, Maryland **SIC code:** 80 **Address:** Howard University Hospital, Dept. of Radiology, 2041 Georgia Ave. N.W., Washington, DC 20060

HAMZEPOUR, SHOKOUFEH
Industry: Healthcare **Born:** December 18, 1936, Shiraz, Iran **Univ./degree:** M.D., University of Geneva, Switzerland, 1963; Board Certified, Pediatric Anesthesiology, London, England, 1968; Residency, Anesthesia, 1971; Fellowship, Clinical Pharmacology, 1973 University of Miami, Florida; **Current organization:** Med-Ped Associates **Title:** Pediatrician **Type of organization:** Private group practice **Major product:** Patient care **Area of distribution:** Florida **Area of Practice:** General pediatrics; Residency in Pediatrics, University of Missouri, Columbia School of Medicine, 1989-92 **Affiliations:** Fellow, American Academy of Pediatrics; Hospital Chief of Staff, University of Shiraz Medical School, 1979; Clinical Assistant Professor in Neonatology Dept., University of Miami, School of Medicine, 1992-94 **Hob./spts.:** Gardening, landscape design, collecting Persian art and Persian archeology **SIC code:** 80 **Address:** 521 N.W. 107th Ave., Plantation, FL 33324 **E-mail:** emostoufi@aol.com

HANDLIN, DENNIS K.
Industry: Healthcare **Born:** April 16, 1952, Long Beach, New York **Current organization:** Roxbury Open MRI and Surgical Center **Title:** Imaging/Technical Supervisor **Type of organization:** Medical center **Major product:** Surgery, imaging services **Area of distribution:** New Jersey **Area of Practice:** Imaging (MRI, CT scanning, x-ray); Certified Radiologic Technician, Certified C.T., Certified M.R.I. **Affiliations:** American Society of Radiologic Technologists **Hob./spts.:** Boating, woodworking **SIC code:** 80 **Address:** 26 Winona Trail, Lake Hopatcong, NJ 07849

HANEY, W. MICHAEL
Industry: Healthcare **Born:** August 11, 1959, Melborne, Florida **Univ./degree:** M.D., University of South Florida College of Medicine, 1987 **Current organization:** Okaloosa Surgical Associates **Title:** M.D. **Type of organization:** Medical practice **Major product:** Patient care **Area of distribution:** Florida **Area of Practice:** General surgery **Affiliations:** A.C.S. **Hob./spts.:** Triathlon, waterskiing **SIC code:** 80 **Address:** Okaloosa Surgical Associates, 1003 W. College Blvd., Niceville, FL 32578

HANKS, ELAINE H.
Industry: Healthcare **Born:** February 2, 1945, Jefferson, North Carolina **Univ./degree:** R.T., Charlotte Memorial School of X-Ray Technology, 1995 **Current organization:** Ashe Memorial Hospital **Title:** R.T., R.M. **Type of organization:** Hospital **Major product:** Patient care **Area of distribution:** North Carolina **Area of Practice:** Radiology, mammography **Affiliations:** F.D.A.; A.C.R.; American Academy of Radiology **Hob./spts.:** Baseball, reading **SIC code:** 80 **Address:** Ashe Memorial Hospital, 200 Doctor's Ave., Jefferson, NC 28640

HANLEY, WILLIAM JAMES
Industry: Dentistry **Univ./degree:** D.M.D., University of Medicine and Dentistry of New Jersey, 1985 **Current organization:** Dr. William James Hanley **Title:** President **Type of organization:** Dental office **Major product:** General dentistry **Area of distribution:** Hilton Head Island, South Carolina **Area of Practice:** Cosmetic and reconstructive surgery **Honors/awards:** DaVinci Lab Award for Outstanding Works of Cosmetics **Affiliations:** South Carolina Prosthodontics **SIC code:** 80 **Address:**

Dr. William James Hanley, 400 Merchant St., Hilton Head Island, SC 29926 **E-mail:** wjhhhdental.com

HANNA, ADEL F.
Industry: Healthcare **Born:** February 14, 1957, Cairo, Egypt **Univ./degree:** M.D., University of Mexico, 1985 **Current organization:** NSLIJ Healthcare System **Title:** Director, Cardiothoracic Unit **Type of organization:** Hospital **Major product:** Patient care **Area of distribution:** Long Island, New York **Area of Practice:** Critical care medicine **Published works:** Multiple publications **Affiliations:** A.C.C.P. **Hob./spts.:** Chess, tennis, swimming **SIC code:** 80 **Address:** NSLIJ Healthcare System, 300 Community Dr., Manhasset, NY 11030 **E-mail:** hanna8121000@yahoo.com

HANNA, GRETA G.
Industry: Healthcare **Born:** May 20, 1937, El-Fayoum, Egypt **Univ./degree:** M.D., Cairo University, 1962 **Current organization:** Greta G. Hanna, M.D. **Title:** Anesthesiologist **Type of organization:** Private practice **Major product:** Patient care **Area of distribution:** Roslyn, New York **Area of Practice:** Anesthesiology **Affiliations:** American Society of Anesthesiology; New York State Society of Anesthesiology **Hob./spts.:** Pianist, volunteer work **SIC code:** 80 **Address:** 27 Wimbledon Dr., Roslyn, NY 11576

HANNA, SALEM E.
Industry: Healthcare **Born:** May 13, 1963, Venezuela **Univ./degree:** M.D., Damascus Medical College, 1987 **Current organization:** Mountain Comprehensive Health Corp. **Title:** M.D. **Type of organization:** Multi specialty corporate practice **Major product:** Patient care **Area of distribution:** Kentucky **Area of Practice:** Internal medicine **Published works:** 3 articles **Affiliations:** A.M.A.; A.C.P. **Hob./spts.:** Soccer, volleyball, swimming **SIC code:** 80 **Address:** Mountain Comprehensive Health Corp., 226 Medical Plaza, Whitesburg, KY 41858 **E-mail:** sahanna24@hotmail.com

HAQUE, MOINUL
Industry: Healthcare **Born:** October 10, 1959, Bangladesh **Univ./degree:** M.D., Dhaka Medical College, Bangladesh, 1984 **Current organization:** Brooklyn Hospital Center **Title:** M.D. **Type of organization:** Hospital **Major product:** Patient care **Area of distribution:** Brooklyn, New York **Area of Practice:** Pain management, anesthesiology **Affiliations:** A.S.A.; A.M.A; I.S.A. **SIC code:** 80 **Address:** Brooklyn Hospital Center, 121 Dekalb Ave., Brooklyn, NY 11201 **E-mail:** mhaque2002@hotmail.com

HARBER, DANIEL R.
Industry: Healthcare **Born:** January 22, 1960, Ann Arbor, Michigan **Univ./degree:** D.O., Michigan State University, 1988 **Current organization:** Cardiovascular Clinical Associates **Title:** D.O./Director of Cardiac Rehab. **Type of organization:** Private practice **Major product:** General cardiology including pacemaker implantation, cardiac catheterization and transesophogeal echo **Area of distribution:** Michigan **Area of Practice:** Cardiology **Published works:** Multiple publications **Affiliations:** A.C.C.; A.C.O.I.; A.O.A. **Hob./spts.:** Golf, running, weightlifting **SIC code:** 80 **Address:** Cardiovascular Clinical Associates, 30626 Ford Rd., Garden City, MI 48135 **E-mail:** drhnx01@comcast.net

HARD, GORDON C.
Industry: Healthcare **Born:** July 5, 1931 New Zealand **Univ./degree:** BSc; BVSc; Ph.D.; D.Sc., Melbin University **Title:** Dr. **Type of organization:** Private consulting firm **Major product:** Advice in toxicology and pathology **Area of distribution:** Global **Area of Practice:** Toxicology and pathology (kidney, liver, stomach and thyroid) **Published works:** Over 150 scientific papers, editor-in-chief of three journals **Affiliations:** American Association of Cancer Research; Society of Toxicology; Society of Toxicologic Pathology **Hob./spts.:** Squash competitor **SIC code:** 80 **Address:** 203 Paku Dr., PO Box 86, Waikato, Tairua 2853, New Zealand **E-mail:** gordonhard@msn.com

HARDIN, PETER B.
Industry: Healthcare **Born:** November 23, 1965, Fort Bragg, North Carolina **Univ./degree:** M.D., University of Illinois, 1993 **Current organization:** West Michigan Cancer Center **Title:** M.D. **Type of organization:** Free standing cancer center **Major product:** Oncology **Area of distribution:** Kalamazoo, Michigan **Area of Practice:** Radiation Oncology **Published works:** Griem, K., Hardin, P.B., Breast Cancer in Treatment Planning on Radiation Oncology, Edited by F. Khan, R. Potish Baltimore, Williams and Wilkins; Hardin P.B.et al, Patterns of Failure in Locally Advanced (Stage III) Non-small cell Carcinoma of the lung Treated with Combined Modality Therapy (Accepted) **Affiliations:** A.S.T.R.O.; A.C.R.O.; A.B.S.; M.S.M.S.; Professor, Michigan State University **SIC code:** 80 **Address:** West Michigan Cancer Center, 200 North Park St., Kalamazoo, MI 49007 **E-mail:** phardin@wmcc.org **Web address:** www.wmcc.org

HARDIN-COLLINS, LILLIE M.
Industry: Healthcare **Univ./degree:** A.D.N., Malcolm X. College, 1977; B.S.W., Summa Cum Laude, Eastern Michigan University, 1995 **Current organization:** Gilbert Residence **Title:** Quality of Life Nurse/Resident Care Coordinator/Charge Nurse **Type of organization:** Long-term care facility **Major product:** Assisted living and nursing center **Area of distribution:** Michigan **Area of Practice:** Quality of Life Program: Fall/restorative program; Pain and end of life; Skin program; Interim Director of Nursing at Gilbert Residence **Honors/awards:** On Dean's List entire time at Eastern Michigan University; Induction into The Golden Key Society, Apr. 1993; Induction into Phi Kappa Pi Honor Society, Apr. 1994; Recipient of Black Achievement Award of Excellence, Spring 1991 for having GPA of 4.0 **Hob./spts.:** Photography, writing, reading; Sunday School Teacher **SIC code:** 80 **Address:** Gilbert Residence, 203 S. Huron St., Ypsilanti, MI 48197 **E-mail:** lilharcoll@aol.com

HARDY, GERALDINE M.
Industry: Healthcare **Born:** January 24 1929, Greenville, South Carolina **Univ./degree:** B.S., Winthrop College, South Carolina, 1950; M.D., Wayne State University College of Medicine, Michigan, 1955 **Current organization:** Geraldine Hardy, M.D. **Title:** M.D. **Type of organization:** Private medical practice/osteoporosis center **Major product:** Patient care, Internal Medicine **Area of distribution:** Michigan; also has another office located at 4587 Schoenherr, Shelby Township, Michigan 48315 (Fax # (810) 566-1444) **Area of Practice:** Certified Internist **Affiliations:** Diplomate, American Board of Internal Medicine; American Thoracic Society; American Diabetics Society; American College of Physicians **Hob./spts.:** Piano **SIC code:** 80 **Address:** Geraldine Hardy, M.D., 19707 Mack Ave., Grosse Pointe Woods, MI 48236 **E-mail:** ghardy@pol.net

HARDY, J. MICHAEL
Industry: Healthcare **Univ./degree:** D.D.S., University of Washington, 1978 **Current organization:** J. Michael Hardy, DDS **Title:** Dentist **Type of organization:** Private practice **Major product:** Patient dental care **Area of distribution:** Renton, Washington **Area of Practice:** Family dentistry **Affiliations:** A.D.A.; W.S.D.A.; A.A.G.D.; A.A.C.D.; Past President, University of Washington Dental Association; President, Greater Seattle Study Club; Past Board Member, Renton Rotary Club; Board Member, Renton Community Foundation 60975 **SIC code:** 80 **Address:** J. Michael Hardy, DDS, 10700 S.E. 174th St., Suite 104, Renton, WA 98055 **E-mail:** drjmhardy47@yahoo.com

HARES, ROUZANA
Industry: Dentistry **Born:** May 1, 1973, Syria **Univ./degree:** D.D.S., University of Detroit, 1999 **Current organization:** Rouzana Hares, D.D.S. **Title:** Dentist **Type of organization:** Private practice **Major product:** Dental care **Area of distribution:** Hamtramck, Michigan **Area of Practice:** Cosmetic and pediatric dentistry **Affiliations:** A.D.A.; A.G.D.; O.K.U. **Hob./spts.:** Travel **SIC code:** 80 **Address:** Rouzana Hares, D.D.S., 8721 Joseph Campau, Hamtramck, MI 48212 **E-mail:** rharesdds@sbcglobal.net

HARGIS, BETTY J.
Industry: Healthcare **Born:** August 14, 1925, Madison, Indiana **Univ./degree:** Ph.D., Boston University **Current organization:** New England Cryogenic Center **Title:** Ph.D. **Type of organization:** Cryo preservation laboratory **Major product:** Sperm banking/andrology **Area of distribution:** National **Area of Practice:** Laboratory Biologist **Published works:** 48 publications, journals **Affiliations:** American Association of Reproductive Medicine; American Association of Tissue Banks **Hob./spts.:** Skiing, reading **SIC code:** 80 **Address:** New England Cryogenic Center, 665 Beacon St., Boston, MA 02215 **E-mail:** necryo@aol.com **Web address:** www.necryogenic.com

HARPER, MARJORIE
Industry: Healthcare **Born:** December 10, 1953, New York, New York **Univ./degree:** B.S.N.; M.S.N., Management, Dobbs Ferry **Current organization:** Bainbridge Nursing Home **Title:** Director of Nursing **Type of organization:** Nursing home **Major product:** 24 hour geriatric care, rehabilitation medicine **Area of distribution:** National **Area of Practice:** Sub acute care, nurse management **Hob./spts.:** Reading, travel **SIC code:** 80 **Address:** Bainbridge Nursing Home, 3518 Bainbridge Ave., Bronx, NY 10467-1598

HARRELL, AMY C.
Industry: Healthcare **Born:** July 8, 1965, Butler, Alabama **Univ./degree:** B.S., Psychology, Judson College, 1987 **Current organization:** Greater Meridian Health Clinic **Title:** Staff Radiologist Technician **Type of organization:** Medical clinic **Major product:** Patient care **Area of distribution:** Alabama **Area of Practice:** Radiologic technology **Affiliations:** American Society of Radiologic Technologists **SIC code:** 80 **Address:** 4380 Main St., Pennington, AL 36916 **E-mail:** amyharrell@tds.net

HARRIS, D. SUE
Industry: Healthcare **Born:** September 19, 1946, New London, Connecticut **Current organization:** St. Mary's Regional Medical Center **Title:** R.I.S. **Type of organization:** Hospital **Major product:** Patient care **Area of distribution:** Oklahoma **Area of Practice:** Radiology information systems, mammography, bone density, x-ray **Affiliations:** A.R.R.T. **Hob./spts.:** Travel, antiques **SIC code:** 80 **Address:** St. Mary's

Regional Medical Center, Radiology Dept., 305 S. Fifth St., Enid, OK 73701 **E-mail:** sue.harris@uhsinc.com

HARRISON, JANA L.
Industry: Dentistry **Born:** June 19, 1967, Houston, Texas **Univ./degree:** Doctorate, Baylor College of Dentistry, 1994 **Current organization:** Millennium Dental **Title:** Doctor **Type of organization:** Private dental practice **Major product:** Dental care **Area of distribution:** Plano, Texas **Area of Practice:** General and cosmetic dentistry **Affiliations:** A.D.A.; T.D.A.; D.C.D.A. **Hob./spts.:** Reading, travel, art projects **SIC code:** 80 **Address:** Millennium Dental, 6940 Coit Rd., Suite 200, Plano, TX 75023

HART, WAVENEY P.
Industry: Healthcare **Born:** Guyana, South America **Spouse:** Allan Hart (Deceased September 3, 2003) **Children:** Paul, Howard (Deceased May 15, 2003), Gail Hart Pati **Univ./degree:** C.C.R.N., Georgetown Hospital, 1964 **Current organization:** North Shore Medical Center, Queens **Title:** R.N. **Type of organization:** Hospital **Major product:** Patient care **Area of distribution:** Metropolitan New York **Area of practice:** Critical care nursing, Certified Midwife, staff education, contract negotiations; Attended and participated in Critical Care Seminar in the Soviet Union 1985; Also met with doctors and nurses in Egypt, Istanbul, Turkey and Lebanon; Had a nursing seminar at Zodhiates Hospital in Thessalonica, Greece 1986; Travels extensively to Europe and the Middle East including Israel, Cyprus and India and to many West Indian islands **Area of Practice:** Critical care nursing, Certified Midwife, staff education, contract negotiations; Attended and participated in Critical Care Seminar in the Soviet Union 1985; Also met with doctors and nurses in Egypt, Istanbul, Turkey and Lebanon; Had a nursing seminar at Zodhiates Hospital in Thessalonica, Greece 1986; Travels extensively to Europe and the Middle East including Israel, Cyprus and India and to many West Indian islands **Honors/awards:** Article written about her in The Hindu, May, 2005, Bangalore entitled 'Hart in the Right Place' **Affiliations:** Delegate for the Registered Nursing Council for Local 1199 **Career accomplishments:** Mentoring, teaching and financially assisting students who earned their R.N. degrees and Certified Nurses Assistant Certificates **Hob./spts.:** Singing, mentoring, interior decorating **SIC code:** 80 **Address:** 105-25 65th Ave., #1H, Forest Hills, NY 11375

HARTER, DAVID J.
Industry: Healthcare **Born:** April 12, 1942, Milwaukee, Wisconsin **Univ./degree:** B.S., Biology and Chemistry, University of Wisconsin at Madison, 1964; M.D., University of Wisconsin at Madison School of Medicine, 1968 **Current organization:** Port St. Lucie Cancer Center **Title:** Medical Director **Type of organization:** Free standing center **Major product:** Radiation therapy for cancer **Area of distribution:** National **Area of Practice:** Radiation oncology **Honors/awards:** Alpha Omega Alpha **Affiliations:** A.M.A.; A.S.C.O.; A.R.S.; A.S.T.R.O.; A.B.S. **Hob./spts.:** Gardening, motorcycling, genealogy **SIC code:** 80 **Address:** Port St. Lucie Cancer Center, 1780 S.E. Hillmoor Dr., Port St. Lucie, FL 34952 **E-mail:** dharter@gate.net

HARTRICK, NANCY E.
Industry: Healthcare **Born:** February 21, 1955, Royal Oak, Michigan **Univ./degree:** D.D.S., University of Michigan **Current organization:** Hartrick Dental Care **Title:** D.D.S. **Type of organization:** Dental practice **Major product:** Dental care **Area of distribution:** Royal Oak, Michigan **Area of Practice:** General dentistry **Honors/awards:** Distinguished Mentor and Clinical Instructor for John Kois, CRE; Best Dentists in America, 2004 **Affiliations:** A.D.A.; C.D.A.; M.D.A.; C.R.E. **Hob./spts.:** Photography, travel, water sports **SIC code:** 80 **Address:** Hartrick Dental Care, 32609 Woodward Ave., Royal Oak, MI 48073 **E-mail:** nhartrick@msn.com

HASAN, SYED P.
Industry: Medical **Born:** July 10, 1968, Hazaribagh, India **Univ./degree:** M.D., Rajendra Medical College, India, 1991 **Current organization:** Western Missouri Medical Center, Warrensburg, MO **Title:** Chief, Medicine, ICU, Cardiology **Type of organization:** Regional hospital **Major product:** Medical research, patient care, medical education **Area of distribution:** International **Area of Practice:** Hematology, internal medicine, sickle cell disease **Honors/awards:** Contemporary Who's Who, 2003; Marquis Who's Who in Medicine and Healthcare, 2004; American Medal of Honor, 2003, 2004; Man of the Year 2003 by American Biographical Institute; Commander's Award of Excellence 509th Medical Group, Whiteman Air Force Base, Missouri, Sept. 2003; Living Legend and International Health Professional of Year 2004 by International Biographical Centre, Cambridge, U.K.; **Published works:** "Role of elevated Troponin I in diagnosing coronary events in patients with normal coronaries", presented at scientific forum at HUH in Dec. 1999 and bagged 2nd prize. Journal of Southern Medical Assoc., Oct 2000, Vol 93, No 10, pS9, Ravi Akula MD, Syed Hasan MD, FABHP, Deborah Williams MD, Charles Curry MD, Div. of Cardiology, Howard Univ. Hospital, Washington, DC; "Efficacies of diagnostic test in Pulmonary Embolism", presented at ACP-ASIM, annual associates meeting as well as Howard Univ. scientific forum, May 2001, Ravi Akula MD, Syed Hasan MD, Humera Mujahid MD, Sheik Hassan MD, Dept. of Medicine, Howard Univ. Hospital, Washington, DC; "Depression in Sickle Cell Patients", Syed Hasan MD, Shahzad Hashmi MD, Mohammed Alhassen MD, William Lawson MD, Oswaldo Castro MD, Center for Sickle Cell Disease/Dept. of Psychiatry. Manuscript submitted for publication; "EKG changes in Obstructive Sleep Apnea Syndrome", Syed Hasan MD, Jahan Ara Ahmad MD, Kalpana Prakasa MD, Ravi Akula MD, James Diggs MD, accepted for presentation at Howard Univ. scientific forum/ACP-ASIM, DC chapter 2002; "Prevalence of Hepatitis C in Sickle Cell Patients" Syed Hasan MD, Mohammed Hassan MD, Oswaldo Castro MD, Laila Alamgir MD; Book, "The Respiratory System: Easy to Understand"; 20 abstracts and 20 detailed manuscripts in various national and international journals; Various Letters to the Editor **Affiliations:** European Hematology Assoc.; Assoc. of Medical Review Officers; Amer. College of Physicians; Amer. Society of Internal Medicine; International Society for Cellular Therapy; Amer. Society of Hematology; Amer. Society of Clinical Oncology **Hob./spts.:** Gardening, classical music **SIC code:** 80 **Address:** Howard University Hospital, Washington, D.C., 301 N. Beauregard St., #608, Alexandria, VA 22312 **E-mail:** syedphasan@hotmail.com

HASHEMI, SEYED M.
Industry: Healthcare **Born:** September 18, 1967, Tehran, Iran **Univ./degree:** M.D., Istahan Medical College, Iran, 1992 **Current organization:** Pennsylvania Hospital **Title:** M.D. **Type of organization:** Hospital **Major product:** Patient care **Area of distribution:** Pennsylvania **Area of Practice:** Clinical/internal medicine **Published works:** Article **Affiliations:** A.C.P.; A.S.I.M. **SIC code:** 80 **Address:** Pennsylvania Hospital, 800 Spruce St., Philadelphia, PA 19107 **E-mail:** smhashemi@hotmail.com

HASS, JAMES P.
Industry: Healthcare **Born:** April 23, 1956, Milwaukee, Wisconsin **Univ./degree:** B.S., Social Work, University of Wisconsin, 1986 **Current organization:** Lee Memorial Health System **Title:** Computer Tomography Technologist **Type of organization:** Hospital **Major product:** Patient care **Area of distribution:** Florida **Area of Practice:** Computer tomography and all types of radiography **Affiliations:** A.S.R.T. **Hob./spts.:** Family, scuba diving, sailing **SIC code:** 80 **Address:** 1806 S.E. 8th Place, Cape Coral, FL 33990 **E-mail:** jamesp1806@aol.com

HASSAN, ELSAYED A.
Industry: Healthcare **Born:** May 10, 1948, Alexandria, Egypt **Univ./degree:** M.D., University of Alexandria School of Medicine, 1974 **Current organization:** Private office **Title:** Physiatrist, M.D. **Type of organization:** Hospital and private office **Major product:** Medical services **Area of distribution:** International **Area of Practice:** Physical medicine and rehabilitation; practiced as General Surgeon for 25 years **Published works:** 2 peer reviewed journals **Affiliations:** A.M.A.; A.A.P.M.R. **Hob./spts.:** Family, children, soccer, basketball, drawing, painting, computers, reading, photography **SIC code:** 80 **Address:** 74 Pearsall St., Staten Island, NY 10305 **E-mail:** drhassan7@aol.com

HASSAN, MOHAMMED RAQIBUL
Industry: Medical **Born:** October 1, 1957, Bangladesh **Univ./degree:** M.D., Dhaka Medical College, 1983 **Current organization:** Texas Tech University Health Sciences Center **Title:** M.D. **Type of organization:** University hospital **Major product:** Medical services **Area of distribution:** Texas **Area of Practice:** Internal medicine, cardiology **Affiliations:** A.C.C.; Texas Medical Association **Hob./spts.:** Family, fishing, hunting, gardening **SIC code:** 80 **Address:** Texas Tech University, Health Sciences Center, 3401 Fourth St., Lubbock, TX 79403 **E-mail:** mhassan57@yahoo.com

HASSAN, SYED T.
Industry: Healthcare **Born:** January 30, 1939, Bihar, India **Univ./degree:** B.S., General Science, University Bihar, India, 1959; M.S., Glass Engineering, University of Sheffield, UK, 1964 **Current organization:** National Physical Therapy Services **Title:** Administrator **Type of organization:** Private practice **Major product:** Physical therapy **Area of distribution:** National **Area of Practice:** Operations management, glass and ceramics engineering; pioneered tinted glass in Pakistan, 1978 **Honors/awards:** Inbo Asahi Japan Scholarship, 1959 **Affiliations:** Chairman, Pakistan Standard Institute; A.C.S.; G.I. **Hob./spts.:** Family, soccer **SIC code:** 80 **Address:** National Physical Therapy Services, 12701 Telegraph Rd., Suite 209, Taylor, MI 48180 **E-mail:** tahirgilani@yahoo.com

HASSANIN, HANAN M.
Industry: Medical **Born:** September 20, 1964, Cairo, Egypt **Univ./degree:** M.S., Cairo University; M.D., Cairo University School of Medicine, 1987 **Current organization:** Hanan M. Hassanin, M.D./Albert Einstein College of Medicine **Title:** M.D./Assistant Professor **Type of organization:** Private practice/university **Major product:** Patient care, medical education **Area of distribution:** New York **Area of Practice:** Adult, child and adolescent psychiatry **Affiliations:** A.P.A. **Hob./spts.:** Reading, travel **SIC code:** 80 **Address:** 99-72 66th Rd., #1-C, Rego Park, NY 11374 **E-mail:** hhassanin@aol.com

HATCHER, ANTHONY CREEL
Industry: Healthcare **Born:** April 1, 1959, Glasgow, Kentucky **Univ./degree:** M.S., Biology, Western Kentucky University, 1994 **Current organization:** Southern Medical Laboratory **Title:** Laboratory Manager **Type of organization:** Medical laboratory

Major product: Research **Area of distribution:** Glasgow, Kentucky **Area of Practice:** Microbiology **Affiliations:** American Society of Chemical Pathologists; National Certification Agency for Medical Laboratory Personnel **Hob./spts.:** Weightlifting, hiking **SIC code:** 80 **Address:** Southern Medical Laboratory, 1330 N. Race St., Glasgow, KY 42141 **E-mail:** achatcher@glasgow-ky.com

HAUSWIRTH, CHRISTINE

Industry: Healthcare **Born:** April 23, 1951, Providence, Rhode Island **Univ./degree:** R.N., Newport Hospital School of Nursing, 1972 **Current organization:** Kindred Hospital Arlington, Texas **Title:** R.N./Director, Case Management & Utilization Management **Type of organization:** Hospital **Major product:** Patient care **Area of distribution:** Arlington, Texas **Area of Practice:** Certified case manager **Hob./spts.:** Tennis, reading **SIC code:** 80 **Address:** Kindred Hospital Arlington, Texas, 1000 N. Cooper, Arlington, TX 76011

HAWK, STEPHEN M.

Industry: Healthcare **Born:** November 29, 1968, Kansas City, Missouri **Univ./degree:** D.O., Kansas City University School of Medicine & Bio Sciences, 1995 **Current organization:** Bay Area Behavioral Health Associates **Title:** D.O. **Type of organization:** Medical office **Major product:** Patient care **Area of distribution:** Largo, Florida **Area of Practice:** Psychiatry **Affiliations:** Greater Tampa Bay Psychiatric Society; American Psychiatric Association **Hob./spts.:** Sailing, travel, computers **SIC code:** 80 **Address:** Bay Area Behavioral Health Associates, 10225 Ulmerton Rd., Suite 4A, Largo, FL 33771 **E-mail:** jeparham@tampabay.rr.com **Web address:** www.bayarea.yourmd.com/hawk

HAWKINS, JAMES K.

Industry: Healthcare **Born:** June 10, 1945, Bainbridge, New York **Univ./degree:** B.S., Southern Illinois university, 1977; M.A., Human Resource Development Education, George Washington University, 1989 **Current organization:** Sodexho Health Services at Knapp Medical Center **Title:** General Manager, Plant Operations **Type of organization:** Hospital **Major product:** Patient care **Area of distribution:** Texas **Area of Practice:** Engineering, Certified Plant Engineer, Certified Healthcare Facility Manager **Published works:** "Reach Client First-An Innovation in Customer Service" **Affiliations:** N.F.P.A.; Association of Facilities Engineers; American Society of Healthcare Engineering **Hob./spts.:** Golf, reading **SIC code:** 80 **Address:** Sodexho Health Services at Knapp Medical Center, 1401 E. Eighth St., Weslaco, TX 78596 **E-mail:** jhawkins@knappmed.org

HAWKINS, MARY E.

Industry: Healthcare **Born:** September 5, 1939, Henderson, North Carolina **Univ./degree:** B.S., St. Francis College, 1977 **Current organization:** Rockville Nursing Center **Title:** R.N. **Type of organization:** Nursing home **Major product:** Geriatric resident care **Area of distribution:** Rockville Centre, New York **Area of Practice:** Rehabilitation and pressure sore management **Affiliations:** Chi Eta Phi Nurses Sorority, Inc.; National Council of Negro Women, Inc. **SIC code:** 80 **Address:** Rockville Nursing Center, 41 Maine Ave., Rockville Centre, NY 11570

HAZELBAKER, KIMBERLYN

Industry: Healthcare **Born:** August 14, 1953, Amarillo, Texas **Univ./degree:** B.A., Biology, West Texas A&M University, 1975 **Current organization:** Harrington Cancer Center **Title:** MT(ASCP)QCYM-Director of Lab **Type of organization:** Nonprofit cancer center (out-patient) **Major product:** Oncology, hematology **Area of distribution:** Texas, New Mexico, Oklahoma, Kansas **Area of Practice:** Clinical laboratory **Affiliations:** A.S.C.P. **Hob./spts.:** Teaching jewelry class **SIC code:** 80 **Address:** Harrington Cancer Center, 1500 Wallace Blvd., Amarillo, TX 79106 **E-mail:** khazelbaker@harringtoncc.org

HEDGE, THOMAS K.

Industry: Healthcare **Born:** February 5, 1961, Mentor, Ohio **Univ./degree:** D.D.S., Ohio State University, 1987 **Current organization:** Thomas K. Hedge, DDS **Title:** Dentist **Type of organization:** Private practice **Major product:** Dentistry **Area of distribution:** West Chester, Ohio **Area of Practice:** General dentistry **Affiliations:** F.A.C.E.; A.D.A.; O.D.A. **Hob./spts.:** Travel **SIC code:** 80 **Address:** Thomas K. Hedge, DDS, 7908 Cincinnati Dayton Rd., Suite Y, West Chester, OH 45069 **E-mail:** tomhedge@msn.com

HEDRICK, JERRY A.

Industry: Healthcare **Born:** May 12, 1961, Hickory, North Carolina **Univ./degree:** B.S., Chemistry, E. Carolina University, 1983; Licensed Massage Therapist, Casey Riley School of Massage, 1993; D.C., Sherman College of Straight Chiropractic, 1999 **Current organization:** Bayside Chiropractic **Title:** D.C. **Type of organization:** Chiropractic clinic/wellness center **Major product:** Chiropractic care **Area of distribution:** Virginia **Area of Practice:** Hands on chiropractic, trained in healing touch and energy medicine **Affiliations:** Association for Research and Enlightenment **Hob./spts.:** Stand-up comedy **SIC code:** 80 **Address:** Bayside Chiropractic, 1658 Pleasure House Rd., Virginia Beach, VA 23455 **E-mail:** jerrydc@doctor.com

HEERDT, ALEXANDRA S.

Industry: Healthcare **Born:** August 4, 1965, Pennsylvania **Univ./degree:** B.S., Biology, Pennsylvania State University, 1985; M.D., Jefferson College of Medicine, 1987; M.P.H., Columbia University, 1996 **Current organization:** Memorial Sloan-Kettering Cancer Center **Title:** M.D., M.P.H. **Type of organization:** Hospital **Major product:** Patient care **Area of distribution:** New York **Area of Practice:** Breast cancer surgery **Honors/awards:** Finalist, Resident Essay Award, Society of Surgical Oncology, 1992; Outstanding Young Women of America Award, 1988; Janet M. Glasgow American Medical Women's Association Award, 1987; William Potter Memorial Prize in Clinical Medicine, 1987; Paul D. Zimskind Memorial Prize in Urology, 1987; Alpha Omega Honor Medical Society, 1987; Warren C. Batroff Scholarship Award, 1985; Lange Medical Publications Prize, 1987; Melvin I. Katzman Pathology Prize, 1986 **Published works:** Numerous book chapters and peer-reviewed publications including: Heerdt, A.S., Insertion of mediport catheters in: Multidisciplinary Atlas of Breast Surgery. Kinne, D.W., ed. Philadelphia: Lippincott-Raven Publishers, 1997; Heerdt, A.S., Borgen, P.I., Current status of Tomoxifen use: an update for the surgical oncologist. J Surg Onc 1999;72:42-49; Abstracts: Heerst, A.S., Senie, R.T., Cohen, M.A., Tran, K.N., Borgen, P.I., Factors associated with inability to conserve the breast. 1998, Society of Surgical Oncology; Quan, M.L., Heerdt, A., Sclafani, L., Fey, J., Morris, E., Borgen, P.I., Magnetic resonance imaging (MRI) of the breast detects unsuspected disease in patients with infiltrating lobular cancer. 2003, Society of Surgical Oncology. (Submitted) **Affiliations:** Society of Surgical Oncology; American Society for Breast Disease; American Cancer Society; Member, Advisory Committee, Cost Effectiveness of Breast Cancer Control for African Americans (Funded: NCI) 2001-02; Member, Advisory Committee, Breast Examination Center of Harlem, 1994-02 **Hob./spts.:** Family **SIC code:** 80 **Address:** Memorial Sloan-Kettering Cancer Center, 1275 York Ave., New York, NY 10021 **E-mail:** heerdta@mskcc.org **Web address:** www.mskcc.org

HEGGERS, JOHN P.

Industry: Medical **Born:** February 8, 1933, Brooklyn, New York **Univ./degree:** B.A., Bacteriology, University of Montana, 1958; M.S., Microbiology, University of Maryland, 1965; Ph.D., Bacteriology and Public Health, Washington State University, 1972 **Current organization:** University of Texas Medical Branch/Shriners Burns Hospital **Title:** Professor of Surgery (Plastic)/Microbiology and Immunology, UTMB and Director, Clinical Microbiology **Type of organization:** Teaching hospital **Major product:** Treatment of pediatric burns, education **Area of distribution:** International **Area of Practice:** Clinical microbiology, bacteriology **Honors/awards:** Numerous including, Fisher Award in Medical Technology 1982 and Technologist of the Year 1983, Amer. Medical Technologists; At-Large Award 1986, Curtis P. Artz Distinguished Service Award 1996 and Robert B. Lindberg Award 1991, 1992, 2004, Amer. Burn Assoc.; Dr. Stanley Reitman Memorial Award for Outstanding Achievement 1987; Who's Who in the South & Southwest 1992; Who's Who in Science & Engineering 1991, 1994, 2003-04; Int'l Order of Merit, The Int'l Biog. Centre 1992; Washington State Univ. Alumni Achievement Award 1993; Univ. of Montana Distinguished Alumni Award 1994 **Published works:** 211 articles, 46 books and book chapters, 181 abstracts **Affiliations:** Many including, Fellow, Amer. Acad. of Microbiology; Fellow, New York Acad. of Science; Diplomate, Amer. Acad. of Wound Management (CWS); 2nd Vice Pres., Amer. Burn Assoc. Board of Trustee's; Amer. Soc. of Plastic & Reconstructive Surgeons; Editorial Advisory Board, Journal of Burn Care & Rehabilitation and Journal of Phytotherapy Research; Editorial Board, Journal of Burns, 1st Website Journal; Board of Education Training Ad-hoc Reviewer, Amer. Soc. for Microbiology; Southern Region Board of Dir. of AAB, Chrm, Continuing Education **Hob./spts.:** Bowling, scuba diving **SIC code:** 80 **Address:** University of Texas Medical Branch, Shriners Burns Hospital, 815 Market St., Galveston, TX 77550 **E-mail:** jphegger@utmb.edu

HEILBRONER, PETER L.

Industry: Healthcare **Born:** June 24, 1954, New York, New York **Univ./degree:** Ph.D., Anthropology, Columbia University, 1987; M.D., University of Medicine and Dentistry of New Jersey, 1993 **Current organization:** Neurology Group of Bergen County, P.A. **Title:** M.D., Ph.D. **Type of organization:** Group practice **Major product:** Patient care **Area of distribution:** New Jersey **Area of Practice:** Pediatric neurology **Published works:** 1 book, "Pediatric Neurology-Essentials for General Practice" **Affiliations:** American Academy of Pediatrics; Child Neurology Society; American Academy of Neurology **Hob./spts.:** Playing jazz guitar **SIC code:** 80 **Address:** Neurology Group of Bergen County, P.A., 1200 E. Ridgewood Ave., Ridgewood, NJ 07454 **E-mail:** pheilbroner@neurobergen.com **Web address:** www.neurobergen.com

HEKIER, RON J.

Industry: Healthcare **Born:** January 7, 1970 **Univ./degree:** B.A., Cellular and Molecular Biology, California State University at Northridge; M.D., Tufts University School of Medicine, Boston **Current organization:** Precision Surgery **Title:** M.D. **Type of organization:** Group practice **Major product:** Patient care **Area of distribution:** Texarkana, Texas **Area of Practice:** Surgery, breast cancer, weight reduction **Honors/awards:** Alpha Omega Alpha Society **Affiliations:** American Society of Breast Surgeons; American Society of Breast Diseases; Michael E. DeBakey International Surgical Society **Hob./spts.:** Antique map collecting **SIC code:** 80 **Address:** Precision Surgery, 2717 Summerhill Rd., Texarkana, TX 75503

HELMS, LORI A.
Industry: Healthcare **Born:** October 21, 1962, Concord, North Carolina **Univ./degree:** Radiology Certifications **Current organization:** Copperfield Ob/Gyn **Title:** (RT)R **Type of organization:** Medical office **Major product:** Patient care **Area of distribution:** North Carolina **Area of Practice:** Radiology - bone density and ultrasound **Published works:** Published photos in the Independent Tribune **Affiliations:** A.R.R.T.; A.S.R.T.; N.C.S.R.T. **Hob./spts.:** Photography, physical fitness, outdoor activities, pet care **SIC code:** 80 **Address:** Copperfield Ob/Gyn, 349 Penny Lane, Concord, NC 28025

HELSEL, STEPHANIE A.
Industry: Healthcare **Born:** October 9, 1967, Pratt, Kansas **Univ./degree:** R.N., Pratt Community College **Current organization:** Cancer & Blood Care, P.C. **Title:** R.N., Medical Staff Manager, Oncology Nurse **Type of organization:** Clinic **Major product:** Patient care **Area of distribution:** Ponca City, Oklahoma **Area of Practice:** Chemotherapy; OCN Certified **Affiliations:** O.N.S.; Kansas Nursing Society; Strathmore's Who's Who **Hob./spts.:** Walking, reading, movies **SIC code:** 80 **Address:** Cancer & Blood Care, P.C., 609 Virginia Ave., Ponca City, OK 74601 **E-mail:** stephaniecbc@cable1.net

HENDERSON, MARY A.
Industry: Healthcare **Born:** March 26, 1936, Rochester, New York **Univ./degree:** B.S.N., Nazareth College, New York, 1958 **Current organization:** Lemuel Shattuck Hospital **Title:** R.N. **Type of organization:** Hospital **Major product:** Patient care **Area of distribution:** Franklin, Massachusetts **Area of Practice:** Supervision (medical surgical, intensive care, oncology) **Affiliations:** National and local chapters, A.N.A. **Hob./spts.:** Family, cooking, gardening **SIC code:** 80 **Address:** 144 Stone Ridge Rd., Franklin, MA 02038 **E-mail:** mollyetwilliam@netscape.net

HENDRICKSON, CONSTANCE C.
Industry: Mental health **Born:** August 12, 1926, New York, New York **Univ./degree:** Ph.D. in Clinical Social Work, Catholic University of America, Washington, D.C., 1985 **Current organization:** Constance C. Hendrickson, Ph.D. **Title:** Doctor **Type of organization:** Private practice Psychotherapy **Major product:** Mental health **Area of distribution:** Bethesda, Maryland and Washington, D.C. **Area of Practice:** Troubled adults, families **Affiliations:** NFCSW.; Greater Washington Society Clinical Social Work **Hob./spts.:** Singing, church, hiking, reading **SIC code:** 80 **Address:** Constance C. Hendrickson, Ph.D., 3000 Connecticut Ave. N.W., Suite 201, Washington, DC 20008 **E-mail:** chendr3000@aol.com

HENDRY, JOHN A.
Industry: Healthcare **Born:** May 14, 1949, Neptune, New Jersey **Spouse:** Cheryl Woodson **Married:** June 18, 1977 **Univ./degree:** B.S., Biology, Spring Hill College, 1971; D.D.S., Louisiana State University School of Dentistry, 1977/LSU, Pediatric Dentistry, 1979 **Current organization:** John A. Hendry. D.D.S. **Title:** D.D.S. Pediatric Dentistry **Area of distribution:** National **Area of practice:** Pediatric dentistry (Board Certified, 1984) **Area of Practice:** Pediatric dentistry (Board Certified, 1984) **Published works:** 2 articles **Affiliations:** A.D.A., National Spokesperson; Fellow, A.A.P.D., 1984; Fellow, A.D.P.D., 1997; L.D.A.; A.S.D.C.; Pierre Fauchard Academy; President and Chair, Louisiana Open, Inc.; Board of Trustees, Spring Hill College, 2004-present **Hob./spts.:** Golf **SIC code:** 80 **Address:** 185 S. Beadle Rd., Lafayette, LA 70508 **E-mail:** drjohn@drjohnhendry.com **Web address:** www.drjohnhendry.com

HENIN, KRISTINE J.
Industry: Healthcare **Born:** December 6, 1966, Tulsa, Oklahoma **Univ./degree:** L.P.N., Kiamichi Technology Center, 2000 **Current organization:** Brookside Nursing Center **Title:** LPN **Type of organization:** Nursing home **Major product:** Long-term care, rehab services **Area of distribution:** Madill, Oklahoma **Area of Practice:** MDS Coordinator **Affiliations:** O.N.A. **Hob./spts.:** Family, reading, swimming, boating, physical fitness **SIC code:** 80 **Address:** Brookside Nursing Center, P.O. Box 848, Madill, OK 73446 **E-mail:** khenin@madillok.net

HENION, JULIA S.
Industry: Healthcare **Born:** June 29, 1946, Rolla, Missouri **Univ./degree:** M.B.A., Our Lady of the Lake University, San Antonio, Texas; R.N., Incarnate Word University, San Antonio, Texas **Current organization:** Driscoll Children's Hospital **Title:** V.P./Chief Nursing Officer **Type of organization:** Hospital **Major product:** Patient care **Area of distribution:** National **Area of Practice:** Pediatric nursing and administration **Honors/awards:** Administrator of Excellence, Santa Rose Health Center, 1992; Alumni of Distinction, Incarnate Word University; Administrator of Excellence, Harborview Medical Center, 1993 **Affiliations:** Diplomate, A.C.H.E.; C.H.C.A.; A.N.A.; T.N.A.; **Hob./spts.:** Swimming, photography, video games, reading **SIC code:** 80 **Address:** Driscoll Children's Hospital, 3533 S. Alameda St., Corpus Christi, TX 78411 **E-mail:** Julia.henion@dchstx.org

HENLEY, CARL E.
Industry: Healthcare **Univ./degree:** D.D.S.; Northwestern University Dental School **Current organization:** Center for Advanced Dentistry **Title:** President/Dental Director **Type of organization:** Dental facility **Major product:** Dentistry **Area of distribution:** Naperville, Illinois **Area of Practice:** Cosmetic and reconstructive dentistry **Affiliations:** I.C.C.N.O.; C.D.S.; A.D.A.; A.G.D.; A.A.C.D. **SIC code:** 80 **Address:** Center for Advanced Dentistry, 931 W. 75th St., Suite 107, Naperville, IL 60565

HENN, CARMEN E.
Industry: Healthcare **Univ./degree:** M.D., University of Puerto Rico Medical School, 1984 **Current organization:** V.A. Medical Center-Puerto Rico **Title:** M.D./Chief of Ophthalmology **Type of organization:** Medical center **Major product:** Patient care **Area of distribution:** San Juan, Puerto Rico **Area of Practice:** Ophthalmology **Published works:** Articles **Affiliations:** A.A.O., Puerto Rico Chapter; P.R.M.A. **Hob./spts.:** Family **SIC code:** 80 **Address:** Paseo San Juan, La Garita #E9, San Juan, PR 00926

HENRY, DAVID S.
Industry: Healthcare **Born:** January 1, 1962, Kingston, Jamaica **Univ./degree:** M.D., University of West Indies, Jamaica, 1988 **Current organization:** Access Healthcare P.C. **Title:** M.D. **Type of organization:** Private practice **Major product:** Patient care **Area of distribution:** Connecticut **Area of Practice:** Internal medicine, cardiology **Published works:** 3 articles **Affiliations:** A.C.C.; A.C.P; C.S.M.S; H.C.M.S. **Hob./spts.:** Tennis, fishing **SIC code:** 80 **Address:** Access Healthcare P.C., 1229 Albany Ave., Hartford, CT 06112

HENSLEY, TAMMY
Industry: Healthcare **Title:** Home Health Director **Type of organization:** Home health agency **Major product:** Home healthcare services **SIC code:** 80 **Address:** Bradley County Home Health Agency, 404 South Bradley St., Warren, AZ 71671 **E-mail:** thensley@bcmed.org

HERMANSEN, BRUCE ALLEN
Industry: Healthcare **Born:** September 21, 1954, Minneapolis, Minnesota **Univ./degree:** M.D., University of Minnesota, 1982 **Current organization:** Health Partners **Title:** M.D. **Type of organization:** Health maintenance organization **Major product:** Medical care **Area of distribution:** St. Paul, Minnesota **Area of Practice:** Adult psychiatry **Affiliations:** American Psychiatric Association **Hob./spts.:** Tennis, cross country skiing, Cub Scouts, family **SIC code:** 80 **Address:** Health Partners, 640 Jackson St., St. Paul, MN 55101 **E-mail:** bruce.a.hermansen@healthpartners.com

HERNANDEZ, MARTA L.
Industry: Healthcare **Born:** March 26, 1952, Lincoln, Nebraska **Univ./degree:** B.S., University of Nebraska, 1971; M.D., University of Southern California, 1980 **Current organization:** King-Drew Medical Center **Title:** Staff Perinatologist/M.D. **Type of organization:** Hospital **Major product:** Women's healthcare **Area of distribution:** Los Angeles, California **Area of Practice:** Perintalogist, Ob/Gyn **Honors/awards:** Special Commendation for Outstanding Support for Adolescent Health and Teen Clinic in South Central Los Angeles, 1994; Best Attending of the Year, King-Drew Medical Center, Dept of Ob/Gyn, 1987; Distinguished Alumni Award, Lincoln High School, Lincoln, Nebraska, 1986; Best Graduating Resident, King-Drew Medical Center, 1984; Executive Chief Resident, King-Drew Medical Center, 1984; National Mortar Board Honor Society, 1974; National Honor Society, 1970 **Published works:** Abstracts on medical complications of pregnancy **Affiliations:** Fellow, S.I.F.M.; A.P.G.O.; A.S.H.G.; S.C.A.R.M. **Hob./spts.:** Reading, crafts, embroidery **SIC code:** 80 **Address:** King-Drew Medical Center, 12021 S. Wilmington Ave., Los Angeles, CA 90240 **E-mail:** drmarta@juno.com

HERNANDEZ, NELSON D.
Industry: Healthcare **Born:** May 14, 1955, Cuba **Univ./degree:** M.D., San Pedro de Macorix, Dominican Republic, 1982 **Current organization:** Dr. Nelson D. Hernandez, P.A. **Title:** M.D./Psychaitrist **Type of organization:** Private practice **Major product:** Mental healthcare **Area of distribution:** Miami, Florida **Area of Practice:** General psychiatry **Published works:** Article **Affiliations:** A.P.A.; A.M.A.; Southern Medical Association, Southern Florida Psychiatric Association **Hob./spts.:** Music, reading **SIC code:** 80 **Address:** Dr. Nelson D. Hernandez, M.D., 8917 N.W. 171st Lane, Miami, FL 33018 **E-mail:** nisdhernandez@aol.com

HERNANDEZ, ROSE P.
Industry: Medical **Born:** May 12, Saginaw, Michigan **Univ./degree:** D.O., Michigan State, 1979 **Current organization:** Clinica Adelante, Inc. **Title:** D.O. **Type of organization:** Medical practice **Major product:** Patient care **Area of distribution:** Surprise, Arizona **Area of Practice:** Family practice **Affiliations:** A.O.A.; A.C.O.F.P.; A.O.M.A. **Hob./spts.:** Reading, tennis, hiking, theatre, dancing **SIC code:** 80 **Address:** Clinica Adelante, Inc., 16560 N. Dysart Rd., Surprise, AZ 85374

HERNANDEZ MICHELS, ANGELA T.
Industry: Healthcare **Born:** July 22, 1947, Dominican Republic **Univ./degree:** M.D., University of Puerto Rico School of Medicine, 1971 **Current organization:** Triple-S-Blue Shield of P.R. **Title:** M.D./Medical Director **Type of organization:** Health insurance services **Major product:** Health services and plans **Area of distribution:** Puerto Rico **Area of Practice:** Public health and pediatrics **Published works:** "Genetics", Pediatric Journal **Affiliations:** A.M.A. (National and Local Chapter) **SIC code:** 80 **Address:** P.O. Box 149199, San Juan, PR 00936 **E-mail:** ahernand@edp.ssspr.com

HERRIN, JOHN T.
Industry: Healthcare **Born:** February 19, 1936, Rutherglen Victoria, Australia **Univ./degree:** M.B.B.S. **Current organization:** Children's Hospital, Div. of Nephrology **Title:** Director of Clinical Services **Type of organization:** Hospital **Major product:** Patient care **Area of distribution:** International **Area of Practice:** Pediatric nephrology **Published works:** Articles **Affiliations:** American Society of Nephrology; International Society of Pediatric Nephrology **Hob./spts.:** Reading, music **SIC code:** 80 **Address:** Children's Hospital, Div. of Nephrology, 360 Longwood Ave., HUN 3, Boston, MA 02115 **E-mail:** john.herrin@tch.harvard.edu

HERSKOVIC, ARNOLD M.
Industry: Healthcare **Born:** July 30, 1943, Baltimore, Maryland **Univ./degree:** M.D., University of Maryland, 1969 **Current organization:** Northwest Community Hospital **Title:** M.D./Medical Director **Type of organization:** Hospital **Major product:** Patient care **Area of distribution:** National **Area of Practice:** Radiation, oncology **Published works:** Multiple publications **Affiliations:** A.M.A.; A.S.T.R.O.; F.A.C.R. **Hob./spts.:** Pilot **SIC code:** 80 **Address:** Northwest Community Hospital, 800 W. Central Ave., Arlington Heights, IL 60005 **E-mail:** arnoldh134@aol.com

HESHMATI, HEIDAR G.
Industry: Healthcare **Born:** February 23, 1944, Iran **Univ./degree:** M.D., Tehran University, 1968; M.P.H., University of Central Florida, 1985; Ph.D., Southland University, 1989 **Current organization:** Brevard County Health Dept. **Title:** MD, MPH, PhD **Type of organization:** Health department **Major product:** Medical services **Area of distribution:** Florida **Area of Practice:** Preventative medicine, public health, orthopedics **Affiliations:** A.M.A.; F.M.A.; B.C.M.S.; A.C.P.H.P.M. **Hob./spts.:** Gardening, travel **SIC code:** 80 **Address:** Brevard County Health Dept., 2575 N. Courtenay Pkwy., Merritt Island, FL 32953

HESS, NATALIE B.
Industry: Education/writing/TESOL **Born:** February 3, 1936, Pjotrkow, Poland **Univ./degree:** B.S., English/French, Indiana State University, 1957; M.S., Education, Harvard University, 1963; Ph.D., English, University of Arizona at Tucson, 1993 **Current organization:** University of Northern Arizona at Yuma **Title:** Professor **Type of organization:** University **Major product:** Education/writing **Area of distribution:** National **Area of Practice:** TESOL **Published works:** 24 articles, 6 books **Affiliations:** Board Member, Arizona Teachers of English TSOL **SIC code:** 80 **Address:** University of Northern Arizona at Yuma, ESL-BME Program, 9500 S. Ave. Eight, East, Yuma, AZ 85365 **E-mail:** natalie.hess@nau.edu

HICKS, JEANNE E.
Industry: Healthcare **Born:** August 20, 1940, Montclair, New Jersey **Univ./degree:** B.S., Biology, Georgian Court College, New Jersey, 1962; M.D., University of Tennessee School of Medicine, 1966 **Current organization:** Medical Consultants **Title:** M.D./Director/President **Type of organization:** Private practice **Major product:** Medical consultations **Area of distribution:** North Carolina **Area of Practice:** Rehabilitation, rheumatology **Published works:** 130+ articles, 2 books **Affiliations:** F.A.C.R.; Board Member, Mt. Sinai Association Advisory Board **Hob./spts.:** Music, various media of painting, piano, organ, travel **SIC code:** 80 **Address:** Medical Consultants, 6410 Harrison Rd., Charlotte, NC 28270 **E-mail:** jehicks999@aol.com

HIESIGER, EMILE M.
Industry: Healthcare **Born:** October 18, 1949, New York, New York **Univ./degree:** B.A., Political Science, 1970; M.A., Political Science, 1971, New York University; M.D., New York Medical College, 1978; Fellowship, Neurology, Memorial Sloan Kettering Hospital, 1985 **Current organization:** NYU Medical Center **Title:** M.D. **Type of organization:** Hospital **Major product:** Medical services **Area of distribution:** New York **Area of Practice:** Interventional pain management, neurology **Affiliations:** Fellow, A.A.N.; N.Y.S.M.S.; A.P.A.; E.P.A.; A.M.A. **Hob./spts.:** Flying, painting, drawing **SIC code:** 80 **Address:** NYU Medical Center, 530 First Ave., Suite 9S, New York, NY 10016 **E-mail:** doctor@hiesiger.com **Web address:** www.hiesiger.com

HIGBEE, NANCY K.
Industry: Healthcare **Born:** October 28, 1954, St. Louis, Missouri **Univ./degree:** B.S., Nursing, St. Louis University **Current organization:** Anthony L. Jordan Health Center **Title:** Director, Clinical Operations **Type of organization:** Community health center **Major product:** Patient care **Area of distribution:** Rochester, New York **Area of Practice:** Nursing **Hob./spts.:** Gardening, boating, camping **SIC code:** 80 **Address:** Anthony L. Jordan Health Center, 82 Holland St., Rochester, NY 14605 **E-mail:** nhigbee@jordanhealth.org

HIGGINBOTHAM, EDITH ARLEANE
Industry: Healthcare **Born:** September 14, 1946, New Orleans, Louisiana **Univ./degree:** M.S., Chemistry, 1971; M.D., 1974, Howard University **Current organization:** James Valley Imaging, Ltd. **Title:** M.D. **Type of organization:** Radiology firm **Major product:** Radiology **Area of distribution:** Mitchell, South Dakota **Area of Practice:** Radiology **Published works:** 15 articles **Affiliations:** A.C.R.; S.N.M.; R.S.N.A. **Hob./spts.:** Aerobics, piano, walking, reading **SIC code:** 80 **Address:** 1015 Circle Dr., Mitchell, SD 57301 **E-mail:** edith@santel.net

HIGGS, GEOFFREY B.
Industry: Healthcare **Born:** March 9, 1960, Bermuda **Univ./degree:** B.S., University of Virginia; M.D., Columbia University, 1988; Fellowship, Harvard University; Residency, Columbia University **Current organization:** Advanced Orthopaedic Centers **Title:** Orthopaedic Surgeon, Fellowship Co-Director **Type of organization:** Medical practice **Major product:** Orthopaedic sports medicine, shoulder and knee surgery **Area of distribution:** Mid Atlantic Region **Area of Practice:** Sports medicine, shoulder and knee specialist **Honors/awards:** Frank Stinchfield Award; Orren Baus Award; Several Research Awards; National Leadership Award **Published works:** 25 scientific publications **Affiliations:** F.A.A.O.S.; A.O.S.S.M.; A.A.N.A.; I.S.A.K.O.S.; A.B.O.S.; A.C.S.M.; R.A.M.; V.O.S.; M.S.M.; 38th Parallel Medical Society; German-American Medical Society; National Football Foundation; College Football Hall of Fame **Hob./spts.:** Artist (sculpting), skiing **SIC code:** 80 **Address:** Advanced Orthopaedic Centers, 7650 Parham Rd., Richmond, VA 23294 **E-mail:** geoffhiggs@yahoo.com

HIGHTOWER, CURTIS E.
Industry: Medical **Born:** January 14, 1955, Wichita, Kansas **Univ./degree:** D.V.M., Kansas State University, 1979; M.D., Case Western Reserve University, 1984 **Current organization:** M.D. Anderson Cancer Center **Title:** M.D./Assistant Professor of Anesthesia **Type of organization:** Hospital/university **Major product:** Medical services, cancer treatment **Area of distribution:** International **Area of Practice:** Anesthesia, exercise physiology **Affiliations:** A.M.A.; A.S.A.; A.V.M.A. **Hob./spts.:** Target shooting, kayaking, sailing **SIC code:** 80 **Address:** M.D. Anderson Cancer Center, 1515 Holcombe Blvd., Box 042, Houston, TX 77030 **E-mail:** chightow@mdanderson.org

HIJAZI, ZIYAD M.
Industry: Medical **Born:** June 1, 1958, Madaba, Jordan **Univ./degree:** M.D., University of Jordan; M.P.H., Yale University **Current organization:** University of Chicago **Title:** Chief of Pediatric Cardiology **Type of organization:** Teaching hospital **Major product:** Medical services (pediatric cardiology, clinical and education) **Area of distribution:** International **Area of Practice:** Interventional pediatric cardiology **Affiliations:** F.A.C.C.; F.A.A.P. **Hob./spts.:** Jogging **SIC code:** 80 **Address:** University of Chicago, 5841 S. Maryland Ave., MC 4051, Chicago, IL 60637

HILLS, DONA JOANNE
Industry: Healthcare **Univ./degree:** M.D., Rutgers University, 1977 **Current organization:** Queens Long Island Medical Group **Title:** Director of Ultrasound **Type of organization:** Medical group **Major product:** Patient care **Area of distribution:** Long Island, New York **Area of Practice:** Obstetrics, gynecology, radiology, ultrasound **Affiliations:** A.M.A.; A.I.U.M.; Women in Medicine **SIC code:** 80 **Address:** Queens Long Island Medical Group, 308 Bay Shore Rd., North Babylon, NY 11703 **E-mail:** sonodoc@aol.com

HILLSMAN, REGINA O.
Industry: Healthcare **Univ./degree:** B.A., 1972; M.D., 1977, George Washington University **Current organization:** Regina O. Hillsman MD, PC **Title:** M.D. **Type of organization:** Private practice **Major product:** Surgery, rehabilitation **Area of distribution:** National **Area of Practice:** Orthopaedic surgery (Board Certified) specializing in sports injuries **Published works:** Lecturing and public speaking **Affiliations:** International Orthoscopic Society **SIC code:** 80 **Address:** Regina O. Hillsman MD, PC, 1183 New Haven Rd., Naupatuck, CT 06770 **Web address:** www.drhillsman.com

HINKLE, KATHLEEN S.
Industry: Healthcare **Born:** February 19, 1960, Columbia, South Carolina **Univ./degree:** B.S.N., Clemson University, 1983 **Current organization:** Lexington Medical Center **Title:** RN, Admissions Nurse **Type of organization:** Medical center **Major product:** Patient care **Area of distribution:** Lexington, South Carolina **Area of Practice:** Geriatrics **Hob./spts.:** Reading, crossword puzzles, painting, baking, cross stitching **SIC code:** 80 **Address:** Lexington Medical Center, 815 Old Cherokee Rd., Lexington, SC 29072

HINTON, LORI
Industry: Law/healthcare **Born:** August 26, 1942, Wynot, Nebraska **Univ./degree:** B.S., Mount Marty College, 1964; M.P.H.; University of Minnesota, 1976; Ph.D., University of Texas, 1984 **Current organization:** American Case Management **Title:**

President **Type of organization:** Legal consultation **Major product:** Legal nurse consulting, expert witness, litigation **Area of distribution:** National **Area of Practice:** Nursing, life care planning **Published works:** 20 publications **Affiliations:** A.N.A.; T.X.N.A.; International Academy of Life Care Planners; American Association of Legal Nurse Consultants; Association of Rehabilitation Nurses; International Association of Rehabilitation Professionals; Texas Association of Rehabilitation Professionals; Review Panel Member for 2004 Grant Process, Rehabilitation Nursing Foundation; Adjunct Professor, University of Texas **Hob./spts.:** Oil painting, flower arranging, reading, travel, home decorating **SIC code:** 80 **Address:** American Case Management, 1330 Post Oak Blvd., Suite 2990, Houston, TX 77056 **E-mail:** lhinton@hintonlaw.com

HIRSCH, RICK M.
Industry: Medical **Born:** August 18, 1963, Chicago, Illinois **Univ./degree:** D.O., Western University, 1997 **Current organization:** Western University of Health Sciences **Title:** Assistant Professor of Family Medicine **Type of organization:** University **Major product:** Patient care, medical education **Area of distribution:** Pomona, California **Area of Practice:** Family medicine **Affiliations:** A.O.A.; American Academy of Family Physicians; American College of Sports Medicine **Hob./spts.:** Sports medicine **SIC code:** 80 **Address:** Western University of Health Sciences, 309 E. Second St., Pomona, CA 91766 **E-mail:** rhirsch@westernu.edu

HMIEL, S. PAUL
Industry: Medical **Born:** October 2, 1958, Beaver, Pennsylvania **Univ./degree:** M.D., Ph.D., Case Western Reserve University, 1987 **Current organization:** Washington University **Title:** M.D., Ph.D. **Type of organization:** University **Major product:** Patient care, medical education **Area of distribution:** National **Area of Practice:** Pediatrics, nephrology **Affiliations:** Fellow, A.A.P.; A.S.T.; A.S.P.N.; A.S.N. **Hob./spts.:** Computers, running **SIC code:** 80 **Address:** Washington University, 1 Children's Place, Suite 8116, St. Louis, MO 63110 **E-mail:** hmiel@kids.wustl.edu

HO, JOHN S.
Industry: Medical **Born:** February 16, 1966, New York, New York **Univ./degree:** M.D., University of Texas Medical Branch, Galveston, Texas, 1997 **Current organization:** St. Luke's Episcopal Hospital/Texas Heart Institute **Title:** M.D. **Type of organization:** University hospital **Major product:** Patient care, medical education **Area of distribution:** Pearland, Texas **Area of Practice:** Cardiology **Affiliations:** A.M.A; A.C.C.; A.C.P. **Hob./spts.:** Tennis, travel, stamp collecting **SIC code:** 80 **Address:** St. Luke's Episcopal Hospital/Texas Heart Institute, 3247 Southdown Dr., Pearland, TX 77584 **E-mail:** johnandcindiho@netscape.net

HOBBS, THOMAS R.
Industry: Healthcare **Born:** August 26, 1934, Forrest City, Pennsylvania **Univ./degree:** Ph.D., 1968, M.D., 1969, West Virginia University **Current organization:** Pennsylvania Medical Society **Title:** Medical Director, Physician Health Program **Type of organization:** Medical society **Major product:** Aid to physicians with professional impairment **Area of distribution:** Harrisburg, Pennsylvania **Area of Practice:** Addiction medicine **Honors/awards:** Nominated, Work Group of the National Alliance for Drug Laws **Affiliations:** P.M.S.; F.A.S.A.M.; F.A.C.F.M. **Hob./spts.:** Hunting, fishing, boating, photography **SIC code:** 80 **Address:** Pennsylvania Medical Society, 777 E. Park Dr., Harrisburg, PA 17105 **E-mail:** t.hobbs@pamed.soc.com

HOCHSTADT, RON J.
Industry: Healthcare **Born:** December 4, 1955, New York **Current organization:** Diana Fischer, M.D., P.A. **Title:** Business Manager **Type of organization:** Private medical practice **Major product:** Psychiatric healthcare **Area of distribution:** Lake Worth, Florida **Area of Practice:** Business management **Hob./spts.:** Travel, photography **SIC code:** 80 **Address:** Diana Fischer, M.D., P.A., 7556 Lake Worth Rd., #101, Lake Worth, FL 33467 **E-mail:** ronsterh@bellsouth.net

HODYL, THOMAS W.
Industry: Healthcare **Born:** January 7, 1971, Long Island, New York **Univ./degree:** B.S., Biology, Adelphi University, 1993; M.D., Wayne State University School of Medicine, 1997 **Current organization:** Thomas W. Hodyl, M.D., P.C **Title:** M.D. **Type of organization:** Private practice **Major product:** Patient care **Area of distribution:** Long Island, New York **Area of Practice:** Family practice **Affiliations:** A.A.F.P.; New York Medical Society **Hob./spts.:** Computers, sports **SIC code:** 80 **Address:** Thomas W. Hodyl, M.D., P.C, 517 Oak St., Suite C, Copiague, NY 11726

HOFFMAN, TIMOTHY M.
Industry: Medical **Univ./degree:** M.D., West Virginia University School o Medicine, 1992; Residency, West Virginia University; Pediatric Cardiology Fellowship and Cardiac Critical Care and Organ Transplant Fellowship, Children's Hospital of Philadelphia **Current organization:** Columbus Children's Hospital, Division of Cardiology **Title:** M.D./Medical Director, Heart Transplant Program/Staff Cardiologist, Cardiac Critical Care Medicine **Type of organization:** University hospital **Major product:** Pediatric cardiology, heart transplant and heart failure program, medical education **Area of distribution:** National **Area of Practice:** Pediatric cardiology, cardiac critical care medicine, thoracic organ transplant **Honors/awards:** Outstanding Resident Teaching Award, Dept. of Pediatrics WVU School of Medicine, 1995; Outstanding Resident Research Award, Dept. of Pediatrics, WVU School of Medicine, 1996; Aaron Morton Endowed Fellowship, Children's Hospital of Philadelphia, University of Pennsylvania School of Medicine, 1999-2000; Best Doctors In America, 2003-04 **Published works:** Hoffman TM, Rhodes LA, Wieand TS, Spray TL, Bridges ND. Arrhythmias After Pediatric Lung Transplantation, Pediatric Transplantation, 2001;5(5):349-52; Fleenor JT, Hoffman TM, Bush DM, Paridon SM, Clark BJ, Spray TL, Bridges ND, Pneumatosis Intestinalis after Pediatric Thoracic Organ Transplant, Pediatrics, 2002;109(5):e78-8; book chapters, Hoffman TM, The Cardiology Laboratory, Clinical Handbook of Pediatrics, 2e Schwartz, Williams and Wilkins, Philadelphia, PA 1998; Hoffman TM, Rheumatic Fever. The 5 Minute Pediatric Consult, 3e Schwartz, Williams and Wilkins, Philadelphia, PA 2003 **Affiliations:** F.A.C.C.; A.H.A.; I.S.H.L.T. **SIC code:** 80 **Address:** Columbus Children's Hospital, Division of Pediatric Cardiology, 700 Children's Dr., Room 628 ED, Columbus, OH 43205-2664 **E-mail:** thoffman@chi.osu.edu

HOHN, DAVID C.
Industry: Healthcare **Born:** February 24, 1942, Tucson, Arizona **Univ./degree:** B.S., Chemistry, University of Illinois at Urbana, 1964; M.D., University of Illinois School of Medicine, 1970 **Current organization:** Roswell Park Cancer Institute **Title:** M.D., President, CEO **Type of organization:** Research institute **Major product:** Medical research **Area of distribution:** International **Area of Practice:** Cancer research **Published works:** 60-75 articles and book chapters **Affiliations:** Board Member, Roswell Park Alliance Foundation; Board Member, Roswell Park Cancer Institute **Hob./spts.:** Music, gardening, house restoration **SIC code:** 80 **Address:** Roswell Park Cancer Institute, Elm & Carlton, Buffalo, NY 14263 **E-mail:** david.hohn@roswellpark.org

HOLCOMB, LILLIAN P.
Industry: Mental Health **Born:** July, 15, 1944, Newport, Rhode Island **Univ./degree:** B.A., Elmira College, 1969; M.A.T., Cornell University, 1971; Ph.D., Syracuse University, 1974 **Current organization:** Lillian P. Holcomb, Ph.D. **Title:** Licensed Psychologist **Type of organization:** Psychologist's clinic **Major product:** Psychotherapy **Area of distribution:** Hawaii **Area of Practice:** Women, gender, minority issues, midlife, aging and disability crisis, poverty concerns **Honors/awards:** 1st Legally Blind Psychologist to sit for State Licensure Exam, 1979; Diplomate, Clinical Forensic Counseling, 2003; First psychological consultant during opening year of the women's prison in Kailua, 1977 **Published works:** Co-editor, "Women With Disabilities: Found Voices", 1993; 1 journal article, "Coping With Challenges; College Experiences of Older Women and Women with Disabilities in textbook "Variations on a Theme: Diversity and the Psychology of Women", SUNY Press, 1955; 1 article, "Disabled Women: A New Issue in Education" published in Journal of Rehabilitation, 1984 **Affiliations:** International Council of Psychologists; American Psychological Association (membership divisions on women, aging, religion, rehabilitation/disability); Association for Women in Psychology; Hawaii Psychological Association; Hawaii Island Psychologists' Association; Mental Health Association in Hawaii County; Charter Member, Prescribing Psychologists' Register; ASPPB Mobility Program-Senior Psychologists; American Academy of Pain Management **SIC code:** 80 **Address:** Lillian P. Holcomb, Ph.D., 190 Keawe St., Suite 15, Hilo, HI 96720

HOLFELNER, BARBARA A.
Industry: Healthcare **Born:** November 8, 1947, Philadelphia, Pennsylvania **Univ./degree:** M.S.N., Nursing, University of Pennsylvania, 1980 **Current organization:** Our Lady of Lourdes Medical Center **Title:** Vice President, Patient Care Services **Type of organization:** Medical center **Major product:** Patient care **Area of distribution:** New Jersey **Area of Practice:** Risk management, nursing **Honors/awards:** Sigma Theta Tau **Published works:** 2 articles **Affiliations:** American Organization of Nurse Executives; New Jersey State Nursing Association **Hob./spts.:** Golf, reading **SIC code:** 80 **Address:** Our Lady of Lourdes Medical Center, 1600 Haddon Ave., Camden, NJ 08103 **E-mail:** holfelnerb@lourdesnet.org

HONDA, YASUHIRO
Industry: Medical **Born:** January 7, 1964, Japan **Univ./degree:** M.D., Kyoto University, Faculty of Medicine, 1990 **Current organization:** Stanford University **Title:** M.D./Assistant Director, Cardiovascular Core Analysis Laboratory **Type of organization:** University **Major product:** Medical services **Area of distribution:** International **Area of Practice:** Cardiology **Published works:** 80+ articles **Affiliations:** American College of Cardiology **SIC code:** 80 **Address:** Stanford University, Dept. of Medicine, Div. of Cardiovascular Medicine, 300 Pasteur Dr., Room H3554, Stanford, CA 94305 **E-mail:** yshonda@crci.stanford.edu **Web address:** www.stanford.edu

HONG, JAMES W.
Industry: Healthcare **Born:** May 10, 1951, Baltimore, Maryland **Univ./degree:** B.A., Biological Sciences, University of Maryland, Baltimore County, 1973; M.S., Microbiology, University of Maryland at Baltimore, 1984 **Current organization:** Quest Diagnostics, Inc. **Title:** Manager, Microbiology, Virology, Molecular Biology

Type of organization: Private laboratory **Major product:** Clinical laboratory services **Area of distribution:** National **Area of Practice:** Infectious diseases **Honors/awards:** Corp., Best Practice Team, Largest Clinical Supplier in U.S. **Published works:** Hong, James W. and Austin P. Platt (1975), Critical Photoperiod and Daylength Threshold Differences Between Northern and Southern Populations of the Butterfly "Limenitis archippus, Journal of Insect Physiology", vol. 21, pp. 1159-1165; Hong J.W., Wagner L.G.: Comparison of Two Media for the Isolation of Corynebacterium JK. "Abstracts of the General Meeting of the American Society for Microbiology", May 1990; Yu, C., Turner, D., Lilli, H., Hong, J.: Antibiotic Susceptibility testing of Stenotrophomonas maltophilia with trimethoprim/sulfamethoxazole using the Phoenix System. "Abstracts of the European Congress of Clinical Microbiology and Infectious Diseases", March 1999; Wiles, T., Turner, D., Brasso, W., Hong, J., Reuben, J.: Rapid Antimicrobial Susceptibility Testing in Phoenix. "Abstracts of the General Meeting of the American Society for Microbiology", May 1999; Turner, D., Turng, B., Wiles, T., Hong, J., Reuben, J.: Detection of Gram-negative Resistance to Fluoroquinolone agents in the Phoenix Automated System. "Abstracts of the Interscience Conference on Antimicrobial agents and Chemotherapy", September 1999; Turng, B., Hong, J., Wulff, S., O'Rourke, S., Fischbein, K.: Detection of Gram-negative Resistance to Amino glycosides with Phoenix 100 System. "Abstracts of the European Congress of Clinical Microbiology and Infectious Diseases, May 2000 **Affiliations:** Consortium of Clinical Microbiologists; Central Pennsylvania Microbiology Association; American Society of Clinical Pathologists; American Society of Microbiology **Hob./spts.:** Travel, jogging, research education **SIC code:** 80 **Address:** Quest Diagnostics, Inc., 1901 Sulphur Spring Rd., Baltimore, MA 21227 **E-mail:** jamesw.hong@questdiagnostics.com

HOOK, JEANETTE L.
Industry: Healthcare **Born:** October 9, 1936, Kentucky **Univ./degree:** B.S.N., McKendree College, 1997 **Current organization:** White County Medical Center **Title:** Vice President Patient Services **Type of organization:** Hospital **Major product:** Patient care **Area of distribution:** Illinois **Area of Practice:** Administration **Affiliations:** I.O.N.L., I.N.A.; A.N.A.; Member, Rotary International **Hob./spts.:** Family, church, reading **SIC code:** 80 **Address:** White County Medical Center, 400 Plum St., Carmi, IL 62821 **E-mail:** grannyj404@yahoo.com

HORBELT, CARLTON V.
Industry: Healthcare **Born:** November 27, 1954, Galveston, Texas **Univ./degree:** D.D.S., University of Texas Dental Branch, 1981 **Current organization:** Arlington Developmental Center; University of Tennessee College of Dentistry in Memphis **Title:** DDS, FACD, FADPD, Diplomate, American Board of Special Care Dentistry **Type of organization:** Institutional/Educational **Major product:** Dental care **Area of distribution:** Tennessee **Area of Practice:** Special care dentistry **Honors/awards:** Harold Berk Award; Distinguished Practitioner-National Academy of Practice in Dentistry; Omicron Kappa Upsilon **Published works:** Published in Pediatric Dentistry Today, EP Magazine, InterFace, Special Care in Dentistry, Journal of the Greater Houston Dental Society **Affiliations:** ABSCD; SCD; ADPD; ACD; AADMD; NAP; SAID; ADA; IADH **SIC code:** 80 **Address:** Arlington Developmental Center, c/o Dental Clinic, P.O. Box 586, Arlington, TN 38002 **E-mail:** lucs@bellsouth.net

HOROVITZ, LEN
Industry: Healthcare **Univ./degree:** M.D., New York University School of Medicine, 1976 **Current organization:** Carnegie Medical, P.C. **Title:** M.D./Director **Type of organization:** Medical practice **Major product:** Patient care **Area of distribution:** New York **Area of Practice:** Board Certified, Internal Medicine; lung specialist **Affiliations:** Founding Member, Independent Doctors of New York **Hob./spts.:** Concert pianist; breeding African cichlids **SIC code:** 80 **Address:** Carnegie Medical, P.C., 47 E. 77th St., New York, NY 10021 **E-mail:** drlenhorowitz@aol.com

HORTON, KAREN M.
Industry: Medical **Univ./degree:** B.S., 1994; M.Sc., 1996, Queens University; M.D., University of Toronto, 2000 **Current organization:** University of Manitoba, Section of Plastic Surgery **Title:** Chief Resident, Plastic Surgery **Type of organization:** University hospital **Major product:** Medical services **Area of Practice:** Plastic surgery **Affiliations:** American Society of Plastic Surgery; Canadian Society of Plastic Surgery **SIC code:** 80 **Address:** 1658 Wellington Crescent, Winnipeg, MB R3NOB4, Canada **E-mail:** drkarenhorton@hotmail.com

HORTON, PHILIP A.
Industry: Healthcare **Born:** September 21, 1952, Rochester, New York **Univ./degree:** M.D., Medical College of Georgia, 1986; Residency, Internal Medicine 1986-89; Residency, Psychiatry 1989-92 **Current organization:** East Central Mental Health Center **Title:** Medical Director/Acting CEO **Type of organization:** County mental health center **Major product:** Patient care **Area of distribution:** Georgia **Area of Practice:** Internal medicine, psychiatry **Affiliations:** F.A.C.P.-A.S.I.M.; A.M.A.; Southern Medical Association; National Alliance for the Mentally Ill **Hob./spts.:** Automobiles, reading, writing (fiction) **SIC code:** 80 **Address:** East Central Mental Health Center, 3421 Mike Padgett Hwy., Augusta, GA 30906 **E-mail:** ltyson@bellsouth.net

HORVATH, ANNETTE
Industry: Healthcare **Born:** March 12, 1963, Bronx, New York **Univ./degree:** M.S., Health Services Administration, Iona College, New Rochelle, New York, 1999 **Current organization:** Excellent Home Care **Title:** CEO **Type of organization:** Certified home care agency **Major product:** Homecare services **Area of distribution:** New York **Area of Practice:** Homecare, operations, budgets, board meetings **Affiliations:** President, New York Chapter, Association for Nurses in Aides Care; Board Member, Vice Chairwoman, NYS Health Care Providers; Membership Committee, Women in Health Management **Hob./spts.:** Reading **SIC code:** 80 **Address:** 1508 Library Ave., Bronx, NY 10465 **E-mail:** ahorvath28@yahoo.com

HORVILLEUR, RENÉ
Industry: Healthcare - Dentistry **Born:** November 1, 1954, Logan, Utah **Univ./degree:** D.D.S., New York University and National University of Nicaragua **Current organization:** René Horvilleur, D.D.S. **Title:** Dentist **Type of organization:** Dental Office **Major product:** Dental care **Area of distribution:** US **Area of Practice:** Prosthodontics, Implant Dentistry **Honors/awards:** AIA - Honor for Exceptional Dedication, Implant Dentistry, 2002 **Affiliations:** A.D.A.; First District Dental Society of New York; International Congress of Oral Implantology; Sociedad Española of Dental Implantes **Hob./spts.:** Horseback riding **SIC code:** 80 **Address:** René Horvilleur, D.D.S., 420 Lexington Ave., Suite 228, New York, NY 10170 **E-mail:** rhorvilleur@onsiteaccess.com

HORWICH, MARK S.
Industry: Healthcare **Born:** March 3, 1942, Middletown, New York **Univ./degree:** M.D., Harvard University, 1967 **Current organization:** Mark S. Horwich, M.D. **Title:** M.D. **Type of organization:** Private practice **Major product:** Patient care **Area of distribution:** New York **Area of Practice:** Neurology **Published works:** Articles **Affiliations:** American Academy of Neurology; American Headache Society **Hob./spts.:** Golf, scuba diving **SIC code:** 80 **Address:** Mark S. Horwich, M.D., 523 E. 72nd St., New York, NY 10021 **E-mail:** mark.horwich.63@alum.dartmouth.org

HOTHERSALL, LORETTA A.
Industry: Healthcare **Born:** July 23, 1952, Brooklyn, New York **Univ./degree:** M.S.N., Simmons College **Current organization:** Maine Center for Endocrinology & Diabetes **Title:** Family Nurse Practitioner **Type of organization:** Ambulatory clinic (hospital associated) **Major product:** Healthcare delivery systems **Area of distribution:** Maine **Area of Practice:** Nursing/diabetes **Affiliations:** A.A.N.P.; P.C.N.A. **Hob./spts.:** Gardening, flower arrangements **SIC code:** 80 **Address:** Maine Center for Endocrinology & Diabetes, 100 US Route One, Suite 116, Scarborough, ME 04074

HOWELL, DORIS A.
Industry: Healthcare **Born:** December 2, 1923, Brooklyn, New York **Univ./degree:** M.D., McGill University, 1949 **Current organization:** University of California, San Diego **Title:** M.D./Professor Emeritus **Type of organization:** University hospital **Major product:** Patient care, research, medical education **Area of distribution:** San Diego, California **Area of Practice:** Pediatrics, hematology/oncology, women's healthcare **Published works:** Multiple articles **Affiliations:** F.A.P.S.; F.S.P.R.; F.A.A.P. **Hob./spts.:** Cooking, symphony music **SIC code:** 80 **Address:** 3890 Nobel Dr., Apt. 404, San Diego, CA 92122-5786 **E-mail:** poechsle@ucsd.edu

HTAIK, TUN T.
Industry: Medical **Born:** August 18, 1956, Burma **Univ./degree:** M.B., B.S., Institute of Medicine I, Ragoon; FRCSEd, Royal College of Surgeons of Edinburgh **Current organization:** Hahnemann University hospital **Title:** M.D. **Type of organization:** University hospital **Major product:** Medical services **Area of distribution:** Pennsylvania **Area of Practice:** Radiology **Hob./spts.:** Tennis, martial arts, soccer **SIC code:** 80 **Address:** Hahnemann University Hospital, 344 Avon Rd., #L338, Devon, PA 19333 **E-mail:** htaik@att.net

HUANG, MARK XIAOGU
Industry: Healthcare **Born:** February 27, 1956, Shanghai, China **Univ./degree:** M.D., Shanghai Second Medical University, 1982; Drexel University, 1992 **Current organization:** Advantage Medical Healthcare, LLC **Title:** M.D./Director/Owner **Type of organization:** Private practice **Major product:** Patient care **Area of distribution:** New York **Area of Practice:** Physical medicine and rehabilitation **Affiliations:** American Academy of Physical Medicine & Rehabilitation; American Academy of Pain Management; Attending Physician, M.S., NYU Downtown Hospital/NYU Rusk Institute of Rehabilitation Medicine **Hob./spts.:** Swimming, tennis, music, movies, travel **SIC code:** 80 **Address:** Advantage Medical Healthcare, LLC, 136-19 41st Ave., 4th floor & 5th floors, Flushing, NY 11355 **E-mail:** m.huang@email.com

HUANG, XUDONG
Industry: Healthcare **Born:** January 31, 1965, Fuzhou, China **Univ./degree:** M.S., Chemistry, Tufts University, 1990; Ph.D., Massachusetts Institute of Technology, 1995 **Current organization:** MGH/Harvard Medical School, Genetics & Aging Research Unit **Title:** Assistant Professor of Psychiatry **Type of organization:** Hospital **Major**

product: Research **Area of distribution:** Charlestown, Massachusetts **Area of Practice:** Aging and Neurological Disorders such as Alzheimer's Disease **Published works:** Research articles **Affiliations:** American Chemical Society; Society for Neuroscience; Sigma Xi; Phi Lambda Epsilon **Hob./spts.:** Flying, reading, golf, travel **SIC code:** 80 **Address:** MGH/Harvard Medical School, Genetics & Aging Research Unit, 114 16th St., Charlestown, MA 02129 **E-mail:** huangx@helix.mgh.harvard.edu

HUGHES, SYLVIA S.
Industry: Healthcare **Born:** June 18, 1954, Collins, Mississippi **Univ./degree:** B.S., Medical Technology, Southern University, 1978; M.Div., Counseling and Ministry, New Orleans Baptist Seminary **Current organization:** Memorial Hermann at S.W. Hospital **Title:** Microbiology Manager (for 6 hospitals) **Type of organization:** Medical center **Major product:** Patient care **Area of distribution:** Texas **Area of Practice:** Operations, quality assurance, quality control, training, MLT training program, teaching, laboratory management **Affiliations:** A.S.C.P. **Hob./spts.:** Singing, reading, gardening, sewing, floral design **SIC code:** 80 **Address:** Memorial Hermann at S.W. Hospital, 7600 Beechnut, 2nd floor Lab, Houston, TX 77074 **E-mail:** sylvia.hughes@memorialhermann.org **Web address:** www.memorialhermann.org

HUGHES, WANDA G.
Industry: Healthcare **Born:** March 8, 1954, Baton Rouge, Louisiana **Univ./degree:** M.S., Nursing Administration, Southeastern Louisiana University, 1991 **Current organization:** Baton Rouge General Hospital **Title:** Director, Performance Improvement **Type of organization:** Hospital **Major product:** Patient care **Area of distribution:** Louisiana **Area of Practice:** Nursing **Affiliations:** A.O.N.E.; I.A.J.C.S.C. **Hob./spts.:** Quilting, football **SIC code:** 80 **Address:** Baton Rouge General Hospital, 8590 Picardy Ave., Baton Rouge, LA 70809 **E-mail:** wanda_hughes@generalhealth.org

HULCHER, FRANK HOPE
Industry: Medical **Univ./degree:** Ph.D., Virginia Tech Institute, 1957 **Current organization:** Wake Forest University School of Medicine **Title:** Professor of Biochemistry (Retired) **Type of organization:** School of medicine **Major product:** Medical education, patient care **Area of distribution:** National **Area of Practice:** Biochemistry **Published works:** 55 papers, 1 patent **Affiliations:** A.C.B.C. **SIC code:** 80 **Address:** Wake Forest University School of Medicine, Medical Center Blvd., Biochemistry Dept., Winston Salem, NC 27103

HULETT, DONNA R.
Industry: Healthcare **Born:** July 13, 1952, Milan, Missouri **Univ./degree:** A.S., Trenton University, 1978 **Current organization:** Stover's Residential Care Facility **Title:** Owner/Operator **Type of organization:** Assisted living facility **Major product:** Assisted living and healthcare **Area of distribution:** Milan, Missouri **Area of Practice:** Care for senior citizens and persons with mental illness and/or behavioral problems **Honors/awards:** Business Woman of the Year, National Republican Association **Affiliations:** National Republican Association **Hob./spts.:** Bowling, hunting **SIC code:** 80 **Address:** Stover's Residential Care Facility, 520 E. Fifth St., Milan, MO 63556 **E-mail:** hulett@nemr.net

HUNT, ANDREA
Industry: Healthcare **Born:** March 31, 1955, Cincinnati, Ohio **Univ./degree:** Certified Legal Assistant, SUNY, 1981; L.P.N., Roanoke Memorial Hospital, 1982 **Current organization:** ABC Medical Reserve Corps. **Title:** Administrative Director **Type of organization:** Medical surge capacity **Major product:** Patient care **Area of distribution:** National **Area of Practice:** Designing programs, drafting employees (funded through homeland security) **Published works:** Lectures at the National Conference for the Medical Reserve Corps. **SIC code:** 80 **Address:** ABC Medical Reserve Corps., 1401 Blackburn Ave., Ashland, KY 41101 **E-mail:** ahunt@abcem.hunt

HUNTER, HELI M.
Industry: Healthcare **Born:** July 13, 1959, Tampere, Finland **Univ./degree:** B.S.N., University of Texas Medical Branch; M.S.N., Vanderbilt University **Current organization:** Advanced Neurosciences Institute **Title:** Nurse Practitioner **Type of organization:** Neurological institute **Major product:** Patient care **Area of distribution:** Tennessee **Area of Practice:** Multiple Sclerosis Certified Nurse **Affiliations:** International Organization of Multiple Sclerosis Nurses; Sigma Theta Tau **Hob./spts.:** Travel, reading **SIC code:** 80 **Address:** Advanced Neurosciences Institute, 4230 Harding Pike, Suite 605, Nashville, TN 57205

HURTADO, ANDREINA F.
Industry: Healthcare **Born:** November 5, 1964, Punto Fijo, Venezuela **Univ./degree:** M.D., Central University of Venezuela, 1995 **Current organization:** Miami Dade Health & Rehabilitation Services **Title:** Ophthalmologist **Type of organization:** Medical clinics **Major product:** Eye care **Area of distribution:** Miami, Florida **Area of Practice:** Eye physician **Affiliations:** American Academy of Ophthalmology; Venezuelan-American Medical Association; Florida Society of Opthalmology; American Medical Association **SIC code:** 80 **Address:** 1111 Brickell Ave., Suite 2650, Miami, FL 33131 **E-mail:** ahurt3@email.msn.com

HURTADO-LORENZO, ANDRES
Industry: Medical **Born:** March 3, 1972, Colombia **Univ./degree:** Ph.D., Molecular Medicine & Gene Therapy, University of Manchester, England **Current organization:** Massachusetts General Hospital/Harvard Medical School **Title:** Research Fellow in Medicine **Type of organization:** Research hospital/medial school **Major product:** Medical research **Area of distribution:** National **Area of Practice:** Molecular medicine, gene therapy, cell biology **Published works:** 8 publications **Affiliations:** American Society for Cell Biology; American Society of Gene Therapy; American Society for Biochemistry and Molecular Biology **Hob./spts.:** Salsa dancing, soccer, hiking **SIC code:** 80 **Address:** Massachusetts General Hospital/Harvard Medical School, Program in Membrane Biology & Renal Unit, Bldg. 149, 13th St., Renal Unit, 8th floor, Charlestown, MA 02129 **E-mail:** andres_hurtado-lorenzo@hms.harper.edu

HURWITZ, DENNIS J.
Industry: Healthcare **Born:** June 8, 1946, Baltimore, Maryland **Univ./degree:** B.S., Zoology, 1966; M.D., 1970, University of Maryland School of Medicine **Current organization:** Hurwitz Center for Plastic Surgery **Title:** M.D. **Type of organization:** Private practice **Major product:** Patient care **Area of distribution:** International **Area of Practice:** General and cosmetic surgery; national and international lecturing on body contouring after weight loss; Plastic Surgery (Board Certified) **Honors/awards:** Omicron Kappa Upsilon, National Dental Association, 2001 **Published works:** 125 articles, chapters and books including, "Total Body Lift" 2005 **Affiliations:** F.A.C.S.; A.S.P.S.; A.M.A.; Clinical Professor of Surgery, University of Pittsburgh **SIC code:** 80 **Address:** Hurwitz Center for Plastic Surgery, 3109 Forbes Ave., Suite 500, Pittsburgh, PA 15213 **E-mail:** drhurwitz@hurwitzcenter.com **Web address:** www.hurwitzcenter.com

HUSAR, WALTER G.
Industry: Healthcare **Born:** September 24, 1956, Jersey City, New Jersey **Univ./degree:** M.D., New Jersey Medical School at Newark, 1988 **Current organization:** Central Morris Neurology, P.A. **Title:** M.D./Vice President **Type of organization:** Medical facility **Major product:** Patient care **Area of distribution:** Denville, New Jersey **Area of Practice:** Neurology **Published works:** 6 research articles, 8 abstracts **Affiliations:** American Medical Association; American Academy of Neurology **SIC code:** 80 **Address:** Central Morris Neurology, P.A., 145 Diamond Spring Rd., Denville, NJ 07834 **E-mail:** whusar@optonline.net

HUSSAIN, HAMID
Industry: Healthcare **Univ./degree:** M.D., Khyber Medical College, Pakistan, 1987 **Current organization:** Suffolk Allergy & Asthma Center **Title:** M.D. **Type of organization:** Private medical practice **Major product:** Allergy, asthma treatment **Area of distribution:** New York **Area of Practice:** Allergy, sinusitis, asthma **Honors/awards:** Best Resident of the Year, 1991-1992 **Published works:** Co-authored: "Drug reactions and desensitization in AIDS", Immunology and Allergy Clinics of North America, 1997; 17:319-337; "Drug Reactions in HIV/AIDS", Western Journal of Medicine, 1997; 167(5):344; "Prevalence of food allergy in 137 latex-allergic patients", Allergy and Asthma Proceedings, 1999; 20:95-97 **Affiliations:** Stony Brook University Hospital **Hob./spts.:** Reading **SIC code:** 80 **Address:** Suffolk Allergy & Asthma Center, 620 Belle Terre Rd., Port Jefferson, NY 11777 **E-mail:** humza@dnamail.com

HUTCHEON, DAVID F.
Industry: Healthcare **Born:** August 12, 1947, Englewood, New Jersey **Univ./degree:** M.D., Columbia University **Current organization:** Grrazak, Tucker & Hutcheon M.D., P.A. **Title:** Physician/Partner **Type of organization:** Medical group practice **Major product:** Gastroenterology **Area of distribution:** Maryland, Virginia, Washington, D.C. **Area of Practice:** General gastroenterology **Affiliations:** Assistant Professor, Johns Hopkins University **Hob./spts.:** Wine collecting, skiing **SIC code:** 80 **Address:** Grrazak, Tucker & Hutcheon M.D., P.A., 10751 Falls Rd., Baltimore, MD 21093 **E-mail:** dhutche@jhmi.edu

HUTCHESON, ANNE L.
Industry: Healthcare **Univ./degree:** B.S., Microbiology, Mississippi University for Women, 1963; M.T.(ASCP), Emory University, 1964 **Current organization:** Delta Regional Medical Center **Title:** Micro Supervisor **Type of organization:** Hospital **Major product:** Patient care **Area of distribution:** Greenville, Mississippi **Area of Practice:** Microbiology, laboratory services **Affiliations:** American Society of Clinical Pathologists **SIC code:** 80 **Address:** 127 Wildwood Dr., Greenville, MS 38701 **E-mail:** ahutcheson@deltaregional.com **Web address:** www.deltaregional.com

HUTCHISON, BRUCE R.
Industry: Healthcare **Born:** May 26, 1954, Butler, Pennsylvania **Univ./degree:** D.D.S., Georgetown University, 1981 **Current organization:** Bruce R. Hutchison, D.D.S., P.C. **Title:** D.D.S. **Type of organization:** Private dental practice **Major product:** Patient care **Area of distribution:** Centerville, Virginia **Area of Practice:** Family dentistry **Honors/awards:** Fellow, I.N.C.D. **Affiliations:** President Elect, A.D.A.; F.I.N.C.D. **Hob./spts.:** Golf, skiing, shooting **SIC code:** 80 **Address:** Bruce R. Hutchison, D.D.S., P.C., 14245-P Centreville Square, Centreville, VA 20121 **E-mail:** bhutchdds@aol.com

HVIDDING, JOSEPH L.
Industry: Dentistry **Born:** September 5, 1951, Seattle, Washington **Univ./degree:** D.M.D., Fairleigh Dickinson Dental School **Current organization:** Joseph L. Hvidding, D.M.D., F.A.G.D., PA **Title:** Dentist **Type of organization:** Private dental practice **Major product:** Dental care **Area of distribution:** Regional **Area of Practice:** Restorative dentistry **Affiliations:** F.A.G.D.; A.C.D.N.A.; F.D.I.; O.K.U. **Hob./spts.:** Photography, mountain climbing **SIC code:** 80 **Address:** Joseph L. Hvidding, D.M.D., F.A.G.D., PA, 3100 Highway 138, Wall, NJ 07719 **E-mail:** newsmile@earthlink.net

IAKOVIDIS, PANAGIOTIS
Industry: Healthcare **Born:** July 12, 1959, Thessaloniki, Greece **Univ./degree:** M.D., University of Texas at Houston **Current organization:** Bond Clinic **Title:** M.D. **Type of organization:** Medical clinic **Major product:** Patient care **Area of distribution:** Florida **Area of Practice:** Vascular and thoracic surgery **Published works:** Multiple publications **Affiliations:** A.M.A.; F.M.A.; A.A.T.S. **Hob./spts.:** Writing poetry **SIC code:** 80 **Address:** Bond Clinic, 500 E. Central Ave., Winter Haven, FL 33880 **E-mail:** piakovidis@aol.com

IDEYI, STEVE C.
Industry: Healthcare **Univ./degree:** M.D., University of Nigeria, College of Medicine, 1988 **Current organization:** Bronx Lebanon Hospital/Albert Einstein College of Medicine, New York **Title:** M.D. **Type of organization:** Hospital/university **Major product:** Medical services **Area of distribution:** International **Area of Practice:** Radiology, surgery **Published works:** Articles **Affiliations:** A.M.A.; Radiologic Society of North America **Hob./spts.:** Soccer, tennis, swimming **SIC code:** 80 **Address:** Bronx-Lebanon Hospital/Albert Einstein College of Medicine, New York, 1650 Grand Concourse, Bronx, NY 10457 **E-mail:** stevechyke@hotmail.com

IGOE, PETER CHRISTOPHER
Industry: Healthcare **Born:** April 23, 1969, Patchogue, New York **Univ./degree:** D.D.S., Case Western Reserve University, 1995 **Current organization:** Peter C. Igoe, D.D.S. **Title:** D.D.S. **Type of organization:** Private practice **Major product:** Family and laser dentistry with orthodontics **Area of distribution:** Medina, New York **Area of Practice:** General dentistry, orthodontics, cosmetic and reconstructive surgery **Affiliations:** A.D.A.; A.G.D.; President, Orleans County Dental Society **Hob./spts.:** Golf, ice hockey, tennis **SIC code:** 80 **Address:** Peter C. Igoe, D.D.S., 511 West Ave., Medina, NY 14103 **Web address:** www.drigoe.com

INFANTINO, MICHAEL N.
Industry: Healthcare **Born:** April 6, 1954, Brooklyn, New York **Univ./degree:** M.D., State University of New York Downstate, 1981 **Current organization:** St. Vincent's Medical Center **Title:** Chief of Coronary Care Unit **Type of organization:** Medical center **Major product:** Patient care **Area of distribution:** New York **Area of Practice:** Cardiology **Published works:** Multiple articles **Affiliations:** F.A.C.C.; American Society of Eco Cardiology; Nuclear Cardiology Association **Hob./spts.:** Carpentry, gardening, golf **SIC code:** 80 **Address:** St. Vincent's Medical Center, 32 W. 18th St., New York, NY 10011 **E-mail:** minfan406@aol.com

INGENITO, ANTHONY C.
Industry: Healthcare **Born:** August 2, 1963, Paterson, New Jersey **Univ./degree:** M.D., University of Medicine & Dentistry of New Jersey, 1991 **Current organization:** Hackensack University Medical Center **Title:** Administrative Director **Type of organization:** Hospital **Major product:** Medical care **Area of distribution:** New Jersey **Area of Practice:** Radiation oncology **Affiliations:** American Medical Association; American Academy of Radiology; A.S.T.R.O.; Oncology Society of New Jersey. **Hob./spts.:** Jogging, physical fitness **SIC code:** 80 **Address:** Hackensack University Medical Center, 30 Prospect Ave., Dept. of Radiation & Oncology, Hackensack, NJ 07601 **E-mail:** aingenito@humed.com

INOYATOVA, INNA I.
Industry: Healthcare **Born:** July 26, 1962, Moscow, Russia **Univ./degree:** M.D., Moscow Medical University, 1985 **Current organization:** Professional Medical Plaza **Title:** M.D. **Type of organization:** Medical clinic **Major product:** Patient care **Area of distribution:** Brooklyn, New York **Area of Practice:** Board Certified, Internal Medicine, 2000 **Published works:** 12 articles **Affiliations:** A.M.A.; Lutheran Medical Center; Maimondes Medical Center; Beth Israel Medical Center **SIC code:** 80 **Address:** Professional Medical Plaza, 2269 Ocean Ave., Brooklyn, NY 11229 **E-mail:** slavinigor@hotmail.com

IPPOLITO-FATA, JUSTINE P.
Industry: Healthcare **Born:** January 2, 1966, Bronx, New York **Univ./degree:** B.S.M., Cum Laude, Chemistry, Fordham University, 1987; D.D.S., Georgetown University School of Dentistry, 1990 **Current organization:** Victoria Dental Center **Title:** Dentist/Owner **Type of organization:** Private practice **Major product:** Patient care **Area of distribution:** Bronx, New York **Area of Practice:** Pediatric to geriatric general dentistry **Honors/awards:** Award for Outstanding Service to Patients with High Risk Status, United Bronx Parents Association, 1996 **Affiliations:** A.D.A.; Academy of General Dentistry; American Academy of Oral Medicine; Director of Dentistry, Murray Weigel Hall Nursing Home, Fordham University **SIC code:** 80 **Address:** Victoria Dental Center, 2466 Arthur Ave., Bronx, NY 10458 **E-mail:** vdc94@aol.com

IQBAL, ATIF
Industry: Medical/research **Born:** December 31, 1979 **Univ./degree:** M.D., King Edward Medical College **Current organization:** University of Missouri - Columbia, Dept. of Surgery **Title:** M.D. **Type of organization:** University hospital **Major product:** Patient care, medical education, research **Area of distribution:** National **Area of Practice:** General surgery, research **Honors/awards:** 4 times in the Top 3 Position, Toastmasters International **Published works:** 10 journal articles **Affiliations:** A.C.S.; A.M.A.; A.A.A.S.; M.S.M.A. **Hob./spts.:** Reading, playing cricket **SIC code:** 80 **Address:** University of Missouri - Columbia, Dept. of Surgery, 1 Hospital Dr., Columbia, MO 65212 **E-mail:** iqbalat@health.missouri.edu **Web address:** www.surgery.missouri.edu

IQBAL, SHAMAH QASIM
Industry: Healthcare **Born:** December 3, 1952, Kashmir, India **Univ./degree:** M.D., University of Kashmir, 1976 **Current organization:** Interfaith Medical Center **Title:** Attending Pathologist **Type of organization:** Medical center **Major product:** Patient care **Area of distribution:** Brooklyn, New York **Area of Practice:** Pathology **Hob./spts.:** Knitting, needlework **SIC code:** 80 **Address:** Interfaith Medical Center, 555 Prospect Place, Brooklyn, NY 11238

IRANI, ADIL NOSHIR
Industry: Medical **Born:** April 11, 1969, Bombay, India **Univ./degree:** M.B.B.S., Krishna Institute of Medical Science, India, 1992 **Current organization:** University of Southern California and Los Angeles County **Title:** M.D. **Type of organization:** University hospital **Major product:** Patient care, research, education **Area of distribution:** Glendale, California **Area of Practice:** Cardiology, internal medicine **Honors/awards:** Best Outgoing Resident of the Year, Internal Medicine Program of L. A. County and University of Southern California Medical Center; In top decile of the Country in Board Certification exam, American Board of Internal Medicine **Published works:** 10 articles, 10 abstracts, published research work in medical journals and presented at international forums **Affiliations:** A.C.C.; A.H.A.; S.C.C.M.; A.M.A.; A.C.P.; Association of Physicians of India; American Board of Internal Medicine **Hob./spts.:** Cricket, ping-pong, physical fitness **SIC code:** 80 **Address:** 1630 Calle Vaquero, Apt. 201, Glendale, CA 81206 **E-mail:** adilirani@hotmail.com

IRIZARRY-PEREZ, LUIS A.
Industry: Healthcare **Born:** June 9, 1922, Ponce, Puerto Rico **Univ./degree:** M.D., University of Arkansas **Current organization:** Luis A. Irizarry-Perez **Title:** M.D. **Type of organization:** Private practice **Major product:** Patient care and house calls **Area of distribution:** Ponce, Puerto Rico **Area of Practice:** Family medicine **Published works:** Column, Family Medicine, published in "Perla del Sur", Colegio Cirujano de Puerto Rico, Academia Medica del Sur **Affiliations:** A.M.A.; International College of Physicians and Surgeons **Hob./spts.:** Jogging, running, writing (urban forestry, conservation of trees), oil painting collection **SIC code:** 80 **Address:** Mendez Vigo #63-B, P.O. Box 7684, Ponce, PR 00732

ISAACS, JEFFREY D.
Industry: Healthcare **Born:** December 14, 1946, Johannesburg, South Africa **Univ./degree:** M.D., University of Witwatersrand, South Africa, 1971 **Current organization:** Southwest Hematology Oncology P.C. **Title:** President/Oncologist **Type of organization:** Group practice **Major product:** Patient care **Area of distribution:** Phoenix, Arizona **Area of Practice:** Oncology, hematology **Honors/awards:** Nominated, Top Oncologist in the Phoenix, Arizona area **Published works:** "Proceedings of the National Academy of Science" **Affiliations:** A.S.H.; A.S.C.O; A.S.N.O. **Hob./spts.:** Art, theatre **SIC code:** 80 **Address:** Southwest Hematology Oncology P.C., 10565 N. Tatum Blvd., Suite B116, Paradise Valley, AZ 85253

ISAYEVA, ELEONORA
Industry: Healthcare **Born:** September 19, 1939, Russia **Univ./degree:** M.D., New York College of Osteopathic Medicine, 1998 **Current organization:** Dr. E. Isayeva Service **Title:** M.D. **Type of organization:** Private practice **Major product:** Patient care **Area of distribution:** Manalapan, New Jersey **Area of Practice:** Pediatric care **Published works:** 100+ articles **Affiliations:** A.A.P; A.M.A.; A.O.A. **Hob./spts.:** Travel, theatre **SIC code:** 80 **Address:** Dr. E. Isayeva Service, 224 Taylors Mills Rd., Manalapan, NJ 07726 **E-mail:** goldshmid-isayeva@msn.com

ISKANDER, SHERIF SAAD
Industry: Healthcare **Born:** October 10, 1963, Alexandria, Egypt **Univ./degree:** M.D., Alexandria University, 1990 **Current organization:** Cardiovascular Associates of East Texas **Title:** M.D. **Type of organization:** Medical center **Major product:** Patient care **Area of distribution:** National **Area of Practice:** Cardiology, research and development, clinical management, therapeutic methodologies focusing on nuclear cardiology **Published works:** Articles, journals **Affiliations:** S.E.C.; A.C.C.; S.N.C. **Hob./spts.:**

Tennis, golf, reading, church activities **SIC code:** 80 **Address:** Cardiovascular Associates of East Texas, 1505 Grande Blvd., #103, Tyler, TX 75703 **E-mail:** sssiskander@yahoo.com

ISSA, EBRAHIM S.
Industry: Healthcare **Born:** India **Univ./degree:** M.D., Marathwada University, India, 1981 **Current organization:** North Jersey Heart P.A. **Title:** M.D. **Type of organization:** Medical practice **Major product:** Patient care **Area of distribution:** National **Area of Practice:** Cardiology **Honors/awards:** Nominated Best Student, Class of 1976, India **Affiliations:** Board Member, Kenya, Mombasa, F.A.C.C.; **Hob./spts.:** Travel **SIC code:** 80 **Address:** 205 Sunrise Ct., River Vale, NJ 07675 **E-mail:** njheart@optonline.net

IVAN, MIRCEA
Industry: Medical **Univ./degree:** M.D., University of Medicine & Pharmacy, Romania, 1993; Ph.D., Cancer Research, University of Wales College of Medicine, 1997 **Current organization:** Tufts - New England Medical Center **Title:** M.D., Ph.D. **Type of organization:** University/hospital **Major product:** Medical services **Area of distribution:** National **Area of Practice:** Cancer biology, research **Honors/awards:** AACR Award for Pancreatic Cancer Research 2005-07 **Published works:** 18 publications **Affiliations:** A.A.C.R.; A.A.A.S. **SIC code:** 80 **Address:** Dana-Farber Cancer Institute/Harvard Medical School, 44 Binney St., Mayer 455, Boston, MA 02115 **E-mail:** mivan@tufts-nemc.org

IZIMA, NDUBISI E.
Industry: Healthcare **Born:** December 28, 1950 **Univ./degree:** D.O., Michigan State University, 1983 **Current organization:** Abby & Izima, D.O., P.C. **Title:** D.O. **Type of organization:** Private practice **Major product:** Patient care **Area of distribution:** Michigan **Area of Practice:** Internal medicine, gastroenterology **Affiliations:** A.M.A.; A.O.A **SIC code:** 80 **Address:** Abby & Izima, D.O., P.C., 1931 Horton Rd., Suite 12, Jackson, MI 49203

JACA, IGNACIO J.
Industry: Medical **Born:** November 6, 1968, San Juan, Puerto Rico **Univ./degree:** M.D., New York Medical College, 1995 **Current organization:** University of Miami **Title:** M.D. **Type of organization:** University **Major product:** Medical services **Area of distribution:** Florida **Area of Practice:** Gastroenterology **Honors/awards:** Alpha Omega Alpha Honor's society **Affiliations:** A.G.A.; A.S.G.E.; A.M.A. **Hob./spts.:** Basketball, baseball, reading **SIC code:** 80 **Address:** 1500 Bay Rd., #1158, Miami Beach, FL 33139 **E-mail:** ignaciojjaca@cs.com

JACKSON, EVERN N.
Industry: Medical **Born:** August 3, 1978, Richmond, Virginia **Univ./degree:** A.A., Radiology Technology, Delaware Technical Community College, 2001 **Current organization:** Hospital of the University of Pennsylvania **Title:** MRI Technologist **Type of organization:** University hospital **Major product:** Patient care, diagnostic imaging **Area of distribution:** Pennsylvania **Area of Practice:** Imaging technology **Hob./spts.:** Dancing **SIC code:** 80 **Address:** Hospital of the University of Pennsylvania, 3400 Spruce St., Philadelphia, PA 19104

JACKSON, KRISTIN M.
Industry: Healthcare **Born:** September 20, 1971, Philadelphia, Pennsylvania **Univ./degree:** M.D., Hahnemann University, 1997 **Current organization:** GCSF OB/GYN Associates **Title:** M.D. **Type of organization:** Private medical practice **Major product:** Patient care **Area of distribution:** Pennsylvania **Area of Practice:** Ob/Gyn **Honors/awards:** Rosenfield Research Award, 2000; Rebecca Hoague Award, 2001; Outstanding Resident **Affiliations:** A.C.O.G.; A.M.A.; P.M.D. **Hob./spts.:** Scuba diving, cooking **SIC code:** 80 **Address:** GCSF OB/GYN Associates, 2300 Computer Rd., E-25, Willow Grove, PA 19001 **E-mail:** jjax4@hotmail.com

JACKSON, LARRY
Industry: Healthcare **Born:** February 23, 1941, Connersville, Indiana **Current organization:** Veterans Affairs Medical Center **Title:** Chief, Supply, Processing and Distributing **Type of organization:** Hospital **Major product:** Patient care **Area of distribution:** National **Area of Practice:** Sterile processing **Hob./spts.:** Church activities **SIC code:** 80 **Address:** Veterans Affairs Medical Center, 4100 W. Third St., Mailstop 90E, Dayton, OH 45428 **E-mail:** larry.jackson@med.va.gov

JACKSON, THERESA A.
Industry: Healthcare **Born:** January 29, 1953, Pontiac, Michigan **Current organization:** Heartland Health Care **Title:** P.C.C./L.P.N. **Type of organization:** Healthcare provider **Major product:** Home healthcare **Area of distribution:** Michigan **Area of Practice:** Licensed Practical Nurse; coordinating patient care, wound care, motivational speaking, training and development **Honors/awards:** Wound Care Certified, 2005 **Hob./spts.:** Horses, gardening, birds **SIC code:** 80 **Address:** Heartland Health Care, 1058 Coleman St., Ypsilanti, MI 48198-6308

JACKSON, TINA MARIE
Industry: Healthcare **Born:** December 23, 1961, Paragould, Arkansas **Univ./degree:** R.N., Arkansas State University **Current organization:** NEA Medical Center **Title:** R.N./House Supervisor **Type of organization:** Community hospital **Major product:** Patient care **Area of distribution:** Jonesboro, Arkansas **Area of Practice:** Intensive care nursing and supervisory **Affiliations:** A.A.C.N. **Hob./spts.:** Spending time with family, decorating, fishing, duck hunting **SIC code:** 80 **Address:** NEA Medical Center, 3024 Stadium Blvd., Jonesboro, AR 72401 **E-mail:** tinaj@grnco.net

JACOB, ROJYMON
Industry: Medical **Born:** Trivandrum, Kerala **Univ./degree:** M.D., University of Kerala, 1990 **Current organization:** University of California, Davis **Title:** M.D., F.R.C.R. **Type of organization:** University cancer center **Major product:** Patient care, medical education **Area of distribution:** International **Area of Practice:** Radiation oncology, clinical research **Published works:** 30 peer reviewed articles **Affiliations:** American Society of Radiological Oncologists; European Society of Radiological Oncologists; A.R.O.I.; U.I.C.C.; Royal College of Radiologists **Hob./spts.:** Hiking, photography **SIC code:** 80 **Address:** University of California, Davis, 4501 X Street, Sacramento, CA 95834 **E-mail:** rojymon.jacob@ucdmc.ucdavis.edu

JACOBS, IAN N.
Industry: Healthcare **Born:** May 13, 1960, Yonkers, New York **Univ./degree:** M.D., Mt Sinai Medical School, 1986 **Current organization:** Children's Surgical Associates **Title:** Assistant Professor of Otolaryngology-Head and Neck Surgery **Type of organization:** Academic practice **Major product:** Ear, nose and throat care for children **Area of distribution:** Pennsylvania and New Jersey **Area of Practice:** Pediatric Otolaryngology **Affiliations:** A.S.P.O.; A.M.A.; A.B.E.A. **Hob./spts.:** Tri-athlete, weightlifting **SIC code:** 80 **Address:** Children's Surgical Associates, Ltd., First floor (Wood Bldg.), 34th St. & Civic Center Blvd., Philadelphia, PA 19104 **E-mail:** jacobsi@email.chop.edu

JACOBS, MARY KATHRYN
Industry: Healthcare **Born:** October 20, 1947, Sioux City, Iowa **Univ./degree:** R.N., Methodist Hospital School of Nursing, 1968 **Current organization:** Avera McKennan **Title:** Safety Officer **Type of organization:** Hospital **Major product:** Acute and long term care, behavioral health and ambulatory care and clinics **Area of distribution:** South Dakota, Iowa, Minnesota, Nebraska **Area of Practice:** Nursing management, safety **Affiliations:** A.S.H.E., 1999-present; A.A.O.H.N., 2002 **Hob./spts.:** Reading mystery stories, golf, gardening **SIC code:** 80 **Address:** Avera McKennan, 800 E. 21st St., Sioux Falls, SD 57117 **E-mail:** kathy.jacobs@mckennan.org

JACOBSON, DONALD M.
Industry: Healthcare **Born:** June 23, 1955, Chicago, Illinois **Univ./degree:** B.S., M.S., German Literature, Northeastern University, 1977; M.D., Vanderbilt University School of Medicine, 1981 **Current organization:** Donald M. Jacobson, MD, SC **Title:** Psychiatrist **Type of organization:** Solo practice and correctional facility **Major product:** Mental healthcare **Area of distribution:** Illinois **Area of Practice:** Affective and anxiety disorders, mood disorders **Affiliations:** Racine Youth Offenders Correctional Facility **Hob./spts.:** Foreign languages, music, reading **SIC code:** 80 **Address:** Donald M. Jacobson, MD, SC, 3701 Durand Ave., Suite 325, Racine, WI 53405 **E-mail:** djacobson6@wi.rr.com

JACOBSON, LAWRENCE M.
Industry: Healthcare **Born:** November 5, 1962, Boston, Massachusetts **Univ./degree:** M.D., Tuffs University, 1991 **Current organization:** Comprehensive Eye Care **Title:** M.D. **Type of organization:** Private practice **Major product:** Patient eye care **Area of distribution:** New York, New York **Area of Practice:** Ophthalmology **Honors/awards:** Research Grant, 1995 **Published works:** American Journal of Ophthalmology **Affiliations:** A.A.O.; A.R.V.O.; C.L.A.O.; President & Medical Director, Governor's Hospital **Hob./spts.:** Computers, sailing, hockey **SIC code:** 80 **Address:** Comprehensive Eye Care, 107 W. 82nd St., Suite 108, New York, NY 10024 **E-mail:** ljacob@gte.net

JACQUIN, KIMBERLY A.
Industry: Healthcare **Born:** September 7, 1977, Washington, Missouri **Univ./degree:** D.C., Logan College of Chiropractic, 2003 **Current organization:** Franklin County Chiropractic **Title:** D.C. **Type of organization:** Medical office **Major product:** Chiropractic care **Area of distribution:** Union, Missouri **Area of Practice:** Muscle work, acupuncture, activator, diversified **Hob./spts.:** Running **SIC code:** 80 **Address:** Franklin County Chiropractic, 1004 Vondera Ave., Bldg. 2, Suite 204, Union, MO 63084

JAEGER, ROBERT M.
Industry: Healthcare **Born:** June 1, 1969, Queens, New York **Univ./degree:** B.S., Biology, Queens College, 1991; D.O., New York College of Osteopathic Medicine, 1996 **Current organization:** Robert M. Jaeger, D.O. **Title:** D.O. **Type of organization:** Private practice **Major product:** Patient care **Area of distribution:** New York

Area of Practice: Family practice **Affiliations:** A.A.F.P.; A.O.A.; A.C.O.P.; Suffolk Medical Society **Hob./spts.:** Baseball, tennis, Star Trek **SIC code:** 80 **Address:** Robert M. Jaeger, D.O., 126 E. Main St., East Islip, NY 11730

JALAL, PRASUN K.
Industry: Healthcare **Univ./degree:** M.D., Institute of Medical Education and Research, India, 1994 **Current organization:** Long Island Jewish Hospital **Title:** M.D. **Type of organization:** Hospital **Major product:** Patient care **Area of distribution:** New York **Area of Practice:** Gastroenterology **Affiliations:** A.M.A.; American Gastroenterological Association; American College of Gastroenterology **Hob./spts.:** Travel **SIC code:** 80 **Address:** Long Island Jewish Hospital, 27005 76th Ave., New Hyde Park, NY 11040 **E-mail:** pkjalal@msn.com

JALALI, ZIBA
Industry: Healthcare **Born:** March 13, 1973, Tehran, Iran **Univ./degree:** M.D., 1997; Ph.D., 1998, University of Cologne, Germany **Current organization:** Montefiore Medical Center **Title:** M.D. **Type of organization:** Hospital **Major product:** Patient care **Area of distribution:** New York **Area of Practice:** Infectious diseases, HIV medicine **Published works:** 7 publications including, Co-author, "Apoptosis: pathophysiology and therapeutic implications for the cardiovascular surgeon", Ann.Thorac.Surg. 2004, 78(3):1109-1118; "Should we offer operative management to the septuagenarians and octogenarians with acute type A aortic dissection?", Chest 2002, 122(4):111S; "Cardiocyte apoptosis in congestive heart failure: what are the implications for the cardiovascular surgeons?", Chest 2002, 122(4):125S **Affiliations:** I.D.S.A.; A.M.A.; A.C.P./A.S.I.M. **Hob./spts.:** Painting, music-guitar **SIC code:** 80 **Address:** Montefiore Medical Center, 111 E. 20th St., Bronx, NY 10467 **E-mail:** zibajalali@yahoo.com

JALIL, QAMAR
Industry: Healthcare **Univ./degree:** M.D., King Edward Medical College at Lahore, Pakistan, 1970 **Current organization:** Central Dupage Health **Title:** M.D. **Type of organization:** Hospital/clinic **Major product:** Patient care **Area of distribution:** Illinois **Area of Practice:** Internal medicine **Affiliations:** A.M.A.; Dupage Medical Society **Hob./spts.:** Reading **SIC code:** 80 **Address:** Central Dupage Health, 1130 W. Stearns Rd., Bartlett, IL 60103 **E-mail:** qamar_jalil@cdh.org

JAMES, TERRANCE A.
Industry: Healthcare **Born:** August 9, 1959, Mobile, Alabama **Current organization:** PA Hospital **Title:** Mechanical Systems Specialist **Type of organization:** Hospital **Major product:** Patient care, emergency services **Area of distribution:** Ardmore, Pennsylvania **Area of Practice:** Engineering **SIC code:** 80 **Address:** 2710 Chestnut Ave., Ardmore, PA 19003 **E-mail:** tjames9838@aol.com

JAN, M. FUAD
Industry: Medical **Born:** May 9, 1974, India **Univ./degree:** M.D., 2000, GMC, Srinagar **Current organization:** Drexel University **Title:** Assistant Professor of Medicine **Type of organization:** University **Major product:** Patient care, medical education **Area of distribution:** Wyndmoor, Pennsylvania **Area of Practice:** Internal medicine **Affiliations:** A.M.A.; A.C.P.; S.G.I.M. **Hob./spts.:** Poetry, politics, cricket, soccer **SIC code:** 80 **Address:** Drexel University, 8765 Duveen Dr., Wyndmoor, PA 19038 **E-mail:** fuadfehmi@rediffmail.com

JANES, JANET E.
Industry: Medical **Current organization:** Owens Medical College **Title:** Professor (Retired from Medical College of Ohio Hospital) **Type of organization:** Hospital/community college **Major product:** Medical services **Area of distribution:** Ohio **Area of Practice:** Administration, education, operating room, sterile processing **Affiliations:** Governor's Commission of Nursing; President, A.O.R.N.; Member, Board of Regents **Hob./spts.:** Gardening **SIC code:** 80 **Address:** 3278 Cragmoor Ave., Toledo, OH 43614 **E-mail:** hayden1@buckeye-express.com

JANI, SUSHMA
Industry: Healthcare **Born:** September 26, 1959, India **Univ./degree:** M.D., B.J. Medical College, India 1983 **Current organization:** Riverside Hospital **Title:** Medical Director **Type of organization:** Hospital **Major product:** Psychiatry **Area of distribution:** Washington, D.C. **Area of Practice:** Child and adolescent psychiatry **Honors/awards:** Best Teacher Award; Muncie Award; Americas Top Pediatricians 2002-2003; Who's Who Worldwide **Affiliations:** A.M.A.; A.P.A. **Hob./spts.:** Reading, cooking, travel, knitting, swimming **SIC code:** 80 **Address:** Riverside Hospital, 4460 MacArthur Blvd., Washington, DC 20007 **E-mail:** sushmajani@hotmail.com

JARSTAD, JOHN S.
Industry: Healthcare **Born:** September 7, 1955, Seattle, Washington **Univ./degree:** M.D., University of Washington, 1984 **Current organization:** Evergreen Eye Centers, Inc. **Title:** President/CEO **Type of organization:** Private medical practice **Major product:** Cataract, retina and laser eye surgery **Area of distribution:** Federal Way, Washington **Area of Practice:** Laser vision correction **Honors/awards:** Lecturing Medal from the University of Indonesia, 1995; Outstanding Instructor, Mayo Clinic, 1987; Humanitarian of the Year, Washington Academy of Eye Physicians and Surgeons, 2001 **Published works:** Ophthalmology Management; Ocular Surgery News **Affiliations:** A.M.A.; A.S.C.R.S.; President, W.A.E.P.S.; A.A.O. **Hob./spts.:** Skiing, fishing **SIC code:** 80 **Address:** Evergreen Eye Centers, Inc., 34719 Sixth Ave. South, Federal Way, WA 98003 **E-mail:** drjarstad@aol.com **Web address:** www.evergreeneyecenter.com

JASZCZAK, STANLEY E.
Industry: Healthcare **Born:** July 10, 1933, Seroczyn, Poland **Univ./degree:** M.D., 1959; Ph.D., 1964, University of Warsaw, Poland **Current organization:** Metro Medical Practice **Title:** M.D., Clinical Associate Professor **Type of organization:** Group practice **Major product:** Patient care **Area of distribution:** International **Area of Practice:** Ob/gyn, reproductive physiology, congenital abnormalities of the central nervous system **Published works:** 100 articles, 11 book chapters **Affiliations:** F.A.C.O.G. **Hob./spts.:** Travel, reading **SIC code:** 80 **Address:** Metro Medical Practice, 34770 Dequinore, Sterling Heights, MI 48310

JEAN-BAPTISTE, DEMESVAR A.
Industry: Healthcare **Born:** January 3, 1973 **Univ./degree:** M.D., State University of New York, 1998 **Current organization:** St. Francis Center for Advanced Weight Loss **Title:** M.D. **Type of organization:** Medical center **Major product:** Patient care **Area of distribution:** New Jersey **Area of Practice:** Bariatric surgery, laparoscopic surgery **Hob./spts.:** Tennis, IT **SIC code:** 80 **Address:** St. Francis Center for Advanced Weight Loss, 1345 Kuser Rd., Suite 1, Trenton, NJ 08619

JEAN-JACQUES, ANTHONY
Industry: Healthcare **Born:** May 13, 1938, Haiti **Univ./degree:** M.D., State University of Haiti, 1964 **Current organization:** Polk Family Clinic **Title:** M.D. **Type of organization:** Medical practice **Major product:** Patient care **Area of distribution:** Florida **Area of Practice:** Board Certified, general surgery and family practice **Affiliations:** F.A.C.S.; A.M.A. **Hob./spts.:** Soccer **SIC code:** 80 **Address:** Polk Family Clinic, 1263 E. Main St., Bartow, FL 33830

JEANLOUIE, ODLER R.
Industry: Healthcare **Born:** Port-au-Prince, Haiti **Univ./degree:** M.D., State University of Haiti, 1985 **Current organization:** The Health Institute **Title:** Medical Director **Type of organization:** Medical institute **Major product:** Patient care and health education **Area of distribution:** Essex County, New Jersey **Area of Practice:** Internal medicine, nephrology, hypertension, critical care **Affiliations:** A.M.A.; A.S.N.; S.C.C.M.; A.C.P. **Hob./spts.:** Travel, photography, creative writing **SIC code:** 80 **Address:** The Health Institute, 60 Northfield Ave., West Orange, NJ 07051 **Phone:** (973)731-1919 **Fax:** (973)731-0408 **E-mail:** ojeanlouie2@medscape.com **Web address:** www.medcross.com

JEANNITON, EVELYNE M.
Industry: Healthcare **Born:** December 27, 1946, Haiti **Univ./degree:** M.D., Grace University, St. Kitts, W.I.; Ph.D., La Salle University, 1987 **Current organization:** Health & Hospital Corp./CHS and USAR **Title:** Healthcare Assessor/Coordinator **Type of organization:** Healthcare provider and assessor **Major product:** Assessor of care to inmates, Provider of healthcare to soldiers in the United States Army Reserve **Area of distribution:** New York **Area of Practice:** Healthcare administration, management, coordinator of psychotherapy, drug counseling and coordinates physical rehabilitation to athletes (colleges, institutions) **Affiliations:** L.T.C. U.S.A.R.; Community affiliation: Executive Director, Military Women & Friends (501C3) **Hob./spts.:** Gardening, community service to homeless veterans **SIC code:** 80 **Address:** 213-34 28th Ave., Bayside, NY 11360

JEEVANANDAM, VALLUVAN
Industry: Medical **Univ./degree:** M.D., Columbia University, 1984 **Current organization:** University of Chicago Section of Cardiac & Thoracic Surgery **Title:** M.D. **Type of organization:** University **Major product:** Patient care, medical education **Area of distribution:** Chicago, Illinois **Area of Practice:** Cardiac surgery **Affiliations:** A.H.A.; S.T.S.; A.A.T.S. **Hob./spts.:** Tennis, jogging **SIC code:** 80 **Address:** University of Chicago Section of Cardiac & Thoracic Surgery, 5812 S. Ellis Avenue, Chicago, IL 60637 **E-mail:** jeevan@surgery.bsd.uchicago.edu

JENKINS, FLORENCE B.
Industry: Healthcare **Born:** March 26, Africa **Univ./degree:** L.P.N., HMI Regency School of Practical Nursing **Title:** LPN **Major product:** Patient care **Area of distribution:** Philadelphia, Pennsylvania **Hob./spts.:** Reading **SIC code:** 80 **Address:** 2635 S. 70th St., Philadelphia, PA 19142 **E-mail:** florencebabyjenkins@yahoo.com

JENKINS, JERRY H.
Industry: Healthcare **Born:** June 9, 1968, Irving, Texas **Univ./degree:** M.D., Utah State University, 1994 **Current organization:** Jerry H. Jenkins, M.D., P.A. **Title:** M.D. **Type of organization:** Family practice **Major product:** Patient care **Area of distribution:** Lufkin, Texas **Area of Practice:** Family medicine **Affiliations:** A.A.F.P.;

T.A.F.P.; A.M.A.; T.M.A. **Hob./spts.:** Physical fitness, bicycling, bird hunting **SIC code:** 80 **Address:** Jerry H. Jenkins, M.D., P.A., 1105 W. Frank St., Suite 290, Lufkin, TX 75904 **E-mail:** jjenkinsmd@consolidated.net

JENKINS, TESSY CHINYERE
Industry: Healthcare **Born:** April 16, 1961, Portharcourt, Nigeria **Univ./degree:** M.D., University of Jos Nigeria, 1984 **Current organization:** Henry Ford Hospital **Title:** M.D. **Type of organization:** Hospital **Major product:** Patient care **Area of distribution:** Detroit, Michigan **Area of Practice:** Neurology, epileptology **Honors/awards:** Scholarship from the Federal Government of Nigeria, 1973; Vice President of Medical Students Association; Residence Teaching Excellence Award, 1994; Diplomate of the American Board of Psychiatry and Neurology, 1999 **Affiliations:** A.M.A.; A.A.N.; A.E.S.; Henry Ford Alumni Association **Hob./spts.:** Gardening, swimming, walking **SIC code:** 80 **Address:** Henry Ford Hospital, 2799 West Grand Blvd., Detroit, MI 48202 **E-mail:** jenkinst@pol.net

JENKINS LEE, AUDREY
Industry: Healthcare **Born:** April 9, 1958, Waynesboro, Georgia **Univ./degree:** M.S.H.C., Central Michigan University, 1994 **Current organization:** Eisenhower Army Medical Center **Title:** Senior MRI Technologist, RT(R) (MR) (CT) **Type of organization:** Hospital **Major product:** Patient care **Area of distribution:** Georgia **Area of Practice:** MRI technology **Affiliations:** A.R.R.T. **Hob./spts.:** Sightseeing, travel, gardening **SIC code:** 80 **Address:** 3207 Cheshire Dr., Augusta, GA 30906 **E-mail:** magneticmrs2003@yahoo.com

JENSON, ROBERT D.
Industry: Healthcare **Born:** September 22, 1961, Dubuque, Iowa **Univ./degree:** B.S., Clinical Lab Science and Chemistry, South Dakota State University, 1985 **Current organization:** Prairie Lakes Healthcare Systems **Title:** MT(ASCP) **Type of organization:** Hospital **Major product:** Patient care **Area of distribution:** Watertown, South Dakota **Area of Practice:** Microbiology, serology **Affiliations:** A.S.C.P.; A.S.M.; A.S.C.L.S. **Hob./spts.:** Camping, biking, classical music concerts **SIC code:** 80 **Address:** Prairie Lakes Healthcare Systems, 401 9th Ave. N.W., Watertown, SD 57201 **E-mail:** bob.jenson@prairielakes.com **Web address:** www.prairielakes.com

JHAVERI, MEENAKSHI K.
Industry: Healthcare **Born:** June 9, 1946, Bombay, India **Univ./degree:** M.D. **Current organization:** North Shore University Hospital **Title:** M.D. **Type of organization:** University hospital **Major product:** Patient care **Area of distribution:** International **Area of Practice:** Neonatology **Honors/awards:** TV Show: You and Your Baby **Published works:** 17 articles **Affiliations:** American Academy of Pediatrics **Hob./spts.:** Writing poetry and stories in Hindi, playing the sitar **SIC code:** 80 **Address:** 55 Hitchcock Lane, Old Westbury, NY 11568 **E-mail:** drmkj@hotmail.com

JIMERSON, ANN BLAKLEY
Industry: Healthcare **Born:** December 3, 1964, Houston, Texas **Univ./degree:** M.D., Texas Tech University, 1994 **Current organization:** IU Medical Group **Title:** M.D. **Type of organization:** Multispecialty group **Major product:** Patient care **Area of distribution:** Indiana **Area of Practice:** General pediatrics **Honors/awards:** Who's Who of Medical Professionals; Pediatric Advisors Award, 2000 **Affiliations:** A.A.P.; A.M.A.; Alpha Omega Alpha **Hob./spts.:** Racquetball, sky diving **SIC code:** 80 **Address:** IU Medical Group, 9443 E. 38th St., Indianapolis, IN 46235 **E-mail:** ajimerson@inpui.edu

JIVA, TAJ M.
Industry: Healthcare **Univ./degree:** M.D., State University of New York Downstate, 1999; M.P.H., Medical College of Wisconsin, 2004 **Current organization:** Phoenix Rising Medical, PC **Title:** M.D./M.P.H. **Type of organization:** Solo practice **Major product:** Patient care **Area of distribution:** Buffalo, New York **Area of Practice:** Critical care, pulmonary, sleep medicine, behavioral sleep medicine, forensic medicine **Published works:** Editor, Rotary International Magazine **Affiliations:** Fellow, American College of Physicians.; Fellow, American College of Chest Physicians; A.C.O.E.M; D.A.B.S.M., Citizens' Corps; Hope for Tomorrow Foundations; Master Mason; Rotary Club **Hob./spts.:** Target shooting, music **SIC code:** 80 **Address:** Buffalo Medical Group, PC, 85 High St., Buffalo, NY 14203 **E-mail:** sarahmarium@adelphi.net

JOHN, EUNICE G.
Industry: Medical **Born:** May 8, 1939, India **Univ./degree:** M.D., Christian Medical University, India, 1964 **Current organization:** University of Illinois College of Medicine **Title:** M.D., F.A.A.P., Director of Pediatric Nephrology **Type of organization:** University hospital **Major product:** Patient care, medical education **Area of distribution:** Illinois **Area of Practice:** Pediatric nephrology **Affiliations:** American Society of Nephrology; International Society of Nephrology; American Society of Pediatric Nephrology; International Society of Pediatric Nephrology; American Academy of Pediatrics; International Society of Pediatric Transplants; Chicago Pediatric Society **Hob./spts.:** Music, art **SIC code:** 80 **Address:** University of Illinois College of Medicine, Dept. of Pediatrics, 840 S. Wood St., MC856, Chicago, IL 60612 **E-mail:** ejohn@ulc.edu

JOHN, KARLA S.
Industry: Healthcare **Born:** October 18, 1963, Urbana, Ohio **Univ./degree:** B.S.M.T., Medical Technology, Ball State University, 1987 **Current organization:** Central Indiana Regional Blood Center **Title:** NAT Lab Manager **Area of distribution:** International **Honors/awards:** Strathmore's Who's Who **Published works:** 12+ peer-reviewed journals, 30+ abstracts, 1 chapter **Affiliations:** A.S.C.P. **Hob./spts.:** Lead singer in a barbershop quartet, crochet, quilting **SIC code:** 80 **Address:** Central Indiana Regional Blood Center, 3450 N. Meridan St., Indianapolis, IN 46208 **E-mail:** kjohn@cirbc.org

JOHNA, SAMIR D.
Industry: Medical **Born:** November 22, 1958, Baghdad, Iraq **Univ./degree:** M.D., University of Baghdad, 1983 **Current organization:** Loma Linda University Medical Center **Title:** Assistant Professor, General Surgery, Trauma **Type of organization:** Medical university **Major product:** Medical services **Area of distribution:** National **Area of Practice:** General surgery **Honors/awards:** Founder, Assyrian Medical Society; Best Teacher in Surgery, 1998 **Published works:** 20+ articles **Affiliations:** A.M.A.; S.A.G.E.S.; A.C.S.; S.L.S.; A.A.S.; A.M.S. **SIC code:** 80 **Address:** Loma Linda University Medical Center, Dept. of Surgery, 11175 Coleman Pavillion, Suite 21111 L, Loma Linda, CA 92350 **E-mail:** sjohna@verizon.net

JOHNSON, CANDACE S.
Industry: Healthcare/research **Born:** April 10, 1949, Columbus, Ohio **Univ./degree:** B.S.; M.S., 1974; Ph.D., Immunology, 1977, Ohio State University **Current organization:** Roswell Park Cancer Institute **Title:** Senior VP for Translational Research, Professor of Pharmaceutical Sciences **Type of organization:** Cancer research institute **Major product:** Cancer research **Area of distribution:** International **Area of Practice:** Immunology **Published works:** 120+ articles and chapters **Affiliations:** American Association for Cancer Research; American Society of Clinical Oncology **Hob./spts.:** Golf **SIC code:** 80 **Address:** Roswell Park Cancer Institute, Elm & Carlton, Buffalo, NY 14263 **E-mail:** candace.johnson@roswellpark.org

JOHNSON, DEBRA J.
Industry: Healthcare **Born:** August 29, 1956, Silsbee, Texas **Univ./degree:** A.S., Lamar University, 1994 **Current organization:** Southeast Texas Home Care Specialist **Title:** R.N./D.O.N. **Type of organization:** Home healthcare facility **Major product:** Home healthcare **Area of distribution:** Texas **Area of Practice:** Case management, Nurse Advocate and Pt. Advocate **Hob./spts.:** Gardening, reading **SIC code:** 80 **Address:** 1715 Redbud St., Vidor, TX 77662

JOHNSON, DONNA
Industry: Healthcare **Born:** June 11, 1961, Dayton, Ohio **Univ./degree:** M.D., Ohio State University, 1987 **Current organization:** Crystal Park Pediatrics **Title:** M.D. **Type of organization:** Private practice **Major product:** Patient care **Area of distribution:** Oklahoma City, Oklahoma **Area of Practice:** Pediatrics **Affiliations:** A.M.A.; American Academy of Pediatrics **Hob./spts.:** Baseball, basketball, scrap booking, quilting **SIC code:** 80 **Address:** Crystal Park Pediatrics, 8100 S. Walker, Suite 200, Oklahoma City, OK 73139 **E-mail:** donnajohnson@coxinet.net

JOHNSON, KRISTEN L.
Industry: Healthcare **Born:** November 22, 1970, Guymon, Oklahoma **Univ./degree:** RRT Degree, University of Tulsa, Oklahoma, 1992 **Current organization:** Mountain View Clinical Research, Inc. **Title:** President/Owner **Type of organization:** Research **Major product:** Pharmaceutical research **Area of distribution:** Colorado **Area of Practice:** Respiratory therapy **Affiliations:** Volunteer, Community Resources, Inc., Colorado Donor Alliance; board member, Arts For All **Hob./spts.:** Golf, skiing **SIC code:** 80 **Address:** Mountain View Clinical Research, Inc., 3865 Cherry Creek Dr., Suite 140, Denver, CO 80209 **E-mail:** mtnviewresearch@aol.com

JOHNSON, MARTIN C.
Industry: Healthcare **Born:** November 16, 1933, Santa Fe, New Mexico **Univ./degree:** M.D., Stanford University Medical School, California, 1959 **Current organization:** Pacific Northwest Neurosurgical Associates, P.C. **Title:** M.D., F.A.C.S., F.A.A.P. **Type of organization:** Surgical consulting **Major product:** Pediatric neurological surgery **Area of distribution:** National **Area of Practice:** Medicine/surgery, pediatric neurology **Affiliations:** Fellow, A.C.S.; Fellow, A.A.P.; Fellow, F.M.E. **Hob./spts.:** Fly-fishing, reading, coin collecting, former pilot **SIC code:** 80 **Address:** Pacific Northwest Neurosurgical Associates, P.C., 31870 S.W. Country View Lane, Wilsonville, OR 97070 **E-mail:** martinc33@hotmail.com

JOHNSON, MICHAEL PAUL
Industry: Healthcare **Born:** June 15, 1967, Denver, Colorado **Univ./degree:** M.D., Creighton University **Current organization:** Cohen & Womack, PC **Title:** M.D. **Type of organization:** Private practice **Major product:** Patient care **Area of distribution:**

Lakewood, Colorado **Area of Practice:** Ob/Gyn **Affiliations:** A.C.O.G.; Colorado Medical Society; Clear Creek Valley Medical Society **Hob./spts.:** Golf, skiing, home brewing beer, landscaping, family **SIC code:** 80 **Address:** Cohen & Womack, PC, 255 Union Blvd. #200, Lakewood, CO 80228 **E-mail:** cowojo@aol.com

JOHNSON, ROBERT A.
Industry: Healthcare **Born:** September 28, 1945, Alexandria, Virginia **Univ./degree:** Medical College of Virginia, Richmond, 1971 **Current organization:** Robert A. Johnson, D.D.S. **Title:** D.D.S. **Type of organization:** Private practice **Major product:** Patient care **Area of distribution:** Restorative dentistry **Area of Practice:** Tappahannock, Virginia **Affiliations:** Fellow, Academy of General Dentistry; American Dental Association; Virginia Dental Association **Hob./spts.:** Fishing, gardening **SIC code:** 80 **Address:** Robert A. Johnson, D.D.S., 139 Prince St., Tappahannock, VA 22560 **E-mail:** docraj@verizon.net

JOHNSON, WILLIAM E.
Industry: Healthcare **Born:** December 23, 1962, Oakland, California **Univ./degree:** M.D., University of Southern California, 1989 **Current organization:** Surgical Associates **Title:** Surgeon **Type of organization:** Clinic **Major product:** Surgery (thoracic) **Area of distribution:** International **Area of Practice:** General surgery, teaching residents **Affiliations:** Fellow, A.C.S. and International C.S./A.C.S. Oncology Group **Hob./spts.:** Weightlifting, travel, medical management **SIC code:** 80 **Address:** Surgical Associates, 9155 S.W. Banks Rd., Suite 304, Portland, OR 97225

JOHNSON, WILLIAM H.
Industry: Healthcare **Born:** August 25, 1928, Duck Town, Tennessee **Univ./degree:** D.D.S., University of Tennessee, 1954 **Current organization:** William H. Johnson, DDS, MAGD **Title:** D.D.S. **Type of organization:** Dental office **Major product:** Patient care **Area of distribution:** Anaheim, California **Area of Practice:** Reconstructive, cosmetic and general dentistry **Affiliations:** O.C.D.S.; C.D.A.; A.D.A.; A.G.D. **Hob./spts.:** Scuba diving, golf, fishing **SIC code:** 80 **Address:** 4029 E. Country Canyon Rd., Anaheim, CA 92807-3408 **E-mail:** drjohnson24@hotmail.com

JOHNSON II, GLENN T.
Industry: Healthcare **Born:** November 28, 1966, West Virginia **Univ./degree:** M.D., University of Kentucky, 1992 **Current organization:** Tri-State Orthopedic Surgeons **Title:** M.D. **Type of organization:** Private practice, single specialty group **Major product:** Patient care **Area of distribution:** Evansville, Indiana **Area of Practice:** Orthopedic/upper extremity surgery **Published works:** 1 article **Affiliations:** Fellow, A.A.O.S.; A.M.A.; I.S.M.A. **Hob./spts.:** Golf, camping **SIC code:** 80 **Address:** Tri-State Orthopedic Surgeons, 1101 Professional Blvd., Evansville, IN 47714 **E-mail:** bonedocj@aol.com

JOHNSTON, FEROL L.
Industry: Healthcare **Born:** July 23, 1929, Delta, Colorado **Current organization:** Golden Orchard, Inc. **Title:** Administrator **Type of organization:** Assisted-living homes for the elderly **Major product:** Elderly care **Area of distribution:** Centennial, Colorado **Area of Practice:** Marketing **Affiliations:** Alzheimer's Association; Gerontological Association **Hob./spts.:** Travel **SIC code:** 80 **Address:** Golden Orchard, Inc., 890 E. Orchard Rd., Centennial, CO 80121 **E-mail:** feroljohn@aol.com **Web address:** www.goldenorchard.com

JOHNSTONE, JEAN DOBSON
Industry: Healthcare **Born:** January 27, 1956 **Univ./degree:** M.S., Public Administration, Pennsylvania State University **Current organization:** Bon Secours Hospital **Title:** Mission Coordinator/Vice President **Type of organization:** Hospital **Major product:** Patient care **Area of distribution:** National **Area of Practice:** Administration **Hob./spts.:** Reading, hiking, gardening **SIC code:** 80 **Address:** Bon Secours Hospital, 2500 Seventh Ave., Altoona, PA 16602 **E-mail:** jjohnstone@altoonaregional.org

JONAS, ANDREW S.
Industry: Healthcare **Born:** February 6, 1952, Atlanta, Georgia **Univ./degree:** B.S., Chemistry, Emory University; M.D., University of Miami, 1979 **Current organization:** Andrew S. Jonas M.D., P.C. **Title:** Chief of Pathology **Type of organization:** Private practice **Major product:** Patient care, anatomic and clinical pathology **Area of distribution:** Florida **Area of Practice:** Expert surgical pathologist, specialize in cytopathology **Affiliations:** F.C.A.P.; I.A.P. **SIC code:** 80 **Address:** Andrew S. Jonas M.D., P.C., 14000 Fivay Rd., Hudson, FL 34667 **E-mail:** ajonas99@aol.com

JONES, DAN
Industry: Healthcare **Born:** August 26, 1961, Reading, Pennsylvania **Univ./degree:** M.D., Loma Linda University, California, 1989 **Current organization:** Jones Neurology, LTD **Title:** M.D. **Type of organization:** Private practice **Major product:** Neurological consultation, EMG **Area of distribution:** Ohio **Area of Practice:** Movement disorders and sleep **Published works:** Columbus Monthly **Affiliations:** A.M.A. A.A.N.; A.A.E.N.; A.S.D.A. **Hob./spts.:** Aikido, playing guitar/keyboard, beach volleyball **SIC code:** 80 **Address:** Jones Neurology, LTD, 737 Enterprise Dr., Suite 3, Westerville, OH 43081 **E-mail:** djonesmd@columbus.rr.com

JONES, DAVID A.
Industry: Healthcare **Born:** December 21, 1954 **Univ./degree:** M.D., Ohio State University College of Medicine, 1980 **Current organization:** Capital Health Plan **Title:** M.D. **Type of organization:** HMO **Major product:** Patient care **Area of distribution:** Florida **Area of Practice:** Pediatrics **Published works:** "Resolution of hypoxemia in a liver transplant recipient after ligation of a portosystemic shunt", L. Terry Spencer MD, Max R. Langham MD, Mark H. Hoyer MD, David A. Jones MD, et al, J. Pediatrics 2000, 137: 575-7 **Affiliations:** American Academy of Pediatrics; Florida Pediatrics Society; Capital Medical Society; Florida Medical Association; Courtesy Assistant Professor of Pediatrics, Florida State College of Medicine; Board of Directors, Big Bend Hospice **Hob./spts.:** Sports, playing tuba, church activities **SIC code:** 80 **Address:** Capital Health Plan, 2140 Centerville Place, Tallahassee, FL 32308

JONES, LARRY M.
Industry: Healthcare **Born:** May 21, 1956, Chatham, Virginia **Univ./degree:** M.D., University of Health Sciences, Kansa City, Missouri **Current organization:** Pro Med Emergency Care Centers **Title:** M.D. **Type of organization:** Hospital **Major product:** Patient care **Area of distribution:** Charlotte, North Carolina **Area of Practice:** Emergency physician **Affiliations:** A.M.A.; A.C.P. **Hob./spts.:** Chess, golf **SIC code:** 80 **Address:** Pro Med Emergency Care Centers, 7238 Canyon Dr., Charlotte, NC 28262 **E-mail:** lvu2380@msn.com

JORAPUR, VINOD
Industry: Medical **Univ./degree:** M.D., Sri Venkateswara Medical College, Tirupati, India, 1990 **Current organization:** Our Lady of Mercy University Hospital **Title:** M.D. **Type of organization:** University hospital **Major product:** Medical services **Area of distribution:** Bronx, New York **Area of Practice:** Interventional cardiology/patient care/acute care **Published works:** 18 publications **Affiliations:** A.C.P.; Cardiology Society of India; American Heart Association **Hob./spts.:** Travel, photography, reading **SIC code:** 80 **Address:** Our Lady of Mercy University Hospital, Dept. of Medicine, 600 233rd St., Bronx, NY 10466

JOSEPH, RAYMOND E.
Industry: Government/medical/research **Born:** February 8, 1946, Bordman, Ohio **Univ./degree:** M.D., George Washington School of Medicine, 1972 **Current organization:** Center for biologic evaluation and research **Title:** M.D./ F.A.C.P./F.A.C.G. **Type of organization:** Government **Major product:** Therapeutics **Area of distribution:** Rockville, Maryland **Area of Practice:** Gastroenterology, hematology **Honors/awards:** Kentucky Colonel Award presented by Governor Patton, 1996 **Published works:** Lancit Gastroenterology **Affiliations:** A.G.A.; John's Hopkins Medical Association **Hob./spts.:** Sailing, golf **SIC code:** 80 **Address:** CBER/FDA, 1401 Rockville Pike, Rockville, MD 20852 **E-mail:** josephr@cber.fda.gov

JOSHI, HARISH C.
Industry: Medical **Born:** February 14, 1957, Maia, Almora, India **Univ./degree:** Ph.D., University of Delhi, India, 1983 **Current organization:** Emory University School of Medicine, Dept. of Cell Biology **Title:** Associate Professor **Type of organization:** University **Major product:** Higher education **Area of distribution:** International **Area of Practice:** Cancer and cell cycle research **Honors/awards:** Best Membership, Emory University, 2001 **Affiliations:** A.S.C.B. **Hob./spts.:** Squash, science, travel, sky diving **SIC code:** 80 **Address:** Emory University School of Medicine, Dept. of Cell Biology, 1648 Pierce Dr., Atlanta, GA 30322 **E-mail:** joshi@cellbio.emory.edu

JULIEN-BRIZAN, VERN M.
Industry: Healthcare **Born:** March 17, 1943, Trinidad **Univ./degree:** B.S.N., City College of New York; M.P.A., C.W. Post; M.S., Molloy College **Current organization:** Caribbean American Family Health Center **Title:** Family Nurse Practitioner **Type of organization:** Medical practice **Major product:** Patient care **Area of distribution:** Brooklyn, New York **Area of Practice:** Family health **Honors/awards:** Chairperson, Relay for Life, American Cancer Society, 2004-05; Nominated, Nurse Practitioner of the Year Award, New York State Nurse Practitioners Association **Affiliations:** American Diabetes Association; Nurse Practitioners Association; American Academy of Nurse Practitioners **Hob./spts.:** Baseball, reading, active in her community **SIC code:** 80 **Address:** 810 Midwood St., #2G, Brooklyn, NY 11203 **E-mail:** vjbrizan@earthlink.net

JUNGE, DAVID A.
Industry: Healthcare **Born:** October 8, 1943, Grosse Pointe, Michigan **Univ./degree:** M.D., University of Michigan Medical School, 1968 **Current organization:** David A. Junge, M.D. **Title:** M.D./Director **Type of organization:** Private practice/Endometrial Ablation center **Major product:** Health services **Area of distribution:** Midland, Michigan **Area of Practice:** In-office hysteroscopy and endometrial ablation, Ob/Gyn **Affiliations:** A.M.A.; American College of Obstetrics and Gynecology; Michigan State

Medical Society **Hob./spts.:** Golf, football **SIC code:** 80 **Address:** David A. Junge, M.D., 4009 Orchard Dr., Suite 3025, Midland, MI 48640-6111

JUNGÉ, SANDRA H.
Industry: Medical **Born:** September 6, 1959, Albany, Georgia **Univ./degree:** B.S. Communication Services Disorder, Brescia College, 1991; M.S., Communication Sciences/Speech Pathology, University of Alabama, 1992 **Current organization:** Medical Studies Group Inc. **Title:** C.M.E. Director **Type of organization:** Conferences/travel **Major product:** Continuing medical education **Area of distribution:** National **Area of Practice:** Education **Hob./spts.:** Arts, crafts **SIC code:** 80 **Address:** Medical Studies Group Inc., 3116 E. Morgan Ave., Suite B, Evansville, IN 47711 **E-mail:** cmetravelplanner@sbcglobal.net

KABNICK, LOWELL S.
Industry: Healthcare **Univ./degree:** M.D., George Washington University **Current organization:** Vein Institute of New Jersey **Title:** M.D. **Type of organization:** Physician/surgeon office **Major product:** Quality specialized medical care **Area of distribution:** International **Area of Practice:** Vascular Surgeon, Phlebologist **Affiliations:** Fellow, American College of Surgeons **Hob./spts.:** Sailboat racing, sculpting **SIC code:** 80 **Address:** Vein Institute of New Jersey, 95 Madison Ave., Suite 109, Morristown, NJ 07960 **E-mail:** doctlc@aol.com

KADAYIFCI, SINAN
Industry: Healthcare **Born:** May 11, 1961, Turkey **Univ./degree:** M.D., Turkey **Current organization:** Island Heart Associates **Title:** M.D./Cardiologist **Type of organization:** Medical practice **Major product:** Patient care **Area of distribution:** International **Area of Practice:** Cardiology **Affiliations:** F.A.C.C.; F.A.M.A.; F.A.S.N.C.; A.N.A.; T.M.A. **Hob./spts.:** Chess, swimming **SIC code:** 80 **Address:** 33 Lanier Lane, Bay Shore, NY 11706 **E-mail:** ssnmk1@hotmail.com

KAHN, ASHFAQ A.
Industry: Medical **Born:** September 11, 1968, Lahore, Pakistan **Univ./degree:** M.D., University of Malta, 1992 **Current organization:** University of Minnesota **Title:** M.D. **Type of organization:** University **Major product:** Patient care, medical education **Area of distribution:** Minneapolis, Minnesota **Area of Practice:** Cardiology **Published works:** Book chapter on ecocardiology **Affiliations:** A.C.C.; V.B.W.G.; C.O.A.C.H. **Hob./spts.:** Tennis, swimming, rollerblading **SIC code:** 80 **Address:** University of Minnesota, 420 Delaware St. S.E., MMC 508, Minneapolis, MN 55455 **E-mail:** ashfaqkhan2000@hotmail.com

KALASSIAN, KENNETH G.
Industry: Healthcare **Born:** April 25, 1960, Boston, Massachusetts **Univ./degree:** M.D., Stanford University, 1991 **Current organization:** Georgia Lung Associates **Title:** M.D. **Type of organization:** Medical group **Major product:** Patient care **Area of distribution:** Georgia **Area of Practice:** Critical care medicine **Published works:** 20 publications **Affiliations:** F.A.C.P.; F.A.C.C.P.; Society of Critical Care Medicine **SIC code:** 80 **Address:** Georgia Lung Associates, 1700 Hospital South Dr., Suite 202, Austell, GA 30106 **E-mail:** kkalassian@hotmail.com

KALLIS, JOHN N.
Industry: Dental **Born:** November 30, 1960, New York, New York **Univ./degree:** B.S., Biology, 1981; D.M.D., 1985, Fairleigh Dickinson University **Current organization:** Palisades Oral Surgeons, P.A. **Title:** D.M.D. **Type of organization:** Dental practice **Major product:** Oral and maxillofacial surgery **Area of distribution:** New Jersey **Area of Practice:** Dental surgery **Affiliations:** A.A.O.M.S.; New Jersey Association of Oral and Maxillofacial Surgeons **Hob./spts.:** Sports, fishing **SIC code:** 80 **Address:** Palisade Oral Surgeons P.A., 1534 Palisades Ave., Ft. Lee, NJ 07024

KALLOS, NILZA
Industry: Healthcare **Born:** July 26, 1944 **Univ./degree:** M.S., Liberal Arts, Sao Paulo, Brazil, 1966; M.D., University of Pennsylvania School of Medicine, 1970 **Current organization:** Breast Health Center & Diagnostic Ultrasound, P.A. **Title:** M.D. **Type of organization:** Women's diagnostic center **Major product:** Breast cancer diagnosis and wellness **Area of distribution:** National **Area of Practice:** Radiologist (breast specialist) **Affiliations:** F.A.C.R.; N.A.R.S.; Dade County Medical Association; Past President, American Cancer Society, Dade County Chapter **SIC code:** 80 **Address:** Breast Health Center & Diagnostic Ultrasound, P.A., 6280 Sunset Dr., Suite 603, Miami, FL 33143

KAMINSKI, LEEAN M.
Industry: Healthcare **Born:** October 8, 1962, Pittsburgh, Pennsylvania **Univ./degree:** R.N., Ohio Valley General Hospital **Current organization:** Moran's Home **Title:** Administrator/COO **Type of organization:** Nursing home **Major product:** Long-term patient care **Area of distribution:** Pennsylvania **Area of Practice:** Administration **Affiliations:** American Medical Directors Association **Hob./spts.:** Reading, rose gardening, music (piano, organ, piccolo, flute), ice hockey **SIC code:** 80 **Address:** Moran's Home, 402 Maple Ave., Bellwood, PA 16617 **E-mail:** MORANHOME@aol.com

KANAKAMEDALA, USHA V.
Industry: Healthcare **Univ./degree:** M.D., SUNY Health Science Center at Brooklyn, 1992 **Current organization:** Jeannette District Memorial Hospital **Title:** Director, Women's Imaging Center, Department of Radiology **Type of organization:** Hospital **Major product:** Patient care **Area of distribution:** Jeannette, Pennsylvania **Area of Practice:** Women's Imaging, Diagnostic Radiology **Affiliations:** R.S.N.A.; Pennsylvania Medical Society; American College of Radiology; Society for Advancement of Women's Imagery (SAWI) **SIC code:** 80 **Address:** Jeannette District Memorial Hospital, 600 Jefferson Ave., Jeannette, PA 15644

KANJWAL, MOHAMMED Y.
Industry: Medical **Born:** Kashmir, India **Univ./degree:** M.D., University of Kashmir, 1979 **Current organization:** Medical College of Ohio **Title:** MD **Type of organization:** University hospital **Major product:** Patient care, medical education **Area of distribution:** Ohio **Area of Practice:** Cardiac Electro-physiology **Published works:** 12 publications **Affiliations:** F.A.C.C.; A.M.A.; N.A.S.P.E. **Hob./spts.:** Listening to old classical music **SIC code:** 80 **Address:** Medical College of Ohio, 3000 Arlington Ave., Toledo, OH 43614 **E-mail:** ykanjwal@mco.edu

KAPLAN, IDIDA A.
Industry: Healthcare **Born:** March 23, 1955, Jerusalem, Israel **Univ./degree:** B.A., Barnard College, 1975; B.S., Biology, Columbia University, Summa Cum Laude, 1975; M.D., Mount Sinai School of Medicine, 1979 **Current organization:** Idida A. Kaplan, M.D. **Title:** M.D. **Type of organization:** Ophthalmology office **Major product:** Eye care, medical surgical **Area of distribution:** Great Neck, New York **Area of Practice:** Glaucoma **Affiliations:** F.A.A.O; F.A.C.S.; H.E.E.B.; N.Y.P.B. **Hob./spts.:** Theatre, travel **SIC code:** 80 **Address:** Idida A. Kaplan, M.D., 935 Northern Blvd., Suite 204, Great Neck, NY 11021

KAPLAN, LEWIS J.
Industry: Medical **Born:** August 29, 1962, Philadelphia, Pennsylvania **Univ./degree:** M.D., Robertwood Johnson Medical School,1988 **Current organization:** Yale University Hospital **Title:** M.D./Associate Professor of Surgery **Type of organization:** University hospital **Major product:** Medical services **Area of distribution:** National **Area of Practice:** Trauma and surgical critical care **Affiliations:** American College of Surgeons; Society of Critical Care Medicine; Eastern Association for the Surgery of Trauma **Hob./spts.:** Ninjutsu **SIC code:** 80 **Address:** Yale University Hospital, 330 Cedar St. BB-310, New Haven, CT 06520 **E-mail:** lewis.kaplan@yale.edu **Web address:** www.yale.edu

KAPLAN, MICHAEL S.
Industry: Healthcare **Born:** May 1, 1955, Everett, Massachusetts **Univ./degree:** M.D., Baylor College of Medicine, 1981 **Current organization:** Michael S. Kaplan, M.D., Ltd. **Title:** President **Type of organization:** Private practice **Major product:** Patient care **Area of distribution:** Henderson, Nevada **Area of Practice:** Urology **Honors/awards:** Phi Betta Kappa, UCLA, 1977; Top Urologist, Las Vegas Life Magazine, 2000 **Affiliations:** A.U.A.; A.M.A.; C.C.M.A. **Hob./spts.:** Racquetball, golf, physical fitness, ping pong **SIC code:** 80 **Address:** Michael S. Kaplan, M.D., Ltd., 4 Sunset Way B-6, Henderson, NV 89014

KAPLAN, MITCHELL ALAN
Industry: Healthcare **Born:** January 26, 1954, Brooklyn, New York **Univ./degree:** B.A. (Hons.), Long Island Univ., Brooklyn Center, NY, 1976; M.A., Sociology, New School for Social Research, NY, 1979; M.Phil. Sociology, City Univ. of New York Graduate Center, 1985; Ph.D., Sociology, City Univ. of New York Graduate School, 1987 **Current organization:** Beth Israel Medical Center **Title:** Ph.D./Project Manager **Type of organization:** Medical center **Major product:** Improved healthcare outcomes for patients from underserved patient populations **Area of distribution:** New York **Area of Practice:** Behavioral science research, substance abuse treatment and HIV/AIDS studies, evaluation of social and vocational rehabilitation service programs for persons with disabilities, pain and palliative care patient outcome studies; Certified Professional Sociological Practitioner by the Certification Commission, American Academy of Professional Sociological Practitioners 1997 Cert. #1129 **Honors/awards:** Who's Who in Science and Engineering 1993-94; Who's Who in the East 1994-95; Recipient National Institute on Drug Abuse Postdoctoral Research Training Fellowship 1987-89; Graduated from Long Island University Brooklyn Center Cum Laude 1976; Received Long Island University Departmental Certificate of Award for Outstanding Academic Achievement in the Fields of Sociology and Anthropology; Member, Pi Gamma Mu, National Social Science Honor Society **Published works:** Articles published in peer review professional journals including, Co-author, "The Unintended Consequences of the Restructuring of the Division of AIDS Services in New York City", Clinical Sociology Review, 16, 29-42, 1998; Abstracts, book chapters; Passik, S.D., Whitcomb, L., Kaplan, M.A., Kirsh, K.L., Schein, J.R. Dodd, S., Kleinman, L. Katz, N.P., & Portnoy, R.K. (2006) Monitoring Outcomes During Long-Term Opioid

Therapy for Non-cancer Pain: Results with the Pain Assessment and Documentation Tool "Journal of Opioid Management" (in press). **Affiliations:** American Sociological Association; American Public Health Association: National Rehabilitation Association; Society for Disability Studies; New York Academy of Sciences; American Association for Public Opinion Research **Hob./spts.:** Spending time with friends, reading, movies **SIC code:** 80 **Address:** 2540 Batchelder St., #7N, Brooklyn, NY 11235 **E-mail:** DrMKaplan@aol.com

KAR, SAIBAL
Industry: Healthcare **Born:** September 15, 1960, India **Univ./degree:** M.D., University of Calcutta, 1986 **Current organization:** Cedars-Sinai Medical Center, Division of Cardiology **Title:** Cardiologist **Type of organization:** Hospital **Major product:** Patient care **Area of distribution:** International **Area of Practice:** Interventional cardiology **Published works:** 60 abstracts, 16 articles **Affiliations:** F.A.C.C.; F.A.H.A.; A.C.P.; A.M.A. **Hob./spts.:** Table tennis, movies, travel, shows, art, calligraphy **SIC code:** 80 **Address:** Cedars-Sinai Medical Center, Division of Cardiology, 8631 W. Third St., Suite 415E, Los Angeles, CA 90048 **E-mail:** karsk@cshs.org

KARANJIA, PERCY N.
Industry: Healthcare **Born:** July 6, 1946, Bombay, India **Univ./degree:** M.D., University of Bombay, India, 1973 **Current organization:** Marshfield Clinic Dept. of Neurology **Title:** M.D., Researcher **Type of organization:** Clinic **Major product:** Patient care, research **Area of distribution:** International **Area of Practice:** Neurology, cerebrovascular disorders, Board Certified, MRCP, 1975 **Affiliations:** A.S.A.; A.A.N. **Hob./spts.:** Music **SIC code:** 80 **Address:** Marshfield Clinic Dept. of Neurology, 1000 N. Oak, Marshfield, WI 54449 **E-mail:** karanjip@mfldclin.edu

KARDOS, AUDREY S.
Industry: Healthcare **Born:** July 9, 1935, Spotsylvania, Virginia **Univ./degree:** B.S.N., University of Virginia, 1957 **Current organization:** University of Virginia **Title:** RN, BSN (Retired) **Type of organization:** Hospital **Major product:** Patient care **Area of distribution:** Virginia **Area of Practice:** Nursing **Affiliations:** University of Virginia School of Nursing; University of Virginia; Spotsylvania County Daughters of American Revolution; Ladies Auxiliary of National Association of Letter Carriers **Hob./spts.:** Knitting, sewing, travel, grandchildren **SIC code:** 80 **Address:** P.O. Box 6002, Charlottesville, VA 22906 **E-mail:** akardos@firstva.com

KATARIYA, KUSHAGRA
Industry: Medical **Born:** July 8, 1964, New Delhi, India **Univ./degree:** M.D., University of Delhi, India **Current organization:** University of Miami School of Medicine **Title:** M.D., F.A.C.S. **Type of organization:** University **Major product:** Medical services, education **Area of distribution:** Florida **Area of Practice:** Thoracic Surgery **Published works:** 25 papers **Affiliations:** Fellow, American College of Surgeons; Society of University Surgeons; Society of Thoracic Surgeons; Southern Thoracic Surgeons Association; Florida Society of Cardiothoracic Surgeons; Society of VA Surgeons **SIC code:** 80 **Address:** University of Miami School of Medicine, 1611 N.W. 12th Ave., Miami, FL 33136 **E-mail:** kkatariya@med.miami.edu

KATKOVSKY, DIMITRIY
Industry: Healthcare **Born:** March 14, 1960, Moscow, Russia **Univ./degree:** M.D., New York College of Osteopathic Medicine, 1997 **Current organization:** Beth Israel Medical Center **Title:** D.O. **Type of organization:** Hospital **Major product:** Patient care **Area of distribution:** Brooklyn, New York **Area of Practice:** Emergency medicine **Published works:** 40 articles **Affiliations:** A.O.A.; A.M.A.; A.C.O.M. **Hob./spts.:** Gardening, tennis, swimming, travel **SIC code:** 80 **Address:** Beth Israel Medical Center, 3201 Kings Hwy., Brooklyn, NY 10467 **E-mail:** dmitriyk@prodigy.net

KAUSHIK, RAJ R.
Industry: Healthcare **Univ./degree:** M.B.B.S., Topiwala National Medical College, University of Bombay, 1979 **Current organization:** Cardiovascular Surgical Associates, P.A. **Title:** M.D. **Type of organization:** Medical practice **Major product:** Cardiovascular care, surgery **Area of distribution:** New Jersey **Area of Practice:** Beating heart surgery, minimally invasive heart surgery including a-fib **Published works:** 20+ publications **Affiliations:** F.A.C.S.; F.A.C.C; S.T.S.; Heart Rhythm Society **Hob./spts.:** Scuba diving, squash, tennis **SIC code:** 80 **Address:** Cardiovascular Surgical Associates, P.A., 350 Boulevard, Suite 130, Passaic, NJ 07055 **E-mail:** cardiosurg99@comcast.net

KAWIECKI, JACALYN A.
Industry: Healthcare **Univ./degree:** M.D., 1997; M.H.A., 1994, University of Minnesota **Current organization:** Courage Center - Medical Director **Title:** Medical Director **Type of organization:** Rehabilitation center **Major product:** Patient care **Area of distribution:** Golden Valley, Minnesota **Area of Practice:** Physical medicine, rehabilitation **Affiliations:** A.A.P.M.R.; A.A.P.; A.C.R.M.; A.M.A. **SIC code:** 80 **Address:** Courage Center - Medical Director, 3915 Golden Valley Rd., Golden Valley, MN 55422 **E-mail:** jackie.kawiecki@courage.org **Web address:** www.courage.org

KAY, LYNDA LEE
Industry: Healthcare **Born:** January 7, 1954, Rangoon, Burma **Univ./degree:** M.D., Institute of Medicine, Burma, 1979 **Current organization:** Bristol Park Medical **Title:** M.D. **Type of organization:** Medical center/hospital **Major product:** Patient care **Area of distribution:** Fountain Valley, California **Area of Practice:** Medical services **Honors/awards:** Distinction award, 1972; Surgery Award, 1976; Obstetrics/Gynecology Award, 1978; Honor Award in Residency, 1993 **Affiliations:** A.B.F.P. **Hob./spts.:** Music, running **SIC code:** 80 **Address:** 11420 Warner Ave., Fountain Valley, CA 92708 **E-mail:** dbestfamdoc.yahoo.com

KAYALEH, RAOUF ANTOINE
Industry: Healthcare **Born:** February 12, 1956, Beirut, Lebanon **Univ./degree:** M.D., American University of Beirut, Lebanon **Current organization:** Raouf A. Kayaleh, M.D. **Title:** M.D. **Type of organization:** Private medical practice **Major product:** Patient care **Area of distribution:** California **Area of Practice:** Pulmonary and critical care **Affiliations:** A.C.C.P. **Hob./spts.:** Music, biking **SIC code:** 80 **Address:** Raouf A. Kayaleh, M.D., 1125 E. 17th St., Suite E-109, Santa Ana, CA 92701 **E-mail:** rafksz@aol.com

KAYMAKTCHIEV, SIMEON C.
Industry: Healthcare **Born:** August 31, 1956 **Univ./degree:** B.A., Bulgaria, 1980 **Current organization:** Port Chester Nursing and Rehabilitation Center **Title:** Physical Therapist Assistant **Type of organization:** Skilled nursing and rehab center **Major product:** Physical therapy treatment **Area of distribution:** Port Chester, New York **Area of Practice:** Physical therapy **Published works:** Papers, articles, textbook chapter **Affiliations:** American Physical Therapists Association **Hob./spts.:** Swimming, jogging, hiking **SIC code:** 80 **Address:** Port Chester Nursing and Rehabilitation Center, 1000 High St., Port Chester, NY 10573 **E-mail:** kaymaktchiev@yahoo.com

KAZANJIAN, POWEL H.
Industry: Medical **Born:** May 27, 1953, Newport, Rhode Island **Univ./degree:** M.D., Tufts University, 1979 **Current organization:** University of Michigan Health System **Title:** M.D. **Type of organization:** University hospital **Major product:** Medical services **Area of distribution:** Michigan **Area of Practice:** Infectious diseases/HIV **Affiliations:** I.D.S.A.; A.S.M. **Hob./spts.:** History **SIC code:** 80 **Address:** University of Michigan Health System, 3120 Taubman Center, Ann Arbor, MI 48109-0378 **E-mail:** pkazanji@umich.edu

KEEL, CLINT KESLAR
Industry: Healthcare **Born:** May 2, 1976, Memphis, Tennessee **Univ./degree:** B.S.N., University of Mississippi, 2000 **Current organization:** University Medical Center **Title:** R.N./Nurse Manager **Type of organization:** Medical center **Major product:** Patient care **Area of distribution:** Mississippi **Area of Practice:** Nursing management **Honors/awards:** Psi Kappa Psi; Sigma Delta Tau **Published works:** 1 article, American Journal of Nursing **Hob./spts.:** Singing, playing the piano **SIC code:** 80 **Address:** University Medical Center, Nursing Services, 2500 N. State St., Jackson, MS 39216 **E-mail:** ckeel@nurseunmed.edu **Web address:** www.umed.edu

KELLY, MICHAEL THOMAS
Industry: Healthcare **Born:** October 2, 1946, Fort Dodge, Iowa **Univ./degree:** B.A., English/Philosophy, University of New Mexico, 1972; R.N., Merritt College, Oakland, California, 1990 **Current organization:** St. Rose Hospital **Title:** RN, C **Type of organization:** Hospital **Major product:** Patient care **Area of distribution:** California **Area of Practice:** Registered Nurse - Certified, Medical/Surgical **Published works:** 6 books **Affiliations:** American Nurses Association; American Emergency Nurses Association **Hob./spts.:** Poetry, philosophy **SIC code:** 80 **Address:** St. Rose Hospital, 27200 Calanoga Ave., Haywood, CA 94545 **E-mail:** mikellyrn@hotmail.com

KELLY, MICHAEL W.
Industry: Healthcare **Born:** November 6, 1956, Lubbock, Texas **Univ./degree:** M.D., University of Texas, 1983 **Current organization:** The Kelly Eye Center **Title:** M.D. **Type of organization:** Private practice **Major product:** Patient care **Area of distribution:** Raleigh, North Carolina **Area of Practice:** Ophthalmology **Affiliations:** A.M.A.; I.S.R.S. **Hob./spts.:** Skiing **SIC code:** 80 **Address:** The Kelly Eye Center, 4201 Lake Boone Trail, #104, Raleigh, NC 27607 **E-mail:** mwk@kellyeyecenter.com

KELLY II, MICHAEL V.
Industry: Healthcare **Univ./degree:** M.D., University of Texas, Southwest Medical School **Current organization:** Aesthetic Surgery Center of Houston **Title:** M.D. **Type of organization:** Surgery center **Major product:** Plastic and aesthetic surgery **Area of distribution:** National **Area of Practice:** Plastic surgery **Honors/awards:** President Elect, Harris County Medical Society **Published works:** 30+ articles and journals **Affiliations:** H.S.P.S.; A.M.A.; T.S.P.S. **SIC code:** 80 **Address:** Aesthetic Surgery Center of Houston, 17070 Red Oak Dr., Suite 303, Houston, TX 77090 **E-mail:** drkelly@houstonplasticsurgery.com **Web address:** www.houstonplasticsurgeon.com

KEMPA, PETRA C.
Industry: Healthcare **Born:** September 30, 1962, Nuremberg, Germany **Univ./degree:** M.H.S.A., Armstrong Atlantic State University, 2000 **Current organization:** Select Specialty Hospital **Title:** Director, Provider Relations **Type of organization:** Hospital **Major product:** Long term acute care hospital services **Area of distribution:** Georgia **Area of Practice:** Marketing and business development **Affiliations:** A.A.R.C.; N.B.R.C. **Hob./spts.:** The outdoors, time with family, kayaking, canoeing **SIC code:** 80 **Address:** 39 River Bluff Dr., Savannah, GA 31406 **E-mail:** petrakempa@selectmedicalcorp.com

KENDALL, MICHAEL W.
Industry: Healthcare **Born:** January 30, 1943, Glendale, Arizona **Univ./degree:** B.S., Biology, University of Northern Iowa, 1965; M.S., Biology; Ph.D., Human Anatomy, 1972, University of Louisville, Graduate School of Medicine; D.P.M., California College of Podiatric Medicine, 1984 **Current organization:** Kendall Foot Clinic **Title:** Podiatrist **Type of organization:** Private practice **Major product:** Podiatric surgery and medicine **Area of distribution:** National **Area of Practice:** Innovative heel spur and bunion surgery; Ellman's electrosurgical instrumentation technique; Podiatric Medicine and Orthopedics (Board Certified); Podiatric Surgery (Board Certified) **Published works:** 13 scientific articles **Affiliations:** American Podiatric Medical Association; Texas Podiatric Medical Association **Hob./spts.:** Champion trap shooter, competitive runner, racquetball, woodcarving **SIC code:** 80 **Address:** Kendall Foot Clinic, 702 Quail Creek, Amarillo, TX 79124 **E-mail:** kendallfootclinic@wtxcoxmail.com

KENNEDY, COLLEEN I.
Industry: Healthcare **Born:** December, Port Arthur, Texas **Univ./degree:** M.D., Jefferson Medical College, 1996; Residency, General Surgery, Medical College of Virginia; Fellowship, Laparoscopic and Bariatric Surgery, Cleveland Clinic, 2004 **Current organization:** Ochsner Medical Center, Dept. of Surgery **Title:** Director, Bariatric Surgery **Type of organization:** Multi specialty clinic **Major product:** Patient care **Area of distribution:** National **Area of Practice:** Bariatric Surgery (running the obesity program) **Published works:** 10 journal articles, 2 book chapters **Affiliations:** American Society for Bariatric Surgery; Society of American Gastrointestinal and Endoscopic Surgeons **SIC code:** 80 **Address:** Ochsner Medical Center, Dept. of Surgery, 1514 Jefferson Hwy., T-8, New Orleans, LA 70121 **E-mail:** cokennedy@ochsner.org **Web address:** www.ochsner.org

KERNBERG, PAULINA F.
Industry: Healthcare **Born:** January 10, 1935, Santiago, Chile **Univ./degree:** B.S., Biology, University of Chile, 1956; M.D., University of Chile School of Medicine, 1958 **Current organization:** New York Presbyterian Hospital, Westchester Division **Title:** Psychiatrist **Type of organization:** Hospital **Major product:** Patient care, research **Area of distribution:** International **Area of Practice:** Child and adolescent psychiatry **Published works:** 100+ peer reviewed journals, 3 books **Affiliations:** F.A.A.C.P.; A.P.A.; I.P.A.; G.T.A.; A.C.P. **Hob./spts.:** Art, swimming **SIC code:** 80 **Address:** New York Presbyterian Hospital, Westchester Division, 21 Bloomingdale Rd., White Plains, NY 10605

KESSLER, DEBRA B.
Industry: Healthcare **Born:** March 1, 1953, Kingston, Pennsylvania **Univ./degree:** M.D., University of Pennsylvania School of Medicine, 1989; Ph.D., Bioengineering, University of Pennsylvania, 1987 **Current organization:** Debra B. Kessler M.D., P.C. **Title:** President **Type of organization:** Radiology firm **Major product:** Radiology **Area of distribution:** New York **Area of Practice:** General diagnostic radiology, nuclear medicine **Honors/awards:** Alliance for Engineering in Medicine and Biology, Paul Mayer Research Award; NASA/COSMOS Space Flight Group Achievement Award, 1987 **Published works:** 7 articles, 100+ abstracts **Affiliations:** I.E.E.E.; Radiological Society of North America; Society of Nuclear Medicine; American College of Radiology **Hob./spts.:** Golf, painting (water colors), cross country skiing, photography **SIC code:** 80 **Address:** Debra B. Kessler M.D., P.C., 74 Teakettle Spout Rd., Mahopac, NY 10541 **E-mail:** dkessler@powerview.com

KESWANI, SANJAY C.
Industry: Medical **Born:** November 19, 1969, London England **Univ./degree:** M.D., Bartholemew Hospital School of Medicine, London 1994 **Current organization:** Johns Hopkins University School of Medicine **Title:** M.D. **Type of organization:** University/hospital **Major product:** Medical services **Area of distribution:** Maryland **Area of Practice:** Neurology **Published works:** 10 Articles **Affiliations:** American Academy of Neurology; Peripheral Nervous System **Hob./spts.:** Reading, squash, hiking **SIC code:** 80 **Address:** Johns Hopkins University School of Medicine, Dept. of Neurology, 600 N. Wolf St., Baltimore, MD 21287 **E-mail:** skeswani@jhmi.edu

KHADRA, SUHAIL HELMI
Industry: Medical **Born:** April 29, 1955, Damascus, Syria **Univ./degree:** M.D., University of Damascus, 1979 **Current organization:** Stroger Hospital of Cook County **Title:** M.D./Chairman, Cardiovascular Sub-Committee **Type of organization:** Academic hospital **Major product:** Patient services, medical education **Area of distribution:** Illinois **Area of Practice:** Internal medicine, cardiology, interventional cardiology (all Board Certified) **Published works:** 5 articles **Affiliations:** American College of Cardiology **Hob./spts.:** Tennis, swimming, chess **SIC code:** 80 **Address:** Stroger Hospital of Cook County, 1901 W. Harrison St., #3620, Chicago, IL 60612 **E-mail:** skdra@aol.com **Web address:** www.ccbhs.org

KHALEEQ, GHULAM
Industry: Healthcare **Born:** March, 3, 1975, Pakistan **Univ./degree:** M.D., Drexel University **Current organization:** Albert Einstein Medical Center **Title:** M.D. **Type of organization:** Hospital **Major product:** Patient care **Area of distribution:** National **Area of Practice:** Pulmonary disease and critical care medicine; Treatment of Sarcoidosis with Infliximab **Affiliations:** American Thoracic Society; Society of Critical Care Medicine; American College of Chest Physicians; American College of Physicians; American Medical Society **Hob./spts.:** Golf, fishing, hiking, mountain climbing **SIC code:** 80 **Address:** Albert Einstein Medical Center, 5501 Old York Rd., Suite 331, Philadelphia, PA 19141 **E-mail:** khaleeqg@einstein.edu

KHALID, SYED M.
Industry: Healthcare **Univ./degree:** M.D., King Edward Medical College, 1990 **Current organization:** Consultants in Gastroenterology **Title:** M.D. **Type of organization:** Medical practice **Major product:** Patient care **Area of distribution:** Lees Summit, Missouri **Area of Practice:** Gastroenterology **Affiliations:** A.M.S.G.E.; A.C.P. **Hob./spts.:** Fishing **SIC code:** 80 **Address:** 437 N.E. Tara Dr., Lees Summit, MO 64064 **E-mail:** syed.khalid@lycos.com

KHAMVONGSA, PETER A.
Industry: Healthcare **Born:** November 20, 1965, Washington, D.C. **Univ./degree:** B.S., Biology and Psychology; Residency/Internship National Naval Medical Center; M.D., Georgetown University School of Medicine, 1990 **Current organization:** Baptist Hospital of Miami **Title:** Attending Obstetrician/Gynecologist **Type of organization:** Hospital/group practice **Major product:** Patient care **Area of distribution:** Florida **Area of Practice:** Advanced laparoscopy, pelvic reconstruction, tri lingual; OB/GYN (Board Certified) **Honors/awards:** Outstanding Teacher, Georgetown University; Galloway Fellowship, Memorial Sloane Kettering, New York, 1993 **Affiliations:** Fellow, American College of Obstetrics and Gynecology; Fellow, American College of Surgeons; Product Review Committee, Baptist Hospital **Hob./spts.:** Bicycling, billiard, travel **SIC code:** 80 **Address:** Baptist Hospital of Miami, 8950 N. Kendall Dr., Medical Arts Bldg., Suite 302, Miami, FL 33176 **E-mail:** drpeterak@aol.com **Web address:** www.drkobgyn.medem.com

KHAN, AMID
Industry: Healthcare/education **Born:** December 16, 1964, Bangladesh **Univ./degree:** MB.BS, (Bachelor of Medicine & Bachelor of Surgery), Dhaka, Bangladesh, 1988; M.R.C.P., United Kingdom, 1994; Diploma in Cardiology, London University, 1996 **Current organization:** Lankenau Hospital **Title:** M.D.; Director, Interventional Cardiology **Type of organization:** Hospital **Major product:** Patient care **Area of distribution:** International **Area of Practice:** Interventional cardiology, stenting, angioplasty **Honors/awards:** Travel Award to attend Transcatheter Cardiovascular Therapeutics Conference in Washington, DC, Sept., 2002, sponsored by the Spectranetics Corporation, USA; Travel Award to attend 17th Scientific Meeting of The International Society of Hypertension in Amsterdam, Netherlands; June 1998, sponsored by Parke-Davis Pharmaceuticals, UK **Published works:** Numerous articles including, "Excimer Laser-assisted Coronary Angioplasty in Acute ST Elevation Myocardial Infarction", Khan A, Patel NC, Cavros NC, American Journal of Cardiology, 2002; 90(suppl 6A) 109H; "Hormonal Management of Prostatic Cancer", Jolobe OMP, Khan A, British Journal of Hospital Medicine, 1993, Vol 50, No 8; "Prognostic Implications of a Normal Exercise Versus a Normal Dobutamine Stress Echocardiographic Study", Qureshi EA, Khan A, Saeed A, Burhan U, Cohen R, Yao SS, Cahudhury FA, Journal of the American Society of Echocardiography, 2003; 16(5):548; ICU Handbook "Introduction to the ICU", Editor, Amid Khan, The Lankenau Hospital Department of Medicine **Affiliations:** Diplomate, Royal College of Physicians of United Kingdom; American Society of Nuclear Cardiology; American College of Cardiology; American College of Physicians; American Society of Internal Medicine; American Medical Association **Hob./spts.:** Golf, reading, watching movies, travel **SIC code:** 80 **Address:** Lankenau Hospital, 100 Lancaster Ave., Medical Office Bldg., Suite 558, Wynne, PA 19096 **E-mail:** aarkhan@aol.com

KHAN, AYESHA
Industry: Healthcare **Born:** May 2, 1948, Eau Claire, Wisconsin **Univ./degree:** M.D., Dow Medical College **Current organization:** Marshfield Clinic **Title:** M.D. **Type of organization:** Multi-specialty group practice **Major product:** Patient care **Area of distribution:** National **Area of Practice:** Pediatric medicine **Affiliations:** Wisconsin Medical Society **SIC code:** 80 **Address:** Marshfield Clinic, 2116 Craig Rd., Eau Claire, WI 54701 **E-mail:** khan.ayesha@marshfieldclinic.org

KHAN, HUSMAN
Industry: Healthcare **Born:** May 2, 1946, Georgetown, Guyana **Univ./degree:** M.D., Agra Medical College, India, 1972 **Current organization:** Husman Khan, M.D., P.A. **Title:** M.D. **Type of organization:** Private practice **Major product:** Patient care **Area of distribution:** Fort Lauderdale, Florida **Area of Practice:** Internal medicine, geriatrics **Honors/awards:** Who's Who of American Universities and Colleges **Published works:** Articles in medical journals **Affiliations:** F.A.C.P.; A.M.A.; F.M.A.; Broward County Medical Association **Hob./spts.:** Community work **SIC code:** 80 **Address:** 16 S.E. 18th St., Ft. Lauderdale, FL 33316 **E-mail:** dochkahn@mediaone.net

KHAN, M. FAISAL
Industry: Medical **Univ./degree:** M.B.B.S., United Medical & Dental Schools of Guy's & St. Thomas's Hospitals, London, England **Current organization:** Boston Medical Center **Title:** M.D., M.R.C.P. **Type of organization:** Teaching/academic hospital **Major product:** Patient care, medical education **Area of distribution:** Boston Massachusetts **Area of Practice:** Cardiology **Honors/awards:** ARC Medal **Published works:** Review articles, book chapters, abstracts **Affiliations:** Member, Royal College of Physicians, London, England; British Medical Association; American Heart Association; American College of Cardiology **Hob./spts.:** Hiking, biking, squash, gardening **SIC code:** 80 **Address:** Boston Medical Center, Dept. of Cardiology, D8, 88 E. Newton St., Boston, MA 02118 **E-mail:** faisal.khan@comcast.net

KHAN, MOHAMED H.
Industry: Healthcare **Born:** October 29, 1954, Boksburg North, Republic of South Africa **Univ./degree:** M.D., University of Alexandria, Egypt, 1983 **Current organization:** Cardiovascular Institute of the South **Title:** M.D./F.A.C.C./Clinical Hypertension Specialist **Type of organization:** Private medical practice **Major product:** Patient care **Area of distribution:** National **Area of Practice:** Interventional cardiology **Honors/awards:** United Nations Scholarship **Published works:** Articles **Affiliations:** F.A.C.C.; F.A.C.A., F.A.C.A. & I **Hob./spts.:** Soccer, travel, work **SIC code:** 80 **Address:** Cardiovascular Institute of the South, 1270 Attakapas Dr., Suite 501, Opelousas, LA 70570 **E-mail:** mohamed.khan@cardio.com

KHAN, NUSRAT (NESS) A.
Industry: Healthcare **Born:** November 12, 1962, Karachi, Pakistan **Univ./degree:** B.S., Biology, Davidson College, 1991; M.D., East Carolina University **Title:** M.D. **Type of organization:** Private practice **Major product:** Patient care, research **Area of distribution:** National **Area of Practice:** Board Certified, Pediatrics and Internal Medicine, 2002 **Published works:** 10 articles **Affiliations:** F.A.C.P.-A.S.I.M.; F.A.A.P.; F.A.A.H.P.; Former Chief Resident, Cleveland Clinic Foundation; Former Vice Chair, North Carolina Rural Health Coalition **Hob./spts.:** Family **SIC code:** 80 **Address:** 765 Double Jack St., Bourbonnais, IL 60914 **E-mail:** nesskhan@rsh.net

KHAN, QAISAR M
Industry: Healthcare **Born:** June 11, 1976, Karachi, Pakistan **Univ./degree:** H.S.S.C., Lawrence College, 1994; M.D., Aga Khan University, 1999 **Current organization:** University of Arkansas for Medical Sciences **Title:** M.D. **Type of organization:** Hospital **Major product:** Patient care **Area of distribution:** International **Area of Practice:** Cardiac catheterization **Affiliations:** American Heart Association; American College of Cardiology **Hob./spts.:** International travel, dining **SIC code:** 80 **Address:** 13111 West Markham, #57, Little Rock, AR 72211 **E-mail:** qmkhan@uams.edu

KHAN, ZANA N.
Industry: Medical **Univ./degree:** M.S., Pathology, Texas A&M University, 1978 **Current organization:** Temple University Hospital **Title:** Supervisor **Type of organization:** Hospital **Major product:** Patient care **Area of distribution:** Pennsylvania **Area of Practice:** Laboratory management, troubleshooting **Affiliations:** A.S.C.P.; N.S.H. **Hob./spts.:** Tropical fish, house plants **SIC code:** 80 **Address:** 202 Mill Pond Dr., Exton, PA 19341 **E-mail:** khanzn@tuhs.temple.edu

KHANEJA, SATISH C.
Industry: Healthcare **Born:** May 9, 1946, India **Univ./degree:** M.D., All India Institute of Technology, 1967 **Current organization:** Bronx-Lebanon Hospital **Title:** M.D., F.A.C.S. **Type of organization:** Hospital **Major product:** Patient care, surgery **Area of distribution:** New York **Area of Practice:** Thoracic surgery **Published works:** 15 articles **Affiliations:** F.A.C.S.; American Association of Trauma Surgeons **SIC code:** 80 **Address:** Bronx-Lebanon Hospital, 1650 Selwyn Ave., Suite 5A, Bronx, NY 10457

KHASHU, BUSHAN L.
Industry: Healthcare **Born:** January 12, 1942, Kashmir, India **Univ./degree:** M.D., University of Calcutta, India, 1964 **Current organization:** North Shore - LIJ Health System/Albert Einstein College of Medicine **Title:** M.D., Assistant Professor, Director Mens Health **Type of organization:** Hospital **Major product:** Patient care **Area of distribution:** National **Area of Practice:** Urology **Published works:** Multiple publications **Affiliations:** F.A.C.S.; F.R.C.S.; A.U.A; Nassau Academy of Medicine **Hob./spts.:** Long distance bicycling, racquetball **SIC code:** 80 **Address:** North Shore - LIJ Health System, 102-01 66th Rd., Forest Hills, NY 11375 **E-mail:** bushankhashu@aol.com

KHASNIS, ATUL ASHOK
Industry: Medical **Born:** October 8, 1974, Bombay, India **Univ./degree:** M.D., University of Bombay, India, 2002 **Current organization:** Michigan State University **Title:** M.D. **Type of organization:** University/clinical center **Major product:** Patient care, medical education **Area of distribution:** National **Area of Practice:** Internal medicine **Affiliations:** A.C.P./A.S.I.M.; N.M.A. **SIC code:** 80 **Address:** Michigan State University, B301 M.S.U. Clinical Center, East Lansing, MI 48824 **E-mail:** akhas@hotmail.com

KHATTAK, TASLIM A.
Industry: Healthcare **Born:** Karak, Pakistan **Univ./degree:** M.B.B.S., Khyber Medical College, 1984; Residency, Internal Medicine, Methodist Hospital, Memphis, Tennessee **Current organization:** Prime Medical Group, PC **Title:** Director **Type of organization:** Group practice **Major product:** Internal medicine **Area of distribution:** Tennessee **Area of Practice:** Internal medicine (Board Certified), Ob/Gyn, counseling **Affiliations:** American College of Physicians; American Heart Association **Hob./spts.:** Cooking, reading, physical fitness, travel **SIC code:** 80 **Address:** Prime Medical Group, PC, 6006 Park Ave., Suite 433B, Memphis, TN 38119 **E-mail:** takhattak@hotmail.com

KHDAIR, ADNAN M.
Industry: Medical **Born:** July 16, 1954, Baghdad, Iraq **Univ./degree:** M.D., College of Medicine, Baghdad, Iraq, 1978 **Current organization:** Long Island College Hospital Faculty Practice **Title:** M.D. **Type of organization:** College hospital **Major product:** Medical services **Area of distribution:** New York **Area of Practice:** Assistant Professor of Medicine **Affiliations:** A.M.A.; American College of Physicians; American College of Gastroenterologists **Hob./spts.:** Swimming, chess **SIC code:** 80 **Address:** Long Island College Hospital Faculty Practice, 97 Amity St., Brooklyn, NY 11201 **E-mail:** akhdair@aol.com

KHODADADIAN, PARVIZ
Industry: Healthcare **Univ./degree:** M.D., Tehran Medical School, 1965 **Current organization:** Zwanger Pesiri Radiology Group **Title:** M.D./Partner/Director Neuro Surgery **Type of organization:** Private practice **Major product:** Radiology services **Area of distribution:** New York **Area of Practice:** Radiology **Affiliations:** A.M.A.; F.A.C.R.; Nassau Medical Association **SIC code:** 80 **Address:** Zwanger Pesiri Radiology Group, 126 Hicksville Rd., Massapequa, NY 11758 **Web address:** www.zwanger-pesiri.com

KHODR, DOLORES A.
Industry: Healthcare **Born:** May 7, 1939, Oklahoma City, Oklahoma **Univ./degree:** B.S.; M.Ed. **Current organization:** Maxim **Title:** R.N. **Type of organization:** Healthcare placement agency **Major product:** Nursing **Area of distribution:** Oklahoma **Area of Practice:** Medical/surgical nursing, home healthcare **Hob./spts.:** Reading **SIC code:** 80 **Address:** 2420 N.W. 109th St., Oklahoma City, OK 73120-7212 **E-mail:** kdolly39@aol.com

KHOURI, CHARLES H.
Industry: Healthcare **Born:** January 2, 1942, Miami, Florida **Univ./degree:** M.D., American University of Beirut, 1968 **Current organization:** Diabetes Eye Center **Title:** M.D. **Type of organization:** Medical practice **Area of distribution:** International **Area of Practice:** Ophthalmology **Affiliations:** American Academy of Ophthalmology **Hob./spts.:** Computers, medical research **SIC code:** 80 **Address:** Diabetes Eye Center, 9000 S.W. 87 Ct., Suite 206-207, Miami, FL 33176 **E-mail:** drk@dogparalysis.com

KHULPATEEA, NEEKIANUND
Industry: Healthcare **Born:** November 1, 1943, New Grove, Mauritius **Univ./degree:** M.D., Hebrew University, Jerusalem, 1971 **Current organization:** Maimonides Medical Center **Title:** M.D., Director Gyn. Div. **Type of organization:** Hospital **Major product:** Patient care **Area of distribution:** Brooklyn, New York **Area of Practice:** Gynecology, gynecological surgery **Honors/awards:** CREOZ Teaching Award, 1995, 1998, 2000; Excellent Teaching Award, A.P.G.O., 1996; Attending of the Year, 1981-2001; Scholarship to Medical School from 1963-69 **Affiliations:** A.M.A.; A.C.O.G.; A.A.G.O.; S.L.S.; New York Gynecologic Society; Brooklyn Gynecologic Society **Hob./spts.:** Gardening, travel **SIC code:** 80 **Address:** Maimonides Medical Center, Division of Gynecology, 953 49th St., 2nd floor, Brooklyn, NY 11219

KHULPATEEA, TARULATA
Industry: Healthcare **Born:** May 7, 1944, Kalol, India **Univ./degree:** M.D., Bombay University Medical School, 1969 **Current organization:** Nassau Suffolk Ob/Gyn **Title:** M.D., F.A.C.O.G., Co-Owner **Type of organization:** Private group medical practice **Major product:** Patient care **Area of distribution:** New York **Area of Practice:** Ob/Gyn **Affiliations:** Fellow, American College of Gynecologists; Brooklyn Gynecological Society; Nassau County Gynecological and Obstetrics Society; **Hob./**

spts.: Reading, cooking, travel **SIC code:** 80 **Address:** Nassau Suffolk Ob/Gyn, 4200 Sunrise Hwy., Massapequa, NY 11758

KIA, ALI
Industry: Healthcare **Born:** March 3, 1974, Tehran, Iran **Univ./degree:** M.D., Roth University, 2002 **Current organization:** Rancho Internal Medicine Group **Title:** M.D./ Clinician **Type of organization:** Hospital **Major product:** Internal medicine **Area of distribution:** Las Vegas, Nevada **Area of Practice:** Clinical medicine **Affiliations:** A.M.S.A.; A.M.A.; A.C.P.; A.H.C.A.P. **Hob./spts.:** Yoga, snowboarding, car restoration, hiking **SIC code:** 80 **Address:** Rancho Internal Medicine Group, 2705 Sun Cactus Ct., Las Vegas, NV 89106 **E-mail:** ah33174@yahoo.com

KIM, GARY O.
Industry: Healthcare **Born:** August 19, 1931, Kae Sung, Korea **Univ./degree:** M.D., University of California at Irvine College of Medicine, 1966 **Current organization:** Gary O. Kim, M.D. **Title:** M.D. **Type of organization:** Private practice **Major product:** Patient care **Area of distribution:** Arcadia, California **Area of Practice:** Internal medicine **Affiliations:** A.M.A.; Diplomate, A.C.F.M. **Hob./spts.:** Golf **SIC code:** 80 **Address:** Gary O. Kim, M.D., 612 W. Duarte Rd., #501, Arcadia, CA 91007 **E-mail:** garyokim@hotmail.com

KIM, JOHN J.
Industry: Healthcare **Born:** Seoul, Korea **Univ./degree:** Bachelor of Liberal Arts, DePaul University; M.S., Health Sciences, University of Illinois, Chicago, 2000 **Current organization:** Health Benefits Pain Management Service **Title:** Director of Operations **Type of organization:** Pain management clinic **Major product:** Patient care **Area of distribution:** Chicago, Illinois **Area of Practice:** Chronic pain management **Affiliations:** A.P.S.; American College of Sports Medicine; Chicago Council on Foreign Relations **Hob./spts.:** Running, weight training **SIC code:** 80 **Address:** Health Benefits Pain Management Service, 25 E. Washington St., Suite 1329, Chicago, IL 60620 **E-mail:** hbpain@sbcglobal.net

KIM, OWEN
Industry: Healthcare **Born:** January 17, 1955, Seoul, Korea **Univ./degree:** M.D., University of California at Los Angeles, 1981 **Current organization:** Cancer Treatment Center **Title:** M.D./Medical Director **Type of organization:** Medical practice **Major product:** Patient care **Area of distribution:** Porterville, California **Area of Practice:** Cancer treatment and hospice **Affiliations:** A.B.R.; A.B.H.P.M. **Hob./spts.:** Studying international religions **SIC code:** 80 **Address:** Cancer Treatment Center, 465 W. Putnam Ave., Porterville, CA 93257 **E-mail:** syar@ocsnet.net

KIM, TAEK Y.
Industry: Healthcare **Born:** March 15, 1941, Korea **Univ./degree:** M.D., Yonsei Medical College, Korea, 1966 **Current organization:** Taek Y. Kim, M.D.S.C. **Title:** M.D./President **Type of organization:** Private practice **Major product:** Patient care **Area of distribution:** Illinois **Area of Practice:** Obstetrics/gynecology, infertility, gyne urology, cosmetic skin laser surgery **Published works:** Write-ups **Affiliations:** F.A.C.O.G; I.M.S.; A.M.A. **SIC code:** 80 **Address:** Taek Y. Kim, M.D.S.C., 6800 S. Main St., Suite 218, Downers Grove, IL 60516

KIPPER, DAVID A.
Industry: Healthcare consulting **Univ./degree:** Ph.D., Durham University, England **Current organization:** Executive Psychological Consulting, Ltd. **Title:** Ph.D. **Type of organization:** Consulting **Major product:** Psychological consulting **Area of distribution:** International **Area of Practice:** Psychology, family business mediation **Published works:** 70+ articles, 1 book **Affiliations:** A.P.A. **SIC code:** 80 **Address:** Executive Psychological Consulting, Ltd., 142 E. Ontario, Suite 550, Chicago, IL 60611 **E-mail:** kipperda@aol.com

KIRCHNER, JOHN R.
Industry: Healthcare **Born:** March 16, 1935, Omaha, Nebraska **Univ./degree:** B.S., Biology, Creighton University, 1957; M.D., University of Nebraska School of Medicine, 1961 **Current organization:** Kirchner Headache Clinic **Title:** M.D./Director **Type of organization:** Private medical clinic **Major product:** Patient services **Area of distribution:** National **Area of Practice:** Board Certified, Headache Management **Honors/awards:** Served in Active Duty U.S. Army from 1962-1964 - Retired as a Captain **Published works:** 2 articles **Affiliations:** A.H.S.; I.H.S. **SIC code:** 80 **Address:** Kirchner Headache Clinic, 13906 Gold Circle, Suite 104, Omaha, NE 68144 **Web address:** www.kirchnerheadacheclinic.com

KIRSNER, JOSEPH BARNETT
Industry: Medical **Born:** September 21, 1909, Boston, Massachusetts **Univ./degree:** M.D., Tufts University, 1935; Ph.D., University of Chicago, 1942 **Current organization:** University of Chicago Hospitals **Title:** M.D., Ph.D. **Type of organization:** University Hospital **Major product:** Healthcare, medical education **Area of distribution:** International **Area of Practice:** Inflammatory bowel disease **Published works:** 730 scientific papers, edited 17 textbooks **Affiliations:** A.S.C.I.; A.A.P.; A.G.I.A.; Co-Founder, A.S.G.E.; Founder, Gastrology Research Group **Hob./spts.:** Classical music **SIC code:** 80 **Address:** University of Chicago Hospitals, 5805 S. Dorchester Ave., Top C, Chicago, IL 60637 **E-mail:** jkirsner@medicine.bsd.uchicago.edu

KISBERG, STEPHEN
Industry: Healthcare **Born:** May 14, 1943, Brooklyn, New York **Univ./degree:** B.S., Biology, Long Island University, 1966; D.P.M., New York College of Podiatric Medicine, 1970 **Current organization:** South Shore Podiatry **Title:** Podiatrist **Type of organization:** Private practice **Major product:** Podiatric medicine **Area of distribution:** New York **Area of Practice:** Podiatric medicine **Affiliations:** P.P.S. **SIC code:** 80 **Address:** South Shore Podiatry, 11 Franklin Place, Woodmere, NY 11598

KISLING, CHERYL L.
Industry: Healthcare **Born:** August 10, 1955, Lincoln, Nebraska **Current organization:** Mosaic **Title:** R.N. **Type of organization:** Hospital **Major product:** Patient care **Area of distribution:** Beatrice, Nebraska **Area of Practice:** Director of Nursing **Hob./spts.:** Family time, bowling **SIC code:** 80 **Address:** Mosaic, 722 S. 12th St., Beatrice, NE 68310

KITE, CARL J.
Industry: Healthcare **Univ./degree:** M.D., West Virginia University, 1976 **Current organization:** Health Plan of Upper Ohio Valley **Title:** M.D. **Type of organization:** Private practice **Major product:** Patient care **Area of distribution:** West Virginia **Area of Practice:** Internal medicine **Affiliations:** Fellow, A.C.S. **SIC code:** 80 **Address:** Health Plan of Upper Ohio Valley, 953 National Rd., Suite 127, Wheeling, WV 26003 **E-mail:** boobsurg@aol.com

KLAINER, PETER S.
Industry: Healthcare **Born:** September 9, 1962, Boston, Massachusetts **Univ./degree:** M.D., Columbia University College of Physicians and Surgeons, 1988 **Current organization:** Chrysalis Plastic Surgery **Title:** M.D., F.A.C.S. **Type of organization:** Private practice **Major product:** Plastic, aesthetic and reconstructive surgery **Area of distribution:** Virginia **Area of Practice:** Breast augmentation, liposuction, abdominoplasty, facial surgery, lasers **Published works:** 8 articles **Affiliations:** A.M.A.; A.S.P.S.; A.S.L.M.S. **Hob./spts.:** Bowling (National League) **SIC code:** 80 **Address:** Chrysalis Plastic Surgery, 21495 Ridgetop Circle, #201, Sterling, VA 20166 **E-mail:** chrysalisplastic@prodigy.net

KLETZKER, G. ROBERT
Industry: Healthcare **Born:** February 20, 1952, St. Louis, Missouri **Univ./degree:** M.D., University of Missouri School of Medicine, 1984 **Current organization:** Ear Care & Skull Base Surgery **Title:** M.D. **Type of organization:** Private practice **Major product:** Patient care **Area of distribution:** Missouri **Area of Practice:** Otology, neurotology, skull base surgery **Affiliations:** A.A.O.H.N.S.; A.N.S.; N.A.S.B.S. **Hob./spts.:** Golf, sailing, water sports **SIC code:** 80 **Address:** 621 South New Ballas Road, Suite 611-A, St. Louis, MO 63141 **E-mail:** earcare@sprintmail.com

KNOX, THOMAS I.
Industry: Healthcare **Born:** December 28, 1970, Danbury, Connecticut **Univ./degree:** M.D., Tuft University, 1996 **Current organization:** Thomas I. Knox, M.D. **Title:** M.D./ Cardiologist **Type of organization:** Private practice **Major product:** Patient care **Area of distribution:** West Hartford, Connecticut **Area of Practice:** Cardiology **Honors/awards:** Doctor Elliot Award, 1993 **Affiliations:** A.M.A.; M.M.S.; A.C.C.; A.S.N.C. **SIC code:** 80 **Address:** Thomas I. Knox, M.D., 118 Fuller Dr., West Hartford, CT 06117 **E-mail:** knoxy@attbi.com

KOCH, TODD B.
Industry: Healthcare **Born:** June 25, 1951, Brooklyn, New York **Univ./degree:** M.D., University of Buffalo, 1977 **Current organization:** Todd B. Koch, MD **Title:** M.D. **Type of organization:** Private practice **Major product:** Patient care **Area of distribution:** Williamsville, New York **Area of Practice:** Cosmetic surgery **Affiliations:** A.S.P.S.; A.S.A.P.S.; A.M.A; New York State Medical Society; Erie County Medical Society; Assistant Clinical Professor, SUNY Buffalo **Hob./spts.:** Running, weight lifting, biking, skiing **SIC code:** 80 **Address:** Todd B. Koch, MD, 6315 Sheridan Dr., Buffalo, NY 14221 **E-mail:** tbkochmd@aol.com

KOKKALERA, UTHAIAH P.
Industry: Healthcare **Born:** Bangalore, India **Univ./degree:** M.D., Bangalore Medical College, 1996 **Current organization:** UMass Memorial Medical Center, Dept. of General and Laparoscopic Surgery **Title:** M.D., F.A.C.S. **Type of organization:** University medical center **Major product:** Patient care, medical education, research **Area of distribution:** Worcester, Massachusetts **Area of Practice:** Laparoscopic surgery, general surgery and bariatrics **Affiliations:** F.A.C.P.; S.A.G.E.S.; S.L.S. **Hob./spts.:** Music, playing drums, guitar and harmonica **SIC code:** 80 **Address:** UMass Memorial Medical Center, Dept. of General & Laparoscopic Surgery, 55 Lake Ave. North, Worcester, MA 01606 **E-mail:** uthaiah470@hotmail.com

KOLESNIKOV, SERGEI
Industry: Medical **Born:** February 22, 1961, Ukraine **Univ./degree:** M.D., Ukraine, 1984 **Current organization:** SUNY at Buffalo **Title:** M.D. **Type of organization:** University hospital **Major product:** Patient care **Area of distribution:** National **Area of Practice:** Anesthesiology **Published works:** Articles **Affiliations:** A.M.A.; A.P.A.; New York Society of Anesthesiologists **Hob./spts.:** Chess, downhill skiing **SIC code:** 80 **Address:** 32 Greystone Lane, Orchard Park, NY 14127 **E-mail:** sk38@acsu.buffalo.edu

KOLOZSVARY, JOHN A.
Industry: Healthcare **Born:** Detroit, Michigan **Univ./degree:** B.S., Health Systems Management, Lake Superior State University, 1979; M.S., Health Service Administration, Central Michigan University, 1993 **Current organization:** POH Medical Center **Title:** Director Ambulatory Care **Type of organization:** Hospital **Major product:** Patient care **Area of distribution:** Michigan **Area of Practice:** Business operations and development **Affiliations:** H.F.M.A.; M.G.M.A. **Hob./spts.:** Golf, biking **SIC code:** 80 **Address:** POH Medical Center, 385 N. Lapeer Rd., Oxford, MI 48390 **E-mail:** jkolozsvar@aol.com

KOLTZOVA, YULIA K.
Industry: Healthcare **Born:** October 20, 1972, San Mateo, California **Univ./degree:** B.A., Biology; B.A., Russian, Johns Hopkins University, 1994; M.D., University of Rochester, 1998 **Current organization:** Cohen & Huffurd MDs, Inc. **Title:** M.D. **Type of organization:** Private practice **Major product:** Patient care **Area of distribution:** California **Area of Practice:** Internal medicine **Honors/awards:** Golden Key National Honor Society, Psi Chi Honor Society, Johns Hopkins University **Affiliations:** A.C.P.; A.M.A. **Hob./spts.:** Cooking, travel **SIC code:** 80 **Address:** Cohen & Huffurd MDs, Inc., 3838 California St. #707, San Francisco, CA 94118 **E-mail:** ykoltzova@hotmail.com

KOMARI, HABIB JOHN
Industry: Healthcare **Born:** December 20, 1954, Al Hasakah, Syria **Univ./degree:** M.D., Aleppo University, Syria, 1978; Internal Medicine/Cornell Medical College, Affiliated Hospital, Englewood, New Jersey, 1988; Cardiology Fellow, Tufts Medical School, BVMC, Boston, Massachusetts, 1991; Nuclear Cardiology, Harvard Medical School, Ms, **Current organization:** Indiana Cardiac and Vascular Consultants (ICVC) **Title:** MD/Chairman/CEO **Type of organization:** Medical group practice **Major product:** Cardiovascular care, disease prevention and medical consulting **Area of distribution:** National **Area of Practice:** Board Certified, Internal Medicine, Cardiology, Nuclear Cardiology; disease prevention, lecturing and public speaking, medical practice administration and management **Honors/awards:** Listed in the National Directory of Who's Who in Executive and Professions; America's Top Physician Award **Affiliations:** F.A.C.P.E.; F.A.C.C.; F.A.C.P.; F.C.C.P.; A.M.A.; I.S.M.A.; Dudley White Society; Nuclear Cardiology Society **Hob./spts.:** Family, soccer, table tennis, Chairman of "Core Care", a mobile vascular laboratory and MSOI, a consultancy providing assistance to physicians **SIC code:** 80 **Address:** Indiana Cardiac and Vascular Consultants, 1350 E. County Line Rd., Suite H, Indianapolis, IN 46227 **E-mail:** icvc001@aol.comicvckomari@aol.com **Web address:** www.icvc.com

KOMODROMOS, THEMIS
Industry: Healthcare **Born:** November 19, 1970, Cyprus **Univ./degree:** M.D., Hungary, Albert Szent Gyorgyi Medical University, 1998 **Current organization:** Michael Reese Hospital **Title:** M.D. **Type of organization:** Hospital **Major product:** Patient care **Area of distribution:** Chicago, Illinois **Area of Practice:** Internal medicine, Cardiovascular Disease Fellow **Honors/awards:** Summa Cum Laude; Alfred Pick Award for Academic Excellence, 2000-2001 **Published works:** Articles in medical journals **Affiliations:** American College of Cardiology **SIC code:** 80 **Address:** 2901 S. King Dr., #1511, Chicago, IL 60616 **E-mail:** theko@hotmail.com

KONTRAS, DANA G.
Industry: Healthcare **Born:** September 15, 1960, Cleveland, Ohio **Univ./degree:** M.S.N., University of Phoenix, 2002 **Current organization:** Mayo Clinic Jacksonville **Title:** RN, MSN, CCRP Supervisor **Type of organization:** Hospital **Major product:** Patient care, education, research **Area of distribution:** Florida **Area of Practice:** Research **Affiliations:** S.C.C.A.; M.U.S.C.A.; N.A.N.A.I.N.A.; Sigma Theta Tau **Hob./spts.:** Assisting American Indian people in eliminating health disparity; music **SIC code:** 80 **Address:** 1575 Parkwood St., Jacksonville, FL 32207 **E-mail:** kontras@bellsouth.net

KOPPARTHI, ROM MOHAN
Industry: Healthcare **Born:** August 11, 1951, Vijayawada, India **Univ./degree:** M.D., Kurnool University of Health Sciences, India, 1978 **Current organization:** Advocate Neonatology Group **Title:** Medical Director of I.C.U. **Type of organization:** Hospital based medical practice **Major product:** Patient care **Area of distribution:** Illinois **Area of Practice:** Neonatology **Honors/awards:** Gold Medal, Top Pediatric Physician of the Year, Washington D.C., 2002 **Published works:** 1 article **Affiliations:** F.A.A.P.; A.A.P.I. **Hob./spts.:** Tennis, golf **SIC code:** 80 **Address:** 1480 Radcliff Lane, Aurora, IL 60504 **E-mail:** rommohan@yahoo.com

KORKMAZSKY, YELENA
Industry: Healthcare **Born:** January 19, 1961, Russia **Univ./degree:** M.D., Saratov Medical School, Russia, 1984 **Current organization:** Springfield Pediatrics **Title:** M.D. **Type of organization:** Private practice **Major product:** Patient care **Area of distribution:** Springfield, New Jersey **Area of Practice:** Pediatrics **Affiliations:** A.A.P. **Hob./spts.:** Hiking, skiing **SIC code:** 80 **Address:** Springfield Pediatrics, 190 Meisel Ave., Springfield, NJ 07081 **E-mail:** yelenak@mail.com

KORNMEHL, CAROL L.
Industry: Healthcare **Born:** April 14, 1959, Brooklyn, New York **Univ./degree:** M.D., State University of New York at Downstate, 1984 **Current organization:** New Jersey Radiation Therapy **Title:** M.D. **Type of organization:** Medical practice **Major product:** Patient care **Area of distribution:** Brick, New Jersey **Area of Practice:** Radiation oncology **Published works:** 4 articles **Affiliations:** A.S.T.R.O.; A.C.R.; N.J.O.S. **Hob./spts.:** Music **SIC code:** 80 **Address:** New Jersey Radiation Therapy, 455 Jack Martin Blvd., Brick, NJ 08724 **E-mail:** ckornmehl@sonixmr.com

KOZIKOWSKI, LORI-ANN
Industry: Healthcare **Born:** January 2, 1963, Springfield, Massachusetts **Univ./degree:** A.S.N. with Highest Honors, Holyoke Community College, 1994 **Current organization:** Bay state Medical Center **Title:** RN, CCRC **Type of organization:** Teaching hospital **Major product:** Patient care, level I trauma center **Area of distribution:** Springfield, Massachusetts **Area of Practice:** Research Coordinator **Honors/awards:** Elaine Marieb Scholarship; Bay state Legend; Phi Theta Kappa **Published works:** Co-author, 1abstract: Activated Protein C Therapy in Patients with ARDS/ALI and Severe Sepsis. Critical Care Medicine 7.003; 30: A10Z **Affiliations:** Association of Clinical Research Professionals **SIC code:** 80 **Address:** Baystate Medical Center, 759 Chestnut St., Springfield, MA 01199 **E-mail:** lori-ann.kozikowski@bhs.org

KRANIAS, GEORGE
Industry: Healthcare **Born:** November 19, 1941, Salonika, Greece **Univ./degree:** M.D., Medical School of Salonika, Greece, 1968 **Current organization:** Tri State Eye Care **Title:** Clinical Professor of Ophthalmology **Type of organization:** Group practice **Major product:** Patient care **Area of distribution:** Ohio **Area of Practice:** Vitreo-Retinal Surgeon **Published works:** Articles, abstracts, journals **Affiliations:** American Academy of Ophthalmology; Vitreous Society **Hob./spts.:** General Manager, Clifton Investment Company **SIC code:** 80 **Address:** Tri State Eye Care, 2230 Auburn Ave., Cincinnati, OH 45219 **E-mail:** gkranias@yahoo.com

KRIEGER, BEN-ZION
Industry: Healthcare **Born:** July 31, 1951, Israel **Univ./degree:** M.D., University of Bologna, Italy **Current organization:** Ben-Zion Krieger, M.D. **Title:** Associate Clinical Professor, State University of New York **Type of organization:** Group practice **Major product:** Patient care **Area of distribution:** Brooklyn, New York **Area of Practice:** Pediatrics/allergy and immunology **Honors/awards:** Helped pass a law to enable pregnant women to obtain an HIV test **Published works:** Articles **Affiliations:** F.A.A.P.; A.M.A.; Brooklyn Pediatric Association **Hob./spts.:** Baseball fan (Yankees), collecting baseball cards **SIC code:** 80 **Address:** Ben-Zion Krieger, M.D., 1365 48th St., Brooklyn, NY 11219 **E-mail:** dudie48@aol.com

KRING, BRUNHILD
Industry: Medical **Born:** July 14, 1952, Wehrheim, Germany **Univ./degree:** M.D., University of Frankfurt, Germany, 1978; Residency, Albert Einstein College of Medicine, Bronx, New York, 1983 **Current organization:** Lincoln Medical & Mental Health Center **Title:** Director of Residency Training **Type of organization:** University affiliated hospital **Major product:** Medical services **Area of distribution:** International **Area of Practice:** Psychiatry **Honors/awards:** Excellence Teacher Award, Cornell University, 2001; Best Teacher of the Year, Cornell University Medical Center **Published works:** 3+ articles **Affiliations:** American Psychiatric Association; Society of Sex Therapy & Research **Hob./spts.:** Academic advancement **SIC code:** 80 **Address:** Lincoln Medical & Mental Health Center, 234 E. 149th St., Bronx, NY 10451

KRISHNAMURTHY, MAHESH
Industry: Healthcare **Born:** Tamil Nadu, India **Univ./degree:** M.D., St. John's Medical College of India; Fellowship, New York University **Current organization:** Academic Faculty, Dept. of Internal Medicine, Easton Hospital **Title:** M.D. **Type of organization:** Hospital **Major product:** Patient care **Area of distribution:** Pennsylvania **Area of Practice:** Geriatrics and internal medicine **Published works:** 10 peer-reviewed articles for medical journals **Affiliations:** A.M.A.; American College of Physicians; American Geriatric Society **Hob./spts.:** Basketball, reading, travel **SIC code:** 80 **Address:** Academic Faculty, Dept. of Internal Medicine, Easton Hospital, 2040 Lehigh St., Suite 321, Easton, PA 18042 **E-mail:** krishm01@med.nyu.edu

KRISHNAMURTHY, VENKATARAMU

Industry: Healthcare **Born:** May 10, 1971, Sagar, India **Univ./degree:** M.D., Post Graduate Institute of Medical Education and Research, Chandigarh, India, 1997; Residency, Radiology, India, 1994 **Current organization:** University of Michigan/VA Hospital **Title:** M.D./Radiologist/Clinical Assistant Professor **Type of organization:** University/VA hospital **Major product:** Medical education/VA patient care **Area of distribution:** International **Area of Practice:** Interventional radiology, interventional oncology, peripheral vascular interventions; Radiology (Board Certified) **Honors/awards:** Silver Medal for Diagnostic Radiology, PGI; Henry H. Lerner Award, Teaching Excellence, University of Michigan, 2005; Fellowship, Abdominal Imaging, University of Miami, 2001; Fellowship, Vascular Interventional Radiology, Indiana University Hospital, 2001-02 **Published works:** 10 publications, 1 book chapter **Affiliations:** Radiological Society of North America; I.R. Lexicon Committee; American Roentgen Ray Society **Hob./spts.:** Reading **SIC code:** 80 **Address:** University of Michigan/VA Hospital, UHB1 D530, 1500 East Medical Center Dr., Ann Arbor, MI 48109 **E-mail:** venkatking@hotmail.com

KRISHT, ALI F.

Industry: Medical **Born:** September 17, 1959, Kano, Nigeria **Univ./degree:** M.D., Emery University, 1985 **Current organization:** University of Arkansas for Medical Sciences **Title:** M.D., F.A.C.S. **Type of organization:** University hospital **Major product:** Patient care **Area of distribution:** International **Area of Practice:** Neurosurgery **Published works:** Book, "Pituitary Disorders: Comprehensive Management"; Editor, "Contemporary Neurosurgery" **Affiliations:** Fellow, American College of Surgeons; American Association of Neurological Surgery **Hob./spts.:** Soccer **SIC code:** 80 **Address:** University of Arkansas for Medical Sciences, 4301 W. Markham, Slot 507, Little Rock, AR 72205 **E-mail:** krishtali@uams.edu

KROHN, MICHAEL J.

Industry: Healthcare **Born:** January 2, 1948, Milwaukee, Wisconsin **Univ./degree:** B.S., Nuclear Medicine, University of Iowa **Current organization:** V.A. Medical Center **Title:** Nuclear Medicine Technologist **Type of organization:** Hospital **Major product:** Patient care **Area of distribution:** Wisconsin **Area of Practice:** Nuclear medicine **Affiliations:** Society of Nuclear Medicine **Hob./spts.:** Sailing **SIC code:** 80 **Address:** V.A. Medical Center, 5149 N. Santa Monica Blvd., Whitefish Bay, WI 53217

KROLICK, MERRILL A.

Industry: Healthcare **Born:** October 14, 1959, New York, New York **Univ./degree:** D.O., College of Osteopathic Medicine, 1985 **Current organization:** Heart and Vascular Institute of Florida **Title:** D.O. **Type of organization:** Medical institute **Major product:** Patient care **Area of distribution:** National **Area of Practice:** Cardiology (interventional) **Affiliations:** F.A.C.C.; F.A.C.P.; A.O.A.; A.M.A.; S.C.E.I. **Hob./spts.:** Football **SIC code:** 80 **Address:** 7664 Hunter Lane, Pinellas Park, FL 33782 **E-mail:** m.krolick@tampabay.rr.com

KRPAN, MARKO F.

Industry: Healthcare **Univ./degree:** B.S., Agustana College,1988; M.D., Des Moines University Osteopathic Medical Center, 1998 **Current organization:** Mercy Health Systems **Title:** D.O./Orthopaedic Surgeon **Type of organization:** Group practice **Major product:** Patient care **Area of distribution:** Illinois **Area of Practice:** Orthopaedic surgery **Affiliations:** A.O.S.; A.O.O.S. **SIC code:** 80 **Address:** Mercy Health Systems, 350 Congress Pkwy., Suite E, Crystal Lake, IL 60014 **E-mail:** mkrpan@mhsjvc.org

KRUMPOS, GERALD L.

Industry: Healthcare **Born:** January 11, 1964, Green Bay, Wisconsin **Univ./degree:** M.D., University of Wisconsin, 1991 **Current organization:** Portage Clinic, Ltd. **Title:** M.D. **Type of organization:** Medical practice **Major product:** Patient care **Area of distribution:** Portage, Wisconsin **Area of Practice:** Family practice (Board Certified), obstetrics **Affiliations:** A.M.A.; A.A.F.P.; Tri-County Medical Society; State Medical Society of Wisconsin **Hob./spts.:** Baseball, deep-sea fishing **SIC code:** 80 **Address:** Portage Clinic, Ltd., St. Mary's Ventures, 916 Silver Lake Rd., Portage, WI 53901

KRUSE, CARL R.

Industry: Healthcare **Born:** January 26, 1933, Hannibal, Missouri **Univ./degree:** M.D., University of Iowa, 1966 **Current organization:** Mark Twain Area Counseling Center **Title:** M.D./Medical Director **Type of organization:** Community counseling center **Major product:** Counseling and psychiatric evaluation **Area of distribution:** Hannibal, Missouri **Area of Practice:** Psychiatry **Affiliations:** A.M.A.; President, Missouri State Medical Association **Hob./spts.:** Woodworking **SIC code:** 80 **Address:** Mark Twain Area Counseling Center, 917 Broadway, Hannibal, MO 63401

KUKEC, VAL B.

Industry: Healthcare **Born:** March 9, 1950, Germany **Univ./degree:** A.A.S., Architectural Engineering, 1976; A.S., Building Technology, 1979; College of Dupage; B.S., Civil Engineering, Kensington University, 1986 **Current organization:** Oak Forest Hospital of Cook County **Title:** Director of Materials Management **Type of organization:** Hospital **Major product:** Patient care **Area of distribution:** Oak Forest, Illinois **Area of Practice:** Construction management, materials management, civil engineering, architectural engineering, materials management **Affiliations:** American Society for Testing Materials; Construction Specifications Institute; Society for Maintenance and Reliability Professionals; American Society for Hospital Engineering **Hob./spts.:** Photography, fishing, golf **SIC code:** 80 **Address:** Oak Forest Hospital, 15900 South Cicero Ave., Oak Forest, IL 60452 **E-mail:** saxon57germ@yahoo.com

KUMAR, SHASHI

Industry: Healthcare **Born:** August 20, 1956, India **Univ./degree:** M.D., Banaras Hindu University, India, 1981 **Current organization:** Southwest Gastroenterology Assoc. **Title:** M.D. **Type of organization:** Medical practice **Major product:** Patient care **Area of distribution:** Clairton, Pennsylvania **Area of Practice:** Gastroenterology **Published works:** Articles **Affiliations:** A.M.A.; A.G.A.; P.M.S. **Hob./spts.:** Swimming, golf, volleyball **SIC code:** 80 **Address:** Southwest Gastroenterology Assoc., 1200 Brooks Lane, Suite 260, Clairton, PA 15025 **E-mail:** ina925@aol.com

KUNCHAPPA, KARTHY

Industry: Healthcare **Born:** August 24, 1961, Ooty, India **Univ./degree:** B.P.T., Sri Ramakrishna Institute of Paramedical Science, 1991 **Current organization:** Jackson's Preferred Rehab. Care Inc. **Title:** President, Physical Therapist **Type of organization:** Clinics **Major product:** Rehabilitation, wellness **Area of distribution:** Central Michigan **Area of Practice:** Manual physical therapy, myofacial release, soft tissue massage, vestibular rehabilitation **Affiliations:** American Physical Therapy Association; Jackson and Leslie Chambers of Commerce **Hob./spts.:** Knitting, fabric painting **SIC code:** 80 **Address:** Jackson's Preferred Rehab. Care Inc., 2545 Spring Arbor Rd., Jackson, MI 49203 **E-mail:** srishankar@comcast.net

MEDICAL

KUPPUSWAMY, BAIRAVA S.

Industry: Medical **Born:** November 17, 1968, Banglor, India **Univ./degree:** M.B.B.S., J.J.M. Medical College, 1994 **Current organization:** Camden Clark Memorial Hospital **Title:** Internist-Consultant Physician **Type of organization:** Teaching hospital **Major product:** Patient care, medical education **Area of distribution:** Parkersburg West Virginia and Mid Ohio Valley **Area of Practice:** Internal Medicine and care of elderly **Honors/awards:** Best Resident of the Year, Brookdale University Medical Center 2003, Chief Resident of Medicine 2004 **Published works:** 2 case reports (in gastroenterology and hepatology) **Affiliations:** American College of Physicians; American Medical Association; Member, Royal College of Physicians, U.K., 2000 **Hob./spts.:** Chess, meditation, motorcycle rallies, music **SIC code:** 80 **Address:** 2610 Camden Ave., Parkersburg, WV 26104 **E-mail:** bairavs@hotmail.com

KUTCH SR., STEPHEN M.

Industry: Healthcare **Born:** May 18, 1940, Connellsville, Pennsylvania **Univ./degree:** Air Force Certification, Electrical Engineering, 1960 **Current organization:** Presbyterian Healthcare Services **Title:** Supervisor Facility Services **Type of organization:** Hospital **Major product:** Patient care **Area of distribution:** New Mexico **Area of practice:** Facilities engineering **Area of Practice:** Facilities engineering **Hob./spts.:** Walking, fishing, hunting **SIC code:** 80 **Address:** 1027 Dorothy St. N.E., Albuquerque, NM 87112 **E-mail:** skutch@phs.org **Web address:** www.phs.org

KUURE, BOJAN M.

Industry: Healthcare **Born:** November 14, 1942, Finland **Univ./degree:** Surgery and Anesthesia, University of Helsinki, Finland (Specialty Nurse in Operating Room with Management Degree) **Current organization:** Island Hospital **Title:** R.N./Director of Surgical Services **Type of organization:** Hospital **Major product:** Patient care **Area of distribution:** Washington, International (Third World Countries) **Area of Practice:** Director of OR, PACU, OP, CS & Pain clinic **Honors/awards:** Paul Harris Award; Soroptimist International, "Women Helping Women Award", 2003 **Affiliations:** A.O.R.N., N.W.O.N.E.; Interplast; Healing the Children, West Coast and Midlantic Chapters **Hob./spts.:** Volunteer work around the world, travel **SIC code:** 80 **Address:** Island Hospital, 1211 24th St., Anacortes, WA 98221 **E-mail:** bkuure@islandhospital.org **Web address:** www.islandhospital.org

KUZNETSOV, VALERY

Industry: Healthcare **Born:** January 11, 1958 **Univ./degree:** M.D., First Moscow Medical Institute, 1981 **Current organization:** Dr. Valery Kuznetsov Cardiologist, P.C. **Title:** M.D. **Type of organization:** Private practice **Major product:** Patient care **Area of Practice:** Cardiology **Published works:** 10 publications **Affiliations:** Fellow, American College of Cardiology; New York State Medical Society **SIC code:** 80 **Address:** Dr. Valery Kuznetsov Cardiologist, P.C., 202 Foster Ave., Suite D, Brooklyn, NY 11230 **E-mail:** kuz100@yahoo.com

KWAI BEN, VALERIE C.

Industry: Healthcare **Born:** May 26, 1963, Panama **Univ./degree:** M.D., Medical College of Wisconsin, 1990 **Current organization:** The Permanente Medical Group **Title:** M.D./Chief of Pharmacy and Therapeutics/Director, Echocardiography Lab **Type of**

organization: Hospital **Major product:** Patient care, cardiovascular disease treatment **Area of distribution:** San Jose, California **Area of Practice:** Cardiology **Affiliations:** F.A.C.C.; A.M.A.; S.C.C.M.A. **Hob./spts.:** Racquetball, gardening **SIC code:** 80 **Address:** The Permanente Medical Group, 270 International Circle Two North, Second floor, San Jose, CA 95119-1110 **E-mail:** valerie.kwaiben@kp.org

KWITEROVICH JR., PETER O.
Industry: Medical **Born:** June 24, 1940, Danville, Pennsylvania **Univ./degree:** B.S., Holy Cross, 1962; M.D., Johns Hopkins University School of Medicine, 1966 **Current organization:** Johns Hopkins University School of Medicine **Title:** M.D./Professor **Type of organization:** University hospital **Major product:** Medical education/research **Area of distribution:** International **Area of Practice:** Cholesterol **Published works:** 300+ articles and chapters, 150 abstracts, 1 book **Affiliations:** American Society for Clinical Investigation; Society of Pediatric Research **Hob./spts.:** Family, boating, fishing, running **SIC code:** 80 **Address:** Johns Hopkins University School of Medicine, 550 N. Broadway, Baltimore, MD 21205 **E-mail:** pkwitero@jhmi.edu

KYLE, MARIE E.
Industry: Healthcare **Born:** July 26, 1955, Ohio **Univ./degree:** B.S., Bowling Green State University, 1977 **Current organization:** Med Synergies, Inc. **Title:** Practice Manger **Type of organization:** Multi specialty practice **Major product:** Ophthalmology, oculoplastic surgery **Area of distribution:** Orlando, Florida **Area of Practice:** Personnel management **Published works:** Articles, National Peddle Sports Magazine **Affiliations:** American Academy of Ophthalmology **Hob./spts.:** Reading, computers **SIC code:** 80 **Address:** Med Synergies, Inc., Dr. Bates, Parker & Haas, 16 West Columbia Street, Orlando, FL 32806 **E-mail:** kyle3872@aol.com

LACSON, ATILANO G.
Industry: Healthcare **Born:** October 5, 1948 **Univ./degree:** B.S., Pre-Medicine, 1968; M.D., 1972, University of Philippines, Manila **Current organization:** All Children's Hospital **Title:** MD, FRCPC **Type of organization:** Hospital **Major product:** Patient care **Area of distribution:** Oldsmar, Florida **Area of Practice:** Pediatric pathology, neuropathology and diagnostic services **Affiliations:** Fellow, American Society of Clinical Pathologists; College of American Pathologists **SIC code:** 80 **Address:** All Children's Hospital, 4970 Pointe Circle, Oldsmar, FL 34677 **E-mail:** alacson1@tampabay.rr.com

LAGON, MANUEL GALASINAO
Industry: Healthcare **Born:** December 25, 1931, Manila, Philippines **Univ./degree:** M.D., Philippines, 1956 **Current organization:** Texas Medical Associates **Title:** M.D. **Type of organization:** Private practice **Major product:** Patient care **Area of distribution:** Texas **Area of Practice:** Colon and rectal surgery **Hob./spts.:** Painting, waterskiing, golf, yard work **SIC code:** 80 **Address:** Texas Medical Associates, 901 Eighth Ave., Ft. Worth, TX 76104 **E-mail:** lagonmg@aol.com

LAIRD, THOMAS R.
Industry: Healthcare **Born:** February 2, 1938, Hastings, Nebraska **Univ./degree:** B.S., University of Nebraska at Lincoln, 1959; M.D., University of Nebraska School of Medicine, 1964 **Current organization:** Thomas R. Laird, M.D. **Title:** M.D. **Type of organization:** Private practice/hospital **Major product:** Patient care **Area of distribution:** Missouri **Area of Practice:** Emergency medicine **Honors/awards:** Eagle Scout with 3 Palms; Silver Beaver Award, BSA **Affiliations:** Life member, A.C.E.P.; Past Member, N.S.M.A.; Admiral, Great Navy State of Nebraska; Former President and Cornhusker Council, BSA; Former President George Bush's physician on visit to National BSA Jamboree; Former Vice President, North Central Region BSA; Former Chair, YMCA; Camp Kitaki Committee **Hob./spts.:** Gardening, woodworking, sailing, travel **SIC code:** 80 **Address:** Thomas R. Laird, M.D., 2035 S. Highway 65, Marshall, MO 65340 **E-mail:** docme@webtv.net

LAM, KENNETH M.
Industry: Healthcare **Born:** August 25, 1954, Hong Kong **Univ./degree:** M.D., Hong Kong University, 1980 **Current organization:** Huntington Hospital **Title:** Doctor **Type of organization:** Hospital **Major product:** Patient care **Area of distribution:** Pasadena, California **Area of Practice:** Prostate cancer, oncology **Affiliations:** American College of Radiation Oncology; President, Southern California Radiation Oncology Society **Hob./spts.:** Fishing, golf **SIC code:** 80 **Address:** Huntington Hospital, 100 W. California Blvd., Pasadena, CA 91105 **E-mail:** kenneth.lam@huntingtonhospital.com **Web address:** www.huntingtonhospital.com

LAMBRIGHT, JO
Industry: Healthcare **Born:** Ardmore, Oklahoma **Current organization:** Northwest Texas Hospital **Title:** Purchasing Agent **Type of organization:** Hospital **Major product:** Patient care **Area of distribution:** Amarillo, Texas **Area of Practice:** Purchasing, strategic planning, project management **Affiliations:** Hospital Purchasing Agency **Hob./spts.:** Golf, Dallas Cowboys football fan **SIC code:** 80 **Address:** Northwest Texas Hospital, 1501 Coulter Rd., Amarillo, TX 79106 **E-mail:** jo-lambright@nwths.com

LANDRY, JEROME CARL
Industry: Healthcare **Born:** February 3, 1956, Chicago, Illinois **Univ./degree:** M.D., Harvard University School of Medicine **Current organization:** Emory Clinic **Title:** M.D./Associate Professor **Type of organization:** Medical practice **Major product:** Patient care **Area of distribution:** Georgia **Area of Practice:** Radiation treatment of cancer **Affiliations:** A.S.C.O.; A.S.T.R.O. **Hob./spts.:** Travel **SIC code:** 80 **Address:** Emory Clinic, 1365 Clifton Rd., Atlanta, GA 30322 **E-mail:** jla2468@aol.com

LANG, DAVID J.
Industry: Healthcare **Born:** September 24, 1932, New York **Univ./degree:** B.S., Swarthmore, 1954; M.D., Harvard School of Medicine, 1958 **Current organization:** Children's Hospital of Orange County **Title:** M.D., Director, Infectious Diseases **Type of organization:** Hospital **Major product:** Patient care **Area of distribution:** California **Area of Practice:** Infectious diseases, developmental disabilities **Published works:** 90 articles; editor, book and chapters **Affiliations:** A.A.P.; Society of Pediatric Research **SIC code:** 80 **Address:** Children's Hospital of Orange County, Director Infectious Diseases, 455 S. Main St., Orange, CA 92868 **E-mail:** dlidpeds@aol.com

LANTZ, MELINDA S.
Industry: Medical **Born:** July 23, 1960, New Brunswick, New Jersey **Univ./degree:** M.D., U.M.D.M.J. **Current organization:** Beth Israel Medical Center/Melinda S. Lantz, M.D. **Title:** Chief of Geriatric Psychiatry **Type of organization:** University hospital **Major product:** Patient care/education/research **Area of distribution:** New York **Area of Practice:** Geriatric psychiatry **Published works:** 25+ publications, journal articles **Affiliations:** Chair of Education, A.A.G.P.; A.M.A.; A.P.A. **Hob./spts.:** Sewing, painting **SIC code:** 80 **Address:** Beth Israel Medical Center/Melinda S. Lantz, M.D., 1st Ave. at 16th St., 2B49, New York, NY 10003 **E-mail:** mlantz@chpnet.org

LANTZ II, PERICLES JOHN
Industry: Medical **Born:** March 7, 1974, New York, New York **Univ./degree:** M.D., Mt. Sinai Medical Center, 2000 **Current organization:** New York University - Mt. Sinai Healthcare System **Title:** M.D. **Type of organization:** University hospital **Major product:** Medical services **Area of distribution:** New York **Area of Practice:** Biotechnology and medical technology **Honors/awards:** Sigma Xi Research Award, 1994 **Affiliations:** A.C.P. **Hob./spts.:** Martial arts **SIC code:** 80 **Address:** 108 E. 96th St., Apt. 5E, New York, NY 10128 **E-mail:** pericles@usa.net

LAPITE, OLADAPO
Industry: Healthcare **Born:** July 20, 1962, Lagos, Nigeria **Univ./degree:** M.D., Lagos University, Nigeria, 1988 **Current organization:** Lapite Family Practice **Title:** M.D./F.A.A.F.P. **Type of organization:** Private medical practice **Major product:** Patient care **Area of distribution:** Monroe, Louisiana **Area of Practice:** Family practice **Published works:** Co-authored 1 book, 4 papers **Affiliations:** A.M.A.; L.S.M.S. **Hob./spts.:** Golf, travel, reading **SIC code:** 80 **Address:** Lapite Family Practice, 850 S. Second St., Monroe, LA 71202 **E-mail:** dapoebun@aol.com

LAPORTA, MARIA
Industry: Healthcare **Born:** July 9, 1954, Italy **Univ./degree:** M.D., Loyola University, 1982 **Current organization:** Rockford Anesthesiologist Associates **Title:** Vice President **Type of organization:** Medical group **Major product:** Patient care **Area of distribution:** Freeport, Illinois **Area of Practice:** Anesthesiology **Affiliations:** A.S.A.; I.S.A.; A.M.A.; Illinois State Medical Society **Hob./spts.:** Physical fitness, reading **SIC code:** 80 **Address:** Rockford Anesthesiologist Associates, 2202 Harlem Rd., Suite 200, Loves Park, IL 61111

LARACUENTE, RITA
Industry: Healthcare **Born:** October 5, 1956, New York, New York **Univ./degree:** M.D., University of Puerto Rico Medical School, 1981 **Current organization:** Central Florida Wound & Skin Consultants **Title:** M.D./Owner **Type of organization:** Home healthcare **Major product:** Home visiting for geriatrics, wound and skin consulting **Area of distribution:** Central Florida **Area of Practice:** Physician specializing in geriatric care **Affiliations:** American Medical Association **Hob./spts.:** Reading **SIC code:** 80 **Address:** Central Florida Wound & Skin Consultants and Rita Laracuente MD, PA, 14325 Bending Branch Court, Orlando, FL 32824 **E-mail:** centralfloridawoundandskinconsultants@hotmail.com **Web address:** www.homestead.com/woundandskin.com

LAROCHELLE, PATRICIA A.
Industry: Healthcare **Born:** April 21, 1952, Bath, Maine **Univ./degree:** B.A., Medical Technology, University of Maine at Orono **Current organization:** Mercy/WSK Lab **Title:** Senior Medical Technologist **Type of organization:** Hospital **Major product:** Medical lab services **Area of distribution:** Maine **Area of Practice:** General laboratory procedures **Affiliations:** Clinical Lab Managers Association **Hob./spts.:** Hiking, kayaking, volunteer Windham football, monthly platelet donor **SIC code:** 80 **Address:** Mercy/WSK Lab, 40 Park Rd., Westbrook, ME 04092 **E-mail:** larochellep@mercyme.com

LAROIA, NIRUPAMA
Industry: Medical **Born:** India **Univ./degree:** M.B.B.S.; M.D., Christian Medical College, India, 1980 **Current organization:** University of Rochester Medical Center **Title:** M.B.B.S., M.D. **Type of organization:** Hospital/university **Major product:** Patient care, medical education **Area of distribution:** New York **Area of Practice:** Pediatrics **Published works:** 6 articles **Affiliations:** A.A.P.; Board Member, National Networking Forum **Hob./spts.:** Walking, tennis, cooking **SIC code:** 80 **Address:** University of Rochester Medical Center, 601 Elmwood Ave., Box 651, Rochester, NY 14642 **E-mail:** nirupama-laroia@urmc.rochester.edu **Web address:** www.urmc.rochester.edu

LASZEWSKI, ZOFIA
Industry: Healthcare **Born:** Poland **Univ./degree:** M.D., University of Aberdeen School of Medicine, Scotland, 1951 **Current organization:** Institute of Preventive & Nutritional Medicine, Inc. **Title:** Director **Type of organization:** Medical practice **Major product:** Cancer research, anti-aging and chelation therapy practice **Area of distribution:** International **Area of Practice:** Laboratory **Published works:** 5 articles **Affiliations:** A.C.A.M.; A.A.P.M. **Hob./spts.:** Art, gardening, cultural events, tennis, swimming **SIC code:** 80 **Address:** Institute of Preventive & Nutritional Medicine, Inc., P.O. Box 733, 11 Money Hill Rd., Chepachet, RI 02814 **E-mail:** instzlmd@aol.com

LATIFF-BOLET, LIGIA
Industry: Healthcare **Born:** Panama **Univ./degree:** Ph.D., Carlos Albizu University, Puerto Rico **Current organization:** South Carolina Dept. of Mental Health **Title:** Ph.D./Director, Division of Quality Management **Type of organization:** State psychiatric hospitals and community mental health centers **Major product:** Mental healthcare **Area of distribution:** South Carolina **Area of Practice:** Clinical psychology **Published works:** 2 papers **Affiliations:** A.P.A.; taught at Interamerican University and the Caribbean Center for Advanced Studies in Puerto Rico **Hob./spts.:** Swimming, jogging, reading **SIC code:** 80 **Address:** South Carolina Dept. of Mental Health, 2414 Bull St., Columbia, SC 29202 **E-mail:** lbolet.@aol.com

LATORTUE, KARL E.
Industry: Healthcare **Born:** March 23, 1959, Haiti **Univ./degree:** M.D., University of Tampico, 1988 **Current organization:** Community Healthcare Network **Title:** M.D. **Type of organization:** Community based organization **Major product:** Patient care **Area of distribution:** Brooklyn, New York **Area of Practice:** Internal medicine, H.I.V. Specialist **Affiliations:** A.M.A.; Kings County Medical Center **Hob./spts.:** Golf, tennis **SIC code:** 80 **Address:** Community Healthcare Network, 1167 Nostrand Ave., Brooklyn, NY 11225 **E-mail:** klatortuemd@aol.com

LAU, DARYL T.-Y.
Industry: Medical **Born:** April 15, 1962, Macau, China **Univ./degree:** M.D., McGill University, Montreal, Canada, 1986 **Current organization:** University of Texas Medical Branch at Galveston **Title:** M.D. **Type of organization:** University hospital **Major product:** Patient care, medical education, scientific researh **Area of distribution:** National **Area of Practice:** Hepatology **Honors/awards:** N.I.H. Award **Published works:** Articles, abstracts, book chapters **Affiliations:** A.A.S.L.D.; H.E.A.; American Liver Foundation **Hob./spts.:** Collecting antiques and art, music **SIC code:** 80 **Address:** University of Texas Medical Branch at Galveston, 4.106 McCullough Bldg., 301 University Blvd., Galveston, TX 77555-0764 **E-mail:** dalau@utmb.edu

LAUNIUS, BEATRICE K.
Industry: Medical **Born:** December 14, 1954, Chiseldon, England **Univ./degree:** M.S.N., Northwestern State University of Louisiana **Current organization:** Louisiana State University Health Sciences Center **Title:** Acute Care Nurse Practitioner **Type of organization:** University medical center **Major product:** Medical services **Area of distribution:** Louisiana **Area of Practice:** Heart transplant care **Affiliations:** A.A.C.N.; L.A.N.P.; A.C.N.P. **Hob./spts.:** Running, needlework, cycling, bird watching, scrabble **SIC code:** 80 **Address:** 3015 Oliver St., Bossier, LA 71112 **E-mail:** blaunius@bellsouth.net

LAXOVA, RENATA
Industry: Medical **Born:** Czechoslovakia **Univ./degree:** M.D.; Ph.D., Masaryk University, Czechoslovakia **Current organization:** University of Wisconsin Medical School **Title:** Professor Emerita **Type of organization:** University **Major product:** Patient care, medical education, research **Area of distribution:** International **Area of Practice:** Medical/clinical genetics, pediatrics **Published works:** 105 articles, chapters, 1 book "Letter to Alexander" **Affiliations:** American Society for Human Genetics; American College of Medical Genetics **Hob./spts.:** Music, walking, reading, gardening **SIC code:** 80 **Address:** 714 Delladonna Way, Madison, WI 53704

LE, KIM N.
Industry: Healthcare **Born:** March 14, 1970, Binh Buong, Viet Nam **Univ./degree:** B.S.; D.D.S., Baylor College of Dentistry, 1998 **Current organization:** Kim N. Le, D.D.S. **Title:** D.D.S. **Type of organization:** Private practice **Major product:** Dental care **Area of distribution:** Texas **Area of Practice:** Implants, dentures, cosmetics **Affiliations:** A.D.A.; A.C.P. **Hob./spts.:** Swimming, hiking **SIC code:** 80 **Address:** Kim N. Le, D.D.S., 990 U.S. Hwy. 287N, #112, Mansfield, TX 76063 **E-mail:** drngale99@yahoo.com

LEADLEY, RUTH E.
Industry: Healthcare **Born:** January 25, 1958, Hackensack, New Jersey **Univ./degree:** B.S.; O.T.R., Boston University, 1980; Certified C.H.T, 1993 **Current organization:** Capital District Hand & Occupational Therapy Services P.C. **Title:** O.T.R., C.H.T. **Type of organization:** Medical office, clinic **Major product:** Hand therapy **Area of distribution:** National **Area of Practice:** Occupational therapy/Certified hand therapy (Specialist) **Affiliations:** American Society of Hand Therapists, New York Occupational Therapy Association **Hob./spts.:** Skiing, travel **SIC code:** 80 **Address:** Capital District Hand & Occupational Therapy Services P.C., 1201 Nott St., Suite 105A, Schenectady, NY 12308 **E-mail:** rel112756@aol.com

LEAVELL-HAYES, LILI A.
Industry: Healthcare **Born:** October 10, 1959, Anderson, Indiana **Univ./degree:** M.D., Indiana University, 1986 **Current organization:** Lili A. Leavell-Hayes, M.D. **Title:** M.D. **Type of organization:** Private practice **Major product:** Patient care **Area of distribution:** Indiana **Area of Practice:** Anesthesiology **Honors/awards:** 1 patent **Affiliations:** A.S.A.; A.M.A.; N.M.A.; Society of Police Surgeons; Indiana Society of Anesthesiologists **Hob./spts.:** Tennis, golf, bicycling **SIC code:** 80 **Address:** Lili A. Leavell-Hayes, M.D., 8420 Galley Ct., Indianapolis, IN 46236 **E-mail:** llhmd1010@netscape.net

LEE, JERRY L.
Industry: Healthcare **Born:** June 1, 1953, Augusta, Georgia **Univ./degree:** City College of Chicago, 1979; Augusta Technical University, 1989 **Current organization:** East Central Regional Hospital of Augusta **Title:** L.P.N. on Forensic Mental Health Unit/SFC 91C 40 US Army Reserve 22 years, 11 months (Retired) **Type of organization:** Hospital **Major product:** Patient care **Area of distribution:** Georgia **Area of Practice:** Psychiatry/Military expertise: EMT, EMS, supervised and managed hospital reserve unit **Honors/awards:** 1 Meritorious Service Medal, 3 Army Commendation Medals, 3 Army Achievement Medals, numerous Letters of Appreciation for Outstanding Performances for Professionalism, for Training, Dedication and Leadership as Ward-master **Affiliations:** L.P.N.A.; Church Youth Director **Hob./spts.:** Fishing, travel, woodworking, gardening and lawn work **SIC code:** 80 **Address:** 3207 Cheshire Dr., Augusta, GA 30906 **E-mail:** Jerryaud5@aol.com

LEE, MEICHI
Industry: Healthcare **Born:** March 8, 1959, Taipei, Taiwan **Univ./degree:** M.A., Education, University of Kansas, 1985; M.S., Health Administration, Central Texas University, 1993 **Current organization:** Prime Medical **Title:** Administrator **Type of organization:** Medical practice **Major product:** Patient care **Area of distribution:** Louisiana **Area of Practice:** Healthcare administration **Hob./spts.:** Drawing, painting, reading **SIC code:** 80 **Address:** Prime Medical, 6723 N. Woodgate Ct., Baton Rouge, LA 70808 **E-mail:** chenmeichi@hotmail.com

LEE, YICK MOON
Industry: Healthcare **Born:** June 2, 1970, New York, New York **Univ./degree:** M.D., Mount Sinai, 1995 **Current organization:** Dr. Yick Moon Lee, Pediatrician **Title:** Associate Director of Maimonides Children's Hospital **Type of organization:** Hospital **Major product:** Patient care **Area of distribution:** New York **Area of Practice:** Pediatrics **Affiliations:** American Academy of Pediatrics; Chinese American Medical Society **Hob./spts.:** Fishing **SIC code:** 80 **Address:** Dr. Yick Moon Lee, Pediatrician, 80 Bowery, Suite 303, New York, NY 10013 **E-mail:** pediatrics.303@hotmail.com

LEE-ROBINSON, AYSE L.
Industry: Healthcare **Born:** November 17, 1956, St. Louis, Missouri **Univ./degree:** B.A., Biology/Chemistry (Cum Laude), Miami University, Oxford, Ohio; M.D., University of Cincinnati College of Medicine, 1982; Board Certifications: American Board of Physical Medicine and Rehabilitation; American Board of Electrodiagnostic Medicine **Current organization:** American Academy of Physical Medicine & Rehabilitation/American Academy of Electrodiagnostic Medicine/Academy of Medicine/American Medical Association **Title:** M.D./Partner **Type of organization:** Private group practice **Major product:** Rehabilitation and Electrodiagnostic Studies **Area of distribution:** Cincinnati, Ohio **Area of Practice:** Electrodiagnostic Medicine for diagnosis of Carpal Tunnel Syndrome, Radiculopathies & Neuropathy, Inpatient and Outpatient treatment of disorders such as Rehabilitation for Stroke, Joint replacements, Arthritis, Neuropathy and Debility **Honors/awards:** Class Representative, University of Cincinnati; Member, Executive Committee, University of Cincinnati; Barry Spore Memorial Award of Excellence in field of PM&R, 1982; Medical Honorary - M.U./AO; Ohio State Record for 110 ft hurdles - girls, 1994; AAU Nationals, track and field, 1974: 4th Place, 100 meter hurdles; Semifinalist - running long jump **Published works:** Article, Ultrasound Therapy: A Comparative Study of Difference Coupling Media - Archives of PM&R; March 1986; Vol 67 #3 Pg 147 **Affiliations:** A.M.A.; O.S.M.A.; C.M.A.; A.M.W.A. **Hob./spts.:** Hiking, snorkeling, swimming, gardening, travel, track and field **SIC code:** 80 **Address:** Rehabilitation and Electrodiagnostic

Medicine, 6200 Pfeiffer Rd., Suite 390, Cincinnati, OH 45242 **Phone:** (513)891-3373 **Fax:** (513)985-6793 **E-mail:** ayselee@yahoo.com

LEETUN, DARIN T.
Industry: Healthcare **Born:** March 8, 1965, Kasper, Wyoming **Univ./degree:** M.D., University of Virginia, 1992 **Current organization:** Bone & Joint Clinic **Title:** M.D. **Type of organization:** Private clinic **Major product:** Orthopaedic sports medicine **Area of distribution:** Bismarck, North Dakota **Area of Practice:** Orthopaedics **Published works:** Multiple articles **Affiliations:** A.M.A.; A.C.S.M. **Hob./spts.:** Woodworking, hockey, tennis **SIC code:** 80 **Address:** Bone & Joint Clinic, P.O. Box 1397, Bismarck, ND 58502 **E-mail:** dleetun@bone-joint.com

LEEVY, CARROLL MOTON
Industry: Medical **Born:** October 13, 1920, Columbia, South Carolina **Univ./degree:** M.D., University of Michigan Medical School, 1944 **Current organization:** U.M.D.N.J. New Jersey Medical School Liver Center **Title:** Distinguished Professor & Director **Type of organization:** Medical school/hospital **Major product:** Medical education, patient care **Area of distribution:** International **Area of Practice:** Hepatology **Affiliations:** A.A.S.L.; A.C.P./A.S.I.M.; N.M.A. **SIC code:** 80 **Address:** U.M.D.N.J., New Jersey Medical School Liver Center, 100 Bergen St., Newark, NJ 07103

LEFEBER JR., EDWARD J.
Industry: Medical **Born:** January 12, 1941, Galveston, Texas **Univ./degree:** B.S., University of the South, Tennessee, 1962; M.D., University of Texas at Galveston School of Medicine, 1966 **Current organization:** University of Texas, Health Science Center **Title:** MD, FACP **Type of organization:** University **Major product:** Medical services **Area of distribution:** Texas **Area of Practice:** Internal medicine/geriatrics **Published works:** Articles **Affiliations:** Colonel in Army Reserves, 2/67-1/01; Retired Officers Association; Alpha Omega Alpha **Hob./spts.:** Civil War history and history of medicine **SIC code:** 80 **Address:** University of Texas, Health Science Center, 4647 Medical Dr., San Antonio, TX 78229 **E-mail:** elefeber@juno.com

LEFTWICH, OWEN B.
Industry: Healthcare **Univ./degree:** M.D., Louisiana State University **Current organization:** Westside Eye Clinic **Title:** M.D. **Type of organization:** Medical practice **Major product:** Medical and surgical treatment for eyes **Area of distribution:** Louisiana **Area of Practice:** Ophthalmology **Affiliations:** A.A.O.; Louisiana State Medical Society; New Orleans Academy of Ophthalmology **SIC code:** 80 **Address:** Westside Eye Clinic, 4601 Wichers Dr., Marrero, LA 70072

LEJEUNE JR., FRANCIS E.
Industry: Healthcare **Born:** January 3, 1929, New Orleans, Louisiana **Univ./degree:** M.D., Tulane University, 1953 **Current organization:** Ochsner Clinic Foundation **Title:** Physician Emeritus **Type of organization:** Medical clinic **Major product:** Patient care, head/neck/larynx surgery **Area of distribution:** River Ridge, Louisiana **Area of Practice:** Otolaryngology **Affiliations:** American Medical Association; American College of Surgeons **Hob./spts.:** Woodwork, fishing **SIC code:** 80 **Address:** 334 Garden Rd., River Ridge, LA 70123 **E-mail:** flejeune@cox.net

LEMASTER, JOHN P.
Industry: Dentistry **Born:** March 14, 1960, Lexington, Kentucky **Univ./degree:** B.A., Biology, Transylvania University, Kentucky, 1982; D.M.D., University of Kentucky, 1990; Mastership, Academy of General Dentistry, 2002 **Current organization:** John P. LeMaster, D.M.D., MAGD, P.A. **Title:** Dentist/Forensic Consultant **Type of organization:** Private practice **Major product:** General, reconstructive and cosmetic dentistry **Area of distribution:** North Carolina **Area of Practice:** Forensic dentistry, expert witnessing; Certified Medical Investigator, Level 5; Certified in Homeland Security, Level 3; Certified Forensic Consultant **Honors/awards:** North Carolina Caring Dentist Program Meritorious Award for Outstanding Dedication, 1999, 2000 & 2001; NRCC 2000 and 2002 Businessman of the Year Award **Published works:** "Chemical Dependency in the Dental Office: Let the Stigma Cease", American Dental Association News, 01/02 **Affiliations:** Diplomate, American Board of Forensic Dentistry; Diplomate, American Board of Forensic Medicine; Fellow, American Association of Integrative Medicine; Academy of General Dentistry; American Academy of Cosmetic Dentistry; American College of Forensic Examiners International; American Dental Association; American Dental Society of Anesthesiology; Forsyth County Dental Society; North Carolina Dental Society; Second district Dental Association; Member, Advisory Board, American College of Forensic Examiners International - American Board of Forensic Dentistry; Member, Advisory Board, American Association of Integrative Medicine **Hob./spts.:** Mountain biking, scuba diving **SIC code:** 80 **Address:** John P. LeMaster, D.M.D., MAGD, P.A., 112 Harmon Lane, Suite A, Kernersville, NC 27284 **Web address:** www.piedmontsmiles.com

LEON, MILTIADIS N.
Industry: Healthcare **Born:** October 26, 1965, Patras, Greece **Univ./degree:** M.D., 1990; Ph.D., 2001, University of Patras School of Medicine, Greece **Current organization:** Odessa Heart Institute **Title:** M.D. **Type of organization:** Medical institute **Major product:** Cardiovascular medicine **Area of distribution:** National **Area of Practice:** Interventional cardiology, R&D, program design and implementation; is an active lecturer and public speaker **Published works:** Several articles and journals **Affiliations:** A.C.C.; A.C.P.; A.M.A.; Clinical Associate Professor of Medicine, Texas Tech University **Hob./spts.:** Tennis, swimming **SIC code:** 80 **Address:** Odessa Heart Institute, 720 N. Golder Ave., Odessa, TX 79761 **E-mail:** miltosl@hotmail.com

LEONARD, ROBERT I.
Industry: Healthcare **Born:** February 6, 1965, Cumberland, Maryland **Current organization:** Maniilaq Health Center **Title:** Facilities Director **Type of organization:** Hospital **Major product:** Patient care **Area of distribution:** Alaska **Area of Practice:** Facilities management, maintenance engineering, building automation, computer technology, staff training **Affiliations:** A.S.H.E.; N.F.P.E. **Hob./spts.:** Boating, fishing, hunting, snowmobiling, piloting aircraft **SIC code:** 80 **Address:** Maniilaq Health Center, 479 D-1, P.O. Box 82, Kotzebue, AK 99752 **E-mail:** bleonard@maniilaq.org

LEONG, MARY
Industry: Healthcare **Born:** March 7, 1953, New York, New York **Univ./degree:** M.D., New York University, 1978 **Current organization:** Long Island Jewish Medical Center **Title:** M.D. **Type of organization:** Hospital **Major product:** Patient care **Area of distribution:** Long Island, New York **Area of Practice:** Obstetrics/gynecology **Published works:** Articles **Affiliations:** American Association of Gynecologic Laparoscopy **SIC code:** 80 **Address:** Long Island Jewish Medical Center, 270-05 76th Ave., New Hyde Park, NY 11040 **E-mail:** mleong@lij.edu

LEON-GARCIA, ROSEMARY
Industry: Healthcare **Born:** July 16, 1954, Salamanca, New York **Univ./degree:** A.A., Nursing, Mission College; Licensed Psychiatric Tech., Gavalin College, 1988 **Current organization:** Royal Oaks Convalescent Hospital **Title:** L.V.N. Supervisor **Type of organization:** Hospital **Major product:** Patient care **Area of distribution:** Galt, California **Area of Practice:** Skilled nursing, administration, geriatrics, hospice and consulting **Hob./spts.:** Raising Boer goats, horseback riding, loving animals **SIC code:** 80 **Address:** 10481 E. Liberty Rd., Galt, CA 95632

LEUZZI, SAM A.
Industry: Healthcare **Born:** September 4, 1957, Woodbury, New Jersey **Univ./degree:** B.S.; M.D., University of Rome School of Medicine, Italy, 1986 **Current organization:** Cromwell Pediatrics **Title:** M.D. **Type of organization:** Private practice **Major product:** Patient care **Area of distribution:** New York **Area of Practice:** Pediatrics **Published works:** Write-ups **Affiliations:** A.A.P.; Staten Island Medical Society **SIC code:** 80 **Address:** Cromwell Pediatrics, 78 Cromwell Ave., Staten Island, NY 10304

LEVENTHAL, MARVIN R.
Industry: Healthcare **Born:** March 2, 1955, Chattanooga, Tennessee **Univ./degree:** B.S., University of Tennessee at Knoxville, 1977; M.D., University of Tennessee School of Medicine, 1981 **Current organization:** Memphis Orthopedic Group **Title:** MD, FACS **Type of organization:** Orthopedic surgery group **Major product:** Patient care **Area of distribution:** Tennessee **Area of Practice:** Orthopedic surgery **Honors/awards:** Alpha Omega Alpha **Affiliations:** Fellow, American Academy of Orthopedic Surgeons; Fellow, American College of Surgeons **Hob./spts.:** Golf, hunting, skiing **SIC code:** 80 **Address:** Memphis Orthopedic Group, 7655 Poplar Ave., Suite 250, Germantown, TN 38138 **E-mail:** mleventhl@midsouth.rr.com

LEVIN, NATHAN
Industry: Healthcare **Univ./degree:** M.D., Lvov Medical School **Current organization:** Nathan Levin Physician, PC **Title:** M.D. **Type of organization:** Private practice **Major product:** Patient care **Area of distribution:** New York **Area of Practice:** Internal medicine **Honors/awards:** Articles, journals **Affiliations:** A.M.A.; A.C.P. **SIC code:** 80 **Address:** Nathan Levin Physician, PC, 500 Brightwater Ct., Brooklyn, NY 11235 **E-mail:** drnlevin@aol.com

LEVITAN, WILLIAM S.
Industry: Healthcare **Born:** March 29, 1954, Chicago, Illinois **Univ./degree:** D.D.S., University of Illinois College of Dentistry, 1980 **Current organization:** William S. Levitan, D.D.S. **Title:** D.D.S. **Type of organization:** Private practice **Major product:** Dental care **Area of distribution:** Skokie, Illinois **Area of Practice:** General dentistry **Affiliations:** A.D.A. **SIC code:** 80 **Address:** William S. Levitan, D.D.S., 3834 W. Dempster, Skokie, IL 60076 **E-mail:** wmslev@aol.com

LEVITIN, GREGORY
Industry: Healthcare **Univ./degree:** M.D., University of North Carolina at Chapel Hill, 1997 **Current organization:** Vascular Birthmark Institute of New York **Title:** M.D., F.A.C.S. **Type of organization:** Private practice **Major product:** Adult and pediatric patient care **Area of distribution:** International **Area of Practice:** Ear, nose and throat doctor, birth defect removal, plastic surgery **Affiliations:** American College of Surgeons; American Osteopathic College of Otolaryngology **SIC code:** 80 **Address:**

Vascular Birthmark Institute of New York, 126 W. 60th St., New York, NY 10023 **E-mail:** glevitin@gmail.com **Web address:** www.birthmarks.org

LEVY, MICHÈLE
Industry: Healthcare **Univ./degree:** B.S., French, Lycée Francais University, 1975; O.D., New England College of Optometry, 1984 **Current organization:** Michèle Levy, OD., FAAO **Title:** O.D., FAAO **Type of organization:** Private medical practice **Major product:** Eye exams, contact lenses, treatment **Area of distribution:** Greenwich, Connecticut **Area of Practice:** Family optometry, ocular diseases **Affiliations:** American Academy of Optometry; American Optometric Association; Connecticut Association of Optometrists **SIC code:** 80 **Address:** Michèle Levy, OD., FAAO, 2 Lafayette Ct., Greenwich, CT 06830

LEVY, SUSANNA A.
Industry: Healthcare **Born:** March 29, 1954, Budapest, Hungary **Univ./degree:** B.S., Chemical Engineering, Polytechnic University of Budapest, 1957; M.S., Analytical/Physical Chemistry, Hebrew University, 1961; Ph.D., Polytechnic University of New York, 1968 **Current organization:** Queens Health Network Elmhurst Hospital **Title:** Regional Director of Chemistry/Immunology **Type of organization:** University hospital **Major product:** Patient care, medical education **Area of distribution:** New York, New York **Area of Practice:** Clinical chemistry, immunology **Published works:** 40 publications **Affiliations:** American Association of Clinical Chemists; American Chemical Society; New York Academy of Science **SIC code:** 80 **Address:** Queens Health Network, Elmhurst Hospital, 7901 Broadway, New York, NY 11373 **E-mail:** shosh34@aol.com

LEVY, TERRIE L.
Industry: Healthcare **Born:** June 2, 1955, Augusta, Georgia **Univ./degree:** A.S., Nursing, Augusta College **Current organization:** St. Joseph Hospital Wound Healing Center **Title:** Clinical Manager **Type of organization:** Wound healing center **Major product:** Patient care **Area of distribution:** Augusta, Georgia **Area of Practice:** Wound care **Affiliations:** A.N.A.; O.C.N.; American Cancer Society **Hob./spts.:** Gardening, basketball **SIC code:** 80 **Address:** St. Joseph Wound Healing Center, 2258 Wrightsboro Rd., Suite 170, Augusta, GA 30904 **E-mail:** terriel@stjoshosp.org

LEWIS, KATHLEEN A.
Industry: Healthcare **Born:** May 12, 1947, Erie, Pennsylvania **Univ./degree:** Oncology Certification **Current organization:** Regional Cancer Center **Title:** RN/OCN/Medical Oncology Coordinator **Type of organization:** Cancer center **Major product:** Outpatient radiation/Medical oncology **Area of distribution:** Pennsylvania **Area of Practice:** Medical oncology **Affiliations:** American Cancer Society; Army Reserve (First Lt.) **Hob./spts.:** Bowling, teaching **SIC code:** 80 **Address:** Regional Cancer Center, 2500 W. 12th Street, Erie, PA 16505 **E-mail:** klewis@trcc.org

LEWIS, LULA TATE
Industry: Healthcare **Born:** August 20, 1953, Helena, Arkansas **Univ./degree:** B.S., Biology and Chemistry, Oakwood College, Alabama, 1977; B.H.S., University of Kentucky, 1983 **Current organization:** Samaritan Hospital **Title:** Supervisor **Type of organization:** Hospital **Major product:** Patient care **Area of distribution:** Kentucky **Area of Practice:** Medical technologist - supervisor **Affiliations:** American Society of Clinical Pathologists **Hob./spts.:** Physical fitness, bicycling, walking, youth programs **SIC code:** 80 **Address:** Samaritan Hospital, 310 S. Limestone, Lexington, KY 40508 **E-mail:** lula777@alltel.net

LEWIS, NANCY A.
Industry: Healthcare **Born:** April 1, 1950, Zanesville, Ohio **Univ./degree:** Diploma, Albany Medical Center School of Nursing, 1972; B.S., Nursing, Pennsylvania State University, 1981; M.S.N., University of Pittsburgh Graduate School of Nursing, 1985 **Current organization:** HealthSouth Harmarville Rehabilitation Hospital **Title:** R.N./Case Manager **Type of organization:** Hospital **Major product:** Patient care, rehabilitation **Area of distribution:** Pennsylvania **Area of Practice:** Clinical Nurse Specialist, spinal cord injury **Honors/awards:** The Expanded Role Award for Excellence in SCI Nursing from American Association of Spinal Cord Injury Nurses, 2001 **Published works:** Lewis, N.A. (1986), "Functional gains in CVA patients: A nursing approach", Rehabilitation Nursing, 11(2), 25-27; Passarella, P.M. & Lewis, N.A. (1987), "Nursing application of Bobath Principles in stroke care", The Journal of Neuroscience Nursing, 19(2), 106-109; Lewis, N.A. (1988), "Nursing management of altered pattern of elimination", Journal of Home Health Care Practice, 1(1), 35-42; Lewis, N.A. (1995), "Implementing a bladder ultrasound program", Rehabilitation Nursing, 20(4), 215-216; Lewis, N.A. (1999), "This one's juuust right", Advance for Directors in Rehabilitation, 8(6), 19-20; Konety, B.R., Nguyen, T.T., Brenes, G., Sholder, A., Lewis, N., Bastacky, S., Potter, D.M. & Getzenberg, R.H. (2000), "Clinical usefulness of the novel marker BLCA-4 for the detection of bladder cancer", The Journal of Urology, 164, 634-639 **Affiliations:** A.R.N.; A.N.A.; A.A.S.C.I.N. **Hob./spts.:** Health sports program for the disabled **SIC code:** 80 **Address:** HealthSouth Harmarville Rehabilitation Hospital, P.O. Box 11460, Guys Run Rd., Pittsburgh, PA 15238-0460 **E-mail:** nal14@comcast.net

LI, YONG-TONG
Industry: Medical **Born:** China **Univ./degree:** M.D., Beijing University School of Medicine, 1986 **Current organization:** Pennsylvania Hospital - University of Pennsylvania Health System **Title:** M.D. **Type of organization:** University/hospital **Major product:** Medical services **Area of distribution:** Pennsylvania **Area of Practice:** Psychiatry **Published works:** 10 articles **Affiliations:** A.P.A.; American Geriatric Psychiatry Association **Hob./spts.:** Fine art **SIC code:** 80 **Address:** Pennsylvania Hospital, University of Pennsylvania Health System, 800 Spruce St., Philadelphia, PA 19107 **E-mail:** yongtongli@yahoo.com

LIAKEAS, GEORGE P.
Industry: Healthcare **Born:** May 22, 1971, New York, New York **Univ./degree:** B.S., Sociology/Biochemistry, Honors College at University of New York, 1994; M.D., Albert Einstein College of Medicine, 1997 **Current organization:** George P. Liakeas, M.D. **Title:** M.D. **Type of organization:** Private practice **Major product:** Outstanding patient care **Area of distribution:** New York **Area of Practice:** Family practice, medical aesthetics **Affiliations:** A.M.A.; A.C.P.; H.M.S.; B.I.M.C.; M.S.S.N.Y.; N.Y.M.C. **SIC code:** 80 **Address:** George P. Liakeas, M.D., 686 Lexington Ave., New York, NY 10022 **E-mail:** liakeasmd@aol.com

LIANG, PING
Industry: Healthcare/education **Born:** Huitong, Hunan, China, 1964 **Univ./degree:** M.S., Cell Biology, Chinese Academy of Sciences, 1985; Ph.D., Molecular Biology, Dalhousie University, 1998 **Current organization:** Roswell Park Cancer Institute **Title:** Assistant Professor/Director of Bioinformation Core Facility **Type of organization:** Nonprofit cancer institute **Major product:** Biomedical research, cancer treatment and research **Area of distribution:** National **Area of Practice:** Bioinformatics software and databases, human genetics research **Published works:** 40 journal articles, 2 book chapters **Affiliations:** American Society of Human Genetics; Human Genome Variation Society; International Society of Computational Biology; Human Genome Organization **Hob./spts.:** Ping-Pong, piano **SIC code:** 80 **Address:** Roswell Park Cancer Institute, Elm and Carlton Streets, Buffalo, NY 14263 **E-mail:** ping.liang@roswellpark.org **Web address:** falcon.roswellpark.org

LIEN, JANE M.
Industry: Medical **Born:** July 7, 1967 City, State **Univ./degree:** M.D., University of Puerto Rico at San Juan, 1993 **Current organization:** Carolina University Hospital, Medical Science Campus **Title:** M.D. **Type of organization:** University hospital **Major product:** Medical services **Area of distribution:** San Juan, Puerto Rico **Area of Practice:** Ob/Gyn **Published works:** Multiple publications **Affiliations:** A.C.O.G.; Medical Association of Puerto Rico **Hob./spts.:** Family **SIC code:** 80 **Address:** Urb Borinquen Gardens, D5 Calle Azalea, San Juan, PR 00926

LIGHT, GERALD S.
Industry: Healthcare **Univ./degree:** M.D., Saskatchewan Canada University **Current organization:** Kidney Care & Hypertension **Title:** M.D. **Type of organization:** Private practice **Major product:** Patient care **Area of distribution:** Georgia **Area of Practice:** Nephrology **Affiliations:** American Renal Association **SIC code:** 80 **Address:** Kidney Care & Hypertension, 3564 N. Crossing Circle, Suite B, Valdosta, GA 31602 **Web address:** www.kidneycare.com

LIMLE, ANDREW J.
Industry: Healthcare **Born:** June 16, 1976, Cincinnati, Ohio **Univ./degree:** D.C., National University of Health Science, 2002 **Current organization:** Cincinnati Chiropractic **Title:** Owner **Type of organization:** Private chiropractic office **Major product:** Chiropractic services **Area of distribution:** Cincinnati, Ohio **Area of Practice:** General chiropractic care and sports therapy; Certified Chiropractic Sports Physician **Published works:** 1 article **Affiliations:** Cincinnati Chiropractic Association **Hob./spts.:** Skiing, backpacking, bicycling, the outdoors **SIC code:** 80 **Address:** Cincinnati Chiropractic, 4021 Harrison Ave., Cincinnati, OH 45211 **E-mail:** drlimle@cincinnatichiropractic.com **Web address:** www.cincinnatichiropractic.com

LIN, ALEXANDER S.
Industry: Healthcare **Born:** October 24, 1942, Tokyo, Japan **Univ./degree:** B.S., National Taiwan University, 1967; M.S., University of Pittsburgh, 1969; Ph.D., Stanford University, 1974; M.D., University of Miami School of Medicine, 1977 **Current organization:** Lin & Wilson Radiology Medical Group, Inc. **Title:** M.D., Ph.D. **Type of organization:** Group practice **Major product:** Diagnostic medical services **Area of distribution:** California **Area of Practice:** Radiology **Honors/awards:** Sigma Chi **Published works:** Articles, chapters **Affiliations:** American Physical Society; American Radiology of North America; Association of Neuro Medicine; Past Member, I.E.E.E. **SIC code:** 80 **Address:** Lin & Wilson Radiology Medical Group, Inc., 301 Victoria St., Costa Mesa, CA 92627 **E-mail:** dralexlin@aol.com

LIN, FRANK S.
Industry: Healthcare **Born:** January 12, 1942, Peng Fu, Taiwan **Current organization:** St. Mary's Hospital **Title:** Chief Engineer **Type of organization:** Hospital **Major**

product: Patient care **Area of distribution:** New Jersey **Area of Practice:** Engineering **Hob./spts.:** Family, baseball, football, politics **SIC code:** 80 **Address:** St. Mary's Hospital, 211 Pennington Ave., Passaic, NJ 07055

LINGERFELT, ALICE J.
Industry: Healthcare **Born:** September 3, 1950, Athens, Tennessee **Current organization:** Downtown Health Plaza of Baptist Hospital, Radiology Dept. **Title:** Chief Technologist **Type of organization:** Outpatient clinical facility which is affiliated with Wake Forest University Baptist Medical Center in Winston-Salem, NC **Major product:** Patient care **Area of distribution:** North Carolina **Area of Practice:** Registered Radiologic Technologist, Certified in Mammography by American Registry of Radiologic Technologists (ARRT); responsibilities include good quality radiographs for interpretation by Radiologist at the hospital, performing Mammogram exams and all quality control **Honors/awards:** 2001 Employee of Year at Downtown Health Plaza, the first time this honor was given **Affiliations:** American Society of Radiologist Technologists (ASRT); North Carolina Society of Radiologic Technologists (NCSRT); Order of the Eastern Star; Pine Grove United Methodist Church (Organist and Choir Director) **Hob./spts.:** Ballroom dancing and competing (Fred Astaire Dance Studios), football and basketball (college and professional), knitting, gospel music **SIC code:** 80 **Address:** 317 Linville Springs Rd., Kernersville, NC 27284 **E-mail:** alingerf@wfubmc.edu

LINMAN, SINA
Industry: Healthcare **Born:** April 2, 1953, Ida Grove, Iowa **Univ./degree:** M.A., University of Iowa, 1988 **Current organization:** Methodist Physician Clinic **Title:** Pediatric Nurse Practitioner **Type of organization:** Clinic **Major product:** Patient care **Area of distribution:** Council Bluffs **Area of Practice:** Pediatric nursing **Affiliations:** A.N.A., N.A.P.N.P.; I.P.N.A., S.C.N.S.; Flying Physicians Association **Hob./spts.:** Marathon running **SIC code:** 80 **Address:** Methodist Physician Clinic, 933 E. Pierce St., Council Bluffs, IA 51503-4626 **E-mail:** sina.linman@nmhs.org

LIPOW, KENNETH I.
Industry: Healthcare **Born:** January 31, 1951, New York, New York **Univ./degree:** M.D., Albert Einstein School of Medicine, 1978 **Current organization:** Connecticut Neurosurgical Specialists, P.C. **Title:** M.D., President **Type of organization:** Group practice **Major product:** Advanced neurosurgical care **Area of distribution:** International **Area of Practice:** Neurological surgery **Published works:** Articles, book chapter **Affiliations:** A.A.N.S.; C.N.S. **Hob./spts.:** Music, electronics **SIC code:** 80 **Address:** Connecticut Neurosurgical Specialists, P.C., 267 Grant St., Bridgeport, CT 06610 **E-mail:** cyberken@optonline.net

LISAK, ROBERT P.
Industry: Medical **Born:** March 17, 1941, Brooklyn, New York **Univ./degree:** B.A., History, New York University, 1961; M.D., Columbia University School of Medicine, 1965; Training in Internal Medicine, Montefiore Medical Center and Bronx Municipal Medical Center; Neurochemistry, Neuroimmunology, National Institute of Mental Health **Current organization:** Wayne State University School of Medicine **Title:** Parker Webber Chair, Neurology; Professor and Chair, Neurology; Professor of Immunology/Microbiology **Type of organization:** University hospital **Major product:** Patient care, education **Area of distribution:** International **Area of Practice:** Neuroimmunology including basic and clinical research related to multiple sclerosis, myasthenia gravis and other autoimmune diseases affecting the nervous systems and muscles **Honors/awards:** Fulbright Scholar **Published works:** Author or co-author of 191 articles, 116 books, chapters, editorials and reviews, 204 abstracts **Affiliations:** American Neurology Association; American Academy of Neurology; Editor, Journal of Neurological Sciences; served or serves on grant and research committees including the National Multiple Sclerosis Society, NINDS and MGFA; GBS Foundation **Hob./spts.:** Family, tennis, travel, food & wine **SIC code:** 80 **Address:** Wayne State University School of Medicine, Dept. of Neurology, 4201 St. Antoine, 8 David University Health Center, Detroit, MI 48201 **E-mail:** rlisak@med.wayne.edu **Web address:** www.med.wayne.edu

LISS, DONALD
Industry: Healthcare **Born:** June 17, 1955, New York, New York **Univ./degree:** M.D., Wayne State University, 1979 **Current organization:** The Physical Medicine and Rehabilitation Center, P.A. **Title:** M.D. **Type of organization:** Outpatient rehabilitation facility **Major product:** Sports medicine **Area of distribution:** New Jersey **Area of Practice:** Rehabilitation medicine, pain management **Affiliations:** A.M.A.; A.A.P.M.R.; A.C.S.M. **Hob./spts.:** Weightlifting, hiking, travel, wildlife **SIC code:** 80 **Address:** The Physical Medicine &, Rehabilitation Center, P.A., 15 Engle St., Suite 205, Englewood, NJ 07631 **E-mail:** dlissmd@aol.com

LITTLE, TONYA E.
Industry: Healthcare **Born:** December 28, 1968, Jacksonville, Arkansas **Univ./degree:** M.D., St. Louis University, 1995 **Current organization:** Tonya E. Little, M.D., P.A. **Title:** M.D. **Type of organization:** Medical office/clinic **Major product:** Patient care **Area of distribution:** Heber Springs, Arkansas **Area of Practice:** Family medicine **Affiliations:** A.A.F.P.; A.M.A. **Hob./spts.:** Fishing, music, reading, hiking **SIC code:** 80 **Address:** Tonya E. Little, M.D., P.A., 1511 Hwy. 25B North, P.O. Box 1198, Heber Springs, AR 72543 **E-mail:** telittle@cox-internet.com

LITTLETON, J.D.
Industry: Government/Health **Born:** August 3, 1954, Hazlehurst, Mississippi **Univ./degree:** D.O., Nova Southeastern University, 1992 **Current organization:** U.S. Army, Blanch Field Army Community Hospital **Title:** Chief of Internal Medicine/Lt. Colonel, U.S. Army **Type of organization:** Hospital **Major product:** Patient care **Area of distribution:** International **Area of Practice:** Internal medicine **Published works:** "Focal Distonia" **Affiliations:** P.T.C.; O.A. **Hob./spts.:** Body building **SIC code:** 80 **Address:** 3319 Greenspoint Dr., Clarksville, TN 37042-7272 **E-mail:** doctorjd@bellsouth.net

LIU, PAUL I.
Industry: Medical **Born:** November 23, 1932 **Univ./degree:** M.D.; Ph.D., San Louise, Mississippi, 1969 **Current organization:** Olive View - UCLA Medical Center **Title:** M.D. **Type of organization:** University hospital **Major product:** Patient care, medical education **Area of distribution:** International **Area of Practice:** Laboratory medicine **Honors/awards:** Teaching Awards **Published works:** Editor, medical journal; Book: "How to Select & Interpret Lab Results" **Affiliations:** Lifetime Member, A.M.A.; American Society of Clinical Pathology **SIC code:** 80 **Address:** Olive View - UCLA Medical Center, 14445 Olive View Dr., Sylmar, CA 91342 **E-mail:** piliu@dhs.co.la.ca.us

LIZARRIBAR, JOSE
Industry: Healthcare **Univ./degree:** M.D., University of Puerto Rico, 1980 **Current organization:** Odessa Regional Hospital **Title:** Medical Director **Type of organization:** Hospital **Major product:** Patient care **Area of distribution:** Odessa, Texas **Area of Practice:** Emergency healthcare **Affiliations:** F.A.C.P. **SIC code:** 80 **Address:** Odessa Regional Hospital, 520 E. Sixth St., Odessa, TX 79761 **E-mail:** drjoselizarribar@yahoo.com

LOBATI, FREDERICK NTUM
Industry: Healthcare **Born:** October 10, 1960, Mankon Bamenda, Cameroon, Africa **Spouse:** Winifred **Married:** May 12, 1991 **Children:** Verena, April 16, 1992; Vida-lea, July 18, 1996; Erika, January 31, 2000 **Univ./degree:** German Language and Preliminary University Medical Studies, 1980-82; M.D., University of Cologne, Germany, 1988; Pre-Clinical Medical Studies, University of Dusseldorf, W. Germany, 1982-84; Diploma in Tropical Medicine & Community Healthcare **Current organization:** Mercy St. John's Health System, Internal Medicine - Fremont **Title:** M.D./Internal Medicine Physician, Subspecialist in Infectious Diseases **Type of organization:** Hospital **Major product:** Medical services **Area of distribution:** National **Area of Practice:** Board Certified, Internal Medicine; Board Certified, Infectious Diseases **Honors/awards:** 3 Physicians' Recognition Awards, A.M.A. (one with commendation); Travel Grant Award to Participate at the North American Region of the International Union Against Tuberculosis and Lung Disease at its 10th Annual Meeting, Chicago, IL **Published works:** "Osteomyelitis: etiology, diagnosis, treatment and outcome in a public vs. a private institution", published in European Journal Infection, 2001 **Affiliations:** American College of Physicians; Infectious Diseases Society of America; A.M.A.; Missouri State Medical Association; Kansas City Metropolitan Medical Society; Ozark Medical Association; Greene County Medical Society **Hob./spts.:** Reading; active member of the local church in Ozark, MO **SIC code:** 80 **Address:** Mercy St. John's Health System, Internal Medicine - Fremont, 1965 S. Fremont, Suite 350, Springfield, MO 65804 **E-mail:** flobatimd@sprg.mercy.net **Web address:** www.mercy.net and www.stjohns.net

LOBE, THOM E.
Industry: Medical **Univ./degree:** M.D., University of Maryland, 1975; J.D., LaSalle University, 1994 **Current organization:** Le Bonheur Children's Medical Center **Title:** M.D., F.A.C.S., J.D. **Type of organization:** University hospital **Major product:** Children's healthcare **Area of distribution:** Tennessee **Area of Practice:** Pediatric surgery, Director of complementary alternative medicine **Honors/awards:** Healthcare Man of the Year, Memphis Business Journal, 2003 **Published works:** 3+ books **Affiliations:** F.A.C.S. **Hob./spts.:** Flyfishing, sailing **SIC code:** 80 **Address:** 6403 River Tide Dr., Memphis, TN 38120 **E-mail:** tlobe@utmem.edu

LODHA, SURESH
Industry: Healthcare **Univ./degree:** M.D., Rnd Medical College, India, 1968 **Current organization:** Suresh Lodha M.D. Inc. **Title:** President, M.D. **Type of organization:** Private practice **Major product:** Internal medicine **Area of distribution:** Santa Maria, Claifornia **Area of Practice:** Pulmonary/internal medicine **Published works:** 13 publications **Affiliations:** A.M.A.; California Medical Association **SIC code:** 80 **Address:** Suresh Lodha M.D. Inc., 214 S. Stratford Ave., Santa Maria, CA 93454

LOEB, ELIZABETH M.
Industry: Healthcare **Born:** May 30, 1956, Iowa **Univ./degree:** B.S.; M.S.; M.D., 1982, University of Iowa **Current organization:** Iowa City Family Practice Clinic

Title: M.D. **Type of organization:** Medical clinic **Major product:** Patient care **Area of distribution:** Iowa **Area of Practice:** Family practice **Affiliations:** A.M.A. **SIC code:** 80 **Address:** Iowa City Family Practice Clinic, 269 N. First Ave., Iowa City, IA 52245 **E-mail:** sank.mari@aol.com

LOESSIN, SCOTT J.
Industry: Healthcare **Born:** March 19, 1962, Milwaukee, Wisconsin **Univ./degree:** M.D., University of Wisconsin, 1988 **Current organization:** Scott J. Loessin, M.D. **Title:** M.D. **Type of organization:** Private practice **Major product:** Facial cosmetic surgery **Area of distribution:** Daytona Beach, Florida **Area of Practice:** Plastic surgery **Published works:** co-author of books, multi-journal publications **Affiliations:** F.A.C.S.; A.S.P.S. **Hob./spts.:** Art, tennis **SIC code:** 80 **Address:** Scott J. Loessin, M.D., 311 N. Clyde Morris Blvd., Suite 360, Daytona Beach, FL 32114 **E-mail:** docloessin@aol.com

LOMBARDI, JOSEPH S.
Industry: Healthcare **Born:** August 2, 1950, Newark, New Jersey **Univ./degree:** M.D., New Jersey College of Medicine, 1978 **Current organization:** Edison-Metuchen Orthopedic Group **Title:** M.D. **Type of organization:** Private medical practice **Major product:** Orthopaedic surgery **Area of distribution:** National **Area of Practice:** Spinal surgery **Published works:** Articles **Affiliations:** A.M.A.; National Spine Association **SIC code:** 80 **Address:** Edison-Metuchen Orthopedic Group, 10 Parsonage Rd., Suite 500, Edison, NJ 08837 **E-mail:** lombardi@starband.net

LOMBOY, CHARLES M.
Industry: Healthcare **Born:** Fort McCarthy, San Pedro, California **Univ./degree:** El Camino College, Chapman University **Current organization:** City of Angels Medical Center **Title:** Director of Engineering **Type of organization:** Medical center **Major product:** Patient care **Area of distribution:** Los Angeles, California **Area of Practice:** Facilities management for two facilities including environmental services, security and grounds; Chair, Environment of Care; Safety Officer, OSHPD projects, JCAHO, DHS and Title 22 **Affiliations:** California Society of Healthcare Engineering; Served 4 years in U.S. Navy **Hob./spts.:** Bowling, softball, camping, water sports, bicycling, salsa dancing **SIC code:** 80 **Address:** City of Angels Medical Center, Engineering Dept., 1711 W. Temple St., Los Angeles, CA 90026 **E-mail:** engr@cofamc.org

LONG, FREDERICK R.
Industry: Healthcare **Born:** June 20, 1960, Euclid, Ohio **Univ./degree:** M.D., Yale University, 1988 **Current organization:** Children's Radiological Institute, Columbus Children's Hospital **Title:** Chief of Body and CTR Imaging **Type of organization:** Hospital/university **Major product:** Radiological services **Area of distribution:** Columbus, Ohio **Area of Practice:** Pediatric radiology **Published works:** 20 articles, 2 book chapters **Affiliations:** A.C.R.; R.S.N.A.; Society for Thoracic Radiology; American Roentgen Ray Society **Hob./spts.:** Chess, rowing, running **SIC code:** 80 **Address:** Children's Radiological Institute, Columbus Children's Hospital, 700 Children's Dr., Columbus, OH 43205 **E-mail:** flong@chi.osu.edu **Web address:** www.chi.osu.edu

LONG, SANDRA H.
Industry: Healthcare **Univ./degree:** A.S., Medical Laboratory Science, Alamance Community College, 1993 **Current organization:** Regional Hematology Oncology **Title:** Supervisor, Laboratory Services **Type of organization:** Physician's office **Major product:** Oncology, hematology **Area of distribution:** Durham, North Carolina **Area of Practice:** Clinical laboratory **Affiliations:** American Society of Clinical Pathologists; American Medical Technologists **SIC code:** 80 **Address:** Regional Hematology Oncology, 4411 Ben Franklin Blvd., Durham, NC 27704 **E-mail:** sandra.long@usoncology.com

LOPEZ, GLADYS H.
Industry: Healthcare **Born:** January 12, 1970, Cali, Colombia **Univ./degree:** M.D., National University of Colombia, 1993 **Current organization:** Metropolitan Hospital **Title:** M.D. **Type of organization:** Hospital **Major product:** Patient care **Area of distribution:** New York, New York **Area of Practice:** Internal medicine, emergency medicine **Affiliations:** A.M.A. **Hob./spts.:** Hiking, skiing, rock climbing **SIC code:** 80 **Address:** Metropolitan Hospital, Dept. of Emergency Medicine, 1901 First Ave., 2nd floor, New York, NY 10029 **E-mail:** gladyshelenal1@aol.com

LOPEZ, J. ANTONIO G.
Industry: Healthcare **Born:** September 27, 1955, San Diego, California **Univ./degree:** M.D., Harvard University, Massachusetts, 1983 **Current organization:** Desert Cardiology Center **Title:** M.D./Director of Lipid Clinic/Clinical Associate Professor, Internal Medicine, Southern Illinois University School of Medicine **Type of organization:** Cardiology group practice **Major product:** Preventive cardiology and cardiovascular rehabilitation **Area of distribution:** Illinois **Area of Practice:** Internal Medicine, cardiovascular diseases, lipid disorders, invasive cardiology, transesophageal echocardiography, cardiovascular intensive care, cardiovascular physiology, electron beam CT coronary artery imaging **Honors/awards:** Finalist, Young Investigators Award, American College of Chest Physicians, 1989; National Trainee Award, American Federation of Clinical Research, 1989; Finalist, Alfred Soffer Research Award, American College of Chest Physicians, 1988; Midwest-Trainee Award, American Federation for Clinical Research, 1987; Veterans Administration Associate Investigators Award, 1987; Henry J. Kaiser Family Foundation Merit Scholar, 1983 **Published works:** Multiple publications, 34 abstracts, 23 papers, 12 book chapters and 18 reviews **Affiliations:** Fellow, American College of Cardiology; Fellow, American College of Physicians; Fellow, American College of Chest Physicians; Fellow, American College of Angiology; Fellow, Council on Clinical Cardiology; American Heart Association; Fellow, Council on Arteriosclerosis; American Heart Association; Associate Fellow, Council on Epidemiology and Prevention; American Heart Association; Fellow, Inter American College of Physicians and Surgeons; American Medical Association **Hob./spts.:** Jazz, trombone, tennis **SIC code:** 80 **Address:** Desert Cardiology Center, Hal B. Wallis Building, 3900 Bob Hope Drive, Rancho Mirage, CA 92270-3221 **E-mail:** jantoniolopez@msn.com

LOPEZ DEL POZO, JORGE J.
Industry: Healthcare **Born:** January 24, 1960, Ponce, Puerto Rico **Univ./degree:** M.D., San Pedro University, Dominican Republic, 1982 **Current organization:** Sociedad Drs. Lopez Del Pozo **Title:** M.D. **Type of organization:** Hospital **Major product:** Patient care **Area of Practice:** Internal medicine **Affiliations:** American Medical Society; American College of Physicians **Hob./spts.:** Boating, golf **SIC code:** 80 **Address:** Sociedad Drs. Lopez Del Pozo, 8169 Concordia St., Ponce, PR 00717-1554 **E-mail:** kraysea@cogui.net

LOPEZ-DAVILA, LIANA E.
Industry: Healthcare **Born:** July 1, 1963, San Juan, Puerto Rico **Univ./degree:** M.D., University of Puerto Rico, 1990 **Current organization:** Somascan, Inc. **Title:** M.D. **Type of organization:** Radiology center **Major product:** Patient care **Area of distribution:** Puerto Rico **Area of Practice:** Diagnostic radiology **Honors/awards:** Fellowship, 1991-95, Beth Israel, New York; Fellowship, New England Medical Center, 1995-96 **Affiliations:** A.M.A.; Radiological Society of North America, Puerto Rico Chapter; American College of Radiology **Hob./spts.:** Swimming, running, cooking **SIC code:** 80 **Address:** 1924 Sauco St., Santa Maria, Rio Piedras, PR 00927-1518 **E-mail:** llopezdavila@aol.com

LOPEZ-URIZAR, GLADYS I.
Industry: Healthcare **Title:** M.D. **Type of organization:** Private practice **Major product:** Patient care **Area of Practice:** Pediatrics **SIC code:** 80 **Address:** Coral Reef Pediatrics, 9299 SW 152nd St., Suite 206, Miami, FL 33157

LORENZ, KEVIN M.
Industry: Healthcare **Born:** November 1, 1960, Langdon, North Dakota **Univ./degree:** M.D., Saint Louis University School of Medicine, 1987 **Current organization:** The Eye Clinic of North Dakota **Title:** M.D. **Type of organization:** Private practice **Major product:** Eye surgery **Area of distribution:** North Dakota **Area of Practice:** Ophthalmology - refractive and cataract surgery **Affiliations:** American College of Surgeons; American Academy of Ophthalmology **Hob./spts.:** Hunting, fishing, golf **SIC code:** 80 **Address:** The Eye Clinic of North Dakota, 620 N. 9th St., Bismarck, ND 58501 **E-mail:** ecnd@btinet.net

LORENZINI, RONALD N.
Industry: Healthcare **Born:** December 12, 1935, Illinois **Univ./degree:** B.S., University of Notre Dame, 1957; M.D., Loyola University School of Medicine, 1960 **Current organization:** Dr's Lorenzini, Senica & Bruneau Ltd. **Title:** M.D. **Type of organization:** Medical practice **Major product:** Patient care **Area of distribution:** Illinois **Area of Practice:** Obstetrics, gynecology **Published works:** Article **Affiliations:** F.A.C.O.G.; F.A.C.S. **Hob./spts.:** Golf **SIC code:** 80 **Address:** Dr's Lorenzini, Senica & Bruneau Ltd., 5207 S. Main St., Downers Grove, IL 60515

LORIO, MELISSA J.
Industry: Healthcare **Born:** New Orleans, Louisiana **Univ./degree:** B.S.N., Louisiana State University Health Sciences Center **Current organization:** Ochsner Clinic Foundation **Title:** Unit Director, R.N. **Type of organization:** Ambulatory surgery center **Major product:** Patient care **Area of distribution:** New Orleans, Louisiana **Area of Practice:** Ambulatory Surgery Certified **Affiliations:** A.O.R.N. **Hob./spts.:** Travel, tennis **SIC code:** 80 **Address:** Ochsner Clinic Foundation, 1516 Jefferson Hwy., New Orleans, LA 70005 **E-mail:** mlorio@ochsner.org

LOUGHRIDGE, BILLY P.
Industry: Healthcare **Born:** April 19, 1935, Oklahoma **Univ./degree:** M.D., University of Oklahoma, School of Medicine, 1961 **Current organization:** Cardiovascular Surgery, Inc./Health Design, Inc. **Title:** M.D./President **Type of organization:** Private practice **Major product:** Patient care **Area of distribution:** Oklahoma **Area of Practice:** Thoracic and cardiovascular surgery **Honors/awards:** Fullbright Scholar to Sweden **Published works:** 15 publications; 2 books: "The Cardiac Surgeons Diet and Health Design", "Every Breath You Take" **Affiliations:** A.C.S.; A.C.C.; S.T.S. **Hob./spts.:** Reading, golf, flyfishing **SIC code:** 80 **Address:** Cardiovascular Surgery, Inc./

Health Design, Inc., 2624 E. 21st St., Suite 4, Tulsa, OK 74114 **E-mail:** bllridge@aol.com **Web address:** www.dietandhealthdesign.com

LOUIS, BERTIN MAGLIORE
Industry: Healthcare **Born:** September 5, 1936, Haiti **Univ./degree:** B.S.; M.D., State University of Haiti, 1964 **Current organization:** Maimonides Medical Center **Title:** M.D./Director of Nephrology **Type of organization:** Hospital **Major product:** Patient care **Area of distribution:** Brooklyn, New York **Area of Practice:** Internal medicine and nephrology (Board Certified), kidney diseases and severe hypertension **Honors/awards:** New York Best Doctors (3years) **Published works:** 25+ articles **Affiliations:** F.A.C.N.; A.S.N. **Hob./spts.:** Family, classical music **SIC code:** 80 **Address:** Maimonides Medical Center, 4802 Tenth Ave., Brooklyn, NY 11219

LOULMET, DIDIER F.
Industry: Healthcare **Born:** July 21, 1960, Cahors, France **Univ./degree:** M.D., Toulouse University, 1984 **Current organization:** Lenox Hill Hospital **Title:** Chief, Minimally Invasive Robotic Cardiac Surgery **Type of organization:** Private hospital **Major product:** Cardiac surgery **Area of distribution:** National **Area of Practice:** Robotics, minimal access, endoscopic bypass, valves repair **Published works:** Articles **Affiliations:** A.M.A.; International Society of Minimally Invasive Cardiac Surgery **Hob./spts.:** Skiing, windsurfing, tennis **SIC code:** 80 **Address:** Lenox Hill Hospital, 130 E. 77th St., Fourth floor, New York, NY 10021 **E-mail:** loulmetd@aol.com

LOVELACE, JANE B.
Industry: Healthcare **Born:** Chattanooga, Tennessee **Univ./degree:** Certified Dietary Manager, Chattanooga State University, 1997 **Current organization:** Erlanger (North) Medical Center **Title:** CDM/CFPP **Type of organization:** Hospital **Major product:** Patient care **Area of distribution:** Tennessee **Area of Practice:** Dietary management **Affiliations:** National Dietary Managers Association; Tennessee Dietary Managers Association; Stage manager/Board Member, Flo Summit Theatre at Oak Street Playhouse; Member/Officer/board member, Pilot Club of Chattanooga; Chattanooga Chapter of Dietary Managers Association; Served as Task Force Member, Dietary Managers Program; First Centenary United Methodist Church, Chattanooga, Tennessee; Member, Morgan Class **Hob./spts.:** Physical fitness, walking, reading, needlepoint, spending time with friends **SIC code:** 80 **Address:** Erlanger (North) Medical Center, 632 Morrison Springs Rd., Chattanooga, TN 37415 **E-mail:** lovelajb@erlanger.org

LOVETT, JEFFREY E.
Industry: Healthcare **Born:** March 8, 1961, Binghamton, New York **Univ./degree:** M.S., Business Administration, University of North Florida, 1987 **Current organization:** Mayo Clinic **Title:** Contract Administrator **Type of organization:** Hospital and physician clinic **Major product:** Patient care **Area of distribution:** National **Area of Practice:** Finance **Affiliations:** Healthcare Financial Management Association; American & Florida Institute for Certified Public Accountants **SIC code:** 80 **Address:** Mayo Clinic, 4500 San Pablo Rd., Jacksonville, FL 32224 **E-mail:** lovett.jeffrey@mayo.edu **Web address:** www.mayo.edu

LOVRIEN, FRED C.
Industry: Healthcare **Born:** February 11, 1948, Fort Dodge, Iowa **Univ./degree:** M.D., University of Iowa, 1973 **Current organization:** Nuclear Medicine and Thyroidology **Title:** M.D., Owner **Type of organization:** Private practice **Major product:** Patient care **Area of distribution:** National **Area of Practice:** Nuclear medicine, thyroid practice **Honors/awards:** Listed, Best Physicians in America and Who's Who in Medicine; Best Teacher Awards from local hospitals **Published works:** Articles **Affiliations:** A.C.N.P.; F.A.C.P.; A.M.A.; Society of Nuclear Medicine; American Diabetes Association; State and local medical societies **Hob./spts.:** Medicine, reading, tennis **SIC code:** 80 **Address:** Nuclear Medicine and Thyroidology, 109 S. Petro Ave., Sioux Falls, SD 57107 **E-mail:** flovrien@dtgnet.com

LOWDER, FRIEDA MILLER
Industry: Healthcare/management **Born:** July 25, 1961, Germany **Univ./degree:** B.A., Business, Montreat University, North Carolina, 2003 **Current organization:** Physicians Network/Northeast Medical Center **Title:** Vice President **Type of organization:** Hospital **Major product:** Patient care **Area of distribution:** North Carolina **Area of Practice:** Healthcare management **Honors/awards:** Listed in Who's Who of America's Students **Published works:** 2 articles **Affiliations:** M.G.M.A. **Hob./spts.:** Golf, travel **SIC code:** 80 **Address:** Physicians Network, Northeast Medical Center, 920 Church St. North, Concord, NC 28025

LOWENTHAL, DAVID T.
Industry: Medical **Born:** April 2, 1941, Philadelphia, Pennsylvania **Univ./degree:** M.D., 1966; Ph.D., Exercise Physiology, 1986, Temple University **Current organization:** University of Florida College of Medicine/VA Medical Center **Title:** Professor of Medicine, Pharmacology and Exercise Science, University of Florida College of Medicine/Director Emeritus, Geriatric Research Education and Clinical Center, VA Medical Center, Gainesville, FL **Type of organization:** University/hospital **Major product:** Medical education/patient care **Area of distribution:** Florida **Area of Practice:** Clinical pharmacology cardiovascular/renal and hypertension clinical research, exercise physiology research in the elderly, stroke rehab in the elderly **Published works:** 320 papers, 18 books and 150 abstracts **Affiliations:** Fellow, American College of Physicians (FACP); Fellow, American College of Clinical Pharmacology (FCCP); Visiting Professorships: University of Perugia, School of Medicine, Institute of Gerontology and Geriatrics, Perugia, Italy; Ben Gurion University School of Medicine, Beersheba, Israel, Division of Hypertension and Dept. of Pharmacology **Hob./spts.:** Competitive distance running, track and field **SIC code:** 80 **Address:** 4430 S.W. 84th Way, Gainesville, FL 32608 **E-mail:** dlowen4241@aol.com

LUBA, KATARZYNA
Industry: Medical **Born:** December 20, 1956, Warsaw, Poland **Univ./degree:** M.D., Akademia Medyczna w Warszawie, Warsaw, Poland **Current organization:** The University of Chicago, Dept. of Anesthesia & Critical Care **Title:** M.D. **Type of organization:** University medical center **Major product:** Medical services **Area of distribution:** Illinois **Area of Practice:** Anesthesiology/critical care **Published works:** "Perioperative Management of the Patient with Muscular Dystrophy", In Atlee J (ed.); "Complications in Anesthesia" 2nd ed, Elsevier (submitted); Co-Author, "Recent Changes in the Management of Intracranial Hypertension" Int Anesth Clin 38(4):69-85, 2000; Co-Author, "Carcinoma of the Ampulla of Vater Treated by Radical Pancreatectomy", Pol Surg Rev 54:7-8, 539-41, 1982 **Hob./spts.:** Travel, reading, cooking, music, gardening **SIC code:** 80 **Address:** The University of Chicago, Dept. of Anesthesia & Critical Care, 9323 Springfield Ave., Evanston, IL 60203 **E-mail:** kluba@dacc.uchicago.edu

LUM, GARY M.
Industry: Medical **Born:** May 19, 1948, El Paso, Texas **Univ./degree:** B.S., University of North Dakota, 1966; M.D., Bowman Gray School of Medicine, North Carolina, 1970 **Current organization:** University of Colorado Health Sciences Center, The Children's Hospital **Title:** M.D. **Type of organization:** University hospital **Major product:** Patient care, medical education **Area of distribution:** Colorado **Area of Practice:** Pediatric nephrology **Published works:** 150 articles, chapters and edited books **Affiliations:** A.S.P.N.; A.S.N. **SIC code:** 80 **Address:** University of Colorado Health Sciences Center, The Children's Hospital, 1056 E. 19th St., Denver, CO 80218 **E-mail:** lum.gary@tchden.org **Web address:** www.tchden.org

LYMBERIS, MARIA T.
Industry: Healthcare **Born:** August 7, 1938, Athens, Greece **Univ./degree:** M.D., University of Southern California, School of Medicine, 1964 **Current organization:** UCLA **Title:** Clinical Professor of Psychiatry **Type of organization:** University/private practice **Major product:** Patient care **Area of distribution:** Santa Monica, California **Area of Practice:** Psychiatry **Honors/awards:** Life Fellow, A.P.A. and A.C.P. **SIC code:** 80 **Address:** UCLA, 1500 Montana Ave., Suite 204, Santa Monica, CA 90403 **E-mail:** maria@lymberis.com **Web address:** www.lymberis.com

MAATOUK, ISSAM MOUSSA
Industry: Healthcare **Born:** 1960, Homs, Syria **Univ./degree:** M.D., Damascus University Medical School, Syria, 1985 **Current organization:** Southeastern Medical Centers, S.C. **Title:** C.E.O. and Medical Director **Type of organization:** Healthcare Services Provider **Major product:** Industrial and Physical medicine, Multi-Specialty Medical Centers, Occupational and Rehabilitation Medical Services **Area of distribution:** Chicago, Illinois and Northwest Indiana **Area of Practice:** Internal medicine, Intensivist/Critical Care Medicine, Trauma and Emergency Medicine and Business Medical Administration **Published works:** Articles, Research Papers **Affiliations:** American Medical Association (AMA); American Association for the Advancement of Science (AAAS); American College of Physicians-American Society of Internal Medicine (ACP-ASIM); New York Academy of Science (NYAS); Illinois State Medical Society (ISMS); Chicago Medical Society (CMS); National Arab American Medical Association (NAAMA) **Hob./spts.:** Music (play Violin and Lute), Chess and Research **SIC code:** 80 **Address:** 5630 W. Lyons St., Morton Grove, IL 60053 **E-mail:** issmaat@yahoo.com

MACGILLIVRAY, JOHN D.
Industry: Healthcare **Univ./degree:** M.D., Tufts University, School of Medicine, 1990 **Current organization:** Hospital for Special Surgery **Title:** M.D. **Type of organization:** Hospital **Major product:** Patient care **Area of distribution:** International **Area of Practice:** Orthopaedic surgery, sports medicine, works with U.S. ski team and high school athletic teams **Affiliations:** A.O.S.S.M.; A.A.N.A.; A.M.A. **Hob./spts.:** Skiing, tennis, running **SIC code:** 80 **Address:** Hospital for Special Surgery, 535 E. 70th St., New York, NY 10021 **E-mail:** macgillivrayj@hss.edu

MADISON III, JAMES B.
Industry: Healthcare **Born:** December 30, 1932, Washington, D.C. **Univ./degree:** B.S., Zoology, University of Miami, 1955; M.D., Tulane University School of Medicine, 1959 **Current organization:** Oviedo Orthopaedics **Title:** Orthopaedic Surgeon **Type of organization:** Private group practice **Major product:** Patient care **Area of distribution:** Central Florida **Area of Practice:** Spine disorders, general orthopae-

dics **Honors/awards:** Outstanding Physician, Florida Medical Association, 1990; Citizen of the Year, Winter Park Chamber of Commerce, 1991 **Affiliations:** F.A.C.S.; American Medical Association; North American Lake Management Association; Pan American Medical Association; Florida Medical Association; Past President, Winter Park Chamber of Commerce; Chief of Medical Staff, Winter Park Hospital **Hob./spts.:** Sailing, restoration of Florida's lakes and waterways **SIC code:** 80 **Address:** Oviedo Orthopaedics, 8000 Red Bug Lake Rd., Suite 100, Oviedo, FL 32756 **E-mail:** james.madison@flhosp.org

MADOC-JONES, HYWEL
Industry: Healthcare **Born:** November 7, 1938, Cardiff, Whales **Univ./degree:** M.D., University of Chicago, 1973; Ph.D., University of London, 1965 **Current organization:** Caritas Norwood Hospital, Southwood Campus **Title:** M.D. **Type of organization:** Hospital **Major product:** Patient care **Area of distribution:** Norfolk, Massachusetts **Area of Practice:** Radiation oncology specialist **Published works:** Books **Affiliations:** Fellow, American College of Radiology; Assistant Secretary Treasurer, Massachusetts Medical Society **Hob./spts.:** Music (opera, orchestra, choral), skiing, sailing **SIC code:** 80 **Address:** Caritas Norwood Hospital, Southwood Campus, 111 Dedham St., Norfolk, MA 02056-1666 **E-mail:** hywelmadoc-jones@cchcs.org

MAGNINO, MATTHEW J.
Industry: Healthcare **Univ./degree:** B.S., California State College, San Bernardino, 1982; M.D. **Current organization:** Anesthesia Care Specialists **Title:** M.D. **Type of organization:** Group practice **Major product:** Patient care **Area of distribution:** Nebraska **Area of Practice:** Anesthesia, pain management **Affiliations:** A.S.A.; A.M.A. **SIC code:** 80 **Address:** Anesthesia Care Specialists, 300 E. 23rd St., Fremont, NE 68025 **E-mail:** mmagnino@neb.rr.com

MAHAFZAH, MAHMOUD
Industry: Healthcare **Born:** September 10, 1954, Jordon **Univ./degree:** M.D., Jordon Medical College, 1972; Ph.D., Biology and Chemistry, SUNY at Buffalo, 1985 **Current organization:** Mahafzah Medical Center **Title:** M.D., Ph.D. **Type of organization:** Private medical practice **Major product:** Patient care **Area of distribution:** Illinois **Area of Practice:** Internal medicine, hematology/oncology **Published works:** 7 papers, 7 abstracts **Affiliations:** A.M.A.; A.C.P. **Hob./spts.:** Reading **SIC code:** 80 **Address:** Mahafzah Medical Center, 5669 W. 95th St., Oak Lawn, IL 60453

MAHALATI, KATHY M.
Industry: Healthcare **Born:** October 27, 1964, Iran **Univ./degree:** M.D., University of Maryland, Baltimore, 1995 **Current organization:** Women's First Ob/Gyn Associates **Title:** M.D. **Type of organization:** Hospital clinic **Major product:** Patient care, research **Area of distribution:** Maryland **Area of Practice:** Obstetrics and gynecology **Affiliations:** American Federation for Medical Research; Southern Medical Association; American College of Obstetricians and Gynecologists **Hob./spts.:** Playing the piano, walking **SIC code:** 80 **Address:** Women's First Ob/Gyn Associates, 11016 New Hampshire Ave., Silver Spring, MD 20904 **E-mail:** katayoon@bellatlantic.net

MAHMOUD, FADE AZIZ
Industry: Healthcare **Born:** April 7, 1973, Syria **Univ./degree:** M.D., Tishreen University School of Medicine, Syria, 1996; Postgraduate Degree, Internal Medicine, Damascus University Hospitals, Syria, 1999 **Current organization:** Cleveland Clinic Foundation, The Taussig Center Dept. of Hematology & Oncology **Title:** M.D. **Type of organization:** Medical Institution **Major product:** Patient care, research **Area of distribution:** Ohio **Area of Practice:** Hematology and oncology **Affiliations:** American Society of Clinical Oncology; European Society of Medical Oncology; Multinational Association of Supportive Care in Cancer **Hob./spts.:** Reading, music, sports **SIC code:** 80 **Address:** Cleveland Clinic Foundation, The Taussig Center, Dept. of Hematology & Oncology, 9500 Euclid Ave., M76, Cleveland, OH 44195 **Phone:** (216)445-1246 **E-mail:** mahmouf@cc.ccf.org

MAIER, MARGARET D.
Industry: Healthcare **Born:** Suffolk County, New York **Univ./degree:** A.S., Nursing, Suffolk Community College **Current organization:** Able Health Care Services Inc. **Title:** ADPS (Assistant Director of Patient Services) **Type of organization:** Home healthcare **Major product:** Home healthcare services **Area of distribution:** New York **Area of Practice:** Management, HBOC computer trainer; Certified Med/Surg Nursing **Affiliations:** A.N.A.A. **Hob./spts.:** Stained glass artisan **SIC code:** 80 **Address:** 291 Central Ave., Bohemia, NY 11716 **E-mail:** mmaierrnc@aol.com

MAINI, ATUL
Industry: Medical **Born:** April 11, 1966, Ludhiana, India **Univ./degree:** M.D. **Current organization:** Brookdale Hospital and Medical Center **Title:** Chief Resident **Type of organization:** Teaching hospital **Major product:** Patient care **Area of distribution:** New York **Area of Practice:** Internal medicine **Hob./spts.:** Travel **SIC code:** 80 **Address:** 660 E. 98th St., #2H, Brooklyn, NY 11236 **E-mail:** amaini2000@yahoo.com

MAIZEL, DAVID R.
Industry: Healthcare **Born:** December 25, 1948, Paterson, New Jersey **Univ./degree:** M.D., University of Medicine and Dentistry of New Jersey, 1974 **Current organization:** Sentara Medical Group **Title:** Executive Medical Director **Type of organization:** Medical group **Major product:** Patient care **Area of distribution:** Virginia Beach, Virginia **Area of Practice:** Family practice **Affiliations:** A.A.F.P.; A.C.P.E. **Hob./spts.:** Music, cycling **SIC code:** 80 **Address:** Sentara Medical Group, 5555 Greenwich Rd, Suite 600, Virginia Beach, VA 23462 **E-mail:** drmaizel@sentara.com

MALANI, ASHOK K.
Industry: Healthcare **Born:** December 17, 1969, Jabcharla, India **Univ./degree:** Biology, St. Joseph Junior College, Hyderabad, India, 1986; M.B.B.S., Osmania University, India, 1992 **Current organization:** Heartland Regional Medical Center **Title:** M.D./M.S./F.R.C.S. **Type of organization:** Hospital **Major product:** Patient care **Area of distribution:** St. Joseph, Missouri **Area of Practice:** Hematology, oncology, treatment of cancer and blood disorders **Hob./spts.:** Writing, movies, tennis, photography **SIC code:** 80 **Address:** Heartland Regional Medical Center, 53 Faraon St., St. Joseph, MO 64506

MALDONADO, MARIANNA
Industry: Healthcare **Born:** February 13, 1945, Hayward, California **Univ./degree:** M.D., University of Puerto Rico Medical School, 1969 **Current organization:** Marianna Maldonado, M.D. **Title:** M.D. **Type of organization:** Medical practice **Major product:** Treatment of anxiety and depression (therapy and pharmacotherapy) **Area of distribution:** Columbia, South Carolina **Area of Practice:** General psychiatry, child and adolescent psychiatry **Affiliations:** A.P.A.; A.M.A.; American Academy of Child & Adolescent Psychiatry **Hob./spts.:** Sewing, gardening **SIC code:** 80 **Address:** Marianna Maldonado, M.D., 1 Harbison Way, #108, Columbia, SC 29212

MALETIC, VLADIMIR
Industry: Healthcare **Born:** July 4, 1956, Belgrade, Yugoslavia **Univ./degree:** M.D., University of Belgrade **Current organization:** Greenville Psychiatry, P.A. **Title:** M.D., Psychiatrist **Type of organization:** Psychiatry practice **Major product:** Patient care **Area of distribution:** National **Area of Practice:** Child, adolescent and adult psychiatry **Honors/awards:** Double Residency and Double Board Certified **Published works:** 15 articles, two book chapters, 30 C.M.S. presentations, 300+ speaking engagements per year **Affiliations:** C.M.E.; S.C.P.A. **Hob./spts.:** Hiking, sailing, tennis, skiing **SIC code:** 80 **Address:** Greenville Psychiatry, P.A., 9A Caledon Ct., Greenville, SC 29615 **E-mail:** vladimir96@charter.net

MALIK, S.
Industry: Healthcare **Born:** April 14, 1963, Rawalpindi, Pakistan **Univ./degree:** M.D., SUNY at Stony Brook, 1989 **Current organization:** S. Malik M.D., P.C. **Title:** M.D **Type of organization:** Private practice **Major product:** Eye care **Area of distribution:** New York **Area of Practice:** Ophthalmology **Affiliations:** A.M.A.; A.A.O. **Hob./spts.:** Dancing, billiards, swimming **SIC code:** 80 **Address:** S. Malik M.D., P.C., 185 Woodbury Rd., Hicksville, NY 11801

MALLIK, SAROJA
Industry: Healthcare **Born:** December 13, 1939 **Univ./degree:** M.D., India, 1962 **Current organization:** Saroja Mallik, M.D. **Title:** M.D., F.A.C.O.G. **Type of organization:** Private practice **Major product:** Women's healthcare **Area of distribution:** New Jersey **Area of Practice:** OB/GYN **Honors/awards:** A.M.A. Award **Affiliations:** A.M.A. **Hob./spts.:** Music, travel, gardening **SIC code:** 80 **Address:** Saroja Mallik, M.D., 2025 Hamburg Tpke., Suite K, Wayne, NJ 07470 **E-mail:** malliks@mindspring.com

MALLOY, ELIZABETH A.
Industry: Healthcare **Current organization:** St. Peter's Hospital (Breast Center) **Title:** Lead Sonographer **Type of organization:** Hospital **Major product:** Patient care **Area of Practice:** Board Certified, CAT scan, radiological technology and ultrasound **SIC code:** 80 **Address:** 725 East Rd., Clarksburg, MA 01247 **E-mail:** emalloy@worldnet.att.net

MANCINI, MARY C.
Industry: Medical **Born:** December 15, 1953, Scranton, Pennsylvania **Univ./degree:** M.D., University of Pittsburgh, Pennsylvania, 1978; Ph.D. Louisiana State University, 2000 **Current organization:** LSU Health Sciences Center **Title:** M.D. **Type of organization:** University hospital **Major product:** Patient care **Area of distribution:** National **Area of Practice:** Cardiothoracic surgery, transplantation **Published works:** Multiple publications **Affiliations:** F.A.C.S.; I.S.H.L.T. **Hob./spts.:** Skiing, gardening, writing **SIC code:** 80 **Address:** LSU Health Sciences Center, 1501 Kings Hwy., Shreveport, LA 71130 **E-mail:** mmanci@lsuhsc.edu

MANGAT, DEVINDER S.
Industry: Healthcare **Born:** September 16, 1947, Kisumu, Kenya **Univ./degree:** M.D., University of Kentucky, 1973; Residency, University of Oklahoma **Current organiza-**

tion: Mangat - Kuy Plastic Surgery Center **Title:** M.D. **Type of organization:** Surgery center **Major product:** Cosmetic surgery **Area of distribution:** International **Area of Practice:** Facial plastic and cosmetic surgery **Published works:** 50 publications **Affiliations:** Fellow, A.C.S.; A.M.A.; Past President, A.A.F.P.R.S.; Vice President, A.B.F.P.R.S. **Hob./spts.:** Running, cycling, skiing, mountain climbing **SIC code:** 80 **Address:** Mangat - Kuy Plastic Surgery Center, 8044 Mongomery Rd., Suite 230, Cincinnati, OH 45236 **E-mail:** mangat@renewyourlooks.com **Web address:** www.renewyourlooks.com

MANLEY, JACK C.
Industry: Healthcare **Born:** May 16, 1935, Toledo, Ohio **Univ./degree:** M.D., St. Louis University School of Medicine,1959 **Current organization:** Wisconsin Heart & Vascular Clinic, S.C. **Title:** M.D. **Type of organization:** Medical clinic **Major product:** Patient care **Area of distribution:** Wisconsin **Area of Practice:** Interventional cardiology and cardiovascular disease **Affiliations:** F.A.C.C.; F.A.H.A. **Hob./spts.:** Farming, skiing, fly fishing **SIC code:** 80 **Address:** Wisconsin Heart & Vascular Clinic, S.C., 2801 W. Kinnickinnic River Pkwy., Milwaukee, WI 53215

MANNAN, MOHAMMAD Y.
Industry: Healthcare **Born:** January 9, 1957, Bangladesh **Univ./degree:** M.D., University of Dhaka, Dhaka Medical College, Bangladesh, 1983 **Current organization:** Long Island Jewish Medical Center **Title:** M.D. **Type of organization:** Hospital **Major product:** Patient care **Area of distribution:** New York **Area of Practice:** Infectious diseases, geriatrics and internal medicine **Published works:** "Identifying Issues of Distress Affecting Family Members and Care Giver in Long-term Care", American geriatric Society Journal, May 2001 **Affiliations:** A.M.A.; A.C.P.; I.D.S.A.; A.G.S. **Hob./spts.:** Soccer, basketball **SIC code:** 80 **Address:** Long Island Jewish Medical Center, Division of Infectious Disease, 270-05 76th Ave., New Hyde Park, NY 11040 **E-mail:** doctor.mannan@aol.com

MANUEL-ACKER, SHIRLEY A.
Industry: Medical **Born:** December 9, 1949, Lafayette, Louisiana **Univ./degree:** A.S.N., 1980; B.S.N., 1988, Lamar University; M.S., Health Education, University of Texas at Galveston, 1997 **Current organization:** University of Texas at Galveston, Medical Branch **Title:** Director of Nurses **Type of organization:** University hospital **Major product:** Medical services **Area of distribution:** Texas **Area of Practice:** Nursing, administration **Published works:** 1 book **Affiliations:** National Association of University Women **Hob./spts.:** Reading, church **SIC code:** 80 **Address:** 4040 Crow Rd, #1205, Beaumont, TX 77706 **E-mail:** jsks4846@aol.com

MARCANO, BRENDA V.
Industry: Healthcare **Born:** November 8, 1967, Puerto Rico **Univ./degree:** M.D., St. George's University, Granada, 1995 **Current organization:** Schneider Children's Hospital of North Shore **Title:** M.D. **Type of organization:** Hospital **Major product:** Children's healthcare **Area of distribution:** New York **Area of Practice:** Pediatric critical care **Affiliations:** A.A.P. **Hob./spts.:** Skiing **SIC code:** 80 **Address:** Schneider Children's Hospital of North Shore, LIJ Dept. of Pediatric Critical Care, 269-01 76th Ave., New Hyde Park, NY 11040 **E-mail:** brenda1@pol.net

MARCIAL, VICTOR A.
Industry: Healthcare **Born:** february 24, 1924 San Juan, Puerto Rico **Univ./degree:** M.D., Harvard University, Massachusetts, 1949 **Current organization:** Marcial Radiation Oncology **Title:** M.D., F.A.C.R., Director **Type of organization:** Medical practice **Major product:** Oncology **Area of distribution:** Puerto Rico, Caribbean **Area of Practice:** Radiation Oncology **Affiliations:** Founder, Radiation Oncology Group; Past Director, Cancer Control Program; Founder, Puerto Rico Division, American Cancer Society; Puerto Rico Dept. of Health **SIC code:** 80 **Address:** Marcial Radiation Oncology, 400 Roosevelt Ave., Suite 109, San Juan, PR 00918

MARGASSERY, SURESH KUMAR
Industry: Medical **Born:** August 24, 1961, Trichur, India **Univ./degree:** M.B.B.S., Thanjavur University Medical School, 1986; M.D., Coimbatore University Medical School, India, 1991; M.R.C.P., Royal College of Physicians, London, UK, 1995 **Current organization:** St. Louis University Health Science Center **Title:** M.D., Assistant Professor **Type of organization:** University hospital/medical school **Major product:** Medical services/education **Area of distribution:** Missouri **Area of Practice:** Nephrology, internal medicine **Honors/awards:** Gold Medal, Cardiology; Gold Medal, Internal Medicine, Coimbatore University, 1990 **Published works:** Journal of Nephrology, 2001 **Affiliations:** A.S.N.; I.S.N.; A.C.P.; A.S.D.I.N. **SIC code:** 80 **Address:** St. Louis University Health Science Center, Division of Nephrology, 3635 Vista at S. Grand, St. Louis, MO 63123 **E-mail:** margassk@slu.edu

MARGENTHALER, JULIE A.
Industry: Medical **Born:** August 10, 1971, Pinckneyville, Illinois **Univ./degree:** M.D., Southern Illinois University, 1997 **Current organization:** Washington University School of Medicine **Title:** M.D. **Type of organization:** University hospital **Major product:** Medical services **Area of distribution:** International **Area of Practice:** General surgery **Honors/awards:** Phi Beta Kappa; Alpha Omega Alpha, Strathmore's Who's Who **Published works:** 20 publications **Affiliations:** A.M.A.; A.C.S.; A.W.S.; M.S.M.A.; S.T.L.S.S. **Hob./spts.:** Travel, piano, swimming, snorkeling **SIC code:** 80 **Address:** 4400 Lindell Blvd., #12C, St. Louis, MO 63108 **E-mail:** margenthaler@msnotes.wustl.edu

MARHEINE-MAXEY, CONSTANCE C.
Industry: Healthcare **Born:** August 18, 1954, Kansas City, Missouri **Univ./degree:** M.S.N., Marquette University **Current organization:** BJC Health Care **Title:** Consultant **Type of organization:** Hospital **Major product:** Patient care **Area of distribution:** St. Louis, Missouri **Area of Practice:** Nursing education/critical care **Affiliations:** A.A.C.N.; National Nursing Staff Development Organization **Hob./spts.:** Stained glass, carpentry **SIC code:** 80 **Address:** BJC Health Care, 8201 Waddell Ave., St. Louis, MO 63125 **E-mail:** ccm2084@bjc.org

MARJAMA-LYONS, JILL
Industry: Healthcare **Born:** September 21, 1962, Alexandria, Virginia **Univ./degree:** B.A. Honors, Psychology, Univ. of North Carolina at Chapel Hill, 1984; M.D., S.U.N.Y. Health Science Center-Syracuse, 1988; Residencies, Univ. of Rochester, Univ. of Arizona; Fellowship, Univ. of Kansas **Current organization:** University of Florida, Dept. of Neurology **Title:** Assistant Professor of Neurology/Medical Director of Parkinson & Movement Disorder Center, Shands Jacksonville, FL/Assistant Medical Director, National Parkinson Foundation Five Care Centers, FL **Type of organization:** University hospital **Major product:** Patient care, clinical research **Area of distribution:** Florida **Area of Practice:** Movement Disorder Specialist **Honors/awards:** Who's Who Among American High School Students 1979; Phi Eta Sigma Honor Society 1980; Phi Beta Kappa 1983; R1 Dinner Club Co-founders Recognition Award 1989; Medical School Award for Excellence in Teaching 1993; 93% Neurology In-Service Exam 1993; International Who's Who Among Professionals 1996; Excellence in Healthcare Award for the Shands Parkinson's Center 2000 **Published works:** Numerous including, Co-author, "Marchiafava-Bignami Disease: Premortem Diagnosis of an Acute Case Utilizing MRI", J.Neuroimaging, 4:106-109, 1994; "Psychogenic Movement Disorders in Differential Diagnosis and Treatment of Movement Disorders", pg. 127-136, 1998; "Tremor-Predominant Parkinson's Disease" Approaches To Treatment, Drug & Aging, 2000 Apr. 16 (4):273-278 **Affiliations:** American Academy of Neurology; Movement Disorders Society; American Medical Association; Greater Albuquerque Medical Association; Co-founder, Florida Movement Disorder Society **Hob./spts.:** Martial arts, kick boxing, tennis, skiing, fishing, sketching, scuba diving/snorkeling **SIC code:** 80 **Address:** University of Florida, Dept. of Neurology, 655 W. Eighth St., Parkinson Center, Jacksonville, FL 32209 **E-mail:** jm.lyons@jax.ufl.edu

MARKHAM, KATRINA C.
Industry: Healthcare **Title:** Branch Manager **Type of organization:** Homecare **Major product:** In-home healthcare **Area of Practice:** Management **SIC code:** 80 **Address:** American Homecare Management, 501 E. Main St., Suite C, Park Hills, MO 63601 **E-mail:** katrina_markham@hotmail.com

MARKIN, RODNEY S.
Industry: Medical **Univ./degree:** M.D., University of Nebraska Medical Center, 1983 **Current organization:** University of Nebraska Medical Center **Title:** M.D., Ph.D. **Type of organization:** University medical center **Major product:** Patient care, medical education **Area of distribution:** International **Area of Practice:** Pathology **Affiliations:** A.M.A.; American Association for Clinical Chemistry; National Academy of Clinical Biochemistry; American Society of Clinical Pathologists **SIC code:** 80 **Address:** University of Nebraska Medical Center, 983135 Nebraska Medical Center, Omaha, NE 68198-3135 **E-mail:** rmarkin@unmc.edu

MARKLEY, JOHN G.
Industry: Healthcare **Born:** June 15, 1963, Gardenia, California **Univ./degree:** M.D., Medical College of Wisconsin, 1992 **Current organization:** Harry S. Truman Veterans Memorial Hospital **Title:** M.D. **Type of organization:** Hospital **Major product:** Patient care **Area of distribution:** National **Area of Practice:** Cardiothoracic surgery **Published works:** 4 articles, abstracts **Affiliations:** Society of Thoracic Surgeons **Hob./spts.:** Health and fitness, music, home theater, computers **SIC code:** 80 **Address:** Harry S. Truman Veterans Memorial Hospital, Cardiothoracic Surgery Room, 800 Hospital Dr., Columbia, MO 65201 **E-mail:** john.markley2@med.va.gov

MARKS, CINDY
Industry: Healthcare **Univ./degree:** B.S., University of St. Francis, 2002 **Current organization:** Swedish American Health System **Title:** PACS Administrator **Type of organization:** Hospital **Major product:** Imaging services **Area of distribution:** Northern Illinois and Southern Wisconsin **Area of Practice:** Digital Imaging **Affiliations:** A.S.R.T.; S.C.A.R.; Co-Founder, Emageon User Group **Hob./spts.:** Gardening, travel **SIC code:** 80 **Address:** Swedish American Health System, 1401 E. State St., Rockford, IL 61104 **E-mail:** c.marks@insightbb.com

MARSHALL, TERESA J.
Industry: Healthcare **Born:** March 1, 1949, Red Cloud, Nebraska **Univ./degree:** Ph.D., Clinical Psychology, 1985; M.A., Counseling and Guidance **Current organization:** Theresa J. Marshall Psychological Services LLC **Title:** Doctor of Psychology/ Clinical Director **Type of organization:** Private practice **Major product:** Individual therapy, mental healthcare **Area of distribution:** International **Area of Practice:** Individual therapy **Affiliations:** Vice President, Pueblo Rape Crisis Center; E.M.D.R.I.A. **Hob./spts.:** Family activities, reading **SIC code:** 80 **Address:** Theresa J. Marshall Psychological Services LLC, 56 Club Manor Dr., Suite 100, Pueblo, CO 81008 **E-mail:** drtjmarshall@earthlink.net

MARSHALL JR., HARRY P.
Industry: Medical **Born:** July 2, 1958, Washington, DC **Univ./degree:** M.D., Morehouse College, 1984 **Current organization:** Georgetown University Hospital **Title:** M.D./F.A.C.S./Assistant Professor of Surgery **Type of organization:** University hospital **Major product:** Medical services **Area of distribution:** International **Area of Practice:** Advanced surgical technology training, virtual reality systems **Published works:** Journals, science articles **Affiliations:** A.M.C.S.; S.E.S.C. **Hob./spts.:** Family, golf **SIC code:** 80 **Address:** 436 15th St. S.E., Washington, DC 20003 **E-mail:** marshall@gunet.georgetown.edu

MARTIN, BRENDA M.
Industry: Healthcare **Title:** Lab Manager **Type of organization:** Private healthcare center **Major product:** Patient cancer care **Area of Practice:** Hematology lab testing **SIC code:** 80 **Address:** Missouri Cancer Associates, 105 Keene St., #200, Columbia, MO 65201 **E-mail:** brenda.martin@usoncology.com

MARTIN, CAROLINE
Industry: Healthcare **Born:** December 18, 1940, Hermon, Maine **Univ./degree:** B.S., Nursing; M.A., Health and Hospital Administration, MCV-VCU **Current organization:** Riverside Health System **Title:** Executive Vice President **Type of organization:** Non-profit integrated health system **Major product:** Patient care **Area of distribution:** Southeast Virginia **Area of Practice:** Executive management, registered nurse, strategic planning, wellness operations **Affiliations:** A.C.H.E.; Board Member, V.H.H.A.; Campaign Chair, United Way; Phi Kappa Phi; Phi Beta Kappa **Hob./spts.:** Reading, cooking, skiing **SIC code:** 80 **Address:** Riverside Health System, 606 Denbigh Blvd., Suite 601, Newport News, VA 23608-4442 **E-mail:** caroline.martin@rivhs.com **Web address:** www.rivhs.com

MARTIN, CHERYL L.
Industry: Healthcare **Born:** September 19, 1954, Geneva, New York **Univ./degree:** M.S., Nursing, Iona College, 1997; Paralegal Degree, Kaplan College, 2002 **Current organization:** Westchester Medical Center, Joslin Diabetes Center **Title:** Administrative Director, Director of Risk Management Dept. **Type of organization:** Hospital **Major product:** Patient care, education **Area of distribution:** New York **Area of Practice:** Nursing **Published works:** Abstracts **Affiliations:** A.P.A.; A.A.A.C.N. **Hob./spts.:** Crocheting, reading, grandchildren **SIC code:** 80 **Address:** Westchester Medical Center, Joslin Diabetes Center, Cedarwood Hall, Lower Level, Valhalla, NY 10595 **E-mail:** martinc@wcmc.com

MARTIN, DOUGLAS W.
Industry: Healthcare **Born:** March 14, 1965, Tecumseh, Nebraska **Univ./degree:** M.D., University of Nebraska, 1991 **Current organization:** St. Lukes Occupational Health **Title:** Medical Director **Type of organization:** Medical center **Major product:** Patient care **Area of distribution:** National **Area of Practice:** Occupational medicine **Affiliations:** A.A.D.E.P.; A.C.O.E.M.; I.A.F.P. **Hob./spts.:** Family **SIC code:** 80 **Address:** St. Lukes Occupational Health, 224 N. Derby Lane, North Sioux City, SD 57049 **E-mail:** martindw@stlukes.org

MARTIN, PAMELA K.
Industry: Nursing **Born:** February 5, 1949, Longview, Texas **Univ./degree:** B.S.N., University of Mary Hardin-Baylor, 1970; M.S.N.,1981; Ph.D., 1995, Texas Women's University **Current organization:** The University of Texas at Tyler College of Nursing **Title:** Ph.D., R.N., Associate Professor, Associate Dean for Undergraduate Nursing Programs **Type of organization:** University **Major product:** Nursing education **Area of distribution:** Texas **Area of Practice:** Maternity **Published works:** 4 articles **Affiliations:** American Nurses Association; Sigma Theta Tau International; Southern Nursing Research Society **Hob./spts.:** Gardening, sewing **SIC code:** 80 **Address:** The University of Texas at Tyler, College of Nursing, 3900 University Blvd., Tyler, TX 75799 **E-mail:** pmartin@mail.uttyl.edu **Web address:** www.uttyler.edu/nursing

MARTIN, UBALDO J.
Industry: Medical **Born:** October 20, 1968 Guatemala City, Guatemala **Univ./degree:** M.D., University of Francisco Marroquín, Guatemala, 1994 **Current organization:** The Temple Long Center at Temple University Hospital **Title:** M.D. **Type of organization:** University hospital **Major product:** Patient care, medical education **Area of distribution:** Philadelphia, Pennsylvania **Area of Practice:** Pulmonary, critical care medicine **Affiliations:** A.M.A.; American Thoracic Society **Hob./spts.:** Racquetball, wine tasting **SIC code:** 80 **Address:** The Temple Long Center at Temple University Hospital, 3401 N. Broad St., 7PP, Philadelphia, PA 19140 **E-mail:** martinu@tuhs.temple.edu

MARTIN SR., ALVIN M.
Industry: Healthcare **Born:** February 14, 1962, Conway, North Carolina **Univ./degree:** B.S. Biology/Chemistry, East Carolina State University, 1984; M.S., Project Management, Western Carolina University, 2003 **Current organization:** Family Health International **Title:** Laboratory Manager **Type of organization:** Nonprofit independent testing facility **Major product:** Testing of contraceptive devices **Area of distribution:** International **Area of Practice:** Quality control/quality assurance **Hob./spts.:** Weightlifting, golf **SIC code:** 80 **Address:** Family Health International, 2810 Meridian Pkwy., Suite 110, Durham, NC 27709 **E-mail:** amartin@fhi.org

MARTINEZ, FERNANDO R.
Industry: Healthcare **Born:** September 29, 1963, Ponce, Puerto Rico **Univ./degree:** M.D., San Juan Bautista University, Puerto Rico, 1993 **Current organization:** San Juan de Capestrano Hospital **Title:** M.D. **Type of organization:** Hospital **Major product:** Patient care **Area of distribution:** San Juan, Puerto Rico **Area of Practice:** Psychiatry **Affiliations:** A.P.A. **Hob./spts.:** Scuba diving, reading, listening to classical music **SIC code:** 80 **Address:** San Juan de Capestrano Hospital, PMB 535, 89 De Diego, Suite 105, San Juan, PR 00927-6346

MARTY, BENITO I.
Industry: Healthcare **Born:** May 7, 1965, Seattle, Washington **Univ./degree:** M.D., Philippines, 1989 **Current organization:** Ann Klein Forensic Center **Title:** M.D. **Type of organization:** State hospital **Major product:** Patient care **Area of distribution:** West Trenton, New Jersey **Area of Practice:** Psychiatry **Affiliations:** American Psychiatric Association **SIC code:** 80 **Address:** Ann Klein Forensic Center, P.O. Box 7717, West Trenton, NJ 08628

MARU, DIPEN
Industry: Healthcare **Born:** September 30, 1966, Gurat, India **Univ./degree:** M.B.B.S., India, 1989 **Current organization:** M.D. Anderson Cancer Center **Title:** M.D. **Type of organization:** Hospital **Major product:** Patient care, research **Area of distribution:** Texas **Area of Practice:** Oncopathology, clinical and anatomical pathology **Published works:** 7 articles, 50 abstracts/presentations **Affiliations:** C.A.P.; A.S.C.R.; A.G.A.; A.S.C.; A.S.C.P.; A.M.D.A. **Hob./spts.:** Tennis, reading, writing **SIC code:** 80 **Address:** 7300 Brompton St., Apt. 5826, Houston, TX 77025 **E-mail:** dmaru@mdanderson.org **Web address:** www.mdanderson.org

MARWAH, ONKARJIT SINGH
Industry: Medical **Born:** November 14, 1961, Punjab, India **Univ./degree:** M.D., Punjab University, India, 1985 **Current organization:** USC School of Medicine, Los Angeles **Title:** Clinical Assistant Professor, M.D. **Type of organization:** University/ hospital **Major product:** Medical services **Area of distribution:** National **Area of Practice:** Cardiology, angioplasty, interventional cardiology **Published works:** Articles **Affiliations:** F.A.C.C.; A.M.A.; A.C.P.-A.S.I.M.; American Heart Association; Indian Medical Association **Hob./spts.:** Tennis, golf, travel **SIC code:** 80 **Address:** 801 S. Chevy Chase Blvd., Suite 101, Glendale, CA 91205 **Phone:** (818)243-9600 **Fax:** (323)664-4121

MARX, GERALD R.
Industry: Healthcare **Born:** March 11, 1950, New York, New York **Univ./degree:** M.D., UCLA School of Medicine, 1976 **Current organization:** Boston Children's Hospital **Title:** M.D. **Type of organization:** Hospital **Major product:** Pediatric cardiology **Area of distribution:** International **Area of Practice:** Pediatric cardiology **Published works:** Articles, chapters, books **Affiliations:** American Heart Association; American College of Cardiology; American Society of Echocardiography; Harvard School of Medicine **Hob./spts.:** Spending time with his children **SIC code:** 80 **Address:** Boston Children's Hospital, 300 Longwood Ave., Boston, MA 02115 **E-mail:** marx@cardio.tch.harvard.edu

MASAKAYAN, RAUL JOSE
Industry: Healthcare **Born:** November 18, 1960, Philippines **Univ./degree:** B.S., Psychology, University of Philippines, 1981; M.D., University of Philippines Medical School, 1985 **Current organization:** Raul Jose Masakayan M.D. **Title:** MD **Type of organization:** Private practice **Major product:** Patient care **Area of distribution:** New York **Area of Practice:** Anesthesiology **Honors/awards:** Teacher of the Year, 2000-2002, SUNY Stony Brook, Dept. of Anesthesiology **Affiliations:** A.C.P.; American Society of Anesthesiology; Assistant Professor, SUNY Stony Brook **Hob./spts.:** Family, music, sports, reading **SIC code:** 80 **Address:** Raul Jose Masakayan M.D., 32 Setalcott Place, Setauket, NY 11733 **E-mail:** rjm85@optonline.net

MASHTARE, THERESA CARBAJAL
Industry: Healthcare **Born:** January 10, 1964, Pampanga, Philippines **Univ./degree:** L.P.N. **Current organization:** Abbott Professional Nursing Care **Title:** Director of Operations **Type of organization:** Home healthcare **Major product:** In home LPN's, RN's and care givers for the sick and elderly **Area of distribution:** Virginia **Area of Practice:** Management, administration, team building; Clinical Instructor at Abbott Education Center **Hob./spts.:** Tennis, volleyball **SIC code:** 80 **Address:** Abbott Professional Nursing Care, 5441 Virginia Beach Blvd., Suite 107, Virginia Beach, VA 23462 **E-mail:** theresa_abbottpnc@worldnet.att.net

MASI, PAUL E.
Industry: Healthcare **Born:** July 31, 1957, Bridgeport, Connecticut **Univ./degree:** M.D., New York Medical College, 1984 **Current organization:** The Eye Center **Title:** M.D. **Type of organization:** Group ophthalmology practice **Major product:** Ophthalmology **Area of distribution:** Connecticut **Area of Practice:** Cateract surgery, diabetic retinopathy **Honors/awards:** Medical School Honors, AOA **Affiliations:** A.M.A.; A.A.O; A.S.C.R.S.; C.S.M.S. **Hob./spts.:** Running, golf **SIC code:** 80 **Address:** The Eye Center, 2880 Old Dixwell Ave., Hamden, CT 06518 **E-mail:** idoceye.doc.40@aol.com

MASI, ROBERT JOHN
Industry: Healthcare **Born:** October 25, 1945, New York, New York **Univ./degree:** B.S., Mathematics, Fordham University, 1967; M.D., New York Medical College, 1972 **Current organization:** Eye Medical Clinic of Santa Clara Valley **Title:** M.D. **Type of organization:** Private practice **Major product:** Ophthalmology **Area of distribution:** California **Area of Practice:** Eye surgery **Published works:** 12 articles **Affiliations:** American Association of Ophthalmology; American Society of Cataract & Refractive Surgery **Hob./spts.:** Gardening, wine, travel **SIC code:** 80 **Address:** Eye Medical Clinic of Santa Clara Valley, 220 Meridian Ave., San Jose, CA 95126 **E-mail:** rjm.md@skineye.us

MASON, MARIA K. S.
Industry: Healthcare **Born:** September 6, 1952, Washington, D.C. **Univ./degree:** L.P.N., Margaret Murray Washington, 1982 **Current organization:** Veterans Hospital **Title:** L.P.N. **Type of organization:** Hospital **Major product:** Patient care **Area of distribution:** Washington, D.C. **Area of Practice:** Geriatrics **Affiliations:** D.C.L.P.N.A.; N.A.P.N.E.S. **Hob./spts.:** Casinos, travel **SIC code:** 80 **Address:** 1230 Rhode Island Ave. N.E., Washington, DC 20018 **E-mail:** mariamason202@aol.com

MASSAQUOI, SIDIBRIMA J.
Industry: Healthcare **Born:** August 20, 1949, Blama-Massaquoi, Sierra Leone, West Africa **Univ./degree:** B.Sc., Medical Technology, Lawrence University of Technology (Formerly, Detroit Institute of Technology), 1975 **Current organization:** Quest Diagnostics **Title:** Medical Technologist **Type of organization:** Laboratory **Major product:** Medical testing **Area of distribution:** Trenton, New Jersey **Area of Practice:** Phlebotomy, medical technologies **Affiliations:** International Society for Laboratory Technology; American Association of Bioanalysts; American Society for Medical Technologists; Michigan Society for Medical Technologists; Detroit Society for Medical Technologists **Hob./spts.:** Reading, dancing, movies **SIC code:** 80 **Address:** Quest Diagnostics, 795 Parkway Ave., Trenton, NJ 18618

MASSON, LISA M.
Industry: Healthcare **Univ./degree:** M.D., University of Southern California **Current organization:** Gould Medical Group **Title:** M.D. **Type of organization:** Group medical practice **Major product:** Patient care **Area of distribution:** Modesto, California **Area of Practice:** Adolescence and sports medicine **Honors/awards:** Board of Governors of Gould Medical Foundation **Affiliations:** A.A.F.P.; North American Menopause Society; American College of Quality Assurance; Educational Counselor of MIT **Hob./spts.:** Snow skiing, juggling, unicycling **SIC code:** 80 **Address:** Gould Medical Group, 1329 Spanos Ct., #B4, Modesto, CA 95355

MASTERSON, THOMAS E.
Industry: Healthcare **Born:** March 10, 1949, Windom, Minnesota **Univ./degree:** M.D., University of Minnesota, 1975 **Current organization:** Medical X-Ray Center **Title:** M.D. **Type of organization:** Medical facility **Major product:** Patient care **Area of distribution:** Sioux Falls, South Dakota **Area of Practice:** Interventional radiology **Affiliations:** S.I.R.; A.C.R; R.S.N.A.; A.M.A.; S.D.M.A. **Hob./spts.:** Reading, basketball **SIC code:** 80 **Address:** 1417 S. Minnesota Ave., Sioux Falls, SD 57105 **E-mail:** tmasterson@sio.midco.com

MATOS, MANUEL A.
Industry: Healthcare **Born:** September 11, 1950, San Juan, Puerto Rico **Univ./degree:** M.D., Universidad Central del Este, San Pedro, 1976 **Current organization:** GMG Anesthesia Services Inc. **Title:** M.D. **Type of organization:** Hospital **Major product:** Patient care **Area of distribution:** Puerto Rico **Area of Practice:** Anesthesia, pain management **Affiliations:** A.M.A.; P.R.M.A.; C.M.C. **Hob./spts.:** Race car driving **SIC code:** 80 **Address:** GMG Anesthesia Services Inc., P.O. Box 696, Arecibo, PR 00613 **E-mail:** matos@xsn.net

MATTIX, AMBREA M.
Industry: Healthcare **Born:** January 5, 1957, Jonesboro, Arkansas **Univ./degree:** A.S., Arkansas State University **Current organization:** NEA Medical Center **Title:** House Supervisor; LPN; RN **Type of organization:** Hospital **Major product:** Patient care **Area of distribution:** Jonesboro, Arkansas **Area of Practice:** Certified: ACLS, NALS, BLS, PALS, MALS **Affiliations:** American Nurses Association; American Cancer Society **SIC code:** 80 **Address:** 619 W. College, Jonesboro, AR 72401 **E-mail:** sassepantz@aol.com

MATZINGER, CAROLYN ANNE
Industry: Healthcare **Born:** September 29, 1961, Lockport, New York **Univ./degree:** M.D., Wright State University School of Medicine, 1987 **Current organization:** Women's Care Center and Private Practice **Title:** M.D. **Type of organization:** Outpatient clinic and private practice **Major product:** Women's healthcare and Internal Medicine **Area of distribution:** Henderson, Nevada **Area of Practice:** Internal medicine **Honors/awards:** Community awards for professional mentoring of youth in the community; Named as one of the Top 100 Black Female Physicians in the Country, Essence Magazine, 1995 **Affiliations:** Clark County Medical Society; Television Health Correspondent on the 12 noon news in Columbus, Ohio, 1994-1995; Television Health Correspondent for local Las Vegas, Nevada morning television program; Executive Leadership Coach, Landmark Education Corp.; Physician Consultant/Lecturer, Legacy for Life Corp.; Clark County Medical Society; A.C.P.; Wright State University Alumni Assoc.; American College of Physicians; Diplomate, American Board of Internal Medicine **Hob./spts.:** Physical fitness, community volunteering, family time **SIC code:** 80 **Address:** Women's Care Center and Private Practice, 10620 Southern Highlands Pkwy., Suite 110-419, Las Vegas, NV 89141 **E-mail:** cscm@aol.com

MAURER, GLENDA M.
Industry: Healthcare **Born:** April 30, 1958, Saskatchewan, Canada **Univ./degree:** M.D., University of Saskatchewan, 1985 **Current organization:** Norton County Hospital **Title:** M.D. **Type of organization:** County hospital **Major product:** Patient care/education **Area of distribution:** Norton, Kansas **Area of Practice:** Family practice with obstetrics and emergency room services **Affiliations:** A.M.A.; S.C.O.G.; Kansas Medical Society **Hob./spts.:** Gardening, traveling **SIC code:** 80 **Address:** Norton County Hospital, Dept. of Family Medicine, 711 N. Norton Ave., Norton, KS 67654 **E-mail:** gmaurer@ntcohosp.com

MAURER, HAROLD M.
Industry: Medical **Univ./degree:** M.D., SUNY, 1961 **Current organization:** University of Nebraska Medical Center **Title:** Chancellor **Type of organization:** University, medical center **Major product:** Medical education, patient care **Area of distribution:** International **Area of Practice:** Pediatric hematology, oncology **Affiliations:** A.A.H.C.; A.S.C.O.; A.A.M.C.; S.P.R.; I.S.P.O. **SIC code:** 80 **Address:** University of Nebraska Medical Center, Chancellor's Office, 986605 Nebraska Medical Center, Omaha, NE 68198-6605 **E-mail:** hmmaurer@unmc.edu **Web address:** www.unmc.edu

MAW MAW, NINA K.
Industry: Medical **Born:** Yangon, Myanmar **Univ./degree:** M.D., Ladx Hardinge Medical College, Delhi, India, 1997 **Current organization:** ETSU - Memorial - Chattanooga, Center for Family Medicine **Title:** M.D. **Type of organization:** ETSU - Family Practice Residency Program **Major product:** Patient care, medical education **Area of distribution:** Chattanooga, Tennessee **Area of Practice:** Family practice physician **Affiliations:** A.M.A.; A.A.F.P.; T.A.F.P. **Hob./spts.:** Interior decorating, music, oil painting **SIC code:** 80 **Address:** ETSU - Memorial - Chattanooga, Center for Family Medicine, 2525 deSales Ave., Chattanooga, TN 37404 **E-mail:** ninamawmaw@aol.com

MAXFIELD, WILLIAM S.
Industry: Healthcare **Born:** May 9, 1930, Waco, Texas **Univ./degree:** M.D., Baylor University, 1954 **Current organization:** Manatee Diagnostic Center/ CAT Scan 2000 **Title:** National Medical Director/Chief of Radiology, CAT Scan 2000 and M.D.C., Chief of Nuclear Medicine and Breast Service **Type of organization:** Medical imaging **Major product:** General medical imaging, mobile CT screening for the heart, lungs, abdomen, pelvis **Area of distribution:** National **Area of Practice:** Radiology, nuclear medicine and hyperbaric medicine **Published works:** Radiology/American Journal of Radiology/Journal of Nuclear Medicine/Southern Medical Journal 51:320 March 1958, Treatment of bone metastasis with P32 and Testosterone, Cancer Research 31:166 Feb 1971. Synergism between radiation and estrogen in breast cancer. Supportive Care in Cancer 9:283 June 2001, The Value of Hyperbaric Oxygen in Cancer Care **Affiliations:** Fellow, A.C.N.M.; A.C.R.; A.C.H.M.; A.M.A.; S.N.M.; A.C.N.M.; R.S.N.A. & Roentgen Ray Society **Hob./spts.:** Sailing, woodworking, art, gardening **SIC code:** 80 **Address:** CAT Scan 2000, 19995 U.S. Hwy. North, Clearwater, FL 33764 **E-mail:** wsm3304@pol.net

MAYERHOFF, DAVID I.
Industry: Healthcare **Born:** September 3, 1958, Brooklyn, New York **Univ./degree:** M.D., SUNY Downstate, 1983 **Current organization:** Greystone Park Psychiatric Hospital **Title:** M.D. **Type of organization:** State facility **Major product:** Long term patient care **Area of distribution:** New Jersey **Area of Practice:** Psychiatry, treatment of schizophrenia, clinical research **Published works:** 30+ publications **Affiliations:** A.M.A.; American Psychiatric Organization; New Jersey Psychiatric Association **Hob./spts.:** Museums, travel, yoga, classical music, sports **SIC code:** 80 **Address:** 5 Marie Terrace, West Orange, NJ 07052 **E-mail:** drsyke@aol.com

MAYFIELD, DONALD D.
Industry: Healthcare **Born:** October 29, 1937, Mannington, West Virginia **Univ./degree:** N.M.D., Great Lakes College **Current organization:** The First Resort Nature Apothic Medical Clinic **Title:** NMD, DOM, Physician **Type of organization:** Natural health clinic **Major product:** Patient care **Area of distribution:** International **Area of Practice:** Natural healing **Affiliations:** A.N.M.A. **Hob./spts.:** Reading, travel **SIC code:** 80 **Address:** Mayfield Health Center, 5023 S. Highway 17-92, Casselberry, FL 32707 **E-mail:** donltron@aol.com

MAYORGA, RENE N.
Industry: Healthcare **Born:** August 30, 1956, Nicaragua **Univ./degree:** M.D., National Autonomous University, Nicaragua **Current organization:** Country Walk Family Medicine **Title:** M.D. **Type of organization:** Private practice **Major product:** Patient care **Area of distribution:** Miami, Florida **Area of Practice:** Family medicine **Affiliations:** A.A.F.M.; F.A.A.F.P. **Hob./spts.:** Fishing **SIC code:** 80 **Address:** Country Walk Family Medicine, 13721 S.W. 152nd St., Miami, FL 33177

MAZZA, MICHAEL A.
Industry: Healthcare **Born:** April 22, 1957, New York, New York **Univ./degree:** M.D., Universidad Central del Este, Dominican Republic, 1983 **Current organization:** Brooklyn Hospital Dept. of Pediatrics **Title:** M.D., F.A.A.P. **Type of organization:** Hospital **Major product:** Patient care **Area of distribution:** Brooklyn, New York **Area of Practice:** Pediatrics **Affiliations:** F.A.A.P.; B.P.S. **Hob./spts.:** Tennis, golf **SIC code:** 80 **Address:** Brooklyn Hospital Dept. of Pediatrics, 121 DeKalb Ave., Brooklyn, NY 11201

MCADAMS, MARIA H.
Industry: Healthcare **Born:** April 28, 1955, Delhi, New York **Univ./degree:** L.P.N., BOCES, 1990 **Current organization:** DBA - Flexible Team Player **Title:** L.P.N., Respite Nurse **Type of organization:** DBA **Major product:** Home healthcare **Area of distribution:** New York Tri-County Area **Area of Practice:** Nursing, home healthcare **Affiliations:** Nursing Association **Hob./spts.:** Arts and crafts, church **SIC code:** 80 **Address:** P.O. Box 272, Margaretville, NY 12455 **E-mail:** maria_mc_adams@yahoo.com

MCALISTER, MARILYNN B.
Industry: Healthcare **Born:** December 13, 1941, Dalhart, Texas **Univ./degree:** A.A.S., Medical Office Administration, Amarillo Community College, 1980 **Current organization:** Ron Mansolo, M.D., P.A. **Title:** Practice Manager **Type of organization:** Medical clinic **Major product:** Patient care **Area of distribution:** Cedar Park, Texas **Area of Practice:** Practice administration **Honors/awards:** Office Manager of the Year, 2005 from PAHCOM **Affiliations:** Founder/Former President, PAHCOM; Board Member, Virginia Institute, College of Medical Office; Professional Association of Healthcare Managers **Hob./spts.:** Running, hiking, mountain climbing **SIC code:** 80 **Address:** 515 Palm Valley Blvd., #1417, Round Rock, TX 78664 **E-mail:** marilynn.m@cox-internet.com **Web address:** www.hcfamilyhealth.yourmd.com

MCAVENEY, KEVIN M.
Industry: Healthcare **Born:** November 11, 1960, Philadelphia, Pennsylvania **Univ./degree:** B.S., Chemistry, St. Joseph's University, Pennsylvania, 1982; D.O., Philadelphia School of Osteopathic Medicine, 1992 **Current organization:** Mercy Suburban Hospital **Title:** D.O. **Type of organization:** Hospital **Major product:** Patient care **Area of distribution:** Pennsylvania **Area of Practice:** Emergency medicine, family practice **Affiliations:** A.O.A.; A.A.C.P.; A.E.M.S.; Strathmore's Who's Who **SIC code:** 80 **Address:** Mercy Suburban Hospital, Emergency Dept., 2701 Dekalb Pike, Norristown, PA 19401 **E-mail:** mcaveney@msn.com

MCAVOY, SANDRA J.
Industry: Healthcare **Born:** September 4, 1963, Poughkeepsie, New York **Univ./degree:** L.P.N., Duchess County Boces Tech Center, 1994 **Current organization:** Northeast Center for Special Care **Title:** L.P.N./Charge Nurse **Type of organization:** Specialty hospital/nursing home **Major product:** Patient care **Area of distribution:** New York **Area of Practice:** Behavioral health **Honors/awards:** BOCES High Honor Award and Award for Most Academic Achievements **Hob./spts.:** Reading, swimming, relaxing at home, gardening, time with pets, grandchildren and family events **SIC code:** 80 **Address:** Northeast Center for Special Care, 300 Grant Ave., Lake Katrine, NY 12449 **E-mail:** coronabird2006@msn.com

MCCABE, PATRICK J.
Industry: Healthcare **Born:** September 27, 1952, Bayonne, New Jersey **Univ./degree:** B.S., University of Arizona, 1975 **Current organization:** Christ Hospital **Title:** Pharmacy Manager **Type of organization:** Hospital **Major product:** Patient care **Area of distribution:** New Jersey **Area of Practice:** Pharmaceutical management **Affiliations:** Vice President, Christ Hospital Credit Union; Co-Chairman, Patient Safety Committee; Director, Medication Error Reporting Team with Christ Hospital; Hudson County Pharmaceutical Association; New Jersey Society of Hospital Pharmacists **Hob./spts.:** Coaching baseball **SIC code:** 80 **Address:** 87 W. Ninth St., Bayonne, NJ 07002 **E-mail:** pmccabe@christhospital.org

MCCARTY, BETTY E.
Industry: Healthcare **Born:** June 15, 1959, Chambersburg, Pennsylvania **Univ./degree:** A.S., Radiologic Technologist, Medical College of Georgia, 1979 **Current organization:** Crawford Long Hospital of Emory University **Title:** CT Technologist **Type of organization:** Teaching hospital **Major product:** Patient care **Area of distribution:** Atlanta, Georgia **Area of Practice:** CT technology **Affiliations:** A.R.R.T. **Hob./spts.:** Yoga, weight-training, NASCAR **SIC code:** 80 **Address:** Crawford Long Hospital of Emory University, 550 Peach Tree St. N.E., Atlanta, GA 30308 **E-mail:** betty_mccarty@emory.edu **Web address:** www.emory.edu

MCDONALD, JOANNE E.
Industry: Healthcare **Born:** August 15, 1954, Fort Worth, Texas **Univ./degree:** A.S., Nursing, Tarrant County College, 1993 **Current organization:** Kindred Hospital Tarrant County Fort Worth S.W. **Title:** R.N./CIC **Type of organization:** Hospital **Major product:** Patient care **Area of distribution:** Fort Worth, Texas **Area of Practice:** Infection control; CIC Certified **Affiliations:** A.C.L.S.; A.P.I.C.; P.I.C.C.; BLS (Basic Life Support) Instructor **Hob./spts.:** Spending time with her grandchildren, sports, basketball, horseback riding, walking, reading, stained glass **SIC code:** 80 **Address:** Kindred Hospital of Tarrant County, Fort Worth S.W., 7800 Oakmont Blvd., Ft. Worth, TX 76132

MCGILLEN, JOHN J.
Industry: Healthcare **Born:** January 18, 1947, Chicago, Illinois **Univ./degree:** M.D., Northwestern University, Chicago, 1973 **Current organization:** Northwest Community Hospital **Title:** Chief of Medicine **Type of organization:** Hospital **Major product:** Patient care **Area of distribution:** Illinois **Area of Practice:** Infectious diseases, internal medicine **Affiliations:** F.A.C.P; A.M.A.; I.D.S.A.; Illinois Medical Society **Hob./spts.:** Golf, philosophy **SIC code:** 80 **Address:** Northwest Community Hospital, 1300 E. Central Rd., Suite C, 2nd floor, Arlington Heights, IL 60005 **E-mail:** johnmcmd@msn.com

MCGRAW, DAVE D.
Industry: Healthcare **Born:** July 19, 1959, Marion, Indiana **Univ./degree:** A.S., HVAC Engineering, Denver Institute of Technology **Current organization:** Spanish Peaks Regional Health Center **Title:** Support Services Director **Type of organization:** Hospital/nursing home **Major product:** Patient care **Area of Practice:** Staff supervision, budget **Published works:** Designed and presents safety programs to employees **Affiliations:** N.F.P.A.; N.W.T.F.; C.B.H.A. **Hob./spts.:** Certified Taxidermist, hunting, hiking, camping **SIC code:** 80 **Address:** Spanish Peaks Regional Health Center, 23500 U.S. Hwy. 160, Walsenburg, CO 81089 **E-mail:** dmcgraw@sprhc.org

MCGRORY, MICHELE A.
Industry: Healthcare **Born:** March 28, 1967, Syracuse, New York **Univ./degree:** B.A., Biology, Lemoyne College; Certificate in Surgical Technology, Onondaga Community College **Current organization:** Specialists' One-Day Surgery, LLC **Title:** Materials Manager **Type of organization:** Surgery center **Major product:** Orthopedics **Area of distribution:** Syracuse, New York **Area of Practice:** Purchasing **Hob./spts.:** Camping, embroidery, reading **SIC code:** 80 **Address:** Specialists' One-Day Surgery, LLC, 190 Intrepid Lane, Syracuse, NY 13205 **E-mail:** mmcgrory@sosbones.com

MCLARTY, ALLISON J.
Industry: Medical **Born:** June 16, 1962, Jamaica **Univ./degree:** M.D., Columbia University, 1988 **Current organization:** University Hospital/SUNY at Stony Brook **Title:** Cardio-Thoracic Surgeon **Type of organization:** University hospital **Major product:** Medical services **Area of distribution:** Stony Brook, New York **Area of Practice:** Cardio-thoracic surgery **Honors/awards:** O.T. Clagget Award, Mayo Clinic, 1997 **Published works:** Annals of Thoracic Surgery; Circulation; Journal of Thoracic and Cardio-Vascular Surgery **Affiliations:** F.A.C.S.; A.H.A.; NYSTS; Women Thoracic Surgeons **Hob./spts.:** Ballroom dancing, painting **SIC code:** 80 **Address:** University Hospital/SUNY at Stony Brook, Health Science Center, 19th floor, Room 080, Stony Brook, NY 11798 **E-mail:** allison.mclarty@sunysb.edu

MCMINN, MELINDA BETH
Industry: Healthcare **Born:** February 4, 1970, Fredonia, New York **Univ./degree:** M.D., SUNY Syracuse, 1996 **Current organization:** St. Joseph's Hospital Health Center **Title:** M.D. **Type of organization:** Not-for-profit hospital **Major product:** Patient

care **Area of distribution:** New York **Area of Practice:** Family medicine **Affiliations:** A.M.A.; American Academy of Family Practice **Hob./spts.:** Weightlifting, rock climbing, hiking **SIC code:** 80 **Address:** St. Joseph's Hospital Health Center, 3452 State Route 31, Baldwinsville, NY 13027 **E-mail:** melinda.mcminn@sjhsey.org

MCMURRAY, STEPHEN D.
Industry: Healthcare **Univ./degree:** M.D., Indiana University, 1972 **Current organization:** Indiana Medical Associates **Title:** M.D. **Type of organization:** Private medical practice **Major product:** Patient care **Area of distribution:** National **Area of Practice:** Nephrology **Published works:** 25+ articles **Affiliations:** Fellow; American College of Physicians; Reno Nephrology Association **SIC code:** 80 **Address:** Indiana Medical Associates, 7900 W. Jefferson Blvd., Suite 201, Ft. Wayne, IN 46804 **E-mail:** steve@ehsfwa.com

MCNIEL, JANET SNOW
Industry: Healthcare **Born:** March 25, 1942, Portland, Oregon **Univ./degree:** B.A., Biology, Walla Walla College, Washington, 1963; M.D., Loma Linda University School of Medicine, California, 1967 **Current organization:** East Tennessee Physician's Care **Title:** M.D. **Type of organization:** Private practice/clinic **Major product:** Patient care **Area of distribution:** Knoxville, Tennessee **Area of Practice:** General family practice, environmental medicine, nutrition, detoxification, pain management and natural hormone replacement, thyroid problems, fluent in Spanish **Honors/awards:** Physicians' Recognition Award, A.M.A. **Affiliations:** Fellow, American Academy of Family Practitioners; Diplomate, American Academy of Pain Management; Tennessee Medical Association **Hob./spts.:** Church activities, bird watching, playing piano **SIC code:** 80 **Address:** East Tennessee Physician's Care, 5917 Rutledge Pike, Knoxville, TN 37924 **Phone:** (865)525-2121 **E-mail:** etpcdr@aol.com

MCPARTLAND, SHEILA A.
Industry: Healthcare **Born:** December 19, 1965, Alamogordo, New Mexico **Univ./degree:** R.N. **Current organization:** Good Samaritan Hospital **Title:** Nurse Manager **Type of organization:** Hospital **Major product:** Patient care **Area of distribution:** California **Area of Practice:** Cardiac nursing, nurse management **Hob./spts.:** Hiking, reading, the beach **SIC code:** 80 **Address:** 467 Tovar Dr., San Jose, CA 95123 **E-mail:** samrnplus3@aol.com

MEAGHER, BRIAN D.
Industry: Healthcare **Born:** August 17, 1956, Bronx, New York **Univ./degree:** B.A., Neurobiology and Behavior, Cornell University Ithaca, New York, 1978; M.D., Georgetown University School of Medicine, Washington, D.C., 1982 **Current organization:** Jamestown Radiology, P.C. **Title:** M.D. **Type of organization:** Hospital based practice **Major product:** Patient care **Area of distribution:** New York **Area of Practice:** Radiology (CT, MRI, ultrasound) **Honors/awards:** Alpha Omega Alpha Honor Society, appointed 1981 **Affiliations:** American College of Radiology; American Roentgen Ray Society; Radiological Society of North America; Past President, Oswego County Medical Society; U.S. Air Force (4 years Reserves, 7 years Active Duty, 1978-89), Retired as Major **Hob./spts.:** Downhill skiing, snowmobiling **SIC code:** 80 **Address:** 204 Sanbury Rd., Jamestown, NY 14701 **E-mail:** madrad@hughes.net

MEDRANO, MARCELINA L.
Industry: Healthcare **Univ./degree:** M.D., University of Santo Thomas, 1965 **Current organization:** Staten Island Medical Group **Title:** M.D. **Type of organization:** Medical facility **Major product:** Patient care **Area of distribution:** Staten Island **Area of Practice:** Pediatrics **Published works:** Articles **Affiliations:** Member, Board of Directors, P.A.C.C.C.S.I.; President, A.U.R.O.R.A. **Hob./spts.:** Bowling **SIC code:** 80 **Address:** Staten Island Medical Group, 1050 Clove Rd., Staten Island, NY 10301

MEHDI, SYED A.
Industry: Medical **Univ./degree:** M.D., Dow Medical College, Karachi, Pakistan, 1984; Residency & Fellowship, Upstate University Syracuse, New York **Current organization:** Veterans Affairs Medical Center/UND **Title:** MD, FACP **Type of organization:** Teaching hospital **Major product:** Patient care, medical education **Area of distribution:** National **Area of Practice:** Hematology/oncology **Published works:** Peer reviewed journals **Affiliations:** A.C.P.; A.S.C.O.; A.S.H.; A.O.A. **Hob./spts.:** Reading **SIC code:** 80 **Address:** Veterans Affairs Medical Center, 11-C (Hem/Onc) Elm St., Fargo, ND 58102 **E-mail:** smehdi@aol.com

MEHTA, GAURAV
Industry: Healthcare **Born:** June 8, 1977, Bombay, India **Univ./degree:** M.D., K.J. Somaiya Medical College, University of Bombay, 2001; Residency, Transitional Medicine, Frankfurt Hospital, 2002-2003; Residency, Internal Medicine, Graduate Hospital, 2003-2006 **Current organization:** Albert Einstein Hospital **Title:** Fellow in Hepatology **Type of organization:** Hospital **Major product:** Patient care **Area of distribution:** Pennsylvania **Area of Practice:** Liver transplants, clinical and research work **Honors/awards:** Chairman's Award, Graduate Hospital, 2004; Director's Award as Outstanding Resident, Graduate Hospital, 2006 **Affiliations:** American Association for the Study of Liver Diseases; American Gastroenterological Association **Hob./spts.:** Tennis, playing electric guitar, reading, club instructor **SIC code:** 80 **Address:** Albert Einstein Hospital, 5501 Old York Rd., Philadelphia, PA 19141 **E-mail:** gauravapp2002@yahoo.com

MEHTA, MUKESH N.
Industry: Healthcare **Born:** June 21, 1962, India **Univ./degree:** M.D., Shah Medical College, Jamnager, India, 1986 **Current organization:** Mukesh N. Mehta , M.D., P.A. **Title:** M.D. **Type of organization:** Group practice **Major product:** Patient care **Area of distribution:** Texas **Area of Practice:** Internal medicine **Honors/awards:** National Merit Scholarship, 1984 **Affiliations:** A.A.P.I.; American College of Physicians **Hob./spts.:** Golf, tennis, reading, travel **SIC code:** 80 **Address:** Mukesh N. Mehta , M.D., P.A., 5618 Medical Center Dr., Suite 104, Katy, TX 77494 **E-mail:** mukeshm22@aol.com

MEHTA, PRAFUL C.
Industry: Healthcare **Born:** January 14, 1949, India **Univ./degree:** M.D., Baroda Medical College **Current organization:** Piedmont Psychiatric Associates **Title:** President **Type of organization:** Medical practice **Major product:** Mental healthcare **Area of distribution:** North Carolina **Area of Practice:** Psychiatry **Affiliations:** G.S.A.P.; C.N.C.A.P.; A.P.A.; A.M.A.; N.C.M.A.; S.M.A.; N.C.P.A.; L.A.P.A. **Hob./spts.:** Travel **SIC code:** 80 **Address:** Piedmont Psychiatric Associates, 459 N. Wendover Rd., Charlotte, NC 28211 **E-mail:** mehtapcmd@yahoo.com

MEILLIER, DAVID E.
Industry: Healthcare **Born:** August 19, 1924, Rice County, Minnesota **Univ./degree:** B.S., Accounting, University of St. Thomas, 1962 **Current organization:** Pleasant Manor, Inc. **Title:** President **Type of organization:** Assisted living skilled nursing facility **Major product:** Long term nursing **Area of distribution:** Minnesota **Area of Practice:** Accounting **Affiliations:** C.P.M.N.; Past Treasurer, N.A.H.C.F.; Knights of Columbus; U.S. Army Corp of Engineers **Hob./spts.:** Golf **SIC code:** 80 **Address:** Pleasant Manor, Inc., 27 Brand Ave., Fairbault, MN 55021

MEIROWITZ, ROBERT F.
Industry: Healthcare **Born:** December 18, 1957, New York, New York **Univ./degree:** M.D., New York Medical College at Valhalla, 1984 **Current organization:** Princeton Gastroenterology Associates; Chief of Endoscopy, Medical Center of Princeton; Clinical Professor, Robert Wood Johnson Medical School **Title:** Senior Partner, President **Type of organization:** Medical group **Major product:** Cancer screening and colonoscopy **Area of distribution:** New Jersey **Area of Practice:** Gastroenterology **Affiliations:** A.M.A.; A.C.G.; A.G.A.; Director of Gastroenterology, Medical Center of Princeton **Hob./spts.:** Lacrosse, coaching, sports memorabilia **SIC code:** 80 **Address:** Princeton Gastroenterology Associates, 281 Witherspoon St., Suite 230, Princeton, NJ 08542

MEJIAS, MIGUEL FIGUEROA
Industry: Healthcare **Born:** February 12, 1939, Aguada, Puerto Rico **Univ./degree:** M.D., Occupational Specialist, 1984; Ph.D., Education, 1984, Western University, Florida; B.S.A.; Ph.D., Agriculture **Current organization:** Workmen's Compensation (Medical Dept.) **Title:** M.D, Ph.D. **Type of organization:** Hospital **Major product:** Patient care, physical examinations **Area of distribution:** Puerto Rico **Area of Practice:** Education, HIV counseling, industrial medicine **Published works:** Articles **Affiliations:** A.M.A.; P.R.M.A.; Colonel, Puerto Rico National Guard; Vietnam Vet (Dept. of Defense 7 years) **Hob./spts.:** Scuba diving **SIC code:** 80 **Address:** Workmen's Compensation (Medical Dept.), Road #2 in front of the Cascados, P.O. Box 837, Aguadilla, PR 00603 **E-mail:** nazareno@caribe.net

MELLER, JANET
Industry: Healthcare **Born:** March 16, 1955, Illinois, Chicago **Univ./degree:** B.S., Biology, Minor in Math, University of Miami, 1976; M.D., Chicago Medical School, 1980 **Current organization:** Midwest Pediatric Surgical Associates **Title:** M.D./Surgeon **Type of organization:** Private practice **Major product:** Pediatric surgery **Area of distribution:** Illinois **Area of Practice:** Pediatric surgery **Published works:** 20 journals, 10 book chapters, conference papers and abstracts **Affiliations:** F.A.C.S.; F.A.A.P.; A.M.A.; A.S.C.C.; Chicago Surgeons Society **SIC code:** 80 **Address:** Midwest Pediatric Surgical Associates, 4400 W. 95th St., #108, Oak Lawn, IL 60453 **E-mail:** pedsurg16@aol.com

MELLOW, ELLEN
Industry: Healthcare **Born:** December 5, 1953, New York, New York **Univ./degree:** M.D., Cornell Medical College, 1980 **Current organization:** Ellen Mellow, MD **Title:** M.D. **Type of organization:** Private practice **Major product:** Patient care/consulting **Area of distribution:** New York, New York **Area of Practice:** Internal medicine, cardiology, renal, liver and pancreas transplants **Published works:** Multiple abstracts **Affiliations:** F.A.C.C.; A.H.A. **Hob./spts.:** Music, family **SIC code:** 80 **Address:** Ellen Mellow, MD, 860 Fifth Ave., New York, NY 10021

MELOY, LINDA D.
Industry: Medical **Univ./degree:** M.D. **Current organization:** Virginia Commonwealth University **Title:** Associate Professor of Pediatrics **Type of organization:** University, research center **Major product:** Patient care, medical education and research **Area of distribution:** International **Area of Practice:** Pediatrics, charity **Hob./spts.:** Photography **SIC code:** 80 **Address:** Virginia Commonwealth University, 11920 Blandfield St., Richmond, VA 23233

MENARD, RALPH G.
Industry: Healthcare **Born:** July 25, 1952, Roseburg, Oregon **Univ./degree:** M.D., Medical College of Georgia, 1982 **Current organization:** Ralph G. Menard M.D. **Title:** M.D. **Type of organization:** Private practice **Major product:** Patient care **Area of distribution:** National **Area of Practice:** Anesthesiology/Pain Management **Affiliations:** A.A.P.M.; A.S.I.P.P.; American Pain Society; Founding Member, Texas Pain Society **Hob./spts.:** Hunting, reading, travel, photography **SIC code:** 80 **Address:** Ralph G. Menard M.D., 4742 N. Loop 289, Suite 209, Lubbock, TX 79416 **E-mail:** paindoc@ralphmenardmd.com

MENDESZOON, MICHAEL H.
Industry: Healthcare **Born:** July 23, 1960, Brooklyn, New York **Univ./degree:** M.D., SUNY Health Sciences Center, Brooklyn, 1986; Baruch/Mount Sinai Program in Healthcare Administration, 2002 **Current organization:** Kings County Hospital Center **Title:** M.D. **Type of organization:** Hospital **Major product:** Medical services **Area of distribution:** New York **Area of Practice:** Anesthesiology **Affiliations:** Fellow, New York Academy of Medicine; Treasurer, New York Society of Anesthesiologists; American College of Physician Executives; A.S.A.; A.M.A. **Hob./spts.:** Martial arts, Tae Kwon Do, Kung Fu, reading, plays, films, **SIC code:** 80 **Address:** Kings County Hospital Center, 451 Clarkson Ave., B Bldg., Room 2175, Brooklyn, NY 11203 **E-mail:** mendeszoon@mindspring.com

MENDEZ, DEBRA J.
Industry: Healthcare **Born:** May 18, 1964, Chicago, Illinois **Univ./degree:** Business Certificate, Robert Morris College **Current organization:** Northwestern Memorial Hospital **Title:** Manager **Type of organization:** Academic medical center (Level I Trauma) **Major product:** Medical services, sterile surgical instruments **Area of distribution:** Illinois **Area of Practice:** Central sterile supply **Affiliations:** C.P.B.S.P.D. **Hob./spts.:** Baseball, softball, refinishing antiques **SIC code:** 80 **Address:** Northwestern Memorial Hospital, 251 E. Huron St., Chicago, IL 60611 **E-mail:** dmendez@nmh.org **Web address:** www.nmh.org

MENDIETA, CONSTANTINO G.
Industry: Healthcare **Born:** December 6, 1963, Los Angeles, California **Univ./degree:** M.D., Creighton Medical School, 1989 **Current organization:** Canstantino Mandieta, M.D., FACS **Title:** M.D. **Type of organization:** Private practice **Major product:** Patient care **Area of distribution:** National **Area of Practice:** Plastic surgery **Published works:** T.V. Bravo "Miami Slice"; CBS News, Fox, New York Times, book published **Affiliations:** American Medical Association; American College of Surgeons **Hob./spts.:** Movies, books, dancing, travel, water sports **SIC code:** 80 **Address:** Constantino Mandieta, M.D., FACS, 2310 S. Dixie Hwy., Miami, FL 33133 **E-mail:** cmendi@aol.com

MENDOZA, CARMEL M.
Industry: Healthcare **Univ./degree:** B.S., Nursing, William Paterson University, 1984 **Current organization:** Delray Medical Center **Title:** Bariatric and Joint Replacement Program Manager **Type of organization:** Hospital **Major product:** Patient care **Area of Practice:** Critical care nursing, bariatric/orthopedic surgery **Affiliations:** American Society for Bariatric Surgery; American Association for Critical-Care Nurses **Hob./spts.:** Family, travel, music **SIC code:** 80 **Address:** Delray Medical Center, 5352 Linton Blvd., Delray Beach, FL 33484 **E-mail:** carmel.mendoza@tenethealth.com

MENDOZA, SHERRIE L.
Industry: Healthcare **Univ./degree:** B.S.N., Weber State University, Utah, 1992 **Current organization:** HMH Management, Lynwood Manor **Title:** Director of Nursing Services **Type of organization:** Long-term healthcare facility **Major product:** Patient care **Area of distribution:** Washington **Area of Practice:** Geriatrics, infection control, nursing management; Certified Advanced IV Practitioner, Crowne Point Indian Hospital, 1997 **Affiliations:** A.P.I.C.; I.N.S. **Hob./spts.:** Reading, needlecrafts, naturalist/herbologist **SIC code:** 80 **Address:** 15320 Mill Creek Blvd., #BB101, Mill Creek, WA 98012 **E-mail:** orcas.one@verizon.net

MENHINICK, DENISE C.
Industry: Healthcare **Born:** December 1, 1965, Searcy, Arkansas **Univ./degree:** M.T., University of Central Arkansas, 1994; M.H.A. Candidate, University of Arkansas **Current organization:** Arkansas Surgical Hospital **Title:** Administrative Manager **Type of organization:** Hospital **Major product:** Patient care **Area of distribution:** Arkansas **Area of Practice:** Medical technology, phlebotomy, training, laboratory management **Affiliations:** Clinical Laboratory Managers Association; American Society of Clinical Pathologists **Hob./spts.:** Crafts, reading **SIC code:** 80 **Address:** Arkansas Surgical Hospital, 5201 N. Shore Dr., North Little Rock, AR 72118 **E-mail:** dmenhinick@arksurgicalhospital.com **Web address:** www.arksurgicalhospital.com

MESSANY, FRANKLIN L.
Industry: Healthcare **Born:** April 6, 1933, Kalamazoo, Michigan **Univ./degree:** D.O., Kirksville College of Osteopathic Medicine, 1966 **Current organization:** Michigan Dept. of Corrections/Muskegon Correctional Facility **Title:** D.O./Chief of Staff at Heritage Hospital **Type of organization:** State dept. of corrections **Major product:** Medical services **Area of distribution:** Muskegon, Michigan **Area of Practice:** Internal medicine, correctional medicine **Honors/awards:** Colonel in the Army Medical Corp. **Affiliations:** A.O.A.; M.O.A. **Hob./spts.:** Scuba diving **SIC code:** 80 **Address:** Michigan Dept. of Corrections, 2400 S. Sheridan, Muskegon, MI 49442 **E-mail:** fmess28641@aol.com

MESSINA, JOHN J.
Industry: Healthcare **Born:** December 20, 1960, Brooklyn, New York **Univ./degree:** M.D., St. George's University, 1986 **Current organization:** St. Joseph's Children's Hospital **Title:** M.D./Chief, Pediatric Cardiology/Pediatric Intensivist **Type of organization:** Hospital **Major product:** Patient care **Area of distribution:** Paterson, New Jersey **Area of Practice:** Pediatric cardiology **Honors/awards:** New Jersey List of Top Doctors, 2001; Teaching Award, St. Joseph's Children's Hospital, 1997-99 **Published works:** 5 published articles **Affiliations:** A.C.C.; A.A.P.; S.C.C.M. **SIC code:** 80 **Address:** St. Joseph Children's Hospital, 703 Main St., Paterson, NJ 07503

METTU, KRISHNA KANTH REDDY
Industry: Medical **Born:** January 1, 1976, Andhra Pradesh, India **Univ./degree:** M.D., BLDEA Shri B M Patil Medical College, India; M.S., University of La Verne, California **Current organization:** University of Missouri, Columbia **Title:** M.D., M.S. **Type of organization:** University **Major product:** Patient care, medical education **Area of distribution:** Columbia, Missouri **Area of Practice:** Neurology, gerontology **Honors/awards:** A.A.N. Resident Scholarship, Recipient of Multiple Sclerosis Comprehensive Treatment Program; Mahendra Memorial Award in Secondary school **Published works:** A.A.N.; A.H.S.; A.A.N.E.M.; A.A.P.M.; A.R.N.M.D.; A.M.A.; A.A.P.I.; G.S.A.; N.P.F.; A.H.A. ; A.A.S.M.; American Society on Aging; American Stroke Association **Affiliations:** American Academy of Neurology; American Academy of Gerontology; American Headache Society; Society for Ethics **Hob./spts.:** Travel, fishing, hiking, cruises, water sports, reading, kite flying **SIC code:** 80 **Address:** University of Missouri, Columbia, 1 Hospital Dr., M-178 DC047.00, Dept. of Neurology, Columbia, MO 65212 **E-mail:** kk_mettu@yahoo.com

METZINGER, STEPHEN E.
Industry: Medical **Born:** September 4, 1960, New Orleans, Louisiana **Univ./degree:** M.D., Louisiana State University, 1987; Reconstructive Surgery, Johns Hopkins University, 1996; Residency in Plastic Surgery, Otalaryngology, General Surgery; Fellowship, American Academy of Facial Plastic & Reconstructive Surgery, Birmingham, AL, 1994 **Current organization:** LSU Health Sciences Center/Dept. of Otalaryngology & Dept. of Surgery, Division of Plastic and Reconstructive Surgery **Title:** M.D./Associate Professor **Type of organization:** University hospital **Major product:** Plastic and reconstructive surgery, medical education and otalaryngology **Area of distribution:** National **Area of Practice:** Plastic reconstructive and maxillofacial surgery **Published works:** 17 articles **Affiliations:** A.S.P.S.; A.A.O.-H.N.S.; A.S.M.S. **Hob./spts.:** Sailing, swimming, running **SIC code:** 80 **Address:** LSU Health Sciences Center, 533 Bolivar, Fifth floor, New Orleans, LA 70112 **E-mail:** smetzi@lsuhsc.edu

MICIANO, ARMANDO S.
Industry: Healthcare **Born:** March 30, 1962, Manila, Philippines **Univ./degree:** M.D., University of South Florida at Tampa, 1993 **Current organization:** Pain & Rehabilitation Center **Title:** M.D. **Type of organization:** Private practice **Major product:** Patient care **Area of distribution:** National **Area of Practice:** Pain management, rehabilitation, public speaking **Affiliations:** A.M.A.; A.A.P.M.R.; Nevada Medical Society **Hob./spts.:** Volleyball, water sports **SIC code:** 80 **Address:** Pain & Rehabilitation Center, 7500 W. Lake Mead, #9611, Las Vegas, NV 89128

MIERES, JENNIFER H.
Industry: Medical **Born:** March 29, 1960, Trinidad **Univ./degree:** B.S., Chemistry and Psychology, Bennington College, 1982; M.D., Boston University School of Medicine, 1983 **Current organization:** North Shore University Hospital **Title:** M.D. **Type of organization:** Hospital **Major product:** Patient care, medical education **Area of distribution:** New York **Area of Practice:** Cardiology **Honors/awards:** New York State Govenors Award for excellence in heart disese in women received 03-02; American Heart Association Award received 06-01through 06-02; Long Island Fund for women and girls received 11-02 **Published works:** 8 abstracts, 3 manuscripts - Documentary on women and heart disease shown on PBS. **Affiliations:** F.A.C.C.; American Heart Association **Hob./spts.:** Family, skiing, tennis, reading, writing **SIC code:** 80 **Address:** North Shore University Hospital, Division of Cardiology, 300 Community Dr., Manhasset, NY 11030 **E-mail:** jmieres@nshs.edu **Web address:** www.nshs.com

MIHAESCU, EDITH E.
Industry: Mental healthcare **Born:** June 13, 1936, Bucharest, Romania **Univ./degree:** M.D., Bucharest Medical School, Romania, 1959; Psychiatric Residency, Johns Hopkins, 1980-82 **Current organization:** Edith Mihaescu, M.D., Psychiatry **Title:** Psychiatrist **Type of organization:** Private practice **Major product:** Psychotherapy **Area of distribution:** Maryland **Area of Practice:** Medication psychotherapy, children to seniors **Honors/awards:** Fellowship, Psychiatric Research, Maryland Research Center **Affiliations:** American Psychiatric Association **Hob./spts.:** Reading, travel, gardening **SIC code:** 80 **Address:** Edith Mihaescu, M.D., Psychiatry, 902 Washington Rd., Suite G, Westminster, MD 21157

MILES-YOUNG, NARVA
Industry: Healthcare **Born:** August 15, 1946, Gilmer, Texas **Univ./degree:** B.S., Nursing, Texas Woman's University, 1973 **Current organization:** Superior Family Care Inc. **Title:** CNO/COO **Type of organization:** Hospital staffing, nurses (temporary and permanent) to area hospitals and medical facilities within the DFW metroplex **Major product:** Patient care **Area of distribution:** Texas **Area of Practice:** Nursing **Affiliations:** A.C.C.N.; Black Business Association; Black Nurses Association; Better Business Bureau **Hob./spts.:** Bowling, swimming **SIC code:** 80 **Address:** Superior Family Care Inc., 2321 S. Beltline Rd., Suite 138, Grand Prairie, TX 75051 **E-mail:** narva@superiorfamilycare.com

MILLER, DIANE M.
Industry: Healthcare **Born:** January 5, 1956, Waynesboro, Pennsylvania **Univ./degree:** A.S., Nursing, Hagerstown Community College, 1975 **Current organization:** Ashley Valley Medical Center **Title:** R.N. **Type of organization:** Hospital **Major product:** Patient care, emergency room nurse **Area of distribution:** Utah **Area of Practice:** Emergency room nursing, Certified, neonatal resuscitation, taking Forensic Nursing course **Affiliations:** A.C.L.S.; T.N.T.C.; P.A.L.S.; B.L.S. **Hob./spts.:** Singing camping, the outdoors, bead collecting (old beads) **SIC code:** 80 **Address:** 291 W. 200 South, Vernal, UT 84078 **E-mail:** nursedi75@hotmail.com

MILLER, GARY D.
Industry: Healthcare **Born:** November 11, 1958, Bartlesville, Oklahoma **Univ./degree:** B.S.N., Northeastern Missouri State University, 1989 **Current organization:** Piedmont Medical Center, Tenet Healthcare **Title:** R.N., B.S.N., W.O.C.N. **Type of organization:** Medical center **Major product:** Patient care **Area of distribution:** South Carolina **Area of Practice:** Cardiac catheterization, coronary angiography, peripheral angiography, wound care **SIC code:** 80 **Address:** Piedmont Medical Center-Cath Lab., 222 Herlong Ave., Rock Hill, SC 29732

MILLER, JEFFREY N.
Industry: Healthcare **Born:** May 3, 1961, Springfield, Massachusetts **Univ./degree:** M.D., State University of New York, Syracuse, 1988 **Current organization:** University Plaza Obstetrics & Gynecology, LLP **Title:** M.D. **Type of organization:** Medical practice **Major product:** Women's healthcare **Area of distribution:** Long Island, New York **Area of Practice:** Ob/Gyn **Affiliations:** A.C.O.G.; New York State Ob/Gyn Society **Hob./spts.:** Tennis, Weightlifting **SIC code:** 80 **Address:** University Plaza Obstetrics & Gynecology, LLP, 877 Stewart Ave., Suite 7, Garden City, NY 11530

MILLER, JOHN R.
Industry: Healthcare **Univ./degree:** M.D., University of Padova, Italy, 1966 **Current organization:** Doctor's Care **Title:** M.D. **Type of organization:** Professional corporation **Major product:** Patient care **Area of distribution:** Linden, New Jersey **Area of Practice:** Orthopedics **SIC code:** 80 **Address:** Doctor's Care, 10 North Ave., Linden, NJ 07036

MILLER, MARY L.
Industry: Healthcare **Born:** March 30, 1941, Hicksville, Ohio **Univ./degree:** R.N., Clark State College, 1985 **Current organization:** Loving Care Hospice and Home Health **Title:** R.N. **Type of organization:** Hospice **Major product:** Patient care **Area of distribution:** Ohio **Area of Practice:** Compassionate care and nursing of the terminally ill **Hob./spts.:** Crocheting, volunteer work, sports spectator **SIC code:** 80 **Address:** 11449 Lafayette P.C. Rd., Plain City, OH 43064 **E-mail:** mlmnurs@aol.com

MILLER, RUSSELL P.
Industry: Healthcare **Born:** December 20, 1967, Spangler, Pennsylvania **Univ./degree:** M.D., Pennsylvania State College of Medicine at Hershey, 1994 **Current organization:** Russell P. Miller, M.D. **Title:** M.D. **Type of organization:** Medical practice **Major product:** Patient care **Area of distribution:** Patton, Pennsylvania **Area of Practice:** Family practice **Affiliations:** A.M.A.; American Board of Family Practice (Board Certified) **Hob./spts.:** Gardening, reading, playing the bagpipes **SIC code:** 80 **Address:** Russell P. Miller, M.D., 456 Magee Ave., Patton, PA 16668 **E-mail:** taliesin@uplink.net

MINAKER, KENNETH L.
Industry: Healthcare **Born:** May 14, 1948, Toronto, Ontario, Canada **Univ./degree:** M.D., 1972; FRCP(C), 1979; CSC(GM), 1985, University of Toronto **Current organization:** Massachusetts General Hospital **Title:** Chief of Geriatrics **Type of organization:** Hospital **Major product:** Patient care **Area of distribution:** International **Area of Practice:** Geriatric care **Honors/awards:** American Geriatrics Society Nascher Manning Award; First Fellow trained in aging, Harvard Medical School; Alpha Omega Alpha **Published works:** 125 journal articles, 19 books, 48 chapters and reviews related to aging in health and neuroendocrine aspects of aging **Affiliations:** Director of Research, Division on Aging, Harvard Medical School; Associate Professor in Medicine, Harvard Medical School; Director, Program for Lifelong Health Education, Harvard University Health Service **Hob./spts.:** Sailing, hiking **SIC code:** 80 **Address:** Massachusetts General Hospital, MGH Senior Health, 5th floor, 100 Charles River Plaza, Boston, MA 02114 **Web address:** www.massgeneral.org/seniorhealth

MINEO, MARIA J.
Industry: Healthcare **Born:** April 15, 1970, Queens, New York **Univ./degree:** M.D., Creighton University, 1998 **Current organization:** Branch Pediatrics **Title:** M.D. **Type of organization:** Private practice **Major product:** Children's healthcare **Area of distribution:** Long Island, New York **Area of Practice:** Pediatrics **Affiliations:** A.A.P.; Suffolk Pediatric Society **SIC code:** 80 **Address:** Branch Pediatrics, 300 E. Main St., Suite 5, Smithtown, NY 11787 **E-mail:** brnped@optonline.net

MINNICK, KATRINA L.
Industry: Healthcare **Born:** October 19, 1959, Ada, Oklahoma **Univ./degree:** A.A., Radiologic Technology, Rose State College, 1993 **Current organization:** Mary Mahoney Memorial Health Center **Title:** Mammographer/Case Manager **Type of organization:** Community health center **Major product:** Patient care **Area of distribution:** Oklahoma **Area of Practice:** Diagnostic radiography and mammography **Published works:** Project Woman **Affiliations:** American Registry of Radiologic Technologists; Oklahoma Society of Radiologic Technologists; Bethel Christian Center Outreach **Hob./spts.:** Drama, mystery, comedy, movies, walking **SIC code:** 80 **Address:** Mary Mahoney Memorial Health Center, 12716 Northeast 36th St., Oklahoma City, OK 73140 **E-mail:** katrina.ninnick@tds.net **Web address:** www.mmmhc.org

MINTZ-HITTNER, HELEN
Industry: Medical **Born:** August 12, 1944, Houston, Texas **Univ./degree:** B.A., Rice University, 1965; M.D., Baylor College of Medicine, 1969 **Current organization:** University of Texas, Houston Medical School **Title:** Pediatric Ophthalmologist **Type of organization:** University hospital **Major product:** Medical services **Area of distribution:** International **Area of Practice:** Pediatric ophthalmology **Published works:** 100+ articles **Affiliations:** A.A.O.; A.A.P.O.S.; A.M.A. **Hob./spts.:** Spending time with grandchildren **SIC code:** 80 **Address:** 6410 Fannin St., Suite 920, Houston, TX 77030 **E-mail:** helen.a.mintz-hittner@uth.tmc.edu **Web address:** www.mintz-hittner-md.com

MIRACLE, KIMBERLY A.
Industry: Healthcare **Born:** June 14, 1952, Madison, Indiana **Univ./degree:** B.S.N., University of Evansville, 1974; M.S.N., Bellarmine University, Kentucky, 1989 **Current organization:** Jewish Hospital **Title:** Clinical Coordinator **Type of organization:** Nonprofit acute care hospital **Major product:** Patient care **Area of distribution:** Kentucky **Area of Practice:** Nursing **Affiliations:** Sigma Theta Tau **Hob./spts.:** Reading, crafts **SIC code:** 80 **Address:** Jewish Hospital, 217 E. Chestnut St., Louisville, KY 40202 **E-mail:** kamiracle@insightbb.com

MIRANDA, LUIS DA GRAÇA
Industry: Healthcare **Born:** September 9, 1942, India **Univ./degree:** M.D., Goa Medical College, India, 1965 **Current organization:** Luis da Graca Miranda, M.D. **Title:** M.D. **Type of organization:** Private practice **Major product:** Patient care **Area of distribution:** New York **Area of Practice:** Erectile dysfunction, Urology (Board Certified) **Affiliations:** New York State Medical Association, President, Richmond County Medical Society **Hob./spts.:** Founder and President, Richmond County Symphony Orchestra, Violin **SIC code:** 80 **Address:** Luis da Graça Miranda, M.D., 11 Ralph Place, Suite 202, Staten Island, NY 10304 **E-mail:** siteoym@aol.com

MIRRIONE, KATHLEEN M.
Industry: Healthcare **Born:** June 2, 1960, Brooklyn, New York **Univ./degree:** B.A., Magna Cum Laude, Physical Education, 1982; M.P.S., Leisure and Recreation Management, Adelphi University, 1984 **Current organization:** Regal Heights Rehab. & Health Care Center **Title:** C.T.R.S./Director, Therapeutic Recreation **Type of organization:** Rehabilitation center and long-term care **Major product:** Therapeutic recreation services **Area of distribution:** Queens, New York **Area of Practice:** Certified Therapeutic Recreation Specialist; patient care **Honors/awards:** Received the Special Recognition Award from the Metropolitan New York Recreation & Park Society, 1995; completed board approved 100-hour pre-licensure course for Nursing Home Administrator's at C.W. Post College, was the 1st Therapeutic Recreation Specialist to complete this course **Published works:** Abstract, "Communication Through

Music and Rhythm for CVA-Aphasic Patients", published in The Archives of Physical Medicine and Rehabilitation, Sept. 1994 edition **Affiliations:** A.T.R.A.; N.T.R.S.; N.Y.S.R.P.S.; M.E.T.R.O. **Career accomplishments:** Presented workshop entitled "First Things First: Assessment and Documentation" at the Eger Health Care Center in Staten Island, 1993; presented workshop for the United Hospital Fund, entitled, "Leadership Skills: How to Lead Recreation Programs in Long-Term Care Facilities" at Fairview Nursing Home, 1994; presented a workshop entitled, "Therapies in Long Term Care" for the Nursing Home Administrator's 100-hour pre-approved course at C.W. Post College, 1998 **Hob./spts.:** Reading, theatre, movies, various team sports **SIC code:** 80 **Address:** Regal Heights Rehab. & Health Care Center, 70-05 35th Ave., Jackson Heights, NY 11372 **E-mail:** kmirrone@regalheightsrehab.com **Web address:** www.regalheightsrehab.com

MIRZA, SHIRWAN A.
Industry: Healthcare **Born:** Sulamanya, Iraq **Univ./degree:** M.D., University of Baghdad, College of Medicine **Current organization:** Endocrinology, Diabetes and Metabolism, PLCC **Title:** M.D. **Type of organization:** Medical office **Major product:** Patient care **Area of distribution:** Auburn, New York **Area of Practice:** Endocrinology and Internal Medicine **Published works:** Journal articles, 3 book chapters **Affiliations:** American Medical Association; American College of Physicians; American College of Endocrinologists; Clinical Assistant Professor of Medicine, Upstate Medical University, Syracuse, NY **SIC code:** 80 **Address:** Endocrinology, Diabetes and Metabolism, PLCC, 37 W. Garden St., Auburn, NY 13021 **E-mail:** leopol@thumpernet.COM

MIRZA, ZAFAR K.
Industry: Medical **Born:** October 20, 1967, Pakistan **Univ./degree:** M.D., King Edward Medical College, Pakistan, 1991 **Current organization:** UMDNJ - Robert Wood Johnson Medical School, Dept. of Medicine **Title:** M.D. **Type of organization:** University hospital **Major product:** Patient care, medical education **Area of distribution:** New Brunswick, New Jersey **Area of Practice:** Internal medicine, gastroenterology **Published works:** Numerous abstracts and papers including: Mirza, Z. Murthy, U., Nizam, R., Linscheer, W., "Iron Deficiency Anemia With No Overt Gastrointestinal Source of Blood Loss: Long-Term Outcome", American Journal of Gastroenterology 1196; 91(9): A1993; Mirza, Z., Prasad S., Das, K., Mohan, V. "Colonoscopy to Evaluate Weight Loss. Is it Worth Doing?", American Journal of Gastroenterology 1999; 94(9): A2679; Miza, Z., Kosa, E., Prasad, S., Griffel, L., Das, K., "Infliximab Therapy for Fistulizing Crohn's Disease", American Journal of Gastroenterology 2000; 95(9): A2635; Zafar, K. Mirza, Peter S. Amenta, Louis H. Griffel, Laura Ramsundar, Jason Slate, Saket Prasad, Kinichi Yokota, Hiroki Tanabe, Tomonobu Sato, Yukata Kohgo, Kiron M. Das, "Gastric Intestinal Metaplasia With Colonic Phenotype, as Detected by a Novel Biomarker, is Highly Associated With Gastric Carcinoma (submitted to Gastroenterology) **Affiliations:** A.C.P.; A.C.G.; A.G.A. **Hob./spts.:** Reading **SIC code:** 80 **Address:** UMDNJ - Robert Wood Johnson Medical School, Dept. of Medicine, 1 Robert Wood Johnson Place, New Brunswick, NJ 08903 **E-mail:** zmirza@excite.com

MISHRICK, ABDALLAH S.
Industry: Healthcare **Born:** November 28, 1928, Lebanon **Univ./degree:** M.D., St. Mary's, Cambridge, England **Current organization:** NS-LIJ Health System **Title:** Medical Director/MD, FACS, FRCS(E), DABS, FRCS(C), FICS, FRSM **Type of organization:** Hospital **Major product:** Patient care **Area of distribution:** New York **Area of Practice:** General surgery/administration **Hob./spts.:** Family, reading, duck hunting, skeet shooting, collecting **SIC code:** 80 **Address:** NS-LIJ Health System, 221 Jericho Tpke., Syosset, NY 11791

MITCHELL, KAREN L.
Industry: Healthcare **Univ./degree:** B.S., Saint Francis University, 1998 **Current organization:** Memorial Medical Center **Title:** Business Services Manager **Type of organization:** Medical center **Major product:** Patient care **Area of distribution:** Springfield, Illinois **Area of Practice:** Radiology services **Affiliations:** A.R.R.T. **SIC code:** 80 **Address:** Memorial Medical Center, Dept. of Radiology, 701 N. First St., Springfield, IL 62781 **E-mail:** mitchell.karen@mhsil.com

MIYAZAWA, JEFFREY K.
Industry: Dentistry **Born:** May 19, 1969, Honolulu, Hawaii **Univ./degree:** D.D.S., Creighton University, 1994 **Current organization:** Jeffrey K. Miyazawa, D.D.S. **Title:** Dentist **Type of organization:** Private practice **Major product:** Dental care **Area of distribution:** Kaneohe, Hawaii **Area of Practice:** Cosmetic and reconstructive dentistry **Affiliations:** A.D.A.; H.D.A.; A.A.C.D. **Hob./spts.:** Golf, baseball **SIC code:** 80 **Address:** Jeffrey K. Miyazawa, D.D.S., 45-480 Kaneohe Bay Dr., Kaneohe, HI 96744 **E-mail:** jkmdds@aol.com

MOBLEY, NORMA D.
Industry: Healthcare **Born:** February 14, 1962, Jackson, Michigan **Univ./degree:** B.S., Psychology, Michigan State University, 1985; M.B., Emory University School of Medicine, 1988; M.D., Morehouse School of Medicine at Atlanta, Georgia, 1997 **Current organization:** Franklin Primary Healthcare, Inc. **Title:** M.D./Assistant Professor at U.S.A. (Board Certified) **Type of organization:** Community health center **Major product:** Patient care for the indigent population **Area of distribution:** Alabama **Area of Practice:** Pediatrics **Honors/awards:** Who's Who Among Young Professionals, 1990-91; National Health Service Corps Scholar, 1993-97; Emory Pediatric Residency Advisory Committee, 1998-2000; Mary Brady Award, Emory University, 2000; Teacher of the Year P.A. Program, South Alabama University, 2003 **Published works:** Presentations: "The Pediatrician's Approach to Contraception in the Adolescent Patient", 2000; "Diagnostic Approach and Management of Gastrointestinal Complaints", 1999; "Diagnostic Approach and Management of Respiratory Complaints", 1999; "Persistent Tachycardia in a Neonate", 1999; "Child Presenting with a Limp", 1999; "Cross Cultural Communication: Treating the Whole Patient", 1997; "Parasomnias in Children", 1996 & 1998; "Brain Death in Children: A Diagnostic Dilemma", 1996; "Promote Breastfeeding in Our Community for Healthier Babies", 1996; "Sickle Cell Disease in Pregnancy: Complications and Management", 1996 **Affiliations:** A.M.A.; M.P.S., A.A.P., G.A.A.P.; Mobile Bay Area Medical Society; National Medical Association **Hob./spts.:** Singing **SIC code:** 80 **Address:** Franklin Primary Healthcare, Inc., 1217 Government St., Mobile, AL 36604 **E-mail:** tank2768@aol.com

MODROW, PATRICIA C.
Industry: Government/military/healthcare **Born:** December 24, 1952, Worcester, Massachusetts **Univ./degree:** Ph.D., New York State University at Buffalo, 1980 **Current organization:** United States Army Medical Research & Material Command **Title:** Program Manager, Department of Defense Ovarian Cancer Research Program **Type of organization:** Government research center **Major product:** Cancer prevention and treatment **Area of distribution:** Frederick, Maryland **Area of Practice:** Program and science administration **Published works:** 60 papers, 50 abstracts **Affiliations:** American Physiological Society; New York Academy of Sciences **Hob./spts.:** Gardening, bicycling, volunteer work **SIC code:** 80 **Address:** United States Army Medical Research & Material Command, 1077 Patchel Street, Frederick, MD 271702 **E-mail:** patricia.modrow@amedd.army.mil

MOE, JERRY J.
Industry: Healthcare **Born:** June 30, 1955, San Francisco, California **Univ./degree:** B.S., Sociology, 1978; M.A., Education Counseling, 1981, San Francisco State University **Current organization:** Betty Ford Center **Title:** National Director of Children's Services **Type of organization:** Hospital/clinic **Major product:** Alcohol and drug addiction treatment and related family counseling **Area of distribution:** International **Area of Practice:** Administration, counseling **Honors/awards:** 2000 Ackerman/Black Award, National Association for Children of Alcoholics; 1995 Promise Award in Texas; Marty Mann Award, 1993 **Published works:** Books include: "Kids' Power: Healing Games for Children of Alcoholics", "Conducting Support Groups for Elementary Children", "Discovery. . Finding the Buried Treasure", "Kids' Power Too: Words to Grow By", "The Children's Place . . At the Heart of Recovery" **Affiliations:** National Association for Children of Alcoholics; National Association of Alcoholism & Drug Abuse Counselors **Hob./spts.:** Sports, music, family **SIC code:** 80 **Address:** Betty Ford Center, 39000 Bob Hope Dr., Rancho Mirage, CA 92270 **E-mail:** jmoe@bettyfordcenter.org **Web address:** www.bettyfordcenter.org

MOHAN, CHANDER
Industry: Healthcare **Born:** February 19, 1952, Fazila, India **Univ./degree:** M.D., MGM Medical College, Jamshedpur, India, 1979 **Current organization:** Chander Mohan, M.D., Inc. **Title:** M.D. **Type of organization:** Private practice **Major product:** Patient care **Area of distribution:** National **Area of Practice:** General and geriatric psychiatry, psychotherapy, medication management **Affiliations:** American Psychiatric Association; Member, Board of Trustees, University of Akron **SIC code:** 80 **Address:** Chander Mohan, M.D., Inc., 275 Graham Rd., Suite 5, Cuyahoga Falls, OH 44223 **E-mail:** ilovebailey@aol.com

MOHL, ALLAN S.
Industry: Mental healthcare **Born:** February 10, 1933, Passaic, New Jersey **Univ./degree:** M.A., 1956; M.S.S., 1960, New York University; Ph.D., Columbia Pacific University, 1991 **Current organization:** Committee on Special Education, District 28, NYC Board of Ed. **Title:** Social Worker (Retired) **Type of organization:** Education, NYC Board of Education **Major product:** Counseling, psychotherapy **Area of distribution:** Ardsley, New York; Queens, New York **Area of Practice:** Counseling for adults and children **Affiliations:** International Society of Poets; National Association of Social Workers; New York Association for Marriage and Family Therapy; New York State Society of Clinical Social Workers; The New York Academy of Sciences **Hob./spts.:** Football (Jets fan), hunting, poetry, playing piano by ear, theatre, music, science, movies, politics **SIC code:** 80 **Address:** , 8 Shorthill Rd., Ardsley, NY 10502-2020 **E-mail:** amohl@msn.com

MOHR, BARBARA H.
Industry: Healthcare **Born:** New York, New York **Univ./degree:** B.S., Biology, Caldwell College **Current organization:** VWMC (Volunteer Women's Medical Clinic) **Title:** Lab Manager **Type of organization:** Clinic **Major product:** Patient care **Area of distribution:** Tennessee **Area of Practice:** Biology, chemistry **Affiliations:**

A.S.A.P. **Hob./spts.:** Reading, opera, symphony, theatre **SIC code:** 80 **Address:** VWMC (Volunteer Women's Medical Clinic), 313 Concord St., Knoxville, TN 37919

MOJARAD, MOHAMMAD
Industry: Healthcare **Born:** April 6, 1943, Iran **Univ./degree:** M.D., University of Tehran, 1971 **Current organization:** Eisenhower Medical Center **Title:** M.D. **Type of organization:** Hospital **Major product:** Patient care **Area of distribution:** National **Area of Practice:** Internal medicine, pulmonary, critical care **Published works:** Articles, journals **Affiliations:** F.C.C.P.; A.M.A.; C.M.A.; A.C.P. **Hob./spts.:** Hiking, horseback riding, classical music **SIC code:** 80 **Address:** Eisenhower Medical Center, 39000 Bob Hope Dr., Rancho Mirage, CA 92270 **E-mail:** mojared@earthlink.net

MOLINA, MANUEL A.
Industry: Healthcare **Univ./degree:** M.D., Panama **Current organization:** SUNY Downstate Medical Center **Title:** M.D. **Type of organization:** Hospital **Major product:** Medical services **Area of distribution:** National **Area of Practice:** Surgery **Affiliations:** A.M.A. **SIC code:** 80 **Address:** SUNY Downstate Medical Center, 345 E. 80th St., New York, NY 10021-0643 **E-mail:** manmolina@hotmail.com

MOMIN, FEROZE A.
Industry: Healthcare **Born:** March 6, 1949, Pune, India **Univ./degree:** M.D., University of Pune, 1974; Fellowship, Wayne State University **Current organization:** Oakwood Hospital **Title:** M.D.; Director, Stem Cell Transplant Program **Type of organization:** Hospital/medical center **Major product:** Patient care **Area of distribution:** International **Area of Practice:** Hematology, stem cell transplants; Cancer Specialist **Affiliations:** A.C.P.; A.S.C.O.; A.S.B.M.T. **Hob./spts.:** Landscape photography **SIC code:** 80 **Address:** Oakland Hospital, Stem Cell Transplant Program, 18101 Oakwood Blvd., P.O. Box 2500, Dearborn, MI 48123 **E-mail:** mominf@oakwood.org **Web address:** www.oakwood.org

MOMPOINT, DANIEL J.
Industry: Healthcare **Born:** May 22, 1953 Port-au-Prince, Haiti **Univ./degree:** M.D., University of Haiti School of Medicine, 1978 **Current organization:** Daniel J. Mompoint, M.D. **Title:** M.D./Obstetrician/Gynecologist **Type of organization:** Private practice **Major product:** Patient care **Area of distribution:** Gretna, Louisiana **Area of Practice:** Laparoscopy **Honors/awards:** Top 50 Doctors in New Orleans **Published works:** Write-ups **Affiliations:** American Gynecologic Association; Jefferson Parrish Medical Society **Hob./spts.:** Photography, languages (French and Spanish) **SIC code:** 80 **Address:** Daniel J. Mompoint, M.D., OB/GYN, 230 Meadowcrest St., Gretna, LA 70056 **E-mail:** dmompoint@myhealth.com **Web address:** www.myhealth.com

MONASTERIO, JOSE RAMIRO
Industry: Healthcare **Born:** April 13, 1944, Santa Cruz, Bolivia **Univ./degree:** B.S., Humanities, American Institute, 1960; M.D., San Miguel de Tucuman School of Medicine, Argentina, 1968 **Current organization:** Brandywine Surgical Associates, P.C. **Title:** M.D. General Surgical & Vascular **Type of organization:** Private practice **Major product:** Patient care **Area of distribution:** Pennsylvania **Area of Practice:** General and vascular surgery **Affiliations:** F.I.C.S.; F.A.S.A.S.; Fellow, Society of Laparoendoscopic Surgeons; Fellow, American Society of General Surgeons **Hob./spts.:** Family, horseback riding, ranching, soccer, travel **SIC code:** 80 **Address:** 901 Stargazers Rd., Coatesville, PA 19320 **E-mail:** pepe901@aol.com

MONROE, RICKIE K.
Industry: Healthcare **Born:** October 23, 1960 Richmond, Virginia **Univ./degree:** M.D., Meharry Medical College, Tennessee 1988 **Current organization:** Associates in Anesthesiology, Inc. **Title:** M.D. **Type of organization:** Hospital **Major product:** Anesthesia **Area of distribution:** Ohio **Area of Practice:** Anesthesiology **Honors/awards:** Recipient of Scholarships **Affiliations:** A.M.A.; American Society of Anesthesiologists **Hob./spts.:** Golf, gardening, jazz music, travel, tennis **SIC code:** 80 **Address:** 5755 Logan Arms Dr., Girard, OH 44420 **E-mail:** rmdrkm@aol.com

MONTANIEL, NECITO LUCIANO
Industry: Healthcare **Born:** October 30, 1933, Manila, Philippines **Univ./degree:** M.D., Far Eastern University, 1959 **Current organization:** Spirit Lake Medical Center **Title:** M.D., Clinical Director **Type of organization:** Medical center **Major product:** Patient care **Area of distribution:** North Dakota **Area of Practice:** General surgery, family practice, pathology, trauma critical care, laser surgery, laparoscopy **Honors/awards:** Recognition Award, North Dakota Medical Association, 1994-2000; Certification of Appreciation, LYT Medical Society Association, 1994 **Affiliations:** A.M.A.; A.S.G.S.; F.A.C.S.; Lifetime Member, Phi Kappa Phi **Hob./spts.:** Riding horses, boating, printing, singing, racing **SIC code:** 80 **Address:** Spirit Lake Medical Center, P.O. Box 309, Ft. Totten, ND 58335

MONTESCLAROS, GILBERT
Industry: Healthcare **Born:** January 24, 1951, Cebu City, Philippines **Univ./degree:** B.S., M.T., Southwestern University, 1971; S.H. Certified, 1985; C.L.S., 2006 **Current organization:** Inova Fair Oaks Hospital **Title:** Hematology Supervisor **Type of organization:** Hospital **Major product:** Patient care **Area of distribution:** Virginia **Area of Practice:** Hematological services and procedures, coagulation **Honors/awards:** Achievement Service Award, Inova Fair Oaks Hospital **Affiliations:** American Society of Clinical Pathologists; Canadian Society for Laboratory Medical Science; International Commission on Healthcare Professionals **SIC code:** 80 **Address:** Inova Fair Oaks Hospital, 3600 Joseph Sieweck Dr., Fairfax, VA 22033 **E-mail:** gilbert.montesclaros@inova.com **Web address:** www.inova.com

MOONEY, MICHAEL D.
Industry: Healthcare **Born:** February 27, 1949, Kalamazoo, Michigan **Univ./degree:** D.M.D., University of Alabama, 1976 **Current organization:** Michael D. Mooney, DMD **Title:** D.M.D. **Type of organization:** Private dental practice **Major product:** Dental services **Area of distribution:** Asheville, North Carolina **Area of Practice:** Oral reconstruction, dental implants **Affiliations:** Fellow, Academy of General Dentistry; Fellow, American Academy of Implant Dentistry **SIC code:** 80 **Address:** Michael D. Mooney, DMD, 627 Haywood Rd., Asheville, NC 28806 **E-mail:** michaelmooney@bellsouth.net

MOORE, GERALDINE L.
Industry: Healthcare **Born:** September 10, 1948, New York, New York **Univ./degree:** M.S., Nursing, Marymount University, Arlington, Virginia **Current organization:** Correction Medical Services **Title:** Family Nurse Practitioner (Board Certified) **Type of organization:** Medical facility **Major product:** Patient care **Area of distribution:** Decatur, Georgia **Area of Practice:** Family medicine **Affiliations:** C.H.E.S.; American Heart Association; Board Member, American Diabetes Association **Hob./spts.:** Reading, travel **SIC code:** 80 **Address:** Correction Medical Services, 4425 Memorial Dr., Decatur, GA 30087 **E-mail:** gerril969@aol.com

MOORE, MICHAEL C.
Industry: Government/Healthcare **Born:** July 22, 1966, Lancaster, Pennsylvania **Univ./degree:** B.A., Biology, La Salle University, 1988; D.O., Philadelphia College of Osteopathic Medicine, 1992 **Current organization:** U.S. Army 18th Aviation Brigade **Title:** Flight Surgeon **Type of organization:** Military **Major product:** Defense, healthcare **Area of distribution:** International **Area of Practice:** Flight surgeon, family physician **Affiliations:** U.S.A.F.P.; A.A.F.P.; U.S.A.F.S.S. **Hob./spts.:** Sports medicine, triathlons, soccer coach, swimming **SIC code:** 80 **Address:** HHC, 18th (AVN) Brigade, Ft. Bragg, NC 28307 **E-mail:** mooremich@bragg.army.mil

MOORTHI, K.M.L.S.T.
Industry: Healthcare **Born:** August 2, 1973, Madros, India **Univ./degree:** M.D., Stanley Medical College **Current organization:** St. Francis Hospital **Title:** M.D. **Type of organization:** Hospital **Major product:** Patient care **Area of distribution:** Evanston, Illinois **Area of Practice:** Internal medicine **Honors/awards:** Intern of the Year Award, 2000; Resident of the Year, 2001, St. Francis Hospital **Published works:** Books: "Picture Eests in Internal Medicine", 2001; "Review of Biochemistry", 1999; Journal of Internal Medicine **Affiliations:** A.C.P.; A.M.A. **Hob./spts.:** Photography **SIC code:** 80 **Address:** St. Francis Hospital, 701 Austin St., #1E, Evanston, IL 60202847 **E-mail:** kmlstmoorthi@yahoo.com

MOOTOO, KEITH I.H.
Industry: Healthcare **Born:** January 30, Guyana **Univ./degree:** M.D., Middlesex Hospital Medical School, England, 1974; Fellowship, Nephrology, State University of New York, Stony Brook, Meadowbrook Hospital, 1980 **Current organization:** Atlantic Avenue Medical Clinic Inc. **Title:** MD, FACP **Type of organization:** Multidisciplinary medical practice **Major product:** Patient care **Area of distribution:** California **Area of Practice:** Nephrology, internal medicine **Affiliations:** F.A.C.P.; N.S.I.M.; C.M.A.; A.M.A.; A.S.N.; L.A.C.M.A. **SIC code:** 80 **Address:** Atlantic Avenue Medical Clinic Inc., 7503 Atlantic Ave., Suite D, Cudahy, CA 90201 **E-mail:** kmootoo1@mpowercom.net

MORALES, JAMES R.
Industry: Medical **Born:** March 8, 1970, Bronx, New York **Univ./degree:** B.S., Biology, University of Michigan, 1992; M.D., Robert Wood Johnson Medical School, 1997 **Current organization:** Robert Wood Johnson University Hospital **Title:** M.D. **Type of organization:** University hospital **Major product:** Medical services **Area of distribution:** International **Area of Practice:** Sports medicine; Attending Sports Medicine Physician for Princeton & Rutgers Athletes **Published works:** 4 conference papers/abstracts, 1 peer reviewed journal **Affiliations:** A.C.S.M.; A.M.S.S.M.; A.M.A.; A.A.F.P. **Hob./spts.:** Fitness training, wrestling, piano, travel **SIC code:** 80 **Address:** Robert Wood Johnson University Hospital, 1 Robert Wood Johnson Place, New Brunswick, NJ 08901 **E-mail:** jamesrmorales@aol.com

MORALES, JAVIER
Industry: Healthcare **Born:** Puerto Rico **Univ./degree:** M.D. **Current organization:** Schwechter & Morales **Title:** M.D. **Type of organization:** Health clinic **Major product:** Patient care **Area of distribution:** Mineola, New York **Area of Practice:**

Internal medicine, quadrilingual **SIC code:** 80 **Address:** Schwechter & Morales, 80 East Jericho Tpke., Suite 201, Mineola, NY 11501 **E-mail:** saxodoc@optonline.net

MORELAND, RAE ANN
Industry: Healthcare **Born:** September 22, 1960, Waterbury, Connecticut **Univ./degree:** B.S., Chemistry, Elon College, 1982 **Current organization:** Laboratory Corporation of America **Title:** Research & Development Chemist **Type of organization:** Clinical diagnostic testing laboratory **Major product:** Diagnostic testing **Area of distribution:** International **Area of Practice:** Evaluation/implementation of new tests and procedures **Honors/awards:** Laboratory Corporation of America, National Chairman's Award, 2000 **Affiliations:** American Chemical Society **Hob./spts.:** Family, singing, crafts **SIC code:** 80 **Address:** Laboratory Corporation of America, 1447 York Ct., Burlington, NC 27215 **E-mail:** tindelr@labcorp.com **Web address:** www.labcorp.com

MORELL DELVALLE, SAMUEL
Industry: Healthcare **Born:** December 6, 1959, Puerto Rico **Univ./degree:** M.D., San Juan Bautista University, 1987 **Current organization:** Clinica Dr. Samuel Morell **Title:** M.D. **Type of organization:** Medical office **Major product:** Patient care **Area of distribution:** San Juan, Puerto Rico **Area of Practice:** Internal medicine **Affiliations:** A.C.P.; Local Chapter, A.M.A. **Hob./spts.:** Basketball, racquetball **SIC code:** 80 **Address:** Clinica Dr. Samuel Morell, P.O. Box 362070, San Juan, PR 00936-2070

MORGAN, LEON W.
Industry: Healthcare **Born:** April 12, 1947, Fort Riley, Kansas **Univ./degree:** R.N., St. Margaret Hospital School of Nursing, Kansas, 1969; Graduate, USAF Flight Nursing School, 1970 **Title:** Medical/Surgical Charge Nurse (Retired) **Type of organization:** Medical center **Major product:** Healthcare for federal prisoners **Area of distribution:** National **Area of Practice:** Acute correctional nurse, flight nurse, pediatric nurse, adaptation and improvisation **Affiliations:** Masons, Scottish Rite **Hob./spts.:** Gardening, domestic travel, reading about forensic science **SIC code:** 80 **Address:** 2072 N. Preakness Dr., Nixa, MO 65714 **E-mail:** tupher@aol.com

MORRIS, LINDEN
Industry: Healthcare **Born:** October, 1958, Brooklyn, New York **Univ./degree:** B.S., Facilities Management, State University of New York at Farmingdale **Current organization:** Menorah Home & Hospital **Title:** Director of Engineering **Type of organization:** Hospital, nursing home **Major product:** Patient care **Area of distribution:** Brooklyn, New York **Area of Practice:** Electrical, engineering **Affiliations:** A.S.E., A.S.H.E. **Hob./spts.:** Golf, running **SIC code:** 80 **Address:** Menorah Home & Hospital, 1516 Oriental Blvd., Brooklyn, NY 11235 **E-mail:** lmorris@menorahhome.com

MORRIS, THOMAS R.
Industry: Healthcare **Born:** January 26, 1949, Indianapolis, Indiana **Univ./degree:** D.C., Cleveland College, 1974 **Current organization:** Morris Family Chiropractic Inc. **Title:** D.C. **Type of organization:** Private practice **Major product:** Patient care **Area of distribution:** Arizona **Area of Practice:** Chiropractics **Affiliations:** American Chiropractic Association **Hob./spts.:** Bowling, table tennis **SIC code:** 80 **Address:** Morris Family Chiropractic Inc., 3755 Karicio Lane, Suite 2-A, Prescott, AZ 86303 **E-mail:** tmorris1@cableone.net

MORRONE, LEE ELLEN
Industry: Healthcare **Born:** February 8, 1960, New York, New York **Spouse:** Joseph V. Fierro **Children:** Allegra, December 12, 1990; Joseph, October 21, 1993 **Univ./degree:** B.A., Summa Cum Laude, Biology, Minor, Biochemistry, Barnard College, New York, 1981; M.D., Columbia College of Physicians and Surgeons, New York, 1985; Residency, Obstetrics & Gynecology, Mount Sinai Medical Center, New York, 1989 **Current organization:** Morrone-Kirsch Associates, LLP **Title:** M.D. **Type of organization:** Private practice **Major product:** Women's healthcare **Area of distribution:** New York, New York **Area of Practice:** Obstetrics, gynecology, healthcare for women with special needs and the mentally retarded or disabled, adolescent gynecology, perimenopause, menopause transition years management **Honors/awards:** The Helen Downs Award (awarded to the student who shows the greatest promise of distinction in medicine); The Helen R. Downes Award (awarded by the Honors Committee to an outstanding student based on overall academic record, integrity and good citizenship); Listed in Who's Who of American Women 1998 & 1999; Alpha Omega Alpha; Television Appearances on Lifetime/MSNBC, Oxygen Cable Network, Fox News **Published works:** Article, "Postpartum Care and Breastfeeding Myths", Rosie Magazine, June 2001 **Affiliations:** A.I.U.M.; American College of Obstetrics & Gynecology; Professional Women Physicians; Board Certified Member, Advanced Laproscopic Surgeons of New York; Gusberg Medical Society; Clinical Assistant Professor, Obstetrics & Gynecology, Mount Sinai Medical Center, Mount Sinai Hospital **Hob./spts.:** Gourmet cooking, reading, skiing, tennis, being a mom **SIC code:** 80 **Address:** Morrone-Kirsch Associates, LLP, Attn: Carmen, 62 E. 88th St., Suite 201, New York, NY 10128 **Phone:** (212)860-4800 **Fax:** (212)860-4891 **E-mail:** nyladymd@aol.com

MORROW, DWIGHT W.
Industry: Healthcare **Born:** October 23, 1952, California, Missouri **Univ./degree:** M.D., University of Illinois Medical School, 1978 **Current organization:** Laboratory & Pathology Diagnostics, LLC **Title:** M.D. **Type of organization:** Hospital based pathology group **Major product:** Laboratory services **Area of distribution:** Illinois **Area of Practice:** Pathology **Affiliations:** A.M.A.; I.L.S.M.S.; C.A.P.; A.S.C.P. **Hob./spts.:** Weightlifting, triathlon, singing **SIC code:** 80 **Address:** Laboratory & Pathology Diagnostics, LLC, 801 S. Washington St., Naperville, IL 60540 **E-mail:** dmorrow@edward.org

MOSS, FRED R.
Industry: Healthcare **Born:** March 1, 1958, Detroit, Michigan **Univ./degree:** M.D., Northwestern University, 1988 **Current organization:** Fred R. Moss, M.D., Inc. **Title:** President **Type of organization:** Private practice **Major product:** Patient care **Area of distribution:** Cincinnati, Ohio **Area of Practice:** Psychiatry **Affiliations:** A.M.A.; O.S.M.A.; American Board of Psychiatry and Neurology **Hob./spts.:** Reading, basketball, baseball, rock concerts **SIC code:** 80 **Address:** Fred R. Moss, M.D., Inc., 4144 Crossgate Sq., Cincinnati, OH 45236 **E-mail:** fmoss@cinci.rr.com

MOSS, JOHN S.
Industry: Healthcare **Born:** October 3, 1952, Richmond, Virginia **Univ./degree:** M.D., 1979; Residency, 1984, Medical College of Virginia **Current organization:** Fredericksburg Orthopaedic Assoc. **Title:** M.D. **Type of organization:** Healthcare facility **Major product:** Patient care **Area of distribution:** Fredericksburg, Virginia **Area of Practice:** Orthopaedic surgery, sports medicine, injury **Honors/awards:** Fellowship, Multispecialty, Richmond, Virginia, 1985-89; Fellowship, Arthroscopic Surgery, 1985 **Published works:** Articles **Affiliations:** A.M.A; Fellow, American Academy of Orthopaedic Surgeons; Fellow, American College of Surgeons; Arthroscopy Association of North America **SIC code:** 80 **Address:** Fredericksburg Orthopaedic Assoc., 3310 Fall Hill Ave., Fredericksburg, VA 22401 **E-mail:** jaybenz5@aol.com

MOSTOUFI-MOAB, EBRAHIM
Industry: Healthcare **Born:** October 1, 1943, Iran **Univ./degree:** M.D., Shiraz University, 1970 **Current organization:** Florida Institute for Cardiovascular Care **Title:** M.D./F.A.C.C./F.A.C.P. **Type of organization:** Group practice **Major product:** Patient care **Area of distribution:** International **Area of Practice:** Board Certified, Internal Medicine and Cardiology; nuclear cardiology; electrophyiology cardiology **Published works:** 6 papers **Affiliations:** American College of Cardiologists; American College of Physicians **Hob./spts.:** Hiking, travel, history of civilization, reading **SIC code:** 80 **Address:** Florida Institute for Cardiovascular Care, 3700 Washington St., Suite 300, Hollywood, FL 33021 **E-mail:** emostoufi@aol.com

MOULISWAR, MYSORE P.
Industry: Medical **Born:** February 11, 1951, India **Univ./degree:** M.D., India, 1980 **Current organization:** Center for Aging-UMDNJ, School of Medicine **Title:** Asst. Professor **Type of organization:** University hospital **Major product:** Medical services **Area of distribution:** New Jersey **Area of Practice:** Geriatrics **Published works:** 5 papers **Affiliations:** A.M.A.; A.C.P.; A.G.S. **Hob./spts.:** Meditation, reading **SIC code:** 80 **Address:** Center for Aging-UMDNJ, School of Medicine, 42 Laurel Rd. East, Stratford, NJ 08054

MOUSA, HAYAT M.
Industry: Medical **Born:** January 11, 1958, Homs, Syria **Univ./degree:** M.D., Damascus University, Syria **Current organization:** Ohio State University-Columbus Children's Hospital **Title:** M.D. **Type of organization:** University hospital **Major product:** Medical services **Area of distribution:** Ohio **Area of Practice:** Pediatrics **Affiliations:** A.M.A.; A.A.P.; A.G.A. **Hob./spts.:** Music, piano **SIC code:** 80 **Address:** Ohio State University-Columbus Children's Hospital, 700 Children's Dr., Educational Bldg., Room 426, Columbus, OH 43205-2664 **E-mail:** mousah@pediatrics.ohio-state.edu

MOUSSA, GHIAS
Industry: Healthcare **Univ./degree:** M.D., Damascus Medical School, 1979 **Current organization:** Gias Moussa, M.D. **Title:** M.D., F.A.C.C. **Type of organization:** Hospital **Major product:** Patient care **Area of distribution:** New Jersey **Area of Practice:** Cardiology **Affiliations:** F.A.C.C.; A.M.A. **SIC code:** 80 **Address:** 1850 Kennedy Blvd., Jersey City, NJ 07305 **E-mail:** moussagus@aol.com

MUCCI, JUDITH P.
Industry: Mental health **Born:** October 9, 1950, Massachusetts **Univ./degree:** M.A., Clinical Pastoral Counseling, Emmanuel College, 1985 **Current organization:** Northwestern Human Services NHWS of Philadelphia **Title:** M.A./C.P.R.P./Psychotherapist/FFS **Type of organization:** Counseling services **Major product:** Mental health and substance abuse counseling for individuals, couples, adults and adolescents **Area of distribution:** New Jersey **Area of Practice:** Working with chronic mentally ill, dual diagnosis, loss and grief, stress management, anger management, substance abuse, Certified Addiction Prevention Specialist, Family Mediation Specialist, **Honors/**

awards: Selected to do grief counseling at Liberty Park for 4 days during 9/11 representing Camden County, New Jersey and Dept. of Mental Health **Affiliations:** N.A.M.I.; I.A.M.F.T.; A.S.G.W.; American Counseling Association; National Association of Forensic Counselors **Hob./spts.:** Photography, fishing, racquetball **SIC code:** 80 **Address:** Northwestern Human Services, NHWS of Philadelphia, 11082 Knights Rd., Philadelphia, PA 19154 **E-mail:** jmu1313@comcast.net

MUELLER-CORDERO, LINDA
Industry: Healthcare **Born:** August 14, 1947, Philadelphia, PA **Current organization:** North Shore Hematology, Oncology Assoc., P.C. **Title:** COO **Type of organization:** Private medical practice **Major product:** Patient care **Area of distribution:** Long Island, New York **Area of Practice:** Administration **Published works:** Multiple articles **Affiliations:** M.G.M.A.; A.O.H.A. **Hob./spts.:** Reading, tennis **SIC code:** 80 **Address:** North Shore Hematology/Oncology Assoc., P.C., 181 N. Belle Mead Rd., East Setauket, NY 11733 **E-mail:** lmueller2@juno.com

MUKHERJEE, SHYAMALI
Industry: Education **Born:** June 6, 1953, Calcutta, India **Univ./degree:** B.S. with Honors, Physiology, 1974; M.S., Physiology (Special Paper on Endocrinology), 1976; Ph.D., Physiology, 1984, University of Calcutta, India **Current organization:** Meharry Medical College **Title:** Ph.D./Assistant Professor **Type of organization:** Medical School **Major product:** Training, higher education **Area of distribution:** Tennessee **Area of Practice:** Training medical, dental and graduate students **Published works:** 38 articles, 3 book chapters **Affiliations:** American Society for Biochemistry and Molecular Biology; New York Academy of Science **Hob./spts.:** Cooking, crafts **SIC code:** 80 **Address:** Meharry Medical College, Dept. of Pharmacology, 1005 D.B. Todd Blvd., Nashville, TN 37208 **E-mail:** smukherjee@mmc.edu **Web address:** www.mmc.edu

MUKHOPADHYAY, PARTHA
Industry: Education **Born:** October 30, 1963, Calcutta, India **Univ./degree:** B.S.; M.S., University of Calcutta; Ph.D., Jadavpur University, India, 1996 **Current organization:** University of Louisville, School of Dentistry, Birth Defects Center **Title:** Ph.D., Scientist/Assistant Professor **Type of organization:** University **Major product:** Higher education, medical research **Area of distribution:** International **Area of Practice:** Molecular, cellular and developmental biology **Honors/awards:** Research Fellowship, C.S.I.R., India: Research Fellowship, National Institute of Health **Published works:** 15 articles, 18 abstracts **Affiliations:** Association for Research in Vision and Ophthalmology; President 2002, "TreeNaNeel", The Bengalee Cultural Association of Kentucky; Founder Member, Mid-America Bengalee Association **SIC code:** 80 **Address:** University of Louisville, School of Dentistry, 501 S. Preston St., Bldg ULSD, Room 301, Louisville, KY 40202 **E-mail:** p0mukh0l@louisville.edu

MULK, HUMA T.
Industry: Healthcare **Born:** December 8, 1964, India **Univ./degree:** M.D., Ghandi Medical College, India, 1988 **Current organization:** Medina Health Care **Title:** M.D. **Type of organization:** Private practice/clinic **Major product:** Patient care **Area of distribution:** Sauk Village, Illinois **Area of Practice:** Internal medicine **Hob./spts.:** Cooking **SIC code:** 80 **Address:** Medina Healthcare, 1715 Sauk Trail, Sauk Village, IL 60411

MULLER, SUSAN M.
Industry: Healthcare **Born:** January 18, 1964, Massachusetts **Univ./degree:** M.D., Albany Medical College, 1991 **Current organization:** Saratoga Family Health **Title:** M.D. **Type of organization:** Private practice **Major product:** Patient care **Area of distribution:** Saratoga Springs, New York **Area of Practice:** Family Physician (Board Certified) **Honors/awards:** UpJohn Achievement Award for excellence in outpatient medicine, 1991; Navy Commendation Medal, 1994 & 1997; A.M.A. Physicians Recognition Award, 2002 **Affiliations:** A.A.F.P; A.M.A.; Medical Society of New York **Hob./spts.:** Drawing, painting, sculpting, photography, physical fitness **SIC code:** 80 **Address:** Saratoga Family Health, 119 Lawrence St., Saratoga Springs, NY 12866

MULROW, CYNTHIA D.
Industry: Education/professional service **Born:** May 23, 1953, Edinburg, Texas **Univ./degree:** M.D., Baylor University, 1978; M.Sc., London School of Tropical Medical Hygiene, 1984 **Current organization:** Robert Wood Johnson Foundation **Title:** Clinical Professor of Medicine/Deputy Editor, Annals of Internal Medicine **Type of organization:** Education/publishing **Area of distribution:** International **Area of Practice:** Internist **Published works:** 100 articles **Affiliations:** American Society for Clinical Investigations; American College of Physicians; Society of General Internal Medicine **Hob./spts.:** Reading, swimming **SIC code:** 80 **Address:** Robert Wood Johnson Foundation, 6415 Pemwoods, San Antonio, TX 78240 **E-mail:** mulrow@uthscsa.edu

MUNDEY, KAVITA
Industry: Medical **Born:** October 10, 1971, Wardha, India **Univ./degree:** M.D., All India Institute of Medical Sciences, 1995 **Current organization:** Medical College of Wisconsin **Title:** M.D./Assistant Professor **Type of organization:** University/hospital **Major product:** Patient care, medical education **Area of distribution:** National **Area of Practice:** Internal medicine, pulmonary medicine, critical care, sleep disorders **Affiliations:** A.C.C.P.; A.A.S.M.; A.C.P./A.S.I.M. **Hob./spts.:** Swimming, yoga, music **SIC code:** 80 **Address:** Medical College of Wisconsin, 9200 W. Wisconsin Ave., Milwaukee, WI 53226 **E-mail:** kmundey@mcw.edu

MUNDO-SAGARDIA, JORGE ANGEL
Industry: Medical **Born:** August 13, 1971, San Juan, Puerto Rico **Univ./degree:** B.S., Magna Cum Laude, Biology, University of Puerto Rico, 1993; M.D., University of Puerto Rico School of Medicine, 1997; Residency, University of Puerto Rico School of Medicine University District Hospital **Current organization:** University of Puerto Rico School of Medicine **Title:** M.D. **Type of organization:** University hospital **Major product:** Patient care, medical research **Area of distribution:** Puerto Rico **Area of Practice:** Internal medicine **Published works:** Journal articles **Affiliations:** American Internal Medicine Board Certified **Hob./spts.:** Weights, travel, reading **SIC code:** 80 **Address:** #776 Interamericana St., University Gardens, San Juan, PR 00927 **Phone:** (787)758-2525 **Fax:** (787)754-1739 **E-mail:** evinski@hotmail.com

MURALIDHARAN, VISVANATHAN
Industry: Healthcare **Univ./degree:** M.D., Stanley Medical College, India, 1993; M.R.C.P., Royal College of Medicine, UK, 1997; Board Certified, Internal Medicine, American Board of Internal Medicine, 2003 **Current organization:** Bridgeport Hospital **Title:** M.D. **Type of organization:** Hospital; part of Yale New Haven Health/Yale University Hospital Program **Major product:** Patient care **Area of distribution:** Connecticut **Area of Practice:** Internal medicine, gastroenterology **Published works:** Articles, abstracts **Affiliations:** A.M.A.; A.C.P.; A.G.A. **Hob./spts.:** Cricket, badminton, reading **SIC code:** 80 **Address:** Avalon Gates, #4214 Old Town Rd., Bldg. 4, Trumbull, CT 06611 **E-mail:** vmdharan1@hotmail.com

MURASKAS, ERIK K.
Industry: Healthcare **Born:** February 6, 1956, Chicago, Illinois **Univ./degree:** B.S., Biology, Loyola University, 1978; M.D., Loyola University School of Medicine, 1981 **Current organization:** Eric K. Muraskas, M.D. **Title:** M.D. **Type of organization:** Private property **Major product:** Patient care **Area of distribution:** Illinois **Area of Practice:** OB/GYN **Published works:** Articles **Affiliations:** A.M.A.; F.A.C.O.G. **SIC code:** 80 **Address:** 2160 S. First Ave., Building 103, Maywood, IL 60153

MURCIA, ALVARO M.
Industry: Healthcare **Born:** August 13, 1967, Bogotá, Colombia **Univ./degree:** M.D., Pontificia Universidad Javeriana, 1992 **Current organization:** University Heart Institute **Title:** M.D. **Type of organization:** Medical office **Major product:** Patient care **Area of distribution:** Pembroke Pines, Florida **Area of Practice:** Cardiology **Published works:** 3 papers **Affiliations:** A.C.C., A.H.A. **Hob./spts.:** Travel, reading, chess **SIC code:** 80 **Address:** University Heart Institute, 2301 N. University Dr., Suite 112, Pembroke Pines, FL 33024 **E-mail:** alvaromurcia@yahoo.com

MURPHY III, JOSEPH JAMES
Industry: Healthcare **Born:** August 22, 1970, Meadowbrook, Pennsylvania **Univ./degree:** B.A., Theology, Georgetown University, 1992; M.D., Cum Laude, Jefferson Medical College, 1996 **Current organization:** GCSF Ob/Gyn Associates **Title:** M.D. **Type of organization:** Group practice **Major product:** Patient care **Area of distribution:** Pennsylvania **Area of Practice:** Ob/Gyn **Honors/awards:** A.O.A. Medical Honor Society; Pennsylvania Thomas V. Zachary III Award; Abington Memorial Hospital Faculty Teaching Award, 2001-2002 **Published works:** Write-ups; article, Olie RA, Fenderson, Daley K, Oosterhuis JW, Murphy J, Looijenga LH. "Glycolipids of human primary testicular germ cell tumors" BrJ Cancer, Dec. 1996, 74(11): 1853 **Affiliations:** Pennsylvania Medical Society, Fellow, American College of Obstetrics & Gynecology; member, Pennsylvania Hospital Thomas Bond Society **Hob./spts.:** Family, travel, rowing, skiing **SIC code:** 80 **Address:** GCSF Ob/Gyn Associates, 2300 Computer Rd., E-25, Willow Grove, PA 19001

MURTHY, REVATHY
Industry: Healthcare **Born:** July 23, 1943, Keraki, India **Univ./degree:** M.B.B.S., Lady Harding Medical College, New Delhi, India, 1968 **Current organization:** Revathy Murthy, MD, PA **Title:** M.D. **Type of organization:** Medical practice **Major product:** Patient care **Area of distribution:** National **Area of Practice:** Internal medicine, pulmonary medicine **Honors/awards:** Premed-Price for Chemistry and English; Medical School-Price for Eye/Ent; Outstanding Teacher-1997 Graduating Class **Published works:** Numerous articles, including: Co-author, "Pericardial Effusion in Sarcoidosis", Chest, Vol. 76, p. 476, 1979; "Rapidly Progressive Pulmonary Infiltrate", Chest, Vol. 78, p. 77-78, 1980; "Sarcoidosis-Rare Causes of Superior Vena Cava Obstruction", Pennsylvania Medicine, Vol. 83, p. 31, 1980 **Affiliations:** F.A.C.P.; F.A.C.C.P.; Former President, The Indian American Medical Association **Hob./spts.:** Indian classical music **SIC code:** 80 **Address:** Revathy Murthy, MD, PA, 6130 Landover Rd., Cheverly, MD 20785 **E-mail:** revathymurthy@aol.com

MURTHY, SREENIVASA L.
Industry: Healthcare **Born:** July 3, 1946, India **Univ./degree:** M.D., Institute of Medical Science, 1970 **Current organization:** Sreenivasa L. Murthy, M.D. **Title:** M.D. **Type of organization:** Private practice **Major product:** Patient care **Area of distribution:** Bronx, New York **Area of Practice:** Pediatrics **Published works:** 4 articles **Affiliations:** N.Y.M.S.; A.A.P. **Hob./spts.:** Reading, swimming **SIC code:** 80 **Address:** Sreenivasa L. Murthy, M.D., 2034 Benedict Ave., Bronx, NY 10462

MUSTAFA, TALAL
Industry: Healthcare **Born:** July 8, 1937, Bolivia **Univ./degree:** M.D., Universidad Mayor de San Simon, 1963 **Current organization:** Lutheran General Hospital **Title:** M.D. **Type of organization:** Hospital **Major product:** Patient care **Area of distribution:** Illinois **Area of Practice:** Emergency medicine **Affiliations:** A.C.E.P.; International College of Physicians and Surgeons **Hob./spts.:** Poetry **SIC code:** 80 **Address:** Lutheran General Hospital, 1775 Dempster St., Park Ridge, IL 60068-1143 **E-mail:** blanca@dem.com

MUSZYNSKI, CHERYL A.
Industry: Healthcare **Born:** Detroit, Michigan **Univ./degree:** M.D., Washington University, 1988 **Current organization:** Children's Hospital of Wisconsin **Title:** M.D. **Type of organization:** Hospital **Major product:** Children's healthcare **Area of distribution:** National **Area of Practice:** Pediatric Neurosurgery **Affiliations:** F.A.C.S.; F.A.A.P.; Congress of Neurological Surgeons **Hob./spts.:** Child advocacy **SIC code:** 80 **Address:** Children's Hospital of Wisconsin, Dept. of Neurosurgery, 9000 W. Wisconsin Ave., MS 405, Milwaukee, WI 53201 **E-mail:** cmuszynski@neuroscience.mcw.edu

MWAISELA, FRANCIS J.
Industry: Healthcare **Univ./degree:** M.D., University of Dar Es Salaam, Tanzania, 1976 **Current organization:** Towson Neurology Assoc. **Title:** M.D. **Type of organization:** Group medical practice **Major product:** Patient care **Area of distribution:** Maryland **Area of Practice:** Neurology, clinical neurophysiology **Affiliations:** American Academy of Neurology **SIC code:** 80 **Address:** Towson Neurology Assoc., 120 Sister Pierre Dr., Suite 109, Towson, MD 21204 **E-mail:** mumwaisela@hotmail.com

MYERS, JACQUELINE A.
Industry: Healthcare **Born:** November 3, 1951, Plentywood, Montana **Univ./degree:** R.N., Miles City Community College **Current organization:** Evergreen Healthcare, LLC, Montana **Title:** R.N., Regional Operations Manager **Type of organization:** Healthcare facility **Major product:** Long-term healthcare facilities **Area of distribution:** Billings, Montana **Area of Practice:** Operations management **Affiliations:** Former Member and President, N.O.A. **Hob./spts.:** Golf, oil and watercolor painting, writing, outdoor activities **SIC code:** 80 **Address:** 1870 Gleneagles Blvd., Billings, MT 59105

MYERS, WAYNE A.
Industry: Medical **Born:** December 13, 1931, New York, New York **Univ./degree:** M.D., Columbia University, 1956 **Current organization:** Weill College of Medicine at Cornell University **Title:** M.D./Professor Emeritus **Type of organization:** Private practice **Major product:** Mental healthcare, psychotherapy, couple counseling **Area of distribution:** National **Area of Practice:** Psychiatry **Published works:** 100 publications; 5 books entitled: "Dynamic Therapy of the Older Patient" (1984), New York: Jason Anderson; Co-editor with J.M. Ross, Washington D.C.; American Psychiatric Press, Inc.; "New Concepts in Psychoanalytic Psychotherapy" (1988), Co-editor with J.M. Ross, Washington D.C.; American Psychiatric Press, Inc.; "The Perverse and the Near Perverse in Clinical Practice: New Psychoanalytic Perspectives" (1991), Co-editor with G.I. Fogel, New Haven & London: Yale University Press; "New Techniques in the Psychotherapy of Older Patients" (1991), Editor, American Psychiatric Press, Inc.; "Shrink Dreams"(1992), Simon and Schuster; "Shrink Dreams" (paperback) (1993), New York: Touchstone Press, Inc. **Affiliations:** Life Fellow, A.P.A. **Hob./spts.:** Travel **SIC code:** 80 **Address:** 60 Sutton Place #1CN, New York, NY 10022

MYNATT-WOTEN, KAREN R.
Industry: Healthcare **Born:** November 23, 1956, Knoxville, Tennessee **Univ./degree:** B.S, Health Sciences, University of St. Francis, 2000 **Current organization:** Thompson Cancer Survival Center **Title:** Manager P.E.T. Imaging Center **Type of organization:** Hospital outpatient facility **Major product:** Diagnostic imaging **Area of Practice:** Radiology **Affiliations:** Eastern Tennessee Organization of Nuclear Medicine Technologists **Hob./spts.:** Horses, scuba diving **SIC code:** 80 **Address:** Thompson Cancer Survival Center, 9711 Sherrill Blvd., Knoxville, TN 37932 **E-mail:** kwoten@covhlth.com

MYSOREKAR, UMA V.
Industry: Healthcare/religion/education **Born:** June 27, 1944, India **Univ./degree:** M.D., Grand Medical College, Bombay, India, 1966 **Current organization:** The Hindu Temple Society of North America/Uma V. Mysorekar, M.D. **Title:** President/M.D. **Type of organization:** Religion, cultural education/private practice **Major product:** Community service/patient care **Area of distribution:** New York **Area of Practice:** Promoting interfaith and culture/OB-GYN **Published works:** Write-ups **Affiliations:** F.A.C.O.G. **Hob./spts.:** Music, reading **SIC code:** 80 **Address:** The Hindu Temple Society of North America, 45-57 Bowne St., Flushing, NY 11355 **E-mail:** uvmys@aol.com

NACINOVICH, MARCIA
Industry: Healthcare **Born:** March 2, 1948, Chicago, Illinois **Univ./degree:** R.N., Cook County Hospital, 1970; B.A., Healthcare, University of Redlands, 1976; B.S.N., New York University, 1992 **Current organization:** Fountains at the Carlotta **Title:** Director Health Care Services **Type of organization:** Senior living community **Major product:** Health and wellness **Area of distribution:** California **Area of Practice:** Registered nurse **Hob./spts.:** Reading, camping, travel, crafts, quilting **SIC code:** 80 **Address:** Fountains at the Carlotta, 41505 Carlotta Dr., Palm Desert, CA 92234 **E-mail:** mnacinovich1@dc.rr.com

NADLER, RENATE M.
Industry: Healthcare **Born:** May 17, 1939, Passaic, New Jersey **Univ./degree:** M.D., Ludwig-Maximillion University, Munich, Germany **Current organization:** Saint Louise Regional Hospital **Title:** Emergency Room Physician **Type of organization:** Hospital **Major product:** Patient care **Area of distribution:** California **Area of Practice:** Emergency medicine, trauma care **Honors/awards:** Top Docs in San Jose, 2005 **Affiliations:** American Board of Emergency Medicine **Hob./spts.:** Ballroom dancing, gardening **SIC code:** 80 **Address:** 1610 Salem Dr., Gilroy, CA 95020 **E-mail:** renatenadler@charter.net

NAEF III, ROBERT W.
Industry: Healthcare **Born:** February 1, 1955, Jackson, Mississippi **Univ./degree:** M.D., University of Mississippi Medical Center, 1987 **Current organization:** Pikes Peak Maternal-Fetal Medicine Center **Title:** M.D. **Type of organization:** Hospital-based practice **Major product:** Obstetric healthcare for high risk patients **Area of distribution:** Colorado **Area of Practice:** Maternal fetal medicine **Published works:** 21 abstracts, 21 journal articles, 4 book chapters **Affiliations:** S.M.F.M. **Hob./spts.:** Outdoor activities **SIC code:** 80 **Address:** Pikes Peak Maternal-Fetal Medicine Center, 1400 E. Boulder, Suite 3300, Colorado Springs, CO 80909-5599 **E-mail:** docnaef@aol.com

NAGEL, RONALD L.
Industry: Medical **Born:** January 18, 1936, Santiago, Chile **Univ./degree:** B.S., Biology, University of Chile, 1952; M.D., University of Chile College of Medicine, 1960 **Current organization:** Albert Einstein College of Medicine **Title:** M.D., Head of Hematology **Type of organization:** Medical school **Major product:** Medical education, research, patient care **Area of distribution:** International **Area of Practice:** Hematology **Honors/awards:** Ministry of Education Prize, Chile, 1952; Health Research Council of the City of New York Scientist Award, 1969-75; Foreign Investigator Fellowship Award by Institute National de la Sante et de la Recherche Medicale, Paris, France, 1984; Dr. John Hercules Memorial Address, Boston, Massachusetts, 1994; Dr. John Hercules Memorial Address, Washington, DC, 1998 **Published works:** 300+ reviewed papers; several books including, Genetical, Functional and Physical Studies of Hemoglobins, Editors: Arends, Bemski and Nagel, Karger, Basel, 1971; Camino del Alba, University of Chile Press, Santiago, Chile, 1973; Disorders of Hemoglobin: Genetics, Pathophysiology, Clinical Management, Editors: M.H. Steinberg, B.G. Forget, D.R. Higgs, R.L. Nagel, Cambridge University Press, UK 2000; Hemoglobin Disorders: Molecular Methods and Protocols. Series on Methods in Molecular Medicine. Editor: RL Nagel, MD, Humana Press, NY 2003; numerous book chapters including, Nagel RL and Gibson QH: Mechanism of the Formation of the Hemoglobin-Haptoglobin Complex. In Genetical, Functional and Physical Studies of Hemoglobins. Arends, Bemski and Nagel (eds.), Karger, Basel, 1971; Nagle RL and Ranney HM: Drug-Induced Oxidative Denaturation of Hemoglobin. Semin Hematol 10:269, 1973; Nagel RL and Bookchin RM: Human Hemoglobin Mutants with Abnormal Oxygen Binding. Semin Hematol 11:385, 1974; Nagel RL, Fabry ME and Kaul DK: New Insights on Sickle Cell Anemia. Diagnostic Medicine 7:26-33, 1984; **Affiliations:** Member, Editorial Board, Hemoglobin, International Journal for Hemoglobin Research; Past Member, Editorial Board, Proceedings of the Society for Experimental Biology and Medicine; Past Member, Editorial Board, Blood, Journal of the American Society of Hematology **Hob./spts.:** Travel, opera, instrumental music **SIC code:** 80 **Address:** Albert Einstein College of Medicine, Dept. of Hematology, 1300 Morris Park Ave., Ullmann 921, New York, NY 10461 **E-mail:** nagel@aecom.yu.edu

NAHEEDY, M. HOSSAIN
Industry: Medical **Born:** March 21, 1946, Rezaiyeh, Iran **Univ./degree:** M.D., Tehran University, Iran, 1971 **Current organization:** University Hospital CWRU **Title:** M.D. **Type of organization:** Medical school **Major product:** Patient care, medical education **Area of distribution:** Cleveland, Ohio **Area of Practice:** Neuro-radiology **Published works:** 45 articles, 4 book chapters **Affiliations:** A.S.N.R.; A.U.R.; R.N.S.A.; Cleveland R.A. **Hob./spts.:** Golf, photography **SIC code:** 80 **Address:** University Hospital CWRU, 11100 Euclid Ave., Cleveland, OH 44106 **E-mail:** naheedy@uhrad.com

NAMDARI, HASSAN
Industry: Healthcare **Born:** May 22, 1950, Iran **Univ./degree:** B.S., Medical Technology, 1974, Isfahan University of Technology; M.S., Microbiology, East Tennessee State University, 1978; Ph.D., Microbiology, Rhode Island University, 1987 **Current organization:** Clinical Laboratories, Inc. **Title:** Director of Microbiology **Type of organization:** Clinical laboratory **Major product:** Diagnostic clinical microbiology services **Area of distribution:** Northeastern Pennsylvania **Area of Practice:** Clinical and molecular microbiology **Published works:** 60+ articles, book chapters **Affiliations:** American Society for Microbiology **Hob./spts.:** Golf **SIC code:** 80 **Address:** Clinical Laboratories, Inc., Director of Microbiology, 901 Keystone Industrial Park, Throop, PA 18512 **E-mail:** hnamdari@clinical.com **Web address:** www.clinical.com

NANAVATI, DINESH M.
Industry: Healthcare **Born:** September 15, 1935, Junagadh, India **Univ./degree:** M.D., Kasturba Medical College, India **Current organization:** Unity Health System **Title:** M.D. **Type of organization:** Medical practice **Major product:** Patient care **Area of distribution:** Rochester, (Monroe County) N.Y. **Area of Practice:** General psychiatry **Published works:** Pharmacological journal from the U.K. **Affiliations:** A.M.A.; A.P.A.; A.A.P.I.; M.C.M.S. **Hob./spts.:** Swimming, tennis, coin collecting, reading **SIC code:** 80 **Address:** Unity Health System, 1561 Long Pond Rd., Suite 117, Rochester, NY 14626

NANDIPATI, JAYAPRADA
Industry: Healthcare **Born:** August 18, 1962, Guntur, Andhra Pradesh **Univ./degree:** M.D., OB/GYN, Guntur Medical College, India **Current organization:** Greenville Memorial Hospital **Title:** M.D. **Type of organization:** Hospital **Major product:** Patient care **Area of distribution:** Greenville, South Carolina **Area of Practice:** Family medicine, consultant obstetrician in India **Affiliations:** A.M.A.; A.F.P. **Hob./spts.:** Gardening, cooking, table tennis **SIC code:** 80 **Address:** Greenville Memorial Hospital, 701 Grove Rd., Greenville, SC 29605 **E-mail:** jayanandipati@hotmail.com

NANDYAL, RAJAGOPAL R.
Industry: Healthcare **Born:** April 22, 1948, India **Univ./degree:** M.D., Anhra Medical School, India **Current organization:** Southeastern Neonatology Associates, Ltd. **Title:** Director of Neonatology **Type of organization:** Community hospitals, private practice **Major product:** Newborn/infant care **Area of distribution:** Wisconsin **Area of Practice:** Pediatrics, neonatology **Published works:** 10 articles **Affiliations:** A.M.A.; A.A.P.; St. Luke's Hospital; St. Mary's Hospital **SIC code:** 80 **Address:** Southeastern Neonatology Associates, Ltd., 1320 Wisconsin Ave., Racine, WI 53403 **E-mail:** rajnandyal@aol.com

NASEER, NAUMAN
Industry: Healthcare **Born:** November 10, 1974, Lahore, Pakistan **Univ./degree:** M.B.B.S, King Edward Medical College, Lahore, Pakistan, 1998 **Current organization:** Hospital of the University of Pennsylvania **Title:** M.D. **Type of organization:** Hospital **Major product:** Patient care **Area of distribution:** Pennsylvania **Area of Practice:** Cardiology, interventional cardiology **Affiliations:** Board Certified, American Board of Internal Medicine **Hob./spts.:** Reading, swimming, hiking **SIC code:** 80 **Address:** 2606 Burroughs Mill Circle, Cherry Hill, NJ 08002 **E-mail:** nauman.naseer@uphs.upenn.edu

NASRULLAH, HABIB M.
Industry: Healthcare **Born:** December 3, 1965, Dhaka, Bangladesh **Univ./degree:** M.D., University of Chittagong, Bangladesh **Current organization:** New York Methodist Hospital **Title:** M.D., Directorship Anesthesia Dept., New York Methodist Hospital **Type of organization:** Hospital **Major product:** Patient care **Area of distribution:** National **Area of Practice:** Anesthesiology **Published works:** Abstracts **Affiliations:** A.M.A.; American Society of Anesthesiologists; New York Society of Anesthesiology **Hob./spts.:** Computers, watch collecting, cricket **SIC code:** 80 **Address:** New York Methodist Hospital, 506 Sixth St., Brooklyn, NY 11215 **E-mail:** j.jnj@verizon.net

NASSAR, JOSE A.
Industry: Healthcare **Born:** Puerto Rico **Univ./degree:** M.D., Temple Medical School, 1963 **Current organization:** Jose A. Nassar, M.D. **Title:** M.D. **Type of organization:** Private office **Major product:** Diagnostic radiology **Area of distribution:** Puerto Rico **Area of Practice:** Radiology (Board Certified) **Affiliations:** R.S.N.A.; A.R.R.S.; A.I.U.M.; Puerto Rico Medical Association; Society of Breast Imaging; Society of Radiologists in Ultra Sound; American College of Radiology **SIC code:** 80 **Address:** Jose A. Nassar, M.D., 63 Cruz Ortiz Stella Ave., P.O. Box 9132, Humacao, PR 00792

NASSIF, ANIS SAMI
Industry: Medical **Born:** February 13, 1969, Beirut, Lebanon **Univ./degree:** M.D., St. Louis University **Current organization:** St. Louis University, Dept. of Radiology **Title:** M.D. **Type of organization:** Academic university hospital **Major product:** Patient care, medical education **Area of distribution:** Missouri **Area of Practice:** Medical imaging, neuro imaging and interventions, MR spectroscopy **Affiliations:** A.M.A.; R.S.N.A.; A.C.R.; A.S.N. **Hob./spts.:** Golf, tennis, soccer, opera **SIC code:** 80 **Address:** St. Louis University, Dept. of Radiology, 3635 Vista Ave. at Grand Blvd., 2nd floor, St. Louis, MO 63110 **E-mail:** nassifa@slu.edu

NAUGHTON, JOHN P.
Industry: Medical **Born:** May 20, 1933, West Nanticoke, Pennsylvania **Univ./degree:** M.D., Oklahoma University, 1958 **Current organization:** SUNY Buffalo School of Medicine and Biomedical Sciences **Title:** M.D./Professor/Former Dean and Vice President **Type of organization:** University medical school **Major product:** Patient care, medical education **Area of distribution:** Buffalo, New York **Area of Practice:** Cardiology, internal medicine **Honors/awards:** U Chancellor Norton Medal; Honorary Doctorate, Kosin Medical School **Published works:** Book, "Exercise Testing and Exercise Training, 1973"; Circulation; American Journal of Cardiology; JAMA **Affiliations:** F.A.C.P.; F.A.C.C.; F.A.C.S.M. **Hob./spts.:** Swimming, jogging, walking, reading **SIC code:** 80 **Address:** SUNY Buffalo School of Medicine and, Biomedical Sciences, 128 Farber Hall, 3435 Main St., Buffalo, NY 14214 **E-mail:** jpn@buffalo.edu

NAVARA, DINA J.
Industry: Healthcare **Born:** Kingston, New York **Univ./degree:** A.A., R.N., Ulster Community College, 1998; B.S., Organizational Leadership, Marist College, 2005 **Current organization:** Hospice Inc. **Title:** Team Leader, R.N. **Type of organization:** Hospice **Major product:** Palliative care **Area of distribution:** New York **Area of Practice:** Organizational leadership, healthcare **Affiliations:** H.P.C.N.Y.; National Geriatric Nursing Association **Hob./spts.:** Reading, travel **SIC code:** 80 **Address:** Hospice Inc., P.O. Box 1118, Port Ewen, NY 12446 **E-mail:** nursedina8113@yahoo.com

NAVARRETE, ANNA C.
Industry: Healthcare **Born:** August 24, 1959, Manila, Philippines **Univ./degree:** B.S.B.A., Georgian Court University, 2006 **Current organization:** Meridian Health **Title:** Histology Supervisor **Type of organization:** Hospital **Major product:** Patient care **Area of distribution:** New Jersey **Area of Practice:** Histology **Affiliations:** A.S.C.P., N.S.H. **Hob./spts.:** Running, reading **SIC code:** 80 **Address:** 724 Old Corlies Ave., Neptune, NJ 07753 **E-mail:** anavarrete@meridianhealth.com

NAVARRO, AURORA L.
Industry: Healthcare **Born:** September 23, 1968, Monterrey, Mexico **Univ./degree:** B.S.M.T., University of Texas, Medical Branch, 1994 **Current organization:** Laredo Medical Center **Title:** Lab Supervisor **Type of organization:** Hospital **Major product:** Patient care **Area of distribution:** Laredo, Texas **Area of Practice:** Medical technology, lab testing **Affiliations:** A.S.C.P. Certified **Hob./spts.:** Soccer, Track & Field, gardening **SIC code:** 80 **Address:** 60242, P.O. Box 2068, Laredo, TX 78041

NAWAZ, IRFAN
Industry: Healthcare **Born:** April 17, 1976, Pakistan **Univ./degree:** M.B.B.S., Khyber Medical College, Peshawar, Pakistan, 1999; M.D. (E.C.F.M.) Education Commission for Foreign Medical Graduates; Residency in Internal Medicine, Graduate Hospital, Drexel University, 2003-2006 **Current organization:** Tenet Healthcare Graduate Hospital **Title:** Chief Resident, House Staff **Type of organization:** Hospital **Major product:** Patient care **Area of distribution:** Pennsylvania **Area of Practice:** Internal Medicine (Board Certified); Clinical care residents' education, lecturing on management of G.I. bleeding **Published works:** 3 abstracts, 3 case reports **Affiliations:** American College of Physicians; American College of Gastroenterology; American Medical Association; American Gastroenterological Association **Hob./spts.:** Tennis, hiking, travel **SIC code:** 80 **Address:** Tenet Healthcare Graduate Hospital, 1 Graduate Plaza, Philadelphia, PA 19146 **E-mail:** nawazi1@yahoo.com

NEHRA, AJAY
Industry: Medical **Born:** February 15, 1958, Nairobi, Kenya **Univ./degree:** M.D., All India Institute of Medical Sciences, 1983 **Current organization:** Mayo Clinic, Dept. of Urology **Title:** M.D./Professor of Urology **Type of organization:** Hospital/university **Major product:** Medical services **Area of distribution:** National **Area of Practice:** Urology **Published works:** 65 articles, book chapters, editor of books **Affiliations:** American Urological Association; Board Member, Society of Sexual Medicine **Hob./spts.:** Tennis, squash, basketball **SIC code:** 80 **Address:** Mayo Clinic, Dept. of Urology, 200 First St. S.W., Rochester, MN 55905 **E-mail:** nehra.ajay@mayo.edu **Web address:** www.mayoclinic.org/urology-rst/12370606.htm

NELSON, THEODORA J.
Industry: Healthcare **Born:** March 7, 1964, San Diego, California **Univ./degree:** M.D., University of Vermont, 1991 **Current organization:** Scripps Clinic **Title:** M.D. **Type of organization:** Medical clinic **Major product:** Patient care **Area of distribution:** Santee, California **Area of Practice:** Pediatrics **Honors/awards:** Teaching Award, UCSD, 1994 **Affiliations:** A.A.P. **Hob./spts.:** Horseback riding, swimming **SIC code:** 80 **Address:** Scripps Clinic, 278 Town Center Pkwy., #105, Santee, CA 92071 **E-mail:** tnelson@scrippsclinic.com

NELSON-MAXWELL, JOAN C.
Industry: Healthcare **Born:** December 8, 1946, Charleston, South Carolina **Univ./degree:** M.S., Clinical Chemistry, Medical University of South Carolina **Current organization:** Barnwell County Hospital **Title:** Lab Director **Type of organization:** Hospital **Major product:** Patient care **Area of distribution:** Barnwell, South Carolina **Area of Practice:** Clinical pathology **Affiliations:** A.S.C.P.; S.C.A.C.M.; C.F.P.A. **Hob./spts.:** Horses, reading, writing poetry **SIC code:** 80 **Address:** Barnwell County Hospital, 811 Reynolds Rd., Barnwell, SC 29812 **E-mail:** joanonsc@yahoo.com

NESI, ROLAND M.
Industry: Healthcare **Born:** February 8, 1937, Brooklyn, New York **Univ./degree:** M.D., University of Bologna, 1965 **Current organization:** Frank J. Demento & Associates **Title:** M.D.; F.A.A.D. **Type of organization:** Group practice **Major product:** Dermatology **Area of distribution:** National **Area of Practice:** Diagnosis and treatment of skin cancer, melanoma **Published works:** "Melanoma In The Black Patient" **Affiliations:** New York State Medical Society; Suffolk County Dermatological Society **Hob./spts.:** Drawing, cooking **SIC code:** 80 **Address:** Frank J. Demento & Associates, 520 Franklin Ave., Garden City, NY 11530

NESOFF, AARON
Industry: Healthcare **Born:** May 13, 1944, Bronx, New York **Univ./degree:** M.D., Autonomous University of Guadalajara, Mexico, 1976 **Current organization:** Peninsula Hospital Center **Title:** Director of Family Health Services **Type of organization:** Hospital **Major product:** Patient care **Area of distribution:** New York **Area of Practice:** Family practice, outpatient department **Affiliations:** American Academy of Family Practice, Harley Owners Group **Hob./spts.:** Biking, scuba diving, cooking **SIC code:** 80 **Address:** Peninsula Hospital Center, 51-15 Beach Channel Dr., Far Rockaway, NY 11691 **E-mail:** anesoff@pol.net

NEW, TAMARA N.
Industry: Healthcare **Univ./degree:** M.D., Mount Sinai University, 1996; Fellowship, Columbia University Children's Hospital of New York, 2002 **Current organization:** Harlem Hospital Center **Title:** M.D; Director of Comprehensive Sickle Cell Center; Director of Pediatric Resident Training Program **Type of organization:** Hospital **Major product:** Patient care, teaching, health services **Area of distribution:** New York, New York **Area of Practice:** Pediatric hematology and oncology **Affiliations:** Association of Pediatric Program Directors; American Academy of Pediatrics; American Society of Hematology; American Society of Pediatric Hematology/Oncology **Hob./spts.:** Reading, theatre, movies **SIC code:** 80 **Address:** Harlem Hospital Center, 506 Lenox Ave., MLK 17-110, New York, NY 10037 **E-mail:** tn143@columbia.edu

NEWMAN, ALBERT E.
Industry: Healthcare **Born:** December 11, 1928, Chicago, Illinois **Univ./degree:** B.A., Fisk University, 1949; D.D.S., Meharry Medical College, 1957 **Current organization:** Albert E. Newman, D.D.S., Ltd. **Title:** Dentist **Type of organization:** Private dental practice **Major product:** Dental care **Area of distribution:** Chicago, Illinois **Area of Practice:** Dentistry **Affiliations:** A.D.A.; N.D.A.; Chairman, local Republican Party **Hob./spts.:** Boxing, baseball **SIC code:** 80 **Address:** Albert E. Newman, D.D.S., Ltd., 9101 S. Western Ave., Chicago, IL 60620 **E-mail:** newmantuthdr@aol.com

NEWMAN, NATHAN
Industry: Healthcare **Born:** December 22, 1968, Persia, Iran **Univ./degree:** M.D., Albert Einstein College of Medicine, 1996 **Current organization:** Orchid Surgery Center **Title:** M.D. **Type of organization:** Private practice **Major product:** Cosmetic surgery, dermatology **Area of distribution:** Beverly Hills, California **Area of Practice:** Cosmetic surgery specializing in liposuction, weight management **Published works:** Multiple publications **Affiliations:** A.A.D.; A.A.C.S. **Hob./spts.:** Soccer, basketball, swimming **SIC code:** 80 **Address:** Orchid Surgery Center, 9301 Wilshire Blvd., Suite 303, Beverly Hills, CA 90201 **E-mail:** orchidsurgery@yahoo.com

NEWSOME, JAMES L.
Industry: Healthcare **Born:** October 28, 1955, Marietta, Georgia **Univ./degree:** M.D., Medical College of Georgia, 1980; Fellowship, Surgical Autopsy Pathology, 1986-87; Fellowship, Cytopathology, Sloan Kettering, 1987 **Current organization:** Carraway Methodist Med. Center/Norwood Clinic **Title:** Chair, Dept. of Pathology **Type of organization:** Hospital and clinic **Major product:** Patient care **Area of distribution:** Birmingham, Alabama **Area of Practice:** Anatomic and clinical pathology, hospital administration **Honors/awards:** Physician's Recognition Award, A.M.A. **Published works:** 2 articles in "Birmingham News" **Affiliations:** Fellow, College of American Pathologists; A.M.A.; International Academy of Cytology; Alabama State Medical Association **Hob./spts.:** Orchid cultivation, scuba diving **SIC code:** 80 **Address:** Norwood Clinic, 1528 Carraway Blvd., Birmingham, AL 35234 **E-mail:** jnews91126@aol.com

NEZHAT, FARR R.
Industry: Healthcare **Univ./degree:** M.D., Isfahan University, 1976 **Current organization:** Mount Sinai School of Medicine **Title:** MD, FACOG, FACS **Type of organization:** Medical practice **Major product:** Patient care **Area of distribution:** New York **Area of Practice:** Gyn/Onc **Affiliations:** Fellow, American Obstetrics and Gynecological Association; Fellow, American Society of Gynecology and Oncology; Fellow, American College of Surgeons **SIC code:** 80 **Address:** Mount Sinai School of Medicine, 5 E. 98th St., New York, NY 10019 **E-mail:** fr0250@aol.com

NGAIZA, JUSTINIAN R.
Industry: Healthcare **Born:** August 23, 1955, Bukoba, Tanzania **Univ./degree:** M.D., 1978, University of Dar Es Salaam, Tanzania; M.S., Clinical Tropical Medicine, 1983; Ph.D., Immunoparasitology, 1988, University of London **Current organization:** Hematology Oncology Associates, Ltd. **Title:** Hematologist-Oncologist **Type of organization:** Private medical practice **Major product:** Clinical medicine **Area of distribution:** Virginia **Area of Practice:** Hematology, oncology, clinical tropical medicine **Affiliations:** A.S.C.O.; A.S.H.; A.M.A. **Hob./spts.:** Physical fitness, swimming, jazz, painting **SIC code:** 80 **Address:** Hematology Oncology Associates, Ltd., 5226 Dawes Ave., Alexandria, VA 22311 **E-mail:** ngaiza@aol.com

NGUYEN, THUAN-PHUONG
Industry: Medical **Born:** March 13, 1963, Dalat, Vietnam **Univ./degree:** B.S., Biology, Catholic University, 1985; M.D., Georgetown Medical College, 1989 **Current organization:** West Virginia University Hospital **Title:** M.D. **Type of organization:** University hospital **Major product:** Medical services **Area of distribution:** International **Area of Practice:** Diagnostic radiology **Published works:** Articles on bone tumors and deomoid tumors in the neck **Affiliations:** F.A.C.R.; R.S.N.A.; West Virginia Medical Society **Hob./spts.:** Music, swimming, travel, theatre, hiking **SIC code:** 80 **Address:** West Virginia University Hospitals, Dept. of Diagnostic Radiology, P.O. Box 9235, Morgantown, WV 26505

NICHOLAS, THOMAS A.
Industry: Medical **Current organization:** University of Missouri, Kansas City School of Medicine/Kansas City Southern Railway **Title:** M.D./Professor/Chief Medical Officer **Type of organization:** Medical school and railway **Major product:** Teaching/international railroad system **Area of distribution:** Missouri **Area of Practice:** Medical education **Affiliations:** Society of Teachers of Family Medicine; Missouri State Medical Society; A.M.A. **SIC code:** 80 **Address:** Truman Medical Center Lakewood, 7900 Lee's Summit Rd., Kansas City, MO 64139 **E-mail:** tomnich@att.net

NICHOLS, ADRIENNE L.
Industry: Healthcare **Born:** January 31, 1951, Flint, Michigan **Current organization:** Michigan Diagnostic Imaging **Title:** R.T.(R)(M) **Type of organization:** Diagnostic center **Major product:** Diagnostic imaging services **Area of distribution:** Mount Morris, Michigan **Area of Practice:** Mammography and radiology **Affiliations:** A.R.R.T.; A.S.R.T. **Hob./spts.:** Family, bowling, sports **SIC code:** 80 **Address:** 337 Lincoln Ave., Mount Morris, MI 48458

NICHOLS, RONALD LEE
Industry: Medical **Born:** June 25, 1941, Chicago, Illinois **Univ./degree:** M.D., University of Illinois, 1966 **Current organization:** Tulane University School of Medicine, Dept. of Surgery **Title:** M.D., F.A.C.S. **Type of organization:** University **Major product:** Patient care, medical education **Area of distribution:** International **Area of Practice:** General surgery, surgical infections **Honors/awards:** Numerous including: Owl Club Award, Tulane University School of Medicine, 1983; Douglas Stubbs Lecture Award, The Surgical Section, National Medical Association, 1987; Board of Trustees Award for Research, University of Health Sciences, The Chicago Medical School, 1977; Clinical Professor of the Year, University of Health Sciences, The Chicago Medical School, 1977; Awarded Honorary Fellowship in the Hellenic Surgical Society, Athens, Greece, 1990 **Published works:** Numerous articles including: Nichols RL and Condon RE, Antibiotic preparation of the colon; Failure of commonly used regimens. Surg Clin North Am 51:223-231, 1971; Nichols RL, Thadepalli H and Gorbach SL. Infections following abdominal trauma. Ill Med J 142:50-53, 1972; Nichols RL and Smith JW. Modern Approach to the diagnosis of anaerobic surgical sepsis. Surg Clin North Am 55:51-30 **Affiliations:** Sr. Visiting Surgeon, MCLNO, Tulane University School of Medicine; William Henderson, Professor of Surgery Emeritus, Professor of Microbiology and Immunology **SIC code:** 80 **Address:** Tulane University School of Medicine, Dept. of Surgery, 1430 Tulane Ave., SL-22, New Orleans, LA 70112-2699 **E-mail:** rlnmd@yahoo.com **Web address:** www.som.tulane.edu

NIEWIAROWSKI, EWA K.
Industry: Healthcare **Univ./degree:** M.D., Warsaw Medical Academy, Poland, 1984 **Current organization:** Ewa K. Niewiarowski, MD, PLLC **Title:** M.D. **Type of organization:** Medical clinic **Major product:** Patient care **Area of distribution:** Plano, Texas **Area of Practice:** Family physician **Affiliations:** Texas Medical Association; Texas Academy of Family Physicians **SIC code:** 80 **Address:** Ewa K. Niewiarowski, MD, PLLC, 6124 W. Parker Rd., Medical Office 53, Suite 230, Plano, TX 75093

NIRODY, SHULA A.
Industry: Medical **Born:** November 24, 1947, Bombay, India **Univ./degree:** B.S., Microbiology and Chemistry, Bombay University, India, 1971 **Current organization:** Robert Wood Johnson University Hospital at Rahway **Title:** Lab Systems & Microbiologist **Type of organization:** University hospital **Major product:** Patient care **Area of distribution:** New Jersey **Area of Practice:** Clinical laboratory services, microbiology **Affiliations:** American Society of Clinical Pathologists **Hob./spts.:** Family, travel, cooking, reading, walking **SIC code:** 80 **Address:** Robert Wood Johnson, University Hospital at Rahway, 865 Stone St., Rahway, NJ 07065 **E-mail:** snirody@rwjuhr.com

NOEL, R. BURKE
Industry: Healthcare **Born:** October 16, 1970, Plainview, Texas **Univ./degree:** D.D.S., Baylor College of Dentistry, 1997 **Current organization:** Dundee Family Dental **Title:** D.D.S. **Type of organization:** Private practice **Major product:** Dental care **Area of distribution:** Omaha, Nebraska **Area of Practice:** Family and cosmetic dentistry **Affiliations:** A.D.A.; N.D.A. **Hob./spts.:** Bicycling, hunting, fishing **SIC code:** 80 **Address:** Dundee Family Dental, 5006 Dodge St., Omaha, NE 68117 **E-mail:** dnoel72@msn.com

NOFFSINGER, MARK A.
Industry: Medical **Born:** May 28, 1956, Defiance, Ohio **Univ./degree:** M.D., Indiana University, 1982 **Current organization:** Kalamazoo Orthopaedic Clinic, P.C. **Title:** M.D. **Type of organization:** University/hospital **Major product:** Medical services **Area of distribution:** Michigan **Area of Practice:** Orthopaedic surgery, trauma, joint replacement, inventing **Honors/awards:** Resident Teaching Award, Michigan State University, 1983; Wellmerling Award, American Fracture Association, 1997 **Published works:** Journal of Bone & Joint Surgery, Orthopaedics Today **Affiliations:** A.B.O.S.; A.A.O.S.; A.F.A.; A.M.A.; M.S.M.S.; Mid American Orthopaedic Association **Hob./spts.:** Golf, boating **SIC code:** 80 **Address:** Kalamazoo Orthopaedic Clinic, P.C., 2490 S. 11th St., Kalamazoo, MI 49009 **E-mail:** noffsinm@bronsonng.org

NOLAN, MARC A.
Industry: Healthcare **Univ./degree:** M.D., George Washington University **Current organization:** Progressive Medical Assoc. **Title:** Doctor **Type of organization:** Private practice **Major product:** Patient care **Area of distribution:** New York, New York **Area of Practice:** Cardiology, diagnosis and treatment of adult heart conditions **Published works:** Scholarly articles, peer reviews **Affiliations:** Fellow, American College of Cardiology; Diplomate, The Certification Board of Nuclear Cardiology; Diplomate, American Board of Internal Medicine; American Society of Nuclear Cardiology; American Medical Association **SIC code:** 80 **Address:** Progressive Medical Assoc., 90 East End Ave., New York, NY 10028 **E-mail:** brianbeck911@hotmail.com **Web address:** www.pmanyc.com

NORA, NANCY A.
Industry: Healthcare **Born:** February 28, 1958, Chicago, Illinois **Univ./degree:** B.S., Psychology, St. Louis University, Missouri, 1979; M.D., The Royal College of Surgeons, Ireland, 1985 **Current organization:** David S. Ginsburg, M.D. **Title:** M.D. **Type of organization:** Group private practice **Major product:** Patient care **Area of distribution:** Illinois **Area of Practice:** Nephrology, internal medicine **Affiliations:** F.A.C.P.; A.S.N. **SIC code:** 80 **Address:** David S. Ginsburg, M.D., 750 Homewood Ave., Suite 250, Highland Park, IL 60035

NORDYKE, GREGGORY N.
Industry: Healthcare **Born:** September 1, 1957, Amarillo, Texas **Univ./degree:** B.S.N., West Texas A&M University, 2000 **Current organization:** Northwest Texas Healthcare System **Title:** R.N. **Type of organization:** Hospital **Major product:** Patient care **Area of distribution:** Amarillo, Texas **Area of Practice:** Cardiology **Affiliations:** A.N.A.; Cardiovascular Nurses Society **Hob./spts.:** Spending time with her grandchildren, hunting, fishing, motorcycles **SIC code:** 80 **Address:** 1557 Parr St., Amarillo, TX 79106 **E-mail:** jubalharshaw2@msn.com

NORRELL JR., MILTON G.
Industry: Healthcare **Univ./degree:** M.D., Loma Linda University, 1951 **Current organization:** Norrell Clinic, P.A. **Title:** M.D. **Type of organization:** Private practice **Major product:** Patient care **Area of distribution:** Pell City, Alabama **Area of Practice:** Family practice (Board Certified) **Affiliations:** A.M.A.; A.A.F.P.; Medical Association of the State of Alabama; Southern Medical Association; American Board of Family Practice; Interstate Post Graduate Medical Association **SIC code:** 80 **Address:** Norrell Clinic, P.A., 1716 First Ave. North, Pell City, AL 35125 **E-mail:** mgn@pell.net

NORTON, STEPHEN G.
Industry: Healthcare **Born:** August 19, 1951, Harrisburg, Pennsylvania **Univ./degree:** Bucknell University; D.M.D., University of Pennsylvania School of Dental Medicine; Post Graduate Studies, Northwestern University Evanston Hospital, General Practice Residency **Current organization:** Stephen G. Norton, DMD **Title:** Dentist **Type of organization:** Private practice **Major product:** Dental services **Area of distribution:** Delray Beach, Florida **Area of Practice:** General and cosmetic dentistry **Honors/awards:** Teaching Fellowship, University of Pennsylvania **Affiliations:** A.D.A. **Hob./spts.:** Tennis, golf **SIC code:** 80 **Address:** Stephen G. Norton, DMD, 222 Palm Court, Delray Beach, FL 33444 **Phone:** (561)278-0362

NWANKWO, CECILIA
Industry: Healthcare **Born:** New York, New York **Univ./degree:** M.D., University of Nigeria, 1980 **Current organization:** Capital Pediatrics **Title:** M.D., F.A.A.P. **Type of organization:** Private practice **Major product:** Patient care **Area of distribution:** International **Area of Practice:** Pediatrics **Affiliations:** A.M.A.; American Academy of Pediatrics; Maryland Medical Society **Hob./spts.:** Travel, shopping **SIC code:** 80 **Address:** Capital Pediatrics, 16220 S. Frederick Ave., Suite 427, Gaithersburg, MD 20877 **E-mail:** ceciliaanwankwo@yahoo.com

NWANKWO JR., CHRISTIAN
Industry: Healthcare **Born:** Nigema **Univ./degree:** M.D., University of Ibadan, Nigeria, 1980 **Current organization:** Christian Nwankwo, Jr., M.D., F.A.A.F.P. **Title:** M.D., F.A.A.F.P. **Type of organization:** Private practice **Major product:** Patient care **Area of distribution:** International **Area of Practice:** Family physician **Affiliations:** American Academy of Family Physicians; A.M.A.; MedChi of Maryland **Hob./spts.:** Racquetball, charity walks **SIC code:** 80 **Address:** Christian Nwankwo, Jr., M.D., F.A.A.F.P., 15811 Berryville Rd., Darnestown, MD 20874 **E-mail:** christiannwankwo@aol.com **Web address:** www.capricore.co

O'CONNELL, CAROLYN
Industry: Healthcare **Born:** March 10, 1961, Denver, Colorado **Univ./degree:** A.A., Golden West College, 1994; Cypress College, 1999 **Current organization:** Esthetic Rx **Title:** RN, Founder, Owner **Type of organization:** Organized healthcare systems **Major product:** Aesthetic procedures, aesthetic training for medical professionals **Area of distribution:** California **Area of Practice:** Aesthetic procedures **Affiliations:** California Nursing Association; National League of Nurses **Hob./spts.:** Family **SIC code:** 80 **Address:** Esthetic Rx, 415 Pier Ave., Hermosa Beach, CA 90254

O'DAY, STEVEN JOHN
Industry: Healthcare **Born:** December 20, 1960, San Mateo, California **Univ./degree:** M.D., Johns Hopkins Medical School **Current organization:** John Wayne Cancer Institute **Title:** M.D., Director of Medical Oncology and Medical Oncology Research **Type of organization:** Research Hospital **Major product:** Oncology research **Area of distribution:** International **Area of Practice:** Oncology **Affiliations:** A.S.C.O.; A.S.H.; Society of Surgical Oncology; Southwest Oncology Group **Hob./spts.:** Clinical research in melanoma, piano **SIC code:** 80 **Address:** John Wayne Cancer Institute, 2001 Santa Monica Blvd., Suite 860W, Santa Monica, CA 90404 **E-mail:** odays@jwci.org

OFILI, ELIZABETH O.
Industry: Medical **Born:** March 5, 1956, Kano, Nigeria **Spouse:** Chamberlain Obialo, M.D. **Married:** May 5, 1985 **Children:** Tim Chima, 20; Sharon Shimite, 18; Chris Chinedu, 16; Felicia Nkechi, 14 **Univ./degree:** M.B.B.S., Ahmadu Bello University, Zaria, Nigeria, 1979; M.P.H., Johns Hopkins, University, 1983 **Current organization:** Morehouse School of Medicine **Title:** Associate Dean; Professor and Chief of Cardiology **Type of organization:** University/Clinical Research Center **Major product:** Patient care, medical education and research **Area of distribution:** International **Area of practice:** Cardiology **Area of Practice:** Cardiology **Honors/awards:** Platinum Member, Manchester Who's Who, Executive Professionals; Changing the Face of Medicine: The Rise of America's Women Physicians (National Library of Medicine) Physician of the Year, United States Congress; Outstanding Georgia Citizen; Tall Drums; Nigerians who are Changing America; Woman of the Year: Salute to Black Mothers (Concerned Black Clergy); America's Leading Physicians (Black Enterprise Magazine); Nanette Wenger Award for Health Policy (Women Heart); Daniel Savage Science Award (Association of Black Cardiologists); Black History Month (Johns Hopkins University) **Published works:** 100+ articles and chapters **Affiliations:** American Heart Association; Association of Black Cardiologists; American College of Cardiology; Association of American Medical Colleges **Career accomplishments:** Chief of Cardiology, 1994-2005: advanced public health through practice, research and medical education; First Female President of the 800 member National Association of Black Cardiologists, 2000-02; Outstanding Research on Health Disparities, impacting National Policy; Associate Dean for Clinical Research at Morehouse School of Medicine, leading multidisciplinary research teams and securing multimillion dollars in research awards **Hob./spts.:** Family, reading, cooking, music **SIC code:** 80 **Address:** Morehouse School of Medicine, Dept. of Medicine, 720 Westview Dr. S.W., Atlanta, GA 30310 **E-mail:** ofilie@msm.edu **Web address:** www.msm.edu

O'GRADY, BARBARA VINSON
Industry: Healthcare **Born:** July 6, 1928, Alhambra, California **Univ./degree:** B.S., Public Health, University of California, Los Angeles, 1951; R.N., 1948; M.S., Public Health, 1972, University of Minnesota **Current organization:** Ramsey County Public Health Dept. **Title:** Director of Public Health Nursing (Retired) **Type of organization:**

County health dept. **Major product:** Public health nursing services **Area of distribution:** Santa Ynez, California **Area of Practice:** Nursing, administration **Published works:** Book chapter, articles **Affiliations:** A.N.A; Fellow, American Academy of Nursing **Hob./spts.:** Travel, reading, grandchildren **SIC code:** 80 **Address:** P.O. Box 624, Santa Ynez, CA 93460 **E-mail:** jb@syv.com

OJUTIKU, OLUKAYODE O.
Industry: Healthcare **Born:** July 29, 1945, Nigeria **Univ./degree:** M.D., University of Ibadan, 1969 **Current organization:** A. Holly Patterson Extended Care Facility **Title:** M.D./ Medical Director **Type of organization:** Hospital affiliated nursing home **Major product:** Long term patient care **Area of distribution:** New York **Area of Practice:** Board Certified, Internal Medicine **Published works:** Medical journals **Affiliations:** F.A.C.P.; American Medical Directors Association; Assistant Professor, State University of New York at Stony Brook **Hob./spts.:** Travel, music **SIC code:** 80 **Address:** A. Holly Patterson Extended Care Facility, 875 Jerusalem Ave., Uniondale, NY 11553 **E-mail:** polykay@aol.com **Web address:** www.numc.edu

OKAFOR, IFEANYICHUKWU O.
Industry: Healthcare **Born:** February 20, 1963, Kano, Nigeria **Univ./degree:** M.B.B.S., Ibadan University, Nigeria, 1987; M.D., Internal Medicine, Howard University, 2000 **Current organization:** Scala Medical Clinic **Title:** M.D. **Type of organization:** Medical clinic **Major product:** Patient care **Area of distribution:** North Carolina **Area of Practice:** Internal medicine **Affiliations:** A.M.A.; A.C.P.; A.S.I.M. **Hob./spts.:** Reading **SIC code:** 80 **Address:** Scala Medical Clinic, 630 Clark Dr., Lincolnton, NC 28092 **E-mail:** ifeanyi20@yahoo.com

OKEHIE-COLLINS, TINA
Industry: Healthcare **Born:** February 10, 1956 **Univ./degree:** D.C., 1994 **Current organization:** Pain-Aid Chiropractic & Medical Clinic **Title:** D.C. **Type of organization:** Private practice **Major product:** Patient care **Area of distribution:** Texas **Area of Practice:** Chiropractic medicine **Hob./spts.:** Basketball **SIC code:** 80 **Address:** Pain-Aid Chiropractic & Medical Clinic, 8440 Fondren Rd., Houston, TX 77074 **E-mail:** chidindu@aol.com

OLENYN, PAUL T.
Industry: Dentistry **Born:** November 3, 1948, Brooklyn, New York **Univ./degree:** B.A., Biological Science, Rutgers University; D.D.S., Georgetown Dental School, 1975 **Current organization:** Paul T. Olenyn, D.D.S., Ltd. **Title:** Dentist **Type of organization:** General dentistry **Major product:** Patient care **Area of distribution:** Burke, Virginia **Area of Practice:** Family and cosmetic dentistry **Honors/awards:** National Honor Society for Dentists (OKU); Top Dentist in Washington; Best Dentist in America **Affiliations:** Dental Advisory Council, Metropolitan Life; Psi Omega; American Academy of Dentistry for Children; American Dental Association; North Virginia Implant Society; Fairfax County Dental Society **Hob./spts.:** Jogging, cycling, swimming **SIC code:** 80 **Address:** Paul T. Olenyn, D.D.S., Ltd., 5207-A Lynngate Ct., Burke, VA 22015 **E-mail:** bookkeeper@erols.com

OLSSON, JAY E.
Industry: Healthcare **Univ./degree:** D.O. , Kansas City University of Medicine and Biosciences College of Osteopathic Medicine **Current organization:** Interventional Spine Institute of Florida **Title:** D.O. **Type of organization:** Hospital/clinic **Major product:** Patient care **Area of distribution:** National **Area of Practice:** Rehab and physical medicine, pain medicine **Affiliations:** A.A.P.M.; A.A.P.M.R.; A.O.P.M.R. **Hob./spts.:** Painting, writing, poetry, family **SIC code:** 80 **Address:** Interventional Spine Institute of Florida, 308 S. Harbor City Blvd., Suite A, Melbourne, FL 32901

ONAT, ESRA S.
Industry: Healthcare **Born:** August 13, 1960, Istanbul, Turkey **Univ./degree:** M.D., University of Istanbul School of Medicine **Current organization:** Esra S. Onat, M.D. **Title:** M.D. **Type of organization:** Private practice **Major product:** Patient care **Area of distribution:** New Jersey **Area of Practice:** Family medicine **Affiliations:** American Academy of Family Practice; American College of Advanced Medicine **Hob./spts.:** Tennis, classical music, basketball **SIC code:** 80 **Address:** Esra S. Onat, M.D., 290 Madison Ave., Bldg. #3, Morristown, NJ 07960

ONONYE, CHUBA B.
Industry: Healthcare **Univ./degree:** M.D., St. George's School of Medicine, Grenada, 1980 **Current organization:** Bendel Clinic **Title:** M.D. **Type of organization:** Clinic **Major product:** Patient care **Area of distribution:** Arizona **Area of Practice:** Internal medicine **SIC code:** 80 **Address:** Bendel Clinic, 6550 E. Broadway Rd., Suite 210, Mesa, AZ 85206

OOSTERMAN, STEPHAN E.
Industry: Medical **Born:** September 28, 1952, Worcester, Massachusetts **Univ./degree:** B.S., Biochemistry, Calvin College, 1981; D.O., Michigan State University, 1985 **Current organization:** Shands Jacksonville, University of Florida Health Science Center **Title:** Doctor; Assistant Professor; Medical Director **Type of organization:** University hospital **Major product:** Patient care/medical education **Area of distribution:** Florida **Area of Practice:** Family practice **Honors/awards:** Navy Meritorious Service Medal **Affiliations:** A.F.F.P.; S.T.F.M. **SIC code:** 80 **Address:** Shands Jacksonville, University of Florida Family Practice Center, 1255 Lila Ave., Jacksonville, FL 32208 **E-mail:** stephan.oosterman@jax.ufl.edu

ORLEDGE, JEFFREY D.
Industry: Medical **Born:** February 13, 1966, Coaldale, Pennsylvania **Univ./degree:** M.D., Penn State University, 1994 **Current organization:** Penn State Milton S. Hershey Medical Center **Title:** M.D. **Type of organization:** University hospital **Major product:** Emergency medicine **Area of distribution:** Hershey, Pennsylvania **Area of Practice:** Emergency medicine **Affiliations:** A.C.E.P. **Hob./spts.:** Computers **SIC code:** 80 **Address:** 625 Carroll Dr., Hummelstown, PA 17036 **E-mail:** jorledge@bellatlantic.net

ORLOFF, NATHALIE F.
Industry: Healthcare **Born:** January 27, 1929, Shanghai, China **Univ./degree:** B.S., Microbiology, UCLA, 1953; A.S., Medical Technology, St. Johns Hospital, California; M.D., USC Medical School, 1959; Fellowship in Pathology, Los Angeles County General Hospital, 1964 **Current organization:** St. John's Health Center **Title:** M.D. **Type of organization:** Hospital **Major product:** Patient care **Area of distribution:** California **Area of Practice:** Hematopathology, clinical pathology **Affiliations:** American Medical Association; American Society of Clinical Pathology; American Association of Blood Banks; California Society of Blood Banks; California Medical Association; Los Angeles County Medical Association **Hob./spts.:** Gardening, walking, reading, volunteer work **SIC code:** 80 **Address:** 4848 Elkridge Dr., Rancho Palos Verdes, CA 90275 **E-mail:** nathalie.orloff@stjohns.org **Web address:** www.stjohns.org

ORR, MALCOLM D.
Industry: Medical **Born:** June 26, 1939, Townsville, Queensland, Australia **Univ./degree:** M.B., B.S., University of Queensland, Brisbane, Australia, 1964; Ph.D., Biochemistry, Australian National University, Canberra, Australia, 1969 **Current organization:** University of Texas HSCSA **Title:** Professor of Anesthesiology **Type of organization:** University Health System **Major product:** Medical services **Area of distribution:** San Antonio, Texas **Area of Practice:** Anesthesiology **Honors/awards:** Numerous including, First Place Award, Scientific Exhibit, "The Nicotinic Acetylcholine Receptor II. Structure to Function Relationships at the Myo Neural Junction. Modification of the Cholinesterase". American Society of Anesthesiologists Meeting, San Francisco, Oct. 28-30, 1991; Best Scientific Exhibit Award, "Allosteric Subunit Structure of the Acetylcholine Receptor Protein at the Neuromuscular Junction. A Computer Simulation." 44th Annual Postgraduate Assembly, New York State Society of Anesthesiologists, New York, NY, Dec. 8-12, 1990 **Published works:** Numerous including, Orr MD: "Perioperative hemodilution", Autologous Transfusion and Hemotherapy (Taswell HF, Pineda AA, Eds.), p. 104, Blackwell Scientific Publications, Boston, 1991; Orr MD: "Massive Blood Transfusion", Decision Making in Anesthesiology, 3rd ed. (Bready LL, Mullins RM, Noorily SH, Smith RB, Eds.), Mosby Year Book, Inc, 1999; Orr MD: "Munchausen's Syndrome", Decision Making in Anesthesiology, 3rd ed. (Bready LL, Mullins RM, Noorily SH, Smith RB, Eds.) Mosby Year Book, Inc., 1999 **Affiliations:** American Medical Association; American Society of Anesthesiology; Texas Society of Anesthesiology; San Antonio Northwest Rotary International **Hob./spts.:** Restoration of Corvettes **SIC code:** 80 **Address:** University of Texas HSCSA, 334F Dept. of Anesthesiology, 7703 Floyd Curl Dr., San Antonio, TX 78229-7838 **E-mail:** orr@uthscsa.edu

ORSHER, STUART
Industry: Healthcare **Born:** October 19, 1949, Philadelphia, Pennsylvania **Univ./degree:** M.D., Hahnemann Medical College, Pennsylvania; J.D., Fordham University School of Law, New York **Current organization:** Stuart Orsher, M.D., J.D. **Title:** Physician/Attorney **Type of organization:** Private medical practice **Major product:** Patient care **Area of distribution:** New York, New York **Area of Practice:** Internal medicine, health policies **Affiliations:** American Medical Association; American Bar Association; New York County Medical Society; Past President and Trustee, Medical Society, State of New York **Hob./spts.:** Health policy, travel **SIC code:** 80 **Address:** Stuart Orsher, M.D., J.D., 9 E. 79th St., New York, NY 10021-0123

ORTEGA-ELIAS, MANUEL
Industry: Healthcare **Born:** November 13, 1955, Bayamon, Puerto Rico **Univ./degree:** M.D., University of Puerto Rico School of Medicine **Current organization:** Pediatrix Medical Group **Title:** M.D./Neonatologist **Type of organization:** Medical group **Major product:** Patient care **Area of distribution:** San Juan, Puerto Rico **Area of Practice:** Neonatal intensive care **Affiliations:** F.A.A.P. **Hob./spts.:** Music, Puerto Rican folk music **SIC code:** 80 **Address:** Pediatrix Medical Group, Calle Jilguero 270, San Juan, PR 00926 **E-mail:** mortega@nueworld.com

ORTIZ, HERNANDO
Industry: Healthcare **Born:** May 2, 1940, Medellin, Colombia **Univ./degree:** M.D., Antioquia University Medical School, Colombia, 1965; Specialty: University of

Arizona, University of Puerto Rico, DABR **Current organization:** MROI **Title:** M.D. **Type of organization:** Radiation therapy and oncology institute **Major product:** Patient care **Area of distribution:** San Juan, Puerto Rico **Area of Practice:** Radiation oncology **Affiliations:** R.S.N.A.; A.S.T.R.O.; E.S.T.R.O.; A.C.R.; A.R.S.; Member of I.R.B., Professor at University of Puerto Rico Medical School **Career accomplishments:** Licensee: Colombia, Puerto Rico, Georgia, Florida, Texas **Hob./spts.:** Opera, walking by the sea, museums, foreign travel **SIC code:** 80 **Address:** MROI, 1479 Ashford Ave., #420, San Juan, PR 00907 **E-mail:** hortiz@rtcionline.com

ORTIZ, PEDRO P.
Industry: Medical **Born:** June 29, 1962, Huejuquilla, El Alto, Mexico **Univ./degree:** M.D., University of Guadalajara, Mexico, 1991 **Current organization:** University of Puerto Rico Medical Center **Title:** M.D. **Type of organization:** University/hospital **Major product:** Patient care, medical education **Area of distribution:** Puerto Rico **Area of Practice:** Cardiology **Affiliations:** A.C.P.-A.S.I.M.; A.C.C.; A.M.A. **Hob./spts.:** Skiing, soccer, travel **SIC code:** 80 **Address:** University of Puerto Rico Medical Center, Cardiology Section, San Juan, PR 00925 **E-mail:** pedro2mwm@hotmail.com

ORTIZ, ROBERT
Industry: Healthcare **Born:** January 14, 1961, Bronx, New York **Univ./degree:** B.S., Physiology, Michigan State University, 1984; M.D., Temple University School of Medicine, 1993; Internal Medicine, Beth Israel Medical Center, New York, 1997 **Current organization:** Terra-Therapy, Inc. **Title:** President/CEO **Type of organization:** Health and beauty **Major product:** Health and beauty aids **Area of distribution:** National **Area of Practice:** Internal Medicine **Honors/awards:** 25 Outstanding Seniors Awards, 1984; Academic Excellence Award, 1984; Office of Supportive Services Special Merit Award, 1983; Office of Student Affairs Achievement Award, 1983; Office of Minority Affairs Award, 1982; 1 patent: A Therapeutic After-Shave Care Lotion, Ortiz, R., Fernandez, V. **Published works:** Numerous publications including: Ortiz, R., Alfaro, D.V., Simoni, G.J., "A Simplified Method For Preparing Rabbit Eyes for Experimental Surgical Procedures", Ophthalmic Surgery, 18(9): 691-2, 1987; Ortiz, R. Carlisi, D.J., Imbriolo, A., "The Biological Effects of Combined Herbal Oral and Topical Formulations on Androgenetic Alopecia", 1998; Zimmerman, N.J., Chang, S., Iwamoto, T., Ortiz, R., Ozmert, E., Miller, W.T., Alfaro, D.V., "A New Class of Vitreous Substitutes: Liquid Fluorochemicals", American Academy of Ophthalmology, 1987 **Affiliations:** Fellow, I.C.P.S.; A.M.A.; A.R.V.O.; S.N.M.A.; A.M.S.A.; National Chapter Treasurer, B.H.O.; Chapter Founder & President, Temple University School of Medicine **Hob./spts.:** Competitive volleyball, fencing, tennis, music, travel, Naturopathic/Homeopathic Medicine **SIC code:** 80 **Address:** P.O. Box 746, New York, NY 10150 **E-mail:** bortizmd.@aol.com

ORTIZ BELMONTE, LUIS R.
Industry: Healthcare **Univ./degree:** M.B.A. Candidate, University of Phoenix **Current organization:** Hospital Auxilio Mutuo, Purchasing Dept. **Title:** Purchasing and Material Manager **Type of organization:** Hospital **Major product:** Patient care **Area of distribution:** Hato Rey, Puerto Rico **Area of Practice:** Purchasing and logistics, material logistics, management **SIC code:** 80 **Address:** Hospital Auxilio Mutuo, Purchasing Dept., 725 Stop 27 ½, Hato Rey, PR 00917 **E-mail:** ortiz-belmonte@adelphia.com

O'RYAN, CECILIA
Industry: Healthcare **Born:** December 25, 1946, Oruro, Bolivia **Univ./degree:** B.S., Business Administration, University of Maryland, 1979 **Current organization:** The Bonati Institute **Title:** Administrator **Type of organization:** Ambulatory surgical center **Major product:** Orthopaedics **Area of distribution:** International **Area of Practice:** Business **Hob./spts.:** Horses, opera **SIC code:** 80 **Address:** The Bonati Institute, 7315 Hudson Ave., Hudson, FL 34667 **E-mail:** admin@bonati.net

ORY-GIBSON, CHRISTINA M.
Industry: Medical **Born:** August 13, 1973, Pascagoula, Mississippi **Univ./degree:** B.S., Radiologic Technology, University of Louisiana at Monroe, 2000 **Current organization:** University of Mississippi Medical Center **Title:** Radiology Information Systems Manager **Type of organization:** Hospital **Major product:** Medical services **Area of distribution:** Mississippi **Area of Practice:** Radiological technology **Affiliations:** American Society of Radiologic Technologists **Hob./spts.:** Travel **SIC code:** 80 **Address:** University of Mississippi Medical Center, 2500 N. State St., Jackson, MS 39216 **E-mail:** cgibson@radiology.umsmed.edu

OSBORNE, JULIANNE
Industry: Healthcare **Univ./degree:** A.S., Radiologic Technology, Tacoma University, Washington **Current organization:** Alaska Open Imaging **Title:** RT(R)(M)(CT) **Type of organization:** Medical clinic **Major product:** Radiology **Area of distribution:** Alaska **Area of Practice:** Imaging Technologist **Affiliations:** A.R.R.T.; A.S.R.T. **Hob./spts.:** Family **SIC code:** 80 **Address:** Alaska Open Imaging, 1751 E. Gardner Way, Wasilla, AK 99654 **E-mail:** pub_jules@alaskaopen.com

OSHINSKY, ROB JOAN
Industry: Healthcare **Univ./degree:** Ph.D., Biochemistry, 1982; M.D., 1988, University of Texas **Current organization:** R. Joan Oshinsky, M.D., Ph.D., P.A. **Title:** M.D., Ph.D. **Type of organization:** Private practice **Major product:** Patient care **Area of distribution:** Lanham, Maryland **Area of Practice:** Neurophysiology, multiple sclerosis **Affiliations:** American Neurological Association; Society for Neuroscience **SIC code:** 80 **Address:** R. Joan Oshinsky, M.D., Ph.D., P.A., 9801Greenbelt Rd., Suite 101, Lanham, MD 20706 **E-mail:** oshinsky2, comcast.com

OSHO, JOSEPH A.
Industry: Healthcare **Born:** May 26, 1949, Frun-akoko, Western State, Nigeria **Univ./degree:** M.D., SUNY Downstate Medical Center, 1985 **Current organization:** Joseph A. Osho, M.D., P.C. **Title:** Vice Chairman, Dept. of Ob/Gyn, Brookdale Hospital Medical Center; Assistant Director of Residency Program, Brookdale Hospital Medical Center **Type of organization:** Hospital **Major product:** Patient care **Area of distribution:** International **Area of Practice:** Ob/Gyn **Honors/awards:** Recognition Residency Award **Affiliations:** A.C.O.G.; B.G.S.; N.Y.G.S. **Hob./spts.:** Soccer **SIC code:** 80 **Address:** Joseph A. Osho, M.D., P.C., 9221 Ave. L, Brooklyn, NY 11236

OSMANOVIC, SMAJO
Industry: Healthcare **Born:** June 7, 1954, Belgrade **Univ./degree:** M.D., Belgrade School of Medicine, 1978; Ph.D., Belgrade University, 1984 **Current organization:** Arlington Eye Physicians **Title:** M.D., Ph.D. **Type of organization:** Private practice **Major product:** Eye care **Area of distribution:** Illinois **Area of Practice:** Ophthalmology **Honors/awards:** Fulbright Fellow **Published works:** 40 articles, 2 chapters **Affiliations:** American Association of Ophthalmology; Society of Neuro Science **Hob./spts.:** Running, basketball **SIC code:** 80 **Address:** Arlington Eye Physicians, 1614 W. Central Rd., Arlington Heights, IL 60095 **E-mail:** osmanovic@attbi.com

OSSORIO, JULIO M.
Industry: Healthcare **Born:** September 9, 1948, San Juan, Puerto Rico **Univ./degree:** B.S., 1968; M.D., 1972, University of Puerto Rico **Current organization:** Dahlonega Urology Center **Title:** M.D. **Type of organization:** Private practice **Major product:** Urology **Area of distribution:** National **Area of Practice:** Incontinence, genitourinary conditions **Hob./spts.:** Travel, theatre, baseball **SIC code:** 80 **Address:** Dahlonega Urology Center, 108 Mountain Dr., Suite B, Dahlonega, GA 30533 **E-mail:** Dahlonegaurology@alltel.net

OSUNKWO, IFEYINWA (IFY)
Industry: Healthcare **Born:** June 5, 1972, New York, New York **Univ./degree:** M.D., University of Nigeria, 1993 **Current organization:** Aflac Cancer Center **Title:** M.D./Clinical Operations Director **Type of organization:** Medical Center **Major product:** Patient care **Area of distribution:** International **Area of Practice:** Hematology, oncology **Affiliations:** American Society of Hematology; American Society of Pediatric Hematology/Oncology **Hob./spts.:** Choir singing **SIC code:** 80 **Address:** Aflac Cancer Center, 140 Clifton Rd., Atlanta, GA 30322 **E-mail:** ify.osunkwo@choa.org

OTSUKA, COLLEEN G.
Industry: Healthcare **Born:** Julesburg, Colorado **Current organization:** Denver N.M.R. Inc. **Title:** Radiologic Technologist **Type of organization:** Medical imaging clinic **Major product:** MRI and CT scanning **Area of distribution:** Lakewood, Colorado **Area of Practice:** Certified Radiologic Technologist, Certified, MRI **Affiliations:** A.S.R.T.; A.R.R.T.; Rocky Mountain Imaging Society; Society for Cardiovascular Magnetic Resonance **Hob./spts.:** Stained glass, golf, softball **SIC code:** 80 **Address:** Denver N.M.R. Inc., 990 Garrison St., Lakewood, CO 80215-5867 **E-mail:** cotsuka2@worldnet.att.net

OWENS, TWYMAN R.
Industry: Medical **Univ./degree:** M.D., Michigan State University School of Medicine, 1998 **Current organization:** Martin Luther King/Charles R. Drew Medical Center **Title:** M.D. **Type of organization:** University hospital **Major product:** Patient care, medical education **Area of distribution:** Los Angeles, California **Area of Practice:** Pediatric cardiology, lecturing **Published works:** Books, articles **Hob./spts.:** Sports **SIC code:** 80 **Address:** Martin Luther King/Charles R. Drew Medical Center, 12021 S. Wilmington Ave., Room 5016, Los Angeles, CA 90059 **E-mail:** t.owens@dhs.co.la.ca.us

OWUSU, STEPHEN E.
Industry: Healthcare **Born:** December 18, 1954, Kumasi, Ghana **Univ./degree:** D.P.M., Temple University School of Medicine, Philadelphia, Pennsylvania, 1992 **Current organization:** Mount Zion Podiatry, P.C. **Title:** D.P.M., M.A. **Type of organization:** Private practice **Major product:** Patient care **Area of distribution:** New York **Area of Practice:** Podiatry **Published works:** 2 papers **Affiliations:** A.P.M.A.; N.Y.S.P.M.A. **Hob./spts.:** Soccer, tennis, ping pong **SIC code:** 80 **Address:** Mount Zion Podiatry, P.C., 106 Pennsylvania Ave., Brooklyn, NY 11207

PADRO-YAMET, RAFAEL
Industry: Healthcare **Born:** October 23, 1923, Puerto Rico **Univ./degree:** M.D., University of Salamanca, Spain, 1956 **Current organization:** Rafael Padro-Yumet, M.D. **Title:** Psychiatrist, Psychoanalyst **Type of organization:** Private practice **Major product:** Mental healthcare **Area of distribution:** Puerto Rico **Area of Practice:** Psychiatry, psychoanalysis, teaching **Published works:** Multiple publications **Affiliations:** Research Fellowship, Rockefeller Foundation; President, Puerto Rico Education Council; Medical Director, PAA Psychiatric Hospital; Teaching, Temple University and University of Puerto Rico; American Psychoanalytic Association; International Psychoanalytic Association **SIC code:** 80 **Address:** Rafael Padro-Yumet, M.D., 450 Ponce de Leon, Condominium Torre de la Reina, Suite 201, San Juan, PR 00901 **E-mail:** rafaelpadroyumetmd@prtc.com

PADUA, ANTONIO M.
Industry: Healthcare **Born:** April 15, 1961, Puerto Rico **Univ./degree:** M.D., University of Puerto Rico, 1986 **Current organization:** Centro Meumologico del Oeste **Title:** M.D. **Type of organization:** Healthcare **Major product:** Patient care **Area of distribution:** Mayagucz, Puerto Rico **Area of Practice:** Pulmonary disease, sleep/internal medicine **Affiliations:** American Academy of Sleep Medicine; American Thoracic Society **Hob./spts.:** Boating **SIC code:** 80 **Address:** Centro Meumologico del Oeste, La Palma 1C, Mayaguez, PR 00680

PADUA, HELVETIA ROSARIO
Industry: Healthcare **Born:** October 23, 1963, Ponce, Puerto Rico **Univ./degree:** B.S., Catholic University of Puerto Rico, 1984; M.D., San Juan Medical School, 1987; Residency Cardiovascular Program, Damas and San Bucas Hospital, 1992-95 **Current organization:** La Casa del Médico **Title:** M.D./President **Type of organization:** Private practice **Major product:** Patient care **Area of distribution:** Puerto Rico **Area of Practice:** Cardiology **Published works:** Multiple presentations **Affiliations:** American College of Cardiology.; Asociación de Cardiólogos de Puerto Rico; Colegio de Médicos-Cirujanos de Puerto Rico; President, Academia Médica del Sur; Asociación Médico de Puerto Rico **Hob./spts.:** Water skiing, the beach **SIC code:** 80 **Address:** Helvetia Rosario Padua, M.D., Urb. Alhambra, Obispado 19, Ponce, PR 00731

PAGEL, PAUL S.
Industry: Medical **Born:** December 6, 1957, Madison, Wisconsin **Univ./degree:** B.S., Chemistry & Math, Carroll College, Waukesha, Wisconsin, 1979; M.D., 1986; Ph.D., 1994, Medical College of Wisconsin **Current organization:** Medical College of Wisconsin **Title:** Professor and Director of Cardiac Anesthesiology **Type of organization:** Medical school **Major product:** Medical education, patient care, research **Area of distribution:** National **Area of Practice:** Cardiovascular anesthesiology, cardiovascular pharmacology **Published works:** 150 reference journal and book chapters, 100 conference papers **Affiliations:** F.A.C.C.; F.A.C.C.P.; F.A.H.A. **Hob./spts.:** Family, physical fitness **SIC code:** 80 **Address:** Medical College of Wisconsin, 8701 Watertown Plank Rd., MEB-M4280, Milwaukee, WI 53226 **E-mail:** pspagel@mcw.edu

PAIMANY, BEHZAD
Industry: Healthcare **Born:** February 26, 1967, Tehran, Iran **Univ./degree:** M.D., State University of New York at Brooklyn, 1994 **Current organization:** Long Island Heart Associates **Title:** M.D. **Type of organization:** Private cardiology group **Major product:** Patient care **Area of Practice:** Cardiology, non-invasive stress testing, stress echo, transesophageal echo **Published works:** "Clinical Application of High Sensitive-(CRP) C-reactive Protein", Cardiology Review, 2/02; "Clinical Features of Ventricular Tachycardia", Cardiology Review, 08/02; "3D-Echocardiography Volume Assessment", American Society of Echo, 12/02 **Affiliations:** American College of Physicians; American Medical Association; American College of Cardiology **Hob./spts.:** Swimming, jogging **SIC code:** 80 **Address:** Long Island Heart Associates, 200 Old Country Rd., Suite 278, Mineola, NY 11501 **Phone:** (516)877-0977 **Fax:** (516)294-6861

PALADINO, GABRIELLE M.
Industry: Healthcare **Univ./degree:** M.D., Ross University, 1991; Residency, University of California, San Francisco, 1996 **Current organization:** Atascadero State Hospital **Title:** M.D. **Type of organization:** Hospital **Major product:** Patient care **Area of distribution:** Atascadero, California **Area of Practice:** Forensic psychiatry **Affiliations:** A.M.A.; A.A.P.L.; American Psychiatric Association **SIC code:** 80 **Address:** Atascadero State Hospital, P.O. Box 7001, Atascadero, CA 93423 **E-mail:** gabriellep@charter.net

PALAFOX, BRIAN A.
Industry: Healthcare **Born:** February 9, 1951, Honolulu, Hawaii **Univ./degree:** B.S., Biology, University of Hawaii, 1972; M.D., University of California School of Medicine at Irvine, 1975 **Current organization:** Society of Thoracic Surgeons **Title:** M.D., F.A.C.S. **Type of organization:** Group practice **Major product:** Thoracic surgery - children and adults **Area of distribution:** California **Area of Practice:** Heart, lung, esophageal and endocrine surgery **Published works:** 12 articles **Affiliations:** F.I.C.S.; F.A.C.S. **SIC code:** 80 **Address:** Orange County Thoracic & Cardiovascular Surgeons, 1310 W. Stewart Dr., #503, Orange, CA 92868

PALMER, DENNIS D.
Industry: Healthcare **Born:** November 27, 1945, Grinnell, Iowa **Univ./degree:** B.S., Zoology, Iowa State University, 1965; M.S., Biology, Truman State University, 1971; D.O., Kirksville College of Osteopathic Medicine, 1975 **Current organization:** Mercer Health Center S.C. **Title:** D.O. **Type of organization:** Family practice medicine **Major product:** Patient care **Area of distribution:** Aledo, Illinois **Area of Practice:** Family medicine, geriatrics, surgery, public speaking, consulting **Honors/awards:** Rival Physician of Excellence Award, 2006 **Affiliations:** Former President, Illinois Association of Osteopathic Physicians & Surgeons; Former President, Civic Center Authority; National Health Service Corps **Hob./spts.:** Horses, dogs, road races, triathlons **SIC code:** 80 **Address:** Mercer Health Center S.C., 409 N.W. Fourth St., Aledo, IL 61231 **E-mail:** ddpalmerdo@hotmail.com

PALMER, JOEL M.
Industry: Healthcare **Born:** June 14, 1944, New York, New York **Univ./degree:** B.S., Chemistry, New York University, 1966; M.D., New York University School of Medicine, 1970; Fellowship, Gynecologic Oncology, Metropolitan Hospital **Current organization:** Joel M. Palmer, M.D., P.A./Holy Cross Hospital **Title:** Doctor/Director Ob/Gyn Clinic **Type of organization:** Private practice/hospital **Major product:** Patient care **Area of distribution:** National **Area of Practice:** Gynecologic oncology, laparoscopy, hormone replacement; Ob/Gyn (Board Certified) **Affiliations:** Med Chi Society; Montgomery County Medical Society **Hob./spts.:** Golf, football, chalk artist **SIC code:** 80 **Address:** Joel M. Palmer, M.D., P.A./Holy Cross Hospital, P.O. Box 59622, Potomac, MD 20859-5303 **E-mail:** oncdr@msn.com

PALUMBO, DONNA M.
Industry: Healthcare **Born:** December 26, 1964, Camden, New Jersey **Current organization:** Underwood Hospital **Title:** Angiographer **Type of organization:** Hospital **Major product:** Patient care **Area of distribution:** New Jersey **Area of Practice:** Cardiac cath/angio lab **Affiliations:** A.S.R.T.; A.R.R.T. **Hob./spts.:** Travel, the beach, walking, swimming **SIC code:** 80 **Address:** 700 Erial Rd., Blackwood, NJ 08012 **E-mail:** donnap1264@yahoo.com

PAN, CALVIN Q.
Industry: Healthcare, Medical Research **Born:** March 5, 1963, China **Univ./degree:** M.D., Guangzhou Medical College, China, 1985 **Current organization:** Pan Medicine P.C. **Title:** President, Director of Medical Research **Type of organization:** Digestive disease center/consulting **Major product:** Patient care/clinical research/endoscopy and laser treatment **Area of distribution:** Queens, Long Island, New York City **Area of Practice:** Gastroenterology, hepatology, endoscopy intervention and laser therapy **Published works:** Author, medical scientific research, articles published at the American Journal of Physiology, 1993; Author, medical scientific research, article published at Research Communication of Substance Abuse, 1993; Author, medical scientific research, article published at P.S.E.B.M., 1994; Author, medical scientific research, articles published at Nephron, 1995; Author, medical scientific research, articles published at Nephron, 1995; Author, medical scientific research, articles published at Gastroenterology, 1995; Author, medical scientific research, articles published at Nephron, 1996 **Affiliations:** American College of Physicians; American College of Gastroenterology **Hob./spts.:** Tennis, music, country walk, ballroom dance **SIC code:** 80 **Address:** Pan Medicine P.C., 147-48 Roosevelt Ave., L4, Flushing, NY 11354 **E-mail:** cpan11355@yahoo.com

PAN, YI
Industry: Medical **Born:** October 4, 1955, Beijing, China **Univ./degree:** M.D., Beijing, China, 1982; Ph.D., Howard University, 1992 **Current organization:** St. Louis University Hospital **Title:** M.D./Assistant Professor **Type of organization:** University hospital **Major product:** Neurology **Area of distribution:** St. Louis, Missouri **Area of Practice:** Cerebral vascular disease, clinical neurophysiology, neuro-rehabilitation **Published works:** Contributed Articles to: Journal of Neurological Science and Magnetic Resonance Imaging Journal **Affiliations:** American Academy of Neurology; Society of Neuroscience; American Medical Association **Hob./spts.:** Skiing, swimming **SIC code:** 80 **Address:** St. Louis University Hospital, Dept. of Neurology, 3635 Vista Ave., St. Louis, MO 63110 **E-mail:** pany@slu.edu

PANCHAL, HEMANT K.
Industry: Healthcare **Born:** June 19, Ahmedabad, India **Univ./degree:** M.D., University of Connecticut School of Medicine, Farmington, 1991 **Current organization:** Office of Hemant K. Panchal, M.D. **Title:** M.D. **Type of organization:** Private practice **Major product:** Patient care **Area of distribution:** Connecticut **Area of Practice:** Pediatrics **Affiliations:** Connecticut State Medical Society **Hob./spts.:** Tennis **SIC code:** 80 **Address:** Office of Hemant K. Panchal, M.D., 170 Hazard Ave., Enfield, CT 06082 **E-mail:** hpanchalmd@aol.com

PANDYA, HASIT P.
Industry: Healthcare **Born:** February 16, 1965, Mbeya, Tanzania, Africa **Univ./degree:** M.B.B.S., 1987; M.D., 1992 B.J. Medical College, India **Current organization:** Brookdale Hospital **Title:** M.D. **Type of organization:** Hospital **Major product:**

Patient care, research **Area of distribution:** International **Affiliations:** A.C.P.; A.S.I.M.; Member, Royal College of Physicians **Hob./spts.:** Spending time with family, photography, sight seeing, travel **SIC code:** 80 **Address:** 247-64B 77th Crescent, Bellerose, NY 11426 **E-mail:** arjunhasit@hotmail.com

PANDYA, PARAG A.
Industry: Healthcare **Born:** July 22, 1966, Ahmedabad, India **Univ./degree:** M.B.B.S., 1989; M.S., 1993, Ophthalmic Surgery, B.J. Medical College, Gujarat University, India **Current organization:** Danville Regional Medical Center **Title:** Staff Anesthesiologist **Type of organization:** Hospital **Major product:** Patient care **Area of distribution:** Virginia **Area of Practice:** Pain management, Anesthesia **Affiliations:** A.S.A.; V.S.A.; I.A.R.S.; A.S.R.A. **Hob./spts.:** Tennis, golf, basketball, travel and entertainment **SIC code:** 80 **Address:** Danville Regional Medical Center, 1114 Main St., Danville, VA 24541 **E-mail:** pandyaps@prodigy.net

PANETTA, DEBORAH L.
Industry: Healthcare **Born:** June 28, 1959, Detroit, Michigan **Univ./degree:** B.S., Radiation Therapy Technology, Wayne State University, 1982 **Current organization:** Vassar Brothers Medical Center **Title:** President, Administrative Director **Type of organization:** Hospital **Major product:** Patient care **Area of distribution:** Poughkeepsie, New York **Area of Practice:** Radiation therapy **Affiliations:** A.S.R.T. **Hob./spts.:** Horses, camping **SIC code:** 80 **Address:** Vassar Brothers Medical Center, 45 Reade Place, Poughkeepsie, NY 12601

PANICCO, RICHARD J.
Industry: Healthcare **Born:** February 2, 1947, Pittsburgh, Pennsylvania **Univ./degree:** D.O., Philadelphia College of Osteopathic Medicine **Current organization:** Southwest Gastroenterology Associates **Title:** D.O. **Type of organization:** Medical practice **Major product:** Patient care **Area of distribution:** McMurray, Pennsylvania **Area of Practice:** Gastroenterology **Affiliations:** F.A.C.G.; A.S.G.E.; A.G.A.; A.C.P.; A.M.A. **Hob./spts.:** Football, American Indian art **SIC code:** 80 **Address:** Southwest Gastroenterology Associates, 3515 Washington Rd., McMurray, PA 15317

PANOZZO, ALBERT
Industry: Medical **Univ./degree:** M.D., University of Wales, Australia **Current organization:** NYU Medical Center **Title:** M.D. **Type of organization:** University hospital **Major product:** Medical services **Area of distribution:** New York **Area of Practice:** Orthopedics, upper limb surgery, microsurgery **Affiliations:** F.R.A.C.S. **SIC code:** 80 **Address:** 567 Fort Washington Ave., New York, NY 10033 **E-mail:** albertpanozzo@yahoo.com

PARAGAS, MIGUELA L.
Industry: Healthcare **Born:** September 29, 1950, Manila, Philippines **Univ./degree:** M.D., Far Eastern University, Manila, Philippines, 1976; M.P.H., Tulane University, 1986 **Current organization:** Arlington Pediatrics Inc. **Title:** M.D., M.P.H. **Type of organization:** Solo medical practice **Major product:** Pediatric medicine **Area of distribution:** New Jersey **Area of Practice:** Pediatrics **Affiliations:** F.A.A.P.; New Jersey Medical Society **Hob./spts.:** Travel **SIC code:** 80 **Address:** Arlington Pediatrics Inc., 312 Belleville Pike, 3C, North Arlington, NJ 07031 **E-mail:** mel.paragas@prodigy.net

PARAYATH, PADMAJA
Industry: Healthcare **Born:** March 18, 1955, Kerala, India **Univ./degree:** M.D., Medical College, University of Kerala, Trivandrum, India, 1979 **Current organization:** Padmaja Parayath, M.D./Parayath Medical Associates **Title:** M.D. **Type of organization:** Private practice **Major product:** Patient care **Area of distribution:** Massachusetts **Area of Practice:** Family practice, internal medicine **Hob./spts.:** Travel, reading **SIC code:** 80 **Address:** 150 York St., Stoughton, MA 02072 **E-mail:** kbg@info-tek.com

PARDALOS, JOHN ARRIS
Industry: Healthcare **Born:** August 12, 1964, Jefferson City, Missouri **Univ./degree:** M.D., University of Missouri, 1990 **Current organization:** University Hospital & Clinics **Title:** M.D. **Type of organization:** Hospital **Major product:** Patient care **Area of distribution:** Columbia, South Carolina **Area of Practice:** Neonatology **Honors/awards:** Outstanding Physician **Affiliations:** American Academy of Pediatrics **SIC code:** 80 **Address:** University Hospital & Clinics, 1 Hospital Dr., Columbia, MO 65212 **E-mail:** pardalosj@health.missouri.edu

PARENS, HENRI
Industry: Medicine **Born:** December 18, 1928, Lodz, Poland **Univ./degree:** M.D., Tulane University **Current organization:** Jefferson Medical College & Psychoanalytic Center of Philadelphia **Title:** Psychiatrist - Psychoanalyst **Type of organization:** Medical college, psychoanalytical institute **Major product:** Patient care, medical education, research **Area of distribution:** Bala Cynwyd, Pennsylvania **Area of Practice:** Psychiatry - Psychoanalysis, adult and child **Honors/awards:** 16 incl. Life Time Achievement Awards (1999, 2004, 2005) **Published works:** 150+ publications, 14 books (7 books authored) **Affiliations:** A.P.A.; A.P.A.A.; I.P.A.A.; A.C.A.P.; C.A.P. **Hob./spts.:** Musician **SIC code:** 80 **Address:** Jefferson Medical College & Psychoanalytic, Center of Philadelphia, 111 Presidential Blvd., Suite 133, Bala Cynwyd, PA 19004 **E-mail:** hparens@verizon.net

PARK, SUNMIN
Industry: Healthcare **Born:** Seoul, South Korea **Univ./degree:** M.D., Medical College of Wisconsin, 1991 **Current organization:** Sunmin Park M.D., Eye Physician & Surgeon **Title:** M.D. **Type of organization:** Private practice **Major product:** Patient care **Area of distribution:** Torrance, California **Area of Practice:** Cornea and refractive surgery **Affiliations:** A.A.O.; A.B.O.; A.M.A.; California Medical Association **Hob./spts.:** Kayaking **SIC code:** 80 **Address:** Sunmin Park M.D., Eye Physician & Surgeon, 3440 Lomita Blvd, #242, Torrance, CA 90505

PARKER, LYNN P.
Industry: Medical **Univ./degree:** M.D., University of Missouri, 1992; Residency, University of Oklahoma, 1997 **Current organization:** University of Louisville **Title:** Director of Gynecologic Oncology **Type of organization:** University, hospital **Major product:** Patient care, medical education **Area of distribution:** National **Area of Practice:** Gynecologic oncology, research **Affiliations:** Gynecologic Oncology Group; Society of Gynecologic Oncologists **Hob./spts.:** Riding horseback **SIC code:** 80 **Address:** University of Louisville, 529 S. Jackson St., Louisville, KY 40202 **E-mail:** lppark02@gwise.louisville.edu

PASPULATI, RAJ MOHAN
Industry: Medical **Born:** March 8, 1960, India **Univ./degree:** M.D., Osmania Medical College, India, 1983 **Current organization:** University Hospitals of Cleveland **Title:** M.D. **Type of organization:** University hospital **Major product:** Medical services **Area of distribution:** Ohio **Area of Practice:** Radiology **Published works:** Several articles **Affiliations:** Member, A.I.U.M.; Member, A.R.R.S.; Member, I.S.M.R.M.; Radiological Society of North America; Canadian Association of Radiologists **Hob./spts.:** Tennis, reading **SIC code:** 80 **Address:** University Hospitals of Cleveland, Radiology Dept., 11100 Euclid Ave., Cleveland, OH 44106 **E-mail:** prajmohan@hotmail.com

PASUPULETI, DEVAKINANDA V.
Industry: Medical **Born:** August 27, 1953, India **Univ./degree:** M.D., Andhra University, India, 1976 **Current organization:** Michigan State University; Hurley Medical Center; McLaren Hospital; Consultant with Genesee Health Systems **Title:** Director of Neurology **Type of organization:** Hospital/university **Major product:** Patient care/education **Area of distribution:** Michigan **Area of Practice:** Electromyography, neurology **Published works:** Book, "Happiness for Everyone/Finding Everlasting Contentment Through the Five Golden Rules", 1st Books, 2004, ISBN: 1-4140-1263-2; Articles **Affiliations:** American Medical Association; American Neurological Association; Genessee County Medical Society; Michigan State Medical Society; Clinical Professor at Michigan State University **Hob./spts.:** Swimming, tennis, reading, family **SIC code:** 80 **Address:** 2370 S. Linden Rd., Flint, MI 48532 **E-mail:** dpasupu1@hurley.mc.com

PATEL, KANDARP B.
Industry: Healthcare **Univ./degree:** M.B.B.S., Doctoral Training, Baroda Medical College, Maharaja Sayajirao University of Baroda **Current organization:** Care South **Title:** M.D. **Type of organization:** Hospital **Major product:** Patient care/non-invasive cardiology services **Area of distribution:** National **Area of Practice:** Cardiology **Affiliations:** F.A.C.C.; A.M.A.; A.A.C.I.O.; A.H.A.; I.M.C.; A.C.H.P.; T.M.A.; T.C.A.C.M.; V.B.W.G **SIC code:** 80 **Address:** Care South, 1203 Vann Dr., Jackson, TN 38305 **E-mail:** kbpatel@pol.net **Web address:** www.mydoctor.com\kanpatel

PATEL, SARITA
Industry: Healthcare **Born:** September 13, 1962, India **Univ./degree:** M.D., India, 1989 **Current organization:** Bronx Lebanon Hospital Center **Title:** M.D. **Type of organization:** Hospital **Major product:** Patient care **Area of distribution:** Bronx, New York **Area of Practice:** Internal medicine **Affiliations:** A.M.A.; A.C.P.; Albert Einstein College of Medicine **Hob./spts.:** Teaching yoga and meditation **SIC code:** 80 **Address:** Bronx Lebanon Hospital Center, General Medicine Clinic, 1265 Franklin Ave., Bronx, NY 10456 **E-mail:** omguru13@aol.com

PATTERSON, JAMES W.
Industry: Medical **Born:** December 29, 1946, Tacoma Park, Washington **Univ./degree:** M.D., Virginia Commonwealth University, 1972 **Current organization:** University of Virginia Health System **Title:** M.D., Professor of Pathology **Type of organization:** University medical center **Major product:** Patient care, medical education **Area of distribution:** National **Area of Practice:** Dermatopathology **Affiliations:** A.A.D.; A.C.P. **Hob./spts.:** Baseball, golf **SIC code:** 80 **Address:** University of Virginia Health System, , 1215 Lee St., Room 3018, Charlottesville, VA 22908 **E-mail:** jwp9e@virginia.edu

PATTERSON, STEPHEN G.
Industry: Healthcare **Born:** March 20, 1966, Fort Lauderdale, Florida **Univ./degree:** B.S., University of Notre Dame, 1988; M.D., University of South Florida, 1992 **Current organization:** H. Lee Moffitt Cancer Center **Title:** M.D. **Type of organization:** Academic practice **Major product:** Patient care **Area of distribution:** Tampa, Florida **Area of Practice:** Medical oncology **Published works:** Several abstracts and publications including: Patterson, S., Fishman, M., Ewbank, D., DeFelice, J., Rago, R. (deceased). Thalidomide plus daily oral dexamethasone for mestatic hormone refractory prostate cancer (HRPC) in patients previously treated with cytotoxic chemotherapy Submitted ASCO 2003; Patterson, S., Baldacci, L., The Book of Job: A 2,500 year old Current Guide to the practice of Oncology; The Nexus of Medicine and Spirituality. Journal of Cancer Education, Vol. 17, No. 4, Pgs. 237-241, Winter 2002; Patterson, S.G., Baldacci, L.B., Pow-Sang, J.M., Controversies Surrounding Androgen Deprivation for Prostate Cancer. Cancer Control, Vol. 9, No. 4, July/August, Pgs. 315-325, 2002; Greene, G., Patterson, S.G., Warner, E., Ingestion of Angel's Trumpet: An increasingly common source of toxicity. Southern Medical Journal, Volume 89, Number 4, pgs. 365-369, 1996; Helfet, D.L., Koval, K.J., Hissa, E.A., Patterson, S.G., DiPasquale, T., Sanders, R., Intraoperative somatosensory evoked potential monitoring during acute pelvic fracture surgery; Journal of Orthopedic Trauma, Volume 9, Number 1, Pgs. 28-34, 1993 **Hob./spts.:** Golf, tennis, running, swimming **SIC code:** 80 **Address:** H. Lee Moffitt Cancer Center, GU-PROG, 12902 Magnolia Dr., Tampa, FL 33612 **E-mail:** sgpattsn@tampabay.rr.com

PATTON, KATHY A.
Industry: Healthcare **Born:** December 19, 1955, Bellflower, California **Univ./degree:** A.S.N., Bakersfield College, 1977; B.S.N., University of Washington, 1995; M.S.N., University of Phoenix, 2002 **Current organization:** Olympic Medical Center **Title:** Director of Critical Care Unit **Type of organization:** Hospital **Major product:** Patient care **Area of distribution:** Washington **Area of Practice:** Critical care nursing, management **Honors/awards:** Sigma Theta Tau **Affiliations:** A.A.C.N. **Hob./spts.:** Biking, gardening, hiking **SIC code:** 80 **Address:** Olympic Medical Center, 939 Caroline St., Port Angeles, WA 98362 **E-mail:** kpatton@olympicmedical.org

PEABODY, SYLVIA R.
Industry: Healthcare **Born:** June 12, 1919, Chester, Vermont **Univ./degree:** B.S.N., Public Health Nursing, Columbia University, 1946; M.S.N., Public Health Administration, Simmons College, 1954 **Current organization:** Visiting nurse service of Newport **Title:** R.N. (Retired) **Type of organization:** Home care **Major product:** Nursing, home care services **Area of distribution:** Massachusetts **Area of Practice:** Public health nursing, pediatrics **Published works:** Articles **Affiliations:** A.P.H.A.; National League for Nursing **Hob./spts.:** Painting, church activities **SIC code:** 80 **Address:** 50 Broadlawn Park, Apt. 111, Chestnut Hill, MA 02467-3524 **E-mail:** sylviarp@att.net

PEARSON, CRAIG B.
Industry: Healthcare **Born:** February 3, 1943, Philadelphia, Pennsylvania **Univ./degree:** B.S., Biochemistry, Albright College, Pennsylvania, 1964; M.D., Temple University School of Medicine, Pennsylvania, 1968 **Current organization:** M.D. (Retired) **Title:** Medical Doctor/Philanthropist/Professional Sports Medical Team M.D. **Type of organization:** Consulting, public speaking practice **Major product:** Consulting and public speaking **Area of distribution:** International **Area of Practice:** Sports medicine, involved in airlifts in Ethiopia, Zaire and Bosnia; Board Certified, Family Medicine, National Speaker on Serbia and Bosnia issues **Honors/awards:** Associate Member, Major League Baseball Alumni; Testimonial Luncheon, Prehab; Distinguished Alumni Award, Albright College, Pennsylvania; Honored by St. Sava Church, AZ for donating $400,000 in medical supplies to the Serbs in Bosnia; Independent discoverer of the "Stunned Look" which telegraphs a brain tumor **Affiliations:** Fellow, American Academy of Family Practice; Founding Family, Temple Emanuel; Past Chairman of the Board, Temple Beth Shalom; Benefactor, Sunshine Acres Orphanage; Benefactor, Past Doctor, Prehab; Team Physician for seven major league baseball teams; Holocaust Center; Museum of Tolerance, Los Angeles; Liaison Physician, Philadelphia Eagles (NFL); Former Liaison Physician, Arizona **Hob./spts.:** Family, Philanthropist, coaching basketball, recruiting basketball players, political buttons **SIC code:** 80 **Address:** 945 North Pasadena, #66, Mesa, AL 85201 **E-mail:** pearsonsplace@earthlink.net

PEASE, FRANCIS R.
Industry: Healthcare **Born:** April 27, 1949, Camden, New Jersey **Univ./degree:** Attended Camden Community College, Major in Administration of Justice **Current organization:** Graduate Hospital **Title:** Engineering Supervisor **Type of organization:** Hospital **Major product:** Patient care **Area of distribution:** Pennsylvania **Area of Practice:** Engineering maintenance **Affiliations:** N.F.P.A., Healthcare Facility Manager, Association of Delaware Valley; Hospital Fire Marshall Association; American Legion Post 281 **Hob./spts.:** Golf, time with family **SIC code:** 80 **Address:** Graduate Hospital, 1800 Lombard St., Philadelphia, PA 19146 **E-mail:** francis.pease@tenethealth.com

PECHET, TAINE T.
Industry: Medical **Born:** November 24, 1965, Boston, Massachusetts **Univ./degree:** M.D., Harvard University, 1992 **Current organization:** Jefferson Medical College **Title:** Assistant Professor of Surgery **Type of organization:** Medical college **Major product:** Medical education/healthcare **Area of distribution:** Pennsylvania **Area of Practice:** Thoracic surgery **Published works:** Articles **Affiliations:** A.C.C.P.; A.C.S.; I.S.H.L.T.; S.T.S. **Hob./spts.:** Family, sailing **SIC code:** 80 **Address:** Jefferson Medical College, Div. of Thoracic Surgery, 1025 Walnut St., Suite 605, Philadelphia, PA 19107

PEKAROVICS, SUSAN
Industry: Healthcare **Born:** February 16, 1964, Muncach, Ukraine **Univ./degree:** M.D., Semmelweis Medical University, Budapest,1988; Residency, Internal Medicine, Yale University, 1995; Clinical & Research Fellowship, Endocrinology and Metabolism, UCLA, 1996-1999 **Current organization:** Susan Pekarovics, M.D. **Title:** Medical Doctor **Type of organization:** Private practice **Major product:** Patient care **Area of distribution:** Los Angeles, California **Area of Practice:** Internal medicine, endocrinology, concentration on adult medicine and obesity **Affiliations:** American Diabetes Association; The Endocrine Society **Hob./spts.:** Dance, music, The Arts **SIC code:** 80 **Address:** 6360 Wilshire Blvd., Suite 502, Los Angeles, CA 90048 **E-mail:** dr.susan@verizon.net

PEÑA, RAÚL A.
Industry: Healthcare **Born:** February 14, 1961, McAllen, Texas **Univ./degree:** M.D., University of Monterey, 1987 **Current organization:** Raúl A. Peña, M.D. **Title:** M.D. **Type of organization:** Private practice **Major product:** Patient care **Area of distribution:** McAllen, Texas **Area of Practice:** Optomology **Published works:** Articles in journal **Affiliations:** American Academy of Optomology **Hob./spts.:** Golf, scuba diving, tennis, baseball **SIC code:** 80 **Address:** 1910 S. First St., Suite 100, McAllen, TX 78503 **E-mail:** rospena@msn.com

PENROD, DEBRA S.
Industry: Healthcare **Born:** January 25, 1956, Salem, Indiana **Univ./degree:** M.S., Counseling, Counselor Education, International University **Current organization:** Penrod Counseling Center **Title:** Director/Owner **Type of organization:** Counseling center **Major product:** Counseling **Area of distribution:** Avon, Indiana **Area of Practice:** Mental healthcare **Affiliations:** American Counseling Association; Association for Christian Counselors **Hob./spts.:** Camping, fishing **SIC code:** 80 **Address:** Penrod Counseling Center, 192 N. State Rd., Avon, IN 46123 **E-mail:** shrinkdeb@penrod.com

PEPER, KATHRYN
Industry: Healthcare **Born:** February 1, 1956, Fort Devens, Massachusetts **Univ./degree:** M.D., New York University School of Medicine, 1984 **Current organization:** Morristown Memorial Hospital **Title:** M.D. **Type of organization:** Family health clinic **Major product:** Patient care **Area of distribution:** New Jersey **Area of Practice:** Internal medicine **Affiliations:** F.A.C.P.; A.M.A.; N.J.M.A.; S.G.I.M. **SIC code:** 80 **Address:** Morristown Memorial Hospital, 100 Madison Ave., Morristown, NJ 07960 **E-mail:** kathrynpeper@ahsys.org

PEREZ, GASTON O.
Industry: Healthcare **Born:** September 8, 1957, Havana, Cuba **Univ./degree:** M.D., Uniremhos Medical College, 1988 **Current organization:** Global Family Medicine **Title:** M.D. **Type of organization:** Medical practice **Major product:** Patient care **Area of distribution:** Bluffton, South Carolina **Area of Practice:** Family practice **Affiliations:** A.A.F.P.; A.M.A. **Hob./spts.:** Scuba diving, sailing **SIC code:** 80 **Address:** Global Family Medicine, 25C Sherington Dr., Bluffton, SC 29910 **E-mail:** gustomd@aol.com

PEREZ DIAZ, JOSE R.
Industry: Healthcare **Born:** July 10, 1956, Dominican Republic **Univ./degree:** M.D., CETEC University, Santo Domingo, Dominican Republic, 1983 **Current organization:** Salud Para Todos, Inc. **Title:** M.D., Nutritionist **Type of organization:** Medical practice **Major product:** Natural healthcare products **Area of distribution:** Corona, New York **Area of Practice:** Naturopathic Nutrition **Affiliations:** Hispanic Professional Health Association; Mason Grade 32nd Templar Knight **Hob./spts.:** Baseball **SIC code:** 80 **Address:** Salud Para Todos, Inc., 3773 103rd St., Corona, NY 11368 **E-mail:** eduardo@saludparatodos.com **Web address:** www.saludparatodos.com

PERKINS, THOMAS R.
Industry: Healthcare **Univ./degree:** D.O., Michigan State University, 1995 **Current organization:** Michigan Knee & Shoulder Institute **Title:** D.O. **Type of organization:** Private practice **Major product:** Reconstructive shoulder and knee surgery **Area of distribution:** Auburn Hills, Michigan **Area of Practice:** Orthopedic surgery, sports medicine **Affiliations:** A.O.A.; American Orthopaedic Society for Sports Medicine **Hob./spts.:** Marathon runner **SIC code:** 80 **Address:** Michigan Knee & Shoulder Institute, 3252 University Dr., Suite 140, Auburn Hills, MI 48326 **E-mail:** theperkinsklan@aol.com

PERRY, BEV JEAN
Industry: Healthcare **Current organization:** Clay County Healthcare Authority **Title:** Quality Risk Manager, Compliance Officer **Type of organization:** Hospital **Major product:** Patient care **Area of distribution:** Alabama **Area of Practice:** Risk management, quality, compliance **Hob./spts.:** Animals, crafts, quilting, sewing **SIC code:** 80 **Address:** P.O. Box 292, Wedowee, AL 36278 **E-mail:** bevjperry@yahoo.com

PETERSBURG, GREGORY W.
Industry: Healthcare **Born:** December 11, 1950, Des Moines, Iowa **Univ./degree:** D.O., Michigan State University College of Osteopathic Medicine, 1977 **Current organization:** San Juan Regional Medical Center **Title:** V.P., Medical Affairs **Type of organization:** Medical center **Major product:** Acute care **Area of distribution:** New Mexico, Colorado, Arizona, Utah **Area of Practice:** Family medicine **Affiliations:** A.C.P.E.; A.C.O.F.M.S.; A.C.M.C.M.; A.C.Q.A.U.R.P.; A.O.A.; A.A.A.A.M.; N.M.S.; N.M.S.O.M. **Hob./spts.:** Astronomy, computers, golf, fitness **SIC code:** 80 **Address:** San Juan Regional Medical Center, 801 W. Maple St., Farmington, NM 87401 **E-mail:** gpetersburg@sjrmc.net

PETERSON, CATHERINE C.
Industry: Healthcare **Born:** March 21, 1954 Birmingham, Alabama **Univ./degree:** B.S., University of Alabama, 1976 **Current organization:** Alabama Colon & Rectal Institute P.C. **Title:** Practice Director **Type of organization:** Medical/surgical office **Major product:** Patient care **Area of distribution:** National **Area of Practice:** Management, healthcare **Affiliations:** A.A.A.H.C.; M.G.M.A. **Hob./spts.:** Family, friends, golf, walking **SIC code:** 80 **Address:** Alabama Colon & Rectal Institute P.C., 1317 Fourth Ave. South, Birmingham, AL 35233 **E-mail:** acripc@aol.com

PETRASKO, MARIAN S.
Industry: Healthcare **Born:** July 6, 1958, Presov, Czechoslovakia **Univ./degree:** M.D., Charles University School of Medicine, Prague, Czechoslovakia, 1983; Ph.D., Czechoslavic Academy of Science, 1991 **Current organization:** Muskogee Heart Center **Title:** M.D. **Type of organization:** Private practice **Major product:** Cardiology **Area of distribution:** Oklahoma **Area of Practice:** Cardiology **Published works:** 30+ publications **Affiliations:** F.A.C.C.; A.M.A.; A.C.P. **Hob./spts.:** Music, skiing **SIC code:** 80 **Address:** Muskogee Heart Center, 3340 W. Okmulgee St., Muskogee, OK 74403 **E-mail:** andrea@intellex.com

PFISTER, ALFRED K.
Industry: Healthcare **Born:** September 29, 1936, Wheeling, West Virginia **Univ./degree:** M.D., George Washington University, 1962 **Current organization:** Charleston Area Medical Center **Title:** MD, FACP **Type of organization:** Hospital **Major product:** Patient care **Area of distribution:** West Virginia **Area of Practice:** Internal medicine **Affiliations:** A.C.P.-A.S.I.M.; American Society for Bone and Mineral Research **Hob./spts.:** Running **SIC code:** 80 **Address:** Charleston Area Medical Center, Integrated Health, 4604 McCorkle Ave., Charleston, WV 25304

PHAM, TIMOTHY A.
Industry: Healthcare **Univ./degree:** M.D., University of California at Irvine, 1991 **Current organization:** Timothy A. Pham, M.D. **Title:** M.D. **Type of organization:** Private practice **Major product:** Immunology **Area of distribution:** California **Area of Practice:** Immunology, allergy, asthma **Published works:** 3 publications **Affiliations:** A.M.A.; A.A.P. **Hob./spts.:** Family, golf, tennis **SIC code:** 80 **Address:** Timothy A. Pham, M.D., 65 N. Madison Ave., Suite 707, Pasadena, CA 91101

PHANSE, MOHAN S.
Industry: Healthcare **Born:** December 14, 1944, India **Univ./degree:** M.D., India, 1967 **Current organization:** Southwest Gastroenterology Associates **Title:** M.D. **Type of organization:** Medical practice **Major product:** Patient care **Area of distribution:** Pennsylvania **Area of Practice:** Gastroenterology **Published works:** Multiple publications **Affiliations:** A.M.A.; P.M.S. **Hob./spts.:** Golf **SIC code:** 80 **Address:** Southwest Gastroenterology Associates, 3515 Washington Rd., McMurray, PA 15317 **E-mail:** swgastrol.yahoo.com

PHILBRICK, DOUGLAS R.
Industry: Healthcare/education **Born:** March 17, 1942, St. Louis, Missouri **Univ./degree:** Education Specialist, University of South Dakota, 1992 **Current organization:** Desert Visions **Title:** Teacher **Type of organization:** Drug and alcohol abuse treatment center **Major product:** Substance abuse treatment **Area of distribution:** National **Area of Practice:** Education and treatment for youth **Affiliations:** L.I.U.N.A. **Hob./spts.:** Church activities **SIC code:** 80 **Address:** Desert Visions (I.H.S.), Box 458, Sacaton, AZ 85247

PHILLIPS, DEBRA M.
Industry: Healthcare **Title:** Director of Adult Health **Type of organization:** Hospital **Major product:** Patient care **Area of Practice:** Orthopedic and general post-op care **SIC code:** 80 **Address:** Wayne Memorial Hospital, P.O. Box 8001, Goldsboro, NC 27533 **E-mail:** debbie.phillips@waynehealth.org

PHILLIPS, MICHAEL M.
Industry: Healthcare **Born:** August 20, 1940, Brooklyn, New York **Univ./degree:** B.A., Biology, Brooklyn College, 1962; M.D., SUNY Buffalo, 1967 **Current organization:** Michael M. Phillips M.D., P.C. **Title:** M.D. **Type of organization:** Private medical practice **Major product:** Patient care **Area of distribution:** Washington D.C. **Area of Practice:** Gastroenterology **Honors/awards:** Who's Who in the World, since 2001; Best Doctors in the Southeast United States, since 1995; Washingtonian Magazine's "Top Doctors" issue, since 1994; New York State Regents College Scholarship, 1958 **Published works:** Editorial Consultant and contributor to Oakstone Publications (Education Reviews in Gastroenterology), since 1989 **Affiliations:** F.A.C.P.; A.G.A.; Diplomate, American Board of Internal Medicine; American Association for the Study of Liver Disease; William Earl Clark Society **Hob./spts.:** Oenology (wine tasting) **SIC code:** 80 **Address:** Michael M. Phillips M.D., P.C., 2021 K Street N.W., #412, Washington, DC 20006 **E-mail:** barmike@bellatlantic.net

PHILLIPS, STELLA PAULINE
Industry: Medical **Born:** November 12, 1963, Yonkers, New York **Univ./degree:** B.S., Iona College, 1985 **Current organization:** New York University School of Medicine **Title:** Administrator, Neurology Dept. **Type of organization:** Hospital/Medical School **Major product:** Medical services/education **Area of distribution:** New York **Area of Practice:** Accounting, management, administration **Hob./spts.:** Needlepoint, bicycle riding, income taxes **SIC code:** 80 **Address:** New Yorl University School of Medicine, 462 First Ave., New York, NY 10016 **E-mail:** Stella.Phillips@med.nyu.edu **Web address:** www.med.nyu.edu

PICHARDO-MATOS, ELSA
Industry: Healthcare **Born:** November 28, 1934, Santo Domingo, Dominican Republic **Univ./degree:** M.D., University of Santo Domingo, 1959 **Current organization:** Americare Medical Center **Title:** M.D. **Type of organization:** Clinic **Major product:** Patient care **Area of distribution:** Florida **Area of Practice:** General practitioner **Affiliations:** A.M.A.; Florida Medical Association **Hob./spts.:** Bible reading **SIC code:** 80 **Address:** Americare Medical Center, 3161 Riverland Rd., Ft. Lauderdale, FL 33312 **E-mail:** enpm@aol.com

PICKARD, GAIL
Industry: Healthcare **Current organization:** Valdez Senior Citizens Center **Title:** Program Manager **Type of organization:** Senior citizens center **Major product:** Healthcare and well-being **Area of distribution:** Alaska **Area of Practice:** Program management **Published works:** Monthly newsletter **Affiliations:** V.N.W. **SIC code:** 80 **Address:** Valdez Senior Citizens Center, 1300 E. Hanagita Place, P.O. Box 1635, Valdez, AK 99686 **E-mail:** vsccsr@alaska.net

PICONE, LUCY C.
Industry: Dentistry **Born:** September 1, 1951, New York, New York **Univ./degree:** D.D.S., University of California at Los Angeles **Current organization:** Lucy C. Picone, D.D.S., Holistic Dentistry **Title:** President/Dentist **Type of organization:** Holistic dental office **Major product:** Holistic health, cosmetics, Invisalign braces **Area of distribution:** California **Area of Practice:** Mercury removal, Invisalign braces, cosmetic dentistry; extensive training in alternative health **Honors/awards:** National Team Speed Skating, 1979 **Affiliations:** D.O.C.S.; C.D.S.; I.M.O. **Hob./spts.:** Speed skating, skiing, rollerblading **SIC code:** 80 **Address:** Lucy C. Picone, D.D.S., Holistic Dentistry, 1501 S. Catalina Ave., Redondo Beach, CA 90277 **E-mail:** picone.dds@verizon.net **Web address:** www.drpicone.com

PIERCE, MICHAEL NORMAN
Industry: Healthcare **Born:** May 1, 1955, New York, New York **Univ./degree:** M.D., University of Vermont ,1982 **Current organization:** St. Luke's Roosevelt Hospital Center **Title:** M.D. **Type of organization:** Hospital **Major product:** Patient care **Area of distribution:** New York **Area of Practice:** Internal medicine, HIV medicine **Honors/awards:** Fellow, A.C.P.-A.S.I.M. **Hob./spts.:** Music, fine arts and cuisine **SIC code:** 80 **Address:** St. Luke's Roosevelt Hospital Center, Samuel Center, 1000 Tenth Ave., Suite 2T, New York, NY 10019

PIERRE, JEANIQUE M.
Industry: Medical **Born:** July 4, 1972, New York, New York **Univ./degree:** M.S., Public Health and Hospital Relations, New York University **Current organization:** New York University Medical Center **Title:** Evening MRI Supervisor **Type of organization:** Hospital **Major product:** Patient care, medical education **Area of distribution:** New York **Area of Practice:** Supervision, training, MRI **Affiliations:** A.A.R.T.; A.S.R.T.; MRI Society **SIC code:** 80 **Address:** New York University Medical Center, 530 First Ave., New York, NY 10010 **E-mail:** jeanique.pierre@nyuhealth.org **Web address:** www.nyuhealth.org

PIETRANTONI, MARCELLO
Industry: Healthcare **Born:** September 10, 1955, South America **Univ./degree:** M.D., University of Guadalajara, 1982; M.D., University of Buffalo, 1984 **Current organization:** University of Louisville **Title:** M.D./Associate Professor **Type of orga-**

nization: University hospital **Major product:** Women's healthcare **Area of distribution:** Louisville, Kentucky **Area of Practice:** Maternal fetal medicine **Affiliations:** F.A.C.O.G.; A.M.A.; S.P.M.; American Diabetes Association **Hob./spts.:** Motorcycles **SIC code:** 80 **Address:** University of Louisville, Dept. of Obstetrics & Gynecology, 550 S. Jackson, Louisville, KY 40202

PINNEY, EDWARD L.
Industry: Healthcare **Univ./degree:** M.D., Washington University, 1949 **Current organization:** Edward L. Pinney, M.D. **Title:** MD **Type of organization:** Private practice **Major product:** Psychiatry **Area of distribution:** Puerto Rico **Area of Practice:** Research, teaching **Published works:** Several books **Affiliations:** A.M.A.; A.P.A. **Hob./spts.:** Swimming, sailing **SIC code:** 80 **Address:** #3 Playa Azul Beach, #1301, Luquillo, PR 00773 **E-mail:** efpinney@pinacolada.net

PINTEA, ADRIAN IOAN
Industry: Healthcare **Born:** October 23, 1947, Sibiu, Romania **Univ./degree:** M.A., Psychology and Nursing, Babes-Bolyay State University, Romania; Ph.D. Candidate **Current organization:** FJHHC, Inc. **Title:** Director of Nursing **Type of organization:** Home healthcare agency **Major product:** Home healthcare services per nurses and therapists **Area of distribution:** Chicago, Illinois **Area of Practice:** Psychology, nursing **Published works:** Thesis, "Stress in the Home Healthcare Industry, A Dynamic Approach" **Affiliations:** American Nurses Association; American Home Health Association **Hob./spts.:** Hiking, music, poetry **SIC code:** 80 **Address:** FJHHC, Inc., 5254 W. Dakin St., Floor One, Chicago, IL 60641 **E-mail:** adrianioanpintea@yahoo.com

PINTER, RUTH C.
Industry: Healthcare **Born:** March 7, 1952, San Francisco, California **Univ./degree:** B.S.N., California State University at Chico **Current organization:** U. S. Bioservices **Title:** Director of Nursing **Type of organization:** Specialty pharmacy for manufacturers, physicians, payers and patients **Major product:** Home infusion and injectable medications **Area of distribution:** California, Nevada, Arizona **Area of Practice:** Nursing **Honors/awards:** Southern California Cancer Pain Initiative Award of Excellence, 2002 **Affiliations:** Infusion Nurses Society **Hob./spts.:** Family, swimming, horseback riding, archery **SIC code:** 80 **Address:** U. S. Bioservices, 15017 Califa St., Van Nuys, CA 91411 **E-mail:** ruth.pinter@usbioservices.com

PIPOVSKI, LAZO SLAVKO
Industry: Healthcare **Born:** March 6, 1958, Struga, Yugoslavia **Univ./degree:** M.D., Belgrade, Yugoslavia **Current organization:** Gulf Coast Kidney Associates **Title:** M.D. **Type of organization:** Private practice **Major product:** Patient care **Area of distribution:** Sarasota, Florida **Area of Practice:** Nephrology, internal medicine **Honors/awards:** 2 Year Fellowship at Cornell **Affiliations:** A.S.N.; A.M.A. **Hob./spts.:** Tennis, classical guitar **SIC code:** 80 **Address:** Gulf Coast Kidney Associates, 1921 Waldemere St., Sarasota, FL 34239 **E-mail:** lp3658@yahoo.com

PISANO, RICHARD ROCCO
Industry: Healthcare **Born:** August 16, 1944, New York, New York **Univ./degree:** M.D., University of Bologna, Italy, 1973 **Current organization:** Richard R. Pisano, M.D. **Title:** M.D. **Type of organization:** Private practice **Major product:** Patient care **Area of distribution:** New Rochelle, New York **Area of Practice:** Internal medicine **Affiliations:** New York State Medical Society; American College of Physicians; Westchester County Medical Society; President, Medical Board Sound Shore Medical Center, New Rochelle, New York **SIC code:** 80 **Address:** Richard R. Pisano, M.D., 175 Memorial Hwy. 2-7, New Rochelle, NY 10801 **E-mail:** rrpkp@aol.com

PITTENGER, MARK F.
Industry: Biotechnology **Born:** February 9, 1956, Havertown, Pennsylvania **Univ./degree:** Ph.D., Johns Hopkins School of Medicine, 1986 **Current organization:** Osiris Therapeutics Inc. **Title:** Director, Discovery Research **Type of organization:** Research, development and manufacturing of cell products **Major product:** Adult stem cells for biology and tissue engineering **Area of distribution:** International **Area of Practice:** Research in cell biology and tissue engineering **Affiliations:** A.S.C.B.; S.R.M. **Hob./spts.:** Sailing, sports **SIC code:** 80 **Address:** Osiris Therapeutics Inc., 2001 Aliceanna St., Baltimore, MD 21231 **E-mail:** mpittenger@osiristx.com

PIZZO, SALVATORE V.
Industry: Healthcare **Born:** June 22, 1944, Philadelphia, Pennsylvania **Univ./degree:** M.D., Duke University, 1973; Ph.D., Duke University, 1972 **Current organization:** Duke University Medical Center **Title:** Professor/Chairman **Type of organization:** University hospital **Major product:** Patient care, research, medical education **Area of distribution:** National **Area of Practice:** Pathology, biochemistry **Honors/awards:** Elected to Association of University Pathologists, 1985 and The American Society for Clinical Investigation, 1988; Discovery Research Group Award Winner, 1998; Elected Fellow, American Association for the Advancement of Science, 1999 **Published works:** 360 papers and abstracts, several patents **Affiliations:** A.A.A.S.; A.S.C.I.; A.U.P.; A.S.M.B.B.C.; A.S.H.; A.C.S.; A.A.C.R. **Hob./spts.:** Wine collecting, cooking, history **SIC code:** 80 **Address:** Duke University Medical Center, Dept. of Pathology, M301 Davison Bldg., Durham, NC 27710 **E-mail:** pizzo001@mc.duke.edu

PLAZA, LAURA C.
Industry: Healthcare **Born:** July 8, 1962, Ponce, Puerto Rico **Univ./degree:** M.D., University of Puerto Rico School of Medicine, 1989 **Current organization:** Fisiatria y Medicina Alternativa, CSP **Title:** M.D. **Type of organization:** Clinic **Major product:** Medical services **Area of distribution:** San Juan, Puerto Rico **Area of practice:** Physical medicine/rehab medicine **Area of Practice:** Physical medicine/rehab medicine **Honors/awards:** Interview at Puerto Rico television, Channel 30; Interview by El Nuevo Dia, a Puerto Rico newspaper **Published works:** Collaboration to sports publications, 2001-03 **Affiliations:** President, Acupuncture Association of Puerto Rico; American Academy of Physical Medicine and Rehabilitation; American Paraplegic Society; Faculty Member, Puerto Rico Medical Acupuncture Society **Hob./spts.:** Aerobic exercise, Latin American literature **SIC code:** 80 **Address:** Fisiatria y Medicina Alternativa, CSP, 359 Calle San Claudio, Suite 313, San Juan, PR 00926 **E-mail:** lauracplaza@aol.com

PLEMENTOSH, NICKY
Industry: Healthcare **Born:** August 31, 1956, Owosso, Michigan **Univ./degree:** M.D., University of Alabama **Current organization:** Nicky Plementosh, MD, LLC **Title:** M.D. **Type of organization:** Private practice **Major product:** Women's healthcare **Area of distribution:** Poplar Bluff, Missouri **Area of Practice:** Obstetrics/gynecology **Affiliations:** F.A.C.O.G.; Missouri State Medical Society; Christian Medical Society **Hob./spts.:** Breeding Old English Sheep Dogs **SIC code:** 80 **Address:** Nicky Plementosh, MD, LLC, 2725 N. Westwood Blvd., Suite 2, Hillsdale Plaza, Poplar Bluff, MO 63901 **Phone:** (573)785-3087 **Fax:** (573)785-3506

PODGORSKA, HELENA
Industry: Healthcare **Born:** October 21, 1952, Ujsie Jezuickie, Poland **Univ./degree:** M.D., Nicholas Copernicus Medical Academy, 1982 **Current organization:** Resurrection Health Plan **Title:** M.D. **Major product:** Healthcare **Area of distribution:** Illinois **Area of Practice:** Family medicine **Affiliations:** Board Certified Family Practice **Hob./spts.:** Family, tennis, coin collecting **SIC code:** 80 **Address:** Resurrection Health Plan, 838 N. Forestview, Park Ridge, IL 60068

POE, LENORA MADISON
Industry: Mental healthcare **Born:** January 3, 1934, Newbern, Alabama **Univ./degree:** Ph.D., Center for Psychological Studies, Albany, California, 1991 **Current organization:** State Coalition of Grand Parent/Relative Caregivers **Title:** Chairperson **Type of organization:** State coalition **Major product:** To provide service and support for caregivers of children whose parents are unable or unwilling to parent their children **Area of distribution:** International **Area of Practice:** Psychotherapy, support services **Published works:** 5 articles, 1 book **Hob./spts.:** Spending time with her children and grandchildren, reading, travel **SIC code:** 80 **Address:** State Coalition of Grand Parent/Relative Caregivers, 2034 Blake St., #1, Berkeley, CA 94704 **E-mail:** lenorapoe@aol.com

POGO, GUSTAVE J.
Industry: Healthcare **Born:** February 7, 1957, Buenos Aires, Argentina **Univ./degree:** M.D., New York University, 1983 **Current organization:** North Shore University Hospital **Title:** M.D. **Type of organization:** Hospital **Major product:** Patient care **Area of distribution:** Manhasset, New York **Area of Practice:** Cardiothoracic surgery **Affiliations:** A.M.A.; American College of Surgeons **SIC code:** 80 **Address:** North Shore University Hospital, 300 Community Dr., Manhasset, NY 11030

POLLAK, KEVIN H.
Industry: Healthcare **Born:** June 2, 1960, Mt. Vernon, New York **Univ./degree:** M.D., Ross University, 1991 **Current organization:** Anesthesia Providers **Title:** M.D. **Type of organization:** Private practice **Major product:** Anesthesiology **Area of distribution:** Pennsylvania **Area of Practice:** Anesthesiology **Affiliations:** A.M.A.; A.S.A. **Hob./spts.:** Theatre, the arts **SIC code:** 80 **Address:** Anesthesia Providers, 18 Meadow Lane, Lansdale, PA 19446 **E-mail:** kevinpollack@msn.com

POMEROY, BRUCE M.
Industry: Healthcare **Born:** July 11, 1959, East St. Louis, Illinois **Univ./degree:** A.S.N., 1979; B.S.N., 1981; M.S.N., St. Louis University, 1992 **Current organization:** Forest Park Hospital/Deaconess College of Nursing **Title:** Administrative Nursing Supervisor/Clinical Instructor **Type of organization:** Hospital/College **Major product:** Healthcare, teaching of healthcare **Area of distribution:** Illinois **Area of Practice:** Cardiopulmonary nursing **Affiliations:** A.A.C.C.N.; Sigma Theta Tau; Phi Theta Kappa; Sigma Zeta **Hob./spts.:** Raising tropical plants-orchids **SIC code:** 80 **Address:** St. Joseph's Hospital, 9515 Holy Cross Lane, Breese, IL 62230 **E-mail:** pomeroy205@aol.com

POMPA, DOMINIC A.
Industry: Healthcare **Univ./degree:** M.D., New York Medical College, 1969 **Current organization:** Dominic A. Pompa, M.D. **Title:** M.D. **Type of organization:** Private medical practice **Major product:** Patient care **Area of Practice:** Board Certified, Internal Medicine **Published works:** Articles **SIC code:** 80 **Address:** 1419 Richmond Rd., Staten Island, NY 10304 **E-mail:** domenlo@aol.com

POPA, EMIL LIVIU
Industry: Healthcare **Born:** July 9, 1960, Cluj, Romania **Univ./degree:** M.D., Cluj Medical University, Romania, 1985 **Current organization:** Mt. Sinai Services at Queens Hospital Center **Title:** M.D. **Type of organization:** Hospital **Major product:** Patient care **Area of distribution:** New York **Area of Practice:** General surgery **Published works:** Articles **Affiliations:** A.M.A.; New York Medical Association **Hob./spts.:** Travel, home electronics **SIC code:** 80 **Address:** 8615 Ava Place, #4E, Jamaica, NY 11432

POREMBKA, DAVID
Industry: Medical **Born:** November 28, 1953, Latrobe, Pennsylvania **Univ./degree:** M.D., Michigan State University, 1981 **Current organization:** University of Cincinnati College of Medicine **Title:** Professor of Anesthesia, Surgery, Internal Medicine (Cardiology), Director of Preoperative Echocardiology, Associate Director of Surgical Interim Care **Type of organization:** University **Major product:** Medical services **Area of distribution:** International **Area of Practice:** Anesthesiology, trauma, transesophageal echocardiography **Honors/awards:** Outstanding Physician, Cincinnati; Presidential Citation, SCCM; Who's Who in America **Affiliations:** S.C.C.M.; I.A.R.S.; A.S.E.; A.S.E. **Hob./spts.:** Golf, sky diving, fossil hunting, photography **SIC code:** 80 **Address:** University of Cincinnati College of Medicine, 231 Albert Sabin Way, Cincinnati, OH 45267 **E-mail:** david.porembka@uc.edu **Web address:** www.uc.edu

PORTER, LILLY M.
Industry: Healthcare **Born:** January 16, 1945, Ashland, Kentucky **Univ./degree:** R.N., King's Daughters Medical Center, 1966 **Current organization:** King's Daughters Medical Center **Title:** Nurse Educator **Type of organization:** Medical center **Major product:** Patient care **Area of distribution:** Kentucky **Area of Practice:** Clinical educator in cardiac nursing **Honors/awards:** Edna Monk Nursing Award, 1988 **Hob./spts.:** Oil painting, animals **SIC code:** 80 **Address:** 902 Milton Ave., Ashland, KY 41102 **E-mail:** lporter@kdmc.net **Web address:** www.kdmc.net

POTEET, JOSEPH J.
Industry: Healthcare **Title:** Psychotherapist **Type of organization:** Mental health center **Major product:** Mental health services, addiction medicine, pain medicine **Area of Practice:** Psychotherapy, medical psychology, behavioral medicine **SIC code:** 80 **Address:** Catholic Charities of Central Florida, Counseling Center, 790 Powder Horn Row, Lakeland, FL 33809 **E-mail:** jpoteet@cc.lakeland.org **Web address:** www.cc.orlando.org

POWELL, ELLEN E.
Industry: Healthcare **Born:** June 16, 1938, Corsicana, Texas **Univ./degree:** L.V.N., Medical Arts School, 1958 **Current organization:** Rossmoor Medical Center **Title:** L.V.N. **Type of organization:** Medical clinic **Major product:** Patient care **Area of distribution:** California **Area of Practice:** Specialist Nurse **Hob./spts.:** Family, reading, sewing **SIC code:** 80 **Address:** 305 Jacinto, Pittsburg, CA 94565

POWERS-MOORE, ANNEMARIE
Industry: Healthcare **Born:** January 21, 1957, Brandenburg, Germany **Univ./degree:** B.S., Psychiatry, Southern Connecticut State University, 1982 **Current organization:** Gentiva Health Services **Title:** Director, Clinical Management **Type of organization:** Hospital, home care **Major product:** Patient and home care services **Area of distribution:** Connecticut **Area of Practice:** Marketing, daily operations, behavioral health **Affiliations:** A.N.A.; Connecticut Association for Home Care **Hob./spts.:** Hiking, biking, tennis, violin, her 10 year old son **SIC code:** 80 **Address:** Gentiva Health Services, 1 Evergreen Ave., Hamden, CT 06518 **Web address:** www.gentiva.com

PRABHAT, MEERA
Industry: Healthcare **Born:** January 7, 1943, Madras, India **Univ./degree:** M.B.B.S., India, 1966 **Current organization:** Meera Prabhat Physician, P.C. **Title:** MD, FACOG **Type of organization:** Private practice **Major product:** Patient care **Area of distribution:** New York **Area of Practice:** Ob/Gyn (Board Certified) **Affiliations:** F.A.C.O.G. **Hob./spts.:** Reading **SIC code:** 80 **Address:** Meera Prabhat Physician, P.C., 144-16 Holly Ave., Flushing, NY 11355

PREIS, ODED
Industry: Healthcare **Born:** June 9, 1947, Haifa, Israel **Univ./degree:** M.D., Hebrew University, Jerusalem, Israel **Current organization:** Office of Dr. Oded Preis, M.D. **Title:** M.D. **Type of organization:** Private medical practice **Major product:** Patient care **Area of distribution:** Brooklyn, New York **Area of Practice:** Pediatrics, neonatology, critical care **Honors/awards:** Castle Connelly Registry **Published works:** Journal of Pediatrics; Pediatric Research **Affiliations:** F.A.A.P.; F.A.C.F.E. **Hob./spts.:** Skiing, handcrafts **SIC code:** 80 **Address:** Office of Dr. Oded Preis, M.D., 1729 E. 12th St., Brooklyn, NY 11229 **E-mail:** opidoci@aol.com

PRESS JR., HARRY C.
Industry: Medical **Born:** August 22, 1931, Chesapeake, Virginia **Univ./degree:** M.D., Virginia Union University, 1957 **Current organization:** Howard University, Dept. of Radiology **Title:** M.D./Professor of Radiology **Type of organization:** University hospital **Major product:** Medical education, diagnostic, radiology **Area of distribution:** Washington D.C. **Area of Practice:** Radiology **Affiliations:** F.A.C.R.; R.S.N.A. **Hob./spts.:** Gardening, tennis **SIC code:** 80 **Address:** Harry C. Press Jr., MD, 2041 Georgia Ave. N.W., Washington, DC 20060

PRICE, ALLAN E.
Industry: Healthcare **Born:** May 26, 1941, Vernon, Texas **Univ./degree:** B.S., Biology, University of Texas at Arlington, 1962; M.D., University of Texas Medical Branch at Galveston, 1965; M.P.H., Texas A&M School of Pubic Health, 2006 **Current organization:** Central Texas Veterans Healthcare System **Title:** M.D./Chief of Cardiology **Type of organization:** Hospital **Major product:** Patient care **Area of distribution:** Texas **Area of Practice:** Cardiology, administration **Affiliations:** A.H.A.; A.M.A.; A.C.P.; Past President, A.H.A., Dallas Chapter and Ten-Bel Chapter **Hob./spts.:** Stamp collecting, golf **SIC code:** 80 **Address:** Central Texas Veterans Healthcare System, 1901 S. First, Temple, TX 96504 **E-mail:** aepmhp714@aol.com

PRIKHOJAN, ALEXANDER
Industry: Healthcare **Born:** April 2, 1959, Moscow, Russia **Univ./degree:** M.D., Moscow Medical School, 1982; Ph.D., Academy of Medical Science, 1987 **Current organization:** Midwood Family Doctors, P.C. **Title:** Psychiatrist **Type of organization:** Multispecialty medical group (Geared to the Russian speaking community) **Major product:** Psychopharmacology **Area of distribution:** Brooklyn, New York **Area of Practice:** Psychiatry **Honors/awards:** Outstanding Resident Award, National Institute of Mental Health, 1997; Fellowship, New York Psychoanalytic Institute; additional awards from pharmaceutical companies: Bayer Corp., Janssen Corp., Wyeth Ayerst **Published works:** Book, "Transient Pharmacology of Neurotransmission", 1987; Chapter, "Synaptosomal Release of Excitatory Amino Acid Neurotransmitters"; Book, "Current Issues in the Psychopharmacology of Schizophrenia"; Chapter, "Dementia in Schizophrenia"; Contributed to "Directions in Psychiatry-The Journal of Nervous & Mental Diseases-Brain Research" **Affiliations:** New York State Psychiatric Institute; American Psychiatric Association; Beth Israel Medical Center; Mount Sinai Medical Center; Principal Investor of Clinical Grants in America **Hob./spts.:** Opera, photography **SIC code:** 80 **Address:** Midwood Family Doctors, P.C., 1915 Ocean Ave., Brooklyn, NY 11230

PSALTIS, HELEN
Industry: Healthcare **Born:** November 27, 1931, Rockford, Illinois **Univ./degree:** R.N., 1953, St. Margaret Mercy; B.S., 1961, DePaul University; M.S., 1971, Purdue University; M.S.N., 1988, Purdue Calumet University **Current organization:** St. Margaret Mercy Health Centers **Title:** Registered Nurse **Type of organization:** Hospital **Major product:** Healthcare services **Area of distribution:** National **Area of Practice:** Cardiac nursing, training, teaching; School, Clinical and Head Nurse **Affiliations:** A.N.A.; Sigma Theta Tau; N.L.N. **Hob./spts.:** Reading, walking, art appreciation, music appreciation **SIC code:** 80 **Address:** St. Margaret Mercy Health Centers, 5454 Hohman Ave., Hammond, IN 46320

PUGMAN, ALEX
Industry: Healthcare **Univ./degree:** B.S.N., Thomas Jefferson University, 1996 **Current organization:** Home Care Hospice **Title:** Owner/Hospice Director **Type of organization:** Hospice **Major product:** Hospice care **Area of distribution:** Pennsylvania **Area of Practice:** Hospice nursing, administration **Affiliations:** National Hospice and Palliative Care; Member, Board of Directors, Jewish National Fund **Hob./spts.:** Family **SIC code:** 80 **Address:** Home Care Hospice, 1810 Grant Ave., Philadelphia, PA 19115 **E-mail:** apug@homecarehospice.com

PUIG, GILBERTO
Industry: Healthcare **Born:** January 4, 1961, Puerto Rico **Univ./degree:** B.S., Chemistry, University of Puerto Rico, 1983; M.D., University of Puerto Rico School of Medicine, 1987 **Current organization:** Grupo Intensivo Pediatrico **Title:** M.D. **Type of organization:** Private practice **Major product:** Medical services **Area of distribution:** Puerto Rico **Area of Practice:** Pediatric intensive care **Published works:** Write-ups **Affiliations:** Society for Critical Care Medicine; American Academy of Pediatrics **SIC code:** 80 **Address:** Grupo Intensivo Pediatrico, Condesa del Mar, #804, Carolina, PR 00979 **E-mail:** puigramos@hotmail.com

QUARTUCCI, JENNIFER L.
Industry: Healthcare **Born:** April 26, 1953, Portsmouth, Virginia **Current organization:** Sentara Health Care Corp. **Title:** R.T.(R)(M)(MR) **Type of organization:** Hospital

Major product: Patient care, MRI medical services **Area of distribution:** International **Area of Practice:** MRI technology **Published works:** 3 articles **Affiliations:** A.R.R.T.; A.S.R.T.; S.M.R.T.; C.M.R.S. **Hob./spts.:** Sports mom, travel **SIC code:** 80 **Address:** 2725 Bunch Walnuts Rd., Chesapeake, VA 23322 **E-mail:** jlquartu@sentara.com

QUATTLEBAUM, ROBERT BASKIN
Industry: Professional service **Born:** March 6, 1933, Roanoke, Alabama **Univ./degree:** M.D., University of Alabama, 1961 **Current organization:** The Urology Clinic **Title:** M.D. **Type of organization:** Medical facility **Major product:** Patient care **Area of distribution:** Savannah, Georgia **Area of Practice:** Urology **Honors/awards:** S.E. Section, American Neurological Society **Published works:** Articles **Affiliations:** A.U.A.; A.M.A. **Hob./spts.:** Golf, bass fishing, quail shooting and dining out **SIC code:** 80 **Address:** The Urology Clinic, 5354 Reynolds St., Suite 416, Savannah, GA 31405 **E-mail:** rbqsav@aol.com **Web address:** www.drquattlebaum.com

QUATTROMANI, ANTONELLA
Industry: Healthcare **Born:** January, 14, 1958, Perugia, Italy **Univ./degree:** M.D., University of Perugia; M.B.A., St. Louis University **Current organization:** Sisters of St. Mary's Medical Group **Title:** M.D. **Type of organization:** Hospital **Major product:** Patient care **Area of distribution:** Missouri **Area of Practice:** Electrophysiology, cardiology **Affiliations:** American College of Cardiology; Heart Rhythm Society **Hob./spts.:** Skiing, traveling, hiking **SIC code:** 80 **Address:** Sisters of St. Mary's Medical Group, 1035 Bellevue Ave., St. Louis, MO 63117 **E-mail:** antonellaq@aol.com **Web address:** www.antonella_quattromani@ssmhs.org

QUEEN, KIMLYN N.
Industry: Healthcare **Born:** June 15, 1971, Marion, Ohio **Univ./degree:** M.S.M., Mount Vernon Nazarene University, 2005 **Current organization:** Marion General Hospital/ Marion Ancillary Services **Title:** Director of Imaging Services **Type of organization:** Hospital **Major product:** Patient care/diagnostic imaging **Area of distribution:** Ohio **Area of Practice:** Certified Radiology Administrator (CRA); RT(R); CTMR **Honors/awards:** Lifetime Member of Strathmore's Who's Who (for Leadership and Achievement in her profession) **Affiliations:** A.R.R.T.; A.H.R.A. **Hob./spts.:** Family, sports, reading, the outdoors **SIC code:** 80 **Address:** Marion General Hospital/Marion Ancillary Services, 1000 McKinley Park Dr., Marion, OH 43302 **E-mail:** kqueen@adelphia.net

QUIMBO, RICARDO VICTORIO S.
Industry: Healthcare **Born:** December 18, 1967, Manila, Philippines **Univ./degree:** M.D., University of the Philippines **Current organization:** St. Vincents Catholic Medical Centers of New York (Manhattan) **Title:** M.D. **Type of organization:** Hospital **Major product:** Patient care **Area of distribution:** New York, New York **Area of Practice:** Pathology **Affiliations:** C.A.P.; A.S.C.P.; A.M.A. **Hob./spts.:** Art, photography **SIC code:** 80 **Address:** St. Vincents Catholic Medical Centers of New York (Manhattan), 107 W. 15th St., #1KN, New York, NY 10011 **E-mail:** drquimbo@yahoo.com

QUIROZ, BRIAN B.
Industry: Healthcare **Born:** April 27, 1976, El Paso, Texas **Univ./degree:** A.S., El Centro Junior College, 2000 **Current organization:** Parkland Health and Hospital System **Title:** RT(R)(MR)(ARRT) **Type of organization:** Hospital **Major product:** Patient care **Area of distribution:** Texas **Area of Practice:** M.R.I.'s, radiology **Affiliations:** A.S.R.T.; A.R.R.T. **Hob./spts.:** Family, ministry, music **SIC code:** 80 **Address:** Parkland Health and Hospital System, 14400 Montford Dr., Suite 1003, Dallas, TX 75254 **E-mail:** quirozrock@yahoo.com

QUIVERS SR., WILLIAM W.
Industry: Healthcare **Born:** September 14, 1919, Phoebus, Virginia **Univ./degree:** B.S., Physical Education/Science, Hampton Institute, 1942; M.D., Meharry Medical College, Tennessee, 1953 **Current organization:** Provident Hospital **Title:** Director of Pediatrics (Retired) **Type of organization:** Hospital **Major product:** Patient care **Area of distribution:** Maryland **Area of Practice:** Pediatric cardiology **Honors/awards:** First African American to practice pediatric cardiology in Baltimore, Maryland **Published works:** 5 articles **Hob./spts.:** Football, basketball, reading, family and children **SIC code:** 80 **Address:** 6110 Benhurst Rd., Baltimore, MD 21209-3805

RADER, RACHEL S.
Industry: Healthcare **Born:** May 16, 1973, Trinidad, Tobago **Univ./degree:** D.P.M., Barry University **Current organization:** Choice Podiatry Center **Title:** D.P.M. **Type of organization:** Private practice **Major product:** Patient care **Area of distribution:** Cumming, Georgia **Area of Practice:** Diabetic and wound care specialist (Board Qualified) **Affiliations:** A.D.A.; A.B.P.O.P.P.M. **Hob./spts.:** Decorating, poetry **SIC code:** 80 **Address:** 2450 Atlanta Hwy., Suite 402, Cumming, GA 30040 **E-mail:** rachelrader@bellsouth.net

RADFAR, FARIDEH
Industry: Healthcare **Born:** May 8, 1946, Tehran, Iran **Univ./degree:** M.S.W., University of Tehran, 1975; Ph.D., Psychology, Florida Institute of Technology, 1984 **Current organization:** RAD Corp. **Title:** CEO, PhD **Type of organization:** Private practice **Major product:** Mental health services **Area of distribution:** Indian Harbor Beach, Florida **Area of Practice:** Licensed Clinical Psychologist, Certified Family Mediator **Published works:** Multiple publications **Affiliations:** F.M.A.; Florida Psychological Association; Florida Associate of Professional Family Mediators; American College of Forensic Examiners; International College of Prescribing Psychologists **Hob./spts.:** Piano, reading **SIC code:** 80 **Address:** RAD Corp., 2040 Hwy. A1A, Suite 208, Indian Harbour Beach, FL 32937 **E-mail:** buzyeducation@aol.com

RAGNO, PHILIP D.
Industry: Healthcare **Univ./degree:** M.D., State University of New York at Stonybrook, 1984 **Current organization:** Island Cardiac Specialists **Title:** M.D. **Type of organization:** Private practice **Major product:** Cardiology/patient care **Area of distribution:** Mineola, New York **Area of Practice:** Cardiology **Affiliations:** American College of Cardiology **SIC code:** 80 **Address:** Island Cardiac Specialists, 80 E. Jericho Tpke., Mineola, NY 11501

RAGOTHAMAN, RAMESH
Industry: Healthcare **Born:** September 16, 1967, India **Univ./degree:** M.B.B.S., 1989; M.D., Pediatrics, 1995, Armed Forces Medical College, Pune, India **Current organization:** Virtua Hospitals **Title:** M.D., FAAP **Type of organization:** Hospital **Major product:** Patient care **Area of distribution:** New Jersey **Area of Practice:** Pediatrics **Published works:** Peer-reviewed articles **Affiliations:** Fellow, American Academy of Pediatrics; Indian Academy of Pediatrics **Hob./spts.:** Travel, computers, reading **SIC code:** 80 **Address:** Virtua Hospitals, One Carnie Blvd., Voorhees, NJ 08043 **E-mail:** rramesh67@yahoo.com

RAGUKONIS, THOMAS P.
Industry: Healthcare **Born:** May 16, 1965, Glen Ridge, New Jersey **Univ./degree:** M.D., University of Medicine and Dentistry of New Jersey **Current organization:** Bergen Pain Management **Title:** M.D. **Type of organization:** Medical practice **Major product:** Pain management **Area of distribution:** New Jersey **Area of Practice:** Anesthesiology and pain management **Affiliations:** A.A.P.M.; North American Spine Society **SIC code:** 80 **Address:** Bergen Pain Management, 30 W. Century Rd., Paramus, NJ 07652

RAISSI, SHARO S.
Industry: Medical **Born:** May 15, 1952, Yerevan, Armenia **Univ./degree:** M.D., Tehran University School of Medicine, 1978; Downstate New York Medical College, 1979 **Current organization:** Cedars-Sinai Medical Center, Cardiac Surgery Group **Title:** M.D. **Type of organization:** University hospital **Major product:** Patient care, medical education **Area of distribution:** California **Area of Practice:** Cardiac surgery **Honors/awards:** F.A.C.S.; F.S.T.S. **Published works:** 12 articles **Affiliations:** Society of Thoracic Surgeons **Hob./spts.:** Sailing, tennis, golf **SIC code:** 80 **Address:** Cedars-Sinai Medical Center, Cardiac Surgery Group, 8700 Beverly Blvd. #6215N., Los Angeles, CA 90048 **E-mail:** sharo.raissi@cshs.org **Web address:** www.cshs.org

RAK, RAMIN
Industry: Healthcare **Born:** January 20, 1966, Tehran, Iran **Univ./degree:** M.D., Free University of Brussels, 1993 **Current organization:** Mid-Atlantic Brain & Spine Institute **Title:** M.D. **Type of organization:** Private practice **Major product:** Patient care **Area of distribution:** National **Area of Practice:** Neurosurgery; involved in neuro-regeneration projects **Affiliations:** American Association of Neurological Surgeons; Congress of Neurological Surgery **Hob./spts.:** Philosophy, tennis **SIC code:** 80 **Address:** Mid-Atlantic Brain & Spine Institute, 5779 Burketowne Ct., Burke, VA 22015 **E-mail:** raminrak@aol.com

RAKOWITZ, FREDERIC
Industry: Healthcare **Born:** December 19, 1945, Brooklyn, New York **Univ./degree:** Ph.D., Experimental Biology, New York University, 1973; M.D., Albany Medical College, 1978 **Current organization:** Frederic Rakowitz M.D., Ph.D., P.C. **Title:** M.D., Ph.D. **Type of organization:** Private practice **Major product:** Patient care **Area of distribution:** Great Neck, New York **Area of Practice:** Internal medicine **Affiliations:** A.M.A.; A.C.P.; New York State Medical Society; Nassau County Medical Society **Hob./spts.:** American history, civil war, travel, sports **SIC code:** 80 **Address:** Frederic Rakowitz M.D., Ph.D., P.C., 295 Northern Blvd., Suite 208, Great Neck, NY 11021

RALSTON JR., JOHN C.
Industry: Healthcare **Born:** April 23, 1928, Fort Atkinson, Wisconsin **Univ./degree:** MD, Indiana University, 1953; MPH, UCLA, 1968 **Current organization:** Medical Office of Dr. John C. Ralston, Jr. **Title:** MD/MPH **Type of organization:** General medical practice **Major product:** Charity general medical practice **Area of distribution:** Licensed in 5 states: Indiana, Oregon, California, Virginia and Arizona **Area of Practice:** General practice, Aerospace Medicine **Honors/awards:** Air Medal; Flight

Surgeon, Medical Corps, U.S. Navy **Affiliations:** AMA; FAsMA; FACPM; California Medical Association; Aerospace Medical Association; Maricopa County Medical Society; Arizona Medical Association **Hob./spts.:** Golf, reading, family-12 grandchildren, 2 great grandchildren **SIC code:** 80 **Address:** 18330 N. 79th Ave., #2082, Glendale, AZ 85308 **E-mail:** johnr42328@aol.com

RAMAN, A. ANANTH

Industry: Medical **Born:** January 10, 1949, Mysore, India **Univ./degree:** M.B.B.S., University of Misore, 1974; M.D., University of Rochester, 1979 **Current organization:** Lung Associates **Title:** M.D./Clinical Professor of Medicine, University of Pittsburgh Medical Center/Director, Pulmonary Medicine, St. Francis Medical Center **Type of organization:** Hospital/university **Major product:** Patient care **Area of distribution:** Allison Park, Pennsylvania **Area of Practice:** Pulmonary Physician **Honors/awards:** "Best Teacher", Golden Apple Award for Teaching; Best Preceptor Award for Outstanding Teacher, American College of Physicians; Board Certified in Internal Medicine, Pulmonary Medicine and Critical Care Medicine **Affiliations:** Fellow, American College of Chest Physicians **Hob./spts.:** Music, traveling **SIC code:** 80 **Address:** Lung Associates, 3903 Shadowood Circle, Allison Park, PA 15101

RAMAN, SUBHA

Industry: Medical **Born:** June 5, 1973, Chennai, India **Univ./degree:** M.D., Beaumont Hospitals, Michigan; M.B.B.S., University of Mumbai, India **Current organization:** University of Massachusetts Memorial Medical Center **Title:** Radiology Fellow **Type of organization:** Teaching hospital **Major product:** Patient care, medical education **Area of distribution:** International **Area of Practice:** Nuclear medicine, radiology **Published works:** "F-18 FDG Image of an Aortic Aneurysmal Thrombus", Clinical Nuclear Medicine, March 2002 vol. 27 pg 213-14; "Another Scintigraphic Pattern of a Post-surgical Bile Leak", Clinical Nuclear Medicine, July 2002 vol.27 pg 518-19; "Evaluating Y90-glass Microsphere Treatment Response of Unresectable Colorectal Liver Metastases By F-18 FDG PET: A Comparison with CT or MRI", European J Nuclear Medicine, 2002 vol.29 pg 815-820; "Head and Neck Malignancy: Is PET/CT More Accurate than PET or CT Alone?", Radiology, May 2005 vol.235(2)pg 580-586; "Whole-body PET/CT - Spectrum of Physiological Variants, Artifacts and Interpretative Pitfalls in Cancer Patients", review paper in the Nuclear Medicine Communications (pub. of the British Nucl. Med. Society), Aug 2005 Vol.26 (8) pg 671-687 **Affiliations:** Society of Nuclear Medicine; American College of Radiology; Radiological Society of North America; American Society of Nuclear Cardiology **Hob./spts.:** Reading, travel, cooking **SIC code:** 80 **Address:** 111 John Olds Dr, #110, Manchester, CT 06042 **E-mail:** as2su@hotmail.com

RAMANATHAN, DEVBALA

Industry: Healthcare **Born:** March 20, 1954, Up, India **Univ./degree:** M.D., India **Current organization:** Devbala Ramanathan, M.D. **Title:** M.D., F.A.C.O.G., Diplomate **Type of organization:** Private practice **Major product:** Patient care **Area of distribution:** New York **Area of Practice:** Ob/Gyn **Honors/awards:** Diplomate **Published works:** 6 papers **Affiliations:** F.A.C.O.G.; Flushing Hospital Medical Center **Hob./spts.:** Writing poems, Hindi literature, table tennis **SIC code:** 80 **Address:** 43-49 Smart St., Flushing, NY 11355

RAMANATHAN, RAMESH C.

Industry: Medical **Born:** September 9, 1965, Madrasi, India **Univ./degree:** M.D., Royal College of Surgeons **Current organization:** University of Pittsburgh Medical Center **Title:** M.D. **Type of organization:** University hospital **Major product:** Medical services **Area of distribution:** National **Area of Practice:** Surgical oncology **Hob./spts.:** Travel, reading, sports **SIC code:** 80 **Address:** 501 Oaklynn Ct., #2A, Pittsburgh, PA 15220 **E-mail:** ramanathanrc@msx.upmc.edu

RAMASWAMY, DHARMARAJAN

Industry: Healthcare **Univ./degree:** M.D., University of Madras, India, 1992 **Current organization:** Lincoln Hospital **Title:** M.D. **Type of organization:** Hospital **Major product:** Patient care **Area of distribution:** New York **Area of Practice:** Rheumatology, internal medicine **Published works:** 4 publications **Affiliations:** American College of Rheumatology; American College of Physicians **SIC code:** 80 **Address:** 300 S. Central Ave., #A-24, Hartsdale, NY 10530 **E-mail:** dranaswamy@msn.com

RAMIREZ, IRMA

Industry: Healthcare **Born:** June 6, 1941, Mayaguez, Puerto Rico **Univ./degree:** M.D., University of Puerto Rico, San Juan School of Medicine, 1967 **Current organization:** University of Texas M.D. Anderson Cancer Center **Title:** Associate Professor of Pediatrics **Type of organization:** Hospital **Major product:** Patient care **Area of distribution:** Houston, Texas **Area of Practice:** Pediatric hematology/oncology, leukemia and lymphoma **Published works:** Journal of Immunology; Medical Pediatric Oncology; Cancer & Chemotherapy Leukemia/Blood, American Journal of Hematology **Affiliations:** A.M.W.A.; A.M.A.; A.A.C.R.; Texas Medical Association; Harris County Medical Society; The Association for Women in Science **Hob./spts.:** Gardening **SIC code:** 80 **Address:** University of Texas M.D. Anderson Cancer Center, 1515 Holcombe, Houston, TX 77096 **E-mail:** Iramirez@md.anderson.org

RAMIREZ, OSCAR M.

Industry: Healthcare **Born:** September 12, 1949, Peru **Univ./degree:** M.D., San Marcus University, Lima, Peru, 1976 **Current organization:** Oscar M. Ramirez, M.D., P.A. **Title:** M.D. **Type of organization:** Private practice **Major product:** Patient care **Area of distribution:** National **Area of Practice:** Cosmetic and plastic surgery, facial beautification and rejuvenation **Published works:** 120 articles, 2 books **Affiliations:** The American Society for Aesthetic Plastic Surgery; International Society of Aesthetic Plastic Surgery **Hob./spts.:** Playing professional soccer **SIC code:** 80 **Address:** Oscar M. Ramirez, M.D., P.A., 2219 York Rd., Suite 100, Timonium, MD 21093 **E-mail:** drramirez@ramirezmd.com **Web address:** www.ramirezmd.com

RAMIREZ-FERRER, LUIS O.

Industry: Healthcare **Born:** San German, Puerto Rico **Univ./degree:** M.D., University of Puerto Rico School of Medicine, 1973 **Current organization:** Diaz, Ramirez & Duran, Cirujanos C.S.P. **Title:** M.D., F.A.C.S. **Type of organization:** Private practice **Major product:** Patient care **Area of distribution:** Mayaguez, Puerto Rico **Area of Practice:** General surgery, peripheral vascular surgery **Published works:** 10+ publications **Affiliations:** Fellow, American College of Surgeons; Puerto Rico Medical Association **Hob./spts.:** Fishing **SIC code:** 80 **Address:** Diaz, Ramirez & Duran, Cirujanos C.S.P., Pablo Maiz St. #13, Mayaguez, PR 00681 **E-mail:** luisramfer@hotmail.com

RAMNARINE, JOTIR A.

Industry: Healthcare **Born:** June 30, 1961, Guyana **Univ./degree:** M.D., Almustsiryah University, 1988; 5 year Internship in Guyana; 3 year Residency Marsten Memorial; 2 year Fellowship, Infectious Diseases, Beth Israel, 1997-99 **Current organization:** 32 BJ (Local) **Title:** M.D. **Type of organization:** Hospital **Major product:** Patient care **Area of distribution:** International **Area of Practice:** Infectious diseases, internal medicine **Published works:** 1 abstract **Affiliations:** A.M.A.; A.C.P.; I.D.S.A.; N.Y.M.S. **Hob./spts.:** Swimming, tennis, reading **SIC code:** 80 **Address:** 32 BJ (Local), 101 Avenue of the Americas, New York, NY 10013 **E-mail:** jotirus@yahoo.com

RAMOS, MARIA E.

Industry: Healthcare **Born:** March 21, 1967, San Juan, Puerto Rico **Univ./degree:** B.A. Communication and Speech Disorders Science, Magna Cum Laude, Universidad de Puerto Rico, Medical Campus, 1988; M.D., Universidad Central del Caribe, 1995 **Current organization:** Ramos & Borges Cardiology Office **Title:** Invasive and Non-invasive Adult Cardiologist **Type of organization:** Private practice **Major product:** Women's healthcare (high risk, geriatric, pregnancy) **Area of distribution:** Puerto Rico **Area of Practice:** Adult cardiology, cardiac non-invasive and invasive procedures, consulting for cardiac risk and clearance prior to surgical procedures, preventive medicine and education **Honors/awards:** Cardiology Fellowship, San Juan Veterans Hospital; Internal Medicine Board Certificate, 2000; Cardiovascular Disease Board Certificate, 2004 **Published works:** Datos epidemiológicos y prevención de la enfermedad cardiovascular en la mujer; Los Contraceptivos orales y la hipertención arterial **Affiliations:** A.C.C.; A.H.A.; La Asociación de Cardiólogas de Puerto Rico; Sociedad Puertorriqueña del Corazon **Hob./spts.:** Water sports, classical music, Flamenco dancing, violin **SIC code:** 80 **Address:** 3011 Avenue Alejandrino, #1603, Guaynabo, PR 00969-7006 **E-mail:** mariaramos1984@yahoo.com

RAMOS, VICTOR M.

Industry: Healthcare **Born:** May 24, 1972, Puerto Rico **Univ./degree:** M.D., University of Puerto Rico **Current organization:** Puerto Rico Medical College **Title:** M.D. **Type of organization:** Medical college **Major product:** Medical services **Area of distribution:** Rio Piedras, Puerto Rico **Area of Practice:** Pediatrics **Published works:** Articles **Affiliations:** Puerto Rico Medical College of Physicians **Hob./spts.:** Movies, theatre **SIC code:** 80 **Address:** Hospital San Francisco Pediatric Dept., Ave de Diego 371, Second floor, Rio Piedras, PR 00923 **E-mail:** ramnormandia@yahoo.com

RAMOS-GONZALEZ, RIGOBERTO

Industry: Healthcare **Born:** January 15, 1961, Ponce, Puerto Rico **Univ./degree:** B.S., Magna Cum Laude, Biology, University of Puerto Rico, 1982; M.D., University of Puerto Rico School of Medicine at San Juan, 1986 **Current organization:** Rigoberto Ramos-Gonzalez, M.D. **Title:** M.D. **Type of organization:** Private practice **Major product:** Patient care **Area of distribution:** Adjuntas, Puerto Rico **Area of Practice:** Invasive and non-invasive cardiology, internal medicine **Honors/awards:** UPR, BS, Magna Cum Laude; UPR, Beta Beta Beta-Biological Honor Society; Frank G. Brooks Award for Excellence in Student Research; BBB, Caribbean Region Convention, 1982; Beta Beta Beta, Active Member Award, 1982 **Published works:** "The Polysome and RNA of Spider Fibroin", C.G. Candelas, O.M. Rodriguez, R. Ramos, N.A. Ortiz, Journal of Cell Biology, November , 1982 **Affiliations:** A.C.C.; A.C.P.; A.H.A.; A.M.A.; American Society of Echocardiography; Society of Diagnostic Medical Sonographers; Society of Vascular Technology **Hob./spts.:** Fishing, radio controlled cars and planes, family **SIC code:** 80 **Address:** Rigoberto Ramos Gonzalez, M.D., Ave. Tito Castro 609, Suite 102, PMB 261, Ponce, PR 00716-2232 **E-mail:** rigo@coqui.net

RAMSAKAL, ASHA
Industry: Medical **Born:** May 4, 1960, Trinidad, West Indies **Univ./degree:** D.O., Nova Southeastern, 1997; Board Certified, American Board of Internal Medicine, 2001 **Current organization:** James A. Haley V.A. Hospital **Title:** D.O., Assistant Clinical Professor of Medicine, University of South Florida **Type of organization:** University/federal government hospital **Major product:** Medical services/education **Area of distribution:** Tampa, Florida **Area of Practice:** Internal medicine **Honors/awards:** National Dean's List, Nova Southeastern University, 1994; President's List, Nova Southeastern University, 1994; Janet M. Glasgow Memorial Achievement Citation for Scholastic Achievement, 1997 **Published works:** "A Potentially Fatal Effect of Topical Anesthesia", Hosp. Practice, 36:6, 2001 **Affiliations:** A.C.P.; A.B.I.M.; A.M.A.; A.M.W.A. **Hob./spts.:** Chess, tennis, badminton **SIC code:** 80 **Address:** James A. Haley V.A. Hospital, 1300 Bruce B Downs Blvd., Tampa, FL 33612 **E-mail:** asha.ramsakal@med.va.gov

RAMSEY, PHILIP M.
Industry: Healthcare **Born:** August 16, 1958, Beverly Hills, California **Univ./degree:** A.A.S., Radiologic Technology, Medical University of South Carolina, 1983 **Current organization:** U.C.I. Medical Affiliates, Inc. **Title:** Supervisor of Radiology **Type of organization:** Urgent care/family practice **Major product:** Medical care **Area of distribution:** South Carolina **Area of Practice:** Diagnostic Radiography **Affiliations:** A.R.R.T. **Hob./spts.:** Reading, birdwatching, studying, museums **SIC code:** 80 **Address:** U.C.I. Medical Affiliates, Inc., 1851 Sam Rittenberg Blvd., Charleston, SC 29407

RANGANATHAN, PAVITHRA
Industry: Healthcare **Born:** July 10, 1977, India **Univ./degree:** M.D., Annamalai University, India, 1998 **Current organization:** NYU Medical Center **Title:** M.D. **Type of organization:** Hospital **Major product:** Medical services **Area of distribution:** New York **Area of Practice:** Anesthesiology **Published works:** Numerous publications and abstracts including, Co-author, "Endotracheal Tube Puncture during Ventriculoatrial Shunt Procedure", Journal of Clinical Anesthesia, Oct. 2004; "Fertility After Cancer, a prospective review of assisted reproductive outcome with banked semen specimens", Fertility and Sterility, Feb. 2004; "The Electrocardiogram in predicting cardiac function and hypertensive end organ damage", Society for Technology in Anesthesia, 2004 **Affiliations:** A.S.A.; I.A.R.S.; S.T.A. **Hob./spts.:** Painting **SIC code:** 80 **Address:** NYU Medical Center, 320 E. 42nd St., #2504, New York, NY 10017 **E-mail:** pavithra.ranganathan@med.nyu.edu

RANSON, CHARLES THOMAS
Industry: Healthcare **Born:** January 12, 1955, Pittsburgh, Pennsylvania **Univ./degree:** B.S., Marketing, Robert Morris University **Current organization:** Haemonitics Inc. **Title:** Territory Named Account Representative **Type of organization:** Marketing **Area of distribution:** International **Area of Practice:** Marketing **Affiliations:** American Marketing Association; Hospital Council of America **Hob./spts.:** Educational seminars, tennis, golf, theatre **SIC code:** 80 **Address:** 343 Alamo Dr., Pittsburgh, PA 15241 **E-mail:** charlescranso@aol.com

RAO, JAYANTH G.
Industry: Healthcare **Born:** May 25, 1953, India **Univ./degree:** Pre-Medicine, with honors, Osmania University, 1971; M.D., with honors, Gandhi Medical College, Osmania University, India, 1977 **Current organization:** Cancer Treatment Center; Ocala Community Cancer Center, 3201 S.W. 33rd Rd., Ocala, Florida, 34474 **Title:** M.D. **Type of organization:** Medical center **Major product:** Patient care **Area of distribution:** Florida **Area of Practice:** Radiation oncology **Honors/awards:** Guest speaker at 17th International Prostate Cancer Symposium and Workshop at the Hyatt, Kissimmee, Orlando, 1999; guest speaker and moderator at 18th International Prostate Cancer Workshop, Long Beach, California, April 2003 **Published works:** High Dose Rate Brachytherapy for Prostate Cancer: "New Trends, Technical Innovations"; HDR Prostate Collaborative Group Recommendations - ASTRO abstract, Internal Journal of Radiation Oncology **Affiliations:** A.M.A.; F.M.A.; R.C.P.; Citrus County Medical Society; American Association of Physician Specialists; American Brachytherapy Society; International Brachytherapy/Endocurietherapy Society **Hob./spts.:** Tennis, golf **SIC code:** 80 **Address:** Cancer Treatment Center, 3406 N. Lecanto Hwy., Suite A, Beverly Hills, FL 34465 **E-mail:** raojayanth@hotmail.com

RAO, RAMAA V.
Industry: Medical **Born:** September 15, 1955 **Univ./degree:** M.D., Kurnool Medical College Venkateswara University , 1977 **Current organization:** Healing Touch Family Acupuncture **Title:** M.D., Lic. Acupuncturist **Type of organization:** Healthcare provider **Major product:** Healing **Area of distribution:** Massachusetts **Area of Practice:** Acupuncture, anesthesiologist, Reiki healer **Published works:** Indian Journal of Opthalmology "Opthalmoplegia" Vol 28 No. 1;1980 **Affiliations:** A.M.A.; Acupuncture Society of Mass. **Hob./spts.:** Painting, poetry **SIC code:** 80 **Address:** Healing Touch Family Acupuncture, 50 North St., Medfield, MA 02052 **E-mail:** ramaavrao@aol.com

RASTEGAR, RAYMONDA H.
Industry: Healthcare **Born:** April 19, 1964, Tehran, Iran **Univ./degree:** B.S., Chemistry/Physics, Hunter College, 1986; M.D., Mount Sinai School of Medicine, 1990 **Current organization:** Raymonda H. Rastegar, M.D., F.A.C.C. **Title:** M.D., F.A.C.C. **Type of organization:** Private practice **Major product:** Cardiovascular diseases **Area of distribution:** New York, New York **Area of Practice:** Arteriosclerosis, valvular disease, echocardiography **Published works:** 10 articles **Affiliations:** F.A.C.C.; American Society of Echocardiography **Hob./spts.:** Music **SIC code:** 80 **Address:** 109 E. 38th St., New York, NY 10016 **E-mail:** raymonda_1999@yahoo.com

RAVICHANDRAN, PASALA S.
Industry: Medical **Born:** June 29, 1955, Madras, India **Univ./degree:** M.D., Madras Medical College, 1979 **Current organization:** Oregon Health Sciences University/VA Medical Center **Title:** M.D. **Type of organization:** University hospital **Major product:** Medical services **Area of distribution:** Oregon **Area of Practice:** Cardiothoracic surgery **Published works:** 25 articles **Affiliations:** F.A.C.C., F.A.C.S; Western Thoracic Society of America **Hob./spts.:** Skiing **SIC code:** 80 **Address:** Oregon Health Sciences University/VA Medical Center, 3181 S.W. Sam Jackson Park Rd. (L353), Portland, OR 97201 **E-mail:** ravichan@ohsu.edu **Web address:** www.ohsu.edu

RAY, MUKUNDA B.
Industry: Medical **Born:** November 15, 1942, Calcutta, India **Univ./degree:** M.D., University of Dacca, Bangladesh, 1967; Ph.D., Hepatitis B, Catholic University of Leuven, Belgium, 1978 **Current organization:** University of Louisville Medical Hospital, Dept. of Pathology **Title:** Professor/Director **Type of organization:** University hospital **Major product:** Patient care **Area of distribution:** International **Area of Practice:** Anatomical and general pathology **Affiliations:** C.A.P.; I.A.P.; Member, Royal College of Pathology, England **SIC code:** 80 **Address:** University of Louisville Medical Hospital, Dept. of Pathology, 530 S. Jackson St., Louisville, KY 40202 **E-mail:** mbray001@gwise.louisville.edu

RAZAVI, ALI
Industry: Healthcare **Born:** January 1, 1944, Kashan, Iran **Univ./degree:** M.D., Pahlavi University, Shiraz, Iran, 1971 **Current organization:** Cardiology Associates of Cincinnati **Title:** M.D. **Type of organization:** Group practice **Major product:** Patient care **Area of distribution:** Cincinnati, Ohio **Area of Practice:** Cardiology **Published works:** Lancet Medical Journal **Affiliations:** F.A.C.C.; A.M.A.; Cincinnati Medical Association **Hob./spts.:** Skiing **SIC code:** 80 **Address:** Cardiology Associates of Cincinnati, 3219 Clifton Ave., Suite 400, Cincinnati, OH 45220 **E-mail:** alirazavimd@hotmail.com

RAZZAQ, KHURSHID B.
Industry: Healthcare **Born:** September 6, 1933, Lahore, Punjab **Univ./degree:** M.D., Pakistan Punjab University **Current organization:** Connecticut Valley Hospital **Title:** M.D. **Type of organization:** Hospital **Major product:** Patient care **Area of distribution:** Connecticut **Area of Practice:** Psychiatry **Hob./spts.:** Travel, cooking, gardening **SIC code:** 80 **Address:** Connecticut Valley Hospital, Silver St. P.O. Box 351, Middletown, CT 06457

REDDY, JYOTHSNA M.
Industry: Healthcare **Univ./degree:** M.D., S V University, 1981 **Current organization:** NWFP **Title:** M.D. **Type of organization:** Clinic **Major product:** Patient care **Area of distribution:** Crystal, Minnesota **Area of Practice:** Family practice **Affiliations:** A.A.F.P.; A.M.A. **SIC code:** 80 **Address:** NWFP, 5502 W. Broadway Ave., Crystal, MN 55428

REDDY, NEELIMA G.
Industry: Medical **Born:** April 27, 1975, Madanapalle, India **Univ./degree:** M.D., Gandhi Medical College, 1997 **Current organization:** University of Alabama at Birmingham **Title:** M.D. **Type of organization:** University **Major product:** Medical services **Area of distribution:** Alabama **Area of Practice:** Internal medicine **Honors/awards:** The UAB Award for Alabama for the UBIM **Published works:** 2 Abstracts **Affiliations:** A.C.P.E.; A.A.P.I. **SIC code:** 80 **Address:** 3201 Hargrove Rd. East, Apt 504, Tuscaloosa, AL 35405 **E-mail:** neelima_greddy@yahoo.com

REDNAM, KRISHNARAO V.
Industry: Healthcare **Born:** August 1, 1949, Visakhapatnam, India **Univ./degree:** M.D., Andhra Medical College, 1973 **Current organization:** St. Louis Eye Clinic **Title:** M.D. **Type of organization:** Clinic group practice **Major product:** Eye care services **Area of distribution:** Missouri **Area of Practice:** Ophthalmology, vitreo retinal surgery **Affiliations:** A.M.A.; A.A.O.; A.C.S.; International College of Surgeons **Hob./spts.:** Spending time with family, tennis **SIC code:** 80 **Address:** St. Louis Eye Clinic, 135 W. Adams, #302, Kirkwood, MO 63122

REED, DENNIS J.
Industry: Healthcare **Born:** November 16, 1955, Warren, Ohio **Univ./degree:** M.D., University of Cincinnati, 1986 **Current organization:** Group Health Associates **Title:**

M.D. **Type of organization:** Multi-specialty group **Major product:** Patient care **Area of distribution:** Cincinnati, Ohio **Area of Practice:** Ob/Gyn **Honors/awards:** The Robert Swain Award, University of Cincinnati, 1982 **Affiliations:** A.M.A.; O.M.A.; A.I.U.M. **SIC code:** 80 **Address:** Group Health Associates, 9905 Pheasantwalk Ct., Cincinnati, OH 45241 **E-mail:** doxtar@quixnet.net

REED, GAYLE W.
Industry: Healthcare **Univ./degree:** B.S., P.T., Daemen College; M.A., P.T., New York University **Current organization:** Realhab, Inc. **Title:** President **Type of organization:** Outpatient Physical Therapy and Rehabilitation **Major product:** Physical Therapy and Rehabilitation **Area of distribution:** National **Area of Practice:** Physical Therapy and Rehabilitation **Honors/awards:** Physical Therapy Political Action Committee (PTPAC) 2005 PT-PAC Platinum Eagle Award; National Republican Congressional Committee 2006 National Leadership Award **Affiliations:** American Physical Therapy Association; Daughters of the American Revolution **Hob./spts.:** Swimming, tennis, glass blowing, Mastiff dogs **SIC code:** 80 **Address:** Realhab, Inc., 8263 US Hwy. 301 North, Parrish, FL 34219-8670 **E-mail:** realhabinc@tampabay.rr.com

REED, KATHRYN E.
Industry: Mental health **Born:** December 18, 1952, Detroit, Michigan **Univ./degree:** M.A., Guidance Counselor, Central Michigan University, 1985 **Current organization:** Life Skills Enrichment Center, P.C. **Title:** Family Counselor **Type of organization:** Private practice **Major product:** Counseling **Area of distribution:** Midland, Michigan **Area of Practice:** Families, divorce, adolescence **Affiliations:** Diplomate, American Psychotherapy Association; American Counseling Association **Hob./spts.:** Classical music, jazz, reading **SIC code:** 80 **Address:** Life Skills Enrichment Center, P.C., 3596 E. Mary Jane Dr., Midland, MI 48642

REED, MARY K.
Industry: Healthcare **Born:** July 10, 1954, Memphis, Tennessee **Univ./degree:** M.D., Boston University, 1980 **Current organization:** Bronx Lebanon Hospital **Title:** M.D. **Type of organization:** Hospital **Major product:** Patient care **Area of distribution:** National **Area of Practice:** Oncology/hematology **Published works:** Multiple articles **Affiliations:** A.S.C.O.; A.C.P. **SIC code:** 80 **Address:** Bronx Lebanon Hospital, 1650 Grand Concourse, Bronx, NY 10457 **E-mail:** mksreed@yahoo.com

REED, PATRICE C.
Industry: Healthcare **Born:** May 6, 1960, Clarksville, Tennessee **Univ./degree:** M.D., University of Tennessee, 1991 **Current organization:** Memphis Pediatrics PLLC **Title:** M.D. **Type of organization:** Private practice **Major product:** Children's healthcare **Area of distribution:** Tennessee **Area of Practice:** Pediatrics **Affiliations:** F.A.A.P.; Vice President, Memphis-Shelby County Pediatric Society **Hob./spts.:** Arts and crafts, physical fitness, family **SIC code:** 80 **Address:** Memphis Pediatrics PLLC, 6401 Poplar, Suite 410, Memphis, TN 38119

REEDY, R. GRAHAM
Industry: Healthcare **Born:** November 23, 1937, Kalamazoo, Michigan **Univ./degree:** M.D., University of California at Irvine College of Medicine, 1966 **Current organization:** Rainier Foothills Medical Center **Title:** M.D. **Type of organization:** Private medical practice **Major product:** Patient care **Area of distribution:** Washington **Area of Practice:** Family practice/sports medicine **Affiliations:** F.A.C.S.M.; F.A.A.F.P. **Hob./spts.:** Golf, music **SIC code:** 80 **Address:** Rainier Foothills Medical Center, 1314 8th St. NE, Suite 101, Auburn, WA 98002 **E-mail:** reedyrg@aol.com

REEDY, YVONNE B.
Industry: Healthcare **Born:** May 20, 1947, Danville, Pennsylvania **Univ./degree:** Ph.D., School Psychology, Pennsylvania State University, 1994 **Current organization:** Cen-Clear Child Services, Inc. **Title:** Ph.D., Mental Health Director **Type of organization:** Nonprofit corporation **Major product:** Mental health services **Area of distribution:** Pennsylvania **Area of Practice:** Psychology **Affiliations:** N.A.S.P.; Council for Exceptional Children; Past President, Pennsylvania Association for Play Therapy; Association for Play Therapy **Hob./spts.:** Yoga **SIC code:** 80 **Address:** RR 1 Box 537, Tyrone, PA 16686 **E-mail:** ybreedy@usa.net

REESAL, MICHAEL R.
Industry: Healthcare **Born:** September 24, 1927, Trinidad, Wisconsin **Univ./degree:** B.S.C., Honors, 1948; M.S.C., 1950, Ph.D., McGill University, Canada, 1967; M.D., Queens College, Ireland, 1955 **Current organization:** Reesal Medical Clinic **Title:** M.D./Director of Medicine, North Carolina State Veterans Nursing Home **Type of organization:** Medical consultation service **Major product:** Patient care, disability evaluation **Area of distribution:** North Carolina **Area of Practice:** Medicine, pathology, occupational medicine **Published works:** 50+ articles and chapters **Affiliations:** A.M.A.; American Society of Occupational Medicine; academic positions: Associate Professor, McGill University, 1968, Assistant Professor, Harvard University, 1977, Professor of Medicine, University of Alberta, Canada, 1983 **Hob./spts.:** Tennis, reading **SIC code:** 80 **Address:** Reesal Medical Clinic, 2404 Rolling Hill Rd., Fayetteville, NC 28304 **E-mail:** reesalmedical1@earthlink.net

REEVES, CARLA M.
Industry: Healthcare **Born:** June 25, 1949, San Francisco, California **Univ./degree:** M.S., University of Kentucky, 1975 **Current organization:** Palo Alto Medical Foundation **Title:** Certified Nurse Midwife **Type of organization:** Private medical group **Major product:** Patient care **Area of distribution:** Fremont, California **Area of Practice:** Nurse midwifery, women's healthcare **Honors/awards:** Meritorious Service Medal with Oak Leaf Cluster; State of Arizona Outstanding Achievement - PMH Physicians Office Nurse, 1992 **Affiliations:** American College of Nurse Midwives; Education Affiliate, American College of Obstetrics and Gynecology **Hob./spts.:** Photography, gardening, home improvement **SIC code:** 80 **Address:** Palo Alto Medical Foundation, 3200 Kearney St., Fremont, CA 94538 **E-mail:** reevesc@pamf.org

REHMAN, ASIF M.
Industry: Healthcare **Born:** June 9, 1963, Kashmir, Pakistan **Univ./degree:** M.D., Nishtar Medical College, 1987 **Current organization:** St. Francis Hospital **Title:** M.D. **Type of organization:** Hospital **Major product:** Patient care **Area of distribution:** New York **Area of Practice:** Cardiology/interventional cardiology **Published works:** Numerous journal articles and abstracts **Affiliations:** F.A.C.C.; American College of Physicians; American College of Cardiology; Long Island Heart Council **SIC code:** 80 **Address:** St. Francis Hospital, 100 Port Washington Blvd., Roslyn, NY 11576

REN, XING J.
Industry: Healthcare **Born:** Shanghai, China **Univ./degree:** M.D., Shanghai Medical College **Current organization:** Scripps Clinic **Title:** M.D. **Type of organization:** Medical clinic **Major product:** Patient care **Area of distribution:** California **Area of Practice:** Internal medicine and geriatrics **Honors/awards:** Fellow, American College of Physicians **Published works:** 2 papers **Affiliations:** American Geriatrics Society; Assistant Clinical Professor, University of California at San Diego **Hob./spts.:** Playing violin, music, travel, tennis **SIC code:** 80 **Address:** Scripps Clinic, 2020 Genesee Ave., San Diego, CA 92123

REUL, ROSS MICHAEL
Industry: Healthcare **Born:** January 22, 1967, Milwaukee, Wisconsin **Univ./degree:** B.A., Biology, University of Texas, 1989; M.D., Cum Laude, Baylor College of Medicine, 1993 **Current organization:** Surgical Associates of Texas/Texas Heart Institute **Title:** M.D./Director of Surgical Innovations, St. Luke's Episcopal Hospital **Type of organization:** Hospital **Major product:** Patient care **Area of distribution:** International **Area of Practice:** Cardiothoracic and vascular surgery **Honors/awards:** Excellence in Teaching Award from the Harvard Medical Students, Harvard Medical School, 1997-98; Young Investigator Award, American Society of Transplant Physicians, 1997; Genetech Travel Grant, American Heart Association 69th Scientific Sessions, 1996; Junior Resident Teaching Award from the Harvard Medical Students, Harvard Medical School, 1994-95; Baylor Medical Alumni Association Outstanding Student Award, Baylor College of Medicine, 1993; Alpha Omega Alpha, 1992 **Published works:** Numerous including: Ross. M. Reul and Lawrence H. Cohn: Mitral valve reconstruction for mitral insufficiency. Progress in Cardiovascular Disease 1997; 39: 567-599; Ross M. Reul and Lawrence H. Cohn: Aortic valve disease. In Daniel P. McKellar, Richard B. Reiling, Ben Eiseman (eds.) Prognosis and Outcomes Expectancy of Surgical Disease. Quality Medical Publishing, Inc., St. Louis, MO, 1999. p 78-81 **Affiliations:** American College of Cardiology; American College of Surgeons; American Medical Association; Denton A Cooley Cardiovascular Surgery Society; Cooley Hands Society; Harris County Medical Society; International Society for Minimally Invasive Cardiac Surgery **Hob./spts.:** Family, water skiing **SIC code:** 80 **Address:** Surgical Associates of Texas/Texas Heart Institute, 1101 Bates Ave., Suite P-514, Houston, TX 77030 **E-mail:** rreul@yahoo.com

REY, AYLED
Industry: Medical **Univ./degree:** M.D., Universidad Central Del Este, 1976 **Current organization:** Dept. of Veterans Affairs Medical Center **Title:** M.D., Chief Section of Internal Medicine **Type of organization:** University hospital **Major product:** Patient care **Area of distribution:** San Juan, Puerto Rico **Area of practice:** Internal Medicine, Nephrology **Area of Practice:** Internal Medicine, Nephrology **Hob./spts.:** Family **SIC code:** 80 **Address:** Dept. of Veterans Affairs Medical Center, 1 Veterans Plaza, San Juan, PR 00927

REYES CABEZA, VICTOR S.
Industry: Healthcare **Born:** May 25, 1951, San Juan, Puerto Rico **Univ./degree:** B.S., Biology, Pontifical Catholic University of Puerto Rico, 1973; M.D., Polytechnic Institute of Mexico School of Medicine, 1980 **Current organization:** Policlinica Las Americas Inc. **Title:** Medical Director **Type of organization:** Group practice **Major product:** Patient care **Area of distribution:** Puerto Rico **Area of Practice:** General medicine/administration **Hob./spts.:** Sailing, scuba diving, travel **SIC code:** 80 **Address:** Policlinica Las Americas, Inc., 1903 Ave. Las Americas, Ponce, PR 00728-1815 **E-mail:** vitovita@prtc.net

RHODES, JEFFREY M.
Industry: Medical **Born:** October 12, 1964, Buffalo, New York **Univ./degree:** M.D., University of Rochester School of Medicine and Dentistry, 1991 **Current organization:** University of Rochester School of Medicine **Title:** Assistant Professor of Surgery **Type of organization:** University **Major product:** Patient care, medical education **Area of distribution:** National **Area of Practice:** Vascular surgery **Published works:** Articles: Rhodes JM, Gloviczki P. Canton LG, Rooke TW, Lewis BD, Lindsey JR. "Factors affecting clinical outcome following endoscopic perforator vein ablation", Am J. Surg 1998; 176: 162-7; Rhodes JM, Gloviczki P, Canton L, Heaser TV, Rooke TW, Endoscopic perforator division with ablation of superficial reflux improves venous hemodynamics. J Vasc Surg 1998; 28: 839-47; Rhodes JM, Gloviczki P. "Endoscopic perforating vein surgery" Surg Clin N Am 1999; 79:667-681; Rhodes JM, Gloviczki P, Bower TC, Panneton JM, Canton LG, Toomey BJ "The benefits of secondary interventions in patients with failing or failed pedal bypass grafts" Am J Surg 1999; 178:151-155; Book chapters: Gloviczki P, Rhodes JM. The management of perforating vein incompetence. In: "Vascular Surgery" 5th Ed., Rutherford RB (ed). Philadelphia, WB Saunders, 2002; Rhodes JM, Gloviczki P. Subfascial endoscopic perforating vein surgery. In: "The Handbook of Venous Disorders: Guidelines of the American Venous Forum" 2nd Ed. Gloviczki P, Yao JST (eds.). London. Arnold Publishing, 2001 **Affiliations:** American College of Surgeons; Society for Clinical Vascular Surgery; Association for Academic Surgery **Hob./spts.:** Ice-hockey **SIC code:** 80 **Address:** University of Rochester School of Medicine, 601 Elmwood Ave., Box 652, Rochester, NY 14642 **E-mail:** jeffrey_rhodes@urmc.rochester.edu

RICCIARDI, DANIEL D.
Industry: Healthcare **Born:** February 3, 1953, Brooklyn, New York **Univ./degree:** B.S., Biology, SUNY Stony Brook, 1975; M.D., St. George's School of Medicine, 1981 **Current organization:** Long Island College Hospital **Title:** Chief of Rheumatology **Type of organization:** Hospital/private practice **Major product:** Patient care **Area of distribution:** New York **Area of Practice:** Rheumatology **Affiliations:** F.A.C.R.; A.S.I.M.; Past President, New York Rheumatism Association; Board Member, Board of Mental Health, City of New York; Board Member, Health & Hospital Corp.; N.Y.P.D. Surgeon **Hob./spts.:** Politics, theatre, music **SIC code:** 80 **Address:** Long Island College Hospital, 100 Clinton St., Brooklyn, NY 11201 **E-mail:** drricciardi@aol.com

RICE, STUART G.
Industry: Healthcare **Born:** February 15, 1960, Seattle, Washington **Univ./degree:** B.S., Biology, University of North Dakota, 1983; M.D., Medical College of Wisconsin, 1987 **Current organization:** Neurosurgical Associates **Title:** M.D., F.A.C.S. **Type of organization:** Clinic **Major product:** Patient care, neurological services **Area of distribution:** Regional **Area of Practice:** Neurosurgeon, author **Published works:** 2 books, Scientific novel and a Medical mystery **Affiliations:** Fellow, American College of Surgeons; American Association of Neurological Surgeons; Congress of Neurological Surgeons **Hob./spts.:** Golf, tennis, writing **SIC code:** 80 **Address:** Neurosurgical Associates, 2805 Fifth St., Suite 110, Rapid City, SD 57701 **E-mail:** neurotron1@aol.com

RICHARD, ANGELIA B.
Industry: Healthcare **Born:** January 4, 1961, New Iberia, Louisiana **Univ./degree:** R.N., Excelsior College, Albany, New York, 2004 **Current organization:** Crowley American Legion Hospital **Title:** R.N. **Type of organization:** Hospital **Major product:** Patient care **Area of distribution:** Crowley, Louisiana **Area of Practice:** Medical surgical nursing; C.N.A. Instructor through Medicaid **Affiliations:** Louisiana Nurses Association **Hob./spts.:** Baseball **SIC code:** 80 **Address:** 25734 Chestnut Rd., Kaplan, LA 70548 **E-mail:** angeliarichard@cs.com

RICHARDSON, MARY K.
Industry: Healthcare/psychology **Univ./degree:** Ph.D., Psychology, U.M.K.C., 1987 **Current organization:** Mary K. Richardson, P.C. **Title:** Psychologist **Type of organization:** Private Practice **Major product:** Wellness **Area of distribution:** Missouri **Area of Practice:** Depression, anxiety, career, family, marriage and family **Affiliations:** American Psychological Association; Kansas City Psychological Association **Hob./spts.:** Gardening **SIC code:** 80 **Address:** Mary K. Richardson P.C., 4901 Main St., Suite 401, Kansas City, MO 64112 **E-mail:** cpa-01@swbell.net

RIENHARDT, CHERYL D.
Industry: Healthcare **Born:** June 18, 1969, Baytown, Texas **Univ./degree:** A.S., Tyler Junior College, 1989 **Current organization:** Trinity Mother Frances Hospital **Title:** Ultrasound Specialist **Type of organization:** Hospital **Major product:** Patient care **Area of distribution:** Texas **Area of Practice:** Ultrasound **Affiliations:** A.R.R.T.; S.D.M.S.; S.V.U.; Tyler Junior College Ultrasound Program (Advisory and Admissions Committees) **Hob./spts.:** Scrapbooking, outdoor activities **SIC code:** 80 **Address:** Trinity Mother Frances Hospital, 800 E. Dawson, Tyler, TX 75708 **E-mail:** endr3@aol.com

RIGGS, PATRICK N.
Industry: Healthcare **Univ./degree:** M.D., Wake Forest University Bowman Gray School of Medicine, 1989 **Current organization:** Via Health **Title:** M.D. **Type of organization:** Hospital **Major product:** Patient care **Area of distribution:** Rochester, New York **Area of Practice:** Vascular surgery **Affiliations:** Monroe County Medical Society; International Society of Cardiovascular Surgeons **Hob./spts.:** Family **SIC code:** 80 **Address:** Via Health, 1445 Portland Ave., Parnall Bldg., Suite 108, Rochester, NY 14621

RIKHER, KIRILL V.
Industry: Healthcare **Born:** October 4, 1954, Moscow, Russia **Univ./degree:** M.D., 1977; Ph.D., 1988, First Moscow Medical School, Moscow **Current organization:** Empire Family Medicine, P.C. **Title:** M.D. **Type of organization:** Medical group **Major product:** Patient care **Area of distribution:** Brooklyn, New York **Area of Practice:** Family medicine **Published works:** 125 scientific publications **Affiliations:** A.A.F.P.; New York State Academy of Family Physicians **Hob./spts.:** Basketball, computers **SIC code:** 80 **Address:** Empire Family Medicine, PC, 3060 Ocean Ave., #L-A, Brooklyn, NY 11235-3354 **E-mail:** krikher@pol.net

RIOS, MARY M.
Industry: Healthcare **Born:** June 19, 1965, Corpus Christi, Texas **Current organization:** The Methodist Hospital **Title:** Nurse Director **Type of organization:** Hospital **Major product:** Patient care **Area of distribution:** International **Area of Practice:** Administration, acute care, renal and endocrine; ANCC Certified Medical Surgical Nurse **Affiliations:** T.N.A.; A.N.N.A.; A.C.H.E.; N.A.H.N.; N.S.H.P. **SIC code:** 80 **Address:** The Methodist Hospital, 6565 Fannin St., MS A820, Houston, TX 77030 **E-mail:** mrios@tmh.tmc.edu

RIPA, BORIS
Industry: Healthcare **Born:** January 11, 1962, Russia **Univ./degree:** M.D., Stavropoulos University School of Medicine, 1985 **Current organization:** Friendly Pediatrics, P.C. **Title:** M.D., F.A.A.P. **Type of organization:** Private practice **Major product:** Patient care **Area of distribution:** New York **Area of Practice:** Pediatrics **Published works:** 1 article **Affiliations:** F.A.A.P.; American Medical Association **Hob./spts.:** Fishing, swimming, tennis **SIC code:** 80 **Address:** Friendly Pediatrics P.C., 3099 Coney Island Ave., Brooklyn, NY 11235

RIVERA, BLANCA
Industry: Healthcare **Born:** June 8, 1904, Mayaguez, Puerto Rico **Univ./degree:** B.S., Chemistry, Biology, Minor, Physics, University of Puerto Rico, College of Agriculture & Mechanic Arts; M.A., Mathematics, Columbia University, New York; M.D., Medicine & Surgery, Madrid University School of Medicine **Title:** M.D. in Medicine and Surgery **Type of organization:** Hospital **Major product:** Patient care **Area of distribution:** International **Area of Practice:** Internal medicine, respiratory diseases, clinical cardiology **Published works:** New England Journal of Medicine; Cardiology Today; American Thoracic Society Journal of Respiratory and Critical Care Medicine **Affiliations:** A.C.P.; New York Medical Society; Puerto Rico Medical Society; American Thoracic Society; American Heart Association; American Heart Association of Puerto Rico; National Heart Foundation; National Foundation for Cancer Research; Puerto Rico Medical Society, Western District; Colegio Medicos, Cirujanos de Puerto Rico **Hob./spts.:** Music, Broadway theatre, reading, travel **SIC code:** 80 **Address:** 920 M. Maymon St. Rio Cristal, Mayaguez, PR 00680

RIVERA, IVELISSE
Industry: Healthcare **Born:** March 22, 1966, San Juan, Puerto Rico **Univ./degree:** M.D., University Central Caribe, 1993 **Current organization:** Cruz Soto Padilla Nephrologists **Title:** M.D. **Type of organization:** Physicians group **Major product:** Nephrology consulting **Area of distribution:** Dorado, Puerto Rico **Area of Practice:** Nephrology **Affiliations:** American Medical Association; Puerto Rico Nephrology Association; Fellow, University Hospital of San Juan **Hob./spts.:** Guitar, tennis, bicycling **SIC code:** 80 **Address:** Cruz Soto Padilla Nephrologists, Eliari #283, Paseo del Sol, Dorado, PR 00646

RIVERA, JOSE D.
Industry: Healthcare **Born:** January 7, 1956, Puerto Rico **Univ./degree:** M.D., University of Puerto Rico, 1982 **Current organization:** Centro Cardiologico del Norte **Title:** M.D. **Type of organization:** Private practice **Major product:** Cardiovascular services

Area of distribution: Arecibo, Puerto Rico **Area of Practice:** Cardiology **Published works:** 15 publications **Affiliations:** American Medical Association; American College of Cardiology; Puerto Rican Society of Cardiology **Hob./spts.:** Boating **SIC code:** 80 **Address:** Centro Cardiologico del Norte, Jose de Diego Ave. #19, Arecibo, PR 00612 **E-mail:** jdcardio@coque.net

RIZVI, IRFAN
Industry: Healthcare **Born:** September 8, 1971, Karachi, Pakistan **Univ./degree:** M.D., Aga Khan University Medical School, Pakistan **Current organization:** West Virginia University **Title:** M.D., F.R.C.S. **Type of organization:** University **Major product:** Patient care **Area of distribution:** Morgantown, West Virginia **Area of Practice:** General surgery **Affiliations:** Fellow, Royal College of Surgeons, U.K.; American College of Surgeons; American Association of Chest Physicians **Hob./spts.:** Reading, travel, squash **SIC code:** 80 **Address:** West Virginia University, 4 Sunridge Dr., Morgantown, WV 26505 **E-mail:** irizvi@hsc.wvu.edu

RIZZO, MARCO
Industry: Healthcare **Born:** January 29, 1942, Rome, Italy **Univ./degree:** M.D., University of Buenos Aires, 1967 **Current organization:** Plastic Surgery Clinic **Title:** M.D. **Type of organization:** Cosmetic surgery facility **Major product:** Cosmetic surgery **Area of distribution:** Honolulu, Hawaii **Area of Practice:** Asian rynoplasti, Asian breast augmentation **Affiliations:** A.S.P.S.; N.S.C.S.; I.T.R.S.A. **Hob./spts.:** Sailing, yachting, soccer, tennis **SIC code:** 80 **Address:** Plastic Surgery Clinic, 1329 Lusitana St., #401, Honolulu, HI 96813 **E-mail:** rizzo@lava.net

ROBBOY, MERLE S.
Industry: Healthcare **Born:** February 9, 1941, Cleveland, Ohio **Univ./degree:** M.D., Ohio State University, 1965 **Current organization:** Merle S. Robboy, M.D., A Prof. Corp. **Title:** M.D. **Type of organization:** Private practice **Major product:** Patient care **Area of distribution:** Newport Beach, California **Area of Practice:** OB/GYN **Affiliations:** Pacific Coast OB/GYN Society; American College of Obstetricians and Gynecologists **Hob./spts.:** Flowers, Orchids, Dahlias **SIC code:** 80 **Address:** Merle S. Robboy, M.D., A Prof. Corp., 355 Placentia Ave., Suite 308, Newport Beach, CA 92663 **E-mail:** drorkid@sbcglobal.net

ROBERTS, WALTER H.
Industry: Education **Born:** January 24, 1915, British Columbia, Canada **Univ./degree:** M.D., Loma Linda University, 1939 **Current organization:** Loma Linda University Dept. of Human Anatomy **Title:** Professor of Anatomy **Type of organization:** University **Major product:** Higher education **Area of distribution:** California **Area of Practice:** Human anatomy **Affiliations:** A.M.A. **SIC code:** 80 **Address:** Loma Linda University, Dept. of Human Anatomy, 24745 Campus St., Loma Linda, CA 92350

ROBERTSON, RESA L.
Industry: Healthcare **Born:** March 15, 1952, Arkansas City, Kansas **Spouse:** David L. Robertson **Married:** June 4, 1983 **Children:** Joshua Metteal Robertson, DOB February 4, 1985; Jacob Lee Robertson, DOB May 27th, 1987; Jonathan David Robertson, DOB October 23, 1989 **Univ./degree:** B.S.N., Southwestern College, 2002; M.S.N., Family Nurse Practitioner Specialization, Wichita State University, 2005 **Current organization:** Hutchinson Clinic **Title:** A.R.N.P. **Type of organization:** Clinic **Major product:** Patient care **Area of distribution:** Hutchinson, Kansas **Area of Practice:** Oncology, 20 years experience **Honors/awards:** National Society of Collegiate Scholars, 2004; Sigma Theta Tau International, Honor Society of Nursing, 2003 - present; Oncology Nursing Society, 1999 - present **Published works:** Numerous including: Jaffe, M.D., N. Raymond, M.D., K., Robertson R.N. P.N.P., R., Effective of cumulative courses of intra-arterial cis-diammenedichloroplatin-II on the primary tumor in osteosarcoma, CANCER, Vol. 63, No 1, January1, 1989; Jaffe, N., Cangir, A., Wallace, S., Robertson, R., Treatment of pediatric bone and soft tissue sarcoma with intra-arterial cis-diammenedichloroplatin-II (CDP)., Contr. Oncol., Vol. 29, pp. 292-305 **Affiliations:** Sigma Theta Tau; Oncology Nursing Society **Career accomplishments:** Speaker to local college nursing students; Transcriptionist of Kansas and local cancer support groups on cancer awareness and detection of breast cancer. Served as preceptor for the advancement of other nurse practitioner students and physician assistants for the care and management of oncology patients. **Hob./spts.:** Cooking, gardening, walking, outdoor gardening **SIC code:** 80 **Address:** 1120 North Walnut St., Hutchinson, KS 67501 **E-mail:** resalou@cox.net

ROBERTSON, ROBERT CLIO
Industry: Healthcare **Born:** July 28, 1941, Kansas City, Kansas **Univ./degree:** B.A., 1963; M.D., 1967, University of Kansas **Current organization:** Central States Orthopedic Specialists **Title:** M.D. **Type of organization:** Medical practice **Major product:** Orthopedic service and surgery **Area of distribution:** Oklahoma **Area of Practice:** Orthopedic surgery **Published works:** Articles **Affiliations:** Alpha Omega Alpha; American Academy of Orthopedic Surgeons **Hob./spts.:** Tennis, golf, skiing, boating **SIC code:** 80 **Address:** Central States Orthopedic Specialists, 6585 S. Yale, #200, Tulsa, OK 74136 **Web address:** www.csosortho.com

ROBINSON, ALAN J.
Industry: Healthcare **Born:** July 1, 1956, Washington, D.C. **Univ./degree:** B.A., Criminal Justice, Thomas A. Edison State College, New Jersey, 1997 **Current organization:** Atlantic Health System **Title:** Director of Corporate Security **Type of organization:** Hospital **Major product:** Patient care, health services **Area of distribution:** National **Area of Practice:** Security, corporate compliance, executive protection **Affiliations:** Healthcare Compliance Association; Security Management Institute; N.C.M.E.C. **Hob./spts.:** Weightlifting, self defense **SIC code:** 80 **Address:** Atlantic Health System, 325 Columbia Turnpike, P.O. Box 959, Florham Park, NJ 07932-0959 **E-mail:** alan.robinson@ahsys.org

ROBINSON, ALFRED G.
Industry: Healthcare **Born:** June 5, 1917, Sherman, Michigan **Univ./degree:** B.S., Michigan State University; M.D., University of Texas at Galveston, 1953 **Current organization:** American Bariatric Center **Title:** M.D., President **Type of organization:** Weight loss clinic **Major product:** Weight loss control, physical conditioning **Area of distribution:** California **Area of Practice:** Medical weight control and conditioning **Published works:** "Your Body Talks to You About Weight Control" **Affiliations:** F.A.A.F.P.; Diplomate, A.A.B.P.; A.S.B.P **Hob./spts.:** Writing **SIC code:** 80 **Address:** American Bariatric Center, 1037 W Avenue N, Suite 204, Palmdale, CA 93551 **E-mail:** robbie_lois@yahoo.com

ROBINSON, BERNARD
Industry: Healthcare **Born:** August 29, 1945, Plant City, Florida **Univ./degree:** B.A., University of Southern Florida, 1969; M.D., Howard University, 1973 **Current organization:** Kaiser Permanente-Hawaii Region **Title:** M.D. **Type of organization:** Health maintenance **Major product:** Totally integrated healthcare **Area of distribution:** National **Area of Practice:** Neurological surgeon **Affiliations:** N.M.A.; A.M.A. **Hob./spts.:** Gardening, fishing **SIC code:** 80 **Address:** Kaiser Permanente-Hawaii Region, 3288 Moanalua Rd., Honolulu, HI 96819 **E-mail:** bernierob1@aol.com

ROBINSON, CAROLYN G.
Industry: Medical **Born:** November 24, 1950, Marion, Virginia **Univ./degree:** R.N., Whitfield Community College, 1980; B.S.N., Radford University **Current organization:** TCRH **Title:** House Supervisor/RN **Type of organization:** Teaching hospital **Major product:** Patient care, training for nursing students **Area of distribution:** Galax, Virginia **Area of Practice:** Supervision, healthcare **Hob./spts.:** Church activities (Christian education), baked goods, arts and crafts **SIC code:** 80 **Address:** TCRH, 200 Hospital Dr., Galax, VA 24333 **E-mail:** cgr1950@yahoo.com

ROBINSON, CATHY K.
Industry: Healthcare **Current organization:** St. Joseph's Imaging Associates **Title:** Nuclear Medicine Technologist **Type of organization:** Out-patient imaging center **Major product:** Medical imaging **Area of distribution:** New York **Area of Practice:** Nuclear medicine technology **Hob./spts.:** Reading, crafts, soccer **SIC code:** 80 **Address:** 15 Lora Lane, Homer, NY 13077 **E-mail:** ckrobinson80@hotmail.com

ROBINSON, JEANETTE M.
Industry: Healthcare **Born:** August 1, 1950, New Orleans, Louisiana **Univ./degree:** B.S.N., University of Phoenix, Arizona **Current organization:** Miramar Home Health, Inc. **Title:** CEO **Type of organization:** Healthcare agency **Major product:** Home healthcare **Area of distribution:** Kenner, Louisiana **Area of Practice:** Nursing administration; R.N. **Affiliations:** American Society of Nursing **SIC code:** 80 **Address:** Miramar Home Health, Inc., 819 Veterans Memorial Blvd., Suite 201, Kenner, LA 70062

ROBINSON, M. CLIVE
Industry: Healthcare **Born:** November 27, 1945, New Zealand **Univ./degree:** M.B.C.H.B.; M.D., University of Otago, New Zealand, 1970 **Current organization:** Bridgeport Hospital, Dept. of Cardiothoracic Surgery **Title:** M.D./Chief of Cardiothoracic Surgery **Type of organization:** Hospital **Major product:** Patient care, minimally invasive heart surgery **Area of distribution:** National **Area of Practice:** Internationally recognized pioneer of Minimally Invasive and Beating heart Surgery, Inventor of keyhole heart surgery **Published works:** Multiple publications **Affiliations:** Foundation Board Member, International Society of Minimally Invasive Cardiac Surgeons; S.T.S.; R.A.C.S. **Hob./spts.:** Antique tractors, fishing **SIC code:** 80 **Address:** Bridgeport Hospital, Dept. of Cardiothoracic Surgery, 267 Grant St., Schine 8, Bridgeport, CT 06610

ROBINSON, THERESA L.
Industry: Healthcare **Univ./degree:** M.D., Texas State University, 1984 **Current organization:** Theresa L. Robinson, M.D. **Title:** M.D. **Type of organization:** Private practice **Major product:** Women's healthcare **Area of distribution:** Texas **Area of Practice:** Gynecological services, obstetrics **Affiliations:** American College of Obstetricians and Gynecologists **SIC code:** 80 **Address:** Theresa L. Robinson, M.D., The Woman's Professional Bldg., 7580 Fannin St., #235, Houston, TX 77054 **E-mail:** theresal@pdq.net

ROCK, AUGUST DAVID
Industry: Healthcare **Born:** March 3, 1953, Princeton, Indiana **Univ./degree:** A.A. **Current organization:** Quality Lifestyles, Inc. **Title:** Administrator **Type of organization:** Assisted living **Major product:** Elder care **Area of distribution:** West Melbourne, Florida **Area of Practice:** Healthcare administration **Affiliations:** Brevard Administration Association **Hob./spts.:** Painting, floor work **SIC code:** 80 **Address:** Quality Lifestyles, Inc., 2155 Keystone Ave., West Melbourne, FL 32904

RODKEY, MARK L.
Industry: Healthcare **Born:** November 1, 1961, Spokane, Washington **Univ./degree:** B.S., Biology, Computer Science, 1984; B.S., Biology, 1984, Gonzaga University; M.D., Wayne State University Medical School, Michigan, 1990 **Current organization:** Hillcrest Hospital **Title:** Medical Director, Pediatric Emergency Medicine **Type of organization:** Trauma Level II Community Hospital **Major product:** Patient care **Area of distribution:** Ohio **Area of Practice:** Pediatric emergency medicine; Residency, Cleveland Clinic Foundation, 1990-1993 **Affiliations:** Fellow, American Academy of Pediatrics; American Medical Association; Hillcrest Trauma Committee **Hob./spts.:** Snowboarding, 4-wheeling, home renovations **SIC code:** 80 **Address:** Hillcrest Hospital, 6780 Mayfield Rd., Mayfield Heights, OH 44124 **E-mail:** markrodkeymd@aol.com

RODRIGUEZ, AMIRA
Industry: Healthcare **Born:** February 18, 1981, Laredo, Texas **Univ./degree:** Graduate Summa Cum Laude, Laredo Community College, 2001; B.A., M.T., University of Texas, Medical Branch, 2006 **Current organization:** Laredo Medical Center **Title:** M.T. **Type of organization:** Medical center **Major product:** Patient care **Area of distribution:** Laredo, Texas **Area of Practice:** Medical technology **Honors/awards:** Dean's Academic Achievement Award, UTMB, 2005-6; Lambda Mu Tau Member, 2006 **Affiliations:** A.M.T.; A.S.C.P. **Hob./spts.:** Choir, singing, church **SIC code:** 80 **Address:** Laredo Medical Center, 1700 E. Saunders St., Laredo, TX 78041 **E-mail:** amira_o@lycos.com

RODRIGUEZ, JUAN J.
Industry: Healthcare **Born:** October 30, 1953, San Juan, Puerto Rico **Univ./degree:** M.D., Dominican Republic Center of East University **Current organization:** Juan J. Rodriguez, M.D. **Title:** M.D. **Type of organization:** Hospital **Major product:** Patient care **Area of distribution:** Puerto Rico **Area of Practice:** Neuro psychiatry **Hob./spts.:** Golf **SIC code:** 80 **Address:** Juan J. Rodriguez, M.D., Torre San Pablo, Suite 301, Bayamón, PR 00936

RODRIGUEZ-BECERRA, JAVIER J.
Industry: Healthcare **Born:** March 30, 1969, San Juan, Puerto Rico **Univ./degree:** M.D., University of Puerto Rico, 1997 **Current organization:** Clendo Reference Lab **Title:** M.D. **Type of organization:** Laboratory, family practice **Major product:** Laboratory analysis **Area of distribution:** Puerto Rico **Area of Practice:** Pathology **Published works:** Articles **Affiliations:** A.M.A.; A.P.I. **Hob./spts.:** Computer work, wood shop, bicycling, jogging **SIC code:** 80 **Address:** Clendo Reference Lab, P.O. Box 549, Bayamón, PR 00960 **E-mail:** jjrodriguez@clendo.com

RODRIGUEZ-ROSA, RICARDO E.
Industry: Healthcare **Born:** April 16, 1972, Fajardo, Puerto Rico **Univ./degree:** M.D., University of Puerto Rico School of Medicine, 1996 **Current organization:** Bayamon Medical Plaza **Title:** M.D. **Type of organization:** Medical plaza **Major product:** Ophthalmology **Area of distribution:** Luquillo, Puerto Rico **Area of practice:** Pediatric ophthalmology **Area of Practice:** Pediatric ophthalmology **Published works:** Article in the American Journal of Ophthalmology **Affiliations:** A.A.O.; P.R.S.O.; P.R.C.P.; Professor of Ophthalmology, University of Puerto Rico **Hob./spts.:** Playing the Cuatro, tennis **SIC code:** 80 **Address:** Bayamon Medical Plaza, HC02 Box 6432, Suite 301, Luquillo, PR 00773

RODRIQUEZ-DEL RIO, FELIX A.
Industry: Healthcare **Born:** June 14, 1962, Hato Rey, Puerto Rico **Univ./degree:** M.D., University of Puerto Rico, 1998 **Current organization:** Instituto Ortopédico de Cayey **Title:** M.D. **Type of organization:** Hospital **Major product:** Foot and ankle surgery **Area of distribution:** Puerto Rico **Area of Practice:** Orthopedic Surgeon **Affiliations:** American Sports Medicine Association; American Medical Association; A.A.O.S. **Hob./spts.:** Golf, surfing, painting, playing guitar **SIC code:** 80 **Address:** Instituto Ortopédico de Cayey, PMB #233 GPO Box 70344, San Juan, PR 00936 **E-mail:** ffelosurf@aol.com

ROGERS, DONNA M.
Industry: Healthcare **Title:** ARRT(R)(M), Director of Radiology **Type of organization:** Hospital **Major product:** Patient care **Area of Practice:** X-ray services **SIC code:** 80 **Address:** Hill Regional Hospital, 101 Circle Dr., Hillsboro, TX 76645 **E-mail:** donna_rogers@chs.net **Web address:** info.hillsboro.tech.chs.net

ROGERS, NEISHA M.
Industry: Healthcare **Born:** January 3, 1975, Springfield, Missouri **Univ./degree:** L.P.N., Omar Gibbson Vocational School, 1995 **Current organization:** Intelistaff Staffing Agency & Nursefinders Staffing Agency **Title:** L.P.N., Traveling Nurse **Type of organization:** Staffing healthcare agency for hospitals and nursing homes **Major product:** Professional nursing care **Area of distribution:** Missouri **Area of Practice:** Medical, rehabilitation, geriatrics; IV Certified **Hob./spts.:** Family, animals **SIC code:** 80 **Address:** 4219 S. Glenstone, #81, Springfield, MO 65804 **E-mail:** vett2be@juno.com

ROGERS, SHEILA M.
Industry: Healthcare **Born:** July 17, 1918, Glasgow, Scotland **Univ./degree:** D.O., Kirksville College of Osteopathic Medicine, 1939 **Current organization:** Downriver Cardiology **Title:** D.O. (Retired) **Type of organization:** Private practice **Major product:** Patient care **Area of distribution:** Trenton, Michigan **Area of Practice:** Internal medicine, cardiology **Honors/awards:** Detroit Salvation Army Citizen of the Year, 1975 **Affiliations:** F.A.C.O.I.; M.A.O.P. **Hob./spts.:** Choral singing, gardening **SIC code:** 80 **Address:** Downriver Cardiology, 2205 Riverside Dr., Trenton, MI 48138 **E-mail:** jt&smrogers@aol.com

ROMBOLA, ROBERT A.
Industry: Healthcare **Born:** April 23, 1952, Fairmont, West Virginia **Univ./degree:** B.A., West Virginia University, 1975; M.D., West Virginia Medical School, 1979; Internship, 1979-80; Residency, Dept. of Ob/Gyn, 1980-83, Charleston Area Medical Center **Current organization:** Gessler Clinic **Title:** M.D. **Type of organization:** Medical clinic **Major product:** Patient care **Area of distribution:** Winter Haven, Florida **Area of Practice:** Obstetrics and Gynecology (Board Certified) **Affiliations:** F.A.C.O.G.; American Medical Association Florida Medical Association; Polk County Medical Association; Southern Medical Association; Florida Birth Related Neurological Injury Compensation Association; Winter Haven Hospital; Regency Medical Center; Board of Directors, First Commerce Bank of Central Florida **Hob./spts.:** Golf, bowling **SIC code:** 80 **Address:** Gessler Clinic, 601 First St. North, Winter Haven, FL 33881 **Web address:** www.GesslerClinic.com

ROMERO, CECILIA M.
Industry: Medical **Born:** August 19, 1947, Provo, Utah **Univ./degree:** B.S., Biology, New Mexico Highlands University, Las Vegas, 1968; M.D., New Mexico University, 1974 **Current organization:** University of Texas Medical Branch, Dept. of Family Medicine **Title:** M.D./Associate Professor, Dept. of Family Practice **Type of organization:** Medical school **Major product:** Medical services **Area of distribution:** Texas **Area of Practice:** Medical education **Published works:** 50 presentations - chapters **Affiliations:** Society of Teachers of Family Medicine **Hob./spts.:** Reading, walking, hiking **SIC code:** 80 **Address:** University of Texas Medical Branch, Dept. of Family Medicine, 400 Harbor Site Dr., Galveston, TX 77555-1123 **E-mail:** cromero@utmb.edu **Web address:** www.utmb.edu

ROMERO-FISCHMANN, DAVID
Industry: Healthcare/real estate **Univ./degree:** M.D., Universidad Mayor de San Francisco Xavier, 1990 **Current organization:** M.C.C.I./South Winds L.L.C./Benehern L.L.C. **Title:** M.D./ President, Owner **Type of organization:** Private medical practice/ Real estate firm **Major product:** Patient care/ Residential and commercial real estate sales **Area of distribution:** National **Area of Practice:** Pulmonary critical care, sleep medicine, internal medicine/real estate speculation and operations **Affiliations:** A.M.A.; A.C.P.; A.C.C.P. **Hob./spts.:** Water sports, soccer, chess, TaeKwon-Do **SIC code:** 80 **Address:** M.C.C.I./South Winds L.L.C./Benehern L.L.C., 11750 S.W. 40th St., Miami, FL 33175 **E-mail:** darofi70@hotmail.com

ROMEU, JESSE
Industry: Healthcare **Born:** July 22, 1962, New York, New York **Univ./degree:** M.D., Escuela de San Juan Batista, 1988 **Current organization:** Centro Meumologico del Oeste **Title:** M.D. **Type of organization:** Private practice **Major product:** Patient care **Area of Practice:** Critical Care Specialist; pulmonary medicine **Affiliations:** Fellow, College of Chest Physicians; American College of Physicians; Society of Critical Care Medicine **Hob./spts.:** Boxing, basketball, volleyball **SIC code:** 80 **Address:** Urb. Villa Real E-25, Cabo Rojo, PR 00623 **E-mail:** jromeu2262@aol.com

ROSARIO, ISMAEL TORRES
Industry: Healthcare **Born:** January 26, 1956, Honduras, Puerto Rico **Univ./degree:** B.S., 1987; M.D., 1982, San Juan City Hospital **Current organization:** Hato Rey Hematology Oncology Group **Title:** MD **Type of organization:** Group practice **Major product:** Patient care/medical research **Area of distribution:** International **Area of practice:** Oncology **Area of Practice:** Oncology **Affiliations:** F.A.C.P.; American College of Oncology; National Cancer Institute **Hob./spts.:** Family **SIC code:** 80 **Address:** Hato Rey Hematology Oncology Group, C-8 Calle Honduras, Oasis Gardens, Guaynabo, PR 00969-3452 **E-mail:** ismael531@aol.com

ROSARIO-GUARDIOLA, REINALDO
Industry: Healthcare **Born:** September 17, 1948, San Juan, Puerto Rico **Univ./degree:** M.D., University of Puerto Rico Medical School, 1972 **Current organization:** Reinaldo Rosario-Guardiola, M.D. **Title:** M.D. **Type of organization:** Medical practice **Major product:** Patient care **Area of distribution:** San Juan, Puerto Rico **Area of Practice:** Dermatology **Affiliations:** Puerto Rico Dermatological Society; Alpha Omega Alpha **Hob./spts.:** Soccer, baseball **SIC code:** 80 **Address:** Reinaldo Rosario-Guardiola, M.D., 652 Muñoz Rivera Ave., Suite 3170, San Juan, PR 00918-4257 **E-mail:** rrosario@icepr.com

ROSENBERG, GARY SHELDON
Industry: Healthcare **Born:** May 19, 1952, Jersey City, New Jersey **Univ./degree:** M.D., State University of New York Downstate Medical Center, 1977 **Current organization:** University Plaza Obstetrics & Gynecology L.L.P. **Title:** M.D. **Type of organization:** Medical practice **Major product:** Women's healthcare **Area of distribution:** Long Island, New York **Area of Practice:** Obstetrics and gynecology **Affiliations:** A.C.O.G.; A.S.R.M.; A.A.G.L.; N.S.S.; Nassau County Medical Society **SIC code:** 80 **Address:** University Plaza Obstetrics & Gynecology L.L.P., 877 Stewart Ave., Suite 7, Garden City, NY 11530 **E-mail:** garyshros@aol.com

ROSENBERG, JAY H.
Industry: Healthcare **Born:** September 25, 1943, Chicago, Illinois **Univ./degree:** M.D., Chicago Medical School, 1969 **Current organization:** Valley Plastic Surgery Center **Title:** M.D., President/Founder **Type of organization:** Physician offices **Major product:** Surgical procedures **Area of distribution:** West Dundee, Illinois **Area of Practice:** Plastic and reconstructive surgery **Honors/awards:** Freemont Chandler Schlorarship Award **Affiliations:** A.M.A.; C.P.S.S.; A.S.A.P.S. **Hob./spts.:** Painting, sculpture, golf **SIC code:** 80 **Address:** Valley Plastic Surgery Center, 350 S. Eighth St., West Dundee, IL 60118 **E-mail:** vpsc@mindspring.com **Web address:** www.valleyplasticsurgery.com

ROSENBLUM, NORMAN G.
Industry: Healthcare **Born:** June 4, 1948, Philadelphia, Pennsylvania **Univ./degree:** Ph.D., 1975; M.D., 1978; Thomas Jefferson Medical College **Current organization:** Fox Chase Cancer Center **Title:** M.D./Ph.D./Chief, Section of Gynecologic Oncology **Type of organization:** Hospital **Major product:** Surgery **Area of distribution:** Pennsylvania **Area of Practice:** Gynecologic oncology **Affiliations:** American Society of Clinical Oncology; American College of Surgeons; Society of Gynecologic Oncologists **Hob./spts.:** Physical fitness, family **SIC code:** 80 **Address:** Fox Chase Cancer Center, Section of Gynecologic Oncology, 7701 Burholme Ave., Philadelphia, PA 19111 **Web address:** www.fccc.edu

ROSENTHAL, MARK J.
Industry: Healthcare **Born:** December 15, 1951, Los Angeles, California **Univ./degree:** M.D., University of Pennsylvania **Current organization:** Mark J. Rosenthal, M.D./UCLA School of Medicine **Title:** M.D./Associate Professor **Type of organization:** Medical practice/university **Major product:** Patient care/medical education, research **Area of distribution:** Sepulveda/Los Angeles, California **Area of Practice:** Internal Medicine, Diabetes, Geriatrics **Published works:** 85 peer reviewed articles **Affiliations:** American Diabetes Association; American Geriatrics Society; Endocrine Society **SIC code:** 80 **Address:** Mark J. Rosenthal, M.D., 16111 Plummer St., #11E, Bldg. 25, Dept. GRECC, Sepulveda, CA 91343

ROSS, MARC KENNEDY
Industry: Healthcare **Born:** November 22, 1963, New York, New York **Univ./degree:** M.D., New York Medical College, 1989 **Current organization:** Cabrini Medical Center **Title:** M.D., Director of PM & R **Type of organization:** Hospital **Major product:** Patient care **Area of distribution:** New York **Area of Practice:** Physical medicine and rehabilitation **Honors/awards:** Best Doctors in New York **Published works:** Journal, "Advancement for the Directors of Rehabilitation", Co-author, 1 chapter, "The Textbook of Penetrating Trauma" **Affiliations:** A.B.P.M.R.; A.A.P.M.R.; A.M.A.; A.A.P.; New York Medical Society **Hob./spts.:** Family **SIC code:** 80 **Address:** Cabrini Medical Center, 227 E. 19th St., New York, NY 10003 **E-mail:** mross@cabrininy.org

ROUSOU, JOHN A.
Industry: Healthcare **Born:** September 18, 1944, Cyprus, Greece **Univ./degree:** M.D., American University, Beirut, Lebanon, 1971 **Current organization:** Baystate Medical Center **Title:** M.D., Chief of Cardiac Surgery **Type of organization:** Medical center **Major product:** Patient care **Area of distribution:** Massachusetts **Area of Practice:** Cardiac surgery **Affiliations:** American Association of Thoracic Surgeons; American College of Surgeons; American Medical Association; American Heart Association **Hob./spts.:** Golf, boating **SIC code:** 80 **Address:** Baystate Medical Center, 759 Chestnut St., Springfield, MA 01107

ROUSSEAU, JANICE E.
Industry: Healthcare **Born:** October 13, 1949, Lancaster, South Carolina **Univ./degree:** A.A., Respiratory Therapy, Flagler Career Institute, Florida, 1990 **Current organization:** JFK Medical Center **Title:** Supervisor/Blood Gas Coordinator **Type of organization:** Hospital **Major product:** Patient care **Area of distribution:** Florida **Area of Practice:** Administration - blood gas laboratory **Affiliations:** F.S.R.C.; A.A.R.C.; N.B.R.C. **Hob./spts.:** Baseball, reading, sewing, fishing **SIC code:** 80 **Address:** JFK Medical Center, 5301 S. Congress Ave., Atlantis, FL 33462 **E-mail:** evedn@yahoo.com

ROUSSEV, ROUMEN G.
Industry: Reproductive medicine **Born:** February 22, 1952, Bulgaria **Univ./degree:** M.D., Medical College of Bulgaria, 1978; Ph.D., Institute for Emergency Medicine, Bulgaria **Current organization:** Millenova Immunology Laboratories **Title:** Manager/Director **Type of organization:** Private institute, laboratory **Major product:** Reproductive immunology testing **Area of distribution:** International **Area of Practice:** Reproductive immunology, infertility **Published works:** 100+ articles and chapters, 2 books **Affiliations:** American Society for Reproductive Immunology **SIC code:** 80 **Address:** Millenova Immunology Laboratories, 233 E. Erie St., #510, Chicago, IL 60611-5935 **E-mail:** rgroussev@millenova.com **Web address:** www.millenova.com

ROY, P.K.
Industry: Healthcare **Born:** January 4, 1953, Bombay, India **Univ./degree:** M.D., University of Bombay, 1977 **Current organization:** Associated Psychiatric Consultants, Inc. **Title:** M.D. **Type of organization:** Private practice **Major product:** Patient care **Area of distribution:** Texas **Area of Practice:** General Psychiatry **Honors/awards:** T.S.P.P.; A.S.C.P.; F.A.P.A. **Hob./spts.:** Running **SIC code:** 80 **Address:** Associated Psychiatric Consultants, Inc., 2330 Timber Shadows Dr., Suite 106, Kingwood, TX 77339 **E-mail:** pkroymd@aol.com

ROY, RENÉE
Industry: Healthcare **Born:** July 19, 1955, Ottawa, Canada **Univ./degree:** M.D., McGill University, 1984 **Current organization:** Renée Roy, M.D. **Title:** M.D. **Type of organization:** Private practice **Major product:** Patient care **Area of distribution:** Mid West City, Oklahoma **Area of Practice:** Family medicine **Honors/awards:** Honor as Community Teacher for 3rd year Medical Student **Affiliations:** Fellow, American Academy of Family Physicians; Fellow, Canadian College of Family Medicine; Flight Surgeon; Board of Trustees, Oklahoma State Medical Association **Hob./spts.:** Ballroom dancing, swimming, skiing **SIC code:** 80 **Address:** Renée Roy, M.D., 10002 S.E. 15th St., Midwest City, OK 73130 **E-mail:** rroy4@cox.net

ROZEN-KATZMAN, SHULAMIT
Industry: Healthcare **Born:** September 29, 1963, Chicago, Illinois **Univ./degree:** M.D., Sackler Medical School, Tel Aviv, 1989 **Current organization:** Aventura Children's Center **Title:** M.D. **Type of organization:** Medical practice **Major product:** Patient care **Area of distribution:** International **Area of Practice:** Pediatrics **Affiliations:** Fellow, American Academy of Pediatrics **Hob./spts.:** Fluent in English, Hebrew, French, Spanish, Italian **SIC code:** 80 **Address:** Aventura Childrens Center, 19030 N.E. 29th Ave, Aventura, FL 33180 **E-mail:** shula123@aol.com

RUBIN, JAMES M.
Industry: Healthcare **Born:** December 23, 1935, New York **Univ./degree:** M.D., New York Medical College, 1960 **Current organization:** Allergy & Asthma Associates of Murray Hill **Title:** M.D. **Type of organization:** Medical office **Major product:** Patient care **Area of distribution:** National **Area of Practice:** Allergies **Published works:** 12 articles, 3 books **Affiliations:** F.A.A.A.A.I.; F.A.C.A.A.I.; F.A.C.P.; F.A.C.C.P. **Hob./spts.:** Reading, golf **SIC code:** 80 **Address:** Allergy & Asthma Associates of Murray Hill, 35 E. 35th Street, New York, NY 10016 **E-mail:** jmrubinmd@aol.com

RUDIN, ROBERT LAWRENCE
Industry: Healthcare **Born:** December 18, 1956, Philadelphia, Pennsylvania **Univ./degree:** M.D., Hahnemann University, 1986; Internship, Pediatrics, William Beaumont Army Medical Center; Internship and Residency, Internal Medicine, Graduate Hospital **Current organization:** Kress Family Practice **Title:** M.D. **Type of organization:** Private medical practice **Major product:** Family practice **Area of distribution:** Jenkintown, Pennsylvania **Area of Practice:** Internal medicine **Affiliations:** American Medical Association; American College of Physicians; American Society of Internal Medicine; Pennsylvania State Medical Society; Montgomery County Medical Society **Hob./spts.:** Guitar, jogging, reading, foreign languages **SIC code:** 80 **Address:** Kress

Family Practice, 610 Old York Rd., Suite 70, Jenkintown, PA 19046 **E-mail:** docrlr@aol.com

RUIZ, DONNA C.
Industry: Healthcare **Born:** August 9, 1960, New York, New York **Univ./degree:** M.D., University of Santo Tomas, 1986 **Current organization:** Summit Pediatrics, PA **Title:** Doctor of Medicine **Type of organization:** Private practice with hospital affiliation **Major product:** Patient care **Area of distribution:** Bergen County, New Jersey **Area of Practice:** Pediatrics **Published works:** Zuckerman, G.B., Ruiz, D.C., Keller, I.A. Brooks J., 1996. Neurologic Complications Following Intranasal Administration of Heroin in an Adolescent. The Annals of Pharmacotherapy, 30:778-781; Castro, A., Ruiz, D.C., Ivashkiv, L. 1997. IL-4 Induced Alteration of IL-2 Signaling and Stat5 Activation. Keystone Conference Colorado; Castro, A. Ruiz, D.C., Ivashkiv, L., 1999. IL-4 Selectively Inhibits IL-2 Triggered Stat5 Activation, but not Proliferation, in Human T Cells. The Journal of Immunology, 162:1261-1269. **Affiliations:** A.A.P.; A.C.R.; A.M.A.; M.S.N.J.; American Board of Medical Specialties; Northern New Jersey Pediatric Society **Hob./spts.:** Art, modern decorating, fashion **SIC code:** 80 **Address:** Summit Pediatrics, PA, 55 Summit Ave., Hackensack, NJ 07601 **E-mail:** dcruiz@earthlink.net

RULLAN-VARELA, MELINDA
Industry: Healthcare **Born:** San Juan, Puerto Rico **Univ./degree:** M.D., University of Puerto Rico, 1996 **Current organization:** Intensive Care Services **Title:** M.D. **Type of organization:** Private practice **Major product:** Patient care, medical research and consulting **Area of distribution:** Miami, Florida **Area of Practice:** Internal medicine **Published works:** 3 publications **Affiliations:** A.M.A;, Society of Critical Care Medicine; A.C.P. **Hob./spts.:** Painting **SIC code:** 80 **Address:** Intensive Care Services, 8900 N. Candle Dr., Miami, FL 33196 **E-mail:** melindarullan@msn.com

RUN, SHEILA N.
Industry: Healthcare **Born:** September 11, 1940, San Francisco, California **Univ./degree:** M.D., Universita di Bologna Facolta di Medicina e Chirurgia, Italy, 1971 **Current organization:** Cleveland Clinic Foundation **Title:** M.D./Associate Staff **Type of organization:** Multispecialty academic hospital **Major product:** Medical services, pain management **Area of distribution:** Chardon, Ohio **Area of Practice:** Anesthesia, surgery pavilion management **Affiliations:** C.S.A.; O.S.A.; N.S.A. **Hob./spts.:** Stained glass **SIC code:** 80 **Address:** 13050 Coachman Dr., Chardon, OH 44024 **E-mail:** runs.@ccf.org

RUSSELL, MARILYN A.
Industry: Healthcare **Univ./degree:** D.M.D., Medical College of Georgia, Augusta, 1974 **Current organization:** Progressive Periodontics **Title:** Periodontist **Type of organization:** Dental office **Major product:** Periodontal services **Area of distribution:** International **Area of Practice:** Implants, extraction, gum surgery **Affiliations:** President, North Georgia Dental Association **SIC code:** 80 **Address:** Progressive Periodontics, 105 Carnegie Place, Suite 113, Fayetteville, GA 30214 **E-mail:** perio1@mindspring.com **Web address:** www.progressiveperidontics.com

RUSSELL, THOMAS J.
Industry: Healthcare **Born:** July 30, 1954, Connecticut **Univ./degree:** M.S., Microbiology & Forensic Science, University of New Haven, Connecticut, 1981 **Current organization:** Mid State Medical Center **Title:** EMS Coordinator **Type of organization:** Hospital **Major product:** Patient care **Area of distribution:** Meriden, Connecticut **Area of Practice:** Emergency medicine **Affiliations:** N.A.E.M.S.E.; N.A.E.M.S.P. **Hob./spts.:** Child safety **SIC code:** 80 **Address:** Mid State Medical Center, 435 Lewis Ave., Meriden, CT 06451 **E-mail:** tjrusse@harthosp.org

RUSSELL JR., RICHARD O.
Industry: Healthcare **Born:** 1932, Birmingham, Alabama **Univ./degree:** M.D., Vanderbilt University, Tennessee, 1956 **Current organization:** Cardiovascular Associates, Inc. **Title:** M.D. **Type of organization:** Medical group **Major product:** Cardiovascular care **Area of distribution:** Alabama **Area of Practice:** Cardiology **Honors/awards:** Distinguished Fellow, American College of Cardiology **Published works:** Hemodynamic Monitoring; Radiographic Anatomy of Coronary Arteries **Affiliations:** A.C.C.; A.H.A.; A.C.C.P.; United Way; Kiwanis Club, Birmingham **SIC code:** 80 **Address:** Cardiovascular Associates, Inc., 880 Montclair Rd., 1st floor, Birmingham, AL 35213-1971

RUSSO, CHARLES D.
Industry: Healthcare **Univ./degree:** M.D., New York Medical College, 1981; Residency & Fellowship, Hartford Hospital **Current organization:** Cardiology Associates **Title:** M.D., F.A.C.C. **Type of organization:** Cardiology specialty practice **Major product:** Patient care **Area of distribution:** Florida **Area of Practice:** Non-invasive cardiology, nuclear cardiology **Affiliations:** A.H.A.; A.M.A.; Chief Resident, Hartford Hospital; Faculty, University of Miami, 1990-95 **SIC code:** 80 **Address:** Cardiology Associates, 4725 N. Federal Hwy., Suite 401, Ft. Lauderdale, FL 33308 **Web address:** www.cardiology-associates.com

RUTLEDGE, BILLIE
Industry: Healthcare **Born:** October 11, 1961, Carlsbad, New Mexico **Univ./degree:** A.S.N., New Mexico State University, 1994 **Current organization:** Carlsbad Medical Center **Title:** RN,C, Case Manager **Type of organization:** Hospital **Major product:** Patient care **Area of distribution:** New Mexico **Area of Practice:** Case management **SIC code:** 80 **Address:** Carlsbad Medical Center, 303 Valley View, Carlsbad, NM 88220 **E-mail:** billier@caverns.com

RYAN, SHERYL A.
Industry: Medical **Born:** September 6, 1954, Fall River, Massachusetts **Univ./degree:** B.S., Biology, Boston College; M.D., Yale University School of Medicine, 1981 **Current organization:** Yale University School of Medicine, Dept. of Pediatrics **Title:** Associate Professor of Pediatrics; Chief, Section of Adolescent Medicine; Director, Adolescent Clinic in Primary Care Center, Yale - New Haven Hospital **Type of organization:** Medical school/hospital **Major product:** Patient care, medical education **Area of distribution:** National **Area of Practice:** Pediatrics, adolescent medicine, clinic administration, research; Preceptor to residents **Honors/awards:** Young Investigator Award for Research, 1993 (SAM); Phi Beta Kappa, Order of the Cross & the Crown **Published works:** 20+ articles, several chapters **Affiliations:** Fellow, Society for Adolescent Medicine; Fellow, American Academy of Pediatrics **Hob./spts.:** Choral singing (New Haven Chorale) , gardening **SIC code:** 80 **Address:** Yale University School of Medicine Dept. of Pediatrics, P.O. Box 208064, New Haven, CT 06521 **E-mail:** sherly.ryan@yale.edu

RYAN, TIMOTHY J.
Industry: Healthcare **Born:** March 24, 1961, Salt Lake City, Utah **Univ./degree:** B.S., 1983; M.S., Sports Medicine, 1985, Springfield College; M.S., Physical Therapy, Quinnipiac College, Connecticut, 1987; O.D., University of Health Science, Kansas City, Missouri, 1991 **Current organization:** Missouri Valley Physicians **Title:** D.O./Chief of Staff **Type of organization:** Medical clinic **Major product:** Patient care **Area of distribution:** Missouri **Area of Practice:** Osteopathic medicine **Honors/awards:** Resident of the Year, 1992-94; Sirridge Award for Excellence in Clinical Medicine, 1994 **Affiliations:** A.M.A.; A.O.A. **Hob./spts.:** Hunting, fishing, running **SIC code:** 80 **Address:** Missouri Valley Physicians, 2303 S. Highway 65, Marshall, MO 65340 **E-mail:** tryan@socket.net

SABATIER, RICHARD E.
Industry: Healthcare **Born:** February 5, 1949, Baton Rouge, Louisiana **Univ./degree:** M.D., Tulane University, 1973 **Current organization:** Plastic and Reconstructive Surgery **Title:** M.D. **Type of organization:** Medical practice **Major product:** Patient care **Area of distribution:** Louisiana **Area of Practice:** Craniofacial, maxillofacial, orthognathic, neurosurgery, surgical oncology, general and thoracic surgery, microvascular surgery, hand surgery, plastic surgery **Published works:** Multiple publications **Affiliations:** F.A.C.S. **SIC code:** 80 **Address:** Plastic and Reconstructive Surgery, 109 Northpark Blvd., Suite 210, Covington, LA 70433 **E-mail:** resabatier@aol.com

SABHARWAL, VEENA
Industry: Healthcare **Univ./degree:** M.D., University of India **Current organization:** Southwest Pediatrics **Title:** M.D. **Type of organization:** Private practice **Major product:** Patient care **Area of distribution:** Livonia, Michigan **Area of Practice:** Pediatrics **Affiliations:** A.A.P.; A.M.A.; M.A.P.I. **SIC code:** 80 **Address:** Southwest Pediatrics, 37672 Professional Center Dr., Livonia, MI 48154 **E-mail:** swpedsvf@yahoo.com

SADASHIV, SANTHOSH KUKKADI
Industry: Healthcare **Born:** June 17, 1973, Bangalore, India **Univ./degree:** M.D., SRI-SIDD Hartha Medical College, India, 1997; Residency, Brookdale University Hospital **Current organization:** Brookdale University Hospital & Medical Center **Title:** M.D. **Type of organization:** Hospital **Major product:** Patient care, residency training **Area of distribution:** Brooklyn, New York **Area of Practice:** Critical care **Honors/awards:** Best Intern Award, 2000; Best Outstanding Resident M.D. **Published works:** Articles **Affiliations:** A.M.A. **Hob./spts.:** Reading, mountain tracking **SIC code:** 80 **Address:** Brookdale University Hospital & Medical Center, 7 Hegeman Ave., #9A, Brooklyn, NY 11212 **E-mail:** santiacedoc@yahoo.com

SADATY, ANITA F.
Industry: Healthcare **Born:** October 19, 1966, Newark, New Jersey **Univ./degree:** M.D., Cornell University, 1994; Residency, North Shore University Hospital **Current organization:** Great Neck Obstetrics & Gynecology **Title:** M.D. **Type of organization:** Private practice **Major product:** Women's healthcare **Area of distribution:** Long Island, New York **Area of Practice:** Obstetrics/gynecology **Honors/awards:** Alpha Omega Alpha; 2001 Teaching/Physicians Award, North Shore Hospital **Published works:** "Diabetes Impairs the Late Inflammatory Response to Wound Healing", Journal of Surgical Research **Affiliations:** American College of Gynecology; American Medical Women's Association; Nassau County Ob/Gyn; Society of Laparoscopic Surgeons **Hob./spts.:** Boxing, weightlifting, running, photography **SIC code:** 80 **Address:** Great Neck Obstetrics & Gynecology, 900 Northern Blvd., Great Neck, NY 11021 **E-mail:** sadaty@yahoo.com

SADIKOT, SHABBIR
Born: September 17, 1946, Bombay, India **Univ./degree:** M.D., School of Bombay-Grant Medical College, 1971 **Title:** M.D. **Area of Practice:** Geriatric, family practice **Honors/awards:** Diplomate, American Board of Family Practice; Diplomate, American Board of Ethical Physicians; Diplomate, American Board of Hospital Physicians **Affiliations:** South Nassau Communities Hospital, New York; Long Beach Medical Center, New York **Hob./spts.:** Travel, baseball, football **SIC code:** 80 **Address:** Shabbir Sadikot, M.D., 865 Merrick Rd., Suite 206, Baldwin, NY 11510 **E-mail:** nufammed@aol.com

SAENZ, MARY RITA
Industry: Healthcare **Univ./degree:** Certified Laboratory Assistant, Driscoll Children's Hospital, 1962 **Current organization:** South Texas Adult Medicine Assoc. **Title:** CLA **Type of organization:** Clinical lab/medical office **Major product:** Patient care **Area of distribution:** Corpus Christi, Texas **Area of Practice:** Internal medicine **SIC code:** 80 **Address:** South Texas Adult Medicine Assoc., 601 Texan Trail, Suite 200, Corpus Christi, TX 78411

SAFO, MARGARET
Industry: Healthcare **Born:** July 27, 1952, Accra, Ghana **Univ./degree:** M.D., University of Ghana Medical School, 1980 **Current organization:** Margaret Safo, MD, PC **Title:** MD, FAAP, MPH **Type of organization:** Clinic **Major product:** Patient care **Area of distribution:** New York **Area of Practice:** Pediatrics **Affiliations:** Fellow, American Academy of Pediatrics; American Public Health Association; Nassau County Medical Association; Ghana Medical Association of the USA **Hob./spts.:** Sewing, cooking, physical fitness **SIC code:** 80 **Address:** Margaret Safo, MD, PC, 248 Beach 20th St., Far Rockaway, NY 11691 **E-mail:** drmsafo@aol.com

SAGER, DAVID S.
Industry: Healthcare **Univ./degree:** B.A., History, Tufts University, 1969; M.D., University of Illinois Medical School 1973 **Current organization:** Rheumatic Disease Center Physicians S.C. **Title:** M.D./Partner **Type of organization:** Private group practice **Major product:** Patient care **Area of distribution:** Illinois **Area of Practice:** Rheumatology, teaching at Lutheran General Hospital **Published works:** 10 publications **Affiliations:** Fellow, American College of Rheumatology **SIC code:** 80 **Address:** Rheumatic Disease Center Physicians S.C., 150 River Rd., Des Plaines, IL 60016 **E-mail:** docbowtie@aol.com

SAGLIK, METIN
Industry: Healthcare **Born:** December 19, 1937, Turkey **Univ./degree:** M.D., University of Istanbul, 1963 **Current organization:** St. John's Hospital (Emeritus) **Title:** M.D. **Type of organization:** Hospital **Major product:** Patient care **Area of distribution:** St. Claire Shores, Michigan **Area of Practice:** Obstetrics, gynecology **Affiliations:** A.M.A.; A.C.O.G. **SIC code:** 80 **Address:** 3701 Country Club Dr., St. Claire Shores, MI 48082-2953 **E-mail:** msaglik@home.com

SAIDI, JOHN A.
Industry: Healthcare **Univ./degree:** M.D., Kabul University, Afghanistan, 1974 **Current organization:** Complete Care Family Medicine **Title:** M.D. **Type of organization:** Private practice **Major product:** Patient care **Area of distribution:** Oklahoma City, Oklahoma **Area of Practice:** Family medicine **Published works:** Research articles **Affiliations:** A.A.F.P.; A.M.A. **SIC code:** 80 **Address:** Complete Care Family Medicine, 9220 S. Pennsylvania Ave., Suite A, Oklahoma City, OK 73159-6902 **E-mail:** drjsaidi@sbcglobal.net

SALADA, ELIZABETH A.P.
Industry: Healthcare **Born:** August 8, 1965, Phoenix, Arizona **Univ./degree:** M.D., Wake Forest University, Bowman Gray School of Medicine, 1993 **Current organization:** Palomar Medical Group **Title:** M.D., M.P.H. **Type of organization:** Office based private practice **Major product:** Patient care **Area of distribution:** Escondido, California **Area of Practice:** Internal medicine **Honors/awards:** Member, Who's Who; Women of Merit in Escondido, California **Published works:** Research articles **Affiliations:** A.M.A.; F.A.C.P.; A.M.W.A.; Redwood Terrace Medical Director; Committee Member, Palomar Medical Center's Investigation Review Board; Member, Sharp Community Medical Group Pharmacy and Therapeutics Committee; Volunteer, Clinical Faculty/Career Counselor, U.C.S.D. **Hob./spts.:** Running, music, dance, children **SIC code:** 80 **Address:** Palomar Medical Group, 625 E. Grand Ave., Escondido, CA 92025 **Web address:** www.pphs.org

SALAMAH, MEIR
Industry: Healthcare **Title:** M.D. **Type of organization:** Private practice **Major product:** Patient care **Area of Practice:** Pediatrics **SIC code:** 80 **Address:** Meir Salamah Medical Office, 407 Avenue U, Brooklyn, NY 11223 **E-mail:** mesl671@aol.com

SALANOVA, VINCENTA
Industry: Medical **Born:** January 28, 1945, Santo Domingo, Dominican Republic **Univ./degree:** M.D., University of Madrid, Spain, 1968 **Current organization:** Indiana University, University Hospital, Dept. of Neurology **Title:** M.D./Associate Professor **Type of organization:** University hospital **Major product:** Patient care, research, medical education **Area of distribution:** Indianapolis, Indiana **Area of Practice:** Neurology, epilepsy **Affiliations:** A.A.N.; A.E.S.; I.S.M.S. **Hob./spts.:** Classical music, reading, skiing **SIC code:** 80 **Address:** Indiana University, University Hospital, Dept. of Neurology, 550 University Blvd., Room-1711, Indianapolis, IN 46202-5250 **E-mail:** vsalanova@iupui.edu

SALEH, ANTHONY G.
Industry: Healthcare **Born:** October 8, 1959 **Univ./degree:** M.D., St. George's University School of Medicine, 1985 **Current organization:** Anthony G. Saleh, M.D. **Title:** M.D. **Type of organization:** Private practice **Major product:** Patient care **Area of distribution:** New York **Area of Practice:** Internal medicine, pulmonary diseases **Affiliations:** American College of Chest Physicians **Hob./spts.:** Basketball, running **SIC code:** 80 **Address:** Anthony G. Saleh, M.D., 7702 4th Ave., Brooklyn, NY 11209 **E-mail:** anthonylung@aol.com

SALERNO, JOHN
Industry: Healthcare **Born:** February 4, 1960, Jamaica, New York **Univ./degree:** B.S., Biology, Adelphi University, 1982; D.O., New York College of Osteopathic Medicine, 1987 **Current organization:** John Salerno, D.O. **Title:** D.O. **Type of organization:** Private practice **Major product:** Patient care **Area of distribution:** New York **Area of Practice:** Family practice **Affiliations:** F.A.C.O.F.P.; A.O.A.; A.M.A.; A.A.F.P.; A.C.A.M.; A.C.A.A. **Hob./spts.:** Art collector, baseball, outdoor activities, skiing, travel, Broadway plays, reading **SIC code:** 80 **Address:** 72 Marina Way, Islip, NY 11751 **E-mail:** drsalerno@aol.com

SALGADO, CARLOS A.
Industry: Healthcare **Born:** June 18, 1952, Puerto Rico **Univ./degree:** M.D., University of Puerto Rico School of Medicine, 1978 **Current organization:** Centro Cardiovascular de Arecibo **Title:** Cardiologist/Professor **Type of organization:** Medical school **Major product:** Patient care, medical education **Area of distribution:** Arecibo, Puerto Rico **Area of Practice:** Cardiology **Affiliations:** F.A.H.A.; F.A.C.P.; F.A.C.C., F.A.C.A. **Hob./spts.:** Basketball, baseball, collector of racing cars **SIC code:** 80 **Address:** Centro Cardiovascular de Arecibo, P.O. Box 575, Arecibo, PR 00613 **E-mail:** ccvarecibo@hotmail.com

SALINAS, SILVERIO J.
Industry: Healthcare **Born:** July 11, 1962, Cerralvo, Mexico **Univ./degree:** M.D., University of Nuevo Leon **Current organization:** Silverio Salinas Inc. **Title:** President **Type of organization:** Private practice **Major product:** Naturopathic services **Area of distribution:** Corpus Christi, Texas **Area of Practice:** Complementary-alternative medicine/naturopathic doctor/patient care **Published works:** 1 book, "Good-bye Pain (500 Pressure Points on Ear to Relieve Pain)" **Affiliations:** Medical Director, Good-bye Cancer **SIC code:** 80 **Address:** Silverio Salinas Inc., 5225 Bonham St., Corpus Christi, TX 78415 **E-mail:** silveriosalinas@aol.com

SAMADI, DILARA EILEEN
Industry: Healthcare **Born:** January 8, 1960, Washington, D.C. **Univ./degree:** B.S., Randolph & Mason Women's College, Virginia, 1981; M.D., Autonomous College of Medicine, Guatamala, 1985 **Current organization:** Buffalo Medical Group **Title:** M.D. **Type of organization:** Group practice **Major product:** Patient care **Area of distribution:** New York **Area of Practice:** OB-GYN **Affiliations:** F.A.C.O.G.; F.A.C.S. **SIC code:** 80 **Address:** Buffalo Medical Group, Dept. OB/GYN, 295 Essjay Rd., Williamsville, NY 14221

SAMPATH, ANGUS C.
Industry: Medical **Title:** M.D. **Type of organization:** University hospital **Major product:** Patient care **Area of Practice:** Pathology, diagnosis of diseases **SIC code:** 80 **Address:** Harlem Hospital-Columbia University, Dept. of Pathology, 506 Lenox Ave., New York, NY 10037 **E-mail:** acs3@columbia.edu

SAMRAJ, GEORGE
Industry: Medical **Born:** February 16, 1957, Madras, India **Univ./degree:** M.D., Madras University, 1980 **Current organization:** University of Florida **Title:** M.D. **Type of organization:** University **Major product:** Patient care, medical education **Area of distribution:** Florida **Area of Practice:** Family practice, education **Published works:** 15 publications, 5 abstracts **Affiliations:** A.A.F.P.; A.M.A.; S.M.A.; A.D.A.; S.T.F.M. **Hob./spts.:** Photography **SIC code:** 80 **Address:** University of Florida, 625 S.W. Fourth Ave., Gainesville, FL 32601 **E-mail:** georges@ufl.edu

SAMUELS, VERNICE M.
Industry: Healthcare **Born:** June 5, 1948, West Indies, Jamaica **Univ./degree:** B.S., Healthcare Administration, St. Joseph's College, 1995 **Current organization:** Marcus Garvey Nursing Home **Title:** DNS **Type of organization:** Nursing home **Major product:** Patient care **Area of distribution:** New York **Area of Practice:** Nursing/management **Affiliations:** A.N.A. **Hob./spts.:** Music, sports **SIC code:** 80 **Address:**

Marcus Garvey Nursing Home, 810-20 St. Marks Ave., Brooklyn, NY 11213 **E-mail:** vernicesamuels@aol.com

SAMUYLOVA, RAISA
Industry: Dentistry **Born:** July 4, 1950, The Volgograd Region, Russia **Univ./degree:** D.D.S., New York University College of Dentistry, 1993 **Current organization:** Real Dental, LLC; 2nd office location: 5 Manor Dr., Suite 1-C, Newark, NJ 07106 **Title:** D.D.S. **Type of organization:** Private practice **Major product:** Dental care **Area of distribution:** New Jersey **Area of Practice:** Cosmetic and restorative dentistry **Affiliations:** A.D.A.; A.G.D.; N.J.D.A. **Hob./spts.:** Tennis, photography, gardening **SIC code:** 80 **Address:** Real Dental, LLC, 473 Broadway, Suite 200, Bayonne, NJ 07002 **E-mail:** raisasmiler@comcast.net

SANCHEZ, CHERYL P.
Industry: Medical **Born:** March 12, 1961, Philippines **Univ./degree:** M.D., University of the Philippines, 1986 **Current organization:** University of Wisconsin School of Medicine & Public Health **Title:** M.D./Associate Professor of Pediatrics **Type of organization:** University hospital **Major product:** Patient care, medical education **Area of distribution:** International **Area of Practice:** Pediatric nephrology **Affiliations:** American Society of Nephrology; American Society of Pediatric Nephrology **Hob./spts.:** Travel **SIC code:** 80 **Address:** University of Wisconsin School of Medicine & Public Health, 3590 MSC, 1300 University Avenue, Madison, WI 53706 **E-mail:** cpsanchez@wisc.edu

SANCHEZ, CYNTHIA M.
Industry: Healthcare **Born:** March 14, 1975, New York, New York **Univ./degree:** B.A., Health Services, Florida International University, 2000 **Current organization:** American Therapeutic Association **Title:** Owner/Administrator **Type of organization:** Medical clinic **Major product:** Chiropractic **Area of distribution:** Miami, Florida **Area of Practice:** Administration of health services **Hob./spts.:** Reading, basketball **SIC code:** 80 **Address:** American Therapeutic Association, 8324 S.W. Eighth St., Miami, FL 33144 **E-mail:** cindyandboris@aol.com

SÁNCHEZ, ALFREDO RODRIGUEZ
Industry: Healthcare **Born:** September 2, 1956, San Juan, Puerto Rico **Univ./degree:** M.D., Central East University School of Medicine, Dominican Republic **Current organization:** Vega Baja Primary Care Center **Title:** President **Type of organization:** Private practice **Major product:** Patient care **Area of distribution:** Puerto Rico **Area of Practice:** General practice **Affiliations:** P.R.M.C. **Hob./spts.:** Golf, jogging **SIC code:** 80 **Address:** Vega Baja Primary Care Center, Box 4144, Vega Baja, PR 00694

SANCHEZ-LONGO, LUIS P.
Industry: Healthcare **Born:** December 1, 1925, Bayamon, Puerto Rico **Univ./degree:** B.S., Rio University, Puerto Rico; M.D., Jefferson University, Philadelphia **Current organization:** University of Puerto Rico School of Medicine **Title:** Professor Emeritus of Neurology **Type of organization:** Teaching hospital **Major product:** Neurology, clinical education **Area of distribution:** Puerto Rico **Area of Practice:** Treatment of epilepsy, multiple sclerosis, spinal chord problems, herniated discs **Hob./spts.:** Tenor vocalist **SIC code:** 80 **Address:** URB Las Americas, 960 Calle San Salvador, San Juan, PR 00921-2335

SANCHEZ-PENA, RAFAEL A.
Industry: Healthcare/consulting **Born:** October 25, 1947, Santurce, Puerto Rico **Spouse:** Luz **Married:** December 14, 1968 **Children:** Rafael 30, Jose Luis 26, Jose Alberto 25 **Univ./degree:** B.S., Physical Engineering, University of Puerto Rico, 1979 **Current organization:** Puerto Rico Medical Services Administration **Title:** Electrical Systems Manager **Type of organization:** Medical center **Major product:** Healthcare electrical consultant **Area of distribution:** Puerto Rico **Area of Practice:** Electrical engineering, installation, maintenance, training, electrical security **Affiliations:** I.E.E.E.; N.S.P.A.; N.S.S.A.; N.S.P.E. **Hob./spts.:** Antique cars **SIC code:** 80 **Address:** Puerto Rico Medical Services Administration, P.O. Box 2129, San Juan, PR 00922-2129 **E-mail:** rafaelsp4@corp.asempr.org

SANDERS, JESSICA S. (JARROTT)
Industry: Healthcare **Born:** Lubbock, Texas **Univ./degree:** A.S., Radiological Technology, North Arkansas Community College, 1997 **Current organization:** Community Medical Center of Izard County **Title:** Co-Director Radiology **Type of organization:** Hospital **Major product:** Patient care **Area of distribution:** Calico Rock, Arkansas **Area of Practice:** Mammography, CT, ultrasound **Hob./spts.:** Tae Kwon Do, dancing **SIC code:** 80 **Address:** Community Medical Center of Izard County, P.O. Box 438, Calico Rock, AR 72519 **E-mail:** neeko@centurytel.net

SANDY, YVONNE J.
Industry: Healthcare **Born:** July 31, 1939, Trinidad, West Indies **Univ./degree:** B.S.N., Pace University, 1983; M.S.N., St. Joseph's College **Current organization:** St. Mary's Hospital **Title:** Nurse Manager **Type of organization:** Hospital **Major product:** Patient care **Area of distribution:** Brooklyn, New York **Area of Practice:** Medical/surgical **Affiliations:** Nurse Executive Association **Hob./spts.:** Travel **SIC code:** 80 **Address:** St. Mary's Hospital, 170 Buffalo Ave., Brooklyn, NY 11213

SANNER, JUDITH G.
Industry: Healthcare **Born:** January 15, 1959, Dayton, Ohio **Univ./degree:** A.S., Nursing, Columbus Community College, Ohio, 1988; B.S.N., Ashland University, New York, 2004 **Current organization:** Vista Hospital of Dallas **Title:** Director of Surgical Services **Type of organization:** Hospital/surgery center **Major product:** Patient care **Area of distribution:** Texas **Area of Practice:** Surgical operations and management **Affiliations:** A.O.R.N.; T.S.N.B. **Hob./spts.:** Fishing, camping, needlework, sewing **SIC code:** 80 **Address:** Vista Hospital of Dallas, 2696 W. Walnut St., c/o Surgery, Garland, TX 75181 **E-mail:** judith.sanner@vista-dallas.com **Web address:** www.vista-dallas.com

SANSARICQ, CLAUDE
Industry: Healthcare **Born:** May 18, 1929, Jeremie, Haiti **Univ./degree:** M.D., University of Haiti School of Medicine, 1954; M.S., Nutrition, 1982; Ph.D., Nutrition, 1991, Columbia University **Current organization:** Mt. Sinai Medical Center **Title:** Director of Biochemical Genetics/M.D. **Type of organization:** University hospital **Major product:** Patient care, research **Area of distribution:** International **Area of Practice:** Pediatrics, genetics, nutrition **Published works:** 35+ peer review journals, 30 abstracts/conference papers, 3 book chapters **Affiliations:** F.A.C.N.; F.A.A.P. **Hob./spts.:** Reading, travel **SIC code:** 80 **Address:** Mt. Sinai Medical Center, Dept. of Human Genetics, Box 1497, 1 Gustave L. Levy Place, New York, NY 10029 **E-mail:** claude.sansaricq@mssm.edu

SANSON, JERRY L.
Industry: Laboratory **Born:** June 23, 1964, Alexandria, Louisiana **Univ./degree:** Northwestern State University **Title:** Histology Technician **Type of organization:** Hospital laboratory **Major product:** Histology equipment and products **Area of distribution:** Alexandria, Louisiana **Area of Practice:** Histology **Affiliations:** L.S.H.P.; N.A.H.T. **Hob./spts.:** Golf **SIC code:** 80 **Address:** 3330 Masonic Dr., Alexandria, LA 71301 **E-mail:** jlsanson1@yahoo.com

SANTANA-SIERRA, ALBA V.
Industry: Healthcare **Born:** January 22, 1929, San Cristobal, Dominican Republic **Univ./degree:** M.D., Universidad de Santo Tomas, Dominican Republic **Current organization:** Clinica Andres-Grillasca Oncologia **Title:** Chief of Anesthesia **Type of organization:** Hospital **Major product:** Patient care **Area of distribution:** Ponce, Puerto Rico **Area of Practice:** Anesthesia **Affiliations:** Medical Association of Puerto Rico; (SUR); Asociación de Mujeres Medicos Americanos **Hob./spts.:** Reading **SIC code:** 80 **Address:** Calle Caudal F-8 Valle Verde, Ponce, PR 00731 **E-mail:** eyasab@centennialpr.net

SANTIAGO, LUIS R.
Industry: Healthcare **Univ./degree:** M.D., University of Puerto Rico, 1994 **Current organization:** Clinica Oftalmica **Title:** M.D. **Type of organization:** Private practice **Major product:** Eye care **Area of distribution:** Aibonito, Puerto Rico **Area of Practice:** Ophthalmology **Affiliations:** A.A.O.; S.O.P.R. **SIC code:** 80 **Address:** Clinica Oftalmica, P.O. Box 455, Aibonito, PR 00705 **E-mail:** clinicaoftalmica@aol.com

SANTIAGO, YVONNE SANTIAGO
Industry: Healthcare **Born:** September 19, 1971, Mayaguez, Puerto Rico **Univ./degree:** M.D., San Juan Bautista School of Medicine, 1997 **Current organization:** Corporacion del Fondo del Seguro de Estado **Title:** M.D. **Type of organization:** Healthcare facility **Major product:** Patient care **Area of distribution:** Aguada, Puerto Rico **Area of Practice:** Family medicine; Certified in addiction counseling **Affiliations:** ACP **Hob./spts.:** Reading **SIC code:** 80 **Address:** P.O. Box 922, Aguada, PR 00602

SANTIAGO PÉREZ, HÉCTOR MANUEL
Industry: Healthcare **Born:** October 26, 1970, Ponce, Puerto Rico **Univ./degree:** M.D., Ponce School of Medicine **Current organization:** Santiago & Rivera Medical Associates **Title:** M.D. **Type of organization:** Medical practice **Major product:** Patient care **Area of distribution:** San Germán, Puerto Rico **Area of Practice:** Invasive and non-invasive cardiology **Published works:** Articles **Affiliations:** American College of Cardiology; Puerto Rico Society of Cardiology **Hob./spts.:** Music **SIC code:** 80 **Address:** Santiago & Rivera Medical Associates, San Germán Medical Plaza, Suite 211, San Germán, PR 00683 **E-mail:** medicalassoc@prw.net

SANTIAGO-FIGUEROA, JOSE M.
Industry: Healthcare **Born:** December 27, 1959, Puerto Rico **Univ./degree:** M.D., University of Puerto Rico at San Juan, 1986 **Current organization:** Jose M. Santiago-Figueora, M.D. **Title:** M.D. **Type of organization:** Private practice/academic appointment **Major product:** Patient care **Area of distribution:** San Juan, Puerto Rico **Area of Practice:** Orthopaedics and hand surgery **Published works:** Multiple publications **Affiliations:** A.M.A.; F.A.A.O.S.; F.A.S.S.H.; P.R.M.A. **Hob./spts.:** Marathon running

SIC code: 80 **Address:** Jose M. Santiago-Figueroa, M.D., 8th St. G-15, El Mirador, San Juan, PR 00926 **E-mail:** josafi@coqui.net

SANTMANN, THERESA M.
Industry: Healthcare **Current organization:** Little Flower Nursing Home **Title:** Owner/Executive Director **Type of organization:** Skilled nursing home **Major product:** Skilled nursing services, rehabilitation **Area of distribution:** East Islip and Sayville, New York **Area of Practice:** Skilled nursing care for the elderly **Affiliations:** Farmingdale College Foundation **SIC code:** 80 **Address:** Little Flower Nursing Home, 340 East Montauk Hwy., East Islip, NY 11730 **Web address:** www.little-flower.com

SANTOS, CARLOS R.
Industry: Healthcare **Born:** January 14, 1966 Caguas, Puerto Rico **Univ./degree:** M.D., University of Puerto Rico, San Juan, 1989 **Current organization:** Dr. Stewart Bernstein, PA **Title:** M.D. **Type of organization:** Private practice **Major product:** Patient care **Area of distribution:** Florida **Area of Practice:** Pulmonary and critical care medicine **Affiliations:** F.C.C.P.; A.T.S.; Alpha Omega Alpha **Hob./spts.:** Computers **SIC code:** 80 **Address:** Dr. Stewart Bernstein, PA, 21110 Biscayne Blvd., Suite 405, Aventura, FL 33180 **E-mail:** valmar92@yahoo.com

SANTOS, PRESCILLA L.
Industry: Healthcare **Born:** March 1, 1946, Taal, Batangas, Philippines **Univ./degree:** Centro Escolar University, Philippines/B.S., Medical Technology trained at Kansas City General Hospital & Medical Center, Kansas City, MO **Current organization:** Liberty HealthCare System - JCMC **Title:** Section Head Hematology/Chemistry **Type of organization:** Hospital **Major product:** Patient care **Area of distribution:** New Jersey **Area of Practice:** Laboratory management **Affiliations:** A.S.A.P. **Hob./spts.:** Swimming, movies **SIC code:** 80 **Address:** Liberty HealthCare System - JCMC, 355 Grand St. - 3 West, Jersey City, NJ 07302 **E-mail:** psantos@libertyhcs.org

SARABU, MOHAN R.
Industry: Healthcare **Born:** June 10, 1951, Khamman, India **Univ./degree:** M.D., Osmania University, 1973 **Current organization:** Cardiac Surgery Group, P.C. **Title:** M.D., F.A.C.S. **Type of organization:** Medical group **Major product:** Patient care **Area of distribution:** New York **Area of Practice:** Cardiothoracic surgery **Published works:** Annuls of Thoracic Surgery; Journal of Thoracic Cardio Vascular Surgery **Affiliations:** F.A.C.S.; S.T.S.; New York Medical College **SIC code:** 80 **Address:** Cardiac Surgery Group, P.C., Westchester Medical Center, 95 Grasslands Rd., Valhalla, NY 10595 **E-mail:** mohansarabu@hotmail.com

SARACINO, JOSEPH A.
Industry: Healthcare **Born:** June 1, 1960, Newark, New Jersey **Univ./degree:** M.D., University of Medicine and Dentistry of New Jersey, 1987 **Current organization:** Kinston Diagnostic Group **Title:** M.D. **Type of organization:** Multispecialty group **Major product:** Patient care **Area of distribution:** Kinston, North Carolina **Area of Practice:** Gastroenterology **Honors/awards:** Magna Cum Laude **Affiliations:** A.C.P.; A.S.G.E.; A.G.A.; North Carolina Medical Society **Hob./spts.:** Family, travel, swimming **SIC code:** 80 **Address:** Kinston Diagnostic Group, 109 Airport Rd., Kinston, NC 28501 **E-mail:** gijoee99@email.com

SARADAR, RAJA
Industry: Healthcare **Univ./degree:** M.D., Damascus University, 1979 **Current organization:** Silverman & Assoc. **Title:** M.D. **Type of organization:** Private practice **Major product:** Patient care **Area of distribution:** Monroeville, Pennsylvania **Area of Practice:** Pediatrics **Affiliations:** A.M.S.; P.M.S. **SIC code:** 80 **Address:** Silverman & Assoc., 300 Red Oak Ct., Monroeville, PA 15146-3100

SAREMBOCK, IAN J.
Industry: Medical **Born:** June 9, 1951, South Africa **Univ./degree:** M.D., Capetown University School of Medicine, South Africa, 1975 **Current organization:** University of Virginia, Cardiovascular Division **Title:** M.D., F.A.C.C., F.A.C.P. **Type of organization:** University hospital/clinics **Major product:** Medical services, medical education, medical research **Area of distribution:** Virginia **Area of Practice:** Interventional cardiology, vascular biology research **Published works:** 70+ articles and chapters **Affiliations:** F.A.C.C.; F.A.C.P.; American Heart Association **Hob./spts.:** Sports, reading **SIC code:** 80 **Address:** University of Virginia, Room 5614, Private Clinics Bldg., Hospital Dr., Charlottesville, VA 22908-0158 **E-mail:** ijs4s@virginia.edu **Web address:** www.virginia.edu

SARHILL, NABEEL
Industry: Healthcare **Born:** February 8, 1967, Lattakia, Syria **Univ./degree:** M.D., Tishreen University, Syria, 1990 **Current organization:** St. Vincent Charity Hospital **Title:** M.D. **Type of organization:** Hospital **Major product:** Patient care **Area of distribution:** International **Area of Practice:** Internal medicine **Published works:** 15 articles, 50 abstracts **Affiliations:** A.M.A.; American College of Physicians; American Academy Hospice & Palliative Medicine **Hob./spts.:** Soccer **SIC code:** 80 **Address:** St. Vincent Charity Hospital, 7710 Lucerne Dr., #R32, Cleveland, OH 44130 **E-mail:** sarhiln@yahoo.com

SARKAR, KUNAL
Industry: Medical **Born:** June 30, 1976, Bijnor, India **Univ./degree:** M.D., All India Institute of Medical Sciences, 1999; Residency: Internal Medicine, Drexel University, 2004; Fellowship: Cardiology, University of Arkansas for Medical Sciences, 2005 **Current organization:** University of Arkansas for Medical Sciences **Title:** M.D. **Type of organization:** University hospital/Medical school **Major product:** Medical services, research, education **Area of distribution:** International **Area of Practice:** Cardiology, Internal Medicine **Affiliations:** A.H.A.; A.C.C.; A.M.A.; A.A.P.I.; A.C.P. **Hob./spts.:** Filmmaking "The Heartbeat of Medicine" (shown on Indian TV), photography **SIC code:** 80 **Address:** University of Arkansas for Medical Sciences, 13111 W. Markham, #181, Little Rock, AR 72211 **E-mail:** ksarkarmd@gmail.com

SAROSIEK, JERZY
Industry: Medical **Born:** April 13, 1945, Poland **Univ./degree:** M.D., 1969; Ph.D., 1973, Medical School of Bialystok, Poland **Current organization:** University of Kansas Medical Center **Title:** M.D., Ph.D., Research Professor of Medicine, Director of Gastroenterology Research Laboratory **Type of organization:** University/medical center **Major product:** Basic/clinical medical research services **Area of distribution:** Kansas **Area of Practice:** Gastroenterology, biochemistry **Honors/awards:** Two US patents: US005314409 and US005730958 **Published works:** Multiple publications **Affiliations:** A.G.A.; A.C.G.; New York Academy of Sciences **Hob./spts.:** Classical music, swimming, tennis **SIC code:** 80 **Address:** University of Kansas Medical Center, Dept. of Medicine-4035 Delp, 3901 Rainbow Blvd., Kansas City, KS 66160-7350 **E-mail:** jsarosie@kumc.edu

SATALOFF, ROBERT THAYER
Industry: Healthcare **Born:** February 22, 1949, Philadelphia, Pennsylvania **Univ./degree:** M.D., Jefferson Medical College **Current organization:** Robert T. Sataloff, M.D. **Title:** M.D., D.M.A. **Type of organization:** Private practice **Major product:** Patient care, research, education **Area of distribution:** International **Area of Practice:** Neurology **Published works:** 400 articles, 21 books **Affiliations:** A.M.A.; A.A.O.H.N.S.; Voice Foundation **Hob./spts.:** Professional opera singer, music conductor **SIC code:** 80 **Address:** Robert T. Sataloff, M.D., 1721 Pine St., Philadelphia, PA 19103 **E-mail:** rtsataloff@phillyent.com

SAUL-SEHY, CHERYL L.
Industry: Healthcare **Born:** August 27, 1970, Mount Clemens, Michigan **Univ./degree:** M.D., Michigan State University, 1997 **Current organization:** Beverly Hills Pediatrics **Title:** M.D., Partner **Type of organization:** Medical practice **Major product:** Patient care **Area of distribution:** Birmingham, Michigan **Area of Practice:** Pediatrics **Published works:** 1 book **Affiliations:** F.A.A.P.; A.A.P. **Hob./spts.:** Marathon runner, piano **SIC code:** 80 **Address:** Beverly Hills Pediatrics, 1447 Washington Blvd., Birmingham, MI 48009

SAVASAN, SUREYYA
Industry: Medical **Born:** September 11, 1960, Karaman, Turkey **Univ./degree:** M.D., Hacettepe University School of Medicine **Current organization:** Children's Hospital of Michigan/Wayne State University **Title:** M.D. **Type of organization:** University hospital **Major product:** Medical services **Area of distribution:** Michigan **Area of Practice:** Pediatric hematology/oncology **Affiliations:** A.S.H.; Association of Pediatric Hematology/Oncology **Hob./spts.:** Soccer **SIC code:** 80 **Address:** Children's Hospital of Michigan, Hem/Onc, Wayne State University, 3901 Beaubien Blvd., Detroit, MI 48201 **E-mail:** ssavasan@med.wayne.edu

SAYA, SHOAIB H.
Industry: Healthcare **Born:** December 12, 1970, Karachi, Pakistan **Univ./degree:** M.D., Dow Medical College, Pakistan, 1994 **Current organization:** Baptist Hickman Community Hospital **Title:** M.D. **Type of organization:** Hospital **Major product:** Healthcare **Area of distribution:** Centerville, Tennessee **Area of Practice:** Internal medicine/emergency room **Honors/awards:** Director of bariatric unit **Published works:** 2 articles **Affiliations:** A.S.B.A. **Hob./spts.:** Tennis, cricket, music, travel **SIC code:** 80 **Address:** Baptist Hickman Community Hospital, 150 E. Swan Street, Centerville, TN 37033 **E-mail:** shoaibsaya@yahoo.com

SCAUNAS, DORINA S.
Industry: Healthcare **Born:** September 17, 1964, Romania **Univ./degree:** M.D., Loyola University, 1990 **Current organization:** Associates in OB-GYN S.C. **Title:** M.D. **Type of organization:** Private practice **Major product:** Pediatrics, adolescent and women's gynecology **Area of distribution:** Park Ridge, Illinois **Area of Practice:** Obstetrics and gynecology **Published works:** 2 articles **Affiliations:** F.A.C.O.G.; A.M.A.; I.M.S.; N.A.S.A.P.G. **Hob./spts.:** Music, horseback riding **SIC code:** 80 **Address:** Associates in OB-GYN S.C., Parkside Center, Suite 245, 1875 Dempster St., Park Ridge, IL 60068

SCAVO, SUSAN A.
Industry: Healthcare **Born:** September 30, 1969, Long island, New York **Univ./degree:** M.D., State University of New York, Syracuse, 1995 **Current organization:** University Plaza Obstetrics & Gynecology, LLP **Title:** M.D. **Type of organization:** Medical practice **Major product:** Women's healthcare **Area of distribution:** New York **Area of Practice:** Ob/Gyn **Affiliations:** A.C.O.G.; Nassau County Medical Society; Nassau County Ob/Gyn Society **Hob./spts.:** Family **SIC code:** 80 **Address:** University Plaza Obstetrics & Gynecology, LLP, 877 Stewart Ave., Suite 7, Garden City, NY 11530

SCHAAF, CYNTHIA A.
Industry: Healthcare **Univ./degree:** R.N., Lincoln Land Community College, Illinois, 1975, St. Louis University **Current organization:** Capitol Care **Title:** Administrator **Type of organization:** Long-term care nursing home **Major product:** Patient long-term care **Area of distribution:** Illinois **Area of Practice:** Registered Nurse/Healthcare Administrator **Affiliations:** National Association of Healthcare Administrators; Long-Term Care Nurses Association **Hob./spts.:** Family, gardening, music **SIC code:** 80 **Address:** Capitol Care, 555 W. Carpenter, Springfield, IL 62702 **E-mail:** cschaaf@platinumhc.net

SCHAEFER, MARY ANN
Industry: Healthcare **Born:** May 18, 1942, Chicago, Illinois **Univ./degree:** M.B.A., Health Management, Webster University, 1989; J.D., Health Law, Loyola University School of Law, 1993 **Current organization:** Sherman Health **Title:** Director of Women's Services **Type of organization:** Hospital **Major product:** Patient care **Area of Practice:** Women's services: education, maternal and child healthcare; Certified, Inpatient Obstetrics by NCC **Published works:** Editor of newsletter **Affiliations:** Board Member, Illinois Prenatal Association; A.W.H.O.N.N.; St. Francis Hospital School of Nursing **Hob./spts.:** Travel, reading, walking **SIC code:** 80 **Address:** Sherman Health, 934 Center St., Elgin, IL 60120-2198 **E-mail:** maryann.schaefer@shermanhospital.org

SCHAINFELD, ROBERT M.
Industry: Healthcare **Born:** October 22, 1953, Philadelphia, Pennsylvania **Univ./degree:** B.S., Psychobiology, Albright University, 1975; D.O., Western State University Health Science Center, 1984 **Current organization:** St. Elizabeth's Medical Center **Title:** Doctor of Osteopathic Medicine **Type of organization:** Hospital **Major product:** Patient services **Area of distribution:** National **Area of Practice:** Vascular medicine, hypertension, internal medicine **Published works:** 24 articles, 4 book chapters, 36 abstract/conference papers **Affiliations:** F.S.V.M.B.; F.S.C.A.I.; A.C.O.I. **Hob./spts.:** Physical fitness, rollerblading, rowing **SIC code:** 80 **Address:** St. Elizabeth's Medical Center, 736 Cambridge St., Boston, MA 02135 **E-mail:** veindoc@hotmail.com

SCHAPIRO, SALO R.
Industry: Healthcare **Born:** April 22, 1945, Santiago, Chile **Univ./degree:** M.D., Catholic University of Chile, 1973 **Current organization:** Salo R. Schapiro M.D., P.A. **Title:** M.D., Psychiatrist, Child and Adolescent **Type of organization:** Private practice **Major product:** Patient care **Area of distribution:** National **Area of Practice:** Child, adolescent and adult chemical dependency, family psychiatry **Honors/awards:** Fellow, American Psychiatric Association **Affiliations:** A.M.A.; American Academy of Child & Adolescent Psychiatry **SIC code:** 80 **Address:** Salo R. Schapiro M.D., P.A., 2499 Glades Rd., Suite 201, Boca Raton, FL 33431 **E-mail:** saloschapiro@yahoo.com

SCHARENBERG, SANDRA L.
Industry: Healthcare **Born:** March 6, 1960, Miami, Florida **Univ./degree:** A.A., Nursing; R.N., Lima Technical College, Ohio, 1981 **Current organization:** Wilson Memorial Hospital **Title:** R.N. **Type of organization:** Community hospital **Major product:** Multi-specialty acute healthcare **Area of distribution:** Ohio **Area of Practice:** Coronary and critical care nursing **Affiliations:** A.A.C.N. **Hob./spts.:** Golf **SIC code:** 80 **Address:** Wilson Memorial Hospital, 915 W. Michigan Ave., Sidney, OH 45365

SCHARF, JONATHAN
Industry: Dentistry **Born:** July 18, 1947, New York, New York **Univ./degree:** D.M.D., University of Pennsylvania School of Dental Medicine, 1972 **Current organization:** Exton Dental Health Group **Title:** Dentist **Type of organization:** Private practice **Major product:** Dental care **Area of distribution:** International **Area of Practice:** Cosmetic dental care **Honors/awards:** Included in: Who's Who in Medicine, 1990, Who's Who Among Outstanding Americans, 1994, Who's Who in Dentistry, 1995; President's Awards for outstanding contributions to The American Academy of Cosmetic Dentistry; Voted "Best of the Main Line", Main Line Today, 2003; Best Dentists in America:, 2004, 2005, 2006 **Published works:** Interviews and clinical photographs in Glamour, Woman's World, American Health Magazine; Consulting Editor for Cosmetic Dentistry for the GP, Cosmetic Dentistry Update, Dentistry Today; Member of editorial team of the Esthetic Dentistry Research Group, (Reality) **Affiliations:** American Dental Association; Pennsylvania Dental Association; Chester-Delaware County Dental Association; Academy of General Dentistry; International Association for Orthodontics; American Equilibration Society; Past President, American Academy of Cosmetic Dentistry; Diplomate, American Board of Aesthetic Dentistry **Career accomplishments:** Established the American Academy of Cosmetic Dentistry Educational Endowment Fund; Has created smiles for television and media personalities as well as corporate executives throughout the Main Line, Philadelphia and the Greater Delaware Valley; Visiting Associate Professor, Dept. of Esthetic Dentistry, University of Buffalo School of Dental Medicine; Has trained dentists internationally in Cosmetic Dental Technology, Cosmetic Dental Practice Management and Fiber Reinforcement in Dentistry **SIC code:** 80 **Address:** Exton Dental Health Group, 101 J.R. Thomas Dr., Exton, PA 19341-2652 **E-mail:** drjscharf@aol.com

SCHECK, KAREN N.
Industry: Healthcare **Born:** December 25, 1963, Smithtown, New York **Univ./degree:** M.A., Touro College, 1991 **Current organization:** Rothman Therapeutics **Title:** Regional Director **Type of organization:** Medical clinic **Major product:** Patient care **Area of distribution:** New York **Area of Practice:** Physical therapy **Honors/awards:** Nominated, Woman of the Year **Affiliations:** Fundraiser, Catholic Health Services **Hob./spts.:** Marathon running **SIC code:** 80 **Address:** 9 Newton St., Sayville, NY 11782 **E-mail:** karenhugf@earthlink.net

SCHELLACK, JOHN K.
Industry: Healthcare **Born:** March 6, 1921, Eudora, Kansas **Univ./degree:** M.S., Oklahoma State University, 1943; M.D., Tulane University, 1946 **Current organization:** John K. Schellack, M.D. **Title:** M.D., F.A.C.S. **Type of organization:** Private practice **Major product:** Patient care **Area of distribution:** Atlanta, Georgia **Area of Practice:** General surgery **Affiliations:** A.M.A.; A.C.S.; G.S.A.; Former teacher, Emory College **Hob./spts.:** Gardening, hunting **SIC code:** 80 **Address:** 340 Boulevard N.E., Suite 324, Atlanta, GA 30312

SCHLUSSELBERG, MOSHE
Industry: Healthcare **Born:** December 3, 1952, Brooklyn, New York **Univ./degree:** M.D., State University of New York School of Medicine, 1978 **Current organization:** Pediatric Healthcare of Long Island **Title:** M.D. **Type of organization:** Medical group **Major product:** Patient care **Area of distribution:** Woodmere, New York **Area of Practice:** Pediatrics **Hob./spts.:** Weight training, hiking, community service **SIC code:** 80 **Address:** Pediatric Healthcare of Long Island, 115 Franklin Place, Woodmere, NY 11598 **E-mail:** pedsli@aol.com **Web address:** www.pedshcli.com

SCHNEIDER, ANDREW IAN
Industry: Healthcare **Born:** September 20, 1962, Orange, New Jersey **Univ./degree:** M.D., SUNY Downstate Medical Center, 1989 **Current organization:** Orthopaedic Care Specialists **Title:** M.D. **Type of organization:** Private practice **Major product:** Patient care **Area of distribution:** North Palm Beach, Florida **Area of Practice:** Orthopaedic surgery **Published works:** Co-authored articles **Affiliations:** F.A.A.O.S. **Hob./spts.:** Running, wine **SIC code:** 80 **Address:** Orthopaedic Care Specialists, 733 U.S. Hwy. 1, North Palm Beach, FL 33408

SCHNEIDER, TINA M.
Industry: Healthcare **Born:** May 11, 1977, Cleveland, Ohio **Univ./degree:** B.A., Psychology, Wright State University, 1999; M.S., Counseling Exceptional Children, Wright State University, 2003 **Affiliations:** American Counseling Association; Association for Specialists in Group Work; Delta Zeta Sorority Alumnae; member, The Advocates for People with Developmental Disabilities **Hob./spts.:** Skiing, movies, music **SIC code:** 80 **Address:** 160 Cannonbury Court, Apt. J, Kettering, OH 45429 **E-mail:** s004tmp@hotmail.com

SCHNOSE, GREGORY
Industry: Healthcare **Born:** June 11, 1951, Casper, Wyoming **Univ./degree:** M.D., University of Kansas, 1976 **Current organization:** Internal Medicine Group, PA **Title:** Owner/Co-founder **Type of organization:** Medical practice **Major product:** Patient care **Area of distribution:** Lawrence, Kansas **Area of Practice:** Internal medicine **Affiliations:** F.A.C.P. -A.S.I.M.; Kansas Medical Society; American Diabetes Association **Hob./spts.:** Gardening, playing piano, water sports **SIC code:** 80 **Address:** Internal Medicine Group, PA, 2200 Harvard Rd., Lawrence, KS 66049 **E-mail:** gschnose@sbcglobal.net

SCHOCH, NICHOLAS
Industry: Healthcare **Born:** March 1, 1967, Pointe-Claire, Quebec **Univ./degree:** D.O., Michigan State University, 1994 **Current organization:** Orthopedic Sports Medicine **Title:** D.O. **Type of organization:** Healthcare **Major product:** Orthopedic surgery **Area of distribution:** Clinton Township, Michigan **Area of Practice:** Orthopedic surgery **Honors/awards:** Orthopedic Resident Award; Iris Klinkenberg Award **Affiliations:** A.O.A.; Michigan Academy of Physicians and Surgeons; Orthopedic Surgery Society **Hob./spts.:** Basketball, baseball, golf **SIC code:** 80 **Address:** Orthopedic Sports Medicine, 21620 Harrington Blvd., Clinton Township, MI 48036

SCHRAM, VALERIE T.
Industry: Healthcare **Born:** March 26, 1950, Independence, Iowa **Univ./degree:** M.D., University of Nevada Medical School, 1989 **Current organization:** Veterans Administration/Southern Nevada Healthcare System **Title:** M.D. **Type of organization:** V.A./federal hospital **Major product:** Patient care **Area of distribution:** Las Vegas, Nevada **Area of Practice:** Internal medicine **Hob./spts.:** Horseback riding, boating **SIC code:** 80 **Address:** Veterans Administration/Southern Nevada Healthcare System, Attn: Medical Services, 1600 Vegas Dr., Las Vegas, NV 89106

SCHREIBER, ANDREW J.
Industry: Healthcare **Born:** August 1, 1918, Budapest, Hungary **Univ./degree:** Ph.D., Heed University; B.S., M.F.T., Columbia University **Current organization:** Andrew J. Schreiber, Ph.D. **Title:** Psychotherapist **Type of organization:** Solo practice **Major product:** Mental healthcare **Area of distribution:** California **Area of Practice:** Marriage, family, child counseling **Affiliations:** M.M.F.D.; C.T.A. **Hob./spts.:** Art (teaching, professional exhibition) **SIC code:** 80 **Address:** 1658 Via Laguna, San Mateo, CA 94404

SCHUBERT, VICKY LEFF
Industry: Healthcare **Born:** May 7, 1967, Bogota, Colombia **Univ./degree:** B.S., Microbiology, University of Florida, 1989; D.O., Nova Southeastern School of Medicine, 1994 **Current organization:** Pediatric Associates **Title:** D.O. **Type of organization:** Pediatric offices **Major product:** Children's healthcare **Area of distribution:** Florida **Area of Practice:** Pediatrics, lecturing, teaching **Honors/awards:** National Hispanic Honor Society Scholarship, Uniformed Services Professional Health Scholarship Program, 1992-94 **Affiliations:** F.A.A.P., A.O.A.; Broward County Pediatric Society; American College of Osteopathic Pediatricians **Hob./spts.:** Physical fitness, weightlifting, biking **SIC code:** 80 **Address:** Pediatric Associates, 1835 N. Corporate Lakes Blvd., Weston, FL 33326 **E-mail:** nikomen@msn.com

SCHULZ, VALERIE MARIA
Industry: Healthcare **Born:** June 10, 1964, Bayshore, New York **Univ./degree:** M.D., State University of New York Health Science Center at Syracuse, 1989 **Current organization:** Women's Comprehensive Health Center **Title:** Associate Attending **Type of organization:** Women's Comprehensive Health Center **Major product:** Patient care **Area of distribution:** New York **Area of Practice:** Obstetrics and gynecology **Affiliations:** Fellow, American College of Obstetricians and Gynecologists; American Society for Colposcopy and Cervical Pathology; American Medical Association **Hob./spts.:** Gardening, needlework, Yankee baseball fan **SIC code:** 80 **Address:** Women's Comprehensive Health Center, 1554 Northern Blvd., Manhasset, NY 11030

SCHULZE, ROBERT W.
Industry: Medical **Born:** May 15, 1963, Newark, New Jersey **Univ./degree:** B.A., Biology, 1986; M.A., 1988, Boston University; M.D., Boston University School of Medicine, 1992 **Current organization:** S.U.N.Y. Downstate/Kings County Hospital **Title:** Assistant Professor of Surgery/Clinical Assistant Dean Student Affairs **Type of organization:** Medical school/hospital **Major product:** Medical services **Area of distribution:** New York **Area of Practice:** Trauma, surgery, education **Honors/awards:** Hubert Humphrey Research Scholarship, 1989; Department of Health & Human Services, T32 research grant, 1994, 1995 **Published works:** Publications: Schulze RW, Gangopadhyay A, Lazure D, Steele G, Thomas P: Tyrosine Phosphorylation Is Important for Signal Transduction in Endotoxin Stimulated Kupffer Cells. "Hepatology", Vol. 22;4 Part 2, page 305A, October, 1995; Schulze RW, Gangopadhyay A, Cay O, Lazure D, Thomas P: Tyrosine Kinase Activation In LPS Stimulated Rat Kupffer Cells. In Press: "Receptors and Signal Transduction, 1998; Presentations: Tyrosine Phosphorylation is Important for Signal Transduction in Endotoxin Stimulated Kupffer Cells. Presented at the American Association for the Study of Liver Diseases: Chicago, Illinois, November 7, 1995; Gangopadhyay A, Lazure DL, Schulze RW, Jessup JM, Steele G., Thomas P: Carcinoembryonic Antigen induces Signal Transduction in Kupffer Cells. American Association for Cancer Research, 1996 **Affiliations:** F.A.C.S.; Massachusetts Medical Society; Southeastern Surgical Congress; Society of Critical Care Medicine; Eastern Association for the Surgery of Trauma **SIC code:** 80 **Address:** SUNY Downstate/Kings County Hospital, 450 Clarkson Avenue Box 40, Brooklyn, NY 11203 **E-mail:** robert.schulze@downstate.edu

SCHUSTER, MICHAEL P.
Industry: Healthcare **Born:** September 4, 1959, Russia **Univ./degree:** M.D., Magna Cum Laude, Stavropol State Medical School, 1982 **Current organization:** Michael P. Schuster, M.D. **Title:** Physician **Type of organization:** Private practice **Major product:** Patient care **Area of distribution:** Manhattan, Kansas **Area of Practice:** Pain management and rehabilitation **Affiliations:** Medical Director, Mercy Regional Health Center; International Spine Intervention Society; Society of Pain Practice Management **Hob./spts.:** Hiking, fishing **SIC code:** 80 **Address:** Michael P. Schuster, M.D., 4809 Vue Du Lac Place, Suite 205, Manhattan, KS 66503 **E-mail:** bestonedoctor@yahoo.com

SCHWARTZ, JANE S.
Industry: Healthcare **Born:** May 28, 1955, Fall River, Massachusetts **Univ./degree:** B.A., Music, University of Hartford,1976; R.N., Peter Bent Brigham, 1983; M.S.N., Yale University, 1988 **Current organization:** Jane S. Schwartz, MSN, APRN **Title:** Nurse Psychotherapist, M.S.N., C.S., APRN, DAPA **Type of organization:** Private practice **Major product:** Psychiatric treatment **Area of distribution:** Connecticut **Area of Practice:** Psychotherapy, trauma, medication management, severe chronic psychiatric illness **Published works:** 1 article, 1 CD published **Affiliations:** Connecticut Nursing Association; Sigma Theta Tau; Associate Clinical Professor, Yale University School of Nursing; Member, Association for Forensic Counselors; Diplomate, American Psychotherapy Association **Hob./spts.:** Harpsichord, composer, artist **SIC code:** 80 **Address:** Jane S. Schwartz, MSN, APRN, Private Practice, 24 Greenway St., Hamden, CT 06517-1316

SCHWARTZ, PAULA R.
Industry: Healthcare **Born:** October 16, 1952, New York, New York **Univ./degree:** M.D., Downstate Medical School, 1980 **Current organization:** Hematology-Oncology Associates of Long Island; 2nd office - 700 Old Country Rd., Suite 102, Plainview, New York **Title:** M.D. **Type of organization:** Private group practice **Major product:** Hematology/oncology **Area of distribution:** Long Island, New York **Area of Practice:** Hematology/oncology **Honors/awards:** Top Long Island 50 Professional Women **Affiliations:** Chairman, North Shore-Long Island Jewish Healthcare Oncology Performance Improvement Committee for Quality Management; American Society of Clinical Oncology **Hob./spts.:** Singing in choir at synagogue, family **SIC code:** 80 **Address:** Hematology-Oncology Associates of Long Island, 3003 New Hyde Park Rd., Suite 401, New Hyde Park, NY 11042

SCHWEITZ, MICHAEL C.
Industry: Healthcare **Born:** June 7, 1947, Washington, D.C. **Univ./degree:** M.D., George Washington University School of Medicine, 1972; Fellowship in Rheumatology, Georgetown University **Current organization:** Arthritis & Rheumatology Association of Palm Beach **Title:** Rheumatologist **Type of organization:** Medical practice **Major product:** Rheumatology, arthritis, autoimmune disease **Area of distribution:** Florida **Area of Practice:** Rheumatology and Internal Medicine (Board Certified) **Affiliations:** Vice President, Coalition of State Rheumatology Organizations; Past President, Florida Society of Rheumatology; Good Samaritan Hospital in West Palm Beach **Hob./spts.:** Wine collecting, reading **SIC code:** 80 **Address:** Arthritis & Rheumatology Association of Palm Beach, 1515 N. Flagler Dr., Suite 620, West Palm Beach, FL 33401 **E-mail:** mschweitz@gmail.com

SCHWIEDER, V. ANN
Industry: Healthcare **Born:** March 6, 1948, Crawfordsville, Indiana **Univ./degree:** B.S.; D.C., 1995, Palmer College of Chiropractic **Current organization:** Deere Road Chiropractic, Ltd. **Title:** Doctor of Chiropractic/Owner **Type of organization:** Private practice **Major product:** Chiropractic care **Area of distribution:** Illinois **Area of Practice:** Activator Doctor and low force adjustments **Affiliations:** Illinois Prairie State Chiropractic Association; International Chiropractic Association; The Sports Council of Chiropractic; The Pediatric Council of Chiropractic **Hob./spts.:** Golf, reading, gardening **SIC code:** 80 **Address:** Deere Road Chiropractic, Ltd., 5202 38th Ave., Moline, IL 61265

SEABROOK GRIFFIN, LILLIAN
Industry: Healthcare **Univ./degree:** M.A., Nursing Administration; Michigan University **Current organization:** Rockaway Care Center **Title:** Director of Nursing Services **Type of organization:** Nursing home **Major product:** Patient care **Area of distribution:** New York **Area of Practice:** Geriatrics **Affiliations:** NYS & A; American College of Administrators **Hob./spts.:** Physical fitness, church (Mass Choir, Pastor Aid Ministry, Teaching Nurse Ministry) **SIC code:** 80 **Address:** Rockaway Care Center, 353 Beach 48th St., Edgemere, NY 11691 **E-mail:** seabrook8084@compuserve.com

SEDLAK, CHERYL A.
Industry: Healthcare **Born:** September 14, 1958, Pittsburgh, Pennsylvania **Univ./degree:** B.A., Psychology, Grove City College, 1980; M.A., Clinical Psychology, University of Dayton, 1982 **Current organization:** Florida Therapy Services **Title:** Licensed Mental Health Counselor, Addiction Counselor, Certified Criminal Justice Specialist **Type of organization:** Mental health services **Major product:** Substance

abuse, mental health counseling, hypnotherapy, EMDR **Area of distribution:** Panama City, Florida **Area of Practice:** Counseling, hypnotherapy, workshop presenter, interviewed on Channel 7, 1998 **Honors/awards:** Award of Appreciation, Florida Therapy Services, 1998-2001 **Affiliations:** The Mid-West Psychological Association; American Counseling Association; National Guild of Hypnotherapy; American Association of Christian Counselors; National Association of Forensic Counselors **Hob./spts.:** Swimming, reading, tennis, lighthouses **SIC code:** 80 **Address:** Florida Therapy Services, 538 Harmon Ave., Panama City, FL 32405 **E-mail:** cherylpsych@aol.com

SEGAL, BRAHM H.
Industry: Medical **Born:** April 9. 1965, Montreal, Canada **Univ./degree:** B.S., Biology, McGill University, 1988; M.D., Albert Einstein College of Medicine, 1992 **Current organization:** Roswell Park Cancer Institute **Title:** M.D. **Type of organization:** University hospital **Major product:** Patient care **Area of distribution:** Buffalo, New York **Area of Practice:** Infectious diseases in immunocompromise. **Honors/awards:** Henry Christian Award; American Federal Medical Research Award; Roswell Park Cancer Institute Alliance Award ;SUNY Dept. Of Medicine Award Of Research; SUNY Dept. Of Medicine Award Of Teaching **Published works:** Journal of Immunology; Journal of Leukocyte Biology **Affiliations:** I.D.S.A.; A.C.P.; I.C.H.S. **Hob./spts.:** Reading, the outdoors, hiking, camping, chess **SIC code:** 80 **Address:** Roswell Park Cancer Institute, Elm & Carlton Streets, Buffalo, NY 14263 **E-mail:** brahm.segal@roswellpark.org

SEGUROLA JR., ROMUALDO
Industry: Healthcare **Current organization:** South Florida Heart & Lung Institute **Title:** M.D. **Type of organization:** Private practice **Major product:** Patient care **Area of distribution:** Miami, Florida **Area of Practice:** Cardiovascular thoracic surgery **SIC code:** 80 **Address:** South Florida Heart & Lung Institute, 3661 South Miami Ave., Suite 906, Miami, FL 33133 **E-mail:** rspetermd@aol.com

SEKAR, SURYA
Industry: Healthcare **Univ./degree:** M.D., Madras University, India, 1963 **Current organization:** Surya Sekar Ob/Gyn P.C. **Title:** M.D., F.A.C.O.G., F.A.C.S. **Type of organization:** Private practice **Major product:** Women's healthcare **Area of distribution:** New York **Area of Practice:** Obstetrics, gynecology, laparascopy, osteoporosis testing, menopausal care **Honors/awards:** Honored for 25 years of service as a member in the Queens Medical Society **Affiliations:** President, Queens Obstetrics and Gynecologic Society, 2002; Queens New York Medical Society; New York State Medical Society **SIC code:** 80 **Address:** Surya Sekar Ob/Gyn P.C., 83-21 57th Ave., New York, NY 11373-4707

SEKHAR, LALIGAM N.
Industry: Medical **Born:** November 7, 1951, Madras, India **Univ./degree:** M.D., University of Madras, India, 1973 **Current organization:** North Shore University Hospital **Title:** M.D., F.A.C.S. **Type of organization:** University **Major product:** Patient care, medical education **Area of distribution:** International **Area of Practice:** Brain tumor and brain aneurysms and skull base tumors **Honors/awards:** Listed, Top Ten Neurosurgeons **Published works:** 270 published articles, 4 books **Affiliations:** INOVA Fairfax Hospital, GW University Hospital **Hob./spts.:** Tennis, cricket, classical music **SIC code:** 80 **Address:** North Shore University Hospital, 865 Northern Blvd., Suite 302, Great Neck, NY 11021 **E-mail:** lsekhar@aol.com

SELBY, RONALD M.
Industry: Healthcare **Born:** February 24, 1951, New Brunswick, New Jersey **Univ./degree:** M.D., Autonomous University of Guadalajara Medical School, 1979 **Current organization:** Orthopaedic Surgery & Sports Medicine **Title:** M.D./Orthopaedic Surgeon **Type of organization:** Private practice **Major product:** Surgery **Area of distribution:** International **Area of Practice:** Knees, shoulders and elbows **Honors/awards:** Listed in "Guide to America's Top Surgeons", 2002-2003; National Leadership Award, Physician's Advisory Board, The National Republican Congressional Committee; 2001 Order of Merit, Cum Laude, Orthopaedic Research and Education Foundation; Team Physician, Special Olympics, World-Wide Games, North Carolina, June-July, 1999 **Published works:** 12+ articles, Associate editor, Arthroscopy: The Journal of Arthroscopic & Related Surgery **Affiliations:** Diplomate, American Board of Orthopaedic Surgery; F.A.A.O.S.; F.A.C.S.M.; F.R.S.M.; A.O.S.S.M.; A.M.S.S.M. **Hob./spts.:** Golf, tennis **SIC code:** 80 **Address:** Orthopaedic Surgery & Sports Medicine, 901 Fifth Avenue, New York, NY 10021 **E-mail:** rmselbysportsmed@msn.com

SETHI, YASH P.
Industry: Medical **Born:** February 24, 1965, Delhi, India **Univ./degree:** M.D., Delhi University School of Medicine, 1987; Post-Graduate, 1992 **Current organization:** University of Missouri, Columbia; Hospitals & Clinic **Title:** M.D./Assistant Clinical Professor **Type of organization:** University hospital **Major product:** Medical services **Area of distribution:** Missouri **Area of Practice:** Radiology **Honors/awards:** Numerous including, Service Quality Hero Award, Sept. 2004, Univ. of Missouri Health Care, Columbia; Teacher of the Year 2003-04 Award, Dept. of Radiology, Univ. of Missouri Health Care, Columbia; Nominated for Physician of the Year 2002-03 Award, Harry S. Truman Veterans Hospital at Columbia, MO; Teacher of the Year, 2003, Best Conferences, Dept. of Radiology, Univ. of Missouri, Columbia; Listed in America's Top Radiologist, 2002-03 annual listing by National Consumer Council of America, Philadelphia; Service Quality Hero Award of the Month, June 2002, Univ. of Missouri, Health Care Hospitals and Clinics **Published works:** 15 articles **Affiliations:** Radiological Society of North America; American Roentgen Ray Society **SIC code:** 80 **Address:** University of Missouri, Columbia; Hospitals and Clinic, 1 Hospital Dr., Columbia, MO 65212 **E-mail:** ypsethi@hotmail.com

SEWALL, ARLEEN M.
Industry: Healthcare **Born:** February 3, 1956, Trenton, New Jersey **Univ./degree:** R.N., Mercer County Community College **Current organization:** Tropicare Health Systems, Inc. **Title:** R.N., C.A.R.N., Director, Behavioral Sciences **Type of organization:** Healthcare **Major product:** Patient care **Area of distribution:** Clearwater, Florida **Area of Practice:** Psychiatry, addiction certification **Affiliations:** A.N.C.B. **Hob./spts.:** Walking, fishing, gardening **SIC code:** 80 **Address:** Tropicare Health Systems, Inc., 5955 140th Terrace North, Clearwater, FL 33760 **E-mail:** arsewall@aol.com

SFERA, ADONIS
Industry: Healthcare **Born:** October 30, 1955, Belgrade, Yugoslavia **Univ./degree:** M.D., Institul de Medicina, Timisoara, Romania, 1980 **Current organization:** Adonis Sfera, MD, Inc. **Title:** Psychiatrist **Type of organization:** Private practice **Major product:** Patient care **Area of distribution:** National **Area of Practice:** Geriatric psychiatry, Alzheimer's related diseases **Published works:** 4 articles, 3 book chapters, "Sensory Stimulation in Patients with Schiaophrenia Presenting with Negative Symptoms" (Advance for Physical Therapists, 1994) **Affiliations:** Diplomate, American Board of Psychiatry and Neurology; A.P.A.; A.M.A.; A.B.F.E.; A.S.C.P.; A.A.C.A.P.; Diplomate, American Board of Psychiatry and Neurology; Volunteer faculty, University of Southern California School of Medicine **Hob./spts.:** Family, travel, reading, baseball **SIC code:** 80 **Address:** Adonis Sfera, MD, Inc., 515 S. Beach Blvd, Suite K, Anaheim, CA 92804 **E-mail:** sfera@medscape.com

SHAH, AHMED IJAZ
Industry: Healthcare **Born:** November 12, 1970, Pakistan **Univ./degree:** M.D., Allama Iqbal Medical College, Pakistan, 1996 **Current organization:** Mount Sinai Medical Center Dept. of Critical Care Medicine **Title:** M.D. **Type of organization:** Hospital **Major product:** Patient care **Area of distribution:** International **Area of Practice:** Critical care medicine **Published works:** 5 articles, 1 book chapter **Affiliations:** American College of Chest Physicians; Society of Critical Care Medicine; American College of Physicians **Hob./spts.:** Family, photography, travel **SIC code:** 80 **Address:** Mount Sinai Medical Center, Dept. of Critical Care Medicine, 1 Gustave L. Levy Place, New York, NY 10029 **E-mail:** shahji98@hotmail.com

SHAH, MAHENDRA K.
Industry: Healthcare **Born:** July 10, 1942, India **Univ./degree:** M.S., Microbiology, India **Current organization:** New York Eye & Ear Infirmary **Title:** Supervisor **Type of organization:** Hospital **Major product:** Patient care (eye/ear, cosmetic surgery) **Area of distribution:** New York, New York **Area of Practice:** Teaching, research, microbiology **Affiliations:** A.R.V.O.; A.S.M.; A.A.O.; N.C.A. **Hob./spts.:** Baseball, cricket **SIC code:** 80 **Address:** New York Eye & Ear Infirmary, 310 E. 14th St., New York, NY 10003 **E-mail:** mshah@nyee.edu

SHAH, NAYAN C.
Industry: Healthcare **Born:** Ahmadabad, India **Univ./degree:** M.D., Baroda Medical College, Baroda, India, 1979; Fellowship, Gastroenterology, Albany Medical College, 1985 **Current organization:** Eynon Surgery Center **Title:** M.D.; CEO/President **Type of organization:** Outpatient surgery center **Major product:** Patient care **Area of distribution:** Pennsylvania **Area of Practice:** Board Certified, Internal Medicine and Gastroenterology; Crohn's Disease **Affiliations:** American College of Gastroenterology; American Society of Gastrointestinal Endoscopy; Pennsylvania Medical Association; Lackawanna County Medical Association; Director of GI Unit, Chairman of Pharmacy & Therapeutics, Marian Community Hospital; Director of GI Unit, Mid Valley Hospital **SIC code:** 80 **Address:** Eynon Surgery Center, 681 Scranton Carbondale Hwy., Eynon, PA 18403 **E-mail:** drnyanshah@yahoo.com **Web address:** www.eynonsurgery.com

SHAH, RESHMA M.
Industry: Healthcare **Born:** February 9, 1969, Africa **Univ./degree:** B.S., Chemistry, Emory University, 1990; M.D. Ross University Medical School, Dominica, 1995 **Current organization:** Perimeter North Family Medicine **Title:** M.D. **Type of organization:** Group practice **Major product:** Patient care **Area of distribution:** Georgia **Area of Practice:** Family practice **Affiliations:** A.F.P.; A.M.A. **Hob./spts.:** Family, reading, tennis **SIC code:** 80 **Address:** Perimeter North Family Medicine, 4075 Pleasant Hill Rd., Duluth, GA 30096 **E-mail:** rms000@aol.com

SHALAK, LINA F.
Industry: Medical **Born:** November 25, 1970, Beirut, Lebanon **Univ./degree:** M.D., American University, Lebanon, 1995 **Current organization:** University of Texas Southwestern Medical Center **Title:** M.D./Clinical Assistant Professor **Type of organization:** University, medical center **Major product:** Medical services **Area of distribution:** Texas **Area of Practice:** Pediatrics, neonatal intensive care **Honors/awards:** Best Graduating Resident Award, 1998 **Published works:** 18 publications **Affiliations:** A.A.P. **SIC code:** 80 **Address:** University of Texas Southwestern Medical Center, 5323 Harry Hines Blvd., Dallas, TX 75390 **E-mail:** lshalak@hotmail.com

SHAMSHAM, FADI MICHEL
Industry: Healthcare **Born:** November 28, 1968, Beirut, Lebanon **Univ./degree:** M.D., American University of Beirut, 1993 **Current organization:** Medical Group of North Florida **Title:** M.D. **Type of organization:** Private practice **Major product:** Patient care **Area of Practice:** Cardiovascular diseases, nuclear cardiology, interventional cardiology, peripheral vascular interventions **Published works:** 6 publications/newspaper articles, 5 multicenter trials **Affiliations:** American College of Physicians; American College of Cardiology; Society for Cardiovascular Angiography & Interventions **Hob./spts.:** Photography, skiing, fishing **SIC code:** 80 **Address:** Medical Group of North Florida, 2626 Care Dr., Suite 100, Tallahassee, FL 32308 **E-mail:** fshamsham@aol.com

SHANLEY, LEE G.
Industry: Healthcare **Born:** March 12, 1955, Rockville Centre, New York **Univ./degree:** M.S., Safety Engineering, Kennedy Western University, 1999 **Current organization:** Nassau University Medical Center **Title:** Director, Department of Public Safety **Type of organization:** Hospital **Major product:** Patient care **Area of distribution:** New York **Area of Practice:** Safety/compliance & regulations **Affiliations:** Past President, International Association for Health Care Security & Safety; Hospital Fire Marshall's Association; New York State Fire Marshall's Association **Hob./spts.:** Bandmaster & snare drummer in "Tara Pipes & Drums" **SIC code:** 80 **Address:** 9 Oak St., Farmingdale, NY 11735

SHANNON, DENISE
Industry: Healthcare **Born:** July 9, 1963, Denver, Colorado **Univ./degree:** B.A., Nursing, University of Colorado Health Sciences Center, 1992 **Current organization:** Hospice of Metro Denver **Title:** Vice President of Inpatient Services **Type of organization:** Hospice **Major product:** Hospice services **Area of distribution:** Colorado **Area of Practice:** Hospice inpatient long-term care **Hob./spts.:** Gardening, reading, volleyball, walking, hiking **SIC code:** 80 **Address:** 10186 Flower Ct., Westminster, CO 80021 **E-mail:** deniselshannon@aol.com

SHARF, ANDREW G.
Industry: Healthcare **Born:** September 20, 1922, Neustadt, Germany **Univ./degree:** B.A., Albion College, Michigan, 1944; M.D., Wayne State University, Michigan, 1948; Ph.D., Albion College, Michigan, 1988 **Current organization:** Andrew Sharf Clinic **Title:** M.D., Ph.D.; F.A.C.S., F.I.C.S. **Type of organization:** Nonprofit clinic **Major product:** Vascular surgery and vascular disease **Area of distribution:** National **Area of Practice:** General vascular surgery **Honors/awards:** Numerous including, Distinguished Alumni, Albion College; Outstanding Services as CMA Accreditation Surveyor, 1993-96 **Published works:** Numerous including "Surgical indications for Carotid and Vertebral artery obstructive disease" **Affiliations:** Fellow, American College of Surgeons; Founding Member, Society of Clinical Vascular Surgery; Fellow, Southwestern Surgical Congress; International College of Surgeons, U.S. Section, President 1980, International Corporate Secretary 1984-88; California Medical Association; Wayne State Surgical Society; St. Anthony's Society, Wayne State; National Board of Medical Examiners; American Medical Association; Fellow, World Health Association; Queen of Angels-Hollywood Presbyterian Medical Center: President of Medical Staff, 1980 & 1994; Chairman, Dept. of Surgery, 1981-89; Chairman, CME, 1974-87 **Hob./spts.:** Breeding Arabian horses, with wife Maureen Sharf operates Sharf Arabian Horse Ranch, skiing, tennis **SIC code:** 80 **Address:** 4176 Casey Ave., Santa Ynez, CA 93460 **E-mail:** sharf@thegrid.net

SHARMA, ARATI
Industry: Medical **Born:** February 14, Ambala, India **Univ./degree:** Ph.D., Toxicology, Gujaret School of Science, India **Current organization:** Penn State College of Medicine/Hershey Medical Center **Title:** Post Doctorate Fellow **Type of organization:** Teaching hospital **Major product:** Patient care, medical education **Area of distribution:** International **Area of Practice:** Cancer research **Hob./spts.:** Cooking **SIC code:** 80 **Address:** Penn State College of Medicine/Hershey Medical Center, 500 University Dr., Pharmacology Dept. HO78, Hershey, PA 17033 **E-mail:** aks12@psu.edu

SHARMA, DEVESH
Industry: Healthcare **Born:** November 27, 1971, Delhi, India **Univ./degree:** M.D., University of Delhi **Current organization:** Geisinger Medical Center **Title:** M.D. **Type of organization:** Hospital **Major product:** Medical services **Area of distribution:** Danville, Pennsylvania **Area of Practice:** General surgery, plastic surgery **Affiliations:** Association of Plastic Surgeons of India; American College of Surgeons; International Society for Burn Injuries **Hob./spts.:** Music, tennis, photography **SIC code:** 80 **Address:** 107 Orchard Ave., Danville, PA 17821 **E-mail:** devesharma@hotmail.com

SHARMA, KULDIP
Industry: Healthcare **Born:** December 5, 1952, Burma **Univ./degree:** M.B.B.S., Nagpur University, India, 1977 **Current organization:** Medical Associates of Middletown **Title:** M.D. **Type of organization:** Medical practice **Major product:** Patient care **Area of distribution:** Middletown, Ohio **Area of Practice:** Gastroenterology, hepatology **Affiliations:** F.R.C.P.(C); A.G.A.; A.C.G.; A.M.A. **Hob./spts.:** Tennis, camping **SIC code:** 80 **Address:** 4801 Deer Creek, Middletown, OH 45042 **E-mail:** kulu5@msn.com

SHARP, STEPHAN C.
Industry: Healthcare **Born:** March 5, 1961, Memphis, Tennessee **Univ./degree:** B.S., Biology, Southwestern at Memphis (Rhodes College), 1983; M.D., University of Tennessee, 1987 **Current organization:** Levine & Sharp **Title:** M.D. **Type of organization:** Private practice **Major product:** Patient care **Area of distribution:** Nashville, Tennessee **Area of Practice:** Endocrinology, hypertension **Honors/awards:** 3 Grants, National Institutes of Health; Fellow, American College of Endocrinology **Published works:** Numerous abstracts, manuscripts, book chapters and editorials **Affiliations:** Endocrine Society; American Association of Clinical Endocrinologists; American Society of Hypertension; American Board of Internal Medicine, Endocrinology (Board Certified); Tennessee Permanent Medical License; American Academy of Pharmaceutical Physicians; American College of Physicians; American Diabetes Association; American Heart Association Hypertension Council; American Society for Andrology; American Society for Bone and Mineral Research; American Society for Reproductive Medicine; The North American Menopause Society; The Polycystic Ovarian Syndrome Association **Hob./spts.:** Soccer, football, gardening, dogs **SIC code:** 80 **Address:** Levine & Sharp, 2222 State St., Nashville, TN 37203

SHEPPARD, BARRY B.
Industry: Healthcare **Born:** June 27, 1961, Raleigh, North Carolina **Univ./degree:** B.S., University of South Carolina, 1983; M.D., University of South Carolina School of Medicine, 1987 **Current organization:** B.B. Sheppard, M.D., Inc. **Title:** M.D. **Type of organization:** Private practice **Major product:** Surgical services **Area of distribution:** California **Area of Practice:** Cardiac and thoracic oncology surgery **Published works:** 20 articles, 1 book chapter **Affiliations:** Secretary, M.M.A.; Secretary/Treasurer, S.F.S.S. **SIC code:** 80 **Address:** B.B. Sheppard, M.D., Inc., 1828 El Camino Rd., Suite 802, Burlingame, CA 94010 **E-mail:** barakuda@pachill.net

SHIHABUDDIN, LINA
Industry: Medical **Born:** February 7, 1965, Beirut, Lebanon **Univ./degree:** M.D., American University of Beirut, 1989 **Current organization:** Bronx V.A. M.C. **Title:** M.D. **Type of organization:** University/hospital **Major product:** Psychiatry **Area of distribution:** Bronx, New York **Area of Practice:** Geriatric Psychiatry **Honors/awards:** Siever Foundation Fellow, 1995 **Published works:** Archives of Journal of Psychiatry; American Journal of Psychiatry **SIC code:** 80 **Address:** Bronx V.A. M.C., 130 W. Kingsbridge Rd., Bronx, NY 10468 **E-mail:** lina.shihabuddin@med.va.gov

SHIMONY, RONY Y.
Industry: Medicine **Univ./degree:** M.D., State University of New York at Buffalo, 1984 **Current organization:** Lenox Hill Hospital **Title:** M.D. **Type of organization:** Private practice **Major product:** Patient care, cardiology, cardiac electrophysiology **Area of distribution:** National **Area of Practice:** Heart rhythm problems **Honors/awards:** Certificate of Special Congressional Recognition, 1996 **Affiliations:** F.A.C.C. **Hob./spts.:** Family, sports **SIC code:** 80 **Address:** 425 E. 61st St., 4th floor, New York, NY 10021 **Phone:** (212)752-2700 **Fax:** (212)752-2949

SHIRANI, JAMSHID
Industry: Medical **Born:** February 28, 1955, Sanandaj, Iran **Univ./degree:** MD, Shiraz University School of Medicine, Iran, 1980 **Current organization:** Albert Einstein College of Medicine **Title:** Associate Professor of Medicine and Pathology **Type of organization:** Medical school **Major product:** Medical services **Area of distribution:** International **Area of Practice:** Cardiology, internal medicine **Honors/awards:** Physician of the Year, MMC Heart Center, 2003; Distinguished Teacher Award, Division of Cardiology, 2002; Distinguished Leader Award, Division of Cardiology, 2001 **Published works:** 80 articles, 10 books and chapters, 100 abstracts **Affiliations:** F.A.C.C.; F.A.H.A.; F.A.C.P. **SIC code:** 80 **Address:** Albert Einstein College of Medicine, Div. of Cardiology, 1300 Morris Park Ave., Bronx, NY 10461 **E-mail:** jshirani@montefiore.org **Web address:** cardiologyfellowship.org

SHOOKSTER, LINDA A.
Industry: Healthcare **Born:** January 10, 1956, New York, New York **Univ./degree:** M.D., Columbia University, 1981 **Current organization:** Rheumatology Associates of Southern Westchester **Title:** M.D. **Type of organization:** Private practice **Major**

product: Patient care **Area of distribution:** New York **Area of Practice:** Rheumatology **Published works:** Multiple publications **Affiliations:** A.C.R.; A.C.P.-A.S.I.M. **Hob./spts.:** History, medical ethics **SIC code:** 80 **Address:** Rheumatology Associates of Southern Westchester, 421 Huguenot St., New Rochelle, NY 10801 **E-mail:** mrmoose@pol.net

SHORTER, CARRIE J.
Industry: Healthcare **Born:** May 22, 1960, New Orleans, Louisiana **Univ./degree:** M.S.N., University of Phoenix **Current organization:** Eternity Healthcare Staffing, LLC **Title:** Owner **Type of organization:** Staffing agency **Major product:** Healthcare staffing **Area of distribution:** Louisiana **Area of Practice:** Staffing **SIC code:** 80 **Address:** Eternity Healthcare Staffing, LLC, 626 N. Acadian Thruway West, Baton Rouge, LA 70802-2255

SHPITALNIK, VILOR
Industry: Healthcare **Born:** Latvia **Univ./degree:** M.D., Medical School of Russia, 1959; Board Certified in Psychiatry, 1999 **Current organization:** Vilor Shpitalnik, M.D.; 2nd office - 1951 Queens Blvd., Rego Park, New York **Title:** M.D. **Type of organization:** Private practice **Major product:** Psychiatry **Area of distribution:** Brooklyn, New York **Area of Practice:** Psychiatry (Board Certified) **Published works:** 30 publications **Affiliations:** American Association of Psychopharmacology **SIC code:** 80 **Address:** Vilor Shpitalnik, M.D., 581 Ocean Pkwy., Suite 2, Brooklyn, NY 11218

SHWAYDER, JAMES M.
Industry: Healthcare/Law **Born:** November 12, 1951, Greeley, Colorado **Univ./degree:** M.D., University of Colorado; J.D., University of Denver **Current organization:** James M. Shwayder, MD, JD **Title:** Physician/Lawyer **Type of organization:** Private practice **Major product:** Patient care/legal services **Area of distribution:** National **Area of Practice:** Ob/Gyn, laparoscopy, ultrasound/medical malpractice **Hob./spts.:** Running, biking **SIC code:** 80 **Address:** 6920 W. Princeton Ave., Denver, CO 80235 **E-mail:** jshwayder@hotmail.com

SIA, EDWIN O.
Industry: Healthcare **Born:** October 16, 1948, Philippines **Univ./degree:** B.S., Medical Technology, Far Eastern University, Manila, Philippines; Southwestern University, Cebu City, Philippines, Doctor of Medicine **Current organization:** St. John's Biomedical Lab, Inc./Tomoka Medical Lab., Inc. **Title:** Laboratory Director **Type of organization:** Privately owned laboratory **Major product:** Body fluid analysis: microbiology, hematology, serology, chemistry and parasitology **Area of distribution:** National **Area of Practice:** Technical consultant, bioanalyst clinical lab director, clinical consultant **Affiliations:** Member, Board of Directors, Philippines Medical Society; American Board of Bioanalysis; Member, Board of Directors, Philippine-American Association of St. Augustine **Hob./spts.:** Singing, dancing, gardening **SIC code:** 80 **Address:** St. John's Biomedical Lab, Inc., 165 South Park Blvd., Suite A, St. Augustine, FL 32086

SIDDIQUI, ADEEL M.
Industry: Healthcare **Born:** October 10, 1965, Coimbatore, India **Univ./degree:** M.D., Boston University, 1994 **Current organization:** Richmond Internal Medicine/Cardiology and Associates **Title:** M.D. **Type of organization:** Private practice in group setting **Major product:** Patient care **Area of distribution:** Rockingham, North Carolina **Area of Practice:** Internal medicine **Affiliations:** A.M.A.; A.C.P. **Hob./spts.:** Time with family, sports, reading **SIC code:** 80 **Address:** Richmond Internal Medicine/Cardiology and Associates, 110 Grey Fox Run, Rockingham, NC 28379 **E-mail:** adeel@etinternet.net

SIDDIQUI, FOWZIA
Industry: Medical **Born:** September 14, 1966, Karachi, Pakistan **Univ./degree:** M.D., Dow Medical College, Pakistan, 1990 **Current organization:** Brigham & Women's Hospital, Harvard Medical School **Title:** M.D. **Type of organization:** University hospital **Major product:** Medical services **Area of distribution:** National **Area of Practice:** Neurophysiologist/Epileptologist/Neurologist **Affiliations:** American Academy of Neurology **Hob./spts.:** Gardening, reading, skiing **SIC code:** 80 **Address:** Brigham & Women's Hospital, Harvard Medical School, 75 Francis St., Boston, MA 02115 **E-mail:** fsiddiqui@partners.org

SIDHU, JAGMOHAN SINGH
Industry: Healthcare **Born:** January 10, 1955, Punjab, India **Univ./degree:** M.D., Medical College, Patiala, India, 1978 **Current organization:** United Health Services **Title:** Director and Chairman, Department of Pathology and Laboratory Medicine **Type of organization:** Community hospital **Major product:** Patient care **Area of distribution:** Johnson City, New York; Binghamton, New York; Endicott, New York **Area of Practice:** Hematopathology **Published works:** Articles **Affiliations:** A.M.A.; American Society of Clinical Pathology **Hob./spts.:** Writing poetry, oil painting **SIC code:** 80 **Address:** 290 Foster Rd., Vestal, NY 13850 **E-mail:** jagmohan_sidhu@uhs.org

SIEGEL, JUDY FRIED
Industry: Healthcare **Born:** February 13, 1962, New York **Univ./degree:** B.S., Biology, Cornell University, 1984; M.D., University of Vermont School of Medicine, 1988 **Current organization:** A Family Urology Practice, P.C. **Title:** M.D. **Type of organization:** Private practice **Major product:** Patient care **Area of distribution:** New York, Connecticut, New Jersey **Area of Practice:** Urology, female and pediatric urology **Published works:** 32 articles **Affiliations:** Executive Board Member, Society of Women in Urology **SIC code:** 80 **Address:** A Family Urology Practice, P.C., 623 Warburton Ave., Hastings on Hudson, NY 10706-1523

SIEMERS, KENT H.
Industry: Healthcare **Born:** August 12, 1957, Kenmare, North Dakota **Univ./degree:** M.D., University of North Dakota, 1983 **Current organization:** Mid-City Ob/Gyn P.C. **Title:** M.D. **Type of organization:** Private practice **Major product:** Womens' healthcare **Area of distribution:** Omaha, Nebraska **Area of Practice:** Ob/Gyn **Affiliations:** A.M.A.; F.A.C.O.G.; M.O.M.S. **Hob./spts.:** Hunting, running **SIC code:** 80 **Address:** Mid-City Ob/Gyn P.C., 7205 West Center Rd., Suite 200, Omaha, NE 68124

SIEW, SHIRLEY
Industry: Medical **Born:** March 12, 1925, South Africa **Univ./degree:** M.D.; Ph.D., Witwatersrand University, South Africa, 1963 **Current organization:** Michigan State University **Title:** M.D./Ph.D./Professor **Type of organization:** University **Major product:** Medical services **Area of distribution:** International **Area of Practice:** Pathology **Published works:** 90 articles, 3 book chapters **Affiliations:** F.A.C.C.; A.M.A. **SIC code:** 80 **Address:** Michigan State University, Dept. of Pathology, East Fee Hall, A-634, East Lansing, MI 48824 **E-mail:** shirley.siew@ht.msu.edu **Web address:** www.ht.msu.edu

SIGWORTH, KRISTINE L.
Industry: Dentistry **Univ./degree:** D.D.S. **Current organization:** Kristine L. Sigworth, D.D.S. **Title:** D.D.S. **Type of organization:** Dental office **Major product:** Family dentistry **Area of distribution:** Ohio **Area of Practice:** General family dentistry concentrating on prevention, patient education and cosmetic dentistry **Hob./spts.:** Running, reading **SIC code:** 80 **Address:** Kristine L. Sigworth, D.D.S., 2825 S. Union Ave., Alliance, OH 44601 **E-mail:** ksigworth@mfire.com

SIKES, MARY E.
Industry: Healthcare **Born:** June 25, 1964, Centralia, Illinois **Univ./degree:** L.P.N., Vernon Regional Junior College, 1989 **Current organization:** William H. Freeman M.D., P.A. Clinic **Title:** Charge Nurse, L.P.N., L.R.T. **Type of organization:** Family practice clinic **Major product:** Patient care **Area of distribution:** Conway, Arkansas **Area of Practice:** Geriatrics **Hob./spts.:** Golf, bowling, playing pool, fishing **SIC code:** 80 **Address:** William H. Freeman M.D., P.A. Clinic, 410 Denison, Conway, AR 72034 **E-mail:** marellsik2003@yahoo.com

SILBER, ALAN
Industry: Healthcare **Born:** March 7, 1962, Hato Rey, Puerto Rico **Univ./degree:** M.D., San Juan Bautista School of Medicine -1989 **Current organization:** Silber Medical Center **Title:** M.D. **Type of organization:** Medical practice **Major product:** Patient care **Area of distribution:** Guaynabo, Puerto Rico **Area of Practice:** General medicine, acupuncture, laser/cosmetic medicine, intense pulsed light **Published works:** Puerto Rico Association of Medical Acupuncture **Affiliations:** American Society of Laser Medicine & Surgery **Hob./spts.:** Golf **SIC code:** 80 **Address:** Silber Medical Center, 45 Tropical St., Urb Muñoz Rivera, Guaynabo, PR 00969 **E-mail:** drsilber@isla.net

SILVERMAN, BARNEY B.
Industry: Healthcare **Born:** October 17, 1936, Winchester, Kentucky **Univ./degree:** M.D., University of Louisville, Kentucky, 1964 **Current organization:** Westchester Ob/Gyn **Title:** M.D. **Type of organization:** Group practice **Major product:** Women's healthcare **Area of distribution:** White Plains, New York **Area of Practice:** Gynecology, menopause **Published works:** multiple publications **Affiliations:** F.A.C.S.; A.M.A.; F.A.C.O.G. **Hob./spts.:** grandchild, basketball **SIC code:** 80 **Address:** Westchester Ob/Gyn, 170 Maple Ave., White Plains, NY 10601

SILVERMAN, JOEL R.
Industry: Healthcare **Born:** May 4, 1947, New York, New York **Univ./degree:** M.D., University of Oklahoma, 1974 **Current organization:** Patel, Silverman & Chadha **Title:** M.D. **Type of organization:** Group practice **Major product:** Patient care **Area of distribution:** New York **Area of Practice:** Pulmonary medicine **Affiliations:** A.T.S.; A.C.P.; A.C.C.P. **Hob./spts.:** Jazz, tennis **SIC code:** 80 **Address:** Patel, Silverman & Chadha, 111-20 Queens Blvd., Forest Hills, NY 11375

SILVERMAN, MATTHEW N.
Industry: Healthcare **Born:** May 17, 1955, Brooklyn, New York **Univ./degree:** M.D., New York Medical College, 1982 **Current organization:** Boro Park Obstetrics & Gynecology **Title:** M.D. **Type of organization:** Private practice **Major product:** Women's healthcare **Area of distribution:** Brooklyn, New York **Area of Practice:** OB/GYN, infertility **Published works:** 1 article **Affiliations:** F.A.C.O.G.; A.A.L.G. **SIC code:** 80 **Address:** Boro Park Obstetrics & Gynecology, 5925 15th Ave., Brooklyn, NY 11219 **E-mail:** gynomatt@aol.com

SIMON, STEVEN M.
Industry: Healthcare **Born:** August 17, 1947, Kansas City, Missouri **Univ./degree:** B.S., Psychology, University of Missouri; M.D., Ross Medical School, 1983 **Current organization:** Mid America Physiatrists **Title:** Director **Type of organization:** Private practice **Major product:** Rehabilitation, pain management **Area of distribution:** Overland Park, Kansas **Area of Practice:** PMR/pain management **Honors/awards:** Top 200 Physicians of the Year, 2000; Who's Who of America's Physicians **Published works:** "Raj's Textbook of Pain"; "The SI Joint Intervention of Pain Management", chapter 50; "Topics in Neurology", chapter 8; Spacity Journal **Affiliations:** Society of Pain Practice Management **Hob./spts.:** Racquetball **SIC code:** 80 **Address:** Mid America Physiatrists, 4601 W. 109th St., Suite 302, Overland Park, KS 66211 **E-mail:** ssimonmd@yahoo.com

SIMPSON, MARIE
Industry: Healthcare **Born:** Webb, Mississippi **Univ./degree:** L.P.N. II Certification, Pueblo Community College **Current organization:** Sunrise Adult Foster Care of Pueblo, Inc. **Title:** Owner/President **Type of organization:** Healthcare facility **Major product:** Assisted living for the elderly **Area of distribution:** Pueblo, Colorado **Area of Practice:** Nursing **Affiliations:** N.A.A.C.P., Business Women's Network; Martin Luther King Cultural Center **Hob./spts.:** Darts, sewing, writing **SIC code:** 80 **Address:** Sunrise Adult Foster Care of Pueblo, Inc., 1219 Lake Ave., Pueblo, CO 81004 **E-mail:** mississippian70@aol.com

SIMPSON, SUE A.
Industry: Healthcare **Born:** June 7, 1950, Roanoke, Virginia **Univ./degree:** Diploma, Surgical Technician, Carolina Medical Center, 1971 **Current organization:** Health South Surgery Center of Charlotte **Title:** Surgical Technician/Materials Manager **Type of organization:** Outpatient surgery center **Major product:** Patient care **Area of distribution:** North Carolina **Area of Practice:** Materials management; Certified Surgical Technician **Hob./spts.:** Camping, NASCAR racing **SIC code:** 80 **Address:** Health South Surgery Center of Charlotte, 2825 Randolph Rd., Charlotte, NC 28211 **E-mail:** sue.simpson@healthsouth.com **Web address:** www.healthsouth.com

SINGER, PAMELA A.
Industry: Healthcare **Born:** Dickson, Tennessee **Univ./degree:** D.O., Kansas City, 1985 **Current organization:** Dickson Family Medical Group, P.C. **Title:** D.O. **Type of organization:** Medical practice **Major product:** Patient care **Area of distribution:** Dickson, Tennessee **Area of Practice:** Family healthcare **Affiliations:** American Medical Association; American Osteopathic Association; Fellow, American Academy of Family Practice **SIC code:** 80 **Address:** Dickson Family Medical Group, P.C., 118 Hwy. 70E, Dickson, TN 37055 **E-mail:** pamelas@med-pc.com

SINGH, FRANCINA
Industry: Medical **Born:** June 25, 1948, India **Univ./degree:** M.P.H., Columbia University, 1976 **Current organization:** Stony Brook University Hospital **Title:** Co-Director, Health Care Epidemiology Dept. **Type of organization:** University hospital **Major product:** Patient care, education, research **Area of distribution:** National **Area of Practice:** Epidemiology and infection control **Affiliations:** A.P.I.C.; L.I.D.S. **Hob./spts.:** Stamp and coin collecting **SIC code:** 80 **Address:** Stony Brook University Hospital, Nichols Rd., Stony Brook, NY 11794 **E-mail:** fsi@notes.cc.sunysb.edu

SINGH, GURDEV
Industry: Healthcare **Univ./degree:** M.D. University of London, England, 1980 **Current organization:** Stota Institute for Health and Education **Title:** President **Type of organization:** Medical institute **Major product:** Medical services **Area of distribution:** International **Area of Practice:** Internal medicine, general surgery **Affiliations:** Fellow, Royal College of Surgeons in England & Scotland; A.S.I.M.; A.C.P. **SIC code:** 80 **Address:** Stota Institute for Health and Education, 441 S. Livernois Rd., Suite 235, Rochester Hills, MI 48307 **E-mail:** gsingh@aol.com **Web address:** www.stuta.com

SIVASANKARAN, SATISH
Industry: Healthcare **Univ./degree:** M.B.B.S., Stanley Medical College, India **Current organization:** Lahey Clinic **Title:** M.D. **Type of organization:** Hospital **Major product:** Patient care **Area of distribution:** Massachusetts **Area of Practice:** Cardiology **Affiliations:** American Heart Association; American College of Cardiology; Royal College of Physicians, U.K. **SIC code:** 80 **Address:** Lahey Clinic, 48 N. Emerson St., Unit 10, Wakefield, MA 01880 **E-mail:** satsank72@gmail.com

SKANDALAKIS, JOHN E.
Industry: Medical **Born:** January 20, 1920, Molai, Sparta, State of Laconia, Greece **Univ./degree:** M.D., University of Athens; Ph.D., Anatomy, Emory University **Current organization:** Emory University Medical School **Title:** Director of Surgical Anatomy/Chris Carlos Distinguished Professor of Surgical Anatomy & Technique **Type of organization:** University medical school and hospital **Major product:** Patient care, medical education **Area of distribution:** National **Area of Practice:** Author, professor and hospital director **Published works:** 187 articles, several books including "Embryology for Surgeons" **Affiliations:** Past Chair, University of Georgia Board of Regents **SIC code:** 80 **Address:** Emory University Medical School, Dept. of Surgical Anatomy & Technique, 1462 Clifton Rd. N.E., Atlanta, GA 30322

SKEELS, JEANETT R.
Industry: Healthcare **Born:** June 26, 1964, Los Gatos, California **Univ./degree:** Nursing License, Clover Park Technical College, 1984 **Current organization:** Columbia Lutheran Homes **Title:** L.P.N. **Type of organization:** Nursing home **Major product:** Long-term healthcare **Area of distribution:** Lynwood, Washington **Area of Practice:** Hospice, geriatrics **Hob./spts.:** Baseball, gardening, cooking **SIC code:** 80 **Address:** Columbia Lutheran Homes, 4700 Phinney Ave., Seattle, WA 98103 **E-mail:** jrskeels_juno.com

SKINNER, DARLENE A.
Industry: Healthcare **Born:** October 30, 1957, Cheverly, Maryland **Univ./degree:** M.S., Nursing, Catholic University of America, 1991 **Current organization:** Doctors Community Hospital **Title:** Director of Critical Care and Emergency Services **Type of organization:** Hospital **Major product:** Patient care **Area of distribution:** Lanham, Maryland **Area of Practice:** Critical and emergency care **Affiliations:** A.A.C.C.N.; S.C.C.M.; Maryland State Bar Association, Student Division; Sigma Theta Tau **Hob./spts.:** Golf, reading, pets **SIC code:** 80 **Address:** Doctors Community Hospital, 8118 Good Luck Rd., Lanham, MD 20706

SMITH, GLORIA J.
Industry: Healthcare **Born:** February 22, 1962, Roaring Spring, Pennsylvania **Univ./degree:** A.A., Nursing, Mount Aloysius Jr. College, Pennsylvania, 1995 **Current organization:** Fulton County Medical Center **Title:** Chief Nursing Officer **Type of organization:** Hospital with LTC facility attached **Major product:** Patient care **Area of distribution:** Fulton County, Pennsylvania **Area of Practice:** Nursing **Published works:** Article **Affiliations:** Pennsylvania Nursing Association **Hob./spts.:** Motorcycle riding, travel **SIC code:** 80 **Address:** Fulton County Medical Center, 216 S. First St., McConnellsburg, PA 17233 **E-mail:** gsmith@fcmc-pa.org

SMITH, H. MARIE
Industry: Healthcare **Born:** July 27, 1947, Johnstown, Pennsylvania **Univ./degree:** R.N., Latrobe Area Hospital, Pennsylvania, 1969 **Current organization:** Tower Day Surgery **Title:** R.N./Director of Nurses **Type of organization:** Ambulatory surgery center **Major product:** Patient care **Area of distribution:** Oklahoma City, Oklahoma **Area of Practice:** Nursing/Administration **Affiliations:** A.O.R.N. **Hob./spts.:** Spending time with her grandchildren, hiking, reading **SIC code:** 80 **Address:** Tower Day Surgery, 1044 S.W. 44th St., Suite 100, Oklahoma City, OK 73109 **E-mail:** msmith@ortho-ok.com

SMITH, LINDA S.
Industry: Healthcare **Born:** July 24, 1948 **Univ./degree:** R.N., Northwestern Hospital, Minneapolis, Minnesota **Current organization:** Winona Health Nursing Home **Title:** RNC **Type of organization:** Nursing home **Major product:** Long-term care **Area of distribution:** Winona, Minnesota **Area of Practice:** Alzheimer's disease **Hob./spts.:** Crafts, knitting **SIC code:** 80 **Address:** Winona Health, 855 Mankato Ave., Winona, MN 55987 **E-mail:** wgsmith@rconnect.com

SMITH, LORI A.
Industry: Healthcare **Born:** March 23, 1965, Gallatin, Tennessee **Univ./degree:** A.S., Nursing, Lincoln Memorial University, 1986 **Current organization:** East Tennessee Children's Hospital **Title:** Nurse Manager; NRP Regional Trainer **Type of organization:** Hospital **Major product:** Patient care **Area of distribution:** Tennessee **Area of Practice:** Neonatal **Affiliations:** National Association of Neonatal Nurses **Hob./spts.:** Piano, family time **SIC code:** 80 **Address:** East Tennessee Children's Hospital, NICU Dept., 2018 Clinch Ave., Knoxville, TN 37901 **E-mail:** lasmith@etch.com

SMITH, PETER TRENT
Industry: Healthcare **Born:** November 24, 1955, Bay City, Michigan **Univ./degree:** B.S., Pre-med., Saginaw Valley State University, 1981; M.D., American University of the Caribbean, 1987 **Current organization:** Peter Trent Smith, M.D., P.C. **Title:** M.D./ Psychiatrist **Type of organization:** Private practice **Major product:** Patient care **Area of distribution:** Michigan **Area of Practice:** Psychiatry (general disorders, substance abuse, forensics) **Honors/awards:** Physicians' Recognition Award **Affiliations:** A.P.A.; A.M.A.; Michigan State Medical Society **Hob./spts.:** Hockey, golf, college sports, travel, reading, gardening, cooking **SIC code:** 80 **Address:** P.O. Box 814, Bay City, MI 48707 **E-mail:** ptmdsmith@aol.com

SMITH, PORTER
Industry: Healthcare **Born:** April 9, 1951, Illinois **Univ./degree:** M.D., University of Missouri at Columbia, 1977 **Current organization:** Eye Surgery Consultants **Title:** M.D. **Type of organization:** Private practice **Major product:** Patient care, eye surgery **Area of distribution:** Poplar Bluff, Missouri **Area of Practice:** Cataract, laser and glaucoma surgery **Affiliations:** A.M.A.; M.M.A. **Hob./spts.:** Weightlifting, music **SIC code:** 80 **Address:** Eye Surgery Consultants, 2210 Barron Rd., Poplar Bluff, MO 63901 **E-mail:** ada@semo.net

SMITH, STEVE
Industry: Healthcare/Hospitality **Born:** December 21, 1973, Auburn, Alabama **Univ./degree:** A.A., Culinary Arts, Scottsdale Culinary Institute **Current organization:** National Health Care Corp. **Title:** Executive Chef **Type of organization:** Healthcare center **Major product:** Assisted living **Area of distribution:** Tennessee **Area of Practice:** Certified Executive Chef, Certified Dietary Manager **Affiliations:** American Culinary Federation; Dietary Managers Association **SIC code:** 80 **Address:** National Health Care Corp., 120 Cavett Hill Lane, Knoxville, TN 37934 **E-mail:** tntigerchef@f-m.fm

SMITH-MAXWELL, PATRICIA D.
Industry: Healthcare **Born:** August 15, 1955, Detroit, Michigan **Current organization:** Henry Ford Hospital **Title:** Residency Coordinator **Type of organization:** Hospital **Major product:** Patient care **Area of distribution:** International **Area of Practice:** Residency coordinator, OB/GYN department **Affiliations:** Youth program, New Bride Missionary Baptist Church **Hob./spts.:** Bingo, bike riding **SIC code:** 80 **Address:** 1070 Parker St., Flat 2, Detroit, MI 48214 **E-mail:** pmaxwel1@hfhs.org

SMULL, EDNA MARIE
Industry: Healthcare **Born:** February 1, 1939, Phoenix, Arizona **Univ./degree:** B.A., Nursing, Iowa Westland University, 1990 **Current organization:** Great River Medical Center **Title:** V.P. Nursing **Type of organization:** Nonprofit community hospital **Major product:** Patient care **Area of distribution:** West Burlington, Iowa **Area of Practice:** Nursing **Published works:** 1 article **Affiliations:** I.O.N.E.; A.A.C.N.; Red Cross **SIC code:** 80 **Address:** Great River Medical Center, 1221 S. Gear Ave., West Burlington, IA 52655 **E-mail:** esmull@grhs.net

SNOWDEN, ROBERT T.
Industry: Healthcare **Born:** March 29, 1944, Delane, Florida **Univ./degree:** M.D., Vanderbilt University, Tennessee, 1969 **Current organization:** Gulf Coast Orthopaedic Specialists **Title:** M.D. **Type of organization:** Orthopaedic surgery group practice **Major product:** Medical services, surgery **Area of distribution:** Florida **Area of Practice:** Orthopedic surgery, total joint replacement **Published works:** Article, the A.A.O.S., 1969 **Affiliations:** F.A.A.O.S.; C.M.S.; F.M.A.; S.O.A.; A.A.H.K.S. **Hob./spts.:** Skiing, fishing, playing piano, music **SIC code:** 80 **Address:** Gulf Coast Orthopaedic Specialists, 4541 N. Davis Hwy., Suite A, Pensacola, FL 32503 **E-mail:** robertsnowden@cox.net

SNYDER, RICHARD
Industry: Healthcare **Univ./degree:** D.O., Philadelphia College of Osteopathic Medicine; Fellowship, Classical Research, University of Pennsylvania **Current organization:** Lehigh Valley Nephrology Associates **Title:** D.O. **Type of organization:** Hospital **Major product:** Patient care **Area of distribution:** Easton, Pennsylvania **Area of Practice:** Nephrology; A.M.A. Board Certified, Internal Medicine **Published works:** 7 papers **Affiliations:** A.M.A.; National Kidney Foundation; American Osteopathic Association; American Osteopathic Internists **SIC code:** 80 **Address:** Lehigh Valley Nephrology Associates, 30 Community Dr., Easton, PA 18040 **E-mail:** stanniocalcin@hotmail.com

SNYDER JR., WILLIAM E.
Industry: Healthcare **Born:** March 15, 1964, Plymouth, Indiana **Univ./degree:** M.D., Indiana University, 1993 **Current organization:** Neurosurgical Associates **Title:** M.D. **Type of organization:** Medical practice **Major product:** Neurosurgery care **Area of distribution:** Knoxville, Tennessee **Area of Practice:** Neurosurgery with interest in brain tumors, cerebrovascular disease and complex spine disorders **Honors/awards:** Alpha Omega Alpha, Honor Society, 1991; J. Donald Hubbard Award, Outstanding Performance in Pathology, 1993; Pittman Surgical Scholarship Award, 1993 **Published works:** Article: Shappiro, S.A., Snyder, W., "Spinal Instrumentation with Low Complication Rate", Surgical Neurology, 48: 566-574, 1997 **Affiliations:** A.M.A.; T.M.A.; A.A.N.S.; C.N.S. **Hob./spts.:** Golf, basketball **SIC code:** 80 **Address:** Neurosurgical Associates, 1932 Alcoa Hwy., Bldg. C, Suite 550, Knoxville, TN 37920 **E-mail:** wesnyder@mc.utmck.edu

SOLIMAN, IBRAHIM N.
Industry: Healthcare **Born:** April 3, 1959. Cairo, Egypt **Univ./degree:** M.D., Aim Shams Medical School, Cairo Egypt **Current organization:** Lutheran Medical Center **Title:** M.D. **Type of organization:** Medical facility **Major product:** Patient care **Area of distribution:** Brooklyn, New York **Area of Practice:** Internal medicine **Honors/awards:** Chief Resident; Graduate Honors, Medical School **Affiliations:** A.M.A.; A.C.P. **SIC code:** 80 **Address:** 405 78th St., Apt. 4D, Brooklyn, NY 11209 **E-mail:** insoliman@aol.com

SOLIS, ROBERTO E.
Industry: Healthcare **Born:** December 8, 1962, Guatemala, Central America **Univ./degree:** M.D., Francisco Marroquín University, Guatemala, 1987; Residency in Internal Medicine and Cardiology, Texas Tech University **Current organization:** Cardiologists of Lubbock **Title:** M.D. **Type of organization:** Group practice **Major product:** Patient care **Area of distribution:** Lubbock, Texas **Area of Practice:** Internal medicine (Board Certified), interventional cardiology, cardiovascular disease **Honors/awards:** Outstanding Young American Award **Affiliations:** A.M.A.; S.C.A.I.; A.S.I.M.; Lubbock-Garza County Medical Society; American College of Cardiology; American College of Physicians **Hob./spts.:** Soccer, jogging **SIC code:** 80 **Address:** Cardiologists of Lubbock, 3506 21st St., Suite 507, Lubbock, TX 79410 **E-mail:** parvxsw@cox.net

SOMERVILLE, JUDSON J.
Industry: Healthcare **Born:** January 1, 1961, Corpus Christi, Texas **Univ./degree:** M.D., University of Texas, 1980 **Current organization:** The Pain Management Clinic of Laredo **Title:** M.D./Director **Type of organization:** Health clinic **Major product:** Patient care **Area of distribution:** National **Area of Practice:** Pain management; Chief Resident, Anesthesiology, 1994 **Hob./spts.:** Hunting, fishing, collecting Mexican coins **SIC code:** 80 **Address:** The Pain Management Clinic of Laredo, 6801 McPherson, Suite 334, Laredo, TX 78041 **E-mail:** somervillejudson@netscape.net

SON, DANIEL L.
Industry: Healthcare **Born:** June 22, 1950, Wilkes-Barre, Pennsylvania **Univ./degree:** M.D., Guadalajara, Mexico, 1976; Residency Urology, Hahnemann University, Philadelphia, Pennsylvania **Current organization:** Daniel L. Son, M.D. **Title:** M.D. **Type of organization:** Private practice **Major product:** Patient care **Area of distribution:** Hazleton, Pennsylvania **Area of Practice:** Urology **Published works:** Articles pertaining to urologic medicine **Hob./spts.:** Golf, hunting, fishing, trapshooting **SIC code:** 80 **Address:** 668 N. Church St., Hazleton, PA 18201 **Phone:** (570)454-5200 **Fax:** (570)454-9927

SONES, DANIEL J.
Industry: Healthcare **Born:** September 2, 1966, Ventura, California **Univ./degree:** D.D.S., U.C.L.A., 1992; Completed Advanced Education in General Dentistry Residency, U.C.L.A., 1993 **Current organization:** Daniel J. Sones, D.D.S. **Title:** Dentist **Type of organization:** Private practice **Major product:** Dental care **Area of distribution:** California **Area of Practice:** Family dentistry **Affiliations:** C.D.A.; A.D.A.; Venture/Santa Barbara local Dental Society; Ventura Chamber of Commerce; UCLA Alumni Association; Appollonians of the UCLA School of Dentistry; Research Associates of Point Loma Nazarene University; Surfrider Foundation **Hob./spts.:** Surfing, travel, active in church, coach-youth soccer and softball **SIC code:** 80 **Address:** Daniel J. Sones, D.D.S., 3356 Loma Vista Rd., Ventura, CA 93003 **E-mail:** dsondds@adelphi.net

SONG, MI-KYOUNG
Industry: Healthcare **Born:** March 26, 1964, San Francisco, California **Univ./degree:** B.S., Biochemistry, University of California at Berkeley, 1964; M.D., Wayne State School of Medicine, 1994 **Current organization:** Eye Associates of New Mexico **Title:** M.D. **Type of organization:** Group practice **Major product:** Eye healthcare **Area of distribution:** New Mexico **Area of Practice:** Vitreo-retinal specialist **Published works:** Articles **Affiliations:** A.A.O.; New Mexico Ophthalmological Society **SIC code:** 80 **Address:** Eye Associates of New Mexico, 101 Hospital Loop N.E., Albuquerque, NM 87109

SONI, MADHU
Industry: Medical **Born:** December 9, 1968, Toronto, Canada **Univ./degree:** M.D., Northwestern University School of Medicine, 1992 **Current organization:** Midwest Association in Neurology, Rush-Presbyterian-St. Luke's Medical Center **Title:** M.D. **Type of organization:** University medical center/private practice **Major product:** Patient care, medical education **Area of distribution:** Illinois **Area of Practice:** Neurology **Affiliations:** A.M.A.; American Academy of Neurology **Hob./spts.:**

Tennis, music, flowers **SIC code:** 80 **Address:** Midwest Association in Neurology, Rush-Presbyterian-St. Luke's Medical Center, 675 W. North Ave., Suite 214, Melrose Park, IL 60160 **E-mail:** msoni@rush.edu **Web address:** www.rush.edu

SOORI, MOHAMMED K.B.
Industry: Healthcare **Born:** August 29, 1955, Mpoho, Ghana **Univ./degree:** M.D., First Pavlov Medical Institute, St. Petersburg, Russia, 1982 **Current organization:** St. Lukes Roosevelt Hospital **Title:** M.D. **Type of organization:** Hospital **Major product:** Patient care **Area of distribution:** National **Area of Practice:** Psychiatry, family and alternate medicine **Affiliations:** A.M.A.; A.P.A. **Hob./spts.:** Yoga, nature walks, music, swimming **SIC code:** 80 **Address:** St. Lukes Roosevelt Hospital, 66 W. 109th St., #62, New York, NY 10025 **E-mail:** soori01@aol.com

SOPEYIN, TEMITOPE O.
Industry: Healthcare **Born:** May 24, 1963, Nigeria **Univ./degree:** M.D., Nigeria University of Ibagan **Current organization:** Joe Dimaggio Children's Hospital Florida **Title:** M.D. **Type of organization:** Hospital **Major product:** Patient care **Area of distribution:** Florida **Area of Practice:** Pediatric emergency medicine **Published works:** Articles **Affiliations:** A.A.P. **Hob./spts.:** Sports, music **SIC code:** 80 **Address:** Joe Dimaggio Children's Hospital Florida, 3501 Johnson St., Hollywood, FL 33021 **E-mail:** temi@prodigy.net

SOTO, MARTIN
Industry: Healthcare **Born:** June 17, 1966, Miami, Florida **Univ./degree:** M.D., Iberoamerican University, 2000 **Current organization:** Physician Associates **Title:** M.D. **Type of organization:** Medical practice **Major product:** Patient care **Area of distribution:** International **Area of Practice:** Certified, Family Practice **Affiliations:** A.M.A.; American Academy of Family Physicians **Hob./spts.:** Travel, college football, basketball **SIC code:** 80 **Address:** Physician Associates, 779 N. Alafaya Trail, Orlando, FL 32828 **E-mail:** msoto@paof.com **Web address:** www.paof.com

SOTO, VICTOR G.
Industry: Healthcare **Born:** April 12, 1953, Panama City, Panama **Univ./degree:** M.D., 1977 **Current organization:** Gables Diagnostic Imaging Associates **Title:** M.D., F.A.C.C.; F.A.C.P. **Type of organization:** Independent diagnostic testing facility **Major product:** Patient care **Area of distribution:** Florida **Area of Practice:** Internal medicine, cardiology **Published works:** Articles **Affiliations:** A.M.A.; American College of Physicians; American College of Cardiology **Hob./spts.:** Tennis, running, scuba diving **SIC code:** 80 **Address:** Gables Diagnostic Imaging Associates, 495 Biltmore Way, First floor, Coral Gables, FL 33134

SOTUDEH, SHARIAR
Industry: Healthcare **Born:** November 18, 1938, Yazd, Persia **Univ./degree:** M.D., Medical University of Vienna, Austria, 1997 **Current organization:** Mount Vernon Hospital **Title:** M.D., Chief of Orthopaedics **Type of organization:** Hospital **Major product:** Patient care **Area of distribution:** Mount Vernon, New York **Area of Practice:** Orthopedic surgery **Published works:** Articles, journals **Affiliations:** Fellow, American Academy of Orthopaedic Surgeons; President, A.I.O.S.A. **SIC code:** 80 **Address:** Mount Vernon Hospital, P.O. Box 536, Mount Vernon, NY 10552

SOWERS, WILLIAM E.
Industry: Healthcare **Born:** January 9, 1971, Danville, Indiana **Univ./degree:** B.S., Biology/Chemistry, Butler University, 1993; M.D., University of Indiana School of Medicine, 1997 **Current organization:** Family Health Care of Muncie **Title:** M.D. **Type of organization:** Group practice **Major product:** Patient care **Area of distribution:** Indiana **Area of Practice:** Family medicine **Affiliations:** A.A.F.P.; A.M.A. **Hob./spts.:** Family, music, reading, the outdoors, sports **SIC code:** 80 **Address:** Family Health Care of Muncie, 5501 W. Bethel Ave., Muncie, IN 47304 **E-mail:** wsowers@aol.com

SPADA, DOMINICK
Industry: Healthcare **Born:** October 21, 1969, Brooklyn, New York **Univ./degree:** B.S., Pharmacy, LIU, 1992; M.S., Health Administration, Kennedy Western University, 2004 **Current organization:** Ocean Breeze Infusion Care Inc. **Title:** CEO **Type of organization:** Home healthcare **Major product:** Home respiratory care, DME and pharmacy **Area of distribution:** Staten Island, New York **Area of Practice:** Healthcare administration, pharmacy practice **Affiliations:** A.P.H.A.; P.S.S.N.Y.; A.S.H.P. **Hob./spts.:** Golf **SIC code:** 80 **Address:** Ocean Breeze Infusion Care Inc., 27 Brienna Ct., Staten Island, NY 10309 **E-mail:** dspada@siuh.edu

SPANIER, CYNTHIA A.
Industry: Healthcare **Born:** November 16, 1958, Melrose, Minnesota **Univ./degree:** B.S., Magna Cum Laude, 1981; M.S., 1982, Marquette University; Ph.D., University of Pittsburgh, 1997 **Current organization:** Psychological Health & Behavioral Medicine **Title:** Psychologist **Type of organization:** Healthcare provider **Major product:** Psychological consultation, therapy and intervention **Area of distribution:** International **Area of Practice:** Adults, the elderly and families **Honors/awards:** Academic Scholarship Recipient, Marquette University Graduate School, 1981; Student Travel Award, Program Committee, Society for Psychotherapy Research, 1994; First Prize, Clinical Psychology Intern Research Poster, First Annual Research Behavior, Brown University School of Medicine, 1996; Travel Award Fellowship, Program Committee, Association for Clinical Psychosocial Research, 1997; 2001 Item Writer: New Items (Item Bank) in Clinical Health Psychology and Program; 2002 Participant: for the Examination for Professional Practice in Psychology (EPPP), April-August, 2001; Diplomate in sports psychology **Published works:** 20 articles and 4 book chapters **Affiliations:** A.P.A.; S.S.C.P.; A.M.S.P. **Hob./spts.:** Family, writing, books **SIC code:** 80 **Address:** Psychological Health & Behavioral Medicine, 225 Penn Ave., Suite 1028, Pittsburgh, PA 15221 **E-mail:** cyndiespanielr@aol.com

SPARKS, LAURA J.
Industry: Healthcare **Univ./degree:** B.S., Biology, Virginia Tech; B.S.P.T., University of Maryland Medical School **Current organization:** Physiotherapy Associates **Title:** Physical Therapist **Type of organization:** Medical **Major product:** Outpatient orthopedics and sports medicine **Area of distribution:** National **Area of Practice:** Shoulder dysfunction **Affiliations:** Former Member, American Physical Therapy Association; USTA **Hob./spts.:** Tennis, reading, scrapbooking, gardening, family activities **SIC code:** 80 **Address:** Physiotherapy Associates, 100 Mountain View Dr., Suite 100, Cumming, GA 30040 **E-mail:** dlsparks@adelphia.net

SPEARS, ZEPHIA DEE
Industry: Healthcare **Univ./degree:** A.S., Nursing, Amarillo College **Current organization:** Interim Healthcare **Title:** Director of Pediatrics **Type of organization:** Home healthcare agency **Major product:** Home healthcare (Pediatrics) **Area of distribution:** Texas **Area of Practice:** Special needs children's healthcare, foster mother for special needs children **Hob./spts.:** Reading, swimming, painting **SIC code:** 80 **Address:** Interim Healthcare, 6601 I-40 West, Bldg. 2, Amarillo, TX 79106 **E-mail:** dees@interimwesttex.com

SPENCER, JEREMIAH L.
Industry: Medical/religious counseling **Born:** March 5, 1939, Topeka, Kansas **Univ./degree:** St. Thomas University, 1965 **Current organization:** University of Kansas Hospital/Holy Name Catholic Church **Title:** Chaplain/Reverend **Type of organization:** Hospital/Catholic parish **Major product:** Patient care, medical education/religious counseling **Area of distribution:** National **Area of Practice:** Counseling, consulting **Affiliations:** F.B.I. **Hob./spts.:** Travel, sports, reading **SIC code:** 80 **Address:** University of Kansas Hospital/Holy Name Catholic Church, 16 S. Iowa St., Kansas City, KS 66103 **E-mail:** jspencer@kumc.edu

SPREHE, DANIEL J.
Industry: Healthcare/Psychiatry **Born:** February 21, 1932, Oklahoma City, Oklahoma **Univ./degree:** B.S., Zoology, University of Oklahoma, 1954; M.D., University of Oklahoma, School of Medicine, 1957 **Current organization:** University of South Florida Medical School, Dept. of Psychiatry **Title:** M.D. (Retired) **Type of organization:** University medical school **Major product:** Psychiatry, mental health **Area of distribution:** Florida **Area of practice:** Forensic psychiatry, consultant and expert witness testimony **Area of Practice:** Forensic psychiatry, consultant and expert witness testimony **Honors/awards:** Phi Beta Kappa; Alpha Omega Alpha, Honor Medical Society; Named, The Best Doctors in America; Southeast Region, 1996-97; Nominee, FMA/FPS Leadership Award in the Medical Education Board, 1997; Outstanding Clinical Faculty Award, USF Dept, of Psychiatry, 1989; Outstanding Service Award, Department of Psychiatry USF, 1982 Appreciation Award, Criminal Defense Lawyers of Hillsborough County; Recognition Plaque, The Florida Bar Convention, 6/81 **Published works:** Numerous works and presentations including - Presentation for the Workers' Comp Section of the Florida Bar Association, 3/96; Presentation, American Academy of Psychiatric and the Law, Seattle Washington, 10/95; "Psychiatric Validity of Legal Terms in Will Contest", submitted American Academy Psychiatry and Law, 10/93; "Geriatric Psychiatry and the Law", Chapter in Principles and Practice of Forensic Psychology, Chapman & Hall, 1994; "Does the Greenback Poultice Improve Stress Related Trauma", paper presented, AAPL, San Francisco, 10/88 **Affiliations:** Fellow American Psychiatric Association; Fellow American College of Psychiatry; Past Vice President, American Academy of Psychiatry and the Law, 1992-93; A.M.A.; Florida Medical Association; American Academy of Forensic Sciences **Hob./spts.:** Sailboat

racing, ocean racing, mountain climbing, skiing **SIC code:** 80 **Address:** University of South Florida Medical School, 800 West Martin Luther King, Tampa, FL 33603

SQUIERS, FERNE E.
Industry: Healthcare/consulting **Born:** May 7, 1948, Little Falls, New York **Univ./degree:** B.S.N., Indiana University, 1996 **Current organization:** St. Vincent Hospice **Title:** Long Term Care Management Consultant **Type of organization:** Long-term care management consulting firm **Major product:** Management consulting to long-term care facilities **Area of distribution:** Indiana **Area of Practice:** Consulting **Affiliations:** American Nurses Association **Hob./spts.:** Russian literature, history and language; classical music, opera, pro football **SIC code:** 80 **Address:** St. Vincent Hospice, Indianapolis, IN 46261 **E-mail:** fsquiers@msn.com

STAATS, PETER S.
Industry: Healthcare **Born:** May 22, 1963, Phoenix, Arizona **Univ./degree:** M.D., University of Michigan, 1989 **Current organization:** Johns Hopkins University School of Medicine **Title:** M.D. **Type of organization:** University **Major product:** Patient care **Area of distribution:** Baltimore, Maryland **Area of Practice:** Pain medicine/therapics **Published works:** 200+ articles **Affiliations:** A.P.S.; A.A.P.M.; President, S.P.S. **Hob./spts.:** Family **SIC code:** 80 **Address:** Johns Hopkins University School of Medicine, 550 N. Broadway, Suite 301, Baltimore, MD 21205 **E-mail:** pstaats@jhmi.edu

STADNYK, HARRY W.
Industry: Healthcare **Born:** November 26, 1941, Thunder Bay, Ontario, Canada **Univ./degree:** D.D.S., St. Louis University, 1966 **Current organization:** Harry W. Stadnyk, D.D.S. **Title:** D.D.S. **Type of organization:** Private practice **Major product:** Dental care **Area of distribution:** Missouri **Area of Practice:** Laser and cosmetic dentistry **Affiliations:** A.D.A.; A.G.D.; A.O.I.; A.L.D. **Hob./spts.:** Boating **SIC code:** 80 **Address:** Harry W. Stadnyk, D.D.S., 807 Hazelwest Dr., Hazelwood, MO 63042 **E-mail:** docstads1@aol.com

STAHL, JEFFREY A.
Industry: Healthcare **Born:** March 6, 1956, Boston, Massachusetts **Univ./degree:** M.D., Albert Einstein, 1984 **Current organization:** Jeffrey A. Stahl, M.D., F.A.C.C. **Title:** Cardiologist **Type of organization:** Private practice **Major product:** Patient care **Area of distribution:** Manhasset, New York **Area of Practice:** Cardiology, internal medicine (Board Certified) **Published works:** Multiple publications **Affiliations:** F.A.C.P.; F.A.C.C.; F.A.C.C.P. **Hob./spts.:** Travel **SIC code:** 80 **Address:** Jeffrey A. Stahl, M.D., F.A.C.C., 1165 Northern Blvd., Suite 400, Manhasset, NY 11030 **E-mail:** mdcardiac@nymed.net

STAHL, ROSALYN E.
Industry: Healthcare **Born:** April 28, 1952, Patterson, New Jersey **Univ./degree:** B.S., Biology, Stern College Yeshiva, 1973; M.D., Albert Einstein School of Medicine, 1976 **Current organization:** Englewood Pathologists, P.A. **Title:** M.D. **Type of organization:** Pathology Department of Englewood Hospital **Major product:** Patient care **Area of distribution:** New Jersey **Area of Practice:** Pathology **Published works:** 30 + articles, one chapter, co-editor of medical book **Affiliations:** Fellow, American College of Pathology; New York Pathology Society **SIC code:** 80 **Address:** Englewood Pathologists, P.A., c/o Englewood Hospital, 350 Englewood Ave., Englewood, NJ 07631 **E-mail:** leonkozak@aol.com

STANLEY JR., ALFRED W.H.
Industry: Healthcare **Born:** May 20, 1939, Macon, Georgia **Univ./degree:** M.D., University of Florida, 1967 **Current organization:** Alabama Cardiovascular Group **Title:** Interventional Cardiologist **Type of organization:** Private group practice **Major product:** Patient care **Area of distribution:** International **Area of Practice:** Interventional Cardiologist; research **Published works:** 30+ articles **Affiliations:** F.A.C.P.; F.A.H.A., F.A.C.C. **Hob./spts.:** Golf **SIC code:** 80 **Address:** 4401 Fredericksburg Dr., Birmingham, AL 35213 **E-mail:** sylviaalstanley@aol.com

STANZIOLA, FELIX A.
Industry: Healthcare **Born:** December 7, 1958, Republic of Panama **Univ./degree:** M.D., University of Panama School of Medicine, 1983; McGill University, Orthopedic Surgery, 1991 **Current organization:** Felix A. Stanziola, M.D., P.A. **Title:** M.D., Orthopaedic Surgeon **Type of organization:** Private practice **Major product:** Patient care **Area of distribution:** Miami, Florida **Area of Practice:** Orthopaedic surgery **Affiliations:** Fellow, American Academy of Orthopaedic Surgeons; Royal College of Surgeons of Canada **Hob./spts.:** Fishing **SIC code:** 80 **Address:** Felix A. Stanziola, M.D., P.A., 7000 SW 97th Ave., Suite 200, Miami, FL 33173 **E-mail:** rstanzio@aol.com

STARLING, JAY C.
Industry: Healthcare **Born:** July 29, 1949, Detroit, Michigan **Univ./degree:** B.S., University of Maryland, 1972; M.D., University of Maryland, 1976 **Current organization:** Tidewater Eye Centers **Title:** M.D. **Type of organization:** Group practice **Major product:** Patient care **Area of distribution:** Virginia **Area of Practice:** Ophthalmology **Published works:** 3 articles **Affiliations:** F.A.C.E.S.; American Society of Cataract and Refracture Surgery **SIC code:** 80 **Address:** Tidewater Eye Centers, 3603 County St., Portsmouth, VA 23454 **E-mail:** dcobb.tidewatereye.com **Web address:** www.tidewatereye.com

STASSART, JACQUES P.
Industry: Healthcare **Born:** April 24, 1953, Liege, Belgium **Univ./degree:** M.D., Catholic University of Lovain, Belgium, 1977 **Current organization:** Reproductive Medicine & Infertility Associates **Title:** M.D. **Type of organization:** Private practice **Major product:** Patient care **Area of distribution:** St. Paul, Minnesota **Area of Practice:** Reproductive endocrinology **Published works:** Articles **Affiliations:** F.A.S.R.M.; F.A.C.O.G. **Hob./spts.:** Downhill skiing, swimming **SIC code:** 80 **Address:** Reproductive Medicine & Infertility Associates, 360 Sherman St., Suite 350, St. Paul, MN 55102 **E-mail:** drstassart@rmia.com **Web address:** www.rmia.com

STAUB, PATRICIA B.
Industry: Healthcare **Born:** March 9, 1953, Pittsburgh, Pennsylvania **Univ./degree:** B.S., Medical Technology, Penn State University, 1976 **Current organization:** Iredell Memorial Hospital **Title:** Hematology Section Head **Type of organization:** Hospital **Major product:** Patient care **Area of distribution:** North Carolina **Area of Practice:** Hematology **Hob./spts.:** Canoeing **SIC code:** 80 **Address:** 8368 Normandy Rd., Denver, NC 28037-8646 **E-mail:** staubcpk@aol.com

STAUDINGER, EDWARD B.
Industry: Healthcare **Born:** February 11, 1954, Providence, Rhode Island **Univ./degree:** M.D., Tufts University, 1980 **Current organization:** Staudinger & Walsh, LLP **Title:** Surgeon **Type of organization:** Private practice **Major product:** Patient care **Area of distribution:** New Orleans, Louisiana **Area of Practice:** General surgery **Affiliations:** F.A.C.S.; A.B.S. **Hob./spts.:** Golf **SIC code:** 80 **Address:** Staudinger & Walsh, LLP, 2820 Napoleon Ave., Suite 640, New Orleans, LA 70115 **E-mail:** ebsjjw@bellsouth.net

STEBEL, ANDREA
Industry: Healthcare **Born:** November 12, 1952, Cleveland, Ohio **Univ./degree:** M.D., University of Guadalajara, Mexico, 1980 **Current organization:** Newport Breast Care **Title:** M.D. **Type of organization:** Medical office **Major product:** Breast care **Area of distribution:** National **Area of Practice:** Oncology **Affiliations:** American Society of Clinical Oncologists; American Society of Breast Disease **Hob./spts.:** Tennis, music **SIC code:** 80 **Address:** Newport Breast Care, 355 Placentia Ave., #207A, Newport Beach, CA 92663 **Web address:** www.newportbreastcare.com

STEFANICS, CHARLOTTE L.
Industry: Healthcare **Born:** December 30, 1927, Leechburg, Pennsylvania **Univ./degree:** R.N., St. Elizabeth Hospital, Dayton, Ohio, 1948; B.S.N., Seton Hall University, New Jersey, 1968; M.S.N., Ohio State University, 1971; Ed.D., University of Sarasota, Florida, 1982 **Current organization:** Miami Valley Hospital (Retired from Veteran's Affairs Medical Center, Bay Pines, Florida) **Title:** Doctor of Education/ARNP/Catholic Chaplain/Psychiatric-Mental Health Clinical Nurse Specialist **Type of organization:** Community hospital **Major product:** Patient care, Ministers as Chaplain **Area of distribution:** International **Area of practice:** Diplomate in Logotherapy; working with death, dying and bereavement, psychiatric/mental health nursing, teaching, consulting, Catholic religion **Area of Practice:** Diplomate in Logotherapy; working with death, dying and bereavement, psychiatric/mental health nursing, teaching, consulting, Catholic religion **Honors/awards:** Numerous including, Service and Leadership Award from Viktor Frankl Institute of Logotherapy; Nominated Nurse of the Year, FNA #13, St. Petersburg, Florida; Speaker for Recognition Service for Nurses graduation class at Duke University, 1977; Speaker for Graduation, Springfield Community Hospital School of Nursing, 1973 **Published works:** Co-author (with Rosalie Peck, MSW), "Learning to Say Goodbye", 1987; Co-author (with Rev. Father Gerald Niklas), "Ministry to the Sick", 1982 **Affiliations:** Former Teacher, Duke University School of Nursing, North Carolina; Former Therapist, Teacher, Consultant, Veterans Affairs Medical Center; Catholic Chaplain, Miami Valley Hospital; Faculty, Viktor Frankl Institute of Logotherapy; Habitat for Humanity International; Association of Christian Therapists, Nurses Organization Veterans Affairs **Hob./spts.:** Reading, classical music, gardening, going to Hungary to build houses with Habitat for Humanity **SIC code:** 80 **Address:** Miami Valley Hospital, Pastoral Care and Counseling, 128 E. Apple St., Dayton, OH 45409

STEINBERG, RICHARD S.
Industry: Healthcare **Univ./degree:** B.A., Biology, Hofstra University, 1976; M.D., Downstate Medical College, 1980 **Current organization:** Department of Imaging Services, Peninsula Hospital Center **Title:** M.D., D.A.B.R. **Type of organization:** Hospital **Major product:** Radiology **Area of distribution:** Far Rockaway, New York **Area of Practice:** Radiology, US, MRI, CT **Published works:** 5 publications **Affiliations:** North American Spinal Society **SIC code:** 80 **Address:** Department of Imaging Services, Peninsula Hospital Center, 15-15 Beach Channel Dr., Far Rockaway, NY 11691-1042 **E-mail:** rsteinberg@att.net

STENNETT, KEVIN T.
Industry: Healthcare **Born:** October 10, 1960, Lockney, Texas **Univ./degree:** M.D., Texas Technical Health Center, 1987 **Current organization:** Cogdell Clinic & W.J. Mangold Memorial Hospital **Title:** M.D. **Type of organization:** Clinic/hospital **Major product:** Patient care **Area of distribution:** Texas **Area of Practice:** Family practice with obstetrics and some surgery **Affiliations:** Texas Medical Association; American Academy of Family Practice **Hob./spts.:** Pilot, golf, fishing **SIC code:** 80 **Address:** Cogdell Clinic & W.J. Mangold Memorial Hospital, 320 N. Main St., Box 37, Lockney, TX 79241

STERLING, JEFFREY A.
Industry: Healthcare **Born:** October 18, 1976, Bethpage, New York **Univ./degree:** B.S., Biology, University of North Carolina, Chapel Hill, 1998; O.D., Southern College of Optometry, Memphis, 2002 **Current organization:** Doctor's Vision Center **Title:** Optometrist **Type of organization:** Group practice **Major product:** Patient care **Area of distribution:** North Carolina **Area of Practice:** Primary care optometry, surgical co-management **Affiliations:** North Carolina State Optometric Society; American Optometric Association **Hob./spts.:** University of North Carolina Basketball fan **SIC code:** 80 **Address:** Doctor's Vision Center, 901 N. Winstead Ave., Rocky Mount, NC 27858 **E-mail:** ipupil@yahoo.com

STERN, LEON
Industry: Healthcare **Born:** May 5, 1947, Vilnius, Lithuania **Univ./degree:** M.D., Lithuania, 1971 **Current organization:** Medical and Mental Art Center **Title:** M.D. **Type of organization:** Medical center **Major product:** Psychiatry, psychotherapy **Area of distribution:** Brooklyn, New York **Area of Practice:** Psychiatry **Affiliations:** A.P.A. **Hob./spts.:** Tennis, chess, art collecting **SIC code:** 80 **Address:** Medical & Mental Art Center, 307 Ocean View Ave., Brooklyn, NY 11235

STEVENS, SAMUEL E.
Industry: Healthcare **Born:** June 1, 1978, Johnstown, Pennsylvania **Univ./degree:** A.S., Mount Aloysius College **Current organization:** Altoona Regional Health System **Title:** R.N./Staff Nurse **Type of organization:** Hospital **Major product:** Patient care **Area of distribution:** Pennsylvania **Area of Practice:** Critical Care/Cardiac, Emergency Medical Technician, Volunteer Firefighter; ; Pursuing Paramedic Certification and Pre-Hospital Registered Nurse Certification **Affiliations:** Cambria County Volunteer Firemen's Association; Central District Firemen's Association; A.A.C.N. Regional Member **Hob./spts.:** Outdoors, gardening, old cars, antiques, woodworking/crafts, fishing, hunting, baseball, football **SIC code:** 80 **Address:** Altoona Regional Health System, 180 Shoemaker Circle, Portage, PA 15946 **E-mail:** stevens@blaircon.net

STEWART, KAREN LYNN
Industry: Medical **Born:** August 23, 1964, Trenton, New Jersey **Univ./degree:** B.S., Applied Sciences/Radiologic Technology, Thomas Edison State College, 1966 **Current organization:** Robert Wood Johnson University Hospital **Title:** PACS Coordinator **Type of organization:** University hospital **Major product:** Medical services **Area of distribution:** New Jersey **Area of Practice:** Certified, Cardiovascular Interventional Radiology **Affiliations:** A.H.R.A.; A.S.R.T.; S.C.A.R. **SIC code:** 80 **Address:** Robert Wood Johnson University Hospital, 1 Robert Wood Johnson Place, New Brunswick, NJ 08902 **E-mail:** kstew99@yahoo.com

STEWART, WAYNE THOMAS
Industry: Healthcare **Born:** September 1, 1952, Philadelphia, Pennsylvania **Univ./degree:** M.S., Education, Temple University, 1977; M.D., Universidad Central del Este, 1980 **Current organization:** Uintah Basin Medical Center **Title:** M.D., Director of Diagnostic Imaging **Type of organization:** Hospital **Major product:** Patient care **Area of distribution:** International **Area of Practice:** Radiology, MRI, mammography, ultrasound, body imaging, nuclear medicine and computer technology **Affiliations:** A.C.R.; Member, Mammography Society; American Institute of Ultrasound in Medicine; Utah Radiological Society; Designated a Knight of the Holy Sepulcher by the Holy Catholic Church **Hob./spts.:** Photography, computers, travel **SIC code:** 80 **Address:** Uintah Basin Medical Center, 250 W. 300 North, Roosevelt, UT 84066 **E-mail:** stew@ubtanet.com

STILLABOWER, MICHAEL E.
Industry: Healthcare **Born:** February 2, 1944, Columbus, Indiana **Univ./degree:** B.S.E.E., Purdue University, 1966; M.D., Jefferson Medical College, 1976; Fellowship, Cardiology, Virginia Medical Center, Washington, D.C., 1980 **Current organization:** Cardiology Consultants, P.A. **Title:** M.D. **Type of organization:** Private practice **Major product:** Patient care **Area of distribution:** Delaware **Area of Practice:** Interventional Cardiology, clinical research, heart failure, lipid management **Honors/awards:** Lt., U.S. Navy, 1966-1972 **Affiliations:** F.A.H.A.; F.A.C.C.; F.S.C.A.I.; A.M.A.; D.M.S.; N.C.M.S.; Associate Professor, Jefferson Medical College **SIC code:** 80 **Address:** Cardiology Consultants, P.A., 1211 Barley Mill Rd., Wilmington, DE 19807 **E-mail:** michael.stillabower@cardioconsultants.net

STILWELL, JAMES R.
Industry: Healthcare **Born:** August 27, 1929, Birmingham, Alabama **Univ./degree:** B.S., Chemistry/Biology, College of Charleston, 1952; M.D., University of South Carolina School of Medicine, 1956 **Title:** M.D./Plastic Surgeon (Retired) **Type of organization:** Medical practice **Major product:** Patient care **Area of distribution:** International **Area of Practice:** Plastic surgery, cleft lip and pallet repair **Affiliations:** Past President, N.W.S.P.S.; Board Member Emeritus, A.S.P.S. **Hob./spts.:** Skiing **SIC code:** 80 **Address:** 122 Cypress Bend Place, Florence, AL 35630

STOCK, ARABELA C.
Industry: Healthcare **Born:** October 19, 1963, Bucharest, Romania **Univ./degree:** M.D., Institute of Medicine and Pharmacy, Bucharest. Romania, 1989 **Current organization:** Children's Hospital at Montefiore **Title:** M.D. **Type of organization:** Hospital **Major product:** Children's healthcare **Area of distribution:** New York **Area of Practice:** Pediatrics intensive care **Affiliations:** A.A.P.; C.C.P. **Hob./spts.:** Tennis, hiking **SIC code:** 80 **Address:** Children's Hospital at Montefiore, 3415 Bainbridge Ave., Bronx, NY 10467 **E-mail:** astock@montefiore.com

STONEBARGER, SHELLY D.
Industry: Healthcare **Univ./degree:** R.N., Connors State College, 2004 **Current organization:** Amedisys Home Health **Title:** R.N. **Type of organization:** Home healthcare system **Major product:** Patient care **Area of distribution:** Oklahoma **Area of Practice:** Professional in-home healthcare, patient evaluations, in-home treatment **Hob./spts.:** Gardening, youth sports **SIC code:** 80 **Address:** Amedisys Home Health, 309 Main Street, Gore, OK 74435 **Web address:** www.amedisys.com

STOTZ, AIMEE D.
Industry: Medical **Born:** November 19, 1959, Chicago, Illinois **Univ./degree:** D.O., Chicago University, 1992 **Current organization:** Loyola University Medical Center **Title:** D.O. **Type of organization:** University **Major product:** Patient care, medical education **Area of distribution:** Maywood, Illinois **Area of Practice:** Pain management **Affiliations:** A.M.A.; A.S.A.; A.O.A. **Hob./spts.:** Water sports **SIC code:** 80 **Address:** Loyola University Medical Center, 2160 S. First Ave., Maywood, IL 60153 **E-mail:** astotz@lumc.edu

STOUT, DEREK O.
Industry: Healthcare **Born:** April 28, 1971, Indiana **Univ./degree:** D.O., Midwestern University College of Osteopathic Medicine, 2000 **Current organization:** Sarah Busch Lincoln Health Center **Title:** Emergency Room Physician **Type of organization:** Hospital **Major product:** Patient care **Area of distribution:** Indiana **Area of Practice:** Osteopathic medicine, emergency room medicine **Affiliations:** A.C.O.I.; E.M.R.A.; American Osteopathic Association; American College of Emergency Room Physicians **Hob./spts.:** Waterskiing, snow skiing, scuba diving, hiking, camping **SIC code:** 80 **Address:** 5024 Woodbridge Ave., Portage, IN 46368 **E-mail:** kim.derek@verizon.net

STREICH, DENNIS K.
Industry: Healthcare **Born:** January 19, 1957, Phoenix, Arizona **Univ./degree:** D.D.S., Northwestern University, 1983 **Current organization:** Ahwatukee Foothills Village Dental **Title:** Dentist **Type of organization:** Private practice **Major product:** Dental care **Area of distribution:** Arizona **Area of Practice:** Cosmetic dentistry, implants, TM disorders **Affiliations:** A.D.A.; A.A.C.D.; A.G.D. **Hob./spts.:** Skiing **SIC code:** 80 **Address:** Ahwatukee Foothills Village Dental, 4350 E. Ray Rd., Suite 122, Bldg. 5, Phoenix, AZ 85044 **E-mail:** dksdds27@yahoo.com

STREIT, BARRY
Industry: Healthcare **Born:** May 3, 1947, Brooklyn, New York **Univ./degree:** M.D., University of Brussels, Belgium, 1975 **Current organization:** Medical Pulmonary Associates **Title:** M.D. **Type of organization:** Private practice **Major product:** Patient care **Area of distribution:** Florida **Area of Practice:** Pulmonary critical care, internal medicine **Published works:** Weisberg et al. Streit, B., Megestrol Acetate Stimulates Weight Gain and Ventilation in Underweight COPD Patients, Chest:2002:421:1070-1078 **Affiliations:** A.S.C.C.M.; A.C.C.P.; A.T.S. **Hob./spts.:** Tennis, martial arts **SIC code:** 80 **Address:** Medical Pulmonary Associates, 6610 N. University Dr., Suite 220, Tamarac, FL 33321 **E-mail:** pulmd13@aol.com

STRICKLAND, DELOIS L.
Industry: Healthcare **Born:** December 16, 1953, Gulfport, Mississippi **Univ./degree:** A.S., Business, Jefferson Davis Jr. College, 1975 **Current organization:** Orange Grove Family Medical Center **Title:** Practice Administrator **Type of organization:** Medical clinic **Major product:** Patient care **Area of distribution:** Gulfport, Mississippi **Area of Practice:** Management **Affiliations:** A.A.P.A.; A.A.P.C.; A.A.M.F. **Hob./spts.:** The outdoors, reading **SIC code:** 80 **Address:** Orange Grove Family Medical Center, 12330 Ashley Dr., Gulfport, MS 39503 **E-mail:** dlstrickland1450.aol.com

STRICKLAND, JAMES W.
Industry: Healthcare **Born:** January 4, 1936, Indianapolis, Indiana **Univ./degree:** M.D., Indiana University School of Medicine, 1952 **Current organization:** Reconstructive Hand Surgeons of Indiana **Title:** M.D. **Type of organization:** Medical practice **Major product:** Orthopaedic surgery/surgery of the hand **Area of distribution:** Indiana **Area of Practice:** Reconstruction of arthritis hand and wrist **Published works:** 181 Journals **Affiliations:** A.M.A. **Hob./spts.:** Tennis, golf **SIC code:** 80 **Address:** Reconstructive Hand Surgeons of Indiana, 755 W. Carmel Dr., Suite 202, Carmel, IN 46032

STY, JOHN R.
Industry: Healthcare **Born:** April 18, 1944, Chicago, Illinois **Univ./degree:** B.S., Biology, Loyolla University, 1966; M.D., St. Louis University School of Medicine, Missouri, 1970 **Current organization:** Pediatric Radiology Services, S.C., Children's Hospital of Wisconsin **Title:** Chief of Pediatric Radiology **Type of organization:** Hospital **Major product:** Patient care **Area of distribution:** National **Area of Practice:** Pediatric radiology **Honors/awards:** Served in active duty, Captain, U.S. Army 1971-72 **Published works:** 270 peer reviewed articles, five books, 26 book chapters **Affiliations:** F.A.C.R.; A.M.A.; Wisconsin State Medical Association **SIC code:** 80 **Address:** Pediatric Radiologic Services, SC, Childrens Hospital of Wisconsin, 9000 W. Wisconsin Ave., Milwaukee, WI 53226 **E-mail:** jsty@chw.org **Web address:** www.chw.org

SU, SEAN
Industry: Healthcare **Born:** October 31, 1965, Taipei, Taiwan **Univ./degree:** M.D., Medical College of Pennsylvania, 1993 **Current organization:** Hamot Medical Center **Title:** M.D. **Type of organization:** Hospital **Major product:** Patient care **Area of distribution:** Erie, Pennsylvania **Area of Practice:** Psychiatry **Honors/awards:** Who's Who **Affiliations:** American Medical Association; Pennsylvania Medical Society **Hob./spts.:** Surfing the Internet, time with family **SIC code:** 80 **Address:** Hamot Medical Center, 201 State St., Erie, PA 16550 **E-mail:** ssu3882200@aol.com

SUDDLE, MOHAMMED N.
Industry: Healthcare **Univ./degree:** M.D., King Edward Medical College, Pakistan, 1977 **Current organization:** Mohammed N. Suddle, M.D. **Title:** M.D. **Type of organization:** Private practice **Major product:** Patient care **Area of distribution:** Pennsylvania **Area of Practice:** Internal medicine **Affiliations:** A.M.A.; Pennsylvania Medical Society **SIC code:** 80 **Address:** Mohammed N. Suddle, M.D., 214 S. Trenton Ave., Pittsburgh, PA 15122 **E-mail:** msuddle163@c.s.com

SUGARMAN, GILBERT R.
Industry: Healthcare **Born:** May 17, 1926, Bronx, New York **Univ./degree:** M.D., Vanderbuilt University, 1949 **Current organization:** Associates in Female Health Care, P.A. **Title:** M.D. **Type of organization:** Medical group **Major product:** Patient care **Area of distribution:** New Jersey **Area of Practice:** Ob/Gyn **Affiliations:** A.C.O.G.; Essex County Medical Society; New Jersey Ob/Gyn Society; New Jersey Medical Society **Hob./spts.:** Sports, tennis, golf, reading, stamp collecting **SIC code:** 80 **Address:** Associates in Female Health Care, P.A., 235 Millburn Ave., Millburn, NJ 07041

SUITERS, NANCY
Industry: Healthcare **Univ./degree:** B.S.N., Indiana State University, 1980 **Current organization:** St. Vincent Hospital & Health Care Center **Title:** R.N., B.S.N., C.V.N. **Type of organization:** Hospital/healthcare center **Major product:** Patient care **Area of distribution:** Indiana **Area of Practice:** R.N.; compliance, insurance **Affiliations:** Past President, S.V.N.; C.C.R.N.; Nursing Honor Society **Hob./spts.:** Family **SIC code:** 80 **Address:** St. Vincent Hospital & Health Care Center, 8402 Harcourt Rd., Suite 301, Indianapolis, IN 46254 **E-mail:** nancysuiters@earthlink.net

SULE, SACHIN S.
Industry: Medical **Born:** September 23, 1971, Bombay, India **Univ./degree:** M.B.B.S., T.N. Medical University, Bombay, India, 1994 **Current organization:** New York Medical College/Westchester Medical Center **Title:** M.D., Assistant Professor of Medicine **Type of organization:** Medical college **Major product:** Medical services **Area of distribution:** New York **Area of Practice:** Internal medicine **Honors/awards:** Scored within top 10% in the U.S. for American Board of Internal Medicine **Affiliations:** A.C.P.; A.S.I.M.; Diplomate, American Board of Internal Medicine **Hob./spts.:** Music, reading, foreign travel **SIC code:** 80 **Address:** 2009 Crescent Dr., Tarrytown, NY 10591 **E-mail:** sachinsule@hotmail.com **Web address:** www.nymc.edu

SULKOWSKI, EUGENE
Industry: Healthcare/research **Born:** May 22, 1934, Poland **Univ./degree:** Ph.D., Warsaw University, Poland, 1960 **Current organization:** Roswell Park Cancer Institute **Title:** Ph.D., Research Professor **Type of organization:** Hospital **Major product:** Patient care/research **Area of distribution:** International **Area of Practice:** Biotechnology **Published works:** 3 U.S. patents; 80 publications **Affiliations:** A.S.B.C. **SIC code:** 80 **Address:** Roswell Park Cancer Institute, Elm & Carlton St., Buffalo, NY 14263 **E-mail:** diane.tymorek.@roswellpark.org

SULLIVAN, DANIEL Y.
Industry: Healthcare **Born:** February 4, 1948, Providence, Rhode Island **Univ./degree:** D.D.S., Georgetown University **Current organization:** Sullivan & Kaihara, DDS **Title:** D.D.S./Partner **Type of organization:** Private practice **Major product:** Patient care **Area of distribution:** International **Area of Practice:** Dentistry **Published works:** 60 articles, 1 textbook **Affiliations:** F.A.A.E.D.; F.A.O.; F.A.C.P. **Hob./spts.:** Writing, reading, travel **SIC code:** 80 **Address:** Sullivan & Kaihara, DDS, 2440 M. St. N.W., Suite 610, Washington, DC 20037 **E-mail:** drsulli@aol.com

SUN, DEXTER Y.
Industry: Medical **Born:** October 29, 1959, Hangzhou, China **Univ./degree:** M.D., Zhejiang University School of Medicine, China, 1982 **Current organization:** New York Presbyterian Hospital **Title:** M.D. **Type of organization:** University hospital **Major product:** Patient care/medical education **Area of distribution:** National **Area of Practice:** Neurology **Published works:** 10 publications **Affiliations:** Past President, A.A.C.P.; A.A.N. **Hob./spts.:** Tennis, swimming **SIC code:** 80 **Address:** New York Presbyterian Hospital, Dept. of Neurology, 943 Lexington Ave., New York, NY 10021 **E-mail:** sundexter@hotmail.com

SUNG, BIN S.
Industry: Healthcare **Born:** January 23, 1960, Maylasia **Univ./degree:** M.D., National Taiwan University **Current organization:** Sweetwater Pediatrics **Title:** M.D. **Type of organization:** Private practice **Major product:** Patient care **Area of distribution:** Fort Bend County, Texas **Area of Practice:** Pediatrics **Affiliations:** Texas Medical Association; Harris County Medical Society; Chinese American Doctors Association of Houston **Hob./spts.:** Swimming, table tennis, reading, travel **SIC code:** 80 **Address:** Sweetwater Pediatrics, 4780 Sweetwater Blvd., Suite 100, Sugar Land, TX 77479 **E-mail:** bsung20002000@yahoo.com

SUNIL, GOPINATH S.
Industry: Healthcare **Born:** February 8, 1962, Kerala, India **Univ./degree:** M.B.B.S., University of Kerala School of Medicine, 1987 **Title:** M.D. **Major product:** Patient care **Area of distribution:** International **Area of Practice:** Endocrinology, internal medicine **Published works:** 5 articles **Affiliations:** F.A.C.E.; F.A.C.P.; A.D.A. **Hob./spts.:** Tennis, biking, travel, movies **SIC code:** 80 **Address:** 9200 Bonita Beach Rd. S.E., Suite 109, Bonita Springs, FL 34135 **E-mail:** parvathysunil@hotmail.com

SURYA, GERALD
Industry: Healthcare **Born:** June 11, 1970, Toronto, Canada **Univ./degree:** M.D., Mount Sinai School of Medicine, 1995 **Current organization:** JKF Medport, JFK International Airport **Title:** M.D./Director of Medicine **Type of organization:** Medical office **Major product:** Corporate and private medical services **Area of distribution:** Jamaica, New York **Area of Practice:** Internal medicine **Published works:** 2 publications **Affiliations:** A.M.A. **SIC code:** 80 **Address:** JFK Medport, JFK International Airport, Building 14, Suite 14A, Jamaica, NY 11430 **E-mail:** surya@nols.com

SUSTER, VICKI
Industry: Healthcare **Born:** April 6, 1943, Pontiac, Michigan **Univ./degree:** B.S., Nursing, Ursuline College, Ohio, 1998 **Current organization:** Huron Hospital **Title:** Director, Surgical Services **Type of organization:** Hospital (part of the Cleveland Clinic Health System) **Major product:** Patient care **Area of distribution:** Ohio **Area of Practice:** Nursing **Affiliations:** A.O.R.N.; A.S.P.S.N.; A.S.P.A.C.N. **Hob./spts.:** Golf, gardening, travel, lecturing **SIC code:** 80 **Address:** Huron Hospital, 13951 Terrace Rd., East Cleveland, OH 44112 **E-mail:** vsuster@meridia.org

SUTTON, JOSEPHINE A.
Industry: Healthcare **Born:** January 24, 1947, Maxton, North Carolina **Univ./degree:** B.S.N., University of North Carolina, Pembroke, 2001 **Current organization:** Healthcare Connections **Title:** Vice President of Nursing **Type of organization:** Home healthcare agency **Major product:** Nursing services **Area of distribution:** North Carolina **Area of Practice:** Management of 11 offices, supervision of R.N.'s, C.N.A.'s, nursing administration and training **Honors/awards:** Nurse of the Year, Healthcare Connections, 2003 **Affiliations:** American Nursing Association; Minister, Beaver Dam and St. James United Methodist Churches **Hob./spts.:** Gardening, cooking, travel **SIC code:** 80 **Address:** Healthcare Connections, 402 S. Main St., Raeford, NC 28376 **E-mail:** jsutton55@hotmail.com

SWAFFORD, CATHY E.
Industry: Healthcare **Born:** February 18, 1950, Corpus Christi, Texas **Univ./degree:** A.S., Del Mar College, Texas, 1991 **Current organization:** T.P.S. Medical Services **Title:** R.T.(R)(M) **Type of organization:** Medical imaging provider **Major product:** Imaging services **Area of distribution:** Oklahoma **Area of Practice:** Mammography **Affiliations:** A.S.R.T.; A.R.R.T. **Hob./spts.:** Walking, reading **SIC code:** 80 **Address:** 2814 Sandstone Rd., Durant, OK 74701 **E-mail:** cswafford@hotmail.com

SWAMINATHAN, RAJAGOPALA

Industry: Medical **Born:** October 14, 1943, Madras, India **Univ./degree:** M.D., Madras University, India, 1967 **Current organization:** Rajagopala Swaminathan, M.D. **Title:** M.D./Chair, Dept. of Dermatology, University of Illinois College of Medicine at Peoria **Type of organization:** University, private practice **Major product:** Medical services, teaching and research **Area of distribution:** International **Area of Practice:** Dermatology, Dermatopathology and Immunopathology, Principal Investigator (P.I.) in dermatology related research programs **Published works:** Articles, chapters, poster presentations locally and internationally **Affiliations:** Fellow, American Academy of Dermatology; Fellow, American Society of Dermatology; Diplomate, American Board of Dermatology; Diplomate, American Board of Dermapathology; Fellow, Association of Professors of Dermatology; Member, Chicago Dermatological Society; Member, Illinois Dermatological Society; Member, Peoria Medical Society; Member, Council for Nail Disorders; Member, American Contact Dermatitis Society; Member, American College of Physicians; American Society of Internal Medicine **Hob./spts.:** Reading, music, travel, cycling, tennis **SIC code:** 80 **Address:** Rajagopala Swaminathan, M.D., 200 E. Pennsylvania Ave., Suite 204, Peoria, IL 61603

SWANN, RUSSELL E.

Industry: Healthcare **Born:** Jackson, Mississippi **Univ./degree:** M.D., Tulane University of Louisiana, 1975 **Current organization:** Russell E. Swann, MD, FACS **Title:** M.D. **Type of organization:** Private practice **Major product:** Patient care **Area of distribution:** Waco, Texas **Area of Practice:** Medical services, cataract and refractive surgery, glaucoma **Honors/awards:** Best Doctors in America, 2001-2002; Who's Who, 1995-1996 **Affiliations:** A.A.O.; A.S.C.R.S. **Hob./spts.:** Sailing, skiing **SIC code:** 80 **Address:** Russell E. Swann, M.D., F.A.C.S., 405 Londonderry Dr., Suite 301, Waco, TX 76712 **E-mail:** rswann@aol.com

SWEDENBORG, JON ERIC

Industry: Healthcare **Born:** December 14, 1964, Riverside, California **Univ./degree:** M.D., Vanderbilt University School of Medicine, 1990 **Current organization:** Santa Teresa Hospital **Title:** M.D. **Type of organization:** Hospital **Major product:** Patient care **Area of distribution:** San Jose, California **Area of Practice:** Otolaryngology, head and neck surgery **Honors/awards:** Top Doctor, San Jose Magazine **Published works:** Articles **Affiliations:** American Academy of Otolaryngology - Head & Neck Surgeons; California Medical Association **Hob./spts.:** Golf, fishing, tennis **SIC code:** 80 **Address:** Santa Teresa Hospital, 5811 Gleneagles Dr., San Jose, CA 95138 **E-mail:** jswedenborg@msn.com

SWINGLE, DOROTHY E.

Industry: Healthcare **Born:** June 19, 1960, Torrence, California **Univ./degree:** M.D., University of California, 1997 **Current organization:** Northeastern Rural Health Clinics **Title:** M.D. **Type of organization:** Clinic **Major product:** Patient care **Area of distribution:** California **Area of Practice:** Rural medicine and women's healthcare **Published works:** Article **Affiliations:** A.M.A.; A.A.F.P.; Christian Medical and Dental Association **Hob./spts.:** Horseback riding, hiking, canoeing **SIC code:** 80 **Address:** Northeastern Rural Health Clinics, 1306 Riverside Dr., Susanville, CA 96130 **E-mail:** docdori@onemain.com

SZABO, ANDRAS

Industry: Healthcare **Born:** Soprom, Hungary **Univ./degree:** M.D., University of Debrecen, 1993 **Current organization:** Wagner Community Memorial Hospital **Title:** M.D. **Type of organization:** Hospital **Major product:** Patient care **Area of distribution:** South Dakota **Area of Practice:** Internal medicine **Honors/awards:** Who's Who in America; Who's Who in the World; Who's Who in Medicine and Health **Affiliations:** A.C.P.; A.A.P.M.; A.D.A.; A.M.A. **Hob./spts.:** Music, history **SIC code:** 80 **Address:** Wagner Community Memorial Hospital, Third & Walnut St., Wagner, SD 57380 **E-mail:** aszabo@charles-mix.com

TABOADA, JAVIER G.

Industry: Healthcare **Univ./degree:** M.D., National University of Peru, 1966 **Current organization:** Associated Neurologists of New Jersey, Pennsylvania **Title:** M.D., President **Type of organization:** Medical practice **Major product:** Patient care, disability evaluations **Area of distribution:** New Jersey **Area of Practice:** Neurology and psychiatry (Board Certified) **Published works:** Papers and articles **Affiliations:** President, Mercer County Medical Society **SIC code:** 80 **Address:** 1245 White Horse Mercerville Rd., Trenton, NJ 08619 **E-mail:** jtaboada@yahoo.com

TABOR, KIMBERLY A.

Industry: Healthcare **Born:** June 18, 1967, Loraine, Ohio **Univ./degree:** D.O., Michigan State University **Current organization:** Health Star Physicians **Title:** D.O. **Type of organization:** Medical practice **Major product:** Patient care **Area of distribution:** Tennessee **Area of Practice:** Family practice **Affiliations:** A.A.F.P.; A.O.A.; T.O.M.A. **Hob./spts.:** Spending time with family and friends, golf, travel, sports **SIC code:** 80 **Address:** Health Star Physicians, 657 E. Broadway Blvd., Jefferson City, TN 37760

TAKATA, HIROYOSHI

Industry: Healthcare **Born:** December 14, 1940, Kobe, Japan **Univ./degree:** M.D., Kobe School of Medicine, Japan. 1965 **Current organization:** Hartford Thoracic & Cardiovascular Surgeons, P.C. **Title:** M.D., F.A.C.S. **Type of organization:** Private practice **Major product:** Patient care **Area of distribution:** Hartford, Connecticut **Affiliations:** F.A.C.S.; S.T.S. **SIC code:** 80 **Address:** Hartford Thoracic & Cardiovascular Surgeons, P.C., 85 Seymour St., Suite 325, Hartford, CT 06106 **E-mail:** ctvas@snet.net

TALREJA, ASHOK

Industry: Medical **Born:** July 21, 1976, Bombay, India **Univ./degree:** M.B.B.S., All India Institute of Medical Sciences, 1999 **Current organization:** Albert Einstein College of Medicine, Montefiore Medical Center **Title:** M.D. **Type of organization:** University/hospital **Major product:** Medical services **Area of distribution:** International **Area of Practice:** Cardiology; Internal Medicine (Board Certified) **Honors/awards:** Best Teaching Award Residency, 2003; Best Medical Student; Highest Marks, Gold Medals in Biochemistry, Anatomy, Physiology, Ob/Gyn, Pharmacology and Microbiology; Best Undergraduate, 1999 **Affiliations:** A.H.A.; A.C.C. **Hob./spts.:** Chess, table tennis **SIC code:** 80 **Address:** Albert Einstein College of Medicine, Montefiore Medical Center, 111 E. 210th St., Bronx, NY 10467 **E-mail:** talrejaashok@yahoo.com

TAMMERA, GRACE D.

Industry: Healthcare **Born:** April 1, 1957, Newark, New Jersey **Univ./degree:** O.D., Pennsylvania College of Optometry, 1984 **Current organization:** Grace D. Tammera, O.D **Title:** Optometric Physician **Type of organization:** Optometric practice **Major product:** Vision/medical services **Area of distribution:** New Jersey **Area of Practice:** Glaucoma management, contact lens fitting, comprehensive eye examinations **Hob./spts.:** Travel, theatre, music, reading **SIC code:** 80 **Address:** Grace D. Tammera, O.D., 1192 White Horse Rd., Voorhees, NJ 08043 **E-mail:** gdtammera@verizon.net

TAN, DOMINGO C.

Industry: Healthcare **Born:** February 1, 1934, Mendau City, Philippines **Univ./degree:** B.S.; M.D., University of Santo Thomas School of Medicine, Philippines **Current organization:** Newport Hospital **Title:** M.D. **Type of organization:** Hospital **Major product:** Patient care **Area of distribution:** Arkansas **Area of Practice:** General and emergency medicine **Affiliations:** American Academy of Ambulatory Care; Arkansas Medical Society **SIC code:** 80 **Address:** 2212 Shafer Circle, Newport, AR 72112 **E-mail:** lyntan@cox-internet.com

TAN, EDWIN V.

Industry: Healthcare **Born:** February 23, 1965, Philippines **Univ./degree:** M.D., Cebu Institute of Medicine, 1989 **Current organization:** Regional Medical Center of Lubec/Down East Community Hospital **Title:** Medical Director (RMCL)/Head of Dept. of Medicine for Down East Community Hospital **Type of organization:** Medical center **Major product:** Patient care **Area of distribution:** Lubec, Maine; Washington County, Maine **Area of Practice:** Internal Medicine **Honors/awards:** Excellence in the Study of Anatomy; Most Outstanding Post-Graduate Intern; Outstanding Resident **Affiliations:** A.M.A.; A.C.P.; Maine Medical Association **Hob./spts.:** Shooting, hunting **SIC code:** 80 **Address:** Regional Medical Center of Lubec/Down East Community Hospital, 43 South Lubec Rd., Lubec, ME 04652

TAN, MARILOU C.

Industry: Healthcare **Born:** July 25, 1956, Philippines **Univ./degree:** D.D.S., University of the East, Philippines, 1979 **Current organization:** Pioneer Family Dental Practice **Title:** D.D.S. **Type of organization:** Private practice **Major product:** Patient care **Area of distribution:** California **Area of Practice:** General dentistry **Affiliations:** A.D.A.; C.D.A.; S.D.D.S. **Hob./spts.:** Piano, tennis **SIC code:** 80 **Address:** Pioneer Family Dental Practice, 7850 Stockton Blvd., Suite 160, Sacramento, CA 95823

TAN, PATRICIA T.

Industry: Healthcare **Born:** April 7, 1960, Manila, Philippines **Univ./degree:** B.S., Cum Laude (Accelerated Program); M.D., 1984, University of Santo Thomas **Current organization:** South Nassau Hospital **Title:** M.D., Asst. Professor (Stonybrook University Hospital) **Type of organization:** Hospital and rehab center **Major product:** Patient care **Area of distribution:** New York **Area of Practice:** Pediatric and Adult Rehab Medicine, Brain Injury specialist, movement disorder specialist **Honors/awards:** Recipient, Starlight Children's Foundation Grant, Pediatric Rehabilitation; Recipient, Christopher reeve Paralysis Foundation Grant, Spinal Cord Injury **Published works:** Author, "Pediatric Rehabilitation Study Guide for Residents", Stony Brook University Hospital, 1998; Author, "Positioning in Pediatric Patients", Schneider Children's Hospital's Quarterly, 1994 **Affiliations:** American Academy of Pediatrics; American Academy of Physical Medicine & Rehabilitation; American Academy for Cerebral Palsy and Developmental Medicine; New York Society of Physical Medicine & Rehabilitation; Diplomate, American Board of Physical Medicine and Rehabilitation; Founder, Philippine Chinese American Medical Association **Hob./spts.:** Jogging, swimming, arts & crafts **SIC code:** 80 **Address:** 282 Stewart Ave., Garden City, NY 11530 **E-mail:** allcarept@aol.com

TANG, LAURA H.
Industry: Medical **Born:** May 2, 1959, China **Univ./degree:** M.D., China, 1983; Ph.D., Emory University, 1990 **Current organization:** Memorial Sloan-Kettering Cancer Center **Title:** M.D. **Type of organization:** University hospital **Major product:** Medical services **Area of distribution:** New York **Area of Practice:** Pathology **Published works:** 50+ papers **Affiliations:** A.S.G.; U.S.C.A.P. **Hob./spts.:** Squash **SIC code:** 80 **Address:** Memorial Sloan-Kettering Cancer Center, 1275 York Ave., New York, NY 10021 **E-mail:** tangl@mskcc.org

TARLEY PATSCHKE GORBEY, JACQUELINE LANE
Industry: Healthcare **Univ./degree:** RN, Fairmont State University, 1987 **Current organization:** Fairmont General Hospital **Title:** R.N. **Type of organization:** Hospital **Major product:** Patient care **Area of distribution:** West Virginia **Area of Practice:** Cardiac step-down; Nurse Consultant **Affiliations:** C.C.R.N. **Hob./spts.:** Family, girls basketball and baseball **SIC code:** 80 **Address:** Rt. 1 Box 150-A, Fairmont, WV 26554 **E-mail:** nursemeis@aol.com

TAYLOR, GILBERT C.
Industry: Healthcare **Born:** December 28, 1950, Sierra Leone, West Africa **Univ./degree:** B.S., Mechanical Engineering, Kherson State University, U.S.S.R., 1976 **Current organization:** St. Elizabeth's Hospital **Title:** Chief Engineer **Type of organization:** Hospital **Major product:** Patient care **Area of distribution:** Washington D.C. **Area of Practice:** Maintenance, engineering, project management **Hob./spts.:** Soccer, church activities, travel **SIC code:** 80 **Address:** St. Elizabeth's Hospital, Dept. of Mental Health, 2700 MLK Jr. Ave. S.E., Washington, DC 20032 **E-mail:** gilbert.taylor@dc.gov

TAYLOR, JAMES
Industry: Healthcare **Born:** September 21, 1953, Monroe, North Carolina **Univ./degree:** M.D., Medical University of South Carolina, 1984 **Current organization:** St. Francis Hospital **Title:** M.D. **Type of organization:** Private practice **Major product:** Patient care **Area of distribution:** Roslyn, New York **Area of Practice:** Cardiac surgery **Affiliations:** A.M.A.; Alpha Omega Alpha; Society of Thoracic Surgeons **SIC code:** 80 **Address:** St. Francis Hospital, 100 Port Washington Blvd., Room 601, Roslyn, NY 11576

TAYLOR, LYNN S.
Industry: Healthcare **Born:** November 13, 1956, Pennington Gap, Virginia **Current organization:** Lee Regional Medical Center **Title:** R.N. **Type of organization:** Hospital **Major product:** Patient care **Area of distribution:** Virginia **Area of Practice:** ICU **Affiliations:** A.A.C.N.; V.N.A. **Hob./spts.:** Camping, football **SIC code:** 80 **Address:** RR 2 Box 513-N, Pennington Gap, VA 24277 **E-mail:** bigtoots@hotmail.com

TAYLOR, ROSLYN D.
Industry: Medical **Born:** February 14, 1941, Columbia, South Carolina **Univ./degree:** B.S., Biology, Emory College, 1963; M.D., Emory School of Medicine, 1967 **Current organization:** Memorial Health University Medical Center **Title:** M.D./Residency Director **Type of organization:** University medical center **Major product:** Patient care, medical education **Area of distribution:** Georgia **Area of Practice:** Family practice **Honors/awards:** Phi Beta Kappa; Alpha Omega Alpha Medical Honor Society; Physician of the Year, Mayor's Committee on Hiring the Handicapped; Outstanding Family Practice Faculty of the Year: Mercer University School of Medicine, Savannah Campus **Published works:** 2 articles **Affiliations:** A.A.F.P.; Georgia Academy of Family Physicians **Hob./spts.:** Photography, reading, beach combing **SIC code:** 80 **Address:** Memorial Health University Medical Center, 1107 E. 66th St., Savannah, GA 31404 **E-mail:** taylor01@memorialhealth.com **Web address:** www.memorialhealth.com

TAYLOR, TAD W.
Industry: Healthcare **Born:** December 16, 1954, Billings, Montana **Univ./degree:** Ph.D., Chemical Engineering, University of Wisconsin at Madison, 1983; M.D., Yale University, 1994 **Current organization:** Federal Way Medical Center **Title:** M.D., Ph.D. **Type of organization:** Medical clinic **Major product:** Patient care **Area of distribution:** Washington **Area of Practice:** Internal and general medicine **Published works:** Articles, 5 book chapters **Affiliations:** Diplomate, A.M.A.; A.B.I.M. **Hob./spts.:** Cooking, Tae Kwon-Do (Black Belt) **SIC code:** 80 **Address:** 4906 S. 302 Lane, Auburn, WA 98001 **E-mail:** taddoo@worldnet.att.net

TEBCHERANY, DINA J.
Industry: Healthcare **Born:** October 19, 1961, Lebanon **Univ./degree:** M.D., Universidad of Autonomous, 1993 **Current organization:** Dina J. Tebcherany, M.D. **Title:** M.D. **Type of organization:** Private practice **Major product:** Patient care, chemotherapy **Area of distribution:** Texas **Area of Practice:** Medical oncology **Affiliations:** A.M.A.; T.M.A.; A.S.C.O. **Hob./spts.:** Travel, music, skiing **SIC code:** 80 **Address:** 4517 Grand Cypress Dr., Austin, TX 78747 **E-mail:** tebcheranyd@aol.com

TECTOR, ALFRED J.
Industry: Healthcare **Univ./degree:** M.D., St. Louis University School of Medicine, 1963 **Current organization:** Midwest Heart Surgery Institute **Title:** M.D./M.S. **Type of organization:** Health facility **Major product:** Patient care, surgery **Area of distribution:** Milwaukee, Wisconsin **Area of Practice:** Thoracic and cardiovascular surgery **Affiliations:** F.A.C.S.; F.A.C.C.; F.A.H.A.; Society of Thoracic Surgeons; American Association of Thoracic Surgeons **SIC code:** 80 **Address:** Midwest Heart Surgery Institute, 2901 W. Kinnickinnie River Pkwy., Milwaukee, WI 53215 **E-mail:** tector@excecpc.com **Web address:** www.midwestheartsurgery.com

TEGENU, MESFIN
Industry: Healthcare **Born:** March 24, 1956, Addis Ababa, Ethiopia **Univ./degree:** M.S., Pharmacy Administration, St. John's University, 1988 **Current organization:** Keystone Mercy Health Plans **Title:** Vice President of Pharmacy Services **Type of organization:** Healthcare service provider **Major product:** Health plans, medical coverage **Area of distribution:** National **Area of Practice:** Pharmacy administration **Published works:** Article in Managed Executive News **Affiliations:** American Managed Care **Hob./spts.:** Family, basketball, vacationing in Hawaii **SIC code:** 80 **Address:** Keystone Mercy Health Plans, 200 Stevens Dr., Philadelphia, PA 19113 **E-mail:** mesfin.tegenu@kmhp.com

TELLO, CELSO
Industry: Healthcare **Born:** November 10, 1963, Ecuador **Univ./degree:** M.D., Universidad de Cuenca, Ecuador **Current organization:** Glaucoma Associates of New York **Title:** M.D. **Type of organization:** Private practice **Major product:** Patient care **Area of distribution:** International **Area of Practice:** Eye Surgeon specializing in cataracts and glaucoma **Published works:** Peer reviewed articles, 15 chapters in books **Affiliations:** American Academy of Ophthalmology; Pan-American Academy of Ophthalmology; President, New York Society for Clinical Ophthalmology; Association for Research in Vision and Ophthalmology **SIC code:** 80 **Address:** Glaucoma Associates of New York, 310 East 14th St., New York, NY 10003 **E-mail:** ctello@nyee.edu

TEMPLE, H. THOMAS
Industry: Medical **Born:** June 6, 1958, McKeesport, Pennsylvania **Univ./degree:** B.S., Biology, Harvard University, 1980; M.D., Jefferson Medical College, 1986 **Current organization:** University of Miami School of Medicine **Title:** M.D. **Type of organization:** University **Major product:** Patient care, medical education **Area of distribution:** Florida **Area of Practice:** Orthopaedic oncology surgery **Published works:** 70 articles, 15 chapters **Affiliations:** American Orthopaedic Association; American Academy of Orthopaedic Surgeons **SIC code:** 80 **Address:** University of Miami School of Medicine, Dept. of Orthopaedic Surgery, 1611 N.W. 12th Ave., Rehab 303, Miami, FL 33136

TEMPLETON, DEBORAH DENTON
Industry: Healthcare **Born:** April 18, 1957, Naha, Okinawa **Univ./degree:** M.B.A., Marshall University, 1997 **Current organization:** Princeton Community Hospital **Title:** Hematology/LIS Sr. Technician **Type of organization:** Hospital **Major product:** Patient care **Area of distribution:** International **Area of Practice:** Daily operations oversight of laboratory medicine **Affiliations:** Past Member, American Association of Clinical Pathologists **Hob./spts.:** Horseback riding **SIC code:** 80 **Address:** Princeton Community Hospital, 12th St. Extension, Princeton, WV 24740 **E-mail:** dtempleton@pchonline.org

TENORE, PETER L.
Industry: Healthcare **Born:** February 27, 1954, New York, New York **Univ./degree:** M.D., State University of New York at Buffalo, 1981 **Current organization:** Albert Einstein Division of Substance Abuse Treatment **Title:** M.D./Director **Type of organization:** Medical clinic **Major product:** Patient care **Area of distribution:** National **Area of Practice:** Substance abuse and HIV treatment **Published works:** Multiple articles **Affiliations:** A.M.T.A.; A.S.A.M.; New York State Office of Alcoholism and Substance Abuse Services **Hob./spts.:** Writing music, collecting antique furniture, construction **SIC code:** 80 **Address:** Albert Einstein Division of, Substance Abuse Treatment, 1500 Waters Place, Bronx, NY 10461 **E-mail:** picten@aol.com

TERPENNING, MARILOU
Industry: Healthcare **Born:** September 20, 1949, Jersey City, New Jersey **Univ./degree:** M.D., Washington University, St. Louis, 1976; Internship, University of Michigan at Ann Arbor; Fellowship, UCLA Center for the Health Sciences **Current organization:** Santa Monica Hematology-Oncology Consultants **Title:** M.D. **Type of organization:** Private practice **Major product:** Patient care **Area of distribution:** Santa Monica, California **Area of Practice:** Hematology, oncology **Published works:** 7-8 abstracts **Affiliations:** F.A.C.P.; A.S.C.O.; A.M.W.A.; California Medical Association; Los Angeles County Medical Association; Southern California Oncology Association **Hob./spts.:** Hiking, backpacking, swimming **SIC code:** 80 **Address:** Santa Monica Hematology-Oncology Consultants, 2021 Santa Monica Blvd., Suite 400E, Santa Monica, CA 90404 **E-mail:** marilou.terpenning@santamonicaoncology.com

TERRY, DOUGLAS WEEDEN

Industry: Healthcare **Born:** January 12, 1924, Los Angeles, California **Univ./degree:** M.D., University of Texas Medical Branch at Galveston, 1949; M.S., Georgetown University, Washington, D.C.; Internship, Residency & Fellowship, Georgetown University Hospital **Title:** M.D. (Retired) **Type of organization:** Private medical practice **Major product:** Patient care **Area of distribution:** Texas **Area of Practice:** Internal medicine, hematology **Published works:** Journal report in New England Journal of Medicine, abstracts and other journals **Affiliations:** American Society of Internal Medicine; American College of Physicians; American Society of Hematology; International Society of Hematology; Past Instructor in Medicine, Georgetown University; Past Assistant Professor, Creighton University School of Medicine; Texas Medical Association; Travis County Medical Society **Hob./spts.:** Fly-fishing, reading, philosophy, politics, theology, American literature, history, volunteer work for Central Texas Regional Blood Center in Austin **SIC code:** 80 **Address:** 5609 Courtyard Cove, Austin, TX 78713

TESFAMARIAM, SABA W.

Industry: Healthcare **Born:** May 17, 1967, Asmara, Eritrea **Univ./degree:** M.D., Addis Ababa University Medical School, Ethiopia, 1989 **Current organization:** Emergency USA **Title:** M.D. **Type of organization:** Urgent care clinic **Major product:** Patient care **Area of distribution:** Virginia **Area of Practice:** Family medicine **Affiliations:** A.M.A.; A.A.F.P. **Hob./spts.:** Swimming, the outdoors **SIC code:** 80 **Address:** Emergency USA, 12011 Lee Jackson Memorial Hwy., Fairfax, VA 22033-3357

THAKKAR, HEENA N.

Industry: Healthcare **Univ./degree:** M.D., Medical School of Bombay, India **Current organization:** Heena N. Thakkar, M.D., FAAP **Title:** M.D., FA.A.P. **Type of organization:** Private practice **Major product:** Patient care **Area of distribution:** National **Area of Practice:** Pediatrics **Honors/awards:** Physician of the Year, Washington, D.C., 2002 **Published works:** Texas Monthly **Affiliations:** A.M.S.; T.M.A.; A.A.P. **SIC code:** 80 **Address:** Heena N. Thakkar, M.D., FAAP, 1740 W. 27th St., Suite 305, Houston, TX 77008 **E-mail:** thakkarmd@aol.com

THAKUR, ABHASH C.

Industry: Medical **Born:** January 11, 1967, Motipur, Supaul, India **Univ./degree:** M.D., Ranchi University and MGM Memorial Medical College, Jamshedpur, India, 1992 **Current organization:** Long Island College Hospital **Title:** M.D. **Type of organization:** Teaching hospital **Major product:** Patient care, medical education **Area of distribution:** New York **Area of Practice:** Internal medicine, cardiology **Published works:** 19 articles **Affiliations:** A.A.C.I.O.; A.M.A.; A.M.P.A.C.; A.T.S.; A.G.S.; S.C.C.M.; I.S.C.U. **Hob./spts.:** Chess, movies **SIC code:** 80 **Address:** Long Island College Hospital, , 339 Hicks St., Brooklyn, NY 11201 **E-mail:** thakurac@hotmail.com

THAYER, DAVID M.

Industry: Healthcare **Title:** D.C. **Type of organization:** Clinic **Major product:** Patient care **Area of Practice:** Chiropractic, acupuncture **SIC code:** 80 **Address:** Highland Pain Relief, 811 Broadway, Highland, IL 62249 **Web address:** www.drthayer.com

THIBODEAU, PAIGE

Industry: Healthcare **Born:** June 27, 1941, Holyoke, Massachusetts **Univ./degree:** D.C., Palmer College of Chiropractic, 1964; Attended Furman University, 1959-1961 **Current organization:** Scotts Valley Chiropractic **Title:** D.C. **Type of organization:** Private practice **Major product:** Chiropractic services, full service office **Area of distribution:** Scotts Valley, California **Area of Practice:** Chiropractic Activator Methods Technique **Affiliations:** A.C.A.; C.C.A.; A.H.C.; A.P.H.A.; A.A.N.C.; F.C.E.R. **Hob./spts.:** Gardening, spending time with grandchildren **SIC code:** 80 **Address:** Scotts Valley Chiropractic, 4736 Scotts Valley Dr., Scotts Valley, CA 95066 **Web address:** www.scottsvalleychiropractic.com

THOMAS, BERNARD I.L.

Industry: Healthcare **Born:** February 21, 1954, St. Johns, Antigua, West Indies **Univ./degree:** M.S., Fire Safety Engineering, University of Phoenix, 1991 **Current organization:** VA Medical Center **Title:** Safety and Occupational Health Specialist **Type of organization:** Hospital **Major product:** Patient care **Area of distribution:** Waco, Texas **Area of Practice:** Safety, inspection, accident investigation and reconstruction **Affiliations:** Mason, 3rd Degree; U.S. Army (Ret.), 1975-95, Final Rank E-9 **Hob./spts.:** Football, fishing, basketball, golf **SIC code:** 80 **Address:** VA Medical Center, 4800 Memorial Dr., Waco, TX 76711 **E-mail:** bilt44@yahoo.com

THOMAS, KAREN A.

Industry: Healthcare **Born:** November 28, 1954, Brooklyn, New York **Univ./degree:** D.C., New York Chiropractic College, 1987; Acupuncture studies at Pacific Institute of Oriental Medicine **Current organization:** Community Chiropractic & Acupuncture **Title:** D.C./Owner **Type of organization:** Private practice **Major product:** Chiropractic care **Area of distribution:** Brooklyn, New York **Area of Practice:** Chiropractic neurology, acupuncture, homeopathy **Honors/awards:** Diplomate in Chiropractice Neurology **Affiliations:** American Chiropractic Association **Hob./spts.:** Scuba diving, outdoor sports **SIC code:** 80 **Address:** Community Chiropractic & Acupuncture, 71 8th Ave., Brooklyn, NY 11217 **E-mail:** dockat123@aol.com

THOMAS, MACK A.

Industry: Healthcare **Born:** March 18, 1936, Mississippi **Univ./degree:** M.D., Louisiana State University, 1962 **Current organization:** Ochsner Clinic Foundation, LSU Health Science Center **Title:** M.D., F.A.C.S. **Type of organization:** Hospital **Major product:** Professional medical services **Area of distribution:** Metairie, Louisiana **Area of Practice:** Anesthesiology, critical care medicine **Published works:** 14 articles, chapters **Affiliations:** Fellow American College of Surgeons **SIC code:** 80 **Address:** 244 Beverly Dr., Metairie, LA 70001 **E-mail:** accma@aol.com

THOMAS, MAGGIE

Industry: Healthcare **Born:** July 8, 1947, Cassville, Missouri **Univ./degree:** B.S., Biology/Chemistry, University of Colorado, 1968; MT(ASCP), St. John's Hospital, 1970 **Current organization:** Centura Health **Title:** MT(ASCP), Chemistry Supervisor, Purchasing Agent **Type of organization:** Hospital **Major product:** Patient care **Area of distribution:** Colorado **Area of Practice:** Clinical laboratory medicine **Affiliations:** A.S.C.P. **Hob./spts.:** Oil painting **SIC code:** 80 **Address:** Centura Health, St. Mary-Corwin Medical Center, 1008 Minnequa Ave., Pueblo, CO 81004 **E-mail:** maggiethomas3@centura.org

THOMAS, PIERRE L.

Industry: Healthcare **Born:** June 21, 1948, Haiti **Univ./degree:** M.D., University of Bordeaux, France, 1981 **Current organization:** Lincoln Hospital **Title:** M.D./Director **Type of organization:** Hospital **Major product:** Patient care **Area of distribution:** New York **Area of Practice:** Adult psychiatry **Hob./spts.:** Soccer **SIC code:** 80 **Address:** Lincoln Hospital, 234 E. 149th St., Brooklyn, NY 11235

THOMPSON, HEATHER L.

Industry: Healthcare **Born:** February 16, 1978, Casper, Wyoming **Univ./degree:** A.S., Radiographic Sciences, Casper College, 1999; Registered Technologist in Radiography, 1999; Registered in Computed Tomography, 2001 **Current organization:** Wyoming Medical Center **Title:** Radiologic Technologist in the Cardiac Cath Lab **Type of organization:** Hospital **Major product:** Patient Care **Area of distribution:** Casper, Wyoming **Area of Practice:** Radiography, Computed Tomography and Cardiac Interventions **Affiliations:** A.R.R.T.; A.S.R.T.; W.S.R.T. **Hob./spts.:** Scrapbook crafts **SIC code:** 80 **Address:** Wyoming Medical Center, 1233 E. Second St., Casper, WY 82601 **E-mail:** xraychick1@bresnan.net

THOMPSON, JUDITH A.

Industry: Healthcare/counseling **Born:** April 13, 1944, Long Beach, California **Univ./degree:** B.A., Texas A&M University, 1967 **Current organization:** House of Isaiah **Title:** Program Director **Type of organization:** Alcohol/drug recovery center **Major product:** Rehabilitation **Area of distribution:** Texas **Area of Practice:** Alcohol/drug/recovery/12 step education **Hob./spts.:** Crafts, needlework, painting, music **SIC code:** 80 **Address:** House of Isaiah, 5508 Coronado Dr., Garland, TX 75043 **E-mail:** judilcbc@sbcglobal.net

THOMPSON, RITA J.

Industry: Healthcare **Born:** November 27, 1954, Olton, Texas **Univ./degree:** B.S., Nursing, Southwestern Oklahoma State University, 1997 **Current organization:** Hospice of Lubbock **Title:** Clinical Manager, B.S.N., R.N. **Type of organization:** Hospice **Major product:** Hospice patient care **Area of distribution:** Lubbock, Texas **Area of Practice:** Hospice care, clinical management **Hob./spts.:** Crafts **SIC code:** 80 **Address:** Hospice of Lubbock, 2509 59th St., Lubbock, TX 79413

THURBER, GEORGE M.

Industry: Healthcare **Born:** January 30, 1959, Detroit, Michigan **Univ./degree:** M.D., University of Mississippi **Current organization:** The Center for Eye Care **Title:** M.D./President **Type of organization:** Medical clinic **Major product:** Eye care and surgery **Area of distribution:** Mississippi **Area of Practice:** Ophthalmology **Affiliations:** A.M.A.; A.A.O.; A.S.C.R.S. **Hob./spts.:** Judo, Boy Scouts, church, guitar, hunting **SIC code:** 80 **Address:** The Center for Eye Care, 1720-A Medical Park Dr., Suite 330A, Biloxi, MS 39532

TIFFANY MATHER, ELIZABETH G.

Industry: Medical - Allied Health **Born:** October 21, 1928, Philadelphia, Pennsylvania **Univ./degree:** B.S., University of Pennsylvania, 1950; M.E.D., Temple University, 1975 **Current organization:** Temple University **Title:** Associate Professor; Chair, Dept of O.T. Temple University (Retired) **Type of organization:** University College of Allied Health Professions **Major product:** Patient care, medical education **Area of distribution:** International **Area of Practice:** Occupational therapy **Honors/awards:** Fellow, American Occupational Therapy Association **Published works:** Contributor to Smith & Hopkins "Willard & Spackman's Occupational Therapy", Editions V, VI, VII **Affiliations:** A.O.T.A.; P.O.T.A. **Hob./spts.:** Nature conservancy, bird watching, plants **SIC code:** 80 **Address:** 122 Crosslands Dr., Kennett Square, PA 19348 **E-mail:** bantiffmat@aol.com

TIMKO, BRIAN ALLEN
Industry: Healthcare **Born:** April 7, 1970, Plainfield, New Jersey **Univ./degree:** M.D., University of North Carolina School of Medicine, 1998 **Current organization:** Internal Medicine & Family Care **Title:** M.D. **Type of organization:** Group practice **Major product:** Patient care **Area of distribution:** Woodbury, Connecticut **Area of Practice:** Internal medicine **Honors/awards:** Ralph G. Vernon Award **Affiliations:** A.M.A.; New Haven County Medical Association **Hob./spts.:** Landscaping, gardening, running, biking **SIC code:** 80 **Address:** Internal Medicine & Family Care, 40 North Main St., Woodbury, CT 06798 **E-mail:** briantimko@hotmail.com

TIN-U, CAESAR K.
Industry: Healthcare **Born:** September 26, 1960, Rangoon, Burma **Univ./degree:** M.D., Institute of Medicine, Burma, 1985 **Current organization:** Texas Oncology, P.A. **Title:** M.D. **Type of organization:** Oncology physicians' group **Major product:** Patient care **Area of distribution:** Houston, Texas **Area of practice:** Hormone related cancer **Area of Practice:** Hormone related cancer **Affiliations:** A.S.C.O.; A.A.C.R.; A.S.H.M. **SIC code:** 80 **Address:** Texas Oncology, P.A., 7515 S. Main St., Suite 740, Houston, TX 77030 **E-mail:** caesar.tin-u@usoncology.com

TOBORG, R. TED
Industry: Healthcare **Born:** May 21, 1972, Cedar Rapids, Iowa **Univ./degree:** B.S., Physical Therapy, Marquette University, 1994; M.D., University of Iowa School of Medicine, 1998 **Current organization:** Marlette Family Practice **Title:** M.D. **Type of organization:** Private practice **Major product:** Patient care **Area of distribution:** North Carolina **Area of Practice:** Family medicine **Affiliations:** A.M.A.; A.A.F.P.; North Carolina Association of Family Practice; North Carolina Medical Society **Hob./spts.:** Family, golf, volleyball, basketball, travel **SIC code:** 80 **Address:** Marlette Family Practice, 2554 Lewisville-Clemmons Rd., #109, Clemmons, NC 27012 **E-mail:** tedtoborg@aol.com

TOCZEK, MARIA TEKLA
Industry: Healthcare **Univ./degree:** B.A., English, 1983; M.D., 1990, Georgetown University **Title:** M.D. **Type of organization:** Medical **Major product:** Patient care **Area of distribution:** California **Area of Practice:** Neurology, neurological disorders **Affiliations:** American Academy of Neurology; American Epilepsy Society; American Academy of Sleep Medicine **SIC code:** 80 **Address:** 204 W. Kenneth Rd., Glendale, CA 91202-1439 **E-mail:** mttoczek@gmail.com

TODD, MICHAEL D.
Industry: Healthcare **Born:** August 20, 1972, East Tallassee, Alabama **Univ./degree:** B.S., Auburn University, Montgomery Alabama; M.S., Management, Troy University, Montgomery, Alabama **Current organization:** Health Services, Inc. **Title:** Director of Laboratory & Radiology **Type of organization:** Nonprofit community healthcare centers **Major product:** Patient care **Area of distribution:** Montgomery, Alabama **Area of Practice:** Clinical laboratory science **Published works:** 2 articles **Affiliations:** Clinical Laboratory Management Association; American Society for Clinical Pathology **Hob./spts.:** Bowling, art, drawing, painting, tennis **SIC code:** 80 **Address:** Health Services, Inc., 3060 Mobile Hwy., Montgomery, AL 36116 **E-mail:** michael.todd@hservinc.com

TODORAN, IULIU F.
Industry: Healthcare **Born:** April 14, 1938, Cluj, Romania **Univ./degree:** M.D., Cluj Medical School, 1960 **Current organization:** The New York Trade Council and Hotel Association of New York City **Title:** M.D. **Type of organization:** Trade council/hotel organization (Health organization of the Hotel Union of New York City) **Major product:** Patient care **Area of distribution:** New York **Area of Practice:** Internal medicine, pathology, treatment of digestive illnesses including influenza, liver conditions; designs and implements programs for the Trade Council and Hotel Association of New York City **Published works:** Papers and journals **Affiliations:** A.M.A. **Hob./spts.:** Fishing, travel **SIC code:** 80 **Address:** The New York Trade Council and Hotel Association of New York City, 111 Wadsworth Ave., New York, NY 10033

TOLTZIS, ROBERT JOSHUA
Industry: Healthcare **Born:** May 6, 1949, Philadelphia, Pennsylvania **Univ./degree:** B.A., Biology & History, Temple University; M.D., Hahemann School of Medicine, 1974 **Current organization:** The Cincinnati Heart Group **Title:** M.D., F.A.C.C. **Type of organization:** Group practice **Major product:** Patient care **Area of distribution:** Ohio, Kentucky, Indiana **Area of Practice:** Cardiology **Published works:** 30 articles and book chapters **Affiliations:** Alpha Omega Alpha; Fellow, American College of Cardiology; Fellow, American College of Chest Physicians; Fellow, Council on Clinical Cardiology; American Heart Association **SIC code:** 80 **Address:** The Cincinnati Heart Croup, 625 Eden Park Dr., Suite 340, Cincinnati, OH 45202

TON-THAT, QUYNH A.
Industry: Healthcare **Born:** Da Nang, Vietnam **Univ./degree:** M.D., University of Kansas, 1996 **Current organization:** Health Texas IPCU **Title:** M.D. **Type of organization:** Hospital **Major product:** Patient care **Area of distribution:** Texas **Area of Practice:** Internal medicine **Affiliations:** A.M.A.; A.C.P.; American Society of Internal Medicine; American Board of Internal Medicine **SIC code:** 80 **Address:** Health Texas IPCU, 2901 Prestonwood Dr., Plano, TX 75093 **E-mail:** quynh_md@yahoo.com

TOPPIN, ALICE ALONIA
Industry: Healthcare **Born:** October 22, 1947, Dover, Delaware **Univ./degree:** Diploma, Medical Biller & Health Claims Examiner, Star Technical Institute, 2004 **Current organization:** Courtland Manor Nursing Home **Title:** LPN/Charge Nurse **Type of organization:** Nursing home and rehab facility **Major product:** Patient care, rehabilitation **Area of Practice:** Nursing **Affiliations:** Delaware Nurses Association; Hattie B. Hubbard Council of Delaware; Pride of Dover Temple #784 of IBPOE of W **Hob./spts.:** Church, playing bingo, travel **SIC code:** 80 **Address:** Courtland Manor Nursing Home, 889 S. Little Creek Rd., Dover, DE 19901

TORRES, MARK L.
SIC code: 80 **Address:** Four Points Sheraton Hotel, 505 Avenue Q, Lubbock, TX 79401

TORRES-LOPEZ, WANDA I.
Industry: Healthcare **Born:** November 18, 1967, Puerto Rico **Univ./degree:** M.D., University of Puerto Rico, 1994 **Current organization:** Wanda I. Torres-Lopez, M.D. **Title:** M.D. **Type of organization:** Private medical practice/university hospital **Major product:** Patient care **Area of distribution:** Puerto Rico **Area of Practice:** Infectious disease **Affiliations:** Puerto Rico Medical Association; American Medical Association **Hob./spts.:** Reading, tennis **SIC code:** 80 **Address:** Wanda I. Torres-Lopez, M.D., P.O. Box 3384, Guaynabo, PR 00970-3384

TOTH, MIKLOS
Industry: Healthcare **Born:** October 15, 1941, Szekszard, Hungary **Univ./degree:** M.D., Szemelweisc University, Budapest, 1959 **Current organization:** Millennium Health Foundation **Title:** M.D. **Type of organization:** Private practice **Major product:** Patient care, teaching, research **Area of distribution:** International **Area of practice:** Obstetrics/gynecology; laparoscopic surgery **Area of Practice:** Obstetrics/gynecology; laparoscopic surgery **Honors/awards:** Ellis Island Medal of Honor; Man of the Year Award, American Biographic Institute **Published works:** Articles, book chapters **Affiliations:** A.M.A.; Society of Ultrasound in Obstetrics and Gynecology; Infectious Disease Society for Obstetrics and Gynecology; Society of Laparoscopic Surgeons **Hob./spts.:** Art, theatre, dancing **SIC code:** 80 **Address:** Millennium Health Foundation, 1070 Park Ave., #1A, New York, NY 10128 **E-mail:** matzoog@aol.com **Web address:** www.mhsny.org

TRACY III, JERRY J.
Industry: Healthcare **Univ./degree:** M.D., Universidad del Noreste, 1984 **Current organization:** Methodist Pain Management Clinic **Title:** Medical Director **Type of organization:** Hospital **Major product:** Treatment of acute/chronic pain **Area of distribution:** Illinois **Area of Practice:** Multidisciplinary approach to pain **Affiliations:** A.P.S.; A.M.A. **Hob./spts.:** Biking, weight lifting, playing the saxophone **SIC code:** 80 **Address:** 5931 W. Old Orchard Dr., Peoria, IL 61614 **E-mail:** drjjt@prodigy.net

TRAHAN, TAMARA S.
Industry: Healthcare **Born:** June 4, 1966, Pequannock, New Jersey **Univ./degree:** B.S.N., Emory University, 1988 **Current organization:** The Connecticut Hospice **Title:** IV Coordinator/Nurse Educator **Type of organization:** Hospice home care **Major product:** Interdisciplinary healthcare **Area of distribution:** Connecticut **Area of Practice:** Oncology **Affiliations:** I.N.S. **Hob./spts.:** Furniture building, gardening **SIC code:** 80 **Address:** The Connecticut Hospice, 100 Double Beach Rd., Branford, CT 06405 **E-mail:** ttrahan@hospice.com

TRAPPLER, BRIAN
Industry: Healthcare **Univ./degree:** M.D., Witwatersrand, South Africa **Current organization:** Kingsboro Psychiatric Hospital **Title:** M.D. **Type of organization:** Hospital **Major product:** Psychiatry **Area of distribution:** New York **Area of Practice:** Teaching stress management trauma **Published works:** Numerous including, Author, "Clomipramine versus fluoxetine in a very old patient with dementia and cardiac failure", Issue 1, 2002, pg. 7-9, Review Series in Psychiatry; Co-author, "Holocaust survivors in a primary care setting-50 years later", Psychologic Reports, 2002, 91, 545-552; Co-author, "Obsessive-Compulsive Disorder in a Multi-Ethnic Urban Outpatient Clinic: Initial Presentation and Treatment Outcome with Exposure and Ritual Prevention", Behavior Therapy, 34, 397-410, 2003 **Affiliations:** A.P.A.; R.C.P. **SIC code:** 80 **Address:** 501 Montgomery St., Brooklyn, NY 11225 **E-mail:** kbmdbtt@omh.state.ny.us **Web address:** www.omh.state.ny.us

TRAUGOTT, UTE
Industry: Medical **Born:** August 1, 1943, Linz, Austria **Univ./degree:** M.D., University of Vienna School of Medicine, 1970 **Current organization:** Comprehensive MS Care Center **Title:** M.D. **Type of organization:** University hospital **Major product:** Medical services **Area of distribution:** National **Area of Practice:** Neuroimmunology, multiple sclerosis **Published works:** 99+ publications **Affiliations:** A.A.N., A.M.A. **Hob./spts.:** Music, gardening **SIC code:** 80 **Address:** Comprehensive MS Care Center, 303 North St., Suite 202, White Plains, NY 10605 **E-mail:** tannlberg@aol.com

TRAVIS, THERESA RODRIGUEZ
Industry: Healthcare **Born:** September 8, 1952, Cambridgeshire, England **Univ./degree:** B.S., Nursing; M.D., 1983, University of Arkansas **Title:** M.D./Medical Director **Type of organization:** Hospice **Major product:** Patient care/education **Area of distribution:** Little Rock, Arkansas **Area of Practice:** Palliative medicine **Affiliations:** Arkansas Medical Society; American Academy of Family Practice; American Academy of Hospice & Palliative Practice; American Medical Association **SIC code:** 80 **Address:** Hospice Home Care, Inc., 1501 N. University Ave., Suite 500, Little Rock, AR 72207

TREFT, ROBERT L.
Industry: Healthcare **Born:** October 24, 1951, Salt Lake City, Utah **Univ./degree:** M.D., University of Utah, 1981 **Current organization:** Mountain View Eye Center **Title:** M.D. **Type of organization:** Medical center **Major product:** Eye care **Area of distribution:** Utah **Area of practice:** Ophthalmology **Area of Practice:** Ophthalmology **Published works:** Multiple publications **Affiliations:** F.A.A.O.; A.M.A.; U.O.S.; D.C.M.S. **Hob./spts.:** Skiing, scuba diving, Utah Jazz basketball fan **SIC code:** 80 **Address:** Mountain View Eye Center, 1580 W. Antelope Dr., #175, Layton, UT 84041 **E-mail:** drtreft@utaheyedoc.com

TREYZON, YAKOV B.
Industry: Healthcare **Born:** February 15, 1956, Livanai, Latvia **Univ./degree:** M.D., University of Latvia, Riga Medical Center, 1960 **Current organization:** Midway Industrial Healthcare Services **Title:** M.D., Director **Type of organization:** Medical clinic **Major product:** Patient care **Area of distribution:** Los Angeles, California **Area of Practice:** Occupational medicine (Board Certified) **Published works:** 6 articles **Affiliations:** A.M.A.; L.G.S.; A.A.E.P.S. **SIC code:** 80 **Address:** Midway Industrial Healthcare Services, 5901 West Olympic Blvd., Suite 100, Los Angeles, CA 90036 **Phone:** (323)930-1331 **Fax:** (323)930-1354

TRUJILLO, OSCAR
Industry: Healthcare **Born:** March 4, 1941, Palmira, Colombia **Univ./degree:** M.D., University of Cauca Popayan, Colombia **Current organization:** Pathology Lab **Title:** M.D., F.C.A.P. **Type of organization:** Independent laboratory **Major product:** Histopathology, cytopathology **Area of distribution:** Mayaguez, Puerto Rico **Area of Practice:** Pathology **Honors/awards:** Buena Viva, Best Specialty Doctors, 2002 **Published works:** Journal of Medical Association of Puerto Rico **Affiliations:** F.C.A.P.; M.C.P.R. **Hob./spts.:** Coin collecting **SIC code:** 80 **Address:** Pathology Lab, 206 Medical 4 Building, Dr. Basora Street 55 North, Mayaguez, PR 00680 **E-mail:** patlab.@centennialpr.com

TRUMBULL, KATHY A.
Industry: Medical **Born:** October 8, 1961, Oak Park, Illinois **Univ./degree:** M.D., St. Louis University, 1987 **Current organization:** University of Illinois College of Medicine **Title:** M.D. **Type of organization:** University **Major product:** Medical education, patient care **Area of distribution:** Illinois **Area of Practice:** Reproductive endocrinology **Affiliations:** American College of Obstetrics and Gynecology; American Society for Reproductive Medicine **Hob./spts.:** Ballroom dancing, computers **SIC code:** 80 **Address:** University of Illinois College of Medicine, 5401 N. Knoxville, Suite 110, Peoria, IL 61614 **E-mail:** ktrumbul@uic.edu

TRUMP, DONALD L.
Industry: Healthcare **Born:** July 31, 1945, Green Castle, Indiana **Univ./degree:** B.S., Johns Hopkins University, 1967; M.D. Johns Hopkins School of Medicine, 1970 **Current organization:** Roswell Park Cancer Institute **Title:** M.D. **Type of organization:** Clinical care center **Major product:** Cancer research/clinical care **Area of distribution:** National/International **Area of Practice:** Clinical research, new drug development, prostate cancer **Honors/awards:** Secretary Treasurer, American Society Clinical Oncology, 2002, 2003; Pittsburgh Vectors, Man of the Year/Science & Medicine, 2001 **Published works:** 200+ articles, chapters **Affiliations:** A.S.C.O.; A.A.C. Research **Hob./spts.:** Golf **SIC code:** 80 **Address:** Roswell Park Cancer Institute, Elm & Carlton Sts., Buffalo, NY 14263 **E-mail:** donald.trump@roswellpark.org

TSAI, FONG Y.
Industry: Medical/health sciences **Born:** July 11, 1941, Taipei, Taiwan **Univ./degree:** M.D., Taipei Medical University, Taiwan, 1966 **Current organization:** University of California, Irvine, Dept. of Radiological Sciences **Title:** Professor and Chairman, Dept. of Radiological Sciences **Type of organization:** University **Major product:** Medical services **Area of distribution:** California **Area of Practice:** Radiology/neurointerventional surgery **Honors/awards:** F.A.C.R.; Outstanding International Graduate; Hasso brothers Endowed Chair **Published works:** 102 peer-reviewed articles in medical journals; author of 2 books; 19 book chapters **Affiliations:** F.A.C.R.; American Society of Interventional & Therapeutic Neuroradiology **Hob./spts.:** Music, golf **SIC code:** 80 **Address:** University of California, Irvine, 101 The City Dr. South, Orange, CA 92868-3298 **E-mail:** ftsai@uci.edu

TSAU, PEI H.
Industry: Medical **Born:** September 15, 1968, Taipei, Taiwan **Univ./degree:** M.D., University of Arizona, 1994 **Current organization:** University of Arizona Health Science Center **Title:** M.D. **Type of organization:** University hospital **Major product:** Medical services **Area of distribution:** Tucson, Arizona **Area of Practice:** Cardiothoracic surgery **Affiliations:** A.M.A.; A.C.S.; A.C.C. **Hob./spts.:** Family, music, gardening **SIC code:** 80 **Address:** University of Arizona Health Science Center, 1501 N. Campbell Ave., Tucson, AZ 85724 **E-mail:** pht@email.arizona.edu

TSINKER, MARK
Industry: Healthcare **Born:** December 7, 1951, Former Soviet Union **Univ./degree:** M.D., Kauno Medical Institute, Lithuania **Current organization:** Bay Parkway Medical, P.C. **Title:** M.D. **Type of organization:** Medical office **Major product:** Patient care **Area of distribution:** New York **Area of Practice:** Internal medicine **Affiliations:** A.C.P.; A.S.I.M.; New York State Medical Society; Kings County Medical Society **Hob./spts.:** Tennis, reading, chess, basketball **SIC code:** 80 **Address:** Bay Parkway Medical PC, 7701 Bay Pkwy., Suite 1G, Brooklyn, NY 11214

TSUJI, MORIYA
Industry: Medical **Born:** January 1, 1958, Tokyo, Japan **Univ./degree:** M.D., Jikei University, 1983; Ph.D., University of Tokyo, 1987 **Current organization:** New York University School of Medicine **Title:** M.D., Ph.D. **Type of organization:** University **Major product:** Medical science, research, higher education **Area of distribution:** International **Area of Practice:** Immunology, microbiology **Honors/awards:** New York Whitehead President's Award, 1993; American Lung Association of New York Research Award **Published works:** "Progress Toward Malaria Vaccine" **Affiliations:** A.A.A.S.; A.A.T.; I.V.C.; A.T.M.H. **Hob./spts.:** Singing, skiing, playing flute, jogging **SIC code:** 80 **Address:** 341 E. 25th St., New York, NY 10010 **E-mail:** moriya.tsuji@med.nyu.edu **Web address:** www.med.nyu.edu

TU, GENE CHANG
Industry: Healthcare **Born:** January 20, 1968, Chia-Yi, Taiwan **Univ./degree:** M.D., University of California at San Diego, 1994 **Current organization:** Advance Care Medical Group **Title:** C.E.O. **Type of organization:** Clinic/urgent care facility **Major product:** Medical care **Area of distribution:** Rowland Heights, California **Area of Practice:** Family practice **Published works:** 3 papers **Hob./spts.:** Hiking, tennis, bowling, stamp collecting **SIC code:** 80 **Address:** Advance Care Medical Group, 1330 S. Fullerton Rd., Suite 288, Rowland Heights, CA 91748 **E-mail:** genetu@yahoo.com

TUCKER II, PAUL A.
Industry: Healthcare **Born:** July 10, 1962, Houston, Texas **Univ./degree:** M.D., Baylor College of Medicine, 1987 **Current organization:** Texas Cardiovascular Consultants **Title:** M.D. **Type of organization:** Medical practice **Major product:** Patient care **Area of distribution:** Texas **Area of Practice:** Cardiovascular diseases **Honors/awards:** Alpha Omega Alpha **Published works:** 1 article **Affiliations:** A.M.A.; A.C.C.; T.M.A. **Hob./spts.:** Running, travel **SIC code:** 80 **Address:** Texas Cardiovascular Consultants, 4316 James Casey St., Bldg. A, Austin, TX 78745 **E-mail:** paultii@austin.rr.com

TURK, NORMA K.
Industry: Healthcare **Born:** November 17, 1957, Dixon, Illinois **Univ./degree:** M.D., Medical School of Wisconsin at Madison, 1997 **Current organization:** Medical Clinic of Houston **Title:** M.D. **Type of organization:** Specialty clinic **Major product:** Patient care **Area of distribution:** Texas **Area of Practice:** Internal medicine, primary care **Honors/awards:** Sigma Xi, 1988; Top 10% of Graduating Medical School Class; A.M.W.A. Award, 1997 **Published works:** Primary Care Journal Club **Affiliations:** A.S.C.P.; A.S.I.M.; A.O.A.; A.M.A.; Texas Medical Association; Harris County Medical Society **Hob./spts.:** Hiking **SIC code:** 80 **Address:** Medical Clinic of Houston, 1707 Sunset Blvd., Houston, TX 77005 **E-mail:** nturk@mchllp.com

TURLEY, CHRISTINE B.
Industry: Medical **Born:** December 15, 1964, Forest Hills, New York **Univ./degree:** B.S., Biology, University of South Florida, 1984; M.D., University of Miami School of Medicine, 1988 **Current organization:** University of Texas Medical Center **Title:** M.D. **Type of organization:** Academic health center **Major product:** Patient care, medical education **Area of distribution:** Texas **Area of Practice:** Pediatrics, physician administration **Published works:** Abstracts, lectures **Affiliations:** A.A.P.; Ambulatory Pediatric Association **Hob./spts.:** Family **SIC code:** 80 **Address:** University of Texas Medical Center, Dept. of Pediatrics, 301 University Blvd., Rt. 1119, Galveston, TX 77555-1119 **E-mail:** cbturley@utmb.edu **Web address:** www.utmb.edu

TURNER, LILLIAN E.
Industry: Healthcare **Born:** April 22, 1918, Walden, Colorado **Univ./degree:** B.A., Biology/Economics, Colorado State University, 1940; B.S.N., Columbia University, 1945; P.A., University of Utah, 1978 **Current organization:** The Hanna Clinic/The Basin Clinic at Hanna **Title:** Certified Physicians Assistant, RN (Retired) **Major product:** Patient care **Area of distribution:** International **Area of Practice:** Medical and surgical nursing **Honors/awards:** Medal for service in Vietnam, U.S. and Vietnamese Government; National Humanitarian, 1993; Distinguishes Alum, Columbia University, School of Nursing, 1997; International Nursing Advisor **Affiliations:** Life Member, V.F.W.; American Legion; Physicians Assistants Association; Served in active duty, U.S. Army 1946-47 and 1964-75, Retired as Commander; World War II and Vietnam Veteran **Hob./spts.:** University of Wyoming sports teams, college sports, reading, the outdoors **SIC code:** 80 **Address:** P.O. Box 337, Hanna, WY 82327

TURNER, ROD J.
Industry: Healthcare **Born:** August 15, 1961, New Orleans, Louisiana **Univ./degree:** M.D., Tulane University School of Medicine, 1987 **Current organization:** Rod J. Turner, MD, PA **Title:** M.D. **Type of organization:** Private practice **Major product:** Women's healthcare **Area of distribution:** Houston, Texas **Area of Practice:** Obstetrics/gynecology **Honors/awards:** Eagle Scout Award, 1975 **Affiliations:** F.A.C.O.G.; Texas Medical Association **Hob./spts.:** Stamp collecting, coin collecting, tennis **SIC code:** 80 **Address:** Rod J. Turner, MD, PA, 2060 Space Park Dr., #210, Houston, TX 77058 **E-mail:** rod.j.turner@gte.net

TUZIL, TERESA JORDAN
Industry: Healthcare **Univ./degree:** B.S., English, St. John's University, 1970; M.S., Social Work, Hunter College, 1973 **Current organization:** Teresa Jordan Tuzil, A.C.S.W.-R., C.A.S.A.C. **Title:** A.C.S.W.-R., C.A.S.A.C. **Type of organization:** Private practice **Major product:** Psychotherapy **Area of distribution:** Long Island, New York **Area of Practice:** Psychotherapy **Published works:** 2 journals, 2 articles **Affiliations:** N.Y.S.C.S.W.A.; N.A.S.W.; N.A.D.A.C. **SIC code:** 80 **Address:** 3859 Tiana St., Seaford, NY 11783 **E-mail:** tjt3378751@aol.com

TWEARDY, DAVID J.
Industry: Medical **Born:** February 12, 1952, Monessen, Pennsylvania **Univ./degree:** M.D. **Current organization:** Baylor College of Medicine **Title:** M.D./Professor of Medicine and Molecular and Cellular Biology **Type of organization:** Medical College **Major product:** Medical education, biomedical research **Area of distribution:** International **Area of Practice:** Infectious diseases, immunology and research, international lecturing **Published works:** 104 peer reviewed journal articles **Affiliations:** American Clinical and Climatological Association; Fellow, Infectious Diseases Society of America; Association of American Physicians; Clinical Practice, Ben Taub General Hospital **Hob./spts.:** Sports, travel **SIC code:** 80 **Address:** Baylor College of Medicine, 1 Baylor Plaza, Houston, TX 77030 **E-mail:** dtweardy@bcm.edu **Web address:** www.bcm.edu

TYLER, LAMARR B.
Industry: Healthcare **Born:** July 29, 1959, Chicago, Illinois **Univ./degree:** M.D., Chicago College of Osteopathic Medicine, 1986 **Current organization:** Evanston Northwestern Healthcare **Title:** D.O. **Type of organization:** Medical group **Major product:** Women's healthcare **Area of distribution:** Skokie, Illinois **Area of Practice:** Ob/Gyn **Published works:** Multiple publications **Affiliations:** A.C.O.G.; A.A.G.L.; A.M.A. **Hob./spts.:** Golf, basketball, tennis, skiing **SIC code:** 80 **Address:** Evanston Northwestern Healthcare, 9977 Woods Dr., Skokie, IL 60076 **E-mail:** lbtobgyn@attbi.com

TYLKE, JAMES E.
Industry: Healthcare **Born:** September 5, 1964, Milwaukee, Wisconsin **Univ./degree:** M.D., Medical College of Wisconsin, 1991 **Current organization:** Regal Marketing, Inc. **Title:** M.D. **Type of organization:** Private independent practice **Major product:** Anesthesiology, pain management **Area of distribution:** National **Area of Practice:** High acuity anesthesiology **Affiliations:** A.S.A.; F.S.A.; I.A.R.S.; Palm Beach Medical Society **Hob./spts.:** Golf, scuba diving, computers, reading **SIC code:** 80 **Address:** Regal Marketing, Inc., 1068 Sanctuary Cove Dr., North Palm Beach, FL 33410 **E-mail:** jetgas4@msn.com

UBOSI, ANGIE N.
Industry: Healthcare **Born:** August 12, 1952, Enugu, Nigeria **Univ./degree:** B.A., Marketing; Ph.D., International Holistic Medicine University, 1994 **Current organization:** Angie International Holistic Health Center, Inc. **Title:** President **Type of organization:** Holistic health center **Major product:** Nutritional counseling, nutritional products, therapy, massage, reflexology **Area of distribution:** International **Area of Practice:** Holistic health, therapy and counseling **Affiliations:** President, Decatur Toastmaster's Club **Hob./spts.:** Reading, dancing, story telling **SIC code:** 80 **Address:** Angie International Holistic Health Center, Inc., 3554 Covington Hwy., Decatur, GA 30032

UDENZE-UTAH, CHINEDUM N.S.
Industry: Healthcare **Born:** April 23, 1960, Nigeria **Univ./degree:** M.D., University Benin School of Medicine, Nigeria, 1986 **Current organization:** Nelson Medical Group **Title:** M.D. **Type of organization:** Group practice **Major product:** Patient care **Area of distribution:** Pennsylvania **Area of Practice:** Pediatrics **Affiliations:** A.M.A.; American Academy of Pediatrics **SIC code:** 80 **Address:** Nelson Medical Group, 1300 S. 18th St., Philadelphia, PA 19146

UDOBI, KAHDI FERNANDO
Industry: Medical **Born:** August 15, 1958, Santa Isabel, Fernando **Univ./degree:** M.D. University of Ibadan, 1980 **Current organization:** Kansas University School of Medicine **Title:** M.D., F.A.C.S. **Type of organization:** University hospital **Major product:** Patient care, medical education **Area of distribution:** Kansas **Area of Practice:** General surgery **Affiliations:** A.M.A.; S.A.G.E.S. **Hob./spts.:** Walking, squash **SIC code:** 80 **Address:** Kansas University School of Medicine, 3901 Rainbow Blvd., Kansas City, KS 66160

UFFNER, JULIA M.
Industry: Healthcare **Born:** October 25, 1958, Philadelphia, Pennsylvania **Univ./degree:** B.S., Tufts University, 1980; M.D., University of Pennsylvania School of Medicine, 1985 **Current organization:** Julia M. Uffner, M.D. **Title:** M.D. **Type of organization:** Private practice **Major product:** Patient care **Area of distribution:** Pennsylvania **Area of Practice:** Internal medicine **Published works:** Write-ups **Affiliations:** Diplomate, A.C.P. **SIC code:** 80 **Address:** 551 W. Lancaster Ave., Suite 302, Haverford, PA 19041

UGOLIK, LORI LEE
Industry: Healthcare **Born:** September 19, 1963, Bridgeport, Connecticut **Univ./degree:** B.S., Exercise Physiology, Ohio University, 1985; D.C., Life University, 1992 **Current organization:** Ugolik Chiropractic Clinic **Title:** Doctor of Chiropractic **Type of organization:** Chiropractic clinic **Major product:** Chiropractic services **Area of distribution:** Macon, Georgia **Area of Practice:** Chiropractics **Affiliations:** International Chiropractic Association; Georgia Chiropractic Counsel; Rotary; Past President, Greater Macon Women Business Owners **Hob./spts.:** Flying, tennis, travel, photography, animals, politics **SIC code:** 80 **Address:** Ugolik Chiropractic Clinic, 618 Shurling Dr., Macon, GA 31211 **E-mail:** ugolikdc@mindspring.com

UNAY, EDNA E.
Industry: Healthcare **Univ./degree:** B.S.N., University of Santo Tomas, Philippines, 1969 **Current organization:** Valley View Manor **Title:** Owner/Administrator **Type of organization:** Residential healthcare facility for seniors **Major product:** Elder care **Area of distribution:** New Jersey **Area of Practice:** Administration **Hob./spts.:** Reading, travel **SIC code:** 80 **Address:** Valley View Manor, 53 Sparta Ave., Sparta, NJ 07871

USHA, SAMA P.
Industry: Healthcare **Univ./degree:** M.D., B.B.S., D.P.M. **Current organization:** Sama P. Usha, M.D. **Title:** Psychiatrist **Type of organization:** Solo practice **Major product:** Patient care **Area of distribution:** International **Area of Practice:** Consulting, psychotherapy, community psychiatry **Affiliations:** A.C.P.; C.M.P.A. **SIC code:** 80 **Address:** Sama P. Usha, M.D., 220 Dundas St. W. 305, Whitby, ON L1N 8M7, Canada

VACHIRAKORNTONG, VIRUCH
Industry: Healthcare **Univ./degree:** M.D., Mahidol University, 1983; OB-GYN training, Jersey City Medical Center, Seton Hall University, 1995; Certified in American Boards of Obstetrics & Gynecology, 2000 **Current organization:** Viruch Vachirakorntong M.D., Inc. **Title:** M.D. **Type of organization:** Private medical practice **Major product:** Healthcare provider **Area of distribution:** California **Area of Practice:** Obstetrics/Gynecology **Honors/awards:** Outstanding Resident in Gynecology Endoscopy, 1995; Honorary Resident, 1995 **Affiliations:** Fellow, American College of Obstetricians and Gynecologists; High Desert Primary Care, St. Mary Choice Medical Group, Victor Valley IPA, IEHP, Molina, Vantage Medical Group, Medical, Medicare, Family PACT Program **SIC code:** 80 **Address:** Viruch Vachirakorntong M.D., Inc., 309 E. Mountain View, Suite 108, Barstow, CA 92311, and 18484 Hwy. 18, Suite 230, Apple Valley, CA 92307 **Phone:** (760)256-0383 **Fax:** (760)256-3163 **E-mail:** viruch@obgyn.com

VAJDA, DOREEN S.
Industry: Healthcare **Born:** March 7, 1958, Hackensack, New Jersey **Current organization:** The Heart Center, P.C. **Title:** Director of Administration **Type of organization:** Cardiology practice **Major product:** Cardiology **Area of distribution:** New Jersey **Area of Practice:** Administration **Hob./spts.:** Gardening, homemade soaps and lotions (body care products), volleyball **SIC code:** 80 **Address:** The Heart Center, P.C., 1001 US Highway 9, Howell, NJ 07731 **E-mail:** dvajda@cardiologycare.net

VALDES, MARIE E.
Industry: Healthcare **Born:** February 23, 1955, Queens, New York **Univ./degree:** B.S., Biology, College of Mount St. Vincent, 1977; M.D., New York University School of Medicine, 1981 **Current organization:** ENT and Allergy Associates **Title:** Surgeon **Type of organization:** Medical group practice **Major product:** Patient care **Area of distribution:** National **Area of Practice:** Medicine-ENT **Published works:** 3 peer reviewed articles, 3 abstracts **Affiliations:** F.A.C.S.; F.A.B.H.N.S.; A.S.H.N.S.; New York Medical Society **Hob./spts.:** Reading, sailing, scuba diving, gardening, music **SIC code:** 80 **Address:** ENT and Allergy Associates, 185 Route 312, Brewster, NY 10509 **E-mail:** mevmd@yahoo.com

VALDÉS-VEGA, EDEL W.
Industry: Healthcare **Born:** August 26, 1968, San Juan, Puerto Rico **Univ./degree:** B.S., Biology, University of Puerto Rico,1991; M.D., University Central del Caribe, 1995 **Current organization:** ABC Pediatrics **Title:** M.D. **Type of organization:** Healthcare facility **Major product:** Patient care **Area of distribution:** Puerto Rico **Area of Practice:** Pediatrics **Affiliations:** A.A.P. **Hob./spts.:** Music, children **SIC code:** 80 **Address:** ABC Pediatrics, Calle McKinley, #107, Suite 1, Manati, PR 00674 **E-mail:** edelwal@hotmail.com

VALENCIA, MARY B.
Industry: Healthcare **Born:** October 13, 1961, Harlingen, Texas **Univ./degree:** B.A., Business, University of Texas-Pan American **Current organization:** Valley Baptist Family Practice Residency Program **Title:** Assistant Director **Type of organization:** Hospital, residency program **Major product:** Physician practice management **Area of distribution:** Texas **Area of Practice:** Practice management; Certifications: CMOM, CMC **Affiliations:** A.A.P.C.; P.A.H.C.O.M. **Hob./spts.:** Swimming, walking, volunteer work with church youth group **SIC code:** 80 **Address:** Valley Baptist Family Practice, Residency Program, 2222 Benwood St., Harlingen, TX 78550 **E-mail:** mary.valencia@valleybaptist.net

VALENTE, JOHN F.
Industry: Healthcare **Born:** June 23, 1960, San Francisco, California **Univ./degree:** B.S., Biology, 1983; M.D., 1987, University of California at San Francisco **Current organization:** University Hospitals of Cleveland **Title:** Director of Kidney Transplant Program **Type of organization:** Hospital system **Major product:** Surgery **Area of distribution:** Cleveland, Ohio **Area of Practice:** Transplant surgery **Published works:** Over 40 articles, over 40 published presentations and abstracts, book chapters in "Surgery, Basic Science and Clinical Evidence", 2001, Springer Verlag; "Mastery of Surgery", 1997, Boston; "Phagocyte Function: A Guide for Research and Clinical Evaluations", 1998, John Wiley & Sons **Affiliations:** American Society of Transplant Surgeons; American Society of Transplantation; Shock Society; Surgical Infection Society **Hob./spts.:** Rowing, sword and knife collecting **SIC code:** 80 **Address:** University Hospitals of Cleveland, 11100 Euclid Ave., Cleveland, OH 44106 **E-mail:** jvalente@lhs.org

VALLARTA-AST, NELLIE
Industry: Healthcare **Born:** June 16, 1952, Freeport, Illinois **Univ./degree:** University Hospital (X-Ray School), 1974; Clinical Densitometry, University of Wisconsin, 1997 **Current organization:** Middleton Memorial VA Hospital **Title:** Bone Densitrometist **Type of organization:** Veterans' Hospital **Major product:** Bone aquisition and analysis **Area of distribution:** National **Area of Practice:** Bone densitometry, osteoporosis detection and treatment monitoring **Published works:** 2 articles **Affiliations:** A.S.B.M.R.; I.S.C.D.; A.R.R.T. **Hob./spts.:** Travel, biking, gardening **SIC code:** 80 **Address:** Middleton Memorial VA Hospital, 2500 Overlook Terrace, Madison, WI 53705

VAN GELDER, HUGH M.
Industry: Healthcare **Born:** May 3, 1958, London, England **Univ./degree:** M.D., Cornell University, 1985 **Current organization:** Cardiac Surgical Associates **Title:** M.D. **Type of organization:** Medical practice **Major product:** Patient care **Area of distribution:** St. Petersburg, Florida **Area of Practice:** Thoracic cardiac surgery **Honors/awards:** America's Top Surgeon Award; Top Florida Doctors Award, 2002 **Published works:** 10 journals **Affiliations:** F.A.C.S.; F.A.C.C.; F.A.C.P.; F.S.E.S.C.; A.S.T.S.; S.S.T.S. **Hob./spts.:** Golf **SIC code:** 80 **Address:** Cardiac Surgical Associates, 603 Seventh St. South, Suite 450, St. Petersburg, FL 33701 **E-mail:** hmvgcheartsurgery-csa.com

VASHIST, SUDHIR
Industry: Medical **Born:** April 13, 1971, New Delhi, India **Univ./degree:** M.D., Brookdale University Hospital & Medical Center, 2001 **Current organization:** Brookdale University Hospital & Medical Center (an affiliate of SUNY-Brooklyn) **Title:** M.D. **Type of organization:** University hospital **Major product:** Medical services **Area of distribution:** New York **Area of Practice:** Pediatrics **Published works:** 1 abstract, 1 poster presentation, 1 oral presentation **Affiliations:** A.M.A.; American Academy of Pediatrics; Diplomat of American Board of Pediatrics **Hob./spts.:** Table tennis, swimming, badminton **SIC code:** 80 **Address:** Brookdale University Hospital & Medical Center, 1Brookdale Plaza, Brooklyn, NY 11212 **E-mail:** sudhir_vashist@hotmail.com

VATA, KORKUT C.
Industry: Education **Born:** February 12, 1972 **Univ./degree:** M.S., Bilkent University, Ankara, Turkey; Ph.D. Candidate **Current organization:** Duke University **Type of organization:** University **Major product:** Higher education **Area of distribution:** National **Area of Practice:** Pathology/cardiology **Published works:** 3 papers **Affiliations:** Member, American Society of Cell Biology **Hob./spts.:** Basketball, scuba diving **SIC code:** 80 **Address:** Duke University, 1105 Pine Winds Dr., #102, Raleigh, NC 27603 **E-mail:** kcvata@hotmail.com

VAUGHN-MOTLEY, DENITA L.
Industry: Healthcare **Born:** September 21, 1959, Louisville, Kentucky **Univ./degree:** B.A., Biology; B.S., Medical Technology, University of Louisville, 1982 **Current organization:** Baptist Hospital Northeast **Title:** Lab Coordinator **Type of organization:** Hospital **Major product:** Patient care, testing **Area of distribution:** Kentucky **Area of Practice:** Microbiology **Affiliations:** American Society for Clinical Pathology; South Central Association of Clinical Pathologists **Hob./spts.:** Reading, gardening, lawn care, walking **SIC code:** 80 **Address:** 4647 Grand Dell Dr., Crestwood, KY 40031

VAYNER, ELLIOT I.
Industry: Healthcare **Born:** Russia **Univ./degree:** M.D., Ross University, 1999 **Current organization:** Brooklyn Pediatrics **Title:** M.D. **Type of organization:** Private practice **Major product:** Children's healthcare **Area of distribution:** Brooklyn, New York **Area of Practice:** Pediatrics, pharmacology **Affiliations:** A.M.A.; A.A.P.; A.P.A. **SIC code:** 80 **Address:** 1761 E. 12th St., Brooklyn, NY 11229

VAZQUEZ, MILDRED J.
Industry: Healthcare **Born:** April 18, 1955, Bronx, New York **Univ./degree:** M.D., University of Central del Caribe, Residency in Pediatrics, 1981 **Current organization:** Primary Residential Services **Title:** M.D. **Type of organization:** Residential house call services **Major product:** Patient care **Area of distribution:** East Pointe, Michigan **Area of Practice:** Trauma care, pediatrics **Published works:** Articles **Affiliations:** American Academy of Pediatrics; American Board of Pediatrics; American Academy of Pediatrics **Hob./spts.:** Horseback riding **SIC code:** 80 **Address:** Primary Residential Services, 21147 Virginia Ave., East Pointe, MI 48021 **E-mail:** muazquez21668997@aol.com

VAZQUEZ-TANUS, JOSE B.
Industry: Healthcare **Born:** June 17, 1954, Havana, Cuba **Univ./degree:** B.S., University of Puerto Rico, 1979; M.D., University of Puerto Rico School of Medicine, 1983 **Current organization:** Research & Cardiovascular Corp. **Title:** M.D., Principal Investigator **Type of organization:** Ambulatory clinic **Major product:** Patient care, research **Area of distribution:** International **Area of Practice:** Non-invasive cardiology, clinical cardiology, internal medicine **Published works:** 3 articles **Affiliations:** F.A.C.A.; A.H.A.; A.S.E.C.; A.A.P.P.; A.C.C.; A.C.R.P.; Puerto Rico Medical Society **Hob./spts.:** Golf, travel **SIC code:** 80 **Address:** Research & Cardiovascular Corp., Ponce Bypass 2225, Parra Medical Bldg, Suite 707, Ponce, PR 00717-1322 **E-mail:** vazqueztanus@hotmail.com **Web address:** www.unitoday.net/vazquez

VEDANTAM, RAVISHANKAR
Industry: Healthcare **Born:** March 12, 1961, Masulipatnam, India **Univ./degree:** M.B.B.S., University of Poona, 1983 **Current organization:** Orthopedic & Spine Surgery, LLC **Title:** M.D. **Type of organization:** Medical practice **Major product:** Orthopedic and spine surgery **Area of distribution:** Indiana **Area of Practice:** Orthopedic surgery, spinal disorders **Affiliations:** A.M.A.; Indian Orthopedic Association **Hob./spts.:** Yoga, skiing, basketball **SIC code:** 80 **Address:** 1401 Chester Blvd., Suite B-6, Richmond, IN 47374 **E-mail:** rvedantam@earthlink.net

VEGA, HERMAN E.
Industry: Healthcare **Born:** March 24, 1954, Bogota, Colombia **Univ./degree:** Ph.D., North Central University, 1998 **Current organization:** Total Rehab Services **Title:** Clinical Director **Type of organization:** Rehabilitation clinic **Major product:** Psychological and medical rehabilitation **Area of distribution:** Miami, Florida **Area of Practice:** Psychotherapy, acupuncture **Affiliations:** A.A.O.M.; A.A.N.C.; F.S.O.M.A.; F.S.P. **Hob./spts.:** Reading, tennis, stamp collecting **SIC code:** 80 **Address:** Total Rehab Services, 4011 W. Flagler St., Suite 206, Miami, FL 33134 **E-mail:** cyberpoints2000@netzero.net

VELANOVICH, VIC
Industry: Healthcare **Born:** January 17, 1961, Dearborn, Michigan **Univ./degree:** M.D., Wayne State University, 1987 **Current organization:** Henry Ford Hospital **Title:** M.D. **Type of organization:** Hospital **Major product:** Patient care **Area of distribution:** Detroit, Michigan **Area of Practice:** General surgery, oncology **Published works:** 100+ publications **Affiliations:** A.C.S.; S.S.O.; S.A.G.E.S. **Hob./spts.:**

Physical fitness **SIC code:** 80 **Address:** Henry Ford Hospital, Dept. of Surgery, 2799 W. Grand Blvd., Detroit, MI 48202 **E-mail:** vvelano1@hfhs.org

VELARDE, FRANCISCO JAVIER
Industry: Healthcare **Born:** May 8, 1960, Guadalajara, Mexico **Univ./degree:** M.D., University of Guadalajara School of Medicine, Mexico, 1984 **Current organization:** Francisco Javier Velarde, M.D. **Title:** M.D. **Type of organization:** Private practice **Major product:** Patient care **Area of distribution:** Puerto Rico **Area of Practice:** Pediatrics **Affiliations:** American Academy of Pediatrics **Hob./spts.:** Spending time with family, sports, travel **SIC code:** 80 **Address:** Francisco Javier Velarde, M.D., HC-02 Box 7898, Aibonito, PR 00705 **E-mail:** javier@isla.net

VELASCO, JOSE M.
Industry: Healthcare **Born:** March 20, 1947, Valladolid, Spain **Univ./degree:** M.D., University of Valladolid **Current organization:** Rush North Shore Medical Center **Title:** Chair, Dept. of Surgery **Type of organization:** Hospital **Major product:** Patient care **Area of distribution:** Illinois **Area of Practice:** General and oncologic surgery **Published works:** Co-author, Rush Review of Surgery, Fall Edition **Affiliations:** American College of Surgeons; Central Surgical Society; Western Surgical Society **Hob./spts.:** Fly-fishing, mountain biking **SIC code:** 80 **Address:** Rush North Shore Medical Center, Dept of Surgery, 9600 Gross Point Rd., Skokie, IL 60076 **E-mail:** jose_velasco@rush.edu

VELAZQUEZ, LYZETTE E.
Industry: Healthcare **Born:** September 15, 1958, San Juan, Puerto Rico **Univ./degree:** M.D., Ross University School of Medicine, West Indies, 1983 **Current organization:** Neuro Care, L.L.C. **Title:** M.D. **Type of organization:** Private practice **Major product:** Patient care **Area of distribution:** New York **Area of Practice:** Neurology **Affiliations:** A.A.N. **Hob./spts.:** Gardening, needlework **SIC code:** 80 **Address:** Neuro Care, L.L.C., 1811 Hone Ave., Bronx, NY 10462 **E-mail:** lyzettevel@aol.com

VELAZQUEZ, MARCOS A.
Industry: Healthcare **Born:** July 2 , 1956, Puerto Rico **Univ./degree:** M.D., Catholic University of Madre y Maestra School of Medicine, Santiago, Dominican Republic, 1983 **Current organization:** Yaguez Cardiovascular Clinic **Title:** Chief of Cardiology **Type of organization:** Hospital **Major product:** Patient care **Area of distribution:** Puerto Rico **Area of Practice:** Cardiology **Affiliations:** President, Western Area Cardiovascular Association; Puerto Rico Society of Cardiology **Hob./spts.:** Family **SIC code:** 80 **Address:** Yaguez Cardiovascular Clinic, Plaza Yaguez Bldg., Suite 204, McKinley St. 114 E, Mayaguez, PR 00680 **E-mail:** mavelazquez@aol.com

VELÁZQUEZ, MIGUEL
Industry: Healthcare **Born:** September 29, 1965, Arecibo, Puerto Rico **Univ./degree:** B.S., Biology, Washington University, 1988; M.D., St. John the Baptist San Juan Medical School, 1992; Fellowship, Ob/Gyn and Cancer, Memorial Sloan Kettering, New York, 1999 **Current organization:** Centro Cirugia Pelvica y Laparoscopic Avanzada **Title:** MD, CEO **Type of organization:** Medical facility **Major product:** Gynecology and pelvic surgery **Area of distribution:** International **Area of Practice:** Laparoscopic and pelvis reconstructive surgery **Affiliations:** A.U.G.S.; I.U.G.S.; S.P.S.; I.C.S.; M.I.G.L.S.; S.L.E.S. **Hob./spts.:** Tennis **SIC code:** 80 **Address:** Centro Cirugia Pelvica y Laparoscopic Avanzada, Torre San Pablo Del Este, Suite 309, Fajardo, PR 00738 **E-mail:** mjvelaz@prtc.net

VENIS, JOYCE A.
Industry: Psychiatry **Born:** Manville, New Jersey **Univ./degree:** A.D., Nursing Science, Middlesex Community College, 1970 **Current organization:** Princeton Psychiatric Centers **Title:** Nursing Administrator, psychotherapist **Type of organization:** Psychiatric **Major product:** Psychiatric treatment **Area of distribution:** International **Area of Practice:** Women's mental health, perinatal mood disorders **Honors/awards:** Nancy Berchtold Founder's Award, Postpartum Support International, 2006 **Published works:** Articles, currently co-authoring a book **Affiliations:** Advisory Board, Postpartum Support International; Past President, DAD, Inc. **Hob./spts.:** Cars, poetry, dogs, people **SIC code:** 80 **Address:** Princeton Psychiatric Centers, 60 Mount Lucas Rd., Suite 700, Princeton, NJ 08540 **Phone:** (609)683-1000 **Fax:** (609)683-4554 **E-mail:** joycevenis-rnc@verizon.net **Web address:** www.depressionafterdelivery.com

VENTURA, HECTOR O.
Industry: Healthcare **Born:** March 21, 1951, Buenos Aires, Argentina **Univ./degree:** M.D., National University of Buenos Aires, 1975 **Current organization:** Ochsner Clinic Foundation **Title:** M.D. **Type of organization:** Clinic **Major product:** Patient care **Area of distribution:** International **Area of Practice:** Cardiology **Affiliations:** Fellow, American College of Cardiologists; Fellow, American Heart Association; Secretary/Treasurer, Louisiana Chapter, American College of Cardiologists **Hob./spts.:** Tennis, jogging, history **SIC code:** 80 **Address:** Ochsner Clinic Foundation, 1514 Jefferson Hwy., New Orleans, LA 70121 **E-mail:** hventura@ochsner.org

VENTURA, LAURIE Z.
Industry: Healthcare **Univ./degree:** B.S.N., Louisiana State University, 1985 **Current organization:** Oshsner Foundation **Title:** R.N., Lead Clinician Nurse **Type of organization:** Hospital **Major product:** Patient care **Area of distribution:** New Orleans, Louisiana **Area of Practice:** Nursing, cardiovascular care **SIC code:** 80 **Address:** Ochsner Foundation, 1514 Jefferson Hwy., New Orleans, LA 70121 **E-mail:** lventura@ochsner.org

VERBOUT, JAMES P.
Industry: Healthcare **Born:** July 7, 1957, Sterling, Illinois **Univ./degree:** B.S., Recreational Therapy, University of Wisconsin at La Crosse; M.S., Organizational Management, Concordia University, 2003 **Current organization:** Mayo Clinic **Title:** Assistant Supervisor **Type of organization:** Hospital **Major product:** Patient care **Area of distribution:** National **Area of Practice:** Administration, therapeutic recreation **Published works:** 10+ articles, 1 chapter **Affiliations:** A.T.R.A.; Minnesota Recreation Park Association; National Brain Injury Association **Hob./spts.:** Reading, fishing, high school sports **SIC code:** 80 **Address:** Mayo Clinic, 200 First St. S.W., Rochester, MN 55905 **E-mail:** verbout.james@mayo.edu **Web address:** www.mayo.edu

VERNOV, SIMA
Industry: Healthcare **Univ./degree:** M.D., Minsk University, Russia, 1978 **Current organization:** Sima Vernov, M.D. **Title:** M.D. **Type of organization:** Private pediatric office **Major product:** Pediatrics **Area of distribution:** National **Area of Practice:** Pediatrics **Honors/awards:** Best Resident, 1995, 1997 **Affiliations:** A.M.A.; American Academy of Pediatrics **SIC code:** 80 **Address:** Sima Vernov, M.D., 1250 Ocean Pkwy., Brooklyn, NY 11230

VERTKIN, GENE
Industry: Healthcare **Born:** August 19, 1956, Belarus (formerly, the Soviet Union) **Univ./degree:** M.D., Second Moscow Medical School, 1979 **Current organization:** Gene Vertkin, M.D. **Title:** M.D. **Type of organization:** Private practice **Major product:** Patient care **Area of Practice:** Anesthesia **Affiliations:** F.A.S.A. **Hob./spts.:** Motorcycles, diving, flying airplanes, downhill skiing **SIC code:** 80 **Address:** Gene Vertkin, M.D., 6600 Duckweed Rd., Lake Worth, FL 33467 **E-mail:** genevertkin@aol.com

VIDAS, MICHAEL CHARLES
Industry: Healthcare **Born:** September 5, 1952, Berwin, Illinois **Univ./degree:** M.D., University of Chicago, 1978 **Current organization:** Peoria Ear Nose Throat Group **Title:** M.D. **Type of organization:** Group practice **Major product:** Patient care **Area of distribution:** Illinois **Area of Practice:** Otolaryngology **Published works:** 5 articles **Affiliations:** President, Peoria Medical Society; Trustee, Illinois State Medical Society **Hob./spts.:** Tae Kwon Do (Black belt), tennis **SIC code:** 80 **Address:** Peoria Ear Nose Throat Group, 7301 N. Knoxville Ave., Peoria, IL 61614 **E-mail:** mcvidas@aol.com

VIDELL, JARED S.
Industry: Healthcare **Born:** April 9, 1947, Philadelphia, Pennsylvania **Univ./degree:** D.O., University of Pennsylvania School of Medicine, 1976 **Current organization:** North Philadelphia Health System - Girard Medical Center Division **Title:** Physician/Medical Director:CCM (Continuing Care Hospital) **Type of organization:** Medical center/hospital **Major product:** Patient care **Area of distribution:** Philadelphia, Pennsylvania **Area of Practice:** Internal medicine, cardiology, nuclear cardiology **Published works:** Articles **Affiliations:** F.A.C.A.; International Society of Physicians Exec; National Association of Managed Care Physicians, Inc; International Society of Internal Medicine **Hob./spts.:** Fishing, bicycling, coin and stamp collecting **SIC code:** 80 **Address:** North Philadelphia Health System, Girard Medical Center Division, Eighth St. & Girard Ave., Philadelphia, PA 19122 **E-mail:** heartdoc@sprintmail.com

VIERLING, JOHN M.
Industry: Healthcare **Born:** November 20, 1945, Bellflower, California **Univ./degree:** M.D., Stanford University School of Medicine, California, 1972 **Current organization:** Cedars-Sinai Medical Center **Title:** Director of Hepatology/Medial Director, Multi Organ & Transplantation/Professor of Medicine, UCLA Medical School **Type of organization:** Medical center/research institute **Major product:** Clinical care, research, transplantation **Area of distribution:** California **Area of Practice:** Hepatology, organ transplantation, liver diseases, rejection of transplanted livers, infections with hepatitis viruses, directing clinical trial of therapies **Published works:** Author of many research papers, reviews and book chapters **Affiliations:** American Gastroenterological Association; American Association for the Study of Liver Diseases; I.A.S.L. **Hob./spts.:** Tennis, hiking **SIC code:** 80 **Address:** Cedars-Sinai Medical Center, 8635 W. Third Street, Suite 590W, Los Angeles, CA 90048 **E-mail:** vierling@csmc.edu

VIGO, JUAN A.
Industry: Medical **Born:** November 24, 1958, Santiago, Dominican Republic **Univ./degree:** M.D., Santo Domingo University, 1982 **Current organization:** Puerto Rico Medical Center **Title:** M.D. **Type of organization:** University hospital/private practice **Major product:** Medical services **Area of distribution:** Puerto Rico **Area of Practice:**

Pediatric Neurosurgeon **Hob./spts.:** Fishing, boating **SIC code:** 80 **Address:** 52 Kings Court, #1-B, San Juan, PR 00911 **E-mail:** ogivnauj@caribe.net

VILLALTA, JOSUE J.
Industry: Healthcare **Born:** December 25, 1941, Bogotá, Colombia **Univ./degree:** M.D., The Pontifical Xavierian University, Bogotá, Colombia **Current organization:** Westside Gynecology, Inc. **Title:** M.D., M.P.H. **Type of organization:** Private practice **Major product:** Patient care **Area of distribution:** Indiana **Area of Practice:** Gynecology, urogynecology **Published works:** 12 publications **Affiliations:** M.C.M.S.; I.S.M.S.; A.S.M.A.; A.V.A. **Hob./spts.:** Skiing **SIC code:** 80 **Address:** Westside Gynecology, Inc., 6920 Parkdale Pl., Indianapolis, IN 46254

VILLEGAS, SARAH E.
Industry: Healthcare **Born:** January 31, 1946, San Antonio, Texas **Univ./degree:** B.S.N., University at Incarnate Word,San Antonio, Texas, 1984 **Current organization:** Southwest Texas Methodist Hospital System **Title:** Diabetes Education Program Coordinator **Type of organization:** Hospital **Major product:** Diabetes education **Area of distribution:** International **Area of Practice:** Diabetes education **Published works:** Article **Affiliations:** A.A.D.E. **Hob./spts.:** Volleyball, baseball, reading **SIC code:** 80 **Address:** 5411 Princess Donna, San Antonio, TX 78229 **E-mail:** sarah.villegas@mhshealth.com

VINCENT, JANICE M.
Industry: Healthcare **Born:** November 12, 1951 **Univ./degree:** M.S., Total Quality Management, Anna Maria College, Paxton, Massachusetts, 1995 **Current organization:** Saint Anne's Hospital **Title:** Administrative Director, Quality Nursing Systems **Type of organization:** Catholic community hospital **Major product:** Patient care **Area of distribution:** Massachusetts **Area of Practice:** ED, performance improvement, critical care **Hob./spts.:** Photography, reading, writing poetry **SIC code:** 80 **Address:** Saint Anne's Hospital, 795 Middle St., Fall River, MA 02721 **E-mail:** jan_vincent@cchcs.org

VISSCHER, PATRICIA A.
Industry: Healthcare **Born:** August 10, 1946, County Bay City, Michigan **Univ./degree:** B.S., Healthcare Administration, St, Joseph's College, Maine, 1988 **Current organization:** Tawas St. Joseph Hospital **Title:** R.N., Director of Surgical Services **Type of organization:** Hospital **Major product:** Patient care **Area of distribution:** Tawas City, Michigan **Area of Practice:** Surgical services **Affiliations:** A.O.R.N. **Hob./spts.:** Camping, reading **SIC code:** 80 **Address:** Tawas St. Joseph Hospital, Surgical Services Dept., 200 Hemlock, Tawas City, MI 48763 **E-mail:** pvisscher@sjhsys.org **Web address:** www.stjosephhealthsystem.org

VO, TRACY T.
Industry: Healthcare **Born:** May 18, 1969, Vietnam **Univ./degree:** M.D., New York University School of Medicine, 1995 **Current organization:** New York Hospital of Queens **Title:** M.D. **Type of organization:** Hospital/private practice **Major product:** Women's healthcare **Area of distribution:** New York **Area of Practice:** Ob/Gyn (Board Certified) **Affiliations:** F.A.C.O.G.; A.M.A. **Hob./spts.:** Travel **SIC code:** 80 **Address:** New York Hospital of Queens, 163-03 Horace Harding Expwy., Fresh Meadows, NY 11365

VOELKEL, NORBERT F.
Industry: Medical **Born:** December 22, Bayreuth, Germany **Univ./degree:** M.D., University of Hamburg School of Medicine, Germany, 1971 **Current organization:** University of Colorado, Health Sciences Center **Title:** M.D. **Type of organization:** University hospital **Major product:** Medical services **Area of distribution:** Colorado **Area of Practice:** Pulmonary hypertension **Published works:** 250+ articles, 1 book **Affiliations:** A.S.C.I.; A.S.A.A.; Royal Society of Medicine, London **Hob./spts.:** Painting, sculpting **SIC code:** 80 **Address:** University of Colorado, Health Sciences Center, Dept. of Pulmonary Critical Care, 4200 E. 9th Ave., Denver, CO 80262 **E-mail:** norbert.voelkel@uchsc.edu **Web address:** www.uchsc.edu

VU, KENNETH K.
Industry: Medical **Born:** August 1, 1959, Saigon, Vietnam **Univ./degree:** M.D., Loma Linda University, California, 1988 **Current organization:** Hawaii Center For Reproductive Medicine & Surgery **Title:** M.D. **Type of organization:** Hospital and university **Major product:** Medical services, infertility research & academic medicine **Area of distribution:** International **Area of Practice:** Reproductive endocrinology & infertility **Published works:** 4 book chapters; 30+ papers; 90+ articles **Affiliations:** F.A.C.O.G.; A.S.R.M.; S.A.R.T.; A.M.A.; Armed Forces District; Associate Professor, Section of American Colleges of Ob/Gyn **Hob./spts.:** Running, swimming, ceramics, volunteer **SIC code:** 80 **Address:** Hawaii Center For Reproductive Medicine & Surgery, 642 Ulokahki St., Suite 300, Kailua, HI 96734 **E-mail:** doctorkenv@aol.com

WACHOB, DAVID A.
Industry: Healthcare **Born:** July 26, 1948, New Castle, Pennsylvania **Univ./degree:** B.S., Mechanical Engineering, University of Cincinnati, 1971 **Current organization:** Providence Everett Medical Center **Title:** Project Construction Manager **Type of organization:** Hospital **Major product:** Patient care **Area of distribution:** Washington **Area of Practice:** Construction management **Affiliations:** A.S.H.E. **Hob./spts.:** All sports **SIC code:** 80 **Address:** Providence Everett Medical Center, 916 Pacific Ave., Everett, WA 98201 **E-mail:** dwachob@providence.org

WADHWA, PUNIT D.
Industry: Healthcare **Born:** September 30, 1967, Pune, India **Univ./degree:** M.D., B.J. Medical College, India **Current organization:** Metro Health Medical Center **Title:** M.D. **Type of organization:** Hospital **Major product:** Patient care **Area of distribution:** Cleveland, Ohio **Area of Practice:** Hematology, oncology **Honors/awards:** The Angen Fellowship Award, 2001 **Published works:** "Annual Review of Medicine", 2002; Textbook chapter, Cancer Gene Therapy Models, "The Cancer Handbook" **Affiliations:** A.S.H.; A.S.C.O.; E.C.O.G. **Hob./spts.:** Reading, music, travel **SIC code:** 80 **Address:** Metro Health Medical Center, 2500 Metro Health Dr., Cleveland, OH 44109-1998 **E-mail:** punitwadhwa@yahoo.com

WAGNER, CATHERINE M.
Industry: Healthcare **Born:** October 23, 1933, Stowe, Pennsylvania **Univ./degree:** R.N., Chester County Hospital School of Nursing, 1954; Associate degree in Business Management, Elizabethtown College, 1985 **Current organization:** Gulf Coast Treatment Center **Title:** R.N. Supervisor **Type of organization:** Hospital **Major product:** Patient care **Area of distribution:** Florida **Area of Practice:** Management, nursing; Nursing Home Administration License from Pennsylvania; RN license in Florida and Pennsylvania; Surveyor/Inspector of Hospitals, Dept. of Health & Welfare, Division of Hospitals, Eastern Pennsylvania **Honors/awards:** Valedictorian, The Chester County Hospital School of Nursing, Class of 1954; Obstetrics and Pediatrics Awards, The Chester County School of Nursing, 1954 **Affiliations:** Pennsylvania Nurses Association; Sertoma Club; Sons of Italy; NHA, Wetzler Nursing Home; NHA, Ephrata Nursing Home; Administrator and Owner of Palm Krest Manor Personal Care Home, Haines City, Florida; Director of Nursing, Leaders Nursing Home; Director of Inservices, Whitehall Nursing Home; President, Women's XYZ Club, 1976; President, Women's XYZ Club, 1976; Alumni of Chester County Hospital School of Nursing; President and Treasurer of Auxiliary to the American Business Club of Lancaster, Pennsylvania **Hob./spts.:** Reading, playing bridge, dancing, walking, boating **SIC code:** 80 **Address:** 1018 Troon Dr. East, Niceville, FL 32578-4061

WAGNER, V. DOREEN
Industry: Education/healthcare/consulting **Born:** January 22, 1959, Syracuse, New York **Univ./degree:** A.D.N., Tallahassee Community College, 1984; M.S.N., Georgia State University, 1995 **Current organization:** North Georgia College and State University/Wagner Consulting Services **Title:** Assistant Professor/Consultant **Type of organization:** University/healthcare consulting **Major product:** Higher education/patient safety and legal issues **Area of distribution:** International **Area of Practice:** Adult health/nursing/patient safety; R.N. **Honors/awards:** National Award for Perioperative Research, A.O.R.N., 2005 **Affiliations:** S.T.T.I.; A.N.A./G.N.A.; A.O.R.N. **Hob./spts.:** Family time, reading, gardening **SIC code:** 80 **Address:** North Georgia College and State University/, Wagner Consulting Services, 924 Chesterfield Place, Marietta, GA 30064 **E-mail:** doreen1799@aol.com

WAGONER, LINDA R.
Industry: Healthcare **Born:** February 16, 1948, Washington, D.C. **Univ./degree:** B.S., Medical Technology, Duke University, 1971 **Current organization:** Doctors' Hospital Laboratory **Title:** Laboratory Director **Type of organization:** Hospital **Major product:** Patient care, medical lab testing **Area of distribution:** Shreveport, Louisiana **Area of Practice:** Technical, consulting, management **Affiliations:** American Society of Clinical Pathologists; Louisiana Society of Medical Technologists **Hob./spts.:** Fly-fishing, gardening **SIC code:** 80 **Address:** Doctors' Hospital Laboratory, 1130 Louisiana Ave., Shreveport, LA 71101 **E-mail:** lwagoner@dhshreveport.com **Web address:** www.dhshreveport.com

WAISMAN, WARNER
Industry: Healthcare **Born:** April 22, 1931, New York, New York **Univ./degree:** B.S., Biochemistry, Queens College, 1955; B.S., Sociology, Queens College, 1955; B.S., Pharmacy, Long Island University, 1958 **Current organization:** Coler Hospital **Title:** Registered Pharmacist (Retired) **Type of organization:** Hospital **Major product:** Patient care **Area of distribution:** New York **Area of Practice:** Pharmacy and sociology **Hob./spts.:** Travel **SIC code:** 80 **Address:** 132-15 Rico Place, Ozone Park, NY 11417

WALDECK, MARGARET K.
Industry: Healthcare **Born:** March 12, 1953, Clarksburg, West Virginia **Univ./degree:** M.S., West Virginia University, 1978 **Current organization:** United Hospital Center **Title:** Clinical Microbiologist **Type of organization:** Hospital **Major product:** Patient care **Area of distribution:** West Virginia **Area of Practice:** Microbiology **Affiliations:** A.S.M.; National Registry of Microbiologists; Member of American Roller Coaster Enthusiasts; Teacher at Salem College and Fairmont State College; Worship Com-

mittee, First United Methodist Church; Volunteers at Robert C. Byrd High School, Meadowview Manor Nursing Home and Robert C. Byrd High School Band Boosters **Hob./spts.:** Roller coasters, violin reconstruction/repair, playing mandolin **SIC code:** 80 **Address:** United Hospital Center, Rt. 19 S, Clarksburg, WV 26301 **E-mail:** mwaldeck.@aol.com

WALKER, LUCY DORIS
Industry: Education **Born:** May 6, 1951, Ridgeway, North Carolina **Univ./degree:** M.A., Theatre, Montclair State University, 1977 **Current organization:** Teaneck High School **Title:** Teacher **Type of organization:** High school **Major product:** Education **Area of distribution:** Teaneck, New Jersey **Area of Practice:** Performing arts **Hob./spts.:** Painting, design and building, theatrical costumes, hiking, outdoor activities **SIC code:** 80 **Address:** 363 Washington Place, Englewood, NJ 07631 **E-mail:** walkplum@aol.com

WALKER, ROBERT B.
Industry: Medical **Born:** March 30, 1948, St. Petersburg, Florida **Univ./degree:** M.D., University of Florida, 1974; M.S., Marshall University, 1991 **Current organization:** Marshall University, Joan C. Edwards School of Medicine **Title:** Professor/Chair, Family & Community Health **Type of organization:** University **Major product:** Patient care, medical education and delivery **Area of distribution:** National **Area of Practice:** Family practice, geriatrics **Honors/awards:** National Rural Educator of the Year, 2000 **Published works:** Articles, book chapters **Affiliations:** A.M.A.; American Academy of Family Practitioners; National Rural Health Association **SIC code:** 80 **Address:** Marshall University, Joan C. Edwards School of Medicine, Attn: Dept. of Family & Community Health, 1600 Medical Center Dr., Huntington, WV 25701 **E-mail:** walkerrb@marshall.edu

WALL, KAREN L.
Industry: Healthcare **Univ./degree:** M.A., Counseling, University of South Dakota, 1994 **Current organization:** Associates for Psychological & Therapy Services **Title:** Therapist **Type of organization:** Mental health services **Major product:** Patient care **Area of distribution:** National **Area of Practice:** Eating disorders, alcohol and drug abuse, gambling disorders, family and couples therapy **Affiliations:** Iowa Mental Health Counselors Association; National Mental Health Counselors Association; National Board of Certified Counselors; American Counseling Association **SIC code:** 80 **Address:** Associates for Psychological & Therapy Services, 1551 Indian Hills, Suite 221, Sioux City, IA 51104

WALTER, CHARLES H.
Industry: Dentistry/oral and maxillofacial surgery **Born:** March 25, 1953, Ames, Iowa **Univ./degree:** D.D.S., University of Iowa, 1978 **Current organization:** OMS Associates **Title:** D.D.S. **Type of organization:** Private practice **Major product:** Surgery of the jaw and face **Area of distribution:** Washington **Area of Practice:** Oral and maxillofacial surgery **Published works:** Articles **Affiliations:** Director, Mt. Baker Theatre; President, W.S.O.M.F.S.; W.S.S.M.F.S.; Rotary Club; Phi Eta Sigma; Phi Beta Kappa; Omicron Kappa Upsilon; Delta Chi; Amer. Dental Assoc.; Amer. Assoc. of Oral & Maxillofacial Surgeons; Pres., Washington State Society of Oral & Maxillofacial Surgeons; Pres., Western Society of Oral & Maxillofacial Surgeons; Washington Delegate, AAOMS; Member, Rotary International **Hob./spts.:** Golf, waterskiing, snow skiing **SIC code:** 80 **Address:** OMS Associates, 3400 Squalicum Pkwy., Suite 102, Bellingham, WA 98225 **E-mail:** c.walter@attbi.com

WALTERS, ARTHUR SCOTT
Industry: Medical **Born:** February 20, 1943, Baltimore, Maryland **Spouse:** Lesley Gill **Married:** December 19, 1992 **Univ./degree:** B.S., Kalamazoo College; M.D., Wayne State University Medical School, 1972 **Current organization:** New Jersey Neuroscience Institute at JFK Medical Center **Title:** M.D. / Professor of Neuroscience **Type of organization:** University medical center **Major product:** Medical services, research, teaching **Area of distribution:** New Jersey **Area of Practice:** Neurologist, movement disorders and sleep disorders **Honors/awards:** Researcher of the Year Award in Medicine, Seton Hall University, 2003-2004; Michael Aldrich Honorary Sleep Medicine Lectureship for Outstanding Contributions to Patient Care, Education and Research, University of Michigan, 2006 **Published works:** 150+ articles, chapters, 3 books: Ed., "Sleep thief: the restless legs syndrome", Orange Park, FL, Galaxy Books, Inc., pp. 1-316, 1996; Co-author, "Parkinson Disease Handbook", New York, American Parkinson Disease Association Inc., pp. 1-40, 1996; Co-ed., "Sleep and Movement Disorders", 1st Edition, USA, Butterworth Heinemann, pp. 1-546, 2003; "The International Classification of Sleep Disorders", American Academy of Sleep Medicine, Westchester, Illinois, 2005 **Affiliations:** Fellow, A.A.N.; F.A.A.S.M.; Active Member, American Neurological Association; Editorial Board of Sleep Medicine; Editorial Board of Sleep; Professor of Neuroscience, Seton Hall University **Career accomplishments:** Chair of the International Restless Legs Syndrome Study Group comprised of 130 physicians and scientists from around the world dedicated to research of Restless Legs Syndrome and Periodic Limb Movements in Sleep; 1992-98 Chair of the Medical Advisory Board of the Restless Legs Syndrome Foundation, a nationwide support group by and for patients with Restless Legs Syndrome/Periodic Limb Movements in Sleep **Hob./spts.:** Family, music, tennis, racquetball **SIC code:** 80 **Address:** New Jersey Neuroscience Institute, at JFK Medical Center, 65 James St., Edison, NJ 08820 **E-mail:** artumdnj@aol.com **Web address:** www.njneuro.org

WANG, FU NAN
Industry: Healthcare **Born:** August 8, 1952, Taiwan **Univ./degree:** M.D., China Medical College **Current organization:** Fu Nan Wang, M.D. **Title:** M.D., Ph.D., Acupuncturist **Type of organization:** Medical practice **Major product:** Patient care **Area of distribution:** California **Area of Practice:** Obstetrics, gynecology, male/female infertility, reproduction, Oriental medicine, real-time sperm micro-separation technologies, acupuncture **Honors/awards:** Numerous patents **Affiliations:** Charles R. Drew University of Medicine; Los Angeles County, Martin Luther King Jr./Drew Medical Center **Hob./spts.:** Basketball, swimming, horseback riding **SIC code:** 80 **Address:** 2059 Atlantida Dr., Hacienda Heights, CA 91745-4844 **E-mail:** wangtube@gte.net

WARD, BOBBIE GOOCH
Industry: Medical **Born:** March 23, Water Valley, Mississippi **Univ./degree:** B.S., Nursing, 1965; M.S., Nursing, 1974, University of Mississippi **Current organization:** University of Mississippi Medical Center **Title:** Clinical Nursing Coordinator **Type of organization:** University hospital/medical center **Major product:** Medical services **Area of distribution:** Mississippi **Area of Practice:** Nursing education **Honors/awards:** Phi Kappa Phi; Sigma Theta Tau **Affiliations:** American Nurses Association **Hob./spts.:** Reading, classical music, travel, cooking **SIC code:** 80 **Address:** University of Mississippi Medical Center, 2500 N. State St., Jackson, MS 39216

WARD III, E. FRAZIER
Industry: Medical **Born:** August 17, 1939, Crewe, Virginia **Univ./degree:** B.S., Chemistry, Millsaps College, Mississippi, 1961; M.D., University of Mississippi Medical School, 1965 **Current organization:** University of Mississippi Medical Center **Title:** Associate Professor/Orthopedic Surgeon **Type of organization:** University hospital/medical center **Major product:** Medical services **Area of distribution:** Mississippi **Area of Practice:** Orthopedics **Honors/awards:** Listed in "Who's Who of the Best Doctors in the Southeast" **Published works:** 12 peer-reviewed journal articles; Author, first and second edition, "Skeletal Trauma" **Affiliations:** Fellow, American Academy of Orthopedic Surgeons **Hob./spts.:** Rebuilding John Deere tractors, travel, gardening **SIC code:** 80 **Address:** University of Mississippi Medical Center, 2500 N. State St., Jackson, MS 39211

WARD JR., PARKER J.
Industry: Healthcare **Born:** November 1, 1934, Winsted, Connecticut **Univ./degree:** M.D., University of Michigan Medical School, 1959 **Current organization:** Parker J. Ward Jr., M.D., P.C. **Title:** M.D. **Type of organization:** Private practice **Major product:** Patient care **Area of distribution:** Norwich, New York **Area of Practice:** General surgery **Affiliations:** Fellow, American College of Surgeons; A.M.A.; New York State Medical Society **SIC code:** 80 **Address:** Parker J. Ward Jr., M.D., P.C., 157 E. Main St., Norwich, NY 13815 **E-mail:** mdward@frontiernet.net

WARREN, DEBORAHA S.
Industry: Healthcare **Born:** April 13, 1953, Skowhegan, Maine **Univ./degree:** A.S., Medical Technology, Kennebec Valley Technical Institute, 1980 **Current organization:** Redington-Fairview General Hospital **Title:** Chemistry Supervisor **Type of organization:** Hospital **Major product:** Patient care **Area of distribution:** Maine **Area of Practice:** Laboratory services and chemistry, instrumentation **Affiliations:** American Society of Clinical Pathologists **Hob./spts.:** Art, biking, kayaking **SIC code:** 80 **Address:** Redington-Fairview General Hospital, Laboratory Dept., 41 Fairview Ave., Skowhegan, ME 04976 **E-mail:** dswarren2004@yahoo.com

WASIK, JOHN H.
Industry: Healthcare **Born:** August 13, 1958, New Britain, Connecticut **Univ./degree:** Electronics Studies, Hartford State Technical Institute **Current organization:** Waterbury Hospital **Title:** Senior Biomedical Technician **Type of organization:** Hospital **Major product:** Patient care **Area of distribution:** Connecticut **Area of Practice:** Electronic Engineer; medical electronic equipment repair; training to technicians and residents **Honors/awards:** U.S. Army, 1977, graduated with distinguished honors in radar and helicopter equipment class **Affiliations:** New England Society of Clinical Engineering **Hob./spts.:** Weightlifting, fishing, gardening **SIC code:** 80 **Address:** Waterbury Hospital, Clinical Emergency Dept., 64 Robbins St., Waterbury, CT 06721 **E-mail:** waitlifter13@aol.com

WASSERMAN, HARVEY M.
Industry: Healthcare **Born:** June 20, 1951, New York, New York **Univ./degree:** B.A., Speech/Theatre, Long Island University, 1972; D.C., Life College, Atlanta, Georgia, 1990 **Current organization:** All About Health Chiropractic Center **Title:** Chiropractor **Type of organization:** Chiropractic holistic health center **Major product:** Patient care **Area of distribution:** Florida **Area of Practice:** Chiropractic, holistic health **Published works:** Lectures, presentations **Affiliations:** Past Member, Pediatric Society; Florida

Chiropractic Association **Hob./spts.:** Martial arts, rollerblading, vegetarian cooking, holistic health **SIC code:** 80 **Address:** All About Health Chiropractic Center, 960 Arthur Godfrey Rd., Suite 120, Miami Beach, FL 33140 **E-mail:** allabouthealthch@aol.com

WATERFALLEN, JOHN W.
Industry: Healthcare **Born:** March 20, 1952, Okmulgee, Oklahoma **Univ./degree:** M.D., Louisiana State University Medical Center, Shreveport **Current organization:** Ob/Gyn Associates of Shreveport **Title:** M.D. **Type of organization:** Medical practice **Major product:** Patient care **Area of distribution:** Louisiana **Area of Practice:** Obstetrics/gynecology **Affiliations:** A.M.A.; F.A.C.O.G. **Hob./spts.:** His children and their sports, football, fishing **SIC code:** 80 **Address:** Ob/Gyn Associates of Shreveport, 7941 Youree Dr., Shreveport, LA 71105

WAWRZYNIAK, ZYGMUNT T.
Industry: Healthcare **Born:** May 11, 1948, Przedborz, Poland **Univ./degree:** M.D., Warsaw Medical School, Poland, 1975 **Current organization:** Zygmunt T. Wawrzyniak, M.D., PCP **Title:** M.D. **Type of organization:** Private practice **Major product:** Patient care, emergency medicine **Area of distribution:** Linden, New Jersey **Area of Practice:** Internal medicine **Affiliations:** A.M.A. **Hob./spts.:** Metal sculpting, bicycling **SIC code:** 80 **Address:** Zygmunt T. Wawrzyniak, M.D., PCP, 911 Northwood Ave., Linden, NJ 07036 **Phone:** (908)925-7425 **Fax:** (908)925-6520 **E-mail:** zygmuntw@home.com

WAYMIRE, BONNIE G.
Industry: Healthcare **Born:** December 16, 1954, Williamsport, Indiana **Univ./degree:** B.A., Business Administration, Indiana Institute of Technology; B.S.N., Lakeview College of Nursing, 2000 **Current organization:** Interim Occupational Health **Title:** R.N. **Type of organization:** Healthcare facility **Major product:** Patient care **Area of distribution:** Indiana **Area of Practice:** Nursing **Hob./spts.:** Collecting Star Trek memorabilia, coins and stamps **SIC code:** 80 **Address:** Interim Occupational Health, 6429 Atlanta Dr., Indianapolis, IN 46241

WEAVER, DENISE C.
Industry: Healthcare **Born:** February 18, 1959, Chicago, Illinois **Univ./degree:** B.S., Biology, Northwestern University, 1981; M.D., Rush University, St. Lukes Presbyterian School of Medicine, 1986 **Current organization:** Medical Specialist **Title:** M.D. **Type of organization:** Private practice **Major product:** Patient care **Area of distribution:** Indiana **Area of Practice:** Infectious diseases **Published works:** 10 articles **Affiliations:** I.D.S.A. **SIC code:** 80 **Address:** Medical Specialist, 761 45th St., Munster, IN 46321

WEBB JR., SCOTT P.
Industry: Healthcare **Born:** January 1, 1947, Huntington, West Virginia **Univ./degree:** Associate in Applied Science, Marshall University, 1990 **Current organization:** Veterans Area Medical Center **Title:** Maintenance and Operations Manager **Type of organization:** Hospital **Major product:** Patient care **Area of distribution:** West Virginia **Area of Practice:** Engineering and maintenance, CPD **Honors/awards:** 3 Performance Awards, 5 Special Contributions Awards and 25 Suggestion Awards for designing, improving and installing plumbing, heating and sprinkler piping systems within the Veterans Area Medical Center **Affiliations:** American Society of Sanitary Engineers; American Society of Plumbing Engineers; International Association of Plumbing and Mechanical Officials; American Backflow Prevention Association; United Association of Plumbers and Pipefitters; Interdenominational Christ Temple-Director of First Impressions Ministry **Hob./spts.:** Football, fishing, track and field, walking **SIC code:** 80 **Address:** Veterans Area Medical Center, 1540 Spring Valley Dr., Dept. 138, Huntington, WV 25704-9588 **E-mail:** Scott.Webb@Med.VA.gov

WEBSTER, TATJANA
Industry: Medical **Univ./degree:** M.D., Summa Cum Laude (with Highest Honors), University of Belgrade, 1967 **Current organization:** University of South Florida, College of Medicine **Title:** Assistant Professor of Internal Medicine **Type of organization:** University **Major product:** Patient care, medical education **Area of distribution:** International **Area of Practice:** Internal medicine **Published works:** 13 papers **Affiliations:** A.C.P.; A.S.I.M.; A.M.A.; N.Y.A.S.; S.S.I.M.; S.W.A. **Hob./spts.:** Art, piano, literature, aerobic exercises **SIC code:** 80 **Address:** VA Medical Center Bay Pines, Dept. of Medicine, 10,000 Bay Pines Blvd., St. Petersburg, FL 33708 **E-mail:** tatjana.webster@med.va.gov **Web address:** www.med.va.gov

WEEMS, LANELLE L.
Industry: Healthcare **Born:** April 16, 1961, Mississippi **Univ./degree:** M.S.N., University of Mississippi Medical Center, 2002 **Current organization:** Woman's Hospital at River Oaks **Title:** Vice President of Patient Care **Type of organization:** Hospital **Major product:** Patient care **Area of distribution:** Mississippi **Area of Practice:** Nursing **Honors/awards:** Phi Kappa Phi **Affiliations:** A.O.N.E.; A.W.H.O.N.N. **Hob./spts.:** Swimming, tennis **SIC code:** 80 **Address:** Woman's Hospital at River Oaks, 1026 N. Flowood Dr., Jackson, MS 39232 **E-mail:** lanelleweems@roh.hma-corp.com

WEIGLE, AMY LYNN
Industry: Healthcare **Born:** May 30, 1979, Ransom, Kansas **Univ./degree:** B.S., Medical Diagnostic Imaging, Fort Hays State University, 2001 **Current organization:** North Colorado Medical Center **Title:** MRI Technologist **Type of organization:** Hospital **Major product:** Patient care **Area of Practice:** MRI, radiologic technology **Affiliations:** A.R.R.T. **SIC code:** 80 **Address:** North Colorado Medical Center, 1801 16th St., Greeley, CO 80631 **E-mail:** aimeslw@yahoo.com

WEINBERG, HOLLY E.
Industry: Healthcare **Born:** August 6, 1952, Billings, Montana **Univ./degree:** B.S., Whitworth College, 1974 **Current organization:** St. Luke's Regional Medical Center **Title:** Supervisor, Hematology/Homeostasis/Flow Cytometry **Type of organization:** Hospital/clinical laboratory **Major product:** Patient care, laboratory work **Area of distribution:** Idaho **Area of Practice:** Hematology, homeostasis, flow cytometry **Affiliations:** A.S.C.P.; A.S.C.L.S. **Hob./spts.:** Gardening, camping **SIC code:** 80 **Address:** St. Luke's Regional Medical Center, 190 E. Bannock, Boise, ID 83712 **E-mail:** weinbergh@slrmc.org

WEINER, LESLIE P.
Industry: Medical **Born:** March 17, 1936, Brooklyn, New York **Univ./degree:** M.D., University of Cincinnati, 1961 **Current organization:** Keck School of Medicine of the University of Southern California **Title:** Professor, Dept. of Neurology **Type of organization:** University, school of medicine **Major product:** Medical services **Area of distribution:** California **Area of Practice:** Medicine, neurology **Affiliations:** A.A.N.; A.N.A.; A.A.A.S.; International Society for Stem Cell Research **Hob./spts.:** Music, reading **SIC code:** 80 **Address:** Keck School of Medicine of the University of Southern California, 2025 Zonal RMR 506, Los Angeles, CA 90033

WEINGART, CAROL JAYNE
Industry: Healthcare **Born:** October 2, 1943, Schenectady, New York **Univ./degree:** Ph.D., Marriage and Family Counseling, University of Louisiana, 1995 **Current organization:** Morrisville Center **Title:** Ph.D. **Type of organization:** Nursing home **Major product:** Long-term healthcare **Area of distribution:** Vermont **Area of Practice:** Staff development, legal nurse consulting, psychotherapy **Affiliations:** Vermont State Nursing Association **Hob./spts.:** Family, reading, travel, knitting, sewing **SIC code:** 80 **Address:** Morrisville Center, 293 E. Main St., North Troy, VT 05859 **E-mail:** drmom@together.net

WEINMAN, EFIM
Industry: Healthcare **Born:** May 17, 1944, Former USSR **Univ./degree:** M.D., Kiev Medical School, 1955 **Current organization:** Franklin Square Hospital - Bay Region Psychiatric Service **Title:** Psychiatrist **Type of organization:** Hospital **Major product:** Patient care **Area of distribution:** National and local **Area of Practice:** Psychiatry **Affiliations:** Association for Convulsive Therapy; American Society for Clinical Psychopharmacology; American Association for Geriatric Psychiatry **Hob./spts.:** Medicine **SIC code:** 80 **Address:** 3123 Old Post Dr., Baltimore, MD 21208

WELLER, KATHY
Industry: Healthcare **Born:** May 26, 1948, Baltimore, Maryland **Univ./degree:** Ph.D., Administration, Columbia University, 1997 **Current organization:** Montgomery Hospital **Title:** Ph.D., R.N./Release Supervisor **Type of organization:** Hospital **Major product:** Patient care **Area of distribution:** Olney, Maryland **Area of Practice:** Nursing **Affiliations:** A.A.C.N.; A.N.A.; M.T.N. **Hob./spts.:** Reading, stamping **SIC code:** 80 **Address:** Montgomery Hospital, 18101 Pince Philip Dr., Olney, MD 20686 **E-mail:** jkn0554@aol.com

WELZ, EDWARD J.
Industry: Healthcare **Born:** March 19, 1957, Chicago, Illinois **Univ./degree:** M.B.A., Cal-State University, 1984 **Current organization:** Wellcare Enterprises, Inc. **Title:** President **Type of organization:** Home healthcare **Major product:** Patient care **Area of distribution:** National **Area of Practice:** Management, marketing **Affiliations:** Y.P.O.; Texas Home Health Association **Hob./spts.:** Golf, waterskiing, skiing, physical fitness **SIC code:** 80 **Address:** Wellcare Enterprises, Inc., 671 S. Mesa Hills Dr., Suite 1, El Paso, TX 79913 **E-mail:** edw@wellcare-inc.com

WEST, JEFFREY CHARLES
Industry: Healthcare **Born:** May 5, 1956, Alliance, Ohio **Univ./degree:** M.D., Columbia University College of Physicians and Surgeons, 1993 **Current organization:** Danbury Hospital **Title:** M.D./Pathologist **Type of organization:** Hospital **Major product:** Patient care **Area of distribution:** Connecticut **Area of Practice:** Atomic and clinical pathology **Affiliations:** College of American Pathologists; American Society of Clinical Pathologists; U.S. Society of Pathology; Canadian Society of Pathology **Hob./spts.:** Music **SIC code:** 80 **Address:** Danbury Hospital, 24 Hospital Rd., Danbury, CT 06810 **E-mail:** jeffrey.west@danhosp.org

WESTMORELAND, CANDICE R.
Industry: Healthcare **Born:** May 24, 1981, Morganton, North Carolina **Univ./degree:** B.S., Clinical Lab Sciences, West Carolina University, 2003 **Current organization:** Blue Ridge Health Care, Microbiology Lab **Title:** Microbiology Section Head **Type of organization:** Laboratory **Major product:** Patient care **Area of distribution:** Morgantown, North Carolina **Area of Practice:** Daily operations oversight **Affiliations:** A.S.C.P. **Hob./spts.:** Family **SIC code:** 80 **Address:** Blue Ridge Health Care, Microbiology Lab, 2201 S. Sterling St., Morgantown, NC 28655 **E-mail:** cwestmoreland@blueridgehealth.org

WESTMORELAND, IRENA S.
Industry: Healthcare **Born:** May 11, 1942, U.S.S.R. **Univ./degree:** M.D., Lenigrad Medical School, USSR (Former)-1965 and 4 years Internship and Residency in Psychiatry - Arizona, USA **Current organization:** Verdugo Mental Health Center, DiDi Hirsch Mental Health Center **Title:** M.D./Psychiatrist **Type of organization:** Mental health clinic **Major product:** Evaluation and treatment of the mentally ill **Area of distribution:** California **Area of Practice:** Psychiatry **Affiliations:** A.P.A.; South California Psychiatric Society; A.S.A.M.; C.A.M.S.; A.P.P.A. **Hob./spts.:** Classical music, ballet, yoga, nature, animals, the ocean, alternative medicine **SIC code:** 80 **Address:** Verdugo Mental Health Center, 1540 E. Colorado St., Glendale, CA 91205-1514

WETZLER, GRACIELA
Industry: Healthcare **Born:** November 9, 1959, Buenos Aires, Argentina **Univ./degree:** M.D., University of Buenos Aires Medical School, 1984 **Current organization:** Maimonides Medical Center **Title:** M.D./Co-Director **Type of organization:** Hospital **Major product:** Patient care **Area of distribution:** New York **Area of Practice:** Pediatric gastroenterology and nutrition **Published works:** Column for YourBaby.com **Affiliations:** A.A.P.; National Society for Pediatrics, Gastroenterology and Nutrition **Hob./spts.:** Family, music, movies **SIC code:** 80 **Address:** Maimonides Medical Center, Pediatric Gastroenterology & Nutrition, 4802 10th Ave., Brooklyn, NY 11209 **Web address:** www.yourbaby.com

WEYRAUCH, BONITA
Industry: Healthcare **Born:** April 3, 1957, Altona, Pennsylvania **Univ./degree:** B.A., Business, Penn State University, 1988 **Current organization:** Dermatology Nurses Assoc. **Title:** President **Type of organization:** International nursing organization **Major product:** Education **Area of distribution:** International **Area of Practice:** Dermatology (preventative and action oriented) **Affiliations:** Board of Directors, Dermatology Nurses Association; American Nurses Association **Hob./spts.:** Travel, reading **SIC code:** 80 **Address:** Dermatology Nurses Assoc., 216 Wilde Ave., Drexel Hill, PA 19026 **E-mail:** bonitak@prodigy.net

WHEELER, DOTTIE L.
Industry: Healthcare **Born:** July 19, 1965, Ironton, Ohio **Univ./degree:** A.A. Candidate, Business, Lima Technical College **Current organization:** Martin A. Kassan, M.D. **Title:** Office Manager **Type of organization:** Medical office **Major product:** Cosmetic/plastic surgery, hand surgery **Area of distribution:** Kentucky **Area of Practice:** Patient coordinator, billing, management **Affiliations:** P.S.A.A.; American Cancer Society Specialty Projects **Hob./spts.:** Cross-stitching, fishing, camping, family, son's sports (basketball, football) **SIC code:** 80 **Address:** Martin A. Kassan, M.D., 617 23rd St., Suite 7, Ashland, KY 41101 **E-mail:** kassansoffice@aol.com **Web address:** www.martinkassanmd.com, dwhee@adelphia.net

WHEELER, JOE ELLIS
Industry: Healthcare **Born:** October 16, 1938, Cone, Texas **Univ./degree:** M.D., University of Texas at Galveston, 1964; M.D., Neurosurgery, Tulane University, 1991 **Current organization:** Drs. Smith & Wheeler, M.D., P.A. **Title:** M.D. **Type of organization:** Private medical practice **Major product:** Neurological surgery **Area of distribution:** International **Area of Practice:** Neurological surgery **Affiliations:** F.A.C.S.; F.I.C.S.; International College of Surgeons; Congress of Neurological Surgeons **Hob./spts.:** Photography, hunting, fishing, licensed pilot **SIC code:** 80 **Address:** Drs. Smith & Wheeler, M.D., P.A., 750 Eighth Ave., Suite 530, Ft. Worth, TX 76104 **E-mail:** wheelerns1@aol.com **Web address:** www.wheelerjoemd.medem.com

WHEELER, RONALD D.
Industry: Healthcare **Born:** November 10, 1944, Pucatello, Idaho **Univ./degree:** M.D., Mount Sinai School of Medicine, New York, 1974 **Current organization:** Eastern Idaho Orthopedics & Sports Medicine Center **Title:** M.D. **Type of organization:** Medical practice **Major product:** Orthopedics **Area of distribution:** Idaho **Area of Practice:** Orthopedics **Published works:** A.A.O.S. **Affiliations:** A.M.A.; Idaho Medical Association; Alpha Omega Alpha **Hob./spts.:** Sports, basketball **SIC code:** 80 **Address:** Eastern Idaho Orthopedics & Sports Medicine Center, 2860 Channing Way, #116, Idaho Falls, ID 83404

WHIGHAM-REYNOLDS, DOROTHY T.
Industry: Healthcare **Born:** August 5, 1924, Louisiana **Univ./degree:** R.N., Mobile Infirmary, 1945 **Title:** RN/Director of Nursing, Washington County Hospital (Retired) **Type of organization:** Hospital **Major product:** Patient care **Area of distribution:** Alabama **Area of Practice:** Teaching nursing trainees **Honors/awards:** Humanitarian of the Year, 1992 **Hob./spts.:** Baking **SIC code:** 80 **Address:** P.O. Box 475, Chatom, AL 36518

WHISLER, SANDRA L.
Industry: Healthcare **Born:** May 15, 1957, Albuquerque, New Mexico **Univ./degree:** B.S., Biology, Baylor University, Texas, 1979; M.S., Cell Biology, University of New Mexico, 1984; M.D., University of New Mexico School of Medicine, 1989 **Current organization:** University of New Mexico School of Medicine **Title:** M.D., FAAP, Associate Professor **Type of organization:** Medical school/Hospital **Major product:** Medical services, education **Area of distribution:** New Mexico **Area of Practice:** Pediatrics, children with special needs **Honors/awards:** Numerous including: America's Top Pediatricians; National Registry of Who's Who; Strathmore's Who's Who; Physician Recognition Award, 1999-2001, 1996-1998, 1993-1995 **Published works:** Co-Author, "Pediatrics, 700 Questions & Answers" 9th Edition; Co-Author, "Why Do Babies Cry?"; Original research and articles in refereed journals **Affiliations:** F.A.A.P.; A.M.A.; N.M.M.S.; N.M.P.S.; G.A.M.A.; A.A.C.P.D.M. **Hob./spts.:** Boston Terriers (obedience train and show), dance-ballet and jazz, perform Nutcracker, New Mexico Ballet Company **SIC code:** 80 **Address:** University of New Mexico School of Medicine, 11216 Desert Classic Lane, Albuquerque, NM 87111 **E-mail:** slwhisler@worldnet.att.net

WHITE, PAUL V.
Industry: Healthcare **Born:** May 20, 1949, Salem, Massachusetts **Univ./degree:** A.S., Chemistry, North Shore Community College, 1970; B.S., Chemical Biological Technology, Northeastern University, 1980 **Current organization:** Health Resources Inc. **Title:** Laboratory Manager **Type of organization:** Occupational health company **Major product:** Occupational health and medical management **Area of distribution:** International **Area of Practice:** Forensic chemistry, laboratory management, consulting, lab set-ups **Honors/awards:** First Presenter at AMT Conference in Boston, 1982 **Affiliations:** American Society for Clinical Pathology; Past Chair, Massachusetts Association of Medical Technologists **Hob./spts.:** Water sports, fishing, antique cars **SIC code:** 80 **Address:** Health Resources Inc., 2 Rehabilitation Way, Woburn, MA 01801 **E-mail:** pwhite@hlthres.com **Web address:** www.healthresourcescorp.com

WICKS, MARK S.
Industry: Healthcare **Born:** October 25, 1941, Chicago, Illinois **Univ./degree:** M.D., Louisiana State University; Ph.D., University of Mississippi, 1973 **Current organization:** Suburban Pulmonary & Sleep Associates **Title:** M.D. **Type of organization:** Group private practice **Major product:** Patient care **Area of distribution:** Illinois **Area of Practice:** Pulmonary care **Affiliations:** American College of Physicians; American Thoracic Society; Chicago Lung Association **Hob./spts.:** Jogging, swimming **SIC code:** 80 **Address:** Suburban Pulmonary & Sleep Associates, 700 E. Ogden Ave., Westmont, IL 60559

WIESELMAN, ALEX
Industry: Mental health **Born:** October 15, 1956, Tangiers, Morocco **Univ./degree:** Ed.S., Seton Hall University, 1994 **Current organization:** Bedminster Far Hills Counseling Center, LLP **Title:** Ed.S./Individual Marriage and Family Therapist **Type of organization:** Private counseling center **Major product:** Mental health services **Area of distribution:** New Jersey **Area of Practice:** Individual, marriage and family counseling and psychotherapy **Affiliations:** N.J.S.L.E.O.A. **Hob./spts.:** Volunteer lecturing, single parent studies, gay and lesbian studies, cars, gardening, tennis **SIC code:** 80 **Address:** Bedminster Far Hills Counseling Center, LLP, 43 U.S. Hwy., #202, Far Hills, NJ 07931 **E-mail:** bfhcc1@aol.com

WIJETILAKA, ROHAN L.
Industry: Healthcare **Univ./degree:** M.D., Sri Lanka University **Current organization:** Rohan Wijetilaka, M.D. **Title:** M.D. **Type of organization:** Private medical practice **Major product:** Patient care, medical services **Area of distribution:** Yonkers, New York **Area of Practice:** Internal medicine, cardiology **Affiliations:** Fellow, American College of Cardiology; Fellow, American College of Physicians; Assistant Clinical Professor of Medicine, Columbia University, New York **SIC code:** 80 **Address:** Rohan Wijetilaka, M.D., 944 N. Broadway, Suite 203, Yonkers, NY 10701 **E-mail:** ruviniw@aol.com

WILCOX, PHILISIE
Industry: Healthcare **Born:** January 26, 1958, Dickson, Tennessee **Univ./degree:** B.S.N., 1995; M.S.N., 1998, Tennessee State University **Current organization:** Carthage Family Medical Center **Title:** Nurse Practitioner **Type of organization:** Medical center **Major product:** Patient care **Area of distribution:** Smith Co., Jackson Co., Trousdale Co., Macon Co. **Area of Practice:** Family healthcare **Honors/awards:** Tennessee Square Dance Champion **Affiliations:** American Nurses Association; Tennessee Nurses Association; Phi Kappa Phi; Sigma Theta Tau **Hob./spts.:** Football, square dancing, horseback riding **SIC code:** 80 **Address:** Carthage Family Medical

Center, 168 Wilburn Hollow Rd., Riddleton, TN 37151 **E-mail:** phmwilcox@yahoo.com

WILDFORSTER, BARBARA
Industry: Healthcare **Born:** January 8, 1953, Denver, Colorado **Univ./degree:** A.S., Nursing, Front Range Community College, 1992 **Current organization:** Health In Home Nursing **Title:** R.N. **Type of organization:** Home health agency **Major product:** Home healthcare **Area of distribution:** Colorado **Area of Practice:** Geriatrics **Hob./spts.:** Camping, kayaking, fishing **SIC code:** 80 **Address:** 5148 E. Galena Ave., Castle Rock, CO 80104

WILEN, HOWARD O.
Industry: Healthcare **Born:** July 20, 1951, Brooklyn, New York **Univ./degree:** M.D., American University of the Caribbean School of Medicine, 1978 **Current organization:** Southwest Gastroenterology Assoc. **Title:** M.D. **Type of organization:** Healthcare facility **Major product:** Patient care **Area of distribution:** Clairton, Pennsylvania **Area of Practice:** Gastroenterology **Affiliations:** A.M.A.; A.C.P. **Hob./spts.:** Tennis, skiing **SIC code:** 80 **Address:** Southwest Gastroenterology Assoc., 1200 Brooks Lane, Suite 260, Clairton, PA 15025

WILLIAMS, DARRELL P.
Industry: Healthcare **Born:** November 7, 1953, Denver, Colorado **Univ./degree:** M.D., Vanderbilt University School of Medicine **Current organization:** Trinity Regional Eye Care - Williams Center **Title:** M.D. **Type of organization:** Hospital affiliate **Major product:** Ophthalmology **Area of distribution:** National **Area of Practice:** Cataract/refractive surgery **Affiliations:** A.M.A.; A.S.C.R.S. **Hob./spts.:** Missions, physical fitness, family **SIC code:** 80 **Address:** Trinity Regional Eye Care - Williams Center, 120 Burdick Expressway E., Minot, ND 58701 **E-mail:** darrell.williams@trinityhealth.org **Web address:** www.trinityhealth.org

WILLIAMS, DAVID J.
Industry: Healthcare **Born:** December 30, 1953, Memphis, Tennessee **Univ./degree:** M.D., University of Mississippi, Jackson, 1982 **Current organization:** Women's Clinic of New Albany, P.C. **Title:** M.D., F.A.C.O.G. **Type of organization:** Private practice **Major product:** Ob/Gyn **Area of distribution:** Mississippi **Area of Practice:** Infertility **Affiliations:** Fellow, A.C.O.G.; A.M.P.; A.R.S.M. **Hob./spts.:** Golf, running, college sports **SIC code:** 80 **Address:** Women's Clinic of New Albany, P.C., 460 W. Bankhead St., New Albany, MS 38652 **E-mail:** rebdr@bellsouth.net

WILLIAMS, H.R. (BILL)
Industry: Healthcare **Univ./degree:** D.D.S., University of Texas Health Center, 1973 **Current organization:** H.R. Williams, D.D.S. **Title:** President **Type of organization:** Private dental practice **Major product:** Patient care **Area of distribution:** Texas **Area of Practice:** Cosmetic dentistry, surgery, family dentistry **SIC code:** 80 **Address:** H.R. Williams, D.D.S., 1715 Weston Brent, El Paso, TX 79935 **E-mail:** hr.pr.williams2th-doc@aol.com

WILLIAMS, JODY
Industry: Healthcare **Born:** January 29, 1959, Sulphur, Louisiana **Univ./degree:** M.S.W., Louisiana State University, 1994 **Current organization:** Charter Home Health, LLC **Title:** CEO **Type of organization:** Home healthcare **Major product:** Assisted living for seniors **Area of distribution:** Denham Springs, Louisiana **Area of Practice:** Geriatrics, nursing, therapy, social work **Affiliations:** Louisiana Healthcare Review **Hob./spts.:** Playing piano, saxophone, decorating **SIC code:** 80 **Address:** Charter Home Health, LLC, 2550 Florida Blvd. S.W., Denham Springs, LA 70726 **E-mail:** jodywilliams@charterhomehealth.com

WILLIAMS, LARRY R.
Industry: Healthcare **Born:** July 20, 1952, Murphysboro, Illinois **Univ./degree:** M.D., University of Illinois, 1978 **Current organization:** Lee & Williams, P.A. **Title:** Vascular Surgeon **Type of organization:** Surgical practice **Major product:** Patient care **Area of distribution:** St. Petersburg, Florida **Area of Practice:** Vascular surgery **Published works:** 35+ articles on vascular surgery **Affiliations:** Florida Vascular Society; A.C.S.; F.M.A. **Hob./spts.:** Golf **SIC code:** 80 **Address:** Lee & Williams, P.A., 1111 Seventh Ave. North, Suite 105, St. Petersburg, FL 33705

WILLIAMS, PATRICIA S.
Industry: Healthcare **Born:** July 17, 1950, Albemarle, Stanley County, North Carolina **Univ./degree:** B.S.N., University of North Carolina, 2003 **Current organization:** First Health Richmond Memorial Hospital **Title:** Director of Nursing, Palmer-Hinson Acute Care Division **Type of organization:** Hospital **Major product:** Patient care **Area of distribution:** Rockingham, North Carolina **Area of Practice:** Administration, regulatory compliance, quality assurance **Affiliations:** N.A.D.D.O.N.A.; Alpha Sigma Lambda **Hob./spts.:** Music **SIC code:** 80 **Address:** First Health Richmond Memorial Hospital, 925 Long Dr., Rockingham, NC 28379 **E-mail:** pwilliams15@nc.rr.com

WILLIAMSON, STEPHEN K.
Industry: Medical **Born:** June 1, 1954, Wichita, Kansas **Univ./degree:** M.D., University of Kansas, 1979 **Current organization:** University of Kansas, Cancer Center **Title:** M.D., Professor of Medicine **Type of organization:** University/cancer center **Major product:** Cancer care and research **Area of distribution:** Kansas **Area of Practice:** Clinical trials, lung cancer research and education; actively involved in public speaking and consulting to pharmaceutical companies **Published works:** 30+ manuscripts **Affiliations:** A.S.C.O.; A.C.P. **Hob./spts.:** Spending time with family, swimming, reading, travel **SIC code:** 80 **Address:** University of Kansas, Cancer Center, 3901 Rainbow, Kansas City, KS 66160

WILSEY, BRENDA J.
Industry: Healthcare **Univ./degree:** B.S.N., Syracuse University, 1997 **Current organization:** Tripler Army Medical Center **Title:** Nurse Manager **Type of organization:** Hospital **Major product:** Leadership, initiative and follow through **Area of distribution:** Hawaii **Area of Practice:** Perioperative Nurse Manager **Honors/awards:** Outstanding Junior Officer; Nominee Nurse of Distinction; Deans List, Syracuse University; Nominee, Who's Who in Colleges & Universities; Veteran, Desert Storm **Affiliations:** Sigma Theta Tau; A.O.R.N.; V.F.W.; American Legion; Women's Memorial Foundation **Hob./spts.:** Hiking, travel, golf, kayaking **SIC code:** 80 **Address:** 47-336 Walhee Rd., Kaneohe, HI 96744 **E-mail:** bwilsey@hotmail.com

WILSEY JR., MICHAEL JOHN
Industry: Healthcare **Born:** November 21, 1969, Hollywood, Florida **Univ./degree:** M.D., University of Miami School of Medicine, 1996 **Current organization:** Baylor College of Medicine **Title:** M.D. **Type of organization:** Hospital **Major product:** Patient care **Area of distribution:** National **Area of Practice:** Pediatric gastroenterology, hepatology, nutrition **Published works:** 1 article **Affiliations:** North American Society for Pediatric Gastroenterology, Hepatitis & Nutrition; American Academy of Pediatrics **SIC code:** 80 **Address:** Pediatric GI Nutrition, 4726 N. Habana Ave., Suite 101, Tampa, FL 33614 **E-mail:** michaelw@bcm.tmc.edu

WILSON, GARY FRANCISCO
Industry: Healthcare **Born:** February 2, 1969, Manila, Philippines **Univ./degree:** B.S., Clinical Management and Leadership, George Washington University, 2003 **Current organization:** Piedmont Hospital **Title:** Interventional Radiology Supervisor **Type of organization:** Hospital **Major product:** Patient care **Area of distribution:** Atlanta, Georgia **Area of Practice:** Interventional radiology **Affiliations:** A.V.I.R.; A.S.R.T.; A.R.R.T. **Hob./spts.:** Softball **SIC code:** 80 **Address:** Piedmont Hospital, Interventional Radiology Dept., 1968 Peachtree Rd. N.W., Atlanta, GA 30309 **E-mail:** gary.wilson@piedmont.org

WILSON, LARRY D.
Industry: Healthcare **Born:** January 26, 1953, Tulsa, Oklahoma **Univ./degree:** M.D., University of Oklahoma, 1985 **Current organization:** Concentra Medical Centers **Title:** M.D./Center Medical Director **Type of organization:** Medical group **Major product:** Patient care **Area of distribution:** Round Rock, Texas **Area of Practice:** Occupational medicine **Affiliations:** A.A.F.P.; Texas Medical Association; Texas Academy of Family Physicians **Hob./spts.:** Scuba diving, snorkeling **SIC code:** 80 **Address:** Concentra Medical Centers, 117-B Louis Henna Blvd., Suite 200, Round Rock, TX 78664

WILSON, MICHELLE L.
Industry: Medical **Born:** October 2, 1958, Colorado Springs, Colorado **Univ./degree:** D.O., West Virginia School of Osteopathic Medicine, 1992 **Current organization:** Memorial Health University Medical Center **Title:** D.O./Associate Director of Internal Medicine Dept. **Type of organization:** University medical center **Major product:** Medical services **Area of distribution:** Georgia **Area of Practice:** Internal medicine **Affiliations:** A.M.A.; A.O.A.; A.C.P.; F.A.B.H.P.; Assistant Professor, Mercer Medical School **Hob./spts.:** Travel, boating, hiking **SIC code:** 80 **Address:** 8 Off Shore Rd., Savannah, GA 31410 **E-mail:** wilsondocshelly1@aol.com

WILT, SONYA M.
Industry: Healthcare **Born:** March 7, 1937, Charleroi, Pennsylvania **Univ./degree:** Ph.D., Interpersonal Communications, University of Pittsburgh, 1975 **Current organization:** Communication Specialists **Title:** Ph.D. **Type of organization:** Private practice **Major product:** Rehabilitation services **Area of distribution:** Pennsylvania **Area of Practice:** Speech/Language Pathology; cognitive rehabilitation for traumatic brain injury and C.V.A. **Affiliations:** A.S.H.L.A.; A.V.A.N.T.A. **Hob./spts.:** Travel **SIC code:** 80 **Address:** Communication Specialists, 262 Leech Rd., Greenville, PA 16125 **E-mail:** sonya7@neo.rr.com

WIMMER, MICHELE L.
Industry: Healthcare **Born:** April 6, 1958, Milwaukee, Wisconsin **Univ./degree:** B.S., Pre-Veterinary Medicine, California State Polytechnic University-Pomona, 1980 **Current organization:** The Senior Connection, Inc. **Title:** Director, In-Home Support Services **Type of organization:** Home health care provider **Major product:** In home

support service for seniors **Area of distribution:** California **Area of Practice:** Medical, business **Affiliations:** N.S.O.; CSA, Society of Certified Senior Advisors **Hob./spts.:** Skiing, gardening, building dollhouses, quilting **SIC code:** 80 **Address:** The Senior Connection, Inc., 993 Playground Dr., Crestline, CA 92325 **E-mail:** theseniorconnection@charter.net **Web address:** www.mountainseniorservices.com

WINDSOR, JOHN H.
Industry: Healthcare **Born:** September 4, 1958, Tucson, Arizona **Univ./degree:** D.O., Nova-Southeastern University, 1989 **Current organization:** Heart & Lung Clinic **Title:** Doctor **Type of organization:** Multispecialty group medical practice **Major product:** Cardiology **Area of distribution:** North Dakota, South Dakota, Montana **Area of Practice:** Interventional cardiology **Honors/awards:** Trainee Investigator Award, A.P.S.; Cardiovascular Guest-Fellow Program, A.H.A.; Outstanding Young Men in America **Published works:** Co-author of abstracts for journals and presentations **Affiliations:** A.O.A.; A.M.A.; F.A.C.C.; F.A.C.C.P.; Clinical Associate Professor, College of Osteopathic Medicine and Surgery; Adjunct Professor, University of Mary School of Nursing; Clinical Assistant Professor, University of North Dakota Medical School **SIC code:** 80 **Address:** Heart and Lung Clinic, 311 N. Ninth St., Bismarck, ND 58501 **E-mail:** jwindsor@primecare.org

WINTERS, KAREN P.
Industry: Medical/Nursing **Born:** January 28, 1957, Jackson, Mississippi **Univ./degree:** B.S.N., Texas Christian University, 1979; M.S.N., University of Alabama; Ph.D., University of Mississippi, 2004 **Current organization:** University of Mississippi Medical Center School of Nursing **Title:** Ph.D. **Type of organization:** University medical center **Major product:** Patient care, medical education **Area of distribution:** Mississippi **Area of Practice:** Nursing **Affiliations:** Mississippi Nursing Association; Eliza Pillars Nursing Association **Hob./spts.:** Reading **SIC code:** 80 **Address:** University of Mississippi Medical Center, School of Nursing, 2500 N. State St., Jackson, MS 39216 **E-mail:** kwinters@ums.med.edu **Web address:** www.ums.med.edu

WITTENBERG, IAN S.
Industry: Healthcare **Born:** October 20, 1967, New York, New York **Univ./degree:** M.D., Mt. Sinai Medical School, 1995 **Current organization:** Bronx Lebanon Hospital **Title:** M.D. **Type of organization:** Hospital **Major product:** Patient care **Area of distribution:** New York **Area of Practice:** Pediatrics **Affiliations:** F.A.A.P.; Alpha Omega Alpha **Hob./spts.:** Reading, cooking, fishing **SIC code:** 80 **Address:** Bronx Lebanon Hospital, 1560 Selwyn Ave., 6th floor, Bronx, NY 10457 **E-mail:** iwmd2000@yahoo.com

WITTENBERG, STEPHEN W.
Industry: Healthcare **Born:** August 12, 1942, Detroit, Michigan **Univ./degree:** DPM, Ohio College of Podiatric Medicine, 1969 **Current organization:** Dr. Stephen Wittenberg DPM/PC **Title:** Podiatrist **Type of organization:** Private practice **Major product:** Patient care **Area of distribution:** Michigan **Area of Practice:** Podiatry, orthopedic, general surgery **Affiliations:** American Podiatric Medical Association; Michigan Podiatric Medical Association; Orthopedic Medical Society; American Council of Certified Podiatric Physicians & Surgeons **Hob./spts.:** Boating **SIC code:** 80 **Address:** Dr. Stephen Wittenberg DPM/PC, 28037 Dequindre Rd., Madison Heights, MI 48071

WOLF, CHRIS A.
Industry: Healthcare **Born:** May 11, 1951, Bayard, Iowa **Univ./degree:** B.S., Leisure Services, Iowa State University, 1979; N.H.A., Des Moines Community College, 1987 **Current organization:** Heritage Care Center **Title:** Administrator **Type of organization:** Long term care facility **Major product:** Nursing and skilled nursing for long term elder care **Area of distribution:** Iowa Falls, Iowa **Area of Practice:** Administration, training and lecturing on healthcare administration; Quality assurance program development; **Honors/awards:** Governor's Award for Quality Care, 2006; Malcolm Baldrige Step 1 Quality Award, 2006 **Affiliations:** President, Iowa Falls Business and Professional Women; Board Member, Lion's Club; Advisory Board, Hospice **Hob./spts.:** Drawing, painting, woodworking, crafts **SIC code:** 80 **Address:** Heritage Care Center, 2320 Washington Ave., Iowa Falls, IA 50126 **E-mail:** cwolf@vhsmail.com **Web address:** www.heritagecarecenter.com

WOLF, SHARON A.
Industry: Healthcare **Born:** May 13, 1951, Dallas, Texas **Univ./degree:** Ph.D., Union Graduate School, Cincinnati, Ohio, 1989 **Current organization:** Sharon A. Wolf, Ph.D. **Title:** Licensed Mental Health Counselor **Type of organization:** Private practice **Major product:** Treatment for mental health, domestic violence, eating disorders **Area of distribution:** Tilton, New Hampshire **Area of Practice:** Individual/family psychotherapy **Affiliations:** American Counseling Association; New Hampshire Counseling Association **Hob./spts.:** Family, flowers, birds **SIC code:** 80 **Address:** Sharon A. Wolf, Ph.D., P.O. Box 253, Tilton, NH 03276 **Phone:** (603)286-7647

WOLSTEIN, KAREN JILL
Industry: Healthcare **Univ./degree:** B.S., Marketing, Florida State University, 1986; M.S., Sports Medicine, University of Miami, 1988; D.C., Life College, Atlanta, Georgia, 1993 **Current organization:** Suncoast Spinal Medical & Rehabilitation Centers **Title:** Chiropractor **Type of organization:** Medical and rehabilitation practice **Major product:** Patient care **Area of distribution:** Florida **Area of Practice:** Back, spine, rehabilitation **Affiliations:** A.C.A. Council on Diagnostic Imaging; American Chiropractic Association Florida Chiropractic Association; Florida Chiropractic Association of Sports Injury Council **Hob./spts.:** Yoga, physical fitness, chess, reading **SIC code:** 80 **Address:** Suncoast Spinal Medical & Rehabilitation Centers, 24945 US Highway 19 N, Clearwater, FL 33763

WON, JONATHAN R.
Industry: Health insurance **Born:** October 2, 1942, Honolulu, Hawaii **Univ./degree:** M.P.H., University of Hawaii, 1969 **Current organization:** Hawaii Dental Service **Title:** President/CEO **Type of organization:** Insurance provider **Major product:** Dental insurance **Area of distribution:** Hawaii **Area of Practice:** Management **Affiliations:** Honolulu Executives Association; Hawaii Employers Council **Hob./spts.:** Karate instructor, surfing, playing slack-key guitar **SIC code:** 80 **Address:** Hawaii Dental Service, 700 Bishop St., Suite 700, Honolulu, HI 96813 **E-mail:** jwon@hdsonline.org

WONG, BARON C.K.W.
Industry: Healthcare **Born:** December 1, 1970, Kailua, Hawaii **Univ./degree:** B.S. with Distinction, Biology, University of Hawaii, 1992; M.D., John A. Burns School of Medicine, 1997; Training: Internal Medicine Residency, Geriatric Fellowship Program, 2001 **Current organization:** Wahiawa Specialty Clinic **Title:** M.D./Consultant at Wahiawa General Hospital **Type of organization:** Hospital, medical centers, clinics **Major product:** Patient care **Area of distribution:** Hawaii **Area of Practice:** American Board of Geriatric Medicine (Board Certified, 2001); American Board of Internal Medicine (Board Certified, 2000); Diplomate of the American Board of Hospital Physicians; Diplomate of the American College of Ethical Physicians; American Board of Medical Specialties; Member and Fellow of the American Board of Hospital Physicians **Honors/awards:** Home Care Physician of the Year, Healthcare Association of Hawaii, Homecare and Hospice Division, 2004; America's Top Physicians Award, 2003; Inclusion, State License Documentation, 2003 and 2006; 2000 Outstanding Intellectuals of the 21st Century, 2004; Outstanding Physician Nominee, The Queen's Medical Center, 2002; Physician's Recognition Award, 2002-03, American Medical Association; James A. Orbison Resident of the Year Award, 1999-2000, University of Hawaii Internal Medicine Residency Program; Mission Effectiveness Award, St. Francis Medical Center **Published works:** Numerous articles and presentations at state/institutional meetings **Affiliations:** American Medical Association; American College of Physicians-American Society of Internal Medicine; American Geriatric Association; Alpha Omega Alpha Medical Honor Society; Hawaii Medical Association; Honolulu County Medical Society; American Association of Family Physicians; American Medical Association-Political Action Committee; Diplomate, Fellow and Member of the American Board of Hospital Physicians; Diplomate of American College of Ethical Physicians, American Board of Medical Specialties, American Biographical Institute, International Biographical Centre **Career accomplishments:** Clinical Teaching for Geriatric Fellows, Medical Residents and Medical Students **Hob./spts.:** Tennis, reading, jogging, spending time with family **SIC code:** 80 **Address:** Wahiawa Specialty Clinic, 128 Lehua St., Ground floor, Wahiawa, HI 96786 **E-mail:** baronwong@hotmail.com

WONG, CARSON
Industry: Medical **Univ./degree:** M.D., University of Western Ontario, Canada, 1995 **Current organization:** The University of Oklahoma Health Sciences Center **Title:** M.D.; Assistant Professor and Director, Section of Endourologic, Laparoscopic and Minimally Invasive Surgery, Dept. of Urology, The University of Oklahoma Health Sciences Center **Type of organization:** University/hospital **Major product:** Patient care, medical education, research **Area of distribution:** Oklahoma, Texas, Arkansas, Kansas, New Mexico **Area of Practice:** Laparoscopy, Endourology and Minimally Invasive Surgery **Honors/awards:** Fellow, Royal College of Physicians and Surgeons of Canada (FRCSC) Urology; Diplomate, American Board of Urology; Fellow, American College of Surgeons (FACS) **Published works:** Numerous peer-reviewed publications and national/international presentations **Affiliations:** American Urological Association; Endourological Society; Canadian Urological Association; Society of Laparoendoscopic Surgeons; American Association for Cancer Research; Societe Internationale d'Urologie; Society of University Urologists **SIC code:** 80 **Address:**

The University of Oklahoma Health Sciences Center, 920 Stanton L. Young Blvd., Suite WP 3150, Oklahoma City, OK 73104 **E-mail:** carson-wong@ouhsc.edu

WOOD, R. WILLIAM
Industry: Healthcare **Born:** June 24, 1943 **Univ./degree:** D.D.S., Washington University School of Dental Medicine **Current organization:** R. William Wood, D.D.S. **Title:** D.D.S. **Type of organization:** Private practice **Major product:** Dental care **Area of distribution:** International **Area of Practice:** Restorative cosmetic dentist and ceramist **Affiliations:** A.D.A.; M.D.A. **Hob./spts.:** Golf, gourmet cooking **SIC code:** 80 **Address:** R. William Wood, D.D.S., 5640 Maple Rd., Suite 303, West Bloomfield, MI 48322 **E-mail:** rwood37262@aol.com

WOODARD, EDNA L.
Industry: Healthcare **Born:** May 30, 1956, Nashville, Tennessee **Univ./degree:** M.S., West Kentucky University, 2001 **Current organization:** Woodard Family Healthcare **Title:** President **Type of organization:** Healthcare clinic **Major product:** Patient care **Area of distribution:** National **Area of Practice:** Family health **Affiliations:** American Nurses Association; Tennessee Nurses Association **Hob./spts.:** Bluegrass and gospel music, softball **SIC code:** 80 **Address:** Woodard Family Healthcare, 109 Damascus Ave., Hartsville, TN 37074-1501 **E-mail:** edna1971@aol.com

WOODARD, MARK DOWNING
Industry: Healthcare **Born:** January 21, 1956, Boise, Idaho **Univ./degree:** M.D., University of Colorado, 1982 **Current organization:** Lander Valley Medical Center **Title:** Pathologist **Type of organization:** Hospital **Major product:** Patient care **Area of distribution:** Lander, Wyoming **Area of Practice:** Pathology (anatomic and clinical) **Affiliations:** F.A.C.P.; F.A.S.C.P.; F.N.A.M.E.; Phi Betta Kappa **Hob./spts.:** Fishing, hunting, photography, backpacking **SIC code:** 80 **Address:** Lander Valley Medical Center, 1320 Bishop Randall Dr., Lander, WY 82520 **E-mail:** woodard@rmisp.com

WOODWARD, NEIL W.
Industry: Healthcare **Univ./degree:** M.D., University of Oklahoma, 1956 **Current organization:** Advanced Colon & Rectal Surgery **Title:** M.D. **Type of organization:** Private medical practice **Major product:** Health services **Area of distribution:** Oklahoma **Area of Practice:** Colon and rectal surgery **Affiliations:** Delegate, Oklahoma State Medical Association; Oklahoma County Medical Society **Hob./spts.:** Pilot instructor **SIC code:** 80 **Address:** Advanced Colon & Rectal Surgery, 4200 W. Memorial Rd., Suite 909, Oklahoma City, OK 73120 **E-mail:** drnww@aol.com

WORSHAM, GEORGE FREDERICK
Industry: Healthcare **Born:** November 19, 1948, Charleston, South Carolina **Univ./degree:** M.D., Medical University of South Carolina, 1974 **Current organization:** Charleston Pathology, Dept. of Pathology, Roper Hospital **Title:** M.D. **Type of organization:** Medical practice with hospital, laboratory relationship **Major product:** Diagnostic medical services **Area of distribution:** South Carolina **Area of Practice:** Pathology **Affiliations:** Arthur Purdy Stout Society of Surgical Pathologists; C.A.P. **Hob./spts.:** Tennis, skiing, running **SIC code:** 80 **Address:** Charleston Pathology, Dept. of Pathology, Roper Hospital, 316 Calhoun St., Charleston, SC 29401 **E-mail:** gfworsh@aol.com

WORTHINGTON-WHITE, DIANA A.
Industry: Medical **Born:** January 7, 1956, Cleveland, Ohio **Univ./degree:** M.E.d., University of Cincinnati, 1978 **Current organization:** Children's Healthcare of Atlanta **Title:** Director, Cellular Therapies Laboratory **Type of organization:** Hospital (teaching hospital of Emory University) **Major product:** Medical services, bone marrow and blood transplantation **Area of distribution:** Georgia **Area of Practice:** Cellular therapies, oncology, bone marrow transplant, pediatrics **Honors/awards:** Excellence in Research from University of Florida, 1984; International Woman of the Year, 1994; International Who's Who in Medicine, 1995; Who's Who in Science & Engineering, 1997; Who's Who in America, 1998, 2000, 2003 **Published works:** American Journal of Clinical Nutrition, International Journal of Cancer, Experimental Hematology, Blood, Progress in Clinical & Biological Research, Journal of Cellular Physiology, Cytotherapy, Clinical Immunology & Immunotherapy **Affiliations:** A.A.A.S.; A.M.W.A.; C.S.E.; Founding Member, I.S.C.T. **Hob./spts.:** Semi-professional flute player, freelance medical editor **SIC code:** 80 **Address:** Children's Healthcare of Atlanta, 1405 Clifton Rd. N.E., Atlanta, GA 30322 **E-mail:** diana.worthington-white@choa.org

WREN, V. RICK
Industry: Healthcare **Born:** August 7, 1955, Springtown, Texas **Univ./degree:** Pre-Med Studies, Western Texas University; D.C., Texas Chiropractic College, 1980 **Current organization:** Wren Chiropractic Center **Title:** President **Type of organization:** Private practice **Major product:** Chiropractic care **Area of distribution:** National **Area of Practice:** Impulse adjusting, lecturing **Honors/awards:** Centarion Award, 2001; Chiropractor of the year, 1990 **Published works:** Co-author, "Say Yes to Chiropractic Success" **Affiliations:** Chiropractic Emergency Response Volunteers; National Director, American Chiropractic Association; Texas Chiropractic Association **Hob./spts.:** Sports enthusiast **SIC code:** 80 **Address:** Wren Chiropractic Center, 4020 Texoma Pkwy., Sherman, TX 75090 **E-mail:** wren@texoma.net **Web address:** www.wrenchiropracticcenter.com

WRIGHT, FRANCES J.
Industry: Healthcare **Born:** December 22, 1943, Los Angeles, California **Univ./degree:** Ed.D., Educational Psychology, Brigham Young University, 1980 **Current organization:** Liberty Care Services **Title:** Program Manager **Type of organization:** Private mental health clinic **Major product:** Mental health services, counseling **Area of distribution:** Idaho **Area of Practice:** Staff management, program design, counseling; LCPC License, 2002 **Affiliations:** A.C.A.; A.C.L.D. **Hob./spts.:** Crafts, reading, community work **SIC code:** 80 **Address:** Liberty Care Services, , Twin Falls, ID 83301 **E-mail:** libertycare@onewest.net

WRIGHT, MARY D.
Industry: Healthcare **Born:** December 12, 1943, Wendell, North Carolina **Univ./degree:** M.D., Howard University, 1974 **Current organization:** The Family Medicine Center **Title:** M.D. **Type of organization:** Private practice **Major product:** Family practice, patient care **Area of distribution:** Bronx, New York **Area of Practice:** Family physician **Affiliations:** A.M.A. **Hob./spts.:** Gardening, gourmet cooking, interior design **SIC code:** 80 **Address:** The Family Medicine Center, 1590 Undercliff Ave., #3M, Bronx, NY 10453 **E-mail:** mwrig7@aol.com

WU, JOSEPHINE
Industry: Medical **Univ./degree:** D.D.S., University of Southern California, 1998 **Current organization:** Mount Sinai School of Medicine **Title:** Assistant Professor **Type of organization:** Academic hospital **Major product:** Patient care, medical education **Area of distribution:** National **Area of Practice:** Molecular pathology **Affiliations:** A.M.P. **SIC code:** 80 **Address:** 1324 Lexington Ave., Suite 222, New York, NY 10128 **E-mail:** josephine.wu@mssm.edu

WU, SUYING
Industry: Medical **Born:** January 7, 1955, China **Univ./degree:** M.D., Tohgji Medical University, China, 1983 **Current organization:** University of Arkansas for Medical Sciences **Title:** M.D. **Type of organization:** Medical university **Major product:** Patient care **Area of distribution:** Arkansas **Area of Practice:** Neurology **Published works:** Numerous, incuding: (1996) Potentiation of IPSCs by nitric oxide in immature rat sympathetic preganglionic neurons in vitro. J. Physiol. 495.2, 479-490; (1998) Release of nociceptin-like substances from the rat spinal cord dorsal horn. Neurosci Lett. 244(3); (1990) Characterisation of 5-HT responses in rat motoneuron. Soc. Neurosci. Abst. 16, 35.9 **Affiliations:** Society for Neuroscience; American Academy of Neurology **Hob./spts.:** Swimming **SIC code:** 80 **Address:** Elkhart Clinic, , 303 S. Nappanee St., Elkhart, IN 46514 **E-mail:** suyingw@yahoo.com

WU, WEN-CHIH HANK
Industry: Healthcare **Born:** May 9, 1971, Kaohsiung, Taiwan **Univ./degree:** M.D., University of Costa Rica, 1995 **Current organization:** Lifespan - Rhode Island Hospital **Title:** M.D. **Type of organization:** Hospital **Major product:** Medicine **Area of distribution:** Warwick, Rhode Island **Area of Practice:** Cardiology **Published works:** Article on transfusions **Affiliations:** American College of Cardiology; American College of Physicians **Hob./spts.:** Basketball, outdoor activities **SIC code:** 80 **Address:** 830 Chalkstone Ave., Providence, RI 02908 **E-mail:** wenchihwu@hotmail.com

WU, WILLIAM C.L.
Industry: Healthcare **Univ./degree:** M.D., Kaohsiung Medical University, Taiwan, 1982; M.P.H. in Epidemiology, Johns Hopkins University, 1984 **Current organization:** Central Cardiovascular Institute of San Antonio **Title:** M.D. **Type of organization:** Healthcare organization **Major product:** Patient care **Area of distribution:** San Antonio, Texas **Area of Practice:** Interventional cardiology **Published works:** Numerous articles, presentations, abstracts **Affiliations:** F.A.C.C.; F.A.C.P.; F.S.C.A.I.; President/CEO, Central Cardiovascular Institute of San Antonio; President/CEO, Heart Center of Central San Antonio; Clinical Assistant Professor, Cardiology, University of Texas Health Science Center at San Antonio; Chair, Dept. of Medicine, Texas Heart Hospital; Top Physician, Research Council of America **SIC code:** 80 **Address:** Central Cardiovascular Institute of San Antonio, 927 McCullough Ave., San Antonio, TX 78216 **E-mail:** williamclwu@msn.com

WUNDERLICH JR., RAY C.
Industry: Healthcare **Born:** August 11, 1929, St. Petersburg, Florida **Univ./degree:** M.D., Columbia College of Physicians and Surgeons, 1975; Ph.D., English Literature, University of South Florida, 2002 **Current organization:** Wunderlich Center **Title:** M.D., Ph.D. **Type of organization:** Private practice **Major product:** Patient care **Area of distribution:** Florida **Area of Practice:** Nutritional medicine **Published works:** 200+ articles and chapters, 3 books **Affiliations:** A.M.A.; Florida Medical Society **SIC code:** 80 **Address:** Wunderlich Center, 1152 94th Ave. North, St. Petersburg, FL 33702

WYNTER, CLIVE I.
Industry: Education **Born:** August 6, 1938, Kingston, Jamaica **Univ./degree:** B.S., Chemistry, McGill University, 1962; M.S., Chemistry, 1966; Ph.D., Chemistry, 1967, Howard University **Current organization:** Nassau Community College **Title:** Professor **Type of organization:** Community college **Major product:** Higher education, research **Area of distribution:** International **Area of Practice:** Organometallic compounds **Honors/awards:** Who's Who Among U.S. Teachers, 9th and 10th editions; Chancellor's Award, Scholarship for Creativity, SUNY, 2004 **Affiliations:** American Chemical Society, Division of Molecular Chemistry and Technology; Core Director, Nassau Mossbauer Conference; Sickle Cell Anemia, Nitrous Oxide Research **Hob./spts.:** Jazz, classical music, cricket, soccer, track **SIC code:** 80 **Address:** Nassau Community College, 1 Education Dr., Garden City, NY 11530 **E-mail:** wynterc@ncc.edu **Web address:** www.ncc.edu

WYSOKI, RANDEE SUE
Industry: Healthcare **Born:** June 12, 1956, New York, New York **Univ./degree:** M.D., Georgetown University, 1982 **Current organization:** Westchester Gynecologists & Obstetricians P.C. **Title:** M.D. **Type of organization:** Private practice **Major product:** Patient care **Area of distribution:** New York **Area of Practice:** Ob/Gyn **Published works:** Article **Affiliations:** A.C.O.B.G.Y.N.; A.M.A.; W.C.M.S. **Hob./spts.:** Crafts, sewing, needlepoint **SIC code:** 80 **Address:** Westchester Gynecologists & Obstetricians P.C., 170 Maple Ave., White Plains, NY 10601

YALAMANCHILI, KIRAN K.
Industry: Medical **Born:** December 4, 1974, India **Current organization:** New York Medical College/Westchester County Jail **Title:** Assistant Professor/M.D. **Type of organization:** Medical college/county jail **Major product:** Patient care, medical education **Area of distribution:** Yonkers, New York **Area of Practice:** Internal medicine, research **Affiliations:** A.C.P. **Hob./spts.:** Bicycling, skiing **SIC code:** 80 **Address:** 34 Beaumont Circle, #2, Yonkers, NY 10710 **E-mail:** yalamn@yahoo.com

YANCEY, GRACE C.
Industry: Healthcare **Born:** January 23, 1967, Richmond, Virginia **Univ./degree:** Nursing, South Regional Medical, 1997 **Current organization:** Discover Home Care **Title:** Administrator **Type of organization:** Home healthcare **Major product:** Long-term care, elder care **Area of distribution:** Virginia **Area of Practice:** Personal care **Affiliations:** Chamber of Commerce **SIC code:** 80 **Address:** Discover Home Care, 3660 Blvd., Suite E, Colonial Heights, VA 23834 **E-mail:** discoverhomecare@verizon.net

YANG, WEN C.
Industry: Healthcare **Univ./degree:** M.D., Taiwan University Medical School, 1966 **Current organization:** Beth Israel Medical Center **Title:** M.D. **Type of organization:** Hospital **Major product:** Patient care **Area of distribution:** New York City, New York **Area of Practice:** Neuroradiology, radiology **Affiliations:** A.M.A.; Radiological Society of North America; American Society of Neuroradiology; American Roentgen Ray Society; American Society of Spine Radiology; American College of Radiology **SIC code:** 80 **Address:** Beth Israel Medical Center, Dept. of Radiology, 1st Ave. at 16th St., New York, NY 10003 **E-mail:** wyang@chpnet.org

YANKAH, DE-GRAFT H.
Industry: Healthcare **Born:** January 27, 1953, Africa **Univ./degree:** M.D., University of Ghana, Africa, 1978 **Current organization:** Central Alabama Urology Services **Title:** M.D. **Type of organization:** Private practice **Major product:** Urology **Area of distribution:** Selma, Alabama **Area of Practice:** Urological surgery **Published works:** Multiple publications **Affiliations:** F.R.C.S.; A.U.A.; A.M.A.; Alabama Medical Association **Hob./spts.:** Reading, music, tennis **SIC code:** 80 **Address:** Central Alabama Urology Services, 1023 Medical Center Pkwy., Suite 310, Selma, AL 36701 **E-mail:** dhyankah@aol.com

YANONG, PROCOPIO U.
Industry: Healthcare **Born:** March 1, 1936, Cebu, Philippines **Univ./degree:** M.D., Southwest University, Philippines, 1982; Residency, Cook County, Chicago **Current organization:** Advocate Health Center **Title:** M.D., F.A.A.P. **Type of organization:** Medical facility **Major product:** Patient care **Area of distribution:** Chicago, Illinois **Area of Practice:** Pediatrics **Honors/awards:** Philanthropy Award, Am. Fed., New York **Affiliations:** American Academy of Pediatrics; Philippines Medical Association **Hob./spts.:** Boating, church activities **SIC code:** 80 **Address:** 3046 W. Hollywood Ave., Chicago, IL 60659 **E-mail:** puyanong@hotmail.com

YAO, RUIJIN
Industry: Medical **Univ./degree:** M.D., Fujin Medical University, China, 1982; Ph.D., Microbiology, Immunology, Wayne State University, 1991 **Current organization:** Montefiore Medical Center, The University Hospital for the Albert Einstein College of Medicine **Title:** M.D., Ph.D. **Type of organization:** University hospital **Major product:** Medical services; academic program of residency training **Area of distribution:** National **Area of Practice:** Physical medicine and rehabilitation **Published works:** 2 book chapters **Affiliations:** A.A.P.M.R.; A.B.E.D.M.; A.S.I.P.P. **SIC code:** 80 **Address:** Montefiore Medical Center, 111 E. 210th St., Bronx, NY 10467 **E-mail:** ruijinyao@yahoo.com

YASMIN, SARAH
Industry: Medical **Born:** July 18, 1974, Lahore, Pakistan **Univ./degree:** M.D., Aga Khan University, Karachi, Pakistan, 1997; M.S. Candidate, Public Health, University of Massachusetts **Current organization:** University of Massachusetts Medical School **Title:** M.D. **Type of organization:** University hospital **Major product:** Patient care **Area of distribution:** Worcester, Massachusetts **Area of Practice:** Psychiatry **Published works:** Co-authored book: "Biological Psychiatry", 3 articles **Affiliations:** A.P.A.; M.P.S.; P.M.D.C. (Pakistani association) **Hob./spts.:** Biking, reading, swimming **SIC code:** 80 **Address:** University of Massachusetts Medical School, Office of Psychiatric Education, 55 Lake Ave. North, Worcester, MA 01655 **E-mail:** syasmin@bigfoot.com

YASSIN, MONA
Industry: Healthcare **Born:** 1954, Suez, Egypt **Univ./degree:** M.D. **Current organization:** Sunshine Pediatrics, Inc. **Title:** M.D., Owner **Type of organization:** Private practice **Major product:** Patient care **Area of distribution:** St. Louis, Missouri **Area of Practice:** Pediatrics **Honors/awards:** Fellowship, Washington University **Affiliations:** A.A.P.; American Medical Association **Hob./spts.:** Travel, home improvement **SIC code:** 80 **Address:** Sunshine Pediatrics, Inc., 3009 N. Ballas Rd., Suite 259C, St. Louis, MO 63131-2322 **E-mail:** drmona@cbn.stl.com

YAVORKOVSKY, LEONID L.
Industry: Healthcare **Born:** March 8, 1955, Riga, Latvia **Univ./degree:** M.D., Riga Medical Institute, Latvia, 1978; Ph.D., Hematology, 1985; D.Med.Sci., 1993, Latvian Hematology Academy of Medicine **Current organization:** The Permanente Medical Group, Inc. **Title:** MD, PhD **Type of organization:** Hospital **Major product:** Patient care **Area of distribution:** California **Area of Practice:** Oncology, hematology **Affiliations:** American Society of Hematology **Hob./spts.:** Music, stamp collecting **SIC code:** 80 **Address:** The Permanente Medical Group, Inc., 270 International Circle, San Jose, CA 95119 **E-mail:** yav_leo@hotmail.com

YE, JIAN JIM
Industry: Healthcare **Born:** May 9, 1962, Shanghai, China **Univ./degree:** M.D., Shanghai Medical University **Current organization:** Laser & Skin Disease Center **Title:** M.D. **Type of organization:** Medical office **Major product:** Skin laser surgery **Area of distribution:** Los Angeles, California **Area of Practice:** Laser medicine and surgery **Affiliations:** A.C.O.P.; A.A.D. **Hob./spts.:** Swimming **SIC code:** 80 **Address:** Laser & Skin Disease Center, 1950 Sawtelle Blvd., Suite 145, Los Angeles, CA 90025

YEH, MING-NENG
Industry: Medical **Born:** October 13, 1938, Taiwan **Univ./degree:** M.D., National Taiwan University School of Medicine, 1964 **Current organization:** Columbia University/New York Presbyterian Medical Center **Title:** M.D. **Type of organization:** University hospital **Major product:** Medical services **Area of distribution:** National **Area of Practice:** Obstetrics, gynecology **Published works:** 25+ articles, 1 book chapter **Affiliations:** F.A.C.O.G.; New York Academy of Medicine **Hob./spts.:** Reading, swimming, music **SIC code:** 80 **Address:** Columbia University/New York Presbyterian Medical Center, 161 Fort Washington Ave., Suite 621, New York, NY 10032

YOUNG, ANGELA M.
Industry: Healthcare **Univ./degree:** B.A., Business Administration, Hanover College **Current organization:** Thorton Terrance Health Campus **Title:** Executive Director **Type of organization:** Assisted living facility **Major product:** Long-term care **Area of distribution:** Hanover, Indiana **Area of Practice:** Business **Affiliations:** Chamber of Commerce **SIC code:** 80 **Address:** Thorton Terrance Health Campus, 188 Thornton Rd., Hanover, IN 47143

YOUNG, MELVIN W.
Industry: Healthcare **Born:** January 7, 1938, New York **Univ./degree:** M.D., Chicago Medical School, 1963 **Current organization:** Long Island Cardiology Group **Title:** M.D. **Type of organization:** Private practice **Major product:** Patient care **Area of distribution:** Long Island, New York **Area of Practice:** Cardiovascular disease **Honors/awards:** First Honorary Humanitarian Award, St. John's Episcopal Hospital **Published works:** 14+ articles **Affiliations:** A.C.C.; A.C.P.; New York Cardiology Society; President, Medical Board, St. John's Episcopal Hospital **Hob./spts.:** Music, tennis, skiing **SIC code:** 80 **Address:** Long Island Cardiology Group, 123 Grove Ave., Cedarhurst, NY 11516 **E-mail:** melyoung38@hotmail.com

YOUNG, SARAH M.
Industry: Consulting/health **Born:** June 10, 1947, Galveston, Texas **Univ./degree:** Ed.D., Ph.D., California Coast University, 1989 **Current organization:** Successno Therapy ™ **Title:** Founder **Type of organization:** Consulting **Major product:** Hypnotherapy, success and health products and technology for success **Area of distribu-**

tion: National **Area of Practice:** Hypnotherapy success coaching **Published works:** Articles **Affiliations:** National Association of Female Executives; Associate, A.S.B.S. **SIC code:** 80 **Address:** Successno Therapy ™, Next Generation Business Resources, (Productivity Telecommunications Products), 10257 Trails End Circle, San Diego, CA 92126-3517 **E-mail:** sarah@drsarahmyoung.net **Web address:** www.drsarahmyoung.net

YOUNG III, SAMUEL D.
Industry: Healthcare **Born:** April 1, 1973, El Paso, Texas **Univ./degree:** M.D., University of Texas Southwestern Medical School, 1999 **Current organization:** Hospital of the University of Pennsylvania **Title:** M.D. **Type of organization:** Hospital **Major product:** Patient care **Area of distribution:** Philadelphia, Pennsylvania **Area of Practice:** Orthopedic surgery **Affiliations:** American Academy of Orthopedic Surgeons; Pennsylvania Medical Society **Hob./spts.:** Golf, skiing, drawing, playing guitar, recreational flying **SIC code:** 80 **Address:** 204 Valley Forge Lookout Place, Radnor, PA 19087 **E-mail:** young.sam@att.net

YOUNGERMAN, JAY S.
Industry: Healthcare **Born:** April 12, 1954, Bronx, New York **Univ./degree:** M.D., Medical College of Virginia, 1979 **Current organization:** Long Island ENT Associates **Title:** M.D. **Type of organization:** Medical practice **Major product:** ENT services **Area of distribution:** New York **Area of Practice:** Otolaryngology, head and neck surgery **Affiliations:** Fellow, American College of Surgeons; Past President, Long Island Society of Otolaryngology Head & Neck Surgery; Board of Governors; A.A.O.H.N.S.; Chief Division of Otolaryngology, North Shore University Hospital at Plainview **Hob./spts.:** Tennis, art collecting **SIC code:** 80 **Address:** Long Island ENT Associates, 875 Old Country Road, Plainview, NY 11803 **E-mail:** jyent@aol.com

YOVANOF, SILVANA
Industry: Healthcare **Univ./degree:** M.D., American University of the Caribbean, 1985 **Current organization:** Medical & Endocrinology Associates, P.C. **Title:** M.D. **Type of organization:** Medical practice **Major product:** Medical services **Area of distribution:** Pennsylvania **Area of Practice:** Medicine, endocrinology **Affiliations:** American College of Physicians; A.S.C.E. **Hob./spts.:** Travel **SIC code:** 80 **Address:** Medical & Endocrinology Associates, P.C., 420 W. Main St., Monongahela, PA 15063 **E-mail:** syovanof@ipninet.com

YURASEK, FRANK A.
Industry: Healthcare **Born:** October 30, 1939 **Univ./degree:** B.A., 1961; M.A., 1963, University of Notre Dame; Ph.D., Mid West College, Guangzhou University of China, 2002 **Current organization:** Eastern Wellness Group, Inc. **Title:** President **Type of organization:** Alternative medicine clinic **Major product:** Patient care **Area of distribution:** Chicago, Illinois and South Bend, Indiana **Area of Practice:** Acupuncture/herbs, teaching **Published works:** Publisher, Oriental Medicine Journal **Affiliations:** President, American Board of Eastern Medicine; Past Director of Education, National Qi Gong Association; Professional Member, American Herbalist Guild; Member, Japanese oriental Medicine Society; Professor, Midwest College of Oriental medicine **SIC code:** 80 **Address:** Eastern Wellness Group, Inc., 7773 Lake St., River Forest, IL 60305 **E-mail:** eastwell@ameritech.net

ZABUKOVEC, DALE M.
Industry: Healthcare **Born:** October 27, 1951, Cleveland, Ohio **Univ./degree:** B.S., Biology, Cleveland State University, 1974; Medical Technology, Mt. Sinai School of Medical Technology, 1975 **Current organization:** Euclid Hospital **Title:** Team Leader **Type of organization:** Hospital **Major product:** Patient care **Area of distribution:** Euclid, Ohio **Area of Practice:** Medical Laboratory Testing, including C.A.P. Standards Inspector and Medical Technical Writing **Published works:** "The Effect of a Clot-Promoting Reagent in Therapeutic Drug Monitoring of Theophylline and Digoxin", 1993, ITC Commercial Group **Affiliations:** American Society of Clinical Pathologists (104968); College of American Pathologists; Society for Technical Communications **Hob./spts.:** Racquetball, sailing, skiing, refinishing antiques **SIC code:** 80 **Address:** Euclid Hospital, 18901 Lake Shore Rd., Laboratory, first floor, Euclid, OH 44119 **E-mail:** dzabukov@cchseast.org and dmzabukovec@hotmail.com **Web address:** www.cchseast.org

ZALDUONDO DUBNER, FERNANDO M.
Industry: Healthcare **Born:** November 13, 1963, Killen, Texas **Children:** Andrés, 10; Pablo, 6 **Univ./degree:** B.A., Psychology, Cum Laude, Princeton University, 1985; M.D., Columbia College of Physicians & Surgeons, 1989 **Current organization:** San Patricio MRI & CT Center **Title:** Medical Director/Owner **Type of organization:** Medical office/imaging center **Major product:** Perform and interpret advanced computed tomography and magnetic resonance imaging studies **Area of distribution:** San Juan, Puerto Rico **Area of Practice:** Neuroradiology **Honors/awards:** Caribbean Business 40 under 40 Award, 2003 **Affiliations:** President, Sociedad Radiológica de Puerto Rico; Senior Member, American Society of Neuroradiology; Neuroradiology MR-accredited, Clinical Magnetic Resonance Society; Radiological Society of North America; Colegio de Médicos-Cirujanos de Puerto Rico; American Roentgen Ray Society; American College of Radiology; American Medical Association **Hob./spts.:** Race car driving **SIC code:** 80 **Address:** San Patricio MRI & CT Center, 1508 Roosevelt Ave., Suite 103, San Juan, PR 00920 **E-mail:** zalduondo@sanpatriciomrict.com

ZAPARINUK, BELINDA L.
Industry: Healthcare **Born:** October 21, 1964, Pittsburg, Kansas **Univ./degree:** A.S., Labbette Community College, Parsons, Kansas, 1985 **Current organization:** John F. Kennedy Hospital, Indio, CA **Title:** R.T. (R)(M) **Type of organization:** Hospital **Major product:** Patient care/education **Area of distribution:** California **Area of Practice:** Mammography; teaching physicians, technologists and patient education and awareness of breast care **Honors/awards:** Chairperson, Breast Imaging Symposium **Published works:** 2 articles for Breast Imaging Symposium **Affiliations:** A.R.R.T.; C.R.T.; American Society Radiologic Technology **Hob./spts.:** Rock climbing, travel, music **SIC code:** 80 **Address:** 79-095 Kristen Ct., La Quinta, CA 92253 **E-mail:** zapfest1@aol.com

ZAPATA ROSARIO, ARNALDO IVAN
Industry: Healthcare **Born:** May 31, 1959, New York, New York **Univ./degree:** B.S., Biology, University of Puerto Rico at Mayaguez, 1980; M.D., Ponce School of Medicine, Puerto Rico, 1984 **Current organization:** Hospital Santa Rosa **Title:** Director of Invasive and Non-Invasive Cardiology **Type of organization:** In hospital private practice **Major product:** Patient care **Area of distribution:** Puerto Rico **Area of Practice:** Invasive and non-invasive cardiology, internal medicine **Published works:** 3 articles **Affiliations:** A.M.A. **Hob./spts.:** Scuba diving, community volunteering, missionary travel and free healthcare overseas **SIC code:** 80 **Address:** Hospital Santa Rosa, Invasive and Non-invasive Cardiology Dept's., Avenida Los Veteranos, Guayama, PR 00785 **E-mail:** arnaldozapata@yahoo.com

ZAPPASODI, JOSEPH V.
Industry: Healthcare **Born:** June 3, 1933, Philadelphia, Pennsylvania **Univ./degree:** B.S., Temple University School of Pharmacy, 1954; D.O., Philadelphia College of Osteopathic Medicine, 1967 **Current organization:** Joseph V. Zappasodi, D.O. **Title:** Physician **Type of organization:** Solo practice **Major product:** Patient care **Area of distribution:** New Jersey **Area of Practice:** General medicine/geriatrics; Past Medical Director, Correctional Medicine Dept. of Corrections State of New Jersey **Honors/awards:** Courier Post Award, 1997 "One of the Best Doctors in South Jersey" **Affiliations:** A.O.A.; N.J.O.A.; N.J.T.B.A. **Hob./spts.:** Thoroughbred owner, trainer, breeder race horse, football, baseball **SIC code:** 80 **Address:** Joseph V. Zappasodi, D.O., 198 Jarvis Rd., Sicklerville, NJ 08081 **E-mail:** www.JZappasodi@aol.com

ZASADIL, MARY LEE
Industry: Medical **Born:** December 14, 1966, Waukegan, Illinois **Univ./degree:** B.S., Biology, Northern Illinois University, 1989; M.D., St. George's University School of Medicine at Grenada, 1998 **Current organization:** University of Wisconsin at Madison **Title:** M.D. **Type of organization:** University hospital **Major product:** Medical services **Area of distribution:** Wisconsin **Area of Practice:** Cardiology **Published works:** 1 article **Affiliations:** A.M.A.; A.C.C. **Hob./spts.:** Biking, skiing **SIC code:** 80 **Address:** University of Wisconsin at Madison, Dept. of Cardiology, 600 Highland Ave., Madison, WI 53792

ZELKOWITZ, MARVIN
Industry: Healthcare **Born:** December 9, 1944, Brooklyn, New York **Univ./degree:** M.D., Medical College of Virginia, 1970 **Current organization:** South Suburban Neurology, Ltd. **Title:** President **Type of organization:** Medical practice **Major product:** Patient care **Area of distribution:** Flossmoor, Illinois **Area of Practice:** Neurology **Published works:** Multiple publications **Affiliations:** A.M.D.A.; A.A.N.; C.N.S.; A.A.P. **Hob./spts.:** Trains, guitar, skiing **SIC code:** 80 **Address:** South Suburban Neurology, Ltd., 3235 Vollmer Rd., Suite 110, Flossmoor, IL 60422 **E-mail:** marvzelk@hotmail.com

ZELMAN, VLADIMIR
Industry: Medical **Born:** October 17, 1935, Ukraine **Univ./degree:** Ph.D., Siberia **Current organization:** Keck School of Medicine, University of Southern California **Title:** M.D., Ph.D., Clinical Chairman **Type of organization:** University hospital **Major product:** Patient care, medical education **Area of distribution:** Los Angeles, California **Area of Practice:** Anesthesiology, critical care **Affiliations:** A.A.N.S.; California Society of Anesthesiologists **Hob./spts.:** Swimming, archeology **SIC code:** 80 **Address:** Keck School of Medicine, University of Southern California, 1200 N. State St., Los Angeles, CA 90033 **E-mail:** vzelman@usc.edu

ZELMAN, VLADIMIR L.

Industry: Medical **Born:** October 17, 1935, Skvira, Ukraine **Univ./degree:** M.D.,1959; Ph.D., 1965, Novo Si Birsk Medical School, Siberia **Current organization:** USC Keck School of Medicine **Title:** M.D./Clinical Chairman/Professor **Type of organization:** University medical school **Major product:** Medical services **Area of distribution:** California **Area of Practice:** Anesthesiology **Published works:** Multiple publications **Affiliations:** A.S.A.; C.S.A. **Hob./spts.:** History, art, swimming, travel **SIC code:** 80 **Address:** USC Keck School of Medicine, Dept. of Anesthesiology, 1200 N. State St., Los Angeles, CA 90033

ZHANG, JING

Industry: Healthcare **Born:** December 27, 1960, Shung Hai, China **Univ./degree:** M.D., Shung Hai Medical University, 1983 **Current organization:** Staten Island Medical Group **Title:** M.D. **Type of organization:** Medical group **Major product:** Patient care **Area of distribution:** Staten Island, New York **Area of Practice:** Internal medicine **Honors/awards:** Resident of the Year, St. Vincent's Medical Center, N.Y. Medical College, 1997 **Affiliations:** A.C.P.; Richmond Medical Society **Hob./spts.:** Dancing, home decorating **SIC code:** 80 **Address:** Staten Island Medical Group, 1050 Clove Rd., Staten Island, NY 10301

ZHANG, MANCONG

Industry: Healthcare **Born:** June 28, 1965, China **Univ./degree:** M.D., Shanghai Medical School, China, 1985; Residency and Fellowship, Massachusetts General Hospital, 2003 **Current organization:** InCyte Pathology **Title:** M.D./Pathologist **Type of organization:** Pathology laboratory **Major product:** Anatomic and clinical pathology, dermatopathology services **Area of distribution:** Washington **Area of Practice:** Pathology **Published works:** Peer-reviewed articles in medical journals **Affiliations:** College of American Pathologists; Washington State Pathology Association **Hob./spts.:** Reading, cooking, gardening, travel **SIC code:** 80 **Address:** InCyte Pathology, 13103 E. Mansfield, P.O. Box 3405, Spokane, WA 99220-3405 **E-mail:** mzhang@incytepathology.com

ZIAS, ELIAS A.

Industry: Medical **Born:** June 6, 1962, Greece **Univ./degree:** M.D., New York Medical College, 1989 **Current organization:** Westchester Medical Center/New York Medical College **Title:** M.D. **Type of organization:** Hospital/medical school **Major product:** Patient care, medical education **Area of distribution:** National **Area of Practice:** Cardiothoracic Surgery **Affiliations:** F.A.C.S.; F.A.C.C.; S.T.S. **SIC code:** 80 **Address:** Westchester Medical Center/New York Medical College, Macy Pavilion, 95 Grasslands Rd., Suite 114, Valhalla, NY 10595 **E-mail:** ziase@wcmc.com

ZIEM, GRACE E.

Industry: Healthcare **Born:** November 17, 1943, Marshfield, Wisconsin **Univ./degree:** M.D., University of Kansas School of Medicine, 1967; M.P.H., Johns Hopkins University, 1971; D.P.H., Harvard University School of Public Health, 1977 **Current organization:** Grace E. Ziem, M.D., D.P.H. **Title:** Occupational Medicine Physician **Type of organization:** Private practice **Major product:** Patient care, teaching, preventing chemical injury **Area of distribution:** National **Area of Practice:** Treating chemically injured patients, toxicology, medicine and biochemistry of healing chemical injury, international expert **Affiliations:** American Public Health Association; Society for Occupational and Environmental Health **Hob./spts.:** Music, reading, nature **SIC code:** 80 **Address:** Grace E. Ziem, M.D., D.P.H., 16926 Eylers Valley Rd., Emmitsburg, MD 21727 **Web address:** www.chemicalinjury.net

ZIMMER, MICHAEL A.

Industry: Healthcare **Born:** December 5, 1963, New York, New York **Univ./degree:** M.D., Jefferson Medical College, 1989 **Current organization:** Michael A. Zimmer, M.D. **Title:** M.D. **Type of organization:** Private practice **Major product:** Patient care **Area of distribution:** St. Petersburg, Florida **Area of Practice:** Internal medicine **Affiliations:** A.C.P.; A.M.A.; F.M.A. **Hob./spts.:** Golf, flying, running **SIC code:** 80 **Address:** Michael A. Zimmer, M.D., 1099 5th Ave. N., Suite 110, St. Petersburg, FL 33705

ZIMMERMAN II, G. RICHARD

Industry: Healthcare **Born:** January 21, 1968, Washington, Pennsylvania **Univ./degree:** M.D., Hahnemann University, Pennsylvania **Current organization:** Pittsburgh Internal Medicine Associates **Title:** M.D. **Type of organization:** Medical practice **Major product:** Patient care **Area of distribution:** Pittsburgh, Pennsylvania **Area of Practice:** Internal medicine **Affiliations:** A.M.A. **Hob./spts.:** Running, snow skiing **SIC code:** 80 **Address:** Pittsburgh Internal Medicine Associates, 3089 Sussex Ave., Pittsburgh, PA 15226

ZOROWITZ, RICHARD D.

Industry: Medical **Born:** November 23, 1958, Teaneck, New Jersey **Spouse:** Candace Stair **Married:** June 25, 1989 **Children:** Sam, 11; Joel, 9 **Univ./degree:** B.S., Northwestern University, 1981; M.D., Tulane University, 1985; Internship, Internal Medicine at the Long Island Jewish Medical Center; Residency, Northwestern University, 1989 **Current organization:** University of Pennsylvania **Title:** M.D./Director of Stroke Rehabilitation/Medical Director of the Piersol Rehabilitation Unit/Associate Professor of Physical Medicine and Rehabilitation **Type of organization:** University hospital **Major product:** Medical services **Area of distribution:** Pennsylvania **Area of Practice:** Physical medicine and rehabilitation **Honors/awards:** Excellence in Stroke Education Citation, National Stroke Association, 2000; Recognition Award, University of Pennsylvania Stroke Center, Southeastern Pennsylvania Region of the American Stroke Association, 2001; Inducted into Visionary in Practice Society of the National Stroke Association, 2001; Outstanding Leadership Award, American Stroke Association, Southeastern Pennsylvania Region, 2002; Who's Who in America, 2002, 2003; Top Doctors in America, 2002; Who's Who in Science and Engineering, 2003; Best Doctors, 2002, 2004; Who's Who in Medicine & Healthcare, 2004 **Published works:** Articles in peer reviewed journals; Book chapters about stroke rehabilitation **Affiliations:** A.A.P.M&.R.; A.A.P.; American Heart Association Stroke Council; Chair, Rehabilitation & Professional Advisory Boards of the National Stroke Association **Career accomplishments:** He has research interests in rehabilitation outcomes, dysphagia, spasticity and the hemiplegic shoulder. He currently is researching effects of percutaneous intramuscular stimulation for post-stroke glenohumeral subluxation, treatment of intrathecal baclofen for post-stroke spasticity and the effectiveness of post-stroke rehabilitation. **Hob./spts.:** Music, theatre, camping **SIC code:** 80 **Address:** University of Pennsylvania, 5 W. Gates 3400 Spruce St., Philadelphia, PA 19104 **E-mail:** richard.zorowitz@uphs.upenn.edu **Web address:** php.med.upenn.edu/providers/index.pcgi?scre

ZYADEH, NADIM T.

Industry: Medical **Born:** June 9, 1970, Beirut, Lebanon **Univ./degree:** M.D., Lebanon University, 1996 **Current organization:** SUNY Downstate Medical Center **Title:** M.D. **Type of organization:** University **Major product:** Patient care **Area of distribution:** Staten Island, New York **Area of Practice:** Gastroenterology **Published works:** Papers **Affiliations:** A.G.A.; A.S.G.E. **Hob./spts.:** Tennis, skiing **SIC code:** 80 **Address:** SUNY Downstate Medical Center, 74 Jefferson Ave., Staten Island, NY 10306 **E-mail:** nade60@aol.com

ZYLSTRA, SAMUEL

Industry: Medical **Born:** July 5, 1948, Sneek, Holland **Univ./degree:** M.D., University of Europe, 1980; M.S., Public Health, University of Massachusetts, 1999 **Current organization:** Milford Regional Medical Center, University of Massachusetts **Title:** Physician **Type of organization:** University medical center **Major product:** Patient care, education **Area of distribution:** National **Area of Practice:** Obstetrics, gynecology, urogynecology **Affiliations:** I.S.P.I.N.; I.S.N.M.; V.A.U.A.; American College of Obstetricians and Gynecologists **Hob./spts.:** Gardening, reading **SIC code:** 80 **Address:** Milford Regional Medical Center, University of Massachusetts, 140 Sutton St., Uxbridge, MA 01569 **E-mail:** szylstra@milreg.org

Legal Services

ALLEN, THOMAS PHILIP
Industry: Law **Born:** February 15, 1943, New York, New York **Univ./degree:** B.S., Union College, New York, 1964; J.D., Southwestern University School of Law, California, 1978 **Current organization:** The Law Office of Thomas P. Allen **Title:** Attorney at Law **Type of organization:** Law firm **Major product:** Legal services **Area of distribution:** Florida **Area of Practice:** Social Security disability law **Affiliations:** F.B.A.; L.P.B.A.; N.O.S.S.C.R.; Served in active duty, U.S. Air Force and U.S. Army; Retired as Lieutenant Colonel **Hob./spts.:** Commercial piloting **SIC code:** 81 **Address:** The Law Office of Thomas P. Allen, P.O. Box 81-4612, Hollywood, FL 33020 **E-mail:** dibattorney@aol.com

ALMARAZ JR., ROSENDO
Industry: Law **Born:** October 27, 1973, Weslaco, Texas **Univ./degree:** J.D., St. Mary's University, San Antonio, Texas **Current organization:** The Almaraz Law Firm **Title:** Attorney **Type of organization:** Law firm **Major product:** Legal services **Area of distribution:** International **Area of Practice:** Personal injury litigation **Published works:** Journals, papers **Affiliations:** T.T.L.A.; S.T.L.A.; A.B.A.; H.C.B.A.; C.C.B.A.; T.S.B.A. **Hob./spts.:** Football, art collecting, golf, music **SIC code:** 81 **Address:** The Almaraz Law Firm, 260 S. Texas Blvd., Suite 300, Weslaco, TX 78596 **E-mail:** rajr@almadrazlaw.com

AMARO JR., LUIS J.
Industry: Law **Born:** November 12, 1972, Jersey City, New Jersey **Univ./degree:** J.D., Boston College, !997 **Current organization:** Cole, Schotz, Meisel, Forman & Leonard, P.A. **Title:** Attorney **Type of organization:** Law firm **Major product:** Legal services **Area of distribution:** National **Area of Practice:** Litigation, personal injury, labor litigation **Affiliations:** A.B.A.; New Jersey Bar Association; North Hudson Lawyers Club **Hob./spts.:** Travel **SIC code:** 81 **Address:** Cole, Schotz, Meisel, Forman & Leonard, P.A., 25 Main St., Hackensack, NJ 07602 **E-mail:** lamaro@coleschotz.com

ANDERSON, LARA
Industry: Law **Born:** August 19, 1967, Chicago, Illinois **Univ./degree:** J.D., Northern Illinois University College of Law, 1992 **Current organization:** Tressler, Soderstrom, Maloney & Priess, LLP **Title:** Attorney **Type of organization:** Law firm **Major product:** Legal services **Area of distribution:** Bolingbrook, Illinois **Area of Practice:** Condominium and municipal law **Affiliations:** A.B.A.; Illinois State Bar Association; School Board Council **SIC code:** 81 **Address:** Tressler, Soderstrom, Maloney & Priess, LLP, 305 W. Briarcliff Rd., Suite 201, Bolingbrook, IL 60440 **E-mail:** landerson@tsmp.com

ANWYL-DAVIES, MARCUS J.
Industry: Law **Univ./degree:** M.A., Christ Church, Oxford **Title:** His Honour Judge: Appointment: Queen's Counsel **Type of organization:** Law **Major product:** Judiciary duties **Area of distribution:** National **Area of Practice:** Civil litigation, arbitration **Honors/awards:** President, Her Majesty's Council of Circuit Judges, 1990 **Published works:** "False Imprisonment and Malicious Persecution", Halsbury's Laws of England, 2nd Edition; "Agency", Halsbury's Encyclopedia of Forms and Precedents **Affiliations:** Fellow of the Chartered Institute of Arbitrators; Honourable Society of the Inner Temple **SIC code:** 81 **Address:** 16624 Calle Arbolada, Pacific Palisades, CA 90272-1923

ARANEDA, JORGELINA E.
Industry: Law **Born:** January 11, 1962, Rosario, Argentina **Univ./degree:** J.D., University of North Carolina, 1989; LL.M., George Washington University, 1992 **Current organization:** Araneda Law Firm **Title:** Attorney **Type of organization:** Law firm **Major product:** Legal services **Area of distribution:** International **Area of Practice:** Immigration law **Honors/awards:** 2004 Business Woman of the Year by NRCC Business Advisory Council **Affiliations:** A.B.A.; American Immigration Lawyers Association; North Carolina State Bar Association **SIC code:** 81 **Address:** Araneda Law Firm, 4600 Marriott Dr., Suite 35, Raleigh, NC 27612 **E-mail:** JEA@aranedalaw.com **Web address:** www.aranedalaw.com

ARBIDE, Z. SUZANNE
Industry: Law **Born:** March 21, 1956, Lima, Peru **Univ./degree:** J.D., University of Miami, 1997 **Current organization:** Pyszka Blackmon Levy Mowers & Kelley **Title:** Attorney **Type of organization:** Law firm **Major product:** Legal services **Area of distribution:** Florida **Area of Practice:** State and Federal civil litigation, insurance coverage, errors and omissions, commercial litigation, community association **Affiliations:** The Florida Bar; American Bar Association; Dade County Defense Bar Association **Hob./spts.:** Playing guitar and flute **SIC code:** 81 **Address:** Pyszka Blackmon Levy Mowers & Kelley, 14750 N.W. 77th Ct., Suite 300, Miami Lakes, FL 33016 **E-mail:** sarbide@pblmklaw.com **Web address:** www.pblmklaw.lawoffice.com

ARDALAN, P. CHRISTOPHER
Industry: Law **Born:** August 26, 1973, Iran **Univ./degree:** B.A., California State University at Northridge; J.D., Loyola University **Current organization:** Ardalan & Associates **Title:** President **Type of organization:** Law firm **Major product:** Litigation **Area of distribution:** California **Area of Practice:** Criminal and family law **Hob./spts.:** Children's basketball **SIC code:** 81 **Address:** Ardalan & Associates, 15060 Ventura Blvd., Suite 201, Sherman Oaks, CA 91403 **E-mail:** pca@ardalanlaw.com **Web address:** www.ardalanlaw.com

ASHNAULT, WALLACE F.
Industry: Law **Born:** March 26, 1932, North Conway, New Hampshire **Univ./degree:** J.D., Boston University School of Law **Current organization:** Wickins & Ashnault **Title:** Attorney **Type of organization:** Law firm (since 1958) **Major product:** Legal services **Area of distribution:** New York **Area of Practice:** Estate planning **Honors/awards:** "AV" rated, Martindale-Hubbell **Affiliations:** New York State Bar; American Bar Association **Hob./spts.:** Skiing, golf, tennis, hunting **SIC code:** 81 **Address:** Wickins & Ashnault, 1828 Penfield Rd., Penfield, NY 14526

ASHTON, FRANK A.
Industry: Law **Born:** Santa Monica, California **Univ./degree:** B.A., Magna Cum Laude, University of California, 1979; J.D. with High Honors, University of Florida, 1986 **Current organization:** Peek, Cobb, Edwards & Ashton, P.A. **Title:** Partner **Type of organization:** Law firm **Major product:** Legal services **Area of distribution:** National **Area of Practice:** Personal Injury, Medical Malpractice, Nursing Home Negligence, Insurance Litigation, Products Liability, Automobile Accidents and Injuries; Admitted: 1986, Florida and U.S. District Court, Southern and Middle Districts of Florida; 1992, U.S. Court of Appeals, Eleventh Circuit **Honors/awards:** AV Peer Review rated by Martindale-Hubbell; Order of the Coif; Phi Kappa Phi; Recipient, American Jurisprudence Awards in Civil Procedure, Contracts and Property Law; Articles Editor, University of Florida Law Review, 1986; Assistant State Attorney, Fourth Judicial Circuit, 1988-91; Felony Division Chief and Homicide Prosecutor; Chairman, Jacksonville Historic Preservation Commission; Queens Council, American College of Barristers **Affiliations:** Jacksonville Bar Association; American Bar Association; The Florida Bar; Association of Trial Lawyers of America; Academy of Florida Trial Lawyers; Jacksonville Trial Lawyers Association (Sec./Treas., 2001-02; President, 2003); National Association of Elder Law Attorneys; Million Dollar Advocates Forum (Member); Military: Commander, U.S. Navy Reserves (Retired) **SIC code:** 81 **Address:** Peek, Cobb, Edwards & Ashton, P.A., 1301 Riverplace Blvd., Suite 1609, Jacksonville, FL 32207 **Web address:** www.peekcobb.com

AWAD, JOSEPH P.
Industry: Law **Born:** September 26, 1954, Oneida, New York **Univ./degree:** J.D., Union University Albany Law School, 1981 **Current organization:** Silberstein, Awad & Miklos, P.C. **Title:** Senior Partner **Type of organization:** Law firm **Major product:** Trial and appellate civil litigation **Area of distribution:** New York **Area of Practice:** Medical malpractice, complex personal injury, matrimonial **Affiliations:** V.P., New York State Trial Lawyers Association; Member, Board of Directors, National Crime Victims Association; Officer/Director, Long Island Affiliate **Hob./spts.:** Tennis, travel **SIC code:** 81 **Address:** Silberstein, Awad & Miklos, P.C., 600 Old Country Rd., Garden City, NY 11530 **E-mail:** jawad@askysam.net

BADAWI, SUZANNE
Industry: Law **Born:** November 20, 1971, Beruit, Lebannon **Univ./degree:** B.A., Philosophy, University of Maryland, 1993; J.D., Syracuse University, 1996 **Current organization:** Luce, Forward, Hamilton & Scripps LLP **Title:** Attorney **Type of organization:** Law firm **Major product:** Legal services **Area of distribution:** California **Area of Practice:** Business and commercial law, bankruptcy work, insurance litigation **Published works:** Multiple articles; One publication-" For The Record" **Affiliations:** A.B.A. **Hob./spts.:** Tennis, lacrosse, screen play writing **SIC code:** 81 **Address:** Luce, Forward, Hamilton & Scripps LLP, 777 S. Figueroa St., Suite 3600, Los Angeles, CA 90017 **E-mail:** suzbadawi@yahoo.com

BAGLEY III, PHILIP J.
Industry: Law **Born:** November 24, 1941, Richmond, Virginia **Univ./degree:** B.A., University of Richmond, 1963; J.D., University of Virginia, 1966 **Current organization:** Troutman Sanders LLP **Title:** Partner **Type of organization:** Law firm **Major product:** Legal services **Area of distribution:** National **Area of Practice:** Commercial real estate law **Honors/awards:** "AV" rated, Martindale-Hubbell **Published works:** 12 law review articles **Affiliations:** Immediate Past Chairman, American Bar Association, Section of Real Property, Probate and Trust Law; President, Richmond Real Estate Group; Past President, A.C.R.E.L. **SIC code:** 81 **Address:** Troutman Sanders LLP, 1111 E. Main St., Richmond, VA 23219 **E-mail:** phil.bagley@troutmansanders.com **Web address:** www.troutmansanders.com

BAKER JR., WALTER W.
Industry: Law **Born:** July 27, 1942, Raleigh, North Carolina **Univ./degree:** J.D., University of North Carolina at Chapel Hill **Current organization:** Baker Law Offices **Title:** Attorney/Founder **Type of organization:** Law firm **Major product:** Legal services/justice **Area of distribution:** High Point, North Carolina **Affiliations:** Past President, North Carolina Trial Lawyers Association; N.B.L.; A.T.L.A.; A.B.A. **Hob./**

spts.: Teaching **SIC code:** 81 **Address:** Baker Law Offices, 820 N. Elm St., High Point, NC 27262 **E-mail:** bbbaker@northstate.net

BALDWIN, EDWIN S.
Industry: Law **Born:** May 5, 1932, St. Louis, Missouri **Univ./degree:** LL.B., Harvard Law School, 1957 **Current organization:** Armstrong Teasdale LLP **Title:** Of Counsel **Type of organization:** Law firm **Major product:** Legal services **Area of distribution:** Missouri **Area of Practice:** Estate and trust **Affiliations:** A.C.T.E.C.; A.B.A.; M.O.B.A. **Hob./spts.:** Golf, bridge **SIC code:** 81 **Address:** Armstrong Teasdale LLP, 1 Metropolitan Square, Suite 2600, St. Louis, MO 63102 **E-mail:** tbaldwin@armstrongteasdale.com **Web address:** www.armstrongteasdale.com

BALLIRO, JULIANE
Industry: Law **Born:** August 1, 1956, Cambridge, Massachusetts **Univ./degree:** J.D., Boston College, 1981 **Current organization:** Perkins, Smith & Cohen, LLP **Title:** Partner **Type of organization:** Law firm **Major product:** Litigation **Area of distribution:** Boston, Massachusetts **Area of Practice:** Labor, employment, white collar crime **Honors/awards:** Best Lawyers of America **Published works:** Massachusetts Superior Court Criminal Practice Manual; Massachusetts Employment Law Manual; Massachusetts District Court Criminal Defense Manual; "Trying Drug Cases in Massachusetts"; "Pre-Trial Motions in Criminal Law" **Affiliations:** A.B.A.; Massachusetts Bar Association; Boston Bar Association; Past President, M.A.W.L.; Board Member, M.A.C.D.L. **Hob./spts.:** Physical fitness, dogs **SIC code:** 81 **Address:** Perkins, Smith & Cohen, LLP, 1 Beacon St., 30th floor, Boston, MA 02108 **E-mail:** juliane_balliro@pscboston.com

BANKSTON, JEFFREY R.
Industry: Law **Univ./degree:** B.A., Political Science, Auburn University, 1985; J.D., Samford University Cumberland School of Law, 1988; LL.M., Tax, University of Florida College of Law, 1989 **Current organization:** Buschman Ahern Persons & Bankston **Title:** Esquire **Type of organization:** Law firm **Major product:** Legal services **Area of distribution:** Florida **Area of Practice:** Civil and jury trials, complex estate planning **Affiliations:** A.F.T.L.; F.B.A.; Owner of a franchise motorcycle dealership, Bankston's Kawasaki Aprilia of Daytona Beach **Hob./spts.:** Judo, motorcycles **SIC code:** 81 **Address:** Buschman Ahern Persons & Bankston, 2215 S. Third St., Suite 101, Jacksonville, FL 32250 **E-mail:** jbankston@bapblaw.com

BARBER II, JENSEN E.
Industry: Law **Born:** May 22, 1945, Ashville, North Carolina **Univ./degree:** J.D., Catholic University **Current organization:** Law Offices of J.E. Barber, PC **Title:** President **Type of organization:** Law firm **Major product:** Legal services **Area of distribution:** International **Area of Practice:** Criminal defense, medical malpractice **Affiliations:** N.A.C.D.L.; Georgetown Club; American Society of Barristers **Hob./spts.:** Sailboat racing, skiing, travel **SIC code:** 81 **Address:** Law Offices of J.E. Barber, PC, 400 Seventh St. N.W., Suite 400, Washington, DC 20004-2242 **E-mail:** jebarberpc@aol.com **Web address:** www.jebarbercriminallaw.com

BARNES II, WALTON J.
Industry: Law **Born:** October 9, 1945, Fort Worth, Texas **Univ./degree:** J.D., Louisiana State University Law School, 1970 **Current organization:** Barnes and Greenfield **Title:** Attorney **Type of organization:** Law firm **Major product:** Legal services **Area of distribution:** Louisiana **Area of Practice:** Family law, personal injury, commercial law **Affiliations:** Member, Family Law Council, Louisiana State Bar Association **Hob./spts.:** Aerobics, weightlifting, team penning **SIC code:** 81 **Address:** Barnes and Greenfield, 351 St. Ferdinand, Baton Rouge, LA 70802

BARON, JOANNA E.
Industry: Law **Born:** January 10, 1977, Columbus, Ohio **Univ./degree:** J.D., Capitol University Law School, 2002 **Current organization:** Law Office of J. Baron **Title:** Attorney at Law **Type of organization:** Law firm **Major product:** Legal services **Area of distribution:** Ohio **Area of Practice:** General practice **Affiliations:** O.H.B.A.; A.T.L.A.; T.B.A.; A.C.L.U. **Hob./spts.:** Riding horses **SIC code:** 81 **Address:** Law Office of J. Baron, 1900 Monroe St., Suite 113, Toledo, OH 43624-1781 **E-mail:** jnnbaron@sbcglobal.net

BASSEN, NED H.
Industry: Law **Born:** June 8, 1948, Far Rockaway, New York **Univ./degree:** J.D., Cornell Law School, 1973 **Current organization:** Hughes Hubbard & Reed LLP **Title:** Attorney **Type of organization:** Law firm "AV" rated, Martindale-Hubbell **Major product:** Legal services **Area of distribution:** National **Area of Practice:** Labor and employment law **Honors/awards:** "AV" rated, Martindale-Hubbell, The Best Lawyers in America, Cornell Law Review, Note and Comment Editor **Published works:** "EEO Compensation Alert for Government Contractors," Of The Metropolitan Corporate Counsel 18 (1999); "What Can an Employer Do To Help Protect Against Sexual Harassment Lawsuits?", 37 Public Relations Quarterly 26 (1992); "Synopsis of State Laws Regulating Employment of the Handicapped", Journal of College and University Law 293 (1977); The Effect of Strikes Upon Vocations", 57 Cornell Law Review 633 (1972) **Affiliations:** U.S. 2nd Circuit Court of Appeals; U.S. 11th Circuit Court of Appeals; New York State and Federal Courts **SIC code:** 81 **Address:** Hughes Hubbard & Reed LLP, 1 Battery Park Plaza, New York, NY 10004-1482 **E-mail:** bassen@hugheshubbard.com **Web address:** www.hugheshubbard.com

BATTÉ, LESLIE K.
Industry: Law **Born:** February 21, 1967, Elmhurst, Illinois **Univ./degree:** B.A., Political Science, University of Wisconsin-Madison; J.D., University of Notre Dame Law School; LL.M. with Honors, Intellectual Property, The John Marshall Law School **Current organization:** The Mihlbaugh Law Firm, LLP **Title:** Partner **Type of organization:** Law firm **Major product:** Legal services **Area of distribution:** National **Area of Practice:** Intellectual Property, Trademark and Copyright Law **Affiliations:** U.S. Supreme Court; Supreme Court of the State of Ohio; Supreme Court of the State of Illinois; U.S. District Court for the Northern District of Ohio; U.S. District Court for the Southern District of Ohio; U.S. District Court for the Northern District of Illinois; U.S. Court of Appeals for the Sixth Circuit; U.S. Court of Appeals for the Seventh Circuit; U.S. Court of Appeals for the Federal Circuit; International Trademark Association (INTA) **Hob./spts.:** Culinary arts, international travel **SIC code:** 81 **Address:** The Mihlbaugh Law Firm, LLP, P.O. Box 1141, Lima, OH 45802 **E-mail:** mihlbaughlawfirm@earthlink.net

BEAMER, KEKUAILOHIA M.
Industry: Law **Born:** February 23, 1968, Wahiawa, Hawaii **Univ./degree:** B.A., English and Sociology, University of California, Berkeley, 1989; J.D., University of Hawaii, 1994 **Current organization:** Law Office of Kekuailohia M. Beamer **Title:** Attorney **Type of organization:** Law firm **Major product:** Legal services **Area of distribution:** National **Area of Practice:** Business and civil litigation **Affiliations:** Association of Trial Lawyers of America; American Bar Association; Hawaii State Bar Association; U.S. District Court of Appeals, 9th Circuit **Hob./spts.:** Coaching tennis **SIC code:** 81 **Address:** Law Office of Kekuailohia M. Beamer, 550 Halekauwila St., Suite 106, Honolulu, HI 96813 **E-mail:** kbeamerlaw@msn.com

BELL, RICHARD T.
Industry: Law **Born:** August 31, 1972, Houston, Texas **Univ./degree:** J.D., South Texas College of Law, 1997 **Current organization:** Cease & Bell, P.L.L.C. **Title:** General partner **Type of organization:** Law firm **Major product:** Legal services **Area of distribution:** Sugar Land, Texas **Area of Practice:** Litigation (family) **Published works:** Who's Who in American Teachers **Affiliations:** A.T.L.A.; N.C.D.A.; T.C.D.A.; President, Portman County Bar Association **Hob./spts.:** Physical fitness, golf, Sunday school teacher **SIC code:** 81 **Address:** Cease & Bell, P.L.L.C., 1 Sugar Creek Blvd., Suite 4200, Sugar Land, TX 77478 **E-mail:** rickbell@alltel.net

BENASSI, JOHN M.
Industry: Law **Univ./degree:** J.D., George Washington University, Washington D.C., 1974 **Current organization:** Paul, Hastings, Janofsky & Walker **Title:** Managing Partner **Type of organization:** Law firm **Major product:** Legal services **Area of distribution:** International **Area of Practice:** Patent and intellectual property litigation **Affiliations:** San Diego Bar Association; Federal Bar Association **SIC code:** 81 **Address:** Brobeck, 12390 El Camino Real, San Diego, CA 92130 **E-mail:** johnbenassi@paulhastings.com

BENNICK, DONNA E.
Industry: Law **Born:** April 16, 1959, Concord, North Carolina **Univ./degree:** J.D., University of North Carolina at Chapel Hill **Current organization:** Donna E. Bennick, P.C. **Title:** President **Type of organization:** Law firm **Major product:** Legal services **Area of distribution:** North Carolina **Area of Practice:** Family law **Affiliations:** North Carolina Academy of Trial Lawyers; North Carolina Bar Association; Orange County Bar Association; New York State Bar Association; North Carolina Association of Women Attorneys; The Family Violence Prevention Center; Rape Crisis Center **Hob./spts.:** Gardening, swimming, travel **SIC code:** 81 **Address:** Donna E. Bennick, P.C., 1829 E. Franklin St., Bldg. 600, Chapel Hill, NC 27514 **E-mail:** donnabennick@yahoo.com **Web address:** www.donnabennickpc.com

BERMAN, BARRIE D.
Industry: Law **Born:** December 31, 1960, New York, New York **Univ./degree:** J.D., Washington University, St. Louis, Missouri, 1986 **Current organization:** Manatt, Phelps & Phillips, LLP **Title:** Partner **Type of organization:** Law firm **Major product:** Legal services **Area of distribution:** National **Area of Practice:** Corporate law **Affiliations:** A.B.A.; District of Columbia Bar Association **Hob./spts.:** Reading, physical fitness **SIC code:** 81 **Address:** Manatt, Phelps & Phillips, LLP, 1501 M Street N.W., Suite 700, Washington, DC 20005 **E-mail:** bberman@manatt.com

BLACKMORE, ADELE M.
Industry: Law **Born:** June 27, 1958 **Univ./degree:** J.D., University of Dayton School of Law **Current organization:** Law Offices of Blackmore & Blackmore **Title:** Partner **Type of organization:** Law firm **Major product:** Legal services **Area of distribution:** International **Area of Practice:** Personal injury; Board Certified Civil Trial Lawyer

Honors/awards: "AV" rated, Martindale-Hubbell **Affiliations:** The Florida Bar; Federal Bar Association **Hob./spts.:** Reading, gardening, tennis **SIC code:** 81 **Address:** Law Offices of Blackmore & Blackmore, 320 S.E. Tenth Ct., Ft. Lauderdale, FL 33316 **E-mail:** adelelaw@bellsouth.net **Web address:** www.blackmorelaw.com

BLOUNT III, MARVIN K.
Industry: Law **Univ./degree:** J.D., Wake Forest School of Law, 1996 **Current organization:** The Blount Law Firm, P.A. **Title:** Attorney **Type of organization:** Private law firm **Major product:** Legal services **Area of distribution:** Greenville, North Carolina **Area of Practice:** Civil litigation **Affiliations:** North Carolina Board of Transportation; North Carolina Bar Association; East Carolina University Board of Visitors; North Carolina Head of Trial Lawyers; American Trial Lawyers Association **SIC code:** 81 **Address:** The Blount Law Firm, P.A., 400 W. First St., Greenville, NC 27834

BLUESTEIN, HAROLD
Industry: Law **Univ./degree:** J.D., University of Miami, 1975 **Current organization:** Bluestein, Wayne and Weintraub, P.A. **Title:** Attorney **Type of organization:** Law firm **Major product:** Legal services **Area of distribution:** Florida **Area of Practice:** Family, marital and trial law **Affiliations:** American Bar Association; The Florida Bar; American Trial Lawyers Association **SIC code:** 81 **Address:** Bluestein, Wayne and Weintraub, P.A., 2665 South Bayshore Dr., Suite 1204, Miami, FL 33133 **E-mail:** hbluestein@bw-pa.com

BODKIN, ROBERT THOMAS
Industry: Law **Born:** January 26, 1945, Anderson, Indiana **Univ./degree:** J.D., Indiana University, 1973 **Current organization:** Bamberger Foreman Oswald & Hahn LLP **Title:** Partner/Attorney **Type of organization:** Law firm **Major product:** Legal services **Area of distribution:** Indiana **Area of Practice:** Medical malpractice defense **Published works:** Numerous including, "Four Elements of Damage", Condemnation: The Bottom Line, ICLEF, 1997; "Section 1983 Liability for Indiana Sheriffs After McMillian vs. Monroe County", Defense Forum, Defense Trial Counsel of Indiana, 1998; "Cahoon v. Cummings Defines Spoliation", Indiana Lawyer: Vol. 11, No. 19, Dec. 2000; "Supreme Court Settles Wrongful Act Issues", Indiana Lawyer: Vol. 12, No. 3, Apr. 2001 **Affiliations:** A.A.D.A.; Diplomate, D.T.C.I.; I.A.D.C. **Hob./spts.:** Reading, gardening **SIC code:** 81 **Address:** Bamberger Foreman Oswald & Hahn LLP, 20 N.W. Fourth St., Evansville, IN 47708 **E-mail:** tbodkin@bamberger.com

BOLANOWSKI, EUGENE R.
Industry: Law **Born:** July 2, 1941, Detroit, Michigan **Univ./degree:** Classical A.B. Degree, University of Detroit, 1963; J.D. with Honors, University of Detroit School of Law, 1966 **Current organization:** Gene Bolanowski & Associates **Title:** Senior Attorney **Type of organization:** Law firm **Major product:** Legal services **Area of distribution:** Michigan **Area of Practice:** Labor relations law and litigation, AV rated by Martindale Hubbell (Register of Pre-eminent Lawyers Civil Litigation 1994); Represented both management and labor, heavy emphasis in management in private sector and labor in public sector; Experience in handling complex labor matters **Honors/awards:** Numerous complex and significant litigation matters; Created First Citizens Conference for Macomb County Michigan Bar Association; Designated Best Projects Award by American Bar Association, 1985 **Affiliations:** Director, Secretary Treasurer, President Elect and President, Macomb County Bar Association; Committees, Michigan State Bar Association; Presently Director, Macomb County Bar Foundation **Hob./spts.:** Community involvement, baseball, travel, fishing **SIC code:** 81 **Address:** Gene Bolanowski & Associates, 16931 19 Mile Rd., Suite 110, Clinton Township, MI 48038 **E-mail:** bolanowskifirm@netscape.net

BOMMARITO, SALVATORE
Industry: Law **Born:** February 1, 1971, Brooklyn, New York **Univ./degree:** J.D., Syracuse University, 2002 **Current organization:** Law Offices of Salvatore Bommarito **Title:** Attorney at Law **Type of organization:** Law firm **Major product:** Legal services **Area of distribution:** California **Area of Practice:** Business law, estate planning, family law **Affiliations:** American Bar Association **Hob./spts.:** Physical fitness, basketball, golf **SIC code:** 81 **Address:** Law Offices of Salvatore Bommarito, 225 S. Civic Dr., Suite 1-3, Palm Springs, CA 92262 **E-mail:** sbommarito34@hotmail.com

BOND, ROBIN FRYE
Industry: Law **Born:** September 23, 1957, Beaver Falls, Pennsylvania **Univ./degree:** J.D., University of Pittsburgh School of Law, 1982 **Current organization:** Transition Strategies, Inc. **Title:** President **Type of organization:** Law firm **Major product:** Consulting **Area of distribution:** Wayne, Pennsylvania **Area of Practice:** Employment and severance agreement negotiations for executives **Honors/awards:** Phi Beta Kappa; Volunteer of the Year,The Junior League of Philadelphia, 2000 **Published works:** Health Law Practice Guide, Volume 1, Chapter 1 **Affiliations:** P.B.A.; S.H.R.M.; B.L.N. **Hob./spts.:** Charity work **SIC code:** 81 **Address:** Transition Strategies, Inc., 88 Militia Hill Drive, Wayne, PA 19087 **E-mail:** call2robin@aol.com

BONDONNO, FRANKLIN E.
Industry: Law **Born:** February 17, 1942, San Francisco, California **Univ./degree:** J.D., University of Santa Clara Law School, 1970 **Current organization:** Popelka Allard, A.P.C. **Title:** J.D., President **Type of organization:** Law firm **Major product:** Legal services **Area of distribution:** San Jose, California **Area of Practice:** Civil litigation **Honors/awards:** James Emory Scholarship, 1968-70; Outstanding Community Service Award, 1970, University of Santa Clara; Winner of University of Santa Clara Law School Moot Court Competition, 1968 **Published works:** Author, Shipyard/Sailor Industry Source Book, 1991 **Affiliations:** American Bar Association; Association of Defense Counsel; Association of Trial Lawyers of America; Northern California Mediation Association; Santa Clara Bar Association; Society of Professionals in Dispute Resolution; California State Bar Association; The Chartered Institute of Arbitration (UK); National Arbitration Forum - International Arbitration; NAM - International Arbitration and Mediation **Hob./spts.:** British history **SIC code:** 81 **Address:** Popelka Allard, A.P.C., 1 Almaden Blvd., Eighth floor, San Jose, CA 95113-2215 **Phone:** (408)491-4850 **Fax:** (408)275-0814 **E-mail:** fbondonno@popelka.com **Web address:** www.popelka.com

BONFIGLIO, RICHARD S.
Industry: Law **Born:** January 22, 1952, Brooklyn, New York **Univ./degree:** B.A., Accounting and Tax, Pace University, 1973; J.D. Fordham University School of Law, 1984 **Current organization:** The Law Firm of Richard S. Bonfiglio, Esq. **Title:** Attorney **Type of organization:** Law firm **Major product:** Legal services **Area of distribution:** New York **Area of Practice:** Civil trial, tax, trusts, estates **Affiliations:** American Bar Association; New York State Bar Association; New York State Trial Lawyers Association; American Trial Lawyers Association **Hob./spts.:** Family, golf, deep sea fishing **SIC code:** 81 **Address:** The Law Firm of Richard S. Bonfiglio, Esq., 238-92nd St., Brooklyn, NY 11209-5702 **E-mail:** suedoctor@aol.com

BONNELL, NANCY M.
Industry: Law **Born:** December 8, 1968, Anchorage, Alaska **Univ./degree:** J.D., Hamline University, 1995 **Current organization:** Dallimore & Bonnell, LLP **Title:** Partner **Type of organization:** Law firm **Major product:** Legal services **Area of distribution:** Phoenix, Arizona **Area of Practice:** Antitrust, commercial litigation **Affiliations:** Arizona Women Lawyers' Association; Arizona Builders Alliance **Hob./spts.:** Coach, high school mock teams, Jr. Achievement instructor, golf **SIC code:** 81 **Address:** Dallimore & Bonnell, LLP, 2200 E. Camelback Rd., Suite 106, Phoenix, AZ 85016 **E-mail:** dandbllp@aol.com

BOOP, ARLENE F.
Industry: Law **Born:** June 30, 1948, Darby, Pennsylvania **Univ./degree:** J.D., New York University, 1975 **Current organization:** Alterman & Boop, P.C. **Title:** Attorney at Law **Type of organization:** Law firm **Major product:** Legal services **Area of distribution:** New York **Area of Practice:** Plaintiff's employment decision and Executive buyouts **Published works:** Articles **Affiliations:** National Employment Lawyers Association; National Lawyers Guild **Hob./spts.:** Hiking, kayaking, playing the violin **SIC code:** 81 **Address:** Alterman & Boop, P.C., 35 Worth St., New York, NY 10013 **E-mail:** a.boop@altermanboop.com

BOREN, JASON D.
Industry: Law **Born:** June 24, 1970, Ogden, Utah **Univ./degree:** J.D., University of Utah, 1997 **Current organization:** Burbidge & Mitchell **Title:** Attorney **Type of organization:** Law firm **Major product:** Legal services **Area of distribution:** Utah **Area of Practice:** civil litigation (complex commercial) **Affiliations:** A.B.A.; A.T.L.A.; Salt Lake County Bar Association, Utah Trial Lawyers Association **Hob./spts.:** Waterskiing **SIC code:** 81 **Address:** Burbidge & Mitchell, 215 S. State St., Suite 920, Salt Lake City, UT 84111 **E-mail:** jboren@burbidgeandmitchell.com

BOSWELL, JOHN H.
Industry: Law **Born:** March 22, 1932, Houston Texas **Univ./degree:** J.D., University of Houston Law Center **Current organization:** Adams & Boswell, P.C., Attorneys at Law **Title:** Chairman/Named Shareholder **Type of organization:** Law firm **Major product:** Legal services **Area of distribution:** Texas **Area of Practice:** Court litigation **Hob./spts.:** Domestic and international travel, flying airplanes (former Navy pilot) **SIC code:** 81 **Address:** Adams & Boswell, P.C., Attorneys at Law, 1010 Lamar St., Suite 1800, Houston, TX 77002

BOUDREAU, JAMES N.
Industry: Law **Born:** September 29, 1965, Hartford, Connecticut **Univ./degree:** J.D., University of Minnesota **Current organization:** Littler Mendelson P.C. **Title:** Attorney/Shareholder **Type of organization:** Law firm **Major product:** Legal services **Area of distribution:** National **Area of Practice:** Labor and employment law, management side **Affiliations:** A.B.A.; Philadelphia Bar Association **Hob./spts.:** Golf, baseball **SIC code:** 81 **Address:** Littler Mendelson P.C., Three Parkway, 1601 Cherry St., Suite 1400, Philadelphia, PA 19102 **E-mail:** jboudreau@littler.com

BOYDEN, CHRISTOPHER W.
Industry: Law **Born:** January 4, 1952, Orange, California **Univ./degree:** B.A., Magna Cum Laude, Fairleigh Dickinson University, 1975; J.D., Cum Laude, Seton Hall University School of Law, 1978 **Current organization:** Law Offices of Christopher W. Boyden **Title:** Attorney at Law **Type of organization:** Law firm **Major product:** Legal services **Area of distribution:** Florida **Area of Practice:** Civil litigation **Honors/awards:** 2002 President's Award for Literary Excellence; Best Poems of the 90's, National Library of Poetry; Awarded an Athletic and Academic Scholarship, Phillips Andover Academy, 1965 **Published works:** Poetry Anthologies: "A Moment In Time", 1995, National Library of Poetry; "Lyrical Heritage", 1996, National Library of Poetry; "The Best Poems of 1996", National Library of Poetry; "Outstanding Poets of 1998", National Library of Poetry; "A Celebration of Poets", 1998, International Library of Poetry; "The Best Poems and Poets of 2001", International Library of Poetry; "Awakenings", 2002, Illiad Press; "The Best Poems and Poets of 2002", International Library of Poetry; "Outlooks", 2003, Illiad Press; "The Best Poems and Poets of 2004", International Library of Poetry **Hob./spts.:** Certified scuba diver **SIC code:** 81 **Address:** Christopher W. Boyden, Attorney at Law, 222 N. US 1, Suite 213, Tequesta, FL 33469 **E-mail:** uniquedata@aol.com

BOYER, TYRIE A.
Industry: Law **Born:** September 10, 1924, Williston, Florida **Univ./degree:** J.D., University of Florida, 1954 **Current organization:** Boyer, Tanzler & Sussman, P.A. **Title:** Lawyer **Type of organization:** Law firm **Major product:** Legal services **Area of distribution:** Florida **Area of Practice:** General practice **Honors/awards:** Phi Beta Kappa; Order of the Coif **Affiliations:** A.B.T.A.; A.B.A.; J.B.A.; F.B.A.; A.F.T.L.A. **Hob./spts.:** Big game hunting **SIC code:** 81 **Address:** Boyer, Tanzler & Sussman, P.A., 210 E. Forsyth St., Jacksonville, FL 32202

BRACH, SUSAN KUSS
Industry: Law **Univ./degree:** B.S. with Distinction, Political Science, University of Wisconsin, 1984; J.D., Memphis State University, 1987 **Current organization:** Susan L. Brach, LLC **Title:** Attorney **Type of organization:** Law firm **Major product:** Legal services **Area of distribution:** National **Area of Practice:** Labor and employment law, state and federal litigation **Published works:** (Cases): Eckles v. Conrail et al, 890 F. Supp. 1391 (S.D. Indiana, 1995), affirmed 94 F.3rd 1041 (11th Cir. 1996); Parker v. Noble Romans, 22 A.D.D. 1184 (S.D. Indiana, 1996); Agee v. Central Soya Co., Inc., 695 N.E.2nd 624 (Ind. Ct. App. 1998); Adler v. Wallace, 202 F.R.D. 666 (N.D. Georgia, 2001) **Affiliations:** Licensed in Georgia, Illinois and Indiana in state and federal courts and admitted to practice before the U.S. Supreme Court; Member, American Bar Association, Sections Member Labor & Employment and Litigation; Georgia State Bar Association, Section Member Labor & Employment; Society for Human Resource Management (SHRM) **Hob./spts.:** Under water photography **SIC code:** 81 **Address:** Susan L. Brach, LLC, 14 Westbury Park Way, Suite 100, Bluffton, SC 29910-7461 **Phone:** (843)706-5977 **Fax:** (843)706-5979 **E-mail:** sbrach@brachlaw.com

BRADEN, EVERETTE A.
Industry: Law **Univ./degree:** J.D., John Marshall Law School **Current organization:** Zedrick T. Braden & Assoc. **Title:** Attorney/Judge (Retired) **Type of organization:** Law firm **Major product:** Legal services **Area of distribution:** Chicago, Illinois **Area of Practice:** Probate, family law **Affiliations:** C.B.A.; C.C.B.A.; I.S.B.A.; I.J.A.; I.J.C; Mason I.J.F. **Hob./spts.:** Travel **SIC code:** 81 **Address:** Zedrick T. Braden & Assoc., 8 South Michigan, Suite 1401, Chicago, IL 60603

BRAUN, LESLIE A.
Industry: Law **Born:** July 2, 1960, Inglewood, California **Univ./degree:** B.A., Western State University, 1993; J.D., Thomas Jefferson School of Law, 1995 **Current organization:** Simpson Delmore Greene LLP **Title:** Attorney **Type of organization:** Law firm **Major product:** Legal services **Area of distribution:** San Diego, California **Area of Practice:** Current practice: Civil Litigation-Complex Litigation: Construction Defect Defense and Insurance Coverage for Developers; Past practice: Employment Law Plaintiff-Civil Rights Cases: Racial Discrimination, Gender Discrimination, Religious Discrimination, Disability Discrimination, Age Discrimination, Sexual Harassment, Retaliation, Failure to Hire, Constructive Discharge and Wrongful Termination **Honors/awards:** Delta Theta Chi-Tau Chapter Academic Scholarship, 1993; National Dean's List, 1994-95; Honor Roll, Fall 1994 **Affiliations:** San Diego Bar Association; State Bar of California; American Bar Association; Consumer Attorneys of California; University of San Diego School of Law: Judge, First-Year Moot Court, 2002-04, Legal Eagle Mentor Program, 2004 **Hob./spts.:** Collecting antiques, interior design, gardening, physical fitness **SIC code:** 81 **Address:** Simpson Delmore Greene LLP, 600 W. Broadway, 28th floor, San Diego, CA 92101 **E-mail:** lbraun@sdgllp.com **Web address:** www.sdgllp.com

BRENNAN, THERESA M.
Industry: Law **Born:** August 31, 1964, Hazleton, Pennsylvania **Univ./degree:** B.S., Penn State University, 1986; J.D., Temple University School of Law, 1989 **Current organization:** Brennan Legal Services **Title:** Attorney/Owner **Type of organization:** Law firm **Major product:** Legal services **Area of distribution:** National **Area of Practice:** Real estate and business law specializing in corporate and governance contract drafting, stock purchases and agreements, industrial and commercial real estate law; frequent lecturer and part- time educator at Penn State University **Affiliations:** A.B.A.; P.B.A.; Director, Volleyball Tournament for the Helping Hand Society; Certified Instructor, with the I.R.W.A. **Hob./spts.:** Church activities, CCD 2nd grade educator and Eucharist Administrator **SIC code:** 81 **Address:** Brennan Legal Services, 124 E. Broad St., Hazleton, PA 18201 **E-mail:** tmb@brennanlegal.com **Web address:** www.brennanlegal.com

BRESCHER JR., JOHN B.
Industry: Law **Born:** July 8, 1947, Elizabeth, New Jersey **Univ./degree:** B.S., Accounting and Finance, Lehigh University, 1969; J.D., 1972; L.L.M., 1976, Georgetown School of Law **Current organization:** McCarter & English **Title:** Partner **Type of organization:** Law firm **Major product:** Legal services **Area of distribution:** National **Area of Practice:** Tax law, estates, employee benefits, corporate law **Published works:** Contributing editor, "New Jersey Transactions", Matthew Bender & Co.; Co-author, "ERISA Section 404© Requirements: A Primer for Plan Sponsors and Investment Advisors", The Journal of Investment Consulting, September/October, 1999; Co-author, "Use of Brokerage Accounts to Company with ERISA Section 404(c)," The Journal of Investment Consulting, November, 1999; Author, "Fiduciary Duties of Directed Trustees", Property and Probate, July/August, 2002; "COBRA Draconian Penalties", Employee Relations Law Journal, Volume 14, 1988 **Affiliations:** E.S.O.P.A.; American Bar Association; Member, New Jersey Bar Association; District of New Jersey Bar; District of Columbia Bar **Hob./spts.:** Jogging, reading **SIC code:** 81 **Address:** McCarter & English, 4 Gateway Center, 100 Mulberry St., Newark, NJ 07102 **E-mail:** jbrescher@mccarter.com **Web address:** www.mccarter.com

BROCKETT, DANIEL L.
Industry: Law **Born:** May 10, 1956, Honolulu, Hawaii **Univ./degree:** B.S., Philosophy, Kent State University, 1979; J.D., University of Pittsburgh School of Law, 1982 **Current organization:** Squire, Sanders & Dempsey LLP **Title:** Partner **Type of organization:** Law firm **Major product:** Legal services **Area of distribution:** International **Area of Practice:** Business litigation **Published works:** 12 articles **Affiliations:** Ohio State Bar Association; New York State Bar Association; Cleveland Bar Association **Hob./spts.:** Family **SIC code:** 81 **Address:** Squire, Sanders & Dempsey LLP, 4900 Key Tower, 127 Public Square, Cleveland, OH 44114 **E-mail:** dbrockett@ssd.com **Web address:** www.ssd.com

BROWN, REBECCA C.
Industry: Law **Born:** February 12, 1954, Ashland, Kentucky **Univ./degree:** J.D., Northern Kentucky University - Salmon P. Chase College of Law **Current organization:** Bailes, Craig & Yon **Title:** Partner **Type of organization:** Law firm **Major product:** Legal services **Area of distribution:** Huntington, Washington **Area of Practice:** General law, medical malpractice **Affiliations:** A.B.A.; West Virginia Bar Association; Kentucky Bar Association **SIC code:** 81 **Address:** Bailes, Craig & Yon, 401 Tenth St., Suite 500, Huntington, WV 25701 **E-mail:** rcb@bcyon.com

BROWN, RICHARD I.
Industry: Law **Born:** August 31, 1949, Chicago, Illinois **Univ./degree:** J.D., University of Denver College of Law, 1974 **Current organization:** Lottner Rubin Fishman Brown & Saul, P.C. **Title:** Attorney at Law **Type of organization:** Law firm **Major product:** Legal services **Area of distribution:** National **Area of Practice:** Commercial litigation, real estate **Published works:** Articles **Affiliations:** C.B.A.; A.B.A.; C.T.L.A.; A.T.L.A. **Hob./spts.:** Golf, physical fitness, motorcycles **SIC code:** 81 **Address:** Lottner Rubin Fishman Brown & Saul, P.C, 633-17th St., Suite 2700, Denver, CO 80202 **E-mail:** rbrown@lrflegal.com

BRUNEMAN, STEVEN W.
Industry: Law **Born:** June 15, 1956, Dallas, Texas **Univ./degree:** B.B.A., University of Texas, 1978; J.D., St. Mary's University, 1981 **Current organization:** The Law Office of Steven W. Bruneman **Title:** Attorney **Type of organization:** Law firm **Major product:** Legal services **Area of distribution:** Texas **Area of Practice:** Family law, divorce, child custody and property issues **Affiliations:** State Bar of Texas; Texas Academy of Family Law; Dallas Bar Association; American Bar Association, Family Law Section **Hob./spts.:** Spending time with family, boating, skiing **SIC code:** 81 **Address:** The Law Office of Steven W. Bruneman, 900 Jackson St., Suite 310, Dallas, TX 75202 **E-mail:** steve@brunemanlaw.com

BUCHANAN, DAWN MARIE BATES
Industry: Law **Title:** Managing Attorney **Type of organization:** Law firm **Major product:** Not for profit legal aid **Area of Practice:** Family/matrimonial law **SIC code:** 81 **Address:** Community Legal Services of Mid-Florida, 128-A Orange Ave., Daytona Beach, FL 32114 **E-mail:** dawnb@clsmf.org

BUENTE, DAVID T.
Industry: Law **Born:** October 23, 1946, Pittsburgh, Pennsylvania **Univ./degree:** B.S., Business and Accounting, Lehigh University, 1968; J.D., University of Pennsylvania

School of Law, 1975 **Current organization:** Sidley Austin Brown & Wood, LLP **Title:** Partner **Type of organization:** Law firm **Major product:** Legal services **Area of distribution:** National **Area of Practice:** Environmental law **Published works:** Articles **Affiliations:** A.B.A.; Environmental Law Institute **Hob./spts.:** Music, cooking, physical fitness **SIC code:** 81 **Address:** Sidley Austin Brown & Wood, LLP, 1501 K St. N.W., Washington, DC 20005 **E-mail:** dbuente@sidley.com

BUONCRISTIANI, DAVID M.
Industry: Law **Born:** September 26, 1946, San Francisco, California **Univ./degree:** B.A., Philosophy, University of San Francisco, 1968; J.D., University of California, Hastings College of Law, 1971 **Current organization:** Thelen Reid & Priest **Title:** Partner **Type of organization:** Law firm **Major product:** Legal services **Area of distribution:** International **Area of Practice:** Construction industry litigation, disputes on large projects and commercial disputes **Honors/awards:** Order of the Coif; Managing Editor, the Hastings Law Journal, 1970-71; Thurston Honor Society; "AV" rated, Martindale-Hubbell **Published works:** Contributing Editor, Construction Litigation Formbook (Wiley Publications, 1990); Contributing Editor, Construction Litigation: Representing the Contractor (Wiley Publications, 1992); Contributing Editor, Proving and Pricing Construction Claims (Wiley Publications, 1996) **Affiliations:** Public Contract and Litigation Sections, American Bar Association Forum on Construction Industry; Associated General Contractors Legal Advisory Committee, State Bar of California; San Francisco Bar Association; The Olympic Club; American College of Construction Lawyers **Hob./spts.:** Family, golf **SIC code:** 81 **Address:** Thelen Reid, Two Embarcadero Center, San Francisco, CA 94111 **E-mail:** dbuoncristiani@thelenreid.com

BURGESS, JOHN A.
Industry: Law **Born:** February 6, 1951, Waltham, Massachusetts **Univ./degree:** J.D., Harvard University, 1976 **Current organization:** Hale and Dorr LLP **Title:** Senior Partner **Type of organization:** Law firm **Major product:** General law services **Area of distribution:** International **Area of Practice:** Corporate and international law **Honors/awards:** Phi Betta Kappa **Published works:** Article in book **Affiliations:** A.B.A.; U.S. Naval Institute; Council on Foreign Affairs **Hob./spts.:** Naval history, hiking **SIC code:** 81 **Address:** Hale and Dorr LLP, 60 State St., Boston, MA 02019 **E-mail:** john.burgess@haledorr.com

BUSCARINI, CARRIE A.
Industry: Law **Born:** June 14, 1975, Scranton, Pennsylvania **Univ./degree:** J.D., Widener University School of Law, 2000 **Current organization:** Law Offices of Eugene D. Sperazza **Title:** Attorney **Type of organization:** Law firm **Major product:** Legal services **Area of distribution:** National **Area of Practice:** Personal injury law **Honors/awards:** Graduated Magna Cum Laude from the University of Pittsburgh, 1997; President of Trial Advocacy Honor Society (Widener University School of Law); Recipient, Trial Advocacy Award; Certificates of Achievement in Pennsylvania Criminal Practice and Federal Courts (for highest grade in class); Former Assistant District Attorney, Philadelphia, 2000-04 **Affiliations:** P.B.A.; PA.T.L.A.; A.T.L.A.; Wilkes-Barre Law and Library Association **Hob./spts.:** Fishing, hiking, horseback riding, reading a good book, watching a good comedy **SIC code:** 81 **Address:** Law Offices of Eugene D. Sperazza, 525 Wyoming Ave., Kingston, PA 18704 **E-mail:** cajjd@adelphia.net **Web address:** www.adelphia.net

BUTLER, HOWARD G.
Industry: Law **Univ./degree:** J.D., Stetson College of Law, 1985 **Current organization:** Ossi, Butler, Najem & Rosario **Title:** Senior Partner **Type of organization:** Law firm **Major product:** Legal services **Area of distribution:** Florida **Area of Practice:** Civil and entertainment law **Honors/awards:** "AV" rated, Martindale-Hubbell **Affiliations:** A.F.T.L.; A.I.E.G.; The Million Dollar Advocates Forum; Bar Register of Pre-Eminent Lawyers **Hob./spts.:** Travel, golf **SIC code:** 81 **Address:** Ossi, Butler, Najem and Rosario, 1506 Prudential Dr., Jacksonville, FL 32207 **E-mail:** hobutler@bellsouth.net

BUTLER SR., ROBERT STEPHEN
Industry: Law **Born:** January 6, 1951, Memphis, Tennessee **Univ./degree:** B.B.A., Marketing, 1973; J.D., 1976, Memphis State University **Current organization:** Steve Butler, Attorney At Law **Title:** Attorney at Law **Type of organization:** Law firm **Major product:** Legal services **Area of distribution:** National **Area of Practice:** Trial law/criminal law **Affiliations:** A.T.L.A.; Tennessee Bar Association; Tennessee Supreme Court Bar; 6th & 3rd U.S. Circuit Court of Appeals **Hob./spts.:** Birddogs **SIC code:** 81 **Address:** Steve Butler, Attorney At Law, 11002 Highway 64, Arlington, TN 38002 **E-mail:** rsbutler@applelinks.net

BYRD, SONYIA CLAY
Industry: Law **Born:** September 4, 1960, Fort Worth, Texas **Univ./degree:** B.A., North Texas University, 1982; J.D., Southern Methodist University, 1988 **Current organization:** Sonyia Byrd, Attorney at Law **Title:** Attorney **Type of organization:** Law firm **Major product:** Legal services **Area of distribution:** Texas **Area of Practice:** Probate, personal injury, social security, disability **Affiliations:** Tarrant County Bar Association; Tarrant County Black Bar Association; Secretary, United Community Center **Hob./spts.:** Christian church activities **SIC code:** 81 **Address:** Sonyia Byrd, Attorney at Law, 1407 Texas St., Suite 103, Ft. Worth, TX 76102 **E-mail:** sonyiabyrd@sbcglobal.net

CACOULIDIS, GEORGE
Industry: Law **Born:** May 7, 1961, Queens, New York **Univ./degree:** J.D., Vermont School of Law, 1988 **Current organization:** The Law Offices of George Cocoulidis **Title:** Attorney (Owner) **Type of organization:** Law firm **Major product:** Legal services **Area of distribution:** International **Area of Practice:** Motor sport law, corporate and real estate law **Affiliations:** Association of the Bar of the City of New York **Hob./spts.:** Motor sports **SIC code:** 81 **Address:** Law Offices of George Cocoulidis, 590 Madison Ave., 21st floor, New York, NY 10022

CALABRIA, CHAD A.
Industry: Law **Born:** January 7, 1971, Westwood, California **Univ./degree:** J.D., California Western University, 1996 **Current organization:** Law Offices of Chad A. Calabria **Title:** Attorney at Law **Type of organization:** :aw firm **Major product:** Legal services **Area of distribution:** Encino, California **Area of Practice:** Criminal Defense **Affiliations:** N.A.C.D.L. **SIC code:** 81 **Address:** Law Offices of Chad A. Calabria, 16133 Ventura Blvd., Suite 600, Encino, CA 91436 **E-mail:** harpua007@earthlink.net

CALLOWAY, ROBERT WILLIAM
Industry: Law **Born:** September 7, 1934, Wills Point, Texas **Children:** Marlyn, 42; Christopher, 39; Robert William Jr., 32 **Univ./degree:** B.S., 1955; J.D., 1958, Southern Methodist University, Texas **Current organization:** Calloway, Norris, Burdette & Weber **Title:** Attorney/Partner **Type of organization:** Law firm **Major product:** Probate and estate planning **Area of distribution:** National **Area of Practice:** Probate law, AV rated, Martindale-Hubbell **Honors/awards:** Best Lawyer of America since 1984 **Affiliations:** Fellow, Dallas Bar Association; Fellow, Texas Bar Foundation; American Bar Association **Hob./spts.:** Family, hunting, fishing, golf **SIC code:** 81 **Address:** Turner, Rodgers, Calloway & Norris, 3811 Turtle Creek Blvd., Suite 400, Dallas, TX 75219 **E-mail:** rwcalloway@cnbwlaw.com

CAMERON, F. MORTON
Industry: Law **Born:** April 4, 1918, San Diego, California **Univ./degree:** B.A., Economics, Political Science, San Diego State University, 1940; J.D., University of California at Berkeley, 1946 **Current organization:** Law Offices of F. Morton Cameron **Title:** Esquire **Type of organization:** Law firm **Major product:** Legal services **Area of distribution:** Real property, business and probate law **Area of Practice:** California **Affiliations:** American Bar Association; State Bar of California **Hob./spts.:** Flying planes, hunting, fishing, outdoor activities **SIC code:** 81 **Address:** Law Offices of F. Morton Cameron, 2550 Fifth Ave., #710, San Diego, CA 92103

CANDIDO, KRISTINA M.
Industry: Law **Born:** August 2, 1970, Springfield, Massachusetts **Univ./degree:** University of Massachusetts, 1993; J.D., Nova Southeastern University, 1999 **Current organization:** Arnstein & Lehr, LLP **Title:** Esquire **Type of organization:** Law firm **Major product:** Legal services **Area of distribution:** Florida **Area of Practice:** Commercial litigation and family law **Honors/awards:** Krupnick, Campbell, et al, Award for Trial Advocacy and Trial Competitions; Award for Best Oralist in the Burton D. Wechlser First Amendment Moot Court Competition **Affiliations:** U.S. District Court, Northern, Middle and Southern Districts of Florida; U.S. Court of Appeals, Eleventh Circuit; Palm Beach County Bar Association, Family Law Practices Committee, Palm Beach County Judicial Relations Committee; Palm Beach County Bar Association Young Lawyers Section Executive Committee Member; Arnstein & Lehr Health Law Committee; Florida Federation of Business & Professional Women's Clubs, Inc. **Hob./spts.:** Scuba diving, skiing, hiking **SIC code:** 81 **Address:** Arnstein & Lehr, LLP, 515 N. Flagler Dr., Suite 600, West Palm Beach, FL 33401 **E-mail:** kmcandido@arnstein.com

CANEPA, JOSEPH G.
Industry: Law **Born:** September 3, 1959, New York, New York **Univ./degree:** J.D., Brooklyn Law School, 1988 **Current organization:** Joseph G. Canepa, PLLC **Title:** Esquire **Type of organization:** Law firm **Major product:** Legal services **Area of distribution:** National **Area of Practice:** General practice **Honors/awards:** Army Commendation **Affiliations:** New York Criminal & Civil Courts Bar Association; Army Reserves **Hob./spts.:** Chess, jogging, television **SIC code:** 81 **Address:** Joseph G. Canepa, PLLC, 78-27 37th Ave., Suite 2, Jackson Heights, NY 11372 **E-mail:** jcanepa@1800elabogado.com

CANNELLA, NICHOLAS M.
Industry: Law **Born:** July 13, 1951, New York **Univ./degree:** J.D., St. John's University, 1975 **Current organization:** Fitzpatrick, Cella, Harper & Scinto **Title:** Attorney at Law **Type of organization:** Law firm **Major product:** Legal services **Area of distribution:** International **Area of Practice:** Patent law **Affiliations:** A.B.A.; American Intellectual Property Law Association **SIC code:** 81 **Address:** Fitzpatrick,

Cella, Harper & Scinto, 30 Rockefeller Plaza, 39th floor, New York, NY 10112 **E-mail:** ncannella@fchs.com **Web address:** www.fitzpatrickcella.com

CARON, RONALD J.
Industry: Law **Born:** October 9, 1956 **Univ./degree:** J.D., Washburn University, 1982 **Current organization:** Brennan, Caron, Lenehan & Iacopino **Title:** Attorney **Type of organization:** Law firm **Major product:** Legal services **Area of distribution:** New Hampshire **Area of Practice:** Civil litigation, criminal defense, domestic law **Published works:** Article **Affiliations:** New Hampshire Bar Association **SIC code:** 81 **Address:** Brennan, Caron, Lenehan & Iacopino, 85 Brook St., Manchester, NH 03104 **E-mail:** rcaron@bclilaw.com **Web address:** www.bclilaw.com

CARTWRIGHT, WENDY A.
Industry: Law **Born:** November 7, 1964, Washington, D.C. **Univ./degree:** J.D., University of Maryland School of Law, 1989 **Current organization:** Wendy A. Cartwright & Assoc., PC **Title:** Honorable/Attorney at Law **Type of organization:** Law firm **Major product:** Legal services **Area of distribution:** Maryland **Area of Practice:** Professional service as attorney and chief judge **Affiliations:** M.D.B.A.; N.A.W.J. **Hob./spts.:** Playing the violin, films, started church chamber group, sports, reading legal novels and mysteries **SIC code:** 81 **Address:** Wendy A. Cartwright & Assoc., PC, 10111 Martin Luther King Jr. Hwy., Suite 101, Bowie, MD 20720

CASTILLO-JOHNSON, CORINA F.
Industry: Law **Born:** August 26, 1975, Edinburg, Texas **Univ./degree:** J.D., South Texas College of Law **Current organization:** Mateer & Harbert, P.A. **Title:** Esquire **Type of organization:** Law firm **Major product:** Legal services **Area of distribution:** Orlando, Florida **Area of Practice:** Real estate and construction law **Affiliations:** Association of Trial Lawyers of America; Florida State Bar **Hob./spts.:** Reading, travel, photography **SIC code:** 81 **Address:** Mateer & Harbert, P.A., 225 E. Robinson, Suite 600, Orlando, FL 32801 **E-mail:** cjohnson@mateerharbert.com **Web address:** www.mateerharbert.com/attorneys/cjohnson.ht

CATES, JOHN L.
Industry: Law **Born:** December 19, 1953, Madison, Wisconsin **Univ./degree:** B.S., History/Political Science, University of Rochester, 1976; J.D., University of Wisconsin School of Law, 1980 **Current organization:** Gingras, Cates & Luebke, S.C. **Title:** Attorney/Partner **Type of organization:** Law firm **Major product:** Legal services **Area of distribution:** Wisconsin **Area of Practice:** Civil litigation, medical malpractice, product liability **Honors/awards:** Board of Governors, Wisconsin State Bar; Board of Directors, Wisconsin Academy of Trial Lawyers **Affiliations:** Wisconsin State Bar Association; Dane County Bar Association **Hob./spts.:** Family, basketball, running **SIC code:** 81 **Address:** Gingras, Cates & Luebke, S.C., 8150 Excelsior Dr., Madison, WI 53717 **E-mail:** cates@gcllawyers.com **Web address:** www.gcllawyers.com

CHESNUTT, MARCUS W.
Industry: Law **Born:** August 31, 1953, Lumberton, North Carolina **Univ./degree:** B.A., History, Duke University, Chapel Hill, North Carolina, 1975; J.D., Samford University, Birmingham, Alabama, 1978 **Current organization:** Chesnutt, Clemmons, Thomas & Peacock, PC **Title:** Esquire/Managing Partner **Type of organization:** Law firm **Major product:** Legal services **Area of distribution:** North Carolina **Area of Practice:** Criminal trial **Honors/awards:** A Rating, Martindale-Hubbell **Affiliations:** A.T.L.A.; N.C.B.A.; C.C.B.A.; N.C.A.T.L.; 3rd Judicial Bar Association; Federal Court Clerk, Eastern District, North Carolina, 1978-79 **SIC code:** 81 **Address:** Chesnutt, Clemmons, Thomas & Peacock, PC, 225 C Broad St., New Bern, NC 28560 **E-mail:** gary@nclegalnet.com **Web address:** www.nclegalnet.com

CICCONE, KELLY
Industry: Law **Born:** June 27, 1959, Seneca Falls, New York **Univ./degree:** J.D., Syracuse University College of Law, 1999 **Current organization:** Self-employed **Title:** Esquire **Type of organization:** Law firm **Major product:** Legal services **Area of distribution:** Rochester, New York **Area of Practice:** Family law **Affiliations:** N.Y.S.B.A.; M.C.B.A.; Association of Collaborative Family Law Attorneys **Hob./spts.:** Travel, writing, fine arts **SIC code:** 81 **Address:** 19 W. Main St., Suite 600, Rochester, NY 14614 **E-mail:** kmcicconeesq@yahoo.com **Web address:** www.kellyciccone.com

CLARK, MICHAEL E.
Industry: Law **Born:** September 11, 1956, Falls Church, Virginia **Univ./degree:** J.D., South Texas College of Law, 1982; LL.M., Tax, 1996; LL.M., Health, 2000, University of Houston **Current organization:** Hamel Bowers & Clark LLP **Title:** Partner **Type of organization:** Law firm **Major product:** Legal services **Area of distribution:** National **Area of Practice:** Federal litigation **Hob./spts.:** Writing, publishing **SIC code:** 81 **Address:** Hamel Bowers & Clark LLP, 5300 Memorial Dr., Suite 900, Houston, TX 77007 **E-mail:** mclark@hbctrial.com

COBB, DAVID L.
Industry: Law **Born:** May 6, 1940, Eunice, Louisiana **Univ./degree:** J.D., Mississippi College School of Law, 1969 **Current organization:** Allen, Vaughn, Cobb & Hood, P.A. **Title:** Attorney **Type of organization:** Law firm **Major product:** Legal services **Area of distribution:** National **Area of Practice:** Insurance defense **Affiliations:** M.D.L.A.; D.R.I. **Hob./spts.:** Golf, racquetball, fishing **SIC code:** 81 **Address:** Allen, Vaughn, Cobb & Hood, P.A., 1 Hancock Plaza, 12th floor, Gulfport, MS 39501 **E-mail:** dcobb@avchlaw.com **Web address:** www.avchlaw.com

COCKRELL III, M.W. "TREY"
Industry: Law **Born:** March 6, 1973, Houston, Texas **Univ./degree:** J.D., South Texas College of Law, 2000 **Current organization:** Cockrell Law Firm PLLC **Title:** Attorney **Type of organization:** Law firm **Major product:** Legal services **Area of distribution:** South Carolina **Area of Practice:** Personal injury, family law **Affiliations:** A.T.L.A.; S.C.T.L.A.; South Carolina Bar Association; Association of Citadel Lawyers; President, Carolina Chapter of STCL Alumni **Hob./spts.:** Fishing, camping, golf **SIC code:** 81 **Address:** Cockrell Law Firm PLLC, 159 Main St., Chesterfield, SC 29709 **E-mail:** cockrell@justice.com

COFFEY, SHIRLEY A.
Industry: Law **Born:** August 15, 1959, Tallahassee, Florida **Univ./degree:** B.A. Summa Cum Laude, Music Education, University of Cincinnati Conservatory of Music, 1980; J.D., University of Cincinnati College of Law, 1992 **Current organization:** Shea & Associates **Title:** Senior Associate **Type of organization:** Law firm **Major product:** Legal services **Area of distribution:** Ohio **Area of Practice:** Medical malpractice **Honors/awards:** 1 of Ohio's Super Lawyers, 2004-05, Chosen by Peer Group **Published works:** Law Review article on bankruptcy **Affiliations:** A.T.L.A.; Jury Instruction Committee of Ohio State Bar Association; Kentucky Bar Association; American Bar Association; Ohio Academy of Trial Lawyers **Hob./spts.:** Musician-plays violin and trombone, photography **SIC code:** 81 **Address:** Shea & Associates, 250 E. Fifth St., Suite 444, Cincinnati, OH 45202 **E-mail:** scoffey@shea-associates.com

COFIÑO, PEDRO ALEJANDRO
Industry: Law **Born:** June 13, 1952, Havana, Cuba **Univ./degree:** A.A., with Honors, Miami Dade Community College, 1975; B.A., Business Administration, Major in Accounting, Magna Cum Laude (emphasis in Economics and Psychology), University of Miami, 1977; J.D., Nova University School of Law, 1980 **Current organization:** Cofiño & Associates **Title:** Attorney At Law **Type of organization:** Law firm **Major product:** Legal services **Area of distribution:** International **Area of practice:** Civil litigation/personal injury/family law **Area of Practice:** Civil litigation/personal injury/family law **Honors/awards:** July 1972-April 1974, United States Army, Highest Rank Specialist; 4 Awards: National Defense Medal, Good Conduct Medal, letters of commendation and certificates of achievements. Assigned to United States Third Army, subsequent to TRADOC **Affiliations:** F.T.L.A.; President, Miami Beach Bar Association; The Florida Bar; Southern & Middle Federal District, Florida; 11th Circuit Court of Appeals Tax Court; Florida Supreme Court Bar; Honor Society Beta Alpha Psi National Accounting Fraternity; Phi Pheta Kappa National Honor Fraternity of the Junior College; Beta Gamma Sigma, Honor Society; Phi Kappa Phi, Honor Society; The International Law Society, Nova University Law Center **Hob./spts.:** Breeding nationally ranked champion German Shepherds **SIC code:** 81 **Address:** Cofiño & Associates, 407 Lincoln Rd., Suite 2B, Miami Beach, FL 33139 **E-mail:** cofino@bellsouth.net **Web address:** www.miamibeachlawyers.com

COHEN, ROBERT A.
Industry: Law **Born:** July 23, 1929, Pittsburgh, Pennsylvania **Univ./degree:** J.D., Harvard University, 1954 **Current organization:** Cohen Legal Services, LLC **Title:** Attorney **Type of organization:** Law firm **Major product:** Legal services **Area of distribution:** Pennsylvania **Area of Practice:** Medical malpractice, personal injury, stock broker negligence **Affiliations:** A.B.A.; P.B.A.; A.C.B.A.; F.B.A. **Hob./spts.:** Reading, gardening **SIC code:** 81 **Address:** 205 Oak Heights Dr., Oakdale, PA 15071 **E-mail:** bobberlaw@yahoo.com

COOK, DAVID C.
Industry: Law **Born:** September 17, 1947, New York, New York **Univ./degree:** B.A., Economics, New York University, 1968; J.D., Brooklyn Law School, 1972 **Current organization:** Kreindler & Kreindler, LLP **Title:** Partner **Type of organization:** Law firm **Major product:** Legal services **Area of distribution:** National and International **Area of Practice:** Aviation disaster law; wrongful death and severe personal injury litigation and trial including medical malpractice, automobile and transportation matters; insurance and property fire, flood and disaster law; consumer protection class action law **Published works:** Co-Author, 3 volume treatise New York Law of Torts **Affiliations:** A.B.A.; A.T.L.A.; N.Y.S.B.A.; N.Y.S.T.L.A.; Prior Member of the TICL Executive Committee of the N.Y.S.B.A. and Chair of Fire and Property Insurance Section **SIC code:** 81 **Address:** Kreindler & Kreindler, LLP, 100 Park Ave., New York, NY 10017 **E-mail:** Dcook@kreindler.com **Web address:** www.kreindler.com

COOKE, ROBERT F.
Industry: Law **Univ./degree:** J.D., University of Miami, 2001 **Current organization:** George, Hartz, Lundeen, Fulmer, Johnstone, King & Stevens P.A. **Title:** Attorney **Type of organization:** Law firm **Major product:** Legal services **Area of distribution:** Flor-

ida **Area of Practice:** Commercial/consumer litigation **Affiliations:** F.B.A.; A.T.L.A.; A.B.A. **Hob./spts.:** Diving, fishing, golf, pilot **SIC code:** 81 **Address:** George, Hartz, Lundeen, Fulmer, Johnstone, King & Stevens P.A., 4800 Le Juene Rd., Coral Gables, FL 33146 **E-mail:** robert.cooke@georgehartz.com

COOPER, MARNELL ALLAN
Industry: Law **Born:** January 7, 1970, Baltimore City, Maryland **Univ./degree:** B.A., Philosophy, University of Maryland, 1997; J.D., University of Maryland-School of Law, 2002 **Current organization:** Resnick & Abraham, LLC **Title:** Esquire **Type of organization:** Law firm **Major product:** Legal services **Area of distribution:** National **Area of Practice:** Creditors' rights and personal injury **Affiliations:** Maryland State Bar Association; Maryland Trial Lawyers Association; Fuel Fund of Maryland **Hob./spts.:** Travel, physical fitness, cigars and scotch **SIC code:** 81 **Address:** Resnick & Abraham, LLC, 1 E. Franklin St., Suite 200, Baltimore, MD 21202

CORETTE III, JOHN E.
Industry: Law **Born:** June 24, 1936, Montana **Univ./degree:** B.S., Business, University of Montana, 1958; J.D., University of Virginia, 1961 **Current organization:** Piper Rudnick, LLP **Title:** Partner **Type of organization:** Law Firm **Major product:** Legal services **Area of distribution:** National **Area of Practice:** International law, corporate mergers, acquisitions, borrowing and business transactions **Published works:** Articles **Affiliations:** A.B.A.; C.B.A.; D.C.B.A.; M.B.A.; Columbia Country Club; University of Montana Athletics Board **Hob./spts.:** Tennis, skiing, golf **SIC code:** 81 **Address:** Piper Rudnick, LLP, 1200 19th St. N.W., Suite 700, Washington, DC 20036 **E-mail:** shaun.corette@piperrudnick.com

COTNER, DAVID B.
Industry: Law **Born:** August 5, 1957, Fort Lewis, Washington **Univ./degree:** B.S., B.A. with Honors, 1980; J.D. with Honors, University of Montana School of Law, 1983 **Current organization:** Datsopoulos, MacDonald & Lind, P.C. **Title:** Shareholder **Type of organization:** Law firm **Major product:** Legal services **Area of distribution:** Montana **Area of Practice:** Commercial litigation, trial work, arbitration **Honors/awards:** "AV" rated, Martindale-Hubbell; Listed in Best Lawyers in America since 2000 **Affiliations:** A.T.L.A.; Montana Trial Lawyers Association; Board Member, Max & Betty Swanson Foundation **Hob./spts.:** Golf **SIC code:** 81 **Address:** Datsopoulos, MacDonald & Lind, P.C., 201 W. Main St., Suite 201, Missoula, MT 50802 **E-mail:** dcotner@dmllaw.com

COTTLE, ROBERT W.
Industry: Law **Born:** March 11, 1962, Provo, Utah **Univ./degree:** B.A., University of Utah, 1986; J.D., Loyola Marymount University, 1989 **Current organization:** Mainor Eglet Cottle **Title:** Attorney **Type of organization:** Law firm **Major product:** Legal services **Area of distribution:** National **Area of Practice:** Personal injury, wrongful death, nursing home negligence, toxic tort class actions, products liability, medical malpractice, construction defect, insurance bad faith **Honors/awards:** Phi Delta Phi; Member, St. Thomas Law Honor Society **Published works:** Author, "Product Defect Litigation in Nevada" **Affiliations:** Utah State Bar; State Bar of Nevada; Nevada Trial Lawyers Association Pillar of Justice **Hob./spts.:** Golf, skiing, family **SIC code:** 81 **Address:** Mainor Eglet Cottle, 400 S. Fourth St., #600, Las Vegas, NV 89101

COURTNEY, SCOT R.
Industry: Law **Born:** November 16, 1965, Houston, Texas **Univ./degree:** B.S., Political Science & Geography, Southwestern Texas State University, 1990; J.D., Thurgood Marshall School of Law, 1994 **Current organization:** Scardino & Courtney L.L.P. **Title:** Attorney **Type of organization:** Law firm **Major product:** Legal services **Area of distribution:** Houston, Texas **Area of Practice:** Criminal trial defense **Affiliations:** A.T.L.A.; U. S. Supreme Court Bar Association; Texas Criminal Defense Lawyers Association **Hob./spts.:** Golf **SIC code:** 81 **Address:** Scardino & Courtney L.L.P., 1004 Congress St., 3rd Floor, Houston, TX 77002 **E-mail:** scotcourtney@sbcglobal.net

COUTURE, ANDREW J.
Industry: Law **Born:** September 24, 1977, Gardner, Massachusetts **Univ./degree:** J.D., Massachusetts School of Law, 2006 **Current organization:** Massachusetts School of Law **Title:** Attorney **Type of organization:** Law school **Major product:** Legal services **Area of distribution:** Massachusetts **Area of Practice:** General law **Hob./spts.:** Literature, martial arts, outdoor activities **SIC code:** 81 **Address:** 28 Spring St., Fitchburg, MA 01420 **E-mail:** andrewc1977@msn.com

CRABTREE, LARRY DOUGLAS
Industry: Law **Born:** May 14, 1951, Kingsport, Tennessee **Univ./degree:** B.A., Management, Tennessee Technological University, 1973; J.D., University of Tennessee School of Law, 1975 **Current organization:** King & Ballow **Title:** Attorney/Partner **Type of organization:** Law firm **Major product:** Legal services **Area of distribution:** Tennessee **Area of Practice:** ERISA, employee benefits and pensions **Published works:** Seminars **Affiliations:** American Bar Association; Tennessee State Bar Association; Nashville Bar Association **Hob./spts.:** Sports, Crabtree Ridge Farm (for rescue of injured and abandoned animals) **SIC code:** 81 **Address:** King & Ballow, 315 Union St., Suite 1100, Nashville, TN 37201 **E-mail:** lcrabtree@king-ballow.com **Web address:** www.king.ballow.com

CREWS JR., WILLIAM P.
Industry: Law **Born:** June 7, 1931, Shreveport, Louisiana **Univ./degree:** J.D., Loyola University **Current organization:** William P. Crews, Jr., LLC **Title:** Attorney **Type of organization:** Law firm **Major product:** Legal services **Area of distribution:** Louisiana **Area of Practice:** Medical malpractice **Affiliations:** American Trail Lawyers Association **Hob./spts.:** Fishing, hunting **SIC code:** 81 **Address:** William P. Crews, Jr., LLC, 129 Rue St. Denis St., Natchitoches, LA 71457 **E-mail:** billcrews@cp-tel.net

CUNEO, JONATHAN W.
Industry: Law **Born:** September 10, 1952, New York, New York **Univ./degree:** A.B., Economics, Columbia University, 1974; J.D., Cornell Law School, 1977 **Current organization:** Cuneo, Gilbert & LaDuca, LLP **Title:** Senior Partner **Type of organization:** Law firm **Major product:** Legal services **Area of distribution:** National **Area of Practice:** Commercial and civil litigation, legislative advocacy **Honors/awards:** Trial Lawyer of the Year Finalist, Trial Lawyers for Public Justice, 2006 **Published works:** 8 publications **Affiliations:** Board Member, American Antitrust Institute; Board Member, Violence Policy Center; American Bar Association **Hob./spts.:** Recreational boxing, charity work **SIC code:** 81 **Address:** Cuneo, Gilbert & LaDuca, LLP, 507 C. St. N.E., Washington, DC 20002 **E-mail:** jonc@cuneolaw.com **Web address:** www.cuneolaw.com

CURPHEY, WILLIAM E.
Industry: Law **Born:** April 28, 1948, Cleveland, Ohio **Univ./degree:** J.D., Cleveland University, 1973 **Current organization:** William E. Curphey & Associates, P.A. **Title:** Managing Attorney **Type of organization:** Law firm **Major product:** Legal services **Area of distribution:** National **Area of Practice:** Corporate Defense, Litigator, Immigration Law, Labor and Employment Law **Affiliations:** A.B.A.; A.T.L.A.; F.B.A. **Hob./spts.:** Model trains, backpacking, hiking **SIC code:** 81 **Address:** William E. Curphey & Associates, P.A., 2605 Enterprise Rd E., Suite 155, Clearwater, FL 33759 **E-mail:** wcurphey@curpheylaw.com

CURTIS, PATRICIA J.
Industry: Law **Born:** February 12, 1956, Des Moines, Iowa **Univ./degree:** J.D., Boston College, 1981 **Current organization:** Shell & Wilmer, LLP **Title:** Attorney/Partner **Type of organization:** Law firm **Major product:** Legal services **Area of distribution:** National **Area of Practice:** Real estate/finance **Affiliations:** A.B.A.; N.A.I.O.P.; Nevada State Bar; Clark County Bar Association; Urban Land Inst. **Hob./spts.:** Family, community work **SIC code:** 81 **Address:** Shell & Wilmer, LLP, 3800 Howard Hughes Pkwy., #1900, Las Vegas, NV 89109 **E-mail:** pcurtis@swlaw.com

D'AMATO, ALEXA B.
Industry: Law **Born:** August 22, 1976, Atlantic City, New Jersey **Univ./degree:** B.S., Psychology, Richard Stockton University; J.D., Rutgers University School of Law, 2001 **Current organization:** D'Amato & D'Amato P.C. **Title:** Attorney **Type of organization:** Law firm **Major product:** Legal services **Area of distribution:** New Jersey **Area of Practice:** Personal injury **Honors/awards:** Listed in Who's Who: American Law Students, "AV" rated, Martindale-Hubbell **Affiliations:** American Association of University Women; ATLA; ATLA of New Jersey-Board of Governors; ATLA New Lawyers Division-Board of Governors-Regional Captain; American Bar Association; New Jersey State Bar Association; National Institute of Trial Advocacy; Atlantic County Bar Association-Member and Chair of the Young Lawyers Division; Camden County Bar Association; Trial Lawyers for Public Justice; National Institute of Trial Advocacy; UNICO; LPGA Classic Partners **SIC code:** 81 **Address:** D'Amato & D'Amato P.C., 401 New Rd., Suite 103, Linwood, NJ 08221 **E-mail:** alexa@damatolawfirm.com **Web address:** www.damatolawfirm.com

DATTA, RAJBIR SINGH
Industry: Law/Advocacy **Born:** January 17, 1982, Pittsburgh, Pennsylvania **Univ./degree:** B.A., Political Science, Temple University, 2005 **Current organization:** Sikh American Legal Defense and Education Fund **Title:** Director **Type of organization:** Nonprofit legal advocacy **Major product:** Legal and educational services for the American-Sikh community **Area of distribution:** National **Area of Practice:** Civil rights **Affiliations:** Leadership Conference for Civil Rights; National Hate Crimes Associations; National Council of Asian Pacific Americans **Hob./spts.:** Golf, hockey, physical fitness **SIC code:** 81 **Address:** Sikh American Legal Defense and Education Fund, 1413 K St. N.W., 5th floor, Washington, DC 20005 **E-mail:** rdatta@saldef.org

DAVIS, REUBEN
Industry: Law **Born:** November 5, 1943, Muskogee, Oklahoma **Univ./degree:** J.D., University of Oklahoma, 1973 **Current organization:** Boone, Smith, Davis, Hurst & Dickman **Title:** Esquire **Type of organization:** Law firm **Major product:** Legal services **Area of distribution:** National **Area of Practice:** Business litigation **Honors/awards:** Outstanding Lawyers of America; Best Lawyers in America **Affiliations:**

American Bar Association; Oklahoma Bar Association; Tulsa County Bar Association; Defense Research Institute **Hob./spts.:** Golf, Boy Scouts **SIC code:** 81 **Address:** Boone, Smith, Davis, Hurst & Dickman, 500 ONEOK Plaza, 100 W. 5th St., Tulsa, OK 74103 **E-mail:** rdavis@boonesmith.com

DECKERT, PAUL B.
Industry: Law **Born:** New Orleans, Louisiana **Univ./degree:** J.D., Loyola University New Orleans School of Law, 1999 **Current organization:** Paul B. Deckert, A.P.L.C. **Title:** Attorney **Type of organization:** Law firm **Major product:** Legal services **Area of distribution:** Louisiana **Area of Practice:** Collections Attorney **Affiliations:** C.L.L.A.; Louisiana State Bar Association; American Bar Association; New Orleans Bar Association; Federal Bar Association; Lt. Col. Marine Corps Reserves **Hob./spts.:** Hunting, fishing, **SIC code:** 81 **Address:** Paul B. Deckert, A.P.L.C., 6506 Spanish Fort Blvd., Suite 100, New Orleans, LA 70124 **E-mail:** bubba@pbdeckertaplc.com

DEDERICK, RONALD O.
Industry: Law **Born:** August 26, 1935, Chicago, Illinois **Univ./degree:** B.A., International Affairs, University of Virginia, 1957; J.D., University of Virginia School of Law, 1962 **Current organization:** Day, Berry & Howard, LLP **Title:** Partner **Type of organization:** Law firm **Major product:** Legal services **Area of distribution:** International **Area of Practice:** Trusts, estates and tax law **Published works:** Various articles in bar journals **Affiliations:** Fellow, A.B.F.; Fellow, C.B.F.; I.B.A., I.S.T.E.C.; Past Chairman, Probate Section, Connecticut Bar Association; Connecticut Bar Association; New York State Bar Association; Greenwich Bar Association **Hob./spts.:** Golf, fishing, theatre **SIC code:** 81 **Address:** Day, Berry & Howard, LLP, 1 East Putnam Ave., Greenwich, CT 06801 **E-mail:** rodederick@dbh.com **Web address:** www.dbh.com

DEFOREST III, WALTER P.
Industry: Law **Born:** December 4, 1944, Oklahoma **Univ./degree:** J.D., Harvard Law School, 1969 **Current organization:** DeForest Koscelnik Yokitis & Kaplan **Title:** Founder/Attorney **Type of organization:** Law firm **Major product:** Legal services **Area of distribution:** National **Area of Practice:** Labor law **Affiliations:** A.B.A.; P.B.A.; Ohio Bar Association; West Virginia State Bar **Hob./spts.:** Running marathons **SIC code:** 81 **Address:** DeForest Koscelnik Yokitis & Kaplan, Koppers Bldg., 30th floor, 436 Seventh Ave., Pittsburgh, PA 15219 **E-mail:** deforest@dkyk.com **Web address:** www.dkyk.com

DELINSKY, STEPHEN R.
Industry: Law **Born:** August 13, 1944, Hartford, Connecticut **Univ./degree:** B.A., Tufts University, 1966; J.D., Boston College Law School, 1970 **Current organization:** Eckert Seamans Cherin & Mellott, LLC **Title:** Attorney **Type of organization:** Law firm **Major product:** Legal services **Area of distribution:** International **Area of Practice:** White collar criminal defense **Honors/awards:** "AV" rated, Martindale-Hubbell **Published works:** 5 articles **Affiliations:** A.B.A.; Massachusetts Bar Association; National Association of Criminal Defense Lawyers; Massachusetts Association of Criminal Defense Lawyers **Hob./spts.:** Boating, power walking, weight lifting, physical fitness **SIC code:** 81 **Address:** Eckert Seamans Cherin & Mellott, LLC, 1 International Place, Boston, MA 02110 **E-mail:** srd@escm.com **Web address:** www.escm.com

DEMPSEY, THOMAS M.
Industry: Law **Born:** February 29, 1940, Los Angeles, California **Univ./degree:** J.D., University of Oregon, 1968 **Current organization:** Law Offices of Thomas M. Dempsey **Title:** Trial/Civil Lawyer **Type of organization:** Law firm **Major product:** Legal services **Area of distribution:** Los Angeles, California **Area of Practice:** Special needs of the mentally handicapped, personal injury (specializing in brain injuries), professional negligence, products liability **Honors/awards:** Ted Horn Memorial Award, 1994; Certificate of Appreciation for Litigation Section of the L.A. County Bar Association; Outstanding Chapter President from the CTLA,1983 **Published works:** Trial; The Advocate; The Forum; L.A. Lawyer; Trial Digest; Trial Lawyer for Public Justice **Affiliations:** A.T.L.A.; C.A.O.T.; C.A.A.L.A.; A.B.T.A.; Member, Board of Trustees, L.A.C.B.A.; Past President, Consumer Attorneys of L.A. **Hob./spts.:** Skiing, photography, running **SIC code:** 81 **Address:** Law Offices of Thomas M. Dempsey, 10990 Wilshire Blvd., Suite 1200, Los Angeles, CA 90024 **E-mail:** glozorozo@aol.com

DENOCE, KEVIN G.
Industry: Law **Born:** May 21, 1960, Teaneck, New Jersey **Univ./degree:** B.A., University of Colorado at Boulder; J.D., Pepperdine University **Current organization:** Law Offices of Kevin G. De Noce **Title:** Attorney **Type of organization:** Law firm **Major product:** Legal services **Area of distribution:** California **Area of Practice:** Criminal law, DUI defense, plaintiff personal injury **Honors/awards:** Outstanding Prosecutor of the Year Award, Ventura County District Attorney's Office, 1988; Outstanding Prosecutor of the Year Award, Mothers Against Drunk Driving, 1989; Joyce Yoshoika Award, Ventura County Criminal Defense Bar Association, 2002; Santa Barbara Independent News Local Heroes Annual Honor Roll, 2001 **Published works:** Published decision, In re Efren Cruz, B154156; Published decisions before the California Supreme Court and Court of Appeal **Affiliations:** President, Ventura County Deputy District Attorney's Association, 1995 Former Senior Ventura County Deputy District Attorney; President/Chief Negotiator, the Union known as the Criminal Justice Attorney's Association of Ventura County, 1995-96 **Hob./spts.:** Reading, jogging, swimming **SIC code:** 81 **Address:** Law Offices of Kevin G. Denoce, 6401 Telephone Rd., Suite 130, Ventura, CA 93003 **E-mail:** internetlaw@aol.com **Web address:** www.denoce.com

DESANTIS, PASQUALE
Industry: Law **Born:** October 6, 1954, Pettorano Sul-Gicio, Italy **Univ./degree:** J.D., Magna Cum Laude, Suffolk University, 1987 **Current organization:** Prince Lobel Glovsky & Tye, LLP **Title:** Esquire **Type of organization:** Law firm **Major product:** Legal services **Area of distribution:** Boston, Massachusetts **Area of Practice:** Domestic relations law, civil litigation **Honors/awards:** "The Safety Net", a television program on domestic relationships broadcast by Brookline Access Television; Magna Cum Laude **Published works:** NBI booklet **Affiliations:** Boston Bar Association; Massachusetts Bar Association; Justinian Law Society **Hob./spts.:** Coaching soccer, fluent in Italian, snow skiing **SIC code:** 81 **Address:** Prince Lobel Glovsky & Tye, LLP, 585 Commercial St., Boston, MA 02109 **E-mail:** pdesantis@plgt.com

DIAZ JR., MICHAEL
Industry: Law **Born:** November 24, 1960, Havana, Cuba **Univ./degree:** B.S., Business/International Finance, 1983; J.D., 1986, University of Miami **Current organization:** Law Offices of Michael Diaz Jr. **Title:** Attorney **Type of organization:** Law firm **Major product:** Legal services/consulting **Area of distribution:** International **Area of Practice:** Complex civil and criminal litigation **Affiliations:** Cuban American Bar Association; Hispanic Bar Association **Hob./spts.:** Coaching Little League baseball, boating **SIC code:** 81 **Address:** Law Offices of Michael Diaz Jr., 100 S.E. Second Street, Suite 3400, Miami, FL 33131 **E-mail:** info@michaeldiazjr.com

DIXON, PHINEAS S.
Industry: Law **Univ./degree:** LL.B., University of Baltimore, Maryland, 1962 **Current organization:** Phineas S. Dixon, Esq. **Title:** Attorney **Type of organization:** Law firm **Major product:** Legal services **Area of distribution:** Maryland **Area of Practice:** Civil and criminal law **Affiliations:** Maryland State Bar Association; Baltimore County Bar Association; Howard County Bar Association **Hob./spts.:** Family, golf, fishing **SIC code:** 81 **Address:** Phineas S. Dixon, Esq., 401 Frederick Rd., Catonsville, MD 21228

DOLCE-HARKINS, MARY A.
Industry: Law **Born:** July 21, 1964, Brooklyn, New York **Univ./degree:** Legal Secretary, Drake Business School,1989; Wagner College **Current organization:** Frank J. Santo, P.C. **Title:** Legal Assistant/Office Manager **Type of organization:** Law firm **Major product:** Legal assistance **Area of distribution:** International **Area of Practice:** Criminal/personal injury/trusts and estates **Affiliations:** Past Treasurer and President, Alpha Delta Pi **Hob./spts.:** Painting, softball, camping **SIC code:** 81 **Address:** 48 Dewey Ave., Staten Island, NY 10308 **E-mail:** m.harkins@si.rr.com

DORRIS, DAVID V.
Industry: Law **Univ./degree:** B.A., History, Blackburn College; J.D., University of Illinois, 1973 **Current organization:** Dorris Law Firm, P.C. **Title:** Attorney **Type of organization:** Law firm **Major product:** Legal services **Area of distribution:** Bloomington, Illinois **Area of Practice:** Personal injury litigation, client relations **Affiliations:** A.T.L.A.; Head of C.L.U. Committee Forum, Illinois Trial Lawyers Association; Illinois State Bar Association **Hob./spts.:** Genealogy, politics **SIC code:** 81 **Address:** Dorris Law Firm, P.C., 207 W. Jefferson St., Suite 601, Bloomington, IL 61752 **E-mail:** dvdstoy@aol.com

DOUGHERTY, JAMES RICHARD
Industry: Law **Born:** April 4, 1976, Hinsdale, Illinois **Univ./degree:** B.A., History, Eastern Illinois University, 1999; J.D., John Marshall Law School, 2002 **Current organization:** Wilson, Elser, Moskowitz, Edelman & Dicker, LLP **Title:** Attorney at Law **Type of organization:** Law firm **Major product:** Legal services **Area of distribution:** International **Area of Practice:** Litigation, product liability **Affiliations:** U.S. Circuit Court of Appeals, 7th Circuit; Supreme Court of Illinois; Illinois State Bar Association; Chicago Bar Association; A.B.A. **Hob./spts.:** Weightlifting, basketball, martial arts **SIC code:** 81 **Address:** Wilson, Elser, Moskowitz, Edelman & Dicker, LLP, 120 N. LaSalle St., 26th floor, Chicago, IL 60602 **E-mail:** doughertyj@wemed.com **Web address:** www.wemed.com

DRAPER, JAMES W.
Industry: Law **Born:** December 26, 1926, Grosse Pointe Farms, Michigan **Univ./degree:** J.D., University of Michigan **Current organization:** Dykema Gossett (Retired member) **Title:** Attorney **Type of organization:** Law firm **Major product:** Legal services **Area of distribution:** Michigan **Area of Practice:** Savings and loan, real estate **Published works:** Articles, papers **Affiliations:** American College of Real Estate Lawyers **Hob./spts.:** Golf, sailing **SIC code:** 81 **Address:** 113 Merriweather Rd., Grosse Pointe Farms, MI 48236

DREIZE, LIVIA R.
Industry: Law **Univ./degree:** B.S., Florida International University, 1988; J.D., Pontifical Catholic University of Puerto Rico, 1992 **Current organization:** Damera & Dreize, P.A. **Title:** Managing Partner **Type of organization:** Law firm **Major product:** Legal services **Area of distribution:** International **Area of Practice:** Corporate, immigration, traffic and criminal law **Affiliations:** Dade County Bar Association **Hob./spts.:** Arts, music **SIC code:** 81 **Address:** Damera & Dreize, P.A., 2701 Le Jeune Rd., Suite 406, Coral Gables, FL 33134 **Phone:** (305)446-6760 **Fax:** (305)446-9991 **E-mail:** briefdc@aol.com

DUFFY, ANTHONY CARL
Industry: Law **Born:** February 4, 1947, Seattle, Washington **Univ./degree:** A.B., with Honors, Political Science, Stanford University, California, 1968; J.D., Yale Law School, 1971 **Current organization:** The Duffy Law Firm **Title:** Attorney at Law **Type of organization:** Law firm **Major product:** Legal services **Area of distribution:** International **Area of Practice:** Business litigation, real estate **Published works:** Co-authored 1 book **Affiliations:** A.B.A.; A.S.C.D.C., State Bar of California; Orange County Bar Association; U.S. Court of Appeals, 9th Circuit; Phi Beta Kappa; Captain, U.S. Army Reserves (Retired), 1968-76 **Hob./spts.:** Golf, scuba diving, travel, theatre, music, politics **SIC code:** 81 **Address:** The Duffy Law Firm, 4675 MacArthur Ct., Suite 550, Newport Beach, CA 92660 **E-mail:** acd@duffylawfirm.com

DUZAN, JAMES R.
Industry: Law **Born:** August 7, 1946, Westphalia, Indiana **Univ./degree:** B.S., Mechanical Engineering, Rose Hulman Polytechnic Institute, 1968; J.D., Indiana University, 1972; M.B.A., Oklahoma City University, 1983 **Current organization:** Trask Britt **Title:** Partner **Type of organization:** Law firm **Major product:** Intellectual property law **Area of distribution:** International **Area of Practice:** Patent law, Internet law **Affiliations:** American Bar Association; D.C. Bar Association; Utah Bar Association; American Intellectual Property Law Association; Indiana State Bar Association **Hob./spts.:** Automobiles, hunting, shooting **SIC code:** 81 **Address:** Trask Britt, 230 S. 500 East, Suite 300, Salt Lake City, UT 84102 **E-mail:** jrduzan@traskbritt.com **Web address:** www.frankbritt.com

DWYER, ELIZABETH MALC
Industry: Law **Born:** February 9, 1964, Painesville, Ohio **Univ./degree:** B.A., Political Science, Allegheny College, 1986; J.D., University of Toledo College of Law, 1990 **Current organization:** Elizabeth Malc Dwyer, Attorney at Law **Title:** Attorney **Type of organization:** Law firm **Major product:** Legal services **Area of distribution:** Erie, Pennsylvania **Area of Practice:** Family Law **Hob./spts.:** Gardening, landscape design **SIC code:** 81 **Address:** Elizabeth Malc Dwyer, Attorney at Law, 337 West Sixth St., Erie, PA 16507

EAGAN, WILLIAM L.
Industry: Law **Born:** February 10, 1928, Tampa, Florida **Univ./degree:** J.D. with Honors, University of Florida School of Law, 1961 **Current organization:** Arnold, Matheny & Eagan, P.A. **Title:** Of Counsel Attorney **Type of organization:** Law firm **Major product:** Legal services **Area of distribution:** National **Area of Practice:** Comprehensive law firm servicing agriculture, business, real estate transactions, Florida Bar Certified Civil Litigator, 1984-2004; Leading Florida Attorneys Network **Affiliations:** The Florida Bar; Middle and Southern Federal Districts of Florida; 11th and 5th Circuit U.S. Court of Appeals; Order of the Coif; Phi Kappa Phi; Phi Alpha Delta **Hob./spts.:** Hunting, fishing, boating **SIC code:** 81 **Address:** Arnold, Matheny & Eagan, P.A., 605 E. Robinson St., Suite 730, Orlando, FL 32801 **Web address:** www.weagan@ameorl.com

EDDY, RAND C.
Industry: Law **Born:** August 5, 1961, New York, New York **Univ./degree:** J.D., Oklahoma City University School of Law, 1986 **Current organization:** Eddy & Jones, P.C. **Title:** Attorney at Law **Type of organization:** Law firm **Major product:** Legal services **Area of distribution:** Oklahoma **Area of Practice:** Employment/discrimination/civil rights **Honors/awards:** Listed in Best Lawyers in America and Society of Outstanding Lawyers of America **Published works:** 2 Law Review articles, 2 Oklahoma Bar Journal articles **Affiliations:** O.C.B.A.; A.B.A.; N.E.L.A. **Hob./spts.:** Family, golf, football, physical fitness **SIC code:** 81 **Address:** Eddy & Jones, P.C., 228 R.S. Kerr, Suite 220, Oklahoma City, OK 73102 **E-mail:** rand@eddyjoneslaw.com

EHRHARDT, ERIK A.
Industry: Law **Born:** January 25, 1971, Gainesville, Florida **Univ./degree:** B.S., Political Science/Russian Studies, Stetson University, 1993; J.D., University of Florida School of Law, 1996 **Current organization:** Office of Public Defender-10th Circuit **Title:** Attorney at Law **Type of organization:** Public defenders office **Major product:** Legal services **Area of distribution:** Lakeland, Florida **Area of Practice:** Juvenile/criminal law **Affiliations:** The Florida Bar **SIC code:** 81 **Address:** 5428 Struthers Rd., Winter Haven, FL 33884 **E-mail:** erikehrhardt@hotmail.com

EKLUND-EASLEY, MOLLY S.
Industry: Law **Born:** August, 1953, Benton Harbor, Michigan **Univ./degree:** B.S., Political Science, Grand Valley University, 1975; J.D., University of Detroit Law School, 1979 **Current organization:** Eklund-Easley & Associates **Title:** Attorney **Type of organization:** Law firm **Major product:** Legal services **Area of distribution:** National **Area of Practice:** Divorce, family law, probate, real estate, criminal and traffic **Affiliations:** A.B.A.; State Bar of Michigan **SIC code:** 81 **Address:** Eklund-Easley & Associates, 19111 W. Ten Mile Rd., Suite 106, Southfield, MI 48075 **E-mail:** scionmee@msn.com **Web address:** www.eklund-easleyassociates.com

EPSTEIN, ROBERT H.
Industry: Law **Born:** June 22, 1958, St. Louis, Missouri **Univ./degree:** J.D., Washington University, 1983 **Current organization:** Gallop, Johnson & Neuman, L.C. **Title:** Attorney **Type of organization:** Group law firm **Major product:** Legal services **Area of distribution:** Missouri **Area of Practice:** Real estate, corporate, environmental law **Affiliations:** Missouri Bar; Metro Bar of St. Louis **Hob./spts.:** Sports, golf, politics **SIC code:** 81 **Address:** Gallop, Johnson & Neuman, L.C., 101 South Hanley, Suite 1700, St. Louis, MO 63105 **E-mail:** rhepstein@gjn.com **Web address:** www.gjn.com

ESTES, TIM
Industry: Law **Born:** Shreveport, Louisiana **Univ./degree:** Louisiana Nursing School, 1946; Louisiana Real Estate, 1984; Louisiana Civil Law Notary, 1985 **Current organization:** Professional Civil Law Notary Assoc. **Title:** Founder/President **Type of organization:** Law **Major product:** Civil law services **Area of distribution:** Shreveport, Louisiana **Area of Practice:** Management **Published works:** 5 poems **Affiliations:** Notary Ambassador for Louisiana, 2001 and 2003; Louisiana Real Estate Association; Louisiana Notary Association; Greater Shreveport Chamber of Commerce; United State Power Squadron; Beefmasters Breeders Universal Association; Founder/Officer of Greater Shreveport /Bossier City Notary Chapter of Louisiana Notary Association **Hob./spts.:** Music, poetry **SIC code:** 81 **Address:** Professional Civil Law Notary Assoc., 1848 S. Brookwood Dr., Shreveport, LA 71118 **E-mail:** timestes@sport.rr.com **Web address:** www.pclna.org

EVANS, CHARLES E.
Industry: Law **Born:** November 23, 1942, New Brighton, Pennsylvania **Univ./degree:** J.D., Du Quesne University **Current organization:** Evans, Portnoy & Quinn **Title:** Partner **Type of organization:** Law firm **Major product:** Legal services **Area of distribution:** Pennsylvania **Area of Practice:** Civil trial law **Honors/awards:** Best Lawyers in American, 1993-present **Affiliations:** President, Western Chapter, American Board of Trial Advocates; Past President, Pennsylvania Trial Lawyers Association **Hob./spts.:** Politics, sports **SIC code:** 81 **Address:** Evans, Portnoy & Quinn, 1 Oxford Centre, 36th floor, Pittsburgh, PA 15219 **E-mail:** ceevans@stargate.net

FANCHER, C. LARRY
Industry: Law **Born:** August 6, 1942, Auburn, Washington **Univ./degree:** B.A., Industrial Education, Central Washington State University; M.A., Industrial Education, California State University, Long Beach; J.D., Western State University College of Law (Fullerton), 1981 **Current organization:** Law Office of C. Larry Fancher **Title:** Esquire/Attorney at Law **Type of organization:** Law firm **Major product:** Legal services **Area of distribution:** California **Area of Practice:** Family law **Affiliations:** O.C.B.A.; State Bar of California **Hob./spts.:** Deep-sea fishing **SIC code:** 81 **Address:** Law Office of C. Larry Fancher, 440 E. La Habra Blvd., La Habra, CA 90631 **E-mail:** clarryfancher@yahoo.com

FARZANEH, AMIR M.
Industry: Law **Born:** June 6, 1963, Tehran, Iran **Univ./degree:** J.D., Oklahoma City University, 1995 **Current organization:** McKinney & Stinger **Title:** Attorney **Type of organization:** Law firm **Major product:** Legal services **Area of distribution:** National **Area of Practice:** Immigration law **Affiliations:** A.B.A.; A.I.L.A.; President, South Oklahoma City Lawyers Association **Hob./spts.:** Judo **SIC code:** 81 **Address:** McKinney & Stinger, 101 N. Robinsin, Suite 1300, Oklahoma City, OK 73102 **E-mail:** amir@farzaneh.com

FELLHAUER, DANIEL
Industry: Law **Born:** July 11, 1973, Columbus, Ohio **Univ./degree:** J.D., University of Toledo **Current organization:** Boucher, Hutton, & Graham, P.C. **Title:** Attorney **Type of organization:** Law firm **Major product:** Legal services **Area of distribution:** Virginia **Area of Practice:** Bankruptcy and criminal **Affiliations:** Virginia State Bar; Washington County Bar Association **Hob./spts.:** Travel, golf **SIC code:** 81 **Address:** Boucher, Hutton, & Graham, P.C., 131 E. Valley St., Abingdon, VA 24210 **E-mail:** fellhauer@abingdon-law.com

FERRUCCI, JOSEPH ANTHONY
Industry: Law **Born:** January 13, 1969, New Haven, Connecticut **Univ./degree:** J.D., Pepperdine University School of Law, 1996 **Current organization:** Law Offices of Joseph A. Ferrucci, P.C. **Title:** Attorney **Type of organization:** Law firm **Major product:** Legal services **Area of distribution:** Irvine, California **Area of Practice:**

Business, corporate, real estate and construction law **Affiliations:** Orange County Bar Association **Hob./spts.:** Golf **SIC code:** 81 **Address:** Law Offices of Joseph A. Ferrucci, P.C., 420 Exchange, Suite 270, Irvine, CA 92602 **E-mail:** jferrucci@jaf-law.com

FILITTI, GERARD
Industry: Law **Born:** New York, New York **Univ./degree:** M.A., University of London, 1998; J.D., University of Michigan, 2003 **Current organization:** Drinker Biddle & Reath, LLP **Title:** Attorney **Type of organization:** Law firm **Major product:** Legal services **Area of distribution:** National **Area of Practice:** Commercial litigation **Affiliations:** A.T.L.A.; N.Y.S.B.A.; N.J.B.A. **Hob./spts.:** Golf, tennis, motocross and rally racing **SIC code:** 81 **Address:** Drinker Biddle & Reath, LLP, 500 Campus Dr., Florham Park, NJ 07932 **E-mail:** gerard.filitti@dbr.com

FINN, FRANK
Industry: Law **Born:** September 20, 1928, Dallas, Texas **Univ./degree:** B.A., University of Notre Dame, Indiana; LL.B., University of Texas at Austin **Current organization:** Thompson & Knight, LLP **Title:** Senior Counsel **Type of organization:** Law firm **Major product:** Legal services **Area of distribution:** National **Area of Practice:** General civil trial, mediation and arbitration, business litigation, general corporation representation and intellectual property **Affiliations:** State Bar of Texas; Texas Federal Courts; Fifth Circuit and U.S. Supreme Court **Hob./spts.:** Notre Dame football **SIC code:** 81 **Address:** Thompson & Knight, LLP, 1700 Pacific Ave., Suite 3300, Dallas, TX 75201 **E-mail:** frank.finn@tklaw.com **Web address:** www.tklaw.com

FITZPATRICK, MICHAEL T.
Industry: Law **Univ./degree:** J.D., Thomas Cody Law School, 1994 **Current organization:** Michael Fitzpatrick Law Office **Title:** Esquire **Type of organization:** Law firm **Major product:** Legal services **Area of distribution:** National **Area of Practice:** Social Security Disability Law **Published works:** 2 publications **Affiliations:** N.A.D.R.; A.T.L.A.; National Organization for Social Security Reps. **Hob./spts.:** Travel, golf, reading **SIC code:** 81 **Address:** Michael Fitzpatrick Law Office, 316 E. Silver Spring Dr., Suite 220, Milwaukee, WI 53217 **E-mail:** mike@fitzpatricklawoffice.com

FLAHERTY, JOHN J.
Industry: Law **Born:** December 19, 1956, Buffalo, New York **Univ./degree:** J.D., Thomas Cooley Law School, 1985 **Current organization:** John J. Flaherty, Attorney at Law **Title:** Attorney **Type of organization:** Law firm **Major product:** Legal services **Area of distribution:** New York **Area of Practice:** Motor vehicle accidents **Affiliations:** A.T.L.A.; Erie County Bar Association; New York State Bar Association; Lions Club **Hob./spts.:** Golf, coaching Little League basketball and baseball, pool, studying jazz piano **SIC code:** 81 **Address:** John J. Flaherty, Attorney at Law, 5500 Main St., Suite 100, Williamsville, NY 14221 **E-mail:** jjf_esq@yahoo.com

FORTUNATO, ANNAMARIE
Industry: Law **Born:** July 19, 1969, Brooklyn, New York **Univ./degree:** B.A., Political Science, Boston College; J.D., Hofstra University School of Law, 1994 **Current organization:** Fortunato & Fortunato, PLLC **Title:** Attorney at Law **Type of organization:** Law firm **Major product:** Legal services **Area of distribution:** Brooklyn, New York **Area of Practice:** Personal injury, negligence, labor law **Affiliations:** N.Y.S.B.A.; A.B.A.; Columbian Law Association; Christ Law Association **Hob./spts.:** Travel, swimming, reading **SIC code:** 81 **Address:** Fortunato & Fortunato, PLLC, 26 Court St., Suite 1301, Brooklyn, NY 11234

FOURNIER, NICOLE M.
Industry: Law **Born:** March 6, 1971, Providence, Rhode Island **Univ./degree:** J.D., Quinnipiac University, 1997 **Current organization:** Lynch, Traub, Keefe & Errante **Title:** Attorney **Type of organization:** Law firm **Major product:** Legal services **Area of distribution:** New Haven, Connecticut **Area of Practice:** Civil defense **Honors/awards:** Young Lawyers; Women in the Law; Outstanding Legal Scholarship Award, 1997; Distinguished Academic Achievement Award for Business Organization/Legal Skills; Honorary Scholarship from Law School, 1994-97 **Affiliations:** C.B.A., Federal Practice Section; A.B.A.; C.C.D.L; New Haven County Bar Association **Hob./spts.:** Reading, fitness **SIC code:** 81 **Address:** P.O. Box 1612, New Haven, CT 06506 **E-mail:** n.fournier@ltke.com

FREEDMAN, ROBERTA
Industry: Law **Born:** June 22, 1958, Chanute Air force Base, Illinois **Univ./degree:** J.D., University of Baltimore, 1983 **Current organization:** Pederson & Freedman, LLP **Title:** Attorney/Managing Partner **Type of organization:** Law firm **Major product:** Legal services **Area of distribution:** Washington D.C. **Area of Practice:** Immigration law **Affiliations:** A.I.L.A.; A.B.A. **SIC code:** 81 **Address:** Pederson & Freedman, LLP, 2001 L St. N.W., Suite 601, Washington, DC 20036 **E-mail:** rfreedman@usvisainfo.com

FRENCH, THOMAS M.
Industry: Law **Born:** November 15, 1934, Muskegon, Michigan **Univ./degree:** J.D., University of Wisconsin **Current organization:** Thomas M. French, Attorney-at-Law **Title:** Attorney **Type of organization:** Law firm **Major product:** Legal services **Area of distribution:** Brattleboro, Vermont **Area of Practice:** General law practice **Published works:** 5 papers **Affiliations:** Windham County Bar Association; A.T.L.A.; A.B.A.; Vermont Bar Association **Hob./spts.:** Fruit trees, map collecting, tennis **SIC code:** 81 **Address:** Thomas M. French, Attorney-at-Law, 919 Western Ave., P.O. Box 492, Brattleboro, VT 05302-0492 **E-mail:** sfwta@aol.com

FROMAN-BETTENCOURT, RACHEL J.
Industry: Law **Univ./degree:** J.D., Boston College Law School, 1994 **Current organization:** Law Offices of Rachel J.F. Bettencourt **Title:** Esquire **Type of organization:** Private law office **Major product:** Legal services **Area of distribution:** Massachusetts **Area of Practice:** Children's advocacy **Affiliations:** A.B.A.; Massachusetts Supreme Court **SIC code:** 81 **Address:** Law Offices of Rachel J.F. Bettencourt, P.O. Box 533, Leominster, MA 01453 **E-mail:** rachbetten@netzero.com

FULTON, PHILIP J.
Industry: Law **Born:** March 8, 1955, Columbus, Ohio **Univ./degree:** B.A., Ohio State University, 1977; J.D., Capitol University School of Law, 1980 **Current organization:** Philip J. Fulton Law Office **Title:** Attorney **Type of organization:** Law firm **Major product:** Legal services **Area of distribution:** Ohio **Area of Practice:** Workmen's compensation **Honors/awards:** Ohio Academy of Trial Lawyers Workers' Compensation Hall of Fame; Best Lawyers in America **Published works:** 1 book and articles; Author, Ohio Workers Compensation Law, Anderson Publishing Co., 1991, 1998 **Affiliations:** Ohio State Bar Association; American Bar Association; Vice President, Ohio Academy of Trial Lawyers, 2003-2004 **Hob./spts.:** Family, golf **SIC code:** 81 **Address:** Philip J. Fulton Law Office, 89 E. Nationwide Blvd., Suite 300, Columbus, OH 43215 **E-mail:** phil@fultonlaw.com **Web address:** www.fultonlaw.com

GAMBOURG, ROMAN V.
Industry: Law **Univ./degree:** J.D., Hofstra University School of Law, 2000 **Current organization:** Roman V. Gambourg, P.C. **Title:** Attorney **Type of organization:** Law firm **Major product:** Legal services **Area of distribution:** International **Area of Practice:** Real estate law, corporate law **Affiliations:** A.B.A.; A.T.L.A. **SIC code:** 81 **Address:** Roman V. Gambourg, P.C., 2185 Lemoine Ave., Ft. Lee, NJ 07024

GERARDIN, KARIN S.
Industry: Law **Born:** July 11, 1965, Baltimore, Maryland **Univ./degree:** B.A., Marketing, Florida International University, 1995; J.D., St. Thomas University School of Law, 1998 **Current organization:** Law Offices of Karin S. Gerardin, PA **Title:** Attorney at Law **Type of organization:** Law firm **Major product:** Legal services **Area of distribution:** International **Area of Practice:** Immigration and family law **Published works:** 1 article **Affiliations:** A.I.L.A.; President, B.N.I. (southern district of Florida); The Florida Bar **Hob./spts.:** Cooking, reading, community work **SIC code:** 81 **Address:** Law Offices of Karin S. Gerardin, PA, 633 N.E. 167th St., Suite 501, North Miami Beach, FL 33162 **E-mail:** ksg@gerardinlaw.com **Web address:** www.gerardinlaw.com

GERBER, EDWARD F.
Industry: Law **Born:** October 10, 1932, Houston, Texas **Univ./degree:** L.L.B., J.D., Syracuse University, 1960 **Current organization:** Alli, Pappas, Cox **Title:** Of Counsel to Firm **Type of organization:** Law firm **Major product:** Legal services **Area of distribution:** National **Area of Practice:** Defense of white collar crime **Affiliations:** A.C.T.L.; U.S.T.L.A.; President, Bar Foundation; President, Upstate Trial Lawyers Association **Hob./spts.:** Golf **SIC code:** 81 **Address:** Alli, Pappas, Cox, 614 James St., Suite 100, Syracuse, NY 13203 **E-mail:** efgesq@yahoo.com

GERVAIS-GRUEN, ELIZABETH
Industry: Immigration Law **Born:** February 4, Hungary **Spouse:** Rudolph Gruen (1934), Ralph Gervais (1970) **Children:** Richard Gruen, Robert Gruen, S. Daniel Gruen, David J. Gruen **Univ./degree:** LL.B., St. John's University, 1934 **Current organization:** Law Office of Elizabeth Gervais-Gruen **Title:** Immigration Attorney **Type of organization:** Immigration law firm **Major product:** Obtaining legal immigration status for immigrant clients **Area of distribution:** Representing immigrants with the Homeland Security (formerly INS. Now INS authority has been transferred to Homeland Security within 3 Bureaus): 1) US Citizenship and Immigration, 2) Immigration and Customs Enforcement, 3) US Customs & Border Protection **Area of Practice:** Immigration and Naturalization Law **Honors/awards:** American Immigration Lawyers Association-North Carolina Chapter Established Award; Elizabeth Gervais-Gruen Mentor Award; Received 1st Elizabeth Gervais-Gruen Mentor Award; American Immigration Lawyers Association, Sam Williamson Mentor Award; American Immigration Law Foundation, Honorary Fellow Award; American Immigration Lawyers Association, President's Commendation; Sara and Mutt Evans Award for Service to the Jewish Community **Affiliations:** Board Member, American Immigration Lawyers Association; Founding Member, American Immigration Lawyers Association Carolinas Chapter; Chair of

Immigration and Nationality Committee, North Carolina Bar Association; American Bar Association; Orange County Bar Association; North Carolina Association of Women Lawyers; Durham Orange Women's Association; Executive Committee of Central Carolina Mineral Club; Triangle Stamp Club; North Carolina Botanical Garden Wildflower **Career accomplishments:** Successful immigration law practice **Hob./spts.:** Reading immigration law, collecting minerals and fossils, gardening, collecting Judaic artifacts **SIC code:** 81 **Address:** Law Office of Elizabeth Gervais-Gruen, 914 Crestwood Lane, Chapel Hill, NC 27517 **E-mail:** egervaisgruen@nc.rr.com

GHAZNAVI, JAHANGIR H.
Industry: Healthcare **Born:** October 11, 1953, Sylhet, Bangladesh **Univ./degree:** M.D., Sylhet Medical College, Bangladesh, 1990; Internship, Internal Medicine, University of Oklahoma Sciences Center **Current organization:** Red Rock Behavioral Health Services **Title:** M.D./Medical Director **Type of organization:** Mental health center **Major product:** Mental health services **Area of distribution:** Oklahoma **Area of Practice:** General psychiatry, schizophrenia, major depression mood disorder, administration **Honors/awards:** Outstanding Medical Director, Red Rock Geriatric Service, 1994-9 **Affiliations:** Diplomate, American Board of Forensic Medicine; Diplomate, American Association of Psychiatric Medicine; Oklahoma Psychiatric Physicians Association; American College of Forensic Examiners **Hob./spts.:** Gardening, fishing, travel, music **SIC code:** 81 **Address:** Red Rock Behavioral Health Services, 4400 N. Lincoln Blvd., Oklahoma City, OK 73105 **E-mail:** sufijhg@yahoo.com

GILES, DARREN C.
Industry: Law **Born:** October 23, 1972, Hammond, Louisiana **Univ./degree:** J.D., Mississippi College, 1999 **Current organization:** F.Q. Hood Jr., APLC **Title:** Attorney **Type of organization:** Law firm **Major product:** Legal services **Area of distribution:** Bossier City, Louisiana **Area of Practice:** Trial practice **Affiliations:** Louisiana Bar Association **Hob./spts.:** Gardening, golf **SIC code:** 81 **Address:** F.Q. Hood Jr., APLC, 1503 Doctors Dr., Bossier City, LA 71111

GIOIA, DANIEL A.
Industry: Law **Univ./degree:** B.A., Georgetown University, 1972; J.D., The American University, Washington D.C., 1975 **Current organization:** Spangler, Jennings & Dougherty, P.C. **Title:** Attorney at Law, Managing Partner **Type of organization:** Law firm **Major product:** Legal services **Area of distribution:** Valparaiso, Indiana **Area of Practice:** Defense law, mediation **Affiliations:** Indiana State Bar Association **Hob./spts.:** Soccer referee **SIC code:** 81 **Address:** Spangler, Jennings & Dougherty, P.C., 8396 Mississippi St., Merriville, IN 46410-6316 **E-mail:** dgioia@sjdlaw.com

GLADSTONE, M. BRETT
Industry: Law **Born:** September 28, 1957, New York, New York **Univ./degree:** J.D., Duke University Law School, 1983 **Current organization:** Gladstone & Associates **Title:** Partner/Attorney **Type of organization:** Law firm **Major product:** Legal services **Area of distribution:** National **Area of Practice:** Real estate law **Affiliations:** San Francisco Planning and Urban Research; Residential Builders Association; University Club of San Francisco **Hob./spts.:** Jazz piano, squash **SIC code:** 81 **Address:** Gladstone & Associates, 177 Post St., Penthouse, San Francisco, CA 94108 **E-mail:** brett@gladstoneassociates.com

GLICKSMAN, ELLIOT A.
Industry: Law **Univ./degree:** B.A., Psychology, University of Wisconsin, 1976; J.D. with High Distinction, University of Arizona, 1979; Order of the Coif. **Current organization:** Stompoly, Stroud, Glicksman & Erickson, P.C. **Title:** Attorney at Law **Type of organization:** Law firm **Major product:** Legal services **Area of distribution:** National **Area of Practice:** Personal Injury and Wrongful Death, Certified Specialist, State Bar of Arizona **Published works:** Lead Counsel: Webster v. Culbertson, 158 Ariz 159, 761 P2d 1063 (1988); Vermillion vs. AAA Pro Movers, 146 Ariz 215, 704 P2d 1360 (Ariz. App. 1985); Rhoads v. Harvey Publishing, Inc. 131 Ariz 267, 640 P2d 198 (Ariz. App. 1982) **Affiliations:** Arizona Trial Lawyers Association **SIC code:** 81 **Address:** Stompoly, Stroud, Glicksman & Erickson, P.C., 1 S. Church Ave., Suite 1640, Tucson, AZ 85701 **E-mail:** elliotglicksman@qwest.net

GLINN, FRANKLYN B.
Industry: Law **Born:** October 22, 1943, Newark, New Jersey **Univ./degree:** J.D., University of Florida **Current organization:** Glinn & Somera **Title:** Attorney/Partner **Type of organization:** Law firm **Major product:** Legal services **Area of distribution:** National **Area of Practice:** Personal injury, medical malpractice **Affiliations:** A.T.L.A.; A.F.T.L.; A.B.A. **SIC code:** 81 **Address:** Glinn & Somera, P.A., 2100 Coral Way, Suite 401, Miami, FL 33145 **E-mail:** glinnsomera@aol.com

GLOCKHOFF, ROY H.
Industry: Law **Born:** June 18, 1912, Rock Island, Illinois **Univ./degree:** Attended Augustana College; A.B., University of Illinois, 1934; LL.B., University of Illinois, 1937 **Current organization:** Glockhoff and Haytcher **Title:** Attorney at Law/Owner **Type of organization:** Law firm **Major product:** Legal services **Area of distribution:** National **Area of Practice:** General practice **Affiliations:** A.B.A.; Illinois State Bar Association; Rock Island County Bar Association; Rotary International; City Attorney, East Moline, IL; Village Attorney, Colona, IL, Illini Hospital District, all municipal organizations and Community Savings and Loan Association **Hob./spts.:** Travel, gardening **SIC code:** 81 **Address:** Glockhoff and Haytcher, 912-15th Ave., East Moline, IL 61244 **Phone:** (309)752-2600 **Fax:** (309)752-2604

GOLDBERG, JEFFREY M.
Industry: Law **Born:** March 8, 1948, Chicago, Illinois **Univ./degree:** J.D., John Marshall Law School, 1974 **Current organization:** Jeffrey M. Goldberg & Associates **Title:** Owner/President/Founder/Principal Attorney **Type of organization:** Law firm **Major product:** Legal services **Area of distribution:** National **Area of Practice:** Birth trauma, medical malpractice, personal injury **Published works:** 15 articles, public speaking (nationally) **Affiliations:** A.T.L.A.; Illinois Trial Lawyers' Association; Trial Lawyers for Public Justice **Hob./spts.:** Motorcycling, sailing, skiing **SIC code:** 81 **Address:** Jeffrey M. Goldberg & Associates, 20 N. Clark St., Suite 3100, Chicago, IL 60602 **E-mail:** jgoldberg@goldberg

GONZALEZ, DANIEL R.
Industry: Law **Born:** October 20, 1955, Simi Valley, California **Univ./degree:** J.D., Loyola Law School, 1983 **Current organization:** Law Offices of Daniel Gonzalez **Title:** Attorney **Type of organization:** Law firm **Major product:** Legal services **Area of distribution:** Simi Valley, California **Area of Practice:** Family law, criminal law **Affiliations:** A.B.A.; Ventura County Bar Association; Ventura County Mexican/American Bar Association **Hob./spts.:** Fishing, tennis, scuba diving, backpacking, motorcycles **SIC code:** 81 **Address:** Law Offices of Daniel Gonzalez, 4266 E. Los Angeles, Suite 205, Simi Valley, CA 93063 **E-mail:** dangonzalez@earthlink.net

GONZALEZ, JOE M.
Industry: Law **Born:** Tampa, Florida **Univ./degree:** J.D., Gonzaga University School of Law, 1980; LL.M., Georgetown University Law School, 1981 **Current organization:** Joe M. Gonzalez, P.A. **Title:** Attorney **Type of organization:** Law firm **Major product:** Legal services **Area of distribution:** Florida **Area of Practice:** Estate planning, probate, corporate, matrimonial **Honors/awards:** City of Tampa Hispanic Advisory Council, 1983 (Chairman since 1993); University of South Florida, Hispanic Advisory Board, 1999-2001; President, Tampa Hispanic Heritage, Inc., 1985-93; Founder, Carnavale en Tampa, Inc., 1986-90 **Affiliations:** Association of Trial Lawyers of America; Supreme Court of the United States; United States Tax Court; Lambda Chi Alpha Fraternity **Hob./spts.:** Boating, tennis, waterskiing **SIC code:** 81 **Address:** Joe M. Gonzalez, P.A., 304 S. Willow Ave., Tampa, FL 33606 **E-mail:** joegonzalezpa@aol.com

GOOCH, J. CHRISTOPHER
Industry: Law **Born:** September 20, 1970, Newport Beach, California **Univ./degree:** B.A., Magna Cum Laude, Economics/Architectural Structure, Claremont McKenna College, 1995; J.D., University of Arizona, College of Law, 1998 **Current organization:** Cohen Kennedy Dowd & Quigley P.C. **Title:** Esquire **Type of organization:** Law firm **Major product:** Commercial, real estate and technology litigation **Area of distribution:** Arizona and Southwestern U.S. **Area of Practice:** Complex commercial, real estate and technology litigation **Published works:** "The Internet, Personal Jurisdiction and the Federal Long Arm Statue: Rethinking the Concept of Jurisdiction" **Affiliations:** A.B.A.; State Bar of Arizona; Instructor, Institute of Paralegal Education and National Business Institute **Hob./spts.:** Bonsai, basketball, art **SIC code:** 81 **Address:** Cohen Kennedy Dowd & Quigley P.C., 2425 E. Camelback Rd., Suite 1100, Phoenix, AZ 85016 **E-mail:** cgooch@ckdqlaw.com **Web address:** www.ckdqlaw.com

GORDON, ROBERTA G.
Industry: Law **Born:** May 8, New York, New York **Univ./degree:** B.A. with Highest Honors, Chemistry, Environmental Planning and Public Policy, University California at Santa Cruz, 1981; J.D., Yale Law School, 1986 **Current organization:** Bryan Cave, LLP **Title:** Esquire **Type of organization:** Law firm **Major product:** Legal services **Area of distribution:** International **Area of Practice:** Environmental law; Lead case attorney for September 11, 2001 World Trade Center attacks picked by Trial Lawyers Care **Honors/awards:** Valedictorian, Highest Honors and Thesis Honors, University of California **Published works:** Past Senior Editor, Yale Law Journal; The Emerging Environmental Insurance Market, Nov. 2004, New Solutions to Environmental Problems in Business and Real Setae Deals 2004, Practicing Law Institute (and faculty member); The Emerging Environmental Insurance Market, Nov. 2003, New Solutions to Environmental Problems in Business and Real Estate Deals 2004, Practicing Law Institute (and faculty member); Risk Management Techniques: Tools Applied to Assess Business Transactions Reach New Maturity, Oct. 25, 1999, N.Y.L.J., Environmental Law Section, S4; **Affiliations:** A.B.A.; Association of the Bar of the City of New York; New York State Bar Association; Former Director, Yale Environmental Litigation Program **Hob./spts.:** Cooking, travel, music **SIC code:** 81 **Address:** Bryan Cave, LLP, 1290 Avenue of the Americas, New York, NY 10104 **E-mail:** rggordon@bryancave.com **Web address:** www.bryancave.com

GORMAN, ELLEN R.
Industry: Law **Born:** New York, New York **Univ./degree:** B.A., State University of New York at Albany, 1974; J.D., Northeast School of Law, Massachusetts, 1992 **Current organization:** Gorman Miotke & Associates, P.A. **Title:** Attorney/President **Type of organization:** Law firm **Major product:** Legal services **Area of distribution:** Florida **Area of Practice:** Immigration law **Published works:** Articles **Affiliations:** Florida State Bar; U.S. Supreme Court Bar **Hob./spts.:** Family, church **SIC code:** 81 **Address:** Gorman Miotke & Associates, P.A., 9800 Fourth St. North, Suite 403, St. Petersburg, FL 33702 **E-mail:** gormanlaw@yahoo.com

GOZA, SHIRLEY E.
Industry: Law **Born:** April 24, 1957, Garnett, Kansas **Univ./degree:** J.D., University of Kansas, 1982 **Current organization:** Shook, Hardy & Bacon **Title:** Attorney **Type of organization:** Law firm **Major product:** Legal services **Area of distribution:** National **Area of Practice:** Employment and labor law **Affiliations:** Missouri Bar **Hob./spts.:** Tennis, Running **SIC code:** 81 **Address:** Shook, Hardy & Bacon, 1 Kansas City Place, 1200 Main St., Kansas City, MO 64105-4118 **E-mail:** sgoza@shb.com

GRAVENHORST, PAUL S.
Industry: Law **Born:** October 4, 1950, New York **Univ./degree:** J.D., Gonzaga University, 1977; L.L.M., New York University, 1978 **Current organization:** Holland & Knight, LLP **Title:** Attorney/Partner **Type of organization:** Law firm **Major product:** Legal services/advice **Area of distribution:** National **Area of Practice:** Estate, tax planning **Affiliations:** A.B.A.; F.B.A. **Hob./spts.:** Golf, boating **SIC code:** 81 **Address:** Holland & Knight, LLP, 1 E. Broward Blvd., Suite 1300, Ft. Lauderdale, FL 33301 **E-mail:** pgravenh@hklaw.com

GRAVES, JOHN H.
Industry: Law **Born:** December 21, 1977, Oklahoma City, Oklahoma **Univ./degree:** B.A., University of Oklahoma, 2000; J.D., University of Oklahoma School of Law, 2003 **Current organization:** Don G. Pope and Associates, P.C. **Title:** Attorney **Type of organization:** Law firm **Major product:** Environmental litigation **Area of distribution:** Oklahoma **Area of Practice:** Environmental law **Affiliations:** A.T.L.A.; Oklahoma Trial Lawyers Association; Oklahoma Bar Association **Hob./spts.:** Watching Oklahoma University sports, hunting, family **SIC code:** 81 **Address:** Don G. Pope and Associates, P.C., 2424 Springer Dr., Suite 201, Norman, OK 73069

GRAY III, JAMES A.
Industry: Law **Born:** September 23, 1970, Orangeburg, South Carolina **Univ./degree:** J.D., University of Houston **Current organization:** The Gray Firm, LLC **Title:** Attorney **Type of organization:** Law firm **Major product:** Legal services **Area of distribution:** Louisiana **Area of Practice:** Personal injury and real estate **Published works:** 2 articles **Affiliations:** A.B.A.; National Bar Association; Louisiana State Bar Association; State Bar of Texas; American Trial Lawyers Association; Louisiana Trial Lawyers Association **Hob./spts.:** Active participant in all sports activities **SIC code:** 81 **Address:** The Gray Firm, LLC, 1100 Poydras, Suite 2620, New Orleans, LA 70163 **E-mail:** james.gray.iii@gmail.com

GREER, RAYMOND W.
Industry: Law **Born:** July 20, 1954, Port Arthur, Texas **Univ./degree:** J.D., University of Houston, Bates College of Law, 1981 **Current organization:** Rigg & Greer **Title:** Partner **Type of organization:** Law firm **Major product:** Legal services **Area of distribution:** Sugarland, Texas **Area of Practice:** Civil trial **Honors/awards:** Outstanding Alumni Award, English Dept., Sam Houston State University; Alpha-Chi, Sam Houston State University; Who's Who in American Law; Who's Who in the World; Man of Achievement, 14th Edition; Who's Who in Finance & Industry; 2000 Outstanding Intellectuals of the 21st Century, 1st Edition **Affiliations:** A.B.A.; State Bar Association of Texas; Houston Bar Association; Fort Bend County Bar Association **Hob./spts.:** Reading, golf **SIC code:** 81 **Address:** Rigg & Greer, 13333 Southwest Freeway, Suite 100, Sugar Land, TX 77478

GRENADIER, ILONA E.
Industry: Law **Univ./degree:** J.D., Cum Laude, George Washington University, 1967 **Current organization:** Grenadier, Anderson, Simpson, Starace & Duffett, PC **Title:** Esquire **Type of organization:** Law firm **Major product:** Legal services **Area of distribution:** Virginia **Area of Practice:** Domestic relations **Honors/awards:** Order of the Coif **Affiliations:** American Bar Association; Virginia State Bar; American Academy of Matrimonial Lawyers; International Academy of Matrimonial Lawyers; Virginia Bar Association; Alexandria Bar Association; Fairfax Bar Association; Virginia Trial Lawyers Association **SIC code:** 81 **Address:** Grenadier, Anderson, Simpson, Starace & Duffett, PC, 649 S. Washington St., Alexandria, VA 22314 **E-mail:** igrenadier@vafamilylaw.com

GRIECO, JENNIFER M.
Industry: Law **Born:** July 15, 1971, Frankfurt, Germany **Univ./degree:** B.A., Political Science/minor-History, 1993; J.D., 1997, University of Toledo, Ohio **Current organization:** Sommers, Schwartz, Silver & Schwartz, P.C. **Title:** Shareholder **Type of organization:** Law firm **Major product:** Legal services **Area of distribution:** National **Area of Practice:** Plaintiffs personal injury - medical malpractice, product liability, toxic tort, including mold litigation **Honors/awards:** Recognized as 2004 Up and Coming Lawyers (1 of 5) by Michigan Lawyers Weekly; Speaking engagements at professional conferences and seminars on such topics as "Mold Creates New Cause of Action", "Environmental Law", "Solving Water Intrusion and Mold Problems in Michigan", "The Resident Standard of Care in Medical Malpractice" **Published works:** Articles/Journals: Michigan Trial Lawyers Association White Paper "Making the Case Against the Resident-The Resident Standard of Care in Michigan"; "Mold Grows in Michigan", Negligence Law Section Quarterly, Spring 2001; "Mold Creates New Cause of Action: Failure to Diagnose Sick Homes", MTLA Quarterly, Winter 2001 **Affiliations:** President, Women's Bar Association of Oakland County (2003-04); Executive Board Member, Michigan Trial Lawyer's Association, since Fall 2002; Director, Oakland County Bar Association, Board of Directors, elected Spring 2003; State Bar of Michigan Representative Assembly, elected Spring 2004; Member, American Trial Lawyers Association **Hob./spts.:** Hiking, camping, gardening **SIC code:** 81 **Address:** Sommers, Schwartz, Silver & Schwartz, P.C., 2000 Town Center, Suite 900, Southfield, MI 48075 **E-mail:** Jgrieco@sommerspc.com **Web address:** www.sommerspc.com

GRIFFITH, EMLYN I.
Industry: Law **Born:** May 13, 1923, Utica, New York **Univ./degree:** B.A., Colgate University, 1942; J.D., Cornell University, 1950 **Current organization:** Griffith Law Office **Title:** Attorney/State Regent Emeritus **Type of organization:** Law firm **Major product:** Legal services **Area of distribution:** Central New York **Area of Practice:** Estate planning, probate and real estate **Honors/awards:** Phi Alpha Delta, Selden Society, England; 10 Honorary Doctorates from Institutions in the U.S. and U.K.; Life Fellow, New York Bar Foundation and American Bar Foundation **Published works:** 15 articles in New York State Bar Journal **SIC code:** 81 **Address:** Griffith Law Office, 225 N. Washington St., Rome, NY 13440

GROSS, LEONARD A.
Industry: Law **Univ./degree:** B.S., University of California, 1940; J.D., Golden Gate College, 1961 **Current organization:** Leonard A. Gross P.C. **Title:** President **Type of organization:** Law firm **Major product:** Legal services **Area of distribution:** Oakland, California **Area of Practice:** Estate planning, tax law **Affiliations:** A.B.A. **Hob./spts.:** Golf **SIC code:** 81 **Address:** Leonard A. Gross P.C., 1999 Harrison St., Suite 1650, Oakland, CA 94612 **E-mail:** leonardagross@aol.com

GURWELL, KARIN EASTER
Industry: Law **Born:** December 15, 1948, Independence, Missouri **Univ./degree:** J.D., Southwestern University, 1976 **Current organization:** Law Office Of Karin Easter Gurwell **Title:** Attorney at Law **Type of organization:** Law firm **Major product:** Legal services **Area of distribution:** Huntington Beach, California **Area of Practice:** Business litigation **Affiliations:** California State Bar Association; Orange County Bar Association **Hob./spts.:** Saddleback College Master Circle **SIC code:** 81 **Address:** Law Office of Karin Easter Gurwell, 7755 Center Ave., 11th floor, Huntington Beach, CA 92647 **E-mail:** kgurwell@aol.com

GUSS, AMY J.
Industry: Law **Born:** September 27, 1963, Englewood, New Jersey **Univ./degree:** J.D. **Current organization:** Satterlee Stephens Burke & Burke, LLP **Title:** Esquire **Type of organization:** Law firm **Major product:** Legal services **Area of distribution:** International **Area of Practice:** Estate planning, tax planning, administration **Affiliations:** A.B.A.; New York State Bar **SIC code:** 81 **Address:** Satterlee Stephens Burke & Burke, LLP, 230 Park Ave., Suite 1130, New York, NY 10169 **E-mail:** aguss@ssbb.com

GWILLIAM, J. GARY
Industry: Law **Born:** May 18, 1937, Utah **Univ./degree:** LL.B., University of California at Berkeley, Boalt Hall School of Law, 1962 **Current organization:** Gwilliam, Ivary, Chiosso, Cavalli & Brewer **Title:** Senior Partner **Type of organization:** Law firm **Major product:** Legal services **Area of distribution:** National **Area of Practice:** Civil litigation, employment law **Published works:** "Are Lawyers Becoming Extinct?", 1999; "Trial By Fear", 2000 **Affiliations:** President, Trial Lawyers for Public Justice **SIC code:** 81 **Address:** Gwilliam, Ivary, Chiosso, Cavalli & Brewer, 1999 Harrison St., Suite 1600, Oakland, CA 94612-3528 **E-mail:** ggwilliam@giccb.com **Web address:** www.giccb.com

HALL, PATRICK Q.
Industry: Law **Born:** February 27, 1955, Mississippi **Univ./degree:** J.D. **Current organization:** Seltzer, Caplan, McMahon, Vitek **Title:** Partner **Type of organization:** Law firm **Major product:** Legal services **Area of distribution:** National **Area of Practice:** Criminal defense **Affiliations:** National Association of Criminal Defense Lawyers **Hob./spts.:** Swimming, golf, tennis **SIC code:** 81 **Address:** Seltzer, Caplan, McMahon, Vitek, 750 B. St., Suite 2100, San Diego, CA 92101 **E-mail:** hall@scmv.com

HALLORAN, DANIEL J.
Industry: Law **Born:** March 16, 1971, Queens, New York **Univ./degree:** J.D., 2000; LL.M., 2001, St. John's University **Current organization:** Palmieri & Castiglione, LLP **Title:** Attorney **Type of organization:** Law firm **Major product:** Legal services **Area of distribution:** New York **Area of Practice:** Criminal law **Affiliations:** N.A.T.L.; I.B.A.; N.Y.S.C.D.A; N.R.A. **Hob./spts.:** Camping, Eagle Scout **SIC code:** 81 **Address:** Palmieri & Castiglione, LLP, 250 Mineola Blvd., Mineola, NY 11501 **E-mail:** omisson@nysbar.com

HARDEN, SHAWN M.
Industry: Law **Born:** Marengo, Iowa **Univ./degree:** B.A., Summa Cum Laude, Criminal Justice, Mount Mercy College, 2000; J.D., with Honors, Drake University **Current organization:** Harden Law Office **Title:** Attorney and Judicial Magistrate, 1st Judicial District **Type of organization:** Law office **Major product:** Legal services **Area of distribution:** Iowa **Area of Practice:** Criminal, juvenile and family law **Affiliations:** American Bar Association; I.S.B.A.; I.A.M.; Alpha Phi Sigma; American Civil Liberties Union; Amnesty International; Association of Trial Lawyers of America; Buchanan County Bar Association; Iowa Bar Association; Iowa Trial Lawyers Association; Iowa Public Defenders Association; Kappa Gamma Pi; National Association of Criminal Defense Attorneys **SIC code:** 81 **Address:** Harden Law Office, 322 First Street East, P.O. Box 33, Independence, IA 50644-0331 **E-mail:** sharden@indytel.com

HARDY, C. SHANNON
Industry: Law **Born:** September 29, 1965, Montgomery, Alabama **Univ./degree:** J.D., Louisiana State University, 1990 **Current organization:** Penny & Hardy, APLC **Title:** Attorney **Type of organization:** Law firm **Major product:** Legal services **Area of distribution:** Louisiana **Area of Practice:** Insurance defense **Affiliations:** A.B.A.; D.R.I.; L.A.D.C.; Louisiana State Bar Association; Lafayette Parish Bar Association **Hob./spts.:** Family, golf **SIC code:** 81 **Address:** Penny & Hardy, APLC, 100 E. Vermilion St., Suite 301, Lafayette, LA 70501 **E-mail:** shannon@pennyhardy.com

HARNER, SHANNON R.
Industry: Law **Born:** Neubrucke, Germany **Univ./degree:** J.D., Georgetown University **Current organization:** Hoppe & Harner, LLP **Title:** Attorney **Type of organization:** Law firm **Major product:** Legal services **Area of distribution:** Nebraska **Area of Practice:** Real estate law **Published works:** Journals **Affiliations:** American Bar Association; Nebraska Association of Trial Lawyers; Nebraska State Bar Association; Massachusetts Bar Association **Hob./spts.:** Visual and performing arts **SIC code:** 81 **Address:** Hoppe & Harner, LLP, 5631 S. 48th St., Suite 220, Lincoln, NE 68516-4107 **E-mail:** shannon@hoppeharner.com

HARRINGTON, CURTIS R.
Industry: Law **Born:** December 25, 1953 **Univ./degree:** J.D., Louisiana State University, 1978 **Current organization:** C. Rodney Harrington Law Office **Title:** Founder/Attorney **Type of organization:** Law firm **Major product:** Legal services **Area of distribution:** Louisiana **Area of Practice:** Personal injury, bankruptcy **Affiliations:** Louisiana State Bar Association; L.T.L.A.; W.D.B.B. **Hob./spts.:** Music (owns a band called "Johnny Earthquake and the Moonshiners") **SIC code:** 81 **Address:** C. Rodney Harrington Law Office, 459 Jefferson, Natchitoches, LA 71457 **E-mail:** crodney50@yahoo.com

HARRISON III, ORRIN L.
Industry: Law **Born:** July 1, 1949, Dallas, Texas **Univ./degree:** B.A., Political Science, University of the South, Tennessee, 1971; J.D., Southern Methodist University, Texas, 1974 **Current organization:** Akin Gump Strauss Hauer & Feld LLP **Title:** Attorney **Type of organization:** Law firm **Major product:** Legal services **Area of distribution:** National **Area of Practice:** Securities, anti trust litigation **Affiliations:** State Bar of Texas; Admitted to practice before the U.S. Supreme Court, 5th Circuit and 11th Circuit **Hob./spts.:** Family, skiing **SIC code:** 81 **Address:** Akin Gump Strauss Hauer & Feld LLP, 1700 Pacific Ave., Suite 4100, Dallas, TX 75201 **E-mail:** oharrison@akingump.com

HART IV, WALTER L.
Industry: Law **Born:** June 1, 1961, Grand Forks, North Dakota **Univ./degree:** J.D., West Virginia College School of Law, 1986 **Current organization:** Walter L. Hart IV, Esq. **Title:** Attorney at Law **Type of organization:** Law firm **Major product:** Legal services **Area of distribution:** North Carolina **Area of Practice:** Plaintiff's civil litigation **Published works:** Trying Wrongful Death Claims in North Carolina; Analysis of Patterson vs. Craig **Affiliations:** W.V.S.B.A.; A.B.A.; N.C.A.T.L.; North Carolina Bar Association; American Trial Lawyers Association **Hob./spts.:** Running, golf, racquetball **SIC code:** 81 **Address:** Chandler & Hart, 1508 E. Fourth St., Charlotte, NC 28204 **E-mail:** bhart@charlottelawoffice.com

HARTMANN, ROBERT MARK
Industry: Law **Born:** April 21, 1960, Encino, California **Univ./degree:** B.S., Political Science, UCLA, 1982; J.D., Loyola Law School, California,1986 **Current organization:** Hartmann & Miller **Title:** Attorney at Law **Type of organization:** Law firm **Major product:** Legal services **Area of distribution:** California **Area of Practice:** White-collar criminal defense in state and federal courts **Honors/awards:** Judge Pro Tempore for the Orange County Supreme Court; Who's Who in Executives and Professionals; Martindale-Hubbell; 2001 Republican of the Year **Published works:** Article, Law Review **Affiliations:** State Bar of California, U.S. Supreme Court, Ninth Circuit Court of Appeals, various federal district courts **Hob./spts.:** Computers, sports **SIC code:** 81 **Address:** Hartmann & Miller, 1912 N. Broadway, Suite 350, Santa Ana, CA 92706 **E-mail:** bob@hartmannandmiller.com **Web address:** www.hartmannandmiller.com

HAWKINS, MICHAEL L.
Industry: Law **Univ./degree:** J.D., Salmon P. Chase College of Law, 1995 **Current organization:** Michael L. Hawkins & Associates PLLC **Title:** Attorney **Type of organization:** Law firm **Major product:** Legal services **Area of distribution:** Kentucky **Area of Practice:** Personal injury, family law, medical negligence **Affiliations:** K.A.T.A.; A.B.A.; K.B.A.; A.T.L.A. **SIC code:** 81 **Address:** Michael L. Hawkins & Associates PLLC, 420 Ann St., Frankfort, KY 40601 **E-mail:** hawklaw1@bellsouth.net

HECHT, F. THOMAS
Industry: Law **Born:** June 18, 1944, Ann Arbor, Michigan **Univ./degree:** J.D., University of Chicago, 1975 **Current organization:** Ungaretti & Harris **Title:** Partner **Type of organization:** Law firm **Major product:** Legal counseling **Area of distribution:** Illinois **Area of Practice:** Litigation, corporate internal investigation **Affiliations:** American Association of Trial Lawyers **Hob./spts.:** Photography, hiking, reading **SIC code:** 81 **Address:** Ungaretti & Harris, Three First National Plaza, Chicago, IL 60602 **E-mail:** fthecht@uhlaw.com

HEISKELL, MATTHEW P.
Industry: Law **Born:** Chicago, IL **Univ./degree:** J.D., Duquesne University,1998 **Current organization:** Beatie & Osborn LLP **Title:** Attorney **Type of organization:** Law firm **Major product:** Legal services **Area of distribution:** New York **Area of Practice:** Litigation **Affiliations:** City of New York Bar **SIC code:** 81 **Address:** Beatie & Osborn LLP, 521 Fifth Ave., Suite 3400, New York, NY 10175 **E-mail:** mheiskell@bandolaw.com

HENRY, CAROLYN M.
Industry: Law **Born:** April 17, 1964, Buffalo, New York **Univ./degree:** B.A., Business Administration and Finance, SUNY Buffalo, 1986; J.D., SUNY Buffalo School of Law, 1989 **Current organization:** Independent Health Association **Title:** Attorney at Law/Assistant General Counsel **Type of organization:** Health organization **Major product:** Professional legal services **Area of distribution:** National **Area of Practice:** Health law **Affiliations:** New York State Bar Association; Women's Bar Association; Erie County Bar Association **Hob./spts.:** Photography **SIC code:** 81 **Address:** Independent Health Association, 511 Farber Lakes Dr., Williamsville, NY 14221 **E-mail:** chenry@independenthealth.com

HERMAN, GREGG E.
Industry: Law **Born:** January 27, 1955, Detroit, Michigan **Univ./degree:** B.B.A. with Distinction, University of Michigan Graduate School of Business Administration, 1976; J.D., Cum Laude, Detroit College of Law, 1980 **Current organization:** Gregg E. Herman, P.C. **Title:** Attorney **Type of organization:** Law firm **Major product:** Legal services **Area of distribution:** Michigan **Area of Practice:** Civil litigation, medical malpractice; guest appearances on local radio and television programming, guest speaker at legal seminars **Honors/awards:** Lifetime Member, Kingston's National Registry of Who's Who, 2002 **Affiliations:** State Bar of Michigan; Michigan Trial Lawyers Association (MTLA); American Trial Lawyers Association (ATLA); Oakland County Bar Association (OCBA); American College of Legal Medicine; Brain Injury Association of Michigan; Wayne County Mediation Tribunal; Negligence Section of State Bar of Michigan **SIC code:** 81 **Address:** Gregg E. Herman, P.C., 30850 Telegraph Rd., #250, Bingham Farms, MI 48025

HERSHBERGER, RICHARD B.
Industry: Law **Born:** February 11, 1930, Los Angeles, California **Univ./degree:** J.D., University of California at Los Angeles School of Law, 1957 **Title:** Attorney at Law (Retired), Former Senior Trial Deputy District Attorney **Type of organization:** Law firm **Major product:** Legal services **Area of distribution:** California **Area of Practice:** General and litigation (never lost a murder case-either prosecuting or defense) **Affiliations:** Footprinters; Optimists Club; Alumni Advisor, Sigma Alpha Epsilon; President of 3 different SAE Alumni Associations; Former President, Los Angeles High School Alumni Association; Air Force Veteran **Hob./spts.:** Watching basketball and football **SIC code:** 81 **Address:** Richard B. Hershberger, Attorney at Law, 419 N. Larchmont Blvd, Los Angeles, CA 90004

HETZEL, OTTO J.
Industry: Law/consulting **Born:** June 2, 1933, New York, New York **Univ./degree:** B.A., Pennsylvania State University; J.D., Yale University, Connecticut; LL.M.,

Harvard University, Massachusetts **Current organization:** Otto J. Hetzel, Esq./Wayne State University Law School **Title:** Attorney at Law/Professor of Law Emeritus, Wayne State University Law School **Type of organization:** Private law firm/university **Major product:** Legal representation, urban affairs consulting/legal education **Area of distribution:** International **Area of Practice:** Housing and community development, legislative law, administrative law **Published works:** Various books and articles **Affiliations:** American Bar Association; American Law Institute; Housing and Development Reporter; Advisory Board, National Housing Conference **Hob./spts.:** Sailing, tennis **SIC code:** 81 **Address:** 5015 Allan Rd., Bethesda, MD 20816 **E-mail:** otto@hetzelesq.com

HODDINOTT, COLIN J.
Industry: Law **Univ./degree:** J.D., Quinnipiac College, 1999 **Current organization:** Law Offices of Angelo Cicchiello **Title:** Attorney **Type of organization:** Law firm **Major product:** Legal services **Area of distribution:** Connecticut **Area of Practice:** Workers compensation litigation, personal injury **Affiliations:** A.B.A.; A.T.L.A.; Hartford County Bar; Connecticut Bar Workers Compensation Section **SIC code:** 81 **Address:** 367 Plains Rd., Haddam, CT 06438 **E-mail:** choddinott@aol.com **Web address:** www.cicchiellolaw.com

HOFFMAN, GEORGE B.
Industry: Law **Born:** St. Louis, Missouri **Univ./degree:** J.D., Abraham Lincoln School of Law, 2004 **Current organization:** George B. Hoffman, Attorney at Law **Title:** Attorney **Type of organization:** Law firm **Major product:** Legal services **Area of distribution:** California **Area of Practice:** Estate planning **Hob./spts.:** Sailing, golf, travel **SIC code:** 81 **Address:** George B. Hoffman, Attorney at Law, 5000 Birch St., #3000 West, Newport, CA 92660 **E-mail:** retirement_plan@msn.com

HOLLAND, JAMES R.
Industry: Law **Born:** June 20, 1962, Albuquerque, New Mexico **Univ./degree:** B.A., University of Alabama; M.F.A., University of Southern California; J.D., University of Alabama, 1992 **Current organization:** Weltermark, Holland, Keith & Barber **Title:** Lawyer/Partner **Type of organization:** Law firm **Major product:** Legal services for railroad employees **Area of distribution:** Southeast Florida **Area of Practice:** Railroad law **Honors/awards:** Al Cone Trial Seminar, Board of Directors, Board Certified **Published works:** 1 article **Affiliations:** A.F.T.L.; A.T.L.A.; A.R.L.A.; G.T.L.A. **Hob./spts.:** Family, skiing, fishing **SIC code:** 81 **Address:** Weltermark, Holland, Keith & Barber, 1 Independent Dr., Suite 3100, Jacksonville, FL 32202 **E-mail:** felawyer@msn.com

HOLSER, DEREK P.
Industry: Law **Born:** June 30, 1973, Berlin, Germany **Univ./degree:** M.A., Regent University, 2003 **Current organization:** Advocatus, LLC **Title:** President **Type of organization:** Law firm **Major product:** Legal services (represents nonprofit organizations) **Area of distribution:** Virginia **Area of Practice:** Marketing, leadership development **Affiliations:** A.B.A. **Hob./spts.:** Basketball, reading, comedy films **SIC code:** 81 **Address:** Advocatus, LLC, 448 Viking Dr., Suite 370, Virginia Beach, VA 23452

HOSSLER, DAVID J.
Industry: Law **Born:** October 18, 1940, Mesa. Arizona **Univ./degree:** B.A., 1969; J.D., 1972, University of Arizona **Current organization:** Hunt, Kenworthy and Hossler **Title:** Attorney **Type of organization:** Law firm **Major product:** Legal services **Area of distribution:** Arizona **Area of Practice:** Personal injury, wrongful death, domestic relations, commercial litigation **Honors/awards:** Phi Delta Phi (Outstanding Graduate, Province XI, 1972); Recipient, Rotary International Service Above Self Award **Published works:** Editor-in-Chief, Arizona Advocate, 1971-1972 **Affiliations:** Adjunct Professor, University of Arizona, Agricultural Law; Member, City of Yuma Board of Adjustment, 1976-1980; University of Arizona Alumni Association; U.S. Navy, 1962-1967; Yuma County and American Bar Associations; State Bar of Arizona; American Judicature Society; Arizona Trial Lawyers Association; Association of Trial Lawyers of America; State Bar Free Arbitration Committee **SIC code:** 81 **Address:** Hunt, Kenworthy & Hossler, 330 W. 24th St., Yuma, AZ 85364 **E-mail:** dhossler@mindspring.com

HOUSE, ROBERT L.
Industry: Law **Born:** August 2, 1939, Bakersfield, California **Univ./degree:** B.S., University of California, Berkeley; J.D., University of California-Hastings College of Law **Current organization:** Lavorato, House, Chilton, Lavorato & Lavorato **Title:** Attorney **Type of organization:** Law firm **Major product:** Legal services **Area of distribution:** California **Area of Practice:** Certified Specialist in Estate Planning, Trust and Probate Law, The State of California Board of Legal Specialization **Honors/awards:** Chief Justice Gibson Award for Community Service & Ethics, 1993; Salinas Area Citizen of the Year, 1994 **Affiliations:** A.B.A.; C.B.A.; N.A.E.P. **Hob./spts.:** Jogging (ran the Boston Marathon) **SIC code:** 81 **Address:** Lavorato, House, Chilton, Lavorato & Lavorato, 310 Capitol St., Salinas, CA 93901 **Phone:** (831)758-2786 **Fax:** (831)758-0566 **E-mail:** rhouse@lavohouse.com

HOWE, DONALD H.
Industry: Law **Born:** June 12, 1957, Charleston, South Carolina **Univ./degree:** J.D., University of South Carolina, 1983 **Current organization:** Howe & Wyndham LLP **Title:** Esquire **Type of organization:** Law firm **Major product:** Legal services **Area of distribution:** Charleston, South Carolina **Area of Practice:** Litigation **Affiliations:** A.B.A.; N.A.C.D.L.; American Trial Lawyers Association **Hob./spts.:** Travel **SIC code:** 81 **Address:** Howe & Wyndham LLP, 47 State St., Charleston, SC 29401 **E-mail:** howewyndham@bellsouth.net

HUDSON SR., ROGER J.
Industry: Law **Born:** February 13, 1943, Des Moines, Iowa **Univ./degree:** J.D., Drake University, 1972 **Current organization:** Hudson, Mallaney & Shindler **Title:** President **Type of organization:** Law firm **Major product:** Legal services **Area of distribution:** Iowa **Area of Practice:** Litigation, real estate law, family law, personal injury **Affiliations:** Iowa State Bar Association; American Bar Association; American Trial Lawyers Association **SIC code:** 81 **Address:** Hudson, Mallaney & Shindler, 5015 Grand Ridge Dr., #100, West Des Moines, IA 50265 **E-mail:** rhudson@hudsonlaw.net

HUGHES, CINDY H.
Industry: Law **Born:** August 2, 1978, Corpus Christi, Texas **Univ./degree:** J.D., Dedman School of Law at Southern Methodist University **Current organization:** Law Offices of Eric Cedillo, P.C. **Title:** Attorney **Type of organization:** Law firm **Major product:** Legal services **Area of distribution:** Dallas, Texas **Area of Practice:** Personal injury, malpractice **Affiliations:** A.T.L.A.; T.T.L.A.; T.Y.O.A.; State Bar of Texas **Hob./spts.:** Softball, volleyball **SIC code:** 81 **Address:** Law Offices of Eric Cedillo, P.C., 2600 State St., Dallas, TX 75204 **E-mail:** ch@cedillolaw.com

HUGHES, TIMOTHY A.
Industry: Law **Born:** August 1, 1963, Mobile, Alabama **Univ./degree:** J.D., Birmingham School of Law, 1991 **Current organization:** Law Office of Timothy A. Hughes **Title:** Attorney **Type of organization:** Law firm **Major product:** Legal services **Area of distribution:** Alabama **Area of Practice:** Personal injury, mass torts **Affiliations:** American Bar Association; Alabama State Bar Association; Association of Trial Lawyers of America **Hob./spts.:** Music, sports, antiques **SIC code:** 81 **Address:** Law Office of Timothy A. Hughes, 2107 Fifth Ave. North, Suite 300, Birmingham, AL 35203 **Web address:** www.timhugheslaw.com

HULT, CATHERINE DAY
Industry: Law **Born:** February 4, 1964, Chicago, Illinois **Univ./degree:** J.D., Loyola University School of Law, Chicago, Illinois **Current organization:** Joseph F. Pippen, Jr. and Associates **Title:** Attorney at Law **Type of organization:** Law firm **Major product:** Legal services **Area of distribution:** International **Area of Practice:** Family law, estate planning and real estate litigation **Affiliations:** Illinois State Bar Association; Florida Bar; American Bar Association **Hob./spts.:** Running, biking, swimming, boating, antiquing, music composition **SIC code:** 81 **Address:** Joseph F. Pippen, Jr. and Associates, 10225 Ulmerton Rd., Bldg. 11, Largo, FL 33771 **E-mail:** attyhult@tampabay.rr.com

ILES, R. SCOTT
Industry: Law **Born:** July 18, 1964, Deridder, Louisiana **Univ./degree:** J.D., Louisiana State University, 1989 **Current organization:** Law Office of R. Scott Iles **Title:** Attorney **Type of organization:** Law firm **Major product:** Legal services **Area of distribution:** Louisiana **Area of Practice:** Medical malpractice **Affiliations:** A.T.L.A.; L.T.L.A.; B.O.G. **SIC code:** 81 **Address:** Law Office of R. Scott Iles, 1200 West University Ave., Lafayette, LA 70506-3465 **E-mail:** rsiles@bellsouth.net **Web address:** www.scottileslaw.com

INGERSOLL, MARC W.
Industry: Law **Univ./degree:** J.D., Wake Forest University, 1990 **Current organization:** Ingersoll & Associates, PLLC **Title:** Esquire **Type of organization:** Law firm **Major product:** Legal services **Area of distribution:** North Carolina **Area of Practice:** Elder law, estate planning **Affiliations:** N.A.E.L.A.; N.C.B.A.; A.B.A.; Board Member, Winston-Salem Estate Planning Council; Board Member, Winston-Salem Rescue Mission **Hob./spts.:** Civil War history, golf **SIC code:** 81 **Address:** Ingersoll & Associates, PLLC, 1590 Westbrook Plaza Dr., Suite 203, Winston-Salem, NC 27103 **E-mail:** marc@ingersollfirm.com

IRWIN, GARY R.
Industry: Law **Born:** March 28, 1957, Middletown, Ohio **Univ./degree:** B.A., Economics/History, Southern Illinois University, 1979; J.D., University of Wisconsin Law School, 1984 **Current organization:** Edgerton Weaver & Irwin, LLC **Title:** Shareholder **Type of organization:** Law firm **Major product:** Legal services **Area of distribution:** National **Area of Practice:** Securities litigation, arbitration and mediation **Affiliations:** State Bar of Wisconsin; Minnesota State Bar Association; Florida Bar Association **Hob./spts.:** Tennis, golf, ballet, opera, reading **SIC code:** 81 **Address:** Edgerton Weaver & Irwin, LLC, 5050 Lincoln Dr., #480, Minneapolis, MN 55436 **E-mail:** girwin@neilaw.com **Web address:** www.girwinlaw.com

JACOBSON, MARTIN
Industry: Law **Born:** June 10, 1947 **Univ./degree:** B.S., 1969; M.B.A., 1973, New York University Business School; J.D., University of Chicago, 1976 **Current organization:** Simpson Thacher & Bartlett **Title:** Partner, Attorney at Law **Type of organization:** Law firm **Major product:** Legal services **Area of distribution:** International **Area of Practice:** Structured and project finance **Honors/awards:** "AV" rated, Martindale-Hubbell **Affiliations:** Founding Chair, Project Finance Committee Section of New York City Bar Association; New York State Bar Association **SIC code:** 81 **Address:** Simpson Thacher & Bartlett, 425 Lexington Ave., New York, NY 10017 **E-mail:** mjacobson@stblaw.com **Web address:** www.stblaw.com

JEFFERIES, T. WADE
Industry: Law **Born:** December 4, 1968, Dallas, Texas **Univ./degree:** J.D., University of Texas, 1994 **Current organization:** Hohmann, Taube & Summers, L.L.P. **Title:** Attorney **Type of organization:** Law firm **Major product:** Legal services **Area of distribution:** Texas **Area of Practice:** Commercial litigation, family law and construction law **Affiliations:** State Bar of Texas; U.S. District Court for Northern, Southern, Eastern and Western Districts of Texas; U.S. Court of Appeals for the Fifth Circuit **Hob./spts.:** Water sports, camping **SIC code:** 81 **Address:** Hohmann, Taube & Summers, L.L.P., 100 Congress Ave., Suite 1600, Austin, TX 78701

JEZ, G. SEAN
Industry: Law **Born:** November 9, 1969, Weimar, Texas **Univ./degree:** B.A., University of Texas at Austin, 1992; J.D., University of Houston, 1996 **Current organization:** Fleming & Associates L.L.P. **Title:** Attorney **Type of organization:** Law firm **Major product:** Legal services **Area of distribution:** National **Area of Practice:** Civil litigation, medical malpractice **Affiliations:** A.T.L.A.; A.B.A.; Houston Bar Association; Texas Trial Lawyers Association **SIC code:** 81 **Address:** Fleming & Associates L.L.P., 1330 Post Oak Blvd., Suite 3030, Houston, TX 77056 **E-mail:** sean_jez@fleming-law.com **Web address:** www.fleming-law.com

JIMERSON, HERMAN L.
Industry: Law **Born:** May 31, 1957, Missouri **Univ./degree:** B.S., George Williams/Aurora University, 1979; J.D. University of Missouri-Columbia School of Law, 1986 **Current organization:** Jimerson Law Firm **Title:** Attorney at Law **Type of organization:** Law firm **Major product:** Legal services **Area of distribution:** Regional **Area of Practice:** Litigation, small business development, criminal defense **Published works:** Poetry **Affiliations:** Metropolitan St. Louis Bar Association; American Trial Lawyers Association **Hob./spts.:** Reading, writing **SIC code:** 81 **Address:** Jimerson Law Firm, 225 S. Meramec Ave., Suite 508, St. Louis, MO 63105 **E-mail:** herman@jimersonlawfirm.com **Web address:** www.jimersonlawfirm.com

JOHNSON, JENNIFER R.
Industry: Law **Born:** December 24, 1959, Springfield, Missouri **Univ./degree:** A.A., Nursing, Mesa Community College, 1987; J.D., University of Arizona, 1992 **Current organization:** Lopez, Hodes, Restaino, Milman & Skikos **Title:** Esquire **Type of organization:** Law firm **Major product:** Legal services **Area of distribution:** National **Area of Practice:** Product liability, medical malpractice **Published works:** "From the Dark Side", 2002 **Affiliations:** Board Member, Orange City Trial Lawyers Association; American Trial Lawyers Association **Hob./spts.:** Golf, choir member **SIC code:** 81 **Address:** Lopez, Hodes, Restaino, Milman & Skikos, 450 Newport Center Dr., 2nd floor, Newport Beach, CA 92660 **E-mail:** jjohnson@lopez-hodes.com **Web address:** www.lopez-hodes.com

JOHNSON, ROBERT ALLEN
Industry: Law **Born:** January 22, 1975, Alexandria, Louisiana **Univ./degree:** J.D., Loyola University, 2000 **Current organization:** Johnson Law Firm **Title:** Attorney **Type of organization:** Law firm **Major product:** Legal services **Area of distribution:** Louisiana **Area of Practice:** General litigation, domestic law **Affiliations:** A.B.A.; L.T.L.A. **SIC code:** 81 **Address:** Johnson Law Firm, 502 Tunica Dr. East, Marksville, LA 71351 **E-mail:** rowbear@kricket.net

JONES, ROGER J.
Industry: Law **Born:** January 17, 1951, Buffalo, New York **Spouse:** Karen Krawczyk **Married:** May 2, 1970 **Children:** Robert E. Jones, 1970; Deanna E. Mustafa, 1977; 4 grandchildren **Univ./degree:** B.A., Mathematics and History, 1973; M.A., History, 1976; Ph.D., History, 1979; J.D., 1983, State University of New York at Buffalo **Current organization:** Latham & Watkins, LLP **Title:** Partner **Type of organization:** Law firm **Major product:** Legal services, general practice **Area of distribution:** International **Area of practice:** Federal and state tax law, tax litigation, appellate advocacy **Area of Practice:** Federal and state tax law, tax litigation, appellate advocacy **Honors/awards:** Chambers USA-America's Leading Lawyers for Business, 2004-2007; Illinois Super Lawyers, 2005, 2006, 2007; International Tax Review, World Directory of Tax Advisors, 2001; Phi Beta Kappa, 1973; Sea Grant Fellowship, 1981-83; Teaching Fellowships, 1973-75, 1982-83 **Published works:** "The Life of John Morton, Archbishop of Canterbury and Chancellor of England", "Intercompany Pricing: Getting it Right and What Happens if You Don't", "Staying out of the Lion's Den - U.S. Tax Practice" **Affiliations:** American Bar Association; Illinois Bar Association; New York Bar Association; admitted in Illinois, New York; admitted to U.S. Supreme Court; U.S. Courts of Appeals - 2nd, 6th, 7th, 8th, 9th, 10th and 11th Circuits; U.S. Tax Court, Court of Federal Claims **Career accomplishments:** Frequent speaker at seminars, symposia and conferences on varied tax topics; Editor, International Trade and Business Law Annual 1999-present; Member, Dean's Advisory Council, John Lord O'Brien Law School, S.U.N.Y. at Buffalo 1999-present; have litigated more than 45 Federal and state tax cases, including The Limited, Inc. v. Commissioner, Nestlé Holdings Inc. v. Commissioner, Tele-Communications Inc. v. Commissioner, Westreco Inc. v. Commissioner and Continental Illinois Corp. v. Commissioner **Hob./spts.:** Horseback riding, skiing, hiking **SIC code:** 81 **Address:** Latham & Watkins, LLP, Sears Tower, Suite 5800, 233 South Wacker Dr., Chicago, IL 60806-6401 **E-mail:** roger.jones@lw.com **Web address:** www.lw.com

JUNG, MICHELE L.
Industry: Law **Born:** November 23, 1955, Passaic, New Jersey **Univ./degree:** B.A., William Patterson College, 1977; J.D., Ohio Northern University, 1981 **Current organization:** Michele L. Jung, P.C. **Title:** Attorney at Law **Type of organization:** Law firm **Major product:** Legal services **Area of distribution:** National **Area of Practice:** General practice **Honors/awards:** Prince William County Bar Association Commendation for Distinguished Services as Guardian ad litem, 1994 **Affiliations:** Virginia State Bar; Special Justice 31st Judicial Circuit; U.S. Court of Appeals (4th Circuit); Virginia Trial Lawyers Association; Prince William County Bar Association **Hob./spts.:** Spending time with family, volunteer activities, crossword puzzles, reading **SIC code:** 81 **Address:** Michele L. Jung, P.C., P.O. Box 2324, Manassas, VA 20108 **E-mail:** mjungesq@verizon.net

KALBERG, CHRISTOPHER L.
Industry: Law **Born:** August 8, 1971, St. Louis, Missouri **Univ./degree:** B.S., History, Kansas State University, 1997; J.D., University of Missouri Law School, Kansas City 2002 **Current organization:** Kalberg Law Office, L.L.C. **Title:** Attorney-at-Law **Type of organization:** Law firm **Major product:** Legal services **Area of distribution:** Kansas **Area of Practice:** Civil litigation and criminal defense **Affiliations:** Missouri State Bar Association; Kansas State Bar Association **Hob./spts.:** Boating, swimming **SIC code:** 81 **Address:** Kalberg Law Office, L.L.C., 11184 Antioch, #355, Overland Park, KS 66210 **E-mail:** kalberglaw@everestkc.net

KAPLAN, JOEL A.
Industry: Law **Born:** February 10, 1949, Philadelphia, Pennsylvania **Univ./degree:** B.S., Business, Florida State University, 1970; J.D., Cumberland School of Law, 1974 **Current organization:** Kaplan & Freedman P.A. **Title:** Attorney **Type of organization:** Law firm **Major product:** Legal services **Area of distribution:** Florida **Area of Practice:** Catastrophic and personal injury, wrongful death, medical malpractice **Published works:** Text book chapter **Affiliations:** American Board of Trial Advocates; Eagle Member, Academy of Florida Trial Lawyers **Hob./spts.:** Golf, travel, boating **SIC code:** 81 **Address:** Kaplan & Freedman P.A., 9410 S.W. 77th Ave., Miami, FL 33156 **E-mail:** jkaplan@kaplanfreedman.com **Web address:** www.kaplanfreedman.com

KATZ, BERNARD N.
Industry: Law **Born:** Philadelphia, Pennsylvania **Univ./degree:** B.S., Business and Public Administration, Temple University, 1950; J.D., Temple University School of Law, 1953 **Current organization:** Meranze & Katz, PC **Title:** J.D./Partner **Type of organization:** Law firm **Major product:** Legal services **Area of distribution:** National **Area of Practice:** Labor Law and the Representation of Unions **Affiliations:** United States Navy, Aerographer's Mate First Class, 1945-47 **Hob./spts.:** Swimming, skiing, physical fitness, opera, classical music **SIC code:** 81 **Address:** Meranze & Katz, PC, North American Bldg., 121 South Broad St., 13th Floor, Philadelphia, PA 19127 **E-mail:** april@meranzekatz.com

KEINER, JEFFREY
Industry: Law **Born:** October 11, 1946, St. Louis, Missouri **Univ./degree:** J.D., University of Michigan **Current organization:** Gray Robinson **Title:** Attorney **Type of organization:** Law firm **Major product:** Legal services **Area of distribution:** National **Area of Practice:** Construction litigation, patents and trademarks **Published works:** 20 papers **Affiliations:** A.T.L.A.; Florida State Bar **Hob./spts.:** Driving

racecars **SIC code:** 81 **Address:** Gray Robinson, 30 E. Pine St., Orlando, FL 32802 **E-mail:** jkeiner@grayrobinson.com

KELLY, KEVIN D.
Industry: Law **Born:** August 26, 1953, El Dorado, Arkansas **Univ./degree:** B.A., English, La Salle University, 1975; J.D., Southern Texas College of Law, Houston, 1978; Diplomate of Municipal Law, Rutgers University, 1992 **Current organization:** Kelly & Ward, LLC **Title:** Attorney **Type of organization:** Law firm **Major product:** Legal services **Area of distribution:** New Jersey **Area of Practice:** Municipal law, land use and development **Affiliations:** New Jersey Bar; Pennsylvania Bar Association; Supreme Court Bar; Board Member, Sussex County Bar; Board Member, Sussex Chamber of Commerce; Board Member, United Way **Hob./spts.:** Family, children, basketball, baseball, coaching sports **SIC code:** 81 **Address:** Kelly & Ward, LLC, 93 Spring St., Newton, NJ 07860 **E-mail:** firm@kellyandward.com

KELLY, P. TIMOTHY
Industry: Law **Born:** November 23, 1958, Scranton, Pennsylvania **Univ./degree:** J.D., Villanova University, 1982 **Current organization:** Mattise & Kelly PC **Title:** Esquire **Type of organization:** Law firm **Major product:** Legal services **Area of distribution:** Pennsylvania **Area of Practice:** Personal injury **Affiliations:** Fellow, Roscoe Pound Institute; Pennsylvania Bar Association; Pennsylvania Trial Lawyers Association **Hob./spts.:** Skiing **SIC code:** 81 **Address:** Mattise & Kelly PC, 108 N. Washington Ave., Suite 400, Scranton, PA 18503

KEY, CARLO R.
Industry: Law **Born:** Marshall, Texas **Univ./degree:** J.D., Baylor Law School **Current organization:** Law Office of Carlo Key **Title:** Attorney **Type of organization:** Law firm **Major product:** Legal services **Area of distribution:** San Antonio, Texas **Area of Practice:** Criminal defense, DWI **Affiliations:** Texas Criminal Defense Lawyers Association **SIC code:** 81 **Address:** Law Office of Carlo Key, 401 S. Presa, San Antonio, TX 78205 **E-mail:** carlo@keylawfirm.com

KEYES, KEVIN M.
Industry: Law **Born:** March 15, 1956, Cleveland, Ohio **Univ./degree:** J.D., Case Western Reservation University, 1983 **Current organization:** Fried, Frank, Harris, Shriver & Jacobson **Title:** Partner **Type of organization:** Law firm **Major product:** Tax planning **Area of distribution:** International **Area of Practice:** Tax law **Published works:** Federal Taxation Financial Instruments & Taxes **Affiliations:** Washington D.C. Bar Association; American Bar Association; Financial Transaction Sub Committee **SIC code:** 81 **Address:** Fried, Frank, Harris, Shriver & Jacobson, 1001 Pennsylvania Ave. N.W., Suite 800, Washington, DC 20004-2505 **E-mail:** kevin.keyes@ffhsj.com

KIA, MARYAM
Industry: Law **Univ./degree:** B.A., Liberal Studies (Sociology and Chemistry), University of Calilfornia at Riverside, 1998; M.S.W., 2001; M.P.A., 2002, University of Southern California at Los Angeles; J.D., Whittier Law School, Costa Mesa, California, 2005 **Current organization:** Alarm One, Inc./Law Offices of Steve Levy & Assoc. **Title:** Attorney **Type of organization:** Corporation **Major product:** Legal services **Area of distribution:** Costa Mesa, California **Area of Practice:** Legal representation/ Expert Reviewer, Journal of the National Association of Social Workers, Washington, D.C.; Fluent in Farisi (Persian), some Spanish and Arabic **Published works:** Journal of the **Affiliations:** A.B.A.; C.B.A.; O.C.B.A;, N.S.W;, A.S.P.A.; N.A.S.W. **SIC code:** 81 **Address:** Alarm One, Inc./Law Offices of Steve Levy & Assoc., 2855 Pinecreeks Dr., #F428, Costa Mesa, CA 92626 **E-mail:** liquidmk@msn.com

KILBANE, THOMAS S.
Industry: Law **Born:** March 7, 1941, Cleveland, Ohio **Univ./degree:** B.S., Valedictorian, John Carroll University, 1963; J.D., Northwestern University, 1966 **Current organization:** Squire, Sanders & Dempsey, L.L.P. **Title:** Managing Partner Litigation **Type of organization:** Law firm **Major product:** Legal services **Area of distribution:** International **Area of Practice:** Trial law **Honors/awards:** Listed in all editions, "The Best Lawyers in America" **Published works:** Inside the Minds: Leading Litigators: "Litigation Challenges in the 21st Century" **Affiliations:** Center for Public Resources, Master Barrister; Fellow, American College of Trial Lawyers; International Academy of Trial Lawyers; American Bar Foundation **Hob./spts.:** International travel **SIC code:** 81 **Address:** Squire, Sanders & Dempsey, L.L.P., 4900 Key Tower, 127 Public Square, Cleveland, OH 44114 **E-mail:** tkilbane@ssd.com

KINCADE, MICHAEL J.
Industry: Law **Born:** August 14, 1956, Boston, Massachusetts **Univ./degree:** B.A., J.D., Loyola University **Current organization:** Michael J. Kincade, PLC **Title:** President **Type of organization:** Law firm **Major product:** Legal services **Area of distribution:** National **Area of Practice:** Maritime law, admiralty, Longshore and Harbor Worker's Compensation Act, State Worker's Compensation (PA and LA), insurance defense, subregulation (maritime and civil); Admitted to Bar 1981 Pennsylvania, 1982 Louisiana **Affiliations:** Admitted before: U.S. District Court, Eastern, Middle and Western Districts of Louisiana; U.S. Court of Appeals, Fifth Circuit and Supreme Court of the Commonwealth of Pennsylvania; Member, Philadelphia Bar Association; Pennsylvania Bar Association; Fifth Federal Circuit Bar Association; Louisiana State Bar Association; American Bar Association; Mariners Club of the Port of New Orleans; Louisiana Association of Defense Counsel; St. Thomas More Catholic Lawyers Association; Certified Louisiana Arbitrator Agent and Advisor, National Football League Players' Association (since 1989) **Hob./spts.:** Physical fitness, assistant-coaching high school wrestling, golf **SIC code:** 81 **Address:** Michael J. Kincade, PLC, 3445 N. Causeway Blvd., Suite 520, Metairie, LA 70002 **E-mail:** kincade8@bellsouth.net

KING, STUART H.
Industry: Law **Born:** January 12, 1961, Springfield, Missouri **Univ./degree:** J.D., University of Missouri **Current organization:** McDonald Hosmer King & Royce **Title:** Managing partner **Type of organization:** Law firm **Major product:** Legal services **Area of distribution:** Missouri **Area of Practice:** Business and corporate law **Affiliations:** M.B.A.; A.B.A.; S.B.A. **Hob./spts.:** Sports, golf, scuba diving **SIC code:** 81 **Address:** McDonald Hosmer King & Royce, 300 S. Jefferson, Suite 600, Springfield, MO 65806 **E-mail:** stuart.king@mhkr.com

KISER, CHERIE R.
Industry: Law **Univ./degree:** J.D., Catholic University of America, Columbia School of Law, 1987 **Current organization:** Mintz, Levin, Cohn, Ferris, Glovsky and Popeo, P.C. **Title:** Partner/Managing Partner **Type of organization:** Law firm **Major product:** Legal services **Area of distribution:** International **Area of Practice:** Communications law, telecommunication, telephony **Published works:** 4 articles **Affiliations:** A.B.A.; Computer Law Association; Federal Communications Bar Association **SIC code:** 81 **Address:** Mintz, Levin, Cohn, Ferris, Glovsky and Popeo, P.C., 701 Pennsylvania Ave. N.W., Washington, DC 20004 **E-mail:** crkiser@mintz.com

KLOK, RHETT DANIEL
Industry: Law **Born:** February 9, 1967, New York, New York **Univ./degree:** J.D., Loyola University New Orleans - College of Law, 1992 **Current organization:** Motley Rice, LLC **Title:** Attorney **Type of organization:** Law firm **Major product:** Legal services **Area of distribution:** International **Area of Practice:** Plaintiff protection, pharmaceutical, car products, medical devices, aviation **Affiliations:** A.B.A.; A.T.L.A.; S.C.A.T.L.A. **Hob./spts.:** Skiing, tennis **SIC code:** 81 **Address:** Motley Rice, LLC, 28 Bridgeside Blvd., Mount Pleasant, SC 29465 **E-mail:** rklok@motleyrice.com

KNIGHT, DAVID W.
Industry: Law **Born:** August 6, 1954, Wiesbaden Air Force Base, Germany **Univ./degree:** J.D., University of Oklahoma, 1982 **Current organization:** David W. Knight, Attorney at Law **Title:** Attorney **Type of organization:** Law firm **Major product:** Legal services **Area of distribution:** Texas and Oklahoma **Area of Practice:** Business litigation **Affiliations:** Oklahoma Bar Association; State Bar of Texas **Hob./spts.:** Weightlifting, photography **SIC code:** 81 **Address:** David W. Knight, Attorney at Law, 4726 Jacksboro Hwy., Suite G, Wichita Falls, TX 76302 **E-mail:** dknight@wf.net

KNOLL, TRISTON
Industry: Law **Born:** June 4, 1971, New Orleans, Louisiana **Univ./degree:** J.D., Loyola Law School, 1996 **Current organization:** The Knoll Law Firm **Title:** Attorney/Partner **Type of organization:** Law firm **Major product:** Legal services **Area of distribution:** Louisiana **Area of Practice:** Personal injury, family law **Affiliations:** L.T.L.A. **Hob./spts.:** Football, baseball, skiing, boating **SIC code:** 81 **Address:** The Knoll Law Firm, 233 S. Main St., Marksville, LA 71351 **Phone:** (318)253-6200 **Fax:** (318)253-4044 **Web address:** www.knollawfirm.com

KNOLL JR., JEROLD EDWARD
Industry: Law **Born:** July 26, 1975, Alexandria, Louisiana **Univ./degree:** J.D., Loyola University, 2000 **Current organization:** Knoll & Spruill, LLC **Title:** Attorney **Type of organization:** Law firm **Major product:** Legal services **Area of distribution:** Marksville, Louisiana **Area of Practice:** Real estate, personal injury, banking **Affiliations:** A.B.A.; A.T.L.A.; L.T.L.A. **Hob./spts.:** Hunting, fishing, baseball **SIC code:** 81 **Address:** Knoll & Spruill, L.L.C., 233 S. Main St., Marksville, LA 71351 **E-mail:** eknoll2@aol.com

KNOX, ALISON DOUGLAS
Industry: Law **Born:** October 21, 1933, New York, New York **Univ./degree:** J.D., University of Pennsylvania, 1977 **Current organization:** Alison Douglas Knox, Attorney at Law **Title:** Attorney **Type of organization:** Law firm **Major product:** Legal services **Area of distribution:** Philadelphia, Pennsylvania **Area of Practice:** Copyright litigation, creditor representation **Affiliations:** P.B.A.; Historical Society of Pennsylvania **Hob./spts.:** Bridge **SIC code:** 81 **Address:** Alison Douglas Knox, Attorney at Law, 2025 Delancey Place, Philadelphia, PA 19103

KOCH, GREGORY M.
Industry: Law **Born:** May 9, 1977, Jamaica, New York **Univ./degree:** B.A., Political Science, State University of New York at Binghamton, 1999; J.D., St. John's Law School, New York, 2002 **Current organization:** Cullen and Dykman, LLP **Title:**

Attorney **Type of organization:** Law firm **Major product:** Legal services **Area of distribution:** New York **Area of Practice:** Litigation **Affiliations:** New York State Bar Association; A.B.A.; A.T.L.A.; Nassau County Bar Association **Hob./spts.:** Baseball, coaching, golf **SIC code:** 81 **Address:** Cullen and Dykman, LLP, 177 Montague St., Brooklyn, NY 11201 **E-mail:** gkoch@cullenanddykman.com

KOHLER, DONALD W.
Industry: Law **Univ./degree:** B.A., Metropolitan State University, 1990; J.D., Hamline University School of Law, 1998 **Current organization:** Law Office of Donald W. Kohler **Title:** Attorney **Type of organization:** Law firm **Major product:** Legal services **Area of distribution:** Minnesota **Area of Practice:** Workers' compensation, real estate, estate planning, personal injury **Affiliations:** M.T.L.A.; Minnesota State Bar Association; Ramsey County Bar Association **Hob./spts.:** Reading, fishing, hunting **SIC code:** 81 **Address:** Law Offices of Donald W. Kohler, 3500 Willow Lake Blvd., #800, White Bear Lake, MN 55110 **E-mail:** dkohler@klaw.us **Web address:** www.kohlerlaw.com

KULESA, THADDEUS E.
Industry: Law **Born:** July 21, 1948, Buffalo, New York **Univ./degree:** B.S., B.A., State University of New York at Buffalo, 1971 **Current organization:** Searcy Denney Scarola Barnhart & Shipley **Title:** Paralegal **Type of organization:** Law firm **Major product:** Legal services **Area of distribution:** National **Area of Practice:** Personal injury law **Affiliations:** Florida A.T.L.; New York National Guard (2 years); US Army Reserves (4 years) **Hob./spts.:** Minor and major league baseball, golf **SIC code:** 81 **Address:** Searcy Denney Scarola Barnhart & Shipley, 2139 Palm Beach Lakes Blvd., West Palm Beach, FL 33409 **E-mail:** tek@searcylaw.com **Web address:** www.searcylaw.com

KURTZ-PHELAN, JAMES L.
Industry: Law **Born:** July 13, 1946, El Paso, Texas **Univ./degree:** B.S., University of Texas, 1968; J.D., Yale School of Law, 1972 **Current organization:** Berenbaum, Weinshienk & Eason, P.C. **Title:** Esquire **Type of organization:** Law firm **Major product:** Legal services **Area of distribution:** Colorado **Area of Practice:** Real estate development **Honors/awards:** Order of the Coif **Affiliations:** D.B.A.; C.B.A.; A.B.A.; Board Member, Anti-Defamation League; Board, Jewish Community Centers of Denver **Hob./spts.:** Biking **SIC code:** 81 **Address:** Berenbaum, Weinshienk & Eason, P.C., 370 17th St., Suite 4800, Denver, CO 80202 **E-mail:** kurtzphe@bw-legal.com **Web address:** www.bwelaw.com

LAING, R. SCOTT
Industry: Law **Current organization:** Law Offices of R. Scott Laing **Title:** Attorney/Owner **Type of organization:** Law firm **Major product:** Legal services **Area of distribution:** West Palm Beach, Florida **Area of Practice:** Litigation, collections, estate planning **SIC code:** 81 **Address:** Law Offices of R. Scott Laing, 200 Butler St., Lakeview Suite, West Palm Beach, FL 33407 **E-mail:** imgator1@att.net

LAMACCHIA, SALLY F.
Industry: Law **Born:** February 8, 1956, Los Angeles, California **Univ./degree:** J.D., Magna Cum Laude, South California Institute of Law, 1994 **Current organization:** Law Office of Sally F. LaMacchia **Title:** Attorney **Type of organization:** Law office **Major product:** Legal services **Area of distribution:** National **Area of Practice:** Federal worker's compensation/disability retirement - injured federal workers under federal employee compensation acts - discrimination **Honors/awards:** Board of Directors, South California Institute of Law; Officer of Alumni Association **Affiliations:** Adjunct Professor, USCB; Management Labor Relations Class; Federal US Court of Appeals 9th Circuit; State Bar of California; US State Federal Circuit **Hob./spts.:** Avid swimmer, rollerblading, kayaking, mother of four **SIC code:** 81 **Address:** Law Office of Sally F. LaMacchia, 1779 E. Main St., Ventura, CA 93001-3410 **E-mail:** lamacchialaw@aol.com

LANCE, JAMES R.
Industry: Law **Born:** January 24, 1961, St. Charles, Missouri **Univ./degree:** B.S., Summa Cum Laude, Political Science, Southwest Missouri State University; J.D., Magna Cum Laude, Washington & Lee University School of Law **Current organization:** Post Kirby Noonan & Sweat, LLP **Title:** Esquire, Partner **Type of organization:** Law firm **Major product:** Legal services **Area of distribution:** California **Area of Practice:** Commercial litigation, real estate **Honors/awards:** Order of the Coif **Published works:** Editor, Trial Bar News, San Diego **Affiliations:** C.D.C.B.A.; C.A.S.D.; A.T.L.A.; C.A.O.C. **Hob./spts.:** Snow skiing, mountain biking, weightlifting **SIC code:** 81 **Address:** Post Kirby Noonan & Sweat, LLP, 600 West Broadway, Suite 1100, San Diego, CA 92101 **E-mail:** jlance@pkns.com **Web address:** www.pkns.com

LANDERO IV, REY RAINIER B.
Industry: Law **Born:** December 24, 1969, Carson, California **Univ./degree:** B.A., Political Science, California State University at Northridge, 2000; J.D., Thomas M. Cooley Law School, 1998 **Current organization:** Law Office of Rey R. Landero IV **Title:** Attorney **Type of organization:** Law firm **Major product:** Legal services **Area of distribution:** National **Area of Practice:** Immigration and personal injury **Affiliations:** A.I.L.A.; C.A.B.A.R.; A.B.A. **Hob./spts.:** Family, coaching basketball, snowboarding, golf, bowling **SIC code:** 81 **Address:** Law Office of Rey R. Landero IV, 23243 S. Main St., Carson, CA 90745 **E-mail:** rey4esq@sbcglobal.net

LANGDALE III, WILLIAM P.
Industry: Law **Born:** October 29, 1967, Valdosta, Georgia **Univ./degree:** J.D., 1992 University of Georgia **Current organization:** Langdale, Valloton & Linahan **Title:** Attorney/Partner **Type of organization:** Law firm **Major product:** Legal services **Area of distribution:** Georgia **Area of Practice:** Litigation **Published works:** Article **Affiliations:** A.T.L.A.; G.T.L.A. **Hob./spts.:** Fishing, hunting **SIC code:** 81 **Address:** Langdale, Valloton & Linahan, 1007 N. Patterson St., Valdosta, GA 31602 **E-mail:** popelangdale@langdalevalloton.com **Web address:** www.lvlw-law.com

LANGLEY, KOBY J.
Industry: Law/Federal Litigation **Univ./degree:** J.D., University of Colorado, Harvard Law Mediation **Current organization:** Federal Mediation & Litigation Associates **Title:** Litigation Attorney/Certified Mediator **Type of organization:** Law firm **Major product:** Federal mediation and litigation **Area of distribution:** National **Area of Practice:** Plaintiff Civil Litigation and Mediation **Affiliations:** Michigan State Bar; District of Columbia Bar **Hob./spts.:** Charity 5/10K races, public speaking **SIC code:** 81 **Address:** Federal Mediation & Litigation Associates, 1200 Wisconsin Ave., Suite 106, Washington, DC 20016 **E-mail:** koby.langley@fmala.com

LAROCCA, FRANK J.
Industry: Law **Born:** October 9, 1964, Bronx, New York **Univ./degree:** J.D., Pace University School of Law, 1995 **Current organization:** Spinato, Conte & LaRocca, PC **Title:** Esquire **Type of organization:** Law firm **Major product:** Legal services **Area of distribution:** Glen Rock, New Jersey **Area of Practice:** Divorce and family law **Published works:** Article, trade publication **Affiliations:** Association of Trial Lawyers of America; New Jersey Bar Association; Monmouth County Bar Association **SIC code:** 81 **Address:** Spinato, Conte & LaRocca, PC, 266 Harristown Rd., Glen Rock, NJ 07652 **E-mail:** flarocca@divorcelawnj.com **Web address:** www.divorcelawnj.com

LAUGESEN, RICHARD W.
Industry: Law/education **Born:** February 28, 1933, Crawford, Nebraska **Univ./degree:** Colorado State College, 1956; J.D., University of Denver Law School, 1962 **Current organization:** Richard Laugesen, Attorney/University of Denver Law School **Title:** Attorney/Professor of Law **Type of organization:** Law firm/University law school **Major product:** Legal services/law education **Area of distribution:** Colorado **Area of Practice:** Insurance law, insurance consultation and litigation **Published works:** Colorado Litigation Forms and Analysis (3 Vols. 1995-updated annually, West Publishing); Annual Survey of Colorado Insurance Law (1975 to date - Colorado Bar Association); Colorado Motor Vehicle Insurance (1975 annually to date, University of Denver Law School/CBA Publication); Insurance General Considerations (University of Denver Law School 1991 - updated annually) **Affiliations:** American Bar Association; Colorado Bar Association; Denver Bar Association; American College of Trial Lawyers **Hob./spts.:** Writing, woodworking, physical fitness **SIC code:** 81 **Address:** 1830 S. Monroe St., Denver, CO 80210 **E-mail:** laugesen@indra.com

LAVALLEE, RAYMOND G.
Industry: Law **Born:** July 6, 1930, Queens, New York **Univ./degree:** J.D., St. Johns University, 1960 **Current organization:** Lavallee & Lavallee **Title:** Attorney **Type of organization:** Law firm **Major product:** Legal services **Area of distribution:** Long Island, New York **Area of Practice:** Criminal, personal injury, labor **Affiliations:** Nassau County Bar Association; New York State Bar Association **Hob./spts.:** Tennis, golf **SIC code:** 81 **Address:** Lavallee & Lavallee, 4 W. Gate Rd., Farmingdale, NY 11735

LAWSON, CORLISS S.
Industry: Law **Born:** November 4, 1962, Topeka, Kansas **Univ./degree:** J.D., Vanderbilt University **Current organization:** Corliss & Associates, P.C. **Title:** Attorney **Type of organization:** Law firm **Major product:** Legal services **Area of distribution:** International **Area of Practice:** Complex commercial litigation **Affiliations:** A.B.A.; G.W.B.C.; G.A.B.W.A.; State Bar of Georgia; **Hob./spts.:** Shopping, home design, jewelry design **SIC code:** 81 **Address:** Corliss & Associates, P.C., 275 Lee St., Fayetteville, GA 30214 **E-mail:** clawson@corlisslaw.com

LÁZARO, VINCENT A.
Industry: Law **Born:** July 6, 1962, San Antonio, Texas **Univ./degree:** B.A., Yale University, 1984; M.A., Public Administration, University of Texas, 1986; J.D., St. Mary's Law School, 1989; M.Ed., Harvard University, 1990; B.A., Berklee College of Music, 1993; J.D., Columbia University, 1993 **Current organization:** Law Office of Vincent A. Lázaro, P.C. **Title:** President/CEO **Type of organization:** Law firm **Major product:** Legal services **Area of distribution:** Texas **Area of Practice:** Plaintiff employment/labor/education **Published works:** Numerous articles, 2 book chapters **Affiliations:** A.T.L.A.; A.B.A. **Hob./spts.:** Playing the trumpet **SIC code:** 81 **Address:**

Law Office of Vincent A. Lázaro, P.C., 115 E. Travis St., Suite 706, San Antonio, TX 78205 **E-mail:** vincent_lazaro@yahoo.com

LEAVY, LORANE G.
Industry: Law **Born:** March 26, 1945, Brooklyn, New York **Univ./degree:** J.D., Regent University, Virginia **Current organization:** Morris and St. Clair, P.C. **Title:** Associate **Type of organization:** Law firm **Major product:** Legal services **Area of distribution:** Virginia **Area of Practice:** Medical negligence/malpractice **Affiliations:** American Trial Lawyers Association **Hob./spts.:** Spending time with her grandchildren, gourmet cooking, reading **SIC code:** 81 **Address:** 828 Linbay Dr., Virginia Beach, VA 23451 **E-mail:** lorane6@msn.com

LEFRANC ROMERO, ROBERTO
Industry: Law **Born:** February 20, 1942, San Juan, Puerto Rico **Univ./degree:** J.D., University of Puerto Rico **Current organization:** Martinez Alvarez, Menendez Cortada & Lefranc Romero, P.S.C. **Title:** Esquire **Type of organization:** Law firm **Major product:** Legal services **Area of distribution:** San Juan, Puerto Rico **Area of Practice:** Labor law, construction law, contracts, equine law **Affiliations:** American Association of Labor Practitioners; Associated General Contractors **Hob./spts.:** Deep sea fishing, horse racing **SIC code:** 81 **Address:** Martinez Alvarez, Menendez Cortada & Lefranc Romero, P.S.C., 701 Ponce de Leon Ave., Suite 407, San Juan, PR 00907

LEGLER III, KENNEDY
Industry: Law **Born:** April 21, 1948, Dayton, Ohio **Univ./degree:** J.D., University of Dayton, 1978 **Current organization:** Legler & Flynn **Title:** Esquire **Type of organization:** Law firm **Major product:** Legal services **Area of distribution:** National **Area of Practice:** Trial practice **Published works:** Articles, seminars **Affiliations:** F.B.A.; A.B.A.; O.B.A.; A.F.T.L.; A.T.L.A. **Hob./spts.:** Sailing, golf, softball, basketball, fishing **SIC code:** 81 **Address:** Legler & Flynn, 2027 Manatee Ave. West, Bradenton, FL 34205

LEHANE, DANIEL PATRICK
Industry: Law **Born:** October 5, 1960, Murfreesboro, Tennessee **Univ./degree:** B.S., Education, Auburn University, 1986; J.D., Birmingham School of Law, 1993 **Current organization:** Daniel Patrick Lehane, Attorney at Law **Title:** Attorney **Type of organization:** Law firm **Major product:** Legal services **Area of distribution:** Alabama **Area of Practice:** Trial law **Honors/awards:** Listed in Who's Who of America's Professionals, Lexington Who's Who, Who's Who of America's Educators **Published works:** 1 article **Affiliations:** Alabama State Bar; Birmingham Bar Association; Lettermen's Club (basketball), Southeastern College, Florida **Hob./spts.:** Family, athletics, running **SIC code:** 81 **Address:** Daniel Patrick Lehane, Attorney at Law, 1629 11th Ave. South, Birmingham, AL 35205 **E-mail:** d.lehane@lehanelaw.com **Web address:** www.lehanelaw.com

LEVINE, LISA S.
Industry: Law **Born:** March 21, 1960, Far Rockaway, New York **Univ./degree:** J.D., University of Miami **Current organization:** Lisa S. Levine, P.A. **Title:** President **Type of organization:** Law firm **Major product:** Legal services **Area of distribution:** Florida **Area of Practice:** Medical malpractice, personal injury **Affiliations:** A.F.T.L.; F.B.A.; A.B.A.; A.T.L.A.; B.C.B.A.; D.C.B.A. **Hob./spts.:** Singing, swimming, skiing, boating, fishing **SIC code:** 81 **Address:** Lisa S. Levine, P.A., 2665 Executive Park Dr., Suite 2, Weston, FL 33331 **E-mail:** lisa@thefemalesideoflaw.com **Web address:** www.thefemalesideoflaw.com

LEWIS, JOHN B.
Industry: Law **Univ./degree:** Hastings College of Law, 1954 **Current organization:** John B. Lewis, Attorney at Law **Title:** Attorney **Type of organization:** Law firm **Major product:** Legal services **Area of distribution:** Sacramento, California **Area of Practice:** Personal injury, workers compensation **Affiliations:** American Board of Trial Advocates **Hob./spts.:** Golf **SIC code:** 81 **Address:** John B. Lewis, Attorney at Law, 1006 Fourth St., 10th Floor, Sacramento, CA 95814

LIDDLE, JEFFREY L.
Industry: Law **Born:** April 21, 1949, Aurora, Illinois **Univ./degree:** B.S., Industrial Labor Relations, Cornell University, 1971; J.D., Root-Tilden-Kern Scholar, New York University Law School, 1976 **Current organization:** Liddle & Robinson, LLP **Title:** Partner **Type of organization:** Law firm **Major product:** Corporate securities and commercial litigation **Area of distribution:** National **Area of Practice:** Business litigation, lecturing on securities, industry arbitration **Affiliations:** New York State Bar Association; American Bar Association **Hob./spts.:** Tennis, reading, travel **SIC code:** 81 **Address:** Liddle & Robinson, LLP, 800 Third Ave., New York, NY 10022 **E-mail:** jliddle@liddlerobinson.com **Web address:** www.liddlerobinson.com

LINDENMUTH, NOEL C.
Industry: Legal services **Born:** November 27, 1940, Chicago, Illinois **Spouse:** Krystyna M. Lindenmuth (Ochman) M.D. **Married:** April 6, 1990 **Children:** Eric Jon, 39; Steve Paul, 38; Robert E. Gadjecki, 33 **Univ./degree:** J.D., Loyola University School of Law, 1970 **Current organization:** Larry D. Lee, P.C./Anesi, Ozmon, Rodin, Novak & Kohen, Ltd. **Title:** Of Counsel **Type of organization:** Law firm **Major product:** Personal injury representation of the plaintiff **Area of distribution:** Colorado, Illinois **Area of Practice:** Complex jury cases work-related heart attacks, medical malpractice, product defect, workers' compensation and automobile litigation; Admitted: Illinois, 1970, U.S. District Court, 1970, U.S. Supreme Court, 1977, Colorado, 1996 **Honors/awards:** "AV" rated, Martindale-Hubbell; Who's Who in American Law; Who's Who in the World **Affiliations:** A.A.J.; Colorado Bar Association; Boulder County Bar Association; Colorado Trial Lawyers Association; American Arbitration Association; Former Board Member, Attention Homes in Boulder; Advisory Board, University of Colorado Medical School's Cardiovascular Institute; Opera Colorado **Hob./spts.:** Fly-fishing, power boating, golf **SIC code:** 81 **Address:** Larry D. Lee, P.C., 1790 38th St., Suite 205, Boulder, CO 80301 **Web address:** www.leelawpc.com; www.anesilaw.com

LINDLEY, HAMILTON P.
Industry: Law **Univ./degree:** B.B.A., Baylor University; J.D., Baylor University, 2004 **Current organization:** Provost Umphrey, LLP **Title:** Attorney **Type of organization:** Law firm **Major product:** Legal services **Area of distribution:** National **Area of Practice:** Securities and patent litigation **Affiliations:** Dallas Bar Association; American Trial Lawyers Association **Hob./spts.:** Sailing, hunting **SIC code:** 81 **Address:** Provost Umphrey, LLP, 3232 McKinney, Suite 700, Dallas, TX 75204 **E-mail:** hlindley@provostumphrey.com

LOCASCIO, ANTHONY V.
Industry: Law **Born:** October 27, 1973, Livingston, New Jersey **Univ./degree:** J.D., Seton Hall School of Law, 1998 **Current organization:** Gold, Albanese, Barletti, Velazquez Law Office **Title:** Esquire **Type of organization:** Full service law firm **Major product:** Legal services **Area of distribution:** National **Area of Practice:** Civil trial practice **Published works:** Author, "Legally Speaking" column, monthly 7 town periodical; Regular legal commentation, Court TV, "Closing Arguments" Nancy Grace, "Both Sides" Kimberly Newsome; CNN, Nancy Grace, Weekend/Morning Edition **SIC code:** 81 **Address:** Gold, Albanese, Barletti, Velazquez Law Office, 58 Maple Ave., Red Bank, NJ 07701 **E-mail:** anthony@goldandalbanese.com

LOEB, ETHAN J.
Industry: Law **Born:** November 1, 1977, Houston, Texas **Univ./degree:** J.D., Stetson College of Law, 2003 **Current organization:** Bricklemyer Smolker & Bolves, P.A. **Title:** Attorney **Type of organization:** Law firm **Major product:** Legal services **Area of distribution:** National **Area of Practice:** Land use and environmental law, civil rights law, litigation **Affiliations:** A.B.A.; A.T.L.A.; Federal Society; The Florida Bar **SIC code:** 81 **Address:** Bricklemyer Smolker & Bolves, P.A., 500 E. Kennedy Blvd., Suite 200, Tampa, FL 33602 **E-mail:** ethanl@bsbfirm.com

LONEY, ERIC J.
Industry: Law **Born:** June 5, 1975, Dubuque, Iowa **Univ./degree:** J.D., Drake University, 2001 **Title:** Attorney **Type of organization:** Law firm **Major product:** Legal services **Area of distribution:** Iowa **Area of Practice:** Personal injury, workers comp., real estate **Affiliations:** Iowa Bar Association; American Bar Association **Hob./spts.:** Basketball, kayaking, the outdoors **SIC code:** 81 **Address:** 1000 73rd St., Suite 24, Windsor Heights, IA 50311 **E-mail:** eric@walklaw.com **Web address:** www.walklaw.com

LONGFELLOW, VICTORIA F.
Industry: Law **Born:** September 11, 1965, Holbrook, Arizona **Univ./degree:** B.S., Finance, Santa Clara University, 1987; J.D., Arizona State University School of Law, 1992 **Current organization:** Rayndon & Longfellow, P.C. **Title:** Attorney/Shareholder **Type of organization:** Law Firm **Major product:** Legal services **Area of distribution:** Arizona **Area of Practice:** Commercial transactions, commercial real estate, corporate and business law, limited liability companies partnerships **Affiliations:** "AV" rated, Martindale-Hubbell; State Bar of Arizona; Maricopa County Bar Association **Hob./spts.:** Horses, equestrian sports, skiing, reading, hiking **SIC code:** 81 **Address:** Rayndon & Longfellow, P.C., 5001 N. Granite Reef Rd., Scottsdale, AZ 85250 **E-mail:** vlongfellow@rayndon.com

LONGMIRE, WENDY L.
Industry: Law **Born:** Columbus, Ohio **Univ./degree:** B.A., Journalism, University of Mississippi; J.D., University of Kentucky **Current organization:** Ortale, Kelley, Herbert & Crawford **Title:** Partner **Type of organization:** Law firm **Major product:** Legal services **Area of distribution:** Tennessee **Area of Practice:** Board Certified, National Board of Trial Advocacy Defense; Certified, Civil Trial Advocacy Specialist **Affiliations:** Nashville Bar Association; Tennessee Bar Association; A.B.A.; Tennessee Defense Lawyers Association; A.T.C.A.; Lawyers Association for Women; Fellow, Nashville Bar Association; A.B.O.T.A. **SIC code:** 81 **Address:** Ortale, Kelley, Herbert & Crawford, 200 Fourth Ave. North, Noel Place, 3rd floor, Nashville, TN 37219 **E-mail:** wlongmire@ortalekelley.com **Web address:** www.ortalekelley.com

LOWE, SHERRY L.
Industry: Law **Born:** May 10, 1955, Smyrna, Tennessee **Univ./degree:** J.D., University of Mississippi, 1996 **Current organization:** Sherry Lowe, Attorney at Law **Title:** President **Type of organization:** Law firm **Major product:** Legal services **Area of distribution:** Mississippi **Area of Practice:** General law **Affiliations:** M.B.A.; A.B.A. **Hob./spts.:** Music composition, guitar **SIC code:** 81 **Address:** 109 Poplar St., P.O. Box 550, Sandersville, MS 39477 **E-mail:** sherrylowe@comcast.net

LOWRY, DAVID B.
Industry: Law **Born:** November 6, 1943, Bronxville, New York **Univ./degree:** J.D., University of Arizona, 1969 **Current organization:** David Burton Lowry, Esq. **Title:** Attorney **Type of organization:** Law firm **Major product:** Legal services **Area of distribution:** Portland, Oregon **Area of Practice:** Disability law **Affiliations:** National Association of Administrative Law Judges; American Bar Association; Association of Trial Lawyers of America **Hob./spts.:** Golf, Greyhound dogs **SIC code:** 81 **Address:** David B. Lowry, Esquire, 10211 S.W. Barbur Blvd., #112A, Portland, OR 97223

LYNCH, KYLE T.
Industry: Law **Born:** Glen Cove, New York, 1974 **Univ./degree:** B.A., Hartwick College, 1996; A.S., Applied Science of Culinary Arts, Johnson & Wales University, 1998; J.D., Hofstra University, New York, 2003 **Current organization:** Lynch Legal Associates, LLP **Title:** Attorney/Partner **Type of organization:** Law firm **Major product:** Legal services **Area of distribution:** New York **Area of Practice:** General practice **Affiliations:** A.T.L.A.; N.Y.S.T.L.A.; N.Y.C.B.A.; A.B.A.; N.Y.S.B.A.; National Institute of Trial Advocacy; Lexis-Nexis Trained, Westlaw Training **SIC code:** 81 **Address:** Lynch Legal Associates, LLP, 431 Willis Ave., Williston Park, NY 11596 **E-mail:** kylelynch@lynchlegal.com **Web address:** www.lynchlegal.com

LYTLE, THOMAS F.
Industry: Law **Univ./degree:** J.D., University of San Francisco, 1961 **Current organization:** Law Office of Thomas F. Lytle **Title:** Attorney **Type of organization:** Law firm **Major product:** Legal services **Area of distribution:** Sacramento, California **Area of Practice:** Trial of Civil Cases **Affiliations:** A.B.O.T.A.; A.T.L.A.; California Consumer Attorneys **SIC code:** 81 **Address:** Law Office of Thomas F. Lytle, 1220 25th St., Sacramento, CA 95816-5005 **E-mail:** tomlytle@sbcglobal.net

MALLOY, TIMOTHY J.
Industry: Law **Born:** April 7, 1944, Hattiesburg, Mississippi **Univ./degree:** J.D., University of Notre Dame, 1969 **Current organization:** McAndrews, Held & Malloy, Ltd. **Title:** Attorney/Partner **Type of organization:** Law firm **Major product:** Legal services **Area of distribution:** International **Area of Practice:** Litigation of intellectual property **Affiliations:** A.B.A.; A.I.P.L.A. **SIC code:** 81 **Address:** McAndrews, Held & Malloy, Ltd., 500 W. Madison St., Suite 3400, Chicago, IL 60661 **E-mail:** tmalloy@mhmlaw.com

MANDELL, JENNIFER E.
Industry: Law **Born:** January 16, 1965, Wiesbaden, Germany **Univ./degree:** B.A., George Mason University; J.D., Catholic University of America **Current organization:** Jennifer E. Mandell, Attorney-at-Law **Title:** Attorney & Counsellor at Law **Type of organization:** Law firm **Major product:** Legal services **Area of distribution:** Virginia and Washington, D.C. **Area of Practice:** Major area of practice: Family law (divorce, custody, visitation, spousal support, child support, property division, separation/settlement agreements, modification and enforcement) **Affiliations:** Virginia State Bar (Member, Family Law Section); Fairfax Bar Association (Member, Family Law Section); District of Columbia Bar; U.S. District Court for the Eastern District of Virginia; Northern Virginia Chapter of the Federal Bar Association; Phi Mu Fraternity (Alumni); CUA National Moot Court Team (Alumni) **Hob./spts.:** Skiing, music, creative writing **SIC code:** 81 **Address:** Jennifer E. Mandell, Attorney-at-Law, P.O. Box 430, Fairfax, VA 22038-0430, Office location: 10521 Judicial Dr., Suite 204, Fairfax, VA 22030 **Phone:** (703)352-5185 **Fax:** (703)352-5750 **E-mail:** jenmandell@aol.com

MANISCALCO, JOSEPH S.
Industry: Law **Born:** July 24, 1970, Brooklyn, New York **Univ./degree:** B.A., Magna Cum Laude, Journalism, Fordham University, 1992; J.D., Hofstra University School of Law, 1995 **Current organization:** LaMonica Herbst & Maniscalco, LLP **Title:** Partner **Type of organization:** Law firm **Major product:** Legal services **Area of distribution:** New York **Area of Practice:** Bankruptcy, litigation **Honors/awards:** First Place, Hofstra Law Review Article on Bankruptcy and Environmental Law, 1995 **Published works:** 8+ articles **Affiliations:** Chairman, Bankruptcy Committee, Nassau County Bar Association; American Bankruptcy Institution; Credit Abuse Resistance Education (CARE) **Hob./spts.:** Coaching baseball, Kenpo martial arts (3rd Degree Brown Belt) **SIC code:** 81 **Address:** LaMonica Herbst & Maniscalco, LLP, 3305 Jerusalem Ave., Suite 201, Wantagh, NY 11793 **E-mail:** jsm@lhmlawfirm.com **Web address:** www.lhmlawfirm.com

MANN, PHYLLIS E.
Industry: Law **Born:** September 6, 1961, Dallas, Texas **Univ./degree:** B.A., Career Arts, Dallas Baptist University, 1989; J.D., Southern Methodist University, Texas, 1993 **Current organization:** Law Office of Phyllis E. Mann **Title:** Attorney **Type of organization:** Law firm **Major product:** Legal services **Area of distribution:** Louisiana **Area of Practice:** Criminal defense **Published works:** Law journals **Affiliations:** Louisiana State Bar Association; American Bar Association; State Bar of Texas **SIC code:** 81 **Address:** Law Office of Phyllis E. Mann, P.O. Box 705, Alexandria, LA 71309 **E-mail:** phyllis@kricket.net

MANTA, ROBYN A.
Industry: Law **Born:** January 8, 1964, Wilkes-Barre, Pennsylvania **Spouse:** Jude Roth **Married:** October 22, 1994 **Univ./degree:** Certified, Paralegal, Penn State University, 1996; A.S., Business Management, Center for Degree Studies, 2003 **Current organization:** Anzalone Law Offices **Title:** Office Manager/Paralegal **Type of organization:** Law firm **Major product:** Legal services **Area of distribution:** National **Area of Practice:** Paralegal, IT consultation, office management, Notary Public **Honors/awards:** Numerous including, "Name the Employee Newsletter" contest winner, Hourigan, Kluger, Spohrer & Quinn; Distinguished Typing Award from Lisa Gialanella, Wilkes-College Nursing Dept.; Letter of Appreciation from Gerard McHugh Jr., Esquire re. coordinating and scheduling legal agenda; Letter of Appreciation from Nancy Wozniak, Administrative Assistant, Hourigan, Kluger, Spohrer & Quinn re. extra effort given during phone crisis; Acknowledgement and Thank You from Wilkes-Barre Chapter of UNICO Annual East-West Football Game **Affiliations:** Paralegal Division, A.T.L.A.; Pennsylvania Association of Notaries; Advisory/Scholarship Board **Hob./spts.:** Reading **SIC code:** 81 **Address:** Anzalone Law Offices, 98 S. Franklin St., Wilkes-Barre, PA 18701 **E-mail:** robyn.manta@anzalonelaw.com **Web address:** www.anzalonelaw.com

MARINO SR., CHARLES J.
Industry: Law **Born:** May 30, 1926, Gillespie, Illinois **Univ./degree:** B.S.; M.A., Commerce Law, St. Louis University; B.A., Management, Webster University; J.D., St. Louis University **Current organization:** Charles J. Marino, Sr., Esq. **Title:** Arbitrator **Type of organization:** Private law firm **Major product:** Legal services **Area of distribution:** Missouri **Area of Practice:** Alternative dispute resolution, labor law **Published works:** 100+ published cases **Affiliations:** A.A.A.; A.B.A.; A.T.L.A.; A.S.P.A.; National Arbitration Forum **Hob./spts.:** Fishing, hunting **SIC code:** 81 **Address:** Charles J. Marino Sr. Esq., 7161 Lindenwood Place, St. Louis, MO 63109-1111 **E-mail:** charlesjmarino@aol.com

MARTIN, JAY G.
Industry: Law **Born:** October 13, 1951, Washington, D.C. **Univ./degree:** B.B.A., Southern Methodist University, 1973; J.D., M.P.A., 1976, Southern Methodist University, **Current organization:** Winstead, Sechrest & Minick **Title:** Shareholder **Type of organization:** Law firm **Major product:** Legal services **Area of distribution:** International **Area of Practice:** Energy, public utility and corporate law **Honors/awards:** Euromoney Publication, Outstanding Energy Lawyer, 1997, 1999 and 2000 **Published works:** Co-author, 3 books, 50+ articles **Affiliations:** Texas State Bar Association; Washington D.C. Bar Association; American Bar Association; Trustee, R.M.M.L.F.; Member, Corporate Council, Texas State Bar Association **Hob./spts.:** Reading, golf, tennis, jogging **SIC code:** 81 **Address:** Baker Huges, Inc., 3900 Essex Lane, Suite 1200, Houston, TX 77027-5177 **E-mail:** jmartin@winstead.com **Web address:** www.winstead.com

MASIAKOS, JORDAN
Industry: Law **Born:** January 30, 1967, Queens, New York **Univ./degree:** B.S., Hofstra University, 1988; J.D., Thomas Cooley School of Law, 1991 **Current organization:** Jordan Masiakos, P.C. **Title:** Attorney **Type of organization:** Law firm **Major product:** Legal services **Area of distribution:** New York **Area of Practice:** Personal injury **Affiliations:** New York State Bar Association; Nassau County Bar Association **Hob./spts.:** Family, computers, music **SIC code:** 81 **Address:** Jordan Masiakos P.C., 200 Willis Ave., Mineola, NY 11501 **E-mail:** masiakoslaw@aol.com **Web address:** www.nysti.org

MASON, RICHARD W.
Industry: Law **Born:** December 17, 1937, Missouri **Univ./degree:** J.D., University of Michigan, 1963 **Current organization:** Richard W. Mason Law Offices **Title:** Attorney at Law **Type of organization:** Law firm **Major product:** Legal services **Area of distribution:** Missouri **Area of Practice:** Family law, civil litigation **Affiliations:** M.O.B.A.; A.B.A. **Hob./spts.:** Boating, fishing, skiing **SIC code:** 81 **Address:** Richard W. Mason Law Offices, 9233 Ward Pkwy., Suite 240, Kansas City, MO 64114 **E-mail:** rwmason@quixnet.net

MATTHEWS, STEWART D.
Industry: Law **Born:** Tulsa, Oklahoma **Univ./degree:** J.D., Texas Wesleyan University School of Law **Current organization:** Matthews Law Firm **Title:** Attorney **Type of organization:** Law firm **Major product:** Legal services **Area of distribution:** National **Area of Practice:** Product liability, personal injury, wrongful death **Affiliations:** A.T.L.A.; T.T.L.A.; D.T.L.A.; Plano Bar; Dallas Bar; Cullen County Bar; State Bar of Texas **Hob./spts.:** Scuba diving, church activities, mock trial competitions, moot court competitions **SIC code:** 81 **Address:** Matthews Law Firm, 3010 Elderberry Dr., Wylie, TX 75098 **E-mail:** productslawyer@aol.com

MAYER, KEVIN C.
Industry: Law **Born:** April 3, 1959, San Francisco, California **Univ./degree:** J.D., University of California, Hastings College of Law, 1984 **Current organization:** Steptoe & Johnson LLP **Title:** Partner **Type of organization:** Law firm **Major product:** Legal services **Area of distribution:** National/international **Area of Practice:** Toxic tort, environmental products liability trials **Affiliations:** Defense Research Institute; Association for Environmental Health and Sciences **Hob./spts.:** Travel **SIC code:** 81 **Address:** Steptoe & Johnson LLP, 633 W. Fifth St., Suite 700, Los Angeles, CA 90071 **E-mail:** kmayer@steptoe.com

MAZAWEY, RICHARD SAMUEL
Industry: Law **Born:** September 17, 1953, Jersey City, New Jersey **Univ./degree:** B.S., Political Science, Rutgers University, 1975; J.D., Hofstra University School of Law, 1978 **Current organization:** Law Office of Richard S. Mazawey & Associates **Title:** Attorney at Law/Owner/Proprietor **Type of organization:** Law firm **Major product:** Legal services **Area of distribution:** National **Area of Practice:** Trial litigation **Published works:** 10+ articles **Affiliations:** A.B.A.; A.T.L.A.; N.J.T.L.A.; N.J.B.A.; 3rd Circuit US Court of Appeals Bar; US Supreme Court Bar **Hob./spts.:** Family, coaching basketball, New Jersey Nets, health and physical fitness **SIC code:** 81 **Address:** Law Office of Richard S. Mazawey & Associates, 1135 Broad St., Suite 211, Clifton, NJ 07013 **E-mail:** rsmlaw1953@aol.com

MCCALEB, JOE W.
Industry: Law **Born:** December 9, 1941, Nashville, Tennessee **Univ./degree:** M.St., Environmental Law, cum laude, Vermont Law School, 1995; J.D., University of Memphis, 1970; B.A., Union University, 1964 **Current organization:** McCaleb and Associates **Title:** Attorney at Law **Type of organization:** Small law firm **Major product:** Environmental litigation in the public interest and American Indian law **Area of distribution:** Tennessee **Area of Practice:** Environmental law **Honors/awards:** Who's Who in American Law 2002-03, 2004-05; National Registry of Who's Who, 2001; Eagle Award, Aniyunweya Nation, Tennessee, 2001; Sarah Hines Award, TN Chapter Sierra Club, 1985; Environmental Advocacy Award, TN Environmental Council, 1988 **Published works:** Co-author: "S.A.B.P. v. U.S. Fish and Wildlife Service, Failure to Designate Critical Habitat for Endangered Species is a 'Continuing Violation' of the Endangered Species Act," Endangered Species Update, University of Michigan, January-February, 2002; Author: "Stewardship of Public Lands and Cultural Resources in the Tennessee Valley: A Critique of the Tennessee Valley Authority," Res Communes, Vermont Journal of the Environment, Vol. One, Winter 1999 **Affiliations:** Tennessee Bar Association; Sumner County Bar Association **Hob./spts.:** Backpacking, photography **SIC code:** 81 **Address:** McCaleb and Associates, 315 W. Main St., Suite 112, Hendersonville, TN 37075 **E-mail:** jwmccaleb@bellsouth.net

MCCLURE, WILLIAM P.
Industry: Law **Univ./degree:** J.D., George Washington University, 1952 **Current organization:** White & Case LLP **Title:** J.D./Attorney **Type of organization:** Law firm **Major product:** Legal services **Area of distribution:** National **Area of Practice:** Taxation **Honors/awards:** "AV" rated, Martindale-Hubbell **Affiliations:** A.B.A.; D.C.B.A. **SIC code:** 81 **Address:** White & Case LLP, 601 13th St. N.W., Suite 600S, Washington, DC 20005 **E-mail:** wmcclure@whitecase.com

MCCOLLOUGH, JASON E.
Industry: Law **Born:** Midwest City, Oklahoma **Univ./degree:** B.A., Political Science/International Relations, 2001; J.D., Drake University Law School, 2003 **Current organization:** Wandro, Baer & Appel, P.C. **Title:** Attorney **Type of organization:** Law firm **Major product:** Legal services **Area of distribution:** National **Area of Practice:** General law practice **Published works:** "State Tort Liability for Failure to Protect Against Bioterrorism", 8 Drake J. Agric. L. 743, 2003 **Affiliations:** A.T.L.A.; A.B.A.; Iowa State Bar Association; Iowa Trial Lawyers Association **Hob./spts.:** Volunteer firefighter and E.M.T. **SIC code:** 81 **Address:** Wandro, Baer & Appel, P.C., 2501 Grand Ave., Suite B, Des Moines, IA 50312 **E-mail:** jmccoll@2501grand.com **Web address:** www.wba.com

MCDYER, DANIEL P.
Industry: Law **Univ./degree:** J.D., Duquesne University, Pittsburgh, Pennsylvania, 1974 **Current organization:** Anstandig McDyer **Title:** Attorney **Type of organization:** Law firm **Major product:** Legal representation, Lexicographical Evidence in the Third Circuit, Liaison Counsel with manufactured products, Toxic Litigation on a national basis; Trademark Litigation; insurance litigation; employment litigation **Area of distribution:** National **Area of Practice:** Litigation **Honors/awards:** "AV" rated, Martindale-Hubbell **Affiliations:** A.B.A.; Federal Circuit Bar Association; Pennsylvania Bar Association; Judicial Merit Committee; West Virginia Federal Courts; Third Court State of Appeals, US Supreme Courts; Allegheny Bar Association; West Virginia State Bar; Civil Litigation Committee **Hob./spts.:** Skiing, jogging, coaching juvenile sports, boating **SIC code:** 81 **Address:** Anstandig McDyer, 707 Grant St., 1300 Gulf Tower, Pittsburgh, PA 15219 **E-mail:** ambylaw.usaor.net

MCHARD, SAM S.
Industry: Law **Born:** November 20, 1951, Aledo, Illinois **Univ./degree:** J.D., Northwestern University School of Law, Chicago **Current organization:** The Law Office of Sam S. McHard, PC **Title:** President **Type of organization:** Law firm **Major product:** Litigation **Area of distribution:** National **Area of Practice:** Personal injury and commercial **Hob./spts.:** Running, farming **SIC code:** 81 **Address:** The Law Office of Sam S. McHard, PC, 1800 Third Ave., Suite 515, Rock Island, IL 61201 **E-mail:** smchard@mchardlaw.com

MCINTOSH, CAROLYN L.
Industry: Law **Born:** December 10, 1955, Boulder, Colorado **Univ./degree:** J.D., University of Colorado, 1980 **Current organization:** Patton Boggs LLP **Title:** Administrative Partner **Type of organization:** Law firm **Major product:** Environment permits, client advisory **Area of distribution:** Colorado **Area of Practice:** Environmental, corporations and individuals **Published works:** Articles on storm water management **Affiliations:** Alliance Program of Professional Women; American Bar Association; Colorado Bar Association **Hob./spts.:** Hiking, politics **SIC code:** 81 **Address:** Patton Boggs LLP, 1660 Lincoln St., Suite 1900, Denver, CO 80264 **E-mail:** cmcintosh@pattonboggs.cm

MCMAHON, DAWN M.
Industry: Law **Born:** February 26, 1977, Cincinnati, Ohio **Univ./degree:** Attended Miami University, Oxford, Ohio; B.S., Business Management, Thematic Sequence, Political Science, 1998; J.D., Nova Southeastern University, Ft. Lauderdale, Florida, 2001 **Current organization:** Coleman & Associates, P.A. **Title:** Lawyer **Type of organization:** Law firm **Major product:** Legal services **Area of distribution:** Florida **Area of Practice:** General civil litigation specializing in attorney malpractice, real estate litigation, insurance defense **Honors/awards:** Buck Rogers Leadership Award, 1998 **Published works:** Frengut v. Vanderpol, 927 So. 2d 148 (Fla. 4th DCA 2006); Vanderpol v. Frengut, citation not yet available (Fla 4th DCA 2006) **Affiliations:** American Trial Lawyers Association (ATLA), American Young Lawyers Division (AYLD); 2005 Member of U.S.D.C. for the Southern District of Florida **Hob./spts.:** Tennis, salsa dancing **SIC code:** 81 **Address:** Coleman & Associates, P.A., 120 E. Palmetto Park Rd., Suite 150, Boca Raton, FL 33432 **E-mail:** dmm@colemanattorneys.com

MEANOR, H. CURTIS
Industry: Law **Born:** October 6, 1929, Cleveland, Ohio **Univ./degree:** LL.B., Rutgers University Law School, 1955 **Current organization:** Podvey, Sachs, Meanor, Catenacci, Hildner & Cocoziello **Title:** Attorney **Type of organization:** Law firm **Major product:** Legal services **Area of distribution:** New Jersey and New York metropolitan area **Area of Practice:** Arbitration and mediation of complex cases **Honors/awards:** When nominated to the U.S. District Court, District of New Jersey, was rated exceptionally well-qualified by unanimous vote by the American Bar Association Committee on Judiciary **Affiliations:** Life Member, American Law Institute; A.A.A.; C.P.R.; Judge of the Superior Court, Law Division (4 years); Judge of the Superior Court, Appellate Division (1 year); Judge of the U.S. District Court, District of New Jersey (8½ years) **Hob./spts.:** Golf **SIC code:** 81 **Address:** Podvey, Sachs, Meanor, Catenacci, Hildner, Cocoziello & Chattman, 1 Riverfront Plaza, 8th floor, Newark, NJ 07102 **E-mail:** hmeanor@podveysachs.com

MEDINA, YOLANDA M.
Industry: Law **Born:** Santa Ana, California **Univ./degree:** J.D., Whittier School of Law, 2002 **Current organization:** Law Offices of Federico Castelan Sayre **Title:** Attorney **Type of organization:** Law firm **Major product:** Legal services **Area of distribution:** National **Area of Practice:** Civil litigation **Affiliations:** H.B.A.; O.C.T.L.A.; A.T.L.A.; C.A.C **Hob./spts.:** Hiking **SIC code:** 81 **Address:** Law Offices of Federico Castelan Sayre, 900 N. Broadway, 4th floor, Santa Ana, CA 92701 **E-mail:** ymmedina@yahoo.com

MEEKINS, RALPH W.
Industry: Law **Born:** Charlotte, North Carolina **Univ./degree:** B.S., Psychology and Physical Education, University of North Carolina at Chapel Hill; J.D., Campbell Law School, 1986 **Current organization:** Teddy & Meekins, LLC **Title:** Attorney **Type of organization:** Law firm **Major product:** Legal services **Area of distribution:** National **Area of Practice:** Personal injury, workers compensation, civil litigation; Board Certified in Civil Trial Advocacy by the National Board of Trial Advocacy; Board Certified Mediator **Honors/awards:** Recipient of a merit scholarship at Campbell Law School; Inducted into Omicron Delta Kappa and Phi Kappa Phi Honorary Fraternities **Published works:** Written articles and lectured throughout North Carolina on topics including, but not limited to, Premises Liability, Professional Negligence, Nursing Home Malpractice, Professionalism, Auto Accident Trials and the proper evaluation of tort cases **Affiliations:** North Carolina Board of Governors for the North Carolina Bar Association; Cleveland County Bar Association; North Carolina Academy of Trial Lawyers; Admitted to practice before the North Carolina Supreme Court and the U.S. District Court for the Eastern, Middle and Western Districts; Chairman of the Board for the Cleveland County YMCA **Hob./spts.:** Sunday School teacher and a trained Stephen Minister in his church **SIC code:** 81 **Address:** Teddy & Meekins, LLC, 1219 Fallston Rd., Shelby, NC 28150 **E-mail:** rmeekins@teddyandmeekins.com **Web address:** www.teddyandmeekins.com

MEISEL, STACEY L.
Industry: Law **Born:** August 18, 1969, Schenectady, New York **Univ./degree:** J.D., Villanova University, 1994 **Current organization:** Becker Meisel LLC **Title:** Attorney **Type of organization:** Law firm **Major product:** Legal services **Area of distribution:** New Jersey **Area of Practice:** Bankruptcy, debtor/creditor, commercial **Affiliations:** New Jersey State Bar Association; Lecturer for Continuing Education, I.C.L.E.; Pro-Bono Work for Essex County Volunteer Lawyer's Association **Hob./spts.:** Reading, running, travel, her dog **SIC code:** 81 **Address:** Becker Meisel LLC, 354 Eisenhower Pkwy., Suite 2800, Livingston, NJ 07042 **E-mail:** slmeisel@beckermeisel.com

MEYER, RICHARD F.
Industry: Law **Born:** May 15, 1955, Springfield, Ohio **Univ./degree:** J.D., Capital University, 1980 **Current organization:** Browning & Meyer Co., LPA **Title:** Esquire **Type of organization:** Law firm **Major product:** Legal services **Area of distribution:** Ohio **Area of Practice:** Estate planning, trusts and probate **Honors/awards:** "AV" rated, Martindale-Hubbell; O.S.B.A. Certified Specialist, Estate Planning, Trusts and Probate **Affiliations:** Ohio State Bar Association; Columbus Bar Association; Elder Law Committee **SIC code:** 81 **Address:** Browning & Meyer Co., LPA, 8101 N. High St., Suite 370, Columbus, OH 43235 **E-mail:** rmeyer@elderlaw.us **Web address:** www.elderlaw.us

MILLER, JOSEPH
Industry: Law **Born:** January 23, 1969, Brooklyn, New York **Univ./degree:** B.A., History, University of Scranton, Magna Cum Laude, 1991; J.D., Pace University School of Law, Dean's List, 1994 **Current organization:** Cullen & Dykman LLP **Title:** Partner/Attorney **Type of organization:** Law firm **Major product:** Legal services **Area of distribution:** National **Area of Practice:** Tort defense litigation; insurance coverage; appellate litigation **Published works:** Extending Extraterritorial Abduction Beyond Its Limits: United States v. Alvarez-Machain, 6 Pace Int'l L. Rev. 221 (1994) **Affiliations:** New York State Bar Association, Tort and Insurance and Trial Lawyers Sections; American Bar Association; National Institute for Trial Advocacy, Patron and Past Participant; Defense Association of New York **Hob./spts.:** Rugby, cycling, hiking, physical fitness **SIC code:** 81 **Address:** Cullen & Dykman LLP, 177 Montague St., Brooklyn, NY 11201 **E-mail:** jmiller@cullenanddykman.com **Web address:** www.cullenanddykman.com

MILLER, KEITH A.
Industry: Law **Born:** August 21, 1953, Jacksonville, North Carolina **Univ./degree:** J.D., Syracuse University, 1989 **Current organization:** Law Offices of Keith Miller **Title:** Attorney **Type of organization:** Law firm **Major product:** Legal services **Area of distribution:** National **Area of Practice:** Veterans law, gaming law **Published works:** multiple articles **Affiliations:** Oregon State Bar, Federal bar of DC **Hob./spts.:** Stamp collecting **SIC code:** 81 **Address:** Law Offices of Keith Miller, 1262 Main St., Sweet Home, OR 97386 **E-mail:** sulaw@attbi.com

MILLS, WILLIAM S.
Industry: Law **Born:** November 12, 1952, Roanoke, Virginia **Univ./degree:** J.D., University of North Carolina at Chapel Hill **Current organization:** Glenn, Mills & Fisher, PA **Title:** Partner **Type of organization:** Law firm **Major product:** Legal services **Area of distribution:** North Carolina **Area of Practice:** Litigation, civil, plaintiff **Affiliations:** A.C.I.A.; N.C.B.A.; A.T.L.A.; A.B.T.A.; N.B.T.A.; Past President, N.C.A.T.L.; Trial Advocacy Professor, Duke University and UNC - Chapel Hill School of Law **Hob./spts.:** Water sports, backpacking, golf, boating **SIC code:** 81 **Address:** Glenn, Mills & Fisher, PA, 400 W. Main St., Suite 709, Durham, NC 27701 **E-mail:** wmills@gmf-law.com

MINASIAN, LAWRENCE D.
Industry: Law **Born:** October 16, 1969, Orange, New Jersey **Univ./degree:** J.D., Seton Hall University School of Law, 1994 **Current organization:** Sluka & Minasian, LLC **Title:** Attorney **Type of organization:** Law firm **Major product:** Legal services **Area of distribution:** New Jersey **Area of Practice:** Personal injury **Honors/awards:** Listed in Who's Who Among American Lawyers **Affiliations:** New Jersey Bar Association; Barrister, Inn of Court; West Orange Rotary Club **Hob./spts.:** Golf **SIC code:** 81 **Address:** Sluka & Minasian, LLC, 80 Main St., West Orange, NJ 07052

MISHAEL, DAVID B.
Industry: Law **Born:** July 22, 1958, Coral Gables, Florida **Univ./degree:** J.D., University of Florida, 1983 **Current organization:** David B. Mishael P.A. **Title:** Attorney **Type of organization:** Law firm **Major product:** Civil, trial law **Area of distribution:** International **Area of Practice:** Medical malpractice, personal injury **Honors/awards:** "AV" rated, Martindale-Hubbell **Affiliations:** A.F.T.L.; A.T.L.A.; Dade County Trial Lawyers Association **Hob./spts.:** Family, sport fishing, golf, tennis **SIC code:** 81 **Address:** David B. Mishael P.A., 8603 S. Dixie Hwy., Suite 315, Miami, FL 33143 **E-mail:** dmishael@aol.com

MITCHELL, DANIEL P.
Industry: Law **Current organization:** Gray, Harris & Robinson, P.A. **Title:** Attorney/Shareholder **Type of organization:** Law firm **Major product:** Legal services **Area of distribution:** Tampa, Florida **Area of Practice:** Insurance law, commercial and civil litigation, personal injury, professional liability, transportation law **Affiliations:** American Bar Association; The Florida Bar; American Arbitration Association; Defense Research Institute; Florida Defense Lawyers' Association (Chair, Products Liability Committee, 2002-); Florida Supreme Court Committee on Standard Jury Instructions in Civil Cases (2000-); American Board of Trial Advocacy ("Advocate" Rank), Federation of Defense and Corporate Counsel **SIC code:** 81 **Address:** Gray, Harris & Robinson, P.A., 201 N. Franklin St., Suite 2200, Tampa, FL 33602 **Phone:** (813)273-5000 **Fax:** (813)273-5145 **E-mail:** dmitchell@grayharris.com

MOAK, SAM A.
Industry: Law **Born:** January 18, 1966, Houston, Texas **Univ./degree:** J.D., South Texas College of Law **Current organization:** Moak & Moak, P.C. **Title:** President/Attorney **Type of organization:** Law firm **Major product:** Legal services **Area of distribution:** Huntsville, Texas **Area of Practice:** Real estate law **Published works:** Weekly newspaper, "The Legal Corner" **Affiliations:** T.T.L.A.; State Bar of Texas; Waller County Bar Association **Hob./spts.:** Hunting, fishing, the Houston Astros **SIC code:** 81 **Address:** Moak & Moak, P.C., 1305 Eleventh St., Huntsville, TX 77340 **Web address:** www.moakandmoak.com

MOELLER, WILLIAM D.
Industry: Law **Born:** November 17, 1957, Davenport, Iowa **Univ./degree:** J.D., University of Iowa, 1985; L.L.M., Georgetown University, 1995 **Current organization:** Stuart, Biolchini, Turner & Givray **Title:** Attorney **Type of organization:** Law firm **Major product:** Legal services **Area of distribution:** International **Area of Practice:** Corporate and commercial law **Affiliations:** Oklahoma Bar Association; Texas State Bar Association; American Bar Association; Houston Bar Association; Tulsa County Bar Association **Hob./spts.:** Junior Warden at St. Jerome's church **SIC code:** 81 **Address:** Stuart, Biolchini, Turner & Givray, 15 E. Fifth St., Suite 3300, Tulsa, OK 74103 **E-mail:** wdmoeller@aol.com

MOLLOY, JOHN F.
Industry: Law **Born:** August 18, 1917, Los Angeles, California **Spouse:** Barbara (Bobbi) Boyer **Married:** September 13, 2002 **Children:** John Joseph Molloy, Eva Josephine Bansner (deceased), Marjorie Letson, Karen Sebring, Thomas A. Molloy, M.D., Craig William Molloy **Univ./degree:** B.A., with Distinction, 1939; J.D. with High Distinction, 1944, University of Arizona, J.D., with Distinction, University of Kansas City, 1939 **Current organization:** Board of Directors, Emeritus - The National Law Center for Inter-American Free Trade **Title:** Judge/Author **Major product:** Legal services **Area of distribution:** Arizona **Area of Practice:** Trial law, writing **Honors/awards:** Honorary Doctor of Laws, University of Arizona, 1986; Distinguished Citizen Award, University of Arizona, 1994 **Published works:** Book, "The Fraternity", Lawyers and Judges in Collusion, published by Paragon House; Authored over 300 decisions for the Arizona Court of Appeals as well as the final Miranda decision for the

Arizona Supreme Court **Affiliations:** A.B.A.; Arizona Bar Association; American Trial Lawyers Association; American Board of Trial Advocates **Career accomplishments:** Founded Pima County Court of Conciliation, 1960; President of Arizona Judges Association, 1965; President of the Marshall Foundation for 26 years; President of the Tucson YMCA, 1966-1968; Appointed to the State Board of Regents by Governor Raul Castro, 1976; Commander of American Legion Post 7, 1949-1951; Visiting Professor of the University of Arizona Law School; Served on the Boards on the Arizona Health Sciences Center, The Sarver Heart Center, The Little Chapel of All Nations, El Pueblo Health Center, Arizona Children's Home, Child Guidance Clinic and the St. Elizabeth of Hungary Clinic; President of the largest law firm in the State of Arizona **Hob./spts.:** Tennis, hunting **SIC code:** 81 **Address:** 404 S. Via de los Campos, Tucson, AZ 85711 **E-mail:** johnfmolloy@aol.com

MOORE, THOMAS C.
Industry: Law **Born:** June 21, 1943, Mountainair, New Mexico **Univ./degree:** J.D., South Texas College of Law, 1972 **Current organization:** Moore, Lewis & Russwurm, P.C. **Title:** Esquire **Type of organization:** Law firm **Major product:** Legal services **Area of distribution:** Dumas, Texas **Area of Practice:** General law **Hob./spts.:** Backpacking, snorkeling, hunting, fishing **SIC code:** 81 **Address:** Moore, Lewis & Russwurm, P.C., 713 Bliss Ave., Dumas, TX 79029 **E-mail:** tmoore@arn.net

MOORE JR., HOWARD
Industry: Law **Born:** February 28, 1932, Atlanta, Georgia **Univ./degree:** J.D., Boston University, 1960 **Current organization:** Moore & Moore **Title:** Attorney-at-Law **Type of organization:** Law firm **Major product:** Legal services **Area of distribution:** National **Area of Practice:** Litigation, employment discrimination, civil rights **Affiliations:** A.T.L.A.; N.C.B.L. **SIC code:** 81 **Address:** Moore & Moore, 445 Bellevue Ave., 2nd floor, Oakland, CA 94610-4924 **E-mail:** moorlaw@aol.com

MORGAN, KERMIT J.
Industry: Law **Born:** February 13, 1914, Henderson, Iowa **Univ./degree:** J.D., University of Southern California at Los Angeles, 1937 **Current organization:** Private practice **Title:** Attorney **Type of organization:** Law firm **Major product:** Legal services **Area of distribution:** National **Affiliations:** Past Board Member, Board of Southern California Defense Council; International Association of Insurance Council; State Bar of California; Los Angeles Bar Association; Association of Attorney-Mediators; American Board of Trial Advocates **SIC code:** 81 **Address:** 2108 Stradella Rd., Los Angeles, CA 90077

MORGAN, RICHARD G.
Industry: Law **Born:** December 23, 1943, Houston, Texas **Univ./degree:** B.A., History, Princeton University, 1966; J.D., University of Texas School of Law, 1969 **Current organization:** Shook, Hardy & Bacon, L.L.P. **Title:** Managing Partner **Type of organization:** Law firm **Major product:** Legal services, product liability defense **Area of distribution:** International **Area of Practice:** Energy law (oil, gas, chemical, electric) **Published works:** 50+ articles, 7 book chapters **Affiliations:** A.B.A.; State Bar of Texas; Southern District, State Bar of Texas; District of Columbia Bar; Minnesota State Bar Association; **Hob./spts.:** Tennis, reading, writing fiction, travel, amateur theatre **SIC code:** 81 **Address:** Shook, Hardy & Bacon, L.L.P., 600 Travis St., Suite 600, Houston, TX 77002 **E-mail:** rgmorgan@shb.com **Web address:** www.shb.com

MORLITZ, GERALD
Industry: Law **Born:** August 3, 1945, New York **Univ./degree:** J.D., Temple University, 1971 **Current organization:** Gerald Morlitz, J.D., C.F.P. **Title:** Attorney **Type of organization:** Law firm **Major product:** Legal services, financial planning **Area of distribution:** New York **Area of Practice:** Legal and estate planning **Affiliations:** New York State Bar Association; Director, Estate Planning Council of New York; President, Financial Planning Association of New York, 2000; Chair, Financial Planning Association of New York **Hob./spts.:** Toy trains **SIC code:** 81 **Address:** Gerald Morlitz, J.D., C.F.P., 530 Fifth Ave., 14th floor, New York, NY 10036 **E-mail:** gerry@morlitz.com

MORRISON, SUSAN MARIE
Industry: Law **Born:** September 22, 1962, Boston, Massachusetts **Univ./degree:** B.A., Political Science, College of New Rochelle, 1984; J.D., Suffolk University, 1988 **Current organization:** Fitzhugh, Parker & Alvaro, LLP **Title:** Senior Associate **Type of organization:** Law firm **Major product:** Legal services **Area of distribution:** National **Area of Practice:** Insurance defense litigation, environmental (lead paint and asbestos) defense litigation, defense product liability, defense/personal injury litigation, medical records evaluation and review **Affiliations:** Federal Bar Association; Catholic Lawyers Guild; Voice of the Faithful; Chernobyl Children Project U.S.A.; Reverend Robert J. Dwyer Scholarship Committee; American Bar Association; Kappa Gamma Pi **Hob./spts.:** Writing, snorkeling, reading, travel, lector-Church of the Blessed Sacrament, Walpole, MA **SIC code:** 81 **Address:** Fitzhugh, Parker & Alvaro, LLP, 155 Federal St., Suite 1700, Boston, MA 02110 **E-mail:** smorrison@fitzhughlaw.com **Web address:** www.fitzhughlaw.com

MULLMAN JR., RAYMOND P.
Industry: Law **Born:** January 3, 1969, Rockville Centre, New York **Univ./degree:** J.D., University of South Carolina School of Law, 1995 **Current organization:** Poliakoff & Assoc. **Title:** Associate **Type of organization:** Law firm **Major product:** Legal services **Area of distribution:** South Carolina **Area of Practice:** Environmental **Affiliations:** Association of Trial Lawyers of America; South Carolina Trial Lawyers Association **SIC code:** 81 **Address:** Poliakoff & Assoc., 215 Magnolia St., Spartanburg, SC 29304 **E-mail:** rmullmanjr@aol.com

MURPHY, ERIN
Industry: Law **Born:** June 10, 1978, Pittsburgh, Pennsylvania **Univ./degree:** B.S., Stephen F. Austin State University, 2000; J.D., South Texas College of Law, 2003 **Current organization:** The Mostyn Law Firm **Title:** Attorney **Type of organization:** Law firm **Major product:** Legal services **Area of distribution:** Texas **Area of Practice:** Commercial litigation **Affiliations:** American Trial Lawyers Association; Texas Young Lawyers Association; Houston Young Lawyers Association; Texas State Bar; Houston Bar Association; Texas Trial Lawyers Association **SIC code:** 81 **Address:** The Mostyn Law Firm, 200 Westcott St., Houston, TX 77007 **E-mail:** ecmurphy@mostynlaw.com **Web address:** www.mostynlaw.com

MURPHY, KEVIN C.
Industry: Law **Born:** Brooklyn, New York **Univ./degree:** B.S., Economics, Syracuse University, 1975; J.D., University of Virginia, 1979 **Current organization:** Devorsetz, Stinziano, Gilberti, Heintz & Smith, P.C. **Title:** Esquire **Type of organization:** Law firm **Major product:** Legal services **Area of distribution:** Syracuse, New York **Area of Practice:** Environmental litigation, client relations **Affiliations:** A.B.A.; New York State Bar Association; Environmental Law Institute **SIC code:** 81 **Address:** Devorsetz, Stinziano, Gilberti, Heintz and Smith, P.C., 555 E. Genesee St., Syracuse, NY 13202 **E-mail:** kmurphy@gilbertilaw.com

MUTTER, JOHN A.
Industry: Law **Born:** March 27, 1927 **Univ./degree:** B.A., Providence College, 1949; J.D., Boston University, 1957 **Current organization:** Rhode Island Family Court **Title:** Associate Justice **Type of organization:** Court **Major product:** Judiciary duties **Area of distribution:** Rhode Island **Area of Practice:** Family relations **Published works:** Co-writer, co-director: "That Summer in Philadelphia", educational film **Affiliations:** Past President, American Judges Association **Hob./spts.:** President Province County Kennel Club, theatre, pastel painting **SIC code:** 81 **Address:** Rhode Island Family Court, 1 Dorrance St., Providence, RI 03903 **E-mail:** jmutter@courts.state.ri.us

NEELON, DANIEL P.
Industry: Law **Univ./degree:** J.D., University of Virginia, 1983 **Current organization:** Neelon Wilder LLC **Title:** Attorney **Type of organization:** Law firm **Major product:** Legal services **Area of distribution:** International **Area of Practice:** Business law and litigation; Licensed in Texas and Massachusetts **Affiliations:** M.B.A.; B.B.A.; Million Dollar Advocates Forum; Texas Bar Foundation **Hob./spts.:** Martial arts **SIC code:** 81 **Address:** Neelon Wilder LLC, 325 Route 149, Marstons Mills, MA 02648 **E-mail:** dneelon@neelonwilder.com

NEFF, MICHAEL A.
Industry: Law **Born:** September 4, 1940, Springfield, Illinois **Univ./degree:** J.D., Columbia University **Current organization:** Michael A. Neff, P.C. **Title:** President **Type of organization:** Law firm **Major product:** Legal services **Area of distribution:** New York, New York **Area of Practice:** Adoption law **Affiliations:** American Bar Association (Family Law Section); National Association of Council for Children; American Association of Adoption Attorneys (Pending) **Hob./spts.:** Writing, training **SIC code:** 81 **Address:** Michael A. Neff, P.C., 5 W. 86th St., #6B, New York, NY 10024 **E-mail:** maneffpc@aol.com

NELON, ROBERT D.
Industry: Law **Born:** August 8, 1946, Shawnee, Oklahoma **Univ./degree:** J.D., University of Oklahoma, 1971 **Current organization:** Hall Estill Hardwick Gable Golden & Nelson **Title:** Partner/Attorney **Type of organization:** Law firm **Major product:** Legal services **Area of distribution:** International **Area of Practice:** Communications law **Affiliations:** A.B.A.; O.B.A.; O.C.B.A. **Hob./spts.:** Reading, golf, tennis **SIC code:** 81 **Address:** Hall Estill Hardwick Gable Golden & Nelson, 100 N. Broadway Ave., Suite 2900, Oklahoma City, OK 73102 **E-mail:** bnelon@hallestill.com

NELSON, ROBERT J.
Industry: Law **Born:** New York, New York **Univ./degree:** J.D., New York University **Current organization:** Lieff, Cabraser, Heimann & Bernstein, LLP **Title:** Attorney **Type of organization:** Law firm **Major product:** Legal services **Area of distribution:** International **Area of Practice:** Class action, mass tort, litigation for plaintiffs **Published works:** 4 articles **Affiliations:** A.T.L.A.; A.B.A.; State Bar of California; New York State Bar Association; District of Columbia Bar; Bar Association of San Francisco **Hob./spts.:** Running, mountaineering, tennis, golf **SIC code:** 81 **Address:**

Lieff, Cabraser, Heimann & Bernstein, LLP, 275 Battery St., 30th floor, San Francisco, CA 94111

NESSEN, MAURICE N.
Industry: Law **Born:** January 28, 1927, Boston, Massachusetts **Univ./degree:** B.A., History, 1950; J.D., 1953, Yale University **Title:** Independent Practitioner of the Law **Major product:** Legal services **Area of distribution:** International **Area of Practice:** Court room, civil and criminal litigation, human rights and business law **Affiliations:** A.B.A.; New York State Bar Association; New York City and County Lawyers Associations; Adjunct Lecturer, Harvard Law School; Past Presidents' Committee of the Legal Aid Society of New York; Trustee of Learning Through the Arts; Advisor to the President of the Royal Conservatory of Music (Canada); Emeritus Board Member of the Manhattan School of Music **Hob./spts.:** Skiing, opera, bicycling, writing **SIC code:** 81 **Address:** Maurice N. Nessen, Esq., 499 Park Ave., New York 10022, 215 W. Smuggler St., Aspen, CO 81677 **E-mail:** mnessen@nyc.rr.com

NEWSOME, C. RICHARD
Industry: Law **Univ./degree:** B.A., Political Science and Economics, Florida State University, 1986; J.D., University of Florida, 1989 **Current organization:** Newsome & Didier, P.A. **Title:** Esquire **Type of organization:** Law firm **Major product:** Legal services **Area of distribution:** National **Area of Practice:** Automotive product liability; trial litigation **Honors/awards:** Chancellor of Honor, National Moot Court, 1988 **Affiliations:** Board Member, F.A.T.L.A.; Board Member, A.T.L.A.; Founder, C.F.T.L.A. **SIC code:** 81 **Address:** Newsome & Didier, P.A., 20 N. Orange Ave., Suite 800, Orlando, FL 32801 **E-mail:** newsome@productsliability.net

NEWTON, PATRICK D.
Industry: Law **Born:** Charlotte, North Carolina **Univ./degree:** B.A., Business Management, University of North Carolina at Greensboro, 1997; J.D., Wake Forest University, 2000 **Current organization:** Webb & Graves, PLLC **Title:** J.D. **Type of organization:** Law firm **Major product:** Legal services **Area of distribution:** Aberdeen, North Carolina **Area of Practice:** Tax and estate planning **Affiliations:** A.B.A.; Tax Section, North Carolina Bar Association **SIC code:** 81 **Address:** Webb & Graves, PLLC, 910 N. Sandhills Blvd., Aberdeen, NC 28315 **E-mail:** patrick.newton@webbandgraves.com

NIESEN JR., FRANK JOSEPH
Industry: Law **Born:** April 8, 1953, St. Louis, Missouri **Univ./degree:** B.S., Political Science, Springhill College, 1974; J.D. St. Louis University, 1977 **Current organization:** Frank J. Niesen Jr. **Title:** Attorney **Type of organization:** Law firm **Major product:** Legal services **Area of distribution:** Missouri **Area of Practice:** Trial Attorney; workmen's comp., personal injury, social security **Affiliations:** A.T.L.A.; A.B.A.; Bar Association of Metropolitan St. Louis; Missouri Bar **Hob./spts.:** Family, golf, hunting **SIC code:** 81 **Address:** Frank J. Niesen Jr., Attorney at Law, 319 N. Fourth St., #200, St. Louis, MO 63102 **E-mail:** niesen@worldnet.att.net

NORWOOD, DEBRA L.
Industry: Law **Univ./degree:** B.S., John Jay College **Current organization:** Huston & Schuller, P.C. **Title:** Paralegal **Type of organization:** Law firm **Major product:** Legal services **Area of distribution:** New York **Area of Practice:** Personal injury, medical malpractice, product liability **Affiliations:** Association of Trial Lawyers of America-Paralegal Affiliate (ATLA) **SIC code:** 81 **Address:** 1818 Newkirk Ave., #5J, Brooklyn, NY 11226 **E-mail:** debra.norwood@att.net

NOVAK, EDWARD F.
Industry: Law **Born:** September 25, 1947, Berwyn, Illinois **Univ./degree:** B.A., Political Science, Knox College, 1969; J.D., DePaul University School of Law, 1976 **Current organization:** Quarles & Brady Streich Lang **Title:** Attorney **Type of organization:** Law firm **Major product:** Legal services **Area of distribution:** Arizona **Published works:** 12 articles **Affiliations:** A.B.A.; Board of Governor's; State Bar of Arizona **Hob./spts.:** Family, weightlifting, hiking **SIC code:** 81 **Address:** Quarles & Brady Streich Lang, Renaissance One, 2 N. Central Ave., Phoenix, AZ 85004 **E-mail:** enovak@quarles.com **Web address:** www.quarles.com

NUSBAUM, JOSEPH N.
Industry: Law **Born:** April 27, 1971, West Palm Beach, Florida **Univ./degree:** B.A., English & History, University of Miami, 1993; J.D., Nova University School of Law, 1997 **Current organization:** Brotman, Nusbaum & Fox **Title:** Attorney at Law **Type of organization:** Law firm **Major product:** Legal services **Area of distribution:** National **Area of Practice:** Medical malpractice, personal injury **Honors/awards:** Palm Beach County Legal Aid Society Lawyer of the Year, 2002 **Affiliations:** A.T.L.A.; A.B.A.; Florida Bar; Florida Trial Lawyers Association **SIC code:** 81 **Address:** Brotman, Nusbaum & Fox, 7000 W. Palmetto Park Rd., #300, Boca Raton, FL 33433 **E-mail:** jnn@bnflaw.com **Web address:** www.bnflaw.com

O'BRIEN, APRIL A.
Industry: Law **Born:** March 28, 1955, Kenosha, Wisconsin **Univ./degree:** B.S., University of Wisconsin, 1983; J.D., Arizona State University School of Law, 1995 **Current organization:** O'Brien & Nelson Chart' D **Title:** Attorney/President **Type of organization:** Law firm **Major product:** Legal services **Area of distribution:** Nevada **Area of Practice:** Employment law, commercial, personal injury, family law **Affiliations:** A.T.L.A.; Nevada State Bar; Clark County Bar Association **Hob./spts.:** Spending time with her daughter, golf, hiking **SIC code:** 81 **Address:** O'Brien & Nelson Chart' D, 1640 Alta Dr., Suite 12, Las Vegas, NV 89106 **E-mail:** aprilobrien_nelson.com **Web address:** www.obrien_nelson.com

O'BRIEN, MICHELLE NADEAU
Industry: Law **Born:** August 4, 1960, Biddeford, Maine **Univ./degree:** B.S.Ed. Magna Cum Laude, Lesley College, 1982; J.D., Cum Laude, Suffolk University Law School, 1990 **Current organization:** Mackie Shea O'Brien, PC **Title:** Shareholder **Type of organization:** Boutique law firm **Major product:** Legal services **Area of distribution:** Massachusetts **Area of Practice:** Environmental and land use permitting, litigation **Honors/awards:** Lesley University Alumni Achievement Award, 2004 **Affiliations:** Co-Chair, Environmental Section, Boston Bar Association; Past President, Lesley University Alumni Association; Lesley University Corporator; Member, Society for Women Environmental Professionals, Massachusetts Chapter; Associate Member, Licensed Site Professional Association **Hob./spts.:** Golf **SIC code:** 81 **Address:** Mackie Shea O'Brien, PC, 137 Newbury St., 6th floor, Boston, MA 02116 **E-mail:** mno@lawmso.com

O'CONNOR JR., EDWARD V.
Industry: Law **Born:** November 9, 1952, Yokosuka, Japan **Univ./degree:** J.D., New York Law School, 1981 **Current organization:** Edward V. O'Connor, Jr., P.C. **Title:** President **Type of organization:** Law firm **Major product:** Legal services **Area of distribution:** Virginia **Area of Practice:** Family law **Honors/awards:** James Keith Public Service Award, Legal Services; Northern Virginia Attorney of the Year, Fairfax County **Affiliations:** Fairfax Bar Association; Virginia State Bar; District of Columbia Bar **Hob./spts.:** Baseball, basketball, swimming **SIC code:** 81 **Address:** Edward V. O'Connor, Jr., P.C., 10650 Main St., Suite 201, Fairfax, VA 22030 **E-mail:** evojr@cox.net

OLIVER, GEORGE J.
Industry: Law **Born:** April 9, 1943, South Carolina **Univ./degree:** J.D., University of Tennessee, 1973 **Current organization:** Smith Moore LLP **Title:** Attorney **Type of organization:** Law firm **Major product:** Legal services **Area of distribution:** North Carolina **Area of Practice:** Labor and employment law **Affiliations:** N.C.B.A.; D.C.B.A.; W.V.C.A.; T.U.W. **Hob./spts.:** Golf, tennis, outdoor activities **SIC code:** 81 **Address:** Smith Moore LLP, 2800 Two Hannover Square, Raleigh, NC 27601 **E-mail:** jerry.oliver@smithmoorelaw.com **Web address:** www.smithmoorelaw.com

OLIVER, JODY H.
Industry: Law **Born:** August 30, 1957, West Palm Beach, Florida **Univ./degree:** J.D., University of Florida School of Law, 1981 **Current organization:** Gary, Dytrych & Ryan, P.A. **Title:** Esquire/Partner **Type of organization:** Law firm **Major product:** Legal services **Area of distribution:** Florida **Area of Practice:** Estate planning and estate administration **Affiliations:** Palm Beach County Bar Association; American Association of Trial Lawyers; National Association of Women Lawyers **Hob./spts.:** Water sports **SIC code:** 81 **Address:** Gary, Dytrych & Ryan, P.A., 701 U.S. Hwy. One, Suite 402, North Palm Beach, FL 33408 **E-mail:** jholiver@gdr-law.com

OXLEY, PERRY W.
Industry: Law **Born:** September 9, 1970, South Charleston, West Virginia **Univ./degree:** J.D., West Virginia University, 1996 **Current organization:** Offutt, Fisher & Nord **Title:** Attorney **Type of organization:** Private practice **Major product:** Legal services **Area of distribution:** National **Area of Practice:** Medical malpractice **Affiliations:** Ohio State Bar Association; Kentucky Bar Association; West Virginia State Bar; Oklahoma Bar Association **Hob./spts.:** Tennis **SIC code:** 81 **Address:** 6119 Fairview Dr., Huntington, WV 25705 **E-mail:** pwoxley@ofnlaw.com

PAJCIC, CURTIS S.
Industry: Law **Born:** June 3, 1968, Tallahassee, Florida **Univ./degree:** J.D. with Honors, Florida State University, 1995 **Current organization:** Pajcic & Pajcic, P.A. **Title:** Attorney at Law **Type of organization:** Law practice **Major product:** Legal services **Area of distribution:** National **Area of Practice:** Plaintiffs civil litigation **Affiliations:** American Bar Association; The Florida Bar; Association of Florida Trial Lawyers **SIC code:** 81 **Address:** Pajcic & Pajcic, P.A., 1 Independent Dr., Suite 1900, Jacksonville, FL 32202-5023

PALMER II, WILLIAM BERRY
Industry: Law **Born:** January 15, 1954, Phoenix, Arizona **Univ./degree:** J.D., San Diego School of Law **Current organization:** Palmer & Associates, P.C. **Title:** Attorney **Type of organization:** Law firm **Major product:** Legal services **Area of distribution:** Nevada **Area of Practice:** Personal injury litigation, criminal law, workers' compensation **Affiliations:** A.T.L.A., N.V.T.L.A. **SIC code:** 81 **Address:** Palmer & Associates,

P.C., 2496 W. Charleston Blvd., Las Vegas, NV 89102 **E-mail:** wpalmer@wbpalmer.com

PALUZZI, VINCENT J.
Industry: Law **Born:** January 25, 1956 Newark, New Jersey **Univ./degree:** B.A., with Honors, The Johns Hopkins University, 1978; J.D., with Honors, Seton Hall University School of Law, 1981 **Current organization:** Sterns & Weinroth, P.C. **Title:** VP and Secretary, Shareholder **Type of organization:** Law firm **Major product:** Legal services **Area of distribution:** National **Area of Practice:** Intellectual property, corporate and construction law **Honors/awards:** Member, Seton Hall Law Review, 1979-80; Associate Editor, 1980-81 **Affiliations:** A.B.A., PTC Committees 204, 205, IPL Committee 306; New Jersey State Bar Association; Mercer County Bar Association **Hob./spts.:** Tennis, baseball, horses **SIC code:** 81 **Address:** Sterns & Weinroth, P.C., 50 W. State St., Suite 1400, Trenton, NJ 08607-1298 **E-mail:** vpaluzzi@sternslaw.com

PAPERA JR., JOHN L.
Industry: Law **Born:** August 2, 1969, Boonton, New Jersey **Univ./degree:** B.A., Administrative Justice, Rutgers University, 1992; J.D., Nova Southeastern University, 1996 **Current organization:** John L. Papera Jr., P.A. **Title:** President/Attorney **Type of organization:** Law firm/title company **Major product:** Legal services **Area of distribution:** Florida, New Jersey **Area of Practice:** Corporate law, real estate, title **Affiliations:** A.B.A.; New Jersey Bar Association; The Florida Bar **Hob./spts.:** Family, charities **SIC code:** 81 **Address:** John L. Papera Jr., P.A., 8000 N. Federal Hwy., Suite 105, Boca Raton, FL 33487 **E-mail:** jlpapera@bellsouth.net

PAPPAS, CHRISTOPHER J.
Industry: Law **Univ./degree:** J.D., Quinnipiac University School of Law **Current organization:** Carbutti & Pappas, LLC **Title:** Attorney **Type of organization:** Law firm **Major product:** Legal services **Area of distribution:** Connecticut **Area of Practice:** Real estate and civil litigation **Hob./spts.:** Golf **SIC code:** 81 **Address:** Carbutti & Pappas, LLC, 147 Prince St., Wallingford, CT 06492 **E-mail:** cpappas@lawcp.com **Web address:** www.lawcp.com

PARKER, HAROLD HOLT
Industry: Law **Born:** August 6, 1933, Tucumcari, New Mexico **Univ./degree:** B.A., Abilene Christian University; M.A., Harding University; J.D., University of New Mexico, 1967 **Current organization:** Law Offices of Harold Holt Parker **Title:** Attorney **Type of organization:** Law firm **Major product:** Legal services **Area of distribution:** Tennessee **Area of Practice:** Elder and family law **Honors/awards:** Who's Who in Ontario **Affiliations:** A.B.A.; National Academy of Elder law Attorneys; State Bar of New Mexico; Tennessee Bar Association; Association of Trial Lawyers of America; Rutherford/Cannon County Bar; permitted to practice in New York and New Mexico **Hob./spts.:** Books, travel **SIC code:** 81 **Address:** Law Offices of Harold Holt Parker, 301 N. Walnut St., Suite 3, Murfreesboro, TN 37130 **Phone:** (615)417-2177 **Fax:** (615)895-0795 **E-mail:** hparker8996@comcast.net **Web address:** www.lawyers.com/haroldholtparker/

PARKER, WILLIAM MAXWELL "MAX"
Industry: Law **Born:** November 17, 1951, Comanche, Texas **Univ./degree:** J.D., University of Texas at Austin, 1976 **Current organization:** Webb Stokes and Sparks, L.L.P., Law Office **Title:** Attorney at Law **Type of organization:** Law firm **Major product:** Legal services **Area of distribution:** Texas **Area of Practice:** Personal injury law **Published works:** Articles from CLE seminars **Affiliations:** A.B.O.T.A.; N.B.T.A.; T.B.L.S.; T.T.L.A.; A.T.L.A.; A.B.A.; Board Certified, National Board of Trial Advocates in Civil Trial Advocacy; Board Certified, Texas Board of Legal Specification **Hob./spts.:** Tennis, snow skiing, scuba diving, cycling, coaching youth baseball and basketball **SIC code:** 81 **Address:** Webb Stokes and Sparks, L.L.P., Law Office, 314 W. Harris Ave., San Angelo, TX 76902 **E-mail:** mparker@webbstokessparks.com **Web address:** www.webbstokessparks.com

PASSONNEAU, POLLY N.
Industry: Law. **Born:** November 4, 1956, St. Louis, Missouri **Univ./degree:** B.A., Washington University, 1978; J.D., University of North Carolina at Chapel Hill **Current organization:** Polly N. Passonneau, P.C. **Title:** Attorney **Type of organization:** Law firm **Major product:** Legal services **Area of distribution:** New York **Area of Practice:** Criminal defense and matrimonial **Affiliations:** New York State Bar Association; National Association of Criminal Defense Lawyers **Hob./spts.:** Writing fiction, art, literature, scuba diving **SIC code:** 81 **Address:** Polly N. Passonneau, P.C., 20 Vesey St., Suite 400, New York, NY 10007 **E-mail:** PNPassonneau@att.net

PASULKA, DAVID P.
Industry: Law **Univ./degree:** J.D., University of San Diego, 1984 **Current organization:** Pasulka & White, LLC **Title:** Attorney **Type of organization:** Law firm **Major product:** Legal services **Area of distribution:** Chicago, Illinois **Area of Practice:** Family law **Affiliations:** Illinois State Bar Association, Family Law Section Council; American Academy of Matrimonial Lawyers **Hob./spts.:** Family, **SIC code:** 81 **Address:** Pasulka & White, LLC, 70 W. Madison St., Suite 650, Chicago, IL 60602 **E-mail:** pasulka@pasulkalaw.com

PATRICK, GEORGE C.
Industry: Law **Born:** January 17, 1967, Lafayette, Indiana **Univ./degree:** B.S., Northwestern University, 1989; J.D., Valparaiso University School of Law, 1992 **Current organization:** Patrick & Associates **Title:** Attorney **Type of organization:** Law firm **Major product:** Legal services **Area of distribution:** Crown Point, Indiana **Area of Practice:** Workers' compensation, employee representation **Published works:** 4 articles **Affiliations:** Workplace Injury Litigation; Indiana State Bar Association **Hob./spts.:** Family, horseback riding **SIC code:** 81 **Address:** Patrick & Associates, 190 S. West, Crown Point, IN 46307 **E-mail:** george@georgepatrick.com **Web address:** www.georgepatrick.com

PAYNE, L. HOWARD
Industry: Law **Born:** December 4, 1933, New York, New York **Univ./degree:** LL.B., Cornell Law School, 1959 **Current organization:** Kirk Pinkerton **Title:** Attorney at Law **Type of organization:** Law firm **Major product:** Legal services **Area of distribution:** Sarasota, Florida **Area of Practice:** Estate planning and administration **Affiliations:** F.B.A.; F.A.C.T.E.C.; New York Bar Association **Hob./spts.:** Sailing, snow skiing, woodworking, reading **SIC code:** 81 **Address:** Kirk Pinkerton, 720 S. Orange Ave., Sarasota, FL 34236 **E-mail:** howardpayne@kirkpinkerton.com

PEÑA JR., HORACIO
Industry: Law **Born:** March 8, 1957, Mission, Texas **Univ./degree:** J.D., St. Mary's University **Current organization:** Law Office of Horacio Peña, Jr. **Title:** Attorney at Law **Type of organization:** Law firm **Major product:** Legal services **Area of distribution:** Texas **Area of Practice:** Federal and state criminal, family law, estate law and personal injury **Affiliations:** State Bar of Texas; Texas Defense Lawyers Association; Hidalgo County Bar Association **Hob./spts.:** Fishing, baseball, coaching, working with children **SIC code:** 81 **Address:** Law Office of Horacio Peña, Jr., 900 N. Bryan Rd., Suite 202, Mission, TX 78572 **E-mail:** hpenajr@sbcglobal.net

PEPPER, JERRY F.
Industry: Law **Title:** Attorney at Law **Type of organization:** Law firm **Major product:** Legal services **Area of Practice:** Complex commercial litigation **SIC code:** 81 **Address:** Jerry F. Pepper, APLC, 3909 Plaza Tower Dr., Baton Rouge, LA 70816-4356 **E-mail:** jfpepper@i-55.com

PERESICH, RONALD G.
Industry: Law **Born:** May 18, 1943 **Univ./degree:** J.D., University of Mississippi, 1968 **Current organization:** Page, Mannino, Peresich & McDermott, PLLC **Title:** Member/Lawyer **Type of organization:** Law firm **Major product:** Litigation **Area of distribution:** National **Area of Practice:** Defense of personal injury and commercial claims **Affiliations:** Fellow, American College of Trial Lawyers; International Association of Defense Counsel; Massachusetts Bar Association; American Bar Association; National Defense Research Institute; Mississippi Bar Foundation **SIC code:** 81 **Address:** Page, Mannino, Peresich & McDermott, PLLC, 759 Vieux Marché Mall, Biloxi, MS 39530 **E-mail:** rgp@pmp.org **Web address:** www.pmp.org

PERKINS, DARLENE J.
Industry: Law **Current organization:** The Minton Firm **Title:** Administrator **Type of organization:** Law firm **Major product:** Legal services **Area of distribution:** Chicago, Illinois **Area of Practice:** Family law **Hob./spts.:** Beading, graphing **SIC code:** 81 **Address:** The Minton Firm, 222 N. LaSalle St., Suite 1950, Chicago, IL 60458 **E-mail:** darlene@mintonoffices.com

PERLSTEIN, LISA B.
Industry: Law **Born:** May 15, 1975, Rochester, New York **Univ./degree:** B.A., Magna Cum Laude, Political Science, Washington University, 1997; J.D., Emory University, 2000 **Current organization:** Trey-Inman & Associates **Title:** Esquire **Type of organization:** Law firm **Major product:** Legal services **Area of distribution:** Atlanta, Georgia **Area of Practice:** Environmental and real property litigation **Honors/awards:** Georgia Super Lawyers Rising Star; Pi Sigma Alpha National Political Science Honor Society, 1996 **Affiliations:** State Bar of Georgia, Environmental Section; The Doghouse Rescue and Adoption, Inc. **Hob./spts.:** Dog rescue, hiking, swimming **SIC code:** 81 **Address:** 163 Vidal Blvd., Decatur, GA 30030

PETERS, KEVIN T.
Industry: Law **Univ./degree:** J.D., Suffolk University of Law, 1987 **Current organization:** Todd & Weld, LLP **Title:** Attorney **Type of organization:** Law firm **Major product:** Legal services **Area of distribution:** National **Area of Practice:** Personal injury, business law and complex litigation **Affiliations:** A.B.A.; B.B.A.; M.B.A.; A.T.L.A. **SIC code:** 81 **Address:** Todd & Weld, LLP, 28 State St., Boston, MA 02109 **E-mail:** kpeters@toddweld.com

PETERSON, HOLLY C.
Industry: Law **Born:** September 7, 1970, Galveston, Texas **Univ./degree:** J.D., Seton Hall University, 2003 **Current organization:** Levy Phillips & Konigsberg **Title:** Esquire **Type of organization:** Law firm **Major product:** Legal services **Area of distribution:** New Jersey **Area of Practice:** Litigation **Affiliations:** A.B.A.; A.T.L.A.; N.A.W.L.; N.Y.S.B.A; N.Y.S.T.L.A.; A.B.C.N.Y.; N.J.S.B.A.; N.Y.C.L.A. **Hob./spts.:** Travel **SIC code:** 81 **Address:** Holly C. Peterson Esq., 1 Court Plaza South, 21 Main St., Hackensack, NJ 07601 **E-mail:** hollypeterson@earthlink.net

PHILIPS, BEN B.
Industry: Law **Univ./degree:** J.D., Mercer Law School, 1974 **Current organization:** Philips Branch **Title:** President/Attorney **Type of organization:** Law firm **Major product:** Legal services **Area of distribution:** Georgia **Area of Practice:** Medical malpractice, personal injury **Affiliations:** G.T.L.A.; A.T.L.A.; C.L.C. **SIC code:** 81 **Address:** Philips Branch, P.O.B. 2808, Columbus, GA 31902

PHILLIPS, GERALD F.
Industry: Law **Born:** May 3, 1925, New York, New York **Univ./degree:** A.B., 1947; Dartmouth College; M.B.A., Amos Tuck School of Business Management, 1947; J.D., Cornell Law School, 1950 **Current organization:** Gerald Phillips **Title:** Arbitrator, Mediator (of Counsel to Phillips, Lerner & Lauzon, L.L.P.) **Type of organization:** Law firm **Major product:** Legal services **Area of distribution:** International **Area of Practice:** Ethics, entertainment law, ADR **Honors/awards:** Listed among the 50 Top Neutrals in California, Dec. 1, 2003 by the Los Angeles Daily Journal; Recipient of Griffin Bell Volunteer Service Award by Dispute Resolution Service Inc., May 6, 2004 **Published works:** Numerous publications and speaking engagements including, "Resolving Entertainment Disputes Through Mediation and Arbitration", UCLA Extension Seminar, 5/17/03; "Is Creeping Legalism Infecting Arbitration?", Dispute Resolution Journal, Feb.-Apr. 2003; "A Client's Bill of Rights", California Lawyer, Feb. 2003; "The Client Has the Right to Be Advised by Counsel about ADR", DRS Newsletter, Winter 2002; "Moving Forward", Daily Journal, 11/18/02; "Building a Better Client-Attorney Relationship Through the Retainer Agreement", The Century City Lawyer, Aug. 2002 **Affiliations:** Co-Founder, College of Commercial Arbitrators; Board Member, C.D.R.C.; Chair, Entertainment Dispute Section of A.B.A.; President, Dispute Resolution Service (DRS) **Hob./spts.:** Tennis, music **SIC code:** 81 **Address:** 2029 Century Park East, Suite 1200, Los Angeles, CA 90067 **E-mail:** gphillips@pll-law.com

PITCHFORD, MALCOLM J.
Industry: Law **Born:** August 17, 1945, Wallasey, England **Univ./degree:** J.D., University of Florida, 1974 **Current organization:** Abel, Band, Russell, Collier, Pitchford & Gordon, Chartered **Title:** Vice President, Esquire **Type of organization:** Law firm **Major product:** Legal services **Area of distribution:** Florida **Area of Practice:** Banking, Finance and Real Property Law **Honors/awards:** "AV" rated, Martindale-Hubbell **Affiliations:** F.B.; A.B.A.; I.B.A.; Fellow, American College of Mortgage Attorneys; United States District Court, Middle District of Florida **Hob./spts.:** Golf, tennis, writing **SIC code:** 81 **Address:** Abel, Band, Russell, Collier, Pitchford & Gordon, Chartered, 240 S. Pineapple Ave., 8th Floor, Sarasota, FL 34230 **E-mail:** mpitchford@abelband.com **Web address:** www.abelband.com

PITZNER, RICHARD W.
Industry: Law **Born:** September 19, 1946, Fond Du Lac, Wisconsin **Univ./degree:** B.B.A., 1968; M.B.A., 1969; J.D., 1972, University of Wisconsin; C.P.A. Certified, 1976 **Current organization:** Murphy & Desmond, S.C. **Title:** Partner **Type of organization:** Law firm **Major product:** Legal services **Area of distribution:** Madison, Wisconsin **Area of Practice:** Business, tax, mergers and acquisitions, estate planning **Honors/awards:** Gold Medal Honor, CPA, 1969; Order of the COIF Top 10% **Affiliations:** A.B.A.; A.I.C.P.A.; State Bar Association of Wisconsin **Hob./spts.:** Golf, all spectator sports **SIC code:** 81 **Address:** Murphy & Desmond, S.C., 2 E. Mifflin St., Madison, WI 53703 **E-mail:** rpitzner@murphydesmond.com

PODVEY, ROBERT L.
Industry: Law **Born:** November 23, 1940, Philadelphia, Pennsylvania **Univ./degree:** J.D., New York University, 1964 **Current organization:** Podvey, Sachs, Meanor, Catenacci, Hildner & Cocoziello **Title:** Attorney **Type of organization:** Law firm **Major product:** Legal services **Area of distribution:** New Jersey **Area of Practice:** Business litigation, transactions, law firm operations **Affiliations:** A.B.A. **Hob./spts.:** Golf **SIC code:** 81 **Address:** Podvey, Sachs, Meanor, Catenacci, Hildner and Cocoziello, One Riverfront Plaza, 8th floor, Newark, NJ 07102 **E-mail:** rpodvey@podveysachs.com

POLLARD V, HENRY R.
Industry: Law **Born:** December 20, 1965, Richmond, Virginia **Univ./degree:** J.D., University of Richmond, 1992 **Current organization:** Christian & Barton, LLP **Title:** Partner/Attorney **Type of organization:** Law firm **Major product:** Legal services **Area of distribution:** Richmond, Virginia **Area of Practice:** Environmental law, water supply law **Affiliations:** Virginia State Bar; Bar Association of the City of Richmond **Hob./spts.:** Sports, reading **SIC code:** 81 **Address:** Christian & Barton, LLP, 909 E. Main St., Suite 1200, Richmond, VA 23219 **E-mail:** hpollard@cblaw.com **Web address:** www.cblaw.com

PORTEUS, JUDITH HODGE
Industry: Law **Born:** September 20, 1939, Providence, Rhode Island **Univ./degree:** A.B., Brown University, 1961; J.D., Boston University School of Law, 1964 **Current organization:** Judith Hodge Porteus, Esq. **Title:** Attorney **Type of organization:** Law office **Major product:** Legal representation **Area of distribution:** Providence, Rhode Island **Area of Practice:** Real estate, probate, Block Island titles **Honors/awards:** First Woman Land Clerk, Supreme Court, State of Rhode Island; Finalist, Boston City Council Race **Published works:** Re-wrote Boston Zoning Code for Back Bay and Beacon Hill **Affiliations:** A.B.A.; Rhode Island Bar Association, Chairman of Zoning Committee, Back Bay Neighborhood Association; Deputy Field Director, Eliot Richardson Senate; Gallery Instructor, Museum of Fine Arts **Hob./spts.:** Politics **SIC code:** 81 **Address:** Judith Hodge Porteus, Esq., 56 Pine St., Providence, RI 02903

POWERS, BILL
Industry: Law **Born:** September 13, 1965, Illinois **Univ./degree:** J.D., Campbell University Law School, 1992 **Current organization:** Bush & Powers **Title:** Esquire **Type of organization:** Law firm **Major product:** Legal services **Area of distribution:** Charlotte, North Carolina **Area of Practice:** DWI, traffic and criminal **Published works:** 3 DWI publications **Affiliations:** American Trial Lawyers Association **Hob./spts.:** flying **SIC code:** 81 **Address:** Bush & Powers, 821 East Blvd., Charlotte, NC 28203 **E-mail:** bowties@mindspring.com

PURDIE, ALAN M.
Industry: Law **Born:** August 6, 1954, Grenada, Mississippi **Univ./degree:** J.D., University of Mississippi **Current organization:** Gore, Kilpatrick, Purdie, Metz & Adcock **Title:** Attorney **Type of organization:** Law firm **Major product:** Legal services **Area of distribution:** Mississippi **Area of Practice:** Civil litigation **Affiliations:** A.B.A. **Hob./spts.:** Music **SIC code:** 81 **Address:** Gore, Kilpatrick, Purdie, Metz & Adcock, 402 Legacy Park, Ridgeland, MS 39157 **E-mail:** apurdie@hgglaw.com

QUINN, DEREK
Industry: Law **Born:** January 6, 1967, Mobile, Alabama **Univ./degree:** J.D., Michigan State University, 1995 **Current organization:** Derek Quinn, Attorney at Law **Title:** Attorney **Type of organization:** Law firm **Major product:** Legal services **Area of distribution:** Alabama **Area of Practice:** Criminal defense, corporate and property law **Affiliations:** A.T.L.A.; N.A.C.D.L.; A.C.L.U. **Hob./spts.:** Running, hiking, motorcycling, horseback riding **SIC code:** 81 **Address:** Derek Quinn, Attorney at Law, 1755 Eastridge Dr., Birmingham, AL 35235 **E-mail:** dereksjustice@yahoo.com

RAKESTRAW, GREGORY A.
Industry: Law **Born:** January 20, 1949, Findlay, Ohio **Univ./degree:** J.D., Ohio Northern University School of Law, 1974 **Current organization:** Rakestraw & Rakestraw **Title:** Attorney **Type of organization:** Law firm **Major product:** Legal services **Area of distribution:** Ohio **Area of Practice:** Litigation **Published works:** Contributed to book **Affiliations:** A.B.A.; O.B.A. **Hob./spts.:** Boating, remodeling of historical homes **SIC code:** 81 **Address:** Rakestraw & Rakestraw, 119 E. Crawford St., Findlay, OH 45840

RAND, ANGELA K.
Industry: Law **Born:** Silver Spring, Maryland **Univ./degree:** J.D., Rutgers University, 2002 **Current organization:** Rand & Associates, LLC **Title:** Attorney **Type of organization:** Law firm **Major product:** Legal services **Area of distribution:** Maryland **Area of Practice:** Real estate law, property management **Affiliations:** M.S.B.A.; F.C.B.A.; D.C.B.A.; A.B.A.; A.T.L.A. **Hob./spts.:** Cycling, fishing **SIC code:** 81 **Address:** Rand & Associates, LLC, 200A Monroe St., #104, Rockville, MD 20850 **E-mail:** angela.rand@randassociates.com

READ II, JOHN H.
Industry: Law **Born:** August 30, 1948, Galveston, Texas **Univ./degree:** J.D., Southern Methodist University, 1979 **Current organization:** Read & Associates, Attorneys & Counselors **Title:** Attorney at Law **Type of organization:** Law firm **Major product:** Legal services **Area of distribution:** Texas **Area of Practice:** Criminal defense, personal injury **Affiliations:** N.A.C.D.L.; A.T.L.A. **Hob./spts.:** Martial arts **SIC code:** 81 **Address:** Read & Associates, Attorneys & Counselors, 900 N. Zang Blvd., Dallas, TX 75208 **E-mail:** attyread@flash.net

REEVES, FREDERICK T.
Industry: Law **Born:** October 10, 1959, Tallahassee, Florida **Univ./degree:** University of Florida **Current organization:** Frederick T. Reeves, P.A. **Title:** P.A. **Type of organization:** Law firm **Major product:** Legal services **Area of distribution:** Florida **Area of Practice:** Commercial and industrial litigation **Affiliations:** F.B.A.; W.P.B.A. **Hob./spts.:** Bird hunting, tennis **SIC code:** 81 **Address:** Frederick T. Reeves, P.A., 5709 Tidalwave Dr., New Port Richie, FL 34652 **E-mail:** freeves@tbaylaw.com

REEVES, MICHAEL S.
Industry: Law **Born:** January 23, 1956, Salt Lake City, Utah **Univ./degree:** B.S.; J.D., University of Utah **Current organization:** Reeves & Associates **Title:** Attorney **Type of organization:** Law firm **Major product:** Legal services **Area of distribution:** Arizona **Area of Practice:** Business consulting, white collar crimes **Hob./spts.:** Mountain biking, golf **SIC code:** 81 **Address:** Reeves & Associates, 1212 E. Osborn Rd., Phoenix, AZ 85014-5533 **E-mail:** michael.reeves@azbar.org

REID, JAMES E.
Industry: Law **Born:** August 8, 1951, Baltimore, Maryland **Univ./degree:** J.D., Syracuse University **Current organization:** Advocates Forum Inc. **Title:** President **Type of organization:** Law firm/independent arbitrator **Major product:** Legal services including case resolution/settlement **Area of distribution:** New York **Area of Practice:** Arbitration/mediation/trial law/litigation **Hob./spts.:** Family activities **SIC code:** 81 **Address:** Advocates Forum Inc., 173 Intrepid Lane, Syracuse, NY 13205

REILLY, DANIEL M.
Industry: Law **Born:** March 21, 1953, Groton, Connecticut **Univ./degree:** J.D., University of Denver College of Law, 1981 **Current organization:** Hoffman Reilly Pozner & Williamson LLP **Title:** Attorney **Type of organization:** Law firm **Major product:** Legal services **Area of distribution:** Colorado **Area of Practice:** Civil litigation **Affiliations:** A.B.A; A.T.L.A.; Colorado Bar Association; American Inns of Court **Hob./spts.:** Running, basketball, football, surfing **SIC code:** 81 **Address:** Hoffman Reilly Pozner & Williamson LLP, 511 16th St., Suite 700, Denver, CO 80202 **E-mail:** dreilly@hrpwlaw.com

REITER, ARNOLD E.
Industry: Law **Born:** June 26, 1947, Newark, New Jersey **Univ./degree:** J.D., Rutgers University, 1983 **Current organization:** Reiter & Zipern, Attorneys **Title:** Managing Partner **Type of organization:** Law firm **Major product:** Legal services **Area of distribution:** National **Area of Practice:** Estates and wills, trusts, taxation, banking **Affiliations:** A.B.A.; New Jersey State Bar Association; New York State Bar Association; District of Columbia Bar Association; Founder, The Bank of Saddle River **Hob./spts.:** Wine collecting, marathon running, community service **SIC code:** 81 **Address:** Reiter & Zipern, Attorneys, 75 Montebello Rd., Suffern, NY 10901 **E-mail:** areiter747@aol.com

RENTSCHLER, JUDITH J.
Industry: Law **Born:** March 2, 1951, South Bend, Indiana **Univ./degree:** B.A., Chinese History, Michigan State University, 1974; J.D., Hastings College of Law, California, 1977 **Current organization:** Rentschler, Tursi, Guastamachio, LLP **Title:** Attorney **Type of organization:** Law firm **Major product:** Legal services **Area of distribution:** National **Area of Practice:** Commercial real estate, finance **Published works:** Articles on Personal Injury **Affiliations:** California Bar Association; S.F.B.A.; S.M.B.A. **Hob./spts.:** Glass fusing, sailing; 2nd degree Black Belt, Tae Kwon Do **SIC code:** 81 **Address:** Rentschler, Tursi Guastamachio, LLP, 989 E. Hillsdale Blvd., Suite 160, Foster City, CA 94404 **E-mail:** jjrentschler@landlaws.com

RETAMAR, RICHARD E.
Industry: Law **Born:** March 28, 1964 **Univ./degree:** J.D., St. Thomas University **Current organization:** Retamar Law Firm **Title:** Senior Partner/President **Type of organization:** Law firm **Major product:** Legal services **Area of distribution:** Florida **Area of Practice:** Personal injury/medical malpractice **Honors/awards:** "AV" rated, Martindale-Hubbell **Published works:** Local journal articles **Affiliations:** The Florida Bar; Hispanic Bar Association; Palm Beach Trial Lawyers Association **Hob./spts.:** Fishing, tennis, basketball **SIC code:** 81 **Address:** Retamar Law Firm, 2424 N. Federal Hwy. #460, Boca Raton, FL 33431 **E-mail:** retamar@retamarlaw.com **Web address:** www.retamarlaw.com

RICH, NANCY J.
Industry: Law **Born:** June 11, 1959, Chicago, Illinois **Univ./degree:** J.D., Whaler University, 1984 **Current organization:** Katten Muchin Rosenman, LLP **Title:** Environmental Partner **Type of organization:** Law firm **Major product:** Legal services **Area of distribution:** National **Area of Practice:** Environmental law and litigation **Affiliations:** A.B.A.; Chicago Bar Association; **Hob./spts.:** History research, biking **SIC code:** 81 **Address:** Katten Muchin Rosenman, LLP, 525 W. Monroe St., Suite 1900, Chicago, IL 60661 **E-mail:** nancy.rich@kattenlaw.com

RICHARDS, SUZANNE K.
Industry: Law **Born:** May 19, 1947, Akron, Ohio **Univ./degree:** B.S., History, Humanistic Studies, St. Mary's College at Notre Dame, 1969; J.D., Ohio State University College of Law, 1974 **Current organization:** Vorys, Sater, Seymour and Pease LLP **Title:** Attorney **Type of organization:** Law firm **Major product:** Legal services **Area of distribution:** Ohio **Area of Practice:** Litigation **Published works:** 1 article, seminars **Affiliations:** A.B.A; Columbus Bar Association; Ohio State Bar Association; Federal Bar Association **SIC code:** 81 **Address:** Vorys, Sater, Seymour and Pease LLP, 52 E. Gay St., Columbus, OH 43215 **E-mail:** skrichards@vssp.com **Web address:** www.vssp.com

ROACH II, JAMES
Industry: Law **Born:** September 18, 1959, Muskegon, Michigan **Univ./degree:** B.B.A., University of Kentucky, 1972; J.D., Tulane University, 1975; LL.M., Tax, Georgetown University **Current organization:** James Roach II, Professional Corp. **Title:** Esquire **Type of organization:** Law firm **Major product:** Legal services **Area of distribution:** National **Area of Practice:** Mergers, acquisitions, taxation **Affiliations:** K.B.A.; S.B.A.; S.B.M. **Hob./spts.:** Family, golf, community service **SIC code:** 81 **Address:** James Roach II, P.C., 8700 E. Vista Bonita Dr., Suite 236, Scottsdale, AZ 85255 **E-mail:** james.roach@azbar.org

ROBERTS, CHARLES BREN
Industry: Law **Born:** October 28, 1949, Washington D.C. **Univ./degree:** Certificate of Law Studies, Harvard University, 1983 **Current organization:** Charles B. Roberts & Associates, P.C. **Title:** Esquire **Type of organization:** Law firm **Major product:** Legal services **Area of distribution:** National **Area of Practice:** Personal injury **Affiliations:** A.B.A.; Virginia Trial Lawyers Association; Federal Bar Association; Association of Trial Lawyers of America **Hob./spts.:** Basketball, politics **SIC code:** 81 **Address:** Charles B. Roberts & Associates, P.C., 1308 Devils Reach Rd., Suite 303, Woodbridge, VA 22192 **E-mail:** info@charlesrobertslaw.com **Web address:** www.charlesrobertslaw.com

ROBERTS, JEFFERY A.
Industry: Law **Born:** October 7, 1965, Mayfield, Kentucky **Univ./degree:** B.S., Criminal Justice, Murray State University, 1985; J.D., Southern Illinois University School of Law, 1992 **Current organization:** Roberts Law Office **Title:** Attorney at Law **Type of organization:** Law firm **Major product:** Legal services **Area of distribution:** Kentucky **Area of Practice:** Workers' compensation **Published works:** Editor, The Workman Compensation Review, Kentucky **Affiliations:** Member, Board of Governors, Kentucky Academy of Trial Attorneys; National Organization of Social Security Claimants' Representatives **Hob./spts.:** Church Deacon, community involvement, cooking, physical fitness **SIC code:** 81 **Address:** Roberts Law Office, 509 Main St., Murray, KY 42071 **E-mail:** jeff@jeffrobertslaw.com **Web address:** www.jeffrobertslaw.com

RODRIGUEZ JR., JULIAN
Industry: Law **Born:** February 25, 1964, San Marcos, Texas **Univ./degree:** B.S.; J.D., Wayne State University School of Law **Current organization:** Julian Rodriguez, Jr. & Associates **Title:** Attorney **Type of organization:** Law firm **Major product:** Legal services **Area of distribution:** Texas **Area of Practice:** Family and general practice **Affiliations:** State Bar of Texas: Hidalgo County Bar Association **Hob./spts.:** Travel, reading, biking **SIC code:** 81 **Address:** Julian Rodriguez, Jr. & Associates, 10113 N. Tenth St., Suite C, McAllen, TX 78504 **E-mail:** jrodlaw1@aol.com

RODRIGUEZ-CHOI, JORGE
Industry: Law **Born:** October 19, 1967, Santiago, Chile **Univ./degree:** B.A., Ethic Studies, 1992; J.D., University of California at Berkeley, 1995 **Current organization:** Law Offices of Jorge Rodriguez-Choi **Title:** Attorney/Owner **Type of organization:** Law firm **Major product:** Legal services **Area of distribution:** International **Area of Practice:** Immigration issues, deportation, defense, appeals **Published works:** Several articles, papers **Affiliations:** A.C.L.U.; A.I.L.A. **Hob./spts.:** Spending time with family, reading, biking **SIC code:** 81 **Address:** Law Offices of Jorge Rodriguez-Choi, 369 Broadway St., Suite 102, San Francisco, CA 94133 **E-mail:** jrodriguezchoi@yahoo.com

ROESLER, ROBERT C.
Industry: Law **Born:** February 3, 1944, Pensacola, Florida **Univ./degree:** B.S., History, Williams College, 1966; J.D., University of Colorado, 1969 **Current organization:** Roesler Whittlesey Meekins & Amidon **Title:** President/Attorney **Type of organization:** Law firm **Major product:** Legal services **Area of distribution:** Vermont **Area of Practice:** Business law **Affiliations:** A.B.A.; V.B.A. **Hob./spts.:** Golf, skiing, tennis **SIC code:** 81 **Address:** Roesler Whittlesey Meekins & Amidon, 84 Pine St., Burlington, VT 05402 **E-mail:** broesler@rwmalaw.com **Web address:** www.rwmalaw.com

ROTHELL, BONNIE YVETTE HOCHMAN
Industry: Law **Born:** January 20, 1963, Brooklyn, New York **Univ./degree:** B.A., English; B.A., Sociology, Brandeis University, 1985; J.D., Cum Laude, University of Miami School of Law, 1988 **Current organization:** Krooth & Altman, LLP **Title:** Esquire **Type of organization:** Law firm **Major product:** Legal services **Area of distribution:** National **Area of Practice:** Litigation; employment law; specialized real estate and finance litigation **Affiliations:** A.T.L.A.; N.E.L.A. **SIC code:** 81 **Address:** Krooth & Altman, LLP, 1850 M St. N.W., Suite 400, Washington, DC 20036 **E-mail:** brothell@krooth.com **Web address:** www.krooth.com

RUSSO JR., ANTHONY J.
Industry: Law **Born:** February 3, 1966, Bronxville, New York **Univ./degree:** B.A., Political Science, History, State University of New York, Albany, 1988; J.D., Nova, Southeastern University, School of Law, 1994 **Current organization:** Freedland, Farmer, Russo & Sheller **Title:** Partner **Type of organization:** Law Firm **Major product:** Trial litigation **Area of distribution:** National **Area of Practice:** Serious personal injury, wrong death and motor vehicle accident litigation **Affiliations:** Academy of Florida Trial Lawyers; American Trial Lawyers Association; Broward County Trial Lawyers Association; Florida Lawyers Action Group; Broward County Candidate Recruitment Task Force; Rotary Club of Weston **Hob./spts.:** Travel **SIC code:** 81 **Address:** Freedland, Farmer, Russo & Sheller, 2665 Executive Park Dr., Suite 3, Weston, FL 33331 **E-mail:** anthony@westonlawyers.com

SAEED, SHEILA
Industry: Law **Born:** April 10, 1970, Tehran, Iran **Univ./degree:** B.S., Finance, Pennsylvania State University, 1991; M.I.S., University of Colorado, 1995; J.D., University of Denver, 1999 **Current organization:** Kerr Brosseau Bartlett O'Brien **Title:** Attorney **Type of organization:** Law firm **Major product:** Legal services **Area of distribution:** National **Area of Practice:** Commercial litigation **Affiliations:** A.B.A.; Denver Bar Association; Internet Chamber of Commerce; Colorado Bar Association **Hob./spts.:** Scuba diving **SIC code:** 81 **Address:** 6450 E. Prentice Place, Englewood, CO 80111 **E-mail:** ssaeed@kbbolaw.com

SAKAI, PETER A.
Industry: Law **Born:** Texas **Univ./degree:** J.D., University of Texas at Austin, 1979 **Current organization:** Bexar County Courthouse **Title:** Judge **Type of organization:** Court **Major product:** Legal services **Area of distribution:** Bexar County, Texas **Area of Practice:** Family law **Honors/awards:** Texas State Foster Parents Association Recognition Award; San Antonio Children's Shelter Recognition Award; Dr. Dale Wood Award, Recognition of Outstanding Achievement **Published works:** San Antonio Magazine; San Antonio Medical Society Magazine; San Antonio Business Journal **Affiliations:** A.B.A.; Texas Bar Association; San Antonio Bar Association **Hob./spts.:** Sports **SIC code:** 81 **Address:** Bexar County Courthouse, , San Antonio, TX 78205

SALDAÑA, VAL W.
Industry: Law **Born:** Selma, California **Univ./degree:** J.D., University of California, Davis **Current organization:** Lang Richert & Patch **Title:** Attorney **Type of organization:** Law firm **Major product:** Legal services **Area of distribution:** National **Area of Practice:** Construction and business litigation **Affiliations:** Board of Directors, A.B.T.L.A.; A.G.C.A; A.T.L.A.; California State Bar **Hob./spts.:** Golf, music **SIC code:** 81 **Address:** Lang Richert & Patch, 5200 N. Palm, Suite 401, Fresno, CA 93704 **E-mail:** vws@lrplaw.net

SALINAS, SHIREE D.
Industry: Law **Born:** March 22, 1965, Detroit, Michigan **Univ./degree:** B. A., Political Science, University of Texas at Austin; J.D., Saint Mary's Law School **Current organization:** Salinas and Sahadi, LLP **Title:** Attorney **Type of organization:** Law firm **Major product:** Legal services **Area of distribution:** International **Area of Practice:** Civil law, product liability **Affiliations:** A.T.L.A.; State Bar of Texas **SIC code:** 81 **Address:** Salinas and Sahadi, LLP, 5401 N. Tenth St., Suite 215, McAllen, TX 78504 **E-mail:** sdslaw@rgv.rr.com

SALOOM, JOSEPH M.
Industry: Law **Born:** January 4, 1950, Enterprise, Alabama **Univ./degree:** B.S., Chemistry, Birmingham Southern College, 1972; J.D., Jones University School of Law, 1999 **Current organization:** Rountree & Associates, LLC **Title:** Attorney **Type of organization:** Law firm **Major product:** Legal services **Area of distribution:** Alabama **Area of Practice:** Family/domestic law **Affiliations:** A.L.T.L.A.; A.F.T.E.; A.L.B.A.; Montgomery Rotary Club; North/South Skirmish Association **Hob./spts.:** Private pilot, Civil Air Patrol **SIC code:** 81 **Address:** Rountree & Associates, LLC, 448 St. Lukes Dr., Montgomery, AL 36117 **E-mail:** jsra@knology.net

SALZMAN, GARY S.
Industry: Law **Born:** Port Chester, New York **Univ./degree:** J.D., University of Miami **Current organization:** Gray Robinson, P.A. **Title:** Attorney **Type of organization:** Law firm **Major product:** Legal services **Area of distribution:** Florida **Area of Practice:** Business, commercial and real estate litigation, mediation and arbitration **Honors/awards:** Legal Elite, Florida Trend Magazine, 2005; Best of the Bar, Orlando Business Journal, 2004 **Affiliations:** The Florida Bar; The Colorado Bar; Orange County Bar Association; Business Law Section of Florida Bar; Business Litigation Committee; Director, First Central Florida Inns of Court; American Arbitration Association; National Arbitration Forum; Former Chair and Member, Business Litigation Certification Committee for the Florida Bar **Hob./spts.:** Ice hockey, skiing, Tae Kwon Do **SIC code:** 81 **Address:** Gray Robinson, P.A., 301 E. Pine St., Suite 1400, Orlando, FL 32801 **E-mail:** gsalzman@gray-robinson.com

SARSFIELD, TIMOTHY J.
Industry: Law **Born:** March 18, 1959, Kalamazoo, Michigan **Univ./degree:** J.D., Summa Cum Laude, Southern Illinois University, 1986 **Current organization:** Thompson Coburn LLP **Title:** Attorney/Partner **Type of organization:** Law firm **Major product:** Legal services **Area of distribution:** St. Louis, Missouri **Area of Practice:** Labor and employment law (management) **Published works:** 3 publications **Affiliations:** D.R.I.; M.O.D.L.; Knights of Columbus **Hob./spts.:** Football, weightlifting **SIC code:** 81 **Address:** Thompson Coburn LLP, 1 US Bank, 28th floor, St. Louis, MO 63101 **E-mail:** tsarsfield@thompsoncoburn.com

SAUNDERS, BRIAN
Industry: Law **Born:** December 26, 1955, New York, New York **Univ./degree:** B.S., Political Science and Economics, Brown University, 1977; J.D., University of Pennsylvania Law School, 1980 **Current organization:** The Saunders Law Group **Title:** Principal **Type of organization:** Law firm **Major product:** Legal services **Area of distribution:** California, Oregon, Washington, Alaska **Area of Practice:** Criminal and civil litigation **Published works:** Articles; chapter in "The Toxic Torts Book" **Affiliations:** A.B.A., Environmental Committee; Los Angeles County Bar Association; Corona Royal Families Kids Camp; Founding Member, Simi Valley Vikings Association; A.T.L.A.; California State Bar Association **Hob./spts.:** Golf, woodworking, reading **SIC code:** 81 **Address:** The Saunders Law Group, 2275 Sampson Ave., Suite 115, Corona, CA 92879-3400 **E-mail:** brian_saunderslaw@sbcglobal.net **Web address:** www.saunderslaw.com

SAVAGE, ARTHUR V.
Industry: Law **Born:** December 24, 1926, New York, New York **Univ./degree:** B.A., History, With Honors, Princeton University; J.D., Harvard University, Massachusetts, 1952 **Current organization:** Patton, Eakins, Lipsett, Holbrook & Savage **Title:** Partner **Type of organization:** Law firm **Major product:** Legal services **Area of distribution:** New York **Area of practice:** Environmental law, trust and estate law **Area of Practice:** Environmental law, trust and estate law **Honors/awards:** Founder's Award, Adirondack Museum, 2002; George W. Perkins Award, New York Parks and Conservation Association, 2003 **Published works:** Adirondack Park Agency Act, Albany Law Review 447, 1976 **Affiliations:** New York State Bar Association; 1st Chairman, Environmental Commission, American Bar Association **Hob./spts.:** Reading, golf, hiking, music **SIC code:** 81 **Address:** Patton, Eakins, Lipsett, Holbrook & Savage, 420 Lexington Ave., Suite 2805, New York, NY 10170 **Phone:** (212)867-8280 **Fax:** (212)599-0342

SCHALK, ROBERT P.
Industry: Law **Born:** June 20, 1931, Pueblo, Colorado **Univ./degree:** B.S., Accounting, University of Colorado, 1953; J.D., U.S.C., 1962 **Current organization:** Robert P. Schalk, Attorney at Law **Title:** C.P.A. **Type of organization:** Law firm **Major product:** Legal services **Area of distribution:** Santa Cruz, California **Area of Practice:** Licensed Attorney, Certified Specialty & Taxation **Honors/awards:** Northern California Super Lawyers, 2005 **Affiliations:** State Bar of California **Hob./spts.:** Golf, football, (San Francisco 49er's), baseball (San Francisco Giants) **SIC code:** 81 **Address:** Robert P. Schalk, Attorney at Law, 550 Water St., F-3, Santa Cruz, CA 95060 **E-mail:** rbtschalk@sbcglobal.net

SCHANBACHER, DAVID C.
Industry: Law **Born:** September 4, 1961, Williamsport, Pennsylvania **Univ./degree:** J.D., Duquesne University, 1986 **Current organization:** Hoffmeyer & Semmelman LLP **Title:** Esquire/Partner **Type of organization:** Law firm **Major product:** Legal services **Area of distribution:** Pennsylvania **Area of Practice:** Family law **Published works:** "ERISA/REA Landmines in Waiver of Survivor Benefits," published by Pennsylvania Bar Institute **Affiliations:** Family Law Section, P.B.A. **Hob./spts.:** Football, cycling, physical fitness **SIC code:** 81 **Address:** Hoffmeyer & Semmelman LLP, 30 N. George St., York, PA 17401 **E-mail:** dschanbacher@hoffsemm.com

SCHLINDRA, MARIE A.
Industry: Law **Born:** December 10, 1971, Ridgewood, New York **Univ./degree:** J.D., New York Law School, 1997 **Current organization:** Pryor Cashman Sherman & Flynn, LLP **Title:** Attorney **Type of organization:** Law firm **Major product:** Legal services **Area of distribution:** National **Area of Practice:** Commercial real estate **Affiliations:** A.B.A.; New York State Bar Association **Hob./spts.:** Photography, skiing

SIC code: 81 **Address:** Pryor Cashman Sherman & Flynn, LLP, 410 Park Ave., New York, NY 10022 **E-mail:** mschlindra@pryorcashman.com

SCHROEDER, RICHARD J.
Industry: Law **Born:** January 15, 1961, Madison, Wisconsin **Univ./degree:** B.S., University of Wisconsin1985; J.D., Hamlin University School of Law, 1992 **Current organization:** Burke & Thomas **Title:** Partner/Attorney **Type of organization:** Law firm **Major product:** Legal services **Area of distribution:** Minnesota **Area of Practice:** Personal injury **Affiliations:** A.T.L.A.; M.T.L.A.; W.A.T.L. **Hob./spts.:** Motorcycles, classic cars **SIC code:** 81 **Address:** Burke & Thomas, 3900 Northwoods Dr., Suite 200, St. Paul, MN 55112 **E-mail:** rjschroeder@msn.com **Web address:** www/burkeandthomas.com

SCHUERING JR., LEO H.
Industry: Law **Born:** July 30, 1942, Sacramento, California **Univ./degree:** J.D., University of California, 1967 **Current organization:** Schuering, Zimmerman & Scully **Title:** Managing Partner **Type of organization:** Law firm **Major product:** Trial work **Area of distribution:** California **Area of Practice:** Medical malpractice defense **Published works:** Articles **Affiliations:** D.R.I.; A.R.A.; "A" Rated in Martindale & Hubbel **Hob./spts.:** Skiing, duck hunting **SIC code:** 81 **Address:** Schuering, Zimmerman & Scully, 400 University Ave., Sacramento, CA 95825-6502

SCHULTZ, JOHN G.
Industry: Law **Born:** July 14, 1962, St. Louis, Missouri **Univ./degree:** J.D., University of Missouri, 1987 **Current organization:** Franke & Schultz, P.C. **Title:** President **Type of organization:** Law firm **Major product:** Litigation **Area of distribution:** Missouri **Area of Practice:** Litigation, insurance **Affiliations:** Missouri Bar Association; Missouri Organization of Defense Lawyers **Hob./spts.:** Golf **SIC code:** 81 **Address:** Franke & Schultz, P.C., 911 Main St., 21st floor, Kansas City, MO 64105

SEGALLA, THOMAS F.
Industry: Law **Born:** April 7, 1943, Lee, Massachusetts **Univ./degree:** J.D., State University of New York at Buffalo, 1972 **Current organization:** Goldberg Segalla LLP **Title:** Founding Partner **Type of organization:** Law firm **Major product:** Legal services **Area of distribution:** National **Area of Practice:** Insurance, bad faith law **Published works:** Couch on Insurance 3d (West) **Affiliations:** D.R.I.; Federation of Insurance & Corporate Counsel **Hob./spts.:** Author of legal papers **SIC code:** 81 **Address:** Goldberg Segalla, LLP, 120 Delaware Ave., Buffalo, NY 14202 **Phone:** (716)566-5400 **Fax:** (716)566-5401

SEIBERT, HENRY E. (NED)
Industry: Law **Born:** December 8, 1942, Columbus, Ohio **Univ./degree:** B. A. History, Princeton University, 1965; J.D., Duke University School of Law, 1968 **Current organization:** Spieth, Bell, McCurdy & Newell Co., L.P.A. **Title:** Principal **Type of organization:** Law firm **Major product:** Legal services **Area of distribution:** Ohio **Area of Practice:** Corporate, business, real estate, oil and gas, hospitality law **Affiliations:** American Bar Association; Ohio State Bar Association; Cleveland Bar Association; Association for Corporate Growth **Hob./spts.:** Reading, history, boating **SIC code:** 81 **Address:** Spieth, Bell, McCurdy & Newell Co., L.P.A., 925 Euclid Ave., Suite 2005, Cleveland, OH 44115

SEKAS, NICHOLAS G.
Industry: Law **Univ./degree:** J.D., Pace University, 1986 **Current organization:** Sekas & Associates, LLC **Title:** Managing Member **Type of organization:** Law firm **Major product:** Legal services **Area of distribution:** New York, New Jersey **Area of Practice:** Personal Injury, Real Estate and Commercial Litigation **Honors/awards:** Award from Martindale-Hubbell; The Peer Review for Ethical Standards, 2006; **Affiliations:** New Jersey Bar Association; New Jersey Trial Lawyers Association; Bergen County Bar Association; New York Bar Association; Connecticut Bar Association; Federal Court of Appeals Second and Third Circuit Court; Federal District Court of Newark; Eastern District Court of New York; Southern District Court of New York; American Trial Lawyers Association; Englewood Cliffs Chamber of Commerce; Honored Member, National Directory of Who's Who, 1994 **Hob./spts.:** Golf, spectator sports; Fluent in Greek and conversational Spanish **SIC code:** 81 **Address:** Sekas & Associates, LLC, 521 Fifth Ave., New York, NY 10175 **E-mail:** nsekas@sekaslaw.com

SHACKELFORD, JASON A.
Industry: Law **Univ./degree:** J.D., Regent University **Current organization:** The Law Offices of Jason Shackelford, P.C. **Title:** Attorney **Type of organization:** Law firm **Major product:** Legal services **Area of distribution:** Missouri **Area of Practice:** Contracts, property, torts **Affiliations:** A.T.L.A.; Boone County Bar Association; Missouri Bar; East and West U.S. Federal District Courts **Hob./spts.:** Sailing **SIC code:** 81 **Address:** The Law Offices of Jason Shackelford, P.C., 1397 E. Highway 22, Centralia, MO 65240 **E-mail:** shackelford@lycos.com

SHAMIEH, ELIAS Z.
Industry: Law **Born:** March 19, 1955, Ramallah, Palestine **Univ./degree:** J.D., New College of California, 1987 **Current organization:** Law Offices of Elias Z. Shamieh **Title:** Attorney at Law **Type of organization:** Law firm **Major product:** Legal services **Area of distribution:** International **Area of Practice:** Immigration law, bankruptcy **Affiliations:** A.I.L.A.; A.B.A.; A.T.L.A. **Hob./spts.:** Soccer, fishing, travel **SIC code:** 81 **Address:** Law Offices of Elias Z. Shamieh, 703 Market St., #1700, San Francisco, CA 94103 **E-mail:** shamiehatlaw@yahoo.com

SHAPIRO, GARY M.
Industry: Law **Born:** June 22, 1956, New Rochelle, New York **Univ./degree:** B.S., Business Management, Cornell University, 1978; J.D., Emory University School of Law, 1983 **Current organization:** Law Offices of Gary M. Shapiro, P.C. **Title:** Esquire **Type of organization:** Law firm **Major product:** Legal services **Area of distribution:** Georgia **Area of Practice:** Trial litigation, catastrophic injury, wrongful death, corporate reorganization **Published works:** 1 book **Affiliations:** A.T.L.A. **SIC code:** 81 **Address:** Law Offices of Gary M. Shapiro, P.C., 400 Galleria Pkwy., Suite 1500-20, Atlanta, GA 30339 **E-mail:** shapirolaw@aol.com **Web address:** www.garyshapiro.com

SHAUB, HENRY Z.
Industry: Law **Born:** May 5, 1955, New York, New York **Current organization:** Shaub, Ahmuty, Citron & Spratt, LLP **Title:** Senior Partner **Type of organization:** Law firm **Major product:** Legal services **Area of distribution:** Metropolitan area **Area of Practice:** Litigation **Affiliations:** N.Y.T.L.A; Nassau County Bar Association; Nassau-Suffolk T.L.A. **SIC code:** 81 **Address:** Shaub, Ahmuty, Citron & Spratt, LLP, 1983 Marcus Ave., Lake Success, NY 11042 **E-mail:** hshaub@sacslaw.com

SHEA III, JOSEPH W.
Industry: Law **Born:** January 3, 1947, Cincinnati, Ohio **Univ./degree:** J.D., University of Northern Kentucky, 1973 **Current organization:** Shea & Associates **Title:** Principal **Type of organization:** Law firm **Major product:** Legal services **Area of distribution:** Ohio **Area of Practice:** Medical legal services representing the plaintiff; national speaker on civil litigation **Honors/awards:** Professional Achievement Award, Outstanding University of Kentucky Graduate, 1998; Top 50 Lawyers in Cincinnati, Super Lawyers Magazine, 2004 **Published works:** 2 books, "Ohio Civil Procedures" and "Ohio Evidence Manual" **Affiliations:** American College of Trial Lawyers; International Society of Barristers; American Board of Trial Advocates **SIC code:** 81 **Address:** Shea & Associates, 250 E. Fifth St., Suite 444, Cincinnati, OH 45202

SHENKMAN, DAVID M.
Industry: Law **Born:** New York **Univ./degree:** J.D., Whittier Law School, 1981 **Current organization:** Law Offices David M. Shenkman, P.A. **Title:** Attorney **Type of organization:** Law firm **Major product:** Legal services **Area of distribution:** Miami, Florida **Area of Practice:** Personal injury, wrongful death **Affiliations:** A.B.A.; The Florida Bar **Hob./spts.:** Skiing, martial arts **SIC code:** 81 **Address:** Law Offices of David M. Shenkman, P.A. 2701 So. Bayshore Drive, 2701 So. Bayshore Drive, Suite 602, Miami, FL 33133 **E-mail:** litig8dms@aol.com

SHIPWASH, MICHAEL S.
Industry: Law **Born:** September 30, 1969, Titusville, Florida **Univ./degree:** J.D., University of Memphis, 1998 **Current organization:** Leitner, Williams, Dooley & Napolitan, P.L.L.C. **Title:** Attorney at Law **Type of organization:** Law firm **Major product:** Legal services **Area of distribution:** International **Area of Practice:** Corporate & trucking defense **Affiliations:** A.B.A.; T.B.A.; K.B.A.; Tennessee Bar Association **Hob./spts.:** Pro-bono work, football **SIC code:** 81 **Address:** Leitner, Williams, Dooley & Napolitan, P.L.L.C., 507 S. Gay St., Suite 1130, Knoxville, TN 37902 **E-mail:** mshipwash@leitnerfirm.com **Web address:** www.leitnerfirm.com

SHIVERS, NANCY TAYLOR
Industry: Law **Born:** August 24, 1948, Lawrence, Kansas **Univ./degree:** B.A., English, University of Kansas, 1970; J.D., University of Houston Law Center, 1977 **Current organization:** Shivers & Shivers **Title:** Attorney **Type of organization:** Law firm **Major product:** Legal services **Area of distribution:** International **Area of Practice:** Immigration and nationality law **Honors/awards:** Best Lawyers in America, since 1992 **Published works:** Articles, seminars **Affiliations:** American Immigration Lawyers Association; Member, Board of Governors, 1986-90; 5th Circuit U.S. State of Appeals; San Antonio Bar Association; State and Federal Jurisdiction, Western District, Texas **Hob./spts.:** Texas public radio, symphony and the arts **SIC code:** 81 **Address:** Shivers & Shivers, 1146 South Alamo St., San Antonio, TX 78210 **E-mail:** ntshivers@aol.com

SICO, STEVEN J.
Industry: Law **Born:** May 26, 1970, Paterson, New Jersey **Univ./degree:** B.A., Psychology, Seton Hall University, 1992; J.D., CUNY School of Law, Queens College, 1997 **Current organization:** Law Office of Steven J. Sico **Title:** Attorney at Law **Type of organization:** Law firm **Major product:** Legal services **Area of distribution:** New

Jersey **Area of Practice:** Litigation, real estate **Affiliations:** A.T.L.A.; N.Y.S.B.A.; A.T.L.A. - N.J. **Hob./spts.:** Baseball, collecting music and handguns **SIC code:** 81 **Address:** Law Office of Steven J. Sico, 234 Main St., 2nd floor, Woodbridge, NJ 07095 **E-mail:** stevensico@aol.com **Web address:** www.stevensico.com

SILVERSTEIN, BENNETT I.
Industry: Law **Born:** November 15, 1952, Bronx, New York **Univ./degree:** J.D., Brooklyn Law School, 1990 **Current organization:** Fischer Brothers **Title:** Attorney **Type of organization:** Law firm **Major product:** Legal services **Area of distribution:** New York, New York **Area of Practice:** Workers' compensation **Affiliations:** New York County Lawyers Association **Hob./spts.:** Organist **SIC code:** 81 **Address:** Fischer Brothers, 217 Broadway, New York, NY 10007

SIMMS, WILLIAM A.
Industry: Law **Born:** February 18, 1946, Lebanon, Tennessee **Univ./degree:** B.A., Political Science, University of the South, Sewanee, Tennessee, 1969; J.D., University of Tennessee Law School, Knoxville, Tennessee, 1971 **Current organization:** Arnett, Draper & Hagood **Title:** Managing Partner **Type of organization:** Law firm **Major product:** Legal services **Area of distribution:** Tennessee **Area of Practice:** Trial practice, product liability, insurance defense, construction, aviation **Honors/awards:** Best Lawyers in America, 2007; Strathmore's Who's Who **Published works:** "A Practical Guide to Discovery and Personal Injury Cases", Tennessee Bar Association sponsored seminar on Practical Discovery, November, 1966; "Discovery Tactics and Tips: Depositions", Knoxville Bar Association sponsored seminar, October, 2002; "Ethical Considerations", National Business Institute sponsored seminar entitled Litigating to Win Through Advanced Trial Advocacy, June, 2007 **Affiliations:** I.A.D.C.; F.D.C.C.; President, Tennessee A.B.O.T.A., 2004; T.D.L.A.; A.B.A.; T.B.A.; K.B.A.; Fellow, Tennessee Bar Foundation and Knoxville Bar Foundation **Hob./spts.:** Hunting, shooting, fishing **SIC code:** 81 **Address:** Arnett, Draper & Hagood, 2300 First Tennessee Plaza, Knoxville, TN 37929 **E-mail:** bsimms@adhknox.com **Web address:** www.adhknox.com

SIMON, JEFFREY B.
Industry: Law **Born:** January 7, 1968, Fort Worth, Texas **Univ./degree:** B.A., Magna Cum Laude, Colgate University, 1990; J.D., University of Texas, 1993 **Current organization:** Waters & Kraus, LLP **Title:** Partner **Type of organization:** Law firm **Major product:** Legal services **Area of distribution:** National **Area of Practice:** Civil trial law **Honors/awards:** Best Lawyers Under 40 in Dallas, D Magazine, 2002 **Affiliations:** A.T.L.A.; T.X.T.L.A.; A.B.A.; Trial Lawyers for Public Justice; Phi Beta Kappa **Hob./spts.:** Running, tennis, travel **SIC code:** 81 **Address:** Waters & Kraus, LLP, 3219 McKinney Ave., Suite 3000, Dallas, TX 75204 **E-mail:** simon@awpk.com **Web address:** www.waters-kraus.com

SINGER, DONALD S.
Industry: Law **Born:** February 24, 1946, St. Louis, Missouri **Univ./degree:** J.D., University of Missouri **Current organization:** The Singer Law Firm, PC **Title:** Attorney **Type of organization:** Law firm **Major product:** Civil litigation, real estate law **Area of distribution:** Midwest **Area of Practice:** Trial law, eminent domain **Hob./spts.:** Licensed Soccer Federation coach and referee **SIC code:** 81 **Address:** The Singer Law Firm, PC, 6963 Waterman Ave., St. Louis, MO 63130 **E-mail:** singerslaw@aol.com

SLATTERY, ROBERT A.
Industry: Law **Born:** December 12, 1936, Milwaukee, Wisconsin **Univ./degree:** J.D. Marquette University Law School, 1960 **Current organization:** Slattery & Duffey, Ltd. **Title:** Shareholder **Type of organization:** Law firm **Major product:** Legal services **Area of distribution:** National **Area of Practice:** Personal injury, product liability, legal instructor, seminars on auto defects **Affiliations:** Fellow, International Academy of Trial Lawyers; Board of Directors, International Society of Primerus Law Firms **Hob./spts.:** Golf **SIC code:** 81 **Address:** Slattery & Duffey, Ltd., W240 N1221 Pewaukee Rd., Waukesha, WI 53188 **E-mail:** rslattery@slatteryduffey.com

SLICKER, FREDERICK K.
Industry: Law **Born:** August 21, 1943, Tulsa, Oklahoma **Univ./degree:** B.A., 1965; J.D. (Highest Distinction), 1968, University of Kansas; LL.M., 1973, Harvard Law School **Current organization:** Slicker Law Firm, P.C. **Title:** President/Attorney **Type of organization:** Law firm **Major product:** Legal services **Area of distribution:** Midwestern U.S. **Area of Practice:** Business law, securities law, franchise law, mediation services **Honors/awards:** Who's Who in Practicing Attorneys; Preeminent Lawyers in the U.S.; "AV" rated by Martindale-Hubbell; Peer Selected for the Best Lawyers in America; Kiwanis Layman of the Year, 2000 and 2005; Kansas Phi Delta Phi Law School Graduate of the Year, 1968 **Published works:** Legal Publications: "Secondary Defendants in Securities Fraud Litigation Rejoice", 65 Okla. B. J. 2597, 7/30/94; "A Practical Guide to Church Bond Financing", 1985 (Self-Published); "Survey of State Securities Laws on Church Bonds", CCH Blue Sky Reporter, No. 755, Part II, 11/21/85; "A Reconsideration of the Doctrine of Successorship-A Step Toward a Rational Approach", 57 Minn. L. Rev. 1051, 1973; "An Evolving Concept of Federal Power Commission Jurisdiction-Will Royalty Owners be Next?", 16 Kan. L. Rev. 378, 1967; Other Publications: "Seeking God's Heart", Christian Publishing Services, Tulsa, 2004; "Angels All Around", 1999 (Self-Published); Numerous Continuing Legal Education Presentations **Affiliations:** American Bar Association; Oklahoma Bar Association; Tulsa County Bar Association, Board of Directors 2004-05, Chairman of Grievance Committee 2004-05, Chairman of Business Law Section 2001-02; numerous church and civic activities **SIC code:** 81 **Address:** Slicker Law Firm, P.C., 4444 E. 66th St., Suite 201, Tulsa, OK 74136 **E-mail:** fslicker@swbell.net **Web address:** www.slickerlawfirm.com

SMITH, ADRIAN P.
Industry: Law **Born:** November 3, 1975, Hammond, Indiana **Univ./degree:** J.D., Valparaiso University, Indiana **Current organization:** Chuhak & Tecson **Title:** Attorney **Type of organization:** Law firm **Major product:** Legal services **Area of distribution:** Indiana **Area of Practice:** Small business, contracts, torts, appellate **Honors/awards:** Trial Lawyer of the Year, I.T.L.A., 2004 **Published works:** Co-author, "Handbook for Indiana Trial Lawyers" **Affiliations:** C.B.A.; I.B.A.; I.L.B.A. **Hob./spts.:** Reading, writing **SIC code:** 81 **Address:** Smith & DeBonis, LLC, 9696 Gordon Dr., Highland, IN 46307 **E-mail:** adriansmith@hotmail.com

SMITH, JASON A. B.
Industry: Law **Born:** August 21, 1971, Washington, D.C. **Univ./degree:** J.D., New York University, 1996 **Current organization:** Weil, Gotshal & Manges, LLP **Title:** Attorney **Type of organization:** Law firm **Major product:** Legal services **Area of distribution:** National **Area of Practice:** Structured finance/securitization **Affiliations:** A.B.A.; New York State Bar Association **Hob./spts.:** Wine **SIC code:** 81 **Address:** Weil, Gotshal & Manges, LLP, 767 Fifth Ave., New York, NY 10153 **E-mail:** jason.smith@weil.com

SMITH, TERRAL R.
Industry: Law **Born:** September 29, 1945, New Rochelle, New York **Univ./degree:** J.D., University of Texas Law School, 1973 **Current organization:** Locke, Liddell & Sapp **Title:** Attorney/Partner **Type of organization:** Law firm **Major product:** Legal services **Area of distribution:** National **Area of Practice:** Political consulting, state and federal law **Affiliations:** State Bar of Texas; District of Columbia Bar **Hob./spts.:** Golf **SIC code:** 81 **Address:** Locke, Liddell & Sapp, 100 Congress Ave., Suite 300, Austin, TX 78701 **E-mail:** tsmith@lockeliddell.com

SMITH-GORDON, SALESIA V.
Industry: Law **Univ./degree:** J.D., Florida State University, College of Law, 1992; Florida A&M University College of Pharmacy **Current organization:** Law Office of Salesia V. Smith Gordon **Title:** Esq. **Type of organization:** Law office **Major product:** Legal services **Area of distribution:** International **Area of Practice:** Personal injury litigation **Affiliations:** Association of Trial Lawyers of America; Palm Beach County Association of Trial Lawyers **SIC code:** 81 **Address:** Law Office of Salesia V. Smith Gordon, 922 Second St., West Palm Beach, FL 33401

SMOAK SR., GERALD C.
Industry: Law **Born:** September 18, 1930, Walterboro, South Carolina **Univ./degree:** B.A., History, University of South Carolina, 1951; J.D., University of South Carolina Law School, 1956 **Current organization:** Gerald C. Smoak, Attorney **Title:** Judge (Retired), Lawyer **Type of organization:** Law firm **Major product:** Legal services **Area of distribution:** South Carolina **Area of Practice:** Judge, Attorney **Affiliations:** American Bar Association; South Carolina Bar Association **Hob./spts.:** Family (10 grandchildren), golf, hunting-quail, birds **SIC code:** 81 **Address:** Gerald C. Smoak, Attorney, 4462 Downing Place Way, Mount Pleasant, SC 29466 **E-mail:** mdwlaw@knology.net

SNODGRASS, TERESA M.
Industry: Law **Born:** July 24, 1953, Orange, California **Univ./degree:** B.A., Literature, emphasis in French, University of California, San Diego, 1975; J.D., University of La Verne **Current organization:** Law Office of the Public Defender **Title:** Deputy Public Defender **Type of organization:** Law firm **Major product:** Criminal defense **Area of distribution:** California **Area of Practice:** Capital case litigation **Affiliations:** State Bar of California; Association of Defense Counsel; The Hague. Netherlands **Hob./spts.:** Golf, travel, French **SIC code:** 81 **Address:** Law Office of Public Defender, 8303 Haven Ave., 3rd floor, Rancho Cucamonga, CA 91730 **E-mail:** tsnodgrass@pd.sbcounty.gov

SOBOLEVSKY, ANDRE
Industry: Law **Born:** May 17, 1958, Moscow, Russia **Univ./degree:** B.A., Syracuse University, J.D., Syracuse University College of Law **Current organization:** Sobolevsky & Associates, LLP **Title:** Partner **Type of organization:** Law firm **Major product:** Legal services **Area of distribution:** National **Area of Practice:** Immigration law with an emphasis on handling Russian clients, background in real estate issues and appellate work **Affiliations:** American Immigration Lawyers Association **Hob./spts.:** Spending time with family, chess, travel, sailing **SIC code:** 81 **Address:**

Sobolevsky & Associates, LLP, 305 Madison Ave., Suite 449, New York, NY 10165 **E-mail:** asobolevsky@aol.com

SOLEY, CHARLES H.
Industry: Law **Born:** April 7, 1945, San Mateo, California **Univ./degree:** J.D., University of California at Berkeley, 1970 **Current organization:** Charles H. Soley, Inc. **Title:** Attorney/Mediator **Type of organization:** Law firm **Major product:** Legal services **Area of distribution:** Fresno, California **Area of Practice:** Family law; Trained law enforcement agencies in enforcement of child custody orders; Judge protemp sitting **Honors/awards:** Phi Beta Kappa, Distinction and General Scholarship **Affiliations:** A.B.A.; C.V.C.L.A.; F.C.A.C. **Hob./spts.:** Sailing, woodworking **SIC code:** 81 **Address:** Charles H. Soley, Inc., 1551 E. Shaw Ave., Suite 122, Fresno, CA 93710 **E-mail:** csoley@aol.com

SOLOTOFF, ERIC S.
Industry: Law **Born:** July 8, 1967, Brooklyn, New York **Spouse:** Tamara **Univ./degree:** B.A., Cum Laude, Psychology, State University of New York at Albany, 1989; J.D., 1992; LL.M., Taxation, 1994, Widener University School of Law **Current organization:** Donahue, Hagan, Klein, Newsome & O'Donnell, P.C. **Title:** Attorney **Type of organization:** Law firm **Major product:** Legal services, family and matrimonial law **Area of distribution:** New Jersey **Area of practice:** Matrimonial and family law **Area of Practice:** Matrimonial and family law **Honors/awards:** 'AV' rated, Martindale-Hubbell; 10 Under 40 Family and Matrimonial Law Attorneys, 2003; 10 Leaders Matrimonial & Divorce Law Under Age 45, Northern New Jersey, 2004; Ten Leaders in Morris County, 2005 **Published works:** Law in the Fifty States, (contributor to New Jersey report), ABA Family Law Quarterly, 1994-95, 1995-96, 2001-02, 2002-03 **Affiliations:** Family Law Section, Law Practice Management Section, Litigation Section, American Bar Association; Family Law Section, New Jersey Bar Association; Family Law Committee, Morris County Bar Association; Family Law Section, Essex County Bar Association; New Jersey Family Law Section, American Trial Lawyers of America; Barrister, Northern New Jersey Family Law Inns of Court **SIC code:** 81 **Address:** Donahue, Hagan, Klein, Newsome & O'Donnell, P.C., 636 Morris Tpke., Suite C, Short Hills, NJ 07028 **E-mail:** esolotoff@dhkno.com **Web address:** www.divorces-nj.com

SOMOS, TOM
Industry: Law **Born:** February 13, 1970, Toronto, Ontario, Canada **Univ./degree:** B.A., Criminal Justice, University of Toronto, 1994; J.D., Capital University Law School, Ohio, 1997 **Current organization:** Robert D. Erney & Associates Co., LPA **Title:** Attorney **Type of organization:** Law firm **Major product:** Legal services **Area of distribution:** Ohio **Area of Practice:** Personal injury, collection law, business insurance law **Affiliations:** A.B.A.; A.T.L.A.; Ohio Academy of Trail Lawyers; Franklin County Bar Association **Hob./spts.:** Family (2 children), tennis, hockey **SIC code:** 81 **Address:** Robert D. Erney & Associates Co., LPA, 1654 E. Broad St., Columbus, OH 43205 **E-mail:** tom.somos@erneylaw.com

SOULE JR., AUGUSTUS W.
Industry: Law **Born:** December 13, 1918, Boston, Massachusetts **Spouse:** Mary Whitner Rogers **Married:** April 26, 1947 **Children:** Augustus W. Soule III, 49; Martha R. Soule, 47; Robert G. Soule, 42 **Univ./degree:** LL.B., Harvard University, Massachusetts **Current organization:** Sullivan & Worcester LLP **Title:** Of Counsel **Type of organization:** Law firm **Major product:** Legal services **Area of distribution:** Massachusetts **Area of Practice:** Probate law **Honors/awards:** Listed in Best Lawyers of America **Affiliations:** A.C.T.E.C.; Boston Bar Association; American Bar Association **Hob./spts.:** Football, swimming **SIC code:** 81 **Address:** Sullivan & Worcester LLP, 1 Post Office Square, Boston, MA 02109

SPEER, JOHN E.
Industry: Law **Born:** March 19, 1956, Conrad, Montana **Univ./degree:** M.S., Counseling, 1994; B.S., Psychology, 1996, University of Great Falls **Current organization:** Private practice **Title:** Freelance Paraprofessional (Paralegal, Counselor) **Type of organization:** Counseling **Major product:** Legal research, court appearances **Area of distribution:** Montana **Area of Practice:** Family and tribal law, medical **Published works:** Newspaper article **Affiliations:** Co-Founder, V.W.A.S. **Hob./spts.:** Camping, hiking **SIC code:** 81 **Address:** P.O. Box 206, Great Falls, MT 59403-0206

STEWART, IAN A.
Industry: Law **Born:** March 12, 1971, St. Louis, Missouri **Univ./degree:** J.D., St. Louis University, 1996 **Current organization:** Wilson, Elser, Moskowitz, Edelman & Dicker, LLP **Title:** Attorney **Type of organization:** Law firm **Major product:** Legal services **Area of distribution:** Chicago, Illinois **Area of Practice:** Professional liability defense **Honors/awards:** "AV" rated, Martindale-Hubbell **Published works:** Article, National Business Institute **Affiliations:** C.B.A.; Illinois State Bar Association **SIC code:** 81 **Address:** Wilson, Elser, Moskowitz, Edelman & Dicker, LLP, 120 N. LaSalle, Suite 2600, Chicago, IL 60606 **E-mail:** stewarti@wemed.com **Web address:** www.wemed.com

STIDHAM, MICHAEL A.
Industry: Law **Born:** April 17, 1948, Old Blue Diamond, Kentucky **Univ./degree:** B.A., Education, University of Kentucky, 1970; J.D. with Distinction, University of Kentucky School of Law, 1972 **Current organization:** Stidham Law Offices **Title:** J.D./Attorney **Type of organization:** Law firm **Major product:** Legal services **Area of distribution:** Kentucky **Area of Practice:** Personal injury, criminal, product liability, medical malpractice **Affiliations:** American Bar Association; Kentucky Bar Association; Kentucky Trial Lawyers Association **Hob./spts.:** Golf, swimming, basketball, football **SIC code:** 81 **Address:** Stidham Law Offices, P.O. Box 732, Jackson, KY 41339

STREHLE, PHILLIP A.
Industry: Law **Born:** August 1, 1957, Michigan **Univ./degree:** J.D., Thomas Cooley **Current organization:** Law Office of Phillip Strehle, P.C. **Title:** Attorney **Type of organization:** Law firm **Major product:** Legal services **Area of distribution:** Southeastern Michigan **Area of Practice:** Personal injury, real estate, probate, contract law **Affiliations:** State Bar of Michigan **Hob./spts.:** Reading, travel, woodworking **SIC code:** 81 **Address:** Law Office of Phillip A. Strehle, P.C., 255 N. Telegraph Rd., Suite 201, Waterford, MI 48328 **E-mail:** phillipstrehle@yahoo.com

STROTHERS, DWAYNE BERNARD
Industry: Law **Born:** December 26, 1960, Suffolk, Virginia **Univ./degree:** B.A., Management, Western Illinois University, 1990 **Current organization:** The Law Office of Dwayne B. Strothers **Title:** Attorney **Type of organization:** Law firm **Major product:** Legal services **Area of distribution:** Virginia **Area of Practice:** Criminal defense, family law, civil litigation **Affiliations:** A.B.A.; N.A.C.D.L.; A.T.L.A. **Hob./spts.:** Basketball, travel **SIC code:** 81 **Address:** The Law Office of Dwayne B. Strothers, 130 Commerce St., Suffolk, VA 23439 **E-mail:** ceagle2b@aol.com

STUBER, JAMES A.
Industry: Law **Born:** July 17, 1948, Warren, Ohio **Univ./degree:** B.A., University of Pennsylvania, 1970; M.A., Columbia University, 1973; J.D., Georgetown University, 1976 **Current organization:** Law Offices of James A. Stuber, P.A. **Title:** Attorney at Law **Type of organization:** Law firm **Major product:** Legal services **Area of distribution:** International **Area of Practice:** Immigration law (Board Certified), business law **Affiliations:** American Immigration Lawyers Association; Former CEO, Cyroflex, Inc. **Hob./spts.:** Kairos Prison Ministry **SIC code:** 81 **Address:** Law Offices of James A. Stuber, P.A., 222 Lakeview Ave., Suite 160-311, West Palm Beach, FL 33401 **E-mail:** jstuber@riversideventures.com

SWAIN, JONATHAN T.
Industry: Law **Born:** August 13, 1950, Waukegan, Illinois **Univ./degree:** J.D., Marquette University, Wisconsin, 1975 **Current organization:** Lindner & Marsack, S.C. **Title:** Attorney **Type of organization:** Law firm **Major product:** Legal services **Area of distribution:** National **Area of Practice:** Labor and employment law; management **Published works:** 2 books; co-author, 1 article **Affiliations:** American Bar Association, Labor and Employment Section; Milwaukee Bar Association **Hob./spts.:** Golf, sailing **SIC code:** 81 **Address:** Lindner & Marsack, S.C., 411 E. Wisconsin Ave., Suite 1000, Milwaukee, WI 53202 **E-mail:** jswain@lindner-marsack.com **Web address:** www.lindner-marsack.com

SWINNEN, BENOIT M.J.
Industry: Law **Born:** January 7, 1961, Liege, Belgium **Univ./degree:** J.D., Magna Cum Laude, University of Brussels, Belgium, 1984; M.B.A., Cum Laude, 1986; J.D., Cum Laude, 1998, Southern Methodist University **Current organization:** Schroer, Rice, P.A. **Title:** Managing Partner **Type of organization:** Law firm **Major product:** Legal services **Area of distribution:** National **Area of Practice:** Personal injury, commercial litigation **Published works:** 1 article **Affiliations:** A.B.A.; A.T.L.A.; Kansas Bar Association; Missouri Bar; Federal District of Kansas, 10th Circuit U.S. Court of Appeals; West Federal District Missouri **Hob./spts.:** Horses, Jumping **SIC code:** 81 **Address:** Schroer, Rice, P.A., 2913 S.W. Maupin Lane, Topeka, KS 66614 **E-mail:** bswinnen@schroerrice.com **Web address:** www.schroerrice.com

TACKETT, STEVEN J.
Industry: Law **Born:** November 24, 1944, Crowell, Texas **Univ./degree:** B.A., Government, University of Texas at Austin, 1968; J.D., University of Texas at Austin Law School, 1971 **Current organization:** Giordani Schurig Beckett Tackett, LLP **Title:** Attorney/Partner **Type of organization:** Law firm **Major product:** Legal services **Area of distribution:** Texas **Area of Practice:** Estate planning and probate law/taxation **Published works:** Article **Affiliations:** A.B.A.; State Bar of Texas; American College of Trust & Estate Counsel; Central Texas Estate Planning Council; National Committee on Planned Giving, Central Texas **Hob./spts.:** The outdoors, hiking, travel **SIC code:** 81 **Address:** Giordani Schurig Beckett Tackett, LLP, 301 Congress Ave., Suite 1900, Austin, TX 78701 **E-mail:** stackett@gsbtlaw.com **Web address:** www.gsbtlaw.com

TALBERT II, BONFORD R.
Industry: Law **Born:** July 28, 1929, Cincinnati, Ohio **Univ./degree:** B.S., Business Administration, Bowling Green State University, 1951; J.D., Ohio State University School of Law, 1956 **Current organization:** Harry Pavilack & Associates **Title:** Judge (Retired), Attorney **Type of organization:** Law firm **Major product:** Legal services **Area of distribution:** South Carolina **Area of Practice:** Disability, injury, plaintiff **Honors/awards:** A.B.A. Traffic Court **Affiliations:** A.B.A.; South Carolina Bar Association; Ohio State Bar Association; Faculty, Nevada Judicial College; Faculty, Ohio Judicial College; President, Judges Association **Hob./spts.:** Ohio State football (Buckeyes), golf **SIC code:** 81 **Address:** Harry Pavilack & Associates, 603 N. Kings Hwy., Myrtle Beach, SC 29577 **E-mail:** pavilack@pavilack.com **Web address:** www.pavilack.com

TALBOTT JR., BEN JOHNSON
Industry: Law **Born:** February 2, 1940, Louisville, Kentucky **Univ./degree:** A.B., History, Xavier University, 1961; LL.B., Harvard University, 1964 **Current organization:** Talbott & Talbott, PLLC **Title:** Attorney/Managing Partner **Type of organization:** Law firm, professional limited liability corporation **Major product:** Legal services **Area of distribution:** Kentucky **Area of Practice:** Commercial litigation, contracts **Published works:** 3 articles **Affiliations:** A.B.A.; Kentucky State Bar Association **Hob./spts.:** Golf, tennis, skiing, fishing **SIC code:** 81 **Address:** Talbott & Talbott, PLLC, 501 S. Second St., Louisville, KY 40202 **E-mail:** bjtalbott@mindspring.com

TALLEY JR., PATRICK A.
Industry: Law **Born:** July 3, 1955 **Univ./degree:** J.D., Louisiana State University, 1982; LL.M., Tulane University, 1993 **Current organization:** Frilot Partridge Law Firm **Title:** Esquire **Type of organization:** Law firm **Major product:** Legal services **Area of distribution:** National **Area of Practice:** Energy and environmental law **Affiliations:** N.A.R.T.C.; M.T.L.A.; L.B.A.; A.B.A. **SIC code:** 81 **Address:** Frilot Partridge Law Firm, 1100 Poydras St., New Orleans, LA 70163 **E-mail:** ptalley@frilotpartridge.com **Web address:** www.frilotpartridge.com

TANICK, MARSHALL H.
Industry: Law **Born:** May 9, 1947, Minneapolis, Minnesota **Univ./degree:** B.A., Journalism, University of Minnesota, 1969; J.D., Stanford University, California, 1973 **Current organization:** Mansfield, Tanick & Cohen, P.A. **Title:** Attorney **Type of organization:** Law firm **Major product:** Legal services, litigation **Area of distribution:** National **Area of Practice:** Employment law **Affiliations:** American Bar Association; Minnesota Bar Association **Hob./spts.:** Bicycling, basketball **SIC code:** 81 **Address:** Mansfield, Tanick & Cohen, P.A., 1560 International Center, 900 Second Ave. South, Minneapolis, MN 55402 **E-mail:** mtanick@mansfieldtanick.com

TANNER, DEE B.
Industry: Law/farming **Born:** January 16, 1913, Provo, Utah **Univ./degree:** J.D., Pacific Coast Law School **Current organization:** Rancho Polo **Title:** Attorney/Farmer **Type of organization:** Law firm/ranch **Major product:** Legal services **Area of distribution:** Pasadena, California **Area of practice:** Law **Area of Practice:** Law **Honors/awards:** Listed in Who's Who in American Law, 1996-1997 and 2002-2003 **Published works:** Law briefs **Affiliations:** Los Angeles Bar Association **Hob./spts.:** Owner, Rancho Polo; gardening, swimming **SIC code:** 81 **Address:** 1720 Lombardy Rd., Pasadena, CA 91106 **E-mail:** rpltd@aol.com

TEJA, G. DAVE
Industry: Law **Born:** May 27, 1934, Auburn, California **Univ./degree:** J.D., M.P.A., University of San Francisco **Current organization:** G. Dave Teja, Attorney at Law **Title:** Attorney **Type of organization:** Law office **Major product:** Legal services **Area of distribution:** Yuba City, California **Area of Practice:** Real estate law **Affiliations:** A.B.A.; Masons; Sons of Norway **Hob./spts.:** Hiking, reading **SIC code:** 81 **Address:** G. Dave Teja, Attorney at Law, 409A Center St., Yuba City, CA 95991-4500 **E-mail:** tejalaw@hotmail.com

TESTINI, GAETANO J.
Industry: Law **Born:** October 21, 1968, Bronx, New York **Univ./degree:** J.D., Gonzaga School of Law,2000 **Current organization:** Wilmer, Messer & Testini, PLC **Title:** Partner **Type of organization:** Law firm **Major product:** Legal services **Area of distribution:** Arizona **Area of Practice:** Workers compensation **Affiliations:** Board of Advisors Gonzaga; Board Liaison for Los Abogados State Chapter, Endowment Fund; Golf Tournament; Member, State Bar Convention Planning Committee **Hob./spts.:** Golf, travel, family **SIC code:** 81 **Address:** Wilmer, Messer & Testini, PLC, 519 E. Thomas Rd., Suite 2, Phoenix, AZ 85012 **E-mail:** gtestini@wmtlegal.com **Web address:** www.wmtlegal.com

THOMAS, RAYMOND L.
Industry: Law **Born:** August 18, 1963, Alpine, Texas **Univ./degree:** B.S., Poly Science, St. Mary's University, 1985; J.D., University of Texas at Austin School of Law, 1988 **Current organization:** Kittleman, Thomas, Ramirez & Gonzales, PLLC **Title:** Trial Lawyer **Type of organization:** Law firm **Major product:** Legal services **Area of distribution:** International **Area of Practice:** Civil trial law **Honors/awards:** President, Texas Young Lawyers Association; Director, State Bar of Texas; Director, Texas Access to Justice Commission; Life Fellow, Texas Bar Foundation; Board Certified, Civil Trial Law, T.B.L.S.; President, McAllen Boys & Girls Club **Published works:** 5 articles **Affiliations:** A.B.A.; A.T.L.A.; T.T.L.A.; S.B. of Texas **Hob./spts.:** Time with family **SIC code:** 81 **Address:** Kittleman, Thomas, Ramirez & Gonzales, PLLC, 4900-B N. Tenth St., McAllen, TX 78504 **E-mail:** thomramz@aol.com

THOMPSON, NEIL H.
Industry: Law **Born:** August 20, 1926, Bismarck, North Dakota **Univ./degree:** J.D., University of North Dakota **Current organization:** Thompson & Thompson, Attorneys at Law **Title:** J.D. **Type of organization:** Law firm **Major product:** Legal services **Area of distribution:** National **Area of Practice:** Personal injury, criminal defense **Affiliations:** A.B.A.; A.T.L.A.; North Dakota State Bar; North Dakota Trial Lawyers Association **SIC code:** 81 **Address:** Thompson & Thompson, Attorneys at Law, 409 Fourth Ave. N.E., Devils Lake, ND 58301-0696

THOMPSON, THOMAS A.
Industry: Law **Born:** Seattle, Washington **Univ./degree:** J.D., University of Washington, 1977 **Current organization:** Walthew Law Firm **Title:** Attorney **Type of organization:** Law firm **Major product:** Legal services **Area of distribution:** Washington **Area of Practice:** Labor and workers' compensation **Affiliations:** A.B.A.; Washington State Trial Lawyers Association **SIC code:** 81 **Address:** Walthew Law Firm, 123 Third Ave. South, Seattle, WA 98104 **E-mail:** garthompson@msn.com

THORBURN, JAMES D.
Industry: Law **Born:** March 4, 1956, Glendale, California **Univ./degree:** B.A., Business, California State University at Northridge, 1987; J.D., University of Denver, 1991 **Current organization:** The Law Office of James D. Thorburn, LLC **Title:** Owner **Type of organization:** Law firm **Major product:** Legal services **Area of distribution:** National **Area of Practice:** Real estate and construction law **Affiliations:** Colorado Bar Association; Chamber of Commerce **Hob./spts.:** Playing piano, auto racing **SIC code:** 81 **Address:** The Law Office of James D. Thorburn, LLC, 133 County Rd. 17, Suite 12, Elizabeth, CO 80107 **E-mail:** jdt@thorburnlaw.com

THORNTON, J. DUKE
Industry: Law **Born:** July 11, 1944, Murray, Kentucky **Univ./degree:** J.D., University of New Mexico, 1969 **Current organization:** Butt, Thornton, & Baehr, Attorney **Title:** Chairman of the Board **Type of organization:** Law firm **Major product:** Legal services **Area of distribution:** National **Area of Practice:** Defense litigation / trial **Honors/awards:** multilple awards **Published works:** Trial Handbook for the New Mexico Lawyers **Affiliations:** A.B.A.; N.C.U.A.; American Board of Trial Lawyers **Hob./spts.:** Flying, driving commercial motor vehicles, golf **SIC code:** 81 **Address:** Butt, Thornton & Baehr, Attorney, 4101 Indian School Rd. N.E., Albuquerque, NM 87110 **E-mail:** jdthornton@btblaw.com **Web address:** www.btblaw.com

THORNTON, LESLIE THOMASINA
Industry: Law **Born:** May 2, 1958, Philadelphia, Pennsylvania **Univ./degree:** B.S., University of Pennsylvania, 1980; J.D., Georgetown University, 1983 **Current organization:** Patton Boggs LLP **Title:** Partner **Type of organization:** Law firm **Major product:** Legal services **Area of distribution:** International **Area of Practice:** Litigation, government, grand jury investigations **Honors/awards:** American Criminal Law Review **Published works:** 30+ articles **Affiliations:** D.S.B.A.; W.B.A.; G.C.W.L.D.; N.B.A.; A.B.A. **Hob./spts.:** Writing, running **SIC code:** 81 **Address:** Patton Boggs LLP, 2550 M St. N.W., Washington, DC 20037 **E-mail:** lthornton@pattonboggs.com **Web address:** www.pattonboggs.com

TOWNSEND, MICHAEL J.
Industry: Law **Born:** March 7, 1952, Bangor, Maine **Univ./degree:** J.D., West New England College School of Law, 1982 **Current organization:** Harris Beach LLP **Title:** Attorney **Type of organization:** Law firm **Major product:** Legal services **Area of distribution:** Rochester, New York **Area of Practice:** Commercial law, municipal finance, mergers and acquisitions **Honors/awards:** "BV" rated, Martindale-Hubbell **Affiliations:** N.Y.S.B.A.; Board member, New York State Power Authority; Montgomery County Bar Association **Hob./spts.:** Coaching Little League, basketball, baseball **SIC code:** 81 **Address:** Harris Beach LLP, 99 Garnsey Rd., Pittsford, NY 14534 **E-mail:** mjtownsend@gatesandadams.com

TRACHTA, S. JON
Industry: Law **Born:** December 6, 1942, Pensacola, Florida **Univ./degree:** J.D., University of Arizona, 1973 **Current organization:** Law Offices of S. Jon Trachta **Title:** Attorney **Type of organization:** Law firm **Major product:** Legal services **Area of distribution:** Arizona **Area of Practice:** Trial law, arbitration, mediation **Honors/awards:** "AV" rated, Martindale-Hubbell **Affiliations:** A.T.L.A.; D.R.I.; American Board of Trial Advocates **Hob./spts.:** Horseback riding, fly-fishing **SIC code:** 81 **Address:** Law Offices of S. Jon Trachta, 2720 E. Broadway, Tucson, AZ 85716 **E-mail:** jon@trachta-law.com

TRONOLONE, TRACEY A.
Industry: Law **Born:** June 25, 1964, New York, New York **Univ./degree:** M.S.W., Hunter College, 1992 **Current organization:** The Children's Law Center **Title:** Director of Social Work **Type of organization:** Not for profit law firm **Major product:** Legal services, representation of children **Area of distribution:** Brooklyn, Bronx, New York **Area of Practice:** Assessment and referrals of social work cases; Certified School Social Worker, New Jersey; Certified Social Worker, New York; Certified L.S.W., New Jersey **Honors/awards:** Listed in Who's Who in America, 2000-2003; Who's Who in the East, 1999-2000 **Affiliations:** N.A.S.W. **Hob./spts.:** Reading **SIC code:** 81 **Address:** The Children's Law Center, 1 Boerum Place, Brooklyn, NY 11201 **E-mail:** traceytron@juno.com

TULLY, BRIAN ANDREW
Industry: Law **Born:** July 19, 1970, Rockville Center, New York **Univ./degree:** B.S., St. John's University, 1993; J.D., Touro Law Center, 1997 **Current organization:** Law Offices of Brian Andrew Tully **Title:** Attorney at Law **Type of organization:** Law firm **Major product:** Legal services **Area of distribution:** Long Island, New York **Area of Practice:** Estate Planning, Elder Law and Asset Preservation; Certified as an Elder Law Attorney by the National Elder Law Foundation; probate and estate litigation **Published works:** Newspaper articles; lectured to public, corporate, human service and professional groups on the benefits of estate and long term planning; interviewed by New 12 Long Island to discuss Elder Care issues **Affiliations:** The New York State, Nassau and Suffolk County Bar Associations and their Estate and Tax Planning and Elder Law Committees; American Bar Association's Estate Planning Committee; National Academy of Elder Law Attorneys; Suffolk County Estate Planning Council; American Society on Aging; NHCCNYS; FRIA; Board of Directors Member, Suffolk County Chapter of the American Parkinson's Disease Association, Inc.; Registered Advocate for the Arthritis Foundation and the Alzheimer's Association; the Long Island Counsel to Pierro & Associates, LLP **Hob./spts.:** Golf, reading **SIC code:** 81 **Address:** Law Offices of Brian Andrew Tully, Attn: Julia, 444 New York Ave., Huntington, NY 11743 **E-mail:** bat@estateplanning-elderlaw.com **Web address:** www.estateplanning-elderlaw.com

TUTTLE, DEBORAH M.
Industry: Law **Born:** May 28, 1956, Ann Arbor, Michigan **Univ./degree:** J.D., DePaul University College of Law, 1981 **Current organization:** Deborah M. Tuttle, Attorney **Title:** Attorney **Type of organization:** Law firm **Major product:** Legal services **Area of distribution:** Indiana **Area of Practice:** Alternative dispute resolution specialist, estate planning **Published works:** Co-author, Indiana Alternative Dispute Resolution Manual, Lawyers Co-op Publishing, 1995 **Affiliations:** Indiana State Bar Association, ADR Section; State Bar of Michigan; Illinois State Bar Association **Hob./spts.:** Golf, fishing, snow and water skiing, family **SIC code:** 81 **Address:** Deborah M. Tuttle, Attorney, Trigon Bldg., 224 W. Jefferson Blvd., South Bend, IN 46601 **Phone:** (574)273-1843 **Fax:** (574)273-2321

UPRIGHT, KIRBY G.
Industry: Law **Born:** September 12, 1946, South Canaan, Pennsylvania **Univ./degree:** B.A., Pennsylvania State University, 1970; J.D., University of Akron, 1973; LL.M., Temple University, 1977 **Current organization:** Young, Upright, Catina & Parker, LLP **Title:** Lawyer **Type of organization:** Law firm **Major product:** Legal services **Area of distribution:** Stroudsburg, Pennsylvania **Area of Practice:** Estate planning, estate and trust administration **Honors/awards:** "AV" rated, Martindale-Hubbell **Affiliations:** A.B.A.; Pennsylvania Bar Association; Chair, Probate and Trust Section, Pennsylvania Bar Association **Hob./spts.:** Boy Scouts, skiing, scuba diving **SIC code:** 81 **Address:** Young, Upright, Catina & Parker, LLP, 300 Stroud Bldg., Stroudsburg, PA 18360 **E-mail:** kupright@pennlawyers.com **Web address:** www.pennlawyers.com

VEIT, R.L.
Industry: Law **Born:** August 16, 1953, Jefferson City, Missouri **Univ./degree:** B.S., Agriculture/Economics, University of Missouri, 1976; J.D., University of Missouri Law School, 1979 **Current organization:** Carson & Coil, P.C. **Title:** President **Type of organization:** Law firm **Major product:** Legal services **Area of distribution:** Missouri **Area of Practice:** Litigation, personal injury, workers compensation, wrongful death, medical malpractice **Affiliations:** Missouri Bar; Cole County Bar Association; M.T.L.A.; A.T.L.A. **Hob./spts.:** Family, fishing, hunting **SIC code:** 81 **Address:** Carson & Coil P.C., 515 E. High St., Jefferson City, MO 65101 **E-mail:** rudy.v@carsoncoil.com **Web address:** www.carsoncoil.com

VINSON JR., ROBERT E.
Industry: Law **Univ./degree:** J.D., Southern Methodist University School of Law, 1987 **Current organization:** Vinson Franchise Law Firm **Title:** Esquire **Type of organization:** Law firm **Major product:** Franchise law services **Area of distribution:** National **Area of Practice:** Franchise law **Affiliations:** A.B.A.; State Bar of California; The Nevada State Bar; State Bar of Texas **SIC code:** 81 **Address:** Vinson Franchise Law Firm, 858 Jennifer St., Incline Village, NV 89451 **E-mail:** rob@franchiselaw.net **Web address:** www.franchiselaw.net

WAGER, DONALD R.
Industry: Law **Born:** March 15, 1936, Rockford, Illinois **Univ./degree:** J.D., Williamette University, 1962 **Current organization:** Law Offices of Donald R. Wager **Title:** Attorney **Type of organization:** Law firm **Major product:** Legal services **Area of distribution:** National **Area of Practice:** Criminal defense **Affiliations:** N.A.C.D.L.; Past President, Los Angeles County Criminal Courts Bar Association; State Bar of California; California Attorneys for Criminal Justice **Hob./spts.:** Travel, walking, opera, theatre **SIC code:** 81 **Address:** Law Offices of Donald R. Wager, 10100 Santa Monica Blvd., Eighth Floor, Los Angeles, CA 90067 **E-mail:** wagerlaw@hotmail.com

WALKER, RANDALL W.
Industry: Law **Univ./degree:** B.S., History, Texas State University, 1984; J.D., Texas Tech Law School, 1986 **Current organization:** Law Office of Randall Walker **Title:** Attorney **Type of organization:** Law firm **Major product:** Legal services **Area of distribution:** Wichita Falls, Texas **Area of Practice:** Family law **Affiliations:** A.B.A. **SIC code:** 81 **Address:** Law Office of Randall Walker, 900 Eighth St., Suite 1400, Wichita Falls, TX 76301 **E-mail:** randall@walkerattorney.com

WALKER, RICHARD K.
Industry: Law **Born:** October 21, 1948, Knoxville, Tennessee **Univ./degree:** B.S., Psychology, University of Kansas, 1970; J.D., University of Kansas, 1975 **Current organization:** Quarles & Brady Streich Lang, LLP **Title:** Attorney **Type of organization:** Law firm **Major product:** Legal services **Area of distribution:** Arizona **Area of Practice:** Labor and employment law litigation **Published works:** 20+ articles **Affiliations:** A.B.A.; State Bar of Arizona; District of Columbia Bar **Hob./spts.:** History, literature, theatre **SIC code:** 81 **Address:** Quarles & Brady Streich Lang, LLP, Renaissance One, Two N. Central Ave., Phoenix, AZ 85004-2391 **E-mail:** rwalker@quarles.com **Web address:** www.quarles.com

WALLACE, BRADLEY W.
Industry: Law **Born:** Tacoma, Washington **Univ./degree:** B.A., Social Sciences, M.Ed., Harding University, Arkansas; J.D., University of Arkansas School of Law **Current organization:** Carr & Carr, Attorneys at Law **Title:** Attorney **Type of organization:** Law firm **Major product:** Legal services **Area of distribution:** Arkansas **Area of Practice:** Personal injury, employment law **Affiliations:** A.B.A.; Arkansas Bar Association; American Trial Lawyers Association; Arkansas Trial Lawyers Association; Sebastian County Bar Association **Hob./spts.:** Rock climbing, chess tournaments **SIC code:** 81 **Address:** Carr & Carr, Attorneys at Law, 14 N. Third St.,, Suite D, Ft. Smith, AR 72901 **E-mail:** bwallace@carrcarr.com **Web address:** www.carrcarr.com

WALLACE, EDNA M.
Industry: Law **Born:** July 22, 1945, Indianapolis, Indiana **Univ./degree:** Certificate with High Honors, American Institute of Paralegal Studies **Current organization:** Whitham, Hebenstreit & Zubek LLP **Title:** Registered Paralegal **Type of organization:** Law firm **Major product:** Legal services **Area of distribution:** National **Area of Practice:** Civil litigation, bankruptcy **Honors/awards:** Paralegal of the Year, I.B.A.,1999; Lifetime Achievement Award, Indiana Paralegal Association, 2002 **Published works:** Numerous articles including; "Professional Conduct and Ethical Considerations for Paralegals", "Liability-Who is Responsible for your Actions?", "The Good, the Bad and the Ugly" **Affiliations:** I.P.A.; I.B.A.; A.B.A.; E.S.A. **Hob./spts.:** Spending time with grandchildren, camping, reading **SIC code:** 81 **Address:** Whitham, Hebenstreit & Zubek LLP, 151 N. Delaware St., Suite 2000, Indianapolis, IN 46204 **E-mail:** emw@whzlaw.com

WALLACE, RICHARD P.
Industry: Law **Born:** April 28, 1941, Troy, New York **Univ./degree:** B.S., Political Science, Brown University, 1963; J.D., Cum Laude, Union University - Albany Law School 1967 **Current organization:** Martin, Shudt, Wallace, DiLorenzo & Johnson **Title:** Managing Partner **Type of organization:** Full service business law firm **Major product:** Legal services **Area of distribution:** New York **Area of Practice:** Trusts, estates, corporate, nonprofit law **Honors/awards:** Russell Taylor Award, New York State Bar Association, 2005; Confidential Law Assistant to the New York State Supreme Court Appellate Division, 3rd Dept., 1968-1969 **Affiliations:** Chair, New York State Bar Association; Continuing Legal Education Committee, Trusts & Estates Law Section; Past President, Trustee, The Albany Academy **SIC code:** 81 **Address:** Martin, Shudt, Wallace, DiLorenzo & Johnson, 279 River St., Troy, NY 12180 **E-mail:** dwallace@martinshudt.com **Web address:** www.martinshudt.com

WARREN, CHARLES S.
Industry: Law **Born:** July 4, 1940, Cleveland, Ohio **Univ./degree:** J.D., Columbia University, 1965 **Current organization:** Bryan Cave, LLP **Title:** Partner **Type of organization:** Law firm **Major product:** Legal services **Area of distribution:** National **Area of Practice:** Environmental law **Affiliations:** A.B.A.; New York State Bar Association; New York League of Conservation Voters; Board Member, Environmental Advocates of New York **Hob./spts.:** Golf **SIC code:** 81 **Address:** Bryan Cave, LLP, 1290 Avenue of the Americas, New York, NY 10104 **E-mail:** cswarren@bryancave.com **Web address:** www.bryancave.com

WARREN, J. STEVE
Industry: Law **Born:** July 15, 1950, Rome, Georgia **Univ./degree:** B.A., Furman University, 1972; J.D., University of South Carolina, 1975 **Current organization:** Jackson Lewis LLP **Title:** Managing Partner **Type of organization:** Law firm **Major product:** Legal services **Area of distribution:** National **Area of Practice:** Labor, employment and immigration law, OSHA issues **Affiliations:** A.B.A.; S.C.B.A.; O.S.H.A.; Greenville Bar Association **SIC code:** 81 **Address:** Jackson Lewis LLP, 2100 Landmark Bldg., 301 N. Main St., 21st floor, Greenville, SC 29601 **E-mail:** warrens@jacksonlewis.com **Web address:** www.jacksonlewis.com

WEBB III, JOHN G.
Industry: Law **Born:** June 1, 1944, Flint, Michigan **Univ./degree:** B.A., English and French, Davidson College, 1966; J.D., Vanderbilt University, 1970 **Current organization:** JGW in Counsel **Title:** Attorney and Interim Counsel **Type of organization:** Law firm **Major product:** Legal services **Area of distribution:** New Jersey **Area of Practice:** Business Law; Trade Regulation; Employment & Benefits; Business Organizations; Intellectual Property; Mergers & Acquisitions; Negotiating **Published works:** Associate Editor, Vanderbilt Law Review; Executive Editor, Vanderbilt Journal of Transnational Law **Affiliations:** A.B.A.; Association of the Bar of the City of New York; New Jersey State Bar Association; Member & Executive Committee, Dept. of Missions, Episcopal Diocese of Newark; Trustee Secretary, Episcopal Community Development Inc., Newark; Trustee, Secretary, Sussex County Community College Foundation; General Counsel, Secretary, Wheelock, Inc. **SIC code:** 81 **Address:** JGW in Counsel, 500 International Dr. North, Suite 125, Mount Olive, NJ 07828 **E-mail:** webbgc@aol.com **Web address:** www.jgwincounsel.com

WEGER, JAMES E.
Industry: Law **Univ./degree:** J.D., University of Oklahoma, 1982 **Current organization:** Jones Givens **Title:** President **Type of organization:** Law firm **Major product:** Legal services **Area of distribution:** National **Area of Practice:** Commercial litigation **Published works:** Article, American Law Journal **Affiliations:** Tulsa County Bar Association **SIC code:** 81 **Address:** Jones Givens, 3800 First Place Tower, 15 E. Fifth St.,, Tulsa, OK 74103-4309 **E-mail:** jweger@jonesgivens.com **Web address:** www.jonesgivens.com

WEILD III, DAVID
Industry: Law **Born:** March 14, Brooklyn, New York **Univ./degree:** B.A., English, Yale University, 1952; LL.B., Yale Law School, 1959 **Current organization:** Fross Zelnick Lehrman & Zissu **Title:** Partner **Type of organization:** Law firm **Major product:** Legal services **Area of distribution:** New York **Area of Practice:** Intellectual property **Affiliations:** City of New York Bar Association; Federal Bar Council **Hob./spts.:** Music **SIC code:** 81 **Address:** Fross Zelnick Lehrman & Zissu, 866 United Nations Plaza, New York, NY 10017 **E-mail:** dweild@fzlz.com **Web address:** www.fzlz.com

WEIMAR, JAN R.
Industry: Law **Born:** West Palm Beach, Florida **Univ./degree:** B.A., Management Accounting, University of Southern Mississippi **Current organization:** Moyle Flanigan Katz Raymond & Sheehan, P.A. **Title:** Director of Administration **Type of organization:** Law firm **Major product:** Legal services **Area of distribution:** Florida **Area of Practice:** Management **Honors/awards:** Management Committee **Affiliations:** A.L.A.; P.B.C.B.A. **Hob./spts.:** Reading, travel, gardening, hiking **SIC code:** 81 **Address:** Moyle Flanigan Katz Raymond & Sheehan, P.A., 625 N. Flagler Dr., 9th floor, West Palm Beach, FL 33401 **E-mail:** jweimar@moylelaw.com

WEINBERG, MICHAEL A.
Industry: Law **Born:** May 5, 1969, Perth Amboy, New Jersey **Univ./degree:** J.D., Capital University, Columbus, Ohio, 1994 **Current organization:** Weinberg McCormick Chatzinoff & Zoll, PA **Title:** Attorney/Adjunct Professor **Type of organization:** Law firm **Major product:** Legal services **Area of distribution:** New Jersey **Area of Practice:** Matrimonial, employment and civil law **Honors/awards:** Multiple Sclerosis Leadership Class of 2003 **Published works:** Co-author of the Bankruptcy and Divorce chapter in New Jersey Family Law Practice, 2002 edition **Affiliations:** New Jersey Bar Association; Pennsylvania Bar Association.; The Florida Bar; Camden County Bar Association; Chair, Membership Committee, Thomas S. Forkins Inns of Court; Matrimonial Early Settlement Panelist in Burlington and Camden County Superior Courts of New Jersey **Hob./spts.:** Reading, boating, skiing **SIC code:** 81 **Address:** Weinberg McCormick Chatzinoff & Zoll, PA, 109 Haddon Ave., Haddonfield, NJ 08033 **E-mail:** mweinberg@weinbergmccormick.com

WEISS, TERRI
Industry: Law **Born:** October 9, 1957, New York **Univ./degree:** B.S., 1978; J.D., 1981, Georgetown University **Current organization:** Marino & Weiss P.C. **Title:** Partner **Type of organization:** Law firm **Major product:** Legal services **Area of distribution:** White Plains, New York **Area of Practice:** Matrimonial law **Honors/awards:** Leahy Prize, Best Overall Advocate, 1981; "AV" rated, Martindale-Hubbell **Published works:** Member, Editorial Board, A.M.L. Journal; Editorial Board, Matrimonial Strategies **Affiliations:** Fellow, A.A.M.L.; I.A.M.L.; N.Y.S.B.A. **Hob./spts.:** Family **SIC code:** 81 **Address:** Marino & Weiss P.C., 162 Grand St., White Plains, NY 10601 **E-mail:** marweil62@aol.com

WELLS, DAVID M.
Industry: Law **Born:** December 15, 1952, Miami Beach, Florida **Univ./degree:** B.S., Summa Cum Laude, Florida International University, 1977; J.D., Magna Cum Laude, University of Miami School of Law, 1980 **Current organization:** McGuire Woods LLP **Title:** Partner **Type of organization:** Law firm **Major product:** Legal services **Area of distribution:** National **Area of Practice:** General complex litigation, commercial litigation, securities liabilities **Honors/awards:** "AV' rated, Martindale-Hubbell **Affiliations:** A.T.L.A.; A.B.A.; The Florida Bar; Florida Academy of Trial Lawyers **SIC code:** 81 **Address:** McGuire Woods LLP, 50 N. Laura St., Suite 3300, Jacksonville, FL 32201 **E-mail:** dwells@mcguirewoods.com **Web address:** www.mcguirewoods.com

WHEELER, RAYMOND L.
Industry: Law **Born:** Fort Sill, Oklahoma **Univ./degree:** J.D., Harvard University School of Law **Current organization:** Morrison & Foerster **Title:** Esquire **Type of organization:** Law firm **Major product:** Legal services **Area of distribution:** National **Area of Practice:** Labor and employment law **Honors/awards:** Martindale-Hubbell **Affiliations:** A.B.A. **Hob./spts.:** Golf, basketball **SIC code:** 81 **Address:** Morrison & Foerster, 755 Page Mill Rd., Palo Alto, CA 94304-1018 **E-mail:** rwheeler@mofo.com

WHITCHER, LYNN A.
Industry: Law **Born:** August 10, 1972, West Union, Iowa **Univ./degree:** J.D., Southwestern University, 1998 **Current organization:** Van Etten Suzumoto & Becket, LLP **Title:** Associate **Type of organization:** Law firm **Major product:** Legal services **Area of distribution:** National **Area of Practice:** Business litigation **Affiliations:** A.T.L.A.; L.A.C.B.A. **Hob./spts.:** Rock climbing, running **SIC code:** 81 **Address:** Van Etten Suzumoto & Becket, LLP, 1620 26th St., Suite 6000 North, Santa Monica, CA 90404 **E-mail:** lwhitcher@vsblaw.com **Web address:** www.vsblaw.com

WHITE, ANTHONY B.
Industry: Law **Born:** July 31, 1969, New York, New York **Univ./degree:** B.A., Clark University; J.D., Nova Southeastern University **Current organization:** Botsford & White **Title:** Partner **Type of organization:** Law firm **Major product:** Legal services **Area of distribution:** Florida **Area of Practice:** Personal injury, civil litigation **Affiliations:** The Florida Bar; A.T.L.A.; Academy of Florida Trial Lawyers; Million Dollar Advocates Forum **Hob./spts.:** Golf, family **SIC code:** 81 **Address:** Botsford & White, 3595 Sheridan St., #208, Hollywood, FL 33021 **E-mail:** awhite@botsfordwhite.com

WHITE, LARRY JAMES
Industry: Law **Born:** April 17, 1951, Danville, Illinois **Univ./degree:** J.D., University of Illinois, 1976 **Current organization:** Smith, White, Sharma & Halpern **Title:** Attorney/Managing Partner **Type of organization:** Law firm **Major product:** Legal services **Area of distribution:** National **Area of Practice:** Business law and wrongful death/malpractice **Affiliations:** A.T.L.A.; Georgia Banking Association **Hob./spts.:** Golf, horseback riding, music **SIC code:** 81 **Address:** Smith, White, Sharma & Halpern, 1126 Ponce de Leon Ave., Atlanta, GA 30306 **E-mail:** swsh1@aol.com

WIEGAND, KIMBERLEY A.
Industry: Law **Born:** August 9, 1963, Detroit, Michigan **Univ./degree:** J.D., Detroit College of Law, 1990 **Current organization:** U.C.A.T./Kimberley A. Wiegand, PC **Title:** Attorney/President, U.C.A.T. **Type of organization:** Community coalition **Major product:** Legal services **Area of distribution:** Michigan **Area of Practice:** Criminal and family law **Affiliations:** State Bar of Michigan; Macome County Bar Association; Women Lawyer's Association **Hob./spts.:** Community activities, antiquing, gardening **SIC code:** 81 **Address:** U.C.A.T./Kimberley A. Wiegand, PC, 40111 Dodge Park Rd., Sterling Heights, MI 48313 **E-mail:** k_wiegand.ameritech.com

WILL, CLARK B.
Industry: Law **Born:** September 17, 1955, San Antonio, Texas **Univ./degree:** J.D., St. Mary's University, 1980 **Current organization:** Quilling Selander, Cummiskey & Lownds, P.C. **Title:** Shareholder/Partner/Attorney **Type of organization:** Law firm **Major product:** Legal services **Area of distribution:** Dallas, Texas **Area of Practice:** Business and commercial litigation **Affiliations:** State Bar of Texas; Dallas Bar Association **Hob./spts.:** Bird hunting (quail and dove) **SIC code:** 81 **Address:** Quilling Selander, Cummiskey & Lownds, P.C., 2001 Bryan St., Suite 1800, Dallas, TX 75201 **E-mail:** cwill@qsclpc.com **Web address:** www.qsclpc.com/qscl/index_2.htm

WILLBANKS, AMY E.
Industry: Law **Born:** December 21, 1973, Columbus, Ohio **Univ./degree:** J.D., University of South Carolina, 2001 **Current organization:** Michael E. Spears, P.A. **Title:** Associate **Type of organization:** Law firm **Major product:** Legal services **Area of distribution:** National **Area of Practice:** Consumer class action, medical malpractice **Published works:** Article, South Carolina Environmental Law Journal **Affiliations:** Association of Trial Lawyers of America; American Bar Association; South Carolina

Bar Association **Hob./spts.:** Skiing, tennis **SIC code:** 81 **Address:** Michael E. Spears, P.A., 215 Magnolia St., Spartanburg, SC 29306 **E-mail:** awillbanks@aol.com

WILLENBROCK, RONALD C.

Industry: Law **Born:** April 22, 1939, St. Louis, Missouri **Spouse:** Madeleine Zuehlke **Married:** December 20, 1975 **Children:** Jerome, 39; Jeffrey, 38; Monique, 34; Paul J, 33; Cynthia Lee, 30; Jason A, 27 **Univ./degree:** B.S., Business Administration, St. Benedicts College, Kansas, 1961; J.D., St. Louis University, Missouri, 1967 **Current organization:** Amelung, Wulff & Willenbrock, P.C. **Title:** Principal/Treasurer/Board of Directors **Type of organization:** Law firm **Major product:** Legal services **Area of distribution:** National **Area of Practice:** General trial and appellate, insurance coverages and statutory regulations, medical malpractice, products liability, architect/agents/attorneys errors and omissions, worker's compensation law **Honors/awards:** AV Rated, Martindale-Hubbell; Award of Merit, Faculty Trial Practice Institute; Who's Who in American Law **Affiliations:** Insurance Committee, Missouri Bar Association; Federation of Insurance and Corporate Counsel; Insurance Law Committee, Defense Research Institute; International Association of Defense Counsel; Board Member, Missouri Organization of Defense Lawyers; Trial Practice Committee, The Bar Association of Metropolitan St. Louis; Association Internationale de Droit de Assurances; Past President, Association of Defense Counsel of St. Louis; Lawyer Association of St. Louis; The Bar Association of St. Louis County; American Judicature Society; General Chairman, Regional Disciplinary Committee for Region XI; Board Member, The Players Club at St. Louis **Hob./spts.:** Golf, trap shooting **SIC code:** 81 **Address:** Amelung, Wulff & Willenbrock, P.C., 515 Olive St., 17th floor, St. Louis, MO 63101-1839 **E-mail:** rcw@awwstl.com

WILLIS, DAVID L.

Industry: Law **Born:** December 31, 1959, San Antonio, Texas **Univ./degree:** J.D., Southern Methodist University **Current organization:** Willis & Wilkins, LLP **Title:** Attorney at Law **Type of organization:** Law firm **Major product:** Legal services **Area of distribution:** Texas **Area of Practice:** Family law, child custody **Affiliations:** State Bar of Texas, Family Law Section; San Antonio Family Law Section; State Bar of Texas; San Antonio Bar Association **Hob./spts.:** Saltwater fishing, golf **SIC code:** 81 **Address:** Willis & Wilkins, LLP, 100 W. Houston St., Suite 1275, San Antonio, TX 78205 **E-mail:** dwillis@stic.net

WILSON, BRENT L.

Industry: Law **Born:** January 1, 1952, New Orleans, Louisiana **Univ./degree:** B.A., Morehouse College, 1973; J.D., University of Georgia, State University of New York at Buffalo, 1976 **Current organization:** Elarbee, Thompson, Sapp & Wilson **Title:** Partner **Type of organization:** Law firm **Major product:** Counseling, trial and appellate practice **Area of distribution:** National **Area of Practice:** Labor relations, employment discrimination law (management exclusively) **Honors/awards:** Named Americas Top Black Lawyers by Black Enterprise Magazine, November Issue **Published works:** Several articles published in Journal of Legal Medicine, interviews; Associate Editor, The Developing Labor Law **Affiliations:** N.E.L.C.; A.B.A.; S.H.R.M.; N.A.A.C.P.; State Bar of Georgia, Co-chair, Georgia Diversity Program; Boys & Girls Clubs of Metro Atlanta; Omega Psi Phi; Phi Alpha Delta; 100 Blackmen of America **Hob./spts.:** Travel, spectator sports **SIC code:** 81 **Address:** Elarbee, Thompson, Sapp & Wilson, 229 Peachtree St. N.E., Suite 800, Atlanta, GA 30303 **E-mail:** bwilson@etsw.com **Web address:** www.etsw.com

WINICK, ANDREW M.

Industry: Law **Born:** June 30, 1970, New York, New York **Univ./degree:** J.D., University of Baltimore School of Law **Current organization:** Brown, Diffenderfer, Kearney LLP **Title:** Esquire **Type of organization:** Law firm **Major product:** Legal services **Area of distribution:** Baltimore, Maryland **Area of Practice:** General litigation, corporate law, contract negotiations, mergers and acquisitions **Affiliations:** Maryland State Bar Association **Hob./spts.:** Skiing, golf, softball **SIC code:** 81 **Address:** Brown, Diffenderfer, Kearney, LLP, 1010 Hull St., Suite 300, Tide Building, Baltimore, MD 21230 **E-mail:** awinick@bdklaw.com

WOOD, ROBERT C.C.

Industry: Law **Univ./degree:** J.D., S.M.U., 1982 **Current organization:** Law Offices of Robert Wood **Title:** J.D. **Type of organization:** Law firm **Major product:** Legal services **Area of distribution:** Texas **Area of Practice:** Corporate litigation **Published works:** Articles **Affiliations:** P.B.A., S.B.T.; Past Board Member, American Cancer Society; Board Member, Crusade Committee, M.E.D.I.S.E.N.D. **Hob./spts.:** Golf, skiing, photography **SIC code:** 81 **Address:** Law Offices of Robert Wood, 5005 Greenville Ave., Suite 200, Dallas, TX 75260 **E-mail:** rccwood@aol.com

WOODS, PAMELA A.

Industry: Law **Univ./degree:** R.N., Bloomfield College, 1989; M.S., Seton Hall University, 1992; J.D., Seton Hall School of Law, 2002 **Current organization:** Drazin & Warshaw **Title:** R.N., J.D. **Type of organization:** Law firm **Major product:** Legal services related to healthcare **Area of distribution:** New Jersey **Area of Practice:** Toxic tort, product liability, nursing home litigation **Affiliations:** A.T.L.A.; E.N.A.; A.B.A.; T.A.N.A.; Monmouth County Bar Association **Hob./spts.:** Martial arts (karate) **SIC code:** 81 **Address:** Drazin & Warshaw, 25 Reckless Place, Red Bank, NJ 07701 **E-mail:** pamw@drazinandwarshaw.com

YAMATE, NOREEN Q.

Industry: Law **Born:** October 16, 1968, Taiwan **Univ./degree:** B.A., English/Asian American, University of California at Berkeley J.D., Santa Clara School of Law, 1994 **Current organization:** McQuaid, Metzler, Bedford & Van Zandt LLP **Title:** Attorney **Type of organization:** Law firm **Major product:** Legal services **Area of distribution:** California **Area of Practice:** Environmental and product liability law **Published works:** Write-ups **Affiliations:** State Bar of California; San Francisco Bar Association **Hob./spts.:** Skiing **SIC code:** 81 **Address:** McQuaid, Metzler, Bedford & Van Zandt, LLP, 221 Main St., 16th floor, San Francisco, CA 94105 **E-mail:** nyamate@mmmvz.com **Web address:** www.mmbvz.com

YETTER, RICHARD

Industry: Law **Born:** March 14, 1929, Rockledge, Pennsylvania **Univ./degree:** B.S., Pennsylvania State University, 1951; J.D., Marquette University,1960 **Current organization:** Law Offices of Richard Yetter **Title:** Attorney **Type of organization:** Law firm **Major product:** Legal services **Area of Practice:** Probate, wills and estate planning **Affiliations:** U.S. Air Force Special Weapons Officer, 1951-1960; State Bar of Texas; State Bar of Wisconsin; Federal Bar of West Texas; Federal Bar of Eastern Wisconsin; The Salvation Army; United Methodist Church; Military Order of World Wars **Hob./spts.:** Family, walking **SIC code:** 81 **Address:** Law Offices of Richard Yetter, 6070 Gateway Blvd. East, Suite 501, El Paso, TX 79905

YOUNG, PENNY R.

Industry: Law **Born:** May 25, 1969, Martinsburg, West Virginia **Current organization:** Santa Barbara Law Offices, P.L.L.C. **Title:** Paralegal **Type of organization:** Law firm **Major product:** Legal services **Area of distribution:** Martinsburg, West Virginia **Area of Practice:** Personal injury, litigation **Affiliations:** West Virginia Trial Lawyers Association; Association of Trial Lawyers of America; Association of West Virginia Paralegals **Hob./spts.:** Knitting, family time **SIC code:** 81 **Address:** Santa Barbara Law Offices, P.L.L.C., 518 W. Stephen St., Martinsburg, WV 25401 **E-mail:** pyoung9900@aol.com and Pyoung@sblawoffice.com **Web address:** www.sblawoffice.com

ZAMBITO, PETER J.

Industry: Law **Born:** September 14, 1935, Manhattan, New York **Univ./degree:** B.A., History, St. Bonaventure University, 1957; J.D., Fordham Law School, 1961 **Current organization:** Dougherty Ryan Giuffra Zambito & Hession **Title:** Partner, Esquire **Type of organization:** Law firm **Major product:** Legal services **Area of distribution:** International **Area of Practice:** Admiralty law **Affiliations:** New York State Bar (Second Dept.); U.S. Court of Appeals, Second Circuit; Supreme Court of the United States; Maritime Law Association of the United States **Hob./spts.:** Eucharistic Minister; Teacher, Confraternity of Christian Doctrine Sts. John & Paul R.C. Church Larchmont, NY 10538; former volunteer attorney for Town of Mamaroneck, NY Volunteer Fire Department; sports; movie buff **SIC code:** 81 **Address:** Dougherty Ryan Giuffra Zambito & Hession, 131 East 38th St., New York, NY 10016 **E-mail:** drgzh@aol.com/peterzambito@aol.com

The Educational Fields

ABBAS, MONTASIR M.

Industry: Education **Univ./degree:** Ph.D., Civil Engineering, Purdue University, 2001 **Current organization:** Texas Transportation Institute, Texas A&M University **Title:** Research Supervisor/Assistant Research Scientist **Type of organization:** University **Major product:** Higher education, research **Area of distribution:** International **Expertise:** Engineering, software **Published works:** 3 journals, 5 CD's **Affiliations:** I.T.E.; A.S.C.E.; C.I.G.M.A.X.I. **Hob./spts.:** Music, poetry, martial arts **SIC code:** 82 **Address:** Texas Transportation Institute, Texas A&M University, CE/TTI Bldg., Suite 310C, College Station, TX 77843-3155 **E-mail:** m-abbas@tamu.edu

ACHOLONU, ALEXANDER D.W.

Industry: Education **Born:** November 30, 1932, Imo State, Nigeria **Univ./degree:** B.S., Howard University, 1958; M.S., Prairie View A&M University, 1961; Ph.D., Colorado State University, 1964; Continuing Education Certificate, Tulane University, School of Public Health, Tropical Medicine and Hygiene, 1994 **Current organization:** Alcorn State University **Title:** PhD, FAS, OON, Professor **Type of organization:** University **Major product:** Higher education **Area of distribution:** Alcorn State, Mississippi **Expertise:** Parasitology, microbiology **Honors/awards:** Top 100 Educators of 2005; International Educators of the Year, 2003; 2000 Outstanding Intellectuals of the 21st Century, 2002 ,U.K.; Cited as a Great Mind of the 21st Century; Universal Award of Accomplishment; Who's Who of American Teachers, 2005; President, Sigma XI Research Honor Society, Southern University Chapter, 1968-69; Beta Beta Beta Biological Honor Society **Published works:** 80+ scientific publications, 2 books, 1 booklet, 4 book chapters **Affiliations:** Vice Chair, Mississippi Academy of Sciences, Zoology and Entomology Section; American Ecological Society; American Society of Parasitologists; Council Member, Executive Board, World Federation of Parasitologists; Nigerian Association of Medical Scientists; Science Association of Nigeria; Nigerian Society for Microbiology; American Society of Parasitologists; Mississippi Academy of Sciences; Ecological Society of America; National Association of African American Studies **Hob./spts.:** Physical fitness, photography, dancing **SIC code:** 82 **Address:** Alcorn State University, Dept. of Biological Science, 1000 ASU Dr., #843, Alcorn State, MS 39096 **E-mail:** chiefacholonu@yahoo.com

ADEL, MIAH M.

Industry: Education **Born:** February 16, 1952, Bhitorbhag, Natore, Bangladesh **Univ./degree:** B.Sc. with Honors, Physics, 1972; M.Sc., Nuclear and Particle Physics, 1974, Rajshahi University, Rajshahi, Bangladesh; Attended American University of Beirut, Lebanon for Nuclear Physics, 1978-80; Ph.D., Space Physics, Louisiana State University, 1988 **Current organization:** University of Arkansas at Pine Bluff **Title:** Ph.D., Professor **Type of organization:** University **Major product:** Higher education, research **Area of distribution:** International **Expertise:** Teaching and research in space, water, air, earth and environmental sciences **Honors/awards:** Outstanding Established Faculty Award for scholarly activities, 2003; Newcomer Award, University of Arkansas at Pine Bluff for outstanding performance in research and other scholarly activities; NATO Fellowship, the NATO Advanced Study Institute in Genesis and Propagation of Cosmic Rays, Ericc, Sicily, Italy **Published works:** 2 books authored "An International Guide to Crescent Sighting"; "Climaice Changes in Northwest Bangladesh (Bengali)". Numerous other publications including: M.M. Adel, "Man-made climatic changes in the Ganges basin", International Journal of Climatology, 22,993-1016, 2002; M.M. Adel, "Chemical agents incineration exhaust fallout and effects", Management of Environmental Quality: An International Journal, Vol. 15 No. 6, 629-655 **Affiliations:** A.C.P.O.; W.F.S.; A.G.U.; WFS; A.M.A.A.S.-U.S.A., Pine Bluff, Arkansas; Emerald Literati Club **Hob./spts.:** Gardening, swimming, writing, troubleshooting electronic equipment **SIC code:** 82 **Address:** University of Arkansas at Pine Bluff, 1200 North University Dr., Pine Bluff, AR 71601 **E-mail:** miah_m@uapb.edu **Web address:** www.uapb.edu

AKER, RUTH B.

Industry: Education **Born:** February 6, 1921, Seymour, Tennessee **Univ./degree:** B.S.,Elementary Education, Lincoln Memorial University, 1966 **Title:** Teacher **Type of organization:** High school **Major product:** Secondary school education **Area of distribution:** Knoxville, Tennessee **Expertise:** Teaching **Affiliations:** Senior Citizens League; Council for Government Reform **Hob./spts.:** Reading **SIC code:** 82 **Address:** Love Tower, 1171 Armstrong Ave. Apt. 210, Knoxville, TN 37917

AKERS, ARTHUR

Industry: Education **Born:** March 27, 1927, Smethwick, England **Univ./degree:** B.S., Physics and Mathematics, 1953; Ph.D., Mechanical Engineering, 1969, University of London **Current organization:** Iowa State University **Title:** Ph.D. **Type of organization:** University **Major product:** Higher education **Area of distribution:** International **Expertise:** Aerospace engineering, mechanical engineering **Published works:** 100+ articles, 3 books **Affiliations:** Fellow, Royal Aeronautical Society; F.A.S.M.E. **Hob./spts.:** Music, hiking **SIC code:** 82 **Address:** 1519 Stone Brooke Rd., Ames, IA 50010 **E-mail:** aakers@iastate.edu

ALEXENKO, ANDREI P.

Industry: Research **Univ./degree:** M.S., Biochemistry, Moscow State University, USSR, 1981; Ph.D., Biology, Institute of Genetics and Selection of Industrial Microorganisms, Moscow, Russia, 1991 **Current organization:** University of Missouri-Columbia **Title:** Ph.D., Research Assistant Professor **Type of organization:** University **Major product:** Research **Area of distribution:** National **Expertise:** Molecular biology, biochemistry **Published works:** Numerous refereed articles, including; Parent, J., Villeneuve, C., Alexenko, A.P., Ealy, A.D. and Fortier, M.A. (2002) Biol. Reprod., 68, 1035-1043; Rosenfeld, C.-S., Alexenko, A.P., Spencer, T.E. and Roberts, R.M. (2002) Biol. Reprod., 67, 847-853; Ealy, A.D., Larson, S.F., Liu, L., Alexenko, A.P., Winkelman, G.L., Kubisch, H.M., Bixby, J.A. and Roberts, R.M. (2001) Endocrinology, 142, 2906-2915; Alexenko, A.P., Ealy, A.D., Bixby, J.A. and Roberts, R. M. (2000) J. Interferon Cytokine Res., 20, 817-22; Arnold, D.R., Binelli, M., Vok, J., Alexenko, A.P., Drost, M. C.J. and Thatcher, W.W. (2000) Domest. Anim. Ednocrinol., 18, 199-216 **Affiliations:** American Society for Biochemistry and Molecular Biology (ASBMB); American Chemical Society (ACS); International Society for Interferon and Cytokine Research (ISICR) **SIC code:** 82 **Address:** University of Missouri-Columbia, 158 Animal Science Research Center, 920 E. Campus Dr.,, Columbia, MO 65211-0001 **E-mail:** alexenkoa@missouri.edu

ALFONSI, FERDINANDO P.

Industry: Education **Born:** October 10, 1928, Arquata del Tronto (AP), Italy **Univ./degree:** M.A., American Literature, Villanova University, 1967; Ph.D., Italian/Comparative Literature, Catholic University, Washington, D.C., 1970 **Current organization:** Fordham University **Title:** Professor/Author **Type of organization:** University **Major product:** Higher education **Area of distribution:** International **Expertise:** Comparative literature: novel, poetry **Published works:** Books: "Alberto Moravia in America: un quarantennio di critica", (1929, 1969). Pp. 176. Catanzaro: Antonio Carello Editore, 1984; "Verso il mare/Toward the Sea", Pp. 120. Catanzaro: Antonio Carello Editore, 1987; "Dictionary of Italo-American Poets" Pp. 164. New York: Peter Lang Publishing, 1989; "Ignazio Silone o della ricerca del permanente. Saggi", Catanzaro: Antonio Carello Editore, 1991. Pp. 96. Articles: "L'elemento sessuale nelle opere di Alberto Moravia giudicato dalla critica americana", Italica, XLIX (Summer 1972), 218-228; "Introduzione" to Luigi Cagliani", Il fiume/The River. Catanzaro: Antonio Carello Editore, 1984; "La poetessa Rose Romano", La Follia, Novembre-Dicembre 1991, p.8; "Pino Lombardi", La Follia, 100 (Gennaio-Febrraio 1992), 18-19; "L'Italese", Almanacco, II (No. 1, primavera 1992), 6-23; "La donna nell'opera di Silone", Il Ponte italo-americano, (Nov-Dic. 1993), 8-9; Reviews: Review in "Italica", L(Spring 1973), 105-108. Vanna Gazzola Stacchini, "La narrativa di Vitaliano Brancati" (Criticism). Firenze: Olschky, 1970; Review in "La Follia", (Settembre-Ottobre 1993), 12-13. Joseph Papaleo, "Picasso at 91" (Harriman: Seaport Poets and Writers Press, 1987); **Affiliations:** American Association of Teachers of Italian; American Association of University Professors **Hob./spts.:** Designing houses **SIC code:** 82 **Address:** 211-65 23rd Ave., Apt. 2H, Bayside, NY 11360-1935 **E-mail:** sanalfonsi@aol.com

ALFONSO, CARMEN J.

Industry: Education **Univ./degree:** M.A., Education, Nova University, 2003 **Current organization:** St. Michael the Archangel School **Title:** Principal **Type of organization:** School **Major product:** Secondary school education **Area of distribution:** Miami, Florida **Expertise:** Administration **Affiliations:** National Association of Secondary School Principals **SIC code:** 82 **Address:** St. Michael the Archangel School, 300 NW 28th Ave., Miami, FL 33125 **E-mail:** calfonso@churchofstmichael.org

ALQADI-SHARARI, SAWSAN

Industry: Education **Born:** May 9, 1965, Kuwait **Univ./degree:** M.A., St. Joseph's University, Lebanon 1992 **Current organization:** MIT/MIT Careers Office **Title:** Computer Administrative Assistant **Type of organization:** University **Major product:** Higher education **Area of distribution:** Massachusetts **Expertise:** Management; teaches Arabic and Middle Eastern cooking **Hob./spts.:** Reading, cooking, travel, website design **SIC code:** 82 **Address:** MIT/MIT Careers Office, 77 Massachusetts Ave. 12-170, Cambridge, MA 02139 **E-mail:** ssharari@mit.edu

AL-SALEM, SALIM S.

Industry: Medical **Born:** December 12, 1940, Jordan **Spouse:** Firdous Butt **Children:** Mohd Osama, MD; Asma, RN; Nurmeen; Shereen; 4 grandchildren **Univ./degree:** M.D., King Edward Medical College, Lahore, Pakistan; Board Certified, Psychiatry; Board Certified, Forensic Medicine **Current organization:** New York Medical College

Title: Psychiatrist/Assistant Professor **Type of organization:** Medical college, hospital **Major product:** Education/healthcare, as a Clinical Assistant Professor/Attending Psychiatrist **Area of distribution:** New York **Expertise:** Psychiatry, forensic medicine **Affiliations:** American Psychiatric Association; Forensic Medicine Association **Hob./spts.:** Jogging, reading **SIC code:** 82 **Address:** New York Medical College, 1901 First Ave., 9W, New York, NY 10029 **Phone:** (212)423-7149 **Fax:** (212)423-8604 **E-mail:** DoctorSalim@aol.com

ANANIAS, JOSÉ

Industry: Education **Born:** August 17, 1929, New York, New York **Univ./degree:** B.A., Political Science, Morehouse College, 1951; M.Ed., City University of New York, 1968 **Current organization:** New York City Board of Education **Title:** School Administrator/Supervisor (Retired) **Type of organization:** Education system **Major product:** Education **Area of distribution:** New York City **Expertise:** Historical writing, lecturing **Honors/awards:** Included in the IBC, International Awards Roster for Lifetime Achievement Award, World Congress of the Arts, Sciences and Communications, 2005; American Medal of Honor, 2002; Listed, the Dictionary of International Biography, 33rd edition, 2006; Delegate to the Inaugural World Forum, St. Catherine's College, Oxford University, England, 2006; Legion of Honor Medal, United Cultural Convention, American Biographical Institute, 2005; Appointed Honorary Director-General, the Americas of the International Biographical Centre, Cambridge, England, 2005; Awarded Ambassadorship, Inaugural World Forum, St. Catherine's College, Oxford, England **Published works:** Manuscript, "History of the Harlem YMCA" **Affiliations:** Harlem YMCA Board of Managers; Service Officer, Veterans of Foreign Wars; American Biographical Institute; International Biographical Centre, Cambridge, England **Hob./spts.:** Spectator sports, jazz **SIC code:** 82 **Address:** 1600 S. Valley View Blvd., Bldg. 11, #1074, Las Vegas, NV 89102 **E-mail:** ananias@iamcarefree.zzn.com **Web address:** www.marquiswhoswho.net/joseananias/

ANDREWS, BILLY F.

Industry: Medical **Born:** September 22, 1932, Graham, North Carolina **Univ./degree:** M.D., Duke University, 1957 **Current organization:** University of Louisville School of Medicine **Title:** Professor Emeritus/Chairman, Dept. of Pediatrics **Type of organization:** University hospital **Major product:** Children's healthcare **Area of distribution:** International **Expertise:** Pediatrics, neonatology, metabolism; nutrition, medical ethics: children's rights, organ transplantation, medical history: pediatrics and Sir William Osler **Honors/awards:** Service Award, University of Louisville, 1989; Member, The Order of International Fellowship, Pro Bono Publico (Cambridge); The International Order of Merit in "Excellentia" (Cambridge); Twentieth Century Award for Achievement, International Biographical Centre, 1996; Twentieth Century Achievement Award, American Biographical Institute, 1997; Alpha Omega Alpha; Clinical Research Award, Kentucky Medical Association, 1971; Visiting Fellow, Green College, Oxford, 1988; Educational Achievement Award, 1997; Who's Who in America; Who's Who in the World; Who's Who in Intellectuals; Who's Who in Technology; Who's Who in Science and Engineering; Who's Who in Health Care; Outstanding Educators of America; The Best Doctors in the U.S.; American Men and Women of Science; Who's Who of Business Leaders; International Who's Who in Medicine; Who's Who in Editors, Writers and Poets; Who's Who in Poetry; Distinguished Alumnus, Wake Forest University, 1983; Wisdom Award of Honor, 1991; The Winston Churchill Medal, The Wisdom Society **Published works:** 8 books on medicine and other areas, 200 articles and abstracts **Affiliations:** Fellow, American College of Physicians; Fellow, American Academy of Pediatrics; Fellow, Royal Society of Medicine; Fellow, The Wisdom Society; Fellow, The International Biographical Association; American Pediatric Society, Society for Pediatric Research, American Osler Society, Irish and American Pediatric Society, American Society of Law, Medicine and Ethics; International Association of Bioethics; American Society for Bioethics and Humanities; American Academy of Pediatrics Section on Bioethics **Hob./spts.:** Gardening, poetry **SIC code:** 82 **Address:** University of Louisville School of Medicine, Dept. of Pediatrics, 571 S. Floyd St., Suite 449, Louisville, KY 40202 **E-mail:** sahabb01@gwise.louisville.edu

ANTONIO, ROCIO

Industry: Education **Born:** November 15, 1966, Tuxpan, Mexico **Univ./degree:** M.A., Escuela Normal Superior **Title:** English Teacher **Type of organization:** Junior high school **Major product:** Education **Area of distribution:** McAllen, Texas **Expertise:** English **Hob./spts.:** Swimming, folklore dancing **SIC code:** 82 **Address:** 3218 Daytona Ave., McAllen, TX 78503 **E-mail:** rocioantonio@yahoo.com

APPEDDU, LISA A.

Industry: Education **Born:** September 19, 1970, Perrysburg, Ohio **Univ./degree:** B.S., Agriculture,1992; M.S., Animal Science, 1994, University of Kentucky; Ph.D., New Mexico State University, 1999 **Current organization:** SWOSU Allied Health **Title:** Assistant Professor **Type of organization:** University **Major product:** Higher education **Area of distribution:** Oklahoma **Expertise:** Animal science education, physiology, microbiology, nutrition **Honors/awards:** Faculty Member of the Year, by student vote, SWOSU, 2006; Congressional Science Fellowship, 1998-2000 **Published works:** 8+ technical papers on animal nutrition **Affiliations:** American Society of Animal Science; Educators' Leadership Academy **Hob./spts.:** Riding horseback, fitness instructor, tennis, travel **SIC code:** 82 **Address:** SWOSU Allied Health, 100 Campus Dr., Weatherford, OK 73096 **E-mail:** lisa.appeddu@swosu.edu **Web address:** www.swosu.edu/alliedhealth

ARCE COLÓN, JOSÉ A.

Industry: Education **Born:** April 29, 1959, San Sebastian, Puerto Rico **Univ./degree:** M.A., Interamericana of Puerto Rico, 1999 **Current organization:** EDP College of Puerto Rico **Title:** Computer Coordinator **Type of organization:** College **Major product:** Higher education **Area of distribution:** Puerto Rico **Expertise:** Computer programming **Honors/awards:** Professor of the Year, 2000 **Affiliations:** A.B.S.A.E. **Hob./spts.:** Family activities, travel, swimming **SIC code:** 82 **Address:** EDP College of Puerto Rico, P.O. Box 1674, San Sebastian, PR 00685 **E-mail:** jarce59@cooui.net **Web address:** www.edpcollege.com

ASGARY, NADER H.

Industry: Education **Born:** October 19, 1948. Ishafan, Iran **Univ./degree:** B.S., Civil Engineering, Texas A&M University, 1978; Ph.D., Economics, University of Houston, 1991 **Current organization:** SUNY Geneseo, Jones School of Business **Title:** Ph.D./Director of Center for International Business **Type of organization:** University **Major product:** Educational services **Area of distribution:** International **Expertise:** International business, economics, finance, globalization policies, civil engineering, project management and education **Honors/awards:** International lecturer on globalization and international economics **Published works:** Several articles and papers **Affiliations:** A.E.A.; I.T.F.A., Business Association of Latin America, Rochester Chamber of Commerce **Hob./spts.:** Basketball, running, swimming, reading, travel **SIC code:** 82 **Address:** Nader Asgary, Ph.D., 1 College Circle, Geneseo, NY 14454 **E-mail:** nader@geneseo.edu **Web address:** www.geneseo.edu

ASHLAY, PAMLA M.

Industry: Education **Born:** April 21, 1949, Owatonna, Minnesota **Spouse:** James McPherson **Married:** September 23, 2006 **Children:** Robert Lewis Twedt, 1974 **Univ./degree:** Morris Pratt Institute; General, Civil Litigation, Real Estate, Corporate, Wills, Trusts & Estates Law Paralegal Degrees, Prof. Career Development Inst.; B.A., Religious Studies, College of Spiritual Science, 1995; University of WI, 2000 **Current organization:** Morris Pratt Institute Association **Title:** Executive Corporate Secretary **Type of organization:** Religious school/seminary **Major product:** Religious education **Area of distribution:** International **Expertise:** Teaching; Mediumship Certification, 1989; Commissioned Healer Certification, 1989; National Spiritualist Teacher Degree, 1990; Ordination, 1990; Missionary, 1992-Present; Reiki I and II Certification; Public Speaking **Published works:** Numerous including- Author, 5 books including "The Soul Book"; "Age of Oneness-A Michael Book"; "The Miracle of the I AM"; Author of 14 Books of Universal Knowledge; articles; compiled a workbook; wrote NSAC Code of Ethics, 2002-2003; public appearances on local and national radio talk shows **Affiliations:** A.A.L.C.U.; National Association of Parliamentarians; National Association of Churches; Public service and volunteer work many organizations including 23 MN Police Depts., the F.B.I.; Bureau of Criminal Apprehension; Suicide Hot Line, Rape Center, Cub Scouts; Board Positions held include- President, Institute of Metaphysical Science; Trustee, Minnesota State Spiritualist Association; Vice President, Mississippi Valley Camp Association; Vice President, Ministerial Association; President, Stow Memorial Foundation; Secretary, Western Wisconsin Camp Association; Trustee, Mississippi Valley Camp Association **Career accomplishments:** Founder and President, Institute of Metaphysical Science; Founded All One Journey, a publishing company for self-publishing books and papers **Hob./spts.:** Reading **SIC code:** 82 **Address:** Morris Pratt Institute Association, 11811 Watertown Plank Rd., Milwaukee, WI 53226 **E-mail:** pamlaashlay@yahoo.com

AU, CHING

Industry: Education/Engineering **Born:** Hong Kong **Univ./degree:** B.Eng. (1st Hon.), Hong Kong Polytechnic University, 1999; S.M., Massachusetts Institute of Technology, 2001; Ph.D., Massachusetts Institute of Technology, 2004 **Current organization:** Massachusetts Institute of Technology **Title:** Graduate Researcher **Type of organization:** University **Major product:** Higher education, research **Area of distribution:** International **Expertise:** Civil/Structural/Material Engineering analysis and design **Honors/awards:** MIT Research Fellowship; China Synergy Program for Outstanding Youth; Sir Edward Youde Memorial Scholar; AIA Foundation Scholar; Bishop Baker Memorial Scholar **Published works:** Analysis & Design of Steel Egg-Shaped Digester; Behavior of FRP-Confined Concrete; Non-Destructive Evaluation of FRP-Confined Concrete Using Microwaves; Use of Advanced Composites in MAGLEV Guideway Systems **Affiliations:** A.S.C.E.; B.S.C.E.; Sigma Xi **Hob./spts.:** Golf, tennis, travel **SIC code:** 82 **Address:** Massachusetts Institute of Technology, Dept. of Civil & Environmental Engineering, 77 Massachusetts Ave., Room 1-053, Cambridge, MA 02139 **E-mail:** auching@mit.edu **Web address:** web.mit.edu

AUCELLA, LAURENCE F.

Industry: Education, research **Born:** July 24, 1959, Waterbury, Connecticut **Univ./degree:** B.A., Behavioral Science, Edu., Anna Maria College, 1982; M.Ed., Dev. and Edu. Psych, Boston College, 1984; CAS, 6th Yr. Counseling, Univ. of Bridgeport, 1992; M.S., Research & Measurement, Southern CT State U., 1996; Ed.D., U. of Bridgeport, 1997 **Current organization:** Crosby High School **Title:** School Counselor **Type of organization:** High school **Major product:** Education, research **Area of distribution:** Waterbury, Connecticut **Expertise:** Counseling, research **Published works:** "Cerebral Dominance, English as a Second Language, Methodologies, Theory, Learning and Acquisition for the Adult ESL Student", 1997, Description: xi, 247 p.: tables, figures; 23cm, Note: Includes bibliographical references p. 239-247, Subject: Cerebral dominance, OCLC # ocm39113526; "Principles of Cerebral Lateralization" (a work in progress) **Affiliations:** A.P.A.; A.C.A.; A.S.A.; President of La Casa Bienvenida in Waterbury, CT; Adjunct Faculty (teaches Thesis Proposal), Albertus Magnus College, New Haven, CT; School Counselor in E.S.L. Program, Waterbury Adult Education, Waterbury, CT **Career accomplishments:** Providing the optimal guidance and knowledge of the entire life development in terms of biological, psychological, spiritual, emotional and philosophical, as it is essential for the school counselor to recognize that organisms react as a whole **Hob./spts.:** Reading, book collecting **SIC code:** 82 **Address:** 90 Oakleaf Dr., Waterbury, CT 06708 **E-mail:** aucella_laurence@hotmail.com

AVERETT-BREWER, ARLENE

Industry: Education **Born:** April 18, 1938, Columbia, Mississippi **Univ./degree:** B.S., Child Development, University of Southern Mississippi, 2004 **Current organization:** Pearl River Opportunity Head Start **Title:** Administrator **Type of organization:** School **Major product:** Childhood education **Area of distribution:** Columbia, Mississippi **Expertise:** Administration, oversight of operations **Honors/awards:** LZ Blankenship Award **Affiliations:** National Association of Education of Young Children **Hob./spts.:** Cooking, visiting the sick **SIC code:** 82 **Address:** Pearl River Opportunity Head Start, 1211 Martin Luther King Dr., Columbia, MS 39429 **E-mail:** arleneaverettbrewer.netzero.net **Web address:** www.prvoinc.org

BABAR, ALMAS

Industry: Education **Univ./degree:** M.S.; Ph.D., St. John's University **Current organization:** AMS College of Pharmacy, Long Island University **Title:** Professor of Pharmaceutics and Industrial Pharmacy **Type of organization:** College **Major product:** Higher education **Area of distribution:** International **Expertise:** Product formulations, cosmetic toiletry, aerosal and pharmaceutical products **Published works:** National and international journals **Affiliations:** Society of Cosmetic Chemists; American Association of the Advancement of Science; American Association of Pharmaceutical Scientists **Hob./spts.:** Music, literature, sports **SIC code:** 82 **Address:** AMS College of Pharmacy, Long Island University, 75 DeKalb Ave., Brooklyn, NY 11201 **E-mail:** almas.babar@liu-edu

BABCOCK, GEORGE F.

Industry: Education **Born:** January 20, 1948, Buffalo, New York **Univ./degree:** Ph.D., Immunology, University of Nebraska Medical School **Current organization:** University of Cincinnati, School of Medicine **Title:** Professor **Type of organization:** University **Major product:** Research and education **Area of distribution:** Ohio **Expertise:** Immunology **Affiliations:** A.A.A.I. **Hob./spts.:** Reading, skiing, scuba diving **SIC code:** 82 **Address:** University of Cincinnati, School of Medicine, 241 Bethesda Ave., Cincinnati, OH 45267-0558 **E-mail:** babcocgf@email.uc.edu

BABU, SUNIL

Industry: Medical **Univ./degree:** M.D., St. Johns Medical College, India, 1996 **Current organization:** New York Medical College **Title:** Assistant Professor/Medical Director **Type of organization:** Medical college **Major product:** Medical education, healthcare **Area of distribution:** New York **Expertise:** Internal medicine; Certified, Corrections Healthcare **Affiliations:** A.M.A.; American College of Physicians **SIC code:** 82 **Address:** New York Medical College, Room 256, Munger Pavilion, Valhalla, NY 10595 **E-mail:** babusunilmail@yahoo.com

BAGHAI-RIDING, NINA L.

Industry: Education **Born:** Pittsburgh, Pennsylvania, 1954 **Univ./degree:** B.S., Geology, 1978; B.S., Botany, 1979, University of Wyoming; M.S., Geology, University of Idaho, 1983; Ph.D., Botany, University of Texas, 1996 **Current organization:** Delta State University **Title:** Associate Professor of Biology and Environmental Science **Type of organization:** University **Major product:** Higher education **Area of distribution:** Mississippi **Expertise:** Biology, paleontology; Teaching biology, general botany, physical geology, environmental geology **Honors/awards:** 2nd Congressional District Award 2005 with Community Pride Grant **Published works:** Publications in American Journal of Botany, Journal of Paleontology, Palaois **Affiliations:** American Association of Stratigraphic Palynologists; Geological Society of America; Botanical Society of America; Sigma Xi; Phi Kappa Phi **Hob./spts.:** Playing the pipe organ, travel, basketball, baseball **SIC code:** 82 **Address:** Delta State University, Div. of Biological & Physical Sciences, P.O. Box 3262, Cleveland, MS 38733 **E-mail:** nbaghai@deltastate.edu

BAICY, JANET KAREN

Industry: Medical **Born:** October 2, 1944 **Univ./degree:** M.S., University of California at Los Angeles, 1971 **Current organization:** Langston University **Title:** Nursing Faculty **Type of organization:** University **Major product:** Nursing education **Area of distribution:** Tulsa, Oklahoma **Expertise:** Advance concept medical cardiology **Hob./spts.:** Horseback riding, gardening, reading **SIC code:** 82 **Address:** Langston University, 3701-A S. Harvard, #319, Tulsa, OK 74135 **E-mail:** scapemay@aol.com

BAILEY II, JAMES B.

Industry: Education/Communications **Born:** April, 17, 1957, Denver, Colorado **Spouse:** Susan Elizabeth Miller **Married:** December 17, 1983 **Children:** Alison O., 19; Trisha A., 18 **Univ./degree:** Business/Education, Western State College, 1977; Federal Aviation Administration Airframe and Powerplant Mechanic licensed Emily Griffith Opportunity School, 1980 **Current organization:** Denver Public Schools Transportation **Title:** Communications Technician Chief **Type of organization:** Large City (Denver) public schools system **Major product:** Transportation, safety and security services; elementary and secondary schools education communication needs **Area of distribution:** Denver, Colorado **Expertise:** Technician (two-way communications); FCC Licensed with Radar Endorsement 1983; Certified NABER Technician 1984; Senior Member, ACT 1988; PCIA Certified Communications Technician 2000; A plus Computer Certified; Maintain Large School public two-way communications systems - currently working on a new radio network to connect all Denver Public Schools to a central security dispatch center and construction of a new Transportation Dispatch Center **Honors/awards:** Communication needs for 7 school districts transportation central command station for World Youth Day with the Pope, John Paul II, 1993 **Published works:** Photographs in: The International Library of Photography; Timeless Treasures Book and America at the Millennium, Best Photos of the 20th Century **Affiliations:** APCO Association of Public-Safety Communication Officials International **Career accomplishments:** Communications at the 1993 PGA Senior Golf Open, Cherry Hills Country Club; Taping golf event with ABC Television; Bill McCartney Promise Keepers 1993 and 1994 Boulder, Colorado; Care to Dare Pathfinders 1994 Bandemare Speedway Colorado; Now working on a new type voice over IP for making computer desktop into a dispatch console via Ethernet; This system will operate two-way radio communications from each school at Denver Public Schools **Hob./spts.:** Photography, bee keeping **SIC code:** 82 **Address:** Denver Public Schools, 2800 W. Seventh Ave., Denver, CO 80204 **E-mail:** busybeeboy@msn.com

BARKER, JAMES C.

Industry: Education **Born:** October 30, 1945, Mount Pleasant, Tennessee **Univ./degree:** Ph.D., Agricultural Engineering, University of Tennessee **Title:** Professor Emeritus, North Carolina State University **Type of organization:** University **Major product:** Higher education **Area of distribution:** National **Expertise:** Engineering **Honors/awards:** National Awards from A.S.A.E., Fellow and Countryside Engineering **Affiliations:** American Society of Agricultural Engineers (ASAE) **Hob./spts.:** Fishing, hiking **SIC code:** 82 **Address:** 906 River Ridge Dr., Asheville, NC 28803

BARR, REGINALD E.

Industry: Education **Born:** December 12, 1931, Brazil, Indiana **Univ./degree:** Ed.D., Secondary Education, University of Arizona, 1972 **Current organization:** Charter Foundation, Inc. **Title:** Superintendent/CEO **Type of organization:** Education foundation **Major product:** Owning and organizing charter schools **Area of distribution:** National **Expertise:** Administration, management **Affiliations:** Life Member, N.E.A.;

A.S.C.D. **Hob./spts.:** Golf **SIC code:** 82 **Address:** Charter Foundation, Inc., 2950 E. Third, Tucson, AZ 85716

BARTLETT, MARGARET WILMER
Industry: Author, Education/Communications, Publishing/Editing **Born:** October 10, 1944, Washington, D.C. **Spouse:** Marshall Prentiss Bartlett **Married:** December 14, 1968 **Children:** John Prentiss Bartlett, 37; Stephen Wilmer Bartlett, 34 **Univ./degree:** B.A., English, Miami University, Oxford, Ohio, 1966; Radcliffe Publishing Procedures Course, Cambridge, Massachusetts, Certificate of Completion, 1966; M.A., International Affairs, Drew University, Madison New Jersey, 1988 **Current organization:** Author preparing for book launches with speeches and book signings **Title:** Author/Teacher/Editor **Type of organization:** School/hospital **Major product:** Author/Teaching/Research **Area of distribution:** International **Expertise:** International Relations/Author/Freelance Editor/Researcher **Honors/awards:** Order of International Fellowship; Suburban Community Music Center Honoree, 2000 **Published works:** Author of "Cyprus, The United Nations and the Quest for Unity" **Affiliations:** Fellow, Academy of Political Science; Member, National Association of Scholars, Princeton, New Jersey; Member, Foreign Policy Association, New York City; Middle East Institute, Washington, D.C. **Career accomplishments:** Author of Cyprus, the United Nations and the Quest for Unity. This book grew out of a paper on the study of Peacekeeping at the United Nations while a student at Drew University. Traveled to Cyprus and interviewed prominent politicians and authors. Researched documents from the University of Cyprus, Centre of Cultural Heritage in Nicosia, Cyprus and National Archives of the United Kingdom, London. The textbook compares two United Nations Peacekeeping Forces, UNEF II in the Sinai and UNFICYP in Cyprus, discusses the Kofi Annan Peace Plan, describes the accession of Cyprus to the European Union and reveals current efforts to resolve the political problem in Cyprus. Certified Substitute Teacher, Editor. **Hob./spts.:** Art, genealogy, golf, travel **SIC code:** 82 **Address:** Young's Rd., P.O. Box 489, New Vernon, NJ 07976 **E-mail:** mpbartl@cs.com

BASHIRI, IRAJ
Industry: Education **Born:** July 31, 1940, Behbahan, Iran **Univ./degree:** B.A., Pahlavi University, Iran, 1963; M.A., Linguistics, University of Michigan, 1968; Ph.D., Iranian Linguistics, University of Michigan, 1972 **Current organization:** University of Minnesota **Title:** Professor of Central Asian Studies **Type of organization:** University **Major product:** Higher education **Area of distribution:** International **Expertise:** Central Asian studies **Honors/awards:** Numerous including Top B.A., Pahlavi University, Shiraz, Iran, 1963; Disting. Tchr., College of Liberal Arts, University of Minnesota, 1980; IREX Res. Scholar, Tajikistan, 1993-94; Hon. Doctorate in History and Culture, Tajikistan State University, 1996; Hon. International Academician, Academy of Science of Tajikistan, 1997 **Published works:** Numerous including The Fiction of Sadeq Hedayat, 1984; Firdowsi's Shahname: 1000 Years After, 1994; The Samanids and the Revival of the Civilization of Iranian Peoples, 1997; Many articles and essay in professional publications **Affiliations:** American Association of Teachers of Slavic and Eastern European Languages; American Association for Advancement of Slavic Studies; American Association for Central Asian Research; American Association for Central Asian Studies **Hob./spts.:** Writing fiction, fishing **SIC code:** 82 **Address:** 518 S.E. 8th St., Minneapolis, MN 55414 **E-mail:** bashi001@maroon.tc.umn.edu **Web address:** www.bashiris.com

BATES JR., CLAYTON W.
Industry: Education **Born:** September 5, 1932, New York, New York **Univ./degree:** B.S.E.E., Manhattan College, 1954; M.S.E.E., Polytechnic University, Brooklyn, 1956; Ph.D., Physics, Washington University, 1966 **Current organization:** Howard University **Title:** Ph.D. **Type of organization:** University **Major product:** Higher education **Area of distribution:** International **Expertise:** Material science and engineering **Honors/awards:** Taught at Stanford University for 22 years **Published works:** 100 journals, articles **Affiliations:** E.A.P.S.; I.E.E.E.; M.R.S.; A.A.A.S. **Hob./spts.:** European history **SIC code:** 82 **Address:** Howard University, 2300 Sixth St. N.W., Room 1016, Washington, DC 20059 **E-mail:** bates@negril.msrce.howard.edu

BAYER, ZEYNEP ERIN
Industry: Medical **Born:** January 24, 1969, Turkey **Univ./degree:** M.D., Cukurova University, Turkey, 1991 **Current organization:** Texas Tech University **Title:** M.D. **Type of organization:** University hospital **Major product:** Medical education **Area of distribution:** National **Expertise:** Anesthesiology **Published works:** Articles, abstracts, journals **Affiliations:** A.S.A.; A.M.A.; A.S.P.P.; S.O.A.P. **Hob./spts.:** Jazz music, swimming **SIC code:** 82 **Address:** Texas Tech University, Dept. of Anesthesiology, 5301 Fourth St., Lubbock, TX 79430 **E-mail:** erinbayer2000@yahoo.com

BEAUCHAMP, LUCY S.
Industry: Education **Born:** September 4, 1949, Arlington, Virginia **Univ./degree:** M.S., Experimental Statistics, North Carolina State University, 1972 **Current organization:** Prince William County School District **Title:** Chairman **Type of organization:** School **Major product:** Education **Area of distribution:** Manassas, Virginia **Expertise:** Experimental statistics **Affiliations:** Prince William United Way **Hob./spts.:** Football, her children's sports **SIC code:** 82 **Address:** Prince William County School District, 9012 Church St., Manassas, VA 20110 **E-mail:** beauchamp@uwnca.org

BENNETT, BYRON L.
Industry: Education **Born:** February 23, 1967, Patrick Air Force Base, Florida **Univ./degree:** B.A., Chemistry, Cedarville College, 1989; Ph.D. Inorganic/Organometallic Chemistry, University of Wyoming, 1997 **Current organization:** University of Nevada-Las Vegas, Dept. of Chemistry **Title:** Professor/Ph.D. **Type of organization:** University **Major product:** Higher education, research **Area of distribution:** National **Expertise:** Chemistry, organometallics, research in organic and inorganic chemistry **Published works:** Research publications **Affiliations:** American Chemical Society; American Cancer Society (Relay for Life) **Hob./spts.:** Rock climbing, golf, karaoke Tae Kwon Do (2nd Degree Black Belt) **SIC code:** 82 **Address:** University of Nevada-Las Vegas, Dept. of Chemistry, 4505 Maryland Pkwy., Las Vegas, NV 89154-4003 **E-mail:** kbennett@unlv.nevada.edu **Web address:** www.unlv.nevada.edu

BERG, PETER C.
Industry: Education **Univ./degree:** B.S.E.E., Case Western Reserve University **Current organization:** University of California **Title:** Principal Engineer **Type of organization:** University **Major product:** Higher education **Area of distribution:** International **Expertise:** Satellite electronics power, DC to DC converters **SIC code:** 82 **Address:** University of California, Space Sciences Lab, 7 Gauss Way, Berkeley, CA 94720 **E-mail:** dc2@pacbell.net

BERNSTORF, EILEEN E.
Industry: Education **Born:** Butler, Indiana **Spouse:** Dr. E. Cranston Bernstorf **Married:** August, 1944 **Children:** Dr. Robert, Kingston, Tennessee; Linda Sullivan, Assistant Head of Montessori Academy; Dr. Steven, Greensboro, North Carolina; James, Harriman, Tennessee **Univ./degree:** B.S., Purdue University; M.Ed., Xavier University, Ohio, 1982 **Current organization:** Montessori Academy, Inc. **Title:** Founder & Headmistress/President (Retired) **Type of organization:** Primary, elementary, middle school and high school **Major product:** Education in the Montessori environment **Area of distribution:** Metro Nashville, Tennessee, Brentwood and surrounding areas **Expertise:** Management, parenting classes **Honors/awards:** Selected as one of five winners in the 2006 Local Hero through the Bank of America Neighborhood Excellence Initiative **Affiliations:** United Methodist Church, Tennessee Montessori Association, American Montessori Society **Career accomplishments:** Purchased 24 acres of undeveloped land in Brentwood, Tennessee and completed the first building phase of the Montessori Academy in 1986; sold Montessori Centre and property; completed third building phase of the Montessori Academy for upper elementary/middle school classrooms and gymnasium; Philosophy is Self-paced learning in multi-aged groups of students which accommodates cultural diversity, music, foreign languages and academic excellence **Hob./spts.:** Reading historical novels, sewing **SIC code:** 82 **Address:** Montessori Academy, Inc., 6021 Cloverland Dr., Brentwood, TN 37027 **E-mail:** ebernstorf@montessoriacad.org **Web address:** www.montessoricad.org

BERRY, MILDRED E.
Industry: Education **Univ./degree:** Ed.D., 1974; M.S., Education, Wayne State University, Michigan; B.S., Paine College, Georgia **Current organization:** Florida Memorial University School of Education **Title:** Interim Dean **Type of organization:** University **Major product:** Higher education **Area of distribution:** Florida **Expertise:** Administration **Published works:** 10 articles **Affiliations:** Kappa Delta Pi; Phi Delta Kappa **Hob./spts.:** Travel **SIC code:** 82 **Address:** Florida Memorial University, School of Education, 15800 N.W. 42nd Ave., Miami Gardens, FL 33054 **E-mail:** mberry@fmuniv.edu

BHUIYAN, LUTFUL BARI
Industry: Education, research **Born:** Barisal, Bangladesh **Univ./degree:** B.Sc. with Honors; M.Sc., Dhaka University, Bangladesh; DIC, Ph.D., Imperial College of Science and Technology **Current organization:** University of Puerto Rico, Rio Piedras campus **Title:** Professor **Type of organization:** University **Major product:** Higher education, research **Area of distribution:** International **Expertise:** Education, research interest in thermodynamics and statistical mechanics of charged fluids-both simple and complex **Published works:** 75+ articles **Affiliations:** A.P.S.; A.C.S. **Hob./spts.:** Cricket **SIC code:** 82 **Address:** University of Puerto Rico, Rio Piedras, Dept. of Physics, Box 23343, Rio Piedras, PR 00931-3343 **E-mail:** beena@beena.cnnet.clu.edu

BLAKE, RICHARD E.
Industry: Education **Born:** February 23, 1943, Philadelphia, Pennsylvania **Univ./degree:** B.F.A., Temple University **Current organization:** Westchester University **Title:** Professor/Sculpture **Type of organization:** University **Major product:** Higher education **Area of distribution:** International **Expertise:** Sculpture/drawing **Published works:** Write-ups **Affiliations:** National Sculpture Society **Hob./spts.:** Family **SIC code:** 82 **Address:** 255 Harristown Rd., Kinzens, PA 17535 **E-mail:** rblake@wcupa.edu **Web address:** www.wcupa.edu

BLUMBERG, AVROM
Industry: Education **Born:** March 3, 1928, Albany, New York **Univ./degree:** Ph.D. **Current organization:** DePaul University **Title:** Professor **Type of organization:** University **Major product:** Higher education **Area of distribution:** International **Expertise:** Physical chemistry, forensic sciences **Hob./spts.:** Classical music **SIC code:** 82 **Address:** 1240 S. State St., Chicago, IL 60605 **E-mail:** ablumber@depaul.edu

BOGGS PARKER, THERESA ANN
Industry: Education **Born:** January 16, 1947, Spencer, West Virginia **Univ./degree:** B.A., Music, Glenville University, 1970; M.A., Special Education, 1991; M.A., Educational Specialist, 1996, Marshall University, College of Graduate Studies **Current organization:** Roane County Schools **Title:** Teacher **Type of organization:** School system **Major product:** Public school education **Area of distribution:** West Virginia **Expertise:** Special education **Published works:** Poems in: Miracles of Nature, Enlightened Shadows, America at the Millennium, Echoes of Yesteryear; The Road That Never Ends, The Best Poems & Poets of 2001, Letters From the Soul **Affiliations:** A.S.C.D.; W.V.P.E. **Hob./spts.:** Reading **SIC code:** 82 **Address:** Roane County Schools, 90 School Dr., Walton, WV 25286 **E-mail:** partheresa6410@aol.com

BORDASH, CYNTHIA ANNE
Industry: Education **Born:** August 24, 1957, Steubenville, Ohio **Univ./degree:** B.A., Fine Arts, Thiel College, 1979; M.S., Administration, Franciscan University, 1999 **Current organization:** Edison Local School District **Title:** Teacher **Type of organization:** Middle school **Major product:** Education **Area of distribution:** Toronto, Ohio **Expertise:** Science **Honors/awards:** Martha Holden Jennings Scholar **Affiliations:** N.S.A. **Hob./spts.:** Camping, the outdoors **SIC code:** 82 **Address:** Edison Local School District, 11653 State Rt., 213 North, Toronto, OH 43964 **E-mail:** bordash@prodigy.net

BORNE, CURTIS J.
Industry: Education **Born:** November 10, 1952, Rayne, Louisiana **Univ./degree:** B.S., Agricultural Education, University of Louisiana at Lafayette, 1974; M.S., Agricultural Education, 1981; Ph.D., 1988, Louisiana State University **Current organization:** Fort Valley State University **Title:** Professor of Agricultural Education **Type of organization:** University **Major product:** Higher education **Area of distribution:** International **Expertise:** Agricultural education, supervision of student teachers; Certifications: agricultural, general science, biology **Honors/awards:** Outstanding Earth Team, State of Georgia, Conservationist of the Year, 1994; Don W. Davidson Outstanding Faculty Award, Fort Valley State, 2004 **Affiliations:** National Association of Agricultural Educators; Georgia Vocational Agriculture Teachers Association; American Association of Colleges for Teacher Education **Hob./spts.:** Horseback riding **SIC code:** 82 **Address:** Fort Valley State University, 1005 State University Dr., Ft. Valley, GA 31030 **E-mail:** bornec@fvsu.edu **Web address:** www.fvsu.edu

BOWDITCH, ANNA H.
Industry: Education **Born:** March 28, 1912, Haverhill, Massachusetts **Univ./degree:** A.B., Botanical Sciences, Wellesley College, 1934; Graduate work, Shady Hill School and University of Illinois **Current organization:** Day Prospect Hill (Retired)/Charter Schools **Title:** Head Mistress **Type of organization:** Secondary school **Major product:** Education **Area of distribution:** Florida, Connecticut, Massachusetts **Expertise:** College counseling **Honors/awards:** NACAC Gayle Wilson Award; Hopkins Award, Hopkins School/Yale; Jean Pond Medal, Bradford; Distinguished Service Award, NEACAC **Published works:** Numerous articles **Affiliations:** N.A.P.S.G.; N.E.A.C.A.C.; N.A.C.A.C. **Hob./spts.:** Fly-fishing, shell collecting, needlepoint **SIC code:** 82 **Address:** P.O. Box 206, Boca Grande, FL 33921

BRADY, ALICE M.
Industry: Education **Born:** November 23, 1957, Ashtabula, Ohio **Univ./degree:** B.S., Library Science, Clarion State College, 1979; M.Ed. with Honors, Mansfield University, 2003 **Current organization:** Clearfield Area School District **Title:** Librarian/Media Coordinator **Type of organization:** Public high school **Major product:** Secondary school education **Area of distribution:** Clearfield, Pennsylvania **Expertise:** Library daily operations, management, media and technology focus for the high school, research, technology mentor **Honors/awards:** Library Recognition as Leader in Technology, 1998; Lambda Sigma Honor Society **Affiliations:** American Library Association; Preservation Committee, Oak Grove Cemetery Association **Hob./spts.:** Gardening, volleyball; church lay speaker **SIC code:** 82 **Address:** Clearfield Area School District, 438 River St., Clearfield, PA 16830 **E-mail:** ambrady@clearfield.org

BRANNAN, CLEO E.
Industry: Education **Born:** February 22, 1924, Turon, Kansas **Univ./degree:** B.S., Education, Fort Hayes State University **Title:** Teacher (Retired) **Type of organization:** Elementary school **Expertise:** Certified elementary education teacher **Published works:** Delta Kappa Gamma Magazine; Articles, Meadowlark Magazine **Affiliations:** AAUW; Delta Kappa Gamma; President, Kansas State Retired Teachers Association; State Friends of Library Board of Directors, 1990-1997; Trustee, Meade Public Library, 10 years; Silver Haired Legislature, 1999 **Hob./spts.:** Reading, travel, collecting china, arranging flowers **SIC code:** 82 **Address:** 416 N. Webb St., Meade, KS 67864

BRESLER, J. LENORA
Industry: Motivational speaking/training **Born:** January 18, 1967, Lakeland, Florida **Univ./degree:** J.D., Stetson University of Law **Current organization:** Bresler Training **Title:** Owner **Type of organization:** Training, consulting, speaking firm **Major product:** Public speaking, leadership, diversity, conflict resolution **Area of distribution:** National **Expertise:** Daily operations oversight; Senior Certified human resource professional **Published works:** 1 book, "Mission Possible" **Affiliations:** Florida Bar; National Speakers Association; Society for Human Resource Management **Hob./spts.:** Performing arts **SIC code:** 82 **Address:** Bresler Training, 987 Lake Hollingsworth Dr., Lakeland, FL 33803 **Web address:** wwww.jenorabresler.com

BRINK, DAVID L.
Industry: Education **Univ./degree:** Ph.D., Chemistry, University of Minnesota, 1954 **Title:** Ph.D. **Major product:** Higher education, chemistry **Area of distribution:** National **Expertise:** Chemistry **Published works:** 104 publications **Affiliations:** A.C.S.; F.P.R.S.; Board Member, Solid Waste Management Committee **SIC code:** 82 **Address:** 1068 Woodside Rd., Berkeley, CA 94708-1721 **E-mail:** dlb@nature.berkely.edu

BROADBENT, H. SMITH
Industry: Education **Born:** July 21, 1920, Snowflake, Arizona **Univ./degree:** Ph.D., University of Iowa, 1946 **Current organization:** Brigham Young University **Title:** Professor of Chemistry Emeritus **Type of organization:** University **Major product:** Higher education **Area of distribution:** International **Expertise:** Chemistry **Affiliations:** N.S.F.; A.C.S. **Hob./spts.:** Backpacking, hiking, gardening, photography **SIC code:** 82 **Address:** 1147 Aspen Ave., Provo, UT 84604 **E-mail:** hsbroadb@juno.com

BROOKS, LYNN ALAN
Industry: Education **Born:** March, 3, 1941, Island Pond, Vermont **Univ./degree:** B.S., General Engineering, U.S. Naval Academy, 1962; J.D., University of Michigan Law School, 1971 **Current organization:** Briarwood College **Title:** President/CEO **Type of organization:** Career and Technical College **Major product:** Higher education **Area of distribution:** Connecticut **Expertise:** Education and policy making, law, finance, management and seminars **Affiliations:** U.S. Navy, 1962-69; Board Member, Intensive Education Academy; Chair, Strategic Planning Committee **Hob./spts.:** Golf, travel **SIC code:** 82 **Address:** Briarwood College, 2279 Mt. Vernon Rd., Southington, CT 06489 **E-mail:** lbrooks@briarwood.edu **Web address:** www.briarwood.edu

BROWDER, JAMES
Industry: Education **Univ./degree:** Ph.D., Physics, University of Florida, 1968 **Current organization:** Jacksonville University **Title:** Professor of Physics **Type of organization:** University **Major product:** Higher education **Area of distribution:** National **Expertise:** Optical Physicist; infrared materials **Published works:** 40 publications **Affiliations:** Optic Society; Sigma Xi; Phi Kappa Phi; Phi Beta Kappa **SIC code:** 82 **Address:** Jacksonville University, 2300 University Blvd. North, Jacksonville, FL 32211 **E-mail:** jbrowde@ju.edu

BROWN, BESSIE M.
Industry: Education **Born:** Starkville, Mississippi **Univ./degree:** B.A., Political Science and History, 1971; M.Ed., 1990, Mississippi State University; Ed. Specialist, Georgia College State University, 1996 **Current organization:** Putnam County Middle School **Title:** Principal **Type of organization:** Middle school **Major product:** Education **Area of distribution:** Putnam County, Georgia **Expertise:** Education, administration, instruction improvement, student achievement, motivational speaking **Honors/awards:** Georgia's Economics Teacher of the Year, 1994 **Affiliations:** Georgia Association of Secondary School Principals; National Education Association; Alpha Kappa Alpha **Hob./spts.:** Music, playing the piano, singing **SIC code:** 82 **Address:** Putnam County Middle School, 314 S. Washington Ave., Eatonton, GA 31024 **E-mail:** bessie_brown@putnam.k12.ga.us **Web address:** www.putnam.k12.ga.us

BROWN, BETTY F.
Industry: Education **Univ./degree:** M.S., University of Tennessee at Knoxville, 1977 **Current organization:** Johnson County High School **Title:** Principal **Type of organization:** High school **Major product:** Secondary school education (9-12 grades)

Area of distribution: Johnson County, Tennessee **Affiliations:** A.S.C.D.; T.A.S.S.A.; Delta Kappa Gamma **Hob./spts.:** Sports **SIC code:** 82 **Address:** Johnson County High School, 510 Fairground Lane, Mountain City, TN 37683

BROWN, EUGENE
Industry: Education **Born:** April, 1931, 1931, New York **Univ./degree:** B.S.; M.S., New York University; Fordham Medical Research, 1960 **Current organization:** Nassau Community College **Title:** Professor **Type of organization:** College **Major product:** Higher education **Area of distribution:** Long Island, New York **Expertise:** Chemistry, nutrition **Honors/awards:** Many VEA Grants; Ph.D. Studies, Eastern Analytical Award; International Conference Alternative Medicine **Published works:** Molecular - Hemoglobin **Affiliations:** Chairman, Long Island Section, American Chemical Society; External Advisory Board, School of Public Health **Hob./spts.:** Organized farming, classic music, opera **SIC code:** 82 **Address:** Nassau Community College, Dept. of Chemistry, 1 Education Dr., Garden City, NY 11530 **E-mail:** ebrown@ncc.org

BROWN, TERENCE J.
Industry: Education **Born:** April 1, 1965, Wauwatosa, Wisconsin **Univ./degree:** B.A., University of Wisconsin; M.B.A., Thunderbird - The Garvin School of International Management **Current organization:** St. Anthony School **Title:** President **Type of organization:** Private school **Major product:** Elementary school education (Pre-K to 8) **Area of distribution:** Milwaukee, Wisconsin **Expertise:** School reform, facility development **Affiliations:** Board Member, Alliance for Choices in Education; Member, Hispanic Council for Reform and Educational Options **SIC code:** 82 **Address:** St. Anthony School, 1727 S. Ninth St., Milwaukee, WI 53204 **E-mail:** brownt@archmil.org

BRYANT, JULIA R.
Industry: Education **Univ./degree:** B.S., Dietetics, Benafe College, 1971; M.S., Institutional Management, Kansas State University, 1971; Ph.D., Institution Administration, University of Maryland, 1987 **Current organization:** Hampton City School District **Title:** Ph.D./ R.D./S.F.N.S./Director, Food and Nutrition Services **Type of organization:** School system **Major product:** Food service **Area of distribution:** Hampton, Virginia **Expertise:** Food preparation, service **Honors/awards:** Home Economics Honor Society **Published works:** Journals, articles, abstracts **Affiliations:** A.D.A.; A.S.F.S.A. **Hob./spts.:** Reading **SIC code:** 82 **Address:** Hampton City School District, 1 Franklin St., Hampton, VA 23669 **E-mail:** jbryant@sbo.hampton.k12.va.us

BUCK, JESSICA L.
Industry: Education and Industrial Setting **Born:** September 26, 1975, Vicksburg, Mississippi **Univ./degree:** M.S.T., 2001; Ph.D. (Tech.), 2003, Mississippi State University **Current organization:** Mississippi State University **Title:** Lecturer/Diversity Trainer **Type of organization:** University **Major product:** Higher and industrial education **Area of distribution:** Mississippi **Expertise:** Industrial technology/technical education **Affiliations:** Phi Delta Kappa Educational Fraternity; Alpha Theta Chi Honorary; Epsilon Pi Tau Technology Honorary; National Association of Industrial Technology **Hob./spts.:** Web page design **SIC code:** 82 **Address:** P.O. Box 6515, Mississippi State, MS 39762 **E-mail:** jlb23@msstate.edu

BUFFENSTEIN, ROCHELLE
Industry: Education **Born:** July 29, 1955, Harare, Zimbabwe **Univ./degree:** Ph.D., Capetown University **Current organization:** City College of New York, Dept. of Biology **Title:** Professor **Type of organization:** University **Major product:** Higher education **Area of distribution:** International **Expertise:** Physiological functions of animals in relationship to their environment **Affiliations:** A.P.S.; A.M.S. **Hob./spts.:** Outdoor activities, hiking **SIC code:** 82 **Address:** City College of New York, Dept. of Biology, 138th St. at Convent Ave., Suite J-526, New York, NY 10031 **E-mail:** rbuffen@sci.ccny.cuny.edu

BUKOWY, STEPHEN J.
Industry: Education **Born:** May 24, 1949, Philadelphia, Pennsylvania **Univ./degree:** B.S., Pennsylvania State University; M.B.A., College of William and Mary, Virginia; M.F.R., Ph.D., University of Georgia **Current organization:** University of North Carolina at Pembroke **Title:** Associate Professor, Accounting **Type of organization:** University **Major product:** Higher education **Area of distribution:** North Carolina **Expertise:** Accounting **Affiliations:** American Accounting Association; American Institute of Certified Public Accountants; Institute of Management Accountants; Society of American Foresters; Reserve Officials Association **SIC code:** 82 **Address:** The University of North Carolina, Pembroke, One University Dr., Pembroke, NC 28372 **E-mail:** stephen.bukowy@uncp.edu

BULLOCK, LAURA S.
Industry: Education **Born:** Edenton, North Carolina **Univ./degree:** B.S., Elementary Education, 1987; M.Ed., Administration, 1993, Southeastern Oklahoma State University **Current organization:** Central Elementary School **Title:** Principal **Type of organization:** Elementary school **Major product:** Education, grades 3,4 and 5 **Area of distribution:** Idabel, Oklahoma **Expertise:** Administration, using "Effective School's" model; Certified, Reading First School Specialist; Certified, Schools Administrator **Hob./spts.:** Water sports, fishing, reading, travel **SIC code:** 82 **Address:** Central Elementary School, 206 S.E. Ave. F, Idabel, OK 74745 **E-mail:** lbullock@idabelps.org **Web address:** www.idabelps.org

BURCH, HERBERT K.
Industry: Education **Born:** April 23, 1953, Fürstenfeld Bruck, West Germany **Univ./degree:** M.S., Aeronautical Engineering, Georgia Institute of Technology, 1984; M.S., Computer Information Systems Management, Webster University, St. Louis, Missouri, 1997 **Current organization:** Ehove Ghrist Adult Career Center **Title:** Computer Technology Training Coordinator **Type of organization:** Adult education **Major product:** Information technology training **Area of distribution:** Ohio **Expertise:** Information systems **Honors/awards:** Graduated Magna Cum Laude **Published works:** Articles, handbook **Affiliations:** A.S.M.E.; A.I.A.A.; Armed Forces; Communications & Electronics Association **Hob./spts.:** Scuba diving, skiing (water & downhill), parachuting, jogging, flying airplanes (mooney) **SIC code:** 82 **Address:** Ehove Ghrist Adult Career Center, P.O. Box 14, Milan, OH 44846 **E-mail:** nickburch@stargate.net

BUSH, JILL A.
Industry: Education **Univ./degree:** M.S., 1995; Ph.D., Penn State University, 1999 **Current organization:** University of Houston **Title:** Assistant Professor **Type of organization:** University **Major product:** Higher education/research **Area of distribution:** International **Expertise:** Endocrine/nutrient/exercise regulation **Published works:** 40 publications **Affiliations:** N.S.C.A.; American Society for Nutritional Sciences; American Physical Society; American College of Sports Medicine **SIC code:** 82 **Address:** University of Houston, 3855 Holman St., 104Q Garrison Gym, Houston, TX 77204 **E-mail:** jbush@uh.edu

BYRD, KIMBERLY
Industry: Education **Born:** January 19, 1967 **Univ./degree:** B.S., Eastern Kentucky University, 2002 **Current organization:** Southeast Kentucky Community & Technical College **Title:** Assistant Professor **Type of organization:** Community College **Major product:** Post secondary education **Area of distribution:** Pineville, Kentucky **Expertise:** Clinical microbiology **Hob./spts.:** Camping **SIC code:** 82 **Address:** Southeast Kentucky Community & Technical College, 3300 South Hwy. 25E, Pineville, KY 40977 **E-mail:** kim.byrd@kctcs.edu **Web address:** www.southeast.kctcs.edu

BYTAUTAS, LAIMUTIS
Industry: Education **Univ./degree:** M.S., Physics, Vilnius University, Lithuania; Ph.D., Physical Chemistry, Vanderbilt University **Current organization:** Iowa State University **Title:** Assistant Scientist **Type of organization:** University **Major product:** Higher education, research **Area of distribution:** International **Expertise:** New methodology in chemical studies, research in computational chemistry and physical chemistry **Published works:** 1 article in: DIMACS Series in Discrete Mathematics and Theoretical Computer Science, L. Bytautas, D.J. Klein, M. Rantic, T. Pisunski, "Foldedness in Linear Polymers: A Difference between Graphical and Euclidean Distances" Volume 51, page 39 (2000); Journal articles: L. Bytautas, K. Ruedenberg, "Correlation Energy Extrapolation by intrinsic scaling. IV. Accurate binding energies of homonuclear diatomic molecules carbon, nitrogen, oxygen and fluorine", Journal of Chemical Physics, volume 122, page 154110 (2005); L. Bytautas, K. Ruedenberg, "Electron pairs, localized orbitals and electron correlation", Molecular Physics, volume 100, page 757 (2002); D.J. Klein, L. Bytautas, "Graphic edges and unpaired pi electron spins", Journal of Physical Chemistry A, volume 103, page 5196 (1999) and others (26 total) **Affiliations:** American Chemical Society **Hob./spts.:** Basketball, soccer **SIC code:** 82 **Address:** Iowa State University, Ames Laboratory, DOE (US), Wilhelm Hall 307, Ames, IA 50011 **E-mail:** bytautas@scl.ameslab.gov **Web address:** www.external.ameslab.gov

CABALLERO, SAN JUANA P.
Industry: Education **Born:** July 18, 1955, Southbend, Indiana **Current organization:** UMOS **Title:** Center Manager **Type of organization:** Education center **Major product:** Educational services **Area of distribution:** National **Expertise:** Administration **Hob./spts.:** Baking **SIC code:** 82 **Address:** UMOS, N2912 State Rd. 22, Montello, WI 53949 **E-mail:** sanjuana.caballero@umos.org

CAMPBELL, FRANCES 'JEAN'
Industry: Education **Univ./degree:** B.A., Missouri Southern State University **Title:** Promotion Director/Coordinator/Advisor, Missouri Southern State College (Retired) **Type of organization:** College **Major product:** Higher education **Area of distribution:** Joplin, Missouri **Expertise:** Event planning, mentoring, development, publications **Honors/awards:** Distinguished Women of Girl Scouts **SIC code:** 82 **Address:** 249 Locust St., La Russell, MO 64848-0034 **E-mail:** jeanbilcamp@mo-net.net

CAMPER, NYAL D.
Industry: Education **Univ./degree:** Ph.D., North Carolina State University, 1967 **Current organization:** Clemson University **Title:** Professor **Type of organization:** University **Major product:** Higher education **Area of distribution:** National **Exper-**

tise: Teaching, research **Honors/awards:** South Carolina Endowed Professor, SC Commission of Higher Education, 1996; Clemson University Board of Trustees Award for Faculty Excellence, 1997; Fellow, Weed Science Society of America, 2000; Teacher of the Year, College of Agriculture, Forestry & Life Sciences, 2005 **Published works:** 75+ articles published in various scientific journals; 7 book chapters **Affiliations:** Weed Science Society of America; American Chemical Society; Sigma Xi **Hob./spts.:** Classic automobiles, antique furniture, photography **SIC code:** 82 **Address:** Clemson University, Dept. of Entomology, Soils and Plant Sciences, Clemson, SC 29634-0315 **E-mail:** dcamper@clemson.edu

CAMPHOR JR., JAMES L.
Industry: Education **Born:** March 16, 1927, Baltimore, Maryland **Univ./degree:** B.A., Education; M.Ed., Coppin State College, 1971 **Current organization:** Coppin State College **Title:** M.Ed./President, Alumni Association **Type of organization:** College **Major product:** Higher education **Area of distribution:** Baltimore, Maryland **Expertise:** Teaching **Affiliations:** N.A.A.C.P.; Black Professional Men; Phi Beta Sigma **Hob./spts.:** Prize fighting, basketball **SIC code:** 82 **Address:** Coppin State College, 2500 North Avenue, Baltimore, MD 21215 **E-mail:** peawin5@aol.com

CANIGLIA, ROSE ANNE
Industry: Education **Born:** New York, New York **Univ./degree:** B.S.; M.A., History & Education, College of Staten Island; Professional Diploma Supervision, Brooklyn College **Current organization:** New York City, Department of Education, The Renaissance Middle School **Title:** Assistant Principal, The Academy of Space and Ocean Exploration **Type of organization:** Public school **Major product:** Elementary and secondary school education **Area of distribution:** South East Queens, New York **Expertise:** Education (gifted and talented students) **Honors/awards:** Who's Who of America's Teachers; Rev. Charles Gray Educational Award; National Junior Honor Society Leadership Award **Affiliations:** Association for Supervision and Curriculum Development; The Marty Lyons Make-A-Wish Foundation; Ronald McDonald Children's Charities; National Association of University Women **Hob./spts.:** Travel, theatre, dance, reading **SIC code:** 82 **Address:** 107 Fifth St., Garden City, NY 11530

CANNON, MAJOR TOM
Industry: Education **Born:** November 11, 1932, Anniston, Alabama **Univ./degree:** M.S., Educational Counseling, University of Georgia, 1968 **Current organization:** CE Murray High School **Title:** Resource Teacher for Learning Disabled **Type of organization:** High school **Major product:** Secondary education **Area of distribution:** Greeleyville, South Carolina **Expertise:** Educational consultation; special education **Published works:** Handbook for Special Education **Affiliations:** Council for Exceptional Children; Kappa Delta Pi **Hob./spts.:** Coin collecting, history, pets **SIC code:** 82 **Address:** CE Murray High School, P.O. Box 188, Greeleyville, SC 29056

CANNON, TINA R.
Industry: Education **Born:** December 19, 1967, Dallas, Texas **Current organization:** Kid's Club Child Development Center **Title:** Director/Owner **Type of organization:** Childcare/education **Major product:** Preschool development program **Area of distribution:** Austin, Texas **Expertise:** Early childhood education/teaching **Hob./spts.:** Skiing, rock climbing, swimming **SIC code:** 82 **Address:** Kid's Club Child Development Center, 12233 RR 620, Suite 201, Austin, TX 78750

CARMICHAEL, RENNARD
Industry: Education **Born:** September 18, 1953, Philadelphia, Pennsylvania **Univ./degree:** A.A., Electronic Engineering, CIT, 1974 **Current organization:** University of Pennsylvania **Title:** Project A/V Engineer **Type of organization:** University **Major product:** Higher education **Area of distribution:** International **Expertise:** Audio/video engineer **Affiliations:** Former Member, I.E.E.E. **SIC code:** 82 **Address:** University of Pennsylvania, 3650 Chestnut St., Suite 221, Philadelphia, PA 19104 **E-mail:** rennardc@isc.upenn.edu **Web address:** www.upenn.edu

CARSON, LINDA F.
Industry: Education **Born:** February 8, 1952, Manchester, Connecticut **Univ./degree:** M.D., George Washington University, 1978 **Current organization:** University of Minnesota **Title:** M.D. **Type of organization:** University **Major product:** Higher education **Area of distribution:** National **Expertise:** Gynecology, oncology **Published works:** 100 articles **Affiliations:** American Academy of OB/GYN; Society of Gynecological Oncology **Hob./spts.:** Gardening, canoeing, fishing **SIC code:** 82 **Address:** University of Minnesota, MMC 395, 420 Delaware St. S.E., Minneapolis, MN 55455 **E-mail:** carso001@tc.umn.edu

CASTRO, FRANCISCO A.
Industry: Education **Born:** December 14, 1948, Santo Domingo, Dominican Republic **Univ./degree:** B.S., Fairleigh Dickinson University **Current organization:** Newark Public Schools **Title:** Supervisor Engineer **Type of organization:** Public school district **Major product:** Education **Area of distribution:** Newark, New Jersey **Expertise:** Engineering **Affiliations:** A.E.E. **Hob./spts.:** Sports **SIC code:** 82 **Address:** Newark Public Schools, 2 Cedar St., Newark, NJ 07102 **E-mail:** fcastro@nps.k12.nj.us

CEGLAREK, DARIUSZ J.
Industry: Education **Born:** January 2, 1963, Stettin, Poland **Univ./degree:** Ph.D., University of Michigan **Current organization:** University of Wisconsin at Madison **Title:** Assistant Professor **Type of organization:** University **Major product:** Higher education **Area of distribution:** International **Expertise:** Manufacturing/design engineering **Affiliations:** A.S.A.M.E.E.; S.M.E.E. **Hob./spts.:** Jogging, bilingual (Russian, Polish, German) **SIC code:** 82 **Address:** University of Wisconsin at Madison, 1513 University Ave., Madison, WI 53706-1572 **E-mail:** darek@engr.wisc.edu

CHANDOR, STEBBINS B.
Industry: Medical **Born:** December 18, 1933, Boston, Massachusetts **Univ./degree:** M.D., Cornell University Medical College **Current organization:** Keck School of Medicine of USC **Title:** Professor Emeritus **Type of organization:** Medical school **Major product:** Medical education **Area of distribution:** California **Expertise:** Pathology **Published works:** 50 peer-reviewed articles in medical journals **Affiliations:** American Society for Clinical Pathology; College of American Pathologists **Hob./spts.:** Golf, tennis, gardening **SIC code:** 82 **Address:** Keck School of Medicine of USC, 2011 Zonal Ave., Los Angeles, CA 90033 **E-mail:** chandor@usc.edu

CHANG, LENG CHEE
Industry: Education **Univ./degree:** Ph.D., Natural Product Chemistry, University of Illinois at Chicago, 1998 **Current organization:** University of Minnesota, Duluth, Dept. of Chemistry & Biology **Title:** Assistant Professor **Type of organization:** University **Major product:** Higher education/research **Area of distribution:** National **Expertise:** Research in natural product chemistry, writing grants, supervision **Honors/awards:** "D. John Faulkner Travel" Award, American Society of Pharmacognosy, 2006 **Affiliations:** American Society of Pharmacognosy; American Chemical Society; Phi Kappa Phi **SIC code:** 82 **Address:** University of Minnesota, Duluth, Dept. of Chemistry & Biology, 1039 University Dr., 246 Chemistry, Duluth, MN 55812 **E-mail:** lcchang@d.umn.edu

CHARALAMBIDES, PANOS G.
Industry: Education **Born:** September 7, 1955, Cyprus, Greece **Univ./degree:** Ph.D., University of Illinois at Champaign-Urbana **Current organization:** Dept. of Engineering/UMBC **Title:** Professor/Chair **Type of organization:** University **Major product:** Higher education, research **Area of distribution:** International **Expertise:** Mechanics of materials, compound materials, micromechanics and finite elements **Published works:** 50+ articles **Affiliations:** A.S.M.E.; American Ceramics Society **Hob./spts.:** Poetry, coaching soccer (son), sports, the outdoors, travel **SIC code:** 82 **Address:** Dept. of Engineering/UMBC, 1000 Hilltop Circle, Baltimore, MD 21250 **E-mail:** panos@umbc.edu **Web address:** www.umbc.edu

CHATO, JOHN C.
Industry: Education/Research **Born:** December 28, 1929, Budapest, Hungary **Univ./degree:** M.E., University of Cincinnati, 1954; M.S., University of Illinois, 1955; Ph.D., Massachusetts of Technology, 1960 **Current organization:** University of Illinois at Urbana-Champaign **Title:** Professor/Assistant Dean Emeritus **Type of organization:** University **Major product:** Higher education, research **Area of distribution:** International **Expertise:** Heat transfer, thermodynamics, fluid mechanics, bioengineering **Honors/awards:** NSF Postdoctoral Fellow, Technische Hochschule Aachen, Germany, 1961-62; Distinguished Engineering Alumnus Award, Univ. of Cincinnati, 1972; Fogarty Senior International Fellow, Institute for Biomedical Engineering of the Federal Technical Univ. of Switzerland (ETH) and of the Univ. of Zurich, 1978-79; Charles Russ Richards Memorial, ASME and Pi Tau Sigma, 1978; Exchange Scholar, Hungary, sponsored by the U.S. and Hungarian Academies of Science, 1978; Russell Scott Memorial Award, Cryogenic Engineering Conference, 1979; Honorary Visiting Professor, Univ. of New South Wales, Kensington, NSW, Australia, 1986; College of Engineering Andersen Consulting Award for Excellence in Advising, 1989; H.R. Lissen Award, Amer. Society of Mechanical Engineers, 1992; Dedicated Service Award, ASME, 2000; Distinguished Alumnus Award, Dept. of Mechanical and Industrial Engineering, Univ. of Illinois, 2005 **Published works:** Over 100 journal articles, books, book chapters **Affiliations:** Fellow, Amer. Society of Mechanical Engineers; Fellow, Amer. Institute for Medical and Biological Engineering; Fellow, Japan Society for the Promotion of Science; Fellow, Amer. Society of Heating, Refrigerating and Air Conditioning Engineers; A.S.E.E.; Sigma Xi **Hob./spts.:** Tennis, birdwatching, kayaking, nature walks **SIC code:** 82 **Address:** 714 W. Vermont Ave., Urbana, IL 61801 **E-mail:** jbchato@uiuc.edu

CHAUHAN, BHARESH K.
Industry: Medical **Univ./degree:** D.Phil. (Oxon), Molecular Biology, University of Oxford, England, 1998 **Current organization:** Albert Einstein College of Medicine Dept. of Ophthal. & Mol. Genetics **Title:** Dr. **Type of organization:** University **Major product:** Higher education, research **Area of distribution:** International **Expertise:** Research scientist **Published works:** 8 papers **Affiliations:** A.A.A.S.; A.S.M.B. **SIC code:** 82 **Address:** Albert Einstein College of Medicine, Dept. of Ophthal. & Mol. Genetics, 1300 Morris Park Ave., Bronx, NY 10461 **E-mail:** chauhan@aecom.yu.edu

CHEEMA, MOHINDAR S.

Industry: Education **Born:** January 15, 1929 **Univ./degree:** Ph.D., Mathematics, UCLA, 1961 **Current organization:** University of Arizona **Title:** Professor Emeritus, Mathematics **Type of organization:** University **Major product:** Higher education, research **Area of distribution:** National **Expertise:** Mathematics **Affiliations:** American Math Society; Mathematical Association of America **Hob./spts.:** Hiking **SIC code:** 82 **Address:** 7401 E. Calle Maicoba, Tucson, AZ 85710 **E-mail:** cheemap@aol.com

CHEN, XI

Industry: Education **Univ./degree:** Ph.D., Harvard University, 2001 **Current organization:** Harvard University, Div. of Engineering and Applied Sciences **Title:** Ph.D. **Type of organization:** University **Major product:** Higher education, research **Area of distribution:** International **Expertise:** Mechanical engineering, solid mechanics, material science **Honors/awards:** Wigner Fellowship Award, Dept. of Energy **Published works:** 30+ technical publications **Affiliations:** American Society of Mechanical Engineers; American Academy of Mechanics; Materials Research Society **SIC code:** 82 **Address:** Harvard University, Div. of Engineering and Applied Sciences, DEAS, 312 Pierce Hall, Cambridge, MA 02138-2901 **E-mail:** chen@esag.harvard.edu

CHENOUDA, DALAL M.

Industry: Education **Born:** May 1, 1960, Egypt, Africa **Univ./degree:** M.D., SUNY Stony Brook, 1994; Residency, Montifiory Medical School, 1997-98 **Current organization:** University of Connecticut Health Science Center **Title:** M.D. **Type of organization:** University clinic **Major product:** Teaching, residency program **Area of distribution:** National **Expertise:** Internal medicine **Hob./spts.:** Travel, children's charities **SIC code:** 82 **Address:** University of Connecticut Health Science Center, 260 Farmington Ave., Suite 200, Dowling South, CT 06001 **E-mail:** dchenouda@aol.com

CHENOWETH SR., DARREL L.

Industry: Education **Born:** November 6, 1941, Indianapolis, Indiana **Univ./degree:** Ph.D. **Current organization:** University of Louisville **Title:** Ph.D./Vice President, Research **Type of organization:** University **Major product:** Higher education **Area of distribution:** National **Expertise:** Educational research, electrical engineering instruction **Affiliations:** Institute of Electrical and Electronics Engineers **Hob./spts.:** Skiing **SIC code:** 82 **Address:** University of Louisville, Office of the Vice President for Research, 2301 S. Third St., Louisville, KY 40292 **E-mail:** dlchen01@aol.com

CHHABRA, AVNEESH

Industry: Medical **Born:** March 3, 1973, Delhi, India **Univ./degree:** M.D., University of Delhi; Radiology degrees from Delhi University and American Board of Radiology **Current organization:** Drexel University College of Medicine **Title:** Staff Radiologist **Type of organization:** University college of medicine **Major product:** Medical education, patient care **Area of distribution:** International **Expertise:** Radiology, MRI **Affiliations:** American Board of Radiology **Hob./spts.:** Badminton, cricket, travel, swimming **SIC code:** 82 **Address:** 2601 Pennsylvania Ave., #148, Philadelphia, PA 19130 **E-mail:** avneesh28@hotmail.com

CHIAPPELLI, FRANCESCO

Industry: Education **Born:** June 11, 1953, Lausanne, Switzerland **Spouse:** Olivia S. Cajulis, D.D.S. **Married:** December 26, 1998 **Univ./degree:** B.A., 1975; M. A., 1981; Ph.D., 1986, University of California at Los Angeles **Current organization:** U.C.L.A. **Title:** Professor **Type of organization:** University **Major product:** Research and research consulting **Area of distribution:** California **Expertise:** Psychoneuroimmunology and evidence based dentistry **Honors/awards:** Alzheimer's Association, 2000 and several other awards **Published works:** Chiappelli F Prolo P Cajulis E Harper S Sunga E Concepcion E. Consciousness, emotional self-regulation and the psychosomatic network: Relevance to Oral Biology and Medicine. In Consciousness, Emotional Self-regulation and the Brain; M. Beauregard, Ed. Advances in Consciousness Research, John Benjamins Publishing Company, 2004; Chapter 9, pp. 253-74; Chiappelli F, Cajulis OS. Psychobiological views on "stress-related oral ulcers". Quintessence International, 2004, 35:223-7; Chiappelli F, Guest Editor-in-Chief, Evidence-Based Research in Dentistry for the Next Decade. Brazilian Journal of Oral Sciences (special issue) 2003 2(5). Book in progress, "Stress in Dentistry" **Affiliations:** President, Psychoneuroimmunology Group, Inc. **Career accomplishments:** 2004 Associate Director, Health Outcomes; NIH-sponsored program on Mind/Brain/Body Interaction and Stress-Related Diseases **Hob./spts.:** Gardening, classical music (German/French and Italian Baroque) **SIC code:** 82 **Address:** U.C.L.A. School of Dentistry, CHS 63-090, Los Angeles, CA 90095-1668 **E-mail:** chiappelli@dent.ucla.edu

CHONG, EDWIN K.P.

Industry: Education **Born:** February 2, 1966, Malaysia **Spouse:** Yat-Yee Chong **Children:** Madeleine, 6; Isaac, 4 **Univ./degree:** B.E., Honors, 1987, University of Adelaide, South Australia; M.A., Electrical Engineering, 1989; Ph.D., Electrical Engineering, 1991, Princeton University **Current organization:** Colorado State University **Title:** Professor, Dept. of Electrical and Computer Engineering/Professor, Dept. of Mathematics **Type of organization:** University **Major product:** Higher education, research **Area of distribution:** International **Expertise:** Electrical and computer engineering **Honors/awards:** Numerous including, Outstanding IEEE Branch Counselor and Advisor Award, 1993; IEEE Section Recognition Award (IEEE Central Indiana Section), 1994; National Science Foundation Faculty Early Career Development Award, 1995; Tarkington Hall Certificate of Appreciation, 1996; Frederick Emmons Terman Award by American Society for Engineering, 1998; Purdue University Faculty Scholar Award, 1999; IEEE Control Systems Society Distinguished Lecturer, 2001-03; Elected to Full Member of Sigma Xi, 2002; Elsevier Best Paper Award, 2004 **Published works:** 2 books, "An Introduction to Optimization", 1996, ISBN 0-471-08949-4, xiii+409 pp and "An Introduction to Optimization, 2nd Edition", 2001, ISBN 0-471-39126-3, xvi+477 pp, John Wiley & Sons Inc., New York, NY; 200 journal papers, conference proceedings and presentations and book chapters; Papers on philosophy, theology and alologetics **Affiliations:** Fellow, I.E.E.E. **SIC code:** 82 **Address:** Colorado State University, 1373 Campus Delivery, Ft. Collins, CO 80523-1373 **E-mail:** ekpchong@yahoo.com **Web address:** www.edwinchong.us

CHRISTMAN, LUTHER P.

Industry: Medical **Born:** February 26, 1915, Summit Hill, Pennsylvania **Univ./degree:** M.S., Clinical Psychology, Temple University, 1950; Ph.D., Sociology/Anthropology, Michigan State University, 1966 **Title:** Professor Emeritus, Vanderbilt University; Dean Emeritus, Rush University **Type of organization:** University **Major product:** Higher education **Area of distribution:** National **Expertise:** Nursing, sociology **Affiliations:** Fellow, American Association for the Advancement of Science; President, American Assembly for Men in Nursing **Career accomplishments:** He was refused admission to the Army Nurse Corps in World War II because he was a man. Despite this, he gained qualifications in psychology and his research led to high level appointments in university nursing faculties. He became the first male to hold the joint appointments of Dean of Nursing and Hospital Director of Nursing. He developed the Rush Model of nursing that gained him an international reputation as a nursing leader. His strategic plans for the development of the nursing profession entailed a critique of its organization, policies, practices, education and female domination that challenged nursing leaders, physicians and hospital administrators alike. **Hob./spts.:** Gardening, wild birds, travel, hiking **SIC code:** 82 **Address:** 5535 Nashville Hwy., Chapel Hill, TN 37034 **E-mail:** lchristman@united.net

CHRONISTER, VIRGINIA A.

Industry: Education **Born:** September 25, 1940, York, Pennsylvania **Univ./degree:** R.N., Harrisburg Hospital, 1961; B.S., Professional Arts, St. Joseph College, 1985; M.S., Education, Pennsylvania State University, 1987; M.Eq., 1988 **Current organization:** West York Area School District **Title:** R.N./Certified School Nurse **Type of organization:** Public school **Major product:** Education **Area of distribution:** York, Pennsylvania **Expertise:** Certified school nursing **Honors/awards:** Cardiac Nursing Award **Affiliations:** P.S.E.A./N.E.A.; A.A.U.W.; N.A.S.N./P.A.S.N.Q.P.; A.A.R.P.; Harrisburg Hospital Nurse Alumni Association; American School Health Association; D.P.S.; United Ostomy Association Inc. **Hob./spts.:** Reading, gardening, sewing, embroidery **SIC code:** 82 **Address:** West York Area School District, 2605 W. Market St., York, PA 17404 **E-mail:** vachronister@wyasd.k12.pa.us

CIRILO, AMELIA

Industry: Educational Consultant **Born:** May 23, 1925 **Univ./degree:** B.S., Chemistry, Biology, Nuclear Engineering, 1950; M.Ed., Secondary & Elementary Education, 1954, University of Houston; Ph.D., Curriculum & Instruction, Nuclear Engineering, 1975, Texas A&M University **Current organization:** Educational Consultant, Motivational Speaker, Comedianne, Substitute Teacher; Self employed, Dallas Independent School District **Title:** Dr. (Ph.D.) **Type of organization:** Education, Speaker, Entertainment **Major product:** Evaluation of Bilingual Programs, Supervision, Teaching, Entertainment **Area of distribution:** National **Expertise:** Supervision, English as a Second Language (ESL-Spanish); Radio Isotope Technology, Science, Math, Motivation, Senior Comedy **Honors/awards:** Marquise Publishers: Who's Who in the World, Who's Who in America, Who's Who of American Women, Who's Who of the Southwest, Who's Who in Education; Selected by International Biographical Centre (IBC), Cambridge, England for 2000 Great Americans of the 20th Century; Outstanding Educator of the Year, Senior Salute, 1996, Senior Salute, NYL and City of Dallas **Published works:** A Comparative Analysis of Evaluative Theory and Practice for the Instructional Component of Bilingual Programs, Arno Press, 1978; Chapter 6, Tri-Ethnic Desegregation: Education and Social Sciences, Harvard University, 1973; Reflections (Poetry) 1983 **Affiliations:** Board of Directors, Methodist Home for the Elderly, 1968, Weslaco TX; Southwestern Educational Authority, 1977, Edinburg, TX; Women's Shelter, 1977 Corpus Christi, TX; National Committee for Domestic Violence, Washington, DC; Women's Political Caucus; Texas Teachers Association; National Educators Association; Texas Association of Bilingual Educators; American Association of University Women; Chemical Society; Pan American Round Table; Rocky Mountain Sociological Association; Metroplex Science Educators Association; League of United Latin American Citizens **Hob./spts.:** Travel, ballroom dancing, comedianne **SIC code:** 82 **Address:** Dallas Public Schools, 2615 Anson Rd., Dallas, TX 75235 **E-mail:** acirilo@earthlink.net

CLARK, BYRON K.

Industry: Education **Born:** January 17, 1964, Indianapolis, Indiana **Univ./degree:** B.A., IUPU, 2005 **Current organization:** IUPUI **Title:** Business Manager **Type of organization:** University **Major product:** Education **Area of distribution:** National **Expertise:** Business management **Affiliations:** Indiana State President, P.T.A.; Sigma Delta Phi; 100 Black Men of America, Inc. **SIC code:** 82 **Address:** IUPUI, 250 University Blvd., Suite 204, Indianapolis, IN 46206 **E-mail:** kclark7003@aol.com

CLARK, MARY E.

Industry: Education **Born:** April 28, 1927, San Francisco, California **Univ./degree:** Ph.D., Berkeley, 1960 **Current organization:** San Diego State University/George Mason University **Title:** Professor (Retired) **Type of organization:** University **Major product:** Higher education **Area of distribution:** National **Expertise:** Biology, conflict resolution **Honors/awards:** 1 biology textbook, 1 book "Ariadnes Thread", 1989 **Affiliations:** Lifetime Fellow, A.A.A.S. **Hob./spts.:** Gardening, piano **SIC code:** 82 **Address:** 780 Girard Ct., Cottage Grove, OR 97424 **E-mail:** meclark@efn.org

CLELAND, JAMES E.

Industry: Education **Born:** April 30, 1953, Evanston, Illinois **Univ./degree:** M.A., Curriculum and Instruction, Loyola University, 1993 **Current organization:** Loyola Academy **Title:** Architectural Design Instructor **Type of organization:** High school **Major product:** Education **Area of distribution:** Wilmette, Illinois **Expertise:** Design, architectural design **Published works:** Articles **Affiliations:** American Institute of Architecture Students **Hob./spts.:** Lecturing on Chicago architecture **SIC code:** 82 **Address:** Loyola University, 1100 Laramie Ave., Wilmette, IL 60091 **E-mail:** jamescleland@mac.com

CLIFFORD, MARIA C.

Industry: Education **Univ./degree:** MA.T., Rollins College, 1993 **Current organization:** Brevard Public Schools-Roy Allen Elementary School **Title:** Educator **Type of organization:** Elementary school **Major product:** Elementary education **Area of distribution:** Brevard, Florida **Expertise:** Mathematics and Science **Honors/awards:** Kappa Delta Pi; Teacher of the Year, 2003 **Affiliations:** N.E.A.; B.F.T.; N.B.C.T.; N.C.T.M.; F.E.A.; F.C.T.M.; N.S.T.A. **Hob./spts.:** Reading, camping, family activities, travel **SIC code:** 82 **Address:** 2081 Fatzler Rd., Melbourne, FL 32935 **E-mail:** iluvny6034@aol.com

COCHRANE, ROBERT L.

Industry: Education **Univ./degree:** Ph.D., University of Wisconsin, 1961 **Current organization:** West Virginia University, Division of Animal and Veterinary Science **Title:** Adjunct Professor **Type of organization:** University **Major product:** Higher education and research **Area of distribution:** West Virginia **Expertise:** Animal and veterinary science fur animal and ruffed grouse specialist **Affiliations:** Society for the Study of Reproduction **SIC code:** 82 **Address:** West Virginia University, Division of Animal and Veterinary Science, P.O. Box 6108, Morgantown, WV 26506-6108

COFFEY, SIMMIE LEE

Industry: Education **Born:** March 8, 1933, Seminole County, Oklahoma **Univ./degree:** A.A., Compton College, 1971; B.A.; M.A., CSUDH; D.D., Institute of Religious Science, 1984 **Current organization:** Rosa Parks Elementary School **Title:** Principal **Type of organization:** Elementary school **Major product:** Elementary school education **Area of distribution:** Lynwood, California **Expertise:** Elementary education, administration **Published works:** Poetry "Gifts of Love", 1982 **Affiliations:** International Poets' Society; International Who's Who; Strathmore's Who's Who, 2004; Minister, Carson Church of Religious Science, Carson, California **Hob./spts.:** Writing poetry **SIC code:** 82 **Address:** Rosa Parks Elementary School, 3900 Agnes St., Lynwood, CA 90262 **E-mail:** scoffey@lynwood.k12.ca.us

COHEN, CRAIG A.

Industry: Education **Born:** September 18, 1965 **Univ./degree:** New York Institute of Technology, 1999 **Current organization:** Wyandanch High School **Title:** Dean of Students **Type of organization:** High school **Major product:** Education **Area of distribution:** Wyandanch, New York **Expertise:** Education, school revival **Honors/awards:** All American Track and Field, 1988 **Hob./spts.:** Track and field, basketball **SIC code:** 82 **Address:** Wyandanch High School, 54 South 32nd, Wyandanch, NY 11798 **E-mail:** gocohengocohen@aol.com

COHEN, DALE

Industry: Education **Born:** June 8, 1949 **Univ./degree:** Cornell University **Current organization:** LaGuardia Community College/City University of New York **Title:** Graphic Designer **Type of organization:** University **Major product:** Education/advertising, publications and public relations **Area of distribution:** New York **Expertise:** Marketing and communications **Hob./spts.:** Tennis, films, skiing, reading **SIC code:** 82 **Address:** LaGuardia Community College/City University of New York, 31-10 Thomson Ave., Room 508, Long Island City, NY 11101

COLBORN, SARAH E. CROCKETT

Industry: Education **Born:** March 3, 1949, Kansas **Univ./degree:** B.A.Mus.Ed., Shorter College, 1972; Certificate Levels I, II, III, Master Class in Orff Approach to Music Ed., Memphis State University, 1987 **Current organization:** Augusta Children's Chorale **Title:** Member, Board of Directors **Type of organization:** Youth community choral group **Major product:** Music education and leadership **Area of distribution:** National **Expertise:** Elementary music educator, teaching Orff Approach, operatic performance **Honors/awards:** Numerous state, regional and national operatic competitions **Affiliations:** Chapter Member, Gamma Delta Kappa; Augusta Opera Chorus **Hob./spts.:** Cooking, geography, travel, opera, dance **SIC code:** 82 **Address:** 178 Creekview Ct., Martinez, GA 30907 **E-mail:** glcolb@yahoo.com **Web address:** www.aosa.com

CONE, MILTON L.

Industry: Education **Born:** May 27, 1945, Sedalia, Missouri **Univ./degree:** Ph.D., Air Force Institute of Technology, 1980 **Current organization:** Embry-Riddle Aeronautical University **Title:** Ph.D. **Type of organization:** University **Major product:** Higher education **Area of distribution:** Arizona **Expertise:** Engineering **Affiliations:** Institute of Electrical and Electronics Engineers **Hob./spts.:** Coaching soccer **SIC code:** 82 **Address:** 1259 E. Pine Ridge, Prescott, AZ 86303 **E-mail:** conec@pr.erau.edu

CONE, ROBERT E.

Industry: Medical **Born:** August 8, 1943, Brooklyn, New York **Univ./degree:** B.S., Biology, Brooklyn College, 1964; M.S., Bacteriology, Florida State University, 1967; Ph.D., Microbiology, University of Michigan, 1970; Postdoctoral Fellow, The Walter and Eliza Institute for Medical Research, Melbourne, Australia, 1971-73 **Current organization:** University of Connecticut Health Center **Title:** Professor **Type of organization:** University **Major product:** Higher education **Area of distribution:** International **Expertise:** Pathology, immunology **Honors/awards:** F.G. Novy Fellow, University of Michigan; Horace Rackham Fellow, University of Michigan; Sigma Chi; Damon Runyon Postdoctoral Fellow; Upjohn Company Basic Research Award, 1980, 1982; Who's Who in American Science; American Men and Women of Science; State of Connecticut Public Service Award, 2003 **Published works:** Author, "Soluble, extracellular antigen-specific T cell immunoproteins", J. Leukocyte Biology 59:605, 1996; Co-author, "Blood mononuclear cells induce regulatory NK thymocytes in anterior chamber-associated immune deviation", J. Leukocyte Biology 69:741, 2001; Numerous other journal articles and book chapters on immunoregulation by T cells; International patent: Immunointeractive molecules and uses thereof-Co-owners, Colin Little M.D. and George Georgiou; abstracts, journal articles, reviews, lectures, book chapters, technical reports **Affiliations:** American Association of Immunologists; American Association for the Advancement of Science; Association of Research In Vision and Ophthalmology; New York Academy of Sciences; Sigma XI **Hob./spts.:** Archaeology, painting, photography **SIC code:** 82 **Address:** University of Connecticut Health Center, Dept. of Pathology, 263 Farmington Ave., Farmington, CT 06030-3105 **E-mail:** cone@idx.uchc.edu

CONNELLY, MARK
Industry: Education **Born:** July 8, 1951, Philadelphia, Pennsylvania **Univ./degree:** Ph.D., English, University of Wisconsin at Milwaukee, 1984 **Current organization:** Milwaukee Area Technical College **Title:** Instructor **Type of organization:** College/ publishing **Major product:** Higher education, books **Area of distribution:** National **Expertise:** English instructor, writer **Published works:** 7 books, including "Deadly Closets: The Fiction of Charles Jackson", 2001; "The Sundance Writer", 2000; "Orwell and Gissing", 1997; "The Sundance Reader", 1996; and "The Diminished Self: Orwell and the Loss of Freedom", 1987 **Affiliations:** Modern Language Association; N.C.T.E. **Hob./spts.:** Irish studies, travel **SIC code:** 82 **Address:** Milwaukee Area Technical College, 700 E. State St., Milwaukee, WI 53233 **E-mail:** markconn@earthlink.net

COOKE, WILLIAM N.
Industry: Education **Born:** February 14, 1948, Alton, Illinois **Univ./degree:** B.S., Economics, Eastern Illinois State University, 1970; M.A., Labor/Industrial Relations, 1973; Ph.D., Labor/Industrial Relations, 1977, University of Illinois **Current organization:** Fraser Center for Workplace Issues/Wayne State University **Title:** Professor **Type of organization:** University **Major product:** Higher education **Area of distribution:** National **Expertise:** Labor and human resource management, corporate strategy, lecturing **Published works:** Book, "Multi National Companies and Global Human Resource Strategies"; articles **Affiliations:** International Industrial Relations Association; served in the U.S. Military during Vietnam **Hob./spts.:** Family, sailing, golf **SIC code:** 82 **Address:** Fraser Center for Workplace Issues, Wayne State University, 255 Reuther Library, Detroit, MI 48202 **E-mail:** wncooke@comcast.net

COOPER, EDWARD S.
Industry: Medical **Born:** December 11, 1926, Columbia, South Carolina **Univ./ degree:** A.B., Lincoln University, Pennsylvania, 1946; M.D. with Highest Honors, Meharry Medical College, Tennessee, 1949 **Current organization:** University of Pennsylvania School of Medicine **Title:** M.D., Emeritus Professor of Medicine **Type of organization:** University **Major product:** Healthcare, teaching, research **Area of distribution:** International **Expertise:** Cardiovascular disease and stroke **Honors/ awards:** Was the first African-American to receive tenure as a full Medical Professor at University of Pennsylvania School of Medicine; Was the first African-American to be elected President of the American Heart Association, 1992-93; Recipient of American Heart Association Award of Merit and Gold Heart Award; the Heart of Philadelphia Award; The Charles Drew Award for Distinguished Contributions to Medical Education; Distinguished Alumnus Awards from Lincoln University and Meharry Medical College **Published works:** Book; numerous articles, reports and reviews for professional journals and committees **Affiliations:** Diplomate and Local Examiner, American Board of Internal Medicine; Past President and chairman of the Stroke Council, American Heart Association; National Medical Association; Blue Cross of Greater Philadelphia; Association of Black Cardiologists; Founding Member and Chair of Executive Committee, American Health Education for African Development and American Foundation of Negro Affairs; American College of Physicians (Master), Board of Trustees, Rockefeller University **Hob./spts.:** Golf, water sports, clarinet **SIC code:** 82 **Address:** University of Pennsylvania School of Medicine, 3400 Spruce St., Philadelphia, PA 19104

COPELAND, JEAN P.
Industry: Education/child care **Born:** June 17, 1936, Petersburg, Virginia **Univ./ degree:** B.S., James Madison University, 1958; M.Ed., Elementary Education, Virginia Commonwealth University, 1968 **Current organization:** The Copeland Schools, Inc. **Title:** President **Type of organization:** Day care/pre-school **Major product:** Preschool education child care for 6 week olds to 12 year olds **Area of distribution:** Virginia **Expertise:** Education, management, financial **Affiliations:** National Child Care Association; National Association for the Education of Young Children; National Association of Child Care Professionals **Hob./spts.:** The beach, gourmet cooking, snow skiing, professional baseball (Braves) **SIC code:** 82 **Address:** The Copeland Schools, Inc., 10107 Krause Rd., Suite 100, Chesterfield, VA 23832 **E-mail:** copelandva@aol.com

CORDUNEANU, CONSTANTIN C.
Industry: Education **Born:** July 26, 1928, Jassy, Romania **Univ./degree:** Ph.D., Mathematics, University of Jassy, Romania-1956 **Current organization:** University of Texas at Arlington **Title:** Emeritus Professor **Type of organization:** University **Major product:** Higher education **Area of distribution:** National **Expertise:** Mathematics **Affiliations:** American Mathematical Society **Hob./spts.:** Statistics, travel **SIC code:** 82 **Address:** 812 S. Collins St., Arlington, TX 76010 **E-mail:** cordun@uta.edu

CROCKER, YUKO KOJI
Industry: Education **Born:** November 4, 1957, Osaka, Japan **Univ./degree:** B.S., Philosophy, Washington University, 2004 **Current organization:** Hawaii Seminar Japanese Language School **Title:** Principal **Type of organization:** School **Major product:** Education, educational development **Area of distribution:** Honolulu, Hawaii **Expertise:** Daily school operations **Hob./spts.:** Golf, gardening **SIC code:** 82 **Address:** Hawaii Seminar Japanese Language School, 3410 Campbell Ave., Honolulu, HI 96815 **Web address:** www.hawaiilanguageschool.com

CROSS, L. ERIC
Industry: Higher education **Born:** August 14, 1923, Morley, England **Univ./degree:** Ph.D., Physics, Leeds University **Current organization:** Pennsylvania State University **Title:** Ph.D. **Type of organization:** University **Major product:** Higher education **Area of distribution:** Pennsylvania **Expertise:** Applied research **Published works:** 20 patents; 640 papers, articles and book chapters **Affiliations:** Fellow, I.E.E.E.; Fellow, A.P.S.; Fellow, American Optical Society; Fellow American Ceramic Society; National Academy of Engineering **SIC code:** 82 **Address:** Pennsylvania State University, Room 187, Materials Research Institute, University Park, PA 16802 **E-mail:** lec3@psu.edu.com **Web address:** www.mri.psu.edu/faculty/lec.asp

CROWTHER, C. RICHARD
Industry: Education **Born:** July 16, 1924, Waterloo, Iowa **Univ./degree:** Ph.D., University of Michigan, 1971 **Current organization:** Michigan Technological University **Title:** Professor Emeritus **Type of organization:** University **Major product:** Higher education **Area of distribution:** Michigan **Expertise:** Forestry, recreation resource management **Published works:** 3 articles **Affiliations:** S.A.F. **SIC code:** 82 **Address:** 6850 N Rd., Escanaba, MI 49829-9524

CRUM, DONNA J.
Industry: Education/associations **Born:** September 27, 1954, Grayling, Michigan **Univ./degree:** B.S. with Honors, Health Science, Western Michigan University, 1997; M.S., Instructional Design, University of Kentucky, 2004 **Current organization:** St. Catharine College/Kentucky Society of Radiologic Technologists **Title:** Program Director, Radiology/President **Type of organization:** College/association **Major product:** Higher education/providing professional growth, education opportunities, quality patient care and to further the welfare of the radiologic profession **Area of distribution:** Kentucky **Expertise:** Radiography curriculum design **Affiliations:** President-Elect, KSRT,Inc. **Hob./spts.:** Audio books, classical and 1950's music **SIC code:** 82 **Address:** St. Catharine College/Kentucky Society of Radiologic Technologists, 2735 Bardstown Rd., St. Catharine, KY 40061 **E-mail:** dcrum@sccky.edu **Web address:** www.sccky.edu

CUMMINGS, JASPER L.
Industry: Education **Born:** September 13, 1936, Snow Hill, North Carolina **Spouse:** Marie R. Cummings **Married:** October 21, 2000 **Children:** Barbara (Deceased), Audrey, Jacqueline, Marie , Michelle, Elaina, Bylinda, 4 Grandchildren, 3 Great Grandchildren **Univ./degree:** A.A., Business Administration, Strayer University, 1973; Attended, University of the District of Columbia, 1983-85; B.A., Magna Cum Laude, Business Administration, Sojourner-Douglass College, 1992; M.A. w/Honors, Administration, World Academy of Letters **Current organization:** Sojourner-Douglass College **Title:** Enrollment Manager **Type of organization:** College **Major product:** Higher education **Area of distribution:** National **Expertise:** Education, finance, accounting **Honors/awards:** Great Minds of the 21st Century; Strathmore's Who's Who; Who's Who in Executives and Professionals Register, Publication, 2006-07; Global Who's Who; World Laureate, ABI; Fellow, ABI; International Peace Prize, World Cultural Society; Lifetime Achievement Award, IBC, Cambridge, England; Outstanding Service Award, National Institutes of Health; Honorable Mention, Saturday Evening Post, Children, Wall of Tolerance, Rosa Parks Co-Chairperson; "The Jasper L. Cummings Foundation" American Biographical Institute, established February 9, 2007 **Affiliations:** American Biographical Institute; International Biographical Association; Past Member, Toastmasters International; Lake Arbor Civic Association; First Baptist Church of Glenarden; International Biographical Centre; 100 Outstanding Administrators, Cambridge, England; Lifetime Member, Sojourner-Douglass College, National Alumni Association; Alpha Nu Omega Fraternity; Past President, South Greene High School Alumni Association; Treasurer, Sojourner-Douglass National Alumni Association **Career accomplishments:** Assisted in the opening of the Sojourner Douglass College, Prince George's County Campus in Lanham, Maryland; Served as Director of Alumni Relations at Sojourner Douglass College **Hob./spts.:** Watching sports, baseball, football, hockey and golf, church involvement (education committee) **SIC code:** 82 **Address:** Sojourner-Douglass College, 8200 Professional Place, Suite 111, Hyattsville, MD 20785 **E-mail:** jcummings@host.sdc.edu **Web address:** www.sdc.edu

CURA, MARCO A.
Industry: Medical **Born:** July 11, 1972, Argentina **Univ./degree:** M.D., 1995 **Current organization:** UTHSCSA **Title:** M.D. **Type of organization:** University **Major product:** Medical education, research **Area of distribution:** International **Expertise:** Interventional radiology **Affiliations:** Radiological Society of North America; Society of Interventional Radiology; American College of Radiology; American Heart Association; Texas Radiological Society **Hob./spts.:** Water sports **SIC code:** 82 **Address:** UTHSCSA, 7703 Floyd Curl Dr., San Antonio, TX 78230 **E-mail:** curam@uthscsa.edu **Web address:** www.uthscsa.edu

CUTKOMP, LAURENCE K.
Industry: Education **Born:** January 24, 1916, Wapello, Iowa **Univ./degree:** Ph.D., Insect Toxicology, Cornell University **Title:** Retired Professor Emeritus, University of Minnesota **Type of organization:** University **Major product:** Higher education, research **Area of distribution:** National **Expertise:** Entomology **Published works:** "Insect Rhythms" in Encyclopedia of Entomology; "Senses and Moves in Insects", "How to Know Immature Insects"; 150+ other publications **Affiliations:** Entomological Society of America **Hob./spts.:** Photography **SIC code:** 82 **Address:** 401 Sibley St., #828, St. Paul, MN 55101 **E-mail:** cutko001@aol.com

DABBAGH, MOHAMED ABDUL-HAY
Industry: Education **Born:** November 21, 1937, Bethlehem **Univ./degree:** A.A., College of San Mateo, California, 1961; B.A., San Jose State University, California, 1963; M.A., University of California at Riverside, 1965; Ph.D., St. Louis University, Missouri, 1974 **Current organization:** Florida Metropolitan University **Title:** Adjunct Faculty **Type of organization:** University **Expertise:** Finance, economics **Honors/awards:** Who's Who in Finance and Industry, 1996-1997 **Published works:** Book, "Analytical Examination of Monetary Resources and the Role of the Central Bank in Lebanon, 1978, Al Risala, Beirut, Lebanon; 80 articles, book review **Affiliations:** American Economic Association; Southern Economic Association; Missouri Valley Economic Association; Midwest Economic Association **Hob./spts.:** Basketball, tennis **SIC code:** 82 **Address:** Florida Metropolitan University, 3319 W. Hillsborough Ave., Tampa, FL 33614 **E-mail:** ma-dabbagh@yahoo.com

DALGLEISH, DONALD DOUGLAS
Industry: Education **Univ./degree:** Ph.D., University of Colorado, 1963 **Current organization:** Arizona State University **Title:** Professor Emeritus of Military Science (Civilian) **Type of organization:** University **Major product:** Higher education **Area of distribution:** National, International **Expertise:** U.S. National defense policy and military history; research, publication and lecturing **Affiliations:** U.S. Naval Institute **Hob./spts.:** Carpentry, horsemanship, swimming **SIC code:** 82 **Address:** 6022 N. 59th Place, Scottsdale, AZ 85253

DAUGHERTY, WILLIAM JAMES
Industry: Education **Univ./degree:** Ph.D., Claremont Graduate School, 1979 **Current organization:** Armstrong Atlantic State University **Title:** Ph.D., Professor **Type of organization:** University **Major product:** Higher education **Area of distribution:** International **Expertise:** Political science (foreign policy) **Published works:** 2 books, 5 journals **Affiliations:** Association of Former Intelligence Officers; U.S. Naval Institute **Hob./spts.:** Tennis, collecting books, travel, scuba diving, private pilot's license **SIC code:** 82 **Address:** Armstrong Atlantic State University, 11935 Aberncorn St., Savannah, GA 31419 **E-mail:** wijid@comcast.net

DAVALOS, JULIO F.
Industry: Education/engineering **Born:** January 12, 1949, Cochabamba, Bolivia **Univ./degree:** B.S.C.E., Civil Engineering, 1985; M.S.C.E., Structural Engineering, 1987, Virginia Tech.; Ph.D., Structural Engineering, Virginia Tech., 1989 **Current organization:** West Virginia University **Title:** Benedum Distinguished Teaching Professor **Type of organization:** University **Major product:** Research, higher education **Area of distribution:** National **Expertise:** Structural engineering and advanced materials **Honors/awards:** Professor of the Year, State of West Virginia, 1998 **Published works:** 70+ journals, 100 papers, 4 book chapters **Affiliations:** A.S.E.E.; S.P.I.; A.S.C.E. **Hob./spts.:** Reading, travel, classical music, theatre **SIC code:** 82 **Address:** Civil and Environmental Engineering, West Virginia University, 611C Engineering Sciences Bldg., Morgantown, WV 26506-6103 **E-mail:** jfdavalos@mail.wvu.edu **Web address:** www.wvu.edu

DAVENPORT, ROBIN DOUGLAS
Industry: Education **Born:** October 6, 1951, Virginia Beach, Virginia **Univ./degree:** M.S., Elementary Education and Administration Endorsement, Old Dominion University, 1978 **Current organization:** Virginia Beach City Public Schools **Title:** Principal **Type of organization:** Elementary school **Major product:** Elementary education **Area of distribution:** Virginia Beach, Virginia **Expertise:** Operations, administration, public speaking **Affiliations:** N.A.E.S.P.; V.A.E.S.P.; President, Ruritan National Foundation **Hob./spts.:** The beach **SIC code:** 82 **Address:** Virginia Beach City Public Schools, 920 Princess Anne Rd., Virginia Beach, VA 23457-1098 **E-mail:** rdavenpo@vbschools.com

DAVINCI-NICHOLS, NINA
Industry: Education **Born:** December 21, 1932, New York, New York **Univ./degree:** Ph.D., New York University **Current organization:** Rutgers University, English Dept. **Title:** Professor **Type of organization:** University **Major product:** Higher education **Area of distribution:** New Jersey **Expertise:** Shakespearean to modern drama **Honors/awards:** Doctoral Award in Shakespeare studies; Grants from the Rockefeller Foundation, the American Academy of Rome **Published works:** Associate Editor, "The Annals of Scholarship"; Editor, Collegiate Press; Articles in Stages, Shakespeare Bulletin, Shakespeare Newsletter, America Oggi, American Book Review, the Journal of the Pirandello Society of America; Books: "Child of the Night", Bantam; "Pirandello and Film", University of Nebraska, 1996; "Ariadne's Lives", Fairleigh Dickinson University Press (New Jersey Associated University Presses, 1995) **Affiliations:** A.C.L.S.; A.A.D.C.; Fellow, International Federation for Theater Research; American Theater Critics Association; Member, Board of Directors, American Foundation for Italian Arts & Letters **SIC code:** 82 **Address:** 305 W. 13th St., New York, NY 10014 **E-mail:** davinci@andromeda.rutgers.edu

DAVIS, DAVID J.
Industry: Medical **Born:** January 12, 1949, Des Moines, Iowa **Univ./degree:** B.S., Mathematics, Biology, University of Northwestern Missouri State, 1972 **Current organization:** University of Colorado HSC **Title:** Lab Manager-Pathology **Type of organization:** University **Major product:** Medical education, clinical pathology, laboratory medicine **Area of distribution:** Colorado **Expertise:** Pathology, histology **Affiliations:** American Society of Clinical Pathologists; National Society for Histotechnology; Colorado Society for Histotechnology; Arizona Society for Histotechnology **Hob./spts.:** Black Belt Karate, water skiing, racquetball, swimming **SIC code:** 82 **Address:** University of Colorado HSC, 4200 E. Ninth Ave., MS 1542, Denver, CO 80262 **E-mail:** david.davis@uchsc.edu

DAWSON, DANA F.
Industry: Education **Univ./degree:** B.S., Education; New Mexico State University, 1977; B.S., Computer Science, University of New Mexico, 1984; M.S., Science Teaching, New Mexico Tech, 2005 **Current organization:** Moriarty Municipal School District **Title:** Educator **Type of organization:** Public school **Major product:** Public school education **Area of distribution:** Edgewood, New Mexico **Expertise:** Secondary education, mathematics **Affiliations:** A.S.C.D.; N.M.A.S.C.D.; N.C.T.M.; Phi Delta Kappa **SIC code:** 82 **Address:** Edgewood Elementary School, 285 Dinkle Rd., Edgewood, NM 87015-9552

DAY, DIANE E.
Industry: Education **Born:** January 14, 1961, Portsmouth, Virginia **Univ./degree:** Ph.D., Biology, Georgia State University, 2003 **Current organization:** Georgia State University **Title:** Ph.D./Lecturer **Type of organization:** University **Major product:** Higher education, research **Area of distribution:** National **Expertise:** Neurobiology and behavior **Published works:** 8 peer-reviewed articles **Affiliations:** Society for Neuroscience; Society for the Study of Ingestive Behavior **Hob./spts.:** Silversmithing, reading, travel, hiking **SIC code:** 82 **Address:** Georgia State University, Dept. of Biology, Room 402, P.O. Box 4010, Atlanta, GA 30302-4010 **E-mail:** deday@gsu.edu

DAY, RICHARD A.
Industry: Education **Born:** April 4, 1931, Kellogg, Iowa **Univ./degree:** B.S., Iowa State University, 1953; Ph.D., Organic Chemistry, Massachusetts Institute of Technology, 1958 **Current organization:** University of Cincinnati **Title:** Professor **Type of organization:** University **Major product:** Higher education, research ("Beta-Lactams") **Area of distribution:** International **Expertise:** Biochemistry **Published works:** 100+ (articles, reviews and book chapters) **Affiliations:** A.C.S.; A.S.M.B.; A.S.M.S. **Hob./spts.:** Archeo-astronomy, music, travel, gardening **SIC code:** 82 **Address:** University of Cincinnati, Dept. of Chemistry, ML 0172, Cincinnati, OH 45221-0172 **E-mail:** richard.day@uc.edu

DE JESUS, GLORIA
Industry: Education **Born:** December 22, 1941, San Juan, Puerto Rico **Univ./degree:** M.A., Special Education; M.A., Supervision and Administration, University of Hartford **Current organization:** Hartford Public Schools **Title:** Director of Assessment, Evaluation and Research **Type of organization:** School administration office **Major product:** Public school education **Area of distribution:** Hartford, Connecticut **Expertise:** Administration, implementation of testing programs, workshops **Honors/awards:** Numerous Recognition Awards at Hartford Public Schools **Published works:** Book: "Enfranchising Urban Learners for the 21st Century" **Affiliations:** Phi-Delta-Kappa **Hob./spts.:** Crafts, fencing, horseback riding, reading **SIC code:** 82 **Address:** Hartford Public Schools, 153 Market St., 9th floor, Hartford, CT 06103 **E-mail:** gdejesu@hartfordschools.org

DE VILLIERS, MELGARDT M.
Industry: Education **Born:** December 1, 1962, Johannesburg, South Africa **Univ./degree:** Ph.D., Pharmaceutics, Potchefstroom University, 1993 **Current organization:** University of Louisiana at Monroe **Title:** Ph.D. **Type of organization:** University **Major product:** Higher education **Area of distribution:** International **Expertise:** Drug delivery **Affiliations:** American Association of Pharmaceutical Sciences; American Chemical Society **Hob./spts.:** Golf, running **SIC code:** 82 **Address:** University of Louisiana at Monroe, College of Pharmacy, Monroe, LA 71209 **E-mail:** pydevilliers@ulm.edu

DE-LEON, ROSA E.
Industry: Education **Born:** August 23, 1973, Roma, Texas **Univ./degree:** B.A., Science & Social Work, University of Texas, 1996 **Current organization:** W.I.S.D. Margo Elementary **Title:** Parent Specialist **Type of organization:** School **Major product:** Elementary school education **Area of distribution:** Weslaco, Texas **Expertise:** Parent programs (student success) **Affiliations:** N.A.S.W. **Hob./spts.:** Sewing, collecting antiques, reading **SIC code:** 82 **Address:** 507 W. 6th St., Apt. C, Weslaco, TX 78596 **E-mail:** budrose23@yahoo.com

DEMAR, KAREN J.
Industry: Education **Born:** March 12, 1946, Rochester, New York **Univ./degree:** B.A., Mathematics, Nazareth College of Rochester, 1968; M.S., Communicative Disorders, Northwestern University, 1972; Continued Advanced Studies, National-Louis University, 1984 **Current organization:** St. Ann Catholic School **Title:** Principal **Type of organization:** Catholic elementary school **Major product:** Pre-K through 8th grade education **Area of distribution:** West Palm Beach, Florida **Expertise:** Administration, special education **Hob./spts.:** Reading, travel **SIC code:** 82 **Address:** St. Ann Catholic School, 324 N. Olive Ave., West Palm Beach, FL 33401 **E-mail:** kdemar@stannwpb.org

DENWORTH, EMIL D.
Industry: Education **Born:** August 17, Philadelphia, Pennsylvania **Univ./degree:** B.A., Latin, Marist College; M.A., History, Salem University; M.A., Administration, Fordham University **Current organization:** St. Agnes Boys High School **Title:** Brother/Chief Librarian **Type of organization:** High school **Major product:** Secondary education **Area of distribution:** New York, New York **Expertise:** Educating inner city students **Hob./spts.:** Opera **SIC code:** 82 **Address:** St. Agnes Boys High School, 555 West End Ave., New York, NY 10024 **E-mail:** emil_denworth@yahoo.com

DETMER, GREGORY MARK
Industry: Medical **Born:** May 22, 1949, Chicago, Illinois **Univ./degree:** B.S., Psychology, Computers, Eastern Michigan University; M.B.A., Central Michigan University **Current organization:** University of Michigan **Title:** Foreman **Type of organization:** University hospital **Major product:** Higher education, patient services **Area of distribution:** Michigan **Expertise:** Project management for the construction services at the University of Michigan Hospital, business development, technical consulting, team leadership, budget planning, computer technology **Affiliations:** A.P.P.A. **Hob./spts.:** Golf, church activities, family, community services (helped to implement diversity) youth activities **SIC code:** 82 **Address:** University of Michigan, 1500 E. Medical Center Dr., Ann Arbor, MI 48109 **E-mail:** detmer@umich.edu

DEVOE, LAWRENCE D.
Industry: Medical **Born:** November 5, 1944, Chicago, Illinois **Spouse:** Anne Hesten **Married:** January 10, 1987 **Children:** Laura, 26 **Univ./degree:** M.D., University of Chicago **Current organization:** Medical College of Georgia **Title:** M.D. **Type of organization:** Medical school/hospital **Major product:** Teaching, research, clinical care **Area of distribution:** Georgia **Expertise:** Medical faculty and clinician, ob/gyn **Published works:** 140 publications **Affiliations:** Fellow, American College of Ob/Gyn; American Medical Association; Society of Maternal Fetal Medicine **Hob./spts.:** Marathon running, opera, sports cars **SIC code:** 82 **Address:** Medical College of Georgia, Dept. of Ob/Gyn, 1120 15th St., Augusta, GA 30912 **E-mail:** ldevoe@mail.mcg.edu

DICKMEYER, DON L.
Industry: Education **Born:** October 6, 1945, Arlington Nebraska **Univ./degree:** Architectural Design, S.E. Community College, 1967 **Current organization:** University of Nebraska Medical Center **Title:** Project Manager **Type of organization:** University **Major product:** Higher education **Area of distribution:** National **Expertise:** Architecture **Hob./spts.:** Golf **SIC code:** 82 **Address:** University of Nebraska Medical Center, 987100 Nebraska Medical Center, Omaha, NE 68198-7100 **E-mail:** ddickmey@unmc.edu

DIGIUSTINI, ANTONETTA A.
Industry: Education **Born:** July 10, 1961, Boston, Massachusetts **Univ./degree:** A.B., Modern European History, Harvard University, 1997 **Current organization:** Harvard University **Type of organization:** University **Major product:** Research and educational academic programs **Area of distribution:** Cambridge, Massachusetts **Expertise:** Non-profit administration, writing **Affiliations:** A.H.A.; A.A.M. **Hob./spts.:** Poetry, photography, running **SIC code:** 82 **Address:** Harvard University, 10 Garden St., Cambridge, MA 02138 **E-mail:** a_digiustini@radcliffe.edu

DIROCCO, PATRICK J.
Industry: Education **Born:** April 23, 1947, Poughkeepsie, New York **Univ./degree:** Ph.D., Motor Development and Adapted Physical Education, University of Oregon; B.S., Physical Education, Ithaca College; M.S., University of Oregon **Current organization:** University of Wisconsin, LaCrosse **Title:** Ph.D., Chair of ESS Dept. **Type of organization:** University **Major product:** Higher education, research **Area of distribution:** Wisconsin **Expertise:** Working with people with disabilities **Affiliations:** American Alliance for Health, Physical Education, Recreation and Dance; National Consortium for Physical Education & Recreation for Individuals with Disabilities **Hob./spts.:** Golf, softball, hiking, reading **SIC code:** 82 **Address:** University of Wisconsin, LaCrosse, 137 Mitchell Hall, UW-L, La Crosse, WI 54601 **E-mail:** dirocco.patr@uwlax.edu

DIXON, ARMENDIA P.
Industry: Education **Univ./degree:** B.A., English, Jackson State College, 1956; M.S., Secondary Administration, Edinboro University of Pennsylvania, 1972; Ph.D., Curriculum & Administration, Kent State University, 1992 **Current organization:** Edinboro University of Pennsylvania **Title:** Chairperson, Academic Support Services **Type of organization:** University **Major product:** Higher education **Area of distribution:** National **Expertise:** Secondary school administration; teaching **Published works:** Numerous including Co-author, "Ebony Genealogy of Sorts"; "Extravaganza: Erie's History in Music, Dance & Drama"; "Meaning Making with Maxine Greene on Her Work as a Philosopher Teacher Educator" **Affiliations:** N.C.T.E.; Alpha Kappa Alpha; Delta Kappa Gamma; Board Member, Edinboro Alumni Association Board; Dr. Martin Luther King Jr. Scholarship Fund, Inc.; Sickle Cell Anemia Foundation; Advisory Committee and Childcare Evaluation Team for International Institute **SIC code:** 82 **Address:** Edinboro University of Pennsylvania, 716 Jefferson St., Meadville, PA 16335 **E-mail:** adixon@edinboro.edu **Web address:** www.edinboro.edu

DIXON-DZIEDZIC, LINDA
Industry: Mental health, counseling, education **Born:** June 2, 1962, Bronx, New York **Univ./degree:** A.A., Beh. Science, Dutchess College, 1980; B.A., Psychology; B.S., Health Science, 1982, SUNY Brockport, 1982; EMT-Specialist, Davenport College, 1983; M.A., Counseling, 1986; C.A.S., School Psychology, 2001, Marist College **Current organization:** Pine Plains Central School District **Title:** School Psychologist **Type of organization:** Public school district **Major product:** Elementary school education **Area of distribution:** Pine Plains, New York **Expertise:** Assessment, consulting, counseling, Certified, first aid and C.P.R., Certified, Aggression Control Techniques **Honors/awards:** Marquis "Who's Who in America", 51st, 52nd, 53rd editions; "Who's Who in Healthcare and Medicine', 1st and 2nd editions, "Who's Who of American Women", 20th and 21st editions; "Who's Who in the World", 15th edition; American Biographical Institute, "International Book of Honor", 5th edition; International Biographical Centre, "The World of Who's Who of Women", 14th edition **Affiliations:** N.Y.A.S.P.; Democratic Ward Delegate, Wapp Falls, New York **Hob./spts.:** Weightlifting **SIC code:** 82 **Address:** Pine Plains Central School District, Rt. 199, Pine Plains, NY 12567 **E-mail:** dziedzic62@wmconnect.com

DLUGOSH, LARRY L.
Industry: Education **Born:** Ord, Nebraska **Univ./degree:** M.Ed., 1975; Ph.D., 1981, University of Nebraska, Lincoln **Current organization:** University of Nebraska, Lincoln **Title:** Ph.D./Chair, Dept. of Administration **Type of organization:** University **Major product:** Higher education **Area of distribution:** Nebraska **Expertise:** Public relations, conflict management **Published works:** 20 publications **Affiliations:** American Educational Research Association; American Association of School Administrators **Hob./spts.:** Golf, travel **SIC code:** 82 **Address:** University of Nebraska (Lincoln), 141 TEAC, Lincoln, NE 68588-0360 **E-mail:** ldlugosh1@unl.edu

DOBROF, ROSE W.
Industry: Education **Born:** November 11, 1924, Denver, Colorado **Univ./degree:** D.S.W., Columbia University, 1976 **Current organization:** Brookdale Center on Aging, Hunter College **Title:** Brookdale Professor of Gerontology **Type of organization:** College **Major product:** Higher education **Area of distribution:** National **Expertise:** Gerontology, social work **Published works:** Numerous including: "Elderly Patients Star on Grandparents Day" (with Jacob Reingold), in "Hospitals", Vol. 38, March 1964; "The Family Relationships and Living Arrangements of Older Women" in "Older Women in New York City Today and Tomorrow", New York: Arno Press, 1979; "The Maintenance of the Family Relationships of Old People in Institutions: Theory and Practice" (with Eugene Litwak), a manual published by the Center of Aging, National Institute on Mental Health, 1977; Editor, "Social Work and Alzheimer's Disease", New York: The Haworth Press, 1986 **Affiliations:** N.A.S.W; Senior Fellow, Brookdale Foundation; Fellow, The New York Academy of Medicine; Co-chair, Committee on Aging of Federation of Jewish Philanthropies; Member, Review Team, The Fund for Improvement of Secondary Education; Gerontological Society of America; National

Council on Aging **Hob./spts.:** Bridge, poker, swimming **SIC code:** 82 **Address:** Brookdale Center on Aging, Hunter College, 1114 Ave. of the Americas, New York, NY 10036 **E-mail:** rdobrof@hunter.sunyedu

DONALSON, MALCOLM D.
Industry: Education **Born:** July 24, 1951, Albany, Georgia **Univ./degree:** Ph.D., Florida State University **Current organization:** Alabama School of Mathematics & Science **Title:** Professor, Foreign Language & History **Type of organization:** College preparatory school **Major product:** College prep education **Area of distribution:** Alabama **Expertise:** Writing **Published works:** "History of the Wolf in Western Civilization", "The Domestic Cat in Roman Civilization", "The Cult of Isis in the Roman Empire" **Affiliations:** American Classical League; North American Patristic Society **Hob./spts.:** Coin collecting **SIC code:** 82 **Address:** Alabama School of Mathematics & Science, 2155 Dauphin St., Mobile, AL 36604 **E-mail:** isisinvicta@aol.com

DONOVAN, WILLARD P.
Industry: Education **Born:** September 1, 1930, Grand Rapids, Michigan **Univ./degree:** B.S.; M.A, Education, 1967, Eastern Michigan University **Current organization:** Warren Consolidated Schools, NY (Retired) **Title:** Teacher **Type of organization:** Elementary school **Major product:** Education **Area of distribution:** Arizona City, Arizona **Expertise:** Remedial classroom, certified K-8, Michigan **Honors/awards:** Decorated Combat Infantry Badge, U.S. Army, Korea, 1947-1950; Purple Heart with Three Clusters, Korean-Japan Service Medal, 1951; Presidential Citation, 1951; Korean Medal with Three Campaign Clusters, 1951; National Defense Service Medal, 1951; Bronze Star; Silver Star **Affiliations:** The Chosen Few Army and Marines Association; The Chosen Few (U.S. Army); 31st Infantry Association; U.S. Army, 1947-1964; Member, N.R.A.; American Quarterhouse Association; Detroit Area Council of Teachers of Math; Met. Detroit School Teachers Association; National Education Association; Michigan Education Association; Warren Education Association **Hob./spts.:** Riding horses, hiking, carpentry, theatre, arts, travel, pistol shooting **SIC code:** 82 **Address:** P.O. Box 563, Arizona City, AZ 85223 **E-mail:** wpdonovan123aol.com

DOODY, JOHN EDWARD
Industry: Education **Born:** March 30, 1925, Chicago, Illinois **Univ./degree:** Ph.D., Physical Chemistry, St. Louis University, 1953 **Current organization:** Christian Brothers University Bx81 **Title:** Ph.D. **Type of organization:** University **Major product:** Higher education **Area of distribution:** National **Expertise:** Assisting faculty, minorities and schools in developing grants. Organizing summer training programs for science teachers in elementary, secondary schools and universities **Honors/awards:** Memphis Chemical Club Education and Service Award; University Maurelian Medal; Lawrence Egbert Distinguished Service Award; Fellow, Tennessee Academy of Science; NASA American Society for Engineering Education Certificate; West Tennessee Science Teachers Certificate of Engineer Award; Selection as Outstanding Educator of America; American Chemical Society Award for furthering the Teaching of High School Chemistry; Memphis Joint Engineering Societies Featured Chemist Award **Affiliations:** Member, Religious Order of the Christian Brothers (aka DeLaSalle Brothers in Europe, Asia and Africa); Director of Field Center for the NSF Chautauqua Short Courses for College Teachers, 1978-2003 **Hob./spts.:** Playing the flute, cooking **SIC code:** 82 **Address:** Christian Brothers University Bx81, 650 E. Parkway South, Memphis, TN 38104 **E-mail:** edoody@cbu.edu

DOWDY, RANDY J.
Industry: Education **Born:** August 29, 1946, Wichita, Kansas **Univ./degree:** A.A.S., Journalism, San Jacinto College, 1966; B.A., History, University of Maryland, 1983; M.P.A., Troy State University, 1993 **Current organization:** Hitchcock Independent School District, Crosby Middle School **Title:** Principal **Type of organization:** Middle school **Major product:** Education, administration **Area of distribution:** Hitchcock, Texas **Expertise:** Education **Honors/awards:** Defense Meritorious Service Medal as U.S. Naval Commanding Officer for the Courier Service in Spain; U.S. Navy 1968-95, retired as Chief Warrant Officer **Published works:** Newspaper reporter, Pasadena Daily News **Affiliations:** Texas Association of Secondary Principals; Association for Supervision and Curriculum Development **Hob./spts.:** Reading history, biographies, travel **SIC code:** 82 **Address:** Crosby Middle School, 7801 Neville Ave., Hitchcock, TX 77563 **E-mail:** rdowdy@hitchcockisd.org

DOYLE, KIMBERLY M.
Industry: Education **Born:** New Prague, Minnesota **Univ./degree:** B.A., Elementary Education, College of St. Benedict, 1980; M.Ed., Administration, 1985; Ed.Specialist, 1994, University of St. Thomas **Current organization:** Blessed Trinity Catholic School **Title:** Principal **Type of organization:** Elementary schools **Major product:** Education of 500 students, pre-school through 8th grade **Area of distribution:** Metro-Minneapolis, Minnesota **Expertise:** Administration, evangelization, literacy development **Affiliations:** Minnesota Non Public School Accreditation Association; Association of Catholic School Principals **SIC code:** 82 **Address:** Blessed Trinity Catholic School, 6720 Nicollet Ave. S., Richfield, MN 55423 **E-mail:** doylek@btcsmn.org **Web address:** www.btcsmn.org

DRECHNEY, MICHAELENE
Industry: Education **Born:** October 13, 1948, Chicago, Illinois **Univ./degree:** M.S., Guidance and Education, Loyola University of Chicago, 1973 **Current organization:** O.A. Thorp Scholastic Academy **Title:** Teacher **Type of organization:** School **Major product:** Education **Area of distribution:** Chicago, Illinois **Expertise:** Teaching 7th and 8th graders **Affiliations:** N.S.T.A.; I.S.T.A. **Hob./spts.:** Travel **SIC code:** 82 **Address:** O.A. Thorp Scholastic Academy, 6024 W. Warwick Ave., Chicago, IL 60634 **E-mail:** miki61@juno.com

DUAN, XIN-RAN
Industry: Education **Univ./degree:** B.S., Xian Jiao Tong University, China, 1968; M.S.M.E., University of Oklahoma, 1992; Ph.D., Administration of Higher Education, Indiana State University, 2003 **Current organization:** Ivy Tech State College **Title:** Chair/Professor **Type of organization:** University (State College) **Major product:** Design technology (mech., arch., CAD/CAM) **Area of distribution:** International **Expertise:** Mechanical engineering, educational administration **Published works:** 15+ public papers **Affiliations:** A.S.M.E.; A.A.U.P.; N.A.I.T.; A.D.D.A.; I.N.E.E.R. **SIC code:** 82 **Address:** Ivy Tech State College, 4475 Central Ave., Columbus, IN 47203-1868

DUBE, JEAN-PIERRE H.
Industry: Education **Born:** August 18, 1972, Kitchener, Ontario, Canada **Univ./degree:** Ph.D., Economics, Northwestern University **Current organization:** University of Chicago Graduate School of Business **Title:** Dr. **Type of organization:** Business school **Major product:** Research, education **Area of distribution:** Illinois **Expertise:** Marketing, economics **Affiliations:** American Marketing Association **Hob./spts.:** Reading, travel **SIC code:** 82 **Address:** University of Chicago Graduate School of Business, 1101 E. 58th St., Chicago, IL 60637 **E-mail:** jdube@gsb.uchicago.edu

DUENO, ERIC EFRAIN
Industry: Education **Born:** March 24, 1968, Omaha, Nebraska **Univ./degree:** Ph.D., Organic Synthesis, University of South Florida, 2004 **Current organization:** Eastern Kentucky University **Title:** Assistant Professor **Type of organization:** University **Major product:** Higher education **Area of distribution:** Kentucky **Expertise:** Synthesis of medicinal compounds **Affiliations:** A.C.S.; Kentucky Academy of Science **Hob./spts.:** Fishing **SIC code:** 82 **Address:** Eastern Kentucky University, Dept. of Chemistry, 521 Lancaster Ave., Richmond, KY 40475 **E-mail:** eric.dueno@eku.edu

DUNCAN, NELLIE R.
Industry: Education **Univ./degree:** Ed.D., Fordham University, 1978 **Current organization:** Self-employed **Title:** District Superintendent, New York City Board of Education (Retired) **Type of organization:** Consulting **Area of distribution:** National **Expertise:** Consulting for the future administrators of America **Affiliations:** Delta Sigma Theta; numerous New York City educational groups **SIC code:** 82 **Address:** 183-04 Camden Ave., St. Albans, NY 11412-1506

DUNNE, PETER B.
Industry: Medical **Born:** October 16, 1933, New York, New York **Univ./degree:** B.S., Harvard University, 1953; M.D., Columbia College of Medicine, 1960 **Current organization:** University of South Florida, College of Medicine **Title:** M.D. **Type of organization:** University **Major product:** Medical education **Area of distribution:** National **Expertise:** Neurology, multiple sclerosis **Published works:** 7 articles **Affiliations:** Society of Clinical Neurology; American Association of Neurology **Hob./spts.:** Family, biking, classical music **SIC code:** 82 **Address:** University of South Florida, College of Medicine, Dept. of Neurology, 12901 Bruce B. Downs Blvd. MDC 55, Tampa, FL 33612 **E-mail:** pdunne@hsc.usf.edu **Web address:** www.hsc.usf.edu

DUR, ERDOGAN
Industry: Education **Born:** April 11, 1966, Turkey **Univ./degree:** M.A., Science, Turkey, 1993 **Current organization:** Brooklyn Amity School **Title:** Science Teacher **Type of organization:** School **Major product:** Secondary school education **Area of distribution:** Brooklyn, New York **Expertise:** Science, chemistry **Affiliations:** National Science Teachers Association **Hob./spts.:** Basketball, reading, movies **SIC code:** 82 **Address:** 1564 Benson Ave., Brooklyn, NY 11228 **E-mail:** durerdogan@hotmail.com

DURKEE, DAVID B.
Industry: Education **Born:** October 4, 1951, Cleveland, Ohio **Univ./degree:** B.S.M.E., Gross City College, 1973; Ph.D., Mechanical Engineering, Northwestern University, 1978 **Current organization:** Lakeland Community College **Title:** Professor/Ph.D./P.E. **Type of organization:** College **Major product:** Higher education **Area of distribution:** Ohio **Expertise:** Engineering **Published works:** Articles **Affiliations:** A.S.M.E. **Hob./spts.:** Chess **SIC code:** 82 **Address:** Lakeland Community College, T-157 Engineering Dept., 7700 Clocktower, Kirtland, OH 44094 **E-mail:** ddurkee@lakelandcc.edu **Web address:** www.lakelandcc.edu

DURR, WILLIE E.

Industry: Education **Born:** July 15, 1956, Abbeville, Alabama **Univ./degree:** M.A., Business Education, Alabama State University, 1993 **Current organization:** Alabama Cooperative Ext. System **Title:** Coordinator **Type of organization:** University **Major product:** Educational assistance **Area of distribution:** Dothan, Alabama **Expertise:** Teaching **Hob./spts.:** Fishing, reading **SIC code:** 82 **Address:** Alabama Cooperative Ext. System, 1699 Ross Clark Circle, Dothan, AL 36301 **E-mail:** wdurr@auburn.edu

DURRICK, GEORGE T.

Industry: Education **Born:** September 14, 1951, Troy, New York **Univ./degree:** MCh.M., Church Music, Fairfax University, 1990; Ph.D., Music Therapy Education, Union Institute, 1994 **Current organization:** Hillsborough County Public Schools **Title:** Music Educator **Type of organization:** School **Major product:** Elementary and secondary school education, music therapy **Area of distribution:** Hillsborough County, Florida **Expertise:** Church music and liturgy, Music therapy in the field of education: Autistic, speech and language impaired, attention deficit disorder, behavior management, emotionally handicapped. Geriatric settings: Alzheimer's, dementia, palliative care, cognitive reconstruction, relaxation, pain abatement, recreation and stress reduction. **Published works:** Handbell curriculum in progress **Affiliations:** N.M.E.C.; American Music Therapists **Hob./spts.:** Swimming, rollerblading, composing electronic music, collectibles, computers **SIC code:** 82 **Address:** Hillsborough County Public Schools, 8207 Tinker St., MacDill AFB, Tampa, FL 33621 **E-mail:** durrick@aol.com

EBOMOYI, E. WILLIAM

Industry: Education **Born:** December 19, 1949, Benin City, Nigeria **Univ./degree:** Ph.D., Community Health, University of Illinois at Urbana-Champaign, 1981 **Current organization:** University of Northern Colorado **Title:** Ph.D. **Type of organization:** University **Major product:** Higher education, research **Area of distribution:** Colorado **Expertise:** Epidemiology **Hob./spts.:** Chess, ping-pong, soccer **SIC code:** 82 **Address:** University of Northern Colorado, Dept. of Community Health, 501 20th St., Greeley, CO 80639

EDEN, MARIO R.

Industry: Research and education **Born:** April 10, 1973, Aabenraa, Denmark **Univ./degree:** M.Sc., Chemical Engineering,1999; Ph.D., Chemical Engineering, 2003, Technical University of Denmark **Current organization:** Auburn University **Title:** Assistant Professor of Chemical Engineering **Type of organization:** University **Major product:** Research and higher education **Area of distribution:** National and international **Expertise:** Process systems engineering, process design, integration and optimization **Honors/awards:** CAREER Award, National Science Foundation, 2006; Auburn Engineering Alumni Council Junior Faculty Research Award, 2006 **Published works:** Eden M.R., Jorgensen S.B., Gani R. (2003). A New Modeling Approach for Future Challenges in Process and Product Design, Computer Aided Chemical Engineering 14, pp. 101-106, Elsevier; Eden, M.R., Jorgensen S.B., Gani R., El-Halwagi M.M. (2003). Reverse Problem Formulation based Techniques for Process and Product Design. Computer Aided Chemical Engineering 15A, pp. 451-456, Elsevier; Eden, M.R., Jorgensen, S.B., Gani R., El-Hawagi M.M. (2003). Property Cluster based Visual Technique for Synthesis and Design Formulations. Computer Aided Chemical Engineering 15B, pp. 1175-1180, Elsevier **Affiliations:** American Institute of Chemical Engineers; American Chemical Society; American Society for Engineering Education; Danish Society for Processing Technology; Danish Society of Chemical Engineers; Society of Danish Engineers **Hob./spts.:** Boating, music, physical fitness, golf, soccer **SIC code:** 82 **Address:** Dept. of Chemical Engineering, Auburn University, Auburn, AL 368-5127 **E-mail:** edenmar@auburn.edu

ELLINGTON, MILDRED L.

Industry: Education **Born:** June 7, 1921, Marion, Ohio **Univ./degree:** B.A., English and French, Olivet Nazarene University, Kankakee, IL, 1943; M.A., French, Ohio State University, OH, 1952; M.A., English, Bowling Green State University, OH, 1964; M.A., Library Science, Rosary College (now Dominican), River Forest, Il, 1975 **Current organization:** Maywood Public Library **Title:** Librarian **Type of organization:** Public library **Major product:** Education, books **Area of distribution:** Maywood, Illinois **Expertise:** Reference Librarian; Literature Teacher **Affiliations:** I.L.A. **Hob./spts.:** Music, opera, reading, travel **SIC code:** 82 **Address:** Maywood Public Library, 121 S. Fifth Ave., Maywood, IL 60153

ELLIS, GILBERT E.

Industry: Education **Born:** February 18, 1943, Brewster, Massachusetts **Univ./degree:** Physiology, Northeast University, Boston, 1979 **Current organization:** Barry University **Title:** Assistant Professor **Type of organization:** University **Major product:** Higher education **Area of distribution:** Florida **Expertise:** Teaching, research, biology, anatomy, physiology **Affiliations:** American Association for the Advancement of Science; National Science Teachers Association; Florida Academy of Sciences **Hob./spts.:** Golf, sailing **SIC code:** 82 **Address:** Barry University, 11300 N.E. 2nd Ave., Miami Shores, FL 33161 **E-mail:** gellis@mail.barry.edu

ELLSWORTH, TAMARA A.

Industry: Education **Born:** April 7, 1914, Michigan **Univ./degree:** M.A., University of Michigan, 1950 **Current organization:** Pontiac School District **Title:** Teacher **Type of organization:** Public school **Major product:** Education **Area of distribution:** Pontiac, Michigan **Expertise:** Teaching, counseling **Affiliations:** Legislature Chairperson, North Oakland Association of Retired School Personnel; Former President, A.A.U.W.; Disabled American Veterans Auxiliary; Co-Founder, Lakeland Players **Hob./spts.:** Tennis, badminton, acting **SIC code:** 82 **Address:** 4736 Pelton Rd., Clarkston, MI 48346-3660

ENGRAM SR., STANLEY

Industry: Education **Univ./degree:** B.S., Music, Concordia University, Nebraska; M.A., Administration, Concordia University, Illinois; Ed. Specialist, University of Missouri; Th.D., Concordia Seminary, 2001 **Current organization:** Central Visual & Performing Arts High School **Title:** Principal **Type of organization:** Performing Arts High School **Major product:** High school education **Area of distribution:** National **Expertise:** Administration of balanced academic and performance excellence, playwright, jazz musician **Affiliations:** National Association of Secondary School Principals **SIC code:** 82 **Address:** Central Visual & Performing Arts H.S., 3125 S. Kings Hwy. Blvd., St. Louis, MO 63139 **E-mail:** stanley.engram@slps.org

EPPRIGHT, MARGARET A.

Industry: Higher education **Born:** April 21, 1913, Manor, Texas **Univ./degree:** M.S., Chemistry; B.S., Organic Chemistry; Ph.D., Biochemistry, University of Texas at Austin, 1945 **Current organization:** Retired **Title:** Ph.D./Professor Emerita **Type of organization:** University **Major product:** Higher education **Area of distribution:** National **Expertise:** Biochemistry, nutrition **Affiliations:** American Chemical Society; Phi Beta Kappa; Sigma Xi; Phi Kappa Phi **Hob./spts.:** Golf, bridge, travel **SIC code:** 82 **Address:** 2517 Hartford Rd., Austin, TX 78703

ERLICH, VICTOR

Industry: Education **Born:** November 22 **Univ./degree:** Ph.D. **Title:** Professor Emeritus **Area of distribution:** National **Honors/awards:** Guggenheim Fellowship **Published works:** 4 books **Affiliations:** American Association of Slovic Studies; Modern Language Association **Hob./spts.:** Theatre, movies **SIC code:** 82 **Address:** 25 Glen Pkwy., Hamden, CT 06517

ESECHIE, HUMPHREY A.

Industry: Education **Born:** Uzedba, Nigeria **Univ./degree:** B.S. with Honors, Crop Science, University of Ibadan, Nigeria; M.S., Agronomy, Kansas State University, 1973; Ph.D., University of Nebraska, 1975 **Current organization:** Sultan Qaboos University **Title:** Professor of Agronomy **Type of organization:** University **Major product:** Higher education **Area of distribution:** International **Expertise:** Environmental physiology; environmental stress **Honors/awards:** Best Research Paper on Salinity Stress, Sultan Qaboos University, 2001 **Published works:** 100 papers on stress physiology **Affiliations:** American Society of Agronomy; Sub Committee, Minorities in Agronomy; Science Teachers Committee, Crop Sciences of America **SIC code:** 82 **Address:** 20406 Cajon Canyon Ct., Katy, TX 77450 **E-mail:** esechie@sbcglobal.net

ESSENHIGH, ROBERT H.

Industry: Education **Born:** April 29, 1928, Hightown, Lancashire, United Kingdom **Univ./degree:** Ph.D., University of Sheffield, United Kingdom, 1959 **Current organization:** Ohio State University **Title:** E.G. Bailey Professor of Energy Conversion/Professor of Mechanical Engineering **Type of organization:** Research, teaching university **Major product:** Higher education, research, science and engineering **Area of distribution:** International **Expertise:** Combustion science, engineering and teaching **Published works:** 100 articles, 20 book chapters **Affiliations:** American Society of Mechanical Engineers; American Association for the Advancement of Science; A.C.S. **Hob./spts.:** Sailing, flying in small planes **SIC code:** 82 **Address:** Ohio State University, Mechanical Engineering Dept., 201 W. 19th Ave., Columbus, OH 43210 **E-mail:** essenhigh.1@osu.edu **Web address:** www.rclsgi.eng.ohio-state.edu/~essenhigh/hier

EUSDEN, JOHN DYKSTRA

Industry: Education, ministry, writing **Born:** July 20, 1922, Holland, Michigan **Univ./degree:** A.B., Harvard University 1943; B.D., 1949; Ph.D., 1954, Yale University **Current organization:** Williams College **Title:** Professor Emeritus, Chaplain **Type of**

organization: University/church **Major product:** Teaching religion and environmental studies; consulting for East Asian programs and China Lingnan Foundation; research and writing in history, aesthetics, healing, ethics; pastoral ministry; administration **Area of distribution:** National and international **Expertise:** Author, editor, lecturer **Honors/awards:** ACLS and Fulbright research awards; Research Award, University of Utrecht, the Netherlands; Research Award, Center for the Study of Japanese Religions, Kyoto; Danforth Campus Ministry Award **Published works:** "Puritans, Lawyers and Politics", 1958, 1968; "William Ames, The Marrow of Theology", 1968, 1971; "Zen and Christian: The Journey Between", 1980; "The Spiritual Life: Learning East and West" (with John H. Westerhoff, III), 1982; "Sensing Beauty: Aesthetics, the Human Spirit and the Church" (with John H. Westerhoff, III), 1998 **Affiliations:** Randolph Mountain Club; Appalachian Mountain Club **Hob./spts.:** Bicycle, cross country ski, downhill ski racing, music, clarinet and recorder **SIC code:** 82 **Address:** 75 Forest Rd., Williamstown, MA 01267 **E-mail:** jeusden@sover.net; jeusden@williams.edu

EVANS, VIVIAN
Industry: Education **Born:** May 4, 1951, Yazoo City, Mississippi **Current organization:** Evans Day & Night Care Inc. **Title:** Vice President **Type of organization:** Child care center **Major product:** Child care **Area of distribution:** Yazoo City, Mississippi **Expertise:** Administration **Honors/awards:** Office for Children & Youth Credentials **Hob./spts.:** Fishing, walking **SIC code:** 82 **Address:** Evans Day & Night Care Inc., 1025 Lamar Ave., Yazoo City, MS 39194 **E-mail:** mackade2002@yahoo.com **Web address:** www.evansdaynightcareinc.com

FAHLMAN, BRADLEY D.
Industry: Education **Born:** November 14, 1972, Regina Saskatchewan, Canada **Univ./degree:** B.Sc. with High Honors, University of Regina, 1996; Ph.D., Inorganic Chemistry, Rice University, 2000 **Current organization:** Central Michigan University **Title:** Associate Professor of Chemistry **Type of organization:** University **Major product:** Higher education, research **Area of distribution:** National **Expertise:** Nanomaterials synthesis and characterization thin film growth via chemical vapor deposition (CVD) **Honors/awards:** Provost's Award for Outstanding Research & Creative Activity, 2005; Research Excellence Fund Award, 2003 **Published works:** 25 articles; textbook in progress, "Materials Chemistry" **Affiliations:** American Chemical Society; Materials Research Society **Hob./spts.:** Golf, travel **SIC code:** 82 **Address:** Central Michigan University, Dow Science 357, Mount Pleasant, MI 48859 **E-mail:** fahlm1b@cmich.edu

FERGUSON, FREDERICK
Industry: Education **Born:** May 8, 1959, Guyana, South America **Univ./degree:** Ph.D., Aerospace Engineering, University of Maryland, 1993 **Current organization:** North Carolina A&T State University **Title:** Associate Professor & Director of Center for Aerospace **Type of organization:** Educational institution **Major product:** Higher education, research, software **Area of distribution:** North Carolina **Expertise:** Engineering **Published works:** 100 articles **Affiliations:** A.S.E.E.; A.I.E.E. **Hob./spts.:** Reading, long walks, soccer **SIC code:** 82 **Address:** North Carolina A&T State University, Dept. of Mechanical Engineering, 1601 E. Market St., Greensboro, NC 27410 **E-mail:** fferguso@ncat.edu **Web address:** www.ncat.edu

FERNANDES, GABRIEL J.
Industry: Education **Born:** March 25, 1936, India **Univ./degree:** Ph.D., University of Bombay, India, 1979 **Current organization:** University of Texas Health Science Center at San Antonio **Title:** Professor **Type of organization:** University **Major product:** Research, higher education **Area of distribution:** International **Expertise:** Nutrition and immunology **Published works:** 160 articles, 70 chapters **Affiliations:** American Association of Immunology; American Association of Nutritional Science **Hob./spts.:** Fishing **SIC code:** 82 **Address:** University of Texas Health Science Center at San Antonio, 7703 Floyd Curl Dr., San Antonio, TX 78229-3900 **E-mail:** fernandes@uthscsa.edu **Web address:** www.uthscsa.edu

FIELD, SUE
Industry: Education **Born:** Duluth, Minnesota **Univ./degree:** B.A., Nursing, College of St. Scholastica, 1978; M.S., Nursing, University of North Dakota, 2002 **Current organization:** Northland Community & Technical College **Title:** Director of Associate Degree Nursing Program **Type of organization:** College **Major product:** Higher education **Area of distribution:** Minnesota **Expertise:** Nursing, asthma, education; Certified Asthma Educator **Affiliations:** N.T.A.; M.N.S.C.U.; Minnesota Asthma Coalition **Hob./spts.:** Skiing, hiking, kayaking, camping **SIC code:** 82 **Address:** Northland Community & Technical College, 1101 Hwy. 1 East, Thief River Falls, MN 56701 **E-mail:** sue.field@northlandcollege.edu **Web address:** www.susanfield.efoliomn2.com

FIORI, KAY L.
Industry: Education **Born:** October 30, 1945, Lockport, Illinois **Univ./degree:** B.M.E., Northern Arizona State University, 1967; M.A., Curriculum, National University, California, 2000 **Current organization:** Corona Norco Unified School District **Title:** Teacher **Type of organization:** Public school **Major product:** Elementary and secondary school education **Area of distribution:** Norco, California **Expertise:** Band, choir, violin **Affiliations:** American Association of University Women; California National Education Association **Hob./spts.:** Family, gardening, music **SIC code:** 82 **Address:** 4170 Mt. Baldi Ct., Norco, CA 92860 **E-mail:** fidler53@sdc.global.net

FISHER, JOHN K.
Industry: Education **Univ./degree:** B.A., Chemistry & Mathematics; M.S., Psychology/Counseling, Alfred University; Ph.D., Education, Administration, Counseling, Research, University of Maryland, 1964 **Current organization:** Norwalk Community College **Title:** Academic Dean **Type of organization:** College **Major product:** Higher education **Area of distribution:** Connecticut **Expertise:** Mathematics, science, psychology **Published works:** 23 journal articles, 2 book chapters **Affiliations:** F.N.S.F.; A.A.H.E.; C.T.S.A.D.C. **Hob./spts.:** Racquetball, basketball **SIC code:** 82 **Address:** Norwalk Community College, 188 Richards Ave., Norwalk, CT 06854 **E-mail:** jfisher@ncc.commnet.edu **Web address:** www.ncc.commnet.edu

FISHER, RODNEY W.
Industry: Medical **Born:** January 14, 1968, Bellefonte, Pennsylvania **Univ./degree:** B.S., Biology, Liberty University of Virginia, 1991; D.O., Ohio University of Osteopathic Medicine, 1995 **Current organization:** West Virginia School of Osteopathic Medicine **Title:** D.O. **Type of organization:** Medical school **Major product:** Medical education **Area of distribution:** West Virginia **Expertise:** Internal medicine, pediatric medicine **Published works:** Abstracts for A.C.P. and A.A.P. **Affiliations:** F.A.A.P.; A.O.A.; A.C.P. **SIC code:** 82 **Address:** West Virginia School of Osteopathic Medicine, 400 N. Lee St., Lewisburg, WV 24901 **E-mail:** rfisher@wvsom.edu **Web address:** www.wvsom.edu

FISHGRAB, BARBARA J.
Industry: Education **Born:** December 13, 1950, Fredonia, Kansas **Univ./degree:** M.A., Counseling, Psychology, Liberty University, Virginia, 1991 **Current organization:** Unified School District **Title:** School Psychologist **Type of organization:** School **Major product:** Education **Area of distribution:** Phoenix, Arizona **Expertise:** Psychology **Affiliations:** Student Member A.P.A.; A.C.A.; A.C.C.A.; **Hob./spts.:** Marshall arts, Tae Kwon Do, swimming, racquetball, horseback riding, rappelling **SIC code:** 82 **Address:** Unified School District, 38201 W. Indian School Rd., Tonopah, AZ 85354

FLANAGAN, JUDY
Industry: Special Events Entertainment/Guest Speaking for Hire **Born:** April 28, 1950, Lubbock, Texas **Univ./degree:** B.S., Ed., Memphis State University, 1972; M.S., Communications, University of Tennessee, 2001- Thesis in progress **Current organization:** University of Tennessee **Title:** Director, Special Events Division **Type of organization:** University, public relations, development, advancement **Major product:** Special events organization, guest speaking engagements **Area of distribution:** Tennessee **Expertise:** Special events services **Affiliations:** International Festivals and Events Association; Tennessee Festivals and Events Association; Who's Who, World Lifetime Achievement **Hob./spts.:** Motorcycles, videotaping, photography, building houses, project management **SIC code:** 82 **Address:** 350 Bruce Rd., Gatlinburg, TN 37738 **E-mail:** Judy_Flanagan@utk.edu

FLORES, WILLIAM V.
Industry: Education **Born:** January 10, 1948, San Diego, California **Univ./degree:** Ph.D., Stanford University, 1987 **Current organization:** New Mexico State University **Title:** Provost **Type of organization:** University **Major product:** Higher education **Area of distribution:** International **Expertise:** Public policy **Honors/awards:** Rockefeller Fellowship in the Humanities; Outstanding Public Service Award; Outstanding Teaching and Research Award (Fresno State) **Published works:** 20 articles, 2 books **Affiliations:** American Association for Higher Education; International Association of University Presidents; Universities Research Association **Hob./spts.:** Biking, hiking, racquetball, music, dancing **SIC code:** 82 **Address:** New Mexico State University, Hadley Hall, Office of the President, P.O. Box 30001, MSC 3445, Las Cruces, NM 88003-8001 **E-mail:** bflores@nmsu.edu **Web address:** www.nmsu.edu

FOLBERG, MARY VINTON
Industry: Education **Born:** March 6, 1940, Mcminnville, Oregon **Univ./degree:** B.A., English Literature and Dance, San Francisco State University, 1964 **Current organization:** The Northwest Academy **Title:** Founder/Head of School **Type of organization:** Independent school **Major product:** Education (grades 6-12) **Area of distribution:** Oregon and Southwest Washington **Expertise:** Academics, art education; Creator of Jefferson Dance Program for Portland Schools; Founding Director of the Jefferson Dancers **Honors/awards:** Metropolitan Arts Comm. Award, 1982; Distinguished Teacher, White House Commission on Presidential Scholars, 1982, 1988, 1989; Featured: Images of Oregon Women and Lears Magazine **Affiliations:** Pacific Northwest Association of Independent Schools **Hob./spts.:** Raising Peruvian horses **SIC code:** 82 **Address:** The Northwest Academy, 1130 S.W. Main, Portland, OR 97205 **Web address:** www.nwacademy.org

FORGOTSON JR., JAMES M.
Industry: Education **Born:** March 17, 1930, Albuquerque, New Mexico **Univ./degree:** Ph.D., Geology, Northwestern University, 1956 **Current organization:** University of Oklahoma **Title:** Professor **Type of organization:** University **Major product:** Higher education **Area of distribution:** National **Expertise:** Gas and oil exploration and production; private consulting **Affiliations:** G.S.A.; A.A.P.G.; S.P.E. **SIC code:** 82 **Address:** University of Oklahoma, School of Geology and Geophysics, SEC 100 E. Boyd, Rm. 810, Norman, OK 73019 **E-mail:** jforgot@ou.edu

FOWLER, ELIZABETH A.
Industry: Education **Born:** August 31, 1946, Prescott, Arizona **Univ./degree:** M.S, Reading, Oswego University, 1974 **Current organization:** Rome City School District (Retired) **Title:** Teacher (Retired) **Type of organization:** Public school **Major product:** Elementary education **Area of distribution:** Rome, New York **Expertise:** Teaching/reading **Honors/awards:** Who's Who Among America's Teachers (2002) **Affiliations:** Representative, R.T.A.; A.F.T.; N.Y.S.U.T.; N.S.T.A.; President, Rome Community Theater **Hob./spts.:** Volunteer with Rome community Theatre and genealogy **SIC code:** 82 **Address:** 807 N. George St., Rome, NY 13440-3409 **E-mail:** efowler1@twcmy.rr.com **Web address:** www.romecommunitytheater.org

FOWLER, WILLIAM B.
Industry: Education **Born:** November 23, 1959, Wilmington, North Carolina **Current organization:** UNC Wilmington **Title:** HVAC Technician **Type of organization:** University **Major product:** Higher education **Area of distribution:** North Carolina **Expertise:** HVAC engineering and design, consulting **Hob./spts.:** Restoring old cars **SIC code:** 82 **Address:** UNC Wilmington, 601 S. College Rd., Wilmington, NC 28403

FRAGOMENI, JAMES M.
Industry: Education **Born:** September 24, 1962, Columbus, Ohio **Univ./degree:** B.S., Metallurgical Engineering, 1985, University of Pittsburgh; M.S.E., Mechanical Engineering, 1989; Ph.D., Mechanical Engineering, 1994, Purdue University **Current organization:** University of Detroit Mercy **Title:** Adjunct Instructor **Type of organization:** University **Major product:** Higher education **Area of distribution:** International **Expertise:** Lightweight alloys for aerospace; Research emphasis is on characterizing the mechanical behavior and microstructures of high strength light weighting aluminum-lithium alloys as a function of the material processing, manufacturing and chemistry **Honors/awards:** Diploma of Expertise, American Biographical Institute, 2005; Marquis Who's Who in Science & Engineering, 8th ed. 2005-06; AcademicKey's Who's Who in Engineering Education, 2002; AFOSR Summer Research Faculty Fellow, 1998; NASA Summer Research Faculty Fellow, 1996, 1997; Order of Engineer, 1989; Honor Societies: Pi Tau Sigma; Sigma Xi; Omicron Delta Kappa; Tau Beta Pi; Phi Eta Sigma; Honors from the American Biographical Institute (ABI): Lifetime Fellow; Lifetime Deputy Governor, 2005 - present; Ambassador of Grand Eminence, A.G.E., 2005-present; Man of the Year, 2005 and 2006; Great Minds of the 21st Century, 2006; American Hall of Fame, 2006; International Peace Prize, 2006; Ambassador General of the United Cultural Convention, 2006-present; Lifetime Achievement Award, United Cultural Convention, 2006 **Published works:** Recent Journal Publications: "Effect of Heat Treating on the Microstructure and Fatigue Behavior of a Ti-6wt.%Al-4wt.%V ELI Alloy", Journal of Advanced Materials, Vol. 33, No. 3, pp. 18-25, July 2001; "Characterizing the Brittle Fracture and the Ductile to Brittle to Ductile Transition of Heat-Treated Binary Aluminum-Lithium Alloys", Engineering Transactions, Vol. 49, No. 4, pp. 573-598, Dec. 2001 **Affiliations:** American Society for Engineering Education; American Society for Materials; Material Society; Engineering Society for Detroit; Society for Manufacturing Engineers; Michigan Education Association; American Society for Quality; American Society for Mechanical Engineers **Career accomplishments:** Advanced research in characterizing the mechanical behavior and microstructures of aluminum lithium aerospace alloys as a function of the material processing, manufacturing and chemistry **Hob./spts.:** Physical fitness, skiing, photography, scuba diving, archery, tennis **SIC code:** 82 **Address:** College Park Station, P.O. Box 211074, Detroit, MI 48221-5074 **E-mail:** jamesmark88@yahoo.com **Web address:** www.jamesmatsci.org

FRANKLIN, GODFREY
Industry: Education **Born:** November 30, 1942, Ghana, West Africa **Univ./degree:** B.D., Theology, Reformed Theological College, Geelong, Victoria, Australia, 1975; Ph.D., Counseling Psychology, University of Alabama, 1983 **Current organization:** The University of West Florida **Title:** Professor/Division Chair of Diversity and Applied Research; Executive Director, Center for Multicultural Studies & International Development **Type of organization:** University **Major product:** Education and research, ministry **Area of distribution:** International **Expertise:** Psychological and philosophical analysis of education/learning **Honors/awards:** Who's Who Among American Teachers, 1996, 1998, 2000; Golden Apple Award, 1993, 2000; Distinguished Teaching Awards, 1993,1998; Outstanding Undergraduate Teaching and Advising Award, 1994 **Published works:** Book, "Analyzing Multicultural Teaching and Learning Styles"; many articles **Affiliations:** N.M.S.A.; American Association of Christian Counselors; African-American Heritage Society; Association for Supervision and Curriculum Development; Florida Association for Multicultural Education; Multiracial Reformed Presbyterian Church **SIC code:** 82 **Address:** The University of West Florida, 11000 University Parkway, Pensacola, FL 32514 **E-mail:** gfrankli@uwf.edu

FRASER JR., MALCOLM JAMES
Industry: Education **Born:** October 20, 1952, Troy, New York **Univ./degree:** Ph.D., Ohio State University, 1981 **Current organization:** University of Notre Dame **Title:** Associate Professor **Type of organization:** University **Major product:** Higher education **Area of distribution:** International **Expertise:** Molecular genetics **Honors/awards:** Recipient of National Institute of Health Research Career Development Award **Affiliations:** A.S.A.; A.S.V. **Hob./spts.:** Skiing, boating, astronomy, music **SIC code:** 82 **Address:** University of Notre Dame, Dept. of Biological Sciences, Notre Dame, IN 46556-0369 **E-mail:** fraser.1@nd.edu

FRAZIER, STANLEY R.
Industry: Education **Born:** January 13, 1953, Charlotte, North Carolina **Univ./degree:** B.A., Johnson C. Smith University, 1975; M.A., Appalachian State University, 1983; Admin. Degree, University of North Carolina at Charlotte, 1985 **Current organization:** Merry Oaks Elementary School **Title:** Principal **Type of organization:** Elementary school **Major product:** Public school education **Area of distribution:** Charlotte, North Carolina **Expertise:** Education **Published works:** Book **Hob./spts.:** Basketball, painting, photography, writing, nature walks **SIC code:** 82 **Address:** Merry Oaks Elementary School, 3508 Draper Ave., Charlotte, NC 28205 **E-mail:** s.frazier@cms.k12.nc.us

FREEMAN, WILLIE
Industry: Education **Born:** January 19, 1953, Brooklyn, New York **Univ./degree:** B.S., St. John's University, 1975; M.S., Long Island University, 1980; Graduate of F.B.I. National Academy 182 Session, 1995 **Current organization:** Newark Public Schools **Title:** Director of Security/Chief Investigator **Type of organization:** Public School District (82 schools, 43,000 students, 8,000 employees) **Major product:** Education **Area of distribution:** Newark, New Jersey **Expertise:** Security management, criminal/civil investigations, law enforcement training; New York City Police Department, 1973-96, Retired as Police Lieutenant **Honors/awards:** Who's Who in Security Industries; Exemplary Service Award-Organization of African American Administrators **Published works:** 4 articles on Security Management **Affiliations:** National Organization of Black Law Enforcement Executives (NOBLE); Chairman of Educational Institutions, American Society of Industrial Security; International Chiefs of Police; Fraternal Order of Police Lodge #12, N.J. Lieutenants Benevolent Association; S.O.A.R.; Superior Officers Association Retired; Committee Member, U.S. Dept. of Education, Safe and Drug Free Schools; National Technical Investigator's Association; Cultured Institution Properties Management **Hob./spts.:** Martial arts, all sports, travel, etc. **SIC code:** 82 **Address:** Newark Public Schools, 2 Cedar St., Room 1007, Newark, NJ 07102 **E-mail:** wfreeman@nps.k12.nj.us

FREESE, MELANIE L.
Industry: Education **Born:** May 12, 1945, Mineola, New York **Univ./degree:** M.A., Elementary Education, Hofstra University, 1969; M.L.S., Library Science, L.I. University, C.W. Post Campus, 1977 **Current organization:** Hofstra University **Title:** Senior Catalog Librarian, Associate Professor of Library Services **Type of organization:** University **Major product:** Higher education **Area of distribution:** Hempstead, New York **Expertise:** Librarianship **Honors/awards:** Woman of the Year, Business Professional Women, 1994; Citizen of the Year, Local Church Community. 1994 **Published works:** PNLA Quarterly, Spring 2002; Library and Archival Security, 1989; Book reviews in Lutheran Libraries **Affiliations:** N.C.L.A.; A.C.R.L.; A.L.A.; Phi Betta Mu; Kappa Delta Pi **Hob./spts.:** Needlecraft, doll making, making afghans **SIC code:** 82 **Address:** Hofstra University, 619 Fulton Ave., Hempstead, NY 11550-4575 **E-mail:** libctmlf@hofstra.edu

FRENKEL, KRYSTYNA
Industry: Education **Born:** March 2, 1941, Poland **Spouse:** Nathan J. Siegel **Married:** February 13, 1977 **Univ./degree:** Ph.D., New York University, 1974 **Current organization:** New York University School of Medicine **Title:** Professor of Environmental Medicine and Pathology **Type of organization:** University **Major product:** Higher education **Area of distribution:** International **Expertise:** Cancer research **Published works:** 100 + articles in scientific journals **Affiliations:** American Association for

Cancer Research; New York Academy of Sciences; International Society for Preventive Oncology; The Oxygen Society; Society of Free Radical Biology & Medicine; American Chemical Society **SIC code:** 82 **Address:** New York University School of Medicine, 550 First Ave., PHL r.802, New York, NY 10016 **E-mail:** krystyna.frenkel@env.med.nyu.edu

FRISCHER, ZELIK
Industry: Medical **Born:** July 17, 1936, Lavig, Riga, Russia **Univ./degree:** M.D., First Medical School (formerly Leningrad Medical School), 1960 **Current organization:** Stony Brook Urology, PC/Stony Brook University Hospital **Title:** Professor **Type of organization:** Medical university **Major product:** Medical services, higher education **Area of distribution:** Stony Brook, New York **Expertise:** Urology and kidney transplantation **Honors/awards:** Best Doctors in New York, 1999-2000 **Published works:** Journal of Urology/Transplantation **Affiliations:** A.S.T.P.; A.S.U.; S.C.U. **Hob./spts.:** Reading, museums **SIC code:** 82 **Address:** Stony Brook University Hospital, Stony Brook Urology, PC, HCS T9 Room 040, Stony Brook, NY 11794-7620 **E-mail:** zfrischer@mail.suny.sb.edu

FRYSZTAK, ROBERT J.
Industry: Education **Born:** May 7, 1961, Chicago, Illinois **Univ./degree:** B.S., Biology, Bradley University, 1983; Ph.D., Anatomy, Loyola University, 1991 **Current organization:** National University of Health Sciences **Title:** Ph.D./Associate Professor **Type of organization:** University **Major product:** Medical education **Area of distribution:** Illinois **Expertise:** Neurophysiology, anatomy **Published works:** 10 articles, abstracts, co-authored 1 chapter **Affiliations:** A.A.A.S.; Society of National Science; Society of Neurosurgeons **Hob./spts.:** Golf, woodworking **SIC code:** 82 **Address:** National University of Health Sciences, Dept. of Physiology, 200 E. Roosevelt Rd., Lombard, IL 60148 **E-mail:** rfrysztak@nuhs.edu **Web address:** www.nuhs.edu

FUSCO, JOSEPH S.
Industry: Education **Born:** November 26, 1950, New York, New York **Univ./degree:** Ph.D., New York University, 2002 **Current organization:** Bergen Catholic High School **Title:** Principal **Type of organization:** Private Catholic secondary school **Major product:** Education for boys grades 9-12 **Area of distribution:** Bergen County, New Jersey **Expertise:** College Preparatory Program (100% of students attend colleges/universities or join the military) **Affiliations:** N.A.S.S.P.; N.N.J.I.L.;A.S.C.D.; F.L.A. **Hob./spts.:** Physical fitness, travel **SIC code:** 82 **Address:** Bergen Catholic High School, 1040 Oradell Ave., Oradell, NJ 07649 **E-mail:** jfusco@bergencatholic.org **Web address:** www.bergencatholic.org

GALARSA, GLORIA
Industry: Education **Univ./degree:** B.S., History; M.S., Education Leadership, California State University, 2001 **Current organization:** Our Lady of the Rosary School **Title:** Principal **Type of organization:** School **Major product:** K-8th grade education **Area of distribution:** Union City, California **Expertise:** Education **Affiliations:** N.E.A. **Hob./spts.:** Reading **SIC code:** 82 **Address:** Our Lady of the Rosary School, 678 B. St., Union City, CA 94587 **E-mail:** ggalarsa@csdo.org **Web address:** www.olrschool.org

GALLINA, ANDREW LOUIS
Industry: Education **Born:** December 11, 1967, Brooklyn, New York **Univ./degree:** A.S., Kingsboro College, 2001 **Current organization:** The Rockefeller University **Title:** Assistant Director **Type of organization:** University **Major product:** Higher education **Area of distribution:** New York, New York **Expertise:** Facilities Manager - budgeting, staffing **Affiliations:** National Fire Protection Association; Facilities Management Association **Hob./spts.:** Boating, camping, Little League baseball coach **SIC code:** 82 **Address:** The Rockefeller University, 1230 York Ave., Box 87, New York, NY 10021 **E-mail:** gallina@mail.rockefeller.edu

GANJIAN, IRAJ
Industry: Education **Born:** April 1, 1944, Tehran, Iran **Univ./degree:** Ph.D., Columbia University **Current organization:** CUNY, Lehman College of New York City **Title:** Professor **Type of organization:** University **Major product:** Education and research **Area of distribution:** New York **Expertise:** Organic chemistry, synthesis and natural products **Published works:** 26 publications **Affiliations:** A.C.S.; Organic Sector of New York **Hob./spts.:** The violin, family **SIC code:** 82 **Address:** 7 Joels Dr., New Fairfield, CT 06812 **E-mail:** iganjian@aol.com

GAO, XIUJIE
Industry: Education **Born:** August 31, 1969, China **Univ./degree:** B.S., Engineering, 1993; Ph.D., 2002 Northwestern University **Current organization:** Northwestern University **Title:** Ph.D. **Type of organization:** University **Major product:** Higher education **Area of distribution:** International **Expertise:** Shape memory materials, finite element, heart treatment **Published works:** Journals, papers **Affiliations:** A.S.M.E.; M.R.S. **Hob./spts.:** Music, running, soccer, swimming, fishing, badminton, travel **SIC code:** 82 **Address:** Northwestern University, Dept. of Mechanical Engineering, 2145 Sheridan Rd., Evanston, IL 60208 **E-mail:** x-gao@northwestern.edu

GARCIA-GUBERN, CARLOS F.
Industry: Medical **Born:** February 3, 1970, Baltimore, Maryland **Spouse:** Lissandra Colon-Rolon, M.D. **Married:** January 5, 2000 **Children:** Paola, 6; Carlos Alberto, 3; Sebastian Andres, 2 months **Univ./degree:** M.D., Ponce School of Medicine, 1996 **Current organization:** University of Puerto Rico School of Medicine **Title:** Emergency Medicine Assistant Residency Director **Type of organization:** University hospital **Major product:** Medical education **Area of distribution:** Puerto Rico **Expertise:** Pediatrics, emergency medicine, education **Affiliations:** A.A.E.M; S.A.E.M.; A.C.E.P.; A.A.E.P.; A.M.A.; P.R.M.A. **Hob./spts.:** Family, basketball, water sports **SIC code:** 82 **Address:** University of Puerto Rico School of Medicine, Emergency Residency Program, Carolina, PR 00926 **E-mail:** prerdoc@yahoo.com

GARLAND, A. GAIL
Industry: Education **Born:** August 8, 1939, Kewanee, Illinois **Univ./degree:** Diploma, West Suburban Hospital School of Nursing, 1960; B.S., Professional Arts, St. Joseph's College, 1986 **Current organization:** Taylor House Assisted Living/Job 1 USA HH Agency **Title:** R.N./B.S.P.A. **Type of organization:** Assisted living/Training in healthcare field **Major product:** Healthcare education **Area of distribution:** McComb, Ohio **Expertise:** Certified RN, Hospice, 1995, Nursing Service Coordinator, HH Nursing **Honors/awards:** Who's Who Among Young Professionals, 1988-1989 **Hob./spts.:** Sewing, needlework **SIC code:** 82 **Address:** 7862 State Rt. 235, McComb, OH 45858-9464 **E-mail:** alco630@aol.com

GARRETT, DONALD B.
Industry: Education **Born:** April 22, 1950, Lubbock, Texas **Univ./degree:** M.S., Fairview A&M University **Current organization:** Waco High School **Title:** Principal **Type of organization:** Public school **Major product:** Secondary education **Area of distribution:** Waco, Texas **Expertise:** Administration/curriculum **Affiliations:** T.A.S.S.P.; A.S.C.D. **Hob./spts.:** Athletics **SIC code:** 82 **Address:** Waco High School, 2020 N. 42nd St., Waco, TX 76710 **E-mail:** dgarrett@wacoisd.org **Web address:** www.wacoisd.org

GARRETT, LORI K.
Industry: Education **Born:** January 27, 1960, Champaign, Illinois **Univ./degree:** M.S., Biology, University of Illinois, 1984 **Current organization:** Danville Area Community College **Title:** Professor **Type of organization:** Community college **Major product:** Higher education **Area of distribution:** Danville, Illinois **Expertise:** Anatomy, physiology **Affiliations:** Human Anatomy and Physiology Society; National Association of Biology Teachers; National Education Association **Hob./spts.:** Gardening, cats **SIC code:** 82 **Address:** Danville Area Community College, 2000 E. Main St., Danville, IL 61832 **E-mail:** lgarrett@dacc.edu

GARZA, ROBERTO J.
Industry: Education **Univ./degree:** Ph.D, Higher Education, Oklahoma State University **Current organization:** University of Texas at Brownsville **Title:** Professor (Retired) **Type of organization:** University **Major product:** Academia **Area of distribution:** Texas **Expertise:** Higher education **Hob./spts.:** Golf, reading, Chicano literature, travel, theatre **SIC code:** 82 **Address:** #2 Alvarado Ave., Rancho Viejo, TX 78575

GEDER, LASZLO
Industry: Healthcare **Born:** August 11, 1932, Hungary **Univ./degree:** M.D., 1956; Ph.D., 1962, University of Debrecen, Hungary **Current organization:** Penn State School of Medicine **Title:** M.D./Associate Professor **Type of organization:** University **Major product:** Patient care, medical education **Area of distribution:** National **Expertise:** Neurology, consulting **Published works:** Multiple publications **Affiliations:** A.A.N.; A.A.N.R. **Hob./spts.:** Reading history, traveling **SIC code:** 82 **Address:** Penn State School of Medicine, 3360 Colebrook Rd., Elizabethtown, PA 17022 **E-mail:** lgeder@aol.com

GEORGE, K.O.
Industry: Education/healthcare/research/dynamic medicine, clinical and academic **Born:** June 30, 1943, Punalur, Kerala, India **Spouse:** Sosamma Eapen, MD(Ht.) **Married:** April 18, 1968 **Children:** Oommen.K., 29 **Univ./degree:** DMS, MBS., CH Medical College and Hosp., Calcutta Univ., India, 1966; US: MA/MSW, American Christian Theological Seminary, 1982; M.D., Hahnemann Medical Soc. of America **Current organization:** Los Angeles Int'l. Univ. of S.H. School of Medicine, Hahnemannian Research Ctr. Inc. **Title:** Pres./Prof. of Medicine and Clinical Health Sciences with Dynamic Pharmacology **Type of organization:** Univ., research ctr., pharmaceutical sciences **Major product:** Educating both allopathic, homoeopathic medical students and scientists under holistic prospective, research in dynamic pharmacology emphasis on chronic degenerative diseases **Area of distribution:** International **Expertise:** Specialist for chronic degenerative diseases, metabolic disorders, endocrine disorders, ophthalmologic diseases, homoeopathic and nutritional medicine; Licensed, FL State Bd. of Homoeopathic Examiners **Honors/awards:** Dean, Dir., Prof. of Homeopathic Medicine with Health Sciences, Samuel Hahnemann School of Homeopathic Medicine; Marquis Who's Who **Published works:** "Advanced Workshop for Physicians,

Nurses and Scientists about the Basic Nature of Three Fundamental Chronic Diseases (Miasma)," HRC Inc., 1989-present **Affiliations:** Hahnemann Medical Soc. of America; FL State Soc. of Homoeopathic Physicians; Int'l. Homoeopathic Medical League; Nat'l. Ctr. for Homoeopathy; Founding Pres., Dir., Homoeopathic Medical Assoc. of America; Contributor, Pres., Hahnemannian Medicine Summit **Hob./spts.:** Reading, writing, teaching, public speaking **SIC code:** 82 **Address:** Los Angeles Int'l Univ. of S.H. School of Medicine, Hahnemannian Research Center Inc., 18818 Teller Ave., Suite 230, Irvine, CA 92612-1680 **E-mail:** laiushshm@aol.com

GEORGE, KIRANRAJ
Industry: Education **Born:** April 25, 1977, India **Univ./degree:** M.E.E., Wright State University **Current organization:** Wright State University **Title:** Researcher **Type of organization:** University **Major product:** Higher education **Area of distribution:** Ohio **Expertise:** Electrical engineering **Affiliations:** I.E.E.E.; M.I.T. **Hob./spts.:** Painting, drawing **SIC code:** 82 **Address:** Wright State University, 1457 Spicetree Circle, #201, Fairborn, OH 45324 **E-mail:** george.19@wright.edu

GETTLEMAN, LAWRENCE
Industry: Medical **Born:** Atlantic City, New Jersey, 1940 **Univ./degree:** B.A., Psychology, Rutgers University, 1962 **Current organization:** University of Louisville, School of Dentistry **Title:** Professor/DMD **Type of organization:** University, school of dentistry **Major product:** Biomaterials research and development **Area of distribution:** International **Expertise:** Biomaterials clinical trials, prosthodontics **Published works:** 64+ articles and book chapters, 127 abstracts **Affiliations:** International Association for Dental Research; American Dental Association **Hob./spts.:** Opera, flying aircraft, greenhousing **SIC code:** 82 **Address:** University of Louisville, School of Dentistry, 501 S. Preston St., Louisville, KY 40292 **E-mail:** gettleman@louisville.edu

GIELEN, UWE P.
Industry: Education **Born:** August 15, 1940, Berlin, Germany **Univ./degree:** M.S., General Psychology, Wake Forest University, 1968; Ph.D., Social Psychology, Harvard University, 1976 **Current organization:** St. Francis College **Title:** Professor of Psychology **Type of organization:** College **Major product:** Higher education **Area of distribution:** International **Expertise:** Cross-cultural psychology; lectured in 29 countries **Published works:** Edited 12 books **Affiliations:** F.A.P.S.; F.A.P.A.; Past President, S.C.C.R.; Past President, I.C.P.; Past Chairman, P.N.Y.A.S.; Executive Director, Institute for International and Cross-Cultural Psychology **Hob./spts.:** Classical music **SIC code:** 82 **Address:** St. Francis College, 180 Remsen St., Brooklyn, NY 11201 **E-mail:** ugielen@hotmail.com

GILLIS, ROY L.
Industry: Education **Born:** September 25, 1951, Cleveland, Ohio **Current organization:** Holland Hall School **Title:** Lead Engineer **Type of organization:** Private college preparatory school **Major product:** Elementary and secondary school education **Area of distribution:** Tulsa, Oklahoma **Expertise:** Engineering, asbestos, HVAC **Hob./spts.:** Reading, landscaping **SIC code:** 82 **Address:** Holland Hall School, 5666 E. 81st St., Tulsa, OK 74137 **E-mail:** rgillis@hollandhall.org

GILMAN, FRANCES H.
Industry: Educational **Born:** May 29, 1952, Newton, Massachusetts **Univ./degree:** M.S., St. Joseph University, Pennsylvania, 1988 **Current organization:** Thomas Jefferson University **Title:** Acting Chair **Type of organization:** University **Major product:** Higher education **Area of distribution:** International **Expertise:** Education, administration **Affiliations:** Board Chair, P.S.R.T.; A.S.R.T. **Hob./spts.:** Travel, reading **SIC code:** 82 **Address:** Thomas Jefferson University, 130 S. Ninth St., Suite 1010, Philadelphia, PA 19107 **E-mail:** frances.gilman@jeffeson.edu

GODSEY, JOHN DREW
Industry: Education **Born:** October 10, 1922, Bristol, Tennessee **Univ./degree:** B.S., Virginia Tech., 1947; B.D., Drew University; 1953; D. Theol., University of Basel, Switzerland, 1960 **Current organization:** Wesley Theological Seminary **Title:** Professor Emeritus, Systematic Theology **Type of organization:** Theological seminary (United Methodist) **Major product:** Theological education **Area of distribution:** International **Expertise:** Teacher of Systematic Theology **Published works:** 6 books **Affiliations:** A.A.R.; American Theological Society; International Bonhoeffer Society **Hob./spts.:** Gardening, photography, reading **SIC code:** 82 **Address:** Wesley Theological Seminary, c/o John D. Godsey, 4500 Massachusetts Ave., N.W., Washington, DC 20016-8605 **Web address:** www.wesleysem.edu

GOEHLER, JOHN S.
Industry: Education **Univ./degree:** CEC, American Culinary Federation **Current organization:** Kent State University **Title:** Assistant Director of Dining Services **Type of organization:** University **Major product:** Higher education **Area of distribution:** Ohio **Expertise:** Chef **Affiliations:** A.C.F. **SIC code:** 82 **Address:** Kent State University, Dining Services, 104 Student Center, Kent, OH 44242 **E-mail:** jgoehler@kent.edu

GOKDEN, MURAT
Industry: Medical **Born:** December 7, 1962, Ankara, Turkey **Univ./degree:** M.D., Dokuz Eylul Medical School, Izmir, Turkey, 1986 **Current organization:** University of Arkansas for Medical Sciences **Title:** M.D., Associate Professor of Pathology **Type of organization:** Academic medical center **Major product:** Patient care, medical education **Area of distribution:** International **Expertise:** Neuropathology, cytopathology, cancer diagnosis, diagnostic techniques in pathology **Published works:** Cetin N. Dienel, G. Gokden M., CD117 expression in glial tumors. Journal of Neuro-Oncology. 75(2):195-202, 2005 Nov.; Gokden M., Shinde A., Recent immunohistochemical markers in the differential diagnosis of primary and metastatic carcinomas of the liver. Diagnostic Cytopathology. 33(3):166-72, 2005 Sep.; Gokden N. Mukunyadzi P., James J.D., Gokden M., Diagnostic utility of renal cell carcinoma marker in cytopathology. Applied Immunohistochemistry & Molecular Morphology. 11(2):116-9, 2003 June **Affiliations:** A.A.N.P.; I.S.N.; A.S.C.; U.S.C.A.P.; I.A.C **Hob./spts.:** Running marathons, chess **SIC code:** 82 **Address:** University of Arkansas for Medical Sciences, 4301 W. Markham St., #517, Dept. of Pathology, Little Rock, AR 72205 **E-mail:** mgokden@uams.edu

GOMEZ-RAMIREZ, FRANCO M.
Industry: Education **Born:** April 12, 1974, Santo Domingo, Dominican Republic **Univ./degree:** Ph.D., University of Illinois, 2001 **Current organization:** University of Illinois at Urbana-Champaign **Title:** Ph.D. **Type of organization:** University **Major product:** Education **Area of distribution:** International **Expertise:** Civil engineering, airport pavement research **Published works:** Articles **Affiliations:** A.S.C.E.; I.A.P.A. **SIC code:** 82 **Address:** University of Illinois at Urbana - Champaign, 205 N. Matthews St., Room 3220, Urbana, IL 61801 **E-mail:** gomezram@uiuc.edu

GONZALES, MARGARITO "MAX"
Industry: Education **Born:** June 10, 1945, Brawley, California **Univ./degree:** A.A., Art; A.A., Social Science; A.A., Law Enforcement; B.A., Sociology, San Jose State University **Current organization:** San Jose Job Corps Center **Title:** Security/Safety Supervisor, Safety Officer **Type of organization:** Live-in training facility **Major product:** Vocational training **Area of distribution:** National **Expertise:** Certified OSHA Instructor **Published works:** Writes for Center's newspaper, "Bridges" **Affiliations:** Retired Deputy Sheriff, 1973-93 **Hob./spts.:** Family, travel, successful artist, teaching art classes for adult education **SIC code:** 82 **Address:** San Jose Job Corps Center, 3485 East Hills Dr., San Jose, CA 95127 **E-mail:** gonzalmax@aol.com

GONZALEZ TUDYK, DIANA
Industry: Education **Univ./degree:** M.S., Education Leadership, Texas A&M University, 1992; M.S., Microbiology, University of Texas Health Science Center, 2000; Ph.D. Candidate, University of Texas at San Antonio **Current organization:** Stonewall Flanders Elementary School **Title:** Principal **Type of organization:** Elementary school **Major product:** Instructional delivery standards **Area of distribution:** San Antonio, Texas **Expertise:** Education leadership **Affiliations:** T.E.P.S.A.; Omicron Delta Kappa; Kappa Delta Pi; American Society for Microbiology **SIC code:** 82 **Address:** Stonewall Flanders Elementary School, 804 Stonewall Ave., San Antonio, TX 78211 **E-mail:** diane.tudyk@ harlandale.net

GOODBODY, JOAN T.
Industry: Library **Born:** July 14, 1949, Richmond, Virginia **Univ./degree:** M.A., Eastern Illinois University, 1986; M.L.S., UNT, 2001 **Current organization:** Michigan Technological University **Title:** Government Document's Coordinator **Type of organization:** Academic library **Major product:** Information, reference services **Area of distribution:** College Station, Texas **Expertise:** Reference and Instruction Librarian **Published works:** Book chapter, articles **Affiliations:** A.L.A.; O.A.H. **Hob./spts.:** Kayaking, horseback riding, needlework, canoeing, volunteer work **SIC code:** 82 **Address:** Michigan Technological University, 1400 Townsend Dr., J. Robert Van Pelt Library, Houghton, MI 49930 **E-mail:** jodyg13@hotmail.com

GOODEN, W. RAY
Industry: Education **Born:** November 25, 1949, Hempstead, Texas **Univ./degree:** B.A., Prairie View A&M University, 1972 **Current organization:** Prairie View A&M University **Title:** Water/Wastewater Manager **Type of organization:** University **Major product:** Higher education **Area of distribution:** Texas **Expertise:** Engineering **Affiliations:** Texas Water Utility Association; American Water Works Association **Hob./spts.:** Sports, fishing, hunting **SIC code:** 82 **Address:** Prairie View A&M University, Lot 31 Meadowview, P.O. Box 2033, Prairie View, TX 77446 **E-mail:** pvamu.edu.gooden

GORBUNOV, MAXIM Y.
Industry: Education **Born:** December 18, 1965, Moscow, Russia **Univ./degree:** Ph.D., Physics, Math, Moscow State University, 1992 **Current organization:** Rutgers University, Dept. of Marine Science **Title:** Professor **Type of organization:** University **Major product:** Higher education, research and development **Area of distribution:** International **Expertise:** Marine science **Published works:** 50+ articles, chapters **Affiliations:** American Optical Society; American Geophysical Union; American Association for the Advancement of Science **Hob./spts.:** Skiing **SIC code:** 82 **Address:** Rutgers Uni-

versity, Dept. of Marine Science, 71 Dudley Rd., New Brunswick, NJ 08901 **E-mail:** gorbunov@imcs.rutgers.edu **Web address:** www.imcs.rutgers.edu

GOTWAY, MICHAEL B.
Industry: Medical **Born:** July 23, 1966, Springfield, Illinois **Univ./degree:** M.D., University of Illinois at Chicago, 1993 **Current organization:** University of California at San Francisco, General Hospital Dept. of Radiology **Title:** Director, Radiology Residency Training Program/Director, Thoracic Imaging **Type of organization:** University hospital **Major product:** Patient care, medical education, research **Area of distribution:** California **Expertise:** Thoracic imaging, radiology **Published works:** 35+ publications **Affiliations:** S.T.R.; A.U.R.; A.P.D.R.; R.S.N.A.; A.R.R.S. **Hob./spts.:** Research **SIC code:** 82 **Address:** University of California at San Francisco, General Hospital Dept. of Radiology, Room 1X55A, Box 1325, San Francisco, CA 94110

GRAHN, LANCE R.
Industry: Education **Born:** December 3, 1952, Denver, Colorado **Univ./degree:** Ph.D., Latin American History, Duke University, 1986 **Current organization:** University of Wisconsin-Stevens Point **Title:** Dean, College of Letters and Science **Type of organization:** University **Major product:** Higher education **Area of distribution:** International **Expertise:** Administration **Published works:** Articles, essays, chapters **Affiliations:** A.H.A.; S.H.A.; C.L.A.H.; L.A.S.A.; A.C.S. **Hob./spts.:** Latin American and Spanish baroque music and architecture **SIC code:** 82 **Address:** University of Wisconsin-Stevens Point, College of Letters & Science, 130 Collins Classroom Center, Stevens Point, WI 54481-3897 **E-mail:** lgrahn@uwsp.edu

GRANDY, REGAN G.
Industry: Education **Born:** November 23, 1971, Driggs, Idaho **Univ./degree:** M.N.S., Geology; Ed.D., Instructional Technology, Idaho State University **Current organization:** Pocatello School District #25/Brigham Young University, Idaho **Title:** Grants Coordinator/Adjunct faculty **Type of organization:** School district/university **Major product:** Secondary education/higher education **Area of distribution:** Idaho **Expertise:** Geological, Instructional Technology **Honors/awards:** Kappa Delta Pi **Affiliations:** A.A.C.E.; N.E.C.C.; G.S.A.; A.G.I.; N.E.S.T.A.; N.S.T.A. **Hob./spts.:** Computers, technology, drumming, mining exploration, geocaching **SIC code:** 82 **Address:** 1076 South 100 West, Victor, ID 83455 **E-mail:** granrega@isu.edu

GRANGER, CHARLES R.
Industry: Education **Born:** September 4, 1939, Marshalltown, Iowa **Univ./degree:** B.S., Biology and Education, Iowa State University; Ph.D., Biology and Science Education, University of Iowa, 1972 **Current organization:** University of Missouri - St. Louis **Title:** Professor of Biology and Education/Curators' Distinguished Teaching Professor **Type of organization:** University **Major product:** Higher education, research **Area of distribution:** International **Expertise:** Science education, curriculum and instruction **Honors/awards:** Presidential Award for Outstanding Teaching; Governor's Award for Excellence in Teaching; Anderson Medal, the Business Higher Education Forum and the American Council of Education; Elected Fellow of the Academy of Science of St. Louis and the Missouri Academy of Science **Published works:** "The Naturalistic Education Theory: In Search of a Unified Learning Theory for Instructional Methodology and Tactical Education" **Affiliations:** National Science Teachers Association; Science Teachers of Missouri; American Association for the Advancement of Science; Academy of Science of St. Louis; Missouri Academy of Science **Hob./spts.:** Collecting primitive antiques and tractors **SIC code:** 82 **Address:** University of Missouri - St. Louis, Dept. of Biology, One University Blvd., St. Louis, MO 63121-4400 **E-mail:** granger@umsl.edu **Web address:** www.umsl.edu

GRANT, GARY K.
Industry: Education **Born:** May 23, 1077, Brooklyn, New York **Univ./degree:** B.A., Early Childhood and Elementary Education, Long Island University, 1998; M.S., Early Childhood Elementary Education, New York University, 2000; Ph.D., Child and Youth Studies, Nova Southeastern University, 2006 **Current organization:** Parkway School **Title:** Director **Type of organization:** School system with 3 annexes **Major product:** Pre-school through 8th grade **Area of distribution:** Brooklyn, New York **Expertise:** Administration of technology, literacy and comprehension, national fundraising **Affiliations:** Partner, Sutlingar Realty **Hob./spts.:** Reading, running **SIC code:** 82 **Address:** Parkway School, 5566 Kings Hwy., Brooklyn, NY 11203 **E-mail:** gkgrant@aol.com **Web address:** www.parkwayschool.org

GREEN, VIVIAN BERRY
Industry: Education **Born:** April 8, 1949, Belglade, Florida **Univ./degree:** Ed.D., Nova Southeastern University, 2003 **Current organization:** School District of Okaloosa County **Title:** Principal **Type of organization:** Middle school **Major product:** Public school education/students and parents **Area of distribution:** National **Expertise:** Administration **Affiliations:** A.K.G.; D.S.F.; D.K.F; A.F.S.A.M. **Hob./spts.:** Children's advocate, reading, stamp collecting **SIC code:** 82 **Address:** School District of Okaloosa County, 120 Lowery Place S.E., Ft. Walton Beach, FL 32548

GREENAMYRE, JOHN W.
Industry: Education **Born:** November 30, 1929, Sarasota, Florida **Univ./degree:** B.A.; M.E.B.; Ed.D. **Current organization:** Christianity Construction Corp. **Title:** Reverend Doctor **Type of organization:** Religious ministry **Major product:** Religious education **Area of distribution:** International **Expertise:** Administration, teaching **Published works:** Author, "Systematic Evangelism" **Affiliations:** American Baptist Association; Chaplain Civil Air Patrol; U.S. Air Force **Hob./spts.:** Communications, TIME WITH FAMILY - Wife Emma, daughter Suzanne Yoder and husband Leon, granddaughter Katherine Yoder **SIC code:** 82 **Address:** Christianity Construction Corp., 12675 Providence Rd., Alpharetta, GA 30004 **E-mail:** jwemg@bellsouth.net **Web address:** www.home.bellsouth.net/p/PWP-JWEMG

GREER, PHILLIP W.
Industry: Education/photography **Born:** September 19, 1944, Chicago, Illinois **Current organization:** Southern Illinois University at Carbondale **Title:** Photojournalist in Residence **Type of organization:** University **Major product:** Higher education **Area of distribution:** International **Expertise:** Teaching photo journalism **Honors/awards:** Pulitzer Prize **Affiliations:** National Press Photographers Association **Hob./spts.:** Reading, jogging, photography **SIC code:** 82 **Address:** 615 Sugar Creek Lane, Goreville, IL 62939 **E-mail:** pgreer1919@aol.com

GRESHAM, JANET L.
Industry: Education **Born:** New Jersey **Univ./degree:** B.A., Psychology and Sociology, St. Martin's College **Current organization:** North Carolina School of Telecommunications **Title:** Department Chair **Type of organization:** Community college **Major product:** Telecommunications educational services **Area of distribution:** North Carolina **Expertise:** Overall operations, administration, training, all aspects of telecommunications; Certified BICSI Trainer **Affiliations:** FOA; BICSI; North Carolina Telecommunications Industry Association **Hob./spts.:** Water sports, working with young authors, horseback riding **SIC code:** 82 **Address:** North Carolina School of Telecommunications, 5910 Clyde Rhyne Dr., Sanford, NC 27330 **E-mail:** jgresham@cccc.edu **Web address:** www.cccc.edu and www.nest.org

GRIFFIN, BOBBY N.
Industry: Education **Born:** March 16, 1950, Ocilla, Georgia **Univ./degree:** B.S., Social Science, 1972, Georgia Southern University; M.Ed., 1975; Ed.S., 1983, Valdosta State University **Current organization:** Berrien County Board of Education **Title:** Superintendent **Type of organization:** County school system **Major product:** Education, grades K-12 **Area of distribution:** Southern Georgia **Expertise:** 32 years in administration **Honors/awards:** National Counseling Advocate, N.C.A., 1990; Georgia Counseling Advocate, 1989 **Affiliations:** Georgia School Superintendents Association; Rotary International; Past Member, Board of Directors, Georgia High School Principals Association **Hob./spts.:** Quarter horses, raising cattle, hunting **SIC code:** 82 **Address:** Berrien County Board of Education, 100 Smith Ave., P.O. Box 625, Nashville, GA 31639 **E-mail:** bgriffin@berrien.k12.ga.us **Web address:** www.berriencountyschools.com

GUARDADO, ANTONIO
Industry: Education **Born:** April 22, 1963, El Paso, Texas **Univ./degree:** A.S., Food Preparation, TVI Institute, 1987 **Current organization:** Sodexho Campus Services UTEP **Title:** Executive Chef **Type of organization:** University **Major product:** Higher education/food services **Area of distribution:** Texas **Expertise:** Culinary arts **Published works:** Articles in newspaper, has appeared on TV programs **Hob./spts.:** Football **SIC code:** 82 **Address:** Sodexho Campus Services UTEP, 500 W. University Ave., El Paso, TX 79968-8900

GUIHER, JOHN H.
Industry: Education **Univ./degree:** B.Ed., Walla Walla College, 1990 **Current organization:** Coyne American Institute **Title:** Maintenance Instructor **Type of organization:** Job Corps **Major product:** Education **Area of distribution:** Chicago, Illinois and Portland, Oregon **Expertise:** Maintenance skills **Hob./spts.:** Wood scroll sawing **SIC code:** 82 **Address:** Coyne American Institute, 1235 W. Fullertone Ave., Chicago, IL 60614-2186 **E-mail:** j.h.guiher@hotmail.com

GUIRARD, BEVERLY M.
Industry: Education **Born:** December 10, 1915, St. Martinsville, Louisiana **Univ./degree:** Ph.D., University of Texas, 1946 **Title:** Biochemist, University of Texas (Retired) **Type of organization:** University **Major product:** Higher education **Area of distribution:** National **Expertise:** Research **Affiliations:** American Chemical Society; Sigma Xi **Hob./spts.:** Reading, gardening, photography **SIC code:** 82 **Address:** 8313 Summer Place Dr., Austin, TX 78759-8220 **E-mail:** b.guirard@mail.utexas.edu

GUNDY, AFAF HELEN
Industry: Education **Born:** October 17, 1952, Alexandria, Egypt **Univ./degree:** M.S., Organic Chemistry, University of California at Santa Barbara, 1980 **Current organization:** Middle College High School, Santa Ana **Title:** Teacher **Type of organization:** High school **Major product:** Education **Area of distribution:** Santa Ana, California

Expertise: Chemistry, physics, health **Affiliations:** Part-time Teacher at Santa Ana College **Hob./spts.:** Reading, sewing **SIC code:** 82 **Address:** 7 Aberdeen St., Irvine, CA 92620 **E-mail:** helengundy@hotmail.com

GURUSIDDAIAH, SARANGAMAT
Industry: Education/consulting **Born:** March 18, 1935, Chitradurga, India **Univ./degree:** Ph.D., Plant Sciences and Chemistry, Washington State University **Title:** Professor/Consultant Scientist, Washington State University (Retired) **Type of organization:** University **Major product:** Higher education **Area of distribution:** International **Expertise:** Scientist; drug discoveries and inventions **Published works:** Numerous patents; 60 journal articles; book (pending) **Affiliations:** American Association of Microbiological Sciences **Hob./spts.:** Gardening (roses, vegetables) **SIC code:** 82 **Address:** 1620 Kenny Dr., Pullman, WA 99163

HAAGA, E.R. VALERIE
Industry: Education **Born:** January 23, 1940, Covington, Louisiana **Univ./degree:** B.A., Art and Social Studies, Notre Dame College, 1962; M.Ed., Administration, Louisiana State University, 1974; Plus 30, University of Tennessee, University of Southwestern Louisiana, Louisiana State University, 1985 **Current organization:** St. Martin Parish School System **Title:** Superintendent **Type of organization:** Parish school system **Major product:** Education, grades K-12 **Area of distribution:** International **Expertise:** Research, education, fine arts, motivational speaker **Honors/awards:** Student Voted Best Teacher; Teacher of the Year; Apple Award; Mr. Harry Community Service Award - National **Affiliations:** Louisiana Association of School Superintendents; Southwest Louisiana Superintendents Association; National School Board Association; Louisiana School Board Association; American Association of School Administrators; Association for Supervision and Curriculum Development; National Art Education Association; Louisiana Art Education Association; Executive Director, Youth Art Council of America **Hob./spts.:** Gardening, painting, travel **SIC code:** 82 **Address:** St. Martin Parish School System, 305 Washington St., St. Martinville, LA 70582 **E-mail:** superintendent@stmartin.k12.la.us **Web address:** www.stmartin.k12.la.us

HAMMILLER, RUTH ELLEN
Industry: Education **Born:** May 6, 1952, Burlington, Wisconsin **Univ./degree:** B.A., Elementary Education, 1974; M.S., Psychology, University of Wisconsin at Whitewater, 1982; Ph.D., Administration, University of Wisconsin at Madison, 1994 **Current organization:** Palmyra Eagle Area School District **Title:** Director of Special Education and Pupil Services **Type of organization:** K-12 school district **Major product:** Education **Area of distribution:** Palmyra, Wisconsin **Expertise:** Administration Director; Nationally Certified School Psychologist **Honors/awards:** Marquis Who's Who in America; Arvil S. Barr Fellowship Recipient, 1993-94; Netzer-Eye Scholarship Recipient, 1992-93 **Published works:** Hammiller, R.E. (1997). Propositions about the school's role in neighborhood-based interagency collaboration. International Studies in Educational Administration, 25, (2), pp. 156-168 **Affiliations:** Executive Board Member, Wisconsin Council of Administrators of Special Services; Council of Administrators of Special Education; American Educational Research Association; National Association of School Psychologists; Wisconsin School Psychologists Association; Phi Delta Kappa; Phi Kappa Phi **Hob./spts.:** Golf, travel, music, reading, writing **SIC code:** 82 **Address:** Palmyra Eagle Area School District, P.O. Box 901, Palmyra, WI 53156 **E-mail:** rhammiller@palmyra.k12.wi.us **Web address:** www.palmyra.k12.wi.us

HARGRAVES II, WILLIAM F.
Industry: Education/military **Born:** August 18, 1932, Cincinnati, Ohio **Univ./degree:** B.S., Mathematics, Physics, Education, 1954; M.S. +12, Physics, 1961, Miami University of Ohio **Current organization:** Central State University/U.S. Air Force **Title:** Assistant Dean of Arts & Sciences/Colonel (Retired) **Type of organization:** University/government **Major product:** Higher education/national defense **Area of distribution:** International **Expertise:** Command pilot, mathematics, physics, computer science and programming **Honors/awards:** Outstanding Black Man, Covington, Kentucky, 1994; Rhodes Scholar Candidate, 1950; Most Popular Professor, 1999-2003; Who's Who Among American Teachers, 1988-2004 **Published works:** 2 articles **Affiliations:** Life Member, Alpha Phi Alpha; Founder of Delta Upsilon; Founder, Pilgrims Baptist Men's Chorus; Phi Beta Kappa (since 1953); Omicron Delta Kappa; Kappa Delta Pi; A.P.A.; A.M.A.; V.F.W.; Math Mentor; Assistant Track Field Coach **Hob./spts.:** FAC Athletic Rep. **SIC code:** 82 **Address:** 123 W. Walnut St., Oxford, OH 45056-1721 **E-mail:** whargraves@csu.ces.edu

HARIJITH, ANANTHA K.
Industry: Medical **Born:** India **Univ./degree:** M.D., Medical College at Trivandrum, India, 1992 **Current organization:** Albert Einstein College of Medicine **Title:** Assistant Professor of Pediatrics **Type of organization:** University medical school **Major product:** Medical education, patient care **Area of distribution:** New York **Expertise:** Pediatric pulmonology **Affiliations:** Royal College of Physicians; Royal College of Pediatrics and Child Health **Hob./spts.:** Ice hockey, tennis **SIC code:** 82 **Address:** Albert Einstein College of Medicine, 1650 Selwyn Ave., Bronx, NY 10457 **E-mail:** harijitha@yahoo.com

HARRIS, MARK D.
Industry: Education **Born:** April 21, 1958, Evansville, Indiana **Univ./degree:** B.S., Elementary Education, 1980; Ed.D., Administration, 1999, Purdue University; M.A., Teaching, DePauw University **Current organization:** Lester B. Sommer Elementary **Title:** Principal **Type of organization:** Elementary school **Major product:** Elementary school education **Area of distribution:** Crawfordsville, Indiana **Expertise:** Administration; literacy **Honors/awards:** Noted as one of the top "Reading Counts" schools in the U.S.; Teacher of the Year, Tippecanoe Schools Corp., 1996 **Published works:** 3 articles **Affiliations:** Indiana Association of School Principals; National Association of Elementary School Principals **Hob./spts.:** Track and field, reading, hiking **SIC code:** 82 **Address:** Lester B. Sommer Elementary, 3794 US Hwy. 136 West, Crawfordsville, IN 47933 **E-mail:** mharris@nm.k12.in.us

HARRIS JR., STANLEY E.
Industry: Education **Univ./degree:** Ph.D., University of Iowa, 1947 **Title:** Professor Emeritus, Southern Illinois University, Carbondale (Retired) **Type of organization:** University **Major product:** Higher education **Area of distribution:** National **Expertise:** Geology, physiography; environmental studies, field trips **Published works:** Articles **Affiliations:** Audubon; Sierra Club **Hob./spts.:** Gardening, walking, wild flowers, habitats **SIC code:** 82 **Address:** 98 Edgewood Lane, Carbondale, IL 62901-5554 **E-mail:** biggrockk@hcis.net

HARRIS-JOHNSON, TRUDI V.
Industry: Education **Born:** January 20, 1949, Georgia **Univ./degree:** Ed.D., Nova Southeastern University, 2000 **Current organization:** Middlesex County College **Title:** Professor/Counselor **Type of organization:** Community college **Major product:** Higher education **Area of distribution:** New Jersey **Expertise:** Adult education **Affiliations:** A.S.C.D.; American Counseling Association - NBCC; Certification **Hob./spts.:** Travel **SIC code:** 82 **Address:** Middlesex County College, 2600 Woodbridge Ave., P.O. Box 3050, Edison, NJ 08818-3050 **E-mail:** lynzigirl85@aol.com

HARTIGAN, GENE
Industry: Education **Born:** February 12, 1943, San Diego, California **Univ./degree:** B.S., Public Administration, California State University, Los Angeles, 1967 **Current organization:** Monrovia United School District **Title:** Director of Maintenance, Operation of Facilities and Transportation **Type of organization:** Public school district **Major product:** Education **Area of distribution:** Monrovia, California **Expertise:** Contracting **Affiliations:** R.E.S.E.S. **Hob./spts.:** Fishing, golf, woodworking **SIC code:** 82 **Address:** Monrovia United School District, 124 S. Madison Ave., Monrovia, CA 91016 **E-mail:** geneh@worldnet.att.com

HARTSAW, WILLIAM O.
Industry: Education/Engineering **Univ./degree:** B.S., Engineering, 1946; M.S. Engineering, Purdue University; Ph.D., Engineering, University of Illinois **Title:** Distinguished Professor Emeritus (Retired), University of Evansville **Type of organization:** University **Major product:** Higher education **Area of distribution:** Evansville, Indiana **Expertise:** Mechanical engineering, Dean of Engineering, teaching, public speaking, consulting **Affiliations:** American Society of Mechanical Engineers; Heating and Refrigeration Association **Hob./spts.:** Solar energy enthusiast **SIC code:** 82 **Address:** 1407 Green Meadow Rd., Evansville, IN 47715 **E-mail:** wo@hartsaw.net

HAVILAND, MARLITA C.
Industry: Education **Univ./degree:** M.A., Northern Arizona University, 1987 **Current organization:** Shonto Preparatory School **Title:** Librarian/Media Specialist **Type of organization:** School **Major product:** Elementary, secondary education **Area of distribution:** Shonto, Arizona **Expertise:** Media specialist (taught first grade) **Affiliations:** Chair, Creditation North Central Association; American Librarian Association; National Science Teachers Association **Hob./spts.:** Computers **SIC code:** 82 **Address:** Shonto Preparatory School, (East of Hwy. 98), P.O. Box 7427, Shonto, AZ 86054 **E-mail:** mchaviland@yahoo.om

HAWKINS, EMMA B.
Industry: Education **Born:** July 28, 1946, Ardmore, Oklahoma **Univ./degree:** Ph.D., English, University of North Texas, 1995 **Current organization:** Lamar University **Title:** Dr. **Type of organization:** University **Major product:** Higher education **Area of distribution:** International **Expertise:** English **Affiliations:** South Central Modern

Language Association; Texas Medieval Association; South Central Conference on Christianity and Literature **Hob./spts.:** Reading, crafts **SIC code:** 82 **Address:** Lamar University, P.O. Box 10023, Beaumont, TX 77710

HAWN, MICAELA
Industry: Education **Born:** July 13, 1945, Mobile, Alabama **Univ./degree:** B.S.; M.A., University of South Alabama, 1972; E.D.S., Barry University, 1995 **Current organization:** Pompano Beach Middle School **Title:** Teacher, Dept. Chair, Gifted Coordinator **Type of organization:** Public middle school **Major product:** Middle school education **Area of distribution:** Broward County, Florida **Expertise:** Math, science, gifted education **Honors/awards:** Outstanding Young Education, Teacher of the Year **Affiliations:** N.C.T.M.; F.C.T.M.; I.S.T.E.; M.E.N.S.A.; A.S.C.D.; A.A.U.W.; F.A.C.E.; Alumi Associations; O.A.K.; Phi Delta Kappa; Methodist **Hob./spts.:** Physical fitness, bridge, orchids, computers **SIC code:** 82 **Address:** 1629 Coral Ridge Dr., Coral Springs, FL 33071 **Phone:** (954)345-1688 **E-mail:** me36963@aol.com

HAYES, ZACHARY J.
Industry: Education **Born:** September 21, 1932, Chicago, Illinois **Univ./degree:** B.A., Philosophy, Quincy University, Illinois, 1956; Th.D., University of Bonn, Germany, 1964 **Current organization:** Catholic Theological Union **Title:** O.F.M., Professor **Type of organization:** School of theology **Major product:** Education of ministers and teachers for churches **Area of distribution:** International **Expertise:** Historical and systematic theology; science and theology **Honors/awards:** Appointed Full Professor, Catholic Theological Union, Chicago, Illinois, 1974; Litt. D., St. Bonaventure University, Olean, NY, 1974; research grant from Association of Theological Schools, 1978; J.C. Murray Award for Distinguished Achievement in Theology, Catholic Theological Society of America, 1985; Litt. D., Quincy University, Quincy, Illinois, 1985; honored by colleagues with Festschrift volume, 1997; named to endowed Duns Scotus Chair of Spirituality, Catholic Theological Union, 1999; Pax et Bonum Award for contribution to the life of the church, Chicago, 2001; Franciscan Institute Medal for contribution to scholarship in Franciscan studies, 2002 **Published works:** 16 books, 55 articles, many reviews **Affiliations:** Catholic Theological Society of America; Society for the Scientific Study of Religion; Medieval Society of Illinois **Career accomplishments:** Lectured and published extensively in theology and on relation of science and religion; Work with environmental groups; Covener for Historical Theology Seminar for the Catholic Theological Society of America; Lectured and conducted faculty seminar at University of Utrecht in the Netherlands; Listed in: Directory of American Scholars, 7th edition; Contemporary Authors, 1984-85; Who's Who in Religion, 4th edition **Hob./spts.:** Classical music, tennis, cycling, alpine skiing **SIC code:** 82 **Address:** Catholic Theological Union, 5401 S. Cornell, Chicago, IL 60615 **E-mail:** zach@ctu.edu

HEATH, MARY ELIZABETH
Industry: Education **Born:** November 19, 1947, Tampa, Florida **Univ./degree:** B.S., Human Development; M.S., Early Childhood; M.Ed., Education Leadership, University of South Carolina; Post Graduate Work, Principalship, Harvard University **Current organization:** St. James Elementary **Title:** Principal **Type of organization:** Elementary school **Major product:** Education **Area of distribution:** Myrtle Beach, South Carolina **Expertise:** Research in early childhood science **Published works:** "Early Childhood Mathematics" **Affiliations:** A.S.C.D.; N.A.E.S.P. **Hob./spts.:** Dogs, gardening, reading **SIC code:** 82 **Address:** St. James Elementary, 9711 St. James St., Myrtle Beach, SC 29588 **Web address:** www.hcs.k12.sc.us

HERBERT, AMANDA K.
Industry: Education **Born:** April 10, 1948, Cleveland, Ohio **Univ./degree:** B.A., Defiance College, 1971; M.Ed., Special Education, Lynchburg College, 1982 **Current organization:** Amherst County High School **Title:** Learning Disabilities Teacher **Type of organization:** County high school **Major product:** High school education, English for students with learning disabilities **Area of distribution:** Amherst County, Virginia **Expertise:** Special education **Honors/awards:** Award Certificate, first Special Ed Teacher to visit China **Affiliations:** N.E.A.; Member, Council for Exceptional Children **Hob./spts.:** Travel, reading **SIC code:** 82 **Address:** 48225, 139 Lancer Lane, Amherst, VA 24521 **E-mail:** aher410@aol.com

HERBSTER, CARL D.
Industry: Association **Born:** Education **Univ./degree:** Ed.D., Bob Jones University, 1981 **Current organization:** American Association of Christian Schools **Title:** President **Type of organization:** Educational association **Major product:** Service to Christian schools **Area of distribution:** International **Expertise:** Educational consulting **Published works:** 3 books **Affiliations:** Council for National Policy; President Bush's Educational Task Force **Hob./spts.:** Private pilot, travel worldwide **SIC code:** 82 **Address:** American Association of Christian Schools, 4500 Little Blue Pkwy., Independence, MO 64057 **E-mail:** cherbster@tri-city.org **Web address:** www.aacs.org

HERNANDEZ, ELIAS
Industry: Education **Univ./degree:** M.A., Administration, University of Texas at San Antonio, 1988 **Current organization:** Bellaire Elementary/Harlandale ISD **Title:** Principal **Type of organization:** Elementary school **Major product:** Educating Pre-K to 5th grade students **Area of distribution:** San Antonio, Texas **Expertise:** Mid-management, elementary education, bilingual education **Honors/awards:** Listed in Strathmore's Who's Who; Who's Who Among Students in American Universities and Colleges, 1981-82; Outstanding Young Men of American, U.S. Jaycees, 1983; Outstanding Young Bilingual Educator, Edgewood District, 1984-85; Teacher of the Year, (Merrill Elementary, Harlandale I.S.D., 1994-1995) **SIC code:** 82 **Address:** Bellaire Elementary/Harlandale ISD, 1150 Babcock #N-5, San Antonio, TX 78201 **E-mail:** elias.hernandez@harlandale.net

HESS, GARY E.
Industry: Education **Born:** August 7, 1951, Cedar Bluff, Virginia **Univ./degree:** M.Ed., Curriculum Instruction, Virginia Tech, 1984 **Current organization:** Honaker Elementary School **Title:** Principal **Type of organization:** Public school **Major product:** Education **Area of distribution:** Russell County, Virginia **Expertise:** Administration **Affiliations:** A.S.C.D; Virginia School Turnaround Specialist Program; Virginia Education Association; National Teachers Association; National Association of Elementary School Principals **Hob./spts.:** Self-improvement **SIC code:** 82 **Address:** Honaker Elementary School, Route 67, Honaker, VA 24260 **E-mail:** ghess@russell.k12.va.us

HEUSCH, CLEMENS A.
Industry: Education **Born:** April 19, 1932, Aachen, Germany **Univ./degree:** Dr.rer. nat., Technical University of Munich, Germany, 1959 **Current organization:** University of California at Santa Cruz **Title:** Dr.rer.nat./Physics Professor **Type of organization:** University **Major product:** Higher education **Area of distribution:** International **Expertise:** Basic sciences with applications, research in elementary particle physics, high-end experimental investigations **Published works:** Direct Measure of the Thermal Conductivity of Various Pyrolytic Graphite Samples, C.A. Heusch, A. Kholodenko, H.G. Moser, submitted to Nucl. Inst. Methods (2000); The Trouble With Inverse Neutrinoless Beta Decay, C.A., Heusch, Int. J. Mod. Phys. A13, 2383 (1998); A Strategy for Discovering Heavy Neutrinos, C.A. Heusch and P. Minkoswki, Phys. Lett. B374, 116 (1996) **Affiliations:** American Physics Society; Humboldt Foundation **Hob./spts.:** Skiing, mountain climbing **SIC code:** 82 **Address:** University of California at Santa Cruz, Santa Cruz Institute for Particle Physics, 1156 High St., Santa Cruz, CA 95064 **E-mail:** heusch@slac.stanford.edu

HIGGINS, SUSAN A.K.
Industry: Education **Univ./degree:** B.S., Medical Technology, 1969; M.S., Clinical Laboratory Sciences, 1996, Michigan State University **Current organization:** Indiana University Northwest **Title:** C.L.S. Program Director/Clinical Assistant Professor **Type of organization:** University **Major product:** Higher education **Area of distribution:** Indiana **Expertise:** Clinical/medical laboratory sciences **Affiliations:** A.S.C.P.; A.C.L.S. **Hob./spts.:** Singing **SIC code:** 82 **Address:** Indiana University Northwest, 3400 Broadway, Gary, IN 46408 **E-mail:** sahiggin@iun.edu **Web address:** www.iun.edu

HILGERT, ARNIE D.
Industry: Education **Born:** February 24, 1944, Detroit, Michigan **Univ./degree:** A.A., General Education, Riverside Community College, 1980; B.A., University of Redlands, 1982; M.B.A., 1984; M.A., Higher Education and Human Development, 1991, Ph.D., Higher Education and Human Development, 1992, Claremont Graduate University **Current organization:** Northern Arizona University **Title:** Associate Professor **Type of organization:** University **Major product:** Higher education **Area of distribution:** International **Expertise:** Management and marketing **Honors/awards:** Academy of Business Administration, Outstanding Teaching Award, 1998; Phi Beta Kappa Honor Society **Affiliations:** Academy of International Business; Literati Club; Literati Club Emerald Management Export Exchange; Center for the Study of Intellectual Development; Claremont Graduate University Women Scholars; Arizona Distance Learning Association **Hob./spts.:** Scuba diving, camping, knitting, hiking, travel **SIC code:** 82 **Address:** 11843 Calle del Cid, Yuma, AZ 85367 **E-mail:** arnie.hilgert@nau.edu

HILLER, LARRY K.
Industry: Education **Born:** April 28, 1941, Morning Sun, Iowa **Univ./degree:** B.S., Agriculture Education, 1963, M.S., Horticulture, 1964, Iowa State University; Ph.D., Carrot Flowering, Cornell University, 1974 **Current organization:** Washington State University, Dept. of Horticulture & Landscape Architecture **Title:** Ph.D. **Type**

of organization: University **Major product:** Higher education and research **Area of distribution:** International **Expertise:** Horticulture (vegetables) **Published works:** 150 articles, 60 abstracts, 3 book chapters **Affiliations:** A.S.H.S.; A.S.P.B.; I.S.H.S.; E.A.P.R.; W.S.S.A.; Director of the Potato Association of America **Hob./spts.:** Photography, camping, golf **SIC code:** 82 **Address:** Washington State University, Dept. of Horticulture & Landscape Architecture, Johnson Hall 149, Pullman, WA 99164-6414 **E-mail:** hillerl@wsu.edu

HOFFMAN, PAUL R.

Industry: Education/human services and government **Born:** January 27, 1929, Hyannis, Massachusetts **Univ./degree:** Ed.D., University of Arizona, 1965 **Current organization:** Office of the Dunn County Board Supervisor **Title:** Prof., Univ. of Wisconsin-Stout, (Ret.)/Exec. Dir., Stout Vocational Rehab. Inst. (Ret.)/Dunn Cty. Bd. Supervisor/Chair, Cty. Health & Human Service Bd./Chair, Cty. Council on Aging/Chair, Cty. Long Term Support Committee/Member, Cty. Exec. Committee **Type of organization:** University/County government, consulting **Major product:** Higher education/Government, consulting **Area of distribution:** National **Expertise:** Education, rehabilitation technology/Administration, consulting **Honors/awards:** Phi Beta Kappa; Phi Delta Kappa; Phi Kappa Phi; Rho Sigma Epsilon; Sigma Mu Sigma; National Honor Society in Psychology, University of Arizona; Distinguished Citizen Award, University of Arizona Alumni, 1970; President's Award, National Rehabilitation Association, 1974; Vocational Evaluation & Work Adjustment Association's Distinguished Service Award named the Paul R. Hoffman Award, 1974; Public Recognition Award, Department of Health Education & Welfare, 1974; Distinguished Service Award, Commission on Accreditation of Rehabilitation Facilities, 1975; Recognition of Dedicated Service Award, White House Conference on Handicapped Individuals, 1977; Citation Award, Association of Rehabilitation Facilities, 1978; Research Support Award, University of Wisconsin Stout, 1987; Outstanding Leadership Award, Vocation Rehabilitation Students, University of Wisconsin Stout, 1988; Meritorious Service Award, Disabled American Veterans, 1989; Distinguished Service Award, Stout Vocational Rehabilitation Institute, 1994; Certificate of Meritorious Service Award, Board of Regents of University of Wisconsin, 1996; Governor's Special Award, State of Wisconsin, 1996; Distinguished Service Award, Dunn County Office on Aging, 1998 **Affiliations:** President, Dunn County Interfaith Volunteers, Inc.; Past Memberships: American Psychological Association, National & Wisconsin Rehabilitation Associations, National & Wisconsin Vocational Evaluation & Work Adjustment Associations **Hob./spts.:** Working with nonprofit organizations, computers, travel **SIC code:** 82 **Address:** 113 W. Second St., N.W., Menomonie, WI 54751 **E-mail:** hoffmanp@uwstout.edu

HOLLAND, ROBERT C.

Industry: Education **Born:** August 16, 1923 **Univ./degree:** Ph.D., University of Wisconsin **Title:** Ph.D. **Type of organization:** Educational **Major product:** Teaching, research publications **Area of distribution:** International **Expertise:** Brain endocrine research **Published works:** Book articles **Affiliations:** A.A.N. **Hob./spts.:** Golf, piano, reading **SIC code:** 82 **Address:** 314 New Crossing Trail, Kennesaw, GA 30144

HOLLEN, EVELYN R.

Industry: Education **Univ./degree:** M.S., University of South Florida, 1992 **Current organization:** Lincoln Avenue Academy **Title:** Principal **Type of organization:** University **Major product:** Higher education **Area of distribution:** International **Expertise:** Education **SIC code:** 82 **Address:** Lincoln Avenue Academy, 1330 N. Lincoln Ave., Lakeland, FL 33805 **E-mail:** evelyn.hollen@polk-fl.net

HOLLI, MELVIN

Industry: Education **Univ./degree:** Ph.D., History, University of Michigan, 1966 **Current organization:** University of Illinois at Chicago **Title:** Professor **Type of organization:** University **Major product:** Higher education **Area of distribution:** Illinois **Expertise:** History **Affiliations:** Finnish History Association **Hob./spts.:** Skiing **SIC code:** 82 **Address:** University of Illinois at Chicago, Dept. of History (M/C 198), 913 University Hall, 601 S. Morgan St., Chicago, IL 60607-7109 **E-mail:** mholli@uic.edu

HOLLOWAY, HARRY

Industry: Education **Born:** August 28, 1925, Seattle, Washington **Univ./degree:** Ph.D., Cornell University, 1958 **Current organization:** University of Oklahoma **Title:** Professor Emeritus **Type of organization:** University **Major product:** Higher education **Area of distribution:** Oklahoma **Expertise:** Political corruption research, books, articles **Published works:** "Bad Times For Good Old Boys", 1993, Oklahoma County Commissioners scandal **Affiliations:** O.P.S.A.; A.S.P.A. **Hob./spts.:** Reading, walking, dogs, bicycling **SIC code:** 82 **Address:** 1029 W. Imhoff Rd., Norman, OK 73072 **E-mail:** harryhy@ionet.net

HOLME, THOMAS A.

Industry: Education **Univ./degree:** B.S., Chemistry/Physics, Loras College, 1983; Ph.D., Chemistry, Rice University, 1987 **Current organization:** University of Wisconsin - Milwaukee **Title:** Professor **Type of organization:** University **Major product:** Higher education, research **Area of distribution:** Wisconsin **Expertise:** Assessment of science learning **Honors/awards:** ACS Award, 1999; TV appearances on WTMJ, NBC Network **Affiliations:** A.C.S.; N.S.T.A.; Sigma Xi **SIC code:** 82 **Address:** University of Wisconsin - Milwaukee, Chemistry Dept., P.O. Box 413, Milwaukee, WI 53201 **E-mail:** tholme@uwm.edu

HOLMES, NATHANIEL J.

Industry: Education **Born:** August 5, 1960, New York, New York **Univ./degree:** M.D., Robert Wood Johnson Medical School, 1987 **Current organization:** Robert Wood Johnson Medical School **Title:** M.D. **Type of organization:** University **Major product:** Medical education **Area of distribution:** National **Expertise:** Colon and rectal surgery **Published works:** Articles, journals, chapter **Affiliations:** American College of Surgeons; American Society of Colon & Rectal Surgeons **Hob./spts.:** Golf, photography **SIC code:** 82 **Address:** Robert Wood Johnson Medical School, 1 RWJ Place, P.O. Box 19, New Brunswick, NJ 08903-0019 **E-mail:** holmesnj@umdnj.edu

HOOVER, WADE P.

Industry: Education **Born:** March 3, 1947, New York, New York **Univ./degree:** Attended Suffolk Community College and State University of New York at Stony Brook **Current organization:** SUNY at Stony Brook **Title:** Plant Utilities Engineer 4 **Type of organization:** University **Major product:** Higher education **Area of distribution:** New York **Expertise:** Engineering **Affiliations:** N.I. U.P.E. **Hob./spts.:** Boating, fishing, walking, woodworking, grandchildren **SIC code:** 82 **Address:** SUNY at Stony Brook, East Campus Heating & Cooling Plant, Stony Brook, NY 11794 **E-mail:** whoover@notes.cc.sunysb.edu

HORSBRUGH, PATRICK

Industry: Education/architecture **Born:** June 21, 1920, Belfast, Northern Ireland **Current organization:** University of Notre Dame, Environic Foundation International, Inc. **Title:** Professor Emeritus/Founder of the EFI, 1970, Doyen **Type of organization:** University **Major product:** Education, design **Area of distribution:** International **Expertise:** Architecture, city and regional planning, landscape design **Affiliations:** Fellow, A.I.A.; Fellow, F.R.S.A.; Fellow, F.B.I.S; R.I.B.A.; R.T.P.I.; A.A.A.S.; A.T.P.I.; A.S.L.A.; A.S.I.D.; R.G.S.; New York Academy of Science **Hob./spts.:** Archaeology, history, painting, art, opera, jazz, classical music, travel **SIC code:** 82 **Address:** Environic Foundation International, Inc., 916 St. Vincent St., South Bend, IN 46617-1443

HRUBY, VICTOR J.

Industry: Education **Born:** December 24, 1938, Valley City, North Dakota **Univ./degree:** B.S., University of North Dakota, 1960; Ph.D., Cornell University, 1965 **Current organization:** University of Arizona **Title:** Regents Professor **Type of organization:** University **Major product:** Higher education **Area of distribution:** National **Expertise:** Chemistry **Published works:** 900 publications **Affiliations:** A.C.S.; A.A.A.S.; New York Academy of Sciences **Hob./spts.:** Philosophy, sociology, opera, theatre, dance, music **SIC code:** 82 **Address:** The University of Arizona, Dept. of Chemistry, 1306 E. University, Tucson, AZ 85721 **E-mail:** hruby@u.arizona.edu

HUANG, JENG-SHENG

Industry: Education **Univ./degree:** Ph.D., Plant Pathology, University of Missouri, 1972 **Current organization:** North Carolina State University **Title:** Professor **Type of organization:** University **Major product:** Higher education **Area of distribution:** National **Expertise:** Plant pathology, research, lectures **Affiliations:** American Phytopathological Society; American Society of Plant Biologists **SIC code:** 82 **Address:** North Carolina State University, Box 7616 1413 Gardner Hall, Raleigh, NC 27695 **E-mail:** jengsheng_huang@ncsu.edu

HUECHTKER, EDWARD D.

Industry: Education **Born:** May 24, 1937, Louisville, Kentucky **Univ./degree:** A.S., State Univ. of New York, Albany, 1977; Physician's Associate, Duke Univ. Medical Ctr., 1975; B.A., Econ., Marymount College, 1979; M.P.A., Health Care Admin., C.W. Post Ctr., Long Island Univ, 1981; Ph.D., Health Admin., Kennedy Western Univ., 2004 **Current organization:** University of Alabama at Birmingham **Title:** Chair, Dept. of Critical Care **Type of organization:** University **Major product:** Higher education **Area of distribution:** National **Expertise:** Health administration; PA-C **Honors/awards:** Pi Alpha Alpha National Honor Society, C.W. Post, 1981; President, Alpha Eta Honor Society, 1995; Selected for Marquis Who's Who in American Medicine and Health Care, Marquis Who's Who in America; Lexington Who's Who and Who's Who Among America's Teachers **Published works:** Numerous presentations and publications including, "Irritable Bowel Syndrome", sponsored by Glaxo, School of Allied Health Sciences at ECU, 2000; "Distance Learning for the Future Workshop", St. Francis College, Loretta, PA, 1999; State of the ECU PA Program, Red Oaks Baptist Church, 1999; Physician Assistants, Partners in Medicine presented to Pitt County Medical Society **Affiliations:** American Society of Physician Assistants; Alabama Rural Health Association; North Carolina Medical Society; Down East Society of Physician Extenders; Central Savannah River Area Physician Assistant Society; Numerous academic and community affiliations **Hob./spts.:** Motorcycling, antique cars **SIC code:** 82 **Address:** University of Alabama at Birmingham, 1530 Third Ave. South, RMSB 483, Birmingham, AL 35294-1212 **E-mail:** Huechtke@uab.edu **Web address:** www.uab.edu

HUFF, SHEILA L.
Industry: Education **Born:** October 29, 1951, Rockport, Indiana **Univ./degree:** M.S., Education, Indiana State University, 1976 **Current organization:** Evansville-Vanderburgh School Corp. **Title:** Middle School Principal **Type of organization:** Public school **Major product:** Elementary and secondary school education **Expertise:** Administration **Affiliations:** N.M.A.; A.S.A.; N.A.S.S.P.; Professor, University of South Indiana **Hob./spts.:** Teaching aerobics class, crossword puzzles **SIC code:** 82 **Address:** 1706 N. Thomas Ave., Evansville, IN 47711-4452

HUGHES III, ROBERT D.
Industry: Education/religion **Born:** February 16, 1943, Boston, Massachusetts **Univ./degree:** B.A., Philosophy, Yale University, 1966; M.A., 1974; Ph.D., Theology, 1980, St. Michael's College, University of Toronto **Current organization:** School of Theology, University of The South **Title:** Professor/Reverend **Type of organization:** University **Major product:** Graduate degrees in theology **Area of distribution:** International **Expertise:** Systematic theology **Honors/awards:** Episcopalian Church Fellow **Published works:** Numerous articles in "Sewanee Theological Review", "Anglican Theological Review" and others **Affiliations:** Society of Anglican and Lutheran Theologians; Society for the Study of Christian Spirituality; American Academy of Religion; American Association of University Professors **Hob./spts.:** Music, sailing **SIC code:** 82 **Address:** School of Theology, University of the South, 335 Tennessee Ave., Sewanee, TN 37383-0001 **E-mail:** rhughes@sewanee.edu **Web address:** www.theology.sewanee.edu

HUMMEL, HELEN J.
Industry: Education **Univ./degree:** M.Ed., Indiana University, Pennsylvania, 1975; M.S.N., Pennsylvania University, 1978 **Current organization:** Lock Haven University of Pennsylvania, Clearfield Campus **Title:** Dean (Retired, 2005) **Type of organization:** University **Major product:** Higher education **Area of distribution:** Pennsylvania **Expertise:** Administration **Honors/awards:** One of 8 individuals honored as founders of the Clearfield Campus **Affiliations:** Member, Delta Kappa Gamma Society International; Sigma Theta Tau International Honor Society of Nursing **Hob./spts.:** Family/grandchildren, ladies basketball, camping, travel **SIC code:** 82 **Address:** Lock Haven University of Pennsylvania, Clearfield Campus, Clearfield, PA 16830 **E-mail:** hhummel@lhup.edu

HUMPHREY, KARALYN J.
Industry: Education **Born:** January 19, 1975 **Univ./degree:** B.S., University of Texas at Dallas, 1997; Ph.D., Baylor University, 2002 **Current organization:** Baylor University **Title:** Laboratory Coordinator **Type of organization:** University **Major product:** Higher education **Area of distribution:** Waco, Texas **Expertise:** Safety, instruction and organizational skills **Hob./spts.:** Hockey **SIC code:** 82 **Address:** Baylor University, 1 Bear Place, #97348, Waco, TX 76798 **E-mail:** karalyn_humphrey@baylor.edu **Web address:** www.baylor.edu

HUSHAK, LEROY J.
Industry: Education **Univ./degree:** Ph.D., University of Chicago, 1968 **Title:** Professor Emeritus **Type of organization:** University **Major product:** Higher education **Area of distribution:** Ohio **Expertise:** Economics **Affiliations:** A.F.S.; B.R.E.I. **SIC code:** 82 **Address:** Ohio State University, 238 Halligan Ave., Worthington, OH 43085 **E-mail:** hushak.1@osu.edu

IATROPOULOS, MICHAEL J.
Industry: Medical **Born:** November 8, 1938, Athens, Greece **Univ./degree:** M.D., 1964; Ph.D., Microscopic Anatomy, 1965, University of Tuebingen, Germany; **Current organization:** New York Medical College, Dept. of Pathology **Title:** Professor of Pathology **Type of organization:** Graduate medical university **Major product:** Medical education, biomedical research **Area of distribution:** International **Expertise:** Toxological pathology, geotoxic compounds, atomic pathology (Board Certified) **Published works:** 150+ peer-reviewed papers; 50+ book contributions **Affiliations:** International Academy of Toxicological Pathology; College of American Pathologists; Japanese Society of Toxopathology **Hob./spts.:** History **SIC code:** 82 **Address:** New York Medical College, Dept. of Pathology, Basic Sciences Bldg., Valhalla, NY 10595 **E-mail:** mjiatropoulos@aol.com

INFANTE, GABRIEL A.
Industry: Education **Born:** November 3, 1945, Havana, Cuba **Univ./degree:** B.S., Chemistry, Catholic University, Puerto Rico, 1967; M.S., Chemistry, University of Puerto Rico at Mayagüez, 1969; Ph.D., Texas A&M University, 1973; Post Doctorate, Carnegie Mellon, Pennsylvania, 1974 **Current organization:** Catholic University of Puerto Rico **Title:** Ph.D./Professor/Director **Type of organization:** University **Major product:** Higher education, research **Area of distribution:** Puerto Rico **Expertise:** Chemistry, environmental chemistry and radiation chemistry **Honors/awards:** American Chemical Society, Puerto Rico Local Section Award, Colegio de Químicos de Puerto Rico Maximum Award, 1983 and others **Published works:** 48 articles and 2 chapters **Affiliations:** American Chemical Society; Colegio de Químicos de Puerto Rico; Society of Research Administrators (SAI) and others **Hob./spts.:** Basketball, baseball, chess, dominoes **SIC code:** 82 **Address:** Catholic University of Puerto Rico, 2250 Las Americas Ave., Suite 608, Ponce, PR 00717 **E-mail:** gainfante@hotmail.com **Web address:** www.cayey.upr.edu

JACOBS, CYNTHIA
Industry: Education **Born:** September 7, 1952, Buffalo, New York **Univ./degree:** M.S., Elementary Education, State University of New York, Buffalo, 1978 **Current organization:** St. John the Baptist School **Title:** Principal **Type of organization:** School **Major product:** Pre K to grade 8 **Area of distribution:** Buffalo, New York **Expertise:** Catholic education **Affiliations:** Phi Delta Kappa; National Catholic Education Association; International Reading Association; Association for Supervision and Curriculum Development; National Council of Social Studies; Catholic School Administrators Association of New York State **Hob./spts.:** Reading mysteries, bowling, Buffalo Sabres, Buffalo Bills **SIC code:** 82 **Address:** St. John the Baptist School, 1085 Englewood Ave., Buffalo, NY 14223 **Web address:** www.sjtbschool.com

JANECKA, MARY ANN
Industry: Education **Born:** March 2, 1967, Hallettsville, Texas **Univ./degree:** M.S., University of Houston **Current organization:** Wharton County Jr. College **Title:** History Instructor **Type of organization:** College **Major product:** Higher education **Area of distribution:** Houston, Texas **Expertise:** History **Affiliations:** Golden Key Honor Society **SIC code:** 82 **Address:** 10300 Wilcrest Dr., Apt. 1103, Houston, TX 77099 **E-mail:** maryannjanecka@aol.com

JARDINE, MURRAY D.
Industry: Education **Born:** October 14, 1954, Regina, Saskatchewan **Univ./degree:** Ph.D., Duke University, 1992 **Current organization:** Auburn University **Title:** Associate Professor **Type of organization:** University **Major product:** Higher education **Area of distribution:** Auburn, Alabama **Expertise:** Political philosophy **Honors/awards:** Auburn University Faculty Teaching Award in the Communication and Social Sciences, 2002; Auburn University Pi Sigma Alpha Outstanding Political Science Professor Award, 2002; LSU Alpha Lambda Delta Freshman Honor Society Award for Superior Instruction of Freshman Students, 1995; Duke University Graduate School Award for Excellence in Teaching, 1990 **Published works:** "The Making and Unmaking of Technological Society: How Christianity Can Save Modernity From Itself", 2004; "Speech and Political Practice" 1998 **Affiliations:** A.P.S.A.; A.A.R.; R.S.A. **Hob./spts.:** Softball **SIC code:** 82 **Address:** Auburn University, Dept. of Political Science, 7080 Haley Center, Auburn, AL 36849-5208 **E-mail:** jardimu@auburn.edu

JAYARAMAN, SUNDARARAJAN
Industry: Education **Born:** September 5, 1948, Thanjavur, India **Univ./degree:** Ph.D., Madurai Kamaraj University, India, 1977 **Current organization:** University of Miami-Diabetes Research Institute **Title:** Assistant Professor **Type of organization:** University, research institute **Major product:** Higher education, research **Area of distribution:** International **Expertise:** Immunology research **Published works:** 35+ articles, 7 chapters **Affiliations:** American Association of Immunology; Indian Immunology Society **Hob./spts.:** Reading, bicycling **SIC code:** 82 **Address:** University of Miami-Diabetes Research Institute, 1450 N.W. Tenth Ave., R-134, Miami, FL 33136 **E-mail:** sjayaram@med.miami.edu

JOHNSON, FRUZSINA K.
Industry: Education **Born:** August 14, 1973, Budapest, Hungary **Univ./degree:** M.D., Semmelweis University, Budapest, Hungary, 1999 **Current organization:** Tulane University **Title:** Instructor **Type of organization:** University **Major product:** Higher education, research **Area of distribution:** Louisiana **Expertise:** Research **Affiliations:** A.P.S.; Council of High Blood Pressure of the American Heart Association **Hob./spts.:** Reading **SIC code:** 82 **Address:** Tulane University, Department of Physiology, 1430 Tulane Ave., SL39, New Orleans, LA 70112 **E-mail:** fjohnso1@tulane.edu

JOHNSON, JENIESA FRANKLIN
Industry: Education **Born:** May 12, Dallas, Texas **Univ./degree:** M.A., Human Relations and Business, Amber University, 1987 **Current organization:** Tarrant County College District **Title:** Associate Professor Health Sciences **Type of organization:** Community college **Major product:** Higher education, allied health **Area of distribution:** Texas **Expertise:** Radiologic technology, X-ray **Affiliations:** T.S.R.T.;

T.A.B.P.H.E.; A.S.R.T.; S.D.M.S.; A.E.R.S. **Hob./spts.:** Reading, sewing, travel **SIC code:** 82 **Address:** Tarrant County College District, 828 Harwood Rd., Hurst, TX 76053 **E-mail:** jeniesa.johnson@tccd.edu

JOHNSON, ROBERT E.
Industry: Education **Born:** November 5, 1950, Farmville, Virginia **Univ./degree:** Ph.D., Southwestern Theological Seminary, 1984 **Current organization:** Central Baptist Theological Seminary **Title:** Professor of Christian Heritage **Type of organization:** Seminary **Major product:** Theological education **Area of distribution:** International **Expertise:** Teaching **Affiliations:** A.H.A.; A.S.C.H.; A.M.S.; A.B.H.S. **Hob./spts.:** Opera, hiking, museums, gardening, reading **SIC code:** 82 **Address:** Central Baptist Theological Seminary, 741 N. 31st St., Kansas City, KS 66102 **E-mail:** rejohnson@cbts.edu **Web address:** www.cbts.edu

JOHNSSON, KENNETH N.
Industry: Education **Born:** November 13, 1964, Chicago, Illinois **Univ./degree:** B.S., Emergency Medicine, Charter Oak State College, 2003 **Current organization:** Phoenix College & EMT Fire Science Dept. **Title:** NREMT-P, Resident Faculty, Program Manager for EMS Program **Type of organization:** Community college **Major product:** Higher education **Area of distribution:** National **Expertise:** Paramedic development, emergency pre-hospital medicine **Published works:** Seminars, textbooks chapters **Affiliations:** F.A.A.P., Emergency Medicine Section; American Association of University Professors; Captain Paramedic, City of Phoenix **Hob./spts.:** Fishing **SIC code:** 82 **Address:** Phoenix College & EMT Fire Science Dept., 1202 W. Thomas Rd., Phoenix, AZ 85013 **E-mail:** ken.johnsson@pcmail.maricopa.edu

JONES, RACHEL
Industry: Education **Born:** June 9, 1945, Beaumont, Texas **Univ./degree:** B.S., Mathematics, Lamar State Technical College; M.S., Guidance and Counseling, 1972; Professional Supervisor, 1976; Professional Mid-Management Administrator, 1986, Lamar University **Current organization:** Price Elementary School **Title:** Principal **Type of organization:** Elementary school **Major product:** Elementary school education **Area of distribution:** Beaumont, Texas **Expertise:** Educator **Honors/awards:** 2006 Honor Roll, Texas Business and Education Coalition; Lamar University Educator Hall of Fame, 2004; Distinguished Principal's Award, Texas Alliance of Black School Educators, 2002 **Affiliations:** Alpha Kappa Alpha; Association of Texas Professional Educators; Scott Olive Baptist Church; Association for Supervision and Curriculum Development; Texas Elementary Principals and Supervisors Association; Beaumont Area Alliance of Black School Educators; Texas Alliance of Black School Educators; National Alliance of Black School Educators **Hob./spts.:** Reading, football **SIC code:** 82 **Address:** Price Elementary School, 7010 Limerick Dr., Beaumont, TX 77706 **E-mail:** rjonesl@beaumont.k12.tx.us

JUHL, LAURA L.
Industry: Education **Born:** Rockford, Illinois **Univ./degree:** M.A.T., Rockford College, 2003 **Current organization:** Harlem School District #122 - Olson Park Elementary School **Title:** Teacher **Type of organization:** School district **Major product:** Elementary school education **Area of distribution:** Machesney Park, Illinois **Expertise:** Third grade teaching, reading specialist **Affiliations:** N.C.T.M.; International Reading Association **SIC code:** 82 **Address:** Harlem School District #122 - Olson Park Elementary School, 144 Minahan Dr., Machesney Park, IL 61115 **E-mail:** ljuhl@harlem122.org

KAISER, HANS E.
Industry: Education **Born:** February 16, 1928, Prague, Czech Republic **Univ./degree:** D.Sc., University of Tuebingen, 1958 **Current organization:** International Society for the Study of Comparative Oncology, Inc. **Title:** Professor of Pathology **Type of organization:** Non-profit society with charitable, educational, scientific and literary purposes **Major product:** Research, education **Area of distribution:** International **Expertise:** Comparative pathology **Honors/awards:** Listed in Who's Who in America **Published works:** In Vivo, the official journal of the International Society of Comparative Oncology, Inc.; Neoplasms-Comparative Pathology of Growth in Animals, Plants and Man, 1981, ed.; Cancer Growth and Progression, 10 volumes 1989-Series Editor; Morphology of the Sirenia, 1972 **Affiliations:** A.C.S **Hob./spts.:** A lifelong dedication to fight against cancer **SIC code:** 82 **Address:** 433 S. West Dr., Silver Spring, MD 20901 **E-mail:** dr.kaiser@erols.com **Web address:** www.iiar-anticancer.org/index2.htm

KARIPPOT, ANOOP
Industry: Medical **Born:** June 4, 1971, Kerala, India **Univ./degree:** M.D., Armed Forces Medical College, University of Pune, India, 1994; Fellowship, Adult and Adolescent Psychiatry, 2003; Fellowship, Sleep Medicine, 2004, University of Louisville, 2004 **Current organization:** University of Louisville School of Medicine **Title:** M.D. **Type of organization:** Medical school, university hospital **Major product:** Education, research, patient care **Area of distribution:** International **Expertise:** Adult, adolescent and child psychiatry, sleep disorders, bipolar, ADSV, insomnia, autism **Affiliations:** A.P.A.; A.A.C.A.P.; A.A.S.M.; K.M.A.; A.M.A. **Hob./spts.:** Golf, chess, reading **SIC code:** 82 **Address:** University of Louisville School of Medicine, Dept. of Psychiatry, BCGC, 200 E. Chestnut St., Louisville, KY 40202 **E-mail:** anoop.karippot@louisville.edu **Web address:** www.louisville.edu

KASTNER, MIRIAM
Industry: Education **Born:** January 22, 1935, Czechoslovakia **Univ./degree:** Ph.D., Harvard University **Current organization:** Scripps Institution of Oceanography **Title:** Ph.D. **Type of organization:** University **Major product:** Research **Area of distribution:** International **Expertise:** Oceanography **Affiliations:** A.A.A.S.; Sigma Xi **Hob./spts.:** Music **SIC code:** 82 **Address:** Scripps Institution of Oceanography, University of California at San Diego, 8615 Discovery Way, La Jolla, CA 92093-0212 **E-mail:** mkastner@ucsd.edu

KATHI, PRADEEP CHANDRA
Industry: Education **Born:** December 15, 1956, Nellore, India **Univ./degree:** B.S., Engineering, India Institute, 1978; Management, Willamette University, 1991; M.S., Public Administration, University of Southern California, 2004 **Current organization:** University of Southern California **Title:** Professor **Type of organization:** University **Major product:** Higher education **Area of distribution:** International **Expertise:** Citizen participation in government and public ethics **Affiliations:** Pi Alpha Alpha; American Society for Public Administration; Public Management Research Association **Hob./spts.:** Tennis, basketball, reading (crime fiction) **SIC code:** 82 **Address:** 3434 S.W. 10th Terrace, Ocala, FL 34474 **E-mail:** kathi@usc.edu **Web address:** www.usc.edu

KATSIGRIS, COSTAS GUS
Industry: Education **Born:** November 7, 1933, Leonidion, Greece **Univ./degree:** A.B.,1955; M.S., Industrial Relations, 1956, Columbia University. **Current organization:** El Centro College and University of North Texas **Title:** Professor Emeritus **Type of organization:** College/University **Major product:** Higher education/training **Area of distribution:** Texas **Expertise:** Food, beverage **Published works:** Author, 2 textbooks **Hob./spts.:** Reading, gardening, travel **SIC code:** 82 **Address:** 3220 Princess Lane, Dallas, TX 75229 **E-mail:** c+k5531@dcccd.edu

KAWAHARA, FRED K.
Industry: Education/research **Born:** Penngrove, California **Univ./degree:** B.S. with Honors, Environmental Chemistry, University of Texas, 1944; Ph.D., Analytical and Organic Analysis, University of Wisconsin-Madison, 1948 **Current organization:** University of Chicago **Title:** Research Scientist (Retired) **Type of organization:** University **Major product:** Higher education, research **Area of distribution:** International **Expertise:** Consulting, chemical research, treatment of oil on a global basis **Honors/awards:** Cambridge Blue Book-Special Biography; Listed in Marquis Who's Who in America **Published works:** 77 publications - many in American Chemical Society Journal **Affiliations:** Fellow, American Institute of Chemists; Fellow, International Biographical Center **Hob./spts.:** Politics, films, baseball, reading, playing Bridge **SIC code:** 82 **Address:** 1632 Cumberland Ave., Ft. Wright, KY 41011

KEENAGHAN, PATRICIA A.
Industry: Education **Born:** January 24, 1951, New York, New York **Univ./degree:** B.S., Political Science, York University; M.S., Secondary Education & Social Services, Queens College of City University of New York, 1975 **Current organization:** Academy of Our Lady **Title:** Principal **Type of organization:** Grade school **Major product:** Pre-K through grade 8 **Area of distribution:** Glen Rock, New Jersey **Expertise:** Administrator **Affiliations:** N.C.E.A.; N.A.A.S.P., N.C.T.M. **Hob./spts.:** Reading, needlework, charity **SIC code:** 82 **Address:** Academy of Our Lady, 180 Rodney St., Glen Rock, NJ 07452 **E-mail:** principal@academyofourlady.org

KEGLER, MARILYN V.
Industry: Education **Born:** September 20, 1955, Lone Oak, Texas **Univ./degree:** M.Ed., Steven F. Foster State University, 1981 **Current organization:** Garrett Primary School **Title:** Principal **Type of organization:** Elementary school **Major product:** Elementary education **Area of distribution:** Lufkin, Texas **Expertise:** School management **Affiliations:** Delta Sigma Theta **Hob./spts.:** Sports **SIC code:** 82 **Address:** 1214 Voyle St., Lufkin, TX 75901 **E-mail:** m1989@consolidated.net

KEHINDE, RONALD O.
Industry: Education **Born:** Lagos, Nigeria **Univ./degree:** B.F.A., Communications, 1978; M.S., Labor and Industry Relations, 1981, New York Institute of Technology; M.A., Human Resources and Manpower Development, The New School for Social Research, 1981 **Current organization:** Bronx Institute for Career Training & Development, Inc. **Title:** President/C.E.O. **Type of organization:** Post secondary career training institute **Major product:** Vocational training **Area of distribution:** International **Expertise:** Immigration, reform, community empowerment **Honors/awards:** Outstanding Young Men of America, 1987 **Affiliations:** American Management Association; National Human Resources Association **SIC code:** 82 **Address:** Bronx Institute for Career, Training & Development, Inc., 962 Ogden Ave., Bronx, NY 10452 **E-mail:** ronaldkehinde@aol.com **Web address:** www.bronxinstitute.org

KEITH, JOHN M.
Industry: Education **Born:** October 22, 1963, Shreveport, Louisiana **Univ./degree:** B.S., Computer Science, Louisiana State University at Shreveport **Current organization:** Caddo Parish School Board **Title:** Systems Analyst **Type of organization:** School **Major product:** Education **Area of distribution:** Shreveport, Louisiana **Expertise:** Mainframe Cobal; SQL; VBA **SIC code:** 82 **Address:** Caddo Parish School Board, 1961 Midway St., Shreveport, LA 71108-2201 **E-mail:** jkeith@caddo.k12.la.us

KELLY, MARY JO
Industry: Education **Born:** November 25, 1947, Baton Rouge, Louisiana **Univ./degree:** Ed.D., Instructional Technology, Louisiana State University, 1980 **Current organization:** Park Forest Elementary School **Title:** Librarian **Type of organization:** Elementary school **Major product:** Education **Expertise:** Instructional technology, storytelling **Affiliations:** N.E.A.; A.S.C.D.; A.E.C.T.; Louisiana Association of School Librarians **Hob./spts.:** Gardening, science fiction, photography **SIC code:** 82 **Address:** Park Forest Elementary, 10717 Elain St., Baton Rouge, LA 70814 **E-mail:** mkelly@ebrpss.k12.la.us

KESIMER, MEHMET
Industry: Healthcare **Born:** September 8, 1963, Devrek, Turkey **Univ./degree:** M.S.A., 2002; Ph.D., 2002, Biochemistry, Gazi University, Turkey **Current organization:** University of North Carolina - Chapel Hill **Title:** Professor **Type of organization:** University **Major product:** Higher education **Area of distribution:** International **Expertise:** Biochemistry **Affiliations:** American Society for Mass Spectrometry; American Society for Biochemistry and Molecular Biology **SIC code:** 82 **Address:** University of North Carolina - Chapel Hill, 4021 Thurston Bowles Bldg., CB#7248, Chapel Hill, NC 27599 **E-mail:** kesimer@med.unc.edu **Web address:** www.med.unc.edu

KHALIMSKY, EFIM
Industry: Education/research **Born:** June 23, 1938, Odessa, Russia **Univ./degree:** Ph.D., Lenin Pedagogical University, Moscow, 1969 **Current organization:** Central State University **Title:** Professor of Mathematics/Scientist **Type of organization:** University **Major product:** Higher education/research **Area of distribution:** National **Expertise:** Mathematics, topology **Published works:** 4 books; 50+ articles **Affiliations:** American Mathematical Society; I.E.E.E. **Hob./spts.:** Classical music, walking, physical fitness **SIC code:** 82 **Address:** 1260 Brentwood Dr., Dayton, OH 45406 **E-mail:** EKhalimsky@centralstate.edu

KHANAFER, KHALIL M.
Industry: Education **Born:** April 4, 1969, Kuwait **Univ./degree:** B.S., 1993; M.S., 1996, Ph.D., 2002 Ohio State University **Current organization:** University of California at Riverside **Title:** Ph.D. **Type of organization:** University **Major product:** Higher education, research **Area of distribution:** National **Expertise:** Mechanical engineering, research and development; has lectured actively at conferences and seminars, transport through porous media, high heat flux, electronics and nanotechnology **Published works:** 28+ journals **Affiliations:** A.S.M.E. **Hob./spts.:** Fishing, biking **SIC code:** 82 **Address:** 10601 Diana Ave., #410, Riverside, CA 92505 **E-mail:** khanafer@engr.ucr.edu

KIENITZ, JEFFREY S.
Industry: Education **Born:** October 25, 1961, Minneapolis, Minnesota **Univ./degree:** B.S., Education, St. Cloud State University, 1989 **Current organization:** Roseau Community Schools **Title:** Technology Coordinator **Type of organization:** School district **Major product:** K-12 education **Area of distribution:** Roseau, Minnesota **Expertise:** Technology, networking, administration; Licensed Power Limited Technician, A+ Certification, Comp-TIA **Honors/awards:** Accommodation Award, International Science Fair; served in the U.S. Army as a Captain for 14 years **Affiliations:** American Legion; Comp-TIA **Hob./spts.:** Outdoor activities, camping, hiking **SIC code:** 82 **Address:** Roseau Community Schools, 509 N.E. Third St., Roseau, MN 56751 **E-mail:** jski@roseau.k12.mn.us **Web address:** www.roseau.k12.mn.us

KIM, GEON U.
Industry: Education **Born:** October 12, 1962, South Korea **Univ./degree:** M.S., Dentistry, 1989; Ph.D., Endodontict Dentistry, 1999, Pusan National University, South Korea **Current organization:** New York University Dental College, Implant Department **Title:** Visiting Researcher/Professor **Type of organization:** University **Major product:** Higher education **Area of distribution:** National **Expertise:** Dentist (Endodontist and Implantologist) **Affiliations:** I.C.O.I.; Korean Academy of Conservative Dentistry; A.O.; K.A.D.A. **Hob./spts.:** Tennis **SIC code:** 82 **Address:** 168 Elmwood Ave., Glen Rock, NJ 07452 **E-mail:** davidgeonkim@aol.com

KIM, KI HANG
Industry: Education **Born:** August 5, 1936, North Korea **Univ./degree:** Ph.D., Mathematics, George Washington University, 1971 **Current organization:** Alabama State University **Title:** Ph.D., Distinguished Professor **Type of organization:** University **Major product:** Higher education **Area of distribution:** International **Expertise:** Mathematics (Teaching experience includes: University of Hartford, George Washington University, Saint Mary's College of Maryland, University of North Carolina, Alabama State University, University of Delhi, University of Lisbon, University of Stuttgart, USSR Academy of Sciences, Chinese Academy of Sciences **Published works:** 8 textbooks; 183 published research papers; Editorships include: Editor-in-Chief, Mathematical Social Sciences, 1981-95; Associate Editor, Hungarian Journal of Pure and Applied Mathematics; Associate Editor, Future Generations Computer Systems **Hob./spts.:** Jogging **SIC code:** 82 **Address:** 416 Arrowhead Dr., Montgomery, AL 36117 **E-mail:** kkim@asunet.alasu.edu

KIM, SOO-YOUL
Industry: Medical **Born:** March 28, 1962, Seoul, South Korea **Univ./degree:** Ph.D., National University in Korea, 1992 **Current organization:** Cornell University/Burke Medical Institute **Title:** Ph.D. **Type of organization:** University and hospital **Major product:** Patient care, medical research, medical education **Area of distribution:** International **Expertise:** Bioscience, medical research **Affiliations:** S.N.S.; S.N.C. **Hob./spts.:** Skiing **SIC code:** 82 **Address:** Cornell University/Burke Medical Institute, 785 Mamaroneck Ave., White Plains, NY 10605 **E-mail:** tgases@hotmail.com

KING, LINDA HUTTO
Industry: Education **Born:** April 17, 1947, Littlefield, Texas **Univ./degree:** B.A., Elementary Education, University of North Texas, 1969; M.A., Texas Tech University, 1971 **Current organization:** Cavazos Junior High School **Title:** Teacher **Type of organization:** Junior high school **Major product:** Education **Area of distribution:** Lubbock, Texas **Expertise:** Piano lab instruction **Published works:** "From Magnolia to Mesquite", 1997 **Affiliations:** N.E.A.; T.S.T.A.; Lubbock Music Teachers Association; Daughters of the Revolution **Hob./spts.:** Gardening, music, reading, sewing, writing **SIC code:** 82 **Address:** Cavazos Junior High School, 210 N. University, Lubbock, TX 79414 **E-mail:** kings4@sbcglobal.net **Web address:** www.mypianolab.com

KINZIE, DORCUS E.
Industry: Education **Born:** May 1, 1944, Colorado **Univ./degree:** B.S., 1966; M.S., 1976, University of North Carolina **Current organization:** Ayres Elementary School **Title:** Principal **Type of organization:** Elementary school (Pre-K - 5th grade) **Major product:** Education **Area of distribution:** Sterling, Colorado **Expertise:** Administration **Affiliations:** National Association of Elementary School Principals **Hob./spts.:** Family, reading **SIC code:** 82 **Address:** Ayres Elementary School, 1812 Robin Rd., Sterling, CO 80751 **E-mail:** kinzied@kci.net

KLEIN, KENNETH K.
Industry: Education **Born:** September 9, 1954, Cleveland, Ohio **Current organization:** Lorain City Schools **Title:** Associate Director of Operations **Type of organization:** City school district **Major product:** Education **Area of distribution:** Lorain, Ohio **Expertise:** Mechanical management **Affiliations:** Lorain Lyons Club **Hob./spts.:** Scuba diving, boating, motorcycling, flying **SIC code:** 82 **Address:** Lorain City Schools, 2350 Pole Ave., Lorain, OH 44052 **E-mail:** kklein@lorainschools.org

KNOLL, GUY LAWRENCE
Industry: Education **Born:** August 18, 1950, Bartlesville, Oklahoma **Univ./degree:** B.A Honors, Economics, Southwest Texas University at Georgetown **Current organization:** Dallas Independent School District **Title:** Recycle Coordinator, District Manager **Type of organization:** School district **Major product:** Education **Area of distribution:** Dallas, Texas **Expertise:** Solid waste disposal and recycling services **Affiliations:** The Odd Fellow Fraternity; Fraternal Order of the Free and Accepted Masons **SIC code:** 82 **Address:** 1866 Green Tree Lane, Duncanville, TX 75137 **E-mail:** guyknoll@sbcglobal.net

KOCH, ROBERT
Industry: Education **Born:** April 7, 1918, New York, New York **Univ./degree:** Ph.D., Yale University, Connecticut, 1957 **Current organization:** Southern Connecticut State University **Title:** Ph.D./Professor Emeritus **Type of organization:** University **Major product:** Higher education **Area of distribution:** National **Expertise:** Art history,

retired author **Honors/awards:** Faculty Scholar Award, SCSU, 1973-74 **Published works:** Louis C. Tiffany: "The Collected Works of Robert Koch", Schiffer Publications, Pennsylvania, 2001; "Will H. Bradley. American Artist in Print", Hudson Hills Press, New York, 2002 **Affiliations:** American Association of University Professors; College Artists Association **Hob./spts.:** Collecting books on antiques **SIC code:** 82 **Address:** Southern Connecticut State University, Stamford, CT 06905

KOGAN, ALEXANDER
Industry: Education **Born:** July 8, 1971, St. Petersburg, Russia **Univ./degree:** B.S., Bucknell University, Pennsylvania, 1994 **Current organization:** Rockefeller University **Title:** Associate Vice President **Type of organization:** University **Major product:** Higher education, research **Area of distribution:** New York **Expertise:** Engineering facility management **Hob./spts.:** Golf, racquet sports **SIC code:** 82 **Address:** Rockefeller University, 1230 York Ave., New York, NY 10021 **E-mail:** kogana@rockefeller.edu

KONCZAK, SANDRA M.
Industry: Education **Born:** Baird, Texas **Univ./degree:** Ed.D., Concordia University, New Hampshire, 2001 **Current organization:** Abilene ISD **Title:** Teacher **Type of organization:** School district **Major product:** Education **Area of distribution:** Texas **Expertise:** Science and computer technology **Affiliations:** A.S.T.A.; N.C.T.M.; Kappa Gamma **Hob./spts.:** Grandchildren, travel, reading, sewing **SIC code:** 82 **Address:** Abilene ISD, 219 Market St., Baird, TX 79504 **E-mail:** skonczak@camalott.com

KOO, SANG-WAHN
Industry: Medical **Born:** May 7, 1963, Soule, Korea **Univ./degree:** Ph.D., Dermatology, Medical School in South Korea, 1988; M.D., Medical School in South Korea, 1997 **Current organization:** University of Pennsylvania **Title:** Fellow / M.D. **Type of organization:** University **Major product:** Patient care, research, education **Area of distribution:** National **Expertise:** Dermatology, skin care, Behcet's disease **Published works:** 30 publications **Affiliations:** A.A.A.S.; K.S.I.D.; K.D.A.; Society of Investigative Dermatology **Hob./spts.:** Classical music, reading, hiking **SIC code:** 82 **Address:** University of Pennsylvania, M-13, Stellar & Chance Lab, 422 Curie Blvd., Philadelphia, PA 19104 **E-mail:** swkoo@mail.med.upenn.edu

KOO, SIMON G.M.
Industry: Education **Born:** January 4, 1974, Hong Kong, China **Univ./degree:** Ph.D., University of San Diego **Current organization:** University of San Diego **Title:** Assistant Professor of Mathematics and Computer Science **Type of organization:** University **Major product:** Higher education, research **Area of distribution:** International **Expertise:** Computer and communication networks **Affiliations:** I.E.E.E.; Sigma Pi **Hob./spts.:** Sports, musicals **SIC code:** 82 **Address:** University of San Diego, 5998 Alcala Park, San Diego, CA 92110 **E-mail:** koo@sandiego.edu **Web address:** www.simonkoo.us

KOOS, BRIAN J.
Industry: Medical **Born:** March 23, 1949, Los Angeles, California **Univ./degree:** M.D., Loma Linda University, California, 1974; Ph.D., Oxford University, England, 1982 **Current organization:** UCLA , Dept. of Obstetrics & Gynecology **Title:** M.D., Professor **Type of organization:** University hospital **Major product:** Patient care, research **Area of distribution:** California **Expertise:** Maternal-fetal medicine **Published works:** 60 publications **Affiliations:** F.A.C.O.G.; P.R.S.; S.G.I. **Hob./spts.:** Surfing, running **SIC code:** 82 **Address:** UCLA Dept. of Obstetrics & Gynecology, 10833 LeConte Ave., Los Angeles, CA 90095-1740 **E-mail:** bkoos@mednet.ucla.edu

KOSHY, THOMAS
Industry: Education **Univ./degree:** B.Sc., Mathematics and Physics, 1962; M.Sc., Mathematics, 1964, University of Kerala, India; Ph.D., Error Correcting Codes, Applied Algebra, Boston University, 1971 **Current organization:** Framingham State College **Title:** Professor **Type of organization:** University **Major product:** Higher education **Area of distribution:** Massachusetts **Expertise:** Applied algebra; course development; advanced study in Combinatorics, Game Theory, Linear Programming, Markov Chains, Graph Theory, Near-Rings and Finite Groups of Automorphisms **Honors/awards:** Numerous including Commonwealth Citation for Outstanding Performance, 1988; Marquis Who's Who in Science and Engineering, 1998; Excellence Award for Outstanding Contributions to Education, Indian American Kerala Cultural and Civic Center, NY, 2004 **Published works:** Over 85 publications including Lattice Points in a Family of Hyperbolas, The Mathematical Gazette and A Generalized Fibonacci Triangular Array, Journal of Recreational Mathematics, 2003-2004 **Affiliations:** Mathematics Association of America; National Council of Teachers of Mathematics **Hob./spts.:** Field hockey, badminton **SIC code:** 82 **Address:** Framingham State College, 100 State St., Framingham, MA 01701 **E-mail:** tkoshy@frc.mass.edu

KOUSSEFF, BORIS G.
Industry: Medical **Born:** March 15, 1935, Berlin, Germany **Univ./degree:** M.D., Academy of Medicine, Sofia, Bulgaria **Current organization:** University of South Florida **Title:** M.D./Professor **Type of organization:** University **Major product:** Medical education **Area of distribution:** National **Expertise:** Human genetics **Published works:** 1 book chapter in "Atlas of Fetal Pathology" entitled "Dysplasae"; Journals: Journal of Pediatrics, Clinical Genetics, American Journal of Medical Genetics **Affiliations:** American Society of Human Genetics; American College of Medical Genetics; International Congress of Human Genetics **Hob./spts.:** Music, tennis, jogging **SIC code:** 82 **Address:** University of South Florida, 1 Davis Blvd., Suite 604, Tampa, FL 33606 **E-mail:** bkoussef@hsc.usf.edu

KREIDER, KEVIN L.
Industry: Education **Born:** March 15, 1959, Baltimore, Maryland **Univ./degree:** Ph.D., Purdue University, 1986 **Current organization:** The University of Akron **Title:** Ph.D. **Type of organization:** University **Major product:** Higher education **Area of distribution:** Ohio **Expertise:** Numerical simulations **Affiliations:** S.I.A.M. **Hob./spts.:** Playing guitar **SIC code:** 82 **Address:** The University of Akron, Dept. of Theoretical and Applied Mathematics, Akron, OH 44325-4002 **E-mail:** kreider@math.uakron.edu **Web address:** www.math.uakron.edu

KRILOV, GORAN
Industry: Education **Univ./degree:** B.S., Chemistry; B.S., Physics, 1997, Drake University; M.S., Chemistry, Physics, 1998; Ph.D., Chemistry, Physics, 2001, Columbia University **Current organization:** Boston College **Title:** Assistant Professor **Type of organization:** University **Major product:** Higher education, research **Area of distribution:** National, international **Expertise:** Theoretical and computational chemistry **Affiliations:** American Chemical Society; American Association for the Advancement of Science **SIC code:** 82 **Address:** Boston College, 2609 Beacon St., Chestnut Hill, MA 02467 **E-mail:** krilov@bc.edu

KRIPALANI, LAKSHMI A.
Industry: Education/consulting **Born:** August 24, 1920, Hydrabad, Pakistan **Univ./degree:** M.Ed., Seton Hall University, 1965 **Current organization:** Montessori Schools **Title:** Montessorian Educator (Retired) **Type of organization:** School **Major product:** Pre-school and elementary school education **Area of distribution:** International **Expertise:** Lecturing, consulting **Affiliations:** American Montessori Association; UNA-USA; Mensa **Hob./spts.:** Gardening, flower arranging **SIC code:** 82 **Address:** 340 N. Fullerton Ave., Upper Montclair, NJ 07043

KRIVEN, WALTRAUD M.
Industry: Education **Born:** April 25, 1949, Eisenstadt, Austria **Univ./degree:** Ph.D., Physical & Inorganic Chemistry, University of Adelaide, Australia, 1976 **Current organization:** University of Illinois at Urbana-Champaign **Title:** Professor **Type of organization:** University **Major product:** Higher education **Area of distribution:** International **Expertise:** Science and engineering **Honors/awards:** Academician, World Academy of Ceramics, 2005; Fellow, American Ceramic Society, 1995 **Published works:** 225 research publications **Affiliations:** American Ceramic Society; Microscopy Society of America; Materials Research Society **Hob./spts.:** Ballroom dancing, cooking, President and owner of Keanetech, LLC **SIC code:** 82 **Address:** University of Illinois at Urbana-Champaign, Dept. of Material Science & Engineering, 1304 W. Green St., Urbana, IL 61801 **E-mail:** kriven@uiuc.edu

KROSWEK, LAWRENCE R.
Industry: Education **Born:** September 12, 1956, Bay City, Michigan **Univ./degree:** B.S., Education, 1981; M.Ed., Administration, 1987, Central Michigan University **Current organization:** Millington Community Schools **Title:** Superintendent **Type of organization:** Public school system **Major product:** Education (K-12) **Area of distribution:** Millington, Missouri **Expertise:** Administration, long-range technology improvement planning, physical education teacher, coach **Published works:** Newsletter contributions **Affiliations:** Michigan Association of Intermediate School Administrators; Tuscola County Superintendents Association **Hob./spts.:** Golf, spectator sports, movies, physical fitness **SIC code:** 82 **Address:** Millington Community Schools, 8780 Dean Dr., Millington, MI 48746 **E-mail:** lawrence.kroswek@mcsdistrict.com **Web address:** www.mcsdistrict.com

KRUEGER, GERHARD R.F.
Industry: Academic Medicine **Born:** November 21, 1936, Berlin, Germany **Univ./degree:** M.D., Ph.D., Free University, Germany, 1962, 1963 **Current organization:** University of Texas, Houston Medical School, Dept. of Pathology **Title:** Professor **Type of organization:** University and hospital **Major product:** Patient care, academic medicine **Area of distribution:** Texas **Expertise:** General pathology and immunopathology, the lymphatic system. herpes virology, computational biomedicine, academic teaching and healthcare administration (former deanship) **Hob./spts.:** Painting (abstract and landscape), classical music, gardening **SIC code:** 82 **Address:** University of Texas, Houston Medical School, Dept. of Pathology & Laboratory Medicine, 6431 Fannin St., MSB 1.126, Houston, TX 77030 **E-mail:** gerhard.krueger@uth.tmc.edu

KRUPINSKI, NANCY L.
Industry: Medical **Born:** March 7, 1939, Bellaire, Ohio **Univ./degree:** A.S., 1987; B.S.N., 1993; M.S., 1995, West Virginia University; Ph.D., Kennedy, California, 2000

Current organization: West Virginia Northern Community College **Title:** Program Director **Type of organization:** College **Major product:** Surgical technology **Area of distribution:** West Virginia **Expertise:** Curriculum organizer, director and lecturer of surgical technology program, Certified Surgical Technician **Honors/awards:** Nominated, West Virginia Teacher of the Year, 2000 **Affiliations:** A.O.R.N.; A.H.A.; American Nursing Association; Association of Surgical Technicians; Association of Operating Room Nurses **Hob./spts.:** Gardening, flowers **SIC code:** 82 **Address:** West Virginia Northern Community College, 1704 Market St., Wheeling, WV 26003 **E-mail:** nkrupinski@northern.wvnet.edu

KUO, CHUNG CHEN
Industry: Education/research **Born:** July 23, 1971, Taiwan **Univ./degree:** Ph.D., Penn State University, 2005 **Current organization:** Penn State University **Title:** Research Assistant **Type of organization:** University **Major product:** Higher education, research **Area of distribution:** National **Expertise:** Flat panel displays, semiconductor process engineering **Affiliations:** I.E.E.E.; S.I.D.; American Physical Society **SIC code:** 82 **Address:** 12-N Graduate Circle, State College, PA 16801 **E-mail:** shelbykuo@gmail.com

KUO LEE, EMILY HWEI-MEI
Industry: Education **Born:** February 4, 1935, Taipei, Taiwan **Univ./degree:** B.S., Speech Pathology, Temple University, 1976 **Current organization:** Hwei-Mei Speech & Hearing Center **Title:** President/owner **Type of organization:** Educational institute **Major product:** Education **Area of distribution:** California **Expertise:** Speech pathology & audiology **Affiliations:** Life Member, U.S. Senatorial Inner Circle Committee; Life Member, Presidential Task Force; Elite Member, National Republican Congressional Committee as a representative from California; Presidential Round Table Member; C.M.T.E. **Hob./spts.:** Travel, flower art, gardening **SIC code:** 82 **Address:** Hwei-Mei Speech & Hearing Center, 1 Montecito Dr., Corona Del Mar, CA 92625 **E-mail:** emikl@yahoo.com

LAMBA, RAM SARUP
Industry: Education **Born:** December 29, 1941, Calcutta, India **Univ./degree:** Ph.D., Commerce Chemistry, Texas A&M University, 1973 **Current organization:** University of Puerto Rico at Cayey **Title:** Ph.D. **Type of organization:** University **Major product:** Education **Area of distribution:** Puerto Rico **Expertise:** Chemistry **Published works:** 15 articles **Affiliations:** American Chemical Society; Royal Society of Chemists **Hob./spts.:** Outdoors, writing proposals **SIC code:** 82 **Address:** University of Puerto Rico at Cayey, Dept. of Chemistry, Barcelona Ave., Cayey, PR 00736

LAN, SHI "STAN"
Industry: Education **Born:** March 4, 1956, Shanghai, China **Univ./degree:** Ph.D., Leadership Theory and Educational Statistics, Colorado State University, 2004 **Current organization:** DeVry University **Title:** Academic Dean of Electronics **Type of organization:** University **Major product:** Higher education **Area of distribution:** National **Expertise:** Electrical engineering, computer technology, educational research **Affiliations:** A.S.E.E.; I.E.E.E.; I.S.A. **SIC code:** 82 **Address:** DeVry University, 3300 N. Campbell Ave., Chicago, IL 60618 **E-mail:** slan@chi.devry.edu

LANGFORD, KELLY E.
Industry: Education **Born:** January 4, 1954, Tucson, Arizona **Univ./degree:** M.Ed., University of Arizona, 1978 **Current organization:** Tucson Unified Schools **Title:** Senior Academic Officer, Student Services **Type of organization:** School, grades k-12 **Major product:** Education **Area of distribution:** Tucson, Arizona **Expertise:** Education, counseling **Affiliations:** Association for Supervision and Curriculum Development; National Black Child Association **Hob./spts.:** Chess, basketball, football **SIC code:** 82 **Address:** 3102 N. Treat Ave., Tucson, AZ 85716 **E-mail:** kelly.langford@tusd1.org **Web address:** www.tusd1.org

LARRAURI, SILVIA M.
Industry: Education **Born:** April 19, Cuba, 1961 **Univ./degree:** B.S., Nova Southeastern University, 1996 **Current organization:** St. Stephen's Episcopal Day School **Title:** Head of School **Type of organization:** Parish Day School **Major product:** Early childhood education **Area of distribution:** National **Expertise:** Pre-K to elementary education **Affiliations:** N.A.I.S.; F.C.I.S.; N.A.E.S.; F.K.C. **Hob./spts.:** Reading, boating, children, family **SIC code:** 82 **Address:** St. Stephen's Episcopal Day School, 3439 Main Hwy., Coconut Grove, FL 33133 **E-mail:** slarrauri@sseds.org **Web address:** www.sseds.org

LARSON, PAUL S.
Industry: Education **Born:** June 24, 1932 **Univ./degree:** D.M.A., Temple University, 1980 **Current organization:** Moravian College, Bach Choir of Bethlehem **Title:** Professor and Archivist **Type of organization:** College **Major product:** Higher education **Area of distribution:** National **Expertise:** Music and art **Published works:** Books, papers, articles **SIC code:** 82 **Address:** Moravian College, 1122 W. Market St., Bethlehem, PA 18018 **E-mail:** larsonplarson@aol.com

LEET, RONALD P.
Industry: Education **Born:** January 18, 1957, San Pedro, California **Univ./degree:** A.S., Harbor College, California **Current organization:** Prairie State College **Title:** Director of Physical Facilities **Type of organization:** College **Major product:** Higher education **Area of distribution:** National **Expertise:** Energy efficiency and conservation, management, maintenance, construction; Universal License HVAC **Honors/awards:** Energy Management Award from Illinois Dept. of Energy & Natural Resources, 1986 **Affiliations:** South Suburban School Maintenance Association **Hob./spts.:** Family, golf, horseback riding **SIC code:** 82 **Address:** Prairie State College, 202 S. Halsted St., K Bldg., Chicago Heights, IL 60411-8226 **E-mail:** rleet@prairiestate.edu **Web address:** www.prairiestate.edu

LEMANSKI, LARRY F.
Industry: Education **Born:** June 5, 1943, Madison, Wisconsin **Univ./degree:** B.S., Biology, University of Wisconsin; M.S., Zoology, 1968; Ph.D., Zoology, Biology, 1971, Arizona State University **Current organization:** Florida Atlantic University **Title:** Vice President for Research/ Professor **Type of organization:** University **Major product:** Higher education, research **Area of distribution:** International **Expertise:** Cell and molecular biology, medicine **Honors/awards:** Lewis & Kate Award, Outstanding Research, New York **Published works:** 300+ **Affiliations:** F.A.A.A.S.; F.A.S.C.B.; F.A.A.C.B. **Hob./spts.:** Fishing, hiking, camping, music **SIC code:** 82 **Address:** Florida Atlantic University, 777 Glades Rd., Boca Raton, FL 33431-0991 **E-mail:** lemanski@fau.edu

LENGEL, LAURA
Industry: Education **Born:** Mount Lebanon, Pennsylvania, 1964 **Univ./degree:** Ph.D., International Communications, Ohio University, 1995 **Current organization:** Bowling Green State University School of Comm. Studies **Title:** Associate Professor **Type of organization:** University **Major product:** Higher education, research **Area of distribution:** International **Expertise:** International communication research **Honors/awards:** Nominated for a National Communication Association Distinguished Scholarship Award by the Division of International & Intercultural Communication Division **Published works:** Author, "Intercultural Communication & Creative Practice: Music, Dance & Women's Cultural Identity", Westport, CT:Praeger; Co-Author, "Casting Gender: Women & Performance in Intercultural Contexts", NY: Peter Lang Press; Co-Author, "Computer Mediated Communication: Social Interaction on the Internet", London: Sage; Author, (ed.) "Culture & Technology in the New Europe: Civic Discourse in Transformation in Post-Communist Nations", Stamford, CT:Ablex **Affiliations:** National Executive Board, Organization for the Study of Communication, Language and Gender; International Communication Association; International Association for Language and International Communication; Executive Board, International & Intercultural Communication Division, National Communication Association **SIC code:** 82 **Address:** Bowling Green State University, 1000 East Wooster St., Bowling Green, OH 43403 **E-mail:** lengell@bgsu.edu

LENZI, LINDA J.
Industry: Education **Title:** Gifted Education Teacher/Liaison **Type of organization:** School district **Major product:** Education **Expertise:** Gifted education **SIC code:** 82 **Address:** Indian Creek School District, 159 Karen Place, Wintersville, OH 43953 **E-mail:** lindajlenzi@excite.com

LEVINE, ALAN B.
Industry: Education **Born:** November 6, 1940, Newark, New Jersey **Univ./degree:** B.S., Rutgers University; D.C., New York Chiropractic College, 1985; D.P.M., New York College of Podiatric Medicine **Current organization:** New York College of Podiatric Medicine **Title:** Associate Professor **Type of organization:** College **Major product:** Higher education, podiatric medicine **Area of distribution:** New York **Expertise:** Neurosciences, infectious diseases, orthopedics **Affiliations:** A.C.A.; Society for Neuroscience **Hob./spts.:** Travel, gardening, photography **SIC code:** 82 **Address:** New York College of Podiatric Medicine, 53 E. 124th St., New York, NY 10035 **E-mail:** docabl@aol.com

LEVITIN, LEV B.
Industry: Education **Born:** September 25, 1935, Moscow, Russia **Univ./degree:** Ph.D., Gorky University, Russia, 1969 **Current organization:** Boston University College of Engineering **Title:** Distinguished Professor of Engineering Science **Type of organization:** University **Major product:** Higher education, research **Area of distribution:** International **Expertise:** Science and engineering **Published works:** 140 publications (journal articles, conference proceedings) **Affiliations:** Fellow, I.E.E.E.; International Academy of Informatics; American Mathematical Society; New York Academy of Sciences; Past Member, A.C.M.; Past Member, S.I.A.M. **Hob./spts.:** Theatre, music, hiking, travel **SIC code:** 82 **Address:** Boston University College of Engineering, 8 Saint Mary's St., Boston, MA 02215 **E-mail:** levitin@bu.edu **Web address:** www.bu.edu

LI, BIAORU
Industry: Medical **Univ./degree:** M.D., 1983; Ph.D., Medical Microbiology, 1993, Shanghai Second Medical University **Current organization:** Case Western Reserve University **Title:** Ph.D., M.D., Assistant Professor **Type of organization:** University **Major product:** Patient care, medical education **Area of distribution:** National **Expertise:** Biology **Affiliations:** American Society for Microbiology; American Society for Cell Biology **SIC code:** 82 **Address:** Case Western Reserve University, Dept. of Biochemistry, 10900 Euclid Ave., Cleveland, OH 44106 **E-mail:** brli1@juno.com

LINDSEY, BRENDA M.
Industry: Education **Univ./degree:** B.S., Education, Troy State University; Ed.S., Auburn University, 1989; Pursuing Doctorate Educational Leadership, 2004-present **Current organization:** Vaughn Road Elementary **Title:** Principal **Type of organization:** Public elementary school **Major product:** Elementary education **Area of distribution:** Montgomery, Alabama **Expertise:** Program and curriculum development, administration, education **Published works:** An Integration of the Arts and the Academic Impact **Affiliations:** N.E.A.; Special Educators of America; Phi Beta Kappa **Hob./spts.:** Reading, tortoise and turtle rescue, herpetology **SIC code:** 82 **Address:** Vaughn Road Elementary, 4407 Vaughn Rd., Montgomery, AL 36054 **E-mail:** brenda.lindsey@mps.k12.al.us

LIPTAK, LAWRENCE J.
Industry: Education **Born:** February 21, 1955, Easton, Pennsylvania **Univ./degree:** A.O.S., Culinary Institute of America, 1974 **Current organization:** Le Cordon Bleu College of Culinary Arts. **Title:** Chef Instructor **Type of organization:** College **Major product:** Professional culinary training and certification **Area of distribution:** International **Expertise:** Education cooking, wine, purchasing, management **Affiliations:** A.C.F. **Hob./spts.:** Basketball **SIC code:** 82 **Address:** Le Cordon Bleu College of Culinary Arts., 3221 Enterprise Way, Miramar, FL 33025-3929 **E-mail:** flliptak@bellsouth.net

LIU, JING
Industry: Education **Born:** September 28, 1957, Beijing, China **Univ./degree:** M.D., Capitol University of Medical Sciences, Beijing, China, 1982; Ph.D., Texas A&M University, 1992 **Current organization:** The University of Texas Medical School at Houston **Title:** Associate Professor/Director of Cytopathology **Type of organization:** University medical school **Major product:** Medical education **Area of distribution:** National **Expertise:** Anatomical and clinical pathology, cytopathology (Board Certified) **Honors/awards:** Project Award for Scientific Technological Advancement, Capitol University of Medical Sciences, Beijing, China; Travel Award from Fifth World Congress for Microcirculation; Travel Award form American Society for Investigative Pathology **Published works:** 75 abstracts, 15 refereed original articles **Affiliations:** College of American Pathologists; US/Canadian Academy of Pathology **Hob./spts.:** Travel, work, community service **SIC code:** 82 **Address:** The University of Texas Medical School at Houston, 6431 Fannin St., MSB 2.136, Houston, TX 77030 **E-mail:** jing.liu.1@uth.tmc.edu

LONGENECKER, JOHN B.
Industry: Education **Born:** Salunga, Pennsylvania **Univ./degree:** B.A., Biochemistry and Mathematics, Franklin & Marshall College, Lancaster, Pennsylvania; Ph.D., Biochemistry & Nutrition, University of Texas at Austin, 1956 **Title:** Professor of Clinical Nutrition, University of North Carolina at Chapel Hill and University of Texas at Austin (Retired) **Type of organization:** Industry and Academia **Major product:** Development of nutritional products, university education and research **Area of distribution:** International **Expertise:** Neutraceuticals for obesity treatment, nutrition education and research to prevent obesity **Published works:** Longenecker, J.B., Israel, R.G. & Israel, K.D., "Nutrition, Exercise and Weight Control for Better Health", University of North Carolina System, Chapel Hill, North Carolina, 1995 (117 pages); Stevens, J. and Longenecker, J.B., (Editors), Proceedings of the International Conference on "The Determination, Treatment and Prevention of Obesity", Journal of Nutritional Biochemostry 9, #9, 487-453, 1998 and numerous other nutrition related publications **Affiliations:** Professor Emeritus, University of Texas at Austin and the University of North Carolina; Lifetime Fellow, American Institute of Nutritional Sciences; New York Academy of Sciences; Advisory Board, Austin/Travis County Hospital Association; Board Member, The University of Texas Blanton Museum; Board Member, City of Austin Gilbert & Solomon Society **Hob./spts.:** Golf, tennis, band and choral music **SIC code:** 82 **Address:** 2305 Preston Trails Cove, Austin, TX 78747

LOPEZ, TERRY ANN
Industry: Education **Born:** May 12, 1952, Santa Fe, New Mexico **Univ./degree:** B.A., Elementary Education, College of Sante Fe; M.A., Educational Administration, University of New Mexico, 1996 **Current organization:** Cristo Rey Catholic School **Title:** Principal **Type of organization:** Elementary school **Major product:** K-8th grade education **Area of distribution:** Santa Fe, New Mexico **Expertise:** Administration, teaching **Honors/awards:** Who's Who Among High School Students, 1970; Who's Who Among Colleges and Universities, 1974; Outstanding Young Women of America, 1980; International Who's Who of Professional Management, 2000; N.C.E.A. Catechetical Leadership Award, 2001-2002 **Affiliations:** A.S.C.D.; N.C.A.; N.C.E.A.; N.M.A.N.S.; Association of the Miraculous Medal; Little Flower Society; Secular Order of Discalced Carmelites; Sacred Heart League **Hob./spts.:** Dancing, tennis **SIC code:** 82 **Address:** Cristo Rey Catholic School, 316 Camino De Lora, Santa Fe, NM 87505 **E-mail:** talopez@quest.net

LORENZO, CARLOS
Industry: Education **Born:** January 29, 1956 **Univ./degree:** M.D., University of Barcelona, 1979; Ph.D., Automous University of Barcelona, 1993 **Current organization:** University of Texas Health Science Center **Title:** M.D., Ph.D. **Type of organization:** University **Major product:** Higher education **Area of distribution:** Texas **Expertise:** Internal medicine, rheumatology **Published works:** 8 publications **Affiliations:** A.M.A.; American College of Physicians **Hob./spts.:** Jogging, reading **SIC code:** 82 **Address:** University of Texas Health Science Center, Dept. of Medicine, 7703 Floyd Curl Dr., San Antonio, TX 78229 **E-mail:** clorenzolanda@hotmail.com

LOSS, RODERICK J.
Industry: Education **Born:** May 14, 1944, Chicago, Illinois **Univ./degree:** M.B.A., Roosevelt University, Chicago, Illinois, 1978 **Current organization:** University of Maryland **Title:** Professor **Type of organization:** University **Major product:** Higher education **Area of distribution:** National **Expertise:** Information systems **Published works:** 200 publications; 4 books **Affiliations:** M.A.D.R.A., F.R.A., F.O.P., A.U.A. **Hob./spts.:** Watching sports, travel **SIC code:** 82 **Address:** University of Maryland, 9805 Wilden Lane, Potomac, MD 20854-2056 **E-mail:** rloss@netzero.net

LOTAKIS, KATINA A.
Industry: Education **Univ./degree:** M.A., Science Education, Edison College, 1972; M.A., Administration, Iona College, 1980 **Current organization:** NYC Board of Education **Title:** Principal **Type of organization:** School **Major product:** Adolescent education **Area of distribution:** Katonah, New York **Expertise:** Science education **Honors/awards:** Women's History Month, September 2006 **Affiliations:** A.C.S.; I.S.C.D.; Who's Who in American Education; Adjunct Professor, Lehman College **SIC code:** 82 **Address:** NYC Board of Education, Michelangelo Middle School, 4 Veronica Place, Katonah, NY 10536 **E-mail:** lot232@optonline.net

LOUGHEED, JACQUELINE I.
Industry: Education **Univ./degree:** Ph.D., Educational Leadership, Wayne State University, 1968 **Current organization:** Oakland University (Retired) **Title:** Ph.D., Professor **Type of organization:** University **Major product:** Higher education **Area of distribution:** Michigan **Expertise:** Education, mission work in Jamaica **Hob./spts.:** Reading, walking, building doll houses **SIC code:** 82 **Address:** 11285 Cedar Cove Ct., Clarkson, MI 48348 **E-mail:** jilougheedladk@aol.com

LOVE, GAYLE MAGALENE
Industry: Education **Born:** July 25, 1953, New Orleans, Louisiana **Univ./degree:** B.S., 1975; M.S. + 30, 1981, Music Education, Loyola University **Current organization:** L.W. Higgins High School, Jefferson Parish Public School System **Title:** Administrator **Type of organization:** Public school system **Major product:** Administration of student discipline **Area of distribution:** Marrero, Louisiana **Expertise:** Educational records and assessments **Honors/awards:** Excellence in Education Award, WB Chamber of Commerce, 1993; Who's Who in American Education **Published works:** "Good Morning, God"; write-ups **Affiliations:** A.S.C.D.; Jefferson Association P.S.E.I./L.A.S.E.; Grand Lady, Knights and Ladies of Peter Claver; Westwego Historical Society; Jefferson Parish Litter Advisory Board; St. Joseph the Worker Parish Council, 2000-2001, 2001-2002 **Hob./spts.:** Church vocalist, reading, public speaking **SIC code:** 82 **Address:** L.W. Higgins High School, Jefferson Parish Public School System, 7201 Lapalco Blvd., Marrero, LA 70072

LOWERY, LAWRENCE F.
Industry: Education **Born:** Oakland, California **Univ./degree:** Ed.D., Education , University of California at Berkeley, 1964 **Title:** Professor Emeritus, University of California at Berkeley **Type of organization:** University **Major product:** Higher education **Area of distribution:** International **Expertise:** Science and mathematics **Published works:** 80 books, 100 articles **Affiliations:** American Educational Research Association; National Science Teachers Association **Hob./spts.:** Collecting children's books **SIC code:** 82 **Address:** 650 Diablo Rd., Danville, CA 94526 **E-mail:** larry@biglittlebooks.com **Web address:** www.llowerybook.com

LUCERO, HOPE T.
Industry: Education **Spouse:** Steve B. Lucero **Married:** January 1, 1978 **Children:** Cynthia Ann Voccio, Sandra Kay Ross, Steve Bart Lucero; Grandchildren: Tiffany, Kristen "Kiki", Leija **Univ./degree:** B.S., Physical Education/Health/Spanish, Sul Ross State University, Texas, 1969; M.A., Guidance Counseling/Administration, New Mexico Highlands University, 1978 **Current organization:** Hope Connection School, Inc. **Title:** Principal/Director **Type of organization:** Private school **Major product:** Education **Area of distribution:** New Mexico **Expertise:** Counseling **Honors/awards:** Nominated for Hall of Fame Women in New Mexico, 2003; Governor's Award for

Outstanding Woman in New Mexico, 2003; John W. Vaughn Excellence in Education Award, 2002; Top 5 Educator in 19 State Region Award, 2002; Top Accredited Private Secondary Schools Award, 2002; Smart, Savvy & Successful Business Woman, 2001; YWCA Women on the Move Award, 1999; Governor's Award for Outstanding Women in New Mexico, 1999; Nominated for Hall of Fame Women in New Mexico, 1999 **Published works:** Students Thrive in Later School Hours; Last Chance High School **Affiliations:** New Mexico State Department of Education; North Central Association of Colleges and Schools; North Central Accreditation; New Mexico School Boards Association **Career accomplishments:** President of the Hope Connection School; Superintendent/Director of the Hope Connection School **Hob./spts.:** Sewing, painting, bowling **SIC code:** 82 **Address:** Hope Connection School, Inc., 4700 Eubank N.E., Albuquerque, NM 87111 **Phone:** (505)237-0844 **Fax:** (505)237-0110 **E-mail:** hopeconnection@comcast.net **Web address:** www.wrldcon.com/hope/

LUCERO, STEVE B.
Industry: Education **Born:** August 11, 1947, Albuquerque, New Mexico **Univ./degree:** M.A., Guidance Counseling, Highlands University, 1978 **Current organization:** Hope Connection School, Inc. **Title:** Assistant Director **Type of organization:** Private school **Major product:** Education **Area of distribution:** Albuquerque, New Mexico **Expertise:** Administration, curriculum design **Hob./spts.:** Sports, hunting, fishing **SIC code:** 82 **Address:** Hope Connection School, Inc., 4700 Eubank Blvd. N.E., Albuquerque, NM 87111-2534 **E-mail:** hopeconnection@comcast.net

LUNDQUIST, KAREN B.
Industry: Education **Born:** May 23, 1947, Jamestown, New York **Univ./degree:** B.S., Health & Physical Education, Akron University, 1969; M.Ed., University of Dayton, 1984 **Current organization:** Edison Local School District **Title:** Health & Physical Education Director **Type of organization:** Middle school **Major product:** Education **Area of distribution:** Toronto, Ohio **Expertise:** Health and physical education; Certified CPR & Lifeguard Instructor **Honors/awards:** Olympic Torch Carrier, 2002; Ohio Health Professional of the Year, 2002; Who's Who Among America's Teachers **Published works:** Future Focus **Affiliations:** N.E.A.; E.L.E.A.; O.E.A.; A.A.H.P.E.R.D.; O.A.H.P.E.R.D.; Instructor for American Red Cross in: Lifeguard, CPR-PR, Sports Medicine, WSI, First Aid **Hob./spts.:** Swimming, walking, photography **SIC code:** 82 **Address:** 1309 Franklin Ave., Apt. A-1, Toronto, OH 43964

MALEK, ESMAIEL
Industry: Education **Born:** Sari, Iran **Univ./degree:** Ph.D., Utah State University **Current organization:** Utah State University **Title:** Ph.D. **Type of organization:** University **Major product:** Higher education, research **Area of distribution:** International **Expertise:** Biometeorology **Published works:** 3 books, journal articles **Affiliations:** American Meteorological Society; American Geophysical Union **Hob./spts.:** Gardening **SIC code:** 82 **Address:** Utah State University, 4820 Old Main Hill, Logan, UT 84322-4820 **E-mail:** emalek@mendel.usu.edu

MALLAPRAGADA, SURYA K.
Industry: Education **Born:** India **Univ./degree:** Ph.D., Purdue University, 1996 **Current organization:** Iowa State University **Title:** Associate Professor **Type of organization:** University **Major product:** Higher education **Area of distribution:** International **Expertise:** Research, plastic for medical applications **Affiliations:** American Chemical Society; American Institute of Chemical Engineers **SIC code:** 82 **Address:** Iowa State University, 3035 Sweeney Hall, Ames, IA 50011 **E-mail:** suryakm@iastate.edu

MANADOM, DORN
Industry: Education **Born:** February 28, 1954, Biafra, Nigeria **Univ./degree:** B.S.N., Emory University **Current organization:** World Outreach Medical Institute **Title:** President/Owner **Type of organization:** Vocational institute **Major product:** Training of medical personnel **Area of distribution:** National **Expertise:** Oncological nursing **Hob./spts.:** Soccer **SIC code:** 82 **Address:** World Outreach Medical Institute, 4650 Memorial Dr., Decatur, GA 30032 **Web address:** www.worldoutreachmi.com

MANNING, RANDOLPH H.
Industry: Education **Born:** December 18, 1947, Bronx, New York **Univ./degree:** A.A., Suffolk Community College; B.A., Psychology; M.A.L.S.; Ph.D., Social Psychology; S.U.N.Y. Stony Brook, 1998 **Current organization:** Suffolk County Community College **Title:** Associate Dean **Type of organization:** Community college **Major product:** Higher education **Area of distribution:** New York **Expertise:** Administration of all business related programs, technology **Honors/awards:** Who's Who Among America's Teachers, 1994; Certificate of Specified Congressional Recognition, 1997; Citation, New York State Assembly, 2000; Proclamation, Suffolk County Executive, 2000 **Published works:** "Student Persistence in the Open Enrollment Community College" **Affiliations:** N.Y.S.S.; A.S.A. **Hob./spts.:** Basketball, golf, music **SIC code:** 82 **Address:** Suffolk County Community College, Business & Technology Dept., 1001 Crooked Hill Rd., Brentwood, NY 11717 **E-mail:** manninr@sunysuffolk.edu

MANSEN, THOM J.
Industry: Education **Born:** August 8, 1950, Holland, Michigan **Univ./degree:** B.S.N., University of Michigan; M.S., University of Utah; Ph.D., Nursing Education, Administration, University of Texas at Austin **Current organization:** University of Utah, College of Nursing **Title:** Associate Professor; Baccalaureate Program Coordinator 2000-05 **Type of organization:** University **Major product:** Higher education **Area of distribution:** National **Expertise:** Assessment, administration, pathophysiology **Honors/awards:** Amy V. Cockcroft Leadership Fellow, 1996-97, University of South Carolina, Columbia , SC **Affiliations:** American Nurses Association; Utah Nurses Association (1st Vice President 1995-97, President 1998-2001, Delegate 1994-2006); Sigma Theta Tau (Gamma Rho), President 1990-92 **Hob./spts.:** Utah opera, piano, playing the organ **SIC code:** 82 **Address:** University of Utah, College of Nursing, 10 S. 2000 E Front, Salt Lake City, UT 84112 **E-mail:** thom.mansen@nurs.utah.edu **Web address:** www.nurs.utah.edu

MARE, W. HAROLD
Industry: Education **Born:** July 23, 1918, Portland, Oregon **Spouse:** Elizabeth Potter **Married:** March 23, 1945 **Children:** Myra A. Ovshak, 54; Sally E. Walke, 50; Nancy L. Hayward, 49; William H. Mare, 46; Judith E. Linton, 41 **Univ./degree:** B.A., M.A., Wheaton College, Illinois; B.D., Faith Seminary; Ph.D., Classical Studies, University of Pennsylvania **Current organization:** Covenant Theological Seminary **Title:** Professor of New Testament **Type of organization:** Seminary **Major product:** Educational training and scientific research **Area of distribution:** International **Expertise:** New Testament, archaeological research; Director, Abila of the Decapolis Excavation, Northern Jordan; Director, Archaeological Institute, Covenant Seminary; President, Abila Archaeological Project, Inc. **Honors/awards:** Graduate with Highest Honor, Wheaton College; Wheaton College Scholastic Honor Society **Published works:** 3 books, N.T. Greek Grammar; Archaeology of the Jerusalem Area; Commentary on 1 Corinthians; in process, Backgrounds of the Bible; numerous articles, including American and overseas publications **Affiliations:** Archaeological Institute of America; Society of Biblical Literature; American Schools of Oriental Research; Near East Archaeological Society; Evangelical Theological Society; Institute for Biblical Research; Classical Club of St. Louis; Missouri Numismatic Society **Career accomplishments:** President, Near East Archaeological Society, 1971-92; President, Archaeological Institute of America, St. Louis Society, 1978-80 **Hob./spts.:** Photography, travel **SIC code:** 82 **Address:** Covenant Theological Seminary, 12330 Conway Road, St. Louis, MO 63141 **E-mail:** whmare@aol.com

MARROW, JERRY R.
Industry: Education **Born:** September 14, 1949, Kearney, Nebraska **Univ./degree:** M.Ed., Kansas State University, 1986 **Current organization:** Kansas State University **Title:** Cable TV Administrator **Type of organization:** University **Major product:** Telecommunication, cable television **Area of distribution:** Manhattan, Kansas **Expertise:** Dial-up technical support **Affiliations:** H.A.H.E.C.T.A. **SIC code:** 82 **Address:** 109 E. Stadium, Manhattan, KS 66506-3102 **E-mail:** jerry@ksu.edu **Web address:** www.telecom.ksu.edu

MARSHALL, MARTHA C.
Industry: Education/writing **Born:** Johnson City, Tennessee **Univ./degree:** B.S., East Tennessee State University; M.A., Peabody College of Vanderbilt University; Ph.D. (Honorary), World University Roundtable, 1999 **Current organization:** Bristol Tennessee High School (Retired) **Title:** Author/Educator **Type of organization:** High school **Major product:** Education/writing **Area of distribution:** National **Expertise:** Writing, teaching, editing, history, lecturing **Honors/awards:** Delta Kappa Gamma; Freedoms Foundation Outstanding Teacher Award, 25 or more Outstanding School Awards, Outstanding History Teacher, DAR (local and state), PTA Life Membership (state); Jefferson Davis UDC Outstanding History Award; American League of American Pen Women, National Life Time Award Pen Woman of the Year for Professional Service; Outstanding Achievement, Early American Society; Outstanding Teacher, State of Tennessee **Published works:** Books: Chronicles of NLAPW in Tennessee; Hundred Year History of NLAPW, Co-Editor (National); Many Patches Ago (Quilt History); Gentle Voices From the Chapel (2 volumes); Autumn in the Mountains; Glimpses From the Hills; Entering a New Century, 1895-1905, Co-editor; A Book, A Rose and A Golden Key; Saga of the Vikings (School History of THS); various articles for magazines and newspapers **Affiliations:** National League of American Pen Women; American Association of University Women; Genealogy Society; Historical Societies **Hob./spts.:** Quilt making, lecturing, research, collecting and various publications **SIC code:** 82 **Address:** 3401 W. Walnut St., Johnson City, TN 37604

MARTEEL-PARRISH, ANNE E.
Industry: Education **Born:** October 23, 1975, Dunkirk, France **Univ./degree:** Ph.D., Chemistry, University of Toledo, Ohio, 2003; Master's, Materials Science, Ecole Universitaire Polytechnique de Lille, France **Current organization:** Washington College **Title:** Professor **Type of organization:** College **Major product:** Higher education, research **Area of distribution:** International **Expertise:** Chemistry, inorganic chemistry, green chemistry, environmentally benign chemistry **Published works:** 8 articles, numerous conference papers **Affiliations:** American Chemical Society (ACS);

Green Chemistry Network; Council on Undergraduate Research; Sigma Xi; IUPAC **Hob./spts.:** Sailing, running, golf **SIC code:** 82 **Address:** Washington College, 300 Washington Ave., Chestertown, MD 21620 **E-mail:** amarteel2@washcoll.edu

MARTINEZ, JUAN A.
Industry: Education **Born:** October 12, 1969, San Juan, Puerto Rico **Univ./degree:** Ph.D., University of Puerto Rico School of Medicine, 2002 **Current organization:** Univ. del Este-Ana G. Mendez Univ. System **Title:** Assistant Professor **Type of organization:** University **Major product:** Higher education **Area of distribution:** Puerto Rico **Expertise:** Biochemistry, cell-molecular, research **Published works:** 1 book chapter, 1 peer-reviewed article **Affiliations:** American Society for Biochemistry **Hob./spts.:** Fishing, basketball **SIC code:** 82 **Address:** Univ. del Este-Ana, P.O. Box 2010, Carolina, PR 00984 **E-mail:** juanchovies@yahoo.com

MARTINEZ, LUIS A.
Industry: Education **Born:** June 1, 1955, Chicago, Illinois **Univ./degree:** B.A., Architecture, University of Illinois, 1978; M.A., Architectural Design, University of Illinois at Urbana, 1980 **Current organization:** City Colleges of Chicago **Title:** Associate Vice Chancellor **Type of organization:** Community college **Major product:** Higher education **Area of distribution:** Illinois **Expertise:** Architecture **Honors/awards:** Latin American Community Service Award, 1992; Superior Public Service Award, 1992; Outstanding Community Service Award, 1990; Leadership Greater Chicago Fellow, 1990; Outstanding Young Men of America Award, 1987; Jennie and Frank B. Long Fellowship, 1980; Chicago Women's Architectural Award, 1979; Nominated for Who's Who in American Colleges and Universities, 1977 **Published works:** Alumni Magazine **Affiliations:** American Institute of Architects; Chicago Council on Urban Affairs; Construction Specification Institute; Trustee, United Puerto Ricans of Chicago; Lincoln Park Restoration Steering Committee; National Organization of Minority Architects **Hob./spts.:** Travel **SIC code:** 82 **Address:** City Colleges of Chicago, 226 W. Jackson St., Suite 1043, Chicago, IL 60606

MASI, MARSHA L.
Industry: Education **Born:** July 1, 1950, Detroit, Michigan **Univ./degree:** M.A., Learning and Counseling, Michigan State University, 1977; Educational Supervision Certification, 1998 **Current organization:** Galena Park High School **Title:** Principal **Type of organization:** High school **Major product:** High school education **Area of distribution:** Galena Park, Texas **Expertise:** Administration, daily operations, education oversight **Honors/awards:** Principal of the Year, 2003 **Affiliations:** Texas Association of Secondary School Principals; National Association of Secondary School Principals; Rotary Club **Hob./spts.:** Gardening, Boy Scouts of America **SIC code:** 82 **Address:** Galena Park High School, 1000 Keene St., Galena Park, TX 77547 **E-mail:** mmasi@galenaparkisd.com

MASTERS, ROGER D.
Industry: Education **Born:** June 8, 1933, Boston, Massachusetts **Married:** Judith A. (Rubin), married June 22, 1956, div. Feb. 6, 1984; Second marriage: Suzanne R. (Putnam), August 26, 1984 **Children:** Seth James, born 1959; William Alan, born 1961; Katherine, born 1971; 4 stepchildren **Univ./degree:** A.B., Summa Cum Laude, Government, Harvard College, 1955; A.M., Political Science, University of Chicago, 1958; Political Science, Institut d'Etudes Politiques, Paris, France, 1959; Ph.D., Political Science, University of Chicago, 1961 **Current organization:** Dartmouth College, Dept. of Government **Title:** Research Professor **Type of organization:** University **Major product:** Research, higher education **Area of distribution:** New Hampshire **Expertise:** Biology and Human Behavior, Neurotoxins, Behavior & Public Policy; Political Philosophy **Honors/awards:** Fulbright Fellowship to France, 1958-59; Joint Yale-S.S.R.C. Fellowship, 1964-65; John Simon Guggenheim Fellowship, 1967-68; John Sloan Dickey Third Century Professor of Government, Dartmouth College, 1979-85; Director d'Etudes Associé, Ecole des Hautes Etudes en Sciences Sociales, Paris, France, 1986; Teaching Award, Dartmouth College, 1998 **Published works:** "The Nation is Burdened" 1967, "The Political Philosophy of Rousseau" 1968, "The Nature of Politics" 1989; "Beyond Relativism: Science, Philosophy and Human Nature" 1993; "Machiavelli, Leonardi and the Science of Power" 1996; "Fortune is a River: Leonardo da Vinci and Niccolï Machiavelli's Magnificent Dream to Change the Course of Florentine History" 1998; Editor, Co-editor of numerous publications; 150+ articles **Affiliations:** American Political Science Association (APSA); Association for Politics & the Life Sciences (APLS); American Association for the Advancement of Science (AAAS) **Career accomplishments:** Editor and co-translator, Collected Writings of Rousseau; Empirical research linking heavy metals and silicofluorides to behavioral dysfunctions (learning disabilities, violent behavior and substance abuse); research on collaboration of Machiavelli and Leonardo da Vinci **Hob./spts.:** Bird watching, cross-country skiing **SIC code:** 82 **Address:** Dartmouth College, Dept. of Government, HB 6108, Hanover, NH 03755 **E-mail:** roger.d.masters@dartmouth.edu

MASTERSON, JAMES F.
Industry: Medical **Born:** March 25, 1926, Philadelphia, Pennsylvania **Univ./degree:** M.D., Jefferson Medical College, 1950 **Current organization:** The Masterson Institute for Psychoanalytic Psychotherapy **Title:** Founder & Director **Type of organization:** Post-graduate training program **Major product:** Higher education **Area of distribution:** New York and California **Expertise:** Psychiatry and Neurology (Board Certified) **Honors/awards:** Psychiatrist of the Year, California Psychiatric Association, 2000 **Published works:** 18 books including "The Personality Disorders: As Viewed Through the Lens of Attachment Theory & New Biological Development of the Cells" **Affiliations:** American Psychiatric Association **Hob./spts.:** Tennis **SIC code:** 82 **Address:** The Masterson Institute for Psychoanalytic Psychotherapy, 60 Sutton Place South, 1 and 2 North, New York, NY 10022 **E-mail:** mastersnin@aol.com **Web address:** www.mastersoninstitute.org

MATA, NANCY R.
Industry: Education **Born:** Pueblo, Colorado **Univ./degree:** B.F.A., West Chester University; M.F.A., Temple University, 2001 **Current organization:** Millersville University **Title:** Assistant Professor **Type of organization:** University **Major product:** Higher education **Area of distribution:** Pennsylvania **Expertise:** Graphic design, interactive media **Affiliations:** A.I.G.A.; Art Directors Club **SIC code:** 82 **Address:** Millersville University, 1 S. George St., Millersville, PA 17551 **E-mail:** nmata@millersville.edu **Web address:** www.millersville.edu

MATHIS, GLENNWOOD
Industry: Education **Born:** January 20, 1934, Beaumont, Mississippi **Univ./degree:** B.S., University of Southern Mississippi, 1964; M.Ed., Mississippi State University, 1969 **Current organization:** Perry County School District **Title:** Special Education Director **Type of organization:** School district **Major product:** Education, service **Area of distribution:** Perry County, Mississippi **Expertise:** Special needs students **Affiliations:** Exchange Club **Hob./spts.:** Fishing, helping people **SIC code:** 82 **Address:** 1513 Bolton Ave., Beaumont, MS 39423

MATLOFF, GREGORY L.
Industry: Education **Univ./degree:** Ph.D., Planetary Atmospheres, New York University, 1976 **Current organization:** New York City College of Technology, CUNY **Title:** Assistant Professor, Physics **Type of organization:** College **Major product:** Higher education **Area of distribution:** International **Expertise:** Course development, physics, astronomy, public speaking, lecturing, consulting **Honors/awards:** Guest Professorship, University of Siena, Italy, 1994 **Published works:** Author, "Deep Space Probes", 2005 **Affiliations:** Hayden Association; American Museum of Natural History; Fellow, British Interplanetary Society; International Academy of Astronautics; The Planetary Society **SIC code:** 82 **Address:** New York City College of Technology, CUNY, 300 Jay St., Brooklyn, NY 11201 **E-mail:** gmatloff@citytech.cuny.edu

MATSUI, DOROTHY N.
Industry: Education **Born:** January 9, 1954, Honolulu, Hawaii **Univ./degree:** B.A., Education, 1979; M.A., Education, 1986, University of Alaska **Current organization:** Anchorage School District **Title:** Educator **Type of organization:** Elementary school **Major product:** Education **Area of distribution:** Anchorage, Alaska **Expertise:** Teaching **Honors/awards:** Who's Who of American Women; Who's Who of Emerging Leaders in America; Who's Who in American Education; The World's Who's Who of Women; Who's Who Among America's Teachers; Five Thousand Personalities of the World; International Leaders in Achievement; Personalities of America; International Directory of Distinguished Leadership; Grand Ambassador of Achievement International **Affiliations:** National Education Association; Alaska Education Association; Alpha Delta Kappa; Smithsonian National Association Program; Smithsonian Air and Space Association; International Platform Association; National Audubon Society; Cousteau Society; Alaska Council for the Social Studies; Alaskan Council for Teachers of Mathematics; United States Olympic Society; University of Alaska Anchorage Alumni Association; National Council for Teachers of Mathematics; Mathematical Association of America; Museum of Flight Foundation; Anchorage Museum of History and Art; Japanese-American National Museum; Association for Supervision and Curriculum Development; Women's Inner Circle Achievement **Hob./spts.:** Reading **SIC code:** 82 **Address:** Anchorage School District, 7001 Cranberry St., Anchorage, AK 99502 **E-mail:** nonchi@alaska.net

MCCANN, ROBERT N.
Industry: Education **Born:** January 22, 1947, Wayne, New Jersey **Univ./degree:** B.A., Paterson State College, 1968; M.A., Institutional Counseling, 1978; M.Ed., 1981, William Paterson College **Current organization:** Hamburg Public School **Title:** Superintendent **Type of organization:** Elementary school **Major product:** K-8 education **Area of distribution:** Hamburg, New Jersey **Expertise:** Administration, education **Honors/awards:** Who's Who Among America's Teachers **Affiliations:** N.J.A.S.A. **Hob./spts.:** Pilot, motorcycle rider, woodworking **SIC code:** 82 **Address:** Hamburg Public School, 30 Linwood Ave., Hamburg, NJ 07419 **E-mail:** rmccann@hamburgschool.com **Web address:** www.hamburgschool.com

MCDANIEL, BARRY LYNN
Industry: Education **Born:** April 19, 1956, Baton Rouge, Louisiana **Univ./degree:** Ph.D., Philosophy, Vocational Education, Louisiana State University, 1989 **Current organization:** Louisiana School for the Visually Impaired **Title:** Ph.D. **Type of orga-**

nization: State school for the blind and visually impaired **Major product:** Educating and serving students **Area of distribution:** Baton Rouge, Louisiana **Expertise:** Education Diagnostician, Vision Specialist **Hob./spts.:** Music, family, sports **SIC code:** 82 **Address:** 6542 Peggy St., Baton Rouge, LA 70808 **E-mail:** bmcdaniel@lsvi.org

MCDONALD, JOHN F.
Industry: Education/research **Born:** January, 14, 1942, Narberth, Pennsylvania **Univ./degree:** B.S.E.E., 1963, Massachusetts Institute of Technology; M.Eng., 1965; Ph.D., Electrical Engineering, 1969, Yale University, Connecticut **Current organization:** Rensselaer Polytechnic Institute **Title:** Professor/Researcher **Type of organization:** University **Major product:** Higher education/research **Area of distribution:** New York **Expertise:** Computer chip, package and board design **Published works:** 209 articles in print **Affiliations:** Institute of Electrical and Electronics Engineers; American Institute of Physics **SIC code:** 82 **Address:** Rensselaer Polytechnic Institute, Center for Integrated Electronics, Room CII-6123, Troy, NY 12181 **E-mail:** mcdonald@unix.cie.rpi.edu **Web address:** www.inp.cie.rpi,edu/research/mcdonald/frisc

MCDOWELL, ORLANDO
Industry: Education/consulting **Born:** September 4, 1963, Chicago, Illinois **Univ./degree:** A.S., Medicine; A.S., Technology Business; B.S., Psychology, Chicago State University **Current organization:** Chicago Board of Education/Chicago Community Policing **Title:** Teacher/CEO **Type of organization:** Education/task force **Major product:** Education/community service **Area of distribution:** Illinois **Expertise:** Engineering technology **Affiliations:** C.C.C.; I.E.E.E.; C.A.F.; Phi Beta Kappa **SIC code:** 82 **Address:** 9034 S. Essex St., Chicago, IL 60617

MCKEAND, PATRICK J.
Industry: Education **Born:** June 10, 1941, Anderson, Indiana **Univ./degree:** B.A., Indiana University; M.A. Ball State University **Current organization:** Indiana University **Title:** Publisher **Type of organization:** University **Major product:** Higher education **Area of distribution:** International **Expertise:** Newspaper publishing **Published works:** Numerous publications **Affiliations:** A.E.J.M.C.; A.P.M.F., Member, National Board of Directors, Society of Professional Journalists, 1999-2001; Society for News Design **Hob./spts.:** Travel, sports, bridge **SIC code:** 82 **Address:** Indiana University, 902 W. New York St., ES4104, Indianapolis, IN 46202 **E-mail:** pmckeand@iupui.edu

MCTAGGART, TIMOTHY T.
Industry: Education/religion **Born:** December 8, 1949, Danville, Pennsylvania **Univ./degree:** B.A., Bloomsberg University, 1971; M.A., Theology, St. Vincent, 1974; Ed.M., Millersville, 1980; Ed.D., Pacific Western University, 1990 **Current organization:** Columbia High School **Title:** Ed.D. **Type of organization:** High school **Major product:** Secondary school education **Area of distribution:** Mount Joy, Pennsylvania **Expertise:** Mathematics, computer science, religion **Affiliations:** N.E.A.; Pennsylvania Education Association **SIC code:** 82 **Address:** Columbia High School, 901 Ironville Pike, Mount Joy, PA 17512 **E-mail:** timmymct@aol.com

MEECH, KAREN J.
Industry: Space science **Born:** July 9, 1959, Denver, Colorado **Univ./degree:** B.S., Space Physics, Rice University, 1981; Ph.D., Planetary Physics, M.I.T., 1987 **Current organization:** Institute for Astronomy **Title:** Ph.D/Astronomer **Type of organization:** University/research institute **Major product:** Higher education/research **Area of distribution:** International **Expertise:** Program development, research, educational outreach, lecturing **Honors/awards:** Urey Prize in Planetary Astronomy, 1994; Annie Jump Cannon Prize, 1988 **Published works:** 100+ publications; 1 book chapter **Affiliations:** President, International Astronomical Union Commission on Bio Astronomy; Board Member, American Association of Variable Star Observers **Hob./spts.:** Scuba diving, kayaking, hiking, piano, gourmet cooking **SIC code:** 82 **Address:** Institute for Astronomy, 2680 Woodlawn Dr., Honolulu, HI 96822 **E-mail:** meech@ifa.hawaii.edu **Web address:** www.ifa.hawaii.edu/~meech

MEHLOTRA, RAJEEV K.
Industry: Education **Born:** September 25, 1963, Patiala, Punjab **Univ./degree:** B.S.; M.S., Lockow University, India; Ph.D., Biochemistry, Central Drug Research Institute, 1991 **Current organization:** Case Western Reserve University School of Medicine **Title:** Senior Instructor **Type of organization:** University **Major product:** Academics and research **Area of distribution:** International **Expertise:** Molecular biologist **Honors/awards:** Outstanding Scientist of the 20th Century **Published works:** 20+ articles, book chapters **Affiliations:** Indian Immunology Society; Indian Parasitology Society; Royal Society of Tropical Medicine and Hygiene **Hob./spts.:** Cricket **SIC code:** 82 **Address:** Case Western Reserve University, School of Medicine, W153, 2109 Adelbert Rd., Cleveland, OH 44106-4983 **E-mail:** rkm@po.cwru.edu

MEIER, ROBERTA M.
Industry: Education **Born:** January 15, 1948, Brooklyn, New York **Univ./degree:** M.Ed., Adelphi University, 1973 **Current organization:** Desert Springs Christian Preschool & Kindergarten **Title:** Director/Co-Founder **Type of organization:** Christian school **Major product:** Early childhood education **Area of distribution:** Scottsdale, Arizona **Expertise:** School operations **Affiliations:** A.C.S.I.; Trainer for Succeeds **Hob./spts.:** Crafts, music, travel **SIC code:** 82 **Address:** Desert Springs Christian Preschool & Kindergarten, 5401 E. Charleston Ave., Scottsdale, AZ 85254 **E-mail:** tromeier@aol.com

MEILE, NATHAN P.
Industry: Education **Born:** December 28, 1978, Kansas **Univ./degree:** B.S., Hotel and Restaurant Management, Kansas State University, 2003 **Current organization:** Kansas State University Housing and Dining Services **Title:** Production Service Manager **Type of organization:** University **Major product:** Higher education, university food service **Area of distribution:** Kansas **Expertise:** Production service and operations **Affiliations:** N.R.A. **Hob./spts.:** Astronomy, hunting **SIC code:** 82 **Address:** 104 Snyder Dr., St. George, KS 66535 **E-mail:** meile@ksu.com

MERLO, PATRICIA A.
Industry: Education **Born:** September 25, 1946, Vidor, Texas **Univ./degree:** B.S.N., California State University, Long Beach, 1983 **Current organization:** Tennessee Technology Center **Title:** Surgical Technology Program Director **Type of organization:** Vocational/technical school **Major product:** Higher education **Area of distribution:** Tennessee **Expertise:** Administration, teaching, program development **Published works:** Book (ready for publication), articles **Affiliations:** A.O.R.N.; A.S.T.; Tennessee State Assembly **Hob./spts.:** Tennis, oil painting, writing **SIC code:** 82 **Address:** Tennessee Technology Center, 241 Vo Tech Dr., McMinnville, TN 37110 **E-mail:** pm413@bellsouth.net

MICHELSON, ALAN E.
Industry: Education **Born:** July 16, 1949, Philadelphia, Pennsylvania **Univ./degree:** M.S.E., Central Missouri State University, 1981 **Current organization:** Cordill-Mason Elementary School **Title:** Principal **Type of organization:** Elementary school **Major product:** Elementary education **Area of distribution:** Blue Springs, Missouri **Expertise:** Administration **Affiliations:** M.A.E.S.P.; Member, Board of Directors, National Association of Elementary School Principals **Hob./spts.:** Reading, golf, travel **SIC code:** 82 **Address:** Cordill-Mason Elementary School, 4001 S.W. Christian Dr., Blue Springs, MO 64014 **E-mail:** amichelson@bssd.net

MILLER, KENNETH B.
Industry: Education **Born:** August 26, 1955, Massachusetts **Current organization:** The Fessenden School **Title:** Food Service Director **Type of organization:** Private boarding school **Major product:** Education **Area of distribution:** Massachusetts **Expertise:** Chef/Food Service Director **Hob./spts.:** Record collecting **SIC code:** 82 **Address:** 62 Forest St., Wakefield, MA 01880 **E-mail:** kmiller@fessenden.org

MILLER, LINCOLN P.
Industry: Medical **Born:** October 27, 1957, New York, New York **Spouse:** Nancy B. Kalkin **Married:** September 22, 1992 **Children:** Graham 9, Georgia 8, Dorothea 4 **Univ./degree:** M.D., University of Tel Aviv Sackler School of Medicine, 1985 **Current organization:** New Jersey Medical School **Title:** Associate Professor **Type of organization:** Medical school **Major product:** Medical education **Area of distribution:** National **Expertise:** Board Certified, Internal Medicine, 1988; Board Certified, Infectious Diseases, 2000 **Honors/awards:** National Research Council; Senior Associateship Award, 1992, 1994 **Affiliations:** American Society of Microbiology; American College of Physicians **Hob./spts.:** Running, bird watching **SIC code:** 82 **Address:** Lincoln P. Miller, M.D., 1500 Pleasant Valley Way, Suite 201, West Orange, NJ 07050 **E-mail:** millerlpnyc@aol.com

MILLER, PETER
Industry: Music Education **Born:** February 5, 1954, Warwick, Rhode Island **Univ./degree:** B.M., Music Education, University of Rhode Island, 1977; M.A.T., Music Performance concentration, Rhode Island College, 1981; additional studies include Universities of Miami, Hartford, South Carolina, Massachusetts, Vermont **Current organization:** Rutland Public Schools, Castleton State College **Title:** Conductor and Teacher **Type of organization:** Educational institutions **Major product:** Music performance and performance education **Area of distribution:** Central Vermont **Expertise:** Orchestra conductor, violinist and violist, educator, professional mentor and motivational speaker **Honors/awards:** 2004 Vermont Arts Educator of the Year, International Who's Who in Music, 1997, 1999; Who's Who in Entertainment, 1996; Who's Who in American Education, 1995; NSOA Distinguished Service Award, 1992; Outstanding Arts Educator Medal, Massachusetts Alliance for Arts Education, 1989 **Published works:** Articles, interviews and columns including the National School Orchestra Association NSOA Journal, American String Teacher, Music Educators Journal **Affiliations:** Numerous including, Past President, NSOA, Co-chair Committee on School Strings and Orchestras, ASTA (American String Teachers Association) Editorial Review Committee and ASTA Teacher Training Symposium Task Force, Membership held: Music Educators National Conference (MENC): International Society for Music Education (ISME); Association for Supervision, Curriculum and Development (ASCD); American Federation of Musicians (AF of M) **SIC code:** 82 **Address:** 46 Chestnut Ave., Rutland, VT 05701 **E-mail:** vtvlnvla@aol.com

MINA, NAIRMEN
Industry: Education **Born:** March 14, 1959, Colombia, South America **Univ./degree:** Ph.D., Physical Chemistry, Baylor University, 1996 **Current organization:** University of Puerto Rico **Title:** Associate Professor **Type of organization:** University **Major product:** Higher education **Area of distribution:** Puerto Rico **Expertise:** Physical chemistry **Published works:** Journals **Affiliations:** A.C.S.; I.M.S.; A.A.N.S. **Hob./spts.:** Swimming **SIC code:** 82 **Address:** Sierra Nevada #183, Mayaguez, PR 00680 **E-mail:** nmma@uprm.edu

MINTZ, HERMAN
Industry: Education **Born:** September 19, 1931, New Jersey **Univ./degree:** B.A., Education; M.A., New Jersey College **Title:** Author/Educator **Type of organization:** Self-employed **Major product:** Writing **Area of distribution:** National **Expertise:** Writing, teaching **Published works:** 11 books **Affiliations:** Knights of Pythias **SIC code:** 82 **Address:** 41 Laurel Ave., Trenton, NJ 08618-4015 **E-mail:** mintz45@msn.com

MISCH, BONNIE L.
Industry: Education **Born:** April 30, 1947, Oneida, New York **Univ./degree:** B.A., Elementary Education, SUNY, Oswego, 1969; Certificate in Advanced Studies, SUNY, Oswego, 1984 **Current organization:** Millard Hawk Primary School **Title:** Elementary Principal **Type of organization:** Elementary school **Major product:** Education **Area of distribution:** Central Square, New York **Expertise:** Academic and character development **Affiliations:** S.A.A.N.Y.S.; A.S.C.D. **Hob./spts.:** Sewing, aerobics **SIC code:** 82 **Address:** Millard Hawk Primary School, 74 School Dr., Central Square, NY 13036 **E-mail:** bmisch@cssd.org

MISIASZEK SR., EDWARD T.
Industry: Education **Univ./degree:** Ph.D., P.E., Clarkson University, 1962 **Title:** Professor/Dean, Undergraduate Studies (Retired) **Type of organization:** University **Major product:** Higher education **Area of distribution:** Pottsdam, New York **Expertise:** Soil mechanics, foundation engineering **Affiliations:** New York State Society of Professional Engineers; Chair, St. Lawrence Red Cross **SIC code:** 82 **Address:** 45 May Rd., Potsdam, NY 13676

MITSCHER, LESTER A.
Industry: Education **Born:** August 20, 1931, Detroit, Michigan **Univ./degree:** Ph.D., Organic Chemistry, Wayne State University in Michigan, 1958 **Current organization:** Kansas University **Title:** University Distinguished Professor **Type of organization:** University **Major product:** Higher education, research **Area of distribution:** International **Expertise:** Chemistry **Published works:** 245 published works, six books **Affiliations:** A.C.S.; J.A.R.A.; B.C.S.; A.A.A.S.; A.S.P. **Hob./spts.:** Stamp collecting, music **SIC code:** 82 **Address:** Kansas University, Dept. of Mechanical Chemistry, 4010 Malott Hall, Lawrence, KS 66045 **E-mail:** lmitscher@ku.edu

MIZUSHIMA, MASATAKA
Industry: Education **Born:** March 30, 1923, Tokyo, Japan **Spouse:** Tsuboi Yoneko **Married:** December, 1955 **Children:** Nanko, 50; Naomi, 48; Nori, 47, Nobuko, 46; Nieret, 43 **Univ./degree:** Degree Rigakushi, Chemistry, 1946; Degree Rigakuhakushi, Sc. Dr. in Physics, 1951; Ph.D., 1952, University of Tokyo; **Current organization:** University of Colorado at Boulder **Title:** Professor of Physics Emeritus **Type of organization:** University **Major product:** Higher education, research **Area of distribution:** International **Expertise:** Physics, general relativity, molecular spectroscopy **Published works:** 86 in molecular spectroscopy including 3 books and 41 in general relativity **Affiliations:** American Chemical Society **Career accomplishments:** 20 Ph.D.'s **Hob./spts.:** Music, geology **SIC code:** 82 **Address:** 523 Theresa Dr., Boulder, CO 80303 **E-mail:** mizushima@colorado.edu **Web address:** www.colorado.edu

MOAG, RODNEY F.
Industry: Education **Born:** October 15, 1936, Warsaw, New York **Univ./degree:** Ph.D., Linguistics, Wisconsin University **Current organization:** University of Texas, Dept. of Asian Studies **Title:** Professor **Type of organization:** University **Major product:** Higher education **Expertise:** Teaching languages of India **Published works:** 2 books, 20 articles **Affiliations:** Lifetime Member, Dravidian Linguistics Association; Association for Asian Studies **Hob./spts.:** Bluegrass and country music **SIC code:** 82 **Address:** 6909 Miranda Dr., Austin, TX 78752 **E-mail:** rmoag@mail.utexas.edu

MOCKFORD, EDWARD L.
Industry: Education **Born:** June 16, 1930, Indianapolis, Indiana **Univ./degree:** Ph.D., University of Illinois, 1960 **Current organization:** Illinois State University, Dept. of Biological Sciences **Title:** Professor Emeritus **Type of organization:** University **Major product:** Information **Area of distribution:** International **Expertise:** Entomology, insect systematics and biology **Affiliations:** American Entomological Society **Hob./spts.:** Bird watching, swimming **SIC code:** 82 **Address:** Illinois State University, Dept. of Biological Sciences, Normal, IL 61790-4120 **E-mail:** elmockf@ilstu.edu

MONTOYA, PAT L.
Industry: Education **Born:** April 27, 1951, Trinidad, Colorado **Univ./degree:** B.A., Elementary Education, 1973; M.A., Educational Leadership, 1990, University of Northern Colorado **Current organization:** Weld County School District #6 **Title:** Principal **Type of organization:** Elementary school **Major product:** Elementary school education **Area of distribution:** Weld County, Colorado **Expertise:** Administration **Hob./spts.:** Reading **SIC code:** 82 **Address:** Weld County School District #6, 1315 4th Ave., Greeley, CO 80631

MOON, DUDLEY G.
Industry: Education **Born:** June 22, 1950, Niagara Falls, New York **Univ./degree:** M.S., Biochemistry, State University of New York, Binghamton, 1979; Ph.D., Physiology and Cell Biology, Albany Medical College, 1983 **Current organization:** Albany College of Pharmacy **Title:** Ph.D., Professor **Type of organization:** College **Major product:** Higher education, research **Area of distribution:** Albany, New York **Expertise:** Hematology **Affiliations:** A.A.A.S.; A.S.P.B.; A.S.C.B. **Hob./spts.:** 8th Degree Black Belt in Karate, laido, played the hammered dulcimer **SIC code:** 82 **Address:** Albany College of Pharmacy, 106 New Scotland Ave., Albany, NY 12208 **E-mail:** moond@acp.edu

MOORE, JOHN J.
Industry: Education **Born:** March 28, 1944, Stourbridge, England **Univ./degree:** Ph.D., Engineering, 1969; D.Eng., 1996, University of Birmingham **Current organization:** Colorado School of Mines **Title:** Trustees' Professor and Head **Type of organization:** University **Major product:** Higher education **Area of distribution:** National **Expertise:** Research and administration **Published works:** 500 papers **Affiliations:** I.M.M.M.; A.S.M. International **Hob./spts.:** Hiking, dancing, soccer **SIC code:** 82 **Address:** Colorado School of Mines, 1500 Illinois St., Golden, CO 80401 **E-mail:** jjmoore@mines.edu

MORGAN, SANDRA
Industry: Education **Born:** August 6, Detroit, Michigan **Univ./degree:** B.S., Andrews University, 1970; M.Ed., Special Education, 1974; M.A., Educational Psychology, 1977; M.A., Counseling, 1980, Wayne State University; Ph.D., University of Southern California, 2002 **Current organization:** Detroit Board of Education **Title:** Ph.D./Psychologist **Type of organization:** School board **Major product:** Education **Area of distribution:** Detroit, Michigan **Expertise:** Counseling, special education **Honors/awards:** Who's Who in America, 1992-93 **Published works:** 3 books **Affiliations:** American Psychotherapy Association; American Counseling Association **Hob./spts.:** Writing poetry, sewing, drawing, music, travel **SIC code:** 82 **Address:** 16239 Lamplighter Ct., #1330, Southfield, MI 48075 **E-mail:** sanmorgan4@juno.com

MORRELL, JUNE ELIZABETH
Industry: Education **Born:** June 20, 1925, Yakima, Washington **Univ./degree:** B.S., Education, Eastern Washington University, 1969 **Current organization:** Camas Valley Christian School **Title:** Principal/Teacher **Type of organization:** Private school **Major product:** Handicapped children **Area of distribution:** Springdale, Washington **Expertise:** Educating and encouraging handicapped children **Hob./spts.:** Reading **SIC code:** 82 **Address:** 4972 Bowler Rd., Springdale, WA 99173

MORTIMER, GREGORY
Industry: Education **Born:** 1951, Denver, Colorado **Univ./degree:** A.A., Cedar Valley Community College, 1993 **Current organization:** Wycliffe International **Title:** Energy Management Supervisor **Type of organization:** College **Major product:** Technology education **Area of distribution:** Texas **Expertise:** Power conservation **Affiliations:** D.W.A.P.P.A.; N.A.T.E.A.; N.T.A.E.E. **Hob./spts.:** Motorcycles **SIC code:** 82 **Address:** Wycliffe International, 7500 W. Camp Wisdom Rd., Dallas, TX 75236 **E-mail:** greg_mortimer@sil.org

MOYANA, AARON T.
Industry: Education **Born:** May 12, 1950, Zimbabwe, Africa **Univ./degree:** B.A., English/French, 1976, Birmingham Southern College; M.Ed., 1979; Ed.D., 1990, University of Alabama **Current organization:** Birmingham City Schools **Title:** Dropout Prevention/School Safety Officer **Type of organization:** City school system **Major product:** Public school education **Area of distribution:** Birmingham, Alabama **Expertise:** Safety and prevention services; Coordinator for Safe and Drug Free Schools Program; Coordinator for the At Risk Grant; Acting Director of the Community Education Dept. **Published works:** Editor, University of Alabama Education Planning Jour-

nal **Affiliations:** International Society for Educational Planning; Phi Delta Kappa; Past Referee and Instructor, U.S. Soccer Federation **Hob./spts.:** Soccer, tennis **SIC code:** 82 **Address:** Birmingham City Schools, 417 29th St. South, Birmingham, AL 35235 **E-mail:** amoyana@bhamcityschools.org **Web address:** www.bhamcityschools.org

MOYÉ II, ULYSSES G.
Industry: Education/music **Born:** April 6, 1942, Kinston, North Carolina **Univ./degree:** B.Mus.Educ., M.Mus.Educ., Dean's List, Howard University; D.Min. Candidate, Trinity College & Seminary **Title:** School Administrator, Fairfax County Virginia Public Schools & Washington, D.C. Public Schools (Retired); Adjunct Professor, George Washington University **Type of organization:** Public school system and university **Major product:** Education **Area of distribution:** Prince George County, Maryland and Washington, D.C. **Expertise:** Education and administration, music education **Honors/awards:** Honorary Doctorate, Sacred Laws and Letters, North Carolina Christian Bible College and Seminary; Who's Who in Religion, 1992; United Black College Fund Award **Published works:** Rejoice Resource Handbook **Affiliations:** A.S.C.D.; M.E.N.C.; N.A.S.S.P.; (5th V.P., Dean, N.C.G.C.C. Inc. USA); M.S.T.A.; Omega Psi Phi; Phi Delta Kappa (Education); Phi Mu Alpha Sinfonia Fraternity (Music); National Alliance of Black School Educators; Prince George's County Educator's Association; Maryland State Teachers Association **Hob./spts.:** Family, sports, church **SIC code:** 82 **Address:** 5243 Kenstan Dr., Temple Hills, MD 20748 **E-mail:** umoye@comcast.net

MUCINO, VICTOR H.
Industry: Education **Born:** January 2, 1952, Mexico City, Mexico **Univ./degree:** Ph.D., University of Wisconsin, 1981 **Current organization:** West Virginia University **Title:** Professor **Type of organization:** University **Major product:** Higher education **Area of distribution:** International **Expertise:** Mechanical engineering design **Published works:** 100 journal articles **Affiliations:** Society of Automotive Engineers; Mexican American Society of Engineers **Hob./spts.:** Music **SIC code:** 82 **Address:** West Virginia University, College of Engineering & Mineral Resource, ESB 127 Evansdale Campus, Morgantown, WV 26506 **E-mail:** vhmucino@mail.wvu.edu

MUELLER, DENNIS W.
Industry: Education **Born:** May 11, 1949, Cook, Nebraska **Univ./degree:** Ph.D., Physics, University of Nebraska, 1982 **Current organization:** University of North Texas/ MetScan Technologies, LLC **Title:** Professor/Director of Research and Development **Type of organization:** University/non-destructive testing and inspection **Major product:** Higher education/advanced instrumentation and services **Area of distribution:** International **Expertise:** Physics, materials science, advanced instrumentation and measurement **Published works:** More than 100 articles and presentations **Affiliations:** AXE; American Physics Society; Materials Research Society; Electro Chemical Society **SIC code:** 82 **Address:** 2436 S. I-35E, #376-192, Denton, TX 76205 **E-mail:** mueller@metscan.com

MUIR, WILLIAM L.
Industry: Education **Born:** March 20, 1948, Norton, Kansas **Univ./degree:** B.A., Business Administration, Kansas State University **Current organization:** Kansas State University **Title:** Assistant Vice President **Type of organization:** University **Major product:** Higher education **Area of distribution:** National **Expertise:** Community relations **Affiliations:** Alpha Tau Omega; Manhattan City Board of Housing Appeals; Board of Trustee, Kansas State University Foundation **Hob./spts.:** Travel **SIC code:** 82 **Address:** Kansas State University, 122 Anderson Hall, KSU, Manhattan, KS 66506 **E-mail:** billmuir@ksu.edu **Web address:** www.ksu.edu

MULDER, PATRICIA M.
Industry: Education **Born:** December 28, 1944, South Bend, Indiana **Spouse:** James **Children:** Todd Alan Mulder; Scott Robert Mulder **Univ./degree:** B.A., Education, Western Michigan University, 1967 **Current organization:** Southwestern Michigan College **Title:** Instructor **Type of organization:** College **Major product:** Higher education **Area of distribution:** Michigan and Indiana **Expertise:** Teaching, photography, freelance writer **Honors/awards:** Award from Noble House Publishers, 2007; Poetry Fellow, 2007; Editor's Choice Award, 2007 **Published works:** Many articles, poetry, newspaper writer **Affiliations:** National Council of Teachers of English (N.C.T.E); International Freelance Photographers Organization (I.F.P.O); Hemingway Society **Hob./spts.:** Oil and watercolor painting, photography **SIC code:** 82 **Address:** 10252 Castner Dr., Berrien Springs, MI 49103 **E-mail:** pmulderm@yahoo.com

MUNCHAUSEN, LINDA L.
Industry: Education **Univ./degree:** Ph.D., Organic Photo Chemistry **Current organization:** Southeastern Louisiana University **Title:** Ph.D./Professor of Chemistry **Type of organization:** University **Major product:** Higher education **Area of distribution:** Hammond, Louisiana **Expertise:** Teaching/organic chemistry **Affiliations:** Louisiana Academy of Sciences; Kiwanis Club; Iota Sigma Pi; Delta Kappa Gamma; American Chemical Society **Hob./spts.:** Pottery, crocheting, knitting, gardening **SIC code:** 82 **Address:** Southeastern Louisiana University, SLU 10878, Hammond, LA 70402 **E-mail:** lmunchausen@selu.edu

MURPHY, JAMES A.
Industry: Education/law enforcement **Born:** April 1, 1973, Buffalo, New York **Current organization:** Canisius College Dept. of Public Safety **Title:** Lieutenant **Type of organization:** University **Major product:** Higher education **Area of distribution:** New York **Expertise:** Law enforcement, public safety **Affiliations:** Crime Prevention Association of Western New York; Community Action Organization (CAO) of Erie County **SIC code:** 82 **Address:** Canisius College Dept. of Public Safety, 2001 Main St., Buffalo, NY 14208 **E-mail:** murphy2@canisius.edu

MYERS, MARSHALL D.
Industry: Education **Title:** Dr. **Type of organization:** University **Major product:** Higher education, undergraduate and graduate degrees **Expertise:** Rhetoric and composition **SIC code:** 82 **Address:** Eastern Kentucky University, 313 Dylan Ct., Richmond, KY 40475 **E-mail:** marshall.myers@eku.edu

MYNBAEV, DJAFAR K.
Industry: Education **Born:** November 7, 1939, Leningrad, USSR **Univ./degree:** Ph.D., V.I. Ul'yanov (Lenin), Leningrad Electrical Engineering Institute, 1969 **Current organization:** New York City College of Technology **Title:** Professor **Type of organization:** University **Major product:** Higher education **Area of distribution:** International **Expertise:** Engineering Professor **Published works:** More than 100 papers, 26 patents and a book **Affiliations:** I.E.E.E. **Hob./spts.:** Tennis, skiing **SIC code:** 82 **Address:** New York City College of Technology, 300 Jay St., V733, Brooklyn, NY 11201 **E-mail:** dmynbaev@citytech.cuny.edu

NACMAN, ALVYN IRWIN
Industry: Education **Univ./degree:** Ph.D., Astrophysics, Washington University, 1979; Ph.D., Astrobiology, Eayard University, Switzerland, 1993 **Title:** Professor, Charter School of Newark and University of Delaware (Retired) **Type of organization:** University **Major product:** Higher education **Expertise:** Astrobiology, cosmology **Affiliations:** A.S.P.; Delaware Astronomical Society **Hob./spts.:** Planetarium, astrobiology, meteorites **SIC code:** 82 **Address:** 48 River Woods Dr., Wilmington, DE 19809-2475 **E-mail:** anacman@worldnet.att.net

NAPIERALA, CHRISTOPHER
Industry: Education **Born:** April 1, 1960, Milwaukee, Wisconsin **Univ./degree:** B.S., University of Wisconsin South, 1982 **Current organization:** Samuel Morse Middle School **Title:** Teacher **Type of organization:** Public school **Major product:** Educational skills in manufacturing **Area of distribution:** Wisconsin **Expertise:** Manufacturing **Honors/awards:** National Teaching Excellence Award, 2005; Superintendent's Teaching Award, 2002; Certificate of Commendation, 2000 **Affiliations:** A.F.S.; A.C.D.; I.T.E.A.; S.P.E.; S.M.E. **Hob./spts.:** Fishing bowling, billiards, travel **SIC code:** 82 **Address:** Samuel Morse Middle School, 4601 N. 84th St., Milwaukee, WI 53225-4958 **E-mail:** napiercx@mailmilwaukee.k12.wi.us **Web address:** www.mailmilwaukee.k12.wi.us

NARASIMHAN, ASHOK
Industry: Education/semiconductors **Born:** February 7, 1980, India **Univ./degree:** M.S., 2003; Ph.D., 2006, University at Buffalo **Current organization:** University at Buffalo **Type of organization:** University/R&D **Major product:** Higher education/cutting edge technology integrated circuits **Area of distribution:** International **Expertise:** Research **Affiliations:** I.E.E.E. **Hob./spts.:** Racing **SIC code:** 82 **Address:** University at Buffalo, 201 Bell Hall, Buffalo, NY 14260 **E-mail:** akn2@cse.buffalo.edu **Web address:** www.cse.buffalo.edu

NARAYANA, PONNADA A.
Industry: Education **Univ./degree:** Ph.D., Physics, Indian Institute of Technology, 1969 **Current organization:** University of Texas Health Science Center **Title:** Professor **Type of organization:** University **Major product:** Higher education, research **Area of distribution:** International **Expertise:** Research, radiology **Published works:** 150 publications **Affiliations:** American Association for the Advancement of Science; American Association of Physicists in Medicine **SIC code:** 82 **Address:** University of Texas Health Science Center, Diagnostic & Intervention Imaging Dept., 6431 Fannin-MSB 2.100, Houston, TX 77030 **E-mail:** ponnada.a.narayana@uth.tmc.edu

NEDZI, LUCIEN ALEXANDER
Industry: Education **Born:** May 24, 1958, Detroit, Michigan **Univ./degree:** M.D., University of California at San Francisco, 1987 **Current organization:** Tulane University, Dept. of Radiation Oncology **Title:** M.D. **Type of organization:** University **Major product:** Higher education **Area of distribution:** National **Expertise:** Radiation oncology, brain tumors **Honors/awards:** ASTRO Residence S.A. Award **Published works:** Peer reviewed journals **Affiliations:** American Society for Therapeutic Radiation & Oncology; European Society for Therapeutic Radiation & Oncology; Society for Neuro-Oncology **Hob./spts.:** Travel **SIC code:** 82 **Address:** Tulane University, Dept. of Radiation Oncology, 150 S. Liberty St., New Orleans, LA 70112 **E-mail:** lnedzi@tulane.edu

NEHER, ROBERT T.
Industry: Education **Born:** November 1, 1930, Mount Morris, Illinois **Univ./degree:** Ph.D., Botany, University of Indiana **Current organization:** University of La Verne **Title:** Chairman of the Natural Sciences Division **Type of organization:** University **Major product:** Higher education **Area of distribution:** International **Expertise:** Education, environmental biology **Published works:** "Ethnobotany of Tagetes", "Monograph of the Genus Tagetes" **Affiliations:** A.A.A.S.; A.A.U.P.; A.S.P.T.; Society of Sigma Xi **Hob./spts.:** Coin collecting, tennis, ethnobotany **SIC code:** 82 **Address:** University of La Verne, Natural Sciences Division, 1950 Third St., La Verne, CA 91750 **E-mail:** neherr@ulv.edu

NELLETT, GAILE HAUSAMAN
Industry: Education **Born:** November 5, 1941, Ottawa, Illinois **Univ./degree:** Ph.D., Loyola University, Chicago, 1998 **Current organization:** University of St. Francis, College of Nursing and Allied Health **Title:** Ph.D./Associate Professor **Type of organization:** University **Major product:** Higher education **Area of distribution:** Illinois **Expertise:** Nursing, research and gerontology **Affiliations:** A.N.A.; N.G.N.A.; M.N.R.S. **Hob./spts.:** Archery, hunting, fishing, quilting, reading **SIC code:** 82 **Address:** 2768 E. 2551st Rd., Marseilles, IL 61341 **E-mail:** gnellett@stfrancis.edu

NELSON, M. JANICE
Industry: Education/nursing **Born:** February 26, 1928, Buffalo, New York **Univ./degree:** Nursing Diploma, St. Joseph Hospital School of Nursing,1960; B.S., Education, Daemen College, 1966; B.S., Nursing, 1968; Ed.M., Nursing Service administration, 1970; Ed.D., Curriculum and Instruction, 1977, Teachers College, Columbia University **Type of organization:** Education **Major product:** Nursing **Expertise:** Nursing **Honors/awards:** Distinguished Alumnae Award, Daemen College, Buffalo, New York; Life Time Achievement Award, New York State Nurses Association; Nursing Hall of Fame, Teachers College, Columbia University; Community Mentor Award, Omicron Alpha Chapter/Sigma Theta Tau, International; Alternate Fellowship Award to "Philosophical Roots of Bioethics", National Endowment for the Humanities, Washington, D.C. **Published works:** "Legal, Ethical and Economic Foundations of the Educational Process", (Chapter) in S.B. Bastable, The Nurse as Educator. Boston: Jones & Bartlett. 1977. [first & second editions] (Winner of the American Journal of Nursing Book of the Year Award, 1998; "Trends in Hospital Nursing", (with M.I. McClure) in L. Aiken. Nursing in the 80's. Published by the American Academy of Nursing; An Existential Viewpoint on Whistelblowing", Should you Tell? Published by the New York State Nurses Association **Affiliations:** Syracuse Home Association; Member, Board Member, Central Counties Professional Nurses Association; Board Member, Foundation of the New York State Nurses Association; Past President, Member Emeritus, Nurses Educational Funds, Inc.; Visiting Nurse Systems of Central New York; Board Member, Chair, Awards Committee **Hob./spts.:** Golf, reading, needlework **SIC code:** 82 **Address:** 482 Summerhaven Dr. North, East Syracuse, NY 13057-3140 **E-mail:** topnurse@twcny.rr.com

NICHOLSON, ROBBIE A.
Industry: Education **Univ./degree:** A.S., American School, Chicago, Illinois, 1968 **Current organization:** School of Materials Science & Engineering **Title:** Technical Services Director / Research Spc. **Type of organization:** University **Major product:** Higher education, woven and non-woven textiles, fiber and film, polymers **Area of distribution:** International **Expertise:** Teaching evaluation of fibers, films, polymers and materials (woven / nonwoven) **Published works:** Articles **Affiliations:** SEMS; SEM; CU Women's Commission; SC State Employees Association; JTAB (Clemson Area Transit Board) **Hob./spts.:** Gardening **SIC code:** 82 **Address:** School of Materials Science and Engineering, Clemson University, 161 Sirrine Hall, Clemson, SC 29634 **E-mail:** nrobbie@clemson.edu

NIEDERMAN, ROBERT A.
Industry: Education **Born:** January 19, 1937, Norwich, Connecticut **Univ./degree:** Ph.D., University of Illinois, 1967 **Current organization:** Rutgers University, Busch Campus **Title:** Professor of Biochemistry **Type of organization:** University/Graduate School **Major product:** Higher education **Area of distribution:** International **Expertise:** Membrane biochemistry **Published works:** 87 publications **Affiliations:** A.S.B.M.B.; A.A.A.S.; I.S.P.R. **Hob./spts.:** Swimming, running cycling **SIC code:** 82 **Address:** Rutgers University, Busch Campus, Nelson Biological Laboratories, Dept. of Molecular Biology & Biochemistry, Piscataway, NJ 08854 **E-mail:** rneiderm@rci.rutgers.edu **Web address:** www.rci.rutgers.edu/~molbio/faculty/niederm

NORGREN, DIANNE L.
Industry: Libraries **Born:** Greeley, Colorado **Univ./degree:** A.S., Veterinarian Technology, Colorado Mountain College **Current organization:** Platteville Public Library **Title:** Director **Type of organization:** Public library **Major product:** Library services **Area of distribution:** Platteville, Colorado **Expertise:** Library services **Affiliations:** American Library Association; 4-H Leaders **SIC code:** 82 **Address:** Platteville Public Library, 504 Marion Ave., P.O. Box 567, Platteville, CO 80651 **E-mail:** dnorgren@weld.lib.co.us **Web address:** www.weld.lib.co.us

NORRIS, KEITH C.
Industry: Healthcare **Born:** April 30, 1957, Paterson, New Jersey **Univ./degree:** M.D., Howard University, 1980 **Current organization:** Charles R. Drew University **Title:** Vice President of Research **Type of organization:** University **Major product:** Higher education **Area of distribution:** International **Expertise:** Nephrology (Educator for the department of health) **Affiliations:** F.A.C.P.; I.S.N.; A.S.H.T.; I.S.H.T.I.B.; A.S.N.; W.P.A.; A.A.K.P.; N.K.E. **Hob./spts.:** Jogging, snowboarding, poetry **SIC code:** 82 **Address:** Charles R. Drew University, 11705 Deputy Yamamoto Pl., Suite B, Lynwood, CA 90262 **E-mail:** knorris@ucla.edu

NORTH, TERESA LYNN
Industry: Education **Univ./degree:** Ph.D., Nutrition, University of California at Davis, 1984; Education Certification, Negotiation and Conflict Resolution, Jones International University, 2003 **Current organization:** Western Illinois University **Title:** Assistant to the Vice President for Student Services **Type of organization:** University **Major product:** Higher education **Area of distribution:** National **Expertise:** Administration, fundraising, strategic planning **Affiliations:** National Association of Student Personnel Administrators; American Council of Professional Administrators **SIC code:** 82 **Address:** Western Illinois University, 1 University Circle, Macomb, IL 61455 **E-mail:** tl-north@wiu.edu **Web address:** www.wiu.edu

NOURI, KEYVAN
Industry: Medical **Born:** September 21, 1967, Tehran, Iran **Univ./degree:** B.A., Summa Cum Laude, Biology, Boston University, 1989; M.D., Boston University, School of Medicine, 1993 **Current organization:** University of Miami School of Medicine **Title:** M.D., Director of Mohs Micrographic Surgery, Dermatologic and Laser Surgery/Director of Surgical Training/Associate Professor **Type of organization:** University **Major product:** Medical services **Area of distribution:** Florida **Expertise:** Mohs Micrographic Laser Surgery **Honors/awards:** Numerous including, Marquis Who's Who in the World 2002; Gaumont Skin Cancer Foundation Scholarship; AAD Scholarships to attend 1999 European Academy of Dermatology and Venereology annual meeting in Amsterdam, Netherlands and 1997 19th World Congress of Dermatology in Sydney, Australia; SID Kligman Fellowship; Phi Beta Kappa; Phi Beta Delta Honor Society; National Golden Key Honor Society; Alpha Epsilon Delta, Premedical Honor Society **Published works:** Textbook, "Techniques in Dermatologic Surgery", Mosby, publication pending; 16 textbook chapters, 26 peer reviewed papers, 4 newspaper and magazine articles, 27 abstracts, 50+ invited presentations (national and international) **Affiliations:** Numerous including, Association of Academic Dermatologic Surgeons; Florida Society of Dermatology; Dermatology Foundation, Florida Chapter; Miami Society for Dermatology and Cultaneous Surgery; Florida Society of Dermatologic Surgeons; Florida Society of Dermatology; International Society of Dermatology; Membership Committee, American Society for Dermatologic Surgery **Career accomplishments:** Supervising and teaching dermatology residents performing Mohs, Dermatologic and Laser Surgeries at Mohs and Laser Center at the University of Miami School of Medicine; Supervision and teaching dermatology residents performing dermatologic surgery at JMH Dermatology Clinic one-half day per month; Preceptor for Skin Cancer, Dermatologic and Laser Surgery for the American Society of Dermatologic Surgery members; Section Editor for Dermatologic Surgery Section of International Journal of Dermatology; Contributing Editor for Dermatologic Surgery; Editor for International Journal of Dermatology; Reviewer for Journal of AAD, British Journal of Dermatology and the Archives for Dermatology **Hob./spts.:** Sports **SIC code:** 82 **Address:** University of Miami School of Medicine, 1475 N.W. 12 Ave., Suite 2175, Miami, FL 33136 **E-mail:** knouri@med.miami.edu

NYGREN, ROBERT J.
Industry: Education **Born:** Saint Paul, Minnesota **Univ./degree:** B.S., Anthropology, University of Minnesota, 1975; Masters Certificate, Project Management, University of Wisconsin, 2002 **Current organization:** The College of St. Catherine **Title:** Director, Facilities Management **Type of organization:** College **Major product:** Higher education **Area of distribution:** Minnesota **Expertise:** Facilities management, safety, security, emergency management, construction management **Affiliations:** A.S.I.S.; I.A.C.L.E.A.; A.P.P.A. **Hob./spts.:** Bluegrass music, guitar, banjo **SIC code:** 82 **Address:** The College of St. Catherine, 2004 Randolph Ave., St. Paul, MN 55105 **E-mail:** rjnygren@stkate.edu **Web address:** www.stkate.edu

NYMEYER-SCHULTZ, PATTI MARIE
Industry: Education **Born:** March 31, 1958, Chicago Heights, Illinois **Univ./degree:** B.S., Olivet Nazarene College, 1981 **Current organization:** Washington Junior High School **Title:** Teacher **Type of organization:** Grade school **Major product:** Education **Area of distribution:** Braidwood, Illinois **Expertise:** Special education, learning disabilities, physical education **Affiliations:** N.E.A.; W.I.B.C.; Women of the Moose Lodge; Board Member, Illinois State 600 Club **Hob./spts.:** Bowling and tournament bowling **SIC code:** 82 **Address:** 597 N. Division St., Braidwood, IL 60408 **E-mail:** pattimnschultz@hotmail.com

ODLE, SUSAN M.
Industry: Education **Born:** February 26, 1960, Birmingham, Alabama **Univ./degree:** B.S., Education, University of Alabama at Tuscaloosa, 1982; M.Ed., University of Alabama at Birmingham, 1984; Ph.D. Candidate, Auburn University **Current organization:** Success Unlimited, LLC **Title:** Founder **Type of organization:** School and tutoring center **Major product:** Education **Area of distribution:** Local and national **Expertise:** Principal K-12, special education oversight, gifted and advanced tutoring, high school completion for adults **Affiliations:** Council for Exceptional Children; Montgomery Chamber of Commerce **SIC code:** 82 **Address:** Success Unlimited, LLC, 2328 Fairlane Dr., Montgomery, AL 36117

O'DOWD, MICHAEL D.
Industry: Education **Born:** November 4, 1965, Denver, Colorado **Univ./degree:** M.A., Administration, University of Nevada, 1992 **Current organization:** Frank Lamping Elementary School **Title:** Principal **Type of organization:** School **Major product:** Childhood education **Area of distribution:** Henderson, Nevada **Expertise:** Elementary school **Affiliations:** N.A.E.S.P.; C.A.S.A.A. **Hob./spts.:** Water skiing **SIC code:** 82 **Address:** Frank Lamping Elementary School, 2551 Summit Grove Dr., Henderson, NV 89052 **E-mail:** mdo256@interact.ccsd.net

OGREN, ROBERT E.
Industry: Education **Born:** February 9, 1922, Jamestown, New York **Univ./degree:** B.A., Wheaton College, Illinois, 1947; M.A., Northwestern University, 1948; Ph.D., University of Illinois, 1953 **Title:** Professor of Biology Emeritus, Wilkes University (Retired) **Type of organization:** University **Major product:** Higher education, research **Area of distribution:** International **Expertise:** Study of flatworms (Platyhelminthes), zoological services and research **Honors/awards:** Darbaker Award for Microscopical Biology, Pennsylvania Academy of Science, 1957, 1961, 1989; Frank B. Shepela, Vol. Award, Northeastern Pennsylvania Heart Association, 1977 **Published works:** Church history; zoological topics **Affiliations:** Fellow, A.A.A.S.; Society for Integrated and Comparative Biology; Society of Protozoologists; Sigma Xi; American Society of Parasitologists; Ecological Society of America; Electron Microscopic Society of America; New York Academy of Science **Hob./spts.:** Travel, hiking, national parks, making model ships, writing, singing **SIC code:** 82 **Address:** 88 Lathrop St., Kingston, PA 18704 **E-mail:** ogrenrobert@hotmail.com

OKA, KAZUHIRO
Industry: Medical **Univ./degree:** Ph.D., Tokyo Institute of Technology, 1982 **Current organization:** Baylor College of Medicine **Title:** Associate Professor **Type of organization:** Medical school **Major product:** Medical education **Area of distribution:** Houston, Texas **Expertise:** Medical science **SIC code:** 82 **Address:** Baylor College of Medicine, 1 Baylor Plaza, Houston, TX 77030 **E-mail:** kazuhiro@bcm.tmc.edu

OLSON, FLOYD L.
Industry: Education **Born:** December 9, 1952, Eau Claire, Wisconsin **Univ./degree:** B.S., M.S., University of Wisconsin; Doctor of Industrial Management with emphasis in academic management, University of Northern Iowa, 1995 **Current organization:** Utah Valley State College **Title:** Associate Professor & Coordinator, Former Dean of Technology, Chair of Manufacturing Engineering Technology, Director of Academic Affairs **Type of organization:** University **Major product:** Education, U.S. military partnerships in post-secondary education, world-class leadership and management, industrial training and education, consulting, seminar and conference presenter **Area of distribution:** International **Expertise:** Project management, quality, post-secondary administrative leadership and management, small business management, manufacturing management in the 21st Century, engineering management, A.B.E.T. accreditation **Honors/awards:** Outstanding Professor, 1988, 1990, 2000; Outstanding Advisor on national level, 1992; First foreign national to serve on Advisory Board for Sichuan Engineering & Technology College, DeYang, China, 2000 **Published works:** World-class management in post-secondary institutions **Affiliations:** Project Management Institute; American Society of Quality; Society of Manufacturing Engineers; American Production and Inventory Control Society **Hob./spts.:** Travel, reading, grandchildren **SIC code:** 82 **Address:** Utah Valley State College, 800 W. University Pkwy., Orem, UT 84058 **E-mail:** olsonfl@uvsc.edu

O'MORCHOE, CHARLES C.C.
Industry: Education **Born:** May 7, 1931, Quetta, Pakistan **Spouse:** Patricia Jean O'Morchoe, M.A., M.D. **Married:** Widowed, July 5, 1953 **Children:** Charles E.C. O'Morchoe, B.A. (Arch.); David J.C. O'Morchoe, M.D. **Univ./degree:** B.A., 1953; M.B., B.Ch. B.A.O., with honors, 1955; M.A., 1959; M.D., 1961; Ph.D., 1969; D.Sc., 1981, University of Dublin, Ireland **Current organization:** University of Illinois at Urbana-Champaign **Title:** Emeritus Professor and Dean **Type of organization:** University **Major product:** Medical education **Area of distribution:** Urbana-Champaign, Illinois **Expertise:** Anatomy, physiology **Honors/awards:** Fellow, Trinity College, 1966; Faculty Teaching Award, Student Council of the University of Maryland School of Medicine, 1971-73; Outstanding Basic Science Teacher of the Year, Loyola University Stritch School of Medicine, 1981; Outstanding Faculty Member of the Year Award, Loyola University of Chicago, 1982; Alpha Omega Alpha, Honor Medical Society; Elected to Emeritus Status in the American Association of Anatomy Chairman, 1989; Cecil K. Drinker Award, North American Society of Lymphology, 1992; Special Recognition Award, University of Illinois College of Medicine at Urbana-Champaign, 1998; Presidential Award, International Society of Lymphology, 2002 **Published works:** Lymphology; American Journal of Physiology; Anatomical Record and other scientific journals **Affiliations:** Director of Placement Service, American Association of Anatomists, 1981-91; American Association of Anatomists, 1989-present; President, International Society of Lymphology, 1993-95; President, North American Society of Lymphology, 1984-86, Secretary, 1993-98; American Medical Association, 1984-98; Illinois State Medical Association, 1984-98; Champaign County Medical Society, 1984-98; Illinois Rural Health Association (Telemedicine Task Force), 1990-98 **Hob./spts.:** Woodworking, gardening, boating **SIC code:** 82 **Address:** 5645 N.E. Lincoln Rd. East, Poulsbo, WA 98370 **E-mail:** cccom@uiuc.edu

O'NEILL, SHANE R.
Industry: Education **Born:** September 6, 1974, Marquette, Michigan **Univ./degree:** B.S., Wood Science, Michigan Technological University, 1997; M.S., Forestry, University of Maine, 2000 **Current organization:** University of Maine, Advanced Engineered Wood Composites Center **Title:** Wood-Plastic Composite Specialist **Type of organization:** University **Major product:** Higher education, wood science and processing **Area of distribution:** International **Expertise:** Wood-plastic composites, product and technology development and commercialization **Published works:** 4 papers, 1 patent in progress **Affiliations:** Society of Plastics Engineers; Forest Products Society; American Chemical Society **SIC code:** 82 **Address:** University of Maine: Advanced Engineered Wood Composites Center, 5793 AEWC Bldg., Orono, ME 04469 **E-mail:** themadhatter@umit.maine.edu

O'ROURKE, JAMES P.
Industry: Education **Born:** August 2, 1944, Worcester, Massachusetts **Univ./degree:** B.S., Electrical Engineering; M.S., Electrical Engineering, Worcester Polytechnic Institute; D.Sc., Astrophysics, Canterbury University, England, 1972 **Current organization:** Worcester Polytechnic Institute **Title:** Manager, ECE Dept. **Type of organization:** University **Major product:** Higher education, research **Area of distribution:** National **Expertise:** Electrical engineering/astrophysics **Affiliations:** I.E.E.E.; Astronomical Society of the Pacific **Hob./spts.:** Family, martial arts, guitar **SIC code:** 82 **Address:** Worcester Polytechnic Institute, 100 Institute Rd., Worcester, MA 01609 **E-mail:** orourke@ece.wpi.edu

OSTROWSKI, MICHAEL M.
Industry: Education **Born:** April 27, 1951, Pittston, Pennsylvania **Univ./degree:** M.S., Special Education, Marywood University, 1976 **Current organization:** Luzerne Intermediate Unit **Title:** Executive Director **Type of organization:** Educational agency **Major product:** Educational services, professional development **Area of distribution:** Pennsylvania **Expertise:** Curriculum in special education, special needs **Affiliations:** P.S.B.A.; A.S.C.D.; A.E.S.A.; P.A.S.B.O.; Phi Delta Kappa **Hob./spts.:** Coaching, basketball, reading **SIC code:** 82 **Address:** Luzerne Intermediate Unit, 368 Tioga Ave., Kingston, PA 18704 **E-mail:** mike.ostrowski@liu18.org

OSUJI, GODSON O.
Industry: Education/scientific research **Born:** June 20, 1943, Nigeria **Univ./degree:** Ph.D., Biochemistry/Molecular Biology, University of East Anglia, Norwich, England, 1975 **Current organization:** CARC, Prairie View A&M University **Title:** Professor/Research Scientist **Type of organization:** University **Major product:** Higher education, scientific research **Area of distribution:** International **Expertise:** Scientific research **Honors/awards:** Award of Achievement in the Food and Agricultural Sciences, 1994, Distinguished Service Award from the President, 1993, Prairie View A&M University; Fulbright Senior Research Fellowship, 1984; United Kingdom Medical Research Council Fellowship, 1976 **Published works:** 50+ articles **Affiliations:** American Society of Plant Biologists; International Society of Plant Molecular Biology **SIC code:** 82 **Address:** CARC, Prairie View A&M University, P.O. Box 4079, Prairie View, TX 77446 **E-mail:** godson_osuji@pvamu.edu

OVASSAPIAN, ANDRANIK
Industry: Medical **Born:** January 27, 1936, Arak, Iran **Univ./degree:** M.D., University of Shiraz School of Medicine, Iran, 1962; Anesthesia Residency, University of Pennsylvania, 1966 **Current organization:** The University of Chicago, Dept. of Anesthesia and Critical Care **Title:** M.D./Professor of Anesthesia **Type of organization:** Univer-

sity **Major product:** Medical education, patient care **Area of distribution:** Chicago, Illinois **Expertise:** Anesthesiologist (Board Certified), management of difficult airway and fiber optic bronchoscopy **Published works:** 3 books, 110 publications **Affiliations:** A.S.A.; I.A.R.S.; Founder, Society for Airway Management **Hob./spts.:** Collecting oriental rugs, playing violin **SIC code:** 82 **Address:** The University of Chicago, Dept. of Anesthesia and Critical Care, 5841 S. Maryland Ave., MC4028, Chicago, IL 60637 **E-mail:** aovassap@airway.uchicago.edu

OVERGAARD, WILLARD M.

Industry: Education **Born:** October 16, 1925, Montpelier, Ohio **Spouse:** Lucia C. (Cochrane) Died: August 10, 2002 **Married:** June 14, 1946 **Children:** Eric Willard, born 1951; Mark Fredrik, born 1957; Alisa Claire, born 1959 **Univ./degree:** B.A., Liberal Arts, University of Oregon, 1949; M.A. Scandinavian Area Studies, University of Wisconsin, 1955; Ph.D., Political Science-Public Law, University of Minnesota, 1969 **Current organization:** Boise State University (Retired 1994) **Title:** Professor Emeritus of Public Law **Type of organization:** College/University and special educational programs **Major product:** Higher education **Area of distribution:** National and international **Expertise:** Public law and public affairs (U.S.A. and international) **Honors/awards:** Numerous including, Selected for Who's Who in America, annually, 1988-2005; Men of Achievement, International Biographical Centre, Cambridge, England, 1977; Fulbright Scholarship, Graduate Study, University of Oslo, Norway, 1949-50 **Published works:** Many including, Co-author, "The Communist Bloc in Europe" 1959; Author, "The Schematic System of Soviet Totalitarianism", 3 vols. 1961 **Affiliations:** Associate Member, A.B.A.-Legal Education, Administrative Law, Alternate Dispute Resolutions Sections; Life Member, Reserve Officers Association (Major, USAR, Retired); American Legion **Career accomplishments:** Organized newly created Dept. of Political Science; Designed and implemented a Master of Public Administration Graduate Degree Program **Hob./spts.:** Research law; foreign languages with general language fluency in Danish, Norwegian, Swedish and German; working knowledge of Russian, Spanish, French and Icelandic **SIC code:** 82 **Address:** 2023 South Five-Mile Rd., Boise, ID 83709-2316 **E-mail:** wgaard@velocitus.net

PADDACK, JOHN N.

Industry: Education/Religion **Born:** July 5, 1949, New York, New York **Univ./degree:** P.D., Administration, St. John's Univ.; M.Div., Theology, St. Joseph's Seminary; M.S., Counseling Psychology, City College of NY; M.A., French Philosophy & Literature, NYU. and Université de Paris; B.A., Modern Languages/Philosophy, Fordham Univ. **Current organization:** Msgr. Farrell High School **Title:** Monsignor **Type of organization:** Private Catholic high school **Major product:** Education **Area of distribution:** Staten Island, New York **Expertise:** Administration, teaching, counseling, religion **Honors/awards:** Service Award, Latino Civic Association **Published works:** 3 articles **Affiliations:** N.C.E.A.; National Association of Secondary School Principals; Catholic School Administrators Association of New York State; Association for Supervision and Curriculum Development **Hob./spts.:** Martial arts, film, travel **SIC code:** 82 **Address:** Msgr. Farrell High School, 2900 Amboy Rd., Staten Island, NY 10306

PAI, REKHA S.

Industry: Education **Born:** May 13, 1976, Bangalore, India **Univ./degree:** M.S., University of Louisville **Current organization:** University of Louisville **Title:** University Fellow **Type of organization:** University **Major product:** Higher education **Area of distribution:** International **Expertise:** Microfluidics **Hob./spts.:** Embroidery, martial arts, travel **SIC code:** 82 **Address:** 2000 Unity Place, #1006, Louisville, KY 40292 **E-mail:** rekha@louisville.edu

PANIKOV, NICOLAI S.

Industry: Education **Born:** March 1, 1950, Irkutsk, Russia **Univ./degree:** M.D., 1972; Ph.D., 1976; Biology/ Mathematics; D.Sci., 1989, Moscow University/Institute of Microbiology **Current organization:** Steven's Institute of Technology **Title:** Professor/Ph.D./D.Sci. **Type of organization:** University **Major product:** Higher education, Biotechnology **Area of distribution:** International **Expertise:** Microbiology, ecology, teaching, mathematical modeling **Honors/awards:** 6+ patents **Published works:** 6 books, 400+ papers **Affiliations:** A.S.M.; A.G.U. **Hob./spts.:** Swimming, tourism/ travel, poetry **SIC code:** 82 **Address:** Steven's Institute of Technology, Castle Point on Hudson, Hoboken, NJ 07030 **E-mail:** npanikov@stevens-tech.edu

PARENT, JASON

Industry: Education **Born:** Fall River, Massachusetts **Univ./degree:** B.A., Literature, University of Massachusetts at Dartmouth, 2000; J.D. Candidate **Current organization:** Barry University School of Law **Title:** Law Student **Type of organization:** University **Major product:** Higher education **Area of distribution:** Florida **Expertise:** Managing Editor, Law Review **Affiliations:** National Honor Society **Hob./spts.:** Writing **SIC code:** 82 **Address:** 3601 Mont Martre Dr., #3213, Orlando, FL 32822 **E-mail:** parentj@bucmail.barry.edu

PARES, PEDRO M.

Industry: Education **Born:** San Juan, Puerto Rico **Univ./degree:** M.S., Business Administration, University of Phoenix, 1999; M.D., State University of Santo Domingo, 1983 **Current organization:** University of Puerto Rico, Medical Sciences Campus **Title:** Professor of Health Sciences **Type of organization:** University **Major product:** Higher education **Area of distribution:** Puerto Rico **Expertise:** Medicine, emergency medical services **Published works:** 7 publications **Affiliations:** Board of Directors, American Red Cross; American Heart Association; Puerto Rico College of Surgeons and Physicians **Hob./spts.:** Community education, writing **SIC code:** 82 **Address:** Pedro M. Pares, M.D., P.O. Box 6677, San Juan, PR 00914-6677 **E-mail:** pedropares@cprs.rcm.upr.edu

PARK, SUNG-JIN

Industry: Education **Univ./degree:** Ph.D., Chemistry, MyongJi University, 1999 **Current organization:** University of Illinois **Title:** Ph.D. **Type of organization:** University **Major product:** Higher education, R&D (plasma science) **Area of distribution:** National **Expertise:** Research **Published works:** 70 publications **Affiliations:** S.I.D.; I.E.E.E.; D.E.P.S. **Hob./spts.:** Movies **SIC code:** 82 **Address:** University of Illinois, 607 E. Healey St., Champaign, IL 61820 **E-mail:** sjinpark@uiuc.edu

PARTON, THOMAS A.

Industry: Education **Born:** August 28, 1961, Decatur, Illinois **Univ./degree:** B.S., Speech Pathology, 1984; M.S., Speech/Language, 1986, Illinois State University **Current organization:** McLean County, Unit 5 **Title:** Speech and Language Pathologist **Type of organization:** Public school **Major product:** Elementary and secondary school education **Area of distribution:** Normal, Illinois **Expertise:** Language, literacy **Published works:** 1 article **Affiliations:** American Language and Hearing Association; Illinois Language and Hearing Association **Hob./spts.:** Playing guitar **SIC code:** 82 **Address:** McLean County, Unit 5, Speech and Language Pathology, 501 N. Parkside Rd., Normal, IL 61761 **E-mail:** parton@insightbb.com

PATEL, SUNIL J.

Industry: Medical **Born:** March 5, 1962, Dar Es Salaam, Tanzania **Univ./degree:** B.S., Physics, Clemson University, 1981; M.D., Medical University of South Carolina, 1985; Fellowship, Neurovascular Surgery, Japan, 1991; Fellowship, Cranial Base Surgery, 1992 and Microsurgery, 1993, Pittsburgh, Pennsylvania **Current organization:** Medical University of South Carolina **Title:** Clinical Chairman, Dept. of Neurosciences/Chief, Division of Neurosurgery **Type of organization:** Medical School **Major product:** Medical education, clinical research **Area of distribution:** International **Expertise:** Neurosurgery, neuro oncology **Affiliations:** A.A.N.S.; F.A.C.S.; C.N.A.; N.A.S.B.S; A.S.H.A. **SIC code:** 82 **Address:** Medical University of South Carolina, 96 Jonathan Lucas St., CSB #428, Charleston, SC 29425 **E-mail:** patels@musc.edu **Web address:** www.musc.com

PAUL, KATHLEEN A.

Industry: Education **Born:** Flint, Michigan **Univ./degree:** B.A., Physical Education, Central Michigan University; M.A., Elementary Administration, Central Michigan University, 1991 **Current organization:** North Elementary School **Title:** Principal **Type of organization:** School **Major product:** Elementary school education **Area of distribution:** Ithaca, Michigan **Expertise:** Education administration, producing seminars for "failing students", special education, students with learning disabilities, title 1, consolidated grants, human sexuality **Affiliations:** Member, State Board, M.E.M.S.P.A.; A.S.C.D.; T.E.P.A.C. Committee; M.H.S.A.A. and Child Advocacy **Hob./spts.:** Volleyball, reading, camping, sports **SIC code:** 82 **Address:** North Elementary School, 201 E. Arcada, Ithaca, MI 48847 **E-mail:** kpaul@ithacaschools.net

PEASLEE, DAVID C.

Industry: Education **Born:** White Plains, New York **Univ./degree:** B.S., Physics, Princeton University; Ph.D., Physics, Massachusetts Institute of Technology **Current organization:** University of Maryland Physics Dept. **Title:** Professor **Type of organization:** University **Major product:** Higher education, research **Area of distribution:** National **Expertise:** Hadron structure **Published works:** 140 publications; 2 books, "Elements of Atomic Physics" and "Science as a Cultural Expression" **Affiliations:** A.P.S. **Hob./spts.:** Music, theatre **SIC code:** 82 **Address:** 4743 Bradley Blvd., #208, Bethesda, MD 20815 **E-mail:** peaslee@physics.umd.edu

PEÑA DE LLORÉNZ, NORMA
Industry: Education **Born:** March 3, 1947, New York, New York **Univ./degree:** B.A., Queens College, City University of New York, 1979; M.A., Columbia University, 1981 **Current organization:** CUNY Hostos Community College **Title:** Deputy Chair **Type of organization:** University **Major product:** Higher education **Area of distribution:** Bronx, New York **Expertise:** Faculty member, taught English through a Spanish radio program **Published works:** Co-authored series of books **Affiliations:** American Association of Professors **Hob./spts.:** Bike riding, chess **SIC code:** 82 **Address:** CUNY Hostos Community College, 500 Grand Concourse, Bronx, NY 10451 **E-mail:** npd.llorenz@att.net **Web address:** www.hostos.cuny.edu

PENLEY, JOHN ALLEN
Industry: Education **Born:** November 1, 1947, Wetumpka, Alabama **Univ./degree:** B.S., Industrial Education, Mankato State University, Minnesota, 1989 **Current organization:** Riverland Community College **Title:** Electrical Instructor **Type of organization:** College **Major product:** Higher education **Area of distribution:** Minnesota **Expertise:** Electricity maintenance and construction, Minnesota "A" Master Wireman License **Honors/awards:** Served in U.S. Navy 1965-71, Honorable Discharge **Affiliations:** M.S.C.F.; N.E.A.; M.E.A.; Instructor of continuing education classes, State Board of Electricity of Minnesota **Hob./spts.:** League softball, fishing, reading **SIC code:** 82 **Address:** Riverland Community College, 2250 Riverland Dr., Albert Lea, MN 56007 **E-mail:** jpenley@river.cc.mn.us

PERALTA, EVERETT F.
Industry: Education **Born:** May 20, 1954, Hermosillo, Mexico **Univ./degree:** B.S., Social Sciences, University of State of New York, Albany, 1985; Post Bachelor, Professional Teacher Education, American Indian College, Phoenix, AZ, 1996; M.A., University of Phoenix, AZ, 2000; Ed.D., Arizona State University at Tempe, 2005 **Current organization:** American Indian College **Title:** Chairman/Professor **Type of organization:** Private college **Major product:** Higher education **Area of distribution:** National **Expertise:** Leadership, change, diversity, history and philosophy, global education and administration K-12 **Honors/awards:** Numerous honors and achievements **Published works:** Dissertation title: "The English Legacy of Joseph Lancaster to the Mexican Philosophy of Education 1825-1925"; Thesis title: "Systemic Discipline Perspective of Improving Student Behavior at a School for the Homeless through Adaptation of a Behavior Discipline Program"; Capstone project: "University of Bridgeport Student Leadership Development Program" **Affiliations:** Assoc. for Supervision and Curriculum Development 2002; National Council for the Social Sciences 2000; National Education Assoc. 2002; Amer. Assoc. of University Professors 2003; Amer. Educational Research Assoc. 2002; Assoc. for Study of Higher Education 2004; Amer. College and University Housing Officers 1992 **Hob./spts.:** Travel, reading, writing, woodworking **SIC code:** 82 **Address:** 10020 North 15th Ave., #115, Phoenix, AZ 85021 **E-mail:** dreverettperalta@hotmail.com

PERRY, CLAUDE A.
Industry: Education/consulting **Born:** July 20, 1920, Houston, Texas **Univ./degree:** B.S., Iowa State University; M.S., Personnel Services, Kean College of New Jersey, 1969; A.B.D., Iowa State University, 1985 **Current organization:** Perry & Perry Educational Consultation **Title:** President **Type of organization:** Consultant to colleges and universities **Major product:** Student counseling **Area of distribution:** National **Expertise:** Marketing students for selective colleges **Published works:** Write-ups **Affiliations:** Alpha Psi Alpha **Hob./spts.:** Conferences and fraternity meetings **SIC code:** 82 **Address:** Perry & Perry Educational Consultation, 4 Dellmead Dr., Livingston, NJ 07039

PERUMAL, JOHN
Industry: Education **Born:** November 27, 1953, Kuching, Malaysia **Univ./degree:** Ph.D., Biology, University of Western Ontario, 1994 **Current organization:** La Sierra University - Biology Dept. **Title:** Ph.D. **Type of organization:** University **Major product:** Higher education and research **Area of distribution:** International **Expertise:** Ecophysiology, deergrass research **Affiliations:** Botanical Society of America; Ecological Society of America; California Native Plant Society **Hob./spts.:** Hiking, camping **SIC code:** 82 **Address:** La Sierra University - Biology Dept., 4500 Riverwalk Pkwy., Riverside, CA 92515 **E-mail:** jperumal@lasierra.edu **Web address:** www.lasierra.edu

PETER, DEANNE F.
Industry: Education **Born:** January 29, 1966, Spokane, Washington **Current organization:** Kids World 2000 **Title:** Director **Type of organization:** School **Major product:** Education, childcare **Area of distribution:** Bellingham, Washington **Expertise:** Program director, management, teaching **Hob./spts.:** Camping, hiking **SIC code:** 82 **Address:** Kids World 2000, 2000 E. Sunset, Bellingham, WA 98226 **E-mail:** deanne@kidsworldinc.us **Web address:** www.kidsworldinc.us

PICKETT, GEORGE E.
Industry: Education **Born:** January 20, 1936, San Bernardino, California **Univ./degree:** M.S., Social Sciences, California State University at Sacramento, 1958 **Current organization:** Elementary Teachers Service **Title:** Owner **Type of organization:** Service provider **Major product:** Continuing education and workshops for K-12 teachers **Area of distribution:** California **Expertise:** Program development, marketing **Affiliations:** Past President, California Council for Social Studies **Hob./spts.:** Sr. league softball **SIC code:** 82 **Address:** Elementary Teachers Service, 162 Winding Canyon Lane, Folsom, CA 95630 **E-mail:** gbhorning@aol.com **Web address:** www.usd-online.org

PILGRIM, WALTER E.
Industry: Education **Born:** March 26, 1934, St. Paul, Minnesota **Univ./degree:** B.A., Social Science & Greek, 1956; Ph.D., New Testament Studies, Princeton University, 1971 **Current organization:** Pacific Lutheran University **Title:** Ph.D. **Type of organization:** University **Major product:** Higher education **Area of distribution:** International **Expertise:** Ethics, community development, religion, program design; served 2 academic terms in Africa **Published works:** 2 books, articles, papers **Affiliations:** S.B.L.; C.B.S. **Hob./spts.:** Skiing, hiking **SIC code:** 82 **Address:** 2410 Western Rd., Steilacoom, WA 98388 **E-mail:** pilgriwe@aol.com

PINKHAM, JEFFREY D.
Industry: Education **Current organization:** Klein Independent School District **Title:** Supervisor of Special Projects **Type of organization:** Public school district **Major product:** k-12 education **Area of distribution:** Klein, Texas **Expertise:** Facilities and equipment **Affiliations:** T.S.F.S.A. **Hob./spts.:** Family **SIC code:** 82 **Address:** Klein Independent School District, Food Service Dept., 16503 Stuebner-Airline Rd., Klein, TX 77379 **E-mail:** jpinkham@klein.1sd.net

PINSON, PAULA
Industry: Education **Born:** October 8, 1952, Des Moines, Iowa **Univ./degree:** M.A., Rehabilitation Counseling, University of Iowa, 1976 **Current organization:** Cristo Rey Catholic School **Title:** Teacher **Type of organization:** Elementary school **Major product:** Education **Area of distribution:** Santa Fe, New Mexico **Expertise:** Math, science, music **Hob./spts.:** Hiking, music **SIC code:** 82 **Address:** Cristo Rey Catholic School, 316 Camino Delora, Santa Fe, NM 87505 **E-mail:** pjppinson@juno.com

POPEK, JAMES W.
Industry: Education **Born:** 1948, Joliet, Illinois **Univ./degree:** A.S., B.S. Candidate **Current organization:** Joliet Junior College **Title:** Instructor/Technician **Type of organization:** Junior college **Major product:** Higher education **Area of distribution:** Illinois **Expertise:** Electrical systems **Honors/awards:** Outstanding Teaching Award, Joliet Junior College, 1998; Listed in Who's Who Among America's Teachers, 2000-2001 **Affiliations:** I.S.A. **Hob./spts.:** Travel, fishing **SIC code:** 82 **Address:** Joliet Junior College, 1215 Houbolt Rd., T 1070, Joliet, IL 60431-8800 **E-mail:** jpopek@jjc.edu **Web address:** www.jjc.edu

PORTER, LILLIAN R.
Industry: Education **Born:** Dallas, Texas **Univ./degree:** M.A., Education, University of Texas **Current organization:** Pease Magnet School **Title:** Principal **Type of organization:** School **Major product:** Elementary school education **Area of distribution:** Midland, Texas **Expertise:** Administration **Affiliations:** T.E.P.S.A.; A.S.C.B. **SIC code:** 82 **Address:** Pease Magnet School, 1700 E. Magnolia, Midland, TX 79705 **E-mail:** liporter@esc18.net

POWELL, C. SUE
Industry: Education **Born:** November 27, 1950, Vina, Alabama **Univ./degree:** Ed.D., Higher Education, Florida State University **Current organization:** Hinds Community College **Title:** Ed.D./Vice President **Type of organization:** Community college **Major product:** Higher education **Area of distribution:** Mississippi **Expertise:** District-wide occupational programs of study **Affiliations:** American Career and Technical Educators Association; Mississippi Career and Technical Educators Association; **Hob./spts.:** Reading, physical fitness **SIC code:** 82 **Address:** Hinds Community College, 3805 Hwy. 80 East, Pearl, MS 39208 **E-mail:** cspowell@hindscc.edu

POWELL, LILLIAN M.
Industry: Education **Born:** June 1, 1927, Deland, Florida **Univ./degree:** M.A., Ohio State University, 1957 **Current organization:** New York City Board of Education (Retired) **Title:** Music Educator/Teacher **Type of organization:** Self-employed **Major product:** Music and theater education, creative musical projects/TV pilot **Area of distribution:** National **Expertise:** Musician-voice, keyboard, creative works and original projects in theatre and music **Affiliations:** New York City Board of Education; Maryland Women In Film And TV **Hob./spts.:** Training horses, horseback riding, astrology, nutrition **SIC code:** 82 **Address:** 4551 College Ave., Ellicott City, MD 21043-6817

PRESCOTT, DAVID J.
Industry: Education **Born:** October 8, 1939, Philadelphia, Pennsylvania **Univ./degree:** Ph.D., University of Pennsylvania, 1967 **Current organization:** Bryn Mawr College **Title:** Ph.D./Professor **Type of organization:** University **Major product:** Higher education **Area of distribution:** Pennsylvania **Expertise:** Biochemistry, envi-

ronmental toxicology, neurochemistry **Published works:** Book chapters **Affiliations:** A.A.A.S. **Hob./spts.:** Restoring historic property, model trains, travel **SIC code:** 82 **Address:** Bryn Mawr College, Biology Dept., 101 N. Merion Ave., Bryn Mawr, PA 19010 **E-mail:** dprescot@brynmawr.edu

PRITCHARD, GEORGE H.
Industry: Education **Born:** November 26, 1945, Columbus, Ohio **Univ./degree:** M.A., University of Dayton at Ohio, 1980 **Current organization:** Bishop Ready High School **Title:** Teacher **Type of organization:** High school **Major product:** Education **Expertise:** Technology, theology, science, administration **Affiliations:** C.T.S. **Hob./spts.:** Hiking **SIC code:** 82 **Address:** Bishop Ready High School, 707 Salisbury Rd., Columbus, OH 43204 **E-mail:** gpritcha@cdeducation.org **Web address:** www.brhs.org/ghp

PROSEN, HARRY
Industry: Medical **Born:** Saskatchewan, Canada **Univ./degree:** M.D., University of Manitoba **Current organization:** Medical College of Wisconsin **Title:** M.D., M.Sc. **Type of organization:** College **Major product:** Medical education, healthcare, psychotherapy **Area of distribution:** Mequon, Wisconsin **Expertise:** Psychiatry, science and education **Honors/awards:** Honorary Member and Past President, Canadian Psychiatric Association; Distinguished Life Fellow, American Psychiatric Association; Distinguished Service Award, Medical College of Wisconsin, 2003; Meritorious Physician Award, Medical College of Wisconsin, 2003 **Published works:** Co-editor, 4 books; 90 papers **Affiliations:** Occupational & Industrial Psychiatric Association; Psychiatric Consultant to Bonobo Species Preservation Society **Hob./spts.:** Fishing, reading, travel **SIC code:** 82 **Address:** 1522 Greenbrier Lane, Mequon, WI 53092 **E-mail:** hprosen@mcw.edu

PRUTZMAN, TROY ALLEN
Industry: Education **Born:** July 17, 1981, Lehighton, Pennsylvania **Univ./degree:** B.S., Electronic Engineering, Pennsylvania State University, 2001 **Current organization:** Bloomsburg University **Title:** Electronic Systems Technician **Type of organization:** University **Major product:** Higher education **Area of distribution:** National **Expertise:** Science laboratory instrumentation - evaluation, design, purchasing, maintenance **Affiliations:** I.E.E.E. **Hob./spts.:** Fishing **SIC code:** 82 **Address:** Bloomsburg University, 400 E. Second St., Bloomsburg, PA 17815 **E-mail:** tprutzma@bloomu.edu **Web address:** www.bloomu.edu

PUTNAM, JEREMIAH L.
Industry: Education **Born:** December 29, 1939 Ft. Worth, Texas **Univ./degree:** Ph.D., Zoology, Texas A&M University, 1970 **Current organization:** Davidson College **Title:** Professor of Biology/Premedical Director **Type of organization:** College **Major product:** Higher education **Area of distribution:** North Carolina **Expertise:** Biology and pre-health advising **Published works:** 15 publications **Affiliations:** N.A.A.H.P.; President , S.E.A.A.H.P. **Hob./spts.:** Genealogy **SIC code:** 82 **Address:** Davidson College, P.O. Box 7135, Davidson, NC 28035 **E-mail:** jeputnam@davidson.edu

RAJAGOPALAN, SUDHA
Industry: Medical **Title:** Ph.D. **Type of organization:** Medical college **Major product:** Medical education, research, patient care **Expertise:** Chemistry, research **SIC code:** 82 **Address:** Albert Einstein College of Medicine, 1300 Morris Park Ave., Room U405, Bronx, NY 10461 **E-mail:** srajagop@aecom.yu.edu

RALLAPALLI, RAMAMURTHI
Industry: Education **Born:** July 27, 1936, Madras, India **Univ./degree:** Ph.D., Sri Venkateswara University, India, 1962 **Current organization:** Clinical Research Center, RWJMS-UMDNJ-Medicine **Title:** Adjunct Associate Professor (Formerly Vice-Chancellor, Sri Venkateswara University) **Type of organization:** University **Major product:** Medical education **Area of distribution:** International **Expertise:** Diseases of the skin, skin care, immunopathology, bioremediation, environment, biodiversity **Honors/awards:** I.F.A.S. Scholar, University of Florida; Fellow of Indian National Science Academy; Millennium Award of Zoroastrian College **Published works:** Articles, books **Hob./spts.:** Tennis, cricket **SIC code:** 82 **Address:** Clinical Research Center, RWJMS-UMDNJ-Medicine- ACB, 1 Robert Wood Johnson Place, New Brunswick, NJ 08903 **E-mail:** rallapali@hotmail.com

RAMAN, JAI SHANKAR
Industry: Education/healthcare **Univ./degree:** M.S., University of Sydney, 1993; Ph.D. **Current organization:** University of Chicago **Title:** Ph.D. **Type of organization:** University **Major product:** Higher education **Area of distribution:** Illinois **Expertise:** Cardiology **Honors/awards:** 54 articles **Affiliations:** American Heart Association **SIC code:** 82 **Address:** University of Chicago, Section of Cardiac Surgery, 5841 S. Maryland Ave. MC5040, Chicago, IL 60637 **E-mail:** jraman@surgerybsduchicago.edu

RAMBERG, JOANNE A.
Industry: Education **Born:** March 1, 1926, Chicago, Illinois **Univ./degree:** Ph.D., University of Kansas, 1984 **Current organization:** Washburn University **Title:** RN/PhD **Type of organization:** University **Major product:** Higher education/consulting **Area of distribution:** International **Expertise:** Human development and sexuality **Honors/awards:** Fellow, American Academy of Clinical Sexologists, original 1988 **Affiliations:** Kansas Association of Psychologists; Program Coordinator, State Program KAN Be Healthy based at Washburn University, September 26, 2005 **Hob./spts.:** Wood carving **SIC code:** 82 **Address:** Washington University Dept. of Continuing Education, 1700 College Ave., Topeka, KS 66621 **E-mail:** jo.ramberg@washburn.edu

RAMLAKHAN, RANI
Industry: Education/Agriculture **Born:** December 13, 1977, Brooklyn, New York **Univ./degree:** B.S., Chemistry, 1999; M.S., Chemistry, 2002, Florida Atlantic University **Current organization:** University of Florida, Institute of Food & Agricultural Sciences, Everglades Research and Education Center **Title:** Chemist **Type of organization:** University research center and laboratory **Major product:** Education, research, soil science **Area of distribution:** Southwest Florida **Expertise:** Soil testing, analytical chemistry and biochemistry **Published works:** Thesis, 1 article **Affiliations:** American Chemical Society **Hob./spts.:** Reading, painting, travel **SIC code:** 82 **Address:** 13661 Persimmon Blvd., Royal Palm Beach, FL 33411 **E-mail:** rramlakhan@cs.com **Web address:** www.ufl.edu

RANA-COLLINS, ARLENE
Industry: Education **Born:** September 7, 1940, Mandan, North Dakota **Univ./degree:** M.A., Administration, Marshall University, 1983 **Current organization:** Poca Middle School **Title:** Teacher (Retired) **Type of organization:** Public School **Major product:** Middle school education **Area of distribution:** Pickerington, Ohio **Expertise:** Teaching **Honors/awards:** Bausch & Lomb Award, 1958 **Affiliations:** A.F.I.; S.I. **Hob./spts.:** Travel, knitting, reading **SIC code:** 82 **Address:** 7292 Fox Den Ct., Pickerington, OH 43147 **E-mail:** ac0907@aol.com

RAO, APPARAO M.
Industry: Education **Born:** February 15, 1961, Bombay, India **Univ./degree:** Ph.D, University of Kentucky **Current organization:** Clemson University **Title:** Professor **Type of organization:** University **Major product:** Higher education, research **Area of distribution:** International **Expertise:** Nano-science technology **Affiliations:** American Association of Scientists **Hob./spts.:** Sports, mentoring **SIC code:** 82 **Address:** Clemson University, 202-C Kinard Lab of Physics, Clemson, SC 29634 **E-mail:** arao@clemson.edu

RAPPORT, MAURICE M.
Industry: Education **Born:** September 23, 1919, New York City, New York **Univ./degree:** Ph.D., Organic Chemistry, California Institute of Technology **Current organization:** Albert Einstein College of Medicine **Title:** Ph.D. **Type of organization:** College **Major product:** Medical education **Area of distribution:** New York **Expertise:** Biology and neurochemistry **Published works:** 180 papers **Affiliations:** American Chemical Society; American Society of Molecular Biology; American Society of Neurochemistry **Hob./spts.:** Reading and history **SIC code:** 82 **Address:** Albert Einstein College of Medicine, 1300 Morris Park Ave., Bronx, NY 10461 **E-mail:** rapport@aecom.yu.edu

RAYMAN, NICK
Industry: Education/telecommunications **Born:** July 17, 1936, Washington, Indiana **Univ./degree:** B.S., Industrial Engineering Technology, Purdue University, 1973 **Current organization:** Purdue University/Nick Rayman, R.C.D.D. **Title:** Consulting Engineer **Type of organization:** University/consulting **Major product:** Higher education/copper and fiber optic engineering **Area of distribution:** National **Expertise:** Engineering **Affiliations:** S.C.T.E., B.I.C.S.I.; Past President, Toastmasters **Hob./spts.:** Golf **SIC code:** 82 **Address:** 1047 Stockton St., Indianapolis, IN 46260 **E-mail:** nickrayman@prodigy.net

RAZA, KASHIF
Industry: Medical **Born:** March 2, 1975, Gujarat, Pakistan **Univ./degree:** M.D., Pakistan, 1998 **Current organization:** University of Pittsburgh **Title:** M.D. **Type of organization:** University **Major product:** Higher education, medical research **Area of distribution:** International **Expertise:** Infectious disease study, research **Affiliations:** American Society of Transplant Surgeons **Hob./spts.:** Squash, table tennis **SIC code:** 82 **Address:** University of Pittsburgh, 8804 Royal Manor Dr., #104, Allison Park, PA 15101 **E-mail:** razak@dan.pitt.edu

RECHTZIGEL, SUZANNE M.
Industry: Education **Born:** May 27, 1947, St. Paul, Minnesota **Univ./degree:** B.A., Psychology/Early Childhood Development, University of Minnesota at Mankato **Current organization:** Lakeside Day Care Center **Title:** Owner/Director **Type of organization:** Child care/development **Major product:** Education **Area of distribution:** Albert Lea, Minnesota **Expertise:** Childhood development, art **Honors/awards:** Many including Who's Who of American Women; Strathmore's Who's Who, 2003-2004; Who's Who of American Education, 1994-1995; National Registries Who's Who of Executives & Professionals, 2004 **Published works:** Artist of original artwork with

exhibits (original paintings in oil, acrylic , pen and watercolors) at hospitals, city centers, regional art centers, businesses and private art showings **Affiliations:** A.A.U.W. **Hob./spts.:** Art, music, hiking, swimming, tennis **SIC code:** 82 **Address:** Lakeside Day Care Center, 1919 Brookside Dr., Albert Lea, MN 56007

REGUEIRO, JOSE O.
Industry: Education **Born:** January 4, 1926, Havana, Cuba **Univ./degree:** M.A., Havana University **Current organization:** Florida National College **Title:** President/CEO **Type of organization:** College **Major product:** Higher education **Area of distribution:** Florida **Expertise:** Administration **Affiliations:** S.A.C.S.; C.O.C. **Hob./spts.:** Fishing **SIC code:** 82 **Address:** Florida National College, 4425 W. 20th Ave., Hialeah, FL 33012 **E-mail:** jregueiro@fnc.edu **Web address:** www.fnc.edu

REICHGELT, HAN
Industry: Education **Born:** September 12, 1958, Bergen op Zoom , Netherlands **Univ./degree:** B.S., Psychology, 1981; M.A., Philosophy; Ph.D., 1985, University of Nijnegen **Current organization:** Georgia Southern University, College of Information Technology **Title:** Ph.D. **Type of organization:** University **Major product:** Higher education **Area of distribution:** International **Expertise:** Information technology, psychology, philosophy **Published works:** 20+ articles **Affiliations:** A.C.M.; A.I.S.; S.I.T.E. **Hob./spts.:** Family, soccer, physical fitness **SIC code:** 82 **Address:** Georgia Southern University, College of Information Technology, Forest Dr., Statesboro, GA 30464 **E-mail:** han@georgiasouthern.edu

REITZ, ELLIOTT D.
Industry: Education **Univ./degree:** B.S., Biology, Clarion University, Pennsylvania, 1963; M.S., Biology, Ohio University, 1965; Ph.D., Biology, SUNY Binghamton **Current organization:** Broome Community College **Title:** Professor **Type of organization:** College **Major product:** Higher education **Area of distribution:** New York **Expertise:** Anatomy, physiology and botany **Honors/awards:** SUNY Chancellor's Award for Excellence in Teaching, 1990; International Botany Educational Trips **Affiliations:** A.A.C.A.; S.C.C.A.; N.E.R.C.; A.C.O.T.A. **Hob./spts.:** Race cars, travel, birding, boating, hiking **SIC code:** 82 **Address:** Broome Community College, 188 E. Maine Rd., Johnson City, NY 13790 **E-mail:** reitz_e@sunybroome.edu

RENNER, BARBARA J.
Industry: Education **Born:** January 1, 1957, Decatur, Indiana **Univ./degree:** B.S., 1979; M. S., 1984, Purdue University **Current organization:** Springs Valley Community Schools **Title:** Teacher **Type of organization:** Junior and senior high school **Major product:** Education services **Area of distribution:** Indiana **Expertise:** Consumer and family science, general science **Honors/awards:** Professional Award, I.V.H.E.A. **Affiliations:** A.C.T.E.; Indiana A.C.T.E.; I.N.D.F.A.C.S.; A.A.F.C.S.; N.M.S.A.; H.A.S.T.I. **Hob./spts.:** Sewing, reading, walking, basketball **SIC code:** 82 **Address:** 8589 W. Skyline Dr., French Lick, IN 47432 **E-mail:** drenner@smithville.net

RIAD, MOURAD Y.
Industry: Education **Born:** November 9, 1968, Alexandria, Egypt **Univ./degree:** B.S.C.E., Alexandria University, 1991; M.S., West Virginia University, 2001; Ph.D., Civil Engineering, West Virginia University, 2005 **Current organization:** West Virginia University **Title:** Engineering Scientist **Type of organization:** University **Major product:** Higher education **Area of distribution:** International **Expertise:** Civil engineering **Published works:** 8 papers **Affiliations:** Member, A.S.C.E.; Affiliate, TRB; Friend, DAWG; Member, West Virginia University Alumni Association **Hob./spts.:** Music, art **SIC code:** 82 **Address:** West Virginia University, Dept. of Civil and Environmental Engineering, P.O. Box 6103, Morgantown, WV 26506 **E-mail:** myriad@mail.wvu.edu **Web address:** www.wvu.edu

RICHARDSON, CARL REED
Industry: Education **Born:** December 20, 1947, Monticello, Kentucky **Univ./degree:** Ph.D., Illinois University, 1976 **Current organization:** Texas Tech University **Title:** Professor **Type of organization:** University **Major product:** Higher education **Area of distribution:** Lubbock, Texas **Expertise:** Ruminant nutrition **Honors/awards:** Texas Tech University Continuing Education Lifetime Achievement Award; Outstanding Researcher Award, 1982; Texas Tech University Teaching Award, 1998 **Published works:** Journal of Animal Science; Feed Science & Technology; Journal of A.R.P.A.S. **Affiliations:** A.S.A.S.; A.D.S.A.; Plains Nutrition Council **Hob./spts.:** Horseback riding **SIC code:** 82 **Address:** Texas Tech University, Dept. Animal Science, Lubbock, TX 79424 **E-mail:** cfire@ttu.edu

RICHARDSON, DONALD M.
Industry: Private publication of personal translations **Born:** December 2, 1923, Portland, Oregon **Univ./degree:** M.A., Oriental Languages, University of California at Berkeley, 1951 **Type of organization:** Literary services **Major product:** Translations of Japanese Literature **Area of distribution:** International **Expertise:** Japanese literature **Hob./spts.:** Botany/rowing **SIC code:** 82 **Address:** 273 North Dr., Winchester, VA 22603-3632

RICHMOND, LARRY R.
Industry: Education **Born:** August 7, 1940, Aurora, Illinois **Univ./degree:** B.S., Chicago Tech., 1967 **Current organization:** Denver Public Schools **Title:** Quality Assurance/Quality Control **Type of organization:** Public school **Major product:** Education **Area of distribution:** Denver, Colorado **Published works:** Interior Magazine **Affiliations:** C.S.I. **Hob./spts.:** Aviation (Crew Chief in Airforce) F1 & F2 Fighters **SIC code:** 82 **Address:** Denver Public Schools, 2800 W. Seventh Ave., Denver, CO 80204 **E-mail:** larryrichmond@dpsk12.org

RIGGS, OMA
Industry: Education **Born:** March 27, 1916, Weiser, Idaho **Univ./degree:** B.A., Pacific University at Forest Grove **Current organization:** Oma Riggs, Inc. **Title:** Reading Consultant **Type of organization:** Developing/distributing of a teaching program **Major product:** Reading programs **Area of distribution:** United States, Canada, Australia **Expertise:** Teaching/reading consulting **Published works:** "How To" Teaching Materials, 1995 **Affiliations:** D.A.R,. **Hob./spts.:** Reading, cooking, gardening, knitting **SIC code:** 82 **Address:** Oma Riggs, Inc., 31 Floral St., #A, Bath, ME 04530

RISIN, SEMYON
Industry: Medical **Title:** Ph.D., M.D. **Type of organization:** Medical school **Major product:** Medical education, research **Expertise:** Pathology **SIC code:** 82 **Address:** UT Houston Medical School, 6431 Fannin, MSB 2.290, Houston, TX 77030 **E-mail:** semyon.a.risin@uth.tmc.edu

RIVAS, JUAN-CARLOS
Industry: Education **Born:** October 21, 1964, Venezuela **Univ./degree:** B.A, Translations and Terminology, Central University of Venezuela, 1989; M.A., Terminology and Translations, University of Laval, Quebec, Canada, 1993 **Current organization:** Monterey Institute of International Studies **Title:** Professor of Translation and Interpretations **Type of organization:** University **Major product:** Higher education **Area of distribution:** International **Expertise:** Project management, software localization, conference interpretations and translations, design of educational programs **Honors/awards:** Professional Consultant and active speaker **Published works:** Several articles and journals **Hob./spts.:** Acting in theatre, opera and musicals, running **SIC code:** 82 **Address:** Monterey Institute of International Studies, 160 Cedar St., San Carlos, CA 94070 **E-mail:** juan-carlos.rivas@miis.edu

RIVERA, MARIA S.
Industry: Education **Univ./degree:** M.A., Business Administration, 1977; M.A., Education Administration and Supervision, 2002, University of Puerto Rico **Current organization:** Action for Progress Day Care Center **Title:** Administrative Director **Type of organization:** Day care center **Major product:** Education, child care **Area of distribution:** New Jersey **Expertise:** Administration, educational consulting **SIC code:** 82 **Address:** 40-3202 Newport Pkwy., Jersey City, NJ 07310 **E-mail:** blackariquena05@aol.com

ROBERTS, EVELYN FREEMAN
Industry: Education in performing arts **Born:** February 13, 1919, Cleveland, Ohio **Spouse:** Thomas S. (Tommy) Roberts **Children:** Evelyn Anita Roberts, Ernest F. Roberts, Lisa F. Roberts (all deceased), Claire E. Freeman, 64 **Univ./degree:** B.A., Music, Cleveland Institute of Music, 1941; Attended U.S.C. and U.C.L.A. **Current organization:** Young Saints Scholarship Foundation (Inc. 1967) **Title:** President/CEO **Type of organization:** Nonprofit (501)(C)(3) **Major product:** Program of free training in performing arts and related technical skills for "at risk" youth **Area of distribution:** Los Angeles, California **Expertise:** Professional musician/educator (training, performing with equal emphasis) **Honors/awards:** Numerous plaques, citations, proclamations from 2 governors, 3 mayors, Congress, state and local officials; Others from community and civic groups; Recipient of Los Angeles Music Week Award, 2003; Induction into the Watts Walk of Fame "Promenade of Prominence", 2006 **Published works:** "Come to Me My True Love" Recorded by Giselle MacKenzie and others); "The Jelly Coal Man" (Recorded by Frankie Laine and others); "Didn't it Rain" and other spirituals **Affiliations:** National Academy of Recording Arts and Sciences (N.A.R.A.S); American Society of Composers, Authors and Publishers (A.S.C.A.P); Songwriters Guild of America; Life Member, American Federation of Musicians (AFL-CIO) **Career accomplishments:** Many recordings, published songs (own publishing, Morrisania music) appearances on TV shows, movies; Successful seminars (4) on the history of black

music **Hob./spts.:** Music, record collecting, lecturing, teaching music history **SIC code:** 82 **Address:** Young Saints Scholarship Foundation (Inc. 1967), 2000 Wellington Rd., Los Angeles, CA 90016-1825 **Phone:** (323)734-5379 **Fax:** (323)734-4997

ROBERTSON, JANET
Industry: Education **Born:** May 29, 1951, Wichita, Kansas **Univ./degree:** B.A, Friends University, 1973 **Current organization:** Corinthian Child Care Center **Title:** Program Director **Type of organization:** Preschool/Day Care Center **Major product:** Child care/education **Area of distribution:** Wichita, Kansas **Expertise:** Early childhood education **Affiliations:** K.A.C.C.R.A.; E.C.D.O.; W.C.A. **Hob./spts.:** Gardening, crafts, antiques **SIC code:** 82 **Address:** Corinthian Child Care Center, 2611 E. Pawnee, Wichita, KS 67211 **E-mail:** janet.preschool@sbcglobal.net **Web address:** www.pacogfamily.org

ROBINSON, PREZELL RUSSELL
Industry: Education **Univ./degree:** Ph.D., Cornell University, 1956 **Current organization:** Saint Augustine's College **Title:** President Emeritus **Type of organization:** College **Major product:** Higher education **Area of distribution:** National **Published works:** Articles **Affiliations:** American Sociological Society; American Anthropological Society **Hob./spts.:** Reading, travel, international relations, writing poetry **SIC code:** 82 **Address:** Saint Augustine's College, 1315 Oakwood Ave., Raleigh, NC 27610 **E-mail:** smcfadden@st.ed

ROBINSON, T. JOAN
Industry: Education **Univ./degree:** Ph.D., Howard University, 1979 **Current organization:** Morgan State University **Title:** Ph.D. **Type of organization:** University **Major product:** Higher education **Area of distribution:** Maryland **Expertise:** Endocrinology, cell biology **Published works:** 20 peer reviewed articles **Affiliations:** A.A.A.S.; American Society for Cell Biology **SIC code:** 82 **Address:** Morgan State University, 1700 E. Cold Spring Lane, Baltimore, MD 21251 **E-mail:** jrobinso@morgan.edu

ROBINSON SR., PRESS L.
Industry: Education **Born:** August 2, 1937, Florence, South Carolina **Univ./degree:** Ph.D., Physical Chemistry, Howard University, 1964 **Current organization:** Southern University at New Orleans **Title:** Ph.D./Chancellor **Type of organization:** University **Major product:** Higher education **Area of distribution:** Louisiana **Expertise:** Physical chemistry, administration **Published works:** 10 articles **Affiliations:** American Chemical Society **Hob./spts.:** Family, bowling, politics **SIC code:** 82 **Address:** Southern University at New Orleans, 6400 Press Dr., New Orleans, LA 70126 **E-mail:** probinso@suno.edu

ROCKLAGE, NORMA M.
Industry: Education **Univ./degree:** Ph.D., St. Louis University, 1965 **Current organization:** Marian College **Title:** OSF/Senior Vice President, Mission Effectiveness and Student Life **Type of organization:** University **Major product:** Higher education **Area of distribution:** International **Expertise:** Administration, teaching **Affiliations:** A.A.H.E.; A.C.H.E.; A.A.C.I.P.; President, I.N.H.E.M; A.C.C.U.; A.F.C.U. **SIC code:** 82 **Address:** Marian College, 3200 Cold Spring Rd., Indianapolis, IN 46222 **E-mail:** nrosf@marian.edu **Web address:** www.marian.edu

RODRIGUE, LYNNETTE A.
Industry: Education **Born:** August 1, 1964, Patrick Air Force Base, Florida **Univ./degree:** B.A., Criminal Justice, Wright State University; M.S., Technical Education, University of Akron **Current organization:** Clark State Community College Police Dept. **Title:** Chief of Police **Type of organization:** Community college **Major product:** Higher education **Area of distribution:** Springfield, Ohio **Expertise:** Law enforcement; Adjunct professor, criminal justice; Police Academy instructor **Affiliations:** Ohio Campus Law Enforcement Association **Hob./spts.:** Sports, basketball, softball, reading **SIC code:** 82 **Address:** Clark State Community College Police Dept., 570 E. Leffel Lane, Springfield, OH 45505 **E-mail:** rodriguel@clarkstate.edu **Web address:** www.clarkstate.edu

ROGAN, THOMAS P.
Industry: Education **Born:** May 23, 1945, Ellenville, New York **Univ./degree:** B.S., Cortland State University, 1967; M.A., Ball State University, 1968 **Current organization:** Hudson Valley Community College **Title:** Professor **Type of organization:** University **Major product:** Higher education **Area of distribution:** New York **Expertise:** Physical education **Hob./spts.:** Marathons, coin collecting, playing Bridge, Special Olympics, racquet sports. triathlons, gardening **SIC code:** 82 **Address:** Hudson Valley Community College, 9 Petticoat Lane, Troy, NY 12180 **E-mail:** rogantho@hvcc.edu **Web address:** www.sportsplexofhalfmoon.com

ROPER, WILLIAM E.
Industry: Education **Univ./degree:** Ph.D., Environmental Engineering, Michigan State University, 1969 **Current organization:** George Washington University **Title:** Ph.D. **Type of organization:** University **Major product:** Higher education, training, R&D **Area of distribution:** Virginia **Expertise:** Geospatial engineering, environmental engineering **Affiliations:** A.S.C.E. **SIC code:** 82 **Address:** George Washington University, 9339 Boothe St., Alexandria, VA 22309 **E-mail:** wroper@seas.gwu.edu

ROSPOND, RAYLENE M.
Industry: Education **Univ./degree:** D.Pharm., University of Texas **Current organization:** Drake University College of Pharmacy **Title:** Dean/Professor **Type of organization:** University **Major product:** Pharmacy education, research **Area of distribution:** International **Expertise:** Program development, chronic pain management **Hob./spts.:** Gardening, soccer **SIC code:** 82 **Address:** Drake University College of Pharmacy, 2507 University Ave., Des Moines, IA 50311 **E-mail:** raylene.rospond@drake.edu

ROSS, MARILYN J.
Industry: Education **Univ./degree:** Ph.D., University of Miami **Current organization:** Florida Memorial University **Title:** Professor **Type of organization:** University **Major product:** Higher education **Area of distribution:** International **Expertise:** English **Affiliations:** A.A.U.W.; A.A.U.P.; N.C.T.E.; M.L.A. **SIC code:** 82 **Address:** 1121 Cranden Blvd., F602, Key Biscayne, FL 33149 **E-mail:** ross1848@bellsouth.net

ROTA, SHERRY PARKS
Industry: Education **Born:** May 11, 1950, Milwaukee, Wisconsin **Univ./degree:** B.S., Education, Farmington University, 1972 **Current organization:** Gardner High School **Title:** Teacher/Dept. Head, Family/Science **Type of organization:** High school **Major product:** Education (grades 9-12) **Area of distribution:** Templeton, Massachusetts **Expertise:** Clothing (sewing), nutrition, early childhood education **Affiliations:** Family & Consumer Science Group **Hob./spts.:** Sports, boating, fishing, camping, skiing, waterskiing, equestrian, one stroke painting (wood and glass), knitting, cooking **SIC code:** 82 **Address:** Gardner High School, 200 Catherine St., Templeton, MA 01440 **E-mail:** peppy@net1.com

ROUNER, DONNA
Industry: Education **Born:** May 31, 1949, Iowa City, Iowa **Univ./degree:** Ph.D., University of Wisconsin **Current organization:** Colorado State University **Title:** Professor **Type of organization:** University **Area of distribution:** Fort Collins, Colorado **Expertise:** Multicultural media, writing **Honors/awards:** University Teaching Award **Published works:** 25 journal articles **Hob./spts.:** Hiking, biking, music, camping **SIC code:** 82 **Address:** 717 Knollwood Circle, Ft. Collins, CO 80524

ROWLEY, MAXINE LEWIS
Industry: Education **Born:** September 23, 1938, Provo, Utah **Univ./degree:** Ph.D., Brigham Young University **Current organization:** Brigham Young University **Title:** Professor **Type of organization:** University **Major product:** Higher education, research **Area of distribution:** International **Expertise:** Research, education **Honors/awards:** National Teacher of the Year, 1978 **Published works:** 100 articles, 15+ books **Affiliations:** Utah Legislative Council (Governor's Health & Wellness Counselor) **Hob./spts.:** Sewing, reading, writing, travel **SIC code:** 82 **Address:** 9801 S. Lampton Circle, South Jordan, UT 84095 **E-mail:** maxine_rowley@byu.edu

RUSSELL, HORACE O.
Industry: Education **Born:** November 3, 1929, Kingston, Jamaica **Univ./degree:** Ph.D., Oxford University, 1972 **Current organization:** Eastern Baptist Theological Seminary **Title:** Professor **Type of organization:** University **Major product:** Higher education **Area of distribution:** International **Expertise:** Teaching and writing **Honors/awards:** multiple honors and awards **Published works:** 3 books **Affiliations:** American Churches Society; Society for Black Religion **Hob./spts.:** Photography **SIC code:** 82 **Address:** Eastern Baptist Theological Seminary, 6 E. Lancaster Ave., Wynnewood, PA 19096-3430 **E-mail:** horussell@aol.com

RYAN, LINDA L.
Industry: Education **Univ./degree:** B.A., Montana State University, 1974; M.A., Central Washington University, Washington, 1979; M.S.A., West Virginia University, 1981; Internationale Academie Für Blinden DeKunst, 1986 **Current organization:** Casper College **Title:** Artist **Type of organization:** University **Major product:** Higher education **Area of distribution:** National **Expertise:** Art/jewelry, sculpture, 3-D art **Honors/awards:** Wyoming grants to Turkey and Greece **Affiliations:** I.S.A.; S.N.A.G.; Co-Curator Consultant for Wyoming State; Co-chair, Arts 500, Wyoming **SIC code:** 82 **Address:** Casper College, 125 College Dr., Casper, WY 82601 **E-mail:** llryan@mac.com

SACCOMAN, STEFANIE A.
Industry: Education **Born:** December 13, 1953, San Francisco, California **Univ./degree:** Ph.D., Education and Psychology, California Coast University **Current organization:** California Polytechnic University **Title:** Project Director **Type of organization:** University **Major product:** Higher education and publication **Area of distribution:** Pomona, California **Hob./spts.:** Travel, gardening **SIC code:** 82 **Address:** 3801 W. Temple Ave., Pomona, CA 91768 **E-mail:** sasaccoman@csupomona.edu

SAGGIO, JOSEPH J.
Industry: Education **Born:** April 9, 1959, Dayton, Ohio **Univ./degree:** B.A., Calif. State Univ., Fresno, 1981; M.A., Ministry, Azusa Pacific Univ., 1985; M.A., Biblical Studies, Vanguard Univ., 1994; Ed.D., Higher/Adult Educ., Arizona State Univ., 2000; Post-doctoral, Mgmt. Dev. Prgm., Harvard Graduate/School of Educ., 2003 **Current organization:** American Indian College **Title:** Academic Dean and Faculty Member (Bible, Ministry and General Education) **Type of organization:** College **Major product:** Higher education **Area of distribution:** National **Expertise:** Education, leadership, Biblical studies and ministry, administration, higher education, multi-culturalism **Published works:** 30 journal articles (most recent, "Assemblies of God higher educational institutions: A means to develop the indigenous church model among Native Americans", Encounter: A Journal for Pentecostal Ministry, 1 (2). E- Journal, 2004), book chapter, conference papers, book reviews, sermon illustrations, workshops, presentations **Affiliations:** Ordained Minister with the General Council of the Assemblies of God; Nationally appointed U.S. Missionary to Native Americans (Assemblies of God); Native American Fellowship of the Assemblies of God; Association for the Study of Higher Education (ASHE) **Hob./spts.:** Travel, music (gospel, jazz, classical) **SIC code:** 82 **Address:** American Indian College, 10020 N. 15th Ave., Phoenix, AZ 85021-2199 **E-mail:** jsaggio@aicag.edu **Web address:** www.aicag.edu

SAHA, MRINAL C.
Industry: Education **Born:** July 10, 1963, Bangladesh, Dhaka **Univ./degree:** Ph.D., Old Dominion University, 2001 **Current organization:** Tuskegee University, Dept. of Mechanical Engineering **Title:** Assistant Professor **Type of organization:** University **Major product:** Higher education/research **Area of distribution:** Alabama **Expertise:** Engineering, composite **Published works:** 10 articles, 20+ conference presentations **Affiliations:** A.S.M.E.; Society for Experimental Mechanics; Sigma Xi **Hob./spts.:** Reading, soccer games, swimming **SIC code:** 82 **Address:** Tuskegee University, Dept. of Mechanical Engineering, Tuskegee, AL 36088 **E-mail:** msaha@tusk.edu **Web address:** www.tusk.edu

SALEH, FARIDA Y.
Industry: Education **Born:** June 17, 1939, Cairo, Egypt **Univ./degree:** Ph.D., University of Texas at Dallas, 1976 **Current organization:** University of North Texas **Title:** Professor (Retired) **Type of organization:** University **Major product:** Higher education **Area of distribution:** National **Expertise:** Environmental chemistry **Honors/awards:** Who's Who in American Scientists; Who's Who in Science & Engineering; Who's Who of American Women; Outstanding Scientists of the 20th Century **Affiliations:** American Chemical Society **Hob./spts.:** Swimming, music, gardening **SIC code:** 82 **Address:** 1314 N. Valley Pkwy., Lewisville, TX 75077 **E-mail:** saleh@unt.edu **Web address:** www.unt.edu

SAMFORD, SALLY J.
Industry: Education **Born:** June 17, 1948, Llano, Texas **Univ./degree:** M.S., Nursing, University of Phoenix, 2002 **Current organization:** Austin Community College **Title:** Vocational Nursing Professor **Type of organization:** Community college **Major product:** Education **Area of distribution:** Texas **Expertise:** Teaching maternal-child nursing and medical-surgical nursing **Affiliations:** N.L.N.; T.A.V.N.E.; T.C.C.T.A. **Hob./spts.:** Spending time with friends, reading **SIC code:** 82 **Address:** 1201 Seward View Rd., Leander, TX 78641 **E-mail:** sjsamford@earthlink.net

SAMSON, LINDA F.
Industry: Education **Born:** December 7, 1949, Miami, Florida **Univ./degree:** Ph.D., University of Pennsylvania, 1989 **Current organization:** College of Health Professions/Governors State University **Title:** Dean **Type of organization:** University **Major product:** Higher education **Area of distribution:** Illinois **Expertise:** Perinatal nursing **Published works:** Book chapters, articles **Hob./spts.:** Water aerobics, travel **SIC code:** 82 **Address:** College of Health Professions/Governors State University, 1 University Pkwy., Steger, IL 60466 **E-mail:** l-samson@govst.edu

SANCHEZ, PAULINO LAUDE
Industry: Education and research **Born:** June 26, 1968, Laguna, Philippines **Univ./degree:** BSc., Plant Breeding, University of the Philippines at Los Banos (UPLB), Los Banos, Laguna, Philippines, 1991; MSc., 2000; PhD., 2003, Plant Breeding and Genetics, Kyushu University, Fukuoka, Japan **Current organization:** University of Arizona **Title:** Research Associate **Type of organization:** University **Major product:** Higher education and research **Area of distribution:** International **Expertise:** Plant breeding and genetics **Honors/awards:** Japan Society for the Promotion of Science Postdoctoral Fellow, 2003-2005; Japanese Government Ministry of Education, Culture and Sports Scholar, 2000-2003; Rotary Yoneyama Fellow, 1999-2000; Outstanding Researcher, Philippine Rice Research Institute (PRRI), 1993; International Rice Research Institute (IRRI), Research Scholar, 1991; University of the Philippines at Los Banos (UPLB), College Scholar, 1989 **SIC code:** 82 **Address:** University of Arizona, Dept. of Plant Sciences, P.O. Box 210036, Tucson, AZ 85721 **E-mail:** psanchez@ag.arizona.edu **Web address:** www.ag.arizona.edu

SANTAELLA DE FIGUEROA, GLORIA M.
Industry: Education **Born:** July 31, 1933 San Juan, Puerto Rico **Univ./degree:** M.D., University of Puerto Rico School of Medicine, 1956 **Current organization:** Inter American University of Puerto Rico **Title:** M.D./ Chair Board Trustee **Type of organization:** University **Major product:** Higher education **Area of distribution:** Puerto Rico **Expertise:** Anesthesiology **Honors/awards:** First woman to preside the Board in history, Inter American University of Puerto Rico **Affiliations:** Puerto Rico Society of Anesthesiology; Museum of Art at Puerto Rico **Hob./spts.:** Cooking, painting **SIC code:** 82 **Address:** Inter American University of Puerto Rico, P.O. Box 363255, San Juan, PR 00936-3255

SANTANA, PAULA
Industry: Education **Univ./degree:** Ed.S., Seton Hall University **Current organization:** Public School No. 11 **Title:** Principal **Type of organization:** Public school **Major product:** Grades 1-8 education **Area of distribution:** Paterson, New Jersey **Expertise:** Teaching **Affiliations:** P.P.A. **SIC code:** 82 **Address:** Public School No. 11, 350 Market St., Paterson, NJ 07501

SAVAGE, GERALD O.
Industry: Education **Born:** January 22, 1943, Wattsville, Virginia **Univ./degree:** M.A., Columbia University; M.B.A., New York University **Current organization:** Essex County College **Title:** Professor of Accounting **Type of organization:** Community college **Major product:** Higher education **Area of distribution:** New Jersey **Expertise:** Instructing accounting **Affiliations:** A.A.A. **Hob./spts.:** Bicycling, singing, body training **SIC code:** 82 **Address:** 33 Howard St., 3rd floor, Irvington, NJ 07111 **E-mail:** savage@essex.edu **Web address:** www.essex.edu

SAVIC, MICHAEL I.
Industry: Education **Born:** August 4, 1929, Belgrade, Former Yugoslavia **Univ./degree:** Dr.Eng.Sc., University of Belgrade, 1963 **Current organization:** Rensselaer Polytechnic Institute **Title:** Professor of Electrical Engineering **Type of organization:** University **Major product:** Education, research **Area of distribution:** International **Expertise:** Electrical engineering **Honors/awards:** 6 patents **Published works:** I.C.A.S.S.B. Journal, 2001 **Affiliations:** I.E.E.E. **Hob./spts.:** Photography **SIC code:** 82 **Address:** Rensselaer Polytechnic Institute, 110 8th St., Troy, NY 12180 **E-mail:** savic@ecse.rpi.edu **Web address:** www.ecse.rpi.edu/homepages/savic

SAWYER, MICHAEL
Industry: Library **Born:** June 8, 1953, Martinez, California **Univ./degree:** M.L.S., University of Pittsburgh, 1976 **Current organization:** Adams County Library System **Title:** Director **Type of organization:** Library **Major product:** Information, public service **Area of distribution:** Adams County, Colorado **Expertise:** Management, oversees Adams County library system **Published works:** Bibliographical index of 5 English mystics; "The Photocopy Machine: How Did It Begin?", Law Library Journal, Winter, 1979; "Albert Lewis Kawter and the Classics: The Man Behind the Gilberton Company", Journal of Popular Culture, Spring, 1987; "Automation Goes to Prison", Computers in Libraries, May, 1989; "I Know What's Best For You: Censorship in Prison", Ohio Libraries, March/April, 1991 **Affiliations:** A.L.A.; C.A.L.; P.L.A. **Hob./spts.:** Bowling, collecting Donald Duck memorabilia **SIC code:** 82 **Address:** 8919 Pearl St., #1819, Thornton, CO 80229 **E-mail:** msawyer@adams.lib.co.us

SAWYER, THOMAS H.
Industry: Education **Born:** April 5, 1946, Oneonta, New York **Univ./degree:** B.S., 1968; M.S., 1971, Springfield College; Ed.D., 1977, Virginia Polytechnic Institute **Current organization:** Indiana State University **Title:** Professor, Physical Education, Recreation and Sport Management **Type of organization:** University **Major product:** Higher education **Area of distribution:** National **Expertise:** Teaching/administration **Honors/awards:** Numerous including, Indiana AHPERD Leadership Award, 1996; Indiana State University's Outstanding Faculty Service Award, 1997; Nominated and Finalist for Indiana State University's Theodore Dreiser's Outstanding Research and Creativity Award, 1999 & 2000; Fellow, North American Society for Health, Physical Education, Recreation, Sport and Dance Professionals, 2000; North Central Association-Committee on Accreditation and School Improvement Ambassador, 2000; Honor Award, Society for the Study of the Legal Aspects of Sport and Physical Activity, 2003; Honor, Award, American Association for the Active Lifestyles and Fitness, 2002-07; American Alliance for Health, Physical Education, Recreation and Dance Honor Award, Apr. 2004 **Published works:** 150 articles, professional journals; author/co-author of 10 books including, "Golf and the Law", Carolina Academic Press, pp. 247, 2005; "Facility management and design for health, physical activity, recreation and sport: concepts and applications", 11th ed., Sagamore Publishing, pp. 566, Aug. 2005; author/co-author of 4 book chapters **Affiliations:** American Alliance for Health, Physical Education, Recreation and Dance; American Association for Active Lifestyles & Fitness; Society for the Study of the Legal Aspects of Sports and Physical Activities; International Association of Facility Management **Hob./spts.:** Woodworking, stamp collecting, reading **SIC code:** 82 **Address:** Indiana State University, Erickson Hall 241, Terre Haute, IN 47802 **E-mail:** pmsawyr@isugw.indstate.edu **Web address:** www.isu.indstate.edu/tsawyer

SCHILLING, LESLIE DONAHUE

Industry: Education/information technology **Born:** August 24, 1952, Jeanerette, Louisiana **Univ./degree:** B.A., University of Louisiana **Current organization:** University of Louisiana at Lafayette **Title:** Director, Resource Center **Type of organization:** University **Major product:** Media design **Area of distribution:** International **Expertise:** Compressed video/presentation development **SIC code:** 82 **Address:** University of Louisiana at Lafayette, P.O. Box 40069, Lafayette, LA 70504-0069 **E-mail:** leslie@louisiana.edu

SCHILPEROORT, SHARON A.

Industry: Education **Born:** April 25, 1947, Tacoma, Washington **Univ./degree:** B.S. English/Education, Evangel College, Springfield, Missouri, 1969; M.A., Heritage College, 1996; Certified Principal, Heritage College, 1997 **Current organization:** Yakima School District **Title:** Educator **Type of organization:** Public School **Major product:** Middle school education **Area of distribution:** Yakima, Washington **Expertise:** Teaching: Paraeducator State Certification test trainer, 2003-present **Affiliations:** Board Member, Yakima County Concert Association, 1992-95; Board Member, Yakima County Health Dept., 1979-80; Member, Admissions/Allocations Board, Yakima City United Way, 1979-80; Bill & Melinda Gates Foundation Grantee, 1999; Member, Harrah Town Council, 1973-80 & 2000-01; Washington St. OSPI Writing Assessment Leadership Team, 2003-present; City University Adjunct Faculty, 2002-present; Yakima Writing Assessment Leadership Team and Workshop Chairman, 2003-present **Hob./spts.:** Travel, reading **SIC code:** 82 **Address:** Yakima School District, 902 S. 44th Ave., Yakima, WA 98933 **E-mail:** schilperoortsharon@ysd.wednet.edu

SCHMIDT-NIELSEN, BODIL M.

Industry: Education **Born:** November 3, 1918, Copenhagen, Denmark **Univ./degree:** D.D.S., 1941; Dr. of Odontology (the first person in Denmark to qualify for this degree), 1946; Dr. Phil., 1955, University of Copenhagen **Current organization:** University of Florida, Dept. of Physiology **Title:** Professor Emeritus **Type of organization:** University **Major product:** Higher education **Area of distribution:** International **Expertise:** Physiology **Honors/awards:** Award from King Christian X Fund of Denmark for her work on the role of saliva in protection against caries, 1945-46; John Simon Guggenheim Memorial Fellow for her research, 1953-54; Established Investigator of AHA, 1954-62; Career Award of NIH, 1962-64; Received honorary degree, D.Sc., from Bates College of Lewiston, Maine, 1983; Recipient of Ray D. Daggs Award, 1989; R.E. Reynolds Award, 1994; The Bodil M. Schmidt-Nielsen Distinguished Mentor and Scientist Award was established by the American Physiological Society to recognize her outstanding contributions to physiological research, 2004 **Published works:** Numerous publications including, Editor, "Urea and the Kidney", Proceedings of an International Colloquy held at Sarasota, Florida, Sept. 1968; Book, "August and Marie Krogh: Lives in Science", published by American Physiological Society, Oxford University Press, 1995 **Affiliations:** Past President (and first woman President), American Physiological Society; Fellow, A.A.A.S.; Fellow, New York Academy of Science; Member, American Society of Nephrology; International Society of Nephrology; International Society of Lymphology; American Society of Zoologists; Former Member, Society for Experimental Biology and Medicine **Hob./spts.:** Swimming, skiing, kayaking **SIC code:** 82 **Address:** 5000 S.W. 25th Blvd., Unit 2118, Gainesville, FL 32608-8901 **E-mail:** bodilmi@aol.com

SCHMITZ, MARIANINA A.

Industry: Education **Born:** June 4, 1951, Des Moines, Iowa **Univ./degree:** B.A. with Honors, English, Minor, ESL & French, University of Northern Iowa, 1973 **Current organization:** Aplington-Parkersburg High School **Title:** English Teacher **Type of organization:** High School **Major product:** Secondary school education **Area of distribution:** Iowa **Expertise:** Drama, English **Honors/awards:** John Philip Sousa Award; State of Iowan Scholar; Purple Key; Chimes; Phi Beta Kappa; NCTE state conference speaker; Governor's Volunteer of the Year Award; ITAG state convention speaker **Affiliations:** N.C.T.E.; I.T.A.G.; Professional Educators of Iowa; A.S.C.D. **Hob./spts.:** Family, music, all sports **SIC code:** 82 **Address:** P.O. Box 6, Kesley, IA 50649

SCHONFELD, RUDOLF L.

Industry: Education **Born:** February 2, 1942, Lapaz, Bolivia, South America **Univ./degree:** Ph.D., Germany, 1972 **Current organization:** Parsippany-Troy Hills Bd. Of Education **Title:** Ph.D. **Type of organization:** Public school district **Major product:** Elementary and secondary school education **Area of distribution:** National **Expertise:** World languages (English as a second language) **Affiliations:** American Council of Teachers of Foreign Languages; Masonic Order **Hob./spts.:** Playing and coaching soccer **SIC code:** 82 **Address:** Parsippany-Troy Hills Bd. Of Education, 5 Lincoln Ave., Lake Hiawatha, NJ 07034 **E-mail:** rudy.s@prodigy.net

SCHULZ, SANDRA ELISE

Industry: Education **Born:** July 2, 1963, Dallas, Texas **Univ./degree:** B.A., Art Education, 1985; M.A., Fine Arts, Sculpting/Drawing and Painting, Texas Women's University, 1990 **Current organization:** Thomas Jefferson High School/Dallas I.S.D. **Title:** Art Teacher **Type of organization:** High school **Major product:** Education **Area of distribution:** Dallas, Texas **Expertise:** Art; Art Club Sponsor, Robotics Team Sponsor **Published works:** Art work published in Arts and Activities Magazine; Illustrations for "Invest in Yourself" published **Affiliations:** Texas Sculptors Education; Texas Cultural Partnership; American Czech. Cultural Association; Dallas Museum of Art; National Art Education Association; Texas Art Education Association; Dallas Art Education Association **Hob./spts.:** Camping, hiking, music, guitar, art **SIC code:** 82 **Address:** Thomas Jefferson High School/Dallas I.S.D., 4001 Walnut Hill Lane, Dallas, TX 75229 **E-mail:** sschulz@flash.net

SCOTT, TERRI M.

Industry: Education **Born:** Ontario, California **Univ./degree:** M.A., Education, Policy & Administration, Pennsylvania State University **Current organization:** Lac Courte Oreilles Ojibwa Community College **Title:** Academic Dean **Type of organization:** Community college **Major product:** Higher education **Area of distribution:** Wisconsin **Expertise:** Education administration **Published works:** Transformation of Nature: From Pattern to Cloth, Cornell University, 1992 **Hob./spts.:** Native American art **SIC code:** 82 **Address:** 13466 W. Trepania Rd., Hayward, WI 54843 **E-mail:** scott@lco-college.edu

SEALOCK, R. WAYNE

Industry: Education **Born:** July 29, 1955, Front Royal, Virginia **Current organization:** Shenandoah University **Title:** Director of Safety and Security **Type of organization:** University **Major product:** Higher education **Area of distribution:** Virginia **Expertise:** Provide security, insure safety regulations, training on safety and security policies **Affiliations:** V.A.C.L.E.A. **Hob./spts.:** Processional/competition tractor pulling **SIC code:** 82 **Address:** Shenandoah University, 1460 University Dr., Winchester, VA 22601 **E-mail:** wsealock@su.edu **Web address:** www.su.edu

SENOPOLE, RICHARD L.

Industry: Education/consulting **Born:** July 17, 1943, Kittanning, Pennsylvania **Univ./degree:** B.A., 1965; B.S., 1965, Pennsylvania State University; M.B.A., University of California at Los Angeles, 1967 **Current organization:** Maricopa Community Colleges, Small Business Development Center **Title:** Center Director **Type of organization:** Professional service and consulting center **Major product:** Technical assistances to businesses **Area of distribution:** International **Expertise:** Leadership, entrepreneurship **Affiliations:** B.R.E.I.; Alpha Kappa Psi; Governor's Workforce Development Board **Hob./spts.:** Travel, collecting art **SIC code:** 82 **Address:** Maricopa Community Colleges, Small Business Development Center, 2400 N. Central Ave., #104, Phoenix, AZ 85004 **E-mail:** rich.senopole@domail.maricopa.edu

SETTELMAIER, ELAINE

Industry: Education **Born:** March 4, 1957 **Univ./degree:** University of Delaware, 1991 **Current organization:** Marion Center Area School District **Title:** Middle School Principal **Type of organization:** Middle school **Major product:** Education **Area of distribution:** Marion Center, Pennsylvania **Expertise:** Administration **Affiliations:** Audubon Society; National Middle School Association; National Association of Elementary School Principals; National Association of Secondary School Principals **Hob./spts.:** Sports, basketball, biking, bird watching, lighthouses **SIC code:** 82 **Address:** 3048 Warren Rd., Indiana, PA 15701 **E-mail:** ecset57@aol.com

SHAFFER, MARCI J.

Industry: Education **Born:** December 19, 1966, Lawrenceville, Illinois **Univ./degree:** B.S., 1989; M.S.Ed., 1992; Specialist in School Psychology, 1994, Southern Illinois University at Carbondale **Current organization:** IYC-Murphysboro Boot Camp **Title:** School Psychologist **Type of organization:** School District 428, Illinois Dept. of Corrections **Major product:** Special education services **Area of distribution:** Illinois **Expertise:** Psychological testing **Affiliations:** N.A.S.P.; I.S.P.A.; S.I.S.P.A. **Hob./spts.:** Special Olympics, Women's Center/domestic violence **SIC code:** 82 **Address:** IYC-Murphysboro Boot Camp, P.O. Box 1507, Boot Camp Rd., Murphysboro, IL 62966 **E-mail:** afreud7@aol.com

SHARAFKHANEH, HOSSEIN

Industry: Medical **Univ./degree:** M.D., Oroumiah University of Medical Sciences, 2001 **Current organization:** Baylor College of Medicine **Title:** Physician/Researcher **Type of organization:** Medical college **Major product:** Medical education, research **Expertise:** Sleep medicine **Published works:** Numerous including: Sharafkhaneh A., Sharafkhaneh H, Bozkurt B., Hirshkowirtz M., Effect of Atrial Overdrive Pacing on Obstructive Sleep Apnea in Patients with Systolic Heart Failure. (Sleep Medicine: January 2007); Sharafkhaneh H. Sharafkhaneh A., Sleep-Related Breathing Disorders and Quality of Life. (Seep Medicine Clinic, December, 2006); Sharafkhaneh A., Sheila Goodnight White, Sharafkhaneh H., Hirshkowitz M., Terry Young, Epidemiology of Sleep-Related Breathing Disorders: Complications with the Veterans Health Administration Databases (Sleep Medicine Clinic; December 2006); Sharafkhaneh H., Sharafkhaneh A., Insomnia (part two): Treatment. (Asheganeh: Association of Iranian Physicians in USA, September 2006); Sharafkhaneh A., Insomnia (part one): definitions, causes and Classifications. (Asheghaneh: Association of Iranian Physicians in USA, August 2006) **Affiliations:** American Academy of Sleep Medicine; Sleep

Research Society; Southern Sleep Society; American Thoracic Society; American College of Chest Physicians; Medical Council, I.R. IRAN **Hob./spts.:** Reading, bicycling, playing football **SIC code:** 82 **Address:** Baylor College of Medicine, MED. VA MC, Sleep Disorders Center, Houston, TX 77030 **E-mail:** hosseins@bcm.tmc.edu

SHEATS, RACHEL G.
Industry: Education **Born:** February 15, 1964, Monett, Missouri **Univ./degree:** B.A., Elementary Education, Missouri Southern State University, 1988; M.A., University of Arkansas at Fayetteville, 1996 **Current organization:** Cassville R-IV Schools **Title:** Educational Technologist **Type of organization:** Public school system and community college **Major product:** Elementary and secondary school education and post secondary **Area of distribution:** Cassville, Missouri **Expertise:** Education and educational technology **Honors/awards:** Member, Who's Who in America, Who's Who in American Education, Who's Who Among American Women, Who's Who Among Young American Professionals, Who's Who Among Women of Business and Who's Who Among Young Educators; Nominee to Disney's Teacher of the Year Awards, 1992; Recognized by the University of Missouri Extension for educational achievement, 1992-93 **Published works:** Created and presented numerous workshops; created and produced a public service announcement video about the Reading Buddies program at Cassville Middle School; produced educational video entitled Let's Start Cooking (which has been used as a part of the curriculum of the Life Skills classes at Cassville Middle School) **Affiliations:** International Society for Technology in Education; Missouri Middle School Association **Hob./spts.:** Reading, travel **SIC code:** 82 **Address:** Cassville R-IV Schools, 1501 Main St., Cassville, MO 65625 **E-mail:** rsheats@mo-net.com **Web address:** www.wildcats.cassville.k12.mo.us

SHELL, JEANNE S.
Industry: Education **Born:** November 20, 1937, Lake City, Tennessee **Univ./degree:** Education, Nova Southeastern University, Bradenton, Florida, 1981 **Current organization:** The Broach School **Title:** Director **Type of organization:** School **Major product:** Education for special needs students **Area of distribution:** National **Expertise:** Teaching, counseling, administration **Hob./spts.:** Education **SIC code:** 82 **Address:** The Broach School, 3005 26th St. West, Bradenton, FL 34205 **E-mail:** jshell@esa-education.com **Web address:** www.esa-education.com

SHELTON, TONI M.
Industry: Education **Born:** May 21, 1965, Denver, Colorado **Univ./degree:** Attended Texas Southern University **Current organization:** Denver Public Schools **Title:** Instructor/Training Coordinator Facilities Management **Type of organization:** School district **Major product:** Public school education **Area of distribution:** Denver, Colorado **Expertise:** Facility training, training and curriculum **Hob./spts.:** Music, movies, horseback riding **SIC code:** 82 **Address:** Denver Public Schools, 2800 W. Seventh Ave., Denver, CO 80204 **E-mail:** toni_shelton@dpsk12.org

SHEN, ANDY HSITIEN
Industry: Education **Born:** 1962, Taiwan **Current organization:** Caltech **Title:** Dr. **Type of organization:** University **Major product:** Higher education **Area of distribution:** National **Expertise:** Gem/mineral, high pressure technology **Affiliations:** A.G.U.; M.S.A. **Hob./spts.:** Classical music, golf, wine tasting, collecting antique pocket watches **SIC code:** 82 **Address:** Caltech, 1200 E. California Blvd., Seismological Laboratory 252-21, Pasadena, CA 91125 **E-mail:** ahshen@caltech.edu

SHEPARD, HELENE M.
Industry: Education **Born:** June 1, 1940, Brooklyn, New York **Univ./degree:** M.Ed., Fordham University, 1965 **Current organization:** St. Mary's Little Lamb Preschool **Title:** Principal **Type of organization:** Preschool **Major product:** Preschool education **Area of distribution:** Washingtonville, New York **Expertise:** Teaching, administration **Affiliations:** N.C.E.A., Catholic Daughters of the Americas; State Regent, Early Childhood Association; Delta Kappa Gamma, Zeta Chapter **SIC code:** 82 **Address:** St. Mary's Little Lamb Preschool, 2 Fr. Tierney Circle, Washingtonville, NY 10992

SHIMER, STANLEY S.
Industry: Education **Born:** August 1, 1938, Indianapolis, Indiana **Univ./degree:** Ed.D., Indiana University, Bloomington, 1979 **Current organization:** Indiana State University, Dept. of Science Education **Title:** Professor of Science Education **Type of organization:** University **Major product:** Higher education **Area of distribution:** National **Expertise:** Earth science, physical science **Honors/awards:** Outstanding Service Award; Outstanding Teacher Award **Published works:** 3 textbooks; 75-200 articles **Affiliations:** N.S.T. **Hob./spts.:** Racquetball, golf, photography **SIC code:** 82 **Address:** Indiana State University, Dept. of Science Education, 300 N. Sixth St., Terre Haute, IN 47809 **E-mail:** stshimer@isugw.indstate.edu

SHORT, ELIZABETH LOUISE
Industry: Education **Born:** October 25, 1948, Laredo, Texas **Univ./degree:** B.S., Divinity, Universal Brotherhood Ministries, 1989; Ph.D., Philosophy/Religion, Universal Life Church, 1990 **Current organization:** American Radionics **Title:** Director **Type of organization:** Education **Major product:** Healing arts **Area of distribution:** International **Expertise:** Education and wellness **Hob./spts.:** Fishing, boating, camping **SIC code:** 82 **Address:** American Radionics, Attn: Janet Mason, 4191 Stilesboro Rd., Kennesaw, GA 30152 **E-mail:** liz@americanradionics.com **Web address:** www.americanradionics.com

SIEGEL, GEORGE J.
Industry: Medical **Born:** August 6, 1936, Bronx, New York **Univ./degree:** M.D., University of Miami, 1961 **Current organization:** Loyola University, Stritch School of Medicine **Title:** Vice Chairman/Professor **Type of organization:** University hospital **Major product:** Patient care, education, research **Area of distribution:** National **Expertise:** Neurology, cell biology, neurochemistry **Published works:** Editor-in-Chief, Basic Neurochemistry: Molecular, Cellular and Medical Aspects **Affiliations:** F.A.A.N.; A.N.A.; Chief of Neurology Services, Edward Hines Jr. Veterans Affair Hospital **Hob./spts.:** Fencing **SIC code:** 82 **Address:** 1530 N. Dearborn Pkwy., Chicago, IL 60610

SIMON, RITA J.
Industry: Education **Born:** November 26, 1931, New York, New York **Univ./degree:** Ph.D., Sociology, University of Chicago, Illinois, 1957 **Current organization:** American University/Women's Freedom Network **Title:** University Professor, School of Public Affairs and the Washington College of Law/President and Founder **Type of organization:** University/Nonprofit **Major product:** Sociological studies/Equality of women **Area of distribution:** National **Expertise:** Sociology, law **Honors/awards:** Fellow, American Society of Criminology, 1986; Fellow to Center for Advanced Study, University of Illinois, 1980-1; Ford Foundation Fellowship, 1970-1; Guggenheim Fellowship, 1966-7 **Published works:** Authored 25 books including "Women's Movements in America: Their Achievements, Disappointments and Aspirations" with Gloria Danziger, 1991, monographs, edited 15+ books including "Neither Victim Nor Enemy: Women's Freedom Network Looks at Gender in America"; Other works have been published in "The Washington Times", "New York Times", "Wall Street Journal" and professional journals **Affiliations:** American Sociological Association; American Criminological Association; Phi Kappa Phi; Editor, Gender Issues; Women and Criminal Justice; Consulting Editor, Journal of Criminal Law and Criminology; Consulting Editor, Social Science Journal **Hob./spts.:** Running **SIC code:** 82 **Address:** American University, 4400 Mass Ave., Washington, DC 20016 **E-mail:** rsimon@american.edu

SIMONOVSKY, FELIX I.
Industry: Education **Born:** Russia **Univ./degree:** M.S., Chemical Engineering, Vladimir Polytechnic Institute; Ph.D., Institute of Chemistry and Technology, Russia,1985 **Current organization:** University of Washington **Title:** Ph.D./Scientist **Type of organization:** University **Major product:** Higher education **Area of distribution:** International **Expertise:** Bio engineering and polymer chemistry **Published works:** 60+ articles, 13 Russian patents **Affiliations:** American Association for the Advancement of Science; Society for Biomaterials; American Chemical Society **SIC code:** 82 **Address:** University of Washington, Dept. of Bioengineering, Box 351720, Bagley Hall, Seattle, WA 98195-1720 **E-mail:** fsimonov@u.washington.edu **Web address:** www.uweb.engr.washington.edu

SIRIBADDANA, RAVEENDRA
Industry: Education **Born:** June 14, 1970, Galle, Sri Lanka **Univ./degree:** M.S.M.E., University of South Florida, 2000; M.S.E.E. Candidate **Current organization:** University of South Florida **Title:** Research Assistant **Type of organization:** University **Major product:** Higher education, research **Area of distribution:** Florida **Expertise:** Finite element analysis **Published works:** 2 articles **Affiliations:** A.S.M.E. **Hob./spts.:** Travel **SIC code:** 82 **Address:** 2818 A. Americana Circle, Tampa, FL 33613 **E-mail:** ravenndra1@msn.com

SLOMCZYNSKI, KAZIMIERZ M.
Industry: Education **Born:** May 10, 1943, Warsaw, Poland **Univ./degree:** Ph.D., Sociology, University of Warsaw, 1971 **Current organization:** Ohio State University **Title:** Professor **Type of organization:** University **Major product:** Higher education **Area of distribution:** International **Expertise:** Educational services, sociology research **Published works:** Articles in American Sociological Review, American Journal of Sociology, Social Forces; books, "Social Structure and Mobility", (Warsaw:IFiS), "Social Structure and Self-Direction (with M. Kohn, Cambridge: Blackwell); editor of volumes, "Social Patterns of Being Political" (Warsaw:IFiS), "Social Structure: Changes and Linkages (Warsaw:IFiS) **Affiliations:** Polish Academy of Sciences; International Sociological Association; American Sociological Association **Hob./spts.:** Writing mystery stories **SIC code:** 82 **Address:** Ohio State University, Dept. of Sociology, 300 Bricker Hall, Columbus, OH 43210 **E-mail:** slomczynski.1@osu.edu

SMITH, EVANGELINE F.
Industry: Education **Univ./degree:** M.B.A., Central Michigan University; Ph.D. Candidate, Educational Leadership, Capella University **Current organization:** Central Carolina Community College **Title:** Literacy Coordinator **Type of organization:** College **Major product:** Higher education **Area of distribution:** Raleigh, North Carolina **Expertise:** Business administration **Honors/awards:** National Republican Congressional Award and Honorary Chairperson **Affiliations:** A.A.W.C.C.; N.E.A.E.A.

SIC code: 82 **Address:** Central Carolina Community College, 5100 North Hills Dr., Raleigh, NC 27612 **E-mail:** esmith4713@nc.rr.com

SMITH, PAUL
Industry: Education **Born:** May 15, 1958, Bronx, New York **Univ./degree:** M.A., Elementary Education/Early Childhood Education, 1995; M.A., Supervision and Administration, 1998 **Current organization:** N.Y.C. Board of Education, P.S. 51 **Title:** Principal **Type of organization:** Public school **Major product:** Elementary school education **Area of distribution:** Bronx, New York **Expertise:** Education. supervision **Hob./spts.:** Musician **SIC code:** 82 **Address:** N.Y.C. Board of Education, P.S. 51, 3200 Jerome Ave., Bronx, NY 10473 **E-mail:** psmith@ecofaith.com

SMITH, PAUL K.
Industry: Education **Born:** April 27, 1961, Brockton, Massachusetts **Univ./degree:** B.A., Boston University; M.A., University of Rochester; Post Masters, Education Administration, University of Connecticut, 1997 **Current organization:** Bolton High School **Title:** Principal **Type of organization:** High school **Major product:** Secondary education **Area of distribution:** Bolton, Connecticut **Expertise:** Educational leadership, creative practices and instruction **Affiliations:** High School Advisory Board, Connecticut American Red Cross; Association for Supervision and Curriculum Development; National Association of Secondary School Principals **Hob./spts.:** Music, theatre and stage directing **SIC code:** 82 **Address:** Bolton High School, 72 Brandy St., Bolton, CT 06043 **E-mail:** paulksmith@boltonct.org

SMITH, REBECCAH P.
Industry: Education/Healthcare **Born:** October 28, 1955, Virginia **Univ./degree:** A.A.S., Radiology and Science, Virginia Western Community College, 1977; B.A., History and Education, Mary Baldwin College, 1999; Student for Principal Masters Program, Radford University **Current organization:** Patrick Henry High School/ Lewis Gale Clinic **Title:** History Teacher/PRN (part time) **Type of organization:** Roanoke City Schools/Physicians Clinic **Major product:** History teacher/patient care **Expertise:** Radiology Technologist 28 years, Certified Medical Assistant; Education, Teacher NK-8, History NK-12 **Honors/awards:** International Who's Who of Professional Management; Who's Who of American High School Students in 1969, 1970 & 1971; National Woman of the Year, 2005 **Affiliations:** V.E.C.; V.S.R.T.; Virginia Educators Society; American Association of Medical Assistants; Part time Homebound Teacher for Botetourt County Schools; Former Medical Program Director at Dominion College; Girl Scout and Boy Scout Leader **Hob./spts.:** Swimming, walking, decorating her house **SIC code:** 82 **Address:** 2231 Byrd Ave. N.E., Roanoke, VA 24012 **E-mail:** babe491@msn.com

SMITH, SUZETTE
Industry: Education **Born:** April 5, 1964, Liberty, Texas **Univ./degree:** B.A., Education, North Texas University, 1987; M.A., Sports Medicine, Indiana University, 1989 **Current organization:** University of Texas Southwestern Medical Center **Title:** Director, Bryan Williams M.D. Student Center **Type of organization:** University **Major product:** Student services and development **Area of distribution:** National **Expertise:** Sports management **Affiliations:** N.I.R.S.A. **Hob./spts.:** Bicycling, volunteer work **SIC code:** 82 **Address:** University of Texas Southwestern Medical Center, 5323 Harry Hines Blvd., Dallas, TX 75390-9001 **E-mail:** suzette.smith@utsouthwestern.edu

SMITH-LEINS, TERRI L.
Industry: Education **Born:** September 19, 1950, Salina, Kansas **Univ./degree:** A.A., Liberal Arts, Stephen's Women's College, Columbia, Missouri; B.S., Math, 1972; M.S., Secondary Education and Mathematics, 1976, Fort Hays State University **Current organization:** University of Arkansas at Fort Smith **Title:** Assistant Professor, College Preparatory **Type of organization:** University **Major product:** Higher education **Area of distribution:** Fort Smith, Arkansas **Expertise:** Mathematics, remediation, general education **Honors/awards:** State Officer, Delta Kappa Gamma; Who's Who in America; Who's Who in American Education; Who's Who among American Women; Who's Who in Science and Engineering; Who's Who in the South and Southwest; Who's Who among America's Teachers; Commendation from the Department of the Army, 1992; Advisor of the Year: Arkansas Black Student Association, 1990 **Affiliations:** N.A.D.E.; ArKADE; Delta Kappa Gamma Society International; Phi Delta Kappa; Member, Black Student Association Advisory Board; Member, Interfaith Community Center Board of Directors **Hob./spts.:** Antique lace, quilts, glass, trains, travel **SIC code:** 82 **Address:** University of Arkansas at Fort Smith, P.O. Box 3649, Ft. Smith, AR 72913-3649 **E-mail:** tleins@uafortsmith.edu **Web address:** www.uafortsmith.edu

SNOW, BEATRICE L.
Industry: Education **Born:** June 9, 1941, Boston, Massachusetts **Univ./degree:** Ph.D., University of New Hampshire, 1971 **Current organization:** Suffolk University Biology Dept. **Title:** Professor/Chairperson **Type of organization:** University **Major product:** Higher education **Area of distribution:** Massachusetts **Expertise:** Genetics **Affiliations:** Colonial Williamsburg Foundation; American Genetic Association; Secretary, New England Biology Conference **Hob./spts.:** Photography, travel **SIC code:** 82 **Address:** Suffolk University Biology Dept., 41 Temple St., Boston, MA 02114 **E-mail:** bsnow@suffolk.edu

SOLBERG, DARRELL D.
Industry: Media consulting/marketing **Univ./degree:** Broadcasting Trade School **Current organization:** DDS Sales Training **Title:** President **Type of organization:** Sales training/marketing **Major product:** Sales training, marketing, management consulting **Area of distribution:** National **Expertise:** Marketing **Published works:** Articles **SIC code:** 82 **Address:** DDS Sales Training, 6904 W. Sagamore Circle, Sioux Falls, SD 57106 **E-mail:** dessales_sio@midco.net

SOLOVIEVA, TATIANA I.
Industry: Education **Univ./degree:** Ed.D., Instructional Design and Technology **Current organization:** VMC Homeland Security Program at West Virginia University **Title:** Lead Instructional Designer **Type of organization:** University/Training and knowledge development organization **Major product:** Design on-line course ware for first and emergency responders for bio terrorism **Area of distribution:** National **Expertise:** Instructional design and technology **Affiliations:** American Public Health Association; American Psychological Association; Sigma Xi Scientific Research Society **Hob./spts.:** Foreign languages **SIC code:** 82 **Address:** 1279 Serene Dr., Fairmont, WV 26544 **E-mail:** tatiana.solovieva@hotmail.com

SONNTAG, HEINZ R.
Industry: Education **Born:** June 19, 1940, Cologne, Germany **Univ./degree:** Ph.D., Bochun University, 1967 **Current organization:** University of Massachusetts at Amherst **Title:** Ph.D. **Type of organization:** University **Major product:** Higher education **Area of distribution:** International **Expertise:** Teaching, research in sociology and consulting, sociology of public policy, sociology of the state, sociology of social movement **Honors/awards:** Gugganheim Fellow, 1999 **Published works:** 60 essays and articles, 20 books in Spanish, German, French and English **Affiliations:** O.C.D.E.; O.E.C.D. **Hob./spts.:** Reading novels **SIC code:** 82 **Address:** University of Massachusetts at Amherst, 27 High St., #1, Amherst, MA 01002-1889 **E-mail:** hrsonntag@earthlink.net

SOPP, ERNEST C.
Industry: Education **Born:** November 1, 1952, Stockton, California **Univ./degree:** M.S., Education Administration, San Diego State University, 1985 **Current organization:** Merced Union High School District **Title:** Principal **Type of organization:** School district **Major product:** Public school education **Area of distribution:** Atwater, California **Expertise:** Educational administration **Affiliations:** American Association of California School Administrators **Hob./spts.:** Golf **SIC code:** 82 **Address:** Merced Union High School District, 1800 Buhach Rd., Atwater, CA 95301 **E-mail:** esopp@muhsd.k12.ca.us

SOSS, MARK N.
Industry: Education **Univ./degree:** B.A., Education; M.A., Education Administration; Certificate of Advanced Studies, SUNY Brockport **Current organization:** Roaring Brook Elementary School **Title:** Principal **Type of organization:** Elementary school **Major product:** Elementary education **Area of distribution:** Chappaqua, New York **Expertise:** Leadership **Affiliations:** Phi Delta Kappa; Co-chair and Founder, Westchester Putnam Elementary School Council **Hob./spts.:** Hiking, photography, travel **SIC code:** 82 **Address:** Roaring Brook Elementary School, 530 Quaker St., Chappaqua, NY 10514 **E-mail:** masoss@ccsd.ws

SPENCER, FRANK COLE
Industry: Education **Born:** December 21, 1925, Haskell, Texas **Univ./degree:** M.D., Vanderbilt University **Current organization:** New York University School of Medicine **Title:** Professor of Surgery **Type of organization:** University **Major product:** Higher education, consulting **Area of distribution:** New York **Expertise:** Cardiac surgery **Affiliations:** American College of Surgeons; Society of Clinical Surgery; American Association for Thoracic Surgery; Southern Surgical Association; American Heart Association **Hob./spts.:** Bass fishing **SIC code:** 82 **Address:** New York University School of Medicine, 550 First Ave., New York, NY 10016 **E-mail:** frank.spencer@msnyuhealth.org

SPENCER BENNETT, MARILYN K.
Industry: Education **Born:** August 18, 1955, Dalhart, Texas **Univ./degree:** B.M.E., Music Education, 1977; M.M.E., Music Education, 1981, Midwestern State University **Current organization:** Munday CISD **Title:** Assistant Band Director **Type of organization:** School district **Major product:** Education **Area of distribution:** Munday, Texas **Expertise:** Music **Honors/awards:** Co-Citizen of the Year, Munday, Texas, 1993; Who's Who Among America's Teachers, 1998, 2002; Who's Who in Mu Phi Epsilon **Affiliations:** A.T.S.S.B.; N.B.A.; W.B.D.I.; T.M.E.A.;T.M.A.A., T.B.A.; M.E.N.C., Chapter Advisor, Honorary Life Member; T.M.E.A. Honor Band Director, 1994, 2000; Delta Kappa Gamma; Tri-M Music Honor Society; Mu Phi Epsilon; Tau Beta Sigma (Life Member) **Hob./spts.:** Reading, needlecraft, gardening, crafts

SIC code: 82 **Address:** Munday CISD, 811 W. D St., Munday, TX 76371 **E-mail:** marilyn.k.bennett@esc9.net

SPIESS, BRUCE D.
Industry: Medical **Born:** June 19, 1954, Pittsburgh, Pennsylvania **Univ./degree:** M.D., Rush Medical College, Illinois, 1980 **Current organization:** Virginia Commonwealth University/Medical College of Virginia **Title:** M.D. **Type of organization:** Medical college **Major product:** Research, medical education/patient care **Expertise:** Cardiovascular anesthesiology **Published works:** 100+ papers, 7 books **Affiliations:** A.S.A.; A.A.B.B.; S.C.A.; F.A.H.A. **Hob./spts.:** Painting, sailing, flyfishing **SIC code:** 82 **Address:** Virginia Commonwealth University/Medical College of Virginia, Dept. of Anesthesiology, 1200 E. Broad St., Box 980695, Richmond, VA 23298-0695 **E-mail:** bdspiess@hsc.vcu.edu

SPINELLI, EVA
Industry: Education **Born:** March 21, 1946, Uzhgorod, Russia **Univ./degree:** M.S., Long Island University **Current organization:** Touro College **Title:** Executive Administrative Dean **Type of organization:** University **Major product:** Higher education **Area of distribution:** New York **Honors/awards:** Most Influential Person in the Russian Community, 1998 **Published works:** "Paper Borders of Africa" **Affiliations:** Charitable organizations **Hob./spts.:** Politics **SIC code:** 82 **Address:** Touro College, 27-33 W. 23rd St., New York, NY 10110 **E-mail:** evaspine@cs.com

STANSBERY, DAVID HONOR
Industry: Research/Teaching **Born:** May 5, 1926, Upper Sandusky, Ohio **Spouse:** Mary Lois Pease **Married:** June 16, 1948 **Children:** Michael D., 54; Mark A., 52; Kathleen M., 50; Linda C., 48 **Univ./degree:** B.S. Cum Laude, 1950; M.S., 1953; Ph.D., Zoology, 1960, Ohio State University **Current organization:** Ohio State University (Retired) **Title:** Professor Emeritus/Curator Emeritus/Ecologist, Malacologist **Type of organization:** University **Major product:** Teaching, research and service **Area of distribution:** International **Expertise:** Teaching, research, publishing, editing, administration **Honors/awards:** The Ohio Conservation Achievement Award, Ohio Dept. of Natural Resources, 1974; The Oak Leaf Award, The Nature Conservancy, 1977; The Osborn Award, The Ohio Biological Survey, 1999; Life Achievement Award, Society for the Conservation of Freshwater Mollusks, 1999 **Published works:** Numerous articles, 4 book chapters, 1 book (in press) **Affiliations:** Fellow, American Association for Advancement of Science; Fellow, Ohio Academy of Science; American Malacological Society; National Board Member, The Nature Conservatory; Visiting Scientist, Smithsonian Institution; Freshwater Mollusk Conservation Society **Career accomplishments:** Numerous offices held, governing boards, etc. for professional organizations; Authored 223 journal articles and reports between 1952 and 1988; Gave 206 presentations, seminars and guest lectures between 1961 and 1988 (detailed records not kept after 1988) **Hob./spts.:** Family, geology, linguistics, history of science **SIC code:** 82 **Address:** 32 Amazon Place, Columbus, OH 43214 **E-mail:** stansbery.1@osu.edu

STAUBER, MARILYN J.
Industry: Education **Born:** February 5, 1938, Duluth, Minnesota **Univ./degree:** B.Ed., 1969; M.Ed., Mathematics, 1977, University of Minnesota at Duluth **Current organization:** Proctor Independent School District **Title:** Teacher/Educational Consultant (Retired) **Type of organization:** Grade school **Major product:** Kindergarten/Elementary/Junior high school education **Area of distribution:** Minnesota **Expertise:** Mathematics (grades K-8); Reading/English (K-8); Certified: Elementary/Secondary Reading Teacher; Remedial Reading Specialist (K-12); Developmental Reading Teacher (K-12); Reading Consultant (K-12) **Affiliations:** N.E.A.; I.R.A.; N.R.A.; Phi Delta Kappa **Hob./spts.:** Travel, reading **SIC code:** 82 **Address:** 6713 Grand Lake Rd., Saginaw, MN 55779

STEELE, JANET E.
Industry: Education **Born:** August 4, 1961, Charleston, Illinois **Univ./degree:** Ph.D., Miami University, 1991 **Current organization:** University of Nebraska at Kearney **Title:** Ph.D. **Type of organization:** University **Major product:** Higher education **Area of distribution:** Kearney, Nebraska **Expertise:** Cardiovascular and renal physiology **Affiliations:** A.P.S.; H.A.P.S.; F.B.R. **Hob./spts.:** Running, gardening **SIC code:** 82 **Address:** University of Nebraska at Kearney, 2401 11th Ave., Kearney, NE 68849 **E-mail:** steelej@unk.edu

STEFANOSKI, STEVCO
Industry: Medical **Born:** April 11, 1978, Macedonia **Univ./degree:** M.D., Wake Forest University School of Medicine, 2005 **Current organization:** Wake Forest University **Title:** M.D. **Type of organization:** University **Major product:** Medical education, healthcare **Area of distribution:** North Carolina **Expertise:** Internal medicine **Published works:** Peer-reviewed articles in medical journals **Affiliations:** American College of Physicians; North Carolina Medical Society; American Medical Association **Hob./spts.:** Racquetball, basketball, opera, theatre **SIC code:** 82 **Address:** Wake Forest University, Medical Center Blvd., Winston-Salem, NC 27103 **E-mail:** stevco20@yahoo.com

STEMBERGER, RICHARD S.
Industry: Education **Title:** Ph.D., Research Associate Professor **Type of organization:** College **Major product:** Higher education **Expertise:** Research, biology **SIC code:** 82 **Address:** Dartmouth College, Biology Dept., Hanover, NH 03755 **E-mail:** stemberger@dartmouth.edu

STEPHENS, JACK E.
Industry: Education/research **Born:** August 17, 1923, Eaton, Ohio **Univ./degree:** Ph.D., Purdue University, 1957 **Current organization:** Connecticut Advanced Pavement Laboratory, University of Connecticut **Title:** Senior Research Advisor **Type of organization:** University **Major product:** Higher education, research on pavement materials **Area of distribution:** National **Expertise:** Engineering, bituminous concrete **Honors/awards:** Teaching Excellence, Western Electric Fund, 1974; University of Connecticut Alumni Association Distinguished Public Service, 1982; University of Connecticut Engineering Alumni Award, 1986; Connecticut Section ASCE Benjamin Wright Award, 1989 **Affiliations:** ASCE; CSPE; AAPT; TRB; CASE; NSPE; ASEE; NEAUPC; NEMEA; ARTBA; ACSM **Hob./spts.:** Owner of 3 Model T Fords **SIC code:** 82 **Address:** 270 S. Eagleville Rd., Storrs, CT 06268 **E-mail:** jack.stephens@uconn.edu

STERPHONE, DAVID
Industry: Education **Born:** June 2, 1955, Gerard, Ohio **Current organization:** Brevard Public Schools **Title:** Building Code Administrator **Type of organization:** School district **Major product:** Public school education **Area of distribution:** Viera, Florida **Expertise:** Certified, State Level; 12 certifications in building coding, review all new construction and renovations for building codes and compliance **Affiliations:** Florida Building Code Officials; N.F.P.A. **Hob./spts.:** Golf, fishing **SIC code:** 82 **Address:** Brevard Public Schools, 1254 S. Florida Ave., Rockledge, FL 32955 **E-mail:** sterphoned@brevard.k12.fl.us

STEWART JR., RICHARD L.
Industry: Education **Born:** June 5, 1969, Indiana, Pennsylvania **Univ./degree:** Ph.D., Ohio State University **Current organization:** Shippensburg University **Title:** Assistant Professor of Biology **Type of organization:** University **Major product:** Higher education **Area of distribution:** Pennsylvania **Expertise:** Biology **Affiliations:** A.S.A.; N.S.T.A. **Hob./spts.:** Fishing, gardening, hunting **SIC code:** 82 **Address:** 988 Ridge Rd., Shippensburg, PA 17257 **E-mail:** rlstew@ship.edu

STOCK, DAVID A.
Industry: Education **Born:** February 8, 1941, Elyria, Ohio **Univ./degree:** B.S., Forestry, Michigan State University, 1963; M.S., North Carolina State University at Raleigh, 1967; Ph.D., Forestry/Genetics, North Carolina State University at Raleigh, 1968 **Current organization:** Stetson University **Title:** Professor of Biology **Type of organization:** University **Major product:** Higher education **Area of distribution:** National **Expertise:** Microbiology, genetics **Published works:** 7+ reviews, chapters, book **Affiliations:** Board Member, Florida Ornithological Society; American Society for Microbiology; American Photobiology Society **Hob./spts.:** Hiking, reading, flower gardening **SIC code:** 82 **Address:** Stetson University, 421 N. Woodland Blvd., Unit 8285, DeLand, FL 32723 **E-mail:** dstock@stetson.edu

STUBICAN, VLADIMIR S.
Industry: Education **Born:** June 1924, Zagreb, Croatia **Univ./degree:** Ph.D., Physical Chemistry/Chemical Engineering, Dipl.Ing., Zagreb University, 1952 **Current organization:** Penn State University **Title:** Professor Emeritus **Type of organization:** University **Major product:** Higher education, research **Area of distribution:** International **Expertise:** Materials science and engineering **Honors/awards:** Fellow, American Chemical Society, American Mineral Society, American Ceramic Society; Distinguished American Bicentennial Era; Case-Western University Centennial Scholar; Cambridge University 2000 Outstanding Scientists **Published works:** 120 papers in scientific journals, 1 book **Affiliations:** A.C.S. **Hob./spts.:** Reading, swimming, tennis **SIC code:** 82 **Address:** 5117 Palm Air Dr., Sarasota, FL 34243 **E-mail:** stubicanvs@msn.com

STURZL, ALICE A.
Industry: Education **Born:** May 22, 1949, Marshfield, Wisconsin **Univ./degree:** B.S., Library Science, University of Wisconsin, Oshkosh, 1971 **Current organization:**

School District of Laona **Title:** Instructional Media Specialist **Type of organization:** School district **Major product:** Education **Area of distribution:** Laona, Wisconsin **Expertise:** Library Director **Published works:** Articles **Affiliations:** A.A.S.L.; N.E.A.; P.L.A.; Past President, Wisconsin Library Association **Hob./spts.:** Reading, bowling, travel, community service, helping others **SIC code:** 82 **Address:** 5170 E. Silver Lake Rd., Laona, WI 54541-9255 **E-mail:** aasturzl@laona.k12.wi.us

SUBLETT, CARL C.
Industry: Education **Born:** February 4, 1919, Paintsville, Kentucky **Univ./degree:** A.S., Liberal Arts, Western Kentucky University **Current organization:** University of Tennessee (Retired) **Title:** Artist **Type of organization:** University **Major product:** Higher education **Area of distribution:** National **Expertise:** Water color, oil art **Honors/awards:** Served in active duty, U.S. Army 1945-53, World War II Veteran **Hob./spts.:** All sports **SIC code:** 82 **Address:** 2104 Lake Ave., Knoxville, TN 37916

SUNDBERG, ARTHUR J.E.
Industry: Education **Born:** December 1, 1940, Bronx, New York **Univ./degree:** A.S., General Electronics, RCA Institute, 1960 **Current organization:** University of Delaware, College of Marine Studies **Title:** Assistant Director, Marine Operations **Type of organization:** University **Major product:** Higher education **Area of distribution:** International **Expertise:** Oceanographic research, instrumentation and field engineering **Published works:** Co-Author, 6 articles **Affiliations:** Marine Technology Society **Hob./spts.:** Scuba diving, fishing, boating **SIC code:** 82 **Address:** University of Delaware, College of Marine Studies, 700 Pilottown Rd., Lewes, DE 19958 **E-mail:** arts@udel.edu

SUNDER, KEERTHY
Industry: Medical **Born:** December 29, 1963, Ranchi, India **Univ./degree:** M.D., University of Rajasthan, 1989 **Current organization:** University of Pittsburgh **Title:** M.D., M.S., DRCOG, Senior Resident Physician **Type of organization:** University, hospital **Major product:** Education, medical research **Area of distribution:** National **Expertise:** Reproductive psychiatry **Honors/awards:** National Young Investigator Award: Development of Evidence-Based Model for Maternal Addictions **Published works:** Mental Fitness; Journal of Clinical Psychiatry **Affiliations:** Fellow, Royal Society of Medicine; American College of Obstetrics and Gynecology; American Psychiatric Association; Royal College of Obstetrics and Gynecology **Hob./spts.:** Meditation yoga, reading, basketball, squash **SIC code:** 82 **Address:** University of Pittsburgh, 3811 O'Hara St., Pittsburgh, PA 15213 **E-mail:** sunderkr@upmc.edu

SWOBODA, DONALD W.
Industry: Education **Born:** March 19, 1944, Norfolk, Nebraska **Univ./degree:** B.S., 1966; M.S., 1968; Ph.D., 1974. University of Nebraska **Current organization:** University of Nebraska at Lincoln, College of Education and Family Science **Title:** Professor **Type of organization:** University **Major product:** Higher education **Area of distribution:** Nebraska **Expertise:** Administrative leadership, continuing and distance education **Published works:** 10 publications **Affiliations:** University of Continuing Education Association (U.C.E.A.); National Association of State Universities and Land-Grant College; Growth Group, Inc. **Hob./spts.:** Family, yard work, woodworking **SIC code:** 82 **Address:** 3810 Cape Charles Ct., Lincoln, NE 68516 **E-mail:** dswoboda1@unl.com

TABAKOFF, WIDEN
Industry: Education/Aerospace Engineering **Born:** December 14, 1919, Bulgaria **Univ./degree:** Ph.D., Engineering, Technical University of Berlin, 1945 **Current organization:** University of Cincinnati, Dept. of Aerospace Engineering **Title:** Professor and Director, Turbomachinery Erosion Laboratory **Type of organization:** University **Major product:** Higher education **Area of distribution:** International **Expertise:** Aerospace engineering and research, turbomachinery in rockets **Published works:** 450+ articles, government reports, book chapters **Affiliations:** Fellow, A.S.M.E.; Fellow, A.I.A.A. **Hob./spts.:** Family, tennis, bicycling, sports **SIC code:** 82 **Address:** University of Cincinnati, Dept. of Aerospace Engineering, P.O. Box 210070, Cincinnati, OH 45221 **E-mail:** widen.tabakoff@uc.edu

TALLEY, DIANE Y.
Industry: Education **Born:** May 8, 1950, Sault Sainte Marie, Michigan **Univ./degree:** M.S., Nova Southeastern University, 2000 **Current organization:** Volusia County Schools **Title:** Special Education Teacher **Type of organization:** Public school **Major product:** Special education students **Area of distribution:** Daytona Beach, Florida **Expertise:** Special education **Honors/awards:** Nominee, Rookie of the Year, ESE; Nominee, Disney Teacher of the Year **Published works:** Hauge Magazine, 1975-1986 **Affiliations:** A.F.T.; N.E.A.; V.T.O.; Audubon Society **Hob./spts.:** Native American crafts, doll collecting, music boxes **SIC code:** 82 **Address:** Volusia County Schools, 155 N. Lanvale, Daytona Beach, FL 32114

TAMEZ, ESMERALDA G.
Industry: Education **Born:** July 22, 1956, Brownsville, Texas **Univ./degree:** Education, University of Texas **Current organization:** Brownsville Independent School District **Title:** Elementary School Principal **Type of organization:** Elementary school **Major product:** Elementary school education **Area of distribution:** Brownsville, Texas **Expertise:** Educational business administration, mid-management **Affiliations:** Texas Association of Brownsville Educators **Hob./spts.:** Scrapbooking, jewelry design, crossword puzzles, reading **SIC code:** 82 **Address:** Brownsville Independent School District, 3201 Lima St., Brownsville, TX 78521 **E-mail:** egtamez@bisd.us

TAN, DONGFENG
Industry: Medical **Born:** Wuhan, China **Univ./degree:** M.D., Tong Ji Medical School, China, 1983 **Current organization:** University of Texas **Title:** M.D. **Type of organization:** University **Major product:** Research, education, clinical services **Area of distribution:** National **Expertise:** Pathology **Affiliations:** U.S. and Canadian Academy of Pathology; American Association for Cancer Research **Hob./spts.:** Reading, fishing, swimming **SIC code:** 82 **Address:** University of Texas, 6431 Fannin St., MSB 2.222, Houston, TX 77030 **E-mail:** dongfeng.tan@uth.tmc.edu

TAYLOR, CLIFFORD O.
Industry: Education **Born:** January 4, 1926, Fort Pierce, Florida **Spouse:** Dorothy Pearce **Married:** December 27, 1952 **Univ./degree:** B.A., Florida State University; M.S., History, University of Illinois **Title:** Professor, Principal (Retired) **Type of organization:** Elementary school - C.O. Taylor/Kirklane Elementary School, Palm Beach County, Florida **Major product:** Education **Area of distribution:** Lake Worth, Florida **Expertise:** Teaching **Honors/awards:** Community Service Award, Lake Worth Community, 2002; In 1991 Kirklane Elementary School was renamed Clifford O. Taylor Kirklane Elementary School **Published works:** Social studies year book, 1954 **Affiliations:** Member, South Florida Pioneer; Lions Club; Southern Association of Colleges and Schools; Phi Delta Kappa; United States Navy 1944-46 **Hob./spts.:** Family, stamp collecting **SIC code:** 82 **Address:** 1811 N. J Terrace, Lake Worth, FL 33460

TAYLOR, JAMES D.
Industry: Educational **Univ./degree:** M.S., Extension Education, University of Tennessee at Knoxville **Title:** County Extension Director (Retired) **Type of organization:** Management Extension Service **Major product:** Education, agriculture, CRD, administration **Area of distribution:** Pulaski, Tennessee **Expertise:** Animal agriculture, marketing, management; Certified Crop Advisor **Affiliations:** Tennessee Association of Agricultural Agents and Specialists; National Association of County Agricultural Agents; Tennessee Agricultural Products Association; Dairy Shrine; Council for Agricultural Science and Technology; American Agronomy Society; Crop Society of America; Soil Society of America; Tennessee Cattlemen's Association; National Cattleman Beef Association; Tennessee Forage and Grassland Council; Southern Middle Tennessee Forestry Association; American Cancer, Diabetes and Heart Association; Tennessee Pork Producers Association; Tennessee Farm Bureau **SIC code:** 82 **Address:** 136 Harmon Dr., Pulaski, TN 38478 **E-mail:** meadowlarkcash@yahoo.com

TEARE, IWAN D.
Industry: Education/Agriculture **Born:** July 24, 1931, Moscow, Idaho **Univ./degree:** B.S., Ag., University of Idaho, 1953; M.S., Ag., Washington State University, 1959; Ph.D., Crop Physiology, Purdue University, 1963 **Current organization:** University of Florida (Retired) **Type of organization:** University **Major product:** Higher education, crop physiology **Area of distribution:** National **Expertise:** Maximization of yield, water relations, integrated pest management **Honors/awards:** Honorary Academic Societies: Sigma Xi, Gamma Sigma Delta, Phi Kappa Gamma; Distinguished Graduate Faculty Award, Kansas State University, 1974; Elected Fellow of American Society of Agronomy, 1986; Appointed to Governor's Art Council in 2001 to present; Aide to Georgia Senator Ragan during Legislative Session, 2001 **Published works:** Book, Crop Water Relations; 3 chapters in books; 200 technical papers (Agronomy); 3 technical papers (Entomological); 34 non-technical papers; 15 invited lectures, seminars or symposia presentations **Affiliations:** American Society of Agronomy; American Society of Crop Science; Kansas Academy of Science; Entomological Society of America; Member, Church of Jesus Christ of Latter Day Saints; Founding Member of Quincy Music Theatre; Member of Syrup City Players **Hob./spts.:** Acting, dancing, collecting Volkswagens **SIC code:** 82 **Address:** 420 Maxwell Dr., Cairo, GA 39828

TEDESCO, JOSEPH W.
Industry: Education **Born:** November, 18, 1948, Woburn, Massachusetts **Univ./degree:** Ph.D., Civil Engineering, Lehigh University, 1982 **Current organization:** University of Florida, **Title:** Professor/Chairman **Type of organization:** University **Major product:** Higher education, research **Area of distribution:** Florida **Expertise:** Engineering **Affiliations:** A.S.C.E.; A.C.I. **Hob./spts.:** Cycling, running **SIC code:** 82 **Address:** University of Florida, Dept. of Civil and Coastal Engineering, 365 Weil Hall, Gainesville, FL 32611-6580 **E-mail:** jtede@ce.ufl.cedu

TERNUS, JEAN ANN
Industry: Medical/nursing **Born:** February 29, 1944, Columbus, Nebraska **Univ./degree:** B.S.N., Mt. Marty College, 1966; M.S., Kansas State University, 1977 **Current organization:** Kansas City, Kansas Community College **Title:** R.N. **Type of organization:** Community College **Major product:** Higher education **Area of**

distribution: Kansas City, Kansas **Expertise:** Nursing, medical/surgical instruction **Honors/awards:** Honorary Recognition, Kansas State Nurses Association **Published works:** 1 article **Affiliations:** A.N.A.; Kansas State Nursing Association; Sigma Theta Tau; N.L.N.; A.A.C.N.; Delta Kappa Gamma; National Gerontological Association; American Heart Association **Hob./spts.:** Music, movies **SIC code:** 82 **Address:** Kansas City, Kansas Community College, 7250 State Ave., Kansas City, KS 66112 **E-mail:** jternus@toto.net

THELIN, PETER CARL
Industry: Education **Born:** June 26, 1945, Wellesley, Massachusetts **Current organization:** West Valley College **Title:** Economics Instructor **Type of organization:** Community college **Major product:** Higher education **Area of distribution:** National **Expertise:** Economic philosophy, natural resource economics **Published works:** 2 books, 28 articles **Affiliations:** A.C.L.U.; Surf Writers **Hob./spts.:** Tai Chi, body surfing, hiking **SIC code:** 82 **Address:** 307 Mott Ave., Santa Cruz, CA 95062

THOMAS, ESTHER M.
Industry: Education **Born:** October 16, 1945, San Diego, California **Univ./degree:** M.S., University of Redlands, 1977 **Current organization:** Cajon Valley Union School District **Title:** Educator **Type of organization:** School **Major product:** Public school education **Area of distribution:** California **Expertise:** Second grade teacher **Published works:** Co-author, "Legends of Lakeside"; Co-author, "Campbell County Treasured Years"; Author, "Individualized Curriculum in the Affective Domain" **Affiliations:** Marine Corp. Museum **Hob./spts.:** Writing country music **SIC code:** 82 **Address:** Cajon Valley Union School District, 1251 Finch St., El Cajon, CA 92020 **E-mail:** estherthomas@gwise.cajon.k12.ca.us

THOMAS, MAJOR JAMES PATRICK
Industry: Education **Univ./degree:** M.A., Public Administration, Troy State University, 1974 **Current organization:** Clark County School District **Title:** Major USAF (Ret.) **Type of organization:** Public school **Major product:** Elementary and secondary school education **Area of distribution:** Henderson, Nevada **Expertise:** Special education **Affiliations:** A.A.R.P. **SIC code:** 82 **Address:** 1929 High Mesa Dr., Henderson, NV 89012 **E-mail:** thomasjimp@aol.com

THOMAS, WIONA W.
Industry: Education **Born:** February 18, 1937, Louisiana **Univ./degree:** B.S., Speech and Social Sciences, Grambling College, 1960; M.Ed., Elementary Education, Southern University, 1968 **Title:** Teacher (Retired) **Type of organization:** Educational **Major product:** Elementary school education **Area of distribution:** Opelousas, Louisiana **Expertise:** Tutoring for K-3 and leap testing **Honors/awards:** Teacher of the Year, Plaisance High School **Affiliations:** National Education Association; American Association of University Women **Hob./spts.:** Reading, involvement **SIC code:** 82 **Address:** 3833 Hwy. 167, Opelousas, LA 70570

THOMPSON, BERNIDA L.
Industry: Education **Born:** July 5, 1946 **Univ./degree:** Ed.D., Nova Southeastern University, 1992 **Current organization:** Roots School System **Title:** Principal/Founder **Type of organization:** School **Major product:** Education **Area of distribution:** International **Expertise:** Early and middle childhood education **Published works:** African-Centered Interdisciplinary Multilevel Hands-On Science Curriculum; Black Adonis & Young Lions: A Rite of Passage for U.S. Black Adolescents **Affiliations:** National Association for the Education of Young Children; National Black Child Development Institute; Association for Supervision and Curriculum Development; World Council for Curriculum Development; National Alliance of Black School Educators **Hob./spts.:** Roller skating, bird watching **SIC code:** 82 **Address:** Roots School System, 15 Kennedy St. N.W., Washington, DC 20011 **E-mail:** bthompson@rootspcs.org **Web address:** www.rootspcs.org

THOMPSON, KATHLEEN A.
Industry: Education **Born:** November 4, 1954, Coldwater, Michigan **Univ./degree:** A.S., Child Development, 1998 **Current organization:** New Friends Daycare & Preschool Center **Title:** Director/Owner **Type of organization:** Daycare center **Major product:** Educational services **Area of distribution:** Rockford, Michigan **Expertise:** Child care, administration **Hob./spts.:** Interior design, restoring antique furniture **SIC code:** 82 **Address:** New Friends Daycare & Preschool Center, 6780 Martinview Dr., Rockford, MI 49341 **E-mail:** trish19742003@yahoo.com

THOMPSON, RAE
Industry: Education **Born:** Detroit, Michigan **Univ./degree:** M.A.-TESL **Current organization:** Tolchii'Kooh, Inc. dba Tolani Lake Elementary School Academy **Title:** Key Teacher/Title I/Technology **Type of organization:** Elementary school **Major product:** Student education (Native American) **Area of distribution:** Winslow, Arizona (Navajo Reservation) **Expertise:** Curriculum, assessments, technology, instruction **Published works:** Book review **Affiliations:** A.S.C.D.; N.C.T.M. **Hob./spts.:** Reading, computers, languages, needlework **SIC code:** 82 **Address:** Tolchii'Kooh, Inc. dba Tolani Lake Elementary School Academy, HC-61, Box 300, Winslow, AZ 86047 **E-mail:** rft5008@yahoo.com

THOMPSON, SANDRA L.
Industry: Education **Born:** Dayton, Ohio **Univ./degree:** B.S., Education, Western Michigan University, 1970; M.S., 1975; Ed.S., Business Education, 1981; Ed.S., School Administration, 1987, Georgia State University **Current organization:** Georgia Association For Career & Technical Education **Title:** Executive Director **Type of organization:** Secondary/post secondary education **Major product:** Educational services/promotion **Area of distribution:** National **Expertise:** Marketing, public relations, consulting **Honors/awards:** Alton B. Parker Liles Award; Outstanding Business Educator, Georgia State University; Future Business Leaders of America, Advisor of the Year, Georgia Department of Education; YWCA Women of Achievement Award, Marietta, Georgia; Teacher of the Year, Lassiter High School, Cobb County School System, Marietta, Georgia **Published works:** Systems for Administrative Office Support, Glencoe, 1994 (college text) **Affiliations:** G.A.C.T.E.; A.C.T.E.; N.E.D.A.; P.A.G.E.; G.A.E.; D.P.E.; N.B.E.A.; S.B.E.A.; G.B.E.A. **Hob./spts.:** Antiques, travel, writing **SIC code:** 82 **Address:** Georgia Association For, Career & Technical Education, P.O. Box 72588, Marietta, GA 30064 **E-mail:** noahthompson@mindspring.com **Web address:** www.gacte.org

THORNTON, H. RICHARD
Industry: Education **Born:** November 15, 1932, Van Etten, New York **Univ./degree:** B.S.; M. S., Alfred University; Ph.D., Ceramic Engineering, University of Illinois, 1963 **Current organization:** Texas A&M University **Title:** Professor Emeritus **Type of organization:** University **Major product:** Higher education **Area of distribution:** National **Expertise:** Mechanical engineering, composite materials and material design **Published works:** 35 articles **Affiliations:** A.S.M.; American Ceramics Society **Hob./spts.:** Coaching, volunteering **SIC code:** 82 **Address:** 2505 Willow Bend Dr., Bryan, TX 77802 **E-mail:** thornton.hr@verizon.net

TOLBERT, BOYD R.
Industry: Education **Born:** August 4, 1959, California **Univ./degree:** B.A., 1981; B.A., Religion, 1982, Vanguard Med Chatham University; Ed.D, Arizona State University **Current organization:** American Indian College **Title:** Ed.D. **Type of organization:** University **Major product:** Higher education **Area of distribution:** Arizona **Expertise:** Education courses **SIC code:** 82 **Address:** American Indian College, 10020 N. 15th Ave., Phoenix, AZ 85021 **E-mail:** btolbert@aicag.edu **Web address:** www.aicag.edu

TORRES, M. LORRAINE
Industry: Education **Born:** November 4, 1958, El Paso, Texas **Univ./degree:** B.S., Biology, 1980; B.S. with Honors, Medical Technology, 1985; M.S., with Honors, Immunology, 1982, University of Texas El Paso; Ed.D. Candidate, University of Phoenix **Current organization:** University of Texas at El Paso **Title:** Education Clinical Contractor **Type of organization:** University **Major product:** Higher education, research **Area of distribution:** Texas **Expertise:** Clinical laboratory science; curriculum coordination; teaching immunology, hematology, serology **Published works:** Prentiss Hall Book Reviewer (texts), 1 article, "Human Herpes - Virus 6" **Affiliations:** American Society of Clinical Pathologists; American Society of Clinical Lab Sciences **Hob./spts.:** Choir director, writes/arranges music, volleyball **SIC code:** 82 **Address:** University of Texas at El Paso, Clinical Lab Science Dept., 1101 N. Campbell St., El Paso, TX 79902 **E-mail:** lorit@utep.edu

TRACY, TRACY E.
Industry: Education **Born:** August 22, 1961, Washington, D.C. **Univ./degree:** B.S., Special Education, Old Dominion University, 1983 **Current organization:** Newport News Public Schools **Title:** Community Based Instruction Program Administrator **Type of organization:** Public school system **Major product:** Education **Area of distribution:** Newport News, Virginia **Expertise:** Liaison between school and community to integrate life skills in the curriculum for special education **Honors/awards:** Outstanding Student in Special Education, Old Dominion University; listed in, Who's Who Among Students in American Universities and Colleges; Outstanding Young Women of America; Who's Who in American Education; Who's Who in America; Who's Who in the World; 2000 Outstanding Scholars of the 21st Century **Affiliations:** Council for Exceptional Children; American Association on Mental Retardation; Newport News Special Olympics Executive Committee; The Arc; Kappa Delta Pi (Nu Eta Chapter); Alpha Chi **Hob./spts.:** Family, Special Olympics volunteer, swimming, soccer **SIC code:** 82 **Address:** Newport News Public Schools, 813 Diligence Dr., Suite 110, Newport News, VA 23606 **E-mail:** ctracywin@cox.net

TRAN, LAC VAN
Industry: Healthcare, research and education **Born:** September 29, 1950, Long An, Viet Nam **Univ./degree:** M.S., Mathematics and Statistics, University of Texas, 1980 **Current organization:** Rush University Medical Center **Title:** Senior Vice President/CIO/Associate Dean **Type of organization:** University medical center **Major product:** Healthcare, system development, telecommunication, education and research **Area**

of distribution: Illinois **Expertise:** Information technology **Affiliations:** College of Healthcare Information Executives; Society for Fiber Optic Engineers **Hob./spts.:** Travel **SIC code:** 82 **Address:** Rush-University Medical Center, 1700 W. Van Buren St., TOB #374, Chicago, IL 60612 **E-mail:** Lac@lpsjjtran.com

TRAYLOR JR., IDRIS R.
Industry: Education **Born:** February 4, 1935, Norman, Oklahoma **Univ./degree:** Ph.D., Duke University, 1965 **Current organization:** Texas Tech University **Title:** Executive Director, Office of International Affairs/Director, International Cultural Center **Type of organization:** University **Major product:** Higher education **Area of distribution:** International **Expertise:** International affairs **Honors/awards:** Honorary Doctorate, Representative for the United Nations Development Program in China **Affiliations:** Former President, W.S.S.A.; Executive Director, A.A.L.S.; A.A.A.S.S. **Hob./spts.:** Travel, coin collecting, bibliofile **SIC code:** 82 **Address:** 3601 63rd Dr., Lubbock, TX 79413 **E-mail:** gay.riggan@ttu.edu

TRITT, TERRY M.
Industry: Education **Born:** August 22, 1956, Highland, North Carolina **Univ./degree:** Ph.D., Clemson University **Current organization:** Clemson University **Title:** Professor; Head of the Complex and Advanced Materials Laboratory **Type of organization:** University **Major product:** Higher education **Area of distribution:** International **Expertise:** Electrical and thermal transport properties and phenomena (especially in measurement and characterization techniques) in new and novel materials including low dimensional systems, quasicrystals, oxides, intermetallics, clathrates and skutterudites; Extensive expertise in measurement science **Published works:** Lead organizer of 3 Materials Research Society Symposia on Advanced Thermoelectrics Materials (MRS Volumes 478, 545, 626); Edited a 3-volume set on "Recent Trends in Thermoelectric Materials Research" for Academic Press Semiconductors and Semimetals series, Volumes 69, 70, 71; Edited a book by Kluwer Press on Thermal Conductivity; 140+ refereed journal publications **Affiliations:** Executive Board Member, International Thermoelectrics Society; Chairman and Host of the 24th International TE Conference, June 2005 **Hob./spts.:** Golf, musician (produced and recorded 4 CD's of his music) **SIC code:** 82 **Address:** Clemson University, Dept. of Physics & Astronomy, 103 Kinard Laboratory, Clemson, SC 29634 **E-mail:** ttritt@clemson.edu **Web address:** www.clemson.edu/caml

TROUTMAN, ELLEN B.
Industry: Education **Born:** May 15, 1966, Salisbury, North Carolina **Univ./degree:** B.S., University of North Carolina at Chapel Hill, 1989 **Current organization:** Rowan-Cabarrus Community College **Title:** B.S., R.T. (R)(M) **Type of organization:** Community college **Major product:** Higher education **Area of distribution:** National **Expertise:** Mammography, radiography **Honors/awards:** Founder of Mammography Program **Affiliations:** A.S.R.T.; N.C.S.R.T.; Lifetime Member, St. Peter's Lutheran Church **Hob./spts.:** Swimming, weightlifting, aerobics, singing and handbells **SIC code:** 82 **Address:** 335 Gold Knob Rd., Salisbury, NC 28146 **E-mail:** troutmane@rccc.cc.nc.us

TRZYNA, CHRIS A.
Industry: Education **Born:** Chicago, Illinois **Univ./degree:** M.S., Education, Northern Illinois University, 1983 **Current organization:** Libertyville High School **Title:** Assistant Athletic Director/Physical Education Teacher/Varsity Girls Volleyball Coach **Type of organization:** High school **Major product:** Secondary school education **Area of distribution:** Illinois **Expertise:** Physical education **Affiliations:** I.A.D.A.; A.A.H.P.E.R.D. **Hob./spts.:** Volleyball, tennis, computers **SIC code:** 82 **Address:** Libertyville High School, 708 W. Park Ave., Libertyville, IL 60048 **E-mail:** trzyna.c@district128.org

ULTRINO, STEVEN R.
Industry: Education **Univ./degree:** B.S., U.S. History & Secondary Education; M.S., Organizational Learning, Suffolk University; C.A.G.S., Educational Leadership, Emmanuel College **Current organization:** St. Mary's High School **Title:** Principal **Type of organization:** High school **Major product:** Education **Area of distribution:** Malden, Massachusetts **Expertise:** Business, economics **Affiliations:** A.S.C.D.; N.B.T.A.; N.A.E.E.; Kiwanis Club **SIC code:** 82 **Address:** 39 Adams St., Malden, MA 02148 **E-mail:** ultrinos@maldencatholic.org

UPTON, EILEEN L.
Industry: Education/healthcare **Born:** August 2, 1925, Helena, Montana **Univ./degree:** RN, Columbus Hospital School of Nursing, Seattle University, Washington, 1947; B.S., Health Sciences, Chapman University, California, 1980; M.S., Education, National University, California, 1985 **Current organization:** California Nursing Education Institute **Title:** RN, BS, MS, Ed.A **Type of organization:** Education institution **Major product:** Nursing education **Area of distribution:** California **Expertise:** Education, nursing consulting, I.V. therapy and phlebotomy instruction **Honors/awards:** Listed in, "Who's Who in American Nurses", "Who's Who in American Teaching"; Women of Distinction Award, Soroptimist Club **Published works:** 2 articles in Infection Control Magazine and Dietary Magazine **Affiliations:** California Nurses Educators Association; member, RNA, Washington State Nurses Association; life member, Phi Delta kappa **Hob./spts.:** Skiing **SIC code:** 82 **Address:** California Nursing Education Institute, 1775 E. Palm Canyon Dr., Suite J, Palm Springs, CA 9264 **E-mail:** eupton_1@juno.com

VAMALA, CHIRANJEEVI
Industry: Education **Born:** August 20, 1978, India **Univ./degree:** M.S., University of Louisiana, 2003 **Current organization:** University of North Texas **Type of organization:** University **Major product:** Higher education **Area of distribution:** Texas **Expertise:** Engineering **Published works:** Thesis **SIC code:** 82 **Address:** 726 Schmitz St., #3, Denton, TX 76209 **E-mail:** chiru777@yahoo.com

VAN APPLEDORN, MARY JEANNE
Industry: Education **Univ./degree:** B.M.,1948; M.M., 1950; Ph.D., 1966, University of Rochester, Eastman School of Music; Studies in computer-synthesized sound techniques at the Massachusetts Institute of Technology, 1982 **Current organization:** Texas Tech University **Title:** Ph.D. **Type of organization:** University **Major product:** Higher education **Area of distribution:** National **Expertise:** Music **Honors/awards:** Paul Whitfield Horn Professorship in Music Composition; ASCAP Standard Panel Award, 1980 to 2005; Who's Who in Music; Who's Who of American Women; Who's Who in the South and Southwest; World Who's Who of Women **Published works:** Compositions published, performed and recorded internationally **Affiliations:** A.S.C.A.P. **SIC code:** 82 **Address:** 1629 16th St., #216, Lubbock, TX 79401-4703 **E-mail:** mary.van-appledorn@ttu.edu

VAN DAELE, DOUGLAS J.
Industry: Education **Born:** February 28, 1969, Oelwein, Iowa **Univ./degree:** B.S., Mechanical Engineering, University of Iowa, 1991; M.D., University of Iowa School of Medicine, 1966 **Current organization:** University of Iowa Healthcare **Title:** M.D. **Type of organization:** University/academic **Major product:** Patient care, medical education **Area of distribution:** Iowa **Expertise:** Otolaryngology **Published works:** 15 articles, 2 chapters **Affiliations:** A.M.A.; American Association of Otolaryngology **Hob./spts.:** Books, mountain biking **SIC code:** 82 **Address:** University of Iowa Healthcare, 200 Hawkins Dr., 21201 PFP, Iowa City, IA 52242 **E-mail:** douglas-vandaele@uiowa.edu **Web address:** www.uiowa.edu

VICKS, JOANN
Industry: Education **Born:** November 3, 1938, Starkville, Mississippi **Univ./degree:** A.A., Education, 1959, Mary Holmes College; B.S., 1961, Tougaloo Collage; M.A. for Teachers in Biology, 1967, Indiana University; Educational Specialist in Secondary Education, 1976; Ed.D. in Secondary Education, 1979, Mississippi State University **Current organization:** East Mississippi Community College **Title:** Professor of Science **Type of organization:** College **Major product:** Higher education **Area of distribution:** Mississippi **Expertise:** Biology, zoology **Honors/awards:** Numerous including, Outstanding Faculty Award on Higher Education in Mississippi, Mary Holmes College, 1990 and 2001; Outstanding Educator of America, 1975; Recognition for participating in the recording session for Voices of Pentecost Mass Choir, Columbus, MS, 1992; Recognition plaque for Outstanding Accomplishment in Education, presented by Second Baptist Church, Starkville, MS, 1979; Appreciation plaques for musical service, presented by the Male Choir, Second Baptist Church, Starkville, MS, 1978, 2000, 2001, 2002 **Published works:** 4 articles including, "The Mommy Managers", Black Child Magazine, Summer 1998, Interrace Publications, pp.12-13 **Affiliations:** Former Member, Phi Delta Kappa Education Fraternity; Mississippi Science Teachers Association; National Biology Teachers Association; American Association for the Advancement of Science **Hob./spts.:** Music (piano and vocal), Bible teaching, writing Christian literature, public speaking, drawing and painting, watching sports events **SIC code:** 82 **Address:** P.O. 604, Starkville, MS 39760 **E-mail:** javicks8@bellsouth.net

VITTIMBERGA, BRUNO M.
Industry: Education **Born:** September 21, 1929, Watertown, Massachusetts **Univ./degree:** Ph.D., Organic Chemistry, University of Illinois, 1957 **Current organization:** University of Rhode Island, Dept. of Chemistry **Title:** Professor/Ph.D. **Type of organization:** University **Major product:** Higher education, research **Area of distribution:** Rhode Island **Expertise:** Organic photo chemistry **Published works:** 70 peer-reviewed articles in chemistry journals **Affiliations:** American Chemical Society; Alpha Kappa Phi; Alpha Chi Sigma **Hob./spts.:** Family, furniture building, theatre, reading **SIC code:** 82 **Address:** University of Rhode Island, Dept. of Chemistry, Kingston, RI 02881 **E-mail:** bvittimberga@chm.uri.edu

VOGEL, GLORIA JEAN HILTS
Industry: Education **Born:** March 24, 1947, Detroit, Michigan **Univ./degree:** B.A., Michigan State University, 1969; M.A., English; Fitchburg State College, 1976 **Current organization:** Leominster High School **Title:** Secondary English Teacher **Type of organization:** High school **Major product:** High school education **Area of distribution:** Townsend, Massachusetts **Expertise:** English education **Honors/awards:** Numerous including, Strathmore's Who's Who , 2002-03, 2003-04; Who's Who in American Education, 6th edition, 2004-05; Top 100 Educators in 2005, International

Biographical Centre, Cambridge, England; United Who's Who Empowering Executives and Professionals (Delray Beach, FL), 2005; Who's Who of American Women, 25th edition, 2006-07; Who's Who in American Education, 7th edition, 2005; Who's Who Among America's Teachers (Austin, TX), 2005; International Who's Who of Professional & Business Women, 8th edition, 2005, American Biographical Institute, Raleigh, NC **Affiliations:** N.E.A.; M.T.A.; L.E.A.; N.C.T.E.; N.E.A.T.E.; A.A.U.W.; B.P.W. **Hob./spts.:** 19th century American art (White Mountain School), Townsend Congregational Church Choir, reading, travel **SIC code:** 82 **Address:** 3 Sycamore Dr., Townsend, MA 01469 **E-mail:** cvogel@net1plus.com

VOO, LIMING M.
Industry: Education **Born:** January 14, 1959, China **Univ./degree:** Ph.D., Medical/Biomedical Engineering, University of Iowa, 1995 **Current organization:** Johns Hopkins University Applied Physics Laboratory **Title:** Ph.D./Senior Research Scientist **Type of organization:** University **Major product:** Higher education/engineering solutions **Area of distribution:** International **Expertise:** Biomedical engineering **Published works:** 50+ articles, conference papers and book chapters **Affiliations:** A.S.M.E.; A.A.A.S.; A.S.T.M.; S.A.E.; American Society of Biomedical Engineers **Hob./spts.:** Family, photography **SIC code:** 82 **Address:** Johns Hopkins University, Applied Physics Laboratory, 11100 Johns Hopkins Rd., Laurel, MD 20723-6099 **E-mail:** liming.voo@jhuapl.edu **Web address:** www.jhuapl.edu

WALDMAN, JACQUELINE
Industry: Education **Born:** February 10, 1953, Basel, Switzerland **Current organization:** Scandinavian Seminar **Title:** CEO **Type of organization:** Nonprofit/educational **Major product:** International education **Area of distribution:** International **Expertise:** Global education **Affiliations:** C.I.E.E.; N.A.F.S.A.; A.R.C.U.S.; N.A.I.S. **Hob./spts.:** Gardening, hiking, cooking **SIC code:** 82 **Address:** Scandinavian Seminar, 24 Dickinson St., Amherst, MA 01002 **E-mail:** waldman@scandinavianseminar.org

WALKER, CAROLYN SMITH
Industry: Education **Born:** May 9, 1946, Atlanta, Georgia **Univ./degree:** M.S., Counseling/Guidance, University of Nebraska, Omaha, 1975 **Current organization:** Atlanta Metropolitan College **Title:** Associate Vice President **Type of organization:** College **Major product:** Higher education **Area of distribution:** Georgia **Expertise:** Senior counseling, alternative dispute and conflict resolution; Principal Examiner **Affiliations:** N.A.D.E.; Alpha Kappa Alpha; Historian for Dogwood Chapter Links Inc. **Hob./spts.:** Horseback riding, tennis, skiing, horticulture **SIC code:** 82 **Address:** Atlanta Metropolitan College, 3511 Toll House Lane S.W., Atlanta, GA 30331 **E-mail:** cwalker@amcmail.atlm.peachnet.edu

WALLISCH, CAROLYN E.
Industry: Education **Born:** August 23, 1939, Denver, Colorado **Univ./degree:** B.Ed., 1961; M.Ed., 1965, University of Northern Colorado **Current organization:** Colorado Christian University **Title:** Adjunct Professor **Type of organization:** University **Major product:** Higher education **Area of distribution:** Colorado **Expertise:** Elementary education **Honors/awards:** Listed in "Who's Who Among American Women", 1999-2001, "International Who's Who of Professionals", 2000-2002; Appeared on National television, "What's Happening in Education", ABC News with Peter Jennings, 1992; Quoted in "Instructor Magazine", 1983 **Published works:** 5 articles **Affiliations:** Principal, Highland Elementary School (Retired) **Hob./spts.:** Golf, tennis, travel, reading **SIC code:** 82 **Address:** 5549 W. Hinsdale Ave., Littleton, CO 80128 **E-mail:** cwallisch@att.net

WALSH, JAN
Industry: Library **Born:** February 2, 1942, Short Hills, New Jersey **Univ./degree:** B.S., Education, Pennsylvania State University, 1964; M.L.S., University of Pittsburgh, PA, 1968 **Current organization:** Washington State Library **Title:** Washington State Librarian **Type of organization:** State library **Major product:** Statewide development of libraries **Area of distribution:** Washington **Expertise:** Library advocacy **Honors/awards:** Washington Library Association, Adovcacy Award, 2002; President, American Library Association, SMLS, PLA, 1999; NCES/NCLIS Annual Lorenz and Keppel Award, 2001-2005; NCES/NCLIS Annual Keppel Award, 1992-2001; Service Quality Executive Mgmt. Award **Affiliations:** American Library Association; Washington Library Association; Washington Reads **Hob./spts.:** Personal trainer **SIC code:** 82 **Address:** Jan Walsh, State Librarian, Office of the Secretary of State, P.O. Box 42460, Olympia, WA 98504-2460 **E-mail:** jwalsh@secstate.wa.gov

WARD, DETRIA M.
Industry: Education **Title:** Manager of Special Projects & Programs **Type of organization:** University **Major product:** Higher education **Expertise:** Project management, program development, student and university events **SIC code:** 82 **Address:** Texas Southern University, Student Services, 3100 Cleburne Ave., Houston, TX 77004 **E-mail:** ward_dm@tsu.edu

WASHBURN, RICHARD W.
Industry: Education **Born:** January 26, 1947, Freeport, Illinois **Univ./degree:** M.S., Mathematics, University of Illinois, 1970 **Current organization:** Antilles Consolidated School System **Title:** Mathematics Teacher **Type of organization:** High school **Major product:** Education **Area of distribution:** Puerto Rico **Expertise:** Mathematics, computers **Honors/awards:** Listed in Marquis Who's Who In American Education **Affiliations:** Mathematical Association of America; National Council of Teachers of Mathematics; Phi Beta Kappa; Phi Kappa Phi **Hob./spts.:** Computers, electronics, woodworking, golf **SIC code:** 82 **Address:** Hwy. 191 km. 25.9, Naguabo, PR 00718-9717 **E-mail:** richwwashburn@cs.com **Web address:** www.cs.com

WATKINS, ROBERT F.
Industry: Education **Born:** May 20, 1927, Pueblo, Colorado **Univ./degree:** P.E.E., U.S. Government Industrial College, 1956; M.B.A., Economics/Finance, 1971; J.D., 1972; Ph.D., Economics/Finance, 1979, California Western University **Current organization:** Pueblo Community College **Title:** Adjunct Professor **Type of organization:** Two year academic and vocational college **Major product:** Higher education **Area of distribution:** International **Expertise:** Defense communications and electronics, 1953-89, (Be.fcrw) Business management including, marketing, finance and economics; Licensed Pastor since 1991 **Honors/awards:** WWII and Korean War Veteran; Various combat service ribbons RFW **Published works:** 20 articles, 2 books **Affiliations:** A.F.C.E.A.; served in active duty, U.S. Navy, 1944-1946, U.S. Navy Reserves, 1946-49, served in active duty, U.S. Navy 1949-50, U.S. Air Force Reserves, 1950-56; Korean War Service, U.S. Air Force, 1951-53; Discharged RFW as Master Sergeant from U.S. Air Force **Hob./spts.:** Biblical research **SIC code:** 82 **Address:** Pueblo Community College, 900 W. Orman Ave., Pueblo, CO 81004 **E-mail:** bob_jan61@msn.com

WATKINS, SHERRY L.
Industry: Education **Born:** October 13, 1944, Indiana **Univ./degree:** M.S., Indiana University, 1968 **Current organization:** Allisonville School **Title:** Teacher, Bargaining Chairperson **Type of organization:** School **Major product:** Elementary and secondary school education **Area of distribution:** Indiana **Expertise:** Teaching **Affiliations:** Delta Kappa Gamma **Hob./spts.:** Travel, theatre, music, reading **SIC code:** 82 **Address:** 7531 Farm View Circle East, Indianapolis, IN 46256 **E-mail:** swatkins@msdwt.k12.in.us

WATROUS, ROBERT T.
Industry: Education **Born:** April 20, 1952, Cleveland, Ohio **Univ./degree:** M.A., Counseling; M.Ed., University of Dayton, 1977 **Current organization:** Kutztown University of Pennsylvania **Title:** Director of Campus Student Life and Student Conduct Standards **Type of organization:** University **Major product:** Higher education **Area of distribution:** National **Expertise:** Student conduct, Town-Gown relations **Affiliations:** National Association of Student Personnel Administrators; Association of Judicial Affairs Officers **Hob./spts.:** Golf, gardening, home improvements **SIC code:** 82 **Address:** Kutztown University of Pennsylvania, 262 McFarland, Student Union Bldg., Kutztown, PA 19530 **E-mail:** watrous@kutztown.edu **Web address:** www.kutztown.edu

WATSON, FRANK R.
Industry: Education **Born:** Birmingham, Alabama **Univ./degree:** B.S., European History, University of Tennessee at Knoxville; M.S./Ed.S., Curriculum/Instruction, University of Alabama at Birmingham; Ed.D., Educational Leadership, Nova Southeastern University, 1995 **Current organization:** Nova Southeastern University **Title:** Adjunct Assistant Professor of Education **Type of organization:** University **Major product:** Higher education **Area of distribution:** Florida **Expertise:** Educational consulting **Published works:** Articles **Affiliations:** Phi Delta Kappa; Kappa Delta Epsilon; Kappa Alpha Psi fraternity, Inc. **Hob./spts.:** Recreational reading, international travel, entertaining, photography/videography **SIC code:** 82 **Address:** Nova Southeastern University, 3530 S. University Drive, Davie, FL 33328 **Phone:** (954)916-0141 **Fax:** (954)916-0145 **E-mail:** frankwatsonf@aol.com

WEAVER, ANDREW AUSTIN
Industry: Education **Born:** July 30, 1950, Atlanta, Georgia **Univ./degree:** B.S., Mercer University, 1998; M.B.A. Candidate **Current organization:** SDS International **Title:** Operations and Training Manager **Type of organization:** Veteran-owned training service **Major product:** Training, modeling, simulation **Area of distribution:** International **Expertise:** BS, MIS, MBA training **Affiliations:** S.E.T.A. **Hob./spts.:** Family, bowling **SIC code:** 82 **Address:** SDS International, 1283 Anderson Way, Atlanta, GA 30330 **E-mail:** andrew.weaver@usa.net

WEBB, ROBERT G.
Industry: Education **Born:** February 18, 1927, Long Beach, California **Univ./degree:** B.S., Zoology; M.S., Zoology, University of Oklahoma; Ph.D., Zoology, University of Kansas, 1960 **Current organization:** The University of Texas, El Paso **Title:** Emeritus Professor of Biological Sciences **Type of organization:** University **Major product:** Higher education **Area of distribution:** National **Expertise:** Research/vertebrate zoology **Published works:** 1 book "Reptiles of Oklahoma", Oklahoma University Press

Affiliations: S.S.A.R.; A.S.I.H.; H.L. **Hob./spts.:** Family **SIC code:** 82 **Address:** The University of Texas, El Paso, Dept. of Biological Sciences, El Paso, TX 79968-0519 **E-mail:** rgwebb@utep.edu **Web address:** www.utep.edu

WEILER, PAUL C.
Industry: Education **Born:** January 28, 1939, Ontario, Canada **Univ./degree:** J.D., Osgood Hall Law School; M.A., Philosophy, University of Toronto; LL.M., Harvard Law School **Current organization:** Harvard Law School **Title:** Henry J. Friendly Professor of Law **Type of organization:** University **Major product:** Higher education **Area of distribution:** International **Expertise:** Creator and director of Harvard's labor and workplace program, sports law program, entertainment and media law program, international lecturer on entertainment, media and sports law, personal injury and tort law, medical malpractice and labor law **Published works:** Author, 15 books including soon to be published "Speaking for Fun and Profit, How the Law Should Be Enhancing Our World of Entertainment", numerous articles and journals **Hob./spts.:** Boston Red Sox Fan, movies, music, family and friends **SIC code:** 82 **Address:** Harvard Law School, Massachusetts Ave., Cambridge, MA 02138 **E-mail:** pweiler@law.harvard.edu

WEINTRAUB, NEIL
Industry: Education **Born:** April 30, 1934, Brooklyn, New York **Univ./degree:** M.Ed., American Intercontinental University, 2004; B.S., ITT Technical Institute **Current organization:** ITT Technical Institute **Title:** Master Instructor **Type of organization:** College **Major product:** Higher education **Area of distribution:** National **Expertise:** Electronic engineering technology, math, physics **Affiliations:** N.A.R.T.E.; E.T.A.; A.S.E.E. **SIC code:** 82 **Address:** ITT Technical Institute, 7955 N.W. 12th St., Miami, FL 33126 **E-mail:** docproff@aol.com

WEMPLE KINDER, SUZANNE F.
Industry: Education **Born:** August 1, 1927, Veszprém, Hungary **Univ./degree:** Ph.D., Medieval History, Columbia University, 1967 **Current organization:** Barnard College & Columbia University (Retired) **Title:** Professor Emeritus **Type of organization:** University **Major product:** Higher education **Area of distribution:** National **Expertise:** Women in political and social history **Published works:** Numerous articles, 3 books including: Women in Frankish Society **Affiliations:** Board Member, L.A.A. **Hob./spts.:** Bridge **SIC code:** 82 **Address:** 102 Moorings Park Dr., #E-104, Naples, FL 34105 **E-mail:** gtkinder@aol.com

WENTZ, CATHERINE J.
Industry: Education **Born:** August 11, 1948, Boise, Idaho **Univ./degree:** M.S., Education, Boise State University, 1975 **Current organization:** Horizon Elementary School **Title:** First Grade Teacher **Type of organization:** Elementary school **Major product:** Education **Area of distribution:** Boise, Idaho **Expertise:** Reading, phonics; Certified Spalding teacher **Affiliations:** I.E.A.; N.E.A.; I.D.A.; Teachers Society **Hob./spts.:** Singing, dancing, tennis **SIC code:** 82 **Address:** Horizon Elementary School, 730 N. Mitchell St., Boise, ID 83704 **E-mail:** catherinewentz@boiseschools.org

WESSELSCHMIDT, QUENTIN F.
Industry: Education/theology **Born:** February 3, 1937, Washington, Missouri **Univ./degree:** M.Div., Concordia Seminary, 1963; M.A., Latin, Marquette University, 1969; Ph.D., Classical Languages, University of Iowa, 1979 **Current organization:** Concordia Seminary, St. Louis **Title:** Professor of Historical Theology **Type of organization:** Seminary **Major product:** Theological education **Expertise:** Historical theology **Honors/awards:** Invited lecturer, Goteborg, Sweden, 2002 **Published works:** Editor, theological journals; 2 book chapters (on theology); Volume Editor, Ancient Christian Commentaries **Affiliations:** Ordained Minister in the Lutheran Church, M-Synod **Hob./spts.:** Biking with his wife **SIC code:** 82 **Address:** 444 Eatherton Valley Rd., Chesterfield, MO 63005 **E-mail:** qfwes@prodigy.net

WEST, ROBERT
Industry: Education **Born:** March 18, 1928, Glen Ridge, New Jersey **Univ./degree:** Ph.D., Inorganic Chemistry, Harvard University, 1954 **Current organization:** University of Wisconsin-Madison **Title:** Professor/Director, Organosilicon Research Center **Type of organization:** University/university research center **Major product:** Higher education, electrolytes, organisilicon compounds **Area of distribution:** National **Expertise:** Chemical research, consulting, editing **Published works:** 620 peer-reviewed articles **Affiliations:** American Chemical Society; Royal Chemical Society **Hob./spts.:** Mountain climbing, flying small airplanes **SIC code:** 82 **Address:** University of Wisconsin-Madison, 1101 University Ave., Madison, WI 53706 **E-mail:** west@chem.wisc.edu

WETZEL, JOAN C.
Industry: Education **Univ./degree:** J.D., Tulane University, 1981; MCM, New Orleans Baptist Theological Seminary (NOBTS), 1995 **Current organization:** New Orleans Baptist Theological Seminary **Title:** Office Manager, Public Relations Office **Type of organization:** Christian Seminary **Major product:** Preparing individuals for Christian ministry **Area of distribution:** International **Expertise:** Public relations/publications; Certified French Teacher; Notary Public for NOBTS; Editor of non-feature material for The Gatekeeper (NOBTS weekly newsletter) **Honors/awards:** Strathmore's Who's Who, 2005-06 **Published works:** Includes: "Day shares his heart, voice in new CD", (NOBTS) Vision, Holiday Edition, 2003; (NOBTS) The Gatekeeper, Vol. 33.18, Jan. 12, 2004; "Opera finds enthusiastic audience in New Orleans seminary production", Baptist Press, May 22, 2001; The Gatekeeper, Vol. 30.35, June 4, 2001; "Hymnology prof honored with personalized hymn", Baptist Press, Feb. 2, 2001; (NOBTS) The Gatekeeper, Vol. 30.21, Feb. 5, 2000; "Draper cites 3 reasons why it's 'worth it' to serve God", Baptist Press, Mar. 3, 1999; The Gatekeeper, Vol. 28.24, Mar. 1, 1999; "An Amazing Year in Korea", Langniappe (JLNO), Spring 1997, pp. 42-44 **Affiliations:** Louisiana State Bar Association; Junior League of New Orleans **Hob./spts.:** Walking, reading, baking **SIC code:** 82 **Address:** New Orleans Baptist Theological Seminary, 3939 Gentilly Blvd., New Orleans, LA 70126 **E-mail:** nobts@nobts.edu **Web address:** www.nobts.edu

WHEELER, DICIREE M.
Industry: Early childhood education **Born:** December 11, 1935, Newbern, Alabama **Univ./degree:** Business Administration, Stillman College Early Childhood Education, Chattanooga State Technical Community College **Current organization:** 21st Century Child Development and Learning Center, Inc. **Title:** Executive Director & Founder **Type of organization:** Education and development center **Major product:** Early childhood care and education **Area of distribution:** Tennessee **Expertise:** Curriculum development and management **Honors/awards:** Outstanding Employer for Hamilton County and the State of Tennessee, South Eastern Consortium, 2003; Certificate Appreciation for the D.A.R.E. Program, Chattanooga Police Dept., 2002, 2001; Award of Excellence, Black Pioneer Women, 1999; Young Entrepreneur of the Year, M.E.D. Week Committee, 1998 **Hob./spts.:** Spending time with her children & grandchildren **SIC code:** 82 **Address:** 21st Century Child Development & Learning Center, Inc., 3315 12th Ave., Chattanooga, TN 37407

WHITACRE, CAROLINE C.
Industry: Education **Born:** November 4, 1949, Cincinnati, Ohio **Univ./degree:** Ph.D., Ohio State University, 1975 **Current organization:** Ohio State University College of Medicine **Title:** Associate Vice President, Health Sciences Research/Vice Dean for Research **Type of organization:** University **Major product:** Higher education, research, biomedical **Area of distribution:** National **Expertise:** Immunology, autoimmune diseases **Published works:** 90 scientific journal articles **Affiliations:** American Society for Microbiology; American Association of Immunologists **SIC code:** 82 **Address:** Ohio State University College of Medicine, 2078 Graves Hall, 333 W. Tenth Ave., Columbus, OH 43210 **E-mail:** whitacre.3@osu.edu

WHITE, DOUGLAS R.
Industry: Education **Born:** 1942, Minneapolis, Minnesota **Univ./degree:** Ph.D., Network Anthropology, University of California, Irvine **Current organization:** School of Social Science at University of California, Irvine **Title:** Professor **Type of organization:** University **Major product:** Higher education **Area of distribution:** International **Expertise:** Network analysis, organizational theory **Honors/awards:** Distinguished U. S. Social Scientist - Alexander Van Humboldt Award, 1990; Who's Who in America, 1999 **Published works:** 103 articles, 2 books **Affiliations:** S.S.H.A.; I.N.S.N.A.; C.S.S., Lifetime Member, Alexander Van Humboldt Foundation **SIC code:** 82 **Address:** School of Social Science at, University of California, Irvine, Irvine, CA 92697 **E-mail:** dr.white@uci.edu **Web address:** www.eclectric.ss.uci.edu

WILKERSON, RITA L.
Industry: Education **Univ./degree:** M.S., Education, University of Central Oklahoma, 1969 **Current organization:** USD #480 Liberal, Kansas **Title:** School Psychologist/Special Education Teacher **Type of organization:** School **Major product:** K-12 education **Area of distribution:** Guymon, Oklahoma **Expertise:** Special education, psychology **Affiliations:** L.N.E.A. **Hob./spts.:** Craft work **SIC code:** 82 **Address:** 616 N. Crumley St., Guymon, OK 73942

WILKIE, DONALD W.
Industry: Education **Born:** June 30, 1931, Vancouver, British Columbia **Univ./degree:** M.S., University of British Columbia, 1966 **Current organization:** University of California San Diego (Retired) **Title:** SIO Aquarium Director Emeritus **Type of organization:** University **Major product:** Higher education **Area of distribution:** California

Expertise: Aquarium biology **Published works:** 20 papers, 1 book **Affiliations:** Past Member, A.A.Z.A.; A.M.E.; A.F.S.; A.S.E. **Hob./spts.:** Skeet shooting, competitive hunting and fishing, dog training **SIC code:** 82 **Address:** 4548 Cather Ave., San Diego, CA 92122 **E-mail:** dwilkie@ucsd.edu **Web address:** www.ucsd.edu

WILLIAM, GERGIS W.
Industry: Education **Born:** August 1, 1973, Alexandria, Egypt **Univ./degree:** B.S.C.E., Alexandria University, Egypt, 1995; M.S.C.E., West Virginia University, 1999; Ph.D., West Virginia University, 2003 **Current organization:** West Virginia University **Title:** Assistant Professor **Type of organization:** University **Major product:** Higher education **Area of distribution:** International **Expertise:** Civil engineering, advanced materials, pavement analysis and bridge design; Registered Professional Engineer, State of Ohio since 2004 **Honors/awards:** Mid-Atlantic Universities Transportation Center (Region 3) Student of the Year, 2003 **Published works:** 35 articles **Affiliations:** A.S.C.E.; Transportation Research Board; Data Analysis Workshop Group **Hob./spts.:** Outdoor activities, fishing, reading, travel **SIC code:** 82 **Address:** West Virginia University, Dept. of Civil & Environmental Engineering, P.O. Box 6103, Morgantown, WV 26506 **E-mail:** gergis.william@mail.wvu.edu

WILLIAMS, BILLY L.
Industry: Education **Born:** November 8, 1952, Knox City, Texas **Univ./degree:** M.S., Computer Information Systems, Arizona State University; Ph.D. **Current organization:** Arizona State University-MBA Online **Title:** Program Manager **Type of organization:** University **Major product:** Education **Area of distribution:** International **Expertise:** Client relations/sales, managing program **Published works:** 1 article **Affiliations:** A.M.C.I.S.; Decision Science Institute **Hob./spts.:** Movies, reading **SIC code:** 82 **Address:** Arizona State University MBA Online, 660 S. Mill Ave., Suite 310A, Tempe, AZ 85281 **E-mail:** billy.williams@asu.edu

WILLIAMS, DURAN O'BRIAN
Industry: Education **Born:** January 24, 1961, Cosby, Tennessee **Univ./degree:** Ed.D., Educational Administration, University of Tennessee, 2003 **Current organization:** Cosby High School **Title:** Principal **Type of organization:** High school **Major product:** Education **Area of distribution:** Cosby, Tennessee **Expertise:** Administration **Affiliations:** N.E.A.; Board Member, T.E.A. **Hob./spts.:** Long distance running **SIC code:** 82 **Address:** Cosby High School, 3320 Cosby Hwy., Cosby, TN 37722 **E-mail:** williamsdob@netscape.net

WILLIAMS, PAUL
Industry: Education **Born:** August 6, 1929, Jacksonville, Illinois **Univ./degree:** B.S., Economics, 1956; Honorary Doctorate of Human Letters, Illinois College **Current organization:** Paul Williams & Associates **Title:** Consultant, Buzan Licensed Instructor **Type of organization:** Training facility **Major product:** Training and education **Area of distribution:** International **Expertise:** Speed reading, mind mapping, range reading **Published works:** Book, "The Execution of Urban Renewal Projects" **Affiliations:** Past President, Kiwanis Club; Rockville Chamber of Commerce; Board Member on the Advisory Committee to the County Executive of Montgomery County **Hob./spts.:** Running, golf, reading, mind development and visual mapping **SIC code:** 82 **Address:** Paul Williams & Associates, 2900 N. Leisure World Blvd., #306, Silver Spring, MD 20906 **E-mail:** owilli7738@aol.com

WILLIAMS-AJALA, ABIMBOLA A.
Industry: Education **Born:** October 18, 1956, Nigeria **Univ./degree:** B.A., University of Ibadan, Nigeria; M.Ed., California State University; Ed.D. Candidate, Nova Southeastern University **Current organization:** Bursch Elementary School, Compton Unified School District **Title:** Principal **Type of organization:** Elementary school **Major product:** Elementary education **Area of distribution:** Compton, California **Expertise:** Educational leadership **Affiliations:** A.C.S.A.; A.C.U.S.A. **Hob./spts.:** Family, travel, dance **SIC code:** 82 **Address:** Bursch Elementary School, Compton Unified School District, 2505 W. 156 St., Compton, CA 90220 **E-mail:** aajala@compton.k12.ca.us **Web address:** www.compton.k12.ca.us

WILLIAMSON, JOYCE J.
Industry: Education **Born:** November 22, 1943, Kendallville, Indiana **Univ./degree:** B.S.+150, Elementary Education, Marion College, 1966 **Current organization:** Edison Local School District **Title:** Teacher **Type of organization:** Middle school **Major product:** Education **Area of distribution:** Toronto, Ohio **Expertise:** Math, science **Affiliations:** Finley Methodist Church; Education Association **Hob./spts.:** Gardening, camping **SIC code:** 82 **Address:** 11653 State Route 213 North, Toronto, OH 43964

WILSON, GRANT I.
Industry: Education **Born:** June 28, 1960, Washington, D.C. **Univ./degree:** B.S., 1986; M.S., 1989, Brigham Young University; Ph.D., Utah State University, 2001 **Current organization:** Dixie State University **Title:** Associate Professor **Type of organization:** University **Major product:** Higher education **Area of distribution:** National **Expertise:** Biology, physiology, anatomy, botany **Honors/awards:** Kodak of Colorado Excellence in Teaching Award, 1999; Aims Community College Favorite Faculty Award, 2001 & 2003 **Published works:** 4 articles **Affiliations:** A.P.S.; E.B.S. **Hob./spts.:** Hiking, tennis, piano **SIC code:** 82 **Address:** 3500 35th Ave., #181, Greeley, CO 80634

WINSLOW, NORMA M.
Industry: Education **Born:** October 18, 1942, Pawling, New York **Univ./degree:** B.S., Castleton State College; M.S., Plattsburgh State University **Current organization:** Hernando Christian Academy **Title:** Director of Student Services **Type of organization:** Private school **Major product:** Education **Area of distribution:** Florida **Expertise:** C.S.E.; A.I.S.; guidance **Honors/awards:** Who's Who in America **Affiliations:** Corinth Central School (Retired); Musical Director, Theatre Guide; Rotary Club; Paul Harris Fellow **Hob./spts.:** Family, music **SIC code:** 82 **Address:** 320 Center St., Corinth, NY 12822 **E-mail:** nwgolf@att.net **Web address:** www.hernandochristian.org

WITMER, JOHN R.
Industry: Education **Born:** December 26, 1949, Dallas, Texas **Univ./degree:** M.S., Library Science, East Texas State University, 1974 **Current organization:** Klein Independent School District **Title:** Librarian **Type of organization:** Public school **Major product:** Elementary and secondary school education **Area of distribution:** Houston, Texas **Expertise:** Audio visual software, equipment and copyright **Affiliations:** Life Member, Texas Library Association **Hob./spts.:** Church work, politics **SIC code:** 82 **Address:** 15114 Runbell Place, Houston, TX 77095 **E-mail:** johnwitmer@juno.com

WOJTCZAK, ANDRZEJ M.
Industry: Healthcare/medical education **Born:** December 12, 1933, Poland **Univ./degree:** M.D., 1955; Ph.D., 1962; D.M.Sc., 1964, Poznan Medical School, Poland **Current organization:** Institute for International Medical Education **Title:** Director **Type of organization:** Research, nonprofit **Major product:** Global essential requirements (competencies) for medical education and tools for their assessment **Area of distribution:** International **Expertise:** Medical Education, International Health, Internal Medicine (Nephrology) **Published works:** Over 300 including Medicine, Medical Education and International Health; Editor of 3 volume Textbook of Internal Medicine, 1983 (in Polish), 2nd edition, 1995 **Affiliations:** Association for Medical Education in Europe; World Health Organization; World Federation for Medical Education **Hob./spts.:** Music, historical and biographical books, tourism **SIC code:** 82 **Address:** Institute for International Medical Education, 106 Corporate Park Dr., Suite 100, White Plains, NY 10604-3817 **Phone:** (914)253-6633 **Fax:** (914)253-6644 **E-mail:** wojtczak@iime.org **Web address:** www.iime.org

WOLFE, DOUGLAS E.
Industry: Education **Born:** January 2, 1972, St. Mary, Pennsylvania **Univ./degree:** Ph.D., Pennsylvania State University, 2001 **Current organization:** The Applied Research Laboratory, Pennsylvania State University **Title:** Research Associate **Type of organization:** University **Major product:** Higher education, research **Area of distribution:** National **Expertise:** Scientist **Published works:** Journal of Materials; Journal of Surface Coatings and Technologies **Affiliations:** A.C.E.R.S.E.; T.M.S. **SIC code:** 82 **Address:** The Applied Research Laboratory, Pennsylvania State University, 119 Materials Research Institute, University Park, PA 16802 **E-mail:** dew125@psu.edu

WOLOSHCHUK, CANDACE D.
Industry: Education **Born:** January 11, 1947, Joliet, Illinois **Univ./degree:** M.Ed., Art Education, University of Hartford, Connecticut, 2002; C.A.G.S., Interdisciplinary Studies, Fitchburg State College **Current organization:** Hampden Wilbraham Regional School **Title:** Visual Arts Specialist/Director of Fine Arts (Fitchburg State College) **Type of organization:** Middle school (grades 7-8) **Major product:** Education **Area of distribution:** Massachusetts **Expertise:** Visual arts **Honors/awards:** Outstanding Visual /Performing Arts Educator of Massachusetts, 1988; Listed in Who's Who in America, 1996-1997, Who's Who in the World, 1997, Who's Who of American Women, 1997-1998 **Affiliations:** Massachusetts Teachers Association; National Art Educators Association **Hob./spts.:** Sailing, painting, needlework, riding and showing Quarter Horses **SIC code:** 82 **Address:** Hampden Wilbraham Regional School, 466 Stony Hill Rd., Wilbraham, MA 01095

WORTH, MARJORIE S.
Industry: Education **Born:** November 10, 1947, Indianapolis, Indiana **Univ./degree:** M.Ed., Indiana State University, 1973 **Current organization:** Rainbow Station Inc. **Title:** Director **Type of organization:** Child care center **Major product:** Child care/education **Area of distribution:** Sarasota, Florida **Expertise:** Teaching **Affiliations:** D.A.R.; N.A.E.Y.C.; National Association of Childcare Professionals **Hob./spts.:** Walking on the beach, family activities **SIC code:** 82 **Address:** Rainbow Station Inc., 3318 Wilkinson Rd., Sarasota, FL 34231 **E-mail:** rbstation@aol.com

WRENN, HOLLY LUND
Industry: Education **Born:** December 18, 1955, Waterbury, Connecticut **Univ./degree:** Educational Specialist Degree **Current organization:** Wolcott Public Schools **Title:** Principal **Type of organization:** Elementary school **Major product:** Elementary school education **Area of distribution:** Waterbury, Connecticut **Expertise:** Adminis-

tration, curriculum development **Hob./spts.:** Golf, bowling, reading, family, children **SIC code:** 82 **Address:** 173 Blanchard St., Waterbury, CT 06705 **E-mail:** wrennh@wolcottps.org **Web address:** www.wolcott.org

WRIGHT, HERBERT F.
Industry: Education **Born:** July 19, 1917, Worcester, Massachusetts **Univ./degree:** Ph.D., Organics and Biochemistry, Cornell University, 1944 **Current organization:** University of New Haven **Title:** Professor Emeritus **Type of organization:** University **Major product:** Teaching, research **Area of distribution:** Westhaven, Connecticut **Expertise:** Nutritional biochemistry **Hob./spts.:** Stock market, oriental alternative electromagnetic medicine **SIC code:** 82 **Address:** University of New Haven, Boston Post Rd., West Haven, CT 06516 **E-mail:** hfwright2000@yahoo.com

WROBLEWSKI, KRZYSZTOF P.
Industry: Education **Born:** February 25, 1952, Lodz, Poland **Univ./degree:** Ph.D., Polish Academy of Sciences, 1985 **Current organization:** University of Pennsylvania **Title:** Professor **Type of organization:** University **Major product:** Higher education **Area of distribution:** International **Expertise:** Biochemistry, biophysics **Honors/awards:** Honorary Membership, Polish Ultrasound Society, 2001 **Published works:** 100+ publications **Affiliations:** N.Y.A.S., I.S.M.R.M., A.M.I.A. **Hob./spts.:** Sailing **SIC code:** 82 **Address:** University of Pennsylvania, Room 96, John Morgan Bldg., Philadelphia, PA 19104 **E-mail:** krzyszto@mail.med.upenn.edu

WU, FEN FEN
Industry: Education **Univ./degree:** Ph.D., University of Pittsburgh, 2001 **Current organization:** University of Texas Southwestern Medical Center **Title:** Ph.D. **Type of organization:** University **Major product:** Higher education, research **Area of distribution:** National **Expertise:** Biomedical science **Honors/awards:** Regional Guest Speaker **Published works:** Journal articles **Affiliations:** A.S.H.G.; A.S.C.B.; S.N.S. **Hob./spts.:** Jogging **SIC code:** 82 **Address:** University of Texas Southwestern Medical Center, NB4 Room 217, 6000 Harry Hines Blvd., Dallas, TX 75390 **E-mail:** wufenfen@hotmail.com

WU, JI
Industry: Education **Univ./degree:** Ph.D., Mechanical Engineering, University of Maryland, 2003 **Current organization:** University of Maryland, Dept. of Mechanical Engineering **Title:** Ph.D. **Type of organization:** University **Major product:** Higher education **Area of distribution:** National **Expertise:** R&D, consulting, engineering **Published works:** 2 book chapters **Affiliations:** I.E.E.E. **SIC code:** 82 **Address:** 8150 Lake Crest Dr., #518, Greenbelt, MD 20770 **E-mail:** jiwu@umd.edu

XU, JUNCHENG
Industry: Education **Born:** January, 1975, Beijing, China **Univ./degree:** M.S., Optical Engineering, Tsinghua University, China, 2000; Ph.D., Electrical Engineering, Virginia Polytechnic Institute, 2005 **Current organization:** Virginia Polytechnic Institute and State University **Title:** Ph.D. **Type of organization:** University **Major product:** Higher education, research **Area of distribution:** Virginia **Expertise:** Engineering, R&D **Affiliations:** I.E.E.E. **Hob./spts.:** Tennis, chess, guitar, travel **SIC code:** 82 **Address:** Virginia Polytechnic Institute and State University, 460 Turner St., Suite 303, Blacksburg, VA 24061 **E-mail:** juxu1@vt.edu

YAKOPEC JR., STEPHEN
Industry: Law **Univ./degree:** A.B., Harvard University, 1980; J.D., University of Pittsburgh Law School, 1984 **Current organization:** Stephen Yakopec Jr., Attorney at Law **Title:** Attorney at Law **Type of organization:** Law firm **Major product:** Legal services **Area of distribution:** Pennsylvania **Expertise:** Municipal, civil, litigation **Published works:** Articles **Affiliations:** A.T.L.A.; Westmoreland County Bar Association; Allegheny Bar Association; West Pennsylvania Bar Association **Hob./spts.:** Family, youth sports, football, soccer **SIC code:** 82 **Address:** Stephen Yakopec Jr., Attorney at Law, 1725 Fifth Avenue, Arnold, PA 15068 **E-mail:** bcylaw@verizon.net

YAKOVLEV, DMITRY Y.
Industry: Education **Born:** May 12, 1952, Moscow, Russia **Univ./degree:** Ph.D., Institute of Bio-Organic Chemistry, 1979 **Current organization:** University of Kansas **Title:** Ph.D. **Type of organization:** University **Major product:** Higher education **Area of distribution:** Kansas **Expertise:** Biochemistry **Affiliations:** American Chemical Society **Hob./spts.:** Boating, listening to music **SIC code:** 82 **Address:** University of Kansas, Dept. of Chemistry, 1251 Wescoe Hall Dr., 6037 Malott Hall, Lawrence, KS 66045 **E-mail:** dyakov@ukans.edu

YAMAMOTO, JANET K.
Industry: Education **Born:** November 9, 1953, Tokyo, Japan **Univ./degree:** Ph.D., Microbiology, University of Texas Medical Branch, Galveston, 1981 **Current organization:** University of Florida, College of Veterinary Medicine, Dept. of Pathobiology **Title:** Professor **Type of organization:** University **Major product:** Higher education, research in AIDS vaccine development **Area of distribution:** International **Expertise:** Immunology and virology **Affiliations:** A.A.I.; New York Academy of Sciences; International AIDS Society; Clinical Immunology Society **Hob./spts.:** Listening to classical music **SIC code:** 82 **Address:** University of Florida, College of Veterinary Medicine, Dept. of Pathobiology, 2015 S.W. 16th Ave., Gainesville, FL 32608 **E-mail:** yamamotoj@mail.vetmed.ufl.edu

YAN, SHIKUI
Industry: Education **Born:** China **Univ./degree:** B.S., Nuclear Physics/Technology 1996; B.S. Economic Management, 1997; M.S., Nuclear Physics/Technology, 1999, University of Science and Technology of China; M.S., Electrical Engineering, 2002; Ph.D. Candidate, Electrical Engineering, Univ. of Connecticut **Current organization:** University of Connecticut **Title:** Research Assistant **Type of organization:** University **Major product:** Higher education **Area of distribution:** International **Expertise:** System engineering; bioinstruments on ultrasound and optics **Honors/awards:** Summer Research Fellowship from Electrical and Computer Department, University of Connecticut, 2002; winner, USTC First Software Competition, 1995 **Published works:** Co-author of numerous papers and articles, including: "Simultaneous near infrared diffusive light and ultrasound imaging", Applied Optics, Vol. 40, No. 34, 6367-6380, Dec., 2001; "The effect of source power on image clarity in optical coherent tomography", J. Dental Res. 80:694, 2001 **Affiliations:** I.E.E.E.; S.P.I.E. **Hob./spts.:** Sports, music, photography **SIC code:** 82 **Address:** University of Connecticut, Electrical & Computer Engineering, 260 Glenbrook Rd., U-157, Storrs, CT 06269 **E-mail:** skyan@engr.uconn.edu

YANG, PING-YI
Industry: Education **Born:** January 12, 1938, Taiwan **Univ./degree:** Ph.D., Oklahoma State University, 1972 **Current organization:** University of Hawaii at Manoa **Title:** Professor of Bioenvironmental Engineering **Type of organization:** University **Major product:** Higher education **Area of distribution:** International **Expertise:** Environmental engineering **Affiliations:** International Water Association; Water Environmental Federation; American Society of Civil Engineers; Association of Environmental Engineering and Science Professors **SIC code:** 82 **Address:** University of Hawaii at Manoa, Dept. of Molecular Biosciences & Bioengineering, 3050 Maile Way, Honolulu, HI 96822 **E-mail:** pingyi@hawaii.edu

YARBROUGH, WILLIAM J.
Industry: Education **Born:** June 5, 1946, Hot Springs, Arkansas **Univ./degree:** A.A., University of Maryland **Current organization:** University of Notre Dame **Title:** Associate Director, Notre Dame Food Services **Type of organization:** University **Major product:** Higher education/food services **Area of distribution:** Indiana **Expertise:** Department operations; Certified Food Management Professional **Affiliations:** N.A.C.U.F.S. **SIC code:** 82 **Address:** University of Notre Dame, P.O. Box 1043, Notre Dame, IN 46556-1043 **E-mail:** wyarbrou@nd.edu

YIN, LI
Industry: Medical **Born:** February 22, 1962, Beijing, China **Univ./degree:** M.D., Beijing Medical University, Beijing, China; Ph.D., University of Strathclyde, Glasgow, Scotland, UK **Current organization:** University of Florida **Title:** Assistant Professor **Type of organization:** University **Major product:** Higher education, research **Area of distribution:** International **Expertise:** Pathology **Hob./spts.:** Gardening **SIC code:** 82 **Address:** 6717 S.W. 81st Terrace, Gainesville, FL 32608 **E-mail:** yin@pathology.ufl.edu

YOCUM, HARRISON G.
Industry: Education **Born:** April 2, 1923, Pennsylvania **Univ./degree:** B.S., Horticulture/Botany, Pennsylvania State University, 1955; M.S., Horticulture/Botany, Rutgers University, 1960 **Current organization:** University of Tennessee/University of Arizona (Ret.) **Title:** Professor Emeritus **Type of organization:** University **Major product:** Higher education **Area of distribution:** International **Expertise:** Horticulture, botany **Honors/awards:** Life Membership Award, The Tucson Botanical Garden, 1975; President's Award, Men's Garden Club, 1991; Sig Boysen Gold Award, 1992; Gardner Award, Arizona - New Mexico Region, 1996; Who's Who in Science and Engineering, 1994-95; "Best of Pima" Achievement Award, 2001; Meritorious Achievement for Horticulture and Botany for Who's Who in the 21st Century, Cambridge, England, 2001; Unique Gardener Award, 2000 **Affiliations:** Numerous including: Deming Mineral Society; Tucson Gem & Mineral Society; Cactus and Succulent Society of America; Member Emeritus, Garden Writers Association of America; American Horticultural Society; President, Men's Garden Club of Tucson, 1991; Charter Member, International Palm Society; National Geographic Society; Life Member, Penn State Alumni Association; Arizona Preservation Foundation; Arizona State Fraternal Order of Police **SIC code:** 82 **Address:** 1628 N. Jefferson Ave., Tucson, AZ 85712-4204

YOUNG, JAMES HARVEY
Industry: Education **Born:** September 8, 1915, Brooklyn, New York **Univ./degree:** Ph.D., American History, University of Illinois, Urbana, 1941 **Current organization:** Emory University **Title:** Candler Professor Emeritus of American Social History **Type of organization:** University **Major product:** Higher education **Area of distribution:** Georgia **Expertise:** Writing, teaching, lecturing **Published works:** Several book

including: "The Toadstool Millionaire", The Medical Messiahs", "American Health Quackery, Collective Essays" **Affiliations:** American Institute of the History of Pharmacy **Hob./spts.:** Family, reading manuscripts and writing **SIC code:** 82 **Address:** 272 Heaton Park Dr., Decatur, GA 30030-1027 **E-mail:** jyouno2@emory.edu

YOUNG, RALPH A.
Industry: Education **Born:** Washington County, Colorado **Univ./degree:** B.S., Agronomy, Colorado State University; Ph.D., Agronomy/Soil Science, Cornell University, 1953 **Title:** Professor of Soil Science Emeritus (Retired), University of Nevada, Reno **Type of organization:** University **Major product:** Higher education **Area of distribution:** Colorado **Expertise:** Teaching, research and administration, soil science and agronomy **Published works:** Journal articles **Affiliations:** American Society of Agronomy; American Soil Science Society; Western Soil Science Society **Hob./spts.:** Volunteer tax work, volunteer work for seniors and low income people **SIC code:** 82 **Address:** 2229 Stagecoach Rd., Grand Junction, CO 81503 **E-mail:** ryoung@acsol.net

YOUNIS, NASHWAN T.
Industry: Education **Born:** August 13, 1955, Mosul, Iraq **Univ./degree:** B.S.M.E., Mosul University, Iraq; M.S., University of Nebraska; Ph.D., Engineering Mechanics, Iowa State University, 1988 **Current organization:** Indiana University-Purdue University Fort Wayne **Title:** Professor **Type of organization:** University **Major product:** Higher Education **Area of distribution:** Indiana **Expertise:** Engineering, experimental stress analysis **Honors/awards:** Outstanding Educator of the Year, A.S.E.E., local chapter **Published works:** Journal articles **Affiliations:** A.S.M.E.; A.S.E.E. **Hob./spts.:** Tennis, running **SIC code:** 82 **Address:** Indiana University-Purdue University Fort Wayne, Engineering Dept., 2101 E. Coliseum Blvd., Ft. Wayne, IN 46805 **E-mail:** younis@engr.ipfw.edu

YOURTEE, DAVID M.
Industry: Education **Born:** October 16, 1937, St. Louis, Missouri **Univ./degree:** B.S., Chemistry, University of Missouri; Ph.D., Pharmacology and Pharmaceutical Science, University of Missouri, 1973 **Current organization:** University of Missouri at Kansas City **Title:** Full Professor of Research; Professor Emeritus **Type of organization:** University **Major product:** Higher education **Expertise:** Toxicore, biomaterial, bio-compatibility testing **Published works:** 110 articles **Affiliations:** International Association of Dental Research, Society for Biomaterials **Hob./spts.:** Backpacking, fishing **SIC code:** 82 **Address:** University of Missouri at Kansas City, 2411 Holmes St., Kansas City, MO 64108-2792 **E-mail:** yourteed@umkc.edu

YU, EDWARD W.
Industry: Education **Born:** November 5, 1963, Hong Kong, China **Univ./degree:** Ph.D., Biophysics, University of Michigan, 1997 **Current organization:** Iowa State University **Title:** Ph.D., Assistant Professor **Type of organization:** University **Major product:** Higher education, research **Area of distribution:** Iowa **Expertise:** Biophysics **Affiliations:** Biophysical Society **Hob./spts.:** Travel, physical fitness, gardening **SIC code:** 82 **Address:** Iowa State University, Dept. of Physics & Astronomy, Suite A115 Physics Hall, Ames, IA 50011 **E-mail:** ewyu@iastate.edu

ZAGAGLIA, ANN MARIE
Industry: Education **Born:** December 19, 1948, Bronx, New York **Univ./degree:** M.S., Education, College of New Rochelle, New York, 1985 **Current organization:** St. Barnabas Elementary School **Title:** Principal **Type of organization:** Catholic elementary school **Major product:** Elementary school education **Area of distribution:** Bronx, New York **Expertise:** Early childhood education, administration **Affiliations:** National Catholic Education Association; Catholic School Administrators Association of New York State; The Middle States Association of Colleges and Schools Accreditation **Hob./spts.:** Music, singing, parish choir **SIC code:** 82 **Address:** St. Barnabas Elementary School, 413 E. 241st St., Bronx, NY 10470 **E-mail:** b229@adnyeducation.org **Web address:** www.stbarnabasschool.org

ZAMBONE, ALANA M.
Industry: Education **Born:** September 17, 1952, Vineland, New Jersey **Univ./degree:** Ph.D., Special Education, Vanderbilt University, 1989 **Current organization:** Educational Development Center, Inc. **Title:** Ph.D. **Type of organization:** Consulting, evaluation, project development **Major product:** Educational research, professional development, publications and materials **Area of distribution:** Massachusetts **Expertise:** Education, special education **Affiliations:** C.E.C.; A.S.C.D.; A.E.R.A. **Hob./spts.:** Scuba diving **SIC code:** 82 **Address:** Educational Development Center, Inc., 55 Chapel St., Newton, MA 02458 **E-mail:** azambone@earthlink.net

ZAVALIANGOS, ANTONIOS
Industry: Education **Born:** March 26, 1963, Volos, Greece **Univ./degree:** B.S., Mechanical Engineering, National Technical University, Greece, 1986; M.S.C.E., Columbia University; Ph.D., Massachusetts Institute of Technology, 1992 **Current organization:** Drexel University, Dept. of Materials Science & Engineering **Title:** Professor **Type of organization:** University **Major product:** Higher education **Area of distribution:** National **Expertise:** Finite element analysis, powder technology; consulting for pharmaceutical industry **Published works:** Journal papers, articles **Affiliations:** A.S.M.E.; A.S.M. International; T.M.S. **Hob./spts.:** Collecting fountain pens **SIC code:** 82 **Address:** Drexel University, Dept. of Materials Science & Engineering, 32nd & Chestnut Sts., Philadelphia, PA 19104 **E-mail:** azavalia@coe.drexel.edu

ZAYAS, MIRIAM
Industry: Education **Born:** September 25, 1950, Puerto Rico **Univ./degree:** B.S., University of Puerto Rico; M.S., Pontificia Universidad Catolica de Puerto Rico; Ed.D., Inter American University, 1995 **Current organization:** Pontifical Catholic University **Title:** Ed.D. **Type of organization:** University **Major product:** Higher education **Area of distribution:** Puerto Rico **Expertise:** Special education, elementary education and curriculum **Honors/awards:** Phi Delta Kappa; A.S.C.D. **Hob./spts.:** Family, reading, water color painting **SIC code:** 82 **Address:** Pontifical Catholic University, Dept. of Education, Graduate School, 2250 Ave. Las Americas, Suite 586, Ponce, PR 00717-0777

ZEIN, JOE
Industry: Medical **Born:** February 27, 1971, Lebanon **Univ./degree:** M.D., Lebanon, 1998 **Current organization:** The University of Oklahoma **Title:** M.D. **Type of organization:** University **Major product:** Higher education, medical research, healthcare services **Area of distribution:** Oklahoma **Affiliations:** A.M.A. **Hob./spts.:** Swimming, fishing **SIC code:** 82 **Address:** 6008 N. Pennsylvania Ave., #16, Oklahoma City, OK 73112 **E-mail:** joezein@hotmail.com

ZELLNER, SHARON MICHELLE
Industry: Education **Born:** September 4, 1958, Cleveland, Ohio **Univ./degree:** B.S., Education, University of Cincinnati, 1981; M.S., Rehabilitation Counseling, Wright State University, 1988 **Current organization:** Xenia Community Schools/McKinley Elementary Schools **Title:** Resource Room Teacher (special needs teacher) **Type of organization:** Elementary school **Major product:** Education (k-5th grade) **Area of distribution:** Xenia, Ohio **Expertise:** Multi-handicapped, special needs children **Affiliations:** C.C.E.; Phi Delta Kappa; Alpha Kappa Alpha; American Association of University Women **Hob./spts.:** Walking, racquetball, reading **SIC code:** 82 **Address:** Xenia Community Schools/McKinley Elementary Schools, 819 Colorado Dr., Xenia, OH 45385 **E-mail:** szkoala@aol.com

ZIEGELMUELLER, GEORGE WILLIAM
Industry: Education **Born:** July 28, 1930, Indianapolis, Indiana **Univ./degree:** B.A., Communications, DePauw University, 1952; M.A., Communications, Southern Illinois University, 1954; Ph.D., Communications, Northwestern University, 1960 **Current organization:** Wayne State University **Title:** Professor **Type of organization:** University **Major product:** Higher education **Area of distribution:** Michigan **Expertise:** Argumentation and debate **Honors/awards:** Distinguished Professor Award; National Communication Association Ecroyd Award as Outstanding College Teacher of Communication, 1998; Carnegie Foundation ACE Award as Outstanding University Professor, State of Michigan, 2000; National Delta Sigma Rhr Tau Kappa Alpha Distinguished Alumni Award; President's Excellence in Teaching Award; American Forensic Association's Ziegelmueller Career Coach Award 1999 **Published works:** 20 articles and chapters and 3 books **Affiliations:** National Communication Association; American Forensic Association; Michigan Speech Communication Association; International Debate Education Association; Central States Communication Association **Hob./spts.:** Travel, reading **SIC code:** 82 **Address:** Dept. of Communications, Detroit, MI 48201 **E-mail:** ziegelmueller@wayne.edu **Web address:** www.wayne.edu

ZVARA, ANDREW A.
Industry: Education **Born:** May 16, 1941, Lorain, Ohio **Univ./degree:** M.A., Philosophy, University of Maryland, 1974 **Current organization:** A.A.Z. Consulting for Education Working for Results **Title:** President/Founder **Type of organization:** Non-profit **Major product:** School development **Area of distribution:** International **Expertise:** Consulting, education, private schools **Published works:** Article in "Philosophical Studies", 1973 **Affiliations:** Leadership Montgomery; Association for Supervision and Curriculum Development; The Family Support Center; Round House Theatre; Green Acres School; Educators Benefit Services **Hob./spts.:** Reading, golf, theatre **SIC code:** 82 **Address:** 12916 Shaw Pl., Silver Spring, MD 20904 **E-mail:** zvara@erols.com

Organizations

ABBATTISTA, STEVEN
Industry: Consulting **Born:** June 9, 1970, Teaneck, New Jersey **Univ./degree:** B.S., Columbia University 1992, M.S., Mechanical Engineering, Stevens Institute of Technology, 1995 **Current organization:** O'Dea, Lynch, Abbattista Consulting Engineers, PC **Title:** Vice President **Type of organization:** Consulting firm **Major product:** Mechanical, electrical, structural, plumbing **Area of distribution:** National **Expertise:** Engineering **Affiliations:** A.S.P.E.; A.I.A. **Hob./spts.:** Golf, football, travel **SIC code:** 87 **Address:** O'Dea, Lynch, Abbattista Consulting Engineers, PC, 50 Broadway, Hawthorne, NY 10532 **E-mail:** sabbattista@olace.com

ABDOU, HOSSAM M.
Industry: Consulting **Born:** November 4, 1959, Cairo, Egypt **Univ./degree:** Ph.D., University of Michigan, 1990 **Current organization:** Alfred Benesch & Co. **Title:** Vice President **Type of organization:** Consulting Firm **Major product:** Structural and civil engineering design **Area of distribution:** Illinois, Michigan, Wisconsin, Pennsylvania **Expertise:** Bridge Engineering **Published works:** 4 articles **Affiliations:** A.C.I.; A.S.C.E.; I.A.B.S.E. **Hob./spts.:** Swimming, volleyball, woodworking **SIC code:** 87 **Address:** Alfred Benesch & Co., 205 N. Michigan Ave., Suite 2400, Chicago, IL 60601 **E-mail:** habdou@benesch.com **Web address:** www.benesch.com

ABELL, LAWRENCE
Industry: Architecture **Born:** September 27, 1941, La Plata, Maryland **Univ./degree:** B.A., Civil Engineering, 1964; M.A., Civil Engineering, 1972, University of Maryland **Current organization:** Lawrence Abell & Associates **Title:** CEO **Type of organization:** Architectural firm **Major product:** Construction and design **Area of distribution:** National **Expertise:** Apartments, housing, colleges, medical facilities, churches, firehouses, shopping centers **Affiliations:** American Institute of Architecture; Natural Council of Architecture **Hob./spts.:** Boating, skiing **SIC code:** 87 **Address:** Lawrence Abell & Associates, 11769 Western View Dr., La Plata, MD 20646 **E-mail:** labell@laa.cc

ABODALO, JAMAL F.
Industry: Consulting **Born:** September 14, 1956, Kuwait **Univ./degree:** M.S., Chemical Engineering, University of Austun, United Kingdom, 1979 **Title:** Vice President, Marketing & Development **Major product:** Provider of engineering and architectural services to high tech industries **Area of distribution:** National **Expertise:** Marketing development **Affiliations:** A.I.C.E.; N.A.C.E.; I.S.P.; T.A.P.P.I. **Hob./spts.:** Deep sea fishing, building model trains **SIC code:** 87 **Address:** 2 Rick Rd., Reading, PA 19607 **E-mail:** jabodalo@uaigroup.com

ABOURAFEH, ISSAM M.
Industry: Engineering **Born:** November 25, 1959, Lebanon **Univ./degree:** M.S., Civil Engineering, West Virginia University, 1984 **Current organization:** IMA Engineering, P.C. **Title:** President **Type of organization:** Engineering firm **Major product:** Residential and commercial architecture and engineering **Area of distribution:** New York **Expertise:** Engineering, consulting **Affiliations:** A.S.C.E.; E.S.T.M. **SIC code:** 87 **Address:** IMA Engineering, P.C., 123-23 82 Ave., Kew Gardens, NY 11415 **E-mail:** issam@ima-architects.com

ABUJAWDEH, SASEEN S.
Industry: Engineering **Univ./degree:** M.E., Structural Engineering; B.E., Stevens Institute of Technology, 1988 **Current organization:** The Cedars Group, Inc. Consulting Engineers **Title:** President **Type of organization:** Consulting engineering firm **Major product:** Structural and civil design **Area of distribution:** New Jersey, New York, Pennsylvania **Expertise:** Engineering; P.E., Planning, P.P. in New York, New Jersey, Pennsylvania, Connecticut, Ohio, Florida **Affiliations:** A.S.C.E.; A.C.I. **Hob./spts.:** Tennis, golf, jogging, basketball, travel **SIC code:** 87 **Address:** The Cedars Group, Inc. Consulting Engineers, 1000 Route 9 North, Suite 205, Woodbridge, NJ 07095 **E-mail:** cgi1@aol.com

ACOSTA, EMMA
Industry: Government **Born:** June 17, 1953, El Paso, Texas **Univ./degree:** M.A., Business Administration, Webster University, 2001 **Current organization:** City of El Paso, Solid Waste Management Dept. **Title:** Deputy Director **Type of organization:** Municipal government **Major product:** Solid waste management **Area of distribution:** Texas **Expertise:** Environment, marketing, human resources **Honors/awards:** Reads Award, YMCA **Published works:** The El Paso Times **Affiliations:** S.W.A.N.A.; M.S.W.M.A.; K.A.B.; K.T.B. **Hob./spts.:** Golf, physical fitness, dance **SIC code:** 87 **Address:** City of El Paso, Solid Waste Management Dept., 7969 San Paulo Dr., El Paso, TX 79907 **E-mail:** aenriquezea@aol.com

ACOSTA, JOSÉ R.
Industry: Government **Born:** December 18, 1955, Aquadilla, Puerto Rico **Univ./degree:** M.S., Systems Engineering, George Mason University **Current organization:** Pension Benefit Guaranty Corp. **Title:** IT Systems Configuration Manager **Type of organization:** Federal corporation **Major product:** Pension benefits, annuity benefits, disability benefits **Area of distribution:** National **Expertise:** Systems engineering, information technology for engineering **Affiliations:** International Society of Configuration Managers **Hob./spts.:** Soccer, tennis, billiards, skiing, oil painting **SIC code:** 87 **Address:** Pension Benefit Guaranty Corp., 1200 K. St. N.W., Washington, DC 20005 **E-mail:** JRacosta@verizon.net

ADAMS, FRANK S.
Industry: Religion **Born:** March 16, 1944, Ludlow, Massachusetts **Univ./degree:** B.S., Nuclear/Metallurgical Engineering, University of Missouri at Rolla, 1966; M.Div., Western School of Theology, 1980; S.T.M., Developmental Psychiatry, Jesuit School of Theology at Berkeley, 1982 **Current organization:** Christ the King American Catholic Church **Title:** Most Reverend Bishop **Type of organization:** Independent Catholic Church **Major product:** Sacraments **Area of distribution:** National **Expertise:** Spiritual counseling **Published works:** "Theological and Nuclear Power Debate", a monograph written for the Theological Science Institute **Affiliations:** Federation of Independent and Orthodox Bishops; American Society of Mechanical Engineers **Hob./spts.:** Fishing, studying economics and nursing **SIC code:** 86 **Address:** 1912 Dakota Court, Ft. Collins, CO 80528 **E-mail:** fadams7330@aol.com

ADAMS, JEFF
Industry: Religion **Born:** January 6, 1967, Shreveport, Louisiana **Univ./degree:** BKZ, Ozark Christian College, 1993; add edu., Houston Baptist University, Summit Theological Seminary, Southeast Christian Church, Louisville; Covey Leadership Center, A.D. Banker & Co. **Current organization:** College Street Christian Church **Title:** Pastor **Type of organization:** Church **Major product:** Religious services and leadership **Area of distribution:** Lacey, Washington **Expertise:** Motivational speaking, consulting, counseling, leadership **Honors/awards:** President, Knights for Christ, 1984-85; Voted Outstanding Leader by peers, 1985; Scholarships granted to Dallas Christian College & Mid-South Christian College, 1981-84; Recognized as an outstanding community service leader, Ozark Christian College, 1988 **Published works:** 4 books, numerous local and national articles, mass-distributed series on Revelation (cassettes); syllabus curriculum, Ozark Christian College and Southeast Houston Bible Institute; various consumer product and automobile reviews; interviewed by Fox News **Affiliations:** Lacey Mid-Day Lion's Club; Executive Board Member, Big Rock Evangelistic Association, 1994-95; Executive Board Member, Southeast Houston Evangelizing Association, 1998-2000; Board of Regents, Dallas Christian College, 1996-2000; Charter Member, The American Association of Christian Counselors, 1993-94; Vice President, Ozark Area Men's Fellowship, 1994-95 **Hob./spts.:** Writing, outdoor activities, sports **SIC code:** 86 **Address:** College Street Christian Church, 3816 College St. S.E., Lacey, WA 98503 **E-mail:** info@cschristian.org **Web address:** www.cschristian.org

ADAMS, MICHAEL K.
Industry: Consulting **Born:** August 7, 1948, Trappe, Maryland **Univ./degree:** M.S., Civil Engineering, University of Maryland, 1982 **Current organization:** Battelle **Title:** Anti-Terrorism/Force Protection Program Manager **Type of organization:** Consulting firm **Major product:** Design and testing, studies and reports **Area of distribution:** National **Expertise:** Environmental engineering **Published works:** 30+ articles **Affiliations:** N.A.E.P.; Association of the U.S. Army; Academy of Board Certified Environmental Professionals, Inc. **SIC code:** 87 **Address:** Battelle Fort McPherson Operation, USARC-G3, Ft. McPherson, GA 30330 **E-mail:** adamsm@battelle.org **Web address:** www.battelle.org

ADAMS, SAMUEL G.
Industry: Biotechnology **Born:** January 12, 1952, Newburgh, Indiana **Univ./degree:** B.S., University of Evansville, 1970 **Current organization:** Vaxgen, Inc. **Title:** Director Procurement **Type of organization:** Research/development/manufacturing **Major product:** Vaccines **Area of distribution:** International **Expertise:** Purchasing, contracts **Published works:** 1 patent **Hob./spts.:** Classical music **SIC code:** 87 **Address:** Vaxgen, Inc., 1000 Marina Blvd., Brisbane, CA 94005-1841 **E-mail:** sadams@vaxgen.com

AHMED, AHMED F. KAMEL
Industry: Engineering/consulting **Born:** January 4, 1940, Alexandria, Egypt **Univ./degree:** M.S., Mechanical Engineering, Alexandria University, 1967 **Current organization:** Radian Inc. **Title:** Project Manager **Type of organization:** Engineering services **Major product:** Research and development, consulting, contracts **Area of distribution:** International **Expertise:** Engineering **Hob./spts.:** Tennis, walking, jogging, swimming **SIC code:** 87 **Address:** Radian Inc., 5845 Richmond Hwy., Alexandria, VA 22303 **E-mail:** akamel@radianinc.com

AHMED, RASHID
Industry: Marine/society **Born:** May 14, 1945, India **Univ./degree:** B.S., Mechanical Engineering, Western Kennedy University, Idaho, 1993 **Current organization:** American Bureau of Shipping **Title:** Classification Surveyor **Type of organization:** Ship classification society **Major product:** Establishment and administration of standards (Rules) for the design, construction and operational maintenance of marine vessels and structures **Area of distribution:** International **Expertise:** Engineering, inspection

and verification; Chief Engineering License, 1973 **Affiliations:** American Society of Mechanical Engineers **Hob./spts.:** Fishing **SIC code:** 86 **Address:** American Bureau of Shipping, 15311 W. Vantagh Pkwy., Suite 220, Houston, TX 77032 **E-mail:** rahmed@eagle.org

ALBRIGHT, NEAL BASIL
Industry: Consulting **Born:** April 14, 1920, Oklahoma **Univ./degree:** B.S., Civil Engineering, University of Arkansas, 1950 **Current organization:** Neal B. Albright, Inc. **Title:** President **Type of organization:** Consulting engineering **Major product:** Structural engineering and civil engineering **Area of distribution:** 4 states (Arkansas, Missouri, Oklahoma, Texas) **Expertise:** Engineering **Published works:** Write-up **Affiliations:** A.S.C.E.; Baptist, **Hob./spts.:** Woodwork, gardening **SIC code:** 87 **Address:** Neal B. Albright, Inc., 2863 Old Missouri Rd., Fayetteville, AR 72703 **E-mail:** neadora@aol.com

ALEXANDER, BENJAMIN R.
Industry: Chemical **Born:** October 12, 1963, Madison, Wisconsin **Univ./degree:** B.S., Computer Science, Pamona College, 1985 **Current organization:** Ar Qule, Inc. **Title:** Senior Scientist **Type of organization:** Research **Major product:** Drug discovery **Area of distribution:** National **Expertise:** Drug discovery, computational chemistry **Published works:** Numerous articles **Affiliations:** A.C.S. **Hob./spts.:** Computer programming, entheogenic research, bovine contemplation **SIC code:** 87 **Address:** Ar Qule, Inc., 15 Sycamore St., Somerville, MA 02143 **E-mail:** bralexander@attbi.com

ALEXANDER, DESMA CATHY
Industry: Engineering **Univ./degree:** B.A., Howard University, 1999; M.A., M.I.T., 2001 **Current organization:** Hovensa, LLC **Title:** Project Engineer **Type of organization:** Architectural/engineering **Major product:** Designs **Area of distribution:** International **Expertise:** Engineering **Honors/awards:** Who's Who of American Students **Published works:** Thesis, poems **Affiliations:** A.S.C.E.; National Society of Black Engineers **SIC code:** 87 **Address:** Calvin Giordano Inc., 1800 Eller Dr., Ft. Lauderdale, FL 33316 **E-mail:** desma@alum.mit.edu

ALFORD, FRANK R.
Industry: Architectural/engineering **Born:** November 23, 1962, Boston, Massachusetts **Current organization:** Alford Design & Drafting **Title:** Owner/Designer **Type of organization:** Architecture, engineering **Major product:** Plans for home or room additions **Area of distribution:** California **Expertise:** Custom home designs; Certifications-AutoCAD Instructor and Designer **Affiliations:** Murrieta Chamber of Commerce **Hob./spts.:** Deep sea fishing, martial arts (Black Belt) **SIC code:** 87 **Address:** Alford Design & Drafting, 41686 Magnolia St., Murrieta, CA 92562 **E-mail:** ADDrafting@aol.com

ALIPIO, ELPIDIO B.
Industry: Automotive/consulting **Born:** December 1, 1946 **Univ./degree:** Ph.D. **Current organization:** Ge Fanuc Automation **Title:** Project Implementation Application Engineer **Type of organization:** Power tran consulting firm **Major product:** Software, CNC, PLC applications **Area of distribution:** International **Expertise:** Engineering **Hob./spts.:** Golf, tennis, scuba diving **SIC code:** 87 **Address:** Ge Fanuc Automation, 25900 Telegraph Rd., Southfield, MI 48034 **E-mail:** elpidio.alipio@gefanuc.com

ALMONTE MEDINA, LEONIDAS
Industry: Testing/paper **Born:** February 20, 1951, Dominican Republic **Univ./degree:** M.S., Mayaguez University, 1995 **Current organization:** Turabo Testing **Title:** Engineer **Type of organization:** Testing lab **Major product:** Paper **Area of distribution:** Puerto Rico **Expertise:** Engineering **Affiliations:** A.S.C.E. **Hob./spts.:** Basketball, Ping-Pong **SIC code:** 87 **Address:** Turabo Testing, P.O. Box 6705, Caguas, PR 00726

ALVES, JOSE F.
Industry: Social services **Born:** November 8, 1970, Brooklyn, New York **Univ./degree:** B.A., City College of New York, 1996 **Current organization:** Lutheran Social Services **Title:** Assistant Director **Type of organization:** Nonprofit social service agency **Major product:** Provide services to mentally ill, substance abusers, formerly homeless, MICA **Area of distribution:** New York, New York **Expertise:** Assistant director, administration; Certificate, Basic Budgeting and Accounting for Real Estate Managers; Certificate, Basic Marketing and Leasing for Real Estate Managers; Certificate, Managing Nonprofit Housing, Institute of Real Estate Management **Hob./spts.:** Jogging, weightlifting, reading **SIC code:** 83 **Address:** Lutheran Social Services, 27 Park Place, New York, NY 10007 **E-mail:** one_in_thought@yahoo.com

AMBRUSO, NESTOR S.
Industry: Architecture and engineering **Born:** January 12, 1936, Bahia Blanca, Argentina **Univ./degree:** B.S., Architecture, National College of Buenos Aires, 1955; M.S., Architecture, University of Buenos Aires, 1962 **Current organization:** Ray Engineers, P.S.C. **Title:** Associate A.I.A., C.A.A.P.P.R.; C.S.I., C.C.S. **Type of organization:** Design, consulting, architecture and engineering **Major product:** Consulting **Area of distribution:** National **Expertise:** Architectural Design and Construction Specifier **Honors/awards:** CSI Institute Director's Award, 2001; CSI Institute Director's Award, 2003; CSI Certificate of Commendation, 2004 **Affiliations:** A.I.A.; C.A.A.P.P.R.; C.S.I.-P.R.; Past President, C.S.I.-P.R. **Hob./spts.:** Tennis, travel, swimming, walking, classical music **SIC code:** 87 **Address:** Ray Engineers, P.S.C., 355 Tetuan St., San Juan, PR 00901 **E-mail:** nambruso@rayae.com **Web address:** www.rayae.com

ANDERSON, GARY J.
Industry: Engineering consulting/petroleum/mining **Born:** September 21, 1936, Salt Lake City, Utah **Univ./degree:** B.S., Business; B.S., Psychology, University of Utah; M.S., Electrical Engineering, UCLA **Current organization:** Thermal Technologies Group **Title:** President **Type of organization:** Consulting **Major product:** Engineering consulting **Area of distribution:** International **Expertise:** F.C.C.U. Operations, refinery engineering **Affiliations:** A.P.I.; A.I.M.E.; National Petroleum Refiners Association **Hob./spts.:** Tennis, golf, duck hunting **SIC code:** 87 **Address:** Thermal Technologies Group, 1451 Arlington Dr., Salt Lake City, UT 84103 **E-mail:** andertrol@mindspring.com

ANDERSON, WILLIAM A.
Industry: Consulting **Born:** October 12, 1959, Magnolia, Arkansas **Univ./degree:** B.S.C.E., University of Arkansas, 1982 **Current organization:** Dowdey Anderson & Associates, Inc. **Title:** President, P.E. **Type of organization:** Engineering firm **Major product:** Land development and municipal services **Area of distribution:** Texas **Expertise:** Civil engineering **Honors/awards:** YMCA, Hiesquite Planning and Zoning Commission **Affiliations:** A.S.C.E.; N.S.P.E.; T.S.P.E.; U.L.I. **Hob./spts.:** Golf, skiing, tennis, basketball, baseball, football **SIC code:** 87 **Address:** Dowdey Anderson & Associates, Inc., 5225 Village Creek Dr., Suite 200, Plano, TX 75093 **Phone:** (972)931-0694 **Fax:** (972)931-9538 **E-mail:** waaeng@attbi.com

ANGIOLI, RENATA M.
Industry: Consulting **Born:** December 14, 1962, New York, New York **Univ./degree:** B.A., Communication, Fordham University, 1984; M.B.A., Management, Wagner College, 1986 **Current organization:** Renata M. Angioli, Agent/Publicist **Title:** Sports Publicist **Type of organization:** Self-employed **Major product:** Publications **Area of distribution:** National **Expertise:** Publicity management **Affiliations:** American Coaster Enthusiasts; Catholic Youth Organization; Fordham Ice Hockey Alumni **Hob./spts.:** Lap swimming - 5 miles/week, world traveler - 5 of 7 continents, Peanuts memorabilia - avid collector **SIC code:** 87 **Address:** 2 Elmwood Park Dr., #710, Staten Island, NY 10314 **E-mail:** rmangioli@aol.com

ANNAN, ROBERT A.
Industry: Laboratory **Born:** June 30, 1955, Accra, Ghana **Univ./degree:** B.S., Pure and Applied Chemistry, Leicester School, 1980 **Current organization:** American Asjay Lab **Title:** Lab Manager **Type of organization:** Laboratory **Major product:** Laboratory testing **Area of distribution:** National/international **Expertise:** Analysis, research **SIC code:** 87 **Address:** American Asjay Lab, 1500 Glendale Ave., Sparks, NV 89431

ANTENUCCI, LAUREN R.
Industry: Engineering **Born:** June 29, 1981, Broomall, Pennsylvania **Univ./degree:** B.S.C.E., Villanova University **Current organization:** Urban Engineering **Title:** Civil Engineer **Type of organization:** Engineering firm **Major product:** Engineering services **Area of distribution:** Pennsylvania **Expertise:** Civil and highway engineering **Honors/awards:** Concrete Canoe Project Award **Affiliations:** A.S.C.E.; S.W.E. **Hob./spts.:** Singing, music, ballet dancing, piano **SIC code:** 87 **Address:** 341 Kent Rd., Broomall, PA 19008 **E-mail:** lauren.antenucci@villanova.edu

ANTWI, GUSTAV BOAKYE
Industry: Government/construction engineering **Born:** January 23, 1959, Accra, Ghana, West Africa **Univ./degree:** B.S., Architecture, Manchester Polytechnic, England; B.S., Civil Engineering, 1994; M.Sc. Candidate, Civil Engineering, California State University **Current organization:** California State-DGS-CSB **Title:** Construction Engineering Supervisor II **Type of organization:** Construction engineering **Major product:** Construction engineering **Area of distribution:** California **Expertise:** Structural Engineering **Affiliations:** F.M.A.; Construction Management Association of America; Professional Engineers in California Government **Hob./spts.:** Soccer **SIC code:** 87 **Address:** California State-DGS-CSB, P.O. Box 580841, Suite 100, Elk Grove, CA 95758 **E-mail:** gustav.antwi@dgs.ca.gov

ARIYO, SAMUEL "WOLE"
Industry: Consulting **Born:** February 2, 1940 **Univ./degree:** M.S., Geology/Petrol Engineering, University of London **Current organization:** Trutec Oil & Gas **Title:** Chief **Type of organization:** Consulting firm **Major product:** Equipment supply, service to small independents **Area of distribution:** International **Expertise:** Oil and gas exploration and production **Affiliations:** N.M.G.S.; S.E.G.; A.A.P.G.; S.P.E.; A.I.M.E.; S.C.E.; N.A.P.E. **Hob./spts.:** Tennis, jazz, playing piano **SIC code:** 87 **Address:** Trutec Oil & Gas, 60 Shakespeare Crescent, London E126LN, United Kingdom

ARJOMAND, LEILI
Industry: Environmental **Born:** July 3, Tehran, Iran **Univ./degree:** B.S.C.E., University of California at Davis, 1992 **Current organization:** Environmental Chemical Corp. **Title:** Science & Engineering Manager **Type of organization:** Consulting firm **Major product:** Environmental remediation, government work **Area of distribution:** International **Expertise:** Civil, structural and environmental engineering, project management, business development, team leadership **Affiliations:** A.S.C.E. **Hob./spts.:** Tennis, biking, home renovations **SIC code:** 87 **Address:** 940 Terrace Dr., Los Altos, CA 94010 **E-mail:** larjomand@ecc.net

ARNDTS, DANIEL R.
Industry: Charitable organizations **Born:** August 14, 1953, Dayton, Ohio **Univ./degree:** A.A., Wright State University, 1979 **Current organization:** United Ancient Order of Druids **Title:** Supreme Secretary **Type of organization:** Fraternal Order/Nonprofit charity **Major product:** Charity **Area of distribution:** International **Expertise:** Secretary and educator **Published works:** Journal proceedings **Affiliations:** Past President, National Union of Paper Workers, Local 1493 **Hob./spts.:** Scuba diving, sheep dogs **SIC code:** 86 **Address:** United Ancient Order of Druids, 4040 Merrimac Ave., Dayton, OH 45405-2315 **E-mail:** danatlowrider@netscape.net

AROS, JOAQUIN
Industry: Automotive **Born:** January 15, 1948, Mexico City, Mexico **Univ./degree:** B.S., Art Center College of Design, 1971 **Current organization:** Aros-Throndson Industrial Designers **Title:** Co-Owner **Type of organization:** Design firm **Major product:** Automotive and product design **Area of distribution:** National **Expertise:** Design **Affiliations:** Society of Mechanical Engineers; International Design Forum **Hob./spts.:** Playing keyboards and guitar **SIC code:** 87 **Address:** Aros-Throndson Industrial Designers, 14001 Garfield Ave., Paramount, CA 90723 **E-mail:** j@arosid.com

ARRIES, BOBBIE E.
Industry: Consulting **Born:** January 3, 1967, Emporia, Kansas **Univ./degree:** B.A., Business, ASU **Current organization:** Neurologic Consultants **Title:** Office Manager **Type of organization:** Specialty physician's office **Area of distribution:** South Miami, Florida **Expertise:** Management **Affiliations:** M.O.M.M.A.; N.A.F.E. **Hob./spts.:** Running, softball, racquetball, walking **SIC code:** 87 **Address:** Neurologic Consultants, 7330 S.W. 62nd Place, #310, South Miami, FL 33143 **E-mail:** bobbiearries@bellsouth.net

ARROWSMITH-LOWE, JANET B.
Industry: Healthcare/consulting **Born:** April 4, 1949, New Orleans, Louisiana **Univ./degree:** M.D., Tulane University, Louisiana, 1979 **Current organization:** Arrowsmith-Lowe Consulting, Inc. **Title:** Partner **Type of organization:** Professional consulting group **Major product:** Pharmaceuticals and biologicals **Area of distribution:** International **Expertise:** Internal medicine, lecturing, Expert Witness **Affiliations:** F.A.C.P.; A.M.A. **Hob./spts.:** Riding Hunter Jumper horses; spending time with her husband, Thomas and children, Eliot and Victoria **SIC code:** 87 **Address:** Arrowsmith-Lowe Consulting, Inc., P.O. Box 3148, Five Eagle Creek Canyon Rd., Ruidoso, NM 88355-3148 **E-mail:** arrowsmith@zianet.com

AVERSANO, VINCE
Industry: Publishing/communications **Born:** New York, New York **Univ./degree:** B.A., Journalism, Marquette University, 1978 **Current organization:** Rotary International **Title:** Communications Division Manager **Type of organization:** Not-for-profit service organization **Major product:** Publishing **Area of distribution:** International **Expertise:** Communications **Published works:** Articles **SIC code:** 86 **Address:** Rotary International, 1560 Sherman Ave., Evanston, IL 60201 **E-mail:** aversanv@rotaryintl.org

AVILES, OSWALDO LAINEZ
Industry: Financial **Born:** April 6, 1966, Nicaragua **Univ./degree:** B.A., Taxation, UNC, 1999 **Current organization:** Lainez & Lainez, Inc. **Title:** Tax Advisor **Type of organization:** Accounting firm **Major product:** Taxation and accounting **Area of distribution:** National **Expertise:** IRS audits and appeals; Entertainment industry **Affiliations:** California Tax and Education Council **Hob./spts.:** Tennis **SIC code:** 87 **Address:** Lainez & Lainez, Inc., 269 S. Beverly Dr., Suite 273, Beverly Hills, CA 90212 **E-mail:** taxlainez@gmail.com

AVITABILE, THOMAS P.
Industry: Architecture/engineering consulting **Born:** July 8, 1952, New York **Univ./degree:** B.S., Architecture **Current organization:** Avitabile Group **Title:** Principal **Type of organization:** Architecture, engineering and consulting firm **Major product:** Residential, commercial, nonprofit design/engineering **Area of distribution:** New York **Expertise:** Architecture/construction consulting **SIC code:** 87 **Address:** Avitabile Group, 113 Elmira St., Staten Island, NY 10306 **E-mail:** avitabile.group@att.net

AYMOND, MARK ANTHONY
Industry: Consulting **Born:** April 10, 1973, Lafayette, Louisiana **Univ./degree:** B.S., Mechanical Engineering, University of Louisiana at Lafayette, 2001 **Current organization:** Associated Design Group, Inc. **Title:** Mechanical Consultant, E.I.T. **Type of organization:** Engineering firm **Major product:** Consulting, engineering **Area of distribution:** National **Expertise:** Commercial HVAC engineered system design, commercial fire protection engineered system design, commercial plumbing engineered system design **Affiliations:** A.S.H.R.A.E. **SIC code:** 87 **Address:** Associated Design Group, Inc., 114 Toledo Dr., Lafayette, LA 70506 **Phone:** (337)234-5710 **Fax:** (337)237-1467 **E-mail:** adginc@adginc.org **Web address:** www.adginc.org

AYOUB, AMY S.
Industry: Consulting **Born:** March 27, 1951, Washington, D.C. **Current organization:** Ayoub & Associates **Title:** President **Type of organization:** Private company **Major product:** Fundraising for nonprofit and political candidates **Area of distribution:** National **Expertise:** Fundraising, administration **Published works:** Newsletters **Affiliations:** Women of Influence **Hob./spts.:** Boxing, dancing **SIC code:** 83 **Address:** Ayoub & Associates, 2265-A Renaissance Dr., Las Vegas, NV 89119 **E-mail:** amyayoub@aol.com

BACULIMA, JAIME R.
Industry: Civil engineering **Born:** March 6, 1955, Cuenca, Ecuador **Univ./degree:** M.S.C.E., Cuenca State University, 1984 **Current organization:** Quality Contracting Inc. **Title:** Civil Engineer **Type of organization:** Manufacturing/consulting **Major product:** Detailing, fabrication **Area of distribution:** New York **Expertise:** Civil engineering; Licensed P.E. in New York **Affiliations:** A.S.C.E.; National Institute of Steel Detailing **SIC code:** 87 **Address:** Quality Contracting Inc., 34-05 111th St., Corona, NY 11368 **E-mail:** baculima@aol.com

BAILEY, BRADFORD E.
Industry: Engineering **Born:** October 6, 1950, Denver, Colorado **Univ./degree:** B.S., Electrical Engineering, Colorado State University, 1978 **Current organization:** BEB Consulting **Title:** Owner **Type of organization:** Consulting **Major product:** Aerospace consulting; military start-up **Area of distribution:** National **Expertise:** Electronics, design, reliability **Published works:** Patents **Hob./spts.:** Fishing, hiking **SIC code:** 87 **Address:** 9039 Harlequin Circle, Longmont, CO 80504 **E-mail:** brad@beb-consulting.com

BAILEY, DAVID A.
Industry: Consulting **Born:** August 17, 1961, Minneapolis, Minnesota **Univ./degree:** M.S., Mechanical Engineering, Rensselear Polytechnic Institute, 1986; M.B.A., Wharton School of Business, University of Pennsylvania, 1991 **Current organization:** Education Transfer **Title:** President **Type of organization:** Nonprofit educational consulting firm **Major product:** Consulting, data processing, printing, specializing in organizing and facilitating outstanding Career Days for schools from elementary to college **Area of distribution:** Delaware **Expertise:** Career event design **Affiliations:** A.S.M.E.; Tao Beta Pi **Hob./spts.:** Windsurfing, skiing, travel **SIC code:** 87 **Address:** Education Transfer, 236 Rushes Dr., Bear, DE 19701 **E-mail:** daveb@educationtransfer.com

BAIRD, ALLAN M.
Industry: Engineering **Univ./degree:** B.S., Humble University, 1970 **Current organization:** A.M. Baird Engineering Inc. **Title:** Owner **Type of organization:** Consulting **Area of distribution:** Fortuna, California **Expertise:** Consulting engineering **Affiliations:** A.S.C.E. **SIC code:** 87 **Address:** A.M. Baird Engineering Inc., 1257 Main St., Fortuna, CA 95540 **E-mail:** ambaird@cox.net

BAIRD, CARY K.
Industry: Consulting **Born:** December 24, 1960, Santa Barbara, California **Univ./degree:** B.S., Urban Design/Landscape Architecture, Arizona State University, 1985 **Current organization:** Stantec Consulting, Inc. **Title:** Senior Associate **Type of organization:** Private consulting firm **Major product:** Engineering, planning, landscape architecture **Area of distribution:** Nevada **Expertise:** Landscape architecture, planning **Affiliations:** A.P.A.; A.S.L.A.; National Recreation and Parks Association **Hob./spts.:** Spending time with family **SIC code:** 87 **Address:** Stantec Consulting, Inc., 7251 W. Charleston Blvd., Las Vegas, NV 89117 **E-mail:** www.stantec.com **Web address:** www.cbaird@stantec.com

BALAZS, ENDRE A.
Industry: Biomedical research **Born:** January 10, 1920, Budapest, Hungary **Univ./degree:** M.D., University of Budapest School of Medicine **Current organization:** Matrix Biology Institute **Title:** Chairman/M.D. **Type of organization:** Nonprofit medical research **Major product:** Research and development **Area of distribution:** International **Expertise:** Biomedical research **Published works:** 350+ articles, 27 U.S. and international patents **SIC code:** 87 **Address:** Matrix Biology Institute, 65 Railroad Ave., Ridgefield, NJ 07657 **E-mail:** eabalazs@matrixha.org **Web address:** www.matrixbiologyinstitute.org

BALBAS, CHRISTINE LOUISE

Industry: Government/social services **Born:** May 23, 1958, Madera, California **Univ./ degree:** B.S., Agricultural Education; M.A., Public Administration, California State University at Fresno **Current organization:** Fresno County Dept. of Employment & Temporary Assistance **Title:** Program Manager/Refugee Services Coordinator **Type of organization:** Government **Major product:** Social services, employment and training services **Area of distribution:** California **Expertise:** Employment and training **Affiliations:** A.C.A.; N.S.D.T.A.; A.P.H.S.A. **Hob./spts.:** Winemaking, gardening, travel (U.S.) **SIC code:** 83 **Address:** Fresno County Dept. of Employment & Temporary Assistance, 4449 E. Kings Canyon Rd., Fresno, CA 93702 **E-mail:** cbalbas@fresno.ca.gov

BANDA VALDEZ, JOSEPHINE S.

Industry: Education **Born:** August 11, 1923, Santa Ana, California **Univ./degree:** B.S., History/Education, Immaculate College, Los Angeles **Current organization:** Association of Mexican-American Educators **Title:** Educator **Type of organization:** Nonprofit organization **Major product:** Educational opportunities and benefits for Mexican-American, Chicano and Latino Students **Area of distribution:** National **Expertise:** Parental skills, educator, bi-lingual education (English/Spanish), ESL **Affiliations:** Delta Kappa Gamma Society International, Omega Chapter; American Business Women's Association; Association of Mexican-American Educators; President, Francisco Rodriguez, Fresno, California **Hob./spts.:** Reading, opera, playing Scrabble, family, travel, Bible study **SIC code:** 86 **Address:** 1160 Seventh St., #2, San Pedro, CA 90731 **Web address:** www.amae.org

BARAL, SURESH R.

Industry: Consulting **Born:** January 1, 1943, Kathmandu, Nepal **Univ./degree:** M.S., Civil Engineering, University of Hawaii, 1974 **Current organization:** Advance Structural Concepts **Title:** P.E., Owner **Type of organization:** Engineering firm **Major product:** Structural engineering **Area of distribution:** National **Expertise:** Architectural and structural services, residential and commercial **Affiliations:** American Iron & Steel Institute; American Society of Civil Engineers; American Concrete Institute **Hob./ spts.:** Swimming, physical fitness, tennis **SIC code:** 87 **Address:** Advance Structural Concepts, 12359 Sunrise Valley Dr., Reston, VA 20191 **E-mail:** sbaral@aol.com

BARENBERG, ERNEST J.

Industry: Engineering/consulting **Born:** April 9, 1929, Rawlins County, Kansas **Univ./ degree:** Ph.D., University of Illinois at Urbana Champaign, 1965 **Current organization:** Ernest Barenberg Consultant **Title:** Professor Emeritus **Type of organization:** Consulting **Major product:** Consulting services, transportation facilities, materials **Area of distribution:** International **Expertise:** Civil engineering **Honors/awards:** Prestigious Awards after receipt pf Ph.D.; Listed in Personalities of the West and Midwest; American Men of Science; Tau Beta Pi; Sigma Xi; Everitt Award for Teaching Excellence, 1973; Listed in National Register of Prominent Americans and International Notables; Listed in Who's Who; Member, International Platform Association; Award of Merit, Illinois Pozzolanic Pavement Association; Faculty Honor Member, Chi Epsilon; Air Transport Division, ASCE Horonjeff Award for "Outstanding Contribution to Airport Pavement Engineering", 1998; Association of American Railroads Award for "Outstanding Service in Directing the AAR Affiliate Program at the University of Illinois", 1998; American Concrete Pavement Association Educator of the Year, 2002 **Published works:** 150+ articles, journals **Affiliations:** Life Member, A.S.C.E.; T.R.B.; University of Illinois **Hob./spts.:** Travel **SIC code:** 87 **Address:** 2245 Nancy Lane, St. Joseph, IL 61873 **E-mail:** ejbm@uiuc.edu

BARLOW, JEREMY P.

Industry: Chemicals **Born:** May 24, 1975, Albuquerque, New Mexico **Univ./degree:** M.S., Synthetic Chemistry, University of New Mexico, 2003 **Current organization:** Adherent Technologies **Title:** Staff Chemist **Type of organization:** R&D **Major product:** Synthetic chemistry **Area of distribution:** National **Expertise:** Synthetic chemistry **Affiliations:** American Chemical Society **Hob./spts.:** Hiking, reading, woodworking **SIC code:** 87 **Address:** Adherent Technologies, 11208 Cochiti SE, Albuquerque, NM 87123 **E-mail:** jbarlow58@hotmail.com

BARNETT, RICHARD W.

Industry: Pharmaceuticals **Born:** November 16, 1955, St. Louis, Missouri **Univ./ degree:** Ph.D., Chemistry, Northwestern University, 1983 **Current organization:** Ligand Pharmaceuticals, Inc. **Title:** Director, Research Planning **Type of organization:** Research and development **Major product:** Pharmaceuticals/therapeutics **Area of distribution:** International **Expertise:** Project management **Hob./spts.:** Golf, softball **SIC code:** 87 **Address:** Ligand Pharmaceuticals, Inc., 10275 Science Center Dr., San Diego, CA 92121 **E-mail:** rbarnett@ligand.com

BARRERA, AGUSTIN J.

Industry: Architecture **Born:** August 21, 1961, Havana, Cuba **Univ./degree:** B.A., Design, University of Florida, 1984; M.Arch., Florida International University, 2005 **Current organization:** Leo A. Daly **Title:** Managing Principal **Type of organization:** Architecture **Major product:** Architecture, planning, design **Area of distribution:** International **Expertise:** Finance, planning, design **Hob./spts.:** Fishing, golf **SIC code:** 87 **Address:** Leo A. Daly, 3390 Mary St., #216, Miami, FL 33133 **E-mail:** ajbarrera@leoadaly.com **Web address:** www.leoadaly.com

BARTELUCE, DANIEL A.

Industry: Architecture **Born:** September 11, 1947, Teaneck, New Jersey **Univ./degree:** B.A., Architecture, University of Oklahoma, 1970 **Current organization:** Barteluce Architects & Assoc. **Title:** Owner/Architect **Type of organization:** Architectural firm **Major product:** Luxury retail stores, religious facilities **Area of distribution:** National **Expertise:** Operations **Affiliations:** A.I.A.; N.C.A.R.B. **Hob./spts.:** Golf **SIC code:** 87 **Address:** Barteluce Architects & Assoc., 36 W. 25th St., 17th Floor, New York, NY 10010 **Web address:** www.bafc.net

BARTH, DELBERT S.

Industry: Consulting **Born:** July 6, 1925, Lawrenceburg, Indiana **Univ./degree:** Ph.D., Biophysics, Ohio State University, 1962 **Current organization:** Self-employed **Title:** Professor Emeritus, University of Nevada, Las Vegas/ Environmental Protection Agency - EPA (Retired) **Type of organization:** Consulting **Major product:** Environmental consulting to government agencies and environmental advocates **Area of distribution:** National **Expertise:** Research and development **Affiliations:** New York Academy of Sciences **Hob./spts.:** Golf, hunting, fishing **SIC code:** 87 **Address:** 1577 Deer Meadow Dr., Henderson, NV 89012-2413 **E-mail:** del1usphs@aol.com

BARTOW, BARBARA J.

Industry: Consulting **Born:** June 26, 1950, Buffalo, New York **Univ./degree:** M.A., Air Force University, 1976 **Current organization:** Barbara J. Bartow **Title:** Consultant **Type of organization:** Consulting **Major product:** Social services consulting **Area of distribution:** International **Expertise:** Social services, veterans services, child advocate **Published works:** Poetry **Affiliations:** D.A.V. **Hob./spts.:** Writing, computers, cooking **SIC code:** 87 **Address:** 1515 Lantern Lane, Sugar Creek Hills, Joliet, IL 60433-2910 **E-mail:** liferpoet1@attbi.com

BASINA, LYNNE M.

Industry: Human services **Born:** May, 7, 1955, Ashland, Wisconsin **Univ./degree:** B.S.W., Mount Senario College; M.Ed., University of Minnesota **Current organization:** First American Prevention Center **Title:** Executive Director **Type of organization:** Not for Profit Community Based Organization **Major product:** Human Relations and Services **Area of distribution:** Bayfield, Wisconsin **Expertise:** Program development, budgets, facilitates teams, counseling, couples education, improving the quality of life for Native American Indians **Hob./spts.:** Writing, drawing and hiking **SIC code:** 83 **Address:** First American Prevention Center, 37525 Dock Rd., Bayfield, WI 54814 **E-mail:** lbasinfapc@charterinternet.net

BATCHELOR, PHILLIP A.

Industry: Engineering **Born:** December 13, 1967, Haleyville, Alabama **Univ./degree:** Attended 2 years, study in Engineering Drafting Technology, Beville State Community College **Current organization:** Gresham, Smith and Partners **Title:** Senior Project Supervisor/Firm Associate **Type of organization:** Consulting firm **Major product:** Consulting (architecture/engineering) **Area of distribution:** National **Expertise:** Roadway engineering **Affiliations:** A.S.C.E.; Served in active duty, U.S. Army, 1986-96 **Hob./spts.:** Family, football, history **SIC code:** 87 **Address:** Gresham, Smith and Partners, 3595 Grandview Pkwy., Suite 300, Birmingham, AL 35243 **E-mail:** pbatc@gspnet.com **Web address:** www.gspnet.com

BATTAGELLO, LINDA K.

Industry: Professional service/education **Born:** Port Huron, Michigan **Univ./degree:** B.A., University of Windsor, Ontario, Canada, 1970 **Current organization:** Goodwill Industries **Title:** C.E.O./C.O.O./Associate Director **Type of organization:** Non-profit rehab facility/retailer **Area of distribution:** Port Huron, Michigan **Expertise:** Finance, sales **Honors/awards:** The Scotty Hanton Award, 1991 **Published works:** Canadian Daily **Affiliations:** Cornerstone Society; President, Quota International; Beacon Society; Port Huron Hospital Foundation **Hob./spts.:** Rollerblading, kickboxing, yoga, meditation **SIC code:** 86 **Address:** Goodwill Industries, 1013 26th St., Port Huron, MI 48060 **E-mail:** lkbattagello@aol.com

BAUCAGE, YILIA M.

Industry: Engineering **Born:** July 11, 1977,. San Juan, Puerto Rico **Univ./degree:** B.S.C.E., 2000; M.S.C.E., 2002, University of Puerto Rico at Mayaguez **Current organization:** CMA Architects & Engineers, LLP **Title:** M.S.C.E./E.I.T. **Type of organization:** Consulting firm **Major product:** Consulting **Area of distribution:** International **Expertise:** Civil engineering (transportation and road design) **Honors/ awards:** Dwight David Eisenhower Transportation Fellowship, 2001-2002 **Published works:** 2 articles **Affiliations:** A.S.C.E.; I.T.E.; C.I.A.P.R. **Hob./spts.:** Snorkeling, travel, reading **SIC code:** 87 **Address:** CMA Architects & Engineers, LLP, 1509 F.D. Roosevelt Ave., San Juan, PR 00920 **E-mail:** ybaucage@yahoo.com **Web address:** www.cma-sjpr.com

BAUCH, DAVID J.
Industry: Social services **Univ./degree:** M.B.A., Finance, City University, 1993 **Current organization:** El Centro de la Raza **Title:** Financial Officer/Controller **Type of organization:** Not for profit **Major product:** Community services **Area of distribution:** International **Expertise:** Accounting **Published works:** Article **Affiliations:** I.M.A.; W.S.C.P.A. **SIC code:** 83 **Address:** El Centro de la Raza, 2524 16th Ave. South, Seattle, WA 98144 **E-mail:** dbauchcpa@netscape.net **Web address:** www.elcentrodelaraza.com

BAUST, JOHN M.
Industry: Biomedical sciences/technology **Born:** June 9, 1974, Dansville, New York **Univ./degree:** B.S., Cornell University, 1998; Ph.D., Binghamton University, 2001; Post Doctorate, Harvard Medical School **Current organization:** BioLife Solutions, Inc. **Title:** Director of Research **Type of organization:** R&D, manufacturing, distribution, consulting **Major product:** Biologic (cell, tissue and organ) preservation solutions **Area of distribution:** International **Expertise:** Research and development-molecular biology, bioengineering **Published works:** 10 articles **Affiliations:** A.S.M.E.; B.M.E.S.; Society for Cryobiology **Hob./spts.:** Football, hockey, hiking, physical fitness, skiing, farming **SIC code:** 87 **Address:** BioLife Solutions, Inc., Science 3, Suite 144 SUNY Park, Binghamton, NY 13902 **E-mail:** jmbaust@biolifesolutions.com

BEASON, FEDLYN A.
Industry: Religion **Born:** December 6, 1941, Calrendon, Jamaica, W.I. **Univ./degree:** Ph.D., D.Div., D.Min.Ed., European Theological Seminary, England **Current organization:** Church of God World Missions **Title:** Caribbean Field Director/General Executive Council **Type of organization:** Religious **Major product:** Religious and spiritual guidance, missions, educational, community development **Area of distribution:** International **Expertise:** Directing world mission projects in 43 countries **Honors/awards:** Justice of the Peace, appointment by Queen Elizabeth II **Affiliations:** Ministry of Health; United Nations Association; Community Council, Public Works, Ministry of Education **Hob./spts.:** Fishing, bird watching **SIC code:** 86 **Address:** Church of God World Missions, 16501 S.W. 18th St., Miramar, FL 33027 **E-mail:** cogcarib@aol.com

BEATO, VALENTIN
Industry: Consulting/engineering **Born:** September 8, 1944, Madrid, Spain **Univ./degree:** M.S., University of Puerto Rico **Current organization:** Beato & Associates **Title:** Partner **Type of organization:** Consulting engineering **Major product:** Pharmaceutical design **Area of distribution:** Guaynabo, Puerto Rico **Expertise:** Engineering **Affiliations:** A.S.C.E. **Hob./spts.:** Tennis, swimming, biking **SIC code:** 87 **Address:** Beato & Associates, Corporate Office Park, PR 20, Cortee Bldg., Suite 101, Guaynabo, PR 00966 **E-mail:** valbeato@caribe.net

BECK, THOMAS M.
Industry: Consulting **Born:** November 18, 1957, Cleveland, Ohio **Univ./degree:** B.S., Mechanical Engineering, Western Michigan University **Current organization:** J.F. Thompson, Inc. **Title:** Project Manager **Type of organization:** Engineering firm **Major product:** Commercial/industrial consulting **Area of distribution:** Texas **Expertise:** Mechanical engineering **Affiliations:** A.S.M.E.; A.S.H.R.A.E. **Hob./spts.:** Golf **SIC code:** 87 **Address:** J.F. Thompson, Inc., 6110 Clarkson Lane, Houston, TX 77055 **E-mail:** tom.beck@jfthompson.com

BECKNELL, LAWRENCE A.
Industry: Consulting/engineering **Born:** December 10, 1948, Phenix City, Alabama **Univ./degree:** M.S., Brigham Young University, 1976 **Current organization:** Stanley Consultants **Title:** President **Type of organization:** Engineering firm **Major product:** Civil engineering/consulting **Area of distribution:** National **Expertise:** Transportation engineering **Published works:** Articles, presentations **Affiliations:** I.T.E.; A.S.C.E. **Hob./spts.:** Golf, racquetball, tennis, travel **SIC code:** 87 **Address:** Stanley Consultants, 5353 S. 960 E., Suite 220, Salt Lake City, UT 84117 **E-mail:** lbecknell@crsengineers.com **Web address:** www.crsengineers.com

BEDI, ANU
Industry: Financial services **Born:** May 28, 1957, Chhindwara, India **Univ./degree:** M.B.A., American Graduate School for International Management, Thunderbird Campus, Arizona **Current organization:** Logitech **Title:** Worldwide Tax Director **Type of organization:** Manufacturing/distributor/retailer **Major product:** Computers **Area of distribution:** International **Expertise:** Worldwide Tax Director **Affiliations:** Tax Executives Institute; American Institute of Certified Pubic Accountants **Hob./spts.:** Reading **SIC code:** 87 **Address:** Logitech Inc., 6505 Kaiser Dr., Fremont, CA 94555 **E-mail:** anu-bedi@logtech.com

BEERS, LARRY F.
Industry: Consulting **Born:** October 17, 1956, Washington, D.C. **Univ./degree:** B.A., Sociology, Binghamton University, 1978 **Current organization:** James E. Rocco Associates, Inc. **Title:** Lead Consultant **Type of organization:** Consulting firm **Major product:** Management services **Area of distribution:** National **Expertise:** Compensation, human resources **Affiliations:** SHRM; PANO; WorldatWork; Blue Hill Troupe **Hob./spts.:** Theater, music, travel **SIC code:** 87 **Address:** James E. Rocco Associates, Inc., 350 Theodore Fremd Ave., Suite 300, Rye, NY 10580 **E-mail:** Lfbeers@rcn.com

BEIGH, PAUL J.
Industry: Architecture **Born:** September 28, 1948, Olympia, Washington **Univ./degree:** Attended California Polytechnic University, San Luis Obispo, California **Current organization:** Homes of Distinction by Paul Beigh, Inc. **Title:** President **Type of organization:** Architectural design firm **Major product:** Architecture **Area of distribution:** National **Expertise:** Custom residential architecture **Honors/awards:** Lifetime Member, Strathmore's Who's Who; Who's Who in Executives & Business; International Who's Who of Professionals **Affiliations:** Williamsburg Foundation Preservation; member, Smithsonian Institution; member, Historical Preservation Society **Hob./spts.:** Water and snow skiing, outdoorsman, world traveler of historical sites **SIC code:** 87 **Address:** Homes of Distinction by Paul Beigh, Inc., 1236 Mt. Estes Dr., Colorado Springs, CO 80921 **Phone:** (805)482-7411 **E-mail:** homesbypb1@aol.com

BELIZAIRE, DEJEAN C.
Industry: Engineering **Born:** Haiti **Univ./degree:** B.S. Civil Engineering, Polytechnic School of Haiti, State University of Haiti, 1961; C.E.S.; M.S., Hydrology/Agricultural Hydraulics, National School of Rural Engineering, Ministry of Agriculture, France, 1964 **Current organization:** Ewell. W. Finley Consulting Engineers, Architects & Surveyors **Title:** Civil Engineer **Type of organization:** Consulting **Major product:** Highway design **Area of distribution:** New York **Expertise:** Design/civil engineering **Honors/awards:** Republican Gold Medal, National Republican Congressional Committee, 2002; Honor and Merit Order Grand Cross, Haitian President Joseph Nerette, 1993 **Published works:** "Le Parlement Haitien Face au Coup du 30 Septembre 1991"-May 2002 **Affiliations:** A.S.C.E.; Member, College National des Ingenieurs et Architectes Haitiens, Port-au-Prince-Haiti; Member, Association des Ingenieurs du Genie Rural des Eaux et Forets, Paris, France **SIC code:** 87 **Address:** 147-37 Charter Rd., Unit 20B, Jamaica, NY 11435

BELL, KATRINA D.
Industry: Human services **Born:** Bessemer, Alabama **Univ./degree:** B.A., Business Management, University of Montevallo, Alabama, 1992 **Current organization:** American Red Cross, Blood Services **Title:** Human Resources Associate **Type of organization:** Nonprofit humanitarian service **Major product:** Blood products **Area of distribution:** National **Expertise:** Human resources **Affiliations:** Society for Human Resource Management; Birmingham Society for Human Resource Management **Hob./spts.:** Singing, children's choir **SIC code:** 86 **Address:** American Red Cross, Blood Services, 1130 22nd St. South, Birmingham, AL 35205 **E-mail:** bellk@usa.redcross.org **Web address:** www.usa.redcross.org

BELL, NATHANIEL (BO)
Industry: Oil & gas **Born:** May 9, 1969, Naples, Florida **Univ./degree:** M.S., Florida Atlantic University, 1988 **Current organization:** In-Depth, Inc. **Title:** President **Type of organization:** Consulting firm **Major product:** Project management **Area of distribution:** International **Expertise:** Deepwater engineering **Published works:** Articles **Affiliations:** A.S.C.E.; Marine Technology Society **Hob./spts.:** Water sports **SIC code:** 87 **Address:** In-Depth, Inc., 5220 Weslayan St., Suite C106, Houston, TX 77005-1079 **E-mail:** bo_bell@msn.com

BELLACE, THOMAS A.
Industry: Engineering **Born:** February 10, 1952, Philadelphia, Pennsylvania **Univ./degree:** B.A., Penn State University, 1975 **Current organization:** Alliance Structural Engineers, LLC **Title:** President **Type of organization:** Design firm **Major product:** Structural engineering **Area of distribution:** National **Expertise:** Chief engineer, business development **Published works:** Articles, technical magazine **Affiliations:** Structural Engineers of Texas; American Society of Civil Engineers **SIC code:** 87 **Address:** Alliance Structural Engineers, LLC, 17355 Village Green Dr., Houston, TX 77004-1004 **E-mail:** aselle@infohwy.com

BENNETT, C. LYNN
Industry: Consulting **Born:** May 21, 1947, Morgantown, West Virginia **Univ./degree:** B.A., Secondary Education, Shepherd University, 1969 **Current organization:** Bennett Educational Consulting **Title:** President **Type of organization:** Consulting **Major product:** Grant writing, program management and development, staff training for educational institutions and nonprofit agencies **Area of distribution:** West Virginia **Expertise:** Education **Affiliations:** N.A.M.T.C.; Phi Delta Kappa **SIC code:** 87 **Address:** Bennett Educational Consulting, 18 Meadow Lane, Bridgeport, WV 26330 **E-mail:** lynnbennettconsulting@yahoo.com

BENNETT, DONALD
Industry: Military/aerospace/telecommunications **Born:** April 9, 1969, Morristown, New Jersey **Current organization:** Garwood Laboratories, Inc. **Title:** Director of Telecom Compliance **Type of organization:** Testing facility **Major product:** Testing services **Area of distribution:** International **Expertise:** Telecommunications **Published works:** Several articles **Affiliations:** O.S.A.; A.T.I.S. **Hob./spts.:** Family,

music (guitar) **SIC code:** 87 **Address:** Garwood Laboratories, Inc., 7829 Industry Ave., Pico Rivera, CA 90660 **E-mail:** donb@garwoodtestlabs.com **Web address:** www.garwoodtestlabs.com

BERGER, DONALD J.
Industry: Construction/engineering **Born:** May 12, 1959 **Univ./degree:** B.S., Civil Engineering, University of Minnesota, 1984; M.S., Civil Engineering, University of Minnesota, 1990 **Current organization:** Yenter Companies, Inc. **Title:** P.E./Senior Project Engineer **Type of organization:** Contractor **Major product:** Geotechnical design, building **Area of distribution:** Colorado **Expertise:** Soil and rock stabilization, drill/blast **Published works:** 12 articles **Affiliations:** A.S.C.E. **Hob./spts.:** Family, skiing, hiking **SIC code:** 87 **Address:** Yenter Companies, Inc., 1512 Grand Ave., Suite 104, Glenwood Springs, CO 81601 **E-mail:** dberger@yenter.com **Web address:** www.yenter.com

BERTRAM, LYNN H.
Industry: Social services **Born:** August 29, 1957, Monroe, North Carolina **Univ./degree:** M.S., Social Work, Florida State University, 1979 **Current organization:** PACE Center for Girls **Title:** Executive Director **Type of organization:** Social work center **Major product:** Delinquency prevention program for at risk girls **Area of distribution:** National **Expertise:** Criminal justice **Affiliations:** National Association of Social Workers; American Association of University Women **Hob./spts.:** Scuba diving, boating, football **SIC code:** 83 **Address:** PACE Center for Girls, 2933 University Blvd., North, Jacksonville, FL 32211 **E-mail:** lbertram@pacejax.org **Web address:** www.pacecenter.org

BETZIG, WILLIAM A.
Industry: Engineering **Born:** January 4, 1964 **Univ./degree:** B.S., University of Wisconsin-Platteville, 1987 **Current organization:** Foth & Van Dyke and Associates, Inc. **Title:** Project Manager **Type of organization:** Consulting engineering firm **Major product:** Public improvement projects **Area of distribution:** National **Expertise:** Transportation and municipal engineering **Honors/awards:** National Excellence Award for Design and Construction in Concrete Pavement, American Concrete Pavement Association, 2002 **Affiliations:** American Society of Civil Engineers **Hob./spts.:** Golf, hunting, fishing, boating, woodworking, home remodeling **SIC code:** 87 **Address:** Foth & Van Dyke and Associates, Inc., 1402 Pankratz St., Suite 300, Madison, WI 53704 **E-mail:** wbetzig@foth.com **Web address:** www.foth.com

BIANCHI, JERRY
Industry: Energy/research **Univ./degree:** A.S., Red Rock College, Golden, Colorado, 1986 **Current organization:** National Renewable Energy Laboratory **Title:** Technician Team Leader **Type of organization:** Research and development **Major product:** Renewable energy systems **Area of distribution:** Colorado **Expertise:** Field engineering **Affiliations:** I.S.A. **Hob./spts.:** Photography **SIC code:** 87 **Address:** 10136 W. Iowa Ave., Lakewood, CO 80232 **E-mail:** gerald_bianchi@nrel.gov

BIANCHI, MARIA
Industry: Consulting **Univ./degree:** M.S., Critical Care Specialist/Administration, Russell Sage College, New York **Current organization:** Trans International Healthcare **Title:** Critical Care Specialist, Adult/Acute Practitioner Mass General Hospital, Boston, MA **Type of organization:** Legal and medical consulting company **Major product:** Medical, legal, education and clinical practice, national consultant and lecturer **Area of distribution:** National **Expertise:** Critical Care Specialist, Consultant, National Lecturer in Critical Care, Pain Management, Documentation, Medio Legal Issues, Advance Practice Issues **Affiliations:** Sigma Theta Tau **SIC code:** 87 **Address:** Trans International Healthcare, P.O. Box 614, Suffield, CT 06078 **E-mail:** mariamtih@aol.com

BILLINGS, MAGGIE
Industry: Consulting **Born:** September 11, Pittsburgh, Pennsylvania **Univ./degree:** A.S., Mechanical Engineering Drafting and Design, New England Institute of Technology, 1994 **Current organization:** SSOE, Inc. **Title:** Process Piping Designer **Type of organization:** Architectural and engineering consulting firm **Major product:** Process design of facilities **Area of distribution:** Ohio **Expertise:** Design of process facilities and technical training; ADDA Professional Drafter Certification **Honors/awards:** Outstanding Public Service Award, St. Jude Children's Research Hospital Lima Telethon, White House Christmas Tree Ornament, Outstanding Volunteer, Family House (homeless shelter), Ohio READS **Published works:** In-house training manuals; Lima Kewpee YMCA Triathlon Design; 1 poem, "Happiness is a Choice" **Affiliations:** Society of Piping Engineers and Designers; American Design Drafting Association (ADDA) **Hob./spts.:** Volunteer work, learning, home decorating **SIC code:** 87 **Address:** P.O. Box 192, Maumee, OH 43537 **E-mail:** sgnillibm@earthlink.net

BINGHAM, KEVIN M.
Industry: Consulting/accounting **Born:** March 17, 1970, Massachusetts **Univ./degree:** B.A., Mathematics, Clarkson University, 1992 **Current organization:** Deloitte & Touche **Title:** Senior Manager **Type of organization:** Accounting firm **Major product:** Insurance, enterprise risk management **Area of distribution:** International **Expertise:** Dynamic financial analysis **Published works:** Published Papers: Implications of Dynamic Financial Analysis on Demutualization; Strategic Insurance Purchasing in the 21st Century; The LIHTC Program and Considerations for Guarantors of Affordable Housing Funds Published Articles: The New Actuary; Demutualization is Contributing to Insurance M&A Activity; To Be or Not to Be, The B2B Actuary; Risk Retention in a Hardening Insurance Market **Affiliations:** A.C.A.S.; M.A.A.A. **Hob./spts.:** Coaching youth hockey **SIC code:** 87 **Address:** Deloitte & Touche, 185 Asylum St., 31st floor, Hartford, CT 06103-3402 **E-mail:** kbingham@deloitte.com

BLACKFORD, BOB
Industry: Biotech **Born:** April 28, 1953, Dayton, Ohio **Univ./degree:** Attended Wright State University, Education **Current organization:** Gene Logic Inc. **Title:** Senior Manager, Health and Safety **Type of organization:** Contract research **Major product:** Pre-clinical toxicology/genomics database **Area of distribution:** International **Expertise:** Lab animal management, health and safety **Published works:** A.A.L.A.S. Trade Journal **Affiliations:** A.A.L.A.S.; A.I.H.A. **Hob./spts.:** Soccer, golf **SIC code:** 87 **Address:** Gene Logic Inc., 15 Firstfield, Gaithersburg, MD 20878 **E-mail:** bblackford@genelogic.com **Web address:** www.genelogic.com

BLACKMAR, TERRI L.
Industry: Engineering consulting **Born:** February 14, 1958, Eagle Bend, Minnesota **Univ./degree:** B.S., Geological Engineering, University of Minnesota, 1985 **Current organization:** Earth Tech, Inc. **Title:** Vice President **Type of organization:** Consulting firm **Major product:** Environmental consulting **Area of distribution:** Illinois **Expertise:** Civil/environmental engineering **Affiliations:** American Society of Civil Engineers; Chemical Engineers/Conservation of Illinois **Hob./spts.:** Family, gardening **SIC code:** 87 **Address:** Earth Tech, Inc., 3121 Butterfield Dr., Oak Brook, IL 60523 **E-mail:** terri_blackmar@earthtech.com

BLACKMON, EARNEST E.
Industry: Religion **Born:** May 22, 1928, Crescent, Oklahoma **Current organization:** Parkrose Deliverance Tabernacle **Title:** Pastor **Type of organization:** Church **Major product:** Religious services and leadership **Area of distribution:** Portland, Oregon **Expertise:** Disciple: preaching, teaching, community outreach, children's programs, sermons, teaching preachers regionally, counseling **Affiliations:** Portland City Bible Church Pastor Prayer Breakfast; Past Union Representative, United Steelworkers of America **Hob./spts.:** Walking, community involvement **SIC code:** 86 **Address:** Parkrose Deliverance Tabernacle, 5740 N.E. Lombard, Portland, OR 97218 **E-mail:** eandlblackmon@netscape.com

BLOCH, ED
Industry: Nonprofit interfaith advocacy **Univ./degree:** B.S.; M.A., Fletcher College **Current organization:** The Interfaith Alliance of NYS Inc. **Title:** Executive Director **Type of organization:** Interfaith advocacy group **Major product:** People of faith working for justice in public policy **Expertise:** Administration and public speaking **Affiliations:** Former International Rep, United Electric, Radio and Machine Workers Union **SIC code:** 83 **Address:** The Interfaith Alliance of NYS Inc., 1 Lear Jet Lane, Suite 1A, Latham, NY 12110-2313 **E-mail:** blocked1@msn.com **Web address:** www.tianys.org

BLOM, KENNETH M.
Industry: Consulting **Born:** Chapman, Kansas **Univ./degree:** B.S., Civil and Structural Engineering, University of Colorado **Current organization:** Structure Components, Inc. **Title:** President **Type of organization:** Consulting **Major product:** Civil and structural engineering consulting **Area of distribution:** Missouri **Expertise:** Engineering **Published works:** 2 patents **Affiliations:** A.S.C.E. **Hob./spts.:** Woodworking **SIC code:** 87 **Address:** Structure Components, Inc., 9600 E. 53rd St., Raytown, MO 64133 **E-mail:** kenblom@sdc-corp.com

BOLAND, JOHN S.
Industry: Marine equipment **Born:** June 18, 1964, Decatur, Alabama **Univ./degree:** B.S., Belhaven College **Current organization:** Boland Industrial Consulting Services Inc. **Title:** President **Type of organization:** Consulting **Major product:** Mechanical reliability services, marine and industrial precision laser alignment **Area of distribution:** National **Expertise:** Vibration analysis, laser alignment, lubrication, filtration **Hob./spts.:** Sailing **SIC code:** 87 **Address:** Boland Industrial Consulting Services Inc., 622 Azalea Rd., Mobile, AL 36609 **E-mail:** bics@bellsouth.net **Web address:** www.bicsinc.com

BOLLINGER-SIMPSON, PAT
Industry: Interior design **Born:** September 29, 1944, Suffolk, Virginia **Univ./degree:** B.A., 1966; B.A., 1987, University of North Carolina, Greensboro **Current organization:** Bollinger Design Group **Title:** Owner **Type of organization:** Consulting firm **Major product:** Residential and multifamily interiors **Area of distribution:** Denver, Colorado **Expertise:** Interior design **Affiliations:** A.S.I.D.; Denver Better Business Bureau **Hob./spts.:** Gardening, cooking, reading **SIC code:** 87 **Address:** Bollinger

Design Group, 670 Grant St., Denver, CO 80203 **E-mail:** pat@bollingerdesign.net **Web address:** www.bollingerdesign.net

BOLOGNA, JOHN A.
Industry: Engineering **Univ./degree:** B.S., Civil Engineering, 1980; M.S., Civil Engineering, 1986, Rice University **Current organization:** Costal Engineering Co., Inc. **Title:** President **Type of organization:** Consulting Engineers **Major product:** Civil/Structural Engineering Consultants **Area of distribution:** Southeastern Massachusetts, Rhode Island, Connecticut **Expertise:** Consulting, civil, structural and marine engineering, land surveying, servicing public, private and institutional clientele **Honors/awards:** Associate of the Year and Special Recognition Award, Home Builders Association of Massachusetts, 2004; Town of Provincetown Historic Restoration Award; Town of Falmouth Historic Preservation Award; Member, Chi Epsilon and Kappa Mu Epsilon **Published works:** Numerous technical and private client reports, including historical structure survey reports for the Town of Provincetown Heritage Museum, Pilgrim Monument and Town of Harwich Brooks Academy **Affiliations:** A.S.C.E.; N.S.P.E.; A.I.S.C.; A.C.I.; A.W.C.; Home Builders Association of Massachusetts **SIC code:** 87 **Address:** Coastal Engineering Co., Inc., 260 Cranberry Hwy., Orleans, MA 02653 **E-mail:** jbologna@ceccapecod.com **Web address:** www.ceccapecod.com

BOND, ROBERT W.
Industry: Aerospace materials testing **Born:** April 30, 1960, Tulsa, Oklahoma **Univ./degree:** B.S., Engineering, University of Alabama **Current organization:** Morgan Research Corp. **Title:** Senior Engineer **Type of organization:** R&D **Major product:** Aerospace materials testing **Area of distribution:** Alabama **Expertise:** Materials research testing **Published works:** U.S. patent **SIC code:** 87 **Address:** Morgan Research Corp., Bldg. 4612, Room 1213, Huntsville, AL 35812 **E-mail:** robert.bond@nasa.gov

BONHAG, WAYNE THOMPSON
Industry: Consulting engineering **Born:** November 30, 1945, Paterson, New Jersey **Univ./degree:** B.S., 1968; M.S., Mechanical Engineering, 1970, University of Vermont **Current organization:** Bonhag Associates, PLLC **Title:** P.E./P.P./Principal **Type of organization:** Mechanical, electrical and engineering firm **Major product:** Planning, designing, problem solving **Area of distribution:** International **Expertise:** Consulting engineering-mechanical, electrical, energy services, professional planner, Licensed Professional Engineer **Honors/awards:** Listed in 'Who's Who in Finance', 'National Registry of Who's Who' **Published works:** Articles **Affiliations:** A.S.M.E.; I.E.E.E.; N.S.P.E.; A.S.H.R.A.E.; B.O.C.A.; N.F.P.A.; A.E.E., A.F.E.; I.S.A.; Order of Engineers **Hob./spts.:** Sailing, photography, tennis **SIC code:** 87 **Address:** Bonhag Associates, PLLC, 314 Poverty Lane, Lebanon, NH 03766-2705 **E-mail:** wbonhag@bonhagassociates.com

BOOB, DANA R.
Industry: Consulting **Born:** May 29, 1948, Bellefonte, Pennsylvania **Univ./degree:** B.S., Environmental Engineering, Pennsylvania State University, 1973 **Current organization:** Dana R. Boob Surveying & Engineering **Title:** Owner **Type of organization:** Consulting engineering **Major product:** Municipal infrastructures **Area of distribution:** Pennsylvania **Expertise:** Civil engineering **Affiliations:** A.S.C.E.; N.S.P.E.; A.W.W.A. **SIC code:** 87 **Address:** Dana R. Boob Surveying & Engineering, 136 W. Main St., Millheim, PA 16854 **E-mail:** drbse@verizon.net

BOPP, ROLAND J.
Industry: Construction **Born:** September 18, 1952, Würzburg, Germany **Univ./degree:** M.B.A., Maximillian University, Würzburg, Germany; M.A., Worchester University **Current organization:** Turner Corp. **Title:** Executive Vice President **Type of organization:** Consulting firm **Major product:** Construction **Area of distribution:** International **Expertise:** Construction development **Honors/awards:** Member, European CEO **Published works:** Several publications **Affiliations:** American Consul in Germany; American Institute for Contemporary German Studies **Hob./spts.:** Golf, skiing, tennis, swimming **SIC code:** 87 **Address:** Turner Corp., 375 Hudson, New York, NY 10014 **E-mail:** rjbopp@yahoo.com

BORNAZYAN, GEORGE GEVORK
Industry: Cardiac and monitoring systems **Born:** November 25, 1955, Yerevan, Armenia **Univ./degree:** M.S., Physics, Yerevan Polytechnic Institute, Armenia **Current organization:** Philips Medical Systems, Cardiac & Monitoring Systems **Title:** Research and Development Engineer **Type of organization:** Manufacturing, R&D **Major product:** Medical systems **Area of distribution:** National **Expertise:** Wireless engineering **Hob./spts.:** Writing poems, soccer **SIC code:** 87 **Address:** 10214 Sully Dr., Sun Valley, CA 91352 **E-mail:** george.bornazyan@att.com

BOYER, NICODEMUS E.
Industry: Consulting **Born:** June 1, 1925, Daugavpils, Latvia **Univ./degree:** B.S., 1951; M.S., 1952; Ph.D., Chemistry, 1955, University of Illinois at Urbana **Current organization:** Delta Scientific Consultants **Title:** Consultant **Type of organization:** Consulting firm **Major product:** Chemistry consulting and translations **Area of distribution:** International **Expertise:** Organic chemistry, cosmology, languages (European) **Affiliations:** Member, Latvian Academy of Sciences; American Chemistry Society; American Association for the Advancement of Science; New York Academy of Sciences; Sigma Xai **Hob./spts.:** Chess, walking, swimming **SIC code:** 87 **Address:** Delta Scientific Consultants, P.O. Box 312, Three Rivers, MI 49093-0312 **E-mail:** studeophile@cs.com

BOYKINS, MICHELLE L.
Industry: Crime prevention **Born:** March 31, 1970, Staten Island, New York **Univ./degree:** B.A., Communication Studies, Virginia Polytechnic Institute and State University, 1992 **Current organization:** National Crime Prevention Council **Title:** Director, Media Campaigns **Type of organization:** Nonprofit **Major product:** Education materials, training **Area of distribution:** National **Expertise:** Media, advertising, public relations **Published works:** Article **Affiliations:** National Broadcasting Association for Community Affairs **Hob./spts.:** Coaching little league baseball, singing **SIC code:** 86 **Address:** National Crime Prevention Council, 1000 Connecticut Ave. N.W., 13th floor, Washington, DC 20036 **E-mail:** mboykins@ncpc.org **Web address:** www.ncpc.org

BRASEL, TREVOR L.
Industry: Research **Born:** July 19, 1978, Sioux Falls, South Dakota **Univ./degree:** Texas Tech University Health Sciences Center **Current organization:** Lovelace Respiratory Research Institute **Title:** Researcher **Type of organization:** Research institute **Major product:** Research **Area of distribution:** National **Expertise:** Microbiology **Affiliations:** American Society for Microbiology **Hob./spts.:** Hiking, fishing, hunting **SIC code:** 87 **Address:** Lovelace Respiratory Research Institute, 2425 Ridgecrest Dr. S.E., Albuquerque, NM 87108-5127 **E-mail:** tbrasel@lrri.org

BRAUN, RONALD R.
Industry: Consulting **Born:** May 19, 1959, Portland, Oregon **Current organization:** Braun Boiler Consultants **Title:** Tech. Rep./Boiler Consultant, Co-Owner **Type of organization:** Consulting firm **Major product:** Ship boiler repair **Area of distribution:** International **Expertise:** Consulting, boiler repair **Hob./spts.:** Surfing, duck hunting **SIC code:** 87 **Address:** Braun Boiler Consultants, 2971 S.E. Risley Ave., Milwaukee, OR 97267

BREINER, MARTIN M.
Industry: Marketing/information technology **Born:** December 20, 1954, Albany, New York **Univ./degree:** J.D., University of Chicago, 1968 **Current organization:** Oedipus, Inc. **Title:** President/ CEO **Type of organization:** Consulting/educational **Major product:** Software development/educational & financial advice **Area of distribution:** National **Expertise:** Training/software **Affiliations:** A.M.A.; Association of Information Technology; Chicago Chamber of Commerce; Northbrook Chamber of Commerce **Hob./spts.:** Cinema **SIC code:** 87 **Address:** Oedipus, Inc., 1360 N. Sandburg Terrace, Suite 1210C, Chicago, IL 60610 **E-mail:** mbguru1360@yahoo.com

BRIDGES, L.W. DAN
Industry: Research **Univ./degree:** A.B., Harvard University, 1954; M.S., 1958; Ph.D., 1962, University of Texas **Current organization:** Bridges Exploration **Title:** Ph. D./Geologist (Retired) **Type of organization:** Independent research **Major product:** Writing **Area of distribution:** International **Expertise:** Oil exploration **Published works:** "Our Expanding Earth: The Ultimate Cause" **Affiliations:** G.S.A.; A.A.P.G. **SIC code:** 87 **Address:** 1925 S. Vaughn Way, Apt. 207, Aurora, CO 80014 **E-mail:** dbrid41775@aol.com

BROADWIN, ALAN
Industry: Consulting **Born:** April 20, 1935, New York, New York **Univ./degree:** B.A., Columbia College, 1956; B.S., Mechanical Engineering, Columbia School of Engineering, 1957; M.S., Industrial Engineering, Stevens Institute of Technology, 1959 **Current organization:** AINSLIE **Title:** Principal/owner **Type of organization:** Quality systems consulting and auditing **Major product:** Medical devices/aerospace **Area of distribution:** International **Expertise:** Engineering, regulatory **Affiliations:** A.S.M.E.; I.E.E.E. **Hob./spts.:** Music, reading **SIC code:** 87 **Address:** AINSLIE, 27 Pine Ridge Rd., Larchmont, NY 10538-2616 **E-mail:** broadwin@ainslie.com **Web address:** www.lawinfo.com/biz/ainslie

BROCK, LARRY R.
Industry: Consulting **Born:** September 24, 1946, Louisville, Kentucky **Current organization:** L. Brock Consulting **Title:** DB Programmer/PC Trainer/Webmaster/ Educator **Type of organization:** Consulting **Major product:** Web design, PC training, DB design, presentations, PC sales **Area of distribution:** National **Expertise:** Project management, computer technology, consulting, business development **Affiliations:** Educator, Arizona Western College **Hob./spts.:** Golf, fishing **SIC code:** 87 **Address:** 3559 E. Moreno Lane, Yuma, AZ 85365 **E-mail:** shopyuma@adelphia.net **Web address:** www.shopyuma.com

BROKAW, JANE
Industry: Pharmaceuticals **Born:** May 2, 1960, Summerville, New Jersey **Univ./ degree:** B.A., Zoology, Drew University, 1982; Ph.D., Microbiology Immunology, Wake Forest University, 1990 **Current organization:** Alexion Pharmaceuticals **Title:** Senior Staff Scientist **Type of organization:** Research and development **Major product:** Biologic development **Area of distribution:** National **Expertise:** Research and development-transgenic cells, microbiology, zoology **Honors/awards:** Magna Cum Laude; Phi Beta Kappa; Dean Fellowship, graduate school **Published works:** Abstracts **Hob./spts.:** Gardening, biking, physical fitness **SIC code:** 87 **Address:** Alexion Pharmaceuticals, 352 Knotter Dr., Cheshire, CT 06410 **E-mail:** brokawj@alxn.com

BROUILLARD, SCOTT L.
Industry: Biopharmaceuticals **Born:** November 17, 1964, Oswego, New York **Univ./ degree:** Industrial Maintenance, Paul Gate Technical Institute, 1982 **Current organization:** AMGEN **Title:** Mechanical Technician **Type of organization:** Research and manufacturing **Major product:** Biopharmaceuticals **Area of distribution:** National **Expertise:** Mechanical and maintenance support **SIC code:** 87 **Address:** 59 Bank St., Hope Valley, RI 02832 **E-mail:** brouils@amgen.com

BROWN, EUNICE
Industry: Consulting/safety and health **Univ./degree:** B.S., Myers University; M.B.A., Baldwin-Wallace College, 1993 **Current organization:** Risk Techs **Title:** President **Type of organization:** Consulting firm **Major product:** Risk management **Area of distribution:** National **Expertise:** Risk management - safety/health/loss prevention and control **Published works:** Magazine on special needs risk management **Affiliations:** Vice President, PRIMA, Ohio Chapter **Hob./spts.:** Skiing, reading, running, vocalist **SIC code:** 87 **Address:** Risk Techs, P.O. Box 43433, Richmond Heights, OH 44143 **E-mail:** emariamab@aol.com

BRUNO, DAVID J.
Industry: Consumer goods **Born:** September 6, 1951, Martins Ferry, Ohio **Univ./ degree:** B.S., Chemical Engineering, Case Institute of Technology, 1973; M.S., Chemical Engineering, University of Cincinnati, 1979 **Current organization:** Procter & Gamble **Title:** Research Fellow **Type of organization:** Research and development **Major product:** Snack foods **Area of distribution:** International **Expertise:** Engineering **Honors/awards:** Developed technology for Olestra **Published works:** 6 patents, technical reports **Affiliations:** American Institute of Chemical Engineers; Institute of Food Technology; American Oil Chemical Society **Hob./spts.:** Boys Scouts of America, Scoutmaster, coaching football **SIC code:** 87 **Address:** Procter & Gamble, 6071 Center Hill Rd., Cincinnati, OH 45224 **E-mail:** bruno.dj@pg.com

BRYANT, GRANT D.
Industry: Consulting/construction **Born:** May 29, 1979, Terre Haute, Indiana **Univ./ degree:** B.S., Engineering **Current organization:** Koch Materials Company (Koch Industries, Inc.) **Title:** Paving Systems Engineer **Type of organization:** Consulting/ construction **Major product:** Refining, providing pavement solutions, petroleum, asphalt **Area of distribution:** National **Expertise:** Engineering **Affiliations:** A.S.C.E. **Hob./spts.:** Golf, hunting, fishing, outdoor activities **SIC code:** 87 **Address:** Koch Materials Company (Koch Industries, Inc.), 415 N. Tenth St., Terre Haute, IN 47807 **E-mail:** bryantg@kochind.com

BUI, NAM
Industry: Biotechnology **Univ./degree:** B.S., University of California, Davis, 1998 **Current organization:** Celera Diagnostics **Title:** Scientist **Type of organization:** Private study **Major product:** Diagnostics **Area of distribution:** International **Expertise:** Research Scientist, international guest speaker **Hob./spts.:** Golf, tennis **SIC code:** 87 **Address:** 941 Shore Point Ct., F114, Alameda, CA 94502 **E-mail:** dnk2000@gmail.com

BULUSU, PRASAD R.
Industry: Engineering consulting/architecture **Born:** May 14, 1948, Vijaywada, India **Univ./degree:** B.S., Electrical Engineering; M.B.A., Osmania University, Hyderabad, India **Current organization:** Pettit Engineers & Architects **Title:** Project Manager **Type of organization:** Engineering/architecture/construction **Major product:** Project management and process design **Area of distribution:** National **Expertise:** Marketing and engineering; QM and ISO Certifications **Published works:** Rural Marketing of Pumps; Mega Marketing **Affiliations:** Member of International Association of Power Generation, Transmission and Distribution **Hob./spts.:** Reading, yoga, music **SIC code:** 87 **Address:** Barrett Takes Blue, Kennesaw, GA 30144 **E-mail:** prasadbrs@hotmail.com

BURGESS, MICHAEL FRANK
Industry: Consulting/development and financial **Born:** November 28, 1941, Livingstone, Zambia **Univ./degree:** B.S.C.E., Howard Durban College, South Africa, 1964; Bachelor of Commerce, University of South Africa, 1974 **Current organization:** Burgess Developments L.L.C. **Title:** President **Type of organization:** Construction management **Major product:** Professional consulting services **Area of distribution:** National **Expertise:** Financing, project administration **Published works:** 9+ articles **Affiliations:** Former Member, Associate of the Institute of Civil Engineers (London); Elected Member, Institute of Structural Engineers (London); Holds P.E. status in South Africa **Hob./spts.:** Golf, long distance running, reading, travel **SIC code:** 87 **Address:** Burgess Developments L.L.C., 1579F Monroe Dr. N.E. 111, Atlanta, GA 30324 **E-mail:** michael.f.burgess@worldnet.att.net

BURKE, JOSEPH W.
Industry: Engineering consulting **Univ./degree:** B.S., US Merchant Marine Academy, 1990 **Current organization:** KP Professional Engineering, PC **Title:** President/Owner **Type of organization:** Engineering firm **Major product:** Mechanical & electrical engineering design drawings and specifications **Area of distribution:** Lindenhurst, New York **Expertise:** Engineering, marketing, business management **Affiliations:** I.E.E.E.; A.S.H.R.A.E.; N.F.P.A.; I.E.S. **SIC code:** 87 **Address:** KP Professional Engineering, PC, 503 S. Fifth St., Lindenhurst, NY 11757 **E-mail:** kpeng90@aol.com

BURNELL, DANIEL K.
Industry: Environmental **Born:** August 1, 1963, Oak Lawn, Illinois **Univ./degree:** B.S., Geology and Mathematics, University of Illinois; M.S., Geophysics; Ph.D., Geophysics, Georgia Tech, 2002 **Current organization:** GeoTrans Inc. **Title:** Senior Hydrologist **Type of organization:** Consulting **Major product:** Ground water cleanup **Area of distribution:** National **Expertise:** Mathematical modeling **Affiliations:** American Geophysical Union; American Mathematics Society **Hob./spts.:** Chess, Little League baseball **SIC code:** 87 **Address:** GeoTrans Inc., 46010 Manekin Plaza, Sterling, VA 20166 **E-mail:** dburnell@geotransinc.com **Web address:** www.geotransinc.com

BURNHAM, DOUGLAS E.
Industry: Hospitality **Born:** July 11, 1958 **Univ./degree:** A.S., University of Maine **Current organization:** Spanish Wells Golf & Country Club **Title:** General Manager **Type of organization:** Country club **Major product:** Golf, tennis courts, fitness center, fine dining **Area of distribution:** Bonita Springs, Florida **Expertise:** Budgeting, construction **Affiliations:** P.G.A.; C.M.A.A. **Hob./spts.:** Golf, boating, deep-sea fishing **SIC code:** 86 **Address:** Spanish Wells Golf & Country Club, 9801 Treasure Cay Lane, Bonita Springs, FL 34135 **E-mail:** dougburnham@spwells.com

BURTON, DAVID R.
Industry: Pharmaceutical/consulting **Born:** August 2, 1969, Kingsport, Tennessee **Univ./degree:** A.A., Nuclear Chemistry Technology, U.S. Navy, 1991 **Current organization:** Commissioning Agents, Inc. **Title:** Validation Specialist **Type of organization:** Commissioning/validation **Major product:** New/remodeled facilities **Area of distribution:** National **Expertise:** Laboratory commissioning **Affiliations:** International Society of Pharmaceutical Engineers **Hob./spts.:** Family, golf, woodworking, travel, reading, history **SIC code:** 87 **Address:** Commissioning Agents, Inc., 5711 Columbia Circle South, Greenwood, IN 46142 **E-mail:** dave.burton@cagents.com

BUSH, MITCHELL L.
Industry: Cultural organization **Born:** February 1, 1936, Syracuse, New York **Current organization:** American Indian Society **Title:** Founder/Editor for Newsletter **Type of organization:** Cultural **Major product:** Newsletter **Area of distribution:** National **Expertise:** Writer **Honors/awards:** American Indian Society Outstanding Elder/Advisor, 1996; Honored by American Indian Community House/Thunderbird American Indian Dancers of NYC, 1991; Honored at the Nanticoke Pow Wow, DE, Pow Wow "Points of Light" Certificate, Dept. of Interior, 1990; Certificate for Outstanding Public Service to the USA, Dept. of Interior, 1990; Maharishi Award conferred by Maharishi University, 1985 **Affiliations:** Member, Virginia Council on Indian Affairs; Board of Directors, Governors' Interstate Indian Council **Hob./spts.:** Reading, sets up information booths at different events and speaks about American Indians **SIC code:** 86 **Address:** American Indian Society, 22258 Cool Water Dr., Ruther Glen, VA 22546 **Web address:** www.aisdc.org

BUSMANN, THOMAS G.
Industry: Consulting **Born:** Buhl, Idaho **Univ./degree:** B.S., University of Idaho, 1980 **Current organization:** Focus Environmental Inc. **Title:** Manager, Process Engineering **Type of organization:** Engineering **Major product:** Environmental and FDA regulatory compliance **Area of distribution:** National **Expertise:** Process engineering **Published works:** 10 articles **Affiliations:** A.I.C.H.E.; A.W.M.A., I.S.A. **Hob./spts.:** Family, computers, travel **SIC code:** 87 **Address:** Focus Environmental Inc., 9050

Executive Park Dr., Suite A-202, Knoxville, TN 37923 **E-mail:** tbusmann@focusenv.com

BUTLER, RAYMOND D.
Industry: Family services **Born:** June 4, 1969, Cleveland, Ohio **Univ./degree:** B.A., Kent State University, 1997 **Current organization:** Janus Development Services, Inc. **Title:** Vice President of Manufacturing **Type of organization:** Not-for-Profit **Major product:** Contract Packaging **Area of distribution:** Indiana **Expertise:** Business operations **Hob./spts.:** Remodeling houses **SIC code:** 86 **Address:** Janus Developmental Services, Inc., 1555 Westfield Rd., Noblesville, IN 46060 **E-mail:** butler@janus-inc.org

BUTSCH, OTTO R.
Industry: Medical/consulting **Born:** November 6, 1936, Columbus, Ohio **Univ./degree:** Ph.D., Mechanical Engineering, Ohio State University, 1980 **Current organization:** OR Butsch & Associates **Title:** President **Type of organization:** Consulting firm **Major product:** Engineering, consulting, development for healthcare **Area of distribution:** National **Expertise:** Engineering **Honors/awards:** 50 patents **Hob./spts.:** Photography **SIC code:** 87 **Address:** OR Butsch & Associates, 1128 E. Yorba Linda Blvd., Placentia, CA 92870 **E-mail:** orbutsch@pacbell.net

CALDERA, GUSTAVO
Industry: Consulting **Born:** July 2, 1961, Zacatecas, Mexico **Univ./degree:** A.S., Engineering, Irvine Valley College, 1984 **Current organization:** FBA Engineering **Title:** Senior Associate **Type of organization:** Consulting, engineering **Major product:** Electrical, fire alarms, telecommunications **Area of distribution:** California **Expertise:** Engineering **Affiliations:** I.E.E.E.; I.E.S. **Hob./spts.:** Soccer **SIC code:** 87 **Address:** FBA Engineering, 3420 Irvine Ave., Suite 200, Newport Beach, CA 92660 **E-mail:** gcaldera@fbaengineering.net

CALDERÓN-SÁNCHEZ, ROBERTO
Industry: Dredging **Born:** July 28, 1930 Carolina, Puerto Rico **Univ./degree:** B.S., Civil Engineering, University of Puerto Rico, 1968 **Current organization:** Scientific Dredging Institute **Title:** Professional Engineer/President/Founder **Type of organization:** Engineering **Major product:** Engineering **Area of distribution:** Puerto Rico **Expertise:** Engineering **Published works:** Book **Affiliations:** A.S.C.E.; International Biography Association; Western Dredging Association, Vancouver, Washington **Hob./spts.:** Presenting poetry by Ruben Dario **SIC code:** 87 **Address:** Urb Santa Maria #6, Azucena Street, San Juan, PR 00927-6731

CAPPS, KEVIN GENE
Industry: Architecture **Born:** April 12, 1963, Bitburgh AFB, Germany **Univ./degree:** B.S., Architecture, University of Texas at Arlington, 1986 **Current organization:** DMS Architects, Inc. **Title:** Architect **Type of organization:** Design firm **Major product:** Architectural design **Area of distribution:** Fort Worth, Texas **Expertise:** Architecture, education facilities **Affiliations:** The American Institute of Architects; Texas Society of Architects **Hob./spts.:** Martial arts **SIC code:** 87 **Address:** 7809 Lake Meredith, Ft. Worth, TX 76104 **E-mail:** kcapps@dmsarch.com **Web address:** www.dmsarch.com

CARLISLE, BRYAN K.
Industry: Telecommunications **Born:** May 18, 1961, Jacinto City, Texas **Univ./degree:** A.A.S., Elementary Education, Mississippi Gulf Coast College, 1999; B.S.E.E., Kennedy-Western University, 2005 **Current organization:** MILCOM Systems Corp. **Title:** Senior Field Engineer **Type of organization:** Federal contractor **Major product:** High frequency electronics, technical and engineering services **Area of distribution:** International **Expertise:** Design, engineering and installation of high frequency electronics; SAGE Certified to teach **Affiliations:** U.S. Navy, 1979-2000, Retired as Aviation Electronics Sr. Chief Petty Officer **Hob./spts.:** Woodcrafting, home redesign, travel, bicycling **SIC code:** 87 **Address:** 206 Vine St., Goose Creek, SC 29445 **E-mail:** bcarlisle@milcom-systems.com

CARPENTER, ROBERT B.
Industry: Social services **Born:** June 7, 1968, Port Thomas, Kentucky **Univ./degree:** M.S., Clinical Psychology, Eastern Kentucky University, 1993 **Current organization:** ENA, Inc. DBA NECCO **Title:** Executive Director/L.P.C.C. **Type of organization:** Family service agency **Major product:** Foster care **Area of distribution:** National **Expertise:** Youth services, crisis intervention **Hob./spts.:** Landscaping **SIC code:** 83 **Address:** ENA, Inc. DBA NECCO, 75 Cavalier Blvd., Suite 110, Florence, KY 41042 **E-mail:** bobc@necco.org

CARR, JONATHAN J.
Industry: Engineering **Born:** October 7, 1972, Auburn, New York **Univ./degree:** B.S., Syracuse University **Current organization:** ManTech MSTC **Title:** Sr. Project Manager **Type of organization:** Consulting engineering/government contractor **Major product:** Security engineering **Area of distribution:** International **Expertise:** Engineering/security **Hob./spts.:** Mountain climbing, mountain biking **SIC code:** 87 **Address:** 305 Patrick St. S.W., Vienna, VA 22180 **E-mail:** carrj@state.gov

CASCONE, JAMES CARLO
Industry: Financial/consulting **Born:** July 14, 1968, Quebec, Montreal **Univ./degree:** B.S., Economics & Management, Concordia University, Canada, 1992 **Current organization:** Deloitte & Touche **Title:** Senior Manager **Type of organization:** Accounting firm **Major product:** Management consulting **Area of distribution:** National **Expertise:** Risk assessments, internal audit; 3 certifications internationally **Honors/awards:** Speaks fluent in Italian, English, French **Affiliations:** I.S.A.C.A.; I.S.C.²; Institute of Internal Auditors **Hob./spts.:** Volleyball, rollerblading, history, astronomy **SIC code:** 87 **Address:** Deloitte & Touche, 350 S. Grand Ave., Los Angeles, CA 90071 **E-mail:** jcascone@cox.net

CASTRO, MILTON
Industry: Consulting **Born:** September 25, 1921, Ponce, Puerto Rico **Univ./degree:** Ph.D., Electrical Engineering, University of Puerto Rico **Current organization:** Milton Castro & Associates **Title:** Electrical Engineer **Type of organization:** Consulting firm **Major product:** Engineering consulting services **Area of distribution:** Puerto Rico **Expertise:** Engineering **Affiliations:** N.S.P.E.; I.E.E.E. **Hob./spts.:** Music, radio **SIC code:** 87 **Address:** Milton Castro & Associates, 1708 Ponce de Leon Ave., Suite 302, San Juan, PR 00909 **E-mail:** mcastro@icepr.com

CÁTALA, MARTA E.
Industry: Religion **Born:** September 25, 1938, Puerto Rico **Univ./degree:** Lehman College, New York, 1961 **Current organization:** Botanica San Miguel **Title:** President **Type of organization:** Social services and religious items **Major product:** Healing oils, incense, candles, natural herbs **Area of distribution:** Miami, Florida **Expertise:** Readings for people **Affiliations:** P.R.O.F.E.S.A. **Hob./spts.:** Painting, floral arrangements **SIC code:** 86 **Address:** Botanica San Miguel, 3533 N.W. 17th Ave., Miami, FL 33142 **Phone:** (305)634-7469

CAVANAUGH, JEAN
Industry: Volunteer Organizations **Born:** June 27, 1924, Lake City, Iowa **Univ./degree:** B.S., Business Administration, 1970; M.S., Guidance and Counseling, 1971, Fort Hays State University; Education Specialist Degree, Hays State University, 1975 **Current organization:** USD #428 School Board/KOOD (Smoky Hills) Public TV Station **Title:** School Board Member **Type of organization:** Volunteer **Major product:** Volunteer work **Area of distribution:** Great Bend, Kansas **Expertise:** Guidance and education **Honors/awards:** Citizen of the Year for Community Service, Chamber of Commerce; Martin Luther King Jr. Award for Community Service **Affiliations:** State School Board Association; Juvenile Service Advisor/Counselor; Pilot International (Past Governors of Missouri and Kansas); Cosmopolitan; Past State President, A.M.A.; Chamber of Commerce; National Middle School Association; Ladies' Study Club **Hob./spts.:** Family-children, soccer, reading, volunteer work **SIC code:** 86 **Address:** 5103 Telstar Lane, Great Bend, KS 67530

CELIA, VICTORIA M.
Industry: Finance/accounting **Univ./degree:** B.S., Accounting, Syracuse University, 1981 **Current organization:** Celia & Allen, LLC & Victoria M. Celia, CPA **Title:** Licensed C.P.A./Partner **Type of organization:** Accounting firm **Major product:** Tax preparation and accounting **Area of distribution:** New Hartford, New York **Expertise:** Certified public accountant **Affiliations:** N.Y.S.S.C.P.A.; A.I.C.P.A.; National Society of Accountants **Hob./spts.:** American Saddlebreds, horseback riding, walking, biking, sporting dogs, reading, community service **SIC code:** 87 **Address:** Celia & Allen, LLC & Victoria M. Celia, CPA, 26 New Hartford Shopping Center, New Hartford, NY 13413 **E-mail:** celiaallen@msn.com

CERQUETTI, JEFFREY
Industry: Power generation **Born:** June 16, 1958, Baltimore, Maryland **Univ./degree:** M.S., Civil Engineering, Johns Hopkins University, 2002; Ph.D. Candidate **Current organization:** Wartsila NA, Inc. **Title:** Chief Design Engineer **Type of organization:** Power plant constructor **Major product:** Electrical generators/power plants **Area of distribution:** International **Expertise:** Civil/ocean engineering **Affiliations:** A.M.S.; A.S.C.E.; A.S.H.R.A. **SIC code:** 87 **Address:** Wartsila NA, Inc., 201 Defense Hwy., Suite 100, Annapolis, MD 21401 **E-mail:** jec@pencilbox.com

CHANG, YIE-HWA
Industry: Biotechnology/biopharmaceuticals **Born:** Chiayi, Taiwan **Univ./degree:** B.S., Organic Chemistry, National Taiwan University, 1977; Ph.D., California Institute of Technology, 1987 **Current organization:** Mediomics, LLC **Title:** President **Type of organization:** R&D, manufacturing **Major product:** CAMP Fluorescence Assay Kit, SAM Fluorescence Assay Kit and Trip Fluorescence **Area of distribution:** National **Expertise:** Proteomics, drug discovery, corporate management, business development **Published works:** 30+ publications **Affiliations:** A.C.S.; A.S.B.M.B.; Society for Neuroscience **Hob./spts.:** Swimming, tennis **SIC code:** 87 **Address:** Mediomics, LLC, 815 Wenneker Dr., St. Louis, MO 63124 **E-mail:** yiechang@mediomics.com

CHAO, TOM
Industry: Construction/engineering **Born:** December 23, 1960, Taiwan **Univ./degree:** B.S.C.E., National Chung-Hsing University, Taiwan, 1983; M.E., 1987; Ph.D. Candidate, Lamar University **Current organization:** Huntley, Nyce & Assoc., Ltd. **Title:** Vice President, Branch Manager **Type of organization:** Civil engineering firm **Major product:** Residential and non-residential land development **Area of distribution:** Virginia, West Virginia, Georgia **Expertise:** Site plan and construction plan designs, stone water quality and controls; Licensed Professional Engineer in Virginia and West Virginia **Hob./spts.:** Reading **SIC code:** 87 **Address:** Huntley, Nyce & Assoc., Ltd., 751 Miller Dr., Suite F-2, Leesburg, VA 20175 **E-mail:** tchao@hna-civil.com **Web address:** www.huntleynyce.com

CHARIFA, RIZALDY D.
Industry: Consulting **Born:** February 28, 1957, Philippines **Univ./degree:** B.S., Civil Engineering; B.S., Sanitary Engineering, Philippines National University, 1978 **Current organization:** Titanium Engineering & Construction **Title:** Consulting Engineer **Type of organization:** Engineering/construction **Major product:** Civil/structural engineering and construction management **Area of distribution:** California **Expertise:** Construction and project management on an international level (residential, commercial, institutional) **Affiliations:** American Society of Civil Engineers (ASCE) **Hob./spts.:** Tennis, swimming, boating, golf **SIC code:** 87 **Address:** Titanium Engineering & Construction, 815 W. Cesar E. Chavez Ave., Suite 205, Los Angeles, CA 90012 **E-mail:** titaniumcompany@sbcglobal.net

CHASI, LUIS
Industry: Consulting **Born:** May 25, 1967, Costa Rica **Univ./degree:** B.S., Civil Engineering, University of Costa Rica; M.S., Texas A & M University; M.B.A., National University, 1991 **Current organization:** Condisa **Title:** General Manager **Type of organization:** Consulting firm **Major product:** Architecture and engineering **Area of distribution:** International **Expertise:** Project management **Affiliations:** C.R.A.; E.P.C.; A.S.C.E.; A.S.H.C.E. **Hob./spts.:** Business reading, tennis **SIC code:** 87 **Address:** Condisa, P.O. Box 025635, Miami, FL 33102 **E-mail:** lchasi@condisa.net

CHAUDHURI, SUBRATA N.
Industry: Consulting **Born:** March 13, 1949, India **Univ./degree:** B.S., Civil Engineering, Jadapur College; M.S., Civil Engineering, Special Structures, Carnegie Mellon University, 1979 **Current organization:** The Louis Berger Group, Inc. **Title:** P.E./Senior Project Engineer **Type of organization:** Consulting firm **Major product:** Engineering (transportation related) **Area of distribution:** International **Expertise:** Structural engineering **Published works:** Report on 7.9 earthquake in India **Affiliations:** A.S.C.E.; B.S.C.E. **Hob./spts.:** Volunteer work **SIC code:** 87 **Address:** The Louis Berger Group, Inc., 75 Second Ave., Suite 700, Needham, MA 02494 **E-mail:** schaudhuri@aol.com

CHEN, SHO LONG
Industry: Semiconductors **Born:** October 19, 1952, Taipei, Taiwan **Univ./degree:** Ph.D., University of Cincinnati, 1981 **Current organization:** VWEB Corp. **Title:** President/CEO/Founder **Type of organization:** Research and development of IC **Major product:** Video compression IC **Area of distribution:** International **Expertise:** Engineering **Affiliations:** I.E.E.E.; I.S.O.M.P.E.G.; Churchill Club; X3L3; CIE **Hob./spts.:** Tennis, karaoke, track and field, art, classical music **SIC code:** 87 **Address:** VWEB Corp., 5300 Stevens Creek Blvd., #3, San Jose, CA 95129 **E-mail:** slchen@vwebcorp.com **Web address:** www.vwebcorp.com

CHENG, WEIDONG
Industry: Engineering **Born:** February 27, 1969, Henan, China **Univ./degree:** Ph.D., Engineering, University of Notre Dame, 2002 **Current organization:** Advantica **Title:** Ph.D./Consulting Engineer **Type of organization:** Consulting **Major product:** Engineering hydraulics **Area of distribution:** International **Expertise:** Engineering/research **Affiliations:** A.S.M.E. **Hob./spts.:** Reading **SIC code:** 87 **Address:** Advantica, 5177 Richmond Ave., Suite 900, Houston, TX 77056-6745 **E-mail:** weidong.cheng@advantica.biz

CHERI, CAREY M.
Industry: Finance **Born:** July 6, 1961, New Orleans, Louisiana **Univ./degree:** M.B.A., Ohio State University, 1989; M.A., Genetic Engineering, Indiana University, 1987 **Current organization:** Accelerent Partners **Title:** Principal **Type of organization:** Financial consulting **Major product:** Consulting services **Area of distribution:** National **Expertise:** Business consulting **Hob./spts.:** Home remodeling **SIC code:** 87 **Address:** Accelerent Partners, 207 Eastmoor Blvd., Columbus, OH 43209 **E-mail:** ccheri@ameritech.net

CHINNAH, ANTHONY D.
Industry: Biotechnology, biopharmaceutical **Born:** January 13, 1950, Danhauser, Republic of South Africa **Univ./degree:** B.Sc., Northeast London Poly., University of East London, U.K.; Ph.D., Vet. Biology, Texas A&M University, 1990 **Current organization:** Delsite Biotechnologies, Inc., R&D **Title:** Research Scientist **Type of organization:** Biopharmaceutical **Major product:** Drug delivery matricies **Area of distribution:** National **Expertise:** Cell biology/biochemistry **Published works:** Several research papers **Affiliations:** A.C.S.; A.A.P.S.; A.A.A.S. **Hob./spts.:** Cooking, art, astronomy, music, gardening **SIC code:** 87 **Address:** Delsite Biotechnologies, Inc., R&D, 1505 Walnut Hill Lane, Irving, TX 75038-3702 **E-mail:** tchinnah@delsitebiotech.com

CHITTENDEN, ROBERT N.
Industry: Engineering **Born:** March 17, 1948, Auburn, California **Univ./degree:** D.Eng., University of California, 1982 (candidate) **Current organization:** Chittenden Engineering **Title:** Principle, D.Eng., P.E. **Type of organization:** Engineering firm **Area of distribution:** National **Expertise:** Structural engineering (seismic); development of building codes, including International Building Code, structural User's Guide to the IBC and MSJC code **Published works:** Co-author, 1 book **Affiliations:** A.S.C.E.; A.C.I.; P.E.I. **Hob./spts.:** Skiing **SIC code:** 87 **Address:** Chittenden Engineering, 1775 Old Airport Rd., Auburn, CA 95602 **E-mail:** bchitten@yahoo.com

CHOUBAH, HALIM A.
Industry: Consulting **Born:** December 28, 1962, Beirut, Lebanon **Univ./degree:** B.S.C.E., University of Massachusetts, 1986 **Current organization:** Hal Choubah, P.E. **Title:** Professional Engineer **Type of organization:** Consulting firm **Major product:** Engineering services **Area of distribution:** National **Expertise:** Civil engineering, site development, subdivision layouts **Affiliations:** A.S.C.E.; P.E., Massachusetts **Hob./spts.:** Travel, biking, swimming **SIC code:** 87 **Address:** Hal Choubah, P.E., 2 Purple Wing Lane, North Dartmouth, MA 02747 **E-mail:** choubah@aol.com

CHOURA, BANA
Industry: Architecture **Univ./degree:** M.A., Architecture/Design, Pratt Institute **Current organization:** Choura Architecture **Title:** President **Type of organization:** Architectural firm **Major product:** Design services **Area of distribution:** International **Expertise:** Residential design **Affiliations:** A.R.A.; S.A.R.A.; W.B.E. **Hob./spts.:** Dancing, skiing **SIC code:** 87 **Address:** Choura Architecture, 1 Barker Ave., White Plains, NY 10601 **E-mail:** chouraarch@yahoo.com

CLARK, ODIS M.
Industry: Religion **Born:** January 23, 1944, Frankfort, Kentucky **Univ./degree:** B.A., Louisville Bible College; M.S.L., Sacred Literature; M.M., Ministry, Kentucky Christian College **Current organization:** Indian Hills Christian Church **Title:** Minister **Type of organization:** Church **Major product:** Religious services, spiritual enlightenment **Area of distribution:** Kentucky **Expertise:** Assisting underprivileged youth through counseling and spiritual guidance; community activities, fund raising, consulting, avid lecturer, public speaker, musical recording artist **Published works:** Several articles in the Christian Standard & The Lookout Magazine **Affiliations:** Chairman, Danville/Boyle County Senior Citizen Committee; Secretary, Danville Rotary Club; Southern Christian Youth Convention **Hob./spts.:** Spending quality time with family and friends, fishing, hunting **SIC code:** 86 **Address:** 516 Grabruck St., Danville, KY 40422 **E-mail:** ihcc@mis.net

CLARK III, SHIELDS E.
Industry: Government **Born:** August 30, 1938, Hattiesburg, Mississippi **Univ./degree:** B.S.C.E., Building Construction, University of Florida, 1963 **Current organization:** Hillsborough County **Title:** Review Team Leader **Type of organization:** Engineering firm **Major product:** Civil engineering, land surveying, flood plain management **Expertise:** Engineering/P.E. **Affiliations:** A.S.C.E.; A.S.F.P. **Hob./spts.:** Family, golf, community volunteering **SIC code:** 87 **Address:** Hillsborough County, P.O. Box 1110, 19th floor, Tampa, FL 33601 **E-mail:** clarks@hillsboroughcounty.org

CLARKE, RAYMOND
Industry: Socio-Economic services **Born:** August 2, 1950, Cincinnati, Ohio **Univ./degree:** B.S., Correctional Administration; M.S., Rehabilitation Administration, University of Arizona, College of Education, 1978 **Current organization:** Tucson Urban League **Title:** President, CEO **Type of organization:** Nonprofit social programs **Major product:** Providing quality programs for individuals **Area of distribution:** National **Expertise:** Business and public administration **Honors/awards:** Scholarship named in honor of Ray Clarke, University of Arizona; Dr. M.L. King Distinguished Leadership Award, University of Arizona; Pima County Distinguished Community Services Award; Tucson Mayor's Copper Letter of Appreciation; Myer & Libby Marmis Humanitarian Award; NAACP Service Award; University of Arizona Black Alumni Outstanding Achievement Award **Affiliations:** Association of Executives - National Urban League **Hob./spts.:** Walking, hiking **SIC code:** 83 **Address:** Tucson Urban League, 2305 S. Park Ave., Tucson, AZ 85713 **E-mail:** rclarke@tucsonurbanleague.net **Web address:** www.tusconurbanleague.net

CLEVELAND, DANIEL J.
Industry: Design/Construction/Architecture **Born:** December 28, 1950, Portland, Oregon **Univ./degree:** B.A., Architecture., University of Idaho, 1972 **Current organization:** Images By Daniel **Title:** President **Type of organization:** Private firm **Major**

product: Residential/industrial construction and design **Area of distribution:** Houston, Texas **Expertise:** Design, auto CAD **Affiliations:** N.A.S.A. **Hob./spts.:** Amateur bicycling, racing **SIC code:** 87 **Address:** Images By Daniel, 10223 Copperwood Dr., Houston, TX 77040-1719 **E-mail:** bikingdan@attglobal.net

COBB, WILLIAM R.
Industry: Engineering **Born:** December 30, 1944, Astoria, New York **Univ./degree:** Business Administration, Communications, State University of New York at Farmingdale **Current organization:** CH2M Hill, Inc. **Title:** Managing Director **Type of organization:** Engineering **Major product:** Engineering services **Area of distribution:** International **Expertise:** Engineering and technology **Affiliations:** Armed Forces Communication and Electronics Association; American Management Presidents Association **Hob./spts.:** Golf, hiking, biking **SIC code:** 87 **Address:** CH2M Hill, Inc., 9189 S. Jamaica St., Englewood, CO 80112-5946 **E-mail:** bcobb@cham.com

COHEN, RICHARD J.
Industry: Engineering consulting **Born:** May 30, 1952, Queens, New York **Univ./degree:** B.S., Civil & Environmental Engineering, 1975; M.S., Civil & Environmental Engineering, University of Rhode Island, 1978 **Current organization:** RJ Cohen Engineering Assoc. **Title:** Owner **Type of organization:** Engineering firm **Major product:** Civil engineering services **Area of distribution:** National **Expertise:** Civil and environmental engineering **Honors/awards:** Lifetime Member, National Registry of Who's Who **Published works:** 4 articles **Affiliations:** National Society of Professional Engineers **SIC code:** 87 **Address:** RJ Cohen Engineering Assoc., 1117 Main St., West Warwick, RI 02893 **E-mail:** rjcohen@riconnect.com

COLEMAN, DREW CLARKE
Industry: Biotechnology **Born:** January 29, 1959, Alameda, California **Univ./degree:** Ph.D., American College, 1988 **Current organization:** ICOS Corp. **Title:** Director of Engineering **Type of organization:** Research and development, manufacturing **Major product:** Human therapeutics **Area of distribution:** International **Expertise:** Process and plant engineering **Affiliations:** International Society of Pharmaceutical Engineers; Chair, Polymer Chemistry Group; American Society of Mechanical Engineers **Hob./spts.:** Judo (Black Belt), woodworking, antique steam engines and boilers **SIC code:** 87 **Address:** ICOS Corp., 22021 20th Ave. S.E., Bothell, WA 98021 **E-mail:** dcoleman@icos.com

COLLINS, CLARE E.
Industry: Social services **Born:** September 23, 1949, Norwalk, Connecticut **Univ./degree:** M.S., Special Education **Current organization:** Sunrise Associates, Inc. **Title:** Executive Director **Type of organization:** Nonprofit **Major product:** Residential support to children with disabilities **Area of distribution:** Maine **Expertise:** Management, administration, clinical **Affiliations:** Board Member, A.V.E.D. **Hob./spts.:** Raising St. Bernard dogs **SIC code:** 83 **Address:** Sunrise Associates, Inc., 62 Portland Rd., Kennebunk, ME 04043 **E-mail:** sunrisemaine@mainecc.com

COMBS JR., IRA
Industry: Human services **Born:** March 21, 1958, Michigan **Current organization:** Christ Centered Homes, Inc. **Title:** Executive Director **Type of organization:** Housing provider **Major product:** Residential care, housing, community support services **Area of distribution:** Michigan **Expertise:** Daily operations oversight **Affiliations:** R.N.C. - T.V. Representative **Hob./spts.:** Golf **SIC code:** 83 **Address:** Christ Centered Homes, Inc., 327 W. Monroe St., Jackson, MI 49202 **E-mail:** ira@modempool.com

CONDITT, MARGARET KAREN
Industry: Consumer goods **Born:** August 7, 1953, Mobile, Alabama **Univ./degree:** Ph.D., Chemistry, University of Colorado at Boulder, 1984 **Current organization:** Procter & Gamble Pharmaceuticals **Title:** Account Executive in Women's Health **Type of organization:** R & D **Major product:** Women's health products **Area of distribution:** International **Expertise:** Professional and scientific relations, final phase education in new product development **Honors/awards:** Teaching Awards, Team Awards **Published works:** 30+ articles **Affiliations:** A.C.S.; North American Menopause Society **Hob./spts.:** Volunteer for the Boy Scouts (Merit Badge Counselor), theological studies, volunteer work **SIC code:** 87 **Address:** Procter & Gamble Pharmaceuticals, 8700 Mason-Montgomery Rd., Mason, OH 45040

CONNOLLY, ÚNA M.
Industry: Social services **Born:** May 15, 1933, Galway, Ireland **Univ./degree:** M.Ed., School Counseling, 1997; M.A., Marriage and Family Counseling, 1983,Loyola Marymount University **Current organization:** Valley Family Center **Title:** Founder **Type of organization:** Counseling center **Major product:** Marriage and family counseling services **Area of distribution:** California **Expertise:** Licensed Marriage and Family Therapist **Honors/awards:** Honored for Outstanding Service to Valley Family Center, 2006, Woman of the Year, Los Angeles County, Supervisor, 2005 **Affiliations:** Professed Sisters of Charity; San Fernando Chamber of Commerce; California Association of Marriage and Family Therapists **SIC code:** 83 **Address:** Valley Family Center, 302 S. Brand Blvd., San Fernando, CA 91340 **E-mail:** valleyfamilycentersf@hotmail.com

CONOVER, JAMES H.
Industry: Pharmaceuticals **Univ./degree:** Ph.D., New York University, 1969 **Current organization:** Endo Pharmaceuticals, Inc. **Title:** VP, Regulatory Affairs **Type of organization:** Pharmaceuticals research and development **Major product:** Drug development **Area of distribution:** National **Expertise:** Regulatory affairs **Honors/awards:** National Cystic Fibrosis Award, 1976-1979 **Published works:** 24+ Articles **Affiliations:** D.I.A. **SIC code:** 87 **Address:** Endo Pharmaceuticals, Inc., 100 Painters Dr., Chadds Ford, PA 19317 **E-mail:** conover.james@endo.com

CONRAD, JAMES L.
Industry: Power generation systems **Born:** January 28, 1948, Houston, Texas **Univ./degree:** B.A., Physics and Math, Rice University, 1970 **Title:** Independent Consultant **Type of organization:** Self-employed **Major product:** Power generation systems **Area of distribution:** International **Expertise:** Sizing of generation systems **Affiliations:** I.E.E.E.; Industrial Applications Society **Hob./spts.:** Houston Tennis Club, jogging, book collecting (technical/historical) **SIC code:** 87 **Address:** 220 W. Helms Rd., Houston, TX 77037 **E-mail:** jameslcusa@netscape.net

CONRAD REGAN, TERRI JO
Industry: Consulting/law **Born:** October 15, 1961, Champaign, Illinois **Univ./degree:** B.B.A., Southern Methodist University, 1983; M.B.A., Pace University, 1986; J.D., Albany Law School, 1990 **Current organization:** UHY Advisors NY, Inc. **Title:** Principal **Type of organization:** Tax and business consultants **Major product:** Financial services **Area of distribution:** National **Expertise:** Taxation **Affiliations:** A.I.C.P.A.; New York State Bar Association; New York Society of Certified Public Accountants **SIC code:** 87 **Address:** UHY Advisors NY, Inc., 66 State St., Albany, NY 12207 **E-mail:** tregan@uhy-us.com **Web address:** www.uhy-us.com

CONSTANTAKOS, SCOTT
Industry: Aerospace & building systems **Born:** August 10, 1953, North Kingston, Rhode Island **Univ./degree:** A.A., Architecture, Palm Beach Community College, 1981; B.S., Program Management, Barry University, 1983; M.B.A., International Business, University of Miami, 1999; M.S. Candidate, University of Miami **Current organization:** United Technologies Pratt & Whitney Advanced Projects **Title:** Project Manager **Type of organization:** Research, manufacturing **Major product:** Rocket and gas turbine engines, building systems **Area of distribution:** International **Expertise:** Project management, engineering; Certified Pollutant Storage Contractor; Florida Real Estate Certificate **Affiliations:** Southern Building Code Congress **SIC code:** 87 **Address:** 1507 Lance Rd., Jupiter, FL 33469 **E-mail:** constan1@pwfl.com

CONWAY, TERRY R.
Industry: Project engineering **Born:** February 4, 1954, Waseca, Minnesota **Univ./degree:** B.S., Mechanical Engineering, Minnesota State University, 2001 **Current organization:** TRC Engineering, LLC **Title:** Owner **Type of organization:** Mechanical design and prototype **Major product:** Mechanical design **Area of distribution:** Minnesota **Expertise:** Engineering **Affiliations:** A.S.M.E. **SIC code:** 87 **Address:** TRC Engineering, LLC, 27603 100th St., Waseca, MN 56093-5900 **E-mail:** terryc@clear.lakes.com

COONES, CHARLES M.
Industry: Engineering **Born:** January 24, 1955, Louisville, Kentucky **Univ./degree:** B.S.C.E., 1977; M.Eng., Civil Engineering, 1978, University of Louisville; M.S., Environmental Engineering, University of Tennessee, 1999 **Current organization:** Donan Engineering Co. **Title:** Senior Forensic Engineer **Type of organization:** Consulting engineering firm **Major product:** Forensic investigation **Area of distribution:** National **Expertise:** Structural, fire protection and safety engineering **Honors/awards:** Westinghouse Quality Award for Program Development, 1991 **Published works:** 2 articles on safety and structural issues **Affiliations:** National Fire Protection Association; Tech . Committee, Fire Protection for Nuclear Facilities; American Society of Civil Engineers **Hob./spts.:** Tennis, target shooting **SIC code:** 87 **Address:** Donan Engineering Co., 1838 Elm Hill Pike, Suite 127, Nashville, TN 37210 **E-mail:** ccoones@donan.com **Web address:** www.donan.com

COONEY, GERRY
Industry: Professional services **Born:** August 4, 1956, New York, New York **Current organization:** F.I.S.T. Foundation **Title:** Chair **Type of organization:** Charitable **Major product:** Fighters' initiative for support and training; helping retired boxers find jobs, medical insurance **Area of distribution:** National **Expertise:** Support and training for boxers, lecturing, advocacy **Honors/awards:** Won international tournaments in England, Wales and Scotland; won 2 New York Golden Gloves Championships, winning both the 1973 160lb Sub-Novice Championship and the 1976 Heavyweight Open Championship; won the 1973 160lb Sub-Novice title and the 1976 Heavyweight Open title **Affiliations:** J.A.B. **Hob./spts.:** Golf, physical fitness, charitable work **SIC code:** 86 **Address:** F.I.S.T. Foundation, 265 W. 14th St., 2nd floor, New York, NY 10011 **E-mail:** jgcooney@comcast.net

COOPER, THOMAS D.
Industry: Aerospace **Born:** April 7, 1932, Dayton, Ohio **Univ./degree:** B.S., Metallurgical Engineering, University of Cincinnati, 1955; M.S., Metallurgical Engineering, The Ohio State University, 1964 **Current organization:** Universal Technology Corp. **Title:** Senior Program Manager **Type of organization:** Aerospace R&D **Major product:** R&D **Area of distribution:** National **Expertise:** Engineering **Honors/awards:** Distinguished Alumnus Award, The College of Engineering, University of Cincinnati, 1972; One of Dayton Area's Outstanding Engineers and Scientists, Affiliate Societies Council of Dayton, 1990 (Recognized by the State of Ohio for this award); Selected to present ASNT's 1991 Mehl Honor Lecture during the Society's 50th Anniversary Conference in Boston; SAE's Franklin W. Kolk Air Transportation Progress Award, 1991; SAE's Arch T. Colwell Cooperative Engineering Gold Medal, 1992 **Published works:** Numerous publications including: Cooper, T.D., "Aluminum and Magnesium", Materials Symposium, WADC TR58-655, July, 1958; Cooper, T.D. and DePierre, V. "Problems and Developments in Primary Processing of Refractory Metals", AFML-TR-64-361; Co-editor of book "Oxide Dispersion Strengthening", with G.S. Ansell and F.W. Lenel, Vol 47, Metallurgical Society Conference, Gordon and Breech, Pub. 1966 **Affiliations:** Fellow, A.S.M.; Basic Fellow, American Institute of Aeronautics and Astronautics; American Society for Nondestructive Testing; Society of Automotive Engineers; Air Force Association **SIC code:** 87 **Address:** Universal Technology Corp., 1270 N. Fairfield Rd., Dayton, OH 45433-2600 **E-mail:** tcooper@utcdayton.com

CORNELISSEN, CHRISTOPHER W.
Industry: Consulting **Born:** July 18, 1963, Bangor, Maine **Univ./degree:** B.S., Civil Engineering, North Carolina State University, 1997 **Current organization:** CTI Consultants Inc. **Title:** P.E. **Type of organization:** Private consulting **Major product:** Geo-environmental engineering **Area of distribution:** Virginia **Expertise:** Engineering **Honors/awards:** Professional Engineer in 4 states **Affiliations:** A.S.C.E. (national and state level) **Hob./spts.:** Sailing, playing baseball with his son **SIC code:** 87 **Address:** CTI Consultants Inc., 11038 Lakeridge Pkwy., Suite 1, Ashland, VA 23005 **E-mail:** ccornelissen@cti-consultants.com

COUGHLIN, CORNELIUS (CONNIE) E.
Industry: Consulting **Born:** September 9, 1927, Boston, Massachusetts **Univ./degree:** B.A., Industrial Management, Northeastern University, Massachusetts **Current organization:** Coughlin Sheff & Associates, PC **Title:** President **Type of organization:** Consulting firm **Major product:** Computer and software consulting, financial and tax consulting **Area of distribution:** New England **Expertise:** Financial consulting **Affiliations:** American Institute of Certified Public Accountants; Massachusetts Society of Certified Public Accountants **Hob./spts.:** Fishing, baseball **SIC code:** 87 **Address:** Coughlin Sheff & Associates, PC, 40 Nagog Park, Acton, MA 01720-3425

COUTIERI, HEIDI M.
Industry: Insurance, risk management **Born:** June 25, 1965, Queens, New York **Univ./degree:** B.A., English Literature, City College of New York **Current organization:** Alpha Risk Management, Inc. **Title:** Senior Vice President **Type of organization:** Consulting **Major product:** Consulting-risk management **Area of distribution:** New York **Expertise:** Real estate **Hob./spts.:** Reading, theatre, travel, cruises **SIC code:** 87 **Address:** Alpha Risk Management, Inc., 60 Cutter Mill Rd., Great Neck, NY 11021 **E-mail:** heidibucher@alpharisk.com **Web address:** www.alpharisk.com

COVARRUBIAS-PIÑA, SALOMÓN
Industry: Religion **Born:** February 4, 1959, Guadalajara, Jalisco, Mexico **Univ./degree:** M.Div., Columbus Ohio School of Divinity, 1991 **Current organization:** St. Peter Claver Parish **Title:** Pastor **Type of organization:** Church **Major product:** Religious services and leadership **Area of distribution:** International **Expertise:** Defender of the bond of sacraments for the office of canonical concerns of the diocese of Yakima, Washington **Hob./spts.:** Reading **SIC code:** 86 **Address:** St. Peter Claver Parish, 509 S. Satus Ave., Wapato, WA 98951 **E-mail:** stpeterclaver@aol.com

COWDEN, RONALD R.
Industry: Basic biomedical research **Born:** July 9, 1931, Memphis, Tennessee **Univ./degree:** Ph.D., Zoology, University of Vienna **Current organization:** Coastal Biomedical Laboratory **Title:** Director/Professor **Type of organization:** Private research **Major product:** Research in cell biology **Area of distribution:** International **Expertise:** Cell biology, cytochemistry **Published works:** 125 publications **Affiliations:** A.S.C.B.; A.S.D.B.; T.H.S.; R.M.S. **Hob./spts.:** Grand opera, big game hunting **SIC code:** 87 **Address:** (In Memoriam), Mobile, AL 36606 **E-mail:** tiffron@comcast.net

COX, ELIZABETH L.
Industry: Research information **Born:** East Orange, New Jersey **Univ./degree:** M.S., Information Science, Pratt University, 1986; M.S., New York University, 2000 **Current organization:** New Jersey Research & Information Service **Title:** Owner/Founder **Type of organization:** Information services **Major product:** Public relations consulting **Area of distribution:** New Jersey **Expertise:** Editing, writing, information specialist, political science **Honors/awards:** Heritage Award, New Jersey Dept. of Community Affairs **Published works:** Booklet, "Who Me? A Politician?"; Newsletters, Summit Republican Committee; Ageing Bulletin, New Jersey Division; American Trade Union **Affiliations:** A.P.S.A.; S.L.A.; N.W.P.C.; Republican National Convention **Hob./spts.:** Politics, women's concerns **SIC code:** 87 **Address:** New Jersey Research & Information Service, 105 New England Ave., Unit 0-4, Summit, NJ 07901 **E-mail:** njresearchi@aol.com

CRIDER, DUSTIN H.
Industry: Engineering **Born:** September 27, 1980 Paducah, Kentucky **Univ./degree:** B.S., Physics, Murray State University, 2002 **Current organization:** Aerospace Testing Alliance **Title:** Scientist **Type of organization:** Engineering **Major product:** Testing and evaluation **Area of distribution:** International **Expertise:** Instrumentation and diagnostics **Affiliations:** A.I.A.A.; S.P.I.E. **SIC code:** 87 **Address:** Aerospace Testing Alliance, 1077 Ave. C, Arnold AFB, TN 37389 **E-mail:** dustin.crider@arnold.af.mil

CROMPTON, LINDA C.
Industry: Financial **Born:** Kent, England **Univ./degree:** B.A., Simon Fraser University, Canada; M.A., University of British Columbia, Canada; M.B.A., University of Kent, United Kingdom **Current organization:** Investor Responsibility Research Center **Title:** President/CEO **Type of organization:** Research **Major product:** Corporate and shareholder issue research **Area of distribution:** International **Expertise:** International finance, corporate social responsibility; frequent lecturer and public speaker **Published works:** Several articles **Hob./spts.:** Distance running, opera, reading, travel **SIC code:** 87 **Address:** Investor Responsibility Research Center, 700-1350 Connecticut Ave. N.W., Washington, DC 20036 **E-mail:** lcrompton@irrc.com **Web address:** www.irrc.com

CROSS, THOMAS E.
Industry: Electronics **Born:** Fort Wayne, Indiana **Current organization:** Contract Specialist **Title:** Senior Product Engineer **Type of organization:** Independent Engineer **Major product:** Power **Area of distribution:** International **Expertise:** Component Engineering, applications of Semiconductors, supply chain, Product Risk assessment and problem resolution; Professional Certification Engineering Technology, National Cryptologic Schools, NSA, 1976 **Hob./spts.:** Photography, writing **SIC code:** 87 **Address:** Motor Appliance Corp., 555 Spirit of St. Louis Blvd., Chesterfield, MO 63005 **E-mail:** thomasecross@hotmail.com

CUMMINGS, ERNST M.
Industry: Educational **Born:** May 24, 1939, Rhode Island **Univ./degree:** B.S., Engineering, Coast Guard Economy, US Naval War College **Current organization:** USS Massachusetts Memorial Committee, Inc. **Title:** Executive Director **Type of organization:** Museum **Major product:** World's largest exhibition of battle ships **Area of distribution:** International **Expertise:** Management, operations, public relations **Hob./spts.:** Golf, sailing **SIC code:** 84 **Address:** USS Massachusetts Memorial Committee, Inc., Battle Ship Cove Museum, 1 Battle Ship Cove, Fall River, MA 02721 **E-mail:** battleship@battleshipcove.org

CURLIN, L. CALVERT
Industry: Chemical/consulting **Born:** October 8, 1941, Chicago, Illinois **Univ./degree:** B.A., Chemistry, Hope College, Holland, Michigan, 1964; M.B.A., Western Michigan University, Kalamazoo, Michigan, 1966 **Current organization:** Curlin Chlor-Alkali Consultants **Title:** President **Type of organization:** Consulting firm **Major product:** Chlorine production technology **Area of distribution:** National and International **Expertise:** Chlorine production technology selection, chlor-alkali plant operations; Expert Witness for lawsuits and arbitrations involving chlorine manufacture and technology **Published works:** U.S. Patent No. 5,137612, Aug., 1992, "Bonded Bus Bar for Diaphragm Cell Cathode"; U.S. Patent No. 4,834,859, May 30, 1989. "Diaphragm Cell Cathode Assembly"; Ullmann's Encyclopedia of Industrial Chemistry, 5th ed., vol. A6, Article "Chlorine", 1986, Wiley-VCH, Weinheim; Kirk-Othmer Encyclopedia of Chemical Technology, 4th ed., vol. 1, "Alkali and Chlorine Products/Chlorine and Sodium Hydroxide", 1991; "Modem Chlor-Alkali Technology", vol. 4, Society of Chemical Industry "POLYRAMIX-A Depositable Replacement for Asbestos Diaphragms", 1990; "Modem Chlor-Alkali Technology", vol. 5, 1992, Society of Chemical Industry "POLYRAMIX Diaphragm-A Commercial Reality", 1992; Ullmann's Encyclopedia of Industrial Chemistry, 6th ed., article, "Chlorine"' Wiley-VCH, Weinheim, 1999; "Chlorine-Principals and Industrial Practice", Wiley-VCH, Weinheim Germany 2000 **Affiliations:** American Institute of Chemical Engineers; American Chemical Society; The Chlorine Institute; Veterans of Foreign Wars; MENSA (The High IQ Society); American Legion; Disabled American Veterans **Hob./spts.:** Coin collecting, computers **SIC code:** 87 **Address:** Curlin Chlor-Alkali Consultants, 2230 Arielle Dr., Unit 1906, Naples, FL 34109 **E-mail:** calcurlin@att.net

CURTIS, PAMELA E.
Industry: Legal/Technical **Born:** September 21, 1963, Washington, D.C. **Current organization:** PC Resources & PC Matrix Designs **Title:** President **Type of organization:** Consulting firm **Major product:** Legal Support, Secretarial, IT Consulting, Paralegal **Area of distribution:** Maryland, D.C. Metropolitan Area **Expertise:** IT Engineering; Paralegal; Secretary **Hob./spts.:** Golf, travel **SIC code:** 87 **Address:**

3937 Elan Ct., Summerfield at Covington, Bowie, MD 20716 **E-mail:** pcmatrixdesigns@msn.com

CURTS, HAROLD LAYNE
Industry: Construction/engineering **Born:** October 30, 1957, Dallas, Texas **Univ./degree:** B.S., LeTourneau University, Longview, Texas, 1992 **Current organization:** Technical Interiors **Title:** President/CEO **Type of organization:** Construction management **Major product:** Construction/design **Area of distribution:** Texas **Expertise:** Engineering **Hob./spts.:** Fishing, travel, skiing **SIC code:** 87 **Address:** Technical Interiors, P.O. Box 14824, Ft. Worth, TX 16117 **E-mail:** pickup83@aol.com

DAILY, JOHN G.
Industry: Consulting **Born:** June 27, 1950, Lafayette, Indiana **Univ./degree:** B.S.M.E., Purdue University, 1972 **Current organization:** Jackson Hole Scientific Investigations Inc. **Title:** President **Type of organization:** Consulting firm **Major product:** Accident investigations **Area of distribution:** International **Expertise:** Traffic crash reconstruction **Published works:** 2 textbooks, 5 SAE papers, numerous articles **Affiliations:** A.S.M.E.; S.A.E. **Hob./spts.:** Hunting, fishing, hiking, golf **SIC code:** 87 **Address:** Jackson Hole Scientific Investigations Inc., P.O. Box 2206, Jackson, WY 83001 **E-mail:** jhsi@rmisp.com **Web address:** www.jhscientific.com

DALEO, ROXANNE E.
Industry: Healthcare/education **Born:** August 28, 1951, Jersey City, New Jersey **Univ./degree:** Ph.D., Behavioral Medicine, Columbia Pacific University **Current organization:** Mindworks for Children, Inc. **Title:** Health Psychologist **Type of organization:** Children's services **Major product:** Child development audio programs for "Special Needs" children **Area of distribution:** International **Expertise:** Child development, relaxation techniques **Affiliations:** A.C.C.H.; C.L.C. **Hob./spts.:** Field hockey, lacrosse, hiking **SIC code:** 83 **Address:** Mindworks for Children, Inc., 14A Eliot St., Cambridge, MA 02138 **E-mail:** dr.roxanne@mindworksforchildren.com

DALTON, JON P.
Industry: Consulting **Born:** September 6, 1966, Sioux City, Iowa **Univ./degree:** B.S., Electrical Engineering, University of Nebraska at Lincoln, 1990 **Current organization:** Davis Design **Title:** Director of Electrical Engineering **Type of organization:** Architecture/engineering **Major product:** Building design **Area of distribution:** Lincoln, Nebraska **Expertise:** Electrical engineering; Professional Engineer in 7+ states **Affiliations:** N.S.P.E., Nebraska Chapter **Hob./spts.:** Spending time with kids, yard work, sports **SIC code:** 87 **Address:** Davis Design, 211 N. 14th St., Lincoln, NE 68508 **E-mail:** jon.dalton@davisdesign.com

DARDET, E. TOMÁS
Industry: Public Relations **Born:** March 7, 1961, Miami, Florida **Univ./degree:** B.S., Marketing, Fairfield University, 1983 **Current organization:** GCI Puerto Rico **Title:** Vice President **Type of organization:** Public relations firm **Major product:** Public Relations **Area of distribution:** National **Expertise:** Public relations, marketing, advertising **Affiliations:** The Association of Public Relations Professionals of Puerto Rico **Hob./spts.:** Skiing, swimming, cooking **SIC code:** 87 **Address:** GCI Puerto Rico, Muñoz Rivera #270, 3rd floor, Hato Rey, PR 00918 **E-mail:** tdardet@gcipuertorico.com **Web address:** www.gcigroup.com

DAREKAR, VIJAY S.
Industry: Electronics **Born:** January 10, 1940, Pune, India **Univ./degree:** Ph.D., Mechanical Engineering, Cornell University, 1991 **Current organization:** American Technocraft **Title:** President **Type of organization:** Consulting firm **Major product:** Technical consultation, design **Area of distribution:** National **Expertise:** Engineering **Hob./spts.:** Travel, audio/video gadgetry, reading **SIC code:** 87 **Address:** American Technocraft, 924 Colony Ridge Ct., Irving, TX 75061 **E-mail:** v.darekar@verizon.net

DAVIS, ELEANOR KAY
Industry: Museum **Born:** November 10, 1935, Rome, Georgia **Univ./degree:** B.A., Biology and Physical Science, Berry College, Georgia, 1957; M.S., Science, Western Maryland University, 1963; Ph.D., Administration, Georgia State University, 1975 **Current organization:** Fernbank Museum of Natural History **Title:** Ph.D./Founder/Executive Director **Type of organization:** Nonprofit museum **Major product:** Culture/educational **Area of distribution:** Georgia **Expertise:** Science administration **Published works:** 12 articles, chapters **Affiliations:** American Association of Museums; American Academy for the Advancement of Science **Hob./spts.:** Travel, reading, swimming **SIC code:** 84 **Address:** Fernbank Museum of Natural History, 767 Clifton Rd., Atlanta, GA 30307 **E-mail:** kay.davis@fernbank.edu **Web address:** www.fernbank.edu

DAVIS, THEAJO
Industry: Nonprofit **Born:** July 21, 1964, Florida **Univ./degree:** Attended North Florida Junior College and Jones College **Current organization:** Tarpon Springs Chamber of Commerce **Title:** Executive Director **Type of organization:** Membership **Major product:** Business services, tourism **Area of distribution:** Sumter County, Florida **Expertise:** Accounting, payroll, staffing, marketing, tourism and relocation **Affiliations:** F.C.A.P. **Hob./spts.:** Spending time with family, boating, fishing, designing graphics **SIC code:** 86 **Address:** Tarpon Springs Chamber of Commerce, 11 E. Orange St., Tarpon Springs, FL 34689 **E-mail:** theajodavis@hotmail.com

DAWOUD, SAM M.
Industry: Consulting engineering **Born:** September 12, 1953, Cairo, Egypt **Univ./degree:** M.S., Mechanical Engineering, Ain Shams University, Egypt, 1977 **Current organization:** Engineering, Planning & Management (EPM), Inc. **Title:** Sr. Fire Protection Engineer **Type of organization:** Consulting / engineering firm **Major product:** Life / fire safety issues (all industries) **Area of distribution:** National **Expertise:** Sr. Fire Protection Engineer **Affiliations:** A.M.A.; N.F.P.A.; A.S.H.R.A.E.; Institute of Petroleum, United Kingdom **Hob./spts.:** Computers **SIC code:** 87 **Address:** Engineering, Planning & Management (EPM), Inc., 20 Speen St., Framingham, MA 01701 **E-mail:** sameh.dawoud@opg.com

DEGHETTO, KENNETH A.
Industry: International consulting **Univ./degree:** B.S.M.E., Rensselaer Polytechnic Institute **Current organization:** Interplan Consulting Inc. **Title:** Chairman **Type of organization:** Management consulting firm **Major product:** International projects **Area of distribution:** International **Expertise:** Project organization, engineering, financing **Honors/awards:** Full Lieutenant, USNR, Graduate US Merchant Marine Academy **Affiliations:** F.A.S.M.E.; B.I.M.E.; Sigma Xi; Tau Beta Pi; Pi Tau Sigma **SIC code:** 87 **Address:** Interplan Consulting Inc., 527 Third Ave., Suite 174, New York, NY 10016 **E-mail:** kendeghetto@worldnet.att.net

DEGRAW, SUPRANEE
Industry: Architecture, engineering **Born:** June 15, 1970, Bangkok, Thailand **Univ./degree:** B.S., Architecture, Kansas State University, 1995 **Current organization:** Jacobs Facilities, Inc. **Title:** Architect **Type of organization:** Design/build **Major product:** Commercial/federal/institutional **Area of distribution:** International **Expertise:** Design, engineering, construction management **Affiliations:** A.I.A.; C.S.I.; N.C.A.R.B. **SIC code:** 87 **Address:** Jacobs Facilities, Inc., 5757 Plaza Dr., Suite 100, Cypress, CA 90630 **E-mail:** supranee.degraw@jacobs.com **Web address:** www.jacobs.com

DELONG, MICHAEL P.
Industry: Engineering **Born:** Kinston, North Carolina **Univ./degree:** B.S., Aeronautical Engineering, U.S. Naval Academy; M.S., Industrial Management, Central Michigan University; Honorary Ph.D., Strategic Intelligence, Joint Military Intelligence College **Current organization:** Shaw Group Inc. **Title:** Executive Vice President, Shaw E&I International / President, Shaw CentCom Services, LLC **Type of organization:** Engineering, construction, manufacturing, environmental, infrastructure **Major product:** Pipelines, power plants, design and build **Area of distribution:** International **Expertise:** Marketing, engineering, security, author **Published works:** 1 book, Inside Centcom: The Unvarnished Truth **Affiliations:** S.A.M.E.; Marine Corps Aviation Association **Hob./spts.:** Raising quarter horses **SIC code:** 87 **Address:** Shaw Group Inc., 4171 Essen Lane, Baton Rouge, LA 70809-2157 **E-mail:** mike.delong@shawgrp.com

DEMARIA, GARY J.
Industry: Construction/consulting **Born:** August 29, 1958, Passaic, New Jersey **Univ./degree:** B.S., with Honors, Construction Engineering, Farleigh Dickinson University, 1980 **Current organization:** Gary DeMaria, Construction Consultant **Title:** Construction Consultant **Type of organization:** Private consulting firm **Major product:** Commercial, residential, healthcare and retail **Area of distribution:** National **Expertise:** Consulting, operations **Affiliations:** Psi Omega Epsilon **Hob./spts.:** Family **SIC code:** 87 **Address:** Gary DeMaria, Construction Consultant, 228 Washington Ave., Suite 4, Miami Beach, FL 33139 **E-mail:** garydemaria@yahoo.com

DEMEO, LISA E.
Industry: Engineering **Born:** April 24, 1959, Haverhill, Massachusetts **Univ./degree:** M.B.A., University of Massachusetts at Lowell **Current organization:** Teweksburg Township **Title:** Town Engineer **Type of organization:** Engineering **Major product:** Civil engineering services **Area of distribution:** North America **Expertise:** Site design, storm water solutions **Affiliations:** A.S.C.E.; Chair of local historical commission; National Association of Women in Construction **Hob./spts.:** History, her children's sports **SIC code:** 87 **Address:** Teweksburg Township, 999 Whipple Rd., Teweksburg, MA 01876 **E-mail:** pjdwile@msn.com

DEMOS, DAVID C.
Industry: Control system integrator **Born:** June 19, 1957, Glendale, California **Univ./degree:** B.S.E.E., Purdue University **Current organization:** System Control Solutions, Inc. **Title:** President **Type of organization:** Consulting **Major product:** Control system integration **Area of distribution:** International **Expertise:** Industrial control systems **Hob./spts.:** Motorcycling, bowling, fishing **SIC code:** 87 **Address:** System Control Solutions, Inc., 3452 S.W. Catskill Dr., Port St. Lucie, FL 34953 **E-mail:** chris@systemcontrolsolutions.com

DEPORTER, FRED
Industry: Aerospace **Born:** March 13, 1952, Tucson, Arizona **Univ./degree:** B.S.E.E., University of Arizona, 1977 **Current organization:** Raytheon **Title:** Senior Principal Engineer **Type of organization:** R&D, Manufacturing **Major product:** Simulations **Area of distribution:** International **Expertise:** Engineering, electronic design, instrumentation, systems integration **Honors/awards:** Corporate Superior Performance Award **Hob./spts.:** Hiking, tennis **SIC code:** 87 **Address:** Raytheon, 1151 E. Hermans Rd., Tucson, AZ 85706 **E-mail:** fdeporter@raytheon.com **Web address:** www.raytheon.com

DERDERIAN JR., JORDAN J.
Industry: Consulting **Born:** March 20, 1946, Massachusetts **Univ./degree:** B.A., Mathematics, Worcester State College; M.A., Special Education, Assumption College, Massachusetts; C.A.E.S., Education Administration/Special Education Administration, Boston College **Current organization:** Self-employed **Title:** Tax Preparer **Type of organization:** Tax service **Major product:** Taxes **Area of distribution:** New Hampshire, Vermont, Massachusetts **Expertise:** Tax preparation **Hob./spts.:** Magician **SIC code:** 87 **Address:** 25 Washington St., Newbury, NH 03255-5905 **E-mail:** jderderian@tds.net

DERRICK, WILLIAM D.
Industry: Consulting **Born:** February 7, 1946, San Diego, California **Univ./degree:** 3 years of college, University of Nebraska; University of Montana **Current organization:** Derrick Enterprises **Title:** Owner **Type of organization:** Consulting/training **Major product:** Consulting, training **Area of distribution:** National **Expertise:** Project management professional # 619 **Published works:** Article **Affiliations:** P.M.I. **SIC code:** 87 **Address:** Derrick Enterprises, P.O. Box 401, Stevensville, MT 59870 **E-mail:** wder789456@msn.com **Web address:** www.derrick@gobizgo.com

DEVINENI, MOHAN RAM P.
Industry: Pharmaceuticals **Born:** August 15, 1957, Hyderabad, India **Spouse:** Nirmala Devineni **Married:** May 21, 1983 **Children:** Ramya Devineni, born 1985; Abhilash Devineni, born 1989 **Univ./degree:** M.S., Pharmacy, Birla Institute of Technology, India, 1980 **Current organization:** Strides, Inc. **Title:** Executive Vice President, Technical Affairs **Type of organization:** Research and development and manufacturing **Major product:** Pharmaceutical dosage forms **Area of distribution:** International **Expertise:** Research and development, quality control, quality assurance, validations, engineering, manufacturing, designing and building pharmaceutical facilities **Honors/awards:** Distinguished Alumni Award by College of Pharmacy, Manipal; Guest of Honor Award by V.V. Puram College of Pharmacy, Bangalore, India **Affiliations:** A.A.P.S.; I.P.A. (India); Chairman, Pharmacon (India) Pvt. Ltd.; Chairman, Dry Cool (India) Pvt. Ltd. **Career accomplishments:** Played a key role in developing an organization from 1 facility with 7 people to 7 facilities with 1000 people; developed several products in tablet, capsule, liquid orals, soft gelatin capsules and parental dosage forms; designed and built 7 world class facilities, supervised the operation of five facilities, traveled to more than 20 countries on business **Hob./spts.:** Oil painting (portraits, landscapes) **SIC code:** 87 **Address:** Strides, Inc., 37 Veronica Ave., Somerset, NJ 08873 **Fax:** (732)249-0225 **E-mail:** dmrp1958@hotmail.com

DIERKS, E. HERBERT
Industry: Consulting **Born:** January 20, 1946, Kansas City, Missouri **Children:** Herb, 24; Joe, 22; Andrew, 20; Becky, 18 **Univ./degree:** B.S.E.E., Colorado State University, 1969 **Current organization:** RVW, Inc. **Title:** Chief Electrical Engineer **Type of organization:** Consulting firm **Major product:** Study, analysis and design reports and drawings, engineering studies and analysis, physical system design with protection schemes, summary reports on power supply and operations **Area of distribution:** Nebraska, Kansas, South Dakota, Iowa **Expertise:** High Voltage and extra high voltage electrical power systems; Missouri, Nebraska, Kansas, Washington, Mississippi Registered Professional Engineer **Honors/awards:** Officer, student chapter, Colorado State University, I.E.E.E.; Special Recognition for participation in long range maintenance planning as a customer of BPA **Affiliations:** National Society of Professional Engineers; Officer, Nebraska Society of Professional Engineers; Institute of Electrical and Electronics Engineers **Hob./spts.:** Golf, sailing, classical music, photography **SIC code:** 87 **Address:** 3611 53rd St., Columbus, NE 68601 **E-mail:** hdierks@rvwinc.com **Web address:** www.rvwinc.com

DIESTEL, CHARLES G.
Industry: Engineering **Born:** November 1, 1948, Chicago, Illinois **Univ./degree:** M.B.A., Valedictorian, Lake Forest Graduate School of Management, 1996 **Current organization:** Sargent & Lundy **Title:** Project Manager **Type of organization:** Consulting, design/engineering **Major product:** Design power stations **Area of distribution:** Domestic and International **Expertise:** Power engineering **Affiliations:** A.S.M.E. **Hob./spts.:** Racquetball, waterskiing **SIC code:** 87 **Address:** Sargent & Lundy, 55 E. Monroe, Chicago, IL 60543

DIETZ, ALMA
Industry: Pharmaceuticals **Born:** November 29, 1922, Holyoke, Massachusetts **Univ./degree:** B.A., American International College; Graduate work in botany, University of Michigan **Current organization:** Independent consultant **Title:** Microbial Taxonomist, Specialty-Actinomycetes **Type of organization:** Private consulting practice **Major product:** Antibiotics **Area of distribution:** International **Expertise:** Microorganisms **Honors/awards:** 2004 AIC Alumni Achievement Award; honored in 1981 with the Upjohn Co.'s prestigious W.E. Upjohn Award for her extensive contributions to the advancement of science through activities associated with culture collections of living organisms **Published works:** 80+ publications, 5 U.S. patents, provided the descriptions and identifications of the strains in 66 other U.S. patents; Editor of the Japanese Journal of Antibiotics **Affiliations:** American Mycological Society; American Society for Microbiology; Society of Industrial Microbiology; Editorial Board of Japanese Journal of Antibiotics; U.S. Federation for Culture Collections; active in local Episcopal Church; served on the Board of Directors of the Arcadia Neighborhood Association in Kalamazoo **Career accomplishments:** Numerous contributions to the field of industrial microbiology **Hob./spts.:** Golf, gardening **SIC code:** 87 **Address:** 2929 Memory Lane, Kalamazoo, MI 49006-5534 **E-mail:** admicrotax@aol.com

DIETZ III, JOSEPH L.
Industry: Hospitality/food services **Born:** April 5, 1962, New Orleans, Louisiana **Univ./degree:** B.A., English, Wayne State University **Current organization:** Bayview Yacht Club **Title:** Executive Chef **Type of organization:** Private club **Major product:** Food and beverage **Area of distribution:** Detroit, Michigan **Expertise:** Culinary arts **Published works:** Has been on television shows **Affiliations:** I.F.S.C. **Hob./spts.:** Football, weightlifting **SIC code:** 86 **Address:** Bayview Yacht Club, 100 Clairpoint St., Detroit, MI 48215-3042 **E-mail:** joechef@byc.com

DIFIORE, VINCENT R.
Industry: Counseling **Born:** July 24, 1943, Lincoln, Nebraska **Univ./degree:** M.A., Piano Performance, Juilliard School of Music **Current organization:** Life Ministry **Title:** Administrator **Type of organization:** Christian counseling center **Major product:** Counseling **Area of distribution:** International **Expertise:** Addiction counseling, support groups, church education **Hob./spts.:** Classical piano **SIC code:** 83 **Address:** Life Ministry, P.O. Box 353, New York, NY 10185 **E-mail:** lifeministry@earthlink.net

DJURIC, RADOMIR
Industry: International development **Born:** December 6, 1959, Croatia **Univ./degree:** M.B.A., University of Toledo, 1992; J.D. equivalent, University of Osijek, 1982 **Current organization:** National Center for State Courts **Title:** Senior Project Manager **Type of organization:** Consulting **Major product:** International development consultancy catering to legal and business sector **Area of distribution:** International **Expertise:** Attorney, international business consultant, legal retail work (prior background as an import/export representative in the textile industry) **Published works:** Several published legal reports **Hob./spts.:** Soccer, travel **SIC code:** 87 **Address:** Radomir Djuric, 1621 T St. N.W., #305, Washington, DC 20009 **E-mail:** radedc@aol.com

DODGENS, JANIE B.
Industry: Religion **Univ./degree:** Ph.D., Theology and Biblical Counseling, Ashwood University, 2006 **Current organization:** Life Under the Son Ministry **Title:** Minister/CEO **Type of organization:** Ministry **Major product:** Religious services, instruction and rehabilitation **Area of distribution:** California **Expertise:** Theology, Biblical counseling, preaching, teaching, religious instruction, social service **Affiliations:** C.A.H.S.H.; Member, Gerontology Board at American River College; Designing Women of Destiny; Registered, Christian Women Speakers' Webpage **Hob./spts.:**

Singing opera, reading, golf **SIC code:** 86 **Address:** Life Under the Son Ministry, 2222 Watt Ave., Suite C8A, Sacramento, CA 95825

DOMJAN, EVELYN
Industry: Art/publishing **Born:** March 25, Budapest, Hungary **Univ./degree:** B.F.A., Hungary Royal Academy of the Fine Arts **Current organization:** Domjan Studio/ Publishing House of Art Books **Title:** Artist/Owner **Type of organization:** Art studio and publishing house **Major product:** Fine art, art books **Area of distribution:** International **Expertise:** Fine art - flower paintings published as greeting cards **Honors/ awards:** Wife of Joseph Domjan known as Master of the Woodcut; received First Prize "Woodcarved Images" Budapest, Gondolat; received National Endowment for the Arts Grant: One Man Shows at the "Little Church on the Hill", Saddle River Valley Cultural Center, New Jersey **Published works:** Books, "Panorama of Hungarian Peasant Painting", "Parta"; illustrated children's books including, "The Dancing Bear", Corvina publishers; exhibited at "City Folk", The Museum of American Folk Art, New York City; Hungarian Heritage Center, New Brunswick, N.J.; The Tuxedo Park Library and Bentley Hall; The Olympia Project, Cultural Center, Demarest **Affiliations:** Ringwood Manor Association of the Arts; Arts Council of Rockland; Metropolitan Museum of Art; Association International Des Arts Plastiques, Unesco, Paris; Salute to Women in the Arts; Society of American Graphic Artists; Print Club of Albany **SIC code:** 84 **Address:** Domjan Studio, 216 West Lake Rd., Tuxedo Park, NY 10987

DOPPALAPUDI, MURALI K.
Industry: Pharmaceuticals **Born:** April, 4, 1965, Nagulapalem, India **Univ./degree:** B.S., Chemistry, Math & Physics, Nagarjuna University, 1985; M.S., Food, Drug & Water Analysis, 1988; Ph.D., Chemistry, 1995, Andhra University **Current organization:** Valogic, LLC **Title:** Sr. Compliance Consultant **Type of organization:** Validation and compliance consultancy **Major product:** Consultation to pharmaceutical and biopharmaceutical companies **Area of distribution:** International **Expertise:** Quality assurance/quality control/validation **Published works:** 15 peer-reviewed journals, 2 abstracts **Affiliations:** A.O.A.C.; P.D.A.; A.C.S.; A.A.P.S. **Hob./spts.:** Travel, reading, music, experimental design, computers and networks **SIC code:** 87 **Address:** Valogic, LLC, 8415 Progress Dr., Suite Y, Frederick, MD 21701 **E-mail:** mkdoppalapudi@hotmail.com

DOTTS, SHARON K.
Industry: Consulting **Born:** February 28, 1964, Malvern, Pennsylvania **Univ./degree:** M.C.E., Villanova University, 1998; B.S.E., Widener University, 1993 **Current organization:** Gilmore & Associates, Inc. **Title:** Project Manager **Type of organization:** Consulting firm **Major product:** Civil engineering and surveying **Area of distribution:** Pennsylvania **Expertise:** Civil engineering **Honors/awards:** Charles E. Hyatt engineering award from Widener University **Affiliations:** A.S.C.E. **Hob./spts.:** Skiing, scuba diving, arts and crafts **SIC code:** 87 **Address:** Gilmore & Associates, Inc., 350 E. Butler Ave., New Britain, PA 18901 **E-mail:** sdotts@gilmore-assoc.com **Web address:** www.gilmore-assoc.com

DRESCHER-LINCOLN, CAROLYN KAY
Industry: Biopharmaceuticals **Born:** April 13, 1950, Columbus, Ohio **Univ./degree:** B.S., Biology, Lebanon Valley College, 1972; Ph.D., Microbiology, University of Pittsburgh School of Medicine and Dental Medicine, 1979; Thesis Committee chaired by Julius S. Youngner, D.Sc. **Current organization:** Bionique Testing Laboratories, Inc. **Title:** Director, Technical Services **Type of organization:** Biotech company **Major product:** Mycoplasma testing and problem solving **Area of distribution:** International **Expertise:** Chief Scientific Officer, medical microbiology, in vitro cell biology **Honors/awards:** Esther Teplitz Award for Teaching Excellence, University of Pittsburgh, 1977; Guest Lecturer for Technical Seminar Series sponsored by Life Technologies, Inc. Johns Hopkins Genetics CORE Research Facility, 1994 **Published works:** 1 chapter in Methods in Cell Biology, Vol. 57; 8 scientific papers; numerous publications and lectures including: Dresher-Lincoln, C.K., P. Jargiello, T.J. Gill III amd H.W. Kunz, 1980 Analysis of the Giemsa-banding patterns of the chromosomes from rats carrying the genes of the growth and reproduction complex (GRC). J. Immunogentics 7:427-430 **Affiliations:** American Society for Microbiology; American Association for the Advancement of Science; International Organization for Mycoplasmology **Career accomplishments:** All of her scientific endeavors, starting with the establishment of her first cell culture lines as part of her senior research project at Lebanon Valley College to the present, have been utilized by others to further scientific discovery and application across specialty boundaries. To date, all of her bench work, whether experimental or analytical, has been repeated and verified by others and then served as a factual foundation for further basic research and/or as factual stepping stones to today's release of numerous cell culture derived biomedical products manufactured by the client companies that she serves. **Hob./spts.:** Family, reading, sketching, home projects/woodworking, baseball, cross-country skiing **SIC code:** 87 **Address:** Bionique Testing Laboratories, Inc., 156 Fay Brook Dr., Saranac Lake, NY 12983 **E-mail:** clincoln65@hotmail.com **Web address:** www.bionique.com

DRISKILL, JONATHAN W.
Industry: Engineering **Born:** June 19, 1958, El Paso, Texas **Univ./degree:** B.S.M.E., University of Tennessee, 1982; M.S.M.E., Boston University, 1993 **Current organization:** Ameresco Federal Solutions (formerly Exelon Services Federal Group and Systems Engineering & Management Corp.) **Title:** Project/Mechanical Engineer **Type of organization:** Energy Services Company (ESCO) **Major product:** Energy consulting and alternative energy services, including providing turnkey design/build projects aimed at reducing energy consumption **Area of distribution:** International **Expertise:** Mechanical engineering (HVAC); Professional Credentials: Professional Engineer (P.E.), TN, 1994; Certified Energy Manager (C.E.M.), 1996 **Honors/awards:** International Who's Who of Professionals, 1995; Strathmore's Who's Who, 2001-03; United Who's Who Registry of Executives and Professionals, 2001-04 **Published works:** Has written numerous Executive Summaries, Training Guides and Survey Reports used to document findings of Energy Audits and Energy Savings Opportunity Studies at numerous U.S. Army, Air Force, Marine Corp and Navy Installations **Affiliations:** American Society of Heating, Refrigeration & Air Conditioning Engineers; Association of Energy Engineers; American Society of Mechanical Engineers; Air Force Association; Community involvement: Member of Property Committee and active volunteer at Messiah Lutheran Church, Knoxville; Volunteer, Cub Scout Den 3, Pack 20, Toqua District, Great Smoky Mountain Council, Boy Scouts of America **Hob./spts.:** Woodworking, home do-it-yourself projects **SIC code:** 87 **Address:** Ameresco Federal Solutions, 1820 Midpark Rd., Suite C, Knoxville, TN 37921 **E-mail:** jdriskill@ameresco.com **Web address:** www.ameresco.com

DROZDZIEL, MARION J.
Industry: Aerospace **Born:** December 21, 1924, Dunkirk, New York **Univ./degree:** B.S., Aero. Engineering, 1947; B.S., Mechanical Engineering, 1948, Tri-State University **Current organization:** Self employed **Title:** Aeronautical Engineer/Consultant **Type of organization:** Personal consultation **Major product:** Consultation-structures, rockets **Area of distribution:** New York **Expertise:** Engineering achievements include: development of criteria and methods of structural analysis extending analyses into the plastic and creep ranges for titanium and columbium rocket nozzle extensions; of criteria and methods of structural analysis for extendable rocket nozzle extensions, including rapid nozzle deployment involving plasticity; of methods of structural analysis for low strength, high ductility steels, aluminums and teflons as positive expulsion devices for zero gravity application in propellant tanks including bellows, reversing heads, rolling diaphragms and devices and collapsing or folding concepts; structural analysis on "X" series of aircraft, on Mercury, Gemini and Apollo spacecraft reaction control and propulsion systems; structural and weight analysis of programs involving rocket engines, propulsion systems, aircraft, air cushion vehicles, surface-effect ships, laser systems avionics, airborne and ground antennae, Army tanks and fighting vehicles. **Honors/awards:** Certificate of Achievement NASA-Apollo, 1972; Certificate of Commendaton, U.K. NATO Program, 1982 **Published works:** Contributed to International Conference on Fracture, Cannes, France, 1981 **Affiliations:** A.A.A.S.; Buffalo Fine Arts Academy; New York Academy of Science; American Institute of Aeronautics and Astronautics; Society of Reliability Engineers; National Space Society; The Planetary Society; Exchange Club; U.S. Navel Institute; American Space Foundation; Nature Conservancy; National Audubon Society; Sierra Club; American Academy of Political and Social Sciences; Academy of Political Science; Union Concerned Scientists; Air Force Association; Society of Allied Weight Engineers; Planetary Society; American Management Association; Biblical Archeology Society **Hob./spts.:** Fishing, golf, bowling, stamp collecting, bicycling **SIC code:** 87 **Address:** Drozdziel Chief Engineering & Consulting, 152 Linwood Avenue, Tonawanda, NY 14150

DRUMGOLE, JOHNNY E.
Industry: Religion **Born:** February 7, 1951, Monroe, Louisiana **Univ./degree:** Honorary Doctorate, Evangel University, 2003 **Current organization:** Liberty Christian Center Ministries **Title:** Pastor **Type of organization:** Church/education facility **Major product:** Religious services, education **Area of distribution:** National **Expertise:** Ministry, teaching, lectures **Affiliations:** Board of Directors, Food Band; Habitat for Humanity; Board of Directors, Nautis House **Hob./spts.:** Golf, tennis, freshwater fishing **SIC code:** 86 **Address:** Liberty Christian Center Ministries, 3220 Hwy. 165, Monroe, LA 71201 **E-mail:** drumgoleministries@yahoo.com

DRUMHELLER, ED
Industry: Aerospace engineering and consulting **Univ./degree:** M.S., California Technical College, 1966 **Current organization:** Northrop, Boeing **Title:** Sr. Aerospace Engineer **Type of organization:** Aerospace Research **Major product:** Aerospace

engineering, research and development, rocket sled test, flight test and wind tunnel engineer **Area of distribution:** International **Expertise:** Flight and field test engineering **Honors/awards:** 3 Caterpillar pins and membership in the Caterpillar Club (for people whose lives have been saved by parachuting from aircraft) operated by the Switlik and Pioneer parachute companies and in the Irvin Parachute Co. Caterpillar Club **Published works:** Air Power Magazine **Affiliations:** A.I.A.A.; S.A.E.; S.A.F.E. **Hob./spts.:** Golf, trapshooting, sport flying (commercial CFI) and hot air ballooning, parachute engineer on 800 mph race car **SIC code:** 87 **Address:** 25238 139th Place S.E., Kent, WA 98042 **E-mail:** hotairpair@aol.com

DUA, SURENDER K.
Industry: General Dynamics Land Systems is a subsidiary of General Dynamics Corporation. It designs, manufactures and supports land and amphibious combat systems for the U.S. Army, the U.S. Marine Corps and allied nations **Born:** April 15, 1947, Jhelum, Pakistan **Univ./degree:** M.S., Mechanical Engineering, Pune University, India, 1983 **Current organization:** General Dynamics Land Systems **Title:** Engineering Specialist **Type of organization:** Defense Contractor **Major product:** Defense vehicles design, prototype development and production **Area of distribution:** U.S. Defense and exports to friendly nations **Expertise:** Mechanical, hydraulic and pneumatic design **Honors/awards:** Best Engineer Award for the Year 1990-91 **Hob./spts.:** Reading, travel, tennis, cricket **SIC code:** 87 **Address:** General Dynamics Land Systems, 640 Seminole Rd., Muskegon, MI 49441 **E-mail:** skdua@att.net

DUDDEN, ALLEN W.
Industry: Testing **Born:** October 27, 1941, Brookings, South Dakota **Current organization:** Gas & Mechanical Laboratory, Inc. **Title:** President **Type of organization:** Laboratory **Major product:** Field testing of gas fired appliances, expert witness **Area of distribution:** International **Expertise:** Dealing with gas appliances & wood burning appliances **Published works:** Article **Affiliations:** C.S.A., C.G.A., G.A.E.S., N.F.P.A. **Hob./spts.:** Fishing, hunting, hiking **SIC code:** 87 **Address:** Gas & Mechanical Laboratory, Inc., 12405 Woodruff Ave., Unit 2, Downey, CA 90241 **E-mail:** allendudden@msn.com

DUFFEY-WROBLESKI, TESA
Industry: Emergency Planning **Univ./degree:** B.S., Emergency Administration and Planning, University of North Texas, 1995 **Current organization:** TDW Consulting **Title:** Owner **Type of organization:** Consulting firm **Major product:** Homeland and business security planning **Area of distribution:** National **Expertise:** Emergency management coordination, WMD, hurricane relief **Affiliations:** Past President, Texas Gulf Coast Emergency Management Association; Emergency Management Association of Texas; Vice President, Regional Homeland Security Council **Hob./spts.:** Tennis, horseback riding, camping **SIC code:** 87 **Address:** 2535 Cliff Dr., San Leon, TX 77539 **E-mail:** tdwconsulting@verizon.net

DUMONT, EDWARD A.
Industry: Architecture **Born:** July 4, 1961, Brooklyn, New York **Univ./degree:** B.A., Architecture, University of Florida, 1984 **Current organization:** Morris Architects **Title:** Senior Associate Project Manager **Type of organization:** Architectural firm **Major product:** Architecture design **Area of distribution:** International **Expertise:** Architecture, planning, interiors **Affiliations:** I.I.D.A. **Hob./spts.:** Furniture, design, photography **SIC code:** 87 **Address:** Morris Architects, 3355 W. Alabama St., Suite 200, Houston, TX 77098 **E-mail:** edward.dumont@morrisarchitects.com

DUNDON, BRIAN P.
Industry: Consulting **Univ./degree:** B.S., Northeastern University, 1988 **Current organization:** Carter & Burgess, Inc. **Title:** Land Development Unit Manager **Type of organization:** Consulting **Major product:** Architecture and civil engineering services **Area of distribution:** National **Expertise:** Civil engineering **Affiliations:** N.S.P.E.; A.S.C.; M.S.P.E.; A.C.I. **SIC code:** 87 **Address:** Carter & Burgess, Inc., 23 East St., Cambridge, MA 02141-1215 **E-mail:** dundonbp@c-b-boston.com

DUNN, ROBERT E.
Industry: Telecommunications/security consulting **Born:** November 15, 1951, New York **Univ./degree:** B.S., Trinity College; B.A., Security Management, Charter Oak State College **Current organization:** DVI Communications, Inc. **Title:** Senior Security Consultant **Type of organization:** Consulting firm **Major product:** Systems design, project management **Area of distribution:** International **Expertise:** Systems design, threat assessments, anti-terrorism, Certified Protection Professional, Certified Protection Officer, Certified Security Professional **Published works:** Security Director Magazine **Affiliations:** A.S.I.S.; I.F.P.O.; N.A.C.O.P.; H.T.C.I.A. **Hob./spts.:** Skiing, weightlifting, sailing **SIC code:** 87 **Address:** DVI Communications, Inc., 170 Broadway, 11th Floor, New York, NY 10038-4154 **E-mail:** rdunn@dvicomm.com

DUTY, CALEB H.
Industry: Country clubs **Born:** November 6, 1974, Marietta, Ohio **Univ./degree:** B.A., Culinary Arts, Hocking College, 1997 **Current organization:** Worthington Hills Country Club **Title:** Executive Chef **Type of organization:** Country club **Major product:** Entertainment **Area of distribution:** Columbus, Ohio **Expertise:** Cooking, plate design **Affiliations:** A.C.F.; Past Member, National Restaurant Association **Hob./spts.:** Outdoors, reading, cooking competitions, hiking, fishing **SIC code:** 86 **Address:** Worthington Hills Country Club, 920 Clubview Blvd. South, Columbus, OH 43235 **E-mail:** chefchd@hotmail.com **Web address:** www.worthingtonhills.com

EARL, LEWIS H.
Industry: Government **Born:** December 17, 1918, Guthrie, Texas **Univ./degree:** B.A., Texas Tech University, 1939; J.D., Georgetown University, 1950 **Current organization:** Garza County Democratic Party **Title:** Chairman **Type of organization:** Local government, public policy activities **Major product:** Economic and management studies **Area of distribution:** International **Expertise:** Economics, U.S. Federal Government, development training programs **SIC code:** 86 **Address:** P.O. Box 580, Post, TX 79356 **E-mail:** lhearl@arn.net

ECKARD, CONNIE
Industry: Public relations and communications **Univ./degree:** B.A., Liberal Arts, Texas A&M, 1957; Ph.D., Communication Management, Pacific Western University, 1985 **Current organization:** Will Communicate for Money/Food **Title:** Vice President **Type of organization:** Communications consultancy **Major product:** Professional support for organizational communications programs **Area of distribution:** National, with Pacific Northwest focus **Expertise:** Employee and management communication programs **Published works:** Articles, journals **Affiliations:** International Association of Business Communicators; Accredited Member, Society of Professional Journalists; National Management Association **Hob./spts.:** Professional Community development activities, theatre **SIC code:** 87 **Address:** 1321 Perkins Ave., Richland, WA 99354-3106 **E-mail:** connie_eckard@msn.com

EDEL, CHRISTIAN
Industry: Communications consulting **Born:** August 12, 1964, Flint, Michigan **Univ./degree:** Speech Communications, Telecommunications and Film, Eastern Michigan University **Current organization:** Edel Communications **Title:** President/Founder **Type of organization:** Communications consulting company **Major product:** Consulting **Area of distribution:** International **Expertise:** Media consulting, speech writing and public speaking **Honors/awards:** Nominated, Prime Contractor of the Year Award, U. S. State Department; Recipient, State Department's Award for Excellence **Hob./spts.:** Snorkeling, tennis, biking, music, theatre **SIC code:** 87 **Address:** Edel Communications, 1401 North Taft St., #1402, Arlington, VA 22201 **E-mail:** Info@EdelCommunications.com

EDMUNDSON, ALLEN B.
Industry: Medical research **Born:** June 16, 1932, Flat River, Missouri **Spouse:** Shelagh Bowman-Edmundson **Married:** August 8, 1987 **Children:** Kathryn L. Edmundson, 41; Carole E. Detherage, 37; Douglas A. Edmundson, 35 **Univ./degree:** Ph.D., Rockefeller University, 1961 **Current organization:** Oklahoma Medical Research Foundation **Title:** Member/Head of Crystallography **Type of organization:** Non-profit **Major product:** Proteins **Area of distribution:** Oklahoma **Expertise:** Protein research **Honors/awards:** Strathmore's Who's Who, V.I.P. Section; Awards from the Biographical Institute: One of "Five Hundred Leaders of Influence", "Twentieth Century Achievement Award", Man of the Year Award, One of the "Outstanding Speakers" of the 20th Century, Universal Award of Accomplishment, One of 500 Leading Intellectuals of the World; Awards from the International Biographical Centre, Cambridge, England: One of the 2000 Outstanding Scientists of the 20th Century, One of 36 individuals to whom the First Edition was dedicated to represent the remainder of the 2000 scientists featured in this publication, One of the Outstanding Speakers of the 20th Century, One of the Outstanding Intellectual's of the 20th Century, One of the One Thousand Great Americans, International Man of the Millennium in Recognition of his services to Science and Education **Published works:** Edmundson, A.B., Tribbick, G., Plompen, S., Geysen, H.M., Yuriev, E., Ramsland, P.A. (2001) Binding of synthetic peptides by a human monoclonal IgM with an unusual combining site structure. J. Mol. Recognit. 14:229-238. Edmundson, A.B., DeWitt, C.R., Goldsteen, B.Z. & Ramsland, P.A. (1999) Packing motifs as predictors of the propensity of antibody fragments to crystallize. J. Cryst Growth. 196, 276-284 **Affiliations:** American Association of Immunologists; Phi Beta Kappa; Sigma Xi; American Society for Biochemistry and Molecular Biology; American Crystallographic Association; New York Academy of Sciences; The Protein Society **Career accomplishments:** Worked with Sir John C. Kendrew in a Nobel Prize

winning project, "Structure of Myoglobin," the sequence of this protein was used to calibrate automated amino acid sequencers for 25 years; Solved one of the first 3-D structures of an antibody fragment and many more since; Introduced and proved concept of induced fit mechanisms of antigen binding by antibodies; Identified aspartame "Equal" as a therapeutic analgesic for humans; Helped develop contemporary field of combinatorial chemistry **Hob./spts.:** Basketball, cricket, softball, tennis **SIC code:** 87 **Address:** Oklahoma Medical Research Foundation, 825 N.E. 13th St., Oklahoma City, OK 73104 **E-mail:** allen-edmundson@omrf.ouhsc.edu

EGGERT SR., ROBERT J.

Industry: Consulting **Born:** Dec. 11, 1913, Little Rock, AR **Spouse:** Annamarie Hayes **Married:** March 19, 1936 **Children:** Robert John; Richard F.; James E. **Univ./degree:** B.S., 1935; M.S., 1936, Univ. of IL; Ph.D. Candidate in Philosophy, 1938, Univ. of MN.; LHD, Honorary, AZ State Univ., 1998 **Current organization:** Eggert Economic Enterprises, Inc. **Title:** Pres./Chief Economist (retired) **Type of organization:** Economic consulting firm **Major product:** Monthly "Blue Chip Economic Indicators" newsletter **Area of distribution:** National **Expertise:** Economic consulting and forecasting **Honors/awards:** Winner, Golden Gloves Boxing, Univ. of IL, 1935; Seer of the Year, Harvard Univ., 1973; AZ Economics Roundtable; Appointed AZ Governor's Commn. of Economic Development **Published works:** "Becoming A Person of Greater Value," Ford Motor Co. **Affiliations:** Fellow, Amer. Statistician Assoc.; Nat'l Assoc. of Business Economists; Past Chairman, Council of Int'l Marketing Research and Planning Directors; Amer. Marketing Assoc.; Past Dir., Amer. Quarter Horse Assoc.; Vice Chairman, Investment Advisory Council, AZ State Retirement System; AZ Chamber of Commerce; Alpha Zeta; Amer. Economists Assoc.; Phoenix Economy Club; Trustee, Marcus J. Lawrence Medical Center; Chairman, Market Research Commission, Governor's Strategic Partnership for Economic Development; Co-Chairman, AZ Senior Industries Cluster **Career accomplishments:** Economic Advisory Bd., U.S. Dept. of Commerce; Census Advisory Committee; Member, Panel of Econ. Advisers, Congl. Budget Office **Hob./spts.:** Racing quarter horses, tennis, traveling **SIC code:** 87 **Address:** Eggert Economic Enterprises, Inc., 790 Rodeo Rd., Sedona, AZ 86336 **E-mail:** eee@sedona.net

EICHBAUM, BARLANE RONALD

Industry: Applied Research & Development **Born:** September 1, 1926, New Brunswick, New Jersey **Spouse:** Beatrice Roth **Married:** August 26, 1950 **Children:** Susanne Bashista, Nancy Radford, Virginia Anderson; Grandchildren: David Bashista, Jimmy Bashista, Kristen Bashista, Timothy Anderson, Brian Chapin; Great Grandchildren: Alex Bashista, Luke Bashista, Dominik Bashista **Univ./degree:** B.S., Rutgers University; M.S., Ceramic Engineering, Texas University; Ph.D., Rutgers University **Title:** Materials Processing Engineer/Scientist and Environmental Scientist **Major product:** Advanced components for: computers, industrial and military equipment; materials processing for new systems; environmental programs and studies to reduce pollution **Area of distribution:** International **Expertise:** Inorganic Materials Science/ Engineering and Environmental Science **Honors/awards:** Foote Minerals 1st Award; Ferro Enamels Award; IBM ERAD Award; Materials in Design Engineering Award; Ford Motor Co. Awards for directing: 1) BIAX High Speed Memory Element Development and Production and 2) Advanced High Speed Thin Film Memory Prototype for NSA; Who's Who in: Electronic Industry; The East; The West; Commerce & Industry; American Men & Women in Science and Royal Blue Book of Great Britain; Fellow, American Institute of Chemists **Published works:** Over 60 publications, patents and presentations in the fields of ceramic and inorganic processing; solid state and electronic component development; studies on external and internal combustion engines and air pollution; automated metal extraction technology and water pollution clean-up studies **Career accomplishments:** His accomplishments have been possible with the help of his GI Bill of Rights for his Engineering education, with prayer to God, working with and with the assistance of many excellent scientific associates. He has had many accomplishments in the field of Applied Research & Development in the development of advanced computers, NASA equipment, military equipment and industrial automated processing equipment **Hob./spts.:** Family activities, genealogy, travel, Christian activities; Founding Member, Reno Christian Fellowship; patriotic events **SIC code:** 87 **Address:** 12065 Stoney Brook Dr., Reno, NV 89511 **E-mail:** eichbaum2@aol.com

ELMAN, SANDRA E.

Industry: Education **Born:** September 15, 1947 **Univ./degree:** Ph.D., University of California at Berkeley, 1982 **Current organization:** Northwest Commission on Colleges & Universities **Title:** President/Ph.D. **Type of organization:** Nonprofit accrediting agency **Major product:** Quality assurance, accreditation **Area of distribution:** International **Expertise:** Public policy **Hob./spts.:** Travel, jazz **SIC code:** 86 **Address:** Northwest Commission on Colleges & Universities, 8060 165th Ave. N.E., Redmond, WA 98052 **E-mail:** selman@nwccu.org **Web address:** www.nwccu.org

ELMER, KIM. W.

Industry: Consulting engineering **Born:** April 10, 1957, Monroe, Wisconsin **Univ./ degree:** A.S., Madison Tech, 1978 **Current organization:** Kimley-Horn & Assoc., Inc. **Title:** Project Manager **Type of organization:** Consulting firm **Major product:** Aviation, land development, transportation **Area of distribution:** Orlando, Florida **Expertise:** Roadway engineer **Affiliations:** F.E.S.; N.S.P.E.; A.S.H.E. **Hob./spts.:** Golf, fishing **SIC code:** 87 **Address:** Kimley-Horn & Assoc., Inc., 3660 Maguire Blvd., Suite 200, Orlando, FL 32803 **E-mail:** kim.elmer@kimley-horn.com

EMERY, EDWARD M.

Industry: Agricultural sciences research **Born:** January 23, 1926, Brooklyn, New York **Univ./degree:** B.S., Chemical Engineering, University of Colorado, 1948; Ph.D., Physical Chemistry, University of Colorado at Boulder, 1952 **Title:** Senior Analytical Consultant, Monsanto Co., (Retired) **Type of organization:** Industrial research **Major product:** Animal nutritional products **Area of distribution:** International **Expertise:** Analytical sciences (research); chromatography, organic spectroscopy **Honors/awards:** Atomic Energy Commission Fellowship; 1981 Award of Merit in Chromatography from Chicago Chromatography Discussion Group **Published works:** 18 technical publications (9 chromatography related) including, "A Quantitative Comparison of Manual Injection vs. Autosampler", Spectra-Physics Chromatography Review, Vol. 1, No. 2, Feb. 1975 and "The Role of New Generation Chromatography Automation in Industrial Research", J. Chrom. Sci. 14, 261, 1976; numerous chromatography talks at technical meetings; 2 patents **Affiliations:** American Chemical Society; Missouri Academy of Science; A.S.T.M. **Hob./spts.:** Travel, walking **SIC code:** 87 **Address:** 7336 Whitehall Colonial Lane, St. Louis, MO 63119 **E-mail:** edot55@aol.com

ENGLERT, JON M.

Industry: Consulting **Born:** December 6, 1939, Chicago, Illinois **Univ./degree:** B.S., Industrial Design, Montana State University, 1962 **Current organization:** Englert Land Co., LLC **Title:** Manager **Type of organization:** Consulting **Major product:** Oil and gas land work, right-of-way **Area of distribution:** National **Expertise:** Easements **Hob./spts.:** Fishing, golf **SIC code:** 87 **Address:** Englert Land Co., LLC, 670 Sapphire Ave., Billings, MT 59105 **E-mail:** mtlandman@aol.com

ENSMINGER, DALE

Industry: Research laboratories **Born:** September 26, 1923, Mount Perry, Ohio **Spouse:** Lois Elizabeth Hamilton **Married:** March 25, 1948 **Children:** Martha Jean Taylor, 50; Laura Lee Francis, 47; Charles Robert, 46; Jonathan Dale, 42; Mary Ann Miller, 41; Daniel Joseph, 31 **Univ./degree:** B.S., Mechanical Engineering; B.S., Electrical Engineering, Ohio State University, 1950 **Current organization:** Battelle Columbus Laboratories **Title:** Senior Research Scientist, Retired **Type of organization:** Independent research and development firm **Major product:** Contract research and development **Area of distribution:** International **Expertise:** Ultrasonics, research and development **Published works:** Numerous books, articles, journals including, "Ultrasonics, Fundamentals, Technology, Applications," 1988, second edition of Ultrasonics - the Low- and High-Intensity Applications, 1973; reviews technical books for Applied Mechanics Reviews **Affiliations:** Ultrasonic Industry Association; Acoustical Society of America; American Society for Nondestructive Testing; Past Dean, Director, Columbus Bible Institute; Board Member, Fundamental Baptist Mission of Trinidad and Tobago; Board Member, The Columbus Prison Association **Career accomplishments:** Has conducted or participated in more than 975 research studies involving both high-intensity and low-intensity applications of ultrasonic energy. These studies have ranged from basic studies of ultrasonic energy and wave propagation to the development of prototype devices for industrial, domestic and military uses. These studies have led to two technical books, two books to which he is a major contributor, books to which he has contributed chapters, over 150 technical articles and patents of applications of ultrasonic energy and a book in preparation for publication tentatively entitled Ultrasonics Data Book of which he is a technical editor and major contributor **Hob./**

spts.: Woodworking **SIC code:** 87 **Address:** Battelle Columbus Laboratories, 198 E. Longview Ave., Columbus, OH 43202 **E-mail:** 104526.2066@compuserve.com

ESTOESTA, FE
Industry: Environmental **Title:** QA Director **Type of organization:** Laboratory **Major product:** Environmental testing **Expertise:** Chemistry **SIC code:** 87 **Address:** James R. Reed & Associates, 770 Pilot House Dr., Newport News, VA 23606 **E-mail:** fpestoesta@jrreed.com

EVILLE, WILLIAM T.
Industry: Cardstock models/alternative medicine **Born:** February 8, 1934, Ohio **Spouse:** Rebecca Holden Eville **Married:** August 8, 1955 **Children:** Nancy Ellen Eville Ehounou, 48 **Univ./degree:** B.S.I.T., Ohio University, 1956 **Current organization:** Paper Aviation Company/Reiki 4U **Title:** Senior Designer, Master Craftsman/Reiki Shinpiden Healer **Type of organization:** Construction, distribution/Energy healing **Major product:** Museum class cardstock models & kits of airplanes and birds/pain relief, healing of trauma and disease **Area of distribution:** National/Northeast Ohio **Expertise:** Designing, engineering/Handling Reiki Force **Honors/awards:** First person to be awarded the B.S.I.T. at Ohio University **Published works:** 1 patent **Affiliations:** Charter Member, New York Central System Historical Society; Charter Member, United States Aviation Museum & Akron Airship Historical Center; Founding Member, The American Air Museum in Britain; Founding Member, The Challenger Foundation; Advisory Board Officer, The Lighter Than-Air Society; Voyager, V.I.P.; Certified Reiki Shinpiden (Master) Practitioner; Member, International Paper and Cardstock Modelers Society; Member, Chapter 325, E.A.A. **Career accomplishments:** Designed: power converter for military X-ray system to take 40G shock load in any direction, cable stripper for test cables used in underground nuclear weapons tests, control cabinets for DC drive of 170 ton dump truck for South African copper mine & Leading Edge Flap Drive for Boeing 747; Designed, inspected and oversaw installation of components of bearing casting line in the Soviet Union **Hob./spts.:** Playing the Australian Didgeridoo, amateur cartoonist **SIC code:** 87 **Address:** Jet Inc., 750 Alpha Dr., Highland Heights, OH 44143-2167 **E-mail:** reikibillevil@yahoo.com

EZRIN, MYER
Industry: Education/Consulting **Univ./degree:** Ph.D., Organic Chemistry, Yale University, 1954 **Current organization:** University of Connecticut, Institute of Materials Science (IMS) **Title:** Director, IMS Associates Program (industrial outreach) **Type of organization:** University **Major product:** Higher education **Area of distribution:** National **Expertise:** Industrial outreach for materials research and development needs and problems; plastics analysis and plastics failure analysis; expert witness-product liability and patent infringement litigation **Honors/awards:** Who's Who in America, 60th edition; Phi Beta Kappa; Fellow, Society of Plastics Engineers; Editorial Board, International Journal of Forensic Engineering **Published works:** Co-author, "Plastics Analysis Guide-Chemical and Instrumental Methods", Hanser, 1983; Author, "Plastics Failure Guide-Cause and Prevention", Hanser, 1996; many papers on plastics analysis and plastics failure analysis **Affiliations:** Society of Plastics Engineers; American Chemical Society **SIC code:** 87 **Address:** 173 Academy Dr., Longmeadow, MA 01106-2158 **E-mail:** mezrin@aol.com

FANJUL, ANDREA N.
Industry: Biotechnology **Born:** January 17, 1961, Argentina **Univ./degree:** M.S., Biology, 1984; Ph.D., Biology, 1991, University of Natural Sciences, Argentina **Current organization:** Maxia Pharmaceutical, Inc. **Title:** Scientist **Type of organization:** Private research **Major product:** Identification of potential chemotherapeutics **Area of distribution:** International **Expertise:** Biology, research **Published works:** 15 journal articles, 40 abstracts/conference papers, 1 book chapter **Affiliations:** Fellow, American Association for the Advancement of Science; American Diabetes Association **Hob./spts.:** Biking, aerobics, travel, reading, theatre, family **SIC code:** 87 **Address:** Maxia Pharmaceutical, Inc., 10835 Altman Row, #250, San Diego, CA 92121 **E-mail:** andrea@maxia.com

FARKAS, LARRY J.
Industry: Consulting engineering **Born:** June 19, 1953, Coatesville, Pennsylvania **Univ./degree:** B.S., Environmental Engineering, Pennsylvania State University, 1977 **Current organization:** Carroll Engineering Corp. **Title:** Project Manager **Type of organization:** Consulting engineering firm **Major product:** Surveying, subdivision and land development, construction specifications, construction management **Area of distribution:** Northeastern United States **Expertise:** Civil engineering, site engineering, surveying **Affiliations:** A.S.C.E.; American Society of Highway Engineers **Hob./spts.:** Family, reading, teaching religious studies, sports **SIC code:** 87 **Address:** Carroll Engineering Corp., 555 Second Ave., Suite G-103, Collegeville, PA 19426

FATZINGER JR., EDWARD CARL
Industry: Engineering/consulting **Born:** March 26, 1974, Allentown, Pennsylvania **Univ./degree:** M.S., Aerospace Engineering, 2001 **Current organization:** Vector Scientific **Title:** Forensic Engineer **Type of organization:** Consulting **Major product:** Engineering, biomechanics, animation consulting **Area of distribution:** International **Expertise:** Accident reconstruction (automotive, motorcycles, heavy trucks, mechanical failure, suspension, dynamics) **Affiliations:** S.A.E.; A.S.M.E.; S.C.C.A.; American Society of Non Destructive Testing; American Motorcycle Association **Hob./spts.:** Racing motorcycles **SIC code:** 87 **Address:** Vector Scientific, 5245 Pacific Concourse Dr., Suite 100, Los Angeles, CA 90045 **E-mail:** efatzinger@vectorscientific.com

FAULKNER, LYNN L.
Industry: Research **Born:** June 24, 1941, Fort Wayne, Indiana **Univ./degree:** Ph.D., Mechanical Engineering (Acoustics), Purdue University, 1969; Postdoctoral Fellowship at Purdue to further pursue scholarly research in engineering acoustics **Current organization:** Battelle Memorial Institute **Title:** Program Manager **Type of organization:** Contract research **Major product:** Research and development **Area of distribution:** International **Expertise:** Acoustics, noise control, machinery dynamics **Honors/awards:** Founding Editor of Marcel Dekker, Inc., N.Y., Mechanical engineering series of textbooks, reference books and handbooks **Published works:** "Handbook of Industrial Noise Control", "Handbook of Machinery Dynamics"; Numerous technical publications; Holds two U.S. patents and has two patents pending **Affiliations:** A.S.A.; Member of Ohio State University Mechanical Engineering Advisory Board; Board Member, Ohio State University Center for Automotive Research; active in community and church organizations **Hob./spts.:** Travel, hunting, fishing, boating, gardening **SIC code:** 87 **Address:** Battelle Memorial Institute, 505 King Ave., Columbus, OH 43201 **E-mail:** faulknel@battelle.org

FENNELL, THOMAS
Industry: Telecommunications IP networks **Univ./degree:** A.S., 1995; A.S., 1997, Heald Institute of Technology **Current organization:** Self-employed **Title:** Systems Engineer **Type of organization:** Consulting **Major product:** Switches, routers, DWDM devices **Area of distribution:** International **Expertise:** Network designs, configurations **Hob./spts.:** Camping, hiking, scuba diving **SIC code:** 87 **Address:** 4282 Indigo Dr., San Jose, CA 95136 **E-mail:** tcfennell@sbcglobal.net

FERNBERGER, MARILYN F.
Industry: Consulting **Born:** August 13, 1927, Philadelphia, Pennsylvania **Spouse:** Edward Fernberger **Married:** June 21, 1947 **Children:** Edward Jr., James Moyer, Ellen Fernberger Shecter **Univ./degree:** B.A., Political Science and English, University of Pennsylvania, 1948 **Current organization:** Global Event Marketing Inc. **Title:** Chairman **Type of organization:** Consulting firm **Major product:** Consulting for sports and art **Area of distribution:** International **Expertise:** Marketing for sports and art world **Published works:** 25 year contributor to in 12 international tennis publications; Book, "History of Tennis in Philadelphia" **Affiliations:** Greater Philadelphia Chamber of Commerce; Lifetime Member Board of Directors, International Tennis Hall of Fame; Board of Directors, Philadelphia Sports Congress; Board of Directors, Philadelphia Museum of Art Associates; Past President, Rodin Museum of Art; Co-chaired the U.S. Pro-Indoor Tennis Championship for 25 years; Lifetime Board of Directors Member and Donor with husband Edward of Tennis Art, Artifacts and Memorabilia **Hob./spts.:** Tennis, art, travel **SIC code:** 87 **Address:** Global Event Marketing Inc., 1112 Penmore Place, Rydal, PA 19046

FERRARIO, SUSAN M.
Industry: Environmental **Born:** October 23, 1962, St. Louis, Missouri **Univ./degree:** B.S., Chemistry, University of Missouri, 2004 **Current organization:** Global Environmental Laboratories **Title:** Chemist/Microscopist **Type of organization:** Independent testing laboratory **Major product:** Industrial asbestos, mold, lead, pollen **Area of distribution:** National **Expertise:** Microscopic analysis **Hob./spts.:** Travel, pottery, physical fitness **SIC code:** 87 **Address:** Global Environmental Laboratories, 11040 Lin-Valle Dr., St. Louis, MO 63123

FEYNBERG, YURI C.
Industry: Healthcare **Born:** August 28, 1943, St. Petersburg, Russia **Univ./degree:** B.S., Special Education, 1970; M.S., Speech Pathology, 1972, University of St. Petersburg, Russia; Ph.D., 1995, New York University **Current organization:** Life Adjustment Center, Inc. **Title:** CEO **Type of organization:** Nonprofit 501(c) (3) organization **Major product:** Services for the mentally and developmentally disabled **Area of distribution:** New York **Expertise:** Healthcare administration **Published works:** "Interventional Strategies for Dyslexic Adolescents", Journal of Speech Pathology, 1971; "Sleep-wake Patterns of Profoundly Retarded Children", Health and Habilitation Studies, NYS, 1985 **Affiliations:** American Association on Mental Retardation **Hob./spts.:** Vintage British sports cars **SIC code:** 83 **Address:** Life Adjustment Center, Inc., 1175 Findlay Ave., Bronx, NY 10456 **E-mail:** ycf@prodigy.net

FILSON, GEORGE DAVID
Industry: Household cleaning products **Born:** October 24, 1941, Fort Wayne, Indiana **Univ./degree:** Attended Indiana University; San Jose State University **Current organization:** Clorox Co. **Title:** Scientist **Type of organization:** Packaging Research & Development **Major product:** Household cleaning products **Area of distribution:** International **Expertise:** Packaging, transportation, handling and warehousing simulation testing **Honors/awards:** Guest Speaker, NWTCA; IOPP; Eagle Scout **Affilia-**

tions: Chair, Northern California Chemical Technicians Division, T.A.G.A.C.S.; Past President, F.S.C.T.Golden Gate Society; Vice President, I.O.P.P., Golden Gate Chapter; past Exploring Commissioner, Golden Gate Council, B.S.A. **Hob./spts.:** Photography, backpacking **SIC code:** 87 **Address:** Clorox Co., 7200 Johnson Dr., Pleasanton, CA 94588 **E-mail:** david.filson@clorox.com

FINDLAYTER, ORLANDO R.
Industry: Religion **Born:** July 9, 1963, Republic of Panama **Current organization:** New Hope Christian Fellowship **Title:** Bishop **Type of organization:** Church **Major product:** Faith and healing **Area of distribution:** International **Expertise:** Mentoring, pastoring **Affiliations:** Churches United to Heal; United Covenant Churches of Christ **Hob./spts.:** Sports **SIC code:** 86 **Address:** New Hope Christian Fellowship, 4615 Church Ave., Brooklyn, NY 11203 **E-mail:** 04hope@aol.com **Web address:** www.insidenewhope.org

FIOL, BRUCE R.
Industry: Religion **Born:** October 4, 1938, Mussoorie, India **Univ./degree:** D.Div., Covenant Theological Seminary **Current organization:** Marco Presbyterian Church **Title:** Rev. Dr. **Type of organization:** Church **Major product:** Religious services **Area of distribution:** National **Expertise:** Preaching, teaching, pastoral ministry **Affiliations:** Suncoast Presbyterian Association; Board Member, Covenant College **Hob./spts.:** Reading, travel **SIC code:** 86 **Address:** Marco Presbyterian Church, 875 West Elkcam Circle, Marco Island, FL 34145 **E-mail:** office@marcochurch.com **Web address:** www.marcochurch.com

FISCHER, KURT H.
Industry: Association/education/consulting **Born:** December 7, 1942 **Univ./degree:** M.A., Culinary Art, Germany, 1972 **Current organization:** The International Food and Beverage Forum **Title:** President **Type of organization:** Association **Major product:** Service for hotels and restaurants **Area of distribution:** International **Expertise:** Food and beverage management **Published works:** Cook book, "Food and Wine-Western Ways" **Affiliations:** International Food and Beverage Association **Hob./spts.:** Tennis **SIC code:** 86 **Address:** The International Food and Beverage Forum, 4228 192nd Ct. S.E., Issaquah, WA 98027 **E-mail:** kurt.fischer@gte.net **Web address:** www.foodbeverageforum.com

FJELLGREN, CHRISTER E.
Industry: Automotive **Born:** June 21, 1950, Sweden **Univ./degree:** Electronics Engineering, Sweden **Current organization:** Thomas Magnete USA, LLC **Title:** President **Type of organization:** Consulting **Major product:** Proportional solenoid valves **Area of distribution:** National **Expertise:** Engineering **Published works:** Articles **Affiliations:** S.A.E.; N.F.P.A. **Hob./spts.:** Family, golf, the outdoors **SIC code:** 87 **Address:** Thomas Magnete USA, LLC, 4465 N. 124th St., Unit F, Brookfield, WI 53005-2537 **E-mail:** info.usa@thomas-magnete.com **Web address:** www.thomas-magnete.com

FLINCHBAUGH, DAVID E.
Industry: Medical **Born:** October 11, 1934, Poughkeepsie, New York **Univ./degree:** B.S., Physics and Math, Union College, New York, 1957; M.S., Physics, 1960; Ph.D., Physics, 1964, University of Connecticut **Current organization:** Health Interventions **Title:** Chairman of the Board of Directors **Type of organization:** Aerospace, defense **Major product:** Medical systems and devices development, marketing, production, distribution, inventions, patents, trademarks, research and product development **Area of distribution:** International **Expertise:** Quantum Physicist, Health Physicist, Medical and Inter-disciplinary Technologist, Licensed Professional Engineer **Honors/awards:** Who's Who in America; Who's Who in the South and Southwest; Who's Who of American Business Leaders; Who's Who, Executive Edition of Sterling Who's Who Directory, 1996; Men of Achievement, International Biographical Society; 500 Leaders of Influence, American Biographical Institute; Entrepreneurial Excellence Award, Jim Moran Institute, 1996; I.E.E.E. Millennium Award, 2000 **Published works:** 151 inventions, 3 books, 10 patents pending in U.S.; 60 patents pending, international **Affiliations:** I.E.E.E., Florida Council; F.C.E.S.; S.M.E.; O.S.A.; A.S.L.M.; Owner/President of Eurosolutions Inc. **Hob./spts.:** Photography, music, swimming, aviation pilot **SIC code:** 87 **Address:** Health Interventions, 5509 Commerce Dr., Suite A, Orlando, FL 32839 **E-mail:** davidf@urosolutions.com **Web address:** www.urosolutions.com

FLINT, STEPHEN E.
Industry: Architecture **Born:** May 2, 1957, Fairburg, Illinois **Univ./degree:** B.S., Architecture, University of Illinois at Chicago, 1984 **Current organization:** Arcon Associates, Inc. **Title:** Principal **Type of organization:** Architectural firm **Major product:** Architecture and design **Area of distribution:** Northern Illinois **Expertise:** K-12 education, recreation, healthcare **Affiliations:** A.I.A.; President, Chamber of Commerce; Planning Committee, Village of Lombard **Hob./spts.:** Family, gardening, bicycling **SIC code:** 87 **Address:** Arcon Associates, Inc., 420 Eisenhower Lane, North, Lombard, IL 60148 **E-mail:** seflint@arconassoc.com **Web address:** www.arconassoc.com

FLOYD, NICOLE S.
Industry: Social services **Born:** March 21, 1970, Henderson, Kentucky **Univ./degree:** A.S., Human Services, Ivy Tech Community College of Indiana, 2006 **Current organization:** Arbor Education/Hurricane Park **Title:** Career Co-coordinator **Type of organization:** Human services **Major product:** Career and life counseling **Area of distribution:** Indianapolis, Indiana **Expertise:** Public and private career and life counseling, welfare to work guidance, educational guidance **Hob./spts.:** Technology, biking **SIC code:** 83 **Address:** 5843 Cedarstone Ct., Indianapolis, IN 46226 **E-mail:** nicolefloyd@arborET.com **Web address:** www.hurricanepark.com

FOERSTEL, EDMUND C.
Industry: Engineering **Born:** May 29, 1923, Los Angeles, California **Univ./degree:** B.S.C.E., University of Southern California, 1950 **Current organization:** Edmund C. Foerstel, Structural Engineer **Title:** President **Type of organization:** Engineering consulting firm **Major product:** Structural and geo technical engineering **Area of distribution:** National **Expertise:** Engineering (registered P.E. in California, Arizona, Hawaii) **Published works:** 1 patent; 1 copyright **Hob./spts.:** Family, restoring a 1929 Model A Ford **SIC code:** 87 **Address:** Edmund C. Foerstel, Structural Engineer, 915-A Calle Amanecer, San Clemente, CA 92673

FORNEY, LOREN J.
Industry: Automotive **Born:** December 15, 1922, Waterloo, Iowa **Univ./degree:** B.S., General Engineering, Iowa State University, 1954 **Current organization:** Tire Consulting Services, Inc. **Title:** President **Type of organization:** Consulting firm **Major product:** Failure analysis of tires and rims **Area of distribution:** National **Expertise:** Representing plaintiffs, deposition, trials **Affiliations:** Former President, General Engineering Society, Iowa State University **Hob./spts.:** Family, NASCAR, English bulldogs **SIC code:** 87 **Address:** Tire Consulting Services, Inc., 433 Brian Dr., Basye, VA 22810 **E-mail:** ltcsinc@aol.com **Web address:** www.tireconsulting.com

FOROUHAR, HAMID R.
Industry: Pharmaceuticals **Born:** July 26, 1960, Tehran, Iran **Univ./degree:** M.S., Microbiology, University of Wisconsin **Current organization:** Irvine Analytical Laboratories **Title:** Quality Control Manager **Type of organization:** Laboratory **Major product:** Laboratory services **Area of distribution:** National, international **Expertise:** Analytical chemistry, chromatography **Affiliations:** A.C.S. **SIC code:** 87 **Address:** Irvine Analytical Laboratories, 10 Vanderbilt, Irvine, CA 92618 **E-mail:** hforouhar@juno.com

FORT, ROBERT B.
Industry: Religion **Born:** December 27, 1948, Portsmouth, Virginia **Univ./degree:** B.A., Religious Studies, Global University of the Assemblies of God, 1976 **Current organization:** United Evangelical Churches **Title:** Reverend, CEO, Board Chairman **Type of organization:** Nonprofit/religious **Major product:** Ministerial fellowship **Area of distribution:** International **Expertise:** Lecturing, seminars, concerts **Published works:** 15 CD's of gospel music **Affiliations:** New York College of Advanced Studies; North American Academy of Arts & Sciences; American Association of Christian Counselors; Board of Administration, Pentecostal/Charismatic Churches of North America **Hob./spts.:** Music **SIC code:** 86 **Address:** United Evangelical Churches, P.O. Box 1000, San Juan Bautista, CA 95045 **E-mail:** rbfort@uecol.org

FOUSHÉE JR., CLARENCE L.
Industry: Aerospace **Born:** April 26, 1921, San Diego, California **Univ./degree:** B.S., Mechanical Engineering, San Diego State University **Current organization:** Materials Consultants **Title:** President **Type of organization:** Consulting firm **Major product:** Non-metallic materials **Area of distribution:** National **Expertise:** Engineering **Affiliations:** Lifetime Member, S.A.E.; A.S.T.M. **Hob./spts.:** Woodworking **SIC code:** 87 **Address:** Materials Consultants, 1814 138th Pl. S.E., Bellevue, WA 98005-4024

FRANCETT, JOHN C.
Industry: Consulting **Born:** February 8, 1951, Easton, Pennsylvania **Univ./degree:** B.A., Hamilton College, Clinton, New York **Current organization:** JBF Incorporated **Title:** President **Type of organization:** Consulting **Major product:** Water utilities **Area of distribution:** International **Expertise:** Engineering **Hob./spts.:** Photography, tennis **SIC code:** 87 **Address:** JBF Incorporated, 696 Corinth Rd., Queensbury, NY 12804 **E-mail:** jcfrancett@hotmail.com

FRANK, GUNNAR K.M.
Industry: Technical consulting and repair of yachts **Born:** April 20, 1956, Sweden **Current organization:** Cruising Consultant & Yacht Repairs, Inc. **Title:** President **Type of organization:** Consulting and repair **Major product:** Boats and engines **Area of distribution:** National **Expertise:** Diesel engines **Honors/awards:** Seldon Mast Award **Published works:** Houston Chronicle, Tell Tales Magazine, Soundings, Mariner Logs, T.V. news **Hob./spts.:** Outdoor adventures **SIC code:** 87 **Address:** Cruising Consultant & Yacht Repair, Inc., 1722 Oak Ridge Dr., Kemah, TX 77565 **E-mail:** gunnarfrank@sprintmail.com

FRANKLIN, CHARLES C.
Industry: Architecture/engineering **Born:** March 6, 1947, Baltimore, Maryland **Univ./degree:** B.S., Electrical Engineering, University of Maryland, 1972 **Current organization:** Ellerbe Becket **Title:** Engineering Principal **Type of organization:** Architectural/engineering **Major product:** Architectural engineering services **Area of distribution:** International **Expertise:** Electrical engineering, telecommunications, security and fire protection **Honors/awards:** Vietnam Veteran, 1968-1971 Captains Citation USS Oriskany; Lighting Design Award, 1984; Electrical Distribution Award, 2003 **Affiliations:** I.E.E.E.; I.E.S.; N.F.P.A.; B.I.S.C.I.; American Arbitration Association-Registered Neutral **Hob./spts.:** AWS Certified Wine Judge, IFPO Master Photographer **SIC code:** 87 **Address:** Ellerbe Becket, 1001 G. Street N.W., Suite 1000, Washington, DC 20001 **E-mail:** Fbutch Franklin@aol.com

FRASER, ALLAN W.
Industry: Religion **Born:** June 18, 1940, Capetown, South Africa **Univ./degree:** B.A., Cross Cultural Counseling, University of South Africa, 1976 **Current organization:** North Warren Church of Christ **Title:** Minister/Elder **Type of organization:** Church **Major product:** Religious services, faith based counseling **Area of distribution:** Michigan **Expertise:** Counseling **Honors/awards:** Paul Harris Fellowship, Rotary Foundation **Affiliations:** Former President, Rotary Club, Durbanville, South Africa; Former Chapter President, Rotary Club, Bloubert, South Africa; Former President, Rotary Club, Goodwood, South Africa; Olympic Games Envoy, Russian team, 1996; Summer Camp Manager, Michigan Youth Camp, Church of Christ Love Ministry **Hob./spts.:** Rugby, yachting, family **SIC code:** 86 **Address:** North Warren Church of Christ, 14150 E. Thirteenth Mile Rd., Warren, MI 48088 **E-mail:** vuurbal@sbcglobal.net **Web address:** www.northwarrencoc.org

FRAY, PAUL G.
Industry: Consulting **Born:** Danbury, Connecticut **Univ./degree:** B.A., Industrial Engineering, University of Bridgeport **Current organization:** ISO Quality Consulting, Inc. **Title:** Owner **Type of organization:** Quality control management company **Major product:** Management system implementation **Area of distribution:** Fort Lauderdale, Florida **Expertise:** Consulting, management **Published works:** Article in "South Florida Small Business Journal", 2002 **Affiliations:** American Society for Quality **Hob./spts.:** Classic music, landscaping **SIC code:** 87 **Address:** ISO Quality Consulting, Inc., 3450 S.W. 25th Ct., Ft. Lauderdale, FL 33312 **E-mail:** paulfray@iqc.bz **Web address:** www.paulfray@iqc.bz

FREEHLING, ALLEN ISAAC
Industry: Religion **Born:** January 8, 1932, Chicago, Illinois **Univ./degree:** Ph.D., Psychology, Kensington University, 1977; D.D., History, Hebrew Union College, 1992 **Current organization:** City of Los Angeles Human Relations Commission **Title:** Executive Director **Type of organization:** Municipal government **Major product:** Intergroup communications **Area of distribution:** International **Expertise:** Multigroup interaction **Honors/awards:** Honorary Doctor of Divinity, Kensington University; "Crystal Achievement Award", AIDS Project Los Angeles; "Bishop Daniel Corrigan Commendation for Spiritual Leadership", the Episcopal Diocese of Southern California; "Silver Angel", Religion in Media; "Humanitarian of the Year", National Conference on Justice and Community; "Social Responsibility Award", Los Angeles Urban League; "Gene LaPrieta Leadership Award", Los Angeles AIDS Hospice Foundation; "National Friendship Award", Parents and Friends of Lesbians and Gays, Inc.; "Sierra Tribute Award", Catholic Archdiocese of Southern California; "Freedom of Religion Honoree", Religious Coalition for Abortion Rights of Southern California; "Citizen of the Year", Brentwood Chamber of Commerce; "Community Recognition Award", Los Angeles-Brentwood Rotary Club; Who's Who in American Education; Who's Who in California; Who's Who in Religion; Who's Who in American Jewry; Who's Who in World Jewry; Who's Who in the West; Who's Who Among Top Executives **Affiliations:** President, Board of Rabbis, Southern California; President, Pacific Region, American Jewish Congress; Chair, Southwest Region's Synagogue Council; Founding Chair, Los Angeles County Commission on AIDS; Founding Chair, AIDS Interfaith Council of Southern California; Chair, Governmental Affairs and Public Affairs Committees of AIDS Project Los Angeles; Founding Chair, International Association of Physicians in AIDS Care and many others **Hob./spts.:** Scuba diving, writer **SIC code:** 86 **Address:** 11960 Sunset Blvd., Los Angeles, CA 90049 **E-mail:** rabbiallenf@mailbox.lacity.org

FRIEDLAN, TERRY
Industry: Environmental **Born:** December 4, 1961, Cody, Wyoming **Univ./degree:** A.S., Northwest College, 1982 **Current organization:** Energy Laboratories, Inc. **Title:** Laboratory Manager **Type of organization:** Environmental analytical laboratory **Area of distribution:** National **Expertise:** Environmental safety (air, water, etc.) **Affiliations:** Society of Petroleum Engineers **Hob./spts.:** Golf, reading **SIC code:** 87 **Address:** Energy Laboratories, Inc., 1105 W. First St., Gillette, WY 82716 **E-mail:** tfriedlan@energylab.com **Web address:** www.energylab.com

FRISBY, PERCY E.
Industry: Engineering **Univ./degree:** M.S., Business Administration, Wallemet University, 1987 **Current organization:** Arctic Pacific Enterprises LLC **Title:** CEO **Type of organization:** Engineering/management **Major product:** Construction management **Area of distribution:** Alaska **Expertise:** Management **Honors/awards:** Best Practices Award, HUD, 1999 **Affiliations:** Director of Energy for State **SIC code:** 87 **Address:** Artic Pacific Enterprises, LLC, 2702 Gambell St., Suite 101, Anchorage, AK 99524 **E-mail:** pfrisby@arcticpacific.com

FRONVILLE, CLAIRE L.
Industry: Foundation/trust **Born:** April 17, 1956, Seattle, Washington **Univ./degree:** B.A., Wellesley College, 1978; M.B.A.; Georgetown University, 1984 **Current organization:** J. Paul Getty Trust **Title:** Assistant to the President for Special Projects **Type of organization:** Foundation/museum **Major product:** Visual arts **Area of distribution:** Los Angeles, California **Expertise:** Project management **Published works:** 1 article, 1984; Report to UNESCO, "The International Creative Sector", Oct. 2003 **Affiliations:** I.C.O.M.; American Association of Museums; Phi Beta Kappa; **Hob./spts.:** Horseback riding, swimming, biking, travel **SIC code:** 84 **Address:** J. Paul Getty Trust, 1200 Getty Center Dr., Los Angeles, CA 90049 **E-mail:** cfronville@getty.edu **Web address:** www.getty.edu

FURMANSKI, GEORGE J.
Industry: Energy **Born:** January 17, 1946, Krakow, Poland **Univ./degree:** M.S., Metallurgical Engineering, School of Mining, Poland, 1970 **Current organization:** CalEnergy **Title:** Sr. Project Engineer **Type of organization:** Leader in the development and production of energy **Major product:** Power generation from geothermal brine **Area of distribution:** International **Expertise:** Engineering **Honors/awards:** Award of Excellence, Institute of Chemical Engineers (Australia) **Affiliations:** I.M.E. **Hob./spts.:** Skiing, tennis **SIC code:** 87 **Address:** CalEnergy, Engineering Dept., 7030 Gentry Rd., Calipatria, CA 92233 **E-mail:** jfurmanski@dc.rr.com

GAGNE, JAMES A.
Industry: Pesticide research and development **Born:** November 25, 1948, Hartford, Connecticut **Spouse:** Cynthia C. Gagne (nee Catt) **Married:** May 31, 1975 **Univ./degree:** Ph.D., Entomology, Texas A&M University, 1980 **Current organization:** BASF Corporation **Title:** Research Fellow, Ecotoxicology **Type of organization:** Pesticide research and development **Major product:** Plant protection products **Area of distribution:** International **Expertise:** Ecotoxicology, ecological risk assessment, product defense, entomology **Published works:** 20+ publications **Affiliations:** Society of Environmental Toxicology and Chemistry; Entomological Society of America; CropLife America **Career accomplishments:** As ecotoxicologist, contributed to the registration or re-registration of 5 major plant protection products, mainly insecticides; Chaired CropLife America technical committee for ecotoxicology and environmental chemistry; Awarded American Cyanamid Co. Scientific Achievement Award for developing field techniques to measure potential effects of an insecticide on birds; As expert witness, successfully defended all testing costs in a cost sharing arbitration for a major insecticide **Hob./spts.:** Golf, music, flyfishing **SIC code:** 87 **Address:** BASF Corporation, 26 Davis Dr., Room E-044, Research Triangle Park, NC 27709 **E-mail:** gagneja@basf-corp.com **Web address:** www.corporate.basf.com

GANAPATHY, SRINIVASAN
Industry: Chemicals **Univ./degree:** Ph.D., Chemistry, Georgetown University **Current organization:** Celanese Ltd. **Title:** Analytical Leader **Type of organization:** Research company **Major product:** Organic chemicals **Area of distribution:** International **Expertise:** Analytical research **Affiliations:** A.C.S. **Hob./spts.:** Gardening **SIC code:** 87 **Address:** Celanese Ltd., Hwy 3057, Bay City, TX 77414 **E-mail:** sganapathy.baycity@celanese.com

GANOE, DAVID W.
Industry: Healthcare/consulting **Born:** May 14, 1939, Pittsburgh, Pennsylvania **Univ./degree:** B.S.M.E., 1962; B.S., 1962, University of Pittsburgh **Current organization:** Self employed **Title:** Healthcare facility consultant **Type of organization:** Personal consulting firm **Major product:** Facility management/engineering services **Area of distribution:** California **Expertise:** Facility and engineering management **Affiliations:** A.S.M.E.; A.S.H.E.; Secretary and Education/Program Chair, California Society of Healthcare Engineering (CSHE) **Hob./spts.:** Family, church, golf, photography, reading fiction **SIC code:** 87 **Address:** 15809 El Tiro Dr., La Mirada, CA 90638 **E-mail:** dganoe@keyway.net

GARCIA, GILBERT M.
Industry: Consulting **Born:** December 15, 1956, Los Angeles, California **Univ./degree:** Sociology Degree, University of Santa Barbara, California, 1980 **Current organization:** Consultants Ink **Title:** Owner **Type of organization:** Consulting firm **Major product:** Full-service consultancy that offers business plans, strategic planning workshops, new business start-ups, grant writing, accounting services; helped develop the Kern County Youth Mariachi Foundation **Area of distribution:** National **Expertise:** Project management, business development, administrative planning, client relations **Affiliations:** Member, M.O.P.A.; Member, A.D.E.L.A.N.T. **Hob./spts.:** Spending time with family, coaching Y.M.C.A. basketball, music, designing programs that promote youth literacy **SIC code:** 87 **Address:** Consultants Ink, 2525 Buena Vista St., Bakersfield, CA 93304 **E-mail:** garciaink@aol.com

GARRETT, RICHARD T.
Industry: Consulting Engineers **Born:** June 29, 1923, Cleveland, Ohio **Univ./degree:** B.S.C.E., University of Michigan, 1948 **Current organization:** Garrett & Associates, Inc. **Title:** President **Type of organization:** Professional engineering **Major product:** Civil engineering services **Area of distribution:** Ohio **Expertise:** Engineering and land surveying **Honors/awards:** Land Surveyor of the Year, 1977 **Affiliations:** Rotary Club; Yacht Club; Cleveland Consulting Engineers; Professional Land Surveyors of Ohio; Cleveland Executives Association **Hob./spts.:** Boating, fishing, camping **SIC code:** 87 **Address:** Garrett & Associates, Inc., 2030 W. 19th St., Cleveland, OH 44113-3549

GARRETT JR., DAVID L.
Industry: Automotive components **Born:** September 22, 1944, San Antonio, Texas **Univ./degree:** Ph.D., University of Iowa **Current organization:** Delphi Corp. **Title:** Chief Materials Engineer **Type of organization:** Engineering/manufacturing/sales **Major product:** Automotive components **Area of distribution:** International **Expertise:** Materials engineering **Honors/awards:** Merrill European Study Travel Fellow **Affiliations:** American Chemical Society; Society of Plastic Engineers; Omega Psi Phi; Alpha Chi Sigma **Hob./spts.:** Golf, bridge **SIC code:** 87 **Address:** Delphi Corp., 1401 Crooks Rd., Troy, MI 48084 **E-mail:** david.l.garrett@delphi.com

GARRISON, DARRELL E.
Industry: Architecture **Born:** November 25, 1962, Indianapolis, Indiana **Univ./degree:** B.A., Ball State University, 1988 **Current organization:** Planning Resources Inc. **Title:** Director of Landscaping Architecture **Type of organization:** Consulting firm **Major product:** Consulting **Area of distribution:** Wheaton, Illinois **Expertise:** Design **Affiliations:** A.S.L.A.; I.A.L.A.; N.O.M.A. **Hob./spts.:** Music **SIC code:** 87 **Address:** Planning Resources Inc., 402 W. Liberty Dr., Wheaton, IL 60187 **E-mail:** dgarrison@planres.com

GATRELL, RUTH BARTON
Industry: Music guild **Born:** December 23, 1921, Farmington, Utah **Univ./degree:** B.A., University of Utah, 1942 **Current organization:** Composer Guild Annual **Title:** President **Type of organization:** Nonprofit, to help composers **Major product:** Sponsoring annual competition contest and 4 concerts of new works by composers; also classes **Area of distribution:** International **Expertise:** Teaching, composition, small publishing company, typesetting music **Hob./spts.:** Photography, hiking, camping, playing the violin, cake decorating, sewing **SIC code:** 86 **Address:** Composer Guild Annual, 40 N. 100 West, Box 586, Farmington, UT 84025

GATTERDAM, PAUL E.
Industry: Pharmaceuticals **Born:** June 27, 1929, La Crosse, Wisconsin **Univ./degree:** Ph.D., University of Wisconsin, 1957 **Current organization:** American Cyanamid Co. (now known as Wyeth) **Title:** Chemist (Retired) **Type of organization:** Chemical laboratory **Major product:** Agricultural chemistry, metabolic chemistry, research **Area of distribution:** International **Expertise:** Medicinal drugs **Hob./spts.:** Historical subjects **SIC code:** 87 **Address:** 20 Stanford Rd. East, Pennington, NJ 08534 **E-mail:** gatterdam2@aol.com

GEORGE, ANDREAS C.
Industry: Laboratory **Born:** April 23, 1931, Clairton, Pennsylvania **Univ./degree:** B.A., Biology, Brooklyn College, 1959; M.A., Civil Engineering, 1972; M.A., Biology, Hunter College, 1960 **Current organization:** Radon Testing Corp. of America **Title:** Lab Director **Type of organization:** Corporation laboratory **Major product:** Research and testing **Area of distribution:** New York **Expertise:** Radon analysis for radioactive gases **Honors/awards:** Meritorious Service Award and Medal, Department of Energy for his pioneering work on radon research in 1987 **Published works:** 1 book, "In the Footsteps of St. Nicholas"; 97 scientific papers on radiation research, measurements and dosimetry **Affiliations:** Fellow Member, Health Physics Society; American Association of Radon Scientists and Technologists **Hob./spts.:** Vegetable farming **SIC code:** 87 **Address:** Radon Testing Corp. of America, 201-27 26th Ave., Bayside, NY 11360 **E-mail:** andycgeo@aol.com

GERDES, CHARLES D.
Industry: Engineering **Univ./degree:** B.S.E.E., DeVry University, 1996 **Current organization:** JT3 **Title:** Telecommunication Engineer **Type of organization:** Government contractor **Major product:** Transmission equipment **Area of distribution:** National **Expertise:** Video data, fiber optics, video surveillance **Affiliations:** I.E.E.E. **SIC code:** 87 **Address:** JT3, 821 Grier Dr., Las Vegas, NV 89119 **E-mail:** charles.gerdes@jt3.com

GHEORGHE, IULIAN
Industry: Aerospace **Univ./degree:** B.S., M.S., Bucharest Polytech Institute; Ph.D., Material Science & Engineering, Clemson University, 2001 **Current organization:** Alu Menziken Aerospace/Universal Alloy Corp. **Title:** Ph.D./Senior R&D Engineer **Type of organization:** Research and development **Major product:** Raw material supplier-aluminum extrusions **Area of distribution:** International **Expertise:** Materials science and engineering, metallurgy **Published works:** 15 papers **Affiliations:** A.S.M., International; T.M.S.; S.A.E. **SIC code:** 87 **Address:** Alu Menziken Aerospace, Universal Alloy Corp., 180 Lamar Haley Pkwy., Canton, GA 30114 **E-mail:** iulian.gheorghe@menzaero.com

GILONSKE, KIMBERLY D.
Industry: Pharmaceuticals **Born:** June 5, 1971, Russellville, Arkansas **Univ./degree:** B.S., Clinical Technology, Arkansas Tech, 1994 **Current organization:** Covance Central Labs **Title:** Manager of Genomics **Type of organization:** C.R.O. **Major product:** Pharmaceutical development **Area of distribution:** National **Expertise:** Genomics, testing, management **Affiliations:** A.S.C.P.; N.C.A.; C.R.S. **Hob./spts.:** Family, clarinet, symphonic orchestra **SIC code:** 87 **Address:** Covance Central Labs, 8211 Scicor Dr., Indianapolis, IN 46214 **E-mail:** kimberly.gilonske@covance.com **Web address:** www.covance.com

GILSON, PAUL D.
Industry: Consulting engineering **Born:** June 19, 1923, Chicago, Illinois **Univ./degree:** B.S., Mechanical Engineering, University of Illinois **Current organization:** Paul Gilson Consulting Associate **Title:** Owner, Associate **Type of organization:** Inspection, maintenance, modifications **Major product:** HVAC, EQMT, lighting, security, service, energy usage **Area of distribution:** Illinois **Expertise:** Engineering, energy **Affiliations:** A.S.H.R.A.E. **Hob./spts.:** Biking, golf, tech meetings **SIC code:** 87 **Address:** 9525 Drake Ave., Evanston, IL 60203 **E-mail:** pdgilson@aol.com

GLENN, CHRISTOPHER C.
Industry: Pharmaceuticals **Born:** June 17, 1965, Covington **Univ./degree:** Ph.D., University of Florida, 1995 **Current organization:** Magellan Pharmaceutical Development **Title:** Ph.D. **Type of organization:** Contract research & development **Major product:** Drug discovery **Area of distribution:** International **Expertise:** Genetics **SIC code:** 87 **Address:** Magellan Pharmaceutical Development, 160 N. Magellan Lab Ct., Morrisville, NC 27560 **E-mail:** chris_glenn@yahoo.com

GOGEL, MICHAEL G.
Industry: Real estate **Born:** December 7, 1982, Phoenix, Arizona **Univ./degree:** A.S., High Tech Institute, 2002 **Current organization:** Precision Design Corp. **Title:** Draftsman **Type of organization:** Engineering and design firm **Major product:** Plot plans, base lots **Area of distribution:** Chandler, Arizona **Expertise:** Drafting **Affiliations:** S.C.A. **SIC code:** 87 **Address:** Precision Design Corp., 135 E. Chilton Dr., Suite 101, Chandler, AZ 85226 **E-mail:** mg73909@cox.net

GOING, RICHARD E.
Industry: Aluminum **Born:** Ashland, Massachusetts **Univ./degree:** Attended MIT **Current organization:** Self employed aluminum consultant **Title:** C.E.F. **Type of organization:** Consulting **Major product:** Cleaning, anodizing, hardcoat and dyeing of aluminum parts **Area of distribution:** National **Expertise:** Type of tanks to be used **Published works:** Articles **Affiliations:** A.E.S.F.; A.A.C. **Hob./spts.:** Woodworking, railroad buff **SIC code:** 87 **Address:** 12 Lyndon Lane, Ashland, MA 01721-2255

GOLDBERG, LAWRENCE D.
Industry: Consulting **Born:** March 13, 1959, San Antonio, Texas **Univ./degree:** B.S., Civil Engineering, Texas A&M University **Current organization:** Landtech Consultants, Inc. **Title:** Director of Engineering **Type of organization:** Engineering firm **Major product:** Civil engineering **Area of distribution:** Texas **Expertise:** General civil design **Affiliations:** Past President, Houston Branch, A.S.C.E. **Hob./spts.:** Volunteer work within the community **SIC code:** 87 **Address:** Landtech Consultants, Inc., 2627 N. Loop West, #224, Houston, TX 77008 **E-mail:** lgoldberg@landtech-inc.com

GOLDIN, MARK A.
Industry: Medical devices **Born:** December 19, 1972, Dayton, Ohio **Univ./degree:** B.S., Mechanical Engineering, University of Cincinnati, 1996; M.S., Mechanical Engineering, University of Cincinnati, 1997 **Current organization:** Ortheon Medical, LLC **Title:** Vice President of R&D and Operations **Type of organization:** Engineering **Major product:** Surgical device development **Area of distribution:** International

Expertise: Engineering/R&D **Hob./spts.:** Family, soccer **SIC code:** 87 **Address:** Ortheon Medical, LLC, 7151 University Blvd., Winter Park, FL 32792 **E-mail:** mark@ortheon.com

GOLDSTEIN, SAUL I.

Industry: Consulting **Born:** 1935, Brooklyn, New York **Univ./degree:** B.S.E.E., Newark College of Engineering; M.S., Business, Pace College **Current organization:** SemiTech **Title:** Electronic Engineering Consultant **Type of organization:** Consulting **Major product:** Electronic engineering **Area of distribution:** International **Expertise:** Electronic engineering consultation **Affiliations:** I.E.E.E. **SIC code:** 87 **Address:** SemiTech, 9215 Clark Circle, Twinsburg, OH 44087 **E-mail:** goldsi@earthlink.net

GOMEZ, DELORES A.

Industry: Assisted living **Born:** August 7, 1936, Birmingham, Alabama **Current organization:** Mason Serenity House, Inc. **Title:** Owner, CEO **Type of organization:** Housing **Major product:** Housing for the elderly **Area of distribution:** Alabama **Expertise:** Geriatrics **Honors/awards:** First African American with the assisted living program **Published works:** 6 newspaper articles **Affiliations:** A.L.S. **Hob./spts.:** Church, travel, reading, writing **SIC code:** 83 **Address:** Mason Serenity House, Inc., 601 Henderson St., P.O. Box 885, Andalusia, AL 36420 **E-mail:** mshinc@hotmail.com

GÓMEZ, ALFONSO

Industry: Engineering **Univ./degree:** M.S., Electrical Engineering, University of Havana, 1955 **Current organization:** A.L. Gómez Inc. **Title:** Electrical Engineer **Type of organization:** Consulting firm **Major product:** Power system analysis, power plant design **Area of distribution:** International **Expertise:** Electrical engineering **Affiliations:** I.E.E.E. **SIC code:** 87 **Address:** A.L. Gómez Inc., 725 49th St. North, St. Petersburg, FL 33710 **E-mail:** algomez@attglobal.net

GORDON, MAXWELL

Industry: Consulting/pharmaceutical **Born:** February 23, 1921, Kamenka, Ukraine **Univ./degree:** B.S., Organic Chemistry, University of the Sciences, 1941, Pennsylvania ; M.S., Organic Chemistry, 1946; Ph.D., Organic Chemistry, 1948, University of Pennsylvania **Current organization:** Gordon Consulting Associates **Title:** President/CEO **Type of organization:** Consulting **Major product:** Pharmaceutical chemistry consulting **Area of distribution:** International **Expertise:** New product development, pharmaceutical chemistry **Honors/awards:** Post Doctorate Fellowship, Swiss Federal Polytechnical Institute, 1949; Post Doctorate Fellowship, Atomic Energy, University of California, Berkeley Radiologic Energy Lab; Post Doctorate Fellowship, Imperial College of Science and Medicine, London, England, 1951; U.S. Navy Normandy Ribbon; U.S. Navy Captain, 1941-1985 **Published works:** 100+ scientific papers, 12+ scientific books, 150+ U.S. and foreign patents in the pharmaceutical field **Affiliations:** A.C.S.; R.S.C.; A.A.A.S.; A.S.M.; Swiss Chemical Society; Squibb Institute for Medical Research, 1951-1955; Director of Congener Research, Smith Kline and French Laboratories, 1955-1970; Director of Research Planning and Licensing, Bristol-Meyers Company, 1970-1986; Chairman and CEO, U.S. Subsidiary of the Japanese company, Ajinomoto Pharmaceuticals, 1986-1996 **Hob./spts.:** Photography, travel **SIC code:** 87 **Address:** Gordon Consulting Associates, 60 East End Ave., Suite 22A, New York, NY 10028 **E-mail:** mgordon523@aol.com

GOSAL, PARNEET

Industry: Healthcare **Born:** March 16, 1975, Chandigarh, India **Univ./degree:** M.B.A., William E. Simon Graduate School of Business, University of Rochester, 1999 **Current organization:** MarketRX, Inc. **Title:** Director, Marketing Strategy **Type of organization:** Consulting **Major product:** Technology **Area of distribution:** International **Expertise:** Marketing strategy and process improvement **Affiliations:** Six Sigma Green Belt **SIC code:** 87 **Address:** MarketRX, Inc., 345 E. 94th St., #25B, New York, NY 10128 **E-mail:** parneet.gosal@gmail.com

GOULDEN, CLYDE EDWARD

Industry: Museums **Born:** November 30, 1936, Kansas City, Kansas **Univ./degree:** B.S., Emporia State University Teachers College; Ph.D., Indiana University, 1962 **Current organization:** Academy of Natural Sciences **Title:** Director, Mongolian Institute **Type of organization:** Museum/research **Major product:** Environmental assessment; exhibitions and activities centering on the environment and its diverse species **Area of distribution:** International **Expertise:** Ecosystem conservation **Published works:** 100 publications **Affiliations:** F.A.A.A.S.; Ecological Society of America **Hob./spts.:** Cooking **SIC code:** 84 **Address:** Academy of Natural Sciences, 1900 Benjamin Franklin Pkwy., Philadelphia, PA 19103 **E-mail:** goulden@acnatsci.org **Web address:** www.acnatsci.org/research/mongolia

GRADY, SCOTT

Industry: Engineering **Born:** March 5, 1968, Jackson, Mississippi **Univ./degree:** B.S.E.E., Mississippi State University, 1990 **Current organization:** Automated Power **Title:** Engineering Manager **Type of organization:** Design, implementation **Major product:** Systems integration, industrial automation **Area of distribution:** National **Expertise:** Control system design, project management **Hob./spts.:** Water sports, travel **SIC code:** 87 **Address:** Automated Power, 4364 Mangum Dr., Flowood, MS 39232 **E-mail:** scott@automatedpower.biz **Web address:** www.automatedpower.biz

GRADY, VERN J.

Industry: Management, Finance, Engineering, Manufacturing, Subcontracting, Marketing **Born:** New Salem, North Dakota **Univ./degree:** B.S., Business Administration/Accounting, University of Southern California, 1981; Certificate, Accounting, University of California Los Angeles, 1969; Passed CPA Examination **Current organization:** Vern J. Grady, CPA **Title:** Principal **Type of organization:** Certified public accountant **Major product:** CPA Services, Consultation/Valuation/Testimony Services to Attorneys, Information Technology Management **Area of distribution:** National **Expertise:** Consulting **Honors/awards:** Phi Beta Kappa; Magna Cum Laude **Affiliations:** A.I.C.P.A.; C.A.C.P.A. **Hob./spts.:** Golf, travel, theatre, movies, physical fitness, education **SIC code:** 87 **Address:** Vern J. Grady, CPA, 246 Bicknell Ave., Suite 3, Santa Monica, CA 90405 **E-mail:** verngrady@aol.com

GRAFFEO, DENISE S.

Industry: Clubs/restaurant **Born:** October 29, 1950, Lynn, Massachusetts **Univ./degree:** A.A.S., Bunker Hill Community College, Massachusetts, 1987; M.A., Education, Cambridge College, Massachusetts, 1990 **Current organization:** Eastern Yacht Club **Title:** Executive Chef **Type of organization:** Private club **Major product:** Food service **Area of distribution:** Marblehead, Massachusetts **Expertise:** Culinary arts **Honors/awards:** Epicurean Club of Boston Chef of the year 2001; Epicurean Club of Boston Presidential Medallion 2000; Chef of the Year Les Dames d'Escoffier 1998 **Published works:** Articles **Affiliations:** Board of Directors, Les Dames d'Escoffier; Clerk (20 years), Epicurean Club of Boston; Member, American Academy of Chefs, 1990; United States Power Squadron; Charter Member, Sons of Italy **Hob./spts.:** Travel, reading, culinary history, boating **SIC code:** 86 **Address:** Eastern Yacht Club, Harbor Ave., Marblehead, MA 01945 **E-mail:** chefde2000@earthlink.net

GRAHAM, ANTHONY M.

Industry: Religion **Born:** February 24, 1965, Port of Spain, Trinidad **Univ./degree:** Ph.D., Georgetown Wesleyan University; D.Min., Bakke Graduate University of Ministry **Current organization:** New Hope Family Worship Center **Title:** Reverend Pastor **Type of organization:** Church **Major product:** Religious services **Area of distribution:** International **Expertise:** Minister of the Gospel, team building **Hob./spts.:** Track, walking **SIC code:** 86 **Address:** New Hope Family Worship Center, 56 Melvin Ave., West Hempstead, NY 11552

GRAHAM, THOMAS K.

Industry: Environmental services **Born:** May 8, 1973, Miami, Oklahoma **Univ./degree:** M.S., Environmental Engineering, Oklahoma State University, 1997 **Current organization:** Air Hygiene International, Inc. **Title:** Project Manager **Type of organization:** Emissions testing **Major product:** Stack testing **Area of distribution:** International **Expertise:** Environmental engineering **Published works:** Thesis **Affiliations:** A.S.C.E.; N.S.P.E.; O.S.P.E. **Hob./spts.:** Band, guitar, piano, body building **SIC code:** 87 **Address:** Air Hygiene International, Inc., 5634 S. 122nd East Ave., Suite F, Tulsa, OK 74146 **E-mail:** tom@airhygiene.com **Web address:** www.airhygiene.com

GRASTY, CHARLES R.

Industry: Religion (Salvation - Eternal Life - Discipleship) **Title:** Pastor **Type of organization:** Southern Baptist Church **Major product:** Worship of Jesus Christ **Expertise:** Pastoral Ministry for 24 years **SIC code:** 86 **Address:** FBC Neches, 200 Anderson St., Neches, TX 75779 **E-mail:** thecountrypastor@aol.com

GRAVELY-MOSS, CAROLYN E.

Industry: Consulting **Born:** April 14, 1948, La Plata, Maryland **Univ./degree:** Ph.D., ABD, Counseling Psychology, Howard University **Current organization:** Crisis Management Introspect **Title:** Director **Type of organization:** Counseling, consulting **Major product:** Seminars, lectures, training **Area of distribution:** National **Expertise:** Counseling supervision, crisis management, suicide training, prevention, critical incident stress management **Published works:** multiple articles on SISM **Affiliations:** A.C.A.; Association for Hostage Negotiators; National Counseling Association; Maryland Counseling Association **Hob./spts.:** Hiking, sewing, hand dancing, singing **SIC code:** 87 **Address:** Crisis Management Introspect, 2314 Minnesota Ave. S.E., Washington, DC 20020 **E-mail:** cmam1448@aol.com

GREEN, KEITH E.

Industry: Geological/petroleum exploration **Born:** July 23, 1929, Pomona, California **Univ./degree:** Ph.D., Ashwood University **Current organization:** Green Geological **Title:** Owner/President **Type of organization:** Consulting, training **Major product:** Paleontological, environmental, stratigraphic, geo supplies **Area of distribution:** International **Expertise:** Micropaleontology **Affiliations:** G.S.A. **SIC code:** 87 **Address:** Green Geological, 6727 Greenleaf Ave., Whittier, CA 90601 **E-mail:** greengeo@aol.com

GREENE, FRANCES
Industry: Social services **Born:** February 7, 1937, Shuqualak, Mississippi **Univ./degree:** B.A., Business Administration and Child Development, **Current organization:** Pittsburg Preschool and Community Council **Title:** Executive Director and Founder **Type of organization:** Nonprofit multi-specialty community outreach, assistance, education and care center **Major product:** Numerous including Senior housing, case management, youth education, job skill training, job placement programs, senior citizen housing, assisted living, ESL classes, literacy programs **Area of distribution:** Pittsburg, California **Expertise:** Executive administration, operations, management **Affiliations:** N.C.D.A.; Board Member, Shelter, Inc., The Healthy Agency; The Pittsburg Art Commission **Hob./spts.:** Cooking, fishing, family **SIC code:** 83 **Address:** Pittsburg Preschool & Community Council, 1760 Chester Dr., Pittsburg, CA 94565-3920

GREENE, KELLY M.
Industry: Membership organization **Born:** November 2, 1961, Orange, New Jersey **Current organization:** Lauderdale Yacht Club **Title:** Executive Chef **Type of organization:** Private club **Major product:** Food/boating **Area of distribution:** Ft. Lauderdale, Florida **Expertise:** Food preparation, food cost analysis **Honors/awards:** Dessert Award, Ft. Lauderdale Museum of Art, 1997 & 1998 **Affiliations:** A.C.F. **Hob./spts.:** Bodybuilding **SIC code:** 86 **Address:** Lauderdale Yacht Club, 1725 S.E. 12th St., Ft. Lauderdale, FL 33316

GREENLEAF, CHRIS J.
Industry: Consulting engineering/environmental **Born:** Winfield, Kansas **Univ./degree:** B.A., Environmental Biology, Emporia State University **Current organization:** Terracon **Title:** Lab Manager **Type of organization:** Testing lab **Major product:** CMT testing **Area of distribution:** National **Expertise:** Soil and concrete, management **Hob./spts.:** Volleyball, golf **SIC code:** 87 **Address:** Terracon, 600 S.W. 7th St., Suite M, Des Moines, IA 50309 **E-mail:** cjgreenleaf@terracon.com **Web address:** www.terracon.com

GREGOR, VILMA ELENA
Industry: Social services **Born:** June 19, 1917, Priekopa, Czechoslovakia **Univ./degree:** A.S.A., Social Work, Psychology **Current organization:** M.O.R.E. Inc. **Title:** Humanitarian Worker **Type of organization:** Embassy/radio **Major product:** Diplomatic functions **Area of distribution:** International **Expertise:** Translator for six languages, humanitarian work, freelance writer, broadcaster **Hob./spts.:** Helping friends and neighbors, history **SIC code:** 83 **Address:** 18 High St., West (Byram), Greenwich, CT 06830 **E-mail:** vilmagregor@aol.com

GREY, FRANCIS J.
Industry: Accounting **Born:** November 30, 1931, Darby, Pennsylvania **Univ./degree:** B.S., Accounting, Villa Nova University, 1958 **Current organization:** Francis J. Grey, CPA **Title:** CPA/Owner **Type of organization:** CPA firm **Major product:** Tax consulting **Area of distribution:** Pennsylvania **Expertise:** Taxation - individual and commercial **Affiliations:** A.I.C.P.A.; P.I.C.A.A. **Hob./spts.:** Basketball **SIC code:** 87 **Address:** Francis J. Grey, CPA, 10 Manchester Ct., Berwyn, PA 19312 **E-mail:** fjgrey@aol.com

GRUNBERG, JEFFREY S.
Industry: Social services **Born:** February 13, 1952, New York, New York **Univ./degree:** Ph.D., Sociology, City University of New York, 1994 **Current organization:** Grand Central Neighborhood Social Services Corp. **Title:** Executive Director **Type of organization:** Social service **Major product:** Assistance to homeless people **Area of distribution:** New York, New York **Expertise:** Board development, funding, administration **Affiliations:** Board Member, Journal of Social Distress **Hob./spts.:** Writing, martial arts, golf **SIC code:** 83 **Address:** Grand Central Neighborhood Social Services Corp., 302 E. 45th St., New York, NY 10017 **E-mail:** gcnexec@aol.com

GUIDO, SANDY L.
Industry: Nonprofit/religious **Born:** July 20, 1932, Reading, Pennsylvania **Current organization:** St. Michael's Convent **Title:** Maintenance Director **Type of organization:** Convent **Major product:** Religion **Area of distribution:** Reading, Pennsylvania **Expertise:** Maintenance, heating, air-conditioning, plumbing, electrical, electronics, carpentry, restoration, planning and design, drawing of blueprints, sub-contracting and estimating; responsible for reports to the administration and provincial council **Hob./spts.:** Family, music, travel, reading **SIC code:** 86 **Address:** St. Michael's Convent, 51 Seminary Ave., Reading, PA 19605

GUTIERREZ, JOSE
Industry: Engineering **Born:** June 26, 1969, Peru **Current organization:** Gopman Consulting Engineers **Title:** Senior Project Manager **Type of organization:** Consulting engineering/design firm **Major product:** Structural engineering **Area of distribution:** National **Expertise:** High-rise design **Affiliations:** S.E.F. **Hob./spts.:** Physical fitness **SIC code:** 87 **Address:** Gopman Consulting Engineers, 192 N.E. 168th St., North Miami Beach, FL 33162 **E-mail:** jg@gopmanconsulting.com

HABERER, JOHN J.
Industry: Engineering **Born:** November 18, 1977, Rome, New York **Univ./degree:** B.S., Civil Engineering, Clarkson University, 1999 **Current organization:** Barton & Loguidice, P.C. **Title:** Assistant Engineer **Type of organization:** Engineering firm **Major product:** Consulting services **Area of distribution:** New York **Expertise:** Bridge design, engineering **Affiliations:** A.B.C.D.; A.S.C.E., Young Members Division, Syracuse Chapter **Hob./spts.:** Golf, softball, volleyball **SIC code:** 87 **Address:** Barton & Loguidice, P.C., 290 Elwood Davis Rd., Liverpool, NY 13088 **E-mail:** jhaberer@bartonandloguidice.com

HABIB, JAMAL N.
Industry: Engineering **Born:** February 22, 1930, Rama, Palestine **Univ./degree:** B.S.C.E., Washington State University, 1956; M.S., 1958; Ph.D., Engineering and Applied Mechanics, 1964, University of California at Los Angeles **Current organization:** Retired **Title:** Manager/Director **Type of organization:** Engineering, project management **Area of distribution:** International **Expertise:** Strategic planning, system engineering, technical management **Affiliations:** A.S.M.E.; A.S.C.E.; N.Y.A.S. **Hob./spts.:** Sub-tropical horticulture, reading, studying world and religious history **SIC code:** 87 **Address:** PO Box 27689, San Diego, CA 92198 **E-mail:** jhabib@san.rr.com

HACK, CARLENE S.
Industry: Social services **Born:** July 7, 1938, Juniata, Pennsylvania **Current organization:** Mifflin-Juniata-Area Agency on Aging, Inc. **Title:** Executive Director **Type of organization:** Not for profit social services agency **Major product:** Social services for senior citizens - in home care, meals (at senior centers and in home), transportation, counseling for the elderly **Area of distribution:** Mifflin and Juniata Counties, Pennsylvania **Expertise:** Leadership, organization **Hob./spts.:** Crafts, theatre, music **SIC code:** 83 **Address:** Mifflin-Juniata-Area Agency on Aging, Inc., 1 Buena Vista Circle, Lewistown, PA 17044 **E-mail:** chack@mjaaa.com

HACKEL, KURT A.
Industry: Consulting/engineering **Born:** September 11, 1930, Tallinn, Estonia **Univ./degree:** M.A., Structural Engineering and Design, Swiss Technical Institute, Switzerland, 1956 **Current organization:** Kurt A. Hackel, M.S.C.E. **Title:** Senior Engineer **Type of organization:** Consulting engineers **Major product:** Construction **Area of distribution:** International **Expertise:** Tunnel construction, reinforced concrete, heavy construction **Affiliations:** A.S.C.E.; Swiss Engineering Society **Hob./spts.:** Horse trainer/rider, sailing **SIC code:** 87 **Address:** 818 S.E. 12th St., Ft. Lauderdale, FL 33316 **E-mail:** alecone@msn.com

HAGEMAN, JIM H.
Industry: Architecture/engineering **Born:** August 26, 1956, Lincoln, Nebraska **Univ./degree:** M.S., Architecture, University of Nebraska, 1981 **Current organization:** Leo A. Daly Co. **Title:** Project Manager **Type of organization:** Architecture and engineering **Major product:** Architecture and engineering services **Area of distribution:** Nebraska **Expertise:** Project management **Affiliations:** A.I.A.; C.S.I. **Hob./spts.:** Waterskiing, golf, camping **SIC code:** 87 **Address:** Leo A. Daly Co., 8600 Indian Hills Dr., Omaha, NE 68114 **E-mail:** jhhageman@leoadaly.com

HAGGARD, DOUGLAS K.
Industry: Healthcare information technology consulting **Born:** April 20, 1962, St. Joseph, Missouri **Univ./degree:** B.S., Medical Technology, Missouri Western State College, 1984 **Current organization:** Cerner Corp. **Title:** Director **Type of organization:** Healthcare informatics/consulting **Major product:** Healthcare software solutions **Area of distribution:** National **Expertise:** Director of Consulting Services **Affiliations:** American Society of Clinical Pathologists **Hob./spts.:** Golf, travel **SIC code:** 87 **Address:** Cerner Corp., 2800 Rockcreek Pkwy., Kansas City, MO 64117 **E-mail:** dhaggard@cerner.com **Web address:** www.cerner.com

HAGMAN, KAREN A.
Industry: Information technology **Born:** March 23, 1962, Mont Clare, Pennsylvania **Univ./degree:** B.S., Quantitative Business Analysis, Pennsylvania State University, 1984 **Current organization:** Information Technology Resources **Title:** Technical Consultant **Type of organization:** Consulting **Major product:** Information technology consulting **Area of distribution:** National **Expertise:** Project management, account management, systems analysis and development **Affiliations:** Lifetime Member, Pennsylvania State Alumni Association **Hob./spts.:** Lacrosse, softball, rock climbing **SIC code:** 87 **Address:** Information Technology Resources, 6722 Orangethorpe Ave., Suite 300, Buena Park, CA 90622 **E-mail:** kahagman@itrweb.com **Web address:** itrweb.com

HAILAB, DAWIT G.
Industry: Wireless communication consulting **Born:** September 30, 1963, Addis Ababa, Ethiopia **Univ./degree:** B.S., Minor in Math, University of Alabama, 1987 **Current organization:** Integrated Wireless Consulting **Title:** Vice President of Engineering **Type of organization:** Service providers **Major product:** Engineering software/hardware, wireless engineering consulting **Area of distribution:** National **Expertise:**

Turnkey solution and wireless network **Affiliations:** I.E.E.E. **Hob./spts.:** Soccer, travel **SIC code:** 87 **Address:** Integrated Wireless Consulting, 801 International Parkway, Suite 5250, Fifth floor, Lake Mary, FL 32746 **E-mail:** dhailab@iwcnet.com

HALBERSTEIN, DANIEL
Industry: Financial **Born:** November 17, 1957, Lima, Peru **Univ./degree:** B.A., Architecture, University of Miami, 1980 **Current organization:** Greater Miami Jewish Foundation **Title:** Principal **Type of organization:** Nonprofit **Major product:** Real estate, financial services **Area of distribution:** Aventura, Florida **Expertise:** Fundraising **Affiliations:** Latin Division of Greater Miami Jewish Foundation **Hob./spts.:** Tennis, travel **SIC code:** 86 **Address:** Greater Miami Jewish Foundation, 18205 Biscayne Blvd., Suite 2202, Aventura, FL 33160 **E-mail:** dhalberstein@bellsouth.net

HALE, GENE
Industry: Healthcare products **Born:** August 11, 1932 **Current organization:** Int'l Aloe Science Council, Inc. **Title:** Executive Director **Type of organization:** Nonprofit **Major product:** Aloe vera products **Area of distribution:** International **Expertise:** Management **Affiliations:** M.P.I. **Hob./spts.:** Golf, gardening **SIC code:** 86 **Address:** Int'l Aloe Science Council, Inc., 415 E. Airport Hwy., #150, Irving, TX 75062 **E-mail:** iasc1@msn.com **Web address:** www.iasc.org

HALE, HARRISON
Industry: Religion **Born:** October 1, 1959, Riverhead, New York **Univ./degree:** D.Div., United Christian College **Current organization:** Church of God in Christ/ Guatemala Ecclesiastical Jurisdiction/Cornerstone Evangelistic Temple **Title:** Bishop, Pastor, CEO **Type of organization:** Church, community centers **Major product:** Spiritual guidance **Area of distribution:** International **Expertise:** Spiritual counseling, administration **Honors/awards:** Congressional Record USA House of Representatives, Suffolk County Boy Scouts of America, Dept. of Veterans Affairs Certificate of Appreciation, New York State Proclamations **Published works:** "Living Life God's Way" and "21 Keys About Knowledge" **Hob./spts.:** Fresh and saltwater fishing **SIC code:** 86 **Address:** Church of God in Christ, 40 Central Pkwy., Medford, NY 11763 **E-mail:** bishophale2@optonline.net

HALL, KEVIN A.
Industry: Engineering **Born:** December 23, 1970, WV **Univ./degree:** B.S., West Virginia Institute of Technology, 1995 **Current organization:** Site-Blauvelt Engineers **Title:** Design Engineer **Type of organization:** Engineering firm **Major product:** Bridge design/highway design **Area of distribution:** Charleston, West Virginia **Expertise:** Engineering **Affiliations:** American Society of Civil Engineers **Hob./spts.:** Hunting, golf **SIC code:** 87 **Address:** Site-Blauvelt Engineers, 1 Kenton Drive, Suite 200, Charleston, WV 25311 **E-mail:** kevinh@site-blauvelt.com

HALL, RICHARD L.
Industry: Consulting engineering **Born:** May 1, 1947, Little Rock, Arkansas **Univ./degree:** B.S., Mechanical Engineering, University of Arkansas, 1970 **Current organization:** Heideman Associates, Inc. **Title:** Associate **Type of organization:** Engineering **Major product:** Building systems designs for all market sectors **Area of distribution:** International **Expertise:** Mechanical, plumbing and fire protection **Affiliations:** A.S.H.R.A.E.; S.F.P.E.; N.F.P.A.; American Society for Healthcare Engineering; Arkansas Academy of Mechanical Engineers **Hob./spts.:** Member, Commemorative Air Force (Arizona Wing); photography, flying, military history **SIC code:** 87 **Address:** Heideman Associates, Inc., 5326 E. Washington St., Suite 4, Phoenix, AZ 85034 **E-mail:** rlhall@zakcompanies.com

HALL, ROBERT L.
Industry: Finance **Born:** July 24 **Univ./degree:** M.B.A., Management, University of Cincinnati, 1977 **Current organization:** Hall & Assoc., Inc. **Title:** President **Type of organization:** CPA firm **Major product:** Financial services **Area of distribution:** Cincinnati, Ohio **Expertise:** Certified Public Accountant **Affiliations:** O.S.C.P.A.; A.I.C.P.A **SIC code:** 87 **Address:** Hall & Assoc., Inc., 7811 Hamilton Ave., Cincinnati, OH 45231 **E-mail:** rhall@hallsr.com

HAND, DONNA
Industry: Business Services **Univ./degree:** A.S., Paralegal/Business Management, Manatee Community College **Current organization:** Help by Hand **Title:** C.E.O. **Type of organization:** Research **Major product:** Research, information **Expertise:** Special knowledge in child support issues **Hob./spts.:** Family, care of grandmother **SIC code:** 87 **Address:** Help by Hand, 2811 Milton Ave., PMB 407, Janesville, WI 53345 **E-mail:** ctdhkk@aol.com

HANKE, DAN H.
Industry: Financial **Born:** December 8, 1941, San Antonio, Texas **Univ./degree:** B.B.A., University of Texas, 1963 **Current organization:** The Hanke Group **Title:** President **Type of organization:** Accounting firm **Major product:** Accounting services and corporate business analysis of complex litigation **Area of distribution:** National **Expertise:** Certified Public Accountant; business development and strategic planning **Published works:** 4 course books for CPA's **Affiliations:** The Episcopal Dioceses of West Texas **Hob./spts.:** Hunting, fishing, reading, active with Texas public radio **SIC code:** 87 **Address:** The Hanke Group, 10101 Reunion Place, Suite 750, San Antonio, TX 78216 **E-mail:** dan.hanke@thehankegroup.com **Web address:** www.thehankegroup.com

HANNS, CHRISTIAN A.
Industry: Consulting **Born:** September 12, 1948, Elizabeth, New Jersey **Univ./degree:** Ph.D., Rutgers University, New Jersey, 1978 **Current organization:** Hanns & Associates **Title:** Founder **Type of organization:** Consulting firm **Major product:** Research, training, writing **Area of distribution:** International **Expertise:** Grant writing, research, technical writing **Published works:** 10 articles, pamphlets, book in progress **Hob./spts.:** Reading, travel **SIC code:** 87 **Address:** Hanns & Associates, 421 Third Ave., Linden, NJ 07036 **E-mail:** channs@damonhouse.org

HARDEE, COSETTE E.
Industry: Social Services/Healthcare/Addiction/Rehabilitation **Born:** October 17, 1947, Columbia, South Carolina **Univ./degree:** B.A., Secondary Education/Spanish, Texas Tech University, 1969; University of South Carolina Graduate School of Foreign Languages, 1973; M.A.C.P., Webster University Graduate School of Counseling, 2002 **Current organization:** Lexington Richland Alcohol Drug Abuse Council (LRADAC) **Title:** Program Director, NCAC II, CFC, CAC II, CDVC, Lexington Program Director (Lexington County); Social Service Provider/Addictions Rehabilitation, Behavior Modification **Type of organization:** County social service provider **Major product:** Addiction, forensic, domestic violence counseling services; Certified Addictions Counselor, Level I and II; National Certified Addictions Counselor, Level I and II; Certified Domestic Violence Counselor; Lexington County Public Defender's Office, Hispanic Service Provider **Area of distribution:** National **Expertise:** Addiction, forensic and domestic violence counseling, parenting and Hispanic services **Honors/awards:** Phoenix Excellence Award for Outstanding Counselor Performance, 1999; SCAADAC Counselor of the Year Award, 2003 **Affiliations:** N.A.A.D.A.C.; C.A.F.C.; N.A.F.C.; N.R.C.F.C.; National Association of Forensic Counselors; Alpha Delta Pi National Sorority **Hob./spts.:** Wildlife, walking, gardening, community service **SIC code:** 83 **Address:** 231 N. Stonehedge Dr., Columbia, SC 29210 **E-mail:** chardee@lradac.org **Web address:** www.lradac.org

HARDING, KEITH R.
Industry: Religion **Univ./degree:** Ed.D., Counseling, 2006 **Current organization:** Florida Conference of Seventh-day Adventists **Title:** Pastor/Dr. **Type of organization:** Church **Major product:** Religious services **Area of distribution:** Florida **Expertise:** Counseling, preaching **Affiliations:** Rotary Club; Chamber of Commerce **Hob./spts.:** Reading, table tennis **SIC code:** 86 **Address:** 2360 Fairmont Ave., Miramar, FL 33025 **E-mail:** kroyh@aol.com

HARDY, RICHARD A.
Industry: Engineering **Born:** July 27, 1950, Queens, New York **Univ./degree:** P.E. **Current organization:** STV, Inc. **Title:** P.E. **Type of organization:** Engineering firm **Major product:** Engineering services **Area of distribution:** International **Expertise:** Civil engineering/bridge inspecting **Affiliations:** A.S.C.E. **SIC code:** 87 **Address:** 84 Whangtown Rd., Carmel, NY 10512 **E-mail:** bridgegy@bestweb.net

HARGIS, HARRY V.
Industry: Religion **Born:** January 18, 1938, Lexington, Kentucky **Current organization:** Stamping Ground Baptist Church **Title:** Pastor (Retired) **Type of organization:** Church **Major product:** Religious services **Area of distribution:** Stamping Ground, Kentucky **Expertise:** Salvation, preaching, teaching **Hob./spts.:** Reading, walking **SIC code:** 86 **Address:** 105 Hurston Ct., Georgetown, KY 40324 **E-mail:** hvhargis@bellsouth.net

HARRIBANCE, LALSINGH "SEAN"
Industry: Parapsychology **Born:** November 11, 1939, Trinidad **Current organization:** Sean Harribance Institute for Parapsychology **Title:** President **Type of organization:** Research institute **Major product:** Parapsychology **Area of distribution:** International **Expertise:** Demonstration of the practical application of parapsychology/ESP Research subject **Published works:** 1 book, "This Man Knows You"; Contributed to over 40 articles published in the following scientific journals: International Journal of Neuroscience, International Journal of Psychophysiology, Journal of Neuropsychiatry and Clinical Neuroscience, Journal of Parapsychology, Journal of the American Society for Psychical Research, Proceedings of the Parapsychologial Association, Research in Parapsychology, Perceptual and Motor Skills **Affiliations:** Honorary Director, the Sean Harribance Institute for Parapsychology Research; Honorary Director, the Sean Harribance Institute of Parapsychology Foundation (Trinidad); Honorary Citizen/Recipient of the key to the city of Baton Rouge; Honorary Lt. Col. Aide-de-camp Alabama State Militia, 1975 **Hob./spts.:** Long-range economic forecast, walking, bird-watching **SIC code:** 87 **Address:** Sean Harribance Institute for Parapsychology, P.O. Box 908, Sugar Land, TX 77487 **E-mail:** harribance@yahoo.com

HARRIGAN, JOCELYN M.
Industry: Childcare services **Born:** November 29, 1964, New Roads, Louisiana **Current organization:** State of Connecticut, Dept. of Children & Families, OFAS/ Susidized Guardianship Unit **Title:** Foster Parent **Type of organization:** Foster care **Major product:** Childcare **Area of distribution:** New London, Connecticut **Expertise:** Childcare **Hob./spts.:** Sewing **SIC code:** 83 **Address:** 37 Woodlawn Rd., New London, CT 06320-2916 **E-mail:** commissioner.dcf@po.state.ct.us

HARRIS, JOHN A.
Industry: Landscaping **Born:** Schenectady, New York **Univ./degree:** A.S., Applied Science in Natural Resources, Morrisville Agricultural &Technical College; B.S., Resources Management and M.S., Forest Economics, College of Environmental Science and Forestry; M.B.A., Organizational Management, Syracuse University **Current organization:** Earth Advisors, Inc. **Title:** President/Founder **Type of organization:** Consulting firm **Major product:** Environmental and landscape consulting, work audits, environmental sight assessments **Area of distribution:** National **Expertise:** Certified Forester; ISA Certified Arborist; ISA-Florida Registered Tree Grader; Certified Landscape Inspector; Certified Mangrove Pruner; Certified Xeriscape Contractor; Registered Tree and Landscape Appraiser **Honors/awards:** Lambda Alpha International Honorary Land Economics Society, 1997 **Published works:** 20+ journal articles including: "Today's Tree Care: It's Not Just Cutting off Branches", "Re-greening: Spring Time is Perfect Time for Landscaping", 1994, "Restoration Program Targets Dade", "Florida ISA Registered Nursery Tree Grader Available for State of Florida Green Industry", 2000, "Pest Control: Ants and Roaches" **Affiliations:** Society of American Foresters; Landscape Inspectors Association of Florida; Land Economics Society **Hob./spts.:** Church, bird watching, skiing **SIC code:** 87 **Address:** Earth Advisors, Inc., 6916 Stirling Rd., Hollywood, FL 33024 **E-mail:** info@earthadvisors.com **Web address:** www.earthadvisors.com and www.landscapeeconomics.

HARRIS, MICHAEL E.
Industry: Management consulting **Born:** November 5, 1949, Ft. Monroe, Virginia **Univ./degree:** D.B.A., LaSalle University; M.B.A., Chadwick University **Current organization:** Harris & Harris, Associates, LLC **Title:** CEO/COO **Type of organization:** Business consulting **Major product:** Analysis/reports to aerospace and construction industries **Area of distribution:** New Jersey **Expertise:** Business process engineering **Affiliations:** N.D.I.A.; I.S.C.M.; P.M.I.; SOLE **Hob./spts.:** Photography, private investigating **SIC code:** 87 **Address:** Harris & Harris, Associates, LLC, 6 Brian Dr., Brown Mills, NJ 08015 **E-mail:** docharris1149@comcast.net

HARRISON, WILLIAM B.
Industry: Ceramic material consulting **Born:** February 27, 1928, Roanoke, Virginia **Univ./degree:** M.S., Ceramic Engineering, Virginia Polytechnic Institute and State University **Current organization:** Harrison Materials Consulting Services **Title:** President **Type of organization:** Consulting **Major product:** Ceramic materials **Area of distribution:** National **Expertise:** Engineering consulting **Published works:** 50 papers **Affiliations:** American Ceramic Society **SIC code:** 87 **Address:** Harrison Materials Consulting Services, 5230 Holiday Rd., Minnetonka, MN 55345 **E-mail:** harrison-times@juno.com

HARVEY, JOHN F.
Industry: Religion **Born:** April 14, 1918, Philadelphia, Pennsylvania **Univ./degree:** M.A., Psychology, Catholic University of America, 1946; S.T.D, Sacred Theology, Catholic University, 1951 **Current organization:** Courage - Archdiocese of New York (Courage is in 60 other dioceses) **Title:** Reverend **Type of organization:** Spiritual support groups for men and women **Major product:** Support group for chastity **Area of distribution:** United States, Australia, New Zealand, Great Britain **Expertise:** Moral theology and counseling **Hob./spts.:** Baseball, football **SIC code:** 86 **Address:** Courage - Archdiocese of New York, 210 W. 31st St., New York, NY 10001 **E-mail:** nycourage@aol.com

HARVEY, MAXINE
Industry: Accounting **Born:** July 4, 1932, Alton, Illinois **Current organization:** H&R Block **Title:** Owner **Type of organization:** Accounting franchise **Major product:** Tax services **Area of distribution:** Florida **Expertise:** Income tax preparation **Affiliations:** B.B.B. **Hob./spts.:** Sewing **SIC code:** 87 **Address:** H&R Block, 873 US Hwy. 331 South, DeFuniak Springs, FL 32435 **E-mail:** mharvey@hrblock.com

HASSAN, TARIQ A.
Industry: Engineering **Born:** July 21, 1973, Karachi, Pakistan **Univ./degree:** B.S.M.E., California State Polytechnical University at Pomona, 1997 **Current organization:** TMAD Engineers **Title:** Mechanical Design Engineer **Type of organization:** Structural, HVAC, mechanical electrical, plumbing, consulting firm **Major product:** Mechanical engineering consulting **Area of distribution:** California **Expertise:** HVAC and mechanical engineering **Affiliations:** ASHRE; AEE **Hob./spts.:** Automotive buff, sci-fi movie fan, travel **SIC code:** 87 **Address:** TMAD Engineers, 500 E. "E" St., Ontario, CA 91764-4226 **E-mail:** tahassan@lycosmail.com **Web address:** www.tmadengineers.com

HAYMAN, CHARLES LEE
Industry: Engineering **Born:** July 23, 1949, Riverside, California **Univ./degree:** M.S.E.E., Utah State University **Current organization:** Hayman's Motion Control Products **Title:** President/Founder **Type of organization:** Engineering consulting **Major product:** Motor drives, controls, power supplies **Area of distribution:** National **Expertise:** Engineering-motor drives, control systems, power supplies **Affiliations:** Reserve Lieutenant, San Diego County Sheriff's Dept. **Hob./spts.:** Racquetball **SIC code:** 87 **Address:** 13654 Sagewood Dr., Poway, CA 92064 **E-mail:** clhayman@hotmail.com

HAZAVEH, NORY
Industry: Architecture and design **Univ./degree:** M.S., Engineering, Brooklyn University; M.S., Architecture, City University of New York **Current organization:** SOSH Architects **Title:** Partner/Principal **Type of organization:** Architecture, planning and interiors firm **Major product:** Superior architecture **Area of distribution:** International **Expertise:** Architecture and design **Affiliations:** American Institute of Architects **SIC code:** 87 **Address:** SOSH Architects, 145 W. 57th St., New York, NY 10019 **E-mail:** nhazaveh@sosharch.com

HAZEL, MYRTHIE A.
Industry: Religion **Born:** September 30, 1959, Caldwell, Texas **Univ./degree:** D.Div., Southern California School of Ministry and the Pentecostal Bible College of Tuskegee, Alabama **Current organization:** Greater Victory World Outreach Center Church **Title:** Senior Pastor **Type of organization:** Church **Major product:** Ministry **Area of distribution:** California **Expertise:** Spirituality, education (k-12th grade) **Honors/awards:** Recognized in the Victorville, California Daily Press for her efforts with the SHARE food program **Published works:** 50+ articles, 50+ papers, 1 book, "We Win the Victory Through Jesus Christ" **Affiliations:** Founder and CEO, Greater Victorville Economic Development Resource Center; Former Assistant Pastor, Adelanto Church of God in Christ; Pastor, George Air Force Base Gospel Services **Hob./spts.:** Family, reading, travel **SIC code:** 86 **Address:** Greater Victory World Outreach Center Church, 15548 Sixth St., Victorville, CA 92392 **E-mail:** gvedrc@earthlink.net **Web address:** www.greatervictory.net

HEE, IVAN A.
Industry: Engineering/consulting **Born:** September 18, 1975, Melaka, Malaysia **Univ./degree:** M.S., Civil Engineering, Virginia Tech., 1998 **Current organization:** GZA Geo Environmental, Inc. **Title:** Assistant Project Manager **Type of organization:** Engineering consulting firm **Major product:** Engineering consulting **Area of distribution:** National **Expertise:** Geotechnical engineering **Affiliations:** A.S.C.E.; B.S.C.E. **Hob./spts.:** Home computer **SIC code:** 87 **Address:** GZA Geo Environmental, Inc., 1 Edgewater Dr., Norwood, MA 02062 **E-mail:** ihee@hotmail.com

HEIL, RICHARD W.
Industry: Engineering **Born:** March 16, 1926, Chicago, Illinois **Univ./degree:** B.S., Civil Engineering, University of Illinois, 1948 **Title:** Professional Engineer (Retired) **Type of organization:** Engineering **Major product:** Bridges **Area of distribution:** National **Expertise:** Design and development of bridges **Affiliations:** Fellow, American Society of Civil Engineers; A.I.C.E.; Chi Epsilon **Hob./spts.:** Genealogy **SIC code:** 87 **Address:** 30 Arthur Ave., Clarendon Hills, FL 60514 **E-mail:** heil.r@sbcglobal.net

HEINING, LEE
Industry: Consulting **Born:** September 17, 1943, Wilmar, Minnesota **Univ./degree:** A.S., Electrical Design, University of Minnesota **Current organization:** Lee's Consulting Services **Title:** Owner **Type of organization:** Consulting firm **Major product:** Electrical consulting **Area of distribution:** National **Expertise:** Electrical design **Hob./spts.:** Golf **SIC code:** 87 **Address:** Lee's Consulting Services, 130 Bar Harbor Ct., Aptos, CA 95003 **E-mail:** heining1@aol.com

HEINS, CONRAD F.
Industry: Consulting/energy **Born:** April 25, 1939, Kolar, India **Univ./degree:** Ph.D., Organic Bio Chemistry, University of Illinois **Current organization:** Renewable Energy Consultant **Title:** Consultant/Retired Professor **Type of organization:** Consulting **Major product:** Renewable energy technology **Area of distribution:** National **Expertise:** Passive solar design, photovoltaics **Published works:** Various journal articles on chemistry and renewable energy **Affiliations:** American Chemical Society; American Solar Energy Association **Hob./spts.:** Gardening, skiing **SIC code:** 87 **Address:** 6300 Ravens Roost Lane, Traverse City, MI 49684 **E-mail:** heinsa@msu.edu

HEINZE, JAMES J.
Industry: Accounting/Consulting **Born:** May 13, 1947, Newark, New Jersey **Univ./degree:** B.S., B.A., Accounting; C.P.A., Seton Hall University, 1969 **Current organization:** J.H. Cohn, LLP **Title:** Partner in charge of New York **Type of organization:** C.P.A. firm **Major product:** Accounting/consulting **Area of distribution:** New York, New Jersey, Connecticut **Expertise:** Accounting and consulting for nonprofit industries, Licensed C.P.A. in New York and New Jersey **Affiliations:** N.Y.S.S.C.P.A.;

N.J.S.S.C.P.A.; N.Y.S.A.E.; A.S.A.E.; N.J.S.A.E.; A.I.C.P.A. **SIC code:** 87 **Address:** J.H. Cohn, LLP, 1212 Ave. of the Americas, 12th Floor, New York, NY 10036 **E-mail:** jheinze@jhcohn.com

HEINZE, JOHN E.
Industry: Public affairs/science consulting **Born:** November 3, 1947, Tulsa, Oklahoma **Univ./degree:** B.S., Summa Cum Laude, Chemistry, Oklahoma Baptist Univ., 1970; M.S., Microbiology, Univ. of Illinois, 1972; Ph.D., Microbiology, Univ. of Illinois at Urbana-Champaign, 1975; Postdoctoral study, Molecular Biology & Genetics, Nat'l Inst. of Health, 1975-77 **Current organization:** John Adams Associates/Environmental Health Research Foundation **Title:** Sr. Vice President for Science/Executive Director **Type of organization:** Public affairs/nonprofit **Major product:** Public affairs/environmental and health research **Area of distribution:** International **Expertise:** Consulting on environmental and health science issues, lecturing presentations **Honors/awards:** Chemical & Engineering News Award of Merit 1970, Wakeman Fellowship, American Society for Microbiology 1973-75 **Published works:** 25+ papers, 2 book chapters **Affiliations:** Past Officer, Arizona Chapter, American Society for Microbiology; Past Chair, Non Animal Testing Subcommittee, Environmental Fate Subcommittee, Soap and Detergent Association **Hob./spts.:** Boating **SIC code:** 87 **Address:** John Adams Associates, Environmental Health Research Foundation, 529 14th St. N.W., Suite 807, Washington, DC 20045 **E-mail:** jheinze@johnadams.com

HEISEY, RANDALL F.
Industry: Facilities management/planning **Born:** Ganado, Arizona **Univ./degree:** B.S.E.E., Villanova University **Current organization:** Johnson Controls **Title:** Instrumentation Engineer **Type of organization:** R&D **Major product:** Pharmaceuticals **Area of distribution:** Collegeville, Pennsylvania **Expertise:** Engineering - instruments and control **Affiliations:** I.S.A.; I.E.E.E. **Hob./spts.:** Golf, motorcycling, radio control models, home improvements **SIC code:** 87 **Address:** Johnson Controls, 1250 S. Collegeville Rd., UP6000B, Collegeville, PA 19426-2990 **E-mail:** rfheisey@netscape.net

HELLEBUST, GARY
Industry: Educational **Univ./degree:** B.S., Agriculture, Kansas State University, 1969 **Current organization:** Kansas State University Foundation **Title:** President/CEO **Type of organization:** 501C(3) nonprofit foundation **Major product:** Fundraising **Area of distribution:** National **Expertise:** Oversees daily operations **Affiliations:** K.A.C.E. **SIC code:** 86 **Address:** Kansas State University Foundation, 2323 Anderson Ave., Manhattan, KS 66520 **E-mail:** garyh@found.ksu.edu

HELMPRECHT, HANS L.
Industry: Consulting **Born:** December 12, 1927, Eschershausen, Germany **Univ./degree:** Ph.D., Chemistry, Western Pacific University, Los Angeles, California **Current organization:** Chemical Consulting of Babylon **Title:** Owner **Type of organization:** Consulting and testing laboratory **Major product:** Chemical analysis of soil and plant tissue **Area of distribution:** Eastern U.S. **Expertise:** Soil analysis, plant tissue analysis **Hob./spts.:** Photography **SIC code:** 87 **Address:** Chemical Consulting of Babylon, 41 E. Main St., Babylon, NY 11702 **E-mail:** chemicalconsulting@yahoo.com

HENKEN, BERNARD S.
Industry: Consultant to attorneys and courts **Born:** May 30, 1919, Everett, Massachusetts **Univ./degree:** Sc.D., Psychology, Calvin Coolidge College, 1955 **Current organization:** Self-employed **Title:** Sc.D. **Type of organization:** Consulting **Major product:** Forensic psychology **Area of distribution:** National **Expertise:** Expert witness testimony in disability cases, cases involving drunk driving, delinquency and sexual disorders **Affiliations:** A.P.A; N.A.S.P.; Past President, M.S.P.A. **Hob./spts.:** Swimming, music **SIC code:** 87 **Address:** 118 Waverly Ave., Melrose, MA 02176

HERNANDEZ, FRANCISCO
Industry: Religion **Born:** December 22, 1966, San Juan, Puerto Rico **Univ./degree:** B.A., Philosophy, St. John's Seminary, Florida, 1990; M.A., Theology, St. Vincent De Paul, Florida, 1994 **Current organization:** St. Mary Star of the Sea Catholic Church **Title:** Reverend, Pastor **Type of organization:** Roman Catholic church **Major product:** Religious services **Area of distribution:** International **Expertise:** Outreach, ministry, management **Honors/awards:** 1st Hispanic Pastor of St. Mary's **Affiliations:** Archdiocese of Miami **Hob./spts.:** Gardening, animals, cooking **SIC code:** 86 **Address:** 1010 Windsor Lane, Key West, FL 33040 **E-mail:** stmarystar@bellsouth.net

HERNANDEZ, JULIO R.
Industry: Healthcare **Born:** August 10, 1956, Caguas, Puerto Rico **Univ./degree:** B.S., Civil Engineering, University of Puerto Rico, 1977; M.D., University of Puerto Rico School of Medicine, 1987 **Current organization:** Julio R. Hernandez, M.D., P.E. **Title:** M.D./Professional Engineer **Type of organization:** Private practice **Major product:** Patient care **Area of distribution:** Puerto Rico **Expertise:** Orthopaedic surgery **Published works:** 1 peer reviewed journal; 2 abstract/conference papers **Affiliations:** F.A.A.O.S. **Hob./spts.:** Water and snow skiing, reading, travel **SIC code:** 87 **Address:** Julio R. Hernandez, M.D., P.E., P.O. Box 70344 PMB #318, San Juan, PR 00936-8344

HERNÁNDEZ, JOSÉ A.
Industry: Consulting engineering **Born:** September 16, 1964, San Juan, Puerto Rico **Univ./degree:** B,S, Chemical Engineering, University of Puerto Rico, 1998; M.S., Occupational Hygiene/Occupational Safety, West Virginia University, 2001 **Current organization:** Panzardi-ERM, Inc. **Title:** Environmental Engineer **Type of organization:** Consulting **Major product:** Wastewater treatment plants evaluation and design; environmental/health/safety compliance; consulting to pharmaceutical/chemical and manufacturing industries **Area of distribution:** National **Expertise:** Environmental engineering **Affiliations:** W.E.F.; N.R.E.P.; N.F.P.A.; A.W.W.A.; C.I.A.P.R. **Hob./spts.:** Basketball, baseball **SIC code:** 87 **Address:** Panzardi-ERM, Inc., P.O. Box 192291, San Juan, PR 00919-2291 **E-mail:** jhernandez@panzardierm.com

HERSHBARGER, LARRY A.
Industry: Engineering **Born:** Newport News, Virginia **Univ./degree:** B.S.E.E., University of Missouri (Columbia), 1990 **Current organization:** Engineering Solutions **Title:** Sr. Engineer **Type of organization:** Manufacturing **Major product:** Product control applications (software) **Area of distribution:** St. Louis, Missouri **Expertise:** Project management, motion and process control **Hob./spts.:** Advit hiking, back packing **SIC code:** 87 **Address:** Engineering Solutions, 6500 Page Ave., St. Louis, MO 63133 **E-mail:** lhersh@engineered-solutions.net

HETTMANSBERGER, JAMES D.
Industry: Automotive lighting **Born:** May 21, 1945, Mineral, Texas **Univ./degree:** 4 Year I.C.S. Correspondence Course **Current organization:** Hella Lighting Corp. North America **Title:** Senior Equipment Engineer **Type of organization:** Manufacturing **Major product:** Automotive lighting (head lamps, fog lamps, off road lamps) **Area of distribution:** International **Expertise:** Assembly equipment engineering; Designed Standard Flexible Quick-Change Workcells and Die Sets for Lean Manufacturing and Assembly of automotive lamps **Hob./spts.:** Going to the beach, time with grandchildren **SIC code:** 87 **Address:** Hella Lighting Corp., 7979 Park Place, East York Industrial Park, York, SC 29745 **E-mail:** jim.hettmansberger@hellausa.com

HEUMANN, CRAIG G.
Industry: Consulting/oil and gas **Born:** November 4, 1952, New Orleans, Louisiana **Univ./degree:** B.S., Civil Engineering, Louisiana State University, 1974 **Current organization:** Global Project Consultants, Inc. **Title:** Vice President **Type of organization:** Consulting **Major product:** Consulting, project and construction management **Area of distribution:** International **Expertise:** Project management **Affiliations:** A.S.C.E.; A.P.I.; M.T.S. **Hob./spts.:** Golf, hunting **SIC code:** 87 **Address:** Global Project Consultants, Inc., 14701 St. Mary's Lane, Suite 600, Houston, TX 77079 **E-mail:** heumannc@globalproject.com

HEUN, RAYMOND C.
Industry: Concrete/construction/consulting **Born:** March 5, 1926, Newark, New Jersey **Univ./degree:** M.S., Structural Engineering, New Jersey Institute of Technology, 1955 **Current organization:** New York Concrete Construction Institute **Title:** Executive Director **Type of organization:** Consulting office and trade association **Major product:** Reinforced concrete **Area of distribution:** New York **Expertise:** Structural engineering **Affiliations:** A.C.I.; N.Y.A.S. **Hob./spts.:** Travel, golf **SIC code:** 87 **Address:** New York Concrete Construction Institute, 49 W. 45th St., New York, NY 10036

HICKTON, LORAN J.
Industry: Public relations/communications **Born:** November 30, 1960, Pittsburgh, Pennsylvania **Univ./degree:** Attended University of Pittsburgh **Current organization:** Salmon Creek Public Relations Inc. **Title:** CEO/President **Type of organization:** Public relations firm **Major product:** Public relations **Area of distribution:** National **Expertise:** Branding, crisis management, product communication, consumer public relations **Affiliations:** P.R.S.A. **Hob./spts.:** Travel, art, his Labrador Retrievers **SIC code:** 87 **Address:** Salmon Creek Public Relations Inc., 109 S.W. First St., Suite 251, Battle Ground, WA 98604 **E-mail:** lhickton@salmoncreekpr.com

HIGHLEY, JOANNE
Industry: Christian counseling **Born:** July 30, 1932, Durant, Oklahoma **Univ./degree:** B.S., Phillips University **Current organization:** L.I.F.E. Inc. **Title:** Founder/Counselor **Type of organization:** Christian counseling center **Major product:** Freedom from homosexuality **Area of distribution:** International **Expertise:** Addiction counseling, support groups and church education **Published works:** The best of "Words of L.I.F.E." **Hob./spts.:** Grandchildren, singing, travel, writing, gardening **SIC code:** 86 **Address:** L.I.F.E. Inc., P.O. Box 353, New York, NY 10185

HILL, JEFFREY R.
Industry: Cutting and machine tools **Born:** November 12, 1954, Merrill, Wisconsin **Univ./degree:** A.S., Machine Tools, NTC, Wausau, Wisconsin, 1974 **Current organization:** Northern States Tool & Cutter **Title:** Sole Proprietor **Type of organization:** Design, manufacturing and service **Major product:** Special application cutting tools for metal, wood and plastics **Area of distribution:** National **Expertise:** Management,

leadership, design engineering, budget, planning courses **Hob./spts.:** Hunting, snow-mobiling, travel **SIC code:** 87 **Address:** Northern States Tool and Cutter, N5333 Hwy. 17, Gleason, WI 54435

HILT, THOMAS H.
Industry: Counseling **Born:** May 19, 1947, Philadelphia, Pennsylvania **Univ./degree:** Ph.D., Christian Counseling, Carolina University of Theology, 1992 **Current organization:** SonHaven Prepartory Academy **Title:** Reverend Doctor **Type of organization:** Nonprofit **Major product:** Counseling, emergency services **Area of distribution:** International **Expertise:** Critical incident stress counseling **Honors/awards:** Merit Award, International Critical Incident Stress Foundation **Affiliations:** International Critical Incident Stress Foundation; American Academy of Experts in Traumatic Stress; National Board of Christian Clinical Therapists; National Christian Counselors Association; American Association of Christian Counselors; International Fellowship of Pastoral Counselors **Hob./spts.:** Family, gardening **SIC code:** 83 **Address:** SonHaven Prepartory Academy, P.O. Box 50517, Sarasota, FL 34232 **E-mail:** thhilt@aol.com

HIPPLER, MICHAEL G.
Industry: Engineering **Born:** March 25, 1962, Lake Bluff, Illinois **Univ./degree:** B.S.E.E., Montana School of Mineral Science & Technology **Current organization:** The Control Systems Group, Inc. **Title:** President **Type of organization:** Design engineering and control systems investigation **Major product:** Engineering services **Area of distribution:** Regional North America **Expertise:** Engineering, project managment **Affiliations:** Chair, Business Advisory Council, NECC **Hob./spts.:** High power rifle, hunting, bench rest competition **SIC code:** 87 **Address:** The Control Systems Group, Inc., 815 Crocker Rd., Suite 3, Cleveland, OH 44145 **E-mail:** mhippler@csginconline.com **Web address:** www.csginconline.com

HIXON, S.B. (DAVE)
Industry: Geology **Born:** September 7, 1930, La Junta, Colorado **Univ./degree:** B.A., Geology, University of Colorado; M.A., Geology, University of Texas; Ph.D., Geology and Mineralogy, University of Michigan, 1964 **Title:** Consultant **Major product:** Geology, mineralogy **Area of distribution:** International **Expertise:** Geology, software engineering; geological mapping geophysical study, aeromagnetic and imagery (Aircraft, Landsat and Radar) interpretation, contract drafting **Honors/awards:** V.P., Engr. Council of Houston, 2006-08; NASA Faculty Fellowship, 1987; Teaching Fellowships, University of Texas and Michigan; Secretary, Sigma Epsilon, Honorary Chapter at University of Michigan **Published works:** Numerous including: "Facies and Petrography of the Cretaceous Buda Limestone of Texas and Northern Mexico", University of Texas 1-1959; "Petrography of the Middle Devonian Bois Blanc Foundation of Michigan and Ontario" 5-1964, University of Michigan; MA and PhD Theses 1959 and 1964; also at University Microfilms, Ann Arbor, Michigan **Affiliations:** Teaching Fellow, Michigan and Texas; Faculty Fellow, NASA Johnson Space Center, 1967; Houston Geological Society; American Association of Petroleum Geologists; American Geological Institute; V.P., Engineering Council of Houston; **Hob./spts.:** Fishing, hunting (NRA), opera **SIC code:** 87 **Address:** 504 Misty Lane, Friendswood, TX 77546

HOAGLIN, DAVID C.
Industry: Applied social research **Born:** March 4, 1944, Charleston, West Virginia **Univ./degree:** B.S., Math, Duke University, 1966; Ph.D., Statistics, Princeton University, 1971 **Current organization:** Abt Associates Inc. **Title:** Principal Scientist **Type of organization:** Research firm **Major product:** Research, policy recommendations **Area of distribution:** National **Expertise:** Statistics **Affiliations:** A.S.A.; I.M.S.; I.S.I. **Hob./spts.:** Amateur radio, travel **SIC code:** 87 **Address:** Abt Associates Inc., 55 Wheeler St., Cambridge, MA 02138 **E-mail:** dave_hoaglin@abtassoc.com **Web address:** www.abtassoc.com

HOFFLEIT, E. DORRIT
Industry: Research **Born:** March 12, 1907, Florence, Alabama **Univ./degree:** A.B., 1928; M.A., 1932; Ph.D., 1938, Radcliffe (now a department of Harvard) **Title:** Senior Research Astronomer, Yale Dept. of Astronomy (Retired) **Type of organization:** University **Major product:** Astronomy research **Area of distribution:** International **Expertise:** Star catalogues, history of astronomy, variable stars **Published works:** Over 450 articles, 1 book: "History of Yale Astronomy" **Affiliations:** International Astronomical Union; American Astronomical Society; American Association of Variable Star Observers; The Meteoritical Society; Connecticut Academy of Arts and Sciences; New York Academy of Sciences; Nantucket Maria Mitchell Society (Director of Observatory 1956-78) **Hob./spts.:** Staying active **SIC code:** 87 **Address:** Yale Dept. of Astronomy, Gibbs Laboratory, 260 Whitney Ave., New Haven, CT 06520-8101

HOFFMANN, DIETGER
Industry: Consulting **Born:** March 16, 1940, Dahlbruch, Germany **Univ./degree:** Diplomate, Engineering, University of Koblenz, Germany, 1969 **Current organization:** Hoffman Consulting **Title:** Owner **Type of organization:** Consulting **Major product:** Underground communication systems in subway, train and street tunnels **Area of distribution:** International **Expertise:** Communication systems **Affiliations:** I.E.E.E. **Hob./spts.:** Swimming **SIC code:** 87 **Address:** Hoffmann Consulting, 7521 Brentcove Circle, Dallas, TX 75214 **E-mail:** maus@mail2.gbronline.com

HOLDER, NEVILLE L.
Industry: Pharmaceutical **Born:** May 28, 1940, St. Joseph, Barbados, West Indies **Univ./degree:** B.Sc., (Hons), 1965; M.Sc., 1968, University of West Indies; Ph.D., University of Waterloo, 1972; M.S., (QA/RA), Temple University, 2002 **Current organization:** Aventis Pharmaceuticals, Inc. **Title:** Ph.D., Research Fellow **Type of organization:** Research and development **Major product:** Ethical pharmaceuticals **Area of distribution:** International **Expertise:** Chromatographic chemist **Affiliations:** American Chemical Society; National Organization for the Professional Advancement of Black Chemists and Chemical Engineers **Hob./spts.:** Bowling, tennis, sports **SIC code:** 87 **Address:** Aventis Pharmaceuticals, Inc., Route 202-206, Bridgewater, NJ 08807 **E-mail:** neville.holder@aventis.com

HOLDER, SUSAN L.
Industry: Education **Born:** December 27, 1952, Clayton, New Mexico **Univ./degree:** B.S., Eastern New Mexico University, 1974; M.S., Texas Tech University, 1976; Ed.D., New Mexico State University, 1990 **Current organization:** Mississippi State University, Extension Service **Title:** State Program Leader-4H **Type of organization:** Mississippi's largest youth organization **Major product:** Youth development **Area of distribution:** National **Expertise:** Leadership development, administration **Hob./spts.:** Travel, writing **SIC code:** 86 **Address:** Mississippi State University, Extension Service, Box 9601, Room 204, Mississippi State, MS 39762 **E-mail:** susanh@ext.msstate.edu

HOLMES, DON PHILIP
Industry: Engineering **Born:** January 1, 1949, Houston, Texas **Univ./degree:** B.S., Mechanical Engineering, University of Texas at Austin, 1972 **Current organization:** URS Corp. **Title:** Senior Engineer **Type of organization:** Engineering/consulting **Major product:** Infrastructure, petro chemicals, environmental, transportation **Area of distribution:** International **Expertise:** Environmental remediation, water/wastewater design, management **Hob./spts.:** Scout Master **SIC code:** 87 **Address:** URS Corp., 9801 Westheimer, Suite 500, Houston, TX 77042 **E-mail:** don_holmes@urscorp.com **Web address:** www.urscorp.com

HOLTERMAN, LUDWIG K.
Industry: Engineering **Born:** May 27, 1932, Bremerhaven, Germany **Univ./degree:** M.A., Engineering, Bremerhaven University, 1956 **Current organization:** Concept Engineering **Title:** Owner **Type of organization:** Engineering firm **Major product:** Heat flux transducers and sensors **Area of distribution:** International **Expertise:** New development/inventions **Affiliations:** I.S.A. **Hob./spts.:** Windsurfing, skiing, ice skating **SIC code:** 87 **Address:** Concept Engineering, 4 Rivers Ridge Rd., Old Saybrook, CT 06475 **E-mail:** concepteng@aol.com **Web address:** www.conceptengineering2000.com

HONG, NORMAN G.Y.
Industry: Architecture **Born:** May 5, 1947, Hon, Hawaii **Univ./degree:** B.A., Architecture, University of Hawaii, 1969 **Current organization:** Group 70 International, Inc. **Title:** Vice Chair, AIA **Type of organization:** Architecture firm **Major product:** Design services **Area of distribution:** International **Expertise:** Architecture, planning, interior design, marketing **Honors/awards:** Design Award, Luxury Residential Project, Point Club, 1991; Award of Excellence, A.I,A, Hawaii Chapter, 1996-97; **Hob./spts.:** Travel **SIC code:** 87 **Address:** Group 70 International, Inc., 925 Bethel St., 5th floor, Honolulu, HI 96813

HORVATH, DEBORAH K.
Industry: Human services **Born:** February 14, 1953, Staten Island, New York **Univ./degree:** M.S., International College, 2005 **Current organization:** American Red Cross - Collier County Chapter **Title:** CEO **Type of organization:** Nonprofit **Major product:** Disaster preparedness **Area of distribution:** International **Expertise:** Executive management **Affiliations:** AFP; PRACC; ABWA; VOAD, Leadership Collier **Hob./spts.:** Horses, snorkeling, crossword puzzles **SIC code:** 83 **Address:** American Red Cross - Collier County Chapter, 2610 Northbrooke Plaza Dr., Naples, FL 34119 **E-mail:** deborahhorvath@hotmail.com **Web address:** www.colliercountyredcross.org

HOWARD, EVERETT A.
Industry: Technology **Born:** August 14, 1966, Rochester, New Hampshire **Univ./degree:** M.E.E., Fayetteville Tech, 1988 **Current organization:** Howard Systems, LLC **Title:** CEO/Chief Engineer **Type of organization:** Technology integration company **Major product:** Technology integration **Area of distribution:** National **Expertise:** Design, sales, service **Affiliations:** N.F.P.A. **Hob./spts.:** Wakeboarding **SIC code:** 87 **Address:** Howard Systems, LLC, 10 Commerce Way, Barrington, NH 03825 **E-mail:** ehoward@howardsystems.net

HOWARD, GARTH A.
Industry: Marketing/customer service **Born:** February 26, 1955, Rexburg, Idaho **Univ./degree:** B.A., Finance, Brigham Young University, Utah, 1981; M.B.A., International Business, University of Utah, 1985 **Current organization:** Convergys Corp. **Title:** President Custom Solutions Group **Type of organization:** Customer service, outsourcing **Major product:** Call center, customer care **Area of distribution:** National/Global **Expertise:** General management **Affiliations:** Board Member, Utah Foundation; Advisory Board Member, C.O.P.C.; State Technology Commission, State of Utah; Executive Committee, Children's Museum of Utah **Hob./spts.:** Sports, running, golf, church activities, Boy Scouts of America **SIC code:** 87 **Address:** Matrixx Marketing Inc., 10975 So. Sterling View Drive, South Jordan, UT 84095 **E-mail:** garth.howard@convergys.com **Web address:** www.convergys.com

HOWELL, DAVID W.
Industry: Consulting **Born:** November 20, 1932, Glen Cove, New York **Univ./degree:** B.S., Mechanical Engineering, Rensselaer Polytechnic Institute, 1959 **Current organization:** Integrated Building Systems **Title:** President **Type of organization:** Engineering firm **Major product:** Design services **Area of distribution:** New York **Expertise:** Consulting **Affiliations:** A.S.H.R.A.E.; N.S.P.E.; New York State Society of Professional Engineers **SIC code:** 87 **Address:** Integrated Building Systems, 73 Troy Rd., East Greenbush, NY 12061-1334 **E-mail:** dhowell@ibseng.com

HOWELL, HARRIS H.
Industry: Religion **Born:** October 21, 1964, St. Elizabeth, Jamaica **Current organization:** Apostolic Worship Center **Title:** Pastor, Overseer **Type of organization:** Multicultural church **Major product:** Religious leadership and refuge **Area of distribution:** International **Expertise:** Religious instruction, preaching **Affiliations:** Church of God in Christ **Hob./spts.:** Fishing, golf **SIC code:** 86 **Address:** Apostolic Worship Center, 540 E. Washington Ave., Bridgeport, CT 06608 **E-mail:** worshipcenter@optonline.net **Web address:** www.apostolicworshipcenter.net

HOYT, DORTHEA L.
Industry: Consulting **Born:** March 4, 1962, Welkon, Republic of South Africa **Univ./degree:** B.S., Geological Engineering, 1985; M.S., Ecological Engineering, 1992, Colorado School of Mines **Current organization:** Gannett Fleming **Title:** Senior Environmental Engineer **Type of organization:** Engineering **Major product:** Consulting **Area of distribution:** National **Expertise:** Ecological engineering **Affiliations:** N.A.E.P.; A.S.C.E.; P.M.I. **Hob./spts.:** Skiing **SIC code:** 87 **Address:** Pacific Western Technology Ltd., 605 Parfet St., Suite 700, Lakewood, CO 80215 **E-mail:** dhoyt@pwt.com

HUANG, JIUNN-RU J.
Industry: Medical and semiconductor research and development **Born:** May 12, 1969, Tai Chung, Taiwan **Univ./degree:** B.S.E.E., National Sun Yat-Sen University, Taiwan; M.S.E.E., Pennsylvania State University, 1996; Ph.D., Electrical Engineering, Pennsylvania State University, 2001 **Current organization:** G.E. Global Research Center **Title:** Ph.D., Process Engineer **Type of organization:** Research and development **Major product:** Semiconductor devices, large area electronics, digital x-ray imagers **Area of distribution:** International **Expertise:** Engineering, physics **Published works:** 18 reference journals, 7 patents/patent disclosures **Affiliations:** I.E.E.E.; M.R.S.; A.I.A.A.; Sigma Xi **Hob./spts.:** Ice skating, walking and sitting meditation **SIC code:** 87 **Address:** G.E. Global Research Center, KWD 270, One Research Circle, Niskayuna, NY 12309 **E-mail:** huangji@research.ge.com **Web address:** www.research.ge.com

HUBER, KENNETH A.
Industry: Consulting **Born:** September 23, 1970, Elizabeth, New Jersey **Univ./degree:** M.S., Civil Engineering, Virginia Polytechnic Institute, 1997 **Current organization:** Langan Engineering and Environmental Services **Title:** Project Manager **Type of organization:** Engineering consulting firm **Major product:** Engineering/consulting services **Area of distribution:** National **Expertise:** Geotechnical engineering **Affiliations:** A.S.C.E.; N.S.P.E.; Board Member, A.C.E. Mentoring Program of Pennsylvania; International Society for Soil Mechanics & Foundation Engineering **Hob./spts.:** Music, reading **SIC code:** 87 **Address:** Langan Engineering and Environmental Services, 30 S. 17th St., Suite 1500, Philadelphia, PA 19103 **E-mail:** khuber@langan.com **Web address:** www.langan.com

HUDSON, CHUCK
Industry: Social services **Born:** July 8, 1963, Halifax, Virginia **Univ./degree:** B.A, 1989; M.B.A., 1994, Averett University **Current organization:** Presbyterian Homes & Family Services **Title:** Marketing Specialist **Type of organization:** Residential care for adolescents **Major product:** Safe, nurturing care to rebuild and reunite residents of the community **Area of distribution:** Virginia **Expertise:** Marketing **Affiliations:** American Marketing Association **Hob./spts.:** Golf **SIC code:** 83 **Address:** Presbyterian Homes & Family Services, 150 Linden Ave., Lynchburg, VA 24503 **E-mail:** chudson@phfs.org **Web address:** www.phfs.org

HUGHES JR., THOMAS P.
Industry: Real estate **Born:** October 7, 1946, Daytona, Florida **Univ./degree:** B.A., University of South Florida, 1976 **Current organization:** Bartram Trail Surveying, Inc. **Title:** President, Owner **Type of organization:** Surveying company **Major product:** All types of land surveying and mapping **Area of distribution:** Green Cove Springs, Florida **Expertise:** GPS; GIS; Boundary surveying **Affiliations:** F.S.L.S.; Green Cove Springs Chamber of Commerce **Hob./spts.:** Coaching football, fishing, hunting **SIC code:** 87 **Address:** Bartram Trail Surveying, Inc., 1501 CR 315, Suite 106, Green Cove Springs, FL 32043 **E-mail:** bartramtrail@bartramtrail.net **Web address:** www.bartramtrail.net

HUNTER, CAROL
Industry: Accounting **Born:** February 13, 1941, Beaver Dam, Virginia **Univ./degree:** Virginia Commonwealth University, 1983 **Current organization:** Accounting by Carol **Title:** Owner **Type of organization:** Accounting firm **Major product:** Accounting services/tax preparation **Area of distribution:** International **Expertise:** Tax preparation and accounting **Honors/awards:** Honorary Chair, National Republican Party; Republican of the Year, 2006 **Affiliations:** National Republican Party **Hob./spts.:** Reading, classic films **SIC code:** 87 **Address:** Accounting by Carol, 1513-C Split Oak Lane, Richmond, VA 23229 **E-mail:** accbcarol@comcast.net

HURREY, EARL T.
Industry: Association/educational **Born:** October 24, 1952, Jacksonville, North Carolina **Univ./degree:** B.A., Music Education, Gettysburg College, 1975 **Current organization:** MENC: The National Association for Music Education **Title:** Assistant Executive Director **Type of organization:** Professional education association **Major product:** Products and action for music education/educators **Area of distribution:** National **Expertise:** Project development, public relations, marketing, government relations **Honors/awards:** Stage/Production Manager for the "President's Own" U.S. Marine Band in Washington, DC - oversaw hundred's of White House ceremonies and performances, 14 national concert tours, 5 European tours and thousands of Marine Band performances around the country and throughout the Washington DC area **Affiliations:** Bands of America; Arts for a Complete Education **Hob./spts.:** Golf **SIC code:** 86 **Address:** MENC: The National Association for Music Education, 1806 Robert Fulton Dr., Reston, VA 20191 **E-mail:** earlh@menc.org **Web address:** www.menc.org

ISDALE, JOE W.
Industry: Engineering **Born:** February 18, 1923, Yoakum, Texas **Univ./degree:** Aero, Texas A&M University, 1940; Math, Houston University; ASTP in Geopolitics, Economics, Loyola LA; History, Schrivenham University, Oxford, England; Mechanical Engineering and Math, Texas University, 1948 **Current organization:** Isdale Engineering **Title:** Owner **Type of organization:** Engineering consulting **Major product:** Writing of engineering principles **Area of distribution:** International **Expertise:** Integration and updating of engineering principles; Registered Professional Engineer, Texas **Published works:** Geophysics, gravity and mapping information, oil well drilling, patent on seal for automation, promoted two oil wells, Wear Away Rock Bit, pending, Flip Submarine Drilling Platform, Design & Development Co. Inc. with 26 programs of innovation, Published, Science Politics and Tomorrow, Houston City-Texas, Super City Now, etc. **Hob./spts.:** Engineering **SIC code:** 87 **Address:** 6445 Sharpview Ave., Houston, TX 77074 **E-mail:** joewisdale@hotmail.com

ISHOY, JAMES F.
Industry: Consulting **Univ./degree:** B.S., Manufacturing Engineering, Brigham Young University, Utah, 1976 **Current organization:** Ishoy & Associates **Title:** President **Type of organization:** Consulting firm **Major product:** Consulting **Area of distribution:** California **Expertise:** Manufacturing **Affiliations:** A.S.Q. **Hob./spts.:** Golf, fishing, photography, travel **SIC code:** 87 **Address:** 1859 Basil Dr., Manteca, CA 95336 **E-mail:** jimishoy@wwdb.org

ISOLDI, DONALD J.
Industry: Consulting **Univ./degree:** B.S., Chemistry, Florida Southern University, 1950 **Current organization:** Polymer Technics L.L.C. **Title:** President **Type of organization:** Consulting, RFD **Major product:** Polymer controlled release technology **Area of distribution:** International **Expertise:** Inventor **Published works:** 24 patents worldwide **Affiliations:** American Chemical Society; Controlled Release Society **Hob./spts.:** Chess **SIC code:** 87 **Address:** Polymer Technics L.L.C., 6928 Sonny Dale Dr., Melbourne, FL 32904 **E-mail:** LI@aol.com

IYER, VENKATRAMAN A.
Industry: Research/engineering **Born:** August 24, 1975, Bombay, India **Univ./degree:** B.S.M.E., Indian Institute of Technology, 1996; M.S.M.E., 1998; Ph.D., Mechanical Engineering, 2001, Purdue University **Current organization:** General Electric **Title:** Ph.D. **Type of organization:** R&D **Major product:** Energy and propulsion systems **Area of distribution:** International **Expertise:** Mechanical engineering, gas turbine and diesel engine combustion **Honors/awards:** Purdue Research Award, Sigma-Xi Scientific Research Society **Published works:** Refereed Publications: Iyer, V. and Abraham, J. "An evaluation of a two-fluid eulerian-liquid eulerian-gas model for Die-

sel sprays," accepted for publication in the Journal of Fluids Engineering (2003); Iyer V., Abraham J. and Magi, V., "Exploring injected droplet size effects on steady liquid penetration in a Diesel spray with a two-fluid model," International Journal of Heat and Mass Transfer, Vol. 45(3), pp. 519-531 (2002); Magi, V., Iyer, V. and Abraham, J., "The k-? model and computed spreading rates in round and plane jets," Numerical Heat Transfer A-Applications, Vol. 40(4), pp. 371-334 (2001); Iyer, V. and Abraham, J., "Penetration and Dispersion of Transient Gas Jets and Sprays," Combust Sci. and Tech., Vol 130, pp. 315-334 (1997) **Affiliations:** A.S.M.E.; S.A.E.; Sigma-Xi **Hob./spts.:** Family, travel, tennis **SIC code:** 87 **Address:** General Electric, 1 Research Circle, Niskayuna, NY 12309 **E-mail:** iyer@crd.ge.com

JAKUBOWSKI, FRANK
Industry: Consulting **Born:** January 10, 1941, Poland **Univ./degree:** B.S., Mechanical Engineering, College of Engineering, Poland, 1972 **Current organization:** FJ Associates **Title:** President/Owner/Design Engineer **Type of organization:** Private practice **Major product:** Consulting-machinery for food production **Area of distribution:** International **Expertise:** Engineering **Affiliations:** Society of Poland Engineers **SIC code:** 87 **Address:** FJ Associates, 69-51 62nd St., Glendale, NY 11385 **E-mail:** frankjak@aol.com

JAMES, BRIAN AVERY ANTHONY
Industry: Architecture **Born:** November 25, 1968, Washington, D.C. **Univ./degree:** B.S., Architecture, University of Houston, Texas, 1995 **Current organization:** SHW Group, Inc. **Title:** Architectural Intern **Type of organization:** Architectural firm **Major product:** Architecture **Area of distribution:** National **Expertise:** Handicap accessibility **Affiliations:** International Building Code Officials; American Institute of Architects **SIC code:** 87 **Address:** SHW Group, Inc., 4000 McEwen Rd. North, Dallas, TX 75244 **E-mail:** bajames@shwgroup.com

JAMES, CHRYSTAL F.
Industry: Architecture **Born:** February 4, 1980, Navaho Reservation Shiprock, New Mexico **Univ./degree:** A.A.S., Architectural Design, Computer Aided Drafting, Hi-Tech Institute, Phoenix, 2000 **Current organization:** Dyron Murphy Architects **Title:** CADD Manager/Project Coordinator **Type of organization:** Native American architectural firm **Major product:** Construction, building for Native American reservations **Area of distribution:** Southwestern United States **Expertise:** CADD management, program customization, training **Affiliations:** AUGIE; Navajo Nation; Autodesk **Hob./spts.:** Running, drawing, painting **SIC code:** 87 **Address:** Dyron Murphy Architects, 5941 Jefferson St. N.E., Suite A, Albuquerque, NM 87109 **E-mail:** cjames@dm-architects.com **Web address:** www.dyronmurphyarchitects.com

JAMES III, EDWIN G.
Industry: Pharmaceuticals **Born:** Baltimore, Maryland **Univ./degree:** A.A., Community College of Baltimore, 1972 **Current organization:** Guilford Pharmaceuticals Inc. **Title:** Senior Director, Facilities Management **Type of organization:** Manufacturing/Research & Development/Sales & Marketing **Major product:** Biopolymer chemotherapeutic wafers for the treatment of brain cancer; anti platelet-inhibitor for the treatment of acute coronary syndrome and novel treatments for Parkinson's disease **Area of distribution:** International **Expertise:** Facilities Management; Startup Bio Tech, Project Management and Professional Security Advisor **Affiliations:** N.A.P.E.; A.F.E.; A.S.I.S. **Hob./spts.:** Saltwater fishing, gardening **SIC code:** 87 **Address:** Guilford Pharmaceuticals Inc., 6611 Tributary St., Baltimore, MD 21224 **E-mail:** jamese@guilfordpharm.com

JANARDHAN, PALANI RAJ
Industry: Consulting **Born:** December 10, 1948, Bangalore, India **Univ./degree:** M.S., Mechanical Engineering, Military College of Electronics & Mechanical Engineering, India, 1979 **Current organization:** United Nations Office of Iraq Program **Title:** Mechanical Engineer **Type of organization:** United Nations **Major product:** Checking the engineering goods exported to Iraq for dual use **Area of distribution:** International **Expertise:** Engineering/dual use **Hob./spts.:** Woodcarving, railroad and aero modeling, landscaping **SIC code:** 87 **Address:** C-407, 61-20 Grand Central Pkwy., Forest Hills, NY 11375 **E-mail:** shamraj24@hotmail.com

JANCZYK, JOHN E.
Industry: Consulting **Univ./degree:** M.S., Criminal Law/Forensic Science, George Washington University, 1976 **Title:** Colonel USAF (Retired), Supervisory Criminal Investigator **Type of organization:** Self-employed **Major product:** Consulting **Area of distribution:** National **Expertise:** Investigations **Honors/awards:** Legion of Merit, Air Force **Affiliations:** Federal Criminal Investigation Association; Fraternal Order, Washington D.C. Police; Air Force Office of Special Investigations **SIC code:** 87 **Address:** Colonel USAF (Ret), 2823 Vixen Lane, Silver Spring, MD 20906-5324

JANECKY, DAVID R.
Industry: Research **Spouse:** Louise Anderson **Children:** Gregg 1988; Grant 1990 **Univ./degree:** A.B. Geology, University of California, Berkeley, 1975; UC Education Abroad Program, Geology, University of Bergen, Norway, 1973-74; Ph.D., Geology, University of Minnesota at Minneapolis, 1982 **Current organization:** Los Alamos National Laboratory **Title:** Deputy Group Leader for Environmental Protection Division, Ecology & Air Quality Group **Type of organization:** U.S. Department of Energy contract laboratory **Major product:** National security, energy, general research **Area of distribution:** National **Expertise:** Geochemistry/environment **Honors/awards:** Numerous including- LANL Director's Development Program; LANL Distinguished Performance Awards, WIPP Project-TRU Waste Characterization/Certification Team **Published works:** Numerous publications and reports including- Janecky, D.R., Seyfried W.E. Jr., 1984, Formation of Oceanic Ridge Crest Massive Sulfide Deposits: Incremental Reaction Models for Mixing Between Hydrothermal Solutions and Seawater. Geochim. Cos. Acta. 48, 2723-2738; Chen S., Dawson S.P., Doolen G.D., Janecky D.R., Lawniczak A., 1995, Lattice Methods and Their Applications to Reacting Systems. Computers & Chemical Engineering, 19, 617-646; Kaszuba J.P., Janecky D.R., Snow M.G., 2003, Carbon dioxide reaction processes in a model brine aquifer at 200 degrees Celsius and 200 bars: Implications for geologic sequestration of carbon. Applied Geochemistry, 18/7, 1065-1080; Clark D.L., Janecky D.R., Lane L.J., 2006, Application of science to actinide remediation actions at Rocky Flats, Physics Today (Sept.), 59, no. 9, 34-40, LAUR-06-4346; Letters & response, Physics Today (Sept.) 60, no. 9, 10 & 12 **Affiliations:** American Geophysical Union; Geochemical Society; American Association for the Advancement of Science (AAAS); Fellow, Society for Economic Geology; The Oceanography Society; Norsk Geologisk Forening (Geological Society of Norway); Order of the Golden Bear, University of California **Career accomplishments:** Research Geochemist; Management and Programmatic Experience highlights- Rocky Flats Environmental Technology Site; Actinide Migration Evaluation; LANL Environmental Management Program; US DOE Basic Energy Sciences; Chemistry, Geoscience and Biosciences Division, Geosciences Programs; LANL TRU Waste Characterization/Certification Program; has served on numerous advisory boards and review committees as well as being a Post Doctoral Scholar sponsor at LANL and a committee member for several Ph.D. students **Hob./spts.:** Skiing, fly-fishing, mountain climbing **SIC code:** 87 **Address:** Los Alamos National Laboratory, Environmental Protection Division, Ecology & Air Quality Group (ENV-EAQ), P.O. Box 1663, MS J978, Los Alamos, NM 87545 **E-mail:** janecky@lanl.gov **Web address:** www.emst.lanl.gov/janecky

JESPHER-DANIEL, JEYAPRAKASH
Industry: Semiconductors **Born:** September, 24, Madras, India **Univ./degree:** M.S., Chemistry, University of Madras, India, 1994; Ph.D., Polymer Science and Micro-Systems, Indian Institute of Technology, 2002 **Current organization:** I.B.M. Almaden Research Center **Title:** Post Doctoral Fellow **Type of organization:** Industrial research center **Major product:** Organic film transistors, micro fluidic devices **Area of distribution:** International **Expertise:** Molecular electronics and nanotechnology **Honors/awards:** D.A.A.D Award 2000, University of Freiburg, Germany; Sir P.T. Thomas Award for Excellence in Chemistry, 1994; First Prize Poster Presentation on Ultrathin and Ultrahydrophobic surfaces, Germany, 2003 **Published works:** 10 international publications **Affiliations:** I.E.E.E., American Chemical Society; Bay Area Nanotechnology Council **Hob./spts.:** Fly-fishing, performing in theatre, travel **SIC code:** 87 **Address:** Advanced Organic Materials Division, I.B.M. Almaden Research Center, 650 Harry Rd. (E-1 244), San Jose, CA 95120 **E-mail:** jpsamuel@us.ibm.com **Web address:** www.research.ibm.com

JOHNSON, ARNOLD IVAN
Industry: Consulting **Born:** June 3, 1919, Madison, Nebraska **Spouse:** Betty L. Spencer **Married:** June 3, 1941 **Children:** Robert Arnold; Bruce Gary; Carmen Sue; 10 grandchildren; 5 great-grandchildren **Univ./degree:** B.A., B.S.C.E., University of Nebraska; Honorary Ph.D., Hacettepe University, Ankara, Turkey **Current organization:** AIJ Water and Soil Consulting **Title:** President **Type of organization:** Private consulting firm **Major product:** Water and soil consulting **Area of distribution:** International, especially Turkey and Middle-East countries **Expertise:** Geohydrology, land subsidence, artificial recharge; Registered Professional Engineer **Honors/awards:** 1996 Outstanding Service Award, ASTM; USGS John Wesley Powell Award; ANSI Finegan standards Award; AIH C.V. Thesis Award; Honorary member, A.S.C.E.; Honorary President, I.A.H.S.; A. Ivan Johnson Outstanding Service Award, ASTM; Listed in Men and Women of Science; Meritorious Service Award, U.S. Dept. of Interior **Published works:** 130 technical articles and books published by U.S. Geological survey and International Societies **Affiliations:** American Society for Testing Materials; American Water Resources Association; American Society of Civil Engineers; International Association of Hydrological Sciences; National Society of Professional Engineers; American Institute of Hydrology; International Association for Hydrologists; National Ground Water Association; American Society Remote Sensing; American Geophysical Union; Life Member, Archaeological Institute of America **Career accomplishments:** Developed many test methods for soil and rock investigations that later became ASTM standards; Solved water problems in many developing countries **Hob./spts.:** Travel, history, reading **SIC code:** 87 **Address:** AIJ Water and Soil Consulting, 7474 Upham Ct., Arvada, CO 80003

JOHNSON, DOUGLAS R.
Industry: Construction/design **Born:** May 10, 1948, Payson, Utah **Univ./degree:** B.S., Civil Engineering, Brigham Young University, 1973 **Current organization:** Project Control Inc. **Title:** Co-owner/Project Manager **Type of organization:** Consulting firm **Major product:** Project management services **Area of distribution:** West Coast **Expertise:** Engineering/project management **Affiliations:** A.S.C.E. **SIC code:** 87 **Address:** Project Control Inc., 3809 S. 300 West, Salt Lake City, UT 84115 **E-mail:** djohnson@projectcontrol-inc.com

JOHNSON, ELIZABETH
Industry: Financial consulting **Born:** April 16, 1961, New York, New York **Univ./degree:** A.A.S., Education, La Guardia College, 1981; Certified American Sign Language, Goldsboro Community College **Current organization:** MEJ Personal Business Services, Inc. **Title:** Vice President **Type of organization:** Consulting **Major product:** Financial consulting/interpreting services **Area of distribution:** National **Expertise:** Sign language, management of the financial and interpreting services **Affiliations:** Registry of Interpreters for the Deaf; National Association of the Deaf **Hob./spts.:** Ice skating, reading, bike riding **SIC code:** 87 **Address:** MEJ Personal Business Services, Inc., 245 E. 116th St., 1st Floor, New York, NY 10029 **E-mail:** elliieZU@aol.com

JOHNSON, THOMAS E.
Industry: Mental health **Born:** July 11, 1945, Dover, New Jersey **Univ./degree:** Attended Newark College of Engineering & College of DuPage **Current organization:** DBSA Aurora (Depression and Bipolar Support Alliance) **Title:** President **Type of organization:** Therapy group **Major product:** Mood disorders support **Area of distribution:** International **Expertise:** Self-support group leader **Affiliations:** Illinois Rt. 66 Association **Hob./spts.:** Grandchildren, biking, country music **SIC code:** 86 **Address:** DBSA Aurora, 1N286 Woods Ave., Carol Stream, IL 60188 **E-mail:** sneezercat@aol.com

JOHNSON-HENDERSON, LORA K.
Industry: Social service housing **Born:** April 15, Marion, Indiana **Univ./degree:** Medical Office Management, Aristotle College, 1998 **Title:** Community Program Director/Property Manager **Type of organization:** Property management **Major product:** Single family, scattered site housing and special program housing **Expertise:** Programs to assist youth, persons at risk of being homeless, pregnant or victims of domestic violence, re-entry (prison based), senior/elder care; Section 8 and Section 42 housing **Honors/awards:** Humanitarian of the Year, 2002; Prodigy Award, Best Community Programs, 2003; Outstanding Achievement 2003 and 2004; Golden Sneaker, JDRF (Juvenile Diabetes Research Foundation), 2005 **Affiliations:** United Way of Central Indiana, Leadership Training for Development and Diversity, 2004 **Hob./spts.:** Reading, baking **SIC code:** 83 **Address:** New Zion Community Development Foundation, 3628 Virginia Ave, Louisville, KY 40211 **E-mail:** lhenderson@vanrooy.com

JONES, GEORGE A.
Industry: Consulting/mining **Born:** June 13, 1952, Lowell, Massachusetts **Univ./degree:** B.S., Business Administration, Southern Utah State College, 1976 **Current organization:** George A. Jones Consulting **Title:** President **Type of organization:** Industrial consulting **Major product:** Machinery operations and maintenance **Area of distribution:** Nevada **Expertise:** Research and development, Certified Welder **Published works:** 2 magazine articles **Hob./spts.:** Golfing, gardening, building houses without power tools, has lived for free since 1987 **SIC code:** 87 **Address:** George A. Jones Consulting, 1905 S. Third East, Ely, NV 89301 **E-mail:** pacegj@directmail.com

JONES, JONATHAN F.
Industry: Consulting **Born:** July 5, 1973, Marietta, Georgia **Univ./degree:** B.S., Civil Engineering, Georgia Tech University **Current organization:** Elite Engineering **Title:** Civil Engineer **Type of organization:** Engineering firm **Major product:** Land planning, civil engineering, surveying **Area of distribution:** Georgia **Expertise:** Civil engineering **Affiliations:** American Society of Civil Engineering **Hob./spts.:** Hunting, fishing **SIC code:** 87 **Address:** Elite Engineering, 276 Hiram Acworth Hwy., Hiram, GA 30141 **E-mail:** jjones@elite-engineering.com **Web address:** www.elite-engineering.com

JONES, WALTER C.
Industry: Social services **Born:** July 14, 1954 **Univ./degree:** M.S., Jackson State University, 1989 **Current organization:** Madison County Human Resource **Title:** Executive Director/Founder of Company (1985) **Type of organization:** Community action agency **Major product:** Human service needs **Area of distribution:** Canton, Mississippi **Expertise:** Social work **Published works:** Article in Transportation Journal **Hob./spts.:** Artist, painting, singing, acting **SIC code:** 83 **Address:** Madison County Human Resource, 3141 S. Liberty St., Canton, MS 39046 **E-mail:** wcjhra2000@aol.com

JOSEPH, JOJI A.
Industry: Medical equipment **Univ./degree:** B.S., Computer Engineering, Stony Brook State University, 2003; M.S. Candidate, New York Institute of Technology **Current organization:** Fonar Corp. **Title:** Design Engineer **Type of organization:** Manufacturing **Major product:** MRI scanners **Area of distribution:** National **Expertise:** Engineering **Affiliations:** Engineering Honorary Society **Hob./spts.:** Robotics, electronic projects **SIC code:** 87 **Address:** Fonar Corp., 110 Marcus Dr., Melville, NY 11747 **E-mail:** jjoseph@fonar.com

JOSEPHSON, HARVEY A.
Industry: Accounting **Born:** April 13, 1945, Brooklyn, New York **Current organization:** Josephson, Luxenberg & Kance CPA's, P.C. **Title:** President **Type of organization:** Accounting firm **Major product:** Accounting, tax and management services **Area of distribution:** National **Expertise:** Tax preparation and management **Affiliations:** A.I.C.P.A.; N.Y.S.C.P.A. **Hob./spts.:** Golf **SIC code:** 87 **Address:** Josephson, Luxenberg & Kance CPA's, P.C., 21 E. 40th St., New York, NY 10016 **E-mail:** hjosephson@aol.com

KAAKOUCH, ZIAD N.
Industry: Engineering **Born:** August 7, 1969, Beirut, Lebanon **Univ./degree:** B.S.C.E., California State Polytechnical University, 1993 **Current organization:** DZ Engineering, Inc. **Title:** Vice President **Type of organization:** Consulting engineering **Major product:** Service **Area of distribution:** Arizona **Expertise:** Civil engineering **Affiliations:** A.S.C.E. **Hob./spts.:** Soccer, hunting, travel **SIC code:** 87 **Address:** DZ Engineering, Inc., 4648 E. Shea Blvd., #A-170, Phoenix, AZ 85028 **E-mail:** dzengineer@earthlink.net

KAPADIA, KIRIT N.
Industry: Consulting **Univ./degree:** M.S., University of Wisconsin **Current organization:** Kapadia Consulting **Title:** Consultant **Type of organization:** Consulting firm **Major product:** Technology consulting **Area of distribution:** National **Expertise:** Manufacturing engineering **Affiliations:** S.M.E. **Hob./spts.:** Woodworking, photography **SIC code:** 87 **Address:** Kapadia Consulting, 3417 Waterpoint Dr., Columbus, OH 43221 **E-mail:** kkapadia@columbus.rr.com

KAPPERS, JEAN M.
Industry: Tax preparation **Born:** March 23, 1951, Wisconsin **Univ./degree:** H&R Block Income Tax Courses **Current organization:** Jean's Income Tax Preparation **Title:** Owner **Type of organization:** Self-employed **Major product:** Preparing tax returns **Area of distribution:** Sheboygan Falls, Wisconsin **Expertise:** Tax preparations **Affiliations:** N.A.T.P. **Hob./spts.:** Sunday school teacher, crafts, grandchildren **SIC code:** 87 **Address:** 643 David Ave., Sheboygan Falls, WI 53085 **E-mail:** kappers@invella.net

KARASTATHIS, KHRISTOS E.
Industry: Architecture **Born:** Volos, Greece **Univ./degree:** B.Arch., Pratt Institute, New York, 1962 **Current organization:** Karastathis Architects and A Design Built Group, Inc. (Construction Management) **Title:** Principal/Owner **Type of organization:** Architectural firm **Major product:** Architectural services **Area of distribution:** International **Expertise:** Architecture, planning and design **Honors/awards:** Queensboro President, Winner of Architectural Competitions in U.S., Iran and Bahrain **Published works:** Schools, houses, "A Look at Home of the Future", "Green Bldgs." **Affiliations:** Columbia University **Hob./spts.:** Tennis, stamp and art collecting, art, photography **SIC code:** 87 **Address:** Karastathis Architects, 410 E. 51st St., New York, NY 10022 **E-mail:** kartisarchitect@yahoo.com

KARBE, FRANK
Industry: Biotechnology **Born:** April 17, 1968, Kassel, Germany **Univ./degree:** M.B.A., The Koblenz School of Corporate Management, With, Germany **Current organization:** Exelixis **Title:** Chief Financial Officer **Type of organization:** Biotechnology **Major product:** Development of cancer drugs **Area of distribution:** International **Expertise:** Administration, finance, lecturing **Honors/awards:** World's Fittest Executive, "Iron Man America", 2005 **Published works:** Several newspaper articles on financial strategy **Affiliations:** Financial Executives International; Board Member, Biopharmaceutical Management Center **Hob./spts.:** Windsurfing, cooking, reading **SIC code:** 87 **Address:** Exelixis, 210 E. Grand Ave., South San Francisco, CA 94083 **E-mail:** fkarbe@exelixis.com **Web address:** www.exelixis.com

KARSH, JEROME W.
Industry: Financial **Born:** January 16, 1936, Denver, Colorado **Univ./degree:** M.B.A., Business Administration, University of Denver, 1967; B.S., Finance, University of Denver **Current organization:** Karsh Consulting P.C. **Title:** Chairman of the Board **Type of organization:** Accounting firm **Major product:** Full service public account-

ing firm **Area of distribution:** National **Expertise:** Business valuations; litigation support; qualified as an Expert Witness in over 2000 court cases; CPA license **Honors/awards:** Reference in "Best Lawyers in America Directory of Experts" **Affiliations:** Colorado Society of Certified Public Accountants; American Institute of Certified Public Accountants **Hob./spts.:** President, U.S. Billiards Association **SIC code:** 87 **Address:** Karsh Consulting P.C., 650 S. Cherry St., Suite 115, Denver, CO 80246 **E-mail:** jkarsh@karshcpa.com

KASHULINES, LESLIE B.
Industry: Financial services **Born:** January 24, 1948, New Hampshire **Univ./degree:** Attended Daniel Webster and Hesser College **Current organization:** LBK Bookkeeping & Accounting **Title:** Owner/Certified Tax Professional **Type of organization:** Professional services **Major product:** Taxes and accounting services **Area of distribution:** National **Expertise:** Taxation **Affiliations:** N.S.T.P.; Past Treasurer, VFW Auxiliary; Member, VFW, American Legion **Hob./spts.:** Race cars, granddaughter, crafts, traveling **SIC code:** 87 **Address:** Lassiter Bookkeeping & Accounting, P.O. Box 589, Dunstable, MA 01827-1703 **E-mail:** payne945@aol.com

KASSAB, HOSSAM
Industry: Consulting engineering **Born:** February 2, 1959, Monsoura, Egypt **Univ./degree:** B.S.M.E., Monsoura University, 1983 **Current organization:** Engineering Maintenance Solutions, Inc. **Title:** President **Type of organization:** Consulting firm **Major product:** Engineering services **Area of distribution:** National **Expertise:** Engineering **Honors/awards:** Certificate of Service, El Salam Hyatt Hotel, Cairo, Egypt; Certificate of Achievement, Refrigeration Service Engineering Society, Movenpick Hotel, Cairo, Egypt **Affiliations:** A.S.M.E.; N.S.P.E. **Hob./spts.:** Tennis, chess, volleyball, travel **SIC code:** 87 **Address:** 21 Marseille Way, Foothill Ranch, CA 92610 **E-mail:** hkassab@thepacificcondo.com

KATSANIS, ANDREW T.
Industry: Religion **Born:** February 26, 1975, Fort Wayne, Indiana **Univ./degree:** B.A., Pastoral Ministry, Warner Southern College, 1995 **Current organization:** Youth for Christ **Title:** Executive Director **Type of organization:** Not for profit youth outreach **Major product:** Relational style outreach **Area of distribution:** Sebring, Florida **Expertise:** Evangelism, public speaking **Hob./spts.:** Golf **SIC code:** 86 **Address:** Youth for Christ, P.O. Box 1526, Sebring, FL 33870

KATZ, ELLEN H.
Industry: Business/Education **Born:** January 7, 1935, Long Beach, New York **Univ./degree:** B.S., Home Economics Education, Brooklyn College, City Univ. of New York, 1956; M.S., Secondary Education, Hofstra Univ., 1962; Ph.D., Home Economics in Higher Education, New York Univ., 1992 **Current organization:** Mentor Talk, Inc. **Title:** President/Partner **Type of organization:** Educational services/career services **Major product:** Career services (career networking, career placement, resume preparation) and educational services (workshops/seminars/classes/research) in career management, career mentoring, career counseling and advice **Area of distribution:** International **Expertise:** Career management and peer review, career mentoring and networking (especially young women), career counseling, career placement, resume preparation, design and implementation of business/education internship programs **Honors/awards:** Assoc. of Home Appliance Manufacturers ALMA Award, 1975, 1976, 1977, 1978; Certificate of Appreciation, Field Study Program, College of Human Ecology, Cornell Univ., 1979; Education Scholastic Research Award, New York Univ., 1988; Certificate of Merit Award, Bureau of Human Services, N.Y. City Public Schools, 1988; Who's Who Among Students in American Univ. and Colleges, 1990; Certificate of Appreciation for Sensitivity and Assistance to Older New Yorkers, N.Y. State Dept. for the Aging, 1990; Honorary Member, Women's Int'l Network of Utility Professionals, 1997; Challenge '96 Team Award Winner, Consolidated Edison Co. of N.Y., 1997 **Published works:** Rowley, M. & Katz., E. (1992), "An Evaluation of Changing Expectations and Perceptions of Professional Organizations", Journal of the Utah Academy of Sciences, Arts and Letters; Katz, E., Dalton, S., Giacquinta, J. (1994), "Status Risk Taking and Receptivity of Home Economics Teachers to a Statewide Curriculum Innovation" (based on doctoral thesis), Home Economics Research Journal; Katz, E., Rowley, M. Eggert, D., Williams, J.D. (pending), "A Model Supporting the Need for Accountability of Professional Organizations in Meeting Different Member Expectations of Benefits", ERIC ED; 31 collective works, articles, journals, papers **Affiliations:** Nat'l Assoc. of Women Business Owners; Nat'l Assoc. of Female Executives; Women's Int'l Network of Utility Professionals; Amer. Assoc. of Family and Consumer Services; Amer. Educ't'l Research Assoc.; Advisory Committee, Eleanor and Lou Gehrig MDA/ALS Center, Columbia Presbyterian Medical Center, NYC; Student/Alumni Networking Events, New York Univ; The Woodhull Institute of Ethical Leadership **Career accomplishments:** Numerous awards and listings from professional organizations and universities **Hob./spts.:** Swimming, reading **SIC code:** 87 **Address:** Mentor Talk, Inc., 96 Fifth Ave., Suite 4D, New York, NY 10011-7607 **E-mail:** katzl@verizon.net **Web address:** www.mentortalk.com

KAWASAKI, GREGORY
Industry: Computer hardware/software **Born:** February 2, 1956, Los Angeles, California **Current organization:** CSC Consulting **Title:** Partner **Type of organization:** IT consulting firm **Major product:** IT needs, assessments, implementations, outsourcing, integration **Area of distribution:** International **Expertise:** Business process, software/hardware integration **Hob./spts.:** Info technology **SIC code:** 87 **Address:** CSC Consulting, 2206 Tall Pine Dr., Duarte, CA 91010 **E-mail:** gkawasaki@csc.com **Web address:** www.csc.com

KEENAN, TERRANCE
Industry: Philanthropy **Born:** February 1, 1924, Philadelphia, Pennsylvania **Univ./degree:** B.A., Yale University, 1950 **Current organization:** The Robert Wood Johnson Foundation **Title:** Special Program Consultant **Type of organization:** Philanthropic foundation **Major product:** Health and healthcare grant making **Area of distribution:** National **Expertise:** Program design and implementation, financial services, business development, project management, communications; frequent lecturer and public speaker on medical education **Honors/awards:** Served in U.S. Naval Air Corps in World War II **Published works:** Articles, journals, short fiction books **Hob./spts.:** Walking, gardening **SIC code:** 86 **Address:** 435 Sterling St., Newtown, PA 18940 **E-mail:** tkeenan@rwjf.org **Web address:** www.rwjf.org

KEILEN, DONALD H.
Industry: Consulting **Born:** October 24, 1931, Portland, Michigan **Univ./degree:** B.S., Radio Engineering, Tri-State College, 1957 **Current organization:** D.H. Keilen Enterprises **Title:** Owner **Type of organization:** Consulting/manufacturing **Major product:** Wireless communication products/GPS components **Area of distribution:** National **Expertise:** Engineering, high surveillance equipment design **Published works:** Several publications, over 25 U.S. patents **Hob./spts.:** Flying and building aircraft, fishing, oldies music **SIC code:** 87 **Address:** D.H. Keilen Enterprises, 1171 Morgan Dr., Kingsburg, CA 93631 **E-mail:** gdkent@netzero.com

KELLY, DAVID R.
Industry: Civil engineering **Born:** September 26, 1967, New York, New York **Univ./degree:** B.S.C.E., Brooklyn Polytechnic Institute, 1992 **Current organization:** Diocese of Rockville Centre **Title:** Capital Project Consultant **Type of organization:** Nonprofit **Major product:** Design and construction of churches, parish centers and schools **Area of distribution:** New York **Expertise:** Capital planning, design and construction management **Honors/awards:** E.I.T. Certification; Member, Chi Epsilon; United Brotherhood of Carpenters, Journey man Certification **Affiliations:** American Society of Civil Engineers **Hob./spts.:** Baseball/carpentry **SIC code:** 86 **Address:** Diocese of Rockville Centre, 50 N. Park Ave., Rockville Centre, NY 11570 **E-mail:** dkelly@drvc.org

KELLY, KATHLEEN M.
Industry: Social services **Born:** September 4, 1950, Paterson, New Jersey **Univ./degree:** B.S., Psychology, University of South Florida, 1989 **Current organization:** The Kimberly Home, Inc. **Title:** Executive Director **Type of organization:** Resource center **Major product:** Support services, infant care, transitional housing **Area of distribution:** Clearwater, Florida **Expertise:** Administration **Affiliations:** President, Tampa Bay Healthcare Collaborators **Hob./spts.:** Walking, running, violin **SIC code:** 83 **Address:** The Kimberly Home, Inc., 1189 N.E. Cleveland St., Clearwater, FL 33755 **E-mail:** kkelly@kimberlyhome.org **Web address:** www.kimberlyhome.org

KELLY-KNIGHT, PHYLLIS M.
Industry: Consulting **Univ./degree:** A.S., Medical Technology, Gaston State Community College, Alabama, 1988; B.S., Mathematics & Biology, University of Alabama, 1992; M.B.A., Samford University, Alabama, 1997; J.D., Birmingham School of

Law, 2004 **Current organization:** Knight Works LLC **Title:** President/CEO **Type of organization:** Consulting, equipment supply and design **Major product:** Hyperbaric turnkey installation and consulting **Area of distribution:** International **Expertise:** Turnkey and consultation for hyperbaric chambers **Affiliations:** A.S.C.P.; A.A.B.E.; N.A.F.T.L.; A.A.T.L. **SIC code:** 87 **Address:** Knight Works LLC, 3004 Arbor Bend, Hoover, AL 35244 **E-mail:** p_kellyknight@bellsouth.net

KEMMER, CHRISTINA
Industry: Consulting **Born:** January 5, 1949, Milwaukee, Wisconsin **Univ./degree:** B.S., Loyola University, 1970 **Current organization:** Communications Pacific, Inc. **Title:** Executive Vice President **Type of organization:** Full service public relations **Major product:** Business services: corporate, marketing, advertising, the internet **Area of distribution:** International **Expertise:** Community building, global lecturing **Hob./spts.:** The open ocean, paddling, travel, art **SIC code:** 87 **Address:** Communications Pacific, Inc., TOPA Financial Center, 745 Fort So. PH., Honolulu, HI 96813 **E-mail:** ckemmer@commpac.com **Web address:** www.commpac.com

KHTEIAN-KEETON, F. "TEDDY"
Industry: Communications/research **Univ./degree:** Ph.D., Social Work, Columbus University; Post Graduate, Federal Grant Law and Public Administration, George Washington University **Type of organization:** Research **Major product:** Research - juvenile program development, strategies and evaluations **Area of distribution:** National **Expertise:** Lecturing, writing, 2004 research, conflict resolution **Honors/awards:** Ronald Reagan Award **Published works:** First guide to basic music in the U.S. (children's book) **Affiliations:** Past Member, The International Society for Prevention of Child Abuse and Neglect **SIC code:** 87 **Address:** 1927 E. 4300 North, Buhl, ID 83316 **E-mail:** tekeeto@research.myrs.net

KILIC, MUSTAFA HAKAN
Industry: Aerospace **Born:** February 20, 1972, Ankara, Turkey **Univ./degree:** Ph.D., Georgia Institute of Technology, Atlanta, Georgia **Current organization:** AdTech Systems Research Inc. **Title:** Research Scientist/Engineer **Type of organization:** Consulting, engineering, R&D firm **Major product:** Testing and analysis of composite materials, software **Area of distribution:** Ohio **Expertise:** Engineering, composite materials **Published works:** Articles **Affiliations:** A.S.C.E.: S.A.M.P.E.; A.S.C.; S.E.I. **SIC code:** 87 **Address:** AdTech Systems Research Inc., 1342 N. Fairfield Rd., Beavercreek, OH 45432 **E-mail:** mhakankilic@yahoo.com

KLINE, BERNARD H.
Industry: Financial **Born:** April 14, 1915, Pennsylvania **Univ./degree:** B.A., The Wharton School of the University of Pennsylvania, 1936 **Current organization:** Kline & Kline PC **Title:** Owner **Type of organization:** CPA firm **Major product:** Accounting, taxes, personal financial planning **Area of distribution:** Pennsylvania **Expertise:** Financial advice/planning **Affiliations:** P.C.P.A.; A.I.C.P.A. **Hob./spts.:** Writing, painting **SIC code:** 87 **Address:** Kline & Kline PC, 87 N. Church St., Hazleton, PA 18201 **E-mail:** rkline@epix.net

KLONTZ, JAMES M.
Industry: Consulting **Born:** May 3, 1920, Kent, Washington **Univ./degree:** B.A., Architecture, University of Washington **Current organization:** Klontz & Associates **Title:** Architect **Type of organization:** Architectural firm **Major product:** Building design **Area of distribution:** International **Expertise:** Industrial building design **Affiliations:** American Institute of Architects **Hob./spts.:** Salmon fishing **SIC code:** 87 **Address:** Klontz & Associates, 4000 Aurora Ave. North, Seattle, WA 98103-7853 **E-mail:** klontz-architect@qwest.net

KNAPP, DONALD D.
Industry: Land surveying/civil engineering **Born:** November 23, 1921, Rio Grande County, Colorado **Current organization:** Knapp Engineering & Surveying Services **Title:** Owner **Type of organization:** Surveying and engineering firm **Major product:** Land surveying and engineering services **Area of distribution:** Alamosa, Colorado **Expertise:** Land surveyor and engineer **Affiliations:** Professional Land Surveyors of Colorado **Hob./spts.:** Reading **SIC code:** 87 **Address:** Knapp Engineering & Surveying Services, 11164 Hwy. 160 E., Alamosa, CO 81101

KOJALO, V. WALTER
Industry: Metal and plastic materials testing **Born:** February 17, 1924, Tapa, Estonia **Univ./degree:** B.S., Chemistry and Pharmacy, University of Bonn, Germany, 1950; Applied Metallurgy, Metal Engineering Institute, 1984 **Current organization:** Massachusetts Materials Research, Inc. **Title:** Quality Assurance Manager **Type of organization:** Testing laboratory **Major product:** Materials test data/results for plastics and metals **Area of distribution:** National **Expertise:** Quality systems, metallurgy **Affiliations:** American Society for Testing and Materials; American Society for Metals International; American Society for Quality Assurance **Hob./spts.:** Reading **SIC code:** 87 **Address:** Massachusetts Materials Research, Inc., 1500 Century Dr., West Boylston, MA 01583-1725 **E-mail:** wkojalo@massmaterials.com

KONG, LARRY M.
Industry: Telecommunications **Born:** January 20, 1962, Beijing **Univ./degree:** Beijing Polytech University, 1988 **Current organization:** Vida Network Technologies, Inc. **Title:** President, CEO **Type of organization:** Research and development **Major product:** Telecommunication, hardware & software **Area of distribution:** International **Expertise:** Management and engineering **Affiliations:** O.S.C. **Hob./spts.:** Golf, tennis **SIC code:** 87 **Address:** Vida Network Technologies, Inc., 31 Debra Dr., Dayton, NJ 08810 **E-mail:** lkong@vidanetwork.com

KORTSCH, WILLIAM J.
Industry: Consulting/real estate **Born:** June 21, 1954, Butte, Montana **Univ./degree:** B.Arch., University of Notre Dame, 1977 **Current organization:** RGA Development Consulting **Title:** Principal/Vice President **Type of organization:** Design/consulting firm **Major product:** Real estate development consulting **Area of distribution:** California **Expertise:** Architecture; CDS Certification **Affiliations:** A.I.A.; American Society of Landscape Architects **SIC code:** 87 **Address:** RGA Development Consulting, 964 Fifth Ave., #509, San Diego, CA 92101 **E-mail:** bill@rga-pd.com

KRAJEWSKI, MICHAEL R.
Industry: Government/forensic chemistry **Born:** Buffalo, New York **Univ./degree:** M.B.A., B.S., Chemistry, Canisius College; M.A., SUNY Buffalo, 1984 **Current organization:** County of Erie, CPS Forensic Lab **Title:** Senior Forensic Chemist **Type of organization:** Government **Major product:** Chemical analysis **Area of distribution:** Buffalo, New York **Expertise:** I.D. of drugs; ignitable liquid analysis **Affiliations:** A.S.T.M.; A.A.F.S.; A.C.S. **Hob./spts.:** Running, fishing, travel **SIC code:** 87 **Address:** County of Erie, CPS Forensic Lab, 45 Elm St., Buffalo, NY 14203 **E-mail:** krajewsm@erie.gov **Web address:** www.erie.gov

KRAUSE, MANFRED O.
Industry: Research **Born:** March 11, 1931, Stuttgart, Germany **Univ./degree:** Ph.D., Stuttgart University, Germany, 1960 **Current organization:** Oakridge National Laboratory **Title:** Senior Scientist (Retired) **Type of organization:** National laboratory **Major product:** Research **Area of distribution:** International **Expertise:** Atomic physics **Published works:** 180 articles, 6 book chapters **Affiliations:** F.A.P.S.; A.A.A.S.; Sigma Xai **Hob./spts.:** Nature conservancy **SIC code:** 87 **Address:** 125 Baltimore Dr., Oak Ridge, TN 37830 **E-mail:** mok@ornl.gov

KRUMMEN, WILLIAM J.
Industry: Technology consulting **Born:** August 22, 1954, Cincinnati, Ohio **Univ./degree:** B.S., Zoology, Miami University, 1976; M.B.A., University of Michigan, 1978 **Current organization:** Hemispheric Center for Environmental Technology **Title:** Assistant Director **Type of organization:** Research center **Major product:** Project management, technical support **Area of distribution:** International **Expertise:** General management and strategy **Published works:** 2 articles **Affiliations:** Board Member, Quail Unlimited; Ducks Unlimited **Hob./spts.:** Conservation **SIC code:** 87 **Address:** Hemispheric Center for Environmental Technology, 105 Mitchell Rd., Oak Ridge, TN 37830 **E-mail:** krummen@hcet.fiu.edu **Web address:** www.hcet.fiu.edu

KUCIEWSKI, PATRICK M.
Industry: Education **Born:** August 20, 1958, Boston, Massachusetts **Univ./degree:** B.F.A., Music Education, SUNY Buffalo, 1980; M.A., Education, Niagara College, 1993 **Current organization:** Niagara Summer Fine Arts Program, Inc. **Title:** Founder/Executive Director **Type of organization:** Not-for-profit **Major product:** Education program/fine arts **Area of distribution:** New York **Expertise:** Theatre, music **Published works:** Write-ups **Affiliations:** A.S.C.A.; M.E.N.C. **Hob./spts.:** Music, theatre, fine arts **SIC code:** 86 **Address:** Niagara Summer Fine Arts Program, Inc., 1337 99th St., Niagara Falls, NY 14304 **E-mail:** nsfapinc@aol.com

KUMAR, SANTOSH KULSHRESTHA
Industry: Community services **Born:** February 2, 1949, Rajasthan, India **Univ./degree:** B.S., Biology, Jodhpur Rajasthan University, 1969; LL.B., with Honors, 1972; LL.M., 1974, AMU, India; A.S., Design & Desktop Publishing, Roosevelt University, Chicago, 1989 **Current organization:** Metropolitan Asian Family Services Organization **Title:** Founding Executive Director **Type of organization:** Non-profit **Major product:** Education, elderly services and counseling **Area of distribution:** Illinois **Expertise:** Administration and law **Affiliations:** Illinois State Bar Association; Board Member/Vice President, C.L.E.S.E.; President, D.S.S.C. **Hob./spts.:** Reading, painting, helping people **SIC code:** 86 **Address:** Metropolitan Asian Family Services Organization, 902 W. Carolyn St., Palatine, IL 60067 **E-mail:** santosh1250@hotmail.com **Web address:** www.mafs.itgo.com

KURTZ JR., RONALD D.
Industry: Architecture **Born:** September 11, 1962, Harrisburg, Pennsylvania **Univ./degree:** B.A., Architecture, Pennsylvania State University, 1987 **Current organization:** Randy Burkett Lighting Design **Title:** Associate and Senior Designer **Type of organization:** Consulting services **Major product:** Lighting design **Area of distribution:** International **Expertise:** Lighting design **Affiliations:** I.A.L.D.; A.E.S.N.A.

Hob./spts.: History, reading **SIC code:** 87 **Address:** Randy Burkett Lighting Design, 609 E. Lockwood Ave., Suite 201, St. Louis, MO 63119 **E-mail:** ron@rbldi.com

KUZIEMSKI, NAOMI E.
Industry: Educational consulting **Born:** December 22, Philadelphia, Pennsylvania **Univ./degree:** B.A., Education, 1945; M.S., 1949, Temple University, Pennsylvania **Current organization:** College Consultants Co. **Title:** Educational Consultant **Type of organization:** Independent consulting **Major product:** Counseling services **Area of distribution:** Philadelphia and Cheltenham, Pennsylvania **Expertise:** College guidance **Affiliations:** American Association of University Women; National Association of College Admission Counselors **Hob./spts.:** Travel **SIC code:** 87 **Address:** College Consultants Co., 7 Lawnside Rd., Cheltenham, PA 19012-1812 **E-mail:** naomikuz@aol.com

KYTE, CHARLES L.
Industry: Pharmaceuticals **Born:** May 1, 1975, Brooklyn, New York **Univ./degree:** M.P.H., Mt. Sinai School of Medicine, 2005 **Current organization:** Schering Plough Research Institute **Title:** Clinical Index Researcher **Type of organization:** Research **Major product:** Compliance **Area of distribution:** International **Expertise:** Clinical documentation, clinical trials **Affiliations:** American College Health Association; American Public Health Association **Hob./spts.:** Iron man competition, travel, physical fitness **SIC code:** 87 **Address:** Schering Plough Research Institute, 50 Lawrence Rd., Springfield, NJ 07081 **E-mail:** charles_kyte@hotmail.com

LACHMAN, LEON
Industry: Consulting **Born:** January 29, 1929, Bronx, New York **Univ./degree:** Ph.D., University of Wisconsin, 1956 **Current organization:** Lachman Consultant Services, Inc. **Title:** President **Type of organization:** Consulting **Major product:** Pharmaceuticals, biotechnology, medical devices, diagnostics **Area of distribution:** International **Expertise:** Regulatory compliance **Honors/awards:** Honorary Doctorate, Columbia University **Published works:** 70+ publications, Journal of Pharmaceutical Science **Affiliations:** P.D.A.; A.P.H.A.; A.A.P.S. **SIC code:** 87 **Address:** Lachman Consultant Services, Inc., 1600 Stewart Ave., Westbury, NY 11590 **E-mail:** llachman@lachmanconsultants.com

LAHTI, DON ROCCO S.
Industry: Engineering/consulting **Born:** November 4, 1948, Duluth, Minnesota **Univ./degree:** B.S.M.E., University of Minnesota at Minneapolis, 1974; M.S.M.E., 1981; Ph.D., 1994, University of Minnesota at Duluth **Current organization:** Fired Heater Specialists, Inc. **Title:** President **Type of organization:** Consulting firm **Major product:** Consulting service for fired heater design, fabrication, erection **Area of distribution:** International **Expertise:** Engineering **Published works:** 30+ articles **Affiliations:** American Chemical Engineering Society **Hob./spts.:** Golf, physical fitness, travel, reading **SIC code:** 87 **Address:** 1520 E. Bowie St., Beeville, TX 78102

LAKHOVA, LERA
Industry: Metal finishing **Born:** September 3, 1952, Nalchik, Russia **Univ./degree:** M.S., Electrical Engineering, St. Petersburg State Polytechnic University of Russia, 1980 **Current organization:** Metal Surfaces Inc. **Title:** Lab Manager, Senior Processing Engineer **Type of organization:** Engineering firm **Major product:** Electroplating, electroless plating **Area of distribution:** International **Expertise:** Electrochemistry **Affiliations:** American Electroplaters and Surface Finishers Society **Hob./spts.:** Travel **SIC code:** 87 **Address:** Metal Surfaces Inc., 6060 Shull St., Bell Gardens, CA 90201-6297 **E-mail:** lbakhova@aol.com **Web address:** www.metalsurfaces.com

LAM, JEROME K.
Industry: Consulting/engineering **Born:** January 4, 1958 Hong Kong, China **Univ./degree:** M.S., University of Southern California, 1981 **Current organization:** Innovative Engineering Group, Inc. (IEG) **Title:** President **Type of organization:** Consulting firm **Major product:** Building design **Area of distribution:** Monterey Park, California **Expertise:** Building consulting, engineering **Affiliations:** N.S.P.E.; L.E.E.D.; A.S.H.R.A.E.; N.F.P.A. **Hob./spts.:** Skiing, deep sea fishing **SIC code:** 87 **Address:** Innovative Engineering Group, Inc. (IEG), 2550 Corporate Place, Suite C100, Monterey Park, CA 91754 **E-mail:** jl@iegeng.com

LAMBRECHT, CHRISTOPHER L.
Industry: Military electronics **Born:** June 18, 1972, St. Joseph, Michigan **Univ./degree:** B.S.E.E., University of Michigan, 1995; M.S.E.E., University of South Florida, 1998 **Current organization:** Raytheon Corp. **Title:** Senior Engineer **Type of organization:** R&D **Major product:** Software **Area of distribution:** National **Expertise:** Digital communications and signal processing in electrical engineering **Honors/awards:** Raytheon Outstanding Achievement Award in 1999, 2000, 2004 **Affiliations:** I.E.E.E. **Hob./spts.:** Softball, physical fitness (running), the outdoors, fluent in Spanish **SIC code:** 87 **Address:** Raytheon Corp., 6049 22nd Ave. North, St. Petersburg, FL 33710 **E-mail:** chris.lambrecht@ieee.org

LANC, JOHN J.
Industry: Engineering **Born:** September 6, 1941, Prague, Czech Republic **Univ./degree:** M.S., Civil Engineering, Czech Republic University, 1963 **Current organization:** Lanc & Tully Engineering and Surveying, P.C. **Title:** P.E./L.S./Partner **Type of organization:** Engineering design firm **Major product:** Site and subdivision plans, infrastructure **Area of distribution:** New York **Expertise:** Civil engineering and land surveying **Affiliations:** F.A.C.S.M.; N.S.P.E.; A.S.C.E.; N.Y.A.P.L.S.; C.S.I. **Hob./spts.:** Snow skiing, scuba diving, sailing **SIC code:** 87 **Address:** Lanc & Tully Engineering and Surveying, P.C., P.O. Box 687, Goshen, NY 10924 **E-mail:** lanc@lanctully.com **Web address:** www.lanctully.com

LANHAM, BRYAN D.
Industry: Medical/clinical/biotechnology diagnostics **Born:** December 3, 1964, Wilmington, Delaware **Univ./degree:** A.S., Electrical Engineering, Delaware Tech, 1987 **Current organization:** Dade Behring Inc. **Title:** Associate Engineer **Type of organization:** Research and development **Major product:** Medical diagnostic equipment **Area of distribution:** International **Expertise:** Product development, electronics, electro/mechanical and optical engineering **Honors/awards:** Who's Who Among American High School Students, 1981-82; Who's Who of Junior College Students, 1987-88; International Who's Who of Professionals, 2002-2003; American Legion Award, 1982; Army Achievement Medal, 1983; Phi Beta Kappa **Hob./spts.:** The outdoors, fishing, shooting, cycling, most sports **SIC code:** 87 **Address:** Dade Behring Inc., Glasgow Business Community, 660 Technology Dr., Newark, DE 19702 **E-mail:** lanhambd@dadebehring.com

LARSEN, K. TIM
Industry: Accounting **Born:** January 20, 1956, Price, Utah **Univ./degree:** M.A., Accounting, Brigham Young University, 1981 **Current organization:** Squire & Co., PC **Title:** President **Type of organization:** Certified Public Accounting firm **Major product:** Tax consulting **Area of distribution:** National **Expertise:** Audits, consulting **Affiliations:** A.I.C.P.A.; U.A.C.P.A.; R.M.A. **Hob./spts.:** Fishing, hunting, golf **SIC code:** 87 **Address:** Squire & Co., PC, 1329 South 800 East, Orem, UT 84097 **E-mail:** timl@squire.com **Web address:** www.squire.com

LASHER, ESTHER LU
Industry: Library/ministry **Born:** June 1, 1923, Denver, Colorado **Univ./degree:** B.A., Music (Violin), University of Denver, 1945; M.A., Christian Education, Eastern Baptist Seminary, 1948; M.L.S., University of Denver, 1968 **Current organization:** The Rutherford Library/Damariscatta Baptist Church **Title:** Librarian/Minister (Nationally Ordained), Educator **Type of organization:** Library/Baptist church **Major product:** Administration and reference/Christian education **Area of distribution:** Maine, Colorado, Indiana **Expertise:** Librarian/Minister **Honors/awards:** Who's Who in America, 2005; Librarian of the Year, 1989; Phi Sigma Iota Language Honorary, 1945; Sigma Alpha Iota, 1944; **Affiliations:** Director, Fulton County Public Library; The Christian Women's Club; Founder, Fulton County Indiana Chapter of Literacy Volunteers of America; Violinist, Mid Coast Community Orchestra **Hob./spts.:** Playing the violin, crafts, positive thinking sermons **SIC code:** 86 **Address:** 2063 State Rte. 129, South Bristol, ME 04568

LATTA, ARLEEN M.
Industry: Associations/healthcare **Born:** November 1, 1931, Old Fort, Laramie, Wyoming **Univ./degree:** B.A., Healthcare and Education, Ottawa University, Kansas **Current organization:** American Association of Nurse Anesthetists **Title:** Director, Dept. of Anesthesia **Type of organization:** Professional association representing more than 30,000 CRNA's nationwide **Major product:** Promulgates education and practice standards and guidelines and affords consultation to both private and governmental entities regarding nurse anesthetists and their practice **Area of distribution:** National **Expertise:** Certified Registered Nurse Anesthetist **Affiliations:** University for Women; American Association of Nurse Anesthetists; Woodhaven Animal Shelter; Best Friends Animal Sanctuary **Hob./spts.:** Hot air ballooning, whitewater rafting, leather tooling **SIC code:** 86 **Address:** 222 S. Prospect Ave., Suite 202, Park Ridge, IL 60068-4001

LAUE, JOHN W.
Industry: Engineering **Born:** October 9, 1947, Kansas **Current organization:** Tetra Tech **Title:** Designer/Civil Engineer **Type of organization:** Consulting engineering **Major product:** Civil engineering services **Area of distribution:** International **Expertise:** Designing, civil engineering **Affiliations:** A.S.C.E. **Hob./spts.:** Fishing, golf **SIC code:** 87 **Address:** Tetra Tech, 501 Soledad, San Antonio, TX 78205 **E-mail:** john.laue@ttisg.com

LE, H. BAO
Industry: Consulting **Born:** July 14, 1956, Saigon, Vietnam **Univ./degree:** B.S., University of Ottawa; M.B.A., University of Toronto **Current organization:** CH2MHill, Inc. **Title:** Senior Vice President **Type of organization:** Engineering **Major product:** Engineering services **Area of distribution:** International **Expertise:** Business Development, Engineering and Technology **Affiliations:** I.E.E.E.; I.S.A.C.A. **Hob./spts.:**

Tennis, golf, skiing **SIC code:** 87 **Address:** CH2MHill, Inc., 9189 S. Jamaica St., Englewood, CO 80112 **E-mail:** bao.le@ch2m.com

LEACH, ROGER D.
Industry: Religion **Univ./degree:** B.S., Agronomy, Science, Fresno State University, 1972 **Current organization:** Valley West Christian Center/Sherman Thomas Charter School **Title:** Senior Pastor/Director/Founder **Type of organization:** Church/charter school **Major product:** Religious services/education **Area of distribution:** International **Expertise:** Lifetime teaching credential, Fresno State University, 1972; program development, preaching, ministries **Hob./spts.:** Basketball, golf, collecting old transistor radios **SIC code:** 86 **Address:** Valley West Christian Center/Sherman Thomas Charter School, 101 W. Adell St., Madera, CA 93638 **E-mail:** pastorrog@madnet.net

LEAHY, DONNA MARIE
Industry: Religion/spiritual care **Born:** January 9, 1950, New Jersey **Univ./degree:** B.S.N., Niagara University, 1971; Shenandoah University, 2002; M.A., Loyola College, 2003 **Current organization:** Manassas Church of Brethren **Title:** Parish Nurse **Type of organization:** Congregation **Major product:** Religious guidance, spiritual care **Area of distribution:** Virginia **Expertise:** Nursing, spiritual care, counseling, bereavement counseling **Affiliations:** Parish Nurse Conference **Hob./spts.:** Travel, golf, music, concerts, cooking **SIC code:** 86 **Address:** 2503 Golden Harvest Ct., Herndon, VA 20171 **E-mail:** dleahy@cox.net

LEBRON, LUIS R.
Industry: Research laboratory **Born:** July 8, 1954, Humacao, Puerto Rico **Univ./degree:** B.S., Medical Technology, University of Puerto Rico; M.S., Environmental Management, Chadwick University; Ph.D., Environmental Engineering, Kennedy Western University **Current organization:** Acualab of Puerto Rico **Title:** President **Type of organization:** Scientific research laboratory **Major product:** Research, analysis for pharmacology, water and wastewater microbiology **Area of distribution:** National **Expertise:** Scientific research **Published works:** 4 books **Affiliations:** Caribbean of Water Associates; College of Medical Technologists of Puerto Rico; Puerto Rico Chamber of Commerce; Society of American Magicians **Hob./spts.:** Pilot, magician **SIC code:** 87 **Address:** Acualab of Puerto Rico, 924 Intersection 926 2.7km, Sector Pitahaya, P.O. Box 625, Humacao, PR 00792 **E-mail:** innovations@acualab.com **Web address:** www.acualab.com

LEE, CHESTER M.
Industry: Engineering **Born:** September 30, 1953, Brooklyn, New York **Univ./degree:** B.S., Electrical Engineering, Cooper University, New York, 1975 **Current organization:** Raytheon Co. **Title:** Senior Principal Engineer **Type of organization:** Defense electronics engineering **Major product:** Radar systems **Area of distribution:** International **Expertise:** Engineering **Affiliations:** Past Member, I.E.E.E. **Hob./spts.:** Family, woodworking, computers **SIC code:** 87 **Address:** Raytheon Co., 528 Boston Post Rd., Sudbury, MA 01776 **E-mail:** chesml@aol.com

LEE, YOUNG H.
Industry: Religion **Born:** February 5, 1949, Korea **Univ./degree:** D.Min., Faith Theological Seminary **Current organization:** New York Presbyterian Church **Title:** Senior Pastor **Type of organization:** Church **Major product:** Religious services, leadership **Area of distribution:** Long Island City, New York **Expertise:** Communication skills **Affiliations:** Korean American Presbyterian Church; Korean Television; KIMNET; SEED International **SIC code:** 86 **Address:** New York Presbyterian Church, 43-23 37th Ave., New York, NY 11101 **E-mail:** yh4949@yahoo.co.kr **Web address:** www.nypc.net

LEON, RICHARD N.
Industry: Engineering/construction **Born:** December 19, 1976, Miami, Florida **Univ./degree:** B.S., Civil Engineering, Ohio University, 1999 **Current organization:** WD Partners **Title:** Civil Engineer **Type of organization:** Architectural/engineering **Major product:** Unit development/construction drawings **Area of distribution:** National **Expertise:** Engineering **Affiliations:** A.S.C.E. **SIC code:** 87 **Address:** WD Partners, 1201 Dublin Rd., Columbus, OH 43228 **E-mail:** rich.leon@wdpartners.com **Web address:** www.wdpartners.com

LEVIN-CUTLER, MARY
Industry: Music **Born:** December 24, Lexington, Kentucky **Univ./degree:** M.A., Music, University of Southern California, 1959 **Current organization:** American Youth Symphony **Title:** President **Type of organization:** Charitable **Major product:** Symphony **Area of distribution:** Beverly Hills, California **Expertise:** Music, politics **Affiliations:** Member, Theatre Center **Hob./spts.:** Music lover **SIC code:** 86 **Address:** American Youth Symphony, 1200 Steven Way, Beverly Hills, CA 90210

LEWIS, JOHN F.
Industry: Consulting **Born:** January 30, 1947, Washington, D.C. **Univ./degree:** M.S., University of Geneva, Switzerland **Current organization:** Lewis Consulting, LLC **Title:** President/CEO **Type of organization:** Consulting **Major product:** Healthcare financial management **Area of distribution:** National **Expertise:** Compliance, reimbursement, collections **Published works:** 1 article **Affiliations:** H.F.M.A.; Health Ethics Trust Committee **Hob./spts.:** Private pilot **SIC code:** 87 **Address:** Lewis Consulting, LLC, P.O. Box 670-Chrisiansted, St. Croix, VI 00821 **E-mail:** johnlewis-consult@netscape.net

LI, LIN
Industry: Environmental consulting **Born:** October 17, 1963, Shijiazhuang, Hebei, China **Univ./degree:** D.Sc., University of Massachusetts at Lowell, 2003 **Current organization:** Environmental Packaging International **Title:** Environmental Policy Analyst **Type of organization:** Environmental consulting company **Major product:** International packaging, WEEE, battery and chemicals regulation compliance guidance **Area of distribution:** International **Expertise:** Environmental policy research, consulting and services **Affiliations:** Professional Association of Chinese Environments **Hob./spts.:** Reading, kayaking, swimming **SIC code:** 87 **Address:** Environmental Packaging International, 41 Narragansett Ave., Jamestown, RI 02835 **E-mail:** lilin123@yahoo.com

LICHTEY, FRANK
Industry: Rubber and plastics **Born:** October 25, 1924, Minehill, New Jersey **Univ./degree:** B.S.C.E., Farleigh Dickerson, 1958; B.S.M.E., New York University, 1962 **Current organization:** Francon **Title:** Consultant, owner **Type of organization:** Consulting **Major product:** Extrusion plastics **Area of distribution:** National **Expertise:** Developing tooling (dies) **Affiliations:** A.S.A.A.S. **Hob./spts.:** Stamp collecting, swimming, painting **SIC code:** 87 **Address:** Frank Lichtey (Francon), 159 Leach Ave., Park Ridge, NJ 07656

LIJINSKY, WILLIAM
Industry: Research, consulting **Born:** August 19, 1928, Dublin, Ireland **Univ./degree:** B.S., 1949; Ph.D., 1951, University of Liverpool, United Kingdom; Post Doctorate, 2 1/2 Years at California Institute of Technology **Current organization:** The Frederick Cancer Center **Title:** Director Emeritus, Carcinogenesis Lab **Type of organization:** Research laboratory **Major product:** Scientific research, publications **Area of distribution:** International **Expertise:** Toxicology and environmental carcinogenesis **Published works:** 440 articles, 1 book **Affiliations:** A.C.S.; A.A.C.R. Emeritus; Biochemistry Society of England **Hob./spts.:** Reading, music, walking **SIC code:** 87 **Address:** 11398 High Hay Dr., Columbia, MD 21044

LISTER, KATHY
Industry: Social services **Born:** February 3, 1929, Trenton, Florida **Current organization:** Meals on Wheels **Title:** Executive Director **Type of organization:** Nonprofit social service agency **Major product:** Wholesome, nutritious food delivered to the elderly and disabled **Area of distribution:** National **Expertise:** Administration, management **Hob./spts.:** Sewing, reading **SIC code:** 83 **Address:** Meals on Wheels, 620 Sixth St. N.W., Winter Haven, FL 33881

LOCKHART, WALTER M.
Industry: Disaster relief **Born:** July 26, 1936, Virginia **Current organization:** Greenbrier Valley Chapter of the American Red Cross **Title:** Executive Director **Type of organization:** Disaster relief agency **Major product:** Relief to victims of disaster including hurricanes, power outages, snowstorms, ice storms, floods and forest fires **Area of distribution:** International **Expertise:** D.S.H.R./administration/personnel **Honors/awards:** U.S. Army Reserves, 31 years, U.S. Navy, 4 years (18 months in Korea) **Affiliations:** Life Member, V.F.W.; American Legion **Hob./spts.:** Stamp collecting **SIC code:** 83 **Address:** Greenbrier Valley Chapter of, the American Red Cross, P.O. Box 189, Lewisburg, WV 24901-0189 **E-mail:** waltlockhart@hotmail.com

LOHAY, SONA R.
Industry: Architecture **Born:** January 2, 1942, Vrbove, Czech Republic **Univ./degree:** M.S., Environmental Design, Technical Institute of Brno, Czech Republic, 1964 **Current organization:** Intex Designs **Title:** Designer/Owner **Type of organization:** Interior and exterior design firm **Major product:** Interior design and landscaping for upper level custom homes **Area of distribution:** California **Expertise:** Architectural design **Affiliations:** Landscape Architecture Association **SIC code:** 87 **Address:** Intex Designs, 19425 Walnut Dr. South, City of Industry, CA 91748

LOSTUTTER, MICHAEL C.
Industry: Consulting **Born:** July 13, 1961, Marion, Indiana **Univ./degree:** B.S., Political Science, Pre-Law, 1983, A.A., Paralegal Administration, 1988, Ball State University **Current organization:** First American Registry **Title:** Paralegal **Type of organization:** Business/real estate law consulting **Major product:** Information and data **Area of distribution:** National **Expertise:** Real estate law, research **Affiliations:** Indiana Association of Paralegals; National Federation of Paralegals Association **Hob./spts.:** History, violin, trombone, weightlifting, yoga **SIC code:** 87 **Address:** 315 Arbor Dr., Bldg. 6, Carmel, IN 46032 **E-mail:** mclient@juno.com

LOTFI, SHAHRAM
Industry: Consulting **Born:** March 31, 1961, Donghan, Iran **Univ./degree:** M.S., Electrical Engineering, S.S.N.Y. of New York, 1986 **Current organization:** EMTG Consultants Inc. **Title:** Professional Engineer/Owner **Type of organization:** Consulting **Major product:** Consulting engineering **Area of distribution:** East Coast **Expertise:** Engineering **Published works:** 4 articles **Affiliations:** N.S.P.E.; I.E.E.E.; N.F.P.A. **Hob./spts.:** Museums, libraries **SIC code:** 87 **Address:** EMTG Consultants Inc., 227 W. 29th St., New York, NY 10001 **E-mail:** EmGCONS@aol.com

LOUEY, CYNTHIA A.
Industry: Healthcare **Born:** August 15, 1956, Malone, New York **Univ./degree:** R.N., with Honors, C.V.P.H. School of Nursing, 1978 **Current organization:** WIC Program/ North Country Children's Clinic **Title:** WIC Coordinator **Type of organization:** Not for profit program **Major product:** Nutritional education for women, infants and children **Area of distribution:** New York **Expertise:** Certified Lactation Consultant; computer programming, nutritional education **Affiliations:** Chairperson, Breast Feeding Council of Malone; Head Start Medical Advisory Committee of Malone; Board Member, Safe Kids Chapter of Franklin County; Board Member, Even Start Program for Franklin County **Hob./spts.:** Raising Labrador Retrievers, travel **SIC code:** 83 **Address:** WIC Program/North Country Children's Clinic, 44 Catherine St., Malone, NY 12953 **E-mail:** ncccfrank@hotmail.com

LOWE, DAVID EDWARD
Industry: Counseling **Born:** February 25, 1957, Los Angeles, California **Univ./degree:** B.A., Counseling, 2005; M.A., Human Services, 2006, Almeda University **Current organization:** Freyhardt & Lowe Counseling Center **Title:** Executive Director **Type of organization:** Partnership counseling center **Major product:** Counseling services **Area of distribution:** California **Expertise:** Marriage, family, drug and alcohol intervention and relapse prevention services **Affiliations:** N.A.A.C.P.; California Association of Alcohol & Drug Educators; Strathmore's Who's Who **Hob./spts.:** Sports, reading **SIC code:** 83 **Address:** Freyhardt and Lowe Counseling Center, 1607 E. Palmdale Blvd., Suite G, Palmdale, CA 93550 **E-mail:** anthonyedward@sbcglobal.net

LOWE, HAROLD A.
Industry: Religion **Born:** August 18, 1930, Panama **Univ./degree:** Theology, IMJ Bible College & Seminary, Chicago **Current organization:** Christ Apostolic Church of God Mission **Title:** Advisory Pastor **Type of organization:** Church **Major product:** Religion, education **Area of distribution:** Brooklyn, New York **Expertise:** Christian teachings **Affiliations:** Paratrooper in the U.S. Army **Hob./spts.:** Reading **SIC code:** 86 **Address:** 55 Goodwin Place, #2M, Brooklyn, NY 11221

LUPO, JOANNE
Industry: Social services **Univ./degree:** B.S., Pace University, 1986 **Current organization:** JCCA **Title:** Director of Nursing **Type of organization:** Child welfare agency **Major product:** Healthcare, foster care and adoption services **Area of distribution:** New York **Expertise:** Pediatric nursing; regional guest speaker **Affiliations:** COFFCA; American Red Cross; Administration for Children Services (ACS); Pediatric Aids Unit (PAU); American Heart Association (AHA) **SIC code:** 83 **Address:** JCCA, 555 Bergen Ave., Bronx, NY 10455 **E-mail:** lupoj@jccany.org

LUTHER, NORRIS B.
Industry: Consulting/metal casting **Born:** March 19, 1922, Akron, Michigan **Spouse:** Barbara Conroy **Married:** December, 1997 **Children:** Ross, Gary, Marcia, Lynn **Univ./degree:** B.S., Mechanical Engineering, General Motors Institute (GMI, now named Kettering University), Flint, Michigan, 1949 **Current organization:** Luther & Associates **Title:** President **Type of organization:** Management and engineering consulting services to metal casting industry **Major product:** Develop and implement new technologies into strategic master plans to modernize foundry production facilities and processes **Area of distribution:** Local & International **Expertise:** Engineering of casting technology and manufacturing facilities and processes **Honors/awards:** American Foundry Society (AFS): AFS Award of Scientific Merit 1985, AFS Pangborn Gold Medalist 1996; Instructor at Cast Metals Institute (CMI) Educational Division of AFS, 1966-2001: CMI Director 1993-97, Chairman, CMI Board of Directors, 1996-7; CMI Directors Award 2000; AFS Engineering Division Distinguished Service Award 1990 (In 2001 this award was named the Norris B. Luther Distinguished Service Award); awarded a Michigan State Scholarship in 4-H HANDICRAFT **Published works:** Numerous articles published include the following 3: Modern Casting periodical, by AFS, Jan. 1988 "Innovation in the Cleaning Room"; Author of "Casting Buyers Guide" published by AFS, May 1988; British Cast Iron Research Association, Birmingham, U.K. Technical Report-"Use of Cold Set Binders in U.S. Foundries" and technical papers presented at AFS Casting Congress's, CMI classes and AFS Chapters throughout the U.S., Canada, England and Mexico **Affiliations:** American Foundry Society, Plant Engineering Committee and Engineering Division Executive Committee; Former Member: Iron and Steel Society of AIME; Society of Die Casting Engineers; Editorial Advisory Panel of "33 Metal Producing" Magazine published by McGraw-Hill; Member, Air Force Association; Life Member, American Legion **Career accomplishments:** Top Management levels achieved as GMC; Gold Medal Award from AFS having the Engineering Division Distinguished Service Award named the Norris B. Luther Distinguished Service Award was a very Special Honor and establishing my own business **Hob./spts.:** Travel, cabinet making, cruises **SIC code:** 87 **Address:** Luther & Associates, 5345 Mission Hill Dr., Tucson, AZ 85718 **E-mail:** NorLuther@aol.com

LYNCH, STEPHEN R.
Industry: Engineering/consulting **Born:** April 6, 1979, Springfield, Illinois **Univ./degree:** B.S., Engineering, Vanderbilt University, 2001 **Current organization:** E.I.T. Patrick Engineering Inc. **Title:** Structural Staff Engineer **Type of organization:** Engineering/consulting **Major product:** Engineering services **Area of distribution:** Midwest **Expertise:** Engineering **Affiliations:** A.S.C.E. **SIC code:** 87 **Address:** E.I.T. Patrick Engineering Inc., 55 E. Monroe St., Suite 3450, Chicago, IL 60603 **E-mail:** slynch@patrickengineering.com

MACHADO, HERNÁN JR.
Industry: Consulting engineering **Univ./degree:** B.S., Recinto Universidad de Mayaguez, 1989 **Current organization:** Hernán Jr. Machado & Associates **Title:** Civil Engineer **Type of organization:** Design firm **Major product:** Engineering **Area of distribution:** Mayaguez, Puerto Rico **Expertise:** Civil engineering **Affiliations:** A.S.C.E.; College of Engineers of Puerto Rico **SIC code:** 87 **Address:** Hernán Jr. Machado & Associates, 15 Peral St., Mayaguez, PR 00680 **E-mail:** jmachado@coqui.net

MACHOVER, CARL
Industry: Consulting **Born:** Brooklyn, New York **Univ./degree:** B.S., Electrical Engineering, Rensselaer Polytechnic Institute, 1951 **Current organization:** Machover Associates Corp. **Title:** President **Type of organization:** Private corporation **Major product:** Computer graphics consulting **Area of distribution:** National **Expertise:** Engineering/CAD CAM **Published works:** 3 books, 180 articles **Affiliations:** I.E.E.E.; A.C.M. **Hob./spts.:** Art, reading **SIC code:** 87 **Address:** Machover Associates Corp., 152A Longview Ave., White Plains, NY 10605 **E-mail:** cmachover@aol.com

MACKIEWICZ III, WILLIAM S.
Industry: Consulting/engineering **Born:** June 20, 1977, New Britain, Connecticut **Univ./degree:** B.S., Georgia Institute of Technology, 2000 **Current organization:** Pharr Engineering, Inc. **Title:** Civil Engineer, E.I.T. **Type of organization:** Civil engineering firm **Major product:** Civil site assessment **Area of distribution:** National **Expertise:** Civil engineer **Affiliations:** A.S.C.E.; Earthquake Engineers Society **SIC code:** 87 **Address:** Pharr Engineering, Inc., 1770 Century Circle, Suite 22, Atlanta, GA 30345 **E-mail:** jbmackiewicz@yahoo.com

MACNEILL JR., JOHN S.
Industry: Engineering **Born:** January 24, 1927, Weehawken, New Jersey **Univ./degree:** B.C.E., Cornell University **Current organization:** John S. MacNeill Jr., P.E. **Title:** P.E./Owner **Type of organization:** Consulting engineering firm **Major product:** Civil-sanitary engineer design **Area of distribution:** Homer, New York **Expertise:** Engineering **Affiliations:** Fellow, American Society of Civil Engineers; National Society of Civil Engineers **Hob./spts.:** Working with rotary exchange students **SIC code:** 87 **Address:** John S. MacNeill Jr., P.E., 12 S. Main St., P.O. Box 226, Homer, NY 13077 **E-mail:** jsmacneill@clarityconnect.com

MADHAVAN, GURUPRASAD
Industry: Biomedical engineering/surgery **Born:** July 19, 1979, Tamilnadu, India **Univ./degree:** MSBME, State University of New York at Stony Brook, 2002 **Current organization:** AFX Inc. and State University of New York **Title:** Consultant Scientist & Doctoral Fellow **Type of organization:** Biomedical engineering, manufacturing **Major product:** Medical devices **Area of distribution:** International **Expertise:** Bioinstrumentation and systems physiology **Published works:** 50 articles **Affiliations:** Associate Fellow, R.S.M.; N.Y.A.M.; Member, I.S.A.; I.E.E.E.; A.H.A.; A.A.M.I.; A.S.M.E.; B.M.E.S.; N.Y.A.S.; A.C.C.E.; I.E.E.; C.M.B.E.S.; N.S.H.S.; A.M.P.I. **Hob./spts.:** Classical music, symphonies, movies, science and technology magazines and books **SIC code:** 87 **Address:** AFX Inc., 47929 Fremont Blvd., Fremont, CA 94538 **E-mail:** madhavprasad@yahoo.com

MAITLAND, JAMES R.
Industry: Environmental **Born:** October 4, 1950, California **Univ./degree:** B.S., Civil Engineering, California State Polytech Institute, 1979; Post Grad, Management, UCI Extension, 1991 **Current organization:** TMAD **Title:** Project Manager **Area of distribution:** California **Honors/awards:** Military Project Award, Air Force, Quality of Design & Production **Affiliations:** A.S.C.E.; B.I.A.; American Military Engineers **Hob./spts.:** History, movies, golf, skiing **SIC code:** 87 **Address:** 5482 Santa Gertrudes, Garden Grove, CA 92845-1032 **E-mail:** jim.maitland@ttisg.com

MALDONADO, ALMA S.
Industry: Human services **Born:** May 1, 1951, Pearsall, Texas **Univ./degree:** Medical Assistant, San Antonio College of Medical & Dental Assistants, 1988 **Current orga-**

nization: Frio Adult Day Care **Title:** President **Type of organization:** Adult cay care center **Major product:** 18 and over activities, outings and meals **Area of distribution:** Pearsall, Texas **Expertise:** Hands-on program management; State licensed medical assistant **Hob./spts.:** Reading, travel casinos **SIC code:** 83 **Address:** Frio Adult Day Care, 2688 BI 35E, Pearsall, TX 78061 **E-mail:** almam1145@awesomenet.net

MANGANO, DAMON A.
Industry: Hospitality **Born:** June 9, 1976, Fort Wayne, Indiana **Univ./degree:** Culinary Degree, Hospitality Management, Akron University, 1998 **Current organization:** Rosemont Country Club **Title:** Executive Chef **Type of organization:** Country club **Major product:** Food, beverage, entertainment (pool grill, golf course and banquet facilities) **Area of distribution:** Ohio **Expertise:** International cuisine, management, purchasing, budget forecasting **Hob./spts.:** Sports **SIC code:** 86 **Address:** Rosemont Country Club, 3777 Rosemont Blvd., Akron, OH 44333 **E-mail:** damonmangano@yahoo.com

MANICKE, CURTIS R.
Industry: Engineering **Born:** September 21, 1978, Waukesha, Wisconsin **Univ./degree:** B.S.M.E., University of South Alabama, 2002 **Current organization:** General Electric Power Systems **Title:** Field Engineer **Type of organization:** Engineering **Major product:** Power systems engineering, field repairs, preventative maintenance **Area of distribution:** International with a regional southeast focus **Expertise:** Mechanical engineering **Affiliations:** A.S.M.E.; S.A.E. **Hob./spts.:** Golf, softball, basketball **SIC code:** 87 **Address:** 912 Van Ave., #335, Daphne, AL 36526 **E-mail:** curtis.manicke@ps.ge.com

MANIGAULT, JUAN A.
Industry: Nonprofit **Born:** October 7, 1952, Charleston, South Carolina **Current organization:** Northern Indiana Workforce Investment Board, Inc. **Title:** President and CEO **Type of organization:** Nonprofit **Major product:** Strategic planning **Area of distribution:** Indiana **Expertise:** Leadership development **Affiliations:** National Association of Workforce Professionals **Hob./spts.:** Golf, tennis **SIC code:** 86 **Address:** Northern Indiana Workforce Investment Board, Inc., 401 E. Colfax Ave., Suite 307, South Bend, IN 46617 **E-mail:** jam200@niwib.com

MANSUKHANI, GUL
Industry: Consulting/food **Born:** April 24, 1938, Hyderabad, West Pakistan **Univ./degree:** B.S., Chemistry **Current organization:** Gul Mansukhani Consultant **Title:** Owner **Type of organization:** Consulting **Major product:** Formulation for food **Area of distribution:** International **Expertise:** Gum base and gum formulas **Hob./spts.:** Travel **SIC code:** 87 **Address:** 97 Petrus Ave., Staten Island, NY 10312 **E-mail:** mansukhanig2002@yahoo.com

MARASCA, SUSAN LEANNE
Industry: Shipbuilding **Univ./degree:** A.S., Structural and Civil Engineering, South Alabama University, 1985 **Current organization:** Northrop Grumman Ship Systems **Title:** Structural Design Specialist **Type of organization:** Defense Contractor **Major product:** Design and development of military ships, destroyers, cruisers, warships **Area of distribution:** International **Expertise:** Structural design, civil engineering **Affiliations:** Society of Naval Architects and Marine Engineers; American Society of Naval Architects and Marine Engineers **Hob./spts.:** Professional bass fishing, cattle ranching **SIC code:** 87 **Address:** 1712 Beth Circle, Gautier, MS 39553 **E-mail:** leanne.marasca@ngc.com

MARAVILLAS, VIRGIL A.
Industry: Construction/consulting **Univ./degree:** Civil Engineering, CEBU Institute of Technology, 1968 **Current organization:** AMPAC Diversified Corp. **Title:** Senior Project Manager **Type of organization:** Consulting **Major product:** General construction **Area of distribution:** California **Expertise:** Civil engineering **Affiliations:** A.S.C.E.; I.C.B.O. **SIC code:** 87 **Address:** 8314 Dempsey Ave., North Hills, CA 91343 **E-mail:** virgil.ampac@verizon.net

MARCHANT, DAVID D.
Industry: Consulting **Born:** May 1, 1943, Murray, Utah **Univ./degree:** Ph.D., Materials Science, M.I.T., 1974 **Current organization:** Marchant's Materials Solutions **Title:** President **Type of organization:** Consulting firm **Major product:** Design and development of bulletproof armor, ceramic product development, ceramic processing and manufacturing **Area of distribution:** International **Expertise:** Engineering **Affiliations:** S.M.E.; D.E.P.S.; A.C.E.R.S. **Hob./spts.:** Golf, gardening **SIC code:** 87 **Address:** 1709 S. Citrus Cove, Mesa, AZ 85204 **Phone:** (480)926-1646 **E-mail:** ceramdoc@aol.com

MARCHESE, FRANK P.
Industry: Chemicals, cosmetics, medicinal and environmental products **Born:** September 15, 1930, New York, New York **Univ./degree:** B.S., Organic Chemistry, Iona College, 1957; M.S., Organic, Physical Chemistry, St. John's University, 1960 **Current organization:** Marchè Image Corp. **Title:** Owner/Director of Research & Development **Type of organization:** Manufacturing/research & development **Major product:** Environmentally safe products, anti aging creams & herbal products **Area of distribution:** International **Expertise:** Organic & physical chemistry, medicinal products **Honors/awards:** 4 product development patents **Published works:** Transpeptidation of Aspartic and Glutamic Acid **Affiliations:** Medical Doctors **Hob./spts.:** Tennis, golf, cycling, trail blazing **SIC code:** 87 **Address:** Marchè Image Corp., 50 Webster Ave., New Rochelle, NY 10801 **E-mail:** marchimage@aol.com

MARINO, CHARLES E.
Industry: Defense contractor/engineering **Univ./degree:** B.S., Electrical Engineering, Louisiana Tech University, 1981; M.S., Electrical Engineering, Southern Methodist University, 1988 **Current organization:** BAE Systems EIS **Title:** Chief Engineer **Type of organization:** Engineering **Major product:** Military aircraft ground support equipment **Area of distribution:** National **Expertise:** Electrical engineering; Registered P.E., Texas **Affiliations:** Senior Member, I.E.E.E. **Hob./spts.:** Family, golf, soccer, coaching youth sports **SIC code:** 87 **Address:** BAE Systems EIS, 6100 Western Place, Suite 200, Ft. Worth, TX 76107 **E-mail:** charles.marino@baesystems.com

MARRERO, JACK L.
Industry: Consulting **Born:** December 12, 1932, Toa Baja, Puerto Rico **Univ./degree:** B.S., Business, Hartwick College, 1959; M.A., Behavioral Science, New York University, 1969 **Current organization:** Princeton Associates, L.L.C. **Title:** President **Type of organization:** Consulting **Major product:** Financial development, brokerage **Area of distribution:** National **Expertise:** Financial development, brokerage and consulting **Affiliations:** President, Princeton Board of Education, 1997-99; Chairman, Kean University of New Jersey, 1996-98; Chairman, New Jersey State Colleges and Universities, 1999; Member of the Board, Beth Israel Medical Center in New York, 1980-2001; The National Conference of Christians and Jews 1969-1998, Executive Director, Brooklyn Region, Vice President for Development, Northeast Region, Executive Director, New Jersey Region, Executive Director, Greater Philadelphia Region, Senior Executive Advisor to the President **Hob./spts.:** Skiing, traveling, reading and writing music, trumpet, singing **SIC code:** 87 **Address:** Princeton Associates, L.L.C., 310 Cherry Hill Rd., Princeton, NJ 08540 **E-mail:** prnctna@aol.com

MARRERO-FIGARELLA, ALBERTO L.
Industry: Engineering **Born:** February 8, 1956, Puerto Rico **Univ./degree:** B.S., University of Puerto Rico, Mayaquez Campus, 1980 **Current organization:** Structural Engineering Consultant **Title:** Structural Engineer **Type of organization:** Structural engineering consultant firm **Major product:** Consulting for bridges and buildings **Area of distribution:** National **Expertise:** Structural engineering consultant **Published works:** Articles **Affiliations:** A.S.C.E.; American Concrete Institute **Hob./spts.:** Family, basketball, reading **SIC code:** 87 **Address:** Structural Engineering Consultant, Anturium 113, Ciudad Jardin I, Toa Alta, PR 00953 **E-mail:** edenpr56@aol.com

MARTINEZ, EVENCIO RODRIGUEZ
Industry: Architecture **Born:** January 11, 1948, Havana, Cuba **Univ./degree:** M.S., Architecture, University of Louisiana, 1970 **Current organization:** Quiñones-Rodriguez **Title:** Architect (Principal) **Type of organization:** Architectural and developing firm **Major product:** Commercial and residential architecture **Area of distribution:** International **Expertise:** Marketing, architecture, development **Affiliations:** Home Builders Association; Association of General Contractors **Hob./spts.:** Fishing **SIC code:** 87 **Address:** Quiñones-Rodriguez, Fernandez Juncos Ave., #811, Miramar Santurce, PR 00907

MARTINEZ, VERONICA I.
Industry: Land development **Born:** February 19, 1974, New York, New York **Univ./degree:** B.S., Civil Engineering, University of Puerto Rico, 1998; M.S. Candidate, Construction Management, Poly Tech **Current organization:** FOG Development, SP **Title:** Civil Engineer **Type of organization:** Development **Major product:** Land development **Area of distribution:** Bayamon, Puerto Rico **Expertise:** Engineering management **Affiliations:** A.S.C.E.; C.I.A.P.R. **Hob./spts.:** Reading, studying **SIC code:** 87 **Address:** FOG Development, SP, 500 Paseo Monaco, Apt. 92, Bayamón, PR 00956 **E-mail:** ingmartinez@hotmail.com

MASON, LINDA A.
Industry: Forensics/fire investigation **Current organization:** Sadler & Associates, Inc. **Title:** President **Type of organization:** Investigation firm **Major product:** Engineering and consulting, arson investigation **Area of distribution:** Michigan and Ohio **Expertise:** Forensic fire investigation; item defect examinations **Affiliations:** N.F.P.A.; I.A.A.I. **Hob./spts.:** Boy Scouts of America **SIC code:** 87 **Address:** Sadler & Associates, Inc., 227 Main St., P.O. Box 249, Luckey, OH 43443 **E-mail:** tolmason@aol.com

MATHISON, THOMAS R.
Industry: Architecture **Univ./degree:** B.S., Architecture, 1973; M.Arch., 1975, University of Michigan **Current organization:** Tower Pinkster Titus Associates, Inc. **Title:** Architect **Type of organization:** Architecture/engineering firm **Major product:**

Architecture/engineering **Area of distribution:** Michigan **Expertise:** Architectural design **Honors/awards:** Design awards 2 time winner-Presidential Award, Grand Valley, 1997 & 2002, A.I.A. Chapters **Affiliations:** A.I.A.; Small Business Association of Michigan **SIC code:** 87 **Address:** Tower Pinkster Titus Associates, Inc., 678 Front Ave. N.W., #255, Grand Rapids, MI 49504 **E-mail:** tmathison@tpta.com

MAUL, GERD G.
Industry: Science **Born:** March 14, 1940, Hoyerswerda, Germany **Univ./degree:** M.S.M., Zoology, Botany and Ecology, Darmstadt Technical University, 1965; Ph.D., Zoology, University of Texas, 1966 **Current organization:** The Wistar Institute **Title:** Ph.D., Professor **Type of organization:** Nonprofit research **Major product:** Research, scientific publications **Area of distribution:** International **Expertise:** Biomedical sciences **Published works:** 140 peer-reviewed articles; book chapters **Affiliations:** American Society for Cell Biology **Hob./spts.:** Sculpting, reading **SIC code:** 87 **Address:** The Wistar Institute, 3601 Spruce St., Philadelphia, PA 19104 **E-mail:** maul@wistar.org

MAYO, TERRY
Industry: Computer software **Born:** October 1, 1965, Atlanta, Georgia **Univ./degree:** B.S., Accounting, Jacksonville State University, 1994 **Current organization:** DataForce Systems, Inc. **Title:** Controller **Type of organization:** Public accounting **Major product:** Software for temporary agencies **Area of distribution:** Georgia **Expertise:** Accounting **Affiliations:** Alabama Society of Certified Public Accountants **SIC code:** 87 **Address:** 163 Jones Bend Rd. N.E., Rome, GA 30165 **E-mail:** tlmayo@dataforcesystems.com

MCCANTS, CARL E.
Industry: High technology **Born:** October 25, 1959, Laredo, Texas **Univ./degree:** Ph.D., Stanford University, 1989 **Current organization:** Agilent Technologies **Title:** Project Manager **Type of organization:** Research & development **Major product:** Optoelectronic devices **Area of distribution:** International **Expertise:** Electrical engineering **Affiliations:** S.P.I.E.; I.E.E.E.; National Society of Black Engineers **Hob./spts.:** Music, playing guitar **SIC code:** 87 **Address:** Booz, Allen, Hamilton Consultants, 3811 N. Fairfax Dr., Suite 600, Arlington, VA 22203 **E-mail:** carl.mccants@agilent.com

MCCHESKEY, JEFFREY T.
Industry: Public service/housing (HUD) **Born:** January 1, 1952, Glendale, West Virginia **Univ./degree:** B.S., Psychology, West Virginia University, 1974 **Current organization:** Jamestown Housing Authority **Title:** Executive Director **Type of organization:** Nonprofit housing corp. **Major product:** Apartment management **Area of distribution:** Jamestown, New York **Expertise:** Administration **Affiliations:** P.H.A.D.A.; N.A.H.R.O.; N.Y.S.P.H.A.D.A. **Hob./spts.:** Woodworking, music **SIC code:** 83 **Address:** Jamestown Housing Authority, 110 W. Third St., Jamestown, NY 14701 **E-mail:** jha@madbbs.com

MCCLELLAN, TIMOTHY J.
Industry: Consulting **Born:** October 16, 1943, Grand Rapids, Michigan **Univ./degree:** M.S., Engineering, Michigan State University, 1971; M.S., Public Administration, Arizona State University, 1991 **Current organization:** Heevy International **Title:** Senior Associate **Type of organization:** Consulting **Major product:** Architectural/engineering **Area of distribution:** National **Expertise:** Criminal justice, schools, office buildings **Affiliations:** A.P.W.A. **Hob./spts.:** Golf, gardening, motorcycles, reading, music **SIC code:** 87 **Address:** Heevy International, 2800 N. Central Ave., Suite 175, Phoenix, AZ 85004-1094

MCCLURE, JOSHUA
Industry: Religion **Born:** October 12, 1931, Brooklyn, New York **Univ./degree:** B.S., Theology and Bible Studies, Barrington College, 1983 **Current organization:** Pleasant Street Baptist Church **Title:** Reverend **Type of organization:** Church **Major product:** Religious leadership, teaching, counseling **Area of distribution:** National **Expertise:** Religious education **Honors/awards:** Biblical Studies Award, 1983; American Baptist Churches of RI Man of the Year, 1980 **Affiliations:** National Grid USA; YMCA; Living Waters Christian Academy **Hob./spts.:** Computers **SIC code:** 86 **Address:** Rev. Joshua McClure, Pleasant Street Baptist Church, 37 Pleasant St., Westerly, RI 02891 **E-mail:** psbch@netzero.net **Web address:** www.psbaptist.org

MCCOLLUM, ODELL
Industry: Religion **Born:** February 16, 1926, Reidsville, North Carolina **Current organization:** The United Holy Church of America, Inc. **Title:** Bishop/General President **Type of organization:** Church **Major product:** Christian service to the world **Area of distribution:** International **Expertise:** Spreading the Christian faith **Published works:** Two papers **Affiliations:** P.C.C.N.A. **SIC code:** 86 **Address:** 707 Woodmark Run, Gahanna, OH 43230

MCCRARY, GILES C.
Industry: Oil and gas/investments **Born:** November 5, 1919, Fort Worth, Texas **Univ./degree:** B.A., Banking/Finance, Washington and Lee University, Lexington, VA **Current organization:** McCrary Ltd. **Title:** President **Type of organization:** Consulting **Major product:** Oil and gas services **Area of distribution:** Post, Texas **Expertise:** Operations, management, consulting **Hob./spts.:** Art, people watching, world wide travel, community service **SIC code:** 87 **Address:** McCrary Ltd., P.O. Box 790, Post, TX 79356 **E-mail:** gilesmccrary@mccraryltyd.com **Web address:** www.mccraryltd.com

MCDANIEL, PATRICIA (TISCH)
Industry: Consulting **Born:** December 4, 1955, Manhattan, Kansas **Current organization:** M&M Advisory Group, Inc. **Title:** President **Type of organization:** Construction management firm **Major product:** Consulting **Area of distribution:** Mississippi, Tennessee, Arkansas **Expertise:** Human resources, Licensed Insurance Agent, safety, workers' compensation **Published works:** "Impression Management" **Affiliations:** Society of Human Resource Executives; National Registry of Who's Who; Strathmore Who's Who; Associated Builders and Contractors; National Association of Insurance and Financial Advisors; Northcreek Golf Course **Hob./spts.:** Golf, writing poetry **SIC code:** 87 **Address:** M&M Advisory Group, Inc., 3830 Esrey Rd., Nesbit, MS 38651 **Phone:** (901)230-6920 **Fax:** (662)429-2463 **E-mail:** tisch@bellsouth.net

MCDONALD, NANCY E.
Industry: Consulting **Univ./degree:** B.S., Biology and Chemistry, University of Central Florida; Attended University of Florida **Current organization:** M&M Consulting & Laboratory, Inc./Tropical Paradise Beverages **Title:** President/Owner **Type of organization:** Consulting and laboratory **Major product:** Beverages consulting and formulation **Area of distribution:** International **Expertise:** R&D, food safety training **Affiliations:** American Chemical Society; Institute of Food Technology **Hob./spts.:** Travel **SIC code:** 87 **Address:** M&M Consulting & Laboratory, Inc., 1825 S. Orange Blossom Trail, Apopka, FL 32703 **E-mail:** nancyemcdl@aol.com

MCGINTY, THOMAS N.
Industry: Counseling **Univ./degree:** M.S., Counseling, Canisius College, 1973 **Current organization:** Orchard Park Youth Bureau **Title:** Executive Director **Type of organization:** Municipal family service agency **Major product:** Youth and family counseling services **Area of distribution:** Orchard Park, New York **Expertise:** Youth counseling and education **Affiliations:** V.E.F.; N.E.A.; Western New York Counselors Association **SIC code:** 83 **Address:** Orchard Park Youth Bureau, 6595 E. Quaker St., Orchard Park, NY 14127 **E-mail:** neilthomas@webtv.net

MCGREEVY, J. PAT
Industry: Human services **Born:** April 21, 1927, Pawtucket, Rhode Island **Univ./degree:** A.B., Philosophy, Providence College, 1950 **Current organization:** Fern House, Inc. **Title:** Executive Director **Type of organization:** 501(c)(3) non-profit residential rehabilitation center **Major product:** Substance abuse counseling **Area of distribution:** Florida **Expertise:** Administration, presentations, fundraising, events **Honors/awards:** Thanks Award to Fern House for Outstanding Community Service, Palm Beach County Public Defender's Office, 2006; One of the Top Achieving Irish Americans in the U.S., Irish American Magazine, 2005/06 **Affiliations:** U.S. Army National Guard **SIC code:** 83 **Address:** Fern House, Inc., 1958 Church St., West Palm Beach, FL 33409 **Web address:** www.fernhouse.org

MCINERNEY JR., JAMES E.
Industry: Military **Born:** August 3, 1930, Springfield, Massachusetts **Univ./degree:** B.S., Military Engineering, U.S. Military Academy, 1952; M.S., Aeronautical Engineering, Princeton University, 1960; M.S., International Affairs, George Washington University, 1970 **Current organization:** National Defense Industrial Association **Title:** Vice President **Type of organization:** Educational association **Major product:** Defense weapons and equipment **Area of distribution:** National/International **Expertise:** Education, membership, lobbying **Affiliations:** British American Business Association; Air Force Association; The Association of the Industrial College of the Armed Forces; National War College Alumni Association **Hob./spts.:** Golf, flying, boating **SIC code:** 86 **Address:** National Defense Industrial Association, 2111 Wilson Blvd., Arlington, VA 22201 **E-mail:** jmcinerney@ndia.org **Web address:** www.ndia.org

MCINTYRE-SMITH, FRANCES E.
Industry: Media **Born:** May 25, Waterbury, Connecticut **Univ./degree:** B.S., Biological Sciences, State University of New York, Westbury, 1992; M.S., Real Estate Development, New York University, 2001 **Current organization:** McIntyre Consultants **Title:** Consultant/Producer **Type of organization:** Consulting/independent producer **Major product:** Linear and non-linear production **Area of distribution:** International **Expertise:** Consulting and producing **Affiliations:** Association of Video & Independent Filmmakers; National Association of Recording Artists; National Association of Female Executives **Hob./spts.:** Arts and crafts, math, music, travel **SIC code:** 87 **Address:** McIntyre Consultants, 436 State St., Brooklyn, NY 11217 **E-mail:** fmcintyres@aol.com

MCKENNA JR., FRANCIS J.
Industry: Environmental **Born:** Summit, New Jersey **Current organization:** Care Environmental Corp. **Title:** President **Type of organization:** Waste disposal/national disaster recovery **Major product:** Hazardous waste disposal **Area of distribution:** National **Expertise:** Operations, management, strategic planning, marketing, business development; Certified Firefighter; Certified Search and Rescue **Affiliations:** N.F.P.A.; N.J.M.C.A.; N.Y.M.C.A.; S.W.A.N.A.; N.P.S.A. **Hob./spts.:** Motorcycle (Harley) **SIC code:** 87 **Address:** Care Environmental Corp., 10 Orben Dr., Landing, NJ 07850

MCKINESS, RICK
Industry: Private security **Born:** December 22, 1955, Aurora, Illinois **Univ./degree:** School of Police Staff & Command, Northwestern University, 2001; FBI National Academy, Quantico, Virginia, 2002 **Current organization:** Moose International, Inc. **Title:** Captain, Kane County Sheriff's Office (Retired)/Director of Security **Type of organization:** Fraternity organization **Major product:** Safety and security **Area of distribution:** Mooseheart Child City, Mooseheart, Illinois; Moosehaven; Orange Park, Florida **Expertise:** 30 years of law enforcement, security and corrections **Honors/awards:** Leadership Medal; 2 Time Life Saving Medal; 2 Time Meritorious Medal; 25 Written Commendations; 64 Letters of Recognition with Kane County Sheriff's Office; Meritorious Service Award, American Jail Association, 1990 **Affiliations:** Loyal Order of the Moose Lodge 682; Fraternal Order of Police; National Crime Prevention Council; Kane County Chiefs of Police Association; FBI National Academy Associates; Past President, Illinois Jail Association **Hob./spts.:** Family, friends **SIC code:** 86 **Address:** Moose International, Inc., 155 International Dr., Mooseheart, IL 60539 **E-mail:** rmckiness@mooseintl.org **Web address:** www.mooseintl.org

MCNEIL, JEAN B.
Industry: Education **Born:** 1951, Christiansburg, Virginia, **Univ./degree:** B.A.; B.S., Mary Baldwin College; M.S., Early Childhood Development, Suffield University **Current organization:** Child Care Solutions **Title:** Partner/Co-Author **Type of organization:** Consulting firm **Major product:** Early childhood education, pre-school curriculum, consulting workshops and conferences **Area of distribution:** National **Expertise:** Pre-school curriculum, early childhood development **Published works:** 8 book set, "Exceed Preschool Curriculum" **Affiliations:** National Association for the Education of Young Children; National Association of Child Care Professionals **Hob./spts.:** Gardening, photography, scrapbooking **SIC code:** 87 **Address:** Child Care Solutions, 7601 Ratling Dr., Midlothian, VA 23112 **E-mail:** jmcneil@exceednow.com **Web address:** www.exceednow.com

MCQUAY, GARY E.
Industry: Plastic packaging **Born:** May 21, 1947, Muncy, Pennsylvania **Univ./degree:** A.S., Pennsylvania Technical College, 1983 **Current organization:** McQuay **Title:** Design Consultant-Plastics **Type of organization:** Consulting **Major product:** Product design **Area of distribution:** National **Expertise:** Design, research and development **Honors/awards:** Ortho McNeill Packaging Award **Published works:** 4 patents **Affiliations:** Society of Plastics Engineers **Hob./spts.:** Family, golf **SIC code:** 87 **Address:** 16350 State Route 405, Watsontown, PA 17777 **E-mail:** gemcquay521@suscom.net

MCQUISTON, DAVID
Industry: Pro-family services **Born:** June 11, 1942, Richmond, Indiana **Univ./degree:** B.S., Indiana Wesleyan University, 1965; D.Min., Religion **Current organization:** Focus on the Family **Title:** D.Min./V.P. **Type of organization:** Non-profit **Major product:** Information **Area of distribution:** National **Expertise:** Family **Affiliations:** Board Member, Equipment Foundation; Board Member, Awakening **Hob./spts.:** Golf, biking **SIC code:** 86 **Address:** Focus on the Family, 8605 Explorer Dr., Colorado Springs, CO 80920 **E-mail:** mcquisdj@fotf.org **Web address:** www.fotf.org

MCRAE, GEORGE E.
Industry: Religion **Born:** August 13, 1941, Florida **Univ./degree:** B.A., Bethune Cookman College, 1976; M.Div., Morehouse School of Religion, 1984; D.Min., Columbia Theological Seminary, 1993 **Current organization:** Mount Tabor Missionary Baptist Church **Title:** Pastor **Type of organization:** Church **Major product:** Religious services, education **Area of distribution:** Miami, Florida **Expertise:** Spiritual leadership **Affiliations:** Florida General Baptist Convention Inc. **Hob./spts.:** Salt and freshwater fishing **SIC code:** 86 **Address:** Mount Tabor Missionary Baptist Church, 1701 N.W. 66th St., Miami, FL 33147 **E-mail:** Tabor1701@aol.com

MEDINA, CARLOS A.
Industry: Engineering/aerospace **Born:** August 19, 1962, Havana, Cuba **Univ./degree:** B.S., With Honors, Electrical Engineering, Florence Nashville University, 1992 **Current organization:** I/O Test, Inc. **Title:** Senior Engineer **Type of organization:** Engineering design **Major product:** Software, hardware systems **Area of distribution:** National **Expertise:** Engineering **Published works:** Several copyrighted programs; U.S. patent for I/O^3 Foot Mouse (a gaming device) **Affiliations:** I.E.E.E. **Hob./spts.:** Spending time with family, playing baseball with his son, fishing **SIC code:** 87 **Address:** I/O Test, Inc., 4717 W. Estrella St., Tampa, FL 33629 **E-mail:** carlos.medina@iotest.net

MEGINLEY, H. JAMES
Industry: Mental healthcare **Univ./degree:** Ph.D., Counseling/Psychology, Southeastern University, 1984 **Current organization:** Alternatives Counseling Associates **Title:** Administrative Director **Type of organization:** Counseling agency **Major product:** Individual, family and group psychotherapy **Area of distribution:** Southeast Tennessee, Northwest Georgia, Northeast Alabama **Expertise:** Marriage, family and sex therapy, substance abuse and other life issues **Published works:** Abstracts **Affiliations:** A.A.S.E.C.T.; Domestic Violence Coalition, State of Tennessee, S.O.T. Board **Hob./spts.:** Musician, scuba diving, woodworking, gardening, water sports, hiking **SIC code:** 83 **Address:** Alternatives Counseling Associates, House of Hope, 2002 Oak St., Chattanooga, TN 37404-2634 **Phone:** (423)624-8535 **Fax:** (423)624-8608 **Web address:** www.homw.earthlink.net/walter2002/

MEIJBOOM, ALBERT F.
Industry: Geology, hydrology and engineering **Born:** February 7, 1948, Netherlands Antilles **Univ./degree:** Doctorate, State University of Leiden, 1973 **Current organization:** Engineering Tectonics P.A. **Title:** Dr. **Type of organization:** Consulting firm **Major product:** Geotechnical, earth and environmental sciences. **Area of distribution:** National **Expertise:** Engineering, geology, hydrology and mining exploration **Hob./spts.:** Soccer, hiking, reading **SIC code:** 87 **Address:** Engineering Tectonics P.A., 1720 Vargrave St., Winston-Salem, NC 27107 **E-mail:** rockdock@hotmail.com

MELNICK, MICHAEL E.
Industry: Construction consulting **Born:** October 4, 1940, Chelsea, Massachusetts **Univ./degree:** M.S., Structural Engineering, Northeastern University, 1971 **Current organization:** Lincoln Consultants, Inc. **Title:** President **Type of organization:** Consulting firm **Major product:** Public schools and facilities **Area of distribution:** Sudbury, Massachusetts **Expertise:** Construction project management **Affiliations:** N.S.P.E.; Boston Society of Civil Engineers; Massachusetts Society of Professional Engineers; Boston Society of Architects; Member, AAA Panel of Arbitration **Hob./spts.:** Gardening **SIC code:** 87 **Address:** Lincoln Consultants, Inc., 97 Lincoln Rd., Sudbury, MA 01776 **E-mail:** memelnick@aol.com

MERRY, STEVEN D.
Industry: DOD contractor **Born:** December 18, 1954, Santa Monica, California **Univ./degree:** B.S.E.E.T., University of Central Florida, 2000 **Current organization:** Gryphon Technologies L.L.C. **Title:** Electrical Systems Engineer **Type of organization:** U.S. government contractor **Major product:** Data collection - acoustic, RF from electro-mech autonomous platforms; circuit design **Area of distribution:** International **Expertise:** Electro-mechanical system integration **Affiliations:** American Legion; Former Member, I.E.E.E. **Hob./spts.:** Fishing, bike riding, gardening **SIC code:** 87 **Address:** 5940 Grissom Pkwy., Cocoa, FL 32927 **E-mail:** smerry@gryphonLC.com

MERTZ, R. PAUL
Industry: Engineering **Born:** December 16, 1962, Kirkwood, Missouri **Univ./degree:** B.S., Civil Engineering, University of Missouri- Rolla, 1985 **Current organization:** P.H. Weis and Associates, Inc. **Title:** Project Engineer **Type of organization:** Consulting firm **Major product:** Building and street design **Area of distribution:** National **Expertise:** Engineering **Hob./spts.:** Baseball, cars, soccer, plants **SIC code:** 87 **Address:** P.H. Weis and Associates, Inc., 410 Sovereign Ct., Suite 11, Ballwin, MO 63011 **Phone:** (636)207-0832 **Fax:** (636)207-0328 **E-mail:** pmertz@phweis.com

METCALFE-RAY, GLADYS
Industry: Interior design **Born:** Kingston, New Hampshire **Univ./degree:** A.A., Interior Design, University of New Hampshire, 1970 **Current organization:** GMR Designs LLC **Title:** Owner **Type of organization:** Manufacturing/consulting **Major product:** Interior design and soft home goods **Area of distribution:** New Hampshire **Expertise:** Fabrication and design of soft home goods **Published works:** Accent Magazine and Window Fashions **Affiliations:** A.B.W.A.; Exeter Portsmouth Chamber; New Hampshire Better Business Bureau **Hob./spts.:** Gardening, cooking, walking, biking **SIC code:** 87 **Address:** GMR Designs LLC, 106 Exeter Rd., Kingston, NH 03848

MICHELSON, SETH G.
Industry: Biotechnology **Born:** August 29, 1950, Miami, Florida **Univ./degree:** B.S., Mathematics, Tulane University, 1972; M.A., Applied Mathematics, 1974; M.S., Biomathematics, 1977, University of California at Berkeley; Ph.D., Biomathematics, U.C.L.A., 1988 **Current organization:** Entelos, Inc. **Title:** Vice President, Silicon R&D **Type of organization:** Contract research **Major product:** Collaborative research, model systems **Area of distribution:** National **Expertise:** Mathematical modeling of human diseases, applied research and simulation **Published works:** 70+ publications **Affiliations:** Adjunct Faculty in Biostatistics, University of California, Berkeley **Hob./spts.:** Photography **SIC code:** 87 **Address:** Entelos, Inc., 110 Marsh Dr., Foster City, CA 94404 **E-mail:** michelson@entelos.com **Web address:** www.entelos.com

MIELENZ, RICHARD C.
Industry: Consulting **Born:** December 18, 1913, Burlingame, California **Univ./degree:** Ph.D., University of California at Berkeley, 1939 **Current organization:** Richard C. Mielenz, P.E., Inc. **Title:** President **Type of organization:** Consulting **Major product:** Petrographic examination of concrete and concrete making materials **Area of distribution:** International **Expertise:** Laboratory and field investigations **Affiliations:** Former President, American Concrete Institute; Geological Society of America; Mineralogical Society of America; American Society for Testing and Materials; National Society of Professional Engineers; Ohio Society of Professional Engineers; Phi Beta Kappa **SIC code:** 87 **Address:** Richard C. Mielenz, P.E., Inc., 112 Woodcrest Dr., Marietta, OH 45750-1352

MIKULICIC, VLADIMIR B.
Industry: Engineering **Univ./degree:** B.S.C.E.; M.S.C.E., University of Zagreb, Croatia, 1975 **Current organization:** Parsons Energy & Chemical **Title:** Civil Engineer, P.E. **Type of organization:** Consulting **Major product:** Project and construction management **Area of distribution:** National **Expertise:** Engineering **Honors/awards:** Listed in Who's Who in Europe **Affiliations:** N.S.P.E.; A.S.C.E. **SIC code:** 87 **Address:** 916 Dewing Ave., Lafayette, CA 94549 **E-mail:** vlado@members.asce.org

MILLER, PAUL E.
Industry: Electrical Engineering **Born:** September 20, 1949, Augusta, Georgia **Current organization:** Black & Veatch **Title:** Senior Electrical Designer **Type of organization:** Engineering design company **Major product:** Electrical design and projects **Area of distribution:** International **Expertise:** Electrical power distribution **Honors/awards:** Electrical Design, J.D. Powers, 2001 **Affiliations:** International Association of Electrical Inspectors; Construction Education Foundation **Hob./spts.:** Scuba diving, golf, his grandchildren **SIC code:** 87 **Address:** Black & Veatch, 10751 Deerwood Park Blvd., Suite 130, Jacksonville, FL 32256 **E-mail:** millerpe@bv.com **Web address:** www.bv.com

MILLER, RONALD E.
Industry: Consulting **Born:** July 19, 1947, Mechanicsburg, Pennsylvania **Univ./degree:** A.A., Electronics Engineering, Penn College, 1969 **Current organization:** REM Consulting **Title:** Owner **Type of organization:** Consulting firm **Major product:** Semiconductor consulting **Area of distribution:** National **Expertise:** Reactive PVD film/aluminum nitride **Published works:** Multiple articles, 4 patents **Hob./spts.:** Fishing, football **SIC code:** 87 **Address:** REM Consulting, 336 Fireline Rd., Kintnersville, PA 18930 **E-mail:** rem47@aol.com

MILLER, VERLYN A.
Industry: Engineering **Born:** October 12, 1969, Alamogordo, New Mexico **Univ./degree:** B.S., Civil Engineering Technology, New Mexico State University, 1992 **Current organization:** Oden-Miller & Associates **Title:** Principal Engineer **Type of organization:** Engineering and consulting firm **Major product:** Consulting engineering specializing in municipal county projects **Area of distribution:** New Mexico **Expertise:** Civil engineering, design and development of drainage and flood control systems **Affiliations:** A.S.C.E.; N.S.P.E. **Hob./spts.:** Golf, football, travel **SIC code:** 87 **Address:** Oden-Miller & Associates, P.O. Box 1976, 200 Central S.E., Moriarty, NM 87035 **E-mail:** vmiller@odenmiller.com **Web address:** www.odenmiller.com

MILLER SR., SAMUEL T.
Industry: Food **Born:** January 2, 1960, Bellefontaine, Ohio **Current organization:** Nestle R&D **Title:** Utilities Supervisor **Type of organization:** Research and development **Major product:** Coffee, confections **Area of distribution:** National **Expertise:** Plant steam, water production and flow **Affiliations:** Boy Scout Master **Hob./spts.:** Family, hunting, fishing, camping **SIC code:** 87 **Address:** Nestle R&D, 809 Collins Ave., Marysville, OH 43040 **E-mail:** samuel.miller@rdoh.nestle.com

MIN, BRYAN B.
Industry: Engineering **Born:** March 13, 1964, Seoul, Korea **Univ./degree:** M.S., System Engineering, Virginia Polytechnic Institute,1996 **Current organization:** Epsilon System Solutions, Inc. **Title:** President/CEO **Type of organization:** Systems engineering **Major product:** Software, management **Expertise:** Systems engineering **Affiliations:** Naval Reserves; Harvard University Alumni Association **Hob./spts.:** Ironman, music, piano, reading, religion **SIC code:** 87 **Address:** Epsilon System Solutions, Inc., 2550 Fifth Ave., Suite 725, San Diego, CA 92103 **E-mail:** bmin@epsilonsystems.com

MINACA, PILAR MARIA
Industry: Aerospace **Born:** October 1, 1973, Springfield, Missouri **Univ./degree:** M.B.A., Southwest Missouri State University, 1996 **Current organization:** International Engineering Online **Title:** President, Founder, Manager **Type of organization:** Engineering/manufacturing **Major product:** Design/engineering/programming **Area of distribution:** International **Expertise:** Design engineering **Honors/awards:** Nationwide Who's Who; International Who's Who of Entrepreneurs **Affiliations:** Society of Manufacturing Engineers **Hob./spts.:** Choreography, house renovating & decorating, gourmet cooking **SIC code:** 87 **Address:** International Engineering Online, 92 Grenada Terrace, Springfield, MA 01108 **E-mail:** minaca@cs.com

MOBIN, PERVEZ
Industry: Consulting engineering **Born:** January 17, 1952, Karachi, Pakistan **Univ./degree:** B.S.E.E., 1974; M.S.E.E., 1976, Georgia Institute of Technology **Current organization:** Consulting Solutions Inc. **Title:** Principal **Type of organization:** Engineering firm **Major product:** Engineering **Area of distribution:** National **Expertise:** Electrical engineering; P.E. **Affiliations:** I.E.E.E. **Hob./spts.:** Tennis, golf, travel, the outdoors **SIC code:** 87 **Address:** Consulting Solutions Inc., 10650 Scripps Ranch Blvd., Suite 210, San Diego, CA 92131 **E-mail:** pmobin@cs-inc.us **Web address:** www.cs-inc.us

MOENS, LUC
Industry: Government/national laboratory **Born:** October 30, 1957, Antwerp, Belgium **Univ./degree:** B.S., Agrochemical Engineering, University of Ghent, Belgium, 1981; Ph.D., Organic Chemistry, University of California at Santa Barbara, 1987 **Current organization:** National Renewable Energy Laboratory **Title:** Senior Scientist **Type of organization:** R&D, U.S. Dept. of Energy **Major product:** Biomass chemistry and processing R&D; Biodiesel chemistry R&D; Solar thermal energy storage fluid development **Area of distribution:** International **Expertise:** Synthetic organic chemistry and electrochemistry **Honors/awards:** Presidents' Green Chemistry Challenge Award, 1999 **Affiliations:** American Chemical Society, 1981-present; Cellist, Denver Philharmonic Orchestra, 2005-present; Cellist and President of the former Rocky Mountain Symphony **Hob./spts.:** Classical music, botany, horticulture, skiing, hiking **SIC code:** 87 **Address:** National Renewable Energy Laboratory, 1617 Cole Blvd., Golden, CO 80401 **E-mail:** luc_moens@nrel.gov **Web address:** www.nrel.gov

MOH, PATRICK
Industry: Research & development/consulting **Univ./degree:** Ph.D., Biochemistry/Physchem, Ohio State University, 1979 **Current organization:** Cambridge Biomedical Research Group (P.O. Box 705, Brookline, MA 02446) **Title:** Vice President/Director R&D/Scientific Director **Type of organization:** Private and university associated **Major product:** R&D, esoteric assay research, development and testing **Area of distribution:** National **Expertise:** Experimental biology, medicine, biochemistry **Published works:** 30 articles, abstract, book chapters **Affiliations:** A.M.P.; American Chemical Society **SIC code:** 87 **Address:** Cambridge Biomedical Research Group, 1256 Soldiers Field Rd., Brighton, MA 02135-1003 **E-mail:** mohpa@aol.com

MOISES, EDWARD TUSAMBA
Industry: Consulting **Born:** August 12, 1963 **Univ./degree:** D.E.S. European Law, Univ. Paris XI, 1994; D.E.S. Diplomatic & Strategic Studies, Centre d'Etudes Diplomatiques et Strategic de Paris, 1996; LL.M. Beasley School of Law, Temple University; Ph.D., International Relations & Diplomacy, Univ. of Paris, 1999 **Current organization:** Institute for Policy, Diplomacy & Global Affairs (I P D G A) **Title:** Chairman/Attorney at Law **Type of organization:** Consulting **Major product:** Training in diplomacy, international politics, strategic studies, trial advocacy, international dispute, leadership programs **Area of distribution:** International **Expertise:** Angola, Central and Southern Africa, Europe, Asia; Lectured and trained high rankings on leadership skills, strategic analysis skills, advocacy skills, international litigation skills, international politics and diplomatic skills **Published works:** Several articles, 1 book, "Legal Issues in Contradictions Surrounding the Question of Peace in Angola" **Affiliations:** American Bar Association; Angolan Bar Association; Angolan Foundation for Peace and Civil Rights; French Association for Diplomatic and Strategic Studies; American Association for Political Science **Hob./spts.:** Tennis, classical music, family activities **SIC code:** 87 **Address:** Institute for Policy, Diplomacy & Global Affairs (I P D G A), 1090 Vermont St. N.W., Suite 800, Washington, DC 20005 **E-mail:** moises@ipdga.org **Web address:** www.ipdga.org

MOLL, JOHN L.
Industry: Consulting **Univ./degree:** Ph.D., Ohio State University, 1952 **Current organization:** Hewlett-Packard (Retired) **Title:** Ph.D. **Type of organization:** Research **Major product:** Semiconductors, software **Area of distribution:** International **Expertise:** Research **Affiliations:** National Academy of Science **Hob./spts.:** Computers **SIC code:** 87 **Address:** 1 W. Edith Ave. 105A, Los Altos, CA 94022-2770 **E-mail:** john1moll@msn.com

MOON, HARRY H.B.
Industry: Religion **Born:** July 3, 1948, South Korea **Univ./degree:** M.Div., Concordia University, 1990 **Current organization:** Korean Social Ministry of O.C. **Title:** Reverend/Pastor/President **Type of organization:** Ministry **Major product:** Mental and spiritual wellness **Area of distribution:** California **Expertise:** Social counseling **Affiliations:** L.C.M.S. **Hob./spts.:** Golf, fishing **SIC code:** 86 **Address:** Korean Social Ministry of O.C., 13121 Brookhurst St., Suite 1, Garden Grove, CA 92844 **E-mail:** harryhmoon@aol.com

MOONEY, ANA C.R.
Industry: Architecture **Born:** San Jose, Costa Rica **Univ./degree:** B.S, Architecture and Interior Design, University of Manitoba **Current organization:** Frederick Architectural Interiors Inc. **Title:** President **Type of organization:** Architectural firm **Major product:** Residential design, new and remodeled **Area of distribution:** Maryland **Expertise:** Residential design, administration **Hob./spts.:** Family, skiing instructor **SIC code:** 87 **Address:** Frederick Architectural Interiors Inc., 10701 Pheasant Dr., Clarksburg, MD 20871 **E-mail:** amooney333@adelphia.net

MOORE, JOY T.
Industry: Financial services **Born:** August 28, 1936, Greenville, Texas **Univ./degree:** Indiana University; Florida University; University of California at Los Angeles **Current organization:** Moore's Bookkeeping and Tax Service **Title:** Principal/Owner **Type of organization:** Accounting firm **Major product:** Bookkeeping and taxes, servicing over 1,000 clients yearly, financial planning **Area of distribution:** International **Expertise:** Executive management, taxes **Honors/awards:** Republican Presidential Medal of Merit; Presidential Honor Rolls Signed by Four Presidents; Outstanding Income Tax Service Plaque, 1986 **Affiliations:** National Association of Tax Practitioners; National Association of Executive Females; National Federation of Independent Business **Career accomplishments:** Started business in home and it is now a $100k+ business with only one associate; Owned the Coin and Stamp shop for ten years while also doing accounting in the back **Hob./spts.:** Music, coin and stamp collecting, hunting, writing **SIC code:** 87 **Address:** Moore's Bookkeeping & Tax Service, 326 County Rd. 2186, Greenville, TX 75402-4977 **E-mail:** jmoore_4826@yahoo.com

MOOREHEAD, LINDA
Industry: Military/aerospace **Born:** October 10, 1951, Holly Springs, Mississippi **Univ./degree:** B.S., Psychology, University of Houston, 1979 **Current organization:** Blackhawk Mgmt. Corp. **Title:** President/CEO **Type of organization:** Engineering **Major product:** Logistics, reverse engineering, I.T. for the Military and N.A.S.A. **Area of distribution:** International **Expertise:** Administration **SIC code:** 87 **Address:** Blackhawk Mgmt. Corp., 1335 Regents Park Dr., Suite 130, Houston, TX 77058 **E-mail:** mooreheadl@blackhawkmgmt.com **Web address:** www.blackhawkmgmt.com

MORALES-TORRES, ANIBAL
Industry: Religion **Born:** June 7, 1966, Arecibo, Puerto Rico **Univ./degree:** M.A., Theology, St. Vincent De Paul Regional Seminary, 1993 **Current organization:** All Saints Catholic Church **Title:** Reverend **Type of organization:** Church **Major product:** Religious teaching and leadership **Area of distribution:** National **Expertise:** Education, theology **Affiliations:** Knights of Columbus **Hob./spts.:** Dance instruction **SIC code:** 86 **Address:** All Saints Catholic Church, 10900 W. Oakland Pk. Blvd., Sunrise, FL 33351 **E-mail:** amorales@allsaintsvillage.com

MORGAN, DWAYNE R.
Industry: Aerospace **Univ./degree:** B.A., Physics, University of North Texas, 1991; M.S., Materials Science, University of North Texas, 2001 **Current organization:** Touchstone Research Laboratory **Title:** Carbon Research Scientist **Type of organization:** Research laboratory **Major product:** CFOAM (Carbon Foam) **Area of distribution:** National **Expertise:** Research Scientist **Hob./spts.:** Family, music, guitar, clarinet **SIC code:** 87 **Address:** Touchstone Research Laboratory, RR 100B, The Millennium Centre, Triadelphia, WV 26059 **E-mail:** dwaynemorgan@hotmail.com

MORRIS, PAM R.
Industry: Insurance/healthcare **Univ./degree:** A.S.R.N., San Juan College, New Mexico; C.R.R.N. Certified, Life Force Rehab, 1993 **Current organization:** P. Morris Consulting **Title:** R.N./President **Type of organization:** Consulting/healthcare insurance **Major product:** Consulting **Area of distribution:** National **Expertise:** Underwriting assessments, insurance case management **Affiliations:** A.R.N.; C.R.R.N **SIC code:** 87 **Address:** P. Morris Consulting, 6509 Veda Lane, Farmington, NM 87402 **E-mail:** pmorris@advantas.net

MORUZA, TITO GANDARILLAS
Industry: Consulting **Born:** February 15, 1921, Santander, Spain **Univ./degree:** B.S., University of California at Berkeley **Title:** Colonel (Retired) **Type of organization:** Consulting firm **Major product:** Consulting **Area of distribution:** International **Expertise:** International law **Affiliations:** Retired Officers Association; U.S. Committee for the Battle of Normandy Museum; D-Day Museum of St. Mere d'Eglise; Charter Member, WW II Memorial; Retired Counter Intelligence Corps Association; World Affairs Council; The Commonwealth Club of California; International House Association **Hob./spts.:** Classical music, skiing, tennis, family, international travel, culture of the Spanish Peninsula **SIC code:** 87 **Address:** 511 Dwight Place, Berkeley, CA 94704-2512

MOSHER, FREDERICK K.
Industry: Consulting engineering **Current organization:** TMG Engineering Inc. **Title:** Vice President **Type of organization:** Design firm **Major product:** Mechanical and electrical systems **Area of distribution:** International **Expertise:** Engineering/marketing **Affiliations:** A.C.S.; A.S.C.E.; I.S.P.E. **Hob./spts.:** Hunting, fishing **SIC code:** 87 **Address:** TMG Engineering Inc., 1090 King Georges Post Rd., Suite 903, Edison, NJ 08837 **E-mail:** fmosher@usa.net

MOULANA, EASA M.
Industry: Engineering/Construction **Born:** July 7, 1937, Iraq **Univ./degree:** B.S., American University, 1962; M.S., University of Cincinnati, 1968 **Current organization:** AEP Engineering **Title:** P.E. (licensed in New York, New Jersey and Ohio) **Type of organization:** Consulting firm **Major product:** Engineering services **Area of distribution:** New York, New Jersey, Connecticut **Expertise:** Commercial and residential buildings, waterfront structures **Honors/awards:** O.S.P.E. **Affiliations:** A.S.C.E. **Hob./spts.:** French and German literature **SIC code:** 87 **Address:** AEP Engineering, 17 Sycamore Dr., Roslyn, NY 11576 **E-mail:** amercanstate@aol.com

MOULDEN JR., FRED A.
Industry: Communications **Univ./degree:** B.S., Illinois Institute of Technology, 1982; M.S., Computer Science, Washington University in St. Louis, 1995 **Current organization:** eSolutions **Title:** Founder **Type of organization:** Consulting **Major product:** Software **Area of distribution:** National **Expertise:** Business improvement, infrastructure, site development, software **Affiliations:** A.C.M. **Hob./spts.:** Martial arts, chess **SIC code:** 87 **Address:** eSolutions, 762 W. Remington Dr., Sunnyvale, CA 94087 **E-mail:** fmoulden@theesolutions.com

MOZELL, HERBERT L.
Industry: Mental health **Born:** February 16, 1963, Miami, Florida **Univ./degree:** B.S., Psychology; M.S., Adult Education, North Carolina A&T State University **Current organization:** Visions of North Carolina, Inc. **Title:** President/Founder **Type of organization:** Not for profit **Major product:** Residential treatment for adolescents with emotional and behavioral disorders **Area of distribution:** North Carolina **Expertise:** Program development, management, administration **Hob./spts.:** Martial arts (4th Degree Black Belt) **SIC code:** 83 **Address:** Visions of North Carolina, Inc., 7607-A Alcorn Rd., Greensboro, NC 27409 **E-mail:** hmozell@hotmail.com

MUELLER, I. LYNN
Industry: Consulting **Born:** February 2, 1941, Cincinnati, Ohio **Spouse:** Maria R. Cavallino **Married:** September 8, 2000 **Children:** Shallah W. Mueller, Geoffrey Koskinen **Univ./degree:** M.B.A., University of Cincinnati **Current organization:** Decisions Strategies Group **Title:** President **Type of organization:** Consulting firm **Major product:** Strategic planning **Area of distribution:** International **Expertise:** Strategic planning **Honors/awards:** Who's Who in the World, 1999-present; Who's Who in the East, 1998-present; Principal Consultant, Governor George Pataki Transition Team, 1994 **Published works:** Contributed book chapter to "Winning Campaigns With The New Politics", 1971; Cover article, "Direct Marketing Magazine", 1971 **Affiliations:** B.C.N.Y., The Planetary Society **Career accomplishments:** Successful entrepreneur in multiple endeavors **Hob./spts.:** Tennis, reading, basketball **SIC code:** 87 **Address:** Decisions Strategies Group, 111 Washington Ave., Suite 409, Albany, NY 12107 **E-mail:** lynnmueller@dsgny.com **Web address:** www.dsgny.com

MULRENNAN JR., JOHN A.
Industry: Entomology consulting **Born:** March 2, 1934, Tallahassee, Florida **Univ./degree:** Ph.D., Entomology, Oklahoma State University, 1968 **Current organization:** Mulrennan & Associates, Inc. **Title:** President **Type of organization:** Consulting **Major product:** Consulting/expert witness **Area of distribution:** Florida **Expertise:** Entomology **Published works:** Scientific journals **Affiliations:** Past President, A.M.C.A.; P.C.A.; F.M.C.A. **Hob./spts.:** Golf, walking, gardening **SIC code:** 87 **Address:** Mulrennan & Associates, Inc., P.O. Box 5321, Jacksonville, FL 32217 **E-mail:** mulrennan9@aol.com

MUNGEKAR, HEMANT P.
Industry: Semiconductors **Born:** Bombay, India **Univ./degree:** Ph.D., Mechanical Engineering, University of Michigan, 2001 **Current organization:** Applied Materials Inc. **Title:** Senior Process Engineer **Type of organization:** R&D, Manufacturing **Major product:** CVD reactors **Area of distribution:** International **Expertise:** Heat transfer, chemically reacting flows, high density plasma, diagnostic techniques **Affiliations:** A.S.M.E., Combustion Institute **SIC code:** 87 **Address:** Applied Materials Inc., 3330 Scott Blvd., M/S 0681, Santa Clara, CA 95054 **E-mail:** hemantmungekar@amat.com

MUNSON, EDWARD D.
Industry: Wastewater **Born:** September 9, 1931, Mexico, Missouri **Univ./degree:** M.S., Sanitary Engineering, University of Missouri, 1960 **Current organization:** Malcolm Pirnie, Inc. **Title:** Senior Project Engineer **Type of organization:** Consulting firm **Major product:** Water, wastewater design **Area of distribution:** National **Expertise:** Engineering **Affiliations:** A.W.W.A.; WE.F. **Hob./spts.:** Fishing, handyman **SIC code:** 87 **Address:** Malcolm Pirnie, Inc., 2170 Highland Ave. S., Suite 250, Birmingham, AL 35205 **E-mail:** emunson@pirnie.com **Web address:** www.pirnie.com

MURPHY, MARCINA M.
Industry: Printing/tax preparation **Born:** August 3, 1951, Chicago, Illinois **Current organization:** Murphy's Tax & Printing Service **Title:** President/CEO **Type of organization:** Tax prep printing specialist/counselor **Major product:** Tax prep & counseling **Area of distribution:** Dixmoor, Illinois **Expertise:** Tax prep, printing, counseling **Affiliations:** National Notary Association; National Payroll Association **Hob./spts.:** Photography, computers **SIC code:** 87 **Address:** Murphy's Tax & Printing Service, Three W. 141st St., Dixmoor, IL 60426 **E-mail:** taxbusiness@sprynet.com

MURPHY, NEIL J.
Industry: Nonprofit/education **Born:** July 25, 1954, Chicago, Illinois **Univ./degree:** B.S., Education, Auburn University, 1976; B.S., Accounting, Florida International University, 1994 **Current organization:** University of Miami Transplant Foundation Inc. **Title:** Accountant **Type of organization:** Nonprofit organization affiliated with the University of Miami School of Medicine **Major product:** Providing services for transplant recipients, increasing organ donation through community education and funding transplant research **Area of distribution:** Florida **Expertise:** Accounting **Honors/awards:** All Southeastern Conference Cross Country Team, Auburn University, 1975; Coach of the Year, The Miami Herald, 1983 **Affiliations:** Chaminade-Madonna College Preparatory High School **Hob./spts.:** Track & Field **SIC code:** 86 **Address:** 6435 Lemon Tree Lane, Miami Lakes, FL 33014-6021

MURPHY, SANDRA A.
Industry: Childcare **Born:** June 13, 1953, Brooklyn, New York **Univ./degree:** Presently enrolled at Empire State College of New York **Current organization:** Sam's Place Child Care **Title:** Director/Owner **Type of organization:** Childcare facility **Major product:** Early childhood education and development **Area of distribution:** Uniondale, New York **Expertise:** Education, development **Affiliations:** N.A.E.Y.C.; C.A.U.; B.W.E.; F.D.C.A.; C.C.C. **Hob./spts.:** Reading, skiing **SIC code:** 83 **Address:** Sam's Place Child Care, 539 Pine Place, Uniondale, NY 11553 **E-mail:** sam539@aol.com

MUSICARO, PATRICIA
Industry: Financial **Univ./degree:** A.S., Business Administration; B.S., Accounting, St. Francis College **Current organization:** Musicaro Business Services **Title:** President **Type of organization:** Accounting and tax agency **Major product:** Accounting, taxes and consulting services **Area of distribution:** National **Expertise:** Taxes **Affiliations:** Instructor/Program Coordinator, Kingsborough Community College **Hob./spts.:** Basketball, arts and crafts, reading **SIC code:** 87 **Address:** P.O. Box 186, Brooklyn, NY 11228 **E-mail:** patriciam@nyc.rr.com

NABHANI, ZIAD A.
Industry: Consulting **Born:** August 18, 1942, Amman, Jordan **Univ./degree:** B.S., Electrical Engineering, Wichita State University **Current organization:** Fluor **Title:** Lead Electrical Engineer **Type of organization:** Engineering, construction firm **Major product:** Design, construction **Area of distribution:** International **Expertise:** Engineering **Affiliations:** I.E.E.E. **Hob./spts.:** Golf, tennis **SIC code:** 87 **Address:** Fluor, 15 Elmwood Dr., Taylors, SC 29687 **E-mail:** ziad.nabhani@fluor.com

NACCARATO, ANTHONY F.
Industry: Construction/engineering **Born:** May 12, 1966, Philadelphia, Pennsylvania **Univ./degree:** B.A., Civil Engineering, Villanova University, 1988 **Current organization:** O'Donnell & Naccarato, Inc. **Title:** Principal, P.E. **Type of organization:** Engineering firm **Major product:** Consulting structural engineering **Area of distribution:** Pennsylvania **Expertise:** Structural engineering **Honors/awards:** Villanova University Engineering Alumni Award **Affiliations:** A.I.A.; D.V.A.S.E.; American Society of civil Engineers **Hob./spts.:** Skiing, golf, playing guitar **SIC code:** 87 **Address:** O'Donnell & Naccarato, Inc., 111 S. Independence Mall East, Suite 950, Philadelphia, PA 19106 **E-mail:** anaccarato@o-n.com

NAIR, A.D.
Industry: Government **Born:** August 9, 1959, India **Univ./degree:** Ph.D., Astronomy/Signal Processing, University of Florida, 1995 **Current organization:** US Technology Resources **Title:** Sr. Consultant **Type of organization:** Consulting **Major product:** E-Commerce application and development **Area of distribution:** International **Expertise:** Management, consulting, new business development **Published works:** 30 Publications, including: A.D. Nair, 1995, PhD Th. 3N, CCD Observing and Dynamical Time Series Analysis of Active Galactic Nuclei; A.D. Nair and Alex C. Smith, 1994, AAS, 185, 4005N, A Test for Nonlinearity in Time Series: Application to 3C 345; A.D. Nair and R.E. Stoner, 1989, BAAS, 21, 777N, Spherical Outflow Interpretation of BAL Quasar Emission Profiles **Affiliations:** I.E.E.E.; A.A.A.I. **SIC code:** 87 **Address:** US Technology Resources, 3649 Emerald St. #119, Torrance, CA 90503 **E-mail:** anair1@socal.rr.com

NANCE, FRANCES LYNNE
Industry: Finance **Born:** November 19, 1923, Memphis, Tennessee **Univ./degree:** A.A., Accounting, Northwestern Junior College, 1982 **Current organization:** C & L Bookkeeping & Tax Service **Title:** Tax Accountant **Type of organization:** Private accounting office **Major product:** Accounting, consulting **Area of distribution:** Tennessee **Expertise:** Certified tax professional/tax consultant **Hob./spts.:** Golf, casino gaming **SIC code:** 87 **Address:** C & L Bookkeeping & Tax Service, 970 Blanchard Rd., Memphis, TN 38116-7013

NANNI, DANILO
Industry: Engineering/construction **Born:** October 10, 1968, Rimini, Italy **Univ./degree:** M.S.C.E., Structural Engineering, Polytechnic University of Milano, Italy/The Polytechnical Institute of Berlin, Germany, (Technische Universitaet Berlin) 1995; M.B.A., University of Miami, Florida, 2002 **Current organization:** Lauris Boulanger, Inc. **Title:** Professional Engineer **Type of organization:** Consulting firm/contractor/construction management **Major product:** Engineering/construction **Area of distribution:** National **Expertise:** Structural engineering, construction management **Honors/awards:** Award of Academic Merit in Graduate Studies for the M.B.A. Degree, University of Miami, 2002 **Affiliations:** A.S.C.E.; Florida, S.E.S.; Lion's Club; Florida Engineering Society **Hob./spts.:** Certified Scuba Diver; parachuting, playing saxophone and flute **SIC code:** 87 **Address:** 19380 Collins Ave., #410B, Sunny Isles, FL 33160 **E-mail:** danilonanni@aol.com

NAYLOR, J. MATTHEW
Industry: Consulting engineering **Born:** April 14, 1957, Cincinnati, Ohio **Univ./degree:** B.S., Civil Engineering, University of Cincinnati, 1993 **Current organization:** Naylor Engineering, Inc. **Title:** P.E. **Type of organization:** Engineering firm **Major product:** Consulting engineering **Area of distribution:** Ohio, Kentucky, Indiana **Expertise:** Geotechnical, foundation structural, storm hydrology **Affiliations:** A.S.C.E.; Structural Engineers; Structural Engineering Institute; Geotechnical Institute **Hob./spts.:** Family, reading, golf, little league **SIC code:** 87 **Address:** Naylor Engineering, Inc., 1007 Eversole Rd., Cincinnati, OH 45230 **E-mail:** jmnaylor@fuse.net

NAZARIO-VELÁZQUEZ, NOEL
Industry: Consulting **Born:** January 13, 1939, Mayaguez, Puerto Rico **Univ./degree:** Ph.D., Civil Engineering, 2001 **Current organization:** R-G Engineering Inc. **Title:** P.E., Ph.D., C.E. **Type of organization:** Engineering **Major product:** Electric power, high voltage **Area of distribution:** Puerto Rico **Expertise:** Engineering **SIC code:** 87 **Address:** R-G Engineering Inc., 605 Condado St., Suite 322, San Juan, PR 00907 **E-mail:** n-nazario@rgepr.com

NEWBY, JOHN R.
Industry: Consulting **Born:** November 17, 1923, Kansas City, Missouri **Univ./degree:** B.S., Chemistry, University of Missouri, 1947; Met.Eng. (Metallurgical Engineering), Colorado School of Mines, 1949; M.S., University of Cincinnati, 1963 **Current organization:** John Newby Consulting **Title:** Principal **Type of organization:** Engineering and consulting **Major product:** Metals **Area of distribution:** Ohio **Expertise:** Failure analysis, accident reconstruction **Honors/awards:** Fellow, American Society for Metals International **Published works:** Articles and books on mechanical testing **Affiliations:** Chairman, Committee E-28 on Mechanical Testing, American Society for Testing & Materials; American Society for Metals International **Hob./spts.:** Art, mixed media, sailing **SIC code:** 87 **Address:** John Newby Consulting, 100 Marymount Court, Middletown, OH 45042-0584 **E-mail:** newbyjohn@aol.com

NEWMAN, JAMES E.
Industry: Consulting **Born:** December 22, 1920, Georgetown, Ohio **Univ./degree:** M.S., Climatology, Ohio State University; Ph.D., Wisconsin University **Current organization:** AGWX Consulting Climatologist **Title:** Climatologist **Type of organization:** Consulting **Major product:** Seasonal climate impacts on agricultural production (cereal grains and oil seeds) worldwide **Area of distribution:** U.S. and Canada **Expertise:** Seasonal weather and climate forecasting **Affiliations:** Editor-in-Chief, 1968-75, Agricultural and Forest Meteorology **Hob./spts.:** Fishing, hunting, travel **SIC code:** 87 **Address:** AGWX Consulting Climatologist, 1100 Hillcrest Rd., West Lafayette, IN 47906-2212 **E-mail:** pjnewman@nlci.com

NEWSLOW, DEBBY L.
Industry: Food/consulting **Born:** Needham, Massachusetts **Univ./degree:** B.S., Food Science, University of Florida, 1973 **Current organization:** D.L. Newslow & Associates **Title:** President **Type of organization:** Consulting firm **Major product:** Food safety training, workshops, quality systems **Area of distribution:** International **Expertise:** Quality systems, consulting **Published works:** 30 articles on food safety, 1 book **Affiliations:** A.S.Q.; I.S.T.; I.A.F.P. **SIC code:** 87 **Address:** D.L. Newslow & Associates, 8260 Cathy Ann St., Orlando, FL 32818 **E-mail:** newsdl@aol.com **Web address:** www.newslow.com

NGUYEN, ANN-LISA Q.
Industry: Consulting **Born:** October 24, 1972, Saigon, Vietnam **Univ./degree:** B.S., Computer Science, Cal Poly San Luis Obispo, 1994; M.S., Business Administration, New York University, 1998 **Title:** Management Consultant/Owner **Type of organization:** Self-employed consultant **Major product:** Software consulting **Area of**

distribution: California **Expertise:** Business operations, business process for CRM and hi-technology innovations **Hob./spts.:** Making espresso drinks, modeling, charity work **SIC code:** 87 **Address:** Ann-Lisa Nguyen, 3566 Minto Ct., San Jose, CA 95132 **E-mail:** lisa_q_nguyen@yahoo.com

NGUYEN, BINH
Industry: Pharmaceuticals **Born:** January 19, 1959, Saigon, Vietnam **Univ./degree:** Ph.D., Georgetown University, 1985; M.D., University of Maryland, 1989 **Current organization:** Eli Lilly & Co. **Title:** M.D., Ph.D. **Type of organization:** Clinical research and development **Major product:** Medical products **Area of distribution:** International **Expertise:** Medical Oncologist **Published works:** 50 articles **Affiliations:** A.S.C.O.; E.S.M.O.; R.A.P.S. **Hob./spts.:** Scuba diving, travel, sailing, photography **SIC code:** 87 **Address:** Eli Lilly & Co., 546 S. Meridian St., Indianapolis, IN 46225 **E-mail:** nguyen_binh@lilly.com

NGUYEN, QUAT T.
Industry: Consulting **Born:** June 26, 1970, Saigon, Vietnam **Univ./degree:** B.S., Civil Engineering/Architectural Engineering, Drexel University, 1996 **Current organization:** Orndorf & Associates, Inc. **Title:** Associate **Type of organization:** Structural engineering firm **Major product:** Designing commercial, industrial, educational, institutional and residential buildings **Area of distribution:** Pennsylvania, New Jersey and Delaware **Expertise:** Engineering **Affiliations:** A.S.C.E.; D.V.A.S.E.; A.I.S.E. **Hob./spts.:** Fishing, camping, tennis, travel **SIC code:** 87 **Address:** Orndorf & Associates, Inc., 112 Cricket Ave., Ardmore, PA 19003 **E-mail:** qnguyen@orndorf.com

NICHOL, YANCY T.
Industry: Consulting engineering **Born:** December 10, 1962, Torrington, Wyoming **Univ./degree:** B.S., University of Wyoming, 1986 **Current organization:** Sopris Engineering, LLC **Title:** Owner **Type of organization:** Consulting firm **Major product:** Civil engineering, surveying **Area of distribution:** Carbondale, Colorado **Expertise:** Engineering, surveying **Affiliations:** A.C.C.E. **Hob./spts.:** Hunting, fishing **SIC code:** 87 **Address:** Sopris Engineering, LLC, 502 Main St., Suite A3, Carbondale, CO 81623 **E-mail:** ynichol@sopriseng.com **Web address:** www.sopriseng.com

NICKELS, KEITH H.
Industry: Utilities/nuclear power **Born:** September 26, 1948, Manitowoc, Wisconsin **Univ./degree:** B.B.A., Silver Lake College, 1990 **Current organization:** Kewaunee Nuclear Power Plant **Title:** Electrical Systems Maintenance Supervisor **Type of organization:** Nuclear power plant **Major product:** Nuclear generated electricity **Area of distribution:** Wisconsin **Expertise:** Nuclear power plant management, electrical systems **Hob./spts.:** Model airplanes, trains, hunting, camping **SIC code:** 87 **Address:** Kewaunee Nuclear Power Plant, N490 Highway 42, Kewaunee, WI 54216 **E-mail:** keith.nickels@nmcco.com

NINNIE, EUGENE D.
Industry: Engineering **Born:** March 18, 1957, Endicott, New York **Univ./degree:** B.S., Architectural Engineering, University of Wyoming, 1982 **Current organization:** Civil Technologies & Engineering P.C. **Title:** President **Type of organization:** Architectural/engineering firm **Major product:** Architecture and engineering **Area of distribution:** National **Expertise:** P.E., design builder, architectural engineering **Affiliations:** A.I.S.C., A.C.I., A.S.C.E., N.S.P.E. **Hob./spts.:** Target shooting **SIC code:** 87 **Address:** Civil Technologies & Engineering P.C., 2622 South Ave., Wappingers Falls, NY 12590 **E-mail:** edn@cte1.com **Web address:** www.cte1.com

NIWAGABA, WILLY K.
Industry: Telecommunications **Born:** September 29, 1954, Kampala, Uganda **Univ./degree:** B.S.E.E., Hons, Makerere University, 1979; M.S.E.E., University of Texas at Arlington, 1989; M.B.A., University of Dallas, 1993 **Current organization:** Global Electro-Comm. Int'l Inc. **Title:** Director, Engineering & Consulting **Type of organization:** Consulting firm **Major product:** Telecommunication consulting and system integration **Area of distribution:** International **Expertise:** Engineering **Published works:** "Range Modernization for Fort Bliss, Texas", May 1992 (H.O. Hall, W.K. Niwagaba & V. Dovydoitis) **Affiliations:** T.S.P.E.; N.S.P.E.; N.Y.A.S.; S.I.E. **Hob./spts.:** Reading, jogging **SIC code:** 87 **Address:** Global Electro-Comm. Int'l Inc., 5720 LBJ Freeway, #470, Dallas, TX 75240 **E-mail:** willy@globalelectrocomm.com

NODEN, RONALD E.
Industry: Consulting **Born:** December 16, 1959, Nebraska **Univ./degree:** B.A., Business, Canterbury University, 1999 **Current organization:** Glenhurst Consulting Group **Title:** Managing Director **Type of organization:** Consulting firm **Major product:** Sales and leadership **Area of distribution:** International **Expertise:** Business growth and consulting **Honors/awards:** National Association of Computer Consulting Business Award, 2002-2003 **Affiliations:** National Speakers Association; National Association of Computer Consulting **Hob./spts.:** Golf, Church Planting, Evangelism **SIC code:** 87 **Address:** Glenhurst Consulting Group, 1240 Lecuyer Circle, Stillwater, MN 55082 **E-mail:** rnoden@glenhurstconsulting.com **Web address:** www.glenhurstconsulting.com

NORMAN, EDWIN J.
Industry: Consulting **Univ./degree:** A.S., Food Service Management, Iowa State University **Current organization:** MVP Services Group, Inc. **Title:** President **Type of organization:** Consulting firm **Major product:** Food facilities planning, management advisory services **Area of distribution:** Midwest U.S. **Expertise:** Consulting **Published works:** "Managing The Supply Chain, A Guide For the Independent Operator", The Consultant, 1998, Vol. 31, #2; "Thrifty Kitchens Don't Burn Dough", Nations Restaurant News, 1999, Vol. 33, #39 **Affiliations:** Food Service Consultants Society International Professional Member **Hob./spts.:** Golf, travel **SIC code:** 87 **Address:** MVP Services Group, Inc., 875 Jackson St., Suite 111, Dubuque, IA 52001 **E-mail:** mvp@galenalink.net **Web address:** www.mvpservicesgroup.com

NORTON, ELIZABETH K.
Industry: Engineering **Univ./degree:** B.S.C.E., Penn State University, 1999 **Current organization:** Pennoni Assoc. **Title:** Staff Engineer **Type of organization:** Consulting engineering firm **Major product:** Utilities design, residential and commercial **Area of distribution:** Northeastern Pennsylvania **Expertise:** Hydrology **Affiliations:** American Society of Civil Engineers; Society of American Military Engineers **Hob./spts.:** Swimming, playing piano , running **SIC code:** 87 **Address:** Pennoni Assoc., 3001 Market St., Philadelphia, PA 19104

NUNN, OSSIE
Industry: Automotive **Born:** August 25, 1945, Arkansas **Univ./degree:** B.S., Central Michigan University, 1982 **Current organization:** Pyramid Quality Solutions and Innovations **Title:** CEO **Type of organization:** Consulting **Major product:** Engineering **Area of distribution:** National **Expertise:** Quality engineering **Hob./spts.:** Golf, gardening **SIC code:** 87 **Address:** 30680 Montpelier, Madison Heights, MI 48071 **E-mail:** onunn@pqsiinc.com

OAKES, THOMAS W.
Industry: Consulting **Born:** June 14, 1950, Danville, Virginia **Univ./degree:** M.S., Nuclear Engineering, Virginia Polytechnic Institute, 1976; M.S., Environmental Engineering, University of Tennessee at Knoxville, 1981 **Current organization:** T30 National Service, Inc. **Title:** President **Type of organization:** Consulting firm **Major product:** Engineering and computers **Area of distribution:** National **Expertise:** Engineering **Affiliations:** A.C.S.; A.A.A.S.; Certified Hazardous Materials Managers **Hob./spts.:** Golf **SIC code:** 87 **Address:** T30 National Service, Inc., 11130 Kingston Pike, Suite I-328, Knoxville, TN 37922 **E-mail:** t30@oakes@inetmail.att.net

OAKS, GLENN S.
Industry: Consulting **Born:** September 20, 1949, Hagerstown, Maryland **Univ./degree:** Thomas Nelson Community College, 1975 **Current organization:** J.P. Harvey Engineering Solutions **Title:** Senior Electrical Designer **Type of organization:** Consulting engineering firm **Major product:** Mechanical electrical plumbing design **Area of distribution:** Virginia **Expertise:** Lighting, power system design, electrical historical design **Honors/awards:** Outstanding Young Americans 1980; Project Awards from Hampton Roads Association for Real Estate Excellence, 2 Design Awards; Preservation Alliance of Virginia, Preservation Award for 2001; Tidewater Region of American Institute of Architects, 2 Design Awards **Affiliations:** I.E.S.; I.E.S.N.A. **Hob./spts.:** Church work, sightseeing, cooking **SIC code:** 87 **Address:** J.P. Harvey Engineering Solutions, 29 N. Kings Way, Hampton, VA 23669-3503 **E-mail:** goaks@jphes.com **Web address:** www.jphes.com

OATES, WILLIE
Industry: Non-profit organizations **Born:** January 14, 1918, Arkansas City, Kansas **Univ./degree:** B.A., Foreign Languages, University of Arkansas, 1941 **Current organization:** Arkansas Division of The American Cancer Society (& 49 other organizations) **Title:** Professional Volunteer **Type of organization:** Non-profit **Major product:** Volunteering **Area of distribution:** National **Expertise:** Motivational skits **Honors/awards:** Little Rock Woman of the Year, 1955; Woman of the Year, Diamond Charter Chapter, ABWA, 1961; Arkansas Traveler Award, Gov. Orval Faubus, 1963; Lady of the Day in Central Arkansas, 1964; Honorary Recruiter in Arkansas for U.S. Army and U.S. Navy, 1968; Awarded Doctor of Aerospaceology by Gen. Jones, USAF Commander, Air Force Easter Test Range, 1968; First Woman Appointee to Grand Jury in Pulaski County; Arkansas Hat Lady; Appointed to the DACOWITS by Secretary of Defense, Robert McNamara; 100 Arkansas Women of Achievement, selected by the Arkansas Press Women **Published works:** Articles **Affiliations:** Little Rock Air Force Base Community Council; Board of Arkansas Division, American Cancer Society; Arkansas Heart Association; March of Dimes; Special Activities Chairperson, Salvation Army Auxiliary; Honorary Life Member, Salvation Army Advisory Board; Fundraiser, City Federation of Women's Clubs; Vice President and Fundraiser, Baptist Medical Center Auxiliary; Public Relations Chairperson and Advisory Board, Arkansas Medical Society Auxiliary; State Legislative Chairman for Business & Professional Women; First Woman President of the Founders Lions Club of Little Rock; Board Member, Multiple Sclerosis; Board Member, United Cerebral Palsy Board; Board Member, Arkansas Division, American Heart Board; Board Member, Alzheimer's Association; Board Member, Ecumenical Prison Ministry; Board Member, Florence

Crittenden Home; Board Member, Altrusa Club; President, Retired Senior Volunteer Program Auxiliary; Member, Little Rock Chapter, DAR; Honorary Member, Beta Sigma Phi **Hob./spts.:** Hat collecting, alumni squad leader, community service **SIC code:** 86 **Address:** 208 Cambridge Place Dr., Little Rock, AR 72227

O'CONNELL, THOMAS A.
Industry: Engineering **Born:** October 24, 1961, Cork, Ireland **Current organization:** Technip **Type of organization:** Contracting firm **Major product:** Engineering **Area of distribution:** International **Expertise:** Engineering **Hob./spts.:** Photography and gardening **SIC code:** 87 **Address:** 5803 Grand Creek Lane, Katy, TX 77450-5470

O'DONNELL, DECLAN JOSEPH
Industry: Membership association/nonprofit/legal **Born:** December 24, 1938, Detroit, Michigan **Univ./degree:** J.D., University of Michigan, 1963 **Current organization:** World Space Bar Association, Inc. **Title:** President **Type of organization:** Legal association **Major product:** Association of professionals **Area of distribution:** International **Expertise:** Trial Lawyer **Published works:** 100 publications **Hob./spts.:** Racquetball, skiing **SIC code:** 86 **Address:** World Space Bar Association, Inc., 499 S. Larkspur Dr., Castle Rock, CO 80104 **E-mail:** djopc@quest.net

OEHME, WOLFGANG
Industry: Architecture/landscaping **Born:** May 18, 1930, Chemnitz, Germany **Univ./degree:** B.S., Landscape Architecture, University of Berlin, 1954 **Current organization:** Oehme, Van Sweden & Associates, Inc. **Title:** C.E.O. **Type of organization:** Architectural firm **Major product:** Landscape planning and design **Area of distribution:** International **Expertise:** Master planning, landscape design **Affiliations:** F.A.S.L.A. **Hob./spts.:** Plants **SIC code:** 87 **Address:** Oehme, Van Sweden & Associates, Inc., 800 G St. S.E., Washington, DC 20003 **E-mail:** ovs@ovsla.com

OHANIAN, RUBINA
Industry: Consulting **Univ./degree:** Ph.D., Master Communications, 1981; Ph.D., Advertising, University of Texas at Austin **Current organization:** Accenture **Title:** Associate Partner **Type of organization:** Consulting firm **Major product:** Communications and High Tech, CRM **Area of distribution:** International **Expertise:** Telecommunications, CRM **Published works:** 30 journal articles **Affiliations:** A.M.A. **Hob./spts.:** Oil painting **SIC code:** 87 **Address:** Accenture, 3475 Oak Valley Rd. NE, Apt. 2910, Atlanta, GA 30326 **E-mail:** rubina.ohanian@accenture.com

O'HARA, CHRISTOPHER E.
Industry: Engineering **Born:** October 4, 1973, Oceanside, New York **Univ./degree:** B.S., Engineering, Notre Dame, 1995 **Current organization:** Loris & Associates, Inc. **Title:** P.E., Senior Structural Engineer **Type of organization:** Consulting firm **Major product:** Buildings, bridges, roads, special structures **Area of distribution:** International **Expertise:** Structural/civil engineering **Affiliations:** A.S.C.E. **Hob./spts.:** Skiing **SIC code:** 87 **Address:** Loris & Assoc., Inc., 1373 Forest Park Circle, #102, Lafayette, CO 80026 **E-mail:** cohara@lorisandassociates.com

OMEL, DAVID R.
Industry: Resort **Born:** November 8, 1953, Long Beach, California **Current organization:** VisionMaker **Title:** Vice President, Operations **Type of organization:** Consulting/development/management **Major product:** Resort/leisure destinations - feasibility studies, development, operations **Area of distribution:** International **Expertise:** Administration **Hob./spts.:** Golf **SIC code:** 87 **Address:** VisionMaker, 600 City Pkwy. West, Suite 320, Orange, CA 92868 **E-mail:** dave.omel@v-maker.com

ONYEAGORO, TONY C.
Industry: Consulting **Univ./degree:** M.S., University of Massachusetts, 1978 **Current organization:** Cole Consulting Corp. **Title:** Director **Type of organization:** Consulting/research/testing **Major product:** Construction materials **Area of distribution:** International **Expertise:** Licensed Professional Engineer **Affiliations:** A.S.C.E.; N.S.P.E.; A.C.I. **SIC code:** 87 **Address:** Cole Consulting Corp., 2269 Saw Mill River Rd., Bldg. 5, Elmsford, NY 10523 **E-mail:** tgoro@coleconsultingcorp.net

OSTERMEIER, KENYA CARINE
Industry: Veterans organization **Born:** March 13, 1942, Mankato, Minnesota **Univ./degree:** B.S., Mankato State University, 1964; Graduate work at the University of Indianapolis and Butler University **Current organization:** American Legion Auxiliary National Headquarters **Title:** Youth Programs/Event Planning Manager **Type of organization:** Non-profit and women's patriotic organization **Major product:** Event planning **Area of distribution:** National **Expertise:** Planning conferences and events, youth citizenship programs i.e. Girls State and Girls Nation **Hob./spts.:** Volunteer, professional church organist and keyboard player, church elder, swimming **SIC code:** 86 **Address:** American Legion Auxiliary National Headquarters, 777 N. Meridian St., Third floor, Indianapolis, IN 46204 **E-mail:** youthprog@legion-aux.org **Web address:** www.legion-aux.org

OSTLIND, DAN A.
Industry: Pharmaceuticals **Born:** June 19, 1936, McPherson, Kansas **Univ./degree:** Ph.D., Kansas State University, 1966 **Title:** Senior Investigator, Merck & Co. Research Laboratories (Retired) **Type of organization:** R&D **Major product:** Veterinary health products **Area of distribution:** International **Expertise:** Basic research **Affiliations:** A.A.V.P.; W.A.A.V.P. **Hob./spts.:** Entomology, sports **SIC code:** 87 **Address:** 94 Dreahook Rd., Whitehouse Station, NJ 08889 **E-mail:** stanton94@earthlink.net

PANAS, RAYMOND MICHAEL
Industry: Pharmaceuticals **Born:** September 12, 1963, Titusville, Pennsylvania **Univ./degree:** M.P.H., University of Pittsburgh, 1991 **Current organization:** Sucampo Pharmaceuticals **Title:** Sr. Clinical Trial Manager **Type of organization:** R&D **Major product:** Drugs, medicines **Area of distribution:** International **Expertise:** Clinical research design, administration **Affiliations:** D.I.A.; A.C.R.P. **SIC code:** 87 **Address:** Sucampo Pharmaceuticals, 4733 Bethesda Ave., Suite 450, Bethesda, MD 20814

PANUCCI, ROCCO
Industry: Membership organization **Born:** September 4, 1963, Pittsburgh, Pennsylvania **Univ./degree:** A.A., Business Management, Robert Morris University, 1983 **Current organization:** Edgewood Country Club **Title:** General Manager **Type of organization:** Country club **Major product:** Food, beverage, golf **Area of distribution:** Pittsburgh, Pennsylvania **Expertise:** Management **Affiliations:** Club Managers Association of America; Rotary Club **Hob./spts.:** Golf **SIC code:** 86 **Address:** Edgewood Country Club, 100 Churchill Rd., Pittsburgh, PA 15235 **E-mail:** rpanucci@eccgolf.com

PASKAUSKY, DAVID F.
Industry: Consulting **Born:** March 1, 1938, Waukegan, Illinois **Univ./degree:** Ph.D., Physical Oceanography, Texas A&M University, 1969 **Current organization:** Wind, Water & Waves **Title:** Owner **Type of organization:** Consulting **Major product:** Consulting, surveillance **Area of distribution:** National **Expertise:** Physical oceanography and surveillance **Published works:** 35 publications **Hob./spts.:** Flyfishing **SIC code:** 87 **Address:** Wind, Water & Waves, 6509 Welch Ave., Ft. Worth, TX 76133-5441 **E-mail:** skymow@aol.com

PATEL, AMRISH A.
Industry: Consulting **Univ./degree:** B.S., India, 1982 **Current organization:** AB Consultants, Inc. **Title:** Professional Engineer/President **Type of organization:** Engineering **Major product:** Engineering, surveying, planning **Area of distribution:** Maryland **Expertise:** Civil engineering **SIC code:** 87 **Address:** AB Consultants, Inc., 9450 Annapolis Rd., Lanham, MD 20706 **E-mail:** amrish@abconsultantsinc.com **Web address:** www_abconsultants.com

PATEL, MAYUR B.
Industry: Construction **Born:** April 16, 1962, Bagalkot, India **Univ./degree:** B.S., Civil and Project Engineering, 1985; M.S., Hydraulic Engineering, MS University, India, 1989 **Current organization:** Eastern Contractors, Inc. **Title:** Chief Estimator **Type of organization:** Industrial and public construction **Major product:** Building construction **Area of distribution:** Massachusetts **Expertise:** Engineering **SIC code:** 87 **Address:** Eastern Contractors, Inc., 571 Union Ave., Framingham, MA 01702 **E-mail:** mayur@easterncontractors.com

PATTERSON, NANCY PEARLE HORD
Industry: Non-profit **Born:** January 19, 1943, Gainesville, Florida **Univ./degree:** Ph.D., Education, University of Florida **Current organization:** National Graves Disease Foundation **Title:** Founder, Executive Director **Type of organization:** Non-profit foundation **Major product:** Support groups for people with thyroid disorder (Graves Disease) **Area of distribution:** National **Expertise:** Management, therapy **Affiliations:** A.N.A.; Association of Independent Psychotherapists **Hob./spts.:** Basket weaving, canoeing **SIC code:** 86 **Address:** National Graves Disease Foundation, 3 Tsiya Court, Brevard, NC 28712 **E-mail:** nancy@ngdf.org **Web address:** www.ngdf.org

PAVULURI, VENKATESWARA RAO
Industry: Pharmaceutical **Univ./degree:** Ph.D., Drug Delivery Systems, Andhra University, Visakhapatnam, India; **Current organization:** Henry Jackson Foundation **Title:** Senior Scientist **Type of organization:** Nonprofit research **Major product:** Drug development and research of diseases for the government and the military **Area of distribution:** International **Expertise:** Development of oral and nasal delivery systems for injectable drugs **Published works:** 4 original research papers and several patents (granted and filed) **Affiliations:** American Association of Pharmaceutical Scientists; American Association for Advancement of Sciences; Life Member, Indian Pharmaceutical Association; American Chemical Society; International Society of Pharmaceutical Engineers **Hob./spts.:** Table tennis **SIC code:** 87 **Address:** Henry Jackson Foundation, 18 Bank Barn Circle, Middletown, MD 21769 **E-mail:** vpavuluri@niaid.nih.gov

PAYO, MARIANO L.
Industry: IT consulting **Born:** Boston, Massachusetts **Univ./degree:** B.A. Candidate, Florida International University **Current organization:** Intelligent Communica-

tion Solutions Inc. **Title:** Executive Director of Marketing **Type of organization:** Procurement firm **Major product:** Network and communication platforms **Area of distribution:** National **Expertise:** Information technologies/network systems **Hob./spts.:** Tennis, golf, fishing, water sports, boating activities **SIC code:** 87 **Address:** Intelligent Communication Solutions Inc., 782 N.W. 42nd Ave., Suite 341, Miami, FL 33126 **E-mail:** mlpayo@oneics.com

PEAK JR., WILLIAM C.
Industry: Engineering **Born:** September 26, 1929, Jacksonville, Florida **Univ./degree:** B.S., Engineering, Louisiana State University, 1958; M.A., Engineering, North Carolina State University, 1964 **Current organization:** CP&F Inc. **Title:** President **Type of organization:** Engineering **Major product:** Engineering solutions **Area of distribution:** Alabama **Expertise:** Engineering sales **Published works:** 15 patents **Hob./spts.:** Shooting instruction, hand-to-hand combat training **SIC code:** 87 **Address:** CP&F Inc., 2317 Starmount Circle, Huntsville, AL 35801 **E-mail:** cpf4you@aol.com **Web address:** www.cpfdixie.com

PECK, ROBERT W.
Industry: Religion **Born:** April 25, 1938, Poultney, Vermont **Univ./degree:** Th.D., Trinity Seminary, 1980 **Current organization:** Presbyterian Church (USA) **Title:** Pastor **Type of organization:** Church **Major product:** Religious services **Area of distribution:** North Tonawanda, New York **Expertise:** Working with problem congregations **Published works:** 1 book, "Genealogy Family Research" **Affiliations:** Clan Ross Association **Hob./spts.:** Writing **SIC code:** 86 **Address:** Presbyterian Church (USA), 309 Shartle Place, North Tonawanda, NY 14120 **E-mail:** pastorp21@verizon.net

PEERCY, MARGARET DEBORAH NIXON
Industry: Membership organization **Univ./degree:** M.B.A., Middle Tennessee State University **Current organization:** Children of the American Colonists **Title:** National Treasurer **Type of organization:** Patriotic/nonprofit **Major product:** Volunteer services, accounting **Area of distribution:** National **Expertise:** Accounting **Honors/awards:** Who's Who in American Colleges and Universities; Outstanding Young Women of America; Outstanding Young Women of the Southeast; SAR Martha Washington Medal for Outstanding Leadership **Affiliations:** American Mensa Ltd; National Society Colonial Dames Seventeenth Century (NSCDXVIIC); Daughters of the American Revolution (NSDAR); Daughters of the American Colonists (NSDAC); Monterey Church of the Nazarene; Judson Baptist Church **Hob./spts.:** Genealogy, needle crafts, piano, computers, jigsaw puzzles, logic puzzles **SIC code:** 86 **Address:** 103 Sheffield Place, Franklin, TN 37067-4428 **E-mail:** peercydn@hotmail.com **Web address:** www.nsdac.org

PELESH, JOHN
Industry: Financial services **Born:** February 5, 1926, Swiatkowa, Poland **Univ./degree:** Attended University of Illinois at Chicago, 1953-54; A.A., Accounting, Bryant & Stratton College, 1955 **Current organization:** Pelesh Consultants, Inc. **Title:** President **Type of organization:** Consulting firm **Major product:** Bookkeeping and income tax services **Expertise:** Auditing, consulting; formerly Public Auditor **Honors/awards:** Recipient of numerous letters of appreciation, including one from President Ronald Reagan, dated Dec. 7, 1984 **Hob./spts.:** History **SIC code:** 87 **Address:** 6902 N. Waukesha Ave., Chicago, IL 60646

PENISTEN, TODD W.
Industry: Consulting **Born:** October 4, 1973, Newton, Iowa **Univ./degree:** B.A., Civil/Environmental Engineering, University of Iowa, 1999 **Current organization:** Veenstra & Kimm, Inc. **Title:** Civil & Environmental Engineer **Type of organization:** Consulting engineering **Major product:** Water and wastewater treatment **Area of distribution:** Iowa **Expertise:** Civil and environmental engineering **Affiliations:** President, Y.M.G.; N.S.P.E.; A.S.C.E. **Hob./spts.:** Travel, football, water skiing, physical fitness **SIC code:** 87 **Address:** 7501 Brookview Dr., Urbandale, IA 50322-8320 **E-mail:** tpenisten@u-k.net

PENNEY, DAVID P.
Industry: Research **Born:** December 11, 1933, Waltham, Massachusetts **Univ./degree:** Ph.D., Boston University, 1962 **Current organization:** Biological Stain Commission, University of Rochester Medical Center **Title:** Treasurer **Type of organization:** Research facility **Major product:** Stains and dyes **Area of distribution:** International **Affiliations:** B.S.C. **Hob./spts.:** Golf, reading **SIC code:** 87 **Address:** Biological Stain Commission, University of Rochester Medical Center, Dept. of Pathology, Box 626, Rochester, NY 14642

PEREZ, ALEJANDRO
Industry: Consulting **Born:** February 22, 1979, Bogotá, Colombia **Univ./degree:** B.S., International Business, Rollins College: M.B.A., Rollins College-Crummer Graduate School of Business **Current organization:** Wilson Learning Andina **Title:** Marketing Generalist **Type of organization:** Consulting firm **Major product:** Consulting (business transformation) **Area of distribution:** International **Expertise:** Marketing **Hob./spts.:** Reading, golf **SIC code:** 87 **Address:** 3080 S. Tuskawilla Rd., Oviedo, FL 32765-8509 **E-mail:** lodger1977@aol.com

PEREZ, ROLANDO
Industry: Chemical **Born:** January 14, 1945, Havana, Cuba **Univ./degree:** B.S., Chemistry, Florida International University, 1995 **Current organization:** ADPEN Labs, Inc. **Title:** President **Type of organization:** Analytical laboratory **Major product:** Analytical services and chemistry **Area of distribution:** International **Expertise:** Food safety, pharmaceuticals, agrochemicals, chemistry **Affiliations:** American Chemical Society; A.O.A.C International **Hob./spts.:** Swimming **SIC code:** 87 **Address:** ADPEN Labs, Inc., 11757 Central Pkwy., Jacksonville, FL 32224 **E-mail:** rp@adpen.com **Web address:** www.adpen.com

PERKINS, PATRICK H.
Industry: Consulting **Born:** August 6, 1938, Marianna, Arizona **Univ./degree:** B.S.E.E., University of Michigan, 1965; M.S.E.E.; University of Colorado, 1972; M.B.A., University of Chicago, 1974 **Current organization:** Perkins Consulting, Inc. **Title:** Owner/President **Type of organization:** Consulting/training **Major product:** Technical training **Area of distribution:** Michigan **Expertise:** Engineering **Hob./spts.:** Reading, physical fitness **SIC code:** 87 **Address:** Perkins Consulting, Inc., 43505 Barclay Way, Canton, MI 48188 **E-mail:** pperkins261058mi@comcast.net

PESERIK, JAMES E.
Industry: Consulting engineering **Born:** September 30, 1945, Beloit, Wisconsin **Univ./degree:** M.A., Public Safety, St. Joseph's University, 1989 **Current organization:** James E. Peserik Associates, Inc. **Title:** President **Type of organization:** Consulting firm **Major product:** Consulting services **Area of distribution:** Worldwide **Expertise:** Electrical and mechanical safety **Honors/awards:** Diplomate, A.C.F.A. (Lifetime Status) **Affiliations:** N.A.F.I.; I.A.A. **Hob./spts.:** Tennis **SIC code:** 87 **Address:** James E. Peserik Assoc. Inc., P.O. Box 181, Coopersburg, PA 18036-0181 **E-mail:** jrpeserik@enter.net

PETERS, JENNIFER J.
Industry: Consulting **Born:** January 2, 1964, Cleveland, Ohio **Univ./degree:** M.E.M., Duke University, 1988 **Current organization:** ICF Consulting **Title:** Project Manager **Type of organization:** Consulting firm **Major product:** Environmental consulting **Area of distribution:** National **Expertise:** Policy analysis - waste and water programs **Published works:** Articles, including "Hazardous Waste Regulations Pose Barriers to Silver Recovery," Photographic Processing Magazine and "Overcoming Barriers to Silvery Recovery," Materials Evaluation, Vol. 56 **Hob./spts.:** Sports, playing drums, travel **SIC code:** 87 **Address:** ICF Consulting, 9300 Lee Hwy., Fairfax, VA 22031 **E-mail:** jpeters@icfconsulting.com

PETERS, KENNETH L.
Industry: Consulting/engineering **Born:** May 24, 1973, Decatur, Georgia **Univ./degree:** B.S., Civil Engineering, Georgia Tech, 1995 **Current organization:** Civil Site Solutions, Inc. **Title:** President **Type of organization:** Engineering consulting firm **Major product:** Land development **Area of distribution:** Georgia **Expertise:** Civil engineering, residential site design **Affiliations:** A.C.E.C.; American Society of Civil Engineers **Hob./spts.:** Fishing, hunting **SIC code:** 87 **Address:** Civil Site Solutions, Inc., P.O. Box 345, Jersey, GA 30018 **E-mail:** kpeters@klpdesign.com

PETERSON, MICHAEL D.
Industry: Nuclear power utility **Born:** March 6, 1962, Fort Bragg, North Carolina **Univ./degree:** B.S., Electrical Engineering, University of Alabama **Current organization:** Entergy Nuclear **Title:** Senior Engineer **Type of organization:** Engineering **Major product:** Nuclear power **Area of distribution:** National **Expertise:** Electrical, I&C systems, central systems **Hob./spts.:** Stock car racing **SIC code:** 87 **Address:** Entergy Nuclear, 17265 River Rd., Kiliona, LA 70057 **E-mail:** mpeters@entergy.com

PETKEWICH, DAVE
Industry: Architecture/engineering **Born:** March 22, 1947, Marblehead, Massachusetts **Univ./degree:** B.S., Civil Engineering, Lowell Tech Institute, Massachusetts, 1974 **Current organization:** Carter & Burgess, Inc. **Title:** Project Manager **Type of organization:** Architecture and engineering firm **Major product:** Engineering **Area of distribution:** National **Expertise:** Civil engineering **Hob./spts.:** Hockey, cars **SIC code:** 87 **Address:** Carter & Burgess, Inc., 23 East Street, Maple Leaf Building, Cambridge, MA 02141 **E-mail:** petkewichdm@c-b.com

PETREVSKI, PETER STOJAN
Industry: Construction **Born:** June 2, 1944, Macedonia, Europe **Univ./degree:** A.A., Fairleigh Dickinson University **Current organization:** KSI Electric, LLC **Title:** Project Engineer **Type of organization:** General contractors **Major product:** Commercial and institutional buildings **Area of distribution:** National **Expertise:** Electrical engineering **Hob./spts.:** Golf, skiing **SIC code:** 87 **Address:** 65 Boonstra Dr., Wayne, NJ 07470 **E-mail:** ppetrevski@keyspanse.com

PETTWAY-HALLBERG, JACQUELINE
Industry: Water resources **Born:** December 20, 1974, Vicksburg, Mississippi **Univ./degree:** M.S., Civil Engineering, Mississippi State University, 2001 **Current organization:** Engineer Research & Development Center **Title:** Research Hydraulic Engineer **Type of organization:** Research and development **Major product:** Consultation, research and development **Expertise:** Engineering **Published works:** Conference proceedings **Affiliations:** A.S.C.E. **Hob./spts.:** Softball, volleyball, woodworking **SIC code:** 87 **Address:** Engineer Research & Development Center, 3909 Halls Ferry Rd., Vicksburg, MS 39180 **E-mail:** hallbej@wes.army.mil

PFEIFER, MICHAEL D.
Industry: Religion **Born:** May 18, 1937, Alamo, Texas **Univ./degree:** D.D., Oblate School of Theology, San Antonio, Texas, 1965 **Current organization:** Catholic Diocese of San Angelo **Title:** Bishop of San Angelo **Type of organization:** Roman Catholic Church **Major product:** Faith, truth, knowledge **Area of distribution:** International **Expertise:** Supervising daily operations of 74 churches in 29 counties **Affiliations:** Oblate of Mary Immaculate; Texas Conference of Churches **Hob./spts.:** Jogging, swimming, gardening **SIC code:** 86 **Address:** Catholic Diocese of San Angelo, 804 Ford St., San Angelo, TX 76905 **E-mail:** mdpomi@aol.com **Web address:** www.san-angelo-diocese.org

PHILLIPS, BRUCE A.
Industry: Consulting **Born:** August 31, 1954, Washington, D.C. **Univ./degree:** M.B.A., Forestry Science, Yale University, 1984 **Current organization:** The NorthBridge Group **Title:** Director **Type of organization:** Consulting **Major product:** Strategic and economic consulting **Area of distribution:** National **Expertise:** Energy industries, electric and gas deregulation **Published works:** "Pricing of Retail Electric Services" **Hob./spts.:** Travel, tennis, basketball, fishing, bird watching **SIC code:** 87 **Address:** The NorthBridge Group, 55 Old Bedford Rd., Lincoln, MA 01773 **E-mail:** bap@nbgroup.com

PILLAY, GAUTAM
Industry: Research **Born:** January 28, 1967, Buffalo, New York **Univ./degree:** B.S., Chemical Engineering, with Honors, New Mexico State University, 1988; Ph.D., Chemical Engineering, Texas A&M University, 1993 **Current organization:** Inland Northwest Research Alliance **Title:** Executive Director **Type of organization:** Non-profit research **Major product:** Research **Area of distribution:** National **Expertise:** Engineering **Honors/awards:** Federal Laboratory Consortium Award for Technology Transfer; 1 patent; Judge, R&D 100 awards **Published works:** 40 presentations and articles **Affiliations:** The Electrochemical Society; American Nuclear Society **Hob./spts.:** Musician, private pilot **SIC code:** 87 **Address:** Inland Northwest Research Alliance, 151 N. Ridge Ave., Suite 140, Idaho Falls, ID 83402

PINO, AMADEO B.
Industry: Architecture **Born:** February 3, 1957, Havana, Cuba **Univ./degree:** B.Arch., University of Miami at Coral Gables **Current organization:** Amadeo Pino Architects **Title:** President **Type of organization:** Architectural **Major product:** Resident and hotel design **Area of distribution:** National **Expertise:** Architecture **Affiliations:** College of Architects; Comite para Desarollo des Oeste **Hob./spts.:** Sailing, water sports **SIC code:** 87 **Address:** Amadeo Pino Architects, KM. 1.7, State Road 349, Mayaguez, PR 00680 **E-mail:** apino@centennialpr.net

PINTER, TIMOTHY E.
Industry: Engineering **Born:** March 20, 1948, Lorain, Ohio **Univ./degree:** B.S.C.E., Ohio University, 1975 **Current organization:** Poggemeyer Design Group, Inc. **Title:** Principal **Type of organization:** Professional service **Major product:** Consulting engineering **Area of distribution:** National **Expertise:** Civil engineering **Honors/awards:** Diplomate, A.C.F.E. **Affiliations:** A.P.W.A.; A.C.E.C.; S.A.M.E.; N.S.P.E. **Hob./spts.:** Family, golf, tennis **SIC code:** 87 **Address:** Poggemeyer Design Group, Inc., 2601 N. Tenaya Way, Las Vegas, NV 89128 **E-mail:** tpinter@pdg-lv.com **Web address:** www.pdg-lv.com

PIRNIA, SIMA
Industry: Engineering **Born:** May 4, 1953, Iran **Univ./degree:** B.S., Civil Engineering, King's College, London, England **Current organization:** Sima H.P. & Friends **Type of organization:** Design and development firm **Major product:** Hydraulics, environmental planning, design, private development **Area of distribution:** Connecticut **Expertise:** "Creation" **Affiliations:** A.S.C.E. **SIC code:** 87 **Address:** 43 Autumn Lane, Stanford, CT 06906

PLUCKNETT, DONALD LOVELLE
Industry: Consulting and research **Univ./degree:** Ph.D., Tropical Soil Science, University of Hawaii, 1961 **Current organization:** Agricultural Research and Development Institute **Title:** Ph.D **Type of organization:** Private consulting firm **Major product:** Technology and research assessments **Area of distribution:** International **Expertise:** Agricultural research, natural resource management **Published works:** 19 books, 200 journal articles **Affiliations:** Fellow, Soil Science Society of America; Fellow, American Society of Agronomy; Linear Society of London **SIC code:** 87 **Address:** Agricultural Research and Development International, 4200 Evergreen Lane, Suite 323, Annandale, VA 22003 **E-mail:** donpluckn@aol.com

PODDER, TARUN K.
Industry: Marine Science and Robotics **Born:** January 16, 1967, Calcutta, India **Univ./degree:** Ph.D., University of Hawaii at Honolulu, 2000 **Current organization:** Monterey Bay Aquarium Research Institute **Title:** Ph.D. **Type of organization:** Marine science research **Major product:** Scientific knowledge **Area of distribution:** Worldwide **Expertise:** Dynamics, control and robotics (engineering) **Honors/awards:** Anton Phillips Award from I.E.E.E. (Best Paper), EE Black Level Scholarship from TRW, National Scholarship from Government of India **Published works:** 6 journals, 11 conferences **Affiliations:** I.E.E.E.; A.S.M.E.; I.S.T.E.; I.E. **Hob./spts.:** Soccer, volleyball, tennis, reading novels, travel **SIC code:** 87 **Address:** Monterey Bay Aquarium Research Institute, 7700 Sandholdt Rd., Moss Landing, CA 95039 **E-mail:** tarun@mbari.org **Web address:** www.mbari.org

POE, CARL M.
Industry: Consulting/technology **Born:** Winston-Salem, North Carolina **Univ./degree:** B.S.E.E.; M.S.E.E., 1984, Clemson University **Current organization:** ETR Solutions, Inc. **Title:** V.P. of Engineering **Type of organization:** Consulting firm **Major product:** Electronic engineering, test and design work **Area of distribution:** North Carolina **Expertise:** Engineering, team building and leadership development **Affiliations:** Cary Chamber of Commerce **Hob./spts.:** Volleyball, classic car restoration **SIC code:** 87 **Address:** ETR Solutions, Inc., 975 Walnut St., Suite 220, Cary, NC 27511 **E-mail:** etrscarlpoe@bellsouth.net

POE, MICHAEL DELWAYNE
Industry: Consulting **Born:** December 12, 1959, Berkeley, California **Univ./degree:** B.B.A., Howard University, Washington, D.C., 1982; M.B.A., University of Michigan at Ann Arbor, 1984 **Current organization:** Tillinghast-Towers Perrin **Title:** Principal **Type of organization:** Management consulting firm **Major product:** Provides actuarial and management consulting to financial services companies and advises other organizations on their self-insurance programs **Area of distribution:** National **Expertise:** Actuarial consulting **Affiliations:** F.C.A.S.; M.A.A.A. **SIC code:** 87 **Address:** 512 Copely Lane, Silver Spring, MD 20904 **E-mail:** michael.poe@tillinghast.com

POLIVKA, KARLA A.
Industry: Research and development **Born:** January 9, 1973, David City, Nebraska **Univ./degree:** M.S., University of Nebraska, Lincoln, 2001 **Current organization:** Midwest Roadside Safety Facility **Title:** Research Associate Engineer **Type of organization:** R&D facility **Major product:** Roadside hardware testing and development **Area of distribution:** National **Expertise:** Engineering, design and testing applications **Published works:** 3 papers **Affiliations:** N.S.P.E.; A.S.M.E. **Hob./spts.:** Outdoor activities, volleyball, sports **SIC code:** 87 **Address:** Midwest Roadside Safety Facility, 527 Nebraska Hall, Lincoln, NE 68588 **E-mail:** kpolivka2@unl.edu

POND, STEVEN P.
Industry: Environmental **Born:** June 5, 1970, Richmond, Virginia **Univ./degree:** B.S., Radford University, 1992 **Current organization:** Schnabel Engineering **Title:** Associate Geologist **Type of organization:** Engineering consulting **Area of distribution:** Virginia **Expertise:** Subsurface exploration, hydrogeology, environmental geology **Affiliations:** A.E.G. **Hob./spts.:** Hunting, metal detecting, fossil hunting, soccer **SIC code:** 87 **Address:** Schnabel Engineering, 1 W. Cary St., Richmond, VA 23220 **E-mail:** spond@schnabel-eng.com **Web address:** www.schnabel-eng.com

POPE, DON A.
Industry: Manufacturing **Born:** February 20, 1954, Boston, Massachusetts **Univ./degree:** B.S., Mechanical Engineering, Tufts University, 1978; M.B.A., Boston University, 1987 **Current organization:** Pope Business Consulting **Title:** President **Type of organization:** Consulting **Major product:** We cultivate business growth and profit by creating strategic implementation plans that integrate the engineering and business needs of a client into profitable technological solutions. **Area of distribution:** National **Expertise:** Strategic and long range planning and business process reengineering **Honors/awards:** Member, Beta Gamma Sigma, National Business Honor Society **Affiliations:** A.S.M.E.; I.M.C. **Hob./spts.:** President, New Bostonian Barbershop Chorus, Waltham, Massachusetts **SIC code:** 87 **Address:** Pope Business Consulting, 56 Main St., Kingston, NH 03848 **E-mail:** dpope@popebusiness.com

PORCHIA SR., EDGAR ALLEN PETER
Industry: Ministry **Born:** December 31, 1925, Buena Vista, Arkansas **Univ./degree:** B.S., Theology, Ouachita Baptist University, 1950; M.Div., Louisiana State University, Monroe, 1956 **Current organization:** CMBS of the State Convention of Arkansas **Title:** Baptist Preacher/Pastor/Teacher **Type of organization:** Religious convention/association **Major product:** Faith-based resources for life **Area of distribution:** International **Expertise:** Praise and productivity in Jesus' name **Affiliations:** 2nd Vice

President, CMBS Convention **Hob./spts.:** Family, reading **SIC code:** 86 **Address:** CMBS of the State Convention of Arkansas, 601 W. Cook, El Dorado, AR 71730

PORTER SR., DEWITT
Industry: Construction **Born:** April 12, 1948, Glenville, Georgia **Univ./degree:** B.S., Civil Engineering, Savannah State University, 1968; B.S., Engineering Science and Mechanics **Current organization:** Fluor Corp. **Title:** Vice President of Operations **Type of organization:** Engineering, construction company **Major product:** Construction, engineering and design services **Area of distribution:** International **Expertise:** Project management, business development, contract negotiations, budget forecasting, program implementation, site development **Affiliations:** P.M.I. **Hob./spts.:** Farming, outdoor activities **SIC code:** 87 **Address:** Fluor Corp., 100 Fluor Daniel Dr., Greenville, SC 29601 **E-mail:** dewitt.porter@fluor.com

POWELL, KARAN HINMAN
Industry: Consulting **Born:** May 25, 1953, Great Lakes, Illinois **Univ./degree:** B.S., Western Illinois University, 1975; M.Div., Loyola University, 1981; Ph.D., George Mason University, 1998 **Current organization:** Powell & Associates, LLC **Title:** President **Type of organization:** Consulting firm **Major product:** Executive development; Organization Change Consulting **Area of distribution:** International **Expertise:** Organizational and executive development, coaching, mergers and acquisitions **Published works:** 20 articles, 5 books, 1 book chapter **Affiliations:** S.H.R.M.; O.D.N.; A.S.T.D.; Academy of Management; Manager, Ashburn Xtreme Hockey Club; Founding Member, St. David Episcopal Church of Ashburn, Virginia; Inaugural Family Member, Ashburn Xtreme Hockey Club **Hob./spts.:** Ice hockey, sailing, reading, travel, music **SIC code:** 87 **Address:** Powell & Associates, LLC, 20773 Ashburn Station Place, Ashburn, VA 20147 **E-mail:** khpowell@aol.com

PRENDERGAST, ROBERT L.
Industry: Consulting/engineering **Born:** April 16, 1936, Galveston, Texas **Univ./degree:** B.S., Electrical Engineering, U.S. Naval Academy; M.A., Education, Pepperdine University, 1974 **Current organization:** Robert Prendergast & Associates **Title:** Owner **Type of organization:** Manufacturing/engineering **Major product:** Factory system design and educational services **Area of distribution:** California **Expertise:** System engineering, factory automation **Honors/awards:** SME 15 Year Service Certificate, Fanul Robotics for Increased Sales, 1999 **Published works:** "A Robotic Material Handling Workcell for the Food & Beverage Industry" Proceeding, Park Alimenteir Conference, Chicago, 1989; "Surface Sonnar Watchstander's Passive Range Predition Manual", Comnavsurf Pac Talmemo 262-1-80, Coronado, CA, 1980 **Affiliations:** Chairman Elect, S.M.E., San Diego; A.G.U.; Kappa Delta Pi **Hob./spts.:** Sailing, skiing, stamp collecting **SIC code:** 87 **Address:** Robert Prendergast & Associates, 16945 Vinaruz Place, San Diego, CA 92128 **E-mail:** rprender@san.rr.com

PRICE, LEANNA
Industry: Education **Born:** March 23, 1940, Opelousas, Louisiana **Current organization:** Honey Bee Learning Academy **Title:** Owner/Director **Type of organization:** Day care center **Major product:** Child care **Area of distribution:** Houston, Texas **Expertise:** Teaching, administration **Affiliations:** National Child Care Association **Hob./spts.:** Home decorating **SIC code:** 83 **Address:** Honey Bee Learning Academy, 6717 St. Augustine, Houston, TX 77021

PRIEST, ROY O.
Industry: Trade associations **Born:** August 13, 1942, Washington, D.C. **Univ./degree:** M.A., American University, Washington D.C., 1984 **Current organization:** National Congress for Community Economic Development **Title:** President/CEO **Type of organization:** Nonprofit/trade association CDC **Major product:** Trade **Area of distribution:** National **Expertise:** Trade **Honors/awards:** Distinguished Service Award, 1995 & 1997 from Secretary U.S. Dept. of HUD **Published works:** Shelter Force Magazine **Affiliations:** USNH/Editorial Board, Housing & Community Development Reporter **Hob./spts.:** Tennis, golf, reading **SIC code:** 86 **Address:** National Congress for Community Economic Development, 1030 15th St. N.W., #325, Washington, DC 20005 **E-mail:** rpriest@ncced.org

PROCTOR, GREGORY O.
Industry: Semiconductor, biomedical, IT **Born:** September 15, 1970, Jackson, Mississippi **Univ./degree:** B.S. Candidate, Business Management, University of Phoenix, 2008 **Current organization:** Prolific-Technology, LLC **Title:** Principal **Type of organization:** Consulting **Major product:** Capital equipment support **Area of distribution:** International **Expertise:** Engineering, technical consulting, new business, capital, equipment, engineering **Hob./spts.:** Running, family **SIC code:** 87 **Address:** Prolific-Technology, LLC, 14011 Rockbasket Terrace, Chester, VA 23836 **E-mail:** greg.proctor@prolific-technology.com **Web address:** www.prolific-technology.com

PROTHRO, DENNIS EVAN
Industry: Financial **Born:** February 12, 1948, Fayetteville, Arkansas **Spouse:** Rosanna Tufts-Prothro (Maiden name: Tufts) **Married:** August 30, 1996 **Children:** Daniel Evan Prothro, 21; Lily Fay Tufts-Prothro, 6 **Univ./degree:** University of Virginia; Thomas Nelson Community College (Dean's List) **Current organization:** Seasons Funding/Seasons Real Estate **Title:** President **Type of organization:** Financial consulting **Major product:** Business notes, mortgage notes **Area of distribution:** National **Expertise:** Certified Capital Specialist, Certified Mortgage Investor **Honors/awards:** Eagle Scout Award 1965; Brotherhood Honor, Order of the Arrow; Pi Mu Fraternity, St. Louis Institute of Music; Master Photographer Regnant, Accredited Photographer of Achievement, International Freelance Photographers Organization; Honorary Appointment, Research Board of Advisors of the American Biographical Institute **Published works:** Photography, poetry **Affiliations:** Colonial Williamsburg Foundation; Smithsonian Associates; Chesapeake Bay Foundation; Presidential Leadership Council, Democratic Party (former member); National Trust for Historic Preservation (former member); National Resource Defense Council (former member); Ecumenicon Fellowship, Trustee **Career accomplishments:** Worked on USS Virginia, America's Bicentennial Ship; Electrical Shop, Brentwood Heavy Repair Facility, Washington, DC; Acting Leadman, Alexandria S&I, Alexandria, VA, West Falls Church S&I, Falls Church, VA and Greenbelt S&I, Beltsville, MD; Acting Supervisor Periodic Inspection, Greenbelt S&I; 1997 Outstanding Achievement Award from the American Public Transit Association; Specialized as a Propulsion System Inspector over the last decade with the Washington Metropolitan Area Transit Authority and ultimately, over 27 years, helped transport over one billion people in the Washington Metropolitan area including assignments at National Airport, Washington DC, Maryland and Virginia **Hob./spts.:** Music, piano, painting, photography, camping, reading, stamp collecting **SIC code:** 87 **Address:** Seasons Funding/Seasons Real Estate, 5808 N. Charles St., Baltimore, MD 21210 **E-mail:** seasonsfunding@verizon.net

PUTNAM, REX G.
Industry: Nuclear power utility **Born:** July 22, 1958, Dallas, Texas **Univ./degree:** M.S., Electrical Engineering, Naval Post Graduate School **Current organization:** Entergy Nuclear **Title:** Systems Engineer Supervisor **Type of organization:** Engineering **Major product:** Waterford 3 nuclear power plant **Area of distribution:** National **Expertise:** I&C systems, control systems **Affiliations:** I.E.E.E.; American Nuclear Society **Hob./spts.:** Sailing **SIC code:** 87 **Address:** Entergy Nuclear, 17265 River Rd., Kiliona, LA 70057 **E-mail:** rputnam@entergy.com

QUINT, BRYAN S.
Industry: Consulting/engineering **Univ./degree:** B.A., History, California State University, Sacramento, 1970; M.S., Systems Management, University of Denver, Colorado, 1972 **Current organization:** Booz Allen Hamilton **Title:** Usstratcom Market Lead **Type of organization:** Consulting firm **Major product:** Systems engineering, modeling and simulation **Area of distribution:** International **Expertise:** Engineering, marketing **Affiliations:** National Contracts Management Association; Armed Forces Communication & Electronics Association **Hob./spts.:** Gardening **SIC code:** 87 **Address:** Booz Allen Hamilton, 1299 Farnam St., Omaha, NE 68102 **E-mail:** quint_skip@bah.com

QUINTANA, ISAAC ALEXANDER
Industry: Engineering **Born:** April 25, 1978, Salt Lake City, Utah **Univ./degree:** B.S., University of Utah, 2002 **Current organization:** Steel Encounters **Title:** E.I.T. **Type of organization:** Engineering firm **Major product:** Design, building plans, construction **Area of distribution:** National **Expertise:** Civil engineering **Honors/awards:** National Hispanic Scholarship **Affiliations:** A.S.C.E. **SIC code:** 87 **Address:** Steel Encounters, 525 E. 300 South, Salt Lake City, UT 84102 **E-mail:** isaac588@yahoo.com

RAGSDALE, WILLIAM L.
Industry: Engineering **Born:** May 19, 1951, Bonne Terre, Missouri **Univ./degree:** B.S., Civil Engineering, Missouri Western College, 1972 **Current organization:** Engineering Design Source, Inc. (EDSI) **Title:** Project Manager/Senior Civil Engineer **Type of organization:** Private engineering firm **Major product:** Civil engineering services **Area of distribution:** Farmington, Missouri **Expertise:** Civil engineering; Registered Professional Engineer **Affiliations:** A.S.C.E.; N.S.P.E. **Hob./spts.:** Weight lifting **SIC code:** 87 **Address:** Engineering Design Source, Inc. (EDSI), 1510 Camillia St., Farmington, MO 63640 **E-mail:** br@engdesignsource.com

RAHE, JOHN H.
Industry: Engineering **Born:** March 19, 1950, Cincinnati, Ohio **Univ./degree:** B.S.C.E., Valparaiso University, Indiana, 1972 **Current organization:** J2FR Engineers **Title:** Professional Civil Engineer **Type of organization:** Consulting and design **Major product:** Engineering services **Area of distribution:** International **Expertise:** Civil and environmental engineering **Affiliations:** A.S.C.E.; Engineering Ministries International **Hob./spts.:** Volunteer engineering in developing world **SIC code:** 87 **Address:** J2FR Engineers, 1070 Youngfield St., Golden, CO 80401 **E-mail:** jhrahe.pe@juno.com

RAINES III, FRANK
Industry: Religion **Born:** September 27, 1958, Detroit, Michigan **Univ./degree:** B.S., Central State University; M.Ed., Elmira College; M.Div., Colgate Seminary **Current organization:** Dexter Ave. Baptist Church **Title:** M.Div./Pastor **Type of organization:** Church **Major product:** Religious services **Area of distribution:** Detroit, Michigan **Expertise:** Sermons, lecturing, serving the congregation **Published works:** Numerous articles **Affiliations:** N.A.A.C.P.; N.B.C., U.S.A., Inc.; Golden Heritage Convention; Wolverine Baptist State Convention; Director, Carver Camp; Vice President, 10th Precinct Clergy **Hob./spts.:** Interacting with the elderly **SIC code:** 86 **Address:** Dexter Ave. Baptist Church, 13500 Dexter Ave., Detroit, MI 48238 **E-mail:** dexterbapt@aol.com

RAMDEO, MAHESH K.
Industry: Engineering **Born:** Georgetown, Guyana **Univ./degree:** B.S.C.E., McMaster University **Current organization:** MWH Americas Inc. **Title:** Engineer **Type of organization:** Consulting firm **Major product:** Consulting **Area of distribution:** International **Expertise:** Construction, project management, water distribution **Affiliations:** A.S.C.E. **SIC code:** 87 **Address:** MWH Americas Inc., 175 W. Jackson Blvd., Chicago, IL 60604 **E-mail:** ramdeom@yahoo.com

RAMÍREZ-MARRERO, MARIA E.
Industry: Consulting **Born:** March 21, 1961, Puerto Rico **Univ./degree:** M.S., University of Puerto Rico **Current organization:** Puerto Rico Chemist Association **Title:** President **Type of organization:** Association for chemist professionals **Major product:** Continuing education program for chemists **Area of distribution:** National **Expertise:** Chemists in the industry, academia, government and private sector **Affiliations:** A.C.S. **Hob./spts.:** Web surfing **SIC code:** 86 **Address:** Puerto Rico Chemist Association, 52 Hatillo St., San Juan, PR 00918 **E-mail:** maria.e.ramirez.marrero@gmail.com

RAMNARINE, ROBERT R.
Industry: Water **Born:** March 1, 1969, San German, Puerto Rico **Univ./degree:** M.S., Chemistry, Florida Atlantic University, 2000 **Current organization:** Broward Testing Laboratory **Title:** Quality Assurance Officer **Type of organization:** Commercial laboratory **Major product:** Water testing, drinking water **Area of distribution:** International **Expertise:** High Performance Liquid Chromatography **Affiliations:** American Chemical Society **SIC code:** 87 **Address:** 4416 N.E. 11th Ave., Ft. Lauderdale, FL 33334 **E-mail:** rramnarine@ntllabs.com

RAMSEY, CHRIS
Industry: Construction/engineering **Born:** March 10, 1975, West Islip, New York **Univ./degree:** B.S., Civil Engineering, University of Cincinnati, 1998 **Current organization:** Richard Goettle, Inc. **Title:** Estimator **Type of organization:** Contractor **Major product:** Deep foundations **Area of distribution:** National **Expertise:** Engineering **Affiliations:** A.S.C.E.; D.F.I. **Hob./spts.:** Sports **SIC code:** 87 **Address:** Richard Goettle, Inc., 12071 Hamilton Ave., Cincinnati, OH 45231 **E-mail:** cramsey@goettle.com **Web address:** www.goettle.com

RANDALL, MATTHEW R.
Industry: Consulting **Born:** December 30, 1975, Portland, Oregon **Univ./degree:** B.S.C.E., Washington State University, 1999; Bible Seminary Graduate Certification, 2000 **Current organization:** KPFF Consulting Engineers **Title:** Civil Designer **Type of organization:** Engineering firm **Major product:** Civil engineering **Area of distribution:** Portland, Oregon **Expertise:** Design **Affiliations:** A.S.C.E. **Hob./spts.:** Baseball, hiking, backpacking, rock climbing, outdoor activities **SIC code:** 87 **Address:** KPFF Consulting Engineers, 111 S.W. Fifth Ave., Suite 2400, Portland, OR 97204 **E-mail:** matthew.randall@kpff.com **Web address:** www.kpff.com

RAS, HENDRIKUS L.
Industry: Design/Construction **Born:** March 21, 1947, Tilburg, The Netherlands **Univ./degree:** B.S., Architectural Engineering, HTS Institute, The Netherlands, 1970 **Current organization:** CETROM, Inc. **Title:** Deputy Director of Architecture **Type of organization:** Architectue, engineering and design build providers **Major product:** A/E services and facilities **Area of distribution:** Gaithersburg, Maryland **Expertise:** Architecture **Honors/awards:** A.I.A. Citation Award **Affiliations:** American Institute of Architecture **Hob./spts.:** Golf **SIC code:** 87 **Address:** CETROM, Inc., 818 W. Diamond Ave., Gaithersburg, MD 20878 **E-mail:** hank.ras@cetrom.com

RAY, JEFFREY D.
Industry: Knowledge management **Born:** November 26, 1953, Niagara Falls, New York **Univ./degree:** B.S., Business Administration, Clemson University, 1974 **Current organization:** Performance Technologies & Site Support, Fluor Corp. **Title:** Director, Performance Technologies **Type of organization:** Consulting **Major product:** Operations and management **Area of distribution:** International **Expertise:** Consulting **Hob./spts.:** Golf **SIC code:** 87 **Address:** Performance Technologies & Site Support, Fluor Corp., 100 Fluor Daniel Dr. (C301J), Greenville, SC 29607-2761 **E-mail:** jeffrey.ray@fluor.com

RAZANI, HOOMAN
Industry: Telecommunications **Born:** March 27, 1965, Tehran, Iran **Univ./degree:** M.S., Applied Physics, The Royal Institute of Technology, Stockholm, Sweden, 1999 **Current organization:** Award Solutions, Inc. **Title:** Senior 3GPP Consultant **Type of organization:** Consulting **Major product:** Optimization, testing, consulting **Area of distribution:** National **Expertise:** Engineering, standards consulting, national seminar speaker **Published works:** 1 thesis on high energy physics **Affiliations:** I.E.E.E.; Global Wireless Education Consortium **Hob./spts.:** Chess, table tennis, travel **SIC code:** 87 **Address:** Award Solutions, Inc., 2100 Lakeside Blvd., Suite 300, Richardson, TX 75082 **E-mail:** hooman@awardsolutions.com **Web address:** www.awardsolutions.com

REEDER, CLINTON B.
Industry: Economics **Born:** April 22, 1939, Pendleton, Oregon **Univ./degree:** Ph.D., Cultural Economics, Purdue University, 1966 **Current organization:** Westfork Natural Resources Research Center **Title:** Owner/Director **Type of organization:** Consulting and contract research **Major product:** Economic research **Area of distribution:** National **Expertise:** Agricultural policy analysis **Hob./spts.:** Photography, research, mountains, beach, hiking **SIC code:** 87 **Address:** 47647 Reeder Rd., Pendleton, OR 97801 **E-mail:** cbreeder@ucinet.com

REICHARD, DAVID D.
Industry: Consulting **Born:** June 23, 1967, Fountain Hill, Pennsylvania **Univ./degree:** M.S., Drexel University, Pennsylvania, 1996 **Current organization:** Haynes Massa & Associates, Inc. **Title:** Project Manager **Type of organization:** Construction service **Major product:** Construction dispute resolution **Area of distribution:** National **Expertise:** Engineering **Published works:** Articles **Affiliations:** American Society of Civil Engineers; National Society of Professional Engineers **Hob./spts.:** Golf, reading **SIC code:** 87 **Address:** Haynes Massa & Associates, Inc., 601 S. Lake Destiny Dr., Suite 110, Maitland, FL 32751 **E-mail:** reichard@haynesmassa.com **Web address:** www.haynesmassa.com

RENGARAJAN, KANNAN
Industry: Facility design engineering **Born:** March 8, 1961, Avinashi, India **Univ./degree:** M.S., Mechanical Engineering, Florida Institute of Technology, 1991 **Current organization:** Cape Design Engineering Co. **Title:** Principal **Type of organization:** Multi-discipline engineering **Major product:** Design engineering and studies **Area of distribution:** Cape Canaveral, Florida **Expertise:** Mechanical engineering **Affiliations:** A.S.P.E.; A.E.E.; N.F.P.A.; A.S.H.R.A.E **Hob./spts.:** Social services, tennis **SIC code:** 87 **Address:** Cape Design Engineering Co., 7001 N. Atlantic Ave., Suite 201, Cape Canaveral, FL 32920 **Web address:** www.cdeco.com

RENKEN, JOHN
Industry: Architecture **Born:** December 4, 1958, Springfield, Illinois **Univ./degree:** B.A., South Illinois University at Carbondale, 1982 **Current organization:** Fitch-Fitzgerald, Inc. **Title:** V.P., Managing Architect **Type of organization:** Chapter C Corporation **Major product:** Architecture, engineering and environmental services, education facilities **Area of distribution:** Springfield, Illinois **Expertise:** Design **Affiliations:** A.I.A. **Hob./spts.:** Coaching youth baseball, hunting **SIC code:** 87 **Address:** Fitch-Fitzgerald, Inc., 1905 Montana Dr., Suite 10, Springfield, IL 62704 **E-mail:** john@fitch-fitzgerald.com

RENTFRO, JANET SUE
Industry: Technical services **Univ./degree:** A.A, Nursing, Lakeland College, 1990 **Current organization:** Computer Sciences Raytheon/US Air Force **Title:** Clinic Supervisor **Type of organization:** Range Technical Services contractor **Major product:** Range Technical Services contractor supporting the U.S. Air Force Space Command's 45th Space Wing at Patrick Air Force Base, Florida **Area of distribution:** National **Expertise:** Nursing, basic cardiac, emergency services **Hob./spts.:** Travel, grandchildren, great-grandchildren **SIC code:** 87 **Address:** RR 1 Box 243, Mode, IL 62444

REUS, DIGNA L.
Industry: Consulting **Born:** October 4, 1964, White Plains, New York **Univ./degree:** Accounting and Marketing, Mercy College; Business Administration and Social Science, Dale Carnegie **Current organization:** RSVP Consulting **Title:** President **Type of organization:** Consulting **Major product:** Consulting, outsourcing billing **Area of distribution:** National **Expertise:** Optimizing operations and finance for firms **Affiliations:** H.I.M.F.A.; A.M.A.; R.B.M.A. **Hob./spts.:** Hiking, walking, biking **SIC code:** 87 **Address:** RSVP Consulting, 214 Mamaroneck Ave., White Plains, NY 10601 **E-mail:** rsvp3@optonline.net

REUS JR., WALDO
Industry: Consulting/billing **Born:** September 3, 1962, New York, New York **Univ./degree:** A.S., Engineering, Westchester Community College, 1985 **Current organization:** RSVP Solutions **Title:** Vice President **Type of organization:** Consulting firm **Major product:** Outsource billing **Area of distribution:** New York **Expertise:**

Finance, benefit packages, staffing **Affiliations:** A.M.A. **Hob./spts.:** Hunting, fishing, boating, golf **SIC code:** 87 **Address:** RSVP Solutions, 214 Mamaroneck Ave., White Plains, NY 10601 **E-mail:** rsvp3@optonline.net **Web address:** www.medical-billing-outsourcing.com

REXACH CINTRÓN, ROBERTO L.
Industry: Engineering **Born:** July 17, 1952, San Juan, Puerto Rico **Univ./degree:** B.S.C.E., University of Massachusetts at Amherst, 1974 **Current organization:** Roberto Rexach Cintrón & Assoc. **Title:** President/Principal **Type of organization:** Engineering/architectural firm **Major product:** Architectural design **Area of distribution:** International **Expertise:** Civil engineering, highways, water/wastewater, drainage **Honors/awards:** Distinguished San Juan Individual, 1998 **Published works:** 3 articles **Affiliations:** A.S.C.E.; N.S.P.E.; Former President, Puerto Rico Institute of Civil Engineers; Engineers Association of Puerto Rico; First Vice President, Engineers College of Puerto Rico; Member, San Juan Power Squadron **Hob./spts.:** Boating, travel **SIC code:** 87 **Address:** Roberto Rexach Cintrón & Assoc., #1271 Americo Miranda Ave., Reparto Metropolitano, San Juan, PR 00921 **E-mail:** rexach@rexach.net **Web address:** www.rexach.net

RHODES, ORAN W.
Industry: Religion **Born:** July 21, 1942, Santa Ana, Texas **Univ./degree:** B.S., McMurry University, 1964; M.A., Hardin-Simmons University, Texas, 1967 **Current organization:** Church of Christ/Sound Words Publications **Title:** Minister/Director/Editor **Type of organization:** Midwestern School of Preaching, Church of Christ **Major product:** Religious publication (in 14th year) **Area of distribution:** National **Expertise:** Religious education, editing, ministry **Honors/awards:** Marquis Who's Who in the Midwest; Dictionary of International Biography **Published works:** 10 books, "God's Way for the Home", "Beatitudes for Living", "Stanzas to Live By", "Assorted Sermon Outlines", "Glimpses into Genesis", "Bits and Pieces", "Mets-A Workbook", "Preaching from the Minor Prophets", "Commentary on Romans", "Esther"; bi-monthly magazine, "Sound Words"; 2 video series, The Book of Daniel, Book of Revelation **Affiliations:** RNC; Heritage Foundation **Hob./spts.:** Travel, genealogy **SIC code:** 86 **Address:** Church of Christ/Sound Words Publications, 17523 E. R.D. Mize Rd., Independence, MO 64057-1540 **E-mail:** orhodes400@aol.com **Web address:** www.sugarcreekchurchofchrist.org

RICHARDS, MARTY G.
Industry: Educational foundation **Born:** July 14, 1962, Spartanburg, South Carolina **Univ./degree:** B.A., English and Political Science, Wofford College; M.A., Public Administration, 1986; M.A., Political Science and Public Policy, 1987, Ohio State University **Current organization:** Spartanburg Technical College Foundation **Title:** Executive Director **Type of organization:** Nonprofit **Major product:** Fundraising for college **Area of distribution:** Spartanburg, South Carolina **Expertise:** Coordinator of events, Fundraising Director **Honors/awards:** Outstanding Local Educator, South Carolina Technical Educ. Assoc., 1996, 1998; Member, Who's Who in America, Who's Who in the South and Southwest and Who's Who in the World **Affiliations:** Presbyterian Church (USA); Board of Directors, Spartanburg Little Theatre and Ballet Spartanburg; Association of Fundraising Professionals, South Carolina Piedmont Chapter; Member, Mount Moriah Foundation Board of Directors; Mayor Bills Barnet's Advisory Committee; Marketing Director for A Dickens of A Christmas; Board Member, Miss South Carolina Pageant Foundation; President, Bill Drake Christmas Music Festival; Member, Board of Commissioners, Spartanburg Memorial Auditorium **Hob./spts.:** Tennis, theater, reading, involved with the community **SIC code:** 86 **Address:** Spartanburg Technical College Foundation, P.O. Box 4386, Spartanburg, SC 29305 **E-mail:** richardsm@stcsc.edu

RICHARDS, RICKY V.
Industry: Consulting **Born:** December 23, 1958, Clifton, Texas **Univ./degree:** B.S.C.E., University of Texas at Austin, 1982 **Current organization:** Norseman Engineering **Title:** Owner, P.E. (Texas) **Type of organization:** Engineering consulting **Major product:** Engineering consulting services/forensic engineering for residential and light commercial businesses **Area of distribution:** Texas **Expertise:** Civil engineering, expert witness work **Honors/awards:** Military Awards: Defense Meritorious Service Medal, Navy Commendation Medal (2), Navy Achievement Medal, National Defense Medal (2) **Published works:** Conference papers **Affiliations:** A.S.C.E. **Hob./spts.:** Camping, hiking, boating, gardening **SIC code:** 87 **Address:** Norseman Engineering, P.O. Box 1683, DeSoto, TX 75123-1683 **E-mail:** norseman.eng@comcast.net

RICKARD, LESTER
Industry: Ceramics **Born:** December 10, 1941, Cuba, New York **Univ./degree:** B.S., Ceramic Engineering, NYS College of Ceramics at Alfred University, 1965; M.B.A., Canisius University, 1978 **Current organization:** LesWal **Title:** Partner **Type of organization:** Consulting **Major product:** Ceramic whitewares, pottery, dinnerware, insulators **Area of distribution:** International **Expertise:** Process engineering, manufacturing, packaging **Affiliations:** American Ceramic Society; Ceramic Association of New York **Hob./spts.:** Hunting, golf, hiking, travel **SIC code:** 87 **Address:** LesWal, S5458 Stilwell Rd., Hamburg, NY 14045 **E-mail:** lesrick@juno.com

RIDER, KATHY T.
Industry: Social work **Born:** April 18, 1945, Roswell, New Mexico **Univ./degree:** M.S.W., University of Texas School of Social Work, 1969 **Current organization:** Private Practice of Clinical Social Work **Title:** Board Certified Social Worker **Type of organization:** Private practice **Major product:** Psychotherapy, clinical social work **Area of distribution:** Austin, Texas **Expertise:** Outpatient mental health **Affiliations:** N.A.S.W.; A.G.P.A.; T.S.C.S.W. **Hob./spts.:** Reading, history, supporter of high school and collegiate education **SIC code:** 83 **Address:** 3724 Jefferson St., Suite 206, Austin, TX 78731 **E-mail:** rider4@austin.rr.com

RILE, ROBERT N.
Industry: Mental health **Born:** September 12, 1947, Ocala, Florida **Univ./degree:** B.S. Forestry; M.A., Urban Development, George Washington University **Current organization:** DSBA Depression/Bipolar Fellowship **Title:** Co-chairman **Type of organization:** Support group **Major product:** Leadership, education and support for individuals suffering from depression and Bipolarity **Area of distribution:** Florida **Expertise:** Leadership/education **Affiliations:** National Association of Mental Health **Hob./spts.:** Writing, public speaking, volunteer work **SIC code:** 83 **Address:** 919 S.E. 14th St., Ocala, FL 34471-3917 **E-mail:** ryry1013@aol.com

RINTALAN, CHRISTOPHER J.
Industry: Consulting **Born:** August 3, 1978, Eugene, Oregon **Univ./degree:** M.S., Tulane University, 2002 **Current organization:** Biomedical Forensics **Title:** Biomedical Engineer **Type of organization:** Consulting firm **Major product:** Consulting **Area of distribution:** Moraga, California **Expertise:** Biomedical and mechanical engineering **Published works:** Journal article **Affiliations:** S.A.M.E.; A.S.M.E.; Biomedical Engineering Society; American Society of Biomedical Mechanics **Hob./spts.:** Football, basketball, skiing, baseball **SIC code:** 87 **Address:** Biomedical Forensics, 1660 School St., #103, Moraga, CA 94556 **E-mail:** crintal@hotmail.com

RIOJAS, ALMA MORALES
Industry: Education **Univ./degree:** B.A., Education, University of Texas, Austin, 1967 **Current organization:** MANA, A National Latina Organization **Title:** President/CEO **Type of organization:** Nonprofit association **Major product:** Leadership development **Area of distribution:** National **Expertise:** Education and economic development **Affiliations:** Executive Women in Government; Member, Board of Directors, Catholic Charities **Hob./spts.:** Reading mystery novels, sewing **SIC code:** 86 **Address:** MANA, A National Latina Organization, 1725 K St. N.W., Suite 501, Washington, DC 20006 **E-mail:** almariojas@yahoo.com

RIOS-DORIA, CARLOS H.
Industry: Consulting **Born:** November 17, 1940, Lima, Peru **Univ./degree:** B.M.E., Lawrence University, Michigan, 1964 **Current organization:** EDS **Title:** Regional Manager **Type of organization:** Consulting **Major product:** Information technology consulting **Area of distribution:** International **Expertise:** Engineering **Affiliations:** A.S.M.E. **Hob./spts.:** Tennis, golf, painting **SIC code:** 87 **Address:** EDS, 4132 Fair Meadow Dr., Plano, TX 75024 **E-mail:** carlos.rios-doria@eds.com

RIPLEY, LINDA S.
Industry: Social Services **Born:** October 31, 1952, Hamilton, New York **Univ./degree:** M.Div., Drew University, 1993 **Current organization:** Our Place Inc. **Title:** Executive Director **Type of organization:** Multi-service drop-in center **Major product:** Religion based social services **Area of distribution:** New Jersey **Affiliations:** American Baptist Church; International Society of Poets **Hob./spts.:** Reading, the outdoors **SIC code:** 83 **Address:** Our Place Inc., 51 Washington St., Morristown, NJ 07960 **Web address:** www.ourplacedropincenter.org

ROBERTS, JOSEPH A.
Industry: Technology **Univ./degree:** A.S., Oakton Community College **Current organization:** Technology Management, Inc. **Title:** Vice President, Engineering **Type of organization:** Consulting Engineering **Major product:** Project Management **Area of distribution:** National, International **Expertise:** Electrical engineering, design and build, telecommunications **Hob./spts.:** Golf, hunting, fresh water fishing **SIC code:** 87 **Address:** Technology Management, Inc., 1911 Rohlwing Rd., Suite E, Rolling Meadows, IL 60008 **E-mail:** jroberts@tmiamerica.com

ROBERTS, LANCE A.
Industry: Consulting engineering **Univ./degree:** M.S.C.E., Structural Engineering, South Dakota School of Mines and Technology, 1999 **Current organization:** TranSystems Corp. **Title:** Bridge Project Engineer **Type of organization:** Consulting firm **Major product:** Transportation design **Area of distribution:** National **Expertise:** Bridge engineering; P.E. **Affiliations:** A.S.C.E.; A.C.I.; A.R.E.M.A. **Hob./spts.:** Hunting, fishing, golf **SIC code:** 87 **Address:** TranSystems Corp., 2400 Pershing Rd., Suite 400, Kansas City, MO 64108 **E-mail:** laroberts@transystems.com

ROBERTSON, JAMES J.
Industry: Engineering **Univ./degree:** B.S.M.E., Kansas State University, 2001 **Current organization:** Knoll's Atomic Power Laboratory **Title:** Nuclear Plant Engineer **Type of organization:** Training and design **Major product:** United States Naval nuclear propulsion **Area of distribution:** National **Expertise:** Nuclear operations training **Affiliations:** A.S.M.E. **Hob./spts.:** Astronomy, soccer, books **SIC code:** 87 **Address:** 98 East Ave., Saratoga Springs, NY 12866 **E-mail:** jjr3497@earthlink.net

RODGERS, JAMES B.
Industry: Religion **Born:** January 1, 1954, Paris, Texas **Univ./degree:** Th.D., Luther Rice Seminary, 1987; Th.D., Texas A&M University **Current organization:** Shiloh Baptist Church **Title:** Senior Pastor **Type of organization:** Church **Major product:** Spiritual development **Area of distribution:** International **Expertise:** Pastoral care **Affiliations:** A.A.C.C.; S.C.E.; N.A.A.C.P.; Faith at Work Ministries **Hob./spts.:** Fishing, horses **SIC code:** 86 **Address:** Shiloh Baptist Church, 3565 9th Ave., Sacramento, CA 95817 **E-mail:** drjbrodgers@sbcglobal.net **Web address:** www.sbcministries.org

RODRIGUEZ, EFRAIN
Industry: Engineering **Born:** March 3, 1972, Bayamon, Puerto Rico **Univ./degree:** B.S., University of Puerto Rico, Mayaguez Campus, 1996 **Current organization:** Thames Water **Title:** Project Manager **Type of organization:** Water and wastewater services **Major product:** Industrial products **Area of distribution:** International **Expertise:** Civil engineering **Honors/awards:** Honor Society **Affiliations:** A.S.C.E.; C.I.A.P.R.; A.W.W.A.; S.I.P.R. **SIC code:** 87 **Address:** Thames Water, P.O. Box 9057, Bayamón, PR 00960-9057 **E-mail:** efrain_rodz@hotmail.com

RODRIGUEZ, ERIC M.
Industry: Human services **Born:** January 24, 1971, Long Island, New York **Univ./degree:** Ph.D., City University of New York Graduate School **Current organization:** Body Positive, Inc. **Title:** Executive Director **Type of organization:** Nonprofit **Major product:** Programs and services for the HIV infected and affected individuals **Area of distribution:** National **Expertise:** Management, administration, research, psychology **Hob./spts.:** Ice hockey, rollerblading, travel **SIC code:** 83 **Address:** Body Positive, Inc., 19 Fulton St., Suite 308B, New York, NY 10038 **E-mail:** erodriguez@bodypos.org **Web address:** www.bodypos.org

RODRÍGUEZ HERNÁNDEZ, CLAUDIO
Industry: Consulting **Born:** November 24, 1943, Sabana Grande, Puerto Rico **Univ./degree:** B.S.C.E., C.A.A.M., Mayaguez, 1970 **Current organization:** Claudio Rodriguez & Associates **Title:** Civil Engineer **Type of organization:** Consulting firm **Major product:** Land development for residential housing projects **Area of distribution:** Hormigueros, Puerto Rico **Expertise:** Housing project development & design **Affiliations:** A.C.I.M.; A.S.C.E.; C.I.A. de Puerto Rico; Lions Club **Hob./spts.:** Chess, dominoes, playing guitar, country music singer **SIC code:** 87 **Address:** Claudio Rodriguez & Associates, P.O. Box 123, Hormigueros, PR 00660-0123 **E-mail:** trh_3@hotmail.com

RODRIGUEZ-CUELLO CAMILO, SANDRA ESTHER
Industry: Consulting/Construction **Univ./degree:** M.A., Architecture, Universidad Autónoma de Santo Domingo, 1985 **Current organization:** Mirsand Town Planning & Architects, Ltd. **Title:** Architect/Co-Owner **Type of organization:** Architecture and engineering firm **Major product:** Architectural design **Area of distribution:** Virgin Islands, The English Caribbean, Dominican Republic **Expertise:** Designer/Urban Planner **Affiliations:** B.V.I. Architect and Engineers Association **Hob./spts.:** Yachting, cooking **SIC code:** 87 **Address:** Mirsand Town Planning & Architects Ltd., Marcy Bldg., 2nd floor, Purcell Estate, P.O. Box 904, Road Town, Tortola, VI 00108 **E-mail:** mirs@surfbvi.com

ROGERS, SCOT D.
Industry: Engineering **Born:** March 7, 1959, Wisconsin **Univ./degree:** B.S., Electrical Engineering, Kansas State University, 1988 **Current organization:** Rogers Labs, Inc. **Title:** President **Type of organization:** Consulting **Major product:** Electrical R.F. design/testing **Area of distribution:** National **Expertise:** Engineering **Affiliations:** N.F.I.B.; I.E.E.E. **Hob./spts.:** Boy Scouts **SIC code:** 87 **Address:** Rogers Labs, Inc., 4405 W. 259th Terrace, Louisburg, KS 66053 **E-mail:** rogers@micoks.net

ROJAS, JESUS JON
Industry: Clinical research **Born:** October 29, 1970, Havana, Cuba **Univ./degree:** B.A., Mobile Intensive Care Paramedic, UCLA, 1988 **Current organization:** Omnicomm Systems, Inc. **Title:** Vice President, Project Management **Type of organization:** Contract research organization **Major product:** Electronic data capture software **Area of distribution:** National **Expertise:** Project management, clinical research **Affiliations:** The Project Management Institute; Association of Clinical Research Professionals; Drug Information Association **Hob./spts.:** Teaching martial arts, surfing, chess **SIC code:** 87 **Address:** Omnicomm Systems, Inc., 2101 West Commercial Blvd., Suite 4000, Sunny Isles Beach, FL 33309 **E-mail:** rojasjonn@aol.com

ROMANKIW, LUBOMYR T.
Industry: Computers and communications **Born:** April 17, 1931, Lviv, Western Ukraine **Univ./degree:** B.Sc., Chemical Engineering, University of Alberta, Canada, 1955; M.Sc., Ph.D., Metallurgy and Materials, Massachusetts Institute of Technology, 1962 **Current organization:** IBM T.J. Watson Research Center **Title:** IBM Fellow/ Chief Scout of Plast-Scout Movement in Ukraine and Diaspora **Type of organization:** Research and development **Major product:** Computers and electronic components **Area of distribution:** International **Expertise:** Electrochemical technology, micro fabrication, magnetics **Honors/awards:** Numerous including the Perkin Gold Medal of the Society of Chemical Industries, 1993 **Published works:** 57 patents, 120+ published inventions, 150+ scientific papers including "Thirty Years of Thin Film Magnetic Heads for the Hard Disk Drives", J. Magn. Soc. Japan, Vol. 24, pp. 1-4, 2000 and "Think Small-One Day It May Be Worth A Billion" Interface (Electrochemical Society), pp. 17-20, 56-57, 1993), 5 book chapters, edited 10 volumes of symposia proceedings in the areas of Magnetic Materials, Processes and Devices and Electrochemistry in Electronics **Affiliations:** Electrochemical Society; ISE; ECS; AESF; IEEE; SPIE; Shevchenko Scientific Society; Ukrainian Engineering Society; Engineering Academy of Ukraine **Career accomplishments:** Dr. Romankiw started the Scout movement for boys and girls in the Ukraine after Ukraine gained independence in 1991. The Scout organization is raising new Western oriented citizens to integrate into the Western world. As Chief Scout, Dr. Romankiw is actively working not only to bring the Ukrainian youth in the world of Scouting traditions of God and country, help to others and obeying Scout laws and leadership, but is engaged in fundraising to support Scouts in Ukraine via the Plast Conference, Inc.-Chief Scout Fund, a USA nonprofit, tax exempt 501(c)(3) organization whose address is: P.O. Box 303, Southfield, NY 10975 **Hob./spts.:** Boy Scouts, fundraising, violin, singing **SIC code:** 87 **Address:** IBM T.J. Watson Research Center, P.O. Box 218, Yorktown Heights, NY 10598 **E-mail:** romankiw@us.ibm.com **Web address:** www.ibm.com

ROME, LARRY
Industry: Geochemical Engineering **Born:** November 4, 1976, New Orleans, Louisiana **Univ./degree:** A.A.S., Industrial Hygiene, Delgado Community College, 1998 **Current organization:** Eustis Engineering Co. **Title:** Operations Manager **Type of organization:** Engineering company **Major product:** Foundation designs, geochemical engineering **Area of distribution:** Louisiana **Expertise:** Management of soil mechanics lab and exploration; Certified Engineering Technologist **Affiliations:** American Society of Certified Engineering Technicians; National Institute for Certification in Engineering Technologies **Hob./spts.:** Family activities **SIC code:** 87 **Address:** Eustis Engineering Co., 3011 28th St., Metairie, LA 70002 **E-mail:** lrome@eustiseng.com **Web address:** www.eustiseng.com

ROSENBLATT, JOEL H.
Industry: Engineering **Born:** September 21, 1924, Baltimore, Maryland **Univ./degree:** B.S., Civil Engineering, University of Maryland **Current organization:** Rosenblatt-Naderi Associates, P.A. **Title:** Vice-President **Type of organization:** Consulting/engineering firm **Major product:** Structural engineering, landscape architectures **Area of distribution:** Florida **Expertise:** Engineering **Published works:** 1 book, "Space on Earth, The Story of Urban Mountain" **Affiliations:** Life Member, A.S.C.E. **Hob./spts.:** Engineering **SIC code:** 87 **Address:** Rosenblatt-Naderi Associates, P.A., P.O. Box 198, Summerland Key, FL 33042 **E-mail:** flakeys@sprynet.com

ROSS, ELEANORA BETSY
Industry: Consulting **Born:** January 3, 1932, Washington, Iowa **Univ./degree:** M.A., University of Iowa **Current organization:** Ray of Hope Ministries, Inc. **Title:** Founder/Director **Type of organization:** Ministries **Major product:** Private and public family counseling **Area of distribution:** National **Expertise:** Counseling **Honors/awards:** American Association of Suicidology **Published works:** Article **Affiliations:** American Association of Suicidology **Hob./spts.:** Sewing, reading, drama **SIC code:** 87 **Address:** Ray of Hope Ministries, Inc., P.O. Box 2323, Iowa City, IA 52244 **E-mail:** ebross1@juno.com

ROSSI, JOHN J.
Industry: Engineering **Born:** June 21, 1948, Ware, Massachusetts **Univ./degree:** B.S., Mechanical Engineering, Central New England College of Technology, Massachusetts, 1978 **Current organization:** Anver Corp. **Title:** Chief Engineer, Custom Lifters **Type of organization:** OEM manufacturing **Major product:** Vacuum lifters and

components **Area of distribution:** International **Expertise:** Mechanical engineering, product design and development **Affiliations:** American Welding Society **Hob./spts.:** Golf, travel, downhill skiing **SIC code:** 87 **Address:** Anver Corp., 36 Parmenter Rd., Hudson, MA 01749 **E-mail:** jjr9000@aol.com

ROY, SUMITA
Industry: Biotechnology **Univ./degree:** Ph.D., Cell Biology, Calcutta University, 1982 **Current organization:** Curis, Inc. **Title:** Associate Director, Research Lab **Type of organization:** Research and development **Major product:** R&D, drug development **Area of distribution:** International **Expertise:** Operations management, purchasing/ordering **Honors/awards:** Outstanding Leadership Award, Genzy, 1998 **Affiliations:** Association of Cytogenetic Technologists; Chair, Environmental Safety Group **Hob./spts.:** Indian vocal music **SIC code:** 87 **Address:** Curis, Inc., 45 Moulton St., Cambridge, MA 02138 **E-mail:** sroy@curis.com

ROZSNYAI, BALAZS F.
Industry: Laboratory **Born:** November 24, 1929, Hungary **Univ./degree:** Ph.D., Nuclear Physics, University of California at Berkeley, 1960 **Current organization:** Lawrence Livermore National Laboratory **Title:** Lab Associate **Type of organization:** National laboratory **Major product:** Theoretical physics, plasma physics **Area of distribution:** International **Expertise:** Plasma physics **Affiliations:** American Physical Society **Hob./spts.:** Skiing, tennis **SIC code:** 87 **Address:** 1104 Ave. de las Palmas, Livermore, CA 94550 **E-mail:** rozsnyai9@aol.com

RUH, EDWIN
Industry: Consulting **Born:** April 22, 1924, Westfield, New Jersey **Univ./degree:** Ph.D., Rutgers University, 1954 **Current organization:** Ruh International Co. **Title:** President **Type of organization:** Consulting firm **Major product:** Consulting, refractories **Area of distribution:** International **Expertise:** Consulting **Published works:** Books **Affiliations:** American Ceramic Society **Hob./spts.:** Antique cars **SIC code:** 87 **Address:** Ruh International Co., 892 Old Hickory Rd., Pittsburgh, PA 15243 **E-mail:** edemruh@adelphia.net

RUHL, CLYDE E.
Industry: Consulting/engineering **Born:** June 4, 1927, Columbus, Montana **Univ./degree:** B.S., Civil Engineering, University of Wyoming, 1956 **Current organization:** CERCO Engineering **Title:** V.P./General Manager **Type of organization:** Consulting engineering firm **Major product:** Engineering and surveying services **Area of distribution:** Alaska **Expertise:** Surveying, civil engineering **Affiliations:** B.S.C.E. **Hob./spts.:** Fishing **SIC code:** 87 **Address:** CERCO Engineering, 325 Hanagita St., Valdez, AK 99686

SAENZ JR., RAMON
Industry: Electric Utility **Born:** Rio Grande City, Texas **Univ./degree:** B.S.E.E., Texas A&M University, 1983 **Current organization:** Patrick Engineering, Inc. **Title:** Senior Manager, P.E. **Type of organization:** Engineering firm **Major product:** Consulting, design, distributing **Area of distribution:** National **Expertise:** Team leadership, leadership development, electric power quality consulting **Published works:** 10 articles **Affiliations:** I.E.E.E.; E.P.R.I.; Chairman, International Power Electronics Conference; International Advisor, National Energy Grid of Poland **Hob./spts.:** Family activities, playing the guitar **SIC code:** 87 **Address:** Patrick Engineering, Inc., 7000 N. Mopac Expwy., 2nd floor, Austin, TX 78731 **E-mail:** rsaenz@patrickengineering.com

SALAMONE, THOMAS
Industry: Consulting/safety/fire prevention **Univ./degree:** B.S., Chemistry, Manhattan College, 1979 **Current organization:** Healthcare & Life Safety Concepts and Life Safety Solutions **Title:** President **Type of organization:** Consulting **Major product:** Accreditation preparation and Environment of Care consulting **Area of distribution:** United States and Canada **Expertise:** Environment of care, safety, life safety, fire prevention and loss prevention, loss control **Affiliations:** N.F.P.A.; S.F.P.E.; A.S.S.E.; A.S.H.E.; H.F.M.A.; A.S.H.R.M.; A.C.H.E.; A.I.H.A.; G.N.Y.H.A. **SIC code:** 87 **Address:** Healthcare & Life Safety Concepts and Life Safety Solutions, 20 Elmwood Circle, Peekskill, NY 10566 **E-mail:** tomsalamone@msn.com

SALOMONE, JOHN ANTHONY
Industry: Financial services/planning **Born:** February 28, 1962, New York, New York **Univ./degree:** B.A., Accounting, Hofstra University, New York, 1984 **Current organization:** John A. Salomone **Title:** Financial Planner **Type of organization:** Private accounting firm **Major product:** Accounting, financial planner **Area of distribution:** New York **Expertise:** Income tax, estate planning **Affiliations:** National Association of Tax Practitioners; National Society of Tax Practitioners; Financial Planners Association; A.A.I.I. **SIC code:** 87 **Address:** John A. Salomone, 44 Family Lane, Levittown, NY 11756 **E-mail:** salomone1040@aol.com **Web address:** www.1040-tax.com

SALTMAN, ROY G.
Industry: Consulting **Born:** New York, New York **Univ./degree:** M.S., Electrical Engineering, M.I.T., 1955; M.A., Public Administration, American University, 1976 **Current organization:** Roy G. Saltman, M.S., M.P.A. **Title:** Owner **Type of organization:** Consulting firm **Major product:** Election policy and technology **Area of distribution:** International **Expertise:** Election policy and technology **Published works:** Reports **SIC code:** 87 **Address:** Roy G. Saltman, M.S., M.P.A., 5025 Broken Oak Lane, Columbia, MD 21044 **E-mail:** rsaltman@alum.mit.edu

SALVATORE, BOB
Industry: Labor organization **Born:** November 14, 1946, New Haven, Connecticut **Univ./degree:** B.S., Management, St. Mary's University, 1980 **Current organization:** San Antonio Building Trades Council **Title:** President **Type of organization:** Non-profit **Major product:** Labor contract negotiations, worker representation **Area of distribution:** Texas **Expertise:** Corporate management, administration, representing workers **Affiliations:** The Texas and Apprenticeship Training Board **Hob./spts.:** Fishing, collecting and repairing diesel motors **SIC code:** 86 **Address:** San Antonio Building Trades Council, 311 S. St. Mary's St., Suite E, 15th floor, San Antonio, TX 78205 **E-mail:** sabtc1@aol.com

SAMPACO, CASAN KING L.
Industry: Consulting **Born:** January 6, 1962, Marawi City, Philippines **Univ./degree:** Ph.D., Civil & Geotechnical Engineering, Utah State University **Current organization:** CH2M Hill, Inc. **Title:** Senior Geotechnical Engineer/Senior Technologist **Type of organization:** Consulting firm **Major product:** Engineering, consulting **Area of distribution:** International **Expertise:** Geotechnical engineering/computer applications in geotechnical engineering **Published works:** 7 professional journals, 38 international conferences, 1 transportation research board circular, 3 research reports **Affiliations:** American Society of Civil Engineers (ASCE); Geo-Institute; Southeast Asian Geotechnical Society (SEAGS); Phi Kappa Phi Honor Society **Hob./spts.:** Listening to jazz music and 70's rock/pop, playing guitar, playing basketball, playing chess, reading **SIC code:** 87 **Address:** CH2M Hill Inc., 777 108th Ave. N.E., Bellevue, WA 98006 **E-mail:** ksampaco@ch2m.com **Web address:** www.ch2m.com

SANCHEZ, JIMMY P.
Industry: Professional service/consulting **Born:** January 13, 1962, Patchsy, California **Univ./degree:** Ph.D., Electrical Engineering, 1997; B.S.M.E., 1984, University of California at Los Angeles **Current organization:** Sanchez Development **Title:** Developer **Type of organization:** Construction **Major product:** Construction/engineering **Area of distribution:** Mojave, California **Expertise:** Engineering **Affiliations:** I.E.E.E.; A.I.A. **SIC code:** 87 **Address:** Sanchez Development, 15824 "M" St., Mojave, CA 93501 **E-mail:** jimmysanchez@antelecom.net

SANDELL, GINGER ANNE
Industry: Certified Public Accounting **Born:** October 8, 1950, Maiden name: Ginger Anne Baxter **Spouse:** Stanley Thronas **Married:** June 22, 2003 **Children:** Dylan Lee Berg, born 1971; Jason Lawrence Powell Martin, born 1975; Lonnie Ira Howard Martin, born 1977; Paul Keanuenue Nicholas Martin, born 1978 **Univ./degree:** B.A., University of Hawaii at Hilo; M.B.A., University of Hawaii at Manoa; Register Investment Representative **Current organization:** Sole proprietor Ginger Sandell, CPA accounting firm **Title:** Owner **Type of organization:** Sole proprietor, CPA accounting firm **Area of distribution:** Hawaii **Expertise:** Tax planning and preparation, financial planning, compilations, reviews, consulting **Honors/awards:** Summa Cum Laude, Beta Gamma Sigma, Wall Street Journal Award **Published works:** Article published in HFMA, 2002 **Affiliations:** A.I.C.P.A.; H.S.C.P.A.; Chamber of Commerce; Kona Executive Association **Career accomplishments:** Progressive growth and responsibility in the financial planning service sector. Began working as a staff accountant for a public accounting firm in 1989 and was promoted to manager in 1993. Began working in private industry in 1996. Started as a controller and was promoted to Chief Financial Officer within 4 months. Promoted to Regional Chief Financial Officer and Regional Compliance Officer in 2000. Started her own CPA firm in 2004 **Hob./spts.:** Ocean swimming, yoga, weightlifting, painting, reading **SIC code:** 87 **Address:** 78-6831 Alii Drive, Suite K-8, Kailua Kona, HI 96740 **E-mail:** gsandell@verizon.net

SANDERFORD, HOWARD D.
Industry: Accounting **Born:** August 11, 1937, Raleigh, North Carolina **Univ./degree:** B.Div., Bible Institute, Ohio, 1975 **Current organization:** Howard Sanderford Accounting &Tax Service **Title:** Owner/Accountant **Type of organization:** Accounting firm **Major product:** Financial statements and tax returns **Area of distribution:** International **Expertise:** Tax returns preparation **Affiliations:** N.S.A.; N.I.P.; A.I.P.B.; Board Member, Homes for the Homeless **Hob./spts.:** Travel, fishing, church treasurer **SIC code:** 87 **Address:** Howard Sanderford Accounting & Tax Service, 1521 Crestwood Circle West, Lehigh Acres, FL 33936 **E-mail:** dsanderfor@cs.com

SANDERSON, JASON H.
Industry: Religion **Born:** April 7, 1966, West Burke, Vermont **Univ./degree:** Theological Training **Current organization:** St. Jude's Liberal Catholic Church **Title:** Father **Type of organization:** Liberal Catholic Church **Major product:** Religious service and outreach programs **Area of distribution:** International **Expertise:** Athletes outreach ministry, African missions **Affiliations:** Member, Masons **Hob./spts.:** Writing, reading

mysteries, wrestling **SIC code:** 86 **Address:** 74 Piscassic Rd., Newfields, NH 03856 **E-mail:** luchepadre@comcast.net

SANDFORD, JOHN LOREN
Industry: Religion **Born:** July 23, 1929, Joplin, Missouri **Univ./degree:** B.A., Drury University, 1951; M.Div., Chicago Theological Seminary, 1958 **Current organization:** Elijah House, Inc. **Title:** Co-Founder/Reverend **Type of organization:** Teaching and Prayer ministry **Major product:** Books, literature **Area of distribution:** International **Expertise:** Teaching, writing, counseling **Published works:** "Why Some Christians Commit Adultery", 1989; "Healing the Nations", 2000; "Elijah Among Us", 2002; Co-authored books: "The Elijah Task", 1977; "Restoring the Christian Family", 1979; "The Transformation of the Inner Man", 1982; "Healing the Wounded Spirit", 1985; "Renewal of the Mind", 1991; "A Comprehensive Guide to Deliverance and Inner Healing", 1992; "Waking the Slumbering Spirit", 1993; "Choosing Forgiveness", 1996; "Prophets Healers and the Emerging Church", 2002 **Affiliations:** Apostolic Council of Prophetic Elders; Apostolic Roundtable of Deliverance Ministries; International Society of Deliverance Ministries"; Elijah House, Inc. USA; The Elijah House in Australia, New Zealand, Finland, Austria, Japan and South Africa **Hob./spts.:** Gardening **SIC code:** 86 **Address:** Elijah House, Inc., 17397 W. Laura Lane, Post Falls, ID 83854-9977 **E-mail:** jlsandford@mac.com **Web address:** www.elijahouse.org

SAPRU, VISHAL
Industry: Power supplies and batteries **Born:** August 19, 1973 **Univ./degree:** Post Graduate Diploma, Market Management, Symbiosis Institute of Business Management, 1998 **Current organization:** Frost & Sullivan **Title:** Research Analyst **Type of organization:** Consulting **Major product:** Research and consulting services **Area of distribution:** International **Expertise:** Power quality and power supplies analysis **Published works:** Technical marketing journals, power quality and power supplies publications, Internet **SIC code:** 87 **Address:** 4000 Horizon Hill Blvd., #2003, San Antonio, TX 78229 **E-mail:** v_sapru@hotmail.com

SARKISIAN, NORAY M.
Industry: Consulting engineers **Born:** May 6, 1951, Detroit, Michigan **Univ./degree:** B.S., Engineering, Eastern Michigan University, 1973 **Current organization:** Sarkison & Associates **Title:** Principal **Type of organization:** Engineering **Major product:** Electrical design of building systems **Area of distribution:** National **Expertise:** Electrical engineering (power) **Affiliations:** I.E.E.E.; National Association of Professional Engineers; National Fire & Protection Association; Grass Valley & Nevada City Chamber of Commerce **Hob./spts.:** Hiking, biking **SIC code:** 87 **Address:** Sarkisian & Associates, 14015 Arrowhead Mine Rd., Grass Valley, CA 95945 **E-mail:** noray@oro.net

SASTRY, SURYANARAYANA C.
Industry: Engineering **Univ./degree:** M.S., Polytec, 1976, Professional Engineer; New York, Illinois and Texas **Current organization:** Chiang, Patel & Yerby, Inc. **Title:** Chief Track Engineer **Type of organization:** Engineering firm **Major product:** Engineering **Area of distribution:** National and International **Expertise:** Railroads and rail transit **Affiliations:** A.S.C.E.; A.R.E.M.A. **SIC code:** 87 **Address:** Chiang, Patel & Yerby, Inc., 1820 Regal Row, Suite 200, Dallas, TX 75235 **E-mail:** ssastry@cpyi.com

SAXTON, RICHARD D.
Industry: Aerospace **Born:** March 27, 1954, Middletown, New York **Univ./degree:** B.S., Physics, Marist College, 1977 **Current organization:** Lockheed Martin Corp. **Title:** Program Manager, Systems Engineering Manager **Type of organization:** Avionics systems integrator **Major product:** Complex systems design, development, integration **Area of distribution:** International **Expertise:** Systems engineering, technical & program management **Affiliations:** I.E.E.E.; A.C.M.; A.I.P.; I.N.C.O.S.E.; P.M.I. **Hob./spts.:** Music, guitar, drums, amateur radio, computing, computers, electronics **SIC code:** 87 **Address:** Lockheed Martin Corp., 1801 State Rt. 17C, M/D 0906, Owego, NY 13827-3998 **Phone:** (607)751-4659 **Fax:** (607)751-3163 **E-mail:** rich.saxton@lmco.com

SCHABIB, JESUS
Industry: Engineering **Born:** June 30, 1950, Bolivia **Univ./degree:** B.S., Engineering, City University of New York, Staten Island **Current organization:** Parsons Brinckerhoff **Title:** Project Manager **Type of organization:** Consulting firm **Major product:** Product design, documents, plans **Area of distribution:** National **Expertise:** Project planning, management of underground tunnels **Hob./spts.:** Bowling, volleyball, disco techs **SIC code:** 87 **Address:** Parsons Brinckerhoff, 469 Seventh Ave., 14th floor, New York, NY 10018 **E-mail:** jschabib@mta-esa.org **Web address:** www.pworld.com

SCHALLER, MATTHEW F.
Industry: Architecture **Born:** November 28, 1953, Denver, Colorado **Univ./degree:** B.S., Engineering, University of Idaho, 1980 **Current organization:** Matthew Schaller, Architect Inc. **Title:** Architect **Type of organization:** Architectural firm **Major product:** Residential and light commercial architecture **Area of distribution:** Hawaii **Expertise:** Architecture - custom homes **Affiliations:** A.S.C.E.; Tau Beta Pi **Hob./spts.:** Golf **SIC code:** 87 **Address:** Matthew Schaller, Architect Inc., P.O. Box 120, Hanalei, HI 96714-0120 **E-mail:** schaller@aloha.net

SCHELLER, ERIK P.
Industry: Civil Engineering **Born:** May 26, 1966, Izmir, Turkey **Univ./degree:** B.S., Civil Engineering, California Polytechnic State University, 1991 **Current organization:** International Drafting Design Source, Inc. **Title:** President **Type of organization:** Engineering/architectural outsourcing **Major product:** Engineering, architectural and construction drafting and/or design collaboration outsourcing services **Area of distribution:** International **Expertise:** Engineering; Registered Professional Engineer in the State of California **Affiliations:** National Society of Professional Engineers; California Society of Professional Engineers; American Society of Civil Engineers; National Peace Corps Association; Friends of Ghana; Rotary International **Hob./spts.:** Travel, collecting die-cast model automobiles, swimming, hiking, camping **SIC code:** 87 **Address:** International Drafting Design Source, Inc., 44 Martin Dr., Novato, CA 94949 **Phone:** (415)260-7006 **Fax:** (415)276-3033 **E-mail:** eriks@iddsource.com **Web address:** www.iddsource.com

SCHIMMOELLER, GERALD M.
Industry: Financial services **Born:** September 2, 1943, Ohio **Univ./degree:** M.B.A., Northeastern University, Boston, 1982 **Current organization:** A.G. Edwards & Sons, Inc. **Title:** Financial consultant **Type of organization:** Financial services **Major product:** Financial planning **Area of distribution:** National **Expertise:** Consulting services **Affiliations:** F.E.I. **Hob./spts.:** Cross country skiing, golf **SIC code:** 87 **Address:** A.G. Edwards & Sons, Inc., 2617 Main St., North Conway, NH 03860 **E-mail:** schimmoellerj@adelphia.net

SCHLOBOHM, DAVID G.
Industry: Consulting **Born:** March 19, 1949, Marianna, Florida **Univ./degree:** M.S., Florida State University, 1974 **Current organization:** Ink Engineering, A Division of LBFH, Inc. **Title:** Client Service Manager **Type of organization:** Engineering consulting firm **Major product:** Civil and environmental engineering and surveying services **Area of distribution:** Florida and Georgia **Expertise:** Engineering and Management **Honors/awards:** Awarded N.R.S.C. Medal of Freedom; ITT Silver Team Award; International Who's Who; Who's Who Worldwide; Outstanding Young Men of America **Published works:** Numerous technical papers **Affiliations:** A.W.W.A.; W.E.F.; A.S.C.E.; N.S.P.E.; N.C.E.E.S.; F.E.S.; F.W.E.A.; G.W. & P.C.A. **Hob./spts.:** College football, travel, outdoor activities, licensed pilot, licensed "ham" radio operator **SIC code:** 87 **Address:** Ink Engineering, A Division of LBFH, Inc., 1400 Colonial Blvd., Suite 31, Ft. Myers, FL 33907 **E-mail:** david-sc@lbfh.com

SCHLUB, TERESA RAE
Industry: Religious counseling **Born:** July 11, 1946, Oak Park, Illinois **Univ./degree:** B.A., Christian Education, Westmar College, 1971; Master of Divinity, Evangelical Theological Seminary, 1974 **Current organization:** Schlub Ministries **Title:** Reverend **Type of organization:** Counseling **Major product:** Religion education, counseling, spiritual formation **Area of distribution:** National **Expertise:** Professional ministering; retail sales for May Kay Cosmetics **Honors/awards:** Who's Who of American Women **Affiliations:** Elder, United Methodist Church **Hob./spts.:** Family, movies, reading **SIC code:** 86 **Address:** Schlub Ministries, 5813 Beechwood Dr., Unit B, Loves Park, IL 61111 **E-mail:** t.r.schlub@att.net **Web address:** www.geocities.com/schlubministries

SCHNEIDER, PETER W.
Industry: President **Born:** May 19, 1937, Davenport, Iowa **Univ./degree:** M.S., Science, Texas A&M University, 1971 **Current organization:** Soil Analysis Center, Inc. **Title:** President and Chief Engineer (N.J.P.E. #26056) **Type of organization:** Engineering company **Major product:** Civil engineering **Area of distribution:** New Jersey **Expertise:** Soil testing, engineering design **Honors/awards:** Phi Kappa Phi Honor Society **Published works:** "UX-6000" **Affiliations:** A.S.C.E. **Hob./spts.:** Aviation **SIC code:** 87 **Address:** Soil Analysis Center, Inc., P.O. Box 588, Wharton, NJ 07885 **E-mail:** pschneider@nac.net

SCHNELL, DEBORAH L.
Industry: Engineering/consulting **Born:** July 31, 1966, Mount Holly, New Jersey **Univ./degree:** B.S.C.E., Lafayette University, Pennsylvania, 1994; M.S.C.E., Geo-environmental Studies, New Jersey Institute of Technology, 1996 **Current organization:** Pneumatic Fracturing Inc. **Title:** President **Type of organization:** Environmental engineering **Major product:** Consulting **Area of distribution:** International **Expertise:** Environmental remediation **Published works:** 6 articles, 5 abstracts/conference papers, 1 book chapter **Affiliations:** A.S.C.E.; S.A.M.E.; S.W.E. **Hob./spts.:** Biking, exercise, softball, reading, travel **SIC code:** 87 **Address:** Pneumatic Fracturing Inc., 1718 Springtown Rd., Alpha, NJ 08865-4634 **E-mail:** pfinc@worldnet.att.net **Web address:** www.pneumaticfracturinginc.com

SCHNOEBELEN, STEVEN C.
Industry: Consulting **Born:** February 20, 1957, Cedar Rapids, Iowa **Univ./degree:** B.A., Economics, Coe College, 1979; M.B.A., Finance, University of Akron, 1983 **Current organization:** PWC Consulting **Title:** Partner **Type of organization:** Consulting **Major product:** Strategy, process and technology consulting **Area of distribution:** International **Expertise:** Finance and supply chain management **Published works:** 5 articles **Affiliations:** I.M.A.; A.P.I.C.S. **Hob./spts.:** Golf, coaching sports teams, travel **SIC code:** 87 **Address:** PWC Consulting, 2304 Hazel Ct., Naperville, IL 60565 **E-mail:** steve.schnoebelen@us.pwcglobal.com

SCHUYLER, ROBERT L.
Industry: Consulting **Born:** March 4, 1936, Burwell, Nebraska **Univ./degree:** M.B.A., Harvard Graduate School of Business, 1960 **Current organization:** The Resource Solutions Group, LLC **Title:** CEO **Type of organization:** Consulting, construction, developers **Major product:** Natural resources **Area of distribution:** New Mexico **Expertise:** Finance, strategic planning **Hob./spts.:** Fly-fishing, golf **SIC code:** 87 **Address:** 37 Saddlehorn Rd., Tubac, AZ 85640 **E-mail:** skysantafe@msn.com

SCHWEB, PROPHET
Industry: Consulting **Univ./degree:** M.B.A., Stanford University, 1981 **Current organization:** ESP Inc. **Title:** President **Type of organization:** Consulting firm **Major product:** Management **Area of distribution:** National **Expertise:** Marketing (show business) **Hob./spts.:** Sailing **SIC code:** 87 **Address:** 114 Serrano Dr., San Francisco, CA 94132

SCHWEGEL, DAVID MASON
Industry: Engineering **Born:** June 12, 1970, Sacramento, California **Univ./degree:** B.S., Civil Engineering, California Polytechnic State University, San Luis Obispo, 1996; B.S., Engineering Science, Pacific Lutheran University, 1996 **Current organization:** Winzler & Kelly Consulting Engineers **Title:** Traffic Engineer **Type of organization:** Consulting engineering **Major product:** Civil Engineering **Area of distribution:** California, Oregon, Washington **Expertise:** Licensed Traffic (California, Oregon) and Civil Engineer (California, Washington) **Published works:** "National Engineers Week to Showcase Awards, Displays, Popsicle Sticks and Engineering Excellence", 2003; "Local Professionals Respond Heroically to the September 11th Terrorist Attacks", 2001 **Affiliations:** Public Relations Chair, Seattle Section, American Society of Civil Engineers; Public Relations Chair and Secretary, Puget Sound Engineering Council; Institute of Transportation Engineers (ITE); National Society of Professional Engineers (NSPE); Registered Traffic Engineers of America (RTEA); International Association of Business Leaders **Career accomplishments:** Cal Poly College of Engineering Alumni Service Award, 2003; Presented "Resolving Seattle's Transportation Crisis in the Wake of Referendum 51", ITE, 2003; "Infrastructure Investment" Testimony, Washington State Legislature, 2000, 2003; Presented "Creating a State-of-the-Art Transportation System for Greater Seattle Within the Constraints of Initiative 695", ITE, 2000; "Transportation Improvements" Testimony, Washington State Blue Ribbon Commission on Transportation, 2000; Presented "Conflict Monitor Operation and Testing", Oregon Traffic Signal Workshop, 1998; Certified Work Zone Safety Specialist, 1998 and Traffic Signal Level 1 Technician, 1998; Dale Carnegie Course Graduate, 1997 and Three-Time Graduate Assistant, 1998-99; Presented "High Speed Trains: Bridging the Time Gaps in Intercity Transportation", American Public Works Association, 1996 **Hob./spts.:** Bicycling - 200 mile Seattle-to-Portland Bicycle Classic, 2000, 2002; 183 mile Ride from Seattle to Vancouver B.C. and Party, 2002, 2003 **SIC code:** 87 **Address:** Barghausen Consulting Engineers, 18215 - 72nd Ave. South, Kent, WA 98032 **Phone:** (425)466-5677 **Fax:** (707)527-8679 **E-mail:** davidschwegel@w-and-k.com **Web address:** www.w-and-k.com

SCOTT, GILBERT L.
Industry: Electronics **Born:** February 21, 1930, Jacksonville, Florida **Spouse:** Donna L. Scott **Married:** February 21, 1962 **Children:** Dawn Truax, Marc Scott (deceased), Gary Scott, Keith Scott, Richard Scott; Grandchildren: Kyle, Brittany, Jake, Audrey; Great-grandchildren: Brielle Walton, Jacqueline Truax **Univ./degree:** B.A., Economics, DePauw University, 1952 **Current organization:** Roche Diagnostics **Title:** Validation Engineer **Type of organization:** Research and development, instrument development **Major product:** Medical instruments **Area of distribution:** Indiana **Expertise:** Reliability engineering **Honors/awards:** American Biographical Institute: Man of the Year 2003; International Biographical Centre, Cambridge, England: Lifetime Achievement Award and DaVinci Diamond for Outstanding Contribution to Reliability Engineering **Published works:** Textbook within company **Career accomplishments:** As a Reliability Engineer he developed field failure rate prediction methods for manufacturing and environmental related field failures; He introduced to Roche Diagnostics techniques for measuring the impact of manufacturing and environment on field failure rates; He also introduced analytical techniques for measuring life test results **Hob./spts.:** Ballroom dancing, water sports **SIC code:** 87 **Address:** 30 Fairwood Dr., Brownsburg, IN 46112-1918

SEELY, NANCY R.
Industry: Marketing **Born:** January 31, Jacksonville, Florida **Univ./degree:** B.S. **Current organization:** The Robin Shepherd Group **Title:** Executive Vice President **Type of organization:** Marketing and communications firm **Major product:** Public relations, strategic planning, corporate identification **Area of distribution:** National **Expertise:** Public relations **Hob./spts.:** Surfing **SIC code:** 87 **Address:** 500 Bishopgate Lane, Jacksonville, FL 32204 **E-mail:** nseely@trsg.net

SEIFERT, SÖNKE
Industry: Chemical **Born:** August 20, 1961, Wilster, Germany **Univ./degree:** Ph.D., Polymer Science, University of Hamburg, Institute for Technical and Micromolecular Chemistry, 1996 **Current organization:** Argonne National Laboratory **Title:** Ph.D./Assistant Scientist **Type of organization:** National laboratory **Major product:** Science, research and technology **Area of distribution:** National **Expertise:** Biology, chemistry, metals, alloys **Affiliations:** German Physical Society **Hob./spts.:** Marathon running, long distance bicycling **SIC code:** 87 **Address:** Argonne National Laboratory, 9700 S. Case Ave., Argonne, IL 60439 **E-mail:** seifert@anl.gov

SEKAVEC, THOMAS L.
Industry: Paper **Born:** April 2, 1949, La Crosse, Kansas **Univ./degree:** B.S., Fort Hayes Kansas State University, 1972 **Current organization:** Pro Tech Consulting **Title:** Agent, Senior Consultant **Type of organization:** Consulting, manufacturing **Major product:** Paper machine optimization services **Expertise:** Paper machine wet end analysis **Published works:** Several articles **Affiliations:** T.A.P.I.; American Chemical Society **Hob./spts.:** Small farm, growing and selling organic wheat, private pilot **SIC code:** 87 **Address:** Pro Tech Consulting, 109 W. Main, Ness City, KS 67560 **E-mail:** tlsekavec@gbta.net

SELAWRY, HELENA P.
Industry: Medical research **Born:** March 28, 1937, Swellendam, South Africa **Univ./degree:** Ph.D., State University of New York at Buffalo, 1970; M.D., South Africa, 1960 **Current organization:** Sertoli Cell Research Institute **Title:** President **Type of organization:** Research laboratory **Major product:** Sertoli cells **Area of distribution:** International **Expertise:** Diabetes research **Published works:** 25 articles, 5 patents **Affiliations:** Diabetes Society; Sigma Xi **Hob./spts.:** Mountain climbing, gardening, travel, theatre, arts **SIC code:** 87 **Address:** Sertoli Cell Research Institute, 386 Beahm Lane, Rileyville, VA 22650 **E-mail:** hselawry@aol.com

SELCUK, SAKIR
Industry: Engineering **Born:** August 1, 1955, Tokat, Turkey **Univ./degree:** Ph.D., University of Minnesota, 1992 **Current organization:** HNTB Corp. **Title:** Project Manager **Type of organization:** Engineering corporation **Major product:** Design and construction management of tunnels and underground structures **Area of distribution:** International **Expertise:** Civil and mining engineering (tunnels) **Published works:** Thesis, 3 papers **Affiliations:** A.S.C.E.; A.S.M.E **Hob./spts.:** Soccer, reading **SIC code:** 87 **Address:** HNTB Corp., 6450 Bloomington Rd., St. Paul, MN 55111 **E-mail:** sselcuk@hntb.com

SEPPER, ALEXANDER
Industry: Nano-technology **Born:** October 10, 1952, T'bilisi, Georgia **Univ./degree:** M.D., Moscow Medical Institute, 1978; M.S.,1979; Ph.D., Oncology and Medical Radiology, 1984, Institute of Oncology **Current organization:** BioNova, Inc. **Title:** Vice President, Research and Development **Type of organization:** Research and development laboratory **Major product:** Pharmaceuticals, cosmoseuticals **Area of distribution:** International **Expertise:** Medical/pharmaceutical science **Published works:** 137 scientific articles, 27 inventions **Hob./spts.:** Classical music, painting **SIC code:** 87 **Address:** BioNova, Inc., 102-05 63 Rd., Suite 1, Forest Hills, NY 11375 **E-mail:** alexsepper@ibionova.com **Web address:** www.bionovalab.com

SEPULVEDA, RENE
Industry: Designs **Born:** February 10, 1975 **Current organization:** Sela Designs **Title:** Lead Designer, Owner **Type of organization:** Design studio **Major product:** Construction documents **Area of distribution:** McAllen, Texas **Expertise:** 3D modeling **Hob./spts.:** Music and art **SIC code:** 87 **Address:** Sela Designs, 3501 W. Hackberry Ave., McAllen, TX 78501 **E-mail:** rene.sepulveda@gmail.com

SERVINO, JOSE S.
Industry: Engineering/consulting **Born:** Philippines **Univ./degree:** B.S., Electronics, Northrup Institute of Technology, 1965; M.B.A., University of Guam, 1975 **Current organization:** Advanced Engineering Consulting Co. **Title:** President **Type of organization:** Consulting firm **Major product:** Electrical and telecommunications **Area of distribution:** International **Expertise:** Electrical engineering, business management **Affiliations:** I.E.E.E.; National Association of Professional Engineers **Hob./spts.:** Computers **SIC code:** 87 **Address:** Advanced Engineering Consulting Co., 454 Ch. Pale Ramon Haya, Yigo, GU 96929 **E-mail:** jservino@vzpacifica.net

SHAMBAYATI, ALI
Industry: Engineering **Univ./degree:** M.S., Electrical Engineering, University of Arizona **Current organization:** Metrics Instruments, Inc. **Title:** President/CEO **Type of organization:** S. Corporation **Major product:** Consulting **Area of distribution:** National **Expertise:** Product design, scientific and industrial instruments **Published works:** 5 patents **SIC code:** 87 **Address:** Metrics Instruments, Inc., 6819 N. 21st Ave., Suite M, Phoenix, AZ 85015 **E-mail:** shambayati@yahoo.com

SHAULYS, JOSEPH P.
Industry: Environmental laboratory **Born:** January 15, 1942, Queens, New York **Univ./degree:** M.B.A.; M.S., Chemistry, Adelphi University **Current organization:** South Mall Analytical Labs Inc. **Title:** President **Type of organization:** Commercial laboratory **Major product:** Analytical services **Area of distribution:** International **Expertise:** Management, strategic planning, public relations, marketing **Affiliations:** American Chemical Society; National Association of Metal Finishers **SIC code:** 87 **Address:** South Mall Analytical Labs Inc., 26 North Mall, Plainview, NY 11803 **E-mail:** js@southmalllabs.com **Web address:** www.southmalllabs.com

SHAY, SHEILA A.
Industry: Youth sports **Born:** October 31, 1962, Erie, Pennsylvania **Univ./degree:** Ohio State University, 1985 **Current organization:** Soccer Association for Youth, USA **Title:** National Executive Director **Type of organization:** Not-for-profit **Major product:** Recreational soccer **Area of distribution:** National **Expertise:** Human resources **Published works:** Articles in USA Today; Soccer America; Touchline **Affiliations:** National Soccer Coaches Association; American Association of Professional Bookkeepers **Hob./spts.:** Gardening, reading, soccer, baseball **SIC code:** 86 **Address:** Soccer Association for Youth, USA, 4050 Executive Park Dr., Suite 100, Cincinnati, OH 45241 **E-mail:** sshay@saysoccer.org **Web address:** www.saysoccer.org

SHEETS, JOHN
Industry: Construction **Current organization:** Pennoni Associates, Inc. **Title:** Steel Inspection Supervisor **Type of organization:** Consulting engineers **Major product:** QA services **Area of distribution:** Pennsylvania **Expertise:** Non-destructive testing of weldments, management, inspections; NDT: magnetic testing plus ICC specialist **Affiliations:** A.W.S.; International Code Council; Member, Board of Directors, Philadelphia American Welding **SIC code:** 87 **Address:** Pennoni Associates, Inc., 3602 Horizon Dr., Suite 160, King of Prussia, PA 19406 **E-mail:** jsheets@pennoni.com

SHERLOCK, JIM
Industry: Legal services **Born:** December 5, 1950, Mobile, Alabama **Univ./degree:** B.S., Troy University **Current organization:** LexisNexis **Title:** Legal Resource Consultant **Type of organization:** Legal consulting/resource services **Major product:** Sources for law, public records, government and business news **Area of distribution:** National **Expertise:** Consulting, resource management **Affiliations:** Board of Directors, Montgomery Kiwanis Club; Montgomery Boys & Girls Club **Hob./spts.:** Baseball, golf, track and field, travel **SIC code:** 87 **Address:** LexisNexis, 9336 Preston Pl., Montgomery, AL 36117 **E-mail:** rocksherlock@hotmail.com

SHI, YUAN
Industry: Biotechnology **Univ./degree:** Ph.D., Chemical Engineering, East China Institute of Chemical Technology, 1988 **Current organization:** Acambis Inc. **Title:** Senior Manager, Viral Fermentation Development **Type of organization:** Research, development, clinical, regulatory, manufacturing, sales, marketing **Major product:** Smallpox Vaccine/Vaccines to prevent and treat infectious disease **Area of distribution:** International **Expertise:** Process development, new technologies **Published works:** 32 articles **Affiliations:** A.C.S.; A.I.C.H.E. **Hob./spts.:** Basketball, soccer, hiking **SIC code:** 87 **Address:** BioVest International, Inc., 25 South St., Hopkinton, MA 01748 **E-mail:** yuan.shi@acambis.com

SHICKLEY, CHARLES DAVID
Industry: Consulting **Born:** September 3, 1959, Salem, Ohio **Univ./degree:** B.S., LeTourneau University, 1983 **Current organization:** EYP Mission Critical Facilities **Title:** Senior Associate **Type of organization:** Engineering/architecture **Major product:** Data center infrastructure design **Area of distribution:** International **Expertise:** Electrical registered professional engineer **Affiliations:** N.S.P.E.; I.E.E.E. **Hob./spts.:** Private pilot, singing in coffee shops, playing the guitar **SIC code:** 87 **Address:** EYP Mission Critical Facilities, 54 State St., Albany, NY 12207-2524 **E-mail:** cshickle@nycap.rr.com

SHIRVINSKI, ADAM J.
Industry: Aerospace, information technology, electronics, defense **Born:** October 25, 1939, Mahanoy City, PA **Univ./degree:** B.S., Engineering, USCG Academy, 1961; M.S. Quantitative Analysis, Naval Postgraduate School, 1970; M.S., Finance, American University, 1987 **Current organization:** Adams' Quality, Inc. (AQI) **Title:** Quality Management Consultant **Type of organization:** Consulting firm **Major product:** Productivity and Process Improvement **Area of distribution:** Washington DC Metro, VA, MD **Expertise:** CQE; CRE; CSQE; CM; ISO-9000: PMBOK; CMMI; Six Sigma **Affiliations:** IEEE; INFORMS; AFCEA; ASQ (Senior) Washington DC Exec Committee **Hob./spts.:** Hunting, Fishing **SIC code:** 87 **Address:** Adams' Quality, Inc. (AQI), 1897 Milboro Dr., Potomac, MD 20854-6123 **Phone:** (301)279-7336

SHUTT, EDWARD L.
Industry: Engineering **Born:** September 25, 1947, Princeton, West Virginia **Univ./degree:** B.S., Civil Engineering, Virginia Polytechnic Institute, 1969 **Current organization:** Stafford Consultants Inc. **Title:** Vice President **Type of organization:** Consulting/design firm **Major product:** Consulting engineering **Area of distribution:** West Virginia **Expertise:** Sanitary engineering; P.E. Certification, 1977 **Affiliations:** National Society of Professional Engineers **Hob./spts.:** Fishing, motorcycle riding **SIC code:** 87 **Address:** Stafford Consultants Inc., RR 3 Box 304 E, Princeton, WV 24740 **E-mail:** sciengrs@inetone.net

SIGUAW, THOMAS R.
Industry: Consulting/energy **Born:** August 1, 1957, Odessa, Texas **Univ./degree:** B.S., Chemical Engineering, University of Texas at Austin, 1979; M.B.A., Centenary College, Louisiana, 1991 **Current organization:** TJ Energy & Marketing **Title:** President **Type of organization:** Energy consulting/project development **Major product:** Energy (oil, natural gas, LPG) **Area of distribution:** Northern Hemisphere **Expertise:** Oil exploration, salt cavern development **Published works:** Write-ups **Affiliations:** Society of Petroleum Engineers; Association of Petroleum Engineers, Gas Providers and Suppliers **Hob./spts.:** Family, reading **SIC code:** 87 **Address:** TJ Energy & Marketing, 12743 Ashford Knoll, Houston, TX 77082 **E-mail:** trsig@aol.com

SILAGHY, FRANK J.
Industry: Engineering **Born:** March 25, 1944, Hungary **Univ./degree:** M.E., Polytechnical University of Budapest, 1967; M.S., Columbia University, 1975 **Current organization:** Foster Wheeler Power Group **Title:** Supervising Systems Engineer **Type of organization:** Engineering constructing/power **Major product:** Engineering services **Area of distribution:** International **Expertise:** Engineering, Professional Engineering Licenses in New York and Pennsylvania **Published works:** Numerous publications, including; "Combustion Turbine Repowering", EPRI AP5493, 1987; "Oxygen Control in Makeup Water for PWRs", EPRI NP-6945, August 1990 **Affiliations:** A.S.M.E.; A.S.H.R.A.E. **Hob./spts.:** Tennis, music **SIC code:** 87 **Address:** Foster Wheeler Power Group, Perryville Corporate Park, Clinton, NJ 08809 **E-mail:** frank_silaghy@fwc.com

SILVA, CHRISTOPHER P.
Industry: Aerospace **Born:** March 17, 1960, Fortuna, California **Univ./degree:** B.S. with Highest Honors Distinction, Electrical Engineering, 1982; M.S., Electrical Engineering, 1985; Ph.D., 1993; University of California at Berkeley **Current organization:** The Aerospace Corp. **Title:** Engineering Specialist **Type of organization:** Federally funded research and development center **Major product:** Technical consultation (not for profit) **Area of distribution:** International **Expertise:** Electrical engineering (nonlinear circuits and systems) **Honors/awards:** Tau Beta Pi; Eta Kappa Nu; Phi Beta Kappa, Aerospace Corporate Presidents, Individual and Team Achievement Awards, University of California Alumni Scholar, NSF Fellowship, Lockheed Leadership Fellowship **Published works:** 40+ publications, 2 book chapters; "The double-hook attractor in Chua's circuit: some analytical results", in Chua's Circuit: A Paradigm for Chaos, R.N. Madon, ed., pp. 671-710, Singapore, World Scientific Inc., 1993; in M.C. Jeruchim, P. Balaban & K.S. Shanmugan, Simulation of Communication Systems, 2nd ed., New York, Kluwer Academic/Plenum Publishers, 2000 **Affiliations:** A.A.A.S.; Senior Member, A.I.A.A.; A.M.S.; Fellow, I.E.E.E.; S.I.A.M. **Hob./spts.:** Reading, desktop publishing, home improvement, traveling **SIC code:** 87 **Address:** The Aerospace Corp., Mail Station M1-111, 2350 E. El Segundo Blvd., El Segundo, CA 90245-4691 **E-mail:** chris.p.silva@aero.org

SINGH, GAJENDRA P.
Industry: Chip design **Born:** August 1, 1970, Bihar, India **Univ./degree:** M.S., Physics, Birla Institute of Technology and Science, Pilani, India, 1992 **Current organization:** Spontey Inc. **Title:** President **Type of organization:** Engineering **Major product:** Chip design services **Area of distribution:** International **Expertise:** Electrical engineering, micro chip design **Honors/awards:** 25-30 patents **Published works:** 6+ articles **Affiliations:** I.E.E.E.E. **Hob./spts.:** Playing soccer, music engineering **SIC code:** 87 **Address:** Spontey Inc., 1045 W. Washington Ave., Suite 9, Sunnyvale, CA 94086 **E-mail:** gpsingh@spontey.com

SINGH, HARDIT
Industry: Engineering **Born:** April 20, 1938, India **Univ./degree:** M.S., Engineering, University of Texas. 1975 **Current organization:** South Texas Engineering, Inc. **Title:** President **Type of organization:** Engineering company **Major product:** Land surveying services **Area of distribution:** San Antonio, Texas **Expertise:** Structural engineering and land surveying **Affiliations:** N.S.P.E.; T.S.P.L.S. **Hob./spts.:** Meditation, charity **SIC code:** 87 **Address:** South Texas Engineering, Inc., 4606 Centerview Dr., San Antonio, TX 78228 **E-mail:** aaurora.ste@sbcglobal.net

SKIFSTROM, EDWARD A.
Industry: Aerospace **Born:** May 11, 1931, Little Fork, Minnesota **Title:** TRW Systems, Engineering Manager, APM (Retired) **Type of organization:** R&D, manufacturing, product design **Major product:** Aerospace research **Expertise:** Engineering **Affiliations:** Veterans of Foreign Wars (VFW) **Hob./spts.:** Body surfing, archery, hunting, fishing in High Sierra, gunsmithing, sky diving, scuba diving, waterskiing, snow skiing, salmon fishing **SIC code:** 87 **Address:** 1601 Voorhees Ave., Manhattan Beach, CA 90266 **E-mail:** patskifs@aol.com **Web address:** www.patskif.com

SLAVIK, WILLIAM B.
Industry: Architecture **Univ./degree:** A.S., Temple Jr. College **Current organization:** William B. Slavik, Architect **Title:** Architect **Type of organization:** Architectural firm **Major product:** Architectural services **Area of distribution:** Cleburne, Texas **Affiliations:** A.I.A.,C.S.I. **Hob./spts.:** Salt water fishing, automobile collecting **SIC code:** 87 **Address:** William B. Slavik, Architect, 813 Hillsboro St., Cleburne, TX 76033 **E-mail:** slavikarchitect@sbcglobal.net

SLOTHOWER, BRIAN K.
Industry: Consulting **Born:** September 13, 1953, Cumberland, Maryland **Univ./degree:** Technical Degree, United Electronic Institute, 1974 **Current organization:** Slothower Industries **Title:** Owner/Engineer **Type of organization:** Electronics lab **Major product:** Electronic technical engineering **Area of distribution:** International **Expertise:** Electronics **Honors/awards:** Strathmore's Who's Who **Published works:** Manuals **Affiliations:** Robotics Society **Hob./spts.:** RV Camper, collectible cars **SIC code:** 87 **Address:** Slothower Industries, 1918 E. El Norte Pkwy., Escondido, CA 92027 **E-mail:** brians01@cox.net

SMALLS, DEBORAH MICHELLE
Industry: Trade Association **Univ./degree:** M.A., Business Administration, Citadel University, 1997 **Current organization:** Waterfront Employers **Title:** Administrator **Type of organization:** Employee benefits **Major product:** Employee benefit plans **Area of distribution:** Charleston, South Carolina **Expertise:** Administration **Affiliations:** International Foundation of Employee Benefit Plans **SIC code:** 86 **Address:** Waterfront Employers, 899 Morrison Dr., Charleston, SC 29403 **E-mail:** chasiladms@aol.com

SMIRNOV, VASILIY I.
Industry: Research and development **Born:** July 17, 1952, Russia **Spouse:** Olga Smirnova **Married:** June 7, 1975 **Children:** Anton, 27; Kseniya, 25 **Univ./degree:** M.S., Material Science, EE, Moscow Technological University, 1975; Ph.D., Physics & Mathematics, Moscow State University, 1986 **Current organization:** Izon Technologies, Inc. **Title:** Ph.D. **Type of organization:** Private company **Major product:** Digital media and video technologies, software and hardware **Area of distribution:** International **Expertise:** Experimental and technical physics, chemical physics, biophysics, applied mathematics, computer vision, image processing, software development **Published works:** Articles in scientific journals, patents **Affiliations:** Moscow State University; Texas Tech University; N.A.S.A.; J&J **Career accomplishments:** Developed experimental facilities and conducted thermodynamic and kinetic investigation of high temperature systems by mass spectrometry of supersonic molecular beams and by spectroscopy methods; developed experimental facilities and conducted optical spectroscopy investigation of species produced in collisions of crossed mass separated ion and molecular beams; developed laser scanning fluorescent microscopy equipment for investigation of pulse ion transport through the heart cell membrane channels; Developed equipment and image processing software and conducted optical investigation of processes at the surfaces of materials used in the biomedical applications; developed original anti-obesity technologies (removing a fat from the human body); developed a new technology and devices for fast intravenous fluid warming; developed a technology for measuring a human body core temperature in the environments with arbitrary external temperature; developed object oriented video compression technology **SIC code:** 87 **Address:** Izon Technologies, Inc., 8200 Nashville, Suite 209, Lubbock, TX 79423 **Phone:** (806)788-0484 **Fax:** (806)722-2029 **E-mail:** vsmirnov@izon.tv

SMITH, BRIAN D.
Industry: Museum **Born:** November 15, 1953, Chicago, Illinois **Univ./degree:** B.S., Criminology, Ohio University, 1978; Valley View Police Academy, 1980 **Current organization:** Columbus Museum of Art **Title:** Manager, Protective Services **Type of organization:** Art museum **Major product:** Art **Area of distribution:** Ohio **Expertise:** Museum security management; safety training and education; Certified in Homeland Security (EMI); Emergency Preparedness Management Certified (FEMA) **Affiliations:** Association of Certified Fraud Examiners; International Foundation for Cultural Property Protection; American Society for Industrial Security; National Association of Chiefs of Police **Hob./spts.:** Reading, coaching youth sports, volunteer EMT **SIC code:** 84 **Address:** Columbus Museum of Art, 480 E. Broad St., Columbus, OH 43215 **E-mail:** bsmith@cmaohio.org **Web address:** www.cmaohio.org

SMITH, DAVID F.
Industry: Engineering/construction **Born:** May 18, 1956, Memphis, Tennessee **Univ./degree:** B.S., Chemical Engineering, South Alabama University, 1985; M.B.A., Louisiana State University, 1999 **Current organization:** U.O. Group **Title:** COO/Executive Vice President **Type of organization:** Engineering and construction **Major product:** Construction for chemical, petrochemical, pulp and paper industries **Area of distribution:** International **Expertise:** Corporate management, chemical engineering, plant operations; Certified Energy Manager **Published works:** Write ups, articles, interviews **Affiliations:** A.I.C.S.; P.M.I.; C.S.I.; Association of Energy Engineers; Instrument Society of America **Hob./spts.:** Spending time with family, golf, church **SIC code:** 87 **Address:** U.O. Group, 6917 Stennis Blvd., Pascagoula, MS 39581 **E-mail:** dsmith@uo-group.com **Web address:** www.uo-group.com

SMITH, DOUG
Industry: Nuclear waste **Born:** Knoxville, Tennessee **Univ./degree:** B.S., Metallurgical Engineering, University of Tennessee **Current organization:** Bechtel, SAIC LLC **Title:** Sr. Technical Specialist **Type of organization:** Design and engineering **Major product:** Waste disposal canisters/high level nuclear waste containers **Area of distribution:** International **Expertise:** Metallurgical engineering **Affiliations:** American Society for Metals; Welding Research Council; American Management Association **Hob./spts.:** Skiing, photography, cooking **SIC code:** 87 **Address:** Bechtel, SAIC LLC, 1180 Town Center Dr., Las Vegas, NV 89144 **E-mail:** sirsmith@cox.net

SMITH, JAMES A.
Industry: Consulting **Born:** April 25, 1925, Bowling Green, Missouri **Univ./degree:** M.S., Electrical Engineering, Union College, Schenectady, New York, 1956 **Current organization:** James A. Smith, Consultant **Title:** Consultant **Type of organization:** Consulting firm **Major product:** Expert witness regarding electrical accidents **Area of distribution:** California **Expertise:** Electrical engineering **Affiliations:** A.M.A.; American Institute of Electrical Engineering **Hob./spts.:** Sailing **SIC code:** 87 **Address:** James A. Smith, Consultant, 2562 Treasure Dr. #4102, Santa Barbara, CA 93105 **E-mail:** jasmith181@aol.com

SMITH, LORA LEE
Industry: Religion **Born:** June 14, 1953, Cleveland, Ohio **Current organization:** Greater Cleveland Baptist Association **Title:** Director of Church & Community Ministries **Type of organization:** Association **Major product:** Religious administration and coordination **Area of distribution:** Ohio **Expertise:** Social ministries and partnerships **Hob./spts.:** Scouts, reading, 4th degree Black Belt **SIC code:** 86 **Address:** Greater Cleveland Baptist Association, 23210 Emery Rd., Cleveland, OH 44128 **E-mail:** lsmith@gcba.cc

SMITH, PAUL R.
Industry: Consulting **Univ./degree:** B.A; M.A., Russian, University of Illinois **Type of organization:** Consulting **Area of distribution:** International **Affiliations:** American Association for the Advancement of Slavic Studies; National Executive Commissioner for the Boy Scouts of America; Served 33 years as a Foreign Service Officer **Hob./spts.:** Travel, photography, camping, hiking, the outdoors **SIC code:** 87 **Address:** 6006 Doris View Dr., Harrisburg, PA 17112 **E-mail:** smithpr@usa.net

SMITH, THOMAS D.
Industry: Research/educational **Born:** October 30, 1939, Cohoes, New York **Univ./degree:** B.S., Marine Engineering, U.S. Coast Guard Academy, 1962; M.S., High Honors, Computer Science, American University, 1971 **Current organization:** Seward Marine Center, University of Alaska, Fairbanks **Title:** Director, Seward Marine Center **Type of organization:** University research center **Major product:** Marine research **Area of distribution:** National **Expertise:** Administration of coastal marine research and presentations **Honors/awards:** Humanitarian Service Medal, Holland America's Prinsendam Rescue Operation, 1983 **Affiliations:** Captain, U.S. Coast Guard, 1962-86; Seward Chamber of Commerce (Retired); U.S.C.G. Academy Alumni Association; American University Alumni Association **Hob./spts.:** Woodworking, photography, cross-country skiing **SIC code:** 87 **Address:** P.O. Box 2484, Seward, AK 99664 **E-mail:** fnts@uaf.edu

SMOLINSKY, STEVEN A.
Industry: Structural engineering **Born:** June 18, 1948, Brooklyn, New York **Univ./degree:** M.S., Civil Engineering, Pennsylvania State University, 1976 **Current organization:** The Office of James Ruderman, LLP **Title:** Partner **Type of organization:** Consulting engineering firm **Major product:** Structural engineering for all types of buildings **Area of distribution:** National **Expertise:** Structural engineering **Affiliations:** A.S.C.E.; N.S.P.E.; S.E.O.N.Y. **Hob./spts.:** Hiking **SIC code:** 87 **Address:** The Office of James Ruderman, LLP, 15 W. 36th St., 13th floor, New York, NY 10018 **Phone:** (212)643-1414 **Fax:** (212)643-1425 **E-mail:** ssmolinsky@jruderman.com

SOHEILA, RAHBARI
Industry: Technology **Born:** October 2, 1958, Tehran, Iran **Univ./degree:** M.S., Drexel University, 1991 **Current organization:** Schoor DePalma **Title:** Senior Project

Manager **Type of organization:** Engineering firm **Major product:** Geotechnical engineering, design **Area of distribution:** International **Expertise:** Geotechnical engineering **Published works:** Articles **Affiliations:** President, New Jersey Chapter, A.S.C.E.; I.E.E.E. **Hob./spts.:** Travel **SIC code:** 87 **Address:** Schoor DePalma, 1101 Laurel Oak Rd., P.O. Box V346, Voorhees, NJ 08043-7346 **E-mail:** srahhari@schoordepalma.com

SOHN, RACHEL A.
Industry: Appliances **Univ./degree:** B.S.M.E., Olivet Nazarene University, 2002 **Current organization:** Whirlpool Corp. **Title:** Design Engineer **Type of organization:** Product design **Major product:** Built-in refrigerators **Area of distribution:** National **Expertise:** Engineering **Hob./spts.:** Photography, gardening **SIC code:** 87 **Address:** Whirlpool Corp., 5401 US Hwy. 41 N., Evansville, IN 47714 **E-mail:** rachel_sohn@yahoo.com

SOLIMANDO JR., DOMINIC A.
Industry: Pharmaceutical consulting/education **Born:** April 4, Brooklyn, New York **Univ./degree:** B.S., Pharmacy/Science, Philadelphia College of Pharmacy and Science, 1976; M.A., Central Michigan University, 1980 **Current organization:** Oncology Pharmacy Services, Inc. **Title:** President **Type of organization:** Pharmaceutical consulting service **Major product:** Clinical/consultative/educational services **Area of distribution:** International **Expertise:** Oncology pharmacy (Board Certified) **Honors/awards:** Rho Chi Pharmaceutical Honor Society, 1988; "A" Proficiency Designator, Office of the Surgeon General, Dept. of the Army, Washington D.C., 1994; Distinguished Achievement Award in Hospital and Institutional Practice, American Pharmaceutical Association, 2001 **Published works:** Drug Information Handbook for Oncology; Lexi-Comp Clinical Reference Library Series **Affiliations:** I.S.O.P.P.; American Pharmacists Association; American Society of Hospital Pharmacists **Hob./spts.:** Cooking, chess, bicycling **SIC code:** 87 **Address:** Oncology Pharmacy Services, Inc., 4201 Wilson Blvd. #110-545, Arlington, VA 22203 **E-mail:** oncrxsvce@aol.com

SOMERS, THOMAS E.
Industry: Consulting/Engineering **Born:** May 2, 1970. Illinois **Univ./degree:** B.S., Civil Engineering, Southern Illinois University, 1990 **Current organization:** Lawrence A. Lipe & Associates **Title:** Project Engineer **Type of organization:** Municipal engineering **Major product:** Highway and roadway construction **Area of distribution:** Benton, Illinois **Expertise:** Project engineering, construction **Affiliations:** N.SP.E. **Hob./spts.:** Golf **SIC code:** 87 **Address:** Lawrence A. Lipe & Associates, 901 N. DuQuoin St., Benton, IL 62812 **E-mail:** lalip@midwest.net

SONENTZ-PAPAZIAN, TATUL
Industry: International humanitarian organization **Born:** June 12, 1928, Egypt **Univ./degree:** M.A., Design, Academie Libanaise des Beaux-Arts, 1948 **Current organization:** Armenian Relief Society, Inc. **Title:** Editor/Director of Publications **Type of organization:** Humanitarian **Major product:** Support of schools, hospitals, cultural organizations **Area of distribution:** International **Expertise:** Design **Affiliations:** Member, United Nations Economic and Social Council **Hob./spts.:** Walking, writing **SIC code:** 86 **Address:** Armenian Relief Society, Inc., 80 Bigelow Ave., Watertown, MA 02472

SOUTHERN, HERBERT B.
Industry: Architecture **Born:** May 21, 1926, Washington, D.C. **Univ./degree:** B.A., Architecture, Howard University, Washington D.C., 1950 **Current organization:** Southern Associates Architects **Title:** Architect/Owner **Type of organization:** Architectural firm **Major product:** Architectural services **Area of distribution:** New Jersey, New York **Expertise:** Architecture **Affiliations:** A.I.A.; N.J.S.A. **SIC code:** 87 **Address:** Southern Associates Architects, 571 E. Hazelwood Ave., Rahway, NJ 07065

SPEAR, JAMES R.
Industry: Geophysical consulting **Born:** July 25, 1946, New York, New York **Univ./degree:** B.S., Physics, University of Delaware; M.S.; Ph.D. **Current organization:** Interactive Interpretation and Training **Title:** Consulting Geophysicist **Type of organization:** Consulting firm **Major product:** Consulting to oil and gas industry; provide mentoring and training to Latin American oil companies **Area of distribution:** International **Expertise:** Reservoir characterization **Published works:** Articles and manuals **Affiliations:** S.E.G.; I.A.A.P. **SIC code:** 87 **Address:** Interactive Interpretation and Training, Consulting Geophysicist, 14819 Hoya Ct., Houston, TX 77070 **E-mail:** spear33@msn.com **Web address:** www.deconpetroleumconsultants.com

SPURGIN, RICHARD E.
Industry: Construction **Born:** Polk County, Iowa **Current organization:** Classic Concrete, L.L.C. **Title:** President **Type of organization:** Consulting Company **Major product:** Commercial/residential concrete construction **Area of distribution:** National **Expertise:** Decorative Construction; Ardex Certified for Decorative Overlay; Alan Engineering System for Floor Finishing **Affiliations:** Masonic Lodge **Hob./spts.:** Hunting and fishing **SIC code:** 87 **Address:** Classic Concrete LLC, 3520 Beaver Ave., Suite D-10, Des Moines, IA 50310

ST. CYR, JOHN A.
Industry: Consulting **Born:** November 26, 1949, Minneapolis, Minnesota **Univ./degree:** M.D., 1980; Ph.D., 1988, University of Minnesota **Current organization:** Jacqmar, Inc. **Title:** M.D., Ph.D. **Type of organization:** Consulting **Major product:** Patient care **Area of distribution:** National **Expertise:** Medical/surgical consulting, research **Published works:** Articles **Affiliations:** A.A.A.S; American Heart Association; New York Academy of Surgeons **Hob./spts.:** Reading, listening to classical music, golf **SIC code:** 87 **Address:** Jacqmar, Inc., 940 Fernbrook Lane North, Minneapolis, MN 55447 **E-mail:** lms94@aol.com

ST. MICHEL, BILL
Industry: Engineering **Univ./degree:** B.S., Mechanical Engineering, California Maritime Academy, 1997 **Current organization:** G.E. Industrial Systems **Title:** Engineer **Type of organization:** Engineering firm **Major product:** Project management, field engineering **Area of distribution:** International **Expertise:** Marine, automation and mechanical engineering **SIC code:** 87 **Address:** G.E. Industrial Systems, 2120 Diamond Blvd., Suite 100, Concord, CA 94520 **E-mail:** william.st.michel@indsys.ge.com

STACK, DORIS BUTLER
Industry: Accounting **Born:** May 31, 1940, Memphis, Tennessee **Univ./degree:** B.S., Purdue University, 1986 **Current organization:** Doris Butler Stack Accounting **Title:** President **Type of organization:** Accounting firm **Major product:** Accounting, taxes, consulting **Area of distribution:** National **Expertise:** General accounting, financial planning **Affiliations:** I.S.P.A.; N.S.A. **Hob./spts.:** Gardening, sewing, reading **SIC code:** 87 **Address:** Doris Butler Stack Accounting, 409 E. Commercial Ave., Lowell, IN 46356

STAFFORD, BETH A.
Industry: Human Services **Born:** July, 15, 1954, Flint, Michigan **Univ./degree:** B.S.W., Social Work, Harding University **Current organization:** Manchester Area Conference of Churches, Inc. **Title:** Executive Director **Type of organization:** Nonprofit **Major product:** Social Services **Area of distribution:** Connecticut **Expertise:** Social Work **Affiliations:** Hartford County Chamber of Commerce; The Rotary Club; C.L.A.S.S.; Manchester Community Service Council; Manchester Church of Christ **Hob./spts.:** Church, community and family activities **SIC code:** 83 **Address:** Manchester Area Conference of Churches, Inc., 466 Main St., Manchester, CT 06040 **E-mail:** bstafford@macc-ct.org **Web address:** www.macc-ct.org

STAMATOVSKI, KRSTO
Industry: Architecture **Born:** September 12, 1953, Macedonia, Yugoslavia **Univ./degree:** M.Arch., Kirilo Metodi University, Yugoslavia, 1981 **Current organization:** Studio K Architects **Title:** President **Type of organization:** Architectural firm **Major product:** Architectural design **Area of distribution:** International **Expertise:** Design **Affiliations:** A.I.A.; Gold Coast Builders **Hob./spts.:** Tennis, travel **SIC code:** 87 **Address:** Studio K Architects, 1499 W. Palmetto Park Rd., Suite 224, Boca Raton, FL 33486 **E-mail:** k@studiokarchitects.com **Web address:** www.studiokarchitects.com

STANBERY, RICHARD L.
Industry: Construction **Born:** December 21, 1947 **Title:** Equipment Manager **Type of organization:** Consulting **Major product:** Highway asphalt construction **Area of distribution:** Oklahoma **Expertise:** Strategic planning, team leadership, quality control, training and education, maintenance and repairs, equipment management **Affiliations:** Association of Equipment Management Professionals; served in the U.S. Coast Guard for 10 years **Hob./spts.:** Spending time with family, football, church **SIC code:** 87 **Address:** Rt. 2, Box 115 AB, Maysville, OK 73057 **E-mail:** 2_4_gospel@wilnet1.com

STARING, CANDY
Industry: Engineering **Univ./degree:** M.S., Environmental Engineering, Oklahoma State University, 1999 **Current organization:** CH2M HILL **Title:** P.E., Project Manager **Type of organization:** Consulting firm **Major product:** Consulting engineering **Area of distribution:** National **Expertise:** Water treatment/resources **Affiliations:** A.W.W.A.; A.P.W.A.; A.S.C.E.; W.E.F. **SIC code:** 87 **Address:** CH2M HILL, 701 N. Broadway Ave., Oklahoma City, OK 73102 **E-mail:** candy.staring@ch2m.com

STERLING, WILLIAM CLARENCE
Industry: Construction/law **Born:** June 10, 1932, Merced, California **Univ./degree:** M.B.A., Madison University, 2002 **Current organization:** Construction Forensics **Title:** Owner **Type of organization:** Consulting firm **Major product:** Construction defects, litigation support and expert witness **Area of distribution:** San Diego, California **Expertise:** Moisture intrusion issues **Affiliations:** C.S.I.; Forensic Consulting Association **Hob./spts.:** Photography **SIC code:** 87 **Address:** Construction Forensics, 13823 Kerry Lane, San Diego, CA 92130 **E-mail:** sbill32@aol.com

STEVENS, MARLA RANDOLPH
Industry: Organizing, public polity **Born:** December 10, 1951, Columbus, Georgia **Univ./degree:** B.A. Music (With Distinction), Vocal Performance, Butler University, 1980 **Current organization:** LGBT Fairness Indiana **Title:** Director of public policy **Type of organization:** NGO/PAC/LDEF **Major product:** LGBT Equality **Area of distribution:** Indiana **Expertise:** Government relations **Published works:** Articles **Hob./spts.:** Reading, garden, railroading, Disney fan **SIC code:** 86 **Address:** LGBT Fairness Indiana, P.O. Box 441396 (627 N. East St.), Indianapolis, IN 46244-1396 **E-mail:** lgbtfair@aol.com

STEWART, FRANKLIN R.
Industry: Insurance **Born:** October 11, 1956, Spokane, Washington **Univ./degree:** B.A., Business, University of Washington, 1979 **Current organization:** Frank Stewart & Associates **Title:** President/Owner **Type of organization:** Consulting firm **Major product:** Consulting **Area of distribution:** Northwest U.S. **Expertise:** After market service, financial consulting **Hob./spts.:** Golf, baseball **SIC code:** 87 **Address:** Frank Stewart & Associates, 18105 N.E. 23rd St., Redmond, WA 98052 **E-mail:** frank_stewart@msn.com

STIGEN, DEBORAH A.
Industry: Quasi-governmental authority **Born:** November 5, 1963, Naha, Okinawa, Japan **Univ./degree:** B.S., Mechanical Engineering, University of Colorado, 2000 **Current organization:** Lowry Redevelopment Authority **Title:** Project Manager **Type of organization:** Development **Major product:** Base closure redevelopment **Area of distribution:** Denver, Colorado **Expertise:** Engineering **Honors/awards:** Special Recognition Award for Leadership, 2000, Employee of the Year, 2000, Lowry Redevelopment Authority **Affiliations:** A.S.M.E.; A.C.I. **Hob./spts.:** Family, skiing, hiking, biking, gardening **SIC code:** 83 **Address:** Lowry Redevelopment Authority, 555 Uinta Way, Denver, CO 80230 **E-mail:** deb.stigen@lowry.org **Web address:** www.lowry.org

STOHL, DON S.
Industry: Financial **Born:** July 18, 1950, West Stewartstown, New Hampshire **Univ./degree:** A.S., Accounting, New Hampshire College, 1972 **Current organization:** Don S. Stohl, Inc. **Title:** President **Type of organization:** Accounting firm **Major product:** Accounting and tax services **Area of distribution:** Regional northeast U.S. **Expertise:** Tax preparation **Affiliations:** N.H.S.A.; V.T.S.T.P.; N.A.E.A.; Board Member, N.E.E.A. **Hob./spts.:** Hiking, family, hunting **SIC code:** 87 **Address:** Don S. Stohl, Inc., 161 Main St., Colebrook, NH 03576 **E-mail:** stohline@verizon.net

STRANNINGER, FRANZ X. J.
Industry: Information technology **Born:** Germany **Current organization:** SAR Automation LP **Title:** Project Manager **Type of organization:** Consulting engineering firm **Major product:** Automation, process and environmental technology, test and measuring technology, IT services, surface application systems **Area of distribution:** International **Expertise:** Design electrical drawings, automated LP, team leader of technical department, quotation planning, human resources **Hob./spts.:** Skiing, gardening, hiking **SIC code:** 87 **Address:** SAR Automation LP, 6830B University Blvd. East, Cottondale, AL 35453 **E-mail:** franz.stranninger@sarlp.com

STREET, RONALD A.
Industry: Consulting **Univ./degree:** B.S.M.E., Villanova University, 1982; Continuing Education, Harvard University **Current organization:** Northstar Advisors, LLC **Title:** Principal **Type of organization:** Project advisor **Major product:** Project/program/construction management **Area of distribution:** National **Expertise:** Project management, business strategy and administration **Affiliations:** A.S.T.M.; I.I.M.A.; Member, Board of Directors, "Please Touch" Museum; Ace Mentoring Program **Hob./spts.:** Family, golf, tennis, community volunteering, pro-bono work **SIC code:** 87 **Address:** Northstar Advisors, LLC, 233 E. Lancaster Ave., Suite 201, Ardmore, PA 19003 **E-mail:** rstreet@northstar-advisors.com **Web address:** www.northstar-advisors.com

STROUD, ALEXIS L.
Industry: Pharmaceuticals **Born:** January 24, 1977, Dover, New Jersey **Univ./degree:** B.S., Psychology/Sociology, Rutgers University, 1999 **Current organization:** CSSC, Inc. **Title:** Validation Scientist **Type of organization:** Validation consulting **Major product:** Validation **Area of distribution:** International **Expertise:** Validation Scientist (computer systems) **Affiliations:** R.A.P.S. **Hob./spts.:** Travel **SIC code:** 87 **Address:** CSSC, Inc., 22 South St., Morristown, NJ 07960 **E-mail:** stroud@csscinc.net **Web address:** www.csscinc.net

SULLIVAN, WILLIAM T.
Industry: Non-profit organizations **Univ./degree:** B.S., Boston College, 1983; M.A., Fordham University, 1995 **Current organization:** Greater New York Councils, Boy Scouts of America **Title:** Director of Development/C.O.O. **Type of organization:** Largest youth non-profit organization in New York City **Major product:** Youth services, administration **Area of distribution:** New York, New York **Expertise:** Marketing, management, finance **Affiliations:** Board Member, James Lenox House, New York City; Board Member, Direct Effect, Rockefeller University **Hob./spts.:** Golf, music, theatre **SIC code:** 86 **Address:** Greater New York Councils, Boy Scouts of America, 350 Fifth Ave., New York, NY 10118 **E-mail:** wsullivan@bsa-gnyc.org

SULLIVAN-HANCOCK, DONNA J.
Industry: Civil Engineering **Born:** December 9, 1957, Hammond, Indiana **Univ./degree:** B.S.C.E., Arizona State University, 1995 **Current organization:** B&R Engineering, Inc. **Title:** Vice President **Type of organization:** Consulting engineering **Major product:** Master plans and infrastructure **Area of distribution:** National **Expertise:** Water resources **Affiliations:** American Society of Civil Engineers; American Council of Engineering Companies **Hob./spts.:** Sailing, Native American Art **SIC code:** 87 **Address:** B&R Engineering, Inc., 9666 E. Riggs Rd., Suite 118, Sun Lakes, AZ 85248 **E-mail:** dhancock@bnraz.com

SUMEGO, DIANNE M.
Industry: Engineering **Born:** July 3, 1965, Akron, Ohio **Univ./degree:** B.S., Civil Engineering, University of Akron **Current organization:** Finkbeiner, Pettis & Strout, Inc. **Title:** Director of Business Development **Type of organization:** Engineering Consultants **Major product:** Environmental and transportation consulting **Area of distribution:** Ohio, Michigan, Virginia, North Carolina **Expertise:** Environmental engineering **Honors/awards:** Select Society of Sanitary Sludge Shovelers (5s), O.W.E.A., 2002; Larry D. Moa Service Award, A.S.C.E., 2002; President's Award, A.S.C.E., 1998 and 2001; Young Civil Engineer Award, A.S.C.E., 1999 **Affiliations:** W.E.F.; A.W.W.A.; A.S.L.E.; A.S.H.E.; Ohio Water Environment Association; Engineer's Week Committee; Engineering Alumni Board, University of Akron (1996-2002) **Hob./spts.:** Volleyball, golf **SIC code:** 87 **Address:** Finkbeiner, Pettis & Strout, Inc., 520 S. Main St., Suite 2400, Akron, OH 44311-1010 **E-mail:** dianne.sumego@fpsengineering.com

SUNDAR, ANAND
Industry: Consulting services **Born:** December 30, 1966, India **Univ./degree:** B.E., Engineering, Anna University, India, 1990; M.S., Manufacturing Engineering, University of Texas at El Paso, 1992 **Current organization:** Infinite Strategies **Title:** President **Type of organization:** Consulting firm **Major product:** Consulting services/system integration **Area of distribution:** International **Expertise:** Supply chain management **Affiliations:** Association of Business Process Management Professionals **Hob./spts.:** Family, travel, movies **SIC code:** 87 **Address:** Infinite Strategies, 1 Smithfield Dr., Boothwyn, PA 19061 **E-mail:** aksundar@yahoo.com

SUNDERMANN, ALEJANDRO
Industry: Environmental infrastructure **Born:** February 16, 1945, El Paso, Texas **Univ./degree:** B.S., Civil Engineering, University of Texas at El Paso, 1968; M.S., Public Administration, University of New Mexico, 1994 **Current organization:** Border Environment Cooperation Commission **Title:** Professional Engineer **Type of organization:** Environmental development **Major product:** Environmental improvement **Area of distribution:** Texas **Expertise:** Engineering management on the design and construction of environmental infrastructure **Affiliations:** A.S.C.E. **Hob./spts.:** Tennis, travel **SIC code:** 87 **Address:** 10405 Omicron Place, El Paso, TX 79924 **E-mail:** asundermann@msn.org

SUTTER, JOHN L.
Industry: Consulting **Born:** March 15, 1947, Slaton, Texas **Univ./degree:** M.S., Mechanical Engineering, University of South Carolina, 1982 **Current organization:** Compliance Services Group, Inc. **Title:** President **Type of organization:** Consulting firm **Major product:** Engineering, project development, scientific **Area of distribution:** International **Expertise:** Engineering **Honors/awards:** Board Chairman, C.S.A.; Board Chairman, C.S.G. Communications; Board Chairman, C.S.G. Healthnet Solutions Inc.; President, C.S.G. International Inc. **Affiliations:** N.F.P.A.; N.S.P.E.; A.S.H.R.A.E. **Hob./spts.:** Skiing, reading **SIC code:** 87 **Address:** Compliance Services Group, Inc., 7619 University Ave., Lubbock, TX 79423-2126 **E-mail:** jlsutter@csg.net

SVETAKA, KURT P.
Industry: Consulting, engineering **Born:** June 16, 1958, Athol, Massachusetts **Univ./degree:** B.S., Chemical Engineering, Rensselaer Polytechnic Institute, 1980 **Current organization:** Trane **Title:** Commercial Sales Manager for Automation Systems and Controls **Type of organization:** Consulting, contracting **Major product:** Facility automation and control systems **Area of distribution:** International **Expertise:** Technical marketing **Affiliations:** American Society of Heating Refrigeration and Heating Engineers; Instrument Society of America; Association of Energy Engineers **Hob./spts.:** Biking, skiing **SIC code:** 87 **Address:** Trane, 225 Wildwood Ave., Woburn, MA 01801 **E-mail:** kpsvetaka@trane.com **Web address:** www.trane.com

SWANSON, ERIK CHRISTIAN
Industry: Museums **Born:** June 17, 1940, Breckenridge, Colorado **Univ./degree:** B.A., Education, University of Northern Colorado, 1973; B.A., History & Language, Royal University, Lund, Sweden **Current organization:** Cripple Creek District Museum **Title:** Director **Type of organization:** Museum **Major product:** History of

Cripple Creek **Area of distribution:** Cripple Creek, Colorado **Expertise:** Operations, administration **Honors/awards:** Served in U.S. Army, 1966-68 **Published works:** Write-ups **Affiliations:** Board Member, Park County Cemetery; Masonic Lodge; Odd Fellows, Elks **Hob./spts.:** Hunting, fishing, hiking, horses **SIC code:** 84 **Address:** Cripple Creek District Museum, 500 E. Bennett, P.O. Box 1210, Cripple Creek, CO 80813 **Web address:** www.cripplecreek.org

SWANSON, ROBERT N.
Industry: Utilities **Born:** February 4, 1932, Ashland, Wisconsin **Univ./degree:** B.S., Chemistry/Mathematics, University of Wisconsin, 1953; M.S., Meteorology, University of Michigan, 1958 **Title:** Certified Consulting Meteorologist **Type of organization:** Self employed (Retired) **Major product:** Applied research **Area of distribution:** National **Expertise:** Expert witness, deposition and court trials, air pollution, alternate energy **Honors/awards:** Fellow, American Meteorological Society (AMS), Royal Meteorological Society (RMS), England **Published works:** Several technical reports **Affiliations:** A.M.S.; R.M.S.; A.A.A.S.; American Weather Association; National Council of Industrial Meteorologists (NCIM) **Hob./spts.:** Travel, cooking, welding, baseball **SIC code:** 87 **Address:** 1216 Babel Lane, Concord, CA 94518 **E-mail:** rswanson1@astound.net

SWEDIN, VERN S.
Industry: Communications **Born:** April 28, 1971, Fort Smith, Arkansas **Univ./degree:** M.S., Sales and Marketing, University of Devonshire **Current organization:** U R On **Title:** Chairman **Type of organization:** Consulting, distributing **Major product:** Communications consulting, distributing **Area of distribution:** International **Expertise:** Consulting, negotiation **Published works:** Monthly leadership article in Broadband Properties Magazine **Affiliations:** Independent Multi-Housing Communications Council **Hob./spts.:** Whitewater rafting guide, golf, racquetball, boating **SIC code:** 87 **Address:** 17678 Cannon City Blvd., Faribault, MN 55021 **E-mail:** vern@uron.cc

SWOFFORD, DEANA K.
Industry: Accounting **Born:** November 1, 1967, Longview, Washington **Univ./degree:** B.A., Accounting, City University, Washington, 1992 **Current organization:** Winlock Tax Service **Title:** Accountant **Type of organization:** Accounting firm **Major product:** Tax preparation **Area of distribution:** Winlock, Washington **Expertise:** Tax preparation **Affiliations:** Better Business Bureau **SIC code:** 87 **Address:** Winlock Tax Service, 311 N.W. Kerron St., Winlock, WA 98596 **E-mail:** deana@localaccess.com

SYMONDS, CURTIS N.
Industry: Consulting **Born:** August 12, 1955, Hamilton, Bermuda **Univ./degree:** B.S., Education, Central Ohio State University **Current organization:** Symonds Synergy Group **Title:** CEO **Type of organization:** Consulting **Major product:** Consulting services **Area of distribution:** National **Expertise:** Marketing **Affiliations:** Cable Positive; Rock & Roll Hall of Fame **Hob./spts.:** Coaching basketball **SIC code:** 87 **Address:** Symonds Synergy Group, 6216 Kilcullen Dr., McLean, VA 22101 **E-mail:** curtissymonds@yahoo.com

SZYMCZAK, CHRISTOPHER M.
Industry: Consulting **Born:** August 30, 1972, Brenham, Texas **Univ./degree:** B.S.C.E., Summa Cum Laude, Texas A&M University, 1995 **Current organization:** Arias & Associates, Inc. **Title:** Geotechnical Operations Manager **Type of organization:** Engineering firm **Major product:** Consulting engineering services **Area of distribution:** San Antonio, Texas **Expertise:** Geotechnical engineering, construction materials testing and observation **Affiliations:** A.S.C.E.; Chi Epsilon; Golden Key; Phi Kappa Phi **Hob./spts.:** Golf, football, basketball **SIC code:** 87 **Address:** Arias & Associates, Inc., 142 Chula Vista Ave., San Antonio, TX 78232 **E-mail:** cszymczak@ariasinc.com **Web address:** www.ariasinc.com

TALLEY, JOSEPH D.
Industry: Consulting/government **Born:** September 3, 1929, Burkeville, Texas **Univ./degree:** B.B.A., University of Houston, Texas, 1952 **Current organization:** Talley Ranch/government (retired) **Title:** Management Analyst **Type of organization:** Consulting service **Area of distribution:** Texas **Expertise:** Engineering, consulting **Affiliations:** President, local Cemetery Association; President, Board of Directors, local rural Water Supply Corp.; President, Board of Directors, local rural Fire District; Secretary/Treasurer, Hunting Club **Hob./spts.:** Hunting, cattle ranch **SIC code:** 87 **Address:** Talley Ranch, 1¼ North Hwy. 87, P.O. Box 87, Burkeville, TX 75932 **E-mail:** jtalley@jas.net

TALYA, SHASHISHEKARA S.
Industry: Power generation, jet engines, healthcare **Born:** September 4, 1975, Bangalore, India **Univ./degree:** B.S.M.E., Indian Institute of Technology, 1996; Ph.D., Arizona State University, 2000 **Current organization:** General Electrical Global Research **Title:** Mechanical Engineer **Type of organization:** Research **Major product:** Jet engines, power plants **Area of distribution:** International **Expertise:** Mechanical engineering, gas turbine design, design optimization, hydro power **Published works:** Journals **Affiliations:** A.S.M.E.; A.I.A.A.; Sigma Xi **Hob./spts.:** Hiking, reading **SIC code:** 87 **Address:** General Electrical Global Research, 1 Research Circle, Bldg. K1, Room 3A26B, Niskayuna, NY 12309 **E-mail:** talya@crd.ge.com

TAMBWEKAR, UNMESH A.
Industry: Consulting **Univ./degree:** B.S., Computer Science, St. Peter's College, 1992; M.E., Engineering, Stephen's Institute of Technology, 1996 **Current organization:** Adroit Software & Consulting **Title:** Management Consultant **Type of organization:** Software consulting company **Major product:** Consulting **Area of distribution:** Tri-state **Expertise:** Engineering, management in areas of operations/streamlining with technology **Published works:** 5 articles, 9 technology/business papers **SIC code:** 87 **Address:** Adroit Software & Consulting, 1109 Green Hollow Dr., Iselin, NJ 08830 **E-mail:** utam@excite.com

TARRANT, ROBERT E.
Industry: Business and finance **Univ./degree:** B.S., Chemistry, University of Delaware, 1982; M.B.A., Monmouth University, 1990 **Current organization:** Techventure **Title:** Principal **Type of organization:** Consulting **Major product:** Strategy, commercial, industrial, utilities **Area of distribution:** New Jersey **Expertise:** Transformational technology **Published works:** 2 journal articles **Affiliations:** I.S.A. **Hob./spts.:** Family **SIC code:** 87 **Address:** 55 Cold Spring Rd., Freehold, NJ 07728 **E-mail:** retarrant1@aol.com

TEAR, HELEN E.
Industry: Healthcare **Born:** October 22, 1940, Goshen, New York **Current organization:** CASA Mia Assisted Living Facility **Title:** Owner/Administrator **Type of organization:** Assisted living facility **Major product:** Resident care and service **Area of distribution:** National **Expertise:** Administration **Affiliations:** A.L.F.; Board Member, Pasco Juvenile Detention Center **Hob./spts.:** Remodeling old homes, gardening, travel **SIC code:** 83 **Address:** CASA Mia Assisted Living Facility, 13935 Eighth St., Dade City, FL 33525 **E-mail:** sassyhdt@aol.com

TERREL, EDDIE D.
Industry: Consulting/oil & gas **Born:** December 19, 1934, Bixby, Oklahoma **Univ./degree:** Attended Oklahoma State University and Kansas State University **Current organization:** Terrel Production Co. **Title:** President **Type of organization:** Consulting **Major product:** Oil and gas drilling and operations **Area of distribution:** International **Expertise:** Drilling, operations **Affiliations:** A.P.I.; Michigan Oil & Gas Association **Hob./spts.:** Camping, travel **SIC code:** 87 **Address:** Terrel Production Co., 7115 Glen Terra Dr., Lansing, MI 48917 **E-mail:** edterrel@cs.com

TERRELL, RITA M.
Industry: Government **Univ./degree:** A.A., Business, Brazosport Community College, 1987 **Current organization:** West Columbia Chamber of Commerce **Title:** President/CEO **Type of organization:** Nonprofit membership **Major product:** Business and industry development and support **Area of distribution:** Texas Gulf Coast **Expertise:** Tourism and revitalization of the downtown historic district **Honors/awards:** Appointed to the Board of the West Columbia Chamber of Commerce, 2002 **Published works:** Editor, "Uptown" (Chamber newsletter) **Affiliations:** Texas Chamber of Commerce Executives; Gulf Coast Chamber of Commerce Executives **Hob./spts.:** Interior design, walking, reading, art galleries, travel **SIC code:** 86 **Address:** West Columbia Chamber of Commerce, 103 S. 16th St., West Columbia, TX 77486 **E-mail:** rita@westcolumbiachamber.org **Web address:** www.westcolumbiachamber.org

TERZIYSKI, ANGUEL G.
Industry: Information technology **Born:** February 23, 1967, Bulgaria **Univ./degree:** M.A., Technical University, Bulgaria, 1991; M.A., Economics, University of Delaware, 1995 **Current organization:** IT Consulting Business **Title:** Senior Software Engineer **Type of organization:** Consulting **Major product:** Software development **Area of distribution:** International **Expertise:** Engineering **SIC code:** 87 **Address:** 9451 Lee Hwy., Apt. 102, Fairfax, VA 22031 **E-mail:** terziiskia@hotmail.com

THEOBALD, DANIEL
Industry: Environmental, Industrial Safety, Public Pool/Spa and Wastewater treatment **Born:** June 21, 1949, Cincinnati, Ohio **Spouse:** Brenda Letterman **Married:** December 7, 1995 **Children:** Darla, 39; Kimberly, 36; Tonya, 33 **Univ./degree:** Accounting, Ferris State University, Michigan **Current organization:** Environmental Services **Title:** President **Type of organization:** Consulting & Training firm **Major product:** Cost reduction services for industrial facilities; training in environmental topics **Area of distribution:** National **Expertise:** Analysis- Developed reporting for analysis & implemented procedures to improve operations; originated an in-house wastewater laboratory and a system of analysis and internal reporting to reduce outside laboratory expense; Cost Reduction- Annual cost reductions are as follows: $120,000 from water conservation, $96,000 from sewer charges and $36,000 from sludge disposal & $16,000 from chemical cost; a one time surcharge expense reduction of $30,000 was realized as well as a one time $45,000 charge averted; Training- Significant accomplishments as Wastewater Operator include the following: trained inexperienced personnel to become seasoned Wastewater Operators; Significant accomplishments as a Wastewater

Trainer include the following: Developed training courses which were delivered statewide throughout South Carolina; first trainer to deliver Wastewater courses via the satellite within the 16 South Carolina Technical Colleges; was the first person to deliver environmental training courses live real time over the internet; sharpened wastewater operator skills through training which empowers each operator to work more effectively; General Consulting- earned four consecutive annual Environmental Awards; Multiple instances of improved work relations between clients and their local regulator; Personal accomplishments include the following: decision making, leadership and organizational & communication skills **Honors/awards:** 4 consecutive annual Environmental Awards **Affiliations:** AWWA; NREP; NESHTA WEF; IBC; ABI **Career accomplishments:** Highest level Licensed Wastewater Operator in multiple states; Nationally certified as Certified Environmental Trainer (CET); Nationally registered as Registered Environmental Professional (REP); Significant accomplishments as Wastewater Operator include the following: He trained inexperienced personnel to become seasoned Wastewater Operators; Developed reporting for analysis and implemented procedures to improve operations; He originated an in-house wastewater laboratory and a system of analysis and internal reporting to reduce outside laboratory expense; Significant accomplishments as a Wastewater Trainer include the following: Developed training courses which were delivered statewide throughout South Carolina; First trainer to deliver Wastewater courses via the satellite with the 16 South Carolina Technical Colleges; He was the first person to deliver environmental training courses live real time over the Internet; Significant accomplishments as a Consultant include the following: Monthly sewer charge reductions of $4,700; Monthly sludge disposal expense is decreased by $1,900; Chemical cost savings of $1,350; A one time surcharge expense reduction of $30,000 was realized; averted a one time $45,000 charge; He has sharpened wastewater operator skills through training which empowers each operator to work more effectively; Multiple instances of improved work relations between his clients and their local regulator resulted from his efforts; Personal accomplishments include decision making, leadership and organizational and communication skills **Hob./spts.:** Baseball, basketball, football **SIC code:** 87 **Address:** Environmental Services, 33-A Ray E. Talley Ct., Simpsonville, SC 29680 **E-mail:** dan@esdlt.com **Web address:** www.esdlt.com

THOMPSON, DOLORES R.
Industry: Job placement **Current organization:** Huntington Station Enrichment Center-Boys & Girls Club of America **Title:** President/Executive Director **Type of organization:** Not for profit organization, training center **Major product:** Programs and sports, home work help **Area of distribution:** Huntington Station, New York **Expertise:** Administration **Affiliations:** N.A.A.C.P. **Hob./spts.:** Reading **SIC code:** 86 **Address:** Huntington Station Enrichment Center, Boys and Girls Club of America, 1264 New York Ave., Huntington Station, NY 11746 **E-mail:** huntse@aol.com

THOMPSON, JEFFREY E.
Industry: Accounting **Born:** Jamaica, West Indies **Univ./degree:** C.P.A., University of the District of Columbia, 1980 **Current organization:** Thompson, Cobb, Bazilio & Associates, PC **Title:** Chairman **Type of organization:** Accounting firm **Major product:** Accounting, management, financial consulting **Area of distribution:** Washington, D.C. **Expertise:** Management consulting **Honors/awards:** Honorary Ph.D., 1997 **Affiliations:** American Institute of Certified Public Accountants; District of Columbia Certified Public Accountants **Hob./spts.:** Reading, swimming, running, jogging **SIC code:** 87 **Address:** Thompson, Cobb, Bazilio & Associates, PC, 1101 15th St. N.W., Suite 400, Washington, DC 20005 **E-mail:** jthompson@pcba.com

THOMPSON, THOMAS J.
Industry: Architecture **Born:** November 13, 1962, Philadelphia, Pennsylvania **Univ./degree:** B.A.E., Pennsylvania State University, 1985 **Current organization:** Thompson + Sears, LLC **Title:** Principal **Type of organization:** Design firm **Major product:** Lighting design firm **Area of distribution:** International **Expertise:** Lighting design **Honors/awards:** IALD 2000, Rodin Museum Pavilion & Plaza, Samsung Headquarters in Seoul, Korea; Lumen 2001, Hoboken Train Station Waiting Room, Hoboken, New Jersey **Affiliations:** I.E.S.; I.A.L.D.; Adjunct Professor, Department of Architecture, MPA Lighting Program, Parsons School of Design **SIC code:** 87 **Address:** Thompson + Sears, LLC, 49 W. 38th St., 16th floor, New York, NY 10018 **E-mail:** tjthompson@ttplus.com

THOMPSON JR., CORNELIUS
Industry: Nuclear power **Born:** December 30, 1969, Macon, Mississippi **Univ./degree:** B.S.M.E., Prairie View A&M University, 1991 **Current organization:** South Texas Project Nuclear Operating Co. **Title:** Systems Engineer **Type of organization:** Nuclear power plant **Major product:** Electricity **Area of distribution:** South Central, Texas **Expertise:** Engineering **Hob./spts.:** Golf, billiards, family **SIC code:** 87 **Address:** South Texas Project Nuclear Operating Co., 8 Miles West of Wadsworth, Wadsworth, TX 77483 **E-mail:** bosso@ev1.net

THOMPSON JR., DALTON E.
Industry: Emergency response/environmental services **Born:** January 6, 1948, Salem, Virginia **Univ./degree:** Business Administration, Virginia Western Community College **Current organization:** LCM Corporation **Title:** Senior Project Manager **Type of organization:** Contracting **Major product:** Remediation/vacuum services/emergency response **Area of distribution:** National **Expertise:** Design engineering, project management **Published works:** 1 article, The Spill Express Publication **Affiliations:** Virginia Association of Hazardous Materials Response Specialists; Virginia State Firefighters Association; Local Emergency Planning Committee (Roanoke); Mid-Atlantic Coastal Area Committee **Hob./spts.:** Golf **SIC code:** 87 **Address:** 1307 Winston Dr., Salem, VA 24034 **E-mail:** et4lcmcorp@aol.com

THREETON, PAMELA
Industry: Fundraising **Born:** November 4, 1973, Hammond, Louisiana **Univ./degree:** B.A., Southwest Louisiana University **Current organization:** Friends of the Cabildo **Title:** Executive Director **Type of organization:** Nonprofit **Major product:** Event planning **Area of distribution:** Louisiana **Expertise:** Museum support **Affiliations:** A.A.A.; L.A.M. **Hob./spts.:** Music, reading, art museum **SIC code:** 84 **Address:** Friends of the Cabildo, 701 Chartres St., New Orleans, LA 70116 **E-mail:** pamela@friendsofthecabildo.org

TITIZER, KORHAN
Industry: Electronics/wireless **Born:** September 8, 1956, Istanbul, Turkey **Univ./degree:** B.S.E.E., University of Surrey, England, 1980; M.S.E.E., University of California, Santa Barbara, 1982 **Current organization:** Aspendos Communications **Title:** CEO **Type of organization:** Engineering/design **Major product:** Semiconductors **Area of distribution:** National **Expertise:** Design engineering, consulting **Published works:** 8 patents pending; several articles **Affiliations:** I.E.E.E.; U.S.T.A. **Hob./spts.:** Tennis, travel **SIC code:** 87 **Address:** Aspendos Communications, 560 S. Winchester Blvd., #500, San Jose, CA 95128 **E-mail:** korhan@aspendoscom.com **Web address:** www.aspendoscom.com

TOCKMAN, RONALD C.
Industry: Accounting **Born:** September 18, 1945, St. Louis, Missouri **Univ./degree:** B.S., Suffolk University, 1971 **Current organization:** Ronald C. Tockman, CPA **Title:** CPA **Type of organization:** Private accounting firm **Major product:** Tax and financial services **Area of distribution:** Canton, Massachusetts **Expertise:** Tax, financial accounting **Affiliations:** Board Director, N.C.C.P.A.; Board Member, Massachusetts C.P.A. Federal And Tax Committees **Hob./spts.:** Family, golf **SIC code:** 87 **Address:** Ronald C. Tockman, CPA, 95 Washington St., Suite 213, Canton, MA 02021 **E-mail:** ronn@rctockmancpa.com **Web address:** www.rctockmancpa.com

TOMASIELLO, A. RICHARD
Industry: Consulting **Born:** August 15, 1937, Chicago, Illinois **Univ./degree:** B.S.E.E., Illinois Institute of Technology, 1962 **Current organization:** Self-employed **Title:** P.E. **Type of organization:** Engineering consulting firm **Major product:** Electrical engineering **Area of distribution:** Nevada **Expertise:** Electrical engineering **SIC code:** 87 **Address:** Hyden Electrical Consultants, Inc., 9585 Teton Diablo Ave., Las Vegas, NV 89117 **E-mail:** puzzzlememe@netzero.com

TOMIC, ERNST A.
Industry: Consulting **Born:** February 1, 1926, Vienna, Austria **Univ./degree:** Ph.D., University of Vienna, 1956 **Current organization:** Retired **Title:** Ph.D. **Type of organization:** Consulting for manufacturing companies **Major product:** Chemicals **Area of distribution:** National **Expertise:** Research **Published works:** 50 publications; patents **Affiliations:** A.C.E.; A.E.S. **Hob./spts.:** Digital photography, tennis **SIC code:** 87 **Address:** 1430 Emory Rd., Wilmington, DE 19803 **E-mail:** eatomic@aol.com

TOURTELLOTTE, JOHN F.
Industry: Consulting **Born:** July 6, 1927, Harvey, Illinois **Univ./degree:** B.S., Chemical Engineering, Northwestern University, 1949; M.S., Chemical Engineering, Illinois Institute of Technology, 1956 **Current organization:** Tourtellotte & Associates, LLC **Title:** President **Type of organization:** Engineering/consulting **Major product:** Creating fuel from biomass **Area of distribution:** International **Expertise:** Chemical engineering; Professional Engineer's Registration, States of Alabama, Michigan, Illinois; Certified Hazardous Materials Site Supervisor Training, 1990; Certified Hazardous Materials Site Technician Training, 1990 **Honors/awards:** Alabama 2003 Businessman of the Year, awarded by NRCC, Washington DC, 2003; Official Registry of Who's Who of American Business Leader, honored 1991, Port Washington, NY; Phi Lambda Upsilon Honorary Chemical Society 1955; Phi Theta Kappa Honor Society Junior College 1947; President, 1945 Senior High School Class; **Published works:** "Terrible Forest Fire Losses!", "If Wildfire Were Electricity", "Assessment of Wood-Based Syngas"; Holder of 10 U.S. Patents **Affiliations:** Member Emeritus, American Institute of Chemical Engineers; Chairman of Birmingham Chapter, AIChE, 2002-03; Past AIChE Committee Chairman, Spray Drying and Evaporation; Founder, Forest Products Division of AIChE; Past Member American Concrete Institute **Hob./spts.:** Golf **SIC code:** 87 **Address:** Tourtellotte & Associates, LLC, 3756 Rockhill Rd., Birmingham, AL 35223 **E-mail:** jft3s@bellsouth.net **Web address:** www.tallcbiomass.com

TRAN, LUAN A.
Industry: Engineering consulting **Univ./degree:** B.S., New Jersey Institute of Technology, 2001 **Current organization:** Burns & Roe Enterprises, Inc. **Title:** Civil/Structural Engineer **Type of organization:** Consulting **Major product:** Power and energy **Area of distribution:** National **Expertise:** Engineering **Affiliations:** A.S.C.E., National Civil Engineers Honor Society **Hob./spts.:** Table tennis, swimming, volleyball **SIC code:** 87 **Address:** 16 Grant St., Little Ferry, NJ 07643 **E-mail:** tranaluan@yahoo.com

TRIPP, LINDA B.
Industry: Religion **Born:** February 11, 1948, Wynne, Arkansas **Current organization:** Angel Ministries **Title:** Founder **Type of organization:** Nonprofit ministry **Major product:** Providing for citizens who do not qualify for state and federal programs, services to the needy and elderly **Area of distribution:** National **Expertise:** Creative ways to provide services to the needy; providing freedom, independence and self sufficiency **Honors/awards:** Republican Executive Committee Eisenhower Commission Award; River City Award of Excellence **Affiliations:** President of American BWA; President and Charter Member, Lake Providence LA Chamber for Commerce; President, Monroe, LA Bata Sigma Phi **SIC code:** 83 **Address:** Angel Ministries, 509 N. Second St., Monroe, LA 71201 **E-mail:** ltripp@caresolutions-inc.com

TRIVEDI, DHARA D.
Industry: Consulting engineering **Born:** May 28, 1975, India **Univ./degree:** B.S., Gujarat University, India, 1996; M.S., with Honors, Griffith University, Australia, 1998, Ph.D., New Jersey Institute of Technology, 2000 **Current organization:** URS Corp. **Title:** Project Engineer **Type of organization:** Consulting environmental firm **Major product:** Environmental and geo-technical consulting **Area of distribution:** International **Expertise:** Environmental engineering **Honors/awards:** First Prize, Presentation at AWWA Conference, Atlantic City, New Jersey, 2000 (Topic: Processing of Dissolved Organic Matter (DOM) fractions using Principal Component Analysis (PCA) with the aid of Spectral Fluorescence Spectroscopy) **Published works:** 2 articles **Affiliations:** A.W.W.A. **Hob./spts.:** Reading, tennis, music **SIC code:** 87 **Address:** URS Corp., 201 Willowbrook Blvd., Wayne, NJ 07470 **E-mail:** dhara_trivedi@urscorp.com

TRIVINO, ESTER L.
Industry: Environmental **Born:** April, 20, 1965, Calama, Chile **Univ./degree:** B.S., Geology, 1989; M.S., Geology, 1995, Loma Linda University **Current organization:** Smith-Emery GeoServices **Title:** Manager of GeoServices **Type of organization:** Consulting **Major product:** Geotechnical, environmental services **Area of distribution:** National **Expertise:** Environmental geology, management consultant **Hob./spts.:** Sports, rock climbing, snow skiing, writing, traveling **SIC code:** 87 **Address:** Smith-Emery GeoServices, 791 E. Washington Blvd., Los Angeles, CA 90021 **E-mail:** etrivino@smithemery.com **Web address:** www.smithemery.com

TROTTER, ERMON
Industry: Union/Automotive **Born:** February 13, 1947, Canton, Mississippi **Univ./degree:** Attended Southern Illinois University for Educational Administration **Current organization:** United Auto Workers/Daimler Chrysler Region 5 Training Center **Title:** Director **Type of organization:** Union/training center **Major product:** Membership benefits/automotive instruction **Area of distribution:** National **Expertise:** Training, finance, development, seminars **Affiliations:** A. Philip Randolph; Treasurer, Masonic Lodge Victorian Chapter #7 **Hob./spts.:** Reading, travel, collecting African art **SIC code:** 86 **Address:** United Auto Workers/Daimler Chrysler, Region 5 Training Center, 958 South Highway Dr., Fenton, MO 63026 **E-mail:** ermontrotter13@yahoo.com

TRUONG, HUAN NGO
Industry: Semiconductors **Born:** March 4, 1976, Saigon, Vietnam **Univ./degree:** B.S., Electrical Engineering, Arizona State University, 1997; M.S., Electrical Engineering, National Technological University, 2005 **Current organization:** Philips Semiconductors **Title:** Senior Analog Applications Engineer **Type of organization:** Engineering, design **Major product:** Semiconductor design, power management, specialty logic **Area of distribution:** National **Expertise:** Analog/logic applications engineering **Honors/awards:** ` **Affiliations:** I.E.E.E. **Hob./spts.:** Table tennis **SIC code:** 87 **Address:** 6541 S. Salt Cedar Place, Chandler, AZ 85249 **E-mail:** analogtek@cox.net

TRUSTY, LEROY A.
Industry: Family Ministries **Univ./degree:** M.Ed., University of Oklahoma **Current organization:** Focus on the Family **Title:** Manager of Safety and Custodial Services **Type of organization:** Nonprofit **Major product:** Publication and constituent response **Area of distribution:** International **Expertise:** Safety, Aviation and Industrial **Affiliations:** American Society of Safety Engineers; World Safety Organization; International Association of Safety Professionals; American Society for Training and Development; Safety System Society **Hob./spts.:** VFW events, golf **SIC code:** 83 **Address:** Focus on the Family, 8605 Explorer Dr., Colorado Springs, CO 80920-1049 **E-mail:** leroy.trusty@fotf.org **Web address:** www.fotf.org

TUDAN, CHRISTOPHER R.
Industry: Pharmaceuticals **Born:** March 2, 1964, Goderich, Ontario, Canada **Univ./degree:** B.S., Honors-Cum Laude, Chemistry, Southern Connecticut State University, 1991; Ph.D., Experimental Medicine, University of British Columbia, 1999 **Current organization:** Advion BioSciences **Title:** Ph.D. **Type of organization:** Contract research **Major product:** Research **Area of distribution:** International **Expertise:** Medical biochemistry **Honors/awards:** Van Arman Excellence in Inflammation Research Award, Inflammation Research Association, 2000; Medical Research Council Studentship Award, 1992-95; Evelynn Martin Cancer Research Fellowship, 1992-93; Alpha Chi Honors Society, 1990; Cheseborough Ponds Chemistry Scholarship for Highest Achieving Chemistry Student, 1990 **Published works:** 17 peer-reviewed papers, 8 patents (novel therapeutics), 1 patent (drug target), 9 patents total **Affiliations:** American Association for the Advancement of Science; Information Research Association; American Chemical Society; Society for Biomolecular Screening **Hob./spts.:** Racing sailboats, astronomy, coaching ice hockey, scuba diving, rowing, golf **SIC code:** 87 **Address:** Advion BioSciences, 15 Catherwood Rd., Ithaca, NY 14859 **E-mail:** ctudan@advion.com

TURNER, BARRY E.
Industry: Research **Univ./degree:** Ph.D., University of California at Berkeley, 1967 **Current organization:** National Radio Astronomy Observatory **Title:** Scientist **Type of organization:** National laboratory under Associated Universities Inc. **Major product:** Research **Area of distribution:** International **Expertise:** Basic research in astrophysics **Affiliations:** American Chemical Society; American Astronomical Society; International Astronomical Society **SIC code:** 87 **Address:** National Radio Astronomy Observatory, 520 Edgemont Rd., Charlottesville, VA 22903 **E-mail:** bturner@nrao.cv.edu

TYLER, DANIEL S.
Industry: Engineering/construction **Born:** November 21, 1979, Cleveland, Ohio **Univ./degree:** B.S., Civil Engineering, Case Western Reserve University, 2002 **Expertise:** Civil engineering, construction management **Honors/awards:** Cleveland Engineering Society 2002 "Engineer of the Year" for Case Western Reserve University, Golden Key International Honor Society, Dean's Honor List, Case Alumni Association Junior/Senior Scholarship, ASCE Student Chapter Service Award, ASCE Outstanding Senior Award, Provost's Scholarship **Affiliations:** ASCE Case Western Reserve Chapter President, Case Men's Glee Club President **Hob./spts.:** Vocal and Instrumental music **SIC code:** 87 **Address:** 300 S. 16th St., #607, Omaha, NE 68102-2218 **E-mail:** dst5@po.cwru.edu

TYNDALE, PETER G.
Industry: Nonprofit **Born:** Mandeville, Jamaica **Univ./degree:** B.B.A., Accounting, City University of New York Bernard Baruch College, 1992 **Current organization:** Council on Foreign Relations **Title:** Director of Finance **Type of organization:** Foreign policy think tank **Major product:** Research **Area of distribution:** International **Expertise:** Accounting/finance **Hob./spts.:** Motorcycles **SIC code:** 86 **Address:** Council on Foreign Relations, 58 E. 68th St., New York, NY 10021 **E-mail:** ptyndale@cfr.org **Web address:** www.cfr.org

UMAR, DURRANI M.
Industry: Engineering **Born:** December 5, 1974, Indianapolis, Indiana **Univ./degree:** B.A., Engineering/Computer Engineering **Current organization:** Ritchie Engineering, Inc. **Title:** Controls Engineer **Type of organization:** OEM, system design and controls **Major product:** Software/hardware design for system **Area of distribution:** International **Expertise:** Robot programming and control design **Affiliations:** I.E.E.E. **Hob./spts.:** Computers **SIC code:** 87 **Address:** 3841 Knickerbocker Place, #1E, Indianapolis, IN 46240 **E-mail:** dmumar@yahoo.com

UTZ, DONALD E.
Industry: Financial **Born:** February 26, 1932, Kansas **Current organization:** Utz Accounting **Title:** President **Type of organization:** Accounting **Major product:** Accounting services **Area of distribution:** Kansas **Expertise:** Accounting **Hob./spts.:** Travel **SIC code:** 87 **Address:** Utz Accounting, 220 S. Stearns St., Haysville, KS 67060 **E-mail:** utzaccounting@sbcglobal.net

VALASTRO, NICHOLAS B.
Industry: Research services **Born:** September 30, 1962, Brooklyn, New York **Univ./degree:** A.A., Business, New York Institute of Technology, 1983 **Current organization:** Valtech Research Inc. **Title:** CEO/President **Type of organization:** Research firm **Major product:** Real estate, corporate and title insurance **Area of distribution:** National **Expertise:** Internet technology and software; lectures nationally **Honors/awards:** Appointed to the National Business Advisory Council, NRCE, 2005 **Published works:** Industry newsletters **Affiliations:** New York Land Title Association; American Land Title Association **Hob./spts.:** Artist, weight training, martial arts **SIC code:** 87 **Address:** Valtech Research Inc., 1 Old Country Rd., Carle Place, NY 11514 **E-mail:** nbv@valtechresearch.com **Web address:** www,valteachresearch.com

VAN TIL, MICHAEL E.
Industry: Mechanical fabricating **Born:** January 4, 1962, Grand Rapids, Michigan **Univ./degree:** B.S., Mechanical Engineering, Western Michigan University, 1988 **Current organization:** Van Til Mechanical Fabricating, Inc. **Title:** President/Engineer **Type of organization:** Manufacturing **Major product:** Domestic booster packages, heat transfer packages **Area of distribution:** International **Expertise:** Mechanical engineering, operations **Affiliations:** A.A.E.E.; A.S.M.E.; A.S.H.R.A.E. **Hob./spts.:** Hockey, golf **SIC code:** 87 **Address:** Van Til Mechanical Fabricating, Inc., 1165 Electric Ave., Wayland, MI 49348 **E-mail:** mevantil@aol.com **Web address:** www.skidpac.com

VANCE, DWIGHT A.
Industry: Pharmacy **Univ./degree:** D.Ph., University of Oklahoma, 1966 **Current organization:** Vance Consulting **Title:** D.Ph. **Type of organization:** Consulting **Major product:** Hospice, pain management **Area of distribution:** Oklahoma **Expertise:** Pharmaceutical consultation **Published works:** Published in International Journal of Pharmaceutical Compounding **Affiliations:** American Pharmaceutical Association; American Society of Health-System Pharmacists **SIC code:** 87 **Address:** Vance Consulting, 101 S. Joshua Ave, Broken Arrow, OK 74012-3124 **E-mail:** dvancedph@cox.net

VANDIVER, RENÉE L. AUBRY
Industry: Consulting **Born:** November 7, 1929, New Iberia, Louisiana **Univ./degree:** B.F.A., Tulane University, 1946 **Current organization:** Renée L. Aubry Vandiver, President, Consultant - Preservation/Interiors **Title:** President/Consultant **Type of organization:** Consulting **Major product:** Interiors and preservation, editing military historical war books **Area of distribution:** International **Expertise:** Layout design, public relations, selling **Hob./spts.:** Travel, family **SIC code:** 87 **Address:** Renée L. Aubry Vandiver, President, Consultant - Preservation/Interiors, P.O. Box 10600, College Station, TX 77842-0600

VARALLO, FRANCIS V.
Industry: Homeowner association **Born:** June 28, 1935, Chicago, Illinois **Univ./degree:** B.S.H., English, Loyola University, Chicago, Illinois, 1958; U.S. Army Command and General Staff College, 1971; National Security Management, National War College, 1972 **Current organization:** Nevada Association of Manufactured Home Owners, Inc. **Title:** President **Type of organization:** Nonprofit **Major product:** Education, assistance and legislative advocacy for manufactured home owners **Area of distribution:** Regional **Expertise:** Management, operation, lobbying **Honors/awards:** NRCC Nevada Businessman of the Year, 2003 and 2004; 2002 and 2003 Republican Gold Medal; 2004 Ronald Reagan Republican Gold Medal; Marquis Who's Who in the West; Strathmore's Who's Who, 2003-04; National Register's Who's Who in Executives and Professionals, 2004-05; Contemporary Who's Who of Professionals, 2004; American Biographical Institute's Man of the Year, 2004 and 2005; Congressional Order of Merit, 2004 and 2005; International Biographical Centre's International Professional of the Year, 2005; International Biographical Centre's 2000 Outstanding Intellectuals of the 21st Century; American Biographical Institute World Medal of Freedom **Affiliations:** (Retired Army Officer as Colonel); Amer. Legion; V.F.W; Disabled Amer. Veterans; Military Officers Assoc. of Amer.; Vietnam Veterans Assoc.; N.R.A.; Freedom Alliance; Heritage Foundation; Selious Foundation; Young America's Foundation; Ronald Reagan Foundation; Colonial Williamsburg Foundation; Senior Congress; Civil War Preservation Trust; NRCC Business Advisory Council; NRCC House Majority Trust; VP, Western Region, Manufactured Home Owners Assoc. of Amer. Inc. **Hob./spts.:** Reading, history, hiking, basketball **SIC code:** 86 **Address:** Nevada Association of Manufactured Home Owners, Inc, 1928 Western, Suite 4, Las Vegas, NV 89102 **E-mail:** namh3@juno.com **Web address:** www.namh-online.com

VASQUEZ, JUAN J.
Industry: Engineering **Born:** August 22, 1971, McAllen, Texas **Univ./degree:** B.S., Architectural Engineering, University of Texas, 1993 **Current organization:** Tomden Engineering **Title:** Associate Project Manager **Type of organization:** Consulting engineering **Major product:** Consulting, engineering and surveying services **Area of distribution:** Texas **Expertise:** Engineering **Affiliations:** A.S.C.E. **Hob./spts.:** Golf, basketball **SIC code:** 87 **Address:** 7905 St. Fillans Lane, Rowlett, TX 75088 **E-mail:** jvasquez@burypartners.com

VAZQUEZ, FERNANDO GARCIA
Industry: Nonprofit **Univ./degree:** M.D., UNDNJ Ponce School of Medicine, 1996 **Current organization:** Valley AIDS Council **Title:** M.D. **Type of organization:** Nonprofit medical clinic **Major product:** Provide care to HIV/AIDS patients **Area of distribution:** Texas **Expertise:** Pediatrics **Honors/awards:** Manager of the Year, Valley AIDS Council, 2000 **Affiliations:** A.C.P.; A.A.P. **SIC code:** 86 **Address:** Valley AIDS Council, 418 E. Tyler Ave., Suite B, Harlingen, TX 78550 **E-mail:** fgarcia.vac@tachc.org

VERBICK, DONALD L.
Industry: Energy **Univ./degree:** B.S.M.E., University of Texas at Austin, 1972; M.S.M.E., University of Houston, Texas, 1979 **Current organization:** Delve Energy Group LLC **Title:** President **Type of organization:** Energy consulting, owner's advisor **Major product:** Project development, due diligence, risk management **Area of distribution:** International **Expertise:** Engineering, executive management **Affiliations:** A.S.M.E.; N.S.P.E.; G.C.P.A.; A.E.E.; A.C.N.W. (nonprofit); Girl Scouts of America; Boy Scouts of America **Hob./spts.:** Family, working with children, church activities, camping, woodworking **SIC code:** 87 **Address:** Delve Energy Group LLC, 855 Foxberry Farms Rd., Medina, MN 55340-9371 **E-mail:** dverbick@scc.net

VERGARA, VIRGILIO S.
Industry: Engineering **Born:** June 28, 1951, Manila, Philippines **Univ./degree:** B.S., Chemical Engineering; M.S., Environmental Engineering, Southwestern University, 1974 **Current organization:** Matrix Desalination, Inc. **Title:** Design & Proposals Manager **Type of organization:** Design and engineering **Major product:** Water and waste water treatment plants **Area of distribution:** International **Expertise:** Engineering and design **Affiliations:** A.I.C.H.E.; A.W.W.A.; F.W.P.C.O.A. **Hob./spts.:** Golf, tennis **SIC code:** 87 **Address:** Matrix Desalination, Inc., 3255 S.W. 11th Ave., Ft. Lauderdale, FL 33315 **E-mail:** virgiliovergara@msn.com

VIDAL, LEONARDO J.
Industry: Consulting **Univ./degree:** B.S., Electrical Engineering, University of Florida, 1970 **Current organization:** Vidal & Associates **Title:** Principal **Type of organization:** Consulting engineering **Major product:** Consulting engineering **Area of distribution:** National **Expertise:** Electrical engineering **Affiliations:** N.R.A. **Hob./spts.:** Boating **SIC code:** 87 **Address:** Vidal & Associates, 844 Calle Esteban Gonzalez, San Juan, PR 00925 **E-mail:** ljvelec@centennialpr.net

VILLANUEVA, MORGAN
Industry: Engineering **Born:** June 27, 1966, Cajamarca, Peru **Univ./degree:** M.S., Civil Engineering/Structural Engineering, Florida International University, Miami, 2000 **Current organization:** Gannett Fleming, Inc. **Title:** Structural Engineer **Type of organization:** Engineering firm **Major product:** Design firm **Area of distribution:** National **Expertise:** Engineering **Honors/awards:** Zhi Epsilon Honor Society of Civil Engineering **Published works:** Company paper **Affiliations:** A.S.C.E.; A.C.I. **Hob./spts.:** Chess **SIC code:** 87 **Address:** Gannett Fleming, Inc., 7300 Corporate Center Dr., Suite 701, Miami, FL 33126 **E-mail:** mvillanueva@gfnet.com

VILLARREAL, AMALIA
Industry: Consulting engineering **Born:** September 26, 1973, Beaumont, Texas **Univ./degree:** B.S., Civil Engineering, Lamar University, 1997 **Current organization:** Carroll & Blackman, Inc. **Title:** Project Manager **Type of organization:** Engineering firm **Major product:** Commercial, residential, municipal development **Area of distribution:** Texas **Expertise:** Civil engineering **Honors/awards:** Young Engineer of the Year, 2004 **Affiliations:** Past President, American Society of Civil Engineers; Local Chapter President, Texas Society of Professional Engineers **Hob./spts.:** Harley Owners' Group **SIC code:** 87 **Address:** Carroll & Blackman, Inc., 3219 26th St., Port Arthur, TX 77642 **E-mail:** molly@cbieng.com **Web address:** www.cbieng.com

VILLEGAS-DÍAZ, HARRY A.
Industry: Consulting/engineering **Born:** Ponce, Puerto Rico **Univ./degree:** B.S., Civil Engineering, University of Puerto Rico **Current organization:** Villegas y Asociados - Ingenieros C.S.P. **Title:** President **Type of organization:** Construction consultants **Major product:** Construction management, QA/QC, qualified inspectors for government requirements **Area of distribution:** San Juan, Puerto Rico **Expertise:** Civil Engineering **Published works:** Articles on construction projects QC/QA, historic paper **Affiliations:** C.I.A.P.R.; A.C.I.; N.S.P.E.; A.S.C.E.; N.F.P.A, **Hob./spts.:** Violin, golf **SIC code:** 87 **Address:** Villegas y Asociados - Ingenieros C.S.P., 1598 Cavalieri Street, Caribe Dev., San Juan, PR 00927-6129 **Phone:** (787)763-4934 **Fax:** (787)753-6403 **E-mail:** havillegas@coqui.net

VIZCAINO, HENRY P.
Industry: Consulting **Born:** August 28, 1918, Hurley, New Mexico **Univ./degree:** M.S., University of New Mexico, 1939 **Current organization:** Henry P. Vizcaino **Title:** Geologist **Type of organization:** Natural resources consulting **Major product:** Consulting and investigation of potential natural resources **Area of distribution:** International **Expertise:** Engineering, geological exploration **Published works:** Article, American Institute of Mining Metallurgy **Hob./spts.:** Stock market, reading **SIC code:** 87 **Address:** 12332 Los Arboles Ave., N.E., Albuquerque, NM 87112-2079

VODEV, EUGENE D.
Industry: Consulting/medical **Univ./degree:** M.A.; Ph.D., Columbia University **Current organization:** Voka Inc. **Title:** President **Type of organization:** Private consulting firm **Major product:** Hospital management consulting **Area of distribution:** International **Expertise:** Hospital management **Published works:** Articles **Affiliations:** A.H.A.; Fellow, American College of Healthcare Executives; Vice President,

New Mexico Hospital Association **SIC code:** 87 **Address:** Voka Inc., 315 Wellington Ave., Lehigh Acres, FL 33972 **E-mail:** evodev@aol.com

VOIGT, KARL E.
Industry: Consulting **Born:** May 23, 1931, Pittsburgh, Pennsylvania **Spouse:** Charlotte Ebert Voigt (Died 2003) **Married:** 1956 **Children:** Karl A., born 1960; Eric M., born 1964; Andrew N., born 1968 **Univ./degree:** B.S., Civil Engineering, Carnegie Mellon University, 1956; U.S. Army Command and General Staff College, Industrial College of the Armed Forces, Air War College **Current organization:** Karl E. Voigt, P.E. **Title:** Engineer **Type of organization:** Consulting **Major product:** Electric related operations, maintenance and construction **Area of distribution:** Western Pennsylvania **Expertise:** Construction engineering, standards and safety **Published works:** 1963, IEEE Conference Paper #63-783, Application of Computer to Overhead Line Ratings **Affiliations:** American Society of Civil Engineers; Engineers Society of Western Pennsylvania; Society of American Military Engineers; Reserve Officers Association of the U.S.; Military Order of the World Wars; Aircraft Owners and Pilots Association; Aero Club of Pittsburgh **Career accomplishments:** Converted several sets of plant records and electric interruption data to computerized systems; Installed and managed a continuing work measurement system for small construction projects to monitor crew performance; Instructed and directed instruction for the reserve Command and General Staff College **Hob./spts.:** Flying **SIC code:** 87 **Address:** Karl E. Voigt, P.E., 1669 Galeton Dr., Verona, PA 15147-2826 **E-mail:** kevoigt@cs.com

VOLZ, PAUL A.
Industry: Research studies **Born:** March 26, 1936, Ann Arbor, Michigan **Univ./degree:** Ph.D. **Current organization:** North Florida Mycology Associates **Title:** Ph.D. **Type of organization:** Research, writing **Major product:** Research, writing **Area of distribution:** International **Expertise:** Mycology, science studies **Published works:** 240 publications **Hob./spts.:** Gardening, classical music, operas **SIC code:** 87 **Address:** North Florida Mycology Associates, 4500 Silverberry Ct., Jacksonville, FL 32224-6836 **E-mail:** pvolz@bellsouth.net

VON ESCHEN, ROBERT L.
Industry: Consulting **Married:** Widowed **Children:** Eric L., Marc A.; Grandchild: Steven A. **Univ./degree:** B.S.E.E., Montana State University; International Law Studies, University of Liberia; US Federal Regulations, Glendale Community College; Computer Programming, Lakeland Community College; Computer Programs, MicroAge Corp. **Current organization:** BWXT Pantex **Title:** Consultant Engineer **Type of organization:** Engineering consulting **Major product:** Facility (O&M) management, engineering **Area of distribution:** International **Expertise:** Technical investigation-audits, inspections, predictive maintenance **Honors/awards:** Listed in Marquis Who's Who-43 publications, 1994 thru 2004; International Biographical Centre (Cambridge, England)-7 publications, 1995 thru 2002; America's Registry, 2002; Many Boy Scouts of America Awards including Silver Beaver **Affiliations:** Institute of Electrical and Electronics Engineers; National Society of Professional Engineers; Texas Society of Professional Engineers; National Defense Industrial Association; Masonic Lodge; Scottish Rite; Shriners; BPO Elks; NRA; Society of American Military Engineers; Association of Former Intelligence Officers **Career accomplishments:** Many technical investigation certifications, a multitude of computer training, plus publication of many manuals, training plans and project standards or Procedures **Hob./spts.:** World travel, writing, coin/stamp collecting **SIC code:** 87 **Address:** 3445 Gladstone Lane, Amarillo, TX 79120-0020 **E-mail:** bobve@amaonline.com

VON FINTEL, LEON
Industry: Engineering/sales **Born:** September 29, 1949, Niederdorff, Switzerland **Univ./degree:** B.S.M.E., 1969; M.S.M.E., 1974, University of Durdan, South Africa **Current organization:** Ystral Inc. **Title:** Project Manager **Type of organization:** Manufacturing and distribution **Major product:** Process equipment **Area of distribution:** International **Expertise:** Engineering (design/evaluation. process engineering) **Affiliations:** E.T.H. **Hob./spts.:** Computer programming, reading, travel, theatre **SIC code:** 87 **Address:** Ystral Inc., 6 E. Washington Ave., Atlantic Highlands, NJ 07716 **E-mail:** ystralinc.usa@verizon.net **Web address:** www.ystral.com

WAINER, RAUL
Industry: Consulting/Engineering **Born:** April 15, 1955, Rio de Janeiro, Brazil **Univ./degree:** B.S., Civil Engineering, I.M.E. Military Institute of Engineering, 1978; M.B.A., P.V.C._R.J., Brazil, 1987; M.S., Environmental Engineering, Florida International University, 2002 **Current organization:** C3TS-Engineers, Architects, Planners **Title:** Engineer **Type of organization:** Consulting firm **Major product:** Civil engineering **Area of distribution:** Florida **Expertise:** Engineering **Affiliations:** American Society of Civil Engineers; Florida Engineering Society **Hob./spts.:** Beach volleyball, fishing **SIC code:** 87 **Address:** C3TS-Engineers, Architects, Planners, 901 Ponce de Leon Blvd., Ste.900, Coral Gables, FL 33134 **E-mail:** raulw@c3ts.com

WALDE, HENDRIK
Industry: Electronics/plasma physics **Born:** Cottbus, Germany **Univ./degree:** M.S., Electronic Engineering with Excellence, Polytechnic Institute, Lvov, Ukraine, 1976 **Current organization:** Advanced Energy Industries **Title:** Senior Staff Engineer **Type of organization:** R&D **Major product:** Plasma power supplies, plasma diagnostics **Area of distribution:** International **Expertise:** Electronics design of plasma sensors **Published works:** 5 articles on plasma processing; 2 personal patents and co-holder of 4 other patents in power and supply measurement and plasma diagnostics **Affiliations:** Society of Vacuum Coaters **Hob./spts.:** Mountain biking, historical reading **SIC code:** 87 **Address:** Advanced Energy Industries, 1625 Sharp Point Dr., Ft. Collins, CO 80525 **E-mail:** hendrick.walde@aei.com **Web address:** www.advanced-energy.com

WALKER, WYATT TEE
Industry: Religion **Born:** August 16, 1929, Montana **Univ./degree:** Ph.D., African American Studies, Colgate University **Current organization:** Canaan Baptist Church of Christ **Title:** Pastor **Type of organization:** Church **Major product:** Human services **Area of distribution:** International **Expertise:** Management **Published works:** 24 books, articles **Hob./spts.:** Yachtsman **SIC code:** 86 **Address:** Canaan Baptist Church of Christ, 52 Delaware Rd., Yonkers, NY 10710 **E-mail:** wyattwalk@ecofaith.com

WALLACE JR., JAMES R.
Industry: Labor unions **Born:** January 18, 1956, East Haven, Connecticut **Current organization:** U.F.C.W. Local 919 **Title:** Secretary/Treasurer **Type of organization:** Union **Major product:** Membership benefits, advocacy **Area of distribution:** National **Expertise:** Negotiations, trustee work **Hob./spts.:** Golf, baseball **SIC code:** 86 **Address:** UFCW Local 919, 6 Hyde Rd., Farmington, CT 06032 **E-mail:** jrw007@sbcglobal.net

WALSH, LONARTA M.
Industry: Petrochemical **Born:** November 29, 1948, Chicago, Illinois **Current organization:** UOP, LLC **Title:** Administrative Assistant **Type of organization:** R&D **Major product:** Technology **Area of distribution:** International **Expertise:** Marketing **Hob./spts.:** Spending time with her grandchildren, antiquing, arts and crafts **SIC code:** 87 **Address:** UOP, LLC, 25 E. Algonquin Rd., Des Plaines, IL 60017 **E-mail:** nard.walsh@uop.com

WALTER, GILBERT C.
Industry: Consulting **Univ./degree:** B.S., Electrical Engineering, Ohio State University **Current organization:** Safety & Compliance Engineering **Title:** President **Type of organization:** Testing and consulting agency **Major product:** Product safety and compliance consulting and testing **Area of distribution:** National **Honors/awards:** Engineering and consulting **Affiliations:** P.S.M.A.; International Association of Electrical Inspectors **SIC code:** 87 **Address:** Safety & Compliance Engineering, 15225 Venetian Way, Morgan Hill, CA 95037

WALTON, DEREK N.
Industry: Electromagnetic compatibility design and testing **Born:** August 23, 1958, Manchester, England **Univ./degree:** Electrical Engineering, Manchester Polytechnic, 1980 **Current organization:** L.F. Research **Title:** Owner **Type of organization:** Design, research and testing lab **Major product:** Electromagnetic compatibility design and test (EMC), calibration **Area of distribution:** International **Expertise:** E.M.C. **Published works:** Papers **Affiliations:** I.E.E.E.; N.A.R.T.E. **Hob./spts.:** Music, badminton, motor racing, model engineering, archery **SIC code:** 87 **Address:** L.F. Research, 12790 Route 76, Poplar Grove, IL 61065 **E-mail:** lfresearch@aol.com

WALTON, VERNA
Industry: Accounting **Born:** March 21, 1946, Everton, Georgia **Current organization:** H&R Block **Title:** Owner **Type of organization:** Accounting **Major product:** Tax services **Area of distribution:** Georgia **Expertise:** Income tax preparation **Hob./spts.:** Fishing **SIC code:** 87 **Address:** H&R Block, 311 Spring St., P.O. Box 1037, Washington, GA 30673 **E-mail:** vwalton@h&rblock.com

WAMIL, ARTUR W.
Industry: Pharmaceutical **Univ./degree:** M.D., Neurology, Psychiatry, 1986; Ph.D., Pharmacology, 1988, Vanderbilt University **Current organization:** Eisai Medical Research & Eisai Global Clinical Development **Title:** Medical Director, Global Clinical Development **Type of organization:** R&D pharmaceutical company **Major product:** Clinical drug development **Area of distribution:** International **Expertise:** Neurology, psychiatry, medicine **Affiliations:** A.M.A.; A.A.N.; A.P.A. **SIC code:** 87 **Address:**

3 Vista Dr., Flanders, NJ 07836 **E-mail:** art_wamil@eisai.com **Web address:** www.eisai.com

WANDOVER, GEORGE
Industry: Engineering **Born:** April 3, 1959, Fairfax, Virginia **Univ./degree:** M.S., Mechanical Engineering, University of Alaska, 1990 **Current organization:** Meinhardt Consulting Engineers **Title:** Senior Associate **Type of organization:** Consulting firm **Major product:** MEP Design **Area of distribution:** International **Expertise:** Commercial, HVAC design **Affiliations:** A.S.H.R.E. **Hob./spts.:** Scuba diving **SIC code:** 87 **Address:** Meinhardt Consulting Engineers, 800 W. Cypress Creek Rd., Ft. Lauderdale, FL 33309 **E-mail:** george.wandover@meinhardtusa.com

WASSERMAN, DEBRA L.
Industry: Advocacy **Born:** September 22, 1968, Brooklyn, New York **Univ./degree:** M.A., Public Administration, Columbia University, 1996 **Current organization:** Israel Policy Forum **Title:** Executive Director **Type of organization:** Nonprofit **Major product:** To support active and sustained American efforts aimed at resolving the conflict between Israel and its Arab neighbors **Area of distribution:** New York, New York **Expertise:** Management, development, strategic planning **Affiliations:** A.I.F. **Hob./spts.:** Jogging, reading, theatre, movies, sports **SIC code:** 86 **Address:** Israel Policy Forum, 165 E. 56th St., 2nd floor, New York, NY 10022 **E-mail:** debipf@aol.com

WATKINS, CONNIE
Industry: Health **Title:** Executive **Type of organization:** Assisted living housing **Major product:** Residence and assistance for the elderly **Expertise:** Administrator **SIC code:** 83 **Address:** Alterra Sterling House, c/o Liz McLaughlin, 2400 N. 14th St., Dodge City, KS 67801

WATSON, CLETUS M.S.
Industry: Religion **Born:** November 3, 1938 **Univ./degree:** B.A., Saint Francis University, Loretto, Pennsylvania, 1962; M.A., LaSalle University, Philadelphia, Pennsylvania, 1974; M.Div., St. Charles Seminary, 1976 **Current organization:** St. Mary Our Lady of Grace Catholic Church **Title:** Pastoral Minister, T.O.R. Franciscan **Type of organization:** Roman Catholic Church **Major product:** Religion **Area of distribution:** National **Expertise:** Pastor, teaching, lecturing **Honors/awards:** Black History Month Award from Jacksonville Naval Base, 1987; One Church/One Child Award, 1990; Citizens Award from Jacksonville, 1991; Alumni Award in Humanities, Saint Francis University, 1992 **Published works:** Many publications including "The Concept of God and the Afro-American", "The Concept of Love and the Human Person", his poetry published in collections by the National Library of Poetry , published articles in several religious periodicals **Affiliations:** K.S.P.C.; Board Member of the Diocese of St. Augustine, Afro-American Board Member of the Diocese; Honorary Member of One Church/One Child, Jacksonville Branch; Knights of St. Peter Claver; Elected to the Board of Trustees for the Franciscan University of Steubenville, 2005; Named Pastor of St. Pius V Catholic Church, 2002, by the Most Rev. Victor B. Galeone, S.T.L. of the Diocese of St. Augustine; Pastor since 1988 of the Church of the Crucifixion, Jacksonville, Florida; Board of Trustees Member, Franciscan Univ. of Steubenville **Hob./spts.:** Movies, reading, walking **SIC code:** 86 **Address:** St. Mary Our Lady of Grace Catholic Church, 515 Fourth St., St. Petersburg, FL 33701

WATSON, JULIA A.
Industry: Social services **Born:** August 1, 1927, Brooklyn, New York **Univ./degree:** B.A., Sociology, Adelphi University; M.S.W., University of Illinois, 1956; Ph.D. Candidate, Fairleigh Dickinson University **Current organization:** Crosswinds Youth Services, Inc. **Title:** Senior counselor **Type of organization:** Counseling center **Major product:** Crisis management/referrals **Area of distribution:** Brevard County, Central Florida **Expertise:** Clinical counseling for at risk youth and families **Affiliations:** National Association of Social Workers; Pastor/Associate Member New Life Christian Fellowship **Hob./spts.:** Reading, writing poetry **SIC code:** 83 **Address:** Crosswinds Youth Services, Inc., 725 Deleon Ave., Titusville, FL 32780 **E-mail:** juliawatson@crosswindsyouthservices.org

WATSON, ROBERT LYNN
Industry: Defense, aerospace **Born:** December 5, 1960, Angeles City, Philippines **Univ./degree:** B.B.A., Faulkner University; M.S., Project Operations Management, University of Arkansas, 2002 **Current organization:** Metric Systems Corp. **Title:** Engineer **Type of organization:** Engineering, manufacturing **Major product:** Defense and aerospace systems for sea, land, air and space **Area of distribution:** International **Expertise:** Engineering **Honors/awards:** Lexington Who's Who **Affiliations:** Nationals Honor Society **Hob./spts.:** Sports memorabilia, fishing, hiking, travel, beach, collecting books, stamps, coins, bank notes **SIC code:** 87 **Address:** Metric Systems Corp., 613 Manchester Rd., Ft. Walton Beach, FL 32547 **E-mail:** bwatson@metricsys.com **Web address:** www.metricsys.com

WAUGH, MICHAEL C.P.
Industry: Consulting **Born:** September 12, 1957, Deep River, Ontario, Canada **Current organization:** Medical IT Pros., LLC **Title:** President/Owner **Type of organization:** Medical consulting firm **Major product:** Sales and support services **Area of distribution:** National **Expertise:** IT **Hob./spts.:** Scuba diving, yachting **SIC code:** 87 **Address:** Medical IT Pros., LLC, 157 3rd Ave., Suite 3C, Westwood, NJ 07675 **E-mail:** mwaugh@meditpros.com **Web address:** www.meditpros.com

WEAVER, DONALD E.
Industry: Architecture **Born:** March 25, 1926, Mt. Vernon, NY **Univ./degree:** B.Arch., University of Oklahoma, 1959 **Current organization:** Donald Weaver + Architect **Title:** Owner **Type of organization:** Architecture firm **Major product:** Architecture services **Area of distribution:** Oklahoma **Expertise:** Architecture **Published works:** Articles **Affiliations:** National & Local Chapter, A.I.A.; National & Local Chapter, C.S.I. **Hob./spts.:** Oil painting **SIC code:** 87 **Address:** Donald Weaver + Architect, 2519 N. Hudson Ave., Oklahoma City, OK 73103 **E-mail:** donaldee@juno.com

WEBB, JAMES B.
Industry: Consulting **Born:** July 20, 1944, St. Louis, Missouri **Univ./degree:** B.A., Education, Lincoln University, 1967 **Current organization:** St. Louis Minority Business Council **Title:** President **Type of organization:** Nonprofit **Major product:** Consulting services **Area of distribution:** National **Expertise:** Minority businesses **Hob./spts.:** Music **SIC code:** 86 **Address:** St. Louis Minority Business Council, 308 N. 21st St., Suite 700, St. Louis, MO 63103 **E-mail:** jwebb@slmbc.org **Web address:** www.slmbc.org

WEBER, WAYLON
Industry: Research **Born:** April 9, 1978, St. Cloud, Minnesota **Univ./degree:** Ph.D., Organic Chemistry, University of New Mexico, 2005 **Current organization:** Loveland Respiratory Research Institute **Title:** Analytical Aerosol Chemist **Type of organization:** Research institute **Major product:** Pharmaceutical research **Area of distribution:** National **Expertise:** Organic synthesis **Published works:** Journal of Toxicology and Environmental Health, Part A **Hob./spts.:** Baseball, hockey, golf, football **SIC code:** 87 **Address:** 415 DeSoto St. S.E., Albuquerque, NM 87123

WEBER, WILLIAM A.
Industry: Educational **Born:** November 16, 1918, New York, New York **Univ./degree:** B.S, Iowa State University; M.S., Washington State University; Ph.D., Plant Taxonomy, Washington State University **Current organization:** University of Colorado **Title:** Professor and Curator Emeritus, Herbarium COLO **Type of organization:** University museum **Major product:** Documentation and study of the natural history and biodiversity of Colorado **Area of distribution:** Boulder, Colorado **Expertise:** Plant taxonomy, flowering plants, lichen, bryophytes, plant geography, biography **Published works:** 22 books, 100+ papers **Affiliations:** F.L.S.; American Society of Plant Taxonomy; International Society of Plant Taxonomy; American Bryological and Lichenological Society; California Botanical Society; Swedish Botanical Society **Hob./spts.:** Ornithology, African art, classical music **SIC code:** 84 **Address:** University of Colorado Museum, Campus Box 265, Boulder, CO 80309 **E-mail:** bill.weber@colorado.edu

WELLS, HARRY M.
Industry: Animal shelter **Current organization:** Crawford County Humane Society **Title:** Vice President/Executive Director **Type of organization:** Not for profit humane society and animal shelter **Major product:** Taking in and caring for animals with no homes **Area of distribution:** Crawford County, Ohio **Expertise:** Business management and fundraising **SIC code:** 86 **Address:** Crawford County Humane Society, P.O. Box 727, Bucyrus, OH 44820 **E-mail:** cchs@cybrtown.com **Web address:** www.crawfordhumane.com

WELSH, CAROL L.
Industry: Native American agency **Born:** April 5, 1957, San Rafael, California **Current organization:** Native American Indian Center of Central Ohio **Title:** Executive Director **Type of organization:** Nonprofit **Major product:** Preserve, protect and promote Native American spirituality, culture and philosophy **Area of distribution:** Ohio **Hob./spts.:** Singing, hand building with clay **SIC code:** 86 **Address:** Native American Indian Center of Central Ohio, 67 E. Innis Ave., Columbus, OH 43207 **E-mail:** zitkana@aol.com

WENNEN, JAMES E.
Industry: Metallurgical engineering/mineral processing **Born:** April 9, 1942, Eveleth, Minnesota **Univ./degree:** M.Sc., Michigan Technological University, 1968 **Current organization:** Self employed **Title:** Consulting Engineer **Type of organization:** Self employed consulting engineering **Major product:** Mineral processing **Area of distribution:** National/International **Expertise:** Engineering, mineral processing **Published works:** Several papers **Affiliations:** Society of Mining Engineers; Canadian Institute of Mining, Metallurgy and Petroleum **Hob./spts.:** Fishing **SIC code:** 87 **Address:** 31506 MacDougal Bay Rd., Grand Rapids, MN 55744 **E-mail:** wennen@uslink.net

WESTBROOK, RONALD
Industry: Video/audio data systems **Born:** June 10, 1949, Birmingham, Alabama **Univ./degree:** B.S., Business, Jacksonville State University **Current organization:**

Westbrook & Assoc. Inc. **Title:** President **Type of organization:** Media consulting **Major product:** Multi-media systems **Area of distribution:** Alabama **Expertise:** Consulting, design and project management **Honors/awards:** Clara Barton Award **Affiliations:** I.C.I.A. **Hob./spts.:** Historical radio, collector of technology **SIC code:** 87 **Address:** Westbrook & Assoc. Inc., 2806 Ruffner Rd., Suite 105A, Birmingham, AL 35210 **E-mail:** ronrwa@bellsouth.net

WEYHRICH, KENNETH L.
Industry: Industrial consulting **Born:** July 18, 1945, Pekin, Illinois **Univ./degree:** Structural Engineering, University of Chicago, 1972 **Current organization:** Industrial Construction Consultants, Inc. **Title:** President **Type of organization:** Consulting services firm **Major product:** Design consulting and construction **Area of distribution:** National **Expertise:** Engineering **Affiliations:** Association of General Contractors **Hob./spts.:** Golf, running, target shooting **SIC code:** 87 **Address:** Industrial Construction Consultants, Inc., 7416 Gadsden Hwy., Trussville, AL 35173 **E-mail:** kensultant@charter.net

WHALEN, JAMES
Industry: Healthcare **Born:** August 3, 1957, Providence, Rhode Island **Univ./degree:** M.D., Brown University, 1989 **Current organization:** AccelRx Research **Title:** M.D. **Type of organization:** Research laboratory **Major product:** Mental health research **Area of distribution:** Lincoln, Rhode Island **Expertise:** Psychiatry **Affiliations:** Fellow, American Psychiatric Association **Hob./spts.:** Pistol shooting, tennis **SIC code:** 87 **Address:** AccelRx Research, 6 Blackstone Valley Pl., Bldg. 4, Suite 401, Lincoln, RI 02865 **E-mail:** jw@accelrx.org **Web address:** www.accelrx.org

WHEATLEY, WILLIAM A.
Industry: Architecture **Born:** September 23, 1944, Knoxville, Tennessee **Univ./degree:** B.A., Philosophy, University of St. Thomas, Texas, 1972 **Current organization:** Wheatley & Associates, Inc. **Title:** Owner **Type of organization:** Architecture firm/consulting services **Major product:** Construction projects **Area of distribution:** International **Expertise:** Architecture, construction management, consulting **Affiliations:** A.I.A.; A.B.A.; A.C.F.E. **Hob./spts.:** Music, singing, playing the piano, art **SIC code:** 87 **Address:** MDC Systems, Inc., 55 West Ave., Wayne, PA 19087-3255 **E-mail:** william.wheatley@wheatleyassociatesinc.com

WHITAKER, JO ANNE
Industry: Healthcare **Born:** February 8, 1927, Bartow, Florida **Univ./degree:** B.S., Florida State University, 1948; M.D., Wake Forest University, 1952 **Title:** M.D., Director/President **Type of organization:** Non-profit **Major product:** Research, education, alternative medicine, Bowen technique and testing for lyme disease **Area of distribution:** National **Expertise:** Pediatric hematology/oncology, Bowen technique expert **Published works:** 60 original papers **Affiliations:** F.A.A.P.; F.L.P.A.; N.P.A.; Bowen Research & Training Institute **Hob./spts.:** Golf champion **SIC code:** 87 **Address:** Bowen Research & Training Institute, 38541 US Highway 19 North, Palm Harbor, FL 34684 **E-mail:** bowenresearch@earthlink.net **Web address:** www.bowen.org

WHITE, DAVID B.
Industry: Consulting engineering **Born:** November 21, 1956, Rockford, Illinois **Univ./degree:** M.S., Petroleum Engineering, Tulane University, 1984 **Current organization:** ReCon Engineering, Inc. **Title:** Vice President, Engineer **Type of organization:** Engineering/management firm **Major product:** Refining, petrochemicals, oil and gas, chemicals **Area of distribution:** Louisiana **Expertise:** Engineering, evaluation, quality assurance **Affiliations:** A.S.C.E.; P.M.I.; Louisiana Engineering Society **Hob./spts.:** Family, track, soccer, golf **SIC code:** 87 **Address:** ReCon Engineering, Inc., 3649 S. Beglis Pkwy., Sulphur, LA 70665 **E-mail:** dwhite@recon-group.com **Web address:** www.recon-group.com

WHITE, DAVID P.
Industry: Pharmaceutical **Born:** March 20, 1966, Johannesburg, South Africa **Univ./degree:** B.Sc. (with distinction); B.Sc. Hons (with distinction); Ph.D., Organometallic Chemistry, University of Witwatersrand, 1993; Post Doctoral, Beckman Institute for Advanced Science and Technology, University of Illinois at Urbana-Champaign, 1996 **Current organization:** aaiPharma **Title:** Senior Director and Head of Discovery Sciences **Type of organization:** Research and development **Major product:** Pharmaceuticals **Area of distribution:** International **Expertise:** Chemistry, administration **Affiliations:** Sigma Xi; Alpha Chi Sigma **Hob./spts.:** Photography, travel, music **SIC code:** 87 **Address:** aaiPharma, 2320 Scientific Park Dr., Wilmington, NC 28405 **E-mail:** david.white@aaipharma.com

WHITTEKER, MARGARET C.
Industry: Social Services **Born:** December 5, 1958, Milford, Delaware **Univ./degree:** Dual M.S., Human Services, Capella University **Current organization:** Aid for Families in Need, Inc. **Title:** Executive Director **Type of organization:** Nonprofit **Major product:** Assistance to low income clients **Area of distribution:** National **Expertise:** Strategic planning, implementation, networking **Affiliations:** Family Liaison, Vietnam Veterans Association, Chapter 37 - Junior, West Virginia **SIC code:** 83 **Address:** Aid for Families in Need, Inc., 21 Country Lane, Amma, WV 25005 **E-mail:** jahrteach@yahoo.com

WICKBOLDT, WALTER C.
Industry: Engineering **Born:** June 2, 1942, New Orleans, Louisiana **Univ./degree:** B.S., Geology, Louisiana State, 1968; M.S.C.E., University of Arizona, 1986 **Current organization:** Walter C. Wickboldt, P.E. **Title:** President/Senior Engineer **Type of organization:** Geotechnical/civil engineering consulting firm **Major product:** Foundation engineering, tunneling, radioactive site contracting for geotechnical services **Area of distribution:** National **Expertise:** Geotechnical site investigations, soil and rock mechanics, project management, ground water studies, well design **Published works:** Many including; "Comprehensive Open-End Contract for Geotechnical Site Investigations", New York District, Corps of Engineers, 1996; "Geotechnical Investigation, Asylum Run Dam Site, Harrisburg, PA", Baltimore District, Corps of Engineers, 1988 **Affiliations:** A.S.C.E.; U.S. Army Civilian Engineering Corps, 1973-96 **Career accomplishments:** Assigned to the design team for the Passaic Tunnel Project - a $2.5 billion structure, 40-feet in diameter and 20-miles long, running from Pompton Plains to Newark Bay, New Jersey. **Hob./spts.:** Sport fishing, hunting, carpentry, reading, gardening, breeding hunting dogs, skeet shooting **SIC code:** 87 **Address:** 3705 Cameron Mills Rd., Alexandria, VA 22305

WILBERT, ROBERT LEWIS
Industry: Consulting **Born:** September 26, 1971, Pensacola, Florida **Univ./degree:** B.S., Mechanical Engineering Technology, SUNY Institute of Technology, 2001 **Current organization:** Proto-Power Corp. **Title:** Engineer I, Mechanical **Type of organization:** Consulting firm **Major product:** Provide architectural/engineering services to the utility industry **Area of distribution:** National **Expertise:** Engineering **Affiliations:** A.S.M.E. **Hob./spts.:** Family, computers, biking, antique cars, woodworking **SIC code:** 87 **Address:** Proto-Power Corp., 15 Thames St., Groton, CT 06340 **E-mail:** rwilbert@protopower.com **Web address:** www.protopower.com

WILKES, DAVID R.
Industry: Food **Born:** October 27, 1922, Providence, Rhode Island **Univ./degree:** D.Sc., Chemistry, Nathaniel Hawthorne University, 1967; LL.M., University of Rhode Island, 1988 **Current organization:** Wilkes Industries Inc. **Title:** President **Type of organization:** Consulting **Major product:** Consulting and product development **Area of distribution:** International **Expertise:** Food flavorings **Affiliations:** S.F.C.; I.F.T. **SIC code:** 87 **Address:** Wilkes Industries Inc., One Kensington Gate, #101, Great Neck, NY 11021 **E-mail:** eeglobe17optimumonline.com

WILLIAMS, CEDERICK L.
Industry: Youth club **Born:** November 4, 1962, Montgomery, Alabama **Univ./degree:** B.S., Education, Alabama State University **Current organization:** Boys & Girls Clubs of South Central Alabama **Title:** President **Type of organization:** Youth club **Major product:** Educational and recreational programs **Area of distribution:** Montgomery, Alabama **Expertise:** Administration; Certified Boys & Girls Club Professional **Honors/awards:** Professional of the State of Alabama, 2003 **Affiliations:** President, Nat King Cole Society; Masons; Rotary Club; Kiwanis Club; Kappa Alpha Psi **Hob./spts.:** Grilling, RV'ing, sports **SIC code:** 86 **Address:** Boys & Girls Clubs of South Central Alabama, P.O. Box 9104, Montgomery, AL 36108 **E-mail:** cwilliams@bgc-sca.org **Web address:** www.bgc-sca.org

WILLIAMS, WILHO E.
Industry: Engineering **Born:** March 7, 1922 **Univ./degree:** B.S., Civil Engineering, Washington State University, 1944; M.S., Structural Engineering, University of Illinois, 1947; Capt. (CEC) USNR (Ret.) **Current organization:** Williams Engineering **Title:** Consultant **Type of organization:** Consulting firm **Major product:** Structural engineering, consulting **Area of distribution:** Idaho, Washington **Expertise:** Structural engineering; P. E. , S.E., Licensed in Oregon, Washington, Idaho (previously licensed in Utah and New Mexico)) **Affiliations:** American Society of Civil Engineers; National Society of Professional Engineers; Structural Engineers Association of Washington **SIC code:** 87 **Address:** Williams Engineering, 2331 East 34th Ave., Spokane, WA 99223 **E-mail:** vawilho@msn.com

WINCH, RICHARD A.
Industry: Engineering **Born:** August 10, 1946, Cantwell, Missouri **Univ./degree:** B.S., Mechanical Engineering , **Current organization:** Power Tek **Title:** President, General Manager **Type of organization:** Engineering consulting **Major product:** Testing, startup and consulting **Area of distribution:** National **Expertise:** Performance and acceptance testing **Affiliations:** A.S.M.E. **Hob./spts.:** Travel **SIC code:** 87 **Address:** Power Tek, P.O. Box 385, Cape Fair, MO 65624 **E-mail:** powertekservices@aol.com

WISE, DONALD LEE
Industry: Chemical engineering **Born:** March 11, 1937, Pittsburgh, Pennsylvania **Univ./degree:** Ph.D., University of Pittsburgh, 1963 **Current organization:** Cambridge Scientific, Inc. **Title:** Chairman **Type of organization:** R&D, manufacturing **Major product:** Biomedical materials, biopolymers **Area of distribution:** International

Expertise: Chemical engineering **Published works:** 40 books, 150+ articles/chapters **Affiliations:** Fellow, American Institute for Medical and Biological Engineering; Fellow, Co-founder, Past President, Society for Environmental Biotechnology **SIC code:** 87 **Address:** Cambridge Scientific, Inc., 180 Fawcett St., Cambridge, MA 02139 **E-mail:** dtrantolo@aol.com

WITHERSPOON, JOHN T.
Industry: Consulting **Born:** June 25, 1947, Springfield, Missouri **Univ./degree:** B.S., Biology and Chemistry,1969; M.S., Biology and Chemistry, S.W. University Missouri State University, 1971; Ph.D., Environmental Sciences, University of Montana, 1975 **Current organization:** Witherspoon Consulting **Title:** Ph.D./Principal **Type of organization:** Consulting firm **Major product:** Drinking water issues **Area of distribution:** Springfield, Missouri **Expertise:** Water resources **Published works:** 25+ journal articles **Affiliations:** Chair, Safe Drinking Water Commission for State of Missouri, 1995 to present; American Waterworks Association; American Society for Testing and Materials; Water Environmental Federation **Hob./spts.:** Guitar, reading, American history (Civil War), golf **SIC code:** 87 **Address:** Witherspoon Consulting, 1927 E. Lark St., Springfield, MO 65804 **E-mail:** jtwithersp@aol.com

WOLFENSON, AZI U.
Industry: Consulting engineering **Born:** August 1, 1933, Riskani, Romania **Spouse:** Rebeca Sterental **Married:** January 10, 1983 **Children:** Ida, born 1958 (deceased 1994); Jeannette, born 1960; Ruth, born 1962; Moises, born 1966; Alex, born 1970; Michael Ben, born 1989; 9 grandchildren **Univ./degree:** Mech. and Elect. Engineer, 1955; Industrial Engineer, 1967, Univ. Nacional de Ingenieria, Peru; M.S., Industrial Engineering, 1966, Univ. of Michigan; Ph.D., Engineering, Mgmt., 1983, Pacific Western Univ.; Ph.D., Engineering Energy, 1985, Century Univ. **Current organization:** Montecristo Editores/La Razon Newspaper **Title:** Ph.D. Engineering/President/Founder-Director **Type of organization:** Engineering consulting **Major product:** Energy, communications **Area of distribution:** International **Expertise:** Energy, management, project promotion and development **Honors/awards:** Numerous state, city and assoc. medals, distinguishes, diplomas and awards including, Appointed Deputy, 1991; Senator, High Chamber, 1996, Int'l Parliament for Safety and Peace; Medal and Diploma for Distinguished Services, Pres. of Peru and Minister of Energy and Mines, 1980; Medal of Recognition, So. Amer. Electrical Development, 1979-80; Exec. of the Year, Gente Magazine, 1979; Medal of Honor from Capítulo de Ingeniería Eléctrica, CIP Peru, Dec. 2003; Special Award, Gente Magazine, Lima, Peru, 2006 **Published works:** Numerous including, El Gran Desafio 1981; co-author, Hacia una Politica Econòmica Alternativa 1982 **Affiliations:** A.S.M.E.; A.I.I.E.; I.I.E.; MTM Assoc.; A.S.E.E.; A.M.A.; A.I.M.; A.E.P.; Amer. Soc. for the Advancement of Science; Institute of Administrative Mgmt.; A.N.S.; Alumni Associations of the Michigan, Pacific Western and Century Universities; F.I.P.E.; F.I.M.E.; F.I.A.M.; F.I.E.E.; Fellow, British Institute of Mgmt.; Peruvian Assoc. of Journalists; PEN Club Int'l; Swiss Assoc. of Writers; Peruvian Circle of Sport Journalists **Career accomplishments:** Dean of Engineering, Executive President of Electro-Peru, responsible for all the electricity in Peru; Founder of very successful newspapers in Peru **Hob./spts.:** Reading, stamp collecting, art collecting, soccer **SIC code:** 87 **Address:** PROA Project Promotion AG, 3601 N.E. 207th St., #1205, Aventura, FL 33180 **E-mail:** aziwolfenson@aol.com

WOLTERS, HUBERT
Industry: Microelectronics system-on-chips **Univ./degree:** B.S., Physics/Engineering, Muenster University, Germany, 1994; M.B.A., San Francisco State University, 2002 **Current organization:** Sonics, Inc. **Title:** Director, Customer Marketing **Type of organization:** R&D, marketing, sales **Major product:** Semiconductors **Area of distribution:** International **Expertise:** Marketing/sales **Published works:** Articles, journals **SIC code:** 87 **Address:** Sonics, Inc., 2440 W. El Camino Real, Suite 600, Mountain View, CA 94041 **E-mail:** hubertwolters@pacbell.net

WONG, RICHARD H.
Industry: Consumer Electronics **Univ./degree:** B.S.E.E., U.S.D. **Current organization:** Sony **Title:** Design Engineer **Type of organization:** R&D **Major product:** High performance semiconductors **Area of distribution:** International **Expertise:** Front end engineering design, product evaluation, quality assurance, project management, system analysis **SIC code:** 87 **Address:** Sony, 3300 Zanker Rd. MS SJ3A3, San Jose, CA 95134 **E-mail:** richard.@mem.sel.sony.com

WONG, YOUNG M.
Industry: Architecture **Univ./degree:** B.Arch., California Polytechnic University, San Luis Obispo, 1984 **Current organization:** MCG Architector **Title:** Director **Type of organization:** Architecture **Major product:** Architectural services **Area of distribution:** National **Expertise:** Marketing/national accounts **Affiliations:** American Institute of Architects; National Council of Shopping Centers **Hob./spts.:** Martial arts, baseball, soccer **SIC code:** 87 **Address:** 785 Market St., San Francisco, CA 94110 **E-mail:** ywong@mcgarchitecture.com

WOOD, DELORIS GRAY
Industry: Membership organization **Born:** November 16, 1943, Missouri **Univ./degree:** B.S., Southwest Michigan State University; M.A., Southern Illinois University, 1976 **Current organization:** Dent County Historical Society **Title:** President/Activist **Type of organization:** Historical society **Major product:** Publications **Area of distribution:** Missouri **Expertise:** Editor/Activist **Published works:** 1 book **Affiliations:** A.E.J.M.C. **Hob./spts.:** Travel, sports, photography **SIC code:** 86 **Address:** RR5 Box 134, Salem, MO 65560 **E-mail:** tomwood@wavecomputers.net

WOOSLEY, JAMES K.
Industry: Aerospace **Born:** August 8, 1958, Bowling Green, Kentucky **Univ./degree:** B.S., Physics, Western Kentucky University, 1979; M.S., Physics, 1983; Ph.D., Physics, 1987, Vanderbilt University **Current organization:** 3D Research Corp. **Title:** Chief Scientist **Type of organization:** Research and development **Major product:** Testing services, safety analysis **Area of distribution:** International **Expertise:** Operations safety, hazardous material management, space systems technology, chemical agents destruction and environmental consulting to the private and public sectors **Published works:** Papers and essays **Affiliations:** A.P.S.; A.C.S.; A.A.A.S. **Hob./spts.:** Church work, reading, collecting textbooks **SIC code:** 87 **Address:** 3D Research Corp., 7057 Old Madison Pike, Huntsville, AL 35806 **E-mail:** jwoosley@3drc.com **Web address:** www.3drc.com

WRONSKA, DANUTA B.
Industry: Biotech/diagnostic **Born:** November 11, 1964, Piotrkow Trybunalski, Poland **Univ./degree:** Undergraduate Degree, Biology, 1989; Ph.D., Immunology, 1993, Jagiellonian University, Krakow, Poland **Current organization:** IGeneX, Inc. **Title:** Research Director **Type of organization:** Reference laboratory **Major product:** Diagnostic tests for tick-borne diseases **Area of distribution:** International **Expertise:** Oversight of R&D department, designing and developing DNA, introducing new technologies and instrumentation, molecular biology, immunology and protein analysis **Published works:** H. Rokita, W. Branicki, D.B. Wronska, L.K. Borysiewicz and A. Koj. 1998. Vaccinia virus-induced changes in cykotine-regulated acute phase plasma protein synthesis by hepatoma cells. Biochemistry and Molecular Biology International. Vol. 44, No. 6. pp1093-1104; D.B. Wronska, T.A. McNearney and D.R. Karp, 1994. Novel HTLV-I genes in patients with autoimmune disorders. British Society for Immunology, Second Annual Congress, L12; J. Kastura, G. Sowa, D. Wronska. 1993, Induction of DNA synthesis by microtubule depolymerization is mediated by actin filaments. Cytobios 76(305), pp57-74 **Hob./spts.:** Ballroom dancing, interior decorating, reading **SIC code:** 87 **Address:** IGeneX, Inc., 797 San Antonio Rd., Palo Alto, CA 94303 **E-mail:** danutabw2000@yahoo.com **Web address:** www.igenex.com

WRONSKI, HELEN M.
Industry: Social services **Born:** July 23, 1948, Milwaukee, Wisconsin **Univ./degree:** B.S., Education, Alverno College, 1970; Post-graduate Teaching Certificate, University of Wisconsin, 1971; Management Certificate, New School for Social Research, 1999; Business Certificate, Wharton School of Business, 2004 **Current organization:** Morris Area Girl Scouts **Title:** Chief Executive Officer **Type of organization:** Human services organization **Major product:** Youth advocacy, girls 5-17 years old **Area of distribution:** National **Expertise:** Policy, finance, change management **Honors/awards:** Paul Harris Fellow, Rotary International **Affiliations:** Life Member, Girl Scouts of America; Life Member, Association of Girl Scouts Executive Staff **Hob./spts.:** Reading, bicycling, travel, movies **SIC code:** 86 **Address:** Morris Area Girl Scouts, 1579 Sussex Tpke., Randolph, NJ 07869 **E-mail:** ceo@magsc.com **Web address:** www.magsc.com

WUTOH, JEFFREY KOBLAH
Industry: Pharmaceuticals **Born:** October 22, 1963, Australia **Univ./degree:** B.S., Biology & Chemistry, 1987 **Current organization:** Pharma Scientific Inc. **Title:** Chairman/CEO **Type of organization:** Distributor, long term care, pharmacy and research, **Major product:** Pharmaceuticals, medical supplies, chemicals **Area of distribution:** International **Expertise:** Research chemist **Published works:** Write ups **Affiliations:** Chamber of Commerce **Hob./spts.:** Music, travel **SIC code:** 87 **Address:** Pharma Scientific Inc., 12075 B Tech Rd., Silver Spring, MD 21227 **E-mail:** jkwutoh@pharmascientific.com **Web address:** www.pharmascientific.com

WYNN, STEVEANNA
Industry: Social services **Born:** September 26, 1946, Princeton, West Virginia **Univ./degree:** A.A., Virginia Intermont College, 1964 **Current organization:** SHARE Food

Program, Inc. **Title:** Executive Director **Type of organization:** Nonprofit **Major product:** Food distribution **Area of distribution:** Pennsylvania **Expertise:** Building community with affordable food **Hob./spts.:** Dragon boat racing, gardening **SIC code:** 83 **Address:** SHARE Food Program, Inc., 2901 W. Hunting Park Ave., Philadelphia, PA 19129 **E-mail:** swynn@sharefoodprogram.org **Web address:** www.sharefoodprogram.org

XU, CHRISTINE RONG
Industry: Biopharmacutical **Born:** China **Univ./degree:** Ph.D., National University of Singapore, 1999 **Current organization:** NeoTherapeutics Inc. **Title:** Research Scientist **Type of organization:** Pharmaceutical company **Major product:** Central nervous system drugs and anticancer drugs **Area of distribution:** National **Expertise:** Pharmaceutical chemistry (Drug Metabolism and Pharmacokinetics) **Honors/awards:** Travel Award APS of 2nd APS/17th IPS meeting, 2001 **Published works:** Journal of Medicinal Chemistry; Electrophoresis; European Journal of Pharmaceutical Sciences; Journal of Bio-Medical Structure Dynamics **Affiliations:** A.A.P.S.; A.P.S.; A.A.C.P. **SIC code:** 87 **Address:** NeoTherapeutics Inc., 157 Technology Dr., Irvine, CA 92618 **E-mail:** cxu@neot.com

YAGI, HARUHIKO
Industry: Government/research **Born:** Sendai, Japan **Univ./degree:** Ph.D., Pharmaceutical Institute of Tohoku, Japan **Current organization:** National Institutes of Health **Title:** Ph.D., Staff Scientist **Type of organization:** Government/research facility **Major product:** Chemical carcinogenesis **Area of distribution:** National **Expertise:** Bioorganic chemistry **Published works:** 500+ papers **Affiliations:** American Chemical Society **Hob./spts.:** Fishing **SIC code:** 87 **Address:** National Institutes of Health, 11 Candlelight Ct., Potomac, MD 20854 **E-mail:** haruhikoy@intra.riddle.nih.gov

YANKELEVICH, MARK A.
Industry: Consulting Engineers (Construction) **Born:** February 27, 1937, Kiev, Ukraine **Univ./degree:** Candidate of Sci., Ukraine Research Institute of Building Structures, 1969; Dr.Sci., Moscow Civil Engineering Institute, 1989 **Current organization:** Weidlinger Associates, Inc. **Title:** Senior Engineer **Type of organization:** Engineering consultants **Major product:** Structural projects **Area of distribution:** International **Expertise:** Professional Engineer, Structural engineering registered in the State of Massachusetts since 1994 **Hob./spts.:** Mountain skiing **SIC code:** 87 **Address:** Weidlinger Associates, Inc., 1 Broadway, 11th floor, Cambridge, MA 02142 **E-mail:** myankelevich@ma.wai.com **Web address:** www.wai.com

YEARICK, CHRISTOPHER J.
Industry: Construction **Born:** October 8, 1970, Oceanside, California **Univ./degree:** B.A., Montana State University, 1996 **Current organization:** Pilari Architects, Inc. **Title:** Principal Architect **Type of organization:** Architectural firm **Major product:** Architecture **Area of distribution:** Bozeman, Montana **Expertise:** Commercial architecture **Affiliations:** A.I.A.; M.C.A.R.B. **Hob./spts.:** Golf, skiing **SIC code:** 87 **Address:** Pilari Architects, Inc., 2011 N. 22nd Ave., Suite 3, Bozeman, MT 59718 **E-mail:** pilariarch@pilari.com **Web address:** www.pilari.com

YGUERABIDE, JUAN
Industry: Biotechnology **Born:** October 9, 1935, Laredo, Texas **Univ./degree:** B.S., Biology and Chemistry, St. Mary's University, 1957; Ph.D., Physical Chemistry, Notre Dame University, 1962 **Current organization:** Genicon Sciences Corp. **Title:** Vice President of Research **Type of organization:** Research and development, manufacturing **Major product:** Medical and laboratory detection products **Area of distribution:** International **Expertise:** Research and development **Published works:** 80 peer-reviewed articles, 5 book chapters, 2 patents, 7 patents pending **Affiliations:** A.A.A.S.; A.C.S.; Biophysical Society; Professor Emeritus, University of California at San Diego **Hob./spts.:** Family, running, fishing **SIC code:** 87 **Address:** Genicon Sciences Corp., 11535 Sorrento Valley Rd., San Diego, CA 92121 **E-mail:** jyguerabide@geniconsciences.com **Web address:** www.geniconsciences.com

YING, Z. CHARLES
Industry: Government/R&D **Born:** September 29, 1960, Shanghai, China **Univ./degree:** B.S., Physics, Peking University; Ph.D., Physics, Cornell University **Current organization:** National Institute of Standards and Technology **Title:** Physicist **Type of organization:** Government R&D laboratory **Major product:** R&D **Area of distribution:** International **Expertise:** Scientist **Affiliations:** A.V.S.; O.S.A. **SIC code:** 87 **Address:** National Institute of Standards and Technology, 100 Bureau Dr., MS 8520, Gaithersburg, MD 20898 **E-mail:** zcharlesying@msn.com

YLLIMORI, RAÚL
Industry: Financial **Born:** March 27, 1960, La Paz, Bolivia **Univ./degree:** Ph.D., Business Administration, Ashford University, 2002 **Current organization:** Y&C Associates CPA **Title:** President **Type of organization:** CPA firm **Major product:** Tax preparation, consulting **Area of distribution:** Virginia **Expertise:** Accounting, consulting **Hob./spts.:** Soccer, golf, chess **SIC code:** 87 **Address:** Y&C Associates CPA, 900 S. Washington, Suite G-17, Falls Church, VA 22046 **E-mail:** info@ycassociates.com **Web address:** www.ycassociates.com

YOUNG, EMMA J.
Industry: Chemical demilitarization **Born:** November 15, 1952, Itta Bena, Mississippi **Univ./degree:** Attended Pine Voc-Tech (SEARK), Dale Carnegie's Management Training, Dale Carnegie's Communication/Management **Current organization:** Washington Group International, Inc. **Title:** Process Supervisor **Type of organization:** Demilitarization **Major product:** Toxic chemical stockpiles **Area of distribution:** Arkansas **Expertise:** Operations **Hob./spts.:** Sewing, fishing, walking, church activities, sports-watching **SIC code:** 87 **Address:** Washington Demilitarization Co., 7013 Dollarway Rd., Pine Bluff, AR 71602-3016

YOUNG, GORDON W.
Industry: Clubs **Born:** June 1, 1960, Pasadena, California **Univ./degree:** B.S., Culinary Arts, California Culinary Academy, 1989 **Current organization:** Pacific Golf & Country Club **Title:** Executive Chef **Type of organization:** Country club **Major product:** Food, beverage, golf **Area of distribution:** San Clemente, California **Expertise:** Regional American cuisine **Hob./spts.:** golf, fishing **SIC code:** 86 **Address:** Pacific Golf & Country Club, 200 Avenida La Pata, San Clemente, CA 92673 **E-mail:** gordonyoung69@hotmail.com

YOUNG, JEFFREY A.
Industry: Internet consulting **Born:** February 23, 1961, Pittsburgh, Pennsylvania **Univ./degree:** M.S., International Management, University of Maryland, 1996; J.D., UCLA, 1986 **Current organization:** Proteus, Inc. **Title:** Chief Operating Officer **Type of organization:** Privately held stock company **Major product:** Software applications **Area of distribution:** National **Expertise:** Strategy, financial and capital administration **Honors/awards:** Technology Achievement, Group Executive Recognition Award **Published works:** Young, J., (July, 1999). Seed Capital: The Key to Urban Technology Development. WWW.BRT-Inc.Org/ Journal Seed Capital The Key to Urban Technology DevelopmentHTM.; Young, J.; (June 1992). Allocating Claims Risk in Employee Relocation. 38 The Practical Lawyer 63.; Young, J., (May 1998) Future Development of the Telecommunications Marketplace. 1 Customer Choice and Utility Competition Report20. **Affiliations:** V.P., Princeton Class of 1983; Advisor, Springboard Org.; Advisor, Horizon Mezzanine Fund, LLP **Hob./spts.:** Basketball, tennis, golf **SIC code:** 87 **Address:** Proteus, Inc., 1101 15th St. N.W. #1010, Washington, DC 20005 **E-mail:** jyoung@proteus.com

YOUNG, SUSAN FRANCES
Industry: Charity **Born:** February 5, 1954, Rochelle, Illinois **Univ./degree:** B.S., Western Illinois University, 1976 **Current organization:** Lions of Illinois Foundation **Title:** Programs/Social Services Coordinator **Type of organization:** Nonprofit **Major product:** Charitable services for the vision/hearing impaired **Area of distribution:** Illinois **Expertise:** Social services **Honors/awards:** Listed in Who's Who of American Women **Affiliations:** Franklin Grove Area Historical Society; Ogle County Farm Bureau Board Business Services Committee; Ogle County Agriculture Literacy Committee; Vince Carney Community Theater; Rochelle Lioness **Hob./spts.:** Travel, walking, hiking, collecting teddy bears, theatre **SIC code:** 83 **Address:** Lions of Illinois Foundation, 2814 Dekalb Ave., Sycamore, IL 60178 **E-mail:** sfy76@tbc.net

YOUTCHEFF, JOHN SHELDON
Industry: Engineering **Born:** April 16, 1925, Newark, New Jersey **Univ./degree:** Ph.D., University of California at Los Angeles, 1953 **Current organization:** Self employed **Title:** Ph.D. **Type of organization:** Consulting **Major product:** Systems effectiveness **Area of distribution:** International **Expertise:** Space systems/defense systems **Affiliations:** A.M.S. **Hob./spts.:** Swimming, hiking, flying **SIC code:** 87 **Address:** 1400 S. Joyce St., #1406, Arlington, VA 22202 **E-mail:** jyoutcheff@earthlink.net

YU, ED K.
Industry: Management consulting **Born:** August 29, 1959, Hong Kong **Univ./degree:** B.S., Mechanical Engineering, University of California at Berkeley, 1983; M.S., M.B.A., Mechanical Engineering/Management, Santa Clara University, 1992 **Current organization:** PRTM **Title:** Director **Type of organization:** Consulting firm **Major product:** Business process implementation to high technology **Area of distribution:** International **Expertise:** Product development **Honors/awards:** 1patent **Published works:** Journals **Affiliations:** P.D.M.A.; P.M.I.; I.D.E.M.A. **SIC code:** 87 **Address:** PRTM, 1503 Grant Rd., Suite 200, Mountain View, CA 94040 **E-mail:** eyu@prtm.com

ZAMBRANA, JAIME R.
Industry: Consulting/Engineering **Born:** June 5, 1975, Cabo Rojo, Puerto Rico **Univ./degree:** B.S.C.E., University of Puerto Rico, 2000 **Current organization:** Jaime R. Zambrana, Private Consultant **Title:** Engineer **Type of organization:** Private consulting **Major product:** Hydraulics and water resources engineering **Area of distribution:** Puerto Rico **Expertise:** Engineering **Honors/awards:** National Collegiate Engineering Award Winner **Affiliations:** A.S.C.E.; Puerto Rico College of Engineering and

Surveying **Hob./spts.:** Golf, reading, mountain biking **SIC code:** 87 **Address:** Jaime R. Zambrana, P.E., Private Consultant, P.O. Box 396, Cabo Rojo, PR 00623 **E-mail:** ss845@yahoo.com

ZAVARZIN, VAL G.
Industry: Medical **Born:** September 21, 1965, Soviet Union **Univ./degree:** Novosibirsk State University, Russia, 1987 **Current organization:** Penn Technologies, Inc. **Title:** Dr. **Type of organization:** Research and development **Major product:** Medical imaging equipment **Area of distribution:** International **Expertise:** Physics **Published works:** 20 papers **Affiliations:** I.E.E.E. **Hob./spts.:** Photography **SIC code:** 87 **Address:** Pem Technologies, Inc., 553 California St., Newton, MA 02460 **E-mail:** zawarzin@bu.edu

ZELLERS, JAMES EDWARD
Industry: Food **Born:** April 19, 1967, Dover, New Jersey **Univ./degree:** A.A.S., Culinary Arts **Current organization:** Lords Valley Country Club **Title:** Executive Chef **Type of organization:** Private club **Major product:** Catering to members only **Area of distribution:** National **Expertise:** Gourmet cuisine **Hob./spts.:** Animals, hiking, dining, travel **SIC code:** 86 **Address:** Lords Valley Country Club, 1004 Hemlock Farms, Lords Valley, PA 18428 **E-mail:** lvccchef@ptd.net

ZHOU, PING
Industry: Research/Aerospace **Born:** April 21, Beijing, China **Univ./degree:** B.S., University of Chemical Technology at Beijing, China, 1969 **Current organization:** Stanford University, Hansen Lab **Title:** Engineer **Type of organization:** University **Major product:** Higher education **Area of distribution:** National **Expertise:** Gravity Probe B Mission, Accelerometers **Honors/awards:** Chinese Academy of Science 2nd Class Achievement **Published works:** Over 40 publications **Affiliations:** ASM-International, Materials Research Society **Hob./spts.:** Reading, hiking **SIC code:** 87 **Address:** Stanford University, Hansen Lab, Stanford, CA 94305 **E-mail:** ping@relgyro.stanford.edu

ZHU, TONG
Industry: Agriculture **Born:** May 11, 1962, Beijing, China **Univ./degree:** Ph.D., Arizona University, 1992 **Current organization:** Torrey Mesa Research Institute, Syngenta **Title:** Principal Scientist **Type of organization:** Research & development **Major product:** Agricultural chemicals, seeds **Area of distribution:** International **Expertise:** Discovery research **Published works:** Articles, book chapters, abstracts **Affiliations:** American Society of Plant Biologists **SIC code:** 87 **Address:** Syngenta, 3054 Corn Wallis Rd, Research Triangle Park, NC 27709 **E-mail:** tong.zhu@syngenta.com

ZIERDT, CHARLES H.
Industry: Healthcare/research **Born:** April 24, 1922, Pittsburgh, Pennsylvania **Univ./degree:** Ph.D., George Washington University, 1967 **Current organization:** National Institute of Health **Title:** Senior Research Associate (Retired) **Major product:** Medical research **Area of distribution:** National **Expertise:** Microbes of medical importance, 40 years of lab research **Published works:** 150 articles **Affiliations:** University of Michigan; Pennsylvania State University **Hob./spts.:** Antique cars, gardening **SIC code:** 87 **Address:** 4100 Norbeck Rd., Rockville, MD 20853

ZLATANIC, SANJA
Industry: Engineering **Born:** May 7, 1963, Tuzla, Yugoslavia **Univ./degree:** B.S., Structural Engineering, School of Civil Engineering, Belgrade, Yugoslavia, 1988 **Current organization:** Parsons Brinckerhoff, Inc. **Title:** Project Manager/Professional Associate **Type of organization:** Consulting firm **Major product:** Project design documents, project management **Area of distribution:** International **Expertise:** Complex underground structures and tunnels **Published works:** 8 articles **Affiliations:** American Society of Civil Engineers **Hob./spts.:** Skiing, tennis **SIC code:** 87 **Address:** Parsons Brinckerhoff, Inc., 469 Seventh Ave., 14th floor, New York, NY 10018 **E-mail:** szlatani@mta-esa.org **Web address:** www.parsonsbrinckerhoff.inc.

ZOOG, G. DEREK
Industry: Engineering **Univ./degree:** B.S.M.E., Drexel University, 1982 **Current organization:** Bonnett Associates, Inc. **Title:** Chief Mechanical Engineer **Type of organization:** Architectural/engineering firm **Major product:** Drawings and specifications **Area of distribution:** Pennsylvania **Expertise:** HVAC; Registered PE, 2004 **Affiliations:** A.S.H.R.A.E.; A.S.P.E. **Hob./spts.:** Fishing, golf **SIC code:** 87 **Address:** Bonnett Associates, Inc., 220 Baldwin Tower Blvd., Eddystone, PA 19022 **E-mail:** dzoog@bonnettassociatesinc.com

ZUCKER-SCHARFF, THOMAS C.
Industry: Healthcare **Born:** March 29, 1959, New York, New York **Univ./degree:** B.S., Elementary Education, Northeastern University **Current organization:** Albert Einstein Cancer Center, Chanin 206 **Title:** Director, Computing & Information Services **Type of organization:** Medical research, education **Major product:** Cancer research and education **Area of distribution:** International **Expertise:** Webmaster, maintenance, security, training; Created the first Albert Einstein website, 1992 **Affiliations:** Association of Information Technology Professionals; Center Info Tech Group **Hob./spts.:** Biking, gardening, Palm Pilots **SIC code:** 87 **Address:** Albert Einstein Cancer Center, Chanin 206, 1300 Morris Park Ave., Bronx, NY 10461 **E-mail:** tzs@cyberdude.com

Miscellaneous

BARBEE, ELSIE A.
Industry: Art **Title:** Artist **Type of organization:** Art studio **Major product:** Paintings **Expertise:** Watercolor and oil paintings **SIC code:** 89 **Address:** Elsie Barbee's Art Works, 113 Golf Club Lane, Springfield, TN 37172

BEGUHN, SANDRA E.
Industry: Poetry **Current organization:** Self employed **Title:** Poet/Writer **Type of organization:** Writing **Major product:** Poetry, publications **Area of distribution:** National **Expertise:** Poetry **Honors/awards:** Multiple awards from American Biographical Institute and International Biographical Association, Cambridge, England; Famous Poets Society Poet of the Year Medallion 2000, Muse of Fire Award 2000 and Medal for Poetry 2002; Senior Olympics Regional 3rd place Medal for Poetry; Listed in Who's Who in the 21st Century, Who's Who in the World 2002; Who's Who in American Women, 2000, 2001, 2002; Certificate of Recognition, Famous Poet for 2002, Famous Poets Society; Shakespeare Award and Medal, 2002; Six Editors Choice Awards, Dec. 2002, International Library of Poetry, poetry.com **Published works:** 90 poems including, The Silent Voice of God, They Call it Aurora Borealis, Earthbound, Just Another Face in the Crowd, Wordsworth's Morning, Roy Rogers Beyond The Sunset, When Angels Descend, Cards, E., Ageless Peace, Teddy Bear's Promise, Saddle Bags, A Canyon Concert, Bessie's Bell, Dude's Opinion, Why, Shaman's Flight, Diana, Cappuccino Cowboy, My Daddy's Eyes, An Audience of One, The Butterfly Outside The Window and Using My Head **Affiliations:** National Library of Poetry; Past President, Mu Chi Sigma Sorority; Famous Poets Society; Sparrowgrass Poetry Society; The Poetry Guild; The Capper's Weekly; Starburst Journal Famous Poets Society; Wyoming Poets; Michigan Poets; Durango Colorado Cowboy Poetry Gathering 5th year; Grace United Methodist Church; Range Writers; Arizona Poets Association **Hob./spts.:** Reading, travel **SIC code:** 89 **Address:** 2115 W. 34th St., Davenport, IA 52806-5301 **E-mail:** xalthim@mchsi.com

BIRKBECK, RAYNES E.
Industry: Fine arts **Born:** February 2, 1956, Bronx, New York **Current organization:** S.A.G.E. **Title:** Painter/Sculptor/Sketch Artist **Type of organization:** Art studio **Major product:** Paintings, drawings, sculptures **Area of distribution:** New York, New York **Expertise:** Sketch artist **Affiliations:** Hudson Guild S.A.G.E.; Gay Men's Health Crisis; South Bridge Senior Center **Hob./spts.:** Museums, theater, reading **SIC code:** 89 **Address:** 102 W. 75th St., Apt. 56, New York, NY 10023-1907 **E-mail:** uraynus01@aol.com **Web address:** www.visualarts.com; www.sage.com; www.gmhc.com

BLOCH, ELEANOR SALESKY SPATER
Industry: Dispute resolution **Born:** May 14, 1936, Boston, Massachusetts **Univ./degree:** B.S., New York University, 1969 **Current organization:** County of Marin **Title:** Mediation Coordinator **Type of organization:** Community mediation program **Major product:** Settlement of disputes **Area of distribution:** Marin County **Expertise:** Mediation coordinating **Affiliations:** A.C.R.; Dispute Resolution Dept. for A.B.A. **Hob./spts.:** 7 grandchildren, 1 great grandchild, music, art, theatre **SIC code:** 89 **Address:** City of Marin, 4 Jeannette Prandi Way, San Rafael, CA 94903 **E-mail:** ebloch@marin.org

BRAUN, WARREN L.
Industry: Writing **Born:** August 11, 1922, Postville, Iowa **Spouse:** Lillian C. Braun **Married:** May 24, 1942 **Children:** Dikki Ciechanski **Univ./degree:** B.S.E.E., Valparaiso Technical Institute, Indiana; Radio Engineering, Capitol Radio Engineering Institute, DC; Business Administration, Alexander Hamilton Institute, New York; Honorary D.Sc., Shenandoah College & Conservatory, 1987 **Title:** Chairman Emeritus of the Board, ComSonics Inc., Professional Engineer, Inventor, Environmentalist, Theologian, Writer **Type of organization:** Self employed writer **Major product:** Books **Area of distribution:** National **Expertise:** Writing, teaching, consulting engineering in following fields-CATV, broadcast systems, audio visual systems, acoustics **Honors/awards:** Jefferson David Medal (UDC), 1961; Engineer of the Year, 1965; Honorary Member, Junior Chamber of Commerce, 1966; Fellow, Audio Engineering Society; Man of the Year, Harrison/Rockingham County Merchants Association; ASE International Award, 1969; E.H. Rietzke Award, 1972; Fellow, International Consular Academy; Distinguished Service Award, VSPE, 1974; Executive of the Year, Professional Secretaries International, 1983; Businessman of the Year, Harrison-Rockingham County Chamber of Commerce, 1985; Virginia Cable Television Association's Hall of Fame Award, 2002 **Published works:** 29 books and papers, 22 patents **Affiliations:** I.E.E.E.; Audio Engineering Society; International Broadcasters Society; American Institute of Electrical Engineers; Acoustical Society of America; National Society of Professional Engineers; Virginia Society of Professional Engineers; Society of Motion Pictures and Television Engineers **Career accomplishments:** In his career he has designed many cable television systems, 2 television stations, 5 AM & FM stations and over a hundred various acoustical projects **Hob./spts.:** Gardening, woodwork, golf **SIC code:** 89 **Address:** 680 New York Ave., Harrisonburg, VA 22801 **E-mail:** wlb81110@ntelos.net

BUCHANAN, ROBERT
Industry: Photography **Born:** August 9, 1949, White Plains, New York **Current organization:** Robert Buchanan Photography **Title:** Owner **Type of organization:** Professional photography service **Major product:** Photography **Area of distribution:** International **Expertise:** Photography, marketing businesses **Affiliations:** C.P.W.N.F. **Hob./spts.:** Fishing, hiking, trap shooting, reading, writing **SIC code:** 89 **Address:** Robert Buchanan Photography, 10 Lafayette Ave., White Plains, NY 10603 **E-mail:** bbucha3458@aol.com **Web address:** www.comm-photog.com

ERIKSON, J. ALDEN
Industry: Writing/nuclear science **Born:** March 3, 1926, Milwaukee, Wisconsin **Univ./degree:** B.S., Chemistry, University of Wisconsin, 1950; Ph.D., Chemistry, Massachusetts Institute of Technology., 1953 **Current organization:** Author House **Title:** Author **Type of organization:** Writing, publishing **Major product:** "Models of Reality" for Static, Nuclei and Atoms **Expertise:** Theoretical nuclear science **Honors/awards:** Presenter of the first paper on static nuclear models, A.C.S. in Chicago, 1967; Man of the Year, American Diagraphical Institute, 2007; Outstanding Professional of the Year, International Biographical Center, England, 2007; Strathmore's Who's Who, 2007 **Published works:** Book, "Models of Reality" for Static, Nuclei and Atoms (introduces the carbon atom as an icosahedron formed from two hydrogen - 3 and two helium three nuclei with two electrons inside the nucleus and four outside providing the valence of 4. Carbon is the core for key elements, isotopes in the periodic table) **Affiliations:** American Chemical Society; U.S. Army, 1944-46; PPG Industries (Retired after 35 year career of making resins, coatings vehicles and 30 U.S. patents) **Hob./spts.:** Gardening, pets, walking **SIC code:** 89 **Address:** 4212 E. Ewalt Rd., Gibsonia, PA 15044

EVRARD, JOHN T.
Industry: Writing **Born:** June 26, 1948, Evansville, Indiana **Univ./degree:** B.A., Arts, University of Illinois, 1970; M.A., English, 1971; Master of Liberal Arts, 1999, University of Chicago; J.D., DePaul University, 1980 **Current organization:** Self-employed writer **Major product:** Books **Area of distribution:** National **Expertise:** Prose fiction, human rights, legal research and editorial assistance **Honors/awards:** Listed in American Directory of American Scholars **Published works:** Novel, "Capitol Partners", 2 book chapters, 7 articles **Affiliations:** Board of Directors, Glen Ellyn Childen's Chorus **Hob./spts.:** Playing the hammer dulcimer, gardening, canoeing **SIC code:** 89 **Address:** 22W274 Glen Park Rd., Glen Ellyn, IL 60137 **E-mail:** j_evrard@msn.com

FEUERMAN, CAROLE A.
Industry: Art **Born:** September 21, 1945, Hartford, Connecticut **Univ./degree:** B.A., Fine Arts, School of Visual Arts, 1967 **Current organization:** Feuerman Studios, Inc. **Title:** President **Type of organization:** Art studio **Major product:** Art, sculptures **Area of distribution:** International **Expertise:** Sculpture **Honors/awards:** Amelia Peabody Award; Betty Parsons Sculpture Award; Lovenzo de Medecci Award, Florence, Italy **Affiliations:** Women's Forum; American Women's Economic Development Corp.; N.C.G.R.; I.S.C.; Who's Who In The World Directory of Distinguished Americans, New York & Co. **Hob./spts.:** Astrology, reading, women's groups; visual arts; museums **SIC code:** 89 **Address:** Feuerman Studios, Inc., 350 Warren St., Eighth floor, Jersey City, NJ 07302 **E-mail:** caroljf@mindspring.com

GASKINS, INA RUTH
Industry: Writings **Born:** December 14, 1920, Nashville, Georgia **Univ./degree:** B.A., Liberal Arts, Cecil College, 1941 **Current organization:** NSDAR (Retired) **Title:** Author **Major product:** Family history books **Area of distribution:** Pennsylvania **Expertise:** Writer **Published works:** 2 books **Affiliations:** DAR **SIC code:** 89 **Address:** 1222 Brittany Pointe, Lansdale, PA 19446 **E-mail:** irgd2000@aol.com

GRITSCH, RUTH CHRISTINE LISA
Industry: Editing, translating **Univ./degree:** B.A., Political Science, New York University, 1953 **Current organization:** Self-employed **Title:** Editor **Type of organization:** Publishing **Major product:** Books, articles **Area of distribution:** National **Expertise:** Editing, translating from German and French **Honors/awards:** Who's Who in America and in the World **Published works:** 8 books **Affiliations:** Adams County Arts Council; League of Women Voters **Hob./spts.:** Art collecting, reading, writing (working on a book) **SIC code:** 89 **Address:** 1 West St., Gettysburg, PA 17325 **E-mail:** ruth@superpa.net

HAFT, SANDY M.
Industry: Fine arts/writing **Born:** December 16, 1943, Brooklyn, New York **Univ./degree:** M.S., Marketing, Adelphi University **Current organization:** Rhymetime Poetry **Title:** Professor Emeritus **Type of organization:** Internet marketing of poetry **Major product:** Custom created poetry **Area of distribution:** National **Expertise:** Writing and marketing poetry **Affiliations:** Vice President, National Computer Club **Hob./spts.:** Poetry **SIC code:** 89 **Address:** 702 Elton Ct., St. James, NY 11780 **E-mail:** prohaft@rhymetime.com **Web address:** www.rhymetime.com

HERRANEN, KATHY
Industry: Art **Born:** Zelienople, Pennsylvania **Univ./degree:** A.A., Scottsdale Community College **Current organization:** K. Herranen Illustrations **Title:** Owner/Artist **Type of organization:** Retail, manufacturing, creating **Major product:** Paintings: pastel, charcoal, pencil, pen and ink, hand-painted and stained-glass wind chimes **Area of distribution:** National **Expertise:** Portraits **Honors/awards:** First Place Award: Phoenix, Arizona, Arts Council (Juried), "Draw the Line", 2003; First Place Award: N.A.S.F. Fine Artists, Phoenix, Arizona, 2001; People's Choice: N.A.S.F. Fine Artists, Phoenix, Arizona, 1996; Merit Award: Winter Juried Exhibition, Arizona Pastel Artists Association, 1995; Juried into Fountain Festival Juried Competitive Exhibition of Fine Arts, Fountain Hills, Arizona, 1994; Honorable Mention: Wildlife Painting Exhibit, Scottsdale Community College, Scottsdale, Arizona, 1993; Second Place: Desert Artists Art Corral, Yuma, Arizona, 1982; First Place Award, Potpourri Art Show, Yuma, Arizona, 1981: Subscriber Award, Butte (MT) Arts Council, 1981; Special Award, Scottsdale Studio 13 (Juried), 1991-92; Merit Award, Scottsdale Studio 13 (Juried), 1993, two in 1994 **Published works:** Numerous including: Arizona Art Alliance Brochure, 2001-05; A Peek at the Peak Magazine, October, 1997, "Here and There in Art", Page 33; FRIENDS Chapter Update, May/June, 1997, "Member Spotlight"; Publicity Mailer for Arizona Women's Caucus for Art "Landscapes Real and Imagined", April, 1996, Front and Back Sides; Southwest Creative Sourcebook: 1996 - Page 179 and Illustrations Page I-183; 1995 - page 156 and illustrations Page I-2; PHOENIX Magazine, "Hungry Mind," September, 1993, Page 40; Ellwood City (PA) Ledger, September 16,1993, Front Page, Page 6, Page 15 and September 19, 1993, Front Page; Scottsdale (AZ) Progress, "Scottsdale Life - Arts & Entertainment Guide", November 28, 1991, Front Page; Arizona Portfolio, 1994, Page 143; 1992, Page 87; 1991, Page 35 **Affiliations:** Officer, Arizona Art Alliance; Arizona Pastel Artists; Desert Sage Artists **Hob./spts.:** Stamp collecting, dancing, acting **SIC code:** 89 **Address:** K. Herranen Illustrations, 4114 E. Union Hills Dr., #1011, Phoenix, AZ 85050 **E-mail:** kathyherranen@aol.com

JACKOBOICE, SANDRA K.
Industry: Art **Born:** July 22, 1936, Detroit, Michigan **Univ./degree:** B.A., Aquinas College, Michigan, 1989 **Current organization:** Color Plus Studio/Gallery **Title:** Artist **Type of organization:** Art Studio **Major product:** Pastel/acrylic paintings **Area of distribution:** National **Expertise:** Acrylic and pastel painting **Honors/awards:** Commissioned Work, West Michigan Iris Society, 1994; Botanical Images Award, 1994-5; Who's Who in America; Who's Who of American Women; Artists and Designers, 2000; Who's Who in the World; Signature Member of Pastel Society of America; A Woman of the Year Award, 2000 **Published works:** Numerous newspaper and magazine articles **Affiliations:** Pastel Instructor, Von Liebig Art Center; Coordinator/Instructor, pastel classes, Grand Rapids Art Museum; Exhibition Coordinator, Peninsular Club; Co-founder, Past President, Great Lakes Pastel Society; Founder and Board Member, Southwest Florida Pastel Society; Developed and directed art program for an educational center in Lowell, Michigan; Membership Chair, Elected, International Association of Pastel Societies **Hob./spts.:** Family, golf, travel, reading **SIC code:** 89 **Address:** Color Plus Studio/Gallery, P.O. Box 6775, Lake Dr. S.E., Grand Rapids, MI 49516 **E-mail:** skjartist@aol.com **Web address:** www.skjackoboice.com

JOHNSON, JANE PENELOPE
Industry: Writing/poetry **Born:** July 1, 1940, Danville, Kentucky **Spouse:** William E. Johnson **Married:** July 15, 1958 **Children:** Buddy Johnson; Robbie Johnson **Univ./degree:** Famous Writers School Graduate, Westport, Connecticut, 1967; Honorary Doctor of Letters, London, England, 1993 **Current organization:** Penny Johnson (Pen Name) Free-Lance Writer **Title:** Freelance Songwriter/World Renowned Poet **Major product:** Poems, songs, gospel songs **Area of distribution:** International **Honors/awards:** Most Admired Woman of the Decade; International Woman of the Year, Cambridge, England; 3 time award winner, Woman of the Year, American Biographical Institute; The National Library of Poetry; Listed, International Who's Who of Intellectuals; "Sing Hosanna" CD sent to U.S. troops in Iraq and around the world, Christmas, 2005; Penny's songs No.1 out of 18, Hilltop Records, Hollywood, California; Who's Who of International Poets "Goldpin" sent to Penny Johnson for excellence in poetry and vision; Appointment - Genius Laureate, USA by Janet M. Evans, President, A.B.I.; Inclusion in 500 Greatest Genius Laureates of the 21st Century; Life Member, American Hall of Fame; Marquis Who's Who in the World, 2007; Lifetime Achievement, A.B.I. **Published works:** Books, "Anthology, Treasured Poems of America"; Noble Laureate" from A.B.I.; "Songs of Honour", worldwide - Penny's poem "Introspection" included according to Nigel Hillary, U.K., 2006-07; "A Penny for Your Thoughts", Penny Johnson, Published by Authorhouse, Bloomington, Indiana, 06-30-04- I.S.B.N. #1-4184-2489-7; Currently in Print-A Poetry book warmly written to lift you up and give you hope **Affiliations:** International Order of Merit; World Literary Academy; Deputy Governor, American Biographical Institute of North Carolina; Laureate Founder - International Society of Poets - Advisor, Nobel House - Empire State Bldg. Poetry Office, U.K. - Paris and Tokyo Publishing **Hob./spts.:** Piano, singing, dancing, walking, swimming **SIC code:** 89 **Address:** P.O. Box 8013, Garden Side Branch, Lexington, KY 40504-3010 **E-mail:** pennyspoems@yahoo.com **Web address:** www.poetry.com

JOHNSON, THERESA W.
Industry: Writing **Born:** October 10, 1934, Newport News, Virginia **Current organization:** TWJ Free Lance **Title:** Freelance Writer **Type of organization:** Self-employed **Major product:** Writing historical biographies **Area of distribution:** Carrollton, Virginia **Expertise:** Freelance writing, editing **Published works:** Work published in newspapers **Hob./spts.:** Travel, fishing, outdoor activities, cooking, entertaining **SIC code:** 89 **Address:** TWJ Free Lance, 15275 Candy Island Lane, Carrollton, VA 23314 **E-mail:** sostartwj@aol.com

KIDWELL, ROBERT S.
Industry: Government/industrial services **Born:** January 27, 1941, Washington, D.C. **Univ./degree:** Attended American University and University of Hawaii; Duke University Senior Executive Program **Current organization:** ManTech Enterprise Integration Center (e-IC) **Title:** Vice President/Senior Technical Director **Type of organization:** Government/commercial technology services **Major product:** Advanced information technology services **Area of distribution:** International **Expertise:** Enterprise information interoperability, standards, Internet technologies **Affiliations:** Government Electronic Information Technology Association (GEIA); Association for Enterprise Integrations (AFEI) **Hob./spts.:** Golf, reading **SIC code:** 89 **Address:** ManTech Enterprise Integration Center (e-IC), 1000 Technology Dr., Suite 3310, Fairmont, WV 26554 **E-mail:** kidwellr@mantech-wva.com **Web address:** www.mantech-wva.com

KNOX, HELENE M.
Industry: Editorial **Univ./degree:** Ph.D., English, University of California at Berkeley; M.Div., Starr King School for the Ministry **Current organization:** ProEditing **Title:** Editor **Type of organization:** Translation/editing service **Major product:** Editorial consulting **Area of distribution:** International **Expertise:** Writing, translation, editing, copy editor **Honors/awards:** 2 Fulbright Grants **Affiliations:** National Writers' Union & PEN; Bioneer **Hob./spts.:** Playing the violin, organic gardening, cultural creatives **SIC code:** 89 **Address:** ProEditing, 2625 Alcatraz Ave., #181, Berkeley, CA 94705-2702 **E-mail:** hknox@juno.com

KRISTIN, KAREN
Industry: Art **Born:** August 27, 1943, Los Angeles, California **Current organization:** Sky Art Karen Kristin, Inc. **Title:** Owner **Type of organization:** Artistic services **Major product:** Paintings, murals, handwriting analysis **Area of distribution:** International **Expertise:** Art, handwriting analysis **Affiliations:** American Handwriting Analysis Foundation; American Association of Handwriting Analysts **Hob./spts.:** Art **SIC code:** 89 **Address:** Sky Art Karen Kristin, Inc., 3051 S. Broadway, Englewood, CO 80110 **Phone:** (303)781-5881 **Fax:** (303)781-5889 **E-mail:** skyartkk@aol.com **Web address:** www.skyartkarenkristin.com

NICOLAÏ, MICHELLE M. (ELLE)
Industry: Nonprofit foundation **Univ./degree:** M.B.A., American Graduate School of International Management **Current organization:** The Salamander Fund **Title:** Philanthropist, Author, Artist **Type of organization:** Private, nonprofit foundation **Major product:** Interdisciplinary research, programs and activities in the fields of health, science, art and consciousness **Area of distribution:** International **Expertise:** Researcher, author, artist, philanthropist, advisor **Published works:** 2 books (international business) "World Business Internet Research Guide", "Multilingual International Trade Lexicon"; 1 book (philosophy/self-improvement/psychology) "The Human Life Book" (a lucid guide to conscious living in the new millennium) Co-authors: James Harvey Stout, Nathan Sassover **SIC code:** 89 **Address:** The Salamander Fund, P.O. Box 1385, Beverly Hills, CA 90213 **E-mail:** michellemnicolai@hotmail.com

OATES, ALICE DURFEE
Industry: Writing **Univ./degree:** B.S., Bryant College, Rhode Island; A.S., University of Alaska, 1984 **Current organization:** Alice Durfee Oates **Title:** Author **Type of organization:** Writing **Major product:** Children's books **Area of distribution:** International **Expertise:** Writing, painting **Published works:** Book, "Chirpy the Squirrel" **Affiliations:** President, V.F.W.; Lions Club **Hob./spts.:** Volunteer work **SIC code:** 89 **Address:** 3282 Adams Dr., Fairbanks, AK 99709 **E-mail:** alice.oates@worldnet.att.net

OLSEN, RICHARD J.
Industry: Art **Born:** November 15, 1935, Milwaukee, Wisconsin **Univ./degree:** M.F.A., University of Wisconsin, 1966 **Current organization:** Thunderbird Studio **Title:** Professor of Art, Emeritus **Type of organization:** Private art studio **Major product:** Oil paintings **Area of distribution:** International, national, regional, local **Expertise:** Studio research/painting (drawings and paintings utilizing a personal expressionistic/abstract style of painting) **Published works:** 6 books **Affiliations:** Military Order of the Purple Heart; Committee Member, Northeast Georgia MOPH Chapter 531; V.F.W.; Vietnam Helicopter Pilots Association; Represented in permanent collections: National Vietnam Vets Art Museum, Chicago, IL; National Museum of Fine Art, Hanoi, Vietnam; Georgia World Congress Center, Atlanta, GA; Complex Carbohydrate Research Center, University of Georgia, Athens, GA **Hob./spts.:** Fishing, fly-tying, running, weightlifting, sports **SIC code:** 89 **Address:** Thunderbird Studio, 165 Springdale St., Athens, GA 30605 **E-mail:** richard.j.olsen@att.net **Web address:** www.mercuryartworks.com

RANGOS SR., JOHN G.
Industry: Car wash/charity **Born:** July 27, 1929, Steubenville, Ohio **Univ./degree:** B.S., Houston **Current organization:** CAR SPA/John G. Rangos Charitable Foundation **Title:** Chairman **Type of organization:** Retail/charitable non-profit **Major product:** Specialized car washing/charity **Area of distribution:** National **Expertise:** Administration, operations **Published works:** Article **Affiliations:** Former CEO, Chambers Dev. Co. **Hob./spts.:** Art collector, athletics, politics **SIC code:** 89 **Address:** CAR SPA & John G. Rangos Sr., Charitable Foundation, 1301 Grandview Ave., Pittsburgh, PA 15211

ROSENAU, ANITA H.
Industry: Literature **Born:** August 25, 1923, Philadelphia, Pennsylvania **Current organization:** Private professional **Title:** Poet/Author/Playwright **Major product:** Literature **Area of distribution:** International **Expertise:** Books, plays, poetry **Honors/awards:** Elected to write original 10 minute play to commemorate 100th anniversary of Mary Shelley's book "Frankenstein" **Published works:** "The Story of David", a retelling; "The Story of Job", a retelling; "The Story of Ruth" (as a CD), a retelling; "Poem and Prayer to God" published in an anthology of poetry, "Ideas on Wings"; Many poems and articles published in "The Christian Science Monitor" and "The Christian Science Journal" **Affiliations:** Dramatists' Guild; Life Member, A.S.C.A.P.; Poetry Society of America; Colorado Dramatists **Hob./spts.:** Writing, travel, bridge **SIC code:** 89 **Address:** 424 Sinclair Rd., Snowmass Village, CO 81615 **E-mail:** ahrosenau@aol.com

SANDERS, MARGARET A.
Industry: Charitable organizations **Born:** November 16, 1910, Canton, Kansas **Univ./degree:** B.A., Journalism, University of Missouri, 1932 **Current organization:** United Way, Women's Resource Center, International Schools **Title:** Outstanding Member of Society **Type of organization:** Charity **Major product:** Charitable fund raising **Area of distribution:** International **Expertise:** Fund raising **Honors/awards:** A.A.I.E. Hall of Fame for Recognition of Outstanding Contribution **Published works:** Various publications **Affiliations:** P.W.C.O.; First Woman Air Traffic Controller for the FAA during WWII; Association for the Advancement of International Education; Member, Alexis de Toqueville Society **Hob./spts.:** Photography, travel **SIC code:** 89 **Address:** 4965 Kestral Pkwy. North, Sarasota, FL 34231-2346 **E-mail:** artistam1@aol.com

SCHNEIDER, HAROLD
Industry: Aerospace **Born:** 1930, Cincinnati, Ohio **Spouse:** Joan S. Brown **Married:** 1959 **Children:** Lynn Groden, 46 and Steven K. Schneider, 42 **Univ./degree:** Ph.D., Physics/Mathematics, University of Cincinnati, 1956 **Current organization:** Retired **Title:** Aerospace Professional and Author **Major product:** 258 page recently published by Dorrance/RoseDog Books, "Board Game Tournaments (BGT) for the Fun, Profit & Professionalism of the Public (Unique!)"; 35 page book "Realistically Starting Board Game Tournaments (BGT) for the Fun, Profit & Professionalism of the Public" New way of making a recreational fun living **Area of distribution:** International **Expertise:** Aerospace physics, mathematics, engineering **Honors/awards:** American Men of Science, 1971; Who's Who in the East; Who's Who in the West; Who's Who in the Frontiers of Science, 1984; Who's Who in Technology Today, 1985-86; Sigma Xi (honorary) MIT Chapter; Aerospace Engineer of 2006 **Published works:** Numerous publications including: "Fourth Symposium on Nonlinear Estimation Theory and its Applications", Sep. 10-12, 1973, Sandi ego, CA, Western Periodicals Co., North Hollywood, Ca.: Integral Solutions to a General Class of Non-Linear Estimation and System Identification Problems", H. Schneider. p. 256; Schneider, H., " Part II Real Time Algorithms for Sensitivity Error Analyses, Spline Estimation and Integration", PLSS Project Technical Memorandum LMSC 19-65-6HS-03 5/4/79, Schneider, H., "Method of Modeling, Parameter and State Estimation of Nonlinear Systems", A1AA Journal of Guidance, Control and Dynamics, March-April, 1980; Schneider, H., Reddy, P., "Spline Method for Non-Linear Optimal Thrust Vector Controls for Atmospheric Interceptor Guidance", A1AA Journal vol. 15 no. 4 April, 1977; Reviewed paper for IEEE Journal, 1976 **Affiliations:** American Institute of Aeronautics and Astronautics; American Men of Science, 1971; New York Academy of Sciences, 1978; Invited Lecture, University of Connecticut, 1975 **Career accomplishments:** "The Exact Analytical Solution (in the limit) for Optimal Nonlinear Parameter & State Estimation/System Identification with n'th Order ODE Constraints", 254 pages of theory and systems applications results including realistic systems simulations and real Aircraft Data results-all as confirmation **Hob./spts.:** Checkers, classical music (baroque), history **SIC code:** 89 **Address:** 3913 N. Virginia Rd., Unit 201, Long Beach, CA 90807 **E-mail:** hjq53@aol.com

SKORUPSKY, YURI OLEKSANDROVYCH
Industry: Arts, collectables **Born:** May 13, 1965, Rava-Ruska, Ukraine **Univ./degree:** B.A., Wood Carving/Sculpture, Ivano-Frankovo College of Woodworking Arts, 1984; M.A., Oil Painting & Graphics, L'viv National Institute of Applied and Decorative Arts, 1991; Fine Arts & Graphics, Moscow National University of Fine Arts, 1987 **Current organization:** Dolya Art, Inc. **Title:** President/Owner **Major product:** Oil paintings, pastels, commissioned portraits, design of miniatures, collectibles and memorabilia, military and fantasy figurines in bronze, silver, gold and resin, sculptures of all types and media, icons and murals **Area of distribution:** International **Expertise:** Impressionist Master of the palette-knife, oil paintings, pastels, restoration, appraisals, woodcarving, iconography, murals, sculpting, design and model-making **Honors/awards:** Grant Award, The Illinois Arts Council, Chicago, Illinois, 1999; World Friendship Award (Certificate), Middfest International Foundation, Cincinnati, Ohio,1993; "Master-Golden Hands" Award, Moscow Medal Winner, Moscow, Russia,1987; Best in Profession, Arts Award, Diploma, Third Place Winner, Yaniv College of Woodworking Arts, 1980 **Published works:** International Art Expo New York, 2003 & 2002 Catalogue; International Art Expo California, San Francisco, 2000 Catalogue; Artists of Ukraine, issue 2. Artistic and Biographical Reference - Book; "Freedom" Art Exhibit commemorating the 5th Anniversary of Ukraine's Independence, Biegas Gallery, Detroit, Catalogue 1995; Fate/Dolya Art's Exhibition Minneapolis, Madison, Chicago, 1991-92 Catalogue; Collections - in public and private, The White House, Washington, D.C.; The Illinois Executive Mansion, Springfield, Illinois Governor's Mansion; Cosmopolitan State Bank and Trust, Chicago, Illinois; General Consulate of Ukraine, Chicago, Illinois; Nativity of the Blessed Virgin Mary Ukrainian Catholic Church, Palos Park, Illinois; The Holy Trinity Russian Orthodox Cathedral in Chicago; Museum of Fine Arts, Rava-Ruska, Ukraine; Ukrainian National Museum, Chicago, Illinois; Ukrainian Institute of Modern Art, Chicago, Illinois; Museum of the College of Woodworking, Ivano-Frankovo, Ukraine **Affiliations:** Honorary Member, Ukrainian National Union of Artists; Member, Oil Painters of America; Chicago Artists Coalition; Founding Member, Dolya Artists' Association, Ukraine **Hob./spts.:** Art Collector, photography, music, nature exploration **SIC code:** 89 **Address:** Dolya Art, Inc., 2228 W. Chicago Ave., Chicago, IL 60622 **Web address:** www.dolyaart.com

STRENGTH, SANDRA B.
Industry: Entertainment/art **Born:** August 30, 1943, North Island, California **Univ./degree:** B.A., Stanford University, 1965; Attended Art Center College of Design, 2 years **Current organization:** Sandra B. Strength, Design Consultant **Title:** Design Consultant **Type of organization:** Self-employed/freelance **Major product:** Movies, sets, paintings, interiors, landscaping **Area of distribution:** International **Expertise:** Colors, designs, projects **Hob./spts.:** Volunteer work with the homeless, rehabilitation, reading, painting, surfing **SIC code:** 89 **Address:** 1944 20th St., #4, Santa Monica, CA 90404

STYX, SHERRIE A.
Industry: Art/education **Born:** September 2, 1956, Chicago, Illinois **Univ./degree:** B.S.A., Western Michigan University (M.A. Candidate) **Current organization:** Styx River Art **Title:** Owner **Type of organization:** Exhibitor/seminars artists **Major product:** Stained glass windows **Area of distribution:** Kalamazoo, Michigan **Expertise:** Sculpture/stained glass **Published works:** Who's Who In Genealogy **Affiliations:** Director, Pregnancy Counseling Center **SIC code:** 89 **Address:** 3721 S. Westnege Ave., Suite 108, Kalamazoo, MI 49008 **E-mail:** styxriverart@yahoo.com

SWIT'ZER, CAROLYN J.
Industry: Art/art education **Born:** April 20, 1931, Petowkey, Michigan **Univ./degree:** B.A.; 1953; M.A., 1964, Art & Philosophy, Michigan State University **Current organization:** The Art Studio of Carolyn J. Swit?zer **Title:** Artist/ Art Educator/ Retired Teacher **Type of organization:** Private studio **Major product:** Fine art **Expertise:** Drawings, oils, acrylics, watercolors **Affiliations:** Zonta International; Detroit Institute of the Arts; Michigan Council of Arts; President, The Arts Study Group of Petoskey (established 1896) **Hob./spts.:** Walking, watching sports; noted mentors (Pailthorp, Gustave Hildebrand, Stanley Kellog) **SIC code:** 89 **Address:** The Art Studio of Carolyn J. Swit?zer, 805 Lindell Ave., Petoskey, MI 49770

SZUEBER, JUNE ALAINE
Industry: Fine art **Born:** March 25, 1925, Wyoming **Univ./degree:** B.A., Art and Education, Blue Mountain College **Current organization:** Self-employed **Title:** Artist/Educator **Major product:** Fine arts education **Area of distribution:** California **Expertise:** Realistic, fantasy paintings; Volunteer teacher, St. James Catholic School **Honors/awards:** Volunteer of the Year, 2005 **Affiliations:** Riverside Community Artists Association **Hob./spts.:** Community volunteering **SIC code:** 89 **Address:** 672

Crystal Creek Rd., Perris, CA 92571 **E-mail:** art.teach@verizon.net **Web address:** www.yessy.com and www.artbyjuneszueber.com

VERBY, JANE CRAWFORD
Industry: Writing **Born:** October 3, 1923, Lacrosse, Wisconsin **Univ./degree:** B.A., Carleton College, 1945 **Current organization:** Self employed **Title:** Author **Type of organization:** General **Major product:** Publications **Area of distribution:** National **Expertise:** Editor **Honors/awards:** Distinguished Achievement Award, Carleton College, 1995 **Published works:** Numerous articles,1 non-fiction book, "How to Talk to Doctors", 1 fiction book, "Patterns", Dorchester, New York (Publisher) **Affiliations:** National League of American Pen Women, Inc. **Hob./spts.:** Physical fitness, swimming **SIC code:** 89 **Address:** 9609 Washburn Ave. South, Bloomington, MN 55431

WAGNER, A. JAMES
Industry: Government **Born:** April 12, 1934, Greenwich, Connecticut **Univ./degree:** B.A., Physics, Wesleyan University, 1956; M.S., Meteorology, M.I.T., 1958 **Current organization:** National Centers for Environmental Prediction, NOAA **Title:** Senior Forecaster **Type of organization:** Government/science service and research **Major product:** Weather and climate forecasts **Area of distribution:** National **Expertise:** Long-range weather forecasts **Published works:** Articles in journals **Affiliations:** Past Board Member, Washington Academy of Science; American Meteorological Society; National Weather Association **Hob./spts.:** Music, reading, photography **SIC code:** 89 **Address:** National Centers for Environmental Prediction, NOAA, 5200 Auth Rd., Camp Springs, MD 20746 **E-mail:** james.wagner@noaa.gov **Web address:** www.ncep.noaa.gov

WOODBRIDGE, NORMA J.
Industry: Writings **Univ./degree:** B.S., Nursing, Temple University, 1958; R.N., University of Pennsylvania **Title:** Author **Major product:** Publications - poetry, novels, plays **Expertise:** Writing **Honors/awards:** Honorary Doctorate, World Academy of Arts & Culture, Egypt, 1990; Yaddo Fellowship, 1988, Poet of the Millennium, International Poets Academy, 2000 **Published works:** 8 books **Affiliations:** A.S.C.A.P.; Peace River Writers Group; New Jersey Poetry Society; Society of American Poets **Hob./spts.:** Fishing, clothing design, knitting, piano, travel **SIC code:** 89 **Address:** 2606 Zoysia Lane, North Ft. Myers, FL 33917 **E-mail:** normawriter@earthlink.net

WRAY, JERRY
Industry: Art **Born:** December 15, 1925, Shreveport, Louisiana **Univ./degree:** B.F.A., Newcomb Art School, Tulane University, 1946 **Current organization:** Self-employed **Title:** Artist **Type of organization:** Art studio **Major product:** Art **Area of distribution:** National **Expertise:** Watercolors **Affiliations:** Signature Member, National Watercolor Society; Bossier Arts Council; The Hoover Watercolor Society **Hob./spts.:** Tennis (ranked 12th in U.S. Senior Tennis Circuit) **SIC code:** 89 **Address:** 573 Spring Lake, Shreveport, LA 71106 **Web address:** www.jerrywray.com

WUNDERBAUM TRAINES, ROSE
Industry: Art **Born:** September 13, 1928, Monroeville, Indiana **Univ./degree:** B.S., Speech and Recreation, Central Michigan University; Attended Indiana State and Michigan State Universities **Current organization:** Self-employed **Title:** Metal Sculptor **Type of organization:** Sculpting **Major product:** Whimsical one of a kind sculptures from metals **Area of distribution:** International **Expertise:** Brazed/welded sculptures **Honors/awards:** Numerous awards including: Central Michigan University Alumni Association's Recognition Award, 1991; Central Michigan University Centennial Award, 1992-93; Allied Artists of America Inc. N.Y. Members and Associates Award, 1996; Salmagundi Club, N.Y. Annual Summer Exhibition, 2003; Members Memorial Award, Copley Society of Boston; Award of Signature, CA (Copley Artist) after sculptor's name; Lifetime of Creative Excellence Award, presented by Hilton Head Island SC Art League, 1998; Northwood University's Artist's Award, Midland Center for the Arts, Midland, MI, 2002; over 50 solo exhibitions and many group shows; sculpt works reside in more than half the U.S. and some foreign countries; presenter of informative, informal, fun lecture programs for galleries, museums, conventions, conferences, universities, organizations, schools, art centers and in workshop/studio **Affiliations:** Salmagundi Club; Allied Artists of America; Copley Society of Boston; Hilton Head Art League, Hilton Head Island, SC; International Sculpture Center; Charter Member, National Museum of Women in the Arts, Washington, D.C.; Brass Latch Gallery, Montpelier, IN; Vero Beach Center for the Arts, FL; Boca Museum of Art, Boca Raton, FL; Art Guild, Boca Raton, FL; Art Reach of Mid-Michigan **Hob./spts.:** Tennis, drums **SIC code:** 89 **Address:** 1151 Nettles Blvd., Jensen, FL 34957 **E-mail:** Fundametal2@webtv.net

ZORNES, J. MILFORD
Industry: Art **Born:** January 25, 1908 **Current organization:** Otis Art Institute **Title:** N.A./Artist/Teacher **Type of organization:** Self-employed **Major product:** Paintings, drawings **Area of distribution:** International **Expertise:** Painting, drawing **Honors/awards:** Has appeared in several magazine articles **Published works:** "Milford Zornes", 1993 **Affiliations:** Member, National Academy of Design; National Watercolor Society; Metropolitan Museum of Art; Former Army Artist, U.S. War Department **Hob./spts.:** Travel, literature, reading on tape **SIC code:** 89 **Address:** 2136 Brescia St., Claremont, CA 91711

Governmental Services

ABERNATHY, MICHAEL C.
Industry: Government **Born:** December 7, 1969, Sheffield, Alabama **Univ./degree:** B.S., Mechanical Engineering, Focus on Material Science, Southern University, 1997; M.S., Mechanical Engineering, LSU, 1999 **Current organization:** U.S. Navy **Title:** Lt. **Type of organization:** Government/National Defense **Major product:** Facility maintenance **Area of distribution:** International **Expertise:** Engineering, finance **Published works:** Simulation of Flow Strength & Microstructure of Titanium Aluminide in Hot Forging, Journal of Materials Science **Affiliations:** A.S.M.E.; A.S.M.; S.A.M.E. **SIC code:** 97 **Address:** U.S. Navy, 1311 Tenth St. Southeast, Suite 102, Washington, DC 20374-5095 **E-mail:** abernathy.michael@pwcwash.navy.mil

ABU, TIJANI J.
Industry: Government **Born:** Auchi, Edo State. Nigeria **Univ./degree:** A.I.S.T., Chemistry/Biochemistry, University of Ibadan/Institute of Science & Technology, London, 1976; B.A., Health Services Administration, 1980; M.P.A., Financial Mgt., 1982, Eastern Washington University; Ed.S., University of Missouri, 1985 **Current organization:** City of Phoenix, Water Services Laboratory **Title:** Chemist **Type of organization:** Municipal government/water and wastewater **Major product:** Process, compliance monitoring and research of water/wastewater **Area of distribution:** National **Expertise:** Chemistry, operations, research; Professional Certifications: ADEQ Grade IV Certifications in Wastewater Collections, ADEQ Grade IV in Wastewater Treatment, ADEQ Grade I in Water Production, ADEQ Grade I in Water Distribution **Affiliations:** A.W.W.A.; Board Member, Atlantic Club of Greater Kansas City, Missouri, 1988-90; Board Member, Arizona Swimming Gauchos, Glendale, Arizona, 2004-06 **Hob./spts.:** Reading, swimming, social events **SIC code:** 95 **Address:** City of Phoenix, Water Services Laboratory, Bldg. 31, 2474 South 22nd Ave., Phoenix, AZ 85009 **E-mail:** Tijani.Abu@phoenix.gov

ADAMS, E. JAMES
Industry: Government **Born:** February 14, 1937, Bixby, Oklahoma **Current organization:** City of Fruita **Title:** Mayor/Business Owner **Type of organization:** Government **Major product:** General government and healthcare services **Area of distribution:** Fruita, Colorado **Expertise:** Administration, public speaking **Hob./spts.:** Hunting, woodworking **SIC code:** 91 **Address:** City of Fruita, 325 E. Aspen, Fruita, CO 81521 **E-mail:** mhopkins@fruita.org **Web address:** www.fruita.org

ADELY, JOHN E.
Industry: Government/engineering **Born:** November 12, 1959, Fuhais, Jordan **Univ./degree:** M.S., Structural Engineering, Manhattan College, 1983 **Current organization:** New York State Thruway Authority **Title:** Professional Engineer **Type of organization:** State government **Major product:** Engineering consulting **Area of distribution:** New York **Expertise:** Engineering **Affiliations:** A.S.C.E. **Hob./spts.:** Computers **SIC code:** 96 **Address:** 20 Dexter Rd., Yonkers, NY 10710 **E-mail:** johnadely@aol.com

AJEMBA, IGNATIUS O.
Industry: Government **Born:** November 17, 1957, Lagos, Nigeria **Univ./degree:** M.S., Howard University, 1984 **Current organization:** D.C. Water & Sewer Authority **Title:** Project Manager **Type of organization:** Government/municipal water and sewer utility **Major product:** Water distribution, sewer and wastewater treatment **Area of distribution:** Lanham, Maryland **Expertise:** Engineering, construction management **Affiliations:** A.S.C.E.; A.C.I. **SIC code:** 95 **Address:** 7604 Newburg Dr., Lanham, MD 20706 **E-mail:** iajemba@dcwasa.com

ALLOCCO, MARCIA A.
Industry: Government/national research laboratory **Born:** June 9, 1967, Buffalo, New York **Univ./degree:** M.S., Environmental Management, University of Maryland, University College, 2002 **Current organization:** Brookhaven National Laboratory **Title:** Staff Engineer **Type of organization:** Federal government/research laboratory **Major product:** Environmental research **Area of distribution:** Upton, New York **Expertise:** Environmental compliance **Honors/awards:** Brookhaven National Laboratory Spotlight Award for 1995, 2000, 2002 **Affiliations:** United States Power Squadrons **Hob./spts.:** Boating, hiking **SIC code:** 95 **Address:** Brookhaven National Laboratory, Bldg. 120, P.O. Box 5000, Upton, NY 11973 **E-mail:** allocco@bnl.gov

ALNAJJAR, MIKHAIL S.
Industry: Research and development **Univ./degree:** B.S., Chemistry, St. Michael's College, Vermont; M.S., Chemistry; Ph.D., Chemistry, State University of New York at Albany, 1983 **Current organization:** Battelle Pacific Northwest National Lab **Title:** Senior Scientist **Type of organization:** Industrial, Environmental and Governmental **Major product:** Research and Intellectual Properties **Area of distribution:** National **Expertise:** Basic Research including Kinetics and Mechanisms of organic free Radical Chemistry **Honors/awards:** Invited on research scholarships to Northwestern University as well as the National Research Council in Canada **Published works:** 70+ authored and co-authored articles, patents and presentations **Affiliations:** American Chemical Society **Hob./spts.:** Soccer, Field & Track, Volleyball, Tennis **SIC code:** 96 **Address:** Battelle Pacific Northwest National Lab, Battelle Blvd., Box 999-K2-57, Richland, WA 99352 **E-mail:** ms.alnajjar@pnl.gov

ANDERSON, JAMES D.
Industry: Government **Born:** August 3, 1941, Des Moines, Iowa **Univ./degree:** B.A., Econ/Bus. Admin., Drake University; M.P.A., Drake University, 1979 **Current organization:** Iowa Dept. of Management **Title:** Senior Fiscal & Policy Analyst **Type of organization:** State government **Major product:** State government planning and finance **Area of distribution:** Iowa **Expertise:** Fiscal and policy planning; Certified Government Financial Manager, CGFM- **Honors/awards:** Honorary Iowa State Trooper; Iowa National Guards Commanders Award for Public Service **Affiliations:** American Society for Public Administration; Section on Public Budgeting and Finance; Association of Government Accountants; Member , P.A.A., National Honor Society in Public Affairs and Administration; Past Scout Leader - received Scouter's Key; Past State Treasurer and Administrative V.P., Iowa Jaycees; Past President, Des Moines Chapter Assoc. of Gov't Accts. **Hob./spts.:** Civil War history and writing, Genealogy **SIC code:** 93 **Address:** Iowa Dept. of Management, 4011 Beaver Ave., Des Moines, IA 50310-2829 **E-mail:** janders5858@aol.com

ANDRUS, MARTHA W.
Industry: Government **Born:** Grambling, Louisiana **Univ./degree:** B.S., Biology, Grambling University, 1960; M.S., Biology, Southern University, 1967 **Current organization:** City of Grambling, Louisiana **Title:** Mayor **Type of organization:** Municipal government **Major product:** Public services **Area of distribution:** Grambling, Louisiana **Expertise:** Administration, teaching **Affiliations:** Delta Sigma Theta Sorority Inc.; Retired Teachers Association; New Rocky Valley BC **Hob./spts.:** Reading, gardening **SIC code:** 91 **Address:** City of Grambling, Louisiana, 2045 Martin Luther King, Jr. Ave., Grambling, LA 71245 **E-mail:** mbwandrus@yahoo.com

ANSCHUTZ, MICHELLE J.
Industry: Government/transportation **Born:** October 16, 1963, Topeka, Kansas **Univ./degree:** B.A., Design and Management, Washburn University, Kansas, 1986; B.S., Engineering, University of Kansas, 1991 **Current organization:** Kansas Dept. of Transportation **Title:** Construction Engineer **Type of organization:** State agency **Major product:** Construction of bridges and highways **Area of distribution:** Kansas, Missouri, Nebraska, Oklahoma, Colorado **Expertise:** Construction engineering **Affiliations:** National Society of Professional Engineers; Kansas Society of Professional Engineers; Zoning Board of Appeals for Horton, Kansas; Planning Board for Horton, Kansas; Horton Lion's Club **Hob./spts.:** Watching movies **SIC code:** 91 **Address:** Kansas Dept. of Transportation, 1686 First Ave. East, Horton, KS 66439-0151 **E-mail:** michelle@ksdot.org

APPELLA, DANIEL H.
Industry: Health sciences **Born:** July 20, 1971, Washington, D.C. **Univ./degree:** Ph.D., Organic Chemistry, University of Wisconsin, 1998 **Current organization:** National Institute of Health, NIDDK **Title:** Principal Investigator **Type of organization:** Government research **Major product:** Basic research **Area of distribution:** National **Expertise:** Organic chemistry **Affiliations:** American Chemical Society **Hob./spts.:** Cooking **SIC code:** 96 **Address:** National Institute of Health, NIDDK, 9000 Rockville Pike, Bldg. A, Room 1A21, Bethesda, MD 20892 **E-mail:** appellad@niddk.nih.gov

ARNOLD, ALLEN W.
Industry: Government/law enforcement **Born:** December 22, 1973, Nashville, Tennessee **Univ./degree:** Tennessee Technical School **Current organization:** Bedford County Jail **Title:** Lieutenant **Type of organization:** County jail **Major product:** Incarceration **Area of distribution:** Bedford County, Tennessee **Expertise:** IT, records **Honors/awards:** Service Certificate for Achievement **Hob./spts.:** Farming, physical fitness **SIC code:** 92 **Address:** Bedford County Jail, 210 N. Spring St., Shelbyville, TN 37160 **E-mail:** arnold303@bellsouth.net

ARONSON, ANNMARIE
Industry: Government/water purification **Born:** September 1, 1951, Orsova, Romania **Univ./degree:** Institute of River & Navigation, Romania, 1975; B.S., M.A., Criminal Justice, Loyola University of Chicago, 1999; J.D., Valparaiso University School of Law, Indiana, 2004 **Current organization:** Metropolitan Water Reclamation District Chicago **Type of organization:** Government agency **Major product:** Water purification **Area of distribution:** Chicago, Illinois **Expertise:** International business **Affiliations:** A.B.A.; International Foreign Relations; Delta Kappa; Illinois State Bar Association **Hob./spts.:** Reading, dancing, music, all sports **SIC code:** 96 **Address:** Metropolitan Water Reclamation District Chicago, 100 E. Erie, Chicago, IL 60611 **E-mail:** annmarie.aronson@valpo.edu

ARRINGTON, FRANK
Industry: Government/construction **Born:** December 10, 1954, Pikeville, Kentucky **Current organization:** Architect of the Capital **Title:** Construction Representative **Type of organization:** Federal government **Major product:** Construction **Area of distribution:** Washington D.C. **Expertise:** Structural and civil engineering, quality control inspection **Hob./spts.:** NASCAR, auto racing, sports **SIC code:** 99 **Address:** Architect of the Capital, 517 Second St., U.S. Capital, Washington, DC 20515 **E-mail:** farringt@aoc.gov

AXLEY, BARBARA J.
Industry: Government/healthcare **Born:** March 28, 1943, Knoxville, Tennessee **Univ./degree:** B.S., Emory University **Current organization:** Cobb/Douglas Counties Boards of Health **Title:** A.P.R.N., B.C. **Type of organization:** County government **Major product:** Health services **Area of distribution:** Austell, Georgia **Expertise:** Women's health **Affiliations:** Georgia Nursing Association **Hob./spts.:** Gardening, reading, hiking, travel, hunting, tennis, swimming, church activities **SIC code:** 94 **Address:** Cobb/Douglas County Boards of Health, 3685 Humphries Hill Rd., Austell, GA 30168

BACON, TERRY W.
Industry: Government/law enforcement **Born:** June 1, 1959, Louisville, Kentucky **Univ./degree:** Criminal Justice, University of Louisville **Current organization:** West Buechel Police Dept. **Title:** Assistant Chief Lieutenant **Type of organization:** Police department **Major product:** Public order, safety and law enforcement **Area of distribution:** West Buechel, Kentucky **Expertise:** Department administration oversight; Cadet Explorers Program **Affiliations:** Fraternal Order of Police, Lodge 32 **Hob./spts.:** Football, basketball **SIC code:** 92 **Address:** West Buechel Police Dept., 3705 Bashford Ave., Louisville, KY 40218-2509 **E-mail:** tbwbpd@yahoo.com

BAGGETT, JESSICA A.
Industry: Government/law **Born:** March 31, 1966, Chicago, Illinois **Univ./degree:** B.A., Women's Studies, Ohio State University, 1988; J.D., Ohio Northern Pettit College of Law, 1993 **Current organization:** Lorain County Juvenile Ct. **Title:** Magistrate, Juvenile Intake Dept. **Type of organization:** Government/county juvenile court **Major product:** Juvenile law **Area of distribution:** Ohio **Expertise:** Domestic relations, juvenile law **Hob./spts.:** Cooking, baking **SIC code:** 92 **Address:** Lorain County Juvenile Ct., 9967 S. Murray Ridge Rd., Elyria, OH 44035 **E-mail:** janae19893@yahoo.com

BAILEY, RANDY H.
Industry: Government/water treatment **Born:** Princeton, West Virginia **Univ./degree:** Certified Water Treatment Licensed **Current organization:** Borough of Tuckerton Water and Sewer Dept. **Title:** Superintendent **Type of organization:** Municipal government **Major product:** Water and wastewater treatment **Area of distribution:** Tuckerton, New Jersey **Expertise:** Overall operations and administration **Affiliations:** American Waterworks Association; New Jersey Water Association; Water Environment Association **Hob./spts.:** Music (bass guitar, guitar) **SIC code:** 95 **Address:** Borough of Tuckerton Water and Sewer Dept., 140 E. Main St., Tuckerton, NJ 08087 **E-mail:** tuckertonwatersewer@comcast.net

BAILEY JR., ROBERT G.
Industry: Government/telecommunications **Born:** May 10, 1952, Gulfport, Mississippi **Univ./degree:** Mississippi State Law Enforcement Academy Graduate, 1977; F.B.I., National Academy Graduate, 1983; B.S., Public Safety and Telecommunications, Jacksonville State University, 2005 **Current organization:** Harrison County Emergency Communications Commission **Title:** Telecommunications Manager **Type of organization:** County government **Major product:** Public safety telecommunications **Area of distribution:** Harrison County, Mississippi **Expertise:** Help establish a countywide public radio system focused on safety telecommunications; lecturing statewide; Certified Telecommunications Instructor **Honors/awards:** The 1st Nationally Certified Emergency Number Prof. in Mississippi **Published works:** Articles, newsletter contributions **Affiliations:** State Chapter President 2002-2004, National Emergency Number Association; Association of Public-Safety Communications Officers **Hob./spts.:** Sailing, cooking, gardening **SIC code:** 96 **Address:** Harrison County Emergency Communications Commission, 15309-B Community Rd., Gulfport, MS 39503 **E-mail:** harrison911@co.harrison.ms.us

BAKER, LOCY L.
Industry: Government **Born:** November 19, 1945, Abbeville, Alabama **Univ./degree:** A.A., Administration, Alabama State University, 1978 **Current organization:** Alabama House of Representatives **Title:** Legislator **Type of organization:** State government **Major product:** Legislation **Area of distribution:** Alabama **Expertise:** Legislation, administration **SIC code:** 91 **Address:** Alabama House of Representatives, 1057 County Rd. 53, Abbeville, AL 36310 **E-mail:** locy@gte.net **Web address:** www.legislature.state.al.us/house/represent

BALDWIN, WILLIAM M.
Industry: Government/law enforcement **Born:** February 22, 1971, Lowell, Massachusetts **Univ./degree:** Attended Franklin Pierce College for Criminal Justice **Current organization:** Atkinson Police Dept. **Title:** Lieutenant **Type of organization:** Municipal government **Major product:** Public order, safety and law enforcement **Area of distribution:** Atkinson, New Hampshire **Expertise:** Administration **Affiliations:** Vice Chair, Timberlane Regional School; Law Enforcement Executive Development Association; Executive Board Member, New Hampshire Traffic Safety Institute **Hob./spts.:** Football, basketball, family **SIC code:** 91 **Address:** Atkinson Police Dept., 27 Academy Ave., Atkinson, NH 03811 **E-mail:** wbaldwin@atkinsonpolice.us

BALL, BRENT
Industry: Government/Law Enforcement **Univ./degree:** B.A., Physical Education & Speech, University of Utah, 1965 **Current organization:** Summit County Sheriff's Office **Title:** Lieutenant **Type of organization:** Sheriff's office **Major product:** Public order and safety, law enforcement **Area of distribution:** Summit County, Utah **Expertise:** Communications, staff oversight **Honors/awards:** Appointed by the Governor to the 911 Committee **Hob./spts.:** Farming **SIC code:** 92 **Address:** Summit County Sheriff's Office, 6300 N. Silver Creek Dr., Park City, UT 84098 **E-mail:** bball@co.summit.ut.us

BARBEE, ANDRIA L.
Industry: Government/health **Born:** October 11, Washington D.C. **Current organization:** D.C. Department of Health **Title:** Special Projects Coordinator **Type of organization:** D.C. Government **Major product:** Community services **Area of distribution:** Washington D.C. **Expertise:** Student internship program **Hob./spts.:** Working with students, helping people **SIC code:** 94 **Address:** D.C. Department of Health, 825 N. Capitol St. N.E., Washington, DC 20002 **E-mail:** albarbee@msn.com

BARKER, PATSY
Industry: Government/public service **Univ./degree:** Leadership courses, University of Tennessee at Obion, 2006 **Current organization:** Town of Obion **Title:** Mayor **Type of organization:** Municipal government **Major product:** Public services - water, sewer, gas **Area of distribution:** Obion, Tennessee **Affiliations:** Mayors Association of Tennessee; Obion County Leadership **Hob./spts.:** Reading, gardening **SIC code:** 95 **Address:** Town of Obion, 137 E. Palestine, Obion, TN 38240 **E-mail:** townofobion@charterinternet.com

BARNES, ARTHUR J.
Industry: Financial **Born:** July 21, 1952, Manila, Alabama **Univ./degree:** B.B.A., Stillman College, 1974 **Current organization:** City of Mobile - Treasury **Title:** Investment - Treasury Officer **Type of organization:** Local government **Major product:** Financial services **Area of distribution:** International **Expertise:** Fiscal management **Honors/awards:** Grad Project Blueprint, 1990; Grad-Leadership Mobile Class, 1992; President's Citation, National Association for Equal Opportunity in Higher Education; Certified Municipal Finance Administrator **Affiliations:** National President, M.T.A.; I.I.A. **Hob./spts.:** Hunting, surfing the internet, travel, reading, fishing **SIC code:** 99 **Address:** City of Mobile - Treasury, 205 Government St., Mobile, AL 36602 **E-mail:** barnes@cityofmobile.org

BASKIN, STEVEN IVAN
Industry: Government/pharmacology/toxicology **Univ./degree:** Pharm.D. with Honors, U.S.C., 1966; Ph.D., Pharmacology/Toxicology, Ohio State University, 1971 **Current organization:** U.S. Army Research Chemical Defense **Title:** Research Fellow **Type of organization:** Government/military **Major product:** Drug discovery, antidotes, analysis, biochemistry **Area of distribution:** International **Expertise:** Cardiovascular, neuro endocrine, chemical terrorism **Honors/awards:** Merck Book Award, 1966; Achievement medal for Civilian Service - 1999 **Published works:** Numerous articles including, Baskin, S.I., Greenberg, M.I., Levy, P.I., Knaub, M., Roberts, J.R. and Kendrick, Z.V.: Use of endotracheal administration of epinephrine. Pharmacology 21:3, 1977; Krusz, C., Dix, R.K. and Baskin, S.I.: Factors that effect endogenous content and uptake of taurine in the rat penial. Fed. Proc. 37:907, 1978; Book, " Principles of Cardiac Toxicology", CRC-Telford Press, FL, 1991 **Affiliations:** Fellow, Academy of Toxicological Sciences; Fellow, American College of Clinical Pharmacology; Fellow, American College of Cardiology; Society of Pharmacology and Experimental Therapeutics; Society of Toxicology **Hob./spts.:** Football, judo **SIC code:** 97 **Address:** U.S. Army Research Chemical Defense, 3100 Ricketts Rd., Aberdeen Proving Ground, MD 21010-5400 **E-mail:** sbaskin@comcast.com

BEALS, DONNA M.
Industry: R&D **Univ./degree:** B.S., Marine Science, University of South Carolina, 1981 **Current organization:** Savannah River National Laboratory **Title:** Fellow Scientist **Type of organization:** National Lab **Major product:** Research **Area of distribution:** National **Expertise:** Environmental and forensic science **Affiliations:** American Society for Testing and Materials **Hob./spts.:** Competing horses **SIC code:** 91 **Address:** Savannah River National Laboratory, Bldg. 735A, Aiken, SC 29808 **E-mail:** donna.beals@srnl.doe.gov

BEAVER, SKIP R.
Industry: Government **Born:** August 21, 1952, Sodus, New York **Univ./degree:** B.A., Business Administration, Empire State College **Current organization:** Town of Greece Police Dept. **Title:** Director of Staff Services/Records **Type of organization:** Local government **Major product:** Law enforcement **Area of distribution:** Rochester, New York **Expertise:** General/project management **Hob./spts.:** Swimming, physical fitness, reading, outdoor activities **SIC code:** 92 **Address:** Town of Greece Police Dept., 400 Island Cottage Rd., Rochester, NY 14612 **E-mail:** sbeaver@rochester.rr.com

BEEFELT, LYLE G.
Industry: Government **Born:** December 10, 1959, Tacoma, Washington **Univ./degree:** B.A., Bringham Young University, 1984 **Current organization:** Prince William County Service Authority **Title:** Senior Financial Analyst **Type of organization:** Government/public authority **Major product:** Water and wastewater management **Area of distribution:** Prince William County, Virginia **Expertise:** Financial management and budgeting **Affiliations:** Association of Financial Professionals **Hob./spts.:** Politics, reading **SIC code:** 95 **Address:** 14856 Keanon Ridge Ct., Manassas, VA 20112 **E-mail:** beefelt@pwcsa.org

BEHM, HANS JOACHIM
Industry: Aerospace **Born:** January 19, 1922, Colonia Independencia, Paraguay **Univ./degree:** M.S., Geology/Geoscience, New York University, 1953 **Title:** Geoscientist (Retired) **Type of organization:** Various scientific research facilities **Major product:** Geology/geoscience research **Area of distribution:** National **Expertise:** Geology, geoscience, petrology, petrography **Honors/awards:** Founder's Award for organizing American Astronautical Society,1958; Election to Sigma Xi, 1953; Fellow, American Association for Advancement of Science, 1961; American Heritage Award, JFK Library for Minorities, 1972 **Published works:** Publications and public speaking: "Geology and Ecology of Ponds and Estuaries", "Remote Sensing", "Water Pollution", "Micropaleontology", "Foraminifera", "Petrology", "Geology of the Moon and Planets", "Meteorology", "The Higher Fungi", "Clouds" **Affiliations:** A.G.I.; A.A.S.; Sigma Xi; S.I.G.S.; S.I.I.A.S.; S.C.A.W.; Greenpeace; W.W.F. Defenders of Wildlife; Friends of Animals: Fund for Animals; P.E.T.A.; Archaeology Society of Staten Island; Protectors of Pine Oak Woods; National Geographic Society; Board Member (Trustee), New York Insitute of Anthropology **Hob./spts.:** Local lecturing **SIC code:** 96 **Address:** 8 Brighton St., #1, Staten Island, NY 10307

BENNETT, CHAUNCEY W.
Industry: Law enforcement **Born:** November 11, 1962, Cortland, New York **Univ./degree:** B.S., Criminal Justice Administration, Almeda University, 2005 **Current organization:** NYS University Police **Title:** Lieutenant **Type of organization:** Police department **Major product:** Safety and law enforcement **Area of distribution:** Cortland, New York **Expertise:** NYS Master Police Instructor Certified, 2006; Certified Radar Instructor; fire arms, interrogation **Affiliations:** International Association of Law Enforcement Fire Arms Instructors; N.E.C.U.S.A. **Hob./spts.:** Playing guitar in band "Taylor Made" **SIC code:** 92 **Address:** NYS University Police, 5345 E. Homer Crossing Rd., Cortland, NY 13045 **E-mail:** chauncey37@hotmail.com

BEREITSCHAFT, FRANK R.
Industry: Government **Born:** December 27, 1945, St. Louis, Missouri **Univ./degree:** M.S., Washington University, 1985 **Current organization:** U.S. Environmental Protection Agency **Title:** Regional Facilities Manager **Type of organization:** Government **Major product:** Public health and safety **Area of distribution:** International **Expertise:** Facilities, safety, health and security management **Published works:** 5 articles **Affiliations:** International Facilities Management Association **SIC code:** 94 **Address:** US Environmental Protection Agency, 1445 Ross Ave., Dallas, TX 75202 **E-mail:** bereitschaft.frank@epa.gov

BERG, MICHAEL R.
Industry: Government/military **Born:** November 23, 1963, Rockford, Illinois **Univ./degree:** B.S., Electrical Engineering, Oklahoma State University, 1986 **Current organization:** Dept. of the U.S. Army **Title:** Chief, Design Branch **Type of organization:** Dept. of Defense **Major product:** Public works **Area of distribution:** Arizona **Expertise:** Engineering **Affiliations:** Society of American Military Engineers **SIC code:** 97 **Address:** Dept. of U.S. Army, Bldg 22422, Sierra Vista, AZ 85635 **E-mail:** michael.berg@hua.army.mil

BERRY, PATRICK L.
Industry: Government **Born:** March 24, 1951, Hillsboro, Ohio **Univ./degree:** B.S., Chemical Engineering, Ohio State University, 1973; M.S., Operations Research, George Washington University, 1986 **Current organization:** U.S. Army Edgewood CB Center **Title:** Technical Architect **Type of organization:** Government/military **Major product:** Defense **Area of distribution:** International **Expertise:** Research and development specializing in technical development of equipment systems designed for biological aerosol detection; Designed and developed the U.S. Army's first fielded bio detection systems (M31/M31A1/M31E2 BIDS) **Honors/awards:** Received three Army R&D Achievement Awards, the Army Meritorious Civilian Service Award and the Army Achievement Medal for Civilian Service; Inducted into Omega Rho and the Honorary Order of the Dragon **Affiliations:** A.I.Ch.E.; A.A.A.R.; I.N.F.O.R.M.S.; I.S.S.S. **Hob./spts.:** Reading, travel, hiking, birding **SIC code:** 97 **Address:** U.S. Army Edgewood CB Center, 5183 Blackhawk Rd., Aberdeen Proving Ground, MD 21010-5424 **E-mail:** patrick.berry@us.army.mil

BETZLER, JOHN R.
Born: July 10, 1927, St. Louis, Missouri **Univ./degree:** B.S., Business Economics, George Washington University, 1950 **Current organization:** North American Aviation, Inc./Military Aircraft Group, McDonnell Douglas Corp. **Title:** Private entrepreneur; Former Eastern Representative, North American Aviation, Inc. and Director of Military Aircraft Group, McDonnell Douglas Corp.; Registered Representative, New York Stock Exchange **Type of organization:** Self employed **Major product:** Inventions, writing, investments **Area of distribution:** National **Expertise:** Marketing, engineering, inventor, author, historian, investments **Hob./spts.:** Sailing, flying airplanes, skiing **SIC code:** 96 **Address:** 1375 Mainsail Dr., #1712, Naples, FL 34114-8808

BHATTACHARYYA, SOMNATH
Industry: Construction/highway design **Born:** May 3, Silver Spring, Maryland **Univ./degree:** B.S., Civil Engineering, Southern Illinois University at Edwardsville, 1998 **Current organization:** Missouri Dept. of Transportation **Title:** Civil Engineer, Highway Designer **Type of organization:** State government **Major product:** Highways, bridge construction, highway design **Area of distribution:** Missouri **Expertise:** Engineering **Honors/awards:** Eagle Award, Boy Scouts, 1984; Red Cross Life Saver Award, 1989; St. Louis Section of the American Society of Civil Engineers Zone III Daniel W. Mead Award for Young Engineers; Deputy Elections Commissioner for Metropolis St. Louis **Published works:** Newsletter articles for Metropolis St. Louis, articles about wine club events and events held for young Indian professionals sponsored through Metropolis St. Louis **Affiliations:** Program Committee, American Society of Civil Engineers; Engineers Club St. Louis; St. Louis International Film Festival; Sangeetha (which promotes classical Indian music in St. Louis) **Career accomplishments:** As a Program Committee Member for American Society of Civil Engineers, he is involved in arranging guest speakers and arranging socials; Through his involvement with the St. Louis International Film Festival, he was able to get Steve Trampe, the owner of Owen Development, to speak at a film festival luncheon showing his documentary, "American Tower"; He also organizes "Celebrate the City" and volunteers for "The Lot" **Hob./spts.:** Reading, writing, physical fitness, travel, international films **SIC code:** 96 **Address:** Missouri Dept. of Transportation, 1590 Woodlake Dr., Chesterfield, MO 63017 **E-mail:** sbhatta27@hotmail.com

BISWAL, NILAMBAR
Industry: Government **Born:** February 20, 1934, Khamar, Orissa, India **Univ./degree:** B.V.Sc., Punjab College of Veterinary Medicine, 1958; M.Sc., Microbiology and Biochemistry, 1963; Ph.D., Microbiology and Virology, 1965, Michigan State University; Post Doctorate, Molecular Virology, University of California at Berkeley, 1967 **Current organization:** USFDA **Title:** Ph.D., Senior Microbiologist **Type of organization:** Government agency **Major product:** Reviewing and approving drugs **Area of distribution:** International **Expertise:** Molecular virology **Published works:** 48 publications on virology **Affiliations:** A.S.M.; A.A.S; Sigma XI; American Cancer Society **Hob./spts.:** Photography, travel **SIC code:** 94 **Address:** 8841 Doves Fly Way, Laurel, MD 20723 **E-mail:** biswal1@comcast.net

BLAKNEY, HAROLD
Industry: Government **Born:** New Hampshire, 1957 **Univ./degree:** A.A.S., Northern Virginia Community College, 1987 **Current organization:** House of Representatives **Title:** Sr. Systems Engineer **Type of organization:** Legislative government **Major product:** Legislation **Area of distribution:** National **Expertise:** Oversees deployment of IT services; Microsoft Product Specialist **Affiliations:** C.N.E. **Hob./spts.:** Water sports **SIC code:** 91 **Address:** House of Representatives, Second and D St. S.W., Washington, DC 20515 **E-mail:** harold.blakney@mail.house.gov

BONAM, JOHN C.
Industry: Government **Born:** June 16, 1949, Jammalamadugu, India **Univ./degree:** M.S., Environmental Engineering, University of New Haven, 1988 **Current organization:** City of Savannah **Title:** Environmental Coordinator **Type of organization:** City government **Major product:** Sanitation **Area of distribution:** Savannah, Georgia **Expertise:** Environmental and civil engineering **Affiliations:** A.S.C.E.; American Public Works Association **Hob./spts.:** Church activities, tennis, basketball **SIC code:** 91 **Address:** 143 Penn Station, Savannah, GA 31410 **E-mail:** jbonam@ci.savannah.ga.us

BOUCHER, DAVID A.
Industry: Government/law enforcement **Born:** May 11, 1951, Santa Maria, California **Univ./degree:** M.A., Public Administration, Utah State University, 2005 **Current organization:** Davis County Sheriff's Office **Title:** Lieutenant **Type of organization:** Sheriff's office **Major product:** Public order, safety and law enforcement **Area of distribution:** Davis County, Utah **Expertise:** Grant writing, statistics, emergency medical services, consulting **Published works:** 2 conference papers **Affiliations:** Lifetime Member, Phi Kappa Phi; American Society for Public Administration **Hob./spts.:** Cycling, flyfishing, skiing instruction **SIC code:** 92 **Address:** Davis County Sheriff's Office, P.O. Box 32, Farmington, UT 84025 **E-mail:** daboucher@msn.com

BRAND, GORDON JAMES
Industry: Government **Born:** July 15, 1952, Oskaloosa, Iowa **Univ./degree:** M.A., University of South Dakota, 1982 **Current organization:** Des Moines Water Works **Title:** Senior Chemist **Type of organization:** Government/water utility **Major prod-**

uct: Potable water **Area of distribution:** Des Moines, Iowa **Expertise:** Water quality **Honors/awards:** Guest Speaker, Mid-West Fish & Wildlife Conference **Published works:** EPA News Notes; CTIC Conference Papers; WQTC proceedings **Affiliations:** A.W.W.A.; Iowa Water Pollution Control Association **Hob./spts.:** Photography **SIC code:** 96 **Address:** Des Moines Water Works, 412 Fleur Dr., Des Moines, IA 50321 **E-mail:** brand@dmww.com

BRAY, PHILIP E.
Industry: Government/law enforcement **Born:** May 6, 1962, Ypsilanti, Michigan **Univ./degree:** A.S., 1994; B.A., Criminal Justice, 1996, Columbia College, Columbia, Missouri **Current organization:** Hanceville Police Dept. **Title:** Chief of Police **Type of organization:** Police department **Major product:** Public order, safety and law enforcement **Area of distribution:** Hanceville, Alabama **Expertise:** 23 years law enforcement and investigative experience; daily operations oversight; loss prevention; investigations; risk analysis; executive protection; fraud detection, theft prevention and physical security; interstate and international background checks; threat and security assessment; hostage/crisis negotiation; Blood Spatter Analyst; Quality Professional Instructor; Anti-Terrorism Advisor **Honors/awards:** Bronze Star Medal; 5 Army Commendation Medals; 7 Good Conduct Medals; Global War on Terrorism Expeditionary Medal; 2 National Defense Service Medals; 2 Meritorious Service Medals; 6 Army Achievement Medals; Armed Forces Expeditionary Medal; Global War on Terrorism Service Medal **Affiliations:** Fraternal Order of Police; Alabama Association of Chiefs of Police; American Legion; Sgt. 1st Class, U.S. Army Criminal Investigation Division **Hob./spts.:** Alpaca farming, raising Great Danes **SIC code:** 92 **Address:** Hanceville Police Dept., 203 Bangor Ave. S.E., Hanceville, AL 35077 **E-mail:** hpdchief@bellsouth.net

BROWN, DENIECE ROBINSON
Industry: Government/social services **Born:** June 15, 1964, Pinewood, South Carolina **Univ./degree:** M.A., Urban Education, Norfolk State University, 2002 **Current organization:** Middlesex County Dept. of Social Services **Title:** Director, Social Services **Type of organization:** Local government agency **Major product:** Social services **Area of distribution:** Local **Expertise:** Social work, administration, child welfare **Affiliations:** B.A.C.W.; V.A.S.W.P. **Hob./spts.:** Reading, travel **SIC code:** 94 **Address:** Middlesex County Dept. of Social Services, P.O. Box 216, Urbanna, VA 23175 **E-mail:** drb119@central.dss.state.va.us

BROWN, LAURICE L.
Industry: Government **Born:** July 15, 1968, Oakland, California **Univ./degree:** B.S., Business Administration, California State University, Hayward **Current organization:** U.S. Dept of Treasury - IRS **Title:** Revenue Agent **Type of organization:** Government **Major product:** Auditing/accounting **Area of distribution:** National **Expertise:** Tax compliance **Hob./spts.:** Reading, travel, investing **SIC code:** 93 **Address:** U.S. Dept of Treasury - IRS, 1301 Clay St., M/S 9905, Oakland, CA 94612 **E-mail:** laurice.brown@irs.gov **Web address:** www.irs.gov

BROWN, SAUNDRA N.
Industry: State Government/correctional facility **Born:** January 25, 1943, Indianapolis, Indiana **Univ./degree:** B.S., Ball State University, 1965; M.S., Secondary Education/English, Indiana University, 1987 **Current organization:** Pendleton Juvenile Correctional Facility **Title:** Teacher **Type of organization:** Indiana Dept. of Correction Maximum Security **Major product:** Education, offender programs **Area of distribution:** Indiana **Expertise:** Teaching English **Honors/awards:** PNJCF Employee of the Quarter, ISTA Minority Educator of the Year, CLD Achievement in Education Award **Affiliations:** NEA; ISTA; PREA; Delta Kappa Gamma **Hob./spts.:** Family, cooking, reading, knitting **SIC code:** 92 **Address:** Pendleton Juvenile Correctional Facility, P.O. Box 900, 9310 S. SR 67, Pendleton, IN 46064 **E-mail:** maka@iquest.net

BROWN, SCOTT R.
Industry: Government **Born:** September 12, 1956, Las Vegas, Nevada **Univ./degree:** B.A., University of Georgia, 1985 **Current organization:** Elko County Nevada **Title:** Director of Planning and Zoning **Type of organization:** Municipality **Major product:** County planning and zoning department **Area of distribution:** Elko County, Nevada **Expertise:** Rural land use planning, master plans for the county, regional presentations **Affiliations:** Emergency Management Institute; Nevada State Board of Professional Engineers and Land Surveyors; American Planning Association; Director Police Athletic League; Floodplain Administrator, Elko County **Hob./spts.:** Fishing, camping **SIC code:** 95 **Address:** Elko County Nevada, 155 S. Ninth St., Elko, NV 89801 **E-mail:** rbrown@elkocountynv.net **Web address:** www.elkocounty.net

BRYANT, JAMES R.
Industry: Government/military **Born:** September 29, 1948, Putnam, Connecticut **Univ./degree:** A.A., Cape Cod Community College; A.S., Community College of Air Force **Current organization:** 10 Fighter Wing **Title:** Wing Weapons Manager **Type of organization:** Military **Major product:** Homeland air defense **Area of distribution:** Massachusetts **Expertise:** Safety **Affiliations:** V.F.W.; Air Force Sergeants Association **Hob./spts.:** Classic cars, running **SIC code:** 97 **Address:** 102 Fighter Wing, 55 Surf Dr., P.O. Box 504, Mashpee, MA 02649-0504 **E-mail:** james.bryant@maotis.ang.af.mil

BURKS JR., CLARENCE H.
Industry: Government **Born:** April 8, 1933, Champaign, Illinois **Univ./degree:** B.S., Science/Education, San Augustine University, 1957; Ph.D., Business Administration, Purdue University, 1968 **Current organization:** Dept. of Public Works **Title:** Supervisor (Retired) **Type of organization:** City organization **Major product:** Community service from inmates **Area of distribution:** National **Expertise:** Supervising functions, advising inmates **Hob./spts.:** Fishing, relaxing **SIC code:** 92 **Address:** 7540 Allenwood Ct., Indianapolis, IN 46268

BURNETT, BRAD
Industry: Government/law **Current organization:** Jefferson County, Texas **Title:** Judge **Type of organization:** Court **Major product:** Justice **Expertise:** Judiciary duties **SIC code:** 92 **Address:** Jefferson County, Texas, 7933 Viterbo Rd., Suite 1, Beaumont, TX 77705 **E-mail:** bburnett@co.jefferson.tx.us

BURNETT, C. DAVID
Industry: Government/law **Born:** August 18, 1941, Blytheville, Arkansas **Univ./degree:** B.A., Political Science, 1964; J.D., 1966, University of Arkansas **Current organization:** Circuit Judge-State of Arkansas **Title:** Honorable **Type of organization:** State government **Major product:** Legal services **Area of distribution:** Arkansas **Expertise:** Circuit Judge **Affiliations:** State Bar of Arkansas; Tennessee Bar Association; Eastern District Court of Arkansas **Hob./spts.:** Hunting, fishing, computers **SIC code:** 92 **Address:** Circuit Judge-State of Arkansas, P.O. Box 1902, Jonesboro, AR 72403 **E-mail:** dburnett@arkansas.net

CALAUTTI, TOMMASO
Industry: Government **Born:** April 19, 1964, Weehawken, New Jersey **Spouse:** Annette **Married:** November 7, 2003 **Univ./degree:** B.S., Construction Engineering, Fairleigh Dickinson University, 1994; M.S. Candidate, St. Peter's College **Current organization:** Town of West New York, Dept. of Public Works **Title:** Project Coordinator/Engineer **Type of organization:** Municipal government **Major product:** Construction for all public facilities, roads and parks **Area of distribution:** West New York, New Jersey **Expertise:** Engineering; construction management **Published works:** Article in Engineering News Record (ENR), Aug. 1998 issue about the project he handled for the City of New York (also quoting and interviewing him) **Affiliations:** A.S.C.E.; C.M.A.A.; B.P.M.I.A. **Career accomplishments:** The success of his construction project for the City of New York and the time frame in which it was completed, was highly recognized by the DEC (Dept. of Design and Construction of New York City) and other firms including Bovis, Inc.; In his present position for the Town of West New York, he has spearheaded all construction, including the restoration and renovation of all the parks as well as the roadways and walkways which currently exist; He continues to work in West New York because of its constant changes and challenges **Hob./spts.:** Reading, weightlifting, hockey, baseball, football; Chief Umpire of West New York Little League **SIC code:** 91 **Address:** 559 Columbia St., New Milford, NJ 07646

CALDWELL, MARCUS N.
Industry: Government/environmental **Born:** January 30, 1973, Smithville, Tennessee **Univ./degree:** A.S., Tennessee Tech, 1994 **Current organization:** DeKalb County Emergency Management Agency **Title:** Deputy Director **Type of organization:** Emergency management **Major product:** WMD/hazardous materials **Area of distribution:** Tennessee **Expertise:** Law enforcement **Affiliations:** E.M.A.` **Hob./spts.:** The outdoors **SIC code:** 95 **Address:** 213 Adams St., Smithville, TN 37166 **E-mail:** caldwellmarcus@yahoo.com

CAMPBELL, RICHARD E.
Industry: Government/law enforcement **Born:** Spokane, Washington **Univ./degree:** B.S., Criminal Justice and Sociology, East Oregon University, 2005 **Current organization:** Cheney Police Dept. **Title:** Lieutenant **Type of organization:** Police department **Major product:** Public order, safety and law enforcement **Area of distribution:** Cheney, Washington **Expertise:** Administration **Affiliations:** W.A.S.P.C.; Fraternal Order of Police; International Association of Chiefs of Police **Hob./spts.:** Boy Scout leader, camping, hiking, reading, church **SIC code:** 92 **Address:** Cheney Police Dept., 215 G. St., Cheney, WA 99004 **E-mail:** rcampbell@cityofcheney.org

CARBERRY-LOUSHAY, MARIAN
Industry: Government **Born:** June 26, 1952, Kyoto, Japan **Univ./degree:** B.S., Information Technology, George Mason University, 1998 **Current organization:** United States Secret Service **Title:** Chief of Property Management Branch **Type of organization:** Government **Major product:** Protecting the nation's leaders, visiting world leaders, national special security events, integrity of the nation's currency and financial systems **Area of distribution:** International **Expertise:** Property management, purchasing and control of service **Affiliations:** Toastmasters **Hob./spts.:** Running, ice skating **SIC code:** 97 **Address:** 5422 Quantas Place, Dale City, VA 22193 **E-mail:** marianloushay@usss.dhs.gov

CARLINI, JOSEPH V.
Industry: Government **Univ./degree:** A.S., Biology, Kingsborough Community College, 1986 **Current organization:** City of Largo, Environmental Services **Title:** Assistant Director **Type of organization:** Government/utilities **Major product:** Environmental control **Area of distribution:** Largo, Florida **Expertise:** Management **Affiliations:** F.W.P.C.O.A. **SIC code:** 95 **Address:** City of Largo, Environmental Services, 5000 150th Ave., Clearwater, FL 33760 **E-mail:** jcarlini@largo.com

CARR, ELAINE G.
Industry: Government **Born:** August 21, 1960, Ventura, California **Current organization:** West Siloam Springs Town City Hall **Title:** Mayor **Type of organization:** Municipality **Major product:** Town management **Area of distribution:** West Siloam Springs, Oklahoma **Expertise:** Second term as Mayor, town development as an entertainment community around the Cherokee Nation Casino **Honors/awards:** Nominated Oklahoma Mayor of the Year, 2003-2006 **Affiliations:** Oklahoma Municipal League; Member, Oklahoma Water Resource Board; Past City Council Member **Hob./spts.:** Music, playing the piano, hiking, the outdoors **SIC code:** 91 **Address:** West Siloam Springs Town, City Hall, 4880 Cedar Dr., West Siloam Springs, OK 74338 **E-mail:** rcarr@CENTRYtel.net

CARROLL, ANDREW R.
Industry: Government/transportation **Born:** June 18, 1948, Dallas, Texas **Univ./degree:** B.S., Civil Engineering, University of Arlington, Texas, 1972 **Title:** Senior Engineer, City of Dallas (Retired) **Type of organization:** City government **Major product:** Transportation services **Area of distribution:** Dallas, Texas **Expertise:** Contract management **Hob./spts.:** Hunting, fishing, Full-time Jeweler, Jewelry by Andy **SIC code:** 91 **Address:** City of Dallas, City Hall L1BN, 1500 Marilla Dr., Dallas, TX 75201 **E-mail:** andy_carroll@sbcglobal.net

CARTER, SHERIAN A.
Industry: Government **Born:** March 24, 1952, San Antonio, Texas **Current organization:** City of Ola **Title:** Mayor **Type of organization:** Municipal government **Major product:** Public services, water **Area of distribution:** City of Ola, Arkansas **Expertise:** Administration; licensed minister **Affiliations:** New Life Outreach; Women's Jail Ministry **Hob./spts.:** Reading **SIC code:** 91 **Address:** City of Ola, 115 W. Pennington, Ola, AR 72853 **E-mail:** sheri@arkwest.com

CASTRO, FEDERICO
Industry: Government/law **Univ./degree:** B.S., University of California, Berkeley, 1954; J.D., University of San Diego School of Law, 1971 **Current organization:** San Diego Superior Court **Title:** Superior Court Judge **Type of organization:** State court **Major product:** Law **Area of distribution:** California **Expertise:** Superior Court Judge **Affiliations:** California Judges Association **Hob./spts.:** Family - spending time with his grandchildren, stock market, reading, history **SIC code:** 92 **Address:** San Diego Superior Court, State of California, 2851 Meadow Lark Dr., San Diego, CA 92123 **E-mail:** federico.castro@sdcourt.ca.gov

CAVALIERI, JOHN D.
Industry: Military **Born:** October 5, 1956, Philadelphia, Pennsylvania **Current organization:** Navy (NSWCCD-Phila) **Title:** Material Handling Team Leader **Type of organization:** Military **Major product:** Defense **Area of distribution:** International **Expertise:** Life cycle manager, Navy In-Service Engineer **Affiliations:** I.E.E.E. **Hob./spts.:** Golf **SIC code:** 97 **Address:** Navy (NSWCCD-Phila), 5001 S. Broad St., Philadelphia, PA 19112 **E-mail:** cavalierijd@nswccd.navy.mil

CETERA, MICHAEL
Industry: Government/architecture **Born:** March 21, 1947, Brooklyn, New York **Univ./degree:** B.A., Architecture, Pratt Institute, 1969 **Current organization:** City of New York/Department of Design & Construction **Title:** Director of Architecture, City of New York **Type of organization:** Government/architecture and planning **Major product:** Architecture design and construction **Area of distribution:** New York, New York **Expertise:** Architecture **Honors/awards:** Excellence in Design **Affiliations:** First Vice Chair, Community Board 9, Brooklyn, New York **Hob./spts.:** Baseball, travel, photography **SIC code:** 91 **Address:** City of New York/Department of Design & Construction, 234 Detroit Ave., Staten Island, NY 10312 **E-mail:** ceteretc@aol.com

CHANDLER, HH
Industry: Government/healthcare **Univ./degree:** B.A., Biology, University of Incarnate Word, 1980 **Current organization:** Virginia Dept. of Health, Eastern Shore Health District **Title:** Medical Technologist **Type of organization:** Department of Health **Major product:** Public healthcare **Area of distribution:** Accomack, Virginia **Expertise:** Clinical laboratory science, phlebotomy and testing, photo-microscopy, management, compliance, safety **Affiliations:** A.S.C.P.; A.S.C.L.S. **Hob./spts.:** Photography, weddings, nature photography, pet portraits **SIC code:** 94 **Address:** 3120 Old Neck Rd., Exmore, VA 23350 **E-mail:** dlc@verizon.com

CHANG, DAVID DAH-CHUNG
Industry: Government **Born:** September 18, 1954, Taiwan **Univ./degree:** B.S./M.S., Civil Engineering, National Cheng Kung University; M.S., Structural Engineering, U.C.L.A. **Current organization:** Building & Safety Dept., City of Los Angeles **Title:** Plan Check Supervisor **Type of organization:** Government/building and construction **Major product:** Building codes and building permits **Area of distribution:** California **Expertise:** Engineering, building codes **Affiliations:** A.S.C.E.; American Concrete Institute; Structural Engineers Association of California; Vice Chair International of Existing Building Code Committee; A.T.C. (Applied Technical Council); E.E.R.I. (Earthquake Engineering Research Institute) **Career accomplishments:** Presentation Speaker for SEAOC Seminars; President of National Cheng Kung University Alumni Association of Southern California; President of National Cheng Kung University Alumni Foundation of Southern California **Hob./spts.:** Physical fitness, reading, travel **SIC code:** 95 **Address:** Building & Safety Dept., City of Los Angeles, 9746 Sunflower St., Alta Loma, CA 91737 **E-mail:** david.chang@lacity.org

CHONG, NATHAN B.N.
Industry: Government **Born:** October 6, 1956 **Univ./degree:** M.S., George Washington University, 1981; B.S.C.E., Purdue University, 1979 **Current organization:** U.S. Army Health Facility Planning Agency **Title:** Director, Project Integration Division **Type of organization:** Government **Major product:** Medical, dental, research facilities **Area of distribution:** International **Expertise:** Engineering **Affiliations:** A.S.C.E.; A.S.H.E. **SIC code:** 94 **Address:** U.S. Army Health Facility Planning Agency, 5109 Leesburg Pike, Suite 679, Falls Church, VA 22041 **E-mail:** nathan.chong@amedd.army.mil

CLAGUE, DAVID L.
Industry: Government/law enforcement **Born:** October 16, Galesburg, Illinois **Univ./degree:** Fellowship Program, FBI National Academy, 2003 **Current organization:** Galesburg Police Dept. **Title:** Lieutenant of Investigations **Type of organization:** City government **Major product:** Public order, safety and law enforcement **Area of distribution:** Galesburg, Illinois **Expertise:** Administration **Affiliations:** Police Benevolent & Protective Association; FBI National Academy Associates **Hob./spts.:** Golf, running **SIC code:** 92 **Address:** Galesburg Police Dept., 150 S. Broad St., Galesburg, IL 61401 **E-mail:** sgtinv@ci.galesburg.il.us

CLARK, DAVID R.
Industry: Transportation **Born:** October 20, 1950, Los Angeles, California **Univ./degree:** B.S.M.E., Pennsylvania State University, 1972 **Current organization:** US Dot/RSPA/OHME **Title:** Environmental Engineer **Type of organization:** Federal government **Major product:** Transportation, compliance **Area of distribution:** National **Expertise:** Environmental engineering **Affiliations:** A.S.M.E.; S.A.E.; A.S.C.E.; Lion's Club **Hob./spts.:** Skiing, golf, Boy Scout Master **SIC code:** 96 **Address:** US Dot/RSPA/OHME, 361 Trappe Lane, Langhorne, PA 19047 **E-mail:** david.clar@rspa.iot.gov **Web address:** www.rspa.dot.gov

CLARK, MARY Y.
Industry: Government **Title:** Mayor **Type of organization:** Municipal government **Major product:** Public services **SIC code:** 91 **Address:** City of Camden, 1000 Lyttleton St., P.O. Box 7002, Camden, SC 29020 **E-mail:** mayor@camdensc.org

CLOHESSY, STEVEN V.
Industry: Government **Born:** December 9, 1952, Staten Island, New York **Univ./degree:** Attended Staten Island Community College, 1971-73 **Current organization:** Housing Preservation & Development N.Y.C. **Title:** Construction Project Manager Level III (Certified) **Type of organization:** City government agency **Major product:** Renovation and restoration of multi-story units for the purpose of housing clients on a transitional basis until permanent housing is located **Area of distribution:** New York **Expertise:** Construction project management **Hob./spts.:** Fishing, boating, travel **SIC code:** 95 **Address:** Housing Preservation & Development N.Y.C., 100 Gold St., New York, NY 10038

COLEMAN, PATRICK S.
Industry: Government/public safety **Born:** July 31, 1975, Lake Charles, Louisiana **Current organization:** Houston River Volunteer Fire Dept. **Title:** Volunteer firefighter **Type of organization:** Volunteer Fire department **Major product:** Fighting fires, fire safety **Area of distribution:** Lake Charles, Louisiana **Expertise:** Volunteer firefighter's

search and rescue; Certified, First Aid, CPR, HAZMAT, Calcasieu Emergency Response Training Center **Affiliations:** Volunteer firefighter for Ward 6 and Carliss Fire Departments **Hob./spts.:** Hunting, fishing, firefighting **SIC code:** 92 **Address:** Houston River Fire Dept., 789 W. Houston Rd., Sulphur, LA 70663 **E-mail:** e911firerescue@aol.com

COLLINS, MARK A.
Industry: Government/law enforcement **Born:** April 10, 1966, Laona, Wisconsin **Univ./degree:** A.S., With Honors, Criminal Justice, Fox Valley Technical College, 1995 **Current organization:** Vilas County Sheriff's Dept. **Title:** Lieutenant **Type of organization:** Sheriff's department **Major product:** Public order, safety and law enforcement **Area of distribution:** Vilas County, Wisconsin **Expertise:** Shift supervision, corrections, dispatch, patrol; Rapid response instructor **Hob./spts.:** Camping, hunting **SIC code:** 92 **Address:** Vilas County Sheriff's Dept., 330 Court St., Eagle River, WI 54521 **E-mail:** macoll@co.vilas.wi.us

COLOMBI, LETITIA G.
Industry: Government **Born:** February 10, 1945, Stamford, Texas **Current organization:** Borough of Haddonfield **Title:** Mayor **Type of organization:** Municipal government **Major product:** Borough services **Area of distribution:** Haddonfield, New Jersey **Expertise:** Public Works **Honors/awards:** Woman of Outstanding Achievement Award, Girl Scouts of America, 2000; Tribute to Women in Industry, Y.W.C.A., 2002; Citizen of the Year, 2000; Alfred E. Driscoll Award for Government **Affiliations:** New Jersey Elected Women Officials; Past President and Member, Camden County Mayors Association, 2005; Past President, New Jersey Mayors Association **Hob./spts.:** Movies, reading, teaching children about government **SIC code:** 91 **Address:** Borough of Haddonfield, P.O. Box 3005, Haddonfield, NJ 08033 **E-mail:** tcolombi@comcast.net

COLONNO, DANIEL JAMES
Industry: Government/law enforcement **Born:** October 2, 1960, Albany, New York **Univ./degree:** B.S., Law Enforcement Management, Madison University, 2006 **Current organization:** Albany NY Police Dept. **Title:** Lieutenant **Type of organization:** City police department **Major product:** Public order, safety and law enforcement **Area of distribution:** Albany, New York **Expertise:** Experienced administrator, law enforcement professional, accomplished Master Police Instructor **Honors/awards:** Life Saving Commendation, Regional Emergency Organization, 2000; Life Saving Medal, Albany Police Dept., 2001 **Affiliations:** Consultant, City of Albany's Corporation Counsel; Dignitary Escort, Soviet-American Law Enforcement Exchange, 1990; Security Consultant/Instructor, International Services Inc., 2002-03 **Hob./spts.:** Family **SIC code:** 92 **Address:** Albany NY Police Dept., 536 Western Ave., Albany, NY 12203 **E-mail:** dcolonno@albany-ny.org **Web address:** www.albany-ny.org

CONNELLY, CHRISTOPHER D.
Industry: Government **Born:** January 25, 1964, Philadelphia, Pennsylvania **Univ./degree:** E.M.T. Degree, Albany Tech Institute; Physics, Drexel University; Defense Acquisition/Logistics Management **Current organization:** Automatic Test Equipment Program Branch **Title:** Project Coordinator **Type of organization:** Military depot **Major product:** Weapon system support **Area of distribution:** International **Expertise:** Automatic test equipment systems development, integration **Hob./spts.:** Scuba diving, travel **SIC code:** 97 **Address:** Automatic Test Equipment Program Branch, 814 Radford Blvd., Suite 20325, Albany, GA 31704-0325 **E-mail:** christopher.connell1@usmc.mil

CONROY, PATRICK J.
Industry: Government water/wastewater utility **Born:** June 8, 1956, New York, New York **Current organization:** Augusta County Service Authority **Title:** Water/wastewater Supervisor **Type of organization:** Municipal utility **Major product:** Drinking water/wastewater treatment **Area of distribution:** Verona, Virginia **Expertise:** S.C.A.D.A. **Affiliations:** S.C. Rural Community Assistance Program; Southeast Rural Community Water Research Committee; Water Environment Federation; Virginia Rural Water Association **Hob./spts.:** Travel **SIC code:** 96 **Address:** Augusta County Service Authority, 18 Government Center Lane, Verona, VA 24482 **E-mail:** pconroy@co.augusta.va.us

COOLEY, LUKE
Industry: Government **Born:** April 3, 1944, Lawton, Oklahoma **Univ./degree:** B.S.W., Florida State University, 1965; M.S.W., University of Alabama; Diplomate, University of Alabama Probate Law School **Current organization:** Houston County **Title:** Judge of Probate **Type of organization:** County government **Major product:** Probate court **Area of distribution:** Houston County, Alabama **Expertise:** Law and legal decision making; Speaker at seminars relating to social work, geriatrics and resource issues **Honors/awards:** Community Leadership Award; Patriotic Employer Award **Published works:** Presentations made to civic groups, church and support groups **Affiliations:** Alabama Probate Judges Association; National Probate Judges Association; National Elections Assistance Commission; Houston County Republican Women; Houston County Republican Executive Committee **Hob./spts.:** Gardening, water sports **SIC code:** 92 **Address:** Houston County, 462 N. Oates St., Dothan, AL 36303 **E-mail:** lbcooley@houstoncounty.org

COOPER, BUEFORD C.
Industry: Government **Born:** December 18, 1922, Bethany, Missouri **Univ./degree:** B.S., University of Missouri, 1950; M.A., Psychology, Ball State University, 1971 **Current organization:** U.S. Air Force, Office of Special Investigations **Title:** Special Agent **Type of organization:** Government **Major product:** National security and defense **Area of distribution:** National **Expertise:** Investigations **Honors/awards:** Inducted in the Hall of Fame, 2005 **Hob./spts.:** Competitive pistol shooting, football, wildlife **SIC code:** 97 **Address:** 25309 E. 250th Ave., Ridgeway, MO 64481 **E-mail:** bcooper@grundyec.net

COUIG, MARY PAT
Industry: Government/healthcare **Born:** August 17, 1956, Evanston, Illinois **Univ./degree:** M.P.H., Johns Hopkins School of Hygiene and Public Health, 1977 **Current organization:** U.S. Public Health Services **Title:** Assistant Surgeon General/Chief Nurse Officer **Type of organization:** Government **Major product:** Public health issues **Area of distribution:** National **Expertise:** Administration, consulting **Published works:** 14 articles **Affiliations:** A.N.A.; A.A.N. **Hob./spts.:** Travel, antiques, the outdoors **SIC code:** 94 **Address:** U.S. Public Health Services, 5600 Fishers Lane, Room 16-85, Rockville, MD 20857 **E-mail:** mcouig@oc.fda.gov

CUETO, LLOYD A.
Industry: Government/law **Born:** April 13, 1951, East St. Louis, Illinois **Univ./degree:** B.A., Political Science, McKendree College, Illinois; J.D., St. Louis University School of Law **Current organization:** State of Illinois **Title:** Circuit Judge **Type of organization:** State government **Major product:** Judiciary duties **Area of distribution:** Illinois **Expertise:** Assigned to major civil cases and complex cases **Honors/awards:** Elected to the position of Circuit Judge in the 20th Judicial Circuit and was sworn in Dec. 1994; Assigned to the Major Felony Division and later became the Presiding Judge of the Felony Division; Was transferred to the Major Civil Division where he has remained until present; Listed in Who's Who of Hispanic America **Affiliations:** Illinois State Bar Association; St. Clair County Bar Association; East St. Louis Bar Association; Illinois Judges Association; Previously served by appointment of the Illinois Supreme Court as a member of the Illinois Judicial Conference Committee on Juvenile Justice; Currently serves by appointment of the Illinois Supreme Court as a member of the Illinois Courts Commission **SIC code:** 92 **Address:** State of Illinois, 10 Public Square, Belleville, IL 62220

CUMMINGS, VIVIAN L.
Industry: Government/Law **Born:** May 30, 1961, Milledgeville, Georgia **Current organization:** Wilkinson County Probate Court **Title:** Probate Judge **Type of organization:** Courthouse **Major product:** Civil law **Area of distribution:** Wilkinson County, Georgia **Expertise:** Small claims, garnishments, wills, FIFA, fire arms, marriage license, traffic **Affiliations:** Judicial Chair of By Laws Committee for State of Georgia **Hob./spts.:** Gospel singing, shopping with daughter (6 year old Makayla) **SIC code:** 92 **Address:** Wilkinson County Probate Court, 100 Bacon St., P.O. Box 201, Irwinton, GA 31042 **E-mail:** judgevivian@hotmail.com

CURRIN III, SAMUEL B.
Industry: Government/law **Born:** July 25, 1946, Oxford, North Carolina **Univ./degree:** J.D., wake Forest University, 1971 **Current organization:** State of North Carolina, Ninth Prosecutorial District **Title:** District Attorney **Type of organization:** Government/Ninth Prosecutorial District of North Carolina **Major product:** Legal services **Area of distribution:** North Carolina **Expertise:** Criminal law **Affiliations:** N.C.C.D.A.; N.C.D.A. **Hob./spts.:** Golf, jogging, reading **SIC code:** 92 **Address:** State of North Carolina, Ninth Prosecutorial District, Granville County Courthouse Annex, Oxford, NC 27565

CUTHBERT, ANDREW J.
Industry: Government **Born:** December 21, 1971, Philadelphia, Pennsylvania **Univ./degree:** B.A., Mechanical Engineering, Temple University, 1999 **Current organization:** USDA **Title:** Mechanical Engineering Technician **Type of organization:** Government/food research **Major product:** Food research **Area of distribution:** International **Expertise:** Engineering **Hob./spts.:** Arts & crafts, house maintenance, reading **SIC code:** 96 **Address:** USDA, 600 E. Mermaid Lane, Wyndmoor, PA 19038

CUZZONE, ANTHONY A.
Industry: Government **Born:** February 12, 1951, Chicago, Illinois **Univ./degree:** Class C EPA Certified Water Operators License; CCCDI Cross Connection Control Device Inspector; IEPA Certified **Current organization:** City of Elmhurst **Title:** Utility Capital Projects Administrator **Type of organization:** Municipal government **Major product:** Public services **Area of distribution:** Elmhurst, Illinois **Expertise:** Sewer and water service **Honors/awards:** Quarter Century Service Award, 2002 **Published works:** 2 articles in American City & County Magazine **Affiliations:** American Waterworks Association; Mid-Central Waterworks Association **Hob./spts.:** Family activities, band drummer, music, travel, fine dining **SIC code:** 91 **Address:** City of Elmhurst, Engineering Division, 209 N. York Rd., Elmhurst, IL 60126 **E-mail:** tony.cuzzone@elmhurst.org

DAVIS, JAMES M.
Industry: Government/financial **Title:** CFE, CEM, District Bank Examiner **Type of organization:** State agency **Major product:** Bank regulation, reports of examination **Expertise:** Supervising bank examiner **Affiliations:** Board Member, Society of Financial Examiners (SOFE) Board of Governors (25 years) **SIC code:** 93 **Address:** Nebraska Dept. of Banking & Finance, 2809 S. 160th St., Suite 308, Omaha, NE 68509 **E-mail:** murleydavis@cox.net

DAWSON, GWENDOLYN B.
Industry: Government **Born:** October 18, 1963, Ocala, Florida **Current organization:** Ocala Housing Authority **Title:** Executive Director **Type of organization:** Government/housing service **Major product:** Housing assistance **Area of distribution:** National **Expertise:** Providing low-income housing **Affiliations:** N.A.F.E.; G.F.O.A.; N.A.H.R.O.; F.A.H.R.O.; N.F.B.P.A. **Hob./spts.:** Reading, volunteering time to community development **SIC code:** 95 **Address:** Ocala Housing Authority, 233 S.W. Third St., Ocala, FL 34474 **E-mail:** ohadawson@aol.com

DELASHMUTT, DEVAN
Industry: Government/education **Born:** May 26, 1971, Pocatello, Idaho **Univ./degree:** B.B.A., Computer Information Systems, Idaho State University, 1995 **Current organization:** Idaho State Dept. of Education **Title:** ISIMS Local Deployment Team Lead/ Educational Technology Specialist **Type of organization:** Government/dept. of education **Major product:** Idaho's educational institutions and public school system **Area of distribution:** Idaho **Expertise:** Educational technology **Affiliations:** I.E.T.A.; P.M.I. **Hob./spts.:** Skiing, mountain biking, hiking **SIC code:** 94 **Address:** 1449 Symphony Ct., Boise, ID 83706

DEVKOTA, LAXMAN M.
Industry: Government/engineering **Born:** January 24, 1955, Nepal **Univ./degree:** B.S., Technology in Civil Engineering, Indian Institute of Technology, New Delhi, India, 1978; M.S., Environmental Engineering, Asian Institute of Technology, Bangkok, Thailand, 1985; Ph.D., Civil (Environmental) Engineering, University of Arizona, 1989 **Current organization:** City of Phoenix, Water Services Dept. **Title:** Research Specialist/Civil Engineer III **Type of organization:** Municipal government **Major product:** Capital improvement programs **Area of distribution:** Phoenix, Arizona **Expertise:** Water and wastewater treatment processes **Honors/awards:** Quentin Mees Research Award, Arizona Water Pollution Control Association, 1996; National Register's Who's Who in Executives and Professionals, 2004-2005 **Published works:** 20 articles **Affiliations:** Past Member, A.S.C.E.; A.W.W.A.; A.W.C.P.A.; Water Environment Federation, Disinfection Committee and Technical Practice Committee for Effluent Disinfection; Golden Key National Honor Society; Committee on Law and Social Sciences, Arizona State University **Hob./spts.:** Family, gardening, poetry **SIC code:** 91 **Address:** City of Phoenix, Water Services Dept., City Hall, 8th Floor, 200 W. Washington, Phoenix, AZ 85003 **E-mail:** laxman.devkota@phoenix.gov **Web address:** www.phoenix.gov

DIAMOND, ANN L.
Industry: Government/law **Born:** 1959, Illinois **Univ./degree:** J.D., Southern Illinois University School of Law **Current organization:** Tarrant County District Attorney's Office **Title:** Chief, Civil Litigation **Type of organization:** Government/District Attorney's office **Major product:** Prosecution **Area of distribution:** Tarrant County, Texas **Expertise:** Litigation, civil issues **Affiliations:** Texas Bar Foundation; Tarrant County Bar Association **Hob./spts.:** Politics, bike riding **SIC code:** 92 **Address:** Tarrant County District Attorney's Office, 401 W. Belknap St., Ft. Worth, TX 76102

DICICCIO, ROBERT JOHN
Industry: Government **Born:** May 16, 1953, Philadelphia, Pennsylvania **Current organization:** U.S. Dept. of Agriculture, Eastern Regional Research Center **Title:** Physical Science Research Technician **Type of organization:** Government agricultural research service **Major product:** U.S.D.A. research, fats, oils and animal co-products (FOAC), also BIODIESEL **Area of distribution:** National **Expertise:** Biodiesel testing, lipid analysis, lipid isolation and fractionation **Hob./spts.:** Musician **SIC code:** 96 **Address:** U.S. Dept. of Agriculture, Eastern Regional Research Center, 600 E. Mermaid Lane, Wyndmoor, PA 19038 **E-mail:** rjdc@excite.com

DICKEY, RORY D.
Industry: Government **Born:** December 14, 1965, Benton Harbor, Michigan **Univ./degree:** Attended Lake Michigan College for Trigonometry **Current organization:** City of St. Joseph **Title:** Superintendent Parks & Grounds **Type of organization:** Department of public works **Major product:** Park system **Area of distribution:** St. Joseph, Michigan **Expertise:** Oversight of parks and grounds, maintenance of city owned buildings, marinas and libraries **Honors/awards:** "Spirit of Blossomtime Award' Festival, 2006 **Affiliations:** I.M.S.A. (Traffic Signal); M.R.P.A.; Board Member, Berrien Teachers Credit Union **Hob./spts.:** Collecting and restoring automobiles **SIC code:** 95 **Address:** City of St. Joseph, 700 Broad St., St. Joseph, MI 49085 **E-mail:** dickey@sjcity.com

DIRICO, ROCCO
Industry: Government/environmental **Born:** March 27, 1957, Queens, New York **Current organization:** N.Y.C. Dept. of Sanitation - Support Services **Title:** Assistant Commissioner **Type of organization:** Municipal government agency **Major product:** Sanitation services **Area of distribution:** New York City, New York **Expertise:** Administration of support services **Affiliations:** S.W.A.N.A.; A.T.A.; Board Member, New York City Columbia Association **SIC code:** 95 **Address:** N.Y.C. Dept. of Sanitation - Support Services, 52-07 58th St., Woodside, NY 11377 **E-mail:** rdirico@dsny.nyc.gov

DOUBT, TIM G.
Industry: Government/law enforcement **Born:** January 3, 1967, Branson, Missouri **Current organization:** Salt Lake City Police Dept. **Title:** Lieutenant **Type of organization:** Police department **Major product:** Public order, safety and law enforcement **Area of distribution:** Salt Lake City, Utah **Expertise:** Administration, narcotics, vice, gangs, S.W.A.T., asset/forfeiture **Affiliations:** National Tactical Officers Association; Special Advisor to the Utah Meth-Amphetamine Initiative; Assistant Division Commander for Special Investigations **Hob./spts.:** Golf **SIC code:** 92 **Address:** Salt Lake City Police Dept., 315 E. 200 South, Salt Lake City, UT 84111 **E-mail:** tim.doubt@slcgov.com

DROPE, NILEANE B.
Industry: Government **Born:** October 14, 1935, Leachville, Arkansas **Current organization:** City of Marmaduke **Title:** Mayor **Type of organization:** Mayor's office **Major product:** Government administration **Area of distribution:** Marmaduke, Arkansas **Expertise:** City management **Affiliations:** B.F.W.; Rotary Club; L.S.N.H.D. **Hob./spts.:** Antiques **SIC code:** 91 **Address:** City of Marmaduke, 104 S. First St., Marmaduke, AR 72443

DUFEK, RONALD D.
Industry: Government **Born:** October 20, 1939, Geddes, South Dakota **Univ./degree:** Vocational Degree in Mechanics, South State Teachers College, 1965 **Current organization:** City of Geddes **Title:** City Councilman **Type of organization:** City government **Major product:** Public services **Area of distribution:** Geddes, South Dakota **Expertise:** Economic development, parks, tourism, historical **Affiliations:** South Dakota Public Power Authority; Athletics Booster; Geddes Chamber of Commerce Economic Development Corp; City Council Historical Development Corp; Fur Traders Group **Hob./spts.:** Sporting events **SIC code:** 91 **Address:** City of Geddes, 222 Main St., Geddes, SD 57342 **E-mail:** dufsdfek@midstatesd.net **Web address:** www.geddes.org

DURANT, CAROLYN FREDERICK
Industry: Government **Born:** November 4, 1947, Washington, Pennsylvania **Univ./degree:** B.A., Chemistry, California State College, 1968 **Current organization:** ADEM **Title:** Chemist **Type of organization:** Environmental state agency **Major product:** Inorganic analysis **Area of distribution:** Alabama **Expertise:** Analysis of metals in water, soil, fish **Hob./spts.:** Bowling, badminton, playing triminos **SIC code:** 95 **Address:** 1559 Birchwood Dr. North, Mobile, AL 36693 **E-mail:** cdurant@adem.state.al.us

DYKES, JAMES BART
Industry: Government/law enforcement **Born:** September 20, 1965, Kingsport, Tennessee **Univ./degree:** Attended Excelsior College and Montgomery College **Current organization:** D.C. Metropolitan Police Dept. **Title:** Lieutenant **Type of organization:** Police department **Major product:** Public order, safety and law enforcement **Area of distribution:** Washington, D.C. **Expertise:** Police science **Honors/awards:** Lieutenant of the Year, 3rd District, 2005 **Affiliations:** Boys and Girls Club, Olney Maryland **Hob./spts.:** Coaching and teaching football and wrestling **SIC code:** 92 **Address:** D.C. Metropolitan Police Dept., 300 Indiana Ave., Washington, DC 20009 **E-mail:** james.dykes@dc.gov

EDWARDS, BERNELL COOK
Industry: Government **Born:** April 12, 1939, Muldrow, Oklahoma **Current organization:** Sequoyah County District Court **Title:** Court Clerk **Type of organization:** District court **Major product:** District justice **Area of distribution:** Oklahoma - 15th Judicial District **Expertise:** Serving third administrative term, budget, training **Honors/awards:** Excellence in Management Award, Supreme Court, 1998 and 2000; Selected Career Woman of the Month, Sequoyah County Business and Professional Women, March 2005 **Affiliations:** Sequoyah County Women's Democratic Association; Oklahoma Court Clerk's Association **Hob./spts.:** Walking, teaching Sunday School, crafts, making floral arrangements **SIC code:** 92 **Address:** Sequoyah County District Court, 120 E. Chickasaw, Suite 205, Sallisaw, OK 74955 **E-mail:** bernell.edwards@oscn.net **Web address:** www.oscn.net

EDWARDS JR., JONATHON
Industry: Government **Born:** March 16, 1979, Birmingham, Alabama **Univ./degree:** B.A., Political Science, Florida State University; J.D., Florida State College of

Law, 2004 **Current organization:** Florida Department of Environmental Protection **Title:** Park Planning Assistant **Type of organization:** Government/regulatory **Major product:** Unit management plans for Florida state park system **Area of distribution:** Florida **Expertise:** Land use and policy research **Hob./spts.:** Reading, dancing, physical fitness **SIC code:** 95 **Address:** Florida Department of Environmental Protection, 2924 Miccosukee Rd., #9A, Tallahassee, FL 32308 **E-mail:** jee4325@fsu.edu

EPSTEIN, DAREN ADAM
Industry: Government/military **Born:** October 17, 1964, Lynn, Massachusetts **Univ./degree:** B.A., Political Science, Auburn University, Alabama, 1995; M.A., National Security Affairs, Naval Postgraduate University, 2003 **Current organization:** United States Army **Title:** Major **Type of organization:** Government **Major product:** Defense **Area of distribution:** National **Expertise:** Strategic planning **Affiliations:** Veterans of Foreign Wars; American Legion; Jewish War Veterans of the USA **Hob./spts.:** Foreign affairs, photography, yoga, kayaking, travel **SIC code:** 97 **Address:** 1024 Pacific Grove Lane, Pacific Grove, CA 93950 **E-mail:** darenadam@darenadam.com **Web address:** www.nationalsecurityasia.com

EVANS, CHARLES
Industry: Government/law enforcement **Born:** December 17, 1962, Andrews, Texas **Univ./degree:** Attended Texarkana Community College **Current organization:** Slaton Police Dept. **Title:** Lieutenant **Type of organization:** Local government **Major product:** Public order, safety and law enforcement **Area of distribution:** Slaton, Texas **Expertise:** Criminal investigation **Honors/awards:** 3 Lifesaving Awards; Medal of Valor; Professional Conduct Award **Affiliations:** Lions Club; Masonic Lodge **Hob./spts.:** Bowling **SIC code:** 92 **Address:** Slaton Police Dept., 175 N. 8th St., Slaton, TX 79364 **E-mail:** cevans102@aol.com

EYRE, DAVID C.
Industry: Government **Born:** January 1, 1960, Caldwell, Idaho **Univ./degree:** B.S., U.S. Army Command and General Staff College, 1998 **Current organization:** Colorado Army National Guard **Title:** Lt. Col., Facility Engineering Manager **Type of organization:** National Guard **Major product:** National defense **Area of distribution:** International **Expertise:** Construction, engineering and government management **Affiliations:** National Society of Professional Engineers; Veterans of Foreign Wars; Association of the U.S. Army; American Legion **Hob./spts.:** Skiing, fishing, hunting **SIC code:** 97 **Address:** Colorado Army National Guard, 6848 S. Revere Pkwy., Centennial, CO 80112 **E-mail:** david.eyre@us.army.mil

FANTAUZZI, EGIDIO
Industry: Government **Born:** November 12, 1963, San Juan, Puerto Rico **Univ./degree:** B.SC.E., University of Puerto Rico-1989 **Current organization:** U.S. General Services Administration **Title:** General Engineer **Type of organization:** Government agency **Major product:** Public building services, new construction, alterations and repairs management **Area of distribution:** San Juan, Puerto Rico **Expertise:** Engineering **Honors/awards:** Corner Stone Award **Affiliations:** N.F.P.A., C.I.A.P.R. **Hob./spts.:** Baseball, martial arts (Japanese karate) **SIC code:** 91 **Address:** U.S. General Services Administration, 150 Chardon St., Federal Bldg., Room 359, Hato Rey, PR 00918 **E-mail:** egidio.fantauzzi@gsa.gov

FEARON, LEE C.
Industry: Government/consulting **Born:** November 22, 1938, Tulsa, Oklahoma **Univ./degree:** B.S., Physics,1961; B.A., Chemistry, 1962; M.S., Analytical Chemistry, 1969,Oklahoma State University **Current organization:** Washington State Dept. of Ecology, Environmental Assessment Program, Lab Accreditation Unit **Title:** Chemist **Type of organization:** Government **Major product:** Laboratory auditing, certification **Area of distribution:** National **Expertise:** Environmental chemist **Honors/awards:** Listed in the following Marquis volumes: Who's Who in America, Who's Who in the World, Who's Who in the West and Who's Who in Science and Engineering; Listed in Strathmore's Who's Who **Published works:** U.S. Patent No. 5,340,406, method for removing organic contaminants from soil, August 23, 1994 **Affiliations:** A.C.S.; A.I.C.; A.A.S. **Hob./spts.:** Photography, travel **SIC code:** 95 **Address:** Lee C. Fearon, Box 514, Manchester, WA 98353-0514 **E-mail:** limafox@wavecable.com

FERN, EMMA E.
Industry: Government/law enforcement **Born:** July 22, 1927, Columbus, Ohio **Univ./degree:** B.S., Criminal Justice, Miami Dade Community College, 1976 **Current organization:** Florida Dept. of Law Enforcement **Title:** Certified Criminal Intelligence Analyst **Type of organization:** State government **Major product:** Law and order **Area of distribution:** Florida **Expertise:** Organized crime **Honors/awards:** U.S. Dept. of Justice Award for Public Service; Florida Dept. of Law Enforcement Contribution to Criminal Justice Award **Affiliations:** Founder and Past President , International Association of Law Enforcement Intelligence Analysts (President, South Florida Chapter) since 1980 **Hob./spts.:** Travel, reading, graphoanalysis, calligraphy **SIC code:** 92 **Address:** 1030 N.W. 111 Ave., Miami, FL 33172 **E-mail:** emmafern@fdle.state.fl.us

FISHER, JOHN R.
Industry: Defense **Born:** December 28, 1924, Columbus, Ohio **Univ./degree:** B.Sc., U.S. Naval Academy, 1946; M.S., Civil Engineering, Rensselaer Polytechnic Institute, 1950 **Current organization:** Navy League of the U.S. **Title:** National President (1999-2001); Currently, Chair, Navy League National Advisory Council **Type of organization:** Civilian organization **Major product:** Civilian support for the sea services **Area of distribution:** International **Expertise:** Civil engineering (34 years in U.S. Navy) **Honors/awards:** Golden Eagle Award, Tau Kappa Epsilon; Superior Public Service Awards, Secretary of the Navy and Commandant of the Coast Guard **Published works:** Articles in Sea Power Magazine **Affiliations:** S.A.M.E.; A.S.C.E. **Hob./spts.:** Tennis, golf **SIC code:** 97 **Address:** 10615 E. Arabian Park Dr., Scottsdale, AZ 85258-6021

FLEAGLE IV, GEORGE BENJAMIN
Industry: Government/transportation **Born:** September 16, 1964, York, Pennsylvania **Univ./degree:** B.S., Engineering, Penn State University, 1994 **Current organization:** Federal Highway Administration **Title:** Highway Engineer **Type of organization:** Government agency **Major product:** Highway funding **Area of distribution:** National **Expertise:** Engineering; P.E. Certified **Affiliations:** A.S.C.E. **Hob./spts.:** Family, motorcycling **SIC code:** 96 **Address:** Federal Highway Administration, 228 Walnut St., Room 536, Harrisburg, PA 17101 **E-mail:** georgefleagle@hotmail.com

FOX, JONATHAN D.
Industry: Government/military **Born:** September 11, 1956, New York, New York **Univ./degree:** B.A., Cum Laude, Rider University, New Jersey; J.D., with honors, Appellate Advocacy, Brooklyn Law School, New York, 1981; Post Graduate, University of Virginia at Charlottesville (School of the Army Judge Advocate General) **Current organization:** Defense Threat Reduction Agency **Title:** Arms Control Advisor **Type of organization:** Department of Defense agency **Major product:** Legal/technical advisor, arms control treaties/export control regimes **Area of distribution:** International **Expertise:** International/treaty law/military law **Honors/awards:** Phi Alpha Theta; Omicron Delta Kappa; Army Commendation Medal; Army Achievement Medal; Army Reserve Component Achievement Medal; Honored Guest of the French Republic, 1993; Delegate to the First Conference on the Establishment of an International Criminal Court, 1993; United States Department of Defense Representative to the Nuclear Suppliers Group, 1998-present **Published works:** "Comment on the Environmental Modification Convention," Proceedings of the United States Naval Institute, 1993; "Technical Ramifications of the Chemical Weapons Conventions," Journal of Nuclear Survivability, 1993; "United States Counterproliferation Policy," Journal of Science and Technology, 1994; "Juridical Observations on the Chemical Weapons Convention," Journal of the Federalist Society, 1996; Editor, "United States Proliferation Policy" **Affiliations:** New York State Bar; Federal Bar; Republican Party of Virginia; World Zionist Congress; National Rifle Association; Jewish Historical Society; Historical Society of the Supreme Court of the United States; New York State, Military & Federal Bars **Hob./spts.:** Music, shortwave radio, animals, firearms **SIC code:** 97 **Address:** D'TRA/ASC, 8725 John J. Kingman Rd., MS6201 MS6201, Ft. Belvoir, VA 22060-6201 **E-mail:** jonathan.fox@dtra.mil

FROCK SR., HAROLD W.
Industry: Government **Born:** April 13, 1959, Havre de Grace, Maryland **Current organization:** City of Crisfield, Public Utilities Dept. **Title:** Superintendent **Type of organization:** Government/utilities **Major product:** Public services **Area of distribution:** Crisfield, Maryland **Expertise:** Water and wastewater; Board of Water Systems Certification, Warwick Tech **Honors/awards:** Achievement Award, Mayor of Crisfield, 2002; Best Operator System of the Year, Maryland Rural Waterworks, 2004 (System of the Year, 2004) **Hob./spts.:** Deer and turkey hunting, motorcycles **SIC code:** 91 **Address:** City of Crisfield, Public Utilities Dept., P.O. Box 270, Crisfield, MD 21817 **E-mail:** wwtpcris@dmv.com

FROST, TERRENCE
Industry: Government/environmental **Born:** April 29, 1921, Concord, New Hampshire **Univ./degree:** M.S., Zoology, University of New Hampshire, 1955 **Current organization:** Southern New Hampshire Resource **Title:** Vice Chairman, Conservation & Development Council **Type of organization:** Government agency **Major product:** Soil conservation **Area of distribution:** New Hampshire **Expertise:** Aquatic biology/oceanography **Honors/awards:** E.P.A. Award (Lifetime Activity) **Affiliations:** Society for the Protection of New Hampshire (Honorary); Appalachian Mountain Club; Phi Sigma (Honorary); Kappa Sigma Social **Hob./spts.:** Hiking **SIC code:** 95 **Address:** 37 Clinton St., Concord, NH 03301 **E-mail:** terrence.frost@comcast.net

FUNKHOUSER, PAUL MONROE
Industry: Government/military/human services **Born:** June 20, 1917, Rantoul, Illinois **Univ./degree:** Blackburn College, Carlinville, IL, 1935-36; A.A., Social Studies; B.S., History, U.S.N.Y., Albany, NY; B.A., Sociology, S.I.U., Edwardsville, IL, 1975 **Current organization:** US Army/Illinois Dept. of Human Services **Title:** Captain, MPC, USAR (Retired) **Type of organization:** Government **Major product:** National defense/social services **Area of distribution:** International **Expertise:** 1st Sgt., Sgt.

Major/social caseworker, medical caseworker **Honors/awards:** Numerous military awards and medals; ACM, AGCM (6), ADSM, ACM, APCM (3 stars), EAMECM, WWIIVM, AOMWWII, MHA, NDSM, AFRM, UNM, 40 AVM (Russia) **Published works:** 5 books: "Coats of Arms for Everyone" (a complete beginners text on the subject of Arms, pedigrees, family trees, lineage and genealogical charts), 4 Family Histories **Affiliations:** Life Member, Reserve Officers Association; V.F.W.; American Legion (PUFL); Clan MacFarlane Society; Scottish-American Military Society; Member, Scottish Society of the Ozark Region; Scottish National Party; Fankhauser-Funkhouser Swiss Family Association; G.O.P. **Hob./spts.:** Music, jewelry crafting, genealogy, heraldry **SIC code:** 97 **Address:** 58 Frank Scott Pkwy. East, Apt. 121, Swansea, IL 62226-2075

GACKSTETTER, CARMEN P.
Industry: Government/law enforcement **Univ./degree:** B.A., Sociology, Criminal Justice, Oakland University, 2005 **Current organization:** Pontiac Police Dept. **Title:** Lieutenant **Type of organization:** Police department **Major product:** Public order, safety and law enforcement **Area of distribution:** Pontiac, Michigan **Expertise:** Community policing **Honors/awards:** Letter of Professional Excellence, 2000; Community Service Award, 2004 **Affiliations:** Alpha Kappa Delta **Hob./spts.:** Playing and watching sports, family activities **SIC code:** 92 **Address:** Pontiac Police Dept., 110 E. Pike St., Pontiac, MI 48342 **E-mail:** cgackstetter@pontiac.mi.us

GANZ, JON D.
Industry: Government/sanitation **Univ./degree:** B.S., Civil Engineering, 1996; M.S., Environmental Engineering, 1996, Stanford University **Current organization:** Los Angeles County Sanitation Districts **Title:** Senior Engineer **Type of organization:** Government/public utility **Major product:** Waste water and solid waste management **Area of distribution:** Los Angeles County **Expertise:** Engineering, construction management **Affiliations:** A.S.C.E.; W.E.F.; President, L.A.B.S. local section of C.W.E.A. **SIC code:** 95 **Address:** Los Angeles County Sanitation Districts, 24501 S. Figueroa St., Carson, CA 90745 **E-mail:** jganz@lacsd.org **Web address:** www.lacsd.org

GARVEY, JOHN E.
Industry: Government **Born:** September 21, 1947, Niagara Falls, New York **Univ./degree:** B.A., Ithaca College, 1969 **Current organization:** Ontario County **Title:** Director of Human Resources **Type of organization:** Local government **Area of distribution:** Canandaigua, New York **Expertise:** Human resources **Affiliations:** Advisory Board, Bank of Geneva; Advisory Board, Blue Cross & Blue Shield **Hob./spts.:** Musician **SIC code:** 91 **Address:** Ontario County, 3019 County Complex Dr., Canandaigua, NY 14424

GAUDET, JAMES R.
Industry: Government/law enforcement **Born:** June 2, 1961, Holyoke, Massachusetts **Univ./degree:** B.S., Criminal Justice, St. Anselm College, 1983 **Current organization:** Litchfield Police Dept. **Title:** Administrative Lieutenant **Type of organization:** Police department **Major product:** Public order, safety and law enforcement **Area of distribution:** Litchfield, New Hampshire **Expertise:** Criminal investigations and prosecutions **Affiliations:** President, Litchfield Police Association; President, Hillsboro County Law Enforcement Association; Past President, New Hampshire Criminal Investigations Association **Hob./spts.:** Genealogy (French Canadian), softball coach and umpire **SIC code:** 92 **Address:** Litchfield Police Dept., 2 Liberty Way, Suite 2, Litchfield, NH 03052 **E-mail:** jgaudet@litchfieldpd.com

GEERKEN, BARNARD J.
Industry: Government/public safety **Born:** September 17, 1971, New Orleans, Louisiana **Current organization:** Nine Mile Point Volunteer Fire Dept. **Title:** Fire Chief **Type of organization:** Fire department **Major product:** Fire fighting and prevention **Area of distribution:** Louisiana **Expertise:** Administration, officer in charge of ladder company; Certified Fire Service Instructor, member first organized urban search and rescue team in Louisiana **Honors/awards:** Firefighter of the Year, V.F.W. **Affiliations:** East Baton Rouge Urban Search & Rescue; Louisiana Fire Chief's Association; Louisiana State Firemen's Association **Hob./spts.:** Fishing, reading, movies **SIC code:** 92 **Address:** Nine Mile Point Volunteer Fire Dept., 1024 Oak Ave., Nine Mile Point, LA 70094 **E-mail:** bgeerken@aol.com

GIBSON, WILLIAM R. "RANDY"
Industry: Government/transportation **Born:** April 10, 1934, Pittsburgh, Pennsylvania **Univ./degree:** B.S, 1957; M.S., Civil Engineering, San Diego State University, 1964 **Title:** Licensed Professional Engineer (Retired) **Type of organization:** State government **Major product:** Roads and Railroads **Area of distribution:** California **Expertise:** Engineering **Published works:** Reports **Affiliations:** Board of Directors, A.S.C.E.; S.A.M.E. **Hob./spts.:** Stamp collecting **SIC code:** 96 **Address:** P.O. Box 80606, San Diego, CA 92138 **E-mail:** wrgengr@worldnet.att.net

GOEDECKE, ROBERT D.
Industry: Government/utilities **Born:** December 15, 1949, Chester, Illinois **Univ./degree:** Attended Southern Illinois University **Current organization:** City of Tacoma-Fleet Services Division **Title:** Heavy Equipment Technician **Type of organization:** City Government repair facility **Major product:** Public utilities services **Area of distribution:** Tacoma, Washington **Expertise:** Diesel engines and equipment tech **Hob./spts.:** Drag racing **SIC code:** 91 **Address:** 14615 88th Ave. N.W., Gig Harbor, WA 98329-8729

GONZALEZ-RIOS, JUAN A.
Industry: Government/law enforcement **Born:** January 4, 1964, San Juan, Puerto Rico **Univ./degree:** B.A., Business Administration, St. Leo University **Current organization:** Newport News Police Dept. **Title:** Master Police Officer **Type of organization:** Police dept. **Major product:** Public safety **Area of distribution:** Newport News, Virginia **Expertise:** Law enforcement; Patrol Officer **Published works:** 1 article, Daily Press, 2003 **Affiliations:** P.B.A.; Life Member, N.R.A.; International Police Association **Hob./spts.:** Family **SIC code:** 92 **Address:** P.O. Box 120526, Newport News, VA 23607 **E-mail:** lonewolf1964@yahoo.com

GRANT III, COLUMBUS
Industry: Government/public works **Univ./degree:** M.S., Public Administration, Old Dominion University, 1998 **Current organization:** City of Elizabeth City, North Carolina **Title:** Director of Public Works **Type of organization:** Municipal government **Major product:** Public service: water, wastewater, solid waste **Area of distribution:** Elizabeth City, North Carolina **Expertise:** Civil engineering **Affiliations:** A.W.W.A.; American Society of Public Administration **SIC code:** 91 **Address:** 511 Cedar St., Elizabeth City, NC 27909 **E-mail:** cgrant@cityofec.com

GREGG HINKLE, SHERRY LYNN
Industry: Government **Born:** January 30, 1962, Beckley, Virginia **Univ./degree:** B.S., Organizational Leadership, Management & Development; A.S., Banking & Finance, Mountain State University, 2001 **Current organization:** Veterans Affairs Medical Center **Title:** CPS **Type of organization:** Medical center/hospital **Major product:** Patient care **Area of distribution:** West Virginia **Expertise:** Computer Specialist **Honors/awards:** Magna Cum Laude Graduate; International Honor Society in Business; Management and Administration from Sigma Beta Delta; National Omricom-PSI Honor Society in recognition of Community Service and Scholastic Promise; USAA All-American Scholar; Federal Woman of the Year, VA Medical Center, Beckley, West Virginia, 2002 **Affiliations:** I.A.A.P.; American Cancer Society **Hob./spts.:** Bowling **SIC code:** 94 **Address:** P.O. Box 484, 103 Hudson St., Mabscott, WV 25871-0484 **E-mail:** sherrylg@cwv.net

GUARINO, MICHAEL J.
Industry: Government/military **Born:** January 5, 1960, New Orleans, Louisiana **Univ./degree:** B.S., Electrical Engineering, Mississippi State University, 1985 **Current organization:** Florida Air National Guard **Title:** Base Civil Engineer **Type of organization:** Air Force **Major product:** National security **Area of distribution:** Florida **Expertise:** Civil engineering, site development, project management, consulting, operations, training, environmental engineering **Affiliations:** I.E.E.E.; A.E.E.; M.O.A.A.; S.A.M.E.; N.F.P.A.; National Guard Association of the U.S. **Hob./spts.:** Reading, fishing, family **SIC code:** 97 **Address:** Florida Air National Guard, 14300 Fang Dr., Jacksonville, FL 32218 **E-mail:** mjgwiz@bellsouth.net

HAGNER, DINAH LYNN
Industry: Government/public service **Univ./degree:** CLT/Med Technologist, Capitol Region Hospital, 1974 **Current organization:** Missouri Dept. of Health and Senior Services **Title:** Senior Public Health Scientist **Type of organization:** Public health and senior services agency **Major product:** Education, medical consulting, public health services **Area of distribution:** International **Expertise:** Medical consulting **Published works:** Assorted articles **Affiliations:** I.A.C.T.; A.S.C.P.; Co-Manager, Breath Alcohol Program **Hob./spts.:** National public speaker **SIC code:** 94 **Address:** 3807 Horseshoe Bend Rd., Jefferson City, MO 65101 **E-mail:** hagned@dhss.mo.gov

HALLENBECK, LOUIS J.
Industry: Government **Born:** August 30, 1965, Phoenicia, New York **Univ./degree:** B.S., Aeronautical Engineering/Geography, State University of New York at Buffalo, 1993 **Current organization:** U.S. Air Force **Title:** Major **Type of organization:** Government/military **Major product:** National defense, delivery of precision weapons **Area of distribution:** International **Expertise:** War/aviator on F-15 Eagle Fighter Bomber **Hob./spts.:** Flyfishing **SIC code:** 97 **Address:** 1439 Long Gulch Rd., Mountain Home, ID 83647

HAMILTON JR., ROGER P.
Industry: Government/law **Born:** St. Martinsville, Louisiana **Univ./degree:** J.D., Louisiana State University **Current organization:** 16th Judicial District Attorney Office **Title:** Assistant District Attorney **Type of organization:** Government **Major product:** Justice **Area of distribution:** New Iberia, Louisiana **Expertise:** Misdemeanors **Affiliations:** Board Member, Louisiana District Attorney Association; Board Member, Iberia Comprehensive Community Health Center; American Bar Association; Louisiana State Bar Association **Hob./spts.:** Golf, collecting baseball cards **SIC code:** 92 **Address:**

16th Judicial District Attorney Office, 300 Iberia St., Suite 200, New Iberia, LA 70563 **E-mail:** paulhouse@prodigy.net

HAMON, DONALD L.
Industry: Government/utilities **Born:** December 9, 1941, W. Frankfort, Kentucky **Current organization:** Dallas County WCID #6 **Title:** General Manager **Type of organization:** County government **Major product:** Water, sewer, solid waste **Area of distribution:** Dallas County **Expertise:** Municipal management **Hob./spts.:** Fishing, preaching, church **SIC code:** 95 **Address:** Dallas County WCID #6, 13503 Alexander Rd., Balch Springs, TX 75180 **E-mail:** dhamon@dc6.org **Web address:** www.dc6.org

HANTUSH, MOHAMED M.
Industry: Government **Born:** March 5, 1962 Baghdad, Iraq **Univ./degree:** B.S., Civil Engineering, Kuwait University, 1985; M.S., Civil Engineering, University of California at Davis, 1988; Ph.D., Civil Engineering, University of California at Davis, 1993 **Current organization:** U.S. EPA, National Risk Management Research Laboratory **Title:** Hydrologist **Type of organization:** Federal government research lab **Major product:** Research reports, technical papers, mathematical and computer models **Area of distribution:** National **Expertise:** Groundwater hydrology, hydrologic and water quality modeling **Honors/awards:** Best Referee ASCE Journal of Irrigation & Drainage Engineering **Published works:** Authored and co-authored more than 30 technical papers and research reports **Affiliations:** A.S.C.E.; A.G.U. **Hob./spts.:** Soccer, jogging, swimming **SIC code:** 96 **Address:** U.S. EPA, 26 W. Martin Luther King Dr., Cincinnati, OH 45268 **E-mail:** hantush.mohamed@epa.gov

HARMON, WILLIAM H.
Industry: Government **Born:** October 13. 1937, Columbia, South Carolina **Univ./degree:** B.S., Civil Engineering, University of South Carolina, 1959; M.S., Management, US Naval Post-Graduate School, 1972 **Current organization:** S.C. Dept. of Corrections **Title:** P.E./Agency Representative/Captain, Civil Engineering Corps, US Navy (retired) **Type of organization:** State government/state prison system **Major product:** Construction, maintenance **Area of distribution:** South Carolina **Expertise:** Civil engineering, Registered professional engineer **Honors/awards:** Honorary Citizen, City of Clarksville, Tennessee; Citation, Governor of Rhode Island, 1982; Who's Who in the South and Southwest, 1984-85; Chairman Emeritus, National Construction Maintenance Institute **Published works:** Write-ups **Affiliations:** Lifetime Member , F.A.S.C.E.; Co-founder, Construction and Maintenance Institute for Civic and Justice Agencies **Hob./spts.:** Licensed commercial pilot, boating, fishing **SIC code:** 92 **Address:** S.C. Dept. of Corrections, 4322 Broad River Rd., Columbia, SC 29036 **E-mail:** snoggyfrog@aol.com

HARRIS, DAVID W.
Industry: Government **Born:** Salisbury, Maryland **Univ./degree:** Ph.D., University of Boulder, Colorado, 1982 **Current organization:** U.S. Bureau of Reclamation **Title:** Group Manager - Materials Engineering Research Laboratory **Type of organization:** Government agency **Major product:** Water delivery, power **Area of distribution:** International **Expertise:** Materials science, model testing **Published works:** 1 Book, 30+ journals **Affiliations:** A.S.C.E.; N.S.P.E.; U.S.S.D.; P.M.A. **SIC code:** 96 **Address:** U.S. Bureau of Reclamation, Materials Engineering Research Laboratory, P.O. Box 25007, Denver, CO 80225 **E-mail:** dwharris@do.usbr.gov **Web address:** www.usbr.gov/merl

HAYTER, WILLIAM L.
Industry: Government **Born:** February 18, 1956, Clinton, Ontario Canada **Univ./degree:** B.S., Urban and Regional Planning, Fanshawe College, 1976 **Current organization:** Tulare County Redevelopment Center **Title:** Manager **Type of organization:** County government/finance **Major product:** Economic development, county promotions, small business development **Area of distribution:** Visalia, California **Expertise:** Finance, project management **Hob./spts.:** Golf **SIC code:** 93 **Address:** Tulare County Redevelopment Center, 5961 S. Mooney Blvd., Visalia, CA 93277 **E-mail:** bhayter@co.tulare.ca.us

HEINTZ, KENNETH E.
Industry: Government **Born:** November 29, 1949, Rochester, New York **Univ./degree:** A.A., B.S., Adult Education, Monroe College, New York, 1978 **Current organization:** New Jersey Dept. of Labor, Division of Public Safety & Occupational Safety & Health **Title:** Mine Safety Education Technician **Type of organization:** State government division **Major product:** Public safety **Area of distribution:** New Jersey **Expertise:** Plant supervision; First Aid/CPR Instructor; MSHA Certified Instructor **Hob./spts.:** Playing oboe, travel, music, theatre **SIC code:** 94 **Address:** New Jersey Dept. of Labor, Public Safety & Occupational Safety & Health Div., P.O. Box 386, Trenton, NJ 08625 **E-mail:** kenneth.heintz@dol.state.nj.us

HENDREN, KYLE E.
Industry: Government **Born:** December 14, 1966, Scottsbluff, Nebraska **Univ./degree:** B.S., Medical Technology, University of Nebraska, 1995 **Current organization:** DHHS, USPHS, IHS **Title:** Microbiology Supervisor **Type of organization:** Government/health and human services **Major product:** Health services **Area of distribution:** Pine Ridge, South Dakota **Expertise:** Clinical Microbiology **Affiliations:** A.S.C.P.; Emergency Preparedness Committee; American Society for Microbiology; Chair, Infectious Control Committee (5 years) **Hob./spts.:** Bow hunting, fishing, family **SIC code:** 94 **Address:** DHHS, USPHS, IHS, E. Highway 118, P.O. Box 1201, Pine Ridge, SD 57770 **E-mail:** khendren@abr.ihs.gov **Web address:** www.abr.ihs.gov

HERNANDEZ, ELIZABETH M.
Industry: Law **Born:** October 18, 1958, Miami, Florida **Univ./degree:** B.A., Economics, Florida International University, 1980; J.D., University of Florida, 1983 **Current organization:** City of Coral Gables **Title:** City Attorney **Type of organization:** City government **Major product:** Legal services **Area of distribution:** National **Expertise:** City, county, local government, national lecturing on constitutional laws, ethics and historic preservation **Honors/awards:** City Attorney of the Year, 2006 **Published works:** 20+ articles **Affiliations:** Historical Society of South Florida; National Historic Association; President, Florida Municipal Attorney's Association; Chair Elect, City, County and Local Government Section, The Florida State Bar **Hob./spts.:** Golf, reading **SIC code:** 91 **Address:** City of Coral Gables, 405 Biltmore Way, Coral Gables, FL 33134 **E-mail:** ehernandez@coralgables.com **Web address:** www.coralgables.com

HERRICK, HOWARD TIM
Industry: Retired Federal Civil Service/U.S. Army Veteran **Born:** Hamilton, Ohio **Univ./degree:** Graduate, Ashland University; Post Graduate, Ohio State University **Area of distribution:** International **Expertise:** Psychology, poetry, writing **Published works:** 4 books **Affiliations:** AMVETS; A.A.R.P.; Y.M.C.A.; American Legion; Rotary International; U.S. Army Reserve; Ohio Army National Guard **Hob./spts.:** Writing, photography, travel, camping, fishing, poetry **SIC code:** 97 **Address:** 1209 Hill Rd. North, Suite 239, Pickerington, OH 43147-8888 **E-mail:** timosha2003@hotmail.com

HILE, ROB
Industry: Government **Born:** October 4, 1963, Torrance, California **Univ./degree:** A.S., Animal Science, 1985; A.S., Mechanical Engineering, Oklahoma State University, 1988 **Current organization:** TAC-Americas, Inc. **Title:** Director of Sales **Type of organization:** Government/sales **Major product:** Turnkey government products/sales **Area of distribution:** International **Expertise:** Federal sales **Affiliations:** Association of Energy Engineers **Hob./spts.:** Hunting, fishing **SIC code:** 99 **Address:** TAC-Americas, Inc., 1650 W. Crosby Rd., Carrollton, TX 75006 **E-mail:** rob_hile@tac-americas.com **Web address:** www.tac-americas.com

HILL JR., H. TOMMY
Industry: Government/Military **Born:** July 15, 1937, Richmond, Virginia **Univ./degree:** B.S., Business Administration, University of Maryland, 1978 **Current organization:** Dept. of the Army (ACES) **Title:** Food Service System Analyst **Type of organization:** Army food service management **Major product:** Management services **Area of distribution:** International **Expertise:** Administration and service management **Honors/awards:** Alpha Phi Alpha; served in active duty U.S. Air Force, 1956-77, retired as a Master Sergeant **Affiliations:** I.F.S.E.A. **Hob./spts.:** Family, sports, travel **SIC code:** 97 **Address:** Dept. of the Army (ACES), Bldg. 5000, 201 22nd St., Ft. Lee, VA 23801 **E-mail:** hillh@lee.army.mil

HIRANO, ANDREW J.
Industry: Government/engineering **Born:** September 26, 1950 ,Honolulu, Hawaii **Univ./degree:** B.S., Electrical Engineering, 1972; M.S., Electrical Engineering, 1974; University of Hawaii **Current organization:** US Air Force, HQ PACAF/CECC **Title:** Electrical Engineer **Type of organization:** Government/Air Force **Major product:** Defense **Area of distribution:** National **Expertise:** Design and construction project management **Affiliations:** S.A.M.E. **Hob./spts.:** Tennis and jogging **SIC code:** 97 **Address:** US Air Force, HQ PACAF/CECC, 25 E. Street, Suite D306, Hickam AFB, HI 96853-5412 **E-mail:** andy.hirano@hickam.af.mil

HOGAN, JEFFERY A.
Industry: Municipal government/public works **Born:** October 6, 1968, Bay City, Michigan **Univ./degree:** B.S., Civil Engineering, Michigan Technological University, 1991; Enrolled: Master's of Public Administration, Midwestern State University, 2002 **Current organization:** City of Wichita Falls, Texas **Title:** City Engineer **Type of organization:** City government **Major product:** Public works projects **Area of distribution:** Wichita Falls, Texas **Expertise:** Civil engineering **Affiliations:** A.S.C.E.; N.S.P.E.; A.P.W.A.; Returned Peace Corps Volunteer, El Salvador **Hob./spts.:** Soccer, bicycling, history, travel **SIC code:** 91 **Address:** City of Wichita Falls, Texas, 1300 Seventh St., P.O. Box 1431, Wichita Falls, TX 76307 **E-mail:** jefferyhogan@hotmail.com

HOLT, JULIANNE M.
Industry: Government/law **Univ./degree:** J.D., South Texas College of Law, 1980 **Current organization:** Hillsborough County Public Defender **Title:** 13th Judicial Circuit Public Defender **Type of organization:** Government law firm **Major product:** Defense service for indigent criminally accused **Area of distribution:** Tampa, Florida

Expertise: Indigent criminal defense **Honors/awards:** Hispanic Women in Government Award, 1994 and 2000; Hank Warren Award, 2000 **Published works:** South Texas Law Journal, 1979 **Affiliations:** A.T.L.A.; N.A.C.D.L.; N.A.D.C.P; Florida Association of Criminal Defense Lawyers **SIC code:** 92 **Address:** Hillsborough County Public Defender, 700 E. Twiggs St., Tampa, FL 33602 **E-mail:** holtj@pd13.state.fl.us

HOPE, GERRI D.
Industry: Government **Born:** Sacramento, California **Univ./degree:** Sierra College, 1977 **Current organization:** State of California Employment Development Dept./Gerrisgift.com (web based gift store) **Title:** Staff Information Systems Analyst Specialist **Type of organization:** Government, corporate, entrepreneurial **Major product:** Telecommunications, voice network security **Area of distribution:** California **Expertise:** Telecommunications, management, analyst and engineering **Published works:** 1 poem, pamphlets, photography **Affiliations:** Board of Directors, Telecommunications Association; Elks **Hob./spts.:** Ceramics, photography, writing, gardening, animal behavior, Christian ministry **SIC code:** 96 **Address:** State of California Employment Development Dept./, Gerrisgift.com (web based gift store), P.O. Box 512, North Highlands, CA 95660-0512 **E-mail:** danisangel767@comcast.net

HOU, CHING
Industry: Government/agriculture **Born:** June 26, 1935, Taiwan **Univ./degree:** Ph.D., Biochemistry, University of Tokyo, 1967 **Current organization:** National Center for Agricultural Utilization Research, USDA **Title:** Lead Scientist **Type of organization:** U.S. government agency **Major product:** Value added agricultural products **Area of distribution:** National **Expertise:** Biochemistry **Affiliations:** Fellow, A.A.M.; S.I.M.; A.O.C.S. **Hob./spts.:** Tennis, soccer **SIC code:** 96 **Address:** National Center for Agricultural Utilization Research, USDA, 1815 N. University St., Peoria, IL 61604 **E-mail:** houct@ncaur.usda.gov

HUSSEIN, MOHAMMED H.
Industry: Government/transportation **Born:** July 8, 1958, Ghana, W. Africa **Univ./degree:** B.S., Electrical Engineering, New York Institute of Technology, 1995 **Current organization:** M.T.A. New York City Transit **Title:** Associate Transit Management Analyst **Type of organization:** Government **Major product:** Mass transit (buses, electric trains and hybrid buses) **Area of distribution:** New York **Expertise:** Electrical engineering **Hob./spts.:** Soccer, research **SIC code:** 96 **Address:** 1456 Townsend Ave., Apt 5F, Bronx, NY 10452 **E-mail:** husseinnycity@yahoo.com

HYDE, RICHARD H.
Industry: Government **Univ./degree:** M.S., Finance, University Illinois; M.S., Administration, Northwest University; M.Ed., DePaul University **Current organization:** City of Waukegan, Illinois **Title:** Mayor **Type of organization:** Municipality **Major product:** City services and maintenance **Area of distribution:** Waukegan, Illinois **Expertise:** Mayoral duties **Hob./spts.:** Sports **SIC code:** 91 **Address:** City of Waukegan, Illinois, 100 MLK Dr., Waukegan, IL 60085

ICENOGLE, GARY D.
Industry: Government/public work construction **Univ./degree:** B.A., Civil Engineering, University of Arkansas, 1975 **Current organization:** Louisiana Dept. of Transportation & Development **Title:** District Construction Engineer **Type of organization:** State government dept. **Major product:** Roads, bridges and related public works **Area of distribution:** Louisiana **Expertise:** Contract administration and engineering **Affiliations:** American Society of Professional Engineers; American Society of Civil Engineers **SIC code:** 96 **Address:** Louisiana Dept. of Transportation & Development, P.O. Box 4068, Monroe, LA 71211 **E-mail:** gicenogle@dotmail.state.la.us

ISAACS, NORETTA J.
Industry: Government **Born:** April 16, 1961, Altus, Oklahoma **Univ./degree:** A.S., Computer Science, Southwest University, 1981 **Current organization:** Cubic Worldwide Technical Services **Title:** Senior ATREP Field Engineer **Type of organization:** Government/ Dept. of Defense **Major product:** Army training aides support **Area of distribution:** International **Expertise:** Alaska training range evolution program **Hob./spts.:** Snow-machining, competitive tomahawk throwing, reading, swimming **SIC code:** 97 **Address:** 1124 Aztec Rd., North Pole, AK 99705 **E-mail:** noretta.isaacs@cubic.com **Web address:** www.cubic.com

ISOM SR., J.M.
Industry: Law enforcement **Born:** March 11, 1963, Leesburg, Florida **Univ./degree:** A.S., Criminal Justice, 1997 **Current organization:** Fruitland Park Police Dept. **Title:** Chief of Police **Type of organization:** Police department **Major product:** Public safety, order and law enforcement **Area of distribution:** Fruitland Park, Florida **Expertise:** Working crimes, traffic **Affiliations:** I.A.C.P.; Florida Chiefs of Police Association; West Central Chiefs of Police Association; Rotary Club, Kiwanis Club **Hob./spts.:** Fishing **SIC code:** 92 **Address:** Fruitland Park Police Dept., 506 W. Berckman St., Fruitland Park, FL 34731 **E-mail:** misom@fruitlandpark.org **Web address:** www.fruitlandpark.org

JACKSON, JEFFREY A.
Industry: Law enforcement **Born:** July 17, 1963, Milford, Delaware **Univ./degree:** A.S. Candidate, Chesapeake Community College **Current organization:** Greensboro Police Dept. **Title:** Chief of Police **Type of organization:** Government/police dept. **Major product:** Law enforcement **Area of distribution:** Greensboro, Maryland **Expertise:** Police administration, patrol functions, training **Affiliations:** International Association of Chiefs of Police; Maryland Chiefs of Police Association **Hob./spts.:** Auto racing, woodworking **SIC code:** 92 **Address:** Greensboro Police Dept., P.O. Box 451, Greensboro, MD 21639 **E-mail:** chief_2760@yahoo.com

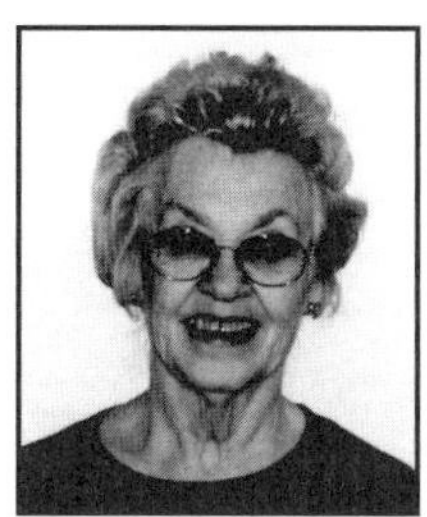

JAMES, JEANNETTE ADELINE
Industry: Government **Born:** November 19, 1929, Maquoketa, Iowa **Spouse:** James Arthur James **Married:** February 16, 1948 **Children:** James Jr., Jeannie, Alice Marie **Univ./degree:** Attended Merritt Davis School of Commerce; University of Alaska **Current organization:** Alaska Legislature, Administration **Title:** Representative, Advisor **Type of organization:** State legislature **Major product:** Legislature, public service **Area of distribution:** Alaska **Expertise:** Accounting, economics, communication, business owner, foster parent **Affiliations:** Rotary; Alaska Miners Association; Greater Fairbanks Chamber of Commerce; North Pole Community Chamber of Commerce; Emblem Club; Women of the Moose **Career accomplishments:** Awards: Arctic Alliance for People, "Community Service Award" 2001; Who's Who in the 21st Century, "Outstanding contribution in the field of business, communication, government" 2001; Alaska Outdoor Council, "Legislator of the Year" 2000; Alaska Chapter of Safari Club Int., "Outstanding courage fighting for continued equality of all Alaska citizens" 2000; National Rifle Assoc., "Defender of Freedom Award" 1994; Golden Heart Shootist Society, Life Membership 2002; University of Alaska-Anchorage, "Tireless Efforts to enact negotiated rulemaking legislation" 2002; Prince William Sound Community College, "Outstanding support" 1996; Alaska Municipal League, "Friend of Municipalities" 1996; International Register of Profiles, 1981; Alaska Psychology Assoc., "Friend of Psychology" 2001; Tanana Valley Sportsmen, "Appreciation-support for rights of Alaskans to protect themselves" 1994; National Federation of Independent Business, "Guardian of Small Business" 1998; Fairbanks Republican Women, "Woman of the Year" 2002; Alaska State Legislature Citation 2003; Alaska Farm Bureau, "Legislator of the Year" 1994; Alaska Farmers Union Life Member 2001; Who's Who in Executives and Professionals 1994-95; Strathmore's Who's Who, Leadership & Achievement Life Member; ABI, "Great Minds of the 21st Century, Business, Communication and Government" 2001 **Hob./spts.:** Bowling, arts and crafts, music, children **SIC code:** 91 **Address:** 3068 Badger Rd., North Pole, AK 99705-6117 **E-mail:** usually@acsalaska,net **Web address:** www.repjames.org

JENKINS, ROBERT G.
Industry: Government **Born:** Charlottesville, Virginia **Univ./degree:** B.S., Animal Science, Virginia Tech College; M.S., Animal Physiology, West Virginia University **Current organization:** U.S. Dept. of Energy **Title:** Director of Aviation Management **Type of organization:** Government **Major product:** Aviation services **Area of distribution:** International **Expertise:** Aviation management **Affiliations:** Order of Daedalians (Military Aviation) **Hob./spts.:** Golf **SIC code:** 95 **Address:** U.S. Dept. of Energy, 1000 Independence Ave. S.W., Suite 4B218, Washington, DC 20585 **E-mail:** RandNJenk@aol.com

JENKINS, WILMA S.
Industry: Correctional facility **Born:** December 31, 1951, Vidalia, Georgia **Univ./degree:** Nursing Diploma, Georgia Baptist School of Nursing **Current organization:** Wheeler Correctional Facility **Title:** Mental Health R.N. **Type of organization:** Correctional facility **Area of distribution:** Alamo, Georgia **Expertise:** Nursing **Honors/awards:** Who's Who in American Nursing, Inaugural Edition, 1984; Who's Who in American Nursing, 1990-1991; International Who's Who of Professional and Business Women, 2000; R.N. of the Year, Wheeler Correctional Facility, 2003 **Affiliations:** A.N.A.; Past Member, A.I.C.N., A.O.R.N., A.A.C.N., G.O.N.E.; A.H.A.; M.A.D.D. **Hob./spts.:** Reading, music **SIC code:** 92 **Address:** Wheeler Correctional Facility, 1100 N. Broad St., Alamo, GA 30411

JOHNSON, FOYE L.
Industry: Government **Born:** October 22, 1949, Lafayette, Georgia **Current organization:** Walker County Courthouse **Title:** Probate Judge **Type of organization:** County court **Major product:** Probate and estate matters **Area of distribution:** Northwest

Georgia **Expertise:** Probate Judge elected 1991, serving Walker County government since 1967 **Affiliations:** Optimist Club; Walker County Chamber of Commerce **Hob./spts.:** Garden crafts, decorating **SIC code:** 92 **Address:** Walker County Courthouse, 103 S. Duke St., Lafayette, GA 30728 **E-mail:** probatecourt@co.walker.ga.us

JOHNSON, PAIGE E.
Industry: Government/defense **Born:** March 4, 1951, Oak Hill, West Virginia **Univ./degree:** Ph.D., Civil Engineering Technology; M.S., Project Management, George Washington University **Current organization:** Ballistic Missile Defense Organization **Title:** National Missile Defense Civil Engineer **Type of organization:** Federal government **Major product:** Engineering services **Area of distribution:** International **Expertise:** Military airfield design and evaluation **Honors/awards:** Member, Defense Acquisition Corps. **Published works:** The Army Aviation Team From A Military Civil Engineer's Perspective **Affiliations:** A.S.C.E.; Society of American Military Engineers; Transportation Research Board **Hob./spts.:** Tractors and farming **SIC code:** 97 **Address:** P.O. Box 125, Compton, MD 20627 **E-mail:** jfarms_pej@yahoo.com

JOHNSON, RICHARD C.
Industry: Government/Law Enforcement **Born:** October 10, 1965, Odessa, Texas **Univ./degree:** B.S., Organized Leadership, Mountain State University, 2006 **Current organization:** Round Rock Police Dept. **Title:** Lieutenant **Type of organization:** Police department **Major product:** Public order and safety, emergency services, emergency management, law enforcement **Area of distribution:** Round Rock, Texas **Expertise:** Administration **Honors/awards:** Who's Who of American College Students **Affiliations:** Texas Gang Investigators Association; Sigma Beta Delta **Hob./spts.:** Breeding horses and Schnauzers **SIC code:** 92 **Address:** Round Rock Police Dept., 615 E. Palm Valley Blvd., Round Rock, TX 78664 **E-mail:** richardj@round-rock.tx.us

JOHNSON, ROBERT
Industry: Government/law enforcement **Title:** Lieutenant **Type of organization:** Police department **Major product:** Public order, safety and law enforcement **SIC code:** 92 **Address:** Crescent City Police Dept., 115 North Summit St., Crescent City, FL 32112 **E-mail:** cclieutenant@netzero.com

JOHNSON, SHEILA A.
Industry: Government **Born:** April 1, 1955, Forest Hills, New York **Univ./degree:** B.A., Cum Laude, Spelman College, 1976; M.L.S., Clark-Atlanta University, Addalso, 1978 **Current organization:** New York State Assembly, Office of Philip Ramos **Type of organization:** Government **Area of distribution:** National **Affiliations:** A.C.L.U.; A.L.A.; N.Y.B.L.C. **Hob./spts.:** Professional cooking, theatre, cultural arts **SIC code:** 91 **Address:** 25 Spruce Rd., Amityville, NY 11701 **E-mail:** sjohnso2@optonline.net

JONES, SHARON M.
Industry: Government/law enforcement **Born:** August 3, 1962, Abington, Pennsylvania **Univ./degree:** B.A., Criminal Justice, St. Leo University, Georgia, 2004; M.P.A., Columbus State University, 2007 **Current organization:** Morrow Police Dept. **Title:** Lieutenant **Type of organization:** Police department **Major product:** Public order, safety and law enforcement **Area of distribution:** Morrow, Georgia **Expertise:** First Responder, administration, instruction **Affiliations:** International Association of Women Police; Police Benevolent Association **Hob./spts.:** Cycling, tennis, boating **SIC code:** 92 **Address:** Morrow Police Dept., 6311-A Murphy Dr., Morrow, GA 30260 **E-mail:** sjones@cityofmorrow.com

KANESHIRO, STACIE Y.
Industry: Government/engineering **Born:** April 29, 1976, Honolulu, Hawaii **Univ./degree:** B.S., Civil Engineering, University of Hawaii, 1999 **Current organization:** U.S. Air Force, Dept. of Defense **Title:** Civil Engineer **Type of organization:** Military installation **Major product:** Civil engineering for the military **Area of distribution:** Hickam AFB, Hawaii **Expertise:** Engineering **Honors/awards:** A.S.C.E. Outstanding Membership Chairperson, 2001; Chi Epsilon, Civil Engineering Honor Society **Affiliations:** Chair, A.S.C.E. Hawaii Section; Member, University of Hawaii Engineering Alumni Association **Hob./spts.:** Softball, golf **SIC code:** 97 **Address:** U.S. Air Force, Dept. of Defense, 75 H St., Bldg. 1200, Hickam AFB, HI 96853 **E-mail:** stacie.kaneshiro@hickam.af.mil

KENNEDY, PATRICK W.
Industry: Government/clinical laboratory science **Born:** March 26, 1968, Houston, Texas **Univ./degree:** B.S., Clinical Laboratory Sciences, University of Nebraska, 1994; M.S., Chapman University, 2002 **Current organization:** 30th Medical Group/U.S. Air Force **Title:** Director, Clinical Laboratory Services **Type of organization:** Hospital **Major product:** Laboratory medicine **Area of distribution:** International **Expertise:** Management, administration **Honors/awards:** District Graduate Officer, Training School; Honor Graduate, Basic Military Training **Hob./spts.:** Basketball, fishing **SIC code:** 97 **Address:** 30th Medical Group/U.S. Air Force, 338 S. Dakota Ave., Vandenberg AFB, CA 93437

KIGHTLINGER, ALAN F.
Industry: Fire department **Born:** July 25, 1949, Los Angeles, California **Univ./degree:** B.S., Agriculture/Journalism, University of Nevada at Reno, 1972 **Current organization:** City of Elko Fire Dept. **Title:** Fire Chief **Type of organization:** Municipal fire department **Major product:** Fire protection and rescue services **Area of distribution:** Elko, Nevada **Expertise:** Firefighting **Affiliations:** National Volunteer Fire Council; National Fire Protection Association; International Association of Arson Investigation; Nevada State Firefighters Association; Nevada Fire Chief's Association **Hob./spts.:** Family, umpire of high school baseball **SIC code:** 92 **Address:** City of Elko Fire Dept., 911 W. Idaho St., Elko, NV 89801 **E-mail:** efd@ci.elko.nv.us **Web address:** www.elkocity.com

KIMBEL, RAYMOND
Industry: Government **Title:** Mayor **Type of organization:** Municipal government **Major product:** Public services **Expertise:** Sewer expansion and water project, campgrounds on small lake (small industrial park) **SIC code:** 91 **Address:** City of Manton, 306 W. Main, Manton, MI 49663

KITCHEN, ROLAND C.
Industry: Government **Born:** November 25, 1934 Marshall, Missouri **Univ./degree:** Attended University of Missouri, College of Agriculture **Current organization:** City of Warrensburg **Title:** Building Official **Type of organization:** City government **Major product:** Building code enforcement **Area of distribution:** Warrensburg, Missouri **Expertise:** Code administration, electric code, training, conducting seminars; Certified Building Official (NICC) **Affiliations:** President, M.A.C.A. **Hob./spts.:** Has built 113 log homes since 1973 **SIC code:** 91 **Address:** City of Warrensburg, 102 S. Holden St., Warrensburg, MO 64093-2331 **E-mail:** rkitchen@warrensburg-mo.com

KITCHENER, KATHRYN R.
Industry: Government **Born:** 1944, Newark, New Jersey **Univ./degree:** B.A., Economics, Douglas College; M.A., Public Administration, Kean University, Union, New Jersey, 1991 **Current organization:** Township of Green Brook **Title:** Administrator/Clerk **Type of organization:** Municipal government **Major product:** Providing public service **Area of distribution:** Green Brook, New Jersey **Expertise:** Management, leadership **Affiliations:** N.J.M.M.A.; I.C.M.A. **Hob./spts.:** Poetry, motorcycles **SIC code:** 91 **Address:** Township of Green Brook, 111 Greenbrook Rd., Green Brook, NJ 08812 **E-mail:** krkitch@aol.com

KLEIN, MICHAEL G.
Industry: Government **Born:** January 14, 1941, Rockford, Illinois **Univ./degree:** Ph.D., University of Wisconsin **Current organization:** USDA- Agricultural Research Service **Title:** Research Entomologist **Type of organization:** Federal government **Major product:** Agricultural research **Area of distribution:** International **Expertise:** Entomology research (Japanese Beetles) **Affiliations:** Society of Invertebrate Pathology; Entomology Society of North America; Wisconsin Entomology Society; International Organization of Biological Control **Hob./spts.:** Golf, hiking **SIC code:** 96 **Address:** USDA- Agricultural Research Service, 1680 Madison Ave., Wooster, OH 44691 **E-mail:** klein.10@osu.edu

KLEIN, SHIRLEY E.
Industry: Government/military **Born:** December 21, 1922, Chicago, Illinois **Univ./degree:** B.S., General Studies, University of Nebraska, 1980; B.S., Social Services/Rehabilitation, American Technological University, 1980; M.A., General Studies, Jacksonville State University, 1987 **Current organization:** United States Army **Title:** CW-4 (Chief Warrant Officer) (Retired) **Type of organization:** Military/animal shelter **Major product:** National defense/animal rescue **Area of distribution:** International **Expertise:** Personnel/receiving and saving animals **Hob./spts.:** Devoted animal rescuer **SIC code:** 97 **Address:** 6100 E. Rancier Ave., Lot #406, Killeen, TX 76543

KNUTSEN, KENNETH C.
Industry: Law **Born:** November 15, 1942, Oneonta, New York **Univ./degree:** A.S., Business Administration, S.U.N.Y., Delhi, New York, 1963; Ph.D., Philosophy, St. Paul's University, 1994 **Current organization:** Town of Schoharie **Title:** Town Justice **Type of organization:** Town Government **Major product:** Judiciary duties **Area of distribution:** Schoharie, New York **Expertise:** Town Justice, appointed in Westford, New York in 1992, re-elected in 2007-2010; Administrative duties, legislature affairs; Independent Non-Denominational Pastor with a Musical Ministry **Affiliations:** New York Magistrates Association; Served as Executive Director to Otsego, New York County chapter; American Red Cross, 1990-1995 **Hob./spts.:** Fishing, photography, camping **SIC code:** 92 **Address:** Town of Schoharie, 300 Main St., Schoharie, NY 12157 **E-mail:** knutsen@yahoo.com

KO, ALBERT
Industry: Government/engineering **Born:** July 1, 1970, San Francisco, California **Univ./degree:** B.S., Civil Engineering, University of California, Berkeley, 1993 **Current organization:** City and County of San Francisco **Title:** Civil Engineer **Type of organization:** Government **Major product:** Management **Area of distribution:**

San Francisco, California **Expertise:** Engineering **Affiliations:** A.S.C.E. **Hob./spts.:** Sports, basketball, travel, biking **SIC code:** 91 **Address:** City and County of San Francisco, 1680 Mission St., San Francisco, CA 94103 **E-mail:** albert_j_ko@ci-sfca-us/agentako88@hotmail.com

KULP, ROBERT R.
Industry: County government **Born:** December 2, 1957, Pottstown, Pennsylvania **Univ./degree:** B.S., Geology, University of Pittsburg, Johnstown, Pennsylvania, 1991 **Current organization:** Montgomery County Parks Department **Title:** Park Ranger **Type of organization:** County parks department **Major product:** Parks and passive recreation **Area of distribution:** Montgomery County, Pennsylvania **Expertise:** Geology and igneous petrology, independent research in the Gettysburg and Newark Basins **Published works:** Book pending, Abstract, "The Existence of Olivine in Several Exposures of Pennsylvania York Haven Type Diabase" 1999 GSA Annual Meeting, Denver, CO; Abstract, "Differentiation of a Rossville Type Diabase Intrusion, Franklin Township, York County Pennsylvania" 2000 GSA Annual Meeting, Reno, NV; Abstract, "Xenoliths of the Triassic Passaic Formation in the Monocacy Hill Diabase Intrusion, Amity Township, Berks County Pennsylvania" 2001 GSA Annual Meeting, Boston, MA **Affiliations:** G.S.A.; Field Conference of Pennsylvania Geologists; Montgomery County Historical Society; Friends of Mineralogy **Hob./spts.:** Rocks and minerals, building wagons, genealogy **SIC code:** 95 **Address:** 2233 Little Rd., Perkiomenville, PA 18074 **E-mail:** rrkanisepa@aol.com

KUPKOWSKI, CHRISTINA L.
Industry: Government/transportation **Born:** December 24, 1976, Sycamore, Illinois **Univ./degree:** B.S., Civil Engineering, University of Iowa, 1999 **Current organization:** Illinois Dept. of Transportation **Title:** Federal Aid Location Engineer **Type of organization:** State government **Major product:** Roadways **Area of distribution:** 6 counties in Northeastern Illinois **Affiliations:** A.S.C.E.; N.S.P.E. **Hob./spts.:** Reading **SIC code:** 96 **Address:** Illinois Dept. of Transportation, 201 W. Center St., Schaumburg, IL 60196

LA FARGE, TIMOTHY
Industry: Government/forestry **Born:** March 14, 1930, New York **Univ./degree:** B.Sc., Forestry, University of Maine; M.F., Yale University School of Forestry; Ph.D., Forestry, Michigan State University **Current organization:** USDA Forest Service (Retired) **Type of organization:** Government **Major product:** Genetically improved forest products, such as timber or pulp and paper; improvements including growth rate, wood quality, resistance to disease, on National Forest land or on private forest land **Area of distribution:** National and private forest land **Expertise:** Forest Genetics, especially analyses of unbalanced progeny test data by a statistical method called Best Linear Prediction, which requires sophisticated computer software **Published works:** 16 proceedings and journal articles **Affiliations:** Society of American Foresters (SAF): American Association for the Advancement of Science (AAAS) **Hob./spts.:** Long distance running, tennis, classical and jazz music **SIC code:** 96 **Address:** 863 Foerster St., San Francisco, CA 94127-2307 **E-mail:** timlaf@comcast.net

LAFERLA, RICHARD T.
Industry: Government **Born:** December 13, 1951, Omaha, Nebraska **Univ./degree:** B.S.E.E., University of Nebraska, 1974 **Current organization:** U.S. Army Corps. Of Engineers **Title:** Electrical Engineer **Type of organization:** Government agency **Major product:** Construction plans and specifications **Area of distribution:** National **Expertise:** Engineering designs, electrical **Affiliations:** I.E.E.E. **Hob./spts.:** Reading, football, shopping **SIC code:** 97 **Address:** U.S. Army Corps. Of Engineers, 106 S. 15th St., Attn: CENWO-ED-DC, Omaha, NE 68102-1258 **E-mail:** richard.t.laferla@usace.army.mil

LARSON, STEVEN H.
Industry: Government **Born:** April 28, 1949, Benson, Minnesota **Univ./degree:** B.A., Technical Illustration, St. Cloud State University, 1972 **Current organization:** City of New Brighton **Title:** Mayor **Type of organization:** Municipal government **Major product:** Public safety, public works, parks and recreation **Area of distribution:** New Brighton, Minnesota **Expertise:** Supervising daily operations of the city **Hob./spts.:** Golf, duplicate bridge **SIC code:** 91 **Address:** City of New Brighton, 2150 Erin Ct., New Brighton, MN 55112 **E-mail:** stevenlarson1@comcast.net

LAUMBACH, RUDOLPH E.
Industry: Government/water and power **Born:** June 16, 1931, Doyleville, Colorado **Univ./degree:** B.S.C.E., New Mexico State University, 1963 **Current organization:** California Dept of Water Resources **Title:** Field Division Chief **Type of organization:** State agency **Major product:** Regulation, conservation and distribution of water **Area of distribution:** California **Expertise:** Engineering, management **Affiliations:** A.S.C.E. **Hob./spts.:** Livestock, ranching **SIC code:** 96 **Address:** California Dept. of Water Resources, 31849 N. Lake Hughes Rd., Castaic, CA 91384 **E-mail:** rel-ajlon84@zianet.com

LEDERER JR., MAX D.
Industry: Government/publishing **Born:** June 21, 1960, Plattsburgh, New York **Univ./degree:** B.A., Marshall University, 1982; J.D., University of Richmond, 1985 **Current organization:** U.S. Dept. of Defense - Stars & Stripes **Title:** Chief Operating Officer & General Counsel **Type of organization:** Government publication **Major product:** Newspaper **Area of distribution:** International **Expertise:** Senior management and intellectual property law **Honors/awards:** Bronze Star, US Army, 1991 **Affiliations:** A.B.A.; P.B.A. **Hob./spts.:** Running, basketball **SIC code:** 96 **Address:** U.S. Dept. of Defense - Stars & Stripes, 529 14th St., Suite 350, Washington, DC 20045 **E-mail:** maxlederer@verizon.net

LEE, NGAR KOK JAMES
Industry: Government/transportation **Born:** August 19, 1953, Hong Kong **Univ./degree:** Ph.D., University of Texas, 1993 **Current organization:** Caltrans **Title:** Researcher/Engineer **Type of organization:** State government dept. **Major product:** Transportation **Area of distribution:** California **Expertise:** Pavement research; Professional Engineer **Published works:** 20+ articles **Affiliations:** A.S.C.E. **Hob./spts.:** Swimming **SIC code:** 96 **Address:** Caltrans, 5900 Folsom Blvd., Sacramento, CA 95819 **E-mail:** james_n_lee@dot.ca.gov

LEE, PHILIP A.
Industry: Government **Univ./degree:** M.S., Biomedical Science, Nottingham Trent University, England, 1994 **Current organization:** Florida Dept. of Health, Bureau of Laboratories **Title:** Microbiologist **Type of organization:** State government/public health **Major product:** Laboratory diagnostics, epidemiology **Area of distribution:** Florida **Expertise:** Microbiology, bio-terrorism defense **Published works:** Peer-reviewed journals **Affiliations:** A.S.M.B.; F.P.H.A.; Past President, JAM **SIC code:** 91 **Address:** Florida Dept. of Health, Bureau of Laboratories, Molecular Biology Dept., 1217 Pearl St., Jacksonville, FL 32202 **E-mail:** phil_lee@doh.state.fl.us

LEONARD JR., AL JACK
Industry: Government **Born:** June 6, 1963, Burlington, North Carolina **Current organization:** Town of Tabor City **Title:** Town Manager **Type of organization:** Municipal government **Major product:** Municipal services **Area of distribution:** Tabor City, North Carolina **Expertise:** Project Management; State of N.C. Licensed Wastewater Treatment Plant Operator; State of N.C . Licensed Water Treatment & Facility Operator; State of N.C. Licensed Plumbing Contractor **Honors/awards:** Lifetime Member, Phi Kappa Honor Society; Gamma Beta Phi Honor Society; Alpha Chi Honor Society; Pi Sigma Alpha Honor Society **Affiliations:** International Who's Who of Public Service **Hob./spts.:** Boating, skiing, college basketball **SIC code:** 91 **Address:** Town of Tabor City, 140 Lake Tabor Dr., Tabor City, NC 28463 **Web address:** www.taborcity.nc.org

LEVIN, HOWARD
Industry: Government **Born:** November 25, 1947, Chicago, Illinois **Univ./degree:** B.S., Accounting, University of Illinois at Chicago, 1970 **Current organization:** United States Environmental Protection Agency **Title:** Accountant **Type of organization:** Federal government agency **Major product:** Environmental protection **Area of distribution:** National **Expertise:** Accounting **Affiliations:** N.S.T.P. **Hob./spts.:** Avid sports fan **SIC code:** 95 **Address:** 3550 N. Lake Shore Dr., #201, Chicago, IL 60657 **E-mail:** rsanto47@aol.com

LEWIS, DON R.
Industry: Government **Born:** February 26, 1929, Bloomington, Indiana **Univ./degree:** M.A., Administration; M.A., Health and Safety; M.A., Counseling Guidance, Indiana State University **Current organization:** Richland Township **Title:** Trustee **Type of organization:** Township government **Major product:** Governing township **Area of distribution:** Richland Township, Indiana **Expertise:** Community relations, government trustee **Affiliations:** President, Monroe County Township; Veteran's Organizations; American Legion; Shriner's; Masons Master **Hob./spts.:** Reading, fishing, hunting, collecting knives and guns **SIC code:** 91 **Address:** Richland Township, 102 S. Park St., Ellettsville, IN 47429

LIDDELL, KENTRELL M.
Industry: Government/justice/medicine/healthcare **Current organization:** Mississippi Dept. of Corrections **Title:** M.D. **Type of organization:** Correctional institution **Major product:** Correctional healthcare **Expertise:** Leadership, business development, healthcare **SIC code:** 92 **Address:** Mississippi Dept. of Corrections, 450 Hillandale Dr., Jackson, MS 39212 **E-mail:** kliddell@mdoc.state.ms.us **Web address:** www.mdoc.state.ms.us

LINN, ROBERT P.
Industry: Government **Born:** December 27, 1908, Pennsylvania **Univ./degree:** B.S., Grove City College, 1931 **Current organization:** Beaver Borough **Title:** Mayor **Type of organization:** Municipal government **Major product:** Politics **Area of distribution:** Beaver, Pennsylvania **Expertise:** Mayor for 57 years **Published works:** Write-ups **Affiliations:** Pennsylvania Mayor's Association; Elective League of Western

Pennsylvania **Hob./spts.:** Sports, family **SIC code:** 92 **Address:** Beaver Borough, 469 3rd St., Beaver, PA 15009 **E-mail:** beaverpolicedeptstargate.net

LIPSCOMB, CLARISSA M.
Industry: Government/environmental **Current organization:** Kerr Lake Regional Water System **Title:** ORC **Type of organization:** Municipal utility **Major product:** Water processing, clean-up **Area of distribution:** Henderson, North Carolina **Expertise:** Operations, management **Affiliations:** North Carolina Waterworks Operators Association; American Water Works Association; West Virginia Rural Water Association **Hob./spts.:** Reading, coaching girls' soccer **SIC code:** 95 **Address:** Kerr Lake Regional Water System, 280 Regional Water Lane, Box 1434, Henderson, NC 27536 **E-mail:** clipscomb@ci.henderson.nc.us

LITTLE, BARBARA A.
Industry: Government/Healthcare **Born:** June 18, 1950, Dora, Alabama **Univ./degree:** R.N., George Corley Wallace College, 1984; Paralegal and Legal Nurse Consultant, College for Professional Studies, 2002; Training by the Federal Centers for Medicaid and Medicare Services in many areas of inspections of care **Current organization:** Alabama Dept. of Public Health, Division of Health Care Facilities **Title:** Complaint Intake Coordinator, R.N., L.N.C., Paralegal **Type of organization:** Government/Federal and State regulatory **Major product:** Healthcare regulatory services, intake of consumer complaints involving Alabama Health Care Facilities, review healthcare facility self reports involving resident/patient abuse, neglect and or other Federal or State mandated reports, onsite complaint investigations in Alabama's health care facilities **Area of distribution:** Alabama **Expertise:** Nursing, complaint and abuse investigations, investigative review and referrals of reports to other Federal and or State agencies or departments, historical experience as director of nursing, quality assurance and infection control in an Alabama based Intermediate Care Facility for the Mentally Retarded and hospital nursing in the field of medical, surgical, pediatric, psychiatric, orthopedic and oncology nursing **Affiliations:** Delta Epsilon Tau International Honor Society; Alabama Public Health Association; Alabama Public Employees Association League **Hob./spts.:** Active in church and civic activities **SIC code:** 94 **Address:** 1290 Cooper Ave., Prattville, AL 36066 **E-mail:** jim.barbara@knology.net

LOCALLO, DANIEL M.
Industry: Government/judiciary **Born:** October 28, 1952, Chicago, Illinois **Univ./degree:** J.D., John Marshall Law School, 1977 **Current organization:** State of Illinois County of Cook **Title:** Circuit Court Judge **Type of organization:** Circuit court **Major product:** Judicial proceedings **Area of distribution:** Chicago, Illinois **Expertise:** Legal decisions **Affiliations:** Illinois State Bar Association; Justinian Society of Lawyers **Hob./spts.:** Golf, coaching youth sports, gardening, reading, history **SIC code:** 92 **Address:** State of Illinois, County of Cook, 2104 Richard J. Daley Center, Chicago, IL 60602 **E-mail:** dmlocal@cookcountygov.com

LOKKA, DUKE G.
Industry: Government **Born:** February 11, 1955, Monrovia, California **Univ./degree:** B.A., University of Southern California, 1977; M.B.A., International Business, American University **Current organization:** U.S. Department of State **Title:** Diplomat (Foreign Service Officer) **Type of organization:** Government **Major product:** Foreign policy (service) **Area of distribution:** International **Expertise:** Policy planning and coordination, budget forecasting, strategic analysis, crisis situations and immigration issues **Hob./spts.:** Spending time with family, music, reading, physical fitness **SIC code:** 91 **Address:** 1515 Laurel Hill Rd., Vienna, VA 22182 **E-mail:** lokkadg@hotmail.com

LOPEZ, ALMA L.
Industry: Government/legal services **Born:** August 17, 1943, Laredo, Texas **Univ./degree:** B.B.A.; Saint Mary's University, 1965; J.D., Saint Mary's University School of Law, 1968 **Current organization:** Fourth Court of Appeals **Title:** Chief Justice **Type of organization:** Appellate court **Major product:** Legal decisions **Area of distribution:** Texas **Expertise:** Judiciary duties **Affiliations:** American Bar Association; Texas Bar Women's Association; Bexar County Bar Association **Hob./spts.:** Reading, stamp collecting **SIC code:** 92 **Address:** Fourth Court of Appeals, 300 Delarosa, Suite 3200, San Antonio, TX 78205 **E-mail:** almallopez@earthlink.net

LOWREY, MAC
Industry: Government/law **Born:** March 13, 1960, Ripley, Mississippi **Univ./degree:** Attended Northeast Mississippi Junior College for Drafting; Graduate, Pearl Police Academy, 1990 **Current organization:** Blue Mountain Police Dept. **Title:** Police Chief **Type of organization:** Police department **Major product:** Public order, safety and law enforcement **Area of distribution:** North Central Mississippi **Expertise:** Administration, lecturing on drug and alcohol abuse, training; Mississippi State Conservation Officer **Published works:** Several articles on wild life and environment **Affiliations:** Master Sgt., Mississippi Wildlife Officer's Association; Mississippi Police Chief's Association **Hob./spts.:** Hunting **SIC code:** 92 **Address:** Blue Mountain Police Dept., 110 Mill St., Blue Mountain, MS 38610

LUCKEYDOO, AMY K.
Industry: Government/healthcare **Born:** March 7, 1971, Nürenberg, Germany **Univ./degree:** M.D., Medical College of Virginia, 1997 **Current organization:** Naval Ambulatory Care Center, Kings Bay **Title:** M.D. **Type of organization:** Government/medical clinic **Major product:** Ambulatory care **Area of distribution:** Kingsland, Georgia **Expertise:** Pediatrics **Honors/awards:** Lieutenant Commander in Navy **Affiliations:** Fellow, American Academy of Pediatrics; Alumni Association of MCV **Hob./spts.:** Handcrafts, jogging, reading, cooking **SIC code:** 94 **Address:** 213 Azalea Ct., Kingsland, GA 31548 **E-mail:** akluckeydoo@sar.med.navy.mil

LUKASZEWSKI, JOHN E.
Industry: Government/public works **Current organization:** Ulster County Dept. of Public Works **Title:** Field Service Operation Manager **Type of organization:** Government **Major product:** Highways and bridges **Area of distribution:** Ulster County, New York **Expertise:** Operations management, road maintenance, snow removal, rebuilding, fabrication; Acting Commissioner **Affiliations:** New York State County Highway Superintendents Association; Ulster County Town Highway Association; Ulster County Volunteer Fire Dept. **SIC code:** 95 **Address:** Ulster County Dept. of Public Works, 317 Shamrock Lane, Kingston, NY 12401

MACDONALD, JOHN M.
Industry: Government/research **Born:** May 1, 1956, Sante Fe, New Mexico **Univ./degree:** A.S., 1982; B.S., Geology, 1984, University of Texas of the Permian Basin **Current organization:** Los Alamos National Laboratory **Title:** Scientist **Type of organization:** Government **Major product:** Research **Area of distribution:** National **Expertise:** Process control and instrumentation, electrical distribution, polymer analysis and computer sciences **Affiliations:** I.S.A.; The Foresight Institute **Hob./spts.:** Fishery, archery, hiking **SIC code:** 96 **Address:** 52887, P.O. Box 1663, M.S. E539, Los Alamos, NM 87545 **E-mail:** jmac@lanl.gov

MADON, MINOO B.
Industry: Government/Special District **Born:** March 6, 1939, Secunderabad, India **Univ./degree:** M.S., Zoology, Osmania University, India, 1960; Entomology, University of Arizona **Current organization:** Greater Los Angeles County Vector Control District **Title:** Scientific Technical Services Director **Type of organization:** Public health/Headquarters office **Major product:** Mosquito & Vector surveillance management **Area of distribution:** California **Expertise:** Public Health; Medical & Veterinary Entomology; epidemiology of vector-borne diseases; venomous arthropods **Honors/awards:** Distinguished Service Award, Society for Vector Ecology, 1996 **Published works:** 35 Publications in scientific Journals, Bulletins and Proceedings; Co-author, 5 chapters in "Arthropods of Public Health Significance in California"; 1 chapter in training manual "Vertebrates of Public Health Importance in California"; Past Editor, Bulletin of the Society for Vector Ecology, 1974-82; Editor, Proceedings & papers of the Mosquito & Vector Control Association of California, 1999 - present **Affiliations:** California Mosquito & Vector Control Association; American Mosquito Control Association; President, Society for Vector Ecology; European Mosquito Control Association; Entomological Society of America, 1970-2000; Board Certified Entomologist; Entomology; Industrial & Urban Entomology, 1972-2000; Vertebrate Pest Council Member since 1978 **SIC code:** 94 **Address:** Greater Los Angeles County Vector Control District, 12545 Florence Ave., Santa Fe Springs, CA 90670-3919 **E-mail:** mmadon@glacvcd.org

MALDONADO, DAVID
Industry: Government **Born:** October 4, 1957, Brooklyn, New York **Univ./degree:** B.A., Architecture, Howard University, 1986 **Current organization:** U.S. General Services Adm. **Title:** Architect **Type of organization:** Government agency **Major product:** Public building services, construction, alterations, repairs **Area of distribution:** Puerto Rico **Expertise:** Architecture, construction **Affiliations:** A.I.A. **Hob./spts.:** Deep sea fishing and diving **SIC code:** 94 **Address:** U.S. General Services Adm., 150 Chardon Ave., Federal Bldg. Room 359, Hato Rey, PR 00918

MALDONADO, RODOLFO J.
Industry: Government/water/energy **Born:** March 18, 1953, Brawley, California **Current organization:** Imperial Irrigation District **Title:** Director, Division 5 **Type of organization:** Public utility **Major product:** Water for agriculture, electricity **Area of distribution:** Imperial, California **Expertise:** Administration (water resources, electricity) **Affiliations:** Chairperson, Calexico New River Committee **SIC code:** 96 **Address:** Imperial Irrigation District, Box 937, Imperial, CA 92251 **E-mail:** rjmaldonado@iid.com

MALINENI, SAYI P.
Industry: Environmental **Born:** September, 13, 1943, Vuyyur, A.P., India **Univ./degree:** M.S., Geology, University of Gauhati, India, 1966 **Current organization:** Entek, Environmental Labs **Title:** Quality Assurance Coordinator **Type of organization:** Analytical testing lab **Major product:** Tests for wastewater, solid waste, wastewater and industrial hygiene **Area of distribution:** Baton Rouge, Louisiana **Expertise:** Quality control in environmental chemistry, petroleum exploration and

production geology **Honors/awards:** Gold Medal winner for graduating at the top of M.S. Geology class **Published works:** Technical articles published in India (oil and gas) **Hob./spts.:** Gardening, Yoga, reading **SIC code:** 95 **Address:** 10350 Dunn Drive, Baton Rouge, LA 70810 **E-mail:** sayi.entek@yahoo.com and spmalineni@yahoo.com **Web address:** spmalineni@yahoo.com

MANN, G.B.
Industry: Government **Univ./degree:** B.S., Civil Engineering, Southern Methodist University, 1941 **Current organization:** Texas Highway Dept. (Retired) **Title:** Senior Design Engineer; Professional Engineer **Type of organization:** State government **Major product:** Maintenance, construction and design of highways **Area of distribution:** Texas **Expertise:** Civil engineering **Affiliations:** Life Member, I.S.P.E.; A.S.C.E.; N.S.P.E. **SIC code:** 96 **Address:** 10007 Lake Gardens Dr., Dallas, TX 75218-2903

MANN, KIMBERLY S.
Industry: Government **Born:** October 29, 1959, Wayne, Nebraska **Univ./degree:** B.S., Architectural Design, University of Nebraska, 1982 **Current organization:** National Park Service **Title:** Historical Architect **Type of organization:** Government/national park **Major product:** Historic preservation **Area of distribution:** National **Expertise:** Architecture/design **Honors/awards:** American Society of Landscape Architects Merit Award; American Society of Architects Merit Award, 2002; Accessibility Award, National Park Service, 2002 **Published works:** Article in Interior Sources, 1993 **Affiliations:** Association for Preservation Technology; National Trust for Historic Preservation **Hob./spts.:** Volleyball, softball, backpacking, sailing **SIC code:** 95 **Address:** National Park Service, 9922 Front St., Empire, MI 49630 **E-mail:** kimberly_mann@nps.gov

MAPLE, THOMAS O.
Industry: Government **Born:** February 20, 1948, Detroit, Michigan **Univ./degree:** B.A., Business, Eastern Michigan Community College/Florida Keys Community College **Current organization:** Naval Air Facility Boca Chica **Title:** Engineering Technician **Type of organization:** Government **Major product:** Structuring contracts **Area of distribution:** National **Expertise:** Engineering **Published works:** Paper on euthanasia **Affiliations:** V.F.W.; American Legion **Hob./spts.:** Golf **SIC code:** 97 **Address:** Naval Air Facility, Commanding Officer, Attn: Code 1882TM, Bldg. A-629, First floor, Key West, FL 33040 **E-mail:** mapleth@naskw.navy.mil

MARA, THOMAS L.
Industry: Government transportation construction **Born:** March 27, 1961, Windham, Connecticut **Current organization:** State of Connecticut, Dept. of Transportation Construction **Title:** Transportation Construction Inspector 2 **Type of organization:** State government **Major product:** Service to roadways, bridges, tunnels **Area of distribution:** Connecticut **Expertise:** Municipality **Hob./spts.:** Playing soccer with his children **SIC code:** 96 **Address:** State of Connecticut, Dept. of Transportation Construction, 171 Salem Tpke, Norwich, CT 06360 **E-mail:** thomasmara@po.state.ct.usa

MARKSBERRY, WILLIAM A.
Industry: Government **Born:** November 3, 1955, Carrollton, Kentucky **Univ./degree:** Certificate, Purdue University **Current organization:** City of Rising Sun **Title:** Mayor **Type of organization:** County government **Major product:** Public service **Area of distribution:** Rising Sun, Indiana **Expertise:** Municipal management **Honors/awards:** Nominated, Outstanding Young Men Under 30 in 1987 **SIC code:** 91 **Address:** City of Rising Sun, 200 N. Walnut St., Rising Sun, IN 47040 **E-mail:** mayor@cityofrisingsun.com

MARTÍ, MIRIAM
Industry: Government/healthcare **Born:** June 12, 1952, Mayaguez, Puerto Rico **Univ./degree:** M.D., University of Puerto Rico School of Medicine, 1976 **Current organization:** San Juan VA Hospital **Title:** M.D. **Type of organization:** Federal Hospital **Major product:** Service to veterans of war, compensation and pension examination **Area of distribution:** San Juan, Puerto Rico and U.S. Virgin Islands **Expertise:** Psychiatry **Honors/awards:** International Who's Who; Strathmore's Who's Who **Affiliations:** A.A.A.S.; A.S.F.E.; A.M.A. American Political Action Committee; New York Academy of Sciences; American Professional Practice Association **Hob./spts.:** Scuba diving, consultant for support groups **SIC code:** 94 **Address:** San Juan VA Hospital, T2-13 Zion St., Urb. Park Gardens, San Juan, PR 00926 **E-mail:** mphcev@yahoo.com

MARTIN, GARY E.
Industry: Aerospace **Born:** May 19, 1948, Dayton, Ohio **Univ./degree:** B.S., Mechanical Engineering, Ohio University, 1971; M.S., Mechanical Engineering, University of Dayton, 1979 **Current organization:** ASC (Aeronautical Systems Center) **Title:** Chief Systems Engineer **Type of organization:** US Air Force, Wright Patterson Air Force Base **Major product:** Military aircraft development and production **Area of distribution:** National **Expertise:** Engineering **Published works:** Internal reports **Affiliations:** A.S.M.E.; N.D.I.A. **Hob./spts.:** Soccer referee, minor league baseball **SIC code:** 97 **Address:** ASC (Aeronautical Systems Control), 1970 Monahan Way, Wright-Patterson AFB, OH 45433 **E-mail:** gary.martin@wpafb.af.mil

MATHEW, M. ABRAHAM
Industry: City government/engineering **Born:** December 9, 1937, India **Univ./degree:** Ph.D., Electrical Engineering, IIT, India, 1977 **Current organization:** DWSD, City of Detroit **Title:** Senior Associate Electrical Engineer **Type of organization:** State City **Major product:** Treatment and distribution of water and treatment of sewage **Area of distribution:** Detroit and suburban cities **Expertise:** Electrical engineering **Published works:** Several research papers and text books **Affiliations:** E.S.D. **Hob./spts.:** Reading **SIC code:** 95 **Address:** DWSD, City of Detroit, 6425 Huber, Detroit, MI 48211 **E-mail:** mmathew@dwsd.org

MCDANIEL III, JOHN PERRY
Industry: Government/law enforcement **Born:** October 9, 1940, Bascom, Florida **Univ./degree:** Attended Chipola Junior College; Law Enforcement Training, Academy Graduate, 1973; FBI Academy Graduate, 1982 **Current organization:** Office of the Sheriff, Jackson County, Florida **Title:** Sheriff of Jackson County, Florida **Type of organization:** Sheriff's office **Major product:** Public safety, order and law enforcement **Area of distribution:** Florida **Expertise:** Law enforcement **Affiliations:** Past Master, Harmony Lodge, Masonic Lodge; Past Board Member, Florida Sheriff's Association; Past Board Member, Florida Youth Ranches; Past Ambassador, Shaddei Temple and Hadji Shrine Temple **Hob./spts.:** Private pilot of fixed wing aircraft, helicopters, scuba diving **SIC code:** 92 **Address:** Office of the Sheriff, Jackson County, Florida, 4012 Lafayette Street, Marianna, FL 32446

MCGARR, BRIAN E.
Industry: Law enforcement **Born:** July 8, 1956, Phenix City, Alabama **Univ./degree:** A.S., Chattahoochee Community College, 1989; Graduated, FBI National Academy for Criminal Justice, 1989 **Current organization:** Phenix City Police Dept. **Title:** Chief of Police **Type of organization:** Police department **Major product:** Protection of citizens and property **Area of distribution:** Phenix City, Alabama **Expertise:** Law enforcement, public service technician **Affiliations:** International Association of Chiefs of Police; Alabama Association of Chiefs of Police; FBI National Academy Associates **Hob./spts.:** Riding Harley Davidson motorcycles, weight lifting **SIC code:** 92 **Address:** Phenix City Police Dept., 1111 Broad St., Phenix City, AL 36867 **E-mail:** bmcgarr@ci.phenix-city.al.us

MCKAY, JOHN
Industry: Government **Born:** November 2, 1948, Ocean Springs, Mississippi **Univ./degree:** B.S., Southern Mississippi University, 1971 **Current organization:** Mississippi Board of Supervisors **Title:** Supervisor, District 5 **Type of organization:** County government **Major product:** Public services **Area of distribution:** Mississippi **Expertise:** District oversight **Affiliations:** N.A.C.O.; V.F.W.; Elks Club; American Legion **Hob./spts.:** Golf, boating **SIC code:** 91 **Address:** 3120 Shadow Wood Dr., Ocean Springs, MS 39564 **E-mail:** john_mckay@co.jackson.ms.us

MCLAUGHLIN, THOMAS F.
Industry: Government/law enforcement **Born:** April 5, 1961, Gardiner, Maine **Univ./degree:** A.S., Criminal Justice, University of Maine, Augusta, 1979 **Current organization:** Maine Dept. of Inland Fisheries & Wildlife/Richmond Police Dept. **Title:** Supervisor/Police Officer **Type of organization:** State/municipal government **Major product:** Wildlife and aquatic conservation, regulation/public order, safety and law enforcement **Area of distribution:** Maine **Expertise:** Administration, law enforcement **Affiliations:** Masons; Assistant Chief, West Gardiner Fire Dept. **Hob./spts.:** Fishing, boating, camping **SIC code:** 92 **Address:** 265 Pond Rd., West Gardiner, ME 04345 **E-mail:** tmclaughlinmestate@prexar.com

MCLEAN, IAN W.
Industry: Government **Born:** September 21, 1943, Durham, North Carolina **Univ./degree:** M.D., University of Michigan, 1969 **Current organization:** Armed Forces Institute of Pathology **Title:** Chief, Division of Ophthalmic Pathology **Type of organization:** Government/pathology institute **Major product:** Pathology reports **Area of distribution:** International **Expertise:** Pathology **Honors/awards:** 1988 Gold Medal, San Paolo **Published works:** 170+ articles and chapters **Affiliations:** A.R.V.O.; America Academy of Ophthalmologists **SIC code:** 94 **Address:** 9110 Kittery Lane, Bethesda, MD 20817 **E-mail:** mclean@afip.osd.mil

MEEHAN, RICHARD K.
Industry: Government **Born:** December 17, 1960, Quincy, Illinois **Current organization:** City of Quincy **Title:** Director of Administrative Services **Type of organization:** City government **Major product:** City services/administration **Area of distribution:** Quincy, Illinois **Expertise:** Labor relations/Dept. Mayor **Affiliations:** Quincy Society of Fine Arts; Historic Quincy Business District Association; Gardner Museum of Art & Design **Hob./spts.:** Archery, wood working, historic reading **SIC code:** 91 **Address:** City of Quincy, 730 Maine St., Quincy, IL 62301 **E-mail:** rmeehan@cl.quincy.il.us

MILES, JOHN T.
Industry: Government/water treatment **Born:** November 10, 1941, Findlay, Ohio **Current organization:** City of Findlay Water Plant **Title:** Master Mechanic **Type of organization:** Government/municipally owned water plant **Major product:** Potable water **Area of distribution:** Findlay, Ohio **Expertise:** Supervisor of maintenance personnel **Hob./spts.:** Walking, bike riding, computers **SIC code:** 96 **Address:** City of Findlay Water Plant, 110 N. Blanchard St., Findlay, OH 45840 **E-mail:** fcwaterboy@aol.com

MILLER, CURTIS L.
Industry: Government/law enforcement **Born:** April 10, 1969, Homer, Illinois **Univ./degree:** B.S., Criminal Justice, MacMurray College, 1991 **Current organization:** Ford County Sheriff's Office **Title:** Lieutenant **Type of organization:** County government **Major product:** Public order, safety and law enforcement **Area of distribution:** Ford County, Illinois **Expertise:** Traffic crash reconstruction, personal defense instruction **Hob./spts.:** Family **SIC code:** 92 **Address:** Ford County Sheriff's Office, 235 North American St., Paxton, IL 60957 **E-mail:** cmiller@fcsheriff.com

MIRANDA, EDWARD G.
Industry: Law enforcement **Born:** January 10, 1961, El Paso, Texas **Current organization:** Anthony Police Dept. **Title:** Chief of Police **Type of organization:** Police department **Major product:** Public order, safety and law enforcement **Area of distribution:** Anthony, Texas **Expertise:** Administration **Honors/awards:** Master Peace Officer **Affiliations:** Chiefs of Police Association of Texas; Wildcat Community Crime Stoppers **Hob./spts.:** Landscaping, golf **SIC code:** 92 **Address:** Anthony Police Dept., 401 Wildcat Dr., Anthony, TX 79821 **E-mail:** chiefmiranda1@yahoo.com

MONAGHAN, MARK W.
Industry: Government/NASA **Born:** November 29, 1954, Superior, Wisconsin **Univ./degree:** B.S.E.E., University of Minnesota at Duluth, 1987; M.S., Technical Management, Embry-Riddle Aeronautical University, 1999 **Current organization:** United Space Alliance **Title:** Engineering Manager **Type of organization:** Prime contractor for NASA **Major product:** Space exploration, electrical, electronic systems **Expertise:** Power engineering **Honors/awards:** Served in active duty, U.S. Coast Guard, 1975-79; U.S. Coast Guard Reserves, 1979-86; U.S. Navy, 1986-99 **Affiliations:** Sr. Member, I.E.E.E.; Knights of Columbus; Sierra Club; Volunteer Pack Leader, Boy Scouts of America Pack 367 **Hob./spts.:** Rebuilding and restoring classic cars, backpacking **SIC code:** 96 **Address:** 2190 Keylime Dr., Titusville, FL 32780 **E-mail:** ce1monag@cfl.rr.com

MOSBY, BRIAN D.
Industry: Government/environmental **Born:** August 12, 1970, Gary, Indiana **Univ./degree:** B.S.C.E., Howard University, 1994 **Current organization:** WSSC Western Branch WWTP **Title:** Plant Superintendent **Type of organization:** Water and wastewater utility **Major product:** Wastewater treatment **Area of distribution:** Baltimore, Maryland and Washington, D.C. **Expertise:** Maintenance, operations management, training **Honors/awards:** General Manager's Award, Competitive Action Program, 2005 **Published works:** 2 books **Affiliations:** Water Environment Federation; CWEA Committee; Steering Team, 1998-2004 **Hob./spts.:** Weightlifting, cruises, boxing **SIC code:** 95 **Address:** WSSC Western Branch WWTP, 6600 Crain Hwy., Upper Marlboro, MD 20772-4136 **E-mail:** bdmosby@hotmail.com

MOYER, ELLEN O.
Industry: Government **Univ./degree:** M.A., Education, 1962 **Current organization:** City of Annapolis **Title:** CEO/Mayor **Type of organization:** Municipal government **Major product:** Government administration **Area of distribution:** Maryland **Expertise:** Governing the City of Annapolis **Honors/awards:** Maryland's Top 100 Women; 1st Woman Mayor of Annapolis; Circle of Excellence **Affiliations:** Board Member, Girl Scouts of America **SIC code:** 91 **Address:** City of Annapolis, 160 Duke of Gloucester St., Annapolis, MD 21401 **E-mail:** mayor@annapolis.gov

MULL, TY J.
Industry: Engineering **Born:** December 24, 1976, Greeley, Colorado **Univ./degree:** B.S., Bioresource and Agricultural Engineering, 1999; M.S., Civil Engineering, Colorado State University, Fort Collins, 2001 **Current organization:** U.S. Bureau of Reclamation **Title:** Hydraulic Engineer **Type of organization:** Government **Major product:** Water planning **Area of distribution:** Western United States **Expertise:** Engineering **Affiliations:** A.S.C.E.; A.S.A.E. **Hob./spts.:** Outdoor activates, snow skiing, hiking, horseback riding, fishing, softball **SIC code:** 95 **Address:** U.S. Bureau of Reclamation, P.O. Box 261305, Lakewood, CO 30226 **E-mail:** tmull@do.usbr.gov

MUNROE, MASSIE
Industry: Government **Born:** March 1, 1954, Tehran, Iran **Univ./degree:** B.S.C.E.; Masters Candidate **Current organization:** Public Works Los Angeles County **Title:** Supervising Civil Engineer Assistant **Type of organization:** Municipal government environmental agency **Major product:** Environmental engineering, science **Area of distribution:** Los Angeles County, California **Expertise:** Civil engineering **Hob./spts.:** Ballet, painting, reading **SIC code:** 95 **Address:** Public Works Los Angeles County, 2167 East Chevy Chase Drive, Glendale, CA 91206

MURAKAMI, MASANORI
Industry: Physics/nuclear energy **Born:** May 16, 1940, Ashiya, Hyogo, Japan **Univ./degree:** Ph.D., MIT, 1970 **Current organization:** Oak Ridge National Laboratory **Title:** Ph.D. **Type of organization:** Government laboratory **Major product:** Nuclear energy, physics research **Area of distribution:** International **Expertise:** Physics research **Published works:** 30 papers, 100+ articles **Affiliations:** Fellow, American Physical Society; Sigma Xi **Hob./spts.:** Hiking, physical fitness, travel **SIC code:** 96 **Address:** Oak Ridge National Laboratory, P.O. Box 2008, Bldg. 5700, Room A307, Oak Ridge, TN 37831 **E-mail:** murakamim@ornl.gov

MURPHY, RAYMOND M.
Industry: Law **Current organization:** Michigan State Senate **Title:** Senator **Type of organization:** State legislation **Major product:** Public service **Area of distribution:** Michigan **Expertise:** Legislation **Affiliations:** A.F.I.D.; President, Federation of Masons; Imperial Council **SIC code:** 91 **Address:** 125 W. Allegan St., Room 715, Lansing, MI 48933 **E-mail:** senrmurphy@senate.state.mi.us

MUSGROVE JR., WAYNE
Industry: Government/law enforcement **Born:** August 3, 1958, Jacksonville, Florida **Univ./degree:** F.B.I. Academy **Current organization:** Suwannee County Sheriff's Office **Title:** Lieutenant **Type of organization:** Sheriff's office **Major product:** Public order, safety and law enforcement **Area of distribution:** Suwannee County, Florida **Expertise:** Sex crimes investigation; SWAT team leader and commander, training **Hob./spts.:** Family, fishing **SIC code:** 92 **Address:** Suwannee County Sheriff's Office, 200 S. Ohio Ave., Live Oak, FL 32060 **E-mail:** wmusgrove@hotmail.com

MYERS, MITCHELL AUSTIN
Industry: Government/utilities **Born:** November 28, 1967, Sacramento, California **Univ./degree:** Attended Sacramento State University (Extension Courses) **Current organization:** Fair Oaks Water District **Title:** Superintendent **Type of organization:** Water district **Major product:** Water distribution **Area of distribution:** Fair Oaks, California **Expertise:** Management, plumbing contracting (grade 4 water distribution operator) **Affiliations:** A.W.W.A. **SIC code:** 96 **Address:** Fair Oaks Water District, 10317 Fair Oaks Blvd., Fair Oaks, CA 95628 **E-mail:** mmyers@fowd.com

NATH, JAYASREE
Industry: Government/defense **Born:** October 22, 1939, Calcutta, India **Univ./degree:** B.S., M.S. with the highest honors, Physiology/Biochemistry, Calcutta University; Ph.D., Indian Institute of Biochemistry and Experimental Medicine, Calcutta, India, 1967 **Current organization:** Walter Reed Army Institute of Research **Title:** Ph.D. **Type of organization:** Premier research institute of the Army/Dept. of Defense **Major product:** Basic and applied research **Area of distribution:** National **Expertise:** Cell biology and biochemical research, oxidative injury mechanisms **Honors/awards:** NSF Center for Excellence Award, University of Virginia; DoD Civilian Achievement Medal, 1994 **Published works:** Numerous articles in major scientific journals including: Journal of Cell Biology, Journal of Biological Chemistry, Journal of Immunology, Toxicology, Critical Care Medicine and Journal of Clinical Investigation **Affiliations:** American Society for Cell Biology; Society for Free Radical Biology and Medicine; A.A.A.S.; Society for Leukocyte Biology; American Federation for Clinical Research; Women in Cell Biology; Co-Founder, Asian Women's Self Help Association (ASHA) **Hob./spts.:** Music, gardening, reading, writing, community service **SIC code:** 97 **Address:** Walter Reed Army Institute of Research, 503 Robert Grant Ave., Room 1A-14, Silver Spring, MD 20910 **E-mail:** jayasree.nath@na.amedd.army.mil

NEGRÓN-MARTINEZ, MILDRED E.
Industry: Government/law **Born:** June 25, 1958, Puerto Rico **Univ./degree:** Ed.D., 1993; M.A., J.D. candidate, Universidad Interamericana de Puerto Rico **Current organization:** Alternative Dispute Resolution Bureau **Title:** Director **Type of organization:** Judicial Power of Puerto Rico **Major product:** Alternative dispute resolution methods (an alternative to going to court), mediation, arbitration, early neutral evaluation **Area of distribution:** National **Expertise:** Psychology, education, counseling, mediation **Published works:** Book: "Un Modelo Puertoriqueño de Mediacion (Lexis Pub.) and several articles on A.D.R. **Affiliations:** The Association for Conflict Resolution **Hob./spts.:** Reading, music **SIC code:** 92 **Address:** Alternative Dispute Resolution Bureau, Supreme Court, San Juan, PR 00919 **E-mail:** mildredn@tld.net

NELSON SR., LARRY W.
Industry: Wastewater treatment **Born:** October 23, 1940, Charleston, West Virginia **Univ./degree:** Attended Indiana Vocational Technical College; Indiana Wastewater Certifications **Current organization:** Sanitary District of Hammond **Title:** Safety Coordinator/Instructor, Wastewater Operator Training Programs **Type of organization:** Wastewater treatment **Major product:** Clean water **Area of distribution:** Hammond, Indiana **Expertise:** Safety and training coordinator **Honors/awards:** Numerous, including; District Award; Safety Award **Affiliations:** A.S.S.E.; W.E.F. **Hob./spts.:**

Fishing, computers **SIC code:** 95 **Address:** Sanitary District of Hammond, 5143 Columbia Ave., Hammond, IN 46327 **E-mail:** wastetreat@hotmail.com **Web address:** www.hmdin.com/sanitarydistrict/index.htm#departmen

NOCE, C. JEFFREY
Industry: Government/wastewater treatment **Born:** August 27, 1955, Syracuse, New York **Univ./degree:** B.S., Chemistry, LeMoyne College-1978 **Current organization:** Onondaga County Dept. Water Environment Protection **Title:** Nutrient Division Supervisor **Type of organization:** Government/county agency **Major product:** Wastewater treatment **Area of distribution:** Onondaga County, New York **Expertise:** Environmental chemistry, wastewater analysis **Hob./spts.:** E.C.A.C. III basketball referee **SIC code:** 95 **Address:** Onondaga County Dept. Water Environment Protection, 650 Hiawatha Blvd., Syracuse, NY 13204 **E-mail:** cjnoce@usadatanet.net

NORFLEET, CHARLES
Industry: Government **Born:** January 11, 1958, Philadelphia, Pennsylvania **Univ./degree:** B.S., Accounting, LaSalle University, 1980 **Current organization:** U.S. General Accounting Office **Title:** Senior Audit Manager **Type of organization:** Federal government **Major product:** Reports to Congress on financial management issues **Area of distribution:** International **Expertise:** Auditing, inspections, assessments; Certified Government Financial Manager; Certified Public Accountant **Honors/awards:** Continuous Improvement Award; Award for Outstanding Achievement and Teamwork; special commendation awards **Affiliations:** A.I.C.P.A; Association of Government Accountants **Hob./spts.:** Family, basketball **SIC code:** 99 **Address:** U.S. General Accounting Office, 441 G. St. N.W., Washington, DC 20548 **E-mail:** norfleet@gao.gov

OCASIO, THOMAS M.
Industry: State Government **Born:** August 7, 1959, Neptune, New Jersey **Current organization:** New Jersey Dept. of Corrections **Title:** Fleet Manager **Type of organization:** Government agency/law enforcement **Major product:** Overseeing correctional institutions of New Jersey **Area of distribution:** New Jersey **Expertise:** Fleet management, vehicle replacements, complaints and repairs (two years of vocational training in automotives) **Affiliations:** N.A.F.A. **Hob./spts.:** Motorcycle drag racing **SIC code:** 92 **Address:** New Jersey Dept. of Corrections, Whittlesey Rd., Trenton, NJ 08625 **E-mail:** thomas.ocasio@doc.state.nj.us

OLIVER, TERESE S.
Industry: Government/law **Born:** October 30, 1952, Riverside, California **Univ./degree:** B.A., Sociology; B.A., History, Salve Regina University, 1975; J.D., Western State University College of Law, 1978 **Current organization:** City of Anaheim **Title:** Deputy City Attorney, Prosecutor **Type of organization:** City government **Major product:** Criminal prosecution **Area of distribution:** Anaheim, California **Expertise:** Domestic violence, code enforcement, criminal law **Honors/awards:** Judge Pro tem, Los Angeles County, 1982; Judge Pro tem, Orange County, 1990-2003 **Affiliations:** Association of University Women, 2000; Garden Grove Soroptimists Club, 2000; Board Member, Friends of the Santa Ana Zoo, 2000-03; Past President and Member, Tustin Branch of the Association of University Women; Orange County Bar Association; Member, Board of Directors and Treasurer, Orange County Women Lawyers **Hob./spts.:** Sewing, walking, reading **SIC code:** 92 **Address:** City of Anaheim, 200 Anaheim Blvd., Suite 303, Anaheim, CA 92805 **E-mail:** toliver@anaheim.net

O'NEIL, LINDA RUSH
Industry: Government **Born:** June 27, 1961, Fort Smith, Arizona **Univ./degree:** M.D., East Temple State University, 1992 **Current organization:** Broward County Medical Examiner's Office **Title:** M.D., Medical Examiner **Type of organization:** Government **Major product:** Autopsies, examinations **Area of distribution:** Broward County, Florida **Expertise:** Forensic pathology **Published works:** Articles **Hob./spts.:** Diving **SIC code:** 94 **Address:** Broward County Medical Examiner's Office, 5301 S.W. 31st Ave., Suite B, Ft. Lauderdale, FL 33312 **E-mail:** lroneil@broward.org

ORTIZ, DIANE THORMAN
Industry: Government/Municipal **Born:** July 22, 1945, Minneapolis, Minnesota **Univ./degree:** B.A., Political Science, University of Nevada, Las Vegas; M.A.-L. in Librarianship, San Jose State University, California; M.P.A., University of Nevada, Las Vegas **Current organization:** Las Vegas Municipal Court, Alternative Sentencing & Education Division **Title:** Management Analyst II **Type of organization:** Municipal Court **Major product:** Criminal justice and sentencing alternatives to incarceration **Area of distribution:** Las Vegas, Nevada Metropolitan Area and other court jurisdictions **Expertise:** Management analysis, library and information science, records and knowledge management, financial and operations management **Honors/awards:** Beta Phi Mu (International Library Science Honor Society); Pi Sigma Alpha (National Political Science Honor Society) **Affiliations:** American Library Association; Special Libraries Association; American Association of Law Libraries; Association of Records Managers and Administrators; National Association for Court Management **Hob./spts.:** Continuing education, current and cultural events, investments, travel, rubber stamp art, walking **SIC code:** 92 **Address:** Las Vegas Municipal Court, Alternative Sentencing & Education Division, 400 Stewart Ave., Las Vegas, NV 89101-2986 **E-mail:** dortiz@ci.las-vegas-nv.us

OSCEOLA, CURTIS
Industry: Government **Born:** February 10, 1953, Miami, Florida **Univ./degree:** B.B.A., Northwood University, 1994; M.B.A. Candidate **Current organization:** South Florida Water Management District **Title:** Specialist Construction Representative **Type of organization:** State government/public works **Major product:** Regional water resource management **Area of distribution:** West Palm Beach, Florida **Expertise:** Project management **Affiliations:** Past Member, A.S.P.O.; A.I.P.A. **Hob./spts.:** Travel, guitar, the outdoors, environmental conservation **SIC code:** 95 **Address:** South Florida Water Management District, 3301 Gun Club Rd., West Palm Beach, FL 33406-3089 **E-mail:** cosceola@sfwmd.gov **Web address:** www.sfwmd.gov

OWENS, JAMES W.
Industry: Government/law enforcement **Born:** January 17, 1954, Rushville, Indiana **Univ./degree:** Attended Ball State University for Criminal Justice; Graduate, Law Enforcement Training Academy,1989; Detective, Indianapolis Police Dept. Detective School, 1990 **Current organization:** Rush County Sheriff's Dept. **Title:** Sheriff **Type of organization:** Sheriff's department **Major product:** Law enforcement administration **Area of distribution:** Southeast Indiana **Expertise:** Program development, training and education of staff, drug elimination; Certified Voice Stress Operator; Indiana Certified Emergency Vehicle Operation Control Instructor **Affiliations:** Indiana Sheriff's Association; American Legion; Knights of Columbus, Eagle's Lodge **Hob./spts.:** Community involvement, boating, fishing, collecting police memorabilia **SIC code:** 92 **Address:** Rush County Sheriff's Dept., 1204 Perkins St., Rushville, IN 46173 **E-mail:** sheriff@spitfire.net

PALMER, DONALD A.
Industry: Government **Born:** August 12, 1943, Perth, Australia **Univ./degree:** B.S., With Honors, Inorganic Chemistry,1964; Ph.D., Chemistry, 1970; University of Western Australia; Post Doc., Inorganic Kinetics, SUNY Buffalo; Post Doc., Coordination Chemistry, University of Frankfurt, Germany **Current organization:** Oak Ridge National Laboratory **Title:** Senior Research Scientist **Type of organization:** Government laboratory **Major product:** Research and development **Area of distribution:** International **Expertise:** Inorganic chemistry **Published works:** 180 peer reviewed journals, 3 book chapters, editor of 2 books **Hob./spts.:** Golf, gardening, travel, theatre **SIC code:** 96 **Address:** Oak Ridge National Laboratory, P.O 2008, Oak Ridge, TN 37831-6110 **E-mail:** palmerda@ornl.gov **Web address:** www.ornl.gov

PANOS, XANTHI B.
Industry: Government **Born:** February 28, 1970, Jamaica, Queens, New York **Univ./degree:** B.S., Civil; Engineering; M.B.A., Webster University, 1996 **Current organization:** City of Yuma **Title:** Project Manager **Type of organization:** Government/municipal **Major product:** Public utilities **Area of distribution:** Yuma, Arizona **Expertise:** Engineering, capital improvement plan, land development **Affiliations:** A.S.C.E.; A.W.W.A.; A.P.W.A.; A.F.M.A. **Hob./spts.:** Family, physical fitness, dancing, travel, hiking **SIC code:** 91 **Address:** City of Yuma, Public Works-Engineering, 155 W. 14th St., Yuma, AZ 85364 **E-mail:** xanthi.lauderdale@ci.yuma.az.us

PARRISH, DARYL J.
Industry: Government **Born:** October 31, 1956, Banning, California **Univ./degree:** M.S., Management, University of Redlands, 1988 **Current organization:** City of Colton **Title:** City Manager **Type of organization:** Municipal government **Major product:** Local government services **Area of distribution:** Colton, California **Expertise:** Administration **Hob./spts.:** Swimming, off-road biking, reading, hiking, games **SIC code:** 91 **Address:** City Manager, City of Colton, 650 N. La Cadena Dr., Colton, CA 92324 **E-mail:** dparrish@ci.colton.ca.us

PASCH, FRANCINE
Industry: Government **Univ./degree:** A.A., Nursing, Mercer Community College, 1987; B.S.N., Immaculate University, 2004 **Current organization:** Garden State Youth Correctional Facility **Title:** R.N. **Type of organization:** Government facility/prison **Area of distribution:** New Jersey **Expertise:** Nursing **Affiliations:** A.P.I.C.; New Jersey State Nursing Association **SIC code:** 92 **Address:** Garden State Youth Correctional Facility, P.O. Box 11401, Yardsville, NJ 08620 **E-mail:** fmpasch@aol.com

PEEPLES, M. WAYNE
Industry: Government/law **Born:** September 14, 1962, St. Mary's, Georgia **Current organization:** Kingsland Police Dept. **Title:** Assistant Police Chief **Type of organization:** Police department **Major product:** Public order, safety and law enforcement **Area of distribution:** Kingsland, Georgia **Expertise:** Police administration **Honors/awards:** 5 Life Saving Awards; 2 Good Samaritan Awards; 4 Officer of the Year Awards **Affiliations:** I.A.C.P.; State of Georgia Coroner's Association **Hob./spts.:** Golf **SIC code:** 92 **Address:** Kingsland Police Dept., 111 S. Seaboard St., Kingsland, GA 31548 **E-mail:** wpeeples@kingslandgeorgia.com

PEPER, CHRIS
Industry: Government laboratories **Born:** August 8, 1946, Boulder, Colorado **Univ./degree:** B.A., Biology; B.S., Medical Technology, Carthage College, Wisconsin, 1973; Blood Banking Newborn Screening, University of Utah, 1976 **Current organization:** Utah Dept. of Health Laboratories **Title:** Supervisor of Specimen Handling **Type of organization:** State government laboratories **Major product:** Health laboratories **Area of distribution:** Utah **Expertise:** Microbiology and newborn screening **Affiliations:** A.S.C.P. **Hob./spts.:** Walking **SIC code:** 94 **Address:** Utah Dept. of Health Laboratories, 46 N. Medical Dr., Salt Lake City, UT 84113 **E-mail:** cpeper@utah.gov

PERDUE, MOSES A.
Industry: Government **Born:** July 16, 1965, Atlanta, Georgia **Univ./degree:** M.A., Public Affairs, Columbus State University, 2005 **Current organization:** Atlanta Police Dept. **Title:** Lieutenant **Type of organization:** Police department **Major product:** Law enforcement **Area of distribution:** National **Expertise:** Management **Affiliations:** N.O.B.L.E. **Hob./spts.:** Football **SIC code:** 92 **Address:** Atlanta Police Dept., 675 Ponce De Leon Ave., Atlanta, GA 30309 **E-mail:** mperdue@atlantaga.gov

PICKERING, ELTON F.
Industry: Government **Born:** December 27, 1942, Fields, Louisiana **Current organization:** Beauregard Parish Police Jury **Title:** Parish Manager **Type of organization:** County government **Major product:** Road and bridge maintenance and repair **Area of distribution:** Beauregard Parish, Louisiana **Expertise:** Engineering **Affiliations:** L.E.P.C.; L.T.A.P. **Hob./spts.:** Antiques **SIC code:** 95 **Address:** Beauregard Parish Police Jury, 203 W. Third St., Deridder, LA 70634-4025 **E-mail:** epickering@beau.org

PIERCE, PETE DOUGLAS
Industry: Government/corrections **Born:** September 30, 1955, Casper, Wyoming **Univ./degree:** B.A., Colorado State University, 1978 **Current organization:** State of Colorado, Dept. of Corrections **Title:** Colorado Work Program Director **Type of organization:** Government **Major product:** Construction and work program education **Area of distribution:** Colorado **Expertise:** Design, engineering and training **Affiliations:** Elks Club; Correctional Peace Officers Foundation **Hob./spts.:** Rock climbing, skiing, camping, hunting, fishing, kayaking, mountain biking **SIC code:** 92 **Address:** State of Colorado Dept. of Corrections, P.O. Box 300, Canon City, CO 81215 **E-mail:** pete.pierce@doc.state.co.us

PINHEIRO, OLIVER M.
Industry: Government **Born:** July 20, 1959, Azores, Portugal **Univ./degree:** A.A., Criminal Justice, College of the Sequoias, 2003 **Current organization:** City of Tulare **Title:** Waster Water Collection Crew Leader **Type of organization:** Government **Major product:** Public service **Area of distribution:** Tulare, California **Expertise:** Oversees routine maintenance, certified instructor for confined space **Honors/awards:** Waste Water Person of the Year, 1984, 1986, 1997, 2001and 2003; President's Award for Distinguished Service from CWEA, 1997 **Affiliations:** California Water Environmental Association (CWEA) **Hob./spts.:** Soccer referee, model plane, car builder **SIC code:** 91 **Address:** City of Tulare, 1875 S. West St., Tulare, CA 93274

PLOCKMEYER, JAMEE SUE
Industry: Government **Univ./degree:** M.B.A., California Lutheran University, 1998; B.S., Civil and Environmental Engineering, University of Rhode Island **Current organization:** US Air Force Headquarters **Title:** Deputy Director, Environmental Division **Type of organization:** Federal government **Major product:** National defense **Area of distribution:** International **Expertise:** Environmental policy/guidance **Affiliations:** Fellow, American Society of Civil Engineers; Society of Women Engineers; Society of American Military Engineers **Hob./spts.:** Gourmet cooking, ballroom dancing **SIC code:** 97 **Address:** US Air Force Headquarters, 1260 Air Force Pentagon, Washington, DC 20330 **E-mail:** jamee.plockmeyer@pentagon.af.mil

PORTER, DONALD L.
Industry: Economic development **Born:** July 25, 1945, Tidewater, Virginia **Univ./degree:** B.S, Norfolk State University, 1968; M.A., Webster University, 1995 **Current organization:** Raeford/Hoke Economic Development **Title:** Executive Director **Type of organization:** Local government **Major product:** Job creation **Area of distribution:** Hoke County, North Carolina **Expertise:** Marketing, business development **Hob./spts.:** Golf **SIC code:** 96 **Address:** Raeford/Hoke Economic Development, 101 N. Main St., Raeford, NC 28376 **E-mail:** dporter@hokecounty.org

PRICE, LINDA R.
Industry: Government **Born:** September 17, 1948, Norman, Oklahoma **Univ./degree:** B.A., History; M.A., Regional City Planning, University of Oklahoma **Current organization:** City of Norman, Oklahoma **Title:** Revitalization Manager **Type of organization:** City government **Major product:** Planning and community development **Area of distribution:** Norman, Oklahoma **Expertise:** Federal grant management code/code compliance **Honors/awards:** Oklahoma Municipal League Honor Roll of Service (25 years), 2001; Oklahoma HUD Best Practice Award for Independent Living Services for Youth, 2000; The World Who's Who of Women, International Biographical Centre; Two Thousand Notable American Women, American Biographical Institute; Who's Who in American Women **Affiliations:** American Planning Association; American Institute of Certified Planners; N.C.D.A.; FEMA Grant Award Committee; Sooner Rotary Club; Board Member, Independent Living Services for Youth, Inc.; Link Norman Stakeholder; Oakhurst Neighborhood Association; League of Women Voters **Hob./spts.:** Softball, travel, reading **SIC code:** 91 **Address:** 1903 Rolling Stone Dr., Norman, OK 73071 **E-mail:** linda.price@ci.norman.ok.us

PROSISE, RAYMOND E.
Industry: Government/sales **Univ./degree:** A.S., Electronics, DeVry Institute, Atlanta, Georgia, 1980 **Current organization:** TAC-America's Inc. **Title:** Account Manager **Type of organization:** Government/sales **Major product:** Energy, turnkey products **Area of distribution:** National **Expertise:** Management of government accounts; Certified Energy Manager (CEM), 2000 **Affiliations:** Association of Energy Engineers **SIC code:** 99 **Address:** 1339 Saddleback Lane, Lewisville, TX 75067 **E-mail:** ray_prosise@tac-americas.com **Web address:** www.tac-americas.com

RAMOS-ALGARIN, RAMON
Industry: Government **Born:** March 10, 1958, Puerto Rico **Univ./degree:** M.A., Architecture, University of Puerto Rico, San Juan, 1982 **Current organization:** U.S. General Services Administration **Title:** Architect **Type of organization:** Government agency **Major product:** Public building services, construction, alterations and repairs management **Area of distribution:** Puerto Rico **Expertise:** Architecture, project management **Affiliations:** A.I.A; Puerto Rico College of Architects **Hob./spts.:** Ceramics, cycling **SIC code:** 91 **Address:** U.S. General Services Administration, 150 Chardon St., Federal Bldg., Room 359, Hato Rey, PR 00918 **E-mail:** ramonramos@gsa.gov

RAMSARRAN, DEODAT
Industry: Government/City **Born:** January 8, 1950, Guyana, West Indies **Univ./degree:** B.S., Civil Engineering, University of the West Indies at Trinidad, 1974 **Current organization:** Dept. of Buildings **Title:** Structural Engineer/Plan Examiner **Type of organization:** City Agency **Major product:** Public service/design and construction of buildings **Area of distribution:** New York, New York **Expertise:** Structural engineering **Affiliations:** A.S.C.E.; Institution of Civil Engineers of London **Hob./spts.:** Sports **SIC code:** 95 **Address:** Dept. of Buildings, 280 Broadway, Third Floor, New York, NY 10007

RANDALL, DWIGHT C.
Industry: Government/law enforcement **Univ./degree:** Certificate, S.P.S.C. **Current organization:** Kane County Sheriff's Office **Title:** Lieutenant **Type of organization:** Police department **Major product:** Public order, safety and law enforcement **Area of distribution:** Kane County, Illinois **Expertise:** Training, special services division, record keeping, traffic division, events, public speaking **Honors/awards:** "Weed & Seed", East Aurora Weed & Seed Committee **Hob./spts.:** Sports, horses, family activities **SIC code:** 92 **Address:** Kane County Sheriff's Office, 777 E. Fabyan Pkwy., Geneva, IL 60134 **E-mail:** randalldwight@co.kane.il.us

RASMUSSEN, JAMES
Industry: Government/law enforcement **Born:** April 30, 1960, Chicago, Illinois **Univ./degree:** Attended Saddle Brook Community College and Riverside Community College **Current organization:** California Highway Patrol **Title:** Lieutenant **Type of organization:** State government **Major product:** Public order, safety and law enforcement **Area of distribution:** California **Expertise:** Area Commander **Honors/awards:** A.A.A. Auto Theft Recovery Award, 1982 and 1984; Officer of the Year, Mission Viejo Kiwanis Club, 1994; Area Commander's Commendation Award, 2000; Division Chief's Commendation, 2001 **Affiliations:** California Police Officers Association; California Dept. of Highway Patrol Association; Needles Rotary Club **Hob./spts.:** Boating, golf **SIC code:** 92 **Address:** California Highway Patrol, 1916 J St., Needles, CA 92363-2634 **E-mail:** jrasmussen@chp.ca.gov

REA, WILLIAM J.
Industry: Government/law **Born:** February 21, 1920, Los Angeles, California **Univ./degree:** University of Colorado, 1949 **Current organization:** U. S. District Court **Title:** U.S. District Judge **Type of organization:** Court **Major product:** Legal decisions **Area of distribution:** National **Expertise:** Trials **Affiliations:** A.B.T.A. **Hob./spts.:** Golf **SIC code:** 92 **Address:** U.S. District Court, 312 N. Spring St., Los Angeles, CA 90012

REDLIN, VICKY J.
Industry: Government **Born:** December 4, 1964. Oshkosh, Wisconsin **Univ./degree:** B.S., Graphic Communications, University of Wisconsin, 1989 **Current organization:** Winnebago County, Wisconsin **Title:** Assistant Manager, Expo Center **Type of organization:** Expo center and fairgrounds **Major product:** Rentals for concerts, horse shows, racing **Area of distribution:** Wisconsin **Expertise:** Marketing **Affiliations:** Women's Division of Oshkosh, Oshkosh Hotel Marketing Group **Hob./spts.:** Yoga, oil

painting **SIC code:** 99 **Address:** Winnebago County, Wisconsin, 625 E. County Rd. Y #500, Oshkosh, WI 54901 **E-mail:** vredlin@co.winnebago.wi.us

REDPATH, JAMES R.
Industry: Government/transportation **Born:** November 22, 1937, Kansas City, Kansas **Univ./degree:** J.D, University of Arkansas,1964 **Current organization:** Office of Arizona Attorney General **Title:** Assistant Attorney General **Type of organization:** Attorney General's office **Major product:** Highway/freeway construction and maintenance **Area of distribution:** Phoenix, Arizona **Expertise:** Eminent domain, tort defense **Honors/awards:** Appreciation Recognition Award, Department of Transportation; Certificate of right of Way, Association of State of Arizona **Hob./spts.:** Reading, fishing, hiking **SIC code:** 96 **Address:** Office of Arizona Attorney General, 1275 W. Washington St., #1, Phoenix, AZ 85007 **E-mail:** jredpath@ag.state.az.us

RICH, KERRY K.
Industry: Law enforcement **Born:** December 11, 1952, Burlington, Colorado **Univ./degree:** Denver Police Academy, 1974 **Current organization:** Denver Police Dept./Front Range Task Force **Title:** Detective **Type of organization:** Police Dept. **Major product:** Law enforcement **Area of distribution:** Colorado **Expertise:** Title III investigations, surveillance technologies, technical investigations, computer technologies, education, lecturing **Honors/awards:** Optimist Club Award; Merit Awards, Commendations, Unit Citations, Denver Police Dept.; Public Safety Award, U.S. Attorney's Office, Organized Crime Drug Enforcement Task Force; Certification of Appreciation, Drug Enforcement Administration; Letter of Recognition, Aurora Police Dept. **Affiliations:** National Technical Investigators Association; Denver Police Protective Association; National Narcotic Officers Associations Coalition; Colorado Drug Investigators Association **Hob./spts.:** Fishing, boating, computers **SIC code:** 92 **Address:** Denver Police Dept./Front Range Task Force, 13900 E. Harvard Ave., Suite 305, Aurora, CO 80014 **E-mail:** kkrich@rmhidta.org

RICKARD, DAVID H.
Industry: Government **Born:** January 3, 1950, Pasadena, California **Univ./degree:** B.A., Speech Communication, Cal Poly, San Luis Obispo; Graduate, Cal State, LA, 1978; M.A., Human Development/Child Psychology, Pacific Oaks College, Pasadena, California, 1983; Ph.D., Crisis Management, Sacramento Regent University, 2005 **Current organization:** Santa Barbara County Offices **Title:** Disaster Recovery Manager - Public Works Project Manager, Santa Barbara County **Type of organization:** County government **Major product:** Public health and safety, crisis planning and management **Area of distribution:** International **Expertise:** Disaster recovery **Published works:** Project Alert: Victory House/s (TX-2-009-249) Treatment Programs (TX-2-992-263) **Affiliations:** National Institute on Drug Abuse; Santa Barbara County Management Association **Hob./spts.:** Golf, Macaw parrots, Porsche Rally's, travel, money collector **SIC code:** 92 **Address:** Disaster Recovery Manager, Public Works Administration/Project Manager, 620 W. Foster Rd., Santa Maria, CA 93455 **E-mail:** drickar@cosbpw.net **Web address:** www.countyofsb.org/pwd/DMA2000.htm

RILEY, MOSES C.
Industry: Government/utilities **Current organization:** Charles County Government **Title:** Maintenance Supervisor **Type of organization:** Government **Major product:** Wastewater treatment **Area of distribution:** Charles County, Maryland **Expertise:** Maintenance **Hob./spts.:** Inventions, equipment rebuilding and trouble shooting **SIC code:** 96 **Address:** P.O. Box 116, 6500 Fire Tower Rd., Welcome, MD 20693 **Phone:** (301)609-9975

RILEY, THOMAS W.
Industry: Government **Born:** October 22, 1953, Iaeger, West Virginia **Univ./degree:** New Jersey State Police Academy, 1982; Western University School of Command and Staff, 1996 **Current organization:** Millville Police Dept. **Title:** Captain **Type of organization:** Police department **Major product:** Public order and safety **Area of distribution:** Millville, New Jersey **Expertise:** Certified, Firearms Instructor; Sub Machine Gun/Assault Weapons Instructor; PR24 (Baton) Instructor; Hostage Negotiator; Bomb Blast Investigator **Affiliations:** New Jersey State Policemen's Benevolent Association; American Legion **Hob./spts.:** Football, sports, travel **SIC code:** 92 **Address:** Millville Police Dept., 18 S. High St., Millville, NJ 08332 **E-mail:** twreagles@aol.com

RIPPE, LYNN E.
Industry: Government **Born:** December 27, 1947, Superior, Nebraska **Univ./degree:** B.A., Economics, Kansas State University, 1969; M.B.A., Southern Illinois University, 1977 **Current organization:** University of California, Lawrence Berkeley National Laboratory **Title:** Subcontracts Manager **Type of organization:** National laboratory **Major product:** Research and development **Area of distribution:** Texas **Expertise:** Contracting **Affiliations:** National Contract Management Association; Beta Gamma Sigma **Hob./spts.:** Reading, crafts **SIC code:** 96 **Address:** 3478 FM 1670, Belton, TX 76513 **E-mail:** lerippe@lbl.gov

RIVENBARK, JOSEPH K.
Industry: Government **Born:** December 1, 1956, Wilmington, North Carolina **Current organization:** Town of Surf City Fire Dept. **Title:** Chief **Type of organization:** Fire department **Major product:** Saving lives and providing safety **Area of distribution:** Surf City, North Carolina **Expertise:** Residential building contractor **Honors/awards:** Fireman of the Year 1989, Penderlea Fire Dept. **Hob./spts.:** Fishing, scuba diving, travel **SIC code:** 92 **Address:** Town of Surf City Fire Dept., 200 Wilmington Ave., Surf City, NC 28445

ROBBINS, DARRELL W.
Industry: Government **Born:** July 7, 1960, Bossier City, Louisiana **Current organization:** City of Waskom **Title:** Public Works Director **Type of organization:** Municipal government/utilities **Major product:** Public services **Area of distribution:** East Harrison County, Texas **Expertise:** Public works, water utilities, supervision of parks, streets and budget; B Certifications in water and wastewater **Affiliations:** Texas Water Utilities Association **Hob./spts.:** Motor cycle touring, physical fitness, football, volunteer firefighter **SIC code:** 96 **Address:** City of Waskom, P.O. Box 730, Waskom, TX 75692 **E-mail:** dwrobbins@eastex.net

ROBERTS, LYNN N.
Industry: Federal civil service employee **Born:** September 17, 1941, Dayton, Ohio **Univ./degree:** B.A. with Honors, English, University of Alabama **Title:** Contract Specialist **Type of organization:** Dept. of Defense (Army) **Major product:** Research & development contracts **Area of distribution:** International **Expertise:** Writing **Honors/awards:** Listed in Who's Who in America **Published works:** Novel, "Souls to Keep" (unpublished); award winning articles, poetry in magazines **Hob./spts.:** Reading, hiking, the outdoors **SIC code:** 97 **Address:** 87 Stoney Brook Dr., Union Grove, AL 35175

ROBERTS, MARK A.
Industry: Government **Univ./degree:** A.S., Butler County Community College, 1991 **Current organization:** City of Douglass **Title:** Mayor **Type of organization:** Municipal government **Major product:** Public services **Area of distribution:** Douglass, Kansas **Expertise:** Leadership, daily operations **Affiliations:** Kansas Mayor's Association; League of Kansas Municipalities; Deputy Fire Chief for local fire department **Hob./spts.:** Golf, fishing, Kansas Jayhawks basketball team **SIC code:** 91 **Address:** City of Douglass, 322 S. Forrest, Douglas, KS 67039 **E-mail:** mroberts@cityofdouglassks.com

ROBERTS, PETER JAMES
Industry: Government **Born:** December 21, 1963, Allentown, Pennsylvania **Univ./degree:** 3 year degree, Electrical Construction, Lehigh Career Technical Institute, 1982 **Current organization:** County of Lehigh, PA, New Court House **Title:** Electrician **Type of organization:** County government **Area of distribution:** Lehigh County, Pennsylvania **Expertise:** Electrician **Hob./spts.:** Karate **SIC code:** 91 **Address:** County of Lehigh, PA, New Court House, 455 Hamilton, Allentown, PA 18101

RODRIGUEZ, ROEL
Industry: Government **Born:** August 12, 1963, San Benito, Texas **Univ./degree:** B.S.C.E., Texas A&M University, Kingsville, 1988 **Current organization:** City of Harlingen **Title:** City Manager **Type of organization:** City government **Major product:** City services **Area of distribution:** Harlingen, Texas **Expertise:** Daily operations of the city; Professional Engineer in Texas and Oklahoma **Affiliations:** A.S.C.E. Texas Society of Professional Engineers; Texas City Management Association **Hob./spts.:** Weight training, running, snow skiing **SIC code:** 91 **Address:** City of Harlingen, P.O. Box 2207, Harlingen, TX 78550 **E-mail:** royrii@hotmail.com

RUSHING, ANN
Industry: Government **Title:** Mayor **Type of organization:** Municipal government **Major product:** Public services **Expertise:** Leadership **SIC code:** 91 **Address:** City of Clarksville, 800 West Main, Clarksville, TX 75426 **E-mail:** abrushing@cebridge.net

RUSSELL, PAUL CURTIS
Industry: Government/law enforcement **Born:** December 19, 1960, Morrilton, Arkansas **Current organization:** Morrilton Police Dept. **Title:** Lieutenant **Type of organization:** Police department **Major product:** Public order, safety and law enforcement **Area of distribution:** Morrilton, Arkansas **Expertise:** Patrol division **Affiliations:** Blue Knights, Masonic Lodge **Hob./spts.:** Drag racing, motorcycles, family **SIC code:** 92 **Address:** Morrilton Police Dept., 212 North Moose St., Morrilton, AR 72110 **E-mail:** ltrussell@morrilton.org

RUSSO, ROBERT J.
Industry: Government/Air Force **Born:** August 22, 1975, Poughkeepsie, New York **Univ./degree:** B.C.E., Civil Engineering, Villanova University, 1997 **Current organization:** U.S. Air Force **Title:** Captain, Chief of Base Development **Type of organization:** Military **Major product:** Defense **Area of distribution:** International **Expertise:**

Civil engineering **Affiliations:** S.A.M.E.; A.S.C.E. **Hob./spts.:** Biking, golfing, surfing **SIC code:** 97 **Address:** 44-251 Mikiola Dr., Kaneohe, HI 96744

SACKMAN, FRANK D.
Industry: Government/Law Enforcement **Born:** March 29, 1972, Soldotna, Alaska **Univ./degree:** A.S., Criminal Justice, University of Alaska, 1997 **Current organization:** Tularosa Police Dept. **Title:** Chief of Police **Type of organization:** Police department **Major product:** Public order and safety, law enforcement **Area of distribution:** Tularosa, New Mexico **Expertise:** Overseeing daily operations of police department **Affiliations:** Duwamish Indian Tribe of Washington State; White Sands Lodge; National Association of Chiefs of Police; Municipal League for Village of Tularosa **Hob./spts.:** Fishing, hiking, hunting, outdoor activities **SIC code:** 92 **Address:** Tularosa Police Dept., 609B St. Francis Dr., Tularosa, NM 88352

SALOMON, DONNA J.
Industry: Government **Born:** January 9, 1940, Chicago, Illinois **Univ./degree:** Diplomate in Christian Education, Trinity College, 1960 **Current organization:** White County Offices **Title:** County Recorder **Type of organization:** County government **Major product:** Public services **Area of distribution:** White County, Indiana **Expertise:** Recording of county records **Hob./spts.:** Fishing, knitting, sewing, painting, church, her grandchildren **SIC code:** 91 **Address:** White County Offices, 2 Oakview Dr., Monticello, IN 47960 **E-mail:** dsalomon@whitecountyindiana.us

SALVADOR, MICHAEL J.
Industry: Law enforcement **Univ./degree:** B.S., Criminology, California State University, Fresno, 1990 **Current organization:** Madera County Sheriff's Office **Title:** Lieutenant **Type of organization:** Sheriff's office **Major product:** Public safety, civil protection **Area of distribution:** Madera County, California **Expertise:** Technology, business practices, supervising operations **Affiliations:** Knights of Columbus; Peace Officers Research Association of California **SIC code:** 92 **Address:** Madera County Sheriff's Office, 14143 Road 28, Madera, CA 93638 **E-mail:** msalvador@madera-county.com

SANCHEZ, BOB P.
Industry: Government **Univ./degree:** B.S.M.E., University of the East, Manila, Philippines, 1977 **Current organization:** Dept. of Health/Public Health Laboratories **Title:** Plant Manager **Type of organization:** Public health laboratories **Major product:** Research **Area of distribution:** Washington **Expertise:** Facility engineering **Published works:** Articles through the American Red Cross **Affiliations:** American Red Cross responder to national disasters; Knights of Columbus #11217; member, I.F.M.A. **SIC code:** 94 **Address:** Dept. of Health/Public Health Laboratories, 1610 N.E. 150th St., Seattle, WA 98166

SANTANA, PETER
Industry: Government **Born:** September 4, 1949, Naguabo, Puerto Rico **Univ./degree:** B.S., Business Administration, Montclair University, 1975 **Current organization:** U.S. Customs Service, Regulatory Audit Division **Title:** Senior Auditor/Computer Audit Specialist/Union Stewart **Type of organization:** U.S. government/customs **Major product:** Auditing of importers/exporters of items **Area of distribution:** International **Expertise:** Auditing, computer auditing specialist **Hob./spts.:** Reading, writing, travel, cooking, automobiles, computers **SIC code:** 99 **Address:** U.S. Customs Service, Regulatory Audit Division, 280 S. First St., Suite 111, San Jose, CA 95113 **E-mail:** whizsantana@earthlink.net

SATO, MOTOAKI
Industry: Government/research **Univ./degree:** Ph.D., Geology, University of Minnesota, 1959; Post Doctorate, Harvard University **Current organization:** U.S. Geological Survey **Title:** Scientist Emeritus **Type of organization:** Federal research agency **Major product:** Research **Area of distribution:** International **Expertise:** Geochemistry **Affiliations:** American Geological Society **Hob./spts.:** Photography **SIC code:** 96 **Address:** U.S. Geological Survey, 11173 Lake Chapel Lane, Reston, VA 20191

SCHMIDT, CARL E.
Industry: Government/law **Born:** February 26, 1941, Buffalo, New York **Univ./degree:** D.O.T., Slidell Baptist Seminary, 1995 **Current organization:** City of Vermilion **Title:** Safety Director **Type of organization:** Police and fire departments **Major product:** Law enforcement, public order and safety **Area of distribution:** Vermilion, Ohio **Expertise:** Public health and safety **Affiliations:** A.R.C., O.S.D.A. **Hob./spts.:** Singing in a Gospel quartet **SIC code:** 92 **Address:** City of Vermilion, 309 Guilford Rd., Vermilion, OH 44089 **E-mail:** spider4541@adelphia.net

SCHWAB, FRANCIS C.
Industry: Government **Born:** Calabasas, California **Univ./degree:** M.S., Stanford University, 1964 **Current organization:** U.S. Government State Dept., Foreign Service Buildings **Title:** Project Director/Contract Officers Representative **Type of organization:** Foreign building construction **Major product:** Embassies/consulates **Area of distribution:** International **Expertise:** Civil engineering **Honors/awards:** Engineer of the Year, Dept. of State **Affiliations:** A.S.C.E.; Amnesty International **SIC code:** 97 **Address:** U.S. Government State Dept., Foreign Service Buildings, Calabasas, CA 91302 **E-mail:** fcsjr@aol.com

SEIFERT, TOMMY-JOHN
Industry: Government/military **Born:** July 23, 1980, Easton, Pennsylvania **Univ./degree:** B.S.M.E., Penn State University, 2002 **Current organization:** United States Navy **Title:** Ensign **Type of organization:** Government **Major product:** National defense **Area of distribution:** International **Expertise:** Nuclear propulsion, engineering **Affiliations:** A.S.M.E. **SIC code:** 97 **Address:** United States Navy, 3357 William Penn Hwy., Easton, PA 18045 **Web address:** www.navy.mil

SHELLEHAMER, GARY L.
Industry: Government/Marketing **Born:** June 14, 1950, Harrisburg **Univ./degree:** B.A., English, B.S., Graphic Design, Pennsylvania State University **Current organization:** Small Business Administration **Title:** Art Director **Type of organization:** Government agency **Major product:** Products and images for print, presentation **Area of distribution:** National **Expertise:** Graphic designs, creative and art direction **Hob./spts.:** Animal rescue, reading **SIC code:** 94 **Address:** Small Business Administration, 409 Third St. S.W., Graphic Concourse, Washington, DC 20416 **E-mail:** gary.shellehamer@sba.gov

SHINDY, WASFY W.
Industry: Government **Born:** August 25, 1958, Cairo, Egypt **Univ./degree:** Ph.D. Environmental Toxicology, University of California at Davis, 1969 **Current organization:** Los Angeles County **Title:** Director, Environmental Toxicology **Type of organization:** Government **Major product:** Service to constituents **Area of distribution:** Los Angeles County, California **Expertise:** Residue analysis **Published works:** 50+ articles **Hob./spts.:** Tennis, sailing **SIC code:** 91 **Address:** Los Angeles County, 11012 B. Garfield Ave., South Gate, CA 90280 **E-mail:** wasfy@acwm.co.la.ca.us

SHOMO, THOMAS E.
Industry: Government/water **Born:** June 28, 1951, Derry, Pennsylvania **Univ./degree:** A.A., Business Management, Duff Business Institute, 1972 **Current organization:** Derry Borough Municipal Authority **Title:** Foreman, Plant Operations **Type of organization:** Municipality **Major product:** Water removal **Area of distribution:** Derry, Pennsylvania **Expertise:** Oversight, management, repairs, replacements and troubleshooting; Certified waste plant operator, Class C1-14 **Affiliations:** Pennsylvania Municipal Authority Association; Pennsylvania Rural Water Association; DEP Partnership, Filtration Rules **Hob./spts.:** Gardening, baseball, family, Collie breeder **SIC code:** 95 **Address:** Derry Borough Municipal Authority, 620 North Chestnut, Derry, PA 15627 **Web address:** www.derrywater.com

SHORE, BRENT D.
Industry: Government **Born:** August 16, 1947, Charlotte, North Carolina **Univ./degree:** B.S.B.A., University of Florida, 1969; J.D., University of Florida Fredric G. Levin College of Law, 1971 **Current organization:** 4th Judicial Circuit, Duval County Courthouse **Title:** Judge **Type of organization:** Court system **Major product:** Judicial decisions **Area of distribution:** Duval County **Expertise:** Civil litigation, criminal law **Affiliations:** Member, Board of Directors, University of North Florida, Pre-law Program; Adjunct Professor, University of North Florida; Jacksonville Bar Association; Florida Bar **SIC code:** 92 **Address:** Duval County Court House, 330 E. Bay St., Jacksonville, FL 32202 **E-mail:** bshore@coj.net

SIEGENTHALER, DEBBIE S.
Industry: Government/healthcare **Born:** August 5, 1969, Argyle, Wisconsin **Univ./degree:** M.S., Healthcare Administration, University of Wisconsin at Madison, 2004 **Current organization:** Lafayette County Health Dept. **Title:** Director/Health Officer **Type of organization:** Government **Major product:** Public health **Area of distribution:** Lafayette County, Wisconsin **Expertise:** Administration **Affiliations:** Wisconsin Public Health Association **SIC code:** 94 **Address:** Lafayette County Health Dept., 729 Clay St., Darlington, WI 53530 **E-mail:** siegdarby@hotmail.com

SIMCOX, GREGORY
Industry: Government/law enforcement **Born:** August 16, 1964, Bristol, Texas **Current organization:** Sullivan County Sheriff's Office **Title:** Captain **Type of organization:** Sheriff's office **Major product:** Public order, safety and law enforcement **Area of distribution:** Sullivan County, Tennessee **Expertise:** Certified in accident reconstruction; Crash investigation, firearms instruction **Hob./spts.:** Family activities, football, target shooting **SIC code:** 91 **Address:** Sullivan County Sheriff's Office, 140 Blountville Bypass, Blountville, TN 37617 **E-mail:** greggs@scsotn.com

SIMES II, L.T.
Industry: Government/law **Born:** September 9, 1950, Poplar Grove, Arkansas **Univ./degree:** J.D., University of Arkansas at Fayetteville, 1974 **Current organization:** Phillips County Court House, First Judicial District **Title:** Circuit Judge **Type of organization:** Court **Major product:** Legal decisions **Area of distribution:** Helena,

Arkansas **Expertise:** Judiciary duties (presides over 6 counties) **Honors/awards:** Law Student of Former President William Jefferson Clinton, University of Arkansas, 1973-74 **Published works:** The Judge's Testimony 2002; Album, "L.T. Simes Gospel Hour" 1995 **Affiliations:** Arkansas Judicial Council **Hob./spts.:** Singing Gospel music **SIC code:** 92 **Address:** Phillips County Court House, First Judicial District, 620 Cherry St., Suite 108, Helena, AR 73342 **E-mail:** ltsimes@hnb.com

SIMPSON, DONALD E.
Industry: Government **Born:** March 8, 1952, Memphis, Tennessee **Univ./degree:** M.S., Civil Engineering, University of Missouri-Rolla, 1988 **Current organization:** U.S. Army Corps of Engineers **Title:** Resident Engineer **Type of organization:** Government **Major product:** Engineering services **Area of distribution:** National **Expertise:** Heavy construction **Affiliations:** S.A.M.E.; A.S.M.E. **Hob./spts.:** Golf, woodworking **SIC code:** 97 **Address:** U.S. Army Corps of Engineers, 1500 County Rd. 202, Shorterville, AL 36373 **E-mail:** simpson@graceba.net

SITTE JR., STEVEN A.
Industry: Government **Born:** February 15, 1970, Park Falls, Wisconsin **Univ./degree:** B.A., University of Wisconsin, 1995 **Current organization:** Wisconsin Army National Guard **Title:** Readiness N.C.O. **Type of organization:** Military **Major product:** Defense **Area of distribution:** International **Expertise:** Protecting borders **Affiliations:** W.N.G.E.A. **Hob./spts.:** Hunting, fishing **SIC code:** 97 **Address:** Wisconsin Army National Guard, 2811 East Park Ave., Chippewa Falls, WI 54729 **E-mail:** steven.sitte@us.army.mil

SMITH, ARTHUR F.
Industry: Government/military **Born:** April 4, 1943, Texarkana, Arkansas **Univ./degree:** M.S., Texas A&M University **Current organization:** Red River Army Depot **Title:** Chief Mechanical and Electronic Inspector **Type of organization:** Government/remanufacturing **Major product:** Mechanical rebuilding **Area of distribution:** International **Expertise:** Electrical, mechanical **Hob./spts.:** Racing cars, music **SIC code:** 97 **Address:** Red River Army Depot, 100 Main Dr., Texarkana, TX 75507-5000 **E-mail:** asmith@txk.com

SMITH, LORRAINE D.
Industry: Government **Born:** June 14, 1927, Hensley, Arkansas **Univ./degree:** M.A., University of Central Arkansas **Current organization:** City of Wrightsville **Title:** Mayor **Type of organization:** Municipal government **Major product:** Municipal services **Area of distribution:** Wrightsville, Arkansas **Expertise:** City management **Affiliations:** Municipal League **Hob./spts.:** Travel, basketball **SIC code:** 91 **Address:** City of Wrightsville, 13024 Hwy. 365, Wrightsville, AR 72183

SMITH, RAYMOND J.
Industry: Government/law enforcement **Born:** May 3, 1968, Fort Benning, Georgia **Univ./degree:** M.S., Psychology, Troy State University, 1996 **Current organization:** Phenix City Police Dept. **Title:** Assistant Chief of Police **Type of organization:** Police department **Major product:** Public order, safety and law enforcement **Area of distribution:** National **Expertise:** Operations command **Affiliations:** International Association of Chiefs of Police; National Tactical Officers Association **Hob./spts.:** Rifle shooting, teaching psychology **SIC code:** 92 **Address:** Phenix City Police Dept., 1111 Broad St., Phenix City, AL 36867 **E-mail:** rsmith@ci.phenix-city/al.us **Web address:** www.phenixcityal.us/publicsafety/police.asp

SMITH JR., GARMON B.
Industry: Government **Born:** October, 5, 1950, Raleigh, North Carolina **Univ./degree:** M.S., Chemistry, University of North Texas, 1976 **Current organization:** United State Environmental Protection Agency **Title:** Safety, Health and Environmental Manager **Type of organization:** Government/environmental **Major product:** Environmental research and development **Area of distribution:** Ada, Oklahoma **Expertise:** Management of solid and hazardous waste, recycling programs **Affiliations:** American Chemical Society ; American Society for Mass Spectrometry; American Society of Safety Engineers; Oklahoma Recycling Association **Hob./spts.:** Lions Club, church activities, vegetable gardening, yard work, volunteer work **SIC code:** 95 **Address:** U.S. Environmental Protection Agency, 919 Kerr Research Dr., P.O. Box 1198, Ada, OK 74820 **E-mail:** smith.garmon@epa.gov **Web address:** www.epa.gov/ada/

SOULE, ADRIENNE D.
Industry: Government/law **Born:** November 16, 1970, Norman, Oklahoma **Univ./degree:** J.D., Florida Coastal School of Law **Current organization:** Office of the State Attorney, 2nd Circuit **Title:** Assistant State Attorney **Type of organization:** Office of the State Attorney **Major product:** Criminal prosecution **Area of distribution:** Florida **Expertise:** Trial law **Affiliations:** A.H.A.; F.P.A.; A.B.A.; Y.L.B.A. **Hob./spts.:** Music, travel, gym, walking, hiking, reading **SIC code:** 92 **Address:** Office of the State Attorney, 2nd Circuit, 3056 Crawfordville Hwy., Crawfordville, FL 32327 **E-mail:** soulea@leoncountyfl.gov

SPARKS, CARL L.
Industry: Government/law enforcement **Born:** November 6, 1940, Bakersfield, California **Current organization:** Kern County Sheriff's Office **Title:** Sheriff **Type of organization:** Sheriff's Dept. **Major product:** Public order and safety **Area of distribution:** Bakersfield, California **Expertise:** Law enforcement **Honors/awards:** Appeared on "Larry King Live" **Published works:** 1 write-up about him, The L.A. Times **Affiliations:** California State Sheriff's Association; National Sheriff's Association **Hob./spts.:** Jogging, weightlifting, bike riding **SIC code:** 92 **Address:** Kern County Sheriff's Office, 1350 Norris Rd., Bakersfield, CA 93308

SPIESS, DANIEL R.
Industry: Government/transportation **Born:** January 15, 1952, Latrobe, Pennsylvania **Univ./degree:** Technical schooling **Current organization:** City of Columbus, Fleet Management **Title:** Supervisor City of Columbus **Type of organization:** City government **Major product:** Maintenance of police, fire and sanitation vehicles **Area of distribution:** Columbus, Ohio **Expertise:** Management, scheduling, planning **Hob./spts.:** Drag racing, motorcycles, hunting **SIC code:** 96 **Address:** City of Columbus, Fleet Management, 423 Short St., Columbus, OH 43215 **E-mail:** drspiess@cmhmetro.net

STACKHOUSE, JOHN E.H.
Industry: Government/Law **Born:** April 3, 1939, New York, New York **Univ./degree:** The Citadel, 1960; J.D., St. John's Law School, 1966 **Current organization:** Supreme Court of New York **Title:** Justice **Type of organization:** Government **Major product:** Judicial proceedings **Area of distribution:** New York **Expertise:** Trials/hearings; guardianship; mental health retention hearings; advocate for elder, disabled and gay/lesbian rights **Published works:** Denial of Justice, Brooklyn L.S. Law Review, 1976 **Affiliations:** New York City Bar Association; New York County Bar Association; Co-Chair, Supreme Court Anti-Bias Committee; Women in the Courts Task Force **Hob./spts.:** Travel, reading, physical fitness **SIC code:** 92 **Address:** Supreme Court of New York, 80 Centre St., New York, NY 10013-4395 **E-mail:** jstackho@courts.state.ny.us

STAGGS, CURTIS M.
Born: August 7, 1953, Dallas, Texas **Univ./degree:** A.S., Electronic Technology, Eastville University, Texas, 1973 **Current organization:** Divconems **Area of distribution:** National **Affiliations:** Association of Energy Engineers **Hob./spts.:** Travel, golf, scuba diving **SIC code:** 99 **Address:** 712 Southwynd Rd., Mesquite, TX 75150 **E-mail:** curtis_staggs@tac-americas.com **Web address:** www.tac-americas.com

STEDELIN, JAMES R.
Industry: Government/agriculture **Born:** June 1, 1955, Centralia, Illinois **Univ./degree:** B.S., Chemistry, Marie State University **Current organization:** Illinois Dept. of Agriculture **Title:** Chemist 3 **Type of organization:** Government **Major product:** Animal health **Area of distribution:** National **Expertise:** Analytical chemistry **Published works:** 8 papers **Affiliations:** A.O.C.S.; A.A.V.L.D.; A.O.A.C.; American Chemical Society **Hob./spts.:** Scuba diving, sailing, jet skiing, golf, cars **SIC code:** 96 **Address:** Illinois Dept. of Agriculture, 9732 Shattuc Rd., Centralia, IL 62801 **E-mail:** jstedelin@agr.state.il.us

STEELE, JOHN R.
Industry: Government **Born:** February 7, 1952, Newark, New Jersey **Univ./degree:** Attended 2 years Hastings College **Current organization:** State Capitol of Nebraska **Title:** Control Systems Operator Tech II **Type of organization:** State government **Major product:** Nebraska legislature **Area of distribution:** Nebraska **Expertise:** Engineering, maintenance of State Capitol of Nebraska, Governor's Mansion, IM Services Building, Executive Building **Affiliations:** Issac Walton Club, Eagles **Hob./spts.:** Fishing, deer hunting, target shooting **SIC code:** 91 **Address:** State Capitol of Nebraska, 16th & K St., Lincoln, NE 68509

STEIN, DAVID E.
Industry: Government **Born:** January 13, 1950, Jacksonville, Florida **Univ./degree:** M.S., Physics, University of Florida, 1977 **Current organization:** CACI **Title:** Defense Analyst **Type of organization:** Government/national defense **Major product:** Defense models and simulations **Area of distribution:** International **Expertise:** Research and strategy **Affiliations:** A.A.P.T.; P.S.W.; Past Officer, A.C.I.S.; World Future Society; World's Fair Council **Career accomplishments:** Identified new atmospheric refractivity effects on low-altitude radar propagation; Extended quantum mechanical computational technique to electromagnetic scattering; Co-pioneered new acquisition sizing methodology for next-generation fighter aircraft; Identified systems acquisition implications of future generic geopolitical scenarios, asymmetric warfare and futuristic technologies; Invented and patented board game; Editor-in-Chief, Applied Computational Electromagnetics Soc. Journal, 1987-93; Co-authored section of the Defense Critical Technologies Plan for the Executive Office of the President; Key Advisor to Air Force Requirements Oversight Council (AFROC); Short course instructor, radar technologies, George Washington Univ.; Associate Editor, Proceedings of the NATO Advanced Research Workshop in Radar Polarimetry, 1988 **Hob./spts.:** Writing, alter-

native medicine **SIC code:** 97 **Address:** CACI, P.O. Box 169, Linthicum Heights, MD 21090 **E-mail:** M742503402@cs.com

STEINHEIMER, CONNIE J.
Industry: Government **Born:** March 12, 1951, Reno, Nevada **Univ./degree:** B.A. Social Psychology, University of Nevada, 1973; J.D., Willamette University School of Law, 1979 **Current organization:** 2nd Judicial District Court, State of Nevada **Title:** Judge **Type of organization:** District court **Major product:** Judicial proceedings **Area of distribution:** Nevada **Expertise:** General jurisdiction of criminal and civil matters; national lecturing on access to justice and technology in the courts **Published works:** Articles **Affiliations:** American Bar Association; Nevada State Bar; Faculty, National Judicial College **SIC code:** 92 **Address:** 2nd Judicial District Court, State of Nevada, 75 Court St., Dept. 4, Reno, NV 89501 **E-mail:** judge.steinheimer@washoecourts.us

STIENMIER, SAUNDRA K.
Industry: Aerospace **Born:** April 27, 1938, Abilene, Kansas **Univ./degree:** Attended Colorado Women's University; Emory Riddle **Current organization:** Rocky Mountain, USAF Flight Training Center **Title:** School Director/Manager **Type of organization:** Government **Major product:** Flight training **Area of distribution:** National **Expertise:** Aviation safety **Affiliations:** N.A.T.A. **Hob./spts.:** Pilot's license and own plane, water color painting **SIC code:** 97 **Address:** Rocky Mountain, USAF Flight Training Center, Hangar 133, P.O. Box 14123, Peterson AFB, CO 80914 **E-mail:** saundra@viawest.net **Web address:** www.petaf.com

STILES, NORMA L.
Industry: Government **Born:** September 18, Miami, Florida **Univ./degree:** Ph.D., Counseling, Jacksonville Theological Seminary, 2005 **Current organization:** Miami-Dade Dept. of Human Services **Title:** Rehabilitative Services Administrator **Type of organization:** Municipal government **Major product:** Out patient treatment, social services **Area of distribution:** Miami-Dade, Florida **Expertise:** Certified Addictions Professional **Affiliations:** Eta Phi Beta; Florida Alcohol & Drug Abuse Association; Alpha Kappa Alpha **Hob./spts.:** Gardening, travel **SIC code:** 94 **Address:** Miami-Dade Dept. of Human Services, 8500 N.W. 27th Ave., Miami, FL 33147 **E-mail:** akajoc@miamidade.gov

STIMPSON, DONNA C.
Industry: Government **Born:** February 20, 1953, Connecticut **Univ./degree:** University of Illinois-MUP-1978 **Current organization:** Ct. Dept. of Mental Health & Addiction Services **Title:** Planning Specialist **Type of organization:** State government **Major product:** Mental and addiction treatment and prevention services **Area of distribution:** National **Expertise:** Planning, grant writing, data analysis **Honors/awards:** CCADV Presidents award-1997 **Affiliations:** President, National Organization of Women; President, YWCA of Connecticut; Catholic Charities **Hob./spts.:** Flyfishing, bird hunting, clay shooting, choir **SIC code:** 94 **Address:** Ct. Dept. of Mental Health & Addiction Services, 410 Capital Ave., P.O. Box 34143, Ms.Pas+4, Hartford, CT 06134 **E-mail:** donna.stimpson@po.state.ct.us

STRAVALLE, ANN R.
Industry: Government/utilities **Born:** January 2, 1957, Greater New York, New York **Univ./degree:** Cum Laude, Boston College, 1980; J.D., Hennessey Scholar, Boston University, 1987; M.B.A., Cum Laude, Rensselaer Polytechnic Institute, 2002 **Current organization:** Connecticut Resources Recovery Authority **Title:** Director of Legal Services (In House Counsel) **Type of organization:** Government **Major product:** Waste management, utilities **Area of distribution:** Connecticut **Expertise:** Contracts, corp. governance, general management, litigation/crises management, strategic planning **Published works:** Many including: "An Appellate Trap for the Unwary", SideBar, Vol. 3, No. 4, 1995; "The Status of Connecticut Law on the Fiduciary Duties of Lenders in Loan Transaction", 60 Conn. Bar J. 363 (Aug. 1995) **Affiliations:** A.C.C.A.; Connecticut Bar Association **Hob./spts.:** Travel, skiing, ice hockey, crew, squash, reading, theatre, opera **SIC code:** 95 **Address:** Connecticut Resources Recovery Authority, 100 Construction Plaza, Hartford, CT 06103 **E-mail:** astravalle@attbi.com

SUDDERTH, SKYLAR BARCLAY
Industry: Government/law **Univ./degree:** J.D., University of Texas at Austin School of Law **Current organization:** Brown County Courthouse **Title:** 35th Judicial District Attorney **Type of organization:** State government **Major product:** Justice **Area of distribution:** Brown County, Texas **Expertise:** Felony Prosecutor **Affiliations:** A.B.A.; Texas State Bar; Medical Technologist, A.M.T.; Clinical Laboratory Scientist, N.C.A. **SIC code:** 92 **Address:** Brown County Courthouse, 200 S. Broadway St., Brownwood, TX 76801

SUTTER, DEBRA J.
Industry: Government/healthcare **Born:** April 9, 1963, Portsmouth, Ohio **Univ./degree:** LPN, Spoon River College, Canton, Illinois; IV Therapy, Illinois Central College, Peoria, Illinois **Current organization:** Illinois Dept. of Corrections **Title:** CMT, LPN **Type of organization:** Correctional facility **Major product:** Inmate healthcare **Area of distribution:** Illinois **Expertise:** Nursing **Affiliations:** National Hot Rod Association (NHRA) **Hob./spts.:** Drag racing fan, interior design, candle collecting, NHRA memorabilia collector **SIC code:** 92 **Address:** Illinois Dept. of Corrections, 711 Kaskaskia St., Menard, IL 62286 **E-mail:** sutter@egyptian.net

SWANN, MADELINE B.
Industry: Government **Born:** July 24, 1951, Washington, D.C. **Univ./degree:** Ph.D., Chemistry, Howard University, 1980 **Current organization:** US Army Research Laboratory **Title:** Chemist **Type of organization:** Government/military **Major product:** Cognitive tools for US soldiers **Area of distribution:** National **Expertise:** Program management **Published works:** 20 publications **Affiliations:** O.B.S.; N.S.B.C.C.E.; Beta Kappa Psi **Hob./spts.:** Reading, travel **SIC code:** 97 **Address:** US Army Research Laboratory, Attn: AMSRL-HR-M, Aberdeen Proving Ground, MD 21005 **E-mail:** mswann@arl.army.mil

SYKES, THOMAS
Industry: Government **Univ./degree:** B.A., Recreation Administration, California State University-Long Beach; M.A., Public Administration, California State University-Northridge **Current organization:** City of Commerce **Title:** City Administrator **Type of organization:** Municipal government **Major product:** Public services and facilities **Area of distribution:** Commerce, California **Expertise:** 31 year employee of the City of Commerce serving as Director and/or President of numerous commissions **Honors/awards:** Man of the Year, Soroptimist International of Commerce/Bell Gardens, 2003; Risk Management Award, California Joint Powers Insurance Authority; Special Recognition Awards from the U.S. Congress, the California State Senate, the California State Assembly, The Los Angeles County Board of Supervisors, the Los Angeles County Sheriff's Dept., Lions International, Kiwanis International, the American Public Transit Association and the cities of Commerce, Walnut and Diamond Bar **Affiliations:** Executive Director, Commerce Community Development Commission; President, Commerce Citadel Development Authority; President, Commerce Joint Powers Financing Authority; Director, Commerce Refuse to Energy Authority; City Council Member and former Mayor (1992, 2000 and 2003) of the City of Walnut **SIC code:** 91 **Address:** City of Commerce, 2535 Commerce Way, Commerce, CA 90040 **E-mail:** smosykes@aol.com

TAFT, JUSTIN
Industry: Farmer, public service **Born:** January 29, 1924, Rochester, Illinois **Univ./degree:** University of Illinois **Title:** Retired County Official and State Official **Type of organization:** Government **Major product:** Public service **Area of distribution:** Illinois **Expertise:** Agriculture **Honors/awards:** "Outstanding Young Farmer", Sangan County **Affiliations:** President, Rochester Historical and Preservation Association; Founder, Lincoln Land Community College; Masonic Orders; Elected Clerk, Illinois Supreme Court **SIC code:** 94 **Address:** 100 Taft Dr., Rochester, IL 62563

TANNER, JAMES C.
Industry: Government **Current organization:** Town of Pawling **Title:** Town Supervisor (Retired) **Type of organization:** Municipal government **Major product:** Local government and services **Area of distribution:** Pawling, New York **Expertise:** Management, financial officer of community, ran Board of Directors for town **Honors/awards:** US Navy WWII veteran **Affiliations:** Mason, United Methodist Church **SIC code:** 91 **Address:** 53 Fairway Dr., Pawling, NY 12564

TAWFIK, EIHAB H.
Industry: Government/healthcare **Born:** September 26, 1974, Cairo Egypt **Univ./degree:** M.D., Ross University **Current organization:** V.A. Medical Center **Title:** M.D. **Type of organization:** Government/veterans hospital **Major product:** Patient care **Area of distribution:** New Jersey **Expertise:** Internal medicine **Affiliations:** A.M.A. **Hob./spts.:** Music, reading **SIC code:** 94 **Address:** 700 Newark Ave., #316, Jersey City, NJ 07306-2812 **E-mail:** eihabtawfik@msn.com

TAYLOR, PAULA J.
Industry: Government **Born:** November 23, 1956, Lansing, Michigan **Univ./degree:** B.S., Social Welfare, West Virginia Wesleyan College, 1979 **Current organization:** West Virginia Dept. of Health & Human Resources **Title:** Child Protective Services Supervisor **Type of organization:** State government/welfare agency **Major product:** Social services **Area of distribution:** West Virginia **Expertise:** Child welfare services **Hob./spts.:** Working with church youth group, reading **SIC code:** 94 **Address:** West Virginia Dept. of Health & Human Resources, P.O. Box 800, Morgantown, WV 26507-0800 **E-mail:** paulataylor@wvdhhr.org

THATCHER, ROBERT C.
Industry: Government/research **Born:** January 11, 1929, Boonville, New York **Univ./degree:** B.S., 1953; M.S. 1954, SUNY College of Forestry; Ph.D., 1971, Auburn University **Title:** Emeritus Scientist, USDA Forest Service Southern Research Station (Retired) **Type of organization:** Government **Major product:** Multiple discipline forest research results **Area of distribution:** National **Expertise:** Integrated pest management **Published works:** Numerous including, Co-author, "Integrated pest management in the South: Highlights of a 5-year program", Agric. Info. Bull. No. 491, Washington,

DC, US Dept. of Agriculture, Forest Service, 1985, 19p; Co-author, "Integrated means of forest protection in the United States", Lesmoye Khoziaystoo, 9:70-74, 1986; Author, "Influence of the pitch-eating weevil, Pachylobius picivorus Germ., on pine regeneration in east Texas", For. Sci. 6:354-361, 1960 **Affiliations:** N.A.R.F.E.; Fellow and Member, Society of American Foresters **Hob./spts.:** Landscaping **SIC code:** 95 **Address:** 12 Bevlyn Dr., Asheville, NC 28803

THOMPSON, ADAM
Industry: Government **Born:** January 13, 1955, Sikeston, Missouri **Current organization:** Topeka Housing Authority **Title:** Maintenance Technician III **Type of organization:** Government/public housing authority **Major product:** Housing for low income families **Area of distribution:** National **Expertise:** Plumbing **Hob./spts.:** Fishing **SIC code:** 95 **Address:** Topeka Housing Authority, 2010 California St. SE, Topeka, KS 66607

TISDALE, BRIAN L.
Industry: Government/transportation **Born:** March 22, 1978, Peoria, Illinois **Univ./degree:** B.S., Bradley University, 2000 **Current organization:** Illinois Dept. of Transportation **Title:** Civil Engineer **Type of organization:** State government **Major product:** Highways **Area of distribution:** Illinois **Expertise:** Engineering **Affiliations:** A.S.C.E. **SIC code:** 96 **Address:** 203 Matthew, Washington, IL 61571 **E-mail:** tisdalebl@nt.dot.state.il.us

TOBIN, PETER C.
Industry: Government/law **Born:** August 25, 1946, Niagara Falls, New York **Current organization:** Ohio Bureau of Criminal Investigation **Title:** Criminal Investigations Administrator, Narcotics Section Chief **Type of organization:** Government law enforcement agency **Major product:** Narcotics enforcement **Area of distribution:** Ohio **Expertise:** Law enforcement **Affiliations:** Ohio Association of Chiefs of Police; Ohio Drug Task Force Commanders Association; Bugeve State Sheriff Association; National Alliance of State Drug Enforcement Agencies; Class Speaker, F.B.I. National Academy **Hob./spts.:** Family, golf, fishing **SIC code:** 97 **Address:** Ohio Bureau of Criminal Investigation, 1560 State Route 56, London, OH 43140 **E-mail:** ptobin@ag.state.oh.us

TOMICH, P. QUENTIN
Industry: Government/animal ecology **Born:** October 11, 1920, Folsom, California **Univ./degree:** Ph.D., University of California, Berkeley, 1959 **Title:** Ph.D. (Retired) **Type of organization:** Government/State Health Dept. **Major product:** Research (public health) **Area of distribution:** Hawaii **Expertise:** Diseases of animals as related to man **Hob./spts.:** Insulator collection, volunteer for State Park service **SIC code:** 94 **Address:** 453292 Ohai St., Honokaa, HI 96727

TRAVIA III, ANTHONY J.
Industry: Government/healthcare **Born:** Brooklyn, New York **Univ./degree:** B.Ch.E., Chemical Engineering, Georgia Institute of Technology, 1986 **Current organization:** U.S. Dept. of Veterans Affairs **Title:** PE, CFM **Type of organization:** Federal government **Major product:** Public service, engineering **Area of distribution:** International **Expertise:** Engineering management **Honors/awards:** Bronze Order of the de Fleury Medal, U.S. Army Corps of Engineers **Published works:** Articles and letters for local and organizational publications **Affiliations:** National Society of Professional Engineers; American Institute of Chemical Engineers; American Society of Civil Engineers; Society of American Military Engineers; International Facility Management Association **SIC code:** 97 **Address:** U.S. Dept. of Veterans Affairs, 4460 Capstan Dr., Hoffman Estates, IL 60195-1006 **E-mail:** anthony.travia@med.va.gov

TRUEBLOOD JR., MARVIN ODELL
Industry: Government/Public Housing **Born:** July 15, 1952, Harrisburg, Pennsylvania **Univ./degree:** B.A., Political Science, Haverford College, 1974 **Current organization:** Harrisburg Housing Authority **Title:** Lead Housing Inspector **Type of organization:** Public housing agency **Major product:** Public housing services **Area of distribution:** Harrisburg, Pennsylvania **Expertise:** Inspections **Honors/awards:** Red Cross Volunteer of the Year, 1996 **Affiliations:** Assistant Scoutmaster, Boy Scout Troop 40, Harrisburg **Hob./spts.:** Scuba diving, travel **SIC code:** 95 **Address:** Harrisburg Housing Authority, 351 Chestnut St., Harrisburg, PA 17103

VAN ZANDT JR., CHARLES R.
Industry: Government/environmental **Born:** January 12, 1959, Fort Belvoir, Virginia **Current organization:** City of Eden **Title:** Superintendent of the Wastewater Plants **Type of organization:** Local government wastewater plant **Major product:** Wastewater treatment **Area of distribution:** Eden, North Carolina **Expertise:** Environmental **Affiliations:** Water Environment Federation; North Carolina Water Environment Association; North Carolina State Firemen's Association; North Carolina Association of Fire Chiefs; North Carolina Pretreatment Consortium **Hob./spts.:** Volunteer firefighter **SIC code:** 95 **Address:** City of Eden, 308 E. Stadium Dr., Eden, NC 27288 **E-mail:** charles.vanzandt@ci.eden.nc.us

VEGA-TORRES, LOURDES
Industry: Government/law enforcement **Born:** April 23, 1956, East Chicago, Indiana **Univ./degree:** B.S., Organizational Management, Calumet College of St. Joseph **Current organization:** East Chicago Police Dept. **Title:** Lieutenant **Type of organization:** Police department **Major product:** Public order, safety and law enforcement **Area of distribution:** East Chicago, Indiana **Expertise:** Law enforcement **Honors/awards:** First female Hispanic to achieve the title of Lieutenant **Affiliations:** Fraternal Order of Police, Lodge #59 **Hob./spts.:** Camping, the outdoors, motorcycles **SIC code:** 92 **Address:** East Chicago Police Dept., 2301 E. Columbus Dr., East Chicago, IN 46312 **E-mail:** lvegatorres@eastchicago.com **Web address:** www.eastchicago.com

VITVITSKY, JACK
Industry: Medical **Born:** March 8, 1945, White Plains, New York **Univ./degree:** B.S., University of Rochester, New York, 1968; RPA-C, Cayuhoga Community College, 1978 **Current organization:** New York Army National Guard **Title:** RPA-C **Type of organization:** Army National Guard **Major product:** Healthcare services **Area of distribution:** New York **Expertise:** Medical care, aviation, writing; PA Certified, NCCPA **Affiliations:** American Academy of Physician Assistants; A.S.P.A. **Hob./spts.:** Skiing, riding horses, pilot, camping, carpentry, mechanics, motorcycle riding **SIC code:** 97 **Address:** Old Military Rd., Lake Placid, NY 12946-1824 **E-mail:** jackvitristsky@juno.com

VONHARDERS, KIMBERLY A.
Industry: Government **Born:** October 6, 1968, Fredericksburg, Virginia **Current organization:** U.S. House of Representatives **Title:** Messaging Systems Branch Manager **Type of organization:** Customer Service Organization for the House **Major product:** Massaging and Fax Systems Infrastructure for the House **Area of distribution:** Washington, D.C. **Expertise:** Management - IT Infrastructure **Honors/awards:** Distinguish Service Award **Hob./spts.:** Family **SIC code:** 91 **Address:** U.S. House of Representatives, 620C Ford House Office Building, Washington, DC 20515 **E-mail:** vonharders@mail.house.gov **Web address:** www.house.gov

WADDINGTON JR., JAMES R.
Industry: Aerospace **Born:** March 31, 1958, Philadelphia, Pennsylvania **Univ./degree:** M.S., Management, La Salle University, 1989 **Current organization:** Lockheed Martin Management & Data Systems (M&DS) **Title:** Director, Communications and Public Affairs **Type of organization:** Information Technology **Major product:** Systems integration, systems engineering, software development **Area of distribution:** National **Expertise:** Communications, public relations **Published works:** Articles **Affiliations:** P.P.R.A.; I.A.B.C.; P.R.S.A. **SIC code:** 96 **Address:** Lockheed Martin Management & Data Systems (M&DS), P.O. Box 8048, Bldg. 100, Room M7047, Philadelphia, PA 19406 **E-mail:** james.r.waddington@lmco.com

WADZINSKI, MARY B.
Industry: Government **Born:** April 26, 1953, Wausau, Wisconsin **Univ./degree:** Attended 2 years North Central Technical Institute **Current organization:** Marathon County Dept. of Social Services **Title:** Office Aide **Type of organization:** Government **Major product:** Social services (social/financial help) **Area of distribution:** Wausau, Wisconsin **Expertise:** Clerical **Honors/awards:** Who's Who in America; Who's Who in the World; Who's Who of American Women; International Biographical Centre of England **Published works:** 2 poetry books: "Pathways", "Treasured Thoughts" **Affiliations:** International Society of Poets; Famous Poets Society **Hob./spts.:** Writing, going to garage sales, singing **SIC code:** 94 **Address:** Marathon County Dept. of Social Services, 400 E. Thomas St., Wausau, WI 54403 **Web address:** www.poets.com

WALTERS, JOHN A.
Industry: Government/military **Born:** May 25, 1939, Diamond Springs, California **Title:** Instructor, Marine Corps Communications & Electronics School (Retired) **Type of organization:** US Marine Corps **Major product:** Military training and preparedness **Area of distribution:** International **Expertise:** Tactical fiber optics training **Affiliations:** E.T.A.I. **Hob./spts.:** Boy Scouts **SIC code:** 97 **Address:** Marine Corps Communications & Electronics School, Bldg. 1748 Room 112, 29 Palms, CA 92278 **E-mail:** jewelrymaker@juno.com

WARREN, MICHAEL R.
Industry: Government/law **Born:** July 15, 1954, Portland, Oregon **Univ./degree:** Graduate, Washington State Police Academy, 1985; A.S., Human Resource Management, George Fox University, Oregon, 1990; Graduate, Northwestern University Center for Public Safety, School of Police Staff and Command, 2006 **Current organization:** Washington State Patrol **Title:** Lieutenant **Type of organization:** State government/law enforcement **Major product:** Public order, safety and law enforcement **Area of distribution:** Washington **Expertise:** Peer support training, incident management **Honors/awards:** Award of Merit, Boy Scouts of America **Affiliations:** Boy Scouts of America **Hob./spts.:** Camping, hiking, muscle cars, trucks **SIC code:** 92 **Address:** Washington State Patrol, 2882 Euclid Ave., Wenatchee, WA 98801 **E-mail:** michael_r_warren@yahoo.com

WAYNE, JOHN W.
Industry: Government/military **Born:** April 30, 1951, Monmouth, Illinois **Current organization:** U.S. Army Corp. of Engineers **Title:** Crane Operator Supervisor **Type of organization:** Federal department **Major product:** Construction, structural maintenance of Rock Island **Area of distribution:** National **Expertise:** Scuba diving safety, crane operation **Hob./spts.:** Scuba and sky diving, motocycles **SIC code:** 95 **Address:** 96 Hwy. 67, P.O. Box 365, Alexis, IL 61412

WEISS, JESSE W.
Industry: Government **Current organization:** Borough of Orwigsburg, Pennsylvania **Title:** Water/Wastewater Supervisor **Type of organization:** Government/public utilities **Major product:** Water, wastewater treatment **Expertise:** Plant operations **SIC code:** 95 **Address:** 88 West Second Mountain Rd., Pottsville, PA 17901

WIEDMAIER, DIANA L.
Industry: Government/law **Born:** April 3, 1946, Clarinda, Iowa **Current organization:** Dekalb City Associated Circuit Court **Title:** Court Clerk (Retired) **Type of organization:** Court **Major product:** Legal administration **Area of distribution:** Clarkesdale, Missouri **Expertise:** Probate matters **Affiliations:** Former A.B.W.A. **Hob./spts.:** Quilting **SIC code:** 92 **Address:** 704 Hilltop Ave., Clarkesdale, MO 64430 **E-mail:** woodnquilt@centurytel.net

WILLIAMS, MARY-PEARL H.
Industry: Government/law **Born:** January 12, 1928, Brownsville, Texas **Univ./degree:** B.A., Government/Spanish; J.D., University of Texas School of Law, 1949 **Current organization:** State of Texas **Title:** Senior Judge **Type of organization:** Texas judicial district court **Major product:** Justice **Area of distribution:** Texas **Expertise:** Civil law, rendering judicial decisions in state court and the Texas Appellate Court **Honors/awards:** First woman judge in Travis County, Texas; Outstanding 50-Year Lawyer Award, presented by the Texas Bar Foundation **Affiliations:** Fellows of the American Bar Foundation, State Bar of Texas, Travis County Bar Association, Travis County Women Lawyer's Association **Hob./spts.:** Family, walking, travel, speaking Spanish **SIC code:** 92 **Address:** 3503 Mt. Barker Dr., Austin, TX 78731-5101 **E-mail:** marypw@mindspring.com

WILLIAMSON, JERRY L.
Industry: Government **Born:** October 19, 1955 **Univ./degree:** Continuing education in Blueprint Reading, Wastewater 2A/2B Water Operations License **Current organization:** Village of Camden **Title:** Superintendent of Public Works **Type of organization:** Local government **Major product:** Wastewater processing, street maintenance, drinking water, budget planning **Area of distribution:** Camden, New York **Expertise:** Providing clean and safe drinking water, oversight of daily operations **Affiliations:** Oneida County Highway Superintendents Association; Cornell Local Roads Program; Jefferson Lewis BOCES **Hob./spts.:** Bass fishing, hunting, shooting sports **SIC code:** 95 **Address:** Village of Camden, 14 Church St., Camden, NY 13316 **E-mail:** big_jerry55@yahoo.com

WILSON, FRANCES E.
Industry: Law enforcement **Born:** August 4, 1955, Keokuk, Iowa **Univ./degree:** B.A., Criminal Justice Administration, St. Ambrose College, 1982; M.A., Law Enforcement Administration, Western Illinois University, 1990 **Current organization:** Davenport Police Dept. **Title:** Sergeant **Type of organization:** Police department **Major product:** Law enforcement **Area of distribution:** Davenport, Iowa **Expertise:** Training **Honors/awards:** Listed in Marquis' Who's Who, American Biographical Institute; Officer of the Year, Iowa Association of Women Police; Law Enforcement Officer of the Year, Noon Optimists, Davenport, Iowa **Published works:** Articles **Affiliations:** American Society of Law Enforcement Trainers; Iowa Association of Women Police; International Association of Women Police; Fraternal Order of Police; American Women's Self Defense Association **Hob./spts.:** Reading, sports **SIC code:** 92 **Address:** Davenport Police Dept., 420 Harrison St., Davenport, IA 52801-1304

WILSON, GLENDA F.
Industry: Government **Born:** April 15, 1951, Natchez, Mississippi **Univ./degree:** B.S., Psychology, University of Southern Mississippi, 1986 **Current organization:** Mississippi Dept. of Vocational Rehabilitation Services for the Blind **Title:** Counselor **Type of organization:** State agency **Major product:** Assisting the blind with employment opportunities **Area of distribution:** Mississippi **Expertise:** Counselor for the blind, licensed social worker **Affiliations:** Civitan International **Hob./spts.:** Reading, woodworking **SIC code:** 94 **Address:** Mississippi Dept. of Vocational Rehabilitation, Services for the Blind, 115 Jeff Davis Blvd., Natchez, MS 39120 **E-mail:** glendawilson52@aol.com

WILSON, GREGORY P.
Industry: Government **Born:** Rochester, New York **Univ./degree:** A.S., Water and Wastewater Technology, Sinclair Community College, 1994 **Current organization:** City of Jackson, Ohio **Title:** Director of Water and Wastewater **Type of organization:** City utilities **Major product:** Water and wastewater **Area of distribution:** Jackson, Ohio **Expertise:** Operations specialist, private consulting **Affiliations:** A.W.W.A.; Water Environment Federation **Hob./spts.:** Riding motorcycles **SIC code:** 95 **Address:** City of Jackson Ohio, 145 Broadway St., Jackson, OH 45640 **E-mail:** ggppww@juno.com

WILSON, JIMMY G.
Industry: Government **Born:** September 11, 1952, Tuscaloosa, Alabama **Current organization:** Montevallo Water & Sewer Board **Title:** Manager **Type of organization:** Municipal government **Major product:** Sewer and water treatment **Area of distribution:** Montevallo, Alabama **Expertise:** Daily operations **Affiliations:** Alabama Rural Water Association; Alabama Water and Pollution Control Association; American Water Works Association **Hob./spts.:** Fishing, hunting **SIC code:** 95 **Address:** Montevallo Water & Sewer Board, 613 Valley St., Montevallo, AL 35115 **E-mail:** jgwilson11@bellsouth.net

WINGATE, MARK E.
Industry: Government **Born:** September 22, 1961, Orange, California **Univ./degree:** B.S., Civil Engineering, California Polytechnic State University **Current organization:** U.S. Army Corps of Engineers **Title:** Disaster Program Manager **Type of organization:** Federal government/emergency response **Major product:** Disaster response, earthquakes, floods, hurricanes, terrorism **Area of distribution:** International **Expertise:** Debris processing, structural safety, counter terrorism **Hob./spts.:** Backpacking, photography **SIC code:** 97 **Address:** U.S. Army Corps of Engineers, 333 Market St., 9th floor, San Francisco, CA 94105 **E-mail:** mark.e.wingate@usace.army.mil

WINTON, GARY J.
Industry: Government **Born:** April 13, 1955, Doylestown, Pennsylvania **Current organization:** Perkasie Borough Authority **Title:** Manager **Type of organization:** Local government **Major product:** Water and sewer service **Area of distribution:** Perkasie, Pennsylvania **Expertise:** Water management **Affiliations:** American Waterworks Authority; Lions Club; Pennsylvania Water Supply Operators Association **Hob./spts.:** Gardening **SIC code:** 91 **Address:** Perkasie Borough Authority, 306 N. Fifth St., P.O. Box 159, Perkasie, PA 18944 **E-mail:** garyjw.garyjw@verizon.net

WOEBKENBERG, MARY LYNN
Industry: Government **Born:** March 7, 1952, Cincinnati, Ohio **Univ./degree:** Ph.D., Analytical Chemistry, University of Cincinnati, 1997 **Current organization:** DHHS/CDC/NIOSH **Title:** Ph.D. **Type of organization:** Government research institute **Major product:** Occupational safety and health research **Area of distribution:** National **Expertise:** Analytical chemistry **Published works:** 40+ peer reviewed articles **Affiliations:** A.C.S.; A.C.G.I.H.; Sweet Adelines International; American Chemical Society; American Conference of Industrial Hygienists **Hob./spts.:** Music, guitar **SIC code:** 99 **Address:** DHHS/CDC/NIOSH, 4676 Columbia Pkwy., Cincinnati, OH 45226 **E-mail:** mwoebkenberg@hhs.gov

WOLTERS, THOMAS E.
Industry: Aerospace **Born:** March 8, 1962, Chester, Illinois **Univ./degree:** B.S.E.E., 1997; M.S., Electrical Engineering, 2002, Old Dominion University **Current organization:** NASA Langley Research Center **Title:** Computer Engineer **Type of organization:** Government research **Major product:** Research simulation of aircraft **Area of distribution:** International **Expertise:** Project management, hardware engineering for systems image generation, general aviation research **Affiliations:** American Institute of Aeronautics and Astronautics **Hob./spts.:** Hunting, saltwater fishing **SIC code:** 96 **Address:** NASA Langley Research Center, 27 W. Taylor St., Mail Stop 125B, Hampton, VA 23681 **E-mail:** t.e.wolters@larc.nasa.gov **Web address:** WWW.NASA.GOV

WOMBLE, SUSAN E.
Industry: Government **Born:** December 28, 1951, Wilmington, Delaware **Univ./degree:** B.S., Chemistry, Grove City College, 1973 **Current organization:** U.S. Environmental Protection Agency **Title:** Center Director **Type of organization:** Government agency **Major product:** Information, education on indoor air quality, BASE study **Area of distribution:** International **Expertise:** Technical information, consumer guidance **Honors/awards:** 1999 Gold Medal for Exceptional Service **Affiliations:** I.S.I.A.Q.; I.S.E.A.; Virgers Guild **Hob./spts.:** Woodworking, universal design for accessible living **SIC code:** 95 **Address:** 1200 Pennsylvania Ave., N.W. 6609J, Washington, DC 20460 **E-mail:** womble.susan@epa.gov

WOOLDRIDGE, LOLA V.
Industry: Government **Born:** Putnam County, Tennessee **Univ./degree:** A.S., Business Administration, University of Tennessee, 1980 **Current organization:** State of Tennessee-Commerce & Insurance **Title:** Consumer Protection Specialist **Type of organization:** Regulatory government agency **Major product:** Consumer protection **Area of distribution:** Tennessee **Expertise:** Consumer complaints **Affiliations:** Vice President, Tennessee Federation; President and Vice President, Davidson County

Democratic Women; National Federation of Democratic Women; Tennessee State Employees Association; American Society of Public Administration **Hob./spts.:** Gardening **SIC code:** 99 **Address:** State of Tennessee-Commerce & Insurance, 500 James Robertson Pkwy., Nashville, TN 37243 **E-mail:** lola.wooldridge@state.tn.us

WYDRA, THOMAS J.
Industry: Government/law enforcement **Born:** July 31, 1970, Milford, Connecticut **Univ./degree:** Attended Sacred Heart University for Business; Meridian Law Enforcement Training Academy, 1993; FBI Academy, 2003 **Current organization:** Hamden Police Dept. **Title:** Deputy Police Chief **Type of organization:** Police department **Major product:** Public order, safety and law enforcement **Area of distribution:** Hamden, Connecticut **Expertise:** Commander of the investigative unit and administration department **Honors/awards:** Hamden Police Officer of the Year, 2004 **Affiliations:** Narcotics Officers Association **Hob./spts.:** Golf, running **SIC code:** 92 **Address:** Hamden Police Dept., 2900 Dixwell Ave., Hamden, CT 06518 **E-mail:** thwydra@hamden.com

YOUNG JR., LLOYD
Industry: Government/court services **Univ./degree:** M.S., Management, Leslie College, Cambridge, Massachusetts, 1992 **Current organization:** Chesapeake Bay Alcohol Safety Action Program **Title:** Executive Director **Type of organization:** Criminal justice agency **Major product:** Intervention services **Area of distribution:** Virginia **Expertise:** Management **Published works:** Articles, newsletters, journals **Affiliations:** President, V.A.S.A.P.D.A. **SIC code:** 94 **Address:** Chesapeake Bay Alcohol Safety Action Program, 868 N. Newtown Rd., Virginia Beach, VA 23462 **E-mail:** lyoung@vaasap.org

ZADE, ISMAIL YAHYA
Industry: Healthcare **Born:** January 6, 1933, Ardebil, Iran **Univ./degree:** M.D., Ankara University, Turkey, 1963 **Current organization:** V.A. Hudson Valley Health Care System **Title:** M.D. **Type of organization:** V.A. Hospital **Major product:** Patient care **Area of distribution:** New York **Expertise:** Pediatrics, pediatric cardiology from England, psychiatry-geriatrics-drug detoxification from U.S.A. **Honors/awards:** Gold Medal from Ankara University; 4 Patents in the U.S.; Inventor of Geripants **Published works:** 3 books, "Vaccination in Children", "Children's' Heart Disease", "Drug Detoxification" **Affiliations:** Established 2 hospitals (Saffeve Hospital, 200 beds in Ardebil and Shah Ismail Hospital, 100 beds in Cazvin) **Hob./spts.:** Reading, writing, chess **SIC code:** 94 **Address:** 25 Larissa Lane, Thornwood, NY 10594

ZAKLUKIEWICZ, PAUL E.
Industry: Government **Born:** October 11, 1966, Allentown, Pennsylvania **Current organization:** U.S. Army **Title:** Leader **Type of organization:** Military **Major product:** National defense **Area of distribution:** International **Expertise:** Computer networking **Honors/awards:** Honor Guard Member, Funerals **Affiliations:** Member, Quick Reaction Force; Force Protection **Hob./spts.:** Softball, baseball, NASCAR **SIC code:** 97 **Address:** U.S. Army, AlphaBattery, 2-18 FA, Ft. Sill, OK 73503 **E-mail:** pzakl@aol.com

ZALTASH, ABDOLREZA
Industry: Government **Born:** May 7, 1959, Tehran, Iran **Univ./degree:** B.S., Chemical Engineering, 1983; M.S., Chemical & Petroleum Engineering, 1985; Ph.D., Chemical & Petroleum Engineering, 1988, University of Pittsburgh **Current organization:** Oak Ridge National Lab **Title:** Chemical Engineer **Type of organization:** Government/research & development lab **Major product:** Cooling, heating & power **Area of distribution:** International **Expertise:** Chemical & petroleum engineering **Honors/awards:** Outstanding Physics Student of the Year, The American Association of Physics Teachers Award, May 7, 1980 **Published works:** 50+ papers **Affiliations:** A.S.M.E. **Hob./spts.:** Backgammon, chess, books, travel **SIC code:** 96 **Address:** Oak Ridge National Lab, 1 Bethel Valley Rd., Mail Stop 6070, Oak Ridge, TN 37831-6070 **Phone:** (865)574-4571 **Fax:** (865)574-9338 **E-mail:** zaltasha@ornl.gov

ZAVER, ALLA G.
Industry: Government/healthcare **Born:** December 26, 1923, Harbin, Manchuria **Univ./degree:** MB. BS (Bachelor of Medicine & Bachelor of Surgery, equivalent to M.D. as per Mass. Medical Board of Registration), Australia University of Queensland Medical School **Current organization:** Social Security Administration **Title:** M.D.; SSA Regional Medical Advisor **Type of organization:** Federal government **Major product:** SSA **Area of distribution:** Region I, New England 6 states, report to Baltimore **Expertise:** Internal medicine, cardiology **Honors/awards:** Outstanding Public Service Award, Social Security Administration, U.S. Dept. of Human Resources (HEW), 1982; Certificate of Appreciation, American Heart Association; Certificate of Appreciation, American Heart Association, Massachusetts Affiliate and Greater Boston, 1989; Active Member Recognition, New York Academy of Sciences, 1984 **Published works:** 8 articles, 5 abstracts including- Zaver, A.G., Nadas, A.S.: Five Congenital Cardiac Defects, A study of the Profile and Natural History, Atrial Septal Defec Secundum Type, Supplement to Circulation 32:#6, 1965, American Heart Association Monography No 12; Zaver, A.G.: Pulmonary Arterial Hypertension, International Anesthesiology Clinics, Pediatric Anesthesia 1:69 August 1962, Little, Brown & Company, Boston, MA; Alla G. Zaver, M.B., B.S., M.R.A.C.P., M.R.C.P. (London), Cardiac Problems in Adolescents, The Medical Clinics of North American, March 1965, Vol 49, No 2, W.B. Saunders Company **Affiliations:** Fellow, Royal Australian College of Physicians MRACP 1956, Fellow PRACP 1973; Member, Royal College of Physicians, London (MRCP), 1957; Fellow, American College of Physicians (FACP), 1965; Fellow, American College of Cardiology (FACC), 1974; American Heart Association; Massachusetts Medical Association; Former Affiliations: British Medical Society; American Association for the Advancement of Science; American Society of Law and Medicine **Career accomplishments:** American Heart Association, chaired many projects and committees while Director of the ICU including Chair of the hospital Quality Assurance Committee **Hob./spts.:** Gardening, nature, music **SIC code:** 94 **Address:** 3 Eliot Hill Rd., South Natick, MA 01760 **E-mail:** agzaver@comcast.net

ZHANG, YANPING
Industry: Government/engineering **Born:** Beijing, China **Univ./degree:** B.S.C.E., Tongji University, 1994; M.S., University of Toledo, 1998 **Current organization:** Prince George's County Government, Maryland **Title:** Engineer **Type of organization:** Government **Major product:** Geo-Storm **Area of distribution:** Largo, Maryland **Expertise:** Civil engineering **Honors/awards:** Registered Professional Engineer (Maryland); Outstanding Achievement (group) **Published works:** Article, Master's thesis **Affiliations:** A.S.C.E. member **Hob./spts.:** Hiking, ice skating, swimming, travel **SIC code:** 91 **Address:** Prince George's County Government, Maryland, 9400 Peppercorn Place, Largo, MD 20774 **E-mail:** yzhang@co.pg.md.us

ZIL, J. S.
Industry: Government/healthcare **Born:** Chicago, Illinois **Univ./degree:** B.S., University of Redlands, 1969; M.D., University of California at San Diego, 1973; M.P.H., Tale University, 1977; J.D., Jefferson University, 1985 **Current organization:** State of California **Title:** Chief Forensic Psychiatrist **Type of organization:** Government courts, prison system **Major product:** Public safety **Area of distribution:** National **Expertise:** Forensic psychiatry **Honors/awards:** Presidential Appointed Commissioner, Physician's Advisory Council, The White House, 2002-2002; Lifetime Achievement Awards, University of California 1996-1996, University of Redlands 1994 **Published works:** 60 books and government monographs; 150 scientific papers **Affiliations:** National President, A.A.M.H.P.C., 1998 **Hob./spts.:** First edition American literature, American history **SIC code:** 92 **Address:** State of California, P.O. Box 160208, Sacramento, CA 95816-0208 **E-mail:** corrmentalhealth@aol.com

SIC Code Directory

AGRICULTURE, FORESTRY AND FISHING 01-09
01 Agricultural Production–Crops
02 Agricultural Production–Livestock
07 Agricultural Services
08 Forestry Services
09 Hunting, Fishing and Trapping

MINING 10-14
10 Metal Mining
12 Coal Mining
13 Oil and Gas Extraction
14 Mining and Quarrying–Nonmetallic Minerals

CONTRACTORS 15-17
15 General Building Contractors
16 Heavy Construction Except Building
17 Construction–Special Trade Contractors

MANUFACTURING 20-39
20 Food and Kindred Products
21 Tobacco Products
22 Textile Mill Products
23 Apparel and Other Finished Products from Fabrics
24 Lumber and Wood Products Except Furniture
25 Furniture and Fixtures
26 Paper and Allied Products
27 Printing, Publishing and Allied Industries
28 Chemical and Allied Products
29 Petroleum Refineries and Related Industries
30 Rubber and Misc. Plastics
31 Leather and Leather Products
32 Stone, Clay, Glass and Concrete Products
33 Primary Metal Industries
34 Fabricated Metal Products Except Machinery and Transportation Equipment
35 Industrial and Commercial Machinery
36 Electronic, Electrical Equipment and Components
37 Transportation Equipment
38 Measuring, Analyzing and Controlling Instruments; Photo, Medical and Optical Goods, Watches, Clocks
39 Misc. Manufacturing Industries

COMMUNICATION, TRANSPORTATION AND UTILITIES 40-49
40 Railroad Transportation
41 Local/Suburban Transit and Highway Passenger Transportation
42 Motor Freight Transportation/Warehouse
43 United States Postal Service (Post Offices)
44 Water Transportation
45 Transportation By Air
46 Pipeline (Oil) Except Natural Gas
47 Transportation Services
48 Communications
49 Electric, Gas and Sanitary Services

WHOLESALERS 50-51
50 Wholesale Trade–Durable Goods
51 Wholesale Trade–Nondurable Goods

RETAILERS 52-59
52 Building Materials, Hardware and Garden Supplies
53 General Merchandise Stores
54 Food Stores
55 Automotive Dealers and Gasoline Service Stations
56 Apparel and Accessory Stores
57 Home Furniture, Furnishings and Equipment
58 Eating and Drinking Places
59 Misc. Retail

FINANCE, INSURANCE AND REAL ESTATE 60-67
60 Depository Institutions
61 Nondepository Credit Institutions
62 Security and Commodity Brokers, Dealers
63 Insurance Carriers
64 Insurance Agents, Brokers and Services
65 Real Estate
67 Holding and Other Investment Offices

SERVICES 70-79
70 Hotels, Rooming Houses, Campgrounds and Other Lodgings
72 Personal Services
73 Business Services
75 Auto Repair and Parking Services
76 Misc. Repair Services
78 Motion Pictures
79 Amusement and Recreation Services

MEDICAL
80 Health Services

LEGAL SERVICES
81 Legal Services

EDUCATIONAL FIELDS
82 Educational Services

ORGANIZATIONS 83-87
83 Social Services
84 Museums, Art Galleries and Botanical Gardens
86 Membership Organizations
87 Engineering, Accounting and Research Services

MISCELLANEOUS
89 Misc. Services N.E.C.

GOVERNMENTAL SERVICES 91-99
91 Executive, Legislative and General Government
92 Justice, Public Order and Safety, Courts
93 Public Finance, Taxation and Monetary Policy
94 Human Resource Programs–Veterans' Affairs, Social Programs, Educational Programs
95 Environmental Programs–Conservation, Waste Management, Urban and Community Development
96 Economic Programs–Regulation of Transportation Programs, Utilities and Agricultural Markets, Space Research and Technology
97 National Security and International Affairs
99 Nonclassifiable Establishments

Alphabetical Index

Geographical Index

ALABAMA

ARKANSAS

CALIFORNIA

COLORADO

CONNECTICUT

DELAWARE

DISTRICT OF COLUMBIA

FLORIDA

HAWAII

IDAHO

ILLINOIS

IOWA

KANSAS

KENTUCKY

LOUISIANA

MARYLAND

MASSACHUSETTS

MISSOURI

NEW HAMPSHIRE

NEW JERSEY

NEW MEXICO

NEW YORK

NORTH CAROLINA

NORTH DAKOTA

OHIO

OKLAHOMA

OREGON

PENNSYLVANIA

SOUTH DAKOTA

TENNESSEE

TEXAS

WEST VIRGINIA

WISCONSIN

UNITED KINGDOM

VIRGIN ISLANDS

ISBN: 978-1-890347-17-8